FIFTH EDITION

HANDEL'S NATIONAL DIRECTORY FOR THE PERFORMING ARTS

VOLUME ONE

ORGANIZATIONS AND FACILITIES

The 5th edition of Handel's NATIONAL DIRECTORY FOR THE PERFORMING ARTS was prepared by R.R. Bowker's Data Base Publishing Group.

Marion Sader, Publisher

Dean Hollister, Director, Data Base Planning
Andrew Grabois, Editorial Director
Elizabeth A. Onaran, Managing Editor
Kimberly A. Willard, Senior Editor
April Messina, Carole J. Rafferty, Stacy A. Stanford, Pu Xiang; Associate Editors
Kimberley B. Jenkins, M. Michelle Mahlstadt, Erica Milowitz; Assistant Editors

Judy Redel, Director, Research
Tanya Hurst, Senior Editor, Research

Peter Simon, Vice President, Data Base Publishing Group

FIFTH EDITION

HANDEL'S NATIONAL DIRECTORY
FOR
THE PERFORMING ARTS

VOLUME ONE

ORGANIZATIONS AND FACILITIES

R.R.BOWKER®

Published by R.R. Bowker, a Reed Reference Publishing Company

International Standard Book Numbers:
2 Vol Set: 0-8352-3250-6
Volume 1:   0-8352-3327-8
Volume 2:   0-8352-3328-6
Library of Congress Catalog Card Number: 73-646635
Printed and bound in the United States of America

ISBN 0 - 8352 - 3250 - 6

9 780835 232500

TABLE OF CONTENTS

VOLUME ONE: ORGANIZATIONS & FACILITIES

STATE INDEX vi

PREFACE vii

AFFILIATIONS viii

ORGANIZATIONS & FACILITIES 1

DANCE INDEX 1529

INSTRUMENTAL MUSIC INDEX 1533

VOCAL MUSIC INDEX 1539

THEATRE INDEX 1543

PERFORMING SERIES INDEX 1551

FACILITY INDEX 1555

GENERAL INDEX 1571

VOLUME TWO: EDUCATIONAL INSTITUTIONS

STATE INDEX vi

PREFACE vii

DEGREES viii

EDUCATIONAL INSTITUTIONS 1

DANCE INDEX 653

MUSIC INDEX 657

THEATRE INDEX 665

GENERAL INSTITUTION INDEX 673

ORGANIZATIONS & FACILITIES - STATE INDEX

ALABAMA 1
ALASKA 13
ARIZONA 25
ARKANSAS 43
CALIFORNIA 55
COLORADO 221
CONNECTICUT 255
DELAWARE 291
DISTRICT OF COLUMBIA 297
FLORIDA 315
GEORGIA 375
HAWAII 401
IDAHO 411
ILLINOIS 419
INDIANA 483
IOWA 507
KANSAS 525
KENTUCKY 539
LOUISIANA 555
MAINE 573
MARYLAND 585
MASSACHUSETTS 601
MICHIGAN 655
MINNESOTA 699
MISSISSIPPI 731
MISSOURI 741
MONTANA 769
NEBRASKA 781
NEVADA 795
NEW HAMPSHIRE 803
NEW JERSEY 815
NEW MEXICO 847
NEW YORK 859
NORTH CAROLINA 1043
NORTH DAKOTA 1083
OHIO 1091
OKLAHOMA 1157
OREGON 1173
PENNSYLVANIA 1193
RHODE ISLAND 1245
SOUTH CAROLINA 1255
SOUTH DAKOTA 1267
TENNESSEE 1277
TEXAS 1303
UTAH 1395
VERMONT 1409
VIRGINIA 1421
WASHINGTON 1445
WEST VIRGINIA 1475
WISCONSIN 1487
WYOMING 1519
PUERTO RICO 1525
VIRGIN ISLANDS 1527

PREFACE

Handel's National Directory for the Performing Arts was first published in 1973 as a result of the vision and energy of Beatrice Handel, who perceived that the explosive growth of the performing arts in all sections of the United States required an authoritative directory to document and encourage that development. From the beginning, the directory's mission has been to "serve as a major and comprehensive resource document for and about the performing arts industry, assisting individuals and organizations in their search for specific information that is qualitative and quantitative relative to their industry." *Handel's* is unique in providing information on both performing arts organizations and facilities as well as information on educational institutions that offer courses and degree programs in the performing arts.

This fifth edition is the first since 1988 and the first to be published by R.R. Bowker, a Reed Reference Publishing Company, a major publisher of directories worldwide. Like its predecessors, it provides current, authoritative information on the status of the performing arts in the United States. Reflecting the continued growth of the field, this edition features more than 900 new organizations and facilities and over 300 new educational programs.

Compilation

Methods used in the compilation of this edition included mail and telephone surveys, updating of fourth edition listings and analysis of published and unpublished sources. More than a year was spent compiling lists of organizations, educational institutions and facilities, retrieving the information needed, and verifying that information. The same process also confirmed the demise or inactivity of organizations, educational institutions and facilities. Information given in response to these requests has been edited to conform to the entry format.

Organization and Contents

Handel's is organized in two volumes, the first covering organizations and facilities, the second educational institutions. The performing arts areas covered in *Volume One* are Dance, Instrumental and Vocal Music, Theatre, and Performing Series. Organizations that do not fit into a specific arts area, such as festivals, sponsoring organizations, historical dramas and community concerts, are included under the general heading Performing Series.

Volume One is arranged alphabetically by state, city within each state, and then arts area. Organization listings contain the names, addresses and phone numbers of the organizations, names of artistic and administrative management, board members, numbers of staff, budget and attendance statistics, founding dates and performance facilities. The Facility listings include the types of facilities and stages, construction and remodeling costs, architects, resident groups, stage dimensions, seating capacities and information on rental availability.

The educational institutions in the second volume are listed alphabetically within the states and contain specific information on their Dance, Music and Theatre departments. Courses, degrees, department heads, numbers of faculty and students, technical training and financial assistance are detailed. Information is also included on each institution's performing groups and series, guest and resident artists, and facilities.

Indexing

Volume One contains separate indices to the Dance, Instrumental Music, Vocal Music, Theatre, and Performing Series organizations as well as a separate index to the Facilities. Additionally, there is a General Index which lists all organizations and facilities alphabetically by name. Similarly, *Volume Two* has separate indices to the Dance, Music and Theatre programs as well as the General Institution Index which lists educational institutions alphabetically by name.

Acknowledgments

The editors wish to thank Bea Handel for her suggestions and guidance for this edition. We are also grateful to all the organizations that took the time to submit information for this directory. Without their help, such an undertaking would not be possible. Comments and suggestions for future editions are always welcome.

AFFILIATIONS

AAA	American Arts Alliance
AACT	American Association of Community Theatres
AAM	American Association of Museums
AATA	American Alliance for Theatre Arts
AATE	American Association of Theatre Educators
AATY	Association of American Theatre for Youth
ACA	American Council for the Arts
ACDA	American Choral Directors Association
ACDFA	American Colleges Dance Festival Association
ACTA	American Community Theatre Association
ACTF	American College Theatre Festival
ACU-I	Association of College Unions - International
ADMA	Alliance for Dance and Movement Arts
ADTA	American Dinner Theatre Association
ADTI	American Dinner Theatre Institute
AEA	Actors' Equity Association
AFM	American Federation of Musicians of the United States and Canada
AFTRA	American Federation of Television and Radio Artists
AGMA	American Guild of Musical Artists
AGO	American Guild of Organists
AGVA	American Guild of Variety Artists
AHA	Association of Hispanic Arts
AMC	American Music Conference
APAC	American Performing Arts Center
APAP	Association of Performing Arts Presenters
ART/NY	Alliance of Resident Theatres/New York
ASCAP	American Society of Composers, Authors and Publishers
ASOL	American Symphony Orchestra League
ASSITEJ	Association Internationale du Theatre pour l'Enfance et de la Jeunesse (International Association of Theatre for Children and Youth)
ATHE	Association for Theatre in Higher Education
BMI	Broadcast Music, Inc.
BOMI	Box Office Management International
CA	Chorus America
CMA	Chamber Music America
CORST	Council of Resident Summer Theatres
COS	Central Opera Service
COST	Council of Stock Theatres
CTAA	Children's Theatre Association of America
DGA	Directors Guild of America
DTW	Dance Theatre Workshop
ECTC	East Coast Theatre Conference
EMA	Early Music America
FACT	Festival of American Community Theatre
FEDAPT	Foundation for the Extension and Development of American Professional Theatre
FIDOF	Federation Internationale des Organisateurs de Festivals (International Federation of Festival Organizations)
GALA Choruses	Gay and Lesbian Association of Choruses
GFA	Guitar Foundation of America
IAAM	International Association of Auditorium Managers
IADMS	International Association for Dance Medicine and Science
IAJE	International Association of Jazz Educators
IATSE	International Alliance of Theatrical Stage Employees and Moving Picture Machine Operators of the United States and Canada
ISPAA	International Society of Performing Arts Administrators

AFFILIATIONS

ITI	International Theatre Institute
LATA	Los Angeles Theatre Alliance
LATP	League of American Theatres and Producers
LCT	League of Chicago Theatres
LMDA	Literary Managers and Dramaturges of America
LOFT	League of Fringe Theatres
LORT	League of Resident Theatres
MAAA	Mid-America Arts Alliance
MENC	Music Educators National Conference
MESA	Middle East Studies Association
MOMA	Museum of Modern Art
NAAO	National Association of Artists Organizations
NACA	National Association for Campus Activities
NALAA	National Association of Local Arts Agencies
NARB	National Association for Regional Ballet
NASAA	National Assembly of State Arts Agencies
NASD	National Association of Schools of Dance
NAST	National Association of Schools of Theatre
NDA	National Dance Association
NDTA	National Dinner Theatre Association
NEA	National Endowment for the Arts
NEAT	New England Area Theatres
NEP	National Education Program
NETC	New England Theatre Conference
NGCSA	National Guild of Community Schools of the Arts, Inc.
NIMT	National Institute for Music Theater
NMTA	National Movement Theatre Association
NOA	National Opera Association
NPN	National Performance Network
NSOA	National Symphony Orchestra Association
NSOL	National Symphony Orchestra League
OA	Opera America
OGI	Opera Guild International
PNWAP	Pacific Northwest Arts Performers
PRBA	Pacific Regional Ballet Association
RDA	Regional Dance America
ROOTS	Rural Organization of Theatres South
SAF	Southern Arts Federation
SEM	Society for Ethno-Musicology
SERBA	Southeast Regional Ballet Association
SETC	Southeastern Theatre Conference
SPEBSQSA	Society for the Preservation and Encouragement of Barbershop Quartets Singing in America, Inc.
SPTA	Small Professional Theatre Association
SSDC	Society for Stage Directors and Choreographers
SWRBA	Southwest Regional Ballet Association
TAAC	The Association for Artists of Color
TCG	Theatre Communications Group
TOG	The Opera Guild
TYA	Theatre for Young Audiences
U/RTA	University/Resident Theatre Association
UNIMA	United International Marionette Association
USA	United Scenic Arts
USITT	United States Institute for Theatre Technology, Inc.
WAAA	Western Alliance of Arts Administrators
WSAF	Western States Arts Federation

ALABAMA

Andalusia

FACILITY

DIXON CENTER FOR THE PERFORMING ARTS
PO Box 1418, Andalusia, AL 36420
(205) 222-6591
FAX: (205) 222-6567
Founded: 1982
Type of Facility: Theatre Complex; Concert Hall; Auditorium; Studio Performance; Performance Center; Theatre House; Room; Loft
Type of Stage: Proscenium
Stage Dimensions: 42'x30'   **Orchestra Pit**
Seating Capacity: 500
Year Built: 1982   **Architect:** Pearson, Humphries, Jones & Associates, Inc.   **Cost:** $900,000
Acoustical Consultant: Electronic Engineers, Inc.
Contact for Rental: Jerry Padgett;   (205) 222-6591, ext. 238
Resident Groups: Junior College Music and Drama Classes

Anniston

THEATRE

ANNISTON COMMUNITY THEATER
PO Box 1454, Anniston, AL 36202
(205) 236-8342
Founded: 1927
Arts Area: Professional; Community
Status: Semi-Professional; Non-Profit
Type: Performing; Resident; Educational
Purpose: To promote dramatic art and culture in the community
Management: Josephine E. Ayers, Producing Artistic Director; Dena Kirkland, Administrative Director
Officers: James Nolen, President; Margaret McNaron, Treasurer; Michael Cassidy, Secretary
Paid Staff: 2   **Volunteer Staff:** 50
Paid Artists: 10   **Non-Paid Artists:** 40
Budget: $50,000 - $100,000
Income Sources: Private Foundations/Grants/Endowments; Business/Corporate Donations; Box Office; Government Grants; Individual Donations
Season: 52 Weeks   **Annual Attendance:** 6,000
Performance Facilities: ACT Playhouse

Birmingham

DANCE

SOUTHERN DANCEWORKS
2829 Second Avenue South, Suite 301, Birmingham, AL 35233
(205) 322-6483
Founded: 1963
Arts Area: Modern; Jazz
Status: Professional; Non-Profit; Commercial
Type: Performing; Educational; Sponsoring
Purpose: To promote performances and the teaching of contemporary dance by local and professional touring artists; to provide a climate where local dancers, teachers, choreographers and artists may realize creative potential; to encourage dance in public education
Management: Joanna Fuller, Director of Development; Mary Foshee, Artistic Director
Officers: Paulette ZanMatre, Chairman of the Board ·
Paid Staff: 2   **Volunteer Staff:** 16
Paid Artists: 6   **Non-Paid Artists:** 6
Utilizes: Guest Artists
Budget: $100,000 - $500,000
Income Sources: Private Foundations/Grants/Endowments; Business/Corporate Donations; Box Office; Government Grants; Individual Donations
Annual Attendance: 6,000

THE STATE OF ALABAMA BALLET/BALLET SOUTH
2001 Park Place North, Birmingham, AL 35203
(205) 252-2475
FAX: (205) 252-2476
    Founded: 1981
    Arts Area: Ballet
    Status: Professional
    Type: Performing; Touring
    Purpose: To offer professional ballet performances to the Southeast
    Management: Catherine Gilmore, Managing Director; Dame Sonia Arova, Artistic Director; Carol H. Cotton, Administrative Assistant; Gail L. Vaughn
    Officers: George G. Lynn, Chair; Mrs. Lee Walls, President; Dr. Morgan Eland, Vice President; Mrs. Harvey Gotlieb, Secretary; Steven Christian, Treasurer
    Paid Staff: 3   **Volunteer Staff:** 25
    Paid Artists: 22   **Non-Paid Artists:** 20
    Utilizes: Guest Artists; Guest Choreographers
    Budget: $500,000 - $1,000,000
    Income Sources: Private Foundations/Grants/Endowments; Business/Corporate Donations; Box Office; Individual Donations
    Season: August - April   **Annual Attendance:** 20,000
    Performance Facilities: Civic Center Theatre and Concert Hall

INSTRUMENTAL MUSIC

ALABAMA SYMPHONY ORCHESTRA
2001 Park Place North, Birmingham, AL 35203
(205) 326-0100
FAX: (205) 521-9069
    Founded: 1933
    Arts Area: Symphony; Orchestra
    Status: Non-Profit
    Type: Performing
    Purpose: To promote, foster and encourage symphonic music and the art of music generally
    Management: Mark Walker, Executive Director
    Officers: Michael Warren, Chairman of the Board; Harold Apolinsky, President; Marvin Engel, Vice President; Peggy Werdehoff, Secretary
    Paid Staff: 15
    Paid Artists: 80
    Utilizes: Guest Conductors; Guest Artists
    Budget: $1,000,000 - $5,000,000
    Income Sources: Private Foundations/Grants/Endowments; Business/Corporate Donations; Government Grants; Individual Donations
    Season: September - May   **Annual Attendance:** 144,000
    Affiliations: ASOL; AFM
    Performance Facilities: Birmingham-Jefferson Civic Center Concert Hall

VOCAL MUSIC

BIRMINGHAM OPERA THEATER
2027 First Avenue North, Commerce Center, Suite 1, Birmingham, AL 35203
(205) 322-6737
FAX: (205) 251-6870
    Founded: 1957
    Arts Area: Grand Opera; Lyric Opera
    Status: Professional; Non-Profit
    Type: Performing; Touring; Educational
    Purpose: To promote opera and American musical dramas through world-class productions and educational tours
    Management: Zane Bradford, Executive Office Administrator
    Officers: J. Ernest Hill, President
    Paid Staff: 2   **Volunteer Staff:** 4
    Paid Artists: 24   **Non-Paid Artists:** 25
    Utilizes: Special Technical Talent; Guest Conductors; Guest Artists; Guest Directors
    Budget: $100,000 - $500,000
    Income Sources: Private Foundations/Grants/Endowments; Business/Corporate Donations; Box Office; Government Grants; Individual Donations
    Season: September - May   **Annual Attendance:** 25,000

Affiliations: Alabama Shakespeare Festival; Atlanta Symphony
Performance Facilities: Birmingham Jefferson Civic Center

THEATRE

BIRMINGHAM CHILDREN'S THEATRE
3 Civic Center Plaza, Birmingham, AL 35203
(205) 324-0470
Founded: 1947
Arts Area: Professional; Theatrical Group
Status: Professional; Non-Profit
Type: Performing; Touring; Resident; Educational; Sponsoring
Purpose: The Birmingham Children's Theatre is a professional company providing quality theatre for young people which incorporates literature, art, music and drama into a medium that is both entertaining and culturally enriching.
Management: James W. Rye, Jr., Managing Director
Officers: Charles D. Perry Jr., President; Barnett Earles, First Vice President; James Moylan, Second Vice President; Felix Drennen III, Third Vice President; Betty H. Pewitt, Secretary; Jean P. Pierce, Treasurer
Paid Staff: 21   **Volunteer Staff:** 80
Paid Artists: 55
Utilizes: Special Technical Talent; Guest Artists; Guest Directors
Budget: $500,000 - $1,000,000
Income Sources: Private Foundations/Grants/Endowments; Business/Corporate Donations; Box Office; Government Grants; Individual Donations
Season: August - May
Annual Attendance: 520,000
Performance Facilities: Civic Center Theatre

TOWN AND GOWN THEATER
1116 South 26th Street, Birmingham, AL 35205
(205) 934-5088
Founded: 1950
Arts Area: Musical; Community; Theatrical Group
Status: Non-Profit
Type: Performing; Touring; Educational
Management: Gary Robertson, Director; Joyce Whitten, Administrative Assistant
Paid Staff: 17   **Volunteer Staff:** 50
Non-Paid Artists: 75
Utilizes: Special Technical Talent; Guest Artists; Guest Directors
Budget: $100,000 - $500,000
Income Sources: Private Foundations/Grants/Endowments; Business/Corporate Donations; Box Office; Individual Donations
Season: October - June   **Annual Attendance:** 33,000
Affiliations: AATA; SETC
Performance Facilities: Clark Memorial Theater

PERFORMING SERIES

BIRMINGHAM FESTIVAL OF ARTS ASSOCIATION
Commerce Center, 2027 First Avenue North, Suite 910, Birmingham, AL 35203
(205) 252-7652
FAX: (205) 252-7656
Founded: 1951
Arts Area: Dance; Vocal Music; Instrumental Music; Theater
Status: Non-Profit
Type: Performing; Educational; Sponsoring
Purpose: A voluntary, non-commercial endeavor to increase international and human understanding by bringing local ethnic groups and foreign citizens together to exhibit the cultural achievements of other nations and peoples
Management: Sara C. Crowder, Executive Director
Officers: Carole Staats, Chairman; David Carder, President
Paid Staff: 2
Utilizes: Special Technical Talent; Guest Conductors; Guest Artists; Guest Directors
Budget: $100,000 - $500,000
Income Sources: Business/Corporate Donations; Box Office; Individual Donations
Season: April - May   **Annual Attendance:** 150,000

FACILITY

BIRMINGHAM-JEFFERSON CIVIC CENTER
1 Civic Center Plaza, Birmingham, AL 35203
(205) 458-8400
FAX: (205) 458-8437
Type of Facility: Civic Center
Year Built: 1976 **Architect:** Geddes, Brecher, Qualls & Cunningham **Cost:** $65,000,000
Acoustical Consultant: Bolt, Beranek & Newman
Contact for Rental: George Pierce; (205) 458-8434
Contains the Coliseum, Concert Hall, Theatre and Exhibition Hall. See separate listings for additional information.

BIRMINGHAM-JEFFERSON CIVIC CENTER - COLISEUM
1 Civic Center Plaza, PO Box 13347, Birmingham, AL 35202-3347
(205) 458-8400
FAX: (205) 458-8437
Type of Facility: Civic Center; Arena
Type of Stage: Flexible; Platform
Seating Capacity: 16,750
Year Built: 1976
Contact for Rental: George Pierce; (205) 458-8434
Resident Groups: Birmingham Bulls (Ice Hockey)

BIRMINGHAM-JEFFERSON CIVIC CENTER - CONCERT HALL
1 Civic Center Plaza, PO Box 13347, Birmingham, AL 35202-3347
(205) 458-8400
FAX: (205) 458-8437
Type of Facility: Concert Hall; Civic Center
Type of Stage: Thrust; Proscenium
Stage Dimensions: 88'Wx84'Dx26'H **Orchestra Pit**
Seating Capacity: 3,000
Year Built: 1974
Contact for Rental: George Pierce; (205) 458-8434
Resident Groups: Alabama Symphony Orchestra

BIRMINGHAM-JEFFERSON CIVIC CENTER - EXHIBITION HALL
1 Civic Center Plaza, PO Box 13347, Birmingham, AL 35202-3347
(205) 458-8400
FAX: (205) 458-8437
Type of Facility: Civic Center; Exhibition Hall
Type of Stage: Flexible
Year Built: 1972
Contact for Rental: George Pierce; (205) 458-8434
220,000 square feet of exhibition space; 70,000 square feet of meeting rooms

BIRMINGHAM-JEFFERSON CIVIC CENTER - THEATRE
1 Civic Center Plaza, PO Box 13347, Birmingham, AL 35202-3347
(205) 458-8400
FAX: (205) 458-8437
Type of Facility: Theatre House; Civic Center
Type of Stage: Thrust; Flexible; Proscenium
Stage Dimensions: 70'Wx46'Dx27'H **Orchestra Pit**
Seating Capacity: 1000
Year Built: 1974
Contact for Rental: George Pierce; (205) 458-8434
Resident Groups: Birmingham Children's Theater

BIRMINGHAM-SOUTHERN COLLEGE THEATRE
900 Arkadelphia Road, Birmingham, AL 35254
(205) 226-4782
Type of Facility: Theatre Complex
Type of Stage: Thrust; Flexible; Proscenium; Arena
Orchestra Pit
Seating Capacity: 390
Year Built: 1968 **Cost:** $1,500,000
Contact for Rental: Matthew Mielke; (205) 226-4785

Decatur

FACILITY

PRINCESS THEATRE
112 Second Avenue, NE, Decatur, AL 35601
(205) 350-1745
    Type of Facility: Performance Center
    Facility Originally: Stable
    Type of Stage: Proscenium
    Stage Dimensions: 34'Wx25'D; 34'Wx16'H proscenium opening   **Orchestra Pit**
    Seating Capacity: 677
    Year Built: 1887
    Year Remodeled: 1983   **Architect:** Frank Neville   **Cost:** $750,000
    Contact for Rental: Manager;   (205) 350-1745
    Resident Groups: Bank Street Players; Professional Series; Travelog Series
    Became Princess Theatre in 1919, remodeled in Art Deco in 1941

Dothan

THEATRE

SOUTHEAST ALABAMA COMMUNITY THEATRE
PO Box 6065, Dothan, AL 36303
(205) 794-0400
    Founded: 1974
    Arts Area: Summer Stock; Community
    Status: Non-Professional; Non-Profit
    Type: Performing
    Purpose: To bring performing theatre to southeast Alabama
    Management: Connie Miller, Business Manager; Marge Wein, General Manager
    Officers: Danny Richards, President; Nancy Robinson, Vice President; Jane Long, Secretary; Connie Miller, Treasurer
    Paid Staff: 2   **Volunteer Staff:** 200
    Budget: $100,000 - $500,000
    Income Sources: Box Office
    Season: 52 Weeks   **Annual Attendance:** 10,000
    Performance Facilities: Dothan Opera House

FACILITY

DOTHAN CIVIC CENTER
North St. Andrews Street, Dothan, AL 36303
(205) 793-0126
    Type of Facility: Auditorium
    Type of Stage: Proscenium
    Stage Dimensions: 54'Wx44'Dx28'H   **Orchestra Pit**
    Seating Capacity: 3100
    Year Built: 1974   **Architect:** Waid & Holmes   **Cost:** $7,000,000
    Contact for Rental: Betty Ellsworth;   (205) 793-0126
    Resident Groups: Southeast Alabama Community Theatre; Community Concerts

Huntsville

DANCE

HUNTSVILLE CIVIC BALLET
620 St. Claire Avenue SW, PO Box 373, Huntsville, AL 35801
(205) 539-0961
    Founded: 1967
    Arts Area: Modern; Ballet; Jazz
    Status: Semi-Professional; Non-Profit
    Type: Touring; Resident
    Purpose: To provide and educate people in Huntsville with dance; to promote arts with master classes
    Management: Floyd Tygett, Artistic Director; David Harriott, Assistant Director
    Officers: Joan May, President; Mrs. T. Craig, First Vice President; Lita Smith, Second Vice President; Betty Soule, Board Member
    Non-Paid Artists: 25

Utilizes: Guest Artists
Budget: $50,000 - $100,000
Income Sources: Private Foundations/Grants/Endowments; Business/Corporate Donations; Box Office; Government Grants; Individual Donations
Season: 52 Weeks

INSTRUMENTAL MUSIC

HUNTSVILLE SYMPHONY ORCHESTRA
PO Box 2400, Huntsville, AL 35804
(205) 539-4818
FAX: (205) 539-4819
Founded: 1953
Arts Area: Symphony
Status: Non-Professional; Non-Profit; Commercial
Type: Performing; Educational; Sponsoring
Purpose: To provide locally-generated, live orchestral music to the community
Management: Gloria Holdman, Executive Director; Taavo Virkhaus, Musical Director
Non-Paid Artists: 75
Utilizes: Guest Conductors; Guest Artists
Budget: $500,000 - $1,000,000
Income Sources: Business/Corporate Donations; Box Office; Government Grants; Individual Donations; Fund-raising
Season: October - May   **Annual Attendance:** 21,000
Affiliations: ASOL
Performance Facilities: Von Braun Civic Center Concert Hall

HUNTSVILLE YOUTH ORCHESTRA
607 Airport Road SW, Huntsville, AL 35802
(205) 882-0774
Founded: 1962
Arts Area: Orchestra; Chamber; Ensemble
Status: Non-Professional; Non-Profit
Type: Performing; Touring; Educational; Sponsoring
Purpose: To provide a rewarding and challenging experience for its members by means of an active participation in the performance of good music; to awaken interest in symphonic literature in young people by giving them an opportunity to play good music and train those young people having outstanding talent for future participation in the performance of good music
Management: Gary Parks, Music Director/Conductor; Johnny Brewer, Administrative Director; Kay Jones, Administrative Assistant
Paid Staff: 4   **Volunteer Staff:** 100
Non-Paid Artists: 270
Utilizes: Guest Conductors; Guest Artists
Budget: $50,000 - $100,000
Income Sources: Private Foundations/Grants/Endowments; Business/Corporate Donations; Box Office; Government Grants; Individual Donations
Season: October - May   **Annual Attendance:** 5,000
Affiliations: ASOL (Youth Orchestra Division); Alabama Federation of Music; Alabama Arts Council
Performance Facilities: Von Braun Civic Center

VOCAL MUSIC

HUNTSVILLE OPERA THEATER
8802 Willow Hills Drive, Huntsville, AL 35802
(205) 881-4796
Founded: 1981
Arts Area: Grand Opera
Status: Non-Profit
Type: Performing
Purpose: To foster the development of young singers, dancers and technicians
Management: Helen Bargetzi, Artistic Director
Officers: Kevin R. Alspaugh, President; Joseph Galloway, Vice President; Jeanne Marlow, Secretary/Treasurer
Budget: $1,000 - $50,000
Income Sources: Private Foundations/Grants/Endowments; Business/Corporate Donations; Box Office; Individual Donations
Season: October - July
Performance Facilities: Von Braun Civic Center Playhouse

THEATRE

HUNTSVILLE LITTLE THEATRE
700 Monroe Street, Huntsville, AL 35801
(205) 533-6565
Founded: 1949
Arts Area: Musical; Community; Theatrical Group
Status: Non-Professional; Non-Profit
Type: Performing
Purpose: To develop, encourage and promote community interest in dramatic arts and to provide a means by which members may broaden and improve their knowledge and proficiency in theatre arts
Officers: Patricia Blackman, President; Elaine Hubbard, Vice President; Ray Cooper, Secretary; Rene Sevigny, Treasurer
Volunteer Staff: 60
Non-Paid Artists: 50
Utilizes: Special Technical Talent; Guest Artists
Budget: $1,000 - $50,000
Income Sources: Private Foundations/Grants/Endowments; Business/Corporate Donations; Box Office; Government Grants; Individual Donations
Season: September - June   **Annual Attendance:** 7,000
Affiliations: Alabama Theatre Conference
Performance Facilities: Von Braun Civic Center

FACILITY

VON BRAUN CIVIC CENTER
700 Monroe Street SW, Huntsville, AL 35801
(205) 533-1953
FAX: (205) 551-2203
Founded: 1975
Type of Facility: Theatre Complex; Concert Hall; Civic Center; Multi-Purpose
Type of Stage: Thrust; Flexible; Proscenium; Platform
Seating Capacity: Arena - 10,106; Playhouse - 502; Concert Hall - 2,171
Year Built: 1975   **Architect:** Smith, Kranert, Tomblin & Associates   **Cost:** $15,500,000
Acoustical Consultant: C.P. Boner & Associates
Contact for Rental: Ronald D. Evans, Executive Director;   (205) 533-1953
The Civic Center contains the Arena, Concert Hall, Exhibit Hall and Playhouse. See separate listings for additional information.

VON BRAUN CIVIC CENTER - ARENA
700 Monroe Street SW, Huntsville, AL 35801
(205) 533-1953
FAX: (205) 551-2203
Founded: 1975
Type of Facility: Arena
Type of Stage: Arena
Seating Capacity: 10,106
Year Built: 1975   **Architect:** Smith, Kranert, Tomblin & Associates   **Cost:** $15,500,000
Contact for Rental: Ronald D. Evans, Executive Director;   (205) 533-1953

VON BRAUN CIVIC CENTER - CONCERT HALL
700 Monroe Street SW, Huntsville, AL 35801
(205) 533-1953
FAX: (205) 551-2203
Type of Facility: Concert Hall
Type of Stage: Proscenium
Stage Dimensions: 54'W   **Orchestra Pit**
Seating Capacity: 2,171
Year Built: 1975
Contact for Rental: Ronald Evans;   (205) 553-1953
Resident Groups: Huntsville Symphony

VON BRAUN CIVIC CENTER - EXHIBIT HALL
700 Monroe Street SW, Huntsville, AL 35801
(205) 533-1953
FAX: (205) 551-2203
Founded: 1975
Type of Facility: Exhibition Hall

Type of Stage: Flexible; Platform
Seating Capacity: 2,000
Year Built: 1975
Contact for Rental: Ronald Evans;   (205) 553-1953
Seats 2,000 banquet-style

VON BRAUN CIVIC CENTER - PLAYHOUSE
700 Monroe Street SW, Huntsville, AL 35801
(205) 533-1953
FAX: (205) 551-2203
Type of Facility: Theatre House
Type of Stage: Thrust; Flexible; Proscenium
Stage Dimensions: 32'W
Seating Capacity: 502, 348, 232
Year Built: 1975
Contact for Rental: Ronald Evans;   (205) 553-1953
Resident Groups: Huntsville Little Theater; Fantasy Playhouse; Twinchenham Repertory Company; University Players; Tennessee Opera Association; Huntsville Literary Association

---

Mobile

VOCAL MUSIC

MOBILE OPERA
PO Box 8366, Mobile, AL 36689
(205) 460-2900
Founded: 1946
Arts Area: Grand Opera
Status: Non-Profit
Type: Performing; Touring; Educational
Purpose: To educate youth and culturally enrich the metropolitan community
Management: Pelham G. Pearce, Jr., General Manager; Ted Taylor, Music Director
Officers: J.B. Horst, President; Wade B. Perry, Vice President
Paid Staff: 5   **Volunteer Staff:** 40
Paid Artists: 20
Utilizes: Special Technical Talent; Guest Artists; Guest Directors
Budget: $100,000 - $500,000
Income Sources: Private Foundations/Grants/Endowments; Business/Corporate Donations; Box Office; Government Grants; Individual Donations
Season: October - March
Annual Attendance: 15,000
Affiliations: OA
Performance Facilities: Mobile Civic Center Theatre

THEATRE

MOBILE THEATRE GUILD
PO Box 1265, Mobile, AL 36633
(205) 433-7513
Founded: 1950
Arts Area: Community; Theatrical Group
Status: Non-Professional
Type: Performing; Educational
Purpose: Community theater specializing in off-Broadway shows
Management: Michael McKee, Director
Officers: Reenie Aldes, President; Barbara Baughman, Vice President/Treasurer; Anne Scott, Secretary
Paid Staff: 1
Budget: $50,000 - $100,000
Income Sources: Private Foundations/Grants/Endowments; Business/Corporate Donations; Box Office; Government Grants; Individual Donations
Season: August - May   **Annual Attendance:** 3,500
Affiliations: FACT

FACILITY

MOBILE CIVIC CENTER
Civic Center Drive, Mobile, AL 36602
(205) 434-7261
FAX: (205) 434-7551
Type of Facility: Civic Center
Year Built: 1964   **Architect:** Slater & Slater   **Cost:** $12,000,000
Contact for Rental: Rick Linio;   (205) 434-7261
Resident Groups: Greater Symphonic Concerts of Mobile; Mobile Municipal Theatre Performing Arts Series;
Mobile Symphonic Pops Orchestra; Mobile Opera; Mobile Ballet
Complex contains the Arena, Exposition Hall and Theatre. See separate listings for additional information.

MOBILE CIVIC CENTER - ARENA
401 Civic Center Drive, Mobile, AL 36602
(205) 434-7261
FAX: (205) 434-7551
Type of Facility: Arena
Type of Stage: Proscenium
Stage Dimensions: 88'Wx40'D
Seating Capacity: 10,680
Year Built: 1964
Contact for Rental: Rick Linio;   (205) 434-7261

MOBILE CIVIC CENTER - EXPOSITION HALL
401 Civic Center Drive, Mobile, AL 33602
(205) 434-7261
FAX: (205) 434-7551
Type of Facility: Exhibition Hall
Type of Stage: Flexible
Year Built: 1964
Contact for Rental: Rick Linio;   (205) 434-7261
Exposition Hall contains 30,000 square feet

MOBILE CIVIC CENTER - THEATRE
410 Civic Center Drive, Mobile, AL 33602
(205) 434-7261
FAX: (205) 435-7551
Type of Facility: Concert Hall; Theatre House
Type of Stage: Proscenium
Stage Dimensions: 42'Wx51'D   **Orchestra Pit**
Seating Capacity: 1,950
Year Built: 1964
Contact for Rental: Rick Linio;   (205) 434-7261

MOBILE THEATRE GUILD
14 North Lafayette Street, Mobile, AL 36607
(205) 433-7513
Type of Facility: Theatre House
Type of Stage: Thrust; Proscenium
Stage Dimensions: 10'x30'x50'
Seating Capacity: 150
Year Built: 1955
Contact for Rental: Mike McKee;   (205) 471-1795

Montgomery

DANCE

MONTGOMERY BALLET
4050 Troy Highway, Montgomery, AL 36116
(205) 288-3110
Founded: 1960
Arts Area: Ballet
Status: Semi-Professional; Non-Profit
Type: Performing; Educational
Purpose: To foster quality ballet in the community, state and region

Management: Don Steffy, Artistic Director; Marylou Hume, Associate Director
Officers: David Kahn, President; Dottye Hannan, President Elect
Paid Staff: 37
Paid Artists: 5
Utilizes: Guest Artists
Budget: $100,000 - $500,000
Income Sources: Private Foundations/Grants/Endowments; Box Office; Government Grants; Individual Donations
Season: 52 Weeks
Affiliations: SERBA
Performance Facilities: Davis Theatre; Alabama Shakespeare Festival; Carolyn Blount Theatre

INSTRUMENTAL MUSIC

MONTGOMERY SYMPHONY ORCHESTRA
220 North Hull Street, Montgomery, AL 36104
(205) 262-5182
Founded: 1976
Arts Area: Symphony; Orchestra
Status: Semi-Professional
Type: Performing; Educational
Purpose: To provide a symphony orchestra in the capital city
Management: Thomas Hinds, Musical Director/Conductor
Officers: Phil Murkett, President, Montgomery Symphony Association
Paid Staff: 2   **Volunteer Staff:** 3
Utilizes: Guest Artists
Budget: $100,000 - $500,000
Income Sources: Private Foundations/Grants/Endowments; Business/Corporate Donations; Box Office;
Individual Donations
Season: October - June   **Annual Attendance:** 15,000
Affiliations: ASOL
Performance Facilities: Daves Theater

PERFORMING SERIES

ALABAMA SHAKESPEARE FESTIVAL
One Festival Drive, Montgomery, AL 36117
(205) 272-1640
Arts Area: Dance; Vocal Music; Instrumental Music; Theater; Festivals
Status: Professional; Non-Profit
Type: Performing; Touring; Resident; Educational; Sponsoring
Purpose: To present the classics as a living and exciting part of our dramatic literature; through the classics, we put a
mirror up to other distant times and, by doing so, shed light on our times and the problems of our lives in the
twentieth century
Management: E. Timothy Langan, Managing Director; Kent Thompson, Artistic Director
Paid Staff: 200
Paid Artists: 47
Utilizes: Special Technical Talent; Guest Artists; Guest Directors
Budget: $1,000,000 - $5,000,000
Income Sources: Private Foundations/Grants/Endowments; Business/Corporate Donations; Box Office; Government
Grants; Individual Donations
Season: 52 Weeks   **Annual Attendance:** 130,000
Performance Facilities: Alabama Shakespeare Festival

FACILITY

ALABAMA SHAKESPEARE FESTIVAL
One Festival Drive, Montgomery, AL 36117
(205) 272-1640
FAX: (205) 271-5348
Type of Facility: Performance Center
Year Built: 1985   **Architect:** Tom Blount   **Cost:** $21,500,000
Acoustical Consultant: ARTEC
Contact for Rental: Beau Williams, General Manager;   (205) 271-5300
Resident Groups: Alabama Shakespeare Festival

ALABAMA SHAKESPEARE FESTIVAL - FESTIVAL STAGE
One Festival Drive, Montgomery, AL 36117
(205) 272-1640
FAX: (205) 271-5348
   Type of Facility: Theatre House
   Type of Stage: Proscenium; Modified Thrust
   Stage Dimensions: 95'7"Wx69'1"D; 60'3"Wx33'3"H proscenium opening   **Orchestra Pit**
   Seating Capacity: 750
   Year Built: 1985
   Contact for Rental: Beau Williams;   (205) 271-5300
   Resident Groups: Alabama Shakespeare Festival

ALABAMA SHAKESPEARE FESTIVAL - OCTAGON
One Festival Drive, Montgomery, AL 36117
(205) 272-1640
FAX: (205) 271-5348
   Type of Facility: Black Box
   Type of Stage: Flexible; Octagonal
   Stage Dimensions: 22'7"N, 28'3"NE, 22'7"E, 28'3"SE, 22'7"S, 28'3"SW, 22'7"W, 28'3"NW
   Seating Capacity: 225
   Year Built: 1985
   Contact for Rental: Beau Williams, General Manager;   (205) 271-5300
   Manager: Beau Williams;   (205) 271-5300
   Resident Groups: Alabama Shakespeare Festival
   Stage dimensions are interior wall lengths of the octagonal space referenced by compass point directions

Tuscaloosa

THEATRE

NEW PLAYWRIGHTS' PROGRAM - UNIVERSITY OF ALABAMA
PO Box 870239, Tuscaloosa, AL 35487
(205) 348-9032
   Founded: 1982
   Arts Area: Theatrical Group
   Status: Professional; Non-Profit
   Type: Touring; Resident; Educational
   Purpose: To develop new plays for production and workshops
   Management: Dr. Paul Castagno, Director
   Officers: Dr. Ed Williams, Department Chair
   Paid Staff: 2
   Paid Artists: 11
   Utilizes: Guest Artists; Guest Directors; Playwrights
   Budget: $50,000 - $100,000
   Income Sources: Private Foundations/Grants/Endowments; Box Office
   Season: August - April
   Affiliations: SETC; ATHE; NAST; LMDA; Dramatist Guild

FACILITY

BAMA THEATRE PERFORMING ARTS CENTER
600 Greensboro Avenue, Tuscaloosa, AL 35401
(205) 758-5195
   Type of Facility: Concert Hall; Theatre House; Opera House
   Facility Originally: Vaudeville; Movie House
   Type of Stage: Modified Apron Proscenium
   Stage Dimensions: 48'Wx30'D; 32'10"Wx24'H proscenium opening
   Seating Capacity: 1,100
   Year Built: 1938   **Architect:** WPA   **Cost:** $150,000
   Year Remodeled: 1985   **Architect:** Fitts & White Architects   **Cost:** $450,000
   Contact for Rental: Gail Skidmore or Danny Smalley;   (205) 758-5195
   Manager: Danny Smalley;   (205) 758-8083
   Resident Groups: Theatre Tuscaloosa; Punch & Judy Players; Tuscaloosa Children's Theatre; Tuscaloosa Community
   Dancers; Tuscaloosa Civic Chorus; Tuscaloosa Chapter, SPEBSQSA
   The Center is a National Historic Landmark. Renovation began in 1976 and was completed in 1985.

UNIVERSITY OF ALABAMA - CONCERT HALL
Frank Moody Music Building, PO Box 2876, Tuscaloosa, AL 35487-2876
(205) 348-7110
    Type of Facility: Concert Hall
    Type of Stage: Concert Stage
    Stage Dimensions: 36'x56'x54'   **Orchestra Pit**
    Seating Capacity: 1000
    Year Built: 1987   **Architect:** Woolen, Molzan & Partners and Fitts & White, Associated Architects   **Cost:** $2,000,000
    Acoustical Consultant: R. Lawrence Kirkegaard & Associates
    Contact for Rental: John Martin;   (205) 348-1471
    Resident Groups: School of Music Ensembles and University Symphony

UNIVERSITY OF ALABAMA - GALLAWAY THEATRE
Department of Theatre and Dance, PO Box 870239, Tuscaloosa, AL 35487-0239
(205) 348-5283
    Type of Facility: Theatre House
    Type of Stage: Proscenium
    Stage Dimensions: 30'Wx30'D; 30'Wx18'D proscenium opening   **Orchestra Pit**
    Seating Capacity: 338
    Year Built: 1956   **Architect:** Van Keuren, Davis & Company   **Cost:** $750,000
    Resident Groups: University Theatre; Dance Alabama

UNIVERSITY OF ALABAMA - HUEY RECITAL HALL
Frank Moody Music Building, PO Box 2876, Tuscaloosa, AL 35487-2876
(205) 348-7110
    Type of Facility: Recital Hall
    Type of Stage: Concert Stage
    Stage Dimensions: 15'x24'x26'
    Seating Capacity: 140
    Year Built: 1987   **Architect:** Woolen, Molzan & Partners and Fitts & White, Associated Architects
    Cost: $360,000
    Acoustical Consultant: R. Lawrence Kirkegaard & Associates
    Contact for Rental: John Martin;   (205) 348-1471
    Resident Groups: Student Recitals

UNIVERSITY OF ALABAMA - MORGAN AUDITORIUM
Department of Theater and Dance, PO Box 870239, Tuscaloosa, AL 35487
(205) 348-5283
    Type of Facility: Auditorium
    Type of Stage: Proscenium
    Stage Dimensions: 30'x29'x50'   **Orchestra Pit**
    Seating Capacity: 716
    Year Built: 1911
    Year Remodeled: 1976   **Cost:** $35,000
    Manager: Edie Barnes, Director
    Resident Groups: Dance Alabama

Tuscumbia

THEATRE

IVY GREEN THEATER
300 West North Commons, Tuscumbia, AL 35674
(205) 383-4066
    Founded: 1961
    Arts Area: Theatrical Group
    Status: Non-Profit
    Type: Performing; Sponsoring
    Purpose: To sponsor an outdoor production of William Gibson's "The Miracle Worker" at the birthplace of Helen Keller in Tuscumbia each summer
    Management: Sue Pilkilton, Manager
    Officers: Rea Mills, Chairman; Lurline Cook, Treasurer
    Paid Staff: 4   **Volunteer Staff:** 36
    Non-Paid Artists: 14
    Utilizes: Guest Directors
    Budget: $1,000 - $50,000
    Income Sources: Box Office
    Season: Mid-June - July   **Annual Attendance:** 5,350

ALASKA

Anchorage

DANCE

ANCHORAGE CONCERT ASSOCIATION INC.
524 West Fourth Avenue, Suite 208, Anchorage, AK 99501
(907) 272-1471
FAX: (907) 272-2519
Arts Area: Modern; Mime; Ballet; Jazz; Ethnic; Folk; Classical
Status: Non-Profit
Type: Presenting
Purpose: To be Alaska's premiere presenter of the arts
Management: Ira Perman, Executive Director
Officers: Tom Gallagher, President of the Board
Budget: $1,000,000 - $5,000,000
Income Sources: Private Foundations/Grants/Endowments; Business/Corporate Donations; Box Office; Government Grants; Individual Donations
Season: 52 Weeks
Performance Facilities: Anchorage Center for Performing Arts

ANCHORAGE FOLK DANCE CONSORTIUM
c/o Shirley Hauck, 2440 East Tudor Road, #342, Anchorage, AK 99507
(907) 345-2699
Founded: 1975
Arts Area: Folk
Status: Non-Professional; Non-Profit
Type: Performing; Educational
Purpose: To teach, perform and promote interest in folk dance, especially dances of Eastern Europe and the Balkans
Management: Shirley Hauck, Ph.D, Teacher and Choreographer
Officers: Barbara Meyer, President; Ahmad Amer, Treasurer; Chris Maack, Member-at-Large
Volunteer Staff: 10
Non-Paid Artists: 10
Budget: $1,000 - $50,000
Income Sources: Private Foundations/Grants/Endowments; Government Grants; Individual Donations
Season: 52 Weeks   **Annual Attendance:** 1,000

BALLET ALASKA
3605 Arctic Boulevard, Suite 267, Anchorage, AK 99503
(907) 346-3200
Founded: 1960
Arts Area: Ballet
Status: Non-Profit
Type: Performing; Educational
Purpose: To bring quality dance to all Alaskans and to provide any Alaskan the opportunity to partake of dance
Management: Lynda Lorimer, Founding Artistic Director; Kathy Fernandez, Executive Director; Earl Sterling, Technical Director
Officers: Karl Thoennes, President
Paid Staff: 5   **Volunteer Staff:** 40
Utilizes: Guest Artists; Guest Directors; Guest Choreographers
Budget: $50,000 - $100,000
Income Sources: Private Foundations/Grants/Endowments; Business/Corporate Donations; Box Office; Government Grants; Individual Donations
Season: September - June   **Annual Attendance:** 7,000
Performance Facilities: Alaska Center for the Arts

INSTRUMENTAL MUSIC

ANCHORAGE SYMPHONY ORCHESTRA
524 West Fourth Avenue, Suite 205, Anchorage, AK 99501
(907) 274-8668
FAX: (907) 272-2519
Founded: 1946
Arts Area: Symphony; Orchestra; Chamber; Ensemble
Status: Non-Profit
Type: Performing; Educational

Purpose: To contribute to the quality of life by providing high-caliber orchestral music for an expanding audience
Management: Sherri Reddick, Executive Director; Stephen Stein, Music Director/Conductor; Wendy Long, Administrative Assistant
Paid Staff: 3   **Volunteer Staff:** 215
Paid Artists: 75
Utilizes: Guest Conductors; Guest Artists
Budget: $100,000 - $500,000
Income Sources: Business/Corporate Donations; Box Office; Government Grants; Individual Donations
Season: October - May   **Annual Attendance:** 15,000
Affiliations: ASOL
Performance Facilities: Anchorage Community College Performing Arts Center

ANCHORAGE YOUTH SYMPHONY
PO Box 240541, Anchorage, AK 99524-0541
(907) 243-1207
Founded: 1965
Arts Area: Symphony; Orchestra
Status: Non-Professional; Non-Profit
Type: Performing; Touring; Educational
Purpose: To rehearse and perform symphonic music of the masters; to tour
Management: Linn Weeda, Music Director/Conductor
Officers: Alan Persons, President
Paid Staff: 1   **Volunteer Staff:** 250
Non-Paid Artists: 210
Utilizes: Guest Artists
Budget: $50,000 - $100,000
Income Sources: Private Foundations/Grants/Endowments; Business/Corporate Donations; Box Office; Individual Donations; Fund-raising
Season: September - May   **Annual Attendance:** 4,000
Affiliations: ASOL (Youth Orchestra Division)
Performance Facilities: West High Auditorium

VOCAL MUSIC

ALASKA LIGHT OPERA THEATRE
639 West International Airport Road, #34, Anchorage, AK 99502
(907) 345-2568
FAX: (907) 561-7515
Founded: 1984
Arts Area: Light Opera
Status: Professional; Non-Profit
Type: Performing; Resident; Educational
Purpose: To produce professional-quality musical theatre; to produce musical-theatre education programs for Alaska school children; to provide professional development to aspiring Alaskan musical-theatre performers through the Resident Artists Program
Management: Gloria Marinacci Allen, General Director; Judy O'Neal, Administrative Assistant
Officers: James Feeney, President; Duane Heyman, Vice President; Frank Danner, Treasurer; Jacquie Turpin, Secretary
Paid Staff: 2   **Volunteer Staff:** 100
Paid Artists: 150
Utilizes: Special Technical Talent; Guest Conductors; Guest Artists; Guest Directors
Budget: $500,000 - $1,000,000
Income Sources: Private Foundations/Grants/Endowments; Business/Corporate Donations; Box Office; Government Grants; Individual Donations
Season: July - September   **Annual Attendance:** 12,000
Performance Facilities: Fourth Avenue Theatre

ANCHORAGE CONCERT CHORUS
PO Box 103738, Anchorage, AK 99510-3738
(907) 274-7464; (907) 561-8000
FAX: (907) 563-5980
Founded: 1947
Arts Area: Choral
Status: Non-Profit
Type: Performing
Purpose: To provide the community with the opportunity to participate in the performance of quality music
Officers: John Brower, President of the Board
Paid Staff: 3
Non-Paid Artists: 160
Utilizes: Guest Conductors

Budget: $50,000 - $100,000
Income Sources: Private Foundations/Grants/Endowments; Business/Corporate Donations; Box Office; Government Grants; Individual Donations
Season: September - April   **Annual Attendance:** 4,000
Affiliations: Anchorage Community College
Performance Facilities: Alaska Center for the Performing Arts

ANCHORAGE OPERA COMPANY
1507 Spar Avenue, Anchorage, AK 99501
(907) 270-2557
FAX: (907) 279-7798
Founded: 1976
Arts Area: Grand Opera; Lyric Opera; Light Opera; Operetta
Status: Professional; Non-Profit
Type: Performing; Resident; Educational
Purpose: To produce professional opera
Management: Margaret Wood, General Manager; Ian D. Hoak, Business Manager; H.E. Hollibaugh, Technical Director; Lisa D. Lind, Administrative Assistant
Officers: Michael F.G. Williams, President
Paid Staff: 4
Paid Artists: 325
Utilizes: Guest Conductors; Guest Artists; Guest Directors
Budget: $500,000 - $1,000,000
Income Sources: Private Foundations/Grants/Endowments; Business/Corporate Donations; Box Office; Government Grants; Individual Donations
Season: September - March; April   **Annual Attendance:** 8,000
Affiliations: OA
Performance Facilities: Discovery Theatre; Alaska Center for the Performing Arts

THEATRE

OUT NORTH THEATRE COMPANY
PO Box 100140, Anchorage, AK 99510
(907) 279-8099
Founded: 1985
Arts Area: Theatrical Group
Status: Semi-Professional
Type: Performing; Educational
Purpose: To be an alternative theatre company producing small-scale productions of contemporary plays and new interpretations of classics
Management: Jay Brause, Managing Director; Gene Dugan, Artistic Director
Paid Staff: 2
Paid Artists: 40
Budget: $100,000 - $500,000
Income Sources: Private Foundations/Grants/Endowments; Business/Corporate Donations; Box Office; Government Grants; Individual Donations; Special Events; Gaming Permit
Season: September - May
Annual Attendance: 5,000
Affiliations: League of Fringe Theatres

PERFORMING SERIES

ANCHORAGE FESTIVAL OF MUSIC
524 West Fourth Avenue, PO Box 10325, Suite 204A, Anchorage, AK 99501
(907) 276-2465
Founded: 1976
Arts Area: Vocal Music; Instrumental Music; Festivals
Status: Professional; Non-Profit
Type: Performing
Purpose: To engage in educational, musical and charitable activities; to plan, coordinate, promote and develop cultural activities in the Anchorage area
Management: David Hagen, General Director
Paid Staff: 1   **Volunteer Staff:** 30
Paid Artists: 50   **Non-Paid Artists:** 30
Utilizes: Guest Conductors; Guest Artists
Budget: $100,000 - $500,000
Income Sources: Private Foundations/Grants/Endowments; Business/Corporate Donations; Box Office; Government Grants; Individual Donations
Season: June - July   **Annual Attendance:** 2,000

SITKA SUMMER MUSIC FESTIVAL
PO Box 201988, Anchorage, AK 99520
(907) 747-6774
>**Founded:** 1972
>**Arts Area:** Instrumental Music; Festivals
>**Status:** Professional; Non-Profit
>**Type:** Performing; Touring
>**Purpose:** To present professional chamber music throughout the state of Alaska
>**Management:** Paul Rosenthal, Music Director; Wendy Kamrass, Administrative Director
>**Officers:** Thad Paulson, President; Charles Bovee, Vice President; Trish White, Secretary; Lowell Tornquist, Treasurer
>**Paid Staff:** 3
>**Paid Artists:** 12   **Non-Paid Artists:** 20
>**Utilizes:** Guest Artists
>**Budget:** $100,000 - $500,000
>**Income Sources:** Private Foundations/Grants/Endowments; Business/Corporate Donations; Box Office; Government Grants; Individual Donations
>**Season:** June, September, February
>**Annual Attendance:** 7,000
>**Affiliations:** CMA
>**Performance Facilities:** Centennial Building; Grant Hall Auditorium

FACILITY

ALASKA CENTER FOR THE PERFORMING ARTS
621 West Sixth Avenue, Anchorage, AK 99501
(907) 263-2900
FAX: (907) 263-2927
>**Founded:** 1988
>**Type of Facility:** Theatre Complex; Concert Hall; Auditorium; Performance Center; Theatre House
>**Type of Stage:** Proscenium
>**Stage Dimensions:** Three theatres: two at 50'x90'; one at 28'x90'
>**Orchestra Pit**
>**Seating Capacity:** 2,000; 702; 350
>**Year Built:** 1988   **Architect:** Hardy, Holzman and Pfeiffer Associates   **Cost:** $70,000,000
>**Acoustical Consultant:** Jaffe
>**Contact for Rental:** Mark Seward;   (907) 263-2918
>**Resident Groups:** Anchorage Concert Association; Anchorage Opera; Anchorage Symphony Orchestra; Anchorage Festival of Music; Alaska Junior Theatre; Alaska Stage Company; Anchorage Community Chorus

WILLIAM A. EGAN CIVIC AND CONVENTION CENTER
555 West Fifth Avenue, Anchorage, AK 99501
(907) 263-2800
>**Type of Facility:** Civic Center
>**Year Built:** 1984   **Cost:** $27,000,000
>**Contact for Rental:**   (907) 263-2800
>*Contains Explorers Hall and Summit Hall. See separate listings for additional information.*

WILLIAM A. EGAN CIVIC AND CONVENTION CENTER - EXPLORERS HALL
555 West Fifth Avenue, Anchorage, AK 99501
(907) 263-2800
>**Type of Facility:** Concert Hall; Auditorium
>**Type of Stage:** Flexible; Platform
>**Seating Capacity:** 2,400
>**Year Built:** 1984
>**Contact for Rental:**   (907) 263-2800

WILLIAM A. EGAN CIVIC AND CONVENTION CENTER - SUMMIT HALL
555 West Fifth Avenue, Anchorage, AK 99501
(907) 263-2800
>**Type of Facility:** Concert Hall; Auditorium
>**Type of Stage:** Flexible; Platform
>**Seating Capacity:** 1,100
>**Year Built:** 1984
>**Contact for Rental:**   (907) 263-2800

Douglas

DANCE

JUNEAU FOLK ENSEMBLE
PO Box 241031, Douglas, AK 99824
(907) 364-2334
>**Founded:** 1980
>**Arts Area:** Ethnic; Folk
>**Status:** Non-Professional; Non-Profit
>**Type:** Performing; Touring; Sponsoring
>**Purpose:** To bring folk dance and related arts to the people of the region (Alaska and the Yukon)
>**Management:** Judy Jones, Artistic Director; Bruce Botelho, Business Manager
>**Volunteer Staff:** 5
>**Non-Paid Artists:** 45
>**Utilizes:** Guest Artists; Guest Directors
>**Budget:** $1,000 - $50,000
>**Income Sources:** Private Foundations/Grants/Endowments; Business/Corporate Donations; Box Office; Government Grants; Individual Donations
>**Season:** 52 Weeks   **Annual Attendance:** 5,000

THEATRE

PERSEVERANCE THEATRE
914 Third Street, Douglas, AK 99824
(907) 364-2421
>**Founded:** 1979
>**Arts Area:** Professional; Theatrical Group
>**Status:** Professional; Non-Profit
>**Type:** Performing; Touring; Resident; Educational
>**Purpose:** To produce quality professional theatre which is by, for and about Alaskans; to train and develop Alaskan actors, directors, designers and playwrights
>**Management:** Molly D. Smith, Artistic Director; Lynette Turner, Producing Director; Vikki Benner, Luan Schooler, Art Rotch, Artistic Team; Rahz Brown, Community Exchange Coordinator; Kate Bowns,Company Manager; Tom Linklater, Outreach Coordinator; Jamie McLean, Training Director; Merry Ellefson, Development Director; Toby Clark, Producing Manager; Nancy Schaufelberger, Office Manager
>**Officers:** Molly D. Smith, Board President
>**Paid Staff:** 12   **Volunteer Staff:** 300
>**Paid Artists:** 277   **Non-Paid Artists:** 279
>**Utilizes:** Guest Artists; Guest Directors
>**Budget:** $1,000,000 - $5,000,000
>**Income Sources:** Private Foundations/Grants/Endowments; Business/Corporate Donations; Box Office; Government Grants; Individual Donations
>**Season:** 52 Weeks   **Annual Attendance:** 19,000
>**Affiliations:** TCG; AAA; WAAA; Alaska Alliance on the Arts
>**Performance Facilities:** Mainstage; Voices Stage; Phoenix Stage

---
Fairbanks

DANCE

NORTH STAR DANCE FOUNDATION
PO Box 73486, Fairbanks, AK 99707
(907) 451-8800
>**Founded:** 1984
>**Arts Area:** Ballet
>**Status:** Non-Professional; Non-Profit
>**Type:** Performing; Touring; Resident; Educational
>**Purpose:** To promote the art of dance in Alaska through education and performance
>**Management:** Norman Shelburne, Artistic Director; Iris Lindsey, Administrative Director
>**Officers:** Paul Kennedy, Board President; Bruce Gordon, Vice President; Freddie Black, Secretary
>**Paid Staff:** 3   **Volunteer Staff:** 4
>**Non-Paid Artists:** 26
>**Utilizes:** Special Technical Talent; Guest Artists; Guest Choreographers; Guest Composers
>**Budget:** $100,000 - $500,000
>**Income Sources:** Private Foundations/Grants/Endowments; Business/Corporate Donations; Box Office; Government Grants; Individual Donations

Season: September - May **Annual Attendance:** 7,000
Performance Facilities: Hering Auditorium

INSTRUMENTAL MUSIC

FAIRBANKS SYMPHONY ASSOCIATION
PO Box 82104, Fairbanks, AK 99708
(907) 479-3407
FAX: (907) 474-6420
Founded: 1969
Arts Area: Symphony; Orchestra; Chamber
Status: Non-Profit
Type: Performing; Touring; Resident; Educational; Sponsoring
Purpose: To support an active and vital symphony orchestra; to promote instrumental music in the schools, a youth orchestra program, orchestra village tours and other related events
Management: Jane Aspnes, General Manager; Dr. Madeline Schatz, Musical Director
Officers: Dietrich Strohmaier, President; Charlotte Barker, Vice President; Ed Peebles, Secretary; Bruce Foote, Treasurer
Paid Staff: 4
Paid Artists: 6
Utilizes: Guest Conductors; Guest Artists
Budget: $100,000 - $500,000
Income Sources: Private Foundations/Grants/Endowments; Business/Corporate Donations; Box Office; Government Grants; Individual Donations
Season: September - May **Annual Attendance:** 12,000
Affiliations: ASOL; Alaska Alliance on the Arts
Performance Facilities: Charles W. Davis Concert Hall

RED HACKLE PIPE BAND
PO Box 82782, Fairbanks, AK 99708-2782
(907) 479-5826
Founded: 1974
Arts Area: Ethnic; Band
Status: Non-Profit
Type: Performing; Educational
Purpose: To offer Scottish music (bagpipe) and Highland dance performances and instruction
Management: Bob White, Pipe Master; Dennis Stephens, Assistant Pipe Master; Arthur L. Robson, Lead Drummer
Officers: John Myers, President; Jennifer Johnston, Vice President; Sandra E. White, Secretary/Treasurer
Volunteer Staff: 30
Non-Paid Artists: 20
Utilizes: Guest Artists
Budget: $1,000 - $50,000
Income Sources: Private Foundations/Grants/Endowments; Business/Corporate Donations; Box Office; Government Grants; Individual Donations
Season: 52 Weeks

VOCAL MUSIC

FAIRBANKS CHORAL SOCIETY, CHILDREN'S CHOIR AND CHORUS!
University of Alaska-Fairbanks, PO Box 900174, Fairbanks, AK 99775
(907) 456-1144
FAX: (907) 456-7464
Founded: 1984
Arts Area: Choral
Status: Non-Professional; Non-Profit
Type: Performing; Educational; Sponsoring
Purpose: To sponsor the Fairbanks Children's Choir, CHORUS! and Sing-It-Yourself Messiah
Management: Dr. Suzanne Summerville, Music Director
Officers: Dr. Carol Diehl, President
Paid Staff: 6
Utilizes: Special Technical Talent; Guest Conductors; Guest Artists; Guest Directors
Income Sources: Private Foundations/Grants/Endowments; Business/Corporate Donations; Box Office; Government Grants; Individual Donations
Season: September - April **Annual Attendance:** 3,000
Performance Facilities: University of Alaska-Fairbanks Concert Hall; Alaskaland

FAIRBANKS LIGHT OPERA THEATRE
PO Box 72787, Fairbanks, AK 99707
(907) 456-3568
Founded: 1969
Arts Area: Light Opera
Status: Non-Professional; Non-Profit
Type: Performing; Touring
Purpose: To bring light opera and musical theatre to our community
Officers: Rusty Gieson, President; Diane Egley, Vice President; Theresa Reed, Vice President; Dot Moravec, Treasurer; Helen Burrell, Corresponding Secretary; Francis Gloria, Recording Secretary
Paid Staff: 1   **Volunteer Staff:** 350
Budget: $100,000 - $500,000
Income Sources: Box Office; Government Grants; Individual Donations
Season: September - March   **Annual Attendance:** 10,000
Performance Facilities: Hering Auditorium; Alaskaland Civic Center

PERFORMING SERIES

FAIRBANKS SUMMER ARTS FESTIVAL
PO Box 80845, Fairbanks, AK 99708
(907) 479-6778
FAX: (907) 479-4329
Founded: 1980
Arts Area: Dance; Vocal Music; Instrumental Music; Theater; Festivals; Grand Opera; Ice Skating; Visual Art
Status: Professional; Semi-Professional; Non-Professional; Non-Profit
Type: Performing; Educational
Purpose: To present a study/performance festival with 56 prestigious guest artists in residence for two weeks
Management: Jo Ryman Scott, Producing Director/Founder; Fred Buda, Artistic Director; Myron Romanul, Music Director
Officers: Jo Scott, Chair; Dick Scott, Vice Chair; Diane Egley, Secretary; Dave Stephenson, Treasurer; Randy Clapp, Jean Mackin, Jo Scotts Center for the Cultural Development, Inc.
Volunteer Staff: 70
Paid Artists: 58
Utilizes: Special Technical Talent; Guest Conductors; Guest Artists; Guest Directors
Budget: $100,000 - $500,000
Income Sources: Business/Corporate Donations; Box Office; Government Grants; Individual Donations; Fundraisers; Registration Fees
Season: July - August   **Annual Attendance:** 12,000
Performance Facilities: University of Alaska at Fairbanks

FACILITY

ALASKALAND CIVIC CENTER
Airport Way and Peger Road, Fairbanks, AK 99701
(907) 452-4244
Type of Facility: Concert Hall; Theatre House; Civic Center; Multi-Purpose; Art Gallery
Type of Stage: Proscenium
Stage Dimensions: 20'x30'x29'   **Orchestra Pit**
Seating Capacity: 354 Fixed, 384 Maximum
Year Built: 1967   **Architect:** Don Stetson   **Cost:** $250,000
Year Remodeled: 1981   **Architect:** Ellerbe
Contact for Rental: Bob Peterson
Resident Groups: Fairbanks Arts Association; Fairbanks Drama Association

UNIVERSITY OF ALASKA - CHARLES W. DAVIS CONCERT HALL
University of Alaska, Fairbanks, AK 99775-1220
(907) 474-7555
Type of Facility: Concert Hall
Type of Stage: Proscenium
Seating Capacity: 1957
Year Built: 1972   **Architect:** Gray, Rogers, Morgan
Acoustical Consultant: Bolt, Beranek & Newman
Contact for Rental: Music Department;   (907) 474-7555
Manager: University of Alaska Music Department

Haines

THEATRE

LYNN CANAL COMMUNITY PLAYERS
PO Box 75, Haines, AK 99827
(907) 766-2425
Founded: 1957
Arts Area: Musical; Community
Status: Non-Professional
Type: Performing
Purpose: To perform in and sponsor all types of theatre; to host the Alaska Community Theatre Festival's biennial, a state-wide drama festival held the spring of odd-numbered years
Officers: Mimi G. Gregg, President; Gail L. Gregg, Vice President; Joanna Egolf, Secretary; Raymond R. Menaker, Treasurer
Utilizes: Special Technical Talent; Guest Artists; Guest Directors
Budget: $1,000 - $50,000
Income Sources: Box Office; Individual Donations
Season: 52 Weeks
Annual Attendance: 1,500
Affiliations: Arts Southeast
Performance Facilities: Chilkat Center for the Arts

PERFORMING SERIES

HAINES ARTS COUNCIL
PO Box 505, Haines, AK 99827
(907) 766-2791
Founded: 1983
Arts Area: Dance; Vocal Music; Instrumental Music; Theater; Festivals; Lyric Opera
Status: Non-Professional; Non-Profit
Type: Performing; Touring; Resident; Educational; Sponsoring
Purpose: To provide an umbrella-type organization for local performing and visual artists; to organize a concert season; to sponsor local festivals
Management: Dr. Suzanne Summerville, Music Director
Officers: John Hunt, President; Heather Lende, Vice President; Mimi Gregg, Secretary; Maisie Jones, Treasurer
Volunteer Staff: 4
Utilizes: Special Technical Talent; Guest Conductors; Guest Artists
Budget: $1,000 - $50,000
Income Sources: Private Foundations/Grants/Endowments; Business/Corporate Donations; Box Office; Government Grants; Individual Donations; Fund-raisers
Season: September - May
Annual Attendance: 2,500
Affiliations: Lynn Community Players; KHNS FM 102;
Performance Facilities: Chilkat Center for the Arts

FACILITY

CHILKAT CENTER FOR THE ARTS
Tower Road and Theatre Lane, Haines, AK 99827
(907) 766-2160, ext. 2162
FAX: (907) 766-2160
Type of Facility: Theatre Complex; Concert Hall; Auditorium; Studio Performance; Performance Center; Civic Center; Multi-Purpose; Room
Type of Stage: Thrust; Flexible; Proscenium; Platform
Stage Dimensions: 22'x36'x40'
Orchestra Pit
Seating Capacity: 300
Year Built: 1901
Year Remodeled: 1982   **Architect:** Wade Hampton   **Cost:** $1,500,000
Contact for Rental: Lee Heinmiller;   (907) 766-2160, ext. 2162
Resident Groups: Chilkat Dancers; KHNS Radio; Lynn Canal Community Players; Haines Schools; Haines Borough; Haines Chamber of Commerce

Homer

THEATRE

PIER ONE THEATRE
PO Box 894, Homer, AK 99603
(907) 235-7333
Founded: 1973
Arts Area: Musical; Dinner; Community; Theatrical Group
Status: Semi-Professional; Non-Profit
Type: Performing; Touring; Resident; Sponsoring
Purpose: To produce and promote the performing arts
Management: Lance Petersen, Artistic Director; Joan Evans, Office Manager; Barbara Petersen, Company Manager
Officers: William Bell, President; Jean McMaster, Vice President; Gwen Neal, Secretary
Paid Staff: 8   **Volunteer Staff:** 16
Paid Artists: 250   **Non-Paid Artists:** 100
Budget: $50,000 - $100,000
Income Sources: Private Foundations/Grants/Endowments; Business/Corporate Donations; Box Office; Government Grants; Individual Donations
Season: 52 Weeks   **Annual Attendance:** 6,000
Performance Facilities: Pier One Theatre; Mariner Theatre

FACILITY

PIER ONE THEATRE
PO Box 894, Homer, AK 99603
(907) 235-7333
Founded: 1973
Type of Facility: Theatre House
Facility Originally: Warehouse
Type of Stage: Flexible; Proscenium; Platform
Stage Dimensions: 36'x30'
Seating Capacity: 120
Year Built: 1955
Year Remodeled: 1986   **Cost:** $10,000
Contact for Rental: Lance Petersen;   (907) 235-7333
Live Performances

Juneau

PERFORMING SERIES

JUNEAU JAZZ AND CLASSICS
PO Box 22152, Juneau, AK 99802
(907) 364-2801
FAX: (907) 586-1938
Founded: 1987
Arts Area: Vocal Music; Instrumental Music; Festivals
Status: Professional; Non-Profit
Type: Educational; Sponsoring
Purpose: To present a music festival featuring world-class jazz and classical artists in Juneau each year
Management: Kitty Sessions, Administrator; Linda Rosenthal, Artistic Director
Paid Staff: 1   **Volunteer Staff:** 1
Paid Artists: 20
Utilizes: Guest Artists
Budget: $50,000 - $100,000
Income Sources: Private Foundations/Grants/Endowments; Business/Corporate Donations; Box Office; Government Grants; Individual Donations
Season: May   **Annual Attendance:** 3,000

FACILITY

CENTENNIAL HALL CONVENTION CENTER
101 Egan Drive, Juneau, AK 99801
(907) 586-5283
FAX: (907) 586-1135
Type of Facility: Concert Hall; Auditorium; Civic Center

Type of Stage: Flexible
Seating Capacity: 1,200
Year Built: 1983
Contact for Rental: Dayle Tennison;   (907) 586-5283

Ketchikan

DANCE

KETCHIKAN THEATRE BALLET SCHOOL
400 Mission, PO Box 6118, Ketchikan, AK 99901
(907) 225-9311
Founded: 1965
Arts Area: Ballet; Jazz
Status: Semi-Professional; Non-Profit
Type: Performing; Touring; Resident; Educational
Purpose: To encourage and promote the serious dance student striving to become a professional
Management: Board of Directors
Officers: Lynn Jorgensen, Penny Luse, Co-Presidents; Elaine Olsen, Secretary; Marcia Lapinski, Treasurer
Paid Staff: 2   **Volunteer Staff:** 4
Utilizes: Guest Artists
Budget: $1,000 - $50,000
Income Sources: Private Foundations/Grants/Endowments; Business/Corporate Donations; Box Office; Government Grants; Individual Donations
Season: September - May   **Annual Attendance:** 2,000
Performance Facilities: Ketchikan High School Auditorium

Kodiak

FACILITY

KODIAK ARTS COUNCIL
PO Box 1792, Kodiak, AK 99615
(907) 486-9251
FAX: (907) 486-6162
Founded: 1963
Type of Facility: Theatre Complex
Type of Stage: Proscenium
Stage Dimensions: 32'x40'   **Orchestra Pit**
Seating Capacity: 750
Year Built: 1985   **Architect:** Sundberg & Associates   **Cost:** $10,500,000
Acoustical Consultant: Gerald C. Wilson
Resident Groups: Kodiak Arts Council; Kodiak Community Theater

Palmer

PERFORMING SERIES

VALLEY PERFORMING ARTS
PO Box 1230, Palmer, AK 99645
(907) 745-2484
Arts Area: Theater
Status: Non-Profit
Type: Performing; Touring; Educational; Sponsoring
Purpose: To provide social and cultural enrichment to the residents of the Matanuska and Susitna Valleys by producing plays which are of the highest artistic excellence
Management: Dean Phipps, Artistic Director
Officers: Grant Olson, President; John Fairfield, Vice President; Larry Bottjen, Treasurer
Volunteer Staff: 20
Paid Artists: 5   **Non-Paid Artists:** 100
Utilizes: Guest Artists; Guest Directors
Budget: $50,000 - $100,000
Income Sources: Private Foundations/Grants/Endowments; Business/Corporate Donations; Box Office; Government Grants; Individual Donations
Season: September - May   **Annual Attendance:** 5,000
Performance Facilities: Colony Theater

Petersburg

THEATRE

MITKOF MUMMERS
PO Box 624, Petersburg, AK 99833
(907) 772-4859
   Founded: 1971
   Arts Area: Musical; Community; Theatrical Group
   Status: Non-Profit
   Type: Performing; Resident; Sponsoring
   Purpose: To provide local actors and actresses an opportunity to perform; to provide the community an opportunity to see live theatre performances
   Management: Vara Wright, Director
   Officers: Penny Baird, President; Peggie Morrison, Secretary/Treasurer; Vara Wright, Historian
   Budget: $1,000 - $50,000
   Income Sources: Box Office; Individual Donations
   Season: September - June   **Annual Attendance:** 1,000
   Affiliations: Petersburg Arts Councils; Little Norway Festival Committee
   Performance Facilities: High School Auditorium

Sitka

FACILITY

SITKA CENTENNIAL BUILDING
330 Harbor Drive, Sitka, AK 99835
(907) 747-3225
   Type of Facility: Concert Hall; Auditorium; Performance Center; Civic Center; Multi-Purpose; Room
   Type of Stage: Proscenium; Platform
   Stage Dimensions: 40'W x 20'D
   Seating Capacity: 500, Dinner 350
   Year Built: 1967   **Architect:** Allen McDonald   **Cost:** $1,295,188
   Contact for Rental: Don Kluting;   (907) 747-3225
   Resident Groups: Theatre Guild; New Archangel Dancers; Summer Music Festival; Sitka Film Society; Sheldon Jackson College Theater Department

ARIZONA

Carefree

PERFORMING SERIES

DESERT FOOTHILLS MUSIC FEST
PO Box 5254, Carefree, AZ 85377
(602) 488-0806
Founded: 1992
Arts Area: Festivals
Status: Professional; Non-Profit
Type: Performing; Educational
Purpose: To assist in making the Arizona High Desert area a major winter cultural center
Management: Paul Perry, Music Director/Conductor; Chet Goldberg, Chairman Cultural Division - Foothills Community Foundation; Ed Spack, Executive Director - Foothills Community Foundation
Paid Staff: 2 **Volunteer Staff:** 150
Paid Artists: 22
Utilizes: Guest Artists
Budget: $50,000 - $100,000
Income Sources: Private Foundations/Grants/Endowments; Business/Corporate Donations; Box Office; Individual Donations; Fund-raising
Season: January **Annual Attendance:** 1,500
Performance Facilities: Cactus Shadows Fine Arts Center

Chandler

FACILITY

CHANDLER CENTER FOR THE ARTS
250 North Arizona Avenue, Chandler, AZ 85224
(602) 786-2996
FAX: (602) 814-0442
Founded: 1989
Type of Facility: Theatre Complex
Type of Stage: Proscenium
Stage Dimensions: 60'x40' **Orchestra Pit**
Year Built: 1989
Architect: Wendell Rossman
Cost: $16,000,000
Contact for Rental: Katrina Mueller; (602) 782-3996

Decatur

PERFORMING SERIES

PRINCESS THEATRE
112 Second Avenue, Decatur, AZ 35601
(205) 350-1745
Founded: 1983
Arts Area: Dance; Vocal Music; Instrumental Music; Theater
Status: Non-Profit
Type: Performing; Educational
Purpose: To present and promote a variety of performing-arts events
Management: Lindy Ashwander, Manager
Paid Staff: 3 **Volunteer Staff:** 400
Budget: $100,000 - $500,000
Income Sources: Private Foundations/Grants/Endowments; Business/Corporate Donations; Box Office; Government Grants; Individual Donations
Season: 52 Weeks **Annual Attendance:** 50,000
Affiliations: APAP; League of Historic American Theatres
Performance Facilities: Princess Theatre

Flagstaff

INSTRUMENTAL MUSIC

FLAGSTAFF SYMPHONY ORCHESTRA
PO Box 122, Flagstaff, AZ 86002
(602) 774-5107
FAX: (602) 774-5109
> **Founded:** 1950
> **Arts Area:** Symphony; Orchestra; Chamber; Ensemble
> **Status:** Semi-Professional; Non-Profit
> **Type:** Performing; Touring; Resident; Educational; Sponsoring
> **Purpose:** To provide a wide-range of symphonic programs for people of all ages in northern Arizona
> **Management:** Harold Weller, Music Director/General Manager; Christine Dicob, Executive Secretary; Erin Murphy, Public Relations Director
> **Officers:** Rita Rose, President, Flagstaff Symphony Association
> **Paid Staff:** 8   **Volunteer Staff:** 1
> **Paid Artists:** 120
> **Utilizes:** Special Technical Talent; Guest Conductors; Guest Artists
> **Budget:** $100,000 - $500,000
> **Income Sources:** Private Foundations/Grants/Endowments; Business/Corporate Donations; Box Office; Government Grants; Individual Donations
> **Season:** 52 Weeks   **Annual Attendance:** 20,000
> **Affiliations:** ASOL; Arizona Commission on the Arts; Flagstaff Arts Council; Arizonans for Cultural Development
> **Performance Facilities:** Ardrey Memorial Auditorium, Northern Arizona University; Poco Diable Resort; Embry Riddle Aeronautical University; Yavapai College Auditorium

PERFORMING SERIES

FLAGSTAFF FESTIVAL OF THE ARTS
PO Box 1607, Flagstaff, AZ 86002
(800) 266-7740; (800) 266-7750
FAX: (602) 774-2600
> **Founded:** 1966
> **Arts Area:** Dance; Vocal Music; Instrumental Music; Theater; Festivals
> **Status:** Professional; Semi-Professional; Non-Profit
> **Type:** Performing; Educational
> **Purpose:** To present professionally-produced, culturally diverse arts programs featuring the finest local, state, national and international artists
> **Management:** Larry Reid, Managing Director; Irwin Hoffman, Orchestra Conductor; Tal Russell, Theatre Artistic Director
> **Officers:** Pat Loven, President; Jose Colchado, Vice President; Red Miles, Secretary; Earl Briggs, Treasurer
> **Paid Staff:** 2   **Volunteer Staff:** 12
> **Paid Artists:** 125
> **Utilizes:** Special Technical Talent; Guest Conductors; Guest Artists; Guest Directors
> **Budget:** $100,000 - $500,000
> **Income Sources:** Private Foundations/Grants/Endowments; Business/Corporate Donations; Box Office; Government Grants; Individual Donations; Fund-raising
> **Season:** July - August   **Annual Attendance:** 20,000
> **Affiliations:** Northern Arizona University
> **Performance Facilities:** Ardrey Auditorium; Creative Arts Theatre; Ashurst Auditorium

FACILITY

COCONINO CENTER FOR THE ARTS
2300 North Fort Valley Road, PO Box 296, Flagstaff, AZ 86002
(602) 779-6921
> **Type of Facility:** Amphitheater
> **Type of Stage:** 3/4 Arena
> **Seating Capacity:** 200
> **Year Built:** 1981
> **Contact for Rental:** Kim O'Meally;   (602) 779-6921

NORTHERN ARIZONA AUDITORIUM - ARDREY MEMORIAL AUDITORIUM
PO Box 6040, Flagstaff, AZ 86011
(602) 523-4120
> **Type of Facility:** Concert Hall; Auditorium; Performance Center; Opera House; Multi-Purpose
> **Type of Stage:** Proscenium
> **Stage Dimensions:** 54'Wx50'D; 54'Wx26'H proscenium opening   **Orchestra Pit**

Seating Capacity: 1,550
Year Built: 1974   **Architect:** T. Atkinson   **Cost:** $3,200,000
Acoustical Consultant: Vern Knudson
Contact for Rental: Jean A. Anderson;   (602) 523-4120
Resident Groups: Flagstaff Symphony; Flagstaff Festival of the Arts; Performing Arts Series

Glendale

FACILITY

GLENDALE COMMUNITY COLLEGE PERFORMING ARTS CENTER
6000 West Olive Avenue, Glendale, AZ 85302
(602) 435-3709
    Type of Facility: Theatre Complex; Concert Hall; Auditorium; Studio Performance; Performance Center; Theatre House
    Type of Stage: Proscenium
    Stage Dimensions: 58'Wx40'D   **Orchestra Pit**
    Seating Capacity: 328
    Year Built: 1977   **Architect:** Varney, Sutton & Sydnor   **Cost:** $3,000,000
    Acoustical Consultant: George Thomas Associates
    Contact for Rental: Jeff Glemba;   (602) 435-3529
    Manager: Virginia Ludders
    Resident Groups: Glendale Community College Theatre Arts and Music Departments
    Available for rent to small productions only. Please contact rental office for details concerning large productions.

Grand Canyon

INSTRUMENTAL MUSIC

GRAND CANYON CHAMBER MUSIC FESTIVAL
PO Box 1332, Grand Canyon, AZ 86023
(602) 638-9215
    Founded: 1984
    Arts Area: Chamber; Ensemble
    Status: Non-Profit
    Type: Presenting
    Purpose: To present a series of concerts in Grand Canyon National Park each September, maintaining high musical standards and diversity of programming; to commission new chamber music from American composers; to give a public service tour to schools in northern Arizona
    Management: Robert Bonfiglio, Festival Director; Clare Hoffman, Artistic Director; Beth Seely, Business Manager
    Officers: Kenneth Bacher, President of the Board; Clare Hoffman, Vice President/Secretary
    Paid Staff: 4   **Volunteer Staff:** 2
    Paid Artists: 18
    Utilizes: Guest Artists
    Budget: $100,000 - $500,000
    Income Sources: Private Foundations/Grants/Endowments; Business/Corporate Donations; Box Office; Government Grants; Individual Donations; Poster Sales
    Season: September - October   **Annual Attendance:** 3,600
    Performance Facilities: Shrine of the Ages; Grand Canyon National Park

Mesa

FACILITY

MESA COMMUNITY CENTER
201 North Center Street, Mesa, AZ 85201
(602) 644-2178
    Type of Facility: Civic Center
    Year Built: 1979   **Architect:** Taliesen West   **Cost:** $2,300,000
    Acoustical Consultant: George Thomas and Associates
    Contact for Rental: Brenda Gravatt;   (602) 644-2178

Manager: Ray Pittman
The Mesa Community Center contains Amphitheatre, Centennial Hall and Conference Center. See separate listings for additional information.

MESA COMMUNITY CENTER - AMPHITHEATRE
201 North Center Street, Mesa, AZ 85201
(602) 644-2178
FAX: (602) 644-2617
Type of Facility: Outdoor (Concert); Amphitheater
Type of Stage: Environmental
Seating Capacity: 4,200
Year Built: 1979
Contact for Rental: Brenda Gravatt;   (602) 644-2178
Manager: Ray Pittman

MESA COMMUNITY CENTER - CENTENNIAL HALL
201 North Center Street, Mesa, AZ 85201
(602) 644-2178
FAX: (602) 644-2617
Type of Facility: Concert Hall
Type of Stage: Flexible; Platform
Stage Dimensions: 24'x40'
Seating Capacity: 1,832
Year Built: 1978
Contact for Rental: Brenda Gravatt;   (602) 644-2178
Manager: Ray Pittman
Resident Groups: Mesa Symphony Orchestra

MESA COMMUNITY CENTER - CONFERENCE CENTER
201 North Center Street, Mesa, AZ 85201
(602) 644-2178
FAX: (602) 644-2617
Type of Facility: Room; Film & Lecture Hall
Type of Stage: Flexible; Platform
Seating Capacity: Conference Theater - 100; Palo Verde Ballroom - 450
Year Remodeled: 1984   **Architect:** CSA Architects   **Cost:** $2,000,000
Acoustical Consultant: George Thomas and Associates
Contact for Rental: Brenda Gravatt;   (602) 644-2178
Manager: Ray Pittman;   (602) 644-2667

Phoenix

DANCE

BALLET ARIZONA
3645 East Indian School Road, Phoenix, AZ 85018
(602) 230-1140
Founded: 1979
Arts Area: Ballet
Status: Professional; Non-Profit
Type: Performing; Touring; Resident; Educational
Purpose: To educate through entertainment by exposing audiences to professional dance
Management: Michael Uthoff, Artistic Director; Julie Dalgleish, Managing Director; Richard Wade, Business Director
Officers: Allen Rosenberg, Chairman; Sharon Ulrich, President
Paid Staff: 4   **Volunteer Staff:** 2
Paid Artists: 45   **Non-Paid Artists:** 5
Utilizes: Guest Conductors; Guest Artists; Guest Directors
Budget: $500,000 - $1,000,000
Income Sources: Private Foundations/Grants/Endowments; Business/Corporate Donations; Box Office; Government Grants; Individual Donations
Season: 52 Weeks   **Annual Attendance:** 95,000
Affiliations: Dance USA; Arts in Mesa

PHOENIX DANCE THEATRE
1528 1/2 East Clarendon, Phoenix, AZ 85014
(602) 266-7131
Founded: 1970

Arts Area: Modern; Ballet; Jazz; Ethnic
Status: Non-Profit
Type: Performing; Educational
Purpose: To entertain and educate
Management: Jean Campbell, Director/Choreographer
Volunteer Staff: 4
Paid Artists: 10   **Non-Paid Artists:** 12
Utilizes: Special Technical Talent; Guest Artists
Budget: $1,000 - $50,000
Income Sources: Individual Donations
Season: 52 Weeks
Affiliations: Royal Academy of Dancing

INSTRUMENTAL MUSIC

PHOENIX CHAMBER MUSIC SOCIETY
PO Box 34235, Phoenix, AZ 85067
(602) 266-3524
Founded: 1959
Arts Area: Chamber
Status: Non-Profit
Type: Sponsoring
Purpose: To bring the finest chamber music ensembles in the world to the Phoenix area
Management: Carol Olsen, Executive Director
Paid Staff: 1
Utilizes: Guest Artists
Budget: $50,000 - $100,000
Income Sources: Private Foundations/Grants/Endowments; Box Office; Individual Donations
Season: Fall - Spring   **Annual Attendance:** 8,000
Performance Facilities: Scottsdale Center for the Arts

PHOENIX SYMPHONY
3707 North Seventh Street, Suite 107, Phoenix, AZ 85014
(602) 277-7291
FAX: (602) 277-7517
Founded: 1947
Arts Area: Symphony; Orchestra; Chamber; Ensemble
Status: Professional; Non-Profit
Type: Performing; Touring; Educational
Purpose: To foster and promote the knowledge and appreciation of music by the public; to establish, maintain, and operate a symphonic performing group in the Phoenix metropolitan area
Management: Howard McCrady, President/Chief Executive Officer; James Sedares, Music Director
Officers: Richard Hill, Chairman, Board of Directors
Paid Staff: 24   **Volunteer Staff:** 972
Paid Artists: 84
Utilizes: Special Technical Talent; Guest Conductors; Guest Artists
Budget: $1,000,000 - $5,000,000
Income Sources: Private Foundations/Grants/Endowments; Business/Corporate Donations; Box Office; Government Grants; Individual Donations
Season: September - June   **Annual Attendance:** 204,000
Affiliations: ASOL
Performance Facilities: Phoenix Symphony Hall; Scottsdale Center for the Arts; Pointe Hilton at Tapatio Cliffs

PHOENIX SYMPHONY YOUTH ORCHESTRA
PO Box 15150, Phoenix, AZ 85060
(602) 820-3310; (602) 902-2356
FAX: (602) 831-1264
Founded: 1952
Arts Area: Symphony; Orchestra
Status: Non-Professional; Non-Profit
Type: Performing; Educational; Sponsoring
Purpose: To stimulate and create a challenge for talented young musicians and an appreciation of good music by participation in the Youth Orchestra, Symphonette Orchestra and the Junior Strings; to select orchestra members by audition
Management: Judy Begun, Director of Orchestral Training; Mark Russell Smith, Conductor, Youth Orchestra; Dr. Walter Temme, Conductor, Symphonette; Dr. Cynthia La Blanc, Conductor, Symphonic Wind Ensemble; Martha Hughes, Conductor, String Orchestra
Officers: Pat Sosnow, President, Phoenix Symphony Guild
Volunteer Staff: 8

Non-Paid Artists: 140
Budget: $1,000 - $50,000
Season: September - May
Annual Attendance: 15,000
Affiliations: ASOL (Youth Orchestra Division)
Performance Facilities: Phoenix Symphony Hall

VOCAL MUSIC

ORPHEUS MALE CHORUS OF PHOENIX
PO Box 217, Phoenix, AZ 85001
(602) 271-9396
Founded: 1929
Arts Area: Choral
Status: Non-Professional; Non-Profit
Type: Performing; Touring
Purpose: To give a singing outlet to men who love to sing; to use music as a means of furthering international and intercultural goodwill
Management: Lloyd Weberg, President; Paul Morrow, Assistant Musical Director
Paid Staff: 2 **Volunteer Staff:** 1
Non-Paid Artists: 112
Utilizes: Special Technical Talent; Guest Artists
Budget: $1,000 - $50,000
Income Sources: Box Office; Individual Donations
Season: September - June
Annual Attendance: 8,000

PHOENIX BOYS CHOIR ASSOCIATION
4621 North 16th Street, Suite B-210, Phoenix, AZ 85016
(602) 264-5328
FAX: (602) 264-6778
Founded: 1949
Arts Area: Choral
Status: Professional; Non-Professional; Non-Profit
Type: Performing; Touring; Educational; Sponsoring
Purpose: To maintain the historic tradition of singing boys; to contribute to local cultural life; to serve as musical ambassadors
Officers: Harvey K. Smith, Artistic Director; Beverly Blanton, Executive Director
Paid Staff: 10 **Volunteer Staff:** 5
Paid Artists: 6 **Non-Paid Artists:** 120
Utilizes: Special Technical Talent; Guest Artists; Guest Directors
Budget: $100,000 - $500,000
Income Sources: Private Foundations/Grants/Endowments; Business/Corporate Donations; Box Office; Government Grants; Individual Donations; Tuition; Fee Engagements
Season: September - June
Annual Attendance: 40,000
Affiliations: CA; ACDA

THEATRE

ACTORS THEATRE OF PHOENIX
815 North First Avenue, # 3W, Phoenix, AZ 85020
(602) 253-6701
Founded: 1985
Arts Area: Professional; Theatrical Group
Status: Professional; Non-Profit
Type: Performing
Purpose: To bring fine professional theatre to Phoenix; to exclusively employ local actors; to build a resident company and a training program
Management: Judith Rollings, Artistic Director; James Pinkerton, Managing Director; Sheila O'Keefe, Marketing Director; Joe Onofrio, Director of Development; Monica Jay Burgess, Production Manager
Officers: Rosemarie Christofalo, Board President; Peter Gerstman, Vice President; George Cohen, Treasurer
Paid Staff: 7
Paid Artists: 40

Utilizes: Special Technical Talent; Guest Artists; Guest Directors
Budget: $100,000 - $500,000
Income Sources: Private Foundations/Grants/Endowments; Business/Corporate Donations; Box Office; Government Grants; Individual Donations; Tuition
Season: September - May   **Annual Attendance:** 14,000
Affiliations: TCG
Performance Facilities: Herberger Theater Center; Stage West

BLACK THEATRE TROUPE
333 East Portland Street, Phoenix, AZ 85004
(602) 258-8128
Founded: 1970
Arts Area: Community
Status: Non-Professional; Non-Profit
Type: Performing; Touring; Resident
Purpose: To make significant contributions to fostering the artistic and theatrical development of the state; to enhance the cultural and artistic nature of the community by providing exposure to Black culture and ideology
Management: Helen Mason, Founder; Joel Coleman, Artistic Director; Brenda Williams, Managing Director
Utilizes: Guest Artists; Guest Directors
Budget: $500,000 - $1,000,000
Income Sources: Private Foundations/Grants/Endowments; Business/Corporate Donations; Box Office; Government Grants; Individual Donations
Season: October - June

PHOENIX LITTLE THEATRE
25 East Coronado Road, Phoenix, AZ 85004
(602) 258-1974
Founded: 1920
Arts Area: Community
Status: Semi-Professional; Non-Professional
Type: Performing; Resident
Purpose: To provide top-quality theatre using the best local talent serving the Phoenix metropolitan area
Management: Chris Swartz, Marketing/Publicity; Peter J. Hill, Producing Director
Paid Staff: 14   **Volunteer Staff:** 200
Paid Artists: 100   **Non-Paid Artists:** 100
Utilizes: Special Technical Talent; Guest Conductors; Guest Artists; Guest Directors
Budget: $500,000 - $1,000,000
Income Sources: Business/Corporate Donations; Box Office; Government Grants; Individual Donations
Season: September - July   **Annual Attendance:** 70,000

FACILITY

JOHN PAUL THEATRE
1202 West Thomas, Phoenix College, Phoenix, AZ 85013
(602) 264-2492
FAX: (602) 285-7700
Type of Facility: Theatre House
Facility Originally: Performing Arts Center
Type of Stage: Thrust
Stage Dimensions: 48'W x 45'D
Seating Capacity: 305
Year Built: 1976   **Architect:** Oberg, Hunt, Gilleland   **Cost:** $1,500,000
Manager: Gary Imel;   (602) 285-7301
Resident Groups: Phoenix College Dramas; Arizona Theatre Company

PHOENIX CIVIC PLAZA
225 East Adams, Phoenix, AZ 85004
(602) 262-6225
Type of Facility: Civic Center
Year Built: 1972   **Architect:** GSAS Architect Planners; Howard, Needles, Tammen & Burgendoff   **Cost:** $28,000,000
Year Remodeled: 1985   **Architect:** GSAS Architect Planners; Howard, Needles, Tammen & Burgendoff
Cost: $55,000,000
Contact for Rental: Maura McCarty, Booking Coordinator;   (602) 262-6225
The Phoenix Civic Center contains Convention Center and Symphony Hall, Exhibition Halls and Grand Ballroom. See separate listings for additional information.

PHOENIX CIVIC PLAZA - CONVENTION CENTER AND SYMPHONY HALL
225 East Adams, Phoenix, AZ 85004
(602) 262-6225
FAX: (602) 495-3608
Founded: 1972
Type of Facility: Concert Hall; Auditorium; Outdoor (Concert); Performance Center; Off Broadway; Theatre House; Opera House; Civic Center; Multi-Purpose; Room
Type of Stage: Flexible; Proscenium; Platform
Stage Dimensions: Symphony Hall and Ballroom - 60'x100' each   **Orchestra Pit**
Seating Capacity: Symphony Hall - 2,599; Ballroom - 3,800; other rooms vary
Year Built: 1972   **Architect:** Charles Luckman & Associates   **Cost:** $28,000,000
Year Remodeled: 1985   **Architect:** GSAS Architect Planners, Inc. with Needles Tammen & Bergendoff
Cost: $55,000,000
Acoustical Consultant: Vern Knudson - original; Howard Smith - expansion
Contact for Rental: Ann Hastings, Maura McCarty, Marilynn Leathers or Kim Gilbert;   (602) 262-6225
Manager: Eric Jones, General Manager;   (602) 262-6225
Resident Groups: Phoenix Symphony; Arizona Opera; Ballet Arizona
Tucson Room - 16,380 square feet; Yuma Room - 17,000 square feet; Phoenix Room - 10,500 square feet; Flagstaff Room - 5,000 square feet; Prescott Room - 3,750 square feet. Seating capacities in meeting rooms can vary from 10 to 2,600 people, depending on configuration.

PHOENIX CIVIC PLAZA - EXHIBITION HALLS
225 East Adams, Phoenix, AZ 85004
(602) 262-6225
FAX: (602) 495-3608
Founded: 1972
Type of Facility: Concert Hall; Civic Center; Exhibition Hall
Type of Stage: Flexible; Proscenium; Platform
Stage Dimensions: Poscenium opening 76'Wx32'H   **Orchestra Pit**
Year Built: 1972
Year Remodeled: 1985
Contact for Rental: Maura McCarty, Sales Manager;   (602) 262-6225
Five halls contain 223,000 square feet

PHOENIX CIVIC PLAZA - GRAND BALLROOM
225 East Adams, Phoenix, AZ 85004
(602) 262-6225
Type of Facility: Concert Hall; Auditorium; Multi-Purpose
Type of Stage: Proscenium
Stage Dimensions: 72'Wx32'H proscenium opening
Seating Capacity: Theater Style - 3,700; Banquet - 2,000
Year Remodeled: 1985
Contact for Rental: Maura McCarty, Booking Coordinator;   (602) 262-6225

Prescott

INSTRUMENTAL MUSIC

YAVAPI SYMPHONY ASSOCIATION
PO Box 2333, Prescott, AZ 86301
(602) 778-0184
Founded: 1966
Arts Area: Symphony
Status: Non-Profit
Type: Sponsoring
Purpose: To provide quality music for the area of Prescott
Management: Lori Bogart, Office
Officers: John B. Schuyler Jr., President; Dana Wingate, A.J. Wilson, Kristi Edwards, Donna Fagan, Officers
Utilizes: Guest Artists
Budget: $1,000 - $50,000
Income Sources: Business/Corporate Donations; Box Office; Government Grants; Individual Donations
Season: September - March   **Annual Attendance:** 3,000
Performance Facilities: Hendrix Auditorium; Yavapi College Community Theatre

---
Scottsdale

INSTRUMENTAL MUSIC

SCOTTSDALE SYMPHONY ORCHESTRA
PO Box 664, Scottsdale, AZ 85252
(602) 945-8071
>**Founded:** 1972
>**Arts Area:** Symphony; Orchestra
>**Status:** Professional; Semi-Professional; Non-Profit
>**Type:** Performing
>**Purpose:** To provide symphonic music to the Scottsdale community
>**Management:** K. Dona Roberson, Business Manager; Irving Fleming, Music Director; Judy Vagis, Financial Director
>**Paid Staff:** 2
>**Non-Paid Artists:** 70
>**Utilizes:** Guest Conductors; Guest Artists
>**Budget:** $100,000 - $500,000
>**Income Sources:** Business/Corporate Donations; Box Office; Individual Donations; Fund-raising
>**Season:** November - June
>**Annual Attendance:** 10,000
>**Affiliations:** ASOL; Scottsdale Chamber of Commerce
>**Performance Facilities:** Scottsdale Center for the Arts

THEATRE

ACTORS LAB ARIZONA
7120 East Fourth Street, Scottsdale, AZ 85251
(602) 990-1731; (602) 990-7898
FAX: (602) 990-0013
>**Founded:** 1980
>**Arts Area:** Theatrical Group
>**Status:** Professional; Non-Profit
>**Type:** Performing; Touring
>**Purpose:** To advance an appreciation of legitimate theater through diverse programming that includes a two-theater complex, educational outreach programs to schools and communities throughout the state, and a school for the performing arts
>**Management:** Jan Rothman-Sickler, Artistic Director; Jerry A. Sickler, Producing Director
>**Paid Staff:** 4
>**Utilizes:** Special Technical Talent; Guest Artists; Guest Directors
>**Budget:** $100,000 - $500,000
>**Income Sources:** Private Foundations/Grants/Endowments; Business/Corporate Donations; Box Office; Government Grants; Individual Donations
>**Season:** October - August
>**Affiliations:** AEA; SPTA
>**Performance Facilities:** Actors Lab

PERFORMING SERIES

DETROIT CONCERT BAND, INC.
7443 East Butherus, Suite 100, Scottsdale, AZ 85260
(602) 948-9870
>**Founded:** 1949
>**Arts Area:** Instrumental Music
>**Status:** Professional; Non-Profit
>**Type:** Performing; Touring
>**Purpose:** To perform concerts
>**Officers:** Leonard B. Smith, President/Executive Director
>**Paid Artists:** 60
>**Utilizes:** Special Technical Talent
>**Budget:** $50,000 - $100,000
>**Income Sources:** Box Office; Individual Donations; Concert Performances
>**Season:** 52 Weeks
>**Affiliations:** AF of M

FACILITY

SCOTTSDALE CENTER FOR THE ARTS
7383 Scottsdale Mall, Scottsdale, AZ 85251
(602) 994-2301
FAX: (602) 994-7728
    Type of Facility: Concert Hall; Theatre House; Civic Center; Exhibition Galleries
    Type of Stage: Thrust; Flexible
    Stage Dimensions: 40'Wx48'D   **Orchestra Pit**
    Seating Capacity: 860
    Year Built: 1975   **Architect:** Bennie Gonzales   **Cost:** $8,500,000
    Year Remodeled: 1986   **Cost:** $500,000
    Acoustical Consultant: AIRO-London; Jaffe Acoustics
    Contact for Rental: Dan Bercovich;   (602) 994-2301
    The Scottsdale Center for the Arts includes the Cinema and Theatre. See separate listings for more information.

SCOTTSDALE CENTER FOR THE ARTS - CINEMA
7383 Scottsdale Mall, Scottsdale, AZ 85251
(602) 994-2301
FAX: (602) 994-7728
    Type of Facility: Film Theatre; Experimental Theatre
    Seating Capacity: 175
    Year Built: 1975
    Contact for Rental: Dan Bercovich;   (602) 994-2301
    Manager: Kathy Hotchner;   (602) 994-2301

SCOTTSDALE CENTER FOR THE ARTS - THEATER
7383 Scottsdale Mall, Scottsdale, AZ 85251
(602) 994-2301
FAX: (602) 994-7728
    Type of Facility: Theatre House
    Type of Stage: Modified Apron Proscenium   **Orchestra Pit**
    Seating Capacity: 800
    Year Built: 1975
    Acoustical Consultant: Jaffe Acoustics
    Contact for Rental: Dan Berkovich;   (602) 994-2301
    Manager: Kathy Hotchner;   (602) 994-2301
    Resident Groups: Scottsdale Symphony; Phoenix Symphony

Sedona

PERFORMING SERIES

SEDONA JAZZ ON THE ROCKS
PO Box 889, Sedona, AZ 86336-0889
(602) 282-1985
    Founded: 1982
    Arts Area: Festivals
    Status: Non-Profit
    Type: Performing; Sponsoring
    Purpose: To sponsor an annual jazz festival; to support education in the area of jazz music
    Management: Ann Briggs, Festival Administrator
    Officers: Ken Fisher, President; Marion Herrman, Vice President; Paula Erwin, Secretary; Chris Frish, Treasurer
    Paid Staff: 1   **Volunteer Staff:** 300
    Paid Artists: 6
    Utilizes: Guest Artists
    Budget: $1,000,000 - $5,000,000
    Income Sources: Private Foundations/Grants/Endowments; Business/Corporate Donations; Box Office; Government Grants; Individual Donations
    Season: September   **Annual Attendance:** 5,000
    Performance Facilities: Hamilton Warren Ampitheatre

Sun City

INSTRUMENTAL MUSIC

SUN CITIES CHAMBER MUSIC SOCIETY
PO Box 1043, Sun City, AZ 85351
(602) 972-0478
Founded: 1976
Arts Area: Chamber; Ensemble
Status: Non-Profit
Type: Sponsoring
Purpose: To present the finest in solo and chamber music and related arts
Officers: Mary Ellen Danley, President; Quillian Ditto, Rebecca O. Johnson, Vice Presidents
Paid Staff: 1
Budget: $50,000 - $100,000
Income Sources: Private Foundations/Grants/Endowments; Business/Corporate Donations; Box Office; Government Grants; Individual Donations
Season: November - April   **Annual Attendance:** 9,500
Affiliations: WAAA; CMA
Performance Facilities: Sundial Auditorium

Sun City West

FACILITY

ARIZONA STATE UNIVERSITY - SUNDOME CENTER FOR THE PERFORMING ARTS
19403 R.H. Johnson Boulevard, Sun City West, AZ 85375
(602) 584-3118
Type of Facility: Performance Center
Type of Stage: Thrust; Proscenium
Stage Dimensions: Thrust/Apron: 67'Wx24'D
Seating Capacity: 7,169
Year Built: 1980   **Architect:** Hawkins, Lindsey, Wilson Associates   **Cost:** $9,600,000
Acoustical Consultant: Coffeen, Anderson & Associates
Contact for Rental: Pat Edwards;   (602) 584-3118
Resident Groups: Sun Cities Symphony

Tempe

DANCE

DESERT DANCE THEATRE
PO Box 25332, Tempe, AZ 85285-5332
(602) 968-4498
Founded: 1979
Arts Area: Modern; Contemporary Dance Theatre
Status: Professional; Non-Profit
Type: Performing; Touring; Educational
Purpose: To develop, promote and present contemporary concert dance through the operation of a contemporary dance company
Management: Lisa R. Chow, Associate Artistic Director/Company Manager; Marion Kirk Jones, Artistic Director; Renee Davis, Rehearsal Director
Officers: Larry Davis, President; Marion Kirk Jones, Vice President; Kay Williams, Secretary; Pat Gosmon, Treasurer
Paid Staff: 2   **Volunteer Staff:** 10
Paid Artists: 10
Utilizes: Special Technical Talent; Guest Artists; Guest Choreographers
Budget: $1,000 - $50,000
Income Sources: Private Foundations/Grants/Endowments; Business/Corporate Donations; Box Office; Government Grants; Individual Donations
Season: September - May   **Annual Attendance:** 10,000
Affiliations: Arizona Commission on the Arts

FACILITY

ARIZONA STATE UNIVERSITY - GAMMAGE CENTER
Tempe, AZ 85287
(602) 965-5062
    Type of Facility: Concert Hall; Auditorium; Performance Center; Theatre House
    Type of Stage: Proscenium   **Orchestra Pit**
    Seating Capacity: 3,029
    Year Built: 1964   **Architect:** Frank Lloyd Wright   **Cost:** $3,400,000
    Acoustical Consultant: Vern Knudsen
    Contact for Rental: Carole Vogt, Scheduling Coordinator;   (602) 965-5602

ARIZONA STATE UNIVERSITY - UNIVERSITY ACTIVITY CENTER
Tempe, AZ 85287-0205
(602) 965-5062
FAX: (602) 965-7663
    Founded: 1885
    Type of Facility: Arena
    Type of Stage: Arena
    Seating Capacity: 14,000-15,000
    Year Built: 1974   **Cost:** $8,000,000
    Contact for Rental: Carole Vogt, Scheduling Coordinator;   (602) 965-5062
    Manager: Colleen Jennings-Roggensack, Director;   (602) 965-5062

Tucson

INSTRUMENTAL MUSIC

TUCSON JAZZ SOCIETY, INC.
PO Box 44163, Tucson, AZ 85733
(602) 743-7347
    Founded: 1978
    Status: Professional; Non-Profit
    Type: Sponsoring
    Purpose: To promote and present jazz
    Management: Yvonne Ervin, Executive Director; Gloria Butler, Volunteer Coordinator; Ben Nead, Technical Director
    Paid Staff: 1   **Volunteer Staff:** 2
    Paid Artists: 19
    Utilizes: Guest Artists; Guest Directors
    Budget: $100,000 - $500,000
    Income Sources: Private Foundations/Grants/Endowments; Business/Corporate Donations; Box Office; Government Grants; Individual Donations
    Season: 52 Weeks   **Annual Attendance:** 25,000
    Affiliations: National Jazz Service Organization; International Association of Jazz Educators

TUCSON SYMPHONY ORCHESTRA
443 South Stone, Tucson, AZ 85701
(602) 792-9155
FAX: (602) 792-9314
    Founded: 1928
    Arts Area: Symphony; Orchestra; Chamber; Ensemble
    Status: Professional
    Type: Performing; Touring; Educational
    Purpose: To present classical, pops, family, chamber, ensemble and educational concerts
    Management: Eric Meyer, General Manager; Robert Bernhardt, Music Director
    Paid Staff: 11   **Volunteer Staff:** 10
    Paid Artists: 86
    Utilizes: Guest Conductors; Guest Artists
    Budget: $500,000 - $1,000,000
    Income Sources: Private Foundations/Grants/Endowments; Business/Corporate Donations; Box Office; Government Grants
    Season: September - May   **Annual Attendance:** 45,000
    Affiliations: ASOL
    Performance Facilities: Tucson Community Center Music Hall

VOCAL MUSIC

ARIZONA OPERA COMPANY
3501 North Mountain Avenue, Tucson, AZ 85719
(602) 293-4336
FAX: (602) 293-5097
Founded: 1972
Arts Area: Grand Opera
Status: Professional; Non-Profit
Type: Performing
Purpose: To present grand opera in Arizona
Management: Glynn Ross, General Director
Officers: Louis Lagomarsino, President; Robert Mueller, Vice President
Paid Staff: 14 **Volunteer Staff:** 4
Paid Artists: 60 **Non-Paid Artists:** 3
Utilizes: Special Technical Talent; Guest Conductors; Guest Artists; Guest Directors
Budget: $1,000,000 - $5,000,000
Income Sources: Private Foundations/Grants/Endowments; Business/Corporate Donations; Box Office; Individual Donations
Season: October - March **Annual Attendance:** 35,000
Affiliations: Tucson Opera Dames; Arizona Opera League; Southern Arizona Opera Guild
Performance Facilities: Tucson Community Center Music Hall; Phoenix Symphony Hall

TUCSON ARIZONA BOYS CHORUS
5770 East Pima, Tucson, AZ 85732
(602) 296-6277
FAX: (602) 296-6751
Founded: 1939
Arts Area: Choral
Status: Professional; Non-Profit
Type: Performing; Touring; Educational
Purpose: To educate and maintain a porfessional boys choir; to tour and perform
Management: Dr. Julien Ackerley, Director; Robin Jablonski-Bryan, Managing Director
Officers: Don Haskell, President of the Board; Bates Butler, Vice President; Mark Cowley, Treasurer; Judy Morriss, Secretary
Paid Staff: 4 **Volunteer Staff:** 2
Paid Artists: 4 **Non-Paid Artists:** 153
Utilizes: Guest Conductors; Guest Artists
Budget: $100,000 - $500,000
Income Sources: Private Foundations/Grants/Endowments; Business/Corporate Donations; Box Office; Government Grants; Individual Donations
Season: September - May **Annual Attendance:** 35,000

UP WITH PEOPLE
3103 North Campbell Avenue, Tucson, AZ 85719
(602) 327-7351
FAX: (602) 325-3716
Founded: 1968
Arts Area: Popular Music with Choreography
Status: Professional; Non-Professional; Non-Profit
Type: Performing; Touring; Educational
Purpose: To encourage understanding among people of all nations through an international educational program involving young men and women from many countries who travel for a year and learn from the people and places they visit while staging a musical show
Management: Bruce L. Erley, Vice President of Scheduling; Glen Shepherd, Vice President of Admissions and Education; Reed W. Thompson, Vice President of Production Services; Jeffrey Stegenga, Chief Financial Officer
Officers: J. Blanton Belk, Founder/Chairman of the Executive Committee; Steven W. Woods, Chairman of the Board/Chief Executive Officer; Dale M. Penny, President/Chief Operating Officer; Hans Chr. Magnus, President, Up With People/Europe; James E. MacLennan, Executive Vice President/Director of Planning
Paid Staff: 204
Non-Paid Artists: 560
Utilizes: Special Technical Talent; Selected Students
Budget: Over 10,000,000
Income Sources: Private Foundations/Grants/Endowments; Business/Corporate Donations; Box Office; Individual Donations; Student Fees; Recordings
Season: August - July **Annual Attendance:** 1,500,000 (live)

THEATRE

ARIZONA THEATRE COMPANY
PO Box 1631, Tucson, AZ 85702
(602) 884-8210
FAX: (602) 628-9129
Founded: 1967
Arts Area: Professional; Theatrical Group
Status: Professional; Non-Profit
Type: Resident
Purpose: To create professional theatre of the highest artistic quality for Arizona that impacts locally and throughout the nation
Management: Ralph Alpaugh, Managing Director; David Ira Goldstein, Artistic Director; Rob Sweibel, Marketing Director; John Tabor, Development Director/Tucson; Douglas Richards, Development Director/Phoenix
Officers: Jon R. Young, President; Dorothy Finley, Vice President/Tucson; Everett L. King, Vice President/Phoenix; Mary K. Sterling, Chairman; William Hawgood II, Secretary; David Ogilvy, Treasurer
Paid Staff: 40
Paid Artists: 60
Utilizes: Special Technical Talent; Guest Artists; Guest Directors
Budget: $1,000,000 - $5,000,000
Income Sources: Private Foundations/Grants/Endowments; Business/Corporate Donations; Box Office; Government Grants; Individual Donations
Season: October - June   **Annual Attendance:** 126,000
Affiliations: LORT; TCG; AEA; SSDC
Performance Facilities: Temple of Music and Art; Herberger Theater Center

BORDERLANDS THEATER/TEATRO FRONTERIZO
166 West Alameda, Tucson, AZ 85701
(602) 882-8607
Founded: 1984
Arts Area: Theatrical Group
Status: Professional; Non-Profit
Type: Performing; Touring; Educational
Purpose: To produce plays that reflect the cultural diversity of the border region; to be an important voice in the region
Management: Debra J.T. Padilla, Managing Director; Barclay Goldsmith, Artistic/Producing Director
Paid Staff: 2   **Volunteer Staff:** 5
Paid Artists: 20
Utilizes: Guest Artists; Guest Directors
Budget: $100,000 - $500,000
Income Sources: Private Foundations/Grants/Endowments; Business/Corporate Donations; Box Office; Government Grants; Individual Donations
Season: 52 Weeks
Annual Attendance: 6,500
Performance Facilities: Pima Community College Center for the Arts

INVISIBLE THEATRE
1400 North First Avenue, Tucson, AZ 85719
(602) 882-9721
Founded: 1971
Arts Area: Theatrical Group
Status: Semi-Professional
Type: Performing
Purpose: To perform adaptations of classics, recent off-Broadway plays and musicals; to encourage new playwrights through full productions and staged readings
Management: Susan Classen, Managing Artistic Director; James Blair, Associate Artistic Director; Deborah Dickey, Literary Manager/Associate Producer; Caroline Reed, Director of Public Relations; Diane Hamra, Business Manager; Gail Fitzhugh, Associate Director; MaryAnn Trombino, Artistic Associate
Officers: Garry Bryant, Franki Levin, Co-Chairs; Ginny Burginger, Secretary; Joan Shillito, Treasurer
Paid Staff: 5   **Volunteer Staff:** 20
Paid Artists: 20
Utilizes: Guest Artists; Guest Directors
Budget: $50,000 - $100,000
Income Sources: Private Foundations/Grants/Endowments; Business/Corporate Donations; Box Office; Government Grants; Individual Donations
Season: September - June
Annual Attendance: 10,000
Affiliations: TCG

NKYIMKYIM STORY THEATRE
2004 East Irvington, #132, Tucson, AZ 85713
(602) 884-7951; (602) 623-9133
Founded: 1980
Arts Area: Professional; Community; Folk
Status: Professional
Type: Performing; Touring; Resident; Educational; Sponsoring
Purpose: To promote the art of storytelling as a means of cultural awareness and exchange
Management: Gloria Myers, Director
Paid Staff: 1
Paid Artists: 1
Utilizes: Special Technical Talent; Guest Artists; Guest Directors
Budget: $1,000 - $50,000
Income Sources: Private Foundations/Grants/Endowments; Business/Corporate Donations; Box Office; Individual Donations
Season: 52 Weeks **Annual Attendance:** 5,000

PERFORMING SERIES

ARIZONA MINI-CONCERTS
2540 Camino La Zorrela, Tucson, AZ 85718
(602) 299-2399
Founded: 1979
Arts Area: Dance; Instrumental Music; Theater; Lyric Opera; Grand Opera
Status: Professional; Non-Profit
Type: Sponsoring
Purpose: To bring high-quality professional concert experiences to outreach audience environments; to showcase local professionals when possible
Management: Louise Spizizen, Artistic Director; Mia Gay, Pat Watrous, Publicity
Officers: Louise Spizizen, President; David Lopez, Secretary; Elaine Baker, Treasurer
Volunteer Staff: 11
Utilizes: Guest Artists
Budget: $1,000 - $50,000
Income Sources: Private Foundations/Grants/Endowments; Business/Corporate Donations; Government Grants
Season: September - June **Annual Attendance:** 5,000
Performance Facilities: El Con Mall; Foothills Mall

TUCSON FESTIVAL SOCIETY
425 West Paseo Redondo, Tucson, AZ 85701
(602) 622-6911
FAX: (602) 622-8838
Founded: 1950
Arts Area: Festivals
Status: Professional; Non-Profit
Type: Performing; Educational; Sponsoring
Purpose: To celebrate and promote Tucson's Native American and Anglo-American cultures and their historic influences on the area through the production of special events
Management: Annette Wallenmeyer, Executive Director; Susan P. Lispron, Assistant to Director
Paid Staff: 4 **Volunteer Staff:** 3,000
Paid Artists: 150
Utilizes: Special Technical Talent; Guest Artists
Budget: $100,000 - $500,000
Income Sources: Private Foundations/Grants/Endowments; Business/Corporate Donations; Government Grants; Individual Donations
Season: April **Annual Attendance:** 200,000
Affiliations: International Festivals Association
Performance Facilities: El Presidio Neighborhood; Fort Lowell Park

FACILITY

TUCSON CONVENTION CENTER
260 South Church Avenue, Tucson, AZ 85701
(602) 791-4101
FAX: (602) 791-5572
Type of Facility: Theatre Complex; Concert Hall; Auditorium; Performance Center; Off Broadway; Opera House; Civic Center; Arena; Multi-Purpose
Type of Stage: Flexible; Platform
Year Built: 1971 **Architect:** Friedman & Jobusch

Year Remodeled: 1987   **Architect:** Anderson, DeBartolo & Pan
Contact for Rental: Joe Rzonca;   (602) 791-4101
Resident Groups: Tucson Symphony Orchestra; Arizona Opera Company; Southern Arizona Light Opera Company; Arizona Dance Company; Ballet Arizona
Contains the Arena, Exhibition Hall, Little Theatre, Music Hall and Theatre. See separate listings for additional information.

TUCSON CONVENTION CENTER - ARENA
260 South Church Avenue, Tucson, AZ 85701
(602) 791-4101
FAX: (602) 791-5572
   Type of Facility: Arena
   Type of Stage: Flexible; Platform; Arena
   Seating Capacity: 9,550
   Contact for Rental: Joe Rzonca;   (602) 791-4101

TUCSON CONVENTION CENTER - EXHIBITION HALL
260 South Church Avenue, Tucson, AZ 85701
(602) 791-4101
FAX: (602) 791-5572
   Type of Facility: Exhibition Hall
   Type of Stage: Flexible; Platform
   Contact for Rental: Joe Rzonca;   (602) 791-4101
   Contains 23,800 square feet of exhibition space

TUCSON CONVENTION CENTER - LITTLE THEATRE
260 South Church Avenue, Tucson, AZ 85701
(602) 791-4101
FAX: (602) 791-5572
   Type of Facility: Theatre House
   Type of Stage: Thrust; 3/4 Arena
   Stage Dimensions: 48'Wx45'D
   Seating Capacity: 526
   Year Built: 1972
   Contact for Rental: Joe Rzonca;   (602) 791-4101

TUCSON CONVENTION CENTER - MUSIC HALL
260 South Church Avenue, Tucson, AZ 85701
(602) 791-4101
FAX: (602) 791-5572
   Type of Facility: Concert Hall; Opera House
   Type of Stage: Proscenium
   Stage Dimensions: 128'Wx49'6"D   **Orchestra Pit**
   Seating Capacity: 2,280
   Contact for Rental: Joe Rzonca;   (602) 791-4101
   Resident Groups: Tucson Symphony Orchestra; Arizona Opera Company; Southern Arizona Light Opera Company; Ballet Arizona

TUCSON CONVENTION CENTER - THEATRE
260 South Church Avenue, Tucson, AZ 85701
(602) 791-4101
FAX: (602) 791-5572
   Type of Facility: Theatre House
   Type of Stage: Thrust
   Stage Dimensions: 130'Wx40'D
   Seating Capacity: 525
   Contact for Rental: Larry Lahaie;   (602) 791-4101

UNIVERSITY OF ARIZONA - CENTENNIAL HALL
Centennial Hall, Building 29, Tucson, AZ 85721
(602) 621-1249
   Type of Facility: Auditorium; Performance Center; Multi-Purpose
   Type of Stage: Proscenium
   Stage Dimensions: 58'Wx46'D   **Orchestra Pit**
   Seating Capacity: 2,454
   Year Built: 1935   **Architect:** Ray Place   **Cost:** $234,260
   Year Remodeled: 1986   **Architect:** John Mascarella & Associates   **Cost:** $4,300,000
   Acoustical Consultant: Initial - Bolt, Beranek & Newman; Sound Renovation - Paoletti Associates

Contact for Rental: Marg Hemmings, Director of Operations;   (602) 621-1249
Resident Groups: University of Arizona Series; University of Arizona Cultural Affairs

UNIVERSITY OF ARIZONA - CROWDER HALL
School of Music, Tucson, AZ 85721
(602) 621-1655
  Type of Facility: Concert Hall
  Type of Stage: Proscenium
  Stage Dimensions: 21'x50'x26'   **Orchestra Pit**
  Seating Capacity: 478
  Year Built: 1956   **Architect:** Place and Place
  Contact for Rental: Dr. Dorothy Payne;   (602) 621-7023
  Resident Groups: School of Music

Yuma

DANCE

YUMA BALLET THEATRE
PO Box 1275, Yuma, AZ 85366
(602) 341-1925
  Founded: 1979
  Arts Area: Ballet
  Status: Non-Professional; Non-Profit; Regional Honor Company
  Type: Performing; Educational
  Purpose: To create, perform and enhance the art of dance within the community
  Management: Jon Cristofori, Kathleen Sinclair, Artistic Directors; Carmen Feriend, Business Manager; David Campbell, Technical Director; Stephanie Jones, Costume; Tom French, Sound
  Paid Staff: 4
  Paid Artists: 2   **Non-Paid Artists:** 40
  Utilizes: Special Technical Talent; Guest Artists; Guest Choreographers
  Budget: $50,000 - $100,000
  Income Sources: Private Foundations/Grants/Endowments; Business/Corporate Donations; Box Office; Government Grants; Individual Donations; Fund-raising
  Season: September - May   **Annual Attendance:** 6,000
  Affiliations: Regional Dance America; Honor Company
  Performance Facilities: Snider Auditorium

FACILITY

YUMA CIVIC AND CONVENTION CENTER - YUMA ROOM
1440 Desert Hills Drive, PO Box 6468, Yuma, AZ 85364
(602) 344-3800
FAX: (602) 344-9121
  Founded: 1973
  Type of Facility: Concert Hall; Civic Center; Room
  Facility Originally: Meeting Hall
  Type of Stage: Flexible; Platform
  Seating Capacity: 2,000
  Year Built: 1973   **Architect:** Benham-Blair & Ditzler   **Cost:** $1,500,000
  Acoustical Consultant: Coffeen & Associates
  Contact for Rental: Suzanne Murray, Director;   (602) 344-3800
  Manager: Suzanne Murray

ARKANSAS

Arkadelphia

FACILITY

OUACHITA BAPTIST UNIVERSITY - DEPARTMENT OF THEATRE & ARTS
Arkadelphia, AR 71998-0001
(501) 245-5000
> **Type of Facility:** Theatre Complex; Theatre House
> **Type of Stage:** Thrust; Proscenium
> **Stage Dimensions:** 28'Wx36'Hx48'D
> **Seating Capacity:** 230
> **Year Built:** 1967   **Architect:** Bruce Anderson   **Cost:** $300,000
> **Contact for Rental:** Scott Holsclaw;   (501) 245-5561
> **Resident Groups:** Ouachita Baptist University Drama Department

Dumas

THEATRE

DUMAS AREA ARTS COUNCIL, INC.
North Main Street, Dumas, AR 71639
(501) 382-6074
> **Founded:** 1979
> **Arts Area:** Musical; Dinner; Community; Theatrical Group
> **Status:** Non-Professional; Non-Profit
> **Type:** Performing; Resident; Educational
> **Purpose:** To provide theatre, music, dance and visual arts to interested performers and attentive audiences
> **Officers:** Brian Payne, President; Sue Gill, Vice President; Tonya Tucker, Secretary; Jimmy Locke, Treasurer
> **Volunteer Staff:** 50
> **Non-Paid Artists:** 100
> **Budget:** $1,000 - $50,000
> **Income Sources:** Private Foundations/Grants/Endowments; Business/Corporate Donations; Box Office; Government Grants; Individual Donations
> **Season:** 52 Weeks   **Annual Attendance:** 1,200
> **Performance Facilities:** Tanenbaum Theatre

FACILITY

DUMAS AREA ARTS COUNCIL, INC.
North Main Street, PO Box 493, Dumas, AR 71639
(501) 382-6713
> **Type of Facility:** Theatre Complex; Multi-Purpose
> **Facility Originally:** Business Facility
> **Type of Stage:** Flexible
> **Seating Capacity:** 200
> **Year Remodeled:** 1986   **Cost:** $50,000
> **Contact for Rental:** Brian Payne;   (501) 382-6836
> **Resident Groups:** Dumas Area Arts Council
> *Rental to Arts-Council sponsored organizations only*

El Dorado

INSTRUMENTAL MUSIC

SOUTH ARKANSAS SYMPHONY
315 East Oak, #206, El Dorado, AR 71730
(501) 862-0521
> **Founded:** 1956
> **Arts Area:** Symphony
> **Status:** Non-Profit
> **Type:** Performing; Educational
> **Purpose:** To provide the highest quality symphonic programs and educational benefits to the largest possible number of people in the South Arkansas Area
> **Management:** Allan Burdick, Executive Director/Music Director & Conductor; Virginia Matthews, Executive Secretary

Officers: Andy Allen, President; John Talpas, First Vice President; Janis Lovell, Second Vice President; Virginia Ray Ellzey, Treasurer; Victoria Harden, Secretary
Paid Staff: 2   **Volunteer Staff:** 35
Paid Artists: 60
Utilizes: Guest Conductors; Guest Artists
Budget: $50,000 - $100,000
Income Sources: Private Foundations/Grants/Endowments; Business/Corporate Donations; Box Office; Government Grants; Individual Donations
Season: September - May   **Annual Attendance:** 3,000
Affiliations: ASOL
Performance Facilities: El Dorado Municipal Auditorium; Harton Theatre

FACILITY

EL DORADO MUNICIPAL AUDITORIUM
100 West Eighth Street, El Dorado, AR 71730
(501) 862-1387
   Type of Facility: Auditorium
   Type of Stage: Proscenium
   Stage Dimensions: 86'Wx35'D   **Orchestra Pit**
   Seating Capacity: 1872
   Year Built: 1959   **Architect:** Herbert Voelcker   **Cost:** $750,000
   Acoustical Consultant: Dr. Joe G. Robbins
   Contact for Rental: John R. Alley;   (501) 862-1387
   Resident Groups: South Arkansas Symphony Association; The South Arkansas Ballet Association; South Arkansas Jubilee

SOUTH ARKANSAS ARTS CENTER
110 East Fifth Street, El Dorado, AR 71730
(501) 862-5474
   Type of Facility: Civic Center; Multi-Purpose
   Facility Originally: National Guard Armory
   Type of Stage: Proscenium
   Stage Dimensions: 20'x36'x46'
   Seating Capacity: 207
   Year Built: 1965   **Architect:** John Abbott   **Cost:** $165,000
   Year Remodeled: 1975   **Architect:** John Abbott   **Cost:** $65,000
   Contact for Rental: Executive Director;   (501) 862-5474
   Manager: Reuben Murray
   Resident Groups: South Arkansas Arts Center Theatre; South Arkansas Arts Center Secondstage

Eureka Springs

THEATRE

ELNA M. SMITH FOUNDATION
PO Box 471, Eureka Springs, AR 72632
(501) 253-9200
   Founded: 1964
   Arts Area: Theatrical Group
   Status: Professional; Non-Profit
   Type: Performing; Sponsoring
   Purpose: To present "The Great Passion Play," an outdoor drama dealing with the life and times of Christ and his passion
   Management: Ken Smith, Production Vice President; Don Berrigan, Director
   Officers: Robert C. Foster, Executive Director; D. Smith, Recording Secretary; Don Robe, Chairman of the Board
   Paid Staff: 14
   Paid Artists: 200
   Budget: $1,000,000 - $5,000,000
   Income Sources: Box Office; Individual Donations
   Season: May - October   **Annual Attendance:** 275,000
   Performance Facilities: Amphitheater

PERFORMING SERIES

INSPIRATION POINT FINE ARTS COLONY
Route 2, PO Box 127, Eureka Springs, AR 73632
(501) 253-8595
   Founded: 1950

Arts Area: Instrumental Music; Lyric Opera; Grand Opera
Status: Non-Professional; Non-Profit
Type: Performing; Educational; Sponsoring
Purpose: To give students the opportunity to experience the real-life opera stage
Officers: James H. Swiggart, General Manager; Carroll Freeman, Artistic Director
Paid Staff: 3
Paid Artists: 28   **Non-Paid Artists:** 50
Utilizes: Special Technical Talent; Guest Conductors; Guest Artists; Guest Directors
Budget: $100,000 - $500,000
Income Sources: Private Foundations/Grants/Endowments; Box Office; Individual Donations
Season: June - July   **Annual Attendance:** 5,500
Affiliations: National Federation of Music Clubs
Performance Facilities: Inspiration Point Fine Arts Colony

Fayetteville

INSTRUMENTAL MUSIC

SYMPHONY SOCIETY OF NORTH ARKANSAS
201 North East Street, Fayetteville, AR 72701
(501) 521-4166
Founded: 1954
Arts Area: Symphony; Orchestra; Chamber; Music Festival
Status: Semi-Professional; Non-Profit
Type: Performing; Educational
Purpose: To offer northwest Arkansas classical and pops concerts in four communities and give educational concerts in the same area
Management: Constance L. Hendrix-Kral, Executive Director
Officers: Mary Nusser, President; Jack Byrd, Vice President; Mitzi Springborn, Secretary; Darlyn Speight, Treasurer
Paid Staff: 3   **Volunteer Staff:** 1
Paid Artists: 52   **Non-Paid Artists:** 23
Utilizes: Guest Conductors; Guest Artists
Budget: $100,000 - $500,000
Income Sources: Private Foundations/Grants/Endowments; Business/Corporate Donations; Box Office; Government Grants; Individual Donations
Season: September - June   **Annual Attendance:** 14,000
Affiliations: University of Arkansas
Performance Facilities: Walton Arts Center

PERFORMING SERIES

MUSIC FESTIVAL OF ARKANSAS
PO Box 1243, Fayetteville, AR 72702
(501) 521-4166
Founded: 1982
Arts Area: Vocal Music; Instrumental Music; Lyric Opera
Status: Professional; Non-Profit
Type: Educational; Sponsoring
Management: Carlton R. Woods, Director; Shea Crain, Festival Manager
Officers: Mary Nusser, President; Jack Byrd, Vice President; Mitzi Springborn, Secretary; Darlyn Speight, Treasurer
Paid Staff: 2
Utilizes: Special Technical Talent; Guest Conductors; Guest Artists
Budget: $50,000 - $100,000
Income Sources: Business/Corporate Donations; Box Office; Government Grants; Individual Donations
Season: June
Performance Facilities: Walton Arts Center

FACILITY

FINE ARTS CONCERT HALL
University of Arkansas, Fayetteville, AR 72701
(501) 575-4175
Type of Facility: Concert Hall
Type of Stage: Thrust
Seating Capacity: 200
Year Built: 1950
Year Remodeled: 1992

Contact for Rental: Dr. C. Johnson; (501) 521-8644
Resident Groups: University of Arkansas Orchestra; Choir; Student and Faculty Recitals

Fort Smith

INSTRUMENTAL MUSIC

FORT SMITH SYMPHONY
405 Central Mall, PO Box 3151, Fort Smith, AR 72913
(501) 452-7575
FAX: (501) 452-8985
Founded: 1923
Arts Area: Symphony; Orchestra; Chamber
Status: Non-Profit
Type: Performing; Resident; Educational
Purpose: To enhance the cultural life in the community
Management: Carol Sue Wooten, Executive Director; John A. Thellman, Music Director/Conductor
Officers: Dr. Benny Gooden, President; Brian McAlpin, First Vice President; John Lange, Second Vice President
Paid Staff: 4
Paid Artists: 60   **Non-Paid Artists:** 2
Utilizes: Guest Artists
Budget: $100,000 - $500,000
Income Sources: Private Foundations/Grants/Endowments; Business/Corporate Donations; Box Office; Government Grants; Individual Donations
Season: September - May   **Annual Attendance:** 6,000
Affiliations: ASOL
Performance Facilities: Southside Auditorium and Civic Center

THEATRE

FORT SMITH LITTLE THEATRE
PO Box 3752, Fort Smith, AR 72913
(501) 783-2966
Founded: 1947
Arts Area: Theatrical Group
Status: Non-Profit
Type: Performing
Volunteer Staff: 15
Non-Paid Artists: 200
Budget: $1,000 - $50,000
Income Sources: Box Office
Season: 52 Weeks   **Annual Attendance:** 10,000
Affiliations: SWTC
Performance Facilities: Fort Smith Little Theatre

FACILITY

FORT SMITH CIVIC CENTER
55 South Seventh Street, Fort Smith, AR 72901
(501) 785-2495
Type of Facility: Civic Center
Year Built: 1966
Acoustical Consultant: Charlie Long
Contact for Rental: Bobbie Sheperd; (501) 785-2495
Manager: Joan Stratmann
One building houses both the exhibition hall and theatre, see separate listing for more information.

FORT SMITH CIVIC CENTER - EXHIBITION HALL
55 South Seventh Street, Fort Smith, AR 72901
(501) 785-2495
Type of Facility: Exhibition Hall
Seating Capacity: 1,000-1,200
Year Built: 1966
Contact for Rental: Bobbie Shepherd; (501) 785-2495

FORT SMITH CIVIC CENTER - THEATER
55 South Seventh Street, Fort Smith, AR 72901
(501) 785-2495
> **Type of Facility:** Concert Hall; Auditorium; Performance Center; Civic Center
> **Type of Stage:** Proscenium
> **Stage Dimensions:** 100'x42' **Orchestra Pit**
> **Seating Capacity:** 1,552
> **Year Built:** 1966
> **Contact for Rental:** Bobbie Shepherd; (501) 785-2495
> **Manager:** Joan Stratmann; (501) 785-2495
> *One building houses both the theatre and exhibition hall*

FORT SMITH LITTLE THEATRE
401 North Sixth Street, Fort Smith, AR 72901
(501) 783-2966
> **Type of Facility:** Theatre House
> **Type of Stage:** 3/4 Arena
> **Stage Dimensions:** 35'Wx20'D
> **Seating Capacity:** 193
> **Year Built:** 1986 **Architect:** Mott, Mobley and McGowan **Cost:** $415,000
> **Contact for Rental:** Manager; (501) 783-2966

WESTARK COMMUNITY COLLEGE - BREEDLOVE AUDITORIUM
PO Box 3649, Fort Smith, AR 72913
(501) 785-7000, ext. 257
> **Type of Facility:** Auditorium
> **Type of Stage:** Flexible
> **Stage Dimensions:** 18'x40'x28' **Orchestra Pit**
> **Seating Capacity:** 440
> **Year Built:** 1976 **Architect:** Ken Cockram **Cost:** $1,500,000
> **Manager:** Stacy Jones; (501) 785-7198
> **Resident Groups:** Fort Smith Symphony

Harrison

PERFORMING SERIES

NORTH CENTRAL ARKANSAS CONCERT ASSOCIATION
PO Box 2117, Harrison, AR 72601
(501) 741-7858
> **Founded:** 1969
> **Arts Area:** Dance; Vocal Music; Instrumental Music; Theater
> **Status:** Non-Profit
> **Type:** Sponsoring
> **Purpose:** To promote culture and education
> **Officers:** Mike Braken, President; Glenna Ragan, Vice President; Betty Shinall, Secretary; Rosalie O'Brien, Treasurer
> **Paid Staff:** 1
> **Budget:** $1,000 - $50,000
> **Income Sources:** Private Foundations/Grants/Endowments; Business/Corporate Donations; Box Office; Government Grants; Individual Donations
> **Season:** October - April **Annual Attendance:** 1,500
> **Affiliations:** Arkansas Arts Council; MAAA
> **Performance Facilities:** Harrison High School Auditorium

Hot Springs

FACILITY

HOT SPRINGS CONVENTION AND VISITORS' BUREAU
PO Box K, Hot Springs, AR 71902
(501) 321-1706
> **Type of Facility:** Auditorium; Civic Center
> **Type of Stage:** Proscenium
> **Stage Dimensions:** 18'x77'x39' **Orchestra Pit**
> **Seating Capacity:** 3,700
> **Year Built:** 1965 **Architect:** I. Granger McDaniel **Cost:** $2,500,000
> **Contact for Rental:** Brenda Bates, Convention Services Manager; (501) 321-2835

Jonesboro

FACILITY

THE FORUM
115 East Monroe, Jonesboro, AR 72401
(501) 935-2726
Founded: 1978
Type of Facility: Concert Hall; Auditorium; Performance Center; Theatre House; Civic Center
Facility Originally: Movie House
Type of Stage: Proscenium   **Orchestra Pit**
Seating Capacity: 690
Year Built: 1926
Year Remodeled: 1978
Contact for Rental: Lynda Bowen;   (501) 935-2726

Little Rock

DANCE

BALLET ARKANSAS
120 Tanglewood, PO Box 7574, Little Rock, AR 72217
(501) 666-4445
Founded: 1978
Arts Area: Ballet
Status: Semi-Professional; Non-Profit
Type: Performing; Touring; Educational; Sponsoring
Purpose: Ballet Arkansas was founded with the objective to provide for and promote the art of dance throughout the state of Arkansas.
Management: Philip Quick, Executive Director; Kirt Hathaway, Artistic Director
Paid Staff: 4   **Volunteer Staff:** 200
Paid Artists: 11   **Non-Paid Artists:** 13
Utilizes: Special Technical Talent; Guest Conductors; Guest Artists; Guest Directors
Budget: $100,000 - $500,000
Income Sources: Private Foundations/Grants/Endowments; Business/Corporate Donations; Box Office; Government Grants; Individual Donations
Annual Attendance: 20,000
Affiliations: SWRBA; NARB
Performance Facilities: Robinson Center Music Hall

INSTRUMENTAL MUSIC

ARKANSAS SYMPHONY ORCHESTRA SOCIETY
PO Box 7328, Little Rock, AR 72217
(501) 666-1761
FAX: (501) 666-3193
Founded: 1966
Arts Area: Symphony; Orchestra; Chamber
Status: Professional; Non-Profit
Type: Performing; Touring; Educational
Purpose: To provide the finest symphonic music to the people of the area
Management: Jo Ann Greene, Executive Director
Officers: George Mitchell, President; John Steari, Vice President; Philip Tappan, Secretary; George Worthen, Treasurer
Paid Staff: 7   **Volunteer Staff:** 3
Paid Artists: 85
Utilizes: Special Technical Talent; Guest Conductors; Guest Artists
Budget: $1,000,000 - $5,000,000
Income Sources: Private Foundations/Grants/Endowments; Business/Corporate Donations; Box Office; Government Grants; Individual Donations
Season: September - July   **Annual Attendance:** 60,000
Affiliations: ASOL; ASCAP
Performance Facilities: Robinson Center Music Hall

VOCAL MUSIC

OPERA THEATRE AT WILDWOOD PARK FOR THE PERFORMING ARTS
PO Box 25202, Little Rock, AR 72221
(501) 821-7275
FAX: (501) 821-7280
  Arts Area: Lyric Opera; Light Opera; Operetta; Musical Theatre
  Status: Professional; Non-Profit
  Type: Performing; Resident
  Purpose: To present operas done in English from standard repertoires as well as world premieres
  Management: Dr. Ann Chotaro, Founder/Artistic Director; Rod Gideons, Education/Tour Director & Artistic Administrator
  Officers: Dr. Aluah Nelson III, President of the Board
  Budget: $500,000 - $1,000,000
  Income Sources: Private Foundations/Grants/Endowments; Business/Corporate Donations; Box Office; Government Grants; Individual Donations
  Season: 52 Weeks
  Performance Facilities: Studio Theatre at Wildwood Park

THEATRE

THE ARKANSAS ARTS CENTER CHILDREN'S THEATER
PO Box 2137, Little Rock, AR 72203
(501) 372-4000
  Founded: 1979
  Arts Area: Professional; Theatrical Group
  Status: Professional; Non-Profit
  Type: Performing; Touring
  Purpose: Family theater
  Management: Bradley D. Anderson, Artistic Director; P.J. Powers, Administrative Manager
  Officers: Curt F. Bradbury, Board President
  Paid Staff: 15
  Utilizes: Special Technical Talent; Guest Artists; Guest Directors
  Budget: $100,000 - $500,000
  Income Sources: Private Foundations/Grants/Endowments; Business/Corporate Donations; Box Office; Government Grants; Individual Donations
  Season: October - May **Annual Attendance:** 124,000
  Affiliations: TCG; ASSITEJ
  Performance Facilities: Arkansas Art Center Theater

ARKANSAS REPERTORY THEATRE
601 Main Street, PO Box 110, Little Rock, AR 72203
(501) 378-0445
FAX: (501) 378-0012
  Founded: 1976
  Arts Area: Professional; Theatrical Group
  Status: Professional; Non-Profit
  Type: Performing; Touring; Resident; Educational; Sponsoring
  Management: Andrew C. Gaupp, Managing Director; Cliff Fannin Baker, Artistic Director; Lynn Frazier, Business Manager; Susan Nichols, Development Associate
  Officers: Maurice Mitchell, Chairman; Don Steely, President; Phil Sutphin, Treasurer; Sandra Cotter, Secretary
  Paid Staff: 25
  Paid Artists: 50
  Utilizes: Special Technical Talent; Guest Artists; Guest Directors; Guest Designers
  Budget: $500,000 - $1,000,000
  Income Sources: Private Foundations/Grants/Endowments; Business/Corporate Donations; Box Office; Government Grants; Individual Donations
  Season: 52 Weeks **Annual Attendance:** 50,000
  Affiliations: TCG; FEDAPT; SWTC; SETC
  Performance Facilities: Arkansas Repertory Theatre

FACILITY

ARKANSAS ARTS CENTER
PO Box 2137, Little Rock, AR 72203
(501) 372-4000
FAX: (501) 375-8053
  Type of Facility: Auditorium; Studio Performance; Theatre House

Type of Stage: Proscenium
Stage Dimensions: 63'Wx42'D   **Orchestra Pit**
Seating Capacity: 389
Year Built: 1962   **Architect:** Cromwell, Neyland, Truemper Millett & Gatchell
Acoustical Consultant: Bolt, Beranek & Newman
Contact for Rental: Ellen Becker;   (501) 372-4000
Manager: Townsend Wolfe
Resident Groups: Arkansas Arts Center Children's Theatre; Arkansas Repertory Theatre

ARKANSAS REPERTORY THEATRE
601 Main Street, Little Rock, AR 72201
(501) 378-0405
Type of Facility: Theatre Complex; Auditorium; Multi-Purpose; Black Box
Facility Originally: Retail Department Store
Type of Stage: Proscenium; Environmental; Modified Apron Proscenium
Stage Dimensions: 42'x23'x41'; 42'x33'x41' with apron   **Orchestra Pit**
Seating Capacity: Auditorium - 362; Black Box - 99
Year Built: 1910   **Architect:** Charles Thompson
Year Remodeled: 1987   **Architect:** Witsell, Evans and Rasco, P.A.   **Cost:** $2,200,000
Acoustical Consultant: Mitchell Kurtz Designs
Contact for Rental: Guy Couch;   (501) 378-0405
Resident Groups: Arkansas Repertory Theatre

ROBINSON CENTER MUSIC HALL
Markham and Broadway, Little Rock, AR 72201
(501) 376-4781
FAX: (501) 374-2255
Type of Facility: Concert Hall; Auditorium; Theatre House; Civic Center; Multi-Purpose
Type of Stage: Proscenium
Stage Dimensions: 35'x60'x40'   **Orchestra Pit**
Seating Capacity: 2,641
Year Built: 1939   **Architect:** WPA Project
Year Remodeled: 1972   **Architect:** Wittenburg, Deloney & Davidson   **Cost:** $3,800,000
Contact for Rental: Phyllis Lucas;   (501) 376-4781
Resident Groups: Arkansas Symphony Orchestra; Ballet Arkansas; Little Rock Community Concerts

UNIVERSITY OF ARKANSAS-LITTLE ROCK - STELLA BOYLE SMITH CONCERT HALL
2801 South University, Little Rock, AR 72204
(501) 569-3296
Type of Stage: Proscenium
Seating Capacity: 719
Year Built: 1965   **Architect:** Cromwell Associates   **Cost:** $350,000
Manager: Dr. Jess Anthony

Mena

THEATRE

OUACHITA LITTLE THEATRE
PO Box 1217, Mena, AR 71953
(501) 394-4436
Founded: 1979
Arts Area: Community; Theatrical Group
Status: Non-Professional; Non-Profit
Type: Performing; Educational
Purpose: Promote theatrical arts, produce plays (dramas, comedies, musicals, children's, educational and community theatre)
Officers: Leda S. Benson, Founder/Coordinator/Past President; Rudy Timmerman, President
Volunteer Staff: 9
Utilizes: Special Technical Talent
Budget: $1,000 - $50,000
Income Sources: Private Foundations/Grants/Endowments; Box Office; Individual Donations
Season: 52 Weeks   **Annual Attendance:** 2,000

Mountain Home

THEATRE

TWIN LAKES PLAYHOUSE
PO Box 482, Mountain Home, AR 72653
(501) 431-5594
    Founded: 1971
    Arts Area: Community
    Status: Semi-Professional; Non-Professional; Non-Profit
    Type: Performing
    Purpose: To provide live theater productions for the area
    Officers: Karin Floyd, Chairman; Glenn Payne, Vice Chairman; Shirley Spitzer, Secretary; Jennifer Baker, Treasurer
    Volunteer Staff: 8
    Non-Paid Artists: 40
    Budget: $1,000 - $50,000
    Income Sources: Business/Corporate Donations; Box Office; Individual Donations
    Season: Spring - Fall   **Annual Attendance:** 1,000

North Little Rock

DANCE

MIRANA MIDDLE EASTERN DANCE COMPANY
257 Plainview Circle, North Little Rock, AR 72116-8913
(501) 753-5122
    Founded: 1985
    Arts Area: Ethnic
    Status: Professional; Non-Profit
    Type: Performing; Educational
    Purpose: To present classic and traditional forms of Middle Eastern dance to the public for education and understanding of the Middle Eastern cultural heritage
    Management: Mirana Thompson, Artistic Director
    Officers: David Martinous, President; Willie Oates, Vice President; Peggy Bowles, Secretary/Treasurer
    Paid Artists: 10   **Non-Paid Artists:** 10
    Utilizes: Special Technical Talent; Guest Artists
    Budget: $1,000 - $50,000
    Income Sources: Private Foundations/Grants/Endowments; Box Office; Individual Donations

Pine Bluff

FACILITY

ARTS AND SCIENCE CENTER OF SOUTHEAST ARKANSAS
220 Martin Street, Pine Bluff, AR 71601
(501) 536-3375
    Type of Facility: Civic Center
    Type of Stage: Proscenium
    Stage Dimensions: 12' x 38' x 24'   **Orchestra Pit**
    Seating Capacity: 191
    Year Built: 1968   **Architect:** Edward Durell Stone
    Contact for Rental: Galen Colbert;   (501) 536-3375
    Resident Groups: Center Stage Players

PINE BLUFF CONVENTION CENTER
500 East Eighth Street, Pine Bluff, AR 71601
(501) 536-7600
    Type of Facility: Civic Center
    Type of Stage: Arena
    Year Built: 1976   **Architect:** Reed, Willis & Burke   **Cost:** $8,000,000
    Contact for Rental: Michael A. Nordine;   (501) 536-7600

PINE BLUFF CONVENTION CENTER - ARENA
500 East Eighth Street, Pine Bluff, AR 71601
(501) 536-7600
    Type of Facility: Arena; Multi-Purpose

Type of Stage: Arena
Seating Capacity: 8,000
Year Built: 1976
Contact for Rental: Michael A. Nordine; (501) 536-7600
Stage area contains 2,300 square feet

PINE BLUFF CONVENTION CENTER - AUDITORIUM
500 East Eighth Street, Pine Bluff, AR 71601
(501) 536-7600
    Type of Facility: Concert Hall; Auditorium; Theatre House; Opera House
    Type of Stage: Proscenium
    Stage Dimensions: 63'Wx93'D; 63'Wx25'H proscenium opening
    Orchestra Pit
    Seating Capacity: 2,027
    Year Built: 1976
    Contact for Rental: Michael A. Nordine; (501) 536-7600

Russellville

FACILITY

ARKANSAS RIVER VALLEY ARTS CENTER
PO Box 2112, Russellville, AR 72801
(501) 968-2452
    Founded: 1990
    Type of Facility: Auditorium
    Facility Originally: School
    Type of Stage: Platform
    Seating Capacity: 300

ARKANSAS TECH UNIVERSITY - WITHERSPOON ARTS AND HUMANITIES BUILDING
Russellville, AR 72801
(501) 968-0274
    Type of Facility: Auditorium
    Type of Stage: Flexible   **Orchestra Pit**
    Seating Capacity: 746
    Year Built: 1972   **Architect:** Dan Cowling & Associates
    Acoustical Consultant: C.P. Boner & Associates
    Contact for Rental: Jimmy Ferguson; (501) 968-0239
    Resident Groups: University Music Department; Little Theatre; Russellville Community Concerts; small group programs

---
Searcy

FACILITY

BENSON AUDITORIUM
900 East Center Street, Searcy, AR 72149-0001
(501) 279-4557
    Founded: 1980
    Type of Facility: Auditorium
    Facility Originally: Auditorium for Harding University
    Type of Stage: Proscenium
    Stage Dimensions: 80'x40'   **Orchestra Pit**
    Seating Capacity: 3,111
    Year Built: 1980

Springdale

FACILITY

ARTS CENTER OF THE OZARKS
214 South Main, Springdale, AR 72765
(501) 751-5441
    Type of Facility: Theatre Complex; Multi-Purpose
    Facility Originally: Church
    Type of Stage: Flexible; Proscenium

Stage Dimensions: 40'Wx25'D
Seating Capacity: 350
Year Built: 1978
Contact for Rental: Harry Blundell; (501) 751-5441
Resident Groups: In-house productions

Stuttgart

PERFORMING SERIES

GRAND PRAIRIE FESTIVAL OF THE ARTS
PO Box 65, Stuttgart, AR 72160
(501) 673-1781; (501) 673-7278
Founded: 1956
Arts Area: Vocal Music; Instrumental Music; Theater
Status: Professional; Non-Professional
Type: Educational; Sponsoring
Purpose: To promote all of the cultural arts in the Grand Prairie area
Officers: Marianne Maynard, Co-Chairperson; Linda Fischer, Co-Chairperson
Volunteer Staff: 25
Utilizes: Guest Artists; Guest Directors
Budget: $1,000 - $50,000
Income Sources: Business/Corporate Donations; Box Office; Government Grants; Individual Donations
Season: September   **Annual Attendance:** 5,000
Affiliations: Grand Prairie Arts Council
Performance Facilities: Grand Prairie War Memorial Auditorium, Grand Prairie Arts Center

FACILITY

GRAND PRAIRIE WAR MEMORIAL AUDITORIUM
600 West 20th, Stuttgart, AR 72160
(501) 673-8585
Type of Facility: Auditorium
Type of Stage: Proscenium
Seating Capacity: 1,000
Contact for Rental: Jo Rowe; (501) 673-8585
Manager: Ronnie Simmons; (501) 673-8585

CALIFORNIA

Anaheim

DANCE

XIPE TOTEC AZTEC DANCERS/VIRGINIA CARMELO
1757 Gardenaire Lane, Anaheim, CA 92804
(714) 491-7510
> **Founded:** 1979
> **Arts Area:** Traditional Aztec
> **Status:** Semi-Professional
> **Type:** Performing; Touring; Educational
> **Purpose:** To retain cultural ties
> **Management:** Virginia Carmelo
> **Budget:** $1,000 - $50,000
> **Income Sources:** Box Office

FACILITY

ANAHEIM CONVENTION CENTER
800 West Katella Avenue, Anaheim, CA 92802
(714) 999-8950
FAX: (714) 999-8965
> **Type of Facility:** Multi-Purpose
> **Year Built:** 1967   **Architect:** Adrian Wilson & Associates   **Cost:** $6,100,000
> **Year Remodeled:** 1982   **Architect:** Howard Needles Tammen & Bergendoff   **Cost:** $17,785,000
> **Contact for Rental:** Lynn Thompson;   (714) 999-8950
> *The Anaheim Convention Center contains the Anaheim Room and the Arena. See separate listings for additional information.*

ANAHEIM CONVENTION CENTER - ANAHEIM ROOM
800 West Katella Avenue, Anaheim, CA 92802
(714) 999-8950
FAX: (714) 999-8965
> **Type of Facility:** Multi-Purpose; Room
> **Type of Stage:** Proscenium
> **Stage Dimensions:** 40'Wx28'D
> **Seating Capacity:** 1,600
> **Contact for Rental:** Lynn Thompson;   (714) 999-8950

ANAHEIM CONVENTION CENTER - ARENA
800 West Katella Avenue, Anaheim, CA 92802
(714) 999-8950
FAX: (714) 999-8965
> **Type of Facility:** Arena
> **Type of Stage:** Arena
> **Seating Capacity:** 8,900
> **Contact for Rental:** Lynn Thompson;   (714) 999-8950

ANAHEIM CULTURAL ARTS CENTER
931 North Harbor Boulevard, Anaheim, CA 92805
(714) 533-3460
> **Type of Facility:** Concert Hall; Auditorium; Studio Performance; Performance Center; Room
> **Facility Originally:** School
> **Type of Stage:** Proscenium
> **Stage Dimensions:** 30'x40'x26'
> **Seating Capacity:** 300
> **Year Built:** 1931   **Cost:** $85,000
> **Year Remodeled:** 1972   **Architect:** Dan Rowland & Associates
> **Contact for Rental:** Sylvia Bula;   (714) 533-3460
> **Resident Groups:** Anaheim Arts Association; Ana-Modjeska Players; Searchers Gem & Mineral Society; Scandinavian Dancers; Strathleven Scottish Country Dancers; Changing Visions Dance Theatre Company

Aptos

DANCE

CRASH, BURN AND DIE DANCE COMPANY
259 Rio Del Mar Boulevard, Aptos, CA 95003
(408) 688-3371
> **Founded:** 1982
> **Arts Area:** Modern
> **Status:** Professional; Non-Profit
> **Type:** Performing; Touring
> **Purpose:** At or over the edge since 1982
> **Management:** Leslie Swaha, Artistic Director
> **Utilizes:** Guest Artists
> **Income Sources:** Private Foundations/Grants/Endowments; Box Office; Individual Donations
> **Season:** 52 Weeks

PERFORMING SERIES

CABRILLO MUSIC FESTIVAL
9053 Soquel, Aptos, CA 95003
(408) 662-2701
> **Founded:** 1963
> **Arts Area:** Vocal Music; Instrumental Music; Festivals
> **Status:** Professional; Non-Profit
> **Type:** Performing; Sponsoring
> **Purpose:** To present the music of living composers, primarily American, to ever-widening audiences
> **Management:** Tom Fredericks, Executive Director; Marin Alsop, Music Director
> **Officers:** Celia Hartman, President
> **Paid Staff:** 2 **Volunteer Staff:** 100
> **Paid Artists:** 70
> **Utilizes:** Guest Conductors; Guest Artists
> **Budget:** $100,000 - $500,000
> **Income Sources:** Private Foundations/Grants/Endowments; Business/Corporate Donations; Box Office; Government Grants; Individual Donations
> **Annual Attendance:** 7,500
> **Performance Facilities:** Santa Cruz Civic Auditorium; Mission San Juan Bautista

FACILITY

CABRILLO COLLEGE THEATER
6500 Soquel Drive, Aptos, CA 95003
(408) 479-6364
FAX: (408) 464-8382
> **Type of Facility:** Theatre House
> **Type of Stage:** Proscenium
> **Stage Dimensions:** 48'Wx40'D; 48'Wx16'H proscenium opening
> **Seating Capacity:** 527
> **Year Built:** 1962 **Architect:** Kump Maston Hurd **Cost:** $1,000,000
> **Contact for Rental:** Bonnie Durham, Facilities Coordinator;   (408) 479-6331
> **Manager:** John Mauceri

Arcata

FACILITY

HUMBOLDT STATE UNIVERSITY
Center Arts, Arcata, CA 95521
(707) 826-4411
> **Type of Facility:** Performance Center
> **Contact for Rental:** Center Arts Production Coordinator;   (707) 826-4411
> *Contains East Gymnasium, Fulkerson Recital Hall, John Van Duzer Theatre and Kate Buchanon Room. See separate listings for additional information.*

HUMBOLDT STATE UNIVERSITY - EAST GYMNASIUM
Center Arts, Arcata, CA 95521
(707) 826-4411
Type of Facility: Basketball Gymnasium
Type of Stage: Platform
Stage Dimensions: 20'x40'
Seating Capacity: 1,800
Contact for Rental: Center Arts Production Coordinator;   (707) 826-4411
Resident Groups: Center Arts

HUMBOLDT STATE UNIVERSITY - FULKERSON RECITAL HALL
Center Arts, Arcata, CA 95521
(707) 826-4411
Type of Facility: Recital Hall
Type of Stage: Proscenium   **Orchestra Pit**
Seating Capacity: 200
Contact for Rental: Center Arts Production Coordinator;   (707) 826-4411
Resident Groups: University Music Department; Center Arts

HUMBOLDT STATE UNIVERSITY - JOHN VAN DUZER THEATRE
Center Arts, Arcata, CA 95521
(707) 826-4411
Type of Facility: Theatre House
Type of Stage: Proscenium   **Orchestra Pit**
Seating Capacity: 750
Contact for Rental: Center Arts Production Coordinator;   (707) 826-4411
Resident Groups: Theater Arts Department; Music Department; Center Arts

HUMBOLDT STATE UNIVERSITY - KATE BUCHANAN ROOM
Center Arts, Arcata, CA 95521
(707) 826-4411
Type of Facility: Multi-Purpose; Room
Type of Stage: Platform
Stage Dimensions: 8'x12'
Seating Capacity: 260
Contact for Rental: Center Arts Production Coordinator;   (707) 826-4411
Resident Groups: Center Arts

Bakersfield

INSTRUMENTAL MUSIC

BAKERSFIELD SYMPHONY ORCHESTRA
1401 19th Street, Suite 130, Bakersfield, CA 93301
(805) 323-7928
FAX: (805) 323-7331
Founded: 1946
Arts Area: Symphony
Status: Professional
Type: Performing
Purpose: To present classical music, educational programs, ballet and pop concerts
Management: A.H. Stanley, Manager
Officers: Donald R. Lindsey, President
Paid Staff: 5   **Volunteer Staff:** 100
Paid Artists: 90
Utilizes: Guest Conductors; Guest Artists
Budget: $100,000 - $500,000
Income Sources: Private Foundations/Grants/Endowments; Business/Corporate Donations; Box Office; Government Grants; Individual Donations
Season: September - May   **Annual Attendance:** 18,500
Affiliations: ASOL; Association of California Symphony Orchestras
Performance Facilities: Bakersfield Civic Auditorium

FACILITY

BAKERSFIELD CIVIC AUDITORIUM
1001 Truxton Avenue, Bakersfield, CA 93301
(805) 327-7553
FAX: (805) 861-9904
    Type of Facility: Concert Hall; Theatre House; Arena; Multi-Purpose
    Type of Stage: Proscenium
    Stage Dimensions: 140'Wx52'D, 25'W proscenium opening   **Orchestra Pit**
    Seating Capacity: Concert Hall 3,041; Festival 6,000
    Year Built: 1962   **Architect:** Wright Metcalf & Parsons   **Cost:** $5,000,000
    Acoustical Consultant: Vern Knudsen
    Contact for Rental: Lee Anderson;   (805) 327-7553

DORE THEATRE - CALIFORNIA STATE UNIVERSITY, BAKERSFIELD
9001 Stockdale Highway, Bakersfield, CA 93311
(805) 664-2221
    Type of Facility: Theatre Complex; Studio Performance
    Type of Stage: Proscenium   **Orchestra Pit**
    Seating Capacity: 492
    Year Built: 1979
    Contact for Rental: Dean of School of Arts and Sciences;   (805) 664-2221
    Resident Groups: California State University, Bakersfield - Fine Arts Department

Bear Valley

PERFORMING SERIES

MUSIC FROM BEAR VALLEY
PO Box 5068, Bear Valley Road, Bear Valley, CA 95223
(209) 753-2574
FAX: (209) 753-2336
    Founded: 1969
    Arts Area: Instrumental Music; Festivals; Grand Opera
    Status: Professional; Non-Profit
    Type: Performing; Resident
    Purpose: To present a sixteen day music fesitval of opera, symphony, pop, and chamber music concerts;
    to present children's concerts and recitals
    Management: Katherine L. Bort, Executive Director; Stewart Comer, General Manager
    Officers: Ann Hicks, President; Daniel P. Hogan, Vice President; Linda Koenig, Secretary; Evelyn Bautista, Treasurer
    Paid Staff: 16   **Volunteer Staff:** 25
    Paid Artists: 110   **Non-Paid Artists:** 38
    Utilizes: Special Technical Talent; Guest Artists
    Budget: $100,000 - $500,000
    Income Sources: Private Foundations/Grants/Endowments; Business/Corporate Donations; Box Office; Government
    Grants; Individual Donations; Auction; Raffle; Product Sales
    Season: July - August   **Annual Attendance:** 10,000
    Affiliations: Association of California Symphony Orchestras

Belvedere

DANCE

THE DANCE ASSOCIATION/RUTH LANGRIDGE DANCE COMPANY
PO Box 692, Belvedere, CA 94920
(415) 435-2771
    Founded: 1979
    Arts Area: Modern; Ballet
    Status: Professional; Non-Profit
    Type: Performing; Touring; Resident; Educational
    Purpose: To provide innovative, contemporary dance performances for the community and on tour; to provide
    high-quality dance training and educational-outreach programs
    Officers: Ruth Langridge, Artistic Director
    Paid Staff: 3   **Volunteer Staff:** 25
    Paid Artists: 8
    Utilizes: Guest Artists; Guest Choreographers
    Budget: $100,000 - $500,000

Income Sources: Private Foundations/Grants/Endowments; Business/Corporate Donations; Box Office; Government Grants; Individual Donations; Tuition; Fund-raising
Season: 52 Weeks
Performance Facilities: New Peformance Gallery

Berkeley

DANCE

BAY AREA REPERTORY DANCE THEATRE (BARD)
c/o David Wood, Department of Dramatic Arts, Berkeley, CA 94720
(510) 642-1677
Founded: 1970
Arts Area: Modern
Status: Non-Professional; Non-Profit
Type: Performing; Educational
Purpose: To offer young dancers an opportunity to gain performance experience; to serve the community in various projects coordinated with educational programs in the arts
Management: Carol Egan, Company Manager; David Wood, Artistic Director; Marni Thomas, General Manager; Barbara Codd, Stage Manager
Paid Staff: 3   **Volunteer Staff:** 2
Non-Paid Artists: 15
Utilizes: Special Technical Talent; Guest Artists
Budget: $1,000 - $50,000
Income Sources: Private Foundations/Grants/Endowments; Box Office; Individual Donations
Season: November - April

BERKELEY CITY BALLET
1800 Dwight Way, Berkeley, CA 94703
(510) 841-8913
Founded: 1974
Arts Area: Ballet
Status: Non-Profit
Type: Performing; Educational
Purpose: To promote and foster dance in the Bay Area by providing training and presenting quality performances
Management: Grace Doty, Artistic Director
Officers: Jim Simonetti, President; Jack Johannes, First Vice President
Paid Staff: 9
Utilizes: Guest Artists; Guest Choreographers
Budget: $100,000 - $500,000
Income Sources: Private Foundations/Grants/Endowments; Business/Corporate Donations; Individual Donations
Season: Spring - Winter   **Annual Attendance:** 15,000
Performance Facilities: Zellerbach Hall; Berkeley Community Theater

WENDY ROGERS/CHOREOGRAPHICS
1187 Shattuck Avenue, Berkeley, CA 94707
(510) 524-8254
Arts Area: Modern
Status: Professional; Non-Profit
Type: Performing; Touring; Resident
Management: Wendy Rogers, Artistic Director
Paid Artists: 5
Utilizes: Guest Artists; Guest Choreographers; Collaborating Artists
Budget: $50,000 - $100,000
Income Sources: Private Foundations/Grants/Endowments; Business/Corporate Donations; Box Office; Government Grants; Individual Donations
Season: 52 Weeks

INSTRUMENTAL MUSIC

BERKELEY SYMPHONY ORCHESTRA
2322 Shattuck Avenue, Berkeley, CA 94704
(510) 841-2800
FAX: (510) 644-2596
Founded: 1969
Arts Area: Symphony; Orchestra

Status: Semi-Professional
Type: Performing
Purpose: To perform contemporary and traditional symphony literature
Management: Kelly Johnson, Executive Director; Elisabeth Beaird, Development Director; Shohei Sawada, Bookeeper/Data Manager; Recardo Antoni, Administrative Assistant; Elizabeth Gibson, Personnel Manager
Officers: Jeffrey Shattuck Leiter, President; John E. Danielsen, Ruth Dorman, Vice Presidents; Janet Maestro, Secretary; Kirk Misaka, Treasurer
Paid Staff: 4 **Volunteer Staff:** 1
Paid Artists: 48 **Non-Paid Artists:** 37
Utilizes: Special Technical Talent; Guest Conductors; Guest Artists
Budget: $500,000 - $1,000,000
Income Sources: Private Foundations/Grants/Endowments; Business/Corporate Donations; Box Office; Government Grants; Individual Donations; Bingo
Season: August - June **Annual Attendance:** 9,000
Performance Facilities: Zellerbach Hall, University of California at Berkeley

CONCERTO AMABILE
c/o San Francisco Early Music Society, PO Box 10151, Berkeley, CA 94709
(510) 528-1725
Arts Area: Chamber; Ensemble; Instrumental Group
Status: Professional; Non-Profit
Type: Performing; Touring
Purpose: To play the best baroque repertoires, especially of lesser-known composers
Management: Kathleen Kraft, Artistic Director
Officers: Kathleen Kraft, President
Budget: $1,000 - $50,000
Income Sources: Private Foundations/Grants/Endowments; Business/Corporate Donations; Box Office; Government Grants; Individual Donations

SAN FRANCISCO EARLY MUSIC SOCIETY
PO Box 10151, Berkeley, CA 94709
(510) 528-1725
Arts Area: Chamber; Ensemble; Ethnic; Folk
Status: Non-Profit
Type: Educational; Sponsoring
Purpose: To serve as an umbrella organization for early music activities in northern California
Management: John Dornenburg, President; Robert Jackson, Executive Director
Budget: $100,000 - $500,000
Income Sources: Private Foundations/Grants/Endowments; Business/Corporate Donations; Box Office; Government Grants; Individual Donations
Season: 52 Weeks
Performance Facilities: First Congregational Church, Berkeley

VOCAL MUSIC

BERKELEY OPERA
715 Arlington, Berkeley, CA 94707
(510) 524-5256
Founded: 1979
Arts Area: Lyric Opera
Status: Semi-Professional
Type: Performing
Purpose: To present opera
Management: Richard Goodman, General Director; Jane Rateaver, Audition Secretary; Bonnie Lockett, Orchestra Manager
Officers: Richard Goodman, President/Treasurer; Jane Rateaver, Vice President; Sue Goodman, Secretary; Edgar Braun, Board Chairman
Volunteer Staff: 20
Paid Artists: 75 **Non-Paid Artists:** 20
Utilizes: Local Talent
Budget: $100,000 - $500,000
Income Sources: Private Foundations/Grants/Endowments; Business/Corporate Donations; Box Office; Government Grants; Individual Donations
Season: February - August **Annual Attendance:** 5,000
Affiliations: Theater Bay Area
Performance Facilities: Julia Morgan Theater; Hillside Club Theater

THEATRE

BERKELEY COMMUNITY THEATRE
1930 Allston Way, Berkeley, CA 94704
(510) 644-6863
FAX: (510) 845-9674
Founded: 1950
Arts Area: Professional; Musical; Community; Theatrical Group
Status: Professional; Non-Professional
Type: Performing; Touring; Educational
Purpose: To provide the community with a professional theatre available for rent to professional, community, and non-profit organizations
Management: Judson H. Owens, Theatre Manager; Lance C. James, Assistant Manager
Paid Staff: 14   **Volunteer Staff:** 70
Utilizes: Special Technical Talent; Guest Conductors; Guest Artists; Guest Directors
Budget: $100,000 - $500,000
Income Sources: Box Office; Government Grants
Season: 52 Weeks   **Annual Attendance:** 200,000

BERKELEY REPERTORY THEATRE
2025 Addison Street, Berkeley, CA 94704
(510) 204-8901
FAX: (510) 841-7711
Founded: 1968
Arts Area: Professional; Theatrical Group
Status: Professional; Non-Profit
Type: Performing; Touring; Resident; Educational
Purpose: To present classical and contemporary plays of major stature, nurturing and stimulating the art form while at the same time stimulating our community
Management: Sharon Ott, Artistic Director; Susan Medak, Managing Director
Officers: Robert W. Burt, President; Edwin C. Shiver, Vice President; Dale Affonso, Secretary; Rick Messman, Treasurer
Paid Staff: 50   **Volunteer Staff:** 20
Paid Artists: 50
Utilizes: Special Technical Talent; Guest Artists; Guest Directors
Budget: $1,000,000 - $5,000,000
Income Sources: Private Foundations/Grants/Endowments; Business/Corporate Donations; Box Office; Government Grants; Individual Donations
Season: September - June   **Annual Attendance:** 160,000
Affiliations: TCG; LORT; AAA; California Confederation of the Arts; California Theatre Council
Performance Facilities: Berkeley Repertory Theatre

BLACK REPERTORY GROUP INC.
3201 Adeline Street, Berkeley, CA 94703
(510) 652-2120
Founded: 1964
Arts Area: Community; Theatrical Group
Status: Non-Professional; Non-Profit
Type: Resident
Purpose: To give youth the opportunity to use drama as a means of discipline and building self-esteem
Management: Nora B. Vaughn, Executive Director
Utilizes: Special Technical Talent; Guest Artists; Guest Directors
Budget: $50,000 - $100,000
Income Sources: Private Foundations/Grants/Endowments; Business/Corporate Donations; Box Office; Government Grants; Individual Donations
Season: November - June

FLORENCE SCHWIMLEY LITTLE THEATRE
2246 Milvia Street, Berkeley, CA 94704
(510) 644-6863
Founded: 1948
Arts Area: Professional; Musical; Community; Theatrical Group
Status: Professional; Non-Professional
Type: Performing; Touring; Educational
Purpose: To provide the community with a professional theatre available for rent to professional, community and non-profit organizations
Management: Judson H. Owens, Theatre Manager; Lance C. James, Assistant Manager
Paid Staff: 3   **Volunteer Staff:** 20

Utilizes: Special Technical Talent; Guest Artists; Guest Directors
Budget: $100,000 - $500,000
Income Sources: Box Office; Government Grants
Season: 52 Weeks   **Annual Attendance:** 20,000

PERFORMING SERIES

BERKELEY SHAKESPEARE FESTIVAL
2531 Ninth Street, Berkeley, CA 94710
(510) 548-3422; (415) 861-3101
Founded: 1973
Arts Area: Theater
Status: Professional; Non-Profit
Type: Performing; Touring; Educational
Purpose: Committed to innovative productions of Shakespearean plays
Management: Maria A. O'Dea, Managing Director; Michael Addison, Artistic Director; Lauren Brown, Development Director; Scott Stuart, Production Manager; Carla Befera, Press Contact
Officers: David Bond, Board President
Paid Staff: 5   **Volunteer Staff:** 90
Paid Artists: 64
Utilizes: Special Technical Talent; Guest Artists; Guest Directors
Budget: $500,000 - $1,000,000
Income Sources: Private Foundations/Grants/Endowments; Business/Corporate Donations; Box Office; Government Grants; Individual Donations
Season: July - November   **Annual Attendance:** 35,000
Affiliations: Theatre/Bay Area; California Arts Council; TCG
Performance Facilities: John Hinkel Park Outdoor Amphitheatre

LA PENA CULTURAL CENTER
3105 Shattuck Avenue, Berkeley, CA 94705
(510) 849-2568
FAX: (510) 849-9397
Founded: 1975
Arts Area: Vocal Music; Instrumental Music
Status: Non-Profit
Type: Educational; Sponsoring
Purpose: To present cultural and educational programs which increase understanding of different cultures and support efforts to build a just society
Management: Paul Chin, Vanessa Whang, Co-Directors; Earthlyn Mannd, Development Director
Officers: Paul Chin, President of the Board
Paid Staff: 7
Utilizes: Special Technical Talent; Guest Artists
Budget: $100,000 - $500,000
Income Sources: Private Foundations/Grants/Endowments; Business/Corporate Donations; Box Office; Government Grants; Individual Donations
Season: 52 Weeks
Annual Attendance: 20,000

UNIVERSITY OF CALIFORNIA - BERKELEY CALIFORNIA PERFORMANCES
101 Zellerbach Hall, Berkeley, CA 94720
(510) 642-0212
FAX: (510) 643-6707
Founded: 1904
Arts Area: Dance; Vocal Music; Instrumental Music; Theater; Classical Music
Status: Non-Profit
Type: Educational; Sponsoring
Purpose: To offer performances at the highest level of content and execution, giving the student an opportunity to form his taste in the arts on a sound foundation
Management: Robert W. Cole, Director
Paid Staff: 25
Budget: $1,000,000 - $5,000,000
Income Sources: Private Foundations/Grants/Endowments; Box Office; Government Grants; Individual Donations
Season: July - June
Affiliations: APAP; ISPAA; WAAA
Performance Facilities: Zellerbach Auditorium, University of California at Berkeley; Zellerbach Playhouse, University of California at Berkeley; Wheeler Auditorium; Hearst Greek Theatre

FACILITY

BERKELEY COMMUNITY THEATRE
1930 Allston Way, Berkeley, CA 94704
(510) 644-6863
  Type of Facility: Theatre Complex; Auditorium; Studio Performance; Theatre House; Civic Center
  Type of Stage: Proscenium
  Orchestra Pit
  Seating Capacity: 3,491
  Year Built: 1950   **Architect:** Will Corlett/Henry Gutterson   **Cost:** $3,000,000
  Contact for Rental: Judson H. Owens;   (510) 644-6863

BERKELEY REPERTORY THEATRE
2025 Addison Street, Berkeley, CA 94704
(510) 204-8901
FAX: (510) 841-7711
  Founded: 1968
  Type of Facility: Theatre House
  Type of Stage: Thrust
  Stage Dimensions: Trapezoidal 25'x15'x20'x30'
  Seating Capacity: 401
  Year Built: 1980   **Architect:** Angell, Lockwood & Associates   **Cost:** $2,000,000
  Acoustical Consultant: James LeBrecht
  Resident Groups: Berkeley Repertory Theatre

UNIVERSITY OF CALIFORNIA-BERKELEY - ALFRED HERTZ MEMORIAL HALL
Department of Music, Berkeley, CA 94720
(510) 642-4864
  Type of Facility: Concert Hall
  Type of Stage: Platform
  Stage Dimensions: 68'x26'
  Seating Capacity: 714
  Year Built: 1958   **Architect:** Gardner Dailey   **Cost:** $1,000,000
  Acoustical Consultant: Vern Knudsen
  Manager: David Whitman
  Resident Groups: University musical organizations

UNIVERSITY OF CALIFORNIA-BERKELEY - HEARST GREEK THEATRE
c/o Cal Performances, 101 Zellerbach Hall, Berkeley, CA 94720
(510) 642-0212
  Type of Facility: Outdoor (Concert); Amphitheater
  Type of Stage: Greek
  Stage Dimensions: 135'x28'   **Orchestra Pit**
  Seating Capacity: 9,000
  Year Built: 1903   **Architect:** John Galen Howard   **Cost:** $40,000
  Year Remodeled: 1957   **Architect:** Ernest Born Associates
  Contact for Rental: David Hillbrand;   (510) 642-0212

UNIVERSITY OF CALIFORNIA-BERKELEY - ZELLERBACH HALL
Berkeley, CA 94720
(510) 642-0212
  Type of Facility: Theatre Complex; Auditorium; Theatre House; Multi-Purpose
  Type of Stage: Proscenium
  Stage Dimensions: 30'x63'x50'   **Orchestra Pit**
  Seating Capacity: 2,015
  Year Built: 1968   **Architect:** Vernon DeMars   **Cost:** $7,000,000
  Acoustical Consultant: Vern Knudsen & W.W. Soroka
  Contact for Rental: Ella Baff or David Hillbrand;   (510) 642-0212
  Manager: Robert Cole;   (510) 642-0212
  Resident Groups: Cal Performances

UNIVERSITY OF CALIFORNIA-BERKELEY - ZELLERBACH PLAYHOUSE
c/o Cal Performances, 101 Zellerbach Hall, Berkeley, CA 94720
(510) 642-0212
  Type of Facility: Theatre Complex; Auditorium; Studio Performance; Theatre House; Arena
  Type of Stage: Thrust; Flexible; Proscenium; Platform; 3/4 Arena; Arena
  Stage Dimensions: 20'x60'x36'   **Orchestra Pit**
  Seating Capacity: 500

Year Built: 1968   **Architect:** Vernon DeMars   **Cost:** $7,000,000
Acoustical Consultant: Vern Knudsen & W.W. Soroka
Contact for Rental: David Hillbrand;   (510) 642-0212
Resident Groups: University Theatre; University Dance; Department of Dramatic Art

Beverly Hills

INSTRUMENTAL MUSIC

BEVERLY HILLS SYMPHONY
PO Box 5429, Beverly Hills, CA 90210
(310) 276-8385
Founded: 1983
Arts Area: Symphony; Orchestra; Chamber; Ensemble
Status: Professional; Non-Profit
Type: Performing; Educational; Sponsoring
Purpose: To be a cultural entity of Beverly Hills, an organization of the highest quality producing first-rate concerts; to further the cultural pursuits of Beverly Hills and enhance the activities of other organizations in the community with our music
Management: Bogidar Avramov, Music Director/Conductor; Razdan Kuymijian, Orchestra Manager
Officers: Debbie Grossman, President
Volunteer Staff: 50
Paid Artists: 65
Utilizes: Guest Artists
Budget: $100,000 - $500,000
Income Sources: Private Foundations/Grants/Endowments; Business/Corporate Donations; Box Office; Government Grants; Individual Donations
Season: 52 Weeks   **Annual Attendance:** 10,000
Affiliations: ASOL; Association of California Symphony Orchestras

LOS ANGELES DOCTORS SYMPHONY
521 North Maple Drive, Beverly Hills, CA 90210
(310) 550-0691
Founded: 1953
Arts Area: Symphony; Orchestra
Status: Non-Professional
Type: Performing
Purpose: To present concert performances to benefit medical charitable organizations locally and internationally
Officers: Simon Gamer DDS, President; Geri Freeland-Soper PhD, Vice President; Nora Graham, Secretary; Harry Dapeer, Treasurer
Paid Staff: 1
Paid Artists: 1   **Non-Paid Artists:** 2
Utilizes: Guest Conductors; Guest Artists
Budget: $1,000 - $50,000
Income Sources: Individual Donations; Charity Organization Donations
Season: September - June   **Annual Attendance:** 3,000

VOCAL MUSIC

LOS ANGELES CONCERT OPERA ASSOCIATION
2250 Gloaming Way, Beverly Hills, CA 90210
(310) 276-2731
Founded: 1987
Arts Area: Lyric Opera
Status: Non-Profit
Type: Performing
Purpose: To give young semiprofessional singers an opportunity to perform
Management: Dr. Loren L. Zachary, General Director
Officers: Richard C. Wulliger, President
Volunteer Staff: 20
Paid Artists: 50
Utilizes: Guest Conductors
Budget: $1,000 - $50,000
Income Sources: Box Office; Individual Donations
Season: January   **Annual Attendance:** 1,200
Performance Facilities: Ambassador Auditorium

THEATRE

THEATRE 40
PO Box 5401, Beverly Hills, CA 90210
(310) 277-4221
FAX: (213) 876-0227
Founded: 1964
Arts Area: Professional; Theatrical Group
Status: Professional
Type: Performing; Educational
Purpose: A professional equity company committed to performing classical and contemporary plays
Management: Charles Arthur, Artistic Director; Lee Ann Holfelder, Business Manager; Diana Hale, Publicity Director
Paid Staff: 4
Utilizes: Guest Directors
Budget: $50,000 - $100,000
Income Sources: Business/Corporate Donations; Box Office; Individual Donations
Season: July - June   **Annual Attendance:** 8,000
Affiliations: Los Angeles Theatre Alliance; League of Producers and Theatres of Greater Los Angeles
Performance Facilities: Theatre 40

PERFORMING SERIES

INTERNATIONAL CONCERTS EXCHANGE
1124 Summit Drive, Beverly Hills, CA 90210
(213) 272-5539
FAX: (213) 272-5539
Founded: 1942
Arts Area: Festivals
Status: Professional; Semi-Professional; Non-Professional; Non-Profit
Type: Performing; Educational
Management: Dr. Irwin Paones, Producer/Managing Director
Paid Staff: 2
Utilizes: Special Technical Talent; Guest Artists
Income Sources: Box Office

PLAYBOY JAZZ FESTIVAL
9242 Beverly Boulevard, Beverly Hills, CA 90210
(310) 246-4000
FAX: (310) 246-4077
Founded: 1979
Arts Area: Vocal Music; Instrumental Music
Status: Professional
Type: Sponsoring
Purpose: To provide a community service; to enable Los Angeles residents to enjoy jazz music
Utilizes: Guest Artists
Budget: $500,000 - $1,000,000
Income Sources: Box Office
Season: June   **Annual Attendance:** 35,000
Performance Facilities: Hollywood Bowl

FACILITY

BEVERLY HILLS PLAYHOUSE
254 South Robertson Boulevard, Beverly Hills, CA 90211
(310) 855-1556
Type of Facility: Theatre House
Type of Stage: Proscenium
Stage Dimensions: 23'Wx18'6"D; 23'Wx12'H proscenium opening
Seating Capacity: 99
Year Built: 1940
Year Remodeled: 1982
Contact for Rental: Adrienne Woody;   (213) 855-1556

Big Bear Lake

FACILITY

BIG BEAR LAKE PERFORMING ARTS CENTER
39707 Big Bear Boulevard, PO Box 2800, Big Bear Lake, CA 92315
(909) 866-5831
FAX: (909) 866-6766
    Founded: 1988
    Type of Facility: Concert Hall; Auditorium; Performance Center; Civic Center
    Type of Stage: Proscenium
    Stage Dimensions: 40'x42'   **Orchestra Pit**
    Seating Capacity: 400
    Year Built: 1977   **Architect:** Wolff, Lang, Christopher and Associates   **Cost:** $5,500,000
    Acoustical Consultant: John von Szelski (theatre)
    Contact for Rental: Colleen J. McBride;   (909) 866-5831

Blue Lake

THEATRE

DELL' ARTE PLAYERS COMPANY
131 H Street, PO Box 816, Blue Lake, CA 95525
(707) 668-5663
    Founded: 1971
    Arts Area: Professional; Theatrical Group
    Status: Professional; Non-Profit
    Type: Performing; Touring
    Purpose: To give artists a chance to live and work in a rural area
    Management: Michael Fields, Managing Director; Donald Forrest, Joan Schirle, Co-Artistic Directors
    Officers: Michael Fields, President; Bobbi Ricca, Secretary/Treasurer
    Paid Staff: 3
    Paid Artists: 5
    Budget: $100,000 - $500,000
    Income Sources: Private Foundations/Grants/Endowments; Business/Corporate Donations; Box Office; Government Grants; Individual Donations
    Season: 52 Weeks
    Affiliations: Humboldt Arts Council; California Theater Council
    Performance Facilities: Dell' Arte Theatre

Brea

FACILITY

CURTIS THEATRE
1 Civic Center Circle, Brea, CA 92621
(714) 990-7722
FAX: (714) 990-2258
    Founded: 1980
    Type of Facility: Theatre House
    Type of Stage: Proscenium
    Stage Dimensions: 50'Wx40'D
    Seating Capacity: 199
    Year Built: 1980   **Cost:** $5,000,000
    Contact for Rental: D. Scott Riordan;   (714) 990-7723
    Resident Groups: Brea's Youth Theatre; Brea Civic Light Opera; Brea Theatre League

---

Burbank

INSTRUMENTAL MUSIC

BURBANK SYMPHONY ASSOCIATION
PO Box 4141, Burbank, CA 91502
(818) 846-5981
    Founded: 1944
    Arts Area: Symphony; Orchestra

Status: Non-Profit
Type: Sponsoring
Purpose: To provide symphonic music for the community
Management: Victor Vener, Conductor/Music Director; Sabina Vener, Orchestra Manager
Officers: Walter Mears, President; Evan Binn, Vice President; Veronica Chavour, Treasurer
Volunteer Staff: 27
Paid Artists: 70
Utilizes: Guest Conductors; Guest Artists
Budget: $1,000 - $50,000
Income Sources: Private Foundations/Grants/Endowments; Business/Corporate Donations; Box Office; Government Grants; Individual Donations
Season: 52 Weeks   **Annual Attendance:** 5,000
Performance Facilities: Hall of Liberty, Forest Lawn; Starlight Amphitheatre

THEATRE

ACME PERFORMANCE GROUP, INC.
1212A North San Fernando, #119, Burbank, CA 91504
Founded: 1991
Arts Area: Professional; Theatrical Group
Status: Professional; Non-Profit
Type: Performing
Purpose: To produce new and unusual American theatrical works
Management: Lee Wochner, Managing Director; Gary Guidinger, Artistic Director; Julie Briggs, Eve Baker, Joe Stafford, Administrative Directors
Paid Staff: 2   **Volunteer Staff:** 5
Paid Artists: 12
Utilizes: Guest Artists; Guest Directors
Budget: $1,000 - $50,000
Income Sources: Private Foundations/Grants/Endowments; Business/Corporate Donations; Box Office; Government Grants; Individual Donations
Season: 52 Weeks

VICTORY THEATRE
3324-26 West Victory, Burbank, CA 91505
(818) 843-9253
Founded: 1979
Arts Area: Professional; Theatrical Group
Status: Professional; Non-Profit
Type: Performing; Educational
Purpose: To encourage the growth of American playwrights; to present original plays
Management: Maria Gobetti, Tom Ormeny, Artistic Directors
Utilizes: Special Technical Talent; Guest Artists; Guest Directors
Budget: $50,000 - $100,000
Income Sources: Private Foundations/Grants/Endowments; Box Office; Individual Donations
Season: 52 Weeks
Affiliations: Los Angeles Theatre Alliance; AEA
Performance Facilities: Victory Theatre

Calabasas

DANCE

KARPATOK HUNGARIAN FOLK ENSEMBLE
4377 Park Carona, Calabasas, CA 91302
(818) 363-2219; (818) 222-2704
FAX: (818) 363-1349
Founded: 1965
Arts Area: Folk
Status: Professional; Non-Profit
Type: Performing; Touring; Educational
Purpose: To contribute to the multi-ethnic American cultural landscape through the perpetuation of the performing arts of the Hungarian people
Management: Mary Beth Treen, Artists' Managment
Officers: Laszlo G. Heredy, President; Dennis Frigyes-Fredricks, Vice President; Marianne Toghia, Secretary; Rosemary Heredy, Treasurer
Paid Staff: 3   **Volunteer Staff:** 2
Paid Artists: 35

Utilizes: Guest Artists; Guest Directors; Guest Choreographers
Budget: $50,000 - $100,000
Income Sources: Private Foundations/Grants/Endowments; Business/Corporate Donations; Government Grants; Individual Donations
Season: 52 Weeks

Canoga Park

DANCE

JAZZ DANCERS, INC.
20314 Lorne Street, Canoga Park, CA 91306
(818) 709-7542
Founded: 1979
Arts Area: Jazz
Status: Professional; Non-Profit
Type: Performing; Touring; Educational
Purpose: To present and preserve the traditions of American jazz dance on a concert level
Management: Dennon Rawles, Managing Director; Nela Fry, Administrative Director
Officers: Charles Hardie CPA, President; Victoria Cashion, Secretary; Thomas Stevens, Treasurer
Paid Staff: 2   **Volunteer Staff:** 2
Paid Artists: 12
Utilizes: Guest Artists; Guest Choreographers; Commissioned Composers
Budget: $1,000 - $50,000
Income Sources: Business/Corporate Donations; Box Office; Government Grants; Individual Donations
Season: 52 Weeks   **Annual Attendance:** 2,000
Performance Facilities: Japan America Theatre

INSTRUMENTAL MUSIC

WEST VALLEY SYMPHONY, DIVISION OF THE LOS ANGELES CIVIC ORCHESTRA
20210 Haynes Street, Canoga Park, CA 91306
(818) 883-6283
Arts Area: Symphony; Orchestra; Chamber; Ethnic
Status: Professional; Semi-Professional; Non-Profit
Type: Performing; Touring; Resident; Educational; Sponsoring
Purpose: To showcase new composers, conductors and soloists; to build classical-music appreciation via affordable and/or free concerts
Management: James Elza Domine, Music Director; Nancy Ross, Associate Conductor
Officers: Jonathan Laurie, President; Leon Wood, Vice President
Paid Staff: 1   **Volunteer Staff:** 12
Paid Artists: 60
Utilizes: Special Technical Talent; Guest Conductors; Guest Artists
Budget: $50,000 - $100,000
Income Sources: Business/Corporate Donations; Box Office; Government Grants; Individual Donations
Season: September - July   **Annual Attendance:** 8,000
Affiliations: Association of California Symphony Orchestras; San Fernando Valley Arts Council
Performance Facilities: Main Stage Theater, Pierce College - Soka Campus

Carmel

INSTRUMENTAL MUSIC

CHAMBER MUSIC SOCIETY OF THE MONTEREY PENISULA
PO Box 6283, Carmel, CA 93921
(408) 625-2212
Founded: 1967
Arts Area: Chamber
Status: Non-Profit
Type: Sponsoring
Purpose: To present high-quality chamber music at a minimum cost; to sponsor an annual competition for young musicians
Officers: Jerry Foote, President; DeForest Sweeney, Vice President; Berenis Tomlinson, Secretary; Harry Handler, Treasurer
Volunteer Staff: 20
Utilizes: Guest Artists
Budget: $1,000 - $50,000

Income Sources: Private Foundations/Grants/Endowments; Business/Corporate Donations; Box Office; Individual Donations
Season: October - May   **Annual Attendance:** 3,000

PERFORMING SERIES

CARMEL BACH FESTIVAL
San Carlos & Ninth, Room 11, PO Box 575, Carmel, CA 93921
(408) 624-1521
    Founded: 1935
    Arts Area: Vocal Music; Instrumental Music; Festivals; Lyric Opera
    Status: Professional; Non-Profit
    Type: Performing; Educational
    Purpose: To perform the music of Johann Sebastian Bach, his predecessors, contemporaries, and successors
    Management: Nana Faridany, Executive Director; Bruno Weil, Music Director/Conductor
    Officers: Davis Factor, President; Roberta Bialek, Vice President; Lee Rosen, Treasurer
    Paid Staff: 4   **Volunteer Staff:** 150
    Paid Artists: 100   **Non-Paid Artists:** 35
    Utilizes: Guest Conductors; Guest Artists
    Budget: $500,000 - $1,000,000
    Income Sources: Private Foundations/Grants/Endowments; Business/Corporate Donations; Box Office; Government Grants; Individual Donations
    Season: July - August   **Annual Attendance:** 17,000
    Performance Facilities: Sunset Cultural Center

FACILITY

SUNSET CENTER THEATRE
PO Box 5066, Carmel, CA 93921
(408) 624-3996
    Type of Facility: Theatre House
    Type of Stage: Proscenium
    Stage Dimensions: 40'x28'x35'   **Orchestra Pit**
    Seating Capacity: 732
    Year Built: 1930
    Contact for Rental: Manager;   (408) 624-3996
    Manager: Brian Donaghue, Director
    Resident Groups: Carmel Bach Festival; Monterey County Symphony Orchestra; Carmel Music Society; Chamber Music Society; Performance Carmel

Carmel-by-the-Sea

INSTRUMENTAL MUSIC

MONTEREY COUNTY SYMPHONY
PO Box 3965, Carmel-by-the-Sea, CA 93921
(408) 624-8511
FAX: (408) 624-3837
    Founded: 1946
    Arts Area: Symphony; Orchestra; Chamber; Ensemble
    Status: Professional; Non-Profit
    Type: Performing
    Purpose: To produce high-quality classical music for the people of Monterey County
    Management: Joseph Truskot, Executive Director; Joan DeVisser, Director of Operations; Celia Perez Martinez, Director of Marketing/Development
    Officers: Sherrie McCullough, President; Susan Schlen, Jeff Craig, Dick Zahm, Vice Presidents; Diane Kelley, Treasurer
    Paid Staff: 5
    Paid Artists: 100
    Utilizes: Special Technical Talent; Guest Conductors; Guest Artists
    Budget: $500,000 - $1,000,000
    Income Sources: Private Foundations/Grants/Endowments; Business/Corporate Donations; Box Office; Government Grants; Individual Donations
    Season: September - August   **Annual Attendance:** 12,500
    Affiliations: Association of California Symphony Orchestras; ASOL
    Performance Facilities: Sunset Theater; Sherwood Hall

Carson

FACILITY

CALIFORNIA STATE UNIVERSITY-DOMINGUEZ HILLS - CONCERT HALL
1000 East Victoria Street, Carson, CA 90747
(310) 516-3543
Type of Facility: Concert Hall
Type of Stage: Flexible
Seating Capacity: 200
Year Built: 1972
Contact for Rental: David Champion, Music Department, Chairman;   (310) 516-3543
Manager: Quincy Jones

CALIFORNIA STATE UNIVERSITY-DOMINGUEZ HILLS - UNIVERSITY THEATRE
1000 East Victoria Street, Carson, CA 90747
(310) 516-3588
Type of Facility: Theatre House
Type of Stage: Proscenium
Stage Dimensions: 65'x80'x40'   **Orchestra Pit**
Seating Capacity: 467
Year Built: 1977   **Architect:** Daniel Dworsky   **Cost:** $2,200,000
Contact for Rental: Stewart Christie;   (310) 516-3898
Manager: Peter Rodney
Resident Groups: Theatre Arts Department

Claremont

FACILITY

THE CLAREMONT COLLEGES - GARRISON THEATRE
Tenth and Dartmouth, Claremont, CA 91711
(714) 621-8000, ext. 3800
Type of Facility: Auditorium; Multi-Purpose
Type of Stage: Proscenium
Stage Dimensions: 35'Wx30'D; 35'Wx18'H proscenium opening   **Orchestra Pit**
Seating Capacity: 690
Year Built: 1963   **Architect:** Sheets
Contact for Rental: Theatre Manager;   (714) 621-8000, ext. 3800
Resident Groups: Pomona College Theatre Department; Claremont Travel Film Series

THE CLAREMONT COLLEGES - MABEL SHAW BRIDGES AUDITORIUM
Fourth Street and College Way, Claremont, CA 91711
(714) 621-8031; (714) 621-8032
FAX: (714) 621-8484
Type of Facility: Concert Hall; Auditorium; Performance Center; Theatre House; Opera House
Type of Stage: Proscenium
Stage Dimensions: 62'Wx38'3"D; 62'Wx36'H proscenium opening   **Orchestra Pit**
Seating Capacity: 2,483
Year Built: 1977   **Architect:** William Templeton Johnson   **Cost:** $600,000
Year Remodeled: 1977   **Architect:** H. Wendell Mounce & Associates   **Cost:** $1,600,000
Acoustical Consultant: Abe Metzler
Contact for Rental: Paula Thatcher;   (714) 621-8031

Columbia

FACILITY

FALLON HOUSE THEATRE
Columbia State Historic Park, PO Box 1079, Columbia, CA 95310
(209) 532-4644
Type of Facility: Theatre Complex; Theatre House
Facility Originally: Meeting Hall; Vaudeville; Movie House; Warehouse
Type of Stage: Proscenium
Stage Dimensions: 42'Wx46'D; 30'Wx9'6"H proscenium opening
Seating Capacity: 277

Year Built: 1862
Year Remodeled: 1983   **Cost:** $1,500,000
Contact for Rental: David G. Purdy;   (209) 532-4644
Manager: Sally Farrington
Resident Groups: Columbia Actors' Repertory
An 1862 Period Theatre, Fallon House Theatre was restored between 1981 and 1983 by the California State Office of Historic Preservation.

Compton

THEATRE

LYNWOOD PERFORMING ARTS
PO Box 4393, Compton, CA 90224
(310) 631-5027
    Arts Area: Community
    Status: Non-Profit
    Type: Performing
    Management: Perry Brents, Director
    Volunteer Staff: 3
    Non-Paid Artists: 60
    Utilizes: Guest Artists
    Budget: $1,000 - $50,000
    Income Sources: Individual Donations
    Season: September - July
    Performance Facilities: Lynwood Civic Center

Concord

THEATRE

CITIARTS THEATRE
1950 Parkside Drive, Concord, CA 94519
(510) 671-3065
FAX: (510) 671-3375
    Founded: 1974
    Arts Area: Professional
    Status: Professional; Non-Profit
    Type: Performing; Resident; Educational
    Purpose: CitiArts Theatre is a small professional theatre committed to producing small musicals and plays as well as rarely produced classics
    Management: Richard H. Elliott, Artistic Director; Andrew F. Holtz, Managing Director; George Evano, Marketing Director; Leslye Asera, Development Director
    Officers: Don Fitzgerald, President; Karen Huckeby, Vice President/Treasurer; Trinna Sheley, Secretary
    Paid Staff: 18   **Volunteer Staff:** 1
    Paid Artists: 178
    Utilizes: Guest Artists; Guest Directors; Designers; Composers; Writers
    Budget: $1,000,000 - $5,000,000
    Income Sources: Private Foundations/Grants/Endowments; Business/Corporate Donations; Box Office; Government Grants; Individual Donations; Tuition; Merchandise Sales
    Season: 52 Weeks
    Affiliations: TCG; Theatre Bay Area; AEA
    Performance Facilities: Willows Theatre; Gasoline Alley Theatre; Centre Concord

FACILITY

CONCORD PAVILION
2000 Kirker Pass Road, Concord, CA 94524
(510) 676-8742
FAX: (510) 676-7262
    Mailing Address: PO Box 6166, Concord, CA 95424
    Type of Facility: Amphitheater
    Type of Stage: Flexible
    Stage Dimensions: 63'Wx60'D   **Orchestra Pit**
    Seating Capacity: 9,019
    Year Built: 1975   **Architect:** Frank O. Gehry   **Cost:** $6,600,000
    Acoustical Consultant: Jaffe Acoustics

Contact for Rental: Doug Warrick, Assistant General Manager; (510) 798-3318
Manager: John Toffoli, Jr.; (510) 671-3275

WILLOWS THEATRE
1975 Diamond Boulevard, Concord, CA 94520
(510) 671-3065
Type of Facility: Studio Performance; Performance Center; Theatre House; Multi-Purpose
Type of Stage: Proscenium
Stage Dimensions: 40'Wx24'D   **Orchestra Pit**
Seating Capacity: 203
Year Built: 1977
Contact for Rental: Bob Webb; (510) 671-3387
Resident Groups: CitiArts Theatre Company

Costa Mesa

DANCE

THE BALLET MONTMARTRE
2632 Santa Ana Avenue, Costa Mesa, CA 92627
(714) 646-7688
Founded: 1972
Arts Area: Modern; Ballet; Jazz
Status: Semi-Professional; Non-Profit
Type: Performing; Resident
Management: Stela Viorica, Artistic Director
Paid Artists: 6   **Non-Paid Artists:** 18
Utilizes: Guest Artists; Guest Choreographers
Budget: $1,000 - $50,000
Income Sources: Private Foundations/Grants/Endowments; Business/Corporate Donations; Box Office;
Individual Donations
Season: 52 Weeks

VOCAL MUSIC

MASTER CHORALE OF ORANGE COUNTY
PO Box 2156, Costa Mesa, CA 92628
(714) 556-6262
FAX: (714) 556-6341
Founded: 1956
Arts Area: Choral
Status: Non-Profit
Type: Performing
Management: Dr. William D. Hall, Music Director; Dr. Thomas Sheets, Associate Music Director; Sheri Sheperd,
Administrative Director; Jean Updegraff, Administrative Assistant
Officers: Dr. Philip Winsor, Chairman; Robert W. Guyett, President; Julia Rappaport, Executive Vice President; Robert J.
Reyes, Vice President Finance; Kenneth Roehrs, Corresponding Secretary
Paid Staff: 5   **Volunteer Staff:** 10
Paid Artists: 10   **Non-Paid Artists:** 140
Utilizes: Guest Artists
Budget: $100,000 - $500,000
Income Sources: Private Foundations/Grants/Endowments; Business/Corporate Donations; Box Office; Government
Grants; Individual Donations
Season: September - May   **Annual Attendance:** 10,000
Performance Facilities: Orange County Performing Arts Center

OPERA PACIFIC
650 Town Center Drive, Suite 400, Costa Mesa, CA 92626
(714) 546-7372
FAX: (714) 662-2796
Founded: 1986
Arts Area: Grand Opera; Light Opera; Musical Theatre
Status: Professional; Non-Profit
Type: Performing; Touring; Resident; Educational
Purpose: To present a broad repertoire of opera and American musicals with the highest artistic standards; to provide op-
portunities for emerging opera talent; to reach out to area communities with educational and performance opportunities
which will stimulate and develop new audiences

Management: Dr. David DiChiera, General Director; Richard H. Owens, Managing Director of Development and Administration; Lori Burrill, Managing Director of Production and Financial Planning
Officers: William H. Roberts, Chairman; Richard G. Engel, President; Michael D. Rubin, Secretary; Robert A. Huber, Treasurer
Paid Staff: 23   **Volunteer Staff:** 60
Paid Artists: 450
Utilizes: Special Technical Talent; Guest Conductors; Guest Artists; Guest Directors
Budget: $1,000,000 - $5,000,000
Income Sources: Private Foundations/Grants/Endowments; Business/Corporate Donations; Box Office; Government Grants; Individual Donations
Season: September - April   **Annual Attendance:** 60,000
Affiliations: OA
Performance Facilities: Orange County Performing Arts Center

THEATRE

PACIFIC AMPHITHEATRE
100 Fair Drive, Costa Mesa, CA 92626
(714) 546-4875
FAX: (714) 850-1157
Founded: 1983
Arts Area: Professional; Musical
Status: Commercial
Type: Performing
Purpose: To maintain an outdoor concert venue open May-October
Management: Susan Rosenbluth, General Manager; Mike Garcia, Theatre Manager; Jo-Ann Armstrong, Operating Manager
Utilizes: Special Technical Talent; Guest Artists
Income Sources: Box Office
Season: May - October

SOUTH COAST REPERTORY
655 Town Center Drive, Costa Mesa, CA 92626
(714) 957-2602
FAX: (714) 545-0391
Founded: 1964
Arts Area: Professional
Status: Professional; Non-Profit
Type: Performing; Touring; Resident; Educational
Purpose: To serve the art of theatre and Orange County audiences in a manner socially relevant and theatrically inventive
Management: David Emmes, Producing Artistic Director; Martin Benson, Artistic Director; Paula Tomei, Business Director; Paul Hammond, Production Director; Louise Cummings, Director of Development; John Mouledoux, Director of Marketing
Officers: Thomas Sutton, President; Lydia Wang Himes, James Henwood, Vice Presidents; Maryann Finley, Secretary; Donald Kennedy, Treasurer
Paid Staff: 51   **Volunteer Staff:** 237
Paid Artists: 150   **Non-Paid Artists:** 15
Utilizes: Guest Artists; Guest Directors
Budget: $1,000,000 - $5,000,000
Income Sources: Private Foundations/Grants/Endowments; Business/Corporate Donations; Box Office; Government Grants; Individual Donations
Season: September - June   **Annual Attendance:** 250,000
Affiliations: LORT; TCG
Performance Facilities: South Coast Repertory Theatre

PERFORMING SERIES

ORANGE COAST COLLEGE
2701 Fairview Road, PO Box 5005, Costa Mesa, CA 92628
(714) 432-5880
FAX: (714) 432-5902
Founded: 1947
Arts Area: Band
Status: Semi-Professional
Type: Performing; Touring; Educational
Purpose: To offer a comprehensive performing-arts season
Management: George Blanc, Dean of Community Services
Paid Staff: 8
Paid Artists: 50

Paid Artists: 50
Utilizes: Guest Artists
Budget: $100,000 - $500,000
Income Sources: Individual Donations
Season: September - June **Annual Attendance:** 46,000
Affiliations: Orange Coast College
Performance Facilities: Robert B. Moore Theatre; Fine Arts Recital Hall

FACILITY

ORANGE COUNTY PERFORMING ARTS CENTER
600 Town Center Drive, Costa Mesa, CA 92626
(714) 556-2121
FAX: (714) 556-0156
Founded: 1986
Type of Facility: Theatre Complex; Concert Hall; Performance Center; Multi-Purpose
Type of Stage: Proscenium **Orchestra Pit**
Year Built: 1986 **Architect:** The Blurock Partnership; CRS **Cost:** $71,000,000
Acoustical Consultant: Jerald Hyde; A. Harold Marshall; Taoletti Lewitz Associates
Contact for Rental: Judith O'Dea Morr, General Manager; (714) 556-2121
Manager: Judith O'Dea Morr; (714) 556-2121
Resident Groups: Pacific Symphony; Opera Pacific; Orange County Philharmonic Society; Pacific Chorale;
Master Chorale of Orange County
Orange County Performing Arts Center contains Founders Hall and Segerstrom Hall. See separate listings for additional information.

ORANGE COUNTY PERFORMING ARTS CENTER - FOUNDERS HALL
600 Town Center Drive, Costa Mesa, CA 92626
(714) 556-2121
Type of Facility: Studio Performance; Black Box
Type of Stage: Flexible
Stage Dimensions: 50'Wx66'L
Seating Capacity: 300
Year Built: 1986
Contact for Rental: Judith O'Dea Morr, General Manager; (714) 556-2121
Manager: Judith O'Dea Morr

ORANGE COUNTY PERFORMING ARTS CENTER - SEGERSTROM HALL
600 Town Center Drive, Costa Mesa, CA 92626
(714) 556-2121
Type of Facility: Concert Hall; Auditorium; Theatre House; Opera House
Type of Stage: Modified Apron Proscenium
Stage Dimensions: 124'10'Wx64'3"D; 68'Wx42'H proscenium opening **Orchestra Pit**
Seating Capacity: 2,994
Year Built: 1986
Contact for Rental: Judith O'Dea Morr, General Manager; (714) 556-2121
Manager: Judith O'Dea Morr
Orchestra pit is two separate screw-jack lifts. Lift A adds 8' and lift B adds 7' to stage depth for a total of 15' when both lifts are at stage level. Each may be used independently for varied stage configurations.

SOUTH COAST REPERTORY
655 Town Center Drive, Costa Mesa, CA 92626
(714) 957-2602
Founded: 1964
Type of Facility: Theatre Complex; Performance Center
Year Built: 1978 **Architect:** Stewart Woodard **Cost:** $3,000,000
Year Remodeled: 1987 **Architect:** Stewart Woodard **Cost:** $1,500,000
Acoustical Consultant: Purcell Noppe & Associates
Resident Groups: South Coast Repertory
South Coast Repertory contains Second Stage and Mainstage (Segerstrom Auditorium). See individual listings for additional information.

SOUTH COAST REPERTORY - SECOND STAGE
655 Town Center Drive, Costa Mesa, CA 92626
(714) 957-2603
Founded: 1964
Type of Facility: Theatre House
Type of Stage: 3/4 Arena

Stage Dimensions: 18'Wx29'D
Seating Capacity: 161
Year Built: 1978
Year Remodeled: 1987
Available for rent

SOUTH COAST REPERTORY - SEGERSTROM AUDITORIUM, MAINSTAGE
655 Town Center Drive, Costa Mesa, CA 92626
(714) 957-2603
Founded: 1964
Type of Facility: Auditorium; Theatre House
Type of Stage: Thrust; Proscenium
Stage Dimensions: 85'Wx41'D; 47'W proscenium opening
Seating Capacity: 507
Year Built: 1978   **Architect:** Stewart Woodard
Year Remodeled: 1987   **Architect:** Stewart Woodard
Contact for Rental: Paul Hammond, Director of Theatre Operations;   (714) 957-2602

Culver City

FACILITY

VETERAN'S MEMORIAL AUDITORIUM
4117 Overland Avenue, Culver City, CA 90230
(310) 837-5211
FAX: (310) 839-6106
Type of Facility: Auditorium
Type of Stage: Proscenium
Stage Dimensions: 50'x60'x30'
Seating Capacity: 1,600
Contact for Rental: Pamela Robinson;   (310) 202-5688
Manager: Kenneth D. Good

Cupertino

DANCE

ABHINAYA DANCE COMPANY
11445 Charsan Lane, Cupertino, CA 95014
(408) 725-2951
FAX: (408) 446-0433
Founded: 1981
Arts Area: Ethnic; Indian
Type: Performing
Purpose: To present classical Indian dance
Management: Mythili Kumar, Artistic Director/Choreographer
Season: 52 Weeks

PERFORMING SERIES

FLINT CENTER FOR THE PERFORMING ARTS
21250 Stevens Creek Boulevard, Cupertino, CA 95050
(408) 864-8820
Founded: 1971
Arts Area: Dance; Vocal Music; Instrumental Music; Theater; Lyric Opera; Popular Artists
Status: Professional; Semi-Professional; Non-Professional; Non-Profit; Commercial
Type: Performing; Touring; Educational; Sponsoring
Purpose: To present and sponsor internationally-renowned artists as well as non-professional performers
Management: Dr. Vicky K. O'Brien, Executive Director; Jaynos Szablya, Operations Manager
Paid Staff: 6
Utilizes: Special Technical Talent; Guest Artists
Budget: $500,000 - $1,000,000
Income Sources: Private Foundations/Grants/Endowments; Business/Corporate Donations; Box Office; Individual Donations
Season: 52 Weeks   **Annual Attendance:** 200,000
Affiliations: WAAA; APAP
Performance Facilities: Flint Center for the Performing Arts

FACILITY

DE ANZA COLLEGE - FLINT CENTER FOR THE PERFORMING ARTS
21250 Stevens Creek Boulevard, Cupertino, CA 95014
(408) 864-8820
> **Type of Facility:** Concert Hall; Theatre House
> **Type of Stage:** Proscenium
> **Stage Dimensions:** 52'Wx32'Hx39'D   **Orchestra Pit**
> **Seating Capacity:** 2,571
> **Year Built:** 1971
> **Contact for Rental:** Dr. Vicky K. O'Brien

Davis

PERFORMING SERIES

UNIVERSITY OF CALIFORNIA-DAVIS - UC DAVIS PRESENTS
University Cultural Programs, Davis, CA 95616
(916) 757-3488
FAX: (916) 757-6815
> **Founded:** 1954
> **Arts Area:** Dance; Vocal Music; Instrumental Music; Theater; Festivals; Grand Opera
> **Status:** Non-Profit
> **Type:** Touring; Educational; Sponsoring
> **Purpose:** To present a broad range of quality performing arts for the Davis campus and the immediate
> geographical region
> **Management:** James Wockenfuss, Director
> **Paid Staff:** 11   **Volunteer Staff:** 50
> **Paid Artists:** 25
> **Utilizes:** Guest Artists
> **Budget:** $500,000 - $1,000,000
> **Income Sources:** Private Foundations/Grants/Endowments; Business/Corporate Donations; Box Office; Government
> Grants; Individual Donations
> **Season:** October - June
> **Annual Attendance:** 30,000
> **Affiliations:** APAP; California Confederation of the Arts; California Presenters
> **Performance Facilities:** Kleiber Hall; Freeborn Hall; Main Theater; Sacramento Convention Center Theater

FACILITY

DAVIS ART CENTER
1919 F Street, Davis, CA 95616
(916) 756-4100
> **Type of Facility:** Multi-Purpose
> **Type of Stage:** Platform
> **Stage Dimensions:** 30'x30'
> **Seating Capacity:** 100
> **Year Built:** 1987   **Architect:** Ken LaGrone/Tandem

VETERANS' MEMORIAL THEATRE
203 East 14th Street, Davis, CA 95616
(916) 758-7839
> **Type of Facility:** Concert Hall; Auditorium; Theatre House
> **Type of Stage:** Thrust; Proscenium
> **Stage Dimensions:** 29'x30'x40'   **Orchestra Pit**
> **Seating Capacity:** 325
> **Year Built:** 1974   **Architect:** Dean F. Unger   **Cost:** $400,000
> **Contact for Rental:** Michael Gerell;   (916) 758-7839
> **Resident Groups:** Davis Comic Opera; Black Repertoire Dance Troupe; Nexus Modern Dance Collective; The Davis Ballet; Davis Art Center

---
Downey

INSTRUMENTAL MUSIC

DOWNEY SYMPHONIC SOCIETY
PO Box 763, Downey, CA 90241
(310) 869-3323
Founded: 1958
Arts Area: Orchestra
Status: Semi-Professional; Non-Profit
Type: Performing
Management: Robert Armer, Music Director
Officers: Lorine Parks, President; Loren DeWind, Vice President; Ruth Hillecke, Secretary; C. Richard Holmes, Treasurer
Paid Staff: 1   **Volunteer Staff:** 22
Paid Artists: 20   **Non-Paid Artists:** 40
Utilizes: Guest Artists
Budget: $1,000 - $50,000
Income Sources: Private Foundations/Grants/Endowments; Business/Corporate Donations; Government Grants; Individual Donations
Season: November - May   **Annual Attendance:** 1,600
Performance Facilities: Downey Community Theater

YOUTH SYMPHONY WEST
7609 Calmcrest Drive, Downey, CA 90240
(310) 927-9455
Founded: 1974
Arts Area: Orchestra
Status: Non-Professional; Non-Profit
Type: Educational
Purpose: To afford young musicians an opportunity to perform orchestral literature in a full symphonic setting
Management: Art Mautner, Conductor; Steve Kerstein, Assistant Conductor
Officers: Mickey Fruchter, University Liaison
Paid Staff: 1   **Volunteer Staff:** 3
Utilizes: Special Technical Talent
Budget: $1,000 - $50,000
Income Sources: Individual Donations
Season: October - July
Affiliations: California State University at Los Angeles; Conservatory of Music
Performance Facilities: California State University at Los Angeles

---
El Cajon

DANCE

SAMAHAN PHILIPPINE DANCE COMPANY
1441 Hillsmont Drive, El Cajon, CA 92020
(619) 444-7528
Founded: 1974
Arts Area: Ethnic; Folk
Status: Semi-Professional; Non-Profit
Type: Performing; Touring; Educational; Sponsoring
Purpose: To preserve, develop and present the cultural performing arts of the Philippines
Management: Lolita D. Carter PhD, Executive Director; Ruby Pearl B. Chiong, Company Manager; George Ragaza, Artistic Director; Juanita Caccam, Music Coordinator
Officers: Tessie Porciuncula, President; Carlos Linayao, Vice President; Estela Garcia, Secretary; Dina Ellorin, Treasurer
Paid Staff: 3   **Volunteer Staff:** 3
Paid Artists: 16   **Non-Paid Artists:** 8
Utilizes: Guest Artists
Budget: $50,000 - $100,000
Income Sources: Private Foundations/Grants/Endowments; Box Office; Government Grants; Individual Donations; Fund-raising
Season: 52 Weeks   **Annual Attendance:** 10,000
Affiliations: San Diego Culture and Dance Alliance

FACILITY

EAST COUNTY PERFORMING ARTS CENTER - THEATRE EAST
210 East Main Street, El Cajon, CA 92020
(619) 440-2277
Type of Facility: Concert Hall; Performance Center; Theatre House
Type of Stage: Thrust; Proscenium
Stage Dimensions: 70'Wx26'D; 70'Wx19'6"H proscenium opening   **Orchestra Pit**
Seating Capacity: 1,200
Year Built: 1977   **Architect:** William Blurock and Art Decker
Contact for Rental: Jane Bender;   (619) 440-0372
Manager: R.M.D. Childs;   (619) 440-0372
Resident Groups: Grossmont Community College

El Granada

PERFORMING SERIES

BACH DANCING AND DYNAMITE SOCIETY GROUP
PO Box 302, El Granada, CA 94018
(415) 726-4143
Founded: 1964
Arts Area: Vocal Music; Instrumental Music; Headliner; Jazz
Status: Professional; Non-Profit
Type: Presenting
Purpose: To present all forms of jazz and classical chamber music
Management: Pete Douglas, Concert Manager
Officers: Bennett Kilpack, President; Tom Morrison, Vice President; Sylvia Way, Secretary/Treasurer
Paid Staff: 3
Utilizes: Guest Artists
Budget: $100,000 - $500,000
Income Sources: Business/Corporate Donations; Government Grants; Individual Donations
Season: February - December   **Annual Attendance:** 10,000
Affiliations: Half Moon Bay
Performance Facilities: Douglass Beach House

Emeryville

DANCE

NANCY KARP AND DANCERS
4250 Horton Street, Studio 6, Emeryville, CA 94608
(510) 653-1195
FAX: (510) 652-0898
Founded: 1976
Arts Area: Modern
Status: Professional; Non-Profit
Type: Performing; Touring
Management: Nancy Karp, Artistic Director
Officers: Laura Kline, President
Paid Staff: 2   **Volunteer Staff:** 2
Paid Artists: 10
Utilizes: Special Technical Talent; Guest Artists
Budget: $50,000 - $100,000
Income Sources: Private Foundations/Grants/Endowments; Business/Corporate Donations; Box Office; Government Grants; Individual Donations
Season: April - October
Performance Facilities: Zellerbach Playhouse, University of California at Berkeley; Laney College Theatre; Theater Artaud

THEATRE

THE BMT THEATER
3617 San Pablo Avenue, #118, Emeryville, CA 94608
(510) 843-7519
FAX: (415) 822-7898
Founded: 1988

Arts Area: Theatrical Group
Status: Semi-Professional; Non-Profit
Type: Performing; Touring; Educational
Management: Ed Bullins, Producing Director
Budget: $1,000 - $50,000
Income Sources: Private Foundations/Grants/Endowments; Box Office; Individual Donations
Season: 52 Weeks

Englewood

DANCE

HANNAH KAHN DANCE COMPANY
4685 South Ogden Street, Englewood, CA 80110
(303) 789-4181
> **Founded:** 1992
> **Arts Area:** Modern
> **Status:** Professional
> **Type:** Performing; Touring
> **Purpose:** To perform the works of Hannah Kahn
> **Management:** Hannah Kahn, Artistic Director
> **Officers:** Hannah Kahn, President; Arthur Best, Secretary
> **Volunteer Staff:** 2
> **Paid Artists:** 8   **Non-Paid Artists:** 1
> **Budget:** $1,000 - $50,000   **Income Sources:** Box Office; Government Grants; Individual Donations

Escondido

THEATRE

LAWRENCE WELK RESORT THEATRE
8860 Lawrence Welk Drive, Escondido, CA 92026
(619) 749-3000
FAX: (619) 749-6182
> **Arts Area:** Professional; Dinner
> **Status:** Professional; Commercial
> **Type:** Performing
> **Management:** Frank Wayne, Artistic Director
> **Officers:** Bud Desantis, Executive Producer
> **Paid Staff:** 33
> **Paid Artists:** 18
> **Utilizes:** Guest Artists
> **Budget:** $500,000 - $1,000,000
> **Income Sources:** Box Office
> **Season:** 52 Weeks
> **Affiliations:** AEA

Ferndale

THEATRE

FERNDALE REPERTORY THEATRE
447 Main Street, PO Box 892, Ferndale, CA 95536
(707) 725-4636
> **Founded:** 1971
> **Arts Area:** Community
> **Status:** Semi-Professional; Non-Profit
> **Type:** Performing
> **Purpose:** To provide North Coast residents and visitors theatrical performances of the highest quality
> **Management:** Clinton Rebik, Artistic Director
> **Officers:** Judith Anderson, President; Robert Tait, Vice President; Janet Frost, Secretary; Dominique Jackson, Treasurer
> **Paid Staff:** 7
> **Paid Artists:** 20   **Non-Paid Artists:** 200
> **Utilizes:** Special Technical Talent; Guest Artists; Guest Directors
> **Budget:** $100,000 - $500,000

Income Sources: Private Foundations/Grants/Endowments; Business/Corporate Donations; Box Office; Government Grants; Individual Donations; Memberships
Season: 52 Weeks   **Annual Attendance:** 16,000
Performance Facilities: Ferndale Repertory Theatre

Fontana

FACILITY

FONTANA PERFORMING ARTS CENTER
9460 Sierra Avenue, Fontana, CA 92335
(909) 350-6741; (909) 350-6734
Type of Facility: Auditorium; Performance Center; Room
Facility Originally: Meeting Hall
Type of Stage: Proscenium
Stage Dimensions: 20'x40'
Seating Capacity: 990
Year Built: 1956   **Architect:** Herman Ruhraw
Year Remodeled: 1985   **Cost:** $310,000
Contact for Rental: Larry Watson;   (714) 350-6741

Fremont

INSTRUMENTAL MUSIC

FREMONT-NEWARK PHILHARMONIC
PO Box 104, Fremont, CA 94537
(510) 794-1652
Founded: 1963
Arts Area: Symphony; Orchestra; Ensemble
Status: Professional; Semi-Professional
Type: Performing; Educational
Purpose: To perform orchestra and chamber concerts
Management: Timothy Zerlang, Executive Director; David Sloss, Music Director
Officers: Eva Maria Tisdale, President; Art Kimber, Treasurer
Paid Staff: 2   **Volunteer Staff:** 30
Paid Artists: 60   **Non-Paid Artists:** 2
Utilizes: Special Technical Talent; Guest Artists
Budget: $100,000 - $500,000
Income Sources: Private Foundations/Grants/Endowments; Business/Corporate Donations; Box Office; Government Grants; Individual Donations
Season: October - May   **Annual Attendance:** 3,500

Fresno

DANCE

FRESNO BALLET
1432 Fulton Street, Fresno, CA 93721
(209) 233-2623
FAX: (209) 233-2670
Founded: 1967
Arts Area: Modern; Ballet; Ethnic
Status: Professional; Non-Profit
Type: Performing; Touring; Educational; Sponsoring
Purpose: To enrich the arts environment of central California through the production and presentation of dance
Management: Donald Bradburn, Artistic Director; Chris Moad, Executive Director
Paid Artists: 20   **Non-Paid Artists:** 30
Utilizes: Special Technical Talent; Guest Conductors; Guest Artists; Guest Directors; Guest Choreographers
Budget: $100,000 - $500,000
Income Sources: Private Foundations/Grants/Endowments; Business/Corporate Donations; Box Office; Government Grants; Individual Donations
Season: December - May; Summer Festival   **Annual Attendance:** 20,000
Performance Facilities: William Saroyan Theatre

JOHN CHOOKASIAN FOLK ENSEMBLE - KING TUT REVUE BELLY DANCE
2511 West Browning, Fresno, CA 93711
(209) 449-1777
>   **Founded:** 1962
>   **Arts Area:** Ethnic; Folk
>   **Status:** Professional; Non-Profit
>   **Type:** Performing; Touring; Educational
>   **Purpose:** To introduce people to the folk music, folk dance and folk instruments of the Middle East, including Armenian, Greek and Persian
>   **Management:** John Chookasian, Artistic Director
>   **Paid Staff:** 1
>   **Paid Artists:** 8
>   **Utilizes:** Guest Artists
>   **Budget:** $1,000 - $50,000
>   **Income Sources:** Private Foundations/Grants/Endowments; Box Office
>   **Season:** 52 Weeks

INSTRUMENTAL MUSIC

FRESNO PHILHARMONIC ASSOCIATION
2610 West Shaw Avenue, Suite 103, Fresno, CA 93711-3332
(209) 261-0600
FAX: (209) 261-0700
>   **Arts Area:** Symphony; Orchestra
>   **Status:** Professional; Non-Profit
>   **Type:** Performing; Educational
>   **Purpose:** To provide quality orchestral music to central California
>   **Management:** Andrew Massey, Music Director; Irene Klug-Nielson, General Manager
>   **Officers:** Dr. Charles Mittman, President
>   **Budget:** $500,000 - $1,000,000
>   **Income Sources:** Private Foundations/Grants/Endowments; Business/Corporate Donations; Box Office; Government Grants; Individual Donations
>   **Performance Facilities:** William Saroyan Theatre

FRESNO PHILHARMONIC ORCHESTRA
1300 North Fresno Street, #201-B, Fresno, CA 93703
(209) 485-3020
>   **Founded:** 1954
>   **Arts Area:** Symphony; Orchestra
>   **Status:** Professional; Non-Profit
>   **Type:** Performing; Touring; Resident
>   **Management:** Andrew Massey, Principal Guest Conductor/Artistic Advisor; Irene Klug Nielsen, General Manager
>   **Officers:** Parker Powell, President, Board of Directors; Larry Balakian, First Vice President; William M. Lyles, Second Vice President; John Dodson, Treasurer; Richardson Herrinton, Assistant Treasurer
>   **Paid Staff:** 5 **Volunteer Staff:** 25
>   **Paid Artists:** 65
>   **Utilizes:** Guest Conductors; Guest Artists
>   **Budget:** $500,000 - $1,000,000
>   **Income Sources:** Private Foundations/Grants/Endowments; Business/Corporate Donations; Box Office; Government Grants; Individual Donations
>   **Season:** October - May **Annual Attendance:** 37,000
>   **Affiliations:** ASOL; Association of California Symphony Orchestras
>   **Performance Facilities:** Saroyan Theatre

THEATRE

GOOD COMPANY PLAYERS
833 East Fern, Fresno, CA 93728
(209) 266-0211
>   **Founded:** 1973
>   **Arts Area:** Community; Theatrical Group
>   **Status:** Non-Professional; Commercial
>   **Type:** Performing; Touring; Educational
>   **Purpose:** To perform original works at local schools, Roger Rocka's Music Hall and the Second Theatre
>   **Management:** Dan Pessano, Managing Director; Linda Thayer, Business Manager
>   **Officers:** Dan Pessano, President; Laurie Pessano, Vice President; Linda Thayer, Secretary/Treasurer
>   **Paid Staff:** 11 **Volunteer Staff:** 40
>   **Utilizes:** Guest Directors

Budget: $1,000 - $50,000
Income Sources: Box Office
Season: 52 Weeks   **Annual Attendance:** 85,000
Affiliations: AACT
Performance Facilities: Roger Rocka's Music Hall; Good Company Players' Second Theatre

FACILITY

CALIFORNIA STATE UNIVERSITY-FRESNO - JOHN WRIGHT THEATRE
5201 North Maple, Fresno, CA 93740
(209) 278-2216
    Type of Facility: Theatre House; Arena
    Type of Stage: Proscenium   **Seating Capacity:** 180
    Year Built: 1960   **Cost:** $1,000,000
    Year Remodeled: 1991   **Cost:** $2,100,000
    Contact for Rental: Pam Dyer;   (209) 278-2216
    Resident Groups: Portable Dance Troupe

CALIFORNIA STATE UNIVERSITY-FRESNO - WAHLBERG RECITAL HALL
2380 East Keats, Fresno, CA 93740-0077
(209) 294-2654
    Type of Facility: Concert Hall
    Facility Originally: School
    Type of Stage: Platform
    Stage Dimensions: 16'x18'
    Seating Capacity: 180
    Year Built: 1960
    Contact for Rental: Beverly Noell;   (209) 294-2654
    Resident Groups: CSUF Faculty String Quartet; CSUF Graduate String Quartet; Opera Workshop; University Wind Ensemble; University Jazz Bands; Presidents Quintet; California Woodwind Quintet; Concert Choir; University Orchestra

FRESNO CONVENTION CENTER THEATRE
700 M Street, Fresno, CA 93721
(209) 498-1511
FAX: (209) 488-4643
    Type of Facility: Theatre House
    Type of Stage: Proscenium
    Stage Dimensions: 30'x52'x52'   **Orchestra Pit**
    Seating Capacity: 2,359
    Year Built: 1966   **Architect:** Robert Stevens Associates   **Cost:** $10,000,000
    Contact for Rental: Karen Thurber;   (209) 498-1511
    Manager: Michael J. Sweeney;   (209) 498-1511

TOWER THEATRE FOR THE PERFORMING ARTS
815 East Olive, Fresno, CA 93728
(209) 485-9050
FAX: (209) 485-3941
    Founded: 1990
    Type of Facility: Concert Hall
    Facility Originally: Movie House
    Type of Stage: Thrust
    Stage Dimensions: 30'Dx40'W
    Seating Capacity: 761
    Year Built: 1939   **Architect:** S. Charles Lee
    Year Remodeled: 1990   **Architect:** Kennedy Lutz Architecture, Inc.   **Cost:** $1,500,000
    Contact for Rental: Ronald D. Eichman;   (209) 485-9050

WARNOR'S THEATER
1400 Fulton Street, Fresno, CA 93721
(209) 233-1157
    Type of Facility: Concert Hall; Performance Center; Theatre House; Opera House
    Type of Stage: Proscenium
    Stage Dimensions: 47'10"Wx30'D   **Orchestra Pit**
    Seating Capacity: 2,164
    Year Built: 1927   **Architect:** B. Marcus Priteca
    Contact for Rental: Marty Schnepp;   (209) 233-1157

Fullerton

DANCE

DANCE REPERTORY THEATRE
California State University, Fullerton, CA 92634
(714) 773-2689
Founded: 1981
Arts Area: Modern; Ballet
Status: Professional; Non-Profit
Type: Performing; Touring; Resident; Educational
Purpose: A professional adjunct to the dance program of California State University at Fullerton,
Dance Repertory Theatre provides professional opportunities for graduating dance majors.
Management: Barbara Arms, Artistic Director
Paid Staff: 3
Paid Artists: 9 **Non-Paid Artists:** 1
Budget: $1,000 - $50,000
Income Sources: Box Office; Individual Donations
Season: February - October
Affiliations: California State University at Fullerton

VOCAL MUSIC

FULLERTON CIVIC LIGHT OPERA
218 West Commonwealth, Fullerton, CA 92632
(714) 526-3832
Founded: 1972
Arts Area: Light Opera; Operetta; Musical Theatre
Status: Semi-Professional; Non-Profit
Type: Performing; Resident
Purpose: To provide entertainment at affordable prices
Management: Griff Duncan, General Manager; Jan Duncan, Artistic Director; Donna Parsons, Production Manager
Officers: Jack Bedell, President; Karen Gallio, Vice-President; Cecil Ricks, Secretary; David MacKain, Treasurer
Paid Staff: 50 **Volunteer Staff:** 50
Paid Artists: 40 **Non-Paid Artists:** 90
Utilizes: Special Technical Talent; Guest Conductors; Guest Artists; Guest Directors
Budget: $500,000 - $1,000,000
Income Sources: Private Foundations/Grants/Endowments; Business/Corporate Donations; Box Office; Government
Grants; Individual Donations; Costume and Scenery Rentals
Season: October - May **Annual Attendance:** 33,000
Performance Facilities: Plummer Auditorium

FACILITY

MUCKENTHALER CULTURAL CENTER
1201 West Malvern Avenue, Fullerton, CA 92633
(714) 738-6595
FAX: (714) 738-6366
Type of Facility: Outdoor (Concert); Studio Performance; Amphitheater; Civic Center; Multi-Purpose
Type of Stage: Platform
Stage Dimensions: 20'x40'
Seating Capacity: 264
Year Built: 1924
Year Remodeled: 1984 **Cost:** $750,000
Contact for Rental: Denise Watson; (714) 738-6595
Resident Groups: Theatre-on-the-Green

PLUMMER AUDITORIUM
201 East Chapman Avenue, Fullerton, CA 92632
(714) 870-3739
FAX: (714) 870-3768
Type of Facility: Concert Hall; Auditorium; Theatre House
Type of Stage: Proscenium
Stage Dimensions: 35'9"x21'9" **Orchestra Pit**
Seating Capacity: 1,334
Year Built: 1930 **Architect:** Carlton Monroe Winslow **Cost:** $295,541
Year Remodeled: 1972 **Architect:** Frick, Frick & Jette
Contact for Rental: Walt De Jong, Theatre Manager; (714) 870-3739

Manager: Walt De Jong
Resident Groups: Community Concerts; Fullerton Civic Light Opera; California State University - Fullerton Pair Series

Garden Grove

INSTRUMENTAL MUSIC

ORANGE COUNTY SYMPHONY
12866 Main Street, Suite 106, Garden Grove, CA 92640
(714) 534-1103
FAX: (714) 537-9652
   Founded: 1985
   Arts Area: Symphony
   Status: Professional
   Type: Performing; Resident; Educational
   Management: Yaakov Dvir-Djerassi, General Manager
   Officers: Richard H. Hain, President; Marion Silverberg, Vice President; Emma Daugherty, Secretary;
   Ian Darley, Treasurer
   Paid Staff: 3   **Volunteer Staff:** 10
   Paid Artists: 85
   Utilizes: Guest Conductors; Guest Artists; Guest Directors
   Budget: $100,000 - $500,000
   Income Sources: Private Foundations/Grants/Endowments; Business/Corporate Donations; Box Office; Government
   Grants; Individual Donations; Fund-raising
   Season: September - June   **Annual Attendance:** 15,000
   Performance Facilities: Don Wash Auditorium

THEATRE

GROVE SHAKESPEARE
12852 Main Street, Garden Grove, CA 92640
(714) 636-7213
FAX: (714) 539-2651
   Founded: 1979
   Arts Area: Professional; Musical; Classical
   Status: Professional; Non-Profit
   Type: Performing
   Purpose: To present classical works from the World Theatre; to present a Shakespeare Festival in summer
   Management: W. Stuart McDowell, Artistic Director; Charles Johanson, Office Manager
   Paid Staff: 8
   Paid Artists: 250
   Utilizes: Special Technical Talent; Guest Artists; Guest Directors
   Budget: $100,000 - $500,000
   Income Sources: Private Foundations/Grants/Endowments; Business/Corporate Donations; Box Office; Government
   Grants; Individual Donations
   Season: 52 Weeks   **Annual Attendance:** 30,000
   Affiliations: TCG; California Theater Council; Orange County Theater Alliance
   Performance Facilities: Gem Theatre; The Festival Amphitheatre

PERFORMING SERIES

THE GROVE SHAKESPEARE FESTIVAL
12852 Main Street, Garden Grove, CA 92640
(714) 636-7213
FAX: (714) 539-2651
   Founded: 1979
   Arts Area: Theater
   Status: Professional; Non-Profit
   Type: Performing; Resident; Educational
   Management: W. Stuart McDowell, Artistic Director; Barbara G. Hammerman, Managing Director
   Paid Staff: 9
   Paid Artists: 15
   Utilizes: Special Technical Talent; Guest Artists; Guest Directors
   Budget: $500,000 - $1,000,000
   Income Sources: Box Office; Government Grants; Individual Donations
   Season: June - September   **Annual Attendance:** 8,000
   Performance Facilities: The Festival Amphitheatre; Gem Theater

Glendale

INSTRUMENTAL MUSIC

GLENDALE SYMPHONY
401 North Brand Boulevard, Suite 520, Glendale, CA 91203
(818) 500-8720
Founded: 1924
Arts Area: Symphony; Orchestra
Status: Professional; Non-Profit
Type: Performing; Educational
Purpose: To educate youth and to bring high-quality familiar classical and light classical music to the community
Management: Shirley Seely, Administrator
Paid Staff: 1   **Volunteer Staff:** 3
Paid Artists: 95
Utilizes: Guest Conductors; Guest Artists
Budget: $100,000 - $500,000
Income Sources: Business/Corporate Donations; Box Office; Government Grants; Individual Donations
Season: October - April   **Annual Attendance:** 30,000
Affiliations: ASOL
Performance Facilities: Dorothy Chandler Pavilion

Glendora

FACILITY

HAUGH PERFORMING ARTS CENTER
1000 West Foothill, Glendora, CA 91740
(818) 914-8845
FAX: (818) 335-4715
Type of Facility: Theatre House
Type of Stage: Proscenium
Stage Dimensions: 28'x54'x70'; grid height 78'   **Orchestra Pit**
Seating Capacity: 1,451
Year Built: 1971   **Architect:** Neptune & Thomas   **Cost:** $2,300,000
Contact for Rental: Greg Hinrichsen, Director of Performing Arts;   (818) 914-8847
Manager: Greg Hinrichsen
Resident Groups: Evenings at Eight/Narrated Film Series; Citrus Singers

Guerneville

PERFORMING SERIES

RUSSIAN RIVER JAZZ FESTIVAL, INC.
16342 Third Street, Guerneville, CA 95446
(707) 869-3940
FAX: (707) 869-0147
Founded: 1976
Arts Area: Vocal Music; Instrumental Music; Festivals
Status: Non-Profit
Type: Performing
Purpose: To bring top name performers in jazz and related musical genres to an outdoor venue to benefit local, community and youth music programs
Management: Kathryn Marceau, Office Manager
Officers: Paul Neel, President; Debbie Padilla, Secretary; Dan Cool, John Hughes, Paul Larkin, Directors
Paid Staff: 1   **Volunteer Staff:** 60
Paid Artists: 14   **Non-Paid Artists:** 5
Utilizes: Special Technical Talent; Guest Artists
Budget: $100,000 - $500,000
Income Sources: Private Foundations/Grants/Endowments; Box Office; Government Grants
Season: June - September   **Annual Attendance:** 8,000

Hayward

FACILITY

CALIFORNIA STATE UNIVERSITY-HAYWARD - MAIN THEATRE
Carlos Bee Boulevard, Hayward, CA 94542
(510) 881-3374
Type of Facility: Theatre House
Type of Stage: Proscenium
Stage Dimensions: 36'Wx40'D; 36'Wx22'H proscenium opening   **Orchestra Pit**
Seating Capacity: 480
Year Built: 1972   **Architect:** Niell Smith & Associates; Anderson Simons Dusel & Campini   **Cost:** $1,500,000
Contact for Rental: Facilities Reservations;   (510) 881-3548
Resident Groups: Theatre Arts Department

CHABOT COLLEGE PERFORMING ARTS CENTER
25555 Hesperian Boulevard, Hayward, CA 94545-2447
(510) 786-6976
FAX: (510) 782-9315
Type of Facility: Theatre Complex; Concert Hall; Auditorium; Performance Center; Black Box
Type of Stage: Flexible; Proscenium
Stage Dimensions: Main Theatre - 46'Wx35'D; Little Theatre - Flexible   **Orchestra Pit**
Seating Capacity: Main Theatre - 1,482; Little Theatre - 208
Year Built: 1968   **Architect:** Johnson, Poole & Storm   **Cost:** $1,869,290
Contact for Rental: Elliott Charnow, Chairman, Humanities Division;   (510) 786-6828
Manager: Roger Noyes;   (510) 786-6976

Hemet

PERFORMING SERIES

RAMONA HILLSIDE PLAYERS
27402 Ramona Bowl Road, Hemet, CA 92544
(909) 658-3111
FAX: (909) 658-2695
Founded: 1941
Arts Area: Vocal Music; Instrumental Music; Theater
Status: Non-Professional; Non-Profit
Type: Performing; Resident; Educational
Purpose: To present quality entertainment and train individuals in all phases of theatre
Management: Peggy L. McQuown, Contact Person
Utilizes: Guest Directors
Budget: $1,000 - $50,000
Income Sources: Box Office; Individual Donations
Season: 52 Weeks   **Annual Attendance:** 5,500
Performance Facilities: Ramona Hillside Playhouse

RAMONA PAGEANT ASSOCIATION
27400 Ramona Bowl Road, Hemet, CA 92544
(909) 658-3111
FAX: (909) 658-2695
Founded: 1923
Arts Area: Dance; Vocal Music; Theater; Community
Status: Professional; Non-Professional; Non-Profit
Type: Performing; Resident; Educational
Purpose: To portray early California history - the coming of white men and its effect on the Spanish and Indian cultures
Management: Roland C. Parker, Executive Director
Officers: Michael McIntyre, President; Daniel T. Donnelly, Vice President; W.P. Ryan, Secretary; J. Robert Eichinger, Treasurer
Paid Staff: 4
Paid Artists: 2   **Non-Paid Artists:** 350
Utilizes: Guest Artists; Guest Directors
Budget: $100,000 - $500,000
Income Sources: Box Office
Season: April - May   **Annual Attendance:** 39,000

Affiliations: Institute of Outdoor Dramas
Performance Facilities: Ramona Bowl Outdoor Theatre

FACILITY

RAMONA BOWL
27400 Ramona Bowl Road, Hemet, CA 92544
(909) 658-3111
FAX: (909) 658-2695
    Type of Facility: Amphitheater
    Type of Stage: Environmental
    Seating Capacity: 6,662
    Contact for Rental: R.C. Parker; (909) 658-3111
    Manager: W.R. Rose

Hollywood

THEATRE

AMERICAN LIVING HISTORY THEATER
PO Box 2677, Hollywood, CA 90078
(213) 876-2202
    Founded: 1975
    Arts Area: Professional
    Status: Professional; Non-Profit
    Type: Performing; Touring; Resident; Educational
    Purpose: To present theatre productions on American historical and literary characters and events
    Management: Dorene Ludwig, Artistic Director/President
    Income Sources: Business/Corporate Donations; Box Office; Government Grants; Individual Donations
    Season: 52 Weeks

THE CAST THEATRE/THE CAST-AT-THE-CIRCLE
804 North El Centro, Hollywood, CA 90038
(213) 462-0265; (213) 462-9872
    Founded: 1974
    Arts Area: Theatrical Group
    Status: Non-Profit
    Type: Performing; Touring
    Purpose: To encourage playwrights; to produce new American plays
    Management: R.T. Schmitt, Producing Artistic Director; Diana Gibson, Associate Artistic Director
    Officers: Doris Koenig, President; Stanley Handman, Secretary
    Paid Staff: 6 **Volunteer Staff:** 5
    Paid Artists: 40
    Utilizes: Special Technical Talent; Guest Artists; Guest Directors
    Budget: $50,000 - $100,000
    Income Sources: Private Foundations/Grants/Endowments; Business/Corporate Donations; Box Office; Government Grants; Individual Donations
    Season: 52 Weeks **Annual Attendance:** 12,000
    Affiliations: TCG; Los Angeles Theatre Alliance; California Theatre Council
    Performance Facilities: The Cast Theatre; The Cast-at-the-Circle Theatre

FRIENDS AND ARTISTS THEATRE ENSEMBLE
1761 North Vermont Avenue, Hollywood, CA 90027
(213) 664-0680
    Founded: 1986
    Arts Area: Professional; Musical; Theatrical Group
    Status: Professional; Semi-Professional; Non-Profit
    Type: Performing; Touring; Resident; Educational
    Purpose: To produce and develop original works; to revive great works of literature
    Management: Pauli Dewitt, Administrative Director; Liz Hipwell, Production Coordinator; Tony Miller, Stage Manager; Steven Ingrassia, Technical Director
    Officers: Sal Romeo, Artistic Director; Laurie Wemdorf, Maria Simpson, Marc Handler, Vice Presidents; Bob Zemtis, Secretary; Michael Mehring, Treasurer
    Paid Staff: 5 **Volunteer Staff:** 50
    Paid Artists: 100 **Non-Paid Artists:** 100
    Utilizes: Special Technical Talent; Guest Conductors; Guest Artists; Guest Directors
    Budget: $50,000 - $100,000

Income Sources: Private Foundations/Grants/Endowments; Business/Corporate Donations; Box Office; Government Grants; Individual Donations
Season: 52 Weeks **Annual Attendance:** 10,000

MCCADDEN PLACE THEATRE
1157 North McCadden Place, Hollywood, CA 90038
(213) 856-0665
Founded: 1981
Arts Area: Professional; Theatrical Group
Status: Professional; Non-Profit
Type: Performing; Educational
Management: Joy Rinaldi, Jay Donohue, Artistic Directors
Utilizes: Special Technical Talent; Guest Artists; Guest Directors
Budget: $1,000 - $50,000
Income Sources: Box Office; Individual Donations
Season: 52 Weeks
Affiliations: AEA
Performance Facilities: McCadden Theatre (scheduled to reopen in 1993)

STAGES THEATRE
1540 North McCadden Place, Hollywood, CA 90028
(213) 465-1010
FAX: (213) 462-2176
Founded: 1981
Arts Area: Professional
Status: Professional; Non-Profit
Type: Performing
Purpose: To expose new or unfamiliar works or styles of theater to Los Angeles audiences; to host unique artists-in-residence who utilize distinctive theatrical styles, such as Theater of the Absurd and Commedia del' Arte
Management: Paul Verdier, Artistic Director; Sonia Lloveras, Managing Director
Officers: Pompea Smith, Chair; Sonia Lloveras, Treasurer
Paid Staff: 1 **Volunteer Staff:** 8
Paid Artists: 3 **Non-Paid Artists:** 3
Utilizes: Guest Artists; Guest Directors
Budget: $50,000 - $100,000
Income Sources: Box Office; Government Grants; Individual Donations
Season: October - September **Annual Attendance:** 6,000
Affiliations: TCG
Performance Facilities: Stages Theatre

THEATRE RAPPORT/HOLLYWOOD THEATRE CLUB
8128 Gould Avenue, Hollywood, CA 90046
(213) 660-0433
Founded: 1967
Arts Area: Theatrical Group
Status: Professional
Type: Performing
Purpose: To present West Coast premieres of contemporary plays to an aware, adventurous audience
Management: Crane Jackson, Artistic Director/Producer
Volunteer Staff: 8
Non-Paid Artists: 30
Utilizes: Guest Directors
Budget: $1,000 - $50,000
Income Sources: Box Office; Individual Donations

UNICORN PLAYERS INC.
1743 North Hudson Avenue, Hollywood, CA 90028
(213) 464-8738
Founded: 1973
Status: Semi-Professional; Non-Profit
Type: Touring
Purpose: To expose as many children as possible to exciting theatrical experiences and examples of their literary heritage
Management: Shirley Adams, General Manager; James Hays, Artistic Director
Officers: James Hays, President; Beth Collier, Secretary
Volunteer Staff: 2
Paid Artists: 5
Utilizes: Special Technical Talent
Budget: $50,000 - $100,000
Income Sources: Touring Fees

Season: October - June   **Annual Attendance:** 100,000
Affiliations: Los Angeles Theatre Alliance

FACILITY

THE COMPLEX
6476 Santa Monica Boulevard, Hollywood, CA 90038
(213) 465-0383
> **Type of Facility:** Theatre Complex
> **Type of Stage:** Proscenium
> **Seating Capacity:** 55 in each of five theatres
> **Contact for Rental:** Matt Chait;   (213) 465-0383
> **Resident Groups:** Theatre 6470; The Blueline Theatre Group
> *1960's conversion to five theatre spaces*

HOLLYWOOD BOWL
2301 North Highland Avenue, Hollywood, CA 90078
(213) 850-2000
> **Type of Facility:** Outdoor (Concert); Amphitheater
> **Type of Stage:** Proscenium; Arena
> **Stage Dimensions:** 106'x55'x48'
> **Seating Capacity:** 17,906
> **Year Built:** 1922
> **Acoustical Consultant:** Elizabeth Cohen
> **Contact for Rental:** Mark Ferber;   (213) 850-2080
> **Manager:** Anne Parsons;   (213) 850-2095
> **Resident Groups:** Los Angeles Philharmonic Association; Hollywood Bowl Orchestra

HOLLYWOOD PALLADIUM
6215 Sunset Boulevard, Hollywood, CA 90028
(213) 962-7600
> **Type of Facility:** Concert Hall; Multi-Purpose; Room
> **Facility Originally:** Ballroom
> **Type of Stage:** Thrust
> **Stage Dimensions:** 25'x65' with 4'x8' extensions
> **Seating Capacity:** Theater-style - 2,400; Festival-style - 4,400
> **Year Built:** 1940   **Architect:** McClellan and Cruz
> **Contact for Rental:** Mark Midgley;   (213) 962-7600

JAMES A. DOOLITTLE THEATRE
1615 North Vine Street, Hollywood, CA 90028
(213) 462-6666
FAX: (213) 926-2936
> **Type of Facility:** Theatre House
> **Type of Stage:** Proscenium
> **Stage Dimensions:** 74'10"Wx34'D; 38'Wx25'2"H proscenium opening   **Orchestra Pit**
> **Seating Capacity:** 1,019
> **Year Built:** 1926
> **Year Remodeled:** 1985   **Architect:** Brian Murphy   **Cost:** $650,000
> **Acoustical Consultant:** Bolt, Beranek & Newman
> **Contact for Rental:** Phil Lipman, UCLA;   (213) 825-9159
> *Rental limited to equity only*

Huntington Beach

THEATRE

HUNTINGTON BEACH PLAYHOUSE
PO Box 451, Huntington Beach, CA 92648
(714) 832-1405
> **Founded:** 1963
> **Arts Area:** Musical; Community; Theatrical Group
> **Status:** Non-Professional; Non-Profit
> **Type:** Performing
> **Purpose:** As a non-profit organization dedicated to community educational and cultural enrichment in dramatic arts, Huntington Beach Playhouse presents dramatic productions, sponsors student scholarships and offers stagecraft workshops.
> **Management:** Phil de Barros, President; Martin G. Eckmann, Technical Director

Officers: Phil de Barros, President; Lana Campbell, Vice President; Orvil Dart, Treasurer; Patricia Powers, Business Manager
Volunteer Staff: 25
Non-Paid Artists: 50
Utilizes: Special Technical Talent; Guest Directors
Budget: $50,000 - $100,000
Income Sources: Business/Corporate Donations; Box Office; Individual Donations
Season: October - August   **Annual Attendance:** 7,000
Affiliations: Huntington Beach Chamber of Commerce
Performance Facilities: Gisler Intermediate School; Huntington Beach Central Library

FACILITY

GOLDEN WEST COLLEGE - MAINSTAGE THEATRE
15744 Golden West Street, Huntington Beach, CA 92647
(714) 895-8772
Type of Facility: Theatre House
Type of Stage: Proscenium
Stage Dimensions: 72'Wx33'D   **Orchestra Pit**
Seating Capacity: 340
Year Built: 1971   **Architect:** William Pereira and Associates   **Cost:** $3,500,000
Year Remodeled: 1992   **Cost:** $85,000
Acoustical Consultant: William Pereira and Associates
Contact for Rental: David Anthony;   (714) 895-8772

Huntington Park

THEATRE

HUNTINGTON PARK CIVIC THEATRE
6952 Salt Lake Avenue, Huntington Park, CA 90255
(213) 584-6215
FAX: (213) 588-4577
Founded: 1947
Arts Area: Musical; Community
Status: Non-Profit
Type: Performing; Resident
Purpose: To develop an interest for drama in the community; to provide a recreational outlet for community members
Management: Board of Directors
Officers: Eileen Gerardi, President; Anne Parks, Vice President; Dorothy Fitzel, Secretary; Esther Hennes, Treasurer
Volunteer Staff: 15
Non-Paid Artists: 40
Utilizes: Guest Artists; Guest Directors
Budget: $1,000 - $50,000
Income Sources: Box Office; Individual Donations
Season: 52 Weeks   **Annual Attendance:** 1,500
Affiliations: Recreation Department
Performance Facilities: Bonelli Center

Idyllwild

PERFORMING SERIES

IDYLLWILD SCHOOL OF MUSIC AND THE ARTS
52500 Temecula Drive, Idyllwild, CA 90210
(909) 659-2171
Founded: 1950
Arts Area: Dance; Vocal Music; Instrumental Music; Theater; Festivals
Status: Professional; Non-Professional; Non-Profit
Type: Performing; Educational
Purpose: To make the arts and arts education available to all people
Management: Steven Fraider Summer, Program Director; William Lowman, Executive Director
Income Sources: Private Foundations/Grants/Endowments; Business/Corporate Donations; Box Office; Government Grants; Individual Donations
Season: June - August
Performance Facilities: Idyllwild Arts Foundation Theatre; Holmes Amphitheatre

Inglewood

FACILITY

THE GREAT WESTERN FORUM
3900 West Manchester Boulevard, Inglewood, CA 90306
(310) 419-3182
FAX: (310) 419-3234
Type of Facility: Arena
Type of Stage: Flexible; Arena
Stage Dimensions: 48'x40'
Seating Capacity: 18,679
Year Built: 1967   **Architect:** Charles Luckman Associates
Contact for Rental: Claire L. Rothman;   (213) 419-3182

Irvine

INSTRUMENTAL MUSIC

ORANGE COUNTY PHILHARMONIC SOCIETY
2082 Business Center Drive, Suite 100, Irvine, CA 92715
(714) 553-2422
FAX: (714) 553-2421
Founded: 1953
Arts Area: Symphony; Orchestra; Chamber; Ensemble; Ethnic; Folk; Instrumental Group
Status: Professional; Non-Profit
Type: Educational; Sponsoring
Purpose: To present the finest classical music; to provide a nationally-recognized network of educational outreach programs for Orange County youth, coordinated and funded in part by the 1,700 members of the Orange County Philharmonic Society's Women's Committees
Management: Erich A. Vollmer, Executive Director; Rebecca A. Menes, Marketing/Communications Manager
Officers: Susan S. Beechner, Chairman of the Board; Steven A. Lupinacci, President
Utilizes: Special Technical Talent; Guest Conductors; Guest Artists; Guest Directors
Budget: $1,000,000 - $5,000,000
Income Sources: Private Foundations/Grants/Endowments; Business/Corporate Donations; Box Office; Government Grants; Individual Donations
Season: September - May
Affiliations: California Arts Council
Performance Facilities: Orange County Performing Arts Center; Irvine Barclay Theatre

PACIFIC SYMPHONY ASSOCIATION
2151 Michelson Drive, Suite 216, Irvine, CA 92715
(714) 474-2109
FAX: (714) 474-2256
Arts Area: Symphony; Orchestra
Status: Professional; Non-Profit
Type: Performing; Educational
Purpose: To provide the Orange County region with symphonic performances of the highest quality through development and maintenance of a nationally-recognized orchestra; to broaden the appreciation of great music by exposing new and diverse audiences to the orchestra's performances
Management: Carl St. Clair, Music Director; Louis G. Spisto, Executive Director
Officers: G. Randolph Johnson, Chairman of the Board; Janice Johnson, President
Budget: $5,000,000 - $10,000,000
Income Sources: Private Foundations/Grants/Endowments; Business/Corporate Donations; Box Office; Government Grants; Individual Donations
Performance Facilities: Orange County Performing Arts Center

VOCAL MUSIC

PACIFIC CHORALE
18218 East McDurmotte, Suite B-1, Irvine, CA 92714
(714) 252-1234
FAX: (714) 252-1885
Arts Area: Choral
Status: Semi-Professional; Non-Profit
Type: Performing; Touring; Educational
Purpose: To provide the finest classical choral performances for Orange County and beyond

Management: John Alexander, Artistic Director/Conductor; Bonnie McClain, Executive Director
Officers: Jay St. Clair, President of the Board
Budget: $500,000 - $1,000,000
Income Sources: Private Foundations/Grants/Endowments; Business/Corporate Donations; Box Office; Government Grants; Individual Donations
Performance Facilities: Orange County Performing Arts Center

PERFORMING SERIES

UCI CULTURAL EVENTS
320 University Tower, University of California, Irvine, CA 92717-5185
(714) 856-5589
FAX: (714) 725-2201
Founded: 1965
Arts Area: Dance; Instrumental Music; Theater
Status: Professional; Non-Profit
Type: Educational; Sponsoring; Presenting
Purpose: To present professional performing artists to the campus and community
Management: Desiree Mallory, Manager of Cultural Events
Paid Staff: 7
Utilizes: Guest Artists
Budget: $100,000 - $500,000
Income Sources: Private Foundations/Grants/Endowments; Business/Corporate Donations; Box Office; Government Grants; Individual Donations
Season: October - June
Performance Facilities: Irvine Barclay Theatre; Bren Events Center; University of California at Irvine Student Center

FACILITY

BREN EVENTS CENTER
University of California, Irvine, CA 92717-1500
(714) 856-5050
FAX: (714) 856-5097
Founded: 1987
Type of Facility: Arena
Type of Stage: Flexible; Platform; 3/4 Arena; Arena
Stage Dimensions: 60'Wx40'D
Seating Capacity: 5,400
Year Built: 1986   **Architect:** Parkin Architects   **Cost:** $17,000,000
Acoustical Consultant: Poaletti/Lewitz/Associates
Contact for Rental: Steven H. Neal;   (714) 856-5050

UNIVERSITY OF CALIFORNIA-IRVINE - VILLAGE THEATRE
University of California, Irvine, CA 92717
(714) 856-4901
Type of Facility: Theatre House
Type of Stage: Proscenium
Stage Dimensions: 60'x120'x40'   **Orchestra Pit**
Seating Capacity: 420
Year Built: 1970   **Architect:** William Pereira and Associates   **Cost:** $1,500,000
Acoustical Consultant: Del Sano
Manager: Production Manager;   (714) 856-4901

Kentfield

INSTRUMENTAL MUSIC

MARIN COMMUNITY COLLEGE SYMPHONY
Kentfield, CA 94904
(415) 485-9460
Founded: 1960
Arts Area: Symphony; Orchestra; Chamber; Instrumental Group
Status: Non-Professional; Non-Profit
Type: Performing; Educational
Purpose: To promote cultural advancement
Management: Norman Masonson, Music Director/Conductor
Paid Staff: 4   **Volunteer Staff:** 60
Utilizes: Special Technical Talent; Guest Artists

Budget: $1,000 - $50,000
Income Sources: Government Grants; Individual Donations
Season: August - December; January - May   **Annual Attendance:** 400
Performance Facilities: Fine Arts Theatre

La Jolla

INSTRUMENTAL MUSIC

LA JOLLA CHAMBER MUSIC SOCIETY
7949 Ivanhoe Street, Suite 319, La Jolla, CA 92037
(619) 459-3724
    Mailing Address: PO Box 2168, La Jolla, CA 92038
    Founded: 1968
    Arts Area: Symphony; Chamber; Ensemble
    Status: Professional; Non-Profit
    Type: Performing
    Purpose: To offer San Diego County audiences classical chamber music of the highest quality through concerts and recitals
    Management: Neale Perl, Executive Director
    Officers: Robert Edmunds, President
    Paid Staff: 3
    Paid Artists: 35
    Utilizes: Guest Artists
    Budget: $500,000 - $1,000,000
    Income Sources: Private Foundations/Grants/Endowments; Business/Corporate Donations; Box Office; Government Grants; Individual Donations
    Season: August - June   **Annual Attendance:** 50,000
    Affiliations: Association of California Symphony Orchestras; Combined Arts Council of San Diego County
    Performance Facilities: Sherwood Auditorium; Civic Theatre

THEATRE

LA JOLLA PLAYHOUSE
PO Box 12039, La Jolla, CA 92039
(619) 534-6760; (619) 534-3960
FAX: (619) 534-7870
    Founded: 1948
    Arts Area: Professional
    Status: Professional; Non-Profit
    Type: Touring; Resident; Educational; Produce
    Purpose: To produce bold and innovative theater of adventurous intent; to provide a summer home for the leading theater artists in America
    Management: Des McAnuff, Artistic Director; Terrance Dwyer, Managing Director; Robert Blacker, Associate Artistic Director; Sidney Baker, Director of Development; Patricia Nicholson, Marketing Director; Constance Harvey, Press Representative; Lisa Peterson, Associate Director
    Officers: Willard VanderLann, Board President
    Paid Staff: 18
    Paid Artists: 75
    Utilizes: Special Technical Talent; Guest Artists; Guest Directors
    Budget: $1,000,000 - $5,000,000
    Income Sources: Private Foundations/Grants/Endowments; Business/Corporate Donations; Box Office; Government Grants; Individual Donations
    Season: May - November   **Annual Attendance:** 120,000
    Affiliations: AEA; LORT; TCG
    Performance Facilities: La Jolla Playhouse; Mandell Weiss Performing Arts Center

PERFORMING SERIES

UNIVERSITY OF CALIFORNIA-SAN DIEGO - UNIVERSITY EVENTS OFFICE
9500 Gilman Drive, La Jolla, CA 92093-0078
(619) 534-4090
FAX: (619) 534-1505
    Founded: 1965
    Arts Area: Dance; Instrumental Music; Theater
    Status: Professional; Non-Profit
    Type: Educational; Sponsoring
    Purpose: To provide events and entertainment for the University and community

Management: Lynne Peterson, Director
Paid Staff: 8   **Volunteer Staff:** 60
Paid Artists: 60
Budget: $100,000 - $500,000
Income Sources: Box Office; Government Grants; Individual Donations
Season: October - June
Annual Attendance: 30,000
Affiliations: WAAA; APAP; California Confederation of the Arts; California Presenters
Performance Facilities: Mandeville Auditorium, University of California at San Diego

FACILITY

MANDELL WEISS PERFORMING ARTS CENTER
2910 La Jolla Village Drive, La Jolla, CA 92037
(619) 534-3791
FAX: (619) 534-1080
Type of Facility: Theatre Complex; Theatre House
Type of Stage: Thrust; Flexible; Proscenium; Three Stages
Stage Dimensions: 80'Wx40'D; 40'Wx24'H proscenium opening   **Orchestra Pit**
Seating Capacity: Forum - 400; Theatre - 500; Forum Studio - 120
Year Built: 1982   **Architect:** Forum-Antoine Predock
Acoustical Consultant: Bolt, Beranek & Newman
Contact for Rental: Mark Loigman
Resident Groups: La Jolla Playhouse (May-September); University of California at San Diego Theatre Department (October-April)
The Mandel Weiss Performing Arts Center contains the Mandell Weiss Forum, the Mandell Weiss Theatre and the Mandell Weiss Forum Studio. For information concerning the Mandell Weiss Performing Arts Center, contact La Jolla Playhouse at (619) 534-6760 or University of California, San Diego at (619) 534-2062.

SHERWOOD AUDITORIUM
Museum of Contemporary Art- San Diego, 700 Prospect Street, La Jolla, CA 92037
(619) 454-3541
Type of Facility: Auditorium
Type of Stage: Proscenium
Stage Dimensions: 40'Wx26'D
Seating Capacity: 500
Year Built: 1959   **Architect:** Mosher & Drew
Contact for Rental: Gwen Fowler;   (619) 454-3541

UNIVERSITY OF CALIFORNIA-SAN DIEGO - MANDEVILLE AUDITORIUM
Mandeville Center for the Performing Arts, La Jolla, CA 92093
(619) 534-2380
Type of Facility: Concert Hall; Auditorium; Theatre House
Type of Stage: Proscenium
Stage Dimensions: 100'Wx40'D   **Orchestra Pit**
Seating Capacity: 788
Year Built: 1975   **Architect:** Quincy Jones
Acoustical Consultant: Dr. Gerald Strang
Contact for Rental: Shirley Pyykko;   (619) 534-2380
The Mandeville Auditorium also includes the 150-seat Recital Hall. Rental is limited to university departments and non-profit organizations.

La Mesa

PERFORMING SERIES

GROSSMONT COMMUNITY CONCERTS
4900 Rosehedge Drive, Unit 213, La Mesa, CA 91941
(619) 465-7545
Founded: 1947
Arts Area: Dance; Vocal Music; Instrumental Music; Lyric Opera
Status: Professional; Non-Profit
Type: Performing
Purpose: To provide excellent concerts for our area at minimal cost
Management: Columbia Artists
Officers: Barbara Oppenheimer, President; Betty Coleman, First Vice President
Paid Staff: 1
Utilizes: Guest Artists

Budget: $1,000 - $50,000
Income Sources: Individual Donations
Season: October - May
Affiliations: Community Concert Association
Performance Facilities: East County Performing Arts Center

La Mirada

THEATRE

LA MIRADA THEATRE FOR THE PERFORMING ARTS
14900 La Mirada Boulevard, La Mirada, CA 90638
(714) 994-6150
Founded: 1977
Arts Area: Professional; Community
Status: Professional; Non-Profit
Type: Performing; Sponsoring
Purpose: To present theatre, music and dance in southern California
Management: Thomas C. Mitze, Executive Director
Paid Staff: 20 **Volunteer Staff:** 100
Paid Artists: 100 **Non-Paid Artists:** 500
Utilizes: Special Technical Talent; Guest Conductors; Guest Artists; Guest Directors
Budget: $1,000,000 - $5,000,000
Income Sources: Box Office; Government Grants
Season: 52 Weeks **Annual Attendance:** 250,000
Performance Facilities: La Mirada Theatre For the Performing Arts

FACILITY

LA MIRADA THEATRE FOR THE PERFORMING ARTS
14900 La Mirada Boulevard, La Mirada, CA 90638
(714) 994-6150
Type of Facility: Theatre House
Facility Originally: Movie House
Type of Stage: Proscenium
Stage Dimensions: 80'Wx40'D **Orchestra Pit**
Seating Capacity: 1,310
Year Built: 1977 **Architect:** Anthony & Langford **Cost:** $3,500,000
Acoustical Consultant: Howard Smith
Contact for Rental: Thomas Mitze; (714) 994-6150
Resident Groups: Broadway Season; La Mirada Playhouse; La Mirada Symphony; Whittier-La Mirada Musical Theatre; Golden State Children's Theatre

Laguna Beach

DANCE

BALLET PACIFICA
PO Box 626, Laguna Beach, CA 92652
(714) 642-9275
FAX: (714) 642-9277
Founded: 1962
Arts Area: Ballet
Status: Professional; Non-Profit
Type: Performing; Touring; Resident
Purpose: To provide entertainment for all ages
Management: Molly Lynch, Artistic Director
Officers: Barbara Stuart, Chairman
Paid Artists: 10 **Non-Paid Artists:** 16
Utilizes: Guest Artists
Budget: $100,000 - $500,000
Income Sources: Private Foundations/Grants/Endowments; Business/Corporate Donations; Box Office; Government Grants; Individual Donations
Season: 52 Weeks
Affiliations: Forum Theatre
Performance Facilities: Laguna Moulton Playhouse; The Forum; Irvine Barclay Theatre

INSTRUMENTAL MUSIC

LAGUNA CHAMBER MUSIC SOCIETY
PO Box 385, Laguna Beach, CA 92652
Founded: 1959
Arts Area: Chamber
Status: Non-Profit
Type: Sponsoring
Purpose: To encourage an interest in classical music by presenting and promoting high-quality chamber music in the community
Management: Glenda Vander Zaag, Executive Director
Officers: Ray Hendrickson, President; Brenda Agren, Vice President; Jacqueline Hanson, Secretary; Curt Blankenbiller, Treasurer
Utilizes: Guest Artists
Budget: $50,000 - $100,000
Income Sources: Private Foundations/Grants/Endowments; Business/Corporate Donations; Box Office; Government Grants; Individual Donations
Season: September - May   **Annual Attendance:** 4,500
Affiliations: Orange County Philharmonic Society
Performance Facilities: Irvine Barclay Theatre

THEATRE

LAGUNA PLAYHOUSE
606 Laguna Canyon Road, Laguna Beach, CA 92651
(714) 494-8022
Founded: 1920
Arts Area: Community; Children's Theatre
Status: Non-Professional; Non-Profit
Type: Performing; Educational
Purpose: Dedicated to excellence in the production of professional-quality theatre
Management: Richard Stein, Executive Director; Andrew Barnicle, Artistic Director
Officers: Joan McGillis, President; Don Crevier, Terry Neptune, Vice Presidents; James Gardiner, Secretary; Carl E. Schwab, Treasurer; Michael C. Miller, Parliamentarian
Paid Staff: 12   **Volunteer Staff:** 50
Paid Artists: 30   **Non-Paid Artists:** 150
Utilizes: Guest Artists
Budget: $1,000,000 - $5,000,000
Income Sources: Private Foundations/Grants/Endowments; Business/Corporate Donations; Box Office; Government Grants; Individual Donations
Season: September - June   **Annual Attendance:** 65,000
Affiliations: Inter-theatre Institute; AATE
Performance Facilities: Moulton Theater

FACILITY

LAGUNA PLAYHOUSE
606 Laguna Canyon Road, Laguna Beach, CA 92651
(714) 494-8022
Type of Facility: Theatre House
Type of Stage: Thrust; Proscenium
Seating Capacity: 418
Year Built: 1969   **Architect:** William Pereira and Associates   **Cost:** $500,000
Year Remodeled: 1985   **Architect:** Thola Productions   **Cost:** $450,000
Contact for Rental: Richard Stein;   (714) 494-8022
Resident Groups: Laguna Playhouse

Long Beach

DANCE

LOS ANGELES CLASSICAL BALLET
1122 Wardlow Road, Long Beach, CA 90807
(310) 424-8498
FAX: (310) 426-2622
Arts Area: Ballet
Status: Professional; Non-Profit
Type: Performing; Touring; Resident

Management: David Wilcox, Artistic Director/Chief Executive Officer
Utilizes: Guest Artists; Guest Choreographers
Income Sources: Private Foundations/Grants/Endowments; Business/Corporate Donations; Box Office; Government Grants; Individual Donations
Season: 52 Weeks
Performance Facilities: Terrace Theater; Long Beach Convention Center

INSTRUMENTAL MUSIC

LONG BEACH SYMPHONY ORCHESTRA
555 East Ocean Boulevard, Suite 106, Long Beach, CA 90892
(310) 436-3203
FAX: (310) 491-3599
Founded: 1935
Arts Area: Symphony; Orchestra
Status: Non-Profit
Type: Performing
Purpose: To present symphonic music
Management: Mary E. Newkirk, Executive Director
Paid Staff: 6   **Volunteer Staff:** 2
Paid Artists: 86
Budget: $1,000,000 - $5,000,000
Income Sources: Private Foundations/Grants/Endowments; Business/Corporate Donations; Box Office; Government Grants; Individual Donations
Annual Attendance: 40,000
Performance Facilities: Terrace Theater

VOCAL MUSIC

LONG BEACH CIVIC LIGHT OPERA
PO Box 20280, Long Beach, CA 90801
(310) 435-7605
Founded: 1950
Arts Area: Light Opera; Operetta
Status: Professional; Non-Profit
Type: Performing
Purpose: To maintain artistic excellence in the presentation and performance of professional musical theatre; to train pre-professionals and youth in musical theatre
Management: Pegge Logefeil, Managing Director; Martin Wiviott, Producer
Officers: James C. Barggren, President, Board of Directors
Paid Staff: 9
Utilizes: Special Technical Talent; Guest Conductors; Guest Artists; Guest Directors
Income Sources: Private Foundations/Grants/Endowments; Business/Corporate Donations; Box Office; Government Grants; Individual Donations
Season: October - August   **Annual Attendance:** 150,000
Performance Facilities: Terrace Theater

LONG BEACH OPERA
6372 Pacific Coast Hwy., Long Beach, CA 90803
(310) 596-5556
FAX: (310) 596-8380
Founded: 1978
Arts Area: Grand Opera; Lyric Opera
Status: Professional; Non-Profit
Type: Performing; Educational
Purpose: To present professional opera productions to southern California audiences; to instill in children a love for opera and the performing arts
Management: Michael Milenski, General Director
Officers: Joseph Sheridan, President, Board of Directors
Volunteer Staff: 10
Paid Artists: 250   **Non-Paid Artists:** 25
Utilizes: Special Technical Talent; Guest Conductors; Guest Artists; Guest Directors
Budget: $500,000 - $1,000,000
Income Sources: Private Foundations/Grants/Endowments; Business/Corporate Donations; Box Office; Government Grants; Individual Donations
Season: October - May   **Annual Attendance:** 25,000
Performance Facilities: Center Theater; Terrace Theater

THEATRE

THE FOUND THEATRE
251 East Seventh Street, Long Beach, CA 90813
(310) 433-3363
Founded: 1974
Arts Area: Theatrical Group
Status: Professional; Non-Profit
Type: Performing
Purpose: To provide professional-quality alternative theatre to the community as inexpensively as possible; to provide a place for actors, directors, and technicians to experiment, refine their craft, and grow as artists
Management: Cynthia Galles, Artistic Managing Director; Virginia DeMoss, Literary Director; Alice Secrist, Music Director
Paid Staff: 1
Budget: $1,000 - $50,000
Income Sources: Private Foundations/Grants/Endowments; Business/Corporate Donations; Box Office; Government Grants; Individual Donations
Season: 52 Weeks   **Annual Attendance:** 2,000
Performance Facilities: The Found Theatre

LONG BEACH JEWISH COMMUNITY CENTER YOUTH SUMMER STOCK
3801 East Willow Street, Long Beach, CA 90815
(310) 426-7601
FAX: (310) 424-3915
Founded: 1949
Arts Area: Summer Stock; Community; Theatrical Group
Status: Non-Profit
Type: Performing
Management: Lynne Rosenstein, Assistant Executive Director
Paid Staff: 3
Non-Paid Artists: 80
Utilizes: Guest Directors; Guest Choreographers
Budget: $1,000 - $50,000
Income Sources: Private Foundations/Grants/Endowments; Box Office
Annual Attendance: 2,000
Affiliations: United Way; Jewish Welfare Board
Performance Facilities: Jewish Community Center

FACILITY

JORDAN THEATRE
6500 Atlantic Avenue, Long Beach, CA 90805
(310) 423-1471, ext. 2150
Type of Facility: Auditorium; Loft
Facility Originally: School
Type of Stage: Proscenium
Stage Dimensions: 125'Wx49'D; 49'Wx26'H proscenium opening   **Orchestra Pit**
Seating Capacity: 1,700
Year Built: 1952   **Cost:** $750,000
Year Remodeled: 1971   **Cost:** $500,000
Acoustical Consultant: David Barclift, Unlimited Production Services
Contact for Rental: Dave Barclift;   (213) 423-1471, ext. x2150

LONG BEACH COMMUNITY PLAYHOUSE - STAGE
5021 East Anaheim Street, Long Beach, CA 90804
(310) 494-1014
Type of Facility: Theatre House
Type of Stage: 3/4 Arena
Stage Dimensions: 40'Wx16'D thrust with 8'D behind proscenium
Seating Capacity: 200
Year Built: 1951
Year Remodeled: 1965
Manager: Elaine Herman, Managing Director

LONG BEACH CONVENTION AND ENTERTAINMENT CENTER
300 East Ocean Boulevard, Long Beach, CA 90802
(310) 436-3636
FAX: (310) 436-9491
  Type of Facility: Theatre Complex
  Type of Stage: Thrust; Proscenium; Arena
  Stage Dimensions: 65'x88'
  Orchestra Pit
  Seating Capacity: Arena - 14,500; Terrace Theater - 3,141; Center Theater - 362
  Year Built: 1962   **Architect:** Kenneth Wing   **Cost:** $8,500,000
  Acoustical Consultant: Jonathan Deans
  Contact for Rental: Tracy Begerow, Booking Manager;   (310) 436-3636
  Resident Groups: Long Beach Symphony; Long Beach Opera; Long Beach Ballet; Long Beach Civic Light Opera

LONG BEACH PLAYHOUSE - MAINSTAGE THEATRE
5021 East Anaheim Street, Long Beach, CA 90804
(213) 494-1014
  Founded: 1929
  Type of Facility: Theatre Complex; Theatre House; Exhibition Gallery
  Type of Stage: Proscenium; 3/4 Arena; Combination
  Stage Dimensions: 19'Wx8'D proscenium opening; 16'x40' thrust (3/4 arena)
  Seating Capacity: 200
  Year Built: 1951   **Architect:** Hugh Gibbs   **Cost:** $125,000
  Year Remodeled: 1965   **Architect:** Francis Huesel   **Cost:** $200,000
  Manager: Elaine Herman, Managing Director;   (213) 494-1014
  1992 marks the 64th year of continuous operation for Long Beach Community Playhouse. The Playhouse contains the Stage and Studio Theatre. See individual listings for additional information.

LONG BEACH PLAYHOUSE - STUDIO THEATRE
5021 East Anaheim Street, Long Beach, CA 90804
(213) 494-1014
  Founded: 1929
  Type of Facility: Theatre Complex; Theatre House
  Type of Stage: Modified Apron Proscenium
  Stage Dimensions: 20'Wx20'D with 30'Wx8'D apron
  Seating Capacity: 99
  Year Built: 1951
  Year Remodeled: 1967
  Manager: Elaine Herman, Managing Director;   (310) 494-1014

WOODROW WILSON HIGH SCHOOL
4400 East Tenth Street, Long Beach, CA 90804
(310) 433-0481
  Type of Facility: Concert Hall; Auditorium
  Facility Originally: School
  Type of Stage: Proscenium
  Stage Dimensions: 22'x44'x36'   **Orchestra Pit**
  Seating Capacity: 1,652
  Year Built: 1926   **Architect:** W. Horace Austin
  Year Remodeled: 1937   **Architect:** W. Horace Austin
  Acoustical Consultant: Glen Clancy/Continental Sound & Acoustics
  Contact for Rental: Ronald W. Mahan;   (310) 433-0481
  Resident Groups: Rainbow Playhouse Players

Los Altos Hills

FACILITY

ROBERT C. SMITHWICK THEATRE
12345 El Monte Road, Los Altos Hills, CA 94022-2921
(415) 949-7252
FAX: (415) 949-7375
  Founded: 1961
  Type of Facility: Auditorium
  Facility Originally: College Theatre
  Type of Stage: Proscenium
  Stage Dimensions: 39'6"Wx15'5"H proscenium opening   **Orchestra Pit**

Seating Capacity: 952
Year Built: 1961   **Architect:** Ernest J. Krump and Maston & Hurd Associated Architects
Contact for Rental: Duncan Graham;   (415) 949-7252
Resident Groups: College Performance Arts Groups

Los Angeles

DANCE

AMAN INTERNATIONAL MUSIC AND DANCE COMPANY
PO Box 5820, Los Angeles, CA 90055-0820
(213) 629-8387
FAX: (213) 629-8396
Founded: 1964
Arts Area: Ethnic; Folk
Status: Professional; Non-Profit
Type: Performing; Touring; Educational
Purpose: To preserve and present America's multicultural heritage as it is found in music, song and dance
Management: Timothy Ney, Managing Director; Barry Glass, Artistic Director
Officers: Hon. William Huss, Chairman
Paid Staff: 5   **Volunteer Staff:** 3
Paid Artists: 36
Utilizes: Special Technical Talent; Guest Directors
Budget: $100,000 - $500,000
Income Sources: Private Foundations/Grants/Endowments; Business/Corporate Donations; Box Office; Government Grants; Individual Donations
Season: September - June   **Annual Attendance:** 100,000
Affiliations: Dance California; Dance USA

BETHUNE THEATREDANSE
8033 Sunset Boulevard, Suite 221, Los Angeles, CA 90046
(213) 874-0481
FAX: (213) 851-2078
Founded: 1980
Arts Area: Modern; Ballet
Status: Professional; Non-Profit
Type: Performing; Touring; Resident; Educational
Purpose: To combine multimedia and dramatic dance to create contemporary theatre art; to utilize stories drawn from screen plays, the literary world and television scripts, involving a broad range of multimedia art forms
Management: Libi Warren, Administrative Director; Zina Bethune, Artistic Director; Rachel Cohen, Booking Contact; Paula Graber, Producer
Officers: Richard Sigler, President; Zita Rahbar, Vice President; Ida Meyers, Secretary; Henry Schiffer, Treasurer
Paid Staff: 3   **Volunteer Staff:** 10
Paid Artists: 20   **Non-Paid Artists:** 8
Utilizes: Special Technical Talent; Guest Artists; Guest Choreographers
Budget: $100,000 - $500,000
Income Sources: Private Foundations/Grants/Endowments; Business/Corporate Donations; Box Office; Government Grants; Individual Donations
Season: September - July   **Annual Attendance:** 10,000
Affiliations: Dance Resource Center; Chamber of Commerce

JAZZ TAP ENSEMBLE
1416 Westwood Boulevard, Suite 206, Los Angeles, CA 90024
(310) 475-4412
Season: 52 Weeks

LACE/LOS ANGELES CONTEMPORARY EXHIBITIONS
1804 Industrial Street, Los Angeles, CA 90021
(213) 624-5650
FAX: (213) 624-6679
Founded: 1977
Arts Area: Modern
Status: Professional; Semi-Professional; Non-Profit
Type: Performing
Purpose: To present art and ideas; to serve as a forum for artists and audiences
Management: Gwen Darien, Executive Director; Tom Dennison, Performance Coordinator
Officers: Coleen Sterritt, Chair; Karen Carson, Vice Chair; Richard Duardo, Secretary; Catherine B. Chester, Treasurer
Paid Staff: 7

Budget: $500,000 - $1,000,000
Income Sources: Private Foundations/Grants/Endowments; Box Office; Government Grants; Individual Donations
Season: April - June

LEWITZKY DANCE COMPANY
700 South Flower Street, Suite 2000, Los Angeles, CA 90017-4207
(213) 627-5555
FAX: (213) 627-9249
Founded: 1966
Arts Area: Modern
Status: Professional; Non-Profit
Type: Performing; Touring; Educational
Purpose: To maintain Lewitzky repertoire, choreograph new works and develop existing and new audiences for dance
Management: Darlene Neel, Company Manager; Bella Lewitzky, Artistic Director; Ruth L. Eliel, Managing Director; Edson Womble, Production Manager
Officers: Douglas L. Dodds, Chairperson of the Board
Paid Staff: 7
Paid Artists: 14
Utilizes: Guest Artists
Budget: $500,000 - $1,000,000
Income Sources: Private Foundations/Grants/Endowments; Business/Corporate Donations; Government Grants; Individual Donations
Season: Mid-August - Mid-July   **Annual Attendance:** 35,000

LOLA MONTES AND HER SPANISH DANCERS
1529 North Commonwealth Avenue, Los Angeles, CA 90027
(213) 664-3288
Founded: 1955
Arts Area: Ethnic
Status: Professional
Type: Performing; Touring; Educational
Purpose: To keep alive Hispanic heritage; to maintain a professional company of high standards; to develop young artists
Management: Lola Montes Foundation for Dances of Spain and the Americas
Officers: Lola Montes, President; Patricia Tashma, Vice President; Caroline Hicks, Secretary/Treasurer
Volunteer Staff: 5
Paid Artists: 10
Utilizes: Special Technical Talent; Guest Artists
Budget: $1,000 - $50,000
Income Sources: Private Foundations/Grants/Endowments; Government Grants; Individual Donations
Season: 52 Weeks   **Annual Attendance:** 50,000
Affiliations: WAAA; California Confederation of the Arts

LORETTA LIVINGSTON AND DANCERS
870 North Occidental Boulevard, #2, Los Angeles, CA 90026
(213) 484-9888
FAX: (213) 484-9888
Founded: 1984
Arts Area: Modern
Status: Professional; Non-Profit
Type: Performing; Touring; Educational
Purpose: To produce Loretta Livingston's choreography and maintain a touring dance company; to provide outreach and educational programs
Management: David Plettner, Managing Director; Loretta Livingston, Artistic Director; Madeline Sogun, Marketing Associate
Paid Staff: 3
Paid Artists: 6
Budget: $100,000 - $500,000
Income Sources: Private Foundations/Grants/Endowments; Business/Corporate Donations; Box Office; Government Grants; Individual Donations
Season: 52 Weeks   **Annual Attendance:** 10,000
Affiliations: Dance/USA
Performance Facilities: Japan America Theatre; UCLA Center for Performing Arts

LOS ANGELES CHAMBER BALLET
503 1/2 North Norton Avenue, Los Angeles, CA 90040
(310) 453-4952
Arts Area: Ballet
Status: Professional; Non-Profit

Type: Performing; Touring; Resident
Management: Victoria Koenig, Raiford Rogers, Artistic Directors
Income Sources: Private Foundations/Grants/Endowments; Business/Corporate Donations; Box Office; Government Grants; Individual Donations

LOS ANGELES CHOREOGRAPHERS AND DANCERS
1807 North Rodney Drive, Los Angeles, CA 90027
(213) 665-5628
Founded: 1979
Arts Area: Modern; Tap
Status: Professional; Non-Profit
Type: Performing; Touring
Purpose: To create performance opportunities for Los Angeles and expand and educate a dance audience; to present the work of Louise Reichlin and Alfred Desio
Management: Louise Reichlin, Artistic/Managing Director
Paid Staff: 10   **Volunteer Staff:** 25
Paid Artists: 15
Utilizes: Special Technical Talent
Budget: $50,000 - $100,000
Income Sources: Private Foundations/Grants/Endowments; Business/Corporate Donations; Box Office; Government Grants; Individual Donations
Season: 52 Weeks   **Annual Attendance:** 27,000
Affiliations: Dance Resource Center; WAAA
Performance Facilities: Bing Theatre at USC; Japan America Theatre

LULA WASHINGTON CONTEMPORARY DANCE FOUNDATION
5179 1/2 West Adams Boulevard, Los Angeles, CA 90016
(213) 936-6591
FAX: (310) 671-4572
Founded: 1980
Arts Area: Modern; Jazz; Ethnic
Status: Professional; Non-Profit
Type: Performing; Touring; Educational; Sponsoring
Purpose: To explore the Black experience through high-quality dance
Management: Lula Washington, Artistic Director; Erwin Washington, Executive Director
Officers: Nina Shaw, Board President; Robert Johnson, Vice President
Paid Staff: 6   **Volunteer Staff:** 1
Paid Artists: 10
Utilizes: Guest Choreographers
Budget: $100,000 - $500,000
Income Sources: Private Foundations/Grants/Endowments; Business/Corporate Donations; Box Office; Government Grants; Individual Donations
Season: 52 Weeks   **Annual Attendance:** 5,000
Affiliations: Black Dance Companies Association

RHAPSODY IN TAPS
1558 North Hoover Street, Los Angeles, CA 90027
(213) 661-2172; (714) 838-3318
FAX: (714) 838-4660
Founded: 1981
Arts Area: Rhythm Tap with Live Jazz
Status: Non-Profit
Type: Performing; Touring
Purpose: To promote and perform the act of rhythm tap dance while exploring new choreographic directions
Management: Kay L. Davis, Administrative Director; Marci Jurls, Administrative Assistant; Anne W. Smith, Development Consultant
Officers: Linda Sohl-Donnell, Persident; Marilyn Gatto, Secretary; O.T. Gatto, Treasurer
Paid Staff: 3   **Volunteer Staff:** 16
Paid Artists: 10
Utilizes: Special Technical Talent; Guest Artists; Guest Choreographers
Budget: $50,000 - $100,000
Income Sources: Private Foundations/Grants/Endowments; Business/Corporate Donations; Box Office; Government Grants; Individual Donations

RUDY PEREZ PERFORMANCE ENSEMBLE
PO Box 36614, Los Angeles, CA 90036
(213) 931-3604
Founded: 1970

Arts Area: Modern
Status: Professional; Non-Profit
Type: Performing; Touring
Purpose: To present and produce experimental dance works
Management: Rudy Perez, Artistic Director/Choreographer
Paid Artists: 5
Utilizes: Special Technical Talent
Budget: $50,000 - $100,000
Income Sources: Private Foundations/Grants/Endowments; Business/Corporate Donations; Box Office; Government Grants; Individual Donations
Season: 52 Weeks

RUTH ST. DENIS FOUNDATION
618 South Sycamore, Los Angeles, CA 90036
(213) 934-8643
Founded: 1948
Arts Area: Modern; Ethnic
Status: Professional; Non-Profit
Type: Performing; Touring; Resident; Educational
Purpose: To teach, perform, and continue the works of Ruth St. Denis and Michio Ito
Management: Karoun Tootikian, Artistic Director; Ronny Cothron, Secretary
Officers: Karoun Tootikian, President; Lonny Cothron, Secretary; Lalla Lezli, Treasurer; Wendy Uyeda, Program Coordinator
Volunteer Staff: 4
Paid Artists: 8
Budget: $1,000 - $50,000
Income Sources: Box Office; Individual Donations
Season: 52 Weeks

TNR-MOEBIUS
4091 West Eighth Street, Los Angeles, CA 90005
(213) 389-4088
FAX: (213) 388-3618
Founded: 1972
Arts Area: Modern
Status: Professional; Non-Profit
Type: Performing; Touring; Resident
Purpose: To create works of ceremony and rituals
Management: Yen Lu Wong, Artistic Director
Paid Staff: 2
Paid Artists: 30 **Non-Paid Artists:** 200
Utilizes: Guest Artists
Budget: $50,000 - $100,000
Income Sources: Private Foundations/Grants/Endowments; Business/Corporate Donations; Box Office; Government Grants; Individual Donations
Season: 52 Weeks

VALENTINA OUMANSKY DRAMATIC DANCE FOUNDATION
3433 Cahuenga Boulevard West, Los Angeles, CA 90068
(213) 850-9497
Founded: 1973
Arts Area: Ballet
Status: Non-Profit
Type: Performing; Touring; Resident; Educational
Management: Valentina Oumansky, Artistic Director
Officers: Robert Y. Takagi, President; Betsy Ross Lueke, Vice President; Marilyn Carter, Treasurer/Secretary
Utilizes: Guest Artists
Budget: $1,000 - $50,000
Income Sources: Private Foundations/Grants/Endowments; Business/Corporate Donations; Individual Donations
Season: 52 Weeks
Performance Facilities: Studio Theatre

ZAPPED TAPS/ALFRED DESIO
1807 North Rodney Drive, Los Angeles, CA 90027
(213) 665-5628
Founded: 1979
Arts Area: Tap
Status: Professional; Non-Profit

Type: Performing; Touring
Purpose: To create and perform new solo tap works, both traditional and using Alfred Desio's invention "Tap-Tronics"
Management: Louise Reichlin, Managing Director
Paid Staff: 1   **Volunteer Staff:** 25
Paid Artists: 7
Utilizes: Special Technical Talent
Budget: $1,000 - $50,000
Income Sources: Private Foundations/Grants/Endowments; Business/Corporate Donations; Box Office; Government Grants; Individual Donations
Season: 52 Weeks
Annual Attendance: 27,000
Affiliations: Dance Resource Center

INSTRUMENTAL MUSIC

CALIFORNIA E.A.R. UNIT FOUNDATION
PO Box 86374, Los Angeles, CA 90086-0734
(213) 488-9788
FAX: (213) 488-9788
Arts Area: Chamber; Electronic & Live Electronic
Status: Professional; Non-Profit
Type: Performing; Touring; Resident; Educational
Purpose: To promote and perform the music of our time
Management: Amy Knoles, Booking Manager; Dorothy Stone, Director
Budget: $50,000 - $100,000
Income Sources: Private Foundations/Grants/Endowments; Business/Corporate Donations; Box Office; Government Grants; Individual Donations
Performance Facilities: Los Angeles County Museum of Art

THE INTERNATIONAL ASSOCIATION OF JAZZ APPRECIATION
PO Box 48146, Los Angeles, CA 90048
(310) 673-7541
FAX: (310) 673-0757
Founded: 1982
Arts Area: Orchestra; Ensemble; Band
Status: Non-Profit
Type: Performing; Educational
Purpose: To preserve jazz music through education and presentation
Officers: Wm. J. Coffey MD, Founder/President
Paid Staff: 2   **Volunteer Staff:** 7
Paid Artists: 100
Utilizes: Guest Artists
Budget: $100,000 - $500,000
Income Sources: Private Foundations/Grants/Endowments; Business/Corporate Donations; Box Office; Government Grants; Individual Donations
Season: 52 Weeks

"KOROYAR" FOLKLORE ENSEMBLE
PO Box 27873, Los Feliz Station, Los Angeles, CA 90027
(909) 627-7150
Founded: 1969
Arts Area: Ethnic; Folk; Instrumental Group
Status: Non-Profit
Type: Performing; Educational
Purpose: To present the music and dance of southeast Europe and the Near East in an entertaining, authentic and educational manner; to reveal and explore other aesthetics
Management: Richard Unciano, Executive Director; Loren Lichty, Administrative Director; Ron Muller, Music Director; Jim Dimitroff, Associate Director
Officers: Richard Unciano, President; Ron Muller, Vice President; Karen Bassett, Secretary
Volunteer Staff: 5
Non-Paid Artists: 14
Utilizes: Guest Artists
Budget: $1,000 - $50,000
Income Sources: Box Office
Season: 52 Weeks
Annual Attendance: 6,000
Affiliations: Folk Dance Federation of California

LOS ANGELES CHAMBER ORCHESTRA
315 West Ninth Street, Suite 801, Los Angeles, CA 90015
(213) 622-7001
FAX: (213) 955-2071
Founded: 1968
Arts Area: Orchestra; Chamber
Status: Professional; Non-Profit
Type: Performing; Touring; Resident
Purpose: To perform literature of the chamber orchestra repertoire; to foster an appreciation of chamber music within the community
Management: Deborah Rutter, Executive Director; Welz Kauffman, General Manager; Robert McMullin, Development Director; George Sebastian, Marketing Director; Gloria Sanchez, Finance Director
Officers: Jennifer Diener, President; David Gersh, Chairman; Douglas Brengal, Ed Zolla, Robert Davidson, Vice Presidents
Paid Staff: 11
Paid Artists: 40
Utilizes: Guest Conductors; Guest Artists; Guest Directors
Budget: $1,000,000 - $5,000,000
Income Sources: Private Foundations/Grants/Endowments; Business/Corporate Donations; Box Office; Government Grants; Individual Donations; Fundraising
Season: October - May
Annual Attendance: 55,000
Affiliations: ASOL; Association of California Symphony Orchestras; AAA; California Arts Alliance
Performance Facilities: Ambassador Auditorium; Royce Hall, UCLA; Japan America Theatre

LOS ANGELES PHILHARMONIC ASSOCIATION
135 North Grand Avenue, Los Angeles, CA 90012
(213) 972-7300
FAX: (213) 617-3065
Founded: 1919
Arts Area: Symphony; Orchestra; Chamber; Ensemble
Status: Professional; Non-Profit
Type: Performing; Touring; Educational; Sponsoring
Purpose: To present symphonic music concerts and other music events; to promote an appreciation of symphonic music in our community
Management: Ernest Fleischmann, Executive Vice President; Bennett McClellan, General Manager; Gene Pasquarelli, Finance Director
Officers: Stanley Beyer, Chairman of the Board; C. Joseph LaBonte, President; Dennis Kent, Treasurer
Utilizes: Special Technical Talent; Guest Conductors; Guest Artists
Budget: Over 10,000,000
Income Sources: Private Foundations/Grants/Endowments; Business/Corporate Donations; Box Office; Government Grants; Individual Donations
Season: 52 Weeks
Annual Attendance: 1,000,000
Performance Facilities: Dorothy Chandler Pavilion; Hollywood Bowl

VIKLARBO CHAMBER EMSEMBLE
7969 West Fourth Street, Los Angeles, CA 90048
(213) 653-3330
Founded: 1978
Arts Area: Chamber; Ensemble; Instrumental Group; New Music
Status: Professional; Non-Profit
Type: Performing; Touring; Educational
Purpose: To perform standard and contemporary works using an ensemble of flexible instrumentation including violin, viola, clarinet, cello and piano
Management: Wendy Prober, Managing Director
Officers: Michael Arlen, Kenneth Hertz, Board Members; Maria Newman, President; Wendy Prober, Chairman; Larry Kohorn, Secretary/Treasurer
Paid Staff: 1   **Volunteer Staff:** 4
Paid Artists: 4
Utilizes: Guest Artists
Budget: $1,000 - $50,000
Income Sources: Private Foundations/Grants/Endowments; Box Office; Government Grants; Individual Donations
Season: 52 Weeks
Annual Attendance: 1,200
Affiliations: CMA; AMC
Performance Facilities: Murphy Hall, Loyola Marymount University; Hancock Auditorium, University of Southern California

VOCAL MUSIC

GUILD OPERA COMPANY, INC.
6425 Hollywood Boulevard, Los Angeles, CA 90028
(213) 463-6593
Founded: 1949
Arts Area: Grand Opera; Lyric Opera; Light Opera
Status: Professional; Non-Profit
Type: Performing; Touring; Educational
Purpose: To provide professional opera, fully staged with orchestra, for young audiences
Management: Gayle Blankenburg, Managing Director; Heinz Blankenburg, Artistic Director
Officers: Steven Siskin, President; Peter Ulrich, Vice President of Administration; Clarke Morrow, Vice President of Education; Carolyn Novin, Secretary; Tess Macaraya, Treasurer
Paid Staff: 2 **Volunteer Staff:** 8
Paid Artists: 50
Utilizes: Special Technical Talent; Guest Artists
Budget: $100,000 - $500,000
Income Sources: Private Foundations/Grants/Endowments; Business/Corporate Donations; Box Office; Government Grants; Individual Donations
Season: March - May **Annual Attendance:** 16,000
Performance Facilities: Royce Hall, UCLA ; Marsee Auditorium; Glendale High School Auditorium

LOS ANGELES MASTER CHORALE ASSOCIATION
135 North Grand Avenue, Los Angeles, CA 90012
(213) 972-7282
FAX: (213) 972-7312
Arts Area: Choral
Status: Professional
Type: Performing; Resident; Educational
Purpose: To educate the public in the art of choral singing and to foster an appreciation of the art form
Management: Paul Salamunovich, Music Director; Roger Wagner, Founder/Music Director Laureate; Maurice Staples, General Manager; Mark Praigg, Assistant to General Manager
Officers: Marshall A. Rutter, Chairman; Clifford A. Miller, Executive Committee Chairman; Edward J. McAniss, President
Paid Staff: 6 **Volunteer Staff:** 1
Paid Artists: 75 **Non-Paid Artists:** 37
Utilizes: Guest Conductors; Guest Artists
Budget: $1,000,000 - $5,000,000
Income Sources: Private Foundations/Grants/Endowments; Business/Corporate Donations; Box Office; Government Grants; Individual Donations
Season: November - April
Annual Attendance: 52,900
Affiliations: CA
Performance Facilities: Dorothy Chandler Pavilion

LOS ANGELES MUSIC CENTER OPERA
135 North Grand Avenue, Los Angeles, CA 90012
(213) 972-7219
FAX: (213) 687-3490
Founded: 1986
Arts Area: Grand Opera
Status: Professional; Non-Profit
Type: Performing; Resident; Educational
Purpose: To present opera at its highest professional standard with international guest artists and a resident company
Management: Peter Hemmings, General Director; Placido Domingo, Artistic Consultant; Patricia Mitchell, Deputy General Director
Paid Staff: 32
Paid Artists: 300
Utilizes: Guest Conductors; Guest Artists; Guest Directors; Guest Designers
Budget: Over 10,000,000
Income Sources: Private Foundations/Grants/Endowments; Business/Corporate Donations; Box Office; Government Grants; Individual Donations
Season: September - June **Annual Attendance:** 120,000
Affiliations: OA
Performance Facilities: Dorothy Chandler Pavilion

UNIVERSITY OF SOUTHERN CALIFORNIA OPERA
Ramo Hall, #208B, University Park, Los Angeles, CA 90089-0851
(213) 740-3109
FAX: (213) 740-3217
Founded: 1940
Arts Area: Grand Opera; Lyric Opera; Light Opera; Operetta
Status: Semi-Professional; Non-Profit
Type: Performing; Touring; Educational
Purpose: To provide a training ground and performance possibilities for aspiring young singers in all areas of performance; to present two full operas and various single scenes
Management: William Williams, Opera Manager/Professor; William Vendice, Resident Director/Conductor; Frans Boerlage, Stage Director
Paid Staff: 7
Non-Paid Artists: 25
Budget: $1,000 - $50,000
Income Sources: University
Season: September - May   **Annual Attendance:** 3,000
Affiliations: University of Southern California
Performance Facilities: Bing Theater

THEATRE

ACTORS FOR THEMSELVES
Matrix Theatre, 7657 Melrose Avenue, Los Angeles, CA 90048
(213) 852-1445
Founded: 1974
Arts Area: Professional; Theatrical Group
Status: Professional; Non-Profit
Type: Performing; Resident; Educational
Purpose: To give actors a chance to practice their craft and the opportunity to control the full process of theater production
Management: Joe Stern, Artistic Director
Paid Staff: 2
Utilizes: Special Technical Talent; Guest Artists; Guest Directors
Budget: $100,000 - $500,000
Income Sources: Private Foundations/Grants/Endowments; Business/Corporate Donations; Box Office; Government Grants; Individual Donations
Season: 52 Weeks
Performance Facilities: Matrix Theatre

ATTIC THEATRE
6562 1/2 Santa Monica Boulevard, Los Angeles, CA 90038
(213) 462-9720
Founded: 1987
Arts Area: Professional; Theatrical Group
Status: Semi-Professional; Commercial
Type: Performing; Resident; Sponsoring
Purpose: To maintain a small commercial theatre with a resident company; to rent the facility to outside productions
Management: James Carey, Artistic Director; Denise Ragan, Business Manager
Paid Staff: 2   **Volunteer Staff:** 7
Utilizes: Special Technical Talent; Guest Directors
Budget: $1,000 - $50,000
Income Sources: Box Office; Individual Donations
Season: February - December
Affiliations: Theatre Los Angeles

BILINGUAL FOUNDATION OF THE ARTS
421 North Avenue 19, Los Angeles, CA 90031
(213) 225-4044
FAX: (213) 225-1250
Founded: 1973
Arts Area: Professional; Theatrical Group
Status: Professional; Non-Profit
Type: Performing; Touring; Educational
Purpose: To celebrate the diversity and the richness of the Hispanic Theater tradition by producing and directing in both the English and the Spanish language
Management: Carmen Zapata, Producing Director; Margarita Galban, Artistic Director; Estela Scar, Los Angeles Theatre Alliance, Production Director; Jim Payne, Managing Director
Officers: Al Mejia, Chairman; Carmen Zapata, President

Paid Staff: 7   **Volunteer Staff:** 40
Paid Artists: 120
Utilizes: Guest Artists; Guest Directors
Budget: $500,000 - $1,000,000
Income Sources: Private Foundations/Grants/Endowments; Business/Corporate Donations; Government Grants; Individual Donations
Season: 52 Weeks   **Annual Attendance:** 80,000
Affiliations: AAA; TCG; California Confederation of the Arts
Performance Facilities: The Bilingual Foundation of the Arts

BOB BAKER PRODUCTIONS
1345 West First Street, Los Angeles, CA 90026
(213) 250-9995
Founded: 1963
Arts Area: Professional; Puppet
Status: Professional
Type: Resident
Purpose: To produce marionette productions, shop tours and birthday parties
Management: Bob Baker, Director; Tina Gainsboro, Theatre Manager
Paid Staff: 20
Budget: $100,000 - $500,000
Income Sources: Box Office
Season: 52 Weeks
Annual Attendance: 100,000

BURBAGE THEATRE ENSEMBLE
2330 Sawtelle Boulevard, Los Angeles, CA 90064
(310) 478-0897
Founded: 1969
Arts Area: Professional
Status: Professional; Non-Profit
Type: Performing; Touring
Purpose: To stimulate the creative growth of the arts in our community
Management: Ivan Spiegel, Andy Griggs, Co-Artistic Directors; Lucas McClure, Production Manager
Officers: Andy Griggs, President; William Mohr, Secretary; Ivan Spiegel, Treasurer
Paid Staff: 4   **Volunteer Staff:** 8
Paid Artists: 25   **Non-Paid Artists:** 15
Budget: $100,000 - $500,000
Income Sources: Private Foundations/Grants/Endowments; Business/Corporate Donations; Box Office; Government Grants; Individual Donations
Season: 52 Weeks
Annual Attendance: 20,000
Affiliations: TCG
Performance Facilities: Burbage Theatre

CELEBRATION THEATRE
4470-107 Sunset Boulevard, #353, Los Angeles, CA 90027
(213) 957-1884
Founded: 1982
Arts Area: Professional
Status: Professional; Non-Profit
Type: Resident; Educational
Purpose: To produce gay and lesbian plays exclusively; to celebrate the positive aspects of gay and lesbian culture
Management: Paul Borden, Executive Director; Ron Edwards, Artistic Director
Volunteer Staff: 12
Non-Paid Artists: 10
Utilizes: Special Technical Talent; Guest Artists; Guest Directors
Budget: $1,000 - $50,000
Income Sources: Box Office; Individual Donations
Season: 52 Weeks
Annual Attendance: 6,000
Affiliations: Los Angeles Theatre Alliance; Gay and Lesbian Theatre Alliance
Performance Facilities: Celebration Theatre

CO-REAL ARTISTS
1811 West 45th Street, Los Angeles, CA 90062
(310) 827-1353
Founded: 1969
Arts Area: Musical; Drama; Dance

Status: Semi-Professional; Non-Profit
Type: Performing; Touring; Educational
Purpose: To prepare and present undiscovered talent through workshops and quality community theater productions
Management: Genie Jackson, Founder/Executive Director
Officers: Genie Jackson, Chairman; Rena Gist, President; Lynn Blount, Administrative Assistant
Paid Staff: 1   **Volunteer Staff:** 13
Paid Artists: 15   **Non-Paid Artists:** 4
Budget: $1,000 - $50,000
Income Sources: Business/Corporate Donations; Box Office; Government Grants; Individual Donations
Annual Attendance: 25,000
Affiliations: California Confederation of the Arts

COLONY THEATRE COMPANY
1944 Riverside Drive, Los Angeles, CA 90039
(213) 665-3011
Founded: 1975
Arts Area: Theatrical Group
Status: Semi-Professional; Non-Profit
Type: Performing; Resident
Management: Barbara Beckley, Producing Director
Officers: Barbara Beckley, President; Michael Wadler, Vice President; Robert Canning, Secretary; Rosser Cole, Treasurer
Utilizes: Special Technical Talent; Guest Artists; Guest Directors
Budget: $50,000 - $100,000
Income Sources: Business/Corporate Donations; Box Office; Government Grants; Individual Donations
Season: July - June
Annual Attendance: 15,000
Affiliations: Equity-Waiver; TCG; California Theatre Council; Glendale Arts Council; AEA
Performance Facilities: Studio Theatre Play House

THE COMPLEX
6476 Santa Monica Boulevard, Los Angeles, CA 90038
(213) 465-0383
Founded: 1990
Arts Area: Professional; Theatrical Group
Status: Semi-Professional; Non-Professional
Type: Performing
Management: Matt Chait, Owner; John Bergantine, Assistant
Paid Staff: 1
Utilizes: Special Technical Talent
Budget: $1,000 - $50,000
Income Sources: Box Office; Individual Donations
Season: 52 Weeks

DILLON STREET PLAYERS
802 North Dillon Street, Los Angeles, CA 90026
(213) 663-1664
FAX: (213) 663-1664
Arts Area: Professional; Repertory
Status: Professional
Management: Scott Crawford, Artistic Director
Volunteer Staff: 6
Non-Paid Artists: 20
Utilizes: Guest Artists; Guest Directors
Budget: $100,000 - $500,000
Income Sources: Private Foundations/Grants/Endowments; Business/Corporate Donations; Box Office; Individual Donations
Affiliations: AEA

EAST WEST PLAYERS
4424 Santa Monica Boulevard, Los Angeles, CA 90029
(213) 660-0366
Founded: 1965
Arts Area: Professional
Status: Professional; Non-Profit
Type: Performing; Touring; Resident; Educational
Purpose: To foster the creation of an Asian-American aesthetic point of view and theatre; to support the development of artists possessing outstanding talent and of new works which address this mission
Management: Nobu McCarty, Artistic Director; Tom Donaldson, General Producer; Lisa Lee, Administrative Director

Officers: Toshizaku Terasawa, Chairman; Jeff Smith, President; John Kobara, Wenda Fong, Vice Presidents; Janie Gates, Secretary
Paid Staff: 8
Paid Artists: 100
Utilizes: Special Technical Talent; Guest Artists; Guest Directors
Budget: $100,000 - $500,000
Income Sources: Private Foundations/Grants/Endowments; Business/Corporate Donations; Box Office; Government Grants; Individual Donations
Season: October - July   **Annual Attendance:** 40,000
Affiliations: TCG; Los Angeles Theatre Alliance; California Confederation of the Arts
Performance Facilities: East West Players Theater

EBONY SHOWCASE THEATRE
4720 West Washington Boulevard, Los Angeles, CA 90016
(213) 936-1107
Founded: 1950
Arts Area: Theatrical Group
Status: Semi-Professional; Non-Profit
Type: Performing; Resident
Purpose: To educate; to foster artistic and cultural enrichment through entertainment
Management: Nick and Edna Stewart, Founders/Managing Directors
Utilizes: Guest Artists; Guest Directors
Budget: $1,000 - $50,000
Income Sources: Box Office; Individual Donations
Season: 52 Weeks
Performance Facilities: Ebony Showcase Theatre

GENE DYNARSKI THEATER ENSEMBLE
5600 Sunset Boulevard, Los Angeles, CA 90028
(213) 465-5600
Founded: 1977
Arts Area: Theater Group
Status: Professional; Non-Profit
Type: Performing
Purpose: To provide high-quality theater directed in an experimental and educational manner
Management: Gene Dynarski, Artistic/Administrative Director
Season: 52 Weeks
Performance Facilities: Gene Dynarski Theater

THE GROUNDLING THEATRE
7307 Melrose Avenue, Los Angeles, CA 90046
(213) 934-4747
Founded: 1972
Arts Area: Theatrical Group
Status: Non-Profit
Type: Performing; Resident
Purpose: To create new comedy talent and new comedy productions
Management: John Gidcomb, Theatre Manager
Paid Staff: 30
Budget: $100,000 - $500,000
Income Sources: Private Foundations/Grants/Endowments; Business/Corporate Donations; Box Office; Government Grants; Individual Donations
Season: 52 Weeks   **Annual Attendance:** 26,000
Performance Facilities: The Groundling Theatre

LOS ANGELES CIVIC LIGHT OPERA
6233 Hollywood Boulevard, Los Angeles, CA 90028
(213) 972-7550
Founded: 1936
Arts Area: Musical Theatre
Status: Non-Profit
Type: Performing
Purpose: To make available top-quality musical theatre in southern California by presenting revivals and originating new productions
Management: James M. Nederlander, Chairman of the Board; Stan Seiden, President; Neil Papiano, Treasurer
Paid Staff: 40
Utilizes: Special Technical Talent; Guest Conductors; Guest Artists; Guest Directors
Budget: $500,000 - $1,000,000
Income Sources: Box Office

Season: May - September   **Annual Attendance:** 130,000
Performance Facilities: Pantages Theatre

THE LOS ANGELES THEATRE ACADEMY
Los Angeles City College, 855 North Vermont Avenue, Los Angeles, CA 90029
(213) 963-4336
      Founded: 1929
      Arts Area: Theatrical Group
      Status: Non-Profit
      Type: Performing; Educational
      Purpose: To provide a professional training program to students in all areas of theatre arts and to support this training with professional-level productions
      Management: Winston Butler, Department Chairperson; Dena M. Paponis, Theatre Manager
      Officers: Greg Sexton, President; Louise Ksoot-Haukkes, Vice President; William Mohr, Secretary; Ivan Spiegel, Treasurer
      Paid Staff: 19
      Non-Paid Artists: 100
      Utilizes: Special Technical Talent; Guest Artists
      Budget: $100,000 - $500,000
      Income Sources: Box Office
      Season: September - June   **Annual Attendance:** 10,000
      Affiliations: Equity-Waiver; Los Angeles Theatre Alliance; SCETA; American College Theatre Festival

LOS ANGELES THEATRE CENTER
514 South Spring Street, Los Angeles, CA 90013
(213) 627-6500
FAX: (213) 624-6096
      Founded: 1975
      Arts Area: Professional
      Status: Professional; Non-Profit
      Type: Touring; Educational
      Purpose: To faciliate the production of performance pieces of all disciplines that further communication between multiethnic communities
      Management: Lee Sweet, Business Manager; Laural Meade, Rental Contact; David MacMurtry, Technical Director
      Paid Staff: 85   **Volunteer Staff:** 500
      Paid Artists: 65
      Utilizes: Special Technical Talent; Guest Artists
      Budget: $1,000,000 - $5,000,000
      Income Sources: Private Foundations/Grants/Endowments; Business/Corporate Donations; Box Office; Government Grants; Individual Donations
      Season: 52 Weeks   **Annual Attendance:** 250,000

MELROSE THEATRE ASSOCIATION
733 Seward Street, Los Angeles, CA 90038
(213) 465-1885
      Founded: 1964
      Arts Area: Professional; Theatrical Group
      Status: Professional; Non-Profit
      Type: Performing; Educational
      Purpose: To provide an extension of the learning process for professional actors; to offer beginning acting classes
      Management: Paul Kent, Artistic Director; Jomarie Ward, Administrator
      Volunteer Staff: 6
      Non-Paid Artists: 20
      Utilizes: Special Technical Talent; Guest Artists; Guest Directors
      Budget: $1,000 - $50,000
      Income Sources: Business/Corporate Donations; Box Office; Individual Donations
      Season: 52 Weeks   **Annual Attendance:** 8,000
      Affiliations: Los Angeles Theatre Alliance
      Performance Facilities: Melrose Theatre

NINE O'CLOCK PLAYERS
1367 North St. Andrews Place, Los Angeles, CA 90028
(213) 469-1973
      Founded: 1929
      Arts Area: Musical; Theatrical Group; Musical Theatre
      Status: Semi-Professional; Non-Profit
      Type: Performing; Touring

Purpose: To provide free musical theater for culturally and physically disadvantaged children as well as paid performances for all children of southern California; to donate proceeds to the services of the Assistance League of Southern California
Management: Assistance League of Southern California
Officers: Ottilie Laybourne, Chairman; Linnette Temple, First Vice Chairman; Doretta Lee, Second Vice Chairman; Suzanna Royse, Third Vice Chairman/Production
Volunteer Staff: 65
Utilizes: Guest Directors
Income Sources: Private Foundations/Grants/Endowments; Business/Corporate Donations; Box Office; Individual Donations
Season: September - May
Annual Attendance: 13,000
Performance Facilities: ALSC Playhouse

ODYSSEY THEATRE ENSEMBLE
2055 South Sepulveda Boulevard, Los Angeles, CA 90025
(310) 477-2055
FAX: (310) 444-0455
Founded: 1969
Arts Area: Professional; Musical; Theatrical Group
Status: Professional; Non-Profit
Type: Performing; Resident; Sponsoring
Purpose: To create an alternative, experimental theatre centre housing an ensemble company; to work towards the creation of an international theatre center
Management: Ron Sossi, Artistic Director; Jason Loewith, Production Manager
Officers: Lynn Miller, President of the Board
Paid Staff: 7 **Volunteer Staff:** 150
Paid Artists: 15 **Non-Paid Artists:** 35
Utilizes: Special Technical Talent; Guest Artists; Guest Directors
Budget: $100,000 - $500,000
Income Sources: Private Foundations/Grants/Endowments; Business/Corporate Donations; Box Office; Government Grants; Individual Donations
Season: 52 Weeks
Annual Attendance: 17,500
Affiliations: Theatre Consortium (Los Angeles Theatre Pass), League of Producers and Theatres of Los Angeles; Los Angeles Theatre Alliance; TCG; California Confederation of the Arts
Performance Facilities: Odyssey Theatre

PADUA HILLS PLAYWRIGHTS WORKSHOP
PO Box 461450, Los Angeles, CA 90046
(213) 913-2636
Arts Area: Professional
Status: Professional; Non-Profit
Type: Performing; Resident; Educational
Purpose: The workshop is a seven-week conference taught by 12 master playwrights. The concurrent Padua Hills Playwrights Festival annually produces premiere works written and directed by resident playwrights and performed by Padua's resident professional acting company.
Management: Murray Mednick, Artistic Director; Cheryl Slean, Managing Director
Officers: Barry Opper, President of the Board
Budget: $50,000 - $100,000
Income Sources: Private Foundations/Grants/Endowments; Box Office; Government Grants; Individual Donations
Season: 52 Weeks

PIPELINE, INC.
11901 Santa Monica Boulevard, #497, Los Angeles, CA 90025
(310) 207-4380
Founded: 1982
Arts Area: Professional
Status: Professional; Non-Profit
Type: Performing; Touring; Resident; Educational
Purpose: To provide innovative and socially relevant theatre using entertainment as a vehicle for education and communication for the audiences and artists of Los Angeles
Management: Scott Kelman, Artistic Director; Aaron Slavin, Executive Director
Officers: Aaron Slavin, Chairman; Isabel Holt, Rob Seltzen, Vice Chairmen
Paid Staff: 5
Paid Artists: 25
Utilizes: Special Technical Talent; Guest Artists; Guest Directors
Budget: $1,000 - $50,000

Income Sources: Private Foundations/Grants/Endowments; Business/Corporate Donations; Box Office; Government Grants; Individual Donations
Season: 52 Weeks   **Annual Attendance:** 20,000

STAGES THEATRE CENTER
1540 North McCadden Place, Los Angeles, CA 90028
(213) 463-5356; (213) 465-1010
FAX: (213) 462-3176
Founded: 1980
Arts Area: Professional
Status: Non-Profit
Type: Performing
Purpose: To present and promote uncelebrated multicultural theatrical works, in English and other languages, at a modest admission, devised, selected and presented by informed and gifted theatre practitioners
Management: Paul Verdier, Artistic Director; Kay Tornborg, Managing Director
Officers: Sonia Lloveras, Board President; Pompea Smith, Board Chair; Hilma Carter, Secretary; Sonia Lloveras, Treasurer
Paid Staff: 4
Utilizes: Guest Directors; Artists-in-Residence
Budget: $100,000 - $500,000
Income Sources: Private Foundations/Grants/Endowments; Business/Corporate Donations; Box Office; Government Grants; Individual Donations
Season: 52 Weeks   **Annual Attendance:** 6,000

THEATRE WEST
3333 Cahuenga Boulevard West, Los Angeles, CA 90068
(213) 851-4839
Founded: 1962
Arts Area: Theatrical Group
Status: Professional; Non-Profit
Type: Performing; Resident; Educational
Purpose: Theatre West conducts weekly theater workshops, produces several plays a year and strives to be a cultural force in the community.
Management: Douglas Marney, Managing Director; Mary Van Arsdel, Administrative Assistant; Norman Cohen, Artistic Moderator
Officers: Timothy J. Noyes, Chairman; Valeri Jackson, Vice Chairperson; Kevin West, Secretary
Paid Staff: 3   **Volunteer Staff:** 7
Paid Artists: 60
Utilizes: Guest Directors
Budget: $100,000 - $500,000
Income Sources: Private Foundations/Grants/Endowments; Business/Corporate Donations; Box Office; Government Grants; Individual Donations
Season: 40 weeks   **Annual Attendance:** 10,000
Affiliations: AEA
Performance Facilities: Theatre West

THE WESTWOOD PLAYHOUSE
10886 Le Conte Avenue, Los Angeles, CA 90024
(310) 208-5454
Founded: 1974
Arts Area: Professional; Musical
Status: Professional; Commercial
Type: Performing; Resident
Purpose: To produce quality theatre in a broad range of presentations of many moods and characters; to present comedy, drama, musicals, new plays, revivals, classics, experimental children's theatre, special events, multimedia
Management: Eric Krebs, Executive Directors
Officers: Paul Morer, General Manager
Utilizes: Special Technical Talent; Guest Artists; Guest Directors
Budget: $100,000 - $500,000
Income Sources: Box Office
Season: 52 Weeks   **Annual Attendance:** 90,000
Performance Facilities: The Westwood Playhouse

THE WORLD'S FIRST INNER-MUSICAL THEATRE
1743 East 122nd Street, Los Angeles, CA 90059
(213) 636-7733
Founded: 1986
Arts Area: Musical; Community; Theatrical Group
Status: Non-Profit

Type: Performing; Touring; Educational
Purpose: To perform theatrical plays, using the inner-music or emotion-mastery acting technique involving expression of emotional punctuation symbols (a new art form)
Management: J.L. Sherman, Director
Officers: J.L. Sherman, President
Volunteer Staff: 3
Non-Paid Artists: 35
Utilizes: Special Technical Talent; Guest Artists; Guest Directors
Budget: $1,000 - $50,000
Income Sources: Box Office; Individual Donations
Season: 52 Weeks
Affiliations: Emotion Mastery Seminars

ZEPHYR THEATRE
7456 Melrose Avenue, Los Angeles, CA 90046
(213) 653-4667
Founded: 1977
Arts Area: Professional
Status: Professional; Commercial
Type: Performing
Purpose: To produce new work
Management: Stephen Barber, General Manager; Lee Sankowicz, Artistic Director
Paid Staff: 5
Paid Artists: 100
Utilizes: Guest Artists; Guest Directors
Budget: $50,000 - $100,000
Income Sources: Box Office
Season: 52 Weeks   **Annual Attendance:** 20,000
Affiliations: Los Angeles League of Theaters and Producers
Performance Facilities: Zephyr Theatre

PERFORMING SERIES

BING CONCERTS
5905 Wilshire Boulevard, Los Angeles, CA 90036
(213) 857-6000
Founded: 1965
Arts Area: Vocal Music; Instrumental Music
Status: Professional; Non-Profit
Type: Performing
Purpose: To present programs as a special benefit for members of the Los Angeles County Museum of Art
Management: Dorrance Stalvey, Director of Music Programs
Paid Staff: 1
Utilizes: Guest Conductors; Guest Artists
Budget: $1,000 - $50,000
Income Sources: Private Foundations/Grants/Endowments; Box Office
Season: July - June   **Annual Attendance:** 5,000
Affiliations: Los Angeles County Museum of Art
Performance Facilities: Leo S. Bing Theatre, Los Angeles County Museum of Art

CHAMBER MUSIC/LA FESTIVAL
3264 Primera Place, Los Angeles, CA 90068
(213) 850-8064
Founded: 1985
Arts Area: Instrumental Music; Festivals
Status: Professional
Type: Performing
Purpose: To promote appreciation and understanding of chamber music
Management: Susanne Glass, Executive Director; Yukiko Kamei, Artistic Director
Officers: James Arkatov, President; Josh Livingston, Vice President; Manya Schaff, Secretary; Mary Archibald, Treasurer
Paid Staff: 2   **Volunteer Staff:** 5
Paid Artists: 20
Utilizes: Guest Artists
Budget: $100,000 - $500,000
Income Sources: Private Foundations/Grants/Endowments; Business/Corporate Donations; Box Office; Government Grants; Individual Donations

Season: May   **Annual Attendance:** 5,000
Performance Facilities: Japan America Theatre

CITY OF LOS ANGELES CULTURAL AFFAIRS DEPARTMENT
433 South Spring Street, 10th Floor, Los Angeles, CA 90013
(213) 485-2433
FAX: (213) 485-6835
Founded: 1980
Arts Area: Dance; Vocal Music; Instrumental Music; Theater; Festivals
Status: Non-Profit
Type: Performing
Purpose: To bring cultural events, both visual and performance-related, to the people of Los Angeles
Management: Adolfo Nodal, General Manager; Rodney Punt, Ann Giagmi, Assistant General Managers
Officers: David Smith, President; Julie A. Sgarzi, Vice President
Paid Staff: 60
Paid Artists: 125
Utilizes: Special Technical Talent; Guest Conductors; Guest Artists; Guest Directors
Budget: $1,000,000 - $5,000,000
Season: 52 Weeks
Annual Attendance: 25,000

FESTIVAL PLAYERS OF CALIFORNIA
3809 DeLongpre Avenue, Los Angeles, CA 90027
(213) 665-6444
Founded: 1957
Arts Area: Dance; Vocal Music; Instrumental Music; Theater; Festivals
Status: Professional; Non-Profit
Type: Performing; Touring; Educational; Sponsoring
Purpose: To present a full spectrum of performing and visual arts experiences, geared to meet the multicultural needs of the southern California community
Management: Dr. Dorye Roettger, Founder/Director; Margaret Bonadurer, Associate Director
Officers: Marion E. Rutger, President; Lewis I. Williams, Vice President; Caryl Warner, Secretary/Treasurer
Utilizes: Special Technical Talent; Guest Artists; Guest Directors
Budget: $1,000 - $50,000
Income Sources: Private Foundations/Grants/Endowments; Business/Corporate Donations; Government Grants; Individual Donations
Season: 52 Weeks

GREEK THEATRE
2700 North Vermont Avenue, Los Angeles, CA 90027
(213) 665-1927
Founded: 1930
Arts Area: Dance; Vocal Music; Instrumental Music; Theater
Status: Commercial
Type: Performing
Purpose: To present a variety of contemporary entertainment including concerts, Broadway plays, and comedy
Management: Susan Rosenbluth, General Manager
Utilizes: Special Technical Talent; Guest Artists
Income Sources: Box Office
Season: May - October
Performance Facilities: Greek Theatre

HOLLYWOOD BOWL SUMMER FESTIVAL
c/o Los Angeles Philharmonic Association, 135 North Grand Avenue, Los Angeles, CA 90012
(213) 972-7300
FAX: (213) 617-3065
Arts Area: Dance; Vocal Music; Instrumental Music; Festivals; Recitals; Jazz
Status: Professional; Non-Profit
Type: Performing; Touring; Resident; Educational; Sponsoring
Purpose: To provide a summer home for the Los Angeles Philharmonic and the Hollywood Bowl Orchestra; to present a summer festival featuring artists in the classical, pop, and jazz fields
Management: Anne Parsons, General Manager; Kathy Henkel, Publicity Assistant; Ernest Fleischmann, Executive Vice President/Managing Director; Esa-Pekka Salonen, Music Director of the Los Angeles Philharmonic; John Mauceri, Conductor of the Hollywood Bowl Orchestra
Officers: Stanley Beyer, Chairman of the Board; C. Joseph LaBonte, President of the Board, Los Angeles Philharmonic
Budget: Over 10,000,000
Season: June - September

Affiliations: Los Angeles Philharmonic
Performance Facilities: Hollywood Bowl

INNER CITY CULTURAL CENTER
North Hyland Avenue, Suite 200, Los Angeles, CA 90028
(213) 962-2102
FAX: (213) 962-2403
Founded: 1966
Arts Area: Dance; Theater
Status: Professional; Non-Profit
Type: Performing; Educational; Sponsoring
Purpose: Through an extensive program of professionally-produced plays, concerts, exhibits and events, we attempt to explore and develop interest in the arts of all people. The Center maintains a multiracial policy in all aspects of its operation.
Management: C. Bernard Jackson, Executive Director
Officers: C. Bernard Jackson, Executive Vice President
Paid Staff: 15
Utilizes: Special Technical Talent; Guest Artists
Budget: $100,000 - $500,000
Income Sources: Business/Corporate Donations; Box Office; Government Grants; Individual Donations
Season: September - June

LOS ANGELES COUNTY MUSEUM OF ART: MUSIC PROGRAMS
5905 Wilshire Boulevard, Los Angeles, CA 90036
(213) 857-6115
FAX: (213) 931-7347
Founded: 1939
Arts Area: Vocal Music; Instrumental Music
Status: Professional; Non-Profit
Type: Performing
Purpose: To produce concerts of chamber music and Jazz
Management: Dorrance Stalvey, Director of Music Programs; Cheryl Tiano, Administration/Promotion
Paid Staff: 2
Utilizes: Special Technical Talent; Guest Conductors; Guest Artists
Budget: $100,000 - $500,000
Income Sources: Private Foundations/Grants/Endowments; Business/Corporate Donations; Box Office; Government Grants; Individual Donations
Season: 52 Weeks   **Annual Attendance:** 28,000
Affiliations: Los Angeles County Museum of Art
Performance Facilities: Leo S. Bing Theater

LOS ANGELES FESTIVAL
PO Box 5210, Los Angeles, CA 90055
(213) 689-8800
Founded: 1985
Arts Area: Dance; Vocal Music; Instrumental Music; Theater; Festivals; Lyric Opera; Grand Opera; Media; Literary; Visual
Status: Professional; Non-Profit
Type: Performing; Sponsoring
Purpose: To present an international festival of the performing arts
Management: Peter Sellars, Artistic Director; Allison Sampson, Executive Director
Officers: Maureen A. Kindel, Chairman of the Board
Utilizes: Special Technical Talent; Guest Conductors; Guest Artists; Guest Directors
Budget: $1,000,000 - $5,000,000
Income Sources: Private Foundations/Grants/Endowments; Business/Corporate Donations; Box Office; Government Grants; Individual Donations
Season: September (biannually)   **Annual Attendance:** 150,000

THE MUSIC CENTER OF LOS ANGELES COUNTY
135 North Grand Avenue, Los Angeles, CA 90012
(213) 972-7570
Founded: 1964
Arts Area: Dance; Vocal Music; Instrumental Music; Theater; Festivals; Grand Opera
Status: Professional; Non-Profit
Type: Performing; Resident; Educational; Sponsoring
Purpose: To sponsor educational outreach programs; to provide fund-raising support for the resident performing companies of the Los Angeles County Music Center

Officers: James A. Thomas, Chairman; Esther Watchell, President; Lyle Marshall, Vice President of Finance/Administration; Susan Pearce, Vice President of the Music Center Unified Fund; Louise Otis, Vice President of Donor Relations; Larry Landre, Vice President of Marketing and Communications; Joan Boyett, Vice President of Education
Paid Staff: 65 **Volunteer Staff:** 1,000
Budget: Over 10,000,000
Income Sources: Private Foundations/Grants/Endowments; Business/Corporate Donations; Box Office; Government Grants; Individual Donations; Retail; Travel Operations
Season: 52 Weeks **Annual Attendance:** 2,000,000
Affiliations: Los Angeles Philharmonic Association; Center Theatre Group; Music Center Opera Association; Los Angeles Master Chorale Association; Music Center Operating Company; Music Center Education Division

OCCIDENTAL COLLEGE ARTIST SERIES
1600 Campus Road, Los Angeles, CA 90041
(213) 259-2737; (213) 259-2922
FAX: (213) 341-4987
Founded: 1887
Arts Area: Dance; Vocal Music; Instrumental Music; Theater; World Music
Status: Non-Profit
Type: Sponsoring
Management: Sandy Robertson, Marketing Consultant; Terri Gens, Technical Director for Theatres
Paid Staff: 2
Season: October - April
Performance Facilities: Thorne Hall; Keck Theater

FACILITY

BOB BAKER MARIONETTE THEATER
1345 West First Street, Los Angeles, CA 90026
(213) 250-9995
Founded: 1963
Type of Facility: Theatre House; Room
Facility Originally: Warehouse
Type of Stage: Proscenium; 3/4 Arena
Seating Capacity: 245
Year Built: 1930
Year Remodeled: 1963
Contact for Rental: Tina Gainsboro; (213) 250-9995
Resident Groups: Bob Baker Marionette Theater

CALIFORNIA PLAZA
300 South Grand Avenue, Suite 3200, Los Angeles, CA 90071
(213) 687-2190
FAX: (213) 687-2191
Founded: 1987
Type of Facility: Outdoor (Concert); Environmental; Amphitheater
Type of Stage: Thrust; Flexible; Greek; Environmental
Stage Dimensions: 1 at 40'x60'; 2 at 26' diameter
Seating Capacity: 350; 550; 1,000
Year Built: 1985 **Architect:** Arthur Erickson
Year Remodeled: 1992 **Architect:** Arthur Erickson
Contact for Rental: Melissa Schwartz; (213) 687-2190

CALIFORNIA STATE UNIVERSITY-LOS ANGELES - MUSIC HALL
5151 State University Drive, Los Angeles, CA 90032
(213) 224-3348
Type of Facility: Concert Hall
Type of Stage: Proscenium
Stage Dimensions: 18'x45'x24' **Orchestra Pit**
Seating Capacity: 195
Year Built: 1957 **Architect:** Architecture Department, State of California **Cost:** $2,500,000
Contact for Rental: Mickey Fruchter; (213) 224-3348
Resident Groups: California State University Music Department

CALIFORNIA STATE UNIVERSITY-LOS ANGELES - PLAYHOUSE
5151 State University Drive, Los Angeles, CA 90032
(213) 224-3345
Type of Facility: Theatre House
Type of Stage: Proscenium

Stage Dimensions: 52'x84'x35'   **Orchestra Pit**
Seating Capacity: 422
Year Built: 1958   **Architect:** Architecture Department, State of California   **Cost:** $2,500,000
Contact for Rental: Ellen Ketchum;   (213) 224-3344
Resident Groups: Theatre Department

CELEBRATION THEATRE
7051B Santa Monica Boulevard, Los Angeles, CA 90028
(213) 957-1884
   Type of Facility: Theatre House
   Facility Originally: Business Facility
   Type of Stage: Arena
   Stage Dimensions: 15'x30'x20'
   Seating Capacity: 50
   Year Built: 1970   **Cost:** $4,000
   Year Remodeled: 1983   **Cost:** $10,000
   Contact for Rental: Chuck Rowland;   (213) 876-4257
   Resident Groups: Celebration Theatre

EAST WEST PLAYERS
4424 Santa Monica Boulevard, Los Angeles, CA 90029
(213) 660-0366
FAX: (213) 666-1929
   Founded: 1967
   Type of Facility: Theatre House
   Facility Originally: Ceramics Factory
   Type of Stage: Flexible; Proscenium
   Seating Capacity: 99
   Year Remodeled: 1972   **Architect:** Rae Creevey   **Cost:** $5,000
   Manager: Nobu McCarthy, Artistic Director

GREEK THEATRE
2700 North Vermont Avenue, Los Angeles, CA 90027
(213) 480-3232
   Type of Facility: Outdoor (Concert); Performance Center; Theatre House; Amphitheater
   Type of Stage: Proscenium
   Stage Dimensions: 54'Wx23'H proscenium opening; 42'Dx60'W   **Orchestra Pit**
   Seating Capacity: 6,187
   Year Built: 1930
   Year Remodeled: 1983   **Architect:** McClellan Cruz Glaylord & Associates   **Cost:** $1,000,000
   Contact for Rental: Susan Rosenbluth;   (213) 665-5857

JAPAN AMERICA THEATER
244 South San Pedro Street, Los Angeles, CA 90012
(213) 680-3700
FAX: (213) 617-8576
   Type of Facility: Theatre Complex; Concert Hall
   Type of Stage: Thrust; Proscenium; Apron - 5' Deep
   Stage Dimensions: 48'Wx36.5'Dx22.5'H   **Orchestra Pit**
   Seating Capacity: 841
   Year Built: 1983   **Architect:** Kajima Architecture
   Contact for Rental: Teusa Koiwai;   (213) 680-3700

LOS ANGELES COUNTY MUSEUM OF ART - LEO S. BING THEATER
5905 Wilshire Boulevard, Los Angeles, CA 90036
(213) 857-6031
FAX: (213) 931-7347
   Type of Facility: Concert Hall; Performance Center; Theatre House; Multi-Purpose
   Type of Stage: Proscenium
   Stage Dimensions: 36'Wx26'Dx18'H
   Seating Capacity: 603
   Year Built: 1965

LOS ANGELES THEATRE CENTER
514 South Spring Street, Los Angeles, CA 90013
(213) 627-6500
FAX: (213) 624-6096
   Type of Facility: Theatre Complex; Performance Center

Facility Originally: Bank
Type of Stage: Thrust; Flexible; Proscenium; Modified Thrust (35'x35')
Stage Dimensions: 40'x45'; 30'x40'; 40'x28'
Seating Capacity: 498; 296; 323; 99
Year Built: 1916   **Architect:** John Parkinson
Year Remodeled: 1985   **Architect:** John Sergio Fisher   **Cost:** $16,000,000
Acoustical Consultant: John Sergio Fisher
Contact for Rental: Chaz McEwan, Laurel Meade;   (213) 627-6500
Contained within the Theatre Center are Theatre 2, Theatre 3, Theatre 4 and Tom Bradley Theatre. See separate listings for additional information.

LOS ANGELES THEATRE CENTER - THEATRE 2
514 South Spring Street, Los Angeles, CA 90013
(213) 627-6500
    Type of Facility: Auditorium
    Type of Stage: Proscenium
    Stage Dimensions: 53'Wx25'D   **Orchestra Pit**
    Seating Capacity: 296
    Contact for Rental: Laurel Meade;   (213) 627-6500

LOS ANGELES THEATRE CENTER - THEATRE 3
514 South Spring Street, Los Angeles, CA 90013
(213) 627-6500
    Type of Facility: Concert Hall
    Type of Stage: Greek
    Stage Dimensions: 40'Wx32'D
    Seating Capacity: 323
    Contact for Rental: Laurel Meade;   (213) 627-6500

LOS ANGELES THEATRE CENTER - THEATRE 4
514 South Spring Street, Los Angeles, CA 90013
(213) 627-6500
    Type of Facility: Multi-Purpose; Room
    Type of Stage: Flexible
    Stage Dimensions: 44'Wx25'D, size of entire room
    Seating Capacity: 99 maximum
    Contact for Rental: Laurel Meade;   (213) 627-6500

LOS ANGELES THEATRE CENTER - TOM BRADLEY THEATRE
514 South Spring Street, Los Angeles, CA 90013
(213) 627-6500
    Type of Facility: Theatre House
    Type of Stage: Thrust
    Stage Dimensions: 38'Wx44'D
    Seating Capacity: 503
    Contact for Rental: Chaz McEwan;   (213) 627-6500

MUNICIPAL ART GALLERY - GALLERY THEATER
Barnsdall Art Park, 4804 Hollywood Boulevard, Los Angeles, CA 90027
(213) 485-2460
    Type of Facility: Theatre House
    Type of Stage: Proscenium; Modified Apron Proscenium
    Stage Dimensions: 50'Wx26'D; 29'Wx15'3"H proscenium opening
    Seating Capacity: 295
    Contact for Rental: Maxene Wolf;   (213) 485-2460

THE MUSIC CENTER OF LOS ANGELES COUNTY
135 North Grand Avenue, Los Angeles, CA 90012
(213) 972-7211
FAX: (213) 972-7474
    Type of Facility: Theatre Complex; Performance Center
    Year Built: 1967   **Architect:** Welton Beckett   **Cost:** $34,500,000
    Acoustical Consultant: R. Lawrence Kirkegaard; Abraham Meltzer
    Contact for Rental: Gordon Jenkins, Booking Manager;   (213) 972-7489
    Resident Groups: Los Angeles Master Chorale; Glendale Symphony Orchestra
Contained within the Music Center are the Ahmanson Theater, Dorothy Chandler Pavilion and Mark Taper Forum. See individual listings for additional information.

THE MUSIC CENTER OF LOS ANGELES COUNTY - AHMANSON THEATER
135 North Grand Avenue, Los Angeles, CA 90012
(213) 972-7211
FAX: (213) 972-7474
    Type of Facility: Theatre House
    Type of Stage: Proscenium
    Stage Dimensions: 109'6"Wx47'Dx67'H; 40'Wx28'6"H proscenium opening   **Orchestra Pit**
    Seating Capacity: 2,071
    Year Built: 1967
    Contact for Rental: Gordon Jenkins, Booking Manager;   (213) 972-7479
    Resident Groups: Center Theater Group

THE MUSIC CENTER OF LOS ANGELES COUNTY - DOROTHY CHANDLER PAVILION
135 North Grand Avenue, Los Angeles, CA 90012
(213) 972-7211
FAX: (213) 972-7474
    Type of Facility: Concert Hall
    Type of Stage: Proscenium
    Stage Dimensions: 121'Wx60'Dx95'H; 58'Wx30'H proscenium opening   **Orchestra Pit**
    Seating Capacity: 3,197
    Year Built: 1967
    Contact for Rental: Gordon Jenkins, Booking Manager;   (213) 972-7489

THE MUSIC CENTER OF LOS ANGELES COUNTY - MARK TAPER FORUM
135 North Grand Avenue, Los Angeles, CA 90012
(213) 972-7211
FAX: (213) 972-7474
    Type of Facility: Theatre House
    Type of Stage: Thrust
    Stage Dimensions: 36'2"Wx30'D
    Seating Capacity: 737
    Year Built: 1967   **Architect:** Welton Beckett
    Acoustical Consultant: R. Lawrence Kirkegaard; Abraham Meltzer
    Contact for Rental: Gordon Jenkins, Booking Manager;   (213) 972-7489
    Resident Groups: Center Theater Group; Los Angeles Master Chorale; Los Angeles Philharmonic Orchestra; Music Center Opera, Education Division

OCCIDENTAL COLLEGE - THORNE HALL
1600 Campus Road, Los Angeles, CA 90041
(213) 259-2737
    Type of Facility: Auditorium
    Type of Stage: Proscenium   **Orchestra Pit**
    Seating Capacity: 960
    Year Built: 1938
    Year Remodeled: 1989
    Contact for Rental: Terri Gens;   (213) 259-2737

SHRINE AUDITORIUM AND EXPOSITION CENTER
649 West Jefferson Boulevard, Los Angeles, CA 90007
(213) 748-5116
FAX: (213) 742-9922
    Type of Facility: Theatre Complex; Concert Hall; Auditorium; Theatre House; Opera House; Civic Center; Multi-Purpose
    Type of Stage: Proscenium   **Orchestra Pit**
    Seating Capacity: 6,300
    Year Built: 1925   **Architect:** John C. Austin
    Year Remodeled: 1986   **Architect:** William D. Coffey & Associates
    Contact for Rental: Douglas Worthington;   (213) 748-5116
    Resident Groups: Soul Train Music Awards; American Music Awards; Ballet Folkloreico De Mexico; Comedy Awards

SHUBERT THEATRE
2020 Avenue of the Stars, Los Angeles, CA 90067
(310) 201-1500; (800) 233-3123
FAX: (310) 201-1585
    Type of Facility: Theatre House
    Type of Stage: Proscenium
    Stage Dimensions: 80'H deck to grid, ; 53'Wx30'H proscenium opening   **Orchestra Pit**
    Seating Capacity: 1,829
    Year Built: 1971   **Architect:** Henry George Greene, AIA

Contact for Rental: Lawrence K. O'Conner;   (213) 201-1500
Manager: Alisa Fishbach

UNIVERSITY OF CALIFORNIA-LOS ANGELES - ROYCE HALL
405 Hilgard Avenue, Los Angeles, CA 90024
(310) 825-8981
    Type of Facility: Theatre House
    Type of Stage: Proscenium
    Stage Dimensions: 80'Wx35'D   **Orchestra Pit**
    Seating Capacity: 1,843
    Year Built: 1929
    Year Remodeled: 1984   **Architect:** Carl Werniche Associates   **Cost:** $10,000,000
    Acoustical Consultant: Bolt, Beranek & Newman
    Contact for Rental: UCLA Center for Performing Arts;   (310) 206-8745
    Manager: James Bates, Technical Director
    Resident Groups: Los Angeles Philharmonic; American Youth Symphony; UCLA Dance Company;
    Los Angeles Chamber Orchestra
    Cultural Events; Film; Lectures

UNIVERSITY OF CALIFORNIA-LOS ANGELES - WADSWORTH THEATER
405 Hilgard Avenue, Los Angeles, CA 90024
(310) 206-8745
    Type of Facility: Theatre House
    Type of Stage: Proscenium
    Seating Capacity: 1,400
    Year Built: 1951
    Year Remodeled: 1983   **Architect:** Brian Murphy Associates
    Contact for Rental: UCLA Center for Performing Arts;   (310) 206-8745
    Manager: James Bates, Technical Director

UNIVERSITY OF SOUTHERN CALIFORNIA - BOVARD AUDITORIUM
Los Angeles, CA 90089
(213) 740-2311
    Type of Facility: Auditorium
    Type of Stage: Thrust; Proscenium
    Seating Capacity: 1,600
    Year Built: 1921
    Year Remodeled: 1980
    Contact for Rental: Joe Singer;   (213) 740-2514
    Resident Groups: University of Southern California Department of Music
    Rental limited to university-sponsored events and time availability

Malibu

INSTRUMENTAL MUSIC

SEAVER COLLEGE COMMUNITY SYMPHONY
c/o Music Department, Malibu, CA 90263
(310) 456-4503
    Founded: 1983
    Arts Area: Symphony
    Status: Semi-Professional
    Type: Performing
    Purpose: To train our students; to provide a good symphonic experience for our audience which includes students
    and people from the community
    Management: Thomas Osborn, Music Director/Conductor
    Paid Staff: 1   **Volunteer Staff:** 2
    Paid Artists: 27   **Non-Paid Artists:** 38
    Utilizes: Guest Artists
    Budget: $1,000 - $50,000
    Season: October - May
    Annual Attendance: 15,000
    Performance Facilities: Smothers Theatre, Pepperdine University; Railt Recital Hall

FACILITY

PEPPERDINE UNIVERSITY - AMPHITHEATRE, FINE ARTS DIVISION
24255 Pacific Coast Highway, Malibu, CA 90263-9605
(310) 456-4264
  Type of Facility: Amphitheater
  Type of Stage: Flexible
  Stage Dimensions: Open 32'x32'
  Seating Capacity: 400
  Year Built: 1972   **Architect:** William Periera and Associates
  Contact for Rental: Director of Auxiliary Services;   (310) 456-4264

PEPPERDINE UNIVERSITY - MINI-THEATRE, FINE ARTS DIVISION
24255 Pacific Coast Highway, Malibu, CA 90263-9605
(310) 456-4264
  Type of Facility: Mini-theatre
  Facility Originally: School
  Type of Stage: Proscenium
  Stage Dimensions: 9'x24'x11'
  Seating Capacity: 48
  Year Built: 1972   **Architect:** William Periera and Associates
  Year Remodeled: 1977   **Cost:** $3,000
  Contact for Rental: Director of Auxiliary Services;   (310) 456-4264
  Manager: Dr. Jerry Henderson

PEPPERDINE UNIVERSITY - SMOTHERS THEATRE
24255 Pacific Coast Highway, Malibu, CA 90263-4522
(213) 456-4558
  Type of Facility: Theatre Complex
  Type of Stage: Proscenium
  Stage Dimensions: 80'x30'   **Orchestra Pit**
  Seating Capacity: 515
  Year Built: 1980   **Architect:** Neptune & Thomas   **Cost:** $3,500,000
  Acoustical Consultant: Purcell & Noppe
  Contact for Rental: Marnie Duke-Mitze, Managing Director;   (213) 456-4558
  Resident Groups: University Theatre and Music Departments

Mendocino

DANCE

MENDOCINO DANCE SERIES
PO Box 453, Mendocino, CA 95460
(707) 937-5611
  Founded: 1982
  Arts Area: Modern; Ballet; Jazz; Ethnic; Folk; Tap
  Status: Non-Profit
  Type: Presenting
  Management: Rhoda Teplow, Executive Director
  Paid Staff: 10   **Volunteer Staff:** 30
  Paid Artists: 100
  Utilizes: Special Technical Talent; Guest Artists; Guest Directors; Guest Choreographers
  Budget: $50,000 - $100,000
  Income Sources: Private Foundations/Grants/Endowments; Business/Corporate Donations; Box Office; Government Grants; Individual Donations
  Season: November - June   **Annual Attendance:** 3,000
  Affiliations: WAAA; AAA; California Presenters
  Performance Facilities: Cotton Auditorium

PERFORMING SERIES

MENDOCINO MUSIC FESTIVAL ASSOCIATION
PO Box 1808, Mendocino, CA 95460
(707) 937-2044
  Founded: 1986
  Arts Area: Vocal Music; Instrumental Music
  Status: Professional; Non-Profit
  Type: Performing

Purpose: To blend the best of several orchestras - music history in the making
Management: Allan Pollack, Musical Director; Carolyn Steinbuck, Executive Manager; Walter Green, Artistic Advisor/Orchestra Manager
Paid Staff: 10
Paid Artists: 45 **Non-Paid Artists:** 22
Utilizes: Special Technical Talent; Guest Artists
Budget: $100,000 - $500,000
Income Sources: Business/Corporate Donations; Box Office; Individual Donations
Season: July - August **Annual Attendance:** 4,200
Performance Facilities: The Grounds of the Ford House

FACILITY

MENDOCINO ART CENTER - HELEN SCHOENI THEATER
45200 Little Lake Road, Mendocino, CA 95460
(707) 937-4477
   Type of Facility: Theatre House
   Type of Stage: Proscenium
   Stage Dimensions: 30'x20'
   Seating Capacity: 81
   Year Built: 1970 **Cost:** $58,000
   Contact for Rental: Diana DeWees, Marjorie Eseppi; (707) 937-4477
   Resident Groups: Mendocino Theatre Company

Mill Valley

INSTRUMENTAL MUSIC

MILL VALLEY CHAMBER MUSIC SOCIETY
PO Box 5121, Mill Valley, CA 94942
(415) 383-7359
   Founded: 1974
   Arts Area: Chamber; Ensemble; Instrumental Group
   Status: Non-Profit
   Type: Educational; Sponsoring
   Purpose: To present an annual subscription series that includes five concerts each season
   Officers: Nelson N. Foote, President; Robert Glasson, Treasurer
   Volunteer Staff: 17
   Paid Artists: 20
   Utilizes: Guest Artists
   Budget: $1,000 - $50,000
   Income Sources: Private Foundations/Grants/Endowments; Business/Corporate Donations; Box Office; Government Grants; Individual Donations
   Season: October - May **Annual Attendance:** 1,600

THEATRE

MARIN THEATRE COMPANY
397 Miller Avenue, Mill Valley, CA 94941
(415) 388-5200
FAX: (415) 381-3724
   Founded: 1966
   Arts Area: Professional; Theatrical Group
   Status: Professional; Non-Profit
   Type: Performing; Resident; Educational; Sponsoring
   Purpose: To present a season of theatrical performances; to foster development of new plays; to provide theatrical training and present other art forms
   Management: Joanne Williams, Public Relations; Lee Sankowich, Artistic Director; Regina Lickteig, Managing Director; Katherine Boneti, Development Director
   Officers: Herb Boyer, Board President
   Paid Staff: 4
   Utilizes: Special Technical Talent; Guest Artists; Guest Directors
   Budget: $1,000,000 - $5,000,000
   Income Sources: Private Foundations/Grants/Endowments; Business/Corporate Donations; Box Office; Government Grants; Individual Donations
   Season: September - June
   Affiliations: TCG
   Performance Facilities: Marin Theatre Company

Mission Hills

THEATRE

LITTLE BROADWAY PRODUCTIONS, INC.
PO Box 5008, Mission Hills, CA 91395-0008
(818) 894-4222; (800) 527-8747
FAX: (818) 891-1813
    Arts Area: Musical; Musical Theatre for Children
    Status: Professional; Non-Profit
    Type: Performing; Touring
    Purpose: To present quality main-stage musical theatre to young audiences
    Management: Jill Shawn Adereth, Executive Producer; Marily Weitz, Artistic Director; Cathy Kelleher,
Office/Tour Manager; Michael Benson, Technical Director
    Officers: Jill Shawn Adereth, Chairman/Treasurer; Marilyn Weitz, President; Mary Jane Evans, John Kelleher, Frank
Barneburg, Members; Marty Sokup, Secretary
    Paid Staff: 4   **Volunteer Staff:** 2
    Paid Artists: 9
    Utilizes: Special Technical Talent; Guest Artists
    Budget: $100,000 - $500,000
    Income Sources: Private Foundations/Grants/Endowments; Business/Corporate Donations; Box Office; Government
Grants
    Season: October - February   **Annual Attendance:** 80,000
    Affiliations: WAAA; Theatre Los Angeles; California Booking Exchange; SCETA; AATE; California Educational
Theatre Association

Modesto

DANCE

MODESTO CIVIC BALLET THEATRE
1328 H Street, PO Box 22, Modesto, CA 95353
(209) 522-6879
    Arts Area: Ballet
    Status: Professional; Non-Profit
    Type: Performing; Touring
    Management: Mavis Dell Seeman, Artistic Director; Carla Fletcher, Assistant Artistic Director
    Paid Artists: 25
    Income Sources: Box Office; Individual Donations
    Performance Facilities: Central Valley Performing Arts Center

INSTRUMENTAL MUSIC

MODESTO SYMPHONY
1700 McHenry Village Way, Suite 10A, Modesto, CA 95350
(209) 523-4156
    Founded: 1931
    Arts Area: Symphony
    Status: Professional; Non-Profit
    Type: Performing; Educational
    Purpose: To provide high-quality symphonic performances; to promote educational opportunities
    Management: Michael Royer, General Manager
    Officers: Ken Berns, President; Dawn Berg, First Vice President; Richard Fisher, Second Vice President; James Beard,
Treasurer
    Paid Staff: 5   **Volunteer Staff:** 55
    Paid Artists: 90
    Utilizes: Special Technical Talent; Guest Artists
    Budget: $500,000 - $1,000,000
    Income Sources: Private Foundations/Grants/Endowments; Business/Corporate Donations; Box Office;
Individual Donations
    Season: September - May   **Annual Attendance:** 3,000
    Affiliations: Association of California Symphony Orchestras; City of Modesto
    Performance Facilities: Modesto Junior College Auditorium

VOCAL MUSIC

TOWNSEND OPERA PLAYERS
1502 Maywood Drive, Modesto, CA 95350
(209) 523-6426
FAX: (209) 579-0532
Founded: 1982
Arts Area: Grand Opera; Lyric Opera; Light Opera; Operetta
Status: Professional; Non-Profit
Type: Performing; Touring; Educational
Purpose: To perform great opera and American musical theatre classics by and for the San Joaquin Valley and beyond
Management: Erik Buck Townsend, Founder/General Director; Erika Townsend, Office Manager
Officers: Alfred Hodder, Board President; Judy Schmidt, Secretary; Lynn Dooley, Treasurer
Paid Staff: 4 **Volunteer Staff:** 210
Paid Artists: 45 **Non-Paid Artists:** 50
Utilizes: Special Technical Talent; Guest Conductors; Guest Artists; Guest Directors
Budget: $100,000 - $500,000
Income Sources: Private Foundations/Grants/Endowments; Business/Corporate Donations; Box Office; Government Grants; Individual Donations
Season: 52 Weeks **Annual Attendance:** 30,000
Affiliations: OA

FACILITY

MODESTO JUNIOR COLLEGE CABARET
Blue Gum Avenue, Modesto, CA 95350
(209) 523-4156
Type of Facility: Theatre House
Facility Originally: Warehouse
Type of Stage: Flexible
Stage Dimensions: 60'x60'
Seating Capacity: 300
Year Built: 1940
Year Remodeled: 1976 **Architect:** James Shade **Cost:** $435,000
Contact for Rental: Mrs. D. King, Facilities Coordinator; (209) 575-6020
Manager: Steve Collins

Montclair

PERFORMING SERIES

STARLITE PATIO THEATER SUMMER SERIES
Montclair Civic Center, Benito and Fremont, Montclair, CA 91763
(909) 626-8571
Founded: 1963
Arts Area: Dance; Theater
Status: Non-Profit
Type: Performing
Purpose: To offer admission-free summer cultural entertainment and special programs every Tuesday
Management: Harve Edwards, Manager/Program Director
Budget: $1,000 - $50,000
Annual Attendance: 2,400
Performance Facilities: The Starlite Patio Theater

FACILITY

MONTCLAIR CIVIC CENTER - STARLITE PATIO THEATRE
Montclair Civic Center, Montclair, CA 91763
(909) 626-8571
Type of Facility: Outdoor (Concert); Civic Center
Type of Stage: Flexible
Stage Dimensions: 12'x24'x20'
Seating Capacity: 350
Year Built: 1957
Year Remodeled: 1977
Contact for Rental: Angie Antonelli, Recreation Director; (909) 626-8571

Manager: Harve Edwards;   (909) 986-4321
Resident Groups: Recreation Department Groups; Starlite Summer Series

---

Monterey

PERFORMING SERIES

MONTEREY JAZZ FESTIVAL
PO Box Jazz, Monterey, CA 93942
(408) 373-3366
FAX: (408) 373-0244
Founded: 1958
Arts Area: Dance; Vocal Music; Instrumental Music; Festivals
Status: Non-Profit
Type: Performing
Purpose: To present jazz artists in an ideal setting
Management: Stella Lepine, Education Coordinator; Jan Plunkett, Executive Secretary
Paid Staff: 3
Utilizes: Special Technical Talent; Guest Conductors; Guest Artists; Guest Directors
Budget: $500,000 - $1,000,000
Income Sources: Box Office; Individual Donations
Season: 52 Weeks
Performance Facilities: Monterey County Fairgrounds

Napa

INSTRUMENTAL MUSIC

NAPA VALLEY SYMPHONY
2407 California Boulevard, Napa, CA 94558
(707) 226-6872
FAX: (707) 226-3046
Founded: 1933
Arts Area: Symphony
Status: Non-Profit
Type: Performing; Educational
Purpose: To provide symphonic music performances at high standards to the Napa Valley and serve youth with music education programs
Management: Jay Goetting, General Manager; Anne Collett, Development Director; Jeanette Doxsee, Marketing Coordinator; Sandra Tront, Administrative Assistant; Asher Raboy, Music Director/Conductor
Officers: Elaine John, President; Terry Robinson, Linda McClimans, Vice Presidents; Frank Takahashi, Treasurer
Volunteer Staff: 35
Paid Artists: 65   **Non-Paid Artists:** 10
Utilizes: Special Technical Talent; Guest Artists
Budget: $500,000 - $1,000,000
Income Sources: Private Foundations/Grants/Endowments; Business/Corporate Donations; Box Office; Government Grants; Individual Donations
Season: October - May   **Annual Attendance:** 21,500
Affiliations: ASOL; Napa Valley Chamber of Commerce; Napa County Arts Council; Association of California Orchestras
Performance Facilities: Lincoln Theatre, Yountville

FACILITY

NAPA VALLEY OPERA HOUSE
PO Box 6297, Napa, CA 94581
(707) 226-7372
Type of Facility: Opera House
Type of Stage: Proscenium
Seating Capacity: 500
Year Built: 1879   **Architect:** Samuel Newsom; Joseph Cather Newsom
The Opera House, currently closed for renovations, is a member of the League of Historic American Theatres.

National City

THEATRE

THE LAMB'S PLAYERS THEATRE
PO Box 26, National City, CA 91951
(619) 474-3385
FAX: (619) 474-6156
Founded: 1973
Arts Area: Professional; Theatrical Group
Status: Professional; Non-Profit
Type: Performing; Touring; Resident; Educational
Purpose: To present a wide variety of theatrical productions which not only entertain but confront values and perspectives of our culture; to present the hope of the historic world viewed through the varied use of the dramatic arts
Management: W. Robert Smyth, Producing Artistic Director; Kerry Meads, Deborah Smyth, Associate Directors
Paid Staff: 3
Utilizes: Special Technical Talent; Guest Artists; Guest Directors
Budget: $500,000 - $1,000,000
Income Sources: Private Foundations/Grants/Endowments; Business/Corporate Donations; Box Office; Individual Donations
Season: February - November
Affiliations: TCG; California Theatre Council

Nevada City

PERFORMING SERIES

MUSIC IN THE MOUNTAINS
401 Spring Street, #101, Nevada City, CA 95959
(916) 265-6124
FAX: (916) 265-3170
Founded: 1981
Arts Area: Vocal Music; Instrumental Music; Festivals
Status: Professional; Non-Profit
Type: Performing; Resident; Educational; Sponsoring
Purpose: To present high-quality classical, pop and Broadway music at affordable prices
Management: Terry M. Brown, Executive Director; Paul Perry, Artistic Director/Conductor
Officers: Marguerite Blickenstaff, President; Marian Gallaher MD, First Vice President; Helen Daggett, Second Vice President; John van der Veen, Treasurer; Mike Hill, Secretary
Paid Staff: 6 **Volunteer Staff:** 315
Paid Artists: 62 **Non-Paid Artists:** 130
Utilizes: Guest Conductors; Guest Artists
Budget: $100,000 - $500,000
Income Sources: Private Foundations/Grants/Endowments; Business/Corporate Donations; Box Office; Government Grants; Individual Donations
Season: 52 Weeks **Annual Attendance:** 13,150
Performance Facilities: Don Baggett Theatre; St. Joseph's Hall; Nevada County Fairgrounds

North Hollywood

VOCAL MUSIC

MUSICAL AMERICA
North Hollywood High School, 5231 Colfax Avenue, North Hollywood, CA 91607
(818) 769-8510, ext. 308
Founded: 1969
Arts Area: Choral
Status: Semi-Professional; Non-Professional
Type: Performing; Touring; Educational
Purpose: To educate with fine choral music; to provide entertainment for the community
Management: Cornelia Korney, Director
Paid Staff: 1 **Volunteer Staff:** 20
Utilizes: Special Technical Talent; Guest Conductors; Guest Artists
Budget: $1,000 - $50,000
Income Sources: Private Foundations/Grants/Endowments; Business/Corporate Donations; Government Grants; Individual Donations
Season: November - June

Affiliations: Los Angeles Unified School District
Performance Facilities: North Hollywood High School

THEATRE

ACTORS ALLEY REPERTORY THEATER
12135 Riverside Drive, North Hollywood, CA 91607
(818) 986-2278
Founded: 1971
Arts Area: Professional
Status: Professional; Non-Profit
Type: Performing; Resident
Purpose: The challenge of a true regional theater is to create and enhance the development of all facets of theater arts within the community in which it lives. Actors Alley Repertory Theater is dedicated to meeting that challenge.
Management: Jeremiah Morris, Artistic Director; Robert Caine, Managing Director
Officers: Thomas H. Cole, President; Carol Rowen, Vice President; Sunny Caine, Secretary
Paid Staff: 6 **Volunteer Staff:** 75
Non-Paid Artists: 65
Utilizes: Special Technical Talent; Guest Directors
Budget: $100,000 - $500,000
Income Sources: Private Foundations/Grants/Endowments; Business/Corporate Donations; Box Office; Individual Donations
Season: 52 Weeks   **Annual Attendance:** 12,000
Affiliations: Los Angeles Theatre Alliance; California Theater Council
Performance Facilities: Actors Alley Repertory Theater

BARRIO PLAYERS - ACTORES DEL BARRIO
12443 Huston Street, North Hollywood, CA 91607
(818) 766-1066
Founded: 1977
Arts Area: Theatrical Group
Status: Semi-Professional; Non-Profit
Type: Performing
Purpose: To find and develop promising young actors and writers in the barrio
Management: Joseph (Pepe) Arciga, Playwright/Founder
Officers: Helen Lopez; Bernadette Cologne; Ruben Garfias
Volunteer Staff: 5
Non-Paid Artists: 10
Budget: $1,000 - $50,000
Income Sources: Box Office; Individual Donations
Annual Attendance: 1,500
Affiliations: Los Angeles Theater Center

GROUP REPERTORY THEATRE
10900 Burbank Boulevard, North Hollywood, CA 91601
(818) 769-7529
Founded: 1973
Arts Area: Theatrical Group
Status: Professional; Non-Profit
Type: Performing
Purpose: To stage five-six productions each year emphasizing new works by playwrights and young actors; to work with the Los Angeles Unified School District to produce theatrical presentations for those learning English as a second language
Management: Lonny Chapman, Artistic Director; Burt Rosario, Assistant Artistic Director
Officers: Larry Eisenberg, President; Geraldine Allen, Treasurer
Budget: $50,000 - $100,000
Income Sources: Business/Corporate Donations; Box Office; Individual Donations
Season: 52 Weeks   **Annual Attendance:** 4,000
Affiliations: Valley Arts Council
Performance Facilities: Group Repertory Theatre

SYNTHAXIS THEATRE COMPANY
6310 Whitsett Avenue, North Hollywood, CA 91607
(213) 877-4726
Founded: 1972
Arts Area: Theatrical Group
Status: Professional; Non-Profit
Type: Performing; Touring; Resident; Educational
Purpose: To present new works and lesser-known material by renowned authors with particular attention to works by women; to present children's shows and benefit performances

Management: Estelle Bush, Executive Director
Paid Staff: 2
Paid Artists: 15
Budget: $1,000 - $50,000
Income Sources: Private Foundations/Grants/Endowments; Business/Corporate Donations; Box Office; Government Grants; Individual Donations
Season: 52 Weeks
Annual Attendance: 10,000
Affiliations: Los Angeles Theatre Alliance; San Fernando Valley Arts Council

THEATRE EXCHANGE
11855 Hart Street, North Hollywood, CA 91605
(818) 765-9005
Founded: 1975
Arts Area: Theatrical Group
Status: Professional
Type: Performing; Educational
Purpose: To seek out and produce the best in American and European drama with a current emphasis on new American full-length plays
Management: Rob Zapple, Managing Director; Matthew Faison, Artistic Director; Alison Evans, Box Office Manager; Carol Monroe, Treasurer
Volunteer Staff: 50
Non-Paid Artists: 50
Utilizes: Guest Directors
Budget: $1,000 - $50,000
Income Sources: Business/Corporate Donations; Box Office; Individual Donations
Season: 52 Weeks
Affiliations: Los Angeles Theatre Alliance

Northridge

PERFORMING SERIES

MULTI-CULTURAL MUSIC AND ART FOUNDATION OF NORTHRIDGE
PO Box 101, Northridge, CA 91328
(818) 349-3400; (818) 349-3431
FAX: (818) 349-0716
Founded: 1990
Arts Area: Dance; Vocal Music; Instrumental Music; Festivals
Status: Non-Profit
Type: Performing; Educational
Purpose: To promote multicultural music, art and dance
Management: Grace Wan Kien Lee, Program Coordinator; Jonathan Green, Music
Paid Staff: 2 **Volunteer Staff:** 5
Utilizes: Special Technical Talent; Guest Artists
Budget: $1,000 - $50,000
Income Sources: Private Foundations/Grants/Endowments; Business/Corporate Donations; Box Office
Season: January; March - April; December
Annual Attendance: 1,000
Performance Facilities: McMafn Theatre

FACILITY

CALIFORNIA STATE UNIVERSITY-NORTHRIDGE - CAMPUS THEATRE
18111 Nordhoff Street, Northridge, CA 91330
(818) 885-3086
Type of Facility: Theatre Complex; Theatre House
Type of Stage: Proscenium
Stage Dimensions: 21'x40'x36'
Orchestra Pit
Seating Capacity: 400
Year Built: 1960
Contact for Rental: Jeffrey Levy;   (818) 885-3091
Resident Groups: Department of Theatre, California State University at Northridge

CALIFORNIA STATE UNIVERSITY-NORTHRIDGE - LITTLE THEATRE
18111 Nordhoff Street, Northridge, CA 91330
(818) 885-3086
>**Type of Facility:** Theatre Complex; Theatre House
>**Type of Stage:** Proscenium
>**Stage Dimensions:** 16'x20'x24'9"
>**Orchestra Pit**
>**Seating Capacity:** 210
>**Year Built:** 1960
>**Contact for Rental:** Jeffrey Levy;   (818) 885-3091
>**Resident Groups:** Department of Theatre, California State University at Northridge

CALIFORNIA STATE UNIVERSITY-NORTHRIDGE - STUDIO THEATRE
18111 Nordhoff Street, Northridge, CA 91330
(818) 885-3086
>**Type of Facility:** Theatre Complex; Studio Performance; Environmental; Theatre House; Arena; Multi-Purpose; Room
>**Type of Stage:** Flexible; Environmental; Arena
>**Stage Dimensions:** 46'5"x50'10"
>**Seating Capacity:** 90-120
>**Year Built:** 1960
>**Contact for Rental:** Jeffrey Levy;   (818) 885-3091
>**Resident Groups:** Department of Theatre, California State University at Northridge

Oakland

DANCE

DANCE BRIGADE
1515 Webster, Oakland, CA 94612
(510) 465-3686
>**Founded:** 1986
>**Arts Area:** Modern; Ethnic
>**Status:** Professional
>**Type:** Performing; Touring; Resident; Sponsoring
>**Purpose:** To present socially-relevant dance to the widest possible audience
>**Management:** Raquel Lopez, Managing Director; Nina Finchter, Krissy Keefer, Artistic Directors
>**Officers:** Jerry Atkin, President; Robert Hanamura; James Orgala
>**Paid Staff:** 3   **Volunteer Staff:** 5
>**Paid Artists:** 6
>**Utilizes:** Special Technical Talent; Guest Conductors; Guest Artists; Guest Choreographers
>**Budget:** $100,000 - $500,000
>**Income Sources:** Private Foundations/Grants/Endowments; Box Office; Government Grants; Individual Donations; Concessions; Performance Fees
>**Annual Attendance:** 15,000

DIMENSIONS DANCE THEATER
606 60th Street, Oakland, CA 94609-1420
(510) 428-2466
FAX: (510) 428-2910
>**Founded:** 1972
>**Arts Area:** Modern; Jazz; Ethnic
>**Status:** Professional; Non-Profit
>**Type:** Performing; Touring; Resident; Educational
>**Purpose:** To promote and perpetuate the knowledge and appreciation of African and African-derived dance
>**Management:** Mlinzi Majigiza, Executive Director; Jim Dees, Shirley Bucher, Agents - J. Dees Presents
>**Officers:** Deborah Stevenson, Chairperson; Paul Johnson, Secretary
>**Paid Staff:** 2
>**Paid Artists:** 17
>**Utilizes:** Special Technical Talent; Guest Artists; Guest Choreographers
>**Budget:** $100,000 - $500,000
>**Income Sources:** Private Foundations/Grants/Endowments; Business/Corporate Donations; Box Office; Government Grants; Individual Donations
>**Season:** October - August
>**Annual Attendance:** 2,200
>**Affiliations:** International Association of Blacks in Dance; Dance Bay Area
>**Performance Facilities:** Scottish Rite Theater Center

ELLEN WEBB DANCE FOUNDATION
2822-A Union Street, Oakland, CA 94608-4426
(510) 452-5919
Founded: 1987
Arts Area: Modern
Status: Professional; Non-Profit
Type: Performing; Touring
Purpose: To change the way people see the world; to tie together three seperate projects—the Ellen Webb Dance Company, the Talking Dance Porject and the Ellen Webb Dance Studio
Management: Ellen Webb, Artistic Director
Budget: $50,000 - $100,000
Income Sources: Private Foundations/Grants/Endowments; Business/Corporate Donations; Box Office; Government Grants; Individual Donations
Annual Attendance: 6,000

OAKLAND BALLET
2025 Broadway, Oakland, CA 94612
(510) 452-9288
Founded: 1965
Arts Area: Ballet
Status: Professional; Non-Profit
Type: Performing; Touring
Purpose: To reconstruct, preserve and present ballets from the Diaghilev era, ballets by American choreogrphers and those by contemporary choreographers
Management: Laird Rodet, General Manager; Todd Perreira, Marketing Director; Carol Tanenbaum, Development Director; Robin Hovis James, Operations Director
Officers: Ronn Guidi, Artistic Director; Ron Thiele, Associate Artistic Director
Paid Staff: 14   **Volunteer Staff:** 25
Paid Artists: 35
Utilizes: Guest Conductors; Guest Artists; Guest Choreographers
Budget: $1,000,000 - $5,000,000
Income Sources: Private Foundations/Grants/Endowments; Business/Corporate Donations; Box Office; Government Grants; Individual Donations; Rentals; Boutique
Season: September - March
Performance Facilities: Paramount Theatre

VOCAL MUSIC

KITKA
1201 Martin Luther King Jr. Way, Oakland, CA 94612
(510) 444-0323
Founded: 1979
Arts Area: Choral; Ethnic
Status: Professional
Type: Performing; Touring
Management: Russ Jennings, Administrative Director
Officers: Bon Brown, Artistic Director
Paid Staff: 2
Paid Artists: 11
Utilizes: Guest Artists
Budget: $100,000 - $500,000
Income Sources: Private Foundations/Grants/Endowments; Box Office; Government Grants; Individual Donations; Performing Fees
Season: 52 Weeks

OAKLAND YOUTH CHORUS
2619 Broadway, Oakland, CA 94612
(510) 832-6080
FAX: (510) 832-2211
Founded: 1974
Arts Area: Choral
Status: Professional; Non-Profit
Type: Performing; Touring; Sponsoring
Purpose: To provide multicultural youth ages 14-21 with professionally-directed training that advances the choral art form
Management: Diana Freeland, General Manager

Officers: Trente Morant, Artistic Director; Elizabeth Min, Conductor
Paid Staff: 6   **Volunteer Staff:** 15
Paid Artists: 26   **Non-Paid Artists:** 80
Utilizes: Guest Conductors; Guest Artists; Guest Directors
Budget: $100,000 - $500,000
Income Sources: Private Foundations/Grants/Endowments; Business/Corporate Donations; Box Office; Government Grants; Individual Donations
Season: September - June
Annual Attendance: 6,000
Performance Facilities: First Presbyterian Church; Calvin Simmons Theater; Paramount Theater

THEATRE

OAKLAND CIVIC THEATRE
1520 Lakeside Drive, Oakland, CA 94612
(510) 452-2909
FAX: (510) 238-2224
Founded: 1968
Arts Area: Community; Theatrical Group
Status: Non-Profit
Type: Performing; Touring; Resident
Purpose: To provide quality entertainment for, and by, the community
Management: Ted Smalley, Director
Paid Staff: 1   **Volunteer Staff:** 90
Utilizes: Special Technical Talent
Budget: $1,000 - $50,000
Income Sources: Private Foundations/Grants/Endowments; Business/Corporate Donations; Box Office; Government Grants; Individual Donations
Season: October - September
Annual Attendance: 4,000
Affiliations: AACT
Performance Facilities: Lakeside Park Garden

OAKLAND ENSEMBLE THEATRE
1428 Alice Street, Suite 289, Oakland, CA 94612
(510) 763-7774
Founded: 1974
Arts Area: Professional; Theatrical Group
Status: Professional; Non-Profit; Commercial
Type: Performing; Touring; Resident
Purpose: To provide insightful and engaging works of contemporary theatre shaped by the sensitivities and sensibilities of African-Americans
Management: Sharon Walton, Producing Director; Kim Euell, Managing Director
Utilizes: Special Technical Talent; Guest Artists; Guest Directors
Budget: $100,000 - $500,000
Income Sources: Box Office; Individual Donations
Season: 52 Weeks

OAKLAND SUMMER THEATRE
1520 Lakeside Drive, Oakland, CA 94612
(510) 658-2085
Founded: 1975
Arts Area: Community
Status: Non-Profit
Type: Performing
Purpose: To provide a performing-arts experience during the summer months for youth and adults
Management: Oakland Office of Parks and Recreation (Drama Section); Ted Smalley, Director
Officers: Rosemary Thomas, President; Theresa Denham, Secretary; James Thomas, Treasurer
Paid Staff: 12   **Volunteer Staff:** 20
Paid Artists: 4   **Non-Paid Artists:** 8
Utilizes: Special Technical Talent
Budget: $1,000 - $50,000
Income Sources: Private Foundations/Grants/Endowments; Box Office
Season: June - August
Annual Attendance: 20,000
Performance Facilities: Laney College Theatre

PERFORMING SERIES

OAKLAND JAZZ ALLIANCE
1330 Broadway, #1030, Oakland, CA 94612
(510) 839-2440
FAX: (510) 268-9065
> **Founded:** 1987
> **Arts Area:** Vocal Music; Instrumental Music; Festivals
> **Status:** Non-Profit
> **Type:** Performing; Educational
> **Purpose:** To preserve, develop and express jazz music; to develop serious young artists
> **Management:** Charla Montgomery, Executive Director
> **Officers:** Buddy Montgomery, President; David Montgomery, Vice President; Majors Harrison, Secretary; Dr. Alan Werblin, Treasurer
> **Paid Staff:** 1   **Volunteer Staff:** 2
> **Non-Paid Artists:** 1
> **Utilizes:** Guest Artists
> **Budget:** $1,000 - $50,000
> **Income Sources:** Private Foundations/Grants/Endowments; Business/Corporate Donations; Box Office; Government Grants; Individual Donations; Charter Memberships
> **Season:** 52 Weeks   **Annual Attendance:** 800

FACILITY

HENRY J. KAISER CONVENTION CENTER
10 Tenth Street, Oakland, CA 94607
(510) 839-7500
> **Type of Facility:** Civic Center
> **Year Built:** 1914   **Architect:** John J. Donovan & W.J. Matthews   **Cost:** $7,000,000
> **Year Remodeled:** 1984   **Cost:** $15,000,000
> **Contact for Rental:** Oakland Convention Center Management;   (415) 839-7500
> **Resident Groups:** Oakland Opera
> *The Convention Center contains the Arena and Calvin Simmons Theatre. See separate listings for additional information.*

HENRY J. KAISER CONVENTION CENTER - ARENA
10 Tenth Street, Oakland, CA 94607
(510) 839-7500
> **Type of Facility:** Auditorium; Arena; Multi-Purpose; Room
> **Type of Stage:** Flexible; Arena
> **Stage Dimensions:** portable stage of 124 sections, each 4'x8'
> **Seating Capacity:** 6,200
> **Year Built:** 1914
> **Year Remodeled:** 1984
> **Contact for Rental:** Oakland Convention Center Management;   (510) 839-7500

HENRY J. KAISER CONVENTION CENTER - CALVIN SIMMONS THEATRE
10 Tenth Street, Oakland, CA 94611
(510) 839-7500
FAX: (510) 839-0356
> **Type of Facility:** Theatre House
> **Type of Stage:** Proscenium
> **Stage Dimensions:** 65'x65'x40'   **Orchestra Pit**
> **Seating Capacity:** 1,924
> **Year Built:** 1914
> **Year Remodeled:** 1984
> **Contact for Rental:** Oakland Convention Center Management;   (510) 839-7500
> **Manager:** Charles J. Pattersen;   (510) 839-7509
> **Resident Groups:** Oakland Chamber Orchestra; Oakland Opera; Oakland Eastbay Symphony

LANEY COLLEGE THEATRE
900 Fallon Street, Oakland, CA 94607
(510) 464-3230
> **Type of Facility:** Theatre House
> **Type of Stage:** Proscenium
> **Stage Dimensions:** 43'Wx35'D with additional wing space   **Orchestra Pit**
> **Seating Capacity:** 325
> **Year Built:** 1975   **Architect:** Skidmore Owings & Merrill   **Cost:** $5,000,000

Contact for Rental: David Hartenstein;   (510) 464-3230
Resident Groups: Bay Area Dance Series

MILLS COLLEGE CONCERT HALL
5000 MacArthur Boulevard, Oakland, CA 94613
(510) 430-2171
Type of Facility: Concert Hall
Type of Stage: Proscenium
Orchestra Pit
Seating Capacity: 540
Year Built: 1928   **Architect:** Walter H. Ratcliff
Contact for Rental: Karen Maggio
Resident Groups: Mills College Music Department; Mills College Center for Contemporary Music;
Mills Chamber Ensemble

PARAMOUNT THEATRE
2025 Broadway, Oakland, CA 94612
(510) 893-2300
Type of Facility: Theatre House
Facility Originally: Movie House
Type of Stage: Proscenium
Stage Dimensions: 66'Wx35'D (angles); 24'D SR; 37'D SL; 66'Wx30'H proscenium opening
Orchestra Pit
Seating Capacity: 2,998
Year Built: 1931   **Architect:** Timothy Pflueger   **Cost:** $3,000,000
Year Remodeled: 1973   **Cost:** $1,000,000
Acoustical Consultant: Jaffe Acoustics
Contact for Rental: Peter J. Botto;   (510) 893-2300
Resident Groups: Oakland Ballet; Paramount Organ Pops Series; Paramount Movie Classics

Ojai

PERFORMING SERIES

OJAI FESTIVALS
201 South Signal Street, Ojai, CA 93023
(805) 646-2094
FAX: (805) 646-6037
Founded: 1947
Arts Area: Vocal Music; Instrumental Music
Status: Professional; Non-Profit
Type: Educational; Sponsoring
Purpose: To emphasize contemporary repertoire
Management: Lawrence Morton, Artistic Director Emeritus; Ara Guzelimian, Artistic Director
Officers: Joan Kemper, President; Dee Palmer, First Vice President; Rick Gould, Second Vice President; Gwen Erickson, Secretary; Al Urban, Treasurer
Paid Staff: 3   **Volunteer Staff:** 4
Paid Artists: 140
Utilizes: Guest Conductors; Guest Artists
Budget: $100,000 - $500,000
Income Sources: Private Foundations/Grants/Endowments; Business/Corporate Donations; Box Office; Government Grants; Individual Donations
Season: May - June   **Annual Attendance:** 5,000
Affiliations: ASOL; California Confederation of the Arts
Performance Facilities: Ojai Festival Bowl

FACILITY

OJAI FESTIVAL BOWL
Libbey Park, Ojai, CA 93023
(805) 646-2094
Type of Facility: Amphitheater
Type of Stage: Proscenium
Seating Capacity: 1,000
Year Built: 1956

Orinda

INSTRUMENTAL MUSIC

EARPLAY
32 Scenic Drive, Orinda, CA 94563
(510) 253-0357
Founded: 1985
Arts Area: Chamber
Status: Professional; Non-Profit
Type: Performing
Purpose: To provide excellent performances of new works by American composers
Officers: Robert Festinger, President; Rachel Winheld, Executive Director
Paid Staff: 1   **Volunteer Staff:** 5
Paid Artists: 8
Utilizes: Guest Conductors; Guest Artists
Budget: $1,000 - $50,000
Income Sources: Private Foundations/Grants/Endowments; Box Office; Government Grants; Individual Donations
Season: October - May   **Annual Attendance:** 1,000
Performance Facilities: Cowell Theater; Fort Mason Center for the Arts

Oroville

FACILITY

OROVILLE STATE THEATER
1489 Myers Street, Oroville, CA 95965
(916) 538-2470
FAX: (916) 538-2426
Type of Facility: Performance Center
Facility Originally: Vaudeville; Movie House
Type of Stage: Proscenium
Stage Dimensions: 39'10"Wx24'D   **Orchestra Pit**
Seating Capacity: 612
Year Built: 1927   **Architect:** Timothy L. Pflueger
Year Remodeled: 1986   **Cost:** $680,000
Acoustical Consultant: Vorin Dornan
Contact for Rental: Amelia Jennings;   (916) 538-2470
Resident Groups: Performings Arts & Family Series; Lecture Series; Travelogue Series; Community Concert Series; Annual Musical

Oxnard

FACILITY

OXNARD CIVIC AUDITORIUM
800 Hobson Way, Oxnard, CA 93030
(805) 486-2424
Type of Facility: Concert Hall; Auditorium; Theatre House; Multi-Purpose
Type of Stage: Proscenium
Stage Dimensions: 52'Wx45'D; 52'Wx25'H proscenium opening   **Orchestra Pit**
Seating Capacity: 1,604
Year Built: 1968   **Architect:** Adrian Wilson & Associates   **Cost:** $2,600,000
Acoustical Consultant: Hughes Sound
Contact for Rental: Jack C. Lavin;   (805) 486-2424
Resident Groups: Ventura County Symphony; Oxnard Community Concert Association; Cabrillo Music Theater

Pacific Palisades

INSTRUMENTAL MUSIC

PALISADES SYMPHONY ORCHESTRA
1081 Palisair Place, Pacific Palisades, CA 90272
(310) 454-8040
Founded: 1966
Arts Area: Symphony; Orchestra

Status: Non-Professional; Non-Profit
Type: Performing; Resident; Educational; Sponsoring
Purpose: To bring high-quality orchestra performances to the community without charge, including major choral works; to give singers and orchestra musicians performance experience; to encourage young musicians at annual young artist concert
Management: Eva Holberg, Manager; Joel Lish, Conductor/Music Director; Sigrid Hofer, Fund Chairman
Officers: Eva Holberg, President; Sigrid Hofer, First Vice President; Francis Murray, Secretary; Melissa Leicester, Treasurer
Utilizes: Guest Artists
Budget: $1,000 - $50,000
Income Sources: Private Foundations/Grants/Endowments; Business/Corporate Donations; Individual Donations
Season: September - June   **Annual Attendance:** 3,000
Affiliations: ASOL; Association of California Symphony Orchestras

Palm Desert

VOCAL MUSIC

WEST COAST OPERA THEATRE
PO Box 166, Palm Desert, CA 92661
(619) 779-0061
Founded: 1962
Arts Area: Grand Opera; Light Opera; Operetta; Musical Theatre
Status: Professional; Non-Profit
Type: Performing; Educational
Purpose: To keep opera and its allied educational opportunities open to young audiences; to provide a training ground for young, aspiring artists
Management: Josephine Lombardo, General Manager/Artistic Director
Officers: Mary Stewart, President; Anita Slater, Vice President; Ron Powers, Secretary
Volunteer Staff: 10
Paid Artists: 150
Utilizes: Special Technical Talent; Guest Conductors; Guest Artists; Guest Directors
Budget: $50,000 - $100,000
Income Sources: Box Office; Individual Donations; Fundraising
Season: November - May   **Annual Attendance:** 3,000
Affiliations: COS
Performance Facilities: Annenberg Theater; McAllum Theatre; Bob Hope Cultural Center

FACILITY

BOB HOPE CULTURAL CENTER - MCALLUM THEATRE
73000 Fred Waring Drive, Palm Desert, CA 92260
(619) 346-6505
FAX: (619) 341-9508
Type of Facility: Theatre House
Type of Stage: Modified Apron Proscenium
Stage Dimensions: 50'Wx40'D with 6'D apron; 50'Wx30'H proscenium   **Orchestra Pit**
Seating Capacity: 1,127
Year Built: 1988   **Architect:** Anthony and Langford   **Cost:** $20,000,000
Acoustical Consultant: Smith Fause Associates
Contact for Rental: Charles Giora, Director of Operations;   (619) 346-6505
Manager: Nancy Dolensek, Executive Director;   (619) 346-6505
Resident Groups: Bob Hope Cultural Center - McAllum Theatre

Palm Springs

VOCAL MUSIC

PALM SPRINGS OPERA GUILD OF THE DESERT
PO Box 1378, Palm Springs, CA 92263
(619) 325-6107
Founded: 1968
Arts Area: Grand Opera; Light Opera
Status: Professional; Non-Profit
Type: Performing; Educational; Sponsoring
Purpose: To present high-quality opera and musical theatre productions to the Palm Springs area
Officers: Robert James, President; Tony Rose, Opera Vice President; Hendrik de Boer, Executive Vice President

Volunteer Staff: 635
Utilizes: Special Technical Talent
Budget: $50,000 - $100,000
Income Sources: Box Office; Individual Donations
Season: September - April **Annual Attendance:** 2,400
Affiliations: COS
Performance Facilities: McAllum Theatre

FACILITY

PALM SPRINGS DESERT MUSEUM/ANNENBERG THEATER
101 Museum Drive, Palm Springs, CA 92262
(619) 325-7186
FAX: (619) 327-5069
Founded: 1938
Type of Facility: Concert Hall; Studio Performance; Performance Center; Theatre House; Multi-Purpose; Movie House
Type of Stage: Proscenium
Stage Dimensions: 50'4"Wx31'Dx18'H proscenium opening
Seating Capacity: 450
Year Built: 1976 **Architect:** E. Stewart Williams **Cost:** $9,000,000
Stage Renovated: 1991 **Architect:** Theatre Products International **Cost:** $460,000
Acoustical Consultant: Theatre Products International
Contact for Rental: Dr. Dale Hearth; (619) 325-7186

Palmdale

VOCAL MUSIC

DESERT OPERA THEATRE
PO Box 900434, Palmdale, CA 93590-0434
(805) 947-9442
Founded: 1971
Arts Area: Grand Opera; Lyric Opera; Light Opera; Operetta; Musical Theatre
Status: Semi-Professional; Non-Profit
Type: Performing; Resident; Educational
Purpose: To bring musical theatre to the Antelope Valley showcasing local talent
Management: David Milligan, General/Artistic Director; Dorothy Lewellin, Business Manager
Paid Staff: 9 **Volunteer Staff:** 50
Paid Artists: 25 **Non-Paid Artists:** 20
Utilizes: Special Technical Talent; Guest Artists; Guest Directors
Budget: $1,000 - $50,000
Income Sources: Private Foundations/Grants/Endowments; Business/Corporate Donations; Box Office; Government Grants; Individual Donations
Season: 52 Weeks **Annual Attendance:** 4,000
Affiliations: California Confederation of the Arts; Antelope Valley Arts Council
Performance Facilities: Palmdale Cultural Center

Palo Alto

INSTRUMENTAL MUSIC

CALIFORNIA YOUTH SYMPHONY
PO Box 1441, Palo Alto, CA 94302
(415) 325-6666
Founded: 1952
Arts Area: Symphony
Status: Non-Professional; Non-Profit
Type: Performing; Educational
Purpose: To provide an opportunity for young musicians to perform in a high quality symphony orchestra
Management: James Hogan, Executive Director; Ruby Seto, Executive Secretary; Leo Eylar, Music Director
Officers: Greg Wheelwright, President
Paid Staff: 4 **Volunteer Staff:** 50
Paid Artists: 7 **Non-Paid Artists:** 300
Budget: $100,000 - $500,000
Income Sources: Private Foundations/Grants/Endowments; Business/Corporate Donations; Box Office; Government Grants; Individual Donations
Season: November - June **Annual Attendance:** 6,000

Affiliations: ASOL (Youth Orchestra Division); Association of California Symphony Orchestras
Performance Facilities: Flint Center for the Performing Arts; San Mateo Performing Arts Center

VOCAL MUSIC

WEST BAY OPERA
PO Box 1714, Palo Alto, CA 94302
(415) 321-3471
Founded: 1955
Arts Area: Grand Opera; Lyric Opera; Light Opera
Status: Semi-Professional; Non-Profit
Type: Performing; Educational
Purpose: To provide high quality opera performances and opportunities for community participation; to provide training for aspiring opera performers
Management: Maria Holt, General Director
Officers: Ben DeBolt, Business Manager; Matthew Gilmartin, Development Officer; Michele Sullivan, Production Manager
Paid Staff: 4   **Volunteer Staff:** 1
Paid Artists: 12   **Non-Paid Artists:** 40
Utilizes: Guest Conductors; Guest Artists; Guest Directors
Budget: $100,000 - $500,000
Income Sources: Private Foundations/Grants/Endowments; Business/Corporate Donations; Box Office; Government Grants; Individual Donations
Season: October - May   **Annual Attendance:** 10,000
Performance Facilities: Lucie Stern Theatre

THEATRE

PALO ALTO CHILDREN'S THEATRE
1305 Middlefield Road, Palo Alto, CA 94301
(415) 329-2216
Founded: 1932
Arts Area: Musical; Theatrical Group
Status: Non-Professional; Non-Profit
Type: Performing; Educational
Management: Patricia Briggs, Director; Michael Litfin, Assistant Director; Andy Hayes, Technical Director/Designer; Alison Williams, Costume Supervisor; Sandy Rankin, Program Assistant
Paid Staff: 20   **Volunteer Staff:** 50
Utilizes: Special Technical Talent; Guest Artists; Guest Directors; Instructors
Budget: $100,000 - $500,000
Income Sources: Private Foundations/Grants/Endowments; Business/Corporate Donations; Government Grants; Individual Donations; Part of City Department
Season: 52 Weeks   **Annual Attendance:** 50,000
Performance Facilities: Palo Alto Children's Theatre

THEATREWORKS
1305 Middlefield Road, Palo Alto, CA 94301
(415) 323-8311
FAX: (415) 323-3311
Founded: 1970
Arts Area: Professional; Musical; Theatrical Group
Status: Semi-Professional; Non-Profit
Type: Performing
Management: Robert Kelley, Artistic Director; Randy Adams, Managing Director
Paid Staff: 9   **Volunteer Staff:** 15
Paid Artists: 350
Utilizes: Special Technical Talent; Guest Artists; Guest Directors
Budget: $1,000,000 - $5,000,000
Income Sources: Private Foundations/Grants/Endowments; Business/Corporate Donations; Box Office; Government Grants; Individual Donations
Season: June - May
Annual Attendance: 58,000
Affiliations: TCG
Performance Facilities: The Lucy Stern Theatre; The Mountain View Center for the Performing Arts; Cubberley Stage II

FACILITY

GUNN HIGH SCHOOL - SPANGENBERG THEATRE
780 Arastradero, Palo Alto, CA 94306
(415) 354-8220
> **Type of Facility:** Theatre House
> **Type of Stage:** Proscenium
> **Stage Dimensions:** 18'x44'x35'   **Orchestra Pit**
> **Seating Capacity:** 1,000
> **Contact for Rental:** Jorgen Wedseltoft, Manager;   (415) 354-8220
> **Manager:** Jorgen Wedseltoft
> **Resident Groups:** Palo Alto Chamber Orchestra; Peninsula Youth Theatre; Korean-American Musical Society Association

Paradise

PERFORMING SERIES

PARADISE AREA ARTS COUNCIL
6686 Brook Way, Paradise, CA 95969
(916) 877-8360
> **Founded:** 1980
> **Arts Area:** Dance; Vocal Music; Theater; Festivals
> **Status:** Semi-Professional; Non-Profit
> **Type:** Performing; Educational; Sponsoring
> **Purpose:** To support the arts in the Paradise area; to be a liaison to local town government
> **Officers:** Thomas E. Wilson, President; Wayne Angel, Vice President; Joan Anderson Hayes, Secretary; Trudi Angel, Treasurer
> **Paid Staff:** 1
> **Utilizes:** Guest Artists
> **Budget:** $1,000 - $50,000
> **Income Sources:** Business/Corporate Donations; Individual Donations
> **Season:** June
> **Affiliations:** National Music Council

Pasadena

DANCE

PASADENA CIVIC BALLET
25 South Sierra Madre Boulevard, Pasadena, CA 91107
(818) 792-0873
> **Founded:** 1980
> **Arts Area:** Modern; Mime; Ballet; Jazz; Ethnic
> **Status:** Semi-Professional; Non-Profit
> **Type:** Performing; Educational
> **Purpose:** To provide a semi-professional ballet experience, assist those who dance as an avocation, give young dancers performance opportunities and provide them with a chance to study abroad to enhance dance in our community
> **Management:** Elly-Charlotte Van Dijk, Artistic Director; Diane DeFranco, Associate Artistic Director
> **Officers:** Holly Davis, President; Dr. John Houseman, Treasurer; Kathy Moscarello, Secretary
> **Volunteer Staff:** 15
> **Paid Artists:** 4   **Non-Paid Artists:** 46
> **Utilizes:** Guest Artists; Guest Choreographers
> **Budget:** $1,000 - $50,000
> **Income Sources:** Business/Corporate Donations; Box Office; Individual Donations
> **Season:** September - June   **Annual Attendance:** 6,000
> **Affiliations:** Pasadena Arts Council
> **Performance Facilities:** San Gabriel Civic Auditorium

TERRI LEWIS DANCE ENSEMBLE
787 Merrett Drive, Pasadena, CA 91104
(818) 798-9853
> **Founded:** 1986
> **Arts Area:** Ballet
> **Status:** Professional; Semi-Professional; Non-Profit
> **Type:** Performing; Touring; Educational
> **Purpose:** To perform contemporary chamber ballet in conjunction with residencies in smaller communities
> **Management:** Terri Lewis, Artistic Director; Aletheia Zaremba, Managing Director

Paid Staff: 2
Paid Artists: 10
Utilizes: Guest Choreographers
Budget: $1,000 - $50,000
Income Sources: Business/Corporate Donations; Box Office; Government Grants; Individual Donations
Season: September - June

INSTRUMENTAL MUSIC

COLEMAN CHAMBER MUSIC ASSOCIATION
202 South Lake Avenue, Suite 201, Pasadena, CA 91101
(818) 793-4191
Founded: 1904
Arts Area: Chamber
Status: Non-Profit
Type: Sponsoring
Purpose: To present the finest international chamber ensembles, both established and emerging
Management: Kathy R. Freeland, Manager
Officers: Dr. Robert Wark, President; Robert Zurbach, First Vice President; Carol Bressler, Second Vice President; Mrs. David Grether, Secretary; Chistopher Harcourt, Treasurer
Paid Staff: 2   **Volunteer Staff:** 50
Utilizes: Guest Artists
Budget: $100,000 - $500,000
Income Sources: Private Foundations/Grants/Endowments; Business/Corporate Donations; Box Office; Government Grants; Individual Donations
Season: October - May   **Annual Attendance:** 4,500
Affiliations: APAP; WAAA; CMA
Performance Facilities: Beckman Auditorium, California Institute of Technology

PASADENA SYMPHONY
117 East Colorado Boulevard, #375, Pasadena, CA 91105
(818) 793-7172
FAX: (818) 793-7180
Founded: 1928
Arts Area: Symphony; Orchestra
Status: Professional
Type: Performing
Purpose: To provide the highest quality symphonic music and educational programs to the people of Pasadena and the greater Los Angeles area
Management: Wayne Shilkret, Executive Director; Gloria Smith, Director of Operations
Officers: Stephen J.M. Morris, President; Robert Zurbach, Executive Vice President; Marvin Schultz, Treasurer; Mary Kay Driscoll, Recording Secretary
Paid Staff: 4
Paid Artists: 100
Utilizes: Guest Artists
Budget: $500,000 - $1,000,000
Income Sources: Private Foundations/Grants/Endowments; Business/Corporate Donations; Box Office; Government Grants; Individual Donations
Season: October - May
Annual Attendance: 2,300
Performance Facilities: Pasadena Civic Auditorium

PERFORMING SERIES

OFFICE OF PUBLIC EVENTS
California Institute of Technology, 1201 East California Boulevard, Pasadena, CA 91125
(818) 356-3834
Founded: 1963
Arts Area: Dance; Instrumental Music; Theater
Status: Non-Profit
Type: Educational; Sponsoring
Purpose: To serve as a performing arts presentation center for Cal. Tech and the surrounding community
Management: Jerry Willis, Public Events Manager
Officers: Dr. Samuel Epstein, Chairman, COIP
Paid Staff: 15
Utilizes: Guest Artists
Budget: $100,000 - $500,000
Income Sources: Box Office
Season: October - May   **Annual Attendance:** 70,000

Affiliations: APAP; IAAM; WAAA; California Presenters
Performance Facilities: Beckman Auditorium; Ramo Auditorium

FACILITY

CALIFORNIA INSTITUTE OF TECHNOLOGY - BECKMAN AUDITORIUM
Office of Public Events, 1201 East California Boulevard, Pasadena, CA 91125
(818) 356-3834
Type of Facility: Auditorium
Type of Stage: Thrust
Stage Dimensions: 43'Wx17'H, depth varies from 12'6" to 21'6"
Seating Capacity: 1,165
Year Built: 1964 **Architect:** Edward Durell Stone **Cost:** $1,300,000
Year Remodeled: 1966 **Cost:** $500,000
Acoustical Consultant: Vern Knudsen
Manager: Jerry Willis; (818) 356-4638
Resident Groups: Coleman Chamber Music Association

CALIFORNIA INSTITUTE OF TECHNOLOGY - RAMO AUDITORIUM
Office of Public Events, Cal Tech, 332-92, Pasadena, CA 91125
(818) 356-3834
FAX: (818) 577-0130
Type of Facility: Concert Hall
Type of Stage: Proscenium
Stage Dimensions: 32'Wx24'D; 32'Wx13'H proscenium opening
Seating Capacity: 423
Year Built: 1971 **Architect:** Robert E. Alexander **Cost:** $600,000
Acoustical Consultant: Paul S. Veneklasen & Associates
Resident Groups: Conejo Symphony Association

PASADENA CIVIC AUDITORIUM
300 East Green Street, Pasadena, CA 91101
(818) 793-2122
FAX: (818) 793-8014
Founded: 1931
Type of Facility: Concert Hall; Auditorium; Theatre House; Opera House; Multi-Purpose
Type of Stage: Proscenium
Stage Dimensions: 110'Wx42'D; 47'Wx32'H proscenium opening **Orchestra Pit**
Seating Capacity: 2,965; 98 removable pit seats
Year Built: 1931 **Architect:** Bergstrom, Bennett, Haskell **Cost:** $1,350,000
Year Remodeled: 1979 **Cost:** $500,000
Contact for Rental: Auditorium Manager; (818) 793-2122
Resident Groups: Pasadena Symphony

PASADENA PLAYHOUSE - BALCONY THEATRE
39 South El Molino Avenue, Pasadena, CA 91101
(818) 792-8672
FAX: (818) 792-7343
Type of Facility: Theatre House
Type of Stage: Thrust
Seating Capacity: 99
Year Built: 1937
Contact for Rental: Lars Hansen, Executive Director; (818) 792-8672
Resident Groups: Pasadena Playhouse

PASADENA PLAYHOUSE - MAINSTAGE THEATRE
39 South El Molino Avenue, Pasadena, CA 91101
(818) 792-8672
FAX: (818) 792-7343
Type of Facility: Theatre House
Type of Stage: Proscenium
Stage Dimensions: 32'6"x43' **Orchestra Pit**
Seating Capacity: 699
Year Built: 1924
Year Remodeled: 1984 **Architect:** Richard McCann
Contact for Rental: Lars Hansen, Executive Director; (818) 792-8672
Resident Groups: Pasadena Playhouse

Pomona
FACILITY

CALIFORNIA POLYTECHNIC UNIVERSITY-POMONA - THEATRE
3801 West Temple Avenue, Pomona, CA 91768
(909) 869-7659
> **Type of Facility:** Auditorium; Theatre House
> **Type of Stage:** Proscenium
> **Stage Dimensions:** 50'x96'x38'   **Orchestra Pit**
> **Seating Capacity:** 500
> **Year Built:** 1964   **Cost:** $1,900,000
> **Contact for Rental:** Dennis A. Logan;   (909) 598-4547

Rancho Santa Fe
INSTRUMENTAL MUSIC

SAN DIEGO CHAMBER ORCHESTRA
PO Box 3333, Rancho Santa Fe, CA 92067
(619) 753-6402
FAX: (619) 753-2089
> **Founded:** 1984
> **Arts Area:** Symphony; Orchestra; Chamber
> **Status:** Professional; Non-Profit
> **Type:** Performing
> **Purpose:** To present chamber orchestra concerts of the highest artistic quality with fine soloists throughout San Diego County
> **Management:** Donald Barra, Music Director; Tamra Saylor, General Manager
> **Officers:** Charles Dierenfield, President; D. Frederick Shefte, Vice President; Frances Pope, Secretary; O. Rea Mowery, Treasurer
> **Paid Staff:** 4
> **Paid Artists:** 36
> **Utilizes:** Guest Conductors; Guest Artists
> **Budget:** $100,000 - $500,000
> **Income Sources:** Private Foundations/Grants/Endowments; Business/Corporate Donations; Box Office; Government Grants; Individual Donations
> **Season:** October - May   **Annual Attendance:** 56,000
> **Affiliations:** ASOL; Association of California Symphony Orchestras
> **Performance Facilities:** Sherwood Hall; Fairbanks Ranch

Redding
INSTRUMENTAL MUSIC

SHASTA SYMPHONY
1065 North Old Oregon Trail, Redding, CA 96099
(916) 241-3523
> **Founded:** 1950
> **Arts Area:** Symphony; Orchestra; Ensemble
> **Status:** Non-Professional; Non-Profit
> **Type:** Performing; Touring; Resident; Educational
> **Purpose:** Shasta Symphony is a college and community orchestra. It serves an educational and entertainment function for the college and community.
> **Management:** Bob Davis, Fine Arts Chairman
> **Officers:** Harry Blaesing, Orchestra President; Pat Chipps, Orchestra Vice President; Mary Farruggia, Orchestra League President
> **Paid Staff:** 2   **Volunteer Staff:** 30
> **Paid Artists:** 2   **Non-Paid Artists:** 65
> **Utilizes:** Guest Conductors; Guest Artists; Guest Directors
> **Budget:** $1,000 - $50,000
> **Income Sources:** Business/Corporate Donations; Box Office; Individual Donations
> **Season:** September - June   **Annual Attendance:** 5,000
> **Affiliations:** Shasta College
> **Performance Facilities:** Shasta College Fine Arts Theatre

FACILITY

REDDING CIVIC AUDITORIUM - TRADE AND CONVENTION CENTER
700 Auditorium Drive, Redding, CA 96099
(916) 225-4130
FAX: (916) 225-4354
> **Founded:** 1970
> **Type of Facility:** Auditorium; Multi-Purpose
> **Type of Stage:** Proscenium
> **Stage Dimensions:** 85'x40'
> **Seating Capacity:** 2,082
> **Year Built:** 1970   **Architect:** Van Bourg/Nakamoura, Smart and Claybough   **Cost:** $3,200,000
> **Contact for Rental:** Pat Foruria;   (916) 225-4130
> **Manager:** John Gorman;   (916) 225-4100
> **Resident Groups:** Shasta Symphony; Community Concerts; Travel Films

SHASTA COLLEGE - FINE ARTS THEATRE
PO Box 6006, Redding, CA 96001
(916) 225-4610
> **Type of Facility:** Theatre Complex; Concert Hall; Theatre House; Amphitheater
> **Type of Stage:** Thrust; Proscenium
> **Stage Dimensions:** 47'Wx50'D   **Orchestra Pit**
> **Seating Capacity:** 471
> **Year Built:** 1968   **Architect:** Woodward/Nicols
> **Contact for Rental:** Dan Howard, Fine Arts Events Coordinator;   (916) 225-4610
> **Manager:** Dan Howard;   (916) 225-4610
> **Resident Groups:** Shasta College Theatre Arts Department; Shasta College Music Department

Redlands

PERFORMING SERIES

REDLANDS BOWL SUMMER MUSIC FESTIVAL
PO Box 466, Redlands, CA 92373
(909) 793-7316
> **Founded:** 1923
> **Arts Area:** Dance; Vocal Music; Instrumental Music; Lyric Opera; Grand Opera
> **Status:** Professional; Non-Profit
> **Type:** Performing; Sponsoring
> **Purpose:** Provide admission-free symphonies, ballets, operas, musicals and recitals
> **Officers:** Conant K. Halsey, President; Florence Beeler, Vice President/Program Director; David B. Raff, Chief Financial Officer; Janet M. Weder, Corporate Secretary
> **Paid Staff:** 4   **Volunteer Staff:** 25
> **Budget:** $100,000 - $500,000
> **Income Sources:** Private Foundations/Grants/Endowments; Business/Corporate Donations; Individual Donations
> **Season:** July - August   **Annual Attendance:** 80,000
> **Performance Facilities:** Open-air Amphitheatre

REDLANDS SYMPHONY ASSOCIATION
1200 East Colton, PO Box 3080, Redlands, CA 92373-0999
(909) 793-2121
FAX: (909) 793-2029
> **Founded:** 1958
> **Arts Area:** Vocal Music; Instrumental Music
> **Status:** Professional; Non-Profit
> **Type:** Performing; Educational
> **Purpose:** To create and maintain a high-quality symphony orchestra with an annual concert series; to coordinate outreach programs
> **Management:** James Keays, Orchestra Manager; Bruce Anderson, Personnel Contractor; Jon Robertson, Conductor/Music Director; Viola Slade, Office Manager
> **Officers:** Barbara Wormser, President; Una Hellyer, Vice President; Helen Nies, Secretary; Phillip Doolittle, Treasurer; Carol Robinson, President Emeritus; Sam Dickey, Controller
> **Paid Staff:** 4   **Volunteer Staff:** 20
> **Paid Artists:** 66   **Non-Paid Artists:** 15
> **Utilizes:** Guest Conductors; Guest Artists
> **Budget:** $100,000 - $500,000
> **Income Sources:** Private Foundations/Grants/Endowments; Business/Corporate Donations; Box Office; Government Grants; Individual Donations

Season: September - May
Annual Attendance: 8,500
Affiliations: ASOL; Association of California Symphony Orchestras
Performance Facilities: Memorial Chapel, University of Redlands

FACILITY

REDLANDS COMMUNITY MUSIC ASSOCIATION, INC.
PO Box 466, 25 Grant Street, Redlands, CA 92373
(909) 793-7316
Founded: 1923
Type of Facility: Amphitheater
Facility Originally: Park
Type of Stage: Proscenium   **Seating Capacity:** 3,750
Year Built: 1930   **Architect:** Herbert J. Powell
Contact for Rental: City of Redlands;   (714) 798-7528
Resident Groups: Redlands Bowl Summer Music Festival

Redondo Beach

INSTRUMENTAL MUSIC

BEACH CITIES SYMPHONY
PO Box 248, Redondo Beach, CA 90277
(310) 541-2877
Founded: 1951
Arts Area: Symphony
Status: Semi-Professional; Non-Profit
Type: Performing
Purpose: To present an annual season of great masterworks for orchestra in the South Bay at no charge to the audience
Management: Margaret Kendziorek, Orchestra Manager; Theodora Hilley, Librarian
Officers: Margaret M. McWilliams, President; Hans Wohlwill, Chairman of the Board
Paid Staff: 2   **Volunteer Staff:** 12
Paid Artists: 3
Utilizes: Guest Artists
Budget: $1,000 - $50,000
Income Sources: Business/Corporate Donations; Government Grants; Individual Donations
Season: Fall - Spring
Annual Attendance: 6,000
Affiliations: ASOL; Symphony League of Los Angeles County
Performance Facilities: Marsee Auditorium, El Camino College

Redway

PERFORMING SERIES

MATEEL COMMUNITY CENTER, INC.
PO Box 1910, Redway, CA 95489
(707) 923-3368
FAX: (707) 923-4660
Founded: 1979
Arts Area: Dance; Vocal Music; Instrumental Music; Theater; Festivals
Status: Non-Profit
Type: Sponsoring
Purpose: To create a facility for the cultural and educational enhancement of the South Humboldt and
North Mendocino area
Management: Carol Bruno, Events Coordinator; Doug Green, Public Relations; Paul Bassis, Hall Manager; Susan
Manttila, Bookkeeper; Charity Green, Office Manager
Officers: Gary Chapman, President; Doug Green, Vice President; Jane Gund, Secretary; Jimmy Dangler, Treasurer
Paid Staff: 3
Utilizes: Guest Artists
Budget: $500,000 - $1,000,000
Income Sources: Private Foundations/Grants/Endowments; Business/Corporate Donations; Box Office; Government
Grants; Individual Donations
Season: 52 Weeks
Annual Attendance: 20,000

Richmond

FACILITY

RICHMOND MEMORIAL CONVENTION CENTER
PO Box 4046, Richmond, CA 94804
(510) 620-6789
FAX: (510) 620-6583
   Type of Facility: Theatre Complex; Concert Hall; Auditorium; Studio Performance; Performance Center; Theatre House; Opera House; Civic Center; Arena; Multi-Purpose
   Facility Originally: Meeting Hall
   Type of Stage: Proscenium; Arena
   Stage Dimensions: 140'Wx60'Dx40'H   **Orchestra Pit**
   Seating Capacity: 3,756
   Year Built: 1951   **Architect:** Milton Pflueger   **Cost:** $1,250,000
   Contact for Rental: Bill Allums, Manager;   (510) 620-6789
   Resident Groups: Community Concerts; Power Pak Productions; Farr Entertainment; Nyarit Promociones; WRA Productions
   Facilities for a host of entertainment programs

Riverside

DANCE

RIVERSIDE BALLET THEATRE
3840 Lemon Street, Riverside, CA 92501
(909) 787-7850
FAX: (909) 683-1284
   Founded: 1968
   Arts Area: Modern; Ballet
   Status: Professional; Non-Profit
   Type: Performing; Educational; Sponsoring
   Purpose: To give the young dancers the opportunity to perform in a professional atmosphere and provide high-calibre productions to the community
   Management: Moira Kamgar, Chief Officer; Fred Arens, Office Manager
   Officers: Glend Carhart-Hensly, Director
   Volunteer Staff: 10
   Paid Artists: 5   **Non-Paid Artists:** 75
   Utilizes: Special Technical Talent; Guest Artists
   Budget: $50,000 - $100,000
   Income Sources: Private Foundations/Grants/Endowments; Business/Corporate Donations; Box Office; Government Grants; Individual Donations
   Season: September - May   **Annual Attendance:** 8,000
   Performance Facilities: Landis Auditorium

INSTRUMENTAL MUSIC

RIVERSIDE COUNTY PHILHARMONIC
PO Box 1601, Riverside, CA 92502
(909) 787-0251
   Founded: 1958
   Arts Area: Symphony; Orchestra
   Status: Professional; Non-Profit
   Type: Performing
   Purpose: To provide the Inland area with symphonic music to the general public and for education
   Management: Helen Norton, General Manager; Patrick Flynn, Musical Director/Conductor
   Paid Staff: 1   **Volunteer Staff:** 10
   Paid Artists: 55
   Budget: $1,000,000 - $5,000,000
   Income Sources: Private Foundations/Grants/Endowments; Business/Corporate Donations; Box Office; Government Grants; Individual Donations
   Season: November - May   **Annual Attendance:** 5,000

Affiliations: ASOL
Performance Facilities: Municipal Auditorium

PERFORMING SERIES

PERFORMING ARTS PRESENTATIONS
University of California, Riverside, CA 92521
(909) 787-4629
FAX: (909) 787-2221
Founded: 1973
Arts Area: Dance; Vocal Music; Instrumental Music; Theater
Status: Professional; Non-Profit
Type: Sponsoring
Purpose: To be a cultural and educational resource to the campus and community
Management: Marnie Duke, Manager
Paid Staff: 3   **Volunteer Staff:** 1
Utilizes: Guest Artists
Budget: $100,000 - $500,000
Income Sources: Private Foundations/Grants/Endowments; Business/Corporate Donations; Box Office; Government
Grants; Individual Donations; University Resources
Season: October - May
Annual Attendance: 10,000
Affiliations: WAAA; APAP; California Presenters
Performance Facilities: University Theatre

FACILITY

RIVERSIDE CONVENTION CENTER AT RAINCROSS SQUARE
3443 Orange Street, Riverside, CA 92506
(909) 787-7950
FAX: (909) 787-4940
Founded: 1975
Type of Facility: Concert Hall; Auditorium; Outdoor (Concert); Civic Center; Arena; Multi-Purpose; Room
Type of Stage: Flexible
Stage Dimensions: 40'x26'D; 40'x32'
Seating Capacity: 2,700
Year Built: 1975   **Architect:** Brown & Rawdon   **Cost:** $7,000,000
Acoustical Consultant: Paul Richardson, House Technician
Contact for Rental: Lisa Snider, Event Services/Catering Manager;   (909) 787-7950
Manager: Joseph Prevratil, President/CEO

RIVERSIDE MUNICIPAL AUDITORIUM
3485 7th Street, Riverside, CA 92501
(909) 787-7950
FAX: (909) 787-4940
Type of Facility: Auditorium
Facility Originally: Meeting Hall; Ballroom; Movie House
Type of Stage: Proscenium
Stage Dimensions: 70'Wx40'D; 40'Wx26'H proscenium opening
Seating Capacity: 1,642
Year Built: 1929   **Architect:** Arthur Benton & Stanley Wilson
Contact for Rental: Bill Harper;   (909) 787-7678

UNIVERSITY OF CALIFORNIA-RIVERSIDE - UNIVERSITY THEATRE
900 University Avenue, PO Box 112, Riverside, CA 92521
(909) 787-3319
Type of Facility: Theatre House
Type of Stage: Proscenium
Stage Dimensions: 60'x62'x47'   **Orchestra Pit**
Seating Capacity: 496
Year Built: 1962   **Architect:** George V. Russel   **Cost:** $1,500,000
Year Remodeled: 1977   **Architect:** Donald O'Neill   **Cost:** $250,000
Contact for Rental: David E. Kellstrand, Facilities Director;   (909) 787-3319

Rolling Hills Estate

FACILITY

NORRIS THEATRE FOR THE PERFORMING ARTS
27570 Crossfield Drive, Rolling Hills Estate, CA 90274
(310) 544-0403
FAX: (310) 544-2473
Founded: 1983
Type of Facility: Auditorium; Performance Center; Theatre House
Type of Stage: Proscenium
Stage Dimensions: 44'x38'   **Orchestra Pit**
Seating Capacity: 450
Year Built: 1983   **Architect:** Anthony - Langford Architects   **Cost:** $6,000,000
Contact for Rental: Ellen Rodney;   (310) 544-0403
Resident Groups: Chamber Orchestra

Sacramento

DANCE

DALE SCHOLL DANCE ART
PO Box 162432, Sacramento, CA 95816
(916) 364-8721; (916) 483-4017
Founded: 1982
Arts Area: Modern; Ballet; Jazz; Theatre; Storytelling
Status: Professional; Non-Profit
Type: Performing; Resident
Purpose: To offer an eclectic mix of dance and theatre
Management: Joan Liddicoat, Manager; Dale Scholl, Artistic Director
Paid Staff: 2
Paid Artists: 7
Utilizes: Guest Artists; Guest Choreographers
Budget: $1,000 - $50,000
Income Sources: Private Foundations/Grants/Endowments; Business/Corporate Donations; Box Office; Government Grants; Individual Donations
Season: September - April
Affiliations: Sacramento Area Dance Alliance
Performance Facilities: 24th Street Theatre

SACRAMENTO BALLET
2791 24th Street, #16, Sacramento, CA 95818
(916) 736-2860
FAX: (916) 452-3445
Founded: 1956
Arts Area: Ballet
Status: Professional; Non-Profit
Type: Performing; Touring; Resident
Purpose: To present professional performances of a wide range of standard and contemporary ballets in the classical mode to diverse audiences
Management: Ernest Phinney, Executive Director; Ron Cunningham, Artistic Director
Officers: Richard N. Frey, President; Claudia Cummings, First Vice President; Dave Molit, Treasurer; Lisa Wright, Secretary
Paid Staff: 10   **Volunteer Staff:** 5
Paid Artists: 18   **Non-Paid Artists:** 40
Utilizes: Special Technical Talent; Guest Conductors; Guest Artists
Budget: $1,000,000 - $5,000,000
Income Sources: Private Foundations/Grants/Endowments; Business/Corporate Donations; Box Office; Government Grants; Individual Donations
Season: August - April   **Annual Attendance:** 75,000
Affiliations: Dance USA; NSFRE; Regional Dance Pacific America
Performance Facilities: Sacramento Community Center Theatre

INSTRUMENTAL MUSIC

CAMELLIA SYMPHONY
PO Box 19786, Sacramento, CA 95819
(916) 344-5844
Founded: 1963
Arts Area: Symphony
Status: Semi-Professional; Non-Profit
Type: Performing
Purpose: To expand the musical growth of the Sacramento area by providing unique repertoire, opportunities for area musicians and composers, and performances at reasonable prices
Management: Lauren Russel, General Manager; Nan Washburn, Music Director/Conductor
Officers: Donald Houser, President; Mary Schneider, Vice President; Margaret Thompson, Secretary; Carl Van Der Camp, Treasurer
Paid Staff: 7
Paid Artists: 6 **Non-Paid Artists:** 73
Utilizes: Guest Conductors; Guest Artists
Budget: $50,000 - $100,000
Income Sources: Private Foundations/Grants/Endowments; Business/Corporate Donations; Box Office; Government Grants; Individual Donations
Season: October - May **Annual Attendance:** 5,000
Affiliations: ASOL; Association of California Symphony Orchestras
Performance Facilities: Hiram Johnson High School Auditorium

SACRAMENTO SYMPHONY ASSOCIATION
77 Cadillac Drive, #B1, Sacramento, CA 95825
(916) 649-0300
FAX: (916) 641-0830
Founded: 1948
Arts Area: Symphony; Orchestra; Chamber; Ensemble
Status: Professional; Non-Profit
Type: Performing; Touring; Educational; Sponsoring
Management: Robert Walker, Executive Director; Alasdair Neale, Music Director; Tracy Davis, Orchestra Manager
Officers: Ernist Lewis, President
Paid Staff: 22
Paid Artists: 39
Utilizes: Guest Conductors; Guest Artists
Budget: $1,000,000 - $5,000,000
Income Sources: Private Foundations/Grants/Endowments; Business/Corporate Donations; Box Office; Government Grants; Individual Donations
Season: September - May **Annual Attendance:** 250,000
Affiliations: ASOL
Performance Facilities: Sacramento Community Center Theater

VOCAL MUSIC

SACRAMENTO MEN'S CHORUS
PO Box 188726, Sacramento, CA 95818
(916) 444-5213
Founded: 1985
Arts Area: Choral
Status: Non-Professional; Non-Profit
Type: Performing; Touring
Management: Frank Lawler, Business Manager
Paid Staff: 2
Non-Paid Artists: 30
Budget: $1,000 - $50,000
Income Sources: Box Office; Individual Donations
Season: September - June **Annual Attendance:** 3,000
Performance Facilities: First United Methodist

SACRAMENTO OPERA
2131 Capital Avenue, Sacramento, CA 95816
(916) 442-4224
FAX: (916) 442-4254
Founded: 1947
Arts Area: Grand Opera
Status: Professional; Non-Profit

Type: Performing; Educational
Purpose: To produce opera of the highest level to the Sacramento community
Management: Marianne H. Oaks, General Director; Gene Sirois, Marketing Director
Officers: Randall Yim, President
Paid Staff: 4 **Volunteer Staff:** 2
Utilizes: Special Technical Talent; Guest Conductors; Guest Artists; Guest Directors
Budget: $500,000 - $1,000,000
Income Sources: Private Foundations/Grants/Endowments; Business/Corporate Donations; Box Office; Government Grants; Individual Donations
Season: September - March **Annual Attendance:** 22,000
Affiliations: OA
Performance Facilities: Sacramento Community Center Theatre

THEATRE

SACRAMENTO MUSIC CIRCUS
1510 J Street, Suite 100, Sacramento, CA 95814
(916) 446-5880; (916) 557-1999
FAX: (916) 446-1370
Founded: 1951
Arts Area: Musical; Theatrical Group
Status: Professional; Non-Profit
Type: Performing; Resident
Purpose: To present a week of musical summer stock in Sacramento, as well as national tours
Management: Russell Lewis, President; Leland Ball, Producing Director; Richard Lewis, Marlene Shire, Managing Directors
Paid Staff: 110 **Volunteer Staff:** 3
Paid Artists: 40 **Non-Paid Artists:** 10
Utilizes: Special Technical Talent; Guest Artists
Budget: $5,000,000 - $10,000,000
Income Sources: Box Office
Season: July - Labor Day
Affiliations: Resident Musical Theatre Association

SACRAMENTO THEATRE COMPANY
1419 H Street, Sacramento, CA 95814
(916) 446-7501
FAX: (916) 446-4066
Founded: 1942
Arts Area: Theatrical Group
Status: Semi-Professional; Non-Profit
Type: Performing; Resident
Purpose: The Sacramento Theatre Company produces 10 productions on its two stages between September and May
Management: Mark Cuddy, Artistic Director
Officers: Susan Peters, President; Barry Kohn, Vice President; Michael Moy, Treasurer; Diane Hazelroth, Secretary
Paid Staff: 17
Paid Artists: 6
Utilizes: Guest Artists; Guest Directors
Budget: $1,000,000 - $5,000,000
Income Sources: Private Foundations/Grants/Endowments; Business/Corporate Donations; Box Office; Government Grants; Individual Donations
Season: September - May
Annual Attendance: 40,000
Affiliations: TCG
Performance Facilities: McClatchey Mainstage and Stage Two

PERFORMING SERIES

CROCKER ART MUSEUM
216 O Street, Sacramento, CA 95814
(916) 264-5423
Founded: 1885
Arts Area: Dance; Vocal Music; Instrumental Music; Theater
Status: Non-Profit
Type: Sponsoring
Purpose: To offer opportunity for artists to perform in a museum—a small and intimate setting
Management: Barbara Gibbs, Museum Director
Officers: Jane Lamb, Music Board Chairman
Paid Staff: 23

Utilizes: Guest Artists
Budget: $500,000 - $1,000,000
Income Sources: Private Foundations/Grants/Endowments; Business/Corporate Donations; Government Grants; Individual Donations
Season: September - June
Annual Attendance: 4,500
Performance Facilities: Crocker Art Museum Ballroom

FESTIVAL OF NEW AMERICAN MUSIC
c/o Music Dept., CSU-Sacramento, 6000 J Street, Sacramento, CA 95819
(916) 278-6514
FAX: (916) 278-7217
Arts Area: Vocal Music; Instrumental Music; Festivals; Chamber Music
Status: Non-Profit
Type: Performing; Educational; Sponsoring
Purpose: To perform works written by American composers from the last ten years
Management: Gene Savage, Festival Director
Budget: $100,000 - $500,000
Income Sources: Private Foundations/Grants/Endowments; Business/Corporate Donations; Government Grants; Individual Donations
Performance Facilities: Music Recital Hall

FINEST ASIAN PERFORMING ARTS, INC.
PO Box 162163, Sacramento, CA 95816
(916) 924-1212; (415) 566-1252
FAX: (916) 924-7212; (415) 566-6005
Alternate Mailing Address: PO Box 22668, San Francisco, CA 94122
Founded: 1988
Arts Area: Dance; Vocal Music; Instrumental Music; Festivals
Status: Professional; Semi-Professional
Type: Performing; Sponsoring
Purpose: To promote Eastern culture through performing arts to the Western world and community
Management: Anna Y. Mayo, Executive Director; Lucy Nemac, Secretary; Yan Zhang, Music Director/Advisor
Officers: Anna Y. Mayo, President; William Ku, Finance Officer; Lucy Nemac, Secretary; Jesse Kaplan, Legal Officer; Cheung Fong DDS, Vice President
Paid Staff: 2   **Volunteer Staff:** 30
Paid Artists: 10   **Non-Paid Artists:** 12
Utilizes: Special Technical Talent; Guest Artists
Budget: $50,000 - $100,000
Income Sources: Private Foundations/Grants/Endowments; Business/Corporate Donations; Government Grants; Individual Donations
Season: August - November   **Annual Attendance:** 5,000
Affiliations: Finest Asian Music Festival

FACILITY

SACRAMENTO COMMUNITY CENTER EXHIBITION HALL
1100 14th Street, Sacramento, CA 95814
(916) 264-5291
FAX: (916) 264-7687
Type of Facility: Exhibition Hall
Type of Stage: Flexible
Seating Capacity: 7,000
Year Built: 1974
Contact for Rental: Michael Stauffer;   (916) 264-5291
Manager: Sam Burns;   (916) 264-5291

SACRAMENTO COMMUNITY CENTER THEATER
1301 L Street, Sacramento, CA 95814
(916) 264-5181
Type of Facility: Theatre House
Type of Stage: Proscenium
Stage Dimensions: 70'x85'x46'3"   **Orchestra Pit**
Seating Capacity: 2,436
Year Built: 1974
Contact for Rental: (916) 264-5291
Manager: Sam Burns;   (916) 264-5291

SACRAMENTO COMMUNITY CONVENTION CENTER
1100 14th Street, Sacramento, CA 95814
(916) 449-5291
FAX: (916) 264-7687
>**Administrative Offices:** 1030 15th Street, Suite 250, Sacramento, CA 95814
>**Type of Facility:** Civic Center
>**Year Built:** 1974   **Architect:** Sacramento Architects Collaboration   **Cost:** $19,100,000
>**Acoustical Consultant:** Bolt, Beranek & Newman
>**Contact for Rental:** Michael Stauffer;   (916) 264-5291
>**Manager:** Sam Burns;   (916) 264-5291
>**Resident Groups:** Sacramento Symphony; Sacramento Ballet; Sacramento Opera

San Anselmo

DANCE

CHHANDAM CHITRESH DAS DANCE COMPANY
PO Box 716, San Anselmo, CA 94979
(415) 453-4305
>**Founded:** 1980
>**Arts Area:** Ethnic
>**Status:** Professional; Non-Profit
>**Type:** Performing; Touring; Resident; Educational; Sponsoring
>**Purpose:** To establish Kathak dance in the United States through teaching, performing and community outreach
>**Management:** Chitresh Das, Artistic Director; Michele Zonka, Manager
>**Officers:** Chitresh Das, Executive Director; Dr. Surjit Singh, President; Shamim Formosa; Doug Flegal
>**Paid Staff:** 2   **Volunteer Staff:** 2
>**Paid Artists:** 10   **Non-Paid Artists:** 5
>**Budget:** $50,000 - $100,000
>**Income Sources:** Private Foundations/Grants/Endowments; Box Office; Government Grants; Individual Donations
>**Season:** September - June

San Bernardino

INSTRUMENTAL MUSIC

INLAND EMPIRE SYMPHONY ASSOCIATION
362 West Court Street, San Bernardino, CA 92401
(909) 381-5388
>**Founded:** 1960
>**Arts Area:** Symphony; Orchestra; Chamber; Ensemble
>**Status:** Professional; Non-Profit
>**Type:** Performing; Touring; Educational; Sponsoring
>**Management:** Susan Feller, Executive Director; Arlette Cardenes, Operations Manager
>**Officers:** Allen Gresham, President; Brian Tomkins, Treasurer; Marilyn Bidney, Secretary; Mary Schnepp, Guild President
>**Paid Staff:** 4   **Volunteer Staff:** 15
>**Paid Artists:** 75
>**Utilizes:** Guest Conductors; Guest Artists
>**Budget:** $500,000 - $1,000,000
>**Income Sources:** Private Foundations/Grants/Endowments; Business/Corporate Donations; Box Office; Government Grants; Individual Donations
>**Season:** September - April   **Annual Attendance:** 80,000
>**Affiliations:** ASOL; Association of California Symphony Orchestras; APAP
>**Performance Facilities:** The California Theatre of Performing Arts

VOCAL MUSIC

SAN BERNARDINO CIVIC LIGHT OPERA ASSOCIATION
1398 North E Street, PO Box 606, San Bernardino, CA 92402
(909) 386-7353
FAX: (909) 386-7358
>**Founded:** 1947
>**Arts Area:** Light Opera; MUSICAL THEATRE
>**Status:** Professional; Non-Profit
>**Type:** Performing; Educational
>**Purpose:** The presentation of live musical theatre with opportunities for professional and non-professionals; educational theatre

Management: C. Dale Jenks, General Manager/Producer/Treasurer
Officers: Evlyn Wilcox, President; Walter Shaidnagle, Carl H. Reitz, Vice Presidents
Utilizes: Special Technical Talent; Guest Conductors; Guest Artists; Guest Directors
Income Sources: Private Foundations/Grants/Endowments; Business/Corporate Donations; Box Office;
Government Grants; Individual Donations
Season: 52 Weeks
Affiliations: AEA
Performance Facilities: The California Theatre of Performing Arts

FACILITY

CALIFORNIA STATE UNIVERSITY - CREATIVE ARTS BUILDING
5500 University Parkway, San Bernardino, CA 92407
(909) 887-7452
Type of Facility: Performance Center
Type of Stage: Thrust
Seating Capacity: 143
Year Built: 1977   **Architect:** Carl Maston   **Cost:** $2,500,000
Acoustical Consultant: Gerald Strang

THE CALIFORNIA THEATRE OF PERFORMING ARTS
562 West Fourth Street, San Bernardino, CA 92402
(909) 386-7361
Type of Facility: Auditorium; Theatre House; Opera House
Facility Originally: Vaudeville
Type of Stage: Proscenium
Stage Dimensions: 60'x60'x30'
Orchestra Pit
Seating Capacity: 1,760
Year Built: 1928   **Architect:** Thomas Lamb
Contact for Rental: C. Dale Jenks
Resident Groups: San Bernardino Civic Light Opera Association; San Bernardino Valley Community Concert
Association; Inland Empire Symphony Orchestra

San Diego

DANCE

CALIFORNIA BALLET COMPANY
8276 Ronson Road, San Diego, CA 92111
(619) 560-5676
Founded: 1967
Arts Area: Ballet
Status: Semi-Professional; Non-Profit
Type: Performing; Touring; Resident
Management: Maxine Mahon, Director; Matt Bean, Production Manager
Paid Staff: 6   **Volunteer Staff:** 20
Utilizes: Guest Artists
Budget: $500,000 - $1,000,000
Income Sources: Private Foundations/Grants/Endowments; Business/Corporate Donations; Box Office; Government
Grants; Individual Donations

MALASHOCK DANCE AND COMPANY
438 Camino del Rio South, #213, San Diego, CA 92108
(619) 298-3304
FAX: (619) 291-6652
Founded: 1988
Arts Area: Modern
Status: Professional
Type: Performing; Touring
Purpose: To create, produce and perform modern dance choreographed by John Malashock
Management: John Malashock, Artistic Director; Victoria Saunders, Managing Director
Paid Staff: 2
Paid Artists: 5
Utilizes: Special Technical Talent; Guest Artists; Guest Choreographers

Budget: $100,000 - $500,000
Income Sources: Private Foundations/Grants/Endowments; Business/Corporate Donations; Box Office; Government Grants; Individual Donations
Season: April - November **Annual Attendance:** 3,000
Performance Facilities: Old Globe Theatre

SAN DIEGO FOUNDATION FOR THE PERFORMING ARTS
625 Broadway, Suite 1006, San Diego, CA 92101
(619) 234-5853
FAX: (619) 234-0521
Founded: 1982
Arts Area: Modern; Ballet; Ethnic
Status: Professional; Non-Profit
Type: Educational; Presenter
Purpose: To act as a catalyst in the development of an appreciation for dance in San Diego
Management: Fred Colby, Executive Director; Nadine Buchner, Development Director; Albert Rodewald, Public Affairs Director; William Conrow, Project Director
Officers: Danah Fayman, President; Jean Hellerich, Vice President; Bob Levy, Secretary
Paid Staff: 9 **Volunteer Staff:** 2
Paid Artists: 20 **Non-Paid Artists:** 250
Utilizes: Guest Artists; Guest Choreographers
Budget: $1,000,000 - $5,000,000
Income Sources: Private Foundations/Grants/Endowments; Business/Corporate Donations; Box Office; Government Grants; Individual Donations
Season: September - June
Annual Attendance: 28,000
Affiliations: APAP: California Presenters; WAAA
Performance Facilities: Spreduls Theatre; Civic Center

SUSHI PERFORMANCE AND VISUAL ART
852 Eighth Avenue, San Diego, CA 92101
(619) 235-8466
FAX: (619) 235-8466
Founded: 1980
Arts Area: Modern
Status: Professional; Non-Profit
Type: Performing; Touring; Educational
Purpose: Sushi is a presenter of contemporary performance and dance by those artists working in experimental and meaningful form and content and whose vision embodies the diversity of our rich cultural, ethnic, sexual and personal backgrounds
Management: Lynn Schurhe, Executive Director; Vicki Wolf, Managing Director
Paid Staff: 5 **Volunteer Staff:** 5
Paid Artists: 75
Utilizes: Guest Artists
Budget: $100,000 - $500,000
Income Sources: Private Foundations/Grants/Endowments; Business/Corporate Donations; Government Grants; Individual Donations; Admissions; Membership
Season: September - June
Annual Attendance: 6,000

INSTRUMENTAL MUSIC

ARIOSO WIND QUARTET
San Diego State University, Department of Music, San Diego, CA 92182
(619) 594-6031
FAX: (619) 594-1692
Arts Area: Chamber; Ensemble; Instrumental Group
Status: Professional; Non-Profit
Type: Performing; Touring; Resident; Educational
Purpose: To increase the number and diversity of chamber music enthusiasts; to perform high-caliber concerts featuring works selected for a specific audience; to educate performers, teachers and audiences now and in the future; to sponsor educational outreach programs and adult multi-cultural concerts locally and in conjunction with touring engagements
Management: Marian Liebowitz, Artistic Director; Constance Mullin, Booking Agent
Budget: $1,000 - $50,000
Income Sources: Private Foundations/Grants/Endowments; Business/Corporate Donations; Government Grants; Individual Donations

SAN DIEGO SYMPHONY ORCHESTRA
1245 Seventh Avenue, San Diego, CA 92101
(619) 699-4200
FAX: (619) 699-4237
Founded: 1910
Arts Area: Symphony; Orchestra
Status: Professional; Non-Profit
Type: Performing; Educational; Sponsoring
Purpose: To present the highest quality performances of classical music and build a superior organization within the San Diego arts community
Management: Wesley Brustad, Executive Director; Yoav Talmi, Music Director; Lynn Hallbacka, General Manager
Paid Staff: 25 **Volunteer Staff:** 500
Paid Artists: 81
Utilizes: Guest Conductors; Guest Artists
Budget: $5,000,000 - $10,000,000
Income Sources: Business/Corporate Donations; Box Office; Individual Donations
Season: October - May **Annual Attendance:** 125,000
Affiliations: ASOL; Association of California Symphony Orchestras
Performance Facilities: Copley Symphony Hall

SAN DIEGO YOUTH SYMPHONY
Casa Del Prado, Balboa Park, San Diego, CA 92101
(619) 233-3232
Founded: 1945
Arts Area: Symphony; Orchestra; Chamber; Ensemble
Status: Non-Professional; Non-Profit
Type: Performing; Touring; Educational
Purpose: To enhance the music in youthful musicians in San Diego County and to provide educational and performance opportunities for youthful musicians
Management: Louis Campiglia, Music Director/Conductor
Officers: Kristine Henyer, President
Volunteer Staff: 12
Non-Paid Artists: 75
Utilizes: Guest Artists
Budget: $100,000 - $500,000
Income Sources: Private Foundations/Grants/Endowments; Business/Corporate Donations; Box Office; Government Grants; Individual Donations; Fundraising
Season: September - July
Annual Attendance: 7,000
Affiliations: ASOL (Youth Orchestra Division); Association of California Symphony Orchestras
Performance Facilities: Balboa Park Club; Westgate Hotel

VOCAL MUSIC

SAN DIEGO COMIC OPERA
526 Market Street, San Diego, CA 92101
(619) 231-5714
FAX: (619) 231-0662
Founded: 1980
Arts Area: Light Opera; Operetta; Musical Theater
Status: Professional; Semi-Professional; Non-Profit
Type: Performing; Touring; Resident; Educational
Purpose: To produce musical theater that provides creative employment for local professional artists and a proving ground for young artists moving toward a professional career
Management: Leon Nataker, Artistic Director; Kathleen Switzer, Managing Director
Officers: John Lasher, President; Bonnie Cogan, Treasurer; Patti Goodwin, Secretary
Paid Staff: 4 **Volunteer Staff:** 100
Paid Artists: 150
Utilizes: Special Technical Talent; Guest Conductors; Guest Directors
Budget: $100,000 - $500,000
Income Sources: Private Foundations/Grants/Endowments; Business/Corporate Donations; Box Office; Government Grants; Individual Donations
Season: March - October
Annual Attendance: 9,000
Affiliations: San Diego Theatre League; OA; San Diego Arts and Culture Coalition; Central City Association
Performance Facilities: Casa del Prado

SAN DIEGO MEN'S CHORUS
PO Box 33825, San Diego, CA 92163
(619) 296-7664
 Founded: 1985
 Arts Area: Choral
 Status: Non-Professional; Non-Profit
 Type: Performing; Touring
 Purpose: To sing, to unite in song and to share our music and unity
 Officers: Del Garrett, Secretary
 Paid Staff: 3 **Volunteer Staff:** 7
 Non-Paid Artists: 50
 Utilizes: Guest Artists
 Budget: $50,000 - $100,000
 Income Sources: Box Office; Individual Donations; Fund-raising
 Season: September - July **Annual Attendance:** 5,000

SAN DIEGO OPERA ASSOCIATION
PO Box 988, San Diego, CA 92112
(619) 232-7636
FAX: (619) 231-6915
 Founded: 1965
 Arts Area: Grand Opera; Operetta
 Status: Professional; Non-Profit
 Type: Performing; Touring; Resident; Educational
 Purpose: To present professional opera, concerts, recitals and educational programs
 Management: Ian D. Campbell, General Director; Marianne Flettner, Artistic Administrator
 Officers: Lee Goldberg, President
 Paid Staff: 22 **Volunteer Staff:** 150
 Paid Artists: 350
 Utilizes: Special Technical Talent; Guest Conductors; Guest Artists; Guest Directors
 Budget: $5,000,000 - $10,000,000
 Income Sources: Private Foundations/Grants/Endowments; Business/Corporate Donations; Box Office; Government Grants; Individual Donations
 Season: October - May **Annual Attendance:** 58,000
 Performance Facilities: Civic Theater

STARLIGHT MUSICAL THEATRE/SAN DIEGO CIVIC LIGHT OPERA ASSOCIATION
1549 El Prado - Balboa Park, San Diego, CA 92101
(619) 544-7800
FAX: (619) 544-0496
 Founded: 1946
 Arts Area: Light Opera; Musical Theatre
 Status: Professional; Non-Profit
 Type: Performing; Educational
 Purpose: To promote and preserve musical theatre as an art form
 Management: C.E. "Bud" Farnks, Executive Director; Don and Bonnie Ward, Producing Artistic Directors
 Officers: James Bowers, President of the Board of Directors
 Paid Staff: 19 **Volunteer Staff:** 1
 Paid Artists: 249
 Utilizes: Special Technical Talent; Guest Conductors; Guest Directors
 Budget: $1,000,000 - $5,000,000
 Income Sources: Private Foundations/Grants/Endowments; Business/Corporate Donations; Box Office; Government Grants; Individual Donations; Memberships
 Season: May - September; October-April **Annual Attendance:** 130,000
 Performance Facilities: Starlight Bowl; Civic Theatre; Spreckles Theatre

THEATRE

BLACKFRIARS THEATRE
PO Box 126957, San Diego, CA 92112
(619) 232-4088
 Founded: 1982
 Arts Area: Professional
 Status: Professional; Non-Profit
 Type: Performing; Resident; Co-Produce Community Projects
 Purpose: To entertain and challange audiences with plays that speak to the American experience, plays whose impact is enhanced by the intimacy of our small theatre space, and whose content is most powerfully communicated by honest, meticulously-crafted performances

Management: Ralph Elias, Artistic Director; Allison Brennan, Executive Producer; Dan C. Campbell, Marketing/Communications Manager
Officers: Ronald L. Styn, President; Terrence L. Bingman, Vice President; Stephen H. Streifer, Treasurer; Linda G. Hack, Secretary
Paid Staff: 5   **Volunteer Staff:** 85
Paid Artists: 50
Utilizes: Guest Artists; Guest Directors; Local Artists and Directors
Budget: $100,000 - $500,000
Income Sources: Private Foundations/Grants/Endowments; Business/Corporate Donations; Box Office; Government Grants; Individual Donations
Season: September - June   **Annual Attendance:** 16,000
Affiliations: AEA; San Diego Theatre League
Performance Facilities: Bristol Court Playhouse; Blackfriars Theatre

GASLAMP QUARTER THEATRE
436 Fourth Avenue, San Diego, CA 92101
(619) 232-9608
Founded: 1980
Arts Area: Professional; Musical; Theatrical Group
Status: Professional; Non-Profit
Type: Performing; Educational; Sponsoring
Purpose: To present professional productions of contemporary off-Broadway type plays, most of which San Diego premiers; to present works which tackle the most pressing social issues in American society with a focus on urban issues
Management: Steve Bevans, Managing Director; Kit Goldman, Adleane Hunter, Will Roberson, Rosina Widdowsen-Reynolds, Artistic Associates
Paid Staff: 8   **Volunteer Staff:** 100
Paid Artists: 50
Utilizes: Guest Artists; Guest Directors
Budget: $500,000 - $1,000,000
Income Sources: Private Foundations/Grants/Endowments; Business/Corporate Donations; Box Office; Government Grants; Individual Donations
Season: September - June   **Annual Attendance:** 40,000
Affiliations: San Diego Theatre League
Performance Facilities: Hahn Cosmopolitan Theatre

INSTITUTE FOR READERS THEATRE
PO Box 178333, San Diego, CA 92117
(619) 276-1948
Founded: 1972
Arts Area: Professional
Status: Commercial
Type: Performing; Touring; Resident; Educational
Purpose: To promote all aspects of Readers Theatre, the fastest-growing innovation in art and education
Management: Dr. William Adams, Director; Rosemary Adams, Assistant Director; William Franklin Smith, Business Manager; Flossie Smith, Technician; Thomas Graves, Manager, Readers Theatre Script Service
Paid Staff: 14
Utilizes: Special Technical Talent; Guest Artists; Guest Directors
Budget: $100,000 - $500,000
Income Sources: Business/Corporate Donations
Affiliations: University of Central Florida

OLD GLOBE THEATRE
1363 Old Globe Way, San Diego, CA 92101
(619) 231-1941
FAX: (619) 231-5879
Mailing Address: PO Box 2171, San Diego, CA 92112
Founded: 1937
Arts Area: Professional; Theatrical Group
Status: Professional; Non-Profit
Type: Performing; Educational; Sponsoring
Purpose: To affirm its commitment to its survival in maintaining the integrity of theatre by producing the highest quality professional theatre; to undertake a wide spectrum of theatrical enterprises with continued emphasis on Shakespeare as well as other world classics and contemporary and new works; to provide theatrical professionals with a challenging and supportive environment condusive to individual and collective artistic growth; to establish a training program which will afford the intern direct involvement in all aspects of the professional theatre; to serve and involve the community in a manner that delights, stimulates, and instructs; to develop audiences through educational, outreach, and touring programs; to provide a forum for promoting an understanding of the unique character of this region; to achieve local, regional and national recognition by a commitment to an American classical standard
Management: Thomas Hall, Managing Director; Craig Noel, Executive Producer; Jack O'Brien, Artistic Director

Officers: Bobbie Quick, President, Board of Directors
Paid Staff: 120
Paid Artists: 150
Utilizes: Special Technical Talent; Guest Artists; Guest Directors
Budget: $5,000,000 - $10,000,000
Income Sources: Private Foundations/Grants/Endowments; Business/Corporate Donations; Box Office; Government Grants; Individual Donations
Season: December - October   **Annual Attendance:** 275,000
Affiliations: TCG; LORT; AAA
Performance Facilities: Old Globe Theatre; Cassius Carter Centre Stage; Lowell Davies Festival Theatre

SAN DIEGO JUNIOR THEATRE
Casa del Prado, #208, Balboa Park, San Diego, CA 92101
(619) 239-1311
Founded: 1948
Arts Area: Theatrical Group
Status: Non-Professional; Non-Profit
Type: Performing; Educational
Purpose: To instruct youth, ages 8-18, in theatre arts for their benefit and enjoyment
Management: Pat Rogers, Executive Director; Michael Erickson, Artistic Director; Jennifer Nash, Education Director; Deborah Sims, Marketing/Public Relations
Officers: Roseanne Luth, President, Board of Directors; Carol Windham, Secretary; Kathy Haber, Treasurer
Paid Staff: 8   **Volunteer Staff:** 15
Paid Artists: 15   **Non-Paid Artists:** 300
Utilizes: Guest Artists; Guest Directors
Budget: $100,000 - $500,000
Income Sources: Private Foundations/Grants/Endowments; Business/Corporate Donations; Box Office; Government Grants; Individual Donations; Tuition
Season: November - August   **Annual Attendance:** 25,000
Affiliations: SCETA; San Diego Theatre League
Performance Facilities: Casa del Prado Theater

SAN DIEGO REPERTORY THEATRE
79 Horton Plaza, San Diego, CA 92101
(619) 231-3586
FAX: (619) 235-0939
Founded: 1976
Arts Area: Professional
Status: Professional; Non-Profit
Type: Performing; Touring; Educational; Sponsoring
Management: Sam Woodhouse, Producing Director; Doug Jacobs, Artistic Director; John Redman, General Manager
Paid Staff: 30
Paid Artists: 60
Utilizes: Guest Directors
Budget: $1,000,000 - $5,000,000
Income Sources: Private Foundations/Grants/Endowments; Business/Corporate Donations; Box Office; Government Grants; Individual Donations
Season: April - January   **Annual Attendance:** 500,000
Affiliations: TCG
Performance Facilities: The Lyceum Theatre

SOUTHEAST COMMUNITY THEATRE
5140 Solola Avenue, San Diego, CA 92114
(619) 262-2817; (619) 264-0698
Founded: 1976
Arts Area: Community; Theatrical Group
Status: Semi-Professional; Non-Profit
Type: Performing; Resident; Sponsoring
Purpose: To mount theatrical productions that promote the works of African-American playwrights by utilizing and showcasing the talent of amateur, semi-professional and professional artists
Management: Floyd Gaffney, Artistic Director; Bonnie J. Ward, Production Manager; Rufus DeWitt, Business Manager
Officers: Kathleen Harmon, President; Henry McClaron, Vice President; Yvette McClaron, Secretary; Robert Matthews, Treasurer
Paid Staff: 3   **Volunteer Staff:** 10
Utilizes: Guest Artists; Guest Directors
Budget: $50,000 - $100,000
Income Sources: Private Foundations/Grants/Endowments; Business/Corporate Donations; Box Office; Government Grants; Individual Donations
Season: September - June   **Annual Attendance:** 8,000

Affiliations: AACT
Performance Facilities: Educational Cultural Complex Performing Arts Theater; Lyceum Space Theatre

PERFORMING SERIES

STARLIGHT-SAN DIEGO CIVIC LIGHT OPERA ASSOCIATION
Balboa Park, 1549 El Drado, #11, San Diego, CA 92101
(619) 544-7800
FAX: (619) 544-0496
Founded: 1946
Arts Area: Theater
Status: Professional; Non-Profit
Type: Performing; Touring; Resident; Educational
Purpose: To present and further the American musical theatre through productions for residents and visitors to the San Diego area in the unique setting of the 4,324-seat Starlight Bowl in Balboa Park
Management: C. E. "Bud" Franks, Executive Director; Don and Bonnie Ward, Co-Artistic Directors
Officers: James L. Bowers, President/Board of Directors; Kent C. Thompson, Secretary; Michael J. Howard, Treasurer
Paid Staff: 23
Paid Artists: 300
Utilizes: Guest Artists; Guest Directors
Budget: $1,000,000 - $5,000,000
Income Sources: Private Foundations/Grants/Endowments; Business/Corporate Donations; Box Office; Government Grants; Individual Donations
Season: June - September
Annual Attendance: 150,000
Performance Facilities: Starlight Bowl/Balboa Park

FACILITY

BLACKFRIARS THEATRE
1057 First Avenue, San Diego, CA 92101
(619) 232-4088
Type of Facility: Theatre House; Room
Facility Originally: Ballroom; Hotel & Meeting Rooms
Type of Stage: Thrust; 3/4 Arena
Stage Dimensions: 25'Wx18'D
Seating Capacity: 99
Year Remodeled: 1985   **Architect:** Kim McCallum   **Cost:** $5,000
Contact for Rental: Dan Campbell;   (619) 232-4088
Resident Groups: The Bowery Theatre
Originally built in the 1920's

CAFE DEL REY MORO
House of Hospitality, 1549 El Prado, San Diego, CA 92101
(619) 234-8511
Type of Facility: Auditorium; Theatre House; Multi-Purpose; Room
Facility Originally: Exhibition Facility Of The 1914 Panama C
Type of Stage: Proscenium
Stage Dimensions: 41'9"Wx18'D
Seating Capacity: 400
Year Built: 1914
Year Remodeled: 1935
Contact for Rental: Cafe del Rey Moro;   (619) 234-8511
Originally the 1914 Foreign Arts Building, the building was remodeled in 1935 for the California Pacific International Exposition.

CASA DEL PRADO THEATRE
Village Place, Balboa Park, San Diego, CA 92101
(619) 235-1105
FAX: (619) 235-1112
Type of Facility: Theatre House
Facility Originally: Meeting Hall; Movie House
Type of Stage: Proscenium
Stage Dimensions: 48'Wx36'D   **Orchestra Pit**
Seating Capacity: 682
Year Built: 1971   **Architect:** Wheeler   **Cost:** $2,500,000
Year Remodeled: 1981   **Cost:** $500,000
Contact for Rental: Inge Dickens;   (619) 235-1105

Resident Groups: San Diego Junior Theatre; San Diego Youth Ballet; San Diego Comic Opera Company; San Diego Parks and Recreation Dance Productions
Rental available on a limited basis only.

COPLEY SYMPHONY HALL
1245 Seventh Avenue, San Diego, CA 92101
(619) 699-4200
FAX: (619) 699-4237
> **Founded:** 1929
> **Type of Facility:** Concert Hall; Performance Center; Theatre House; Multi-Purpose
> **Facility Originally:** Vaudeville
> **Type of Stage:** Proscenium
> **Stage Dimensions:** 50'Wx40'D   **Orchestra Pit**
> **Seating Capacity:** 2,250
> **Year Built:** 1929   **Architect:** Weeks & Day   **Cost:** $2,500,000
> **Year Remodeled:** 1985   **Architect:** Deemes/Lewis & Partners   **Cost:** $6,900,000
> **Acoustical Consultant:** ARTEC
> **Contact for Rental:** Nina Doggrell;   (619) 699-4200
> **Resident Groups:** San Diego Symphony Orchestra

GASLAMP QUARTER THEATRE
444 Fourth Avenue, San Diego, CA 92101
(619) 232-9608
> **Type of Facility:** Theatre House
> **Facility Originally:** Paper Box Factory
> **Type of Stage:** Proscenium
> **Stage Dimensions:** 30'Wx22'6"D, 30'Wx18'H proscenium opening
> **Seating Capacity:** 250
> **Year Remodeled:** 1986   **Architect:** Robert Earl   **Cost:** $3,300,000
> **Contact for Rental:** Ginger Beraha;   (619) 232-9608
> **Manager:** Mark Loigman
> **Resident Groups:** Gaslamp Quarter Theatre Company

THE MARIE HITCHCOCK PUPPET THEATRE IN BALBOA PARK
c/o Balboa Park Management Office, San Diego, CA 92101
(619) 296-5504
FAX: (619) 235-1100
> **Type of Facility:** Puppet Theatre
> **Facility Originally:** Exhibition facility of the 1935 California International Exhibition
> **Type of Stage:** Proscenium
> **Stage Dimensions:** 18'Dx44'W downstage, 24'W upstage
> **Seating Capacity:** 254
> **Year Built:** 1935
> **Year Remodeled:** 1948
> **Contact for Rental:** Balboa Park Management Office;   (619) 235-1100
> **Resident Groups:** San Diego Guild of Puppetry
> *Originally the Palisades Building (Hollywood Hall of Fame), converted to a theatre in 1948*

THE RECITAL HALL - BALBOA PARK
2130 Pan American Road West, San Diego, CA 92101
(619) 235-1100
> **Type of Facility:** Recital Hall
> **Facility Originally:** Exhibition facility of the 1935 California International Exhibition
> **Type of Stage:** Proscenium
> **Stage Dimensions:** 60'Wx22'D
> **Seating Capacity:** 250
> **Year Built:** 1935
> **Contact for Rental:** Balboa Park Management Office;   (619) 235-1100

SAN DIEGO CONCOURSE
202 C Street, San Diego, CA 92101
(619) 236-6500
> **Type of Facility:** Theatre Complex; Civic Center
> **Year Built:** 1964   **Architect:** Frank Hope Jr.   **Cost:** $21,000,000
> **Acoustical Consultant:** Purcell & Knoppe

Contact for Rental: Marika Nieratko;   (619) 236-6500
Manager: Donald Telford
Resident Groups: San Diego Opera; San Diego Playgoers; California Ballet; San Diego Foundation for
the Performing Arts
The Concourse contains the Civic Theatre and Golden Hall. See separate listings for additional information.

SAN DIEGO CONCOURSE - CIVIC THEATRE
202 C Street, San Diego, CA 92101
(619) 236-6500
Type of Facility: Concert Hall; Theatre House
Type of Stage: Proscenium
Stage Dimensions: 129'Wx55'D; 56'Wx29'6"H proscenium opening   **Orchestra Pit**
Seating Capacity: 3,000
Year Built: 1965   **Architect:** Frank Hope Jr.   **Cost:** $4,500,000
Acoustical Consultant: Purcell & Knoppe
Contact for Rental: Marika Nieratko;   (619) 236-6500
Manager: Donald Telford;   (619) 236-6500
Resident Groups: San Diego Opera; San Diego Playgoers; California Ballet; San Diego Foundation for Performing Arts
The Concourse also includes Golden Hall. See separate listing for additional information.

SAN DIEGO CONCOURSE - GOLDEN HALL
202 C Street, San Diego, CA 92101
(619) 236-6500
Type of Facility: Auditorium; Arena; Multi-Purpose
Type of Stage: Hydraulic Lift Stage
Stage Dimensions: 37'6"Wx19'6"D
Seating Capacity: 4,337
Year Built: 1964   **Architect:** Frank Hope Jr.
Acoustical Consultant: Purcell & Knoppe
Contact for Rental: Marika Nieratko;   (619) 236-6500
The Concourse also includes Civic Theatre. See separate listing for additional information.

SIMON EDISON CENTER FOR THE PERFORMING ARTS
Balboa Park, PO Box 2171, San Diego, CA 92112-2171
(619) 231-1941
FAX: (619) 231-5879
Type of Facility: Theatre Complex
Contact for Rental: Thomas Hall;   (619) 231-1941
*The Performing Arts Center contains the Cassius Carter Centre Stage, Lowell Davies Festival Theatre and Old Globe
Theatre. See separate listings for additional information.*

SIMON EDISON CENTER FOR THE PERFORMING ARTS - CASSIUS CARTER CENTRE STAGE
Balboa Park, PO Box 2171, San Diego, CA 92112
(619) 231-1941
FAX: (619) 231-5879
Type of Facility: Studio Performance; Arena
Facility Originally: Restaurant for the 1935 California Pacific International Exhibition
Type of Stage: Arena
Stage Dimensions: 21'x23'
Seating Capacity: 225
Year Built: 1935
Year Remodeled: 1969   **Architect:** Victor Wulff   **Cost:** $350,000
Contact for Rental: Thomas Hall;   (619) 231-1941

SIMON EDISON CENTER FOR THE PERFORMING ARTS - LOWELL DAVIES FESTIVAL THEATRE
Balboa Park, PO Box 2171, San Diego, CA 92112-2171
(619) 231-1941
FAX: (619) 231-5879
Type of Facility: Amphitheater
Type of Stage: Platform; Environmental
Stage Dimensions: 50'Wx50'D
Seating Capacity: 612
Year Built: 1978   **Architect:** Leibhardt, Weston & Associates   **Cost:** $550,000
Year Remodeled: 1985   **Architect:** Leibhardt, Weston & Associates   **Cost:** $2,300,000
Contact for Rental: Thomas Hall;   (619) 231-1941
Original structure burned in 1984, was rebuilt and reopened in 1985.

SIMON EDISON CENTER FOR THE PERFORMING ARTS - OLD GLOBE THEATRE
Balboa Park, PO Box 2171, San Diego, CA 92112-2171
(619) 231-1941
FAX: (619) 231-5879
    Type of Facility: Theatre House
    Facility Originally: Exhibition facility of the 1935 California International Exhibition
    Type of Stage: Modified Stage
    Stage Dimensions: 45'W to 96'W, 48'D
    Seating Capacity: 581
    Year Built: 1935   **Architect:** Thomas Wood Steven
    Year Remodeled: 1982
    Contact for Rental: Thomas Hall;   (619) 231-1941
    Original Theatre burned in 1978, was rebuilt and reopened in 1982.

SPRECKELS ORGAN PAVILION
Balboa Park Administration Building, 2125 Park Boulevard, San Diego, CA 92101-4792
(619) 235-1100
FAX: (619) 235-1112
    Type of Facility: Amphitheater
    Type of Stage: Proscenium
    Stage Dimensions: 69'Wx38'D
    Seating Capacity: 2,400
    Year Built: 1915   **Architect:** Harrison Albright
    Year Remodeled: 1986
    Contact for Rental: Ann-Marie Vavak;   (619) 235-1103
    Pavilion houses a large pipe organ with free performances every Sunday.

STARLIGHT BOWL
Balboa Park, PO Box 3519, San Diego, CA 92163
(619) 544-STAR
    Type of Facility: Environmental; Amphitheater
    Facility Originally: Exhibition facility of the 1935 California International Exhibition
    Type of Stage: Proscenium
    Stage Dimensions: 50'Wx40'D; 50'Wx24'H proscenium opening   **Orchestra Pit**
    Seating Capacity: 4,324
    Year Built: 1935
    Year Remodeled: 1985   **Architect:** Gerald Garapich
    Contact for Rental: Pat Stallard;   (619) 544-7827
    Manager: Bud Franks
    Resident Groups: Starlight - San Diego Civic Light Opera Association
    $1,200,000 has been expended since 1980 in ongoing improvements. Since Starlight Bowl is in the flight path of
    San Diego International Airport, performances are often interrupted by approaching aircraft. Using a stoplight system, a
    spotter halts performances as planes approach and gives a green light when they have passed.

San Francisco

DANCE

ASIAN AMERICAN DANCE PERFORMANCES
2403 16th Street, San Francisco, CA 94103-4210
(415) 552-8980
    Founded: 1975
    Arts Area: Modern
    Status: Professional; Non-Profit
    Type: Performing; Touring; Resident; Educational
    Purpose: To express experiences of Asians in America.
    Management: Anna Sun, Artistic Director; Gayle T. Nishikawa, General Manager
    Officers: Lena Chang, President
    Paid Artists: 7
    Utilizes: Guest Artists; Guest Choreographers
    Budget: $1,000 - $50,000
    Income Sources: Private Foundations/Grants/Endowments; Box Office; Government Grants; Individual Donations
    Season: June - October
    Affiliations: Ethnic Dance Festival

BAILES FLAMENCOS
267 Teresita Boulevard, San Francisco, CA 94127
(415) 824-1960
FAX: (415) 824-1960
Arts Area: Ethnic
Status: Professional; Non-Profit
Type: Performing; Touring; Resident; Educational
Purpose: To advance understanding of the culture and art of Spain in particular the performing arts of flamenco and classical Spanish dance and music
Management: Melanie B. Rainey, Executive Director; Rosa Montoya, Artistic Director
Officers: Carmen Torrico, President of the Board
Budget: $100,000 - $500,000
Income Sources: Private Foundations/Grants/Endowments; Business/Corporate Donations; Box Office; Government Grants; Individual Donations
Performance Facilities: Herbst Theater

CITY CELEBRATION, INC.
Building A, Fort Mason Center, San Francisco, CA 94123
(415) 474-3914
FAX: (415) 474-3922
Founded: 1978
Arts Area: Ethnic; Folk
Status: Non-Profit
Type: Performing; Resident; Educational; Sponsoring
Purpose: To present, promote and celebrate the diverse performing arts of the Bay Area
Management: Robert R. Allen, Executive Director; Joann Knecht, Associate Director; Lily Kharrazi, Program Coordinator; Yasmen Sorab Mehta, Production Coordinator
Officers: Mara Brazer, President; Michael Huerta, Norma Garcia-Kennedy and Larry Giddings, Vice Presidents; Christine Stokes, Treasurer; Susan Tibbons, Secretary
Paid Staff: 7
Paid Artists: 1,000
Utilizes: Guest Artists
Budget: $500,000 - $1,000,000
Income Sources: Private Foundations/Grants/Endowments; Box Office; Government Grants; Individual Donations
Annual Attendance: 18,000
Affiliations: Dance Bay Area; APAP; Dance USA; California Presenters
Performance Facilities: Palace of Fine Arts; Cowell Theater; Golden Gate Bandshell

CONTRABAND
499 Alabama Street, #120, San Francisco, CA 94110
(415) 558-8821
FAX: (415) 864-5437
Founded: 1985
Arts Area: Modern; Contact Improvisation
Status: Professional; Non-Profit
Type: Performing; Touring; Educational
Purpose: Contraband is a team of dancers, artists and musicians committed to the exploration of live theatre forms
Management: Sara Shelton Mann, Artistic Director; Karen Schiller, Administrative Coordinator; Jess Curtis, Production Manager
Officers: Sara Shelton Mann, President
Paid Staff: 3   **Volunteer Staff:** 5
Paid Artists: 8
Budget: $100,000 - $500,000
Income Sources: Private Foundations/Grants/Endowments; Box Office; Government Grants; Individual Donations
Season: September - June
Annual Attendance: 3,000
Affiliations: Dance Bay Area

DANCERS' GROUP
3221 22nd Street, San Francisco, CA 94110
(415) 824-5044
FAX: (415) 824-2873
Founded: 1982
Arts Area: Modern; Performance Art
Status: Professional; Semi-Professional; Non-Professional; Non-Profit
Type: Performing; Educational; Sponsoring
Purpose: To educate the community in dance and the performing arts
Management: Wayne Hazzard, Director; Michael Jones, Manager; Rebecca Lowe, Assistant Manager

Paid Staff: 7   **Volunteer Staff:** 2
Paid Artists: 15
Utilizes: Guest Artists
Budget: $100,000 - $500,000
Income Sources: Private Foundations/Grants/Endowments; Business/Corporate Donations; Box Office; Government Grants; Individual Donations
Season: 52 Weeks   **Annual Attendance:** 5,000
Affiliations: Dance Bay Area

DEBORAH SLATER AND COMPANY
c/o Art of the Matter, 100 Putnam Street, San Francisco, CA 94110
(415) 824-2464
Arts Area: Dance Theater; Experimental
Status: Professional; Non-Profit
Type: Performing; Touring; Resident; Educational
Purpose: To attempt to find meaning in the human experience through dance and theater
Management: Deborah Slater, Director
Officers: Barbara Slotnik, Board President
Budget: $1,000 - $50,000
Income Sources: Private Foundations/Grants/Endowments; Business/Corporate Donations; Box Office; Government Grants; Individual Donations
Performance Facilities: Studio 210

DELLA DAVIDSON DANCE COMPANY
223 Mississippi, San Francisco, CA 94107
(415) 861-5797
Founded: 1976
Arts Area: Modern
Status: Professional; Non-Profit
Type: Performing; Touring
Purpose: Produce the original dance theatre work of Della Davidson
Management: Della Davidson, Artistic Director; John Rush, Executive Director
Officers: Nancy Barlet, President; Derek Dean, Secretary; Suzanne Mayor, Treasurer
Paid Staff: 3   **Volunteer Staff:** 25
Paid Artists: 7
Utilizes: Special Technical Talent; Guest Conductors; Guest Artists; Guest Directors
Budget: $100,000 - $500,000
Income Sources: Private Foundations/Grants/Endowments; Business/Corporate Donations; Box Office; Government Grants; Individual Donations; Tuition; Commissions
Season: September - May   **Annual Attendance:** 20,000
Affiliations: Theatre Artaud
Performance Facilities: Theatre Artaud

ISADORA DUNCAN DANCE CENTER
741 Lakeview Avenue, San Francisco, CA 94112
Founded: 1989
Arts Area: Modern; Historical
Status: Semi-Professional
Type: Performing; Touring; Educational
Officers: Maria Villazana-Ruiz, Director; Madelyn Szepesi, Teacher
Paid Staff: 2   **Volunteer Staff:** 4
Paid Artists: 2   **Non-Paid Artists:** 4
Utilizes: Guest Artists
Budget: $1,000 - $50,000
Income Sources: Box Office; Individual Donations
Season: Spring - Fall   **Annual Attendance:** 2,000
Performance Facilities: Isadora Duncan Dance Center

KHADRA INTERNATIONAL FOLK BALLET
1182 Market Street, Suite 217, San Francisco, CA 94102
(415) 626-7360
FAX: (415) 824-1599
Arts Area: Ethnic; Folk
Status: Semi-Professional; Non-Profit
Type: Performing; Touring; Resident; Educational; Sponsoring
Purpose: To make a unique artistic statement by drawing on traditional folk music and dance; to capture the essence of national character in theatrical presentations
Management: Mari Nijessen, Art; Tricia Dell, General Manager
Officers: F.J. Dale, Chairman of the Board

Budget: $100,000 - $500,000
Income Sources: Private Foundations/Grants/Endowments; Business/Corporate Donations; Box Office; Government Grants; Individual Donations

MARGARET JENKINS DANCE COMPANY
3153 17th Street, San Francisco, CA 94110
(415) 863-1173
Founded: 1972
Arts Area: Modern
Status: Professional; Non-Profit
Type: Performing; Touring; Resident; Educational
Purpose: To perform the work of Artistic Director and choreographer Margaret Jenkins
Management: Steve Jordan, Producing Director
Officers: Margaret Jenkins, President
Paid Staff: 10   **Volunteer Staff:** 10
Paid Artists: 10
Budget: $500,000 - $1,000,000
Income Sources: Private Foundations/Grants/Endowments; Business/Corporate Donations; Box Office; Government Grants; Individual Donations
Annual Attendance: 15,000
Affiliations: California Confederation of the Arts; AAA; Dance USA; Dance California; San Francisco Bay Area Dance Coalition
Performance Facilities: New Performance Gallery; Herbst Theatre; Theatre Arts Auditorium

NEVA RUSSIAN DANCE ENSEMBLE
2450 Sutter Street, San Francisco, CA 94110
(415) 563-7362
Founded: 1983
Arts Area: Ethnic; Folk
Status: Professional; Non-Profit
Type: Performing; Touring; Resident; Educational
Purpose: To present and preserve character/folk dances of northern Russia, Ukraine, Romania and Moldova
Management: Vladimir Riazantsev, Artistic Director; Michal Myers, Business Manager
Officers: Stuart Platt, President of the Board; Nadine Howard, Marie Bergstedt, Board Members; Bob Dettmer, Treasurer
Paid Staff: 1   **Volunteer Staff:** 4
Paid Artists: 2   **Non-Paid Artists:** 2
Utilizes: Special Technical Talent; Guest Artists
Budget: $1,000 - $50,000
Income Sources: Private Foundations/Grants/Endowments; Government Grants; Individual Donations
Performance Facilities: Russian Center of San Francisco

ODC/SAN FRANCISCO
3153 17th Street, San Francisco, CA 94110
(415) 863-6606
FAX: (415) 863-9833
Founded: 1971
Arts Area: Modern
Status: Professional; Non-Profit
Type: Performing; Touring; Resident; Educational
Purpose: To create and perform modern dance
Management: Susan Davis Cushing, Executive Director
Paid Staff: 5
Paid Artists: 12
Utilizes: Special Technical Talent; Guest Conductors; Guest Artists
Budget: $500,000 - $1,000,000
Income Sources: Private Foundations/Grants/Endowments; Business/Corporate Donations; Box Office; Government Grants; Individual Donations
Season: 52 Weeks   **Annual Attendance:** 50,000
Affiliations: Dance USA; San Francisco Bay Area Dance Coalition

SAN FRANCISCO BALLET ASSOCIATION
455 Franklin Street, San Francisco, CA 94102
(415) 861-5600
Founded: 1933
Arts Area: Ballet
Status: Professional; Non-Profit
Type: Performing; Touring; Educational
Purpose: To provide a repertoire of classical and contemporary ballet; provide educational opportunities for the professional training of dancers and choreographers; and excel in ballet, artistic direction and administration

Management: Joyce A. Moffatt, Vice President/General Manager; Helgi Tomasson, Artistic Director; Bonita Borne, Ballet Mistress/Assistant Artistic Director
Officers: Mrs. F. Warren Hellman, Chairman of the Board; Susan S. Briggs, Secretary
Paid Staff: 60 **Volunteer Staff:** 100
Paid Artists: 57
Utilizes: Special Technical Talent; Guest Choreographers
Budget: Over 10,000,000
Income Sources: Private Foundations/Grants/Endowments; Business/Corporate Donations; Box Office; Government Grants; Individual Donations
Season: December - May **Annual Attendance:** 250,000
Affiliations: California Dance Coalition; San Francisco Chamber of Commerce
Performance Facilities: War Memorial Opera House

SAN FRANCISCO JAZZ DANCE COMPANY
PO Box 22336, San Francisco, CA 94122
(415) 456-8053
Founded: 1980
Arts Area: Jazz
Status: Professional; Non-Profit
Type: Performing; Touring; Resident; Educational
Purpose: To perform, preserve and promote the American art form of jazz dance
Management: Allen Habel, Business Manager
Officers: Wendy Ballard, President; Deborah Adams, Vice President; Allen Habel, Secretary; Robert Yastacek, Treasurer
Paid Staff: 1 **Volunteer Staff:** 15
Paid Artists: 9 **Non-Paid Artists:** 2
Utilizes: Guest Artists
Budget: $1,000 - $50,000
Income Sources: Box Office; Individual Donations
Season: September - May **Annual Attendance:** 1,750
Affiliations: WAAA; San Francisco Bay Area Dance Coalition

SAN FRANCISCO PERFORMANCES
500 Sutter Street, Suite 710, San Francisco, CA 94102
(415) 398-6449
FAX: (415) 398-6439
Founded: 1979
Arts Area: Modern; Ethnic
Status: Professional
Type: Sponsoring
Purpose: To present outstanding national, international and emerging artists; to introduce innovative programs; to build new and diversified audiences for the arts
Management: Ruth A. Felt, President/Executive Director; Marian Kohlstedt, Diretor of Public Relations; Nancy Petrisko, Director of Operations/Tickets; Cindy Rasicot, Director of Development
Officers: Amy McCombs, Chair; Clifford Orent, Vice Chair; Dr. Yanek Chiu, Secretary; Barbara Kokesh, Treasurer
Paid Staff: 7 **Volunteer Staff:** 3
Utilizes: Guest Artists
Budget: $1,000,000 - $5,000,000
Income Sources: Private Foundations/Grants/Endowments; Business/Corporate Donations; Box Office; Government Grants; Individual Donations
Season: October - May **Annual Attendance:** 7,100
Affiliations: Dance Bay Area; APAP; ISPAA
Performance Facilities: Herbst Theatre; Cowell Theater at Fort Mason; Palace of Fine Arts Theatre

SAN FRANCISCO'S BALLET CELESTE INTERNATIONAL
25 Taylor Street, Suite 200, San Francisco, CA 94102
(415) 567-0988
FAX: (415) 567-0547
Founded: 1949
Arts Area: Ballet; Jazz; Ethnic; Folk
Status: Non-Professional; Non-Profit
Type: Performing; Touring; Resident
Purpose: To provide a unique performing experience to young artists founded on classical tradition; to present inexpensive concerts for the public
Management: Merriem Lanova, Director; Barbara Owen, Touring Director; John Bischof, Music
Officers: Merriem Lanova, Chief Executive Officer; Stephen Kopel, Secretary; Barbara Owen, Finances; William Holsman, Legal
Paid Staff: 1 **Volunteer Staff:** 30
Non-Paid Artists: 25
Utilizes: Special Technical Talent; Guest Artists; Guest Choreographers

Budget: $50,000 - $100,000
Income Sources: Private Foundations/Grants/Endowments; Business/Corporate Donations; Box Office; Government Grants; Individual Donations
Season: July - August; November-December   **Annual Attendance:** 160,000

TANCE DANZ
347 Dolores Street, #243, San Francisco, CA 94110
(415) 968-5959
Founded: 1980
Arts Area: Modern; Ballet
Status: Professional; Non-Profit
Type: Performing; Touring
Purpose: To extend the horizons of dance through arts interaction - multimedia artists of many disciplines with dance
Management: Tance Johnson, Artistic Director; Carl Sitton, Music Director; Cheryl Elliot, Public Relations
Officers: Margo Sims, President; Wendy Pappas, Vice President; Maggie Merrill, Secretary; Carl Sitton, Treasurer
Paid Staff: 3   **Volunteer Staff:** 10
Paid Artists: 12   **Non-Paid Artists:** 5
Utilizes: Guest Choreographers
Budget: $50,000 - $100,000
Income Sources: Private Foundations/Grants/Endowments; Business/Corporate Donations; Box Office; Government Grants; Individual Donations
Season: 28 Weeks
Affiliations: Dance Action, Inc.; Dance Bay Area

THEATER ARTAUD
2403 16th Street, San Francisco, CA 94103
(415) 621-7641
FAX: (415) 621-7647
Arts Area: Modern; Mime; Ballet; Jazz; Ethnic; Folk; Contemporary Work
Status: Professional
Type: Performing
Purpose: To perform a variety of disciplines; to provide professional technical and administrative services to performing arts companies; to present, produce and collaborate on productions and provide an expansive alternative performance space
Management: Dean Beck-Stewart, Executive Director; Jack Carpenter, Technical Director; Elouise Burrell, Business Manager; Noreen Cooper, Administrative Assistant; Lyndie Riemann, Technical Assistant; Kathleen O'Hara, House Manager; Jennifer Ross, House Manager; Jonny McPhee, Box Office Manager; Janet Adams, Box Office Assistant
Officers: Benjamin Young, President; Sigrid Rupp, Secretary/Treasurer; Dean Beck-Stewart, Executive Director; Melanie Grondel, Elizabeth Spicuzza, Bob Taxin
Paid Staff: 10   **Volunteer Staff:** 2
Paid Artists: 70
Utilizes: Special Technical Talent; Guest Conductors; Guest Artists; Guest Directors; Guest Choreographers
Budget: $500,000 - $1,000,000
Income Sources: Private Foundations/Grants/Endowments; Business/Corporate Donations; Box Office; Government Grants; Individual Donations
Season: 52 Weeks   **Annual Attendance:** 20,000
Affiliations: NPN; California Presenters

THE THEATRE BALLET OF SAN FRANCISCO
25 Taylor Street, Suite 200, San Francisco, CA 94102
(415) 567-0988
FAX: (415) 567-0547
Founded: 1949
Arts Area: Modern; Ballet; Ethnic; Folk
Status: Professional; Semi-Professional; Non-Profit
Type: Performing; Touring
Purpose: To provide as much employment as possible; provide good theater at modest prices; to keep classic traditions alive for both artists and audiences alike
Management: Merriem Lanova, Director; Barbara Owen, Tour Director; John Bischof, Music Librarian
Officers: Merriem Lanova, Chief Executive Officer; Stephan Kopel, Secretary; Barbara Owen, Finances; William Holsman, Attorney
Paid Staff: 10   **Volunteer Staff:** 10
Paid Artists: 45   **Non-Paid Artists:** 20
Utilizes: Special Technical Talent; Guest Conductors; Guest Artists; Guest Choreographers
Budget: $100,000 - $500,000
Income Sources: Private Foundations/Grants/Endowments; Business/Corporate Donations; Box Office; Individual Donations
Season: October - December   **Annual Attendance:** 40,000

INSTRUMENTAL MUSIC

CHAMBER MUSIC WEST FESTIVAL
San Francisco Conservatory of Music, 1201 Ortega Street, San Francisco, CA 94122
(415) 564-8086
FAX: (415) 759-3499
Arts Area: Chamber
Status: Professional; Non-Profit
Type: Performing; Educational
Purpose: To provide advanced students and faculty with the opportunity to perform with outstanding guest artists, continuing the tradition of master artists and gifted young apprentices; To offer Bay Area audiences concerts featuring highly imaginative programming and less cautious, nontraditional interpretations of both traditional and newer repertoire
Management: Colin Murdoch, Artistic Director; Timothy Bach, Festival Coordinator
Officers: Colin Murdoch, Pres. of Conservatory; Michael J. Savage, Chairman of the Board of Conservatory
Budget: $50,000 - $100,000
Income Sources: Private Foundations/Grants/Endowments; Business/Corporate Donations; Box Office; Government Grants; Individual Donations
Season: 52 Weeks
Performance Facilities: Hellman Hall

INTERNATIONAL CREATIVE MUSIC ORCHESTRA
c/o Rova Saxophone Quartet, 332 12th Street, San Francisco, CA 94103
(510) 644-3112; (415) 648-9164
FAX: (510) 704-8350
Arts Area: Jazz Ensemble
Status: Professional; Non-Profit
Type: Performing; Touring
Purpose: An ensemble of musicians from Europe, the US and Canada performing music inspired by jazz and world music
Management: Larry Ochs, Artistic Director; Lawrence Butch Morris, Conductor
Budget: $1,000 - $50,000
Income Sources: Box Office
Season: 52 Weeks

KRONOS QUARTET
1235-A Ninth Avenue, San Francisco, CA 94122
(415) 731-3533
Founded: 1973
Arts Area: Chamber; Ensemble
Status: Professional; Non-Profit
Type: Performing; Touring; Sponsoring
Purpose: To perform and commission new music
Management: Janet Cowperthwaite, Managing Director
Paid Staff: 3   **Volunteer Staff:** 20
Paid Artists: 4
Utilizes: Special Technical Talent; Guest Directors
Budget: $100,000 - $500,000
Income Sources: Private Foundations/Grants/Endowments; Business/Corporate Donations; Box Office; Government Grants; Individual Donations
Season: 52 Weeks

PHILHARMONIA BAROQUE ORCHESTRA
57 Post Street, Suite 705, San Francisco, CA 94104
(415) 391-5252
FAX: (415) 391-3737
Founded: 1981
Arts Area: Orchestra; Historical Performance
Status: Professional; Non-Profit
Type: Performing; Touring
Purpose: To perform 17th and 18th century music on instruments of the period
Management: Nicholas McGegan, Music Director; George Gellas, Executive Director
Utilizes: Guest Conductors; Guest Artists
Budget: $1,000,000 - $5,000,000
Income Sources: Private Foundations/Grants/Endowments; Business/Corporate Donations; Box Office; Government Grants; Individual Donations
Season: September - April
Performance Facilities: Herbst Theatre

SAN FRANCISCO CONSERVATORY OF MUSIC
1201 Ortega Street, San Francisco, CA 94122
(415) 564-8086
FAX: (415) 759-3499
> **Founded:** 1917
> **Arts Area:** Orchestra; Chamber; Ensemble; Electronic & Live Electronic
> **Status:** Non-Profit
> **Type:** Performing; Educational
> **Purpose:** To train classical musicians for professional careers as performers, composers, conductor and teachers
> **Management:** Colin Murdoch, President; Timothy Bach, Acting Dean; Patricia Berkowitz, Director of Administration
> **Officers:** Michael J. Savage, Chairman of the Board
> **Paid Staff:** 35
> **Utilizes:** Special Technical Talent; Guest Conductors; Guest Artists
> **Budget:** $5,000,000 - $10,000,000
> **Income Sources:** Private Foundations/Grants/Endowments; Business/Corporate Donations; Box Office; Government Grants; Individual Donations; Tuition
> **Season:** 52 Weeks
> **Annual Attendance:** 30,000
> **Performance Facilities:** Hellman Hall

SAN FRANCISCO CONTEMPORARY MUSIC PLAYERS
44 Page Street, Suite 604A, San Francisco, CA 94102
(415) 252-6235
FAX: (415) 621-2533
> **Founded:** 1975
> **Arts Area:** Chamber; Ensemble
> **Status:** Professional; Non-Profit
> **Type:** Performing; Touring
> **Purpose:** To professionally perform contemporary chamber music using a mixed ensemble
> **Management:** Stephen L. Mosco, Music Director; Adam L. Frey, Administrator
> **Officers:** Paul Griffin, President; Roy C. Johns, Vice President; T. William Melis, Treasurer
> **Paid Staff:** 3   **Volunteer Staff:** 5
> **Paid Artists:** 12
> **Budget:** $100,000 - $500,000
> **Income Sources:** Private Foundations/Grants/Endowments; Business/Corporate Donations; Box Office; Government Grants; Individual Donations
> **Season:** September - May   **Annual Attendance:** 1,800
> **Affiliations:** CMA
> **Performance Facilities:** Veterans Building

SAN FRANCISCO SYMPHONY ORCHESTRA
Louise M. Davies Symphony Hall, San Francisco, CA 94102
(415) 552-8000
> **Founded:** 1911
> **Arts Area:** Symphony; Orchestra
> **Status:** Professional; Non-Profit
> **Type:** Performing; Touring; Resident; Educational
> **Purpose:** The goals of the San Francisco Symphony Orchestra are: to be a great orchestra; to be recognized as a great orchestra, and to serve the community. These goals are subject to achieving the appropriate balances of financial and organizational strength.
> **Management:** Peter Pastreich, Executive Director; Herbert Blomstedt, Music Director/Conductor; Andrew Massey, Associate Conductor; Leif Bjaland, Exxon Arts Endowment Conductor/Assistant Conductor; Don Roth, General Manager
> **Paid Staff:** 152   **Volunteer Staff:** 1,500
> **Paid Artists:** 105
> **Utilizes:** Guest Conductors; Guest Artists
> **Budget:** Over 10,000,000
> **Income Sources:** Private Foundations/Grants/Endowments; Business/Corporate Donations; Box Office; Government Grants; Individual Donations
> **Season:** September - May
> **Annual Attendance:** 622,000
> **Affiliations:** ASOL; Association of California Symphony Orchestras
> **Performance Facilities:** Louise M. Davies Symphony Hall; Flint Center for the Performing Arts; Stern Grove

SAN FRANCISCO SYMPHONY YOUTH ORCHESTRA
Louise M. Davies Symphony Hall, San Francisco, CA 94102
(415) 552-8000
FAX: (415) 431-6857
> **Founded:** 1981

Arts Area: Symphony; Orchestra
Status: Non-Professional; Non-Profit
Type: Performing; Touring; Resident; Educational; Sponsoring
Purpose: To present the best pre-professional, performance training program for Bay Area, young musicians
Management: Richard L. Bains, Director of Education Programs/Youth Orchestra; Alasdair Neale,
Music Director/Conductor
Paid Staff: 3
Non-Paid Artists: 110
Utilizes: Guest Conductors; Guest Artists
Budget: $100,000 - $500,000
Income Sources: Private Foundations/Grants/Endowments; Business/Corporate Donations; Box Office; Government
Grants; Individual Donations
Season: September - June   **Annual Attendance:** 9,500
Affiliations: ASOL (Youth Orchestra Division)
Performance Facilities: Louise M. Davies Symphony Hall

THE. ART. RE. GRÜP, INC./THE LAB
1807 Divisadero Street, San Francisco, CA 94115
(415) 346-4063
FAX: (415) 346-4567
Arts Area: Chamber; Electronic & Live Electronic; Avant Garde
Status: Professional; Non-Profit
Type: Presenting
Purpose: To support the development of new work in performance, literature, media, visual arts and new music
Management: Laura Brun, Artistic Director; Keesje Fischer, Administrative Director
Officers: Richard Pinegar, Chairman of the Board
Budget: $100,000 - $500,000
Income Sources: Private Foundations/Grants/Endowments; Business/Corporate Donations; Box Office; Government
Grants; Individual Donations
Performance Facilities: The Lab

WOMEN'S PHILHARMONIC
330 Townsend Street, Suite 218, San Francisco, CA 94107
(415) 543-2297
FAX: (415) 543-3244
Founded: 1980
Arts Area: Orchestra; Chamber; Ensemble
Status: Professional; Non-Profit
Type: Performing; Touring; Resident; Educational
Purpose: To promote women composers, conductors and performers through the performance of orchestral and chamber
works, serving as a national resource center for women composers
Management: Miriam Abrams, Executive Director; JoAnn Falletta, Music Director
Officers: Julia Bloomfield, President; Lorraine Gnecco, Vice President; Carol Pierson, Treasurer;
Peggy Bennington, Secretary
Paid Staff: 3   **Volunteer Staff:** 10
Paid Artists: 65
Utilizes: Guest Conductors; Guest Artists
Budget: $100,000 - $500,000
Income Sources: Private Foundations/Grants/Endowments; Business/Corporate Donations; Box Office; Government
Grants; Individual Donations
Season: October - May   **Annual Attendance:** 4,000
Affiliations: ASOL; Association of California Symphony Orchestras; AMC; ASCAP;
League of Women Composers
Performance Facilities: First Congregational Church

VOCAL MUSIC

LAMPLIGHTERS/OPERA WEST FOUNDATION
2350 Turk Boulevard, San Francisco, CA 94118
(415) 752-9813
FAX: (415) 752-9818
Founded: 1952
Arts Area: Light Opera; Operetta
Status: Semi-Professional; Non-Profit
Type: Performing
Purpose: To perform light opera and operettas, especially Gilbert and Sullivan, Lehar, Kalman and Strauss;
to further careers of young singers, designers and musicians
Management: John J. Alecca, General Director; Baker Peeles, Artistic Director

Officers: John Vlahos, President; Nick Tarlson, Treasurer
Paid Staff: 6   **Volunteer Staff:** 180
Paid Artists: 22   **Non-Paid Artists:** 180
Utilizes: Special Technical Talent; Guest Conductors; Guest Artists; Guest Directors
Budget: $500,000 - $1,000,000
Income Sources: Private Foundations/Grants/Endowments; Business/Corporate Donations; Box Office; Government Grants; Individual Donations
Season: March - December
Annual Attendance: 42,000
Affiliations: AFM; California Confederation of the Arts; Theatre Bay Area; California Theatre Council
Performance Facilities: Presentation Theatre

MEROLA OPERA PROGRAM
War Memorial Opera House, San Francisco, CA 94102
(415) 565-6427; (415) 861-4008
FAX: (415) 255-6774
Founded: 1954
Arts Area: Grand Opera; Lyric Opera
Status: Non-Profit
Type: Educational; Sponsoring
Purpose: To discover and develop young professional opera singers; to sponsor the San Francisco Opera Center auditions and the Merola Opera Program at the San Francisco Opera
Management: Rachel Malan, Administrator
Officers: Dr. Jess Shenson, President of the Board
Paid Staff: 16
Utilizes: Special Technical Talent; Guest Conductors; Guest Directors
Budget: $500,000 - $1,000,000
Income Sources: Private Foundations/Grants/Endowments; Business/Corporate Donations; Government Grants; Individual Donations; Fund-raising
Season: June - Mid-August
Annual Attendance: 35,000
Affiliations: COS
Performance Facilities: War Memorial Opera House

PAUL DRESHER ENSEMBLE
c/o Musical Traditions Inc., 235 Surrey Street, San Francisco, CA 94131
(415) 333-4994
FAX: (510) 843-4057
Arts Area: Avant Garde; Electronic Opera
Status: Professional; Non-Profit
Type: Performing; Touring; Educational
Purpose: To create dynamic multi-disciplined musical theatre engaging in varied issues arising from contemporary American life to produce works that range in scale from stage concerts to full-scale productions, becoming a meeting place for art and technology
Management: Paul Dresher, Artistic Director; Robin Kirck, Executive Director
Officers: Paul Dresher, President; Robin Kirck, Vice President
Budget: $100,000 - $500,000
Income Sources: Private Foundations/Grants/Endowments; Business/Corporate Donations; Box Office; Government Grants; Individual Donations; Performance Fees; Sales
Performance Facilities: Theater Artaud; Cowell Theater at Fort Mason

SAN FRANCISCO CHANTICLEER, INC.
650 Fifth Street, Suite 311, San Francisco, CA 94107
(415) 896-5866
FAX: (415) 896-1660
Arts Area: Choral
Status: Professional; Non-Profit
Type: Performing; Touring; Resident; Educational
Purpose: A full-time professional a cappella vocal ensemble of 12 men committed to elevating the standards of choral music through a unique ensemble sound utilizing the full male vocal range from counter-tenor to bass
Management: Louis Botto, Artistic Director; Susan Duncan, Executive Director
Officers: Dr. Richard E. LeBlond Jr., President of the Board
Budget: $1,000,000 - $5,000,000
Income Sources: Private Foundations/Grants/Endowments; Business/Corporate Donations; Box Office; Government Grants; Individual Donations; Recordings
Performance Facilities: Mission Dolores Basilica; Calvary Presbyterian Church; Saint Ignatius Church; Mission Santa Clara

SAN FRANCISCO CHILDREN'S OPERA ASSOCIATION
245 Tenth Avenue, San Francisco, CA 94118
(415) 386-9622
> **Founded:** 1952
> **Arts Area:** Light Opera
> **Status:** Semi-Professional; Non-Profit
> **Type:** Performing; Educational
> **Purpose:** Development of children's enjoyment of music, drama and dance
> **Management:** Dr. Norbert Gingold, Director; Venetia Gingold, Co-Director
> **Officers:** Natalie Stryks, President; Raoul Epling, Vice President; Dr. Linda Angin, Secretary; Raoul Epling, Treasurer
> **Paid Staff:** 12   **Volunteer Staff:** 26
> **Paid Artists:** 16
> **Budget:** $1,000 - $50,000
> **Income Sources:** Private Foundations/Grants/Endowments; Box Office; Individual Donations
> **Season:** November - April
> **Annual Attendance:** 5,000
> **Performance Facilities:** Herbst Theatre

SAN FRANCISCO CHORAL ARTISTS
601 Van Ness Avenue, Suite E 3344, San Francisco, CA 94102
(415) 979-5779
> **Arts Area:** Choral
> **Status:** Professional; Non-Profit
> **Type:** Performing
> **Purpose:** To develop and maintain an outstanding performing choral ensemble dedicated to the art of modern classical music
> **Management:** Claire Giovannetti, Music Director; Doug Wyatt, Associate Conductor; Teresa Byrne, Development Manager; Audrey Wong, Publicity
> **Officers:** Maureen Stone, President of the Board
> **Budget:** $1,000 - $50,000
> **Income Sources:** Private Foundations/Grants/Endowments; Business/Corporate Donations; Box Office; Government Grants; Individual Donations
> **Performance Facilities:** Calvary Presbyterian Church; St. Mark's Episcopal Church, Berkeley; First Presbyterian Church, Palo Alto

SAN FRANCISCO GIRLS CHORAL ASSOCIATION
1100 Ellis Street, San Francisco, CA 94109
(415) 673-1511
FAX: (415) 673-0639
> **Founded:** 1978
> **Arts Area:** Choral
> **Status:** Professional; Non-Professional; Non-Profit
> **Type:** Performing; Touring; Resident; Educational; Sponsoring
> **Purpose:** To make excellent music with young female voices; to provide leadership in the emerging art form of girls choral music
> **Management:** June Wiley, Executive Director; Janet Garvin, Development/Public Relations Director
> **Officers:** Frank Spiller, President; Arthur Perkins, Vice President Finance; James Warren, Vice President Fund-raising; Anne Smith, Vice President Marketing; Emily Mugge, Treasurer; Margaret Haldeman, Secretary
> **Paid Staff:** 6   **Volunteer Staff:** 100
> **Paid Artists:** 16   **Non-Paid Artists:** 200
> **Utilizes:** Guest Artists
> **Budget:** $500,000 - $1,000,000
> **Income Sources:** Private Foundations/Grants/Endowments; Business/Corporate Donations; Box Office; Government Grants; Individual Donations; Tuition; Fees
> **Season:** September - June
> **Annual Attendance:** 106,000
> **Affiliations:** San Francisco Opera

SAN FRANCISCO OPERA ASSOCIATION
301 Van Ness Avenue, San Francisco, CA 94102
(415) 861-4008
FAX: (415) 621-7508
> **Founded:** 1923
> **Arts Area:** Grand Opera
> **Status:** Professional; Non-Profit
> **Type:** Performing; Touring; Resident; Educational; Sponsoring
> **Purpose:** To present international opera performances of the highest quality; to enhance the operatic art form by developing artists, new works and the widest possible audiences

Management: Lotfi Mansouri, General Director; Donald Runnicles, Music Director; Russ Walton, Comapany Manager
Officers: Reid W. Dennis, Chairman; Thomas Tilton, President
Paid Staff: 63
Paid Artists: 340
Utilizes: Special Technical Talent; Guest Conductors; Guest Artists; Guest Directors
Budget: Over 10,000,000
Income Sources: Private Foundations/Grants/Endowments; Business/Corporate Donations; Box Office; Government Grants; Individual Donations
Affiliations: OA; AAA; California Confederation of the Arts
Performance Facilities: War Memorial Opera House

SAN FRANCISCO OPERA CENTER
War Memorial Opera House, 301 Van Ness Avenue, San Francisco, CA 94102
(415) 565-6491; (415) 565-6435
FAX: (415) 255-6774
Founded: 1982
Arts Area: Grand Opera; Lyric Opera; Light Opera; Operetta
Status: Professional; Non-Profit
Type: Performing; Touring; Resident; Educational; Sponsoring
Purpose: To utilize the various affiliate components of the San Francisco Opera Association in a comprehensive and unique professional training program for artists
Management: Christine Bullin, Director; Robin A. Hodgkin, Sales and Marketing Manager/Touring
Paid Staff: 12 **Volunteer Staff:** 20
Paid Artists: 125
Utilizes: Special Technical Talent; Guest Conductors; Guest Artists; Guest Directors; Guest Choreographers
Budget: $1,000,000 - $5,000,000
Income Sources: Private Foundations/Grants/Endowments; Business/Corporate Donations; Box Office; Government Grants; Individual Donations
Season: 52 Weeks **Annual Attendance:** 400,000
Affiliations: San Francisco Opera Association; San Francisco Opera; APAP; Metropolitan Opera Guild; WAAA; CAC; WSAF
Performance Facilities: Theatre Artaud; Herbst Theater

SAN FRANCISCO POCKET OPERA
333 Kearny Street, Suite 703, San Francisco, CA 94108
(415) 989-1853
Founded: 1977
Arts Area: Grand Opera; Lyric Opera; Light Opera; Operetta
Status: Professional; Non-Profit
Type: Performing; Touring; Resident
Purpose: Pocket Opera was created to address the need to preserve and promote accessibility of the broad range of operatic literature for English-speaking audiences at affordable ticket prices.
Management: Donald Pippin, Artistic Director; Judith Whitney, General Manager
Officers: Mel Bachmeier, President; Jim Erhart, Bob Shomler, Vice Presidents
Paid Staff: 4 **Volunteer Staff:** 20
Paid Artists: 90
Utilizes: Guest Artists
Budget: $100,000 - $500,000
Income Sources: Private Foundations/Grants/Endowments; Business/Corporate Donations; Box Office; Government Grants; Individual Donations
Season: 52 Weeks
Annual Attendance: 150,000
Affiliations: COS

SAN FRANCISCO SYMPHONY CHORUS
c/o San Francisco Symphony, Louise M. Davies Symphony Hall, San Francisco, CA 94102
(415) 552-8000
FAX: (415) 431-6857
Arts Area: Symphonic
Status: Professional; Non-Profit
Type: Performing
Purpose: To be a world-class chorus; to perform a varied repertoire of great music under the world's leading conductors
Management: Vance George, Chorus Director; Gregory Boals, Chorus Administrator
Budget: $100,000 - $500,000
Income Sources: Private Foundations/Grants/Endowments; Business/Corporate Donations; Box Office; Government Grants
Performance Facilities: Louise M. Davies Symphony Hall

THEATRE

AFRICAN AMERICAN DRAMA COMPANY
394 5th Avenue, San Francisco, CA 94118
(415) 386-2832
> **Founded:** 1977
> **Arts Area:** Theatrical Group
> **Status:** Professional
> **Type:** Touring
> **Purpose:** To perform African and Black history plays for American audiences
> **Management:** Phillip E. Walker, Ethel Pitts Walker, Executive Directors
> **Paid Staff:** 2
> **Paid Artists:** 5
> **Utilizes:** Guest Directors
> **Budget:** $1,000 - $50,000
> **Income Sources:** Box Office
> **Season:** August - June   **Annual Attendance:** 100,000

AMERICAN CONSERVATORY THEATRE
450 Geary Street, San Francisco, CA 94102
(415) 749-2200
FAX: (415) 771-4859
> **Founded:** 1967
> **Arts Area:** Professional
> **Status:** Professional; Non-Profit
> **Type:** Performing; Resident; Educational
> **Purpose:** To perform classical and contemporary plays concurrently with theatre training
> **Management:** Carey Perloff, Artistic Director; John Sullivan, Managing Director; Susan Stauter, Conservatory Director
> **Officers:** Patrick F. Flannery, President; Shepard P. Pollack, Vice President; Keith B. Williams, Treasurer; Marijke Donat, Secretary
> **Paid Staff:** 52   **Volunteer Staff:** 100
> **Paid Artists:** 60
> **Utilizes:** Special Technical Talent; Guest Artists; Guest Directors
> **Budget:** $5,000,000 - $10,000,000
> **Income Sources:** Private Foundations/Grants/Endowments; Business/Corporate Donations; Box Office; Government Grants; Individual Donations
> **Season:** October - June
> **Annual Attendance:** 250,000
> **Affiliations:** LORT; TCG; AAA; California Confederation of the Arts; National Corporation Theatre Fund
> **Performance Facilities:** Stage Door Theatre; Marines Memorial Theatre; Orpheum Theatre

EL TEATRO DE LA ESPERANZA
PO Box 40578, San Francisco, CA 94140
(415) 255-2320
> **Arts Area:** Theatrical Group
> **Status:** Professional; Non-Profit
> **Type:** Touring; Resident
> **Purpose:** To enhance the theatre movement through the Chicano community with bilingual and bi-cultural plays
> **Management:** Rodrigo Durte Clark, Artistic Director; Eve Donovan, General Manager
> **Officers:** Ruben Castro, President of the Board
> **Budget:** $100,000 - $500,000
> **Income Sources:** Private Foundations/Grants/Endowments; Business/Corporate Donations; Box Office; Government Grants; Individual Donations
> **Performance Facilities:** Mission Culture Center

EUREKA THEATRE COMPANY
340 Townsend Street, #519, San Francisco, CA 94107-1607
(415) 243-9899
> **Founded:** 1972
> **Arts Area:** Professional; Theatrical Group
> **Status:** Professional; Non-Profit
> **Type:** Performing; Resident; Educational
> **Purpose:** To produce contemporary plays that focus directly on political and social issues
> **Officers:** Paul Fagin, Board President
> **Paid Staff:** 10

Utilizes: Special Technical Talent; Guest Artists; Guest Directors
Budget: $100,000 - $500,000
Income Sources: Private Foundations/Grants/Endowments; Business/Corporate Donations; Box Office; Government Grants; Individual Donations
Season: October - June
Affiliations: AEA; Coalition of Bay Area Theatres
Performance Facilities: Eureka Theatre

GEORGE COATES PERFORMANCE WORKS
110 McAllister Street, San Francisco, CA 94102
(415) 863-8520
FAX: (415) 863-7939
Founded: 1977
Arts Area: New Music Theatre
Status: Non-Profit
Type: Performing; Touring; Resident
Purpose: To broaden the boundaries of contemporary performances and the creative experience itself; to explore new relationships between performer and audience; to develop new alliances between arts ensembles, individuals and emerging technology industries; emphasis on contemporary vocal expression and multimedia
Management: George Coates, Artistic Director; Beau Takahara, Executive Director; David Hurd, General Manager; Dan Corr, Production Manager
Officers: Lee Bendekgey, President; Larry Batiste, Vice President; Cookie Marenco, Secretary; Michael McDonell, Treasurer
Paid Staff: 5   **Volunteer Staff:** 10
Paid Artists: 27   **Non-Paid Artists:** 4
Utilizes: Special Technical Talent; Guest Artists; Multimedia
Budget: $500,000 - $1,000,000
Income Sources: Private Foundations/Grants/Endowments; Business/Corporate Donations; Box Office; Government Grants; Individual Donations
Season: September - June
Annual Attendance: 19,000
Performance Facilities: Performance Works

ILLUSTRATED STAGE COMPANY
PO Box 640063, San Francisco, CA 94164
(415) 861-6655
Founded: 1979
Arts Area: Professional; Theatrical Group
Status: Professional; Non-Profit
Type: Performing; Resident
Management: Barbara Malinowski, General Manager
Paid Staff: 2   **Volunteer Staff:** 7
Paid Artists: 4   **Non-Paid Artists:** 1
Utilizes: Guest Artists; Guest Directors
Budget: $100,000 - $500,000
Income Sources: Business/Corporate Donations; Box Office; Individual Donations
Season: 52 Weeks
Annual Attendance: 52,000
Performance Facilities: Alcazar Theatre

THE JULIAN THEATRE
777 Valencia, San Francisco, CA 94110
(415) 626-8986
Founded: 1965
Arts Area: Professional; Theatrical Group
Status: Professional; Non-Profit
Type: Performing; Touring; Resident; Educational; Sponsoring
Purpose: To maintain interest in works that have a social or political sense of the times; multi-cultural theater working with new plays
Management: Richard Reineccius, Artistic/General Director; Veronica Masterson, Library Manager; Jackie Hayes, Development Director; Michael Dingle, Production Manager
Officers: George Crowe, Board Chairman
Paid Staff: 3
Utilizes: Special Technical Talent; Guest Artists; Guest Directors
Budget: $50,000 - $100,000
Income Sources: Box Office; Government Grants
Season: September - June
Affiliations: AEA

LORRAINE HANSBERRY THEATER
500 Sutter Street, Suite 511, San Francisco, CA 94102-1115
(415) 433-9115
FAX: (415) 288-0326
  Arts Area: Professional
  Status: Professional; Non-Profit
  Type: Performing; Educational
  Purpose: To produce plays by America's and the world's leading Black writers; to foster the development of new Black writers through the ongoing activities of the playwrights' workshop
  Management: Stanley Williams, Artistic Director; Quentin Easter, Executive Director
  Budget: $100,000 - $500,000
  Income Sources: Private Foundations/Grants/Endowments; Business/Corporate Donations; Box Office; Government Grants; Individual Donations
  Performance Facilities: Lorraine Hansberry Theater

MAGIC THEATRE
Fort Mason Center, Building D, San Francisco, CA 94123
(415) 441-8001; (415) 441-8822
FAX: (415) 771-5505
  Founded: 1967
  Arts Area: Professional; Theatrical Group
  Status: Professional; Non-Profit
  Type: Performing; Resident; Sponsoring
  Purpose: Devoted exclusively to the development of new plays and playwrights; operates two professional theaters
  Management: Jeff Rowlings, General Manager
  Officers: John St. John, Board Chairman
  Paid Staff: 7 **Volunteer Staff:** 8
  Paid Artists: 130 **Non-Paid Artists:** 20
  Utilizes: Special Technical Talent; Guest Artists; Guest Directors
  Budget: $500,000 - $1,000,000
  Income Sources: Private Foundations/Grants/Endowments; Business/Corporate Donations; Box Office; Government Grants; Individual Donations
  Season: October - June **Annual Attendance:** 25,000
  Affiliations: AEA
  Performance Facilities: Northside Theatre; Southside Theatre

MAKE A CIRCUS
Fort Mason Center, Building C, San Francisco, CA 94123
(415) 776-8477
  Arts Area: Musical; Community; Circus
  Status: Non-Profit
  Type: Performing; Touring; Educational; Participatory
  Purpose: To bring social issues to the arts through participatory circus theater; to perform free in the parks—especially in low-income areas where theater is not accessible; to reach out to high-risk teens by providing them with summer employment
  Management: Peggy Ford, Artistic Director; Mary Anne Cook, Managing Director
  Officers: Jane Herzog, President of the Board
  Budget: $100,000 - $500,000
  Income Sources: Private Foundations/Grants/Endowments; Business/Corporate Donations; Government Grants; Individual Donations

MUSICAL TRADITIONS INC.
235 Surrey Street, San Francisco, CA 94131
(415) 333-4994
FAX: (510) 843-4057
  Arts Area: Professional
  Status: Professional; Non-Profit
  Type: Performing; Touring; Educational
  Management: Carrie Boram, Business Manager
  Budget: $100,000 - $500,000

THE NEW CONSERVATORY CHILDRENS THEATRE COMPANY AND SCHOOL
25 Van Ness, Lower Lobby, San Francisco, CA 94102
(415) 861-4914
FAX: (415) 861-6988
  Founded: 1981
  Arts Area: Professional; Musical; Community; Children's Theatre
  Status: Non-Profit

Type: Performing; Touring; Educational
Purpose: As a professional theatre arts school and performing arts company, we strive to make a positive contribution to our community and to serve as a model for educational theatres across the country.
Management: Ed Decker, Executive Director; Carol Majenski, Executive Assistant; Susan Glenn, Business Manager; Irene Cooper-Basch, Development Associate
Officers: A. Hess, Chairperson; Ed Decker, President; Brad Pence, Treasurer; Wendell Rickets, Secretary
Paid Staff: 14   **Volunteer Staff:** 1
Paid Artists: 16   **Non-Paid Artists:** 1
Utilizes: Guest Directors; Guest Musical Directors
Budget: $100,000 - $500,000
Income Sources: Private Foundations/Grants/Endowments; Business/Corporate Donations; Box Office; Government Grants; Individual Donations; Tuition
Season: October - May   **Annual Attendance:** 2,000
Performance Facilities: The New Conservatory Theatre Center

PERSONA GRATA PRODUCTIONS, INC.
355 15th Avenue, #6, San Francisco, CA 94118
(415) 387-7898
Founded: 1982
Arts Area: Professional; Theatrical Group; Puppet
Status: Professional; Non-Profit
Type: Performing; Educational
Purpose: Cross-cultural and educational
Management: Paul Kwan, Executive Director; Arnold Iger, Artistic Director
Paid Staff: 2
Paid Artists: 8   **Non-Paid Artists:** 4
Utilizes: Special Technical Talent; Guest Artists
Budget: $100,000 - $500,000
Income Sources: Private Foundations/Grants/Endowments; Box Office; Government Grants; Individual Donations

PICKLE FAMILY CIRCUS AND PICKLE FAMILY CIRCUS SCHOOL
400 Missouri Street, San Francisco, CA 94107
(415) 826-0747
FAX: (415) 826-1711
Founded: 1974
Arts Area: Professional; Theatrical Group
Status: Professional; Non-Profit
Type: Performing; Touring; Educational
Purpose: One ring circus, no hype, no animals, just great family entertainment, often works as a fund-raiser for other non-profit organizations. The school teaches both beginning and recreational circus skills and professional level classes, students begin at age 4
Management: Ann Vermel, Executive Director; Lu Yi, Associate Director; Tandy Beal, Artistic Director
Officers: Marc Snyder, Chairman; Jon Carroll, Nancy Pietrafesa, Vice Chairmans
Paid Staff: 6   **Volunteer Staff:** 2
Paid Artists: 20
Utilizes: Special Technical Talent; Guest Artists; Guest Directors
Budget: $1,000,000 - $5,000,000
Income Sources: Private Foundations/Grants/Endowments; Business/Corporate Donations; Box Office; Government Grants; Individual Donations
Season: October - April   **Annual Attendance:** 180,000

SAN FRANCISCO MIME TROUPE
855 Treat Avenue, San Francisco, CA 94110
(415) 285-1717
FAX: (415) 285-1290
Founded: 1959
Arts Area: Professional
Status: Professional; Non-Profit
Type: Performing; Touring; Educational
Purpose: To create socially-relevant, original musical theatre of the highest professional quality; to perform before the broadest possible audience
Management: Patrick L. Osbon, General Manager; Peggy Rose, Financial Manager; Barbara A. Jeppesen, Publicist; Ellen Callas, Production Manager
Paid Staff: 4
Paid Artists: 16
Utilizes: Special Technical Talent; Guest Artists
Budget: $500,000 - $1,000,000

Income Sources: Private Foundations/Grants/Endowments; Business/Corporate Donations; Box Office; Government Grants; Individual Donations
Annual Attendance: 100,000

SOON 3 THEATER
231 Franklin Street, Suite 1, San Francisco, CA 94102
(415) 558-8575
> **Founded:** 1972
> **Arts Area:** Professional; Theatrical Group; Interdisciplinary Experimental
> **Status:** Professional; Non-Profit
> **Type:** Performing
> **Purpose:** To develop innovative forms for presenting theatrical works of social significance
> **Management:** Liz Sizensky, Executive Director
> **Officers:** Alan Finneran, President; John Lion, Vice President; Laurey Finneran, Secretary/Treasurer
> **Paid Staff:** 2   **Volunteer Staff:** 3
> **Paid Artists:** 7
> **Utilizes:** Special Technical Talent; Guest Artists; Guest Directors; Composers; Filmmakers
> **Budget:** $100,000 - $500,000
> **Income Sources:** Private Foundations/Grants/Endowments; Box Office; Government Grants; Individual Donations
> **Season:** May - June   **Annual Attendance:** 4,000
> **Affiliations:** Theater Bay Area

STEVE SILVER PRODUCTIONS
678 Green Street, San Francisco, CA 94133
(415) 421-4284
> **Founded:** 1974
> **Arts Area:** Professional; Musical
> **Status:** Professional; Commercial
> **Type:** Performing; Resident
> **Management:** Steve Silver, Producer/Director/Designer
> **Officers:** Steve Silver, President
> **Paid Staff:** 85
> **Paid Artists:** 30
> **Income Sources:** Box Office
> **Season:** 52 Weeks   **Annual Attendance:** 160,000
> **Affiliations:** San Francisco and California Chambers of Commerce; Theater Bay Area
> **Performance Facilities:** Club Fugazi

THEATER RHINOCERUS, INC.
2926 16th Street, San Francisco, CA 94103
(415) 522-4100
> **Founded:** 1977
> **Arts Area:** Theatrical Group
> **Status:** Professional; Non-Profit
> **Type:** Performing; Resident
> **Purpose:** To present Gay and Lesbian theatre
> **Management:** Adele Prandini, Artistic Director; Judie Ghidinelli, Managing Director; Doug Holsclaw, Associate Artistic Director
> **Officers:** Linda Schneider, Board President
> **Utilizes:** Guest Directors
> **Budget:** $100,000 - $500,000
> **Income Sources:** Private Foundations/Grants/Endowments; Business/Corporate Donations; Box Office; Government Grants; Individual Donations
> **Season:** September - June   **Annual Attendance:** 25,000
> **Affiliations:** TCG; Theatre Bay Area
> **Performance Facilities:** Main Stage; Studio Theater

THEATRE ON THE SQUARE
450 Post Street, San Francisco, CA 94102
(415) 433-6461
FAX: (415) 433-2910
> **Founded:** 1981
> **Arts Area:** Professional; Musical
> **Status:** Professional; Commercial
> **Type:** Performing; Touring
> **Purpose:** To present both original and touring plays
> **Management:** Jonathan Reinis, Owner; Joe Watson, Theatre Manager; Gillian Roth, Treasurer; Judy Karwan, House Manager
> **Officers:** Jonathan Reinis, Owner

Paid Staff: 10
Utilizes: Guest Artists; Guest Directors
Budget: $100,000 - $500,000
Income Sources: Box Office
Season: 52 Weeks   **Annual Attendance:** 75,000
Performance Facilities: Theatre on the Square

THE THESPIAN THEATRICAL CLUB
1750 Clay Street, San Francisco, CA 94109
(415) 474-3516
Founded: 1932
Arts Area: Professional; Musical; Community; Theatrical Group
Status: Non-Profit
Type: Performing; Resident
Management: Rex Waldron, Manager
Officers: Jose Ulloa, Vice President; Jenny Scheck, Recording Secretary; Cynthia Powell, Treasurer; Leone Johns, Finance
Volunteer Staff: 8
Budget: $1,000 - $50,000
Season: 52 Weeks

A TRAVELING JEWISH THEATRE
PO Box 421985, San Francisco, CA 94142-1985
(415) 861-4880
Founded: 1978
Arts Area: Professional; Theatrical Group
Status: Professional; Non-Profit
Type: Performing; Touring; Educational
Purpose: An experimental theatre creating original works of universal concern through the specifics of Jewish experience
Management: Corey Fischer, Albert Greenberg, Naomi Newman, Helen Stoltzfus, Artistic Ensemble; Anna Becker, Managing Director
Officers: Evan Mendelson, Board President; Corey Fischer, Vice President; Mark Jansen, Treasurer; Ursula Sherman, Secretary
Paid Staff: 3
Paid Artists: 4
Utilizes: Special Technical Talent; Guest Artists; Guest Directors
Budget: $100,000 - $500,000
Income Sources: Private Foundations/Grants/Endowments; Box Office; Government Grants; Individual Donations
Annual Attendance: 10,000
Affiliations: TCG

VEERA WIBAUX MIME THEATRE
1536 18th Street, San Francisco, CA 94107
(415) 621-6002
Founded: 1969
Arts Area: Professional
Status: Professional; Non-Profit
Type: Performing; Touring; Resident; Educational
Purpose: Touring performances, workshops, lecture demonstrations
Management: Bert Houle, Veera Wibaux, Artistic Directors
Officers: Bert Houle, President; Veera Wibaux, Vice President
Paid Staff: 2
Paid Artists: 2
Utilizes: Special Technical Talent
Budget: $1,000 - $50,000
Income Sources: Private Foundations/Grants/Endowments; Box Office; Government Grants; Individual Donations
Season: 52 Weeks

PERFORMING SERIES

CITY CELEBRATION ARTS
Fort Mason, Building A, San Francisco, CA 94123
(415) 474-3914
Founded: 1979
Arts Area: Dance; Vocal Music; Instrumental Music; Theater
Status: Professional; Non-Profit
Type: Performing; Sponsoring
Purpose: To present, promote and celebrate the diverse performing arts of the Bay Area
Management: Robert Allen, Executive Director
Officers: Mara Brazer, President

Utilizes: Guest Artists
Income Sources: Private Foundations/Grants/Endowments; Business/Corporate Donations; Box Office; Government Grants; Individual Donations
Season: June - October

MIDSUMMER MOZART
World Trade Center, #280, San Francisco, CA 94111
(415) 781-5931
FAX: (415) 781-6329
      Founded: 1975
      Arts Area: Instrumental Music; Festivals
      Status: Professional; Non-Profit
      Type: Performing
      Purpose: To present orchestral/chamber music of Mozart
      Management: William L. Denton, Executive Director; Marilyn Shaw, Development Director; Jeff Phillips, Administrative Assistant
      Officers: James M. Rockett, Chairman; Wendell Rider, President; Richard Heath, Treasurer
      Paid Staff: 3
      Paid Artists: 40
      Utilizes: Guest Artists
      Budget: $500,000 - $1,000,000
      Income Sources: Private Foundations/Grants/Endowments; Business/Corporate Donations; Box Office; Government Grants; Individual Donations
      Season: July - August
      Annual Attendance: 40,000
      Affiliations: ASOL; California Confederation of the Arts; Association of California Symphony Orchestras

SAN FRANCISCO ARTS COMMISSION
25 Van Ness Avenue, Suite 240, San Francisco, CA 94102
(415) 554-9671
FAX: (415) 621-3868
      Founded: 1932
      Arts Area: Vocal Music; Instrumental Music
      Status: Professional
      Type: Performing; Educational; Sponsoring
      Purpose: To support and advocate for the visual arts and artists of the Bay Area
      Management: Joanne Chow Winship, Director of Cultural Affairs; Maya Rath, Assistant Director
      Paid Staff: 17   **Volunteer Staff:** 8
      Paid Artists: 8   **Non-Paid Artists:** 4
      Utilizes: Special Technical Talent; Guest Conductors; Guest Artists
      Budget: $1,000,000 - $5,000,000
      Income Sources: Private Foundations/Grants/Endowments; Business/Corporate Donations; Box Office; Government Grants; Individual Donations
      Season: 52 Weeks
      Annual Attendance: 500,000
      Affiliations: NALAA; CAC

SAN FRANCISCO JAZZ FESTIVAL
c/o Jazz in the City, 141 Tenth Street, San Francisco, CA 94103
(415) 864-5449
FAX: (415) 863-9462
      Founded: 1983
      Arts Area: Dance; Vocal Music; Instrumental Music; Festivals; Jazz
      Status: Professional; Non-Profit
      Type: Performing; Resident; Educational
      Purpose: Featuring the best of national and Bay Area jazz artists, the San Francisco Jazz Festival performs in venues throughout San Francisco.
      Management: Randall Kline, Director; Shirley Kline, Associate Producer; Ann Dyer, Publicist; Dmitri Matheny, Development Director; Cynthia Taylor, Administrative Production Assistant
      Officers: Kim Fowler, Chairman of the Board; Tom Noonan, President; James P. Mayer, Treasurer; Shirley Kline, Secretary
      Utilizes: Guest Artists
      Budget: $100,000 - $500,000
      Income Sources: Private Foundations/Grants/Endowments; Business/Corporate Donations; Box Office; Government Grants; Individual Donations
      Season: October - November
      Annual Attendance: 25,000

STERN GROVE FESTIVAL ASSOCIATION

44 Page Street, Suite 604D, San Francisco, CA 94102

(415) 252-6252

Founded: 1937
Arts Area: Dance; Vocal Music; Instrumental Music; Theater; Festivals; Lyric Opera; Grand Opera
Status: Professional; Non-Profit
Type: Sponsoring
Purpose: To present free events each summer on Sundays in outdoor Sigmund Stern Grove featuring the finest dance, musical theater, instrumental music, vocal music and jazz
Management: Patricia Kristof Moy, Executive Director; Don O'Brien, Artistic Coordinator
Officers: Mrs. Richard N. Goldman, Chairman; Al H. Nathe, Finance Chairman; Mrs. Robilee Fredrick Deane, Program Chairman
Paid Staff: 20 **Volunteer Staff:** 150
Paid Artists: 500
Utilizes: Guest Conductors; Guest Artists; Guest Directors
Budget: $100,000 - $500,000
Income Sources: Private Foundations/Grants/Endowments; Business/Corporate Donations; Government Grants; Individual Donations
Season: June - August **Annual Attendance:** 150,000
Performance Facilities: Sigmund Stern Grove

FACILITY

THE ALCAZAR THEATRE

650 Geary, San Francisco, CA 94102

(415) 861-6655

Type of Facility: Theatre House
Facility Originally: Shrine Temple
Type of Stage: Thrust
Stage Dimensions: 15'x30'x40'
Seating Capacity: 499
Year Built: 1917
Year Remodeled: 1976 **Architect:** John Gerrity **Cost:** $91,000
Contact for Rental: Steve Dobbins; (415) 861-6655
Manager: Joseph Perrotti

BAYVIEW OPERA HOUSE

4705 Third Street, San Francisco, CA 94124

(415) 824-0386

Type of Facility: Theatre Complex; Concert Hall; Auditorium; Outdoor (Concert); Performance Center; Theatre House; Opera House; Multi-Purpose; Room
Type of Stage: Proscenium
Stage Dimensions: 30'Wx15'D
Seating Capacity: 350
Year Built: 1888
Year Remodeled: 1965
Contact for Rental: Fred McKenzie-Acting Director; (415) 824-0386
Resident Groups: San Francisco Senior Community Choir; Four Visions Theater Company; Bayview Opera House Community Choir
The oldest theater in San Francisco

CENTER FOR AFRICAN AND AFRICAN AMERICAN ART AND CULTURE

762 Fulton Street, San Francisco, CA 94102

(415) 928-8546

Founded: 1990
Type of Facility: Theatre Complex; Concert Hall; Auditorium; Outdoor (Concert); Studio Performance; Performance Center; Off Broadway; Theatre House; Opera House; Civic Center; Multi-Purpose; Room; Loft
Facility Originally: Garage; Business Facility; Warehouse
Type of Stage: Thrust; Platform; 3/4 Arena
Stage Dimensions: 36'x26'x12'
Seating Capacity: 240
Year Built: 1935
Year Remodeled: 1984 **Architect:** Rose Kraus & Broder **Cost:** $500,000
Acoustical Consultant: Community Design Center of UC Berkeley, Chuck Turner
Contact for Rental: Kola Thomas; (415) 928-8546
Resident Groups: Wajumbe Cultural Institution; GO Productions; Cultural Odyssey; BES Children's Educational Theatre; San Francisco African American Historical & Cultural Society
Performances; workshops; seminars; classes; rehearsals; conferences; films

COMMUNITY MUSIC CENTER
544 Capp Street, San Francisco, CA 94110
(415) 647-6015
Founded: 1921
Type of Facility: Concert Hall
Type of Stage: Proscenium
Stage Dimensions: 40'Wx20'D
Seating Capacity: 125
Year Built: 1926
Year Remodeled: 1985 **Architect:** Robert Hersey **Cost:** $150,000
Contact for Rental: Claire Harmon; (415) 647-6015
Recitals, auditions, rehearsals

CURRAN THEATRE
445 Geary Street, San Francisco, CA 94102
(415) 474-3800
Type of Facility: Theatre House
Type of Stage: Proscenium
Orchestra Pit
Seating Capacity: 1,740
Year Built: 1922 **Architect:** Homer Curran
Manager: Shorenstein Hays Nederlander Organizatio

FLORENCE GOULD THEATRE IN THE CALIFORNIA PALACE OF THE LEGION OF HONOR
Lincoln Park, San Francisco, CA 94121
(415) 750-3600
Type of Facility: Concert Hall; Theatre House
Type of Stage: Thrust; Proscenium
Stage Dimensions: 25'Wx13'Hx31'D, includes 5' thrust beyond proscenium
Seating Capacity: 332
Year Built: 1924 **Architect:** George Applegarth
Year Remodeled: 1987 **Architect:** Rosekrans & Broder **Cost:** $1,000,000
Acoustical Consultant: Wilson, Ihrig & Associates
The theatre will be closed for seismic upgrade and renovation through January 1995. No rental inquiries can be accepted until fall 1994.

FORT MASON CENTER - COWELL THEATRE
Fort Mason Center Building A, San Francisco, CA 94123
(415) 941-5706
Founded: 1989
Type of Facility: Theatre Complex; Performance Center; Multi-Purpose
Facility Originally: Army Base
Type of Stage: Proscenium
Stage Dimensions: 41'x30'
Seating Capacity: 440
Year Built: 1989 **Architect:** Robinson, Mills and Williams **Cost:** $2,500,000
Contact for Rental: Robert Martin; (415) 941-5706

GOLDEN GATE THEATRE
#1 at Taylor and Market Street, San Francisco, CA 94102
(415) 776-9211
Type of Facility: Theatre House
Type of Stage: Proscenium
Stage Dimensions: 50'Wx33'D **Orchestra Pit**
Seating Capacity: 2,350
Year Built: 1922 **Architect:** G. Albert Lansburg **Cost:** $2,000,000
Year Remodeled: 1979 **Architect:** G. Albert Lansburg **Cost:** $7,000,000
Contact for Rental: Nederlander Organization; (212) 262-2400

MUSIC AND ARTS INSTITUTE
2622 Jackson Street, San Francisco, CA 94115
(415) 567-1445
Type of Facility: Studio Performance; Room
Facility Originally: School; Ballroom
Type of Stage: Flexible
Seating Capacity: 100
Year Built: 1894 **Architect:** Willis Polk
Contact for Rental: (415) 567-1445

NEW PERFORMANCE GALLERY OF SAN FRANCISCO
3153 17th Street, San Francisco, CA 94110
(415) 626-6745
>**Type of Facility:** Studio Performance
Facility Originally: Warehouse
Type of Stage: Flexible; Loft
Stage Dimensions: 40'x40'
Seating Capacity: 200
Year Remodeled: 1980   **Architect:** Peter Van Dyne
Contact for Rental: K.T. Nelson;   (415) 626-6745
Resident Groups: Oberlin Dance Company - San Francisco; Margaret Jenkins Dance Company

NOB HILL MASONIC CENTER
1111 California Street, San Francisco, CA 94108
(415) 776-4702
>**Type of Facility:** Concert Hall; Auditorium; Exhibit Hall
Facility Originally: Masonic Meeting House
Type of Stage: Thrust
Stage Dimensions: 30'Wx50'D
Seating Capacity: 3,165
Year Built: 1956   **Architect:** Isaiah Roller
Contact for Rental: Ray W. Ward, CFE;   (415) 776-4702
Exhibit Hall is 16,500 square feet.

ORPHEUM THEATER
1192 Market Street, San Francisco, CA 94102
(415) 474-3800
FAX: (415) 775-0309
>**Type of Facility:** Theatre House
Facility Originally: Vaudeville; Movie House
Type of Stage: Proscenium   **Orchestra Pit**
Seating Capacity: 2,500
Year Built: 1926   **Architect:** B. Marcus Priteca   **Cost:** $800,000
Year Remodeled: 1977   **Cost:** $2,000,000
Acoustical Consultant: Tim Purcell
Contact for Rental: Pat Heagy;   (415) 673-6400
Manager: Shorenstein Hays Nederlander Organization;   (415) 673-6400

PALACE OF FINE ARTS
3301 Lyon Street, San Francisco, CA 94123
(415) 563-6504
>**Type of Facility:** Performance Center; Multi-Purpose
Facility Originally: Exhibition Facility Of The 1915 Panama P
Year Built: 1913   **Architect:** Bernard Maybeck   **Cost:** $580,000
Year Remodeled: 1967   **Architect:** Hans Gerson   **Cost:** $7,500,000
Contact for Rental: Kevin J. O'Brien, Executive Director;   (415) 563-6504
The building houses the Palace of Fine Arts Theatre. See separate listing for additional information.

PALACE OF FINE ARTS THEATRE
3301 Lyon Street, San Francisco, CA 94123
(415) 563-6504
FAX: (415) 567-4062
>**Founded:** 1970
Type of Facility: Theatre House; Multi-Purpose
Facility Originally: Exhibit Hall
Type of Stage: Proscenium
Stage Dimensions: 73'Wx52'Dx24'H   **Orchestra Pit**
Seating Capacity: 1,000
Year Built: 1970   **Architect:** Vincent Raney   **Cost:** $750,000
Acoustical Consultant: Dennis Paoletti
Contact for Rental: Kevin J. O'Brien, Executive Director;   (415) 563-6504
Theatre was added to Palace of Fine Arts in 1970.

SAN FRANCISCO CIVIC AUDITORIUM
99 Grove Street, San Francisco, CA 94102
(415) 974-4000
FAX: (415) 974-4084
>**Type of Facility:** Concert Hall; Auditorium

Type of Stage: Platform
Seating Capacity: 7,000
Year Built: 1915
Contact for Rental: Melody Lendaro; (415) 974-4000
Manager: John Adams; (415) 974-4000

SAN FRANCISCO COUNTY FAIR BUILDING
9th & Lincoln, San Francisco, CA 94122
(415) 753-7090
 Type of Facility: Auditorium; Multi-Purpose
 Type of Stage: Regular
 Stage Dimensions: 12'x20'x20'
 Seating Capacity: 400
 Year Built: 1961 **Cost:** $800,000
 Contact for Rental: Elaine Calderon, Reservation Secretary; (415) 753-7090
 Manager: Walden R. Valen; (415) 753-7090

SAN FRANCISCO WAR MEMORIAL AND PERFORMING ARTS CENTER
401 Van Ness Avenue, Suite 110, San Francisco, CA 94102
(415) 621-6600
 Orchestra Pit
 Year Built: 1931 **Architect:** Arthur Brown, Jr. **Cost:** $6,000,000
 Contact for Rental: Margo Cowan; (415) 621-6600
 Resident Groups: San Francisco Symphony; San Francisco Opera; San Francisco Ballet
 The facility contains the Green Room, Herbst Theatre, Louise M. Davies Symphony Hall and War Memorial Opera
 House. See separate listings for additional information.

SAN FRANCISCO WAR MEMORIAL AND PERFORMING ARTS CENTER - GREEN ROOM
401 Van Ness Avenue, Suite 110, San Francisco, CA 94102
(415) 621-6600
FAX: (415) 621-5091
 Founded: 1932
 Type of Facility: Concert Hall; Performance Center; Civic Center; Room
 Facility Originally: Library; Lounge
 Type of Stage: Platform
 Seating Capacity: 350
 Year Built: 1931 **Architect:** Arthur Brown Jr.
 Contact for Rental: Elizabeth Glaze; (415) 621-6600
 Manager: Thelma Shelley
 Resident Groups: San Francisco Contemporary Music Players; Composers, Inc.; D'Addario Foundation for the Perform-
 ing Arts - Guitar Series; Avedis; ARTEA Chamber Orchestra; Pacific Mozart Ensemble

SAN FRANCISCO WAR MEMORIAL AND PERFORMING ARTS CENTER - HERBST THEATRE
401 Van Ness Avenue, Suite 110, San Francisco, CA 94102
(415) 621-6600
FAX: (415) 621-5091
 Founded: 1932
 Type of Facility: Concert Hall; Auditorium; Performance Center; Theatre House; Opera House; Civic Center
 Facility Originally: Meeting Hall; Ballroom; Movie House
 Type of Stage: Proscenium
 Stage Dimensions: 49'1"Wx33'10"D stage; 33'11"Wx24'H proscenium opening
 Orchestra Pit
 Seating Capacity: 928
 Year Built: 1931 **Architect:** Arthur Brown Jr. **Cost:** $1,000,000
 Year Remodeled: 1976 **Architect:** Skidmore Owings Merrill **Cost:** $10,000,000
 Contact for Rental: Margo Cowan; (415) 621-6600
 Manager: Thelma Shelley
 Resident Groups: San Francisco Performances; City Arts and Lectures; San Francisco Children's Opera; Midsummer
 Mozart; Chamber Symphony San Francisco; ODC; Today's Artists; Golden Gate Geographic; San Francisco Museum of
 Modern Art

SAN FRANCISCO WAR MEMORIAL AND PERFORMING ARTS CENTER - LOUISE M. DAVIES SYMPHONY HALL
201 Van Ness Avenue, Suite 110, San Francisco, CA 94102
(415) 621-6600
FAX: (415) 621-5091
 Founded: 1980
 Type of Facility: Concert Hall; Auditorium; Performance Center; Civic Center
 Type of Stage: 3/4 Arena

Orchestra Pit
Seating Capacity: 2743
Year Built: 1980 **Architect:** Skidmore Owings Merrill **Cost:** $36,000,000
Year Remodeled: 1992 **Architect:** Skidmore Owings Merrill **Cost:** $10,000,000
Contact for Rental: Margo Cowan; (415) 621-6600
Manager: Thelma Shelley
Resident Groups: San Francisco Symphony

SAN FRANCISCO WAR MEMORIAL AND PERFORMING ARTS CENTER - WAR MEMORIAL OPERA HOUSE
301 Van Ness Avenue, Suite 110, San Francisco, CA 94102
(415) 621-6600
FAX: (415) 621-5091
Founded: 1932
Type of Facility: Concert Hall; Performance Center; Opera House; Civic Center
Type of Stage: Proscenium
Stage Dimensions: 134'Wx84'6"D stage; 52'Wx51'H proscenium opening **Orchestra Pit**
Seating Capacity: 3,252
Year Built: 1931 **Architect:** Arthur Brown Jr. **Cost:** $2,500,000
Year Remodeled: 1976 **Architect:** Skidmore Owings Merrill **Cost:** $6,000,000
Contact for Rental: Margo Cowan; (415) 621-6600
Manager: Thelma Shelley; (415) 621-6600
Resident Groups: San Francisco Opera; San Francisco Ballet; Merola Opera

TRUSTEES AUDITORIUM - ASIAN ART MUSEUM
Golden Gate Park, San Francisco, CA 94118
(415) 668-6314
Type of Facility: Auditorium
Type of Stage: Platform
Stage Dimensions: 25'x25'x10'
Seating Capacity: 390
Year Built: 1950
Contact for Rental: Alexandra Morgan; (415) 668-6314
Manager: Preston Ni

San Gabriel

FACILITY

SAN GABRIEL CIVIC AUDITORIUM
320 South Mission Drive, San Gabriel, CA 91776
(818) 308-2865
Type of Facility: Auditorium; Performance Center; Theatre House; Multi-Purpose
Type of Stage: Proscenium
Stage Dimensions: 100'Wx75'D; 58'Wx29'6"H proscenium opening **Orchestra Pit**
Seating Capacity: 1,488
Year Built: 1927
Contact for Rental: William D. Shaw; (818) 308-2865
Resident Groups: San Gabriel Valley Civic Light Opera

San Jose

DANCE

SAN JOSE CLEVELAND BALLET
PO Box 1666, San Jose, CA 95109
(408) 993-9531
Founded: 1985
Arts Area: Ballet
Status: Professional; Non-Profit
Type: Performing
Management: Dennis Nahat, Artistic Director
Officers: Carole Minton, President
Paid Staff: 6
Paid Artists: 40
Utilizes: Guest Artists
Budget: $1,000,000 - $5,000,000

Income Sources: Private Foundations/Grants/Endowments; Business/Corporate Donations; Box Office; Individual Donations
Season: October - May
Affiliations: Cleveland Ballet
Performance Facilities: San Jose Center for the Performing Arts

SAN JOSE DANCE THEATRE
753 North 9th Street, Suite 234, San Jose, CA 95112
(408) 293-5665
FAX: (408) 293-0852
Founded: 1965
Arts Area: Ballet
Status: Semi-Professional; Non-Profit
Type: Performing; Touring; Resident; Educational
Purpose: A professional organization that develops the performing arts for young dancers
Management: Paul E. Curtis Jr., Artistic Director
Officers: Carolyne Hui, President; Bob Chortek, First Vice President; Clare Noonan, Secretary; Michael Dertro, Treasurer
Paid Staff: 1   **Volunteer Staff:** 18
Paid Artists: 5   **Non-Paid Artists:** 28
Utilizes: Guest Conductors; Guest Artists
Budget: $500,000 - $1,000,000
Income Sources: Private Foundations/Grants/Endowments; Business/Corporate Donations; Box Office; Government Grants; Individual Donations
Season: September - May   **Annual Attendance:** 15,000
Affiliations: PRBA
Performance Facilities: San Jose Center for the Performing Arts

INSTRUMENTAL MUSIC

SAN JOSE SYMPHONY
99 Almaden Boulevard, #400, San Jose, CA 95113
(408) 287-7383
Founded: 1879
Arts Area: Symphony; Orchestra; Ensemble
Status: Professional; Non-Profit
Type: Performing; Educational
Management: Leonid Grin, Music Director/Conductor
Officers: M. Cathy Peek, Chairman of the Board; Douglas McLendon, President
Paid Staff: 18
Paid Artists: 87
Utilizes: Guest Conductors; Guest Artists
Budget: $1,000,000 - $5,000,000
Income Sources: Private Foundations/Grants/Endowments; Business/Corporate Donations; Box Office; Government Grants; Individual Donations
Season: September - June
Annual Attendance: 50,000
Affiliations: ASOL; Association of California Symphony Orchestras
Performance Facilities: Center for Performing Arts; Flint Center

SAN JOSE TAIKO GROUP
PO Box 26895, San Jose, CA 95159
(408) 293-9344
FAX: (408) 293-9366
Founded: 1973
Arts Area: Ethnic; Instrumental Group
Status: Professional; Semi-Professional; Non-Profit
Type: Performing; Touring; Educational
Purpose: To perform using the taiko (Japanese drum) as the principle instrument in a contemporary performing arts form
Management: Mariko Miho, General Manager; Roy Hirabayashi, Artistic Director
Officers: Jean Shimoguchi, Chairperson; Sharon Noguchi, Secretary; Todd Hirozawa, Treasurer
Paid Staff: 3
Paid Artists: 5   **Non-Paid Artists:** 15
Utilizes: Special Technical Talent; Guest Artists
Budget: $100,000 - $500,000
Income Sources: Private Foundations/Grants/Endowments; Business/Corporate Donations; Box Office; Government Grants; Individual Donations
Season: 52 Weeks

VOCAL MUSIC

OPERA SAN JOSE
12 South First Street, #207, San Jose, CA 95113-2404
(408) 283-4880
   Founded: 1984
   Arts Area: Lyric Opera; Operetta
   Status: Professional; Non-Profit
   Type: Performing; Touring; Educational; Sponsoring
   Purpose: To maintain and enhance a professional opera company of artistic excellence; to provide principally in opera of
   all periods and secondarily in operetta; to provide opera singers with professional development and performance opportuni-
   ties; to develop, educate and entertain
   Management: Irene Dalis, General/Artistic Director; David Rohrbaugh, Musical Director
   Officers: Kitty Spaulding, Chairman; Michael Kalkstein, President
   Paid Staff: 8
   Paid Artists: 149
   Utilizes: Special Technical Talent; Guest Directors
   Budget: $1,000,000 - $5,000,000
   Income Sources: Private Foundations/Grants/Endowments; Business/Corporate Donations; Box Office; Government
   Grants; Individual Donations
   Season: October - June   **Annual Attendance:** 235,000
   Affiliations: OA; COS; Theatre Bay Area
   Performance Facilities: Montgomery Theater

SAN JOSE CIVIC LIGHT OPERA ASSOCIATION INC.
4 North Second Street, Suite 100, San Jose, CA 95113
(408) 297-8811
FAX: (408) 971-4046
   Arts Area: Light Opera; Musical Theater
   Status: Semi-Professional; Non-Profit
   Type: Performing; Resident
   Purpose: Our full-scale, musical-theater production company is one of the largest subscribed musical theater companies
   on the West Coast.
   Management: Dianna Shuster; Stewart Slater, Executive Producer
   Officers: Sunny Claggett, President of the Board
   Income Sources: Private Foundations/Grants/Endowments; Business/Corporate Donations; Box Office; Government
   Grants; Individual Donations
   Performance Facilities: San Jose Center of the Performing Arts

THEATRE

THE NORTHSIDE THEATRE COMPANY
848 East William Street, San Jose, CA 95008
(408) 288-7820
   Arts Area: Theatrical Group
   Status: Non-Profit
   Type: Performing; Touring; Resident; Educational
   Purpose: To provide high quality, theatrical opportunities for youth, regardless of economic, educational, cultural or
   physical limitations
   Management: Richard T. Orlando, Artistic Director; Stu Richel, Development Director; Chriss Zaida, Director of Theater
   Education; Sandra Winslow, Office Manager; Alice Willoughby, Administrative Associate
   Officers: Al Reuter, Chairman of the Board; Kathy Harwood, Secretary; Richard Desmond, Vice Chairman; Bev
   Laflamme, Marketing Chair; Jon Rensen, Treasurer
   Paid Staff: 7   **Volunteer Staff:** 4
   Paid Artists: 1   **Non-Paid Artists:** 10
   Utilizes: Special Technical Talent; Guest Artists
   Budget: $100,000 - $500,000
   Income Sources: Private Foundations/Grants/Endowments; Business/Corporate Donations; Box Office; Government
   Grants; Individual Donations
   Season: October - June   **Annual Attendance:** 6,500
   Affiliations: San Jose Civic Light Opera

SAN JOSE REPERTORY THEATRE
1 North First Street, Suite 1, San Jose, CA 95113
(408) 291-2266; (408) 291-2255
FAX: (408) 995-0737
   Mailing Address: PO Box 2399, San Jose, CA 95109
   Founded: 1980

Arts Area: Professional; Theatrical Group
Status: Professional; Non-Profit
Type: Performing; Resident; Educational
Management: Timothy Near, Artistic Director; Alexandra Boisvert, Managing Director
Officers: Jane Decker, Board President
Paid Staff: 35
Paid Artists: 70
Utilizes: Guest Artists; Guest Directors
Budget: $1,000,000 - $5,000,000
Income Sources: Private Foundations/Grants/Endowments; Business/Corporate Donations; Box Office; Government Grants; Individual Donations
Season: November - August   **Annual Attendance:** 90,000
Affiliations: LORT; TCG
Performance Facilities: Montgomery Theater

TEATRO VISION
271 South 20th Street, San Jose, CA 95116
Founded: 1984
Arts Area: Theatrical Group; Chicano Theatre
Status: Semi-Professional; Non-Profit
Type: Performing; Touring
Purpose: To produce and perform plays with themes that address the Chicano experience
Management: Elisa Marina Gonzalez, Production Manager; Denis Marks, Technical Director
Officers: Norma Ruiz, Board Chair; Elisa Marina Gonzalez, Vice Chair; Jaime Alvarado, Secretary; Rose Mendoza, Treasurer
Volunteer Staff: 25
Utilizes: Guest Artists; Guest Directors
Budget: $50,000 - $100,000
Income Sources: Private Foundations/Grants/Endowments; Business/Corporate Donations; Box Office; Government Grants; Individual Donations
Season: May - December   **Annual Attendance:** 3,000
Affiliations: Movimiento de Arte y Cultura Latinoamericana; Theatre Bay Area

FACILITY

SAN JOSE CITY COLLEGE
2100 Moorpark Avenue, San Jose, CA 95128
(408) 288-3785
Type of Facility: Theatre House
Type of Stage: Proscenium
Stage Dimensions: 16'x32'x36'   **Orchestra Pit**
Seating Capacity: 332
Year Built: 1963   **Architect:** Higgins & Root   **Cost:** $800,000
Contact for Rental: Antoinette Rodriguez;   (408) 288-3756
Manager: Bill Kester;   (408) 288-3785
Resident Groups: San Jose City College Drama Department

SAN JOSE CONVENTION AND CULTURAL FACILITIES
408 Almaden Avenue, San Jose, CA 95110
(408) 277-3925
FAX: (408) 277-3525
Type of Facility: Performance Center
Year Built: 1972   **Architect:** Frank Lloyd Wright   **Cost:** $13,000,000
Contact for Rental: Robin Merriam;   (408) 277-3925
Manager: Ellen Oppenheim
The Convention and Cultural Facilities include the Center for Performing Arts, Civic Auditorium and Montgomery Theater. See separate listings for additional information.

SAN JOSE CONVENTION AND CULTURAL FACILITIES - CENTER FOR THE PERFORMING ARTS
PO Box 90250, San Jose, CA 95109
(408) 277-3925
FAX: (408) 277-3535
Type of Facility: Concert Hall; Opera House
Type of Stage: Proscenium
Stage Dimensions: 144'Wx40'6"D; 60'Wx34'H proscenium opening   **Orchestra Pit**
Seating Capacity: 2,701
Year Built: 1972
Contact for Rental: Robin Merriam;   (408) 277-3925

Manager: Ellen Oppenheim
Resident Groups: San Jose Symphony Association; San Jose Civic Light Opera; San Jose Cleveland Ballet

SAN JOSE CONVENTION AND CULTURAL FACILITIES - CIVIC AUDITORIUM
PO Box 90250, San Jose, CA 95109
(408) 277-3925
FAX: (408) 277-3535
    Type of Facility: Auditorium
    Type of Stage: Proscenium
    Stage Dimensions: 116'Wx36'Dx65'H; 49'9"Wx30'H proscenium opening   **Orchestra Pit**
    Seating Capacity: 3,060
    Year Built: 1972
    Contact for Rental: Robin Merriam;   (408) 277-3925
    Manager: Ellen Oppenheim

SAN JOSE CONVENTION AND CULTURAL FACILITIES - MONTGOMERY THEATER
PO Box 90250, San Jose, CA 95109
(408) 277-3925
FAX: (408) 277-3535
    Type of Facility: Theatre House; Opera House
    Type of Stage: Proscenium
    Stage Dimensions: 50'Wx30'D; 26'Wx14'H proscenium opening
    Seating Capacity: 537
    Year Built: 1972
    Contact for Rental: Robin Merriam;   (408) 277-3925
    Manager: Ellen Oppenheim, Director
    Resident Groups: San Jose Repertory Theatre; Gilbert and Sullivan Society of San Jose; San Jose Children's Musical Theatre; Opera San Jose

SAN JOSE STATE UNIVERSITY - CONCERT HALL
Washington Square, San Jose, CA 95192-0095
(408) 924-4673
FAX: (408) 924-4773
    Type of Facility: Concert Hall
    Type of Stage: Platform
    Seating Capacity: 527
    Year Built: 1953   **Architect:** Architecture Department, State of California
    Contact for Rental: Wanda Butts;   (408) 924-4709
    Resident Groups: San Jose State University Orchestra; San Jose State University Symphonic Band
    Available for rental to non-profit organizations and student groups

SAN JOSE STATE UNIVERSITY - UNIVERSITY THEATRE
One Washington Square, San Jose, CA 95192-0098
(408) 924-4530
FAX: (408) 924-1018
    Type of Facility: Theatre Complex; Theatre House
    Type of Stage: Flexible; Proscenium
    Stage Dimensions: 60'Wx33'D   **Orchestra Pit**
    Seating Capacity: 393
    Year Built: 1955
    Contact for Rental: James Culley;   (408) 924-4552
    Manager: Buddy Butler;   (408) 924-4584

San Juan Bautista

THEATRE

EL TEATRO CAMPESINO
PO Box 1240, San Juan Bautista, CA 95045
(408) 623-2444
FAX: (408) 623-4127
    Arts Area: Professional; Theatrical Group
    Status: Professional; Non-Profit
    Type: Touring; Resident; Educational; Sponsoring
    Purpose: To be one of the nation's pre-eminent Latino/Chicano theaters
    Management: Phillip Esparza, Managing Director; Rosa Maria Escalante, Education/Workdhop Director; Luis Valdez, Artistic Director

Officers: Luis Valdez, Chairman of the Board
Budget: $1,000,000 - $5,000,000
Income Sources: Private Foundations/Grants/Endowments; Business/Corporate Donations; Box Office; Government Grants; Individual Donations
Performance Facilities: El Teatro

San Luis Obispo

INSTRUMENTAL MUSIC

SAN LUIS OBISPO COUNTY SYMPHONY
1160 Marsh, San Luis Obispo, CA 93401
(805) 543-3533
Founded: 1950
Arts Area: Symphony; Chamber
Status: Non-Profit
Type: Performing
Management: Cricket Handler, Executive Director; Michael Nowak, Conductor; Sandy Bear, Marketing Director
Officers: Frank St. Denis, President; Patrick Perry, Chairman of Development
Paid Staff: 3   **Volunteer Staff:** 150
Utilizes: Guest Conductors; Guest Artists
Budget: $100,000 - $500,000
Income Sources: Private Foundations/Grants/Endowments; Business/Corporate Donations; Box Office; Government Grants; Individual Donations
Season: September - May   **Annual Attendance:** 4,500
Affiliations: ASOL; Association of California Symphony Orchestras
Performance Facilities: Church of the Nazarene

PERFORMING SERIES

SAN LUIS OBISPO MOZART FESITVAL
1160 Marsh Street, Suite 310, San Luis Obispo, CA 93401
(805) 543-4580
FAX: (805) 541-5425
Founded: 1970
Arts Area: Vocal Music; Instrumental Music; Festivals; Lyric Opera
Status: Professional; Non-Profit
Type: Performing; Educational
Purpose: To present a classical music festival highlighting Mozart and other classical and contemporary composers
Management: Clifton Swanson, Music Director; Patricia Martin, Executive Director; Jean Ciampi, Public Relations Director
Officers: Jeffrey Kahane, Associate Conductor
Paid Staff: 4   **Volunteer Staff:** 300
Paid Artists: 100
Utilizes: Guest Conductors; Guest Artists; Guest Directors; Guest Lecturers
Budget: $100,000 - $500,000
Income Sources: Private Foundations/Grants/Endowments; Business/Corporate Donations; Box Office; Government Grants; Individual Donations
Season: July - August   **Annual Attendance:** 8,000

FACILITY

CUESTA COLLEGE AUDITORIUM
Cuesta College Campus, PO Box 8106, San Luis Obispo, CA 93403
(805) 546-3100
Type of Facility: Auditorium; Theatre House
Facility Originally: Recreation Hall/gymnasium
Type of Stage: Proscenium
Stage Dimensions: 42'Wx17'6"H
Seating Capacity: 810
Year Built: 1942   **Acoustical Consultant:** Ron McKay of Bolt, Beranek & Newman
Contact for Rental: Community Services;   (805) 544-2943
Resident Groups: San Luis Obispo County Symphony; Pacific Ballet; Pat Jackson's American Dancers
Only rented to non-profit organizations

San Mateo
DANCE

PENINSULA BALLET THEATRE
333 South B Street, San Mateo, CA 94401
(415) 343-8485
Founded: 1967
Arts Area: Ballet
Status: Professional; Non-Profit
Type: Performing; Resident
Purpose: To provide the community with the educational and cultural advantages of a resident ballet company of the highest quality and varied repertoire and to give the artists the enjoyment of community roots not available in touring companies
Management: Anne Bena, Artistic Director; Mary Dahlquist, Company Coordinator
Paid Staff: 2   **Volunteer Staff:** 25
Paid Artists: 30   **Non-Paid Artists:** 15
Utilizes: Special Technical Talent; Guest Conductors; Guest Choreographers
Budget: $100,000 - $500,000
Income Sources: Private Foundations/Grants/Endowments; Business/Corporate Donations; Box Office; Government Grants; Individual Donations
Season: November - June   **Annual Attendance:** 12,000
Performance Facilities: San Mateo Performing Arts Center

FACILITY

SAN MATEO PERFORMING ARTS CENTER
600 North Delaware, San Mateo, CA 94401
(415) 348-8243
Type of Facility: Concert Hall; Performance Center; Theatre House; Opera House
Type of Stage: Proscenium
Stage Dimensions: 100'Wx50'D; 50'W proscenium opening   **Orchestra Pit**
Seating Capacity: 1,600
Year Built: 1953   **Cost:** $800,000
Contact for Rental: Dave LeBlanc;   (415) 348-8243

San Pedro
FACILITY

ANGELS GATE CULTURAL CENTER
3601 South Gaffey Street, PO Box 1471, San Pedro, CA 90731
(310) 519-1874
Type of Facility: Outdoor (Concert); Amphitheater; Multi-Purpose
Facility Originally: Military Base
Type of Stage: 3/4 Arena
Stage Dimensions: 60'x120'
Seating Capacity: 135
Year Built: 1924
Year Remodeled: 1984   **Architect:** Kenneth Darling   **Cost:** $18,000
Acoustical Consultant: David Lamb
Contact for Rental: Besty Lohrer

San Rafael
DANCE

THE MARIN BALLET
100 Elm Street, San Rafael, CA 94901
(415) 453-6705
FAX: (415) 453-5894
Founded: 1963
Arts Area: Modern; Ballet; Jazz; Tap
Status: Non-Profit; Pre-Professional Training
Type: Educational
Purpose: To provide the highest quality dance training in all disciplines at all levels as well as providing performance opportunities to extend the students' experience

Management: Barbara Steele, Business Manager; Margaret Swarthout, Artistic Director
Officers: Nancy Alvarez, President; Diane Parker and Elizabeth Cooper, Vice Presidents; Trish Prokop, Secretary
Paid Staff: 5   **Volunteer Staff:** 30
Paid Artists: 30
Utilizes: Special Technical Talent; Guest Artists; Guest Choreographers
Budget: $500,000 - $1,000,000
Income Sources: Private Foundations/Grants/Endowments; Business/Corporate Donations; Box Office; Individual Donations; Tuition
Season: 52 Weeks   **Annual Attendance:** 20,000
Affiliations: NASD
Performance Facilities: Civic Center

INSTRUMENTAL MUSIC

MARIN SYMPHONY ASSOCIATION
4340 Redwood Highway, Suite 409, San Rafael, CA 94903
(415) 479-8100
FAX: (415) 479-8110
Arts Area: Symphony; Orchestra
Status: Non-Profit
Type: Performing; Educational
Purpose: To provide high-quality musical performances in Marin County; to provide performance opportunities for young people
Management: Jennifer Duston, Executive Director; Gary Sheldon, Music Director
Officers: Howard Creighton, President, Board of Directors
Paid Staff: 8
Utilizes: Guest Artists
Budget: $500,000 - $1,000,000
Income Sources: Private Foundations/Grants/Endowments; Business/Corporate Donations; Box Office; Government Grants; Individual Donations
Season: November - April
Affiliations: California Arts Council; Marin Arts Council; ASOL; Association of California Symphony Orchestras
Performance Facilities: Marin Veterans Memorial Auditorium

MARIN SYMPHONY YOUTH ORCHESTRA
4340 Redwood Highway, Suite 409, San Rafael, CA 94903
(415) 479-8100
Founded: 1954
Arts Area: Symphony; Orchestra; Chamber
Status: Non-Professional; Non-Profit
Type: Performing; Touring; Educational; Sponsoring
Purpose: To provide quality musical training, education and scholarship opportunities for young people in the community
Management: Leslie Stewart, Conductor/Director of MSY Programs.
Paid Staff: 11   **Volunteer Staff:** 1
Non-Paid Artists: 40
Budget: $50,000 - $100,000
Income Sources: Private Foundations/Grants/Endowments; Business/Corporate Donations; Box Office; Individual Donations; Fund-raising
Season: September - May   **Annual Attendance:** 6,300
Affiliations: ASOL (Youth Orchestra Division)
Performance Facilities: San Rafael High School Auditorium

THEATRE

BLAKE STREET HAWKEYES
37 Sirard Lane, San Rafael, CA 94901
(415) 456-4384
Arts Area: Professional
Status: Non-Profit
Type: Performing; Touring; Resident; Educational
Purpose: To promote and create new theater on the edge; to promote new and experimental theater at the grass roots level
Management: Robert Ernst, Jim Cave, Co-Artistic Directors
Budget: $1,000 - $50,000
Income Sources: Private Foundations/Grants/Endowments; Government Grants

FACILITY

DOMINICAN COLLEGE - AUDITORIUM
50 Acacia, San Rafael, CA 94901
(415) 457-4440
> **Type of Facility:** Concert Hall; Auditorium
> **Type of Stage:** Thrust; Proscenium
> **Stage Dimensions:** 20'x36'x22' **Orchestra Pit**
> **Seating Capacity:** 700
> **Year Built:** 1922
> **Contact for Rental:** Manager of College Facilities; (415) 457-4440
> **Manager:** Martin Frick
> **Resident Groups:** College Orchestra and Chorus

MARIN CENTER
Avenue of the Flags, San Rafael, CA 94903
(415) 499-6396
FAX: (415) 499-3700
> **Type of Facility:** Civic Center
> **Year Built:** 1971 **Architect:** Frank Lloyd Wright
> **Acoustical Consultant:** George Izenour
> **Contact for Rental:** Jim Farley; (415) 499-6396
> *Marin Center contains the Showcase Theatre and Veterans Memorial Auditorium. See separate listings for additional information.*

MARIN CENTER - SHOWCASE THEATRE
Avenue of the Flags, San Rafael, CA 94903
(415) 499-6396
FAX: (415) 499-3700
> **Type of Facility:** Theatre House
> **Type of Stage:** Proscenium
> **Stage Dimensions:** 39"9"Wx30'D; 39'9"Wx12'H proscenium opening
> **Seating Capacity:** 309
> **Year Built:** 1976 **Architect:** Frank Lloyd Wright Foundation
> **Contact for Rental:** Jim Farley; (415) 499-6396

MARIN CENTER - VETERANS MEMORIAL AUDITORIUM
Avenue of the Flags, San Rafael, CA 94903
(415) 499-6396
FAX: (415) 499-3700
> **Type of Facility:** Auditorium
> **Type of Stage:** Proscenium
> **Stage Dimensions:** 60'Wx30'D; 60'Wx21'H proscenium opening **Orchestra Pit**
> **Seating Capacity:** 2,086
> **Year Built:** 1971 **Architect:** Frank Lloyd Wright Foundation
> **Acoustical Consultant:** George Izenour
> **Contact for Rental:** Jim Farley; (415) 499-6396

Santa Ana

INSTRUMENTAL MUSIC

SOUTH COAST SYMPHONY
1631 Sunflower Avenue, Suite C-45, Santa Ana, CA 92704
(714) 662-7220
FAX: (714) 641-3898
> **Founded:** 1973
> **Arts Area:** Symphony; Orchestra; Chamber
> **Status:** Professional; Non-Profit
> **Type:** Performing
> **Purpose:** To serve the diverse musical needs of the southern California coastal area
> **Management:** Doreen Hardy, Executive Director
> **Officers:** Arlene Schafer, President; William Crosby, Vice President; Leslie Santana, Recording Secretary; Lorraine Lambeth, Treasurer
> **Paid Staff:** 3 **Volunteer Staff:** 70
> **Paid Artists:** 125
> **Utilizes:** Special Technical Talent; Guest Conductors; Guest Artists

Budget: $100,000 - $500,000
Income Sources: Private Foundations/Grants/Endowments; Business/Corporate Donations; Box Office; Government Grants; Individual Donations
Season: September - May; July - September   **Annual Attendance:** 15,750
Affiliations: ASOL; Association of California Symphony Orchestras
Performance Facilities: Irvine Barclay Theatre; Fairview Park

THEATRE

STOP-GAP
523 North Grand, Santa Ana, CA 92701
(714) 648-0135
FAX: (714) 835-5087
    Founded: 1978
    Arts Area: Professional; Theatrical Group
    Status: Professional; Non-Profit
    Type: Performing; Touring; Educational
    Purpose: We use theater to build bridges between generations thereby reintegrating families and communities. We use drama as a therapeutic tool to improve impaired physical, mental, emotional and social functioning.
    Management: Don Laffoon, Executive Director; Victoria Bryan, Managing Director
    Paid Staff: 4   **Volunteer Staff:** 10
    Paid Artists: 8
    Budget: $100,000 - $500,000
    Income Sources: Private Foundations/Grants/Endowments; Business/Corporate Donations; Box Office; Government Grants; Individual Donations
    Season: 52 Weeks

Santa Barbara

INSTRUMENTAL MUSIC

MUSIC ACADEMY OF THE WEST
1070 Fairway Road, Santa Barbara, CA 93108
(805) 969-4726
FAX: (805) 969-0686
    Founded: 1945
    Arts Area: Symphony; Chamber; Ensemble
    Status: Professional; Non-Professional; Non-Profit
    Type: Performing; Educational; Sponsoring
    Purpose: To maintain a pre-professional instrumental company with vocal instruction
    Management: Robert W. Holmes, President; Carleen Landes, Artistic Manager; Brian Stenfors, Development Director; Ven Holbrook, Marketing Director; Diane Lyytikainen, Controller
    Officers: Mrs. Frank R. Miller, Chairman; Marsha Wayne, First Vice Chairman; Mrs. A. Stevens Halsted, Treasurer; Raymond C. Freeman Jr., Vice Chairman
    Paid Staff: 10   **Volunteer Staff:** 3
    Paid Artists: 33   **Non-Paid Artists:** 145
    Utilizes: Guest Conductors; Guest Artists; Guest Directors
    Budget: $1,000,000 - $5,000,000
    Income Sources: Private Foundations/Grants/Endowments; Business/Corporate Donations; Box Office; Government Grants; Individual Donations
    Season: June - August   **Annual Attendance:** 5,400
    Performance Facilities: Lobero Theatre; Abravanel Hall

SANTA BARBARA SYMPHONY ORCHESTRA
214 East Victoria Street, Santa Barbara, CA 93101
(805) 965-6596
FAX: (805) 963-3510
    Founded: 1954
    Arts Area: Symphony; Orchestra; Ethnic
    Status: Professional; Non-Profit
    Type: Performing; Educational
    Purpose: To provide classical music and music education
    Management: Varujan Kojian, Music Director; James Wright, General Manager
    Officers: Norman Sosner, Board President
    Utilizes: Guest Artists
    Budget: $1,000,000 - $5,000,000
    Income Sources: Private Foundations/Grants/Endowments; Business/Corporate Donations; Box Office; Government Grants; Individual Donations

Season: October - May   **Annual Attendance:** 25,000
Affiliations: ASOL; Association of California Symphony Orchestras
Performance Facilities: Arlington Theatre

WEST COAST CHAMBER ORCHESTRA
1812 La Coronilla Drive, Santa Barbara, CA 93109
(805) 962-6609
Founded: 1966
Arts Area: Symphony; Orchestra; Chamber
Status: Professional; Non-Profit
Type: Performing
Purpose: To provide the finest music at the best price; to employ the finest local musicians available
Management: Storyland Productions; Cielo Foundation for the Performing Arts; P.W. Productions
Officers: Christopher Story VI, President
Volunteer Staff: 5
Paid Artists: 60   **Non-Paid Artists:** 20
Utilizes: Guest Conductors; Guest Artists
Budget: $50,000 - $100,000
Income Sources: Private Foundations/Grants/Endowments; Business/Corporate Donations; Box Office; Government Grants; Individual Donations
Season: October - August   **Annual Attendance:** 4,000
Affiliations: Old Spanish Days Fiesta
Performance Facilities: Courthouse; Sunken Gardens; Lobero Theater; Goleta Valley Community Center

WEST COAST SYMPHONY
1812 La Coronilla Drive, Santa Barbara, CA 93109
(805) 962-6609
Founded: 1966
Arts Area: Symphony; Orchestra; Chamber
Status: Professional; Semi-Professional; Non-Profit
Type: Performing
Purpose: To provide the finest music at the best price and employ the finest local musicians available
Management: Storyland Concerts; Cielo Foundation for the Performing Arts; Piw Productions
Officers: Christopher Story VI, President; Jacqueline Sturgeon, Vice President; Lawrence F. Hilton, Secretary; Gary Gray CPA, Treasurer
Volunteer Staff: 5
Paid Artists: 60   **Non-Paid Artists:** 20
Utilizes: Guest Conductors; Guest Artists
Budget: $50,000 - $100,000
Income Sources: Private Foundations/Grants/Endowments; Business/Corporate Donations; Box Office; Government Grants; Individual Donations
Season: October - August   **Annual Attendance:** 4,000
Affiliations: Old Spanish Days Fiesta
Performance Facilities: Courthouse; Sunken Gardens; Lobero Theatre; Goleta Valley Community Center

THEATRE

SANTA BARBARA CHILDREN'S THEATRE
PO Box 4445, Santa Barbara, CA 93140
(805) 965-8313
Founded: 1976
Arts Area: Theatrical Group
Status: Non-Professional; Non-Profit
Type: Performing; Touring; Educational
Purpose: We are dedicated to the development of theatrical experiences for youth through theater for children by children ages 4-16.
Management: Jan Carter, Artistic Director
Officers: Janice Gaines, President
Paid Staff: 1   **Volunteer Staff:** 150
Non-Paid Artists: 600
Utilizes: Special Technical Talent; Guest Directors
Budget: $1,000 - $50,000
Income Sources: Private Foundations/Grants/Endowments; Business/Corporate Donations; Box Office; Government Grants; Individual Donations; Fund-raising
Season: 52 Weeks   **Annual Attendance:** 3,000
Affiliations: Southern California Educational Theatre Association
Performance Facilities: La Colina Junior High

PERFORMING SERIES

COMMUNITY ARTS AND MUSIC ASSOCIATION OF SANTA BARBARA
924 Anacapa Street, Suite B-1E, Santa Barbara, CA 93101
(805) 966-4324
> **Founded:** 1919
> **Arts Area:** Instrumental Music
> **Status:** Non-Profit
> **Type:** Sponsoring
> **Purpose:** To provide the best symphonic music available to Santa Barbara
> **Management:** Cathy Oliverson, Manager
> **Officers:** James H. Hurley Jr., President; Melville H. Haskell Jr. MD, First Vice President; Mrs. Max E. Meyer, Second Vice President; Frank F. Reed, Treasurer; Ray K. Person Jr., Secretary
> **Paid Staff:** 2 **Volunteer Staff:** 20
> **Utilizes:** Guest Conductors; Guest Artists
> **Budget:** $100,000 - $500,000
> **Income Sources:** Private Foundations/Grants/Endowments; Box Office; Individual Donations
> **Season:** October - May **Annual Attendance:** 12,000
> **Performance Facilities:** Arlington Center for the Performing Arts

UNIVERSITY OF CALIFORNIA AT SANTA BARBARA ARTS & LECTURES
University of California, Santa Barbara, CA 93106
(805) 893-2080
> **Founded:** 1959
> **Arts Area:** Dance; Vocal Music; Instrumental Music; Theater
> **Status:** Professional; Non-Profit
> **Type:** Performing; Educational; Presenting
> **Purpose:** To present a wide variety of professional touring artists and ensembles in dance, theater, classical music, ethnic and traditional arts, film and literature for campus and community audiences
> **Management:** Janet Oetinger, Director
> **Paid Staff:** 11
> **Budget:** $500,000 - $1,000,000
> **Income Sources:** Private Foundations/Grants/Endowments; Box Office; Government Grants; University
> **Season:** October - May **Annual Attendance:** 90,000
> **Affiliations:** WAAA; Arts Presenters; California Presenters
> **Performance Facilities:** Campbell Hall

FACILITY

ARLINGTON CENTER FOR THE PERFORMING ARTS
1317 State Street, Santa Barbara, CA 93101
(805) 963-9589
FAX: (805) 966-4688
> **Type of Facility:** Concert Hall; Performance Center; Theatre House
> **Facility Originally:** Vaudeville; Movie House
> **Type of Stage:** Proscenium
> **Stage Dimensions:** 50'Wx38'Dx27'H **Orchestra Pit**
> **Seating Capacity:** 2,018
> **Year Built:** 1931 **Architect:** Plunkett and Edwards **Cost:** $2,000,000
> **Year Remodeled:** 1976 **Architect:** Grant, Peterson and Phillips **Cost:** $500,000
> **Acoustical Consultant:** Paul Veneklasen
> **Contact for Rental:** Karen Spotten; (805) 963-9589

LOBERO THEATRE
33 East Canon Perdido Street, Santa Barbara, CA 93101
(805) 963-0761
> **Type of Facility:** Concert Hall; Theatre House
> **Type of Stage:** Proscenium
> **Stage Dimensions:** 73'Wx38'D; 36'W proscenium opening **Orchestra Pit**
> **Seating Capacity:** 680
> **Year Built:** 1873 **Architect:** Jose Lobero
> **Year Remodeled:** 1924 **Architect:** George Washington Smith, Lutah Maria Riggs **Cost:** $300,000
> **Acoustical Consultant:** Paul Veneklasen
> **Contact for Rental:** Annette deKnijf; (805) 963-0761

Santa Clara

DANCE

SANTA CLARA BALLET
3123 Millar Avenue, Santa Clara, CA 95051
(408) 247-9178
> **Founded:** 1973
> **Arts Area:** Ballet; Jazz
> **Status:** Semi-Professional; Non-Profit
> **Type:** Performing; Touring; Resident
> **Management:** Benjamin Reyes, Josefa Villanueva, Co-Artistic Directors; Josefa Reyes, Company Manager
> **Officers:** Dennis Mullen, President; Susan Kaplan, Vice President; Maryanne Santos, Secretary/Treasurer
> **Paid Staff:** 2   **Volunteer Staff:** 10
> **Paid Artists:** 2   **Non-Paid Artists:** 10
> **Utilizes:** Guest Artists
> **Budget:** $50,000 - $100,000
> **Income Sources:** Private Foundations/Grants/Endowments; Business/Corporate Donations; Box Office; Government Grants; Individual Donations; Fund-raising
> **Season:** Winter - Summer   **Annual Attendance:** 16,000
> **Affiliations:** Foothill College Performing Arts Alliance

Santa Cruz

DANCE

TANDY BEAL AND COMPANY
500 Seabright Avenue, Suite 101, PO Box 633, Santa Cruz, CA 95061
(408) 429-1324
> **Founded:** 1974
> **Arts Area:** Modern
> **Status:** Professional; Non-Profit
> **Type:** Performing; Touring
> **Purpose:** To perform and produce the choreography of Tandy Beal
> **Management:** Tandy Beal, Artistic Director; Michael Stamp, Managing Director
> **Paid Staff:** 5
> **Paid Artists:** 12
> **Utilizes:** Guest Artists
> **Budget:** $100,000 - $500,000
> **Income Sources:** Private Foundations/Grants/Endowments; Business/Corporate Donations; Box Office; Government Grants; Individual Donations
> **Season:** 52 Weeks
> **Affiliations:** Dance USA; ACA
> **Performance Facilities:** Cabrillo College Theatre

INSTRUMENTAL MUSIC

SANTA CRUZ BRASS QUINTET
216 Alhambra Avenue, Suite C, Santa Cruz, CA 95062
(408) 423-7360
> **Founded:** 1981
> **Arts Area:** Instrumental Group
> **Status:** Semi-Professional; Commercial
> **Type:** Performing; Touring
> **Purpose:** To perform jazz, ragtime, Dixieland, baroque, comtemporary and Renaissance music for audience enjoyment, the quintet plays in various locations including the UC Santa Cruz Arts Festival and the Santa Cruz Summer Arts Concert Series
> **Management:** Scott Harris, Director
> **Paid Artists:** 5
> **Utilizes:** Guest Artists
> **Budget:** $1,000 - $50,000
> **Income Sources:** Box Office
> **Season:** 52 Weeks   **Annual Attendance:** 20,000
> **Affiliations:** AFM; International Trombone Association

SANTA CRUZ COUNTY SYMPHONY
200 Seventh Avenue, Suite 225, Santa Cruz, CA 95062
(408) 462-0553
Founded: 1957
Arts Area: Symphony; Orchestra; Chamber
Status: Professional; Non-Profit
Type: Performing; Educational
Purpose: The mission of the Santa Cruz County Symphony is to serve the diverse Santa Cruz County as a leading musical performing arts group, which fulfills its cultural role by providing a wide variety of fine classical music, entertainment and educational services
Management: John Larry Granger, Music Director/Conductor
Officers: Nancy Hendee, President
Paid Staff: 4 **Volunteer Staff:** 100
Paid Artists: 80
Utilizes: Guest Conductors; Guest Artists
Budget: $100,000 - $500,000
Income Sources: Private Foundations/Grants/Endowments; Business/Corporate Donations; Box Office; Government Grants; Individual Donations
Season: October - May **Annual Attendance:** 10,000
Affiliations: ASOL; Association of California Symphony Orchestras; California Confederation of the Arts
Performance Facilities: Santa Cruz Civic Auditorium

THE SCOTT HARRIS BIG BAND
216 Alhambra Avenue, Suite C, Santa Cruz, CA 95062
(408) 423-7360
Founded: 1980
Arts Area: Instrumental Group; Band
Status: Professional; Commercial
Type: Performing; Touring
Purpose: To present Big Band music of the 1920's-40's purely for audience entertainment
Management: Scott Harris, Director
Paid Artists: 14
Utilizes: Guest Artists
Budget: $1,000 - $50,000
Income Sources: Box Office
Season: 52 Weeks **Annual Attendance:** 15,000

PERFORMING SERIES

SANTA CRUZ BAROQUE FESTIVAL
PO Box 482, Santa Cruz, CA 95061
(408) 336-5731
FAX: (408) 336-2464
Founded: 1974
Arts Area: Festivals
Status: Professional; Non-Profit
Type: Performing; Sponsoring
Purpose: To provide a series of spring concerts featuring early music
Management: Linda K. Fawcett, General Manager; Linda Burman-Hall, Artistic Director
Officers: Charles J. Sutton, President; Jan Jaffe, Vice President; Charles Hall, Treasurer/Secretary
Paid Staff: 2 **Volunteer Staff:** 30
Paid Artists: 28
Utilizes: Guest Artists
Budget: $50,000 - $100,000
Income Sources: Private Foundations/Grants/Endowments; Business/Corporate Donations; Box Office; Government Grants; Individual Donations; Program Ads
Season: February - May **Annual Attendance:** 1,700

FACILITY

KUUMBWA JAZZ CENTER
320-2 Cedar Street, Santa Cruz, CA 95060
(408) 427-2227
Type of Facility: Performance Center
Facility Originally: Business Facility
Type of Stage: Platform
Seating Capacity: 140
Year Remodeled: 1977

Contact for Rental: Tim Jackson; (408) 427-2227
Resident Groups: Kuumbwa Jazz Center

SANTA CRUZ CIVIC AUDITORIUM
307 Church Street, Santa Cruz, CA 95060
(408) 429-3779
FAX: (408) 458-0455
Founded: 1939
Type of Facility: Theatre Complex; Concert Hall; Auditorium; Performance Center; Civic Center; Arena; Multi-Purpose
Type of Stage: Proscenium; Arena
Stage Dimensions: 32'x40'
Seating Capacity: 1,957
Year Built: 1939 **Architect:** Mark Daniels **Cost:** $285,000
Contact for Rental: Eddie Scher; (408) 429-3779

UNIVERSITY OF CALIFORNIA-SANTA CRUZ - PERFORMING ARTS CENTER
Santa Cruz, CA 95064
(408) 459-2147
Type of Facility: Theatre House
Type of Stage: Thrust
Stage Dimensions: 35'x23'
Seating Capacity: 537
Year Built: 1971 **Architect:** Ralph Rapson **Cost:** $2,700,000
Contact for Rental: Scott Anderson; (408) 459-2147
Resident Groups: Theatre Arts Board of Studies; Arts and Lectures Program

Santa Maria

INSTRUMENTAL MUSIC

SANTA MARIA SYMPHONY SOCIETY
110 South Pine Street, Suite 103-B-386, Santa Maria, CA 93454
(805) 937-7652
Founded: 1961
Arts Area: Symphony
Status: Non-Profit
Type: Performing
Purpose: Professional imports for concerts
Management: Karen Breitinger, Executive Director
Officers: Ron Williams, President of Symphony Society
Budget: $1,000 - $50,000
Income Sources: Private Foundations/Grants/Endowments; Business/Corporate Donations; Box Office; Individual Donations
Season: November - June **Annual Attendance:** 1,500
Performance Facilities: First Assembly of God Church

THEATRE

PCPA THEATERFEST
PO Box 1700, Santa Maria, CA 93456
(805) 928-7731
FAX: (805) 928-7506
Founded: 1964
Arts Area: Professional; Theatrical Group
Status: Professional; Semi-Professional; Non-Professional; Non-Profit
Type: Performing; Resident; Educational
Purpose: Professional theater training program (Acting and Technician) and resident professional theater company
Management: Jack Shouse, Managing Artistic Director; Paul Barnes, Conservatory Director/Associate Artistic Director
Officers: Michael O. Brady, Chairman; Linda Kastner, Vice Chairman
Paid Staff: 35
Paid Artists: 6
Utilizes: Special Technical Talent; Guest Artists; Guest Directors
Budget: $1,000,000 - $5,000,000
Income Sources: Private Foundations/Grants/Endowments; Business/Corporate Donations; Box Office; Government Grants; Individual Donations
Season: October - September **Annual Attendance:** 90,000
Affiliations: TCG; AEA; U/RTA
Performance Facilities: Festival Theatre; Marian Theatre; Interim Theater

SOLVANG THEATERFEST
PO Box 1700, Santa Maria, CA 93456
Founded: 1974
Arts Area: Professional; Summer Stock; Musical; Community; Theatrical Group
Status: Professional; Non-Profit
Type: Performing; Resident; Educational
Purpose: Solvang Theaterfest is a unique collaboration of artistic, professional and educational talent.
Management: Jack Shouse, Artistic Director; Paul Barnes, Associate Artistic Director/Conservatory Director
Officers: Mike Brady, Chairman of the Board
Utilizes: Special Technical Talent; Guest Artists; Guest Directors
Budget: $100,000 - $500,000
Income Sources: Private Foundations/Grants/Endowments; Business/Corporate Donations; Box Office; Government Grants; Individual Donations
Season: 52 Weeks
Performance Facilities: Solvang Festival Theatre; Backstage Theater; Marian Performance Theater; Severson Theater

FACILITY

PACIFIC CONSERVATORY OF THE PERFORMING ARTS
800 South College Drive, Santa Maria, CA 93454
(805) 928-7731
Type of Facility: Theatre Complex
Type of Stage: Thrust
Stage Dimensions: 29'x29'
Seating Capacity: 450
Year Built: 1967   **Architect:** Stewart Kerr   **Cost:** $900,000
Contact for Rental: Jack Shouse;   (805) 928-7731
Resident Groups: Pacific Conservatory of the Performing Arts

Santa Monica

THEATRE

ACTORS REPERTORY THEATRE & SANTA MONICA GROUP THEATRE
1211 Fourth Street, Santa Monica, CA 90401
(310) 394-9779
FAX: (310) 393-5573
Founded: 1962
Arts Area: Professional; Summer Stock; Musical; Theatrical Group; Family Theatre (Children's)
Status: Professional; Non-Profit
Type: Performing; Touring; Resident; Educational
Purpose: New plays, touring, educational workshops, young professionals company, resident acting company, international touring
Management: Evelyn Rudie, Artistic Director; Chris De Carlo, Artistic/Managing Director; Elynmarie Kazle, Resident Producer; Cheryl Moffatt, Director of Education/International touring
Paid Staff: 12   **Volunteer Staff:** 3
Non-Paid Artists: 50
Utilizes: Special Technical Talent; Guest Artists
Budget: $100,000 - $500,000
Income Sources: Private Foundations/Grants/Endowments; Business/Corporate Donations; Box Office; Individual Donations
Season: 52 Weeks   **Annual Attendance:** 35,000
Affiliations: TCG; AEA; Theatre Los Angeles
Performance Facilities: Santa Monica Playhouse

SANTA MONICA PLAYHOUSE AND GROUP THEATRE
1211 Fourth Street, Suite E, Santa Monica, CA 90401-1391
(310) 394-9779
Founded: 1962
Arts Area: Professional
Status: Professional; Non-Profit
Type: Performing; Touring; Resident; Educational
Purpose: To provide an alternative for today's television audience
Management: Evelyn Rudie, Chris DeCarlo, Artistic Directors
Paid Staff: 5
Utilizes: Special Technical Talent; Guest Artists; Guest Directors
Budget: $50,000 - $100,000

Income Sources: Private Foundations/Grants/Endowments; Business/Corporate Donations; Box Office; Government Grants; Individual Donations
Season: 52 Weeks   **Annual Attendance:** 40,000
Affiliations: ACTA
Performance Facilities: Santa Monica Playhouse

FACILITY

MORGAN-WIXSON THEATRE
2627 Pico Boulevard, Santa Monica, CA 90405
(310) 828-7519
> **Type of Facility:** Concert Hall; Auditorium; Theatre House
> **Type of Stage:** Proscenium
> **Stage Dimensions:** 30'Wx35'D
> **Seating Capacity:** 201
> **Year Built:** 1964
> **Contact for Rental:** Woodrow Coleman;   (213) 450-4763
> **Resident Groups:** Santa Monica Theatre Guild

SANTA MONICA CIVIC AUDITORIUM
1855 Main Street, Santa Monica, CA 90401
(213) 393-9962
> **Type of Facility:** Auditorium; Theatre House; Opera House; Civic Center; Arena; Multi-Purpose; Room
> **Type of Stage:** Flexible; Proscenium; Arena
> **Stage Dimensions:** 70'x120'x42'   **Orchestra Pit**
> **Seating Capacity:** 3,000 seated; 4,500 festival
> **Year Built:** 1958   **Architect:** Welton Becket   **Cost:** $3,000,000
> **Contact for Rental:** Ellen French, Carole Curtin;   (310) 458-8551

Santa Rosa

INSTRUMENTAL MUSIC

SANTA ROSA SYMPHONY
50 Mark West Springs Road, Santa Rosa, CA 95403
(707) 546-8742
> **Founded:** 1927
> **Arts Area:** Symphony; Orchestra; Chamber; Ensemble
> **Status:** Non-Profit
> **Type:** Performing; Resident; Educational
> **Purpose:** Provide symphonic music to Sonoma County and the Northern Bay Area; to conduct educational projects, youth orchestras, music center in-school demonstrations and youth concerts
> **Management:** Pauline Fisher, Manager; Sarah Obuchowski, Development/Public Relations/Marketing
> **Paid Staff:** 7   **Volunteer Staff:** 40
> **Paid Artists:** 100   **Non-Paid Artists:** 3
> **Utilizes:** Guest Conductors; Guest Artists
> **Budget:** $500,000 - $1,000,000
> **Income Sources:** Private Foundations/Grants/Endowments; Business/Corporate Donations; Box Office; Government Grants; Individual Donations
> **Season:** October - May
> **Performance Facilities:** Luther Burbank Center for the Arts

FACILITY

LUTHER BURBANK CENTER FOR THE ARTS
50 Mark West Springs Road, Santa Rosa, CA 95403
(707) 527-7006
> **Type of Facility:** Performance Center
> **Facility Originally:** Church
> **Year Built:** 1972
> **Contact for Rental:** Scheduling Administrator;   (707) 527-7006

Resident Groups: Baroque Sinfonia; Redwood Empire Lyric Theater; Redwood Empire Theater; Santa Rosa Symphony; Sonoma County Folk Society
The Center contains the Concert Chamber, East Auditorium, Gold Room and Ruth Finley Person Memorial Theatre. See separate listings for additional information.

LUTHER BURBANK CENTER FOR THE ARTS - CONCERT CHAMBER
50 Mark West Springs Road, Santa Rosa, CA 95403
(707) 527-7006
FAX: (707) 545-0518
    Type of Facility: Concert Hall; Performance Center; Theatre House
    Facility Originally: Church
    Type of Stage: Platform
    Stage Dimensions: 16'x35'
    Seating Capacity: 325
    Year Built: 1972
    Contact for Rental: Scheduling Administrator; (707) 527-7006
    Resident Groups: Baroque Sinfonia; Redwood Empire Lyric Theater; Redwood Empire Theater; Santa Rosa Symphony; Sonoma County Folk Society

LUTHER BURBANK CENTER FOR THE ARTS - EAST AUDITORIUM
50 Mark West Springs Road, Santa Rosa, CA 95403
(707) 527-7006
FAX: (707) 545-0518
    Type of Facility: Auditorium
    Facility Originally: Church
    Type of Stage: Platform
    Stage Dimensions: 18'Wx15'D
    Seating Capacity: 425
    Contact for Rental: Scheduling Administrator; (707) 527-7006
    Resident Groups: Baroque Sinfonia; Redwood Empire Lyric Theater; Redwood Empire Theater; Santa Rosa Symphony; Sonoma County Folk Society

LUTHER BURBANK CENTER FOR THE ARTS - GOLD ROOM
50 Mark West Springs Road, Santa Rosa, CA 95403
(707) 527-7006
FAX: (707) 545-0518
    Type of Facility: Room; Dinner Theatre
    Facility Originally: Church
    Type of Stage: Flexible
    Seating Capacity: 100
    Year Built: 1972
    Contact for Rental: Scheduling Administrator; (707) 527-7006
    Resident Groups: Baroque Sinfonia; Redwood Empire Lyric Theater; Redwood Empire Theater; Santa Rosa Symphony; Sonoma County Folk Society

LUTHER BURBANK CENTER FOR THE ARTS - RUTH FINLEY PERSON MEMORIAL THEATRE
50 Mark West Springs Road, Santa Rosa, CA 95403
(707) 527-7006
FAX: (707) 545-0518
    Type of Facility: Performance Center; Theatre House
    Facility Originally: Church
    Type of Stage: Thrust
    Stage Dimensions: 61'Wx40'D
    Seating Capacity: 1,500
    Year Built: 1972
    Contact for Rental: Scheduling Administrator; (707) 527-7006
    Resident Groups: Baroque Sinfonia; Redwood Empire Lyric Theater; Redwood Empire Theater; Santa Rosa Symphony; Sonoma County Folk Society

Saratoga

PERFORMING SERIES

PAUL MASSON SUMMER SERIES
PO Box 2279, Saratoga, CA 95070
(408) 741-5181; (408) 741-5182
    Founded: 1957

Arts Area: Vocal Music; Instrumental Music; Theater
Status: Professional; Non-Profit
Type: Performing; Sponsoring
Purpose: To enhance the cultural atmosphere of the San Francisco Bay Area and generate publicity for Paul Masson Vineyards
Management: Bruce Zabadie, Director of Series; Pat Sjcklocha, Assistant Director
Paid Staff: 2
Utilizes: Special Technical Talent; Guest Artists; Guest Directors
Budget: $1,000,000 - $5,000,000
Income Sources: Business/Corporate Donations; Box Office
Season: June - September
Performance Facilities: Paul Masson Mountain Winery

VILLA MONTALVO CENTER FOR THE ARTS
PO Box 158, Saratoga, CA 95071
(408) 741-3421
Founded: 1930
Arts Area: Dance; Vocal Music; Instrumental Music; Theater; Festivals; Lyric Opera; Grand Opera
Status: Non-Profit
Type: Resident; Educational; Sponsoring
Purpose: To provide cultural and recreational activities for promising students, artists, and the public; to instill an appreciation of the arts and the environment
Management: Elisbeth Challener, Executive Director; Sam Nuccio, Program Director
Officers: J. Michael Patterson, President; Sally Lucas, Vice President; Leigh Weimers, Secretary; Joseph Maglione, Treasurer
Paid Staff: 12   **Volunteer Staff:** 100
Utilizes: Special Technical Talent; Guest Conductors; Guest Artists; Guest Directors
Budget: $500,000 - $1,000,000
Income Sources: Private Foundations/Grants/Endowments; Business/Corporate Donations; Box Office; Government Grants; Individual Donations; Facilities Rentals
Season: April - September   **Annual Attendance:** 26,000
Affiliations: California Connection; APAP
Performance Facilities: Carriage House Theatre; Lilian Fontaine Garden Theatre

FACILITY

VILLA MONTALVO CENTER FOR THE ARTS
PO Box 158, Saratoga, CA 95071
(408) 741-3421
Type of Facility: Outdoor (Concert); Environmental; Performance Center; Theatre House; Amphitheater; Multi-Purpose
Year Built: 1912   **Architect:** Curlett & Son
Contact for Rental: Executive Director;   (408) 741-3421
The Center contains the Carriage House Theatre and Lilian Fontaine Garden Theatre. See individual listings for additional information.

VILLA MONTALVO CENTER FOR THE ARTS - CARRIAGE HOUSE THEATRE
PO Box 158, Saratoga, CA 95071
(408) 741-3421
Type of Facility: Theatre House; Black Box
Facility Originally: Garage
Type of Stage: Thrust; Proscenium
Stage Dimensions: 20'x20'
Seating Capacity: 275
Year Built: 1912
Year Remodeled: 1960   **Architect:** Higgins & Root
Contact for Rental: Executive Director;   (408) 741-3421

VILLA MONTALVO CENTER FOR THE ARTS - LILIAN FONTAINE GARDEN THEATRE
PO Box 158, Saratoga, CA 95071
(408) 741-3421
Type of Facility: Outdoor (Concert); Environmental; Amphitheater
Type of Stage: Thrust; Environmental
Stage Dimensions: 40'x60'   **Orchestra Pit**
Seating Capacity: 800
Year Built: 1960
Year Remodeled: 1987   **Architect:** Design Professionals
Contact for Rental: Executive Director;   (408) 741-3421

Sausalito

THEATRE

ANTENNA THEATER
PO Box 176, Sausalito, CA 94966
(415) 322-4862
FAX: (415) 332-4870
Founded: 1980
Arts Area: Theatrical Group
Status: Professional; Non-Profit
Type: Performing; Touring
Purpose: To stretch the boundaries of contemporary theater by inventing new formats involving nontraditional technologies such as Walkmen, infrared-transmitted sound, 3-D projections, prefabricated environments and audience interaction
Management: Chris Hardman, Artistic Director; Christine Murray, Administrative Director
Paid Staff: 6
Utilizes: Special Technical Talent
Budget: $100,000 - $500,000
Income Sources: Private Foundations/Grants/Endowments; Box Office; Government Grants
Season: 52 Weeks
Affiliations: TCG; California Confederation of the Arts; Theatre Bay Area

Solana Beach

THEATRE

NORTH COAST REPERTORY THEATRE
PO Box 389, Solana Beach, CA 92075
(619) 481-1055
Founded: 1982
Arts Area: Musical; Theatrical Group
Status: Non-Professional; Non-Profit
Type: Performing
Purpose: To educate the public in an appreciation of the theatre arts through stage productions of consistent quality; to provide opportunities for actors and theatre professionals to develop their artistic skills; to evolve into a professional, regional theatre
Management: Olive Blakistone, Artistic Director; Mary Hagan, Operations Manager; Bonnie Barrett, Marketing Manager; John Guth, Box Office Manager; Tom Blakistone, Managing Director; Leslee Baren, Technical Director; Kate King, Development Director
Officers: Edward George, President; Joan Glatthorn, Vice President; Jean Schlinger, Treasurer; Tom Blakistone, Secretary
Paid Staff: 6 **Volunteer Staff:** 120
Non-Paid Artists: 60
Utilizes: Special Technical Talent; Guest Directors
Budget: $100,000 - $500,000
Income Sources: Private Foundations/Grants/Endowments; Business/Corporate Donations; Box Office; Government Grants; Individual Donations
Season: 52 Weeks **Annual Attendance:** 21,000
Affiliations: San Diego Theatre League; CAC
Performance Facilities: Lomas Santa Fe Plaza

South Pasadena

DANCE

AVAZ INTERNATIONAL DANCE THEATRE
1801 Fair Oaks, Suite 209, South Pasadena, CA 91030
(818) 441-1630; (818) 622-6646
Founded: 1977
Arts Area: Folk
Status: Professional; Non-Profit
Type: Performing; Touring; Educational
Purpose: To preserve and perform the traditional dances and music of the Middle East, North Africa and Central Asia
Management: J. Dees Presents
Officers: Conrad Von Bibra, President of the Board; Anthony Shay, Vice President; Keihan Marefat, Treasurer; Bonita Edelberg, Secretary; Boualim Bousouloub, Assistant Treasurer
Paid Staff: 1 **Volunteer Staff:** 4
Paid Artists: 28

Utilizes: Guest Choreographers
Budget: $100,000 - $500,000
Income Sources: Private Foundations/Grants/Endowments; Business/Corporate Donations; Box Office; Government Grants; Individual Donations
Season: 52 Weeks
Annual Attendance: 50,000
Affiliations: Dance/USA; Los Angeles Dance Resource Center

PASADENA DANCE THEATRE
100 West Villa, South Pasadena, CA 91103
(818) 792-4616
FAX: (818) 792-4893
Founded: 1963
Arts Area: Ballet
Status: Semi-Professional; Non-Profit
Type: Performing; Touring; Resident
Management: Phillip Fuller, Artistic Director
Volunteer Staff: 3
Paid Artists: 3   **Non-Paid Artists:** 12
Utilizes: Guest Artists
Budget: $100,000 - $500,000
Income Sources: Private Foundations/Grants/Endowments; Box Office; Government Grants
Season: September - June
Affiliations: NARB

Spring Valley

THEATRE

SAN DIEGO GUILD OF PUPPETRY
3002 Helix Street, Spring Valley, CA 92077
(619) 466-7128
Founded: 1948
Arts Area: Puppet
Status: Professional; Non-Profit
Type: Performing; Resident; Educational
Purpose: To produce shows year-round using hand puppets, rod puppets and marionettes with three shows each Saturday and Sunday; to further the art of puppetry
Management: Marie Hitchcock, Public Relations Director, Guild Coordinator
Volunteer Staff: 7
Non-Paid Artists: 6
Income Sources: Box Office
Season: 52 Weeks
Annual Attendance: 63,000
Affiliations: Puppeteers of America; San Diego Parks & Recreation Department
Performance Facilities: The Marie Hitchcock Puppet Theatre in Balboa Park

Stanford

PERFORMING SERIES

THE LIVELY ARTS AT STANFORD UNIVERSITY
Press Courtyard, Santa Teresa Street, Stanford, CA 94305
(415) 723-2551
FAX: (415) 723-8231
Arts Area: Dance; Vocal Music; Instrumental Music; Theater
Status: Professional; Non-Profit
Type: Resident; Educational; Sponsoring
Purpose: To provide outstanding quality performances for the education and enjoyment of Stanford students, faculty, staff and the surrounding community
Management: Lois Wagner, Director
Paid Staff: 5   **Volunteer Staff:** 30
Paid Artists: 30
Utilizes: Guest Artists
Budget: $500,000 - $1,000,000
Income Sources: Private Foundations/Grants/Endowments; Business/Corporate Donations; Box Office; Government Grants; Individual Donations

Season: October - May   **Annual Attendance:** 40,000
Affiliations: APAP; WAAA; California Confederation of the Arts; ACA
Performance Facilities: Dinkelspiel Auditorium; Memorial Auditorium; Memorial Church; Frost Amphitheater

FACILITY

STANFORD UNIVERSITY - ANNENBURG AUDITORIUM
Press Courtyard, Santa Theresa Street, Stanford, CA 94305-2250
(415) 723-2551
   Type of Facility: Studio Performance; Multi-Purpose; Room
   Type of Stage: Platform
   Stage Dimensions: 25'Wx12'D
   Seating Capacity: 350
   Year Built: 1969   **Architect:** Warnecke & Associates

STANFORD UNIVERSITY - BRAUN RECITAL HALL
Press Courtyard, Santa Theresa Street, Stanford, CA 94305-2250
(415) 723-2551
   Type of Facility: Studio Performance; Room; Recital Hall
   Seating Capacity: 200
   Year Built: 1984   **Architect:** Braun & Associates

STANFORD UNIVERSITY - CAMBLE RECITAL HALL
Press Courtyard, Santa Theresa Street, Stanford, CA 94305-2250
(415) 723-2551
   Type of Facility: Auditorium; Recital Hall
   Type of Stage: Proscenium   Seating Capacity: 225
   Year Built: 1985   **Architect:** Marquis & Associates

STANFORD UNIVERSITY - COVERLY AUDITORIUM
Press Courtyard, Santa Theresa Street, Stanford, CA 94305-2250
(415) 723-2551
   Type of Facility: Auditorium
   Type of Stage: Proscenium
   Stage Dimensions: 30'Wx15'D
   Seating Capacity: 400
   Year Built: 1938
   Architect: Bakerwell and Brown

STANFORD UNIVERSITY - DINKELSPIEL AUDITORIUM
Press Courtyard, Santa Theresa Street, Stanford, CA 94305-2250
(415) 723-2551
   Type of Facility: Auditorium
   Type of Stage: Thrust; Proscenium
   Stage Dimensions: 40'Wx40'D   **Orchestra Pit**
   Seating Capacity: 720
   Year Built: 1957   **Architect:** Milton F. Pflueger

STANFORD UNIVERSITY - MEMORIAL AUDITORIUM
Press Courtyard, Santa Theresa Street, Stanford, CA 94305-2250
(415) 723-2551
   Type of Facility: Auditorium; Performance Center; Theatre House; Multi-Purpose
   Type of Stage: Proscenium   **Orchestra Pit**
   Seating Capacity: 1,714
   Year Built: 1937   **Architect:** Bakerwell and Brown

Stockton

INSTRUMENTAL MUSIC

STOCKTON SYMPHONY ASSOCIATION
37 West Yokuts, Suite C-4, Stockton, CA 95207
(209) 951-0196
FAX: (209) 951-1050
   Founded: 1926
   Arts Area: Symphony; Orchestra
   Status: Professional; Non-Profit

Type: Performing; Educational
Management: Kyung-Soo Won, Music Director/Conductor; George A. Sinclair, Executive Director
Officers: Nancy Schneider, President
Paid Staff: 3   **Volunteer Staff:** 125
Paid Artists: 70
Utilizes: Special Technical Talent; Guest Conductors; Guest Artists
Budget: $500,000 - $1,000,000
Income Sources: Private Foundations/Grants/Endowments; Business/Corporate Donations; Box Office; Government Grants; Individual Donations; Fund-raising
Season: September - May   **Annual Attendance:** 18,000
Affiliations: ASOL; Association of California Symphony Orchestras
Performance Facilities: San Joaquin Delta College

THEATRE

STOCKTON CIVIC THEATRE
2312 Rose Marie Lane, Stockton, CA 95207
(209) 473-2400
FAX: (209) 473-1502
Founded: 1951
Arts Area: Musical; Community; Theatrical Group
Status: Non-Professional; Non-Profit
Type: Performing; Resident
Purpose: To provide quality theatre to the community
Management: Helen Kastner, Executive Director
Officers: George Royston, President; Marge Breezee, Vice President; Frank Whitney, Vice President/Operations
Paid Staff: 1
Utilizes: Guest Artists; Guest Directors
Budget: $100,000 - $500,000
Income Sources: Private Foundations/Grants/Endowments; Business/Corporate Donations; Box Office; Government Grants; Individual Donations
Season: September - May

FACILITY

ATHERTON AUDITORIUM
5151 Pacific Avenue, Stockton, CA 95207
(209) 474-5051
Type of Facility: Theatre Complex; Concert Hall; Auditorium
Type of Stage: Proscenium
Stage Dimensions: 89'x102'x45'   **Orchestra Pit**
Seating Capacity: 1,456
Year Built: 1977   **Architect:** E.J. Kump Associates; Gwathmey Sellier Crosby   **Cost:** $4,700,000
Contact for Rental: Dr. Don Bennett;   (209) 474-5209

UNIVERSITY OF THE PACIFIC - DE MARCUS BROWN STUDIO THEATRE
Stockton, CA 95211
(209) 946-2116
Type of Facility: Studio Performance; Room
Facility Originally: School; Tractor Shop
Type of Stage: Flexible
Stage Dimensions: 38'x42'
Seating Capacity: 110
Year Built: 1977
Resident Groups: University of the Pacific Drama and Dance Department

UNIVERSITY OF THE PACIFIC - FAYE SPANOS CONCERT HALL
Stockton, CA 95211
(209) 946-2415
Type of Facility: Concert Hall; Auditorium
Type of Stage: Proscenium
Orchestra Pit
Seating Capacity: 950
Year Built: 1924   **Architect:** Davis Heller & Pierce
Year Remodeled: 1987   **Architect:** Dean Unger   **Cost:** $1,500,000
Contact for Rental: Joanne Paine;   (209) 946-2415

UNIVERSITY OF THE PACIFIC - LONG THEATRE
Stockton, CA 95211
(209) 946-2116
    Type of Facility: Auditorium
    Type of Stage: Proscenium; Concentric Arch
    Stage Dimensions: 40'Wx24'D   **Orchestra Pit**
    Seating Capacity: 400 fixed seating
    Year Built: 1959   **Architect:** Clowdsley & Whipple
    Year Remodeled: 1979   **Cost:** $210,000
    Acoustical Consultant: Edwin W. Wilson
    Contact for Rental: Jack Pratt;   (209) 946-2054
    Resident Groups: University of the Pacific Drama And Dance Department

UNIVERSITY OF THE PACIFIC - RECITAL HALL
Conservatory of Music, Stockton, CA 95211
(209) 946-2415
    Type of Facility: Recital Hall
    Type of Stage: Platform
    Stage Dimensions: 18'Wx18'D
    Seating Capacity: 119
    Year Built: 1986   **Architect:** Radcliff Associates
    Contact for Rental: Joanne Paine;   (209) 946-2415

Studio City

THEATRE

HOLLYWOOD THEATER COMPANY
12838 Kling Street, Studio City, CA 91604-1127
(310) 984-1867
    Founded: 1972
    Arts Area: Professional; Summer Stock; Dinner
    Status: Professional; Non-Profit
    Type: Performing; Touring
    Purpose: To perform revivals and new plays for diversified Black actors, and on occassion, an integrated entity
    Management: Rai Tasco, Artistic Director; J. Christopher Sullivan, PhD, Co-Manager; Patricia Bell, Production Manager
    Volunteer Staff: 8
    Non-Paid Artists: 16
    Utilizes: Special Technical Talent; Guest Artists; Guest Directors
    Budget: $1,000 - $50,000
    Income Sources: Box Office
    Season: 52 Weeks

THEATRE EAST
17655 Ventura Boulevard, Studio City, CA 91604
(818) 760-4160
    Founded: 1967
    Arts Area: Theatrical Group
    Status: Professional
    Type: Resident
    Purpose: Actors Gymnasium
    Officers: Elaine Welton Hill, Acting President; John Gowans, Secretary; Suzanne Hunt, Treasurer
    Volunteer Staff: 20
    Non-Paid Artists: 125
    Income Sources: Individual Donations

FACILITY

THEATRE EAST
12655 Ventura Boulevard, Studio City, CA 91604
(818) 760-4160
    Type of Facility: Theatre House
    Type of Stage: Proscenium
    Seating Capacity: 99
    Year Built: 1967

Sunnyvale

VOCAL MUSIC

SILICON VALLEY GAY MEN'S CHORUS OF SAN JOSE
PO Box 62151, Sunnyvale, CA 94088
(408) 275-6344
Founded: 1983
Arts Area: Choral
Status: Non-Professional; Non-Profit
Type: Performing
Management: Bob Welton, President; Lynne McLaughlin, Director; Don Giberson, Assistant Director;
Doug McGrath, Accompanist
Paid Staff: 3   **Volunteer Staff:** 7
Non-Paid Artists: 18
Utilizes: Guest Conductors; Guest Artists
Budget: $1,000 - $50,000
Income Sources: Box Office; Individual Donations
Season: September - June   **Annual Attendance:** 1,500
Affiliations: Gay And Lesbian Association Choruses
Performance Facilities: Christ the Good Shepherd Lutheran Church

THEATRE

CALIFORNIA THEATRE CENTER
PO Box 2007, Sunnyvale, CA 94087
(408) 245-2978
FAX: (408) 245-0235
Founded: 1975
Arts Area: Professional; Theatrical Group
Status: Professional; Non-Profit
Type: Performing; Touring
Purpose: To provide quality theater for children and families
Management: Gayle Cornelison, General Director; Will Huddleston, Resident Director; Lynn Pace, Production Director;
Mary Farrow, Production Manager
Paid Staff: 25
Utilizes: Special Technical Talent; Guest Artists; Guest Directors
Budget: $500,000 - $1,000,000
Income Sources: Private Foundations/Grants/Endowments; Business/Corporate Donations; Box Office; Government
Grants; Individual Donations
Season: October - August
Affiliations: AEA
Performance Facilities: The Performing Arts Center

Thousand Oaks

INSTRUMENTAL MUSIC

CONEJO SYMPHONY ORCHESTRA
PO Box 1045, Thousand Oaks, CA 91358
(805) 498-7092
Founded: 1961
Arts Area: Symphony; Chamber
Status: Semi-Professional; Non-Profit
Type: Performing
Purpose: To maintain a non-profit corporation for the education and stimulation of the musical, cultural and social interests of the community, through the medium of a symphony orchestra
Management: Everett Ascher, Executive Director; Susan Ward, Office Manager; Elmer Ramsey, Music Director;
Carol Alexander, Conductor, Youth Symphony; Bonnie Boss, Personnel Manager
Officers: James Thompson, President; Cate Brown, Vice President; Daryl Hill, Secretary; John McLaine, Treasurer
Paid Staff: 5   **Volunteer Staff:** 12
Paid Artists: 50   **Non-Paid Artists:** 37
Utilizes: Special Technical Talent; Guest Conductors; Guest Artists
Budget: $100,000 - $500,000
Income Sources: Private Foundations/Grants/Endowments; Business/Corporate Donations; Box Office;
Individual Donations
Season: June - May   **Annual Attendance:** 7,200

Affiliations: ASOL
Performance Facilities: Preus-Brandt Forum, California Lutheran University

FACILITY

CALIFORNIA LUTHERAN UNIVERSITY - PREUS-BRANDT FORUM
60 West Olsen Road, Thousand Oaks, CA 91360-2787
(805) 493-3195
FAX: (805) 493-3513
Type of Facility: Auditorium; Multi-Purpose
Facility Originally: School
Type of Stage: Proscenium
Stage Dimensions: 14'6"x45'x22'
Seating Capacity: 700
Year Built: 1962
Contact for Rental: Dennis Bryant;   (805) 493-3195

Topanga Canyon

THEATRE

THE WILL GEER THEATRICUM BOTANICUM
1419 North Topanga Canyon Boulevard, Topanga Canyon, CA 90290
(310) 455-2322
Founded: 1973
Arts Area: Theatrical Group
Status: Professional; Non-Profit
Type: Performing; Resident; Educational
Purpose: The Will Geer Theatricum Botanicum is dedicated to the belief that theatre, music and education are integral and necessary parts of life for all individuals to experience on a regular and inexpensive basis.
Management: Kathy Schutzer, General Manager; Ellen Geer, Artistic Director
Paid Staff: 4
Paid Artists: 40
Budget: $100,000 - $500,000
Income Sources: Private Foundations/Grants/Endowments; Business/Corporate Donations; Box Office; Government Grants; Individual Donations
Season: May - October   **Annual Attendance:** 40,000
Performance Facilities: Will Geer Theatricum Botanicum

Torrance

INSTRUMENTAL MUSIC

EL CAMINO COLLEGE - COMMUNITY ORCHESTRA
16007 South Crenshaw Boulevard, Torrance, CA 90506
(310) 532-3670
Founded: 1949
Arts Area: Orchestra
Status: Non-Professional; Non-Profit
Type: Performing; Educational
Purpose: To train college musicians and provide for community musicians to read and perform a greater variety of music than in other local groups
Management: James E. Mack, Music Director/Conductor
Paid Staff: 1
Non-Paid Artists: 50
Utilizes: Guest Artists
Budget: $1,000 - $50,000
Season: September - June   **Annual Attendance:** 2,000
Performance Facilities: Marsee Auditorium

VOCAL MUSIC

LA MARCA AMERICAN VARIETY SINGERS
2424 West Sepulueda Boulevard, Torrance, CA 90501
(310) 325-8708
Founded: 1974
Arts Area: Lyric Opera; Light Opera; Choral; Folk; Show Choirs

Status: Professional; Non-Profit; Commercial
Type: Performing; Touring; Resident; Educational
Purpose: To entertain, educate and promote the arts and the American spirit
Management: Priscilla LaMarca, Director/Manager
Officers: Priscilla LaMarca, President; E. Scottie Brown, Secretary; Barbara Barnes, Treasurer
Volunteer Staff: 4
Utilizes: Special Technical Talent; Original Music
Budget: $1,000 - $50,000
Income Sources: Business/Corporate Donations; Box Office; Individual Donations; Performance Fees; Sponsoring
Season: 52 Weeks   **Annual Attendance:** 10,000
Affiliations: FIDOF

THEATRE

TORRANCE COMMUNITY THEATRE
1522 Cravens Avenue, Torrance, CA 90501
(310) 533-0576
Founded: 1950
Arts Area: Musical; Community; Theatrical Group; Puppet
Status: Non-Profit
Type: Performing
Purpose: To produce live theatre
Officers: Linda Green, President; Jack Drake, Vice President; Shirley Bluman, Secretary
Paid Staff: 2   **Volunteer Staff:** 70
Income Sources: Business/Corporate Donations; Box Office; Individual Donations
Season: 52 Weeks   **Annual Attendance:** 6,000
Performance Facilities: Torrance Community Theatre

PERFORMING SERIES

TORRANCE CULTURAL ARTS CENTER
3330 Civic Center Drive, Torrance, CA 90503
(310) 781-7150
FAX: (310) 781-7199
Founded: 1991
Arts Area: Dance; Vocal Music; Instrumental Music; Theater; Children's Activities
Status: Non-Profit
Type: Sponsoring
Purpose: To enhance community offerings and build audiences; to provide a rental hall for the community
Management: Bob Stewart, Manager
Paid Staff: 26   **Volunteer Staff:** 20
Income Sources: Private Foundations/Grants/Endowments; Business/Corporate Donations; Box Office; Government Grants; Individual Donations
Season: September - June
Affiliations: IAAM; APAP; WAAA
Performance Facilities: Armstrong Theatre

FACILITY

EL CAMINO COLLEGE - SOUTH BAY CENTER FOR THE ARTS
16007 South Crenshaw Boulevard, Torrance, CA 90506
(310) 532-3670
Type of Facility: Auditorium
Type of Stage: Proscenium   **Orchestra Pit**
Seating Capacity: 2,054
Year Built: 1968   **Architect:** Morgridge   **Cost:** $2,500,000
Contact for Rental: Arlene Cabalo;   (310) 715-3485

Turlock

FACILITY

CALIFORNIA STATE UNIVERSITY-STANISLAUS - MAINSTAGE THEATRE
801 West Monte Vista Avenue, Turlock, CA 95380
(209) 667-3451
Type of Facility: Auditorium; Theatre House
Type of Stage: Proscenium
Stage Dimensions: 60'x40'x60'   **Orchestra Pit**

Seating Capacity: 300
Year Built: 1970   **Cost:** $2,500,000
Acoustical Consultant: Landry, Bogen
Contact for Rental: Connie Bratten;   (209) 667-3207
Resident Groups: Drama and Music Departments

Ukiah

THEATRE

UKIAH PLAYERS THEATRE
1041 Low Gap Road, Ukiah, CA 95482
(707) 462-1210
　　Founded: 1977
　　Arts Area: Musical; Community; Theatrical Group
　　Status: Semi-Professional; Non-Profit
　　Type: Performing; Touring; Resident; Educational; Sponsoring
　　Purpose: To provide the general community with a wide range of theatre experiences; to encourage and educate future theatre artists; to serve as a cultural venue
　　Management: Ellen Weed, Artistic Director; Dudley Folks, General Manager; Doug Hundley, Production Manager; Kate Magruder, Associate Director; David Hayes, Associate Technical Director; Dan Hibshman, Publicity Manager
　　Officers: Jeanine Bauman, Board President; Todd Evans, Board Vice President; Christine Webb, Board Secretary; Judy Waterman, Board Treasurer
　　Paid Staff: 7   **Volunteer Staff:** 40
　　Paid Artists: 7   **Non-Paid Artists:** 70
　　Utilizes: Special Technical Talent; Guest Conductors; Guest Artists; Guest Directors
　　Budget: $100,000 - $500,000
　　Income Sources: Private Foundations/Grants/Endowments; Business/Corporate Donations; Box Office; Government Grants; Individual Donations
　　Season: 52 Weeks   **Annual Attendance:** 10,000
　　Affiliations: Theatre Bay Area

Upland

DANCE

CONCERT DANCE THEATRE
2315 West Foothill Boulevard, #7, Upland, CA 91786
(909) 949-4166
　　Founded: 1968
　　Arts Area: Ballet; Jazz
　　Status: Semi-Professional; Non-Profit
　　Type: Performing; Educational
　　Purpose: To educate the community in classical ballet, other types of dance and culture
　　Officers: Mark Amendola, President; Bill Hemphill, Vice President; Frances Maginn, Secretary; Patti Coleman, Treasurer; JoAnn Warner, Artistic Director
　　Paid Staff: 1   **Volunteer Staff:** 5
　　Paid Artists: 12   **Non-Paid Artists:** 40
　　Utilizes: Special Technical Talent; Guest Artists
　　Budget: $1,000 - $50,000
　　Income Sources: Private Foundations/Grants/Endowments; Box Office; Individual Donations
　　Season: March - December   **Annual Attendance:** 3,200

Valencia

INSTRUMENTAL MUSIC

NEW CENTURY PLAYERS
c/o California Institute of the Arts, 24700 McBean Park, Valencia, CA 91355
(805) 253-7817
FAX: (805) 254-8352
　　Arts Area: Symphony; Orchestra; Chamber; Ensemble; Ethnic; Folk; Instrumental Group; Electronic & Live Electronic; Band
　　Status: Professional; Non-Profit
　　Type: Resident

Purpose: The ensemble is comprised of accomplished and versatile musicians who merge high-quality performance with skillfull teaching methods and present concerts versed in traditional chamber music combining performance with commentary.
Management: David Rosenboom, Dean, School of Music/Artistic Director
Budget: $1,000 - $50,000
Income Sources: Private Foundations/Grants/Endowments; Box Office; Government Grants; Individual Donations
Performance Facilities: Roy Disney Music Hall

PERFORMING SERIES

SPRING MUSIC FESTIVAL
c/o California Institute of the Arts, School of Music, 24700 McBean Pkwy, Valencia, CA 91355
(805) 253-7816
FAX: (805) 254-8352
Status: Professional; Non-Profit
Type: Performing; Educational
Purpose: To present the latest in contemporary direction of music and allied arts with a global style and cultural perspectives
Management: David Rosenboom, Dean, School of Music; Bob Clendenen, Production Manager
Budget: $1,000 - $50,000
Income Sources: Private Foundations/Grants/Endowments; Business/Corporate Donations; Government Grants
Performance Facilities: California Institute of the Arts; Japan American Theater

Van Nuys

DANCE

THE FRANCISCO MARTINEZ DANCETHEATRE
6723 Matilija Avenue, Van Nuys, CA 91405
(818) 988-2192
FAX: (310) 821-1163
Founded: 1981
Arts Area: Modern; Ballet
Status: Professional
Type: Performing; Touring; Educational
Purpose: To perform an eclectic repertory for broad audiences and special programs for schools
Officers: David Allen Jones, Executive Director; Lyn Profant, Administrative Assistant; Francisco Martinez, Artistic Director
Volunteer Staff: 15
Paid Artists: 7
Budget: $1,000 - $50,000
Income Sources: Private Foundations/Grants/Endowments; Business/Corporate Donations; Box Office; Government Grants; Individual Donations
Season: September - June   **Annual Attendance:** 5,000
Affiliations: WAAA; Bay Area Dance; Dance Resource Center
Performance Facilities: Plaza de la Raza

THEATRE

PASSAGE THEATRE
6650 Havenhurst Street, Van Nuys, CA 91406
(818) 904-0838
Founded: 1981
Arts Area: Professional
Status: Professional; Non-Profit
Type: Performing; Touring; Educational
Purpose: The purposes of the Passage Theatre are to produce classical plays, to establish a repertory theatre of national importance, and to take performances of the classics to those who might otherwise not have the opportunity to see them.
Management: Scott Guy, Artistic Director; Margaret Scott, Managing Director
Paid Staff: 2
Paid Artists: 50
Utilizes: Special Technical Talent; Guest Directors
Budget: $1,000 - $50,000
Income Sources: Business/Corporate Donations; Box Office; Government Grants; Individual Donations
Season: 52 Weeks   **Annual Attendance:** 21,000
Affiliations: LCT

Venice

THEATRE

HUDSON THEATRE
225 Howland Canal, Venice, CA 90291
(310) 306-1310
    Founded: 1975
    Arts Area: Professional
    Status: Professional; Non-Profit
    Type: Producing In House
    Management: Gary Blumsack and Elizabeth Reilly, Artistic Directors
    Volunteer Staff: 12
    Utilizes: Special Technical Talent; Guest Artists; Guest Directors
    Budget: $1,000 - $50,000
    Income Sources: Box Office
    Season: 52 Weeks
    Performance Facilities: Hudson Theatre; Husdon Backstage

LOS ANGELES THEATRE WORKS
681 Venice Boulevard, Venice, CA 90291
(310) 827-0808
FAX: (310) 827-4949
    Founded: 1974
    Arts Area: Professional
    Status: Professional; Non-Profit
    Type: Touring; Producing
    Purpose: Los Angeles Theatre Works, a pioneering lab for playwrights, directors and other theatre artists, is committed to the exploration of contemporary work in theatre.
    Management: Susan Albert-Loewenberg, Producing Director
    Officers: Doug Jaffe, President; Robert Talcott, Vice President; Genie Shapiro, Secretary; Alan Finkel, Treasurer
    Budget: $100,000 - $500,000
    Income Sources: Private Foundations/Grants/Endowments; Business/Corporate Donations; Box Office; Government Grants; Individual Donations
    Season: 52 Weeks   **Annual Attendance:** 25,000
    Affiliations: TCG; Los Angeles Theatre Alliance; California Confederation of the Arts; California Theatre Council

Ventura

INSTRUMENTAL MUSIC

VENTURA COUNTY SYMPHONY ASSOCIATION
PO Box 1088, Ventura, CA 93002
(805) 643-8646
    Founded: 1962
    Arts Area: Symphony; Chamber; Ensemble
    Status: Professional; Non-Profit
    Type: Performing
    Purpose: To present concerts of classical music for the community; to foster and promote an increased public knowledge and appreciation of concert music
    Management: Ila G. Winterbourne, General Manager; Frank Salazar, Music Director/Conductor; Karine Beesley, Executive Director; Boris Brott, Music Director
    Officers: Gregory Smith, President
    Paid Staff: 6   **Volunteer Staff:** 1
    Paid Artists: 15
    Utilizes: Guest Conductors; Guest Artists
    Budget: $100,000 - $500,000
    Income Sources: Private Foundations/Grants/Endowments; Business/Corporate Donations; Box Office; Government Grants; Individual Donations
    Season: October - June
    Annual Attendance: 10,000
    Performance Facilities: Oxnard Civic Auditorium, Ojai Libbey Bowl

Victorville

FACILITY

VICTOR VALLEY COLLEGE PERFORMING ARTS CENTER
18422 Bear Valley Road, Victorville, CA 92392
(619) 245-4271
FAX: (619) 245-9744
 Type of Facility: Concert Hall; Auditorium; Performance Center; Theatre House; Multi-Purpose
 Type of Stage: Proscenium
 Stage Dimensions: 40'Hx42'D proscenium opening **Orchestra Pit**
 Seating Capacity: 493
 Year Built: 1981 **Architect:** Howard H. Morgridge & Associates **Cost:** $2,600,000
 Acoustical Consultant: Howard G. Smith Associates
 Contact for Rental: Margie Lough; (619) 245-4271, ext. 251

Visalia

INSTRUMENTAL MUSIC

TULARE COUNTY SYMPHONY ORCHESTRA
PO Box 1201, Visalia, CA 93279
(209) 732-8600
 Founded: 1960
 Arts Area: Symphony; Orchestra
 Status: Professional; Non-Profit
 Type: Performing; Resident; Educational
 Purpose: To promote and foster the appreciation of all matters of music; to further adult participation in creative musical activity; to promote the education and development of young musicians
 Management: David Andre, Music Director/Conductor; Anne R. Bernardo, General Manager
 Officers: Thomas A. Akin M.D., President; Pat Finger, Vice President; Christine Richards, Recording Secretary; Martin V. Clevenger, Treasurer
 Paid Staff: 3
 Paid Artists: 75
 Utilizes: Guest Conductors; Guest Artists
 Budget: $100,000 - $500,000
 Income Sources: Private Foundations/Grants/Endowments; Business/Corporate Donations; Box Office; Government Grants; Individual Donations
 Season: September - May
 Annual Attendance: 21,000
 Affiliations: Association of California Symphony Orchestras
 Performance Facilities: L.J. Williams Theatre

FACILITY

VISALIA CONVENTION CENTER - EXHIBIT HALL
303 East Acequia Street, Visalia, CA 93291
(209) 738-3386
FAX: (209) 738-3579
 Type of Facility: Concert Hall; Auditorium; Multi-Purpose; Exhibition Hall
 Seating Capacity: 2,200
 Year Built: 1972 **Architect:** Moring and Hayslett **Cost:** $4,000,000
 Contact for Rental: Mimi McKell; (209) 738-3386

VISALIA CONVENTION CENTER - L.J. WILLIAMS THEATRE
1001 West Main, Visalia, CA 93291
(209) 738-3386
FAX: (209) 738-3574
 Type of Facility: Theatre House
 Facility Originally: School
 Type of Stage: Modified Apron Proscenium
 Stage Dimensions: 65'Wx48'D; 38'Wx21'H proscenium opening **Orchestra Pit**
 Seating Capacity: 1,268
 Year Built: 1940
 Year Remodeled: 1972 **Architect:** Walter Vogel **Cost:** $1,000,000
 Contact for Rental: Mimi McKell; (209) 738-3386
 Resident Groups: Tulare County Symphony

VISALIA CONVENTION CENTER - ROTARY THEATRE
330 South Dollner, Visalia, CA 93291
(209) 738-3386
FAX: (209) 738-3386
> **Type of Facility:** Theatre House
> **Facility Originally:** School
> **Type of Stage:** Thrust; Flexible; Proscenium
> **Stage Dimensions:** 38'Wx18'D; 32'Wx16'D de-mountable thrust
> **Seating Capacity:** 328
> **Year Built:** 1939
> **Year Remodeled:** 1987 **Architect:** Ray Schlick **Cost:** $400,000
> **Contact for Rental:** Mimi McKell; (209) 738-3386

Walnut

DANCE

ANJANI'S KATHAK DANCE OF INDIA
1934 Peaceful Hills Road, Walnut, CA 91789
(909) 595-8934
> **Founded:** 1983
> **Arts Area:** Ethnic
> **Status:** Professional
> **Type:** Performing; Touring
> **Purpose:** To enlighten audiences all over with the unique traditional classical dance of India-Kathak
> **Paid Artists:** 8
> **Utilizes:** Guest Choreographers
> **Budget:** $50,000 - $100,000
> **Income Sources:** Private Foundations/Grants/Endowments; Box Office; Government Grants
> **Season:** 52 Weeks
> **Annual Attendance:** 4,000

Walnut Creek

INSTRUMENTAL MUSIC

THE DIABLO SYMPHONY ORCHESTRA
PO Box 2222, Walnut Creek, CA 94595
(510) 935-7764
> **Founded:** 1969
> **Arts Area:** Symphony; Orchestra
> **Status:** Professional; Non-Profit
> **Type:** Performing; Sponsoring
> **Management:** Joyce Johnson-Hamilton, Music Director/Conductor
> **Officers:** Mary-Margaret Scobey, President, Diablo Symphony Association
> **Paid Staff:** 4 **Volunteer Staff:** 24
> **Non-Paid Artists:** 60
> **Utilizes:** Guest Artists
> **Budget:** $1,000 - $50,000
> **Income Sources:** Private Foundations/Grants/Endowments; Business/Corporate Donations; Individual Donations
> **Season:** September - July **Annual Attendance:** 9,000
> **Affiliations:** ASOL; Association of California Symphony Orchestras
> **Performance Facilities:** Regional Arts Center

YOUNG ARTISTS SYMPHONY ORCHESTRA
PO Box 4849, Walnut Creek, CA 94596
(510) 486-4398
> **Founded:** 1980
> **Arts Area:** Symphony; Orchestra
> **Status:** Non-Professional; Non-Profit
> **Type:** Performing; Touring; Educational; Sponsoring
> **Purpose:** To offer young musicians in Contra Costa and neighboring counties musical education in a teaching and performing group and to participate in a symphony orchestra; to provide social activities; to participate in a biennial tour; to sponsor an annual concerto competition
> **Management:** H.T. Payne, Music Director/Conductor
> **Officers:** Caroline Oliver, President; Dellyn Pacilio, Manager
> **Paid Staff:** 2 **Volunteer Staff:** 20

Non-Paid Artists: 70
Budget: $1,000 - $50,000
Income Sources: Private Foundations/Grants/Endowments; Business/Corporate Donations; Individual Donations; Fund-raising
Season: September - May   **Annual Attendance:** 1,000
Affiliations: ASOL (Youth Orchestra Division)

VOCAL MUSIC

DIABLO LIGHT OPERA COMPANY
PO Box 5034, Walnut Creek, CA 94596
(510) 939-6161; (510) 376-8887
Founded: 1960
Arts Area: Light Opera; Operetta; Musical Theatre
Status: Non-Professional; Non-Profit
Type: Performing; Educational
Purpose: Diablo Light Opera Company (DLOC) is a non-profit community theatre dedicated to providing quality musical and light opera, and to enhancing the lives of our members, audiences and the community.
Management: Rhoda Klitsner, Artistic Advisor; Grete Egan, Producer
Officers: Bobbi Bach, President
Volunteer Staff: 40
Non-Paid Artists: 50
Utilizes: Special Technical Talent; Guest Conductors; Guest Directors; Guest Choreographers; Guest Choreographers
Budget: $100,000 - $500,000
Income Sources: Private Foundations/Grants/Endowments; Business/Corporate Donations; Box Office; Individual Donations
Season: September - June
Annual Attendance: 30,000
Performance Facilities: Regional Center for the Arts

PERFORMING SERIES

REGIONAL CENTER FOR THE ARTS
1601 Civic Drive, Walnut Creek, CA 94596
(510) 295-1400
FAX: (510) 943-7222
Founded: 1965
Arts Area: Dance; Vocal Music; Theater
Status: Non-Profit
Type: Performing
Purpose: Main stage is used for musical theatre; drama, jazz, ballet and films, Stage II is used for drama, lectures and reviews
Management: Scott Denison, Arts Center Manager
Officers: Gary Schaub, Director of Cultural Services
Paid Staff: 12   **Volunteer Staff:** 23
Utilizes: Guest Artists; Guest Directors
Budget: $500,000 - $1,000,000
Income Sources: Government Grants
Season: 52 Weeks   **Annual Attendance:** 100,000
Performance Facilities: Hoffmann Theatre; Dean Lefher Theatre

Weed

FACILITY

COLLEGE OF THE SISKIYOUS - THEATRE
800 College Avenue, Weed, CA 96094
(916) 938-5257
FAX: (916) 938-5227
Type of Facility: Theatre House
Type of Stage: Proscenium
Stage Dimensions: 15'6"x36'6"x24'6" plus apron
Orchestra Pit
Seating Capacity: 604
Year Built: 1969   **Architect:** Allyn Martin   **Cost:** $750,000
Contact for Rental: Carol Kramm;   (916) 938-5206
Manager: Keith Ronee;   (916) 938-5257
Resident Groups: College Drama and Music Departments

West Los Angeles

INSTRUMENTAL MUSIC

AMERICAN YOUTH SYMPHONY
321 Tilden Avenue, West Los Angeles, CA 90049
(310) 476-2825
Founded: 1964
Arts Area: Symphony; Orchestra
Status: Non-Professional; Non-Profit
Type: Performing; Educational
Purpose: To educate tomorrow's professional musicians and to provide free concerts for the community of Los Angeles
Management: Bonnie McClain, Manager; Mehli Mehta, Music Director/Conductor
Paid Staff: 3 **Volunteer Staff:** 50
Non-Paid Artists: 110
Utilizes: Guest Artists
Budget: $100,000 - $500,000
Income Sources: Private Foundations/Grants/Endowments; Business/Corporate Donations; Government Grants; Individual Donations
Season: October - June **Annual Attendance:** 14,000
Affiliations: ASOL (Youth Orchestra Division)
Performance Facilities: Royce Hall, UCLA

Whittier

INSTRUMENTAL MUSIC

RIO HONDO SYMPHONY ASSOCIATION
PO Box 495, Whittier, CA 90608
(310) 695-1102
Founded: 1933
Arts Area: Symphony; Orchestra
Status: Non-Profit
Type: Performing; Resident
Purpose: To provide free concerts of symphonic music to all residents of Whittier and surrounding cities known as the Rio Hondo Area; to encourage young talented musicians through Young Artist Auditions
Management: Wayne Rienecke, Conductor
Officers: Louis Galindo, President
Paid Staff: 5 **Volunteer Staff:** 20
Paid Artists: 60 **Non-Paid Artists:** 25
Utilizes: Guest Artists
Budget: $1,000 - $50,000
Income Sources: Private Foundations/Grants/Endowments; Business/Corporate Donations; Government Grants; Individual Donations
Annual Attendance: 6,000
Affiliations: Rio Hondo Symphony Guild
Performance Facilities: Whittier Union High School Auditorium

THEATRE

WHITTIER JUNIOR THEATRE
7630 South Washington Avenue, Whittier, CA 90602
(310) 945-8207
Founded: 1962
Arts Area: Theatrical Group
Status: Non-Professional; Non-Profit
Type: Performing; Touring; Educational
Purpose: Whittier Junior Theatre is composed of children 9-18 years of age and presents three childrens' theatre productions per year.
Management: Pamela Franklin Bradac, Managing Supervisor
Paid Staff: 10 **Volunteer Staff:** 4
Non-Paid Artists: 150
Utilizes: Guest Directors
Budget: $50,000 - $100,000
Income Sources: Box Office; Individual Donations
Annual Attendance: 3,000
Affiliations: CAC; City of Whittier
Performance Facilities: The Center Theatre

FACILITY

RIO HONDO COLLEGE - MERTON WRAY THEATRE
3600 Workman Mill Road, Whittier, CA 90601
(310) 692-0921
    Type of Facility: Concert Hall; Auditorium; Theatre House
    Type of Stage: Proscenium
    Stage Dimensions: 40'W proscenium opening   **Orchestra Pit**
    Seating Capacity: 320
    Year Built: 1967   **Architect:** Powell, Morgridge, Richards & Goghlan   **Cost:** $2,000,000
    Contact for Rental: Rachel Esqueda;   (310) 908-3426, ext. 301
    Manager: Perry Sites
    Resident Groups: College Student Performing Groups

Woodland

FACILITY

WOODLAND OPERA HOUSE
340 Second Street, Woodland, CA 95695
(916) 666-9617
    Founded: 1895
    Type of Facility: Concert Hall; Auditorium; Performance Center; Theatre House; Opera House; Civic Center;
    Multi-Purpose
    Type of Stage: Proscenium
    Stage Dimensions: 25'x25' playing area   **Orchestra Pit**
    Seating Capacity: 530
    Year Built: 1895
    Year Restored: 1988   **Architect:** Brocchini & Associates   **Cost:** $2,300,000
    Contact for Rental: Elaine Edstrom, General Manager;   (916) 666-9617
    Resident Groups: Theatre Company

Woodland Hills

INSTRUMENTAL MUSIC

THE WEST VALLEY CHAMBER ORCHESTRA
Pierce College Music Department, 6201 Winnetka Avenue, Woodland Hills, CA 91371
(818) 347-0551
    Founded: 1972
    Arts Area: Orchestra
    Status: Non-Professional; Non-Profit
    Type: Performing; Resident; Educational
    Purpose: To offer free concerts to the community year-round
    Management: Rowan Taylor, Conductor; Timothy J. Durand, Assistant Director
    Paid Staff: 1   **Volunteer Staff:** 2
    Non-Paid Artists: 15
    Utilizes: Special Technical Talent; Guest Conductors; Guest Artists
    Budget: $1,000 - $50,000   **Season:** August - June

THEATRE

SHOWBOAT TROUPE
19817 Ventura Boulevard, Woodland Hills, CA 91364
(818) 884-7461
    Founded: 1979
    Arts Area: Musical; Dinner
    Status: Professional; Non-Profit
    Type: Performing; Educational
    Purpose: To provide the only legitimate theatre in the west end of the San Fernando Valley
    Management: Mike Monahan, Managing Director; Cynthia Orme, Business Manager; Ann Mahan,
    Choreographer/Secretary
    Volunteer Staff: 7
    Non-Paid Artists: 100
    Budget: $50,000 - $100,000
    Income Sources: Box Office

Season: 52 Weeks   **Annual Attendance:** 12,000
Performance Facilities: Showboat Dinner Theatre

Yreka

FACILITY

YREKA COMMUNITY THEATRE CENTER
810 North Oregon Street, Yreka, CA 96097
(916) 842-2355
FAX: (916) 842-3628
    Founded: 1976
    Type of Facility: Auditorium; Multi-Purpose
    Type of Stage: Proscenium
    Stage Dimensions: 38'x22'
    Seating Capacity: 307
    Year Built: 1978   **Architect:** Asefth, Jacobs & Schmitz   **Cost:** $1,600,000
    Contact for Rental: Bob Marshall;   (916) 842-2355

COLORADO

Arvada

INSTRUMENTAL MUSIC

ROCKY MOUNTAIN BRASSWORKS
6974 Teller Court, Arvada, CO 80003
(303) 420-6452
   Founded: 1980
   Arts Area: Band
   Status: Non-Professional; Non-Profit
   Type: Performing; Educational
   Purpose: To give the opportunity for the performer and listener to hear the great wealth of brass band music
   Management: Stephen Asheim, Conductor; Rick Argotsinger, Associate Conductor
   Officers: Rick Argostinger, Chairman; Ken Anderson, Vice Chairman; David Ciancio, Treasurer
   Volunteer Staff: 5
   Non-Paid Artists: 38
   Budget: $1,000 - $50,000
   Income Sources: Private Foundations/Grants/Endowments; Business/Corporate Donations; Individual Donations
   Season: September - July   **Annual Attendance:** 3,500

FACILITY

ARVADA CENTER FOR THE ARTS AND HUMANITIES
6901 Wadsworth Boulevard, Arvada, CO 80003
(303) 431-3080
   Type of Facility: Theatre Complex; Concert Hall; Outdoor (Concert); Studio Performance; Performance Center; Amphi-theater; Civic Center; Multi-Purpose
   Type of Stage: Thrust
   Seating Capacity: 500
   Year Built: 1976   **Architect:** Syracuse Lawylor   **Cost:** $3,600,000
   Available for rent.

Aspen

DANCE

DANCE ASPEN
210 AABC, Suite NN, PO Box 8745, Aspen, CO 81611
(303) 925-7718
FAX: (303) 925-3041
   Founded: 1981
   Arts Area: Modern; Ballet; Ethnic
   Status: Non-Profit
   Type: Sponsoring
   Purpose: To present a summer dance festival featuring professional dance companies from the United States and South America
   Management: Jeffrey J. Bentley, Director
   Officers: Andrew V. Hecht, President
   Paid Staff: 5
   Budget: $1,000,000 - $5,000,000
   Income Sources: Private Foundations/Grants/Endowments; Business/Corporate Donations; Box Office; Government Grants; Individual Donations
   Season: July - August   **Annual Attendance:** 9,000
   Affiliations: APAP

PERFORMING SERIES

ASPEN MUSIC FESTIVAL AND SCHOOL
PO Box AA, Aspen, CO 81612
(303) 925-3254
FAX: (303) 925-3802
   Founded: 1949
   Arts Area: Vocal Music; Instrumental Music; Festivals; Lyric Opera; Grand Opera
   Status: Professional; Semi-Professional; Non-Profit

Type: Performing; Resident; Educational
Purpose: To provide the finest supplemental classical music education possible for professionally-oriented students; to produce high-quality concerts for the public
Management: Robert Harth, President/Dean; Lawrence Foster, Music Director; Tom Eirman, General Manager; Martin Verdrager, Artistic Administrator; Debra Ayers, Director of Publicity; Edward Sweeney, Director of Operations
Officers: Fredric Benedict, Chairman; Les Anderson, Vice Chairman; Charles Paterson, Secretary; Noel Congdon, Treasurer
Paid Staff: 400   **Volunteer Staff:** 250
Paid Artists: 200   **Non-Paid Artists:** 965
Utilizes: Special Technical Talent; Guest Conductors; Guest Artists; Guest Directors
Budget: $1,000,000 - $5,000,000
Income Sources: Private Foundations/Grants/Endowments; Business/Corporate Donations; Box Office; Government Grants; Individual Donations
Season: June - August   **Annual Attendance:** 80,000
Performance Facilities: Festival Music Tent

THE DANCE ASPEN FESTIVAL
PO Box 8745, Aspen, CO 81612
(303) 925-7718
Founded: 1981
Arts Area: Ballet
Status: Professional; Non-Profit
Type: Sponsoring
Purpose: To present the finest professional dance companies available in this part of the United States
Management: Jeffrey Bentley, Executive Producing Director
Officers: Andrew V. Hecht, President
Utilizes: Guest Artists
Budget: $500,000 - $1,000,000
Income Sources: Private Foundations/Grants/Endowments; Business/Corporate Donations
Season: July - August   **Annual Attendance:** 11,000
Affiliations: Aspen/Snowmass Arts Council
Performance Facilities: Aspen High School; Performing Arts Center

WHEELER OPERA HOUSE ASSOCIATION
320 East Hyman Avenue, Aspen, CO 81611
(303) 920-2268
FAX: (303) 930-5197
Founded: 1985
Arts Area: Dance; Vocal Music; Instrumental Music; Theatre
Status: Non-Profit
Type: Sponsoring
Management: Heather Tharp, Secretary
Officers: Joyce Semple, President; Denise Jurgens, Treasurer; Robert Murray, Secretary; King Woodward, Treasurer
Utilizes: Special Technical Talent; Guest Artists; Guest Directors
Budget: $100,000 - $500,000
Income Sources: Private Foundations/Grants/Endowments; Business/Corporate Donations; Box Office; Government Grants; Individual Donations
Season: 52 Weeks
Affiliations: APAP
Performance Facilities: Wheeler Opera House

FACILITY

MUSIC TENT
980 North Third Street, Aspen, CO 81611
(303) 925-3254
Type of Facility: Amphitheater; Tent-covered Amphitheatre
Type of Stage: 3/4 Arena
Stage Dimensions: 75'x100'
Seating Capacity: 1731
Year Built: 1949   **Architect:** Eero Saarinen
Year Remodeled: 1965   **Architect:** Herbert Baer
Contact for Rental Director of Operations;   (303) 925-3254
Resident Groups: Aspen Chamber Symphony; Aspen Festival Orchestra; Aspen Concert Orchestra; Sinfonia
Limited availability

WHEELER OPERA HOUSE
320 East Hyman Avenue, Aspen, CO 81611
(303) 925-2750
> **Type of Facility:** Theatre House
> **Type of Stage:** Thrust; Proscenium
> **Stage Dimensions:** 27'11"Wx27'10"D; 27'11"Wx17'3"H proscenium opening   **Orchestra Pit**
> **Seating Capacity:** 502
> **Year Built:** 1889   **Architect:** Edbrook
> **Year Remodeled:** 1984   **Architect:** William Kessler and Associates   **Cost:** $4,500,000
> **Contact for Rental** Robert Murray, Executive Director;   (303) 920-2268
> **Manager:** Leslie Shor
> **Resident Groups:** Aspen Music Festival and School
> *The Wheeler Opera house is a member of the League of Historic American Theatres.*

Aurora

DANCE

AURORA DANCE ARTS
3054 South Laredo Street, Aurora, CO 80013
(303) 699-3911
> **Founded:** 1973
> **Arts Area:** Ballet; Jazz; Tap
> **Status:** Non-Professional
> **Type:** Performing; Resident; Educational
> **Purpose:** To provide instruction in ballet, tap, jazz and pointe for all ages and ability levels and to provide a chance to perform for an audience
> **Management:** Julie Martin, Director; Pam Ziedman, Joy Hines, Office; 13 Dance Instructors
> **Paid Staff:** 16   **Volunteer Staff:** 150
> **Non-Paid Artists:** 50
> **Utilizes:** Special Technical Talent; Guest Artists
> **Budget:** $50,000 - $100,000
> **Income Sources:** Box Office; Government Grants; Individual Donations
> **Season:** 52 Weeks   **Annual Attendance:** 30,000
> **Affiliations:** City of Aurora
> **Performance Facilities:** Central High School; Aurora Fox Arts Center

JAN JUSTIS DANCE COMPANY
11787 East Atlantic Place, Aurora, CO 80014-1106
(302) 369-8687
> **Founded:** 1984
> **Arts Area:** Modern
> **Status:** Professional; Non-Profit
> **Type:** Performing; Touring; Educational
> **Purpose:** To further an appreciation of dance as an art form through cultural and educational programs, concerts, and experimental work, including collaborations with other artists
> **Management:** Jan Justis, Artistic Director/Manager; Rosanne Sterne, Director of Development
> **Officers:** Stephanie Reineke, President; Mark Overmeyer, Vice President; Robin Schaffer, Secretary
> **Paid Staff:** 1   **Volunteer Staff:** 1
> **Paid Artists:** 12
> **Utilizes:** Special Technical Talent; Guest Artists; Guest Choreographers; Composers; Visual Arts
> **Budget:** $1,000 - $50,000
> **Income Sources:** Private Foundations/Grants/Endowments; Business/Corporate Donations; Box Office; Government Grants; Individual Donations
> **Season:** 52 Weeks   **Annual Attendance:** 4,500
> **Affiliations:** Colorado Dance Alliance; Colorado Council on the Arts; Young Audiences of Denver

INSTRUMENTAL MUSIC

AURORA SYMPHONY
9900 East Colfax Avenue, Aurora, CO 80010
(303) 361-2908
> **Founded:** 1979
> **Arts Area:** Symphony
> **Status:** Non-Professional
> **Type:** Performing; Resident
> **Purpose:** To provide Aurora residents a chance to share their musical talents with an audience
> **Management:** Richard Molzer, Conductor/Musical Director; Alice Lee Main, Cultural Arts Administrator

Paid Staff: 1   **Volunteer Staff:** 65
Paid Artists: 4   **Non-Paid Artists:** 65
Utilizes: Guest Artists
Budget: $1,000 - $50,000
Income Sources: Business/Corporate Donations; Box Office; Government Grants; Individual Donations
Season: September - May   **Annual Attendance:** 1,200
Affiliations: City of Aurora
Performance Facilities: Aurora Fox Arts Center

VOCAL MUSIC

AURORA SINGERS
PO Box 9, Fox Arts Center, Aurora, CO 80040
(303) 361-2910; (303) 361-2908
FAX: (303) 361-2952
Founded: 1977
Arts Area: Choral
Status: Non-Professional
Type: Performing; Resident
Purpose: To provide Aurora residents a chance to share their vocal music skills with an audience
Management: Ken Johnson, Conductor/Music Director; Alice Lee Main, Cultural Arts Administrator
Paid Staff: 1   **Volunteer Staff:** 50
Non-Paid Artists: 50
Utilizes: Guest Directors
Budget: $1,000 - $50,000
Income Sources: Business/Corporate Donations; Box Office; Government Grants; Individual Donations
Season: September - May   **Annual Attendance:** 1,600
Affiliations: City of Aurora
Performance Facilities: Aurora Fox Arts Center

THEATRE

AURORA CHILDREN'S THEATRE COMPANY
9900 East Colfax Avenue, Aurora, CO 80010
(303) 361-2910
Founded: 1979
Arts Area: Community
Status: Non-Professional
Type: Performing; Resident; Educational
Purpose: To provide children an opportunity to learn acting skills and perform for an audience
Management: Alice Lee Main, Cultural Arts Administrator; Kim Smith, Theatre Producer; Robert Salisbury, Art Center Director
Paid Staff: 1   **Volunteer Staff:** 400
Non-Paid Artists: 200
Utilizes: Special Technical Talent; Guest Directors
Budget: $1,000 - $50,000
Income Sources: Business/Corporate Donations; Box Office; Government Grants
Season: September - August   **Annual Attendance:** 5,000
Affiliations: City of Aurora
Performance Facilities: Aurora Fox Arts Center

AURORA THEATRE COMPANY
9900 East Colfax Avenue, Aurora, CO 80010
(303) 361-2910
Founded: 1973
Arts Area: Theatrical Group
Status: Non-Professional
Type: Performing; Resident; Educational
Purpose: To provide actors and actresses an opportunity to advance their skills and entertain audiences
Management: Alice Lee Main, Cultural Arts Administrator; Liz Jury, Theatre Producer; Robert Salisbury, Art Center Director
Utilizes: Special Technical Talent; Guest Directors
Budget: $1,000 - $50,000
Income Sources: Business/Corporate Donations; Box Office; Government Grants; Individual Donations
Season: September - May   **Annual Attendance:** 7,000
Affiliations: City of Aurora
Performance Facilities: Aurora Fox Arts Center

FACILITY

AURORA FOX ARTS CENTER
9900 East Colfax, Aurora, CO 80010
(303) 695-7538
> **Founded:** 1985
> **Type of Facility:** Performance Center
> **Facility Originally:** Movie House
> **Type of Stage:** Proscenium
> **Stage Dimensions:** 29'x29' with 10' apron
> **Seating Capacity:** 251 + 4 wheelchair
> **Year Built:** 1946   **Cost:** $100,000
> **Year Remodeled:** 1985   **Architect:** Baer & Hickman Architects   **Cost:** $800,000
> **Acoustical Consultant:** Howard McGregor-Engineering Dynamics
> **Contact for Rental** Robert Salisbury;   (303) 695-7538
> **Resident Groups:** Aurora Theatre Company; Aurora Children's Theatre Company; Aurora Symphony; Aurora Singers; Aurora Dance Arts

BICENTENNIAL ART CENTER
13655 East Alameda, Aurora, CO 80012
(303) 344-1776
> **Type of Facility:** Visual Arts Center
> **Facility Originally:** Military Base
> **Year Built:** 1940
> **Year Remodeled:** 1978   **Cost:** $134,000
> **Resident Groups:** Aurora Potter's Guild
> *Owned by City of Aurora*

Boulder

INSTRUMENTAL MUSIC

BOULDER PHILHARMONIC ORCHESTRA
1722 14th Street, Suite 100, Boulder, CO 80302
(303) 449-1343
FAX: (303) 443-9203
> **Founded:** 1956
> **Arts Area:** Symphony; Orchestra
> **Status:** Non-Professional; Non-Profit
> **Type:** Performing; Sponsoring
> **Purpose:** To provide quality symphonic music to the people of Boulder County and the surrounding region; to take a leadership role in enhancing the cultural environment of Boulder County; to develop an understanding and interest among area residents for fine artistic expression
> **Management:** William Lightfoot, Executive Director; Oswald Lehnert, Conductor/Musical Director
> **Paid Staff:** 3
> **Non-Paid Artists:** 60
> **Utilizes:** Guest Artists
> **Budget:** $100,000 - $500,000
> **Income Sources:** Private Foundations/Grants/Endowments; Business/Corporate Donations; Box Office; Individual Donations
> **Season:** September - April   **Annual Attendance:** 12,000
> **Affiliations:** ASOL; WAAA
> **Performance Facilities:** Macky Auditorium Concert Hall

THEATRE

THE BOULDER REPERTORY COMPANY
3850 Norwood Court, Boulder, CO 80304
(303) 449-7258
> **Founded:** 1975
> **Arts Area:** Theatrical Group
> **Status:** Non-Profit
> **Type:** Performing
> **Purpose:** To perform plays of quality, either classics or the best of contemporary writers, studying people in depth or life in society today; to introduce contemporary plays to the Rocky Mountain region
> **Management:** Frank Georgianna, Artistic Director; Ernestine Georgianna, Administrative Director
> **Officers:** Frank Georgianna, President; Patricia Fitzgerald, Vice President; Susan D'Autremont, Secretary; Ernestine Georgianna, Treasurer

Volunteer Staff: 2
Paid Artists: 15
Utilizes: Special Technical Talent; Guest Artists
Budget: $1,000 - $50,000
Income Sources: Private Foundations/Grants/Endowments; Box Office; Government Grants; Individual Donations
Season: Summer   Annual Attendance: 3,000
Performance Facilities: Guild Theatre, Boulder

PERFORMING SERIES

BOULDER FOLK AND BLUEGRASS ASSOCIATION
2888 Bluff, #492, Boulder, CO 80301
(303) 753-3261
Founded: 1983
Arts Area: Festivals
Status: Non-Profit
Type: Sponsoring
Purpose: Boulder Folk and Bluegrass Association puts on a one-day folk festival annually in September; daytime events are generally free to the public
Management: John Sirkis, Festival Director
Volunteer Staff: 5
Utilizes: Guest Artists
Budget: $1,000 - $50,000
Income Sources: Private Foundations/Grants/Endowments; Business/Corporate Donations; Box Office; Government Grants; Individual Donations
Season: September
Annual Attendance: 5,000

COLORADO DANCE FESTIVAL
PO Box 356, Boulder, CO 80306
(303) 442-7666
Founded: 1979
Arts Area: Dance
Status: Professional; Non-Profit
Type: Performing; Touring; Resident; Educational; Sponsoring
Purpose: To develop new ideas in the arts through innovative dance and arts presentations, research, and education; to be an incubator for the research and development of new work in the area; to present programming of the highest quality that is inspiring and provocative; to respond to the changing needs of emerging artists
Management: Marda Kirn, Artistic Director; Felicia Dryden, Managing Director
Officers: Noel Hefty, President
Paid Staff: 23   Volunteer Staff: 3
Paid Artists: 40
Utilizes: Guest Artists
Budget: $100,000 - $500,000
Income Sources: Private Foundations/Grants/Endowments; Business/Corporate Donations; Box Office; Government Grants; Individual Donations
Season: June - July
Annual Attendance: 5,000
Affiliations: University of Colorado

COLORADO MUSIC FESTIVAL
1035 Pearl Street, Suite 303, Boulder, CO 80302
(303) 449-1397
FAX: (303) 449-0071
Founded: 1977
Arts Area: Instrumental Music
Status: Professional; Non-Profit
Type: Performing
Purpose: To develop and promote an appreciation and love for the musical arts through the operation of an international professional orchestra; to present traditional symphonic literature; to challenge audiences with new or contemporary compositions; to stimulate an intellectual experience
Management: Giora Bernstein, Musical Director; Michael A. Smith, Executive Director
Officers: Carol Kassoy, President; Richard Collins, President - Elect; Robert Bunting, Henry Beer, Timothy Schoecmle, William Phillips, Arthur Smoot, Vice Presidents; Francine Scchauer, Treasurer; Alan Shapely, Secretary
Paid Staff: 10   Volunteer Staff: 20
Paid Artists: 85

Utilizes: Guest Conductors; Guest Artists
Budget: $500,000 - $1,000,000
Income Sources: Private Foundations/Grants/Endowments; Business/Corporate Donations; Box Office; Government Grants; Individual Donations
Season: June - August
Annual Attendance: 30,000
Affiliations: ASOL
Performance Facilities: Chautauqua Auditorium

COLORADO SHAKESPEARE FESTIVAL
University of Colorado, Campus Box 261, Boulder, CO 80309-0261
(303) 492-0554; (303) 492-1527
    Founded: 1958
    Arts Area: Theater
    Status: Professional; Non-Profit
    Type: Performing
    Purpose: To present four full-scale Shakespearean or classical productions in repertory June - August; to promote an appreciation of Shakespeare
    Management: Richard M. Devin, Artistic Director; Patricia B. McFerran, Director of Publicity and Public Relations; Ann Watson, General Manager
    Paid Staff: 50
    Paid Artists: 75   **Non-Paid Artists:** 5
    Utilizes: Special Technical Talent; Guest Artists; Guest Directors
    Budget: $100,000 - $500,000
    Income Sources: Private Foundations/Grants/Endowments; Box Office; Individual Donations
    Season: June - August
    Annual Attendance: 30,000
    Performance Facilities: Outdoor theatre; University Theatre

FACILITY

BOULDER ART CENTER
1750 13th, Boulder, CO 80302
(303) 443-2122
    Type of Facility: Gallery
    Facility Originally: Warehouse
    Type of Stage: Floor space only
    Seating Capacity: 125
    Contact for Rental Angie Lee; (303) 443-2122

THE NAROPA INSTITUTE
2130 Arapahoe Avenue, Boulder, CO 80302
(303) 444-0202
FAX: (303) 444-0410
    Type of Facility: Studio Performance; Environmental; Performance Center; Visual And Performing Arts Classroom
    Facility Originally: Recreation Hall/Gymnasium
    Type of Stage: Environmental
    Year Built: 1920
    Contact for Rental Rebecca Zepp; Phil Jacobson; (303) 444-0202

UNIVERSITY OF COLORADO - MACKY AUDITORIUM CONCERT HALL
Box 285, Boulder, CO 80309
(303) 492-8423
FAX: (303) 492-5105
    Type of Facility: Concert Hall; Multi-Purpose
    Type of Stage: Proscenium
    Stage Dimensions: 39'Wx27'D
    Orchestra Pit
    Seating Capacity: 2,047
    Year Built: 1910 **Architect:** Gove and Walsh **Cost:** $300,000
    Year Remodeled: 1986 **Architect:** Midyette/Seieroe & Associates **Cost:** $2,800,000
    Acoustical Consultant: Lawrence Kirkegaard and Associates
    Contact for Rental Kristin Anderson; (303) 492-8423
    Resident Groups: The Artist Series; The Boulder Philharmonic Orchestra; University of Colorado College of Music Orchestra; Symphonic Band and Choral Groups

---

Breckenridge

THEATRE

BACKSTAGE THEATRE COMPANY
PO Box 297, Breckenridge, CO 80424
(303) 453-0199
Founded: 1974
Arts Area: Musical; Community; Theatrical Group
Status: Semi-Professional; Non-Profit
Type: Performing; Educational
Purpose: To present a wide range of cultural events centered on theatre
Management: Bob and Wendy Moore
Paid Staff: 2   **Volunteer Staff:** 4
Paid Artists: 8
Utilizes: Guest Artists; Guest Directors
Budget: $50,000 - $100,000
Income Sources: Private Foundations/Grants/Endowments; Business/Corporate Donations; Box Office; Government Grants; Individual Donations
Season: Winter; Summer   **Annual Attendance:** 4,500
Affiliations: Rocky Mountain Theatre Guild
Performance Facilities: Backstage Theatre

PERFORMING SERIES

BRECKENRIDGE MUSIC INSTITUTE
130 Ski Hill Road, PO Box 1254, Breckenridge, CO 80424
(303) 453-9142
FAX: (303) 453-1423
Founded: 1980
Arts Area: Vocal Music; Instrumental Music; Festivals
Status: Professional; Non-Profit
Type: Performing; Educational
Purpose: To provide cultural and educational growth and enrichment in music for Summit County residents and visitors
Management: Pamela G. Miller, Executive Director; Peter Bay, Music Advisor; Daniel Schmidt, Festival Administrator; Allison Rouse, Administrative Assistant
Officers: R.H. VanDenburg, President; Charles Simpson, Vice President; James Robertson, Secretary; Richard L. Thomas, Treasurer
Paid Staff: 64   **Volunteer Staff:** 250
Paid Artists: 55
Utilizes: Guest Conductors; Guest Artists
Budget: $100,000 - $500,000
Income Sources: Private Foundations/Grants/Endowments; Business/Corporate Donations; Box Office; Government Grants; Individual Donations
Season: July - August   **Annual Attendance:** 16,000
Performance Facilities: Breckenridge Event Tent

FACILITY

BACKSTAGE THEATRE
PO Box 297, Breckenridge, CO 80424
(303) 453-0199
Type of Facility: Theatre House
Type of Stage: Proscenium
Stage Dimensions: 22'Wx16'D
Seating Capacity: 98
Year Built: 1980   **Architect:** Jon Gunson, AIA
Resident Groups: Backstage Theatre Company

Central City

FACILITY

CENTRAL CITY OPERA HOUSE
Central City, CO 80427
(303) 623-7167
Mailing Address: 621 17th Street, Suite 1601, Denver, CO 80293

Type of Facility: Theatre House; Opera House
Type of Stage: Proscenium
Stage Dimensions: 40'Wx50'D   **Orchestra Pit**
Seating Capacity: 756
Year Built: 1878   **Architect:** Robert Roeschlaub   **Cost:** $23,000
Year Remodeled: 1987   **Architect:** Grammar of Ornament   **Cost:** $80,000
Contact for Rental Daniel Rule;   (303) 623-7167
Resident Groups: Central City Opera
The Opera House has been designated a National Historic Landmark.

Colorado Springs

DANCE

COLORADO SPRINGS DANCE THEATRE
7 East Bijou, Suite 213, Colorado Springs, CO 80903
(719) 630-7434
Founded: 1977
Arts Area: Modern; Ballet; Jazz; Ethnic; Folk; Other Types
Status: Non-Profit
Type: Sponsoring
Purpose: To educate and entertain through dance
Management: Joan Bliss-Pollock, Executive Director; Esther Geoffrey, Artistic Consultant
Officers: Kevin McTernan, President; Maureen Christopher, Vice President; David Parker, Secretary; Mary Pat Sweetman, Treasurer
Paid Staff: 3   **Volunteer Staff:** 2
Utilizes: Guest Artists; Guest Choreographers
Budget: $50,000 - $100,000
Income Sources: Private Foundations/Grants/Endowments; Business/Corporate Donations; Box Office; Government Grants; Individual Donations
Season: September - May   **Annual Attendance:** 7,000
Performance Facilities: Pikes Peak Center; Armstrong Theatre

INSTRUMENTAL MUSIC

COLORADO SPRINGS SYMPHONY ORCHESTRA
PO Box 1692, Colorado Springs, CO 80901
(719) 633-4611
FAX: (719) 633-6699
Founded: 1922
Arts Area: Symphony; Orchestra; Chamber
Status: Professional; Non-Profit
Type: Performing; Educational; Sponsoring
Purpose: To present symphonic music; to sponsor other performing-arts productions and music education in the schools
Management: Daniel J. Hart, Executive Director; Christopher Wilkins, Conductor/Music Director; Douglas Ismail, Director of Marketing and Development
Officers: Richard Nagl, President; Phillip Kendall, Ralph Schauer, Vice Presidents; Susan S. Greene, Secretary; Bruce Kopper, Treasurer
Paid Staff: 16   **Volunteer Staff:** 25
Paid Artists: 87
Utilizes: Guest Conductors; Guest Artists
Budget: $1,000,000 - $5,000,000
Income Sources: Private Foundations/Grants/Endowments; Business/Corporate Donations; Box Office; Government Grants; Individual Donations
Season: September - July   **Annual Attendance:** 256,000
Affiliations: NEA; ASOL; Colorado Council on Humanities
Performance Facilities: Pikes Peak Center

DA VINCI QUARTET
c/o DVC Association, PO Box 7150, Colorado Springs, CO 80923
(719) 593-3331
FAX: (719) 593-3362
Arts Area: Chamber
Status: Professional; Non-Profit
Type: Performing; Touring; Resident; Educational
Purpose: To promote the work of American and women composers as well as the standard repertoire; to maintain a strong educational focus
Management: Madeline Jenkins Millard, Operations Manager

Officers: Brooke Bower, President; Kent Bortes, Vice President
Budget: $50,000 - $100,000
Income Sources: Private Foundations/Grants/Endowments; Business/Corporate Donations; Box Office; Government Grants; Individual Donations
Performance Facilities: Colorado Springs Fine Arts Centre

SOUNDSCAPES
608 Bennett Avenue, Colorado Springs, CO 80909
(719) 634-7470
Arts Area: Chamber; Instrumental Group
Status: Professional; Non-Profit
Type: Performing
Purpose: To bring 20th-century music to the Rocky Mountain area
Management: Sandy Craddock, Artistic Director
Officers: Kathleen Collins, Chairman of the Board
Budget: $1,000 - $50,000
Income Sources: Private Foundations/Grants/Endowments; Government Grants; Individual Donations

VOCAL MUSIC

COLORADO SPRINGS CHORALE
27 South Tejon, PO Box 2304, Colorado Springs, CO 80903
(719) 634-3737
Founded: 1956
Arts Area: Choral
Status: Non-Professional; Non-Profit
Type: Performing; Resident
Purpose: A fully-auditioned community chorus of 130 voices, dedicated to the well-rehearsed performance of great works from the symphonic-choral literature
Management: Jan Boothroyd, General Manager
Officers: Ken Myers, Chairman; Sylvia Hutson, Vice Chairman; Myrtis Thompson, Secretary; James Price, Treasurer
Paid Staff: 2 **Volunteer Staff:** 20
Paid Artists: 2 **Non-Paid Artists:** 130
Utilizes: Guest Conductors; Guest Artists
Budget: $50,000 - $100,000
Income Sources: Private Foundations/Grants/Endowments; Business/Corporate Donations; Box Office; Individual Donations
Season: Fall - Spring **Annual Attendance:** 10,000
Affiliations: CA
Performance Facilities: Pikes Peak Center

MOSAIC
27 South Tejon, PO Box 2304, Colorado Springs, CO 80903
(719) 634-3737
Founded: 1990
Arts Area: Choral
Status: Non-Professional; Non-Profit
Type: Performing; Resident; Educational
Purpose: A representative ensemble of the Colorado Springs Chorale, performing a repertoire of diverse musical styles, performing in schools, service clubs, retirement homes and businesses, and private and public functions
Management: Carolyn Schwartz, Manager
Officers: Ken Myers, Chairman; Sylvia Hutson, Vice Chairman; Myrtis Thompson, Secretary; James Price, Treasurer
Paid Staff: 1 **Volunteer Staff:** 2
Paid Artists: 1 **Non-Paid Artists:** 12
Budget: $1,000 - $50,000
Income Sources: Private Foundations/Grants/Endowments; Business/Corporate Donations; Individual Donations
Season: 52 Weeks

PERFORMING SERIES

COLORADO OPERA FESTIVAL
PO Box 1484, Colorado Springs, CO 80901
(719) 473-0073
Founded: 1971
Arts Area: Grand Opera
Status: Professional; Non-Profit
Type: Performing; Resident
Purpose: To promote and develop the art of opera and knowledge and enjoyment of opera by the public; to carry out public education programs with respect to opera and the commissioning of new works

Management: Elizabeth Lilly, Executive Director; Donald Jenkins, General Director
Officers: Charles Shay, President; Carla Peperzak, Vice President; Penny Sayre, Treasurer
Paid Staff: 4   **Volunteer Staff:** 25
Paid Artists: 20
Utilizes: Special Technical Talent; Guest Conductors; Guest Artists; Guest Directors
Budget: $100,000 - $500,000
Income Sources: Private Foundations/Grants/Endowments; Business/Corporate Donations; Box Office; Government Grants; Individual Donations
Season: July - August   **Annual Attendance:** 6,000
Performance Facilities: Pikes Peak Center

FACILITY

ARNOLD HALL THEATER - UNITED STATES AIR FORCE ACADEMY
HQ/USAFA - CWXRXX, 2302 Cadet Drive, Colorado Springs, CO 80840-5454
(719) 472-4497
FAX: (719) 472-4597
Founded: 1957
Type of Facility: Concert Hall
Type of Stage: Proscenium
Stage Dimensions: 110'Wx44'D
Orchestra Pit
Seating Capacity: 2,808
Year Built: 1958   **Architect:** Skidmore, Owings & Merrill   **Cost:** $2,000,000
Year Remodeled: 1980   **Cost:** $200,000
Acoustical Consultant: Skidmore, Owings & Merrill
Manager: Paula Stamps;   (719) 472-4497
Resident Groups: Academy Band; Blue Bird Cadets

CITY AUDITORIUM
221 East Kiowa Street, Colorado Springs, CO 80903
(719) 578-6652; (719) 578-6640
FAX: (719) 578-6934
Type of Facility: Auditorium; Arena
Type of Stage: Proscenium
Stage Dimensions: 42'x52'x32'; Lon Chaney Theatre - 25'x20'x12'
Seating Capacity: 2,500; Lon Chaney Theatre - 225
Year Built: 1923   **Architect:** Lamar Kelsey   **Cost:** $1,000,000
Year Remodeled: 1975   **Cost:** $142,000
Contact for Rental Michael S. Garcia;   (719) 578-6652
Resident Groups: Star Bar Players

COLORADO COLLEGE - PACKARD HALL
Colorado Springs, CO 80903
(719) 389-6545, ext. X545
FAX: (719) 389-6862
Type of Facility: Concert Hall; Music Performance Hall
Type of Stage: Platform
Stage Dimensions: 30'x25'x15'
Seating Capacity: 350
Year Built: 1976   **Architect:** Edward Larabee Barnes   **Cost:** $3,000,000
Manager: Lyn Doyon;   (719) 389-6545
Resident Groups: Colorado College Music Department

COLORADO SPRINGS FINE ARTS CENTER THEATRE
30 West Dale Street, Colorado Springs, CO 80903
(719) 634-5581
Type of Facility: Civic Center; Multi-Purpose
Type of Stage: Proscenium
Stage Dimensions: 30'x30'x38'
Orchestra Pit
Seating Capacity: 450
Year Built: 1936   **Architect:** John Gaw Meem
Year Remodeled: 1984   **Architect:** Wallace/Nakata   **Cost:** $1,100,000
Contact for Rental Kenneth M. Wohlford, Director of Performing Arts;   (719) 634-5581

PIKES PEAK CENTER
190 South Cascade, Colorado Springs, CO 80903
(719) 520-7453
FAX: (719) 520-7462
   Type of Facility: Theatre Complex; Concert Hall; Auditorium; Studio Performance; Environmental; Theatre House; Opera House; Civic Center; Multi-Purpose
   Type of Stage: Flexible; Proscenium
   Stage Dimensions: 50'x100'   **Orchestra Pit**
   Seating Capacity: 2,000
   Year Built: 1982   **Architect:** John James Wallace & Associates   **Cost:** $13,400,000
   Acoustical Consultant: ARTEC
   Contact for Rental Cindy Ballard;   (719) 520-7453
   Manager: Steve Martin;   (719) 520-7453
   Resident Groups: Colorado Springs Symphony; Colorado Opera Festival; Colorado Springs Chorale; Center Attractions

---

Creede

THEATRE

CREEDE REPERTORY THEATRE
PO Box 269, Creede, CO 81130
(719) 658-2541
FAX: (719) 658-2343
   Founded: 1966
   Arts Area: Professional; Summer Stock; Musical; Theatrical Group
   Status: Professional; Non-Profit
   Type: Performing; Touring; Educational; Sponsoring
   Purpose: To produce five plays in summer in repertory; to promote greater understanding of the performing arts; to raise standards and practice; to make performing arts more accessible to the public
   Management: Richard Baxter, Producing Director; Kay Wyley, Administrative Director; Ken Burt, Business Manager; Julie Purcell, Financial Director
   Officers: Mike Rierson, Chairman of Board; Nell Wyley, Vice President; Dr. Carl Koch, Secretary/Treasurer
   Paid Staff: 3   **Volunteer Staff:** 30
   Paid Artists: 31
   Utilizes: Special Technical Talent; Guest Artists; Guest Directors
   Budget: $100,000 - $500,000
   Income Sources: Private Foundations/Grants/Endowments; Business/Corporate Donations; Box Office; Government Grants; Individual Donations
   Season: Memorial Day - Labor Day   **Annual Attendance:** 15,000
   Performance Facilities: Creede Repertory Theatre

FACILITY

CREEDE REPERTORY THEATRE
PO Box 269, Creede, CO 81130
(719) 658-2541
FAX: (719) 658-2343
   Founded: 1966
   Type of Facility: Performance Center; Theatre House
   Facility Originally: Movie House
   Type of Stage: Proscenium
   Stage Dimensions: 25'x20'
   Seating Capacity: 242
   Year Built: 1935
   Year Remodeled: 1992   **Architect:** Long-Hoeft   **Cost:** $1,100,000
   Manager: Richard Baxter, Producing/Art Director;   (719) 658-2541

Crested Butte

DANCE

DANSWINTER/DANSUMMER
PO Box 506, Crested Butte, CO 81224
(303) 349-6707
   Founded: 1984

Arts Area: Ballet; Jazz; Tap
Status: Semi-Professional; Non-Professional
Type: Resident; Sponsoring
Purpose: To bring dance, enjoyment, technique and style to beginners and intermediates
Management: Heidi Coe DuVal, Artistic Director; Bobbie Reinhardt, Administrative Director
Paid Staff: 2
Paid Artists: 2
Utilizes: Guest Artists
Budget: $1,000 - $50,000
Income Sources: Individual Donations; Tuition
Season: January - February; June-August
Affiliations: Chamber of Commerce; Crested Butte Society for the Arts
Performance Facilities: Indoor Stage; Outdoor Stage

FACILITY

CRESTED BUTTE MOUNTAIN THEATRE
Second and Elk, PO Box 611, Crested Butte, CO 81224
(303) 349-5418
Type of Facility: Performance Center; Theatre House
Facility Originally: Meeting Hall; Movie House
Type of Stage: Flexible
Stage Dimensions: 12'x20'x14'
Seating Capacity: 100
Year Built: 1883   **Architect:** James Kuziak   **Cost:** $25,000
Year Remodeled: 1976
Contact for Rental Cindy Valian;   (303) 349-5418
Manager: Gloria Wojtalik

Cripple Creek

THEATRE

IMPERIAL PLAYERS
123 North Third Street, Cripple Creek, CO 80813
(719) 689-2922
FAX: (719) 689-2922
Founded: 1948
Arts Area: Professional; Musical; Dinner
Status: Professional
Type: Performing; Resident
Purpose: To professionally produce 19th-century melodramas with authentic scripts dating from 1850 to 1900
Management: Imperial Hotel and Casino
Paid Staff: 3
Paid Artists: 14
Utilizes: Special Technical Talent
Budget: $50,000 - $100,000
Income Sources: Box Office
Season: June - September   **Annual Attendance:** 33,000
Affiliations: SWTC
Performance Facilities: Gold Bar Room Theatre

FACILITY

GOLD BAR ROOM THEATRE, IMPERIAL HOTEL
123 North Third Street, PO Box 1003, Cripple Creek, CO 80813
(719) 689-7777
Type of Facility: Multi-Purpose; Historic Hotel & Theatre
Facility Originally: Hotel & Meeting Rooms
Type of Stage: Open 2 Sides
Stage Dimensions: 16'x14'
Seating Capacity: 280
Year Remodeled: 1981
Contact for Rental Imperial Hotel;   (303) 689-2307
Resident Groups: Imperial Players
Opened as a theatre in 1948; remodeled in 1955, 1978 and 1981

Denver

DANCE

ACADEMY OF CREATIVE DANCE AND ELIZABETH MANDEVILLE DANCE COMPANY
3875 Tennyson Street, Denver, CO 80212
(303) 480-1162
>**Founded:** 1975
>**Arts Area:** Modern; Jazz
>**Status:** Commercial
>**Type:** Performing; Educational
>**Purpose:** To train dancers safely and to educate people in dance-injury prevention; to build an interest in modern dance
>**Management:** Elizabeth Mandeville, Director; Lisa Wood, Administrator
>**Paid Staff:** 3
>**Non-Paid Artists:** 6
>**Utilizes:** Special Technical Talent
>**Budget:** $1,000 - $50,000
>**Income Sources:** Box Office
>**Annual Attendance:** 600
>**Performance Facilities:** Shwayder Theatre

BALLET DENVER
3955 Tennyson Street, Denver, CO 80212
(303) 455-4974
>**Founded:** 1973
>**Arts Area:** Modern; Ballet; Folk
>**Status:** Professional; Non-Profit
>**Type:** Performing; Touring; Educational
>**Purpose:** To present an introduction to ballet consisting of classical, romantic, character and modern works; to bring the art of ballet to communities not visited by full companies
>**Management:** Rieke Maria Love, Director; Brian Slota, Company Manager; Janet Hirschfield, Ballet Mistress; Kereen Happe, Rehersal Regisseur; Barbara Hirschfield, Wardrobe Mistress; Scott Bagley, Light Design Technician; Cindy Rowell, Set Design Technician
>**Officers:** Rieke Maria Love, President; Janet Hirschfield, Vice President; Barbara Hirschfield, Secretary/Treasurer
>**Paid Staff:** 1 **Volunteer Staff:** 3
>**Paid Artists:** 7
>**Budget:** $1,000 - $50,000
>**Income Sources:** Box Office; Government Grants; Individual Donations
>**Annual Attendance:** 5,000

CLEO PARKER ROBINSON DANCE ENSEMBLE
119 Park Avenue West, Denver, CO 80205
(303) 295-1759
FAX: (303) 295-1328
>**Founded:** 1972
>**Arts Area:** Modern; Jazz
>**Status:** Professional; Non-Profit
>**Type:** Performing; Touring; Resident; Educational
>**Management:** Cleo Parker Robinson, Executive Artistic Director; Thomas E. Robinson, Business Manager; Sharon Baumgarten, Development Director; Reina Silva, Booking Manager/Operations Director; Keith W. Rice, Technical Director
>**Officers:** Cleo Parker Robinson, Chairman of the Board; Thomas E. Robinson, Secretary
>**Paid Staff:** 4 **Volunteer Staff:** 4
>**Paid Artists:** 35
>**Utilizes:** Guest Artists; Guest Choreographers
>**Budget:** $100,000 - $500,000
>**Income Sources:** Private Foundations/Grants/Endowments; Box Office; Government Grants; Individual Donations
>**Season:** September - June **Annual Attendance:** 35,000
>**Performance Facilities:** The Cleo Parker Robinson Dance Theatre

COLORADO BALLET
999 18th Street, Suite 1645, Denver, CO 80202
(303) 298-0677
FAX: (303) 298-9104
>**Founded:** 1961
>**Arts Area:** Ballet
>**Status:** Professional; Non-Profit
>**Type:** Performing; Touring; Resident; Sponsoring

Purpose: To perform, present, tour and educate classical and contemporary ballet
Management: Jim Harvey, General Manager; Martin Freedmann, Artistic Director; Leanna Clark, Director of Communication
Officers: Colleen Reed, President
Paid Staff: 8
Paid Artists: 18
Utilizes: Special Technical Talent; Guest Artists; Guest Directors
Budget: $500,000 - $1,000,000
Income Sources: Private Foundations/Grants/Endowments; Business/Corporate Donations; Box Office; Government Grants; Individual Donations
Season: October - March   **Annual Attendance:** 50,000
Performance Facilities: Denver Auditorium Theatre; Temple Hoyne Buell Theatre

FLAMENCO FANTASY DANCE THEATRE/GYPSY PRODUCTIONS INC.
600 South Emerson Street, Denver, CO 80209
(303) 722-0054
Founded: 1983
Arts Area: Ethnic; Folk
Status: Professional; Commercial
Type: Performing; Touring; Resident; Educational
Purpose: To further the knowledge and educate the American public about Spanish music and dance
Management: Gypsy Productions, Inc.
Officers: Rene Meredia, Director; Candace Bevior
Paid Staff: 1
Paid Artists: 3   **Non-Paid Artists:** 7
Utilizes: Special Technical Talent; Guest Artists; Guest Choreographers
Budget: $1,000 - $50,000
Income Sources: Box Office
Season: 52 Weeks

INSTRUMENTAL MUSIC

COLORADO SYMPHONY ORCHESTRA
1031 13th Street, Denver, CO 80204
(303) 595-4915
FAX: (303) 595-4935
Founded: 1922
Arts Area: Symphony; Orchestra
Status: Professional; Non-Profit
Type: Performing; Touring; Resident; Educational; Sponsoring
Purpose: To be Colorado's premier full-time professional symphonic music resource
Management: James Copenhaver, Executive Director; David Abosch, Artistic Director; Sandy Lasky, Marketing Director
Paid Staff: 13   **Volunteer Staff:** 35
Utilizes: Guest Conductors; Guest Artists
Budget: $5,000,000 - $10,000,000
Income Sources: Private Foundations/Grants/Endowments; Business/Corporate Donations; Box Office; Government Grants; Individual Donations
Season: 52 Weeks   **Annual Attendance:** 225,000
Performance Facilities: Boettcher Concert Hall

DENVER CHAMBER ORCHESTRA
1616 Glenarm Place, Suite 1360, Denver, CO 80202
(303) 825-4911
Founded: 1968
Arts Area: Orchestra; Chamber
Status: Professional; Non-Profit
Type: Performing; Touring; Educational
Purpose: To provide the highest quality chamber orchestra music to Denver and tour the orchestra throughout the Rocky Mountain Region
Management: Paul Lustiq Dunkel, Music Director/Conductor
Officers: John C. Graff, President; Allan Marter, Treasurer
Paid Staff: 2   **Volunteer Staff:** 50
Paid Artists: 35
Utilizes: Guest Conductors; Guest Artists
Budget: $100,000 - $500,000
Income Sources: Private Foundations/Grants/Endowments; Business/Corporate Donations; Box Office; Government Grants; Individual Donations
Season: September - May   **Annual Attendance:** 20,000
Performance Facilities: Trinity Methodist Church; Paramount Theatre

DENVER MUNICIPAL BAND
3372 South Magnolia Street, Denver, CO 80224
(303) 756-0151
Founded: 1891
Arts Area: Band
Status: Professional
Type: Performing
Purpose: To present free summer concerts in Denver parks
Management: Ed Lenicheck, Conductor; Gerald Endsley, Manager
Officers: Ed Lenicheck, President; Gerald Endsley, Vice President
Paid Staff: 2
Paid Artists: 44
Utilizes: Guest Artists
Budget: $50,000 - $100,000
Income Sources: Private Foundations/Grants/Endowments; Business/Corporate Donations; Government Grants; Individual Donations; Denver Musicians Association
Season: July - August   **Annual Attendance:** 30,000
Affiliations: Association of Concert Bands

FRIENDS OF CHAMBER MUSIC
PO Box 6089, Cherry Creek Station, Denver, CO 80206
Arts Area: Chamber
Status: Non-Profit
Type: Presenting
Purpose: To present five chamber-music concerts annually and sponsor outreach activity including workshops and master classes
Officers: Rosemarie P. Murane, President Board of Directors; Chet Sterne, Vice President; John Lebsack, Treasurer
Volunteer Staff: 15
Utilizes: Guest Artists
Budget: $1,000 - $50,000
Income Sources: Private Foundations/Grants/Endowments; Business/Corporate Donations; Box Office; Individual Donations
Season: October - April   **Annual Attendance:** 2,500

NATIONAL REPERTORY ORCHESTRA
899 Logan Street, Suite 510, Denver, CO 80203
(303) 831-8480
Founded: 1960
Arts Area: Symphony; Orchestra
Status: Professional; Non-Profit
Type: Performing; Touring; Resident
Purpose: To provide an intensive professional internship to musicians, 18-28 years of age, from around the country
Management: Elisa Zimmerman, Director of Development; Edward Birdwell, Orchestra Manager
Officers: Edward Haligman, President of the Board; Richard F. Zellner, President
Paid Staff: 14
Non-Paid Artists: 90
Utilizes: Special Technical Talent; Guest Conductors; Guest Artists
Budget: $100,000 - $500,000
Income Sources: Private Foundations/Grants/Endowments; Business/Corporate Donations; Box Office; Government Grants; Individual Donations
Season: June - August   **Annual Attendance:** 65,000
Affiliations: ASCAP; ASOL; Colorado Council of the Arts; Colorado Music Alliance
Performance Facilities: Keystone Resort; Colorado Front Range Cities

VOCAL MUSIC

CENTRAL CITY OPERA
621 17th Street, Suite 1601, Denver, CO 80293
(303) 292-6500
FAX: (303) 292-4958
Founded: 1932
Arts Area: Grand Opera; Operetta
Status: Professional; Non-Profit
Type: Performing; Educational
Management: John Moriarty, Artistic Director, Administrative/Training Program; Daniel Rule, General Manager
Officers: Nancy Parker, President of the Board
Paid Staff: 8
Paid Artists: 300

Utilizes: Special Technical Talent; Guest Conductors; Guest Artists; Guest Directors
Budget: $1,000,000 - $5,000,000
Income Sources: Private Foundations/Grants/Endowments; Business/Corporate Donations; Box Office; Government Grants; Individual Donations
Season: July - August   **Annual Attendance:** 20,000
Affiliations: OA; Metro Denver Arts Alliance
Performance Facilities: Central City Opera House, Central City

COLORADO CHILDREN'S CHORALE
910 15th Street, Suite 1020, Denver, CO 80202
(303) 892-5600
FAX: (303) 892-0828
     Founded: 1974
     Arts Area: Choral
     Status: Professional; Non-Profit
     Type: Performing; Touring; Educational
     Purpose: To provide the nation a performing-arts group with children as its medium and excellence as its goal
     Management: Duain Wolfe, Artistic Director
     Officers: Stephan Clarke, Chairman; Gregory Glissmann, Vice Chairman; Corry Doty, Treasurer
     Paid Staff: 17   **Volunteer Staff:** 100
     Paid Artists: 10   **Non-Paid Artists:** 350
     Utilizes: Guest Conductors; Guest Artists
     Budget: $500,000 - $1,000,000
     Income Sources: Private Foundations/Grants/Endowments; Business/Corporate Donations; Box Office; Government Grants; Individual Donations
     Season: August - July   **Annual Attendance:** 50,000

THE DENVER CHAMBER CHOIR
12312 West Mississippi Avenue, Denver, CO 80228
(303) 986-7893
     Founded: 1977
     Arts Area: Choral
     Status: Semi-Professional; Non-Profit
     Type: Performing; Resident; Educational
     Purpose: To perform advanced choral repertory from all periods of music history
     Management: Dr. William Jones, Director; Carol Luft, Projects Coordinator
     Officers: Robert Miller, Counsel; Nina Rockley, Secretary
     Volunteer Staff: 2
     Paid Artists: 1   **Non-Paid Artists:** 24
     Utilizes: Guest Artists
     Budget: $1,000 - $50,000
     Income Sources: Private Foundations/Grants/Endowments; Business/Corporate Donations; Government Grants; Individual Donations
     Season: September - July   **Annual Attendance:** 3,500
     Affiliations: CA; ACDA

OPERA COLORADO
695 South Colorado Boulevard, Suite 20, Denver, CO 80222
(303) 778-1500
     Founded: 1981
     Arts Area: Grand Opera
     Status: Professional; Non-Profit
     Type: Performing; Resident; Educational
     Purpose: To produce international quality grand opera in-the-round and to develop appreciation and understanding of opera throughout the community
     Management: Nathaniel Merrill, General Director; William Dickinson, Director of Development
     Officers: Eleanor Caulkins, Chairman of the Board
     Paid Staff: 10   **Volunteer Staff:** 100
     Paid Artists: 250   **Non-Paid Artists:** 75
     Utilizes: Special Technical Talent; Guest Conductors; Guest Artists
     Budget: $1,000,000 - $5,000,000
     Income Sources: Private Foundations/Grants/Endowments; Business/Corporate Donations; Box Office; Government Grants; Individual Donations
     Season: May
     Annual Attendance: 21,000
     Affiliations: OA
     Performance Facilities: Boettcher Concert Hall

THEATRE

CHANGING SCENE THEATER
1527 1/2 Champa Street, Denver, CO 80202
(303) 893-5775
Founded: 1968
Arts Area: Theatrical Group
Status: Non-Profit
Type: Performing; Resident; Educational; Sponsoring
Purpose: To provide a performing space and experience for young artists
Management: Alfred Brooks, President; Maxine Munt, Vice President
Volunteer Staff: 2
Utilizes: Guest Artists; Guest Directors
Budget: $1,000 - $50,000
Income Sources: Box Office; Government Grants; Individual Donations
Season: 52 Weeks

DENVER CENTER THEATER COMPANY
1050 13th Street, Denver, CO 80204
(303) 893-4200
Founded: 1980
Arts Area: Professional; Musical; Theatrical Group
Status: Professional; Non-Profit
Type: Performing; Touring; Resident; Educational
Purpose: We are dedicated to presenting the best of the performing arts to the Rocky Mountain Region
Management: Donovan Markey, Artistic Director; Kevin Maifeld, Executive Director; Barbara Sellers, Producing Director; Tony Church, Dean of the Conservatory
Paid Staff: 30   **Volunteer Staff:** 300
Paid Artists: 275
Utilizes: Special Technical Talent; Guest Artists; Guest Directors
Budget: $5,000,000 - $10,000,000
Income Sources: Private Foundations/Grants/Endowments; Business/Corporate Donations; Box Office; Government Grants; Individual Donations
Season: September - June   **Annual Attendance:** 150,000
Affiliations: The Denver Center; TCG; LORT
Performance Facilities: Denver Center Theatre

EL CENTRO SU TEATRO
4725 High Street, Denver, CO 80216
(303) 296-0219
Founded: 1971
Arts Area: Professional; Musical; Community; Folk; Theatrical Group
Status: Semi-Professional; Non-Profit
Type: Performing; Touring; Resident; Educational; Sponsoring
Management: Anthony J. Garcia, Artistic Director; Rodolfo W. Bustos, Managing Director; Debra Gallegos, Development Director
Officers: Anthony J. Garcia, President; Sherry Candelaria, Secretary
Paid Staff: 2   **Volunteer Staff:** 10
Paid Artists: 8   **Non-Paid Artists:** 12
Utilizes: Guest Artists
Budget: $100,000 - $500,000
Income Sources: Private Foundations/Grants/Endowments; Business/Corporate Donations; Box Office; Government Grants; Individual Donations; Concessions
Season: September - May   **Annual Attendance:** 8,300
Affiliations: Teatro Nacional de Aztlan (TENAZ)

GERMINAL STAGE DENVER
2450 West 44th Avenue, Denver, CO 80211
(303) 455-7108
Founded: 1974
Arts Area: Professional; Theatrical Group
Status: Professional; Non-Profit
Type: Performing
Management: Ed Baierlein, Director/Manager
Officers: Ed Baierlein, President; Ginger Valone, Vice President; Sallie D. Baierlein, Secretary; John C. Seifert, Treasurer
Paid Staff: 2
Paid Artists: 50
Budget: $50,000 - $100,000
Income Sources: Business/Corporate Donations; Box Office; Government Grants

Season: October - August   **Annual Attendance:** 12,000
Affiliations: TCG; Colorado Producers Guild
Performance Facilities: Germinal Stage Denver

STUDIO E THEATRE ENSEMBLE
2715 Welton Street, Denver, CO 80205
(303) 297-9812
Founded: 1982
Arts Area: Theatrical Group
Status: Semi-Professional; Non-Profit
Type: Performing; Touring; Resident; Educational; Sponsoring
Purpose: To perform plays written exclusively by Black playwrights
Management: Jo Bunton Keel, Executive Director
Paid Staff: 2   **Volunteer Staff:** 60
Paid Artists: 100   **Non-Paid Artists:** 30
Budget: $100,000 - $500,000
Income Sources: Private Foundations/Grants/Endowments; Business/Corporate Donations; Box Office; Individual Donations
Season: March - December   **Annual Attendance:** 65,000

SU TEATRO, INC.
4725 High Street, Denver, CO 80216
(303) 296-0219
Arts Area: Community; Theatrical Group
Status: Semi-Professional; Non-Profit
Type: Performing; Touring; Educational; Sponsoring
Purpose: To carry the message of the struggles of the Southwestern barrios; to preserve and perpetuate the Chicano language and culture
Management: Anthony J. Garcia, Artistic Director; Rudolfo W. Bustos, Managing Director; Debra Gallegos, Development Director
Officers: Debra Gallegos, Board Member
Budget: $100,000 - $500,000
Income Sources: Private Foundations/Grants/Endowments; Business/Corporate Donations; Box Office; Government Grants; Individual Donations; Touring Fees
Performance Facilities: El Centro Su Teatro

VICTORIAN THEATRE
4201 Hooker Street, Denver, CO 80211
(303) 433-4343
Founded: 1911
Arts Area: Community; Theatrical Group
Status: Semi-Professional; Non-Profit; Commercial
Type: Performing; Sponsoring
Purpose: To present a five-production season of plays with a variety of drama and comedy
Officers: Michael Hughes, President; Michelle Serries, Vice President; Richard Thompson, Treasurer; Gail Medland Roberts, Secretary
Volunteer Staff: 50
Non-Paid Artists: 30
Utilizes: Guest Artists; Guest Directors
Budget: $1,000 - $50,000
Income Sources: Private Foundations/Grants/Endowments; Business/Corporate Donations; Box Office; Government Grants; Individual Donations
Season: 52 Weeks   **Annual Attendance:** 6,000

PERFORMING SERIES

COLORADO COUNCIL ON THE ARTS
750 Pennsylvania Street, Denver, CO 80203-3699
(303) 894-2617
FAX: (303) 894-2615
Founded: 1967
Arts Area: Dance; Vocal Music; Instrumental Music; Theater; Festivals; Lyric Opera; Grand Opera
Status: Professional; Non-Profit; State Agency
Type: Sponsoring; Grant Making
Purpose: To stimulate arts development in the state; to assist and encourage artists and arts organizations
Management: Barbara Neal, Executive Director; Jim Thompson, Program Director Arts Organizations; Maryo Ewell, Program Director, Community Programs; Daniel Salazar, Program Director, Individual Artists
Officers: Jerry Wartgow, Chair
Paid Staff: 12

Budget: $1,000,000 - $5,000,000
Income Sources: Government Grants
Affiliations: NEA; WSAF; NALAA

FACILITY

AUDITORIUM THEATER - DENVER PERFORMING ARTS COMPLEX
950 13th Street, Denver, CO 80204
(303) 640-2862
FAX: (303) 640-2397
    Founded: 1908
    Type of Facility: Theatre House
    Type of Stage: Proscenium
    Stage Dimensions: 107'Wx48"D; 58'W proscenium opening
    Orchestra Pit
    Seating Capacity: 2,089
    Year Built: 1908   **Architect:** Robert L. Willison   **Cost:** $590,000
    Year Remodeled: 1950   **Architect:** Musik & Musik   **Cost:** $2,000,000
    Contact for Rental Bobbie McFarland, Drew Armstrong;   (303) 640-2862
    Manager: James P. Thompson, Manager;   (303) 640-2862
    Resident Groups: Colorado Contemporary Dance; Colorado Ballet; Robert Garner/Center Attractions

BOETTCHER CONCERT HALL - DENVER PERFORMING ARTS COMPLEX
950 13th Street, Denver, CO 80204
(303) 640-2862
FAX: (303) 640-2397
    Founded: 1978
    Type of Facility: Concert Hall; Opera House
    Type of Stage: In-the-round Capability
    Stage Dimensions: 75'Wx50'D
    Orchestra Pit
    Seating Capacity: 2,629
    Year Built: 1978   **Architect:** Hardy Holtzman Pfieffer   **Cost:** $13,000,000
    Acoustical Consultant: Christopher Jaffe Associates
    Contact for Rental Bobbie McFarland, Drew Armstrong;   (303) 640-2637
    Manager: James P. Thompson;   (303) 640-2862
    Resident Groups: Colorado Symphony Orchestra; Opera Colorado

CHANGING SCENE THEATER
1527 1/2 Champa Street, Denver, CO 80202
(303) 893-5775
    Type of Facility: Off Broadway; Loft
    Facility Originally: Meeting Hall; Movie House
    Type of Stage: Flexible
    Stage Dimensions: 30'x24'
    Seating Capacity: 76
    Year Built: 1900
    Year Remodeled: 1968   **Architect:** John Lucas   **Cost:** $10,000
    Acoustical Consultant: Wesley Wada

DENVER AUDITORIUM - ARENA
1323 Champa Street, Denver, CO 80204
(303) 575-2637
    Type of Facility: Auditorium; Civic Center; Arena; Multi-Purpose
    Type of Stage: Arena
    Stage Dimensions: 20,000 square feet of usable floor area
    Seating Capacity: 7,000
    Year Built: 1952   **Architect:** G. Meredith Musick   **Cost:** $1,200,000
    Contact for Rental Bobbi Niles or Gary Lane;   (303) 575-2637

DENVER AUDITORIUM - CURRIGAN EXHIBITION HALL
1324 Champa Street, Denver, CO 80204
(303) 640-3856
    Type of Facility: Multi-Purpose; Exhibition Hall
    Seating Capacity: 14000
    Year Built: 1969   **Cost:** $7,500,000
    Contact for Rental Bobbi Niles or Gary Lane
    100,800 square feet of space, new hall planned with 300,000 square feet

DENVER AUDITORIUM - MCNICHOLS SPORTS ARENA
1635 Bryant Street, Denver, CO 80204
(303) 572-4700
FAX: (303) 572-4709
    Founded: 1975
    Type of Facility: Arena
    Type of Stage: Arena
    Seating Capacity: 19,000
    Year Built: 1975 **Architect:** Sink-Combs **Cost:** $10,000,000
    Contact for Rental Bobbie McFarland or Gary Lane; (303) 575-2637
    Arena has 20,000 square feet of usable floor area.

DENVER AUDITORIUM - THEATRE
14th and Curtis, Denver, CO 80204
(303) 575-2637
    Type of Facility: Auditorium; Performance Center; Civic Center
    Type of Stage: Proscenium
    Stage Dimensions: 58'x44'
    Seating Capacity: 2,100
    Year Built: 1905 **Architect:** Robert Willison **Cost:** $545,000
    Year Remodeled: 1955 **Architect:** G. Meredith Musick
    Contact for Rental Bobbi Niles or Gary Lane; (303) 575-2637

DENVER COLISEUM
4600 Humboldt Street, Denver, CO 80216
(303) 575-2637
    Founded: 1951
    Type of Facility: Arena
    Type of Stage: Arena
    Seating Capacity: 11,500
    Year Built: 1951 **Cost:** $3,000,000
    Acoustical Consultant: David Adams & Associates
    Contact for Rental Bobbi Niles or Drew Armstrong; (303) 640-2637
    Manager: Bud Quinn; (303) 295-4444
    Coliseum has 25,000 square feet of usable floor area.

DENVER PERFORMING ARTS COMPLEX - BUELL THEATRE
950 13th Street, Denver, CO 80204
(303) 640-2862
FAX: (303) 640-2397
    Type of Facility: Theatre House; Exhibition Hall
    Facility Originally: Arena
    Type of Stage: Flexible; Proscenium
    Stage Dimensions: 115'Wx52'D; 67'-50'Wx41'-30'H proscenium opening **Orchestra Pit**
    Seating Capacity: 2,830
    Year Built: 1991 **Architect:** Van Dijk Johnson - Beyer Blinder Belle **Cost:** $27,500,000
    Acoustical Consultant: Kirkkegaard and Associates
    Contact for Rental Bobbi McFarland, Drew Armstrong; (303) 640-2637
    Manager: James P. Thompson; (303) 640-2862
    Resident Groups: Robert Garner/Center Attractions; Colorado Ballet; Colorado Symphony; Opera Colorado

GERMINAL STAGE DENVER
2450 West 44th Avenue, Denver, CO 80211
(303) 455-7108
    Type of Facility: Theatre House
    Facility Originally: Business Facility
    Type of Stage: 3/4 Arena
    Stage Dimensions: 20'x15'
    Seating Capacity: 100
    Year Built: 1925
    Year Remodeled: 1987 **Architect:** Ron Rinker **Cost:** $60,000
    Resident Groups: Germinal Stage Denver

HOUSTON FINE ARTS CENTER
7111 Montview Boulevard, Denver, CO 80220
(303) 871-6404
FAX: (303) 871-6411
    Type of Facility: Concert Hall; Auditorium; Arena

Facility Originally: School
Type of Stage: Proscenium
Stage Dimensions: 38'x32'
Orchestra Pit
Seating Capacity: 690
Year Built: 1967
Contact for Rental: (303) 871-6873

MAY BONFILS STANTON CENTER FOR THE PERFORMING ARTS
3001 South Federal Boulevard, Denver, CO 80110
(303) 936-8441
Type of Facility: Performance Center
Year Built: 1890
Contact for Rental Rich Harris;   (303) 936-8441
The Center, whose original structure was built in 1890, consists of Little Auditorium, Proscenium Theatre and Stage 2. Additions and remodelings have occurred in 1963 and 1984. See separate listings for additional information.

MAY BONFILS STANTON CENTER FOR THE PERFORMING ARTS - LITTLE AUDITORIUM
3001 South Federal Boulevard, Denver, CO 80110
(303) 936-8441
Type of Facility: Auditorium
Type of Stage: Platform
Seating Capacity: 400
Year Built: 1890
Contact for Rental Rich Harris;   (303) 936-8441

MAY BONFILS STANTON CENTER FOR THE PERFORMING ARTS - PROSCENIUM THEATRE
3001 South Federal Boulevard, Denver, CO 80110
(303) 936-8441
Type of Facility: Theatre House
Type of Stage: Proscenium
Stage Dimensions: 60'Wx40'D
Orchestra Pit
Seating Capacity: 999
Year Built: 1963
Contact for Rental Rich Harris;   (303) 936-8441

MAY BONFILS STANTON CENTER FOR THE PERFORMING ARTS - STAGE 2
3001 South Federal Boulevard, Denver, CO 80110
(303) 936-8441
Type of Facility: Theatre House; Black Box
Type of Stage: Flexible
Stage Dimensions: 48'x60'
Seating Capacity: 180
Year Built: 1984
Contact for Rental Rich Harris;   (303) 936-8441

RED ROCKS AMPHITHEATRE - MORRISON COLORADO
c/o 1380 Lawrence Street, Suite 790, Denver, CO 80204
(303) 640-2637
Type of Facility: Outdoor (Concert); Amphitheater
Type of Stage: Greek
Stage Dimensions: 60'x40' concrete slab
Seating Capacity: 9,000
Year Built: 1941   **Architect:** Burnham Hoyt   **Cost:** $175,000
Year Remodeled: 1958
Contact for Rental Bibbi McFarland or Drew Armstrong;   (303) 640-2637
This 1941 CCC Project turned a small valley into an amphitheater.

VICTORIAN THEATRE
4201 Hooker Street, Denver, CO 80211
(303) 433-4343
Founded: 1911
Type of Facility: Theatre House
Type of Stage: Thrust; Proscenium
Stage Dimensions: 20'Wx16'D
Seating Capacity: 99
Year Built: 1911   **Architect:** George Swartz

Contact for Rental: (303) 433-4343
Manager: Pamela Clifton
Presentation of one-set dramas

Durango

VOCAL MUSIC

DURANGO CHORAL SOCIETY
780 Main Avenue, Suite 214, Durango, CO 81301
(303) 259-3457
Founded: 1961
Arts Area: Choral
Status: Semi-Professional
Type: Performing; Touring; Resident; Educational; Sponsoring
Purpose: DCS exists for the purpose of providing quality choral and orchestral music for the audience and performers of the four-corners region.
Management: Diane Vandenberg, Executive Director/Music Director
Officers: Steven C. Harris, President; Sally Morrissey, Secretary
Paid Staff: 3
Non-Paid Artists: 45
Utilizes: Special Technical Talent; Guest Artists
Budget: $1,000 - $50,000
Income Sources: Private Foundations/Grants/Endowments; Business/Corporate Donations; Box Office; Government Grants; Individual Donations
Season: 52 Weeks   **Annual Attendance:** 3,200
Affiliations: American Choral Directors Association

PERFORMING SERIES

MUSIC IN THE MOUNTAINS, FESTIVAL OF MUSIC AT PURGATORY
PO Box 2082, Durango, CO 81302
(303) 247-9000, ext. 3030
FAX: (303) 385-2107
Founded: 1986
Arts Area: Instrumental Music; Festivals
Status: Professional; Non-Profit
Type: Performing; Educational
Purpose: To provide live classical music of the highest quality to the Four Corners of Colorado, New Mexico, Utah and Arizona
Management: Misha Semanitzky, Music Director; Georg Ann Beauparlant, Festival Coordinator
Officers: Mary Jane Clark, President
Paid Staff: 5   **Volunteer Staff:** 20
Paid Artists: 40
Budget: $100,000 - $500,000
Income Sources: Private Foundations/Grants/Endowments; Business/Corporate Donations; Box Office; Government Grants; Individual Donations
Season: July - August   **Annual Attendance:** 3,000

Englewood

VOCAL MUSIC

CHERRY CREEK CHORALE
c/o 10093 East Weaver Avenue, Englewood, CO 80111
(303) 694-9587
Founded: 1980
Arts Area: Choral
Status: Non-Profit
Type: Performing
Purpose: To provide adults an opportunity to perform varied choral literature; to increase their knowledge and skill
Management: Richard Larson, Executive Director
Officers: Richard Krening, President; John Arenson, Vice President; Lorraine Cooper, Secretary; Elaine Gilley, Treasurer
Paid Staff: 2   **Volunteer Staff:** 60
Utilizes: Special Technical Talent
Budget: $1,000 - $50,000

Income Sources: Private Foundations/Grants/Endowments; Business/Corporate Donations; Box Office; Government Grants; Individual Donations
Season: September - June   **Annual Attendance:** 1,500
Affiliations: Colorado Arts; Metro Denver Arts Alliance

THEATRE

COUNTRY DINNER PLAYHOUSE
6875 South Clinton, Englewood, CO 80112
(303) 790-9311
FAX: (303) 790-2615
Founded: 1970
Arts Area: Professional; Musical; Dinner
Status: Professional
Type: Performing
Management: Bill McHale, Executive Producer/Director
Paid Staff: 24
Paid Artists: 20
Utilizes: Special Technical Talent
Budget: $100,000 - $500,000
Income Sources: Box Office
Season: 52 Weeks

Estes Park

PERFORMING SERIES

ROCKY RIDGE MUSIC CENTER
465 Long's Peak Route, Estes Park, CO 80517
Winter Address: PO Box 81727, Lincoln, NE 68501-1727; (402) 486-4363
Founded: 1942
Arts Area: Instrumental Music; Festivals
Status: Non-Profit
Type: Performing; Educational
Purpose: To offer summer programs of conservatory-level music training for young people, with emphasis on Youth Orchestra, young pianists, chamber music and composition; to offer this program simultaneously with the summer concert series "Music in the Mountains"
Management: Patrick B. Gaines, Executive Director; Jack J. Rinke, Executive Secretary; Gregory Dubinsky, Music in the Mountains Coordinator
Officers: Beth Miller Harrod, Founder/Musical Director; Dr. John Hajdu Heyer, President; Miriam Reitz Baer, Vice President; F.M. Tuttle, Treasurer
Paid Staff: 7   **Volunteer Staff:** 3
Paid Artists: 23   **Non-Paid Artists:** 4
Utilizes: Guest Artists; Guest Conductors
Budget: $50,000 - $100,000
Income Sources: Private Foundations/Grants/Endowments; Box Office; Individual Donations
Season: June - August   **Annual Attendance:** 730

Evergreen

FACILITY

CENTER STAGE AT EVERGREEN
27608 Fireweed Drive, Evergreen, CO 80439
(303) 674-4002
Founded: 1990
Type of Facility: Concert Hall; Auditorium; Performance Center; Theatre House; Opera House; Multi-Purpose
Facility Originally: Church; Meeting Hall
Type of Stage: Thrust; Proscenium
Stage Dimensions: 24'x30'
Seating Capacity: 200
Year Built: 1924
Year Remodeled: 1992   **Architect:** Jack Dysart, AIA   **Cost:** $100,000
Contact for Rental Marcia Phelps;   (303) 674-4002
Resident Groups: Evergreen Chorale, Inc.

Fort Collins

DANCE

THE DANCE CONNECTION
PO Box 2014, Fort Collins, CO 80522
(303) 484-6518
>**Founded:** 1980
>**Arts Area:** Modern
>**Status:** Professional; Non-Profit
>**Type:** Performing; Touring; Educational
>**Purpose:** To communicate the energy and excitement of contemporary dance through quality performances
>**Management:** Linda Green, Business Manager; Eleanor Van Dusen, Sharon Wilson, Co-Artistic Directors
>**Officers:** Roslyn Ruppert, President Board of Directors
>**Paid Staff:** 2 **Volunteer Staff:** 1
>**Paid Artists:** 4
>**Utilizes:** Special Technical Talent; Guest Artists; Guest Choreographers
>**Budget:** $1,000 - $50,000
>**Income Sources:** Private Foundations/Grants/Endowments; Business/Corporate Donations; Box Office; Government Grants; Individual Donations
>**Season:** October - August **Annual Attendance:** 4,000
>**Performance Facilities:** Lincoln Center

INSTRUMENTAL MUSIC

FORT COLLINS SYMPHONY ORCHESTRA
PO Box 1963, Fort Collins, CO 80522
(303) 482-4823
FAX: (303) 482-4858
>**Founded:** 1949
>**Arts Area:** Symphony; Orchestra
>**Status:** Non-Profit
>**Type:** Performing; Educational
>**Purpose:** To further serious music appreciation and general cultural growth in this and neighboring communities
>**Management:** Michael Klesert, General Manager; Merrilee Pouliot, Office Manager; Willfred Schwarz, Conductor
>**Officers:** Kathryn Quan, President; John Clark Pratt, Vice President; Alvin J. Kruckten, Treasurer; Frank Johnson Jr., Secretary
>**Paid Staff:** 4
>**Paid Artists:** 85
>**Utilizes:** Guest Conductors; Guest Artists
>**Budget:** $100,000 - $500,000
>**Income Sources:** Private Foundations/Grants/Endowments; Business/Corporate Donations; Box Office; Government Grants; Individual Donations
>**Season:** September - July **Annual Attendance:** 20,000
>**Affiliations:** ASOL; Fort Collins Chamber of Commerce
>**Performance Facilities:** Lincoln Center

VOCAL MUSIC

THE LARIMER CHORAL SOCIETY
PO Box 884, Fort Collins, CO 80522
(303) 223-2059
>**Founded:** 1978
>**Arts Area:** Choral; Ethnic; Folk; Musicals
>**Status:** Non-Profit
>**Type:** Performing; Resident; Educational
>**Purpose:** To perform the great choral music of the world and to educate the community about choral music
>**Paid Staff:** 3 **Volunteer Staff:** 10
>**Paid Artists:** 10
>**Utilizes:** Guest Artists
>**Budget:** $100,000 - $500,000
>**Income Sources:** Private Foundations/Grants/Endowments; Business/Corporate Donations; Box Office; Individual Donations
>**Season:** August - April **Annual Attendance:** 2,100
>**Performance Facilities:** Lincoln Center

THEATRE

OPENSTAGE THEATRE AND COMPANY, INC.
PO Box 617, 201 South College Avenue, Fort Collins, CO 80522
(303) 484-5237
>**Founded:** 1973
>**Arts Area:** Theatrical Group
>**Status:** Semi-Professional; Non-Profit
>**Type:** Performing
>**Management:** Bruce K. Freestone, Executive Producer; Peter Anthony, Artistic Director; Lisa Rosenhagen, Office Manager
>**Officers:** Mollie Smilie, Chair; Joannah Lyn Merriman, Vice Chair; Neil Petrie, Treasurer; Toni Farquhar, Secretary
>**Paid Staff:** 3
>**Paid Artists:** 60   **Non-Paid Artists:** 25
>**Utilizes:** Special Technical Talent
>**Budget:** $100,000 - $500,000
>**Income Sources:** Business/Corporate Donations; Box Office; Government Grants; Individual Donations
>**Season:** September - June   **Annual Attendance:** 10,000
>**Affiliations:** AACT; Colorado Theatre Producers Guild; Fort Collins Convention and Visitors Bureau; Fort Collins Chamber of Commerce
>**Performance Facilities:** Lincoln Center Mini-Theatre

PERFORMING SERIES

COLORADO STATE UNIVERSITY - OFFICE OF CULTURAL PROGRAMS
Lory Student Center, Fort Collins, CO 80523
(303) 491-6626
FAX: (303) 491-6423
>**Founded:** 1962
>**Arts Area:** Dance; Vocal Music; Instrumental Music; Theater
>**Status:** Non-Profit
>**Type:** Educational; Sponsoring
>**Purpose:** To coordinate the cultural programs for Colorado State University
>**Management:** Mims Harris, Associate Director, Programs; Barb Kistler, Assistant Director, Programs; David Laughlin, Technical Coordinator
>**Paid Staff:** 4   **Volunteer Staff:** 4
>**Utilizes:** Guest Artists
>**Budget:** $50,000 - $100,000
>**Income Sources:** Private Foundations/Grants/Endowments; Box Office
>**Season:** September - May   **Annual Attendance:** 2,000
>**Affiliations:** WSAF; NACA; ACU-I; APAP; WAAA;
>**Performance Facilities:** 670 Theatre

FACILITY

COLORADO STATE UNIVERSITY - UNIVERSITY THEATRE
Fort Collins, CO 80523
(303) 491-5116
>**Type of Facility:** Environmental; Theatre House
>**Facility Originally:** Ballroom; University Student Center
>**Type of Stage:** Proscenium; Environmental
>**Stage Dimensions:** 35'x37' with 14' forestage
>**Seating Capacity:** 320
>**Year Built:** 1937
>**Year Remodeled:** 1964

LINCOLN CENTER
417 West Magnolia, Fort Collins, CO 80521
(303) 221-6735
FAX: (303) 484-0424
>**Type of Facility:** Theatre Complex; Concert Hall; Civic Center; Multi-Purpose
>**Type of Stage:** Thrust; Proscenium
>**Stage Dimensions:** 40'x60'
>**Orchestra Pit**
>**Seating Capacity:** 1180
>**Year Built:** 1978   **Architect:** Stearns-Rogers   **Cost:** $3,000,000
>**Acoustical Consultant:** Jaffe Acoustics
>**Contact for Rental** David Siever, Director;   (303) 221-6733

Resident Groups: Larimer Chorale; Fort Collins Symphony; Openstage Theatre; Fort Collins Civic Theatre
The original structure, a school facility built prior to 1978, became Lincoln Center with new construction and renovations that were completed in 1978.

Golden

INSTRUMENTAL MUSIC

JEFFERSON SYMPHONY ORCHESTRA
1204 1/2 Washington Avenue, Golden, CO 80401
(303) 278-4237
> **Founded:** 1953
> **Arts Area:** Symphony; Orchestra; Ensemble
> **Status:** Semi-Professional; Non-Profit
> **Type:** Performing
> **Purpose:** To provide performing opportunities for serious musicians; to provide good symphonic music; to maintain a position which educates the public of all ages to the pleasure of classical and light classical music
> **Management:** M. Liane McHardy, Office Manager; Eileen Billings, Bookkeeper; Julie Stolt, Fundraiser; Glen DiConstanza, Stage Manager; Jackie Shaffer, Orchestra Personnel Manager; T. Gordon Parks, Music Director/Conductor
> **Officers:** Jack Galland, President; Rod Johnson, Vice President Finance; Helen Leith, Vice President Activities; Joan Havercroft, Vice President Performance; Jean Olhoeft, Secretary; Eileen Beaudrie, Treasurer; Doris McGowan, Vice President Marketing
> **Paid Staff:** 6   **Volunteer Staff:** 50
> **Paid Artists:** 10   **Non-Paid Artists:** 60
> **Utilizes:** Special Technical Talent; Guest Conductors; Guest Artists
> **Budget:** $100,000 - $500,000
> **Income Sources:** Private Foundations/Grants/Endowments; Business/Corporate Donations; Box Office; Government Grants; Individual Donations
> **Season:** October - May   **Annual Attendance:** 8,000
> **Affiliations:** Chamber of Commerces
> **Performance Facilities:** Green Centre, Colorado School of Mines

THEATRE

HERITAGE SQUARE MUSIC HALL
5 Heritage Square, Golden, CO 80401
(303) 279-7800
> **Arts Area:** Professional; Musical; Dinner
> **Status:** Professional; Commercial
> **Type:** Performing; Resident
> **Management:** C.J. Helsley, President; T.J. Mullin, Vice President
> **Paid Staff:** 100
> **Paid Artists:** 15
> **Income Sources:** Box Office
> **Season:** Feburary - December

Grand Junction

INSTRUMENTAL MUSIC

GRAND JUNCTION MUSICAL ARTS ASSOCIATION
130 North Fourth Street, #100, Grand Junction, CO 81501
(303) 243-6787
> **Founded:** 1977
> **Arts Area:** Symphony; Orchestra; Band
> **Status:** Non-Profit
> **Type:** Performing; Touring; Educational; Sponsoring
> **Purpose:** To bring quality classical music to western Colorado
> **Management:** Naomi Shepherd, Manager; Kirk Gustafson, Music Director
> **Officers:** Gudrun Rice, President; John Halvorson, First Vice President; Jack Roberts, Second Vice President; Charles Jones, Secretary; Linda Tice, Treasurer
> **Paid Staff:** 4
> **Paid Artists:** 68
> **Utilizes:** Guest Artists
> **Budget:** $100,000 - $500,000
> **Income Sources:** Private Foundations/Grants/Endowments; Business/Corporate Donations; Box Office; Individual Donations

Season: September - May **Annual Attendance:** 13,500
Performance Facilities: Grand Junction High School Auditorium

FACILITY

MESA COLLEGE - WALTER WALKER AUDITORIUM
PO Box 2647, Grand Junction, CO 81502
(303) 248-1504
Type of Facility: Auditorium
Type of Stage: Thrust
Orchestra Pit
Seating Capacity: 469, (627 with loges)
Year Built: 1969 **Architect:** Van Deusen **Cost:** $800,000
Contact for Rental Lorene Sanford, Building Coordinator; (303) 248-1788
Resident Groups: Mesa College Music Choir; Chamber Choir; Concert Band; Jazz Combos; Mesa College Theatre Department; Mesa College Dance Repertory

Greeley

VOCAL MUSIC

THE GREELEY CHORALE
PO Box 5098, Greeley, CO 80621
(303) 330-1769
Founded: 1964
Arts Area: Operetta; Choral; Ethnic; Folk
Status: Non-Professional; Non-Profit
Type: Performing; Educational; Sponsoring
Purpose: To present a variety of quality choral music for public performance
Management: Bill Howe, Administrator; Carl Gerbrandt, Conductor
Officers: Ken Whitney, President; Stan Peek, Secretary; Sue Varrel, Vice President; Jerry Crews, Treasurer
Paid Staff: 4
Utilizes: Guest Artists
Budget: $50,000 - $100,000
Income Sources: Private Foundations/Grants/Endowments; Business/Corporate Donations; Box Office; Government Grants; Individual Donations
Season: September - May **Annual Attendance:** 3,000
Performance Facilities: Union Colony Civic Center

THEATRE

ALBUNDEGUS ALL-STARS
709 13th Street, Greeley, CO 80631
Founded: 1989
Arts Area: Theatrical Group
Status: Non-Profit
Type: Performing; Workshops; Readings
Purpose: To develop new and original work, expecially works by Colorado playwrights
Management: Michael Baczuk, Artistic Director; David Keyon, Associate Director; Christopher Caldwell, Treasurer
Volunteer Staff: 3
Utilizes: Community Talent
Budget: $1,000 - $50,000
Income Sources: Box Office; Individual Donations
Season: September - May
Performance Facilities: Evans City Hall Auditorium

FACILITY

UNION COLONY CIVIC CENTER
701 Tenth Avenue, Greeley, CO 80631
(303) 350-9450
FAX: (303) 350-9475
Founded: 1988
Type of Facility: Concert Hall; Auditorium; Performance Center; Civic Center
Type of Stage: Proscenium
Stage Dimensions: 50'x60' **Orchestra Pit**
Seating Capacity: 1,667; 220
Year Built: 1988 **Architect:** ARIX - Bob Shreve **Cost:** $9,200,000

Acoustical Consultant: Dave Adams & Associates
Contact for Rental: Joyce Jasurda;   (303) 350-9449

UNIVERSITY OF NORTHERN COLORADO - HELEN LANGWORTHY THEATRE
Frazier Hall, Greeley, CO 80639
(303) 351-2454
FAX: (303) 351-1923
    Type of Facility: Theatre House
    Type of Stage: Proscenium
    Stage Dimensions: 62'Wx32"D   **Orchestra Pit**
    Seating Capacity: 614
    Year Built: 1954   **Architect:** F.W. Ireland   **Cost:** $140,000
    Year Remodeled: 1987
    Acoustical Consultant: Mead and Mount
    Contact for Rental Bill VanLoo;   (303) 351-2454
    Resident Groups: Little Theatre of the Rockies; UNC Opera Theatre; UNC Dance Theatre; UNC Performing Arts

La Junta

THEATRE

PICKETWIRE PLAYERS
Eighth and San Juan, La Junta, CO 81050
(719) 384-8320
    Founded: 1968
    Arts Area: Community; Theatrical Group
    Status: Non-Professional; Non-Profit
    Type: Performing
    Purpose: To provide a good theatre showcase for regional talent in Southeastern Colorado
    Management: Board of Directors
    Officers: Todd Hilstad, President; Rebecca Goodwin, Vice President; Deanna Brown, Secretary; Lindy Nelson, Treasurer
    Volunteer Staff: 9
    Utilizes: Guest Conductors; Guest Artists; Guest Directors
    Budget: $1,000 - $50,000
    Income Sources: Box Office; Individual Donations
    Season: October - July   **Annual Attendance:** 3,600
    Affiliations: La Junta Chamber of Commerce; Colorado Community Theater Coalition
    Performance Facilities: Picketwire Center for the Performing and Visual Arts

FACILITY

OTERO JUNIOR COLLEGE - HUMANITIES CENTER THEATRE
1802 Colorado, La Junta, CO 81050
(719) 384-6870
    Type of Facility: Performance Center
    Type of Stage: Proscenium
    Stage Dimensions: 18'x40'x36'   **Orchestra Pit**
    Seating Capacity: 518
    Year Built: 1971   **Architect:** Joseph Wilson
    Contact for Rental Ed Stafford;   (719) 384-6870
    Resident Groups: Otero Players

PICKETWIRE PLAYERS AND COMMUNITY THEATRE
802 San Juan, La Junta, CO 81050
(719) 384-8320
    Type of Facility: Theatre House
    Facility Originally: School
    Type of Stage: Thrust
    Stage Dimensions: 25'x30'   **Orchestra Pit**
    Seating Capacity: 400
    Year Built: 1934
    Year Remodeled: 1976   **Cost:** $84,000
    Contact for Rental John Spencer, President
    Resident Groups: Picketwire Players

Littleton

DANCE

DAVID TAYLOR DANCE THEATRE
2539 West Main Street, Littleton, CO 80210
(303) 797-6944
Founded: 1980
Arts Area: Modern; Ballet
Status: Professional; Non-Profit
Type: Performing; Touring; Resident; Educational
Purpose: Professional performing contemporary ballet company and school
Management: Gary Lindsey, Artist Services
Officers: Art Binkley, Chairman of Board; Dan Winter, Vice Chairman
Paid Staff: 13   **Volunteer Staff:** 100
Paid Artists: 15   **Non-Paid Artists:** 25
Utilizes: Special Technical Talent; Guest Artists; Guest Choreographers
Budget: $100,000 - $500,000
Income Sources: Private Foundations/Grants/Endowments; Business/Corporate Donations; Box Office; Government Grants; Individual Donations
Season: 52 Weeks
Annual Attendance: 30,000

Longmont

FACILITY

DICKENS OPERA HOUSE
302 Main Street, Longmont, CO 80501
(303) 772-5167
Type of Facility: Studio Performance; Performance Center; Opera House; Multi-Purpose; Room
Type of Stage: Thrust; Proscenium
Stage Dimensions: 44'Wx16'D, thrust 23'6"Wx9'9"D
Seating Capacity: Theater style - 283; Cabaret style - 184
Year Built: 1881   **Architect:** William Dickens
Year Remodeled: 1986   **Architect:** Roger Burton   **Cost:** $500,000
Contact for Rental Dickens Opera House Association;   (303) 772-5167

Pueblo

DANCE

PUEBLO BALLET
431 East Pitkin, Pueblo, CO 81004
(719) 543-7362
Founded: 1974
Arts Area: Ballet
Status: Non-Profit
Type: Performing; Touring; Educational
Purpose: To provide high-quality performance and dance education for Pueblo and southern Colorado
Management: Sharon Conders, Executive Director
Officers: Phyllis Crawford, President; Mary Swearinger, Secretary; Darryl Gurule, Treasurer
Paid Staff: 6   **Volunteer Staff:** 100
Paid Artists: 6   **Non-Paid Artists:** 10
Utilizes: Special Technical Talent; Guest Artists
Budget: $50,000 - $100,000
Income Sources: Private Foundations/Grants/Endowments; Business/Corporate Donations; Box Office; Government Grants; Individual Donations
Season: 52 Weeks   **Annual Attendance:** 5,000
Affiliations: NARB; Colorado Dance Alliance
Performance Facilities: Memorial Hall; Sangre de Cristo Arts and Conference Center

INSTRUMENTAL MUSIC

PUEBLO SYMPHONY ORCHESTRA
503 Noth Main, Thatcher Building, Suite 414, Pueblo, CO 81003
(719) 546-0333
Founded: 1966
Arts Area: Orchestra
Status: Non-Profit
Type: Performing
Management: Tom Christner, Executive Director; Jacob Chi, Musical Director/Conductor
Officers: Richard Moran, President/Executive Board
Paid Staff: 5 **Volunteer Staff:** 4
Paid Artists: 70
Utilizes: Guest Conductors; Guest Artists
Budget: $100,000 - $500,000
Income Sources: Private Foundations/Grants/Endowments; Business/Corporate Donations; Box Office; Individual Donations; Fund-raising
Season: September - May
Affiliations: ASOL
Performance Facilities: Memorial Hall; Hoag Hall, University of Southern Colorado

THEATRE

BROADWAY THEATRE LEAGUE OF PUEBLO
PO Box 3145, Pueblo, CO 81005
(719) 545-4721
FAX: (719) 543-0134
Founded: 1960
Arts Area: Professional
Status: Professional; Non-Profit
Type: Performing; Touring; Sponsoring
Purpose: To bring to the community the opportunity to see professional theatre
Management: Maggie Divelbiss, Manager; David Zupancic, Assistant Manager; Susan Velasco, Administrative Assistant; Cheryl Califano, Box Office Manager
Paid Staff: 2 **Volunteer Staff:** 20
Utilizes: Special Technical Talent
Budget: $100,000 - $500,000
Income Sources: Private Foundations/Grants/Endowments; Business/Corporate Donations; Box Office; Individual Donations
Season: 52 Weeks **Annual Attendance:** 4,500
Performance Facilities: Pueblo Memorial Hall

THE IMPOSSIBLE PLAYERS
PO Box 1005, Pueblo, CO 81002
(719) 542-6969
Founded: 1966
Arts Area: Community; Theatrical Group
Status: Non-Professional; Non-Profit
Type: Performing; Resident; Educational
Purpose: To promote the enjoyment of the performing arts by the public; to further the education of both members and the public in the skills of those arts; to give people an opportunity to perform for the public
Officers: Marlene Schmidt, President; Bill Mattoon, Vice President; Carol Martin, Secretary; Don Warren, Treasurer
Paid Staff: 1
Budget: $1,000 - $50,000
Income Sources: Private Foundations/Grants/Endowments; Business/Corporate Donations; Box Office; Individual Donations
Season: October - April **Annual Attendance:** 28,000
Performance Facilities: Public Community College - The Hoag Theater

PERFORMING SERIES

SANGRE DE CRISTO ARTS AND CONFERENCE CENTER
210 North Santa Fe Avenue, Pueblo, CO 81003
(719) 543-0130
Founded: 1972
Arts Area: Dance; Vocal Music; Instrumental Music; Theater; Festivals; Lyric Opera
Status: Professional; Non-Profit
Type: Performing; Touring; Resident; Educational; Sponsoring

Purpose: To foster and promote the performing and visual arts in a nineteen-county region of southeastern Colorado
Management: Maggie Divelbiss, Director; David Zupancic, Associate Director; Timothy F. Gately, Technical Director
Officers: Assege Abebe, Chairman, Board of Trustees; Keith Lovin, Vice Chairman; Lalonna Meoska, Secretary; Charles Ready, Treasurer
Paid Staff: 50 **Volunteer Staff:** 80
Paid Artists: 10 **Non-Paid Artists:** 75
Utilizes: Special Technical Talent; Guest Artists
Budget: $500,000 - $1,000,000
Income Sources: Private Foundations/Grants/Endowments; Business/Corporate Donations; Box Office; Government Grants; Individual Donations
Season: 52 Weeks **Annual Attendance:** 250,000
Affiliations: APAP; WAAA; Rocky Mountain Theatre Guild
Performance Facilities: Sangre de Cristo Arts and Conference Center

FACILITY

SANGRE DE CRISTO ARTS AND CONFERENCE CENTER
210 North Santa Fe Avenue, Pueblo, CO 81003
(719) 543-0130
FAX: (719) 543-0134
Founded: 1972
Type of Facility: Arts Center
Type of Stage: Thrust
Orchestra Pit
Seating Capacity: 500
Year Built: 1972 **Architect:** Hurtig, Gardner, Froelich **Cost:** $1,300,000
Contact for Rental Jeff Giadone; (719) 543-0130
Resident Groups: Danspectra; Southern Colorado Repertory Theatre (SCRT)

Steamboat Springs

PERFORMING SERIES

STRINGS IN THE MOUNTAINS
PO Box 774627, Steamboat Springs, CO 80477
(303) 879-5056
FAX: (303) 879-5057
Founded: 1988
Arts Area: Vocal Music; Instrumental Music; Festivals
Status: Professional; Non-Profit
Type: Performing
Purpose: To present the finest chamber possible in the inspirational setting of Steamboat Springs
Management: John Sant'Ambrogio, Music Director; Belse Grassby, Executive Director; Kay Clagett, Development Director
Officers: Art Smith, Chairman; Candyce Wither, Treasurer
Paid Staff: 4 **Volunteer Staff:** 25
Paid Artists: 63
Utilizes: Guest Conductors; Guest Artists
Budget: $100,000 - $500,000
Income Sources: Private Foundations/Grants/Endowments; Business/Corporate Donations; Box Office; Government Grants; Individual Donations
Season: July - August **Annual Attendance:** 10,000
Affiliations: ASOL; CMA

Sterling

FACILITY

NORTHEASTERN JUNIOR COLLEGE THEATRE
Northeastern Junior College, Sterling, CO 80751
(303) 522-6600, ext. 666
Type of Facility: Performance Center; Theatre House
Type of Stage: Proscenium; Black Box **Orchestra Pit**
Seating Capacity: 566
Year Built: 1968 **Architect:** Murrin, Kasch, Konn **Cost:** $1,000,000
Contact for Rental Dave Grams; (303) 522-6600
Resident Groups: Northeastern Junior College Players

Telluride

PERFORMING SERIES

TELLURIDE JAZZ CELEBRATION
PO Box 279, Telluride, CO 81435
(303) 728-7009
> **Founded:** 1975
> **Arts Area:** Vocal Music; Instrumental Music; Festivals
> **Status:** Professional; Non-Profit
> **Type:** Sponsoring
> **Purpose:** To keep the Telluride Jazz Festival alive
> **Management:** Paul Machado, Producer/Executive Director
> **Paid Staff:** 25 **Volunteer Staff:** 225
> **Paid Artists:** 10
> **Utilizes:** Special Technical Talent; Guest Artists
> **Budget:** $100,000 - $500,000
> **Income Sources:** Business/Corporate Donations; Box Office; Government Grants; Individual Donations
> **Season:** July
> **Annual Attendance:** 5,500
> **Performance Facilities:** Sheridan Opera House; Telluride Town Park

FACILITY

SHERIDAN OPERA HOUSE
110 North Oak Street, PO Box 2680, Telluride, CO 81435
(303) 728-5182
FAX: (303) 728-6966
> **Type of Facility:** Theatre House; Amphitheater; Civic Center
> **Type of Stage:** Proscenium
> **Stage Dimensions:** 28'Wx12'D; 20'W
> **Seating Capacity:** 240
> **Year Built:** 1914
> **Year Remodeled:** 1985   **Architect:** Johnson-Nimmer   **Cost:** $450,000
> **Contact for Rental** Steven Anderson;   (303) 784-6363
> **Manager:** R.J. White
> **Resident Groups:** Telluride Film Festival; Telluride Jazz Festival; Blue Grass Festival; Mountain Film; Telluride Chamber Music Ensemble; Telluride Institute; Telluride Council for Arts and Humanities
> *The Sheridan Opera House is on the National Register of Historic Places.*

Vail

INSTRUMENTAL MUSIC

BRAVO! COLORADO MUSIC FESTIVAL AT VAIL-BEAVER CREEK
953 South Frontage Road, #104, Vail, CO 81657
(303) 476-0206
FAX: (303) 479-0559
> **Founded:** 1988
> **Arts Area:** Symphony; Orchestra; Chamber; Ethnic
> **Status:** Professional
> **Type:** Performing; Educational
> **Management:** John W. Giovando, Executive Director; Ida Kavafian, Music Director
> **Paid Staff:** 6 **Volunteer Staff:** 125
> **Paid Artists:** 47
> **Utilizes:** Guest Conductors; Guest Artists
> **Budget:** $1,000,000 - $5,000,000
> **Income Sources:** Private Foundations/Grants/Endowments; Business/Corporate Donations; Box Office; Government Grants; Individual Donations
> **Season:** July - August   **Annual Attendance:** 17,100

Westminster

PERFORMING SERIES

WESTMINSTER COMMUNITY ARTIST SERIES
7380 Lowell Boulevard, Westminster, CO 80030
(303) 429-1999
Founded: 1983
Arts Area: Dance; Vocal Music; Instrumental Music; Grand Opera
Status: Non-Profit
Type: Performing
Purpose: To present the finest performing and visual artists from across the nation to Westminster Area audiences
Officers: JoAnne Groff, President; Jeanie Beck, Vice President; Diane Schmidt, Treasurer; William Christopher, Development Director; Wilbur Flachman, Chairman of the Board
Paid Staff: 2 **Volunteer Staff:** 15
Utilizes: Special Technical Talent; Guest Artists
Income Sources: Private Foundations/Grants/Endowments; Business/Corporate Donations; Box Office; Individual Donations
Season: January - December **Annual Attendance:** 17,000

CONNECTICUT

Avon

VOCAL MUSIC

THE HARTFORD CHORALE, INC.
16 Bridgestone Lane, Avon, CT 06001
(203) 673-1341
Founded: 1971
Arts Area: Choral
Status: Non-Professional; Non-Profit
Type: Performing
Purpose: To reach the broadest possible audience with major choral-orchestral literature
Management: Henley Denmead, Music Director
Officers: Dougla Pyrke, President
Paid Staff: 2 **Volunteer Staff:** 14
Non-Paid Artists: 150
Utilizes: Guest Artists
Budget: $50,000 - $100,000
Income Sources: Private Foundations/Grants/Endowments; Business/Corporate Donations; Box Office; Government Grants; Individual Donations
Season: September - July **Annual Attendance:** 9,000
Performance Facilities: Horace Bushnell Memorial Hall

Bloomfield

INSTRUMENTAL MUSIC

HARTFORD JAZZ SOCIETY
116 Cottage Grove Road, Room 204, Bloomfield, CT 06002
(203) 242-6688
Founded: 1960
Arts Area: Jazz
Status: Professional
Type: Sponsoring
Purpose: To promote and keep alive jazz music in this area, we present seven to 11 concerts a year in Hartford, as well as offer community programs on jazz
Management: Betty Ector, President; Bill Sullivan, Program Director
Volunteer Staff: 20
Utilizes: Guest Artists
Budget: $50,000 - $100,000
Income Sources: Private Foundations/Grants/Endowments; Business/Corporate Donations; Box Office; Individual Donations
Season: 52 Weeks **Annual Attendance:** 2,000
Performance Facilities: Hartford Holiday Inn

Bridgeport

INSTRUMENTAL MUSIC

BRIDGEPORT CIVIC ORCHESTRA
Arnold Bernhard Center, University of Bridgeport, Bridgeport, CT 06602
(203) 576-4404
Founded: 1947
Arts Area: Symphony; Orchestra
Status: Non-Professional; Non-Profit
Type: Performing
Purpose: To perform fine orchestral music, bringing together the forces and talents of students, faculty and community members
Management: Daniel D'Addio, Conductor
Paid Staff: 1
Performance Facilities: Arnold Bernhard Center

GREATER BRIDGEPORT SYMPHONY
446 University Avenue, Bridgeport, CT 06604
(203) 576-0263
FAX: (203) 367-0064
Founded: 1945
Arts Area: Symphony; Orchestra; Chamber; Ensemble
Status: Professional; Non-Profit
Type: Performing; Educational
Purpose: To present symphonic and chamber music concerts as well as educational music programs
Management: Jena Maric, General Manager; Glenn Mortimer, Operations Manager
Officers: Nancy Johmann, President; Robert S. Tellalian, Chairman of the Board
Paid Staff: 5   **Volunteer Staff:** 50
Paid Artists: 80
Utilizes: Guest Conductors; Guest Artists
Budget: $100,000 - $500,000
Income Sources: Private Foundations/Grants/Endowments; Business/Corporate Donations; Box Office; Government Grants; Individual Donations
Season: September - June   **Annual Attendance:** 10,000
Affiliations: ASOL
Performance Facilities: Klein Memorial Auditorium

FACILITY

DOWNTOWN CABARET THEATRE
263 Golden Hill Street, Bridgeport, CT 06604
(203) 576-1634
Type of Facility: Cabaret
Facility Originally: YWCA All-purpose Room
Type of Stage: Proscenium   **Stage Dimensions:** 30'x19'
Seating Capacity: 294
Year Built: 1944
Year Remodeled: 1975
Contact for Rental: Bert Bernardi;   (203) 576-1634
Resident Groups: Downtown Cabaret Theatre and Cabaret Children's Company

KLEIN MEMORIAL AUDITORIUM
910 Fairfield Avenue, Bridgeport, CT 06605
(203) 576-8115
Founded: 1940
Type of Facility: Auditorium; Theatre House
Type of Stage: Proscenium
Stage Dimensions: 60'x36'x36'   **Orchestra Pit**
Seating Capacity: 1,500
Year Built: 1940   **Architect:** Leonard Asheim   **Cost:** $500,000
Contact for Rental: Len Alexander, Management Consultants for the Arts, Inc.;   (203) 661-3003
Manager: Len Alexander;   (203) 661-3003
Resident Groups: Connecticut Grand Opera; Connecticut Ballet Theatre

UNIVERSITY OF BRIDGEPORT - BERNHARD CENTER
84 Iranistan Avenue, Bridgeport, CT 06601
(203) 576-4925
Type of Facility: Theatre Complex; Concert Hall; Auditorium; Performance Center
Type of Stage: Proscenium
Stage Dimensions: 40'Wx18'Hx30'D   **Orchestra Pit**
Seating Capacity: 900
Year Built: 1972   **Architect:** Lyons Mater & Lechner   **Cost:** $7,000,000
Contact for Rental: Helen Conlon;   (203) 576-4925
Resident Groups: University of Bridgeport Theatre and Music Departments; Bernhard Center Arts Calendar Events

Cheshire

DANCE

SILO CONCERT DANCERS
855 North Brooksvale Road, Cheshire, CT 06410
(203) 272-9377
Founded: 1985

Arts Area: Modern
Status: Professional; Non-Profit
Type: Performing; Educational
Purpose: To maintain a professional performing company dedicated to presenting the works of Doris Humphrey and preserving their artistic integrity
Management: Ernestine Stodelle, Artistic Director; Gail Corbin, Associate Artistic Director
Paid Staff: 2
Paid Artists: 14
Utilizes: Special Technical Talent; Guest Artists
Budget: $1,000 - $50,000
Income Sources: Box Office; Individual Donations

THEATRE

CHESHIRE COMMUNITY THEATRE
PO Box 149, Cheshire, CT 06410
(203) 271-2903
Founded: 1953
Arts Area: Musical; Community; Theatrical Group
Status: Non-Professional; Non-Profit
Type: Performing; Resident
Officers: Pat Murphy, President
Volunteer Staff: 25
Budget: $1,000 - $50,000
Income Sources: Business/Corporate Donations; Box Office
Season: September - June   **Annual Attendance:** 3,000
Affiliations: New Haven Council of the Arts
Performance Facilities: Cheshire High School

Chester

THEATRE

GOODSPEED-AT-CHESTER/THE NORMA TERRIS THEATRE
North Main Street, Chester, CT 06423
(203) 873-8664
Founded: 1984
Arts Area: Musical
Status: Professional; Non-Profit
Type: Performing; Equity Theater
Purpose: The satellite theatre of the Goodspeed Opera House, Goodspeed-At-Chester/The Norma Terris Theatre is dedicated to developing new works of musical theatre, producing several musicals-in-progress each season.
Management: Michael P. Price, Executive Director; Sue Frost, Producing Associate; Warren Pincus, Casting Director; Michael Sande, Public Relations Director
Officers: Norwood R.G. Goodspeed, Chairman of the Board; Richard Schneller, President
Utilizes: Guest Artists; Guest Directors
Income Sources: Private Foundations/Grants/Endowments; Business/Corporate Donations; Box Office; Government Grants; Individual Donations
Season: May - November   **Annual Attendance:** 20,000

THE NATIONAL THEATRE OF THE DEAF
The Hazel E. Stark Center, Chester, CT 06412
(203) 526-4971
FAX: (203) 526-9732
Founded: 1967
Arts Area: Professional; Theatrical Group
Status: Professional; Non-Profit
Type: Performing; Touring; Educational
Purpose: A professional, international touring company whose productions combine Sign Language and the spoken word
Management: David Hays, Founding Artistic Director; Julianna Fjeld, Co-Artistic Director; Liane Dyer, Director of Public Relations
Paid Staff: 15   **Volunteer Staff:** 2
Paid Artists: 15
Utilizes: Special Technical Talent; Guest Artists; Guest Directors
Budget: $1,000,000 - $5,000,000
Income Sources: Private Foundations/Grants/Endowments; Business/Corporate Donations; Box Office; Government Grants; Individual Donations
Season: 52 Weeks   **Annual Attendance:** 100,000

FACILITY

GOODSPEED-AT-CHESTER/THE NORMA TERRIS THEATRE
North Main Street, Chester, CT 06423
(203) 873-8664
> **Founded:** 1984
> **Type of Facility:** Theatre House
> **Facility Originally:** Factory
> **Type of Stage:** Proscenium
> **Stage Dimensions:** 31'Wx22'6"D   **Orchestra Pit**
> **Seating Capacity:** 200
> **Year Remodeled:** 1984

Danbury

INSTRUMENTAL MUSIC

ASTON MAGNA FOUNDATION FOR MUSIC AND THE HUMANITIES, INC.
PO Box 310, Danbury, CT 06813
(203) 792-4662
FAX: (203) 744-7244
> **Founded:** 1972
> **Arts Area:** Chamber; Early Music
> **Status:** Professional; Non-Profit
> **Type:** Performing; Touring; Educational; Sponsoring
> **Purpose:** To perform baroque and classical music on period instruments; to sponsor educational programs that connect the music with the society and culture in which it was written
> **Management:** Ronnie Boriskin, Executive Director; Daniel Stepner, Artistic Director; Raymond Erickson, Academy/Outreach Director; Amy Poliakoff, Festival Administrator; Constance Baldwin, Academy/Outreach Administrator; Florence Lynch, Business Manager
> **Officers:** Robert B. Strassler, Chairman; Edwin E. McAmis, Treasurer; Richard Bodig, Secretary; Bernard Krainis, Clerk; Dominick Attanasio, Raymond Erickson, Nina Korda, Christopher H. Murray and Sarah Pinchot, Directors
> **Utilizes:** Guest Artists
> **Budget:** $100,000 - $500,000
> **Income Sources:** Private Foundations/Grants/Endowments; Business/Corporate Donations; Box Office; Government Grants; Individual Donations
> **Season:** 52 Weeks
> **Performance Facilities:** St. James Church Festival, Great Barrington, MA

DANBURY MUSIC CENTRE, INC.
256 Main Street, Danbury, CT 06810
(203) 748-1716
> **Founded:** 1935
> **Arts Area:** Symphony; Orchestra; Chamber; Ensemble; Folk
> **Status:** Semi-Professional; Non-Professional; Non-Profit
> **Type:** Performing; Educational; Sponsoring
> **Purpose:** A community organization dedicated to the performance of classical music free to the public
> **Management:** Nancy F. Sudik, Executive Director; James Humphreville, Musical Director, Orchestra; Richard Brooks, Orchestra; Charles Matz, Chorus; Edith Schwab, Symphonette; Julianne LaFond, Nutcracker Director
> **Officers:** James Tegolotti, President; Karen Mattscheck, Vice President; Kris Meier, Secretary; Betsy McIlvaine, Treasurer
> **Paid Staff:** 11   **Volunteer Staff:** 30
> **Paid Artists:** 20   **Non-Paid Artists:** 250
> **Utilizes:** Guest Artists
> **Budget:** $50,000 - $100,000
> **Income Sources:** Private Foundations/Grants/Endowments; Business/Corporate Donations; Individual Donations
> **Season:** September - June   **Annual Attendance:** 8,000

FACILITY

CHARLES IVES CENTER - PAVILION
PO Box 2957, Danbury, CT 06813
(203) 797-4002
FAX: (203) 731-2807
> **Type of Facility:** Environmental; Amphitheater
> **Type of Stage:** Platform; Environmental; Octagonal

Stage Dimensions: 62' diameter octagon with 55'x40' usable stage area
Seating Capacity: 5000
Year Built: 1985
Architect: Kosinsky Associates
Cost: $600,000
Acoustical Consultant: Jaffe Acoustics

Darien

THEATRE

CONNECTICUT'S BROADWAY THEATRE, DARIEN
65 Tokeneke Road, Darien, CT 06820
(203) 655-6812
FAX: (203) 655-9619
Founded: 1977
Arts Area: Professional; Musical; Dinner
Status: Professional; Commercial
Type: Performing; Resident
Purpose: To present professional musical theatre - revivals of vintage pieces and just-released musicals
Management: Jane Bergere, Producer; Donne Shaw, Assistant to the Producer; Paul Squire, Controller
Officers: Phillip Molstre, President
Paid Staff: 50
Paid Artists: 35
Utilizes: Special Technical Talent; Guest Conductors; Guest Artists; Guest Directors
Budget: $100,000 - $500,000
Income Sources: Box Office
Season: 52 Weeks   **Annual Attendance:** 104,000
Affiliations: AEA; SSDC; IATSE; AFM; ADTI

East Haddam

THEATRE

GOODSPEED OPERA HOUSE
Route 82, East Haddam, CT 06423
(203) 873-8664; (203) 873-8668
FAX: (203) 873-2329
Founded: 1963
Arts Area: Musical
Status: Professional; Non-Profit
Type: Performing; Equity Theater
Purpose: The Goodspeed Opera House is one of the only theatres in America dedicated to the heritage of the American musical and the development of new works to add to the repertoire.
Management: Michael P. Price, Executive Director; Sue Frost, Producing Associate; Warren Pincus, Casting Director; Michael Sande, Public Relations Director
Officers: Norwood R.G. Goodspeed, Chairman of the Board; Richard Schneller, President
Utilizes: Guest Artists; Guest Directors
Income Sources: Private Foundations/Grants/Endowments; Business/Corporate Donations; Box Office; Government Grants; Individual Donations
Season: April - December   **Annual Attendance:** 110,000

FACILITY

GOODSPEED OPERA HOUSE
Route 82, East Haddam, CT 06423
(203) 873-8664
Type of Facility: Theatre House; Opera House
Type of Stage: Proscenium
Stage Dimensions: 27'Wx18'D
Orchestra Pit
Seating Capacity: 398
Year Built: 1876   **Architect:** William H. Goodspeed
Year Remodeled: 1962   **Architect:** Frederic Palmer, Henry Sage Goodwin
Manager: Edward Blaschik

East Windsor

THEATRE

COACHLIGHT DINNER THEATRE
266 Main Street, East Windsor, CT 06088
(203) 623-8227
> **Founded:** 1972
> **Arts Area:** Dinner
> **Status:** Professional; Commercial
> **Type:** Performing
> **Management:** Samuel Belkin, Janis Belkin, Ruth Belkin, Producers

Fairfield

INSTRUMENTAL MUSIC

GREATER BRIDGEPORT SYMPHONY YOUTH ORCHESTRA
PO Box 645, Fairfield, CT 06430
(203) 576-0263
> **Founded:** 1970
> **Arts Area:** Symphony; Orchestra
> **Status:** Non-Professional
> **Type:** Performing; Educational
> **Purpose:** To provide a quality orchestral experience for young musicians in the Greater Bridgeport Area
> **Officers:** Beth Harris, President
> **Paid Staff:** 5
> **Budget:** $1,000 - $50,000
> **Income Sources:** Private Foundations/Grants/Endowments; Box Office; Individual Donations
> **Season:** September - May   **Annual Attendance:** 2,000
> **Performance Facilities:** Fairfield High School

Falls Village

PERFORMING SERIES

MUSIC MOUNTAIN
Falls Village, CT 06031
(203) 438-8868
FAX: (203) 438-1769
> **Founded:** 1930
> **Arts Area:** Vocal Music; Instrumental Music
> **Status:** Professional; Non-Profit
> **Type:** Performing; Educational; Sponsoring
> **Purpose:** To bring Connecticut the finest in chamber music; to present the Summer Chamber Music Festival; to broadcast concerts to 200 radio stations
> **Officers:** Nicholas Gordon, President; Jack Amster, Executive Vice President; Louise King, Secretary; Anne Stewart, Treasurer
> **Paid Staff:** 2   **Volunteer Staff:** 15
> **Paid Artists:** 30
> **Utilizes:** Guest Artists
> **Budget:** $50,000 - $100,000
> **Income Sources:** Private Foundations/Grants/Endowments; Business/Corporate Donations; Box Office; Government Grants; Individual Donations
> **Season:** June - September   **Annual Attendance:** 6,000
> **Performance Facilities:** Gordon Hall

Greenwich

INSTRUMENTAL MUSIC

GREENWICH SYMPHONY ORCHESTRA
PO Box 35, Greenwich, CT 06836
(203) 869-2664
> **Founded:** 1958
> **Arts Area:** Symphony

Status: Professional
Type: Performing
Purpose: To present symphonic music performances and a Youth Concert Series for all Greenwich school children in grades 2-7, free of charge
Management: Mrs. Richard W. Radcliffe, President
Officers: Mrs. Richard W. Radcliffe, President; Richard Slagle, First Vice President/Secretary; Harriet Aberle, Publicity; Richard W. Radcliffe, Treasurer
Paid Staff: 3   **Volunteer Staff:** 40
Paid Artists: 95   **Non-Paid Artists:** 2
Utilizes: Guest Artists
Budget: $100,000 - $500,000
Income Sources: Private Foundations/Grants/Endowments; Business/Corporate Donations; Box Office; Individual Donations
Season: October - June   **Annual Attendance:** 12,000
Affiliations: ASOL
Performance Facilities: Greenwich High School

VOCAL MUSIC

GREENWICH CHORAL SOCIETY
PO Box 5, Greenwich, CT 06836
(203) 622-5136
Founded: 1925
Arts Area: Choral
Status: Non-Profit
Type: Performing
Purpose: To make a broad range of choral music available to audiences for their entertainment and education
Management: Wendy Ann Dunkle, Business Administrator
Officers: Curt Carlson, President; Betsy Lawrence, Executive Vice President; Nancy Pierson, Vice President Administration; Susan Deal, Vice President Communications; Tom Casper, Vice President Concert; Roy Pfeil, Vice President Funding; Suzanne Warner, Secretary; Don Lewis, Treasurer
Paid Staff: 1
Utilizes: Guest Artists
Budget: $100,000 - $500,000
Income Sources: Private Foundations/Grants/Endowments; Business/Corporate Donations; Individual Donations
Season: 52 Weeks   **Annual Attendance:** 9,000
Performance Facilities: State University of New York at Purchase

Groton

THEATRE

THE AVERY POINT PLAYERS
University of Connecticut at Avery Point, Groton, CT 06340
(203) 446-1020
FAX: (203) 445-3498
Founded: 1972
Arts Area: Theatrical Group
Status: Non-Professional
Type: Performing; Touring; Educational; Sponsoring
Purpose: To develop programs, performers, leaders and audiences for and in theatre, by and for youth
Management: K.E. Janney, Associate Professor/Producer/Director
Paid Staff: 1
Utilizes: Guest Artists; Guest Directors
Budget: $1,000 - $50,000
Income Sources: Box Office; Individual Donations
Season: September - June   **Annual Attendance:** 2,500

Guilford

INSTRUMENTAL MUSIC

EASTERN BRASS QUINTET
33 Kenneth Circle, Guilford, CT 06437
(203) 481-9226
Founded: 1970
Arts Area: Chamber; Ensemble; Instrumental Group

Status: Professional
Type: Performing; Touring; Educational
Purpose: To perform the best in brass chamber music to a wide variety of audiences
Management: Lisa Sapinkopf, Artist Manager
Officers: Richard Green, Director
Paid Artists: 5
Budget: $50,000 - $100,000
Income Sources: Private Foundations/Grants/Endowments; Individual Donations
Season: 52 Weeks

Hartford

DANCE

ALBANO BALLET COMPANY
15 Girard Avenue, Hartford, CT 06105
(203) 232-8898
Founded: 1972
Arts Area: Modern; Ballet
Status: Professional; Non-Profit
Type: Performing; Touring; Educational
Purpose: To bring quality ballet to the Connecticut area through training and performance
Management: Joseph Albano, Artistic Director
Officers: Julius E. Scheir, President; Herbert Deming, Treasurer; Mrs. Herman Hiebert, Secretary
Utilizes: Guest Artists
Budget: $100,000 - $500,000
Income Sources: Private Foundations/Grants/Endowments; Box Office; Government Grants; Individual Donations
Season: September - May
Affiliations: University of Central Connecticut

HARTFORD BALLET
226 Farmington Avenue, Hartford, CT 06105
(203) 525-9396
FAX: (203) 249-8116
Founded: 1960
Arts Area: Modern; Ballet
Status: Professional; Non-Profit
Type: Performing; Touring; Resident; Educational; Sponsoring
Purpose: To maintain a full-time resident professional dance company and a school for the training of dance teachers and performers
Management: John Simone, Executive Director; Enid Lynn, Director of the School
Officers: Wayne Hauge, President; Robin Pearson, Joan Brown, Vice Presidents
Paid Artists: 22   **Non-Paid Artists:** 12
Utilizes: Special Technical Talent; Guest Artists; Designers
Budget: $1,000,000 - $5,000,000
Income Sources: Private Foundations/Grants/Endowments; Business/Corporate Donations; Box Office; Government Grants; Individual Donations; Tour Fees
Season: August - May   **Annual Attendance:** 80,000
Affiliations: School of the Hartford Ballet
Performance Facilities: The Bushnell Hall

INSTRUMENTAL MUSIC

THE HARTFORD SYMPHONY ORCHESTRA INC.
228 Farmington Road, Hartford, CT 06105
(203) 246-8742
FAX: (203) 247-1720
Arts Area: Symphony; Orchestra; Chamber; Ensemble
Status: Professional; Non-Profit
Type: Performing; Educational
Purpose: To provide the highest quality musical performances to the widest possible audience
Management: Michael Lankester, Music Director; Paul K. Reuter, Executive Director
Officers: Peter S. Burgess, President of the Board
Budget: $1,000,000 - $5,000,000
Income Sources: Private Foundations/Grants/Endowments; Business/Corporate Donations; Box Office; Government Grants; Individual Donations
Performance Facilities: The Bushnell

VOCAL MUSIC

CONNECTICUT OPERA
226 Farmington Avenue, Hartford, CT 06105
(203) 527-0713
FAX: (203) 293-1715
Founded: 1942
Arts Area: Grand Opera; Light Opera; Operetta
Status: Professional
Type: Performing; Touring; Resident; Educational; Sponsoring
Purpose: To present high-quality, professional opera, musical theater and educational services
Management: George D. Osborne, General Director
Officers: John G. Ewen, Chairman; Thomas K. Standish, Vice Chairman; Calvin S. Price, President
Paid Staff: 15 **Volunteer Staff:** 5
Paid Artists: 500 **Non-Paid Artists:** 50
Utilizes: Special Technical Talent; Guest Conductors; Guest Artists; Guest Directors
Budget: $1,000,000 - $5,000,000
Income Sources: Private Foundations/Grants/Endowments; Business/Corporate Donations; Box Office; Government Grants; Individual Donations
Season: September - May
Annual Attendance: 100,000
Affiliations: OA
Performance Facilities: Horace Bushnell Memorial Hall

THEATRE

ARTISTS COLLECTIVE
35 Clark Street, Hartford, CT 06120
(203) 527-3205
Founded: 1970
Arts Area: Theatrical Group
Status: Non-Professional; Non-Profit
Type: Resident
Management: Dollie McLean, Executive Director; Jackie McLean, Creative Consultant
Utilizes: Special Technical Talent; Guest Artists; Guest Directors
Budget: $100,000 - $500,000
Income Sources: Private Foundations/Grants/Endowments; Business/Corporate Donations; Box Office; Government Grants; Individual Donations
Season: September - June

COMPANY ONE
30 Arbor Street, Hartford, CT 06106
(203) 233-4588
FAX: (203) 233-2941
Founded: 1983
Arts Area: Theatrical Group
Status: Professional; Non-Profit
Type: Performing; Touring; Resident; Educational
Purpose: To present evening and matinee performances of full-length plays, staged script readings of new full-length plays (Script Teas), and radio drama (RadioPlaying); to produce new works by emerging artists and developing regional and local artists; to create educational programs which weave theater into the fabric of everyday life
Management: Juanita Rockwell, Artistic Director; Elizabeth Bermel, Managing Director
Officers: Ed Hogan, Board President; Terry O'Conner, First Vice President; Nancy Wolfe, Second Vice President; Jackie Porter, Treasurer; Frederica Brenneman, Secretary
Paid Staff: 5 **Volunteer Staff:** 3
Paid Artists: 50
Utilizes: Special Technical Talent; Guest Artists; Guest Directors
Budget: $50,000 - $100,000
Income Sources: Private Foundations/Grants/Endowments; Business/Corporate Donations; Box Office; Government Grants; Individual Donations
Season: 52 Weeks
Annual Attendance: 7,000
Affiliations: TCG; AEA; New Dramatists Guild
Performance Facilities: The Aetna Theatre at the Wadsworth Atheneum

HARTFORD STAGE COMPANY
50 Church Street, Hartford, CT 06103
(203) 525-5601
FAX: (203) 525-4420
Founded: 1964
Arts Area: Professional
Status: Professional; Non-Profit
Type: Performing; Resident
Purpose: To reinterpret the classics; to discover provocative new plays
Management: Mark Lamos, Artistic Director; David Hawkanson, Managing Director; Michael Ross, Business Manager
Officers: Elliot Gerson, President, Board of Directors
Utilizes: Guest Artists; Guest Directors
Budget: $1,000,000 - $5,000,000
Income Sources: Private Foundations/Grants/Endowments; Business/Corporate Donations; Box Office; Government Grants; Individual Donations
Season: October - June   **Annual Attendance:** 105,000
Affiliations: LORT; TCG; AAA
Performance Facilities: John W. Huntington Theatre

PERFORMING SERIES

AMERICAN MUSIC THEATRE GROUP
487 Main Street, Suite 6, Hartford, CT 06103
(203) 527-2944
Founded: 1978
Arts Area: Vocal Music; Instrumental Music; Lyric Opera
Status: Professional; Non-Profit
Type: Performing; Touring; Educational; Sponsoring
Purpose: To perform American music of all styles and periods
Management: Phillis Bruce, Booking Agent/Program Development Coordinator
Officers: Neely Bruce, President/Artistic Director
Volunteer Staff: 1
Paid Artists: 12
Utilizes: Special Technical Talent; Guest Conductors; Guest Artists; Guest Directors
Budget: $50,000 - $100,000
Income Sources: Private Foundations/Grants/Endowments; Business/Corporate Donations; Box Office; Government Grants; Individual Donations
Season: 52 Weeks   **Annual Attendance:** 3,000
Affiliations: CA
Performance Facilities: Horace Bushnell Memorial Hall

FIRST NIGHT HARTFORD, INC.
c/o Hartford Downtown Council, 250 Constitution Avenue, Hartford, CT 06103
(203) 728-3089
FAX: (203) 527-9696
Founded: 1988
Arts Area: Dance; Vocal Music; Instrumental Music; Theater; Festivals; Lyric Opera; Grand Opera; Major Arts Event
Status: Non-Profit
Type: Performing
Purpose: To provide a New Year's Eve celebration at 25 locations in downtown Hartford
Management: Hartford Downtown Council - Maureen Connolly, Events Manager
Officers: Mayor Perry, President; Christine Austin, Vice President; Anthony Caruso, Secretary; Peter Shapiro, Treasurer
Paid Staff: 2   **Volunteer Staff:** 150
Paid Artists: 250
Utilizes: Special Technical Talent
Budget: $100,000 - $500,000
Income Sources: Private Foundations/Grants/Endowments; Business/Corporate Donations; Individual Donations; Button Sales
Season: New Year's Eve   **Annual Attendance:** 18,000

FACILITY

ALBANO BALLET AND PERFORMING ARTS CENTER
15 Girard Avenue, Hartford, CT 06105
(203) 232-8898
Type of Facility: Performance Center
Type of Stage: Flexible
Stage Dimensions: 12'x30'x25'

Seating Capacity: 185
Year Built: 1900   **Cost:** $125,000
Year Remodeled: 1976   **Cost:** $20,000
Contact for Rental: Joseph Albano;   (303) 232-8898

HARTFORD CIVIC CENTER
One Civic Center Plaza, Hartford, CT 06103
(203) 249-6333
Type of Facility: Concert Hall; Auditorium; Civic Center; Arena; Multi-Purpose
Type of Stage: Flexible; Platform; Arena
Seating Capacity: 16,200
Year Built: 1975   **Architect:** Vincent Kling   **Cost:** $31,000,000
Year Remodeled: 1980   **Cost:** $27,000,000
Contact for Rental: Kathy Martin;   (203) 249-6333
Manager: Gerald Peterson

HARTFORD STAGE COMPANY
50 Church Street, Hartford, CT 06103
(203) 525-5601
Type of Facility: Theatre House
Type of Stage: Thrust
Stage Dimensions: 40'x90'x90'
Seating Capacity: 489
Year Built: 1977   **Architect:** Venturi and Rauch   **Cost:** $2,500,000
Contact for Rental: Candice Chirgotis, Production Manager;   (203) 525-5601
Resident Groups: Hartford Stage Company

HORACE BUSHNELL MEMORIAL HALL
166 Capitol Avenue, Hartford, CT 06106
(203) 527-3123
FAX: (203) 527-4142
Founded: 1928
Type of Facility: Concert Hall; Studio Performance; Performance Center; Opera House; Multi-Purpose; Room
Type of Stage: Thrust; Proscenium
Stage Dimensions: 30'x55'x40'   **Orchestra Pit**
Seating Capacity: 2,819
Year Built: 1930   **Architect:** Helmle, Corbett and Harrison
Year Remodeled: 1974   **Architect:** Venturi and Rauch   **Cost:** $940,000
Contact for Rental: Andrea Rynn;   (203) 527-3123
Manager: Douglas C. Evans;   (203) 527-3123
Resident Groups: Hartford Symphony Orchestra; Connecticut Opera; Hartford Ballet

Manchester

DANCE

CONNECTICUT CONCERT BALLET
280 Garden Grove, Manchester, CT 06040
(203) 643-4796
Founded: 1973
Arts Area: Ballet
Status: Semi-Professional; Non-Profit
Type: Performing; Touring; Resident; Educational; Sponsoring
Purpose: To provide classical training for young dancers and adults
Management: Joyce Karpiej, Director; Dave Fairbanks, Stage Director; Judy McCue, Costume Mistress; Cindy Fairbanks, Production Assistant
Officers: Joyce Karpiej, President; Judy McCue, Vice President; Linda Fraleigh, Secretary; Rosemary Rae, Treasurer
Paid Staff: 4
Paid Artists: 6
Utilizes: Guest Artists; Guest Directors
Budget: $1,000 - $50,000
Income Sources: Private Foundations/Grants/Endowments; Business/Corporate Donations; Box Office; Individual Donations
Season: September - May

INSTRUMENTAL MUSIC

MANCHESTER SYMPHONY ORCHESTRA/CHORALE
PO Box 861, Manchester, CT 06040
(203) 659-8260
Founded: 1960
Arts Area: Symphony; Orchestra; Chorale
Status: Non-Professional; Non-Profit; Volunteer; Community
Type: Performing; Resident
Purpose: To provide a place for talented volunteers to perform; to bring good classical music to the community
Management: Betsy Henderson, Managing Director; Kim Sirois, Publicist
Officers: Charles Morse, President; Ruby Bechtold, Vice President; Nick Mason, Treasurer; Christine Mantie, Secretary
Paid Staff: 2 **Volunteer Staff:** 25
Paid Artists: 4 **Non-Paid Artists:** 150
Utilizes: Guest Conductors; Guest Artists
Budget: $1,000 - $50,000
Income Sources: Private Foundations/Grants/Endowments; Business/Corporate Donations; Box Office; Individual Donations
Season: September - June **Annual Attendance:** 2,500
Affiliations: Artist-in-Residence Manchester High School
Performance Facilities: Manchester High School

THEATRE

MANCHESTER MUSICAL PLAYERS
PO Box 626, Manchester, CT 06045
(203) 649-9065
Founded: 1947
Arts Area: Musical
Status: Semi-Professional; Non-Profit
Type: Performing
Purpose: To produce and present quality musical theatre at reasonable prices and to provide a forum in which our members can perfect and perform their skills
Management: Board of Directors
Officers: Christopher Stone, President; Dianna Burnham, Secretary; William Bengraff, Treasurer; Gail Stone, Fundraising Chairman; Jill Kemp, Publicity Chairman
Volunteer Staff: 33
Non-Paid Artists: 50
Utilizes: Special Technical Talent; Guest Conductors; Guest Directors
Budget: $1,000 - $50,000
Income Sources: Private Foundations/Grants/Endowments; Business/Corporate Donations; Box Office; Individual Donations
Season: April - December **Annual Attendance:** 4,000
Affiliations: East of the River Tourism District
Performance Facilities: Cheney Hall

Middletown

DANCE

DANCES FOR 2
6 Glynn Avenue, Middletown, CT 06457
(203) 346-2210
Founded: 1979
Arts Area: Modern; Ballroom; Ragtime
Status: Professional
Type: Performing; Touring; Educational
Purpose: To perform duet concerts of modern and ballroom choreography using American composers and master teachers of modern technique, composition and ballroom dance
Management: Willie Feuer, Susan Matheke, Artistic Directors
Paid Artists: 2
Utilizes: Guest Artists; Guest Choreographers
Budget: $1,000 - $50,000
Income Sources: Box Office; Individual Donations
Season: 52 Weeks **Annual Attendance:** 1,000
Affiliations: Educational Center for the Arts, Wesleyan University
Performance Facilities: Arts Hall, Wesleyan University

PERFORMING SERIES

WESLEYAN UNIVERSITY CENTER FOR THE ARTS
Wesleyan University, Middletown, CT 06459-0442
(203) 347-9411, ext. 2563
FAX: (203) 344-7948
> **Founded:** 1973
> **Arts Area:** Dance; Vocal Music; Instrumental Music; Theater; Exhibitions
> **Status:** Professional; Non-Profit
> **Type:** Performing; Educational; Sponsoring
> **Purpose:** To provide education in the arts through direct involvement in the artistic process; to enrich and extend the cultural resources of central Connecticut
> **Management:** Jean Shaw, Director
> **Officers:** William M. Chase, President; Raymond Denworth, Chairman, Board of Trustees
> **Paid Staff:** 10 **Volunteer Staff:** 15
> **Paid Artists:** 30
> **Utilizes:** Guest Artists; Guest Directors
> **Budget:** $100,000 - $500,000
> **Income Sources:** Private Foundations/Grants/Endowments; Business/Corporate Donations; Box Office; Government Grants; Individual Donations
> **Season:** September - May **Annual Attendance:** 25,000
> **Performance Facilities:** Wesleyan University Center for the Arts

FACILITY

WESLEYAN UNIVERSITY CENTER FOR THE ARTS
Wesleyan University, Middletown, CT 06459-0442
(203) 347-9411
FAX: (203) 344-7948
> **Founded:** 1973
> **Type of Facility:** Theatre Complex; Concert Hall; Studio Performance; Performance Center; Multi-Purpose; Visual & Performing Arts Classrooms
> **Year Built:** 1970 **Architect:** Roche Dinkeloo Associates **Cost:** $11,900,000
> **Acoustical Consultant:** Bolt, Beranek & Newman
> **Contact for Rental:** University Coordinator;   (203) 347-9411, ext. 2593
> **Manager:** Jean Shaw, Director;   (203) 347-9411, ext. 2563
> *The Center for the Arts is available for rental only on a very limited basis. The 11-building complex is on 6.5 acres and includes the Cinema, Crowell Concert Hall, Theater and World Music Hall. See individual listings for details.*

WESLEYAN UNIVERSITY CENTER FOR THE ARTS - CINEMA
Wesleyan University, Middletown, CT 06459-0442
(203) 347-9411, ext. 2563
FAX: (203) 344-7948
> **Type of Facility:** Film & Lecture Hall
> **Seating Capacity:** 265
> **Contact for Rental:** University Coordinator;   (203) 347-9411, ext. 2593
> **Manager:** Jean Shaw, Director;   (203) 347-9411, ext. 2563
> *Capability for 16mm, 35mm and slides*

WESLEYAN UNIVERSITY CENTER FOR THE ARTS - CROWELL CONCERT HALL
Wesleyan University, Middletown, CT 06459-0442
(203) 347-9411, ext. 2563
FAX: (203) 344-7948
> **Type of Facility:** Concert Hall
> **Type of Stage:** Platform
> **Stage Dimensions:** 48'x23'
> **Seating Capacity:** 400
> **Contact for Rental:** University Coordinator;   (203) 347-9411, ext. 2593
> **Manager:** Jean Shaw, Director;   (203) 347-9411, ext. 2563

WESLEYAN UNIVERSITY CENTER FOR THE ARTS - THEATER
Wesleyan University, Middletown, CT 06459-0442
(203) 347-9411, ext. 2563
FAX: (203) 344-7948
> **Type of Facility:** Theatre House
> **Type of Stage:** Thrust; Flexible; Proscenium; In-the-round Capability
> **Stage Dimensions:** 42'x54'x55'
> **Orchestra Pit**

Seating Capacity: 400-525
Contact for Rental: University Coordinator;   (203) 347-9411, ext. 2593
Manager: Jean Shaw, Director;   (203) 347-9411, ext. 2563

WESLEYAN UNIVERSITY CENTER FOR THE ARTS - WORLD MUSIC HALL
Wesleyan University, Middletown, CT 06459-0442
(203) 347-9411, ext. 2563
FAX: (203) 344-7948
Type of Facility: Concert Hall
Type of Stage: Platform; Carpeted Risers
Seating Capacity: 175
Contact for Rental: University Coordinator;   (203) 347-9411, ext. 2593
Manager: Jean Shaw, Director;   (203) 347-9411, ext. 2563
Originally built to house a Javanese Gamelan Orchestra

New Britain

INSTRUMENTAL MUSIC

NEW BRITAIN SYMPHONY ORCHESTRA
PO Box 1253, New Britain, CT 06050
(203) 621-0316
Founded: 1947
Arts Area: Symphony; Orchestra
Status: Non-Profit
Type: Performing
Management: Jerome Laszloffy, Conductor
Utilizes: Guest Artists
Income Sources: Private Foundations/Grants/Endowments; Business/Corporate Donations; Box Office; Individual Donations
Performance Facilities: Vincent Sala Auditorium, New Britain High School

VOCAL MUSIC

CONNECTICUT CHORALARTISTS, INC.
90 Main Street, New Britain, CT 06051
(603) 224-7500
Founded: 1974
Arts Area: Choral
Status: Professional; Non-Profit
Type: Performing; Touring; Resident; Educational
Purpose: To perform the finest choral music in a professional manner
Management: Catherine Stockuar, Executive Director
Officers: Ray Gialitto, President
Paid Staff: 1   Volunteer Staff: 4
Paid Artists: 50
Utilizes: Guest Conductors
Budget: $100,000 - $500,000
Income Sources: Private Foundations/Grants/Endowments; Business/Corporate Donations; Box Office; Government Grants; Individual Donations
Season: September - June   Annual Attendance: 5,000

GREATER NEW BRITAIN OPERA ASSOCIATION
PO Box 664, New Britain, CT 06050
(203) 223-7557
Founded: 1976
Arts Area: Grand Opera
Status: Professional; Non-Profit
Type: Performing; Resident
Purpose: To showcase young artists in principal roles; to introduce opera to Connecticut youth via work-study programs and class experience
Management: Kenneth A. Larson, General Manager
Officers: Kenneth A. Larson, President; George Zenoble, Vice President; Ursula Gaudette, Secretary; Joseph Geraci, Finance
Volunteer Staff: 40
Paid Artists: 80
Utilizes: Special Technical Talent; Guest Conductors; Guest Directors
Budget: $1,000 - $50,000

Income Sources: Private Foundations/Grants/Endowments; Business/Corporate Donations; Box Office; Government Grants; Individual Donations
Season: September - June

THEATRE

HOLE IN THE WALL THEATRE
10 Harvard Street, New Britain, CT 06051
(203) 229-3049
Founded: 1972
Arts Area: Professional; Musical; Community; Theatrical Group
Status: Professional; Non-Profit
Type: Performing; Resident
Purpose: To bring live theatre to everyone regardless of their ability to pay, donations only at the door
Budget: $1,000 - $50,000
Income Sources: Box Office; Government Grants; Individual Donations
Season: 52 Weeks **Annual Attendance:** 7,000

New Canaan

INSTRUMENTAL MUSIC

THE FAIRFIELD ORCHESTRA
191 Main Street, New Canaan, CT 06840
(203) 972-7400
FAX: (203) 972-7042
Founded: 1981
Arts Area: Orchestra
Status: Professional; Non-Profit
Type: Performing
Purpose: To create, support and develop a classical music orchestra and related ensembles in Fairfield County, Connecticut to be among the finest in the greater New York area; to bring renowned guest artists, modern instrument players and period players to the county; to appeal to all segments of society
Management: Thomas Crawford, Music Director; Amanda C. Fry, Executive Director; Claire Sommers, Production Manager; Andrea Flaks, Box Office Coordinator
Officers: Lawrence D. Pearson, President; Robert E. Enslein, Vice President; John Bartlett, Secretary
Paid Staff: 4 **Volunteer Staff:** 4
Paid Artists: 60
Utilizes: Guest Artists
Budget: $100,000 - $500,000
Income Sources: Private Foundations/Grants/Endowments; Business/Corporate Donations; Box Office; Government Grants; Individual Donations
Season: October - May **Annual Attendance:** 9,000
Performance Facilities: Norwalk Concert Hall

New Fairfield

THEATRE

CANDLEWOOD PLAYHOUSE
Junction of Routes 37 & 39, PO Box 8209, New Fairfield, CT 06812
(203) 746-6557
FAX: (203) 746-6550
Founded: 1983
Arts Area: Professional; Summer Stock; Musical; Theatrical Group
Status: Professional; Non-Profit
Type: Performing; Touring; Resident; Educational
Purpose: To present the finest in musical theatre; to create and develop new works to add to the repertoire
Management: Rick Belzer, Producer
Officers: Rick Belzer, President
Paid Staff: 20 **Volunteer Staff:** 5
Paid Artists: 250 **Non-Paid Artists:** 20
Utilizes: Special Technical Talent; Guest Conductors; Guest Artists; Guest Directors
Budget: $5,000,000 - $10,000,000
Income Sources: Private Foundations/Grants/Endowments; Business/Corporate Donations; Box Office; Individual Donations
Season: June - September **Annual Attendance:** 200,000

New Haven

DANCE

AJDE! FOLK DANCE ENSEMBLE
36 Everit Street, New Haven, CT 06511
(203) 776-2210
Founded: 1965
Arts Area: Folk
Status: Non-Professional; Non-Profit
Type: Performing; Touring
Purpose: To perform traditional European folk dances in authentic costumes
Management: Fred Linton
Non-Paid Artists: 8
Budget: $1,000 - $50,000
Income Sources: Private Foundations/Grants/Endowments
Season: September - June   **Annual Attendance:** 1,500
Affiliations: Arts Council of Greater New Haven

BARBARA FELDMAN AND DANCERS
PO Box 3060, New Haven, CT 06515
(203) 387-0774
Founded: 1981
Arts Area: Modern
Status: Professional
Type: Performing; Touring; Resident; Educational
Purpose: With an emphasis on spirited ensemble dancing and collaborations with composers, BF & D strives to bring innovative modern dance to our audience.
Management: Barbara Feldman, Artistic Director; Tom Haskell, Suzanne Service and Barbara Feldman, Directors
Officers: Barbara Feldman, President; Suzanne Serviss, Secretary
Paid Staff: 2   **Volunteer Staff:** 6
Paid Artists: 6
Utilizes: Special Technical Talent; Guest Artists
Budget: $1,000 - $50,000
Income Sources: Private Foundations/Grants/Endowments; Business/Corporate Donations; Box Office; Government Grants; Individual Donations
Affiliations: Arts Council of Greater New Haven; Connecticut Touring Program; Connecticut Commission on the Arts
Performance Facilities: Educational Center for the Arts; Artspace

INSTRUMENTAL MUSIC

BRASS RING
320 Blatchley Avenue, New Haven, CT 06513
(203) 562-7477
Founded: 1983
Arts Area: Chamber
Status: Professional; Non-Profit
Type: Performing; Touring; Resident; Educational
Purpose: To perform and promote brass chamber music
Management: Hillyer International, New York City - Vincent Wagner
Paid Artists: 5
Utilizes: Guest Artists
Budget: $50,000 - $100,000
Income Sources: Private Foundations/Grants/Endowments; Business/Corporate Donations; Box Office; Government Grants; Individual Donations
Season: September - July   **Annual Attendance:** 5,000
Affiliations: Hartt School of Music; University of Bridgeport

NEW HAVEN CIVIC ORCHESTRA
PO Box 2015, New Haven, CT 06521
(203) 562-0253
Founded: 1940
Arts Area: Symphony; Orchestra; Instrumental Group
Status: Non-Professional; Non-Profit
Type: Performing

Purpose: To give amateur musicians the opportunity to practice and perform good music at a near professional level; to serve the New Haven area with standard, and decidedly non-standard, symphonic repertoire through free concerts
Management: Gordon Emerson, Music Director
Paid Staff: 1
Utilizes: Guest Artists
Budget: $1,000 - $50,000
Income Sources: Private Foundations/Grants/Endowments; Business/Corporate Donations; Individual Donations
Season: September - May
Performance Facilities: Yale University

NEW HAVEN SYMPHONY ORCHESTRA
33 Whitney Avenue, New Haven, CT 06510
(203) 865-0831
FAX: (203) 789-8907
Founded: 1894
Arts Area: Symphony; Orchestra; Ensemble
Status: Professional; Non-Profit
Type: Performing; Touring; Educational; Sponsoring
Purpose: To provide orchestral music to all ages
Management: Catherine Weiskel, General Manager; Michael Palmer, Music Director
Officers: Patrick McFadden, President; John Collaran, Treasurer
Paid Staff: 9   **Volunteer Staff:** 450
Paid Artists: 70
Utilizes: Guest Artists
Budget: $1,000,000 - $5,000,000
Income Sources: Private Foundations/Grants/Endowments; Business/Corporate Donations; Box Office; Government Grants; Individual Donations
Season: October - July
Annual Attendance: 100,000
Performance Facilities: Woolsey Hall

ORCHESTRA NEW ENGLAND
1124 Campbell Avenue, New Haven, CT 06516-2005
(203) 934-8863
FAX: (203) 934-8379
Founded: 1975
Arts Area: Orchestra
Status: Professional; Non-Profit
Type: Performing; Touring
Purpose: To perform the highest quality of music for as many people as possible
Management: James Sinclair, Music Director/Conductor; John McDonald, General Manager
Officers: Walter R. Miller, Chairman; Edward B. Chansky, President
Paid Staff: 3
Budget: $100,000 - $500,000
Income Sources: Private Foundations/Grants/Endowments; Business/Corporate Donations; Box Office; Government Grants; Individual Donations
Season: 52 Weeks
Annual Attendance: 10,000
Affiliations: ASOL
Performance Facilities: Battell Chapel, Yale University

YALE SYMPHONY ORCHESTRA
165 Elm Street, New Haven, CT 06520
(203) 432-4140
Founded: 1965
Arts Area: Symphony; Orchestra
Status: Non-Profit
Type: Performing; Touring; Educational
Purpose: To provide the Yale community a chance both to play and to hear quality classical music
Management: Deborah Gaulrap, Manager; James Russ, Conductor
Paid Staff: 1
Paid Artists: 1   **Non-Paid Artists:** 90
Utilizes: Guest Artists
Budget: $1,000 - $50,000
Season: September - April
Annual Attendance: 12,000
Affiliations: Yale University
Performance Facilities: Woolsey Hall

THEATRE

LONG WHARF THEATRE
222 Sargent Drive, New Haven, CT 06511
(203) 787-4284
FAX: (203) 776-2287
Founded: 1965
Arts Area: Professional
Status: Professional; Non-Profit
Type: Touring; Resident; Educational; Producing
Management: Arvin Brown, Artistic Director; M. Edgar Rosenblum, Executive Director
Officers: G. Newton Schenck, Chairman of Board; Ruth Lord, President; Betty Kubler, Vice President; Patricia Pierce, Treasurer
Paid Staff: 60
Utilizes: Special Technical Talent; Guest Artists; Guest Directors
Budget: $1,000,000 - $5,000,000
Season: October - June
Affiliations: LORT; TCG; Connecticut Commission on the Arts; AEA
Performance Facilities: Long Wharf Theatre

RENAISSANCE THEATER COMPANY
217 Greenwich Avenue, New Haven, CT 06519
(203) 772-2557
Founded: 1978
Arts Area: Theatrical Group
Status: Professional; Non-Profit
Type: Performing; Touring; Educational
Purpose: To produce work of the highest artistic caliber, while promoting understanding, tolerance and friendship among different cultures, races, nationalities and faiths
Management: Dana Sachs, Artistic Director
Officers: Salvatore Pace, President; Alida Engel, Vice President; Kris Sainsbury, Secretary; Dana Sachs, Treasurer
Paid Staff: 2   **Volunteer Staff:** 5
Paid Artists: 6
Utilizes: Guest Artists
Budget: $1,000 - $50,000
Income Sources: Private Foundations/Grants/Endowments; Business/Corporate Donations; Government Grants; Individual Donations
Season: 52 Weeks   **Annual Attendance:** 30,000
Affiliations: New England Foundation for the Arts

YALE REPERTORY THEATRE
222 York Street, New Haven, CT 06520
(203) 432-1515
Founded: 1966
Arts Area: Professional; Theatrical Group
Status: Professional; Non-Profit
Type: Performing; Resident; Educational
Purpose: To produce new American plays, neglected works of the past and classics reviewed through contemporary metaphors
Management: Stan Wojewodski Jr., Artistic Director; Benjamin Mordecai, Managing Director
Utilizes: Guest Artists; Guest Directors
Budget: $1,000,000 - $5,000,000
Income Sources: Private Foundations/Grants/Endowments; Business/Corporate Donations; Box Office; Government Grants; Individual Donations
Season: October - May   **Annual Attendance:** 75,000
Affiliations: AEA; TCG; AAA; LORT; Connecticut Advocates for the Arts
Performance Facilities: Yale Repertory Theatre; University Theatre

FACILITY

LONG WHARF THEATRE
222 Sargent Drive, New Haven, CT 06511
(203) 787-4284
FAX: (203) 776-2287
Type of Facility: Theatre House
Facility Originally: Meat and Produce Terminal
Type of Stage: Thrust; 3/4 Arena
Stage Dimensions: Mainstage - 66'Wx17'D; Thrust - 24'Wx20'Dx18'H

Seating Capacity: 484
Year Remodeled: 1975 **Architect:** Roth and Moore **Cost:** $100,000
Contact for Rental: Janice Muirhead; (203) 787-4284

LONG WHARF THEATRE - STAGE II
222 Sargent Drive, New Haven, CT 06511
(203) 787-4284
Type of Facility: Black Box
Type of Stage: Flexible
Stage Dimensions: 50'x50'x16'
Seating Capacity: 200
Year Built: 1978
Manager: Janice Muirhead

PALACE THEATRE
246-248 College Street, New Haven, CT 06510
(203) 777-3071
Type of Facility: Concert Hall; Performance Center
Facility Originally: Vaudeville
Type of Stage: Thrust; Proscenium
Stage Dimensions: 40'x60'
Orchestra Pit
Seating Capacity: 2,000
Year Remodeled: 1984
Acoustical Consultant: Greg Cocco T.D.
Contact for Rental: (203) 777-3071

SHUBERT PERFORMING ARTS CENTER
247 College Street, New Haven, CT 06510
(203) 624-1825
FAX: (203) 789-2286
Type of Facility: Theatre House
Type of Stage: Proscenium
Stage Dimensions: 91'Wx38'D; 40'Wx30'H proscenium opening
Orchestra Pit
Seating Capacity: 1,629
Year Built: 1914
Year Remodeled: 1984 **Architect:** Bob Wendler **Cost:** $6,000,000
Acoustical Consultant: Jaffe Acoustics
Contact for Rental: Morton Langbord; (203) 624-1825
Manager: Judith Lisi; (203) 624-1825

YALE REPERTORY THEATRE
222 York Street, New Haven, CT 06520
(203) 432-1515
FAX: (203) 432-1550
Type of Facility: Theatre House
Facility Originally: Church
Type of Stage: Thrust; Proscenium
Stage Dimensions: 26'Hx39'Wx20'6"D plus alcove 22'Hx26'Wx18'6"D
Seating Capacity: 487
Year Built: 1872
Year Remodeled: 1975 **Architect:** Patricia Tetrault **Cost:** $500,000
Manager: Benjamin Mordcar
Resident Groups: Yale Repertory Theatre Company

New London

INSTRUMENTAL MUSIC

EASTERN CONNECTICUT SYMPHONY
26 Meridian Street, New London, CT 06320
(203) 443-2876
Founded: 1946
Arts Area: Symphony; Orchestra; Ensemble
Status: Professional
Type: Performing; Educational

Purpose: To provide high-quality musical performances, especially orchestral concerts, to the people of eastern Connecticut
Management: Isabelle G. Singer, Executive Director; Judith Azzinaro, Assistant to the Executive Director; Iris Lampert, Bookkeeper
Officers: Dorothy Askelson, President; Debra Salomonson, Vice President; Tom Castle, Secretary; John Bysko, Treasurer
Paid Staff: 3   **Volunteer Staff:** 6
Utilizes: Special Technical Talent; Guest Conductors; Guest Artists
Budget: $100,000 - $500,000
Income Sources: Private Foundations/Grants/Endowments; Business/Corporate Donations; Box Office; Government Grants; Individual Donations
Season: October - May   **Annual Attendance:** 5,000
Performance Facilities: Garde Arts Center

PERFORMING SERIES

CONNECTICUT EARLY MUSIC FESTIVAL
PO Box 329, New London, CT 06320
(203) 444-2419
Founded: 1983
Arts Area: Dance; Vocal Music; Instrumental Music; Festivals
Status: Professional; Non-Profit
Type: Performing
Purpose: To present an annual fesitval of music from the 1500s to the 1800s, performed on period instruments
Management: Igor Kipnis, John Slocum, Artistic Directors; Richard Wyton, Executive Director
Utilizes: Guest Conductors; Guest Artists
Income Sources: Private Foundations/Grants/Endowments; Business/Corporate Donations; Box Office; Government Grants; Individual Donations
Season: June   **Annual Attendance:** 3,000

CONNETICUT COLLEGE CONCERT AND ARTIST SERIES
PO Box 5331, 270 Mohegan Avenue, New London, CT 06320
Founded: 1939
Arts Area: Dance; Vocal Music; Instrumental Music; Theater; Grand Opera
Status: Professional; Non-Profit
Type: Performing; Presenting
Purpose: To present a varied annual series of the world's great performing artists thereby enriching and enhancing the cultural life of our community
Management: Peggy Middleton, Concert Manager
Officers: John P. Anthony, Chairman Concerts Committee
Paid Staff: 4
Utilizes: Guest Artists
Budget: $100,000 - $500,000
Income Sources: Box Office; Individual Donations; College Subsidy
Season: September - May   **Annual Attendance:** 9,000
Affiliations: APAP; NEP
Performance Facilities: Palmer Auditorium

SUMMER MUSIC, INC.
300 Captain's Walk, Suite 503, New London, CT 06320
(203) 442-9199
FAX: (203) 442-9290
Founded: 1984
Arts Area: Vocal Music; Instrumental Music; Festivals
Status: Non-Profit
Type: Performing
Purpose: To enrich and expand the musical experience of southeastern Connecticut by developing and conducting a summer festival of primarily classical music
Management: Cynde Iverson, Executive Director; Peter Sacco, Music Director; Betsy Carr, General Manager; Keirsten Jenkins, Office Manager; Anne Folino, Box Office Manager
Officers: Jon Kodama, Chairperson; Dr. Lynda Smith, Vice Chairperson; Gail Hamsher, Secretary; Dr. Daniel E. Moalli, Treasurer; Gerald Ceniglio, Executive Committee
Paid Staff: 40   **Volunteer Staff:** 35
Paid Artists: 110
Utilizes: Special Technical Talent; Guest Artists
Budget: $500,000 - $1,000,000
Income Sources: Private Foundations/Grants/Endowments; Business/Corporate Donations; Box Office; Government Grants; Individual Donations
Season: July - August   **Annual Attendance:** 35,000

Affiliations: The Connecticut Orchestra
Performance Facilities: Harkness Park

FACILITY

CONNECTICUT COLLEGE - PALMER AUDITORIUM
270 Mohegan Avenue, PO Box 5331, New London, CT 06320
(203) 439-2787
FAX: (203) 439-2700
    Type of Facility: Concert Hall; Auditorium; Theatre House
    Type of Stage: Proscenium
    Stage Dimensions: 40'x74'x29'   **Orchestra Pit**
    Seating Capacity: 1,298
    Year Built: 1939
    Contact for Rental: Patricia Johnson; (203) 439-2836
    Manager: Peggy Middleton; (203) 439-2708
    Resident Groups: Concert and Artist Series; Theatre One

GARDE ARTS CENTER
325 State Street, New London, CT 06320
(203) 444-6766
FAX: (203) 447-0503
    Founded: 1985
    Type of Facility: Concert Hall; Auditorium; Performance Center; Art Galleries; Office Space
    Facility Originally: Vaudeville; Movie House
    Type of Stage: Proscenium
    Stage Dimensions: 41'x36'   **Orchestra Pit**
    Seating Capacity: 1,545
    Year Built: 1926 **Architect:** Arland Johnson **Cost:** $750,000
    Year Remodeled: 1992 **Architect:** Daniel P. Coffey **Cost:** $10,000,000
    Acoustical Consultant: Jaffe Acoustics
    Contact for Rental: Steve Siegel; (203) 444-6766
    Resident Groups: Eastern Connecticut Symphony Orchestra

New Milford

DANCE

CHILDREN'S DANCE THEATRE OF NEW MILFORD
79 West Street, New Milford, CT 06776
(203) 354-2978
    Founded: 1985
    Arts Area: Modern; Ballet
    Status: Non-Professional; Non-Profit
    Type: Performing; Touring; Educational
    Purpose: To provide performance experience for young dancers; to educate the public; to provide pre-professional training
    Management: Julianne LaFond, Artistic Director; Alexi Tchernichov, Assistant Artistic Director
    Officers: Julianne LaFond, President
    Volunteer Staff: 5
    Non-Paid Artists: 18
    Utilizes: Guest Artists
    Budget: $1,000 - $50,000
    Income Sources: Box Office; Individual Donations
    Season: September - August **Annual Attendance:** 1,000
    Affiliations: LaFond School of Ballet

Newington

THEATRE

NEWINGTON CHILDREN'S THEATRE
131 Cedar Street, Newington, CT 06111
(203) 666-4661
    Founded: 1963
    Arts Area: Musical; Theatrical Group
    Status: Non-Professional; Non-Profit
    Type: Performing; Touring

Purpose: To provide quality theater productions for children by children
Management: Barbara Bianci, Assistant Superintendent of Parks and Recreation
Paid Staff: 3
Non-Paid Artists: 30
Budget: $1,000 - $50,000
Season: February - June **Annual Attendance:** 2,000
Performance Facilities: Newington Auditorium

Norfolk

PERFORMING SERIES

NORFOLK CHAMBER MUSIC FESTIVAL - YALE SUMMER SCHOOL OF MUSIC
Ellen Battell Stoeckel Estate, Norfolk, CT 06058
(203) 542-5537; (203) 432-1966
Founded: 1941
Arts Area: Festivals
Status: Professional; Non-Profit
Type: Performing; Educational
Purpose: To provide chamber-music performances and professional training
Management: Joan Panetti, Executive Director; Michael Geller, Festival Manager
Paid Staff: 10 **Volunteer Staff:** 5
Paid Artists: 45 **Non-Paid Artists:** 5
Budget: $500,000 - $1,000,000
Income Sources: Private Foundations/Grants/Endowments; Business/Corporate Donations; Box Office; Government Grants; Individual Donations; Student Fees
Season: June - August **Annual Attendance:** 12,000
Affiliations: Yale University
Performance Facilities: The Music Shed

Norwalk

INSTRUMENTAL MUSIC

NORWALK SYMPHONY SOCIETY
83 East Avenue, Suite 304, Norwalk, CT 06851
(203) 866-2455
Founded: 1939
Arts Area: Symphony
Status: Semi-Professional; Non-Profit
Type: Performing; Resident
Purpose: To bring quality musical experiences to audiences in southern Connecticut
Management: Rosemary Cook, Executive Director; Jesse Levine, Music Director/Conductor
Officers: J. Robert Flagg, President; Thomas C. Hofstetter, Executive Vice President
Paid Staff: 2 **Volunteer Staff:** 34
Paid Artists: 25 **Non-Paid Artists:** 40
Utilizes: Guest Artists
Budget: $100,000 - $500,000
Income Sources: Private Foundations/Grants/Endowments; Business/Corporate Donations; Box Office; Government Grants; Individual Donations
Season: October - May **Annual Attendance:** 2,500
Affiliations: ASOL
Performance Facilities: Norwalk Concert Hall

NORWALK YOUTH SYMPHONY
PO Box 73, Norwalk, CT 06856-0073
(203) 226-6562
FAX: (203) 227-9494
Founded: 1956
Arts Area: Symphony; Orchestra; Chamber
Status: Non-Profit
Type: Performing; Educational
Purpose: To provide the finest possible orchestral training and performing opportunities for the young people of Fairfield County and surrounding area
Management: Carolyn Monk, Manager
Officers: James Welsch, Chairman; Janet Canning, Eric Lundgren, Vice Chairmen; Sharon Gilbert, Secretary; Maureen Sheehen, Treasurer

Paid Staff: 4   **Volunteer Staff:** 24
Non-Paid Artists: 160
Utilizes: Guest Artists
Budget: $1,000 - $50,000
Income Sources: Private Foundations/Grants/Endowments; Business/Corporate Donations; Box Office; Government Grants; Individual Donations
Season: September - May   **Annual Attendance:** 2,500
Affiliations: ASOL
Performance Facilities: Brien McMahon High School

PERFORMING SERIES

SONO ARTS CELEBRATION, INC.
PO Box 2222, Norwalk, CT 06852
(203) 866-7916
Founded: 1976
Arts Area: Dance; Vocal Music; Instrumental Music; Theater; Festivals
Status: Non-Profit
Type: Performing; Educational
Purpose: To present high-calibre performing and visual arts free to the public; to teach and inspire
Officers: Kathryn Hebert, President; Melissa Pisani, Larry Pisani, Fenn Harvey, Brec Morgan, Marsha Kjoller, Lisa Kohanek, Board Members
Volunteer Staff: 400
Paid Artists: 30
Utilizes: Special Technical Talent; Guest Artists
Budget: $50,000 - $100,000
Income Sources: Private Foundations/Grants/Endowments; Business/Corporate Donations; Individual Donations
Season: August   **Annual Attendance:** 70,000

Oakville

THEATRE

CLOCKWORK REPERTORY THEATRE
133 Main Street, Oakville, CT 06779
(203) 274-7247
Founded: 1977
Arts Area: Theatrical Group
Status: Semi-Professional; Non-Profit
Type: Performing; Resident
Purpose: To produce plays with an emphasis on new American plays depicting controversial events
Management: Harold J. Pantely, Producer; Susan P. Pantely, Artistic Director
Paid Staff: 4   **Volunteer Staff:** 8
Utilizes: Guest Artists; Guest Directors
Budget: $50,000 - $100,000
Income Sources: Private Foundations/Grants/Endowments; Business/Corporate Donations; Box Office; Government Grants; Individual Donations
Season: November - May   **Annual Attendance:** 6,000
Affiliations: NETC

Ridgefield

INSTRUMENTAL MUSIC

RIDGEFIELD SYMPHONY ORCHESTRA
PO Box 613, Ridgefield, CT 06877
(203) 438-3208
Founded: 1964
Arts Area: Symphony
Status: Professional; Non-Profit
Type: Performing
Management: Beatrice Brown, Music Director/Conductor
Officers: Jeanne Cooke, President; William Stopper, Vice President; Frank T. Gellinek, Treasurer
Paid Artists: 68
Utilizes: Guest Conductors; Guest Artists
Budget: $50,000 - $100,000

Income Sources: Private Foundations/Grants/Endowments; Business/Corporate Donations; Box Office; Individual Donations
Season: September - April **Annual Attendance:** 3,600
Affiliations: ASOL; BMI; ASCAP

Salisbury

PERFORMING SERIES

BERKSHIRE HILLS MUSIC AND DANCE ASSOCIATION
PO Box 351, Salisbury, CT 06068
(203) 435-2442
>**Founded:** 1970
>**Arts Area:** Dance; Vocal Music; Instrumental Music
>**Status:** Non-Profit
>**Type:** Sponsoring
>**Purpose:** To foster appreciation of the perfoming arts through the presentation of concerts, recitals and dance attractions of superior quality
>**Officers:** Albert C. Sly, President; Dorothy Massey, Vice President; Heather Schaufele, Secretary; John Estabrook, Treasurer
>**Utilizes:** Guest Artists
>**Budget:** $1,000 - $50,000
>**Income Sources:** Private Foundations/Grants/Endowments; Box Office; Individual Donations
>**Season:** September - April **Annual Attendance:** 1,500

Sharon

THEATRE

EAST-WEST FUSION THEATRE
PO Box 145, Sharon, CT 06069
(203) 364-5220
>**Founded:** 1975
>**Arts Area:** Theatrical Group; Puppet
>**Status:** Professional; Non-Profit
>**Type:** Performing; Touring; Resident; Educational; Sponsoring
>**Purpose:** To bring together artists and scholars from around the world to create a truly international theatre inspired by Asian and other non-Western performing arts and devoted to fusion of the arts
>**Management:** Teviot Fairservis Pourchot, Artistic Director; Dr. Walter A. Fairservis Jr., Producing Director; Amy Schindler, Assistant to the Artistic Director
>**Officers:** Jano Bell Fairservis, President
>**Paid Staff:** 2 **Volunteer Staff:** 50
>**Paid Artists:** 5
>**Utilizes:** Special Technical Talent; Guest Conductors; Guest Artists; Guest Directors
>**Budget:** $50,000 - $100,000
>**Income Sources:** Private Foundations/Grants/Endowments; Business/Corporate Donations; Box Office; Government Grants; Individual Donations
>**Season:** June - August **Annual Attendance:** 8,000
>**Affiliations:** ASSITEJ; ART/NY; DTW
>**Performance Facilities:** Center for East-West Studies

Sherman

THEATRE

SHERMAN PLAYERS
PO Box 404, Sherman, CT 06784
(203) 354-3622
>**Founded:** 1925
>**Arts Area:** Musical; Community; Theatrical Group
>**Status:** Non-Professional; Non-Profit
>**Type:** Performing; Sponsoring
>**Purpose:** To bring high-quality community theatre productions to the area
>**Officers:** George H. Sutton, President; Larry Buoy, Terry Johanesen, Vice Presidents; Betsy Scholze, Treasurer
>**Utilizes:** Special Technical Talent; Guest Directors
>**Budget:** $1,000 - $50,000

Income Sources: Business/Corporate Donations; Box Office; Individual Donations
Season: April - November   **Annual Attendance:** 7,000
Performance Facilities: Sherman Playhouse

FACILITY

SHERMAN PLAYHOUSE
PO Box 471, Sherman, CT 06776
(203) 354-3622
> **Founded:** 1926
> **Type of Facility:** Theatre House
> **Facility Originally:** Church
> **Type of Stage:** Proscenium
> **Seating Capacity:** 120
> **Year Built:** 1832
> **Year Remodeled:** 1974
> **Resident Groups:** Sherman Players

South Windsor

INSTRUMENTAL MUSIC

MANCHESTER PIPE BAND
35 Breezy Hill Road, South Windsor, CT 06074
(203) 644-2709
> **Founded:** 1914
> **Arts Area:** Ethnic; Band
> **Status:** Semi-Professional; Non-Profit
> **Type:** Performing
> **Purpose:** To perform Scottish Pipe Band Music at the highest level of proficiency; to perpetuate this music form
> **Management:** S. Yeomans, President; M. Brannick, Vice President; J. Jones, Secretary; F. Yeomans, Treasurer
> **Officers:** C. Murdoch, Pipe Major; D. Ritchie, Pipe Sargeant; S. Yeomans, Drum Sargeant; D. Ewen, Drum Major
> **Volunteer Staff:** 8
> **Non-Paid Artists:** 20
> **Budget:** $1,000 - $50,000
> **Income Sources:** Business/Corporate Donations; Box Office
> **Season:** 52 Weeks
> **Affiliations:** Eastern U.S. Pipe Band Association

Southington

FACILITY

SOUTHINGTON COMMUNITY THEATRE
PO Box 411, Southington, CT 06489
(203) 621-0071
> **Type of Facility:** Auditorium
> **Type of Stage:** Platform

Stamford

DANCE

CONNECTICUT BALLET THEATRE
PO Box 127, Stamford, CT 06904
(203) 259-3930
> **Founded:** 1981
> **Arts Area:** Modern; Ballet
> **Status:** Professional
> **Type:** Performing; Touring; Educational
> **Purpose:** Classical and contemporary ballet repertory company serving Connecticut and New England
> **Management:** Brett Raphael, Artistic Director
> **Officers:** Ishier Jacobson, Chairman; Brett Raphael, President
> **Paid Staff:** 3   **Volunteer Staff:** 10
> **Paid Artists:** 18

Utilizes: Guest Artists; Guest Choreographers
Budget: $500,000 - $1,000,000
Income Sources: Private Foundations/Grants/Endowments; Business/Corporate Donations; Box Office; Individual Donations
Season: November - May   **Annual Attendance:** 25,000
Performance Facilities: Palace Theatre of the Arts

INSTRUMENTAL MUSIC

STAMFORD SYMPHONY ORCHESTRA
400 Main Street, Stamford, CT 06903
(203) 325-1407
FAX: (203) 325-8762
Founded: 1968
Arts Area: Symphony; Orchestra; Ensemble
Status: Professional; Non-Profit
Type: Performing; Resident; Educational
Purpose: To perform the finest symphony music in the Fairfield County area
Management: Barbara J. Soroca, Executive Director
Officers: Clifford N. Angers, President
Paid Staff: 5   **Volunteer Staff:** 30
Paid Artists: 10
Utilizes: Guest Artists
Budget: $100,000 - $500,000
Income Sources: Private Foundations/Grants/Endowments; Business/Corporate Donations; Box Office; Government Grants; Individual Donations
Season: October - May   **Annual Attendance:** 11,000
Performance Facilities: Palace Theatre of the Arts

THE YOUNG ARTISTS PHILHARMONIC
Ridgeway Station, PO Box 3301, Stamford, CT 06905
(203) 323-0899
Founded: 1960
Arts Area: Orchestra
Status: Non-Professional; Non-Profit
Type: Performing; Educational
Purpose: To develop musical excellence among talented young artists in the area through membership in Young String Ensemble (Elementary), Young People's Orchestra (Middle School) and Young Artists Philharmonic (High School); membership is by audition
Management: Frances Lourie, Manager; Salvatore Princiotti, Musical Director
Paid Staff: 5   **Volunteer Staff:** 30
Non-Paid Artists: 150
Utilizes: Guest Artists
Budget: $1,000 - $50,000
Income Sources: Private Foundations/Grants/Endowments; Business/Corporate Donations; Box Office; Government Grants; Individual Donations
Season: September - May
Performance Facilities: Stamford High School

VOCAL MUSIC

CONNECTICUT GRAND OPERA
61 Atlantic Street, Stamford, CT 06901
(203) 327-2867; (203) 359-0009
Founded: 1978
Arts Area: Grand Opera
Status: Professional
Type: Performing; Resident
Purpose: To develop a permanent professional opera company of international standards in southwestern Connecticut
Management: John Hiddlestone, General Manager
Officers: Sheldon G. Gilgore, Chairman; Frank D. Rich Jr., President; Charles L. Fry, Secretary; Lloyd F. Pierce, Treasurer
Paid Staff: 4
Paid Artists: 120
Utilizes: Special Technical Talent; Guest Conductors; Guest Artists; Guest Directors
Budget: $500,000 - $1,000,000
Income Sources: Private Foundations/Grants/Endowments; Business/Corporate Donations; Box Office; Government Grants; Individual Donations
Season: September - May

Affiliations: AGMA; IATSE
Performance Facilities: Palace Theatre of the Arts; Klein Auditorium

NEW ENGLAND LYRIC OPERETTA
84 West Park Place, Stamford, CT 06901
(203) 324-0240
FAX: (203) 655-0566
Founded: 1986
Status: Professional; Non-Profit
Type: Performing; Resident
Purpose: To perform the full range of European and American operetta
Management: Esme J. Ingledew, General Manager; William H. Edgerton, Artistic Director; Stephen Sulich, Music Director/Conductor; Robert G. Waring, Resident Stage Director
Officers: Ralph L. Rossi, Chairman of the Board; Stephen Pierson, Vice Chairman; William Edgerton, Treasurer
Paid Staff: 3 **Volunteer Staff:** 5
Paid Artists: 75
Utilizes: Special Technical Talent; Guest Artists
Budget: $100,000 - $500,000
Income Sources: Private Foundations/Grants/Endowments; Business/Corporate Donations; Box Office; Government Grants; Individual Donations
Season: September - May **Annual Attendance:** 6,000
Performance Facilities: Palace Theatre

PRO ARTE CHAMBER SINGERS OF CONNECTICUT
PO Box 3635, Stamford, CT 06905
(203) 323-7955
Founded: 1974
Arts Area: Choral
Status: Professional
Type: Performing; Touring
Purpose: To present the range of choral repertoire, from medieval to contemporary times
Management: Cynthia King, Managing Director
Officers: Arthur Congdon, Chairman
Paid Staff: 2 **Volunteer Staff:** 20
Paid Artists: 32
Utilizes: Special Technical Talent
Budget: $50,000 - $100,000
Income Sources: Private Foundations/Grants/Endowments; Business/Corporate Donations; Box Office; Government Grants; Individual Donations
Season: September - June **Annual Attendance:** 1,500
Performance Facilities: First Presbyterian Church

THEATRE

PALACE THEATRE OF THE ARTS
61 Atlantic Street, Stamford, CT 06901
(203) 325-4466
Founded: 1983
Arts Area: Professional; Musical; Theatrical Group
Status: Professional; Commercial
Type: Sponsoring
Management: John Hiddlestone, Facilities Manager; Nancy Koffin, Marketing Director; Vicki Kieffer, House Manager
Paid Staff: 6
Budget: $100,000 - $500,000
Income Sources: Box Office
Season: 52 Weeks
Affiliations: IATSE
Performance Facilities: Palace Theatre

STAMFORD THEATRE WORKS
95 Atlantic Street, Stamford, CT 06901
(203) 359-4414
FAX: (203) 356-1846
Founded: 1988
Arts Area: Professional
Status: Professional; Non-Profit
Type: Performing

Purpose: To produce plays of cultural and social signifigance for the benefit of the greater Stamford area; to build a theatre of regional and national prominence, acclaimed for its innovative productions of contemporary and classical plays
Management: Steve Karp, Artistic/Managing Director; Richard B. Kelley, General Manager; Jane Desy, Literary Manager; Roberta Cohen, Press/Marketing Director
Officers: Steve Karp, President; Robert M. Karp, Vice President; Miriam Burdock Shaw, Secretary/Treasurer; Thomas G. Finck, Chairman of the Board
Paid Staff: 4   **Volunteer Staff:** 10
Paid Artists: 40
Utilizes: Special Technical Talent; Guest Artists; Guest Directors
Budget: $100,000 - $500,000
Income Sources: Private Foundations/Grants/Endowments; Business/Corporate Donations; Box Office; Government Grants; Individual Donations
Season: September - May   **Annual Attendance:** 8,000
Affiliations: AEA; SSDC

FACILITY

PALACE THEATRE - STAMFORD CENTER FOR THE ARTS
61 Atlantic Street, Stamford, CT 06901
(203) 358-0288
Type of Facility: Concert Hall; Theatre House; Opera House
Facility Originally: Vaudeville
Type of Stage: Proscenium
Stage Dimensions: 46'Wx24'D   **Orchestra Pit**
Seating Capacity: 1584
Year Built: 1927   **Architect:** Thomas Lamb
Year Remodeled: 1983   **Architect:** Roger Lang   **Cost:** $2,000,000
Contact for Rental: George Murdock;   (203) 325-0288
Resident Groups: Connecticut Grand Opera; Stamford Symphony Orchestra

Stony Creek

THEATRE

PUPPET HOUSE THEATRE
PO Box 3081, Stony Creek, CT 06405
(203) 488-5752
Founded: 1972
Arts Area: Professional; Summer Stock; Community; Folk; Puppet
Status: Semi-Professional; Non-Professional; Non-Profit
Type: Performing; Touring; Sponsoring
Purpose: To present theatrical programs of community and small professional groups
Management: Barry Fritz, James Weil
Volunteer Staff: 10
Paid Artists: 25   **Non-Paid Artists:** 75
Utilizes: Special Technical Talent; Guest Artists; Guest Directors
Budget: $1,000 - $50,000
Income Sources: Private Foundations/Grants/Endowments; Box Office; Individual Donations
Season: April - December   **Annual Attendance:** 10,000

Storrs

FACILITY

UNIVERSITY OF CONNECTICUT - HARRIET S. JORGENSEN THEATRE
U-127, 802 Bolton Road, Storrs, CT 06269-1127
(203) 486-4025
Type of Facility: Theatre House
Type of Stage: Proscenium
Stage Dimensions: 18'x32'x33'   **Orchestra Pit**
Seating Capacity: 494
Year Built: 1955   **Architect:** Teich   **Cost:** $1,000,000
Acoustical Consultant: Ed Cole
Manager: David R. Kanter, Department Head
Resident Groups: Nutmeg Summer Theatre

UNIVERSITY OF CONNECTICUT - STUDIO THEATRE
Fine Arts Center, Storrs, CT 06269-1127
(203) 486-4025
> **Type of Facility:** Theatre Complex; Studio Performance; Theatre House
> **Type of Stage:** Proscenium
> **Stage Dimensions:** 14'x26'x20'
> **Seating Capacity:** 120
> **Year Built:** 1959   **Architect:** Golden-Storrs Associates
> **Manager:** David R. Kanter, Department Head

Stratford

INSTRUMENTAL MUSIC

THE CLARION BRASS QUINTET
199 College Street, Stratford, CT 06497
(203) 380-2485
> **Founded:** 1976
> **Arts Area:** Chamber; Ensemble; Instrumental Group
> **Status:** Semi-Professional
> **Type:** Performing; Educational
> **Purpose:** To cultivate a deep love of brass music and the desire to bring this music to the people of Connecticut
> **Management:** R. Russell Phillips, Corinne Zanetti, Co-Founders
> **Volunteer Staff:** 5
> **Paid Artists:** 5
> **Utilizes:** Special Technical Talent; Guest Artists
> **Budget:** $1,000 - $50,000
> **Income Sources:** Private Foundations/Grants/Endowments; Business/Corporate Donations; Box Office; Individual Donations
> **Season:** 52 Weeks   **Annual Attendance:** 2,000
> **Affiliations:** Connecticut Touring Program
> **Performance Facilities:** Recital Hall

Torrington

DANCE

NUTMEG BALLET COMPANY
21 Water Street, Torrington, CT 06790
(203) 482-4413
> **Founded:** 1971
> **Arts Area:** Ballet
> **Status:** Semi-Professional; Non-Profit
> **Type:** Performing; Touring; Resident; Educational; Sponsoring
> **Purpose:** To train and provide students with exceptional performance opportunities leading to professional careers in dance and related disciplines
> **Management:** Sharon E. Dante, Artistic Director
> **Officers:** Robert Calabrese, Chairman
> **Paid Staff:** 10   **Volunteer Staff:** 40
> **Paid Artists:** 15   **Non-Paid Artists:** 25
> **Utilizes:** Special Technical Talent; Guest Conductors; Guest Artists; Guest Directors
> **Budget:** $100,000 - $500,000
> **Income Sources:** Private Foundations/Grants/Endowments; Business/Corporate Donations; Box Office; Government Grants; Individual Donations
> **Season:** September - June   **Annual Attendance:** 10,000
> **Performance Facilities:** Warner Theatre/Studio

THEATRE

TORRINGTON CIVIC THEATRE
PO Box 22, Torrington, CT 6790
(203) 482-0073
> **Founded:** 1962
> **Arts Area:** Musical; Community; Theatrical Group
> **Status:** Non-Professional; Non-Profit
> **Type:** Performing
> **Officers:** Chuck Carlin, President

Budget: $1,000 - $50,000
Income Sources: Business/Corporate Donations; Box Office; Individual Donations
Season: November - May Annual Attendance: 1,500
Affiliations: Theatre Guild of Northwest Connecticut
Performance Facilities: Coe Park Civic Center

FACILITY

COE PARK CIVIC CENTER
101 Litchfield Street, Torrington, CT 06790
(203) 489-2274
Type of Facility: Auditorium; Civic Center
Type of Stage: Proscenium
Stage Dimensions: 39'Wx21'D
Seating Capacity: 250
Year Built: 1975 Architect: Tom Babbitt Cost: $450,000
Contact for Rental: John Timm; (203) 489-2274
Resident Groups: Torrington Civic Theatre; T.A.S.S. Theater Group; Rainbow Summer Theater; Torrington Symphony

Wallingford

INSTRUMENTAL MUSIC

WALLINGFORD SYMPHONY ORCHESTRA
333 Christian Street, Wallingford, CT 06492
(203) 269-2699
Founded: 1976
Arts Area: Symphony; Orchestra
Status: Professional; Non-Profit
Type: Performing
Purpose: To provide musical enjoyment for the people of the greater Wallingford area
Officers: Sandra Ulbricht, President
Utilizes: Special Technical Talent; Guest Artists
Budget: $50,000 - $100,000
Income Sources: Private Foundations/Grants/Endowments; Business/Corporate Donations; Box Office; Government Grants; Individual Donations
Season: September - May Annual Attendance: 15,000
Affiliations: Affiliate Artist Program
Performance Facilities: Paul Mellon Arts Center

FACILITY

OAKDALE THEATRE
95 South Turnpike Road, Wallingford, CT 06492
(203) 269-8721
Type of Facility: Concert Hall
Facility Originally: Tent
Type of Stage: In-the-Round
Stage Dimensions: 40'Wx28'D
Seating Capacity: 3184
Year Built: 1953
Year Remodeled: 1973
Contact for Rental: Beau Segal; (203) 269-8721
A wooden dome was constructed over the seating in 1973. No seat in the theatre is more than 70' from the stage.

PAUL MELLON ARTS CENTER
Christian Street, Wallingford, CT 06492
(203) 269-1113
Type of Facility: Concert Hall; Performance Center; Theatre House; Multi-Purpose
Type of Stage: Thrust; Flexible; Proscenium
Stage Dimensions: 90'Wx30'D; 48'Wx36'H proscenium opening Orchestra Pit
Seating Capacity: 850
Year Built: 1972 Architect: I.M. Pei and Partners Cost: $4,700,000

Manager: Terrence Ortwein
The Paul Mellon Arts Center is used by both the Choate School and Rosemary Hall.

Washington

THEATRE

DRAMALITES
PO Box 1117, Washington, CT 06793
 Arts Area: Community
 Status: Non-Professional; Non-Profit
 Type: Performing
 Purpose: To promote community theatre
 Officers: Larry Friedman, President; Mary Adams Childs, Vice President; Phyllis McBride, Secretary; Henry W. Kunhardt, Treasurer
 Budget: $1,000 - $50,000
 Income Sources: Box Office; Individual Donations
 Season: July - August **Annual Attendance:** 1,000
 Performance Facilities: Shepaug Valley Regional School Auditorium

Washington Depot

DANCE

PILOBOLUS DANCE THEATRE
PO Box 388, Washington Depot, CT 06794
(203) 868-0538
 Founded: 1971
 Arts Area: Modern
 Status: Professional; Non-Profit
 Type: Performing; Touring; Resident
 Management: Susan Mandler, Manager; Robby Barnett, Alison Chase, Moses Pendleton, Michael Tracy, Artistic Directors; Jonathan Wolken, Executive Director/Artistic Director
 Paid Staff: 7
 Paid Artists: 5
 Utilizes: Special Technical Talent; Guest Artists
 Budget: $500,000 - $1,000,000
 Income Sources: Private Foundations/Grants/Endowments; Business/Corporate Donations; Box Office; Government Grants; Individual Donations
 Season: September - July
 Performance Facilities: Stamford Center for the Performing Arts

PERFORMING SERIES

ARMSTRONG CHAMBER CONCERTS, INC.
86 Church Hill Road, Washington Depot, CT 06794
(203) 868-0522
 Founded: 1983
 Arts Area: Instrumental Music
 Status: Professional; Non-Profit
 Type: Performing; Touring; Resident; Educational
 Purpose: To perform chamber music of the highest quality, thus broadening the public's understanding of this special kind of music
 Officers: Helen Armstrong, President/Treasurer; Ajit Hutheesing, Vice President; Marvin Ginsky, Secretary
 Paid Staff: 1 **Volunteer Staff:** 4
 Paid Artists: 6
 Utilizes: Guest Artists
 Budget: $1,000 - $50,000
 Income Sources: Private Foundations/Grants/Endowments; Business/Corporate Donations; Box Office; Government Grants; Individual Donations
 Season: October - June **Annual Attendance:** 1,000

Waterbury

INSTRUMENTAL MUSIC

WATERBURY SYMPHONY ORCHESTRA
PO Box 1762, Waterbury, CT 06721
(203) 574-4283
FAX: (203) 756-3507
Founded: 1938
Arts Area: Symphony; Orchestra
Status: Professional
Type: Performing
Purpose: To provide symphonic concerts for the greater Waterbury area
Management: Carol C. Gilbert, Administrative Director
Officers: Direk Barhudt, President; Robert Nocera, Vice President; Robert Griffin, Second Vice President
Paid Staff: 2   **Volunteer Staff:** 100
Paid Artists: 70
Utilizes: Guest Artists
Budget: $100,000 - $500,000
Income Sources: Private Foundations/Grants/Endowments; Business/Corporate Donations; Box Office; Government Grants; Individual Donations
Season: October - May   **Annual Attendance:** 6,000
Performance Facilities: Fine Arts Center, Kennedy High School

---

Waterford

THEATRE

O'NEILL THEATER CENTER
305 Great Neck Road, Waterford, CT 06385
(203) 443-5378
Founded: 1964
Arts Area: Professional; Theatrical Group
Status: Professional; Non-Profit
Type: Performing; Educational; Sponsoring
Management: Sylvia F. Traeger, Manager; Boyd Richards, Artistic Director, National Playwrights Conference
Officers: George C. White, President and Founder
Paid Staff: 30   **Volunteer Staff:** 50
Paid Artists: 75
Utilizes: Guest Artists; Guest Directors
Budget: $1,000,000 - $5,000,000
Income Sources: Private Foundations/Grants/Endowments; Business/Corporate Donations; Box Office; Government Grants; Individual Donations
Season: July - September   **Annual Attendance:** 13,000
Affiliations: LORT
Performance Facilities: O'Neill Theater Center

West Cornwall

DANCE

LOTTE GOSLAR AND COMPANY
39 Town Street, West Cornwall, CT 06796
(203) 672-6042
Arts Area: Modern; Mime; Ballet
Status: Professional; Non-Profit
Type: Performing
Purpose: To perform at colleges, universities and communities; to teach master classes at universities and wherever asked; to give children's concerts and teach children's classes
Officers: Lotte Goslar, Director
Paid Staff: 12
Utilizes: Special Technical Talent
Budget: $100,000 - $500,000
Income Sources: Government Grants
Season: 52 Weeks
Affiliations: NEA Dance Touring Program

West Hartford

INSTRUMENTAL MUSIC

CONNECTICUT STRING ORCHESTRA, INC.
19 Sunset Terrace, West Hartford, CT 06107
(203) 246-9503
Founded: 1968
Arts Area: Orchestra
Status: Non-Professional; Non-Profit
Type: Performing; Resident
Purpose: Community string orchestra
Officers: Thomas P. Kugelman, Librarian; David McMullen, President
Paid Artists: 2 **Non-Paid Artists:** 50
Utilizes: Guest Conductors; Guest Artists
Budget: $1,000 - $50,000
Income Sources: Private Foundations/Grants/Endowments; Business/Corporate Donations; Government Grants; Individual Donations
Season: September - June **Annual Attendance:** 1,000
Performance Facilities: Asylum Hill Congregational Church

PERFORMING SERIES

HARTT SUMMER YOUTH MUSIC FESTIVAL
Hartt School of Music, 200 Bloomfield Avenue, West Hartford, CT 06117
(203) 243-4421
Arts Area: Vocal Music; Instrumental Music
Status: Professional; Non-Profit
Type: Educational; Sponsoring
Purpose: To provide residents of the greater Hartford area with the highest quality musical performances
Management: Neal Smith, Director
Paid Staff: 1
Utilizes: Special Technical Talent; Guest Conductors; Guest Artists
Budget: $50,000 - $100,000
Income Sources: Box Office
Season: June - July
Performance Facilities: Fuller Music Center

FACILITY

LINCOLN THEATER
200 Bloomfield Avenue, West Hartford, CT 06117
(203) 768-4536
FAX: (203) 768-4229
Founded: 1978
Type of Facility: Theatre House
Type of Stage: Thrust; Flexible
Stage Dimensions: 60'x57' **Orchestra Pit**
Seating Capacity: 1,100
Year Built: 1978
Contact for Rental: Raffaella De Gruttola; (203) 768-4536

ROBERTS CENTER THEATRE
170 Kingswood Road, West Hartford, CT 06119
(203) 233-9631
FAX: (203) 232-3843
Type of Facility: Theatre House
Type of Stage: Proscenium
Orchestra Pit
Seating Capacity: 600
Year Built: 1972 **Architect:** Theatre Tech **Cost:** $3,000,000
Contact for Rental: Thomas Burke Jr., Business Manager; (203) 233-9631

Westport

THEATRE

THE FAIRFIELD COUNTY STAGE COMPANY
25 Powers Court, Westport, CT 06880
(203) 227-1072; (203) 227-1290
> **Founded:** 1981
> **Arts Area:** Professional; Theatrical Group
> **Status:** Professional
> **Type:** Performing; Resident
> **Purpose:** Professional regional theatre operating under the Letter of Agreement/LORT "D" Contract with Actors' Equity Association
> **Management:** Burry Fredrick, Artistic Director; Marilyn Hersey, Managing Director; Christopher Cull, Associate Director; Susan Haggstrom, Technical Director
> **Officers:** Rita Fredricks, Board Chairman; Marilyn Hersey, President; Christopher Cull, Secretary; Burry Fredrik, Treasurer
> **Paid Staff:** 11
> **Paid Artists:** 70   **Non-Paid Artists:** 8
> **Utilizes:** Guest Directors
> **Budget:** $500,000 - $1,000,000
> **Income Sources:** Private Foundations/Grants/Endowments; Business/Corporate Donations; Box Office; Government Grants; Individual Donations
> **Season:** October - May
> **Annual Attendance:** 18,000
> **Affiliations:** AEA; SSDC; TCG

WESTPORT COMMUNITY THEATRE
Town Hall, 110 Myrtle Avenue, Westport, CT 06880
(203) 226-1983
> **Founded:** 1956
> **Arts Area:** Community; Theatrical Group
> **Status:** Non-Professional; Non-Profit
> **Type:** Performing
> **Purpose:** To provide entertainment and instruction in the performing art of theatre to the community; to develop an appreciation of theatre amongst our audience
> **Management:** H. Edward Spires, Artistic Manager
> **Officers:** Glenna Kean, Chairman
> **Paid Staff:** 1
> **Utilizes:** Guest Conductors; Guest Directors
> **Budget:** $1,000 - $50,000
> **Income Sources:** Box Office; Individual Donations
> **Season:** 52 Weeks
> **Annual Attendance:** 6,000

WESTPORT COUNTRY PLAYHOUSE
25 Powers Court, PO Box 629, Westport, CT 06880
(203) 227-5137
FAX: (203) 221-7482
> **Founded:** 1930
> **Arts Area:** Professional; Summer Stock
> **Status:** Professional; Non-Profit
> **Type:** Performing; Resident
> **Purpose:** To develop professional theatre in Connecticut
> **Management:** James B. McKenzie, Executive Producer; Julie Monahan, General Manager
> **Officers:** Janet Plotkin, President; Freda Welsh, Vice President; Sharon Giese, Secretary; Wally Meyer, Treasurer
> **Paid Staff:** 50   **Volunteer Staff:** 100
> **Paid Artists:** 100
> **Utilizes:** Guest Artists; Guest Directors
> **Budget:** $1,000,000 - $5,000,000
> **Income Sources:** Private Foundations/Grants/Endowments; Box Office; Individual Donations
> **Season:** June - September
> **Annual Attendance:** 60,000
> **Affiliations:** COST
> **Performance Facilities:** Westport Country Playhouse

PERFORMING SERIES

LEVITT PAVILION FOR THE PERFOMING ARTS
Town Hall, 110 Myrtle Avenue, Westport, CT 06880
(203) 226-7600
FAX: (203) 222-7541
Founded: 1973
Arts Area: Dance; Vocal Music; Instrumental Music; Theater; Lyric Opera
Status: Non-Profit
Type: Performing; Educational
Purpose: To provide 50 nights of high quality entertainment at no admission to audiences of all ages
Management: Michele M. Orris, Managing Director
Officers: Diane Mangano-Cohen, Chairman; Patricia Blaufuss, Vice Chairman; Robert Wettach, Treasurer
Paid Staff: 1 **Volunteer Staff:** 50
Utilizes: Special Technical Talent
Budget: $50,000 - $100,000
Income Sources: Private Foundations/Grants/Endowments; Business/Corporate Donations; Box Office; Government Grants; Individual Donations; Membership; Civic Organizations
Season: June - August **Annual Attendance:** 50,000
Performance Facilities: Levitt Pavilion for the Performing Arts

FACILITY

LEVITT PAVILION FOR THE PERFORMING ARTS
Off Jesup Road, behind New Westport Library, Westport, CT 06880
(203) 226-7600
FAX: (203) 222-7541
Mailing Address: c/o Westport Town Hall, 110 Myrtle Avenue, Westport, CT 06880
Founded: 1973
Type of Facility: Outdoor (Concert); Outdoor Performance Stage; Bandshell
Seating Capacity: 2,500 lawn seating
Year Built: 1973 **Architect:** Bruce Campbell Graham
Year Remodeled: 1992 **Architect:** Bruce Campbell Graham

WESTPORT COMMUNITY THEATRE
110 Myrtle Avenue, Westport, CT 06880
(203) 226-1983
Type of Facility: Auditorium; Environmental
Facility Originally: School
Type of Stage: 3/4 Arena
Stage Dimensions: 26'x23'
Seating Capacity: 185
Year Remodeled: 1978 **Architect:** H. Edward Spires **Cost:** $65,000
Resident Groups: Westport Community Theatre

WESTPORT COUNTRY PLAYHOUSE
25 Powers Court, PO Box 629, Westport, CT 06880
(203) 227-5137
FAX: (203) 221-7482
Founded: 1931
Type of Facility: Theatre House
Facility Originally: Business Facility; Tanning Factory
Type of Stage: Proscenium
Stage Dimensions: 16'x30'x26'
Seating Capacity: 706
Year Built: 1930 **Architect:** Throckmortan **Cost:** $400,000
Contact for Rental: Julie Monahan; (203) 227-5137
Manager: James B. McKenzie; (202) 227-5137

Wilton

THEATRE

THE WILTON PLAYSHOP
15 Lovers Lane, Wilton, CT 06897
(203) 762-7629
Founded: 1937

Arts Area: Theatrical Group
Status: Non-Professional
Type: Performing; Educational
Purpose: To provide fine theatre at reasonable prices; to educate and train members so that quality continues
Management: Carol Albert, President, Board of Directors; Jane Kelly, Business Manager; Pat Gould, Secretary
Officers: Kay Strakosh, President, Board of Trustees; Sigh Schneid, Secretary; Carole Harris, Business Manager
Volunteer Staff: 50
Non-Paid Artists: 300
Utilizes: Guest Artists; Guest Directors
Budget: $1,000 - $50,000
Income Sources: Private Foundations/Grants/Endowments; Business/Corporate Donations; Box Office; Individual Donations
Season: 52 Weeks

DELAWARE

Bear
VOCAL MUSIC

DIAMOND STATE CHORUS OF SWEET ADELINES INTERNATIONAL
42 Craig Road, Bear, DE 19701
(302) 322-6445
FAX: (302) 378-0935
Founded: 1978
Arts Area: Choral
Status: Semi-Professional; Non-Profit
Type: Performing; Educational
Purpose: To entertain and educate the public in the American art form of barber shop harmony
Management: Becky Diamond, Chorus Manager
Officers: Emily Pinder, President; Louisa Leipold, Vice President; Sylvia Taggart, Secretary; Celia Renai, Treasurer
Paid Staff: 1 **Volunteer Staff:** 12
Non-Paid Artists: 50
Utilizes: Special Technical Talent; Guest Artists
Budget: $1,000 - $50,000
Income Sources: Box Office
Season: 52 Weeks

Dover
DANCE

DELAWARE REGIONAL BALLET
1071 Governors Avenue, PO Box 160, Dover, DE 19901
(302) 674-1020
Founded: 1973
Arts Area: Ballet; Jazz
Status: Non-Professional; Non-Profit
Type: Performing
Management: Tatjana Akinfieva-Smith, Artistic Director; Marion Tracy, Administration Director
Officers: Ellie Boone, President
Non-Paid Artists: 35
Utilizes: Guest Artists; Guest Choreographers
Budget: $1,000 - $50,000
Income Sources: Private Foundations/Grants/Endowments; Business/Corporate Donations; Box Office; Individual Donations
Season: September - May

Georgetown
THEATRE

POSSUM POINT PLAYERS
Old Laurel Highway, PO Box 96, Georgetown, DE 19947
(302) 856-3460
Founded: 1973
Arts Area: Musical; Dinner; Community; Theatrical Group
Status: Non-Professional; Non-Profit
Type: Performing; Educational
Purpose: To produce and perform high-quality theatrical productions in Sussex County, Delaware
Management: Andre Beaumont, Executive Director; Mary Cahill, Adminstrative Assistant
Officers: Nina Galerstein, President; Anne Maloney, Vice President; Rhonda Sharman, Secretary; William Thompson, Treasurer
Paid Staff: 1 **Volunteer Staff:** 2
Non-Paid Artists: 50
Utilizes: Guest Directors
Budget: $50,000 - $100,000
Income Sources: Private Foundations/Grants/Endowments; Business/Corporate Donations; Box Office; Government Grants; Individual Donations

Season: 52 Weeks   **Annual Attendance:** 3,800
Affiliations: Delaware Theater Association
Performance Facilities: Possum Hall; Delaware Tech Theater; Millsboro Civic Center

---

Newark

DANCE

THE DANCE NETWORK
East Delaware Avenue and Haines Street, Newark, DE 19711
(302) 368-0365
Founded: 1980
Arts Area: Modern
Status: Semi-Professional; Non-Profit
Type: Performing; Touring; Resident; Educational; Sponsoring
Management: Linda Moores, Director; Dave Fardig, Assistant
Utilizes: Special Technical Talent; Guest Artists; Guest Directors; Guest Choreographers
Budget: $1,000 - $50,000
Income Sources: Private Foundations/Grants/Endowments; Business/Corporate Donations; Box Office; Government Grants; Individual Donations

DELAWARE DANCE COMPANY
22 Prestbury Square Building, Newark, DE 19713
(302) 731-9615
Founded: 1982
Arts Area: Modern; Ballet
Status: Professional; Non-Profit
Type: Performing; Touring; Educational
Purpose: To provide quality dance performances throughout Delaware, Maryland and Pennsylvania while providing a venue for emerging artists (dancers, choreographers and musicians) to hone their professional skills
Management: Priscilla R. Payson, Director; Anne Horgan and Catherine Samardza, Ballet Mistresses; Rick Webster, General Manager; Camille Izard, Artistic Advisor
Officers: Priscilla R. Payson, President; Janan Crouse, Secretary; Jennifer Reynolds, Treasurer
Paid Staff: 2   **Volunteer Staff:** 10
Paid Artists: 6   **Non-Paid Artists:** 30
Utilizes: Special Technical Talent; Guest Artists; Guest Choreographers
Budget: $50,000 - $100,000
Income Sources: Box Office; Individual Donations
Season: September - June   **Annual Attendance:** 10,000
Performance Facilities: Dickinson Theatre; Delaware Theatre Company

INSTRUMENTAL MUSIC

NEWARK SYMPHONY ORCHESTRA
PO Box 7775, Newark, DE 19714
(302) 366-8491
FAX: (302) 368-4419
Founded: 1966
Arts Area: Symphony
Status: Non-Professional; Non-Profit
Type: Performing
Purpose: To provide volunteer musicians the opportunity to play symphonic literature and the community to hear live performances
Officers: Vernon Vernier, President, Board of Directors; Jean Unrun, Vice President; Frank Mazlewski, Treasurer; Carolyn Fuhrman, Secretary
Paid Staff: 3
Paid Artists: 15   **Non-Paid Artists:** 80
Utilizes: Guest Artists
Budget: $1,000 - $50,000
Income Sources: Private Foundations/Grants/Endowments; Business/Corporate Donations; Box Office; Government Grants; Individual Donations
Season: October - May   **Annual Attendance:** 3,500
Affiliations: University of Delaware
Performance Facilities: University of Delaware

Wilmington

INSTRUMENTAL MUSIC

DELAWARE SYMPHONY ASSOCIATION
PO Box 1870, Wilmington, DE 19899
(302) 656-7374
Founded: 1929
Arts Area: Symphony; Orchestra; Chamber; Ensemble; Instrumental Group
Status: Professional; Non-Profit
Type: Performing; Educational
Purpose: To present quality symphonic music which educates, inspires, challenges and entertains a diverse and expanding range of individuals
Management: Curtis Long, Executive Director
Officers: Bernard Lochtenberg, Chairman; Robert B. Rickards, President
Paid Staff: 8
Paid Artists: 85
Utilizes: Guest Conductors; Guest Artists
Budget: $1,000,000 - $5,000,000
Income Sources: Private Foundations/Grants/Endowments; Business/Corporate Donations; Box Office; Government Grants; Individual Donations
Season: September - May   **Annual Attendance:** 60,000
Affiliations: ASOL
Performance Facilities: Grand Opera House

DICKINSON THEATRE ORGAN SOCIETY
1801 Milltown Road, Wilmington, DE 19808
(302) 995-2603
Founded: 1970
Status: Professional; Semi-Professional; Non-Profit
Type: Sponsoring
Purpose: To present theatre organ concerts on the theatre pipe organ in the Dickinson High School Auditorium
Management: Connie Mead, Chairman of Publicity
Officers: Robert E. Dilworth, President; Paul Pringle, Vice President; Karl Keller, Secretary; Rad Mead, Treasurer
Volunteer Staff: 30
Paid Artists: 8
Utilizes: Guest Artists
Budget: $1,000 - $50,000
Income Sources: Private Foundations/Grants/Endowments; Business/Corporate Donations; Box Office; Individual Donations
Season: September - June   **Annual Attendance:** 5,000
Performance Facilities: Dickinson High School Auditorium

VOCAL MUSIC

THE DELAWARE SINGERS
1715 Sycamore Street, Wilmington, DE 19805
(302) 652-2977
Founded: 1984
Arts Area: Choral
Status: Professional
Type: Performing; Touring; Resident; Educational
Purpose: To establish and maintain a standard of choral excellence; to expand awareness of the scope and character of choral music; to encourage the pursuit of professional choral singing
Management: Jean Scalessa, Artistic Director/Founder; Raymond Egan, Music Director/Conductor
Officers: F.L. Peter Stone Esq., President; Sandra Curley-Edstrom, Vice President; Denise Ross, Recording Secretary; Elizabeth Joyce, Treasurer; Joyce Adams, Correspondence
Paid Staff: 2   **Volunteer Staff:** 4
Paid Artists: 16   **Non-Paid Artists:** 24
Utilizes: Guest Conductors; Guest Artists
Budget: $1,000 - $50,000
Income Sources: Private Foundations/Grants/Endowments; Business/Corporate Donations; Box Office; Government Grants; Individual Donations
Season: September - June   **Annual Attendance:** 2,000
Affiliations: CA

MADRIGAL SINGERS OF WILMINGTON
Faith Presbyterian Church, 720 Marsh Road, Wilmington, DE 19803
(215) 358-0946
FAX: (215) 358-5789
> **Founded:** 1959
> **Arts Area:** Choral
> **Status:** Semi-Professional; Non-Profit
> **Type:** Performing; Touring; Educational
> **Purpose:** To present Renaissance and other chamber music, a capella and accompanied, by singers and musicians in period costumes, for the enrichment of the community
> **Management:** Virginia Vaalburg, Director
> **Officers:** Barbara Tilton, President of Board; Carolyn Zoldos-Crowell, Secretary of Board; Brian Hanson, Treasurer of Board
> **Paid Staff:** 1   **Volunteer Staff:** 6
> **Non-Paid Artists:** 20
> **Utilizes:** Guest Artists   **Budget:** $1,000 - $50,000
> **Income Sources:** Private Foundations/Grants/Endowments; Box Office; Government Grants; Individual Donations
> **Season:** 52 Weeks   **Annual Attendance:** 2,000

NORTHERN DELAWARE ORATORIO SOCIETY
2603 Pike Creek Road, Wilmington, DE 19808
(302) 737-1082
> **Founded:** 1970
> **Arts Area:** Choral
> **Status:** Non-Professional; Non-Profit
> **Type:** Performing; Resident; Educational
> **Purpose:** To provide a learning experience for our members; to present reasonably priced, high-level concerts for our audiences
> **Management:** Jean Mosteller, Business Manager; Sheila and Calvin Bourgeault, Artistic Directors
> **Officers:** Robert Mahr, President
> **Paid Staff:** 2   **Volunteer Staff:** 12
> **Paid Artists:** 6   **Non-Paid Artists:** 100
> **Utilizes:** Guest Artists
> **Budget:** $1,000 - $50,000
> **Income Sources:** Box Office; Government Grants; Individual Donations
> **Season:** September - May   **Annual Attendance:** 1,000
> **Performance Facilities:** Grace United Methodist Church

OPERA DELAWARE
St. Andrews Episcopal Church, 719 North Shipley Street, Wilmington, DE 19801-1726
(302) 658-8063
> **Founded:** 1948
> **Arts Area:** Grand Opera
> **Status:** Semi-Professional
> **Type:** Performing; Educational
> **Purpose:** To perform professional grand opera with full orchestra
> **Management:** Eric W. Kjellmark, General Director; Leland Kimball, Artistic Director; Donna Shopa, Public Relations
> **Officers:** Ann Houseman, President; Harry Glaze, Vice President; David Nayes, Treasurer; Geneve Yates, Secretary
> **Paid Staff:** 1   **Volunteer Staff:** 15
> **Paid Artists:** 130   **Non-Paid Artists:** 90
> **Utilizes:** Special Technical Talent; Guest Conductors; Guest Artists; Guest Directors
> **Budget:** $500,000 - $1,000,000
> **Income Sources:** Private Foundations/Grants/Endowments; Business/Corporate Donations; Box Office; Government Grants; Individual Donations
> **Season:** November - May   **Annual Attendance:** 9,000
> **Affiliations:** OA; COS; AAA
> **Performance Facilities:** Grand Opera House

THEATRE

ARTISTS THEATRE ASSOCIATION
PO Box 7258, Wilmington, DE 19803
(302) 798-8775
> **Founded:** 1968
> **Arts Area:** Musical; Community; Theatrical Group
> **Status:** Non-Professional; Non-Profit
> **Type:** Performing

Purpose: To promote the dramatic arts; to encourage the writing of new plays; to present workshop presentations with high school student participation
Officers: Michelle Fay, President; Kathy Bratton, Vice President; Thomas M. Marshall, Treasurer; Barbara Bradbury, Secretary
Volunteer Staff: 100
Non-Paid Artists: 100
Utilizes: Guest Conductors; Guest Directors
Budget: $1,000 - $50,000
Income Sources: Business/Corporate Donations; Box Office; Individual Donations
Season: February - October   **Annual Attendance:** 2,000
Affiliations: Delaware Theatre Association; Delaware Alliance for Arts Education

DELAWARE THEATRE COMPANY
200 Water Street, Wilmington, DE 19801
(302) 594-1104
FAX: (302) 594-1107
Founded: 1978
Arts Area: Professional; Musical; Theatrical Group
Status: Professional; Non-Profit
Type: Performing; Educational
Purpose: The DTC is a cultural, educational, and community service organization whose purpose is to create theatre of the highest professional quality in Delaware.
Management: Cleveland Morris, Artistic Director; David Edelman, Managing Director
Officers: John S. Garrett, Jr., Chairman of the Board; Peter H. Flint, President; Robert C. Forney, Treasurer; Susan Townsend, Secretary
Paid Staff: 10   **Volunteer Staff:** 100
Paid Artists: 35
Utilizes: Guest Artists; Guest Directors
Budget: $1,000,000 - $5,000,000
Income Sources: Private Foundations/Grants/Endowments; Business/Corporate Donations; Box Office; Government Grants; Individual Donations
Season: October - April   **Annual Attendance:** 26,084
Performance Facilities: The Delaware Theatre Company

SHOESTRING PRODUCTIONS, LIMITED
214 West 18th Street, Wilmington, DE 19802
(302) 655-0299
Founded: 1978
Arts Area: Musical; Theatrical Group
Status: Professional
Type: Performing; Touring; Educational
Purpose: To create, produce and tour original musicals for young audiences that entertain and educate
Management: Deborah Dehart, Artistic Director
Officers: Deborah Dehart, President; Charles Conway, Vice President; Judith Conway, Corresponding Secretary; Joseph Kinsolving, Recording Secretary; Susan Zaleski, Treasurer
Volunteer Staff: 3
Paid Artists: 10
Utilizes: New Productions
Budget: $1,000 - $50,000
Income Sources: Private Foundations/Grants/Endowments; Box Office
Season: 52 Weeks   **Annual Attendance:** 22,000

WILMINGTON DRAMA LEAGUE
PO Box 504, Wilmington, DE 19899
(302) 764-1172
Founded: 1933
Arts Area: Community; Theatrical Group
Status: Non-Professional; Non-Profit
Type: Performing; Educational
Purpose: To provide low-cost, quality theatre, theatrical activities, and education to the city of Wilmington and surrounding communities
Management: Laurie Bailey, Ray Jackson, Richard Kane, Judy Marsey, Jack Murphy, Directors at Large; David Reynolds, George Spillane, Ruby Stanley, Bob Winters, Directors at Large; Barbara Reynold, Office Manager
Officers: Bob Evans, President; Jeff Williams, Greg Tigani, Steve Robinson, Rob Tietze, Vice Presidents; Helen Rolph, Bill Rolph, Charles Houghton, Curtis King, Sue Webster, Vice Presidents; Dennis Williams, Treasurer; Sally Waslick, Secretary
Paid Staff: 1
Utilizes: Special Technical Talent
Budget: $50,000 - $100,000

Income Sources: Private Foundations/Grants/Endowments; Business/Corporate Donations; Box Office; Government Grants; Individual Donations
Season: September - June **Annual Attendance:** 10,500
Affiliations: Delaware Arts Council; Delaware Theatre Association; AACT

PERFORMING SERIES

GRAND OPERA HOUSE
818 Market Street, Wilmington, DE 19801
(302) 658-7897
Founded: 1973
Arts Area: Dance; Vocal Music; Instrumental Music; Theater; Lyric Opera; Grand Opera
Status: Professional; Non-Profit
Type: Performing; Educational; Sponsoring
Purpose: To present top-quality international performing artists and showcase local professional performers
Management: David W. Fleming, Executive Director
Officers: Alexander F. Giacco, Chairman of the Board; Philip Syng Reese, President; H. Rodney Sharp III, Vice President; Marilyn R. Hayward, Secretary; Basil L. Anderson, Treasurer
Paid Staff: 23 **Volunteer Staff:** 200
Utilizes: Special Technical Talent; Guest Artists
Budget: $1,000,000 - $5,000,000
Income Sources: Private Foundations/Grants/Endowments; Business/Corporate Donations; Box Office; Government Grants; Individual Donations
Season: September - July **Annual Attendance:** 75,000
Affiliations: APAP; League of Historic American Theatres
Performance Facilities: Grand Opera House

FACILITY

GRAND OPERA HOUSE
818 Market Street, Wilmington, DE 19801
(302) 658-7897
Type of Facility: Concert Hall; Opera House
Type of Stage: Thrust; Proscenium
Stage Dimensions: 70'Wx40'D (12'D thrust); 38'Wx25'H proscenium opening **Orchestra Pit**
Seating Capacity: 1,110
Year Built: 1871 **Architect:** Charles Carson, Thomas Dickson **Cost:** $125,300
Year Remodeled: 1976 **Architect:** Armstrong Child & Grieves **Cost:** $6,500,000
Acoustical Consultant: Roger Morgan
Contact for Rental: Marilyn Bacon; (302) 658-7897
Resident Groups: Opera Delaware; Delaware Symphony
The Opera House is a member of the League of Historic American Theatres.

THE PLAYHOUSE THEATRE
Tenth and Market Streets, DuPont Building, Wilmington, DE 19801
(302) 656-4401
FAX: (302) 656-2145
Type of Facility: Theatre House
Type of Stage: Proscenium
Orchestra Pit
Seating Capacity: 1,250
Year Built: 1913
Contact for Rental: Patricia Dill; (302) 656-4401

DISTRICT OF COLUMBIA

Washington

DANCE

AFRICAN DANCE FESTIVAL FOR KANKOURAN WEST AFRICAN DANCE CO.
c/o Kankouran, 1709 Lang Place NE, Washington, DC 20002
(202) 737-4941; (202) 396-0841
> **Arts Area:** Ethnic
> **Status:** Professional; Non-Profit
> **Type:** Performing
> **Purpose:** To perpetuate and preserve African culture
> **Management:** Assane Konte, Artistic Director; Abbou Kounta, Music Director
> **Budget:** $100,000 - $500,000
> **Income Sources:** Private Foundations/Grants/Endowments; Business/Corporate Donations; Box Office; Government Grants; Individual Donations
> **Performance Facilities:** Stables Art Center

CAPITOL BALLET COMPANY
1200 Delafield Place NW, Washington, DC 20011
(202) 882-4039
> **Founded:** 1961
> **Arts Area:** Ballet
> **Status:** Professional; Non-Profit
> **Type:** Resident
> **Officers:** Audrey Dickerson, President; Shirley Massengale, Vice President
> **Non-Paid Artists:** 12
> **Utilizes:** Special Technical Talent; Guest Artists; Guest Choreographers
> **Budget:** $1,000 - $50,000
> **Income Sources:** Private Foundations/Grants/Endowments; Business/Corporate Donations; Box Office; Individual Donations
> **Season:** September - May

D.C. CONTEMPORARY DANCE THEATRE
1410 Eighth NW, 3rd Floor, Washington, DC 20004
(202) 783-7126
FAX: (202) 393-0156
> **Founded:** 1984
> **Arts Area:** Modern; Ballet; Jazz
> **Status:** Professional; Non-Profit
> **Type:** Performing; Touring; Resident
> **Purpose:** To maintain a multiracial, cross-cultural repertory company perpetuating contemporary American choreography
> **Management:** Miya Hisaka, Artistic Director
> **Paid Staff:** 4
> **Paid Artists:** 10
> **Utilizes:** Guest Artists; Guest Choreographers
> **Budget:** $100,000 - $500,000
> **Income Sources:** Private Foundations/Grants/Endowments; Business/Corporate Donations; Box Office; Government Grants; Individual Donations
> **Season:** September - June

DANCE EXCHANGE
1746-B Kalorama NW, Washington, DC 20009
(202) 232-0833
FAX: (202) 745-7077
> **Arts Area:** Modern
> **Status:** Professional; Non-Profit
> **Type:** Performing; Touring; Resident; Educational
> **Purpose:** An intergenerational dance company, promoting the idea that dance is for everyone
> **Management:** Liz Lerman, Artistic Director; Kimberli Boyd, Associate Artistic Director; Bob Fogelgren, General Manager
> **Officers:** Ronald Eichner, Chairman
> **Budget:** $100,000 - $500,000
> **Income Sources:** Private Foundations/Grants/Endowments; Business/Corporate Donations; Box Office; Government Grants; Individual Donations

DANCE PLACE
3225 Eighth Street NE, Washington, DC 20017
(202) 269-1600
> **Founded:** 1980
> **Arts Area:** Modern; Ethnic
> **Status:** Professional; Non-Profit
> **Type:** Performing; Touring; Resident; Educational; Sponsoring
> **Purpose:** To improve social conditions through educational and cultural programs of contemporary and ethnic dance and arts forms
> **Management:** Carla Perlo, Executive/Artistic Director; Lesa McLaughlin, Associate Artistic Director; Deborah Riley, Public Relations; Sharon Mansur, Development/Box Office; Stefan Johnson, Technical Director; Daniel Burkholder, Associate Technical Director
> **Officers:** Richard Pilkinton, Chairman; David Sparkman, Vice Chairman; Carla Perlo, Secretary; Steve Bloom, President; Phil Schonberger, Capital Campaign Chair
> **Paid Staff:** 7 **Volunteer Staff:** 35
> **Utilizes:** Guest Artists; Guest Choreographers
> **Budget:** $100,000 - $500,000
> **Income Sources:** Private Foundations/Grants/Endowments; Business/Corporate Donations; Box Office; Government Grants; Individual Donations
> **Season:** 52 Weeks

LIZ LERMAN EXCHANGE
1746 Kalorara Road NW, Washington, DC 20009
(202) 232-0833
> **Founded:** 1976
> **Arts Area:** Modern
> **Status:** Professional; Non-Profit
> **Type:** Performing; Touring; Resident; Educational
> **Purpose:** Dance Exchange is based on the belief that the skills, discipline, expression, and beauty of dance can be a part of everyone's life. Two companies, Liz Lerman and the Dance Exchange and The Dancers of the Third Age, have performed at a wide variety of locations in the United States and Europe.
> **Management:** Liz Lerman, Artistic Director; Robert Fogelgren, General Manager; Barbara Greenfield, Executive Director; Kimberli Boyd, Associate Director
> **Officers:** Ronald Eichner, Chairman of the Board
> **Paid Staff:** 5 **Volunteer Staff:** 4
> **Paid Artists:** 19
> **Utilizes:** Special Technical Talent; Guest Choreographers
> **Budget:** $100,000 - $500,000
> **Income Sources:** Private Foundations/Grants/Endowments; Business/Corporate Donations; Box Office; Government Grants; Individual Donations
> **Season:** 52 Weeks   **Annual Attendance:** 100,000
> **Affiliations:** Dance USA; Cultural Alliance of Greater Washington

MICHELLE AVA AND COMPANY
3000 Connecticut Avenue NW, Washington, DC 20008
(202) 328-8092
> **Founded:** 1976
> **Arts Area:** Modern; Jazz
> **Status:** Professional; Non-Profit
> **Type:** Performing; Touring; Educational
> **Purpose:** To promote movement as a healing art
> **Management:** Michelle Ava, Artistic Director
> **Utilizes:** Guest Artists; Guest Choreographers
> **Budget:** $50,000 - $100,000
> **Income Sources:** Private Foundations/Grants/Endowments; Box Office; Individual Donations
> **Season:** September - June
> **Performance Facilities:** Joy of Motion Dance Center

THE WASHINGTON BALLET
3515 Wisconsin Avenue NW, Washington, DC 20016
(202) 362-3606; (202) 362-1683
FAX: (202) 362-1311
> **Founded:** 1976
> **Arts Area:** Ballet
> **Status:** Professional
> **Type:** Performing; Touring
> **Purpose:** To present a unique blend of classical and contemporary ballet

Management: Mary Day, Founder/Artistic Director; Elvi Moore, General Director; Kevin McKenzie,
Lupe Serrano, Artistic Associates
Officers: Frank E. Loy, President
Paid Staff: 18   **Volunteer Staff:** 4
Utilizes: Special Technical Talent; Guest Conductors
Budget: $1,000,000 - $5,000,000
Income Sources: Private Foundations/Grants/Endowments; Business/Corporate Donations; Box Office; Government
Grants; Individual Donations
Season: September - June
Performance Facilities: John F. Kennedy Center for the Performing Arts

INSTRUMENTAL MUSIC

AMERICAN SYMPHONY ORCHESTRA LEAGUE
777 14th Street NW, Suite 500, Washington, DC 20005
(202) 628-0099
FAX: (202) 783-7228
Founded: 1942
Arts Area: Symphony; Orchestra; Chamber
Status: Professional; Non-Profit
Type: Educational; Sponsoring
Purpose: A national service organization serving symphony and chamber orchestras, working to ensure artistic excellence
and administrative effectiveness for large and small orchestras, the ASOL offers a variety of training programs and other
necessary services.
Management: Catherine French, Chief Executive Officer; Donald Thulean, Vice President of Orchestra Services
Officers: Mrs. Ben M. Birkhead
Paid Staff: 38
Budget: $1,000,000 - $5,000,000
Income Sources: Private Foundations/Grants/Endowments; Business/Corporate Donations; Government Grants;
Individual Donations   **Season:** 52 Weeks

CHARLIN JAZZ SOCIETY, INC.
2025 I Street NW, Suite 501, Washington, DC 20006
(202) 331-9404
Founded: 1979
Arts Area: Orchestra; Ensemble; Instrumental Group; Band
Status: Professional; Non-Profit
Type: Performing; Touring; Resident; Educational
Purpose: To nourish jazz as a national treasure
Management: Linda S. Wernick-Cassell, Director
Officers: Charles I. Cassell, President; Julie Van Blarcom, Secretary; Glenn Williams, Treasurer
Paid Staff: 3   **Volunteer Staff:** 3
Utilizes: Guest Artists; Guest Directors
Budget: $100,000 - $500,000
Income Sources: Private Foundations/Grants/Endowments; Business/Corporate Donations; Box Office; Government
Grants; Individual Donations
Season: 52 Weeks   **Annual Attendance:** 10,500
Affiliations: Washington Performing Arts Society; Ellington School of the Arts; WCDU-FM;
George Washington University
Performance Facilities: John F. Kennedy Center for the Performing Arts, Lissner Auditorium;
Ellington School of the Arts

CONTEMPORARY MUSIC FORUM
1690 36th Street NW, Suite 408, Washington, DC 20007
(202) 333-4529
Founded: 1973
Arts Area: Chamber
Status: Non-Profit
Type: Performing; Resident
Purpose: To present contemporary music to the greater Washington area
Management: Helmut Braunlich, Personnel Director; Tony Stark, Program Director
Officers: James McKay, Chairman; Penny Farley, Vice Chairman; Ann Stansbury, Secretary
Paid Staff: 1   **Volunteer Staff:** 20
Paid Artists: 10
Utilizes: Guest Artists   **Budget:** $1,000 - $50,000
Income Sources: Private Foundations/Grants/Endowments; Business/Corporate Donations; Box Office; Government
Grants; Individual Donations
Season: September - May   **Annual Attendance:** 200
Performance Facilities: Armand Hammes Auditorium; Corcoran Gallery

D.C. YOUTH ORCHESTRA PROGRAM, INC.
PO Box 56198, Brightwood Station, Washington, DC 20011
(202) 723-1612
Founded: 1960
Arts Area: Symphony; Orchestra; Chamber
Status: Non-Profit
Type: Performing; Touring; Educational
Purpose: To maintain an instrumental music training center for children ages 5-19
Management: Lyn McLain, Director; Carol Rende, Assistant Director for Administration; Erika Schulte,
Assistant Director for Music; Wing-Chi Chan, Director of Development
Officers: Nsia Opare, President; Patricia Silvey, Vice President; Patricia R. Johnson, Treasurer; Lyn McLain,
Executive Secretary Ex-Officio; Ed Arnold APR; Stuart L. Graham
Utilizes: Guest Artists
Budget: $1,000,000 - $5,000,000
Income Sources: Private Foundations/Grants/Endowments; Business/Corporate Donations; Box Office; Government
Grants; Individual Donations; Fundraising
Annual Attendance: 5,000
Affiliations: ASOL Youth Orchestra Division

NATIONAL GALLERY ORCHESTRA
National Gallery of Art, Washington, DC 20565
(202) 737-4215
FAX: (202) 842-2407
Founded: 1941
Arts Area: Symphony; Orchestra; Chamber; Ensemble
Status: Non-Profit
Type: Performing
Purpose: To provide free concerts for the public at the National Gallery of Art
Management: George Manos, Music Director
Paid Staff: 4
Paid Artists: 55
Utilizes: Guest Artists
Income Sources: Private Foundations/Grants/Endowments; Business/Corporate Donations
Season: October - June   **Annual Attendance:** 6,000
Performance Facilities: Museum Garden Courts, National Gallery

NATIONAL MUSICAL ARTS
2101 Constitution Avenue NW, Washington, DC 20016
(301) 946-0355
Founded: 1980
Arts Area: Chamber; Ensemble
Status: Professional; Non-Profit
Type: Performing; Touring; Resident
Purpose: To present rarely-heard chamber music masterpieces in the context of the traditional repertoire with emphasis on
little-known works and composers of American origin; to collaborate with foreign embassies to present music of specific
countries
Officers: Dr. Charles Cleland, Chairman of the Board; Dr. Patricia Gray, President; James Tavares, Secretary;
Chris Griner, Treasurer
Volunteer Staff: 15
Paid Artists: 10
Utilizes: Special Technical Talent; Guest Conductors; Guest Artists
Budget: $50,000 - $100,000
Income Sources: Private Foundations/Grants/Endowments; Business/Corporate Donations; Government Grants;
Individual Donations
Season: September - May   **Annual Attendance:** 3,500
Affiliations: CMA
Performance Facilities: National Academy of Sciences Auditorium

NATIONAL SYMPHONY ORCHESTRA ASSOCIATION
John F. Kennedy Center for the Performing Arts, Washington, DC 20566
(202) 416-8100
Founded: 1930
Arts Area: Symphony; Orchestra; Chamber
Status: Non-Profit
Type: Performing; Touring
Purpose: To foster, promote and increase the musical knowledge and appreciation of the public by organizing and present-
ing performances of symphonic and other music

Management: Mstislav Rostropovich, Music Director; Stephen Klein, Executive Director
Officers: Albert J. Beveridge III, President; Daniel K. Mayers, Immediate Past President; F. David Fowler, Vice President; Samuel Lehrman, Treasurer/Chairman of Finance Committee; Mrs. John E. Chapoton, Secretary
Paid Staff: 12
Paid Artists: 106
Utilizes: Guest Conductors; Guest Artists
Budget: Over 10,000,000
Income Sources: Private Foundations/Grants/Endowments; Business/Corporate Donations; Box Office; Government Grants; Individual Donations
Season: 52 Weeks
Annual Attendance: 1,000,000
Affiliations: ASOL; John F. Kennedy Center for the Performing Arts
Performance Facilities: John F. Kennedy Center for the Performing Arts - Concert Hall; Wolf Trap Farm Park for the Performing Arts; West Lawn, United States Capitol

THEATER CHAMBER PLAYERS OF THE KENNEDY CENTER
John F. Kennedy Center for the Performing Arts, Washington, DC 20566
(202) 667-4470; (202) 338-3102
Founded: 1968
Arts Area: Chamber
Status: Professional
Type: Performing; Touring; Resident; Educational
Purpose: Presenting outstanding music of the 20th century in relation to the music of the past, the philosophy is that, in our time, new music is best appreciated when heard in company with music of other periods, illustrating lines of continuity between the past and the present.
Management: Leon Fleisher, Dina Koston, Directors; Anita Leong, General Manager
Paid Staff: 1   **Volunteer Staff:** 10
Paid Artists: 27
Season: October - May
Affiliations: CMA; Cultural Alliance of Greater Washington
Performance Facilities: John F. Kennedy Center for the Performing Arts - Terrace Theater

THE UNITED STATES AIR FORCE BAND
Bolling Air Force Base, Washington, DC 20332-6458
(202) 767-4224
FAX: (202) 767-0686
Founded: 1941
Arts Area: Symphony; Orchestra; Chamber; Ensemble; Instrumental Group; Electronic & Live Electronic; Band
Status: Professional; Non-Profit
Type: Performing; Touring
Purpose: The United States Air Force Band performs national and international concert tours to support Air Force and Department of Defense public awareness, community relations objectives and international understanding.
Management: Lieutenant Colonel Alan L. Bonner, Commander/Conductor; Capt. Mark R. Peterson, Vice Commander; Allan P. Waite Jr., The Singing Sergeants Director; Capt. Kevin D. Smith, The Air Force Strings Director; Capt. Robert A. Pouliot, Executive Officer
Paid Staff: 35
Paid Artists: 186
Utilizes: Special Technical Talent; Guest Artists
Season: 52 Weeks
Annual Attendance: 1,800,000
Affiliations: ASOL; MENC; National Bandmasters Association; American Bandmasters Association
Performance Facilities: DAR Constitution Hall

WASHINGTON CHAMBER SYMPHONY
1099 22nd Street NW, #602, Washington, DC 20037
(202) 452-1321
FAX: (202) 728-1134
Arts Area: Symphony; Chamber
Status: Professional; Non-Profit
Type: Performing; Touring; Resident; Educational; Sponsoring
Purpose: To promote classical music; to educate a new generation of audience
Management: Bonnie Ward Simon, Executive Director; Stephen Simon, Music Director/Conductor
Officers: Kathryn Donaldson Baker, Chairman of the Board
Budget: $500,000 - $1,000,000
Income Sources: Private Foundations/Grants/Endowments; Business/Corporate Donations; Box Office; Government Grants; Individual Donations
Performance Facilities: John F. Kennedy Center for the Performing Arts

VOCAL MUSIC

CHORAL ARTS SOCIETY OF WASHINGTON
4321 Wisconsin Avenue NW, Washington, DC 20016
(202) 244-3669
FAX: (202) 244-4244
> **Founded:** 1965
> **Arts Area:** Choral
> **Status:** Non-Professional; Non-Profit
> **Type:** Performing; Resident
> **Purpose:** The Choral Arts Society is dedicated to the highest ideals of excellence in choral programming and performance
> **Management:** Norman Scribner, Music Director; Judith Brophy, Executive Director; Johnnye Egnot, Director of Operations; Robert Schiller, Director of Public Relations and Marketing
> **Officers:** Lou Durden, Chairman; Albert Beveridge, Mrs. Morris C. Hover Jr., Barbara Rossotti, Vice Chairmen; Anne B. Keiser, Secretary; G. Bradford Cook, Treasurer
> **Paid Staff:** 4 **Volunteer Staff:** 2
> **Paid Artists:** 1
> **Utilizes:** Special Technical Talent; Guest Conductors; Guest Artists
> **Budget:** $500,000 - $1,000,000
> **Income Sources:** Private Foundations/Grants/Endowments; Business/Corporate Donations; Box Office; Government Grants; Individual Donations
> **Season:** October - May **Annual Attendance:** 15,000
> **Performance Facilities:** John F. Kennedy Center for the Performing Arts

DISTRICT CURATORS, INC.
PO Box 14197, Washington, DC 20044
(202) 783-0360
FAX: (202) 783-4185
> **Arts Area:** Ethnic
> **Status:** Non-Profit
> **Type:** Presenting
> **Purpose:** To present the finest of the new performing arts to audiences in Washington, DC and the mid-Atlantic region; to advance cultural opportunities for artists and audiences worldwide
> **Management:** Bill Warrell, Executive Director; Katea Stitt, Producer
> **Officers:** Byrne Murphy, Chairman of the Board
> **Budget:** $100,000 - $500,000
> **Income Sources:** Private Foundations/Grants/Endowments; Business/Corporate Donations; Box Office; Government Grants; Individual Donations

NATIONAL LYRIC OPERA COMPANY
5332 Sherrier Place NW, Washington, DC 20016
(202) 244-5041
> **Founded:** 1978
> **Arts Area:** Grand Opera; Lyric Opera; Operetta; Choral
> **Status:** Semi-Professional; Non-Profit
> **Type:** Performing
> **Purpose:** To provide performances to the general public at reasonable prices; to provide a showcase for up-and-coming artists
> **Management:** Nikita Wells, General Manager/Artistic Director; Ruben Vartanyan, Conductor/Music Director; Sidney Yudain, Chairman of the Board
> **Officers:** Armaud Weiss, Business Manager; Michael Reilly, Secretary
> **Volunteer Staff:** 10
> **Paid Artists:** 10 **Non-Paid Artists:** 60
> **Utilizes:** Guest Artists
> **Budget:** $1,000 - $50,000
> **Income Sources:** Private Foundations/Grants/Endowments; Business/Corporate Donations; Box Office; Government Grants; Individual Donations
> **Season:** October - June **Annual Attendance:** 3,000
> **Performance Facilities:** Lisner Auditorium; Warner Theatre

THE PAUL HILL CHORALE/THE WASHINGTON SINGERS
5630 Connecticut Avenue NW, #200, Washington, DC 20015
(202) 364-4321
FAX: (202) 362-2453
> **Founded:** 1967
> **Arts Area:** Choral
> **Status:** Professional; Semi-Professional; Non-Profit
> **Type:** Performing

Purpose: To present choral music concerts
Management: Lunette Arledge, Managing Director; Felicia Burrey, Director of Public Relations; Dennis Martin, Stage Manager/Director of Development; Kathryn Hartzler, Director of Group Sales; Marcia Milleville, Accountant
Officers: John H. Buchanan Jr., Chairman; Robert G. Heiss, President; Jean M. Riddell, Edith W. Seashore, Vice Presidents; Raymond J. Kimball, Secretary; Janene S. Mitchell, Treasurer
Volunteer Staff: 6
Paid Artists: 18   **Non-Paid Artists:** 140
Utilizes: Guest Artists
Budget: $100,000 - $500,000
Income Sources: Private Foundations/Grants/Endowments; Business/Corporate Donations; Box Office; Government Grants; Individual Donations; Events
Season: September - June
Annual Attendance: 14,000
Performance Facilities: John F. Kennedy Center for the Performing Arts - Concert Hall

SUMMER OPERA THEATRE COMPANY
620 Michigan Avenue NE, Washington, DC 20064
(202) 526-1669
Founded: 1978
Arts Area: Grand Opera; Lyric Opera; Operetta
Status: Professional; Non-Profit
Type: Performing; Resident; Educational
Management: Elaine R. Walter PhD, Founder/General Manager
Officers: Constance Donohoe, Chairman of the Board; Thomas L. Helinsk Jr., Vice Chairman; Edith Shubert, Chairman-Emeritus; Dena C. Feeney Esq., Secretary/Treasurer
Paid Staff: 2   **Volunteer Staff:** 2
Paid Artists: 150
Utilizes: Special Technical Talent; Guest Conductors; Guest Artists
Budget: $100,000 - $500,000
Income Sources: Private Foundations/Grants/Endowments; Business/Corporate Donations; Box Office; Government Grants; Individual Donations
Season: July - August
Affiliations: The Catholic University of America
Performance Facilities: Harthe Theatre

WASHINGTON BACH CONSORT
1690 36th Street NW, Washington, DC 20007
(202) 337-1202
FAX: (202) 337-2268
Founded: 1977
Arts Area: Choral; Orchestral
Status: Professional; Non-Profit
Type: Performing; Touring; Educational
Purpose: To present the highest quality performances of the music of J.S. Bach to both national and international audiences; to contribute to the music education of school children
Management: Jane E. Arenberg, General Manager
Officers: Ann Meier, President; Robert Inglis, Treasurer; Craig Hosmer, Secretary
Paid Staff: 2   **Volunteer Staff:** 10
Paid Artists: 66
Utilizes: Guest Artists
Budget: $100,000 - $500,000
Income Sources: Private Foundations/Grants/Endowments; Business/Corporate Donations; Box Office; Government Grants; Individual Donations
Season: October - June   **Annual Attendance:** 5,000

WASHINGTON OPERA
John F. Kennedy Center for the Performing Arts, Washington, DC 20566
(202) 416-7890; (202) 416-7800
FAX: (202) 416-7857
Founded: 1956
Arts Area: Grand Opera; Lyric Opera; Light Opera; Operetta
Status: Professional; Non-Profit
Type: Performing; Resident; Educational
Purpose: To produce opera of the highest standard in the nation's capitol
Management: Martin Feinstein, General Director; Edward Turrington, Administrative Director
Officers: Paul Dragoumis, President; Mrs. Eugene V. Casey, Chairperson, Board of Trustees
Paid Staff: 34   **Volunteer Staff:** 20
Paid Artists: 75
Utilizes: Special Technical Talent; Guest Conductors; Guest Artists; Guest Directors

Budget: Over 10,000,000
Income Sources: Private Foundations/Grants/Endowments; Business/Corporate Donations; Box Office; Government Grants; Individual Donations
Season: November - March   **Annual Attendance:** 97,000
Affiliations: Washington Opera Guild/Educational
Performance Facilities: John F. Kennedy Center for the Performing Arts

WASHINGTON SINGERS
c/o National Choral Foundation, 5630 Connecticut Avenue NW, Suite 200, Washington, DC 20015
(202) 364-4321
FAX: (202) 362-2453
   Arts Area: Choral
   Status: Professional; Non-Profit
   Type: Performing
   Purpose: To present the full range of repertoire for chamber chorus, specializing in 20th-century music
   Management: Paul Hill, Conductor; Lunette Arledge, Managing Director
   Officers: Robert G. Heiss, President of the Board
   Budget: $100,000 - $500,000
   Income Sources: Private Foundations/Grants/Endowments; Business/Corporate Donations; Box Office; Government Grants; Individual Donations

THEATRE

ARENA STAGE
Sixth and Maine Avenue SW, Washington, DC 20024
(202) 554-9066
FAX: (202) 488-4056
   Founded: 1950
   Arts Area: Professional
   Status: Professional; Non-Profit
   Type: Performing; Educational
   Purpose: To perform the best theatre for Washingtonians
   Management: Douglas C. Wager, Artistic Director; Stephen Richard, Executive Director; Guy Bergquist, General Manager; Regan Byrne, Director of Communications
   Officers: Denie S. Weil, President; Carlton D. Lewis, Stephen Richard, Jaan Whitehead, Vice Presidents; Jonathan M. Weisgall, Secretary; Bert I. Helfinstein, Treasurer
   Paid Staff: 150
   Paid Artists: 17
   Utilizes: Guest Directors
   Budget: $5,000,000 - $10,000,000
   Income Sources: Private Foundations/Grants/Endowments; Business/Corporate Donations; Box Office; Government Grants; Individual Donations
   Season: September - June   **Annual Attendance:** 250,000
   Affiliations: AEA; SSDC
   Performance Facilities: Arena Stage: Arena Theater, Kreeger Theater, Old Vat Theatre

FORD'S THEATRE SOCIETY
511 Tenth Street NW, Washington, DC 20004
(202) 638-2941
FAX: (202) 347-6269
   Founded: 1968
   Arts Area: Professional; Musical
   Status: Professional; Non-Profit
   Type: Performing; Educational
   Purpose: To present live theatre productions as a tribute to Abraham Lincoln's love of the performing arts
   Management: Frankie Hewitt, Executive Producer
   Officers: William McSweeny, Chairman
   Paid Staff: 20
   Budget: $1,000,000 - $5,000,000
   Income Sources: Private Foundations/Grants/Endowments; Business/Corporate Donations; Box Office; Government Grants; Individual Donations
   Season: 52 Weeks
   Performance Facilities: Ford's Theatre

GALA HISPANIC THEATRE
PO Box 43209, Washington, DC 20010
(202) 234-7174
   Arts Area: Theatrical Group

Status: Professional; Non-Profit
Type: Resident; Educational
Purpose: To expand and promote Hispanic culture in the United States
Management: Hugo Medrano, Artistic Producing Director; Abel Lopez, Associate Producing Director
Budget: $100,000 - $500,000
Income Sources: Private Foundations/Grants/Endowments; Business/Corporate Donations; Box Office; Government Grants; Individual Donations
Performance Facilities: GALA Hispanic Theatre

HORIZONS THEATRE
PO Box 50204, Washington, DC 20091
(202) 265-6574
Founded: 1976
Arts Area: Theatrical Group
Status: Professional; Non-Profit
Type: Performing; Touring; Resident; Educational
Purpose: To give women artists a forum; to provide women playwrights a broader audience; to offer audiences professional theatre conceived and performed from a woman's viewpoint
Management: Ginger Moss, General Manager; Leslie Jacobson, Artistic Director; Nancy Tartt, Associate Art Director; Marian DiJulio, Literary Manager
Officers: Pat Hawkins, Chairman; Ida Prosky, Vice Chairman; Eda Edgerton, Treasurer
Paid Staff: 3 **Volunteer Staff:** 3
Utilizes: Special Technical Talent; Guest Directors
Budget: $50,000 - $100,000
Income Sources: Private Foundations/Grants/Endowments; Business/Corporate Donations; Box Office; Government Grants; Individual Donations
Season: 52 Weeks **Annual Attendance:** 7,600
Affiliations: League of Washington Theatres; Cultural Alliance of Washington, DC

LIVING STAGE
Sixth Street and Maine Avenue SW, Washington, DC 20024
(202) 554-9066
Founded: 1966
Arts Area: Theatrical Group
Status: Professional; Non-Profit
Type: Resident
Purpose: To bring the art of theatre to people who do not normally have access to the arts
Management: Robert Alexander, Artistic Director; Catherine Irwin, Managing Director
Budget: $100,000 - $500,000
Income Sources: Private Foundations/Grants/Endowments; Business/Corporate Donations; Box Office; Government Grants; Individual Donations
Season: December - June
Performance Facilities: The Living Stage Theatre

NATIONAL THEATRE
1321 Pennsylvania Avenue NW, Washington, DC 20004
(202) 783-6854
Founded: 1835
Arts Area: Professional; Musical; Community; Folk; Puppet
Status: Professional; Non-Profit; Commercial
Type: Educational; Sponsoring
Purpose: To preserve the historic playhouse; to present Class-A legitimate touring productions; to showcase non-professional and professional groups in second stage
Management: Donn B. Murphy, Executive Director; Harry Teter Jr., General Manager
Officers: Donn B. Murphy, President; Jay Adams, Chair
Paid Staff: 10 **Volunteer Staff:** 5
Paid Artists: 500 **Non-Paid Artists:** 100
Utilizes: Special Technical Talent; Guest Artists
Budget: $500,000 - $1,000,000
Income Sources: Private Foundations/Grants/Endowments; Business/Corporate Donations; Box Office; Individual Donations
Season: 52 Weeks **Annual Attendance:** 40,000
Affiliations: AEA; IATSE; The Shubert Organization

THE SHAKESPEARE THEATRE
450 Seventh Street NW, Washington, DC 20004
(202) 547-3230; (202) 393-2700
FAX: (202) 547-0226
Founded: 1970

Arts Area: Professional; Theatrical Group
Status: Professional; Non-Profit
Type: Performing; Resident
Purpose: To present quality classical and Shakespearean productions in an intimate 447-seat theatre
Management: Michael Kahn, Artistic Director; Jessica Andrews, Managing Director; Beth Hauptle,
Director of Public Relations and Marketing
Officers: Lawrence A. Hugh, Chairman; Daniel W. Toohey, Vice Chairman; Emily Malino Scheuer, Secretary;
James B. Adler, Treasurer
Paid Staff: 50
Utilizes: Special Technical Talent; Guest Artists; Guest Directors
Budget: $5,000,000 - $10,000,000
Income Sources: Private Foundations/Grants/Endowments; Business/Corporate Donations; Box Office; Government
Grants; Individual Donations
Season: October - June   Annual Attendance: 60,000
Affiliations: League of Washington Theatres; Cultural Alliance of Greater Washington
Performance Facilities: The Shakespeare Theatre at the Lansburgh

SOURCE THEATRE COMPANY
1835 17th Street NW, Washington, DC 20009
(202) 462-1073
FAX: (202) 462-0676
Founded: 1977
Arts Area: Professional; Theatrical Group
Status: Professional; Non-Profit
Type: Performing; Touring; Resident
Purpose: To provide the community with exciting and innovative productions of new plays as well as contemporary plays
that are particularly relevant to our community; to reinterpret the classics
Management: Pat Murphy Sheehy, Producing Artistic Director; Keith Parker, Literary Manager
Officers: Michael Winston, Chairman; Ted Gay, Vice Chairman; Malcolm Smith, Treasurer; Virginia Knight, Secretary
Paid Staff: 9   Volunteer Staff: 26
Paid Artists: 120   Non-Paid Artists: 320
Utilizes: Special Technical Talent; Guest Artists; Guest Directors; Guest Designers
Budget: $100,000 - $500,000
Income Sources: Private Foundations/Grants/Endowments; Business/Corporate Donations; Box Office; Government
Grants; Individual Donations
Season: 52 Weeks   Annual Attendance: 15,000
Affiliations: TCG; AEA

THE STUDIO THEATRE
1333 P Street NW, Washington, DC 20005
(202) 232-7267
Founded: 1975
Arts Area: Professional; Theatrical Group
Status: Professional; Non-Profit
Type: Performing; Educational; Sponsoring
Purpose: The Studio Theatre is committed to creating the best in contemporary theatre—area premieres of American and
European works, revivals, and solo performance art. The Studio Theatre is an energetic, eclectic urban theatre focused on
the primacy of performance, intimacy between actor and audience, and high production values. The Studio Theatre Second-
stage nutures emerging artists by providing a creative home for them, free of commercial consideration. The Studio Thea-
tre Acting Conservatory trains actors to their fullest potential.
Management: Joy Zinoman, Artistic Director/Managing Director/Founder; Keith Allan Baker,
Associate Managing Director/Artistic Director of Secondstage
Officers: Nancy Linn Patton, Chairperson; Ronald V. McGowan, Vice Chairperson; Irene Harriet Blum,
Chairperson Emeritus
Paid Staff: 20   Volunteer Staff: 250
Paid Artists: 250
Utilizes: Guest Artists; Guest Directors
Budget: $1,000,000 - $5,000,000
Income Sources: Private Foundations/Grants/Endowments; Business/Corporate Donations; Box Office; Government
Grants; Individual Donations; Special Events; Tuition
Season: September - June   Annual Attendance: 50,000
Affiliations: TCG; Cultural Alliance of Greater Washington; League of Washington Theatres
Performance Facilities: The Studio Theatre; The Secondstage

THE WASHINGTON STAGE GUILD
4048 Seventh Street NE, #4, Washington, DC 20017-1939
Founded: 1986
Arts Area: Professional; Theatrical Group
Status: Professional; Non-Profit

Type: Performing; Resident; Educational
Purpose: To perform plays that are often overlooked, including lesser-known works of famous playwrights, classics, and new plays of merit
Management: John MacDonald, Producing Artistic Director; Ann Norton, Executive Director; William Largess, Dramaturge
Paid Staff: 5 **Volunteer Staff:** 10
Paid Artists: 50
Utilizes: Special Technical Talent
Budget: $100,000 - $500,000
Income Sources: Private Foundations/Grants/Endowments; Business/Corporate Donations; Box Office; Government Grants; Individual Donations
Season: September - June **Annual Attendance:** 8,000
Affiliations: AEA; League of Washington Theatres; Cultural Arts Alliance of DC
Performance Facilities: Carroll Hall

WOOLLY MAMMOTH THEATRE COMPANY
1401 Church Street NW, Washington, DC 20005
(202) 393-3939
Founded: 1980
Arts Area: Professional; Musical; Theatrical Group
Status: Professional; Non-Profit
Type: Performing; Resident; Educational
Purpose: To present the most daring and experimental plays in the Washington, DC area.
Management: Howard Shalwitz, Artistic Director; Molly White, Associate Director; Nancy Turner Hensley, Producing Associate
Officers: John Mendonca, President; Sunny Jung Scully, Vice President; Jeffrey B. Stern, Secretary; Sheldon Repp, Treasurer
Paid Staff: 6 **Volunteer Staff:** 400
Paid Artists: 5 **Non-Paid Artists:** 65
Utilizes: Special Technical Talent; Guest Artists; Guest Directors
Budget: $500,000 - $1,000,000
Income Sources: Private Foundations/Grants/Endowments; Business/Corporate Donations; Box Office; Government Grants; Individual Donations
Season: October - July
Annual Attendance: 15,000
Affiliations: TCG
Performance Facilities: Woolly Mammoth Theatre

PERFORMING SERIES

DUMBARTON CONCERT SERIES
3133 Dumbarton Street NW, Washington, DC 20007
(202) 965-2000
FAX: (202) 338-9008
Arts Area: Instrumental Music
Status: Non-Profit
Type: Presenting
Purpose: To present Washinton's best performers in the beautiful historic environment of Dumbarton Church; to promote an extensive outreach program in the community called LIVE MUSIC NOW!
Management: Connie Zimmer, Executive Director; Katy O'Keefe, Producer; Susan Osburn, Associate Producer
Budget: $50,000 - $100,000
Income Sources: Private Foundations/Grants/Endowments; Business/Corporate Donations; Box Office; Government Grants; Individual Donations
Performance Facilities: Dumbarton Church

JOHN F. KENNEDY CENTER FOR THE PERFORMING ARTS
2700 F Street NW, Washington, DC 20566
(202) 872-0466
Authorized: 1958 **Opened:** 1971
Arts Area: Dance; Theater; Grand Opera; Vocal Music; Instrumental Music; Lyric Opera; Musical Theater
Status: Non-Profit; Professional
Purpose: The John F. Kennedy Center for the Performing Arts was authorized by an Act of Congress in 1958 as the National Cultural Center. Since opening its doors in 1971, the Center has operated seven days a week, 365 days a year, and welcomed more than 60 million visitors from all parts of the United States and the world. The Center attracts the most talented national and international stars of dance, theater and music, and entertains, educates and serves millions of Americans across the country through television programs, its touring productions and its education and public service programs.

Board of Trustees: Under the terms of the National Cultural Act of 1958 (as amended in 1964), the Kennedy Center is administered by a Board of Trustees as a separate, independent and self-sustaining bureau of the Smithsonian Institution. This 45-member Board of Trustees is composed of 30 Presidential appointees who serve 10-year overlapping terms. The 15 remaining members are legislatively designated, serving by virtue of their specific public office. The present members of the Board the Board of Trustees are:
Honorary Chairmen: Mrs. George Bush; Mrs. Ronald Reagan; Mrs. Jimmy Carter; Mrs. Gerald R. Ford; Mrs. Richard M. Nixon; Mrs. Lyndon B. Johnson; Mrs. Aristotle Onassis
Officers: James D. Wolfensohn, Chairman; James. H. Evans, Vice Chairman; Leonard L. Silverstein, Vice Chairman; Lawrence J. Wilker, Managing Director; Jean Kennedy Smith, Secretary; Charlotte Woolard, Assistant Secretary; Paul G. Stern, Treasurer; Henry Strong, Assistant Treasurer; Kenneth M. Kaufman, General Counsel; William Becker, Associate Counsel
Members Appointed by the President: Philip F. Anschutz; Mrs. Bennett Archambault; Mrs. Howard H. Baker, Jr.; Mrs. William Cafritz; Ralph P. Davidson; Kenneth Duberstein; James H. Evans; Mrs. Max M. Fisher; Robert Fryer; Mrs. Joseph B. Gildenhorn; Lionel Hampton; Mrs. William Lee Hanley, Jr.; Dina Merrill Hartley; Helen Joan Holt; Caroline Rose Hunt; Mrs. Earle M. Jorgensen; Donald M. Koll; Melvin R. Laird; Mrs. J. Willard Marriott; James A. McClure; Mrs. Abraham A. Ribicoff; Joy A. Silverman; Leonard L. Silverstein; Jean Kennedy Smith; Roger B. Smith; Dennis Stanfill; Roger L. Stevens; Jerry Weintraub; Charles Z. Wick; James D. Wolfensohn
Members Ex-Officio Designated by Act of Congress: Louis Sullivan; Lamar Alexander; Henry E. Catto; Senator Edward M. Kennedy; Senator George J. Mitchell; Senator Mark O. Hatfield; Representative Joseph M. McDade; Representative Charles Wilson; Representative Sidney R. Yates; Sharon Pratt Kelly; Robert McC. Adams; James H. Billington; J. Carter Brown; James M. Ridenour
Utilizes: Special Technical Talent; Guest Conductors; Guest Artists; Guest Directors
Budget: Over $50,000,000
Income Sources: Private Foundations/Grants/Endowments; Business/Corporate Donations; Box Office; Government Grants; Individual Donations
Season: 52 Weeks   **Annual Attendance:** 1,460,507
Since 1971, the Kennedy Center has presented a varied and comprehensive array of programming in dance, drama, musical theater, classical and contemporary music and opera. These performances have been sponsored by the Kennedy Center or by its affiliated constituent (the National Symphony Orchestra) and associated constituents (Washington Opera, American Film Institute and the Washington Performing Arts Society) and independent producers and sponsors.
Affiliations: National Symphony Orchestra; Washington Opera; American Film Institute; Washington Performing Arts Society
Performance Facility: John F. Kennedy Center for the Performing Arts: Concert Hall, Eisenhower Theater, American Film Institute, Opera House; Terrace Theater, Theater Lab. In addition to the performance facilities listed, the Performing Arts Library, a joint undertaking with the Library of Congress, provides video computer access to the nation's most comprehensive collections of films, books recordings and other materials on the performing arts.

NATIONAL GALLERY OF ART/CONCERT SERIES
National Gallery of Art, Washington, DC 20565
(202) 737-4215
> **Founded:** 1941
> **Arts Area:** Vocal Music; Instrumental Music
> **Status:** Non-Profit
> **Type:** Performing
> **Management:** George Manos, Music Director
> **Season:** October - June
> **Performance Facilities:** Museum Garden Courts

SMITHSONIAN INSTITUTION RESIDENT ASSOCIATE PROGRAM
1100 Jefferson Drive SW, Washington, DC 20560
(202) 357-3030
FAX: (202) 786-2034
> **Arts Area:** Dance; Vocal Music; Instrumental Music; Theater
> **Status:** Professional; Non-Profit
> **Type:** Educational; Sponsoring
> **Purpose:** To involve the residents of the Washington metropolitan area in the ongoing activities of the Smithsonian Institution
> **Management:** Janet W. Solinger, Director/RAP (Resident Associate Program); Penelope P. Dann, Program Coordinator; Joan Cole, Public Affairs
> **Officers:** The Board of Regents of the Smithsonian Institution
> **Paid Staff:** 47
> **Paid Artists:** 150
> **Utilizes:** Guest Artists
> **Budget:** $1,000,000 - $5,000,000
> **Income Sources:** Box Office; Memberships
> **Season:** 52 Weeks
> **Annual Attendance:** 22,000
> **Performance Facilities:** Hirshhorn Museum Auditorium; Baird Auditorium; Carmichael Auditorium

WASHINGTON PERFORMING ARTS SOCIETY
2000 L Street NW, #810, Washington, DC 20036
(202) 833-9800
FAX: (202) 331-7678
>   **Founded:** 1966
>   **Arts Area:** Dance; Vocal Music; Instrumental Music; Festivals
>   **Status:** Professional; Non-Profit
>   **Type:** Educational; Sponsoring
>   **Purpose:** To present the world's finest artists in the nation's capital; to present over 100 concerts annually on the major stages, as well as over 800 concerts each year in the schools of the metropolitan Washington area using resident artists
>   **Management:** Douglas H. Wheeler, Managing Director; Craig M. Hosmer, General Manager; Patrick Hayes, Managing Director Emeritus; Linda Coleman Soma, Director of Public Relations and Marketing
>   **Officers:** Lydia Marshall, President
>   **Paid Staff:** 23   **Volunteer Staff:** 10
>   **Utilizes:** Guest Conductors; Guest Artists; Guest Directors
>   **Budget:** $1,000,000 - $5,000,000
>   **Income Sources:** Private Foundations/Grants/Endowments; Business/Corporate Donations; Box Office; Government Grants; Individual Donations
>   **Season:** 52 Weeks   **Annual Attendance:** 250,000
>   **Affiliations:** ISPAA
>   **Performance Facilities:** John F. Kennedy Center for the Performing Arts; DAR Constitution Hall; Lisner Auditorium; George Washington University; Warner Theatre

FACILITY

THE AMERICAN UNIVERSITY - MCDONALD RECITAL HALL
4400 Massachusetts Avenue NW, Washington, DC 20016
(202) 885-3420
FAX: (202) 885-1092
>   **Type of Facility:** Concert Hall; Studio Performance
>   **Type of Stage:** Proscenium
>   **Stage Dimensions:** 40'Wx20'D
>   **Seating Capacity:** 200
>   **Year Built:** 1966
>   **Contact for Rental:** Susan Boyd;   (202) 885-3420

THE AMERICAN UNIVERSITY - NEW LECTURE HALL THEATRE
4400 Massachusetts Avenue NW, Washington, DC 20016
(202) 885-3420
FAX: (202) 885-1092
>   **Type of Facility:** Theatre Complex; Studio Performance; Black Box
>   **Facility Originally:** Lecture Hall
>   **Type of Stage:** Flexible
>   **Seating Capacity:** 200
>   **Year Remodeled:** 1985
>   **Contact for Rental:** Susan Boyd;   (202) 885-3420

ARENA STAGE - FICHANDLER THEATER
Sixth and Maine Avenue SW, Washington, DC 20024
(202) 554-9066
FAX: (202) 488-4056
>   **Founded:** 1950
>   **Type of Facility:** Theatre House
>   **Type of Stage:** Arena
>   **Seating Capacity:** 800
>   **Year Built:** 1960   **Architect:** Harry Weese & Associates   **Cost:** $1,000,000
>   **Contact for Rental:** Production Office;   (202) 554-9066
>   **Resident Groups:** Arena Stage Resident Company

ARENA STAGE - KREEGER THEATER
Sixth and Maine Avenue SW, Washington, DC 20024
(202) 554-9066
FAX: (202) 488-4056
>   **Founded:** 1950
>   **Type of Facility:** Theatre House
>   **Type of Stage:** Thrust; Proscenium; End Stage
>   **Stage Dimensions:** 32'x40'x32'
>   **Seating Capacity:** 500

Year Built: 1970   **Architect:** Harry Weese & Associates   **Cost:** $1,500,000
Contact for Rental: Production Office;   (202) 554-9066
Resident Groups: Arena Stage Resident Company

ARENA STAGE - OLD VAT THEATER
Sixth and Maine Avenue SW, Washington, DC 20024
(202) 554-9066
FAX: (202) 488-4056
Founded: 1950
Type of Facility: Theatre House
Facility Originally: Restaurant
Type of Stage: Flexible; Cabaret-style
Seating Capacity: 165
Year Remodeled: 1976   **Cost:** $21,000
Contact for Rental: Production Office;   (202) 554-9066
Resident Groups: Arena Stage Resident Company

CONSTITUTION HALL
18th and D Streets NW, Washington, DC 20006
(202) 628-4780
Type of Facility: Concert Hall; Auditorium; Multi-Purpose
Type of Stage: Thrust
Stage Dimensions: 52'Wx33'D
Seating Capacity: 3,746
Year Built: 1920   **Architect:** John Russel Pope   **Cost:** $2,000,000
Contact for Rental: George Brooks or Rose Magruder;   (202) 628-4780
Manager: George Brooks;   (202) 628-4780

FORD'S THEATRE
511 Tenth Street NW, Washington, DC 20004
(202) 638-2941
FAX: (202) 347-6269
Founded: 1968
Type of Facility: Theatre House
Facility Originally: Warehouse
Type of Stage: Proscenium
Orchestra Pit
Seating Capacity: 699
Year Built: 1863   **Architect:** James J. Gifford   **Cost:** $75,000
Year Remodeled: 1968   **Cost:** $2,073,600
Manager: Michael Gennaro, Managing Director;   (202) 638-2941
Ford's Theatre was restored to its original appearance after an extensive study. The theatre is available for rent on a very limited basis.

GASTON HALL
37th and "O" Streets NW, Washington, DC 20057
(202) 687-4081
Founded: 1879
Type of Facility: Concert Hall; Auditorium
Facility Originally: Lecture/Concert/Convocation Hall
Stage Dimensions: 50'x20'
Seating Capacity: 734
Year Built: 1879
Contact for Rental: Facilities Coordinator;   (202) 687-4081
Resident Groups: Georgetown Symphony; Cantate Chamber Singers

GEORGE WASHINGTON UNIVERSITY - LISNER AUDITORIUM
730 21st Street NW, Washington, DC 20052
(202) 994-6800
Type of Facility: Concert Hall; Auditorium; Theatre House
Type of Stage: Proscenium
Stage Dimensions: 55'W x 36'D   **Orchestra Pit**
Seating Capacity: 1,495 plus wheelchairs
Year Built: 1945   **Architect:** Waldron Faulkner
Year Remodeled: 1992   **Cost:** $400,000
Acoustical Consultant: Phil Fox, Stage Manager
Contact for Rental: Sylvia L. Kohrn;   (202) 994-6800

Manager: Rosanna Ruscetti, Director;   (202) 994-9120
Resident Groups: The Washington Concert Opera; Masterworks Chorus; Kan-Kouran West African Dance Company

HALL OF NATIONS BLACK BOX THEATRE
1221 36th Street NW, Washington, DC 20057
(202) 687-4081
Founded: 1988
Type of Stage: Flexible
Seating Capacity: 200
Year Built: 1955
Year Remodeled: 1988
Contact for Rental: Facilities Coordinator;   (202) 687-4081
Resident Groups: Student Performance Organizations

JOHN F. KENNEDY CENTER FOR THE PERFORMING ARTS
2700 F Street NW, Washington, DC 20566
(202) 416-8000
Type of Facility: National Cultural Center
Year Built: 1971   **Architect:** Edward Durell Stone   **Cost:** $71,000,000
Acoustical Consultant: Dr. Cyril Harris
Contact for Rental: Helen Hamm, Scheduling Coordinator;   (202) 416-8050
The National Park Service maintains the Kennedy Center as a presidential memorial and is responsible for its security. See individual listings for the American Film Institute, Concert Hall, Eisenhower Theater, Opera House, Terrace Theater and Theater Lab. Under the terms of the National Cultural Center Act of 1958 (as amended in 1964), the Kennedy Center is administered by a Board of Trustees as a separate, independent and self-sustaining bureau of the Smithsonian Institution. This 45-member Board of Trustees is composed of 30 Presidential appointees who serve 10-year overlapping terms. The 15 remaining members are legislatively designated, serving by virtue of their specific public office. For further information reference the Performing Series listing for John F. Kennedy Center for the Performing Arts.

JOHN F. KENNEDY CENTER FOR THE PERFORMING ARTS - AMERICAN FILM INSTITUTE THEATER
2700 F Street NW, Washington, DC 20566
(202) 416-8000
Type of Facility: Film Theater/experimental Theater
Type of Stage: Flexible
Seating Capacity: 224
Year Built: 1973   **Architect:** Lisa Parks
Acoustical Consultant: Dr. Cyril Harris
Contact for Rental: Helen Hamm, Scheduling Coordinator;   (202) 416-8050

JOHN F. KENNEDY CENTER FOR THE PERFORMING ARTS - CONCERT HALL
2700 F Street NW, Washington, DC 20566
(202) 416-8000
Type of Facility: Concert Hall
Type of Stage: Concert Platform
Seating Capacity: 2,759
Year Built: 1971   **Architect:** Edward Durell Stone
Acoustical Consultant: Dr. Cyril Harris
Contact for Rental: Helen Hamm, Scheduling Coordinator;   (202) 416-8050
Manager: Paul D. Simmerman

JOHN F. KENNEDY CENTER FOR THE PERFORMING ARTS - EISENHOWER THEATER
2700 F Street NW, Washington, DC 20566
(202) 416-8200
FAX: (202) 416-8205
Type of Facility: Theatre House
Type of Stage: Proscenium
Stage Dimensions: 75'Wx55'D   **Orchestra Pit**
Seating Capacity: 1,142
Year Built: 1971   **Architect:** Edward Durell Stone
Acoustical Consultant: Dr. Cyril Harris
Contact for Rental: Elizabeth Thomas, Scheduling Coordinator;   (202) 416-8032
Manager: Ed Blacker;   (202) 416-8250

JOHN F. KENNEDY CENTER FOR THE PERFORMING ARTS - OPERA HOUSE
2700 F Street NW, Washington, DC 20566
(202) 872-0466
Type of Facility: Opera House
Type of Stage: Proscenium

Stage Dimensions: 100'Wx65'D   Orchestra Pit
Seating Capacity: 2,318
Year Built: 1971   Architect: Edward Durell Stone
Acoustical Consultant: Dr. Cyril Harris
Contact for Rental: Max A. Woodward, General Manager;   (202) 416-8200
Manager: Richard W. Kidwell;   (202) 416-8159

JOHN F. KENNEDY CENTER FOR THE PERFORMING ARTS - TERRACE THEATER
2700 F Street NW, Washington, DC 20566
(202) 416-8000
Type of Facility: Chamber Hall
Type of Stage: Proscenium
Stage Dimensions: 34'11"Wx17'10 3/4"D
Seating Capacity: 500
Year Built: 1979   Architect: Philip Johnson, Associates
Acoustical Consultant: Dr. Cyril Harris
Contact for Rental: Helen Hamm, Scheduling Coordinator
Manager: Ed Blacker

JOHN F. KENNEDY CENTER FOR THE PERFORMING ARTS - THEATER LAB
2700 F Street NW, Washington, DC 20566
(202) 416-8000
Type of Facility: Multipurpose
Type of Stage: Flexible
Seating Capacity: 100
Year Built: 1971   Architect: Edward Durell Stone
Acoustical Consultant: Dr. Cyril Harris
Contact for Rental: Helen Hamm, Scheduling Coordinator;   (202) 416-8050
Manager: Carole Sullivan

LIBRARY OF CONGRESS
10 First Street SE, Washington, DC 20540
(202) 707-5000
Founded: 1800
Type of Facility: Concert Hall
Type of Stage: Proscenium   Orchestra Pit
Seating Capacity: 500
Year Built: 1925
Year Remodeled: 1992

MASK AND BAUBLE DRAMATIC SOCIETY THEATER
The Leavey Center, Room 316, Washington, DC 20057-1074
(202) 687-3838
Type of Facility: Environmental; Theatre House; Room; Black Box
Facility Originally: Lecture Hall
Type of Stage: Flexible; Environmental
Stage Dimensions: 64'x30'x11'6"
Seating Capacity: 110
Year Built: 1948   Architect: Georgetown University
Year Remodeled: 1976   Architect: Georgetown University
Resident Groups: Mask and Bauble Dramatic Society

NATIONAL THEATRE
1321 Pennsylvania Avenue NW, Washington, DC 20004
(202) 783-6854
Type of Facility: Theatre House
Type of Stage: Modified Apron Proscenium
Stage Dimensions: 80'Wx36'6"D; 39'8"Wx28'H proscenium opening   Orchestra Pit
Seating Capacity: 1,679
Year Remodeled: 1984   Cost: $6,000,000
Contact for Rental: Harry Teter;   (202) 628-6161
Original 1835 construction was destroyed by fire. Renovated in 1984 by Pennsylvania Avenue Foundation

THE SHAKESPEARE THEATRE
450 Seventh Street NW, Washington, DC 20004
(202) 547-3230
Type of Facility: Theatre House
Facility Originally: Department Store

Type of Stage: Proscenium
Stage Dimensions: 36'Wx21'Hx46'D
Seating Capacity: 447
Year Built: 1991   **Architect:** Graham Gund
Contact for Rental: Randy Engels;   (202) 547-3230
Resident Groups: The Shakespeare Theatre

SMITHSONIAN INSTITUTION - BAIRD AUDITORIUM
Tenth and Constitution Avenue NW, Washington, DC 20560
(202) 357-1300
Type of Facility: Auditorium
Seating Capacity: 560
Year Built: 1910   **Architect:** Hornblower and Marshall

SMITHSONIAN INSTITUTION - CARMICHAEL AUDITORIUM
14th and Constitution Avenue NW, Washington, DC 20560
(202) 357-1300
Type of Facility: Auditorium
Seating Capacity: 281
Year Built: 1964   **Architect:** McKim, Meade and White

WARNER THEATRE
PO Box 27280, Washington, DC 20003-7280
(202) 628-1818
FAX: (202) 783-0204
Type of Facility: Concert Hall; Theatre House; Multipurpose
Facility Originally: Vaudeville
Type of Stage: Proscenium
Stage Dimensions: 40'Wx30'D   **Orchestra Pit**
Seating Capacity: 1,987
Year Built: 1924   **Architect:** C. Howard Crane
Year Remodeled: 1992   **Architect:** Shalom Baranes Associates   **Cost:** $8,000,000
Contact for Rental: Jane Podgurski, General Manager;   (202) 628-1818

FLORIDA

Anna Maria

THEATRE

ISLAND PLAYERS
PO Box 2059, Anna Maria, FL 34216
(813) 778-5755
Founded: 1948
Arts Area: Community
Status: Non-Professional; Non-Profit
Type: Performing
Purpose: To provide high-quality community theatre productions for the cultural environment of the area
Officers: Geoffrey Todd, President; Jane Adam, First Vice President; Ruth Stevens, Second Vice President; Patricia Rohrer, Treasurer
Paid Staff: 5
Utilizes: Special Technical Talent; Guest Directors
Budget: $1,000 - $50,000
Income Sources: Private Foundations/Grants/Endowments; Box Office; Individual Donations
Season: October - May   **Annual Attendance:** 11,000
Performance Facilities: Island Players Theatre

FACILITY

ISLAND PLAYERS THEATRE
PO Box 2059, Anna Maria, FL 34216
(813) 778-5755
Type of Facility: Theatre House
Type of Stage: Proscenium
Seating Capacity: 137
Year Built: 1900
Year Remodeled: 1974   **Architect:** John Piercy   **Cost:** $30,000
Resident Groups: Island Players

Belle Glade

FACILITY

DOLLY HAND CULTURAL ARTS CENTER
1977 College Drive, Belle Glade, FL 33430
(407) 992-6160
FAX: (407) 992-6179
Founded: 1992
Type of Facility: Concert Hall; Auditorium; Performance Center; Off Broadway; Theatre House; Multi-Purpose
Type of Stage: Proscenium
Stage Dimensions: 40'Wx16'Hx36'10 1/2"D proscenium opening
Seating Capacity: 468
Year Built: 1982
Contact for Rental: Monika M. Potter;   (407) 992-6160

Boca Raton

VOCAL MUSIC

PICCOLO OPERA COMPANY
24 Del Rio Boulevard, Boca Raton, FL 33432
(800) 282-3161
Founded: 1962
Arts Area: Grand Opera; Lyric Opera; Light Opera; Operetta
Status: Professional; Non-Profit
Type: Performing; Touring; Educational
Purpose: To perform professional operas in English, for adults and children
Management: Lee Jon Associates
Officers: Marjorie Gordon, President; Jack Bean, Vice President; Merry Silber, Secretary; Milton J. Miller, Treasurer

Utilizes: Special Technical Talent; Guest Conductors; Guest Artists; Guest Directors
Budget: $1,000 - $50,000
Income Sources: Performance Sponsors
Season: 52 Weeks
Affiliations: NOA; COS

THEATRE

CALDWELL THEATRE COMPANY
7873 North Federal Highway, Boca Raton, FL 33487
(407) 241-7380
FAX: (407) 997-6917
Founded: 1980
Arts Area: Professional; Theatrical Group
Status: Professional; Non-Profit
Type: Performing; Touring; Resident
Purpose: To present regional professional theater
Management: Michael Hall, Executive Director; Patricia Burdett, Company Manager; Kathy Walton, Marketing Director; Joe Ancker, Director of Development; Chip Latimer, Technical Director
Officers: Donald Giancola, President
Paid Staff: 20
Paid Artists: 15
Utilizes: Guest Artists; Guest Directors; Equity Actors
Budget: $1,000,000 - $5,000,000
Income Sources: Private Foundations/Grants/Endowments; Business/Corporate Donations; Box Office; Government Grants; Individual Donations
Season: 52 Weeks   **Annual Attendance:** 80,000
Affiliations: TCG; Florida Professional Theatre Association

FACILITY

UNIVERSITY CENTER AUDITORIUM
500 NW 20th Street, Boca Raton, FL 33432
(407) 367-3730
FAX: (407) 367-2740
Founded: 1982
Type of Facility: Auditorium; General Purpose Center (fixed seating)
Type of Stage: Thrust
Stage Dimensions: 38'Hx66'W; 24'8" radius
Seating Capacity: 2,400
Year Built: 1982   **Architect:** Stewart Richmond Associates   **Cost:** $2,100,000
Year Remodeled: 1991   **Architect:** Giller and Associates   **Cost:** $250,000
Contact for Rental: Matt Hollander;   (407) 367-3730
Resident Groups: Boca Raton Symphonic Pops; Florida Philharmonic Orchestra; Concert Showcase of Florida

Boynton Beach

INSTRUMENTAL MUSIC

THE JAMES E. BUFFAN GOLD COAST BAND
Freedom Hall Community Center, 128 East Ocean, Boynton Beach, FL 33435
(407) 738-7444
Founded: 1976
Arts Area: Band
Status: Non-Profit
Type: Performing
Purpose: To provide cultural programming for the entire community and promote an opportunity for the development of players. These adult volunteer musicians have played professionally and nonprofessionally.
Management: Devere Fader, Band Director; Debby Banks, Supervisor (Boynton Beach Recreation & Parks Department)
Officers: Al Miller, Arthur Chargois, Marilyn Wilson, Leone Buffan, Band Committee
Paid Staff: 1
Non-Paid Artists: 70
Utilizes: Guest Artists
Budget: $1,000 - $50,000
Income Sources: Individual Donations
Season: October - May   **Annual Attendance:** 4,000
Affiliations: Palm Beach County Council of the Arts
Performance Facilities: Boynton Beach Freedom Hall Community Center

Bradenton

THEATRE

MANATEE PLAYERS/RIVERFRONT THEATRE
102 Old Main Street, Bradenton, FL 33505
(813) 748-0111
Founded: 1948
Arts Area: Community
Status: Non-Profit
Type: Performing; Educational
Purpose: To improve the educational and cultural climate of the community by providing quality live theatre
Management: Nan Alderson, Managing Director; Peter Massey, Artistic Director; Dan Yerman, Technical Director
Officers: Catherine Bonner, President; Bud Douglas, Vice President; Margaret Newsome, Secretary; Ruth Nielson-Rice, Treasurer
Paid Staff: 4 **Volunteer Staff:** 100
Non-Paid Artists: 100
Utilizes: Special Technical Talent; Guest Artists; Guest Directors
Budget: $100,000 - $500,000
Income Sources: Private Foundations/Grants/Endowments; Business/Corporate Donations; Box Office; Government Grants; Individual Donations; Fund-raising Events
Season: 52 Weeks
Affiliations: FACT; AACT; Manatee County Cultural Alliance
Performance Facilities: Riverfront Theatre

Clearwater

DANCE

HIS IMAGE, SACRED DANCE
2037 Edgewater Drive, #4, Clearwater, FL 34615
(813) 443-2133
Founded: 1981
Arts Area: Modern; Ballet
Status: Non-Profit
Type: Performing; Educational
Purpose: Image has sponsored many workshops with professional instructors and performed for the dance-in-school program to stimulate the interest in dance and to help educate and promote modern dance in the Pinellas County Area.
Management: Janet East Beyer, Director
Volunteer Staff: 6
Non-Paid Artists: 8
Utilizes: Guest Artists; Guest Directors
Budget: $1,000 - $50,000
Income Sources: Individual Donations
Season: 52 Weeks **Annual Attendance:** 200
Performance Facilities: Ruth Eckerd Hall, Saint Petersburg Junior College

THEATRE

CITY PLAYERS
Clearwater Parks and Recreation, PO Box 4748, Clearwater, FL 34618
(813) 462-6035
Founded: 1971
Arts Area: Community; Theatrical Group
Status: Non-Professional; Non-Profit
Type: Performing; Educational
Purpose: To bring quality theatre (and education of same) to the public of all ages at very nominal fees
Management: Margo Walbolt, Cultural Arts Supervisor; Phillip Terry, Technical Director; B.J. Pucci, Musical Director
Paid Staff: 4
Paid Artists: 3 **Non-Paid Artists:** 4
Utilizes: Guest Artists
Budget: $1,000 - $50,000

Season: September - August   **Annual Attendance:** 8,000
Performance Facilities: Ruth Eckerd Hall; Saint Petersburg Junior College

SHOWBOAT DINNER THEATRE
3405 Ulmerton Road, Clearwater, FL 34622
(813) 573-3777
FAX: (813) 573-2735
Founded: 1967
Arts Area: Professional; Dinner
Status: Professional; Commercial
Type: Performing
Management: Virginia Sherwood, Owner/President/Producer
Paid Staff: 12
Utilizes: Special Technical Talent; Guest Artists; Guest Directors
Income Sources: Box Office
Season: 52 Weeks

PERFORMING SERIES

PACT-RUTH ECKERD HALL AT THE BAUMGARDNER PERFORMING ARTS CENTER
1111 McMullen Booth Road, Clearwater, FL 34619
(813) 791-7060
FAX: (813) 791-6020
Founded: 1978
Arts Area: Dance; Vocal Music; Instrumental Music; Theater
Status: Non-Profit
Type: Performing; Educational; Sponsoring
Purpose: To present major national and international artists and attractions year-round in a fine acoustic hall; to present educational programming, visual arts exhibits and senior citizen programs
Management: Elissa Getto, Executive Director; Diane Eliades, House Manager; Jan Hickin, Director of Marketing/Publicity
Paid Staff: 40   **Volunteer Staff:** 900
Income Sources: Private Foundations/Grants/Endowments; Business/Corporate Donations; Box Office; Government Grants; Individual Donations
Season: 52 Weeks   **Annual Attendance:** 500,000
Affiliations: APAP; ISPAA
Performance Facilities: Ruth Eckerd Hall

Coconut Creek

FACILITY

OMNI AUDITORIUM - BROWARD COMMUNITY COLLEGE
1000 Coconut Boulevard, Coconut Creek, FL 33066
(305) 973-2233
Type of Facility: Concert Hall; Auditorium; Theatre House; Opera House
Type of Stage: Proscenium
Stage Dimensions: 75'Wx40'D
Seating Capacity: 2,008
Year Built: 1980   **Architect:** Louis Wolffe and Associates
Contact for Rental: Susan Berlin;   (305) 973-2233
Resident Groups: Gold Coast Opera

WYNMOOR RECITAL HALL
1300 Avenue of the Stars, Coconut Creek, FL 33066
(305) 974-2627
Founded: 1974
Type of Facility: Concert Hall
Type of Stage: Thrust
Stage Dimensions: 39'x29'
Seating Capacity: 950
Year Built: 1979   **Cost:** $3,000,000

Coral Gables

DANCE

FREDDICK BRATCHER AND COMPANY
PO Box 140099, Coral Gables, FL 33114-0099
(305) 448-2021
FAX: (305) 445-1412
Founded: 1980
Arts Area: Modern; Jazz
Status: Professional; Non-Profit
Type: Performing; Touring; Educational
Purpose: To provide South Florida with high-quality and innovative contemporary dance theater
Management: Maria Lemus, Managing Director
Officers: Jolie Cummings, President; Aaron Morris, Chairman of the Board; Freddick Bratcher, Artistic Director/Choreographer
Paid Staff: 1   **Volunteer Staff:** 12
Paid Artists: 11
Utilizes: Special Technical Talent; Guest Choreographers
Budget: $50,000 - $100,000
Income Sources: Private Foundations/Grants/Endowments; Business/Corporate Donations; Box Office; Government Grants; Individual Donations
Season: September - June   **Annual Attendance:** 10,000
Performance Facilities: Gusman Center for the Performing Arts; Colony Theater; James L. Knight Center

THEATRE

NEW THEATRE
65 Almeria Avenue, Coral Gables, FL 33134
(305) 443-5909
Founded: 1986
Arts Area: Professional; Theatrical Group
Status: Professional
Type: Performing
Purpose: To present the best of world theatre to South Florida
Management: Rafael DeAcha, Executive Artistic Director; Kimberly Daniel, Company Manager; Maggie Gonzalez, House Manager
Officers: Dianne Joyce, Chairman
Paid Staff: 3
Utilizes: Special Technical Talent; Guest Artists; Guest Directors
Budget: $100,000 - $500,000
Income Sources: Private Foundations/Grants/Endowments; Business/Corporate Donations; Box Office; Government Grants; Individual Donations
Season: 52 Weeks   **Annual Attendance:** 9,000

PERFORMING SERIES

FLORIDA SHAKESPEARE FESTIVAL
232 Minora Avenue, Coral Gables, FL 33134
(305) 446-1116
FAX: (305) 445-8645
Founded: 1979
Arts Area: Theater; Festivals
Status: Professional; Non-Profit
Type: Performing; Touring; Resident; Educational
Purpose: To popularize Shakespeare and other classical dramatist's works in Florida; to educate young audiences to Shakespeare's works
Management: Gail Deschamps, Artistic Director
Officers: Jeanine Goodstein, Chairman of the Board
Paid Staff: 20   **Volunteer Staff:** 100
Paid Artists: 65   **Non-Paid Artists:** 10
Utilizes: Special Technical Talent; Guest Artists; Guest Directors
Budget: $500,000 - $1,000,000
Income Sources: Private Foundations/Grants/Endowments; Business/Corporate Donations; Box Office; Individual Donations
Season: October - May   **Annual Attendance:** 40,000
Performance Facilities: Minora Playhouse

Daytona Beach

INSTRUMENTAL MUSIC

DAYTONA BEACH SYMPHONY SOCIETY
230 South Beach Street, Daytona Beach, FL 32115
(904) 253-2901
FAX: (904) 253-0068
Founded: 1952
Arts Area: Symphony; Orchestra; Chamber
Status: Non-Profit
Type: Sponsoring
Management: Bill Lazarus, Managing Director
Officers: Dorothy Bradley, President; James Finn, First Vice President; Rod Resta, Second Vice President; Dr. Jim Woodward, Third Vice President
Paid Staff: 1   **Volunteer Staff:** 50
Paid Artists: 8
Utilizes: Guest Conductors; Guest Artists; Guest Directors
Budget: $100,000 - $500,000
Income Sources: Private Foundations/Grants/Endowments; Business/Corporate Donations; Box Office; Government Grants; Individual Donations
Season: November - April
Annual Attendance: 10,000
Performance Facilities: Peabody Auditorium

THEATRE

DAYTONA PLAYHOUSE
100 Jessamine Boulevard, Daytona Beach, FL 32118
(904) 255-2431
Founded: 1947
Arts Area: Community
Status: Non-Profit
Type: Performing; Resident
Purpose: Pleasure
Management: James F. Sturgell, Artistic Director
Officers: Dick Vaughan, President; Dave Koch, Treasurer; Louise Murray, Secretary
Paid Staff: 1
Utilizes: Community Volunteers
Budget: $50,000 - $100,000
Income Sources: Box Office; Individual Donations
Season: September - July
Annual Attendance: 10,000
Performance Facilities: Daytona Playhouse

SEASIDE MUSIC THEATER
PO Box 2835, Daytona Beach, FL 32120
(904) 252-3394; (904) 252-6200
FAX: (904) 252-8991
Founded: 1977
Arts Area: Professional; Musical; Dinner; Theatrical Group
Status: Professional; Non-Profit
Type: Performing; Touring; Educational
Purpose: To produce a variety of the best examples of musical theater, operetta and opera in repertory
Management: Lester Malizig, General Manager; Lisa Brooks, Director of Marketing and Sales; Nona Lloyd, Production Manager; Tippen Davidson, Artistic Director/Producer
Paid Staff: 30   **Volunteer Staff:** 25
Paid Artists: 50   **Non-Paid Artists:** 5
Utilizes: Guest Conductors; Guest Artists; Guest Directors
Budget: $1,000,000 - $5,000,000
Income Sources: Private Foundations/Grants/Endowments; Business/Corporate Donations; Box Office; Government Grants; Individual Donations
Season: May - August
Annual Attendance: 35,000
Affiliations: Florida Professional Theatre Association; USITT; SETC
Performance Facilities: Daytona Beach Community College Theatre

PERFORMING SERIES

CENTRAL FLORIDA CULTURAL ENDEAVORS
PO Box 1310, Daytona Beach, FL 32015
(904) 252-1511, ext. 410
> **Founded:** 1982
> **Arts Area:** Dance; Vocal Music; Instrumental Music; Theater; Festivals
> **Status:** Professional; Non-Profit
> **Type:** Sponsoring
> **Purpose:** To provide residents in this area the opportunity to hear quality music by the world's greatest orchestras and chamber groups
> **Management:** Dewey Anderson, General Manager
> **Officers:** Tippen Davidson, President; Georgia Kaney, Treasurer; Nancy Spence, Accountant
> **Paid Staff:** 4
> **Utilizes:** Guest Conductors; Guest Artists
> **Budget:** $500,000 - $1,000,000
> **Income Sources:** Business/Corporate Donations; Box Office; Government Grants
> **Performance Facilities:** Peabody Auditorium

FLORIDA INTERNATIONAL FESITVAL
PO Box 1310, Daytona Beach, FL 32115
(904) 257-7790
FAX: (904) 238-1663
> **Founded:** 1966
> **Arts Area:** Dance; Vocal Music; Instrumental Music; Festivals
> **Status:** Professional
> **Type:** Performing; Educational; Sponsoring
> **Purpose:** To present a biennial festival featuring the London Symphony Orchestra and many other types of performances
> **Management:** Tippen Davidson, Founder and Director; Dewey Anderson, General Manager; Pam Stipsits, Marketing Director
> **Officers:** Tippen Davidson, President
> **Paid Staff:** 15   **Volunteer Staff:** 60
> **Paid Artists:** 150
> **Utilizes:** Guest Conductors; Guest Artists
> **Budget:** $1,000,000 - $5,000,000
> **Income Sources:** Private Foundations/Grants/Endowments; Business/Corporate Donations; Box Office; Government Grants; Individual Donations; Advertising; Souvenirs
> **Season:** July - August   **Annual Attendance:** 35,000
> **Affiliations:** APAP; Florida Arts Presenters
> **Performance Facilities:** Peabody Auditorium; Ocean Center; Ormond Beach PAC

FACILITY

DAYTONA BEACH COMMUNITY COLLEGE - THEATRE CENTER
1200 Volusia Avenue, Daytona Beach, FL 32115
(904) 254-3000
FAX: (904) 254-3044
> **Type of Facility:** Theatre Complex; Auditorium; Performance Center; Theatre House
> **Type of Stage:** Proscenium
> **Stage Dimensions:** 36'W arch; 28' plaster to wall   **Orchestra Pit**
> **Seating Capacity:** 508

DAYTONA PLAYHOUSE
100 Jessamine Boulevard, Daytona Beach, FL 32118
(904) 255-2431
> **Type of Facility:** Theatre House
> **Type of Stage:** Proscenium
> **Stage Dimensions:** 40'x28'x35'   **Orchestra Pit**
> **Year Built:** 1947
> **Manager:** Jim Sturgell

OCEAN CENTER
101 North Atlantic, Daytona Beach, FL 32118
(904) 254-4500
> **Type of Facility:** Civic Center
> **Year Built:** 1985   **Architect:** Ellerbe Builders   **Cost:** $37,000,000
> **Contact for Rental:** Rick Hamilton;   (904) 254-4500
> *Contains the Conference Center and Arena. See separate listings*

OCEAN CENTER - ARENA
101 North Atlantic, Daytona Beach, FL 32118
(904) 254-4500
    Type of Facility: Arena; Multi-Purpose
    Type of Stage: Flexible; Platform
    Seating Capacity: 10,000
    Year Built: 1985   **Architect:** Ellerbe Builders
    Contact for Rental: Rick Hamilton;   (904) 254-4500

OCEAN CENTER - CONFERENCE CENTER
101 North Atlantic, Daytona Beach, FL 32118
(904) 254-4500
    Type of Facility: Multi-Purpose
    Type of Stage: Flexible; Platform
    Year Built: 1985   **Architect:** Ellerbe Builders
    Contact for Rental: Rick Hamilton;   (904) 254-4500
    Conference Center contains 14,000 square feet

PEABODY AUDITORIUM
600 Auditorium, PO Box 551, Daytona Beach, FL 32015
(904) 258-3169
    Type of Facility: Auditorium
    Type of Stage: Proscenium
    Stage Dimensions: 22'x80'x39'
    Orchestra Pit
    Seating Capacity: 2,560
    Year Built: 1948   **Architect:** Francis Walton   **Cost:** $750,000
    Year Remodeled: 1986   **Cost:** $900,000
    Contact for Rental: Janet Ford, Assistant Manager;   (904) 258-3169
    Manager: Owen Davidson;   (904) 258-3169

Delray Beach

THEATRE

DELRAY BEACH PLAYHOUSE
950 NW Ninth Street, PO Box 1056, Delray Beach, FL 33444
(407) 272-1281
    Founded: 1948
    Arts Area: Summer Stock; Community
    Status: Non-Professional; Non-Profit
    Type: Performing; Educational
    Purpose: To provide involvement in performing arts to members of the community
    Management: Randolph del Lago, Artistic Director; Joyce Lunsford, Box Office Manager; Chuck Tisdale, Technical Director; Ann Cadaret, Scenic Director
    Officers: Harvey Brown Jr., President; Ernest G. Simon, Vice President; Yvonne Gugel, Secretary; Jerry McDaniel, Treasurer
    Paid Staff: 4   **Volunteer Staff:** 40
    Non-Paid Artists: 100
    Utilizes: Guest Artists
    Budget: $100,000 - $500,000
    Income Sources: Business/Corporate Donations; Box Office; Individual Donations
    Season: October - June   **Annual Attendance:** 35,000
    Affiliations: Florida Theatre Conference
    Performance Facilities: Delray Beach Playhouse

FACILITY

DELRAY BEACH PLAYHOUSE
950 NW Ninth Street, PO Box 1056, Delray Beach, FL 33444
(305) 272-1281
    Type of Facility: Auditorium
    Type of Stage: Proscenium
    Stage Dimensions: 16'x34'x26'   **Orchestra Pit**
    Seating Capacity: 238
    Year Built: 1948   **Cost:** $50,000
    Year Remodeled: 1978   **Architect:** James Whilden Jr.   **Cost:** $75,000
    Resident Groups: Delray Beach Playhouse

Eustis
THEATRE

BAY STREET PLAYERS
PO Box 1405, Eustis, FL 32726
(904) 357-7777
Founded: 1975
Arts Area: Musical; Community; Theatrical Group
Status: Non-Professional; Non-Profit
Type: Performing; Touring; Educational
Purpose: To develop all aspects of positions in theatre through practical experience gained by doing
Management: Dale R. Carpenter, Executive Director; Deborah Carpenter, Lou Tally, Directors; Michael Lake, Managing Director
Officers: Deborah J. Carpenter, President; Charlie Smith, Secretary; Lou Tally, Comptroller; Timi Lake, Treasurer
Paid Staff: 4   **Volunteer Staff:** 12
Utilizes: Special Technical Talent; Guest Directors
Budget: $50,000 - $100,000
Income Sources: Business/Corporate Donations; Box Office; Individual Donations
Season: 52 Weeks   **Annual Attendance:** 15,000
Performance Facilities: State Theatre

Fort Lauderdale
INSTRUMENTAL MUSIC

PHILHARMONIC ORCHESTRA OF FLORIDA
3401 NW Ninth Avenue, Suite 1, Fort Lauderdale, FL 33309
(305) 561-2997
FAX: (305) 561-1390
Founded: 1949
Arts Area: Symphony
Status: Professional; Non-Profit
Type: Performing; Touring; Resident; Educational
Purpose: To maintain a symphony orchestra for cultural and educational purposes to serve South Florida
Management: John E. Graham, Executive Director; Melinda Hipp, Orchestra Manager; Barbara Fead, Director of Development; Bonnie Arnold, Public Relations; Ed Cambron, Marketing
Officers: John B. Deinhardt, Chairman of the Board; Stanley Marks, President Ft. Lauderdale Symphony Orchestra Foundation; Donald Lyman, President, Boca Raton Board of Trustees; Malcolm Farrel JR., President, Broward Board of Trustees; Mrs. Bobbi Litt and Mrs. Christa Paul Co-Presidents, Dade Board of Trustees; Robert Gunn Esq., President, Palm Beaches Board of Trustees; Melvin T. Goldberger, Treasurer
Paid Staff: 10   **Volunteer Staff:** 1
Paid Artists: 85
Utilizes: Special Technical Talent; Guest Conductors; Guest Artists
Budget: $1,000,000 - $5,000,000
Income Sources: Private Foundations/Grants/Endowments; Business/Corporate Donations; Box Office; Government Grants
Season: October - May   **Annual Attendance:** 200,000
Performance Facilities: War Memorial Auditorium; Florida Atlantic University Auditorium

VOCAL MUSIC

FORT LAUDERDALE OPERA
333 SW Second Street, Fort Lauderdale, FL 33312
Founded: 1945
Arts Area: Grand Opera
Status: Professional; Non-Profit
Type: Performing; Educational; Sponsoring
Management: William H. Martin, General Manager; Marvin David Levy, Artistic Director; G. David Black, Assistant General Manager
Officers: Theodore K. Friedt, President; Bernice Schwenke, First Vice President; Norman F. Codo, Second Vice President; Michael Bienes, Treasurer; Patricia Helmus, Secretary
Paid Staff: 3   **Volunteer Staff:** 350
Utilizes: Special Technical Talent; Guest Conductors; Guest Artists; Guest Directors
Budget: $1,000,000 - $5,000,000
Income Sources: Private Foundations/Grants/Endowments; Business/Corporate Donations; Box Office; Government Grants; Individual Donations

Season: October - May **Annual Attendance:** 10,400
Performance Facilities: Broward Center for the Perfroming Arts

OPERA GUILD
333 SW Second Street, Fort Lauderdale, FL 33312
(305) 728-9700
FAX: (305) 728-9702
Founded: 1944
Arts Area: Grand Opera
Status: Non-Profit
Type: Touring
Purpose: To promote opera and the new performing arts
Management: William H. Martin, General Manager
Paid Staff: 3
Utilizes: Guest Conductors; Guest Artists; Guest Directors
Budget: $100,000 - $500,000
Income Sources: Private Foundations/Grants/Endowments; Business/Corporate Donations; Box Office; Government Grants; Individual Donations
Season: January - April   **Affiliations:** Junior Opera Guild/Children's
Performance Facilities: Broward Center for the Performing Arts

THEATRE

FORT LAUDERDALE CHILDREN'S THEATRE
640 North Andrews Avenue, Fort Lauderdale, FL 33311
(305) 763-6882
Founded: 1959
Arts Area: Community; Theatrical Group
Status: Non-Profit
Type: Performing; Touring; Educational
Purpose: To provide educational courses in theatre arts for area youth; to present performances for children, by children
Management: Carol Ries, Executive Director; Darlene J. Lentz, Education Director; Carol Fretwell, Administrative Director
Officers: Melinda Hord, President; Susan Wedwaldt, First Vice President; Valerie Bailey, Second Vice President; Jill Keesler, Registrar; Louise Roth, Secretary; Michael Roth, Treasurer
Paid Staff: 3 **Volunteer Staff:** 60
Paid Artists: 12 **Non-Paid Artists:** 10
Utilizes: Special Technical Talent; Guest Artists; Guest Directors
Budget: $100,000 - $500,000
Income Sources: Private Foundations/Grants/Endowments; Business/Corporate Donations; Box Office; Government Grants; Individual Donations
Season: 52 Weeks **Annual Attendance:** 25,000
Affiliations: SETC; Florida Theatre Conference; ASSITEJ; American Association of Theatre Educators
Performance Facilities: The Studio; Main Library Theatre

ONE WAY PUPPETS
PO Box 5346, Fort Lauderdale, FL 33310
(305) 491-4221; (305) 444-8842
Founded: 1971
Arts Area: Theatrical Group; Puppet
Status: Professional
Type: Performing; Educational
Purpose: To entertain and educate through the art of puppetry
Management: Bob Dolan, Director
Paid Staff: 2
Paid Artists: 2
Budget: $1,000 - $50,000
Income Sources: Private Foundations/Grants/Endowments; Individual Donations **Season:** 52 Weeks

PERFORMING SERIES

PTG-FLORIDA, INC./PARKER PLAYHOUSE
707 NE Eighth Street, Fort Lauderdale, FL 33304
(305) 764-1441
FAX: (305) 764-0708
Founded: 1967
Arts Area: Dance; Vocal Music; Instrumental Music; Theater
Status: Professional; Semi-Professional; Non-Professional; Non-Profit; Commercial

Type: Performing; Touring
Purpose: To promote a Broadway series; to make the theatre available to other local and professional promoters
Management: Ronald Stokes, Manager; Sheila Turkiewicz, Director of Theatre Operations; Carol Crolla, Box Office Treasurer; Beverly Sapp, Box Office Manager
Paid Staff: 12
Income Sources: Box Office
Season: November - April   **Annual Attendance:** 75,000
Affiliations: Pace Theatrical
Performance Facilities: Broadway Series

FACILITY

BAILEY HALL
3501 SW Davie Road, Fort Lauderdale, FL 33314
(305) 475-6880
FAX: (305) 424-3154
  Founded: 1979
  Type of Facility: Theatre Complex; Concert Hall; Theatre House
  Type of Stage: Proscenium
  Stage Dimensions: 110'Wx40'D   **Orchestra Pit**
  Seating Capacity: 1,201
  Year Built: 1979   **Architect:** William Crawford   **Cost:** $6,000,000
  Year Remodeled: 1986   **Architect:** Southeast Contractors   **Cost:** $20,000
  Contact for Rental: Cindy Garren;   (305) 475-6880
  Resident Groups: Gold Coast Opera; Miami City Ballet; Florida Philharmonic; Broward Friends of Chamber Music

BROWARD CENTER FOR THE PERFORMING ARTS
201 SW Fifth Avenue, Fort Lauderdale, FL 33312
(305) 463-3290
FAX: (305) 462-3541
  Type of Facility: Theatre Complex
  Type of Stage: Proscenium
  Stage Dimensions: 60'x20'; 45'x80'   **Orchestra Pit**
  Seating Capacity: 2,700; 600
  Year Built: 1991   **Architect:** Benjamin Thompson & Associates   **Cost:** $60,000,000
  Acoustical Consultant: Kirkegaard
  Contact for Rental: John D. Vogt;   (305) 468-3290
  Resident Groups: Florida Philharmonic Orchestra; Sinfonia Virtuosi; Greater Miami Opera; Ft. Lauderdale Opera Guild; Miami City Ballet; Concert Association of Florida; Ft. Lauderdale Broadway Series

PARKER PLAYHOUSE
707 NE Eighth Street, PO Box 4603, Fort Lauderdale, FL 33304
(305) 764-1441
  Type of Facility: Theatre Complex; Concert Hall; Auditorium; Off Broadway; Theatre House
  Type of Stage: Proscenium
  Stage Dimensions: 40'Wx33'D; 40'Wx19'H proscenium opening
  Orchestra Pit
  Seating Capacity: 1,200
  Year Built: 1966   **Architect:** John Volk
  Acoustical Consultant: Robert Haskins
  Contact for Rental: Ronald Stokes;   (305) 764-1442
  Resident Groups: Story Theatre Productions; Ft. Lauderdale Broadway Series
  Rentals from late April until mid-December; December - April as available

WAR MEMORIAL AUDITORIUM
800 NE Eighth Street, Fort Lauderdale, FL 33304
(305) 761-5380
  Type of Facility: Theatre Complex; Concert Hall; Auditorium; Theatre House; Opera House; Multi-Purpose; Exhibition Hall
  Type of Stage: Proscenium
  Stage Dimensions: 93'Wx42'D
  Orchestra Pit
  Seating Capacity: 2,110
  Year Built: 1950   **Architect:** Gilroy-Gamble   **Cost:** $650,000
  Year Remodeled: 1983
  Contact for Rental: Robert Stried;   (305) 761-5380

Fort Myers

DANCE

GULFCOAST DANCE
2265 Peck Street, Fort Myers, FL 33902-1593
(813) 334-3274
Founded: 1976
Arts Area: Modern; Ballet; Jazz
Status: Non-Profit
Type: Performing
Purpose: To offer performance opportunities for southwest Florida dancers under professional direction
Management: Jeanne Bochette, Director
Officers: Jeanne Bochette, President; Marc Platt, Vice President; Carol Thagard, Secretary/Treasurer
Non-Paid Artists: 3
Utilizes: Special Technical Talent; Guest Artists
Budget: $1,000 - $50,000
Income Sources: Private Foundations/Grants/Endowments; Business/Corporate Donations; Box Office; Government Grants; Individual Donations
Season: 52 Weeks   **Annual Attendance:** 31,000
Affiliations: State Dance Association of Florida
Performance Facilities: Mann Hall

THEATRE

PENINSULA PLAYERS
1436 Rosada Way, Fort Myers, FL 33901
(813) 334-0780
Founded: 1978
Arts Area: Dinner; Community; Theatrical Group
Status: Non-Profit
Type: Performing
Purpose: To provide the highest quality theatre possible to the people of southwestern Florida
Management: Al Richter, Dan Perry, Directors; Martha Richter, Director/Producer
Budget: $1,000 - $50,000
Income Sources: Box Office
Season: September - June   **Annual Attendance:** 5,000
Affiliations: Lee County Alliance of Arts
Performance Facilities: Peninsula Playhouse

FACILITY

BARBARA B. MANN PERFORMING ARTS HALL
8099 College Parkway SW, Fort Myers, FL 33906
(813) 489-3033
FAX: (813) 481-4849
Founded: 1985
Type of Facility: Concert Hall; Performance Center; Off Broadway; Theatre House; Opera House; Multi-Purpose
Type of Stage: Proscenium
Stage Dimensions: 57'Wx54'D proscenium opening   **Orchestra Pit**
Seating Capacity: 1,776
Year Built: 1985
Acoustical Consultant: Joe Gleason
Contact for Rental: Kevin Frederick;   (813) 489-3033

FORT MYERS HARBORSIDE 3 BUILDINGS
1375 Monroe Street, Fort Myers, FL 33901
(813) 334-6683
FAX: (813) 332-6683
Founded: 1990
Type of Facility: Concert Hall; Auditorium; Civic Center; Arena; Multi-Purpose
Type of Stage: Thrust; Flexible; Proscenium; Platform; Arena
Stage Dimensions: 40'x68'
Seating Capacity: Conv. Hall - 3,088; Exhibit Hall - 1,400; Hall of 50 States - 400
Year Built: 1991   **Architect:** Spillis Camilla and Partners
Contact for Rental: Theresa Joiner;   (813) 334-2073
Multi-purpose facility

Fort Pierce

FACILITY

SAINT LUCIE COUNTY CIVIC CENTER
2300 Virginia Avenue, Fort Pierce, FL 34982
(407) 468-1526
FAX: (407) 468-2132
Type of Facility: Civic Center
Year Built: 1977
Architect: Hank Riegler
Contact for Rental: Rosemary Kelley or Harold Wheeler; (407) 468-1526
Manager: Rosemary Kelley;   (407) 468-1526
Contains the Auditorium and Theater. See separate listings

SAINT LUCIE COUNTY CIVIC CENTER - AUDITORIUM
2300 Virginia Avenue, Fort Pierce, FL 34982
(407) 468-1526
FAX: (407) 268-2132
Type of Facility: Auditorium
Type of Stage: Flexible; Platform
Seating Capacity: 4,000
Year Built: 1977
Architect: Hank Riegler
Contact for Rental: Rosemary Kelley or Harold Wheeler;   (407) 468-1526
Manager: Rosemary Kelley;   (407) 468-1526

SAINT LUCIE COUNTY CIVIC CENTER - THEATER
2300 Virginia Avenue, Fort Pierce, FL 34982
(407) 468-1526
FAX: (407) 468-3132
Type of Facility: Concert Hall; Theatre House; Opera House
Type of Stage: Platform
Stage Dimensions: 40'Wx32'D
Seating Capacity: 2,200
Year Built: 1977   **Architect:** Hank Riegler
Contact for Rental: Rosemary Kelley or Harold Wheeler;   (407) 468-1526
Manager: Rosemary Kelley;   (407) 468-1526
Resident Groups: Treasure Coast Opera; Treasure Coast Concert Association

Fort Walton Beach

DANCE

NORTHWEST FLORIDA BALLET
101 Chicago Avenue, Fort Walton Beach, FL 32548
(904) 664-7787
Founded: 1969
Arts Area: Modern; Ballet; Jazz
Status: Professional; Semi-Professional; Non-Profit
Type: Performing; Touring; Resident; Educational; Sponsoring
Purpose: To perform; to educate the public as well as dancers; to enrich the cultural environment
Management: Bernadette Clements, Director; Fiona Fairrie, Ballet Mistress
Paid Staff: 2
Paid Artists: 6   **Non-Paid Artists:** 12
Utilizes: Guest Artists; Guest Choreographers
Budget: $100,000 - $500,000
Income Sources: Private Foundations/Grants/Endowments; Business/Corporate Donations; Box Office; Government Grants; Individual Donations
Season: September - July
Annual Attendance: 10,000
Affiliations: Florida Dance Association
Performance Facilities: Pensacola-Saenger Theatre; Panama City Marina Civic Center; Fort Walton Beach High Auditorium

---
Gainesville

DANCE

DANCE ALIVE!
1325 NW Second Street, Gainesville, FL 32601
(904) 371-2986
   Founded: 1966
   Arts Area: Modern; Ballet; Jazz
   Status: Professional; Non-Profit
   Type: Performing; Touring; Resident; Educational
   Purpose: To present and perform as a professional dance company; to offer artist residencies and arts-in-
   education residencies; to utilize the work of resident choreographers as well as old masters
   Management: Kim Tuttle, Artistic Director; Judy Skinner, Executive Director; Elaine Funk, Development Director; Ric
   Rose, Production Director
   Officers: Allen Edgar, President; Carl Schwait, President Elect; Linda Sexton, Secretary; Bill Zetrouer, Treasurer; Sheila
   Bilak, Past President
   Paid Staff: 5   **Volunteer Staff:** 5
   Paid Artists: 10   **Non-Paid Artists:** 20
   Utilizes: Special Technical Talent; Guest Conductors; Guest Artists; Guest Choreographers
   Budget: $100,000 - $500,000
   Income Sources: Private Foundations/Grants/Endowments; Business/Corporate Donations; Box Office; Government
   Grants; Individual Donations
   Season: September - May
   Annual Attendance: 20,000
   Affiliations: Siegel Artists Management
   Performance Facilities: Center for the Performing Arts

THEATRE

HIPPODROME STATE THEATRE
25 SE Second Place, Gainesville, FL 32601
(904) 373-5968; (904) 375-4477
   Founded: 1973
   Arts Area: Professional; Theatrical Group
   Status: Professional; Non-Profit
   Type: Performing; Touring; Resident; Educational; Sponsoring
   Purpose: To present the best contemporary theatre possible, and when doing the classics, to reexamine them under our pre-
   sent standards
   Management: Mary Hausch, Producing Director; Carlos Asse, Associate Producing Director
   Paid Staff: 23
   Paid Artists: 30
   Utilizes: Guest Artists; Guest Directors
   Budget: $500,000 - $1,000,000
   Income Sources: Private Foundations/Grants/Endowments; Business/Corporate Donations; Box Office; Government
   Grants; Individual Donations
   Season: 52 Weeks
   Annual Attendance: 50,000
   Affiliations: TCG; LORT; AAA
   Performance Facilities: Hippodrome

FACILITY

HIPPODROME
25 SE Second Place, Gainesville, FL 32601
(904) 373-5968
   Type of Facility: Theatre Complex
   Facility Originally: Post Office
   Type of Stage: Thrust; 3/4 Arena
   Seating Capacity: 266
   Year Built: 1909   **Architect:** Al Dompe   **Cost:** $2,000,000
   Year Remodeled: 1980
   Acoustical Consultant: University of Florida
   Contact for Rental: Shirley Lasseter;   (904) 373-5968

Hialeah

DANCE

BALLET ETUDES
415 West 51st Place, Hialeah, FL 33012
(305) 557-1142
Founded: 1981
Arts Area: Ballet
Status: Semi-Professional; Non-Profit
Type: Performing; Touring; Educational
Purpose: To perform classical and new classical ballet in southeastern Florida
Management: Susana Prieto, Artistic Director
Volunteer Staff: 10
Paid Artists: 15
Utilizes: Guest Artists; Guest Choreographers
Budget: $1,000 - $50,000
Income Sources: Box Office; Individual Donations
Season: September - June
Affiliations: Dance Educators of America
Performance Facilities: Jackie Gleason Theater

Hollywood

THEATRE

THE GOLDEN THESPIANS
900 Tyler Street, Hollywood, FL 33019
(305) 920-5492
Founded: 1965
Arts Area: Musical; Community; Folk; Theatrical Group
Status: Non-Profit
Type: Performing
Purpose: To bring together a senior group of men and women who were professional musicians, singers and dancers in their younger days to perform one-hour vaudeville shows in nursing homes, hospitals and at community affairs
Management: Ellen Bush, President/Director of Shows
Officers: Ellen Bush, President; Gloria Williams, Vice President; Virginia Godfrey, Treasurer; Madeline Barauskas, Secretary
Volunteer Staff: 25
Non-Paid Artists: 25
Utilizes: Guest Artists
Season: September - June
Annual Attendance: 224
Affiliations: President's Council
Performance Facilities: Recreation Center

HOLLYWOOD PLAYHOUSE
2640 Washington Street, Hollywood, FL 33020
(305) 922-0404
Founded: 1948
Arts Area: Musical; Community; Theatrical Group
Status: Semi-Professional; Non-Profit
Type: Performing
Purpose: To bring culture to the community through theatre
Management: Marianne Mavrides, Executive Director; Elaine Trell, Executive Secretary
Officers: Arnold Ilovitch, President; Howard Greenfield, Vice President; Andy Weinman, Treasurer; Abby Frank, Secretary
Paid Staff: 2   **Volunteer Staff:** 80
Utilizes: Guest Conductors
Income Sources: Box Office; Individual Donations
Season: October - July   **Annual Attendance:** 30,000
Affiliations: Florida Theatre Conference

FACILITY

BEACH THEATRE UNDER THE STARS
Johnson Street and Hollywood Beach Boardwalk, Hollywood, FL 33020
(305) 921-3399
FAX: (305) 921-3233
Type of Facility: Outdoor (Concert); Amphitheater
Type of Stage: Proscenium
Stage Dimensions: 30'x20'
Seating Capacity: 900
Year Built: 1965
Contact for Rental: Jerry Estep;   (305) 921-3404

YOUNG CIRCLE PARK AND BANDSHELL
US Highway 1 and Hollywood Boulevard, Hollywood, FL 33020
(305) 921-3399
FAX: (305) 921-3233
Type of Facility: Outdoor (Concert); Amphitheater
Type of Stage: Proscenium
Stage Dimensions: 60'Wx30'D   **Orchestra Pit**
Seating Capacity: 2,400
Year Built: 1952   **Architect:** Ken Spry
Contact for Rental: Irene Devin;   (305) 921-3404
Resident Groups: Greater Hollywood Philharmonic Orchestra

Homestead

THEATRE

ACTORS COMMUNITY THEATRE SHOWCASE
8851 SW 107th Avenue, Homestead, FL 33030
(305) 246-0704
Founded: 1983
Arts Area: Dinner; Community; Theatrical Group
Status: Non-Profit
Type: Performing; Touring; Resident; Educational
Purpose: To let non-professionals in the community be involved in drama; to bring "live" performances to areas that do not normally have the opportunity to see these presentations
Management: David Arisco, Artistic Director; Barbara Stein, Executive Director; Gerald Brow, Director of Development
Officers: Lawrence Stein, President
Volunteer Staff: 10
Non-Paid Artists: 10
Utilizes: Guest Artists; Guest Directors
Budget: $1,000 - $50,000
Income Sources: Business/Corporate Donations; Box Office; Individual Donations
Season: October - May   **Annual Attendance:** 2,000
Affiliations: Homestead Center for the Arts

Indialantic

INSTRUMENTAL MUSIC

MELBOURNE CHAMBER MUSIC SOCIETY
PO Box 33403, Indialantic, FL 32903
(407) 729-3278
FAX: (407) 725-6406
Founded: 1978
Arts Area: Chamber; Ensemble; Instrumental Group
Status: Non-Profit
Type: Sponsoring
Purpose: To bring outstanding professional chamber music to members and the community
Officers: Tom Kabaservice, President; Andy Pavlakos, Vice President; Madeline Herczog, Programs; Roger Uhlhorn, Treasurer
Volunteer Staff: 10
Paid Artists: 20
Utilizes: Guest Artists
Budget: $1,000 - $50,000

Income Sources: Business/Corporate Donations; Box Office; Individual Donations
Season: November - March
Annual Attendance: 750
Performance Facilities: Ascension Luthern Church, Indian Harbor Beach

---

Jacksonville

DANCE

FLORIDA BALLET AT JACKSONVILLE
123 East Forsyth Street, Jacksonville, FL 32202
(904) 353-7518
Founded: 1978
Arts Area: Ballet; Guest Choreographers
Status: Professional; Non-Profit
Type: Performing; Touring; Resident
Purpose: To take a contemporary approach to performance of classical ballet
Management: Laurie Picinich-Byrd, Michael F. Byrd, Artistic Directors
Paid Staff: 5
Paid Artists: 11
Utilizes: Guest Choreographers
Budget: $50,000 - $100,000
Income Sources: Private Foundations/Grants/Endowments; Business/Corporate Donations; Box Office; Government Grants; Individual Donations
Season: September - May
Performance Facilities: Florida Theatre Performing Arts Center

JACKSONVILLE BALLET THEATRE
5516 Keystone Drive South, Jacksonville, FL 32207
(904) 396-5893
Founded: 1970
Arts Area: Modern; Ballet; Jazz
Status: Semi-Professional; Non-Profit
Type: Performing; Educational
Purpose: To further talent in the community by performing and improving technique, acting abilities and audience awareness
Management: Dulce Anaya, Artistic Director
Volunteer Staff: 16
Utilizes: Guest Artists
Income Sources: Private Foundations/Grants/Endowments; Box Office; Individual Donations
Season: September - August
Performance Facilities: Civic Auditorium

INSTRUMENTAL MUSIC

JACKSONVILLE SYMPHONY ORCHESTRA
33 South Hogan Street, Suite 400, Jacksonville, FL 32202
(904) 354-5479
Founded: 1949
Arts Area: Symphony; Orchestra; Chamber
Status: Professional; Non-Profit
Type: Performing; Touring; Educational
Purpose: To provide performances of high artistic quality designed to reach the broadest possible audience; to strive to not only inspire and challenge its audience with classical music, but also provide educational and public service programs
Management: Roger Nierenberg, Music Director/Conductor; David L. Pierson, Executive Director
Officers: Robert T. Shircliff, President; Robert Purcifull, Vice President; Isabelle Davis, Secretary; G. Kennedy Thompson, Treasurer
Paid Staff: 13
Paid Artists: 90
Utilizes: Special Technical Talent; Guest Conductors; Guest Artists
Budget: $1,000,000 - $5,000,000
Income Sources: Private Foundations/Grants/Endowments; Business/Corporate Donations; Box Office; Government Grants; Individual Donations; Fund-raising
Season: September - May   **Annual Attendance:** 250,000
Affiliations: ASOL; Florida Arts Council; Arts Assembly of Jacksonville
Performance Facilities: Florida Theatre Performing Arts Center; Civic Auditorium

THEATRE

ALHAMBRA DINNER THEATRE
12000 Beach Boulevard, Jacksonville, FL 32216
(904) 641-1212
FAX: (904) 642-3505
    Founded: 1967
    Arts Area: Professional; Dinner
    Status: Professional; Commercial
    Type: Performing
    Purpose: To produce the finest in professional theatrical productions
    Management: Tod Booth, Executive Producer
    Officers: Tod Booth, President
    Paid Staff: 75
    Paid Artists: 25
    Utilizes: Guest Artists
    Budget: $1,000,000 - $5,000,000
    Income Sources: Box Office
    Season: 52 Weeks   **Annual Attendance:** 130,000
    Affiliations: AEA; ADTI; SSDC; AFM
    Performance Facilities: Alhambra Dinner Theatre

FACILITY

ALHAMBRA DINNER THEATRE
12000 Beach Boulevard, Jacksonville, FL 32216
(904) 641-1212
FAX: (904) 642-3505
    Type of Facility: Theatre House
    Type of Stage: Thrust
    Stage Dimensions: 18'x22'
    Seating Capacity: 388
    Year Built: 1967
    Contact for Rental: Jack Booth; (904) 641-1212

FLORIDA NATIONAL PAVILION
1410 East Adams Street, Jacksonville, FL 32202
(904) 630-0837
    Type of Facility: Outdoor (Concert)
    Type of Stage: Environmental
    Stage Dimensions: 97'x47'
    Seating Capacity: Concert - 58,000; Theater - 1,875
    Year Built: 1983   **Cost:** $3,000,000
    Contact for Rental: Sharon Brown; (904) 630-0837
    Manager: Dewitt Gibbs
    Resident Groups: Saint John's River City Band; Jacksonville Symphony Orchestra

FLORIDA THEATRE PERFORMING ARTS CENTER
128 East Forsyth Street, Suite 300, Jacksonville, FL 32202
(904) 355-5661
FAX: (904) 358-1874
    Type of Facility: Concert Hall; Theatre House
    Facility Originally: Vaudeville; Movie House
    Type of Stage: Proscenium
    Stage Dimensions: 40'Wx28'H proscenium opening
    Orchestra Pit
    Seating Capacity: 1,978
    Year Built: 1927   **Architect:** Hall & Benjamin
    Year Remodeled: 1983   **Architect:** Herschel Shepard   **Cost:** $5,700,000
    Contact for Rental: Sondra Floyd; (904) 355-5661
    Manager: J. Erik Hart; (904) 355-5661
    Resident Groups: Jacksonville Symphony

JACKSONVILLE CIVIC AUDITORIUM
300 West Water Street, Jacksonville, FL 32202
(904) 630-0701
    Type of Facility: Auditorium
    Type of Stage: Proscenium

Stage Dimensions: 55'Wx30'H proscenium opening
Orchestra Pit
Seating Capacity: 3,200
Year Built: 1962
Contact for Rental: Pat Craig
Contains the Little Theater and Exhibition Hall. See separate listings

JACKSONVILLE CIVIC AUDITORIUM - EXHIBITION HALL
300 West Water Street, Jacksonville, FL 32202
(904) 630-0701
Type of Facility: Exhibition Hall
Year Built: 1962
Contact for Rental: Pat Craig
The Exhibition Hall contains 21,500 square feet

JACKSONVILLE CIVIC AUDITORIUM - LITTLE THEATER
300 West Water Street, Jacksonville, FL 32202
(904) 630-0701
Type of Facility: Theatre House
Type of Stage: Proscenium
Stage Dimensions: 30'Wx28'H proscenium opening
Orchestra Pit
Seating Capacity: 609
Year Built: 1962
Contact for Rental: Pat Craig

Jupiter

THEATRE

COASTAL PLAYERS/JUPITER CIVIC THEATRE
PO Box 1641, Jupiter, FL 33468-1641
(305) 746-6303
Founded: 1964
Arts Area: Community
Status: Non-Professional; Non-Profit
Type: Performing
Purpose: To encourage interest and participation in live theatre; to cultivate community appreciation and support of the theatre
Officers: Don Blaney, President; Royce Emley, Vice President; Jean Menilla, Treasurer; Anna Bell, Secretary
Volunteer Staff: 9
Budget: $1,000 - $50,000
Income Sources: Box Office; Individual Donations
Season: November - March
Annual Attendance: 2,000
Performance Facilities: Jupiter Community Theatre

Key West

THEATRE

KEY WEST PLAYERS
Wall Street Waterfront Playhouse, PO Box 724, Key West, FL 33041
(305) 294-5015
Founded: 1940
Arts Area: Community; Theatrical Group
Status: Non-Profit
Type: Performing; Educational
Purpose: To present live entertainment featuring professional and amateur artists; to provide a teaching experience; to teach all aspects of theater
Officers: Nancy Holt Kamp, President; George Gugleotti, First Vice President; David Bird, Second Vice President; Florence Recher, Treasurer
Volunteer Staff: 20
Utilizes: Special Technical Talent; Guest Artists; Guest Directors
Budget: $50,000 - $100,000
Income Sources: Box Office; Individual Donations
Season: October - May   **Annual Attendance:** 10,000

RED BARN THEATRE
319 Duval Street, Rear Box 707, Key West, FL 33040
(305) 296-9911
>**Founded:** 1979
>**Arts Area:** Professional; Musical; Theatrical Group
>**Status:** Professional; Non-Profit
>**Type:** Performing; Resident; Educational
>**Management:** Joy Hawkins, Co-Artistic Director; Mimi McDonald, Business Manager
>**Paid Staff:** 5
>**Paid Artists:** 60
>**Utilizes:** Guest Artists; Guest Directors
>**Budget:** $100,000 - $500,000
>**Income Sources:** Private Foundations/Grants/Endowments; Business/Corporate Donations; Box Office; Government Grants; Individual Donations
>**Season:** November - June
>**Annual Attendance:** 13,500
>**Affiliations:** TCG
>**Performance Facilities:** Red Barn Theatre

PERFORMING SERIES

TENNESSEE WILLIAMS FINE ARTS CENTER
5901 West College Road, Key West, FL 33040
(305) 296-9081, ext. 299
FAX: (305) 292-5155
>**Founded:** 1977
>**Arts Area:** Dance; Vocal Music; Instrumental Music; Theater; Festivals; Lyric Opera; Grand Opera
>**Status:** Non-Profit
>**Type:** Performing; Sponsoring
>**Purpose:** To expose tourists and residents to a varied program of the arts through in-house productions and sponsored touring productions
>**Management:** Ken Bryant, Theatre Director; Florida Keys Community College Fine Arts Department
>**Paid Staff:** 5
>**Paid Artists:** 400   **Non-Paid Artists:** 100
>**Utilizes:** Guest Conductors; Guest Artists; Guest Directors
>**Season:** October - June
>**Annual Attendance:** 19,000
>**Affiliations:** Florida Keys Community College
>**Performance Facilities:** Tennessee Williams Fine Arts Center

FACILITY

FLORIDA KEYS COMMUNITY COLLEGE - TENNESSEE WILLIAMS THEATRE
Tennessee Williams Fine Arts Center, 5901 West College Road, Key West, FL 33040
(305) 296-1520
>**Type of Facility:** Concert Hall; Theatre House; Opera House
>**Type of Stage:** Proscenium; Hydraulic Lift Stage
>**Stage Dimensions:** 40'Wx20'D;- 40'Wx20'H proscenium opening
>**Orchestra Pit**
>**Seating Capacity:** 490
>**Year Built:** 1977   **Architect:** Carr Smith and Associates
>**Contact for Rental:** Ken Bryant;   (305) 296-9081, ext. 299
>**Resident Groups:** Tennessee Williams Fine Arts Center Presenting Series
>*Southernmost performance facility in the continental United States*

RED BARN THEATRE
319 Duval Street, Rear Box 707, Key West, FL 33040
(305) 296-9911
>**Type of Facility:** Theatre House
>**Facility Originally:** Barn
>**Type of Stage:** Platform
>**Seating Capacity:** 99
>**Year Remodeled:** 1980
>**Contact for Rental:** Joy Hawkins, Mimi McDonald;   (305) 296-9911
>**Resident Groups:** Red Barn Theatre

Kissimmee

THEATRE

OSCEOLA PLAYERS
PO Box 451088, Kissimmee, FL 34745
(407) 846-6257
> **Founded:** 1960
> **Arts Area:** Theatrical Group
> **Status:** Non-Professional; Non-Profit
> **Type:** Performing
> **Purpose:** To promote and foster an interest in the dramatic arts as evidenced through presentations of theatrical works
> **Officers:** Robin DuBois-Borden, President; Sharon Sikorski, Vice President; Terrilea Myers, Vice President; Bob Jones, Treasurer
> **Volunteer Staff:** 15
> **Non-Paid Artists:** 50
> **Utilizes:** Special Technical Talent; Guest Directors
> **Budget:** $1,000 - $50,000
> **Income Sources:** Box Office; Individual Donations
> **Season:** September - May   **Annual Attendance:** 10,000
> **Affiliations:** Florida Theatre Conference
> **Performance Facilities:** Osceola Center for the Arts

FACILITY

OSCEOLA CENTER FOR THE ARTS
PO Box 1195, Kissimmee, FL 32742
(407) 846-6257
> **Founded:** 1966
> **Type of Facility:** Theatre Complex; Multi-Purpose; Art Gallery & Classroom; Music Wing
> **Type of Stage:** Proscenium; C.H. Parsons
> **Stage Dimensions:** 50'Dx30'W   **Orchestra Pit**
> **Seating Capacity:** 249
> **Year Built:** 1968   **Cost:** $85,000
> **Year Remodeled:** 1975   **Architect:** C. H. Parsons   **Cost:** $105,000
> **Contact for Rental:** Pete Edwards, Executive Director;   (407) 846-6257
> **Resident Groups:** Osceola Players; Osceola Choral Society; Osceola Historical Society; Osceola Creative Arts League
> *All but religious or political events*

Lake Worth

FACILITY

PALM BEACH COMMUNITY COLLEGE - WATSON B. DUNCAN III, THEATRE
4200 Congress, Lake Worth, FL 33461
(305) 439-8244
> **Type of Facility:** Theatre Complex; Recital Hall
> **Type of Stage:** Thrust; Proscenium; Hydraulic Lift Stage
> **Stage Dimensions:** 36'dx54'W; 19'Hx42'W proscenium opening   **Orchestra Pit**
> **Seating Capacity:** Main House - 720, Recital Hall - 130
> **Year Built:** 1960
> **Year Remodeled:** 1986   **Architect:** Schwabb & Twitty   **Cost:** $3,100,000
> **Contact for Rental:** W. Lee Bell, Manager;   (305) 439-8244

Lakeland

INSTRUMENTAL MUSIC

IMPERIAL SYMPHONY
217 South Tennessee Avenue, Lakeland, FL 33801
(813) 688-3743
> **Founded:** 1965
> **Arts Area:** Symphony
> **Status:** Non-Profit
> **Type:** Performing; Resident; Educational

Purpose: To provide quality musical experiences to listeners of all ages in Lakeland and audiences in other parts of the area; to enhance the music programs in public schools by providing performance opportunities for advanced students and faculty
Management: Larry Collison, Conductor; Beth Mason, Director
Officers: Susan Cruz, President; Jean Palm, Treasurer
Volunteer Staff: 6
Non-Paid Artists: 65
Utilizes: Guest Artists
Budget: $100,000 - $500,000
Income Sources: Private Foundations/Grants/Endowments; Business/Corporate Donations; Box Office; Government Grants; Individual Donations
Season: September - May
Annual Attendance: 10,000
Affiliations: ASOL
Performance Facilities: Lakeland Civic Center

FACILITY

BRANSCOMB MEMORIAL AUDITORIUM
Florida Southern College, 111 Lake Hollingsworth Drive, Lakeland, FL 33801-5698
(813) 680-4295
FAX: (813) 680-3758
Founded: 1964
Type of Facility: Concert Hall; Auditorium; Performance Center; Theatre House; Opera House
Type of Stage: Proscenium
Stage Dimensions: 40'x28'
Orchestra Pit
Seating Capacity: 1,809
Year Built: 1964   **Architect:** Nils Schweitzer   **Cost:** $1,000,000
Contact for Rental: Anthony C. Harris;   (813) 680-4295
Resident Groups: Robert McDonald, Pianist; Beverly Wolff, Mezzo Soprano; The Clarion Brass; The Hollingsworth Trio; Florida Southern College: Symphony Band; Concert Chorale; Jazz Ensemble; Opera Theatre

FLORIDA SOUTHERN COLLEGE - BUCKNER THEATRE
Lakeland, FL 33801-5986
(813) 680-4226
Type of Facility: Theatre House
Type of Stage: Thrust
Stage Dimensions: 22'x28'x41'
Seating Capacity: 336
Year Built: 1970
Architect: Nils Schweitzer   **Cost:** $750,000
Contact for Rental: Richard LeVene, Manager;   (813) 680-4184
Manager: Richard LeVene;   (813) 680-4184
Resident Groups: Florida Southern College Vagabonds

LAKELAND CIVIC CENTER
700 West Lemon Street, Lakeland, FL 33802
(813) 499-8100
FAX: (813) 499-8101
Founded: 1974
Type of Facility: Theatre Complex; Civic Center
Type of Stage: Thrust
Stage Dimensions: 78'x47'
Orchestra Pit
Seating Capacity: 2,282
Year Built: 1972   **Architect:** Wade Setliff   **Cost:** $12,000,000
Contact for Rental: Allen Johnson;   (813) 499-8100

LAKELAND CIVIC CENTER - ARENA
700 West Lemon Street, Lakeland, FL 33802
(813) 686-7126
Type of Facility: Concert Hall; Arena
Type of Stage: Flexible; Platform
Seating Capacity: 10,000
Year Built: 1974
Contact for Rental: Allen Johnson;   (813) 499-8100

LAKELAND CIVIC CENTER - EXHIBITION HALL
700 West Lemon Street, Lakeland, FL 33802
(813) 499-8100
FAX: (813) 499-8101
　　　Type of Facility: Exhibition Hall
　　　Type of Stage: Flexible; Platform
　　　Year Built: 1974
　　　Contact for Rental: Allen Johnson;　(813) 499-8100
　　　Contains 34,000 square feet of exhibit space

LAKELAND CIVIC CENTER - THEATRE
700 West Lemmon Street, Lakeland, FL 33802
(813) 686-7126
　　　Type of Facility: Concert Hall; Theatre House
　　　Type of Stage: Proscenium
　　　Stage Dimensions: 87'Wx47'D　**Orchestra Pit**
　　　Seating Capacity: 2,282
　　　Year Built: 1974
　　　Contact for Rental: Allen Johnson;　(813) 499-8100
　　　Resident Groups: Imperial Symphony Orchestra

Longboat Key

INSTRUMENTAL MUSIC

SARASOTA-MANATEE COMMUNITY ORCHESTRA
PO Box 8754, Longboat Key, FL 34228
(813) 383-0734
　　　Founded: 1975
　　　Arts Area: Orchestra
　　　Status: Non-Professional; Non-Profit
　　　Type: Performing; Resident
　　　Purpose: To give all those who wish to express themselves musically an opportunity to play in a quality orchestra
　　　Management: Patricia Stenberg, Conductor; Catherine Miller, Librarian
　　　Officers: Carleton Brower, President; Mary Jane Meyer, Corresponding Secretary; C. Vincent Wright, Treasurer; Elizabeth Baritaud, Recording Secretary
　　　Paid Staff: 2　**Volunteer Staff:** 5
　　　Paid Artists: 8　**Non-Paid Artists:** 85
　　　Utilizes: Guest Artists
　　　Budget: $50,000 - $100,000
　　　Income Sources: Private Foundations/Grants/Endowments; Box Office; Individual Donations
　　　Season: October - April　**Annual Attendance:** 7,500
　　　Affiliations: ASOL
　　　Performance Facilities: Van Wezel Performing Arts Hall

Lynn Haven

THEATRE

KALEIDOSCOPE THEATRE
207 East 24th Street, Lynn Haven, FL 32444
(904) 265-3226; (904) 265-3757
　　　Founded: 1972
　　　Arts Area: Musical; Dinner; Community
　　　Status: Non-Professional; Non-Profit
　　　Type: Performing; Educational
　　　Purpose: To enhance the presentational and educational aspects of live theatre for cultural enrichment
　　　Management: Board of Directors: Lois Carter; David Garcia; Inia J. Plumb; Bill Lanier; Barry Brunetti; Blonza Layfield; Martha Laniel; Kerrie Casey; Sue Webb
　　　Officers: Charles Wilson, President; Gail Salsman, Vice President; Drew Casey, Secretary; Nancy Parsons, Treasurer
　　　Volunteer Staff: 20
　　　Non-Paid Artists: 300
　　　Utilizes: Special Technical Talent; Guest Artists; Guest Directors
　　　Budget: $1,000 - $50,000
　　　Income Sources: Private Foundations/Grants/Endowments; Business/Corporate Donations; Box Office; Government Grants; Individual Donations

Season: September - June
Annual Attendance: 6,000
Performance Facilities: Kaleidoscope Theatre

Manalapan

THEATRE

THEATRE CLUB OF THE PALM BEACHES
262 South Ocean Boulevard, Manalapan, FL 33462
(407) 585-3404
FAX: (407) 585-4708
    Arts Area: Professional; Theatrical Group
    Status: Professional
    Type: Performing
    Purpose: To present the best new works by young American playwrights
    Management: Louis Tyrrell, Producing Director; Nancy Barnett, Company Manager; Caroline Breder, Office Manager; Cheryl Dun, Marketing Director; Alison Pruitt, Development Director
    Officers: Richard Rampell, President; David Freese, Mary Montgomery, Vice Presidents; Dan Hall, Treasurer; William Bone, Secretary
    Paid Staff: 14 **Volunteer Staff:** 200
    Paid Artists: 30
    Utilizes: Guest Directors; AEA Actors
    Budget: Over 10,000,000
    Income Sources: Private Foundations/Grants/Endowments; Business/Corporate Donations; Box Office; Government Grants; Individual Donations
    Season: 52 Weeks
    Annual Attendance: 40,000
    Affiliations: AEA; SSDC

Marathon

THEATRE

MARATHON COMMUNITY THEATRE
PO Box 124, Marathon, FL 33050
(305) 743-5277
    Founded: 1957
    Arts Area: Musical; Dinner; Community; Theatrical Group; Puppet
    Status: Non-Profit
    Type: Performing; Sponsoring
    Purpose: To produce quality theatre events for the adult community; to present cultural programs in the local school system
    Officers: Ray Dimarco, President; Joyce Zwart, Vice President; Bud Kreh, Treasurer; Judi Gorman, Secretary
    Non-Paid Artists: 60
    Utilizes: Special Technical Talent; Guest Conductors; Guest Artists; Guest Directors
    Budget: $1,000 - $50,000
    Income Sources: Private Foundations/Grants/Endowments; Business/Corporate Donations; Box Office; Government Grants; Individual Donations
    Season: 52 Weeks
    Annual Attendance: 10,000

Margate

INSTRUMENTAL MUSIC

NORTHWEST SYMPHONIC POPS ORCHESTRA
6009 NW Tenth Street, Margate, FL 33063
(305) 977-9505
    Founded: 1982
    Arts Area: Orchestra
    Status: Non-Professional; Non-Profit
    Type: Performing; Resident
    Purpose: To promote music appreciation and fund-raising through the Seniors Foundation of Northwest Broward County
    Management: Tony Pandy, Music Director/Conductor
    Officers: Anne Oller, President; Henry Katz, Vice President; Joseph Goldstein, Treasurer; Natalie Shrage, Secretary

Volunteer Staff: 100
Paid Artists: 10   **Non-Paid Artists:** 60
Utilizes: Guest Artists
Budget: $1,000 - $50,000
Income Sources: Private Foundations/Grants/Endowments; Business/Corporate Donations; Box Office; Individual Donations
Season: October - March   **Annual Attendance:** 6,000
Performance Facilities: Broward Community College, North Campus

---

Melbourne

THEATRE

MELBOURNE CIVIC THEATRE
625 East New Haven Avenue, Melbourne, FL 32901
(305) 723-6935
  Founded: 1952
  Arts Area: Community; Theatrical Group
  Status: Non-Professional; Non-Profit
  Type: Performing; Educational
  Purpose: To entertain, educate and enrich the community in the theatre arts
  Management: David B. Beyer, Artistic Director; Fran S. Delisle, Business Manager; Patricia England, Technical Director
  Officers: John Warwick, President; Joseph Langlois, Vice President; Darcia Jones-Francey, Secretary; Greg Pollock, Treasurer
  Paid Staff: 3   **Volunteer Staff:** 25
  Non-Paid Artists: 250
  Budget: $100,000 - $500,000
  Income Sources: Business/Corporate Donations; Box Office; Government Grants
  Season: September - June   **Annual Attendance:** 19,000
  Affiliations: Florida Theatre Conference; ACT; SETC
  Performance Facilities: Henegar Center

FACILITY

MAXWELL C. KING CENTER FOR THE PERFORMING ARTS
3865 North Wickham Road, Melbourne, FL 32935
(407) 254-0305, ext. 5100
FAX: (407) 242-2730
  Type of Facility: Theatre Complex
  Type of Stage: Proscenium
  Stage Dimensions: 120'x45'   **Orchestra Pit**
  Seating Capacity: 1,993
  Year Built: 1988   **Architect:** Spillas & Candella   **Cost:** $12,300,000
  Acoustical Consultant: George Eisenhour
  Contact for Rental: Ron McCown;   (407) 254-0305

MELBOURNE AUDITORIUM
625 East Hibiscus Boulevard, Melbourne, FL 32901
(407) 722-6000
  Type of Facility: Auditorium; Multi-Purpose
  Type of Stage: Proscenium
  Stage Dimensions: 60'Wx40'D; 60'Wx17'H proscenium opening
  Seating Capacity: 1,400
  Year Built: 1965   **Cost:** $365,000
  Contact for Rental: Wendi Moon;   (407) 722-6000

Miami

DANCE

BALLET CONCERTO COMPANY OF MIAMI
3410 Coral Way, Miami, FL 33145
(305) 446-7922
  Founded: 1966
  Arts Area: Modern; Ballet; Jazz; Folk
  Status: Semi-Professional; Non-Profit
  Type: Performing; Educational

Purpose: To present dance in all its forms and shapes in performances of the highest quality
Management: Sonia Diaz, Martha Del Pino, Co-Artistic Directors; Vera Dubson, Executive Director
Officers: Nina Saun, Secretary; Noel Puig, Accountant; Mirita Saun, Treasurer
Volunteer Staff: 4
Paid Artists: 15
Utilizes: Guest Artists
Budget: $50,000 - $100,000
Income Sources: Private Foundations/Grants/Endowments; Business/Corporate Donations; Box Office; Government Grants; Individual Donations
Season: October - May   **Annual Attendance:** 30,000
Affiliations: SERBA; Dance Umbrella

BALLET SPECTACULAR/INTERNATIONAL CULTURAL EXCHANGE, INC.
59 NW 25th Avenue, Miami, FL 33125
(305) 642-8000
Founded: 1948
Arts Area: Modern; Mime; Ballet; Jazz; Ethnic; Folk
Status: Professional
Type: Performing; Touring; Resident; Educational; Sponsoring
Management: Francis Mayville, Managing Director; Herschell Munoz, Associate Director; Camilo Giraldo, Director of Public Relations
Paid Staff: 3   **Volunteer Staff:** 10
Paid Artists: 30
Utilizes: Special Technical Talent; Guest Conductors; Guest Artists; Guest Directors; Guest Choreographers
Budget: $100,000 - $500,000
Income Sources: Box Office
Season: January - June
Affiliations: Hungarian Church of Reformation
Performance Facilities: Gusman Center; Jackie Gleason Theatre of the Performing Arts

FLORIDA DANCE ASSOCIATION INC.
300 Northeast Second Avenue, Suite 1412, Miami, FL 33132-2204
(305) 237-3413
FAX: (305) 237-3645
Founded: 1974
Arts Area: Modern; Ballet; Jazz; Ethnic; Folk
Status: Professional; Non-Profit
Type: Educational; Sponsoring; Service
Management: Rebecca Terrell, Executive Director; Thomas E. Thielen, Associate Director
Officers: Toya Dubin, President; Kip Watson, President Elect; Daniel Lewis, Treasurer; Kathryn Cashin, Secretary
Paid Staff: 2
Utilizes: Guest Artists; Guest Choreographers
Budget: $100,000 - $500,000
Income Sources: Private Foundations/Grants/Endowments; Business/Corporate Donations; Box Office; Government Grants; Individual Donations; Technical Assistance Projects

MIAMI DANCE THEATRE
12205 SW 133rd Court, Miami, FL 33165
(305) 238-4362
Founded: 1980
Arts Area: Ballet
Status: Non-Profit
Type: Performing
Purpose: To maintain a classical ballet company for serious students ages 9 through 18
Management: Judith Newman, Mariana Alvarez-Brake, Co-Artistic Directors
Officers: Lana Brown, President; Marcia Stone, Treasurer; Linda Chastine, Secretary
Paid Staff: 3   **Volunteer Staff:** 5
Non-Paid Artists: 27
Utilizes: Special Technical Talent
Budget: $1,000 - $50,000
Income Sources: Private Foundations/Grants/Endowments; Business/Corporate Donations; Box Office; Government Grants; Individual Donations
Season: September - June
Affiliations: SERBA; Dance Umbrella

MOMENTUM DANCE COMPANY
174 East Flagler Street, Miami, FL 33156
(305) 530-8332
Founded: 1982

Arts Area: Modern; Ballet; Jazz
Status: Professional; Non-Profit
Type: Performing; Touring; Resident; Educational
Purpose: To focus on producing new works as well as reconstructing works of historical significance; to act as a modern dance resource for the community though educational programs
Management: Delma Iles, Artistic Director; Diane Guida, Company Manager
Officers: Dr. Michael Newman, President; Delma Iles, Vice President; Laurel Kalser, Secretary/Treasurer
Paid Staff: 2   **Volunteer Staff:** 3
Paid Artists: 11
Utilizes: Special Technical Talent; Guest Artists; Guest Choreographers
Budget: $100,000 - $500,000
Income Sources: Private Foundations/Grants/Endowments; Business/Corporate Donations; Box Office; Government Grants; Individual Donations
Season: September - May   **Annual Attendance:** 15,000
Affiliations: Dance Umbrella; State Dance Association of Florida
Performance Facilities: James L. Knight Center Auditorium

INSTRUMENTAL MUSIC

GREATER MIAMI MERRY MUMMERS STRING BAND
1261 NE 112th Street, Miami, FL 33161
Founded: 1965
Arts Area: Orchestra; Band
Status: Non-Professional; Non-Profit
Type: Performing
Purpose: To do charity work in our community, teach interested folks to play string instruments and bring cheer wherever we go
Officers: George Helker, President; Rhoda Samuels, Vice President; Joe Keilson, Treasurer; Barb Vlugt, Secretary; Joey Dean, Captain; Bob Vlugt, Music Director
Non-Paid Artists: 32
Budget: $1,000 - $50,000
Income Sources: Individual Donations
Season: 52 Weeks   **Annual Attendance:** 25
Affiliations: Philadelphia Mummers Association
Performance Facilities: North Miami Beach Senior High School

MIAMI CHAMBER SYMPHONY
5690 North Kendall Drive, Miami, FL 33156
(305) 662-6600
Founded: 1981
Arts Area: Symphony; Chamber
Status: Professional; Non-Profit
Type: Performing
Purpose: To perform a subscription season of chamber orchestra concerts with famous international artists as well as a series of student concerts
Management: Burton Dines, Music Director/Manager; Jean Bailly, Office Manager
Officers: Patrick R. Sullivan, President; Norris Siert, Vice President; Douglas Archbold, Treasurer
Paid Staff: 2   **Volunteer Staff:** 2
Paid Artists: 40
Utilizes: Guest Conductors; Guest Artists; Guild Activities
Budget: $100,000 - $500,000
Income Sources: Private Foundations/Grants/Endowments; Business/Corporate Donations; Box Office; Government Grants; Individual Donations
Season: October - May   **Annual Attendance:** 4,000
Affiliations: ASOL
Performance Facilities: Gusman Concert Hall

SOUTH FLORIDA YOUTH SYMPHONY
555 NW 152nd Street, Miami, FL 33169
(305) 238-2706
FAX: (305) 252-9876
Founded: 1964
Arts Area: Orchestra; Chamber; Ensemble
Status: Non-Profit
Type: Performing; Educational
Purpose: To broaden the horizons of young talented musicians in the area of symphonic music; to train them in the performance of this music, in conducting and for solos; to offer a junior string training program for beginning students
Officers: Marcia Hencinski, President; Al Babcock, First Vice President; Helaine Clein, Second Vice President
Paid Staff: 2   **Volunteer Staff:** 3

Non-Paid Artists: 3
Utilizes: Guest Artists
Budget: $100,000 - $500,000
Income Sources: Private Foundations/Grants/Endowments; Business/Corporate Donations; Individual Donations
Season: September - June   **Annual Attendance:** 7,300
Affiliations: ASOL; Dade Partners; Barry University Early Credit Program

VOCAL MUSIC

THE GREATER MIAMI OPERA ASSOCIATION
1200 Coral Way, Miami, FL 33145
(305) 854-1643
FAX: (305) 856-1042
Founded: 1941
Arts Area: Grand Opera; Lyric Opera
Status: Professional; Non-Profit
Type: Performing; Touring; Resident; Educational
Management: Robert M. Heuer, General Manager; Willie Anthony Waters, Artistic Director; Paul Lapinski, Assistant General Manager/Production Director
Paid Staff: 26
Utilizes: Special Technical Talent; Guest Conductors; Guest Artists; Guest Directors
Budget: $5,000,000 - $10,000,000
Income Sources: Private Foundations/Grants/Endowments; Business/Corporate Donations; Box Office; Government Grants; Individual Donations
Season: January - May   **Annual Attendance:** 220,000
Performance Facilities: Dade County Auditorium

THEATRE

COCONUT GROVE PLAYHOUSE
3500 Main Highway, PO Box 616, Miami, FL 33133
(305) 442-2662
FAX: (305) 444-6437
Founded: 1956
Arts Area: Professional; Theatrical Group
Status: Professional; Non-Profit
Type: Performing; Touring; Educational
Purpose: To bring good theater to the community; to attempt to expand the knowledge of theater in the community
Management: Arnold Mittelman, Producing Artistic Director; Lynne Peyser, Associate Producer; Mark Sylvester, Director of Marketing; Judith Delgado, Director of Education; Savannah Whaley, Public Relations Manager; Lisa Pearson, Development Director
Paid Staff: 35
Paid Artists: 50
Utilizes: Guest Artists; Guest Directors
Income Sources: Business/Corporate Donations; Box Office; Individual Donations
Season: October - May   **Annual Attendance:** 11,000
Affiliations: TCG
Performance Facilities: Coconut Grove Playhouse

LAS MASCARAS THEATRE
2833 NW Seventh Street, Miami, FL 33125
(305) 649-5301
Founded: 1968
Arts Area: Professional; Summer Stock; Musical; Theatrical Group
Status: Professional; Non-Profit
Type: Performing
Purpose: To perform plays in Spanish by local and international authors
Management: Alfonso Cremata, Salvador Ugarte, Artistic Directors/Lead Actors
Officers: Delia Carballo, President; Consuelo Otero, Vice President; Nina Saun, Secretary
Paid Staff: 4   **Volunteer Staff:** 10
Paid Artists: 20
Utilizes: Guest Artists
Budget: $50,000 - $100,000
Income Sources: Box Office
Season: 52 Weeks   **Annual Attendance:** 25,000
Performance Facilities: Las Mascaras Theatre #1; Las Mascaras Theatre #2

TEATRO AVANTE
742 SW Eighth Street, Miami, FL 33130
(305) 858-4155
FAX: (305) 854-5445
Founded: 1979
Arts Area: Professional; Summer Stock; Theatrical Group
Status: Professional; Non-Profit
Type: Performing; Touring; Educational
Purpose: To promote Hispanic theatre
Management: Mario Ernesto Sanchez, Producing Artistic Director; Rolando Moreno, Resident Director/Designer; Manelo Mina, Technical Coordinator
Officers: Maris Ernest Sanches, President; Edna Schwab, Treasurer; Marilyn Barrot, Secretary
Paid Staff: 5 **Volunteer Staff:** 10
Paid Artists: 30
Utilizes: Special Technical Talent; Guest Artists; Guest Directors
Budget: $100,000 - $500,000
Income Sources: Private Foundations/Grants/Endowments; Business/Corporate Donations; Box Office; Government Grants; Individual Donations
Season: 52 Weeks
Annual Attendance: 25,000
Performance Facilities: El Carruse Theatre

FACILITY

DADE COUNTY AUDITORIUM
2901 West Flagler Street, Miami, FL 33135
(305) 547-5414
FAX: (305) 541-7782
Type of Facility: Auditorium
Type of Stage: Proscenium
Stage Dimensions: 60'Wx40'D; 60'Wx30'H proscenium opening
Orchestra Pit
Seating Capacity: 2,498
Year Built: 1950 **Architect:** Stewart and Skinner **Cost:** $1,500,000
Year Remodeled: 1989 **Architect:** Tilton and Tachi **Cost:** $1,500,000
Acoustical Consultant: Edmunds & Mulgreen
Contact for Rental: Barry Steinman; (305) 547-5414

GUSMAN CENTER FOR THE PERFORMING ARTS
174 East Flagler Street, Miami, FL 33131
(305) 374-2444
FAX: (305) 374-0303
Founded: 1926
Type of Facility: Theatre House; Multi-Purpose
Facility Originally: Movie House
Type of Stage: Proscenium
Stage Dimensions: 41'4"Wx29'H proscenium opening; 66'1"Wx31'D overall; 52' stage depth
Orchestra Pit
Seating Capacity: 1,739
Year Built: 1926 **Architect:** John Eberson **Cost:** $1,500,000
Year Remodeled: 1972 **Architect:** Morris Lapidus Jr.
Contact for Rental: Jeannie Piazza-Zuniga; (305) 374-2444

JAMES L. KNIGHT CENTER
400 SE Second Avenue, Miami, FL 33131
(305) 372-0277
FAX: (305) 372-2919
Founded: 1982
Type of Facility: Multi-Purpose
Type of Stage: Arena; Portable Staging - 16,000 square feet
Stage Dimensions: 56'x36'
Seating Capacity: 5,000
Year Built: 1982 **Cost:** $96,000,000
Acoustical Consultant: Jerry McDonald, Director of Operations
Contact for Rental: Manny Fernandez; (305) 372-0277

Miami Beach

DANCE

MIAMI CITY BALLET
905 Lincoln Road, Miami Beach, FL 33139
(305) 532-4880
> **Founded:** 1985
> **Arts Area:** Ballet
> **Status:** Professional; Non-Profit
> **Type:** Performing; Touring; Resident
> **Purpose:** To maintain Florida's first fully-professional, major, resident ballet company; to provide a variety of performances and outreach services statewide
> **Management:** Edward Villeua, Executive Director; Pam Millor, General Manager
> **Officers:** Rhoda Levitt, President
> **Paid Staff:** 7
> **Paid Artists:** 23
> **Utilizes:** Special Technical Talent; Guest Conductors; Guest Choreographers
> **Budget:** $1,000,000 - $5,000,000
> **Income Sources:** Private Foundations/Grants/Endowments; Business/Corporate Donations; Box Office; Government Grants; Individual Donations
> **Season:** August - May   **Annual Attendance:** 30,000
> **Affiliations:** Dance USA; State Dance Association of Florida
> **Performance Facilities:** Dade County Auditorium

INSTRUMENTAL MUSIC

BROWARD SYMPHONY ORCHESTRA
5225 La Gorce Drive, Miami Beach, FL 33140
(305) 864-7984
FAX: (305) 868-3623
> **Founded:** 1965
> **Arts Area:** Symphony; Orchestra; Chamber; Ensemble; Instrumental Group
> **Status:** Professional; Semi-Professional; Non-Profit
> **Type:** Performing; Touring; Resident; Educational; Sponsoring
> **Purpose:** To provide professional cultural community education
> **Management:** Laurence Gordon Siegel, Music Director
> **Paid Staff:** 1   **Volunteer Staff:** 6
> **Paid Artists:** 6
> **Utilizes:** Guest Conductors; Guest Artists; Guest Directors
> **Budget:** $1,000 - $50,000
> **Income Sources:** Private Foundations/Grants/Endowments; Business/Corporate Donations; Box Office; Individual Donations
> **Season:** October - June
> **Annual Attendance:** 6,000

NEW WORLD SYMPHONY
541 Lincoln Road, Miami Beach, FL 33139
(305) 673-3330
FAX: (305) 673-6749
> **Founded:** 1987
> **Arts Area:** Symphony; Orchestra; Chamber
> **Status:** Professional; Non-Profit
> **Type:** Performing; Touring
> **Purpose:** To maintain a national advanced-training program that prepares gifted young orchestral musicians (ages 21-30) for full-time professional music careers and provides participants the opportunity to study and perform with distinguished conductors and solo artists
> **Management:** Christopher T. Dunworth, Executive Director; John Duffy, Vice President of Operations; Michael Tilson-Thomas, Artistic Advisor/Conductor
> **Officers:** Sherwood Weiser, Chairman; Sheldon Schneider, Treasurer; Diane Sepler, Secretary
> **Paid Staff:** 8
> **Paid Artists:** 75
> **Utilizes:** Guest Conductors
> **Budget:** $1,000,000 - $5,000,000
> **Income Sources:** Private Foundations/Grants/Endowments; Business/Corporate Donations; Box Office; Government Grants; Individual Donations; Fund-raising
> **Season:** October - March   **Affiliations:** ASOL
> **Performance Facilities:** Gusman Center for the Performing Arts

VOCAL MUSIC

PAN-AMERICAN SOCIETY OF ARTISTS INC.
5225 La Gorce Drive, Miami Beach, FL 33140
(305) 864-7984
>**Founded:** 1990
>**Arts Area:** Grand Opera; Lyric Opera; Light Opera; Operetta; Choral; Ethnic; Folk; Symphony; Ballet
>**Status:** Professional; Semi-Professional; Non-Profit
>**Type:** Performing; Touring; Resident; Educational; Sponsoring; Cultural Exchange
>**Management:** Dr. P. Melendez, Development; Maxey Melendez, Public Relations; Lawrence G. Siegel, Music Director
>**Officers:** Luz Morales, President; Dr. F. E. Reyes, Vice President; Mariem Leuiem, Secretary/Treasurer
>**Paid Staff:** 3   **Volunteer Staff:** 10
>**Paid Artists:** 1
>**Utilizes:** Special Technical Talent; Guest Conductors; Guest Artists; Guest Directors
>**Budget:** $50,000 - $100,000
>**Income Sources:** Private Foundations/Grants/Endowments; Business/Corporate Donations; Box Office; Government Grants; Individual Donations
>**Season:** 52 Weeks   **Annual Attendance:** 10,000

THEATRE

GOLD COAST MIME COMPANY
345 West 37th Street, Miami Beach, FL 33140
(305) 538-5500
>**Founded:** 1982
>**Arts Area:** Theatrical Group; Mime
>**Status:** Professional
>**Type:** Performing; Touring; Educational
>**Purpose:** To bring professionalism to mime in South Florida; to extend the limits of creativity
>**Management:** Jude Parry, Director
>**Paid Staff:** 1
>**Paid Artists:** 3
>**Utilizes:** Special Technical Talent
>**Budget:** $1,000 - $50,000
>**Income Sources:** Business/Corporate Donations; Box Office
>**Season:** November - May   **Annual Attendance:** 100,000

FACILITY

JACKIE GLEASON THEATER
1700 Washington Avenue, Miami Beach, FL 33139
(305) 673-7311
FAX: (305) 673-7435
>**Type of Facility:** Concert Hall; Theatre House
>**Type of Stage:** Proscenium
>**Stage Dimensions:** 58'Wx110'D   **Orchestra Pit**
>**Seating Capacity:** 3,023
>**Year Built:** 1950   **Cost:** $2,000,000
>**Year Remodeled:** 1976   **Architect:** Morris Lapidus, Jr.   **Cost:** $7,100,000
>**Acoustical Consultant:** C.P. Boner
>**Contact for Rental:** Steve Clark;   (305) 673-7311
>**Manager:** Norman Litz

Monticello

FACILITY

MONTICELLO OPERA HOUSE
Courthouse Square, PO Box 518, Monticello, FL 32344
(904) 997-4242
>**Founded:** 1890
>**Type of Facility:** Performance Center; Opera House; Ballroom; Meeting Rooms
>**Facility Originally:** Business Facility
>**Type of Stage:** Proscenium
>**Stage Dimensions:** 27'x27'
>**Orchestra Pit**
>**Seating Capacity:** Main Auditorium - 380; Lower Level Bays/Ballroom - 250
>**Year Built:** 1890   **Architect:** John Perkins

Year Remodeled: 1992   **Architect:** Barnett Fronczak Architects   **Cost:** $1,000,000
Contact for Rental: Helen Rouse;   (904) 997-4242
Manager: Camilla Augustine, Program Manager;   (904) 997-7142
Performance season consisting of 8-12 scheduled performances runs from October to April; other special events are held throughout the year.

New Port Richey

VOCAL MUSIC

JUBILLEE MENS CHORUS
5936 Grand Boulevard, New Port Richey, FL 34652
(813) 848-6969
   Founded: 1980
   Arts Area: Light Opera; Operetta; Choral; Ethnic; Folk
   Status: Semi-Professional; Non-Profit
   Type: Performing
   Purpose: To encourage the trained singer to remain an active participant in musical performances
   Management: Dolores K. Long, Director
   Paid Staff: 2   **Volunteer Staff:** 2
   Paid Artists: 4   **Non-Paid Artists:** 2
   Utilizes: Guest Artists
   Budget: $1,000 - $50,000
   Income Sources: Box Office; Individual Donations
   Season: October - June
   Annual Attendance: 1,000

THE THURSDAY MUSICALE
5936 Grand Boulevard, New Port Richey, FL 34652
(813) 848-6969
   Founded: 1947
   Arts Area: Grand Opera; Lyric Opera; Light Opera; Operetta; Choral; Ethnic; Folk
   Status: Semi-Professional; Non-Profit
   Type: Performing; Touring; Sponsoring
   Purpose: To present monthly performances of chorus featuring guest artists; to award two musical scholarships per year, with recipients featured in performances
   Management: Dolores K. Long, Director
   Officers: Lynn Pfieffer, President; Billie Helm, Vice President; Norma Douglass, Secretary; Mildred Ferrari, Treasurer
   Paid Staff: 2   **Volunteer Staff:** 10
   Paid Artists: 8   **Non-Paid Artists:** 1
   Utilizes: Special Technical Talent; Guest Artists
   Budget: $1,000 - $50,000
   Income Sources: Box Office; Individual Donations
   Season: September - June
   Annual Attendance: 6,000
   Performance Facilities: First Baptist Church

New Smyrna Beach

PERFORMING SERIES

ATLANTIC CENTER FOR THE ARTS
1414 Art Center Avenue, New Smyrna Beach, FL 32168
(904) 427-6975
FAX: (904) 427-5669
   Arts Area: Dance; Vocal Music; Instrumental Music; Theater; Performance Art; Installations
   Status: Non-Profit
   Type: Performing
   Purpose: To provide an interdisciplinary artists' community in which master artists and associates collaborate during a three-week project-based or process-based residency
   Management: Ted Potter, Executive Director; James Murphy, Program Director; Suzanne Fetscher, Assistant Program Director; Jenni Mac Innes, Education Coordinator
   Officers: Board of Trustees
   Paid Staff: 10   **Volunteer Staff:** 45
   Paid Artists: 20   **Non-Paid Artists:** 100
   Utilizes: Guest Artists; Master Artists in Residence
   Budget: $500,000 - $1,000,000

Income Sources: Private Foundations/Grants/Endowments; Business/Corporate Donations; Government Grants; Individual Donations; Auction
Season: 52 Weeks
Affiliations: University of Central Florida

North Fort Myers

FACILITY

LEE CIVIC CENTER
11831 Bayshore Road, North Fort Myers, FL 33917
(813) 543-8368
    Type of Facility: Civic Center
    Year Built: 1978
    Contact for Rental: Glenda Dunlap;   (813) 543-8368
    Contains the Arena and Small Theater. See separate listings

LEE CIVIC CENTER - ARENA
11831 Bayshore Road, North Fort Myers, FL 33917
(813) 543-8368
    Type of Facility: Arena
    Type of Stage: Flexible; Platform
    Stage Dimensions: 40'x48'
    Seating Capacity: 8,063
    Contact for Rental: Glenda Dunlap;   (813) 543-8368

LEE CIVIC CENTER - SMALL THEATER
11831 Bayshore Road, North Fort Myers, FL 33917
(813) 543-8368
    Type of Facility: Theatre House
    Type of Stage: Flexible; Platform
    Stage Dimensions: 40'x48'
    Seating Capacity: 3,763
    Contact for Rental: Glenda Dunlap;   (813) 543-8368

North Miami Beach

FACILITY

VICTORY PARK AUDITORIUM
17011 NE 19th Avenue, North Miami Beach, FL 33162
(305) 948-2957
    Type of Facility: Auditorium; Multi-Purpose
    Facility Originally: Recreation Hall; Gymnasium
    Type of Stage: Proscenium
    Stage Dimensions: 28'x35'
    Seating Capacity: 1,394
    Year Built: 1963
    Contact for Rental: North Miami Beach Parks and Recreation Department;   (305) 948-2957
    Manager: Peter S. Kadish
    Resident Groups: North Miami Beach Symphony; South Florida Youth Symphony; Pro Show; Barry University Basketball; Miami Christian College Basketball; Saint Thomas University Basketball

North Palm Beach

THEATRE

THE VILLAGE PLAYERS
501 US Highway 1, North Palm Beach, FL 33408-4906
(407) 626-5310
    Founded: 1980
    Arts Area: Community; Theatrical Group
    Status: Non-Professional; Non-Profit
    Type: Performing; Resident
    Purpose: To provide clean, low cost, quality entertainment for the community; to provide an outlet for talented amateurs
    Management: Roma Smith, Business Manager; Alice Bachman, Liason; Dick Norton, Technical Director

Officers: Caroline Breder, President; Lee Greco, First Vice President; Marilyn Causa, Second Vice President; Roseanne Wolf, Secretary; Terry Elliott, Treasurer
Utilizes: Special Technical Talent; Guest Artists; Guest Directors
Budget: $1,000 - $50,000
Income Sources: Box Office; Individual Donations
Season: August - June
Affiliations: North Palm Beach Recreation
Performance Facilities: North Palm Beach Community Center

Ocala

FACILITY

CENTRAL FLORIDA COMMUNITY COLLEGE - FINE ARTS AUDITORIUM
College Road, PO Box 1388, Ocala, FL 32678
(904) 237-2111, ext. 348
Founded: 1968
Type of Facility: Auditorium
Type of Stage: Proscenium
Orchestra Pit
Seating Capacity: 379
Year Built: 1968 **Architect:** Vance Duncan **Cost:** $300,000
Year Remodeled: 1991 **Cost:** $500,000
Contact for Rental: Daryl Harrison; (904) 237-2111, ext. 348

Orange Park

THEATRE

ORANGE PARK COMMUNITY THEATRE
2900 Moody Avenue, PO Box 391, Orange Park, FL 32065
(904) 276-2599
Founded: 1968
Arts Area: Musical; Community
Status: Non-Professional; Non-Profit
Type: Performing; Educational
Purpose: To perpetuate live theatre in Clay County
Officers: Emma Lee Carpenter, President; Virginia Bell, Vice President; Irving Norton, Secretary; Ray Patterson, Treasurer
Volunteer Staff: 200
Income Sources: Business/Corporate Donations; Box Office; Individual Donations
Season: January - June
Performance Facilities: Lions Club

Orlando

DANCE

SOUTHERN BALLET THEATRE
1111 North Orange Avenue, Orlando, FL 32804
(407) 426-1733
FAX: (407) 426-1734
Founded: 1974
Arts Area: Modern; Ballet; Jazz
Status: Professional; Non-Profit
Type: Performing; Touring; Sponsoring
Purpose: To deliver dance to every corner of the community, from the schools to the theatres - we want our audiences to feel the power and the joy of dance
Management: Kip Watson, General Manager; Barbara Riggins, Artistic Director
Officers: Rosemary O' Shea, President; Pat Anyell, Tony Conway, Candido Seganna, Maria Motes, Michael Brogan, Nancy Jacobson, Vice Presidents; Susan Stucker, President-Elect; Dr. Harry Eisenberg, Secretary; Jim Hutcheson, Treasurer
Paid Staff: 12
Paid Artists: 16
Utilizes: Special Technical Talent; Guest Artists; Guest Choreographers
Budget: $1,000,000 - $5,000,000

Income Sources: Private Foundations/Grants/Endowments; Business/Corporate Donations; Box Office; Government Grants; Individual Donations
Season: September - May   **Annual Attendance:** 40,000
Affiliations: State Dance Association of Florida
Performance Facilities: Bob Carr Performing Arts Center

INSTRUMENTAL MUSIC

FLORIDA SYMPHONY ORCHESTRA
1900 North Mills Avenue, #3, Orlando, FL 32803
(407) 896-0331
FAX: (407) 896-2373
Founded: 1950
Arts Area: Symphony; Orchestra; Chamber
Status: Professional; Non-Profit
Type: Performing; Educational
Purpose: To give concerts; to promote musical education and greater public appreciation of music; to assist in the education of young musicians
Management: Benjamin Greene, Executive Vice President; Kevin Hagen, General Manager; Joseph Silverstein, Music Advisor
Officers: Ann Smith, President; Harvey Massey, President-Elect
Paid Staff: 13
Paid Artists: 72
Utilizes: Guest Conductors; Guest Artists
Budget: $1,000,000 - $5,000,000
Income Sources: Private Foundations/Grants/Endowments; Business/Corporate Donations; Box Office; Government Grants; Individual Donations
Season: September - May   **Annual Attendance:** 150,000
Affiliations: ASOL
Performance Facilities: Bob Carr Performing Arts Center

VOCAL MUSIC

ORLANDO OPERA
1100 North Orange Avenue, PO Box 426-1700, Orlando, FL 32804
(407) 426-1717
FAX: (407) 426-1705
Founded: 1958
Arts Area: Grand Opera
Status: Professional
Type: Performing
Management: Robert Swedberg, General Manager; Barbara Battersby, Director of Development; Alden Brun, Marketing and Advertising
Officers: L.C. Grammer, President; Leyton Yates, President-Elect
Paid Staff: 8   **Volunteer Staff:** 15
Utilizes: Special Technical Talent; Guest Conductors; Guest Artists; Guest Directors
Budget: $100,000 - $500,000
Income Sources: Private Foundations/Grants/Endowments; Business/Corporate Donations; Box Office; Government Grants; Individual Donations
Season: November - April   **Annual Attendance:** 24,000
Affiliations: OA
Performance Facilities: Bob Carr Performing Arts Center

THEATRE

CIVIC THEATRE OF CENTRAL FLORIDA
1001 East Princeton Street, Orlando, FL 32803
(407) 896-7365
FAX: (407) 897-3284
Founded: 1926
Arts Area: Musical; Community; Theatrical Group; Semi-Professional
Status: Semi-Professional; Non-Professional; Non-Profit
Type: Performing; Touring; Educational
Purpose: To serve the community by entertaining, informing, stimulating, educating and providing a forum for artistic expression through live theatre and classroom experiences

Management: Mary Ann Dean, General Manager; Michael Fortner, Artistic Director; Jill Hardester, Theatre for Young People/Second Stage Producer; Julie Bailey, Marketing Director; Ryszard Lukaszewicz, Technical Director
Officers: Ruby Homayssi, President; Jonathan Rich, Linda Santieri, Michael Harding, Vice Presidents; John Holloway, Secretary; Janet Ziomek, Treasurer
Paid Staff: 15
Non-Paid Artists: 1
Utilizes: Special Technical Talent; Guest Conductors; Guest Artists; Guest Directors
Budget: $1,000,000 - $5,000,000
Income Sources: Private Foundations/Grants/Endowments; Business/Corporate Donations; Box Office; Government Grants; Individual Donations
Season: September - June
Annual Attendance: 150,000
Affiliations: AACT; Florida Theatre Conference; United Arts
Performance Facilities: Civic Theatre Complex

MARK TWO DINNER THEATER
3376 Edgewater Drive, Orlando, FL 32804
(407) 843-6275
FAX: (407) 843-1510
Founded: 1986
Arts Area: Professional; Dinner
Status: Professional
Type: Performing
Purpose: To provide Orlando with the best theater and dining possible
Management: Mark Howard, Executive Producer/Director; Scott A. Reeds, General Manager
Officers: Mark Howard, President
Paid Staff: 54
Paid Artists: 10
Utilizes: Guest Artists
Budget: $100,000 - $500,000
Income Sources: Box Office
Season: 52 Weeks
Affiliations: AEA; American Dinner Theatre Association
Performance Facilities: Mark Two Dinner Theater

THEATRE-IN-THE-WORKS
PO Box 532016, Orlando, FL 32853
(407) 365-7235
Founded: 1984
Arts Area: Professional; Theatrical Group
Status: Professional; Non-Profit
Purpose: To develop original plays, musicals and operas witten primarily by Florida authors
Management: Edward Dilks, Producing Director
Paid Staff: 1   **Volunteer Staff:** 6
Utilizes: Guest Artists
Budget: $1,000 - $50,000
Income Sources: Private Foundations/Grants/Endowments; Business/Corporate Donations; Box Office; Government Grants; Individual Donations
Season: March - October

FACILITY

BOB CARR PERFORMING ARTS CENTER
401 West Livingston Street, Orlando, FL 32801
(305) 849-2562
Type of Facility: Concert Hall; Auditorium; Performance Center; Theatre House; Opera House
Type of Stage: Proscenium; Hydraulic Lift Stage
Stage Dimensions: 50'x34'
Orchestra Pit
Seating Capacity: 2,534
Year Built: 1926   **Cost:** $250,000
Year Remodeled: 1978   **Architect:** Don Duer/Tom Price   **Cost:** $3,700,000
Acoustical Consultant: George Izenour
Contact for Rental: Robin Handlin or Bill Becker;   (305) 849-2562
Resident Groups: Florida Symphony Orchestra; Southern Ballet; Orlando Opera; Orlando Broadway Series

ORANGE COUNTY CIVIC CENTER
9800 International Drive, Orlando, FL 32819
(407) 345-9800
FAX: (407) 345-9876
    Type of Facility: Civic Center
    Type of Stage: Platform
    Seating Capacity: 11,000
    Year Built: 1983   **Architect:** Hellman Hurley Charvatt & Peabody   **Cost:** $50,000,000
    Contact for Rental: Elizabeth Forsythe;   (407) 345-9800

VALENCIA COMMUNITY COLLEGE - BLACK BOX THEATRE
701 North Econlockhatchee Trail, Orlando, FL 32825
(407) 299-5000
    Type of Facility: Black Box
    Type of Stage: Flexible
    Stage Dimensions: 50'x50' space
    Seating Capacity: 100-200
    Year Built: 1981
    Contact for Rental: Richard Rietveld;   (407) 299-5000, ext. 2285
    Manager: Que Throm;   (407) 299-5000, ext. 2340

VALENCIA COMMUNITY COLLEGE - PERFORMING ARTS CENTER
701 North Econlockhatchee Trail, Orlando, FL 32817
(407) 299-5000, ext. 2285
    Type of Facility: Theatre Complex
    Type of Stage: Proscenium; Environmental
    Stage Dimensions: 50'x50'; 40'W proscenium opening   **Orchestra Pit**
    Seating Capacity: 588
    Year Built: 1981
    Contact for Rental: Richard Rietveld;   (407) 299-5000, ext. 2285
    Resident Groups: Valencia Character Company

Palm Beach

INSTRUMENTAL MUSIC

GREATER PALM BEACH SYMPHONY
139 North County Road, Palm Beach, FL 33480
(407) 655-2657
FAX: (407) 655-9113
    Founded: 1974
    Arts Area: Symphony
    Status: Professional
    Type: Performing
    Management: Timothy Gilligan, General Manager
    Officers: Ethel S. Stone, Chairman
    Paid Staff: 4   **Volunteer Staff:** 5
    Utilizes: Guest Conductors; Guest Artists
    Budget: $500,000 - $1,000,000
    Income Sources: Private Foundations/Grants/Endowments; Business/Corporate Donations; Box Office; Government Grants; Individual Donations
    Season: November - April
    Performance Facilities: Royal Poinciana Playhouse

FACILITY

THE SOCIETY OF THE FOUR ARTS GALLERY - THEATER
Four Arts Plaza, Palm Beach, FL 33480
(407) 655-7226
FAX: (407) 655-7233
    Founded: 1936
    Type of Facility: Auditorium; Multi-Purpose; Exhibition Galleries
    Facility Originally: Private Club
    Type of Stage: Proscenium
    Stage Dimensions: 25'D, 32'W downstage, 40'W upstage
    Seating Capacity: 718
    Year Built: 1936   **Architect:** Addison Mizner

Year Remodeled: 1947
Two-building complex includes the Gallery Building and Library Building; Auditorium added 1947

Palm Beach Garden

VOCAL MUSIC

THE CHORAL SOCIETY OF THE PALM BEACHES, INC.
PO Box 30831, Palm Beach Garden, FL 33410-7831
(407) 546-7867
Founded: 1963
Arts Area: Choral
Status: Non-Professional; Non-Profit
Type: Performing
Purpose: To strive to meet presentation excellence, public accessability, musical opportunity and public awareness of significant choral literature in Palm Beach County
Management: Calvin Gage, Music Director
Officers: Robert Beaulieu, President
Paid Artists: 2   **Non-Paid Artists:** 45
Utilizes: Guest Artists
Budget: $1,000 - $50,000
Income Sources: Private Foundations/Grants/Endowments; Box Office; Individual Donations
Season: September - May   **Annual Attendance:** 1,500

Pensacola

DANCE

KALEIDOSCOPE DANCE THEATRE BALLET
400 South Jefferson Street, Pensacola, FL 32501
(904) 432-9546
Founded: 1978
Arts Area: Modern; Ballet
Status: Non-Professional; Non-Profit
Type: Performing; Resident; Educational
Purpose: To provide quality training and performing opportunities in classical ballet and modern dance from elementary school through high school
Management: Judy Gomez, Debbie Parrish, Artistic Directors; Patsy Hill, Nannette Whidby, Associate Directors
Officers: Hilda Jones, President; Emily Hill, Vice President; Peggy Nunning, Treasurer; Cane Duch, Secretary
Paid Staff: 7   **Volunteer Staff:** 25
Utilizes: Special Technical Talent; Guest Artists
Budget: $1,000 - $50,000
Income Sources: Private Foundations/Grants/Endowments; Business/Corporate Donations; Box Office; Individual Donations
Season: September - June   **Annual Attendance:** 1,500
Affiliations: Pensacola Dance Alliance

INSTRUMENTAL MUSIC

PENSACOLA SYMPHONY ORCHESTRA
PO Box 1705, Pensacola, FL 32518
(904) 435-2533
FAX: (904) 469-0786
Founded: 1926
Arts Area: Symphony; Orchestra; Chamber
Status: Professional
Type: Performing; Resident; Educational; Sponsoring
Purpose: To provide quality entertainment and assist in educating young minds to appreciate fine music
Management: Brenda Pitts, General Manager; Grier Williams, Music Director; Barbara Gabriel, Personnel Manager
Officers: Dr. Bill Philip Payne, President; John Dunworth, President-Elect; Carlton Proctor, First Vice President; Donna Bloomer, Treasurer
Volunteer Staff: 30
Paid Artists: 72
Utilizes: Special Technical Talent; Guest Conductors; Guest Artists
Budget: $100,000 - $500,000
Income Sources: Private Foundations/Grants/Endowments; Business/Corporate Donations; Box Office; Government Grants; Individual Donations

Season: October - April   **Annual Attendance:** 20,000
Affiliations: ASOL
Performance Facilities: Saenger Theatre

VOCAL MUSIC

CHORAL SOCIETY OF PENSACOLA
1000 College Boulevard, Pensacola, FL 32504
(904) 476-5410, ext. 1800
 Founded: 1935
 Arts Area: Choral
 Status: Semi-Professional; Non-Profit
 Type: Performing; Resident
 Purpose: To perform choral literature
 Management: William Clarke, Conductor/Musical Director
 Officers: Melba Powell, President; Dan Geem Vice President; Ann Cowan, Recording Secretary; Myrna Martin, Corresponding Secretary; John Layman, Treasurer
 Paid Staff: 1   **Volunteer Staff:** 15
 Paid Artists: 50   **Non-Paid Artists:** 82
 Utilizes: Guest Artists
 Budget: $1,000 - $50,000
 Income Sources: Private Foundations/Grants/Endowments; Business/Corporate Donations; Box Office; Government Grants; Individual Donations
 Season: September - May
 Annual Attendance: 2,500
 Affiliations: Arts Council of North West Florida; CA; Florida Cultural Action Alliance
 Performance Facilities: Saenger Theatre; Cokesbury United Methodist Church

THEATRE

PENSACOLA LITTLE THEATRE
PO Box 415, Pensacola, FL 32592
(904) 432-8621; (904) 432-2042
 Founded: 1936
 Arts Area: Community; Children's Theatre
 Status: Non-Professional; Non-Profit
 Type: Performing; Educational; Sponsoring
 Purpose: To stimulate an interest in the performing arts and offer members of the community an opportunity to participate in all phases of live theatre
 Management: Herman Fischer, General Manager
 Officers: Brian K. Spencer, President; Renee C. Ard, Vice President; Jan C. McLendon, Treasurer; Jane Switzer, Secretary
 Paid Staff: 2   **Volunteer Staff:** 30
 Non-Paid Artists: 100
 Budget: $50,000 - $100,000
 Income Sources: Business/Corporate Donations; Box Office; Individual Donations; Season Subscriptions
 Season: 52 Weeks
 Annual Attendance: 15,000
 Affiliations: Florida Theatre Conference; AACT; SETC
 Performance Facilities: Pensacola Little Theatre

PERFORMING SERIES

MUSIC HALL ARTIST SERIES
11000 University Parkway, Pensacola, FL 32514
(904) 474-2147
 Founded: 1969
 Status: Professional
 Type: Sponsoring
 Purpose: To provide the community with high-quality chamber music programs of professional touring groups
 Management: Grier Williams, Chairman
 Paid Staff: 2   **Volunteer Staff:** 3
 Paid Artists: 30
 Utilizes: Guest Artists
 Budget: $1,000 - $50,000
 Income Sources: Private Foundations/Grants/Endowments; Box Office; Government Grants
 Season: October - April
 Annual Attendance: 1,000
 Affiliations: University of West Florida
 Performance Facilities: New Music Hall

FACILITY

PENSACOLA CIVIC CENTER
201 East Gregory Street, Pensacola, FL 32501
(904) 432-0800
> **Type of Facility:** Civic Center; Arena; Multi-Purpose
> **Type of Stage:** Flexible
> **Seating Capacity:** Permanent - 8,200; Floor - 2,300 extra
> **Year Built:** 1985   **Architect:** Sverdrup Architects   **Cost:** $24,000,000
> **Acoustical Consultant:** E.D.I.
> **Contact for Rental:** Carol Pollock;   (904) 432-0800

PENSACOLA JUNIOR COLLEGE, MUSIC AND DRAMA DEPARTMENT
1000 College Boulevard, Pensacola, FL 32504-8998
(904) 484-1800
FAX: (904) 484-1826
> **Founded:** 1948
> **Type of Facility:** Concert Hall; Auditorium
> **Facility Originally:** School
> **Type of Stage:** Proscenium
> **Orchestra Pit**
> **Seating Capacity:** 315
> **Year Built:** 1958
> **Year Remodeled:** 1990

SAENGER THEATRE
118 Palafox Place, Pensacola, FL 32501
(904) 444-7699
FAX: (904) 444-7684
> **Founded:** 1925
> **Type of Facility:** Auditorium; Theatre House
> **Facility Originally:** Vaudeville; Movie House
> **Type of Stage:** Proscenium
> **Orchestra Pit**
> **Seating Capacity:** 1,790
> **Year Built:** 1925   **Cost:** $300,000
> **Year Remodeled:** 1981   **Architect:** Bullock-Graves   **Cost:** $1,600,000
> **Contact for Rental:** Douglas Lee;   (904) 444-7699

UNIVERSITY OF WEST FLORIDA CENTER FOR THE PERFORMING ARTS
11000 University Parkway, Pensacola, FL 32514
(904) 474-2938
FAX: (904) 474-3166
> **Founded:** 1967
> **Type of Facility:** Theatre Complex; Concert Hall; Outdoor (Concert); Studio Performance; Off Broadway; Theatre House; Amphitheater; Multi-Purpose
> **Type of Stage:** Platform
> **Stage Dimensions:** 84'x43'
> **Orchestra Pit**
> **Seating Capacity:** Theatre - 500; Music Hall - 300
> **Year Built:** 1991   **Architect:** Barrett Daffin and Carlan   **Cost:** $8,000,000

Plantation

INSTRUMENTAL MUSIC

BROWARD'S FRIENDS OF CHAMBER MUSIC, INC.
7950 Northwest Fourth Place, Plantation, FL 33324-1950
(305) 473-2353
FAX: (305) 474-1392
> **Founded:** 1980
> **Arts Area:** Chamber
> **Status:** Non-Profit
> **Type:** Performing; Educational
> **Purpose:** To bring chamber groups of international reputation to the community
> **Officers:** Leila G. Winton, President of Board; Robert Hoffman, Vice President of Board; Matthew Carole, Secretary of Board; Aviva Weiss Baer, Board Member; Harold M. Wilton, Treasurer of Board

Volunteer Staff: 4
Paid Artists: 7
Income Sources: Private Foundations/Grants/Endowments; Business/Corporate Donations; Box Office; Government Grants; Individual Donations
Season: December - April   **Annual Attendance:** 5,000
Performance Facilities: Bailey Concert Hall; Broward Community College

THEATRE

PLANTATION THEATRE COMPANY
1829 North Pineland Road, Plantation, FL 33317
(305) 472-6873
Founded: 1975
Arts Area: Musical; Community
Status: Semi-Professional; Non-Professional; Non-Profit
Type: Performing; Educational
Purpose: To afford the community an opportunity to become involved in the performing arts either by participation or by affordable audience participation
Paid Staff: 1   **Volunteer Staff:** 2
Utilizes: Special Technical Talent
Budget: $1,000 - $50,000
Season: 52 Weeks
Performance Facilities: Diecke Auditorium

Pompano Beach

VOCAL MUSIC

GOLD COAST OPERA
1000 Coconut Creek Boulevard, Pompano Beach, FL 33066
(305) 973-2323
FAX: (305) 973-2389
Founded: 1980
Arts Area: Operetta; Muiscal Theatre
Status: Professional; Non-Profit
Type: Performing; Touring; Educational
Purpose: To provide high-quality, fully-staged musical works including musical theatre, comic opera and other operatic productions to Pompano Beach and surrounding communities
Management: Dr. Thomas Cavendish, General Director
Paid Staff: 5
Paid Artists: 40   **Non-Paid Artists:** 20
Utilizes: Special Technical Talent; Guest Artists; Guest Directors
Budget: $100,000 - $500,000
Income Sources: Private Foundations/Grants/Endowments; Business/Corporate Donations; Box Office; Government Grants; Individual Donations
Season: November - April   **Annual Attendance:** 13,000
Affiliations: OA
Performance Facilities: Omni Auditorium; Bailey Hall; Coral Springs Civic Center

THEATRE

POMPANO PLAYERS, INC.
PO Box 2045, Pompano Beach, FL 33061
(305) 946-4646
Founded: 1956
Arts Area: Musical; Community; Theatrical Group
Status: Semi-Professional; Non-Profit
Type: Performing; Resident; Educational
Purpose: To provide live theatre to the community
Management: Penny Manwell, Box Office; David Stockton, Technical; Jerry Sullivan, Technical
Officers: Al Edick, President; Baynor Crane, Vice-President; Don Walters, Treasurer; Dale Petrie, Recording Secretary; Fred Leers, Corresponding Secretary
Paid Staff: 3   **Volunteer Staff:** 8
Utilizes: Special Technical Talent; Guest Artists; Guest Directors
Budget: $50,000 - $100,000
Income Sources: Private Foundations/Grants/Endowments; Business/Corporate Donations; Box Office; Government Grants; Individual Donations
Season: September - May   **Annual Attendance:** 10,400

Affiliations: Florida Theatre Conference
Performance Facilities: Pompano Players Theatre

Port Charlotte

THEATRE

CHARLOTTE PLAYERS
PO Box 2187, Port Charlotte, FL 33949
(813) 743-3229; (813) 627-5393
Founded: 1960
Arts Area: Community; Theatrical Group
Status: Non-Professional; Non-Profit
Type: Performing
Purpose: To provide live, community theater to a growing retirement community; to encourage young people to enjoy theater
Officers: Mark Weiser, President; Rich Schmith, Vice President; Janet Castro, Recording Secretary; Dawn Stuart, Treasurer
Paid Staff: 1
Budget: $50,000 - $100,000
Income Sources: Box Office; Individual Donations
Season: October - June **Annual Attendance:** 10,000
Performance Facilities: Cultural Center Theater

Punta Gorda

FACILITY

CHARLOTTE COUNTY MEMORIAL AUDITORIUM
75 Taylor Street, Punta Gorda, FL 33950
(813) 639-5833; (800) 329-9988
FAX: (813) 639-3814
Type of Facility: Auditorium
Type of Stage: Proscenium
Stage Dimensions: 119'x126'
Seating Capacity: 1,416
Year Built: 1968 **Architect:** Ray Griffith **Cost:** $500,000
Contact for Rental: James Morrison

Saint Augustine

THEATRE

LIMELIGHT DINNER THEATRE
Monson Resort, On The Bayfront, 32 Avenida Menendez, Saint Augustine, FL 32084
(904) 829-2277
FAX: (904) 824-4754
Founded: 1980
Arts Area: Professional; Dinner; Theatrical Group
Status: Professional
Type: Performing
Purpose: To provide professional entertainment to visitors to the Saint Augustine area
Management: Jean Rahner, Anne Kraft, Co-Producers
Paid Staff: 5
Paid Artists: 3
Budget: $1,000 - $50,000
Income Sources: Box Office
Season: 52 Weeks **Annual Attendance:** 4,000
Performance Facilities: Monson Resort

PERFORMING SERIES

FLORIDA'S CROSS AND SWORD
Saint Augustine Amphitheatre, Saint Augustine, FL 32084
(904) 471-1965
Founded: 1965

Arts Area: Theater
Status: Non-Profit
Type: Performing
Purpose: To present an historical drama depicting the founding of Saint Augustine by Don Pedro Manendez de Aviles in 1565
Management: T. Wayne Sims, General Manager
Officers: Dave Judkins, President; Bud Harriss, Vice President; Edward V. Calhoun, Treasurer
Paid Staff: 9
Paid Artists: 75
Budget: $100,000 - $500,000
Income Sources: Private Foundations/Grants/Endowments; Business/Corporate Donations; Box Office; Government Grants; Individual Donations
Season: June - August   **Annual Attendance:** 20,000
Performance Facilities: Saint Augustine Amphitheatre

FACILITY

CROSS AND SWORD AMPHITHEATRE
1340 A1A South, PO Box 1965, Saint Augustine, FL 32085
(904) 471-1965
Founded: 1965
Type of Faciliiy: Amphitheater
Type of Stage: Platform
Stage Dimensions: 75'x55'
Seating Capacity: 2,000
Year Built: 1964   **Architect:** Walker/Parker   **Cost:** $1,000,000
Contact for Rental: T. Wayne Sims, Executive Vice President;   (904) 471-1965
Resident Groups: Florida's Cross and Sword

Saint Petersburg

VOCAL MUSIC

FLORIDA LYRIC OPERA
1183 D, 85th Terrace North, Saint Petersburg, FL 33702
(813) 578-1657
Founded: 1978
Arts Area: Grand Opera; Lyric Opera; Light Opera; Operetta
Status: Professional
Type: Performing; Educational
Purpose: To promote area talent; to direct, train and/or discover talent in every phase of musical performance
Management: Rosalia Maresca, General Manager
Officers: Dr. Walter Afield, President; Marie Hillman, Vice President, Rena Laurenti, Secretary; Rosalia Maresca, Treasurer
Paid Staff: 1
Utilizes: Guest Conductors; Guest Artists; Guest Directors
Budget: $1,000 - $50,000
Income Sources: Box Office; Individual Donations
Annual Attendance: 5,000

THEATRE

AMERICAN STAGE COMPANY
211 Third Street South, PO Box 1560, Saint Petersburg, FL 33731
(813) 823-1600
FAX: (813) 823-7529
Founded: 1979
Arts Area: Professional; Theatrical Group
Status: Professional; Non-Profit
Type: Performing; Touring; Resident; Educational
Purpose: To present and develop the best in theatrical literature, both contemporary and classical
Management: Victoria Holloway, Artistic Director; John A. Berglund, Executive Producer
Officers: Susan Hough, President; Martin Normile, Vice President; Enez Hart, Secretary; Joseph Wheeler, Treasurer
Paid Staff: 9   **Volunteer Staff:** 125
Paid Artists: 105
Utilizes: Special Technical Talent; Guest Directors
Budget: $1,000,000 - $5,000,000
Income Sources: Business/Corporate Donations; Box Office; Government Grants; Individual Donations

Season: November - June
Annual Attendance: 36,100
Affiliations: AEA; TCG; Florida Professional Theatre Association; Pinellas County Arts Council
Performance Facilities: American Stage Company Theatre

VAUDEVILLE PALACE
7951 Ninth Street North, Saint Petersburg, FL 33702
(813) 557-5515
FAX: (813) 578-1024
Founded: 1991
Arts Area: Professional; Dinner; Vaudeville
Status: Professional; Commercial
Type: Performing; Resident
Purpose: To provide amusing entertainment
Management: Buddy Graf, Producer/Director; Carol Graf, General Manager; Skip Lewis, Box Office Manager
Income Sources: Box Office
Season: 52 Weeks   **Annual Attendance:** 36,000
Performance Facilities: Vaudeville Palace

FACILITY

BAYFRONT CENTER COMPLEX
400 First Street South, Saint Petersburg, FL 33701
(813) 892-5798
FAX: (813) 892-5858
Type of Facility: Civic Center
Seating Capacity: Auditorium - 2250; Arena - 8200; Al Lang Stadium - 8,000
Year Built: 1965
Architect: Connell Pierce Garland & Friedman
Cost: $6,300,000
Contact for Rental: Jeff Forman;   (813) 892-5798
Resident Groups: The Florida Orchestra

Sanibel Island

THEATRE

PIRATE PLAYHOUSE
2200 Periwinkle Way, Sanibel Island, FL 33957
(813) 472-0006
Founded: 1985
Arts Area: Professional; Theatrical Group
Status: Professional; Non-Profit
Type: Performing; Touring; Resident; Educational; Sponsoring
Purpose: To present live, professional theatre in Southwest Florida
Management: Carrie Lund, Producing Director; Robert Cacioppo, Artistic Director; Todd Bakerian, Technical Director; Dena Allen, Production Stage Manager; Ricki Cooper, Assistant to the Producers
Officers: John McTavish, President; Jerald Melum, Vice President; Al Leonard, Treasurer; Lois Kessler, Secretary
Paid Staff: 8   **Volunteer Staff:** 150
Paid Artists: 30   **Non-Paid Artists:** 8
Utilizes: Special Technical Talent; Guest Artists; Guest Directors
Budget: $100,000 - $500,000
Income Sources: Private Foundations/Grants/Endowments; Business/Corporate Donations; Box Office; Individual Donations
Season: 52 Weeks
Annual Attendance: 26,000
Performance Facilities: Pirate Playhouse

Sarasota

INSTRUMENTAL MUSIC

FLORIDA BRASS QUINTET
709 North Tamiami Trail, Sarasota, FL 33577
(813) 955-4562
Founded: 1986
Arts Area: Chamber; Ensemble

Status: Professional; Non-Profit
Type: Performing; Touring; Resident; Educational
Purpose: To share the talent of the Florida West Coast Symphony's brass section with residents throughout the community and state
Paid Staff: 14
Paid Artists: 5
Utilizes: Guest Artists
Budget: $50,000 - $100,000
Income Sources: Private Foundations/Grants/Endowments; Business/Corporate Donations; Box Office; Government Grants; Individual Donations
Season: October - May   **Annual Attendance:** 4,000
Affiliations: Florida West Coast Symphony

FLORIDA WEST COAST CHAMBER ORCHESTRA
709 North Tamiami Trail, Sarasota, FL 33577
(813) 953-4562
Founded: 1961
Arts Area: Orchestra; Chamber
Status: Professional; Non-Profit
Type: Performing
Purpose: To provide chamber orchestra programs of the finest quality in the local area, particularly in Manatee and Sarasota counties
Management: Gretchen Serrie, Executive Director; Trevor Cramer, General Manager; Janet Petrecca, Business Manager
Officers: Neil Moody, President; Beatrice Friedman, Vice President; Ernest Rice, Treasurer; Elaine Barnett, Secretary
Paid Staff: 14
Paid Artists: 30
Budget: $1,000 - $50,000
Income Sources: Private Foundations/Grants/Endowments; Business/Corporate Donations; Box Office; Government Grants; Individual Donations
Season: November - January
Annual Attendance: 2,500
Affiliations: Florida West Coast Symphony, Inc.
Performance Facilities: Van Wezel Performing Arts Hall; Lota Mundy Hall

FLORIDA WEST COAST SYMPHONY ORCHESTRA
709 North Tamiami Trail, Sarasota, FL 33577
(813) 953-4252
Founded: 1949
Arts Area: Symphony
Status: Professional; Non-Profit
Type: Performing; Resident
Purpose: To present fine music and musicians to the community, particularly in Manatee and Sarasota counties
Management: Gretchen Serrie, Executive Director; Trevor Cramer, General Manager; Janet Petrecca, Business Manager
Officers: Neil Moody, President; Beatrice Friedman, Vice President; Ernest Rice, Treasurer; Elaine Barnett, Secretary
Paid Staff: 14
Paid Artists: 80
Utilizes: Guest Conductors; Guest Artists
Budget: $1,000,000 - $5,000,000
Income Sources: Private Foundations/Grants/Endowments; Business/Corporate Donations; Box Office; Government Grants; Individual Donations
Season: November - April
Annual Attendance: 20,000
Affiliations: ASOL; Florida West Coast Symphony Inc.
Performance Facilities: Van Wezel Performing Arts Hall

FLORIDA WEST COAST YOUTH ORCHESTRAS
709 North Tamiami Trail, Sarasota, FL 34236
(813) 955-4562
Founded: 1956
Arts Area: Symphony; Orchestra
Status: Non-Professional; Non-Profit
Type: Performing; Educational
Purpose: To provide the finest possible music education and to help create performers and audiences for the future
Management: Chris Confessore, Youth Program Director
Paid Staff: 14
Utilizes: Guest Conductors; Guest Artists

Income Sources: Private Foundations/Grants/Endowments; Business/Corporate Donations; Government Grants; Individual Donations
Season: 52 Weeks
Annual Attendance: 5,000
Affiliations: Florida West Coast Music
Performance Facilities: Florida West Coast Music Center

FLORIDA WIND QUINTET
709 North Tamiami Trail, Sarasota, FL 33577
(813) 955-4562
FAX: (813) 953-3059
Founded: 1985
Arts Area: Ensemble
Status: Professional; Non-Profit
Type: Performing; Resident
Purpose: The resident wind quintet of the Florida West Coast Symphony performs in concert to share its expertise with the community.
Paid Staff: 14
Paid Artists: 5
Utilizes: Guest Artists
Budget: $50,000 - $100,000
Income Sources: Private Foundations/Grants/Endowments; Business/Corporate Donations; Box Office; Government Grants; Individual Donations
Season: October - May
Annual Attendance: 4,000
Affiliations: Florida West Coast Music
Performance Facilities: Florida West Coast Music Center

NEW ARTISTS PIANO QUARTET
709 North Tamiami Trail, Sarasota, FL 33577
(813) 955-4562
Founded: 1991
Arts Area: Ensemble
Status: Professional; Non-Profit
Type: Performing; Resident
Purpose: To showcase new, young pianists from the Florida West Coast Symphony
Management: Trevor Cramer, General Manager, Florida West Coast Symphony
Paid Staff: 14
Paid Artists: 4
Utilizes: Guest Artists
Budget: $50,000 - $100,000
Income Sources: Private Foundations/Grants/Endowments; Business/Corporate Donations; Box Office; Government Grants; Individual Donations
Season: October - May
Annual Attendance: 3,000
Affiliations: Florida West Coast Symphony
Performance Facilities: Florida West Coast Symphony Center

NEW ARTISTS STRING QUARTET
709 North Tamiami Trail, Sarasota, FL 33577
(813) 955-4562
Founded: 1986
Arts Area: Ensemble
Status: Professional; Non-Profit
Type: Performing; Touring; Resident
Purpose: To showcase new, young string players in the Florida West Coast Symphony
Management: Gretchen Seirie, Executive Director; Trevor Cramer, General Manager Florida West Coast Symphony
Officers: Neil Moody, President
Paid Staff: 14
Paid Artists: 4
Utilizes: Guest Artists
Budget: $50,000 - $100,000
Income Sources: Private Foundations/Grants/Endowments; Business/Corporate Donations; Box Office; Government Grants; Individual Donations
Season: October - May
Annual Attendance: 4,000
Affiliations: Florida West Coast Symphony Inc.
Performance Facilities: Van Wezel Performing Arts Hall; Holley Hall; Florida West Coast Symphony Center

VOCAL MUSIC

SARASOTA OPERA ASSOCIATION
61 North Pineapple Avenue, Sarasota, FL 34236
(813) 366-8450
FAX: (813) 955-5571
Founded: 1979
Arts Area: Grand Opera
Status: Professional; Non-Profit
Type: Performing; Educational; Sponsoring
Purpose: To continue to bring quality opera to our community and to showcase it in our own opera house; to educate the general community in an appreciation of opera and send our outreach programs into the schools of both Manatee and Sarasota counties; to offer statewide touring programs
Management: Victor De Renzi, Artistic Director; Deane C. Allyn, Executive Director; Libby Smith, Public Relations; Laurie Clark, House Manager
Officers: Leo M. Rogers and David Pomier, Co-Chairmen; Margaret Wise, President
Paid Staff: 17 **Volunteer Staff:** 225
Paid Artists: 75 **Non-Paid Artists:** 50
Utilizes: Special Technical Talent; Guest Conductors; Guest Artists; Guest Directors
Budget: $1,000,000 - $5,000,000
Income Sources: Private Foundations/Grants/Endowments; Business/Corporate Donations; Box Office; Government Grants; Individual Donations
Season: February - March **Annual Attendance:** 32,000
Affiliations: OA; COS; AGMA
Performance Facilities: Sarasota Opera House

THEATRE

ASOLO CENTER FOR THE PERFORMING ARTS
5555 North Tamiami Trail, Sarasota, FL 34243
(813) 351-9010
FAX: (813) 351-5796
Founded: 1960
Arts Area: Professional; Musical; Theatrical Group
Status: Professional; Non-Profit
Type: Performing; Educational
Purpose: To foster an appreciation for the performing arts in the community, state and country by utilizing live performances as well as television and film; to educate students by placing them with professional actors with whom they may learn the theatrical trade
Management: Margaret Booker, Artistic Director; Lee Warner, Executive Director
Officers: Elizabeth Lindsay, Board President
Paid Staff: 82 **Volunteer Staff:** 567
Paid Artists: 72
Utilizes: Special Technical Talent; Guest Artists; Guest Directors
Budget: $1,000,000 - $5,000,000
Income Sources: Private Foundations/Grants/Endowments; Business/Corporate Donations; Box Office; Government Grants; Individual Donations
Season: September - July **Annual Attendance:** 14,000
Affiliations: TCG; AAA; AEA; LORT
Performance Facilities: Asolo Theater

FLORIDA STUDIO THEATRE
1241 North Palm Avenue, Sarasota, FL 33577
(813) 366-9017
FAX: (813) 955-4137
Founded: 1973
Arts Area: Professional; Theatrical Group
Status: Professional; Non-Profit
Type: Performing; Resident; Educational
Purpose: To produce contemporary theatre with an emphasis on new plays and regional premieres
Officers: Dennis McGillicuddy, Board President
Paid Staff: 10
Paid Artists: 30
Utilizes: Special Technical Talent; Guest Artists; Guest Directors
Budget: $500,000 - $1,000,000

Income Sources: Private Foundations/Grants/Endowments; Business/Corporate Donations; Box Office; Government Grants; Individual Donations
Season: December - July   **Annual Attendance:** 93,000
Affiliations: SPTA; AEA
Performance Facilities: Florida Studio Theatre

GOLDEN APPLE DINNER THEATRE
25 North Pineapple Avenue, Sarasota, FL 34236
(813) 366-2646
FAX: (813) 364-9100
Founded: 1971
Arts Area: Professional; Musical; Dinner
Status: Professional; Commercial
Type: Sponsoring
Purpose: To educate, entertain and enlighten
Management: Robert Turoff, Producer/Director/General Manager
Paid Staff: 30
Paid Artists: 50
Utilizes: Special Technical Talent; Guest Conductors; Guest Artists
Budget: $100,000 - $500,000
Income Sources: Box Office
Season: 52 Weeks   **Annual Attendance:** 65,000
Affiliations: AEA
Performance Facilities: Golden Apple Dinner Theatre

THE PLAYERS OF SARASOTA
838 North Tamiami Trail, Sarasota, FL 34236
(813) 365-2494
Founded: 1930
Arts Area: Musical; Community; Theatrical Group; Puppet
Status: Non-Professional; Non-Profit
Type: Performing; Touring; Educational
Purpose: To be the first and only community theatre in Sarasota offering live entertainment, full orchestra, professional direction and children's theatre
Management: Elizabeth J. DeVivo, Executive Director; Peter Strader, Artistic Director
Officers: Maryann Shorin, President; Barry Miller, Vice President; Ray Suplee, Teasurer; Charlene Knopp, Secretary
Paid Staff: 7   **Volunteer Staff:** 250
Paid Artists: 5   **Non-Paid Artists:** 215
Utilizes: Special Technical Talent; Guest Conductors; Guest Artists; Guest Directors
Budget: $100,000 - $500,000
Income Sources: Private Foundations/Grants/Endowments; Business/Corporate Donations; Box Office; Government Grants; Individual Donations
Season: September - June   **Annual Attendance:** 35,000

PERFORMING SERIES

FLORIDA WEST COAST SYMPHONY
709 North Tamiami Trail, Sarasota, FL 33577
(813) 955-4562
Founded: 1949
Arts Area: Instrumental Music; Festivals
Status: Professional; Non-Profit
Type: Performing; Resident; Educational; Sponsoring
Purpose: To present the Florida West Coast Symphony, Sarasota Music Festival, Florida String Quartet, Florida Wind Quintet, Florida Brass Quintet, New Artists String Quartet, Florida West Coast Chamber Orchestra and Florida West Coast Youth Orchestras
Management: Paul Wolfe, Conductor/Music Director; Gretchen Serrie, Executive Director; Jeff Seloeika, Business Manager; JoAanne Klemart, Marketing Director; Trevor Cramer, General Manager
Officers: Neil Moody, President; Beatrice Friedman, Ruth Robbins, Lionel Williams, Vice Presidents; Elaine Barnett, Secretary; Ernest Rice, Treasurer
Paid Staff: 14
Paid Artists: 80
Utilizes: Guest Conductors; Guest Artists
Budget: $1,000,000 - $5,000,000
Income Sources: Private Foundations/Grants/Endowments; Business/Corporate Donations; Box Office; Government Grants; Individual Donations
Season: September - June   **Annual Attendance:** 50,000
Performance Facilities: Van Wezel Auditorium

SARASOTA MUSIC FESTIVAL
709 North Tamiami Trail, Sarasota, FL 34236
(813) 952-9634
FAX: (813) 953-3059
>**Founded:** 1965
>**Arts Area:** Festivals
>**Status:** Professional; Non-Profit
>**Type:** Performing; Educational
>**Purpose:** To present a teaching and performing festival which will enhance the professional training of young musicians and provide the finest in chamber music performances
>**Management:** Trevor Cramer, Administrative Director
>**Officers:** Neil V. Moody, President; Beatrice Friedman, Lionel Willens, Ruth Robbins, Vice-Presidents; Elaine Barnett, Secretary; Ernest Rice, Treasurer
>**Paid Staff:** 14   **Volunteer Staff:** 50
>**Paid Artists:** 35
>**Utilizes:** Guest Artists
>**Budget:** $100,000 - $500,000
>**Income Sources:** Private Foundations/Grants/Endowments; Business/Corporate Donations; Box Office; Government Grants; Individual Donations
>**Season:** June
>**Annual Attendance:** 10,500
>**Affiliations:** CMA
>**Performance Facilities:** Van Wezel Auditorium; Holley Hall

FACILITY

FLORIDA STUDIO THEATRE
1241 North Palm Avenue, Sarasota, FL 33577
(813) 366-9017
>**Type of Facility:** Theatre House; Black Box
>**Facility Originally:** Meeting Hall; Movie House
>**Stage Dimensions:** Black Box space 30'x35'x25'
>**Seating Capacity:** 165
>**Year Built:** 1913
>**Year Remodeled:** 1987
>**Contact for Rental:** Jayne Dowd;   (813) 366-9017
>**Resident Groups:** Florida Studio Theatre

THE PLAYERS OF SARASOTA THEATRE
838 North Tamiami Trail, Sarasota, FL 34236
(813) 365-2494
>**Type of Facility:** Theatre Complex; Concert Hall; Auditorium; Studio Performance; Performance Center; Off Broadway; Theatre House; Multi-Purpose
>**Type of Stage:** Proscenium
>**Orchestra Pit**
>**Seating Capacity:** 507
>**Year Built:** 1974   **Architect:** Erwin Gremli, II   **Cost:** $550,000
>**Acoustical Consultant:** Davidson and Son
>**Contact for Rental:** Elizabeth De Vivo;   (813) 365-2494

SARASOTA OPERA HOUSE
61 North Pineapple Avenue, Sarasota, FL 34236
(813) 366-8450
FAX: (813) 955-5571
>**Founded:** 1926
>**Type of Facility:** Theatre Complex; Concert Hall; Performance Center; Opera House; Multi-Purpose
>**Facility Originally:** Vaudeville; Movie House
>**Type of Stage:** Flexible; Proscenium; Pit may be covered for additional 10'3"
>**Stage Dimensions:** 36'2"x37'8" stage; 11'6"x30' stage left; 20'3"x30' stage right   **Orchestra Pit**
>**Seating Capacity:** 1,033
>**Year Built:** 1926   **Architect:** Lloyd A. Benjamin   **Cost:** $350,000
>**Year Remodeled:** 1984   **Cost:** $3,000,000
>**Contact for Rental:** Laurie Clark, Manager;   (813) 366-8450
>*Originally the Edwards Theatre, the Sarasota Opera House is on the National Register of Historic Places. Education in Youth Opera; Radio Reading for the Blind; Music Archive*

VAN WEZEL AUDITORIUM
777 North Tamiami Trail, Sarasota, FL 33577
(813) 955-7332
FAX: (813) 951-1449
    Type of Facility: Auditorium
    Type of Stage: Flexible   **Orchestra Pit**
    Seating Capacity: 1,779
    Year Built: 1970   **Architect:** Taliesin   **Cost:** $2,527,000
    Acoustical Consultant: Vern Knudsen
    Contact for Rental: John D. Wikes

Seminole

DANCE

GRUPO FOLKLORICO MEXICANA
11698 Walker Avenue, Seminole, FL 34642
(813) 393-3107 '
    Founded: 1979
    Arts Area: Ethnic; Folk; Mexican
    Status: Semi-Professional
    Type: Performing; Educational
    Purpose: To promote the rich Mexican culture through ethnic folkloric dance, colorful costumes and lively music
    Management: Elena Tellone, Director
    Non-Paid Artists: 10
    Utilizes: Guest Artists
    Budget: $1,000 - $50,000
    Income Sources: Box Office; Individual Donations
    Season: 52 Weeks
    Affiliations: Mexican-American Club; Pinellas County Arts Council; State Dance Association of Florida
    Performance Facilities: Saint Petersburg International Folk Fair

South Miami

DANCE

MIAMI BALLET COMPANY
5818 SW 73rd Street, South Miami, FL 33143
(305) 667-5985
    Founded: 1951
    Arts Area: Ballet
    Status: Non-Professional; Non-Profit
    Type: Performing; Resident
    Purpose: To help young people enjoy and learn ballet before professional experience
    Management: Thomas Armour, Artistic Director
    Non-Paid Artists: 30
    Utilizes: Guest Choreographers
    Budget: $100,000 - $500,000
    Income Sources: Private Foundations/Grants/Endowments; Box Office; Individual Donations
    Season: September - May
    Performance Facilities: Dade County Auditorium

Spring Hill

FACILITY

THE SPRINGSTEAD THEATRE
3300 Mariner Boulevard, Spring Hill, FL 34609
(904) 683-2843
    Founded: 1990
    Type of Facility: Concert Hall; Auditorium; Performance Center; Off Broadway; Theatre House; Opera House; Civic Center
    Type of Stage: Proscenium
    Stage Dimensions: 50'x31'
    Seating Capacity: 606

Year Built: 1990
Architect: Harvard, Jolly and Marcet **Cost:** $2,200,000
Contact for Rental: Tizzy Schoelles; (904) 683-2843
Resident Groups: The Repertory Theatre Company; The Winding Waters Dance Ensemble; The Nature Coast Light Opera; The Hernando Symphony Orchestra

---
Tallahassee

DANCE

TALLAHASSEE BALLET COMPANY
PO Box 772, Tallahassee, FL 32302
(904) 222-1287
Founded: 1972
Arts Area: Modern; Ballet; Jazz
Status: Semi-Professional; Non-Profit
Type: Performing; Resident; Educational
Purpose: To serve as a training ground for professionals; to educate the citizens of Tallahassee and surrounding areas in the dance arts
Management: Joyce Straub, Artistic Director; Kathryn Cashin, Artistic Associate; Helen Earl, Ballet Mistress
Officers: Jan Williams, President; Jan Keshen, Vice President; Deborah Stephens, Treasurer; Nancy Floyd, Secretary
Paid Staff: 5 **Volunteer Staff:** 62
Paid Artists: 15 **Non-Paid Artists:** 45
Utilizes: Special Technical Talent; Guest Artists; Guest Directors; Guest Choreographers
Budget: $100,000 - $500,000
Income Sources: Private Foundations/Grants/Endowments; Business/Corporate Donations; Box Office; Government Grants; Individual Donations
Season: September - May
Annual Attendance: 7,000
Affiliations: Florida Dance Association
Performance Facilities: Ruby Diamond Auditorium; Florida State University; Turner Auditorium; Tallahassee Community College

INSTRUMENTAL MUSIC

TALLAHASSEE SYMPHONY ORCHESTRA
203 North Gadsden Street, Suite 3, Tallahassee, FL 32301
(904) 224-0461
Founded: 1981
Arts Area: Symphony
Status: Semi-Professional; Non-Profit
Type: Performing; Resident
Purpose: To maintain a high-quality symphony orchestra in Tallahassee dedicated to superior quality and to furthering cultural opportunities in the community
Management: Anne Robinson Hodges, General Manager; Julie Maisel, Assistant Manager
Officers: Dot P. Hinson, Chairman; Dr. Robert Glidden, Vice Chairman; Chris Roady, President; W.R. Lindquist, Immediate Past Chairman; Lou Kellenberger, Immediate Past President; John Fons, Treasurer
Paid Staff: 2 **Volunteer Staff:** 3
Paid Artists: 80 **Non-Paid Artists:** 2
Utilizes: Guest Artists
Budget: $100,000 - $500,000
Income Sources: Private Foundations/Grants/Endowments; Business/Corporate Donations; Box Office; Government Grants; Individual Donations
Season: October - April
Annual Attendance: 8,500
Affiliations: ASOL
Performance Facilities: Ruby Diamond Auditorium

VOCAL MUSIC

FLORIDA STATE OPERA AT FLORIDA STATE UNIVERSITY
School of Music, 002 HMU, Tallahassee, FL 32306
(904) 644-5248
FAX: (904) 644-6100
Founded: 1963
Arts Area: Grand Opera; Lyric Opera; Operetta

Status: Semi-Professional; Non-Profit
Type: Performing
Purpose: To provide training for Florida State University students and serve as a cultural resource for the capital and state
Management: Lincoln Clark, Director of Opera
Officers: Dale Nick, President, Florida State University; Jon Piersol, Interim Dean, School of Music
Paid Staff: 6   **Volunteer Staff:** 68
Paid Artists: 5   **Non-Paid Artists:** 200
Utilizes: Special Technical Talent; Guest Conductors; Guest Artists; Guest Directors
Budget: $50,000 - $100,000
Income Sources: Private Foundations/Grants/Endowments; Business/Corporate Donations; Box Office; Government Grants; Individual Donations
Season: November - June
Annual Attendance: 19,000
Affiliations: NOA; COS; TOG
Performance Facilities: Ruby Diamond Auditorium; Opperman Music Hall

THEATRE

YOUNG ACTORS THEATRE
609 Glenview Drive, Tallahassee, FL 32303
(904) 386-6602
  Founded: 1975
  Arts Area: Musical; Community; Theatrical Group
  Status: Semi-Professional; Non-Profit
  Type: Performing; Touring; Educational
  Purpose: To educate youth in theatre arts and performance
  Management: Cristina Williams, Director; Alison Grimes, Musical Director; Alison Busby, Dance Director
  Officers: Terry Mara, President; Thomas Walden, Treasurer; David Van Leuven, Vice President; Tina Williams, Executive Director
  Paid Staff: 9   **Volunteer Staff:** 125
  Paid Artists: 10   **Non-Paid Artists:** 335
  Utilizes: Special Technical Talent; Guest Artists; Guest Directors
  Budget: $50,000 - $100,000
  Income Sources: Private Foundations/Grants/Endowments; Business/Corporate Donations; Box Office; Government Grants; Individual Donations
  Season: December - August
  Annual Attendance: 5,000
  Affiliations: SETC; American Association of Theatre Educators
  Performance Facilities: Young Actors Theatre

FACILITY

FLORIDA A&M UNIVERSITY - CHARLES WINTER WOOD THEATRE
Tallahassee, FL 32307
(904) 599-3394
  Type of Facility: Theatre House
  Type of Stage: Proscenium
  Stage Dimensions: 87'x50'x50'   **Orchestra Pit**
  Seating Capacity: 647
  Year Built: 1956   **Cost:** $1,000,000
  Year Remodeled: 1977   **Architect:** Rowe & Holmes
  Contact for Rental: Ronald O. Davis, Phd.;   (904) 599-3394
  Resident Groups: Florida A&M University/Essential Theatre

TALLAHASSEE-LEON COUNTY CIVIC CENTER
505 West Pensacola Street, Tallahassee, FL 32302
(904) 487-1691
FAX: (904) 222-6947
  Type of Facility: Civic Center; Arena; Multi-Purpose
  Type of Stage: Flexible; Arena
  Stage Dimensions: 6'x8' portable sections, adjustable in height
  Seating Capacity: 3,500-14,000
  Year Built: 1981   **Architect:** Barrett Daffin & Carlan   **Cost:** $33,400,000
  Acoustical Consultant: Bolt, Beranek & Newman
  Contact for Rental: Ron Spencer;   (904) 487-1691

Tampa

INSTRUMENTAL MUSIC

THE FLORIDA ORCHESTRA
1211 North Westshore Boulevard, #512, Tampa, FL 33607
(813) 286-1170
FAX: (813) 286-2316
Founded: 1968
Arts Area: Symphony; Orchestra
Status: Professional; Non-Profit
Type: Performing; Touring; Resident; Educational
Purpose: To serve the Tampa Bay Area and the state of Florida with high-quality symphonic music
Management: Jerry Ferrara, Director of Marketing; Julia Ann Fleming, Director of Development; Donny Rye, Controller; Alan Hopper, Orchestra Manager; John Hyer, President/Chief Executive Officer; Kathryn Holm, Associate Director
Officers: F. Wallace Pope Jr. Esq., Chairman; Jane Peppard, Vice President; Michael J. Lagorac Jr., Vice Chairman; Gerald R. Wicker, Treasurer; Ernie A. Reiner M.D., Secretary
Paid Staff: 19 **Volunteer Staff:** 40
Paid Artists: 110
Utilizes: Guest Conductors; Guest Artists
Budget: $1,000,000 - $5,000,000
Income Sources: Private Foundations/Grants/Endowments; Business/Corporate Donations; Box Office; Government Grants; Individual Donations
Season: September - May **Annual Attendance:** 300,000
Affiliations: ASOL
Performance Facilities: Tampa Bay Performing Arts Center; Ruth Eckerd Hall, Bayfront Center

TAMPA BAY CHAMBER ORCHESTRA
PO Box 10353, Tampa, FL 33679
(813) 874-8367
Founded: 1983
Arts Area: Orchestra; Chamber; Ensemble
Status: Professional; Non-Profit
Type: Performing
Purpose: To provide chamber music and works for chamber orchestra to Florida's west coast
Management: Dennis Herron, Music Director/Conductor; Sally Olsson, Executive Director; David Dillingham, Personnel Manager
Officers: Renate K. Hartman, Chairman; Victor E. Palmer, Vice Chairman; Sheila Seig Griffin Esq., Secretary; W. Haskell Gates, Treasurer
Paid Staff: 2
Paid Artists: 35
Utilizes: Guest Artists
Budget: $1,000 - $50,000
Income Sources: Private Foundations/Grants/Endowments; Business/Corporate Donations; Box Office; Government Grants; Individual Donations
Season: September - June **Annual Attendance:** 1,500
Affiliations: ASOL
Performance Facilities: Tampa Museum of Art

THEATRE

BITS 'N PIECES GIANT PUPPET THEATRE
PO Box 368, Tampa, FL 33601
(813) 228-0702
Founded: 1976
Arts Area: Professional; Puppet
Status: Professional; Non-Profit
Type: Performing; Touring; Resident; Educational
Purpose: To present original, educational musicals with unique nine-foot tall puppets
Management: Jerry Bickel, Executive Director; Holli Rubin, Artistic Director; Jackie Hiendlmayr, Business Director
Paid Staff: 3 **Volunteer Staff:** 3
Paid Artists: 8 **Non-Paid Artists:** 6
Utilizes: Special Technical Talent; Guest Artists
Budget: $100,000 - $500,000
Income Sources: Private Foundations/Grants/Endowments; Business/Corporate Donations; Box Office; Government Grants
Season: 52 Weeks **Annual Attendance:** 175,000

FLORIDA SUNCOAST PUPPET GUILD
7107 North Howard Avenue, Tampa, FL 33604
(813) 932-9252
> **Founded:** 1973
> **Arts Area:** Puppet
> **Status:** Non-Profit
> **Type:** Educational; Sponsoring
> **Purpose:** To promote the art of puppetry through shows, workshops, lectures, demonstrations, meetings and festivals
> **Management:** Norma Bigler, Festival Director
> **Officers:** Jody Wren, President; Priscilla LaKus, Secretary/Treasurer; Bill Weber, Vice President/Program; Celine Mac-Donald, Historian
> **Volunteer Staff:** 4
> **Paid Artists:** 19
> **Utilizes:** Special Technical Talent; Guest Artists
> **Budget:** $1,000 - $50,000
> **Income Sources:** Private Foundations/Grants/Endowments; Box Office; Memberships; Special Festivals
> **Season:** 52 Weeks
> **Annual Attendance:** 12,000
> **Affiliations:** Puppeteers of America

PLAYMAKERS
PO Box 5745, Tampa, FL 33675
(813) 248-6933
> **Founded:** 1981
> **Arts Area:** Professional
> **Status:** Professional; Non-Profit
> **Type:** Resident
> **Purpose:** To provide stimulating, thought-provoking, contemporary theatre that explores the human condition
> **Management:** John Owens, Producing Director
> **Officers:** Steve Bragin, Board Member
> **Paid Staff:** 8 **Volunteer Staff:** 100
> **Utilizes:** Guest Artists; Guest Directors
> **Budget:** $100,000 - $500,000
> **Income Sources:** Private Foundations/Grants/Endowments; Business/Corporate Donations; Box Office; Government Grants; Individual Donations
> **Season:** 52 Weeks
> **Annual Attendance:** 25,000
> **Affiliations:** AEA; TCG; SETC; Florida Professional Theatre Association

SPANISH LYRIC THEATRE
1032 Coral Street, Tampa, FL 33602
(813) 223-7341
> **Founded:** 1959
> **Arts Area:** Musical; Theatrical Group
> **Status:** Semi-Professional; Non-Profit
> **Type:** Performing
> **Purpose:** To further production of Spanish musicals (Zarzuelas); to provide lyric theatre in both Spanish and English
> **Management:** Rene J. Gonzalez, Founder and Artistic Director
> **Officers:** Joel Phillips, Chairman; Armando Dorta Jr., Vice President; Martin A. Favata, Secretary; Oscar Bonis Jr., Treasurer
> **Paid Staff:** 3 **Volunteer Staff:** 5
> **Paid Artists:** 40 **Non-Paid Artists:** 20
> **Utilizes:** Special Technical Talent; Guest Artists
> **Budget:** $100,000 - $500,000
> **Income Sources:** Private Foundations/Grants/Endowments; Box Office; Government Grants; Individual Donations
> **Season:** September - May
> **Performance Facilities:** Tampa Bay Performing Arts Center

THE TAMPA PLAYERS
601 South Florida Avenue, Tampa, FL 33602
(813) 229-1505
> **Founded:** 1926
> **Arts Area:** Professional; Theatrical Group
> **Status:** Professional; Non-Profit
> **Type:** Performing
> **Management:** Bill Leldach, Managing and Artistic Director
> **Paid Staff:** 4 **Volunteer Staff:** 50
> **Paid Artists:** 60

Utilizes: Special Technical Talent; Guest Artists; Guest Directors
Budget: $100,000 - $500,000
Income Sources: Private Foundations/Grants/Endowments; Business/Corporate Donations; Box Office; Government Grants; Individual Donations
Season: September - May
Annual Attendance: 13,500

FACILITY

TAMPA BAY PERFORMING ARTS CENTER
1010 North MacInnes Place, Tampa, FL 33602
(813) 222-1000
FAX: (813) 222-1057
   Founded: 1987
   Type of Facility: Performance Center
   Type of Stage: Flexible; Proscenium; Three-Hall Complex
   Stage Dimensions: Festival Hall - 60'x40'; Playhouse - 40'x30'; Jaeb - 24'x40'   **Orchestra Pit**
   Seating Capacity: Festival Hall - 2,493; Playhouse - 960; Jaeb - 299
   Year Built: 1987   **Cost:** $57,000,000
   Acoustical Consultant: Artec
   Contact for Rental: Lorrin Shepard;   (813) 222-1017
   Resident Groups: The Florida Orchestra; Spanish Lyric Theater

TAMPA BAY PERFORMING ARTS CENTER - FESTIVAL HALL
1010 North MacInnes Place, Tampa, FL 33602
(813) 229-7827
FAX: (813) 222-1057
   Type of Facility: Concert Hall
   Type of Stage: Proscenium
   Stage Dimensions: 60'Wx40'Hx65'D   **Orchestra Pit**
   Seating Capacity: 2,400
   Year Built: 1987
   Contact for Rental: Mrs. Bobbi Warnick;   (813) 222-1017
   Resident Groups: Florida Orchestra

TAMPA BAY PERFORMING ARTS CENTER - JAEB THEATER
1010 North MacInnes Place, Tampa, FL 33602
(813) 229-7827
   Type of Facility: Theatre House; Black Box
   Type of Stage: Proscenium
   Stage Dimensions: 42'Wx24'D   **Orchestra Pit**
   Seating Capacity: 300
   Year Built: 1987
   Contact for Rental: Mrs. Bobbi Warnick;   (813) 222-1017
   Resident Groups: The Playmakers

TAMPA BAY PERFORMING ARTS CENTER - PLAYHOUSE
1010 North MacInnes Place, Tampa, FL 33602
(813) 229-7827
   Type of Facility: Theatre House
   Type of Stage: Proscenium
   Stage Dimensions: 40'Wx50'Dx30'H   **Orchestra Pit**
   Seating Capacity: 900
   Year Built: 1987
   Contact for Rental: Mrs. Bobbi Warnick;   (813) 222-1017
   Resident Groups: Tampa Ballet

TAMPA THEATRE
711 Franklin Street Mall, Tampa, FL 33602
(813) 223-8286
   Type of Facility: Theatre House
   Facility Originally: Vaudeville; Movie House
   Type of Stage: Thrust
   Stage Dimensions: 46'6" Wx25'3"D
   Seating Capacity: 1,446
   Year Built: 1926   **Architect:** John Eberson   **Cost:** $1,250,000
   Year Remodeled: 1977   **Architect:** Joseph Dixon   **Cost:** $1,000,000
   Contact for Rental: John Bell;   (813) 223-8286

UNIVERSITY OF SOUTH FLORIDA - STUDIO THEATRE
TAR 230, Tampa, FL 33620-7450
(813) 974-2701
>   **Type of Facility:** Theatre House; Arena
>   **Type of Stage:** Flexible; Arena
>   **Seating Capacity:** 120
>   **Year Built:** 1968   **Architect:** Jim Green   **Cost:** $668,389
>   **Manager:** Dr. Dennis Calandra

UNIVERSITY OF SOUTH FLORIDA - THEATRE I
TAR 230, Tampa, FL 33620
(813) 974-2701
>   **Type of Facility:** Theatre House
>   **Type of Stage:** Proscenium
>   **Orchestra Pit**
>   **Seating Capacity:** 552
>   **Year Built:** 1961   **Architect:** Gamble Pinell & Gilroy   **Cost:** $537,314
>   **Acoustical Consultant:** George Izenour
>   **Contact for Rental:** Dr. Dennis Calandra
>   *Occasionally available for rent*

UNIVERSITY OF SOUTH FLORIDA - THEATRE II
TAR 230, Tampa, FL 33620-7450
(813) 974-2701
>   **Type of Facility:** Black Box
>   **Stage Dimensions:** Black Box 70'x70'
>   **Seating Capacity:** 150-300
>   **Year Built:** 1984   **Architect:** Randolph Wedding Associates   **Cost:** $1,800,000
>   **Acoustical Consultant:** Russell Johnson Associates; ARTEC
>   **Contact for Rental:** Dr. Dennis Calandra
>   *Occasionally available for rent*

Tequesta

THEATRE

BURT REYNOLDS INSTITUTE FOR THEATRE TRAINING
304 Tequesta Drive, Tequesta, FL 33469
(407) 746-8887
FAX: (407) 743-7452
>   **Founded:** 1979
>   **Arts Area:** Theatrical Group
>   **Status:** Professional; Non-Profit
>   **Type:** Performing; Educational
>   **Purpose:** To provide professional theatre training for developing artists
>   **Management:** Richard Valentine, Executive Director
>   **Officers:** Burt Reynolds, Chairman of the Board
>   **Volunteer Staff:** 22
>   **Paid Artists:** 8   **Non-Paid Artists:** 10
>   **Utilizes:** Guest Artists; Guest Directors
>   **Budget:** $500,000 - $1,000,000
>   **Income Sources:** Private Foundations/Grants/Endowments; Business/Corporate Donations; Box Office; Individual Donations
>   **Season:** 52 Weeks
>   **Annual Attendance:** 14,500
>   **Affiliations:** AEA
>   **Performance Facilities:** Burt Reynolds Institute Theatre

Venice

THEATRE

THE VENICE LITTLE THEATRE
140 West Tampa Avenue, Venice, FL 34285
(813) 488-2419
>   **Founded:** 1950
>   **Arts Area:** Community

Status: Non-Professional; Non-Profit
Type: Performing
Purpose: To present intellectual and instructive entertainment in the performing arts
Management: Lee Linkous, Managing Director
Income Sources: Box Office

FACILITY

VENICE COMMUNITY CENTER
326 South Nokomis Avenue, Venice, FL 34285
(813) 485-6196
    Type of Facility: Civic Center
    Type of Stage: Platform
    Stage Dimensions: 54'x28'
    Seating Capacity: 750
    Year Built: 1976
    Contact for Rental: Diana Finnegan; (813) 485-6196

Vero Beach

THEATRE

THE ACTING COMPANY OF RIVERSIDE THEATRE
3250 Riverside Park Drive, Vero Beach, FL 32963
(407) 231-5860
FAX: (407) 234-5298
    Founded: 1985
    Arts Area: Professional; Theatrical Group
    Status: Professional; Non-Profit
    Type: Performing
    Purpose: To provide audiences of this region with productions that are relevant either by nature of their importance within a particular genre or as socially vital within the changing environment of our culture
    Management: Allen D. Cornell, Artistic Director; Brian Spitler, Production Manager; Ida Spada, Business Manager; Lynn Potter, Development Director; Michael Kint, Director of Education
    Officers: Marilyn Chenault, Board President; Pat Trimble, Board Vice President; Rebecca Allen, Board Treasurer; Judy Balph, Board Secretary
    Paid Staff: 19 **Volunteer Staff:** 2
    Paid Artists: 83 **Non-Paid Artists:** 10
    Utilizes: Guest Artists; Guest Directors
    Budget: $1,000,000 - $5,000,000
    Income Sources: Private Foundations/Grants/Endowments; Business/Corporate Donations; Box Office; Government Grants; Individual Donations; Fund-raising
    Season: October - May **Annual Attendance:** 50,000
    Affiliations: AEA; TCG; Florida Performing Theatre Association
    Performance Facilities: Riverside Theatre

VERO BEACH THEATRE GUILD
PO Box 1502, Vero Beach, FL 32961
(407) 562-8300
    Founded: 1958
    Arts Area: Community
    Status: Non-Professional; Non-Profit
    Type: Performing; Educational
    Purpose: To stimulate interest in dramatic and musical works through the means of community theater; to provide theatrical arts to the people of the Treasure Coast of Florida
    Management: Board of Directors
    Officers: Read Johnson, President; Tony Morely, Vice President; Edna Craven, Secretary; Albert Busck, Treasurer
    Volunteer Staff: 50
    Non-Paid Artists: 200
    Utilizes: Special Technical Talent
    Budget: $100,000 - $500,000
    Income Sources: Private Foundations/Grants/Endowments; Business/Corporate Donations; Box Office; Individual Donations
    Season: September - May **Annual Attendance:** 11,000
    Performance Facilities: Riverside Theatre

FACILITY

RIVERSIDE THEATRE
3250 Riverside Park Drive, Vero Beach, FL 32963
(407) 231-5860
    Mailing Address: PO Box 3788, Vero Beach, FL 32964
    Type of Facility: Theatre House
    Type of Stage: Proscenium
    Stage Dimensions: 25'x50'x25'
    Seating Capacity: 609
    Year Built: 1972

West Palm Beach

DANCE

BALLET FLORIDA
500 Fern Street, West Palm Beach, FL 33401
(407) 659-1212
FAX: (407) 659-2222
    Founded: 1973
    Arts Area: Ballet
    Status: Professional; Non-Profit
    Type: Performing; Touring; Resident; Educational
    Purpose: To achieve a dynamic synthesis of the aspiration of dancers, choreographers, and audiences by challenging all three
    Management: Marie Hale, Artistic Director; A. Harrison Cromer Jr., Executive Director
    Paid Artists: 20
    Utilizes: Guest Artists; Guest Choreographers
    Budget: $1,000,000 - $5,000,000
    Income Sources: Private Foundations/Grants/Endowments; Business/Corporate Donations; Box Office; Individual Donations
    Season: November - April
    Annual Attendance: 50,000
    Affiliations: Dance/USA

VOCAL MUSIC

PALM BEACH OPERA
415 South Olive Avenue, West Palm Beach, FL 33401
(407) 833-7888
FAX: (407) 833-8294
    Founded: 1961
    Arts Area: Grand Opera
    Status: Professional; Non-Profit
    Type: Performing; Touring; Resident; Educational
    Purpose: To produce operas and allied musical performances
    Management: Anton Guadagno, Artistic Director; Herbert Benn, General Director
    Paid Staff: 4   **Volunteer Staff:** 8
    Paid Artists: 55
    Utilizes: Guest Artists
    Budget: $1,000,000 - $5,000,000
    Income Sources: Private Foundations/Grants/Endowments; Business/Corporate Donations; Box Office; Government Grants; Individual Donations
    Season: December - March
    Annual Attendance: 15,000
    Performance Facilities: Kravis Center for the Performing Arts

PERFORMING SERIES

SUNFEST OF PALM BEACH COUNTY, INC.
319 Clematis Street, Suite 701, West Palm Beach, FL 33401
(407) 659-5980
FAX: (407) 659-3567
    Founded: 1982
    Arts Area: Festivals
    Status: Non-Profit

Type: Resident
Purpose: Sunfest, Florida's largest jazz, art and water-events festival, is held annually the first weekend in May in West Palm Beach
Management: Sue A. Twyford, Executive Director; Paul Jamieson, Event Manager; Doreen Poreba, Public Relations Manager; Tamra McCraw, Marketing Manager; Sharvell Becton, Pin Program Coordinator
Officers: Dennis Grady, President; J. Kenneth Brower, President Elect; Dari Bowman, Past President; Robert L. Broadway, Thomas G. Burns Vice Presidents .
Paid Staff: 8 **Volunteer Staff:** 3,000
Utilizes: Guest Artists; Guest Visual Artists
Budget: $1,000,000 - $5,000,000
Income Sources: Private Foundations/Grants/Endowments; Business/Corporate Donations; Admission Fees; Concessions
Season: May
Annual Attendance: 345,000
Affiliations: International Festival Association
Performance Facilities: Along the Intracoastal Waterway, Flagler Drive, West Palm Beach

FACILITY

WEST PALM BEACH AUDITORIUM
1610 Palm Beach Lakes, West Palm Beach, FL 33401
(407) 683-6010
FAX: (407) 687-1687
Founded: 1967
Type of Facility: Multi-Purpose
Type of Stage: Flexible; Proscenium; Platform; Arena
Stage Dimensions: 56'Wx38'D on stage; 88'Wx40'D off stage
Orchestra Pit
Seating Capacity: 6,098
Year Built: 1967
Architect: Bertrand Goldberg
Year Remodeled: 1991
Contact for Rental: Bob Burdett;   (407) 683-6010

White Springs

FACILITY

STEPHEN FOSTER STATE FOLK CULTURE CENTER - AMPHITHEATRE
US 41 North, PO Drawer G, White Springs, FL 32096
(904) 397-2733
Type of Facility: Outdoor (Concert); Amphitheater
Type of Stage: Environmental
Seating Capacity: 5,000
Year Built: 1953
Year Remodeled: 1975   **Architect:** Arthur Rude   **Cost:** $100,000
Contact for Rental: Darrell Krause, Park Office;   (904) 397-2733
Manager: Darrell Krause;   (904) 397-2733
Resident Groups: Florida Folk Life Programs

Winter Haven

THEATRE

THEATRE WINTER HAVEN
210 Cypress Gardens Boulevard, PO Drawer 1230, Winter Haven, FL 33882
(813) 299-2672
Founded: 1970
Arts Area: Community; Theatrical Group
Status: Non-Professional; Non-Profit
Type: Performing; Educational
Purpose: To nurture the cultural growth of the community by providing top-quality live theatre through presentation, participation and training
Management: Norman M. Small, Producing Director; Kim N. Siedentopf, General Manager; Bob Campbell, Technical Director
Paid Staff: 4 **Volunteer Staff:** 300
Paid Artists: 14 **Non-Paid Artists:** 9
Utilizes: Special Technical Talent; Guest Conductors; Guest Artists; Guest Directors

Budget: $100,000 - $500,000
Income Sources: Private Foundations/Grants/Endowments; Business/Corporate Donations; Box Office; Government Grants; Individual Donations
Season: 52 Weeks
Annual Attendance: 18,000
Affiliations: AACT

Winter Park

THEATRE

ANNIE RUSSELL THEATRE
Rollins College, 1000 Holt Avenue - 2735, Winter Park, FL 32789
(407) 646-2145
FAX: (407) 646-2600
    Founded: 1931
    Arts Area: Musical; Theatrical Group; Academic Theatre Program
    Status: Semi-Professional; Non-Professional; Non-Profit; Commercial
    Type: Performing; Resident; Educational; Sponsoring
    Purpose: To provide educational theatre; to book touring events
    Management: S. Joseph Nassif, Director
    Paid Staff: 9   **Volunteer Staff:** 12
    Utilizes: Guest Artists; Guest Directors
    Budget: $100,000 - $500,000
    Income Sources: Private Foundations/Grants/Endowments; Business/Corporate Donations; Box Office; Government Grants; Individual Donations
    Season: 52 Weeks   **Annual Attendance:** 20,000
    Affiliations: APAP; SETC; Florida Theatre Conference
    Performance Facilities: Annie Russell Theatre

FACILITY

ROLLINS COLLEGE - ANNIE RUSSELL THEATRE
1000 Holt Avenue - 2735, Winter Park, FL 32789
(407) 646-2145
FAX: (407) 646-2600
    Type of Facility: Theatre Complex
    Type of Stage: Proscenium
    Stage Dimensions: 27'Wx30'D   **Orchestra Pit**
    Seating Capacity: 375
    Year Built: 1931   **Cost:** $500,000
    Year Remodeled: 1978   **Cost:** $200,000
    Manager: Theatre Department
    Resident Groups: Rollins Players

GEORGIA

Albany

INSTRUMENTAL MUSIC

ALBANY SYMPHONY ASSOCIATION, INC.
PO Box 70065, Albany, GA 31707
(912) 888-8799
Founded: 1964
Arts Area: Symphony; Orchestra; Chamber; Ensemble
Status: Professional
Type: Performing; Educational
Purpose: To provide and promote quality symphonic music for southwest Georgia through the organization of a symphony orchestra and related educational activities
Management: Daphne Burt, General Manager; Claire Fox Hillard, Music Director
Officers: James B. Ligon, President Elect; Mitch Everett, First Vice President; Marilyn Malphurs, Second Vice President; Merrel Callaway, Treasurer; Janet Woods, Secretary
Paid Staff: 3 **Volunteer Staff:** 175
Paid Artists: 75
Utilizes: Guest Artists
Budget: $100,000 - $500,000
Income Sources: Private Foundations/Grants/Endowments; Business/Corporate Donations; Box Office; Government Grants; Individual Donations
Season: September - April **Annual Attendance:** 13,000
Affiliations: ASOL; Albany Arts Council
Performance Facilities: Municipal Auditorium, Albany

THEATRE

THEATRE ALBANY
514 Pine Avenue, Albany, GA 31702
(912) 439-7193
Founded: 1932
Arts Area: Musical; Community; Theatrical Group
Status: Non-Professional; Non-Profit
Type: Performing; Educational
Purpose: To foster live theatre in the community
Management: Mark Costello, Artistic/Managing Director; Walter Thompson, Technical Director; Yvette Foster, Business Manager
Officers: Miriam Gilberg, President; Vic Sullivan III, Vice President; Charles Hancock, Treasurer; Mary Morrison, Recording Secretary
Paid Staff: 5 **Volunteer Staff:** 200
Paid Artists: 6 **Non-Paid Artists:** 60
Utilizes: Guest Directors
Budget: $100,000 - $500,000
Income Sources: Private Foundations/Grants/Endowments; Business/Corporate Donations; Box Office; Individual Donations
Season: October - June **Annual Attendance:** 125,000
Affiliations: AACT; SETC; Georgia Theatre Conference
Performance Facilities: Theatre Albany

FACILITY

ALBANY JAMES H. GRAY SR., CIVIC CENTER
100 West Oglethorpe Boulevard, Albany, GA 31702
(912) 430-5200
FAX: (912) 430-5163
Type of Facility: Civic Center
Year Built: 1983 **Architect:** Taylor and Mathis
Contact for Rental: Matty Goddard; (912) 430-5200
Civic Center contains Arena and Ballroom. See separate listings for additional information.

ALBANY JAMES H. GRAY SR., CIVIC CENTER - ARENA
100 West Oglethorpe Boulevard, Albany, GA 31702
(912) 430-5163
FAX: (912) 430-5163
>**Type of Facility:** Concert Hall; Arena
>**Type of Stage:** Platform
>**Seating Capacity:** 10,240
>**Year Built:** 1983
>**Contact for Rental:** Matty Goddard; (912) 430-5200

ALBANY JAMES H. GRAY SR., CIVIC CENTER - BALLROOM
100 West Oglethorpe Boulevard, Albany, GA 31702
(912) 430-5200
FAX: (912) 430-5163
>**Type of Facility:** Multi-Purpose; Room
>**Type of Stage:** Platform
>**Seating Capacity:** Theatre style - 900; Banquet style - 450
>**Year Built:** 1983
>**Contact for Rental:** Matty Goddard; (912) 430-5200

THEATRE ALBANY
514 Pine Avenue, Albany, GA 31702
(912) 439-7193
>**Type of Facility:** Theatre House
>**Facility Originally:** Private Residence
>**Type of Stage:** Flexible; Proscenium
>**Orchestra Pit**
>**Seating Capacity:** 314
>**Year Built:** 1853
>**Year Remodeled:** 1965
>**Contact for Rental:** Managing Director; (912) 439-7193
>**Resident Groups:** Theatre Albany

Athens

DANCE

ATHENS BALLET
126 Barrington Drive, Athens, GA 30605
(706) 353-2082
>**Founded:** 1973
>**Arts Area:** Ballet
>**Status:** Non-Profit
>**Type:** Performing
>**Purpose:** To promote the opportunity to perform and learn
>**Management:** Mary Ann Hale, Artistic Director
>**Officers:** Ted Baumgartner, President; Randy Kemphouse, Vice President; Kathy Whitaker, Treasurer
>**Non-Paid Artists:** 23
>**Budget:** $1,000 - $50,000
>**Income Sources:** Business/Corporate Donations; Box Office; Individual Donations
>**Season:** September - May
>**Affiliations:** Georgia Council of the Arts
>**Performance Facilities:** Athens School of Ballet

THEATRE

ATHENS PUPPET THEATRE COMPANY
525 West Cloverhurst Avenue, Athens, GA 30606
(706) 354-1860
>**Founded:** 1972
>**Arts Area:** Puppet
>**Status:** Professional; Non-Profit
>**Type:** Performing; Touring; Educational
>**Purpose:** To provide a permanent, professional puppet troupe to tour Northeast Georgia and train puppeteers and encourage puppet skills development in our area
>**Management:** Amburn H. Power, Artistic Director; Karen Gilmore, Business Manager
>**Officers:** Ronnie Norton, President of Board of Directors

Paid Staff: 2   **Volunteer Staff:** 25
Paid Artists: 12
Budget: $1,000 - $50,000
Income Sources: Private Foundations/Grants/Endowments; Business/Corporate Donations; Box Office; Government Grants; Individual Donations
Season: October - April   **Annual Attendance:** 20,000
Affiliations: Puppeteers of America; Georgia Theatre Conference

GABBIES PUPPETS
367 Lexington Heights, Athens, GA 30605
(706) 353-2785
Founded: 1975
Arts Area: Puppet
Status: Professional
Type: Performing; Educational
Purpose: To present and teach language communication skills through the arts of puppets, storytelling, and creative dramatics
Management: Carolyn S. Gabb, Director
Paid Staff: 1
Paid Artists: 1
Utilizes: Special Technical Talent; Guest Artists
Budget: $1,000 - $50,000
Income Sources: Private Foundations/Grants/Endowments
Season: 52 Weeks

Atlanta

DANCE

THE ATLANTA BALLET
477 Peachtree Street NE, Atlanta, GA 30308
(404) 873-5811
FAX: (404) 874-7905
Founded: 1929
Arts Area: Ballet
Status: Professional; Non-Profit
Type: Performing; Touring; Resident
Purpose: To provide professional ballet performances for the people of metropolitan Atlanta and the surrounding area
Management: Chuck Johnston, Executive Director; Robert Barnett, Artistic Director
Officers: Lynda Courts, Chairman of the Board
Paid Staff: 28
Paid Artists: 29
Utilizes: Special Technical Talent; Guest Artists; Guest Directors
Budget: $1,000,000 - $5,000,000
Income Sources: Private Foundations/Grants/Endowments; Business/Corporate Donations; Box Office; Government Grants; Individual Donations
Season: September - May
Affiliations: Dance USA; NARB
Performance Facilities: Atlanta Civic Center

THE RUTH MITCHELL DANCE COMPANY
3509 Northside Parkway, Atlanta, GA 30327
(404) 237-2477
Founded: 1956
Arts Area: Modern; Ballet; Jazz
Status: Professional; Non-Profit
Type: Performing; Touring
Purpose: To provide the community with a small, eclectic company which can perform in places not suited for large ballet companies
Management: Ruth Mitchell, Artistic Director; Courtney Kennedy, Production Manager
Officers: Sandra Ratchford, President, Board of Trustees; Courtney Kennedy, Vice President; Carmen Dillard, Treasurer; Judy Freeman, President of the Guild
Paid Staff: 2   **Volunteer Staff:** 2
Paid Artists: 8
Utilizes: Guest Artists; Guest Choreographers
Budget: $100,000 - $500,000
Income Sources: Private Foundations/Grants/Endowments; Business/Corporate Donations; Box Office; Government Grants; Individual Donations

Season: August - May   **Annual Attendance:** 40,000
Affiliations: NARB; Dance Coalition of Atlanta; Young Audiences of Atlanta
Performance Facilities: 14th Street Playhouse; Cobb Civic Center; Pace Fine Arts

INSTRUMENTAL MUSIC

ATLANTA CHAMBER PLAYERS
68 GSU-Georgia State University, PO Box 4038, Atlanta, GA 30302
(404) 651-1228
  Arts Area: Chamber
  Status: Professional; Non-Profit
  Type: Performing; Touring; Resident; Educational
  Purpose: Atlanta Chamber Players is a professional ensemble of musicians dedicated to providing audiences with world class traditional and contemporary masterpieces as well as commissioned new works
  Management: Paula Peace, Artistic Director; Ed Trafford, Business Manager
  Officers: Cherry Emerson, President of the Board
  Budget: $50,000 - $100,000
  Income Sources: Private Foundations/Grants/Endowments; Business/Corporate Donations; Box Office; Government Grants; Individual Donations
  Performance Facilities: Georgia State University Recital Hall

ATLANTA POPS ORCHESTRA
PO Box 723172-0172, Atlanta, GA 31139-0172
(404) 435-1222
  Founded: 1945
  Arts Area: Orchestra; Pops; Popular Selections
  Status: Professional; Non-Profit
  Type: Performing; Touring
  Purpose: To provide a showcase for amateur guest talent; to give them a chance to grow musically in public performances
  Management: Lorne Coleman, Manager; Albert Coleman, Originator/Director/Conductor
  Officers: Albert Coleman, President; Charles Wills, Vice President; Betty Fitz, Administrative Assistant; Nancy Holland, Publicist
  Paid Staff: 3
  Paid Artists: 55
  Utilizes: Guest Artists
  Budget: $100,000 - $500,000
  Income Sources: Private Foundations/Grants/Endowments; Business/Corporate Donations; Performance Fees
  Season: 52 Weeks   **Annual Attendance:** 40,000
  Performance Facilities: Chastain Park; Stone Mountain; McIntosh Amphitheatre

ATLANTA SYMPHONY ORCHESTRA
1293 Peachtree Street NE, Suite 300, Atlanta, GA 30309
(404) 898-1182
FAX: (404) 898-9557
  Founded: 1945
  Arts Area: Symphony; Orchestra; Chamber
  Status: Professional; Non-Profit
  Type: Performing
  Purpose: To present symphonic concerts for the enjoyment of Atlanta area audiences
  Management: J. Thomas Bacchetti, Executive Director; Robert Shaw, Music Director Emeritus/Conductor Laureate; Yoel Levy, Music Director; George Hanson, Resident Conductor
  Officers: Jay Levine, President; J. Thomas Bacchetti, Vice President
  Paid Staff: 54   **Volunteer Staff:** 1,000
  Paid Artists: 94
  Utilizes: Guest Conductors; Guest Artists
  Budget: Over 10,000,000
  Income Sources: Private Foundations/Grants/Endowments; Business/Corporate Donations; Box Office; Government Grants; Individual Donations
  Season: 52 Weeks   **Annual Attendance:** 600,000
  Affiliations: ASOL
  Performance Facilities: Symphony Hall; Chastain Park Amphitheatre

ATLANTA SYMPHONY YOUTH ORCHESTRA
1293 Peachtree Street NE, Atlanta, GA 30309
(404) 898-1182; (404) 898-9572
FAX: (404) 898-9557
  Founded: 1973
  Arts Area: Symphony; Orchestra

Status: Non-Professional; Non-Profit
Type: Performing; Educational
Management: Cynthia Thomas, Director of Education; Jere Flint, Conductor
Paid Staff: 4
Non-Paid Artists: 110
Utilizes: Guest Conductors
Income Sources: Business/Corporate Donations; Box Office; Individual Donations
Season: September - May **Annual Attendance:** 5,200
Affiliations: ASOL (Youth Orchestra Division); Atlanta Symphony Orchestra
Performance Facilities: Symphony Hall, Robert W. Woodruff Arts Center

VOCAL MUSIC

ATLANTA BACH CHOIR
1026 Ponce de Leon Avenue, Atlanta, GA 30306
(404) 872-2224
Founded: 1980
Arts Area: Choral
Status: Professional; Non-Profit
Type: Performing; Touring; Resident
Purpose: Performance of cantatas, orchestral, chamber and major works of J.S. Bach
Management: Porter Remington, Conductor
Officers: Sue McConner, President; David Miller, Vice President; Deborah Hildebrand, Treasurer
Paid Staff: 1 **Volunteer Staff:** 15
Paid Artists: 102 **Non-Paid Artists:** 33
Utilizes: Guest Artists
Budget: $1,000 - $50,000
Income Sources: Private Foundations/Grants/Endowments; Business/Corporate Donations; Box Office; Government Grants; Individual Donations
Season: September - July **Annual Attendance:** 3,000

THE ATLANTA OPERA
1800 Peachtree Street NW, Suite 620, Atlanta, GA 30309
(404) 355-3311
Founded: 1979
Arts Area: Grand Opera; Lyric Opera
Status: Professional; Non-Profit
Type: Performing; Educational
Purpose: The company is committed to establishing itself as a major artistic presence in the Southeast by combining quality mainstage productions with programs designed to serve community, cultural and educational needs.
Management: William Fred Scott, Artistic Director; Alfred D. Kennedy, General Manager
Officers: Mrs. Shepard B. Ansley, Chairman; Robert Fischer, President
Paid Staff: 7 **Volunteer Staff:** 15
Paid Artists: 6
Utilizes: Special Technical Talent; Guest Conductors; Guest Artists
Budget: $500,000 - $1,000,000
Income Sources: Private Foundations/Grants/Endowments; Business/Corporate Donations; Box Office; Government Grants; Individual Donations
Season: June - August **Annual Attendance:** 15,000
Affiliations: Alliance Theatre
Performance Facilities: Alliance Theatre; Symphony Hall

ATLANTA SYMPHONY CHORUS
c/o Robert W. Woodruff Arts Center, 1292 Peachtree Street NE, Atlanta, GA 30309
(404) 898-1182
FAX: (404) 898-9557
Arts Area: Grand Opera; Operetta; Arias
Status: Non-Professional; Non-Profit; Volunteer
Type: Performing; Touring
Management: Robert Shaw, Conductor; Nola Frank, Choral Administrator
Budget: $50,000 - $100,000
Income Sources: Private Foundations/Grants/Endowments; Business/Corporate Donations; Box Office; Government Grants; Individual Donations
Performance Facilities: Robert W. Woodruff Arts Center Symphony Hall

CHORAL GUILD OF ATLANTA
PO Box 7872, Atlanta, GA 30357
(404) 435-6563
Arts Area: Choral

Status: Semi-Professional; Non-Profit
Type: Performing; Touring
Purpose: To be the pre-eminent large civic chorus in metro Atlanta performing major choral works from the non-standard repertoire while becoming increasingly financially solvent
Management: William Noll, Conductor/Director
Officers: C. William Moody, Chairman of the Board
Budget: $50,000 - $100,000
Income Sources: Business/Corporate Donations; Box Office; Government Grants; Individual Donations

THEATRE

ACADEMY THEATRE
PO Box 191306, Atlanta, GA 31119
(404) 365-8088
Founded: 1956
Arts Area: Professional
Status: Professional; Non-Profit
Type: Performing; Touring; Resident; Educational; Sponsoring
Purpose: To foster an atmosphere that assists the individual in discovering creative resources that will lead to artistic expression of individual feelings and insights and be a forum for ideas, a place to question values, a means to entertain and enhance life
Management: Frank Wittow, Founder/Producing Artistic Director; Lorenne Fey, Managing Director
Officers: Sue L. Symons, Chairman of the Board; Frank Wittow, President
Paid Staff: 5   **Volunteer Staff:** 35
Paid Artists: 40   **Non-Paid Artists:** 30
Utilizes: Special Technical Talent; Guest Conductors; Guest Artists; Guest Directors
Budget: $100,000 - $500,000
Income Sources: Private Foundations/Grants/Endowments; Business/Corporate Donations; Box Office; Government Grants; Individual Donations
Season: 52 Weeks   **Annual Attendance:** 130,000
Affiliations: TCG; Atlanta Theatre Coalition; Atlanta Chamber of Commerce; AATA; ASSITEJ; Georgia Citizens for the Arts

ALLIANCE THEATRE COMPANY
1280 Peachtree Street NE, Atlanta, GA 30309
(404) 898-1132
Founded: 1969
Arts Area: Professional; Theatrical Group
Status: Professional; Non-Profit
Type: Performing; Touring; Resident; Educational
Purpose: To create an environment in which to achieve the highest quality theatre nationally as well as regionally
Management: Edith H. Love, Managing Director; Kenny Leon, Artistic Director; T. Jane Bishop, General Manager
Officers: Robert E. Reiser, President; Kenneth Bernhardt, First Vice President; Chuck Frew, Teasurer
Paid Staff: 203   **Volunteer Staff:** 750
Paid Artists: 200
Utilizes: Special Technical Talent; Guest Artists; Guest Directors
Budget: $5,000,000 - $10,000,000
Income Sources: Private Foundations/Grants/Endowments; Business/Corporate Donations; Box Office; Government Grants; Individual Donations
Season: August - June   **Annual Attendance:** 290,000
Affiliations: AEA; SSDC; LORT; USA
Performance Facilities: Alliance Theatre

ATLANTA SHAKESPEARE COMPANY
PO Box 5436, Atlanta, GA 30307
(404) 874-9219
Founded: 1979
Arts Area: Professional; Theatrical Group
Status: Professional; Non-Profit
Type: Performing; Touring
Purpose: To reinstate the popular appeal inherent, not only in the works of William Shakespeare, but of all living theater
Management: Jeffrey Watkins, Artistic Director; Tony Wright, Marketing Director; Cindy Kearns, Stage Manager
Officers: Jeffrey Watkins, President
Paid Staff: 2   **Volunteer Staff:** 6
Paid Artists: 26
Utilizes: Special Technical Talent; Guest Conductors; Guest Artists; Guest Directors
Budget: $100,000 - $500,000
Income Sources: Business/Corporate Donations; Box Office; Government Grants; Individual Donations

Annual Attendance: 8,000
Affiliations: Atlanta Coalition of Theatres

ATLANTA STREET THEATRE
1660 Moores Mill Road, Atlanta, GA 30327
(404) 355-0020
Founded: 1976
Arts Area: Professional
Status: Professional; Non-Profit
Type: Performing; Touring; Educational
Purpose: To provide relevant theatre to underprivileged youth; to maintain an interracial group at all levels; to use theatre educationally
Management: Michele McNichols, Executive Artistic Director
Officers: Donna Watts-Nunn, Chairman of the Board; John Coleman, Treasurer; Brenda Webb, Secretary
Paid Staff: 1 **Volunteer Staff:** 3
Paid Artists: 10
Budget: $1,000 - $50,000
Income Sources: Private Foundations/Grants/Endowments; Business/Corporate Donations
Season: 52 Weeks **Annual Attendance:** 5,000

CENTER FOR PUPPETRY ARTS
1404 Spring Street NW, Atlanta, GA 30309
(404) 873-3089; (404) 873-3391
FAX: (404) 873-9907
Founded: 1978
Arts Area: Professional; Puppet
Status: Professional; Non-Profit
Type: Performing; Touring; Resident; Educational; Sponsoring
Purpose: Dedicated to expanding the public's awareness of puppetry as a fine art and to expose people to the global aspects of the art form
Management: Vincent Anthony, Executive Director
Officers: Barbara Wylly, Chairman, Board of Trustees
Paid Staff: 22 **Volunteer Staff:** 20
Paid Artists: 30
Utilizes: Special Technical Talent; Guest Artists; Guest Directors
Budget: $1,000,000 - $5,000,000
Income Sources: Private Foundations/Grants/Endowments; Business/Corporate Donations; Box Office; Government Grants; Individual Donations
Season: 52 Weeks **Annual Attendance:** 250,000
Affiliations: TCG; UNIMA; Puppeteers of America; Georgia Citizens for the Arts; Metro Arts
Performance Facilities: Mainstage Theater; Downstairs Theater; Museum Mini Theater; Theater III

GATEWAY PERFORMANCE PRODUCTIONS
PO Box 8062, Atlanta, GA 30306
(404) 222-9884
Founded: 1974
Arts Area: Theatrical Group; MIME
Status: Professional; Non-Profit
Type: Performing; Touring; Resident; Educational
Purpose: To explore and expand the parameters of the art of mime and related movement theatre
Management: Sandra Hughes, Artistic Director; Michael E. Hickey, Company Coordinator
Officers: H. Lamar Mixson, Chairman; Sandra Hughes, President; Michael E. Hickey, Treasurer; Dorothy Sussman, Secretary
Paid Staff: 2
Utilizes: Special Technical Talent; Guest Artists
Budget: $50,000 - $100,000
Income Sources: Private Foundations/Grants/Endowments; Business/Corporate Donations
Season: 52 Weeks

JOMANDI PRODUCTIONS
1444 Mayson Street, Atlanta, GA 30324
(404) 876-6346
Founded: 1978
Arts Area: Theatrical Group
Status: Professional; Non-Profit
Type: Performing; Touring; Resident
Purpose: To nurture the development of new works about the African-American experience and to provide a vehicle for theatre artists to train and perform
Management: Tom Jones, Marsha Jackson, Artistic Directors; Geri Blanchet, Public Relations Director

Officers: Clifton Barber, Chairperson; Herman Reese, Vice Chair; Diana Stevens, Secretary; Andrea Fuller, Treasurer
Utilizes: Special Technical Talent; Guest Artists; Guest Directors
Budget: $50,000 - $100,000
Income Sources: Private Foundations/Grants/Endowments; Business/Corporate Donations; Box Office; Government Grants; Individual Donations
Season: October - June
Performance Facilities: Academy Theatre

JUST US THEATER COMPANY
PO Box 42271, Atlanta, GA 30311-4271
(404) 753-2399
Founded: 1976
Arts Area: Theatrical Group
Status: Professional
Type: Performing; Touring; Resident; Educational
Purpose: Just Us Theater Company is a Black professional company dedicated to the development of minority artists and the presentation of quality arts programs that reflect the diversity of our community; focus on sexism and racism
Management: Pearl Cleage, Artistic Director; Zaron Burnett Jr., Producing Director
Officers: Walter R. Huntley, Board President; Pearle Cleage, Treasurer; Zaron W. Burnett Jr., Secretary
Paid Staff: 4 **Volunteer Staff:** 25
Paid Artists: 70
Utilizes: Special Technical Talent; Guest Artists; Guest Directors
Budget: $100,000 - $500,000
Income Sources: Private Foundations/Grants/Endowments; Business/Corporate Donations; Box Office; Government Grants; Individual Donations
Season: 52 Weeks **Annual Attendance:** 10,000

OMILAMI PRODUCTIONS/PEOPLE'S SURVIVAL THEATRE
8 East Lake Drive NE, Atlanta, GA 30317
(404) 377-6434
FAX: (404) 584-9166
Founded: 1977
Arts Area: Community; Theatrical Group
Status: Semi-Professional; Non-Profit
Type: Performing; Touring; Educational
Purpose: To produce, provide and encourage arts programming for impoverished areas that are not serviced by traditional groups; to stimulate and encourage new playwrights and directors to write and direct for the inner city and rural areas
Management: Elizabeth and Afemo Omilami, Co-Artistic Directors
Paid Staff: 2 **Volunteer Staff:** 3
Paid Artists: 12 **Non-Paid Artists:** 8
Utilizes: Special Technical Talent; Guest Artists; Guest Directors
Budget: $100,000 - $500,000
Income Sources: Private Foundations/Grants/Endowments; Business/Corporate Donations; Box Office; Government Grants; Individual Donations
Season: 52 Weeks **Annual Attendance:** 10,000

SEVEN STAGES
430 Moreland Avenue NE, Atlanta, GA 30307
(404) 522-0911
FAX: (404) 522-0913
Founded: 1978
Arts Area: Professional; Musical; Community; Theatrical Group
Status: Professional; Non-Profit
Type: Performing; Resident
Purpose: To produce new plays which might not otherwise be seen and produce reinterpretations of classics and contemporary theatre
Management: Del Hamilton, Artistic Director; Faye Allen, Producing Director; Lisa Mount, Managing Director; Linda Burgess, Technical Director
Paid Staff: 4 **Volunteer Staff:** 40
Paid Artists: 75
Utilizes: Special Technical Talent; Guest Artists; Guest Directors
Budget: $100,000 - $500,000
Income Sources: Private Foundations/Grants/Endowments; Business/Corporate Donations; Box Office; Government Grants; Individual Donations
Season: 52 Weeks **Annual Attendance:** 10,000
Affiliations: TCG; Alternate Roots
Performance Facilities: Seven Stages

THE SOUTHEASTERN SAVOYARDS
3270 Ivanhoe Drive, Atlanta, GA 30327
(404) 233-7002
Founded: 1980
Arts Area: Musical Theatre
Status: Professional; Non-Profit
Type: Theatrical Group
Purpose: Gilbert & Sullivan repertory company
Management: John H. Stevens, Executive Producer; J. Lynn Thompson, Artistic/Music Director
Officers: John H. Stevens, President; Robert B. Langdon, Vice President; Fern M. Stevens, Treasurer; Marcia Lane, Secretary
Paid Staff: 4 **Volunteer Staff:** 20
Paid Artists: 43
Utilizes: Special Technical Talent; Guest Artists; Guest Directors
Budget: $100,000 - $500,000
Income Sources: Private Foundations/Grants/Endowments; Business/Corporate Donations; Box Office; Government Grants; Individual Donations
Season: October - May **Annual Attendance:** 10,000
Performance Facilities: Center Stage Theater Atlanta

THEATRE GAEL
PO Box 77156, Atlanta, GA 30357
(404) 876-1138
FAX: (404) 892-0355
Founded: 1982
Arts Area: Professional; Theatrical Group; Children's Theatre
Status: Professional; Non-Profit
Type: Performing
Purpose: To perform the plays of Ireland, Scotland and Wales
Management: Aimee Chubb, Managing Director; John Stephens, Artistic Director
Paid Staff: 4 **Volunteer Staff:** 25
Paid Artists: 100 **Non-Paid Artists:** 25
Utilizes: Special Technical Talent; Guest Artists; Guest Directors
Budget: $100,000 - $500,000
Income Sources: Private Foundations/Grants/Endowments; Business/Corporate Donations; Box Office; Government Grants; Individual Donations
Season: 52 Weeks **Annual Attendance:** 60,000
Affiliations: AATA; Alternate ROOTS
Performance Facilities: 14th Street Playhouse

THEATRICAL OUTFIT
1012 Peachtree Street, PO Box 7098, Atlanta, GA 30357
(404) 872-0665
FAX: (404) 872-1164
Founded: 1978
Arts Area: Professional; Musical
Status: Professional; Non-Profit
Type: Performing; Educational
Purpose: Georgia's only theatre that produces new work with music, new musicals, and new adaptations with music
Management: Phillip DePoy, Artistic Director; Robert Hill, General Manager; Robert Teverino, Production Manager; Lori Youngers, Director of Marketing; Chris Cofrin, Volunteer Director of Development
Officers: David Cofrin, Board President
Paid Staff: 4 **Volunteer Staff:** 4
Utilizes: Special Technical Talent; Guest Artists; Guest Directors
Budget: $100,000 - $500,000
Income Sources: Private Foundations/Grants/Endowments; Business/Corporate Donations; Box Office; Government Grants; Individual Donations
Season: 52 Weeks **Annual Attendance:** 30,000
Affiliations: AEA; TCG

PERFORMING SERIES

ATLANTA JAZZ FESTIVAL
c/o Atlanta Bureau of Cultural Affairs, 675 Ponce de Leon, Atlanta, GA 30308
(404) 653-7160
FAX: (404) 658-6945
Arts Area: Dance; Vocal Music; Instrumental Music
Status: Professional; Non-Profit

Type: Performing; Educational
Purpose: To provide an opportunity to showcase local and national talent; to expose the citizens of Atlanta to jazz music
Management: Barbara Bowser, Bureau Director; Jackie Davis, Festivals Manager
Budget: $100,000 - $500,000
Income Sources: Private Foundations/Grants/Endowments; Business/Corporate Donations; Box Office; Government Grants; Individual Donations
Performance Facilities: Grant Park

GEORGIA SHAKESPEARE FESTIVAL
4484 Peachtree Road NE, Atlanta, GA 30319
(404) 264-0020
Founded: 1985
Arts Area: Theater; Festivals
Status: Professional; Non-Profit
Type: Performing; Resident
Purpose: To produce an annual summer Shakespeare festival
Management: Richard Garner, Artistic/Producing Director; Margaret Dickson, Managing Director
Officers: Bruce Callner, President; Eric Bitterman, Treasurer; Barbara Stanton, Secretary
Paid Staff: 3   **Volunteer Staff:** 3
Paid Artists: 20   **Non-Paid Artists:** 7
Utilizes: Guest Artists; Guest Directors
Budget: $100,000 - $500,000
Income Sources: Private Foundations/Grants/Endowments; Business/Corporate Donations; Box Office; Government Grants; Individual Donations
Season: July - August   **Annual Attendance:** 6,100
Affiliations: SETC; Atlanta Theatre Coalition

MONTREUX ATLANTA MUSIC FESTIVAL
c/o Atlanta Bureau of Cultural Affairs, 675 Ponce de Leon, Atlanta, GA 30308
(404) 653-7160
FAX: (404) 658-6945
Arts Area: Vocal Music; Instrumental Music
Status: Professional; Non-Profit
Type: Performing; Educational
Purpose: To expose the citizens of Atlanta to a variety of musical categories including gospel, country, blues, jazz, pop, rhythm and blues and world music; the festival is part of a musical exchange between the cities of Atlanta and Montreux, Switzerland and is a counterpart of the Montreux Jazz Festival
Management: Barbara Bowser, Bureau Director; Jackie Davis, Festivals Manager
Budget: $100,000 - $500,000
Income Sources: Private Foundations/Grants/Endowments; Business/Corporate Donations; Box Office; Government Grants; Individual Donations
Performance Facilities: Piedmont Park

NATIONAL BLACK ARTS FESTIVAL
236 Forsyth Street SW, Suite 400, Atlanta, GA 30303
(404) 730-7315
FAX: (404) 730-7104
Founded: 1987
Arts Area: Dance; Vocal Music; Instrumental Music; Theater; Festivals
Status: Non-Profit
Type: Presenting
Purpose: To showcase and celebrate the works of artists of African descent in eight artistic disciplines
Management: Myrna Anderson-Fuller, Managing Director; Stephanie Hughley, Artistic Director
Officers: Michael Lomax, Chairman of the Board; Nancy Boxill, Vice Chairperson; Milford McGuirt, Treasurer; Sandra Baccus, Secretary
Paid Staff: 8
Paid Artists: 964   **Non-Paid Artists:** 135
Utilizes: Special Technical Talent; Guest Conductors; Guest Artists; Guest Directors; Curators, Choreographers
Budget: $1,000,000 - $5,000,000
Income Sources: Private Foundations/Grants/Endowments; Business/Corporate Donations; Box Office; Government Grants; Individual Donations
Season: August   **Annual Attendance:** 600,000
Affiliations: Fulton County Arts Council

THEATER OF THE STARS
PO Box 11748, Atlanta, GA 30355
(404) 252-8960
Founded: 1953

Arts Area: Dance; Vocal Music; Instrumental Music; Musicals; Plays
Status: Professional; Non-Profit
Type: Performing; Touring; Sponsoring
Management: Christopher Manos, Producer
Paid Staff: 6
Utilizes: Special Technical Talent; Guest Artists; Guest Directors
Income Sources: Business/Corporate Donations; Box Office; Government Grants; Individual Donations
Season: July - August

FACILITY

ACADEMY THEATRE - FIRST STAGE
PO Box 191306, Atlanta, GA 31119
(404) 365-8088
> **Type of Facility:** Black Box
> **Type of Stage:** Flexible
> **Stage Dimensions:** 50'Wx50'Dx16'H
> **Seating Capacity:** 175
> **Year Built:** 1987
> **Contact for Rental:** (404) 365-8088

ACADEMY THEATRE - LAB
173 14th Street, PO Box 191306, Atlanta, GA 31119
(404) 365-8088
> **Type of Facility:** Multi-Purpose; Room
> **Type of Stage:** Flexible
> **Stage Dimensions:** 25'Wx50'D
> **Seating Capacity:** 50
> **Year Built:** 1987
> **Contact for Rental:** (404) 365-8088

ACADEMY THEATRE - PHOEBE THEATRE
PO Box 191306, Atlanta, GA 31119
(404) 365-8088
> **Type of Facility:** Theatre House
> **Type of Stage:** Modified Thrust
> **Stage Dimensions:** 40'Wx44'D
> **Seating Capacity:** 375
> **Year Built:** 1987
> **Contact for Rental:** (404) 365-8088

ATLANTA CIVIC CENTER
395 Piedmont Avenue NE, Atlanta, GA 30308
(404) 523-6275
FAX: (404) 525-4634
> **Type of Facility:** Civic Center
> **Year Built:** 1968   **Architect:** Roberts and Company   **Cost:** $21,000,000
> **Contact for Rental:** Walt Elder;   (404) 523-6275
> *The Civic Center contains Room 104 and Theater Auditorium. See separate listings for additional information.*

ATLANTA CIVIC CENTER - ROOM 104
395 Piedmont Avenue NE, Atlanta, GA 30308
(404) 523-6275
FAX: (404) 525-4634
> **Type of Facility:** Multi-Purpose; Room
> **Type of Stage:** Flexible
> **Seating Capacity:** 800
> **Year Built:** 1968   **Architect:** Roberts and Company
> **Contact for Rental:** Walt Elder;   (404) 523-6275
> **Resident Groups:** Club Zebra

ATLANTA CIVIC CENTER - THEATER AUDITORIUM
395 Piedmont Avenue NE, Atlanta, GA 30308
(404) 523-6275
FAX: (404) 525-4634
> **Type of Facility:** Concert Hall; Auditorium; Theatre House
> **Type of Stage:** Proscenium
> **Stage Dimensions:** 121'8"Wx57'6"D; 86'W proscenium opening   **Orchestra Pit**

Seating Capacity: 4,600
Year Built: 1968   **Architect:** Roberts and Company
Contact for Rental: Walt Elder;   (404) 523-6275
Resident Groups: Atlanta Ballet

14TH STREET PLAYHOUSE
173 14th Street, Atlanta, GA 30309
(404) 892-0103
FAX: (404) 892-0355
Type of Facility: Theatre Complex; Performance Center
Type of Stage: Thrust; Flexible; Proscenium; Three stages
Stage Dimensions: Secondstage - thrust; Stage 3 - flexible; Mainstage - proscenium
Seating Capacity: Mainstage - 400; Secondstage - 200; Stage Three - 100
Year Built: 1987   **Architect:** IA Group   **Cost:** $4,500,000
Acoustical Consultant: Michael Stauffer
Contact for Rental: Robert Putnam;   (404) 892-0103
Resident Groups: Carl Ratcliff Dance Theatre; Jomandi Productions; Theatre Gael; Ruth Mitchell Dance; S.A.M.E.
Performance spaces within the 14th Street Playhouse are Mainstage, Secondstage and Stage 3. See separate listings for additional information.

FOX THEATRE
660 Peachtree Street NE, Atlanta, GA 30365
(404) 881-2100
Type of Facility: Concert Hall; Theatre House; Opera House
Facility Originally: Shrine Temple
Type of Stage: Modified Thrust
Stage Dimensions: 135'Wx39'D; add 19'6"D with 3 hydraulic lift pits at stage level   **Orchestra Pit**
Seating Capacity: 4,518
Year Built: 1929   **Architect:** Mayre Alger Vinour   **Cost:** $3,500,000
Year Remodeled: 1993   **Architect:** Rosser Fabrap International   **Cost:** $8,000,000
Contact for Rental: Edgar Neiss;   (404) 881-2100
The Fox Theatre was originally built to house Yaraab Temple of the Ancient Arabic Order of the Nobles of the Mystic Shrine. A National Historic Landmark, restoration began in 1975. Completion is projected for 1995 with the building remaining open and fully functional during restoration.

GLENN MEMORIAL AUDITORIUM
1652 North Decatur Road NE, Atlanta, GA 30307-1010
(404) 727-6691
FAX: (404) 634-3936
Founded: 1931
Type of Facility: Concert Hall; Auditorium; Multi-Purpose; Church
Facility Originally: Church
Type of Stage: Platform
Stage Dimensions: 44'x40' with extensions
Seating Capacity: 1,250
Year Built: 1931   **Architect:** Hentz, Adler & Shultz   **Cost:** $160,000
Year Remodeled: 1960   **Architect:** Newcomb & Boyd   **Cost:** $300,000
Resident Groups: Emory Music Department

ROBERT W. WOODRUFF ARTS CENTER
1280 Peachtree Street, Atlanta, GA 30309
(404) 892-3600
Type of Facility: Performance Center; Civic Center
Year Built: 1967   **Architect:** Toombs Amisano & Wells; Stevenson & Wilkerson   **Cost:** $13,000,000
Acoustical Consultant: Vern Knudsen
The Arts Center consists of the Alliance Theatre-Main Stage, Alliance Theatre-Studio Theatre, Richard H. Rich Auditorium and Symphony Hall. See separate listings for additional information.

ROBERT W. WOODRUFF ARTS CENTER - ALLIANCE THEATRE-MAIN STAGE
1280 Peachtree Street, Atlanta, GA 30309
(404) 898-1132
FAX: (404) 898-9576
Founded: 1968
Type of Facility: Performance Center; Theatre House
Type of Stage: Proscenium
Stage Dimensions: 94'Wx40'D; 40'Wx28'H proscenium opening   **Orchestra Pit**
Seating Capacity: 784
Year Built: 1967

Acoustical Consultant: Jaffe Acoustics
Contact for Rental: Tom Semans;   (404) 898-1133
Resident Groups: Alliance Theatre Company

ROBERT W. WOODRUFF ARTS CENTER - ALLIANCE THEATRE-STUDIO THEATRE
1280 Peachtree Street, Atlanta, GA 30309
(404) 892-3600
Type of Facility: Black Box
Type of Stage: Flexible
Seating Capacity: 200
Year Built: 1969
Contact for Rental: Tom Semans;   (404) 898-1133

ROBERT W. WOODRUFF ARTS CENTER - RICHARD H. RICH AUDITORIUM
1280 Peachtree Street, Atlanta, GA 30309
(404) 892-3600
Type of Facility: Auditorium
Type of Stage: Proscenium
Stage Dimensions: 35'Wx16'D
Seating Capacity: 437
Year Built: 1967
Contact for Rental: Larry Ahern;   (404) 892-3600, ext. 104

ROBERT W. WOODRUFF ARTS CENTER - SYMPHONY HALL
1280 Peachtree Street, Atlanta, GA 30309
(404) 892-3600
Founded: 1967
Type of Facility: Concert Hall; Theatre House
Type of Stage: Proscenium; Modified Apron Proscenium
Stage Dimensions: 122'6"Wx53'7"D; 65'Wx37'H proscenium opening   **Orchestra Pit**
Seating Capacity: 1,762
Year Built: 1967
Contact for Rental: Maria Williamson;   (404) 898-1182
Resident Groups: Atlanta Symphony Orchestra
Hydraulic lift pit can be raised to stage level. Add 11'D to stage with lift at stage level.

SEVEN STAGES
1105 Euclid Avenue, Atlanta, GA 30307
(404) 522-0911
Type of Facility: Theatre House
Facility Originally: Business Facility
Type of Stage: L-shaped
Stage Dimensions: 30'x30'
Seating Capacity: 96
Year Remodeled: 1983   **Architect:** Community Design Center   **Cost:** $40,000
Acoustical Consultant: Margaret Lemon
Contact for Rental: Del Hamilton;   (404) 523-7647

Augusta

DANCE

AUGUSTA BALLET COMPANY
PO Box 3448, Augusta, GA 30904
(706) 733-5511
Founded: 1964
Arts Area: Ballet; Jazz
Status: Semi-Professional; Non-Profit
Type: Performing; Touring; Resident
Purpose: To present quality dance
Management: Ron Colton, Zanne Beaufort, Artistic Directors
Paid Artists: 20
Utilizes: Guest Artists; Guest Choreographers
Budget: $1,000,000 - $5,000,000
Income Sources: Box Office; Individual Donations
Season: September - May
Performance Facilities: Imperial Community Theater

INSTRUMENTAL MUSIC

AUGUSTA SYMPHONY ORCHESTRA
PO Box 579, Augusta, GA 30903
(706) 826-4705
FAX: (706) 826-4735
> **Founded:** 1945
> **Arts Area:** Symphony
> **Status:** Non-Profit
> **Type:** Performing
> **Management:** Pat Finch, Executive Director; Donald Portnoy, Music Director
> **Paid Staff:** 3
> **Paid Artists:** 75
> **Utilizes:** Guest Conductors; Guest Artists; Guest Directors
> **Budget:** $100,000 - $500,000
> **Income Sources:** Private Foundations/Grants/Endowments; Business/Corporate Donations; Box Office; Government Grants; Individual Donations
> **Season:** September - April   **Annual Attendance:** 5,000
> **Performance Facilities:** Augusta College Performing Arts Theater

VOCAL MUSIC

AUGUSTA OPERA ASSOCIATION
PO Box 3865, Hill Station, Augusta, GA 30904
(706) 826-4710
FAX: (706) 826-4732
> **Founded:** 1967
> **Arts Area:** Grand Opera; Lyric Opera; Light Opera; Operetta
> **Status:** Professional
> **Type:** Performing; Resident; Educational
> **Purpose:** To present operas of young American artists to be performed in English
> **Management:** Edward Bradberry, General Director; Cynthia Hunsucker, Director of Devlopment; Thomas Turner, Director of Marketing; Nancy Gleason, Administrative Assistant
> **Officers:** Dennis G. Sodomka, President; Robert D. Huntley Jr., Treasurer; Stan Marinoff, Secretary
> **Paid Staff:** 4
> **Paid Artists:** 35   **Non-Paid Artists:** 35
> **Utilizes:** Special Technical Talent; Guest Conductors; Guest Artists; Guest Directors
> **Budget:** $500,000 - $1,000,000
> **Income Sources:** Private Foundations/Grants/Endowments; Business/Corporate Donations; Box Office; Government Grants; Individual Donations
> **Season:** September - May   **Annual Attendance:** 21,000
> **Affiliations:** Augusta Symphony and Ballet
> **Performance Facilities:** Imperial Theater

THEATRE

AUGUSTA PLAYERS
PO Box 3541, Augusta, GA 30914
(706) 826-4707
> **Founded:** 1945
> **Arts Area:** Theatrical Group
> **Status:** Non-Professional; Non-Profit
> **Type:** Performing; Educational
> **Management:** Jay Willis, Executive Director
> **Officers:** Helen Symms, President, Board of Trustees, Business and Professional Alliance; Ingrid Titus, President, Board of Directors, Theatre Guild
> **Paid Staff:** 3   **Volunteer Staff:** 30
> **Non-Paid Artists:** 400
> **Utilizes:** Special Technical Talent
> **Budget:** $100,000 - $500,000
> **Income Sources:** Private Foundations/Grants/Endowments; Business/Corporate Donations; Box Office; Government Grants; Individual Donations
> **Season:** 52 Weeks   **Annual Attendance:** 7,000
> **Affiliations:** Georgia Theatre Conference; SETC

FACILITY

AUGUSTA/RICHMOND COUNTY CIVIC CENTER COMPLEX - ARENA
601 Seventh Street, Augusta, GA 30901
(706) 722-3521
  Type of Facility: Civic Center; Arena
  Type of Stage: Flexible; Platform
  Seating Capacity: 8,500
  Year Built: 1979 **Architect:** I.M. Pei and Partners **Cost:** $13,700,000
  Contact for Rental: Larry Rogers
  The Complex also contains a 14,070 square foot Exhibit Hall & Meeting Rooms

IMPERIAL THEATRE
745 Broad Street, Augusta, GA 30903
(706) 722-8290
  Founded: 1990
  Type of Facility: Concert Hall; Auditorium; Theatre House
  Facility Originally: Vaudeville; Movie House
  Type of Stage: Proscenium; Orchestra Pit holds 30 and percussion
  Stage Dimensions: 36'Wx39'D **Orchestra Pit**
  Seating Capacity: 860
  Year Built: 1917 **Architect:** Lloyd Preacher and Howard
  Contact for Rental: M.S. Easterbrook; (706) 722-8293

Cedartown

FACILITY

CEDARTOWN CIVIC AUDITORIUM
205 East Avenue, Cedartown, GA 30125
(706) 748-3220
FAX: (706) 748-8962
  Founded: 1974
  Type of Facility: Auditorium
  Type of Stage: Thrust; Proscenium
  Stage Dimensions: 58'9'Wx36'2"Dx40'W'; 11'6" thrust
  Seating Capacity: 1,012
  Year Built: 1974
  Contact for Rental: Kristy R. Hughes; (706) 748-3220

Columbus

INSTRUMENTAL MUSIC

COLUMBUS SYMPHONY ORCHESTRA
PO Box 5361, Columbus, GA 31906
(706) 323-5059
  Founded: 1855
  Arts Area: Symphony
  Status: Semi-Professional
  Type: Performing; Touring; Resident; Educational; Sponsoring
  Purpose: To provide good music to this area
  Management: Susan Lagg, Executive Director
  Officers: David C. Colby, Board President
  Paid Staff: 7
  Paid Artists: 75 **Non-Paid Artists:** 1
  Utilizes: Guest Conductors; Guest Artists
  Budget: $100,000 - $500,000
  Income Sources: Private Foundations/Grants/Endowments; Business/Corporate Donations; Box Office; Government Grants; Individual Donations
  Season: October - May **Annual Attendance:** 50,000
  Affiliations: ASOL
  Performance Facilities: Three Arts Theatre

THEATRE

SPRINGER OPERA HOUSE/THE STATE THEATER OF GEORGIA
103 Tenth Street, Columbus, GA 31902
(706) 324-1100
> **Founded:** 1961
> **Arts Area:** Community; Theatrical Group
> **Status:** Semi-Professional; Non-Profit
> **Type:** Performing; Touring; Producing
> **Purpose:** To offer high quality productions to the Southeast United States as the Official State Theatre of Georgia
> **Management:** Paul R. Pierce, Managing & Artistic Director
> **Officers:** Tom Austin, President of Board
> **Paid Staff:** 4 **Volunteer Staff:** 200
> **Paid Artists:** 6 **Non-Paid Artists:** 4
> **Utilizes:** Special Technical Talent; Guest Artists; Guest Directors
> **Budget:** $100,000 - $500,000
> **Income Sources:** Private Foundations/Grants/Endowments; Business/Corporate Donations; Box Office; Individual Donations
> **Season:** September - June **Annual Attendance:** 20,000
> **Affiliations:** Georgia Theatre Conference; SETC; League of Historic American Theatres
> **Performance Facilities:** Springer Opera House

PERFORMING SERIES

SOUTHEASTERN MUSIC CENTER
PO Box 8348, Columbus, GA 31908-8348
(706) 568-2465
> **Founded:** 1983
> **Arts Area:** Instrumental Music
> **Status:** Non-Profit
> **Type:** Performing; Resident; Educational
> **Purpose:** To present a four week chamber and orchestra music festival where students study with leading artists in their field
> **Management:** William Bullock, Executive Director; Sharon Faust, Administrative Director; Diana Mann, Administrative Assistant
> **Officers:** James Sigmund, Chairman; Pam White, Vice Chairman
> **Paid Staff:** 3
> **Paid Artists:** 14
> **Utilizes:** Guest Conductors; Guest Artists
> **Budget:** $50,000 - $100,000
> **Income Sources:** Private Foundations/Grants/Endowments; Business/Corporate Donations; Box Office; Government Grants; Individual Donations
> **Season:** July **Annual Attendance:** 1,500

FACILITY

COLUMBUS MUNICIPAL AUDITORIUM
PO Box 1340, Columbus, GA 31902
(706) 571-5890
> **Type of Facility:** Amphitheater
> **Type of Stage:** Proscenium
> **Contact for Rental:** Tony Ford;   (706) 571-5889

SPRINGER OPERA HOUSE - THE STATE THEATRE OF GEORGIA
103 Tenth Street, Columbus, GA 31902
(706) 324-5714
> **Type of Facility:** Theatre House
> **Facility Originally:** Hotel & Meeting Rooms
> **Type of Stage:** Proscenium
> **Stage Dimensions:** 32'Wx50'D   **Orchestra Pit**
> **Seating Capacity:** 749
> **Year Built:** 1871   **Architect:** Daniel Matthew Foley
> **Year Remodeled:** 1965   **Architect:** Edward Neal   **Cost:** $1,300,000
> **Acoustical Consultant:** Abe Feder
> **Contact for Rental:** Deborah Arnette;   (706) 324-5714
> **Manager:** Paul R. Pierce, Managing Art Director

Resident Groups: Springer Opera House; Springer Children's Theatre; Columbus Jazz Society; Springer Guild; Columbus Symphony Chamber Orchestra

The Opera House is listed on the National Register of Historic Places, a National Historic Landmark, a member of the League of Historic American Theatres and is the Official State Theater of Georgia.

THREE ARTS THEATRE
1020 Talbotton Road, Columbus, GA 31901
(706) 571-5893
>**Type of Facility:** Theatre House
>**Type of Stage:** Proscenium
>**Orchestra Pit**
>**Seating Capacity:** 1,668
>**Year Built:** 1925
>**Contact for Rental:** Steve Jackson;   (404) 571-5889

Decatur

DANCE

BEACON DANCE COMPANY
411 West Trinity Place, Decatur, GA 30030
(404) 377-6927
>**Founded:** 1952
>**Arts Area:** Modern; Ballet; Jazz
>**Status:** Semi-Professional; Non-Profit
>**Type:** Performing; Educational
>**Management:** D. Patton White, Artistic Director
>**Officers:** J. Mitchell Bowling Jr., President; Ellen Rosenthal, Secretary; Gregory N. Pierce, Treasurer
>**Paid Staff:** 1   **Volunteer Staff:** 10
>**Paid Artists:** 8   **Non-Paid Artists:** 14
>**Utilizes:** Special Technical Talent; Guest Artists
>**Budget:** $1,000 - $50,000
>**Income Sources:** Private Foundations/Grants/Endowments; Business/Corporate Donations; Box Office; Government Grants; Individual Donations
>**Season:** September - May

VOCAL MUSIC

YOUNG SINGERS OF CALLANWOLDE, INC.
315 West Ponce de Leon Avenue, Suite 915, Decatur, GA 30030
(404) 377-6081
>**Founded:** 1975
>**Arts Area:** Choral
>**Status:** Non-Profit
>**Type:** Performing; Touring; Educational
>**Purpose:** To provide an auditioned children's choir (grades 3-9) based on sound musicianship, vocal training and personal development; credo is "service and growth through singing"
>**Management:** Stephen J. Ortlip, Founder/Musical Director; Jo Ivey, Executive Director; William E. Krape, Accompanist; Doris Ortlip, Instructor; Ellis McIntyre, Financial Secretary
>**Officers:** Leamon R. Scott, President of Board of Directors; Dona Drake, Secretary Board of Directors; Alvin H. Hart, Treasurer Board of Directors
>**Paid Staff:** 5   **Volunteer Staff:** 100
>**Utilizes:** Guest Artists
>**Budget:** $100,000 - $500,000
>**Income Sources:** Private Foundations/Grants/Endowments; Business/Corporate Donations; Box Office; Government Grants; Individual Donations; Tuition
>**Season:** September - May   **Annual Attendance:** 50,000
>**Affiliations:** School of Music, Georgia State University

THEATRE

NEIGHBORHOOD PLAYHOUSE
430 West Trinity Place, Decatur, GA 30030
(404) 373-3904; (404) 373-5311
>**Founded:** 1980
>**Arts Area:** Professional; Theatrical Group
>**Status:** Semi-Professional; Non-Profit
>**Type:** Performing

Purpose: To provide professional quality theatre designed to entertain, educate and challenge our community
Management: Sondra A. Nelson, Artistic/Executive Director; Ken Anderson, Marketing Director; John David Williams, Operations Manager
Officers: Cary Jackson, Secretary; Barry West, Treasurer
Paid Staff: 3 **Volunteer Staff:** 50
Paid Artists: 200
Utilizes: Special Technical Talent; Guest Artists; Guest Directors
Budget: $100,000 - $500,000
Income Sources: Private Foundations/Grants/Endowments; Business/Corporate Donations; Box Office; Government Grants; Individual Donations
Season: 52 Weeks **Annual Attendance:** 25,000
Affiliations: SETC; Atlanta Theatre Coalition; Atlanta Chamber of Commerce; Decatur Business Association; DeKalb Chamber of Commerce

THE PICCADILLY PUPPETS COMPANY
621 Densley Drive, Decatur, GA 30033
(404) 636-0022
Founded: 1970
Arts Area: Professional; Puppet
Status: Professional
Type: Performing; Touring; Educational
Purpose: Puppet theatre for children, mostly educational programs
Management: Carol Daniel, Manager
Officers: Dr. Pat Penn, President; Carol Daniel, Secretary/Treasurer
Paid Staff: 1 **Volunteer Staff:** 2
Paid Artists: 5
Budget: $50,000 - $100,000
Income Sources: Private Foundations/Grants/Endowments; Government Grants; Individual Donations
Season: 52 Weeks **Annual Attendance:** 75,000

FACILITY

GAINES CHAPEL - AGNES SCOTT COLLEGE
Agnes Scott College, Decatur, GA 30030
(404) 371-6000
FAX: (404) 371-6177
Founded: 1889
Type of Facility: Concert Hall; Auditorium; Theatre House
Type of Stage: Proscenium
Stage Dimensions: 32'x28'
Seating Capacity: 825
Year Built: 1940 **Cost:** $275,000
Year Remodeled: 1989
Contact for Rental: Campus Events and Conferences; (404) 371-6408

Gainesville

DANCE

THE GAINESVILLE BALLET
PO Box 1663, Gainesville, GA 30503
(706) 532-4241
Founded: 1974
Arts Area: Modern; Ballet; Jazz
Status: Non-Professional; Non-Profit
Type: Performing; Educational; Sponsoring
Purpose: To further the cause of dance artistry in northeast Georgia through productions of classical, neoclassical, jazz and modern dance
Management: Diane Callahan, Artistic Director; Victoria Burke, Managing Director
Officers: Anne Gress, President
Paid Staff: 5 **Volunteer Staff:** 30
Paid Artists: 8 **Non-Paid Artists:** 35
Utilizes: Special Technical Talent; Guest Artists
Budget: $100,000 - $500,000
Income Sources: Private Foundations/Grants/Endowments; Business/Corporate Donations; Box Office; Government Grants; Individual Donations
Season: August - May **Annual Attendance:** 7,000

Affiliations: Dance Coalition of Metro Atlanta; SERBA
Performance Facilities: Pearce Auditorium

INSTRUMENTAL MUSIC

THE GAINESVILLE SYMPHONY ORCHESTRA
PO Box 162, Gainesville, GA 30503
(706) 532-5727
   Founded: 1982
   Arts Area: Symphony
   Status: Semi-Professional; Non-Profit
   Type: Performing
   Purpose: To provide performances of orchestral music in the Northeast Georgia Area
   Management: Nancy Jacob, Executive Director; Mary Alice Swope, Personnel Manager
   Paid Staff: 1   **Volunteer Staff:** 2
   Paid Artists: 50   **Non-Paid Artists:** 5
   Budget: $50,000 - $100,000
   Income Sources: Private Foundations/Grants/Endowments; Business/Corporate Donations; Box Office; Government Grants; Individual Donations
   Season: November - April   **Annual Attendance:** 1,300
   Affiliations: ASOL
   Performance Facilities: Pearce Auditorium, Brenau College

Jekyll Island

FACILITY

JEKYLL ISLAND AMPHITHEATER
Stable Road, Jekyll Island, GA 31527
(912) 333-5820
   Type of Facility: Amphitheater
   Type of Stage: Proscenium
   Stage Dimensions: 100'Wx40'D
   Seating Capacity: 1,600
   Year Built: 1972   **Architect:** Bull & Kinney   **Cost:** $250,000
   Contact for Rental: Jekyll Island Authority;   (912) 635-2236
   Resident Groups: Jekyll Island Musical Theatre Festival

Macon

INSTRUMENTAL MUSIC

MACON SYMPHONY ORCHESTRA, INCORPORATED
PO Box 5700, Macon, GA 31208
(912) 474-5700
FAX: (912) 477-6146
   Arts Area: Orchestra
   Status: Professional; Non-Profit
   Type: Performing; Resident; Educational
   Purpose: To provide live quality classical music for the enjoyment of the community; to encourage the appreciation of music through educational programs
   Management: Doris Wood, Development Director; Brenda Lipman, General Manager; Adrian Gnam, Music Director/Conductor
   Officers: Ted S. Alexander, President of the Board
   Budget: $100,000 - $500,000
   Income Sources: Private Foundations/Grants/Endowments; Business/Corporate Donations; Box Office; Government Grants; Individual Donations
   Performance Facilities: Porter Auditorium, Wesleyan College

FACILITY

GRAND OPERA HOUSE
651 Mulberry Street, Macon, GA 31201
(912) 749-6580
   Type of Facility: Opera House
   Type of Stage: Proscenium
   Stage Dimensions: 90'Wx58'D; 37'W proscenium opening   **Orchestra Pit**

Seating Capacity: 1057
Year Built: 1884   **Cost:** $75,000
Year Remodeled: 1970   **Architect:** Ella Mae Ellis League   **Cost:** $300,000
Contact for Rental: Bill Preissner;   (912) 749-6580
National Register of Historic Places; charter member, League of Historic American Theatres

WESLEYAN COLLEGE - PORTER AUDITORIUM
4760 Forsyth Road, Macon, GA 31297
(912) 477-1110
FAX: (912) 477-7572
Type of Facility: Theatre Complex; Concert Hall; Auditorium; Theatre House
Type of Stage: Proscenium
Stage Dimensions: 40'Wx27'5"D   **Orchestra Pit**
Seating Capacity: 1,124
Year Built: 1955
Contact for Rental: Frances Van Horn;   (912) 477-1110

Madison

FACILITY

MADISON - MORGAN CULTURAL CENTER
434 South Main Street, Madison, GA 30650
(706) 342-4743
Founded: 1976
Type of Facility: Auditorium
Facility Originally: School
Type of Stage: Proscenium
Stage Dimensions: 26'x25' stage; 72'x67' auditorium
Seating Capacity: 395
Year Built: 1895   **Cost:** $15,000
Year Remodeled: 1975   **Cost:** $450,000
Acoustical Consultant: Magnum Companies
Contact for Rental: Office;   (706) 342-4745

Marietta

DANCE

JAZZ DANCE THEATRE SOUTH
3218 Rimrock Drive, Marietta, GA 30066
(404) 425-1208; (404) 971-1109
Founded: 1986
Arts Area: Jazz
Status: Professional
Type: Performing; Touring; Resident; Educational
Purpose: To educate in jazz dance through performances, classes and lecture demonstrations
Management: Marcus R. Alford, Artistic Director
Paid Staff: 1   **Volunteer Staff:** 3
Paid Artists: 7
Utilizes: Special Technical Talent; Guest Choreographers
Budget: $100,000 - $500,000
Income Sources: Private Foundations/Grants/Endowments; Box Office
Season: 52 Weeks
Performance Facilities: Cobb County Civic Center

THEATRE

PARENTHESIS THEATRE CLUB
4336 Highborne Drive, Marietta, GA 30066
(404) 977-8340
Founded: 1991
Arts Area: Dinner; Theatrical Group
Status: Semi-Professional
Type: Performing; Resident
Purpose: To produce socially relevant ten minute plays and one acts with emphasis on original work
Management: Gregory Blum, Artistic Director; Darrell Wofford, Producing Director

Paid Staff: 9
Paid Artists: 9
Utilizes: Guest Artists
Budget: $1,000 - $50,000
Income Sources: Box Office
Season: 52 Weeks   **Annual Attendance:** 4,000
Performance Facilities: Cabaret Space

THEATRE IN THE SQUARE
11 Whitlock Avenue, Marietta, GA 30064
(404) 422-8369
Founded: 1982
Arts Area: Theatrical Group
Status: Professional
Type: Performing; Touring
Purpose: To present a full variety of live theatre, and provide exciting material and good conditions for theatre professionals to work
Management: Michael W. Horne, Producing Director; Palmer D. Wells, Managing Director
Officers: Cherry Spencer-Stark, Chair
Paid Staff: 5   **Volunteer Staff:** 30
Utilizes: Special Technical Talent; Guest Artists; Guest Directors
Budget: $100,000 - $500,000
Income Sources: Private Foundations/Grants/Endowments; Business/Corporate Donations; Box Office; Government Grants; Individual Donations
Season: 52 Weeks   **Annual Attendance:** 40,000
Performance Facilities: Theatre in the Square

FACILITY

COBB COUNTY CIVIC CENTER
548 South Marietta Parkway, Marietta, GA 30060
(404) 528-8450
FAX: (404) 528-8457
Type of Facility: Civic Center
Year Built: 1975   **Architect:** Cleveland Cail & William Tapp   **Cost:** $3,500,000
Contact for Rental: Bob Ash;   (404) 528-8450
Manager: Liz Fields
The Cobb County Civic Center contains the Jennie T. Anderson Theater and Romeo Hudgins Memorial Hall. See individual listings for more information.

COBB COUNTY CIVIC CENTER - JENNIE T. ANDERSON THEATER
548 South Marietta Parkway, Marietta, GA 30060
(404) 528-8450
FAX: (404) 528-8457
Type of Facility: Concert Hall; Theatre House
Type of Stage: Proscenium; Modified Apron Proscenium
Stage Dimensions: 84'Wx35'D; 50'Wx22'H proscenium opening   **Orchestra Pit**
Seating Capacity: 570
Year Built: 1975
Contact for Rental: Bob Ash;   (404) 404-5280
Manager: Liz Fields

COBB COUNTY CIVIC CENTER - ROMEO HUDGINS MEMORIAL HALL
548 South Marietta Parkway, Marietta, GA 30060
(404) 528-8450
FAX: (404) 528-8457
Type of Facility: Auditorium; Civic Center; Arena; Multi-Purpose
Type of Stage: Flexible
Stage Dimensions: 42'x32'x20'
Seating Capacity: 3,700
Year Built: 1975
Year Remodeled: 1977   **Cost:** $24,000
Contact for Rental: Bob Ash;   (404) 528-8450
Manager: Liz Field

THEATRE IN THE SQUARE
11 Whitlock Avenue, Marietta, GA 30064
(404) 422-8369
FAX: (404) 424-2637
Type of Facility: Theatre House
Facility Originally: Warehouse
Type of Stage: Proscenium
Stage Dimensions: 32'Wx21'D
Seating Capacity: 160
Year Built: 1930
Year Remodeled: 1982   **Architect:** Bill Chegmidden   **Cost:** $65,000
Acoustical Consultant: Warren Short
Contact for Rental: Michael Horne or Palmer Wells;   (404) 422-8369
Resident Groups: Theatre in the Square
Dance recitals; chamber music; comedy; one-person shows

Perry

THEATRE

PERRY PLAYERS, INC.
PO Box 143, Perry, GA 31069
(912) 987-5354
Founded: 1982
Arts Area: Musical; Community; Theatrical Group
Status: Non-Professional; Non-Profit
Purpose: We offer high-quality entertainment and cultural activities to the citizens of middle Georgia; individuals who enjoy acting, singing, dancing and producing cultural entertainment share and improve these skills in a welcoming environment of cooperation and enthusiasm
Officers: Dennis Hooper, President; D. Shawn Kitrell, Vice President; Carol Howard, Secretary; Cathy Stanley, Treasurer
Volunteer Staff: 15
Non-Paid Artists: 30
Utilizes: Special Technical Talent; Guest Artists; Guest Directors
Budget: $1,000 - $50,000
Income Sources: Private Foundations/Grants/Endowments; Business/Corporate Donations; Box Office; Government Grants; Individual Donations
Season: 52 Weeks   **Annual Attendance:** 2,500
Affiliations: Houston County Arts Alliance; Macon Arts Alliance; Perry Chamber of Commerce

Rome

FACILITY

ROME CITY AUDITORIUM
601 Broad Street, Rome, GA 30161
(706) 236-4416
FAX: (706) 236-4549
Type of Facility: Auditorium; Theatre House; Opera House
Type of Stage: Proscenium
Stage Dimensions: 34'8"Dx54'3"L total size including wings; 35'11"x28'4" stage only
Seating Capacity: 1,112
Year Built: 1916   **Architect:** A. Ted Eych Brown   **Cost:** $140,000
Year Remodeled: 1989   **Architect:** Jack McGuffie   **Cost:** $1,200,000
Contact for Rental: Linda Davis;   (706) 236-4416

Savannah

INSTRUMENTAL MUSIC

SAVANNAH SYMPHONY
PO Box 9505, Savannah, GA 31412
(706) 236-9536
Founded: 1953
Arts Area: Symphony; Orchestra; Chamber; Ensemble
Status: Professional; Non-Profit
Type: Performing

Purpose: To provide a wide range of orchestra repertoire in high-quality performances to all segments of our market area; to provide a wide range of educational activities for school-aged and adult members of the community
Management: Gregg Gustafson, General Manager; Katie O'Grady, Marketing Director; Phillip Greenberg, Music Director/Conductor; Laura Hibberts, Development Director; George Council, Operations Manager
Officers: Barbara Murphy, President; Pamela H. Young, Secretary
Paid Staff: 10   **Volunteer Staff:** 500
Paid Artists: 75
Utilizes: Guest Artists
Budget: $500,000 - $1,000,000
Income Sources: Private Foundations/Grants/Endowments; Business/Corporate Donations; Box Office; Government Grants; Individual Donations
Season: September - May   **Annual Attendance:** 50,000
Affiliations: ASOL
Performance Facilities: Savannah Civic Center Theatre

FACILITY

ARMSTRONG STATE COLLEGE FINE ARTS AUDITORIUM
11935 Abercorn Street, Savannah, GA 31419
(912) 927-5329
FAX: (912) 921-5472
Founded: 1975
Type of Facility: Auditorium
Type of Stage: Thrust; Proscenium
Stage Dimensions: 60'x40'
Seating Capacity: 998
Year Built: 1975   **Cost:** $1,800,000
Contact for Rental: Judy Grizzard;   (912) 927-5329
Resident Groups: Armstrong State College: Chorus; Jazz Band; Community Orchestra

SAVANNAH CIVIC CENTER
Montgomery at Liberty, PO Box 726, Savannah, GA 31402
(912) 651-6550
FAX: (912) 651-6552
Type of Facility: Theatre House; Civic Center; Arena; Multi-Purpose
Seating Capacity: 9,600; 2,566
Year Built: 1971   **Cost:** $10,000,000
Acoustical Consultant: Jaffe Acoustics
Contact for Rental: Cynthia Brinson;   (912) 651-6553
Manager: John Lutz, Manager;   (912) 651-6551
Resident Groups: Savannah Symphony Orchestra; Ballet South
The Savannah Civic Center contains the Arena and Theatre. See separate listings for additional information.

SAVANNAH CIVIC CENTER - ARENA
Montgomery at Liberty, PO Box 726, Savannah, GA 31402
(912) 651-6550
FAX: (912) 651-6552
Type of Facility: Arena
Type of Stage: Arena
Seating Capacity: 9,600
Year Built: 1971
Contact for Rental: Cynthia Brinson or John Lutz;   (912) 651-6553
Manager: John Lutz;   (912) 651-6551

SAVANNAH CIVIC CENTER - THEATRE
Montgomery at Liberty, PO Box 726, Savannah, GA 31402
(912) 651-6550
FAX: (912) 651-6552
Type of Facility: Theatre House
Type of Stage: Proscenium
Stage Dimensions: 60'Wx30'D   **Orchestra Pit**
Seating Capacity: 2,566
Year Built: 1971
Contact for Rental: Cynthia Brinson or John Lutz;   (912) 651-6553
Manager: John Lutz;   (912) 651-6551

Sea Island

PERFORMING SERIES

GOLDEN ISLES CHAMBER MUSIC FESTIVAL, INC.
PO Box 1202, Sea Island, GA 31561
(706) 663-4631
>**Founded:** 1988
>**Arts Area:** Instrumental Music
>**Status:** Professional
>**Type:** Performing; Educational
>**Purpose:** To perform the highest quality chamber music
>**Officers:** Susan L. Walters, Musical Director; Jeffrey Moore, Artistic Director
>**Volunteer Staff:** 5
>**Paid Artists:** 13
>**Utilizes:** Guest Artists
>**Budget:** $1,000 - $50,000
>**Income Sources:** Private Foundations/Grants/Endowments; Business/Corporate Donations; Box Office; Government Grants; Individual Donations
>**Season:** May   **Annual Attendance:** 500

Statesboro

FACILITY

GEORGIA SOUTHERN UNIVERSITY - FOY FINE ARTS RECITAL HALL
Department of Music - LB8052, Statesboro, GA 30460
(912) 681-5396
>**Type of Facility:** Concert Hall; Performance Center
>**Type of Stage:** Proscenium
>**Seating Capacity:** 340
>**Year Built:** 1967   **Architect:** Aeck & Associates   **Cost:** $1,250,000
>**Acoustical Consultant:** Bolt, Beranek & Newman
>**Contact for Rental:** Lissa Addington;   (912) 681-5396
>**Resident Groups:** GSU/Music Department

GEORGIA SOUTHERN UNIVERSITY - PUPPET THEATRE
PO Box 8124, Statesboro, GA 30460
(912) 681-5138
>**Type of Facility:** Theatre House
>**Facility Originally:** Skating Rink
>**Type of Stage:** Flexible
>**Seating Capacity:** 100
>**Year Built:** 1972
>**Year Remodeled:** 1985
>**Contact for Rental:** Facilities Office;   (912) 681-5666
>**Resident Groups:** Statesboro/GSU Puppetry Guild

Thomaston

PERFORMING SERIES

THOMASTON-UPSON ARTS COUNCIL
201 South Center Street, PO Box 211, Thomaston, GA 30286
(706) 647-1605
>**Founded:** 1986
>**Arts Area:** Dance; Vocal Music; Instrumental Music; Theater
>**Status:** Non-Profit
>**Type:** Performing; Educational; Sponsoring
>**Paid Staff:** 2
>**Budget:** $50,000 - $100,000
>**Income Sources:** Private Foundations/Grants/Endowments; Business/Corporate Donations; Box Office; Government Grants; Individual Donations

Thomasville

FACILITY

THOMASVILLE CULTURAL CENTER AUDITORIUM
c/o Thomasville Entertainment Foundation, 600 East Washington Street, Thomasville, GA 31792
(706) 226-0588
    Type of Facility: Auditorium
    Facility Originally: School
    Type of Stage: Proscenium
    Seating Capacity: 550
    Year Built: 1915 **Architect:** Frank Galliher **Cost:** $50,000
    Year Remodeled: 1986 **Architect:** Sibley Jennings **Cost:** $3,300,000
    Contact for Rental: (912) 226-0588

Toccoa

INSTRUMENTAL MUSIC

TOCCOA SYMPHONY ORCHESTRA GUILD
PO Box 532, Toccoa, GA 30577
(706) 886-6551
    Founded: 1977
    Arts Area: Symphony
    Status: Semi-Professional; Non-Profit
    Type: Performing; Educational
    Purpose: To promote good symphonic music in our community; to educate our youth to perform with artists
    Management: Dr. Archie Sharretts, Conductor; Mrs. Pinkie Ware, Personnel Manager; Bob Tresly, General Manager
    Officers: Dr. Paul Nichols, President; Toccoa Symphony Orchestra Guild, Board of Managers
    Paid Staff: 25 **Volunteer Staff:** 45
    Paid Artists: 25 **Non-Paid Artists:** 45
    Utilizes: Guest Conductors; Guest Artists; Guest Directors
    Budget: $1,000 - $50,000
    Income Sources: Private Foundations/Grants/Endowments; Business/Corporate Donations; Box Office; Government Grants; Individual Donations
    Season: December - April **Annual Attendance:** 1,500
    Affiliations: Georgia Arts Council
    Performance Facilities: Georgia Baptist Assembly and Theater

Valdosta

THEATRE

JEKYLL ISLAND MUSICAL THEATRE FESTIVAL
Department of Communication Arts, Valdosta, GA 31698
(912) 333-5820
FAX: (912) 333-7408
    Founded: 1990
    Arts Area: Professional; Summer Stock; Musical
    Status: Professional; Non-Profit
    Type: Performing; Touring
    Purpose: To provide high-quality musical theatre for residents of and visitors to Georgia's Golden Isles; to provide professional training to college interns
    Management: Victoria Pennington, Production Supervisor; Robert B. Welch, Dean, School of the Arts
    Officers: Paul Salter, Chairman
    Paid Staff: 14
    Paid Artists: 44
    Utilizes: Special Technical Talent; Guest Directors; Guest Designers
    Budget: $100,000 - $500,000
    Income Sources: Private Foundations/Grants/Endowments; Business/Corporate Donations; Box Office; Government Grants; Individual Donations
    Season: June - August **Annual Attendance:** 20,000
    Affiliations: Valdosta State College
    Performance Facilities: Jekyll Island Amphitheater

FACILITY

VALDOSTA STATE COLLEGE - SAWYER THEATRE
Fine Arts Building, Valdosta, GA 31698
(912) 333-5820
>   **Type of Facility:** Theatre House
>   **Type of Stage:** Proscenium
>   **Seating Capacity:** 250
>   **Year Built:** 1969   **Architect:** Zeb Lackey
>   **Contact for Rental:**   (912) 333-5820
>   **Manager:** Dr. Robert B. Welch

VALDOSTA STATE COLLEGE - WHITEHEAD AUDITORIUM
Fine Arts Building, Valdosta, GA 31698
(912) 333-5816
>   **Type of Facility:** Theatre Complex; Concert Hall; Auditorium; Outdoor (Concert); Theatre House; Amphitheater
>   **Type of Stage:** Proscenium
>   **Stage Dimensions:** 60'Wx40'D   **Orchestra Pit**
>   **Seating Capacity:** 900
>   **Year Built:** 1969   **Architect:** Zeb Lackey   **Cost:** $2,500,000
>   **Contact for Rental:** Dr. Robert B. Welch;   (912) 333-2150

HAWAII

Fort Shafter

THEATRE

ARMY ENTERTAINMENT PROGRAM
USASCH, DPCA, CRD, CSDAB, Entertainment Section, Fort Shafter, HI 96858-5000
(808) 438-1980
FAX: (808) 438-1980
  Founded: 1949
  Arts Area: Musical; Community; Theatrical Group
  Status: Non-Professional; Non-Profit
  Type: Performing; Resident; Educational
  Purpose: The goals of the Army Entertainment Program are to provide interested individuals with a constructive outlet for talents, to maintain a high level of morals and to promote good cultural relations with the local civilian community.
  Management: Vanita Rae Smith, Chief, Army Entertainment; Tom Giza, Technical Director
  Paid Staff: 2 **Volunteer Staff:** 2
  Non-Paid Artists: 30
  Utilizes: Special Technical Talent; Guest Conductors; Guest Directors
  Budget: $100,000 - $500,000
  Income Sources: Private Foundations/Grants/Endowments; Business/Corporate Donations; Box Office; Government Grants; Individual Donations
  Season: 52 Weeks
  Affiliations: AACT; Hawaii State Theatre Council
  Performance Facilities: Richardson Performing Arts Center

Hilo

INSTRUMENTAL MUSIC

HAWAII CONCERT SOCIETY
PO Box 233, Hilo, HI 96721
(808) 935-5831
  Founded: 1956
  Arts Area: Symphony; Orchestra; Chamber; Ensemble; Instrumental Group
  Status: Non-Profit
  Type: Sponsoring
  Purpose: To provide quality classical music to east Hawaii (the Island of Hawaii), performed by professional musicians
  Officers: Tom Geballe, President; Ray Boyea, First Vice President; Judith Wakely, Second Vice President; Bob Fuhrel, Secretary; Emily Spargo-Guerrero, Treasurer
  Volunteer Staff: 14
  Utilizes: Guest Artists
  Budget: $1,000 - $50,000
  Income Sources: Business/Corporate Donations; Box Office; Government Grants; Individual Donations
  Season: September - April **Annual Attendance:** 2,500
  Affiliations: Hawaii Association of Music Societies
  Performance Facilities: Hilo Theatre, University of Hawaii

THEATRE

HILO COMMUNITY PLAYERS
141 Kalakaua Street, Hilo, HI 96720
(808) 935-9155
  Mailing Address: PO Box 46, Hilo, HI 96721
  Founded: 1938
  Arts Area: Community; Theatrical Group
  Status: Non-Professional; Non-Profit
  Type: Performing; Educational
  Purpose: To organize, promote and conduct an educational program of amateur dramatics on the Island of Hawaii
  Management: Paul M. Clark, Business Manager; Peter Schickler, Equipment Manager; Sarah Hilliard, Costume Manager
  Officers: Michael Moore, President; Carl Moon, Treasurer
  Paid Staff: 3
  Paid Artists: 1 **Non-Paid Artists:** 100
  Utilizes: Guest Artists; Guest Directors
  Budget: $1,000 - $50,000

Income Sources: Private Foundations/Grants/Endowments; Box Office; Government Grants; Individual Donations
Season: 52 Weeks   Annual Attendance: 2,500

FACILITY

UNIVERSITY OF HAWAII - HILO THEATRE
523 West Lanikaula Street, Hilo, HI 96720-4091
(808) 933-3310
Type of Facility: Auditorium
Type of Stage: Proscenium
Stage Dimensions: 40'Wx27'D; 40'Wx20'H proscenium opening   **Orchestra Pit**
Seating Capacity: 600
Year Built: 1972   **Architect:** Roehrig Oncdera Kinder
Year Remodeled: 1977   **Architect:** Team Pacific
Contact for Rental: Larry Joseph;   (808) 933-3310
Resident Groups: University of Hawaii at Hilo Performing Arts (Drama/Dance/Music)

Honolulu

DANCE

DANCES WE DANCE
PO Box 22657, Honolulu, HI 96823-2657
(808) 537-2152
FAX: (808) 537-2152
Founded: 1971
Arts Area: Modern; Ballet
Status: Professional; Non-Profit
Type: Performing; Touring; Resident; Educational; Sponsoring
Purpose: To further the appreciation and understanding of dance through cultural and educational services, which include sponsoring performances, Artists-in-the-Schools programs, workshops, professional training, and video projects
Management: Betty Jones, Executive Director; Fritz Ludin, Artistic Director
Officers: Betty Ona, President; Lou Ann Guanson, Vice President; Mary Jo Freshley, Secretary; Denise Miyahana, Treasurer
Paid Staff: 2
Paid Artists: 2
Utilizes: Special Technical Talent; Guest Artists; Guest Choreographers
Budget: $50,000 - $100,000
Income Sources: Private Foundations/Grants/Endowments; Box Office; Government Grants; Individual Donations
Season: 52 Weeks   **Annual Attendance:** 10,000
Affiliations: Artists-in-the-Schools; Hawaii Alliance for Arts in Education
Performance Facilities: Dance Studio

HAWAII STATE BALLET
1418 Copulani Boulevard, Honolulu, HI 96814
(808) 947-2755
Arts Area: Ballet
Status: Professional; Non-Profit
Type: Touring; Resident
Management: John Landovsky, Artistic Director; Gina Surles, Company Manager
Paid Artists: 8
Income Sources: Box Office; Individual Donations

INSTRUMENTAL MUSIC

CHAMBER MUSIC HAWAII
PO Box 61939, Honolulu, HI 96839
(808) 947-1975
FAX: (808) 947-2047
Arts Area: Chamber; Ensemble
Status: Professional; Non-Profit
Type: Presenting
Purpose: To support resident chamber music ensembles and thereby provide chamber music to the people of Hawaii
Management: Amy Walters, Executive Director
Officers: Emery Grantham, Chairman of the Board
Budget: $100,000 - $500,000

Income Sources: Private Foundations/Grants/Endowments; Business/Corporate Donations; Box Office; Government Grants; Individual Donations

HAWAII CHAMBER ORCHESTRA
3810 Maunaloa Avenue, Honolulu, HI 98616
(808) 734-0397
Founded: 1967
Arts Area: Chamber; Ensemble; Opera
Status: Professional; Non-Profit
Type: Performing; Educational
Purpose: To interest the audience in classical music
Management: Herbert Ward, Music Director; Jacqueline Ward, General Manager/Opera Director
Officers: Dorothy Buscemi, President; Henry Klein, Secretary/Treasurer
Budget: $1,000 - $50,000
Season: 52 Weeks

HAWAII YOUTH SYMPHONY ASSOCIATION
1100 University Avenue, Suite 202, Honolulu, HI 96826
(808) 941-9706
FAX: (808) 941-4995
Founded: 1968
Arts Area: Symphony; Orchestra
Status: Non-Profit
Type: Performing; Educational
Purpose: To encourage educational and artistic development of student musicians
Management: Henry Miyamura, Music Director; Michael Nakasone, Director, Concert Orchestra; Louise Ching, Director, String Classes
Officers: F. Robert Springer, President; Leslie Murata, Vice President; Alan Emura, Secretary; Lanny Williams, Treasurer
Paid Staff: 7 **Volunteer Staff:** 50
Paid Artists: 4
Utilizes: Special Technical Talent; Guest Artists
Budget: $100,000 - $500,000
Income Sources: Private Foundations/Grants/Endowments; Business/Corporate Donations; Box Office; Government Grants; Individual Donations
Season: September - May **Annual Attendance:** 12,500
Performance Facilities: Neal S. Blaisdell Center Concert Hall

HONOLULU SYMPHONY SOCIETY
1441 Kapiolani Boulevard, Suite 1515, Honolulu, HI 96814
(808) 942-2200
Founded: 1901
Arts Area: Symphony; Orchestra; Ensemble
Status: Professional; Non-Profit
Type: Performing; Touring; Resident; Educational
Purpose: To bring music in concert to the citizens of Hawaii
Management: Tony H. Bechario, Executive Director
Officers: Richard Hicks, Chairman
Utilizes: Special Technical Talent; Guest Conductors; Guest Artists
Budget: $1,000,000 - $5,000,000
Income Sources: Private Foundations/Grants/Endowments; Business/Corporate Donations; Box Office; Government Grants; Individual Donations
Season: August - April
Affiliations: ASOL
Performance Facilities: Neal S. Blaisdell Center - Concert Hall; Waikiki Shell

MUSIC PROJECTS HONOLULU
905 Spencer Street, #404, Honolulu, HI 96822
(808) 531-6617
FAX: (808) 537-1818
Founded: 1979
Arts Area: Symphony; Orchestra; Chamber; Ensemble; Instrumental Group; Band
Status: Professional; Non-Profit
Type: Performing; Touring; Resident; Educational; Sponsoring
Purpose: To support and present concerts and educational programs by the musicians of the Honolulu Symphony
Management: Amy Walters, Manager; Dianne Wachsman, Publicity
Officers: Paul Barrett, President; Marsha Schweitzer, Vice President/Treasurer; Jean Harling, Secretary
Paid Staff: 2 **Volunteer Staff:** 10
Paid Artists: 60

Utilizes: Guest Conductors; Guest Artists
Budget: $50,000 - $100,000
Income Sources: Private Foundations/Grants/Endowments; Business/Corporate Donations; Box Office; Government Grants; Individual Donations; Benefits; Product Sales
Season: 52 Weeks   **Annual Attendance:** 1,000
Affiliations: Honolulu Symphony Musicians

SPRING WIND QUARTET
905 Spencer Street, #404, Honolulu, HI 96822
(808) 531-6617
Founded: 1974
Arts Area: Chamber; Ensemble; Instrumental Group
Status: Professional
Type: Performing; Touring; Resident; Educational
Purpose: To meet the performer's need to play chamber music; to provide a resident wind quartet to Hawaii
Management: Marsha Schweitzer, Bassoonist
Paid Staff: 1
Paid Artists: 5
Utilizes: Guest Artists
Budget: $1,000 - $50,000
Income Sources: Private Foundations/Grants/Endowments; Business/Corporate Donations; Box Office; Government Grants; Individual Donations
Season: August - May   **Annual Attendance:** 6,000
Affiliations: Chamber Music Hawaii
Performance Facilities: Luthern Church; Honolulu Academy of Arts

UNIVERSITY OF HAWAII AT MANOA,
COLLEGE OF CONTINUING EDUCATION AND COMMUNITY SERVICE
2530 Dole Street, Honolulu, HI 96822
(808) 956-2042
FAX: (808) 956-3364
Founded: 1907
Arts Area: Chamber; Ensemble; Ethnic; Instrumental Group; Solo
Status: Professional
Type: Sponsoring
Purpose: To present quality musical, dance, theater and special attractions throughout Hawaii, including the Honolulu Chamber Music Series
Management: Barbara Furstenberg, Director; Cheryl Kohashi, Marketing/Production Coordinator; Suzanne Shoemaker, Program Specialist; Susan Yokouchi, Secretary
Paid Staff: 4
Utilizes: Guest Artists
Budget: $100,000 - $500,000
Income Sources: Private Foundations/Grants/Endowments; Box Office; Government Grants
Season: September - May   **Annual Attendance:** 30,000
Affiliations: WAAA; APAP
Performance Facilities: Blaisdell Concert Hall; Orvis Auditorium; Kennedy Theatre

VOCAL MUSIC

HAWAII ECUMENICAL CHORALE
3752 Old Pali Road, Honolulu, HI 96817
(808) 595-3447
Founded: 1979
Arts Area: Grand Opera; Choral; Ethnic; Folk
Status: Semi-Professional; Non-Profit
Type: Performing; Resident; Educational
Purpose: To provide an opportunity for local singers to participate in more challenging music than average choirs offer; to sponsor a local choral composition contest to encourage indigenous choral work
Management: Eileen Lum, Artistic Director
Volunteer Staff: 20
Paid Artists: 4   **Non-Paid Artists:** 4
Utilizes: Special Technical Talent; Guest Conductors; Guest Artists; Guest Directors
Budget: $1,000 - $50,000
Income Sources: Private Foundations/Grants/Endowments; Government Grants; Individual Donations
Season: September - June
Affiliations: State Foundation on Culture and the Arts

HAWAII OPERA THEATRE
987 Waimanu Street, Honolulu, HI 96814
(808) 521-6537
Founded: 1962
Arts Area: Grand Opera
Status: Professional; Non-Profit
Type: Performing; Touring; Resident; Educational
Purpose: To produce opera in Hawaii
Management: J. Mario Ramos, General Director
Officers: Peter A. Lee, President; Galen C.K. Leong, Vice President; Michael J. Meagher MD, Treasurer; Charles R. Wade, Recording Secretary; Evelyn Lance, Corresponding Secretary
Paid Staff: 7   **Volunteer Staff:** 250
Utilizes: Guest Conductors; Guest Artists; Guest Directors
Budget: $1,000,000 - $5,000,000
Income Sources: Private Foundations/Grants/Endowments; Business/Corporate Donations; Box Office; Government Grants; Individual Donations
Season: January - March   **Annual Attendance:** 20,000
Affiliations: OA; COS
Performance Facilities: Neal S. Blaisdell Center - Concert Hall

HONOLULU CHILDREN'S OPERA CHORUS
PO Box 22304, Honolulu, HI 96822
(808) 521-2982
Founded: 1961
Arts Area: Grand Opera; Light Opera; Choral; Ethnic
Status: Non-Profit
Type: Performing; Educational
Purpose: To nurture, foster and develop the performing arts through the medium of choral music; to serve as an educational and artistic resource for the state of Hawaii
Management: Nola A. Nahulu, Music Director; Malla Ka'ai, Business Manager; Wendy Chang, Accompanist
Officers: Diane Kurz, President; Frances Goo, First Vice President; Melody Actouka, Second Vice President; Melvin Ah Yo, Treasurer; Donna Tanimura, Recording Secretary; Kela Holt, Corresponding Secretary
Budget: $1,000 - $50,000
Income Sources: Private Foundations/Grants/Endowments; Individual Donations
Season: September - June

THEATRE

DIAMOND HEAD THEATRE
520 Makapuu Avenue, Honolulu, HI 96816
(808) 734-8763; (808) 734-8763
FAX: (808) 735-1250
Founded: 1915
Arts Area: Professional; Musical; Community; Theatrical Group
Status: Non-Professional; Non-Profit
Type: Performing; Educational
Purpose: To present plays and musicals to the community; to hold classes and workshops in acting for all ages; to offer opportunities for all persons interested to participate both on stage and backstage in theatre
Management: Jim Hutchison, Artistic Director; Stan Michaels, Managing Director; Gordon Svec, Technical Director
Officers: Michael Linos, Chairman of the Board; Ed Cassidy, President; Bob Brown, Secretary; David Powell, Treasurer
Paid Staff: 20   **Volunteer Staff:** 350
Paid Artists: 15   **Non-Paid Artists:** 400
Utilizes: Guest Artists; Guest Directors
Budget: $1,000,000 - $5,000,000
Income Sources: Private Foundations/Grants/Endowments; Business/Corporate Donations; Box Office; Government Grants; Individual Donations
Season: 52 Weeks   **Annual Attendance:** 50,000
Affiliations: ACTA; USITT; Hawaii State Theatre Council
Performance Facilities: Diamond Head Theatre

HONOLULU THEATRE FOR YOUTH
2846 Ualena Street, Honolulu, HI 96819-1910
(808) 839-9885
FAX: (808) 839-7018
Founded: 1955
Arts Area: Professional; Theatrical Group
Status: Professional; Non-Profit

Type: Performing; Touring; Resident; Educational
Purpose: To produce professional theatre for a wide range of audiences in the state of Hawaii, specializing in theatre for young audiences
Management: Jane Campbell, Managing Director; Pam Sterling, Artistic Director
Officers: David M. Taylor, President, Board of Trustees; William A. Bonnet, Neil J. Hannahs, Vice Presidents; Nancy Williamson, Corporate Secretary; G. Stephen Holaday, Treasurer
Paid Staff: 19   **Volunteer Staff:** 1
Paid Artists: 24
Utilizes: Special Technical Talent; Guest Artists; Guest Directors
Budget: $1,000,000 - $5,000,000
Income Sources: Private Foundations/Grants/Endowments; Business/Corporate Donations; Box Office; Government Grants; Individual Donations
Season: 52 Weeks   **Annual Attendance:** 140,000
Affiliations: TCG; ASSITEJ; AATY

FACILITY

NEAL S. BLAISDELL CENTER
777 Ward Avenue, Honolulu, HI 96814
(808) 527-5400
Type of Facility: Concert Hall; Auditorium; Outdoor (Concert); Studio Performance; Arena; Multi-Purpose; Room
Year Built: 1963   **Architect:** Adrian Wilson & Associates; Merrill Simms & Roehrig   **Cost:** $8,375,600
Acoustical Consultant: Vern Knudsen
Contact for Rental: Carla W. Coray, Director;   (808) 527-5400
Resident Groups: Honolulu Symphony Society; Hawaii Opera Theatre
Blaisdell Center contains the Arena, Concert Hall and Waikiki Shell. See separate listings for additional information.

NEAL S. BLAISDELL CENTER - ARENA
777 Ward Avenue, Honolulu, HI 96814
(808) 527-5400
Type of Facility: Arena
Type of Stage: Arena
Stage Dimensions: 64'Wx27'D
Orchestra Pit
Seating Capacity: 8,805
Year Built: 1963
Contact for Rental: Carla W. Coray, Director;   (808) 527-5400

NEAL S. BLAISDELL CENTER - CONCERT HALL
777 Ward Avenue, Honolulu, HI 96814
(808) 527-5400
Type of Facility: Concert Hall
Type of Stage: Concert Stage
Stage Dimensions: 80'Wx40'D
Orchestra Pit
Seating Capacity: 2,107
Year Built: 1963
Contact for Rental: Carla W. Coray, Director;   (808) 527-5400

NEAL S. BLAISDELL CENTER - WAIKIKI SHELL
777 Ward Avenue, Honolulu, HI 96814
(808) 527-5400
Type of Facility: Outdoor (Concert)
Type of Stage: Greek
Stage Dimensions: 88'Wx58'D
Seating Capacity: 8,404
Year Built: 1963   **Cost:** $8,375,600
Contact for Rental: Carla W. Coray, Director;   (808) 527-5400

OLD FORT RUGER THEATRE
520 Makapu Avenue, Honolulu, HI 96816
(808) 734-8763
FAX: (808) 735-1250
Type of Facility: Theatre House
Facility Originally: Movie House; Military
Type of Stage: Proscenium
Stage Dimensions: 70'Wx30'D; 70'Wx30'H proscenium opening
Seating Capacity: 500

Year Built: 1940   **Architect:** United States Army   **Cost:** $13,000
Year Remodeled: 1981
Contact for Rental: Stan Michaels, Managing Director;   (808) 734-8763
Resident Groups: Diamond Head Theatre
The theater is also known as Diamond Head Theatre

SAINT LOUIS CENTER FOR THE PERFORMING ARTS - THE MAMIYA THEATRE
3142 Waialae Avenue, Honolulu, HI 96816
(808) 739-7777
FAX: (808) 739-4853
Type of Facility: Theatre Complex
Type of Stage: Proscenium
Stage Dimensions: 35'Wx14'5"D   **Orchestra Pit**
Seating Capacity: 500
Year Built: 1986   **Architect:** LMLI Architects   **Cost:** $38,000,000
Acoustical Consultant: James K.C. Chang, PE
Contact for Rental: David Lewis, Manager;   (808) 739-7777, ext. 821

Kahului

THEATRE

MAUI ACADEMY OF PERFORMING ARTS
107A Wahi Hoola Ha, Kahului, HI 96732
(808) 244-8760
FAX: (808) 244-8762
Founded: 1974
Arts Area: Community; Youth
Status: Non-Profit
Type: Performing; Touring; Educational
Purpose: To present educational performing arts for youths and adults
Management: Frances A. von Tempsky, Managing Director; David C. Johnston, Artistic Director; Stephanie Sheppard, Director of Development
Officers: Joel E. August, President; Alan Yoshioka, Vice President; Linda Howlett, Secretary; Thomas Seif Ph.D., Treasurer
Paid Staff: 10   **Volunteer Staff:** 250
Paid Artists: 8   **Non-Paid Artists:** 200
Utilizes: Guest Artists; Guest Directors
Budget: $100,000 - $500,000
Income Sources: Private Foundations/Grants/Endowments; Business/Corporate Donations; Box Office; Government Grants; Individual Donations
Season: 52 Weeks

Kailua

THEATRE

WINDWARD THEATRE GUILD
PO Box 624, Kailua, HI 96734
(808) 254-1721
Founded: 1956
Arts Area: Musical; Dinner; Community; Theatrical Group
Status: Non-Profit
Type: Performing; Educational
Purpose: To enhance and promote theatrical excellence in all phases of production
Management: Charles Brockman, Manager
Officers: Phil Haff, President; Alex Nishimura, Vice President; Valerie Stubblefield, Treasurer; Margaret Cox, Secretary
Volunteer Staff: 110
Non-Paid Artists: 60
Utilizes: Special Technical Talent; Guest Artists; Guest Directors
Budget: $50,000 - $100,000
Income Sources: Private Foundations/Grants/Endowments; Business/Corporate Donations; Box Office; Government Grants; Individual Donations
Season: October - June   **Annual Attendance:** 9,000
Affiliations: Hawaii State Theatre Council; State Foundation for Culture and the Arts; Alliance for Drama Education
Performance Facilities: Boondocker Theatre; Kaneohe Marine Corps Air Station

Kamuela

THEATRE

KAHILU THEATRE
Mamalahoa Highway, Parker Ranch Shopping Center, Kamuela, HI 96743
(808) 885-6017
FAX: (808) 885-0546
Founded: 1980
Status: Professional; Non-Profit
Type: Performing; Sponsoring
Purpose: To maintain a performing arts center designed to present high-quality national and international artists/groups; to produce two plays annually using local talent under the direction of a professional director
Management: Virginia Pfaff, Managing Director
Officers: Richard P. Smart, President; Warren Gunderson, Vice President/Treasurer; Richard Hendrick, Vice President/Secretary
Paid Staff: 3   **Volunteer Staff:** 54
Paid Artists: 15
Utilizes: Guest Artists; Guest Directors
Budget: $100,000 - $500,000
Income Sources: Business/Corporate Donations; Box Office; Government Grants; Individual Donations
Season: September - May   **Annual Attendance:** 10,000
Affiliations: WAAA; APAP; ISPAA

WAIMEA COMMUNITY THEATRE
PO Box 1387, Kamuela, HI 96743
Founded: 1965
Arts Area: Musical; Dinner; Community; Theatrical Group
Status: Non-Professional; Non-Profit
Type: Performing; Educational
Purpose: To provide quality theatrical entertainment to the north Hawaii area; to provide educational and community support services in areas related to theatrical performance
Officers: Jay West, President; Andy Kunellis, Vice President; Kim Finke, Secretary; Michael Bray, Treasurer
Volunteer Staff: 20
Non-Paid Artists: 50
Utilizes: Special Technical Talent; Guest Artists; Guest Directors
Budget: $1,000 - $50,000
Income Sources: Box Office; Government Grants; Individual Donations
Season: August - June   **Annual Attendance:** 5,000
Affiliations: Hawaii State Theatre Council
Performance Facilities: Parker School Auditorium

Laie

FACILITY

MCKAY AUDITORIUM AT BRIGHAM YOUNG UNIVERSITY HAWAII
Brigham Young University, Laie, HI 96762
(808) 293-3903
Founded: 1959
Type of Facility: Auditorium
Type of Stage: Thrust; Proscenium
Stage Dimensions: 33'x20'x20' proscenium opening   **Orchestra Pit**
Seating Capacity: 655
Year Built: 1959   **Architect:** Carl Burton
Contact for Rental: Craig Ferre;   (808) 293-3903

Wailuku

INSTRUMENTAL MUSIC

MAUI SYMPHONY ORCHESTRA
95 Mahalani Street, PO Box 788, Wailuku, HI 96793
(808) 244-5439
FAX: (808) 242-0812
Founded: 1979
Arts Area: Symphony; Orchestra; Ethnic

Status: Semi-Professional; Non-Profit
Type: Performing
Purpose: To give native musicians an opportunity to perform; to provide the Maui community with a permanent resident orchestra; to provide an opportunity for local performers and choreographers to display their talents through association with the orchestra; to premiere original works
Management: James French, Music Director/Conductor
Officers: Frank Blackwell, President
Paid Staff: 1   **Volunteer Staff:** 40
Paid Artists: 20   **Non-Paid Artists:** 40
Utilizes: Special Technical Talent; Guest Conductors; Guest Artists
Budget: $50,000 - $100,000
Income Sources: Private Foundations/Grants/Endowments; Business/Corporate Donations; Box Office; Government Grants; Individual Donations
Season: September - April   **Annual Attendance:** 15,000
Affiliations: ASOL; Maui Community Arts Council
Performance Facilities: Baldwin Auditorium, Wailuku

IDAHO

Boise

DANCE

AMERICAN FESTIVAL BALLET
Esther Simplot Performing Arts Academy, 516 North Ninth Street, Boise, ID 83702
(208) 343-0556
    Founded: 1971
    Arts Area: Modern; Ballet; Jazz
    Status: Professional
    Type: Performing; Touring; Resident; Educational; Sponsoring
    Management: Esther B. Simplot, Executive Director; Betty Sinow, Assistant Executive Director
    Paid Staff: 5   **Volunteer Staff:** 40
    Paid Artists: 16
    Utilizes: Guest Artists
    Budget: $100,000 - $500,000
    Income Sources: Private Foundations/Grants/Endowments; Business/Corporate Donations; Box Office; Government Grants; Individual Donations
    Season: October - March   **Annual Attendance:** 30,000
    Performance Facilities: Morrison Center for the Performing Arts

OINKARI BASQUE DANCERS
2418 Pendleton, PO Box 1675, Boise, ID 83705
(208) 336-8219
    Arts Area: Ethnic; Folk
    Status: Non-Profit
    Type: Performing; Touring; Educational
    Purpose: To promote and enhance our culture through dance, song, language and education
    Management: John Kirtland, Business Manager; Dan Ansotegui, Boys Dance Director; Toni Ansotegui, Girls Dance Director; Julie Achabal, Historian; Ron Lemmon, Sergeant-at-Arms
    Officers: Lisa Achurra, President
    Paid Staff: 1   **Volunteer Staff:** 7
    Paid Artists: 1   **Non-Paid Artists:** 70
    Utilizes: Special Technical Talent; Guest Artists; Guest Directors
    Budget: $1,000 - $50,000
    Income Sources: Private Foundations/Grants/Endowments; Business/Corporate Donations; Individual Donations
    Season: 52 Weeks   **Annual Attendance:** 25,000
    Affiliations: Euskaldunak
    Performance Facilities: Boise Basque Center

INSTRUMENTAL MUSIC

BOISE PHILHARMONIC
205 North Tenth, Suite 617, Boise, ID 83702
(208) 344-7849
    Founded: 1887
    Arts Area: Symphony; Chamber
    Status: Professional; Non-Profit
    Type: Performing; Educational
    Purpose: The purpose of the Boise Philharmonic is to maintain a symphony orchestra as a high-quality artistic resource for the Treasure Valley. To insure this mission, the association is committed to the highest performance quality and widest community service that finances will allow.
    Management: James Ogle, Artistic Director/Conductor; Margie Stoy Smith, General Manager
    Officers: Richard Roller, President
    Paid Staff: 9
    Paid Artists: 70
    Utilizes: Guest Conductors; Guest Artists
    Budget: $500,000 - $1,000,000
    Income Sources: Private Foundations/Grants/Endowments; Business/Corporate Donations; Box Office; Government Grants; Individual Donations
    Season: September - May   **Annual Attendance:** 50,000
    Affiliations: ASOL
    Performance Facilities: Morrison Center for the Performing Arts, Boise; Brandt Auditorium, Nampa Civic Center

VOCAL MUSIC

BOISE MASTER CHORALE
6925 Copper Drive, Boise, ID 83704
(208) 375-2948
    Arts Area: Choral
    Status: Professional; Semi-Professional; Non-Profit
    Type: Performing
    Purpose: To provide the community with fine choral music and enable people in the community to sing in an outstanding
choral group
    Management: Carson Wong, Conductor; Randall Pierson, Stage Manager
    Officers: Shari Cutshall, President; Katherine Sullivan, Secretary; Emily Riley, Treasurer
    Paid Staff: 10   **Volunteer Staff:** 10
    Non-Paid Artists: 125
    Budget: $1,000 - $50,000
    Income Sources: Private Foundations/Grants/Endowments; Business/Corporate Donations; Box Office; Government
Grants; Individual Donations
    Season: September - May   **Annual Attendance:** 4,000
    Performance Facilities: Saint John's Cathedral; Morrison Center for the Performing Arts

BOISE OPERA
516 South Ninth, Boise, ID 83702
(208) 345-3531
    Founded: 1972
    Arts Area: Grand Opera; Music Theatre
    Status: Professional; Non-Profit
    Type: Performing; Educational
    Management: Michael Winter, Executive Director
    Paid Staff: 1
    Utilizes: Special Technical Talent; Guest Conductors; Guest Artists; Guest Directors
    Budget: $100,000 - $500,000
    Income Sources: Private Foundations/Grants/Endowments; Business/Corporate Donations; Box Office; Individual Dona-
tions
    Season: September - March   **Annual Attendance:** 2,300
    Performance Facilities: Morrison Center for the Performing Arts

THEATRE

IDAHO THEATER FOR YOUTH
Eighth Street Market Place, Suite 232, Boise, ID 83702
(208) 345-0060
FAX: (208) 336-6731
    Mailing Address: PO Box 7926, Boise, ID 83707
    Founded: 1981
    Arts Area: Professional; Theatrical Group
    Status: Professional; Non-Profit
    Type: Performing; Touring; Educational
    Purpose: To provide live, professional theater for the cultural enrichment and theater-arts education of children, young
adults and their families at a cost which makes the programs easily accessible to all
    Management: Cynthia Gaede, Managing Director; David Lee-Painter, Artistic Director; Terri April Dillion, Marketing Di-
rector; Dan Peterson, Associate Artistic Director; Jane Baker, Business Manager
    Officers: Dale Smith, President; David Nevin, Vice President; Gwen Engle, Secretary; Nial Bradshaw, Treasurer
    Paid Staff: 5
    Paid Artists: 12
    Utilizes: Special Technical Talent; Guest Artists; Guest Directors
    Budget: $100,000 - $500,000
    Income Sources: Private Foundations/Grants/Endowments; Business/Corporate Donations; Box Office; Government
Grants; Individual Donations
    Season: September - May   **Annual Attendance:** 100,000
    Performance Facilities: Morrison Center for the Performing Arts

PERFORMING SERIES

IDAHO SHAKESPEARE FESTIVAL
412 South Ninth St., PO Box 9365, Boise, ID 83707
(208) 336-9221
FAX: (208) 336-6731
    Founded: 1976

Arts Area: Theater
Status: Professional; Non-Profit
Type: Performing; Touring; Educational
Management: Charles Fee, Artistic, Director; Vangie Osborn, General Manager
Officers: Charles Davis, President, Board of Trustees
Paid Staff: 4   **Volunteer Staff:** 10
Paid Artists: 12   **Non-Paid Artists:** 10
Utilizes: Guest Artists; Guest Directors
Budget: $100,000 - $500,000
Income Sources: Private Foundations/Grants/Endowments; Business/Corporate Donations; Box Office; Individual Donations
Season: May - September   **Annual Attendance:** 20,000

FACILITY

BOISE STATE UNIVERSITY - MORRISON CENTER FOR THE PERFORMING ARTS
1910 University Drive, Boise, ID 83725
(208) 385-1609
FAX: (208) 385-3021
Type of Facility: Concert Hall; Performance Center; Theatre House; Multi-Purpose
Type of Stage: Proscenium
Stage Dimensions: 120'Wx52'D; 60'Wx30'H proscenium opening   **Orchestra Pit**
Seating Capacity: 2,030
Year Built: 1984   **Architect:** Lombard/Conrad   **Cost:** $18,500,000
Acoustical Consultant: Paeoletti & Levitz
Contact for Rental: Frank Heise;   (208) 385-1609
Resident Groups: Boise Opera; Boise Philharmonic; American Festival Ballet

Caldwell

PERFORMING SERIES

CALDWELL FINE ARTS SERIES
2112 Cleveland Boulevard, Caldwell, ID 83605
(208) 454-1376
FAX: (208) 459-2077
Founded: 1961
Arts Area: Dance; Vocal Music; Instrumental Music; Theater; Grand Opera
Status: Non-Profit
Type: Educational; Sponsoring
Purpose: To present quality performances in all disciplines; to provide educational services for schools in the area; to assist other arts organizations
Management: Sylvia Hunt, Manager
Officers: Beverly Hopper, President; Shirley Marmon, Vice President; Jeanne Skyrm, Secretary; Hanni Hinkle, Treasurer
Paid Staff: 1   **Volunteer Staff:** 40
Paid Artists: 100
Utilizes: Guest Artists
Budget: $50,000 - $100,000
Income Sources: Private Foundations/Grants/Endowments; Business/Corporate Donations; Box Office; Government Grants; Individual Donations
Season: October - April   **Annual Attendance:** 7,500
Affiliations: Pacific Northwest Presenters
Performance Facilities: Jewett Auditorium

Idaho Falls

INSTRUMENTAL MUSIC

IDAHO FALLS SYMPHONY
545 Shoup Avenue, #101, Idaho Falls, ID 83402
(208) 529-1080
Founded: 1955
Arts Area: Symphony; Orchestra
Status: Semi-Professional; Non-Profit
Type: Performing; Resident; Educational
Management: John LoPiccolo, Conductor/Music Director; Linda Waugh, Business Manager
Utilizes: Guest Artists

Budget: $100,000 - $500,000
Income Sources: Business/Corporate Donations; Box Office; Government Grants; Individual Donations
Season: October - May   **Annual Attendance:** 10,000
Affiliations: ASOL
Performance Facilities: Civic Auditorium

FACILITY

CIVIC AUDITORIUM
501 South Holmes, Idaho Falls, ID 83401
(208) 529-1396
    Type of Facility: Concert Hall; Auditorium; Performance Center; Opera House; Civic Center; Multi-Purpose
    Type of Stage: Proscenium
    Stage Dimensions: 84'Wx35'D   **Orchestra Pit**
    Seating Capacity: 1,902
    Year Built: 1951   **Architect:** Fetzer & Fetzer   **Cost:** $1,000,000
    Acoustical Consultant: C.P. Boner & Associates
    Contact for Rental: Roger T. Ralphs;   (208) 529-1396
    Resident Groups: Idaho Falls Symphony; Idaho Falls Opera Theatre; Sounds Choir; Idaho Falls Symphony Chorale; Ballet Society; Idaho Falls Music Club; Community Concerts

Moscow

INSTRUMENTAL MUSIC

WASHINGTON IDAHO SYMPHONY
PO Box 9185, Moscow, ID 83843
(208) 882-6555
    Founded: 1972
    Arts Area: Symphony; Ensemble
    Status: Non-Professional; Non-Profit
    Type: Performing; Resident; Educational
    Purpose: To bring the pleasure of fine music to adults and children while allowing area musicians to participate in an orchestra or chorus
    Management: Cecelia Lund, Executive Director
    Officers: Samuel H. Butterfield, President; Dr. William Cone, First Vice President; Day Bassett, Second Vice President; Bruce Wollenberg, Secretary/Treasurer
    Paid Staff: 8   **Volunteer Staff:** 309
    Paid Artists: 55   **Non-Paid Artists:** 40
    Utilizes: Guest Artists
    Budget: $50,000 - $100,000
    Income Sources: Private Foundations/Grants/Endowments; Business/Corporate Donations; Box Office; Government Grants; Individual Donations
    Season: September - April   **Annual Attendance:** 3,812
    Affiliations: ASOL

THEATRE

IDAHO REPERTORY THEATRE COMPANY
University of Idaho, Moscow, ID 83843
(208) 885-6465
    Founded: 1950
    Arts Area: Professional; Theatrical Group
    Status: Semi-Professional; Non-Profit
    Type: Performing; Educational
    Purpose: To provide high-quality summer theatre for the state of Idaho
    Management: Bruce C. Brockman, Producing Director
    Paid Staff: 3
    Paid Artists: 27
    Utilizes: Special Technical Talent; Guest Artists; Guest Directors
    Budget: $1,000 - $50,000
    Income Sources: Private Foundations/Grants/Endowments; Business/Corporate Donations; Box Office; Government Grants; Individual Donations
    Season: June - August   **Annual Attendance:** 10,000
    Performance Facilities: Hartung Theatre

PERFORMING SERIES

FESTIVAL DANCE AND PERFORMING ARTS
University of Idaho, Moscow, ID 83843
(208) 883-3267
> **Founded:** 1989
> **Arts Area:** Dance; Musical Theatre
> **Status:** Professional; Non-Profit
> **Type:** Performing; Educational; Sponsoring
> **Purpose:** To bring the best of the performing arts to the Inland Northwest through performances, education and outreach programs
> **Management:** Joann Muneta, Executive Director
> **Officers:** Jeff Helbling, Chairman; Paul Smith, Vice Chairman
> **Paid Staff:** 2
> **Paid Artists:** 3
> **Utilizes:** Guest Artists; Guest Companies
> **Budget:** $100,000 - $500,000
> **Income Sources:** Private Foundations/Grants/Endowments; Business/Corporate Donations; Box Office; Government Grants; Individual Donations
> **Season:** 52 Weeks   **Annual Attendance:** 10,000
> **Affiliations:** WAAA; Pacific Northwest Arts Performers
> **Performance Facilities:** Beasly Performing Arts Coliseum, Washington State University

LIONEL HAMPTON, CHEVRON JAZZ FESTIVAL
University of Idaho, Hampton School of Music, Moscow, ID 83843
(208) 835-6765
FAX: (208) 885-6513
> **Founded:** 1968
> **Arts Area:** Festivals
> **Status:** Non-Profit
> **Type:** Performing; Educational; Sponsoring
> **Purpose:** To promote jazz music among the youth of America
> **Management:** Dr. Lynn J. Skinner, Executive Director
> **Paid Staff:** 3   **Volunteer Staff:** 200
> **Paid Artists:** 50
> **Utilizes:** Special Technical Talent; Guest Artists
> **Budget:** $100,000 - $500,000
> **Income Sources:** Private Foundations/Grants/Endowments; Business/Corporate Donations; Box Office; Government Grants; Individual Donations
> **Season:** February - March
> **Annual Attendance:** 45,000

Mountain Home

PERFORMING SERIES

PERFORMING ARTS SERIES OF MOUNTAIN HOME
935 North 12 East, Mountain Home, ID 83647
(208) 587-4821
> **Arts Area:** Dance; Vocal Music; Instrumental Music; Theater
> **Status:** Non-Professional
> **Type:** Performing; Educational
> **Purpose:** To bring culturally enriching performances to our rural community and surrounding areas
> **Management:** Laurie Unrein, Executive Director
> **Officers:** Sher Sellman, President; Tom Bennick, Vice President; Karen Bird, Treasurer; Lorretta Olmstead, Secretary
> **Paid Staff:** 1   **Volunteer Staff:** 12
> **Utilizes:** Guest Artists
> **Budget:** $1,000 - $50,000
> **Income Sources:** Private Foundations/Grants/Endowments; Business/Corporate Donations; Box Office; Government Grants; Individual Donations
> **Season:** September - May
> **Annual Attendance:** 1,400

Pocatello

FACILITY

IDAHO STATE UNIVERSITY - FRAZIER AUDITORIUM
Eighth Street, Pocatello, ID 83209
(208) 236-3695
Type of Facility: Theatre Complex; Auditorium
Type of Stage: Proscenium
Stage Dimensions: 42'Wx20'D **Orchestra Pit**
Seating Capacity: 750
Year Built: 1924
Contact for Rental: Reed Turner, Theater Director; (208) 236-2925

IDAHO STATE UNIVERSITY - GORANSON HALL
Department of Music, PO Box 8099, Pocatello, ID 83209
(208) 236-3636
Type of Facility: Concert Hall
Type of Stage: Proscenium
Seating Capacity: 475
Year Built: 1967 **Cost:** $2,000,000
Contact for Rental: Music Department Secretary; (208) 236-3636
Resident Groups: Idaho State Civic Symphony; University Music Organizations

IDAHO STATE UNIVERSITY - POWELL LITTLE THEATRE
Eighth Street, Pocatello, ID 83209
(208) 236-3695
Type of Facility: Arena; Multi-Purpose; Visual And Performing Classrooms
Facility Originally: Library
Type of Stage: Arena
Stage Dimensions: 20'x30'
Seating Capacity: 150
Year Built: 1924
Contact for Rental: Reed Turner, Theater Director; (208) 236-2925

Rexburg

FACILITY

ELIZA R. SNOW PERFORMING ARTS CENTER
Rexburg, ID 83460-1210
(208) 356-1260
FAX: (208) 356-2390
Type of Facility: Theatre Complex; Concert Hall
Type of Stage: Platform
Stage Dimensions: Drama Theater - 42'x45'; Concert Hall - 54'x30'
Orchestra Pit
Seating Capacity: 700
Year Built: 1980 **Architect:** Collard and Call
Acoustical Consultant: Rein Pirn
Contact for Rental: Ken Howell; (208) 356-1149

Sandpoint

THEATRE

PANIDA THEATER
300 North First Avenue, PO Box 1981, Sandpoint, ID 83864
(208) 263-9191
Founded: 1985
Arts Area: Professional; Musical; Community; Folk; Theatrical Group; Puppet; Dance; Film
Status: Non-Profit
Type: Performing; Resident; Educational; Sponsoring
Purpose: To provide a beautiful and versatile space for organizations and sponsors to present quality performances; to continue efforts to revitalize downtown Sandpoint
Management: Karen Bowers, Manager/Executive Director; Bill Lewis, Technical Director

Officers: Michael Merrell, President; Bruce Millard, Vice President; Barbara Shaver, Secretary/Treasurer; Phyllis Marks, Facilities Chair
Paid Staff: 2   **Volunteer Staff:** 30
Paid Artists: 100   **Non-Paid Artists:** 725
Utilizes: Special Technical Talent; Guest Artists
Budget: $50,000 - $100,000
Income Sources: Private Foundations/Grants/Endowments; Business/Corporate Donations; Box Office; Government Grants; Individual Donations; Theatre Rental
Season: 52 Weeks   **Annual Attendance:** 24,500

PERFORMING SERIES

FESTIVAL AT SANDPOINT
c/o Festival at Sandpoint Inc., PO Box 695, Sandpoint, ID 83864
(208) 265-4554
FAX: (208) 263-9466
Arts Area: Vocal Music; Instrumental Music; Children's Programs
Status: Professional; Commercial
Type: Performing; Educational; Sponsoring
Purpose: To present high-quality musical performances including classical, symphonic, Big Band, ragtime, jazz, country and western, pops, and children's programming; to advance musical education through the Schweitzer Institute of Music
Management: Gunther Schuller, Artistic Director; Constance Berghan, Executive Director
Officers: Bobbie Huguenin, President
Budget: $500,000 - $1,000,000
Income Sources: Private Foundations/Grants/Endowments; Business/Corporate Donations; Box Office; Government Grants; Individual Donations
Performance Facilities: Festival Tent

Sun Valley

PERFORMING SERIES

ELKHORN MUSIC FESTIVAL, INC.
PO Box 1914, Sun Valley, ID 83353
(208) 622-5607
Founded: 1985
Arts Area: Vocal Music; Instrumental Music; Festivals
Status: Professional; Non-Profit
Type: Performing; Educational
Purpose: To present 20 free concerts by Idaho's first and only professional chamber orchestra
Management: Carl Eberl, Music Director/Conductor; Julianne Eberl, Executive Director; Craig Knutson, Stage Manager; Isabel Thompson, Administrative Assistant
Officers: Carl Eberl, President; Rickie Orchin Brady, Vice President; James Hancock, Treasurer; Julianne Eberl, Secretary
Paid Staff: 4
Paid Artists: 40
Utilizes: Guest Artists
Budget: $100,000 - $500,000
Income Sources: Private Foundations/Grants/Endowments; Business/Corporate Donations; Government Grants; Individual Donations; Sale of Specialty Items
Season: August   **Annual Attendance:** 8,000
Affiliations: Sun Valley Chamber of Commerce
Performance Facilities: Elkhorn Plaza Tent

SUN VALLEY CENTER FOR THE ARTS AND HUMANITIES
PO Box 656, Sun Valley, ID 83353
(208) 726-9491
FAX: (208) 726-2344
Arts Area: Dance; Vocal Music; Instrumental Music; Theater
Type: Presenting
Purpose: To present programs highlighting music (classical, chamber, opera, jazz, folk, ethnic and popular), theatre, and dance
Management: Kate Wright, Director of Performing Arts
Budget: $100,000 - $500,000
Season: 52 Weeks
Performance Facilities: Sun Valley Center for the Arts and Humanities

---

Twin Falls

INSTRUMENTAL MUSIC

MAGIC VALLEY SYMPHONY
PO Box 1805, Twin Falls, ID 83303
(208) 733-1079
>**Founded:** 1959
>**Arts Area:** Symphony; Orchestra
>**Status:** Non-Professional; Non-Profit
>**Type:** Performing
>**Purpose:** To enhance the cultural life of the community and provide an outlet for performers
>**Management:** Theodore A. Hadley, Conductor; Edna Thorsen, Business Manager
>**Officers:** Kevin Howard, President; Ernest Moss, Vice President; Judy Call, Secretary
>**Utilizes:** Guest Artists
>**Budget:** $1,000 - $50,000
>**Income Sources:** Business/Corporate Donations; Box Office; Individual Donations
>**Season:** September - May **Annual Attendance:** 1,800
>**Affiliations:** ASOL; BMI; ASCAP
>**Performance Facilities:** College of Southern Idaho Fine Arts Auditorium

---

Wallace

THEATRE

VALLEY COMMUNITY THEATER
PO Box 866, Wallace, ID 83873
(208) 753-5792
>**Founded:** 1966
>**Arts Area:** Musical; Community
>**Status:** Non-Professional; Non-Profit
>**Type:** Performing; Sponsoring
>**Purpose:** Valley Community Theater was founded and is supported by members of the community seriously interested in the performing arts
>**Officers:** Debbie Morris, President; Mary Rae Faraca, Vice President; Ann Wilson, Secretary
>**Volunteer Staff:** 15
>**Non-Paid Artists:** 15
>**Budget:** $1,000 - $50,000

Weiser

FACILITY

INTERMOUNTAIN CULTURAL CENTER AND MUSEUM
2295 Paddock Avenue, Weiser, ID 83672
(208) 549-0205
>**Type of Facility:** Auditorium
>**Facility Originally:** School
>**Type of Stage:** Platform
>**Seating Capacity:** 296
>**Year Built:** 1923
>**Year Remodeled:** 1980
>**Contact for Rental:** Intermountain Cultural Center and Museum; (208) 549-0205

ILLINOIS

Alton

INSTRUMENTAL MUSIC

ALTON SYMPHONY ORCHESTRA
PO Box 1205, Alton, IL 62002-1205
(618) 462-3184
Founded: 1946
Arts Area: Symphony
Status: Non-Professional; Non-Profit
Type: Performing
Purpose: To provide a medium for the further development of instrumental abilities of area musicians; to build an interest in orchestral music; and to present concerts for the public
Management: Dr. Frank M. Boals, Manager
Officers: James S. Reeves, President; Henry B. Lenhardt, Vice President; Jill Zitnick, Secretary; Abby Davison, Treasurer
Paid Artists: 4
Utilizes: Guest Artists
Budget: $1,000 - $50,000
Income Sources: Private Foundations/Grants/Endowments; Business/Corporate Donations; Box Office; Government Grants; Individual Donations
Season: September - May   **Annual Attendance:** 3,000
Affiliations: Illinois Council of Orchestras
Performance Facilities: Hatheway Hall, Lewis and Clark Community College

Argonne

PERFORMING SERIES

ARTS AT ARGONNE
Argonne National Laboratory, 221-D244, Argonne, IL 60439
(708) 252-7160
FAX: (708) 252-5986
Founded: 1988
Arts Area: Instrumental Music
Status: Non-Professional
Type: Sponsoring
Purpose: To enrich the cultural climate at the laboratory by presenting a program of cultural manifestation of the highest artistic quality
Officers: Dr. Hans Kaper, Chairman
Volunteer Staff: 15
Utilizes: Guest Artists
Budget: $1,000 - $50,000
Income Sources: Private Foundations/Grants/Endowments; Box Office
Season: October - May   **Annual Attendance:** 1,500
Affiliations: Chicago Music Alliance
Performance Facilities: Building 362 Auditorium

Aurora

FACILITY

PARAMOUNT ARTS CENTRE
23 East Galena Boulevard, Aurora, IL 60506
(708) 896-7676
Type of Facility: Theatre House
Type of Stage: Proscenium
Stage Dimensions: 48'9"Wx40'Dx30'H   **Orchestra Pit**
Seating Capacity: 1,888
Year Built: 1931   **Architect:** Jules J. Rubens
Year Remodeled: 1976   **Architect:** Prisco & Duffy   **Cost:** $2,950,000
Contact for Rental: James Kampert, Assistant Manager;   (708) 896-7676
In 1980, the Paramount Arts Centre was placed on the National Register of Historic Places.

Batavia

PERFORMING SERIES

FERMILAB ARTS SERIES
Pine Street and Kirk Road, Batavia, IL 60647
(708) 840-2059
FAX: (708) 840-2939
   Arts Area: Dance; Instrumental Music; Theater; Comedy; Jazz
   Status: Non-Profit
   Type: Sponsoring
   Purpose: To provide quality arts presentations to Fermilab and surrounding communities
   Management: Janet Mac Kay, Arts Coordinator; Colleen Choy, Box Office Manager
   Officers: Morris Binkley, Chairman Auditorium Committee
   Paid Staff: 2   **Volunteer Staff:** 30
   Paid Artists: 12   **Non-Paid Artists:** 3
   Utilizes: Guest Artists
   Income Sources: Box Office
   Season: 52 Weeks   **Annual Attendance:** 9,960
   Affiliations: Fermi National Accel Laboratories
   Performance Facilities: Ramsey Auditorium

Belleville

INSTRUMENTAL MUSIC

BELLEVILLE PHILHARMONIC
116 North Jackson, Belleville, IL 62220
(618) 235-5600
   Founded: 1866
   Arts Area: Symphony; Orchestra; Instrumental Group
   Status: Non-Professional; Non-Profit
   Type: Performing; Educational
   Purpose: To serve the interests of music and musicians in Greater Belleville
   Management: Kathleen J. AuBuchon, Administrator; Kathly Albers, Office Manager
   Officers: Audrey Mudd, President; Bill Kniesly, Vice President; Mary Durnell, Secretary; Steve Gondek, Treasurer
   Paid Staff: 3   **Volunteer Staff:** 2
   Paid Artists: 10   **Non-Paid Artists:** 100
   Utilizes: Guest Artists
   Budget: $50,000 - $100,000
   Income Sources: Business/Corporate Donations; Box Office; Government Grants; Individual Donations
   Season: September - May   **Annual Attendance:** 5,000

Bloomington

INSTRUMENTAL MUSIC

BLOOMINGTON-NORMAL SYMPHONY SOCIETY
106 West Monroe, Bloomington, IL 61702-0375
(309) 828-2882
FAX: (309) 827-2726
   Founded: 1944
   Arts Area: Symphony; Orchestra; Chamber
   Status: Semi-Professional; Non-Profit
   Type: Performing; Touring; Resident
   Purpose: To support a symphony orchestra for the purpose of producing high-quality symphonic music for the Bloomington-Normal area.
   Management: Carole M. Ringer, General Manager; Alice D. Morris, Administrative Secretary
   Officers: Susan Smart, President; John Killian, Dr. David Skillrud, Vice Presidents; Kyle C. Sessions, Secretary; Richard Lenahan, Treasurer
   Paid Staff: 2
   Paid Artists: 100
   Utilizes: Guest Conductors; Guest Artists
   Budget: $100,000 - $500,000
   Income Sources: Private Foundations/Grants/Endowments; Business/Corporate Donations; Box Office; Government Grants; Individual Donations
   Season: September - May   **Annual Attendance:** 7,500

Affiliations: Illinois Council of Orchestras; ASOL
Performance Facilities: Braden Auditorium, Illinois State University

FACILITY

ILLINOIS WESLEYAN SCHOOL OF DRAMA - MCPHERSON HALL
302 East Graham, Bloomington, IL 61702
(309) 556-3011
Type of Facility: Theatre Complex; Auditorium; Theatre House
Type of Stage: Flexible
Stage Dimensions: 18'x36'x50' **Orchestra Pit**
Seating Capacity: 279
Year Built: 1962 **Architect:** Shafter Wilson Evans **Cost:** $500,000
Manager: Dr. Jared Brown, Director

ILLINOIS WESLEYAN UNIVERSITY - WESTBROOK AUDITORIUM
Presser Hall, School of Music, Bloomington, IL 61702
(309) 556-3061
Type of Facility: Auditorium
Type of Stage: Proscenium
Orchestra Pit
Seating Capacity: 574
Year Built: 1929 **Architect:** Pillsbury
Year Remodeled: 1970 **Architect:** Evans Associates **Cost:** $129,000
Manager: Dr. Robert A. Kvam
Rental is only on a limited basis.

Champaign

INSTRUMENTAL MUSIC

CHAMPAIGN-URBANA SYMPHONY
44 East Main Street, Room 414, Champaign, IL 61824
(217) 351-9139
FAX: (217) 351-1698
Founded: 1959
Arts Area: Symphony
Status: Professional; Non-Profit
Type: Performing
Management: Paul Vermel, Conductor; Terry I. Benson, Symphony Manager
Utilizes: Guest Artists
Season: September - May
Performance Facilities: Foellinger Great Hall

PERFORMING SERIES

ASSEMBLY HALL
University of Illinois, Champaign, IL 61820
(217) 333-2923
Founded: 1963
Arts Area: Dance; Vocal Music; Instrumental Music; Theater
Status: Professional; Non-Profit
Type: Sponsoring
Purpose: Entertainment and cultural events for university students, the community and the area
Management: Wayne N. Hecht, Director
Paid Staff: 5
Budget: $100,000 - $500,000
Income Sources: Box Office
Affiliations: IAAM; ISPAA; APAP; Big Ten Concert Managers
Performance Facilities: Assembly Hall

THE GREAT AMERICAN PEOPLE SHOW
Station A, Box 2178, Champaign, IL 61820
(217) 367-1900
Founded: 1975
Arts Area: Theater
Status: Non-Profit
Type: Performing; Touring

Purpose: To create historical theatrical pieces using primary materials (letters, diaries, newspaper accounts, poems, and commentary) written or spoken about or by Americans. TGAPS currently produces three historical dramas at Lincoln's New Salem Historical Site.
Management: John Ahart and Rose Buckner Ahart, Co-Artistic Directors; Donna Buzicky, Office Manager
Officers: John Ahart, President; Professor Robert Johannson, Chairman of the Board
Paid Staff: 7 **Volunteer Staff:** 20
Paid Artists: 35
Utilizes: Special Technical Talent; Guest Conductors; Guest Artists
Budget: $100,000 - $500,000
Income Sources: Private Foundations/Grants/Endowments; Box Office; Government Grants; Individual Donations
Season: June - August **Annual Attendance:** 10,000
Affiliations: Illinois Historic Preservation Agency
Performance Facilities: Lincoln's New Salem

Chicago

DANCE

AKASHA AND COMPANY
1016 North Dearborn, Chicago, IL 60657
(312) 266-0039
Founded: 1979
Arts Area: Modern
Status: Professional; Non-Profit
Type: Performing; Touring
Purpose: Akasha: "Spirit Leaping Forth"
Management: Laura Wade, Artistic Director; Jeanne Knowles, General Manager
Paid Staff: 2
Paid Artists: 6
Utilizes: Guest Artists; Guest Choreographers
Budget: $50,000 - $100,000
Income Sources: Private Foundations/Grants/Endowments; Business/Corporate Donations; Box Office; Government Grants; Individual Donations
Season: 52 Weeks

BALLET CHICAGO
222 South Riverside Plaza, Suite 865, Chicago, IL 60606
(312) 993-7575
FAX: (312) 993-1974
Arts Area: Ballet
Status: Professional; Non-Profit
Type: Performing; Touring; Educational
Purpose: To provide metropolitan Chicago and its environs with the finest classical ballet; to develop a diverse repetoire; to educate and develop audiences of all ages and backgrounds
Management: Daniel Duell, Artistic Director; Patricia Blair, Assistant Artistic Director; Gordon Pierce Schmidt, Resident Choreographer
Officers: John C. Staley, Chairman; Peggy Fowler, President
Budget: $1,000,000 - $5,000,000
Income Sources: Private Foundations/Grants/Endowments; Business/Corporate Donations; Box Office; Government Grants; Individual Donations

CHICAGO DANCE COALITION
67 East Madison, Suite 2112, Chicago, IL 60603
(312) 410-8384
Founded: 1981
Status: Professional; Non-Profit
Type: Sponsoring; Service
Purpose: To serve and promote dance in Chicago through publications, hotline, library, seminars, Ruth Page Awards and member services
Management: Lisa Tylke, Executive Director; Lisa Abigai Crampton, Program Coordinator; Valerie Baxley, Membership Services Coordinator
Paid Staff: 3 **Volunteer Staff:** 5
Budget: $100,000 - $500,000
Income Sources: Private Foundations/Grants/Endowments; Business/Corporate Donations; Government Grants; Individual Donations

CHICAGO MOVING COMPANY
1225 West School Street, Chicago, IL 60057
(312) 880-5002
> **Founded:** 1972
> **Arts Area:** Modern
> **Status:** Professional; Non-Profit
> **Type:** Performing; Touring; Educational
> **Purpose:** We believe that art should speak to life; we touch the spirit of the audience, engage them in feeling and reflections, and entertain them
> **Management:** Nana Shineflug, Artistic Director; Dennis Wise, Managing Director
> **Officers:** Bill Gilmore, President; Larry Blust, Vice President
> **Paid Staff:** 1   **Volunteer Staff:** 3
> **Paid Artists:** 10
> **Utilizes:** Special Technical Talent
> **Budget:** $50,000 - $100,000
> **Income Sources:** Private Foundations/Grants/Endowments; Business/Corporate Donations; Box Office; Government Grants; Individual Donations
> **Season:** September - June   **Annual Attendance:** 26,000
> **Performance Facilities:** Columbia Dance Center

THE DANCE CENTER OF COLUMBIA COLLEGE
4730 North Sheridan Road, Chicago, IL 60640
(312) 271-7804
FAX: (312) 271-7046
> **Arts Area:** Modern; Ballet; Jazz; Ethnic; Choreography; Improvisation
> **Status:** Professional; Non-Profit
> **Type:** Performing; Educational
> **Purpose:** To provide dance instruction to a variety of people from culturally diverse backgrounds
> **Management:** Shirley Mordine, Artistic Director
> **Paid Staff:** 18   **Volunteer Staff:** 4
> **Utilizes:** Guest Choreographers
> **Budget:** $500,000 - $1,000,000
> **Income Sources:** Private Foundations/Grants/Endowments; Business/Corporate Donations; Box Office; Government Grants; Individual Donations
> **Season:** August - June   **Annual Attendance:** 24,000
> **Affiliations:** Chicago Dance Coalition; Donors Forum; League of Chicago Theatres
> **Performance Facilities:** Dance Center; Medina Temple; Harold Washington Library Theatre

HUBBARD STREET DANCE COMPANY
218 South Wabash Avenue, Chicago, IL 60604
(312) 663-0853
FAX: (312) 663-9095
> **Founded:** 1977
> **Arts Area:** Ballet-Based Contemporary
> **Status:** Professional
> **Type:** Performing; Touring; Resident; Educational
> **Purpose:** To present the finest of professional dance to our home audiences and on tour
> **Management:** David Foster, John Luckacovic, Columbia Artists Management
> **Officers:** James Peponis, Chairman; William Wood Prince, President; Donald H. Ratner, Treasurer; Jo Hopkins Deutsch, Secretary
> **Paid Staff:** 17   **Volunteer Staff:** 25
> **Paid Artists:** 22
> **Utilizes:** Special Technical Talent; Guest Choreographers; Scenic Designers; Composers
> **Budget:** $5,000,000 - $10,000,000
> **Income Sources:** Private Foundations/Grants/Endowments; Business/Corporate Donations; Box Office; Government Grants; Individual Donations; Merchandise Income
> **Season:** 52 Weeks   **Annual Attendance:** 75,000
> **Affiliations:** Dance USA; APAP; Illinois Arts Alliance; Chicago Dance Coalition; WAAA; NAPAMA; Ohio Regional Association of Concert and Lecture Enterprises; ISPAA
> **Performance Facilities:** Civic Opera House; Ravinia Festival

JAN ERKERT AND COMPANY
2121 West Webster, Chicago, IL 60647
(312) 252-6557
> **Founded:** 1979
> **Arts Area:** Modern
> **Status:** Professional; Non-Profit
> **Type:** Performing; Touring; Resident

Purpose: To make modern dance accessible to a wide audience
Management: Jan Erkert, Artistic Director; Bernt Lewy, Executive Director
Paid Staff: 4
Paid Artists: 8
Utilizes: Guest Artists; Guest Choreographers
Budget: $100,000 - $500,000
Income Sources: Private Foundations/Grants/Endowments; Business/Corporate Donations; Box Office; Government Grants; Individual Donations
Season: September - June

JOEL HALL DANCERS
1225 West School, Chicago, IL 60657
(312) 880-1002
Founded: 1974
Arts Area: Jazz
Status: Professional; Non-Profit
Type: Performing; Touring; Resident; Educational
Management: Joel Hall, Artistic Director; Joseph Ehrenberg, Managing Director
Paid Artists: 12
Utilizes: Guest Artists; Guest Choreographers
Budget: $100,000 - $500,000
Income Sources: Private Foundations/Grants/Endowments; Business/Corporate Donations; Box Office; Government Grants; Individual Donations
Season: 52 Weeks

JOSEPH HOLMES CHICAGO DANCE THEATRE
1935 South Halsted, Chicago, IL 60608
(312) 942-0065
FAX: (312) 942-0815
Founded: 1974
Arts Area: Modern; Jazz
Status: Professional; Non-Profit
Type: Performing; Touring; Educational
Purpose: Chance to Dance Program: to present original choreography to make dance accessible to a large audience
Management: Randy Duncan, Artistic Director; Harriet Ross, Associate Artistic Director; Gary Lindsey, Artist Services; Mary F. Webster, Managing Director; Betsy Whipple, Director of Development
Officers: Kenneth R. Kimbrough, Chairman; Michael S. Kesner, Executive Vice President; Cheryl M. McWorter, Vice President Artistic; Carol Slater, Vice President Special Events
Paid Staff: 4   **Volunteer Staff:** 5
Paid Artists: 14
Utilizes: Guest Artists; Guest Choreographers
Budget: $500,000 - $1,000,000
Income Sources: Private Foundations/Grants/Endowments; Business/Corporate Donations; Box Office; Government Grants; Individual Donations
Season: 52 Weeks
Affiliations: NEA; Chicago Dance Coalition; Arts Midwest; Illinois Arts Alliance
Performance Facilities: Civic Opera House

KAST AND COMPANY
5320 South University Avenue, Chicago, IL 60615
(312) 643-8916
Founded: 1988
Arts Area: Modern; Liturgical
Status: Professional; Non-Profit
Type: Performing
Purpose: To present innovative modern dance as well as dance for worship, schools and community centers
Management: Maggie Kast, Director
Officers: James Jana, President; Jane Siarny, Maggie Kast, Directors
Volunteer Staff: 1
Paid Artists: 3   **Non-Paid Artists:** 1
Budget: $1,000 - $50,000
Income Sources: Box Office; Government Grants; Individual Donations
Annual Attendance: 3,000
Affiliations: Chicago Dance Coalition; Sacred Dance Guild; Phoenix Power and Light

LE BALLET PETIT GUILD
4630 North Francisco, Chicago, IL 60625-3729
(312) 463-3385
Founded: 1962

Arts Area: Mime; Ballet; Jazz; Ethnic; Tap
Status: Non-Professional; Non-Profit
Type: Performing; Resident; Educational
Purpose: To produce traditional and contemporary ballet performance for student participation, and establish and maintain a training facility and a program of scholarship funding
Management: Ida Velez, Director/Choreographer; Delores Schleser, Business Manager
Officers: Margie Dunne, President; Nancy Mason, Secretary; Faith Wilk, Treasurer
Paid Staff: 11 **Volunteer Staff:** 25
Non-Paid Artists: 210
Utilizes: Special Technical Talent; Guest Artists; Guest Choreographers
Budget: $1,000 - $50,000
Income Sources: Box Office; Government Grants; Individual Donations
Season: September - July **Annual Attendance:** 2,000
Performance Facilities: St. Scholastica Theater

MORDINE AND COMPANY DANCE THEATRE
4730 North Sheridan Road, Chicago, IL 60640
(312) 271-7804
FAX: (312) 271-7046
Founded: 1968
Arts Area: Modern
Status: Professional; Non-Profit
Type: Performing; Resident; Educational
Purpose: To perform the works of artistic director, Shirley Mordine; to perform experimental, expansive, architectural and humorous works
Management: Shirley Mordine, Artistic Director; Michael McStraw, General Manager; Elizabeth Hutar, Development Director
Officers: Stephen Marcus, Chairman; Joan Erdman, Vice President; Doe Thornburg, Secretary
Paid Staff: 3
Paid Artists: 7
Utilizes: Special Technical Talent; Guest Artists; Guest Choreographers; Visual Designers; Composers
Budget: $100,000 - $500,000
Income Sources: Private Foundations/Grants/Endowments; Business/Corporate Donations; Box Office; Government Grants; Teaching
Season: October - June **Annual Attendance:** 5,000
Affiliations: APAP; Dance USA; Chicago Dance Coalition
Performance Facilities: The Dance Center of Columbia College

MUNTU DANCE THEATRE
6800 South Wentworth, Suite 3E96, Chicago, IL 60621
(312) 602-1135
FAX: (312) 962-9116
Arts Area: Ethnic
Status: Professional; Non-Profit
Type: Performing; Touring; Resident
Purpose: To perform traditional and contemporary African and African-American dance, music and folklore
Management: Amaniyea Payne, Artistic Director; Mignon McPherson, Administrative Assistant; David K. Smith, Manager of Marketing/Production; Patricia Johnson, Development Officer; Atiba Walker, Assistant Artistic Director
Officers: Joan Gray, President
Budget: $100,000 - $500,000
Income Sources: Private Foundations/Grants/Endowments; Business/Corporate Donations; Box Office; Government Grants; Individual Donations
Performance Facilities: Katherine Dunham Theater, Kennedy-King College

NAJWA DANCE CORPS
1900 West Van Buren, Room 0505, Chicago, IL 60612
(312) 664-7943; (312) 921-4722
Founded: 1975
Arts Area: Modern; Jazz; Ethnic
Status: Professional; Non-Profit
Type: Performing; Touring; Educational
Purpose: The preservation of dance styles and techniques; to dance and entertain with dances of different areas in a historical context
Management: Celeste Harrell, Business Manager; Najwa I, Artistic Director
Officers: Annice Lillard, Jack Ward, Presidents; Sheila Wilkens, Treasurer
Paid Staff: 6
Paid Artists: 15
Utilizes: Special Technical Talent; Guest Artists; Guest Choreographers
Budget: $100,000 - $500,000

Income Sources: Private Foundations/Grants/Endowments; Business/Corporate Donations; Box Office; Government Grants; Individual Donations
Season: 52 Weeks   **Annual Attendance:** 30,000
Affiliations: Chicago Dance Art Coalition; African-American Arts Alliance

INSTRUMENTAL MUSIC

BLACK MUSIC REPERTORY ENSEMBLE
Center for Black Music Research, Columbia College, 600 South Michigan, Chicago, IL 60605-1996
(312) 663-1600, ext. 559
FAX: (213) 663-9019
Founded: 1988
Arts Area: Chamber; Ensemble; Ethnic
Status: Professional; Non-Profit
Type: Performing; Touring
Purpose: To perfrom works by black composers from 1700 to present
Management: Morris A. Phipps, Coordinator of Programs and Services Center for Black Music Research
Officers: Dominique-Rene de Lerma, Director - Center for Black Music Reasearch; Samuel A. Floyd Jr., Artistic Director
Paid Artists: 15
Budget: $100,000 - $500,000
Income Sources: Private Foundations/Grants/Endowments; Business/Corporate Donations; Box Office; Government Grants; Individual Donations
Affiliations: Columbia College, Chicago

CHICAGO BAR ASSOCIATION SYMPHONY ORCHESTRA
321 South Plymouth Court, Chicago, IL 60604
(312) 554-2000
Founded: 1986
Arts Area: Symphony; Orchestra; Chamber
Status: Non-Professional; Non-Profit
Type: Performing; Touring
Purpose: To provide quality orchestral performance experience for legal professionals in the Chicago area
Management: David Katz, Music Director; Julia Nowicki, Founder; Susan Chernoff, Founder; Todd Wiener, Chairman
Paid Staff: 1   **Volunteer Staff:** 3
Paid Artists: 1   **Non-Paid Artists:** 40
Utilizes: Guest Conductors; Guest Artists
Budget: $1,000 - $50,000
Income Sources: Private Foundations/Grants/Endowments; Business/Corporate Donations; Box Office; Individual Donations
Season: September - June   **Annual Attendance:** 1,000
Affiliations: ASOL; Illinois Council of Orchestras

CHICAGO BRASS QUINTET
PO Box 31917, Chicago, IL 60631-0917
(312) 696-1449; (800) 582-7913
FAX: (312) 696-1937
Founded: 1962
Arts Area: Chamber; Ensemble; Instrumental Group
Status: Professional; Non-Profit
Type: Performing; Touring; Resident; Educational; Sponsoring
Purpose: To promote brass chamber music through performance, recordings, broadcasts, educational workshops and commissioning
Management: Diane Dillavou, Artist Manager
Officers: James Mattern, President; Ross Beacraft, Treasurer; Diane Dillavou, Secretary
Paid Staff: 1
Paid Artists: 5
Utilizes: Guest Artists
Budget: $100,000 - $500,000
Income Sources: Private Foundations/Grants/Endowments; Business/Corporate Donations; Box Office; Government Grants; Individual Donations
Season: 52 Weeks

THE CHICAGO CHAMBER ORCHESTRA
410 South Michigan Avenue, Suite 631, Chicago, IL 60605
(312) 922-5570
FAX: (312) 922-5508
Founded: 1952
Arts Area: Orchestra; Chamber

Status: Professional; Non-Profit
Type: Performing
Purpose: To provide regularly scheduled, admission-free performances of great music on a year-round basis and to showcase each distinctive programming through national and international touring
Management: Dr. Dieter Kober, Music Director; Magdalene Lorenz, General Manager; Dorothy Marchi, Secretary
Officers: Frank Williams, President; William Mitchel, Vice President; Sharon Peterson, Treasurer
Paid Staff: 4 **Volunteer Staff:** 15
Paid Artists: 140
Utilizes: Guest Artists
Budget: $100,000 - $500,000
Income Sources: Private Foundations/Grants/Endowments; Business/Corporate Donations; Government Grants; Individual Donations
Season: September - June **Annual Attendance:** 20,000
Affiliations: ASOL; Illinois Council of Orchestras; CMA

CHICAGO PHILHARMONIA
5528 South Hyde Park Boulevard, Suite 1002, Chicago, IL 60637
(312) 493-1915
FAX: (312) 324-6650
Founded: 1985
Arts Area: Symphony; Chamber; Ensemble
Status: Professional; Non-Profit
Type: Performing
Purpose: To present symphonic works for the enjoyment of Chicago area residents
Management: George W. Flynn, Music Administrator; Farobag Homi Cooper, Music Director/Conductor; John Albert, Director of Advertising
Volunteer Staff: 35
Paid Artists: 65
Utilizes: Guest Artists
Budget: $100,000 - $500,000
Income Sources: Private Foundations/Grants/Endowments; Business/Corporate Donations; Box Office; Individual Donations
Season: October - June **Annual Attendance:** 10,000
Performance Facilities: Mandel Hall

CHICAGO STRING ENSEMBLE
3524 West Belmont Avenue, Chicago, IL 60618
(312) 332-0567
FAX: (708) 869-3925
Founded: 1977
Arts Area: Orchestra; Chamber; Ensemble; Instrumental Group
Status: Professional; Non-Profit
Type: Performing; Touring; Educational
Purpose: To develop string orchestra repertoire to its highest level; to bring to Chicago this body of music literature spanning three centuries
Management: Alan Heatherington, Music Director; Mary Jo Deysach, General Manager
Officers: Carl LaMell, President; Art Vallette, James Vogler, Vice Presidents
Utilizes: Guest Artists
Budget: $100,000 - $500,000
Income Sources: Private Foundations/Grants/Endowments; Business/Corporate Donations; Box Office; Government Grants; Individual Donations
Season: September - May
Affiliations: Chicago Music Alliance; ASOL; Illinois Council of Orchestras; Chicago Chamber Consortium
Performance Facilities: Saint Paul's Church; Unitarian Church, Evanston; Elmhurst College

CHICAGO SYMPHONY ORCHESTRA
220 South Michigan Avenue, Chicago, IL 60604
(312) 435-8122
FAX: (312) 786-1207
Founded: 1890
Arts Area: Symphony; Orchestra
Status: Non-Profit
Type: Performing
Management: Henry Fogel, Executive Director; Vanessa Moss, Manager; Martha Gilmer, Artistic Administrator; Joyce Idema, Director of Marketing and Public Relations; Tom Hallett, Director of Finance
Officers: Thomas Eyerman, Vice President for Development
Utilizes: Guest Conductors; Guest Artists

Budget: Over 10,000,000
Income Sources: Private Foundations/Grants/Endowments; Business/Corporate Donations; Box Office; Government Grants; Individual Donations
Season: 52 Weeks
Affiliations: ASOL

CHICAGO YOUTH SYMPHONY
410 South Michigan Avenue, Suite 922, Chicago, IL 60605
(312) 939-2207
Founded: 1946
Arts Area: Symphony; Orchestra; Chamber; Ensemble
Status: Non-Profit
Type: Performing; Touring; Sponsoring
Purpose: To provide the finest quality orchestral training and performance opportunities for Midwestern high school students in a central Chicago location
Management: Jeannette Kreston, Executive Director; Michael Morgan, Music Director/Conductor
Paid Staff: 5 **Volunteer Staff:** 15
Non-Paid Artists: 115
Utilizes: Guest Conductors; Guest Artists; Guest Directors
Budget: $100,000 - $500,000
Income Sources: Private Foundations/Grants/Endowments; Business/Corporate Donations; Box Office; Government Grants; Individual Donations; Tuition
Season: September - May **Annual Attendance:** 13,000
Affiliations: ASOL (Youth Symphony Division); Chicago Music Alliance
Performance Facilities: Orchestra Hall

CIVIC ORCHESTRA OF CHICAGO
220 South Michigan Avenue, Chicago, IL 60604
(312) 435-8159
Founded: 1919
Arts Area: Symphony; Orchestra; Chamber; Ensemble
Status: Non-Professional; Non-Profit
Type: Performing; Educational
Purpose: To train musicians to be professional symphony orchestra members within the environment of a first-rate symphony orchestra such as the Chicago Symphony Orchestra
Management: Henry Fogel, Executive Director; Jeffrey Heggem, Manager
Officers: Henry Fogel, Executive Vice President
Paid Staff: 3
Non-Paid Artists: 110
Utilizes: Guest Conductors; Guest Artists
Budget: $500,000 - $1,000,000
Income Sources: Private Foundations/Grants/Endowments; Business/Corporate Donations; Government Grants; Individual Donations
Season: October - May
Annual Attendance: 16,000
Performance Facilities: Orchestra Hall

MUSIC OF THE BAROQUE
343 South Dearborn, Suite 1716, Chicago, IL 60604
(312) 663-1900; (312) 986-3236
FAX: (312) 347-1490
Founded: 1972
Arts Area: Orchestra; Chamber; Ensemble; Chorus
Status: Professional; Non-Profit
Type: Performing; Educational
Purpose: To provide a chorus and orchestra specializing in music of the 16th through 18th centuries
Management: Kathleen Butera, Executive Director; Thomas Wikman, Music Director
Officers: Jay A. Baylin, Chairman
Paid Staff: 9
Paid Artists: 65
Utilizes: Special Technical Talent; Guest Artists
Budget: $1,000,000 - $5,000,000
Income Sources: Private Foundations/Grants/Endowments; Business/Corporate Donations; Box Office; Government Grants; Individual Donations; Merchandise; Recordings
Season: October - June
Annual Attendance: 13,000
Affiliations: ASOL; CA; Chicago Music Alliance

PERFORMING ARTS CHICAGO
410 South Michigan Avenue, #911, Chicago, IL 60605
(312) 663-1628
FAX: (312) 663-1043
> **Founded:** 1960
> **Arts Area:** Chamber
> **Status:** Professional; Non-Profit
> **Type:** Performing; Resident; Educational; Sponsoring
> **Purpose:** To present artists who explore the creative tension between tradition and innovation, to nurture an environment for and bring to performance new works and new performers, and to remain accountable to its community, furthering support for local artists, engagement and education, not only for its direct audience, but for society at large
> **Management:** Susan Lipman, Executive Director; Heidi Feldman, Director of Marketing and Public Relations
> **Officers:** Lewis Duberman, President; James Peponis, First Vice President of Fund-raising; Drucilla Handy Redinger, Second Vice President of Marketing; Averill Leviton, Third Vice President of Special Events; Norma Stone, Secretary; David Ellis, Treasurer
> **Utilizes:** Guest Artists
> **Budget:** $100,000 - $500,000
> **Income Sources:** Private Foundations/Grants/Endowments; Business/Corporate Donations; Box Office; Government Grants; Individual Donations
> **Season:** September - June   **Annual Attendance:** 9,280
> **Performance Facilities:** The Civic Theatre

STREET MINSTRELS JAZZ SOCIETY
4339 South Berkeley, Chicago, IL 60653
(312) 483-2802
> **Founded:** 1986
> **Arts Area:** Ethnic; Instrumental Group
> **Status:** Non-Professional; Non-Profit
> **Type:** Educational; Sponsoring
> **Purpose:** To capture on film and video local Afro-American jazz musicians performing original works
> **Management:** Edward E. Mead, Founder/Business Manager; Sudan Mahmoud, Public Relations/Media Liason; Edward Rebb, Talent Coordinator
> **Volunteer Staff:** 6
> **Utilizes:** Local Unknown Artists
> **Budget:** $1,000 - $50,000
> **Income Sources:** Individual Donations
> **Season:** June - September   **Annual Attendance:** 300
> **Affiliations:** Arts Midwest
> **Performance Facilities:** Twenty-First Century Bookstore

VOCAL MUSIC

CHAMBER OPERA CHICAGO
500 North Orleans, Chicago, IL 60610
(312) 822-0770
> **Founded:** 1982
> **Arts Area:** Grand Opera; Lyric Opera
> **Status:** Professional; Non-Profit
> **Type:** Performing
> **Purpose:** To present quality opera in English; to provide talented young singers with opportunities to sing major roles
> **Management:** Barre Seid, General Director; Carl Ratner, Artistic Director; Lawrence Rapchak, Administrative/Musical Director
> **Officers:** Barre Seid, President/Treasurer; Lawrence Rapchak, Secretary; Carl Ratner, Arlene Dunn, Kenneth Recu, Directors
> **Paid Staff:** 4
> **Paid Artists:** 100
> **Budget:** $100,000 - $500,000
> **Income Sources:** Private Foundations/Grants/Endowments; Business/Corporate Donations; Box Office; Government Grants; Individual Donations
> **Season:** April - May   **Annual Attendance:** 3,500
> **Performance Facilities:** Ruth Page Auditorium

CHICAGO CHILDREN'S CHOIR
1720 East 54th Street, Chicago, IL 60615
(312) 324-8300
FAX: (312) 324-8333
> **Founded:** 1956
> **Arts Area:** Choral; Folk

Status: Semi-Professional
Type: Performing; Touring; Educational
Purpose: To develop and maintain a high-quality choral training and performance program for children and young people from a variety of cultural, religious, racial and ethnic backgrounds
Management: Nancy Carstedt, Executive Director; Martha O. Swisher, Music Director; Mary E. Adams, Business Manager
Paid Staff: 20
Non-Paid Artists: 110
Utilizes: Guest Artists
Budget: $100,000 - $500,000
Income Sources: Private Foundations/Grants/Endowments; Business/Corporate Donations; Box Office; Government Grants; Individual Donations
Season: September - June   **Annual Attendance:** 55,000
Affiliations: CA

CHICAGO OPERA THEATER
20 East Jackson, Chicago, IL 60604
(312) 663-0555
FAX: (312) 986-3999
Founded: 1974
Arts Area: Lyric Opera
Status: Professional; Non-Profit
Type: Performing; Touring; Educational
Purpose: To make outstanding performances of a broad repertory accessible to the broadest possible audience by offering all operas in English, in an intimate environment, with tickets at reasonable prices
Management: Alan Stone, Artistic Director; Jean Perkins, Managing Director; Tom DeWalle, Director of Development; Lex Poppens, Director of Marketing; Michelle Anderson, Director of Operations
Officers: Marilyn Arado, Chairman; Oreste Boscia, President
Paid Staff: 12   **Volunteer Staff:** 150
Paid Artists: 300
Utilizes: Special Technical Talent; Guest Conductors; Guest Artists; Guest Directors
Budget: $1,000,000 - $5,000,000
Income Sources: Private Foundations/Grants/Endowments; Business/Corporate Donations; Box Office; Individual Donations
Season: mid-February - mid-May   **Annual Attendance:** 20,000
Affiliations: OA; Chicago Music Alliance
Performance Facilities: Athenaeum Theatre

CHICAGO SYMPHONY CHORUS
Orchestra Hall, 220 South Michigan Avenue, Chicago, IL 60604
(312) 435-8712
FAX: (312) 435-0914
Founded: 1957
Arts Area: Choral
Status: Professional; Semi-Professional; Non-Profit
Type: Performing; Touring; Educational
Purpose: To perform with a major symphony orchestra
Management: Joseph Fabbioli, Manager; Margaret Hillis, Founder/Director Artistic Leadership
Paid Staff: 3
Paid Artists: 130   **Non-Paid Artists:** 60
Utilizes: Guest Conductors; Guest Artists; Guest Directors
Income Sources: Private Foundations/Grants/Endowments; Business/Corporate Donations; Box Office; Government Grants; Individual Donations
Season: 52 Weeks   **Annual Attendance:** 100,000
Affiliations: ASOL; CA
Performance Facilities: Orchestra Hall; Ravinia Festival

HUNGARIAN OPERA WORKSHOP
1014 South Michigan Avenue, Chicago, IL 60605
(312) 427-6267
FAX: (312) 427-6677
Founded: 1970
Arts Area: Light Opera; Operetta; Ethnic; Folk
Status: Professional; Non-Profit
Type: Performing; Touring; Resident; Educational
Purpose: To preserve and produce works in their original languages of Hungarian, German or French as well as works translated into English; to present productions to audiences at no charge
Management: Maria D'Albert, Instructor; Susan Kincaid, Executive Director of the Conservatory

Utilizes: Guest Artists
Budget: $1,000 - $50,000
Income Sources: Individual Donations
Season: 52 Weeks   **Annual Attendance:** 600
Performance Facilities: Sherwood Conservatory

LINCOLN OPERA
2456 North Surrey Court, Chicago, IL 60614
(312) 549-3249
Founded: 1983
Arts Area: Grand Opera
Status: Professional; Non-Profit
Type: Performing; Touring; Resident; Educational
Purpose: To perform standard repertoire for all ages at affordable prices; resident company
Management: Norma M. Williams, Artistic Director; Charles Rich, President; Dianna Marks, Executive Consultant; Kevin McMahon, Conductor; Heidi Mayer, Music Director
Officers: Charles Rich, President; Mark Richardson, Treasurer; Babs Lieberman, Director of Education; Louise Biga, Secretary
Paid Staff: 1   **Volunteer Staff:** 42
Paid Artists: 95
Utilizes: Special Technical Talent; Guest Directors
Budget: $100,000 - $500,000
Income Sources: Private Foundations/Grants/Endowments; Business/Corporate Donations; Box Office; Government Grants; Individual Donations
Season: 52 Weeks
Annual Attendance: 20,000

LYRIC OPERA CENTER FOR AMERICAN ARTISTS
20 North Wacker Drive, Chicago, IL 60606
(312) 332-2244
Founded: 1974
Arts Area: Grand Opera; Lyric Opera; Light Opera
Status: Professional; Non-Profit
Type: Performing; Educational
Purpose: To provide final stepping stone for young singers to bridge the transition to a professional career
Management: Andrew Foldi, Director
Officers: Brena Freeman, Chairman of Board; Kip Kelley, President of Board; Irene Antoniov, Vice President of Board; Samuel Budwig Jr., Treasurer of Board
Paid Staff: 4
Paid Artists: 15
Utilizes: Special Technical Talent; Guest Directors
Budget: $500,000 - $1,000,000
Income Sources: Private Foundations/Grants/Endowments; Business/Corporate Donations; Government Grants; Individual Donations
Season: February - August
Affiliations: Lyric Opera of Chicago

LYRIC OPERA OF CHICAGO
20 North Wacker Drive, Chicago, IL 60606
(312) 332-2244
FAX: (312) 419-8345
Founded: 1954
Arts Area: Grand Opera
Status: Professional; Non-Profit
Type: Performing; Sponsoring
Purpose: To bring quality opera to the Chicago area
Management: Ardis Krainik, General Manager
Officers: James Cozad, President/Chief Executive Officer
Paid Staff: 46
Utilizes: Special Technical Talent; Guest Conductors; Guest Artists; Guest Directors
Budget: Over 10,000,000
Income Sources: Private Foundations/Grants/Endowments; Business/Corporate Donations; Box Office; Government Grants; Individual Donations
Season: September - January
Annual Attendance: 240,000
Affiliations: Lyric Opera Center for American Artists
Performance Facilities: Civic Opera House

THE OPERA FACTORY
6161 North Hamilton Avenue, Chicago, IL 60659
(312) 761-1334
FAX: (312) 338-8331
Founded: 1979
Arts Area: Light Opera; Ethnic
Status: Professional; Non-Profit
Type: Performing; Touring; Educational
Purpose: To present Spanish zarazuela, Hispanic song and dance, and plays by Spanish and Hispanic authors with music and dance
Management: Blanche Artis Lewis, Executive Director; Donna Sadlicka, Administrative Assistant; Alex Boas, Director of Development; Roberto Sapier, Artistic Director; Gloria Maria Cruz, Director of Publicity
Officers: Peter Pagratis, Chairman; Terrence Healy, Vice President/Treasurer; Donna Sadlicka, Secretary
Paid Staff: 1   **Volunteer Staff:** 12
Utilizes: Guest Conductors; Guest Artists; Guest Directors
Budget: $1,000 - $50,000
Income Sources: Private Foundations/Grants/Endowments; Business/Corporate Donations; Box Office; Government Grants; Individual Donations; Government of Spain
Season: June   **Annual Attendance:** 800
Affiliations: OA; Chicago Music Alliance
Performance Facilities: Angel Guardian; Northeastern Illinois University

THEATRE

AMERICAN BLUES THEATRE
1225 West Belmont, Chicago, IL 60657
(312) 929-1031
Founded: 1985
Arts Area: Professional
Status: Professional; Non-Profit
Type: Performing
Purpose: To develop and produce new plays by and for the people of the Midwest
Management: Jim Leaming, Kate Buddeke, Co-Artistic Directors
Officers: Doug Laux, Board President
Volunteer Staff: 7
Paid Artists: 50   **Non-Paid Artists:** 125
Budget: $1,000 - $50,000
Income Sources: Business/Corporate Donations; Box Office; Government Grants; Individual Donations
Season: 52 Weeks
Affiliations: League of Chicago Theatres

APOLLO THEATER CENTER
2540 North Lincoln Avenue, Chicago, IL 60614
(312) 935-6100
Founded: 1978
Arts Area: Professional
Status: Professional; Commercial
Type: Sponsoring; Presenting
Purpose: Present local productions of Broadway and off-Broadway shows and serve as a transfer house for smaller off-loop theaters
Management: Leavitt Fox Theatricals
Paid Staff: 12
Budget: $100,000 - $500,000
Income Sources: Box Office
Season: 52 Weeks   **Annual Attendance:** 139,000
Affiliations: League of Chicago Theatres

BAILIWICK REPERTORY
1225 West Belmont, Chicago, IL 60657
(312) 883-1090; (312) 327-5252
FAX: (312) 327-1404
Founded: 1982
Arts Area: Theatrical Group
Status: Professional; Non-Profit
Type: Performing; Sponsoring
Purpose: To provide contemporary theater with a classical core; to produce vivid productions of the greatest dramatists of all times, alongside great works from our time; to serve as host or co-producer for other productions or attractions with similar artistic aims; to present festivals of one act plays; to showcase new directors and gay and lesbian plays

Management: David Zak, Executive Director
Paid Staff: 2 **Volunteer Staff:** 125
Paid Artists: 250
Utilizes: Guest Artists; Guest Directors
Budget: $100,000 - $500,000
Income Sources: Private Foundations/Grants/Endowments; Business/Corporate Donations; Box Office; Government Grants; Individual Donations
Season: 52 Weeks **Annual Attendance:** 50,000
Affiliations: League of Chicago Theatres; TCG; Illinois Theater Association
Performance Facilities: Theatre Building

BLACK ENSEMBLE THEATER
4520 North Beacon, Chicago, IL 60640
(312) 769-5516
Founded: 1975
Arts Area: Professional; Theatrical Group
Status: Professional; Non-Profit
Type: Performing; Touring; Resident; Educational
Purpose: To supply continual employment in the theater for the Black artist and adhere to our philosophy of excellence in the art form of professional theater
Management: Jackie Taylor, Artistic Director/Producer; Ben Morgan, Stage Manager
Officers: Andrea Lyon, President; Bill Gillmore, Vice President; Allen Daniels, Secretary; Jackie Taylor, Treasurer
Paid Staff: 9 **Volunteer Staff:** 5
Paid Artists: 9
Utilizes: Guest Artists; Guest Directors
Budget: $100,000 - $500,000
Income Sources: Private Foundations/Grants/Endowments; Business/Corporate Donations; Box Office; Government Grants; Individual Donations
Season: September - August **Annual Attendance:** 20,000
Affiliations: Black Theater Alliance
Performance Facilities: Leo Lerner Theater

BLIND PARROT PRODUCTIONS
1446 West Berteau, Chicago, IL 60613
(312) 549-3991
Founded: 1983
Arts Area: Theatrical Group
Status: Non-Professional
Type: Performing
Purpose: To produce innovative, intelligent, thought-provoking writing for the stage with a focus on scripts which test the limits of theatrical form; to introduce new concepts; to pursue new relationships between artists and the audience
Management: Clare Nolan-Long and David Perkins, Co-Artistic Directors; Jane Molnar, Executive Director
Officers: Fred Hachmeister, President; Sheri Jones, Secretary; Frank Tourangeau, Treasurer
Volunteer Staff: 4
Non-Paid Artists: 20
Utilizes: Guest Artists; Guest Directors
Budget: $1,000 - $50,000
Income Sources: Private Foundations/Grants/Endowments; Business/Corporate Donations; Box Office; Government Grants; Individual Donations
Season: October - June **Annual Attendance:** 3,500
Affiliations: League of Chicago Theatres

BODY POLITIC THEATRE
2261 North Lincoln Avenue, Chicago, IL 60614
(312) 348-7901
Founded: 1966
Arts Area: Professional
Status: Professional; Non-Profit
Type: Performing; Touring; Resident; Educational
Purpose: The Body Politic Theatre, Chicago's oldest off-loop theatre, provides an intimate forum for the best of classic and contemporary dramatic literature through thought-provoking and entertaining productions.
Management: Albert Pertalion, Artistic Director; Kim Patrick Bitz, Administrative Director; Rick Sheingold, Business Director
Officers: Richard Wier, President
Paid Staff: 4 **Volunteer Staff:** 2
Paid Artists: 40 **Non-Paid Artists:** 10
Utilizes: Guest Directors
Budget: $500,000 - $1,000,000

Income Sources: Private Foundations/Grants/Endowments; Business/Corporate Donations; Box Office; Government Grants; Individual Donations
Season: September - June **Annual Attendance:** 20,000
Affiliations: AEA; USA; League of Chicago Theatres; TCG; Producers Association of Chicago Area Theatres

CENTER THEATER AND THE TRAINING CENTER
1346 West Devon, Chicago, IL 60660
(312) 508-0200; (312) 508-5422
    Founded: 1984
    Arts Area: Theatrical Group
    Status: Professional; Non-Profit
    Type: Performing; Touring; Resident; Educational
    Purpose: To educate, inspire and cultivate theatre audiences; professional theater and ongoing training program for actors
    Management: Dan LaMorte, Artistic Director; R.J. Coleman, General Manager
    Officers: Jerry Proffit, Board President; Diane Tuscher-Ancede, Vice President; Michael A. Africk, Treasurer; Alisa Levy, Secretary
    Paid Staff: 26 **Volunteer Staff:** 20
    Paid Artists: 20 **Non-Paid Artists:** 10
    Utilizes: Guest Artists; Guest Directors
    Budget: $500,000 - $1,000,000
    Income Sources: Private Foundations/Grants/Endowments; Business/Corporate Donations; Box Office; Government Grants; Individual Donations; Tuitions
    Season: September - June **Annual Attendance:** 10,000
    Affiliations: TCG; ASSITEJ
    Performance Facilities: Center Theater

CHICAGO ACTORS ENSEMBLE
941 West Lawrence Avenue, 5th Floor, Chicago, IL 60642
(312) 275-4463
    Founded: 1984
    Arts Area: Professional
    Status: Professional; Non-Profit
    Type: Performing; Touring; Resident
    Management: Richard Helweg, Artistic Director
    Officers: Kit Carson, President
    Utilizes: Special Technical Talent; Guest Directors
    Budget: $1,000 - $50,000
    Income Sources: Private Foundations/Grants/Endowments; Business/Corporate Donations; Box Office; Individual Donations
    Season: October - April **Annual Attendance:** 1,000
    Affiliations: League of Chicago Theatres

CHICAGO CITY THEATRE COMPANY
1225 West School Street, Chicago, IL 60657
(312) 880-1002
    Founded: 1974
    Arts Area: Professional
    Status: Professional; Semi-Professional; Non-Profit
    Type: Performing; Touring; Resident; Educational; Sponsoring
    Purpose: Theatre (Chicago City Theatre), dance (Joel Hall Dancers) and training (New School North), which are multiracial, professional, national and international in scope
    Management: Joseph Ehrenberg and Joel Hall, Co-Directors; Florence Martin, Studio Manager
    Officers: Thomas A. Hajjar, President; David S. Mann, Secretary; Albert D. Beedie, Jr., Treasurer
    Paid Staff: 3 **Volunteer Staff:** 30
    Paid Artists: 25
    Utilizes: Special Technical Talent; Guest Artists; Guest Directors
    Budget: $100,000 - $500,000
    Income Sources: Private Foundations/Grants/Endowments; Business/Corporate Donations; Box Office; Government Grants; Individual Donations
    Season: September - June **Annual Attendance:** 25,000
    Affiliations: League of Chicago Theatres

CHICAGO DRAMATISTS WORKSHOP
1105 West Chicago Avenue, Chicago, IL 60657
(312) 633-0630
    Founded: 1979
    Arts Area: Professional; Theatrical Group
    Status: Professional; Non-Profit
    Type: Performing

Purpose: The Chicago Dramatists Workshop is a professional, non-profit theatre, dedicated to the development of promising, Chicago-area playwrights.
Management: Russ Tutterow, Director; Anita-Joyce Barnes, General Manager
Officers: Gene Jones, Vice President; Gary Brichetto, Treasurer
Paid Staff: 2   **Volunteer Staff:** 5
Utilizes: Guest Artists; Guest Directors
Budget: $1,000 - $50,000
Income Sources: Private Foundations/Grants/Endowments; Business/Corporate Donations; Box Office; Government Grants; Individual Donations
Season: September - August   **Annual Attendance:** 5,000
Affiliations: League of Chicago Theatres

THE CHICAGO MEDIEVAL PLAYERS
International House, 1414 East 59th Street, Chicago, IL 60637
(312) 935-0742
Founded: 1985
Arts Area: Professional; Theatrical Group
Status: Professional; Non-Profit
Type: Performing; Touring
Purpose: The production of Medieval and Renaissance theatre
Management: Ann Faulkner, Artistic Director
Officers: Sheila Chapman, President; Robert Schmidt, Frank Underbriuk, Vice Presidents; Peter Christensen, Secretary
Paid Staff: 2   **Volunteer Staff:** 10
Paid Artists: 20
Utilizes: Guest Artists; Guest Directors
Budget: $1,000 - $50,000
Income Sources: Private Foundations/Grants/Endowments; Box Office; Government Grants; Individual Donations
Season: 52 Weeks
Affiliations: AEA; Societe International pour L'etudier du Theatre Medieval

THE CHICAGO THEATRE COMPANY
500 East 67th Street, Chicago, IL 60637
(312) 493-0901
Founded: 1984
Arts Area: Professional
Status: Professional; Non-Profit
Type: Performing; Resident
Purpose: To provide a professional and creative environment in which local artists may develop their talents, broaden the public's theatrical options, improve economic opportunities for minority artists, and enhance the cultural environment of the inner-city neighborhoods
Management: Douglas Alan Mann, Artistic Director
Officers: Stephanie Davenport, President; Hilton Clark, Vice President; Delia Coy, Treasurer; Marcie Creque, Secretary
Paid Staff: 1
Utilizes: Guest Artists; Guest Directors
Budget: $100,000 - $500,000
Income Sources: Private Foundations/Grants/Endowments; Business/Corporate Donations; Box Office; Government Grants; Individual Donations
Season: September - June
Affiliations: League of Chicago Theatres
Performance Facilities: Parkway Playhouse

CHILD'S PLAY TOURING THEATRE
2650 West Belden, Chicago, IL 60647
(312) 235-8911
FAX: (312) 235-5478
Founded: 1978
Arts Area: Professional; Theatrical Group
Status: Professional; Non-Profit
Type: Performing; Touring; Educational
Purpose: Child's Play Touring Theatre performs only original literature written by children. Its mission is to share, encourage and validate the creative writing of children.
Management: Victor Podagrosi, Artistic Director; June Podagrosi, Executive Director; Valerie Hogan, General Manager
Officers: Joan Mazzonelli, President; June Podagrosi, Mary Bryant, Vice Presidents; Susan Darby, Treasurer; Marie Donovan, Secretary
Paid Staff: 14
Paid Artists: 10
Budget: $50,000 - $100,000

Income Sources: Private Foundations/Grants/Endowments; Business/Corporate Donations; Government Grants; Individual Donations; Touring Fees
Season: September - July   **Annual Attendance:** 175,000

CITY LIT THEATER COMPANY
4753 North Broadway, #618, Chicago, IL 60640
(312) 271-1100
Founded: 1979
Arts Area: Professional
Status: Professional; Non-Profit
Type: Performing; Touring; Resident; Educational
Purpose: City Lit Theater Company's purpose is to adapt literary material for the stage.
Management: Arnold Aprill, Artistic Director; Charles Twichell, General Manager
Officers: Paul Pribbenow, President
Paid Staff: 4
Paid Artists: 20
Budget: $100,000 - $500,000
Income Sources: Private Foundations/Grants/Endowments; Business/Corporate Donations; Box Office; Government Grants; Individual Donations
Season: 52 Weeks   **Annual Attendance:** 38,000
Affiliations: League of Chicago Theatres

CLASSICS ON STAGE! LTD
PO Box 25365, Chicago, IL 60625
(312) 989-0532
Founded: 1982
Arts Area: Professional; Musical; Theatrical Group
Status: Professional; Commercial
Type: Performing; Resident; Educational
Purpose: To provide quality professional live theatre experiences for young audiences in order to develop and sustain live audiences for the future of legitimate theatre for all audiences
Management: Robert D. Boburka, Managing Director; Michele L. Vacca, Artistic Director
Officers: Robert D. Boburka, President and Treasurer; Michele L. Vacca, Vice President and Secretary
Paid Staff: 8
Paid Artists: 14
Utilizes: Special Technical Talent; Guest Artists
Budget: $50,000 - $100,000
Income Sources: Box Office
Season: October - June
Annual Attendance: 50,000
Affiliations: AEA; AATY; League of Chicago Theatres

COURT THEATRE
5535 South Ellis Avenue, Chicago, IL 60637
(312) 702-7005
FAX: (312) 702-5814
Founded: 1954
Arts Area: Professional
Status: Professional; Non-Profit
Type: Performing; Educational
Purpose: To make high quality productions of the world's classic plays available to the people of Chicago and, due to the theatre's association with the University of Chicago, to educate its adult and high school audiences regarding each play
Management: Nicholas Rudall, Executive Director; Sandra Karuschak, Managing Director
Officers: William O'Connor, Chair; Robert McDermott, Vice Chair
Paid Staff: 24
Paid Artists: 70
Utilizes: Special Technical Talent; Guest Artists; Guest Directors
Budget: $1,000,000 - $5,000,000
Income Sources: Private Foundations/Grants/Endowments; Business/Corporate Donations; Box Office; Government Grants; Individual Donations
Season: September - May   **Annual Attendance:** 45,000
Affiliations: AEA; League of Chicago Theatres; TCG; Producers Association of Chicago Area Theatres
Performance Facilities: Court Theatre

DREISKE PERFORMANCE COMPANY
1517 West Fullerton Avenue, Chicago, IL 60614
(312) 281-9075
Founded: 1975

Arts Area: Professional; Theatrical Group
Status: Professional; Non-Profit
Type: Performing; Touring; Resident; Educational
Purpose: Professional touring ensemble, many of whose productions were developed in historic and on-location projects; "The Book of Lear" in the Sahara Desert, "Macondo" in Columbia, South America; currently developing new theater works for performance for international TV and tours
Management: Nicole Dreiske, Artistic Director; Milos Stehlik, Managing Director; Catherine Berkenstein, Literary Manager; John Dreiske, General Manager
Officers: David Edelberg, Chair; Emilye Hunterfields, Secretary
Paid Staff: 18
Paid Artists: 12
Utilizes: Special Technical Talent; Guest Directors
Budget: $500,000 - $1,000,000
Income Sources: Private Foundations/Grants/Endowments; Business/Corporate Donations; Box Office; Government Grants; Individual Donations
Season: February - December
Affiliations: ATHE; ITI; League of Chicago Theatres
Performance Facilities: International Performance Studio

ENSEMBLE ESPANOL
5500 North Saint Louis Avenue, Chicago, IL 60625
(312) 583-4050
Founded: 1976
Arts Area: Professional; Musical; Community; Folk
Status: Professional; Non-Profit
Type: Performing; Touring; Resident; Educational; Sponsoring
Purpose: To share the rich tradition of dance, music, literature, and culture of Spain with all the communities of the United States and to be a center which encourages new artistic creativity
Management: Libby Komaiko Fleming, Director; Jorge D. Perez, Administrative Assistant; Jeanette Lukaszow, Executive Secretary; Flor Dumblao, Accountant
Officers: Dr. Robert Komaiko, President; Angelina Pedroso, Vice President; Janie S. Petersen, Secretary; Edward Garcia, Treasurer
Paid Staff: 4   **Volunteer Staff:** 5
Paid Artists: 20
Utilizes: Guest Artists; Guest Directors
Budget: $100,000 - $500,000
Income Sources: Private Foundations/Grants/Endowments; Business/Corporate Donations; Box Office; Government Grants; Individual Donations
Season: September - August
Annual Attendance: 10,000
Performance Facilities: Northeastern Illinois University, Chicago

ETA CREATIVE ARTS FOUNDATION
7558 So. South Chicago Avenue, Chicago, IL 60619
(312) 752-3955
FAX: (312) 752-8727
Founded: 1971
Arts Area: Professional
Status: Professional; Non-Profit
Type: Performing; Touring; Resident; Educational
Purpose: ETA provides training in the performing and technical aspects of the arts, encouraging the development and employment primarily of Black artists. ETA also works to encourage the development and propagation of the works of Black writers through its productions of original works.
Management: Abena Joan P. Brown, President/Producer; Runako Jahi, Artistic Director; Jerome A. Adams, Director of Development; Teresa A. White, Business Manager; Kenneth Simmons, Building Manager; Darryl Goodman, Technical Director
Officers: Milton Davis, Chairman of the Board; Abena Joan Brown, President; Velma Wilson, Secretary/Treasurer; Wiley Moore, Finance
Paid Staff: 14   **Volunteer Staff:** 450
Paid Artists: 150
Utilizes: Guest Artists; Guest Directors
Budget: $500,000 - $1,000,000
Income Sources: Private Foundations/Grants/Endowments; Business/Corporate Donations; Box Office; Government Grants; Individual Donations
Season: September - July
Annual Attendance: 63,000
Affiliations: Afro-American Arts Alliance; Department of Cultural Affairs; League of Chicago Theatres
Performance Facilities: ETA Square

FREE STREET THEATER
441 West North Avenue, Chicago, IL 60610
(312) 642-1234
Founded: 1969
Arts Area: Professional; Theatrical Group
Status: Professional; Non-Profit
Type: Performing; Touring
Management: David Stein, Artistic Director; Patricia Patton, Marketing Director; Julie Mittman-Glazer, Managing Director
Paid Staff: 3
Paid Artists: 50
Budget: $100,000 - $500,000
Income Sources: Private Foundations/Grants/Endowments; Business/Corporate Donations; Box Office; Government Grants; Individual Donations
Season: 52 Weeks   **Annual Attendance:** 50,000
Affiliations: TCG; Illinois Arts Alliance

GOODMAN THEATRE
200 South Columbus Drive, Chicago, IL 60603
(312) 443-3811
FAX: (312) 263-6004
Founded: 1925
Arts Area: Professional; Musical
Status: Professional; Non-Profit
Type: Performing; Educational; Sponsoring
Purpose: To provide the highest quality professional theatre, both classical and contemporary
Management: Roche Schulfer, Producing Director; Robert Falls, Artistic Director
Paid Staff: 70
Non-Paid Artists: 11
Utilizes: Special Technical Talent; Guest Artists; Guest Directors
Budget: $1,000,000 - $5,000,000
Income Sources: Private Foundations/Grants/Endowments; Business/Corporate Donations; Box Office; Government Grants; Individual Donations
Season: September - July
Affiliations: TCG

IMAGINATION THEATER
1801 West Bryon, Studio 2S, Chicago, IL 60613
(312) 929-4100
Founded: 1966
Arts Area: Professional
Status: Professional; Non-Profit
Type: Performing; Touring; Educational
Purpose: Committed to the value of creative drama as a tool for learning through two basic programs: participatory theater for children, the elderly, and the disabled; and Child Sexual Abuse Prevention Program, a comprehensive program for teachers, parents and students
Management: Warren W. Baumgart Jr., Artistic Director
Paid Staff: 6
Paid Artists: 12
Budget: $100,000 - $500,000
Income Sources: Private Foundations/Grants/Endowments; Business/Corporate Donations; Box Office; Government Grants; Individual Donations
Season: 52 Weeks   **Annual Attendance:** 225,000

LIFELINE THEATRE
6912 North Glenwood, Chicago, IL 60660
(312) 761-4477
Founded: 1982
Arts Area: Theatre Group
Status: Professional; Non-Profit
Type: Performing
Purpose: We at Lifeline believe it is vital to offer an art form that reaffirms the underlying humanity and sense of connection that is essential to all our lives.
Management: Suzanne Plunkett, Managing Director
Officers: Randy Snyder, President; Christina Calvit, Treasurer; Meryl Friedman, Secretary
Paid Staff: 5   **Volunteer Staff:** 10
Paid Artists: 12
Budget: $50,000 - $100,000

Income Sources: Private Foundations/Grants/Endowments; Business/Corporate Donations; Box Office; Government Grants; Individual Donations
Season: September - June **Annual Attendance:** 10,000
Affiliations: League of Chicago Theatres
Performance Facilities: Lifeline Theatre

MAYFAIR THEATRE/"SHEAR MADNESS"
636 South Michigan Avenue, Chicago, IL 60605
(312) 786-9317
Founded: 1982
Arts Area: Theatrical Group
Status: Professional; Commercial
Type: Performing
Purpose: Mayfair Theatre presents "Shear Madness," the comedy whodunit that lets the audience play armchair detective. "Shear Madness" is the longest running play in the history of Chicago theatre.
Management: Deborah Gordon, Company Manager; Marilyn Abrams and Bruce Jordan, Producers
Paid Staff: 10
Paid Artists: 9
Utilizes: Guest Artists
Budget: $500,000 - $1,000,000
Income Sources: Box Office
Season: 52 Weeks **Annual Attendance:** 100,000
Affiliations: League of Chicago Theatres
Performance Facilities: Mayfair Theatre

NEW TUNERS THEATRE
c/o Performance Community, 1225 West Belmont, Chicago, IL 60657
(312) 929-7367
FAX: (312) 327-1404
Arts Area: Professional; Musical
Status: Professional; Non-Profit
Type: Performing; Resident
Purpose: To give new musicals exposure; to support up-and-coming artists of the Chicago area
Management: Ruth Higgins, Joan Mazzonelli, Co-Producers; Alan Chambers, Casting/Drama Director
Officers: Howard Walker, Chairman of the Board
Paid Staff: 10 **Volunteer Staff:** 35
Budget: $500,000 - $1,000,000
Income Sources: Private Foundations/Grants/Endowments; Business/Corporate Donations; Box Office; Government Grants; Individual Donations
Season: 52 Weeks
Affiliations: League of Chicago Theatres; TCG; National Alliance of Theatre Producers
Performance Facilities: New Tuners Theatre Building

ORGANIC THEATER COMPANY
3319 North Clark Street, Chicago, IL 60657
(312) 327-5588
FAX: (312) 327-8947
Founded: 1969
Arts Area: Professional
Status: Professional; Non-Professional; Non-Profit
Type: Performing; Educational
Purpose: To develop and produce new works of theatre and to nurture the artists involved in that process; interested in adventurous, challanging scripts that truly explore the theatrical medium and its possibilities
Management: Richard Fire, Producing Artistic Director; Jeff Neal, General Manager; Sarah Tucker, Literary Manager/Intern Coordinator
Officers: Kathleen B. Gillig, President; Barry Gomberg, Vice President/Secretary; Carl LaMell, Treasurer
Paid Staff: 10 **Volunteer Staff:** 12
Utilizes: Guest Artists; Guest Directors
Budget: $500,000 - $1,000,000
Income Sources: Private Foundations/Grants/Endowments; Business/Corporate Donations; Box Office; Government Grants; Individual Donations
Season: 52 Weeks **Annual Attendance:** 40,000
Affiliations: League of Chicago Theatres; TCG

PEGASUS PLAYERS
Truman College, 1145 West Wilson, Chicago, IL 60640
(312) 878-9761
Founded: 1979

Arts Area: Theatrical Group
Status: Professional; Non-Profit
Type: Performing
Purpose: To provide professional, top-quality theater to the people of Chicago, especially the Uptown Area, at affordable prices and to serve the community with outreach, touring, and educational programs
Management: Arlene Crewdson, Artistic Director; Alan Salzenstein, Managing Director
Paid Staff: 5   **Volunteer Staff:** 5
Paid Artists: 150
Utilizes: Special Technical Talent; Guest Artists; Guest Directors
Budget: $500,000 - $1,000,000
Income Sources: Private Foundations/Grants/Endowments; Business/Corporate Donations; Box Office; Government Grants; Individual Donations
Season: September - August   **Annual Attendance:** 11,000
Affiliations: League of Chicago Theatres
Performance Facilities: O'Rourke Center

PLAYWRIGHTS' CENTER
1222 West Wilson, Chicago, IL 60640
(312) 334-9981
    Founded: 1958
    Arts Area: THEATRE GROUP
    Status: Semi-Professional; Non-Profit
    Type: Educational
    Purpose: To offer a place where a playwright may have a workshop reading and critique of his/her play, followed by a staged reading and a possible production
    Management: James McDowell, Artistic Director; B.L. Robbins, Executive Director
    Budget: $1,000 - $50,000
    Income Sources: Private Foundations/Grants/Endowments; Business/Corporate Donations; Government Grants; Individual Donations
    Performance Facilities: Playwrights' Center

RAVEN THEATRE COMPANY
6931 North Clark Street, Chicago, IL 60626
(312) 338-2177
    Founded: 1983
    Arts Area: Professional; Theatrical Group
    Status: Professional; Non-Profit
    Type: Performing; Resident
    Purpose: To provide professional theatre affordable and accessible to the broadest cross-section of the people of Chicagoland and to provide the opportunity for local theatre artists to develop a showcase for their talents
    Management: Michael Menendian, Executive/Artistic Director; John Munson, Technical Director; Joni Gatz, Production Manager
    Officers: John Munson, President; Barbara King, Vice President; Joni Gatz, Secretary; Ed Bray, Treasurer
    Volunteer Staff: 4
    Paid Artists: 30   **Non-Paid Artists:** 30
    Utilizes: Special Technical Talent; Guest Artists; Guest Directors
    Budget: $50,000 - $100,000
    Income Sources: Private Foundations/Grants/Endowments; Business/Corporate Donations; Box Office; Government Grants; Individual Donations
    Season: 52 Weeks   **Annual Attendance:** 6,000
    Affiliations: League of Chicago Theatres

REMAINS THEATRE
1800 North Clybourn Avenue, Chicago, IL 60614
(312) 335-9595; (312) 335-9800
FAX: (312) 335-0626
    Founded: 1979
    Arts Area: Professional
    Status: Professional; Non-Profit
    Type: Performing; Touring; Educational
    Purpose: The purpose of Remains Theatre is to establish and maintain a theatre company dedicated to presenting work focused in three areas: 1) ensemble-developed original works; 2) provocative contemporary plays; and 3) lesser-known works by eminent writers.
    Management: Larry Sloan, Artistic Director; R.P. Sekon, Producing Director; Janis Post, General Manager
    Officers: Valerie Hoffman, President; David Harvey, Vice President; Elizabeth Hubbard, Secretary
    Paid Staff: 9
    Paid Artists: 20
    Utilizes: Special Technical Talent; Guest Artists; Guest Directors
    Budget: $500,000 - $1,000,000

Income Sources: Private Foundations/Grants/Endowments; Business/Corporate Donations; Box Office; Government Grants; Individual Donations
Season: September - July   **Annual Attendance:** 25,000
Affiliations: TCG; League of Chicago Theatres
Performance Facilities: Remains Theatre

SAINT SEBASTIAN PLAYERS
1641 West Diversey, Chicago, IL 60614
(312) 404-7922
FAX: (312) 728-0496
Founded: 1982
Arts Area: Musical; Community; Theatrical Group
Status: Non-Profit
Type: Performing
Purpose: To enrich the life of the parish community of Saint Bonaventure, as well as that of our surrounding neighborhood
Officers: Chris Andrews, President; Jill Chukerman, Vice President/Secretary; Jim Masini, Treasurer
Volunteer Staff: 10
Non-Paid Artists: 10
Utilizes: Special Technical Talent
Budget: $1,000 - $50,000
Income Sources: Box Office; Individual Donations
Season: May - November   **Annual Attendance:** 750
Affiliations: League of Chicago Theatres
Performance Facilities: Saint Bonaventure Hall

THE SECOND CITY
1616 North Wells, Chicago, IL 60614
(312) 337-3992
FAX: (312) 664-9837
Founded: 1959
Arts Area: Professional
Status: Professional; Commercial
Type: Performing; Touring; Resident; Educational
Purpose: Satirical revue
Management: Andrew Alexander, Executive Producer; Kelly Leonard, Associate Producer
Paid Staff: 43
Paid Artists: 30
Income Sources: Box Office
Season: 52 Weeks
Performance Facilities: Second City; Second City, Etc.

SHAKESPEARE REPERTORY
2140 Lincoln Park West, Suite 1001, Chicago, IL 60614
(312) 281-2101
FAX: (312) 642-8817
Arts Area: Professional; Theatrical Group
Status: Professional; Non-Profit
Type: Performing; Touring; Resident; Educational; Sponsoring
Purpose: To bring accessible Shakespearean productions to Chicago audiences
Management: Barbara Gaines, Artistic Director; Criss Henderson, Producing Director
Officers: Katherine Updike, President of the Board; Sheila Penrose, Executive Vice President of the Board
Budget: $500,000 - $1,000,000
Income Sources: Private Foundations/Grants/Endowments; Business/Corporate Donations; Box Office; Government Grants; Individual Donations
Performance Facilities: Ruth Page Theatre

SHATTERED GLOBE THEATER
2856 North Halsted, Chicago, IL 60657
(312) 404-1237
Founded: 1990
Arts Area: Theatrical Group
Status: Semi-Professional; Commercial
Type: Performing; Resident; Educational
Purpose: The foundation of the Shattered Globe is a core of actors, directors, playwrights, designers and teachers working together as the result of having received similar training in the Sanford Meisner technique.
Management: Brian Pudil, General Manager; Roger Smart, Artistic Director; Joe Forbrich, Associate Director
Officers: Brian Pudil, President; Joe Forbrich, Vice President; Leigh Horsley, Secretary; Linda Reiter, Treasurer
Volunteer Staff: 3

Non-Paid Artists: 15
Utilizes: Special Technical Talent; Guest Artists; Guest Directors; Performance Artists
Budget: $1,000 - $50,000
Income Sources: Box Office; Individual Donations
Season: September - June   **Annual Attendance:** 6,000
Affiliations: League of Chicago Theatres
Performance Facilities: Chicago Actors Project

STAGE LEFT THEATRE
3244 North Clark Street, Chicago, IL 60657
(312) 883-8830
Founded: 1982
Arts Area: Professional; Theatrical Group
Status: Professional; Non-Profit
Type: Performing; Touring; Educational
Purpose: To produce plays that raise the level of debate on political and social issues
Management: Mike Troccoli, Sandra Jean Verthein, Co-Artistic Directors; Drew Martin, Managing Director
Officers: Jay Tarshis, Chairman of the Board; Jeff Cory, Vice Chairman; Sandra Jean Verthein, Secretary; Drew Martin, Treasurer
Volunteer Staff: 10
Paid Artists: 46   **Non-Paid Artists:** 25
Utilizes: Guest Artists; Guest Directors
Budget: $50,000 - $100,000
Income Sources: Private Foundations/Grants/Endowments; Business/Corporate Donations; Box Office; Government Grants; Individual Donations
Season: 52 Weeks
Affiliations: League of Chicago Theatres

STEPPENWOLF THEATRE COMPANY
1650 North Halstead, Chicago, IL 60614
(312) 335-1888
FAX: (312) 335-0440
Founded: 1976
Arts Area: Professional
Status: Professional; Non-Profit
Type: Performing; Resident; Educational
Purpose: The Steppenwolf Theatre Company is comprised of twenty-three actors dedicated to the ensemble approach of dramatic art.
Management: Randall Arney, Artistic Director; Stephen Eich, Managing Director
Paid Staff: 20
Paid Artists: 23
Utilizes: Special Technical Talent; Guest Artists; Guest Directors
Budget: $1,000,000 - $5,000,000
Income Sources: Private Foundations/Grants/Endowments; Business/Corporate Donations; Box Office; Government Grants; Individual Donations
Season: September - July   **Annual Attendance:** 60,000
Affiliations: TCG; AEA; Producers Association of Chicago Theatres
Performance Facilities: Steppenwolf Theater

THEATRE FIRST
6656 Sioux Avenue, Chicago, IL 60646
(312) 792-2226
Founded: 1952
Arts Area: Theatrical Group
Status: Non-Professional
Type: Performing
Management: Joanne Notz, Executive Producer; William Mages, Business Manager
Officers: Edwarc Cavaliere, Chairman of the Board; Dale Marach, Comptroller; Jeaniane Benton, Secretary
Volunteer Staff: 12
Utilizes: Guest Conductors
Budget: $1,000 - $50,000
Income Sources: Private Foundations/Grants/Endowments; Business/Corporate Donations; Box Office; Government Grants; Individual Donations
Season: September - April
Annual Attendance: 10,000
Affiliations: League of Chicago Theatres
Performance Facilities: Athenaeum Theatre

THEATRE II COMPANY
3700 West 103rd Street, Chicago, IL 60655
(312) 779-3300, ext. 475
Founded: 1978
Arts Area: Theatrical Group
Status: Professional; Non-Profit
Type: Performing
Purpose: Theatre II's primary objective is to provide quality live theater to the Southwest Chicago community.
Management: Steve Micotto, Artistic Director; JoAnne Fleming, Managing Director
Paid Staff: 8 **Volunteer Staff:** 8
Paid Artists: 30
Utilizes: Special Technical Talent
Budget: $50,000 - $100,000
Income Sources: Business/Corporate Donations; Box Office; Government Grants; Individual Donations
Season: September - June **Annual Attendance:** 5,000
Affiliations: League of Chicago Theatres; Saint Xavier University
Performance Facilities: McGuire Hall

VICTORY GARDENS THEATER
2257 North Lincoln Avenue, Chicago, IL 60614
(312) 549-5788
Founded: 1974
Arts Area: Professional; Theatrical Group
Status: Professional
Type: Performing; Touring; Resident; Educational
Purpose: Development of Chicago theatre artists, with special emphasis on playwrights
Management: John Walker, Managing Director; Dennis Zacek, Artistic Director; Allyn Pokraka, Administrative Director
Officers: Nancy Breseke, President
Paid Staff: 20
Paid Artists: 20
Utilizes: Special Technical Talent; Guest Artists; Guest Directors
Budget: $1,000,000 - $5,000,000
Income Sources: Private Foundations/Grants/Endowments; Business/Corporate Donations; Box Office; Government Grants; Individual Donations
Season: September - July

WISDOM BRIDGE THEATRE
1559 West Howard Street, Chicago, IL 60626
(312) 743-0486
FAX: (312) 743-1614
Founded: 1974
Arts Area: Professional
Status: Professional; Non-Profit
Type: Performing; Touring; Educational
Purpose: Wisdom Bridge Theatre exists to explore classic literature and address new works within a context of risk-taking and enlightenment.
Management: Jefferey Ortmann, Producing Director; Karl Sullivan, Producing Manager; Sharon Phillips, Director of Program Administration; Terry McCabe, Resident Director
Officers: John Conlon, Jack Johnson, Co-Chairs; Louise Sunderland, Secretary; Ellen Baras, Treasurer
Paid Staff: 12
Utilizes: Special Technical Talent; Guest Artists; Guest Directors
Budget: $1,000,000 - $5,000,000
Income Sources: Private Foundations/Grants/Endowments; Business/Corporate Donations; Box Office; Government Grants; Individual Donations
Season: September - July **Annual Attendance:** 35,000
Affiliations: AEA; League of Chicago Theatres; TCG
Performance Facilities: Wisdom Bridge Theatre

PERFORMING SERIES

AUDITORIUM THEATRE COUNCIL
50 East Congress Parkway, Chicago, IL 60605
(312) 922-4046
Founded: 1960
Arts Area: Dance; Vocal Music; Theater
Status: Professional; Non-Profit
Type: Resident; Educational; Sponsoring

Purpose: To restore the Auditorium Theatre to its original architectural splendor and present dance, music and theatre programs for their cultural and educational value
Management: Robert A. Alsaker, Executive Director; Morton Zolotow, Theatre Manager; Barbara V. Corrigan, Director of Marketing and Group Sales
Utilizes: Special Technical Talent; Guest Conductors; Guest Artists
Performance Facilities: Auditorium Theatre

CRYSTAL BALLROOM CONCERT ASSOCIATION
410 South Michigan Avenue, #521, Chicago, IL 60605
(312) 481-2370
Founded: 1984
Arts Area: Dance; Vocal Music; Instrumental Music; Festivals
Status: Professional; Non-Profit
Type: Performing; Educational; Sponsoring
Purpose: To present nationally and internationally known and young local artists in concert; To promote first world premieres of commissioned works
Management: Beverly DeFries-D'Albert, Executive Secretary/Program Director
Officers: Dr. Francois D'Albert, President; Leslie Kondorossy, Vice President; Beverly DeFries-D'Albert, Treasurer
Volunteer Staff: 10
Paid Artists: 150　**Non-Paid Artists:** 50
Utilizes: Guest Artists
Budget: $1,000 - $50,000
Income Sources: Private Foundations/Grants/Endowments; Box Office; Individual Donations
Season: 52 Weeks
Affiliations: Zoltan Kodaly Academy and Institute
Performance Facilities: Crystal Ballroom

14TH ANNUAL CHICAGO JAZZ FESTIVAL
Mayor's Office of Special Events, 121 North LaSalle Street, Chicago, IL 60602
(312) 744-0576
FAX: (312) 744-8523
Founded: 1979
Arts Area: Vocal Music; Instrumental Music; Jazz
Status: Professional
Type: Performing
Purpose: To present a festival, free to the public featuring jazz in all of its forms
Management: Mayor's Office of Special Events, Producer; Jazz Institute of Chicago, Programmer
Officers: Penny Tyler, Coordinator
Paid Staff: 60　**Paid Artists:** 250
Utilizes: Guest Artists
Budget: $100,000 - $500,000
Income Sources: Business/Corporate Donations
Season: Labor Day Weekend　**Annual Attendance:** 360,000
Performance Facilities: Symphony Music Shell; Petrillo Music Shell

GRANT PARK MUSIC FESTIVAL
425 East McFetridge Drive, Chicago, IL 60605
(312) 294-2420
Founded: 1934
Arts Area: Instrumental Music
Status: Professional; Non-Profit
Type: Performing; Resident; Educational
Purpose: Providing professional symphonic concerts without charge to the people of Chicago
Management: Catherine M. Cahill, General Manager/Artistic Director
Officers: Robert A. Podesta, President; Lucille Burrus, Vice President
Paid Staff: 5　**Volunteer Staff:** 3
Paid Artists: 200　**Non-Paid Artists:** 100
Utilizes: Guest Conductors; Guest Artists
Budget: $1,000,000 - $5,000,000
Income Sources: Government Grants
Season: June - August　**Annual Attendance:** 1,000,000
Performance Facilities: James C. Petrillo Music Shell

FACILITY

ARIE CROWN THEATRE
McCormick Place, Chicago, IL 60616
(312) 791-6516
Type of Facility: Theatre Complex; Theatre House

Type of Stage: Proscenium; Hydraulic Lift Stage
Stage Dimensions: 90'Wx77'D   **Orchestra Pit**
Seating Capacity: 4,319
Year Built: 1971   **Architect:** Gene Summers   **Cost:** $11,000,000
Acoustical Consultant: Klepper Marshall & King
Contact for Rental: Jacqueline A. Huels;   (312) 791-6516

ATHENAEUM THEATRE
2936 North Southport Avenue, Chicago, IL 60657
(312) 935-6860
Type of Facility: Theatre House
Type of Stage: Proscenium
Stage Dimensions: 44'Wx32'Dx20'H plus loft   **Orchestra Pit**
Seating Capacity: 925
Year Built: 1911   **Architect:** Hermann Gaul
Contact for Rental: Clyde Foster;   (312) 935-6860
Resident Groups: Athenaeum Theatre Company; Chicago Opera Theatre

AUDITORIUM THEATRE
50 East Congress Parkway, Chicago, IL 60605
(312) 922-2110
FAX: (312) 922-0347
Type of Facility: Auditorium
Type of Stage: Proscenium
Stage Dimensions: 99'Wx63'D   **Orchestra Pit**
Seating Capacity: 4,000
Year Built: 1889   **Architect:** Dankmar Adler & Louis Sullivan   **Cost:** $3,145,291
Year Remodeled: 1967   **Architect:** Harry M. Weese & Associates   **Cost:** $3,175,000
Contact for Rental: Marie Cali;   (312) 922-4046
Manager: Dolcie Gilmore
Our purpose is to restore the Auditorium Theatre, a National Historic Landmark, to its original splendor

BEVERLY ART CENTER
2153 West 111th Street, Chicago, IL 60643
(312) 445-3838
Founded: 1969
Type of Facility: Visual and Performing Arts Center
Type of Stage: Proscenium
Stage Dimensions: 45'x45'
Seating Capacity: 425
Year Built: 1969   **Architect:** Fugard and Orth Associates   **Cost:** $800,000
Acoustical Consultant: Dan Richardson
Contact for Rental: Rita Moster;   (312) 881-6705
Resident Groups: Beverly Dance Ensemble; Beverly Theatre Guild; Pitt Players; Beverly Hills University Club

CIVIC STAGES CHICAGO
20 North Wacker Drive, Chicago, IL 60606
(312) 346-0270
FAX: (312) 704-6051
Type of Facility: Theatre Complex; Auditorium; Studio Performance; Performance Center; Theatre House; Opera House; Multi-Purpose
Year Built: 1929   **Architect:** Graham Anderson Probst White
Contact for Rental: Fred Solari;   (312) 346-0270
Manager: Randall L. Green
Resident Groups: Lyric Opera of Chicago
The Civic Center contains the Civic Theatre and Opera House. See individual listings for additional information.

CIVIC STAGES CHICAGO - CIVIC THEATRE
20 North Wacker Drive, Chicago, IL 60606
(312) 346-0270
FAX: (312) 704-6051
Type of Facility: Theatre House
Type of Stage: Proscenium
Stage Dimensions: 72'Wx31'D   **Orchestra Pit**
Seating Capacity: 906
Year Built: 1929
Contact for Rental: Fred Solari;   (312) 346-0270
Manager: Randall L. Green

CIVIC STAGES CHICAGO - OPERA HOUSE
20 North Wacker Drive, Chicago, IL 60606
(312) 346-0270
FAX: (312) 704-6051
Type of Facility: Opera House
Type of Stage: Proscenium
Stage Dimensions: 115'Wx75'D
Orchestra Pit
Seating Capacity: 3,486
Year Built: 1929
Contact for Rental: Fred Solari;   (312) 346-0270
Manager: Randall L. Green

CURTISS HALL
410 South Michigan, Chicago, IL 60605
(312) 939-3380
Type of Facility: Concert Hall; Auditorium; Studio Performance; Multi-Purpose; Room
Facility Originally: Recital Hall
Type of Stage: Proscenium
Stage Dimensions: 15'x30'
Seating Capacity: 200
Year Built: 1885   **Architect:** Solon S. Beman
Contact for Rental: Lee Newcomer;   (312) 939-3380

DE PAUL UNIVERSITY - BLACKSTONE THEATRE
60 East Balbo Drive, Chicago, IL 60605
(312) 362-8455
Type of Facility: Theatre House
Type of Stage: Proscenium
Stage Dimensions: 60'6"Wx34'D; 37'10"Wx32'H proscenium opening
Orchestra Pit
Seating Capacity: 1,424
Contact for Rental: Peter Entin;   (212) 944-3700
Manager: The Shubert Organization
Limited availability for rental.

JAMES C. PETRILLO MUSIC SHELL
c/o Grant Park Music Hall, 425 East McSetridge, Chicago, IL 60605
(312) 294-2420
Type of Facility: Outdoor (Concert); Amphitheater
Type of Stage: Concert Shell (outdoor)
Seating Capacity: 5,000 fixed seats, unlimited lawn seating
Year Built: 1978
Acoustical Consultant: Klepper Marshall King Associates, Ltd.
Contact for Rental:
Manager: Catherine Cahill
Resident Groups: Grant Park Symphony Orchestra and Chorus
Available for rental on a limited basis to charity and civic organizations

ORCHESTRA HALL
220 South Michigan Avenue, Chicago, IL 60604
(312) 435-8122
Type of Facility: Concert Hall
Type of Stage: Concert Stage
Stage Dimensions: 73'Wx40'D
Seating Capacity: 2,566
Year Built: 1904   **Architect:** Daniel H. Burnham   **Cost:** $750,000
Year Remodeled: 1981   **Architect:** Skidmore Owings & Merrill   **Cost:** $3,400,000
Acoustical Consultant: R. Lawrence Kirkegaard & Associates
Contact for Rental: Michael Mach;   (312) 435-8122, ext. 8141
Resident Groups: Chicago Symphony Orchestra; Allied Arts Association; Chicago Symphony Chorus; Civic Orchestra of Chicago

PARKWAY PLAYHOUSE
500 East 67th Street, Chicago, IL 60637
(312) 493-0901
Type of Facility: Performance Center; Multi-Purpose

Type of Stage: Thrust
Stage Dimensions: 20'Wx20'D
Seating Capacity: 100
Contact for Rental: Elizabeth Murphy;   (312) 493-0901
Resident Groups: The Chicago Theatre Company

PETRILLO MUSIC SHELL
Columbus Drive and Jackson Boulevard, Chicago, IL 60603
(312) 294-2420
FAX: (312) 616-3719
    Mailing Address: Grant Park Music Festival, 425 East McFetridge Drive, Chicago, IL 60605
    Founded: 1935
    Type of Facility: Outdoor (Concert)
    Type of Stage: Pavilion
    Stage Dimensions: 96'x53'
    Seating Capacity: 5,000
    Year Built: 1978
    Acoustical Consultant: Christopher Jaffe
    Contact for Rental: Marge Frantz;   (312) 294-4772
    Resident Groups: Grant Park Symphony Orchestra and Chorus

PLAYWRIGHTS' CENTER OF CHICAGO
1222 West Wilson Avenue, Chicago, IL 60640
(312) 334-9981
    Type of Facility: Studio Performance; Multi-Purpose; Room
    Facility Originally: Business Facility
    Type of Stage: Flexible
    Stage Dimensions: 24'x14'
    Seating Capacity: 50
    Year Remodeled: 1986   **Architect:** S. Bruce   **Cost:** $1,000
    Acoustical Consultant: S. Bruce
    Contact for Rental: B.L. Robbins;   (312) 975-7711
    Resident Groups: Playwrights' Center
    Suitable for auditions, studio performances, meetings, classes

ROOSEVELT UNIVERSITY - PATRICK L. O'MALLEY THEATRE
430 South Michigan Avenue, Chicago, IL 60605
(312) 341-3719
FAX: (312) 341-3655
    Type of Facility: Theatre House; Multi-Purpose
    Type of Stage: Thrust
    Stage Dimensions: 26'x32'
    Seating Capacity: 336
    Year Built: 1899   **Architect:** Dankmar Adler & Louis Sullivan
    Year Remodeled: 1973   **Architect:** Marion Gutnayer   **Cost:** $140,000
    Resident Groups: Roosevelt University Theatre and Music Theatre Programs

SHUBERT THEATRE
22 West Monroe Street, Chicago, IL 60603
(312) 977-1700
FAX: (312) 977-1740
    Founded: 1906
    Type of Facility: Theatre House
    Facility Originally: Vaudeville
    Type of Stage: Proscenium
    Orchestra Pit
    Seating Capacity: 2,008
    Year Built: 1906   **Architect:** E.R. Krause
    Contact for Rental: Ken Shaw;   (312) 977-1700

THEATRE BUILDING
1225 West Belmont Avenue, Chicago, IL 60657
(312) 929-7367
FAX: (312) 327-1404
    Founded: 1968

Type of Facility: Theatre Complex; Performance Center; Multi-purpose Room
Facility Originally: Warehouse
Type of Stage: Thrust; Flexible; Proscenium
Seating Capacity: 148 in each of three theatres
Year Remodeled: 1977
Contact for Rental: Joan Mazzonelli; (312) 929-7367
Resident Groups: New Tuners Theatre; Illinois Theatre Association; Bailiwick Repertory; American Blues Theatre
Building contains three separate stages

TRUMAN COLLEGE - O'ROURKE CENTER FOR THE PERFORMING ARTS
1145 West Wilson, Chicago, IL 60640
(312) 878-9761
FAX: (312) 271-8057
Type of Facility: Theatre Complex
Type of Stage: Thrust; Proscenium
Stage Dimensions: 38'x34'
Orchestra Pit
Seating Capacity: 250
Year Built: 1980   Cost: $4,000,000
Manager: Arlene Crewdson
Resident Groups: Pegasus Players
Has modest performing arts series

VICTORY GARDENS THEATER
2257 North Lincoln Avenue, Chicago, IL 60614
(312) 549-5788
Type of Facility: Theatre Complex
Facility Originally: Cannery
Type of Stage: Thrust
Seating Capacity: 195
Year Remodeled: 1981   Architect: Sakal & Hood
Acoustical Consultant: R. Lawrence Kirkegaard & Associates
Contact for Rental: John Walker; (312) 549-5788
Resident Groups: Victory Gardens Theater; Body Politic Theatre

Crystal Lake

INSTRUMENTAL MUSIC

MCHENRY COUNTY YOUTH ORCHESTRA
46 South Walkup Avenue, Crystal Lake, IL 60014
(815) 477-4676
Founded: 1980
Arts Area: Symphony; Orchestra; Chamber; Ensemble
Status: Non-Professional; Non-Profit
Type: Performing; Educational; Sponsoring
Purpose: To foster educational, cultural, and musical activities; to support orchestras; to contribute to the cultural life of the community by performances of the orchestras, ensemble and students; to provide private and class instruction in orchestral instruments, piano and voice
Management: Marie Ann Vos, Executive Director
Officers: Tim Warnecke, President; Cathy Braun, First Vice President; Greg Baron, Second Vice President; Joyce Wright, Third Vice President; Cindy Charoenying, Recording Secretary; Deb Rosulek, Corresponding Secretary; N. Landon Hoyt, Treasurer
Paid Staff: 1
Paid Artists: 10   Non-Paid Artists: 135
Utilizes: Guest Artists
Budget: $100,000 - $500,000
Income Sources: Private Foundations/Grants/Endowments; Business/Corporate Donations; Box Office; Government Grants; Individual Donations
Season: September - May
Annual Attendance: 1,200
Affiliations: ASOL; Illinois Council of Orchestras; Illinois Arts Alliance; National Guild Community School of the Arts; Barrington Area Arts Council; Suzuki Association of the Americas; Greater Crystal Lake Chamber of Commerce and Industry

Danville

INSTRUMENTAL MUSIC

DANVILLE SYMPHONY ORCHESTRA
205 1/2 North Walnut Street, Danville, IL 61832
(217) 443-5300
Founded: 1967
Arts Area: Symphony; Orchestra; Chamber
Status: Semi-Professional; Non-Profit
Type: Performing; Educational
Purpose: To provide quality, educational performances to a five-county, two-state area, bringing in top talent and utilizing top local talent
Management: Connie Anderson, Administrative Director; Jeremy A. Swerling, Music Director; Kelly Talsma, Orchestra Manager
Officers: Richard Doyle, President; Steve Foster, Vice President; Dick Cheney, Secretary; M.E. Cary, Treasurer
Paid Staff: 6   **Volunteer Staff:** 25
Paid Artists: 76
Utilizes: Guest Artists
Budget: $50,000 - $100,000
Income Sources: Private Foundations/Grants/Endowments; Business/Corporate Donations; Box Office; Individual Donations
Season: September - March
Annual Attendance: 5,500
Affiliations: Illinois Council of Orchestras; Illinois Presenters Network
Performance Facilities: High School Auditorium; David Palmer Civic Center

De Kalb

DANCE

EMERGENCE DANCE THEATRE
804 1/2 Market Street, PO Box 186, De Kalb, IL 60115
(815) 758-6613
Founded: 1984
Arts Area: Modern; Media
Status: Professional; Non-Profit
Type: Performing; Touring; Educational
Purpose: To promote quality professional dance and media performance in the northern Illinois area
Management: Sandra Schramel, Artistic Director; John Schmitz, Executive Director
Paid Artists: 7
Utilizes: Guest Artists; Guest Choreographers
Budget: $50,000 - $100,000
Income Sources: Private Foundations/Grants/Endowments; Business/Corporate Donations; Box Office; Government Grants; Individual Donations
Season: 52 Weeks
Annual Attendance: 1,200
Performance Facilities: Northern Illinois University Concert Hall

FACILITY

EGYPTIAN THEATRE
135 North Second Street, DeKalb, IL 60115
(815) 758-1215
Founded: 1929
Type of Facility: Concert Hall; Auditorium; Performance Center; Off Broadway; Theatre House
Facility Originally: Vaudeville; Movie House
Type of Stage: Thrust; Proscenium
Stage Dimensions: 30'Dx75'W, including wing space 35' opening
Orchestra Pit
Seating Capacity: 1,483
Year Built: 1929   **Architect:** Elmer F. Behrens   **Cost:** $300,000
Year Remodeled: 1983   **Architect:** Roland Killian of AEC Group, Inc.   **Cost:** $2,125,000
Contact for Rental: Barbara Kummerfeldt, Executive Director;   (815) 758-1215
Resident Groups: Kishwaukee Symphony; Children's Community Theatre; NIU Fine Arts Series
Preservation of the Egyptian Theatre (PET) is an all-volunteer organization formed in 1978 to preserve and operate this historic theatre.

Decatur

VOCAL MUSIC

MILLIKIN UNIVERSITY OPERA THEATRE
1184 West Main Street, Decatur, IL 62522
(217) 424-6209
    Founded: 1955
    Arts Area: Grand Opera; Lyric Opera; Operetta
    Status: Non-Profit
    Type: Educational
    Purpose: To provide performance opportunities for university students and audiences participation for students and community
    Management: Stephen Fiol, General Director; Dr. Wesley Tower, Dean of School of Music
    Officers: Maria Klott, Assistant to the Director
    Paid Staff: 9   **Volunteer Staff:** 10
    Non-Paid Artists: 55
    Utilizes: Guest Directors
    Budget: $1,000 - $50,000
    Season: November - May   **Annual Attendance:** 12,000
    Affiliations: COS; NOA; OA
    Performance Facilities: Kirkland Theater

FACILITY

DECATUR CIVIC CENTER
1 Civic Center Plaza, Decatur, IL 62523
(217) 422-7300
    Type of Facility: Civic Center
    Year Built: 1980   **Architect:** Hellmuth Obata & Kassabaum   **Cost:** $13,800,000
    Acoustical Consultant: Ned Lustig
    Contact for Rental:
    Manager: Ann Brunson
    The Civic Center contains the Arena and Theater. See separate listings for additional information.

DECATUR CIVIC CENTER - ARENA
1 Civic Center Plaza, Decatur, IL 62523
(217) 422-7300
    Type of Facility: Arena
    Type of Stage: Flexible; Platform
    Stage Dimensions: 32'x40'
    Seating Capacity: Bleachers - 1,200; Portable Seating - 1,800
    Year Built: 1980
    Contact for Rental:
    Manager: Ann Brunson

DECATUR CIVIC CENTER - THEATER
1 Civic Center Plaza, Decatur, IL 62523
(217) 422-7300
    Type of Facility: Concert Hall; Theatre House
    Type of Stage: Proscenium
    Stage Dimensions: 40'Wx16'H   **Orchestra Pit**
    Seating Capacity: 460
    Year Built: 1980
    Contact for Rental:
    Manager: Ann Brunson

KIRKLAND FINE ARTS CENTER
1184 West Main Street, Decatur, IL 62522
(217) 424-6253
FAX: (217) 424-3993
    Type of Facility: Performance Center; Fine Arts Center
    Type of Stage: Proscenium   **Orchestra Pit**
    Seating Capacity: 1,944
    Year Built: 1970   **Architect:** Perkins and Will   **Cost:** $3,500,000
    Acoustical Consultant: Bolt, Beranek & Newman
    Contact for Rental: Ken Foster, Managing Director;   (217) 424-6253

Des Plaines

INSTRUMENTAL MUSIC

NORTHWEST SYMPHONY ORCHESTRA
1603 Thacker Street, Des Plaines, IL 60016
(708) 824-1279
Founded: 1951
Arts Area: Symphony; Orchestra; Chamber
Status: Non-Profit
Type: Performing; Educational
Purpose: To provide musical training and a full scale performing symphony for Northwest Suburban Chicago residents
Officers: Sherry Kujala, President; Ann Butler, Treasurer
Volunteer Staff: 15
Paid Artists: 1   **Non-Paid Artists:** 100
Utilizes: Guest Artists
Budget: $1,000 - $50,000
Income Sources: Private Foundations/Grants/Endowments; Business/Corporate Donations; Box Office; Government Grants; Individual Donations
Season: September - June   **Annual Attendance:** 2,000
Affiliations: Maine-Oakton-Niles Adult Evening Education Program
Performance Facilities: Maine West High School

THEATRE

DES PLAINES THEATRE GUILD
620 Lee Street, Des Plaines, IL 60016
(708) 296-1211
Founded: 1946
Arts Area: Community; Theatrical Group
Status: Non-Professional; Non-Profit
Type: Performing
Purpose: To produce professional quality community theatre that will educate and entertain the Northwest Suburban Chicago Area
Officers: Carol Kempiak, President; Marilyn Collignon, Financial Vice President; Jane Berman, Production Vice President; Donald Collignon, Administrative Vice President
Volunteer Staff: 12
Utilizes: Guest Directors
Budget: $50,000 - $100,000
Income Sources: Private Foundations/Grants/Endowments; Business/Corporate Donations; Box Office; Individual Donations
Season: September - June   **Annual Attendance:** 15,000
Performance Facilities: Prairie Lake Community Center

Downers Grove

PERFORMING SERIES

DOWNERS GROVE CONCERT ASSOCIATION
731 59th Street, Downers Grove, IL 60516
(708) 252-7160
FAX: (708) 252-5986
Founded: 1947
Arts Area: Dance; Instrumental Music
Status: Non-Professional
Type: Sponsoring
Purpose: To promote public interest in the performing arts in and about the area of Downers Grove by presenting outstanding professional talent in the sphere of music and dance
Officers: Ellen L. Webb, President; Chris Saricks, Vice President; Robert Durnberger, Secretary; Steven C. Pieper, Treasurer; Hans G. Kaper, Concert Impresario
Volunteer Staff: 20
Utilizes: Guest Artists
Budget: $1,000 - $50,000
Income Sources: Business/Corporate Donations; Box Office; Individual Donations
Season: September - April   **Annual Attendance:** 1,400
Affiliations: Chicago Music Alliance
Performance Facilities: Downers Grove North High School Auditorium

---

Edwardsville

PERFORMING SERIES

SOUTHERN ILLINOIS UNIVERSITY-EDWARDSVILLE
Campus Box 1083, Edwardsville, IL 62026
(618) 692-2626
Arts Area: Dance; Instrumental Music; Theater
Status: Non-Profit
Type: Educational; Sponsoring
Purpose: The Arts and Issues series provides speakers and performance events to the University community to complement the academic programs at the University
Management: Rich Walker, Series Coordinator
Officers: Earl Lazerson, President
Paid Staff: 5
Paid Artists: 32
Utilizes: Guest Artists
Budget: $100,000 - $500,000
Income Sources: Private Foundations/Grants/Endowments; Business/Corporate Donations; Box Office; Government Grants
Season: September - June   **Annual Attendance:** 3,500
Affiliations: APAP
Performance Facilities: University Center and Communications Theater

---

Elgin

INSTRUMENTAL MUSIC

ELGIN AREA YOUTH ORCHESTRA
1700 Spartan Drive, Elgin, IL 60123
(708) 888-7389
FAX: (708) 888-7995
Founded: 1976
Arts Area: Symphony; Orchestra
Status: Non-Professional; Non-Profit
Type: Performing; Educational
Purpose: Provide the finest orchestral performance opportunity to young musicians from schools throughout Illinois' Northern Fox Valley
Management: Elizabeth Prieslozny, Music Director; Martha Henrikson, Assistant Conductor
Officers: Cherie Lee Lewis, President/Elgin Symphony Board; Florence Jacobsen, President/Elgin Symphony League
Paid Staff: 3   **Volunteer Staff:** 3
Paid Artists: 2   **Non-Paid Artists:** 100
Utilizes: Guest Conductors; Guest Artists
Budget: $1,000 - $50,000
Income Sources: Private Foundations/Grants/Endowments; Business/Corporate Donations; Box Office; Government Grants; Individual Donations
Season: September - May   **Annual Attendance:** 3,500
Affiliations: ASOL; MENC; NSOL
Performance Facilities: Hemmens Auditorium

ELGIN SYMPHONY ORCHESTRA
1700 Spartan Drive, Elgin, IL 60123
(708) 888-7389
FAX: (708) 888-7995
Founded: 1950
Arts Area: Symphony; Orchestra
Status: Professional
Type: Performing; Educational
Purpose: To create and provide the finest possible orchestral music serving educational and culutral needs to our entire regional community
Management: Marcene Linstrom, Executive Director; Edith Fitts, Marketing Manager; James Hegarty, Operations Manager; Robert Hanson, Music Director
Officers: Mark Seigle, President of Board; David McClintock, Secretary; Len Rempert, Treasurer; John Snow, Financial Development
Paid Staff: 8
Paid Artists: 69
Utilizes: Guest Conductors; Guest Artists
Budget: $500,000 - $1,000,000

Income Sources: Private Foundations/Grants/Endowments; Business/Corporate Donations; Box Office; Government Grants; Individual Donations
Season: October - May   **Annual Attendance:** 1,100
Performance Facilities: Hemmens Auditorium

Evanston

DANCE

GUS GIORDANO JAZZ DANCE CHICAGO
614 Davis Street, Evanston, IL 60201
(708) 866-6779
> **Founded:** 1968
> **Arts Area:** Modern; Ballet; Jazz
> **Status:** Professional
> **Type:** Performing; Touring; Educational
> **Purpose:** The purpose of Gus Giordano Jazz Dance Chicago is to get audiences excited about dance in general, specifically jazz dance. Contributions will be used for the continued existence and growth of GGJDC so that jazz can continue to be a major art form.
> **Management:** Nan Giordano, Associate Director; Gardner Arts Network, New York City
> **Officers:** Hilary Pender, President; Lloyd Culbertson, Randy Mehrberg, Vice Presidents; A. Steven Crown, Treasurer; William Madden, Secretary
> **Paid Staff:** 2   **Volunteer Staff:** 5
> **Paid Artists:** 12   **Non-Paid Artists:** 3
> **Utilizes:** Special Technical Talent; Guest Artists; Guest Choreographers
> **Budget:** $100,000 - $500,000
> **Income Sources:** Private Foundations/Grants/Endowments; Business/Corporate Donations; Box Office; Government Grants; Individual Donations; Benefits
> **Season:** September - May   **Annual Attendance:** 7,000
> **Affiliations:** Chicago Dance Arts Coalition; Illinois Arts Council; Evanston Arts Council

VOCAL MUSIC

HIS MAJESTIE'S CLERKES
PO Box 1001, Evanston, IL 60204
(708) 866-7464
> **Arts Area:** Choral
> **Status:** Semi-Professional; Non-Profit
> **Type:** Performing
> **Purpose:** To present historically-informed performances of Renaissance masterworks as well as works of the 19th and 20th centuries
> **Management:** Anne Heider, Executive/Art/Music Director
> **Officers:** R. Stephen Warner, President of the Board
> **Budget:** $50,000 - $100,000
> **Income Sources:** Private Foundations/Grants/Endowments; Business/Corporate Donations; Box Office; Government Grants; Individual Donations
> **Season:** 52 Weeks

LIGHT OPERA WORKS
927 Noyes Street, Evanston, IL 60201
(708) 869-6300
FAX: (708) 869-6302
> **Founded:** 1980
> **Arts Area:** Light Opera; Operetta; Musical Comedy
> **Status:** Professional; Non-Profit
> **Type:** Performing
> **Purpose:** Professional production of light opera
> **Management:** Bridget McDonough, Managing Director; Philip A. Kraus, Artistic Director; Tim Pleiman, Business Manager
> **Officers:** Harry Clamor, President; John Auwaerter, Treasurer; Philip A. Kraus, Secretary
> **Paid Staff:** 3   **Volunteer Staff:** 2
> **Paid Artists:** 200
> **Utilizes:** Guest Conductors; Guest Directors
> **Budget:** $100,000 - $500,000
> **Income Sources:** Private Foundations/Grants/Endowments; Business/Corporate Donations; Box Office; Government Grants; Individual Donations
> **Season:** June - December   **Annual Attendance:** 12,000

Affiliations: NOA; OA; League of Chicago Theatres; Chicago Music Alliance
Performance Facilities: Cahn Auditorium

THEATRE

LIVE THEATRE
1234 Sherman Avenue, Evanston, IL 60201
(708) 475-2570
Founded: 1983
Arts Area: Professional
Status: Professional; Non-Profit
Type: Performing
Purpose: "The Focus of Live Theatre," says Artistic Director A.C. Thomas, "is to create a nourishing and challenging environment for our actors and artists in our continued exploration of the human condition."
Management: A.C. Thomas, Artistic Director; Marcia Riegel, Executive Director; Marjorie Cohn, Managing Director; Richard O'Connell and Michael E. Myers, Directors
Officers: Kimberly A. Zeitlin, President; Marcia Riegel, Treasurer
Paid Staff: 4
Paid Artists: 6
Budget: $1,000 - $50,000
Income Sources: Business/Corporate Donations; Box Office; Individual Donations
Season: September - July   **Annual Attendance:** 500
Affiliations: League of Chicago Theatres; Evanston Arts Council
Performance Facilities: Live Theatre

NEXT THEATRE COMPANY
927 Noyes, Evanston, IL 60201
(708) 475-6763
FAX: (708) 475-6767
Founded: 1981
Arts Area: Professional
Status: Professional; Non-Profit
Type: Performing; Resident
Purpose: We believe theatre is a powerful tool for moving, entertaining and provoking people in a positive way. Therefore, the Next Theatre Company devotes itself to producing plays about current social concerns.
Management: Harriet Spizziri, Artistic Director; Jim Keister, Managing Director; Tim Engle, Production Manager; Dexter Bullard, Matt DeCaro, Artistic Associates
Officers: Kate Saccany, President; Alan Leib, Vice President; Charlotte Leib, Secretary; Irwin Noparstak, Treasurer
Paid Staff: 11   **Volunteer Staff:** 20
Paid Artists: 15
Utilizes: Special Technical Talent; Guest Artists; Guest Directors
Budget: $100,000 - $500,000
Income Sources: Private Foundations/Grants/Endowments; Business/Corporate Donations; Box Office; Government Grants; Individual Donations
Season: September - April   **Annual Attendance:** 16,000
Affiliations: AEA; TCG; League of Chicago Theatres; Producers Association of Chicago Area Theatres
Performance Facilities: Noyes Cultural Arts Center

NORTHLIGHT THEATRE AT THE CORONET
817 Chicago Avenue, Evanston, IL 60202
(708) 869-7732; (708) 869-7278
FAX: (708) 869-9445
Founded: 1974
Arts Area: Professional
Status: Professional; Non-Profit
Type: Resident; Producing
Purpose: The theatre's objective is to challenge, as well as entertain, its audiences with a focus to produce compelling new interpretations of contemporary plays drawn from an international repertoire and to create stage adaptions inspired by the full spectrum of artistic disciplines.
Management: Russell Vandenbroucke, Artistic Director; Kimberly C. Sleight, Managing Director
Paid Staff: 15
Paid Artists: 75
Budget: $1,000,000 - $5,000,000
Income Sources: Private Foundations/Grants/Endowments; Business/Corporate Donations; Box Office; Government Grants; Individual Donations
Season: August - May   **Annual Attendance:** 70,000
Affiliations: TCG; LORT; AAA
Performance Facilities: Northlight Theatre at the Coronet

PIVEN THEATRE WORKSHOP
927 Noyes Street, Evanston, IL 60201
(708) 866-6597
    Founded: 1974
    Arts Area: Theatrical Group
    Status: Professional; Non-Profit
    Type: Performing; Educational
    Purpose: A center for training in the performing arts for the child and adult, the novice and the professional, these classes may be ends in themselves or serve to prepare the student for the professional theatre; share work with the public
    Management: Joyce and Byrne Piven, Artistic Directors; Janie Weisenberg, Administrative Director
    Officers: Steve Goranson, President; Bonnie Wilson, Vice President; Ron Saiet, Treasurer
    Paid Staff: 12
    Paid Artists: 8
    Budget: $100,000 - $500,000
    Income Sources: Private Foundations/Grants/Endowments; Business/Corporate Donations; Box Office; Government Grants; Individual Donations
    Season: 52 Weeks   **Annual Attendance:** 10,000
    Affiliations: Illinois Arts Alliance; Evanston Arts Alliance
    Performance Facilities: Noyes Cultural Arts Center

TRINITY SQUARE ENSEMBLE
PO Box 1798, Evanston, IL 60204
(708) 328-0330
    Founded: 1981
    Arts Area: Professional
    Status: Professional
    Type: Performing; Touring; Educational
    Management: Deborah Stewart, Managing Director; Karen L. Erickson, Artistic Director
    Officers: Carl Wesselman, President; Tom Gahlon, Vice President; Glen Rippie, Secretary
    Paid Staff: 1   **Volunteer Staff:** 5
    Paid Artists: 6   **Non-Paid Artists:** 8
    Utilizes: Guest Artists; Guest Directors
    Budget: $50,000 - $100,000
    Income Sources: Private Foundations/Grants/Endowments; Business/Corporate Donations; Box Office; Government Grants; Individual Donations
    Season: 52 Weeks   **Annual Attendance:** 3,000
    Affiliations: League of Chicago Theatres

FACILITY

NATIONAL - LOUIS UNIVERSITY'S WEINSTEIN CENTER FOR THE PERFORMING ARTS
2840 North Sheridan Road, Evanston, IL 60201
(708) 256-5150, ext. 2593
FAX: (708) 256-1047
    Type of Facility: Auditorium; Performance Center
    Facility Originally: Gymnasium
    Type of Stage: Proscenium; Partial Thrust
    Stage Dimensions: 45'Dx60'W, 10' curved apron thrust; 52'x18' proscenium opening
    Seating Capacity: 634
    Year Built: 1925
    Year Remodeled: 1972   **Architect:** Perkins and Will   **Cost:** $100,000
    Contact for Rental: Karin L. Lewis, Director;   (708) 256-5150, ext. 2273

PICK - STAIGER CONCERT HALL
1977 Sheridan Road, Evanston, IL 60208
(708) 332-2373
FAX: (708) 467-1831
    Founded: 1975
    Type of Facility: Concert Hall
    Type of Stage: Thrust
    Stage Dimensions: 57'x38'
    Seating Capacity: 1,003
    Year Built: 1975   **Architect:** Edward D. Dart   **Cost:** $4,000,000
    Acoustical Consultant: Bolt, Beranek and Newman
    Contact for Rental: Jeff Cech;   (708) 491-5441
    Resident Groups: Northwestern University School of Music Performing Organizations

---

Galesburg

INSTRUMENTAL MUSIC

KNOX GALESBURG SYMPHONY
Knox College, PO Box 31, Galesburg, IL 61401
(309) 343-0112, ext. 268
Founded: 1951
Arts Area: Symphony; Orchestra
Status: Non-Profit
Type: Performing
Purpose: To provide symphonic music for the community; to educate
Management: Ruth Ann Baughman, Manager; Bruce Polay, Conductor
Officers: Jim Jackson, President
Paid Staff: 1
Paid Artists: 5
Utilizes: Guest Artists
Budget: $100,000 - $500,000
Income Sources: Private Foundations/Grants/Endowments; Business/Corporate Donations; Box Office; Government Grants; Individual Donations
Season: October - June **Annual Attendance:** 4,000
Performance Facilities: Orpheum Theatre

THEATRE

PRAIRIE PLAYERS CIVIC THEATRE
60 South Kellogg Street, Galesburg, IL 61401
(309) 342-2299
Founded: 1915
Arts Area: Musical; Dinner; Community
Status: Non-Profit
Type: Performing; Touring; Educational
Purpose: As the main community theatre in the Galesburg Area, PPCT provides volunteers and audiences the opportunity to actively participate in, learn about and enjoy all aspects of the theatre arts.
Management: Kathleen Bashem, Youth Theatre Director
Officers: Patricia Conolly, Executive Director
Paid Staff: 2 **Volunteer Staff:** 15
Non-Paid Artists: 50
Budget: $100,000 - $500,000
Income Sources: Private Foundations/Grants/Endowments; Business/Corporate Donations; Box Office; Individual Donations
Season: September - August **Annual Attendance:** 24,000
Affiliations: Illinois Arts Council

FACILITY

KNOX COLLEGE - ELEANOR ABBOTT FORD CENTER FOR THE FINE ARTS
2 East South Street, Galesburg, IL 61401-4999
(309) 343-0112, ext. X408
Type of Facility: Theatre Complex; Concert Hall; Auditorium; Studio Performance; Theatre House; Multi-Purpose
Type of Stage: Thrust; Flexible; Proscenium; Turntable
Stage Dimensions: 65'Wx45'D **Orchestra Pit**
Seating Capacity: Proscenium-598; Thrust-450
Year Built: 1965 **Architect:** Perkins and Will **Cost:** $3,500,000
Acoustical Consultant: Bolt, Beranek & Newman
Contact for Rental: Ivan H. Davidson; (309) 343-0112, ext. x408
Resident Groups: Knox College Theatre; Knox-Galesburg Symphony; Nova Singers; Collegium Musicum

---

Glen Ellyn

INSTRUMENTAL MUSIC

DUPAGE SYMPHONY
PO Box 488, Glen Ellyn, IL 60137
(708) 858-4042
Founded: 1954
Arts Area: Symphony; Orchestra; Chamber; Ensemble
Status: Non-Professional; Non-Profit

Type: Performing; Touring
Purpose: To give citizens of the area the opportunity to hear live music and musicians a chance to play it
Management: Barbara Schubert, Musical Director/Conductor; Doris Purdie, Business Manager
Officers: Wayne Thomas, President; James Kaduk, Vice President; Beri Noble, Secretary; James Swackhamer, Treasurer
Paid Staff: 2
Paid Artists: 1   **Non-Paid Artists:** 65
Utilizes: Guest Conductors; Guest Artists
Budget: $1,000 - $50,000
Income Sources: Business/Corporate Donations; Box Office; Individual Donations
Season: September - August   **Annual Attendance:** 2,000
Affiliations: Illinois Council of Orchestras
Performance Facilities: Dupage County Auditorium

VOCAL MUSIC

GLEN ELLYN CHILDREN'S CHORUS
586 Duane Street, Suite 102, Glen Ellyn, IL 60137
(708) 858-2471
FAX: (708) 858-2476
Arts Area: Choral; Children's
Status: Non-Professional; Non-Profit
Type: Performing; Touring; Educational
Purpose: To provide a music education program for children; to strengthen abilities through performance; to provide an outreach program to sections of the community that would not be able to participate otherwise
Management: Sandra Prodan, Music Director; Linda Madura, Manager
Officers: Thomas Drovin, President of the Board
Budget: $50,000 - $100,000
Income Sources: Private Foundations/Grants/Endowments; Business/Corporate Donations; Box Office; Government Grants; Individual Donations; Tuition
Season: 52 Weeks

FACILITY

COLLEGE OF DUPAGE ARTS CENTER
22nd Street and Park Boulevard, Glen Ellyn, IL 60137-6599
(708) 858-2800, ext. 3008
FAX: (708) 790-9806
Type of Facility: Theatre Complex; Performance Center
Year Built: 1986   **Architect:** Wight and Company   **Cost:** $14,400,000
Acoustical Consultant: Lyle F. Yerges
Contact for Rental: Pat Polonus;   (312) 858-2800, ext. 3009
Manager: Richard Holgate
Resident Groups: New Philharmonic Orchestra; New Classic Singers; Jazz Ensemble; Buffalo Theatre Ensemble
The Arts Center contains the Auditorium, Mainstage, Studio Theatre and Theatre 2. See individual listings for additional information.

COLLEGE OF DUPAGE ARTS CENTER - AUDITORIUM
22nd Street and Park Boulevard, Glen Ellyn, IL 60137-6599
(708) 858-2800, ext. 3008
FAX: (708) 790-9806
Type of Facility: Auditorium
Type of Stage: Proscenium
Seating Capacity: 500
Year Built: 1986
Contact for Rental: Pat Polonus;   (708) 858-2800, ext. 3009
Manager: Richard Holgate
Resident Groups: New Philharmonic Orchestra; New Classic Singers; Jazz Ensemble; Buffalo Theatre Ensemble

COLLEGE OF DUPAGE ARTS CENTER - MAINSTAGE
22nd Street and Park Boulevard, Glen Ellyn, IL 60137-6599
(708) 858-2800, ext. 3008
FAX: (708) 790-9806
Type of Facility: Concert Hall; Theatre House
Type of Stage: Modified Apron Proscenium
Stage Dimensions: 49'Wx25'Hx50'D; add 10'D for hydraulic pit at stage level   **Orchestra Pit**
Seating Capacity: 800
Year Built: 1986

Contact for Rental: Pat Polonus; (708) 858-2800, ext. 3009
Manager: Richard Holgate

COLLEGE OF DUPAGE ARTS CENTER - STUDIO THEATRE
22nd Street and Park Boulevard, Glen Ellyn, IL 60137-6599
(708) 858-2800, ext. 3008
FAX: (708) 858-9806
Type of Facility: Studio Performance; Black Box
Type of Stage: Flexible
Year Built: 1986
Contact for Rental: Pat Polonus; (708) 858-2800, ext. 3009
Manager: Richard Holgate

COLLEGE OF DUPAGE ARTS CENTER - THEATRE 2
22nd Street and Park Boulevard, Glen Ellyn, IL 60137-6599
(708) 858-2800, ext. 3008
FAX: (708) 790-9806
Type of Facility: Theatre House
Type of Stage: Thrust
Stage Dimensions: 30'x30'
Seating Capacity: 200
Year Built: 1986
Contact for Rental: Pat Polonus; (708) 858-2800, ext. 3009
Manager: Richard Holgate

Glencoe

DANCE

MARGOT GRIMMER AMERICAN DANCE COMPANY
970 Vernon Avenue, Glencoe, IL 60022
(708) 835-2556
Founded: 1971
Arts Area: Modern; Ballet; Jazz
Status: Professional; Non-Profit
Type: Performing; Touring
Management: Margot Grimmer, Artistic Director
Paid Staff: 1
Paid Artists: 7
Utilizes: Special Technical Talent; Guest Artists
Budget: $100,000 - $500,000
Income Sources: Private Foundations/Grants/Endowments; Box Office; Individual Donations
Season: August - June

Goodfield

THEATRE

CONKLIN PLAYERS DINNER THEATRE
PO Box 301, Conklin Court, Goodfield, IL 61742
(309) 965-2545
Arts Area: Professional; Dinner; Children's Theatre
Status: Professional; Commercial
Type: Performing; Resident
Purpose: To entertain, educate and spread the word about live performance
Management: Chaunce Conklin, Owner/Producer/Director; Mary Simon, Manager
Officers: Conklin Players Inc.; Chaunce Conklin, President; Mary Simon, Secretary/Treasurer
Paid Staff: 35
Paid Artists: 15
Utilizes: Actors; Singers; Dancers
Budget: $500,000 - $1,000,000
Income Sources: Box Office
Season: January - December   **Annual Attendance:** 70,000

Grayslake

VOCAL MUSIC

LIBERTY FREMONT CHAMBER SINGERS
32600 East Lane, Grayslake, IL 60030
(708) 546-2050
> **Founded:** 1973
> **Arts Area:** Choral
> **Status:** Semi-Professional; Non-Profit
> **Type:** Performing
> **Purpose:** Provide performance opportunities and cultural outreach through fine music
> **Management:** Edwin Kramer, Music Director
> **Paid Staff:** 1   **Volunteer Staff:** 15
> **Paid Artists:** 5   **Non-Paid Artists:** 50
> **Utilizes:** Guest Conductors; Guest Artists; Guest Directors
> **Budget:** $1,000 - $50,000
> **Income Sources:** Private Foundations/Grants/Endowments; Business/Corporate Donations; Box Office; Government Grants; Individual Donations
> **Season:** October - May   **Annual Attendance:** 2,500

Highland Park

THEATRE

THE APPLE TREE THEATRE COMPANY
595 Elm Place, Highland Park, IL 60035
(708) 432-4335
> **Founded:** 1982
> **Arts Area:** Professional; Theatrical Group
> **Status:** Professional; Non-Profit
> **Type:** Performing; Educational
> **Purpose:** To allow new directors, projects and actors a forum in which to perform in a fully professional environment in Chicago
> **Management:** Eileen Boevers, Artistic Director; Scott Slein, General Manager
> **Officers:** Sue Thompson, President; Bryan Gamson, Vice President; June Carrol, Secretary; Diane Rochester, Treasurer
> **Paid Staff:** 3
> **Utilizes:** Guest Artists; Guest Directors
> **Budget:** $100,000 - $500,000
> **Income Sources:** Private Foundations/Grants/Endowments; Business/Corporate Donations; Box Office; Government Grants; Individual Donations
> **Season:** September - May
> **Affiliations:** League of Chicago Theatres

PERFORMING SERIES

RAVINIA FESTIVAL
1575 Oakwood Avenue, Highland Park, IL 60035
(708) 433-8800
> **Founded:** 1935
> **Arts Area:** Dance; Vocal Music; Instrumental Music
> **Status:** Professional; Non-Profit
> **Type:** Performing; Educational
> **Purpose:** Present, at cost, the best music (classical jazz, folk and pop) to the public
> **Utilizes:** Guest Conductors; Guest Artists

FACILITY

APPLE TREE THEATRE
595 Elm Place, Suite 210, Highland Park, IL 60035
(708) 432-4335; (708) 432-8223
> **Type of Facility:** Theatre House
> **Facility Originally:** School
> **Type of Stage:** Thrust
> **Seating Capacity:** 200
> **Year Built:** 1970
> **Manager:** Scott Slein
> **Resident Groups:** The Apple Tree Theatre Company; The Eileen Boevers Performing Arts Workshop

Joliet

FACILITY

RIALTO SQUARE THEATRE
15 East Van Buren Street, Joliet, IL 60431
(815) 726-7171
FAX: (815) 726-0352
Founded: 1926
Type of Facility: Concert Hall; Performance Center; Theatre House
Facility Originally: Vaudeville; Movie House
Type of Stage: Proscenium
Stage Dimensions: 52'Wx23'6"H proscenium opening   **Orchestra Pit**
Seating Capacity: 1,920
Year Built: 1926   **Architect:** C.W. And George Rapp   **Cost:** $3,000,000
Year Remodeled: 1981   **Architect:** Conrad Schmitt Studios   **Cost:** $7,000,000
Contact for Rental: Mary Beth Perros;   (815) 726-7171

Lake Forest

INSTRUMENTAL MUSIC

LAKE FOREST SYMPHONY ASSOCIATION, INC.
225 East Deerpath, Suite 138, Lake Forest, IL 60045
(708) 295-2135
FAX: (708) 295-2747
Arts Area: Orchestra; Ensemble
Status: Professional; Non-Profit
Type: Performing
Purpose: To provide artistically enriching, diverse music programs such as family-oriented concerts, youth programs and classical series that are tailored to suit the cultural needs of the northern Illinois community
Management: Paul Anthony McRae, Music Director; Fran Chaloupka, Director of Marketing/Operations
Officers: Jean Beck, President of the Board
Budget: $500,000 - $1,000,000
Income Sources: Private Foundations/Grants/Endowments; Business/Corporate Donations; Box Office; Government Grants; Individual Donations
Performance Facilities: Rhoades Auditorium, Chicago

Libertyville

FACILITY

DAVID ADLER CULTURAL CENTER
1700 North Milwaukee Avenue, Libertyville, IL 60048
(708) 367-0707
FAX: (708) 367-0804
Founded: 1980
Type of Facility: Concert Hall; Studio Performance; Performance Center; Civic Center; Multi-Purpose
Facility Originally: Historic Home
Type of Stage: Flexible; Platform   **Stage Dimensions:** 5'x14'
Year Built: 1917   **Architect:** David Adler
Year Remodeled: 1980
Acoustical Consultant: Stuart Rosenberg
Contact for Rental: Stuart Rosenberg;   (708) 367-0707
Resident Groups: The Adler Enseble
The Adler Center provides a variety of art workshops, concerts and exhibits.

Lincolnshire

THEATRE

MARRIOTT'S LINCOLNSHIRE THEATRE
10 Marriott Drive, Lincolnshire, IL 60069
(708) 634-0200
Founded: 1975
Arts Area: Musical

Status: Professional; Commercial
Type: Performing; Resident
Purpose: To present five productions each year including classic musicals, seldom-seen musicals, and premiere productions of new works
Management: Dyann Earley, Artistic Director; Kary Walker, Producer; Lauren Johnson, Director of Marketing
Paid Staff: 50
Utilizes: Guest Artists
Budget: $1,000,000 - $5,000,000
Income Sources: Box Office
Season: 52 Weeks   **Annual Attendance:** 300,000
Affiliations: League of Chicago Theatres; ADTI
Performance Facilities: Marriott's Lincolnshire Theatre

Litchfield

THEATRE

ENCORE PLAYERS
222 East Sargent, Litchfield, IL 62056
(217) 326-4414
Founded: 1968
Arts Area: Musical; Dinner; Community; Theatrical Group
Status: Non-Professional; Non-Profit
Type: Performing
Purpose: Promotion of art and development of artistic abilities and other skills in the field of theatrical arts; encouragement of public appreciation of all theatrical arts
Management: Mae Morton, Dennis Plozizka, David Lewey, Tim Price, Directors
Officers: James Wreath, President; David Parsons, Vice President; Teresa Donahoe, Secretary/Treasurer
Volunteer Staff: 30
Utilizes: Guest Directors
Budget: $1,000 - $50,000
Income Sources: Box Office; Individual Donations
Season: 52 Weeks   **Annual Attendance:** 900
Performance Facilities: Community Center

Macomb

THEATRE

SUMMER MUSIC THEATRE
Western Illinois University, Theatre Dep., Brown Hall, Macomb, IL 61455
(309) 298-1543
FAX: (309) 298-2695
Founded: 1972
Arts Area: Summer Stock; Musical
Status: Non-Profit
Type: Performing; Resident; Educational
Purpose: To provide musical theatre for the community and serve as a training ground for students
Management: David Patrick, Managing Director
Paid Staff: 8
Paid Artists: 25
Utilizes: Special Technical Talent; Guest Artists; Guest Directors
Budget: $1,000 - $50,000
Income Sources: Box Office; Individual Donations
Season: June - August   **Annual Attendance:** 6,000
Affiliations: U/RTA
Performance Facilities: Hainline Theatre

FACILITY

WESTERN ILLINOIS UNIVERSITY - HAINLINE THEATRE
Macomb, IL 61455
(309) 298-1543
FAX: (309) 298-2695
Type of Facility: Theatre House
Type of Stage: Proscenium
Stage Dimensions: 64'Wx30'D; 40'Wx16'H proscenium opening   **Orchestra Pit**

Seating Capacity: 387
Year Built: 1957   **Architect:** Lankton-Fregele-Terry
Year Remodeled: 1987   **Architect:** Phillips Swager Associates   **Cost:** $1,200,000
Resident Groups: Summer Music Theatre; University Theatre; Department of Music groups

Marengo

THEATRE

SHADY LANE THEATER
24803 West Grant, Business 20, Marengo, IL 60152
(815) 568-7219
Founded: 1940
Arts Area: Professional; Dinner
Status: Professional; Commercial
Type: Resident
Management: Donna Zeffery, General Manager; Sandra Smith, Artistic Director
Paid Staff: 12
Paid Artists: 75
Utilizes: Special Technical Talent; Guest Artists; Guest Directors
Budget: $100,000 - $500,000
Income Sources: Box Office
Season: March - January   **Annual Attendance:** 40,000
Performance Facilities: Shady Lane Playhouse

Marion

FACILITY

MARION CULTURAL AND CIVIC CENTER
700 Tower Square Plaza, Marion, IL 62959
(618) 997-4030
Founded: 1974
Type of Facility: Concert Hall; Auditorium; Performance Center; Theatre House; Opera House; Civic Center; Multi-Purpose
Facility Originally: Vaudeville; Movie House
Type of Stage: Proscenium
Stage Dimensions: 35'x35'
Seating Capacity: 938
Year Built: 1920
Year Remodeled: 1973   **Cost:** $150,000
Contact for Rental: Ray Reynolds;   (618) 997-4030
Resident Groups: Paradise Alley Players; Volunteers to the Arts

Maywood

THEATRE

COLEMAN PUPPET THEATRE
1516 South Second Avenue, Maywood, IL 60153
(708) 344-2920
Founded: 1947
Arts Area: Puppet
Status: Professional
Type: Performing; Touring
Purpose: To help keep alive classic and modern stories by dramatizing them with puppets
Management: F.R. Coleman, Barbara Coleman, Directors
Paid Staff: 2
Budget: $1,000 - $50,000
Income Sources: Box Office; Private/Corporate Functions
Affiliations: Puppeteers of America; Chicagoland Puppetry Guild; Puppeteers of America

Mendota

THEATRE

MENDOTA COMMUNITY THEATRE
Box 304, Mendota, IL 61342
(312) 344-2920
    Founded: 1953
    Arts Area: Community; Theatrical Group
    Status: Non-Professional; Non-Profit
    Type: Performing; Resident; Educational
    Purpose: To provide and promote theatre and theatre activities in the Tri-County Area
    Management: George Likeness, Treasurer/Business Manager; Rosemary Reger, Audience Relations
    Officers: Darla Cocanour, President; Lori Bieschke, Recording Secretary; Alberta Katthoefer, Corresponding Secretary; George Likeness, Treasurer
    Volunteer Staff: 50
    Non-Paid Artists: 50
    Budget: $1,000 - $50,000   **Income Sources:** Box Office
    Season: September - May   **Annual Attendance:** 2,500
    Performance Facilities: Mendota High School Auditorium

Moline

VOCAL MUSIC

THE MOLINE BOYS CHOIR
3406 54th Street, Moline, IL 61265
(309) 764-3109
    Founded: 1948
    Arts Area: Choral
    Status: Semi-Professional; Non-Profit
    Type: Performing; Touring; Educational
    Purpose: To perform choral literature of a variety of styles; to provide vocal/choral training to boys of talent, interest and ability
    Management: Kermit Wells, Director; Margaret Mangelsdorf, Manager
    Officers: William Barrett, President of Board
    Paid Staff: 5   **Volunteer Staff:** 13
    Non-Paid Artists: 150
    Budget: $50,000 - $100,000
    Income Sources: Business/Corporate Donations; Box Office; Individual Donations
    Season: September - July

Mount Vernon

INSTRUMENTAL MUSIC

CEDARHURST CHAMBER MUSIC
Richview Road, PO Box 907, Mount Vernon, IL 62864
(618) 244-5871
FAX: (618) 244-5871
    Founded: 1979
    Arts Area: Orchestra; Chamber; Ensemble; Ethnic
    Status: Professional; Non-Profit
    Type: Sponsoring
    Purpose: To present a series of chamber music concerts for the broad southern Illinois audience, featuring performers from Illinois, the rest of the United States and overseas
    Management: Carl L. Schweinfurth, Director
    Officers: Catherina Suttle, Operations Manager; Sharon Bradham, Chairman; Joann Nelson, Co-Chair
    Volunteer Staff: 18
    Paid Artists: 50
    Utilizes: Guest Artists
    Budget: $1,000 - $50,000
    Income Sources: Private Foundations/Grants/Endowments; Business/Corporate Donations; Box Office; Government Grants; Individual Donations
    Season: September - May   **Annual Attendance:** 1,600
    Affiliations: CMA; Illinois Presenters Network
    Performance Facilities: Main Gallery, Mitchell Art Museum

---
Naperville

PERFORMING SERIES

NAPERVILLE-NORTH CENTRAL COLLEGE PERFORMING ARTS ASSOCIATION
30 North Brainard Street, Naperville, IL 60566
(312) 420-3309
Founded: 1974
Arts Area: Dance; Vocal Music; Instrumental Music; Theater
Status: Non-Professional; Non-Profit
Type: Sponsoring
Management: James R. Doody, VP Operations
Officers: Norma Ladley, President; James R. Doody, Vice President Operations; Don Hennessy, Secretary; Olive S. Frantz, Treasurer
Volunteer Staff: 33
Utilizes: Guest Artists
Budget: $50,000 - $100,000
Income Sources: Private Foundations/Grants/Endowments; Business/Corporate Donations; Box Office; Government Grants; Individual Donations
Season: September - May   **Annual Attendance:** 5,000
Affiliations: North Central College
Performance Facilities: Pfeiffer Hall

Normal

PERFORMING SERIES

ILLINOIS SHAKESPEARE FESTIVAL
Illinois State University, Box 6901, Normal, IL 61761-6901
(309) 438-2535
FAX: (309) 438-8318
Founded: 1978
Arts Area: Festivals
Status: Non-Profit
Type: Performing; Educational
Management: Barbara Funk, Executive Director; John Sipes, Artistic Director; Peter Guither, General Manager; John Stefano, Managing Director
Paid Staff: 12
Paid Artists: 60
Utilizes: Guest Artists; Guest Directors
Budget: $100,000 - $500,000
Income Sources: Private Foundations/Grants/Endowments; Business/Corporate Donations; Box Office; Government Grants; Individual Donations
Season: June - August   **Annual Attendance:** 12,000
Performance Facilities: Ewing Manor

Northbrook

FACILITY

SHEELY CENTER FOR THE PERFORMING ARTS
2300 Shermer Road, Northbrook, IL 60062
(708) 272-6400, ext. X298
FAX: (708) 272-4330
Type of Facility: Concert Hall; Auditorium
Type of Stage: Proscenium
Stage Dimensions: 55'Wx39'D   **Orchestra Pit**
Seating Capacity: 1,500
Year Built: 1979   **Architect:** Otis Associates   **Cost:** $4,000,000
Acoustical Consultant: Jerit Boies; Bolt, Beranek & Newman

Contact for Rental: Joel A. Monaghan;   (708) 272-6400, ext. x298
Resident Groups: Northbrook Symphony

Oak Park

DANCE

OAK PARK CIVIC BALLET COMPANY
136 North Marion, Oak Park, IL 60301
(708) 383-0361
Founded: 1978
Arts Area: Modern; Ballet
Status: Professional; Non-Profit
Type: Performing; Touring; Resident
Purpose: To bring the great ballets to the public and improve the skills of the performers through constant performances
Management: Eva Lorraine, Artistic Director; Carole Bessler, Len Petrulis, Marketing
Officers: James Bagley, Chairman; Eva Lorraine, President; Geoff Obrzut, Vice President
Paid Staff: 4
Paid Artists: 24
Utilizes: Special Technical Talent; Guest Artists
Budget: $50,000 - $100,000
Income Sources: Box Office; Individual Donations
Season: October - May   **Annual Attendance:** 5,000

THEATRE

OAK PARK FESTIVAL THEATRE
PO Box 4114, Oak Park, IL 60303
(708) 524-2050
Founded: 1975
Arts Area: Professional; Summer Stock
Status: Professional; Non-Profit
Type: Performing
Management: David Darlow, Artistic Director; Susan Levine-Kelley, Managing Director
Paid Staff: 10
Paid Artists: 21
Utilizes: Special Technical Talent; Guest Artists; Guest Directors
Budget: $50,000 - $100,000
Income Sources: Private Foundations/Grants/Endowments; Business/Corporate Donations; Box Office; Individual Donations
Season: July - August   **Annual Attendance:** 5,000
Affiliations: League of Chicago Theatres
Performance Facilities: Austin Gardens

VILLAGE PLAYERS (OAK PARK-RIVER FOREST CIVIC THEATRE, INC.)
1010 Madison Street, Oak Park, IL 60304
(708) 524-1892; (708) 383-9829
Founded: 1961
Arts Area: Community; Theatrical Group
Status: Non-Professional; Non-Profit
Type: Performing; Resident; Educational
Purpose: To promote interest and involvement of the community in the cultural arts and develop their theatrical abilities through education and public performances
Management: Rita Krysko-Harrington, Business Administrator
Officers: Dr. Peter Baker, Chairman; Jerry Le Beda, Vice Chairman; Barbara Hemminger, Secretary; Cathy Madden, Treasurer; Jeff Carey, Charles Cichler, Marcia Mrazek, Board Members
Paid Staff: 1   **Volunteer Staff:** 50
Paid Artists: 10   **Non-Paid Artists:** 90
Utilizes: Special Technical Talent; Guest Artists; Guest Directors
Budget: $100,000 - $500,000
Income Sources: Private Foundations/Grants/Endowments; Business/Corporate Donations; Box Office; Government Grants; Individual Donations
Season: July - June   **Annual Attendance:** 30,000

Oakbrook Terrace

THEATRE

DRURY LANE OAKBROOK TERRACE
100 Drury Lane, Oakbrook Terrace, IL 60181
(708) 530-8300
Founded: 1984
Arts Area: Professional; Musical; Dinner
Status: Professional; Non-Professional; Commercial
Type: Performing; Touring
Purpose: The Drury Lane Oakbrook Terrace presents large-scale musicals as well as comedies that boast some of the top names in theatre both on and off stage.
Management: Diane Van Lente, Managing Director; Hugh Cassidy, General Manager
Paid Staff: 250
Paid Artists: 50
Budget: Over $10,000,000
Income Sources: Box Office
Season: 52 Weeks   **Annual Attendance:** 250,000
Affiliations: ADTA
Performance Facilities: Drury Lane Theater

Park Forest

INSTRUMENTAL MUSIC

ILLINOIS PHILHARMONIC ORCHESTRA ASSOCIATION
210 Illinois Street, Park Forest, IL 60466
(708) 481-6046
Arts Area: Orchestra; Chamber
Status: Professional; Non-Profit
Type: Performing; Educational
Purpose: To provide the citizens of Illinois, particularly the south suburban region, with professional orchestral music
Management: Carmen DeLeone, Music/Artistic Director
Officers: Marilynn Tannebaum, Board President
Budget: $500,000 - $1,000,000
Income Sources: Private Foundations/Grants/Endowments; Business/Corporate Donations; Box Office; Government Grants; Individual Donations
Performance Facilities: Bloom High School Workman Auditorium

THEATRE

ILLINOIS THEATRE CENTER
400A Lakewood Boulevard, Park Forest, IL 60466
(708) 481-3510
Founded: 1976
Arts Area: Professional; Theatrical Group
Status: Professional; Non-Profit
Type: Performing; Touring; Resident; Educational
Purpose: To bring professional, equity productions of new and award winning plays and musicals to residents of the Southland and surrounding communities; to provide a full season of seven productions, each running one month, and two summer productions
Management: Etel Billig, Administrative Director; Steve S. Billig, Artistic Director; Jonathan Roark, Musical Director; Wayne Adams, Assistant Artistic and Technical Director
Officers: Donna Jemilo, Board President
Paid Staff: 12   **Volunteer Staff:** 2
Paid Artists: 48
Utilizes: Special Technical Talent; Guest Artists; Guest Directors
Budget: $100,000 - $500,000
Income Sources: Private Foundations/Grants/Endowments; Business/Corporate Donations; Box Office; Government Grants; Individual Donations
Season: September - August   **Annual Attendance:** 56,000
Affiliations: AEA; TCG; League of Chicago Theatres
Performance Facilities: Illinois Theatre Center

FACILITY

FREEDOM HALL, NATHAN MANILOW THEATRE
410 Lakewood Boulevard, Park Forest, IL 60466
(708) 747-0580
FAX: (708) 503-7713
> **Founded:** 1976
> **Type of Facility:** Theatre House
> **Type of Stage:** Proscenium
> **Stage Dimensions:** 40'x23'x60'
> **Seating Capacity:** 330
> **Year Built:** 1976
> **Contact for Rental:** Naomi Fell;   (708) 747-0580

ILLINOIS THEATRE CENTER
400A Lakewood Boulevard, Park Forest, IL 60466
(708) 481-3510
> **Type of Facility:** Theatre House
> **Facility Originally:** Library
> **Type of Stage:** Thrust
> **Stage Dimensions:** 33'Wx18'D
> **Seating Capacity:** 187
> **Year Built:** 1958   **Architect:** R.H. Norton
> **Year Remodeled:** 1969   **Architect:** R.H. Norton
> **Manager:** Ms. Etel Billig;   (708) 481-3510
> **Resident Groups:** Illinois Theatre Center

Peoria

DANCE

PEORIA CIVIC BALLET
Central College Performing Arts Center, Peoria, IL 61635
(309) 694-5106
> **Arts Area:** Ballet
> **Status:** Professional; Non-Profit
> **Type:** Performing; Touring; Resident
> **Management:** Shirley Shear, Artistic Director
> **Officers:** Steve Staff, President
> **Paid Artists:** 20
> **Income Sources:** Box Office; Individual Donations

INSTRUMENTAL MUSIC

PEORIA SYMPHONY ORCHESTRA
105 East Arcadia, Peoria, IL 61603
(309) 682-6069
> **Founded:** 1897
> **Arts Area:** Symphony; Orchestra
> **Status:** Semi-Professional
> **Type:** Performing; Resident
> **Purpose:** The performance of symphonic music for the enjoyment of residents of Central Illinois
> **Management:** Judy Furniss, Manager; William Wilsen, Music Director/Conductor; Janice N. Hellman, Office Manager
> **Officers:** Karl Kuppler, President; Stanley Butler, Vice President; Thomas Romanowski, Treasurer; Ann Rullman, Secretary
> **Paid Staff:** 9
> **Paid Artists:** 85
> **Utilizes:** Special Technical Talent; Guest Conductors; Guest Artists
> **Budget:** $100,000 - $500,000
> **Income Sources:** Business/Corporate Donations; Box Office; Government Grants; Individual Donations
> **Season:** 52 Weeks   **Annual Attendance:** 20,000
> **Affiliations:** ASOL
> **Performance Facilities:** Peoria Civic Center

VOCAL MUSIC

PEORIA CIVIC OPERA
PO Box 120198, Peoria, IL 61604
(309) 673-0864
Founded: 1973
Arts Area: Grand Opera; Light Opera; Musical Theatre
Status: Professional; Non-Profit
Type: Performing; Educational
Management: Dr. Fiora Contino, Artistic Director/Conductor
Paid Staff: 1 **Volunteer Staff:** 32
Paid Artists: 150 **Non-Paid Artists:** 200
Utilizes: Guest Conductors; Guest Artists; Guest Directors
Budget: $100,000 - $500,000
Income Sources: Private Foundations/Grants/Endowments; Business/Corporate Donations; Box Office; Government Grants; Individual Donations
Season: September - April **Annual Attendance:** 6,000
Performance Facilities: Civic Center Theatre

THEATRE

PEORIA PLAYERS THEATRE
4300 North University, Peoria, IL 61614
(309) 688-4473
Founded: 1919
Arts Area: Community
Status: Non-Professional; Non-Profit
Type: Performing; Resident; Educational
Purpose: The presentation of plays and the study of theatre for and by the community
Management: Rebecca Canty, Theatre Manager
Officers: Arno Loeffler, President; Tom Broderick, Vice President; Gail Anderson, Secretary; Gene Pratt, Treasurer
Paid Staff: 4 **Volunteer Staff:** 300
Budget: $50,000 - $100,000
Income Sources: Private Foundations/Grants/Endowments; Business/Corporate Donations; Box Office; Individual Donations
Season: September - May **Annual Attendance:** 24,000
Affiliations: AACT; Illinois Theatre Association
Performance Facilities: Peoria Players Theatre

PERFORMING SERIES

AMATEUR MUSICAL CLUB OF PEORIA, INC.
416 Hamilton Boulevard, Box 666, Peoria, IL 61652
(309) 674-6516
Founded: 1906
Arts Area: Dance; Vocal Music; Instrumental Music
Status: Professional; Non-Profit
Type: Educational; Sponsoring
Purpose: To offer an annual series of world-class artists
Management: Natalie Casper, Office Manager
Officers: Thomas F. Broderick, President; Tim Bertschy, Vice President; Louise Mueller, Treasurer; Nancy Morgan, Secretary
Paid Staff: 1
Paid Artists: 150 **Non-Paid Artists:** 75
Utilizes: Guest Conductors; Guest Artists; Dance Companies
Budget: $100,000 - $500,000
Income Sources: Private Foundations/Grants/Endowments; Business/Corporate Donations; Box Office; Government Grants; Individual Donations
Season: September - April **Annual Attendance:** 10,000
Affiliations: APAP; Arts Midwest
Performance Facilities: Peoria Civic Center Theatre

FACILITY

PEORIA CIVIC CENTER
201 SW Jefferson Street, Peoria, IL 61602-1448
(309) 673-8900
Type of Facility: Civic Center
Year Built: 1982 **Architect:** Philip Johnson & John Burgee **Cost:** $64,300,000

Acoustical Consultant: Jaffe Acoustics
Contact for Rental: Debbie Ritschell, Booking Manager; (309) 673-8900
Peoria Civic Center contains the Arena, Exhibition Hall and Theatre. See individual listings for additional information.

PEORIA CIVIC CENTER - ARENA
201 Southwest Jefferson Street, Peoria, IL 61602-1448
(309) 673-8900
    Type of Facility: Concert Hall; Arena
    Type of Stage: Flexible
    Stage Dimensions: 60'x40'
    Seating Capacity: 12,400
    Year Built: 1982
    Contact for Rental: Debbie Ritschell, Booking Manager; (309) 673-8900

PEORIA CIVIC CENTER - EXHIBITION HALL
201 SW Jefferson Street, Peoria, IL 61602
(309) 673-8900
    Type of Facility: Exhibition Hall
    Type of Stage: Flexible; Platform
    Year Built: 1982
    Contact for Rental: Debbie Ritschell, Booking Manager; (309) 673-8900
    Exhibition Hall contains 33,000 square feet

PEORIA CIVIC CENTER - THEATRE
201 SW Jefferson Street, Peoria, IL 61602
(309) 673-8900
    Type of Facility: Concert Hall; Theatre House; Opera House
    Type of Stage: Thrust; Proscenium
    Stage Dimensions: 50'Wx26'3"D **Orchestra Pit**
    Seating Capacity: 2,187
    Year Built: 1982
    Contact for Rental: Debbie Ritschell, Booking Manager; (309) 673-8900
    Manager: Jon Smock, Stage Manager; (309) 673-8900, ext. 240
    Resident Groups: Peoria Civic Opera; Peoria Symphony Orchestra; Peoria Civic Ballet; Peoria Area Civic Chorale; Amateur Musical Club; Broadway Theater Series; YouTHeater

PEORIA PLAYERS THEATRE
4300 North University, Peoria, IL 61614
(309) 688-4473
    Type of Facility: Auditorium; Theatre House
    Type of Stage: Proscenium
    Stage Dimensions: 15'x36'x40'
    Seating Capacity: 390
    Year Built: 1956 **Architect:** Leslie Keynon **Cost:** $225,000
    Contact for Rental: Rebecca Canty, Manager; (309) 688-4473
    Manager: Rebecca Canty
    Resident Groups: Peoria Players Theatre
    Musical, dance, lectures

Quincy

INSTRUMENTAL MUSIC

QUINCY SYMPHONY ORCHESTRA
428 Main, Quincy, IL 62301
(217) 222-2856
    Founded: 1947
    Arts Area: Symphony; Orchestra; Chamber
    Status: Non-Professional; Non-Profit
    Type: Performing; Resident; Educational
    Purpose: To bring fine orchestral music to the area, providing local musicians the opportunity to perform; to provide educational programs
    Management: Douglas W. Reeve, General Manager; Vivian Langellier, Executive Secretary
    Officers: Fr. Harry Speakman o.f.m., President
    Paid Staff: 7
    Paid Artists: 25 **Non-Paid Artists:** 45
    Utilizes: Guest Artists
    Budget: $50,000 - $100,000

Income Sources: Private Foundations/Grants/Endowments; Business/Corporate Donations; Box Office; Government Grants; Individual Donations
Season: October - May   **Annual Attendance:** 9,000
Affiliations: ASOL; Illinois Council of Orchestras
Performance Facilities: Quincy Junior High School Auditorium

River Forest

INSTRUMENTAL MUSIC

CHICAGO SINFONIETTA
7900 West Division Street, River Forest, IL 60305
(708) 366-1062
FAX: (708) 366-5419
Founded: 1987
Arts Area: Symphony; Orchestra; Chamber; Ethnic
Status: Professional; Non-Profit
Type: Performing; Touring; Educational
Purpose: To present classical music in original orchestration; to promote ethnic diversity in the concert hall
Management: Camille McGinley, General Manager; Margaret Burk, Director of Development; Derek Scruggs, Operations Coordinator
Officers: Paul Freeman, President; Jim Paglia, Executive Vice President; Bill Kashul and Bettiann Gardner, Vice Presidents; Howard Shapiro, Treasurer; Roger Wilson, Secretary
Paid Staff: 7
Utilizes: Guest Conductors; Guest Artists
Budget: $500,000 - $1,000,000
Income Sources: Private Foundations/Grants/Endowments; Business/Corporate Donations; Box Office; Government Grants; Individual Donations
Season: September - June   **Annual Attendance:** 9,000
Affiliations: Chicago Music Alliance
Performance Facilities: Lund Auditorium, Rosary College

River Grove

FACILITY

RICHARD BURTON PERFORMING ARTS CENTER TRITON COLLEGE
2000 Fifth Avenue, River Grove, IL 60171
(708) 456-0300, ext. 375
FAX: (708) 456-0049
Founded: 1967
Type of Facility: Concert Hall; Auditorium; Performance Center; Theatre House; Multi-Purpose
Facility Originally: Meeting Hall
Type of Stage: Proscenium
Stage Dimensions: 44'Wx20'D proscenium opening   **Orchestra Pit**
Seating Capacity: 412
Year Built: 1981
Year Remodeled: 1982
Contact for Rental: Steven Ginley;   (708) 456-0300, ext. 375; 804
Resident Groups: Triton College Fine Arts Department; AlphaBet Soup Children's Theatre Company

Rock Island

THEATRE

CIRCA '21 DINNER PLAYHOUSE
1828 Third Avenue, Rock Island, IL 61201
(309) 786-2667
FAX: (309) 786-4119
Founded: 1976
Arts Area: Professional; Dinner
Status: Professional; Commercial
Type: Performing; Touring; Resident
Purpose: To provide year-round professional plays and musicals along with high-quality fine dining
Management: Dennis Hitchcock, Producer
Paid Staff: 70

Utilizes: Special Technical Talent; Guest Directors
Budget: $1,000,000 - $5,000,000
Income Sources: Box Office
Season: 52 Weeks   **Annual Attendance:** 75,000

PERFORMING SERIES

QUAD CITY ARTS
1715 Second Avenue, Rock Island, IL 61201
(309) 793-1213
FAX: (309) 793-1265
　　　Founded: 1988
　　　Arts Area: Dance; Vocal Music; Instrumental Music; Theater
　　　Status: Non-Profit
　　　Type: Performing; Educational
　　　Purpose: To present 400 community concerts by professional perfroming artists througout a 100 mile radius of the area; to maintain local and regional visual exhibitions
　　　Management: Diane Sulg, Executive Director; Holly Richard, Director of Visiting Artist Series; Lloyd Schoeneman, Director of Programs; Steve Fors, Gallery Manager
　　　Paid Staff: 14   **Volunteer Staff:** 3
　　　Paid Artists: 50
　　　Utilizes: Guest Artists
　　　Budget: $1,000,000 - $5,000,000
　　　Income Sources: Private Foundations/Grants/Endowments; Business/Corporate Donations; Government Grants; Individual Donations
　　　Season: 52 Weeks   **Annual Attendance:** 150,000
　　　Affiliations: APAP

FACILITY

AUGUSTANA COLLEGE - CENTENNIAL HALL
639 38th Street, Rock Island, IL 61201
(309) 794-7306
FAX: (309) 794-7431
　　　Type of Facility: Auditorium
　　　Type of Stage: Proscenium
　　　Seating Capacity: 1,620
　　　Year Built: 1959   **Cost:** $1,150,000
　　　Manager: Dan Urton, Director
　　　Resident Groups: Augustana Choir; Augustana Concert Band; Augustana Symphony Orchestra; Handel Oratorio Society; Quad-City Symphony Orchestra

Rockford

DANCE

ROCKFORD DANCE COMPANY
711 North Main Street, Rockford, IL 61103
(815) 963-3341
　　　Founded: 1972
　　　Arts Area: Modern; Ballet; Jazz
　　　Status: Semi-Professional; Non-Profit
　　　Type: Performing; Resident; Educational; Sponsoring
　　　Purpose: To serve as an arts resource in dance through presentations, performances and education
　　　Management: Melissa Teske, Executive Director; Joy Xu, Artistic Director
　　　Officers: Grace Wilson, President; L. Paul Harnois, Vice President/Finance; John Holevas, Vice President/Administration; Joyce Lombardozzi, Treasurer; Gail Barton, Secretary
　　　Paid Staff: 3
　　　Paid Artists: 6   **Non-Paid Artists:** 15
　　　Utilizes: Guest Artists; Guest Choreographers
　　　Budget: $100,000 - $500,000

Income Sources: Private Foundations/Grants/Endowments; Business/Corporate Donations; Box Office; Government Grants; Individual Donations
Season: September - May

INSTRUMENTAL MUSIC

ROCKFORD SYMPHONY ORCHESTRA
711 North Main, Rockford, IL 61103
(815) 965-0049
FAX: (815) 965-0042
Arts Area: Symphony
Status: Professional; Non-Profit
Type: Performing
Purpose: To provide symphonic music
Management: Steven Larsen, Music Director; Camille Day, Executive Director
Officers: Robert Fredrickson, President; LoRayne Logan, Vice President; Eugene Engrav, Treasurer; Scott Sullivan, Secretary
Paid Staff: 3
Utilizes: Guest Conductors; Guest Artists
Budget: $100,000 - $500,000
Income Sources: Private Foundations/Grants/Endowments; Business/Corporate Donations; Box Office; Government Grants; Individual Donations
Season: October - May   **Annual Attendance:** 6,000
Affiliations: ASOL
Performance Facilities: Midway Theater; Coronado Theater

THEATRE

NEW AMERICAN THEATER
118 North Main, Rockford, IL 61101
(815) 963-9454
FAX: (815) 963-7215
Founded: 1972
Arts Area: Professional; Theatrical Group
Status: Professional; Non-Profit
Type: Performing; Touring; Resident; Educational
Purpose: To present classic, modern and new work
Management: J.R. Sullivan, Producing Director
Officers: John Pick, President; David Bippus, Vice President of Operations; Mark Murphy, Vice President of Development; Dewayne Fellows, Treasurer
Paid Staff: 14   **Volunteer Staff:** 25
Paid Artists: 10   **Non-Paid Artists:** 20
Utilizes: Special Technical Talent; Guest Artists; Guest Directors
Budget: $1,000,000 - $5,000,000
Income Sources: Private Foundations/Grants/Endowments; Business/Corporate Donations; Box Office; Government Grants; Individual Donations
Season: September - June   **Annual Attendance:** 37,000
Affiliations: TCG
Performance Facilities: New American Theater

FACILITY

MIDWAY THEATRE
721 East State Street, Rockford, IL 61104
(815) 965-2511
FAX: (815) 964-8378
Founded: 1918
Type of Facility: Concert Hall; Auditorium
Facility Originally: Movie House
Type of Stage: Thrust
Stage Dimensions: 40'x90'
Seating Capacity: 1,500
Year Built: 1918   **Architect:** J.E.O. Pridmore
Year Remodeled: 1981   **Architect:** Gary Anderson
Contact for Rental: Mary S. Campbell;   (815) 965-2511
Resident Groups: Rockford Symphony Orchestra

Saint Charles

INSTRUMENTAL MUSIC

ILLINOIS CHAMBER SYMPHONY
12 South First Avenue, Saint Charles, IL 60174
(708) 377-6423
FAX: (708) 377-3105
Founded: 1983
Arts Area: Orchestra; Chamber
Status: Professional; Non-Profit
Type: Performing
Purpose: To promote live classical music of the highest artistic caliber and foster cultural growth in the state of Illinois
Management: Stephen Squires, Music Director; Robert Murphy, Marketing Director; Catherine Squires, Executive Director; Tim Juergensen, Librarian; Amy Scarlato, Personnel Manager
Officers: Charles Brown, President; Jeffrey Hunt, Vice President; William Simmons, Secretary/Treasurer
Paid Staff: 5   **Volunteer Staff:** 2
Paid Artists: 35
Utilizes: Guest Artists
Budget: $50,000 - $100,000
Income Sources: Private Foundations/Grants/Endowments; Business/Corporate Donations; Box Office; Government Grants; Individual Donations
Season: October - May   **Annual Attendance:** 5,000
Affiliations: ICO; Kane County Tourism Association; ASOL; Fox Valley Arts Council
Performance Facilities: Norris Cultural Arts Center; Baker Methodist Church

THEATRE

PHEASANT RUN THEATRE
PO Box 64, Saint Charles, IL 60174
(708) 584-6342
Founded: 1964
Arts Area: Professional; Dinner
Status: Professional; Commercial
Type: Performing
Management: Diana Martinez, Producer/Director
Paid Staff: 12
Paid Artists: 16
Utilizes: Guest Directors
Budget: $100,000 - $500,000
Income Sources: Box Office
Season: 52 Weeks   **Annual Attendance:** 60,000

FACILITY

NORRIS CULTURAL ARTS CENTER
1040 Dunham Road, Saint Charles, IL 60174
(708) 584-9599
FAX: (708) 513-5392
Founded: 1978
Type of Facility: Concert Hall; Performance Center; Theatre House; Gallery
Type of Stage: Proscenium
Stage Dimensions: 40'D (wing space 24'x40'); 30'x50' proscenium opening   **Orchestra Pit**
Seating Capacity: 1,000
Year Built: 1978   **Architect:** Ron Gerritis
Contact for Rental: Patti Harmon-Lind;   (708) 584-9599
Resident Groups: No Center Aisle Theatre Company

Skokie

DANCE

PASCUAL OLIVERA AND ANGELA DEL MORAL'S CELEBRATION OF SPANISH DANCE
7017 Lorel, Skokie, IL 60077
(708) 675-7456
Founded: 1977
Arts Area: Ethnic

Status: Professional
Type: Performing; Touring; Resident; Educational
Purpose: To romantically celebrate Spanish dance from the classical, to the folk, to the Flamenco
Management: Siegel Artist Management
Officers: Ethel Siegel, Liz Silverstein, Jane Curtiss, Co-Directors; Pascual Olivera, Angela Del Moral, Directors
Paid Staff: 2
Paid Artists: 5
Utilizes: Special Technical Talent
Budget: $50,000 - $100,000
Income Sources: Box Office; Touring Fees
Season: 52 Weeks

THEATRE

CENTRE EAST
7701A Lincoln Avenue, Skokie, IL 60077
(708) 673-6305
Founded: 1979
Arts Area: Professional; Musical
Status: Non-Profit
Type: Performing
Purpose: To present and provide the best in the performing arts
Officers: Dorothy S. Litwin, Executive Director
Paid Staff: 10 **Volunteer Staff:** 150
Utilizes: Guest Artists
Budget: $1,000,000 - $5,000,000
Income Sources: Private Foundations/Grants/Endowments; Business/Corporate Donations; Box Office; Government Grants; Individual Donations
Season: September - June

FACILITY

CENTRE EAST
7701A Lincoln Avenue, Skokie, IL 60077
(708) 673-6305
FAX: (708) 673-6327
Founded: 1979
Type of Facility: Theatre Complex; Concert Hall; Auditorium
Facility Originally: School
Type of Stage: Proscenium
Stage Dimensions: 80'Wx40'D **Orchestra Pit**
Seating Capacity: 1,310
Year Built: 1963
Contact for Rental: Jula Radom; (708) 673-6305
Manager: Dorothy Litwin; (708) 673-6305
Resident Groups: Skokie Valley Symphony Orchestra

Springfield

DANCE

SPRINGFIELD BALLET COMPANY
2820 South MacArthur, Springfield, IL 62704
(217) 544-1967
Founded: 1975
Arts Area: Modern; Ballet; Jazz; Folk
Status: Non-Professional; Non-Profit
Type: Performing; Touring; Educational; Sponsoring
Purpose: To foster and promote dance in central Illinois
Management: Grace Luttrell Nanavati, Artistic Director; Julienne Guttas, Ballet Mistress/Manager
Paid Staff: 3 **Volunteer Staff:** 20
Non-Paid Artists: 30
Utilizes: Special Technical Talent; Guest Artists; Guest Directors
Budget: $100,000 - $500,000
Income Sources: Private Foundations/Grants/Endowments; Business/Corporate Donations; Box Office; Government Grants; Individual Donations
Season: June - May **Annual Attendance:** 17,000
Performance Facilities: Sangamon State University

INSTRUMENTAL MUSIC

SPRINGFIELD SYMPHONY ORCHESTRA
524 1/2 East Capitol Avenue, Springfield, IL 62701
(217) 522-2838
FAX: (217) 522-7374
> **Founded:** 1921
> **Arts Area:** Symphony; Orchestra; Chamber; Ensemble
> **Status:** Professional; Non-Profit
> **Type:** Performing; Touring; Resident; Educational
> **Purpose:** To sponsor, promote and assist in the presentation of symphonic concerts; encourage and develop a desire for symphonic music; instruct, assist and develop musical abilities; assist in training and education; provide concerts, musical programs and other entertainment
> **Management:** Linda G. Moore, General Manager; Kenneth Kiesler, Music Director/Conductor; Judith Lampert, Orchestra Manager
> **Paid Staff:** 4 **Volunteer Staff:** 3
> **Paid Artists:** 100
> **Utilizes:** Guest Artists
> **Budget:** $500,000 - $1,000,000
> **Income Sources:** Private Foundations/Grants/Endowments; Business/Corporate Donations; Box Office; Government Grants; Individual Donations; Touring Fees
> **Season:** September - April **Annual Attendance:** 35,000
> **Affiliations:** ASOL; CMA; Illinois Arts Alliance
> **Performance Facilities:** Braden Auditorium-Illinois State University; Sangamon State University Auditorium

FACILITY

SANGAMON STATE UNIVERSITY AUDITORIUM
Sangamon State University, Springfield, IL 62794-9243
(217) 786-6150
FAX: (217) 786-7279
> **Founded:** 1981
> **Type of Facility:** Auditorium
> **Type of Stage:** Proscenium
> **Stage Dimensions:** 120'x44' **Orchestra Pit**
> **Seating Capacity:** 1,951; 60 additional in pit
> **Year Built:** 1980 **Architect:** Ferry & Henderson **Cost:** $18,000,000
> **Acoustical Consultant:** Kirkegaard
> **Contact for Rental:** Ann Schleyhann; (217) 786-6150

SPRINGFIELD COLLEGE - MUSIC HALL
1500 North Fifth Street, Springfield, IL 62702
(217) 525-1420
> **Type of Facility:** Concert Hall; Studio Performance
> **Type of Stage:** Proscenium
> **Stage Dimensions:** 26'x26'
> **Seating Capacity:** 250
> **Year Built:** 1910
> **Contact for Rental:** Fred Greenwald; (217) 525-1420, ext. 33

Summit

THEATRE

CANDLELIGHT DINNER PLAYHOUSE AND FORUM THEATRE
5620 South Harlem, Summit, IL 60501
(708) 496-3000
> **Founded:** 1959
> **Arts Area:** Professional; Musical; Dinner
> **Status:** Professional; Commercial
> **Type:** Performing; Resident
> **Purpose:** America's first dinner theatre prides itself on presenting first-class Broadway musicals year round.
> **Management:** William Pullinsi, Producer/Director; Anthony D'Angelo, Producer/Designer
> **Officers:** William Pullinsi, President
> **Paid Staff:** 150
> **Paid Artists:** 30
> **Utilizes:** Special Technical Talent

Income Sources: Box Office
Season: 52 Weeks
Performance Facilities: Forum Theatre

Urbana

FACILITY

KRANNERT CENTER FOR THE PERFORMING ARTS
500 South Goodwin Avenue, Urbana, IL 61801
(217) 333-6700
FAX: (217) 244-0810
    Type of Facility: Theatre Complex; Performance Center
    Year Built: 1969   **Architect:** Max Abramovitz   **Cost:** $21,000,000
    Acoustical Consultant: Dr. Cyril M. Harris
    Contact for Rental: Janet Taylor; (217) 333-6703
    Manager: Terrence D. Jones
    Resident Groups: Illinois Repertory Theatre; Illinois Opera Theatre; Illinois Dance Theatre; Champaign-Urbana Symphony; Sinfonia da Camera
    The Performing Arts Center contains Colwell Playhouse, Festival Theatre, Foellinger Great Hall and Studio Theatre. See individual listings for additional information.

KRANNERT CENTER FOR THE PERFORMING ARTS - COLWELL PLAYHOUSE
500 South Goodwin Avenue, Urbana, IL 61801
(217) 333-6700
FAX: (217) 244-0810
    Type of Facility: Concert Hall; Theatre House
    Type of Stage: Proscenium; Hydraulic Lift Stage
    Stage Dimensions: 38'Wx33'D, 18'D added with lifts at stage level   **Orchestra Pit**
    Seating Capacity: 675, continental seating
    Contact for Rental: Janet Taylor; (217) 333-6703
    Manager: Terrence D. Jones
    Resident Groups: Illinois Repertory Theatre; Illinois Dance Theatre

KRANNERT CENTER FOR THE PERFORMING ARTS - FESTIVAL THEATRE
500 South Goodwin Avenue, Urbana, IL 61801
(217) 333-6700
FAX: (217) 244-0810
    Type of Facility: Concert Hall; Theatre House
    Type of Stage: Proscenium; Hydraulic Lift Stage
    Stage Dimensions: 40'Wx35'D, 16'D added with lifts at stage level
    Orchestra Pit
    Seating Capacity: 1,000
    Contact for Rental: Terrence D, Jones, Manager; (217) 333-6703
    Manager: Terrence D. Jones; (216) 333-6703
    Resident Groups: Illinois Opera Theatre; Illinois Dance Theatre; Kabuki Theatre with Shozo Sato
    Two hydraulic lifts: 6'Dx40'W and 8'Dx40'W, each operates independently

KRANNERT CENTER FOR THE PERFORMING ARTS - FOELLINGER GREAT HALL
500 South Goodwin Avenue, Urbana, IL 61801
(217) 333-6700
FAX: (217) 244-0810
    Type of Facility: Concert Hall
    Type of Stage: Concert Stage
    Stage Dimensions: 60'Wx48'D, 8'D added with lift at stage level   **Orchestra Pit**
    Seating Capacity: 2,100
    Contact for Rental: Janet Taylor; (217) 333-6703
    Resident Groups: Champaign-Urbana Symphony; Sinfonia da Camera
    One hydraulic lift, 8'Dx60'W

KRANNERT CENTER FOR THE PERFORMING ARTS - STUDIO THEATRE
500 South Goodwin Avenue, Urbana, IL 61801
(217) 333-6700
FAX: (217) 244-0810
    Type of Facility: Studio Performance; Black Box
    Type of Stage: Flexible
    Stage Dimensions: 45'x55' Black Box with 15'H Grid

Seating Capacity: 200
Contact for Rental: Janet Taylor;   (217) 333-6703
Resident Groups: Illinois Repertory Theatre; Illinois Dance Theatre

Waukegan

FACILITY

GOODFELLOW HALL (JACK BENNY CENTER FOR THE ARTS)
39 Jack Benny Drive, Waukegan, IL 60087
(708) 360-4741
FAX: (708) 244-8270
    Founded: 1987
    Type of Facility: Auditorium; Studio Performance; Performance Center; Theatre House; Opera House
    Facility Originally: Meeting Hall; Ballroom
    Type of Stage: Lecture; Recital
    Stage Dimensions: 18'Dx23"W
    Seating Capacity: 100
    Year Built: 1922   **Architect:** Hull House   **Cost:** $1,200
    Year Remodeled: 1987   **Architect:** Waukegan Park District   **Cost:** $18,000
    Contact for Rental: Lynn Schornick;   (708) 360-4741
    Resident Groups: Bowen Park Opera Company; Bowen Park Theatre Company

Western Springs

THEATRE

THEATRE OF WESTERN SPRINGS
4384 Hampton Avenue, Western Springs, IL 60558
(708) 246-4043
    Founded: 1929
    Arts Area: Community; Theatrical Group; Children's Theatre
    Status: Non-Professional; Non-Profit
    Type: Performing; Educational; Sponsoring
    Purpose: To promote, develop and maintain a community theatre producing plays of significance and interest; to provide an open forum for the arts
    Management: Ronn Toebaas, Artistic Director; Jeanne Hopson, Children's Theatre Director
    Officers: Jon Mills, Chairperson
    Paid Staff: 3
    Non-Paid Artists: 250
    Utilizes: Guest Directors
    Budget: $100,000 - $500,000
    Income Sources: Business/Corporate Donations; Box Office; Individual Donations
    Season: September - July
    Affiliations: AACT

Wheaton

INSTRUMENTAL MUSIC

WHEATON SYMPHONY ORCHESTRA
1600 East Roosevelt Road, Wheaton, IL 60187
(708) 668-8585
    Founded: 1959
    Arts Area: Symphony
    Status: Non-Professional
    Type: Performing
    Purpose: To perform the music of 19th and 20th-century composers, composed for large orchestras
    Management: Dr. Donald C. Mattison, General Manager
    Volunteer Staff: 2
    Non-Paid Artists: 2
    Budget: $1,000 - $50,000
    Income Sources: Box Office; Individual Donations
    Season: June - August

Affiliations: ASOL
Performance Facilities: Edman Chapel, Wheaton College

FACILITY

WHEATON COLLEGE - ARENA THEATER
501 East College Avenue, Wheaton, IL 60187
(708) 260-5000
    Type of Facility: Black Box
    Facility Originally: Recreation Hall/gymnasium
    Type of Stage: Flexible
    Stage Dimensions: 60'Wx39'D
    Seating Capacity: 180
    Year Built: 1984
    Contact for Rental: Virginia Kolb
    Resident Groups: Wheaton College Opera Theatre; Wheaton College Players

WHEATON COLLEGE - EDMAN CHAPEL
501 East College Avenue, Wheaton, IL 60187
(708) 752-5000
    Type of Facility: Concert Hall; Auditorium
    Facility Originally: Chapel
    Type of Stage: Proscenium
    Stage Dimensions: 52'x71'x26'
    Seating Capacity: 2,383
    Year Built: 1961   **Architect:** J. Emil Anderson & Son   **Cost:** $1,525,000
    Contact for Rental: Virginia Kolb
    Resident Groups: Wheaton College Concert Choir; Wheaton College Men's Glee Club; Wheaton College Women's Chorale; Wheaton College Wind Ensemble; Wheaton College Symphony Orchestra

Winnetka

THEATRE

T. DANIEL MIME/MOVEMENT THEATRE
1047 Gage, Winnetka, IL 60093
(708) 441-0183
    Founded: 1971
    Arts Area: Professional; Theatrical Group
    Status: Professional
    Type: Performing
    Purpose: To create and present on tour programs on mime and theatre for adults, families and children
    Paid Staff: 1   **Volunteer Staff:** 1
    Paid Artists: 2
    Budget: $1,000 - $50,000
    Income Sources: Box Office; Government Grants
    Season: 52 Weeks   **Annual Attendance:** 100,000

FACILITY

DILLER STREET THEATER
310 Greenbay Road, Winnetka, IL 60093
(708) 446-1978
    Founded: 1980
    Type of Facility: Concert Hall; Auditorium; Theatre House; Multi-Purpose
    Type of Stage: Proscenium
    Stage Dimensions: 40'x30'   **Seating Capacity:** 471
    Year Built: 1926   **Architect:** Edwin Clark
    Year Remodeled: 1991   **Architect:** Schuler and Shook, Consultants
    Contact for Rental: Lisa Tomoleoni;   (312) 446-1978
    Resident Groups: Chicago Children's Theater; North Shore Country Day School

Woodridge

INSTRUMENTAL MUSIC

THE CHINESE CLASSICAL ORCHESTRA
Chinese Music Society of North America, One Heritage Plaza PO Box 5275, Woodridge, IL 60517-0275
(708) 910-1551
FAX: (708) 910-1561
Founded: 1976
Arts Area: Orchestra; Ensemble; Ethnic; Folk
Status: Professional; Non-Profit
Type: Performing; Touring
Purpose: To create music of the 21st century; to perform using the tonal groups of reeded wind, percussion, plucked string and bowed string; to employ just intervals; to tour internationally and in North America year round
Management: Dr. Yuan-Yuan Lee, Director
Officers: Dr. Sin-yan Shen, Music Director; Dr. Yuan-Yuan Lee, Director of Concert and Lecture; Kerry Leung, Production Manager; Billie J. Jefferson, Artistic Administrator
Paid Staff: 10   **Volunteer Staff:** 12
Paid Artists: 28
Utilizes: Special Technical Talent; Guest Conductors; Guest Artists; Guest Directors
Budget: $500,000 - $1,000,000
Income Sources: Private Foundations/Grants/Endowments; Business/Corporate Donations; Box Office; Government Grants; Individual Donations
Season: 52 Weeks
Annual Attendance: 500,000

CHINESE MUSIC EDUCATIONAL PROGRAM
Chinese Music Society of North America, One Heritage Plaza, PO Box 5275, Woodridge, IL 60517-0275
(708) 910-1551
FAX: (708) 910-1561
Founded: 1986
Status: Professional; Non-Profit
Type: Performing; Touring; Educational
Purpose: To provide a national educational program on Chinese music and music of the world, using methods based on musical psychology, thereby eliminating cultural barriers; to provide programs internationally
Management: Dr. Yuan-Yuan Lee, Director Concert and Lecture Department
Officers: Dr. Sin-yan Shen, Music Director; Dr.Yuan-Yuan Lee, Director of Concert and Lecture; Billie J. Jefferson, Artistic Administrator; Scott Conover, Program Manager
Paid Staff: 4   **Volunteer Staff:** 12
Paid Artists: 28
Utilizes: Special Technical Talent; Guest Conductors; Guest Artists; Guest Directors
Budget: $500,000 - $1,000,000
Income Sources: Private Foundations/Grants/Endowments; Business/Corporate Donations; Box Office; Government Grants; Individual Donations
Season: 52 Weeks
Annual Attendance: 500,000

CHINESE MUSIC SOCIETY OF NORTH AMERICA
One Heritage Plaza, PO Box 5275, Woodridge, IL 60517-0275
(708) 910-1551
FAX: (708) 910-1561
Founded: 1976
Arts Area: Symphony; Orchestra; Chamber; Ensemble; Ethnic; Folk; Instrumental Group; Electronic & Live Electronic
Status: Professional; Non-Profit
Type: Performing; Touring; Resident; Educational; Sponsoring
Purpose: The largest Chinese music educational service institution in North America; publishes the Chinese Music Monograph Series, the international journal Chinese Music, and educational material on music and acoustics, and recordings and videos
Management: Dr. Yuan-Yuan Lee, Director Concert and Lecture Department
Officers: Dr. Sin-yan Shen, President; Kok-Koon Ng, Vice President
Paid Staff: 11   **Volunteer Staff:** 30
Paid Artists: 28
Utilizes: Special Technical Talent; Guest Conductors; Guest Artists; Guest Directors
Budget: $500,000 - $1,000,000
Income Sources: Private Foundations/Grants/Endowments; Business/Corporate Donations; Box Office; Government Grants; Individual Donations

Season: 52 Weeks
Annual Attendance: 500,000

THE SILK AND BAMBOO ENSEMBLE
Chinese Music Society of North America, One Heritage Plaza, PO Box 5275, Woodridge, IL 60517-0275
(708) 910-1551
FAX: (708) 910-1561
Founded: 1981
Arts Area: Chamber; Ensemble; Ethnic; Instrumental Group
Status: Professional; Non-Profit
Type: Performing; Touring; Educational
Purpose: To create chamber music of the 21st century; to perform works utilizing silk and bamboo instrumentation and just intervals; to tour internationally and in the U.S. year round
Management: Dr. Yuan-Yuan Lee, Director Concert and Lecture Department
Officers: Dr. Sin-yan Shen, Music Director
Paid Staff: 4   Volunteer Staff: 6
Paid Artists: 5
Utilizes: Special Technical Talent; Guest Conductors; Guest Artists; Guest Directors
Budget: $500,000 - $1,000,000
Income Sources: Private Foundations/Grants/Endowments; Business/Corporate Donations; Box Office; Government Grants; Individual Donations
Season: 52 Weeks
Annual Attendance: 500,000

Woodstock

PERFORMING SERIES

WOODSTOCK OPERA HOUSE
121 Van Buren Street, Woodstock, IL 60098
(815) 338-4212
Founded: 1977
Arts Area: Dance; Vocal Music; Instrumental Music; Theater; Festivals
Status: Non-Profit
Type: Performing; Resident; Educational; Sponsoring
Purpose: To be a cultural center for McHenry County, Illinois, highlighting Illinois, American and international artists; to work closely with the Woodstock community
Management: John Scharres, Executive Director
Paid Staff: 6   Volunteer Staff: 200
Paid Artists: 50   Non-Paid Artists: 50
Utilizes: Special Technical Talent; Guest Conductors; Guest Artists; Guest Directors
Budget: $500,000 - $1,000,000
Income Sources: Private Foundations/Grants/Endowments; Business/Corporate Donations; Box Office; Government Grants; Individual Donations
Season: 52 Weeks   Annual Attendance: 70,000
Affiliations: ISPAA; APAP
Performance Facilities: Woodstock Opera House

FACILITY

WOODSTOCK OPERA HOUSE
121 Van Buren Street, Woodstock, IL 60098
(815) 338-4212
Type of Facility: Opera House
Type of Stage: Proscenium
Stage Dimensions: 24'x15'x26'
Seating Capacity: 429
Year Built: 1890   Architect: Smith Hoag   Cost: $25,000
Year Remodeled: 1977   Architect: John Vincent Anderson   Cost: $500,000
Contact for Rental: Manager;   (815) 338-4212
Resident Groups: Townsquare Players; Judith Svalander Dance Theatre; Woodstock Musical Theatre Company
Woodstock Opera House is a National Historic Landmark

Zion

THEATRE

ZION PASSION PLAY
2500 Dowie Memorial Drive, Zion, IL 60099-2594
(708) 746-2221
FAX: (708) 746-1452
    Founded: 1935
    Arts Area: Musical; Community
    Status: Non-Professional; Non-Profit
    Type: Performing; Resident; Educational
    Purpose: Biblical production of the life of Christ
    Management: Board of Trustees
    Officers: Rev. Roger Ottersen, President; Calvin Weese, Secretary/Treasurer
    Paid Staff: 3   **Volunteer Staff:** 15
    Non-Paid Artists: 200
    Utilizes: Special Technical Talent
    Budget: $1,000 - $50,000
    Income Sources: Box Office; Individual Donations
    Season: Good Friday - May   **Annual Attendance:** 5,200
    Affiliations: Christian Catholic Church
    Performance Facilities: Christian Arts Auditorium

FACILITY

CHRISTIAN ARTS AUDITORIUM
Dowie Memorial Drive, Zion, IL 60099
(708) 746-2221
    Type of Facility: Theatre Complex; Concert Hall; Auditorium
    Facility Originally: Amphitheatre
    Type of Stage: Proscenium
    Stage Dimensions: 90'Wx51'D
    Seating Capacity: 552
    Year Built: 1980   **Architect:** Rehder Rothermel Pekkarin   **Cost:** $994,087
    Acoustical Consultant: Sound, Incorporated
    Resident Groups: Zion Passion Play; Zion Chamber Orchestra; Zion Concert Band; Christian Catholic Church Vesper Service

INDIANA

Anderson

INSTRUMENTAL MUSIC

ANDERSON SYMPHONY ORCHESTRA
PO Box 741, Anderson, IN 46015
(317) 641-4545
Founded: 1978
Arts Area: Symphony
Status: Semi-Professional; Non-Profit
Type: Performing; Resident
Purpose: The production of music and the development of musical culture
Management: Pam Coletti, Manager
Officers: Marion Hovermale, President; John Kane, Treasurer
Paid Staff: 1   **Volunteer Staff:** 5
Paid Artists: 52   **Non-Paid Artists:** 11
Utilizes: Guest Conductors; Guest Artists
Budget: $50,000 - $100,000
Income Sources: Private Foundations/Grants/Endowments; Business/Corporate Donations; Box Office; Government Grants; Individual Donations
Season: October - May   **Annual Attendance:** 9,000
Affiliations: Women's Guild
Performance Facilities: Reardon Auditorium

FACILITY

REARDON AUDITORIUM
1015 East Fifth Street, Anderson, IN 46012
(317) 641-4143
FAX: (317) 641-3851
Founded: 1983
Type of Facility: Auditorium
Type of Stage: Proscenium
Stage Dimensions: 54'x72'   **Orchestra Pit**
Seating Capacity: 2,211
Year Built: 1983   **Architect:** Kent Montgomery   **Cost:** $5,500,000
Contact for Rental: Roger Byrd;   (317) 641-4144

Bedford

THEATRE

BEDFORD LITTLE THEATRE
PO Box 142, Bedford, IN 47421
(812) 279-3009
Founded: 1960
Arts Area: Musical; Community; Theatrical Group
Status: Non-Profit
Type: Performing
Purpose: To provide an opportunity for volunteer performers and directors to entertain our community with theatrical productions
Management: Board of Directors, Executive Committee
Officers: Richard Hahn, President; Jack May, Vice President; Judith Jacobs, Treasurer; Lisa Hardwick, Secretary
Volunteer Staff: 8
Non-Paid Artists: 150
Budget: $1,000 - $50,000
Income Sources: Box Office; Individual Donations
Season: September - June   **Annual Attendance:** 700
Performance Facilities: Little Theatre

Bloomington

INSTRUMENTAL MUSIC

BLOOMINGTON SYMPHONY ORCHESTRA
PO Box 1823, Bloomington, IN 47402
(812) 331-2320
Founded: 1969
Arts Area: Symphony; Orchestra
Status: Non-Profit
Type: Performing; Touring; Educational
Purpose: To present quality performances of orchestra literature to the community of Bloomington and its surrounding areas, fulfilling a function not met by the Indiana University symphonies
Management: Faythe Freese, General Manager; David Pickett, Music Director; Pat Kinzer, Personnel Manager
Officers: Judy Schmid, President; Rodney Young, Vice President; Pat Fell Barker, Treasurer
Volunteer Staff: 14
Non-Paid Artists: 6
Utilizes: Guest Artists
Budget: $50,000 - $100,000
Income Sources: Private Foundations/Grants/Endowments; Business/Corporate Donations; Box Office; Government Grants; Individual Donations
Season: September - May   **Annual Attendance:** 5,000
Affiliations: ASOL
Performance Facilities: St. Mark's Methodist Church

PERFORMING SERIES

INDIANA UNIVERSITY PERFORMING ARTS SERIES
Indiana University Auditorium, Bloomington, IN 47405-5501
(812) 855-9528
FAX: (812) 855-4244
Founded: 1820
Arts Area: Dance; Instrumental Music; Theater
Status: Professional; Non-Profit
Type: Educational; Sponsoring
Purpose: To present to the University community the best available professional performing arts programs
Management: James Holland, Director
Paid Staff: 13   **Volunteer Staff:** 150
Budget: $100,000 - $500,000
Income Sources: Private Foundations/Grants/Endowments; Box Office; Government Grants
Season: September - April
Affiliations: IAAM; APAP
Performance Facilities: Indiana University Auditorium

FACILITY

INDIANA UNIVERSITY AUDITORIUM
Indiana University, Bloomington, IN 47405-5501
(812) 855-9528
FAX: (812) 855-4244
Type of Facility: Concert Hall; Auditorium; Performance Center; Theatre House; Opera House
Type of Stage: Proscenium
Stage Dimensions: 104'Wx40'D   **Orchestra Pit**
Seating Capacity: 3,760
Year Built: 1939   **Architect:** Eggers & Higgins   **Cost:** $1,125,000
Acoustical Consultant: John Ditamore
Contact for Rental: Elise Kushigian;   (812) 855-0170
Manager: James C. Holland, Director;   (812) 855-9528
Our purpose is to present the finest in the performing arts

INDIANA UNIVERSITY MUSICAL ARTS CENTER
Indiana University, School of Music, Bloomington, IN 47405
(812) 335-9053
Type of Facility: Concert Hall; Opera House
Type of Stage: Flexible; Proscenium
Stage Dimensions: 90'Wx60'D   **Orchestra Pit**
Seating Capacity: 1,460
Year Built: 1971   **Architect:** Woolen Associates   **Cost:** $11,300,000

Acoustical Consultant: Bolt, Beranek & Newman
Resident Groups: Indiana University Orchestras; Indiana University Opera Theater; Indiana University Ballet Theater

INDIANA UNIVERSITY THEATRE
Theatre 200, Indiana University, Bloomington, IN 47405
(812) 855-4535
FAX: (812) 855-4704
Type of Facility: Theatre House; Black Box
Type of Stage: Flexible; Proscenium
Orchestra Pit
Seating Capacity: Mainstage - 383; Black Box - 66
Year Built: 1941   **Architect:** Strauss Eggers & Higgins
Acoustical Consultant: Lee Simonson
Manager: R. Keith Michael, Chairman

Brazil

THEATRE

COMMUNITY THEATRE OF CLAY COUNTY
8 East National, Brazil, IN 47834
(812) 443-8012
Founded: 1983
Arts Area: Musical; Dinner; Community; Theatrical Group
Status: Non-Professional; Non-Profit
Type: Performing; Educational
Purpose: To provide opportunities for involvement in the arts in Clay County for all ages, by presenting dinner theatre, musicals, children's workshops, senior citizens programs, and sponsoring drama scholarships
Officers: Susan M. Bradbury, President; John Berry, Vice President; Lois Myers, Secretary/Treasurer
Volunteer Staff: 11
Non-Paid Artists: 200
Utilizes: Special Technical Talent; Guest Conductors; Guest Artists; Guest Directors
Budget: $1,000 - $50,000
Income Sources: Private Foundations/Grants/Endowments; Business/Corporate Donations; Box Office; Individual Donations
Season: 52 Weeks   **Annual Attendance:** 2,000
Affiliations: Arts Illiana; ITA

Bristol

THEATRE

ELKHART CIVIC THEATRE
Bristol Opera House, 210 East Vistula, PO Box 252, Bristol, IN 46507
(219) 848-4116
Founded: 1946
Arts Area: Musical; Community; Theatrical Group
Status: Non-Professional; Non-Profit
Type: Performing; Resident; Educational
Purpose: To provide a high quality theatre experience to audience and participants, including eight major productions per year plus workshops in acting, voice, dance and technical theatre
Management: Frank F. Brush, Manager; Leslie K. Torok, Artistic Director
Officers: William Lavery, President; Kevin Egelsky, Vice President; Brad Gilbert, Treasurer; Frank Brush, Secretary
Paid Staff: 2   **Volunteer Staff:** 10
Non-Paid Artists: 80
Utilizes: Guest Directors
Budget: $100,000 - $500,000
Income Sources: Private Foundations/Grants/Endowments; Business/Corporate Donations; Box Office; Government Grants; Individual Donations
Season: 52 Weeks   **Annual Attendance:** 14,000
Affiliations: Indiana Community Theatre Association; AACT
Performance Facilities: The Bristol Opera House

Brownstown

THEATRE

JACKSON COUNTY COMMUNITY THEATRE
121 West Walnut Street, PO Box 65, Brownstown, IN 47220
(812) 358-2812
    Founded: 1971
    Arts Area: Dinner; Community; Theatrical Group
    Status: Non-Professional; Non-Profit
    Type: Performing; Educational
    Purpose: Produce live plays and bring cultural programs to the community
    Management: Marianne Green, Artistic Director
    Officers: Fred Lewis, President; Mark Coggeshall, Vice President; John Lewis, Secretary; Sarah McGill, Treasurer
    Utilizes: Guest Artists; Guest Directors
    Budget: $1,000 - $50,000
    Income Sources: Business/Corporate Donations; Government Grants; Individual Donations
    Season: September - May   **Annual Attendance:** 2,000
    Affiliations: Indiana Theatre Association
    Performance Facilities: Royal Office Square Theatre

Clarksville

THEATRE

DERBY DINNER PLAYHOUSE
525 Marriott Drive, Clarksville, IN 47129
(812) 288-2632
FAX: (812) 288-2636
    Founded: 1975
    Arts Area: Dinner
    Status: Professional; Commercial
    Type: Performing
    Purpose: Professional dinner entertainment
    Management: Bekki Jo Schneider, Producer; Carolyn Lamb, General Manager
    Paid Staff: 50
    Utilizes: Special Technical Talent; Guest Artists; Guest Directors
    Budget: $100,000 - $500,000
    Income Sources: Business/Corporate Donations; Box Office; Individual Donations
    Season: 52 Weeks
    Performance Facilities: Derby Dinner Playhouse

Columbus

INSTRUMENTAL MUSIC

COLUMBUS PRO MUSICA
302 Washington Street, Columbus, IN 47201
(812) 376-2638
FAX: (812) 376-2567
    Founded: 1971
    Arts Area: Symphony
    Status: Semi-Professional; Non-Profit
    Type: Performing; Educational; Sponsoring
    Purpose: To promote and encourage an active interest in music; to promote and facilitate instruction, study and performing of instrumental music; to work toward providing necessary facilities and equipment; to widen the availability of music instruction; sponsor and present performances
    Management: Alice O. Jolly, Manager; Kaye Ellen Connor, Administrative Assistant; David Bowden, Music Director
    Officers: Robert S. Kasper, President; Nancy Morris, Vice President; Richard A. Stenner, Treasurer; Lori Phillips, Secretary
    Paid Staff: 3
    Utilizes: Guest Artists
    Budget: $100,000 - $500,000
    Income Sources: Private Foundations/Grants/Endowments; Business/Corporate Donations; Box Office; Government Grants; Individual Donations
    Season: September - June   **Annual Attendance:** 15,000
    Affiliations: ASOL; Indiana Orchestra Consort; Indiana Arts Commission; Columbus Area Arts Council

---

Cromwell

THEATRE

ENCHANTED HILLS PLAYHOUSE
9358 East Wizard of Oz Way, PO Box 41, Cromwell, IN 46732
(219) 856-2328
Founded: 1960
Arts Area: Professional; Summer Stock; Musical
Status: Professional; Non-Profit
Type: Performing; Touring; Resident; Educational
Purpose: The mission of Enchanted Hills Playhouse is to produce quality theatre in Kosciusko County and serve as the cultural leader in the area and to provide positive influences on the community.
Management: Robert O. Decker, Executive Producer; Jerry O'Boyle, Associate Producer
Paid Staff: 21   **Volunteer Staff:** 3
Paid Artists: 25
Utilizes: Guest Artists; Guest Directors
Budget: $100,000 - $500,000
Income Sources: Private Foundations/Grants/Endowments; Business/Corporate Donations; Box Office; Government Grants; Individual Donations
Season: June - August   **Annual Attendance:** 15,000
Affiliations: Indiana Theatre Association; Ohio Theatre Alliance; Michigan Theatre Association; Michigan Arts and Sciences Council Inc.
Performance Facilities: Enchanted Hills Playhouse

East Chicago

DANCE

BALLET FOLKLORICO OF EAST CHICAGO, INDIANA
210 East Columbus Drive, East Chicago, IN 46312
(219) 391-4122
FAX: (219) 391-4155
Arts Area: Ballet; Ethnic; Folk
Status: Non-Profit
Type: Performing; Educational
Purpose: To depict the various dances and music of Mexico
Management: Dr. Jose Arredondo, Assistant Superintendent/Director
Paid Artists: 1
Budget: $1,000 - $50,000
Income Sources: Private Foundations/Grants/Endowments; Business/Corporate Donations
Season: 52 Weeks   **Annual Attendance:** 3,000
Performance Facilities: Central High School

Elkhard

PERFORMING SERIES

ELKHART CONCERT CLUB
53336 Old Farm Road, Elkhard, IN 46514
Founded: 1952
Arts Area: Dance; Vocal Music; Theater; Grand Opera
Status: Professional
Type: Performing; Educational
Volunteer Staff: 30
Utilizes: Guest Artists
Budget: $50,000 - $100,000
Income Sources: Private Foundations/Grants/Endowments; Business/Corporate Donations; Box Office; Individual Donations
Season: September - May   **Annual Attendance:** 5,000

Evansville

DANCE

EVANSVILLE DANCE THEATRE
333-E North Plaza East Boulevard, Evansville, IN 47715
(812) 473-8937
Founded: 1981
Arts Area: Ballet
Status: Professional; Non-Profit
Type: Performing; Touring; Resident; Educational
Management: Myron Taylor, Director; David Keener, Deena Laska, Artistic Directors; Patty Muenchen, General Director
Officers: Terry Haynie, President
Paid Artists: 7 **Non-Paid Artists:** 13
Utilizes: Guest Artists; Guest Choreographers
Budget: $1,000 - $50,000
Income Sources: Business/Corporate Donations
Season: September - May

INSTRUMENTAL MUSIC

EVANSVILLE PHILHARMONIC ORCHESTRA
318 Main Street, Suite 218, Evansville, IN 47708
(812) 425-5050
FAX: (812) 426-7008
Founded: 1934
Arts Area: Symphony; Orchestra; Chamber; Ensemble
Status: Professional
Type: Performing; Educational
Purpose: To provide symphonic music of the highest quality for the Tri-State Area of Southern Indiana, Illinois and Kentucky, both for adult audiences and students in the school systems
Management: James W. Palermi, General Manager
Officers: Nancy Hartley Gaunt, President; Thomas H. Bryan, President-Elect; Joan David, Vice President; Charles Schuger, Secretary; Jay Hargis, Treasurer
Paid Staff: 7 **Volunteer Staff:** 200
Paid Artists: 80
Utilizes: Guest Conductors; Guest Artists
Budget: $500,000 - $1,000,000
Income Sources: Private Foundations/Grants/Endowments; Business/Corporate Donations; Box Office; Government Grants; Individual Donations
Season: September - May **Annual Attendance:** 23,400
Affiliations: ASOL; IOC; Evansville Arts and Education Council
Performance Facilities: Vanderburgh Auditorium

THEATRE

REPERTORY PEOPLE OF EVANSVILLE
Old Courthouse Building, Room 200, PO Box 3555, Evansville, IN 47708
(812) 423-2060
Founded: 1975
Arts Area: Theatrical Group
Status: Non-Professional; Non-Profit
Type: Performing; Resident
Purpose: Majority of plays are serious American dramas with occasional comedies
Management: Jim Jackson, Artistic Director; Tom Angermeier, Executive Producer
Paid Staff: 2 **Volunteer Staff:** 15
Budget: $1,000 - $50,000
Income Sources: Private Foundations/Grants/Endowments; Business/Corporate Donations; Box Office; Government Grants; Individual Donations
Season: September - June **Annual Attendance:** 6,000

PERFORMING SERIES

EVANSVILLE ARTIST EDUCATION COUNCIL
123 NW Fourth Street, Suite 312, Evansville, IN 47708
(812) 422-2111
Founded: 1969
Arts Area: Festivals

Status: Professional; Non-Profit
Type: Educational; Sponsoring
Purpose: To promote development of the arts to arts audiences
Management: Lorie Clouser, Executive Director; Kim Setzer, Program Coordinator
Officers: Joe Meyer, President; Tom Fitzsimmons, Vice President; Danny Bateman, Treasurer; Mary Schepper, Secretary
Paid Staff: 4
Utilizes: Special Technical Talent; Guest Artists
Income Sources: Private Foundations/Grants/Endowments; Business/Corporate Donations; Box Office; Government Grants; Individual Donations
Season: 52 Weeks
Affiliations: NALAA; ACA; Alliance for Arts Education

FACILITY

VANDERBURGH AUDITORIUM CONVENTION CENTER
715 Locust Street, Evansville, IN 47708
(812) 426-2270
Type of Facility: Auditorium; Multi-Purpose
Type of Stage: Proscenium
Stage Dimensions: 102'Wx46'Dx22'H   **Orchestra Pit**
Seating Capacity: 2,001
Year Built: 1967   **Architect:** Virgil Miller   **Cost:** $2,500,000
Manager: Sandra Toton
Resident Groups: Evansville Philharmonic Orchestra

Fort Wayne

DANCE

FORT WAYNE BALLET
324 Penn, Fort Wayne, IN 46805
(219) 484-9646
FAX: (219) 484-9647
Founded: 1955
Arts Area: Modern; Ballet; Jazz
Status: Semi-Professional; Non-Profit
Type: Performing; Educational
Purpose: Fort Wayne Ballet is both a teaching and performing company.
Management: Michael Tevlin, Artistic Director
Officers: Ron Cassidente, President
Paid Staff: 14   **Volunteer Staff:** 135
Paid Artists: 5   **Non-Paid Artists:** 17
Utilizes: Special Technical Talent; Guest Artists; Guest Directors
Budget: $100,000 - $500,000
Income Sources: Private Foundations/Grants/Endowments; Business/Corporate Donations; Box Office; Individual Donations
Season: October - May
Affiliations: IAC; Fine Arts Foundation; Mid States Regional Ballet
Performance Facilities: Performing Arts Center

FORT WAYNE DANCE COLLECTIVE
437 East Berry Street, Fort Wayne, IN 46802
(219) 424-6574
Founded: 1979
Arts Area: Modern
Status: Professional; Non-Profit
Type: Performing; Educational; Sponsoring; Video Producer for Public Access
Purpose: To create an interest and appreciation for the art of modern dance
Management: Liz Monnier, Artistic Director
Officers: John H. Brandt, President; James Prickett, Vice President; Lois Schmidt, Secretary; Lisa Isenberger, Treasurer
Paid Staff: 9   **Volunteer Staff:** 15
Paid Artists: 4   **Non-Paid Artists:** 3
Utilizes: Guest Artists; Guest Choreographers
Budget: $100,000 - $500,000
Income Sources: Private Foundations/Grants/Endowments; Business/Corporate Donations; Box Office; Government Grants; Individual Donations
Season: September - June   **Annual Attendance:** 1,400

Affiliations: Chicago Dance Art Coalition; Arts United of Greater Fort Wayne
Performance Facilities: Performing Arts Center

INSTRUMENTAL MUSIC

FORT WAYNE PHILHARMONIC ORCHESTRA
2340 Fairfield Avenue, Fort Wayne, IN 46807
(219) 744-1700
  Founded: 1943
  Arts Area: Symphony; Orchestra; Chamber; Ensemble
  Status: Professional; Non-Profit
  Type: Performing; Touring; Resident; Educational
  Purpose: To present music of the master composers and significant music of our time in Fort Wayne and Northern Indiana
  Management: Christopher D. Guerin, General Manager; Ronald Ondrejka, Music Director; David Crowe, Assistant Conductor
  Officers: Leonard M. Goldstein, President; Michael McCollum, Vice President; William C. Lee, Secretary; David A. Haist, Treasurer
  Paid Staff: 12   **Volunteer Staff:** 300
  Paid Artists: 92
  Utilizes: Guest Conductors; Guest Artists; Guest Directors
  Budget: $1,000,000 - $5,000,000
  Income Sources: Private Foundations/Grants/Endowments; Business/Corporate Donations; Box Office; Government Grants; Individual Donations
  Season: September - May   **Annual Attendance:** 36,000
  Affiliations: ASOL; MOMA; Fine Arts Foundation
  Performance Facilities: Embassy Theatre

THEATRE

ARENA DINNER THEATRE
7820 Schwartz Road, Fort Wayne, IN 46835
(219) 493-1384
  Founded: 1974
  Arts Area: Dinner; Community
  Status: Non-Professional
  Type: Performing
  Purpose: To give another option for theatre-goers and actors in the community
  Officers: Darrell Monroe, President; Brad Beauchamp, Vice President; Marlene Niccum, Treasurer; Stan Volz, Secretary
  Paid Staff: 1   **Volunteer Staff:** 20
  Non-Paid Artists: 50
  Budget: $50,000 - $100,000
  Income Sources: Private Foundations/Grants/Endowments; Business/Corporate Donations; Box Office; Government Grants; Individual Donations
  Season: September - May   **Annual Attendance:** 4,200
  Affiliations: IAC; Fine Arts Foundation; ITA

FIRST PRESBYTERIAN THEATER
300 West Wayne Street, Fort Wayne, IN 46802
(219) 422-6329
  Founded: 1968
  Arts Area: Dinner; Community
  Status: Non-Profit
  Type: Performing; Educational
  Purpose: To provide supportive group atmosphere for participants in production of classical and provocative contemporary drama
  Management: Mary Yarnelle, Director/Theatre Manager
  Officers: Myra McFarland, Church Drama Committee Chairman
  Paid Staff: 3   **Volunteer Staff:** 100
  Paid Artists: 2   **Non-Paid Artists:** 100
  Utilizes: Guest Directors
  Budget: $1,000 - $50,000
  Income Sources: Private Foundations/Grants/Endowments; Box Office; Individual Donations
  Season: September - May   **Annual Attendance:** 6,400
  Affiliations: Fort Wayne Community Arts Council

FORT WAYNE CIVIC THEATRE
303 East Main Street, Fort Wayne, IN 46802
(219) 422-8641
  Arts Area: Community

Status: Non-Professional; Non-Profit
Type: Resident
Purpose: Dedicated to strengthening itself as a significant cultural force in the Fort Wayne area through excellence in programming, theatre education and development of talent in the disciplines of theatre and the related performing arts
Management: Michael Mitchell, Executive Director; Mickie Martin, Business Manager
Officers: Michael McMath, President; Carolyn Pictor, Vice President; Chuck Schimper, Treasurer; Denise Lapsley, Secretary
Utilizes: Guest Directors; Guest Designers
Budget: $500,000 - $1,000,000
Income Sources: Private Foundations/Grants/Endowments; Business/Corporate Donations; Box Office; Individual Donations
Season: 52 Weeks   **Annual Attendance:** 45,000
Performance Facilities: The Performing Arts Center

FACILITY

EMBASSY THEATRE
1107 South Harrison Street, Fort Wayne, IN 46802
(219) 424-6287
> **Type of Facility:** Theatre House
> **Facility Originally:** Show Palace
> **Type of Stage:** Proscenium
> **Stage Dimensions:** 55'Wx26'D; 55'Wx29'6"H proscenium opening   **Orchestra Pit**
> **Seating Capacity:** 2,750
> **Year Built:** 1928   **Architect:** A.M. Strauss   **Cost:** $1,500,000
> **Year Remodeled:** 1987   **Cost:** $1,000,000
> **Contact for Rental:** Doris Stovall, Manager;   (219) 424-6287
> **Manager:** Doris Stovall
> *Original Page Pipe Organ is in facility. Remodeling is in progress.*

FOELLINGER THEATER IN FRANKE PARK
705 East State Boulevard, Fort Wayne, IN 46805
(219) 483-0057
> **Type of Facility:** Theatre Complex; Concert Hall; Auditorium; Outdoor (Concert); Theatre House; Amphitheater; Opera House
> **Type of Stage:** Proscenium
> **Stage Dimensions:** 27'x56'x55'   **Orchestra Pit**
> **Seating Capacity:** 2,715
> **Year Built:** 1949   **Architect:** Shoaff   **Cost:** $100,000
> **Year Remodeled:** 1976   **Architect:** Grinsfelder   **Cost:** $300,000
> **Acoustical Consultant:** K.L.F.
> **Contact for Rental:** Betty Khan;   (219) 483-0057
> **Resident Groups:** Foellinger Theatre Group
> *Summer theater only, June 1 through September 30*

PERFORMING ARTS CENTER
303 East Main Street, Fort Wayne, IN 46802
(219) 423-4349
> **Type of Facility:** Theatre House
> **Type of Stage:** Proscenium
> **Stage Dimensions:** 28'x60'x42'   **Orchestra Pit**
> **Seating Capacity:** 682
> **Year Built:** 1973   **Architect:** Louis Kahn   **Cost:** $4,500,000
> **Acoustical Consultant:** George C. Izenour
> **Contact for Rental:** Janet McCauley;   (219) 423-4349
> **Resident Groups:** Civic Theatre; Fort Wayne Ballet; Philharmonic Orchestra; Youth Theatre
> *John Wainwright, Technical Director*

SCOTTISH RITE AUDITORIUM
431 West Berry Street, Fort Wayne, IN 46802
(219) 423-2593
FAX: (219) 426-4126
> **Type of Facility:** Auditorium; Theatre House
> **Type of Stage:** Thrust; Flexible; Proscenium
> **Stage Dimensions:** 65'x65'x35'   **Orchestra Pit**
> **Seating Capacity:** 2,197
> **Year Built:** 1925
> **Year Remodeled:** 1958
> **Contact for Rental:** James De Monde;   (219) 423-2593

Manager: James De Mond
Resident Groups: Ancient Accepted Scottish Rite of Freemasonry
Family entertainment only

French Lick

THEATRE

FLS ENTERTAINMENT
French Lick Springs Resort, French Lick, IN 47432
(812) 936-9300, ext. 1003
Founded: 1992
Arts Area: Professional; Musical; Theatrical Group
Status: Professional
Type: Performing; Resident; Educational
Purpose: To present original theatre to the populus and cultivate new talent
Management: Chris Bundy, Director of Entertainment; Steve Gorman, Assistant Director of Entertainment
Paid Staff: 2
Paid Artists: 15
Utilizes: Special Technical Talent; Guest Artists
Income Sources: Private Foundations/Grants/Endowments; Business/Corporate Donations; Box Office; Individual Donations
Season: 52 Weeks

Gary

PERFORMING SERIES

I.U. DONS, INC.
PO Box M622, Gary, IN 46401
(219) 887-2041
Founded: 1969
Arts Area: Dance; Vocal Music; Theater
Status: Non-Profit
Type: Educational; Sponsoring
Purpose: To promote educational attainment
Officers: Dr. Vernon G. Smith, President
Volunteer Staff: 20
Utilizes: Guest Artists
Budget: $1,000 - $50,000
Income Sources: Private Foundations/Grants/Endowments; Individual Donations
Season: September - December   **Annual Attendance:** 2,000

Goshen

THEATRE

THE BRIDGEWORK THEATER
113 1/2 East Lincoln Avenue, Goshen, IN 46526
(219) 534-1085
Founded: 1979
Arts Area: Theatrical Group
Status: Professional; Non-Profit
Type: Performing; Touring
Purpose: To create and perform issue-oriented plays for children in the Great Lakes Region
Management: Donald C. Yost, Director
Officers: Ruth Hollinger, Board President; Shirley Lint, Vice President; Cheryl Cooper, Treasurer; Lynn Miller, Secretary
Paid Staff: 4
Paid Artists: 12
Utilizes: Guest Directors
Budget: $100,000 - $500,000
Income Sources: Private Foundations/Grants/Endowments; Business/Corporate Donations; Box Office; Government Grants; Individual Donations; Royalty Income
Season: September - May   **Annual Attendance:** 45,000
Affiliations: ITA

FACILITY

GOSHEN COLLEGE - JOHN S. UMBLE CENTER
1700 South Main, Goshen, IN 46526
(219) 533-3161
    Type of Facility: Theatre House
    Type of Stage: Thrust; Flexible; Proscenium
    Stage Dimensions: 60'Wx47'6"Dx29'H
    Seating Capacity: 410
    Year Built: 1977 **Architect:** Weldon Pries **Cost:** $1,400,000
    Acoustical Consultant: William Cavanaugh
    Contact for Rental: Judy Hollar; (219) 533-3161
    Manager: Lauren Friesen, Director
    Very limited rental use

Hagerstown

THEATRE

NETTLE CREEK PLAYERS
98 East Main Street, PO Box 23, Hagerstown, IN 47346
(317) 489-5214
    Founded: 1971
    Arts Area: Summer Stock; Musical; Community; Theatrical Group
    Status: Semi-Professional; Non-Professional; Non-Profit
    Type: Performing
    Purpose: Summer stock season also consists of training program in musical theatre for ten resident performers
    Management: Alan Montgomery, Artistic Director
    Officers: W.E. Stackhouse, Jr., President
    Paid Staff: 2 **Volunteer Staff:** 1
    Paid Artists: 21 **Non-Paid Artists:** 40
    Utilizes: Guest Directors
    Budget: $50,000 - $100,000
    Income Sources: Private Foundations/Grants/Endowments; Business/Corporate Donations; Box Office; Government Grants; Individual Donations
    Season: June - August **Annual Attendance:** 10,000
    Affiliations: ITA; SETC
    Performance Facilities: Nettle Creek Playhouse

Highland

THEATRE

MAIN SQUARE PLAYERS
8749 Idlewild, Highland, IN 46322
(219) 838-1052
    Founded: 1980
    Arts Area: Professional; Musical
    Status: Semi-Professional; Non-Profit
    Type: Performing; Educational
    Purpose: To introduce new forms of theatre as far as nonconventional space and multi-age backgrounds
    Management: Gregory J. Ladd, Director/Producer
    Paid Staff: 3 **Volunteer Staff:** 8
    Paid Artists: 2 **Non-Paid Artists:** 50
    Utilizes: Special Technical Talent
    Budget: $1,000 - $50,000
    Income Sources: Business/Corporate Donations; Box Office; Individual Donations
    Season: 52 Weeks
    Affiliations: LCT
    Performance Facilities: Saint Thomas More Church, Westminster Presbyterian Church

Indianapolis

DANCE

DANCE KALEIDOSCOPE
429 Vermont Street, Indianapolis, IN 46202
(317) 634-8484
Founded: 1972
Arts Area: Modern; Contemporary
Status: Professional; Non-Profit
Type: Performing; Touring; Resident
Management: David Hochoy, Artistic Director
Officers: Gerda Fogle, President
Paid Staff: 10
Paid Artists: 8
Utilizes: Guest Artists; Guest Choreographers
Budget: $100,000 - $500,000
Income Sources: Private Foundations/Grants/Endowments; Business/Corporate Donations; Box Office; Individual Donations
Season: August - June
Performance Facilities: Indiana Repertory Theatre; Civic Theatre

INDIANAPOLIS BALLET THEATRE
411 East Michigan Street, Indianapolis, IN 46204
(317) 637-8979
Founded: 1973
Arts Area: Modern; Ballet; Jazz
Status: Professional
Type: Performing; Touring; Resident; Educational; Sponsoring
Purpose: To present a total theatrical experience, offer a variety of styles, bring the medium of dance to a wider range of audiences and develop future audiences and artists through school performances; features guest musicians, composers, vocalists and choreographers
Management: Kathryn Stephenson, Executive Director; Dace Dindonis, Artistic Director; Barbara Turner, Development Director; Tim Moore, Public Relations/Marketing Director; Tim Hubbard, Tour Director; Michele Hankins, Costume Mistress; Nancy Baney, Accounting Manager; Doris Hartman, Administrative Assistant; Michael Stephenson, Assistant Artistic Director; Dale Shield, Repetiteur
Officers: Frederick W. Ruebeck, President; Mrs. Evan L. Noyes, Past President; Mrs. W. Taylor Wilson, Robert G. Risk, Larry K. Pitts and Mary Gallagher, Vice Presidents; Myra Selby, Secretary; Robert Rawlings, Treasurer
Paid Staff: 12
Paid Artists: 20   **Non-Paid Artists:** 2
Utilizes: Guest Conductors; Guest Artists; Guest Choreographers
Budget: $500,000 - $1,000,000
Income Sources: Private Foundations/Grants/Endowments; Business/Corporate Donations; Box Office; Government Grants; Individual Donations
Season: July - May   **Annual Attendance:** 160,000
Affiliations: APAP; Arts Midwest; ASOL; IPN; ISPAA; Indiana Advocates for the Arts
Performance Facilities: Clowes Memorial Hall, Butler University; Warren Performing Arts Center

INSTRUMENTAL MUSIC

THE ENSEMBLE MUSIC SOCIETY
PO Box 40188, Indianapolis, IN 46240-0188
(317) 254-8915
Founded: 1944
Arts Area: Chamber
Status: Professional; Non-Profit
Type: Sponsoring
Purpose: To present nationally and internationally known chamber music groups to adult and student audiences
Management: Pamela Steele, Administrative Chief; Julie Marks, Artistic Director; Judith Moore, Production Manager
Officers: Pamela Steele, President; Julie Marks, Vice President; Sylvia Peacock, Secretary; Richard Parker, Treasurer
Volunteer Staff: 6
Paid Artists: 30
Utilizes: Guest Artists
Budget: $1,000 - $50,000
Income Sources: Private Foundations/Grants/Endowments; Business/Corporate Donations; Box Office; Government Grants; Individual Donations

Season: October - April   **Annual Attendance:** 1,700
Affiliations: CMA
Performance Facilities: Lilly Theatre at Children's Muesum

INDIANA JAZZ
PO Box 39013, Indianapolis, IN 46239
(317) 862-4479
    Founded: 1984
    Arts Area: Jazz
    Status: Non-Profit
    Type: Performing; Educational
    Purpose: To promote Indiana music and musicians both in the state and out-of-state
    Management: Kathyrn Stephenson, Executive Director; George C. Verdak, Artistic Director; Roberta Donahue, Business Manager; Jason Smith, Development Director; Mary Bashaw, Public Relations/Marketing Director; Claire Braswell, Tour Director
    Officers: James A. Clark, President; Josephine Weathers, Secretary; Reginald A. DuValle, Treasurer
    Volunteer Staff: 20
    Utilizes: Guest Conductors; Guest Writers
    Budget: $1,000 - $50,000
    Income Sources: Private Foundations/Grants/Endowments; Business/Corporate Donations; Box Office; Government Grants; Individual Donations

INDIANAPOLIS SYMPHONY ORCHESTRA
45 Monument Circle, Indianapolis, IN 46204-2919
(317) 262-1100
FAX: (317) 637-1917
    Founded: 1930
    Arts Area: Symphony; Orchestra; Chamber; Ensemble
    Status: Professional; Non-Profit
    Type: Performing; Touring; Resident; Educational
    Purpose: To provide the finest musical performances to audiences locally, nationally, and internationally
    Management: Robert C. Jones, President; Thomas R. Ramsey, Vice President/General Manager; Herbert L. Jones, Vice President for Development; Susan L. Prenatt, Director of Finance/Administration; Robert Bruce Gold, Director of Marketing; Thomas N. Akins, Director of Public Relations; Paul Hogle, Director of Development
    Officers: Rolla E. McAdams, Chairman of the Board; Mrs. Vaughn D. Bryson, Richard C. Notebaert, Vice Chairmans; Robert C. Jones, President; Mrs. Boris E. Meditch, Secretary; Steven A. Wagner, Treasurer; Dr. Arthur G. Hanson, Immediate Past Chairman
    Paid Staff: 40   **Volunteer Staff:** 3,400
    Paid Artists: 100
    Utilizes: Special Technical Talent; Guest Conductors; Guest Artists
    Budget: Over 10,000,000
    Income Sources: Private Foundations/Grants/Endowments; Business/Corporate Donations; Box Office; Government Grants; Individual Donations
    Season: 52 Weeks   **Annual Attendance:** 425,000
    Affiliations: ASOL
    Performance Facilities: Circle Theatre

PHILHARMONIC ORCHESTRA OF INDIANAPOLIS
PO Box 503, Indianapolis, IN 46206
(317) 283-5242
    Founded: 1940
    Arts Area: Symphony; Orchestra; Chamber
    Status: Non-Professional; Non-Profit
    Type: Performing; Resident; Educational
    Purpose: Community symphony offering concerts at low prices, performed by volunteer musicians, some of whom are soloists from time to time, and/or paid soloists
    Management: Carl Henn Jr., General Manager; Allan Dennis, Music Director
    Officers: Edward Staubach, President; Lorelei Faxlow, Vice President; Marty Frank, Treasurer; Bill Bryan, Secretary
    Paid Staff: 2   **Volunteer Staff:** 4
    Non-Paid Artists: 65
    Utilizes: Guest Conductors; Guest Artists
    Budget: $1,000 - $50,000
    Income Sources: Private Foundations/Grants/Endowments; Business/Corporate Donations; Box Office; Government Grants; Individual Donations
    Season: September - June
    Annual Attendance: 4,000
    Performance Facilities: Caleb Mills Hall

VOCAL MUSIC

INDIANAPOLIS OPERA
250 East 38th Street, Indianapolis, IN 46205
(317) 283-3531
FAX: (317) 923-5611
Arts Area: Grand Opera; Lyric Opera; Light Opera; Operetta
Status: Professional; Non-Profit
Type: Performing; Touring; Resident; Educational; Sponsoring
Management: Durand L. Pope, General Director; James H. Coraher, Acting Artistic Director
Officers: Mrs. Thomas Reilly, President; Mr. Rob Knapp, Executive Vice President
Paid Staff: 9   **Volunteer Staff:** 170
Paid Artists: 250
Utilizes: Special Technical Talent; Guest Conductors; Guest Artists; Guest Directors
Budget: $1,000,000 - $5,000,000
Income Sources: Private Foundations/Grants/Endowments; Business/Corporate Donations; Box Office; Government Grants; Individual Donations
Affiliations: Opera America
Performance Facilities: Clowes Memorial Hall, Butler University

MACALLISTER
PO Box 1941, Indianapolis, IN 46206
(317) 636-7372
FAX: (317) 543-0310
Founded: 1980
Arts Area: Grand Opera; Lyric Opera; Light Opera; Operetta; Competition
Status: Professional; Non-Profit
Type: Performing; Touring; Sponsoring
Purpose: To provide opera opportunities for young artists through opera productions and sponsorship of the MacAllister Awards, the largest sponsored, nonrestricted opera competition on the continent; to provide, through productions, training for young artists, both artistic and technical; Affiliate Artist program will include young conductors and stage directors
Management: Elaine Bookwalter, General Director; P.E. MacAllister, President, Board of Directors
Officers: P.E. MacAllister, President; Melvin Carroway, Vice President; Dawn Smith, Treasurer; Greg Jordan, Secretary
Paid Staff: 1   **Volunteer Staff:** 3
Utilizes: Special Technical Talent; Guest Conductors; Guest Artists; Guest Directors
Budget: $100,000 - $500,000
Income Sources: Private Foundations/Grants/Endowments; Business/Corporate Donations; Box Office; Government Grants; Individual Donations
Season: August   **Annual Attendance:** 6,000
Affiliations: COS; Butler University Romantic Festival
Performance Facilities: Frederic M. Ayers Auditorium

THEATRE

BEEF AND BOARDS DINNER THEATRE
9301 North Michigan Road, Indianapolis, IN 46268
(317) 872-9664
Founded: 1971
Arts Area: Professional; Dinner
Status: Professional
Type: Performing
Management: Robert Zehr, Managing Director; Douglas Stark, Artistic Director
Officers: Robert Zehr, President; Douglas Stark, Secretary/Treasurer
Paid Staff: 80
Paid Artists: 15
Income Sources: Box Office
Season: 52 Weeks   **Annual Attendance:** 160,000
Affiliations: NDTA; ADTI
Performance Facilities: Beef and Boards Dinner Theatre

INDIANA REPERTORY THEATRE
140 West Washington, Indianapolis, IN 46204
(317) 635-5277
FAX: (317) 236-0767
Founded: 1971
Arts Area: Professional
Status: Professional; Non-Profit
Type: Performing; Resident; Educational

Purpose: Through innovative productions of classic and contemporary plays, the Indiana Repertory Theatre creates high quality, professional theatre of consistent artistic and cultural significance; the theatre offers student programs that enables students the opportunity to experience live theatre as a performing art form

Management: Victoria Nolan, Managing Director; Libby Appel, Artistic Director; Janet Allen, Associate Artistic Director

Officers: Robert A. Anker, Chairman of the Board; David H. Kleiman, President; Michael M. Sample, Vice President; Jack R. Shaw, Vice President; Lorene Burkhart, Secretary; R. Brentson Smith, Treasurer

Paid Staff: 65 **Volunteer Staff:** 500

Paid Artists: 90

Utilizes: Special Technical Talent; Guest Artists; Guest Directors

Budget: $1,000,000 - $5,000,000

Income Sources: Private Foundations/Grants/Endowments; Business/Corporate Donations; Box Office; Government Grants; Individual Donations

Season: October - May **Annual Attendance:** 110,000

Affiliations: LORT

Performance Facilities: Indiana Theatre

PHOENIX THEATRE
749 North Park Avenue, Indianapolis, IN 46202
(317) 635-7529
FAX: (317) 635-7529

Founded: 1983

Arts Area: Community; Theatrical Group

Status: Semi-Professional; Non-Profit

Type: Performing

Purpose: To nurture the professional growth and development of local actors, directors, playwrights and other theatre artists

Management: Bryan D. Fonseca, Artistic Director; Karen E. Farley, Business Manager

Officers: Betty LaClare, Board Chairman

Paid Staff: 4 **Volunteer Staff:** 3

Utilizes: Special Technical Talent; Guest Artists; Guest Directors

Budget: $100,000 - $500,000

Income Sources: Private Foundations/Grants/Endowments; Business/Corporate Donations; Box Office; Government Grants; Individual Donations

Season: 52 Weeks **Annual Attendance:** 10,000

Affiliations: AATA; ITA

PERFORMING SERIES

CLOWES MEMORIAL HALL
Butler University, 4600 Sunset Avenue, Indianapolis, IN 46208
(317) 283-9696

Founded: 1963

Arts Area: Dance; Vocal Music; Instrumental Music; Theater; Festivals

Status: Non-Profit

Type: Touring; Educational; Sponsoring

Purpose: Booking and presenting cultural and entertainment attractions in the Indianapolis area

Management: Michael Sells, General Manager/Dean of Jordan College of Fine Arts, Butler University

Officers: Board of Trustees, Butler University; Kathryn Betley, Chair of Clowes Memorial Hall Committee

Paid Staff: 9 **Volunteer Staff:** 300

Utilizes: Guest Artists

Budget: $100,000 - $500,000

Income Sources: Private Foundations/Grants/Endowments; Business/Corporate Donations; Box Office; Individual Donations

Season: September - June

Affiliations: Butler University

Performance Facilities: Clowes Memorial Hall, Butler University

FACILITY

CLOWES MEMORIAL HALL OF BUTLER UNIVERSITY
4600 Sunset Avenue, Indianapolis, IN 46208
(317) 283-9696
FAX: (317) 283-9820

Founded: 1963

Type of Facility: Theatre House; Opera House; Multi-Purpose

Type of Stage: Proscenium

Stage Dimensions: 52'Wx60'Dx35'H; 80' grid **Orchestra Pit**

Seating Capacity: 2,182

Year Built: 1963 **Architect:** John Johanson and Evans Woollen **Cost:** $3,500,000

Acoustical Consultant: Bolt Beranek and Newman, Inc.
Contact for Rental: Linda Neal, Business Manager;   (317) 283-9696
Manager: Tom McTamney, Manager;   (317) 283-9696
Resident Groups: Jordan College of Fine Arts; Indianapolis Opera Company; Indianapolis Ballet Theatre; Indianapolis Chamber Orchestra; INB Broadway Series; Kiwanis Travelogues; Town Hall Lectures
Presents a subscription series of 13-15 events annually

WARREN PERFORMING ARTS CENTER
9301 East 18th Street, Indianapolis, IN 46229
(317) 898-8061
Type of Facility: Performance Center
Year Built: 1983   **Architect:** Daverman Associates   **Cost:** $5,500,000
Acoustical Consultant: Bureky & Brennen
Contact for Rental: Penny Mitchell;   (317) 898-8061
Contains Esch Auditorium and Studio Theater. See separate listings

WARREN PERFORMING ARTS CENTER - ESCH AUDITORIUM
9301 East 18th Street, Indianapolis, IN 46229
(317) 898-8061
Type of Facility: Concert Hall; Auditorium
Type of Stage: Proscenium
Stage Dimensions: 48'Wx59'10"D; 48'Wx25'H proscenium opening   **Orchestra Pit**
Seating Capacity: 1,033
Year Built: 1983
Contact for Rental: Penny Mitchell
Resident Groups: Warren Central High School Music and Theater Departments

WARREN PERFORMING ARTS CENTER - STUDIO THEATER
9301 East 18th Street, Indianapolis, IN 46229
(317) 898-8061
Type of Facility: Room; Rehearsal Studio
Type of Stage: Flexible; Platform
Seating Capacity: 120
Year Built: 1983
Contact for Rental: Penny Mitchell
Resident Groups: Warren High School Theater Department

Jasper

FACILITY

JASPER CIVIC AUDITORIUM
951 College Avenue, Jasper, IN 47546
(812) 482-3070
Founded: 1977
Type of Facility: Concert Hall; Auditorium; Studio Performance; Civic Center; Multi-Purpose; Room; Dance Studio; Art Gallery; Meeting Rooms
Type of Stage: Proscenium
Stage Dimensions: 40'W proscenium; 50' wood; 40'D   **Orchestra Pit**
Seating Capacity: 700
Year Built: 1977   **Architect:** Wayne Seufert   **Cost:** $1,000,000
Year Remodeled: 1982   **Architect:** Wayne Seufert   **Cost:** $100,000
Acoustical Consultant: Bolt, Baranek and Newman
Contact for Rental: Doreen Lechner;   (812) 482-3070
Resident Groups: Jasper Community Players; Dubois County Art Guild; Strings in Jasper

Kokomo

INSTRUMENTAL MUSIC

KOKOMO SYMPHONY
PO Box 6115, Kokomo, IN 46902
(317) 455-1659
Founded: 1971
Arts Area: Symphony; Orchestra; Chamber
Status: Non-Profit
Type: Performing; Touring; Resident; Educational; Sponsoring

Purpose: To provide the highest quality of music performed by our local orchestra under the direction of a capable conductor; to maintain an orchestra, chorus and youth orchestra
Management: Barbara M. Cassis, Executive Director
Paid Staff: 2 **Volunteer Staff:** 300
Paid Artists: 20 **Non-Paid Artists:** 40
Utilizes: Guest Artists
Budget: $100,000 - $500,000
Income Sources: Private Foundations/Grants/Endowments; Business/Corporate Donations; Box Office; Government Grants; Individual Donations
Season: September - May **Annual Attendance:** 650
Affiliations: ASOL; IOC; Indiana Advocates for the Arts
Performance Facilities: Havens Auditorium

Lafayette

INSTRUMENTAL MUSIC

LAFAYETTE SYMPHONY
111 North Sixth, PO Box 52, Lafayette, IN 47902
(317) 742-6463
Founded: 1951
Arts Area: Symphony; Orchestra
Status: Semi-Professional; Non-Profit
Type: Performing; Educational
Purpose: To provide symphonic literature for the enjoyment and education of the Greater Lafayette Area
Management: Michael Cunningham, General Manager
Officers: Bill Bonsignore, President
Paid Staff: 4
Paid Artists: 65
Utilizes: Guest Conductors; Guest Artists
Budget: $100,000 - $500,000
Income Sources: Private Foundations/Grants/Endowments; Business/Corporate Donations; Box Office; Government Grants; Individual Donations
Season: September - May **Annual Attendance:** 8,000
Affiliations: ASOL; IOC
Performance Facilities: Long Center for the Performing Arts

FACILITY

LONG CENTER FOR THE PERFORMING ARTS
111 North Sixth Street, Lafayette, IN 47905
(317) 742-5664
Founded: 1978
Type of Facility: Theatre Complex; Performance Center; Theatre House; Loft
Facility Originally: Vaudeville; Movie House
Type of Stage: Proscenium
Stage Dimensions: 38'Wx37'D
Seating Capacity: 1,200
Year Built: 1921 **Architect:** Scholer Architects
Year Remodeled: 1978 **Architect:** Scholer Architects **Cost:** $900,000
Contact for Rental: C.H. Copeland; (317) 742-5664
Resident Groups: Lafayette Symphony Orchestra

Lawrenceburg

THEATRE

RIVERTOWN PLAYERS
PO Box 454, Lawrenceburg, IN 47025
(812) 537-0751
FAX: (812) 537-5618
Founded: 1982
Arts Area: Community; Theatrical Group
Status: Non-Professional; Non-Profit
Type: Performing
Purpose: To promote, encourage, and develop the enjoyment, appreciation, and participation in theatre through production and performance of plays and musicals

Management: Janice Hizer, Production Manager
Budget: $1,000 - $50,000
Income Sources: Box Office; Individual Donations
Season: 52 Weeks **Annual Attendance:** 3,000
Affiliations: Indiana Theatre Association
Performance Facilities: Lawrenceburg High School Auditorium

Marion

INSTRUMENTAL MUSIC

MARION PHILHARMONIC ORCHESTRA
215 South Adams, PO Box 272, Marion, IN 46952
(317) 662-0012
FAX: (317) 668-5443
Founded: 1969
Arts Area: Orchestra
Status: Non-Profit
Type: Performing
Purpose: To further the cultural and educational development of the Grant County area
Management: Sue Wanninger, Business Manager; Neal Gittleman, Music Director/Conductor
Officers: Jerry Albrecht, President; Jim Fordham, Vice President; Susan Munn, Secretary; Bob Hogan, Treasurer
Paid Staff: 2
Paid Artists: 50
Utilizes: Guest Conductors; Guest Artists
Budget: $100,000 - $500,000
Income Sources: Private Foundations/Grants/Endowments; Business/Corporate Donations; Box Office; Government Grants; Individual Donations
Season: September - May **Annual Attendance:** 5,000
Performance Facilities: Marion High School Auditorium

Muncie

INSTRUMENTAL MUSIC

MUNCIE SYMPHONY ORCHESTRA
310 North McKinley Avenue, Muncie, IN 47306
(317) 285-5531
Founded: 1948
Arts Area: Symphony
Status: Semi-Professional; Non-Profit
Type: Performing; Educational
Purpose: To encourage the performance, development, and appreciation of fine music in east central Indiana by means of combined university and community support of the Muncie Symphony Orchestra
Management: Joan McKee, Business Manager
Officers: Thomas Sargent, President; Julie Skinner, Vice President; Robert Gibiser, Treasurer; Nanette Rushton, Secretary
Paid Staff: 4 **Volunteer Staff:** 1
Paid Artists: 85
Utilizes: Guest Conductors; Guest Artists
Budget: $100,000 - $500,000
Income Sources: Private Foundations/Grants/Endowments; Business/Corporate Donations; Box Office; Government Grants; Individual Donations
Season: September - June **Annual Attendance:** 18,000
Affiliations: ASOL; ASCAP; BMI; IOC; ACA; Indiana Advocates for the Arts
Performance Facilities: Emens Auditorium

Munster

INSTRUMENTAL MUSIC

NORTHWEST INDIANA SYMPHONY SOCIETY
1040 Ridge Road, Munster, IN 46321
(219) 836-0525
Founded: 1941
Arts Area: Symphony; Orchestra; Chamber; Ensemble
Status: Professional; Non-Profit

Type: Performing; Resident; Educational
Purpose: Presentation of subscription, special, and children's concerts and maintenance of Youth Orchestra and Chorus
Management: Richard Scharf, General Manager; Robert Vodnoy, Music Director; Kevin McMahon, Youth Orchestra Conductor; Joe Burt, Chorus Director
Officers: Michael Schrage, President; Richard Combs, Vice Presidents; Barbara Haas, Secretary; Joseph F. Glotzbach, Treasurer
Paid Staff: 4
Paid Artists: 75
Utilizes: Special Technical Talent; Guest Conductors; Guest Artists
Budget: $500,000 - $1,000,000
Income Sources: Private Foundations/Grants/Endowments; Business/Corporate Donations; Box Office; Government Grants; Individual Donations
Season: October - May   **Annual Attendance:** 35,000
Affiliations: ASOL; IOC; Chicago Music Alliance
Performance Facilities: Star Plaza Theatre, Merrillville

North Manchester

FACILITY

MANCHESTER COLLEGE - CORDIER AUDITORIUM
604 College Avenue, North Manchester, IN 46962
(219) 982-5247
FAX: (219) 982-6868
Founded: 1978
Type of Facility: Concert Hall; Auditorium; Performance Center; Multi-Purpose
Type of Stage: Proscenium
Stage Dimensions: 60'Wx39'Dx21'H   **Orchestra Pit**
Seating Capacity: 1,300
Year Built: 1978   **Architect:** The Maguire and Shook Corporation
Contact for Rental: Karl F. Merritt;   (219) 982-5247

Peru

THEATRE

OLE OLSEN MEMORIAL THEATRE
8 Wallace Row, PO Box 580, Peru, IN 46970
(317) 473-9937
Founded: 1963
Arts Area: Community; Theatrical Group
Status: Non-Professional; Non-Profit
Type: Performing
Purpose: Purpose of this organization shall be to promote and encourage interest in the theatrical arts on a non-profit basis
Officers: Bonnie Chilcatt, President; Lynn Bockover, Executive Vice President; William Gornto, First Vice President; Kurt Krauskopf, Second Vice President; Ann Hubbard, Third Vice President; TyAnn Snyder, Secretary; Bob Radel, Treasurer
Budget: $1,000 - $50,000
Income Sources: Box Office; Individual Donations
Season: October - June   **Annual Attendance:** 1,500
Affiliations: Indiana Community Theatre League; Division of Indiana Theaters
Performance Facilities: High School Auditorium

Richmond

INSTRUMENTAL MUSIC

CHANTICLEER STRING QUARTET
944 Woods Road, Richmond, IN 47374
(317) 966-6214
Founded: 1977

Arts Area: Chamber
Status: Professional; Non-Profit
Type: Performing; Touring; Educational
Purpose: To share in creative ways the beauty of chamber music with people in all walks of life and of all ages
Management: Caroline Klemperer Green, Founder/Violinist/Agent
Paid Staff: 1
Paid Artists: 6
Utilizes: Guest Artists
Budget: $1,000 - $50,000
Income Sources: Private Foundations/Grants/Endowments; Business/Corporate Donations; Government Grants; Individual Donations
Annual Attendance: 15,000

RICHMOND SYMPHONY ORCHESTRA
300 Hub Etchison Parkway, PO Box 982, Richmond, IN 47375
(317) 966-5181
FAX: (317) 962-9723
Founded: 1908
Arts Area: Symphony; Orchestra; Chamber; Ensemble
Status: Professional; Non-Profit
Type: Performing; Resident; Educational
Purpose: To present a full repertoire of symphonic literature; to present educational programs; to present performance opportunities to area musicians
Management: William Perrin, Executive Director; Daniel Graves, Choral Conductor; Evelyn Woolard, Personnel Manager; Cynthia Jackson, Office Manager
Officers: Lynn Mayer, President; Nancy Mulick, Maxine Hampton, Vice Presidents; Daniel Braewley, Treasurer; Karen Niersbach, Secretary
Paid Staff: 3   **Volunteer Staff:** 6
Utilizes: Special Technical Talent; Guest Artists
Budget: $100,000 - $500,000
Income Sources: Private Foundations/Grants/Endowments; Business/Corporate Donations; Box Office; Government Grants; Individual Donations
Season: October - May
Annual Attendance: 5,000
Affiliations: ASOL; IOC
Performance Facilities: Civic Auditorium

VOCAL MUSIC

WHITEWATER OPERA COMPANY
805 Promenade, PO Box 633, Richmond, IN 47375
(317) 962-7106
Founded: 1972
Arts Area: Grand Opera; Lyric Opera; Light Opera; Operetta
Status: Professional; Non-Profit
Type: Performing; Touring; Educational
Purpose: To present full-length and one-act operas, locally and on tour, and to present educational operatic programs for schools and organizations
Management: Charles Combopiano, General Manager/Artistic Director; Elsie Klute, Administrative Assistant; Claire Combodiano, Interim Development/Marketing Director; Beverly Senese, Bookkeeper
Officers: Gail Toedebusch, President; James Miller, Vice President; Elsie Klute, Secretary; Beverly Senese, Treasurer
Paid Staff: 3   **Volunteer Staff:** 54
Paid Artists: 175
Utilizes: Special Technical Talent; Guest Conductors; Guest Artists; Guest Directors
Budget: $100,000 - $500,000
Income Sources: Private Foundations/Grants/Endowments; Business/Corporate Donations; Box Office; Government Grants; Individual Donations; Rentals
Season: October - June
Annual Attendance: 4,500
Affiliations: OA; NOA; IPN; Sorg Opera Company
Performance Facilities: Don Kehoe Performing Arts Center; Sorg Opera House

FACILITY

RICHMOND CIVIC THEATRE
1003 East Main Street, Richmond, IN 47374
(317) 962-1816
Type of Facility: Auditorium; Theatre House

Facility Originally: Vaudeville
Type of Stage: Proscenium
Stage Dimensions: 39'6"Wx27'6"D
Orchestra Pit
Seating Capacity: 610
Year Built: 1909 **Architect:** Fred Elliot **Cost:** $40,000
Year Remodeled: 1987 **Architect:** Phil Uhl **Cost:** $150,000
Resident Groups: Richmond Civic Theatre; Richmond Junior Players

South Bend

INSTRUMENTAL MUSIC

SOUTH BEND SYMPHONY
120 West LaSalle, Suite 602, South Bend, IN 46601
(219) 232-6343
FAX: (219) 232-6343
Founded: 1933
Arts Area: Symphony; Chamber; Ensemble; Pops
Status: Non-Profit
Type: Performing; Educational
Management: Lee Ellen Hveem, General Manager
Officers: Mrs. Judd Leighton, Chairman of the Board; Donald A. Dake, Vice Chairman of the Board; Thomas P. Bergin, President
Paid Staff: 4 **Volunteer Staff:** 1
Paid Artists: 100 **Non-Paid Artists:** 120
Utilizes: Guest Conductors; Guest Artists
Budget: $500,000 - $1,000,000
Income Sources: Private Foundations/Grants/Endowments; Business/Corporate Donations; Box Office; Government Grants; Individual Donations
Season: September - May
Annual Attendance: 12,500
Affiliations: ASOL
Performance Facilities: Morris Civic Auditorium

PERFORMING SERIES

FIREFLY FESTIVAL FOR THE PERFORMING ARTS
202 South Michigan, Suite 845, South Bend, IN 46601-2012
(219) 288-3472
Founded: 1981
Arts Area: Dance; Vocal Music; Instrumental Music; Theater; Festivals
Status: Professional; Semi-Professional; Non-Professional; Non-Profit
Type: Performing; Educational
Purpose: To present outstanding music, dance and theatre in an outdoor setting; to promote the performing arts and enrich the cultural scene in Michigan
Management: Carol Weiss Rosenberg, Executive Director; Carol B. Privette, Administrative Assistant; David Homann, Office Assistant; Bill Soderberg, Production Manager; Loretta Baker, House Manger
Officers: Helen V. Hepler, President; Michael B. Watkins, First Vice President; Pam Jarrett, Second Vice President; Candace Butler, Secretary; John M. Schmitt, Treasurer
Paid Staff: 5 **Volunteer Staff:** 392
Paid Artists: 124 **Non-Paid Artists:** 87
Utilizes: Special Technical Talent; Guest Conductors; Guest Artists; Guest Directors
Budget: $100,000 - $500,000
Income Sources: Private Foundations/Grants/Endowments; Business/Corporate Donations; Box Office; Individual Donations
Season: June - August
Annual Attendance: 23,000
Affiliations: APAP; Indiana Arts Commission; Indiana Presenters Network
Performance Facilities: Robert J. Fischgrund Center for the Performing Arts

FACILITY

CENTURY CENTER
120 South St. Joseph Street, South Bend, IN 46601
(219) 235-9711
FAX: (219) 235-9185
Type of Facility: Civic Center

Year Built: 1977   Architect: Philip Johnson and John Burgee
Contact for Rental: Sandy Lee, Director of Sales

CENTURY CENTER - BENDIX THEATRE
120 South St. Joseph Street, South Bend, IN 46601
(219) 235-9711
    Type of Facility: Theatre House
    Type of Stage: Thrust
    Stage Dimensions: 32'Wx39'10"D
    Seating Capacity: 694
    Year Built: 1977
    Contact for Rental: Sandra Lee, Director of Sales;   (219) 235-9711

CENTURY CENTER - CONVENTION HALL
120 South St. Joseph Street, South Bend, IN 46601
(219) 235-9711
    Type of Facility: Multi-Purpose; Room; Exhibition Hall
    Type of Stage: Flexible; Platform
    Seating Capacity: 3,000
    Year Built: 1977   Architect: Philip Johnson; John Burgee
    Contact for Rental: Sandra Lee, Director of Sales;   (219) 235-9711

CENTURY CENTER - RECITAL HALL
120 South St. Joseph Street, South Bend, IN 46601
(219) 235-9711
    Type of Facility: Concert Hall; Recital Hall
    Type of Stage: Thrust
    Stage Dimensions: 25'5"Wx16'1"D
    Seating Capacity: 166
    Year Built: 1977
    Contact for Rental: Sandra Lee, Director of Sales;   (219) 235-9711

MORRIS CIVIC AUDITORIUM
211 North Michigan, South Bend, IN 46601
(219) 284-9198
FAX: (219) 284-9892
    Founded: 1922
    Type of Facility: Theatre House
    Facility Originally: Vaudeville
    Type of Stage: Proscenium
    Stage Dimensions: 54'Wx27'Dx25'H
    Seating Capacity: 2,468
    Year Built: 1922   Architect: Jacob Aroner   Cost: $1,150,000
    Acoustical Consultant: Kirkegard
    Contact for Rental: Dale Balsbaugh;   (219) 284-9198
    Resident Groups: South Bend Symphony; Broadway Theatre League

Terre Haute

INSTRUMENTAL MUSIC

TERRE HAUTE SYMPHONY ORCHESTRA
25 North Sixth Street, Terre Haute, IN 47807
(812) 234-6060
    Founded: 1926
    Arts Area: Symphony; Orchestra; Ensemble
    Status: Semi-Professional
    Type: Performing; Educational; Run-Outs
    Purpose: To maintain an orchestra dedicated to excellent performances of symphonic literature for the enjoyment and cultural enrichment of audiences from the Wabash Valley area
    Management: Susan E. Bunce, General Manager; Shelley Criss, Personnel Manager and Administrative Assistant; Dan Powers, Librarian

Officers: Barbara Passmore, President; Martin Morrow, Vice President for Development; Joyce Keenan, Vice President for Marketing; James Colligan, Vice President for Long Range Planning; Susan Brattain, Secretary; Don Schillson, Treasurer; Marian Pettus, Member at Large
Paid Staff: 4   **Volunteer Staff:** 3
Paid Artists: 85
Utilizes: Guest Conductors; Guest Artists
Budget: $100,000 - $500,000
Income Sources: Private Foundations/Grants/Endowments; Business/Corporate Donations; Box Office; Government Grants; Individual Donations; Indiana State University
Season: September - May
Annual Attendance: 15,000
Affiliations: Indiana State University
Performance Facilities: Tilson Auditorium, Indiana State University

FACILITY

COMMUNITY THEATRE OF TERRE HAUTE
1431 South 25th Street, Terre Haute, IN 47803
(812) 232-7172
Type of Facility: Theatre Complex; Auditorium; Performance Center; Theatre House; Multi-Purpose
Type of Stage: Thrust; Proscenium; Platform
Stage Dimensions: 61'Wx35'D; 25'Wx15'H proscenium opening
Seating Capacity: 375
Year Built: 1940
Year Remodeled: 1954
Resident Groups: Terre Haute International Film Series; Community Theatre

Vincennes

THEATRE

VINCENNES UNIVERSITY SUMMER THEATRE
1002 North First, Vincennes, IN 47591
(812) 885-4256
FAX: (812) 885-5868
Founded: 1968
Arts Area: Summer Stock; Musical
Status: Semi-Professional; Non-Profit
Type: Performing; Resident; Educational
Purpose: To provide quality theatrical entertainment for Vincennes and the surrounding area during the summer months
Management: James J. Spurrier, PhD, Managing/Artistic Director
Officers: Phillip M. Summers, PhD, President, Vincennes University
Utilizes: Special Technical Talent; Guest Artists
Budget: $50,000 - $100,000
Income Sources: Private Foundations/Grants/Endowments; Business/Corporate Donations; Box Office; Government Grants; Individual Donations
Season: June - August
Annual Attendance: 5,400
Performance Facilities: Shircliff Theatre

West Lafayette

THEATRE

PURDUE PROFESSIONAL SUMMER THEATRE
1376 Stewart Center, Room 85, West Lafayette, IN 47907
(317) 494-3082
FAX: (317) 494-3660
Founded: 1958

Status: Professional; Non-Profit
Type: Performing
Purpose: Interested in newer American plays both comedic and dramatic
Management: Jim O'Connor, Division of Theater
Paid Staff: 20   **Volunteer Staff:** 10
Paid Artists: 20
Utilizes: Special Technical Talent; Guest Directors
Budget: $1,000 - $50,000
Income Sources: Box Office
Season: June - August   **Annual Attendance:** 5,000
Affiliations: Purdue University
Performance Facilities: Experimental Theater

FACILITY

ELLIOTT HALL OF MUSIC
Purdue University, West Lafayette, IN 47906
(317) 494-3920
FAX: (317) 494-6621
Founded: 1940
Type of Facility: Concert Hall; Auditorium; Theatre House
Type of Stage: Proscenium
Stage Dimensions: 100'Wx35'D   **Orchestra Pit**
Seating Capacity: 6,027
Year Built: 1940   **Architect:** Walter Scholer and Associates   **Cost:** $1,200,000
Year Remodeled: 1991   **Cost:** $1,200,000
Contact for Rental: Stephen D. Hall;   (317) 494-3937

IOWA

Ames

DANCE

CO'MOTION DANCE THEATER
129 East Seventh Street, Ames, IA 50010
(515) 232-7374
FAX: (515) 232-7374
Founded: 1978
Arts Area: Modern
Status: Professional; Non-Profit
Type: Performing; Touring; Resident; Educational
Purpose: Co'Motion Dance exists to bring high-caliber professional dance to Midwestern sponsors at affordable prices and to offer the highest quality in dance education to its students.
Management: Valerie Williams, Director; J. Thomas Kidd, General Manager
Officers: Dana Schumacher, President; Deb Felton, Vice President; J. Thomas Kidd, Secretary/Treasurer
Paid Staff: 1
Paid Artists: 4
Utilizes: Special Technical Talent; Guest Artists; Guest Choreographers
Budget: $50,000 - $100,000
Income Sources: Private Foundations/Grants/Endowments; Box Office; Government Grants; Individual Donations; Presenter Fees
Season: September - May

INSTRUMENTAL MUSIC

AMES TOWN AND GOWN CHAMBER MUSIC ASSOCIATION
c/o Art Staniforth, 1634 Crestwood Circle, Ames, IA 50010
Founded: 1950
Arts Area: Chamber; Ensemble; Instrumental Group
Status: Non-Profit
Type: Sponsoring
Purpose: To present four to six chamber music concerts per year
Officers: Art Staniforth, President; Paula Helmath, Vice President; Herbert T. David, Secretary; George Karas, Treasurer
Volunteer Staff: 17
Utilizes: Guest Artists
Budget: $1,000 - $50,000
Income Sources: Private Foundations/Grants/Endowments; Business/Corporate Donations; Box Office; Government Grants; Individual Donations; Fundraising
Season: September - May   **Annual Attendance:** 1,400
Affiliations: Iowa State University Music Department
Performance Facilities: Iowa State University Music Hall Recital Hall; Ames City Hall Auditorium

PERFORMING SERIES

AMES INTERNATIONAL ORCHESTRA FESTIVAL ASSOCIATION
PO Box 1243, Ames, IA 50010
(515) 294-3213
Founded: 1969
Arts Area: Dance; Vocal Music; Instrumental Music; Theater; Festivals
Status: Non-Professional; Non-Profit
Type: Educational; Sponsoring
Purpose: To promote, assist and encourage the presentation of symphony orchestras, national and international, and associated events in a festival setting
Management: Robert E. Maxham, Executive Director
Officers: E. Douglas Brown, President; Thomas Griswold, President-Elect; Norman Riis, First Vice President; George Hinshaw, Second Vice President; Carol Torrents, Secretary; Ken Anderson, Treasurer
Paid Staff: 1
Utilizes: Guest Conductors; Guest Artists; Guest Directors
Budget: $100,000 - $500,000
Income Sources: Private Foundations/Grants/Endowments; Business/Corporate Donations; Box Office; Individual Donations
Season: September - May

Affiliations: ASOL
Performance Facilities: C.Y. Stephens Auditorium, Iowa State University

FACILITY

IOWA STATE UNIVERSITY-IOWA STATE CENTER
Suite 4, Scheman Building, Ames, IA 50011-1112
(515) 294-3347
FAX: (515) 294-3349
 Type of Facility: Concert Hall; Auditorium; Theatre House; Arena; Multi-Purpose
 Type of Stage: Proscenium; 3/4 Arena; Arena   **Orchestra Pit**
 Seating Capacity: Variable
 Year Built: 1975
 Contact for Rental: Beth A. Lindquist;   (515) 294-3347
 Manager: Joseph Romano
 Resident Groups: Iowa State University Theatre
 Iowa State Center contains Benton Auditorium, C.Y. Stephens Auditorium, Hilton Coliseum and J.W. Fisher Auditorium.
 See separate listings for additional information.

IOWA STATE UNIVERSITY-IOWA STATE CENTER - BENTON AUDITORIUM
Suite 4, Scheman Building, Ames, IA 50011
(515) 294-3347
 Type of Facility: Auditorium
 Type of Stage: Platform
 Stage Dimensions: 38'x20'
 Seating Capacity: 464
 Year Built: 1975   **Architect:** Crites & McConnell; Brooks Borg & Skiles
 Manager: Joe Romano, Director

IOWA STATE UNIVERSITY-IOWA STATE CENTER - C.Y. STEPHENS AUDITORIUM
Suite 4, Scheman Building, Ames, IA 50011
(515) 294-3347
 Type of Facility: Auditorium
 Type of Stage: Proscenium
 Stage Dimensions: 80'Wx56'D; 80'Wx30'H proscenium opening   **Orchestra Pit**
 Seating Capacity: 2,749
 Year Built: 1972
 Architect: Crites & McConnell; Brooks Borg & Skiles
 Cost: $4,925,000
 Contact for Rental: David M. Olson;   (515) 294-3347
 Manager: Joe Romano

IOWA STATE UNIVERSITY-IOWA STATE CENTER - HILTON COLISEUM
Suite 4, Scheman Building, Ames, IA 50011
(515) 294-3347
 Type of Facility: Arena; Multi-Purpose
 Type of Stage: Flexible; Platform
 Stage Dimensions: 40'x60'
 Seating Capacity: 14,000
 Year Built: 1971
 Architect: Crites & McConnell; Brooks Borg & Skiles
 Cost: $8,165,000
 Acoustical Consultant: Paul S. Veneklasen
 Contact for Rental: David M. Olson;   (515) 294-3347
 Manager: Joe Romano

IOWA STATE UNIVERSITY -IOWA STATE CENTER - J.W. FISHER AUDITORIUM
Suite 4, Scheman Building, Ames, IA 50011
(515) 294-3347
 Type of Facility: Theatre House
 Type of Stage: Proscenium
 Stage Dimensions: 36'x18'x36'   **Orchestra Pit**
 Seating Capacity: 454
 Year Built: 1974   **Architect:** Crites & McConnell; Brooks Borg & Skiles   **Cost:** $900,000
 Contact for Rental: David M. Olson;   (515) 294-3347

Manager: Joe Romano
Resident Groups: Iowa State Theatre

Bettendorf

FACILITY

LINCOLN CENTER FOR THE CULTURAL ARTS
951 27th Street, Bettendorf, IA 52722
(319) 355-8626
    Type of Facility: Performance Center; Multi-Purpose; Cultural Arts
    Facility Originally: School
    Type of Stage: Thrust; Proscenium
    Stage Dimensions: 40'x35'
    Seating Capacity: 350
    Year Built: 1920
    Year Remodeled: 1954
    Contact for Rental: Nancy Sann;   (319) 355-8626

Cedar Falls

FACILITY

UNIVERSITY OF NORTHERN IOWA - OLD AUDITORIUM
Cedar Falls, IA 50614-0358
(319) 273-2725
FAX: (319) 273-2731
    Mailing Address: Artists Series Committee, University of Northern Iowa, CAC 269, Cedar Falls, IA 50614-0358
    Type of Facility: Auditorium
    Type of Stage: Proscenium
    Stage Dimensions: 34'x32'
    Seating Capacity: 1,025
    Year Built: 1900
    Year Remodeled: 1987
    Contact for Rental: Maucker Union Office;   (319) 273-2257

UNIVERSITY OF NORTHERN IOWA - RUSSELL HALL
Cedar Falls, IA 50614
(319) 273-2024
    Type of Facility: Concert Hall
    Type of Stage: Proscenium   **Orchestra Pit**
    Seating Capacity: 600
    Year Built: 1960   **Architect:** Thorson
    Manager: Robert Byrnes, Administrative Assistant
    Resident Groups: UNI/Music Groups

UNIVERSITY OF NORTHERN IOWA - STRAYER-WOOD THEATRE
Cedar Falls, IA 50614-0371
(319) 273-6386
    Type of Facility: Theatre Complex
    Year Built: 1978   **Architect:** Thorson-Brom   **Cost:** $2,000,000
    Acoustical Consultant: Bolt, Beranek & Newman
    Contact for Rental: Greta Berghammer;   (319) 273-6386
    Resident Groups: Theatre UNI
    Strayer-Wood Theatre contains Black Box and Main Stage. See separate listings for additional information.

UNIVERSITY OF NORTHERN IOWA - STRAYER-WOOD THEATRE-BLACK BOX
Cedar Falls, IA 50614-0371
(319) 273-6386
FAX: (319) 273-2731
    Type of Facility: Theatre Complex; Studio Performance; Black Box
    Type of Stage: Flexible   **Orchestra Pit**
    Seating Capacity: 500
    Year Built: 1978
    Contact for Rental: Gretta Berghammer;   (319) 273-6386
    Manager: Paul Sannerud;   (319) 273-2500

UNIVERSITY OF NORTHERN IOWA - STRAYER-WOOD THEATRE-MAIN STAGE
Cedar Falls, IA 50614-0371
(319) 273-6386
Type of Facility: Theatre House
Type of Stage: Proscenium
Stage Dimensions: 22'x84'x39'   **Orchestra Pit**
Seating Capacity: 508
Year Built: 1978
Contact for Rental: Greta Berghammer;   (319) 273-6386

Cedar Rapids

INSTRUMENTAL MUSIC

CEDAR RAPIDS SYMPHONY ORCHESTRA
205 Second Avenue SE, Cedar Rapids, IA 52401
(319) 366-8203
FAX: (319) 366-5206
Founded: 1922
Arts Area: Symphony; Orchestra; Chamber; Ensemble
Status: Professional; Non-Profit
Type: Performing; Educational
Management: Marc D. Levy, Executive Director; Christian Tiemeyer, Music Director/Conductor
Officers: John Smith, President; Thomas Pitner, Vice President/President Elect; Lynn Olsen, Secretary; David McIrvin, Treasurer
Paid Staff: 7
Paid Artists: 85
Utilizes: Guest Artists
Budget: $1,000,000 - $5,000,000
Income Sources: Private Foundations/Grants/Endowments; Business/Corporate Donations; Box Office; Government Grants; Individual Donations
Season: September - May
Affiliations: ASOL
Performance Facilities: Paramount Theatre

PERFORMING SERIES

THE DRAWING LEGION
1103 Third Street SE, Cedar Rapids, IA 52401
(319) 364-1580
FAX: (319) 365-7502
Founded: 1981
Arts Area: Dance; Instrumental Music; Theater
Status: Semi-Professional; Non-Profit
Type: Performing; Touring; Sponsoring
Purpose: To serve as a progressive, multidisciplinary company, producing original performance art and running CSPS, an alternative gallery and performance space
Management: Mel Andringa, Artistic Director; F. John Herbert, Project Director
Paid Staff: 2   **Volunteer Staff:** 3
Utilizes: Guest Artists
Budget: $50,000 - $100,000
Income Sources: Private Foundations/Grants/Endowments; Business/Corporate Donations; Box Office; Government Grants; Individual Donations
Season: 52 Weeks
Affiliations: APAP; NAAO

FACILITY

FIVE SEASONS CENTER ARENA
370 First Avenue NE, Cedar Rapids, IA 52401
(319) 398-5211
FAX: (319) 362-2102
Type of Facility: Concert Hall; Arena; Multi-Purpose
Type of Stage: Flexible; Platform
Seating Capacity: 10,000
Year Built: 1979   **Architect:** Leo Peiffer Associates

Contact for Rental: Sharon Cummins, Chris Werner;   (319) 398-5211
Manager: Ann Larson;   (319) 398-5211

PARAMOUNT THEATRE FOR THE PERFORMING ARTS
370 First Avenue NE, Cedar Rapids, IA 52401
(319) 398-5211
FAX: (319) 362-2102
        Type of Facility: Concert Hall; Off Broadway; Theatre House
        Type of Stage: Proscenium
        Stage Dimensions: 44'Wx27'H proscenium opening   **Orchestra Pit**
        Seating Capacity: 1,913
        Year Built: 1928   **Architect:** Peacock and Frank
        Year Remodeled: 1987   **Architect:** Leo Peiffer & Associates
        Contact for Rental: Sharon Cummins, Chris Werner;   (319) 398-5211
        Manager: Ann Larson;   (319) 398-5211
        Resident Groups: Cedar Rapids Symphony Orchestra; Community Concerts Association; The Cedar Rapids Theater Organ Society

Council Bluffs

THEATRE

CHANTICLEER
PO Box 363, Council Bluffs, IA 51502
(712) 323-9955; (712) 322-9751
        Founded: 1952
        Arts Area: Community
        Status: Non-Profit
        Type: Performing
        Purpose: To promote and educate theatrical performers and performances
        Management: Kay Esancy, Office Manager; Joyce Sheehan, Business Manager; Dixie Price, House Manager
        Officers: John Myers, President/Vice President; Kay Esancy, Secretary/Treasurer
        Paid Staff: 3
        Utilizes: Special Technical Talent; Guest Directors
        Budget: $50,000 - $100,000
        Income Sources: Private Foundations/Grants/Endowments; Business/Corporate Donations; Box Office; Individual Donations
        Season: September - June   **Annual Attendance:** 8,000

Davenport

INSTRUMENTAL MUSIC

QUAD CITY SYMPHONY ORCHESTRA
PO Box 1144, Davenport, IA 52805
(319) 322-0931
FAX: (319) 322-6864
        Founded: 1915
        Arts Area: Symphony; Orchestra
        Status: Professional; Non-Profit
        Type: Performing; Educational
        Purpose: To support symphonic performances and to foster, stimulate and encourage orchestral ensemble and other music through developmental programs and scholarships for talented persons
        Management: Lance O. Willett, Executive Director; Dennis Loftin, Operations Manager; James Dixon, Music Director/Conductor
        Officers: Joyce Bawden, President; John Kindschuk, Executive Vice President; June Stimac, Secretary; Charles Brooke, Treasurer; Elsie von Maur, Honorary Chairman
        Paid Staff: 7   **Volunteer Staff:** 350
        Paid Artists: 95
        Utilizes: Guest Artists
        Budget: $500,000 - $1,000,000
        Income Sources: Private Foundations/Grants/Endowments; Business/Corporate Donations; Box Office; Government Grants; Individual Donations
        Season: September - May   **Annual Attendance:** 56,000
        Affiliations: ASOL; Illinois Council of Orchestras
        Performance Facilities: Centennial Hall, Rock Island; Adler Theater, Davenport

QUAD CITY YOUTH SYMPHONY ORCHESTRA
PO Box 1144, Davenport, IA 52805
(319) 322-0931
> **Founded:** 1958
> **Arts Area:** Symphony; Orchestra; Chamber; Ensemble
> **Status:** Non-Professional; Non-Profit
> **Type:** Performing; Educational
> **Management:** Daniel Culver, Music Director/Conductor
> **Officers:** Eloise Smit, Chairperson
> **Non-Paid Artists:** 82
> **Utilizes:** Guest Artists
> **Budget:** $1,000 - $50,000
> **Income Sources:** Box Office; Individual Donations
> **Season:** September - June   **Annual Attendance:** 5,000
> **Affiliations:** ASOL(Youth Symphony Division); Quad City Symphony Orchestra
> **Performance Facilities:** Centennial Hall, Rock Island; Masonic Temple Auditorium

THEATRE

JUNIOR THEATRE
2822 Eastern Avenue, PO Box 130, Davenport, IA 52803
(319) 326-7862
> **Founded:** 1953
> **Arts Area:** Community; Puppet
> **Status:** Non-Profit
> **Type:** Performing; Touring; Educational
> **Purpose:** Classes in creative drama and play production for students five years old through high school. All students perform each semester and do technical work. Five major productions, 28 touring productions
> **Management:** Parks and Recreation Department of City of Davenport; Bonnie F. Guenther, Cultural Arts Supervisor
> **Officers:** Marlene Miller, President; Carole Kucharo, Vice President; Beverly Rosenbohm, Secretary; Carol Jorgensen, Treasurer
> **Paid Staff:** 12   **Volunteer Staff:** 30
> **Budget:** $50,000 - $100,000
> **Income Sources:** Business/Corporate Donations; Government Grants; City of Davenport Funding
> **Season:** September - August   **Annual Attendance:** 40,000
> **Affiliations:** Iowa Community Theatres; AATE
> **Performance Facilities:** Mary Fluhrer Nighswander Junior Theatre

PERFORMING SERIES

BROADWAY THEATRE LEAGUE OF THE QUAD-CITIES
PO Box 130, Davenport, IA 52805
(319) 326-1916
> **Founded:** 1960
> **Status:** Non-Profit
> **Type:** Sponsoring
> **Purpose:** To sponsor touring New York productions, bus and truck companies, of major Broadway Shows
> **Officers:** Norman J. Kelinson, President & Manager; Leone Bredbeck, Vice President; Suzie Lewis, Secretary; Jim Victor, Treasurer
> **Paid Staff:** 1   **Volunteer Staff:** 35
> **Utilizes:** Guest Artists
> **Budget:** $100,000 - $500,000
> **Income Sources:** Box Office
> **Season:** September - May   **Annual Attendance:** 40,000
> **Performance Facilities:** Adler Theatre

SAINT AMBROSE COLLEGE - GALVIN FINE ARTS CENTER
518 West Locust, Davenport, IA 52803
(319) 383-8878
> **Founded:** 1969
> **Arts Area:** Dance; Vocal Music; Instrumental Music; Theater; Festivals
> **Status:** Non-Profit
> **Type:** Performing; Touring; Educational; Sponsoring
> **Purpose:** To present quality cultural programs for the college and community; to create a positive educational arts experience
> **Management:** Nancy Cerny, Marketing Coordinator; Lance Sadlek, Director
> **Paid Staff:** 32
> **Utilizes:** Special Technical Talent; Guest Conductors; Guest Artists; Guest Directors
> **Budget:** $100,000 - $500,000

Income Sources: Box Office; Government Grants
Season: 52 Weeks **Annual Attendance:** 60,000
Affiliations: APAP; USITT; Iowa Arts Council; Illinois Arts Council

FACILITY

MARYCREST COLLEGE - UPHAM AUDITORIUM
1607 West 12th Street, Davenport, IA 52804
(319) 326-9343
Type of Facility: Concert Hall; Auditorium
Facility Originally: School
Type of Stage: Proscenium; 50' Foot Thrust
Stage Dimensions: 26'Wx16'D
Seating Capacity: 300
Year Built: 1942
Contact for Rental: Communication, Fine and Performing Arts Division;   (319) 326-9221
Resident Groups: Marycrest Performing Arts Series

SAINT AMBROSE COLLEGE - ALLAERT HALL
Galvin Fine Arts Center, 518 West Locust Street, Davenport, IA 52803
(319) 383-8878
FAX: (319) 383-8791
Type of Facility: Auditorium; Performance Center; Theatre House
Type of Stage: Proscenium
Stage Dimensions: 64'x70'   **Orchestra Pit**
Seating Capacity: 1,236
Year Built: 1969   **Architect:** Braecke-Hayes-Miller   **Cost:** $1,500,000
Acoustical Consultant: Wess Ling Beling Engineering Company
Contact for Rental: Lance Sadler;   (319) 383-8878
Manager: Terry Miller;   (319) 383-8878
Resident Groups: Children's Theatre Company

Decorah

VOCAL MUSIC

DORIAN OPERA THEATRE
Decorah, IA 52101
(319) 382-3389
Founded: 1985
Arts Area: Lyric Opera; Light Opera; Operetta
Status: Semi-Professional; Non-Profit
Type: Touring; Resident; Educational
Purpose: To offer performance experience for young professionals and student artists
Management: David Greedy, Douglas Meyer, Co-Directors
Officers: Karen Gray, President; Vicki Donhowe, Vice President; Jack Nelson, Secretary/Treasurer
Paid Staff: 12 **Volunteer Staff:** 12
Paid Artists: 4 **Non-Paid Artists:** 25
Utilizes: Special Technical Talent; Guest Artists
Budget: $50,000 - $100,000
Income Sources: Private Foundations/Grants/Endowments; Business/Corporate Donations; Box Office; Government Grants; Individual Donations
Season: June - July   **Annual Attendance:** 4,000
Performance Facilities: Luther College Center for Faith and Life

PERFORMING SERIES

DECORAH COMMUNITY CONCERT ASSOCIATION
123 West Water Street, Decorah, IA 52101
(319) 382-2665; (319) 382-4504
Founded: 1941
Arts Area: Dance; Vocal Music; Instrumental Music; Lyric Opera; Ballet
Status: Non-Profit
Type: Performing; Educational
Purpose: To provide opportunities to the community to hear and see the best in music and entertainment
Officers: W.G. Linnevold, President; Mrs. F. Peterson, Secretary/Campaign Supervisor; John Hess, Treasurer
Utilizes: Guest Artists
Budget: $1,000 - $50,000

Season: September - May   **Annual Attendance:** 3,500
Affiliations: CCA
Performance Facilities: Center for Faith and Life, Luther College

---

Des Moines

DANCE

IOWA DANCE THEATRE
6720 Hickman Road, Des Moines, IA 50322
(515) 276-2694
Founded: 1983
Arts Area: Modern; Ballet; Jazz
Status: Semi-Professional; Non-Profit
Type: Performing; Touring; Educational
Purpose: To support a company of dancers who will perform and promote dance as an art form
Management: Mary Joyce Lind, Artistic Director; Janice Baker-Haines, Robert Thomas, Co-Directors
Volunteer Staff: 10
Utilizes: Guest Artists
Budget: $1,000 - $50,000
Income Sources: Individual Donations
Annual Attendance: 1,400
Performance Facilities: Performing Arts Hall, Drake University

INSTRUMENTAL MUSIC

DES MOINES SYMPHONY
530 42nd Street, Des Moines, IA 50312
(515) 255-2343
Founded: 1937
Arts Area: Symphony; Orchestra; Chamber; Ensemble
Status: Professional; Non-Profit
Type: Performing; Educational
Management: Paul Ferrone, Executive Director; Joseph Giunta, Music Director and Conductor
Paid Staff: 5
Paid Artists: 84
Utilizes: Guest Conductors; Guest Artists
Budget: $500,000 - $1,000,000
Income Sources: Private Foundations/Grants/Endowments; Business/Corporate Donations; Box Office; Government Grants; Individual Donations; Fund-raising
Season: September - May   **Annual Attendance:** 30,000
Affiliations: ASOL
Performance Facilities: Civic Center of Greater Des Moines

FACILITY

CIVIC CENTER OF GREATER DES MOINES
221 Walnut, Des Moines, IA 50309
(515) 243-0766
FAX: (515) 243-1179
Type of Facility: Concert Hall; Auditorium; Studio Performance; Performance Center; Off Broadway; Theatre House; Opera House; Black Box
Type of Stage: Flexible; Proscenium; Stoner Studio Theatre
Stage Dimensions: 76'Wx30'D; 76'Wx28'H proscenium opening   **Orchestra Pit**
Seating Capacity: 2,735; Stoner Studio Theatre - 200
Year Built: 1979   **Architect:** Charles Herbert & Associates   **Cost:** $9,500,000
Acoustical Consultant: Paul Veneklasen
Contact for Rental: David Olson;   (515) 243-0766
Manager: Gordon D. Smith, Manager
Resident Groups: Des Moines Symphony; Ballet Iowa; Civic Music Association; Drama Workshop
Rental available for all types of musical, theatrical, dance and seminar events

DES MOINES WOMEN'S CLUB
Hoyt Sherman Place, 1501 Woodland, Des Moines, IA 50309
(515) 243-0913
Type of Facility: Concert Hall; Auditorium; Studio Performance; Theatre House
Type of Stage: Proscenium
Stage Dimensions: 35'Wx20'D   **Orchestra Pit**

Seating Capacity: 1,400
Year Built: 1922
Year Remodeled: 1950
Contact for Rental: A.B. Wonders;   (515) 243-0913
Dramas, concerts, seminars, speakers (no rock)

DRAKE UNIVERSITY - HALL OF PERFORMING ARTS, HARMON FINE ARTS CENTER
26th Street & Carpenter Avenue, Des Moines, IA 50311
(515) 271-2018
FAX: (515) 271-3977
    Founded: 1881
    Type of Facility: Concert Hall; Performance Center
    Type of Stage: Proscenium
    Stage Dimensions: 40'Wx32'D   **Orchestra Pit**
    Seating Capacity: 460
    Year Built: 1972   **Architect:** Harry Weese & Associates
    Year Remodeled: 1992   **Architect:** RDG Bussard/Dikis Associates Ltd.   **Cost:** $100,000
    Contact for Rental: Myron Marty;   (515) 271-3939
    Resident Groups: Drake University Theatre Arts and Music Departments

DRAKE UNIVERISTY - OLD MAIN AUDITORIUM
Des Moines, IA 50311
(515) 271-3939
FAX: (515) 271-3977
    Founded: 1881
    Type of Facility: Concert Hall; Auditorium
    Facility Originally: Chapel; Auditorium
    Type of Stage: Platform
    Stage Dimensions: 36'W at front; 30'W at rear; 32'D
    Seating Capacity: 775
    Year Built: 1900   **Cost:** $20,000
    Year Remodeled: 1992   **Architect:** Baldwin Clause Architects PC   **Cost:** $3,800,000
    Acoustical Consultant: Talaske
    Contact for Rental: Myron Marty;   (515) 271-3939
    Resident Groups: Drake University Music Department

Dubuque

INSTRUMENTAL MUSIC

DUBUQUE SYMPHONY ORCHESTRA
1072 Locust Street, PO Box 881, Dubuque, IA 52004-0881
(319) 557-1677
    Founded: 1959
    Arts Area: Symphony; Orchestra; Chamber; Ensemble
    Status: Semi-Professional; Non-Profit
    Type: Performing; Resident; Educational; Sponsoring
    Purpose: To present quality performances and educational programs in the field of classical music
    Management: Robert A. Birman, General Manager; Mary Ellen Rogers, Operations Manager; Tracey Rush, Librarian
    Officers: David Howell, President; Jean Dunn, Secretary; William Skemp, Treasurer
    Paid Staff: 2
    Paid Artists: 4
    Utilizes: Guest Artists
    Budget: $100,000 - $500,000
    Income Sources: Private Foundations/Grants/Endowments; Business/Corporate Donations; Box Office; Government Grants; Individual Donations
    Season: August - May   **Annual Attendance:** 15,000
    Affiliations: Symphony League
    Performance Facilities: Five Flags Center - Theatre

THEATRE

BARN COMMUNITY THEATRE
135 Eighth Street, Dubuque, IA 52001
(319) 588-1305
    Founded: 1971
    Arts Area: Musical; Community
    Status: Non-Professional; Non-Profit

Type: Performing; Educational
Purpose: To provide quality entertainment through live performances and educational experiences thus contributing to the cultural and economic growth of the community
Management: Sue Riedel, Theatre Manager; Helen Johnston, Office Manager
Officers: Dave Grable, President; Daryl Barklow, Vice President; Sue Reilly, Secretary; Melanie Olson, Treasurer
Paid Staff: 8   **Volunteer Staff:** 600
Paid Artists: 45   **Non-Paid Artists:** 200
Utilizes: Guest Artists; Guest Directors
Budget: $100,000 - $500,000
Income Sources: Private Foundations/Grants/Endowments; Business/Corporate Donations; Box Office; Government Grants; Individual Donations
Season: 52 Weeks
Affiliations: ACT; Iowa Community Theatre Association; Dubuque Arts Alliance; Dubuque Area, Galena and Dyersville Area Chambers of Commerce
Performance Facilities: Grand Opera House

FACILITY

FIVE FLAGS CENTER
Fourth and Main Streets, PO Box 628, Dubuque, IA 52001
(319) 556-4369
 Type of Facility: Civic Center
 Year Built: 1979
 Contact for Rental: Carole Barry;   (319) 589-4254
 Five Flags Center contains the Arena and Theatre. See separate listings for additional information.

FIVE FLAGS CENTER - ARENA
Fourth and Main Streets, PO Box 628, Dubuque, IA 52001
(319) 556-4369
 Type of Facility: Concert Hall; Arena
 Type of Stage: Flexible; Platform
 Stage Dimensions: 85'x40'
 Seating Capacity: 5,200
 Year Built: 1979
 Contact for Rental: Carole Barry;   (319) 589-4254
 The arena is also used for ice hockey

FIVE FLAGS CENTER - THEATRE
Fourth and Main Streets, PO Box 628, Dubuque, IA 52001
(319) 556-4369
 Type of Facility: Concert Hall; Theatre House
 Type of Stage: Proscenium
 Stage Dimensions: 32'Wx27'5"D; 32'Wx29'H proscenium opening   **Orchestra Pit**
 Seating Capacity: 717
 Year Built: 1910   **Architect:** Rapp & Rapp
 Year Remodeled: 1976   **Cost:** $1,000,000
 Contact for Rental: Carole Barry;   (319) 589-4254

Forest City

PERFORMING SERIES

WALDORF COMMUNITY ARTISTS SERIES
Waldorf College, 106 South Sixth Street, Forest City, IA 50436
(515) 582-8177
FAX: (515) 582-8111
 Founded: 1988
 Arts Area: Dance; Vocal Music; Instrumental Music; Theater; Lyric Opera; Grand Opera
 Status: Non-Profit
 Type: Sponsoring
 Purpose: To bring high quality performing arts to Waldorf and Forest City
 Management: Steven B. Thompson, Chair Waldorf Community Artist Series
 Paid Staff: 2   **Volunteer Staff:** 12
 Utilizes: Guest Artists
 Budget: $1,000 - $50,000
 Income Sources: Private Foundations/Grants/Endowments; Business/Corporate Donations; Box Office; Government Grants

Season: September - April   **Annual Attendance:** 5,000
Affiliations: Waldorf College

Fort Dodge

INSTRUMENTAL MUSIC

FORT DODGE AREA SYMPHONY ORCHESTRA
Box 1291, Fort Dodge, IA 50501
(515) 573-4224
    Arts Area: Symphony
    Status: Non-Profit
    Type: Performing
    Purpose: To provide live classical music to the community
    Management: Ardella Hein, Personnel Manager
    Officers: Laurel Mors, President; Doris Porter, Vice President; John Mors, Treasurer; Judy Gunderson, Secretary
    Paid Staff: 1   **Volunteer Staff:** 21
    Paid Artists: 3
    Utilizes: Guest Artists
    Budget: $1,000 - $50,000
    Income Sources: Private Foundations/Grants/Endowments; Business/Corporate Donations; Box Office; Government Grants; Individual Donations
    Season: October - April
    Annual Attendance: 3,000
    Performance Facilities: Phillips Middle School Auditorium

---

Garrison

THEATRE

THE OLD CREAMERY THEATRE COMPANY
PO Box 160, Garrison, IA 52229
(319) 477-3925
    Founded: 1971
    Arts Area: Professional; Theatrical Group
    Status: Professional; Non-Profit
    Type: Performing; Touring; Resident; Educational
    Purpose: To bring live theater to as many people as possible in rural Iowa
    Management: Thomas Peter Johnson, Producing Director; Blaine Stephens, Associate Artistic Director
    Officers: Rod Geist, Board President
    Paid Staff: 6
    Utilizes: Special Technical Talent; Guest Artists; Guest Directors
    Budget: $100,000 - $500,000
    Income Sources: Private Foundations/Grants/Endowments; Business/Corporate Donations; Box Office; Government Grants; Individual Donations
    Season: May - December
    Annual Attendance: 40,000
    Affiliations: AEA; TCG
    Performance Facilities: The Old Creamery Theatre (Garrison and Amana)
    Also located at the Amana Colonies Visitors Center, Amana, Iowa

FACILITY

THE OLD CREAMERY THEATRE
PO Box 160, Garrison, IA 52229
(319) 477-3925
    Type of Facility: Theatre Complex; Studio Performance; Theatre House
    Type of Stage: Thrust; Flexible
    Stage Dimensions: 32'Wx22'D
    Seating Capacity: 262
    Year Built: 1899
    Year Remodeled: 1976   **Cost:** $15,000
    Contact for Rental: Thomas P. Johnson;   (319) 477-3925
    Resident Groups: The Old Creamery Theatre Company
    Brenton Stage - studio theatre added in 1981 - seats 135, flexible stage

Indianola

VOCAL MUSIC

DES MOINES METRO OPERA
106 West Boston, Indianola, IA 50125
(515) 961-6221
FAX: (515) 961-2994
Founded: 1973
Arts Area: Grand Opera; Lyric Opera
Status: Professional; Non-Profit
Type: Performing; Touring; Resident; Educational
Purpose: To provide a stage for young American artists, produce high quality performances and educate audiences to opera in the Midwest
Management: Robert L. Larsen, Artistic Director; Jerilee M. Mace, Managing Director
Officers: Don Easter, President; Cherie Shreck, Vice President/President-Elect; Richard Calkins, Vice President/Development; LaDonna Mathes, Secretary; Charles Farr, Treasurer
Paid Staff: 6
Paid Artists: 20 **Non-Paid Artists:** 45
Budget: $1,000,000 - $5,000,000
Income Sources: Private Foundations/Grants/Endowments; Business/Corporate Donations; Box Office; Government Grants; Individual Donations
Season: June - July
Affiliations: OA
Performance Facilities: Blank Performing Arts Center

Iowa City

THEATRE

RIVERSIDE THEATRE
PO Box 1651, Iowa City, IA 52244
(319) 338-7672
Founded: 1981
Arts Area: Theatrical Group
Status: Semi-Professional; Non-Profit
Type: Performing; Touring; Resident; Educational; Sponsoring
Purpose: To provide a season of shows ranging from the classics to premieres of new plays; to sponsor other theatre groups; to provide education and a touring season throughout the Midwest
Management: Jody Hovland, Managing Director; Ron Clark, Artistic Director
Officers: Janice Wilson, Chairman; Tom Walsh, Vice Chairman
Paid Staff: 1
Utilizes: Special Technical Talent; Guest Artists; Guest Directors
Budget: $100,000 - $500,000
Income Sources: Business/Corporate Donations; Box Office; Government Grants; Individual Donations
Season: September - March **Annual Attendance:** 3,000
Performance Facilities: Riverside Theatre

FACILITY

THE UNIVERSITY OF IOWA - HANCHER AUDITORIUM
Iowa City, IA 52242
(319) 335-1160
Type of Facility: Auditorium
Type of Stage: Proscenium
Stage Dimensions: 170'Wx85'Hx55'D **Orchestra Pit**
Seating Capacity: 2,684
Year Built: 1972 **Architect:** Max Abramovitz **Cost:** $7,000,000
Acoustical Consultant: Paul Veneklasen
Contact for Rental: Wally Chappel

Mason City

FACILITY

NORTH IOWA COMMUNITY AUDITORIUM
500 College Drive, Mason City, IA 50401
(515) 421-4240
Type of Facility: Theatre Complex; Concert Hall; Auditorium; Theatre House
Type of Stage: Thrust; Proscenium
Orchestra Pit
Seating Capacity: 1,167
Year Built: 1980   **Architect:** Tom Wagner   **Cost:** $1,800,000
Contact for Rental: Robert A. Davis;   (515) 421-4241

Mount Pleasant

INSTRUMENTAL MUSIC

SOUTHEAST IOWA SYMPHONY ORCHESTRA
601 North Main, Mount Pleasant, IA 52641
(319) 385-6352
FAX: (319) 385-6296
Founded: 1950
Arts Area: Symphony; Orchestra
Status: Non-Professional; Non-Profit
Type: Performing
Purpose: To educate, encourage and perform orchestral music in southeast Iowa
Management: Robert McConnell, Conductor/Music Director; Joy Rayman Anderson, Manager
Officers: Judy Blommer, President; Elaine Cederquist, Vice President; Bobby K. Wilson, Secretary; Ruth Sein, Treasurer
Paid Staff: 4   **Volunteer Staff:** 50
Paid Artists: 20   **Non-Paid Artists:** 40
Utilizes: Guest Artists
Budget: $50,000 - $100,000
Income Sources: Private Foundations/Grants/Endowments; Business/Corporate Donations; Box Office; Government Grants; Individual Donations
Season: September - March   **Annual Attendance:** 5,000
Affiliations: ASOL; BMI; ASCAP
Performance Facilities: James Madison Auditorium; Iowa Wesleyan Chapel Auditorium; Saint John Auditorium

Orange City

FACILITY

NORTHWESTERN COLLEGE
101 Seventh Street SW, Orange City, IA 51041
(712) 737-4821
FAX: (712) 737-8847
Type of Facility: Theatre House; Multi-Purpose
Facility Originally: Church
Type of Stage: Thrust; Proscenium; Two Spaces
Seating Capacity: 224; 175
Year Built: 1925
Contact for Rental: Tres Jacobsma;   (712) 737-4821

Sioux City

DANCE

SIOUXLAND CIVIC DANCE ASSOCIATION
813 Pearl Street, Sioux City, IA 51101
(712) 255-0972
Founded: 1971
Arts Area: Ballet; Jazz
Status: Non-Profit
Type: Performing; Touring; Sponsoring

Officers: Jan King, President; Marge Herbold, Vice President; Karen Eberle, Secretary; Hess Roorda, Treasurer; Shirley Dill, Artistic Director
Volunteer Staff: 20
Non-Paid Artists: 50
Utilizes: Guest Artists; Guest Choreographers
Budget: $1,000 - $50,000
Income Sources: Private Foundations/Grants/Endowments; Business/Corporate Donations; Box Office; Government Grants; Individual Donations
Season: September - May   **Annual Attendance:** 5,000

INSTRUMENTAL MUSIC

SIOUX CITY SYMPHONY ORCHESTRA
258 Orpheum Building, PO Box 754, Sioux City, IA 51102
(712) 277-2111
FAX: (712) 252-0224
    Founded: 1923
    Arts Area: Symphony; Orchestra; Ensemble
    Status: Professional; Non-Profit
    Type: Performing; Resident; Educational
    Purpose: To perform at concerts
    Management: Dr. John E. Luebke, Executive Director; Dr. Alan L. Arnold, Operations Manager/Office Manager; Sandra Lehmberg, Marketing Assistant
    Officers: Michael Zimmerman, President; Thomas Borchert, Dr. Jeffrey Williams, Vice Presidents; David Silverberg, CFP, Treasurer; Linda Bowden, Secretary
    Paid Staff: 4
    Paid Artists: 85
    Utilizes: Guest Conductors; Guest Artists
    Budget: $100,000 - $500,000
    Income Sources: Private Foundations/Grants/Endowments; Business/Corporate Donations; Box Office; Government Grants; Individual Donations
    Season: October - April   **Annual Attendance:** 15,000
    Affiliations: ASOL
    Performance Facilities: Eppley Auditorium

THEATRE

SIOUX CITY COMMUNITY THEATRE
PO Box 512, Sioux City, IA 51102
(712) 233-2719
    Founded: 1948
    Arts Area: Community; Theatrical Group
    Status: Non-Professional
    Type: Performing
    Purpose: Outlet for those interested in producing theatrical productions and educational tool in teaching theatre crafts
    Management: Tom Peterson, General Manager; C. Ann Falkenberg, Operations Manager
    Officers: Gregg Galloway, President; A. Frank Baron, Vice President; Keith Roeper, Treasurer; Kristi Quinn, Secretary
    Paid Staff: 1
    Budget: $50,000 - $100,000
    Income Sources: Private Foundations/Grants/Endowments; Business/Corporate Donations; Box Office; Individual Donations
    Season: October - June   **Annual Attendance:** 1,500
    Affiliations: ACT: Iowa Community Theatre Association
    Performance Facilities: Shore Acres

Spirit Lake

FACILITY

OKOBOJI SUMMER THEATRE
PO Box 341, Spirit Lake, IA 51360
(712) 332-7277
    Type of Facility: Theatre House
    Facility Originally: Airplane Hangar
    Type of Stage: Proscenium
    Stage Dimensions: 120'Wx120'D
    Seating Capacity: 450
    Year Built: 1930

Year Remodeled: 1965 **Architect:** Chin **Cost:** $20,000
Manager: Addison Myers; (314) 876-7193

Waterloo

INSTRUMENTAL MUSIC

WATERLOO-CEDAR FALLS SYMPHONY ORCHESTRA
225 Commercial Street, Waterloo, IA 50702
(319) 235-6331
FAX: (319) 235-6332
   Founded: 1930
   Arts Area: Symphony; Orchestra; Chamber; Ensemble
   Status: Non-Profit
   Type: Performing
   Purpose: To meet the musical needs of the Northeast Iowa community
   Management: Kevin S. Taylor, General Manager; Joseph Giunta, Conductor Laureate
   Officers: Joani Hollen, President; Wes Heitzman, Vice President; Louis Fettkether, Treasurer; Joan Diamond, Secretary
   Paid Staff: 3 **Volunteer Staff:** 500
   Paid Artists: 80
   Utilizes: Guest Conductors; Guest Artists
   Budget: $100,000 - $500,000
   Income Sources: Private Foundations/Grants/Endowments; Business/Corporate Donations; Box Office; Government Grants; Individual Donations
   Season: September - May
   Affiliations: ASOL; ASCAP; BMI
   Performance Facilities: Kersenbrock Auditorium

THEATRE

WATERLOO COMMUNITY PLAYHOUSE/BLACK HAWK CHILDREN'S THEATRE
225 Cedar Street, Waterloo, IA 50701
(319) 235-0367
   Founded: 1916
   Arts Area: Musical; Community
   Status: Non-Professional; Non-Profit
   Type: Performing; Educational; Sponsoring
   Purpose: To provide high quality theatre productions and education for the cultural and creative growth of the northeast Iowa community
   Management: Charles Stilwill, Managing Director; Roger Crimmins, Development Director; Mark Rockwell, Business Manager; Thomas Ballmer, Children's Theatre Director
   Officers: Thomas Lauglas, President; Betty Steege, President-Elect; David Richter, Treasurer; Linda Schipper, Secretary
   Paid Staff: 15 **Volunteer Staff:** 475
   Paid Artists: 10 **Non-Paid Artists:** 175
   Utilizes: Special Technical Talent; Guest Conductors; Guest Artists; Guest Directors
   Budget: $100,000 - $500,000
   Income Sources: Private Foundations/Grants/Endowments; Business/Corporate Donations; Box Office; Government Grants; Individual Donations
   Season: 52 Weeks **Annual Attendance:** 40,000
   Affiliations: ACT; AATY; Waterloo, Cedar Falls and Waverly Chambers of Commerce; Iowa Community Theatre Association; Cedar Arts Forum
   Performance Facilities: Hope Martin Theatre

FACILITY

HOPE MARTIN THEATRE
225 Commercial, Waterloo, IA 50701
(319) 291-4494
   Type of Facility: Performance Center
   Type of Stage: Proscenium
   Stage Dimensions: 14'x32'x28' **Orchestra Pit**
   Seating Capacity: 368
   Year Built: 1965 **Architect:** Thorson, Brom & Broshar **Cost:** $100,000
   Year Remodeled: 1976 **Architect:** Thorson, Brom & Broshar **Cost:** $2,500
   Contact for Rental: Marlene Ackerman; (319) 291-4491
   Resident Groups: Waterloo Community Playhouse; Black Hawk Children's Theatre; Metro Dance Theatre

Waverly

PERFORMING SERIES

WARTBURG COLLEGE ARTISTS SERIES
222 Ninth Street NW, PO Box 1003, Waverly, IA 50677
(319) 352-8328
Arts Area: Dance; Vocal Music; Instrumental Music; Theater; Lyric Opera; Grand Opera
Status: Non-Profit; College
Type: Sponsoring
Purpose: To present the arts for educational uses and community service
Management: Franklin E. Williams, Director; Tony Lutz, Technical Director
Paid Staff: 1
Utilizes: Guest Artists
Budget: $50,000 - $100,000
Income Sources: Box Office; College Support
Season: September - April
Performance Facilities: Neumann Auditorium

FACILITY

WARTBURG COLLEGE - NEUMANN AUDITORIUM
222 Ninth Street NW, PO Box 1003, Waverly, IA 50677
(319) 352-8286
FAX: (319) 352-8394
Type of Facility: Auditorium
Facility Originally: Church
Type of Stage: Flexible; Proscenium
Stage Dimensions: 42'Wx18'Hx25'D; 35' from edge to back wall   **Orchestra Pit**
Seating Capacity: 1343
Year Built: 1959   **Architect:** Woodburn & O'Neil   **Cost:** $342,996
Year Remodeled: 1985   **Architect:** Thorson, Brom, Broshar, Snyder   **Cost:** $152,788
Acoustical Consultant: Woodburn & O'Neil
Contact for Rental: Karen Funk;   (319) 352-8286
Manager: Tom Lutz;   (319) 352-8216
Resident Groups: Wartburg Community Symphony Orchestra; Wartburg Choral Groups and Bands; Wartburg College Artist Series
Programs by educational and cultural organizations on and off campus

West Des Moines

DANCE

BALLET IOWA
2020 Grand Avenue, West Des Moines, IA 50265
(515) 222-0698
Founded: 1966
Arts Area: Ballet
Status: Professional; Non-Profit
Type: Performing; Touring; Resident; Educational; Sponsoring
Management: Konstantin Uralsky, Artistic Director
Paid Staff: 10
Paid Artists: 20
Utilizes: Special Technical Talent; Guest Artists
Budget: $500,000 - $1,000,000
Income Sources: Private Foundations/Grants/Endowments; Business/Corporate Donations; Box Office; Government Grants; Individual Donations
Season: August - April   **Annual Attendance:** 15,000
Performance Facilities: Civic Center of Greater Des Moines; Stephens Auditorium

BALLET IOWA ASSOCIATION
2020 Grand Avenue, West Des Moines, IA 50265
(515) 222-0698
Founded: 1966
Arts Area: Ballet
Status: Professional; Non-Profit
Type: Performing; Touring; Resident; Educational

Purpose: To support and promote through education and performance a high quality school of dance and professional company

Management: Konstantin Uralsky, Artistic Director; Lynn Lavin, Education Director; Steven Crick, Production Director

Officers: Cynthia Lidgett, President; Chuck Johnson, President-Elect

Paid Staff: 10

Paid Artists: 18

Utilizes: Special Technical Talent; Guest Conductors; Guest Artists; Guest Choreographers

Budget: $500,000 - $1,000,000

Income Sources: Private Foundations/Grants/Endowments; Business/Corporate Donations; Box Office; Government Grants; Individual Donations

Season: October - June   **Annual Attendance:** 20,000

Performance Facilities: Civic Center of Greater Des Moines

KANSAS

Chanute

THEATRE

CHANUTE COMMUNITY THEATRE
PO Box 371, Chanute, KS 66720
(316) 431-3213
Founded: 1978
Arts Area: Musical; Dinner; Community; Theatrical Group
Status: Non-Professional; Non-Profit
Type: Performing; Resident; Educational
Purpose: To provide wide-based theatrical entertainment to the community
Officers: Rick Bushnell, President; Bruce LaRue, Vice President; Cindy Crowl, Treasurer; Cindy Fairchild, Secretary
Volunteer Staff: 12
Budget: $1,000 - $50,000
Income Sources: Private Foundations/Grants/Endowments; Business/Corporate Donations; Box Office; Government Grants; Individual Donations
Season: August - May   **Annual Attendance:** 2,000
Affiliations: Association of Kansas Theatres
Performance Facilities: Memorial Auditorium; Chanute Country Club

FACILITY

MEMORIAL AUDITORIUM
First and Lincoln, Chanute, KS 66720
(316) 431-3213; (316) 431-5200
Type of Facility: Auditorium
Type of Stage: Proscenium
Stage Dimensions: 60'Wx40'D   **Orchestra Pit**
Seating Capacity: 1,800
Year Remodeled: 1978
Contact for Rental: City of Chanute;   (316) 431-9300
Resident Groups: Chanute Community Theatre

Coffeyville

THEATRE

COFFEYVILLE COMMUNITY THEATRE
PO Box 317, Coffeyville, KS 67337
(316) 251-1164
Founded: 1945
Arts Area: Musical; Dinner; Community; Theatrical Group
Status: Non-Professional; Non-Profit
Type: Performing
Purpose: To provide live theatre entertainment to the community
Officers: Sally Kimball, President; Andy Medford, Vice President; Lois Hendrix, Treasurer; Nancy Reinecker, Secretary
Paid Staff: 3   **Volunteer Staff:** 40
Non-Paid Artists: 35
Utilizes: Guest Artists
Budget: $1,000 - $50,000
Income Sources: Private Foundations/Grants/Endowments; Business/Corporate Donations; Box Office; Individual Donations
Season: 52 Weeks   **Annual Attendance:** 1,000
Affiliations: Association of Kansas Theatres; Kansas Arts Council
Performance Facilities: Floral Hall

FACILITY

FLORAL HALL
PO Box 1629, Coffeyville, KS 67337
(316) 252-6108
Type of Facility: Theatre House
Type of Stage: Proscenium; Platform

Stage Dimensions: 50'Wx30'D
Seating Capacity: 150
Contact for Rental: City of Coffeyville;   (316) 252-6108
Manager: Mike Maier, Parks Director
Resident Groups: Coffeyville Community Theatre

Concordia

THEATRE

BROWN GRAND THEATRE
310 West Sixth, PO Box 341, Concordia, KS 66901-0341
(913) 243-2553
Founded: 1907
Arts Area: Professional; Musical; Community; Folk; Theatrical Group; Puppet
Status: Non-Profit
Type: Performing; Educational; Sponsoring
Purpose: To maintain the historic Brown Grand Theatre; to enrich the cultural lives of area residents by providing quality live theatre and other entertainment
Management: Susan Haver, Theatre Manager
Officers: Susan Sutton, President; Robert Boardman, Vice President; Everett Miller, Secretary; Wonda Brunkow, Treasurer
Paid Staff: 4   Volunteer Staff: 8
Utilizes: Special Technical Talent; Guest Conductors; Guest Artists; Guest Directors
Budget: $50,000 - $100,000
Income Sources: Private Foundations/Grants/Endowments; Business/Corporate Donations; Box Office; Government Grants; Individual Donations
Season: September - May   Annual Attendance: 11,900
Affiliations: MAAA

Dodge City

FACILITY

DODGE CITY CIVIC CENTER
705 First Avenue, Dodge City, KS 67801
(316) 225-8150
Type of Facility: Theatre Complex; Auditorium; Off Broadway; Multi-Purpose; Exhibit Space
Type of Stage: Proscenium
Stage Dimensions: 60'x43'; 30' ceiling
Seating Capacity: 3,178
Year Built: 1954
Contact for Rental: Jim Bowlin, Director;   (316) 225-8150
Resident Groups: Junior College Basketball

Garden City

THEATRE

THE ARTS PROGRAM, GARDEN CITY RECREATION COMMISSION
PO Box 637, 1101 Kansas Plaza, Garden City, KS 67846
(316) 276-1200
Founded: 1976
Arts Area: Community
Status: Non-Profit; Community
Type: Resident
Purpose: To provide community arts and theatre for the Garden City community and southwest Kansas
Management: Mark Hays, Arts Program Director
Paid Staff: 1
Utilizes: Community Volunteers
Budget: $1,000 - $50,000
Income Sources: Box Office; User Fees; Class Fees
Season: June - August
Affiliations: Association of Community Arts Agencies of Kansas
Performance Facilities: Garden City Community College Fine Arts Theatre

---
Hays

INSTRUMENTAL MUSIC

HAYS SYMPHONY ORCHESTRA
Fort Hays State University, Hays, KS 67601
(913) 628-5360
FAX: (913) 628-4096
> **Founded:** 1920
> **Arts Area:** Symphony; Orchestra
> **Status:** Non-Profit
> **Type:** Performing; Educational
> **Purpose:** To provide western Kansas with musical and culture activities; to provide music students with educational and artistic opportunities
> **Management:** Christine Webber, Conductor/Music Director
> **Officers:** Lyle Dilley, President; Esther Halling, Past President; Ann Pflughoft, Vice President; William Miller, Treasurer; Connie Wilson, Secretary
> **Paid Staff:** 1 **Volunteer Staff:** 20
> **Paid Artists:** 2 **Non-Paid Artists:** 2
> **Utilizes:** Special Technical Talent; Guest Artists
> **Budget:** $1,000 - $50,000
> **Income Sources:** Business/Corporate Donations; Box Office; Government Grants; Individual Donations
> **Season:** September - May **Annual Attendance:** 2,500
> **Affiliations:** ASCAP; ASOL
> **Performance Facilities:** Beach/Schmidt Performing Arts Center

FACILITY

FORT HAYS STATE UNIVERSITY-FELTON - START THEATRE
600 Park Street, Hays, KS 67601-4099
(913) 628-5365
> **Type of Facility:** Theatre Complex
> **Type of Stage:** Proscenium; Modified Apron Proscenium
> **Stage Dimensions:** 40'Wx40'D, 15'D apron; 40'Wx17'H proscenium opening **Orchestra Pit**
> **Seating Capacity:** 316
> **Year Built:** 1965 **Architect:** Woods & Starr
> **Year Remodeled:** 1983
> **Contact for Rental:** Tomme Williams; (913) 628-5365
> **Resident Groups:** Fort Hays State Players; Hays Symphony Orchestra; Encore Series; Fort Hayes Singers; Fort Hayes Concert Choir

---
Hesston

PERFORMING SERIES

HESSTON PERFORMING ARTS SERIES
PO Box 3000, Hesston, KS 67062
(316) 327-8206
> **Founded:** 1982
> **Arts Area:** Vocal Music; Instrumental Music
> **Status:** Non-Profit
> **Type:** Sponsoring
> **Management:** Kathy Goering, Secretary to Hesston Performing Arts Community
> **Volunteer Staff:** 25
> **Paid Artists:** 5
> **Utilizes:** Guest Artists
> **Budget:** $1,000 - $50,000
> **Income Sources:** Business/Corporate Donations; Box Office; Government Grants; Individual Donations
> **Annual Attendance:** 4,500
> **Performance Facilities:** Yost Center, Hesston College

Hutchinson

INSTRUMENTAL MUSIC

HUTCHINSON SYMPHONY
PO Box 1241, Hutchinson, KS 67504
(316) 663-8000
Founded: 1948
Arts Area: Symphony; Chamber
Status: Semi-Professional; Non-Profit
Type: Performing
Purpose: To present concerts locally
Management: Terry L. David, General Manager; Dr. Leon Buske III, Conductor/Musical Director
Officers: Amy Carcy, President; Peg Stephens, Vice President; Linda Dillon, Secretary
Paid Staff: 2
Paid Artists: 60
Utilizes: Guest Conductors; Guest Artists
Budget: $50,000 - $100,000
Income Sources: Private Foundations/Grants/Endowments; Business/Corporate Donations; Box Office; Government Grants; Individual Donations
Season: October - April   **Annual Attendance:** 3,500
Performance Facilities: Hutchinson Fine Arts Center

FACILITY

KANSAS STATE FAIR - GRANDSTAND
2000 North Poplar, Hutchinson, KS 67502
(316) 669-3600
Type of Facility: Outdoor (Concert)
Type of Stage: Platform
Stage Dimensions: 40'Dx60'Wx6'H
Seating Capacity: 10,550
Year Built: 1928
Contact for Rental: Kansas State Fair;   (316) 669-3600
Remodeling completed; dirt race track adjacent

Iola

FACILITY

BOWLUS FINE ARTS CENTER
205 East Madison, Iola, KS 66749
(316) 365-6101
Type of Facility: Auditorium; Performance Center; Multi-Purpose
Type of Stage: Proscenium
Stage Dimensions: 42'Wx37'D
Seating Capacity: 752
Year Built: 1964   **Architect:** Brink & Dunwoody   **Cost:** $1,250,000
Contact for Rental: Manager/Director;   (316) 365-6101
Resident Groups: Iola Community Theatre; Iola Area Symphony; Iola City Band; Southeast Shavers
Non-profit, educational entertainment

Kingman

THEATRE

PRAIRIE PLAYERS, INC.
233 North Main, PO Box 291, Kingman, KS 67068-0291
(316) 532-3321
Founded: 1974
Arts Area: Dinner; Community; Theatrical Group; Puppet
Status: Non-Professional; Non-Profit; Community Theatre
Type: Performing; Resident
Purpose: To maintain live theatre arts within a rural setting
Management: Dennis Lee Hoppes, Trustee
Officers: Rob Monk, President; Sandre Pearson, Vice President; Dennis Lee Hoppes, Secretary/Treasurer; Elizabeth Sheldon; Julie Page

Volunteer Staff: 50
Utilizes: Special Technical Talent; Guest Artists; Guest Directors
Budget: $1,000 - $50,000
Income Sources: Private Foundations/Grants/Endowments; Business/Corporate Donations; Box Office; Government Grants; Individual Donations
Season: April-May; September - October
Affiliations: Association of Kansas Theatres

Lawrence

INSTRUMENTAL MUSIC

KANSAS UNIVERSITY SYMPHONY ORCHESTRA
Murphy Hall, University of Kansas, Lawrence, KS 66045
(913) 864-3436
> **Founded:** 1935
> **Arts Area:** Symphony; Orchestra
> **Status:** Non-Profit
> **Type:** Performing; Educational; Sponsoring
> **Purpose:** To present orchestral performances for the community; to provide orchestral training for advanced students
> **Management:** Brian Priestman, Conductor
> **Paid Staff:** 3
> **Paid Artists:** 1   **Non-Paid Artists:** 4
> **Utilizes:** Guest Conductors; Guest Artists
> **Budget:** $1,000 - $50,000
> **Season:** September - May   **Annual Attendance:** 4,000
> **Affiliations:** University of Kansas
> **Performance Facilities:** Crafton-Preyer Theatre, University of Kansas

FACILITY

UNIVERSITY OF KANSAS - CRAFTON-PREYER THEATRE
Lawrence, KS 66045
(913) 864-3469
> **Type of Facility:** Concert Hall; Theatre House
> **Type of Stage:** Proscenium; Turntable
> **Stage Dimensions:** 40'Wx70'D; 40'Wx20'H proscenium opening; 40'Wx10'D hydraulic lift pit   **Orchestra Pit**
> **Seating Capacity:** 1,188
> **Year Built:** 1957
> **Contact for Rental:** Jack Wright;   (913) 864-3381
> **Resident Groups:** Kansas University Theatre; Kansas University Theatre for Young People

---

Leavenworth

FACILITY

SAINT MARY COLLEGE - XAVIER HALL THEATRE
Leavenworth, KS 66048
(913) 682-5151
> **Type of Facility:** Studio Performance; Theatre House; Multi-Purpose
> **Type of Stage:** Proscenium
> **Stage Dimensions:** 28'x30'
> **Seating Capacity:** 440
> **Year Built:** 1923
> **Year Remodeled:** 1985
> **Contact for Rental:** Van Ibsen;   (913) 682-5151

Lindsborg

PERFORMING SERIES

MESSIAH FESTIVAL OF MUSIC
Bethany College, 421 North First Street, Lindsborg, KS 67456-1897
(913) 227-3311
> **Founded:** 1882

Arts Area: Vocal Music; Instrumental Music
Status: Non-Profit
Type: Performing; Sponsoring
Management: Gregory Aune, Conductor; A. John Pearson, Public Relations and Information
Utilizes: Guest Artists
Income Sources: Box Office
Season: Palm Sunday - Easter
Annual Attendance: 8,000
Affiliations: Bethany College
Performance Facilities: Presser Hall Auditorium

FACILITY

BETHANY COLLEGE - BURNETT CENTER FOR PERFORMING ARTS
Lindsborg, KS 67456
(913) 227-3311, ext. X257
Type of Facility: Auditorium; Performance Center
Type of Stage: Thrust
Stage Dimensions: 36'x40'
Seating Capacity: 243
Year Built: 1973   Architect: The Shaver Partnership   Cost: $300,519
Contact for Rental: Tricia Hawk, Special Programs;   (913) 227-3311, ext. 132
Manager: Norman E. Schroder;   (913) 227-3311, ext. 257
Resident Groups: Bethany College Theatre Program

Manhattan

PERFORMING SERIES

MANHATTAN ARTS COUNCIL
PO Box 74, Manhattan, KS 66502
(913) 539-3276
Founded: 1972
Arts Area: Vocal Music; Instrumental Music; Theater; Festivals
Status: Non-Profit
Type: Educational; Sponsoring
Purpose: To foster and support the knowledge, appreciation, and practice of the arts in the community via education, programming, and funding for arts programs
Management: John Biggs, Executive Director; Dale Clore, Administrative Assistant
Paid Staff: 2   Volunteer Staff: 50
Utilizes: Guest Artists
Budget: $50,000 - $100,000
Income Sources: Private Foundations/Grants/Endowments; Business/Corporate Donations; Government Grants; Individual Donations
Season: 52 Weeks
Affiliations: Association of Community Arts Agencies of Kansas

FACILITY

KANSAS STATE UNIVERSITY - MCCAIN AUDITORIUM
Manhattan, KS 66506
(913) 532-6425
FAX: (913) 532-7114
Type of Facility: Performance Center
Type of Stage: Flexible
Stage Dimensions: 60'Wx36'D   Orchestra Pit
Seating Capacity: 1,800
Year Built: 1970   Architect: Canole & Hale; Wolfenbarger & McCulley
Cost: $3,035,933
Acoustical Consultant: Bolt, Beranek & Newman
Contact for Rental: Richard P. Martin;   (913) 532-6425

McPherson

FACILITY

MCPHERSON COLLEGE - BROWN AUDITORIUM
1600 East Euclid, McPherson, KS 67460
(316) 241-0731
FAX: (316) 241-0731
  Type of Facility: Concert Hall; Auditorium; Studio Performance; Theatre House
  Type of Stage: Proscenium
  Stage Dimensions: 40'Wx14'Dx19'H   **Orchestra Pit**
  Seating Capacity: 1,224
  Year Built: 1960   **Architect:** Mann & Company
  Contact for Rental: Rick Tyler;   (316) 241-0731
  Resident Groups: McPherson College Choir
  Used for band concerts, theatre, community orchestras and convocations

Neodesha

FACILITY

NEODESHA ARTS ASSOCIATION
200 North Fifth Street, PO Box 65, Neodesha, KS 66757
(316) 325-3422
  Founded: 1973
  Type of Facility: Performance Center
  Facility Originally: Church
  Type of Stage: Proscenium
  Seating Capacity: 150
  Year Built: 1914
  Year Remodeled: 1973
  Manager: Zanada Overpeck, Director;   (316) 325-4322

Ottawa

FACILITY

OTTAWA MUNICIPAL AUDITORIUM
PO Box 452, Ottawa, KS 66067
(913) 242-8810
  Type of Facility: Concert Hall; Auditorium; Performance Center; Theatre House; Multi-Purpose
  Facility Originally: Opera House
  Type of Stage: Proscenium
  Stage Dimensions: 65'x40'   **Orchestra Pit**
  Seating Capacity: 839
  Year Built: 1919
  Year Remodeled: 1978   **Architect:** Earl DeVore   **Cost:** $750,000
  Contact for Rental: Dick Smith;   (913) 242-8810

Overland Park

DANCE

AMERICAN YOUTH BALLET
11728 Quivira Road, Shawnee Mission Area, Overland Park, KS 66210
(913) 451-9292
  Founded: 1979
  Arts Area: Modern; Mime; Ballet; Ethnic
  Status: Non-Professional; Non-Profit
  Type: Performing; Touring; Educational
  Purpose: To establish an outlet for aspiring young dancers to learn, practice, and perform all forms of dance in a professional atmosphere
  Management: Kathy and Dennis Landsman, Artistic Directors
  Officers: Kathy Landsman, President; Dennis Landsman, Vice President; Linda Smith, Secretary; Elizabeth Eike, Treasurer
  Paid Staff: 2   **Volunteer Staff:** 20

Non-Paid Artists: 27
Utilizes: Guest Artists; Guest Choreographers
Budget: $1,000 - $50,000
Income Sources: Private Foundations/Grants/Endowments; Business/Corporate Donations; Box Office; Individual Donations
Season: September - May   **Annual Attendance:** 6,000
Performance Facilities: Johnson County Community College Cultural Education Center

THEATRE

THE NEW THEATER COMPANY
9229 Foster, Overland Park, KS 66202
(913) 649-0103
Founded: 1992
Arts Area: Professional; Dinner
Status: Professional
Type: Performing
Management: Dennis D. Hennessy, Richard Carrothers, Executive Producers; Jay Kingwill, Associate Producer
Officers: Donn Miller, Vice President of Operations; Mary Hay, Vice President of Marketing; Cindy Beatty, Company Comptroller
Paid Staff: 10
Utilizes: Guest Artists
Budget: $1,000,000 - $5,000,000
Income Sources: Box Office
Season: 52 Weeks   **Annual Attendance:** 120,000
Performance Facilities: The New Theater Company

Pittsburg

FACILITY

MEMORIAL AUDITORIUM AND CONVENTION CENTER
503 North Pine, Pittsburg, KS 66762
(316) 231-7827
Type of Facility: Concert Hall; Auditorium; Theatre House; Civic Center; Multi-Purpose; Exhibition Hall
Type of Stage: Proscenium
Stage Dimensions: 90'Wx37'D   **Orchestra Pit**
Seating Capacity: 1,588
Year Built: 1925   **Architect:** Thomas W. Williamson   **Cost:** $262,450
Year Remodeled: 1983   **Architect:** Seidler, Owsley & Associates   **Cost:** $3,400,000
Acoustical Consultant: Coffeen, Anderson, Fricke & Associates
Contact for Rental: Pat Ashmore, Mariann David;   (316) 231-7827
Manager: Pat Ashmore, Supervisor
Resident Groups: Pittsburg Arts Council; Pittsburg Community Theater
Professional performances; art exhibits; meetings; and conventions

Prairie Village

INSTRUMENTAL MUSIC

YOUTH SYMPHONY OF KANSAS CITY
5209 West 83rd Street, Prairie Village, KS 66208
(913) 642-7141
FAX: (913) 642-6183
Founded: 1958
Arts Area: Symphony; Orchestra
Status: Non-Professional; Non-Profit
Type: Performing; Touring; Educational; Sponsoring
Purpose: To give talented young musicians of the Kansas City area an opportunity to perform standard symphonic literature; to encourage students to broaden the horizons of their own musicianship and to help them and their audiences to become truly appreciative listeners
Management: Carolyn Holtman, Business Manager; Dr. Glenn A. Block, Music Director/Conductor
Officers: John Schramm, President; Jan Ericson, Vice President; Marian Reeves, Secretary; Elaine Minden, Treasurer
Paid Staff: 4   **Volunteer Staff:** 40
Non-Paid Artists: 183
Utilizes: Guest Conductors; Guest Artists; Guest Directors
Budget: $50,000 - $100,000

Income Sources: Private Foundations/Grants/Endowments; Business/Corporate Donations; Box Office; Government Grants; Individual Donations
Season: November - May **Annual Attendance:** 4,000
Affiliations: ASOL (Youth Orchestra Division); Missouri Citizens for the Arts
Performance Facilities: White Recital Hall, University of Missouri-Kansas City; Conservatory of Music

---

Salina

THEATRE

SALINA COMMUNITY THEATRE
303 East Iron, PO Box 2305, Salina, KS 67402
(913) 827-6126
   Founded: 1960
   Arts Area: Musical; Community; Theatrical Group
   Status: Non-Professional; Non-Profit
   Type: Performing; Sponsoring
   Purpose: To provide entertainment for the community and recreation for volunteers who like to participate
   Management: Charles Kephart, Managing Director
   Officers: Jamie Hall, President; Jerry Hinrikus, Vice President; Pat Sampson, Treasurer
   Paid Staff: 3 **Volunteer Staff:** 200
   Non-Paid Artists: 50
   Utilizes: Guest Artists; Guest Directors
   Budget: $100,000 - $500,000
   Income Sources: Private Foundations/Grants/Endowments; Business/Corporate Donations; Box Office; Government Grants; Individual Donations
   Season: October - July **Annual Attendance:** 12,000

FACILITY

SALINA BICENTENNIAL CENTER
PO Box 1727, Salina, KS 67402-1727
(913) 826-7200
FAX: (913) 826-7207
   Type of Facility: Auditorium; Civic Center; Arena; Multi-Purpose
   Type of Stage: Flexible; 3/4 Arena; Arena
   Stage Dimensions: Flexible varies to 60'x40'
   Seating Capacity: 8,000
   Year Built: 1979 **Architect:** Bucher Willis & Ratliff **Cost:** $6,500,000
   Acoustical Consultant: McClellan Sound
   Contact for Rental: Karen Fallis; (913) 826-7200
   Manager: Phil Shamoff; (913) 826-7200

Shawnee Mission

THEATRE

THE BARN PLAYERS THEATRE
PO Box 12767, Shawnee Mission, KS 66282-2767
(913) 381-4004
   Founded: 1956
   Arts Area: Community; Theatrical Group
   Status: Non-Profit
   Type: Performing
   Purpose: To promote artistic excellence through theatre; to produce community theatre productions; to encourage participation by interested persons; to promote theatre interest in the community
   Management: Margaret Godfrey, Managing Director; Max Beatty, Artistic Director
   Officers: Margaret Godfrey, President; Shirley Wagner, Vice President; Martha Coulter, Secretary
   Volunteer Staff: 50
   Utilizes: Special Technical Talent
   Budget: $1,000 - $50,000
   Income Sources: Business/Corporate Donations; Box Office; Individual Donations
   Season: August - September **Annual Attendance:** 1,000

Affiliations: Association of Kansas Theatres; AACT
Performance Facilities: Overland Theatre

THE SENIOR BARN PLAYERS
PO Box 12767, Shawnee Mission, KS 66212-2767
(913) 381-4004; (913) 681-8446
Founded: 1977
Arts Area: Community; Theatrical Group; One-Act Comedies
Status: Non-Professional; Non-Profit
Type: Performing; Touring
Purpose: To perform one-act comedies from a repertoire of six plays as well as a variety show; to provide theatre opportunities for persons 55 or older
Officers: Martha Coulter, Chairman; Russ Shepherd, Vice Chairman; Eleanor Tarson, Treasurer; Monte Woodruff, Secretary; Francis Moore, Manager of Office Volunteers
Volunteer Staff: 20
Non-Paid Artists: 45
Utilizes: Volunteer Directors/Actors
Budget: $1,000 - $50,000
Income Sources: Private Foundations/Grants/Endowments; Booking Donations
Season: September - June   **Annual Attendance:** 15,000

Topeka

INSTRUMENTAL MUSIC

TOPEKA JAZZ WORKSHOP
1725 South West Gage, Topeka, KS 66604
(913) 273-0186
Founded: 1968
Arts Area: Orchestra; Instrumental Group; Band
Status: Non-Profit
Type: Performing; Educational
Purpose: To promote interest in jazz through sponsorship of concerts, clinics and scholarships
Officers: James A. Monroe, President; Gerald L. Goodell, Secretary; Jim Parker, Treasurer
Volunteer Staff: 18
Paid Artists: 32   **Non-Paid Artists:** 57
Utilizes: Guest Artists; Guest Directors
Budget: $1,000 - $50,000
Income Sources: Box Office
Season: August - April   **Annual Attendance:** 2,000
Performance Facilities: Topeka Civic Theatre

THEATRE

TOPEKA CIVIC THEATRE
534 1/2 North Kansas Avenue, Topeka, KS 66608
(913) 357-5213
FAX: (913) 357-0719
Founded: 1936
Arts Area: Musical; Dinner; Community
Status: Non-Professional; Non-Profit
Type: Performing
Purpose: To stimulate, entertain, educate and serve our community; to provide opportunities for performance and development of theatrical skills
Management: Michael Wainstein, Producing Artistic Director; Brett Landow, Business Manager; Donna Jenks, Box Office Manager
Paid Staff: 5   **Volunteer Staff:** 200
Non-Paid Artists: 100
Utilizes: Guest Conductors; Guest Directors
Budget: $500,000 - $1,000,000
Income Sources: Business/Corporate Donations; Box Office; Individual Donations
Season: 52 Weeks   **Annual Attendance:** 25,000
Affiliations: AACT; Association of Kansas Theatres; Kansas Community Theatre Conference
Performance Facilities: Topeka Civic Theatre

FACILITY

TOPEKA PERFORMING ARTS CENTER
214 East Eighth, Topeka, KS 66603
(913) 234-2787
FAX: (913) 295-3752
Founded: 1987
Type of Facility: Theatre Complex; Concert Hall; Performance Center; Civic Center; Multi-Purpose
Facility Originally: Arena
Type of Stage: Thrust; Proscenium
Stage Dimensions: 50'x35'; 50'x61' with Thrust   **Orchestra Pit**
Seating Capacity: 2,600
Year Built: 1939   **Architect:** Grist & Co.   **Cost:** $2,000,000
Year Remodeled: 1987   **Architect:** Bradley   **Cost:** $10,000,000
Acoustical Consultant: Coffeen
Contact for Rental: Morey Sullivan;   (913) 234-2787

Waterville

THEATRE

WATERVILLE SUMMER THEATRE CORPORATION
Waterville, KS 66548
(913) 785-2323
Founded: 1973
Arts Area: Community; Theatrical Group
Status: Non-Professional; Non-Profit
Type: Performing
Purpose: To bring live theater to a small Kansas community
Officers: Yvonne Larson, President; Eunice Larson, Secretary/Treasurer
Budget: $1,000 - $50,000
Income Sources: Private Foundations/Grants/Endowments; Box Office
Season: May - September   **Annual Attendance:** 2,500
Affiliations: Association of Kansas Theatres
Performance Facilities: Waterville Opera House

FACILITY

WATERVILLE OPERA HOUSE
204 East Front Street, Waterville, KS 66548
(913) 785-2766
Type of Facility: Opera House
Type of Stage: Platform
Stage Dimensions: 22'x36'   **Orchestra Pit**
Seating Capacity: 340
Year Built: 1903   **Cost:** $7,000
Contact for Rental: City of Waterville;   (913) 785-2367
Manager: Beverly Roepke;   (913) 785-2766
Resident Groups: Waterville Summer Theatre Corporation
Owned by the city of Waterville

Wichita

INSTRUMENTAL MUSIC

WICHITA SYMPHONY
Century II Concert Hall, 225 West Douglas, Wichita, KS 67202
(316) 267-5259
FAX: (316) 267-1937
Founded: 1944
Arts Area: Symphony; Orchestra; Chamber
Status: Professional; Non-Profit
Type: Performing; Touring; Educational; Sponsoring
Management: Mitchell Berman, General Manager; Meistro Zouhuang Chen, Music Director/Conductor
Paid Staff: 10   **Volunteer Staff:** 400

Paid Artists: 86
Utilizes: Guest Artists
Income Sources: Private Foundations/Grants/Endowments; Business/Corporate Donations; Box Office; Government Grants; Individual Donations
Season: October - April   **Annual Attendance:** 250,000
Affiliations: ASOL; Wichita Arts Council; Kansas Arts Council
Performance Facilities: Century II Concert Hall

WICHITA YOUTH ORCHESTRA
Century II Concert Hall, 225 West Douglas, Wichita, KS 67202
(316) 267-5259
Founded: 1947
Arts Area: Symphony; Orchestra; Ensemble
Status: Non-Professional; Non-Profit
Type: Performing; Educational
Management: Ann Trechak, Manager; Steve Luttrell, Conductor of Youth Symphony; Gary Burrow, Conductor of Repertory Orchestra
Paid Staff: 6
Non-Paid Artists: 200
Season: November - March   **Annual Attendance:** 3,000
Affiliations: Wichita Symphony; ASOL (Youth Orchestra Division)
Performance Facilities: Century II Concert Hall

THEATRE

WICHITA COMMUNITY THEATRE
258 North Fountain, Wichita, KS 67208
(316) 686-1282
Founded: 1946
Arts Area: Theatrical Group
Status: Non-Professional; Non-Profit
Type: Performing
Purpose: To provide a wide variety of theatrical entertainment to the community; to provide opportunities for theatre performers and technicians at the amateur level
Management: Scott Marshall, Business Manager
Officers: Dr. R.L. Sifford, President; Betty Johnston, Vice President; Ed Francis, Treasurer
Paid Staff: 2   **Volunteer Staff:** 1
Paid Artists: 1
Utilizes: Guest Artists
Budget: $50,000 - $100,000
Income Sources: Private Foundations/Grants/Endowments; Business/Corporate Donations; Box Office; Individual Donations
Season: 52 Weeks   **Annual Attendance:** 12,000
Affiliations: Association of Kansas Theatres
Performance Facilities: Century II Civic Center; Workshop

PERFORMING SERIES

MUSIC THEATRE OF WICHITA
225 West Douglas, Suite 202, Wichita, KS 67202
(316) 265-3253
FAX: (316) 265-8708
Founded: 1971
Arts Area: Theater
Status: Professional; Non-Profit
Type: Performing; Educational
Management: Wayne Bryan, Producing Director
Paid Staff: 3   **Volunteer Staff:** 150
Paid Artists: 160   **Non-Paid Artists:** 50
Budget: $500,000 - $1,000,000
Income Sources: Private Foundations/Grants/Endowments; Business/Corporate Donations; Box Office; Government Grants; Individual Donations
Season: June - August   **Annual Attendance:** 54,000
Affiliations: Association of Kansas Theatres; Kansas Arts Council
Performance Facilities: Century II Concert Hall

FACILITY

CENTURY II CIVIC CENTER
225 West Douglas Avenue, Wichita, KS 67202
(316) 264-9121
>**Founded:** 1969
>**Type of Facility:** Theatre Complex; Concert Hall; Theatre House; Civic Center; Multi-Purpose
>**Type of Stage:** Proscenium
>**Seating Capacity:** See separate listings
>**Year Built:** 1969   **Architect:** Varenhorst   **Cost:** $15,000,000
>**Acoustical Consultant:** Coffeen & Associates
>**Contact for Rental:** Judy Eggleston;   (316) 264-9121
>**Resident Groups:** Wichita Symphony; Music Theatre of Wichita; Wichita Community Theatre; Wichita Children's Theatre; Music Theatre for Young People; Metro Ballet
>*The Century II Civic Center contains the Concert Hall, Convention Hall, Exhibition Hall and Theatre. See separate listings for further information.*

CENTURY II CIVIC CENTER - CONCERT HALL
225 West Douglas Avenue, Wichita, KS 67202
(316) 264-9121
>**Type of Facility:** Concert Hall; Civic Center
>**Type of Stage:** Proscenium
>**Stage Dimensions:** 60'Wx29'Hx49'D   **Orchestra Pit**
>**Seating Capacity:** 2,187
>**Year Built:** 1969
>**Acoustical Consultant:** Coffeen & Associates
>**Contact for Rental:** Judy Eggleston;   (316) 264-9121
>**Manager:** James Hess;   (316) 264-9121
>**Resident Groups:** Wichita Symphony; Music Theatre of Wichita; Metropolitan Ballet

CENTURY II CIVIC CENTER - CONVENTION HALL
225 West Douglas Avenue, Wichita, KS 67202
(316) 264-9121
>**Type of Facility:** Auditorium; Civic Center
>**Type of Stage:** Proscenium
>**Stage Dimensions:** 60'Wx29'Hx33'D
>**Seating Capacity:** 5,244
>**Year Built:** 1969
>**Acoustical Consultant:** Coffeen & Associates
>**Contact for Rental:** Judy Eggleston;   (316) 264-9121
>**Manager:** James Hess;   (316) 264-9121

CENTURY II CIVIC CENTER - EXHIBITION HALL
225 West Douglas Avenue, Wichita, KS 67202
(316) 264-9121
>**Type of Facility:** Civic Center; Exhibition Hall
>**Type of Stage:** Platform
>**Stage Dimensions:** 60'Wx30'D
>**Seating Capacity:** Banquet style - 2,400
>**Year Built:** 1986   **Architect:** Schaeffer & Associates
>**Contact for Rental:** Judy Eggleston;   (316) 264-9121
>**Manager:** James Hess;   (316) 264-9121
>**Resident Groups:** Wichita Theatre Organ

CENTURY II CIVIC CENTER - THEATRE
225 West Douglas Avenue, Wichita, KS 67202
(316) 264-9121
>**Type of Facility:** Theatre House
>**Type of Stage:** Proscenium
>**Stage Dimensions:** 72'Wx40'Dx30'H   **Orchestra Pit**
>**Seating Capacity:** 661
>**Year Built:** 1969
>**Acoustical Consultant:** Coffeen & Associates
>**Contact for Rental:** Judy Eggleston;   (316) 264-9121
>**Resident Groups:** Wichita Community Theatre; Wichita Children's Theatre; Music Theatre for Young People

KENTUCKY

Anchorage

THEATRE

ANCHOR THEATRE
PO Box 23545, Anchorage, KY 40223
(502) 245-4327
Founded: 1984
Arts Area: Community; Theatrical Group
Status: Non-Professional; Non-Profit
Type: Performing; Sponsoring
Purpose: To produce non-musical plays in the theatre; to tour with small casts to local nursing homes and country clubs; to sponsor the Producer's Review
Officers: William J. Aiken, President; Anne Rives, Vice President
Volunteer Staff: 11
Non-Paid Artists: 59
Utilizes: Special Technical Talent; Guest Directors
Budget: $1,000 - $50,000
Income Sources: Private Foundations/Grants/Endowments; Business/Corporate Donations; Box Office; Government Grants; Individual Donations
Season: August - December   **Annual Attendance:** 4,000

Ashland

FACILITY

PARAMOUNT ARTS CENTER
1300 Winchester Avenue, Ashland, KY 41101
(606) 324-3175
Founded: 1972
Type of Facility: Performance Center
Facility Originally: Movie House
Type of Stage: Thrust; Proscenium
Stage Dimensions: 45'x22'
Seating Capacity: 1,308
Year Built: 1931   **Cost:** $450,000
Year Remodeled: 1976   **Architect:** Alan Schatz
Acoustical Consultant: David Portugal
Contact for Rental: Panda Powell;   (606) 324-3175
Manager: Kathleen L. Timmons, Executive Director;   (606) 324-2441
Resident Groups: Ashland Youth Ballet; Backstage Players

Bardstown

PERFORMING SERIES

STEPHEN FOSTER DRAMA ASSOCIATION
US 150 East, PO Box 546, Bardstown, KY 40004
(502) 348-5971; (800) 626-1563
Founded: 1959
Arts Area: Dance; Vocal Music; Theater
Status: Professional; Semi-Professional; Non-Profit
Type: Performing
Purpose: To foster cultural activities in the area
Management: Carlene Offutt, General Manager; Scott Ray, Director/Choreographer; David Brown, Musical Director
Officers: John S. Kelley, Chairman; Donald Busick, Vice Chairman
Paid Staff: 76   **Volunteer Staff:** 50
Paid Artists: 53
Utilizes: Special Technical Talent; Guest Artists
Budget: $500,000 - $1,000,000
Income Sources: Box Office
Season: June - September   **Annual Attendance:** 75,000
Performance Facilities: J. Dan Talbott Amphitheatre

Berea

FACILITY

PHELPS - STOKES AUDITORIUM
Berea College Campus, Berea, KY 40404
(606) 986-9341
    Founded: 1904
    Type of Facility: Concert Hall; Auditorium; Multi-Purpose
    Type of Stage: Platform
    Stage Dimensions: 16'6"x36'10"
    Seating Capacity: 1,585
    Year Built: 1904
    Contact for Rental: Office of Special Programs;   (606) 986-9341, ext. 6830

Bowling Green

INSTRUMENTAL MUSIC

BOWLING GREEN-WESTERN SYMPHONY ORCHESTRA
416 East Main Street, Bowling Green, KY 42101
(502) 745-3751
    Founded: 1982
    Arts Area: Symphony; Orchestra; Chamber
    Status: Semi-Professional; Non-Profit
    Type: Performing; Resident; Educational
    Purpose: To provide classical music for the people of southern Kentucky
    Management: Christopher Norton, Music Director/Conductor
    Officers: Jack Haberkorn, President
    Volunteer Staff: 25
    Paid Artists: 22   **Non-Paid Artists:** 35
    Utilizes: Guest Artists
    Budget: $1,000 - $50,000
    Income Sources: Private Foundations/Grants/Endowments; Business/Corporate Donations; Box Office; Government Grants; Individual Donations
    Season: September - April   **Annual Attendance:** 3,500
    Affiliations: ASOL
    Performance Facilities: Van Meter Auditorium

THEATRE

FOUNTAIN SQUARE PLAYERS
416 East Main Street, Bowling Green, KY 42101
(502) 782-2787
    Founded: 1978
    Arts Area: Community; Theatrical Group
    Status: Non-Professional; Non-Profit
    Type: Performing
    Purpose: To provide for the production, appreciation and enjoyment of all phases of the theatre outside of and in addition to that provided by our school systems
    Officers: Jerry Wallace, President; Whit Crawford, Secretary; William B. Russell, Treasurer; Pat Sprouse, Membership
    Volunteer Staff: 50
    Non-Paid Artists: 150
    Budget: $1,000 - $50,000
    Income Sources: Box Office; Individual Donations; Program Advertisements
    Season: October - August   **Annual Attendance:** 7,000
    Affiliations: AAA
    Performance Facilities: Capitol Arts Center

PERFORMING SERIES

BG-WC ARTS COMMISSION
416 East Main, Bowling Green, KY 42101
(502) 782-2787
FAX: (502) 782-2804
    Founded: 1979
    Arts Area: Dance; Vocal Music; Instrumental Music; Theater; Festivals

Status: Non-Profit
Type: Educational; Sponsoring; Rental
Purpose: To provide a regional arts center for the performing and visual arts
Management: Martha A. Hills, Executive Director; Ginger Cleary, Marketing Director; Stephanie Stottman, Program Director; Ace Raymond, Technical Director; Janice Renusch, Office Manager
Officers: Jeane Robertson, President; Michael Bachmann, Vice President; John Grider, Treasurer; Regina Newell, Secretary; Jerry Martin, Parliamentarian
Paid Staff: 6   **Volunteer Staff:** 22
Utilizes: Guest Artists
Budget: $500,000 - $1,000,000
Income Sources: Private Foundations/Grants/Endowments; Business/Corporate Donations; Box Office; Government Grants; Individual Donations
Season: September - May   **Annual Attendance:** 7,800
Performance Facilities: Capitol Arts Center

FACILITY

CAPITOL ARTS CENTER
416 East Main Street, Bowling Green, KY 42101
(502) 782-2787
FAX: (502) 782-2804
Type of Facility: Performance Center
Facility Originally: Vaudeville
Type of Stage: Proscenium
Stage Dimensions: 45'2"Wx37'8"D; 29'3"Wx20'H proscenium opening   **Orchestra Pit**
Seating Capacity: 850
Year Built: 1900
Year Remodeled: 1981   **Architect:** William G. Moore Jr.   **Cost:** $1,300,000
Contact for Rental: Janice Renusch;   (502) 782-2787
Resident Groups: Fountain Square Players

Danville

THEATRE

PIONEER PLAYHOUSE OF KENTUCKY
Danville, KY 40422
(606) 236-2747
Founded: 1950
Arts Area: Professional; Summer Stock; Musical; Dinner
Status: Professional; Non-Profit
Type: Performing; Resident; Educational
Purpose: To maintain an arts center for vocational training using professionals as teachers and performers
Management: Colonel Eben Henson, Founder/Producer
Officers: Colonel Eben Henson, President; Charlotte Henson, Vice President/Secretary
Paid Staff: 10   **Volunteer Staff:** 20
Paid Artists: 25   **Non-Paid Artists:** 30
Budget: $100,000 - $500,000
Income Sources: Box Office; Government Grants
Season: 52 Weeks
Affiliations: SETC; Kentucky Theatre Association
Performance Facilities: Colonel Eben Henson Amphitheatre

FACILITY

NORTON CENTER FOR THE ARTS
Centre College, Danville, KY 40422
(606) 236-4692
FAX: (606) 236-9610
Founded: 1973
Type of Facility: Theatre Complex; Auditorium
Type of Stage: Thrust; Proscenium
Stage Dimensions: 50'x40' proscenium; 30'x30' thrust   **Orchestra Pit**
Seating Capacity: 1,440; 360
Year Built: 1973   **Architect:** William Wesley Peters   **Cost:** $8,000,000
Acoustical Consultant: Vern O. Knudson
Contact for Rental: Alice Davis;   (606) 236-4692
Resident Groups: Centre College Music and Theatre Performing Groups

---

Falmouth

THEATRE

KINCAID REGIONAL THEATRE
211 West Shelby Street, PO Box 208, Falmouth, KY 41040
(800) 647-7409; (606) 654-2636
FAX: (606) 654-6143
Founded: 1983
Arts Area: Professional; Musical; Theatrical Group
Status: Professional; Non-Profit
Type: Performing; Resident; Educational; Sponsoring
Purpose: To offer quality entertainment and employ talented actors and technicians from the region (northern Kentucky, southwestern Ohio and southeastern Indiana)
Management: Charles Kondek, Artistic Director; Terry Lee Stump, Production Manager; Bob Myers, Musical Director; Linda Dietrich, Public Relations
Officers: Patsy Hampton, Chairman; Julia McClanahan, Vice Chairman; Clifford Wallace, Secretary/Treasurer
Paid Staff: 30   **Volunteer Staff:** 100
Paid Artists: 50
Utilizes: Special Technical Talent; Guest Conductors; Guest Artists; Guest Directors
Budget: $100,000 - $500,000
Income Sources: Private Foundations/Grants/Endowments; Business/Corporate Donations; Box Office; Government Grants; Individual Donations
Season: June - September   **Annual Attendance:** 14,000
Affiliations: SETC
Performance Facilities: Falmouth Auditorium

Georgetown

THEATRE

GEORGETOWN CHILDREN'S THEATRE
Georgetown College, PO Box 258, Georgetown, KY 40324
(502) 863-8162
Founded: 1985
Arts Area: Theatrical Group
Status: Non-Profit
Type: Performing
Purpose: To promote interest in drama and opportunities to participate in theatre to local children
Officers: George J. McGee Jr., President; Margaret Greynolds, Vice President; Cathy McGee, Secretary
Volunteer Staff: 10
Paid Artists: 3   **Non-Paid Artists:** 30
Budget: $1,000 - $50,000
Income Sources: Private Foundations/Grants/Endowments; Box Office; Government Grants
Annual Attendance: 4,000
Affiliations: SETC
Performance Facilities: Hill Chapel

Glasgow

THEATRE

THE FAR-OFF BROADWAY PLAYERS
2110 Hall Street, Glasgow, KY 42141
(502) 651-8612
Founded: 1980
Arts Area: Community; Theatrical Group
Status: Non-Professional; Non-Profit
Type: Performing; Resident
Purpose: To study and perform amateur drama
Officers: Eve Harris, President; Louise Bachelor, Vice President; Pat Hazelip, Secretary; Phillip Patton, Treasurer
Non-Paid Artists: 40
Income Sources: Business/Corporate Donations; Box Office; Individual Donations

Greenville

THEATRE

MUHLENBERG COMMUNITY THEATRE
PO Box 505, Greenville, KY 42345
(502) 754-1935
Founded: 1980
Arts Area: Professional; Musical; Dinner; Community; Theatrical Group
Status: Semi-Professional; Non-Profit
Type: Performing; Touring; Resident; Educational
Purpose: To provide and promote the theatrical arts
Management: Karen Willis, Managing Director
Officers: Larry Willis, President; David Eplett, Vice President; Karen Willis, Secretary; Terry Jessup, Treasurer
Volunteer Staff: 10
Non-Paid Artists: 20
Utilizes: Special Technical Talent; Guest Conductors; Guest Directors
Budget: $1,000 - $50,000
Income Sources: Business/Corporate Donations; Box Office; Government Grants; Individual Donations
Season: 52 Weeks   **Annual Attendance:** 1,600
Affiliations: AACT
Performance Facilities: Palace Theatre

Hopkinsville

THEATRE

COMMUNITY PLAYERS
30-B Pennyrile, Hopkinsville, KY 42240
(502) 886-5455
Founded: 1977
Arts Area: Community; Theatrical Group
Status: Non-Professional; Non-Profit
Type: Performing
Purpose: To bring current Broadway shows to the Hopkinsville community
Management: Paulette Stamps, Director; Shirley Shelton, Assistant Director
Officers: Linda Torain Pearson, NingPing Brooks, Sarah Nance, James Jordon, Hugh Northington, Thelma Moore, Lillian Boyd, Board Members
Volunteer Staff: 36
Non-Paid Artists: 36
Utilizes: Guest Directors
Budget: $1,000 - $50,000
Income Sources: Private Foundations/Grants/Endowments; Government Grants
Season: Fall - Spring   **Annual Attendance:** 400
Performance Facilities: Alhambra Theatre

PENNYRILE PLAYERS
2007 South Main, Hopkinsville, KY 42240
(502) 885-2401
Founded: 1972
Arts Area: Musical; Dinner; Community; Theatrical Group; Puppet
Status: Non-Profit
Type: Performing; Touring; Resident; Educational; Sponsoring
Purpose: To provide live theatrical entertainment while helping to develop and promote the talents of an ever-growing group of participants in theatre arts
Management: Marjanna J. Frising, Producer; Juanita Peacock, Artistic Director; Tim Meredith, Building Security; Rhea Kidd, Technical Director
Officers: Kat Peterson, President; Connie Sloan, Vice President; Marjanna J. Frising, Secretary/Treasurer
Volunteer Staff: 5
Utilizes: Special Technical Talent; Guest Artists; Guest Directors
Budget: $1,000 - $50,000
Income Sources: Private Foundations/Grants/Endowments; Business/Corporate Donations; Box Office; Government Grants; Individual Donations
Season: 52 Weeks
Affiliations: Kentucky Arts Council

Horse Cave

THEATRE

HORSE CAVE THEATRE
107-109 Main Street, PO Box 215, Horse Cave, KY 42749
(502) 786-1200; (800) 342-2177
Founded: 1977
Arts Area: Professional; Theatrical Group
Status: Professional; Non-Profit
Type: Performing; Touring; Resident; Educational
Purpose: To be the only resident professional theater outside of metropolitan Louisville that provides a forum for Kentucky writers to produce their works; to present an annual Shakespeare production that assists in meeting the needs of students where schools cannot
Management: Warren Hammack, Director; Pamela White, Associate Director
Officers: Carol Glaser, Board President
Paid Staff: 5
Paid Artists: 25
Utilizes: Special Technical Talent; Guest Artists; Guest Directors
Budget: $100,000 - $500,000
Income Sources: Private Foundations/Grants/Endowments; Business/Corporate Donations; Box Office; Government Grants; Individual Donations
Season: July - August   **Annual Attendance:** 14,000
Affiliations: AEA; TCG; Kentucky Arts Council
Performance Facilities: Horse Cave Theatre

Lexington

DANCE

LEXINGTON BALLET
161 North Mill Street, Lexington, KY 40507
(606) 233-3925; (606) 257-4929
FAX: (606) 255-2787
Founded: 1974
Arts Area: Ballet
Status: Semi-Professional; Non-Profit
Type: Performing; Resident
Purpose: To offer a variety of presentations in contemporary and classical dance; to educate with a strong emphasis on classical ballet
Management: Karl Kaufman, Artistic Director; Rosemary Miles, Associate Artistic Director; Sylvia Grace, Executive Director
Officers: David Smith Jr., President, Board of Directors
Paid Artists: 2   **Non-Paid Artists:** 16
Utilizes: Guest Artists; Guest Choreographers
Budget: $100,000 - $500,000
Income Sources: Private Foundations/Grants/Endowments; Business/Corporate Donations; Box Office; Individual Donations
Season: October - May
Performance Facilities: The Opera House

INSTRUMENTAL MUSIC

LEXINGTON PHILHARMONIC SOCIETY
161 North Mill Street, Lexington, KY 40507
(606) 233-4226
Arts Area: Symphony; Chamber; Ensemble
Status: Non-Profit
Type: Performing
Purpose: To provide entertainment for the local community
Management: George Zack, Music Director; Barry Auman, Executive Director
Income Sources: Private Foundations/Grants/Endowments; Business/Corporate Donations; Box Office; Government Grants; Individual Donations
Performance Facilities: Singletary Center for the Arts

THEATRE

LEXINGTON CHILDREN'S THEATRE
161 North Mill Street, Lexington, KY 40507
(606) 254-4546
>**Founded:** 1938
>**Arts Area:** Professional; Theatrical Group
>**Status:** Professional; Non-Profit
>**Type:** Performing; Touring; Resident; Educational
>**Purpose:** To provide professional-quality theatrical experiences and education to the young people of Kentucky at affordable prices
>**Management:** Larry E. Snipes, Producing Director; Ronald K. Shull, General Manager; Vivian Robin Snipes, Production Manager
>**Officers:** Michelle Gardner, President; Lorie Morgan, President Elect; Kim Knight, Secretary; Tracy Rivette, Treasurer
>**Paid Staff:** 6
>**Paid Artists:** 19
>**Utilizes:** Guest Artists; Guest Directors
>**Budget:** $100,000 - $500,000
>**Income Sources:** Private Foundations/Grants/Endowments; Business/Corporate Donations; Box Office; Government Grants; Individual Donations; Tuition
>**Season:** September - May   **Annual Attendance:** 40,000
>**Affiliations:** AATY; SETC; Kentucky Theatre Association
>**Performance Facilities:** Lexington Opera House; Arts Place

FACILITY

LEXINGTON OPERA HOUSE
c/o Lexington Center, 430 West Vine, Lexington, KY 40507
(606) 233-4567
>**Founded:** 1886
>**Type of Facility:** Theatre House; Opera House
>**Type of Stage:** Proscenium
>**Stage Dimensions:** 45'x37'x30'   **Orchestra Pit**
>**Seating Capacity:** 1,100
>**Year Built:** 1887   **Architect:** Cobb of Chicago
>**Year Remodeled:** 1976   **Architect:** James Ross
>**Contact for Rental:** Manager;   (606) 233-4567
>**Resident Groups:** Lexington Ballet; Lexington Children's Theatre; Lexington Musical Theatre

OTIS A. SINGLETARY CENTER FOR THE ARTS
University of Kentucky, Lexington, KY 40502-0241
(606) 257-1706
FAX: (606) 257-1433
>**Founded:** 1979
>**Type of Facility:** Concert Hall; Performance Center; Recital Hall
>**Type of Stage:** Proscenium
>**Stage Dimensions:** 74'x50'   **Orchestra Pit**
>**Seating Capacity:** Concert Hall - 1,500; Recital Hall - 392
>**Year Built:** 1979   **Architect:** Johnson/Romanowitz Architect   **Cost:** $6,300,000
>**Acoustical Consultant:** Paul S. Veneklasen
>**Contact for Rental:** Holly Salisbury;   (606) 257-1706
>**Resident Groups:** Lexington Philharmonic Orchestra; Central Kentucky Youth Orchestra; University of Kentucky School of Music Ensembles; Chamber Music Society; The Guitar Society; The Lexington Singers

TRANSYLVANIA UNIVERSITY
300 North Broadway, Lexington, KY 40508
(606) 233-8141
>**Type of Facility:** Auditorium; Performance Center
>**Type of Stage:** Thrust; Proscenium
>**Stage Dimensions:** Haggin Auditorium & Carrick Theatre - 87'x32'; Coleman Recital Hall - 35'x18'
>**Seating Capacity:** Haggin Auditorium - 1,050; Carrick Theatre - 300; Coleman Recital Hall - 172
>**Year Built:** 1969   **Architect:** John T. Gillig   **Cost:** $2,800,000
>**Contact for Rental:** Devon Query;   (606) 233-8141
>*Includes Haggin Auditorium, Carrick Theatre and Coleman Recital Hall*

London

PERFORMING SERIES

SUE BENNETT COLLEGE, APPALACHIAN FOLK FESTIVAL
151 College Street, London, KY 40741
(606) 864-2238
FAX: (606) 864-8475
> **Founded:** 1973
> **Arts Area:** Vocal Music; Festivals
> **Status:** Non-Profit
> **Type:** Performing; Educational
> **Purpose:** To preserve Appalachian cultural heritage, music, folklore and arts and crafts
> **Management:** Madge Chestnut, Chairperson
> **Officers:** Linda Mathies, Jan Mayes, Co-Chairs, Arts and Crafts Show
> **Volunteer Staff:** 20
> **Paid Artists:** 12
> **Utilizes:** Guest Artists
> **Budget:** $1,000 - $50,000
> **Income Sources:** Private Foundations/Grants/Endowments; Sue Bennett College
> **Season:** April   **Annual Attendance:** 3,000
> **Performance Facilities:** Sue Bennett College Auditorium

Louisville

DANCE

GENESIS ARTS/KENTUCKY INC.
3726 West Broadway, Louisville, KY 40211
(502) 776-5715
> **Founded:** 1984
> **Arts Area:** Modern; Ballet; Jazz; Ethnic; Tap
> **Status:** Professional; Non-Profit
> **Type:** Performing; Resident; Educational; Sponsoring
> **Purpose:** To promote cultural enterprises presented by minorities; to provide disadvantaged children and youth with an avenue to artistic expression and dance through theatre arts, creative writing, boys choir and art
> **Management:** Dolores White, Executive Director
> **Officers:** Vadra Henderson, President; Patricia E. Tobin, Secretary; Susan Post; Richard Beal
> **Volunteer Staff:** 3
> **Paid Artists:** 4   **Non-Paid Artists:** 3
> **Utilizes:** Special Technical Talent; Guest Artists; Guest Choreographers
> **Budget:** $1,000 - $50,000
> **Income Sources:** Private Foundations/Grants/Endowments; Business/Corporate Donations; Box Office; Government Grants; Individual Donations
> **Season:** 52 Weeks   **Annual Attendance:** 900
> **Performance Facilities:** First Unitarian Church; Kathrine Spalding Auditorium; R.E. Jones United Methodist Church

LOUISVILLE BALLET
1300 Bardstown Road, Louisville, KY 40204
(502) 456-4520
> **Founded:** 1952
> **Arts Area:** Modern; Ballet; Jazz
> **Status:** Professional; Non-Profit
> **Type:** Performing; Touring; Resident; Educational; Sponsoring
> **Purpose:** To bring high-quality professional dance to a broad audience
> **Management:** Debra Humes Hoffer, Executive Director; Alan Jones, Artistic Director
> **Paid Staff:** 8   **Volunteer Staff:** 200
> **Paid Artists:** 40   **Non-Paid Artists:** 120
> **Utilizes:** Special Technical Talent; Guest Conductors; Guest Artists; Guest Directors
> **Budget:** $1,000,000 - $5,000,000
> **Income Sources:** Private Foundations/Grants/Endowments; Business/Corporate Donations; Box Office; Government Grants; Individual Donations
> **Season:** August - May   **Annual Attendance:** 65,000
> **Affiliations:** Dance USA; SERBA
> **Performance Facilities:** Kentucky Center For The Arts

INSTRUMENTAL MUSIC

KENTUCKY CENTER CHAMBER PLAYERS
c/o Kentucky Center For The Arts, 5 Riverfront Plaza, Louisville, KY 40202
(502) 584-7777; (502) 893-0052
> **Founded:** 1984
> **Arts Area:** Chamber
> **Status:** Professional; Non-Profit
> **Type:** Performing; Touring
> **Purpose:** To present a mixed instrumental ensemble performing traditional and unusual works
> **Management:** Kentucky Center For The Arts
> **Officers:** Joanna Goldstein, President
> **Utilizes:** Guest Artists
> **Budget:** $1,000 - $50,000
> **Income Sources:** Private Foundations/Grants/Endowments; Business/Corporate Donations; Box Office; Individual Donations
> **Season:** September - April   **Annual Attendance:** 1,000
> **Performance Facilities:** University of Louisville; Kentucky Center For The Arts

LOUISVILLE BACH SOCIETY
4607 Hanford Lane, Louisville, KY 40207
(502) 893-7954
> **Founded:** 1964
> **Arts Area:** Orchestra; Choral
> **Status:** Non-Profit
> **Type:** Performing; Touring; Resident; Educational
> **Purpose:** To perform choral and orchestral music of Bach, with other baroque, modern, classical and romantic composers also emphasized
> **Management:** Melvin Dickinson, Musical Director
> **Officers:** Michele Wiggins, President; Tom Diener, Vice President; Robert Myers, Secretary; Milton Moore, Treasurer
> **Paid Staff:** 4   **Volunteer Staff:** 80
> **Paid Artists:** 12   **Non-Paid Artists:** 80
> **Utilizes:** Guest Artists
> **Budget:** $50,000 - $100,000
> **Income Sources:** Private Foundations/Grants/Endowments; Business/Corporate Donations; Box Office; Government Grants; Individual Donations
> **Season:** October - June   **Annual Attendance:** 10,000
> **Affiliations:** Kentucky Arts Council; Greater Louisville Fund for the Arts; AFM
> **Performance Facilities:** University of Louisville

THE LOUISVILLE ORCHESTRA
611 West Main Street, Louisville, KY 40202
(502) 587-8681
FAX: (502) 589-7870
> **Founded:** 1937
> **Arts Area:** Symphony; Orchestra; Chamber
> **Status:** Professional; Non-Profit
> **Type:** Performing; Touring; Educational; Sponsoring
> **Purpose:** To bring the finest orchestral music to our region; to provide an educational resource; to maintain our own recording company that commissions, performs and records new music for our time
> **Management:** Wayne S. Brown, Executive Director; Nora Steinschulte, Director of Public Affairs; Lawrence Leighton Smith, Music Director/Conductor; Albert George, Resident Conductor
> **Paid Staff:** 15   **Volunteer Staff:** 600
> **Paid Artists:** 90
> **Utilizes:** Special Technical Talent; Guest Conductors; Guest Artists
> **Budget:** $1,000,000 - $5,000,000
> **Income Sources:** Private Foundations/Grants/Endowments; Business/Corporate Donations; Box Office; Government Grants; Individual Donations
> **Season:** September - May; June - July   **Annual Attendance:** 180,000
> **Affiliations:** ASOL; AAA; Greater Louisville Fund for the Arts
> **Performance Facilities:** Whitney Hall; Macauley Auditorium; Louisville Gardens; Louisville Zoo

LOUISVILLE YOUTH ORCHESTRA
623 West Main, Louisville, KY 40208
(502) 582-0135
FAX: (502) 582-0149
> **Founded:** 1958
> **Arts Area:** Orchestra

Status: Non-Profit
Type: Performing; Educational
Purpose: To offer a high-quality musical experience to youngsters ages 8-21
Management: Daniel Spurlock, Music Director; Melody Welsh, Executive Director
Officers: Paul Shoemaker, President; Ken Weissteck, Vice President; Jerri Barnsteable, Secretary; Rodney Henderson, Treasurer
Paid Staff: 7   **Volunteer Staff:** 30
Utilizes: Guest Conductors; Guest Artists
Budget: $50,000 - $100,000
Income Sources: Private Foundations/Grants/Endowments; Business/Corporate Donations; Box Office; Government Grants; Individual Donations
Season: September - May   **Annual Attendance:** 10,000
Affiliations: Greater Louisville Fund for the Arts; Youth Performing Arts Council
Performance Facilities: Youth Performing Arts Center

VOCAL MUSIC

KENTUCKY OPERA
631 South Fifth Street, Louisville, KY 40202
(502) 584-4500
FAX: (502) 584-7484
Founded: 1952
Arts Area: Grand Opera; Lyric Opera; Light Opera; Operetta
Status: Professional; Non-Profit
Type: Performing; Touring; Educational
Purpose: To provide quality opera
Management: Thomson Smillie, General Director; Mary Ann Krebs, Executive Director
Officers: Mrs. Charles C. Boyer, Chairman of the Board; John Bridgendall, President; Ronald J. Murphy, Stephen T. Bow, Vice Presidents; Mrs. John Holtman, Secretary; Garrison Cox, Treasurer
Paid Staff: 17   **Volunteer Staff:** 300
Paid Artists: 600   **Non-Paid Artists:** 200
Utilizes: Special Technical Talent; Guest Conductors; Guest Artists; Guest Directors
Budget: $1,000,000 - $5,000,000
Income Sources: Private Foundations/Grants/Endowments; Business/Corporate Donations; Box Office; Government Grants; Individual Donations; Fundraising
Season: October - May   **Annual Attendance:** 25,000
Affiliations: OA
Performance Facilities: Kentucky Center for the Arts; Macauley Theatre

THE LOUISVILLE CHORUS
204 Breckinridge Lane, Louisville, KY 40207
(502) 895-7070
Founded: 1939
Arts Area: Choral
Status: Semi-Professional; Non-Profit
Type: Performing; Touring; Educational; Sponsoring
Purpose: To foster the art of vocal music; to provide a high-quality musical experience, representing a wide variety of styles from the Renaissance to the present
Management: Daniel Spurlock, Music Director; Therese Davis, Managing Director
Officers: Lester Blank, President Board of Directors; Rebecca Greenwell, Secretary; Jena Tippin, Treasurer
Paid Staff: 2   **Volunteer Staff:** 3
Utilizes: Guest Conductors; Guest Artists
Income Sources: Private Foundations/Grants/Endowments; Business/Corporate Donations; Box Office; Individual Donations; Guest Appearances
Season: August - June   **Annual Attendance:** 90,000
Affiliations: Community and State Arts Councils
Performance Facilities: Kentucky Center for the Arts

THEATRE

ACTORS THEATRE OF LOUISVILLE
316-320 West Main Street, Louisville, KY 40202-4218
(502) 584-1265
FAX: (502) 561-3300
Founded: 1964
Arts Area: Professional
Status: Professional; Non-Profit
Type: Performing; Resident

Purpose: To present top-quality professional entertainment to as wide an audience as possible at reasonable prices and at the same time operate in a fiscally responsible manner

Management: Jon Jory, Producing Director; Alexander Speer, Executive Director; Marilee Hebert-Slater, Associate Director

Officers: Caldwell R. Willig, President; Neville Blakemore Jr., Vice President; David W. Hughes, Treasurer; Rande Nortof Swann, Secretary

Paid Staff: 45

Paid Artists: 90

Utilizes: Special Technical Talent; Guest Artists; Guest Directors

Budget: $1,000,000 - $5,000,000

Income Sources: Private Foundations/Grants/Endowments; Business/Corporate Donations; Box Office; Government Grants; Individual Donations

Season: October - May   **Annual Attendance:** 190,000

Affiliations: LORT

STAGE ONE THE LOUISVILLE CHILDREN'S THEATRE
425 West Market Street, Louisville, KY 40202
(502) 589-5946
FAX: (502) 589-5779

Founded: 1946

Arts Area: Professional; Theatrical Group

Status: Professional

Type: Performing; Touring; Educational

Purpose: To provide high-quality, professional live theatre for young people and their families

Management: Moses Goldberg, Producing Director; G. Jane Jarrett, Managing Director

Officers: Mary Michael Steele, President; Sam Corbett, Vice President of Fund-raising; William T. Tyrrell, Vice President of Administration; Mike Keene, Treasurer

Paid Staff: 32   **Volunteer Staff:** 55

Paid Artists: 23   **Non-Paid Artists:** 1

Utilizes: Special Technical Talent; Guest Artists; Guest Directors

Budget: $500,000 - $1,000,000

Income Sources: Private Foundations/Grants/Endowments; Business/Corporate Donations; Box Office; Government Grants; Individual Donations

Season: September - May   **Annual Attendance:** 124,000

Affiliations: AEA

Performance Facilities: Kentucky Center for the Arts; Louisville Gardens

PERFORMING SERIES

SHAKESPEARE IN CENTRAL PARK - KENTUCKY SHAKESPEARE FESTIVAL
520 West Magnolia, Louisville, KY 40208
(502) 634-8237

Founded: 1960

Arts Area: Theater; Festivals

Status: Professional; Non-Profit

Type: Performing; Educational

Purpose: To keep the works of William Shakespeare alive and meaningful for all, regardless of their ability to pay; to remain a dynamic statewide educational resource for Elizabethan studies

Management: Curt L. Tostelend, Producing Director

Officers: Lee Davis, President of the Board

Paid Staff: 3   **Volunteer Staff:** 20

Paid Artists: 30   **Non-Paid Artists:** 10

Utilizes: Special Technical Talent; Guest Artists; Guest Directors

Budget: $100,000 - $500,000

Income Sources: Private Foundations/Grants/Endowments; Business/Corporate Donations; Government Grants; Individual Donations

Season: June - August   **Annual Attendance:** 25,000

Affiliations: AEA

FACILITY

KENTUCKY CENTER FOR THE ARTS
5 Riverfront Plaza, Louisville, KY 40202
(502) 562-0100

Type of Facility: Theatre Complex; Concert Hall; Performance Center; Theatre House; Opera House; Multi-Purpose

Year Built: 1983   **Architect:** Caudill Rowlett Scott   **Cost:** $33,500,000

Acoustical Consultant: Jaffe & Associates

Contact for Rental: Thomas Roberts;   (502) 562-0100

Resident Groups: Louisville Ballet; The Louisville Orchestra; Kentucky Opera; Broadway Series (Louisville Theatrical Association); Stage One; Louisville Children's Theatre
The Center contains the Bomhard Theater, Boyd Martin Experimental Theater and Whitney Hall. See individual listings for additional information.

KENTUCKY CENTER FOR THE ARTS - BOMHARD THEATER
5 Riverfront Plaza, Louisville, KY 40202
(502) 562-0100
Type of Facility: Theatre House; Opera House
Type of Stage: Modified Thrust
Stage Dimensions: 120'Wx30'D; 36'Wx20'H proscenium opening   **Orchestra Pit**
Seating Capacity: 626
Contact for Rental: Thomas Roberts;   (502) 562-0100

KENTUCKY CENTER FOR THE ARTS - BOYD MARTIN EXPERIMENTAL THEATER
5 Riverfront Plaza, Louisville, KY 40202
(502) 562-0100
Type of Facility: Multi-Purpose; Black Box
Type of Stage: Flexible
Stage Dimensions: 42'6"x37'x15'6"H
Seating Capacity: 135
Year Remodeled: 1987   **Architect:** Steve Barry   **Cost:** $277,000
Contact for Rental: Thomas Roberts;   (502) 562-0100
Resident Groups: Boathouse Troupe; Necessary Theater; Walden Theater; Kentucky Playwrights Theater; Creation Theater
Technical Director - Keith Kimmel

KENTUCKY CENTER FOR THE ARTS - WHITNEY HALL
5 Riverfront Plaza, Louisville, KY 40202
(502) 562-0100
Type of Facility: Concert Hall; Theatre House; Opera House
Type of Stage: Modified Thrust
Stage Dimensions: 160'Wx60'D; 56'Wx30'H proscenium opening   **Orchestra Pit**
Seating Capacity: 2,400
Contact for Rental: Thomas Roberts;   (502) 562-0100

LOUISVILLE MEMORIAL AUDITORIUM
970 South Fourth Street, Louisville, KY 40203
(502) 584-4911
FAX: (502) 625-4130
Type of Facility: Auditorium
Type of Stage: Proscenium
Stage Dimensions: 85'Wx39'D; 85'Wx36'H proscenium opening   **Orchestra Pit**
Seating Capacity: 2,000
Year Built: 1929   **Cost:** $2,000,000
Year Remodeled: 1986   **Cost:** $800,000
Contact for Rental: Basil P. Caummisar;   (502) 584-4911
Manager: Dale Royer;   (502) 584-4911
Auditorium has the world's largest Pilcher Organ with 588 pipes.

MACAULEY THEATRE
315 West Broadway, Louisville, KY 40202
(502) 562-0194
FAX: (502) 562-0188
Type of Facility: Theatre House
Type of Stage: Proscenium
Stage Dimensions: 90'Wx38'D   **Orchestra Pit**
Seating Capacity: 1,453
Year Built: 1925   **Architect:** Preston-Bradshaw
Year Remodeled: 1972
Contact for Rental: Jonathan Smillie;   (502) 562-0194
Resident Groups: Theater Workshop of Louisville; Louisville Orhcestra

SOUTHERN BAPTIST THEOLOGICAL SEMINARY - ALUMNI MEMORIAL CHAPEL
2825 Lexington Road, Louisville, KY 40206
(502) 897-4115
Type of Facility: Auditorium
Type of Stage: Flexible

Seating Capacity: 1,600
Year Built: 1950   **Architect:** Joseph Kolbrook   **Cost:** $1,500,000
Acoustical Consultant: Bolt, Beranek & Newman
Manager: Dr. Milburn Price
Resident Groups: Seminary Oratorio Chorus and Orchestra; Male Chorale; Seminary Choir; Collegium Musicum

SOUTHERN BAPTIST THEOLOGICAL SEMINARY - HEEREN RECITAL HALL
2825 Lexington Road, Louisville, KY 40280
(502) 897-4115
Type of Facility: Concert Hall
Type of Stage: Thrust
Seating Capacity: 255
Year Built: 1971   **Architect:** John Grossman   **Cost:** $250,000
Acoustical Consultant: Bolt, Beranek & Newman
Manager: Dr. Milburn Price

Murray

PERFORMING SERIES

MURRAY CIVIC MUSIC ASSOCIATION
College of Fine Arts and Communication, University Station, Murray, KY 42071
(502) 762-6339, ext. 4669
Founded: 1959
Arts Area: Dance; Vocal Music; Instrumental Music; Theater; Lyric Opera; Grand Opera
Status: Non-Profit
Type: Sponsoring
Purpose: To bring outstanding performing arts attractions to the region
Officers: Roger E. Reichmuth, President
Volunteer Staff: 18
Paid Artists: 94
Utilizes: Guest Artists
Budget: $1,000 - $50,000
Income Sources: Business/Corporate Donations; Box Office; Government Grants; Individual Donations
Season: September - May   **Annual Attendance:** 6,000
Performance Facilities: Lovett Auditorium, Murray State University

FACILITY

MURRAY STATE UNIVERSITY - LOVETT AUDITORIUM
College of Fine Arts and Communication, Murray, KY 42071
(502) 762-4516
FAX: (502) 762-6335
Type of Facility: Auditorium
Facility Originally: Recreation Hall; Gymnasium
Type of Stage: Proscenium
Stage Dimensions: 79'6"Wx53'Dx20'H
Seating Capacity: 2,100
Year Built: 1934
Year Remodeled: 1938
Contact for Rental: Gary Hunt;   (502) 762-4516

Owensboro

INSTRUMENTAL MUSIC

OWENSBORO SYMPHONY ORCHESTRA
122 East Eighteenth Street, Owensboro, KY 42301
(502) 684-0661
Founded: 1966
Arts Area: Symphony; Orchestra
Status: Professional; Non-Profit
Type: Performing; Touring; Resident; Educational
Purpose: The Owensboro Symphony Orchestra performs symphonic music to enhance the cultural environment of western Kentucky.
Management: G. Dan Griffith, General Manager; Michael Luxner, Music Director; Paula Hudson, Office Manager
Paid Staff: 7   **Volunteer Staff:** 3

Paid Artists: 90   **Non-Paid Artists:** 2
Utilizes: Guest Conductors; Guest Artists
Budget: $100,000 - $500,000
Income Sources: Private Foundations/Grants/Endowments; Business/Corporate Donations; Box Office; Government Grants; Individual Donations
Season: September - April   **Annual Attendance:** 14,000
Affiliations: ASOL
Performance Facilities: River Park Center

THEATRE

THEATRE WORKSHOP OF OWENSBORO
407 West Fifth Street, PO Box 170, Owensboro, KY 42302
(502) 683-5003
Founded: 1955
Arts Area: Musical; Community; Theatrical Group; Youth Theatre
Status: Non-Professional; Non-Profit
Type: Performing; Resident
Purpose: To provide the Owensboro area with high-quality amateur theatre; to provide an outlet for area performers and technicians to practice their craft
Management: Nestra McFarland, Office Manager
Officers: Robert Wagner, President Board of Directors; Betty Taylor, Vice President; Mary Martin, Secretary; Terry Walker, Treasurer
Paid Staff: 2   **Volunteer Staff:** 75
Utilizes: Guest Conductors; Guest Directors
Budget: $50,000 - $100,000
Income Sources: Business/Corporate Donations; Box Office; Government Grants; Individual Donations
Season: 52 Weeks   **Annual Attendance:** 5,500
Affiliations: AACT; Kentucky Theatre Association
Performance Facilities: Old Trinity Centre; River Park Center

Paducah

THEATRE

MARKET HOUSE THEATRE
141 Kentucky Avenue, Paducah, KY 42003
(502) 444-6828
Founded: 1964
Arts Area: Community
Status: Non-Professional; Non-Profit
Type: Performing; Touring; Educational
Purpose: To enrich the community's cultural and artistic life through the production of a diverse season as well as educational and touring programs
Management: April S. Cochran, Artistic/Executive Director; Michael L. Cochran, Technical Director
Officers: Martha Emmons, President; Sherry Shadle, Vice President; Lana Sirk, Secretary; Lars Blythe, Treasurer
Paid Staff: 4
Non-Paid Artists: 120
Utilizes: Special Technical Talent; Guest Artists; Guest Directors
Budget: $100,000 - $500,000
Income Sources: Private Foundations/Grants/Endowments; Business/Corporate Donations; Box Office; Government Grants; Individual Donations
Season: 52 Weeks   **Annual Attendance:** 12,000
Performance Facilities: Market House Theatre

Radcliff

THEATRE

HARDIN COUNTY PLAYHOUSE
PO Box 394, Radcliff, KY 40160
(502) 351-0577
Founded: 1969
Arts Area: Musical; Community; Theatrical Group
Status: Semi-Professional; Non-Professional; Non-Profit
Type: Performing
Purpose: To present performing arts to the community

Management: Hardin County Playhouse Board of Directors
Officers: Deborah Hibberd, President; Duane Clug, Vice President; Christine Reich, Secretary; Michael Laughlin, Treasurer
Volunteer Staff: 100
Utilizes: Special Technical Talent; Guest Artists; Guest Directors
Budget: $1,000 - $50,000
Income Sources: Private Foundations/Grants/Endowments; Business/Corporate Donations; Box Office; Individual Donations
Season: 52 Weeks **Annual Attendance:** 1,800
Performance Facilities: Hardin County Playhouse

Richmond

THEATRE

RICHMOND CHILDREN'S THEATRE
321 North Second Street, Richmond, KY 40475
(606) 623-8753
Founded: 1978
Arts Area: Musical; Community; Theatrical Group
Status: Non-Professional; Non-Profit
Type: Performing; Touring; Educational
Purpose: To offer to all youth, ages 8-18, the opportunity to participate in the theatre arts through the avenues of workshops, performances, stagecraft and crew
Officers: Kathie Bettler, President; Jo Wernegreen, Vice President Finance; Jeanette Duncan, Secretary; Sandy Johnstone, Treasurer
Volunteer Staff: 30
Paid Artists: 5
Utilizes: Special Technical Talent; Guest Directors
Budget: $1,000 - $50,000
Income Sources: Business/Corporate Donations; Box Office; Government Grants; Individual Donations
Season: September - May **Annual Attendance:** 1,500
Affiliations: Richmond Parks and Recreation Department
Performance Facilities: Eastern Kentucky University Campus Theatre

Whitesburg

THEATRE

ROADSIDE THEATER
306 Madison Street, Whitesburg, KY 41858
(606) 633-0108
Founded: 1975
Arts Area: Professional; Theatrical Group
Status: Professional; Non-Profit
Type: Performing; Touring; Educational
Purpose: To create original plays about central Appalachia and its people
Management: Dudley Cocke, Director; Donna Porterfield, Managing Director; Ron Short, Artistic Director; Valeria Craft, Marketing Director
Paid Staff: 7
Utilizes: Special Technical Talent; Guest Artists; Guest Directors
Budget: $100,000 - $500,000
Income Sources: Private Foundations/Grants/Endowments; Business/Corporate Donations; Box Office; Government Grants; Individual Donations
Season: 52 Weeks
Affiliations: TCG; Alternate ROOTS
Performance Facilities: Appalshop Theatre

LOUISIANA

Baton Rouge

DANCE

BATON ROUGE BALLET THEATRE
301 Main Street, Baton Rouge, LA 70801
(504) 336-0544
  Arts Area: Ballet
  Status: Professional; Non-Profit
  Type: Performing; Touring; Resident
  Management: Sharon Mathews, Molly Boehmann, Artistic Directors
  Paid Artists: 25
  Income Sources: Box Office; Individual Donations
  Performance Facilities: Centroplex Theater for the Performing Arts

INSTRUMENTAL MUSIC

BATON ROUGE SYMPHONY ORCHESTRA
1 America Place, Suite 620, Baton Rouge, LA 70825
(504) 387-2776
FAX: (504) 387-5445
  Founded: 1947
  Arts Area: Symphony; Orchestra; Chamber; Ensemble
  Status: Non-Profit
  Type: Performing
  Purpose: To provide professional quality orchestral performance in symphony and related arts
  Management: Douglas Gerhert, Executive Director
  Officers: George Ballars, President; Charles Lamar, Vice President; Sharon Rochford, Treasurer; Robert Hawthorne, Secretary; Beth Fuller, Immediate Past President
  Paid Staff: 4   **Volunteer Staff:** 150
  Paid Artists: 80
  Utilizes: Guest Artists
  Budget: $500,000 - $1,000,000
  Income Sources: Private Foundations/Grants/Endowments; Business/Corporate Donations; Box Office; Government Grants; Individual Donations
  Season: September - May   **Annual Attendance:** 16,000
  Performance Facilities: Riverside/Centroplex Theatre for Performing Arts

VOCAL MUSIC

BATON ROUGE GILBERT AND SULLIVAN SOCIETY
PO Box 80099, Baton Rouge, LA 70898
(504) 291-7236
  Founded: 1975
  Arts Area: Operetta
  Status: Non-Professional; Non-Profit
  Type: Performing
  Purpose: To perform in full, and in excerpts, the operettas of W.S. Gilbert and Arthur Sullivan
  Officers: Lance Parker, President
  Volunteer Staff: 11
  Paid Artists: 5   **Non-Paid Artists:** 35
  Utilizes: Guest Conductors; Guest Directors
  Budget: $1,000 - $50,000
  Income Sources: Private Foundations/Grants/Endowments; Business/Corporate Donations; Box Office; Government Grants; Individual Donations
  Annual Attendance: 1,400
  Performance Facilities: Baton Rouge Little Theatre

BATON ROUGE OPERA
PO Box 2269, Baton Rouge, LA 70821
(504) 922-9936
  Founded: 1982
  Arts Area: Grand Opera; Light Opera
  Status: Professional; Non-Profit
  Type: Performing; Educational

Management: Marioara Trifan, Artistic Director; Samuel Gray, General Director; Lynn Allen, Office Manager
Officers: Marlene Weyand, President; William Newman, Vice President; Don DeVille, Treasurer; Ellen Hill, Secretary
Paid Staff: 3
Paid Artists: 76   **Non-Paid Artists:** 12
Utilizes: Special Technical Talent; Guest Conductors; Guest Artists; Guest Directors
Budget: $100,000 - $500,000
Income Sources: Private Foundations/Grants/Endowments; Business/Corporate Donations; Box Office; Government Grants; Individual Donations
Season: October - June   **Annual Attendance:** 7,500
Affiliations: Arts and Humanities Council of Baton Rouge; OA
Performance Facilities: Union Theatre, Louisiana State University

THEATRE

BATON ROUGE LITTLE THEATRE
7155 Florida Boulevard, Baton Rouge, LA 70806
(504) 924-6496
Founded: 1946
Arts Area: Musical; Community
Status: Non-Professional; Non-Profit
Type: Performing; Educational
Purpose: To entertain, educate and provide an artistic outlet
Management: Henry Avery, Managing/Artistic Director
Paid Staff: 7   **Volunteer Staff:** 100
Paid Artists: 40   **Non-Paid Artists:** 100
Utilizes: Guest Conductors; Guest Directors
Budget: $100,000 - $500,000
Income Sources: Private Foundations/Grants/Endowments; Box Office; Individual Donations
Season: October - May; July   **Annual Attendance:** 25,000

FACILITY

LSU UNION THEATER
Highland Road, LSU Campus, Baton Rouge, LA 70894
(504) 388-5728
FAX: (504) 388-4329
Founded: 1964
Type of Facility: Theatre Complex; Concert Hall; Auditorium; Off Broadway; Theatre House; Opera House
Type of Stage: Proscenium
Stage Dimensions: 44'Wx30'Dx22'H proscenium opening   **Orchestra Pit**
Seating Capacity: 1,262
Year Built: 1964   **Architect:** John Desmond Associates   **Cost:** $3,500,000
Contact for Rental: Michael R. Derr, Director;   (504) 388-5782
Resident Groups: Baton Rouge Opera; LSU Symphony Orchestra

RIVERSIDE CENTROPLEX
PO Box 4047, Baton Rouge, LA 70821
(504) 389-3030
Type of Facility: Civic Center
Year Built: 1977   **Architect:** Bradley Mermont   **Cost:** $25,000,000
Contact for Rental: Mike Pierce, Executive Director;   (504) 389-3030
The Centroplex contains an Arena, Exhibition Hall and Theatre. See separate listings for further information.

RIVERSIDE CENTROPLEX - ARENA
PO Box 4047, Baton Rouge, LA 70821
(504) 389-3030
FAX: (504) 389-4954
Type of Facility: Concert Hall; Arena
Type of Stage: Flexible; Platform
Seating Capacity: 12,813
Year Built: 1977
Contact for Rental: Mike Pierce, Executive Director;   (504) 389-3030

RIVERSIDE CENTROPLEX - EXHIBITION HALL
PO Box 4047, Baton Rouge, LA 70821
(504) 389-3030
FAX: (504) 389-4954
Type of Facility: Exhibition Hall

Type of Stage: Flexible; Platform
Year Built: 1977
Contact for Rental: Mike Pierce, Executive Director; (504) 389-3030

RIVERSIDE CENTROPLEX - THEATRE FOR PERFORMING ARTS
PO Box 4047, Baton Rouge, LA 70821
(504) 389-3030
FAX: (504) 389-4954
    Type of Facility: Concert Hall; Theatre House; Opera House
    Type of Stage: Proscenium
    Stage Dimensions: 57'9"Wx47'D; 57'9"Wx28'H proscenium opening; 20' wings left and right   **Orchestra Pit**
    Seating Capacity: 2,011
    Year Built: 1980
    Contact for Rental: Mike Pierce, Executive Director; (504) 389-3030
    Resident Groups: Baton Rouge Symphony Orchestra; Baton Rouge Ballet; Baton Rouge Opera

Eunice

THEATRE

EUNICE PLAYERS THEATRE
PO Box 306, Eunice, LA 70535
(318) 457-3330
    Founded: 1969
    Arts Area: Musical; Community
    Status: Non-Professional; Non-Profit
    Type: Performing
    Purpose: To continue to provide quality live theater to Eunice and the surrounding area
    Officers: John Cobb, President; Jody Powell, Secretary; Joan Kerstein, Treasurer
    Volunteer Staff: 16
    Non-Paid Artists: 100
    Budget: $1,000 - $50,000
    Income Sources: Business/Corporate Donations; Box Office; Individual Donations
    Season: 52 Weeks   **Annual Attendance:** 1,800
    Affiliations: Acadiana Arts Council; Saint Landry Arts Association; Eunice Chamber of Commerce

FACILITY

EUNICE PLAYERS THEATRE
PO Box 306, Eunice, LA 70535
(318) 457-3330
    Type of Facility: Studio Performance
    Facility Originally: Business Facility
    Type of Stage: Proscenium
    Stage Dimensions: 22'x20'
    Seating Capacity: 112
    Year Remodeled: 1970
    Contact for Rental: Joanie Kurstein; (318) 457-3330
    Resident Groups: Eunice Players Theatre

Hammond

FACILITY

SOUTHEASTERN LOUISIANA UNIVERSITY - VONNIE BORDEN THEATRE
Hammond, LA 70402
(504) 549-2105
    Type of Facility: Theatre House
    Type of Stage: Proscenium
    Stage Dimensions: 40'x80'

Seating Capacity: 450
Year Built: 1971   **Architect:** Oliver-Frantz, AIA   **Cost:** $2,000,000

Lafayette

INSTRUMENTAL MUSIC

LAFAYETTE CONCERT BAND
PO Box 53762, Lafayette, LA 70505
(318) 233-7060
Founded: 1982
Arts Area: Band
Status: Semi-Professional; Non-Profit
Type: Performing; Touring; Resident; Educational; Sponsoring
Purpose: To provide a competent, well-rehearsed organization which would introduce the unique repertoire for wind ensemble to the people of Southwest Louisiana and to provide a performance outlet for the musical talents of band instrumentalists
Management: Dr. George Sparks, Music Director
Volunteer Staff: 5
Non-Paid Artists: 65
Utilizes: Special Technical Talent; Guest Conductors; Guest Artists
Budget: $1,000 - $50,000
Income Sources: Private Foundations/Grants/Endowments; Business/Corporate Donations; Box Office; Government Grants; Individual Donations
Season: 52 Weeks   **Annual Attendance:** 8,000
Affiliations: National Association of Concert Bands

THEATRE

LAFAYETTE COMMUNITY THEATRE
504 Plaza Village, Lafayette, LA 70506
(318) 235-1532
Founded: 1981
Arts Area: Community; Theatrical Group
Status: Non-Professional; Non-Profit
Type: Performing; Touring; Resident
Purpose: To produce quality drama for local citizens; to encourage participation in all activities by interested residents; to educate citizens regarding theatre and train them in theatre arts
Management: Jack Reedy, Business Manager; John Fiero, Artistic Director; Charles Manns, Technical Director
Officers: Roma Hepburn, President; Maureen Brennan, Vice President; Alozia St. Julien, Secretary; Jack Reedy, Treasurer
Budget: $1,000 - $50,000
Income Sources: Private Foundations/Grants/Endowments; Business/Corporate Donations; Box Office; Individual Donations
Season: 52 Weeks   **Annual Attendance:** 5,000

FACILITY

HEYMANN PERFORMING ARTS AND CONVENTION CENTER
1373 South College Road, Lafayette, LA 70503
(318) 268-5540
FAX: (318) 268-5580
Founded: 1960
Type of Facility: Performance Center; Convention Center
Type of Stage: Proscenium
Stage Dimensions: 107'x49'   **Orchestra Pit**
Seating Capacity: 2,230
Year Built: 1960   **Architect:** Hayes Town   **Cost:** $1,200,000
Year Remodeled: 1989   **Architect:** Wayne Corme   **Cost:** $3,500,000
Acoustical Consultant: Dave Nieblieu
Contact for Rental: Frank Bradshaw;   (318) 268-5540

LAFAYETTE COMMUNITY THEATRE
529 Jefferson Street, Lafayette, LA 70501
(318) 235-1532
Type of Facility: Theatre House
Facility Originally: Business Facility
Type of Stage: Flexible; Proscenium
Stage Dimensions: 40'Wx18'Dx15'H

Seating Capacity: 90
Year Remodeled: 1986   **Architect:** Bob Bennet   **Cost:** $25,000
Contact for Rental: John Fiero;   (318) 234-8210
Resident Groups: Lafayette Community Theatre

Lake Charles

DANCE

LAKE CHARLES BALLET SOCIETY
PO Box 5515, Lake Charles, LA 70606
(318) 436-0160
> **Founded:** 1963
> **Arts Area:** Ballet; Jazz
> **Status:** Non-Professional; Non-Profit
> **Type:** Performing; Resident; Educational; Sponsoring
> **Purpose:** To provide Southwest Louisiana with the highest quality of dance programs, concert series, resident performing companies, dance in schools, and the sponsorship of professional dance companies
> **Management:** Ida Clarke, Artistic Director; Cissie Clarke, Assistant Director/Ballet Mistress
> **Officers:** Marie McCreedy, President; Maureen Cannon, Vice President, Membership; Janet Postell, Secretary; Zippy Scott, Treasurer
> **Volunteer Staff:** 25
> **Paid Artists:** 2   **Non-Paid Artists:** 16
> **Utilizes:** Guest Artists
> **Budget:** $50,000 - $100,000
> **Income Sources:** Private Foundations/Grants/Endowments; Business/Corporate Donations; Box Office; Individual Donations
> **Season:** October - April
> **Performance Facilities:** Lake Charles Civic Center

LAKE CHARLES SOCIETY FOR BALLET JOYEUX
140 West 18th Street, Lake Charles, LA 70601
(318) 436-5217
> **Founded:** 1963
> **Arts Area:** Ballet
> **Status:** Non-Professional; Non-Profit
> **Type:** Performing; Touring; Resident
> **Management:** Cissie Clark, Acting Director
> **Non-Paid Artists:** 20
> **Utilizes:** Guest Artists; Guest Choreographers
> **Budget:** $50,000 - $100,000
> **Income Sources:** Private Foundations/Grants/Endowments; Business/Corporate Donations; Box Office; Individual Donations
> **Season:** September - June
> **Performance Facilities:** Lake Charles Civic Center

THEATRE

ARTISTS CIVIC THEATRE AND STUDIO
One Reid Street, PO Box 278, Lake Charles, LA 70602
(318) 433-2287
> **Founded:** 1966
> **Arts Area:** Musical; Dinner; Community; Theatrical Group; Children's
> **Status:** Non-Professional; Non-Profit
> **Type:** Performing; Touring; Resident; Educational
> **Purpose:** To give local talent a place to work under the direction of a trained professional director where production values are maintained at a high level; to offer formal classes in various aspects of theatre
> **Management:** Marc Pettaway, Executive Director
> **Officers:** Dr. Charles Woodard, President
> **Paid Staff:** 2   **Volunteer Staff:** 40
> **Paid Artists:** 2   **Non-Paid Artists:** 70
> **Utilizes:** Special Technical Talent
> **Budget:** $50,000 - $100,000
> **Income Sources:** Box Office
> **Season:** 52 Weeks   **Annual Attendance:** 8,000
> **Affiliations:** SWTC
> **Performance Facilities:** ACTS' One Reid Street Theatre

PERFORMING SERIES

LAKE CHARLES LITTLE THEATRE
813 Enterprise Boulevard, Lake Charles, LA 70601
(318) 433-7988
Founded: 1926
Arts Area: Theater
Status: Non-Professional; Non-Profit
Type: Performing
Management: Adley Cormier, Artistic Director; Paul Draughn and John Hogan, Board Members
Officers: Bob Michael, President; James Johnson, Vice President; Mathilde Gano, Secretary; Waverlyn Bayard, Treasurer
Paid Staff: 1
Utilizes: Guest Directors
Budget: $1,000 - $50,000
Income Sources: Private Foundations/Grants/Endowments; Business/Corporate Donations; Box Office; Individual Donations
Season: September - May   **Annual Attendance:** 3,500

FACILITY

LAKE CHARLES CIVIC CENTER
900 Lakeshore Drive, PO Box 900, Lake Charles, LA 70602
(318) 491-1256
FAX: (318) 491-1534
Type of Facility: Civic Center
Year Built: 1972   **Architect:** J.T. Platt   **Cost:** $16,000,000
Contact for Rental: Al Harris;   (318) 491-1256
Civic Center contains the Coliseum, Exhibition Hall and Rosa Hart Theatre. See separate listings for further information.

LAKE CHARLES CIVIC CENTER - COLISEUM
900 Lakeshore Drive, PO Box 900, Lake Charles, LA 70602
(318) 491-1256
FAX: (318) 491-1534
Type of Facility: Concert Hall; Arena
Type of Stage: Flexible; Platform
Seating Capacity: 8,000
Year Built: 1972   **Architect:** J.T. Platt
Contact for Rental: Al Harris;   (318) 491-1256

LAKE CHARLES CIVIC CENTER - EXHIBITION HALL
900 Lakeshore Drive, PO Box 900, Lake Charles, LA 70602
(318) 491-1256
FAX: (318) 491-1534
Type of Facility: Exhibition Hall
Type of Stage: Flexible
Year Built: 1972   **Architect:** J.T. Platt
Contact for Rental: Al Harris;   (318) 491-1256
18,000 square feet of hall space

LAKE CHARLES CIVIC CENTER - ROSA HART THEATRE
900 Lakeshore Drive, PO Box 900, Lake Charles, LA 70602
(318) 491-1256
FAX: (318) 491-1534
Type of Facility: Concert Hall; Theatre House
Type of Stage: Proscenium
Stage Dimensions: 65'3"Wx28'Hx60'D   **Orchestra Pit**
Seating Capacity: 2,704
Year Built: 1972   **Architect:** J.T. Platt
Contact for Rental: Al Harris;   (318) 491-1256
Resident Groups: Lake Charles Symphony; Lake Charles Civic Ballet; Southwest Louisiana Concert Association

ONE REID STREET THEATRE
One Reid Street, PO Box 278, Lake Charles, LA 70602
(318) 433-2287
Type of Facility: Theatre Complex
Type of Stage: Proscenium
Stage Dimensions: 44'x25'
Seating Capacity: 200

Year Remodeled: 1987 **Architect:** Gus Quinn; Blair Stoker
Contact for Rental: Marc Pettaway; (318) 433-2287
Resident Groups: Artists Civic Theatre & Studio

Mamou

PERFORMING SERIES

MAMOU CAJUN MUSIC FESTIVAL ASSOCIATION
420 East Street, Apt. 1, Mamou, LA 70554
(318) 468-2258
> **Founded:** 1972
> **Arts Area:** Vocal Music; Festivals
> **Status:** Non-Profit
> **Type:** Performing; Resident; Educational
> **Purpose:** To promote authentic and traditional cajun music, food and games
> **Officers:** Eric Fontenot, President; Donald Landreneau, Vice President; Roy Chamberlin, Secretary; Norris Fontenot, Treasurer
> **Volunteer Staff:** 65
> **Paid Artists:** 40
> **Utilizes:** Special Technical Talent; Guest Artists; Paid Performers
> **Budget:** $1,000 - $50,000
> **Income Sources:** Private Foundations/Grants/Endowments; Box Office; Concessions
> **Season:** June   **Annual Attendance:** 15,000

Metairie

DANCE

CRESCENT BALLET COMPANY
3211 Taft Park, Metairie, LA 70002
(504) 885-2352
> **Founded:** 1970
> **Arts Area:** Ballet
> **Status:** Non-Professional; Non-Profit
> **Type:** Performing; Resident
> **Management:** Patricia LeClercq, Director
> **Non-Paid Artists:** 20
> **Utilizes:** Guest Artists; Guest Choreographers
> **Budget:** $1,000 - $50,000
> **Income Sources:** Private Foundations/Grants/Endowments; Business/Corporate Donations; Box Office; Individual Donations
> **Season:** September - June

DELTA FESTIVAL BALLET
3850 North Causeway Boulevard, Metairie, LA 70003
(504) 836-7166
> **Founded:** 1969
> **Arts Area:** Ballet
> **Status:** Professional; Non-Profit
> **Type:** Performing; Touring; Resident; Educational
> **Purpose:** To promote the art of dance through professional performance, education, cultural outreach and community involvement
> **Management:** Joseph and Maria Giacobbe, Artistic Directors; Christines Hodgins, Administrative Director
> **Officers:** Dr. R. V. Hamsa, President; Thomas Bernard, Vice President; John Bruno, Secretary; Terri Fishbein, Treasurer
> **Paid Staff:** 7   **Volunteer Staff:** 20
> **Paid Artists:** 20   **Non-Paid Artists:** 15
> **Utilizes:** Special Technical Talent; Guest Conductors; Guest Artists; Guest Directors
> **Budget:** $100,000 - $500,000
> **Income Sources:** Private Foundations/Grants/Endowments; Business/Corporate Donations; Box Office; Government Grants; Individual Donations
> **Season:** September - May   **Annual Attendance:** 100,000
> **Affiliations:** NARB

PERFORMING SERIES

JEFFERSON PERFORMING ARTS SOCIETY
PO Box 704, Metairie, LA 70004
(504) 834-5727
FAX: (504) 834-5741
> **Founded:** 1978
> **Arts Area:** Dance; Vocal Music; Instrumental Music; Theater; Festivals; Grand Opera
> **Status:** Professional; Semi-Professional; Non-Professional; Non-Profit
> **Type:** Performing; Educational
> **Purpose:** To create a better community through high-quality art education (especially youth), performance and competitions; to develop schools for the arts in the parish
> **Management:** Dennis G. Assaf Founder/Executive Director/Artistic Director; Carol Artery, Development Association
> **Officers:** Hannah Cunningham, Chairman; Teresa Guzzutta, President; John Brooks, Vice President; Dean Wilson, Secretary
> **Paid Staff:** 4 **Volunteer Staff:** 8
> **Paid Artists:** 35 **Non-Paid Artists:** 100
> **Budget:** $500,000 - $1,000,000
> **Income Sources:** Business/Corporate Donations; Box Office; Government Grants; Individual Donations
> **Season:** September - May
> **Affiliations:** CA

Monroe

INSTRUMENTAL MUSIC

MONROE SYMPHONY ORCHESTRA
PO Box 4353, Monroe, LA 71211-4353
(318) 329-8085
> **Founded:** 1971
> **Arts Area:** Symphony; Orchestra; Chamber; Ensemble
> **Status:** Semi-Professional; Non-Profit
> **Type:** Performing; Educational
> **Purpose:** To present cultural music to the community and to educate students through a program of music in the schools
> **Management:** Dr. Doug Baer, Business Manager
> **Officers:** Chris Cheshier, President; K. Katz, Past President; John Kelly, First Vice President
> **Paid Staff:** 1 **Volunteer Staff:** 8
> **Paid Artists:** 60
> **Utilizes:** Guest Conductors; Guest Artists
> **Budget:** $50,000 - $100,000
> **Income Sources:** Business/Corporate Donations; Box Office; Government Grants
> **Annual Attendance:** 2,000
> **Performance Facilities:** Monroe Civic Center

PERFORMING SERIES

NORTHEAST LOUISIANA UNIVERSITY CONCERTS
Northeast Louisiana University, Monroe, LA 71209
(318) 342-1000
FAX: (318) 342-1034
> **Arts Area:** Dance; Vocal Music; Instrumental Music; Theater
> **Status:** Non-Profit
> **Type:** Performing; Sponsoring
> **Purpose:** To bring to students and townspeople the best in professional cultural entertainment
> **Management:** Jerry D. Holmes, Chairman
> **Paid Staff:** 1 **Volunteer Staff:** 2
> **Utilizes:** Guest Artists
> **Budget:** $50,000 - $100,000
> **Income Sources:** Private Foundations/Grants/Endowments; Box Office
> **Season:** October - April **Annual Attendance:** 2,200
> **Performance Facilities:** Civic Center Theater; Brown Auditorium

FACILITY

MONROE CIVIC CENTER
401 Lea Joyner Boulevard, PO Box 1853, Monroe, LA 71210
(318) 329-2225
FAX: (318) 329-2548
 Type of Facility: Civic Center
 Year Built: 1967 **Architect:** Johns & Neel **Cost:** $13,000,000
 Acoustical Consultant: Tracor
 Contact for Rental: Obie Webser, Stan Lockridge; (318) 329-2225
 Civic Center contains the Arena, Theater, and Conference Hall. See separate listings for further information.

MONROE CIVIC CENTER - ARENA
401 Lea Joyner Boulevard, PO Box 1853, Monroe, LA 71210
(318) 329-2225
FAX: (318) 329-2548
 Type of Facility: Arena
 Type of Stage: Proscenium; Platform
 Stage Dimensions: 48'x72'
 Seating Capacity: 8,000
 Year Built: 1967
 Contact for Rental: Obie Webser, Stan Lockridge; (318) 329-2225

MONROE CIVIC CENTER - THEATER
401 Lea Joyner Boulevard, PO Box 300, Monroe, LA 71201
(318) 329-2225
 Type of Facility: Theatre House
 Type of Stage: Proscenium; Platform
 Stage Dimensions: 56'x72' **Orchestra Pit**
 Seating Capacity: 2,250
 Year Built: 1967
 Contact for Rental: Obie Webster; (318) 329-2225
 Manager: Stan Lockridge; (318) 329-2225

New Orleans

DANCE

NEW ORLEANS BALLET ASSOCIATION
821 Gravier Street, Suite 610, New Orleans, LA 70112
(504) 522-0996
FAX: (504) 595-8454
 Founded: 1971
 Arts Area: Modern; Ballet; Jazz
 Status: Non-Profit
 Type: Sponsoring; Presenting
 Purpose: To present professional dance in the greater New Orleans area
 Management: Jon H. Teeuwissen, Executive Director
 Officers: Phyllis Taylor, President; John Reidy, Vice President; Elizabeth Ryan, Secretary; Curt Queyrouze, Treasurer
 Paid Staff: 7 **Volunteer Staff:** 200
 Paid Artists: 12
 Utilizes: Guest Artists; Guest Choreographers; Guest Companies
 Budget: $500,000 - $1,000,000
 Income Sources: Private Foundations/Grants/Endowments; Business/Corporate Donations; Box Office; Government Grants; Individual Donations
 Season: September - April **Annual Attendance:** 28,000
 Affiliations: Dance USA
 Performance Facilities: Theatre for the Perfroming Arts; Saenger Theatre; Orpheum Theatre; St. Bernard Cultural Center

INSTRUMENTAL MUSIC

LOUISIANA JAZZ FEDERATION
333 Saint Charles Avenue, Suite 613, New Orleans, LA 70130
(504) 522-3154
FAX: (504) 522-3154
 Founded: 1980
 Arts Area: Ensemble; Ethnic; Band

Status: Semi-Professional; Non-Profit
Type: Performing; Educational; Sponsoring
Purpose: To promote the development and unification of the jazz community in Louisiana
Management: Jason Patterson, Executive Director; Patrice Fisher, Development Director; Amber Wallace, JAM Coordinator
Officers: Tim Green, President; Harold Battiste, Vice President; Lorraine Farr, Secretary; Eric Glaser, Treasurer
Paid Staff: 3 **Volunteer Staff:** 18
Paid Artists: 120
Utilizes: Guest Artists
Budget: $50,000 - $100,000
Income Sources: Private Foundations/Grants/Endowments; Business/Corporate Donations; Box Office; Government Grants; Individual Donations
Season: 52 Weeks **Annual Attendance:** 12,000

NEW ORLEANS CONCERT BAND
2200 Lake Oaks Parkway, New Orleans, LA 70122
(504) 282-8609
Founded: 1974
Arts Area: Band
Status: Professional; Non-Professional
Type: Resident
Management: Milton Bush, Conductor/Manager; Ed Barnhart, Property Manager
Officers: Lisa McDonald, President; John Risey, Vice President; Maureen Haney, Secretary; Nicholas Woolverton, Treasurer
Volunteer Staff: 10
Non-Paid Artists: 65
Budget: $1,000 - $50,000
Income Sources: Private Foundations/Grants/Endowments; Individual Donations
Season: September - July **Annual Attendance:** 4,000
Performance Facilities: Saint Charles Avenue Baptist Church

NEW ORLEANS FRIENDS OF MUSIC
1035 Eleanore Street, New Orleans, LA 70115
(504) 897-3491; (504) 895-0690
Founded: 1956
Arts Area: Chamber
Status: Non-Profit
Type: Sponsoring
Purpose: To bring the best chamber music possible to the people of New Orleans at a reasonable ticket price
Management: Marcie Scheurmann, Subscription Manager
Officers: Dr. Stuart D. Farber, President; Lawrence M. Lehmann, Vice President; Dr. Teal F. Bennett, Secretary; Dr. Anne S. Bradburn, Treasurer
Volunteer Staff: 30
Utilizes: Guest Artists
Budget: $1,000 - $50,000
Income Sources: Private Foundations/Grants/Endowments; Business/Corporate Donations; Box Office; Individual Donations
Season: September - April **Annual Attendance:** 5,000
Performance Facilities: Dixon Hall

VOCAL MUSIC

THE B SHARP MUSIC CLUB OF NEW ORLEANS
2724 Mexico Street, New Orleans, LA 70122
(504) 288-0959
Founded: 1917
Arts Area: Light Opera; Operetta
Status: Non-Profit
Type: Performing; Sponsoring
Purpose: To foster the preservation of music from including classical, Negro spirituals and contemporary pieces; to encourage youthful talent by giving scholarship aid and providing the opportunity for youth to perform; to develop followship among music patrons and musicians
Management: Lillian D. Perry, Volunteer Director
Officers: Audrey C. Robertson, President; Lillian Dunn Perry, President Emeritus; Elise Dunn Cain, Vice President; Sylvia N. Oliver, Corresponding Secretary; Leona H. Dawson, Financial Secretary; Sharon Auguillard, Recording Secretary; Junealee Populus, Treasurer

Budget: $1,000 - $50,000
Income Sources: Individual Donations
Season: October - June
Affiliations: National Association of Negro Musicians

NEW ORLEANS OPERA ASSOCIATION
333 Saint Charles Avenue, #907, New Orleans, LA 70130
(504) 529-2278; (504) 524-1018
FAX: (504) 529-7668
Founded: 1943
Arts Area: Grand Opera
Status: Professional; Non-Profit
Type: Performing; Resident; Educational
Purpose: To produce and present the finest in grand opera to Louisiana and the surrounding area
Management: Arthur G. Cosenza, General Director; Garold Whisler, Music Administrator/Chorus Master; Mollie B. Anderson, Senior Studio Administrator
Officers: Joseph Young Jr., President; H. Lloyd Hawkins Jr., Executive Vice President; John G. Panzeca, Treasurer; Owen Q. Niehaus, Secretary
Paid Staff: 10
Paid Artists: 300
Utilizes: Special Technical Talent; Guest Conductors; Guest Artists; Guest Directors
Budget: $1,000,000 - $5,000,000
Income Sources: Private Foundations/Grants/Endowments; Business/Corporate Donations; Box Office; Government Grants; Individual Donations
Season: October - March   **Annual Attendance:** 30,000
Performance Facilities: New Orleans Theatre of Performing Arts

WOMEN'S GUILD OF THE NEW ORLEANS OPERA ASSOCIATION
2504 Prytania Street, New Orleans, LA 70130
(504) 899-1945
Founded: 1942
Status: Professional; Non-Profit
Type: Educational; Sponsoring
Purpose: To support the New Orleans Opera Association through fund-raising; to educate
Officers: Veronica Porteous Scheinuk, President
Paid Staff: 1   **Volunteer Staff:** 10
Utilizes: Special Technical Talent; Guest Conductors; Guest Artists; Guest Directors
Budget: $100,000 - $500,000
Income Sources: Private Foundations/Grants/Endowments; Business/Corporate Donations; Box Office
Season: 52 Weeks

THEATRE

CONTEMPORARY ART CENTER
900 Camp Street, PO Box 30498, New Orleans, LA 70130
(504) 523-1216
FAX: (504) 528-3828
Founded: 1977
Arts Area: Professional; Theatrical Group
Status: Professional; Non-Profit
Type: Performing; Touring; Educational
Purpose: Contemporary Arts Center serves contemporary visual and performing artists and their audiences and provides exhibitions, performances, facilities, education and promotes development for artists in the community
Management: Annette Dimeo Carlozzi, Executive Director
Officers: Martha Jane Murray, President; Jan Gilbert, Vice President-Arts Policy; Thomas Mann, Vice President-Building; Bob Scott, Vice President-Corporate and Foundation Relations; Patricia Chandler, Vice President-Marketing; Nannette Smith-Goins, Vice President-Membership; Suzanne Mestayer, Treasurer; Barbara Lemann, Secretary
Paid Staff: 26   **Volunteer Staff:** 150
Paid Artists: 100
Utilizes: Guest Artists; Guest Directors
Budget: $500,000 - $1,000,000
Income Sources: Private Foundations/Grants/Endowments; Business/Corporate Donations; Box Office; Government Grants; Individual Donations
Season: 52 Weeks   **Annual Attendance:** 50,000
Affiliations: Arts Council of New Orleans
Performance Facilities: Contemporary Arts Center

JUNEBUG PRODUCTIONS INC.
1061 Camp Street, Suite D, New Orleans, LA 70130
(504) 524-8257
FAX: (504) 529-5403
Founded: 1980
Arts Area: Professional
Status: Professional; Non-Profit
Type: Performing; Touring; Educational; Sponsoring
Purpose: To support and inspire efforts to end the exploitation of people and the environment
Management: John O'Neal, Artistic Director; James B. Borders, Managing Director
Officers: Wallace Young, Chairman; John O'Neal, President; Lolis Elie, Vice President; Theresa Holden, Treasurer; John T. Scott, Secretary
Paid Staff: 4
Paid Artists: 4
Utilizes: Special Technical Talent; Guest Artists; Guest Directors; Guest Composers
Budget: $100,000 - $500,000
Income Sources: Private Foundations/Grants/Endowments; Business/Corporate Donations; Box Office; Government Grants; Individual Donations
Season: 52 Weeks   **Annual Attendance:** 40,000
Affiliations: Alternate ROOTS

UNIVERSITY OF NEW ORLEANS RESIDENT ACTING COMPANY
Lakefront, New Orleans, LA 70148
(504) 286-6317
FAX: (504) 286-6098
Founded: 1969
Arts Area: Professional
Status: Professional; Non-Profit
Type: Performing; Resident; Educational
Purpose: Create an ensemble theatrical, television and film performance group to assist in instruction of classes as well as represent the university in the community
Management: Phil Karnell, Managing Director
Officers: Dr. Kevin L. Graves, Chairman
Paid Staff: 3
Paid Artists: 7
Utilizes: Special Technical Talent; Guest Artists; Guest Directors
Budget: $1,000 - $50,000
Income Sources: Private Foundations/Grants/Endowments; Government Grants
Season: August - May   **Annual Attendance:** 8,000
Performance Facilities: University of New Orleans Performing Arts Center

PERFORMING SERIES

NEW ORLEANS JAZZ AND HERITAGE FESTIVAL
142 North Alexander Street, New Orleans, LA 70119
(504) 522-4786
FAX: (504) 522-5456
Founded: 1970
Arts Area: Festivals
Status: Non-Profit
Type: Performing
Purpose: To present and preserve Louisiana music and culture
Management: Quint Davis, Producer/Director
Paid Staff: 50
Paid Artists: 7,000
Budget: $1,000,000 - $5,000,000
Income Sources: Business/Corporate Donations; Box Office; Concession Sales; Sponsorship
Season: April - May   **Annual Attendance:** 300,000

FACILITY

LE PETIT THEATRE DU VIEUX CARRE
616 St. Peter Street, New Orleans, LA 70116
(504) 522-9958
Type of Facility: Theatre House
Type of Stage: Proscenium
Seating Capacity: 460
Year Built: 1797

LOYOLA UNIVERSITY - LOUIS J. ROUSSEL PERFORMANCE HALL
6363 St. Charles Avenue, New Orleans, LA 70118
(504) 865-2148
    Type of Facility: Concert Hall
    Type of Stage: Flexible
    Stage Dimensions: 50'x36' **Orchestra Pit**
    Seating Capacity: 592
    Year Built: 1985 **Architect:** The Mathes Group
    Acoustical Consultant: C.P. Boner and Associates
    Contact for Rental: Stewart Becnel; (504) 865-2148

LOYOLA UNIVERSITY - MARQUETTE THEATRE
6363 St. Charles Avenue, New Orleans, LA 70118
(504) 865-2170
    Type of Facility: Theatre House
    Type of Stage: Proscenium
    Seating Capacity: 155
    Contact for Rental: Ernest Ferlita, SJ

NEW ORLEANS MUNICIPAL AUDITORIUM
1201 St. Peter Street, New Orleans, LA 70016
(504) 565-7470
    Type of Facility: Auditorium
    Year Built: 1929 **Architect:** Mathes Bergman & Associates

NEW ORLEANS THEATRE OF THE PERFORMING ARTS
801 North Rampart, New Orleans, LA 70116
(504) 522-0592
    Type of Facility: Theatre House
    Type of Stage: Proscenium
    Stage Dimensions: 32'x60'x80' **Orchestra Pit**
    Seating Capacity: 2,316
    Year Built: 1973 **Architect:** William Bergman **Cost:** $7,000,000
    Acoustical Consultant: Bolt, Beranek & Newman
    Contact for Rental: Sharon Sheridan
    Resident Groups: New Orleans Philharmonic Symphony

ORPHEUM THEATER
129 University Place, New Orleans, LA 70112
(504) 524-3285
FAX: (504) 524-3286
    Type of Facility: Concert Hall; Multi-Purpose
    Type of Stage: Proscenium
    Stage Dimensions: 77'Wx45'D; 45'Wx27'H proscenium opening **Orchestra Pit**
    Seating Capacity: 1,925
    Year Built: 1921 **Architect:** G. Albert Landsburgh; Samuel Stone **Cost:** $600,000
    Year Remodeled: 1982 **Architect:** Jack Stewart **Cost:** $3,100,000
    Acoustical Consultant: Jaffe Acoustics
    Contact for Rental: Jeff Montalbano, General Manager; (504) 524-3285
    Manager: Peter Pfeil; (504) 524-3288
    Resident Groups: Louisiana Philharmonic Orchestra
Listed on the National Register of Historic Places, the Orpheum has the largest expanse of polychrome terra cotta on its facade in the city of New Orleans.

SAENGER PERFORMING ARTS CENTER
143 North Rampart, New Orleans, LA 70112
(504) 525-1052
FAX: (504) 569-1533
    Type of Facility: Performance Center; Theatre House
    Type of Stage: Proscenium
    Stage Dimensions: 81'9"Wx36'3"D; 51'9"Wx36'3"D proscenium opening **Orchestra Pit**
    Seating Capacity: 3,000
    Year Built: 1927 **Architect:** Emil Weil
    Year Remodeled: 1980 **Cost:** $1,500,000

Contact for Rental: Dale Harris;   (504) 525-1052
Manager: Marks Chowning;   (504) 525-1052

TULANE UNIVERSITY - ALBERT I. LUPIN MEMORIAL EXPERIMENTAL THEATRE
Brandt V.B. Dixon Performing Arts Center, New Orleans, LA 70118
(504) 865-5360
Type of Facility: Theatre Complex; Studio Performance; Arena; Multi-Purpose
Type of Stage: Flexible
Seating Capacity: 150
Year Built: 1984   **Architect:** George Leake & David Leake   **Cost:** $500,000
Acoustical Consultant: David Leake
Resident Groups: Tulane University Theatre; Center Stage at Tulane

UNIVERSITY OF NEW ORLEANS PERFORMING ARTS CENTER
Lakefront, New Orleans, LA 70148
(504) 286-6317
Type of Facility: Theatre Complex; Concert Hall; Studio Performance; Performance Center; Theatre House; Arena; Multi-Purpose
Type of Stage: Thrust; Flexible; Proscenium; Arena
Seating Capacity: 180
Year Built: 1972   **Architect:** Custis & Davis   **Cost:** $3,000,000
Resident Groups: UNO Video; Opera Workshop; Resident Acting Company; UNO Department of Music; UNO Department of Drama and Communications

---

Reserve

THEATRE

ST. JOHN THEATRE
103-205 West Fourth Street, Reserve, LA 70084
(504) 536-2410
Founded: 1931
Arts Area: Musical; Community
Status: Non-Professional; Non-Profit; Community
Type: Performing; Educational
Purpose: To provide live theatre to our community, especially to our schools and students
Management: Jack S. Snowdy, Managing Director
Officers: Lucien Cambre, President; Sterling Snowdy, Vice President; Donna Laurent, Secretary; Richard Oubre, Treasurer
Paid Staff: 2   **Volunteer Staff:** 10
Non-Paid Artists: 50
Utilizes: Special Technical Talent; Guest Artists; Guest Directors; High School Drama Departments
Budget: $1,000 - $50,000
Income Sources: Private Foundations/Grants/Endowments; Business/Corporate Donations; Box Office; Individual Donations
Season: 52 Weeks   **Annual Attendance:** 8,000
Performance Facilities: St. John Theatre Stage

Ruston

FACILITY

LOUISIANA TECH - HOWARD AUDITORIUM CENTER FOR THE PERFORMING ARTS
Arizona & Adams, PO Box 3033 T.S., Ruston, LA 71272
(318) 257-4109
Founded: 1945
Type of Facility: Auditorium; Performance Center; Theatre House; Opera House; Multi-Purpose
Type of Stage: Proscenium   **Orchestra Pit**
Seating Capacity: 1,126
Year Remodeled: 1982
Contact for Rental: David Wylie, Director;   (318) 257-4109

Shreveport

DANCE

SHREVEPORT METROPOLITAN BALLET
6040 Fairfield Avenue, Shreveport, LA 71106
(318) 865-8242
> **Founded:** 1973
> **Arts Area:** Ballet
> **Status:** Non-Professional; Non-Profit
> **Type:** Performing; Resident; Educational
> **Purpose:** An educational vehicle for area young people to learn and perform ballet
> **Management:** Marion Mills, Artistic Director
> **Non-Paid Artists:** 30
> **Utilizes:** Guest Artists; Guest Choreographers
> **Budget:** $1,000 - $50,000
> **Income Sources:** Private Foundations/Grants/Endowments; Business/Corporate Donations; Box Office; Government Grants; Individual Donations
> **Season:** September - June
> **Performance Facilities:** The Shreveport Civic Theatre

INSTRUMENTAL MUSIC

SHREVEPORT SYMPHONY ORCHESTRA
619 Louisiana Avenue, Suite 400, Shreveport, LA 71101
(318) 222-7496
FAX: (318) 222-7490
> **Founded:** 1947
> **Arts Area:** Symphony; Orchestra; Chamber; Ensemble
> **Status:** Professional; Non-Profit
> **Type:** Performing; Touring; Educational
> **Purpose:** To supply the three-state area with the highest possible quality musical performances
> **Management:** Cornelia Mason, General Manager; Jean Ellis, Director of Development; Peter Leonard, Music Director
> **Officers:** Sybil Patten, President; Robert Neff, Treasurer; Dr. Kathy Upham, Secretary
> **Paid Staff:** 8 **Volunteer Staff:** 130
> **Paid Artists:** 65
> **Utilizes:** Guest Conductors; Guest Artists
> **Budget:** $1,000,000 - $5,000,000
> **Income Sources:** Private Foundations/Grants/Endowments; Business/Corporate Donations; Box Office; Government Grants; Individual Donations
> **Season:** 52 Weeks **Annual Attendance:** 150,000
> **Affiliations:** ASOL
> **Performance Facilities:** Civic Theatre

VOCAL MUSIC

SHREVEPORT OPERA
212 Texas Street, Suite 101, Shreveport, LA 71101-3249
(318) 227-9503
> **Founded:** 1949
> **Arts Area:** Grand Opera; Lyric Opera; Light Opera; Operetta
> **Status:** Professional; Non-Profit
> **Type:** Performing; Touring; Resident; Educational
> **Purpose:** To provide professional music theatre to the region
> **Management:** Robert Murray, General Director
> **Officers:** Merritt B. Chastain Jr., President
> **Paid Staff:** 1 **Volunteer Staff:** 200
> **Paid Artists:** 423 **Non-Paid Artists:** 735
> **Utilizes:** Special Technical Talent; Guest Conductors; Guest Artists; Guest Directors
> **Budget:** $100,000 - $500,000
> **Income Sources:** Private Foundations/Grants/Endowments; Business/Corporate Donations; Box Office; Government Grants; Individual Donations; Guild Projects
> **Season:** Fall - Spring
> **Affiliations:** OA; NOA; Shreveport, Bossier Chambers of Commerce
> **Performance Facilities:** Shreveport Civic Theatre; Strand Theatre

THEATRE

THE GAS LIGHT PLAYERS
PO Box 271, Shreveport, LA 71162
(318) 635-8273
> **Founded:** 1959
> **Arts Area:** Theatrical Group
> **Status:** Non-Profit
> **Type:** Performing
> **Purpose:** Community theater whose primary performances will be early melodrama or original works of melodrama style
> **Officers:** C. Marvin Cox, President; George Sewell, Vice President; Nita Renshaw, Treasurer; Anna Aslin, Secretary
> **Volunteer Staff:** 15
> **Budget:** $1,000 - $50,000
> **Income Sources:** Private Foundations/Grants/Endowments; Business/Corporate Donations; Box Office; Individual Donations
> **Season:** June - October   **Annual Attendance:** 11,000

SHREVEPORT LITTLE THEATRE
812 Margaret Place, Shreveport, LA 71101
(318) 424-4439
> **Founded:** 1921
> **Arts Area:** Community
> **Status:** Non-Professional; Non-Profit
> **Type:** Performing; Touring
> **Purpose:** Committed to produce a variety of quality live theatre with predominantly volunteer participation from the community, with the guidance of trained artistic and managerial leadership, for entertainment, enlightenment and growth of audience awareness and pride
> **Management:** John C. Mitchell, Managing Director
> **Officers:** Paul Jordan, President
> **Paid Staff:** 1   **Volunteer Staff:** 30
> **Utilizes:** Guest Directors
> **Budget:** $100,000 - $500,000
> **Income Sources:** Private Foundations/Grants/Endowments; Business/Corporate Donations; Box Office; Individual Donations
> **Season:** September - July   **Annual Attendance:** 8,000

PERFORMING SERIES

THEATRE OF THE PERFORMING ARTS
400 North Dale Avenue, Shreveport, LA 71101
(318) 221-7964
> **Founded:** 1975
> **Arts Area:** Dance; Vocal Music; Instrumental Music; Theater; Festivals
> **Status:** Professional; Non-Profit
> **Type:** Performing; Touring; Sponsoring
> **Purpose:** Multi-discipline organization whose mission is to foster the culture of Afro-America
> **Management:** Gloria J. Christopher Gibson, Artistic Director/Founder
> **Officers:** Willie B. Meyers, President
> **Paid Staff:** 3
> **Utilizes:** Special Technical Talent; Guest Conductors; Guest Artists; Guest Directors
> **Budget:** $50,000 - $100,000
> **Income Sources:** Private Foundations/Grants/Endowments; Business/Corporate Donations; Box Office; Government Grants; Individual Donations
> **Season:** 52 Weeks
> **Affiliations:** Louisiana Black Culture Commission

FACILITY

CENTENARY COLLEGE - RECITAL HALL
Hurley School of Music, Shreveport, LA 71134
(318) 869-5235
> **Type of Facility:** Concert Hall
> **Type of Stage:** Proscenium
> **Seating Capacity:** 315
> **Year Built:** 1964
> **Resident Groups:** Camerata; Opera Theater; Symphony Orchestra; Wind Ensemble; Jazz Band

HIRSCH MEMORIAL COLISEUM
Louisiana State Fair, PO Box 9100, Shreveport, LA 71139-9100
(318) 635-1361
FAX: (318) 631-4909
> **Type of Facility:** Arena
> **Type of Stage:** Platform; Arena
> **Stage Dimensions:** 60'x40'
> **Seating Capacity:** 10,200
> **Year Built:** 1954   **Architect:** E.M. Freeman & Associates
> **Contact for Rental:** Cecil M. Faries;   (318) 635-1361

SHREVEPORT CIVIC THEATRE
400 Clyde Fant Parkway, Shreveport, LA 71101
(318) 673-5100
FAX: (318) 673-5100
> **Type of Facility:** Theatre House
> **Facility Originally:** Meeting Hall; Movie House
> **Type of Stage:** Proscenium
> **Stage Dimensions:** 49'8"Wx23'5"D   **Orchestra Pit**
> **Seating Capacity:** 1,737
> **Year Built:** 1965   **Architect:** Somdal, Sorenson, Smitherman & Associates
> **Acoustical Consultant:** Local 298 IATSE
> **Contact for Rental:** Sharron Killen;   (318) 673-5100
> **Manager:** James B. Hobbs Jr.;   (318) 673-5100
> **Resident Groups:** Shreveport Metropolitan Ballet; Shreveport Symphony; Shreveport Opera

SHREVEPORT MUNICIPAL AUDITORIUM
705 Grand Avenue, Shreveport, LA 71101
(318) 673-5100
FAX: (318) 673-5100
> **Founded:** 1929
> **Type of Facility:** Theatre Complex; Auditorium; Off Broadway; Theatre House; Opera House; Arena; Multi-Purpose
> **Facility Originally:** Meeting Hall
> **Type of Stage:** Proscenium
> **Stage Dimensions:** 58'5"Wx37'5"D
> **Seating Capacity:** 3,293
> **Year Built:** 1928   **Architect:** Weiner
> **Acoustical Consultant:** Local 298 IATSE
> **Contact for Rental:** Sharron Killen;   (318) 673-5100
> **Manager:** James B. Hobbs Jr.;   (318) 673-5100

STRAND THEATRE
619 Louisiana Avenue, PO Box 1547, Shreveport, LA 71165-1547
(318) 226-2924
> **Type of Facility:** Concert Hall; Theatre House
> **Type of Stage:** Proscenium
> **Stage Dimensions:** 35'Dx80'W; 44'Wx27'H proscenium opening   **Orchestra Pit**
> **Seating Capacity:** 1,640
> **Year Built:** 1925   **Architect:** Emil Weil   **Cost:** $850,000
> **Year Remodeled:** 1984   **Architect:** Haas & Massey Architects   **Cost:** $4,300,000
> **Acoustical Consultant:** C.P. Boner & Associates
> **Contact for Rental:** Craig Young;   (318) 226-1481
> **Resident Groups:** Shreveport Symphony

MAINE

Augusta

INSTRUMENTAL MUSIC

AUGUSTA SYMPHONY
PO Box 481, Augusta, ME 04330
(207) 622-5998
>**Founded:** 1920
>**Arts Area:** Symphony; Band
>**Status:** Non-Professional; Non-Profit
>**Type:** Performing
>**Purpose:** To present concerts; to hold rehearsals
>**Officers:** Lynne Burney, President; Timothy Paulin, Vice President; Joan Passle, Secretary; Robert McGuire, Treasurer
>**Volunteer Staff:** 24
>**Paid Artists:** 1   **Non-Paid Artists:** 180
>**Budget:** $1,000 - $50,000
>**Income Sources:** Box Office; Individual Donations
>**Season:** September - June   **Annual Attendance:** 4,000

PERFORMING SERIES

NEW MUSIK DIRECTIONS
67 Green Street, Augusta, ME 04330
(207) 623-1941
>**Founded:** 1981
>**Arts Area:** Festivals
>**Status:** Professional; Commercial
>**Type:** Performing; Educational; Sponsoring
>**Purpose:** To provide a vehicle for the performance of new music, film and video
>**Management:** Joseph Baltar, Director
>**Paid Staff:** 1
>**Utilizes:** Guest Artists
>**Budget:** $1,000 - $50,000
>**Income Sources:** Private Foundations/Grants/Endowments; Business/Corporate Donations; Box Office; Government Grants; Individual Donations
>**Season:** 52 Weeks   **Annual Attendance:** 500

FACILITY

AUGUSTA CIVIC CENTER
Community Drive, Augusta, ME 04330
(207) 626-2405
FAX: (207) 626-5968
>**Type of Facility:** Civic Center; Multi-Purpose
>**Year Built:** 1973   **Architect:** Bunker & Savage   **Cost:** $4,000,000
>**Year Remodeled:** 1978   **Cost:** $3,500,000
>**Acoustical Consultant:** Canfield
>**Contact for Rental:** Bob Howard;   (207) 626-2405
>*The Civic Center contains the Arena and North Hall, a 1978 addition to the Center. See individual listings for additional information.*

AUGUSTA CIVIC CENTER - ARENA
Community Drive, Augusta, ME 04330
(207) 626-2405
FAX: (207) 626-5968
>**Founded:** 1973
>**Type of Facility:** Arena
>**Type of Stage:** Flexible; Platform
>**Stage Dimensions:** 40'x60'
>**Seating Capacity:** Full House - 6,800; Half House - 3,000
>**Year Built:** 1973
>**Contact for Rental:** Bob Howard;   (207) 626-2405

AUGUSTA CIVIC CENTER - NORTH HALL
Community Drive, Augusta, ME 04330
(207) 626-2405
FAX: (207) 626-5968
Type of Facility: Multi-Purpose; Room
Type of Stage: Platform
Stage Dimensions: 20'x20'
Seating Capacity: 500
Year Remodeled: 1978   **Cost:** $3,500,000
Contact for Rental: Bob Howard;   (207) 626-2405

Bangor

INSTRUMENTAL MUSIC

BANGOR SYMPHONY ORCHESTRA
PO Box 1441, Bangor, ME 04401
(207) 942-5555
FAX: (207) 942-9278
Founded: 1896
Arts Area: Symphony; Orchestra; Chamber; Ensemble
Status: Professional; Non-Profit
Type: Performing; Touring; Resident; Sponsoring
Purpose: As the oldest community orchestra in the United States offering continuous service at the community level, the Bangor Symphony Orchestra performs for local audiences as well as on tour.
Management: Robert Bahr, General Manager; Werner Torkanowsky, Music Director/Conductor
Paid Staff: 3   **Volunteer Staff:** 200
Paid Artists: 80   **Non-Paid Artists:** 2
Utilizes: Guest Conductors; Guest Artists; Guest Directors
Budget: $100,000 - $500,000
Income Sources: Private Foundations/Grants/Endowments; Business/Corporate Donations; Box Office; Government Grants; Individual Donations
Season: September - May
Affiliations: ASOL; Greater Bangor Arts Council
Performance Facilities: Bangor Opera House

THEATRE

PENOBSCOT THEATRE COMPANY
183 Main Street, Bangor, ME 04401
(207) 942-3333
Founded: 1974
Arts Area: Professional
Status: Professional; Non-Profit
Type: Performing; Touring; Resident; Sponsoring
Purpose: To provide a resident regional theatre for the Bangor Area; to host and support local arts organizations; to broaden the area's cultural life and activities
Management: Mark Torres, Producing/Artistic Director
Paid Staff: 4   **Volunteer Staff:** 4
Paid Artists: 8   **Non-Paid Artists:** 8
Utilizes: Special Technical Talent; Guest Artists; Guest Directors
Budget: $50,000 - $100,000
Income Sources: Business/Corporate Donations; Box Office; Government Grants; Individual Donations
Season: October - March   **Annual Attendance:** 10,000

FACILITY

BANGOR AUDITORIUM
100 Dutton Street, Bangor, ME 04401
(207) 942-9000
FAX: (207) 947-5105
Type of Facility: Auditorium; Arena
Type of Stage: Arena
Stage Dimensions: 40'x60'; sound wings available
Seating Capacity: 7,000
Year Built: 1953   **Architect:** Eaton/Tarbell   **Cost:** $1,400,000
Contact for Rental: Kurt Rogerson;   (207) 942-9000

BANGOR CIVIC CENTER
100 Dutton Street, Bangor, ME 04401
(207) 942-9000
FAX: (207) 947-5105
Type of Facility: Civic Center
Type of Stage: Flexible; Platform
Stage Dimensions: 40'x60'; sound wings available
Seating Capacity: 1,600
Year Built: 1978 **Architect:** Eaton/Tarbell **Cost:** $1,225,000
Contact for Rental: Kurt Rogerson;   (207) 942-9000

Bar Harbor

PERFORMING SERIES

ARCADY MUSIC SOCIETY
PO Box 780, Bar Harbor, ME 04609
(207) 288-3151
Founded: 1981
Arts Area: Vocal Music; Instrumental Music; Festivals
Status: Professional; Non-Profit
Type: Performing; Educational; Sponsoring
Purpose: To bring high-quality classical and contemporary music to central, northern, and Downeast Maine through live performances, with an emphasis on chamber music and programs for young people
Management: Masanobu Ikemiya, Artistic Director; Melba Wilson, Executive Director
Officers: Etel Thomas, President; Marie Nolb, First Vice President; John Hoelter, Secretary; Richard Fox, Treasurer
Paid Staff: 4 **Volunteer Staff:** 50
Utilizes: Guest Conductors; Guest Artists
Budget: $100,000 - $500,000
Income Sources: Private Foundations/Grants/Endowments; Business/Corporate Donations; Box Office; Government Grants; Individual Donations
Season: 52 Weeks **Annual Attendance:** 3,000
Affiliations: CMA

BAR HARBOR MUSIC FESTIVAL
The Rodick Building, 59 Cottage Street, Bar Harbor, ME 04609
(207) 288-5744
Founded: 1967
Arts Area: Vocal Music; Instrumental Music; Festivals; New Composers
Status: Professional; Non-Profit
Type: Performing; Touring; Resident; Educational; Sponsoring
Purpose: To create performance opportunities for young artists through an annual summer festival and tours
Management: Francis Fortier, Artistic Director
Officers: Francis Fortier, President; J. Philip Benkard, Vice President
Paid Staff: 6 **Volunteer Staff:** 10
Paid Artists: 30
Utilizes: Special Technical Talent; Guest Conductors; Guest Artists
Budget: $100,000 - $500,000
Income Sources: Private Foundations/Grants/Endowments; Business/Corporate Donations; Box Office; Government Grants; Individual Donations
Season: July - August **Annual Attendance:** 10,000
Performance Facilities: Congregational Church; Kebo Valley Golf Club Auditorium

Brunswick

THEATRE

MAINE STATE MUSIC THEATER
PO Box 656, Brunswick, ME 04011
(207) 725-8769
FAX: (207) 725-1199
Founded: 1959
Arts Area: Professional; Summer Stock; Musical
Status: Professional; Non-Profit
Type: Performing; Resident; Educational

Purpose: To educate young theatre professionals; to present quality musical theatre; to preserve the American musical
Management: Chuck Abbott, Artistic Director; Billings Lapierre, General Manager
Officers: Janet Wilk, President; Thomas Pierce, Vice President; Sara McMahan, Secretary; Peter Chandler, Treasurer
Paid Staff: 50   **Volunteer Staff:** 35
Paid Artists: 25   **Non-Paid Artists:** 15
Utilizes: Special Technical Talent; Guest Artists; Guest Directors
Budget: $500,000 - $1,000,000
Income Sources: Box Office; Individual Donations
Season: June - August   **Annual Attendance:** 45,000
Affiliations: AEA

FACILITY

PICKARD THEATRE
Memorial Hall, Bowdoin College, Brunswick, ME 04011
(207) 725-3000; (207) 725-1199
Type of Facility: Theatre House
Facility Originally: School
Type of Stage: Proscenium
Stage Dimensions: 52'Wx35'D   **Orchestra Pit**
Seating Capacity: 600
Year Built: 1865   **Architect:** Stanford White
Year Remodeled: 1955
Resident Groups: Brunswick Summer Music Theater; Maine State Music Theater

Camden

PERFORMING SERIES

BAY CHAMBER CONCERTS
PO Box 191, Camden, ME 04843
(207) 236-2823
Founded: 1960
Arts Area: Instrumental Music
Status: Professional
Type: Performing
Purpose: To encourage the appreciation of music, especially chamber music, in the state of Maine
Management: Thomas Wolf, Artistic Director; Jean Freedman, Administrative Director
Officers: Marvin Garner, President; Bill May, Vice President; Carroll Roberts Jr., Secretary; Steve McAllister, Treasurer
Paid Staff: 2
Utilizes: Guest Artists
Budget: $50,000 - $100,000
Income Sources: Private Foundations/Grants/Endowments; Business/Corporate Donations; Box Office; Government Grants; Individual Donations
Season: July - May   **Annual Attendance:** 5,700
Performance Facilities: Rockport Opera House

FACILITY

CAMDEN OPERA HOUSE
29 Elm Street, Camden, ME 04843
(207) 236-3353
Type of Facility: Concert Hall
Type of Stage: Proscenium
Stage Dimensions: 25'x20'x15'   **Orchestra Pit**
Seating Capacity: 550
Year Built: 1893   **Cost:** $40,000
Year Remodeled: 1930
Contact for Rental: Nancy Hayes;   (207) 236-3353
Resident Groups: Camden Civic Theatre

Freeport

THEATRE

FIGURES OF SPEECH THEATRE
Rural Route 4, PO Box 4277, Freeport, ME 05032
(207) 865-6355
Management: Carol Llewelyn
Season: 52 Weeks

Hancock

PERFORMING SERIES

THE PIERRE MONTEUX SCHOOL
Route 1, PO Box 157, Hancock, ME 04640
(207) 422-3931
FAX: (207) 422-9122
Founded: 1943
Arts Area: Instrumental Music; Symphony
Status: Professional; Non-Profit
Type: Performing; Educational
Purpose: To acquaint young conductors and future orchestra musicians with the full symphonic repertoire
Management: Nancie Monteux-Barendse, Administrative President; Michael Jinbo, Marc David, Assistant Conductors; Charles Bruck, Director/Maestro
Paid Staff: 2
Budget: $50,000 - $100,000
Income Sources: Private Foundations/Grants/Endowments; Business/Corporate Donations; Government Grants; Individual Donations
Season: June - July   **Annual Attendance:** 1,200

Lewiston

PERFORMING SERIES

BATES DANCE FESTIVAL
Lane Hall, Bates College, Lewiston, ME
(207) 786-6077
FAX: (207) 786-6123
Founded: 1982
Arts Area: Dance
Status: Professional
Type: Resident; Educational; Sponsoring
Purpose: To support education, performance and the creation of new works by providing a non-competitive, high-quality dance program
Management: Laura Faure, Director; Larissa Vigue, Administrative Assistant; Linda Stimpson, Development Assistant
Paid Staff: 4   **Volunteer Staff:** 8
Paid Artists: 40
Utilizes: Special Technical Talent; Guest Artists; Guest Choreographers
Budget: $100,000 - $500,000
Income Sources: Private Foundations/Grants/Endowments; Business/Corporate Donations; Box Office; Government Grants; Individual Donations
Season: July - August   **Annual Attendance:** 3,000
Performance Facilities: Schaeffer Theatre

LA ARTS
234 Lisbon Street, Lewiston, ME 04210
(207) 782-7228
Founded: 1973
Arts Area: Dance; Vocal Music; Instrumental Music; Theater; Festivals
Status: Professional; Non-Profit
Type: Performing; Educational; Sponsoring
Purpose: To integrate the arts into the fabric of everyday life in central Maine
Management: Katherine Knowles, Executive Director
Paid Staff: 4
Paid Artists: 40

Budget: $100,000 - $500,000
Income Sources: Private Foundations/Grants/Endowments; Business/Corporate Donations; Box Office; Government Grants; Individual Donations
Season: September - June   **Annual Attendance:** 12,000
Affiliations: APAP; Maine Arts Sponsor Association

FACILITY

BATES COLLEGE - CONCERT HALL
Olin Arts Center, Lewiston, ME 04240
(207) 786-6255
Type of Facility: Concert Hall
Type of Stage: Semicircular
Stage Dimensions: 40'Wx24'D
Seating Capacity: 300
Manager: Mark Howard;   (207) 786-6135

BATES COLLEGE - OLIN ARTS CENTER
Lewiston, ME 04240
(207) 786-6255
Type of Facility: Studio Performance; Performance Center; Multi-Purpose
Year Built: 1986   **Architect:** The Architects Collaborative   **Cost:** $4,300,000
Acoustical Consultant: Cavanaugh Tocci Associates
Manager: Mark Howard;   (207) 786-6135
Resident Groups: Bates College activities

Machias

PERFORMING SERIES

MACHIAS BAY CHAMBER CONCERTS, INC.
PO Box 332, Machias, ME 04654
Founded: 1969
Arts Area: Instrumental Music
Status: Professional; Non-Profit
Type: Sponsoring
Purpose: To present chamber music concerts; to encourage music appreciation; to perform in schools and the community
Officers: Dorothy Day, President; Mrs. Wallace Greenwood, Vice President; Mrs. Hollis Ingalls, Secretary; Richard Shaw, Treasurer
Volunteer Staff: 20
Utilizes: Guest Artists
Income Sources: Private Foundations/Grants/Endowments; Business/Corporate Donations; Box Office; Government Grants; Individual Donations
Season: July - August   **Annual Attendance:** 1,000
Affiliations: Maine Art Sponsors Association

STAGE FRONT: THE ARTS DOWNEAST
University of Maine, O'Brien Avenue, Machias, ME 04654
(207) 255-3313
FAX: (207) 255-4864
Founded: 1969
Arts Area: Dance; Vocal Music; Instrumental Music; Theater; Festivals; Children's Program
Status: Non-Profit
Type: Performing; Educational; Sponsoring
Purpose: Stage Front is the arts organization of the University of Maine at Machias. It presents all areas of the visual and performing arts.
Management: Joan Chamberlain, Program Coordinator for Performing Arts
Paid Staff: 2   **Volunteer Staff:** 25
Utilizes: Special Technical Talent; Guest Artists
Budget: $1,000 - $50,000
Income Sources: Business/Corporate Donations; Box Office; Government Grants; Individual Donations
Season: September - May   **Annual Attendance:** 5,000
Affiliations: Maine Arts Sponsors; New Brunswick Arts Council
Performance Facilities: Powers Hall/Performing Arts Center

FACILITY

UNIVERSITY OF MAINE AT MACHIAS - STAGE FRONT
The Arts Downeast, #9 O'Brien Avenue, Machias, ME 04654
(207) 255-3313
>   **Type of Facility:** Concert Hall; Auditorium; Performance Center; Theatre House
>   **Facility Originally:** Recreation Hall; Gymnasium
>   **Type of Stage:** Thrust; Proscenium
>   **Stage Dimensions:** Proscenium - 40'x17'; Thrust - 40'x18'
>   **Seating Capacity:** 400
>   **Year Built:** 1936 **Architect:** Bunker & Savage
>   **Year Remodeled:** 1982 **Architect:** Alonzo J. Harriman **Cost:** $125,000
>   **Acoustical Consultant:** Alonzo J. Harriman & Associates
>   **Manager:** Joan Chamberlain, Director; (207) 255-3314
>   **Resident Groups:** The Bad Little Falls Players

Monmouth

THEATRE

THE THEATER AT MONMOUTH
Main Street, PO Box 385, Monmouth, ME 04259
(207) 933-2952
>   **Founded:** 1969
>   **Arts Area:** Professional; Summer Stock; Theatrical Group
>   **Status:** Professional; Non-Profit
>   **Type:** Performing; Touring; Resident; Educational
>   **Purpose:** To offer a classical repertory season; to present educational productions utilizing the plays of Shakespeare during the school year; to sponsor special events and children's productions
>   **Management:** Richard C. Sewell, Artistic Director; M. George Carlson, Managing Director; Christopher Rock, Associate Artistic Director
>   **Officers:** Edward N. Hersley, President; Ralph Conant, Vice President; Jeff Smith, Treasurer; Robert V. Schauer, Executive Producer
>   **Paid Staff:** 40 **Volunteer Staff:** 20
>   **Paid Artists:** 20 **Non-Paid Artists:** 5
>   **Utilizes:** Special Technical Talent; Guest Artists; Guest Directors
>   **Budget:** $100,000 - $500,000
>   **Income Sources:** Private Foundations/Grants/Endowments; Business/Corporate Donations; Box Office; Government Grants; Individual Donations
>   **Season:** June - August **Annual Attendance:** 12,000
>   **Affiliations:** TCG; NETC; Maine Arts Sponsors Association
>   **Performance Facilities:** Cumston Hall

FACILITY

CUMSTON HALL
Main Street, PO Box 385, Monmouth, ME 04259
(207) 933-2952
>   **Type of Facility:** Theatre House; Opera House
>   **Facility Originally:** Library; Meeting Hall; Theater; Town Office
>   **Type of Stage:** Thrust; Proscenium
>   **Seating Capacity:** 275
>   **Year Built:** 1900 **Architect:** Harry Cochrane
>   **Resident Groups:** The Theater at Monmouth
>   *Available for rent in winter only*

Northeast Harbor

PERFORMING SERIES

MOUNT DESERT FESTIVAL OF CHAMBER MUSIC
Neighborhood House, PO Box 862, Northeast Harbor, ME 04662
(212) 362-1870
>   **Founded:** 1963
>   **Arts Area:** Festivals
>   **Status:** Professional
>   **Type:** Resident

Purpose: To present a series of five Tuesday-evening concerts using the Composers String Quartet as a nucleus and guest artists
Paid Staff: 2
Paid Artists: 28
Utilizes: Guest Artists
Budget: $1,000 - $50,000
Income Sources: Box Office; Individual Donations
Season: July - August   **Annual Attendance:** 1,500
Performance Facilities: Neighborhood House

Ogunquit-by-the-Sea

THEATRE

OGUNQUIT PLAYHOUSE
PO Box 915, Ogunquit-by-the-Sea, ME 03907
(207) 646-2402
Founded: 1933
Arts Area: Professional
Status: Professional; Commercial
Type: Sponsoring
Management: John Lane, Producer
Paid Staff: 30
Paid Artists: 150
Income Sources: Box Office
Season: June - September   **Annual Attendance:** 55,000
Performance Facilities: Ogunquit Playhouse

FACILITY

OGUNQUIT PLAYHOUSE
PO Box 915, Ogunquit-by-the-Sea, ME 03907
(207) 646-2402
Type of Facility: Theatre House
Type of Stage: Proscenium
Stage Dimensions: 18'x34'x50'   **Orchestra Pit**
Seating Capacity: 750
Year Built: 1932   **Architect:** Wycoft   **Cost:** $100,000

Orono

THEATRE

MARSH ISLAND STAGE
37 Penobscot Street, Orono, ME 04473
(207) 866-5647
Founded: 1984
Arts Area: Theatrical Group
Status: Non-Profit
Type: Performing
Purpose: To bring contemporary playwrights' works to Maine
Management: Christopher Bates, Artistic Director; Susan Camp, Graphic Arts
Officers: Dick Brucher, Carlene Hirsch, Chris Luthin, Board of Directors
Volunteer Staff: 12
Utilizes: Guest Directors
Budget: $1,000 - $50,000
Income Sources: Box Office; Individual Donations
Season: September - June   **Annual Attendance:** 1,000
Performance Facilities: The Ram's Horn

THEATRE OF THE ENCHANTED FOREST
PO Box 336, Orono, ME 04473
(207) 945-0800
Founded: 1974
Arts Area: Professional; Theatrical Group; Family
Status: Professional; Non-Profit
Type: Performing; Touring; Resident; Educational; Sponsoring

Purpose: To bring Maine families the very best that live theatre has to offer; to respect the intelligence and integrity of all audience members, no matter what age; to provide theatre that is not simple-minded nor condescending, but poses plausible dilemmas

Management: Christopher E. Rock, Artistic Director; Sandra Zuk Cyrus, Producing Director; Bronwyn W. Kortge, Associate Producer

Officers: Carol Woodcock, President; Adrian Humphreys, Vice President; Nancy Grover, Secretary; Sandy Ervin, Treasurer

Paid Staff: 3

Paid Artists: 15

Utilizes: Special Technical Talent; Guest Artists; Guest Directors

Budget: $50,000 - $100,000

Income Sources: Business/Corporate Donations; Box Office; Government Grants; Individual Donations

Season: November - July   **Annual Attendance:** 2,500

Performance Facilities: Pavilion Theatre, University of Maine at Orono

FACILITY

UNIVERSITY OF MAINE - MAINE CENTER FOR THE ARTS
Orono, ME 04469
(207) 581-1805

Type of Facility: Concert Hall; Auditorium; Performance Center; Theatre House; Opera House

Type of Stage: Flexible; Proscenium

Stage Dimensions: 70'x30'   **Orchestra Pit**

Seating Capacity: 1,628

Year Built: 1986   **Architect:** Eaton W. Tarbell   **Cost:** $7,500,000

Acoustical Consultant: Bolt, Beranek & Newman

Contact for Rental: John I. Patches;   (207) 581-1805

Portland

DANCE

RAM ISLAND DANCE
25A Forest Avenue, Portland, ME 04101
(207) 773-2562

Arts Area: Modern; Ballet; Inter-arts

Status: Non-Profit

Type: Performing; Touring; Resident; Educational

Purpose: To promote contemporary dance; to support artists living and working in the region

Management: Daniel McCusker, Artistic Director/Choreographer; Linda Pervier, Managing Director

Officers: Sandra I. Lovell, Board President

Budget: $1,000 - $50,000

Income Sources: Private Foundations/Grants/Endowments; Business/Corporate Donations; Box Office; Government Grants; Individual Donations

INSTRUMENTAL MUSIC

LARK SOCIETY FOR CHAMBER MUSIC
PO Box 11, Portland, ME 04112
(207) 761-1522

Arts Area: Chamber; Ensemble

Status: Professional

Type: Performing; Touring; Resident; Educational

Purpose: To support and present a Portland concert series as well as educational presentations by the Portland String Quartet

Management: Barbara Duff Management

Officers: Nancy Aldrich, Executive Director

Paid Staff: 1

Paid Artists: 4

Utilizes: Guest Artists

Budget: $50,000 - $100,000

Income Sources: Private Foundations/Grants/Endowments; Business/Corporate Donations; Box Office; Government Grants; Individual Donations

Season: 52 Weeks
Affiliations: CMA

PORTLAND SYMPHONY ORCHESTRA
30 Myrtle Street, Portland, ME 04111
(207) 773-8191
FAX: (207) 773-6089
Founded: 1924
Arts Area: Symphony; Orchestra
Status: Non-Profit
Type: Performing
Management: Jane E. Hunter, Executive Director
Paid Staff: 10
Utilizes: Guest Artists
Budget: $1,000,000 - $5,000,000
Income Sources: Private Foundations/Grants/Endowments; Business/Corporate Donations; Box Office; Government Grants; Individual Donations
Season: October - April; July
Performance Facilities: Portland City Hall Auditorium

THEATRE

PORTLAND STAGE COMPANY
25A Forest Avenue, Box 1458, Portland, ME 04104
(207) 774-1043
FAX: (207) 774-0576
Founded: 1974
Arts Area: Professional; Theatrical Group
Status: Professional; Non-Profit
Type: Performing; Resident; Educational
Purpose: To produce and develop high-quality work and programs that explore basic human issues and concerns, the purpose of which is to entertain, educate, and engage the audience
Management: Greg Leaming, Artistic Director; William Chance, Managing Director
Officers: Peggy Siegle, President; Margaret Pusch, Vice President of Administration; A. Leroy Greason, Vice President of Development; Deborah Locke, Secretary; Robert F. Wade, Treasurer
Paid Staff: 26   Volunteer Staff: 150
Paid Artists: 45
Utilizes: Special Technical Talent; Guest Artists; Guest Directors
Budget: $500,000 - $1,000,000
Income Sources: Private Foundations/Grants/Endowments; Business/Corporate Donations; Box Office; Government Grants; Individual Donations
Season: November - May   Annual Attendance: 42,000
Affiliations: LORT; TCG
Performance Facilities: Portland Performing Arts Center

PERFORMING SERIES

THE MAINE FESTIVAL
582 Congers Street, Portland, ME 04101
(207) 772-9012
FAX: (207) 772-3995
Founded: 1977
Arts Area: Dance; Vocal Music; Instrumental Music; Theater; Festivals
Status: Professional; Non-Profit
Type: Sponsoring
Purpose: To provide artistic opportunities and to encourage the advancement of the performing and the visual arts in Maine through the presentation of a public program of services to artists
Management: Burl Hash, Artistic Director; Diane Briggs, Fund-raising Coordinator; Bruce Hazard, Executive Director
Paid Staff: 7   Volunteer Staff: 300
Paid Artists: 1,000
Utilizes: Guest Artists
Budget: $500,000 - $1,000,000
Income Sources: Private Foundations/Grants/Endowments; Business/Corporate Donations; Box Office; Government Grants; Individual Donations
Season: August - September   Annual Attendance: 30,000
Affiliations: Bowdoin College; APAP
Performance Facilities: Portland Performing Arts Center; Thomas Point Beach

PORTLAND PERFORMING ARTS CENTER, INC.
25A Forest Avenue, Portland, ME 04101
(207) 761-0591
FAX: (207) 761-0576
  Arts Area: Vocal Music; Instrumental Music
  Status: Professional; Non-Profit
  Type: Performing
  Purpose: To support alternative artists, primarily traditional and ethnic performers but also international artists
  Management: Phyllis O'Neill, Executive Director; Bau Graves, Artistic Director
  Officers: Everett Ingalls, Chairman
  Budget: $100,000 - $500,000
  Income Sources: Private Foundations/Grants/Endowments; Business/Corporate Donations; Box Office; Government Grants; Individual Donations
  Performance Facilities: Portland Performing Arts Center

FACILITY

CUMBERLAND COUNTY CIVIC CENTER
1 Civic Center Square, Portland, ME 04101
(207) 775-3481
FAX: (207) 828-1920
  Type of Facility: Civic Center; Arena
  Type of Stage: Arena
  Seating Capacity: 9,500
  Year Built: 1977   **Architect:** Eduardo Catalano   **Cost:** $6,000,000
  Contact for Rental: Steven Rosenblatt;   (207) 775-3481

PORTLAND EXPOSITION BUILDING
239 Park Avenue, Portland, ME 04102
(207) 874-8200
FAX: (207) 874-8130
  Type of Facility: Arena
  Type of Stage: Arena
  Seating Capacity: 3,000
  Year Built: 1915   **Cost:** $3,000,000
  Year Remodeled: 1983   **Cost:** $300,000
  Acoustical Consultant: Bolt, Beranek & Newman
  Contact for Rental: Frank P. LaTorre;   (207) 874-8200
  Concerts, ballet, theatre, environmental

PORTLAND PERFORMING ARTS CENTER
25A Forest Avenue, Portland, ME 04101
(207) 761-0591
  Type of Facility: Theatre Complex; Studio Performance; Performance Center; Theatre House
  Facility Originally: Meeting Hall; Movie House
  Type of Stage: Thrust; Proscenium
  Stage Dimensions: 31'x21'
  Seating Capacity: 290
  Year Remodeled: 1983   **Architect:** Winton Scott Associates
  Contact for Rental: Manager;   (207) 761-0591

Rockport

FACILITY

ROCKPORT OPERA HOUSE - TOWN OF ROCKPORT
Central Street, PO Box 10, Rockport, ME 04856
(207) 236-9648
  Type of Facility: Concert Hall; Auditorium; Theatre House; Opera House
  Type of Stage: Proscenium
  Stage Dimensions: 22'x24'
  Seating Capacity: 400
  Year Built: 1891
  Year Remodeled: 1972
  Contact for Rental: Nancy Dowling;   (207) 236-9648, ext. 22
  Resident Groups: Bay Chamber Concerts Inc.; Rockport Folk Festival

---
South Paris

FACILITY

CELEBRATION BARN THEATER
RD 1, PO Box 236, Stockfarm Road, South Paris, ME 04281
(207) 743-8452
> **Founded:** 1972
> **Type of Facility:** Theatre Complex; Outdoor (Concert); Studio Performance; Theater School
> **Type of Stage:** Proscenium
> **Seating Capacity:** 100-125
> **Year Built:** 1902
> **Year Remodeled:** 1989
> **Contact for Rental:** Carolyn Brett;   (207) 743-8452
> *The theater is used primarily for workshops and other theater-related activities as well as small conferences.*

Waterville

FACILITY

COLBY COLLEGE - GIVEN AUDITORIUM
Waterville, ME 04901
(207) 872-3000
FAX: (207) 872-3555
> **Type of Facility:** Auditorium
> **Type of Stage:** Proscenium
> **Seating Capacity:** 397
> **Year Built:** 1950
> **Resident Groups:** Colby College musical organizations

MARYLAND

Annapolis

DANCE

BALLET THEATRE OF ANNAPOLIS
PO Box 3311, Annapolis, MD 21403
(410) 263-2909
Founded: 1978
Arts Area: Ballet
Status: Professional; Non-Profit
Type: Touring; Resident
Management: Edward Stewart, Artistic Director; Deboran H. Harris, General Manager
Paid Artists: 14   **Non-Paid Artists:** 27
Utilizes: Guest Artists; Guest Choreographers
Budget: $1,000,000 - $5,000,000
Income Sources: Box Office; Individual Donations
Season: December - January; April - May
Performance Facilities: Maryland Hall for the Creative Arts

VOCAL MUSIC

ANNAPOLIS OPERA
PO Box 24, Annapolis, MD 21404
(410) 267-8135
Founded: 1973
Arts Area: Grand Opera; Light Opera; Operetta
Status: Professional; Non-Professional; Non-Profit
Type: Performing; Educational
Purpose: To present light and grand opera, thus contributing to the educational, cultural and artistic development of the community
Officers: Harry Lindauer, President; Jean Jackson, Vice President; Marie Hampton, Recording Secretary
Volunteer Staff: 10
Paid Artists: 40   **Non-Paid Artists:** 30
Utilizes: Guest Conductors; Guest Artists; Guest Directors
Budget: $100,000 - $500,000
Income Sources: Private Foundations/Grants/Endowments; Business/Corporate Donations; Box Office; Government Grants; Individual Donations
Season: September - May   **Annual Attendance:** 4,500
Performance Facilities: Annapolis Senior High School; Maryland Hall

FACILITY

FRANCIS SCOTT KEY AUDITORIUM
60 College Avenue, Annapolis, MD 21401
(410) 626-2547
FAX: (410) 263-4828
Type of Facility: Theatre Complex; Auditorium
Seating Capacity: 600
Year Built: 1960
Year Remodeled: 1989
Contact for Rental: Jeanette Hoffman;   (410) 626-2547

MARYLAND HALL FOR THE CREATIVE ARTS
801 Chase Street, Annapolis, MD 21401
(410) 263-5544
FAX: (410) 263-5114
Founded: 1979
Type of Facility: Auditorium; Multi-Purpose; Recital Halls; Meeting Space; Galleries
Facility Originally: School
Type of Stage: Proscenium
Stage Dimensions: 30'x40'
Seating Capacity: 855
Year Built: 1932
Year Remodeled: 1980   **Architect:** Riggs Architecture   **Cost:** $3,500,000
Acoustical Consultant: Bolt, Beranek & Newman

Contact for Rental: Denise Bailey-Jackson;   (410) 263-5544
Resident Groups: Maryland Hall Story Theatre; Ballet Theatre of Annapolis; Annapolis Symphony Orchestra; Annapolis Chorale

---

Arnold

INSTRUMENTAL MUSIC

BRASS CHAMBER MUSIC SOCIETY OF ANNAPOLIS
PO Box 161, Arnold, MD 21012
(410) 235-4302
FAX: (410) 235-4302
Founded: 1980
Arts Area: Chamber; Ensemble; Instrumental Group
Status: Non-Profit
Type: Performing; Educational; Sponsoring
Purpose: To promote brass chamber music through concert series and educational outreach programs
Officers: George Rinehart, Chair; Joan Machinchick, Secretary; Maria Coughlin, Treasurer; Robert Posten, Artistic Director
Volunteer Staff: 8
Utilizes: Guest Artists
Budget: $1,000 - $50,000
Income Sources: Private Foundations/Grants/Endowments; Business/Corporate Donations; Box Office; Government Grants; Individual Donations
Season: October - May   **Annual Attendance:** 1,460
Performance Facilities: Anne Arundel Community College

Baltimore

DANCE

BALTIMORE DANCE THEATRE
c/o Auty Associates, 15 Charles Plaza, Suite 306, Baltimore, MD 21201
(410) 685-1313
FAX: (410) 997-3899
Founded: 1975
Arts Area: Modern
Status: Professional; Commercial
Type: Performing; Touring
Purpose: The Baltimore Dance Theatre, the performing group of the Eva Anderson Dancers, sponsors a professional dance company presenting modern ballets.
Management: Auty Associates; Eva Anderson, Artistic Director
Paid Staff: 1
Paid Artists: 8
Utilizes: Guest Artists; Guest Choreographers
Budget: $100,000 - $500,000
Income Sources: Private Foundations/Grants/Endowments; Business/Corporate Donations; Box Office; Government Grants; Individual Donations
Season: 52 Weeks

DOWNTOWN DANCE COMPANY
TSU 8000 York Road, Baltimore, MD 21204-7083
(410) 830-3369
Founded: 1986
Arts Area: Modern; Ballet
Status: Professional; Non-Profit
Type: Sponsoring
Purpose: To present the best new work being created in the modern, ballet and movement theatre genres
Management: Claire Braswell, Managing Director
Officers: Bryon Mollica, Chairman
Paid Staff: 2   **Volunteer Staff:** 20
Budget: $50,000 - $100,000
Income Sources: Private Foundations/Grants/Endowments; Business/Corporate Donations; Box Office; Government Grants; Individual Donations; Program Advertisements
Season: September - May   **Annual Attendance:** 4,000
Affiliations: Baltimore Area Contemporary Arts Presenters
Performance Facilities: Stephens Hall Theatre

THE MARYLAND BALLET
PO Box 26150, Baltimore, MD 21210
(410) 467-8495
>**Founded:** 1986
>**Arts Area:** Ballet
>**Status:** Professional; Non-Profit
>**Type:** Performing; Touring; Resident; Educational; Sponsoring
>**Purpose:** To present the finest in classical ballet as the resident professional ballet company of Maryland
>**Management:** Phillip B. Carman, Artistic Director; Daniel J. Kane, Executive Director
>**Paid Staff:** 4 **Volunteer Staff:** 13
>**Paid Artists:** 28 **Non-Paid Artists:** 4
>**Utilizes:** Special Technical Talent; Guest Conductors; Guest Artists; Guest Choreographers
>**Budget:** $100,000 - $500,000
>**Income Sources:** Private Foundations/Grants/Endowments; Business/Corporate Donations; Box Office; Government Grants; Individual Donations
>**Season:** 52 Weeks **Annual Attendance:** 35,000
>**Performance Facilities:** The Lyric Opera House

INSTRUMENTAL MUSIC

BALTIMORE SYMPHONY ORCHESTRA
1212 Cathedral Street, Baltimore, MD 21201
(410) 783-8100
FAX: (410) 783-8077; (410) 783-8078
>**Founded:** 1916
>**Arts Area:** Symphony
>**Status:** Professional
>**Type:** Performing
>**Management:** John Gidwitz, Executive Director; George Alexsovich, General Manager; Patricia Purcell, Director of Development and Community Affairs; Paul Dupree, Director of Marketing and Publications; Thomas D. May, Finance Director
>**Officers:** Geaorge V. McGowan, Chairman of the Board; Calman J. Zamoisky, President/Chief Executive Officer
>**Paid Staff:** 32 **Volunteer Staff:** 100
>**Paid Artists:** 100
>**Utilizes:** Guest Conductors; Guest Artists
>**Budget:** Over 10,000,000
>**Income Sources:** Private Foundations/Grants/Endowments; Business/Corporate Donations; Box Office; Government Grants; Individual Donations
>**Season:** 52 Weeks **Annual Attendance:** 350,000
>**Affiliations:** ASOL; AAA
>**Performance Facilities:** Joseph Meyerhoff Symphony Hall

CHAMBER MUSIC SOCIETY OF BALTIMORE
2909 Woodvalley Drive, Baltimore, MD 21208
(410) 486-1140
>**Founded:** 1949
>**Arts Area:** Chamber; Ensemble; Electronic & Live Electronic
>**Status:** Professional; Non-Profit
>**Type:** Performing; Educational; Sponsoring
>**Purpose:** To present the finest chamber artists performing a mixture of standard repertory and new work, concentrating on contemporary American pieces
>**Management:** Anthony Stark, Managing Director; Robert Hall Lewis, Music Director
>**Officers:** Randolph S. Rothschild, President; Gordon Cyr, Vice President
>**Paid Staff:** 1 **Volunteer Staff:** 20
>**Non-Paid Artists:** 1
>**Utilizes:** Guest Artists
>**Budget:** $1,000 - $50,000
>**Income Sources:** Private Foundations/Grants/Endowments; Business/Corporate Donations; Box Office; Government Grants; Individual Donations
>**Season:** Autumn - Spring **Annual Attendance:** 2,000
>**Performance Facilities:** Baltimore Museum of Art; Joseph Meyerhoff Symphony Hall

GETTYSBURG SYMPHONY ORCHESTRA
4707 Renwick Avenue, Baltimore, MD 21206
(410) 458-4011
>**Founded:** 1958
>**Arts Area:** Symphony; Orchestra
>**Status:** Professional; Non-Profit

Type: Performing; Educational
Purpose: To produce educational concerts for youth as well as full symphonic performances for adults
Management: Raphael Faraco, Conductor/Music Director and Manager
Officers: John Renneberg, President; Daniel S. Sullivan Jr., Treasurer/Secretary; Charles A. Bodie Jr.; Z. John Levay MD
Budget: $1,000 - $50,000
Income Sources: Private Foundations/Grants/Endowments
Performance Facilities: Loch Raven Senior High School Auditorium

VOCAL MUSIC

BALTIMORE CHORAL ARTS SOCIETY
1316 Park Avenue, Baltimore, MD 21217
(410) 523-7070
Founded: 1966
Arts Area: Choral
Status: Semi-Professional; Non-Profit
Type: Performing; Touring; Educational; Sponsoring
Purpose: To present classical and choral music at the highest professional level
Management: Tom Hall, Music Director; Mary Schretlen, Executive Director; Nancy Hall, Development Director
Officers: John H. Laporte, President; Anita Kreeger, Vice President; Wes Poling, Treasurer; M. Carter Warren, Secretary
Paid Staff: 4 **Volunteer Staff:** 2
Paid Artists: 60 **Non-Paid Artists:** 70
Utilizes: Guest Conductors; Guest Artists; Guest Emsembles
Budget: $100,000 - $500,000
Income Sources: Private Foundations/Grants/Endowments; Business/Corporate Donations; Box Office; Government Grants; Individual Donations; Run Outs
Season: October - May **Annual Attendance:** 9,000
Performance Facilities: Joseph Meyerhoff Symphony Hall; Kraushaar Auditorium

BALTIMORE MEN'S CHORUS
1 East Pratt Street, Baltimore, MD 21202
(410) 547-8610
Founded: 1984
Arts Area: Choral
Status: Non-Profit
Type: Performing
Management: William Garrison, Music Director
Officers: George Rogers, President; Robert Greenfield, Vice President; Stephen Phillips, Secretary; Alan Baumgarten, Treasurer
Volunteer Staff: 5
Non-Paid Artists: 33
Utilizes: Special Technical Talent; Guest Artists
Budget: $1,000 - $50,000
Income Sources: Individual Donations
Season: September - June **Annual Attendance:** 2,000

BALTIMORE OPERA COMPANY
101 West Read Street, Suite 605, Baltimore, MD 21201
(410) 727-0592
FAX: (410) 727-7854
Founded: 1950
Arts Area: Grand Opera; Lyric Opera
Status: Professional; Non-Profit
Type: Performing; Touring; Educational
Purpose: To produce the highest level of artistic performance within our economic means; to educate the public, particularly the youth
Management: Michael Harrison, General Manager; Patricia Elizabeth McMahon, Director of Public Relations and Marketing; William Yannuzzi, Music Director
Officers: Lowell R. Bowen, Chairman; John R. Young, President
Paid Staff: 15 **Volunteer Staff:** 125
Paid Artists: 400
Utilizes: Special Technical Talent; Guest Conductors; Guest Artists; Guest Directors
Budget: $1,000,000 - $5,000,000
Income Sources: Private Foundations/Grants/Endowments; Business/Corporate Donations; Box Office; Government Grants; Individual Donations
Season: October - April **Annual Attendance:** 21,000

Affiliations: OA
Performance Facilities: Lyric Opera House

BALTIMORE SYMPHONY CHORUS
c/o Baltimore Symphony Orchestra Inc., 1212 Cathedral Street, Baltimore, MD 21201
(410) 783-8100
FAX: (410) 783-8077
Arts Area: Choral
Status: Non-Profit; Volunteer
Type: Performing
Purpose: The choir is the choral arm of the Baltimore Symphony and performs when the Symphony needs singers.
Management: Edward Polochick, Director; Felice Homann, Manager
Officers: Richard Holland, Chorus Representative
Budget: $50,000 - $100,000
Income Sources: Private Foundations/Grants/Endowments; Business/Corporate Donations; Box Office; Government Grants; Individual Donations
Performance Facilities: Joseph Meyerhoff Symphony Hall

THEATRE

ARENA PLAYERS
801 McCulloh Street, Baltimore, MD 21201
(410) 728-6500
FAX: (410) 728-6515
Founded: 1953
Arts Area: Community; Theatrical Group
Status: Non-Professional; Non-Profit
Type: Performing; Touring; Educational
Purpose: To discover, foster and showcase talent from the community
Management: Samuel H. Wilson, Artistic Director; Gerald Catus, Managing Director; Catherine B. Orange, Youth Program Director
Officers: Quentin Lawson, Chairman of the Board; Dr. Hilbert Stanley, Vice Chairman, Advisory Board
Utilizes: Guest Artists; Guest Directors
Income Sources: Private Foundations/Grants/Endowments; Business/Corporate Donations; Box Office; Government Grants; Individual Donations
Season: September - August
Affiliations: NEA; Maryland State Arts Council; Mayor's Committee

BALTIMORE ACTORS' THEATRE, INC.
The Dumbarton House, 300 Dumbarton Road, Baltimore, MD 21212
(410) 337-8519
Founded: 1959
Arts Area: Musical; Dinner; Theatrical Group; Children's
Status: Semi-Professional; Non-Profit
Type: Performing; Touring; Educational
Purpose: To teach and perform the arts on a professional level
Management: Helen M. Grigal, Artistic Director; Walter E. Anderson, Executive Director
Officers: Helen M. Grigal, President; Walter E. Anderson, Vice President; Victor L. Grigal, Secretary/Treasurer
Paid Staff: 20 **Volunteer Staff:** 100
Budget: $100,000 - $500,000
Income Sources: Private Foundations/Grants/Endowments; Box Office; Individual Donations
Season: 52 Weeks

CENTER STAGE
700 North Calvert Street, Baltimore, MD 21202
(410) 685-3200
FAX: (410) 539-3912
Founded: 1963
Arts Area: Professional; Theatrical Group
Status: Professional; Non-Profit
Type: Performing; Resident; Educational
Purpose: Center Stage is the official theatrical company of Maryland
Management: Peter Culman, Managing Director; Irene Lewis, Artistic Director
Paid Staff: 40 **Volunteer Staff:** 100
Paid Artists: 54
Utilizes: Guest Artists; Guest Directors
Budget: $1,000,000 - $5,000,000

Income Sources: Private Foundations/Grants/Endowments; Business/Corporate Donations; Box Office; Government Grants; Individual Donations
Season: September - June   **Annual Attendance:** 80,023
Performance Facilities: Center Stage

CHILDREN'S THEATER ASSOCIATION
121 McMechen Street, Baltimore, MD 21217
(410) 225-0052
   Founded: 1943
   Arts Area: Children's Theatre
   Status: Professional; Non-Profit
   Type: Performing; Touring; Educational
   Purpose: To stimulate the creativity of young minds through theatre performances and creative drama classes
   Management: Kevin R. Daly, Managing Director; Roz Byus, Administrative Assistant
   Officers: Linda Dalsimer, President; Clarence Shelley, Vice President of Special Events; Marley Willard, Vice President of Education; Dorothy Potts, Vice President of Finance; Deborah Dickerson, Secretary; Jeffrey Collier, Treasurer
   Paid Staff: 3
   Paid Artists: 27   **Non-Paid Artists:** 200
   Budget: $100,000 - $500,000
   Income Sources: Private Foundations/Grants/Endowments; Business/Corporate Donations; Box Office; Government Grants; Individual Donations
   Season: October - June   **Annual Attendance:** 110,000

THEATRE PROJECT
45 West Preston Street, Baltimore, MD 21201
(410) 539-3091
   Founded: 1971
   Arts Area: Musical; Theatrical Group; Puppet
   Status: Professional; Non-Profit
   Type: Sponsoring
   Purpose: To support national and international new works and innovative forms of expression; to continue as the entry point for international performing companies; to further promote new performance opportunities for them throughout North America
   Management: Philip Arnoult, Director
   Paid Staff: 5   **Volunteer Staff:** 100
   Paid Artists: 100
   Utilizes: Guest Artists
   Budget: $100,000 - $500,000
   Income Sources: Private Foundations/Grants/Endowments; Business/Corporate Donations; Box Office; Government Grants; Individual Donations
   Season: September - May   **Annual Attendance:** 23,500
   Affiliations: TCG; International Theatre Institute; Towson State University
   Performance Facilities: Theatre Project

PERFORMING SERIES

YOUNG AUDIENCES OF MARYLAND
927 North Calvert Street, Baltimore, MD 21202
(410) 837-7577
   Founded: 1950
   Arts Area: Dance; Vocal Music; Instrumental Music; Theater; Lyric Opera
   Status: Professional; Non-Profit
   Type: Performing; Educational; Sponsoring
   Purpose: To present performing arts-in-education programs in schools and elsewhere throughout the community to both children and adults—Young Audiences of Maryland presents 1,100 programs to 300,000 people annually
   Management: Patricia M. Thomas, Executive Director
   Officers: Dr. Michael L. Mark, President; E. Scott Johnson, Donna Hamilton, Vice Presidents; Helen M. Schlossberg Cohen, Secretary; Eric M. Pripstein, Treasurer
   Paid Staff: 5   **Volunteer Staff:** 20
   Paid Artists: 98
   Utilizes: Guest Artists
   Budget: $100,000 - $500,000
   Income Sources: Private Foundations/Grants/Endowments; Business/Corporate Donations; Government Grants; Individual Donations
   Season: 52 Weeks   **Annual Attendance:** 300,000
   Affiliations: Maryland Alliance for Arts Education; National Young Audiences

FACILITY

ARENA PLAYERS
801 McCulloh Street, Baltimore, MD 21201
(410) 728-6500
FAX: (410) 728-6515
Type of Facility: Auditorium; Theatre House; Arena; Multi-Purpose
Facility Originally: Warehouse
Type of Stage: Thrust; Platform; Arena
Seating Capacity: 300
Year Remodeled: 1973   **Architect:** Bridges & Trionfo   **Cost:** $10,000
Contact for Rental: Gerard W. Catus;   (410) 728-6500
Resident Groups: Arena Players; Youtheater; Main Stage Performers; Studio 801; The Road Company

BALTIMORE MUSEUM OF ART - AUDITORIUM
Art Museum Drive, Baltimore, MD 21218
(410) 396-7100
FAX: (410) 396-6562
Type of Facility: Auditorium; Multi-Purpose
Type of Stage: Proscenium
Stage Dimensions: 36'Wx33'D
Seating Capacity: 375
Year Remodeled: 1982   **Architect:** Bower Lewis & Thrower
Acoustical Consultant: Frink & Beuchat
Contact for Rental: Deborah Tunney;   (410) 396-6314
Resident Groups: Baltimore Film Forum; Pro Musica Rara; Chamber Music Society of Baltimore
The Auditorium was built as part of the 1982 expansion/renovation program of the museum. Total cost of this project was $13,500,000.

CENTER STAGE
700 North Calvert Street, Baltimore, MD 21202
(410) 685-3200
FAX: (410) 539-3912
Founded: 1963
Type of Facility: Theatre House
Facility Originally: School
Type of Stage: Thrust; Flexible; Proscenium; Flexible Stage & Seating in Head Theater
Stage Dimensions: 54'Wx11'D, add 6'D for thrust
Orchestra Pit
Seating Capacity: 541 - Flexible
Year Built: 1866
Year Remodeled: 1975   **Architect:** James Grieves, Roger Morgan   **Cost:** $1,800,000
Year of Head Theatre Renovation: 1991   **Architect:** Ziger, Hoopes & Snead
Contact for Rental: Joe Rooney;   (301) 685-3200
Resident Groups: Center Stage, The State Theatre of Maryland
Two stages - Pearlstone and Head Theaters

DUNBAR PERFORMING ARTS CENTER
1400 Orleans Street, Baltimore, MD 21231
(410) 396-9474
Type of Facility: Concert Hall; Performance Center; Theatre House
Seating Capacity: 800
Year Built: 1974   **Architect:** Cochran Stephenson Donkervoert
Contact for Rental: Charlotte Dunbar, Principal, Dunbar High School;   (410) 396-9478
Resident Groups: Urban Services Cultural Arts Program

THE JOHNS HOPKINS UNIVERSITY - THE MERRICK BARN
3400 North Charles Street, Baltimore, MD 21218
(410) 516-7159
Type of Facility: Theatre House
Facility Originally: Barn
Type of Stage: Proscenium
Stage Dimensions: 14'x28'
Seating Capacity: 106
Year Built: 1803
Year Remodeled: 1982
Resident Groups: Theatre Hopkins
Redesigned as a theatre in the 1920's

LYRIC INC./LYRIC OPERA HOUSE
1404 Maryland Avenue, Baltimore, MD 21201
(410) 685-5086
FAX: (410) 332-8234
Founded: 1894
Type of Facility: Concert Hall; Auditorium; Performance Center; Off Broadway; Opera House
Type of Stage: Proscenium
Stage Dimensions: 30'x50'x36'   **Orchestra Pit**
Seating Capacity: 2,564
Year Built: 1894   **Architect:** Griffin & Randall
Year Remodeled: 1992   **Architect:** Richter Cornbrooks Gribble, Inc.   **Cost:** $22,500,000
Contact for Rental: Robert M. Pomory, President;   (410) 685-5087
Manager: John T. Kroneberger;   (410) 685-5086
Resident Groups: Baltimore Opera Company

THEATRE PROJECT
45 West Preston Street, Baltimore, MD 21201
(410) 539-3091
FAX: (410) 539-2137
Type of Facility: Performance Center
Facility Originally: Meeting Hall; Movie House
Type of Stage: Flexible
Stage Dimensions: 37'Wx37'Dx21'H
Seating Capacity: 157
Year Built: 1896
Year Remodeled: 1984   **Architect:** Gould Associates   **Cost:** $2,000,000
Contact for Rental: Robert Mrozek;   (410) 539-3091
Short-term rentals only, not available for long-run productions

---

Bowie

FACILITY

BOWIE STATE COLLEGE - MARTIN LUTHER KING JR., COMMUNICATION ARTS CENTER
Bowie, MD 20715
(301) 464-3441
Founded: 1865
Type of Facility: Auditorium
Type of Stage: Proscenium
Orchestra Pit
Seating Capacity: 1,000
Year Built: 1973   **Architect:** Anthony Johns   **Cost:** $5,200,000
Contact for Rental: Dr. Amos White IV, Department of Humanities & Fine Arts;   (301) 464-7286

Chevy Chase

VOCAL MUSIC

CHILDREN'S OPERA THEATER
3203 Pickwick Lane, Chevy Chase, MD 20815
(301) 656-2442
Founded: 1976
Arts Area: Light Opera; Choral
Status: Professional; Non-Profit
Type: Touring; Educational
Purpose: To introduce and involve young people in opera; to provide employment opportunities for artists in the transitional phase of their careers from apprentice to professional
Management: Michael Kaye, Artistic Director
Paid Staff: 6
Paid Artists: 20
Budget: $50,000 - $100,000
Income Sources: Private Foundations/Grants/Endowments; Business/Corporate Donations; Individual Donations
Season: 52 Weeks   **Annual Attendance:** 20,000

College Park

PERFORMING SERIES

MARYLAND HANDEL FESTIVAL
University of Maryland, College Park, MD 20742
(301) 405-5571
Founded: 1981
Arts Area: Vocal Music; Instrumental Music; Theater; Festivals
Status: Non-Profit
Type: Performing; Educational
Purpose: To focus on the music of Handel; to foster research into Handel and 18th-century topics; to practice performing in the style of that period
Management: Jesse Parker, General Manager/Artistic Staff; Paul Traver, Artistic Director; Howard Serwer, Associate Director
Season: 52 Weeks

UNIVERSITY OF MARYLAND INTERNATIONAL PIANO FESTIVAL AND WILLIAM KAPELL COMPETITION
Summer Programs, University of Maryland, College Park, MD 20740
(301) 454-5276
FAX: (301) 314-9572
Founded: 1971
Arts Area: Instrumental Music; Festivals
Status: Non-Profit
Type: Educational; Sponsoring
Purpose: To sponsor a major biennial international festival featuring master classes, lecture-recitals, recitals, symposia and the William Kapell Piano Competition
Management: George Moquin, Executive Director
Utilizes: Guest Artists
Budget: $100,000 - $500,000
Income Sources: Private Foundations/Grants/Endowments; Business/Corporate Donations; Box Office; Individual Donations
Season: July
Affiliations: University of Maryland
Performance Facilities: Tawes Fine Arts Center

Columbia

DANCE

EVA ANDERSON DANCERS LTD.
5452 High Tor Hill, Columbia, MD 21045
(410) 997-3899
FAX: (410) 730-7411
Founded: 1974
Arts Area: Modern; Ethnic
Status: Professional
Type: Performing; Touring; Educational
Purpose: To create dance based on the American experience with special emphasis on African-American experiences
Management: Eva Anderson, Artistic Director; Yvette Shipley, Assistant Artistic Director
Officers: Doris Williams, President; Ernest Miller, Vice President; Yvette Shipley, Secretary; Troy Burman, Treasurer
Paid Staff: 2 **Volunteer Staff:** 5
Paid Artists: 10
Utilizes: Special Technical Talent; Guest Artists; Guest Choreographers
Budget: $50,000 - $100,000
Income Sources: Private Foundations/Grants/Endowments; Business/Corporate Donations; Box Office; Government Grants; Individual Donations
Season: September - July

PERFORMING SERIES

CANDLELIGHT CONCERT SOCIETY, INC.
5829 Banneker Road, Columbia, MD 21044
(410) 720-1027; (301) 596-6203
Founded: 1974
Arts Area: Vocal Music; Instrumental Music; Chamber Music; Children
Status: Professional; Non-Profit

Type: Performing; Sponsoring
Purpose: To present the finest chamber music artists available to audiences of central Maryland
Management: Bonita J. Bush, Managing Director
Officers: Charles E. Thomas, Acting President of the Board; Will Cook, Secretary of the Board
Paid Staff: 1   **Volunteer Staff:** 150
Utilizes: Guest Artists
Budget: $100,000 - $500,000
Income Sources: Private Foundations/Grants/Endowments; Business/Corporate Donations; Box Office; Government Grants; Individual Donations
Season: October - May   **Annual Attendance:** 15,000
Affiliations: CMA
Performance Facilities: Smith Theatre, Howard Community College

COLUMBIA FESTIVAL, INC.
9861 Broken Land Parkway, Suite 300, Columbia, MD 21117
(410) 381-0520
FAX: (401) 381-4530
Founded: 1988
Arts Area: Dance; Vocal Music; Instrumental Music; Theater; Festivals
Status: Non-Profit
Type: Presenting
Purpose: To present a variety of art forms and to make these accessible to the public
Management: Lynne Nemeth, Managing Director; Donald Hicken, Artistic Director; Alexandria Lippincott, Assistant Managing Director
Officers: Padraic M. Kennedy, President; Jean F. Moon, Vice President; Lynne Nemeth, Secretary; Richard G. McCauley Esq., Treasurer; Harvey B. Steinman Esq., Counsel
Paid Staff: 17   **Volunteer Staff:** 400
Paid Artists: 450
Utilizes: Special Technical Talent; Guest Artists
Budget: $500,000 - $1,000,000
Income Sources: Private Foundations/Grants/Endowments; Business/Corporate Donations; Box Office; Government Grants; Individual Donations
Season: June - July   **Annual Attendance:** 30,000
Performance Facilities: Merriweather Post Pavilion

FACILITY

TOBY'S DINNER THEATRE
PO Box 1003, Columbia, MD 21044
(410) 730-8311
Type of Facility: Dinner Theatre
Type of Stage: Arena
Stage Dimensions: 20'x20'   **Orchestra Pit**
Seating Capacity: 360
Year Built: 1968
Year Remodeled: 1981

Fort Washington

FACILITY

JOHN ADDISON CONCERT HALL
Harmony Hall Regional Center, 10701 Livingston Road, Fort Washington, MD 20744
(301) 292-8331
FAX: (301) 292-7856
Founded: 1989
Type of Facility: Concert Hall; Performance Center; Multi-Purpose
Facility Originally: School
Type of Stage: Proscenium
Stage Dimensions: 37'x41'
Seating Capacity: 209
Year Built: 1965
Year Remodeled: 1989   **Cost:** $1,900,000

Contact for Rental: Dr. Carolyn Bock; (301) 292-8331
Resident Groups: Stratford Chamber Players; Monumental Brass Quintet; Heritage Singers

---

Hagerstown

INSTRUMENTAL MUSIC

MARYLAND SYMPHONY ORCHESTRA
12 Rochester Place, Hagerstown, MD 21740
(301) 797-4000
> **Founded:** 1982
> **Arts Area:** Symphony
> **Status:** Professional
> **Type:** Performing
> **Management:** Cassandra Wantz, Managing Director; Carolyn Bryant, Operations Manager; Barbara Wetzel, Marketing Director; Kathleen Dayhoff, Secretary
> **Paid Staff:** 4
> **Paid Artists:** 150
> **Utilizes:** Special Technical Talent; Guest Conductors; Guest Artists
> **Budget:** $500,000 - $1,000,000
> **Income Sources:** Private Foundations/Grants/Endowments; Business/Corporate Donations; Box Office; Government Grants; Individual Donations
> **Season:** October - March   **Annual Attendance:** 45,000
> **Affiliations:** ASOL
> **Performance Facilities:** Maryland Theatre

THEATRE

MARYLAND THEATRE
21 South Potomac Street, Hagerstown, MD 21740-5512
(301) 790-3500
FAX: (301) 791-6114
> **Founded:** 1976
> **Arts Area:** Professional; Musical; Community; Theatrical Group
> **Status:** Non-Profit
> **Type:** Performing; Touring; Sponsoring
> **Purpose:** To restore and maintain this historic structure and present the performing arts
> **Management:** Paul A. Frank III, Executive Director; Barbara L. Cushwa, Box Office Manager; Donna DeWitt, Administrative Assistant; Michael J. Snabley, Stage Manager
> **Officers:** Susan Elliot, President; Mary Dabbwa, Vice President of Programming; Suzanne Kass, Secretary; Jim Baker, Treasurer
> **Paid Staff:** 4   **Volunteer Staff:** 100
> **Utilizes:** Special Technical Talent; Guest Artists
> **Budget:** $500,000 - $1,000,000
> **Income Sources:** Private Foundations/Grants/Endowments; Business/Corporate Donations; Box Office; Government Grants; Individual Donations
> **Season:** 52 Weeks   **Annual Attendance:** 70,000
> **Performance Facilities:** The Maryland Theatre

FACILITY

MARYLAND THEATRE
21 South Potomac Street, Hagerstown, MD 21740-5512
(301) 790-3500
FAX: (301) 791-6114
> **Type of Facility:** Theatre House
> **Facility Originally:** Vaudeville
> **Type of Stage:** Modified Apron Proscenium
> **Stage Dimensions:** 66'Wx39'D with 15'D apron; 33'9"Wx25'H proscenium opening   **Orchestra Pit**
> **Seating Capacity:** 1,403
> **Year Built:** 1915   **Architect:** Thomas Lamb   **Cost:** $200,000
> **Year Remodeled:** 1976   **Cost:** $1,500,000
> **Contact for Rental:** Paul Frank; (301) 790-3500
> **Resident Groups:** Maryland Symphony Orchestra; Miss Maryland Scholarship Pageant; Community Concerts
> *The Maryland Theatre has been designated a National Historic Landmark.*

Laurel
THEATRE

PETRUCCI'S DINNER THEATRE
312 Main Street, Laurel, MD 20707
(301) 725-5226
Founded: 1977
Arts Area: Dinner
Status: Commercial
Type: Performing
Management: C. David Petrucci, Angela Jo Leonard, Producers
Paid Staff: 7
Paid Artists: 20
Budget: $1,000 - $50,000
Income Sources: Box Office
Season: 52 Weeks **Annual Attendance:** 40,000
Affiliations: NDTA

Mt. Rainier
DANCE

THE FIDDLE PUPPET DANCERS
PO Box 207, Mt. Rainier, MD 20712
(301) 277-5915
FAX: (301) 277-5915
Founded: 1979
Arts Area: Percussive Dance
Status: Professional
Type: Performing
Purpose: To perform percussive dances including tap, step dancing and clogging, in the U.S. and abroad
Management: Laura Lewis, Manager; Eileen Carson, Artistic Director; New Music Times - Agent
Paid Staff: 2
Paid Artists: 7
Utilizes: Special Technical Talent; Guest Artists
Budget: $50,000 - $100,000
Income Sources: Private Foundations/Grants/Endowments; Box Office; Individual Donations
Season: March - November **Annual Attendance:** 500,000

Ocean City
FACILITY

OCEAN CITY CONVENTION CENTER
4001 Coastal Highway, Ocean City, MD 21863
(410) 289-8311
Type of Facility: Auditorium; Civic Center; Arena; Multi-Purpose; Room
Facility Originally: Meeting Hall; Movie House
Type of Stage: Proscenium
Stage Dimensions: 40'x60'
Seating Capacity: 3600
Year Built: 1969 **Cost:** $3,000,000
Contact for Rental: Bob Rothermel; (410) 289-8311

Olney
THEATRE

OLNEY THEATRE/NATIONAL PLAYERS
2001 Olney-Sandy Spring Road, Olney, MD 20832
(301) 924-4485
Founded: 1952
Arts Area: Professional; Summer Stock
Status: Professional; Non-Profit
Type: Performing; Touring; Educational

Management: James A. Petosh, General Manager; Bill Graham Jr., Managing Director
Officers: William H. Graham, President; Harry Teter, Vice President; William P. Roche, Secretary/Treasurer
Paid Staff: 30 **Volunteer Staff:** 120
Paid Artists: 70
Budget: $1,000,000 - $5,000,000
Income Sources: Private Foundations/Grants/Endowments; Business/Corporate Donations; Box Office; Government Grants; Individual Donations
Season: May - November **Annual Attendance:** 70,000
Affiliations: AEA; SSDC
Performance Facilities: Olney Theatre

Rockville

INSTRUMENTAL MUSIC

NATIONAL CHAMBER ORCHESTRA SOCIETY, INC.
15209 Frederick Road, Suite 207, Rockville, MD 20850
(301) 762-8580
Arts Area: Orchestra; Chamber
Status: Professional; Non-Profit
Type: Resident
Purpose: To cultivate an appreciation for great classical music through concerts and programs
Management: Wing Chi-Chan, Executive Director; Piotr Ghaewski, Conductor/Music Director
Officers: Robert Bourne, President of the Board
Budget: $100,000 - $500,000
Income Sources: Private Foundations/Grants/Endowments; Business/Corporate Donations; Box Office; Government Grants; Individual Donations
Performance Facilities: Duke Ellington School of the Arts; F. Scott Theatre

FACILITY

KREEGER FINE ARTS AUDITORIUM
6125 Montrose Road, Rockville, MD 20852
(301) 881-0100
Type of Facility: Auditorium
Type of Stage: Proscenium
Stage Dimensions: 35'Wx30'Dx30'H; 30'Wx16'H proscenium opening
Seating Capacity: 300
Year Built: 1969
Contact for Rental: Felice Kornberg; (301) 881-0100
Resident Groups: Jewish Community Center Orchestra; Center Dance Ensemble; Kinor Dance Troup; Washington Jewish Theatre

Salisbury

FACILITY

WICOMICO YOUTH AND CIVIC CENTER
500 Glen Avenue, Salisbury, MD 21801
(410) 548-4906
FAX: (410) 546-0490
Type of Facility: Civic Center; Arena; Multi-Purpose
Type of Stage: Arena
Seating Capacity: 6,800
Year Built: 1980 **Cost:** $13,000,000
Contact for Rental: Robert C. Wagoner; (410) 548-4906

Silver Spring

DANCE

AMERICAN YOUTH BALLET COMPANY
10111 Colesville Road, Suite 112, Silver Spring, MD 20901
(301) 587-7807
Founded: 1991
Arts Area: Ballet

Status: Non-Professional; Non-Profit
Type: Performing; Resident
Management: Lauri Dickmann, Artistic Director
Non-Paid Artists: 30
Utilizes: Guest Artists; Guest Choreographers
Budget: $1,000 - $50,000
Income Sources: Private Foundations/Grants/Endowments; Box Office; Individual Donations
Season: September - July

THEATRE

ROUND HOUSE THEATRE
12210 Bushey Drive, Silver Spring, MD 20902
(301) 217-6770
FAX: (301) 217-6819
Founded: 1978
Arts Area: Professional; Theatrical Group
Status: Professional; Non-Profit
Type: Performing; Touring; Resident; Educational
Purpose: To engage and envolve the community by addressing contemporary social issues through a wide range of entertaining and provocative theatre experiences; to offer audiences, students and professionals rewarding experiences in live theatre and related educational activities
Management: Tony Elliot, Producing Associate; Barbara Payne, Production Office Manager; Jerry B. Whiddon, Artistic Director; Frank Kirby, Box Office Manager; Geri Olsen, Director of Public Relations
Officers: Jeff Davis, President; Andy Zvara, Vice President; Nancee Simonson, Treasurer
Paid Staff: 12   **Volunteer Staff:** 150
Paid Artists: 45
Utilizes: Special Technical Talent; Guest Artists; Guest Directors
Budget: $500,000 - $1,000,000
Income Sources: Private Foundations/Grants/Endowments; Business/Corporate Donations; Government Grants; Individual Donations
Season: September - June
Affiliations: AEA; SPT
Performance Facilities: Round House Theatre

Stevenson

FACILITY

VILLA JULIA COLLEGE - INSCAPE THEATRE
(410) 486-7000
Type of Facility: Theatre Complex; Studio Performance; Arena; Multi-Purpose; Video Studio
Type of Stage: Thrust; Flexible; 3/4 Arena; Arena
Stage Dimensions: 22'x22'
Seating Capacity: 150
Year Built: 1970   **Architect:** Carl Buck
Contact for Rental: Sally Harris;   (410) 486-7000

Towson

DANCE

DANCE ON THE EDGE
8000 York Road, Stephen Annex, Towson, MD 21204
(410) 830-3369
Arts Area: Modern
Status: Non-Profit
Type: Sponsoring
Purpose: To present new and innovative dance, stretching the boundaries of ballet, modern and contemporary work
Officers: Bryon Mollica, President
Budget: $50,000 - $100,000
Income Sources: Private Foundations/Grants/Endowments; Business/Corporate Donations; Box Office; Government Grants; Individual Donations
Performance Facilities: Stephen Hall Theatre

FACILITY

TOWSON STATE UNIVERSITY - STEPHENS AUDITORIUM
Towson, MD 21204
(410) 830-3289
    Type of Facility: Auditorium
    Type of Stage: Proscenium **Orchestra Pit**
    Seating Capacity: 701
    Year Built: 1925 **Architect:** Fenten Lichtig
    Resident Groups: University Opera Workshop; University Dance Company; Towson Ensemble Dancers; Dance on The Edge

TOWSON STATE UNIVERSITY FINE ARTS CENTER
Towson, MD 21204
(410) 830-3289
    Type of Facility: Theatre Complex; Concert Hall; Studio Performance; Theatre House; Black Box
    Seating Capacity: Concert Hall - 518; Mainstage Theatre - 348; Black Box - 121
    Year Built: 1973 **Architect:** Fenten Lichtig **Cost:** $7,000,000
    Contact for Rental: Events & Conference Services; (410) 830-2244
    Manager: Gilbert Brungardt
    Resident Groups: Towson State University Departments of Dance, Art, Music and Theatre Arts
    The Fine Arts Center contains the Concert Hall, Main Stage and Studio Theatre. See individual listings for additional information.

TOWSON STATE UNIVERSITY FINE ARTS CENTER - CONCERT HALL
Towson, MD 21204
(410) 830-3289
    Type of Facility: Concert Hall; Recital Hall
    Type of Stage: Platform
    Stage Dimensions: 25'x56'
    Seating Capacity: 504
    Year Built: 1973
    Contact for Rental: Events & Conference Services; (410) 830-2244

TOWSON STATE UNIVERSITY FINE ARTS CENTER - MAIN STAGE
Towson, MD 21204
(410) 830-3289
    Type of Facility: Concert Hall; Theatre House
    Type of Stage: Modified Apron Proscenium
    Stage Dimensions: 46'Wx40'D **Orchestra Pit**
    Year Built: 1973
    Contact for Rental: Events & Conference Services; (410) 830-2244

TOWSON STATE UNIVERSITY FINE ARTS CENTER - STUDIO THEATRE
Towson, MD 21204
(410) 830-3289
    Type of Facility: Studio Performance; Black Box
    Type of Stage: Flexible
    Stage Dimensions: 25'x25'
    Year Built: 1973 **Architect:** Fenten Lichtig
    Contact for Rental: Events & Conference Services; (410) 830-2244

MASSACHUSETTS

Allston

THEATRE

DOUBLE EDGE THEATRE PRODUCTIONS INC.
5 Saint Luke's Road, Allston, MA 02134
(617) 254-4228
FAX: (617) 547-7032
Arts Area: Theatrical Group
Status: Professional; Non-Profit
Type: Touring; Resident
Purpose: The Double Edge Theatre, founded in 1982, is a laboratory theatre composed of directors, actors, musicians, designers, scholars and technicians from Israel, Poland, Indonesia and the U.S., committed to the development of a "living culture" in this country.
Management: Stacy Klein, Artistic Director; David Flaxman, Managing Director
Budget: $50,000 - $100,000
Income Sources: Private Foundations/Grants/Endowments; Business/Corporate Donations; Box Office; Government Grants; Individual Donations
Performance Facilities: Double

Amherst

DANCE

AMHERST BALLET THEATRE COMPANY
29 Strong Street, Amherst, MA 01002
(413) 549-1555
Founded: 1977
Arts Area: Modern; Ballet; Jazz; Ethnic
Status: Non-Professional; Non-Profit
Type: Performing; Touring; Educational
Purpose: To train young people to perform for young people bringing an awareness of diversity and art through dance to educate young audiences
Management: Therese Brady Donohue, Artistic Director; Kira Lamb, School Director
Officers: Louis Raboin, President; Gladys Martin, Secretary; Sandra Sacco, Treasurer
Paid Staff: 2 **Volunteer Staff:** 12
Non-Paid Artists: 21
Utilizes: Special Technical Talent; Guest Choreographers
Budget: $1,000 - $50,000
Income Sources: Private Foundations/Grants/Endowments; Business/Corporate Donations; Box Office; Government Grants; Individual Donations
Season: September - June **Annual Attendance:** 3,000
Performance Facilities: Bowker Auditorium; Fine Arts Center; Concert Hall; University of Massachusetts

VOCAL MUSIC

VALLEY LIGHT OPERA
PO Box 2143, Amherst, MA 01004
(413) 549-1098
Founded: 1975
Arts Area: Light Opera
Status: Non-Professional; Non-Profit
Type: Performing
Purpose: To prepare and produce light opera for the enjoyment of both participants and audiences
Management: Sally Venman, Bill Venman, General Managers
Officers: Carol Flandowgh, President; Louis Mold, Vice President; Melton Miller, Treasurer; Lucy Robinson, Clerk
Non-Paid Artists: 100
Budget: $1,000 - $50,000
Income Sources: Box Office; Government Grants; Individual Donations
Season: November - February **Annual Attendance:** 4,000
Performance Facilities: Amherst High School Auditorium

THEATRE

MOLE END PUPPETRY PRODUCTIONS INC.
45 Ward Street, Amherst, MA 01002
(413) 256-0453
    Arts Area: Puppet
    Status: Professional; Non-Profit
    Type: Educational; Sponsoring; Presenting
    Purpose: To present storytelling arts in the western Massachusetts area
    Management: Steve Stoia, Executive Director
    Officers: John Morrison, Chair
    Budget: $100,000 - $500,000
    Income Sources: Private Foundations/Grants/Endowments; Business/Corporate Donations; Box Office; Government Grants; Individual Donations
    Performance Facilities: Paramount Theater

FACILITY

UNIVERSITY OF MASSACHUSETTS - BOWKER AUDITORIUM
Stockbridge Hall, Amherst, MA 01003
(413) 545-0190
    Type of Facility: Auditorium
    Type of Stage: Proscenium
    Stage Dimensions: 35'Wx20'D
    Seating Capacity: 700
    Year Built: 1914
    Year Remodeled: 1985
    Manager: Barbara Aldrich
    Resident Groups: Music and Dance Departments; Concert Series

UNIVERSITY OF MASSACHUSETTS - CONCERT HALL
205 Hasbrouck Lab, Amherst, MA 01003
(413) 545-0190
FAX: (413) 545-0132
    Founded: 1975
    Type of Facility: Theatre Complex; Concert Hall; Performance Center; Multi-Purpose
    Type of Stage: Proscenium
    Stage Dimensions: 58'Wx41'D **Orchestra Pit**
    Seating Capacity: 2,000
    Year Built: 1974 **Architect:** Roche Dinkeloo Associates **Cost:** $16,000,000
    Acoustical Consultant: Bolt, Beranek & Newman
    Contact for Rental: Barbara Aldrich; (413) 545-0190

Arlington

THEATRE

UNDERGROUND RAILWAY THEATER
41 Foster Street, Arlington, MA 02174
(617) 643-6916
    Founded: 1976
    Arts Area: Professional; Musical; Puppet
    Status: Professional; Non-Profit
    Type: Performing; Touring; Educational
    Purpose: Combining puppets, actors and music, URT creates and tours new works including political cabaret, family theatre, and spectacles for symphony orchestras.
    Management: Mara Youdelman, General Manager; Debra Wise, Executive Director; Wes Sanders, Artistic Director; Carl Wieting, Technical Director
    Officers: Downing Cless, President
    Paid Staff: 4 **Volunteer Staff:** 8
    Paid Artists: 4 **Non-Paid Artists:** 4
    Utilizes: Guest Artists
    Budget: $100,000 - $500,000

Income Sources: Private Foundations/Grants/Endowments; Business/Corporate Donations; Box Office; Government Grants; Individual Donations
Season: 52 Weeks

Becket

DANCE

JACOB'S PILLOW DANCE FESTIVAL
George Carter Road, Becket, MA 01223
(413) 637-1322
Founded: 1932
Arts Area: Modern; Mime; Ballet; Jazz; Ethnic
Status: Professional; Non-Profit
Type: Performing; Resident; Educational; Sponsoring
Purpose: To encourage, support, nurture and sustain the art and artists of dance
Management: Samuel A. Miller, Executive Director; William C. Yehle, General Manager
Paid Staff: 25   **Volunteer Staff:** 25
Paid Artists: 100
Utilizes: Special Technical Talent; Guest Artists
Budget: $1,000,000 - $5,000,000
Income Sources: Private Foundations/Grants/Endowments; Business/Corporate Donations; Box Office; Government Grants; Individual Donations
Season: June - September   **Annual Attendance:** 35,000
Affiliations: Dance USA
Performance Facilities: Ted Shawn Theatre

Belmont

THEATRE

BELMONT CHILDREN'S THEATRE
226 Beech Street, Belmont, MA 02178
(617) 489-4380
Founded: 1982
Arts Area: Musical; Community
Status: Non-Professional
Type: Performing; Educational
Purpose: To provide a stimulating educational experience for young people who have an interest in theatre
Management: Laura Kalo, Artistic Director
Officers: Jacqueline Rossi, Faculty; Keith Kirkpatrick, Musician
Paid Staff: 1
Paid Artists: 2
Utilizes: Special Technical Talent
Budget: $1,000 - $50,000
Income Sources: Private Foundations/Grants/Endowments; Business/Corporate Donations; Box Office; Government Grants
Season: September - June   **Annual Attendance:** 1,000

BELMONT DRAMATIC CLUB
58 Harriet Avenue, Belmont, MA 02178
(617) 484-9174
Founded: 1903
Arts Area: Musical; Community; Theatrical Group
Status: Non-Professional; Non-Profit
Type: Performing
Purpose: To bring good drama to the community
Officers: Stephanie Cloutier, President; Cornie Bosse, Carolyn Hickok, Vice Presidents; Willa Rockett, Correspondence Secretary; Marcus Hatch, Treasurer
Utilizes: Guest Directors
Income Sources: Business/Corporate Donations; Box Office; Individual Donations
Season: September - May   **Annual Attendance:** 900
Performance Facilities: Belmont Town Hall, Hendall School

Beverly

THEATRE

NORTH SHORE MUSIC THEATRE
Dunham Road, PO Box 62, Beverly, MA 01915
(508) 922-8500
FAX: (508) 921-0793
    Founded: 1955
    Arts Area: Professional; Musical; Theatrical Group
    Status: Professional; Non-Profit
    Type: Performing; Touring; Educational
    Purpose: North Shore Music Theatre presents the art of musical theatre to the greater Boston community and, in so doing, contributes to the cultural and educational lives of audiences, theatre artists and students.
    Management: Jon Kimbell, Executive Producer; James K. Polese, General Manager; Jim Alberghini, Production Manager; David James, Marketing Director
    Officers: John P. Drislane, President; Donald J. Short, Vice President; Wendell P. Wood, Treasurer
    Paid Staff: 20   **Volunteer Staff:** 150
    Paid Artists: 200
    Utilizes: Guest Artists; Guest Directors
    Budget: $1,000,000 - $5,000,000
    Income Sources: Private Foundations/Grants/Endowments; Business/Corporate Donations; Box Office; Government Grants; Individual Donations
    Season: 52 Weeks   **Annual Attendance:** 310,000
    Affiliations: COST; Massachusetts Cultural Alliance
    Performance Facilities: North Shore Music Theatre

FACILITY

NORTH SHORE MUSIC THEATRE
Dunham Road, PO Box 62, Beverly, MA 01915
(508) 922-8220
FAX: (508) 921-0793
    Type of Facility: Theatre House; Arena
    Type of Stage: Arena   **Orchestra Pit**
    Seating Capacity: 1,790
    Year Built: 1955   **Architect:** Irving Salsberg & Ralph LeBlanc
    Contact for Rental: James K. Polese, General Manager/John Kimbell, Executive Producer;   (617) 922-8220
    Manager: James K. Polese, General Manager
    Resident Groups: North Shore Music Theatre

Boston

DANCE

BOSTON BALLET COMPANY
19 Clarendon Street, Boston, MA 02116
(617) 695-6950
FAX: (617) 695-6995
    Founded: 1963
    Arts Area: Ballet
    Status: Professional; Non-Profit
    Type: Performing
    Purpose: Professional ballet company
    Management: Bruce Marks, Artistic Director; Bruce Wells, Associate Director; D. David Brown, General Manager
    Officers: John W. Humphrey, Chairman; Jill Goldweitz, Morris Hamilburg, Richard Pollard, Vice Presidents
    Paid Staff: 39
    Paid Artists: 83
    Utilizes: Special Technical Talent; Guest Artists
    Budget: $1,000,000 - $5,000,000
    Income Sources: Private Foundations/Grants/Endowments; Business/Corporate Donations; Box Office; Government Grants; Individual Donations

Season: September - May   **Annual Attendance:** 300,000
Performance Facilities: The Wang Center for the Performing Arts

BOSTON BALLET II
19 Clarendon Street, Boston, MA 02116
(617) 695-6950
FAX: (617) 695-6995
Founded: 1980
Arts Area: Ballet
Status: Professional; Non-Profit
Type: Performing; Touring; Educational
Purpose: To educate audiences and young professional dancers through community outreach and children's programming
Management: Susan Larson, Compnay Manager; Laura Young, Director
Paid Staff: 4
Paid Artists: 15
Utilizes: Guest Choreographers
Budget: $100,000 - $500,000
Income Sources: Private Foundations/Grants/Endowments; Business/Corporate Donations; Box Office; Individual Donations
Season: 32 Weeks

DANCE PROJECTS INC./BETH SOLL AND COMPANY
PO Box 825, Prudential Station, Boston, MA 02199
(617) 547-8771
Arts Area: Modern
Status: Professional; Non-Profit
Type: Performing; Touring; Educational
Purpose: To embody the inventive and compelling choreographic style of Beth Soll
Management: Sally Fabens, Managing Director; Beth Soll, Artistic Director
Officers: Lawrence Kunz, President of the Board
Budget: $50,000 - $100,000
Income Sources: Private Foundations/Grants/Endowments; Business/Corporate Donations; Box Office; Government Grants; Individual Donations
Season: 52 Weeks

MARCUS SCHULKIND DANCE COMPANY
352 West Newton Street, #3, Boston, MA 02116
(617) 536-2962
Founded: 1975
Arts Area: Modern
Status: Professional
Type: Performing; Touring; Resident; Educational
Management: Maria Schwartz, Co-Manager; Marcus Schulkind, Artistic Director
Paid Staff: 1   **Volunteer Staff:** 4
Paid Artists: 6   **Non-Paid Artists:** 2
Utilizes: Guest Choreographers
Budget: $1,000 - $50,000
Income Sources: Private Foundations/Grants/Endowments; Business/Corporate Donations; Box Office; Government Grants; Individual Donations
Season: July - October   **Annual Attendance:** 5,000

MJT DANCE COMPANY
Studio: Boston Center For The Arts, Boston, MA 02116
(617) 482-0351
Founded: 1974
Arts Area: Modern
Status: Professional; Non-Profit
Type: Performing; Touring; Educational
Purpose: To educate and enrich through modern dance people of all ages through performances, classes, and outreach
Management: Margie J. Topf, Artistic Director; Brenda Lee Tracey, Business Manager
Officers: Kube Thurston, Board Chairman; Stuart M. Rose, Treasurer
Paid Staff: 5   **Volunteer Staff:** 20
Paid Artists: 15   **Non-Paid Artists:** 10
Utilizes: Guest Artists
Budget: $50,000 - $100,000
Income Sources: Private Foundations/Grants/Endowments; Business/Corporate Donations; Box Office; Individual Donations
Season: September - June   **Annual Attendance:** 5,000

MASSACHUSETTS - Boston

SPANISH DANCE THEATRE
791 Tremont Street, Boston, MA 02118
(619) 266-2120
   Arts Area: Ethnic
   Status: Professional; Non-Profit
   Type: Performing; Touring; Resident; Educational
   Purpose: To promote the enjoyment and understanding of Flamenco Dance technique through performance and education
   Management: Ramon de los Reyes, Artistic Director; Clara Ramona, Chief Choreographer
   Budget: $50,000 - $100,000
   Income Sources: Private Foundations/Grants/Endowments; Business/Corporate Donations; Box Office; Government Grants; Individual Donations

INSTRUMENTAL MUSIC

ALEA III
855 Commonwealth Avenue, Boston, MA 02215
(617) 353-3340
FAX: (617) 353-9551
   Founded: 1979
   Arts Area: Chamber; Ensemble; Electronic & Live Electronic
   Status: Professional; Non-Profit
   Type: Performing; Resident
   Purpose: To play and promote twentieth century classical music and to support the work of contemporary composers
   Management: Synneve Carlino, Executive Administrator; Theodore Antoniou, Music Director
   Officers: Keith Botsford, Chairman; George and Ellen Demeter, Co-Presidents; Electra Cardona, Treasurer
   Paid Staff: 3
   Utilizes: Guest Conductors; Guest Artists; Guest Directors; Guest Speakers
   Budget: $50,000 - $100,000
   Income Sources: Private Foundations/Grants/Endowments; Business/Corporate Donations; Box Office; Government Grants; Individual Donations; University Monies
   Season: September - May   **Annual Attendance:** 700
   Affiliations: Boston University
   Performance Facilities: Tsai Performance Center

BOSTON CLASSICAL ORCHESTRA
551 Tremont Street, Boston, MA 02116
(617) 426-2387
   Founded: 1978
   Arts Area: Symphony; Orchestra; Chamber
   Status: Professional; Non-Profit
   Type: Performing
   Purpose: To perform the classics and music rooted in the classic tradition
   Management: Robert Brink, Executive Secretary; Quindara Dodge, Manager; Harry Ellis Dickson, Music Director
   Officers: Dorothy Bearak, President; Robert M. Leavy, Treasurer; Peter B. Finn, Secretary
   Paid Staff: 1   **Volunteer Staff:** 8
   Paid Artists: 30
   Utilizes: Guest Artists
   Budget: $50,000 - $100,000
   Income Sources: Private Foundations/Grants/Endowments; Business/Corporate Donations; Box Office; Government Grants; Individual Donations
   Season: October - June   **Annual Attendance:** 6,000
   Performance Facilities: Faneuil Hall

BOSTON MUSICA VIVA
25 Huntington Avenue, Suite 612, Boston, MA 02116-5713
(617) 353-0556
FAX: (617) 353-0893
   Founded: 1969
   Arts Area: Chamber; New Music
   Status: Professional
   Type: Performing; Touring; Educational
   Purpose: To champion the work of living American composers along with comtemporary classics
   Management: Hilary Field, General Manager
   Officers: Richard Pittman, Music Director
   Paid Staff: 1   **Volunteer Staff:** 20
   Paid Artists: 6
   Utilizes: Guest Artists; Multi-Media Collaborations
   Budget: $100,000 - $500,000

Income Sources: Private Foundations/Grants/Endowments; Business/Corporate Donations; Box Office; Government Grants; Individual Donations
Season: September - May
Annual Attendance: 4,000
Performance Facilities: Edward Pickman Hall; Blackman Auditorium; Tsai Center

BOSTON POPS
Symphony Hall, 301 Massachusetts Avenue, Boston, MA 02115
(617) 266-1492
FAX: (617) 638-9223
   Arts Area: Orchestra; Pops; Popular Selections
   Status: Professional; Non-Profit
   Type: Performing; Touring
   Management: John Williams, Conductor
   Performance Facilities: Symphony Hall

BOSTON SYMPHONY CHAMBER PLAYERS
Symphony Hall, 301 Massachusetts Avenue, Boston, MA 02115
(617) 266-1492
   Founded: 1964
   Arts Area: Chamber; Ensemble
   Status: Professional; Commercial
   Type: Performing; Touring
   Purpose: The Chamber Players comprise the 12 first-chair players of the Boston Symphony Orchestra. They present programs of standard and contemporary literature not only in Boston and at Tanglewood, but on tour throughout this country and abroad, especially to audiences in locations which would not ordinarily be able to hear the Boston Symphony Orchestra in person.
   Management: Daniel R. Gustin, Manager; Richard Ortner, Assistant Manager
   Paid Staff: 2
   Paid Artists: 12
   Utilizes: Guest Artists
   Budget: $100,000 - $500,000
   Income Sources: Box Office
   Season: Winter; - Spring
   Affiliations: Boston Symphony Orchestra
   Performance Facilities: Jordan Hall; Tanglewood

BOSTON SYMPHONY ORCHESTRA
Symphony Hall, 301 Massachusetts Avenue, Boston, MA 02115
(617) 266-1492
   Founded: 1881
   Arts Area: Symphony; Orchestra; Chamber; Ensemble
   Status: Professional; Non-Profit
   Type: Performing; Touring; Resident; Educational
   Purpose: To bring great music to the widest possible audience; the Boston Symphony Orchestra, Inc. is the parent organization of the Boston Symphony Orchestra, the Boston Pops, the Boston Symphony Chamber Players, Tanglewood and the Tanglewood Music Center
   Management: Kenneth Haas, Managing Director; Daniel R. Gustin, Assistant Managing Director/Manager of Tanglewood; Michael G. McDonough, Director of Finance and Business Affairs; Evans Mirageas, Artistic Administrator; Caroline Smedvig, Director of Public Relations and Marketing; Josiah Stevenson, Director of Development; Ray F. Wellbaum, Orchestra Manager
   Officers: Nelson J. Darling Jr., Chairman Emeritus; J.P. Barger, Chairman; Mrs. Lewis S. Dabney, Mrs. John H. Fitzpatrick, Vice Chairmans; George H. Kidder, President; Archie C. Epps, Vice Chairman; William J. Poorvu, Vice Chairman/Treasurer
   Utilizes: Special Technical Talent; Guest Conductors; Guest Artists
   Budget: Over $10,000,000
   Income Sources: Private Foundations/Grants/Endowments; Business/Corporate Donations; Box Office; Government Grants; Individual Donations
   Season: 52 Weeks
   Performance Facilities: Symphony Hall

DINOSAUR ANNEX MUSIC ENSEMBLE
PO Box 5824, Boston, MA 02114
(617) 643-6627
   Arts Area: Orchestra; Chamber; Ensemble; Instrumental Group; Electronic & Live Electronic
   Status: Professional; Non-Profit
   Type: Performing
   Purpose: To play the best in contemporary music for chamber ensemble
   Management: Scott Wheeler, Artistic Director

Officers: Vance Koven, Chairman of the Board
Budget: $1,000 - $50,000
Income Sources: Private Foundations/Grants/Endowments; Business/Corporate Donations; Box Office; Government Grants; Individual Donations
Performance Facilities: First and Second Church, Boston

GREATER BOSTON YOUTH SYMPHONY ORCHESTRAS
855 Commonwealth Avenue, Boston, MA 02215
(617) 353-3348
FAX: (617) 353-2053
Founded: 1958
Arts Area: Symphony; Orchestra; Chamber
Status: Non-Professional; Non-Profit
Type: Performing; Touring; Resident; Educational
Purpose: To provide quality music education programs; to bring the music of young performers before a wide audience
Management: Parker Monroe, Executive Director; David Commanday, Music Director; Cathy Cotton, Orchestra Manager; Charles Sumner, Director of Public Relations
Officers: Tom Draper, President
Paid Staff: 7
Non-Paid Artists: 250
Budget: $100,000 - $500,000
Income Sources: Private Foundations/Grants/Endowments; Business/Corporate Donations; Box Office; Government Grants; Individual Donations
Season: September - June
Affiliations: Boston University

HANDEL AND HAYDN SOCIETY
300 Massachusetts Avenue, Boston, MA 02115
(617) 266-3605
FAX: (617) 266-4217
Founded: 1815
Arts Area: Chamber; Ensemble; Choral
Status: Professional; Non-Profit
Type: Performing; Touring; Educational; Sponsoring
Purpose: To promote the performance, study, composition and appreciation of music
Management: Christopher Hogwood, Artistic Director; Mary Deissler, Executive Director
Utilizes: Guest Conductors; Guest Artists; Guest Directors
Budget: $500,000 - $1,000,000
Income Sources: Private Foundations/Grants/Endowments; Business/Corporate Donations; Box Office; Government Grants; Individual Donations
Season: September - May   **Annual Attendance:** 55,000
Performance Facilities: Symphony Hall; Jordan Hall

MASSACHUSETTS YOUTH WIND ENSEMBLE
290 Huntington Avenue, Boston, MA 02115
(617) 262-1120, ext. 350
Founded: 1970
Arts Area: Chamber; Ensemble; Instrumental Group; Band
Status: Non-Profit
Type: Performing; Touring; Educational
Purpose: To offer exceptionally talented high school musicians an opportunity to study and perform the quality literature written for wind, brass, and percussion instruments
Management: Daniel J. Riley, Music Director/Conductor; Mark Churchill, Extension Division Director, New England Conservatory
Paid Staff: 14   **Volunteer Staff:** 5
Utilizes: Special Technical Talent; Guest Conductors; Guest Artists; Guest Directors
Budget: $1,000 - $50,000
Income Sources: Business/Corporate Donations; Individual Donations
Season: September - May   **Annual Attendance:** 5,000
Affiliations: New England Conservatory
Performance Facilities: Jordon Hall

SHIRIM KLEZMER ORCHESTRA
15 Perkins Square, #7, Boston, MA 02130
(617) 247-1606
FAX: (617) 524-5425
Founded: 1982
Arts Area: Ethnic; Folk

Status: Professional; Commercial
Type: Performing; Touring; Educational
Purpose: To perform music in the traditions of Eastern European Klezmer, Yiddish Theatre and Yiddish Folk Music
Management: Margaret Pash, Vintage Entertainment
Officers: Glenn Dickson, Owner
Paid Staff: 1
Paid Artists: 8
Budget: $50,000 - $100,000
Income Sources: Box Office; Individual Donations
Season: 52 Weeks

VOCAL MUSIC

BOSTON LYRIC OPERA COMPANY
114 State Street, Boston, MA 02109
(617) 248-8811; (617) 248-8660
FAX: (617) 248-8810
Founded: 1976
Arts Area: Lyric Opera
Status: Professional
Type: Performing
Purpose: To present a varied reportoire of works accessible to a broad segment of the community, productions featuring both young American artists of promise and the most highly-regarded figures in the world of opera
Management: Jan Del Sesto, Managing Director; Thomas Dreeze, Artistic Administrator; David Coolidge, Director of Finance; Laurie Way, Box Office Manager
Officers: Horace H. Irvine II, Chairman Board of Directors; Randolph Fuller, President; Akiba Herman, Treasurer; Michael Lytton, Clerk
Paid Staff: 7   **Volunteer Staff:** 2
Paid Artists: 100
Utilizes: Special Technical Talent; Guest Conductors; Guest Artists; Guest Directors
Budget: $1,000,000 - $5,000,000
Income Sources: Private Foundations/Grants/Endowments; Business/Corporate Donations; Box Office; Government Grants; Individual Donations
Season: September - March   **Annual Attendance:** 11,000
Affiliations: OA
Performance Facilities: Emerson Majestic Theatre

BOSTON OPERA ASSOCIATION
Four Copley Place, Suite 140, Boston, MA 02116
(617) 437-1316
Founded: 1937
Arts Area: Grand Opera; Lyric Opera; Light Opera; Operetta
Status: Professional; Non-Profit
Type: Performing; Educational; Sponsoring
Purpose: To bring opera and operatic performances of high quality to the Boston and New England community that would not otherwise be available
Management: John W. Brewer, Administrator
Officers: William I. Cowin Esq., President
Paid Staff: 1   **Volunteer Staff:** 75
Utilizes: Guest Conductors; Guest Artists
Budget: $500,000 - $1,000,000
Income Sources: Private Foundations/Grants/Endowments; Business/Corporate Donations; Box Office; Individual Donations
Season: September - May   **Annual Attendance:** 20,000
Performance Facilities: The Wang Center for The Performing Arts and Symphony Hall

OPERA COMPANY OF BOSTON
539 Washington Street, PO Box 50, Boston, MA 02112
(617) 426-5300
Founded: 1958
Arts Area: Grand Opera
Status: Professional
Type: Performing; Educational
Purpose: Opera Company of Boston is a professional, performing opera company. Opera New England is the touring arm of Opera Company of Boston.
Management: Sarah Caldwell, Artistic Director; Clifford Brooks, Manager
Paid Staff: 15   **Volunteer Staff:** 10
Utilizes: Special Technical Talent; Guest Conductors; Guest Artists; Guest Directors

Budget: $1,000,000 - $5,000,000
Income Sources: Private Foundations/Grants/Endowments; Business/Corporate Donations; Box Office; Government Grants; Individual Donations
Season: January - June **Annual Attendance:** 52,000
Performance Facilities: Boston Opera House

OPERA NEW ENGLAND
539 Washington Street, Boston, MA 02111
(617) 426-5300
   Founded: 1973
   Arts Area: Grand Opera
   Status: Professional; Non-Profit
   Type: Performing; Touring; Educational
   Purpose: As the touring arm of Opera Company of Boston, Opera New England disseminates opera through productions on tour.
   Management: Sarah Caldwell, Artistic Director; Clifford Brooks, Manager
   Officers: Helen Closson, President; Lucille Johnson, Vice President; Linda Cabot Black, Second Vice President; Demetre Steffon, Treasurer
   Paid Staff: 2 **Volunteer Staff:** 18
   Utilizes: Guest Conductors; Guest Artists; Guest Directors
   Budget: $100,000 - $500,000
   Income Sources: Private Foundations/Grants/Endowments; Business/Corporate Donations; Box Office; Government Grants; Individual Donations
   Season: October - May **Annual Attendance:** 18,000
   Affiliations: OA

THEATRE

BOSTON CHILDREN'S THEATRE
93 Massachusetts Avenue, Boston, MA 02115
(617) 424-6634
   Founded: 1951
   Arts Area: Professional; Theatrical Group
   Status: Professional; Non-Profit
   Type: Performing
   Purpose: To promote live theatre for children, by children; "Enchanted Forest," hosted at the Franklin Park Zoo in October
   Management: Patricia M. Gleeson, Executive Director
   Paid Staff: 2
   Paid Artists: 8 **Non-Paid Artists:** 20
   Utilizes: Special Technical Talent; Guest Artists; Guest Directors
   Budget: $100,000 - $500,000
   Income Sources: Private Foundations/Grants/Endowments; Business/Corporate Donations; Box Office; Government Grants; Individual Donations
   Season: November - May **Annual Attendance:** 21,000
   Affiliations: NETC; AATY; Massachusetts Cultural Alliance
   Performance Facilities: New England Life Hall

CITY STAGE COMPANY
539 Tremont Street, Boston, MA 02116
(617) 542-2291
FAX: (617) 426-5336
   Founded: 1974
   Arts Area: Professional; Theatrical Group
   Status: Professional
   Type: Performing; Touring; Educational
   Purpose: To bring innovative theater and educational programs to specifically defined groups and audiences
   Management: Tom Roulston, Susan Gassett, Artistic Co-Directors; Larry Coen, Associate Director
   Officers: Richard Warren, Chairman; Tom Roulston, President; Susan Gassett, Secretary/Treasurer
   Paid Staff: 3
   Paid Artists: 100
   Utilizes: Special Technical Talent
   Budget: $100,000 - $500,000
   Income Sources: Private Foundations/Grants/Endowments; Business/Corporate Donations; Box Office; Government Grants; Individual Donations
   Season: 52 Weeks **Annual Attendance:** 100,000
   Affiliations: Massachusetts Cultural Alliance

HUNTINGTON THEATRE COMPANY
252 Huntington Avenue, Boston, MA 02115
(617) 353-3320
Founded: 1982
Arts Area: Professional; Theatrical Group
Status: Professional; Non-Profit
Type: Performing; Resident
Purpose: Presenting classic works in their true spirit, and to respond to today's issues and emotions by presenting literate, trenchant, contemporary plays new to Boston
Management: Michael Maso, Managing Director; Peter Altman, Producing Director
Officers: Gerald J. Gross, President; Charles W. Smith, Treasurer
Paid Staff: 25
Paid Artists: 100
Utilizes: Special Technical Talent; Guest Conductors; Guest Artists; Guest Directors
Budget: $1,000,000 - $5,000,000
Income Sources: Private Foundations/Grants/Endowments; Business/Corporate Donations; Box Office; Government Grants; Individual Donations
Season: September - June   **Annual Attendance:** 100,000
Affiliations: Boston University
Performance Facilities: Boston University Theatre

LYRIC STAGE
140 Clarendon Street, Boston, MA 02116
(617) 437-7172
Founded: 1973
Arts Area: Professional; Theatrical Group
Status: Professional; Non-Profit
Type: Performing
Purpose: To present high-quality, professional theatre at low-cost prices to audiences who would otherwise never have known their theatrical heritage
Management: Ron Ritchell, Artistic Director; Polly Ritchell, Producer; James Denietolis, Subscription/Box Office Manager; Carolyn Ridgway, Marketing/Public Relations; Anne Fletcher, Group Sales
Officers: S. Michael Bates, President; Frick Jones, Vice President; Jane Salloway, Treasurer; Kathleen Bates, Clerk
Paid Staff: 6   **Volunteer Staff:** 10
Paid Artists: 50
Utilizes: Special Technical Talent; Guest Directors
Budget: $100,000 - $500,000
Income Sources: Private Foundations/Grants/Endowments; Business/Corporate Donations; Box Office; Individual Donations
Season: September - June   **Annual Attendance:** 25,000
Affiliations: AEA; New England Area Theatres

NEW THEATRE
755 Boyleston, Boston, MA 02116
Founded: 1980
Arts Area: Professional; Theatrical Group
Status: Semi-Professional; Non-Profit
Type: Performing; Resident; Educational
Purpose: To develop new plays, new interpretations of plays and Massachusetts theatre artists
Management: Richard W. Freeman, Artistic Director; John Hennessy, General Manager; Ruth Polleys, Production Manager; Deborah Scaglione, Development Director; Kathleen Canzano, Business Manager; David J. Lima, Box Office
Paid Staff: 6   **Volunteer Staff:** 15
Paid Artists: 80   **Non-Paid Artists:** 7
Budget: $100,000 - $500,000
Income Sources: Private Foundations/Grants/Endowments; Business/Corporate Donations; Box Office; Government Grants; Individual Donations
Season: September - June   **Annual Attendance:** 15,000
Affiliations: Boston Regional Theatre Association

THE PUBLICK THEATRE
11 Ridgemont Street, Boston, MA 02134
(617) 782-5425
Founded: 1970
Arts Area: Professional; Musical; Theatrical Group
Status: Professional; Non-Profit
Type: Performing; Touring; Resident; Sponsoring
Purpose: To discover, develop and showcase Boston-area theatrical talent in programs of professional quality that are accessible to a diverse audience
Management: Spiro Veloudos, Artistic Director; Deborah Schoenberg, Marketing/Development Director

Officers: Michael McDermott, President; Randall Filer, Treasurer
Paid Staff: 7   **Volunteer Staff:** 7
Paid Artists: 50
Utilizes: Guest Artists; Guest Directors
Budget: $100,000 - $500,000
Income Sources: Private Foundations/Grants/Endowments; Business/Corporate Donations; Box Office; Government Grants; Individual Donations
Season: June - Labor Day
Annual Attendance: 10,000
Performance Facilities: The Publick Theatre

PERFORMING SERIES

BOSTON EARLY MUSIC FESTIVAL AND EXHIBITION, INC.
729 Boylston Street, Suite 600, Boston, MA 02116
(617) 661-1812; (617) 262-0650
FAX: (617) 267-6539
Founded: 1980
Arts Area: Dance; Vocal Music; Instrumental Music; Festivals; Lyric Opera; Grand Opera; Early Music Festival
Status: Non-Profit
Type: Performing; Touring; Educational; Sponsoring
Purpose: To discover and reproduce, insofar as possible, the way early music originally sounded to a composer and his audience; to produce a biennial international festival in Boston; to educate youth
Management: Kathleen Fay, Executive Director
Officers: E.S. Whitney Thompson, President; Richard Hester, Vice President; Howard V. Wagner, Treasurer; Richard Portars, Clerk
Paid Staff: 2   **Volunteer Staff:** 200
Paid Artists: 250
Utilizes: Special Technical Talent; Guest Conductors; Guest Artists; Guest Directors
Budget: $500,000 - $1,000,000
Income Sources: Private Foundations/Grants/Endowments; Business/Corporate Donations; Box Office; Government Grants; Individual Donations
Season: 52 Weeks
Annual Attendance: 11,000

CELEBRITY SERIES OF BOSTON, INC.
20 Park Plaza, Suite 832, Boston, MA 02116
(617) 482-2595
FAX: (617) 482-3208
Founded: 1938
Arts Area: Dance; Vocal Music; Instrumental Music; Theater
Status: Non-Profit
Type: Presenting
Purpose: To bring Boston the world's greatest performing artists
Management: Walter Pierce, Executive Director; Martha Jones, General Manager; Kathleen Panoff, Development Director; Michael Botte, Comptroller
Officers: Arnold Zetcher, President; Joop Spanjaard, Chairman Finance
Paid Staff: 12   **Volunteer Staff:** 60
Paid Artists: 200
Utilizes: Guest Artists
Budget: $1,000,000 - $5,000,000
Income Sources: Private Foundations/Grants/Endowments; Business/Corporate Donations
Season: September - May
Annual Attendance: 150,000
Affiliations: ISPAA
Performance Facilities: Symphony Hall; Wang Center; Jordan Hall

FIRST NIGHT, INC.
20 Park Plaza, Suite 927, Boston, MA 02116
(617) 542-1399
FAX: (617) 426-9531
Founded: 1976
Arts Area: Dance; Vocal Music; Theater
Status: Non-Profit
Type: Art Presenter
Purpose: To broaden and deepen the public's appreciation for the visual and performing arts

Management: Zeren Earls, President; Deborah Kittredge, General Manager
Officers: Sam Frankenheim, Chairman; Rosamond Vaule, Vice Chair; Zeren Earls, President; Rina Spence, Treasurer; Randi Ingerman, Clerk
Paid Staff: 10   **Volunteer Staff:** 800
Paid Artists: 1,000
Utilizes: Guest Conductors; Guest Artists; Guest Directors
Budget: $500,000 - $1,000,000
Income Sources: Private Foundations/Grants/Endowments; Government Grants; Buttons; Admissions
Season: New Year's Eve   **Annual Attendance:** 600,000

ISABELLA STEWART GARDNER MUSEUM
280 The Fenway, Boston, MA 02115
(617) 566-1401
FAX: (617) 232-8039
Founded: 1900
Arts Area: Vocal Music; Instrumental Music; Theater; Lyric Opera
Status: Non-Profit
Type: Sponsoring
Purpose: Art Museum
Management: Anne Hawley, Director; Susan Davy, Director of Operations & Finance; Hilliard Goldfarb, Curator
Paid Staff: 85   **Volunteer Staff:** 12
Paid Artists: 75
Utilizes: Guest Conductors; Guest Artists
Budget: $1,000 - $50,000
Income Sources: Private Foundations/Grants/Endowments; Business/Corporate Donations; Box Office; Government Grants; Individual Donations
Season: September - June
Annual Attendance: 130,000
Performance Facilities: Isabella Stewart Gardner Museum

KING'S CHAPEL CONCERT SERIES
58 Tremont Street, Boston, MA 02108
(617) 876-8375
Founded: 1958
Arts Area: Vocal Music; Instrumental Music
Status: Professional
Type: Performing
Purpose: To present chamber works and works for small chorus, especially baroque and contemporary selections
Management: Daniel Pinkham, Music Director
Paid Staff: 1   **Volunteer Staff:** 8
Paid Artists: 30
Utilizes: Special Technical Talent; Guest Artists
Budget: $1,000 - $50,000
Income Sources: Individual Donations
Season: September - February
Performance Facilities: King's Chapel

TANGLEWOOD FESTIVAL
c/o Boston Symphony Orchestra Inc., 301 Massachusetts Avenue, Boston, MA 02115
(617) 266-1492
FAX: (617) 638-9288
Arts Area: Vocal Music; Instrumental Music; Festivals; Orchestral
Status: Professional; Non-Profit
Type: Performing; Educational
Purpose: Tanglewood is the summer home of the Boston Symphony Orchestra and is one of the world's preeminent summer music schools.
Management: Seiji Ozawa, Music Director; Kenneth Haas, Managing Director; Daniel Gustin, Assistant Managing Director of Boston Symphony and Tanglewood
Officers: J.P. Barger, Chairman of the Board; George Kidder, President of the Board
Paid Staff: 100   **Volunteer Staff:** 1,000
Utilizes: Special Technical Talent; Guest Conductors; Guest Artists
Budget: $5,000,000 - $10,000,000
Income Sources: Private Foundations/Grants/Endowments; Business/Corporate Donations; Box Office; Government Grants; Individual Donations
Season: June - August
Annual Attendance: 300,000
Performance Facilities: Tanglewood

FACILITY

BOSTON CENTER FOR THE ARTS - CYCLORAMA
539 Tremont Street, Boston, MA 02116
(617) 426-5000
FAX: (617) 426-5336
   Type of Facility: Multi-Purpose; Exhibition Hall
   Facility Originally: Cyclorama
   Type of Stage: Rotunda
   Stage Dimensions: 125' diameter brick floor
   Year Built: 1884   **Architect:** Cummings & Sears
   Year Remodeled: 1923   **Cost:** $80,000
   Contact for Rental: Harlan Jones;   (617) 426-5000

BOSTON CENTER FOR THE ARTS - THE NATIONAL THEATRE
539 Tremont Street, Boston, MA 02116
(617) 426-5000
FAX: (617) 426-5336
   Type of Facility: Concert Hall; Performance Center; Theatre House; Opera House
   Facility Originally: Opera House
   Type of Stage: Thrust; Proscenium
   Stage Dimensions: 40'Wx25'D   **Orchestra Pit**
   Seating Capacity: 2,500
   Year Built: 1911   **Architect:** Clarence Howard Blackall
   Year Remodeled: 1986   **Architect:** Hidell-Eyster & Associates   **Cost:** $3,500,000
   Contact for Rental: Harlan Jones;   (617) 426-5000

BOSTON OPERA HOUSE
539 Washington Street, Boston, MA 02111
(617) 426-5300
   Type of Facility: Concert Hall; Theatre House; Opera House
   Facility Originally: Vaudeville
   Type of Stage: Modified Apron Proscenium   **Orchestra Pit**
   Seating Capacity: 2,600
   Year Built: 1928   **Architect:** Charles Lamb
   Year Remodeled: 1977
   Contact for Rental: Jim DeVeer or Nancy Talbot;   (617) 426-5300
   Resident Groups: Opera Company of Boston

BOSTON UNIVERSITY SCHOOL FOR THE ARTS - CONCERT HALL
855 Commonwealth Avenue, Boston, MA 02115
(617) 353-3385
   Type of Facility: Concert Hall
   Type of Stage: Platform; Concert Stage
   Stage Dimensions: 1,507 square feet
   Seating Capacity: 450
   Year Built: 1957   **Architect:** George Sherwood
   Acoustical Consultant: Bolt, Beranek & Newman
   Contact for Rental: David Cross;   (617) 353-3831

BOSTON UNIVERSITY THEATRE
264 Huntington Avenue, Boston, MA 02115
(617) 266-7900
FAX: (617) 363-8300
   Type of Facility: Theatre Complex
   Type of Stage: Proscenium   **Orchestra Pit**
   Seating Capacity: 850
   Year Built: 1926   **Architect:** J. William Beal & Sons   **Cost:** $1,000,000
   Year Remodeled: 1973   **Architect:** Harry Weese & Associates   **Cost:** $500,000
   Contact for Rental: Roger Meeker;   (617) 266-7900
   Resident Groups: Huntington Theatre Company; School of Theatre Arts; School of Music (Opera Workshop)
   Boston University Theatre contains the Main Stage and Studio 210. See individual listings for additional information.

BOSTON UNIVERSITY THEATRE - MAIN STAGE
264 Huntington Avenue, Boston, MA 02115
(617) 266-7900
FAX: (617) 363-8300
   Type of Facility: Auditorium; Theatre House

Type of Stage: Proscenium
Stage Dimensions: 76'Wx33'D; 36'Wx24'H proscenium opening   **Orchestra Pit**
Seating Capacity: 856
Year Built: 1926
Year Remodeled: 1973
Contact for Rental: Roger Meeker;   (617) 266-7900
Resident Groups: Huntington Theatre Company; School of Theatre Arts; School of Music (Opera Workshop)

BOSTON UNIVERSITY THEATRE - STUDIO 210
264 Huntington Avenue, Boston, MA 02115
(617) 266-7900
FAX: (617) 363-8300
 Type of Facility: Studio Performance; Black Box
 Type of Stage: Flexible
 Stage Dimensions: 35'Wx75'Lx14'H
 Seating Capacity: 100
 Year Built: 1926
 Year Remodeled: 1973
 Contact for Rental: Roger Meeker;   (617) 266-7900
 Resident Groups: Huntington Theatre Company; School of Theatre Arts

EMERSON MAJESTIC THEATRE
219 Tremont Street, Boston, MA 02116
(617) 578-8727
FAX: (617) 578-8725
 Type of Facility: Theatre House
 Type of Stage: Proscenium
 Stage Dimensions: 38'Wx35'D   **Orchestra Pit**
 Seating Capacity: 850
 Year Built: 1903   **Architect:** John Galen Howard   **Cost:** $135,000
 Year Remodeled: 1988
 Contact for Rental: (617) 578-8727

ISABELLA STEWART GARDNER MUSEUM
280 The Fenway, Boston, MA 02115
(617) 566-1401
FAX: (617) 232-8039
 Type of Facility: Multi-Purpose; Room; Museum Gallery
 Type of Stage: Flexible; Platform
 Seating Capacity: 325
 Year Built: 1900
 Manager: Scott Nickrenz, Music Director;   (617) 566-1401

JORDAN HALL AT NEW ENGLAND CONSERVATORY
30 Gainsboro Street, Boston, MA 02115
(617) 262-1120
FAX: (617) 262-0500
 Founded: 1903
 Type of Facility: Concert Hall; Auditorium
 Type of Stage: Proscenium
 Stage Dimensions: 40'Wx29'D
 Seating Capacity: 1,019
 Year Built: 1903
 Year Remodeled: 1938
 Contact for Rental: Jon Wulp;   (617) 262-1120, ext. 268
 Resident Groups: New England Conservatory Performers

ORPHEUM THEATRE
Hamilton Place, Boston, MA 02108
(617) 482-0651
 Type of Facility: Theatre House
 Type of Stage: Proscenium
 Stage Dimensions: 44'Wx39'D
 Seating Capacity: 2,763
 Year Built: 1900   **Architect:** Charles Lamb
 Contact for Rental: Bruce Montgomery;   (617) 482-0651

SHUBERT THEATRE
265 Tremont Street, Boston, MA 02116
(617) 426-4520
  Type of Facility: Theatre House
  Type of Stage: Proscenium
  Stage Dimensions: 78'Wx42'6'D; 40'Wx30'H proscenium opening   **Orchestra Pit**
  Seating Capacity: 1,696
  Contact for Rental: Peter Entin;   (212) 944-3700
  Manager: The Shubert Organization;   (212) 944-3700
  Limited availability for rental

SYMPHONY HALL
301 Massachusetts Avenue, Boston, MA 02115
(617) 266-1492
  Type of Facility: Concert Hall
  Type of Stage: Proscenium
  Stage Dimensions: 50'x36'x34'
  Seating Capacity: 2,625
  Year Built: 1900   **Architect:** McKim, Meade, White
  Acoustical Consultant: Wallace Sabine
  Contact for Rental: Functions Manager;   (617) 266-1492
  Manager: James Whitaker;   (413) 637-1600
  Resident Groups: Boston Symphony Orchestra; Boston Pops Orchestra

THE WANG CENTER FOR THE PERFORMING ARTS
270 Tremont Street, Boston, MA 02116
(617) 482-9393
  Type of Facility: Concert Hall; Auditorium; Performance Center; Theatre House; Opera House
  Facility Originally: Vaudeville
  Type of Stage: Proscenium
  Stage Dimensions: 60'3"Wx36'1"Hx60'D   **Orchestra Pit**
  Seating Capacity: 4,000
  Year Built: 1927
  Year Remodeled: 1980
  Contact for Rental: Sandy Chapiro;   (617) 482-9393
  Resident Groups: Boston Ballet

Braintree

VOCAL MUSIC

BRAINTREE CHORAL SOCIETY
263 West Street, Braintree, MA 02184
(617) 848-0084
  Founded: 1923
  Arts Area: Choral
  Status: Non-Professional; Non-Profit
  Type: Performing
  Purpose: To promote interest and participation in choral music in the community
  Management: Steven Young, Director; Blanche Blazo, Membership Chairman
  Paid Staff: 1   **Volunteer Staff:** 10
  Paid Artists: 6   **Non-Paid Artists:** 4
  Utilizes: Special Technical Talent; Guest Artists
  Budget: $1,000 - $50,000
  Income Sources: Business/Corporate Donations; Box Office; Government Grants; Individual Donations
  Season: September - May   **Annual Attendance:** 200

Brookline

THEATRE

PUPPET SHOWPLACE THEATRE
32 Station Street, Brookline, MA 02146
(617) 731-6400
  Founded: 1974
  Arts Area: Puppet
  Status: Professional; Non-Profit

Type: Performing; Touring; Resident; Sponsoring
Management: Mary Churchill, Executive Director; Paul Vincent-Davis, Artistic Director
Officers: Claire Dilleo, President; Margaret Keiley, Treasurer; Julie Kronenberg, Clerk
Paid Staff: 4
Paid Artists: 21
Utilizes: Guest Artists
Budget: $100,000 - $500,000
Income Sources: Private Foundations/Grants/Endowments; Box Office
Season: 52 Weeks   **Annual Attendance:** 15,000
Affiliations: Puppeteers of America; UNIMA

Brookline Village

INSTRUMENTAL MUSIC

JAZZ COMPOSERS ALLIANCE
PO Box 752, Brookline Village, MA 02147
(617) 964-5471
   Founded: 1986
   Arts Area: Ensemble; Band; Jazz
   Status: Professional; Non-Profit
   Type: Performing; Sponsoring
   Purpose: To advance the art of jazz composition by featuring the work of established and emerging composers
   Officers: Darrell Katz, Director; Duane Johnson, Treasurer; Susan Calkins, Art Work; Bob Pilkington, Secretary
   Paid Artists: 25
   Utilizes: Special Technical Talent; Guest Artists
   Budget: $1,000 - $50,000
   Income Sources: Private Foundations/Grants/Endowments; Business/Corporate Donations; Box Office; Government Grants; Individual Donations; Advertising
   Season: September - June   **Annual Attendance:** 1,000

Burlington

INSTRUMENTAL MUSIC

CAMBRIDGE FOLK ORCHESTRA
6 Tami Lane, Burlington, MA 01803
(617) 272-0396
   Founded: 1966
   Arts Area: Orchestra; Ensemble; Ethnic; Folk; Instrumental Group; Band
   Status: Professional; Semi-Professional; Commercial
   Type: Performing; Resident; Educational
   Purpose: The orchestra plays for folk dances, parties, workshops, festivals, weddings and social events with most of the selections being ethnic dance music from many countries.
   Management: Calvin R. Howard, Business Manager; Aubry Jaffer, Orchestra Leader
   Paid Artists: 9   **Non-Paid Artists:** 9
   Utilizes: Guest Artists
   Budget: $1,000 - $50,000
   Income Sources: Box Office; Individual Donations
   Season: 52 Weeks

Cambridge

DANCE

BOSTON FLAMENCO BALLET
79 Rice Street, Cambridge, MA 02140
(617) 354-8608; (800) 435-8687
   Founded: 1973
   Arts Area: Mime; Ballet; Ethnic; Folk
   Status: Professional; Non-Profit
   Type: Performing; Touring; Educational
   Purpose: To educate students and adults about Spanish and Hispanic culture and history through dance and music

Management: Simon Blasco, Artistic Director
Officers: Heda Skiotis, President; Jose Alcaraz, Treasurer; Maria E. Calderon, Clerk
Paid Staff: 2   **Volunteer Staff:** 1
Paid Artists: 15
Utilizes: Special Technical Talent; Guest Artists
Budget: $100,000 - $500,000
Income Sources: Box Office
Season: September - December; February-April   **Annual Attendance:** 50,000

DANCE UMBRELLA, BOSTON, INC.
380 Green Street, Cambridge, MA 02139
(617) 492-7578
FAX: (617) 354-1603
        Founded: 1979
        Arts Area: Modern; Mime; Ballet; Jazz; Ethnic; Folk; Performance Art; Dance Theatre
        Status: Professional; Non-Profit
        Type: Performing; Resident; Educational; Presenting
        Purpose: To present the best contemporary and culturally diverse artists from around the world; to nurture dance by commissioning new work; to provide educational programs for the public; to provide services to the local dance community
        Management: Jeremy Alliger, Executive Director/Producer; Kara Keller, General Manager
        Officers: Gordon Orloff Esq., Chairman of the Board; Libby Chiu, President
        Paid Staff: 11
        Utilizes: Guest Artists; Guest Choreographers
        Budget: $1,000,000 - $5,000,000
        Income Sources: Private Foundations/Grants/Endowments; Business/Corporate Donations; Box Office; Government Grants; Individual Donations
        Season: October - June
        Annual Attendance: 30,000
        Affiliations: National Performance Network; APAP; Dance USA

HARVARD SUMMER DANCE CENTER
51 Brattle Street, Cambridge, MA 02138
(617) 495-5535
FAX: (617) 495-9176
        Founded: 1973
        Arts Area: Modern; Ballet; Jazz; Tap
        Status: Non-Profit
        Type: Educational
        Purpose: To bring together students and a distinguished faculty of teacher/artists in a six-week program of classics and performances, films and lectures on the world of dance
        Management: Iris Fanger, Director; Regina Boyland, Coordinator
        Paid Staff: 8
        Paid Artists: 20
        Utilizes: Special Technical Talent; Guest Artists
        Budget: $100,000 - $500,000
        Income Sources: Private Foundations/Grants/Endowments; Business/Corporate Donations; Box Office; Government Grants; Individual Donations
        Annual Attendance: 2,400

MANDALA FOLK DANCE ENSEMBLE
PO Box 246, Cambridge, MA 02139
(617) 868-3641
        Founded: 1965
        Arts Area: Ethnic; Folk
        Status: Professional; Semi-Professional; Non-Profit
        Type: Performing; Touring; Resident; Educational
        Purpose: To research, preserve and perform traditional folk dance and music from around the world; to broaden cross-cultural awareness; to introduce accessible dance to a broad audience
        Paid Staff: 3   **Volunteer Staff:** 10
        Non-Paid Artists: 35
        Utilizes: Special Technical Talent; Guest Choreographers
        Budget: $100,000 - $500,000
        Income Sources: Private Foundations/Grants/Endowments; Business/Corporate Donations; Box Office; Government Grants; Individual Donations
        Season: November - July   **Annual Attendance:** 30,000
        Affiliations: Massachusetts Council on the Arts; New England Foundation Tour Program; NEA Dance Program
        Performance Facilities: John Hancock Hall

INSTRUMENTAL MUSIC

BOSTON BAROQUE
PO Box 380190, Cambridge, MA 02238
(617) 641-1310
FAX: (617) 641-1322
Founded: 1973
Arts Area: Orchestra; Chorus
Status: Professional; Non-Profit
Type: Performing; Touring; Resident
Purpose: To perform Baroque and classical music using period instruments and chorus
Management: Martin Pearlman, Music Director; Carole Friedman, Executive Director
Officers: Marshall Goldman, President; Charles Christenson, Vice President; Thomas R. Kolb, Clerk; John A. Gunnarson, Treasurer
Paid Staff: 4
Paid Artists: 50
Utilizes: Guest Artists
Budget: $100,000 - $500,000
Income Sources: Private Foundations/Grants/Endowments; Business/Corporate Donations; Box Office; Government Grants; Individual Donations
Season: October - June   **Annual Attendance:** 10,000
Performance Facilities: Jordan Hall

BOSTON PHILHARMONIC
PO Box 3000, Cambridge, MA 02218
(617) 861-8530
FAX: (617) 861-8530
Founded: 1979
Arts Area: Symphony; Orchestra
Status: Professional; Semi-Professional; Non-Profit
Type: Performing; Touring
Management: Benjamin Zander, Music Director/Conductor; Mary S. Jaffee, Manager
Officers: Seymour Rothchild, President; Urs Gauchat, Vice President; Gary Seligson, Treasurer; Ira Deitsch, Clerk
Paid Staff: 3   **Volunteer Staff:** 4
Paid Artists: 30   **Non-Paid Artists:** 55
Utilizes: Guest Artists
Budget: $100,000 - $500,000
Income Sources: Private Foundations/Grants/Endowments; Business/Corporate Donations; Box Office; Government Grants; Individual Donations; Fund-raising
Season: November - May   **Annual Attendance:** 10,000
Affiliations: Arts Boston
Performance Facilities: Jordan Hall; Sanders Theater; Symphony Hall

KLEZMER CONSERVATORY BAND
83 Inman, Cambridge, MA 02139
(617) 354-2884
Founded: 1980
Arts Area: Ethnic; Folk; Band
Status: Professional
Type: Performing; Touring
Purpose: Yiddish instrumental and vocal music with many influences (Jazz, Dixieland, Ragtime, Broadway, Latin)
Management: Aaron Concert Management, Boston Mass.; James Guttmann, Business Manager
Officers: Hankus Netsky, President
Paid Staff: 2
Paid Artists: 15
Income Sources: Box Office
Season: September - June

NEW ENGLAND PHILHARMONIC
1972 Massachusetts Avenue, 4th Floor, Cambridge, MA 02140
(617) 868-1222
Founded: 1976
Arts Area: Orchestra
Status: Non-Professional
Type: Performing; Resident
Purpose: To foster and encourage enjoyment and appreciation of new and unusual orchestral music; to perform standard orchestral literature in community locations
Management: Elisa Birdseye, Executive Director; Jeffrey Rink, Music Director; Dick Yoder, Personnel Manager

Officers: Nancy Hawkins, President; Constance Wark, Vice President; Susan Browse, Treasurer
Volunteer Staff: 3
Paid Artists: 3   **Non-Paid Artists:** 65
Utilizes: Guest Artists; Composer-in-Residence
Budget: $1,000 - $50,000
Income Sources: Private Foundations/Grants/Endowments; Business/Corporate Donations; Box Office; Government Grants; Individual Donations
Season: September - May
Annual Attendance: 2,000
Affiliations: ASOL
Performance Facilities: Sanders Theatre, Cambridge; Dwight Hall, Framingham

PRO ARTE CHAMBER ORCHESTRA
1950 Massachusetts Aveneue, Cambridge, MA 02140
(617) 661-7067
FAX: (617) 661-7067
Founded: 1978
Arts Area: Orchestra; Chamber
Status: Professional; Non-Profit
Type: Performing
Purpose: To perform a self-produced yearly series of orchestral works, classical and contemporary, for chamber orchestra
Management: Evelyn Dueck, General Manager
Officers: William Moyer, President; W. Easley Hamner, Secretary; John Porter, Treasurer
Paid Staff: 2   **Volunteer Staff:** 20
Paid Artists: 40
Utilizes: Guest Conductors; Guest Artists; Guest Directors
Budget: $100,000 - $500,000
Income Sources: Private Foundations/Grants/Endowments; Business/Corporate Donations; Box Office; Government Grants; Individual Donations
Season: September - May   **Annual Attendance:** 6,000
Affiliations: Harvard University
Performance Facilities: Sanders Theater

WATER MUSIC
12 Arrow Street, Cambridge, MA 02138
(617) 876-8742
FAX: (617) 876-6036
Founded: 1971
Arts Area: Ensemble; Instrumental Group
Status: Professional; Commercial
Type: Sponsoring
Purpose: To produce music cruises, concerts and special events
Management: Fenton Hollander, Program and Publicity Director
Officers: Fenton Hollander, President
Paid Staff: 5
Paid Artists: 350
Utilizes: Special Technical Talent; Guest Artists
Budget: $100,000 - $500,000
Income Sources: Box Office
Season: 52 Weeks   **Annual Attendance:** 28,000

VOCAL MUSIC

OPERA NEW ENGLAND
5 Hilliard Place, Cambridge, MA 02138
(617) 354-0451
Founded: 1973
Arts Area: Lyric Opera; Light Opera
Status: Professional; Non-Profit
Type: Educational; Sponsoring
Purpose: To present seasons of opera for children and for general audiences. As the regional development program of The Opera Company of Boston, we present productions prepared by The Opera Company of Boston. Since 1983, our chapter has presented only productions for children.
Management: Linda C. Black, Founder
Officers: Linda C. Black, President; Barbara Barclay, Hagnette Cumitz, Norma Peterson, Sonya Schopick, Vice Presidents; Anne Chemiavsky, Secretary; Robert W. Burmester, Treasurer
Volunteer Staff: 1
Paid Artists: 2
Budget: $1,000 - $50,000

Income Sources: Private Foundations/Grants/Endowments; Business/Corporate Donations; Box Office; Government Grants; Individual Donations
Season: September - November   **Annual Attendance:** 8,000
Affiliations: Opera Company of Boston

REVELS INC.
One Kendall Square, Building 600, Cambridge, MA 02139
(617) 621-0505
FAX: (617) 621-1709
Founded: 1971
Arts Area: Musical Theatre
Status: Non-Profit
Type: Performing; Educational
Purpose: To promote education, understanding and appreciation of traditional music, songs, rituals and customs through the mediums of performance and recordings
Management: Gayle Rich, Executive Director; John Langstaff, Artistic Director; Alan Casso, General Manager; William Scheick, Business Manager
Officers: David Mortensen, President; Paul Rahmeier, Vice President; Joseph H. Bragden, Treasurer
Paid Staff: 6   **Volunteer Staff:** 35
Paid Artists: 20   **Non-Paid Artists:** 60
Utilizes: Guest Artists
Budget: $500,000 - $1,000,000
Income Sources: Private Foundations/Grants/Endowments; Business/Corporate Donations; Box Office; Government Grants; Individual Donations
Season: December   **Annual Attendance:** 18,500
Performance Facilities: Sanders Theatre, Harvard University

THEATRE

AMERICAN REPERTORY THEATRE
Harvard University, 64 Brattle Street, Cambridge, MA 02138
(617) 495-2668
FAX: (617) 495-1705
Founded: 1980
Arts Area: Professional
Status: Professional; Non-Profit
Type: Performing; Touring; Resident; Educational
Purpose: The American Repertory Theatre is a separately incorporated not-for-profit organization chartered to provide a service to the widest possible public in the Boston/Cambridge community and to the theatre world in general.
Management: Robert Brustein, Artistic Director; Robert J. Orchard, Managing Director; Ron Daniels, Associate Artistic Director
Paid Staff: 249   **Volunteer Staff:** 458
Paid Artists: 203   **Non-Paid Artists:** 7
Utilizes: Guest Directors
Budget: $5,000,000 - $10,000,000
Income Sources: Private Foundations/Grants/Endowments; Business/Corporate Donations; Box Office; Government Grants; Individual Donations
Annual Attendance: 130,610
Affiliations: AEA; LORT
Performance Facilities: Loeb Drama Center

FACILITY

LOEB DRAMA CENTER
64 Brattle Street, Cambridge, MA 02138
(617) 495-2668
FAX: (617) 495-1705
Type of Facility: Theatre House
Type of Stage: Thrust; Flexible; Proscenium
Orchestra Pit
Seating Capacity: 556
Year Built: 1960   **Architect:** Hugh Stubbins   **Cost:** $1,700,000
Acoustical Consultant: Bolt, Beranek & Newman
Contact for Rental: Production Manager;   (617) 495-2668

Manager: Robert J. Orchard
Resident Groups: American Repertory Theatre; Harvard/Radcliffe Dramatic Club

RADCLIFFE COLLEGE - AGASSIZ THEATER
10 Garden Street, Cambridge, MA 02138
(617) 495-8676
Type of Facility: Theatre House
Facility Originally: Meeting Hall; Movie House
Type of Stage: Proscenium   Orchestra Pit
Seating Capacity: 350
Year Built: 1902   Architect: A.W. Longfellow   Cost: $200,000
Year Remodeled: 1983   Architect: Goody, Clancey & Associates   Cost: $2,000,000
Acoustical Consultant: Cavanaugh & Jucci
Rental is for Harvard and Radcliffe groups only.

RADCLIFFE COLLEGE - LYMAN COMMON ROOM
10 Garden Street, Cambridge, MA 02138
(617) 495-8676
Type of Facility: Room
Facility Originally: Ballroom
Type of Stage: Flexible
Seating Capacity: 150
Year Built: 1902   Architect: A.W. Longfellow   Cost: $200,000
Year Remodeled: 1983   Architect: Goody, Clancey & Associates   Cost: $2,000,000
Rental is for Harvard and Radcliffe groups only.

SANDERS THEATRE
Quincy and Kirkland Streets, Cambridge, MA 02138
(617) 495-4968
FAX: (617) 495-2420
Mailing Address: Harvard Real Estate, 1350 Massachusetts Avenue, Cambridge, MA 02138
Founded: 1876
Type of Facility: Concert Hall; Auditorium; Performance Center
Type of Stage: Semi-Proscenium, no curtain
Stage Dimensions: 59'x27'
Seating Capacity: 1,224
Year Built: 1876   Architect: Ware and Van Brunt
Contact for Rental: Ann Dumaresq;   (617) 495-4968
Resident Groups: Boston Philharmonic; Pro Arte Chamber Orchestra; The Boston Chamber Music Society

---

Charlestown

THEATRE

CHARLESTOWN WORKING THEATER
442 Bunker Hill Street, Charlestown, MA 02129
(617) 242-3534
Founded: 1972
Arts Area: Professional; Summer Stock; Community; Theatrical Group; Puppet
Status: Professional; Semi-Professional; Non-Professional; Non-Profit
Type: Performing; Touring; Resident; Educational; Sponsoring
Purpose: To produce a quality of life that can be felt and understood through the artistic process involving a community of people participating in a world of their own making
Management: Kristen Johnson, Managing Director
Officers: Randall Warren, President; John McKelway, Vice President; Christopher Burnett, Secretary
Paid Staff: 1   Volunteer Staff: 60
Utilizes: Special Technical Talent; Guest Artists; Guest Directors
Budget: $1,000 - $50,000
Income Sources: Private Foundations/Grants/Endowments; Business/Corporate Donations; Box Office; Government Grants; Individual Donations
Season: October - May
Affiliations: Massachusetts Council on the Arts and Humanities

Chilmark

FACILITY

BARN THEATRE
PO Box 405, Chilmark, MA 02535
(508) 645-9662
    Type of Facility: Theatre Complex; Performance Center; Multi-Purpose
    Facility Originally: Barn
    Type of Stage: Modified Apron Proscenium
    Stage Dimensions: 36'Wx27'D
    Seating Capacity: 100
    Year Remodeled: 1983   **Architect:** Ben Moore
    Contact for Rental: John Dodson; (508) 645-9662
    Resident Groups: The Yard

Concord

INSTRUMENTAL MUSIC

THE CONCORD BAND
PO Box 302, Concord, MA 01742
    Founded: 1959
    Arts Area: Band
    Status: Non-Professional; Non-Profit
    Type: Performing
    Management: Wilheim Toland, Music Director; J. Kemson, Manager/Librarian; L. Matson, Fundraising
    Officers: B. P. Troup, President; J. Grace, Treasurer
    Paid Staff: 2   **Volunteer Staff:** 7
    Paid Artists: 1   **Non-Paid Artists:** 70
    Utilizes: Guest Conductors; Guest Artists
    Budget: $1,000 - $50,000
    Income Sources: Private Foundations/Grants/Endowments; Business/Corporate Donations; Box Office; Government Grants; Individual Donations
    Season: September - August
    Affiliations: Association of Concert Bands
    Performance Facilities: 51 Walden

CONCORD ORCHESTRA
PO Box 381, Concord, MA 01742
(508) 369-4967
    Founded: 1952
    Arts Area: Symphony; Orchestra
    Status: Non-Professional; Non-Profit
    Type: Performing
    Purpose: Amateur orchestra dedicated to enjoyment of playing music by its members and providing good music to the community
    Management: Richard Pittman, Conductor
    Officers: Fan-Chia Tao, President; Nancy McCarthy, Vice President; Priscilla Derananian, Secretary; David Powell, Treasurer
    Paid Staff: 1   **Volunteer Staff:** 8
    Paid Artists: 2   **Non-Paid Artists:** 70
    Utilizes: Guest Artists
    Budget: $1,000 - $50,000
    Income Sources: Box Office; Government Grants; Individual Donations
    Season: September - May   **Annual Attendance:** 3,600
    Affiliations: ASOL

FACILITY

THE FRIENDS OF THE PERFORMING ARTS IN CONCORD - 51 WALDEN
51 Walden Street, PO Box 251, Concord, MA 01742
(508) 369-7911
    Type of Facility: Theatre Complex; Concert Hall; Auditorium
    Facility Originally: Meeting Hall; Movie House
    Type of Stage: Flexible; Proscenium
    Stage Dimensions: 26'x24'
    Seating Capacity: 400

Year Built: 1885
Year Remodeled: 1974   **Architect:** Joseph Schiffer   **Cost:** $300,000
Acoustical Consultant: G. Anderson
Contact for Rental: Kathleen Chick;   (508) 369-7911
Resident Groups: The Concord Players; The Concord Orchestra; The Concord Band

---

Deerfield

INSTRUMENTAL MUSIC

MUSIC IN DEERFIELD
PO Box 264, Deerfield, MA 01342
(413) 772-0241, ext. 3327
FAX: (413) 774-6629
Founded: 1979
Arts Area: Chamber; Ensemble; Instrumental Group
Status: Semi-Professional; Non-Profit
Type: Sponsoring
Purpose: To bring to Franklin County the finest chamber music artists of national and international reputation
Management: David C. Howell, President; Priscilla Butterworth, Treasurer
Volunteer Staff: 18
Paid Artists: 15
Utilizes: Guest Artists
Budget: $50,000 - $100,000
Income Sources: Private Foundations/Grants/Endowments; Business/Corporate Donations; Box Office; Government Grants; Individual Donations
Season: September - May   **Annual Attendance:** 1,500
Affiliations: CMA; New England Presenters
Performance Facilities: Brick Church Meeting House

Dennis

THEATRE

CAPE PLAYHOUSE OF THE RAYMOND MOORE FOUNDATION
Route 6A, Dennis, MA 02638
(508) 385-3838
FAX: (508) 385-8162
Founded: 1927
Arts Area: Professional; Summer Stock
Status: Professional; Non-Profit
Type: Performing
Purpose: Established by the Raymond Moore Foundation and chartered by the Commonwealth of Massachusetts in 1948, Cape Playhouse operates for educational and charitable purposes as well as presenting top summer entertainment with stars of stage, screen and television.
Management: Carleton Davis, Managing Director
Officers: Emily Levine, President; James Julian, Vice President; J. Lee Marchildon, Treasurer; Avard Craig, Secretary
Paid Staff: 45   **Volunteer Staff:** 8
Paid Artists: 90
Budget: $500,000 - $1,000,000
Income Sources: Private Foundations/Grants/Endowments; Box Office
Season: June - September   **Annual Attendance:** 50,000
Performance Facilities: Cape Playhouse

FACILITY

CAPE PLAYHOUSE
Route 6A, Dennis, MA 02638
(508) 385-3838
Founded: 1927
Type of Facility: Theatre House
Facility Originally: Church; Meeting Hall; Movie House
Type of Stage: Proscenium
Stage Dimensions: 80'Wx50'D
Seating Capacity: 607
Year Built: 1820
Year Remodeled: 1927   **Architect:** Cleon Throckmorton

Dorchester

INSTRUMENTAL MUSIC

ASHMONT HILL CHAMBER MUSIC
67 Ocean Street, Dorchester, MA 02124
(617) 288-3697
FAX: (617) 825-9789
Founded: 1985
Arts Area: Chamber
Status: Professional
Type: Performing; Touring
Purpose: To perfrom high quality chamber music concerts from a repertoire that spans the centuries; to combine seldom heard and classical works; to educate new audiences about chamber music
Officers: Rachel Goodwin, Artistic Director; Andrea Dietrich, Treasurer; Cetta DiCara, Secretary
Volunteer Staff: 5
Non-Paid Artists: 13
Utilizes: Guest Artists
Budget: $1,000 - $50,000
Income Sources: Private Foundations/Grants/Endowments; Box Office; Government Grants; Individual Donations
Season: September - May **Annual Attendance:** 600
Affiliations: CMA
Performance Facilities: Peabody Hall; All Saints Church

THEATRE

BOSTON THEATER GROUP
26 Eastman Street, Dorchester, MA 02125
(617) 288-3085
Founded: 1978
Arts Area: Professional; Theatrical Group
Status: Semi-Professional; Non-Profit
Type: Performing; Touring; Educational
Purpose: Founded by a small core of actors to create original works for the stage, each piece evolves through the collective work of the actors together with the director, writers, designers and musicians.
Management: Thomas C. Henry, Artistic Director and Administrative Co-Director; Karen S. Henry, Administrative Co-Director; Cornelia Boniface, Booking Manager
Officers: John Hoffman, Chairman, Karen S. Henry, President; Eleanor Shay, Treasurer
Paid Staff: 3 **Volunteer Staff:** 10
Paid Artists: 5
Budget: $1,000 - $50,000
Income Sources: Private Foundations/Grants/Endowments; Business/Corporate Donations; Box Office; Government Grants; Individual Donations
Season: September - June **Annual Attendance:** 5,000

Dover

PERFORMING SERIES

CHARLES RIVER CREATIVE ARTS PROGRAM
56 Centre Street, Box 339, Dover, MA 02054
(508) 785-1260
Founded: 1970
Arts Area: Dance; Vocal Music; Instrumental Music; Theater; Festivals
Status: Non-Professional; Non-Profit
Type: Performing; Resident; Educational; Sponsoring
Purpose: To promote dance, drama, music, art and media among boys and girls ages 8-15, both as creators and performers; to sponsor two 4-week sessions each summer, producing two Arts Festivals
Management: Talbot Dewey, Jr., Director; Liz Callahan, Theatre Director; Bob Ingari, Music Director; Peter D. Dewey, Technical Director; Mary Tsiongas, Art Director; Anne Carey, Dance Director; Anna Jones, Director of the Charles River School; Priscilla B. Dewey, Arts Consultant
Officers: Frank Sola, Chairman of the Board
Paid Staff: 58
Paid Artists: 40
Utilizes: Special Technical Talent; Guest Artists; Guest Directors
Budget: $100,000 - $500,000
Income Sources: Private Foundations/Grants/Endowments; Business/Corporate Donations; Box Office; Government Grants; Individual Donations

Season: June - August   Annual Attendance: 2,000
Affiliations: NETC; Charles River School
Performance Facilities: Festival Theatre

FACILITY

FESTIVAL THEATRE
56 Centre Street, Dover, MA 02030
(508) 785-1260
Type of Facility: Outdoor (Concert); Multi-Purpose
Type of Stage: Thrust; Environmental; Elizabethan
Stage Dimensions: 17'x34'x20'   Orchestra Pit
Seating Capacity: 500
Year Built: 1977   Architect: Dan Veaner   Cost: $7,000
Year Remodeled: 1992   Cost: $50,000
Acoustical Consultant: Peter D. Dewey
Contact for Rental: Talbot Dewey, Jr.;   (617) 785-1260
Resident Groups: Charles River Creative Arts Program; Freelance Players
Occasionally available for rental

East Wareham

THEATRE

THE GATEWAY PLAYERS
PO Box 369, East Wareham, MA 02538
(617) 295-6768
Founded: 1972
Arts Area: Theatrical Group
Status: Semi-Professional; Non-Profit
Type: Performing; Touring; Resident; Educational
Purpose: To provide theater on a year-round basis to the people in Southeastern Massachusetts
Management: Robin Vontura, Directors
Officers: George Hayden, Chairman; Raymond David Cardoza, Vice Chairman; Paul Arthur Wirth, Recording Secretary;
Irene Zook, Corresponding Secretary; Dolores Rinko, Treasurer
Paid Staff: 1   Volunteer Staff: 3
Paid Artists: 3   Non-Paid Artists: 28
Utilizes: Special Technical Talent; Guest Conductors; Guest Artists; Guest Directors
Budget: $1,000 - $50,000
Income Sources: Private Foundations/Grants/Endowments; Business/Corporate Donations; Box Office; Government
Grants; Individual Donations
Season: 52 Weeks   Annual Attendance: 6,000

Fall River

INSTRUMENTAL MUSIC

GREATER FALL RIVER SYMPHONY SOCIETY
PO Box 2101, Fall River, MA 02722
(508) 673-2022
Founded: 1925
Arts Area: Symphony
Status: Professional; Non-Professional; Non-Profit
Type: Performing
Purpose: Cultural resource for over sixty years
Management: Faust D. Fiore, Music Conductor
Officers: Bruce E. Rex, President; Hazel L. Costa, Vice President; Loretta Pacheco, Secretary
Volunteer Staff: 4
Paid Artists: 2   Non-Paid Artists: 2
Utilizes: Guest Artists
Budget: $1,000 - $50,000
Income Sources: Private Foundations/Grants/Endowments; Business/Corporate Donations; Box Office; Government
Grants; Individual Donations
Season: September - April   Annual Attendance: 1,500

Falmouth

VOCAL MUSIC

COLLEGE LIGHT OPERA COMPANY
PO Drawer F, Falmouth, MA 02541
(508) 548-0668; (508) 774-8485
Founded: 1969
Arts Area: Light Opera; Operetta; Musical Theatre
Status: Non-Professional; Non-Profit
Type: Performing; Resident; Educational
Management: Robert A. Haslun, Producer/General Manager; Ursula R. Haslun, Producer/Business Manager
Officers: DeWitt C. Jones III, President; Robert A. Haslun, Treasurer; Ursula R. Haslun, Secretary
Paid Staff: 10 **Volunteer Staff:** 5
Non-Paid Artists: 55
Utilizes: Guest Conductors; Guest Directors
Budget: $100,000 - $500,000
Income Sources: Private Foundations/Grants/Endowments; Business/Corporate Donations; Box Office; Individual Donations
Season: July - September **Annual Attendance:** 15,000
Performance Facilities: Highfield Theatre

FACILITY

HIGHFIELD THEATRE
PO Drawer F, Falmouth, MA 02541
(508) 548-2211
Type of Facility: Theatre House
Facility Originally: Barn
Type of Stage: Proscenium
Stage Dimensions: 20'x30'x15' **Orchestra Pit**
Seating Capacity: 302
Year Built: 1890
Year Remodeled: 1948 **Cost:** $38,000
Manager: Robert Haslun; (508) 548-2211
Resident Groups: The Falmouth Theatre Guild; The College Light Opera Company

Gloucester

THEATRE

GLOUCESTER STAGE COMPANY
267 East Main Street, Gloucester, MA 01930
(508) 281-4099
FAX: (508) 283-5150
Founded: 1979
Arts Area: Professional; Theatrical Group
Status: Professional; Non-Profit
Type: Performing; Resident; Educational; Sponsoring; Producing
Purpose: Through support and performance of drama by contemporary playwrights, Gloucester Stage Company does staged readings of new works-in-process and fun productions of new and important plays.
Management: Mary John Boylan, Business Director; Heidi J. Dallin, Publicity Director; Janet Howes, Production Stage Manager; Israel Horovitz, Artistic Director; Keri Ellis Cahill, Production Coordinator; Robbie Chasitz, Assistant Artistic Director; Rob Duggan, Technical Director
Officers: Barry Y. Wainer Esq., President; Thomas S. Grilk Esq., Vice President; James Dunne, Treasurer; Elaine Conway, Secretary
Paid Staff: 6 **Volunteer Staff:** 30
Paid Artists: 40
Utilizes: Special Technical Talent; Guest Artists; Guest Directors
Budget: $100,000 - $500,000
Income Sources: Private Foundations/Grants/Endowments; Business/Corporate Donations; Box Office; Government Grants; Individual Donations
Season: 40 weeks **Annual Attendance:** 20,000

Great Barrington

DANCE

OLGA DUNN DANCE COMPANY
321 Main Street, PO Box 157, Great Barrington, MA 01230
(413) 528-9674
Founded: 1978
Arts Area: Modern; Ballet; Jazz
Status: Semi-Professional; Non-Profit
Type: Performing; Touring; Educational; Sponsoring
Purpose: To promote dance through outreach programs, school lecture demonstrations and full-length concerts; to train professional-level dancers; to develop original choreography in collaboration with music and theater; to feature local and guest talent
Management: Joan Nikitas, Business Manager; Brian Burke, Development Director; Cora Portnoff, Booking/Travel Coordinator; Marie Care, Administrative Assistant
Officers: Olga Dunn, President; Merrill Sanderson, Secretary; Diana Moxon, Treasurer
Paid Staff: 6 **Volunteer Staff:** 32
Paid Artists: 4 **Non-Paid Artists:** 7
Utilizes: Guest Artists; Guest Choreographers
Budget: $1,000 - $50,000
Income Sources: Private Foundations/Grants/Endowments; Business/Corporate Donations; Box Office; Government Grants; Individual Donations
Season: 52 Weeks **Annual Attendance:** 5,000
Affiliations: Mahaiwe Theater
Performance Facilities: Mahaiwe Theater

Greenfield

THEATRE

ARENA CIVIC THEATRE
Shea Theatre, Avenue A, PO Box 744, Greenfield, MA 01302
(413) 774-5898
Founded: 1971
Arts Area: Community; Theatrical Group
Status: Non-Professional; Non-Profit
Type: Performing
Purpose: Arena Civic Theatre is a volunteer community organization which recognizes the unique spiritual fulfillment and opportunity for personal growth that theatre provides its participants.
Officers: Kimberley Morin, President; Alan Maynard, Vice President; Sondra Radosh, Treasurer; Wendy Fydenkevez, Secretary
Volunteer Staff: 15
Non-Paid Artists: 70
Utilizes: Special Technical Talent; Guest Directors
Budget: $1,000 - $50,000
Income Sources: Business/Corporate Donations; Box Office; Government Grants; Individual Donations
Season: 52 Weeks **Annual Attendance:** 7,500
Affiliations: NALAA; Mohawk Trail Association
Performance Facilities: Shea Theater, Turner Falls, MA

Groton

FACILITY

LAWRENCE ACADEMY THEATRE
Powderhouse Road, Groton, MA 01450
(508) 448-6535
Type of Facility: Theatre House
Type of Stage: Proscenium
Stage Dimensions: 30'x30'
Seating Capacity: 400
Year Built: 1965
Contact for Rental: Donna Tyrrell;   (508) 448-6535

Hingham

THEATRE

HINGHAM CIVIC MUSIC THEATRE
Box 50, Hingham, MA 02043
(617) 749-0934
FAX: (617) 426-3180
    Founded: 1935
    Arts Area: Musical; Dinner; Community; Theatrical Group .
    Status: Non-Professional; Non-Profit
    Type: Performing; Resident; Educational
    Purpose: To foster and promote educational and practical aspects of music and theatre arts in the community
    Utilizes: Special Technical Talent; Guest Conductors; Guest Directors
    Budget: $1,000 - $50,000
    Income Sources: Box Office
    Season: September - June   **Annual Attendance:** 4,000
    Performance Facilities: Hingham High School Auditorium

FACILITY

HINGHAM HIGH SCHOOL - AUDITORIUM
41 Pleasant Street, Hingham, MA 02043
(617) 749-2160
    Type of Facility: Auditorium
    Type of Stage: Proscenium
    Seating Capacity: 750
    Year Built: 1940
    Contact for Rental: Nancy Stinson;   (617) 749-2160
    Resident Groups: Hingham Civic Music Theatre; Hingham Civic Orchestra

Holliston

DANCE

LITHUANIAN FOLK DANCE GROUP OF BOSTON
24 Mitchell Road, Holliston, MA 01746
(508) 429-7567
FAX: (508) 429-3298
    Founded: 1937
    Arts Area: Ethnic; Folk
    Status: Non-Profit
    Type: Performing
    Purpose: To preserve and promote Lithuanian culture
    Management: Ruta Mickunas, Instructor/Choreographer; Gema Phillips, Administrator
    Officers: Gema Phillips, Chairman of the Board
    Volunteer Staff: 6
    Non-Paid Artists: 40
    Budget: $1,000 - $50,000
    Income Sources: Individual Donations
    Season: October - July

Ipswich

PERFORMING SERIES

CASTLE HILL FESTIVAL
Castle Hill Foundation, PO Box 563, Ipswich, MA 01938
(508) 356-4351
FAX: (508) 356-2143
    Founded: 1951
    Arts Area: Vocal Music; Instrumental Music; Festivals
    Status: Professional; Non-Profit
    Type: Performing; Educational; Sponsoring
    Purpose: Presentation of the performing arts in a historic location, the R.T. Crane Estate
    Management: Elizabeth Ann Hathaway, Public Programs Manager

Officers: Glenn Dickson, President; Jim LaFitte, Treasurer
Paid Staff: 7   **Volunteer Staff:** 200
Paid Artists: 121
Utilizes: Special Technical Talent; Guest Conductors; Guest Artists
Budget: $100,000 - $500,000
Income Sources: Private Foundations/Grants/Endowments; Business/Corporate Donations; Box Office; Government Grants; Individual Donations
Season: July - August   **Annual Attendance:** 16,000
Affiliations: APAP; Massachusetts Cultural Alliance
Performance Facilities: Crane Memorial Reservation

Jamaica Plain

THEATRE

THE FOOTLIGHT CLUB
Eliot Hall, PO Box 114, Jamaica Plain, MA 02130
(617) 524-6506
Founded: 1877
Arts Area: Community; Theatrical Group
Status: Non-Professional; Non-Profit
Type: Performing; Resident
Purpose: To provide quality theatre as an integral component of a vital arts community and to offer involvement to anyone interested in theatre
Officers: John Thomann, President; Jane Yoffe, Vice President; Patti Darssigny, Secretary; Lisa Macmillan, Treasurer
Volunteer Staff: 200
Non-Paid Artists: 200
Budget: $1,000 - $50,000
Income Sources: Business/Corporate Donations; Box Office; Individual Donations
Season: 52 Weeks   **Annual Attendance:** 3,000
Performance Facilities: Eliot Hall

Lee

VOCAL MUSIC

BERKSHIRE OPERA COMPANY, INC.
17 Main Street, Box 598, Lee, MA 01238
(413) 243-1343
Founded: 1985
Arts Area: Lyric Opera; Chamber Opera
Status: Professional; Non-Profit
Type: Performing; Touring; Resident; Educational
Purpose: To provide opera fully staged in English to residents and tourists in the Berkshires
Management: Rex Hearn, General Director; Joseph Bascetta, Artistic Director; Joel Revzen, Music Director; Barbara Martin, Administrator
Officers: L.D. Cohen MD, Chairman; R.A. Hearn, President
Paid Staff: 4   **Volunteer Staff:** 12
Paid Artists: 60
Utilizes: Special Technical Talent; Guest Artists; Guest Directors
Budget: $100,000 - $500,000
Income Sources: Private Foundations/Grants/Endowments; Business/Corporate Donations; Box Office; Individual Donations; Program Advertising
Season: July - August   **Annual Attendance:** 4,000
Affiliations: Berkshire Hills Visitors Bureau
Performance Facilities: Cranwell Opera House

Lexington

VOCAL MUSIC

THE MASTER SINGERS
PO Box 172, Lexington, MA 02173
(617) 275-8498
Founded: 1967
Arts Area: Choral

Status: Non-Profit
Type: Performing; Touring
Purpose: To present the chamber chorus repertoire of all eras in an intimate setting aimed at maximum enjoyment for both singers and listeners
Management: James Oleson, Music Director
Officers: Sarah Getty, President; Shaylor Lindsay, Treasurer; Virginia Fitzgerald, Secretary
Volunteer Staff: 6
Paid Artists: 2   **Non-Paid Artists:** 30
Utilizes: Guest Artists
Budget: $1,000 - $50,000
Income Sources: Private Foundations/Grants/Endowments; Business/Corporate Donations; Box Office; Government Grants; Individual Donations
Season: September - June   **Annual Attendance:** 1,000
Affiliations: Massachusetts Cultural Alliance
Performance Facilities: First Parish Church, Lexington

Lowell

THEATRE

MERRIMACK REPERTORY THEATRE
Liberty Hall, 50 East Merrimack, Lowell, MA 01852
(508) 454-6324
Founded: 1979
Arts Area: Professional; Theatrical Group
Status: Professional; Non-Profit
Type: Performing; Resident
Purpose: To engage our audience in a theatrically vital process of communication; to enjoy, together, the resonance of romantic arts
Management: David G. Kent, Artistic Director
Officers: Jack O'Conner, Board President
Paid Staff: 16
Utilizes: Special Technical Talent; Guest Directors
Budget: $500,000 - $1,000,000
Income Sources: Private Foundations/Grants/Endowments; Business/Corporate Donations; Box Office; Government Grants; Individual Donations
Season: November - May
Affiliations: AEA; LORT
Performance Facilities: Liberty Hall

FACILITY

UNIVERSITY OF LOWELL - CENTER FOR THE ARTS
One University Avenue, Lowell, MA 01854
(508) 452-5000
Type of Facility: Performance Center
Type of Stage: Proscenium
Stage Dimensions: 37'Dx40'H proscenium opening   **Orchestra Pit**
Seating Capacity: Theater - 970; Recital Hall - 200
Contact for Rental: Oliver Chamberlain;   (508) 934-4444

Lynn

FACILITY

LYNN CITY HALL MEMORIAL AUDITORIUM
3 City Hall Square, Lynn, MA 01901
(617) 598-4000, ext. 133
FAX: (617) 592-9411
Type of Facility: Auditorium
Type of Stage: Proscenium
Stage Dimensions: 84'Wx31'D   **Orchestra Pit**
Seating Capacity: 2,072
Year Built: 1947   **Architect:** M.A. Dyer Company
Contact for Rental: James I. Starratt, Building Commissioner;   (617) 598-4000

Mansfield

FACILITY

GREAT WOODS CENTER FOR THE PERFORMING ARTS
PO Box 810, Mansfield, MA 02048
(508) 339-2331
  Type of Facility: Amphitheater
  Type of Stage: Environmental
  Seating Capacity: Permanent - 7,000; Lawn Seating- 8,000
  Year Built: 1986
  Contact for Rental: Bruce Montgomery, General Manager;   (508) 339-2331
  Resident Groups: Summer Home of the Pittsburg Symphony Orchestra

Marblehead

INSTRUMENTAL MUSIC

NORTH SHORE PHILHARMONIC ORCHESTRA
PO Box 1131, Marblehead, MA 01945
(617) 631-6513
  Founded: 1948
  Arts Area: Symphony; Orchestra
  Status: Semi-Professional; Non-Profit
  Type: Performing; Resident
  Purpose: To present quality affordable music performances at the local level to a broad cross-section of audiences
  Management: Herbert A. Cohen, Manager; Max Hobart, Music Director
  Officers: Robert Marra, President; Janine M. Grillo, Secretary; Donald Melino, Treasurer
  Volunteer Staff: 10
  Paid Artists: 40   **Non-Paid Artists:** 35
  Utilizes: Guest Artists
  Budget: $1,000 - $50,000
  Income Sources: Private Foundations/Grants/Endowments; Business/Corporate Donations; Box Office; Government Grants; Individual Donations
  Season: September - May   **Annual Attendance:** 10,000

Marlboro

THEATRE

MARLBORO CULTURAL AFFAIRS
255 Main Street, Marlboro, MA 01752
(508) 481-8104
FAX: (508) 624-6397
  Founded: 1978
  Arts Area: Musical; Dinner; Community; Puppet
  Status: Non-Profit
  Type: Performing; Sponsoring
  Purpose: To provide professional leadership in promoting, educating and creating awareness of quality cultural activities in the greater Marlboro area
  Officers: Cecile Sharon, Chairman of the Board
  Paid Staff: 5   **Volunteer Staff:** 75
  Paid Artists: 30   **Non-Paid Artists:** 10
  Utilizes: Special Technical Talent; Guest Conductors; Guest Artists; Guest Directors
  Budget: $100,000 - $500,000
  Income Sources: Private Foundations/Grants/Endowments; Business/Corporate Donations; Box Office; Government Grants; Individual Donations
  Season: 52 Weeks   **Annual Attendance:** 80,000
  Performance Facilities: Johnson Auditorium

Medford

THEATRE

THE MAGIC CIRCLE THEATER
Tufts University, Balch Arena Theater, Medford, MA 02155
(617) 627-3493
  Founded: 1944
  Arts Area: Summer Stock; Theatrical Group
  Status: Non-Profit; Children, Ages 11-15
  Type: Performing; Resident; Educational
  Purpose: To entertain and educate
  Management: Paula Samson, Artistic Director; Sherwood Collins, Executive Director; Joanne Barnett, Business Manager
  Paid Staff: 25   **Volunteer Staff:** 9
  Paid Artists: 15
  Utilizes: Guest Directors
  Budget: $1,000 - $50,000
  Income Sources: Box Office
  Season: June - August
  Affiliations: Tufts University
  Performance Facilities: Arena Theatre

FACILITY

TUFTS UNIVERSITY - BALCH ARENA THEATER
Medford, MA 02155
(617) 627-3493
  Type of Facility: Theatre House
  Type of Stage: Arena
  Stage Dimensions: 18'x23'
  Seating Capacity: 211
  Year Built: 1991   **Architect:** CBT
  Manager: Joanne Barnett
  Resident Groups: Tufts University Theater; Magic Circle Children's Theater; Pen, Paint and Pretzels

Melrose

INSTRUMENTAL MUSIC

MELROSE ORCHESTRAL ASSOCIATION
PO Box 175, Melrose, MA 02176
(617) 662-0641
  Founded: 1918
  Arts Area: Symphony; Orchestra
  Status: Non-Profit
  Type: Performing
  Purpose: To provide classical music to the community and provide a place for community individuals and students to perform
  Officers: Millie Rich, President/CEO; Anne Fremont-Smith, First Vice President; Alice C. Gross, Second Vice President; Caroline Soule, Secretary; Albert J. Traveis, Treasurer
  Volunteer Staff: 20
  Paid Artists: 1   **Non-Paid Artists:** 72
  Utilizes: Guest Artists
  Budget: $1,000 - $50,000
  Income Sources: Private Foundations/Grants/Endowments; Business/Corporate Donations; Box Office; Government Grants; Individual Donations
  Season: September - May   **Annual Attendance:** 2,500
  Performance Facilities: Memorial Building, Melrose

Milton

INSTRUMENTAL MUSIC

ROSALIE GERUT AND FRIENDS
15 Parkway Crescent, Milton, MA 02186
(617) 698-9806
  Founded: 1985

Arts Area: Chamber; Ethnic; Folk; Instrumental Group
Status: Professional
Type: Performing; Touring; Educational
Purpose: To present authentic concerts of Jewish music drawing on folk, Yiddish theater, Klezmer, Hebrew and original music; to preserve this culture by means of recording this music; Rosalie Gerut is the daughter of a folk musician from Lithuania and learned folk music of the Jewish tradition from him
Management: Steve Netsky, Boston Agent; Jewish Lecture Bureau, New York Agent
Officers: Rosalie Gerut, Director/Composer/Singer; Cam Sawzin, Cellist; Robin Miller, Flute/Recorders; Jim Guttman, Upright Bass; Jeff Warschauer, Guitar/Mandolin
Paid Staff: 2
Paid Artists: 5
Budget: $1,000 - $50,000
Season: 52 Weeks
Affiliations: ASCAP

Nantucket

THEATRE

ACTORS THEATRE OF NANTUCKET
18 Hinckley Lane, Nantucket, MA 02554
(508) 228-6325
Founded: 1985
Arts Area: Professional; Musical; Theatrical Group; Children's Theatre
Status: Professional; Non-Profit; Non-Equity
Type: Performing; Resident; Educational; Sponsoring
Purpose: To provide professional theatre for Nantucket Island
Management: Richard Cary, Producing Artistic Director; Tori Haring-Smith, Associate Director
Officers: Bill Hourihan, President; Bob Lang, Vice President; Roger Seitz, Secretary; Richard Cary, Treasurer
Paid Staff: 8 **Volunteer Staff:** 2
Paid Artists: 15
Utilizes: Special Technical Talent; Guest Artists; Guest Directors; Resident Professionals
Budget: $100,000 - $500,000
Income Sources: Private Foundations/Grants/Endowments; Business/Corporate Donations; Box Office; Government Grants; Individual Donations
Season: June - October **Annual Attendance:** 8,000

THE THEATRE WORKSHOP OF NANTUCKET, INC.
2 Twin Street, PO Box 1297, Nantucket, MA 02554
(508) 228-4655; (508) 228-4305
Founded: 1956
Arts Area: Community
Status: Non-Professional; Non-Profit
Type: Performing; Educational
Purpose: To bring theatrical stage entertainment to the community using local talent; to offer year-round productions
Management: Edgar A. Anderson, Business Manager; S. Warren Krebs, Artistic Director
Officers: Elizabeth Gilbert, President; Marie Giffin, Treasurer
Volunteer Staff: 6
Non-Paid Artists: 25
Utilizes: Guest Directors
Budget: $50,000 - $100,000
Income Sources: Private Foundations/Grants/Endowments; Business/Corporate Donations; Box Office; Individual Donations
Annual Attendance: 6,000
Performance Facilities: Bennett Hall

New Bedford

THEATRE

ZEITERION THEATRE
684 Purchase Street, PO Box 4084, New Bedford, MA 02741
(508) 997-5664
FAX: (508) 999-5956
Founded: 1982
Arts Area: Professional
Status: Professional; Non-Profit

Type: Performing; Touring; Sponsoring
Purpose: To present a broad range of quality performing arts programs for the community
Management: Alan C. Liddell, Executive Director
Officers: Philip M. Carney, President; Ben Baker, Vice President; Doug Rodrigues, Treasurer
Paid Staff: 12   **Volunteer Staff:** 100
Budget: $500,000 - $1,000,000
Income Sources: Private Foundations/Grants/Endowments; Business/Corporate Donations; Box Office; Government Grants; Individual Donations
Season: 52 Weeks   **Annual Attendance:** 65,000
Affiliations: New England Presenters
Performance Facilities: Zeiterion Theatre

FACILITY

ZEITERION THEATRE
684 Purchase Street, PO Box 4084, New Bedford, MA 02741
(508) 997-5664
FAX: (508) 999-5956
    Type of Facility: Concert Hall; Performance Center; Theatre House
    Facility Originally: Vaudeville
    Type of Stage: Proscenium
    Stage Dimensions: 80'Wx27'D   **Orchestra Pit**
    Seating Capacity: 1,267
    Year Built: 1923   **Architect:** Leary & Walker   **Cost:** $800,000
    Year Remodeled: 1982   **Architect:** Dyer & Brown Associates   **Cost:** $1,300,000
    Contact for Rental: Christopher LeBlanc;   (508) 997-5664
    Resident Groups: New Bedford Symphony; Miss Massachusetts Pageant; New Bedford Festival Theatre

Newburyport

DANCE

JOPPA JAZZ DANCE COMPANY
"The Tannery", 12 Federal Street, Newburyport, MA 01950
(508) 465-1485
    Founded: 1983
    Arts Area: Jazz
    Status: Non-Profit
    Type: Performing; Educational
    Purpose: To provide performance experience for aspiring dancers, and to educate the public on the beauty and benefits of dance
    Management: Irene L. Weiss, Artistic Director
    Officers: Carole Wagan, President; Claudia Stein, Secretary; Donn Kerrjan, Treasurer
    Volunteer Staff: 2
    Non-Paid Artists: 15
    Utilizes: Special Technical Talent; Guest Artists; Guest Choreographers
    Budget: $1,000 - $50,000
    Income Sources: Private Foundations/Grants/Endowments; Box Office; Government Grants; Individual Donations
    Season: 52 Weeks   **Annual Attendance:** 1,000

PERFORMING SERIES

NEWBURYPORT FAMILY YMCA
76 State, Newburyport, MA 01950
(508) 462-6711
    Founded: 1874
    Arts Area: Dance; Theater; Festivals
    Status: Non-Professional; Non-Profit
    Type: Performing; Educational; Sponsoring
    Purpose: To enrich the lives of the citizens in this area through physical, cultural and academic means
    Management: Jane P. Breaker, Executive Director; Kurt Anderson, Program Director
    Officers: Chip Wyser, President; Mae Bradshaw, Vice President; James Hughes, Treasurer
    Paid Staff: 6   **Volunteer Staff:** 5
    Utilizes: Special Technical Talent; Guest Artists; Guest Directors
    Budget: $50,000 - $100,000
    Income Sources: Private Foundations/Grants/Endowments; Business/Corporate Donations; Individual Donations
    Season: 52 Weeks

Newton

INSTRUMENTAL MUSIC

NEWTON SYMPHONY ORCHESTRA
PO Box 124, Newton, MA 02168
(617) 965-2555
>**Founded:** 1965
>**Arts Area:** Symphony; Orchestra
>**Status:** Non-Profit; Community
>**Type:** Performing
>**Purpose:** To provide outstanding music experience and perform a program from a broad repertoire at affordable prices
>**Management:** Constance G. Kantar, General Manager; Adrienne Hartzell, Personnel Manager/Librarian; Ronald Knudsen, Music Director/Conductor
>**Officers:** Judith Abrams, President; Linda Clarke, Vice President; Sally Baker, Secretary; George Hughes, Treasurer
>**Paid Staff:** 4   **Volunteer Staff:** 25
>**Paid Artists:** 21   **Non-Paid Artists:** 70
>**Utilizes:** Guest Artists
>**Budget:** $50,000 - $100,000
>**Income Sources:** Private Foundations/Grants/Endowments; Business/Corporate Donations; Box Office; Government Grants; Individual Donations
>**Season:** November - May   **Annual Attendance:** 3,600
>**Affiliations:** Newton Public Schools
>**Performance Facilities:** Aquinas College

VOCAL MUSIC

MASTERWORKS CHORALE
PO Box 620692, Newton, MA 02162
>**Founded:** 1940
>**Arts Area:** Choral
>**Status:** Semi-Professional; Non-Profit
>**Type:** Performing; Touring
>**Purpose:** To perform major choral works
>**Management:** Maria D. Hagigeorges, General Manager
>**Officers:** Julia Fox, President; Keivan Towfigh, Vice President; Doreen Fairbairn, Treasurer
>**Paid Staff:** 6   **Volunteer Staff:** 25
>**Paid Artists:** 2   **Non-Paid Artists:** 120
>**Budget:** $100,000 - $500,000
>**Income Sources:** Private Foundations/Grants/Endowments; Business/Corporate Donations; Box Office; Government Grants; Individual Donations; Performance Fees; Member Dues
>**Season:** October - May   **Annual Attendance:** 10,000
>**Performance Facilities:** Sanders Theatre, Harvard University

Newton Centre

ZAMIR CHORALE OF BOSTON
PO Box 126, Newton Centre, MA 02159
(617) 965-6522
>**Founded:** 1969
>**Arts Area:** Choral; Ethnic
>**Status:** Non-Professional; Non-Profit
>**Type:** Performing; Touring; Resident; Educational
>**Purpose:** To perfrom and preserve music arising from the Jewish people and tradition
>**Management:** Mark Miller, Manager; Joshua Jacobson, Music Director; Karen Harvey, Accompanist
>**Officers:** Jules Rosenberg, President; Jeffrey Levine, Vice President; Michael Haselkorn, Treasurer
>**Paid Staff:** 1   **Volunteer Staff:** 10
>**Paid Artists:** 2   **Non-Paid Artists:** 45
>**Utilizes:** Guest Artists
>**Budget:** $50,000 - $100,000
>**Income Sources:** Box Office; Government Grants; Individual Donations
>**Season:** September - July   **Annual Attendance:** 5,000
>**Affiliations:** CA

North Falmouth

THEATRE

FALMOUTH PLAYHOUSE
Off Boxberry Hill Road, PO Box 350, North Falmouth, MA 02556
(508) 563-5922
FAX: (508) 564-4546
Founded: 1949
Arts Area: Professional; Musical; Theatrical Group
Status: Professional; Commercial
Type: Touring; Educational; Producing
Purpose: To produce quality musical theatre, assist in offering young people professional experience, and be profit-making
Management: Jade Curtain Ltd., Hubert Fryman, Producer
Paid Staff: 50   **Volunteer Staff:** 30
Paid Artists: 250
Utilizes: Guest Directors
Budget: $50,000 - $100,000
Income Sources: Box Office
Season: June - October
Performance Facilities: Falmouth Playhouse

FACILITY

FALMOUTH PLAYHOUSE
Off Route 151, PO Box 350, North Falmouth, MA 02556
(508) 563-5922
Type of Facility: Theatre House; Multi-Purpose
Facility Originally: Private Club
Type of Stage: Proscenium
Orchestra Pit
Seating Capacity: 564
Year Built: 1932   **Architect:** E. Gunnar Peterson
Year Remodeled: 1949
Contact for Rental: Hubert Fryman;   (508) 564-4546
Manager: Robert Zeida
A restaurant and bar are attached to the theater.

Northampton

VOCAL MUSIC

COMMONWEALTH OPERA
160 Main Street, Northampton, MA 01060
(413) 586-5026
Founded: 1977
Arts Area: Grand Opera; Lyric Opera
Status: Semi-Professional
Type: Performing; Touring
Purpose: To further the enjoyment and professional opportunities of grand opera regionally
Management: Richard R. Rescia, Artistic Director
Officers: Nancy Gregg, President; Robert Reed, Vice President; Allan Smith, Treasurer; Helen K. Gallivan, Guild President
Volunteer Staff: 10
Budget: $50,000 - $100,000
Income Sources: Private Foundations/Grants/Endowments; Business/Corporate Donations; Box Office; Government Grants; Individual Donations
Season: September - May
Performance Facilities: Academy of Music; Congden Auditorium

THEATRE

NO THEATRE
c/o Available Potential Enterprises, Thornes Market, 150 Main Street, Northampton, MA 01060
(413) 586-5553
Arts Area: Professional; Theatrical Group
Status: Professional; Non-Profit

Type: Touring; Resident; Sponsoring
Purpose: To create original works for the stage using the vocabulary of various media
Management: Gordon G. Thorne, Executive Director; Roy Faudree, Artistic Director of NO Theatre
Officers: Gordon G. Thorne, President
Budget: $100,000 - $500,000
Income Sources: Private Foundations/Grants/Endowments; Business/Corporate Donations; Box Office; Government Grants; Individual Donations
Performance Facilities: Third Floor Thornes

Orleans

THEATRE

ACADEMY OF PERFORMING ARTS, INC.
120 Main Street, PO Box 1843, Orleans, MA 02653
(508) 255-5510; (508) 255-1963
>**Founded:** 1975
>**Arts Area:** Musical; Community; Theatrical Group
>**Status:** Professional; Semi-Professional; Non-Professional; Non-Profit
>**Type:** Performing; Touring; Educational; Sponsoring
>**Purpose:** School for the arts as well as a community theatre offering year-round opportunities in education and performance
>**Management:** Gail Meyers Sharman, Managing Director
>**Officers:** Patricia N. Silverman, President; Ann-Marie Litchfield, Vice President; C. Page McMahan, Treasurer
>**Paid Staff:** 22   **Volunteer Staff:** 20
>**Non-Paid Artists:** 100
>**Utilizes:** Special Technical Talent; Guest Conductors; Guest Artists; Guest Directors
>**Budget:** $100,000 - $500,000
>**Income Sources:** Private Foundations/Grants/Endowments; Business/Corporate Donations; Box Office; Government Grants; Individual Donations
>**Season:** 52 Weeks   **Annual Attendance:** 17,000
>**Performance Facilities:** Academy Playhouse

PERFORMING SERIES

THE CAPE AND ISLANDS CHAMBER MUSIC FESTIVAL
PO Box 2721, Orleans, MA 02653
(508) 349-7709
>**Founded:** 1979
>**Arts Area:** Festivals
>**Status:** Professional; Non-Profit
>**Type:** Performing; Educational
>**Purpose:** To produce a three-week chamber music festival presenting world-famous artists and rising young stars; to offer master classes and open rehearsals; to present new works by composers-in-residence each season
>**Management:** Samuel Sanders and Brian Zeger, Co-Artistic Directors; Joan Stevens, Administrative Director
>**Officers:** Robert Wright, President/Treasurer
>**Paid Staff:** 3
>**Utilizes:** Guest Artists
>**Budget:** $50,000 - $100,000
>**Income Sources:** Private Foundations/Grants/Endowments; Business/Corporate Donations; Box Office; Government Grants; Individual Donations
>**Season:** July - August   **Annual Attendance:** 2,000

FACILITY

ACADEMY PLAYHOUSE
120 Main Street, Orleans, MA 02653
(508) 255-1963
>**Type of Facility:** Theatre House
>**Facility Originally:** Town Hall
>**Type of Stage:** Flexible
>**Seating Capacity:** 172
>**Year Built:** 1873
>**Year Remodeled:** 1955
>**Manager:** Gail Meyers Sharman
>*Available for rent*

Osterville

INSTRUMENTAL MUSIC

CAPE COD SYMPHONY ORCHESTRA
1080 Main Street, Osterville, MA 02655
(508) 428-3577
Founded: 1961
Arts Area: Symphony; Orchestra
Status: Semi-Professional
Type: Performing
Purpose: To foster, promote and increase music knowledge and appreciation
Management: Wesley DeLacy, Executive Director; Christine Wells, Production/Promotion; Royston Nash, Music Director/Conductor
Officers: Fredrick Plumb, President; Gardiner Bridge, Leona Penn, Vice Presidents; Marjorie Burling, Secretary; Robert Barnet, Treasurer
Paid Staff: 4   **Volunteer Staff:** 1
Paid Artists: 70   **Non-Paid Artists:** 25
Utilizes: Guest Artists
Budget: $100,000 - $500,000
Income Sources: Private Foundations/Grants/Endowments; Business/Corporate Donations; Box Office; Government Grants; Individual Donations
Season: October - May   **Annual Attendance:** 30,000
Affiliations: ASOL
Performance Facilities: Mattacheese School, West Yarmouth

Pittsfield

VOCAL MUSIC

BERKSHIRE LYRIC THEATRE
PO Box 347, Pittsfield, MA 01202
(413) 499-8233
Founded: 1964
Arts Area: Light Opera; Choral
Status: Non-Profit
Type: Performing
Purpose: Light opera and choral concerts
Officers: Donald Phipps, President; Sharyl Noroian, Tom Sherer, Vice Presidents; Sue Burke, Secretary; Kathleen Kelley, Treasurer
Volunteer Staff: 50
Paid Artists: 20   **Non-Paid Artists:** 40
Utilizes: Special Technical Talent; Guest Artists
Budget: $1,000 - $50,000
Income Sources: Private Foundations/Grants/Endowments; Business/Corporate Donations; Box Office; Government Grants; Individual Donations
Season: September - June   **Annual Attendance:** 2,000

THEATRE

THE BERKSHIRE PUBLIC THEATRE COMPANY
30 Union Street, PO Box 860, Pittsfield, MA 01202
(413) 445-4631
FAX: (413) 445-4640
Founded: 1976
Arts Area: Professional; Theatrical Group
Status: Professional; Non-Profit
Type: Performing; Resident
Purpose: To provide affordable access to the performing arts, including theatre, music and dance for the Berkshire audience year round
Management: Frank Besell, Artistic Director; Iris Besell, Managing Director
Officers: Maria Caccaviello, Board President
Paid Staff: 10   **Volunteer Staff:** 200
Paid Artists: 50   **Non-Paid Artists:** 50
Utilizes: Guest Artists; Guest Directors
Budget: $100,000 - $500,000
Income Sources: Private Foundations/Grants/Endowments; Business/Corporate Donations; Box Office; Government Grants; Individual Donations

Season: 52 Weeks   **Annual Attendance:** 40,000
Affiliations: TCG
Performance Facilities: The Berkshire Public Theatre

PERFORMING SERIES

SOUTH MOUNTAIN ASSOCIATION
PO Box 23, Pittsfield, MA 01202
(413) 442-2106
    Founded: 1918
    Arts Area: Instrumental Music
    Status: Non-Profit
    Type: Sponsoring
    Purpose: Sponsor of chamber music concerts
    Management: Lou R. Steigler, Director
    Paid Staff: 1
    Paid Artists: 20
    Utilizes: Guest Artists
    Budget: $50,000 - $100,000
    Income Sources: Private Foundations/Grants/Endowments; Business/Corporate Donations; Box Office; Individual Donations
    Season: August - October   **Annual Attendance:** 1,900
    Performance Facilities: Concert Hall

FACILITY

BERKSHIRE COMMUNITY COLLEGE - KOUSSEVITZKY ARTS CENTER
1350 West Street, Pittsfield, MA 01201
(413) 499-0886
    Type of Facility: Theatre House
    Type of Stage: Thrust; Proscenium; Arena
    Stage Dimensions: 40'Wx46'Dx64'H   **Orchestra Pit**
    Seating Capacity: 510
    Year Built: 1970   **Cost:** $2,500,000
    Contact for Rental: Sam Slack;   (413) 499-0886
    Resident Groups: Pittsfield Town Players; Berkshire Ballet

---

Plymouth

INSTRUMENTAL MUSIC

PLYMOUTH PHILHARMONIC ORCHESTRA
130 Court Street, Plymouth, MA 02361
(508) 746-8008
FAX: (508) 746-0115
    Founded: 1913
    Arts Area: Symphony; Orchestra; Chamber; Ensemble
    Status: Professional; Semi-Professional; Non-Profit
    Type: Performing; Educational; Sponsoring
    Purpose: To perform symphonic music for southeastern Massachusetts audiences
    Management: Roberta J. Otto, Managing Director; Susan Lawrenson, Administrative Assistant
    Officers: Marcella Stanton, President; Robert Dawley, Judith Ingram, Vice Presidents; Diane Hilker, Secretary/Clerk; Ronald Orleans, Treasurer
    Paid Staff: 3
    Paid Artists: 68   **Non-Paid Artists:** 7
    Utilizes: Special Technical Talent; Guest Artists
    Budget: $100,000 - $500,000
    Income Sources: Private Foundations/Grants/Endowments; Business/Corporate Donations; Box Office; Government Grants; Individual Donations; Benefit Events
    Season: October - May   **Annual Attendance:** 8,000
    Affiliations: ASOL; Plymouth County Development Council; Plymouth Area Chamber of Commerce
    Performance Facilities: Memorial Hall

Richmond

THEATRE

ROBBINS - ZUST FAMILY MARIONETTES
East Road, Richmond, MA 01254
(413) 698-2591
Founded: 1971
Arts Area: Professional; Theatrical Group; Puppet
Status: Professional
Type: Performing; Touring
Purpose: To share our classic, richly-traditional tales and stories with new audiences and to develop and train those new audiences
Officers: Richard L Robbins, President; Maia Robbins-Zust, Vice President; Genie Zust, Secretary/Treasurer
Paid Staff: 6
Paid Artists: 6
Utilizes: Special Technical Talent; Guest Artists; Guest Directors
Budget: $1,000 - $50,000
Income Sources: Private Foundations/Grants/Endowments; Box Office; Individual Donations
Season: 52 Weeks **Annual Attendance:** 10,000
Performance Facilities: Berkshire Public Theatre

Rockport

INSTRUMENTAL MUSIC

ROCKPORT CHAMBER MUSIC FESTIVAL
PO Box 312, Rockport, MA 01966
(508) 546-7391; (212) 533-2429
Arts Area: Chamber
Status: Professional; Non-Profit
Type: Presenting
Purpose: To present eight chamber ensembles performing alone and in collaboration in a 16-concert series in June
Management: Lila Deis, Artistic Director
Officers: Warren Salinger, President of the Board
Budget: $50,000 - $100,000
Income Sources: Private Foundations/Grants/Endowments; Business/Corporate Donations; Government Grants; Individual Donations; Advertising/ Product Sales
Season: June
Performance Facilities: Rockport Art Association

Roslindale

THEATRE

POOBLEY GREEGY PUPPET THEATRE
106 Kittredge Street, Roslindale, MA 02131
(617) 325-5620
Founded: 1974
Arts Area: Puppet
Status: Professional; Non-Profit
Type: Performing; Touring; Educational
Purpose: To apply the art of puppetry to nonfictional subjects like dinosaurs, whaling, Ancient Egypt and elephants
Management: Janice and Stephen Babcock
Officers: Stephen Babcock, President; Janice Babcock, Treasurer
Paid Staff: 2
Paid Artists: 2
Utilizes: Special Technical Talent
Budget: $1,000 - $50,000
Income Sources: Private Foundations/Grants/Endowments; Box Office
Season: 52 Weeks **Annual Attendance:** 30,000
Affiliations: Arts Institute; New England Foundation for the Arts

---
Salem

VOCAL MUSIC

PAUL MADORE CHORALE
PO Box 992, Salem, MA 01970
(508) 774-7981
>**Founded:** 1966
>**Arts Area:** Lyric Opera; Choral; American Music
>**Status:** Semi-Professional; Non-Profit
>**Type:** Performing
>**Purpose:** To perform choral masterpieces toward the cultural pleasure and advancement of music throughout the North Shore and Boston areas
>**Management:** Paul Madore, Director
>**Officers:** Jacqueline Opie, President; Pauline Maher, Vice President; Roger Dugas, Treasurer; Ann Michaud, Recording Secretary; Nadine Sippel, Cooresponding Secretary; Josephine Kennedy, Librarian
>**Paid Staff:** 1   **Volunteer Staff:** 10
>**Paid Artists:** 12   **Non-Paid Artists:** 6
>**Budget:** $1,000 - $50,000
>**Income Sources:** Private Foundations/Grants/Endowments; Box Office; Individual Donations
>**Season:** September - June   **Annual Attendance:** 2,000
>**Affiliations:** Salem Chamber of Commerce; Nash-Patterson Opera Guild

---
Sharon

THEATRE

SHARON COMMUNITY THEATRE, INC.
53 High Street, Sharon, MA 02067
(617) 784-3721
>**Founded:** 1975
>**Arts Area:** Community; Theatrical Group
>**Status:** Non-Profit
>**Type:** Performing; Educational
>**Purpose:** Produce high quality, family-oriented, local entertainment (mainly play productions) at reasonable prices in the South Shore area
>**Management:** Tina Koppel, Business Manager; Dick Leemon, Publicity
>**Officers:** Eric Kahn, President; Mark Anderson, Vice President; Janet Abrahamson, Secretary; Jo Zagieboylo, Treasurer; Leon Saperstein, Past President; Ed Bolster, Historian
>**Volunteer Staff:** 65
>**Non-Paid Artists:** 60
>**Utilizes:** Special Technical Talent; Guest Directors
>**Budget:** $1,000 - $50,000
>**Income Sources:** Private Foundations/Grants/Endowments; Business/Corporate Donations; Box Office; Government Grants; Individual Donations
>**Season:** September - June   **Annual Attendance:** 1,000
>**Affiliations:** NETC
>**Performance Facilities:** Sharon Recreation Department Mini-Theatre

---
Sheffield

VOCAL MUSIC

BERKSHIRE CHORAL INSTITUTE
Berkshire School, 245 North Undermountain Road, Sheffield, MA 01257
(413) 229-8526
>**Founded:** 1982
>**Arts Area:** Choral
>**Status:** Non-Profit
>**Type:** Performing
>**Purpose:** To provide a summer workshop for amateur choral singers devoted to preparing and performing great choral works
>**Management:** Richard P. Unsworth, Executive Director; Linda Dufault, Business Manager
>**Officers:** John Hoyt Stookey, Founder/President
>**Utilizes:** Guest Conductors; Guest Artists
>**Season:** July - August

Shelburne

PERFORMING SERIES

MOHAWK TRAIL CONCERTS
PO Box 75, Shelburne, MA 01370
(413) 625-9511
> **Founded:** 1970
> **Arts Area:** Vocal Music; Instrumental Music; Festivals
> **Status:** Professional; Non-Profit
> **Type:** Performing; Touring; Resident; Educational; Sponsoring
> **Purpose:** To provide outstanding chamber music in our summer/fall concert series in the Berkshires and our in-school music programs
> **Management:** Cynthia Stetson, Office Manager; Arnold Black, Artistic Director
> **Officers:** Helen Spencer, President; Frederick Purnell, Treasurer
> **Paid Staff:** 1   **Volunteer Staff:** 150
> **Paid Artists:** 200
> **Utilizes:** Guest Artists
> **Budget:** $50,000 - $100,000
> **Income Sources:** Private Foundations/Grants/Endowments; Business/Corporate Donations; Box Office; Government Grants; Individual Donations
> **Season:** July - August
> **Performance Facilities:** Federated Church

Sherborn

INSTRUMENTAL MUSIC

STAN MCDONALD'S BLUE HORIZON JAZZ BAND
25 Farm Road, Sherborn, MA 01770
(508) 653-7247
> **Founded:** 1981
> **Arts Area:** Ensemble; Instrumental Group; Band
> **Status:** Professional
> **Type:** Performing; Touring
> **Purpose:** To preserve, in spirited performance, America's original contribution to the performing arts: the blues, jazz standards, pop tunes, ballads and rags of the early 1900's (especially the 1920's and 1930's)
> **Management:** Stan McDonald, Leader; Ellen McDonald, Manager
> **Paid Staff:** 1
> **Paid Artists:** 7
> **Utilizes:** Guest Artists
> **Income Sources:** Fees
> **Season:** 52 Weeks
> **Affiliations:** Cape Cod Jazz Society; Potomac River Jazz Society; Jazz Appreciation Society of Syracuse; Greater Boston Convention and Visitors Bureau

Somerville

DANCE

ART OF BLACK DANCE AND MUSIC
PO Box 362, Somerville, MA 02144
(617) 666-1859
> **Founded:** 1975
> **Arts Area:** Ethnic
> **Status:** Professional; Non-Profit
> **Type:** Performing; Touring; Resident; Educational
> **Purpose:** To teach the common history of mankind through dance, music and folklore to educate and entertain audiences using the culturally diverse expressions of our African heritage
> **Management:** De Ama Battle, Executive Director
> **Officers:** William Taylor; Roberta Jackson
> **Paid Staff:** 2   **Volunteer Staff:** 1
> **Paid Artists:** 8
> **Utilizes:** Special Technical Talent; Guest Artists; Guest Choreographers
> **Budget:** $50,000 - $100,000
> **Income Sources:** Private Foundations/Grants/Endowments; Business/Corporate Donations; Box Office; Individual Donations; Tuition

Season: September - June   **Annual Attendance:** 30,000
Affiliations: Cambridge Multicultural Arts Center; Boston Cultural Partnership

THEATRE

STUDEBAKER MOVEMENT THEATER COMPANY
1 Fitchburg Street, B450, Somerville, MA 02143
(617) 666-1819
Founded: 1978
Arts Area: Professional; Theatrical Group; Performance
Status: Professional
Type: Performing; Touring; Resident; Sponsoring
Purpose: To create new works in performance
Management: John Bay, Tour Manager
Officers: M.B, Flanders, President; Caroline D'Agincourt, Treasurer
Paid Staff: 2   **Volunteer Staff:** 6
Paid Artists: 6   **Non-Paid Artists:** 10
Utilizes: Special Technical Talent; Guest Artists; Guest Directors
Budget: $1,000 - $50,000
Income Sources: Private Foundations/Grants/Endowments; Business/Corporate Donations; Box Office; Government Grants; Individual Donations
Season: September - May   **Annual Attendance:** 6,000
Affiliations: NMTA
Performance Facilities: Performance Place

South Hadley

PERFORMING SERIES

THE MUSICORDA SUMMER STRING PROGRAM AND FESTIVAL
PO Box 557, South Hadley, MA 01075
(413) 532-0607
FAX: (413) 538-2828
Arts Area: Instrumental Music
Status: Professional; Non-Profit
Type: Performing; Touring; Resident; Educational
Purpose: To provide advanced training and performance experience for gifted string students; to sponsor a performing festival in western Massachusetts
Management: Leopold Teraspulsky, Artistic Director; Jacqueline Melnick, Administrative Director
Budget: $100,000 - $500,000
Income Sources: Private Foundations/Grants/Endowments; Business/Corporate Donations; Box Office; Government Grants; Individual Donations
Performance Facilities: Chapin Auditorium, Mount Holyoke College

South Lancaster

INSTRUMENTAL MUSIC

THAYER SYMPHONY ORCHESTRA
PO Box 271, Main Street, South Lancaster, MA 01561
(508) 368-0041
FAX: (508) 368-0041
Founded: 1973
Arts Area: Symphony
Status: Semi-Professional; Non-Profit
Type: Performing; Educational
Purpose: To provide musical concerts for the residents of Eastern Massachusetts
Management: Francis Wada, General Manager
Officers: Ron Ansin, President; Linda Esposito, Vice President; John Davis, Second Vice President; William Jacobson, Clerk
Paid Staff: 1   **Volunteer Staff:** 120
Paid Artists: 40   **Non-Paid Artists:** 20
Utilizes: Guest Conductors; Guest Artists
Budget: $100,000 - $500,000
Income Sources: Private Foundations/Grants/Endowments; Business/Corporate Donations; Box Office; Government Grants; Individual Donations
Season: October - June   **Annual Attendance:** 9,500

Affiliations: ASOL; North Central Massachusetts Chamber of Commerce
Performance Facilities: Machlan Auditorium, Atlantic Union College

---

South Weymouth

VOCAL MUSIC

FINE ARTS CHORALE
779 Main Street, South Weymouth, MA 02190
(617) 337-3023
Founded: 1966
Arts Area: Choral
Status: Non-Professional; Non-Profit
Type: Performing
Purpose: The authentic performances of sacred choral masterworks using professional orchestra and soloists; no dues required
Management: Peter L. Edwards, Musical Director/Founder
Officers: Deborah Kohl, President; Kate Lacatell, Vice President; Eleanor MacDonald, Secretary; Louise Bacon, Treasurer
Paid Staff: 1   **Volunteer Staff:** 26
Paid Artists: 100   **Non-Paid Artists:** 130
Utilizes: Guest Artists
Budget: $1,000 - $50,000
Income Sources: Private Foundations/Grants/Endowments; Business/Corporate Donations; Box Office; Government Grants; Individual Donations
Season: September - May   **Annual Attendance:** 2,000

Springfield

INSTRUMENTAL MUSIC

SPRINGFIELD ORCHESTRA ASSOCIATION
1391 Main Street, Suite 1006, Springfield, MA 01103
(413) 733-0636
FAX: (413) 781-4129
Arts Area: Symphony
Status: Professional; Non-Profit
Type: Performing; Touring; Educational
Purpose: To foster among the residents of western Massachusetts an appreciation for symphonic music and to provide this and other musical entertainment
Management: Raymond Harvey, Music Director; Robert Stiles, Executive Director
Officers: Peter Carando, President of the Board
Budget: $1,000,000 - $5,000,000
Income Sources: Private Foundations/Grants/Endowments; Business/Corporate Donations; Box Office; Government Grants; Individual Donations
Performance Facilities: Springfield Symphony Hall

WESTERN MASSACHUSETTS YOUNG PEOPLE'S SYMPHONY/PHILHARMONIA
1391 Main Street, Suite 1006, Springfield, MA 01103
(413) 733-0636
FAX: (413) 781-4129
Founded: 1944
Arts Area: Symphony; Orchestra
Status: Non-Professional; Non-Profit
Type: Performing; Educational; Sponsoring
Purpose: To give aspiring and talented young musicians of western Massachusetts and northern Connecticut the opportunity to perform symphonic repertoire, especially important to those whose schools have no formal symphony orchestras or orchestral programs; to cultivate excellence in performance through active participation in a continuous, weekly experience
Management: Elel Thomas, Youth Orchestras Coordinator
Officers: Yek Cheng, Mely Cheng, Co-Presidents; Judy Mish, Vice President; Daniel Dress, Treasurer; Mayme Lajoie, Historian
Paid Staff: 2
Non-Paid Artists: 110
Utilizes: Guest Conductors
Budget: $1,000 - $50,000
Income Sources: Box Office; Government Grants; Individual Donations
Season: September - May   **Annual Attendance:** 1,500
Performance Facilities: Springfield Symphony Hall

THEATRE

STAGEWEST
One Columbus Center, Springfield, MA 01103
(413) 781-4470
FAX: (413) 781-3741
Founded: 1967
Arts Area: Professional
Status: Professional; Non-Profit
Type: Performing; Resident; Educational
Purpose: Professional resident theatre education and outreach research and development of new work and revitalized classics
Management: Eric Hill, Artistic Director; Martha Richards, Managing Director; Catherine Mandel, Artistic Administrator; Rebecca Strang, Marketing/Public Relations
Officers: Rand Gesing, President; Marie Stebbins, Vice President; Malcolm George, Secretary; Barbara Wallace, Treasurer
Paid Staff: 50 **Volunteer Staff:** 10
Paid Artists: 35 **Non-Paid Artists:** 10
Utilizes: Special Technical Talent; Guest Conductors; Guest Artists; Guest Directors
Budget: $1,000,000 - $5,000,000
Income Sources: Private Foundations/Grants/Endowments; Business/Corporate Donations; Box Office; Government Grants; Individual Donations
Season: October - April
Annual Attendance: 95,000
Affiliations: TCG; AAA; LORT
Performance Facilities: S. Prestley Blake Theatre; Winifred Arms Studio Theatre

FACILITY

SPRAGUE - GRISWOLD CULTURAL ART CENTER
American International College, 1000 State Street, Springfield, MA 01109
(413) 747-6393; (413) 747-6394
FAX: (413) 737-2803
Founded: 1885
Type of Facility: Theatre Complex; Performance Center
Type of Stage: Platform
Stage Dimensions: 24'x40'
Seating Capacity: 504
Year Built: 1984 **Architect:** Studio One/Alvin Paige **Cost:** $2,000,000
Contact for Rental: Alvin Paige; (413) 747-6393
Resident Groups: Berkshire Ballet; Community Music School

SPRINGFIELD CIVIC CENTER
1277 Main Street, Springfield, MA 01103
(413) 787-6610
FAX: (413) 787-6645
Founded: 1972
Type of Facility: Concert Hall; Civic Center; Arena; Multi-Purpose
Type of Stage: Flexible; Arena
Seating Capacity: 10,000
Year Built: 1972 **Architect:** Edwardo Catalano **Cost:** $10,200,000
Contact for Rental: Michael J. Graney; (413) 787-6610, ext. 224
Resident Groups: Springfield Indians Hockey Club (AHL)

SPRINGFIELD SYMPHONY HALL
Court Square, Springfield, MA 01103
(413) 787-6610
Type of Facility: Theatre Complex; Concert Hall; Auditorium; Opera House
Type of Stage: Proscenium
Stage Dimensions: 36'x63'x57' **Orchestra Pit**
Seating Capacity: 2,589
Year Built: 1913
Year Remodeled: 1980 **Architect:** Reinhardt Associates **Cost:** $1,000,000
Contact for Rental: Michael J. Graney, Executive Director; (413) 787-6610
Resident Groups: Springfield Symphony Orchestra

Stockbridge

PERFORMING SERIES

BERKSHIRE THEATRE FESTIVAL
East Main Street, PO Box 797, Stockbridge, MA 01262
(413) 298-5536
    Founded: 1928
    Arts Area: Theater; Festivals
    Status: Professional; Non-Profit
    Type: Performing; Resident; Educational; Sponsoring
    Purpose: To provide thought-provoking summer entertainment
    Management: Dick Dunlop, Artistic Director; Chuck Still, Managing Director
    Officers: Jane Fitzpatrick, President; Fredric Rutburg, Secretary; DeKay Palmer, Treasurer
    Paid Staff: 7   **Volunteer Staff:** 25
    Paid Artists: 22   **Non-Paid Artists:** 12
    Utilizes: Special Technical Talent; Guest Artists; Guest Directors
    Budget: $500,000 - $1,000,000
    Income Sources: Private Foundations/Grants/Endowments; Business/Corporate Donations; Box Office; Government Grants; Individual Donations
    Season: June - August   **Annual Attendance:** 30,000
    Affiliations: AEA; CORST

STOCKBRIDGE CHAMBER CONCERTS
Box 164, Stockbridge, MA 01262
(413) 442-7711
    Founded: 1975
    Arts Area: Vocal Music; Instrumental Music; Festivals
    Status: Professional; Non-Profit
    Type: Performing; Touring; Resident; Educational; Sponsoring
    Purpose: For the exclusively charitable and educational purposes of supporting the art of music by sponsoring concerts, lectures and recitals to encourage the cultural education of the public and individual students of music alike
    Management: Elizabeth A. Hagenah, Artistic Director
    Officers: Elizabeth A. Hagenah, President; Jean MacGaffey, First Vice President; Elizabeth C. Erston, Second Vice President; Patricia Webber, Clerk; Ruth Beers, Treasurer; Jean MacGaffey, Jane Shanahan, Assistant Treasurers; Norma Thompson, Chsirman of Gala Receptions
    Volunteer Staff: 12
    Paid Artists: 17
    Utilizes: Guest Artists
    Budget: $1,000 - $50,000
    Income Sources: Private Foundations/Grants/Endowments; Business/Corporate Donations; Box Office; Individual Donations
    Annual Attendance: 1,000
    Affiliations: CMA

FACILITY

BERKSHIRE THEATRE FESTIVAL
East Main Street, PO Box 797, Stockbridge, MA 01262
(413) 298-5536
    Type of Facility: Theatre Complex
    Facility Originally: Private Club
    Type of Stage: Proscenium
    Seating Capacity: 915
    Year Built: 1887   **Architect:** Stamford White
    Contact for Rental:
    Resident Groups: Berkshire Theatre Festival; Unicorn Acting Company
    To present revivals, new plays and musicals

Tisbury

FACILITY

KATHARINE CORNELL MEMORIAL THEATRE
21 Spring Street, PO Box 1239, Tisbury, MA 02568
(508) 696-4200
    Type of Facility: Concert Hall; Theatre House
    Facility Originally: Church

Type of Stage: Thrust
Stage Dimensions: 40'x100'
Seating Capacity: 195
Year Built: 1844
Year Remodeled: 1971   **Architect:** William Katzenbach   **Cost:** $250,000
Contact for Rental: Aase Jones, Secretary;   (617) 693-4200

Waltham

INSTRUMENTAL MUSIC

BRANDEIS UNIVERSITY DEPARTMENT OF MUSIC
South Street, PO Box 9110, Waltham, MA 02254-9110
(617) 736-3331
Founded: 1940
Arts Area: Orchestra; Chamber; Ensemble; Instrumental Group; Electronic & Live Electronic
Status: Professional; Non-Professional; Non-Profit
Type: Performing; Resident
Purpose: University concert series including Professional Series, Concerts at Noon and student performances
Officers: Sarah Mead, Concert Coordinator/Artist in Residence; Lydrian String Quartet, Ensemble in Residence
Paid Staff: 1
Utilizes: Guest Conductors; Guest Artists
Budget: $1,000 - $50,000
Income Sources: Private Foundations/Grants/Endowments
Season: September - May
Performance Facilities: Slosberg Recital Hall

PERFORMING SERIES

BRANDEIS SUMMER MUSIC FESTIVAL
Sydeman Hall, Room 108, Brandeis University, Waltham, MA 02254
(617) 736-3424
Founded: 1989
Arts Area: Instrumental Music
Status: Professional; Non-Professional
Type: Performing; Resident; Educational
Purpose: To present a concert series by the Lydian Quartet and a three-week chamber music course for young professional musicians
Officers: Rhonda Rider and Sanford Lotter, Directors; Gwenn Smaxwill, Administrator
Paid Staff: 7   **Volunteer Staff:** 10
Paid Artists: 6
Utilizes: Guest Artists
Budget: $1,000 - $50,000
Income Sources: Private Foundations/Grants/Endowments; Box Office; Individual Donations
Season: June   **Annual Attendance:** 400
Performance Facilities: Slosberg Hall, Brandeis University

SPINGOLD THEATER CENTER
Brandeis University, PO Box 9110, Waltham, MA 02254-9110
(617) 736-3400
FAX: (617) 736-3389
Founded: 1964
Arts Area: Theater
Status: Professional; Non-Profit
Type: Performing; Educational
Purpose: To blend an educational program with resident professionals and booked programming; to make as broad a training program as possible
Management: John-Edward Hill, General Manager; Michael Murray, Director of the Theatre Arts Program
Officers: Brandeis University Board of Trustees
Paid Staff: 4
Utilizes: Guest Artists; Guest Directors
Budget: $100,000 - $500,000
Income Sources: Private Foundations/Grants/Endowments; Box Office; Individual Donations
Season: October - May   **Annual Attendance:** 28,000
Affiliations: NETC; Massachusetts Cultural Alliance
Performance Facilities: Spingold Theater Center

FACILITY

BRANDEIS UNIVERSITY - SPINGOLD THEATER CENTER
Waltham, MA 02254
(617) 736-3400
FAX: (617) 736-3389
    Founded: 1966
    Type of Facility: Theatre House
    Type of Stage: Proscenium
    Stage Dimensions: 36'Wx40'L   **Orchestra Pit**
    Seating Capacity: 747
    Year Built: 1964 **Architect:** Max Abramowitz
    Contact for Rental: John Edward Hill; (617) 736-3400
    Resident Groups: Theatre Arts Department; Brandeis Gilbert and Sullivan Society

Watertown

THEATRE

HISTORY MAKING PRODUCTIONS
100 Summer, Suite 3-6, Watertown, MA 02172
(617) 924-4430
    Founded: 1976
    Arts Area: Professional; Theatrical Group
    Status: Professional; Non-Profit
    Type: Performing; Touring; Educational
    Purpose: To tour live, professional plays which dramatize historical events and people; to bring literature to life; to spark critical thinking and thoughtful discussion on gender, race, social diversity and social change in our adult and youth audiences
    Management: Linda Myer, Director
    Officers: Lisa Gregory, Board Chairwoman; Judith Einach, Secretary Clerk; Richard Freedberg, Treasurer
    Paid Staff: 1 **Volunteer Staff:** 5
    Paid Artists: 4
    Utilizes: Special Technical Talent; Guest Directors
    Budget: $1,000 - $50,000
    Income Sources: Business/Corporate Donations; Box Office; Individual Donations
    Season: August - June **Annual Attendance:** 18,000
    Affiliations: Massachusetts Advocates for Arts, Sciences and Humanities; Stage Source

West Newton

VOCAL MUSIC

YOUTH PRO MUSICA
1075 Washington Street, West Newton, MA 02165
(617) 965-5899
    Founded: 1970
    Arts Area: Choral
    Status: Non-Professional; Non-Profit
    Type: Performing; Educational
    Purpose: An hundred-member organization divided into three choruses providing choral experience of professional quality to promising young singers and exposing them to a wide variety of choral literature
    Management: Roberta Humez, Music Director; Tom Anderson, Administrator
    Officers: Margo Connoe, President; Peter Witt, Vice President/Clerk
    Paid Staff: 3 **Volunteer Staff:** 4
    Paid Artists: 2
    Utilizes: Guest Conductors
    Budget: $1,000 - $50,000
    Income Sources: Private Foundations/Grants/Endowments; Business/Corporate Donations; Government Grants; Individual Donations
    Season: September - June **Annual Attendance:** 10,000
    Affiliations: Massachusetts Cultural Alliance; American Boychoir Federation

West Springfield

FACILITY

HORACE A. MOSES BUILDING
1305 Memorial Avenue, West Springfield, MA 01089
(413) 737-2443
  Type of Facility: Theatre House
  Facility Originally: 4-H Dormitory and Auditorium
  Year Built: 1925
  Year Remodeled: 1967   **Cost:** $40,000
  Contact for Rental: Susan Lavoie;   (413) 737-2443
  Resident Groups: StageWest
  Located on Eastern States Exposition Grounds; used as a 4-H and FFA participants' dormitory during the Big E each September

Weston

PERFORMING SERIES

CONCERTS-AT-THE-COMMON (HARVARD UNITARIAN CHURCH)
c/o Bernard J. Fine, 32 Coburn Road, Weston, MA 02193
(617) 899-7331
  Founded: 1979
  Arts Area: Vocal Music; Instrumental Music
  Status: Non-Profit
  Type: Sponsoring
  Purpose: To present community concerts
  Officers: Bernard J. Fine, Concert Series Director
  Volunteer Staff: 1
  Utilizes: Guest Artists
  Budget: $1,000 - $50,000
  Income Sources: Business/Corporate Donations; Box Office; Individual Donations
  Annual Attendance: 750

Whitehorse Beach

FACILITY

PRISCILLA BEACH THEATER SCHOOL
PO Box 424, Whitehorse Beach, MA 02381
(508) 224-4888
  Type of Facility: Theatre Complex; Studio Performance; Performance Center; Theatre House; Multi-Purpose
  Facility Originally: Private Residence
  Type of Stage: Thrust; Visual And Performing Arts Classrooms
  Stage Dimensions: 30'x40'   **Orchestra Pit**
  Seating Capacity: 300
  Year Built: 1850
  Year Remodeled: 1932   **Architect:** Dr. Franklin Trask   **Cost:** $50,000
  Anne Joelle, Producer
  Resident Groups: American Association of Dramatic Arts
  It is the first and oldest barn theatre in America

Williamstown

INSTRUMENTAL MUSIC

BERKSHIRE SYMPHONY
Williams College, Williamstown, MA 01267
(413) 597-2127
  Founded: 1944
  Arts Area: Symphony; Orchestra
  Status: Professional; Non-Professional; Non-Profit; Student
  Type: Performing; Resident; Educational
  Purpose: To encourage participation in and enjoyment of old and new symphonic literature
  Management: Kristine Johnson, Concert Manager

Paid Staff: 2
Paid Artists: 35 **Non-Paid Artists:** 40
Utilizes: Special Technical Talent; Guest Artists
Budget: $1,000 - $50,000
Income Sources: Private Foundations/Grants/Endowments; Business/Corporate Donations; Box Office; Individual Donations
Season: October - May
Affiliations: ASOL
Performance Facilities: Chapin Hall, Williams College

THE WILLIAMS TRIO
Williams College, Williamstown, MA 01267
(413) 597-2127
Founded: 1970
Arts Area: Chamber
Status: Professional; Non-Profit
Type: Performing; Touring; Resident
Purpose: To bring high-quality performance of piano trio repertoire to Williams students and the community-at-large at home and on tour
Management: Douglas Moore, Manager
Paid Artists: 3
Utilizes: Guest Artists
Budget: $1,000 - $50,000
Season: 52 Weeks
Performance Facilities: Brooks-Rogers Recital Hall; Bernhard Music Center

THEATRE

THE NEW PHOENIX
42 Cold Spring Road, Williamstown, MA 01267
(413) 458-5235
Founded: 1975
Arts Area: Theatrical Group
Status: Professional; Semi-Professional; Non-Profit
Type: Performing; Touring; Educational; Sponsoring
Purpose: To produce a diversity of small-cast, transportable theatre pieces; special interest in Samuel Beckett, mono dramas, psychological thrillers and black comedies
Management: Ralph Hammann, Artistic Director/Producer; Ed DiNicola, Douglas Bradburd, Associate Director
Officers: Ralph Hamman, President; Dana Swanson, Vice President
Paid Staff: 1
Paid Artists: 3
Utilizes: Guest Artists; Guest Directors
Budget: $1,000 - $50,000
Income Sources: Box Office; Individual Donations

WILLIAMSTOWN THEATRE FESTIVAL
PO Box 517, Williamstown, MA 01267
(413) 597-3377; (413) 458-3200
FAX: (413) 458-3147
Founded: 1955
Arts Area: Professional; Musical; Theatrical Group
Status: Professional; Non-Profit
Type: Performing
Purpose: Outstanding production of modern classics on the main stage and development of new writing, acting, and musical talent at large
Management: William Stewart, Managing Director; Christopher Boll, Production Manager; Peter Hunt, Artistic Director; Steven Lawson, Rachel Davidson Associate Artistic Directors
Officers: Dr. William Everett, President; Ralph Renzi, Vice President; Fred A. Windover, Secretary; Henry N. Flynt, Jr., Treasurer
Paid Staff: 35 **Volunteer Staff:** 70
Paid Artists: 50
Utilizes: Special Technical Talent; Guest Artists; Guest Directors
Budget: $1,000,000 - $5,000,000
Income Sources: Private Foundations/Grants/Endowments; Business/Corporate Donations; Box Office; Government Grants; Individual Donations
Season: June - August **Annual Attendance:** 23,000
Affiliations: AEA
Performance Facilities: Adams Memorial Theater; The Other Stage

FACILITY

WILLIAMS COLLEGE - CHAPIN HALL
Williamstown, MA 01267
(413) 597-2127
    Type of Facility: Concert Hall
    Type of Stage: Proscenium
    Seating Capacity: 1,050
    Resident Groups: Berkshire Symphony; Williams College Jazz Ensemble

Worcester

THEATRE

WORCESTER CHILDREN'S THEATRE
6 Chatman Street, Worcester, MA 01609
(508) 752-7537
    Founded: 1968
    Arts Area: Children's Theatre
    Status: Professional; Semi-Professional; Non-Profit
    Type: Performing; Touring; Educational
    Purpose: To teach children about theatre through performance and educational programming
    Management: Mary Pantano, Director of Programs and Development; Liz Humphreys, Managing Director; Steven Braddock, Artistic Director
    Officers: Angeles Baldanza, President; Kristine Johnson, Donna Clough, Vice Presidents; Ann Shea, Secretary; Mark Edoff, Treasurer; Mayo Morgan, Assistant Treasurer
    Paid Staff: 3
    Utilizes: Guest Artists; Guest Directors
    Budget: $100,000 - $500,000
    Income Sources: Private Foundations/Grants/Endowments; Business/Corporate Donations; Box Office; Government Grants; Individual Donations
    Annual Attendance: 6,000
    Performance Facilities: Worcester State College, Administration Building Theatre

WORCESTER FOOTHILLS THEATRE COMPANY
74 Worcester Center, 100 Front Street, Worcester, MA 01608
(508) 754-4018
    Founded: 1974
    Arts Area: Professional; Theatrical Group
    Status: Professional; Non-Profit
    Type: Performing
    Purpose: To provide professional regional theatre for Worcester and the Central New England Region and serve the region by providing many ancillary services including a theatre conservatory, intern/apprentice programs, youth services, services for the communicatively and physically disabled and more
    Management: Marc P. Smith, Executive Producer/Artistic Director; Doug Landrum, Associate Producer, Production; Susan L. Smith, Associate Producer/Public Relations & Marketing
    Officers: Dr. Tamara A. Bethel, President; James F. Goulet, Treasurer; Hon. Mel Greenberg, Clerk
    Paid Staff: 40   **Volunteer Staff:** 180
    Paid Artists: 50
    Utilizes: Special Technical Talent; Guest Artists; Guest Directors
    Budget: $500,000 - $1,000,000
    Income Sources: Private Foundations/Grants/Endowments; Business/Corporate Donations; Box Office; Government Grants; Individual Donations
    Season: October - May   **Annual Attendance:** 52,000
    Affiliations: AEA
    Performance Facilities: Worcester Foothills Theatre

FACILITY

MECHANICS HALL
321 Main Street, Worcester, MA 06108
(508) 752-5608
FAX: (508) 752-4408
    Type of Facility: Concert Hall; Multi-Purpose
    Facility Originally: Meeting Hall
    Stage Dimensions: 46'8"Wx16'9"D (can be extended to 54'Wx28'9"D)
    Seating Capacity: 1,500
    Year Built: 1857   **Architect:** Eldridge Boyden   **Cost:** $101,000

Year Remodeled: 1976   **Architect:** Anderson, Notter & Feingold Inc.   **Cost:** $5,000,000
Acoustical Consultant: Cavanaugh, Tocci Associates
Contact for Rental: Norma J. Sandison, Director;   (508) 752-5608
Resident Groups: Worcester County Music Association; International Artists Series

WORCESTER MEMORIAL AUDITORIUM
Lincoln Square, Worcester, MA 06108
(508) 755-6600
  Type of Facility: Concert Hall; Auditorium
  Type of Stage: Proscenium
  Stage Dimensions: 67'Wx44'D   **Orchestra Pit**
  Seating Capacity: 3,000
  Year Built: 1933   **Architect:** Lucius Briggs & Frederick Hirons   **Cost:** $2,000,000
  Contact for Rental: Gregg Tassone;   (508) 755-6600

Worthington

PERFORMING SERIES

SEVENARS CONCERTS
South Worthington Academy, Worthington, MA 01098
(413) 238-5854
  Winter Address: 3A, 30 East End Avenue, New York, NY 10028
  Arts Area: Vocal Music; Instrumental Music; Festivals
  Status: Professional; Non-Profit
  Type: Performing; Educational
  Purpose: To develop classical-music artists and audiences
  Utilizes: Guest Artists; Guest Conductors
  Budget: $1,000 - $50,000
  Income Sources: Private Foundations; Business/Corporate Donations; Box Office; Government Grants; Individual Donations
  Season: July - August   **Annual Attendance:** 2,400

MICHIGAN

Adrian

INSTRUMENTAL MUSIC

ADRIAN SYMPHONY ORCHESTRA
110 South Madison Street, Adrian, MI 49221
(517) 264-3121
FAX: (517) 264-3331
Founded: 1981
Arts Area: Symphony; Orchestra; Chamber; Ensemble
Status: Professional; Non-Profit
Type: Performing; Touring; Resident; Educational
Purpose: To remain Lenawee County's premiere musical ensemble and Adrian College's professional orchestra-in-residence; to perform classical, family, holiday, pops, chamber and young peoples' concerts
Management: David Katz, Music Director/Principal Conductor; Susan Hoffman, Executive Director; Nancy Wagner, Administrative Assistant
Officers: Muriel Bell, President; Hon. Henry Newlin, Vice President; Dr. Roger Fechner, Past President
Paid Staff: 5 **Volunteer Staff:** 10
Paid Artists: 65 **Non-Paid Artists:** 5
Utilizes: Guest Conductors; Guest Artists
Budget: $100,000 - $500,000
Income Sources: Private Foundations/Grants/Endowments; Business/Corporate Donations; Box Office; Government Grants; Individual Donations
Season: September - May **Annual Attendance:** 10,000
Affiliations: ASOL; Michigan Orchestra Association
Performance Facilities: Dawson Auditorium

VOCAL MUSIC

FRIEDRICH SCHORR MEMORIAL PERFORMANCE PRIZE IN VOICE
110 South Madison Street, Adrian, MI 49221
(517) 264-3121
FAX: (517) 264-3331
Founded: 1989
Arts Area: Grand Opera; Lyric Opera; Operetta
Status: Professional; Non-Profit
Type: Sponsoring; Vocal Competition
Purpose: To sponsor an annual international competition which awards performance prizes and stipends in excess of $10,000 annually
Management: David Katz, Robert Soller, Artistic Directors
Officers: Charles Nelson Reilly, Honorary Chairman; Mrs. Friedrich Schorr, Founder
Paid Staff: 4 **Volunteer Staff:** 4
Paid Artists: 10
Utilizes: Guest Artists
Budget: $50,000 - $100,000
Income Sources: Private Foundations/Grants/Endowments; Business/Corporate Donations; Box Office; Individual Donations
Season: October - April **Annual Attendance:** 5,000
Affiliations: NOA; OA
Performance Facilities: Croswell Opera House

OPERA! LEWANEE
110 South Madison Street, Adrian, MI 49221
(517) 264-3121
FAX: (517) 264-3331
Founded: 1989
Arts Area: Grand Opera; Lyric Opera; Operetta
Status: Professional; Non-Profit
Type: Performing; Resident; Educational
Purpose: To create grand opera performances for the citizens of Lenawee County, Michigan; to sponsor the Friedrich Schorr Memorial Performance Prize in Voice; to collaborate between the Adrian Symphony and the Croswell Opera House
Management: David Katz, Music Director; Robert Soller, Stage Director; Susan Hoffman, Jimmy Hilburger, Producers
Officers: Robert and Muriel Bell, Co-Chairs
Paid Staff: 8 **Volunteer Staff:** 15

Paid Artists: 50
Utilizes: Special Technical Talent; Guest Artists
Budget: $100,000 - $500,000
Income Sources: Private Foundations/Grants/Endowments; Business/Corporate Donations; Box Office; Individual Donations
Season: October - April   **Annual Attendance:** 5,000
Affiliations: NOA; OA
Performance Facilities: Croswell Opera House

FACILITY

ADRIAN COLLEGE
110 South Madison, Rush Union, Adrian, MI 49221
(517) 264-3156
FAX: (517) 264-3331
Founded: 1859
Type of Facility: Theatre Complex; Concert Hall; Auditorium; Theatre House
Facility Originally: Auditorium
Type of Stage: Proscenium
Seating Capacity: 1,185
Year Built: 1964
Contact for Rental: Office of Conferences and Campus Programs;   (517) 264-3156

Alpena

THEATRE

THUNDER BAY THEATRE
400 North Second Avenue, Alpena, MI 49707
(517) 354-2267
Founded: 1977
Arts Area: Professional; Summer Stock; Musical; Theatrical Group
Status: Professional; Non-Profit; Non-Equity
Type: Performing; Resident; Educational
Purpose: To signify and positively affect the cultural climate of northeast Michigan
Management: David P. Drobot, Artistic Director; Jodi Prahler, Assistant Artistic Director; Ann M. Seymour, Administrative Assistant
Officers: Robert E. Haltiner, President; Carol Witherbee, Vice President; Grace Bachwich, Secretary; Jerry Lamb, Treasurer
Paid Staff: 6   **Volunteer Staff:** 25
Paid Artists: 30
Utilizes: Special Technical Talent; Guest Directors
Budget: $100,000 - $500,000
Income Sources: Private Foundations/Grants/Endowments; Business/Corporate Donations; Box Office; Government Grants; Individual Donations
Season: 52 Weeks   **Annual Attendance:** 10,000
Performance Facilities: Thunder Bay Theatre

PERFORMING SERIES

THUNDER BAY ARTS COUNCIL
312 East Chisholm Street, Alpena, MI 49766
(517) 356-6678
Founded: 1967
Arts Area: Dance; Vocal Music; Instrumental Music; Theater; Lyric Opera
Status: Professional; Non-Profit
Type: Educational; Sponsoring
Purpose: To foster, encourage, and promote cultural arts; to serve as a coordinating agency in scheduling area presentations by other art groups; to enhance the quality of life
Management: Thunder Bay Arts Council Board of Directors
Officers: Peggy Kusler, President; Adelaide Ammon, First Vice President; Elaine Mandenberg, Second Vice President; Alice Silver, Secretary; Nathalie Szczukowski, Treasurer
Paid Staff: 1   **Volunteer Staff:** 27
Utilizes: Special Technical Talent; Guest Conductors; Guest Artists; Guest Directors
Budget: $1,000 - $50,000
Income Sources: Private Foundations/Grants/Endowments; Business/Corporate Donations; Box Office; Government Grants; Individual Donations

Season: 52 Weeks   **Annual Attendance:** 21,000
Performance Facilities: High School Auditorium; Alpena Fine Arts Shell

Ann Arbor

DANCE

ANN ARBOR BALLET THEATRE
548 Church Street, Ann Arbor, MI 48104
(313) 662-2942
Founded: 1980
Arts Area: Ballet; Guest Choreographers
Status: Semi-Professional; Non-Profit
Type: Performing; Touring; Educational
Purpose: To promote local interest and appreciation of classical Russian ballet, combined with live music and theatre
Management: Carol A. Sharp-Radovic, Artistic Director; Kathryn E. Sharp, Assistant Director; Gail Etter, Gen. Manager
Volunteer Staff: 6
Non-Paid Artists: 35
Utilizes: Special Technical Talent; Guest Conductors; Guest Artists; Guest Choreographers
Budget: $1,000 - $50,000
Income Sources: Private Foundations/Grants/Endowments; Business/Corporate Donations; Box Office; Government Grants; Individual Donations
Season: September - June   **Annual Attendance:** 6,000
Affiliations: Michigan Dance Association; Washtenaw Council for the Arts; Washtenaw Dance Association
Performance Facilities: Power Center for Performing Arts; Michigan Theatre; Lydia Mendelssohn

ANN ARBOR CIVIC BALLET
525 East Liberty Street, Ann Arbor, MI 48103
(313) 668-8066
Founded: 1958
Arts Area: Ballet
Status: Non-Profit
Type: Performing; Resident; Educational
Purpose: To encourage young people in the area of dance; to bring guest performers to the community
Management: Sylvia Hamer, Founder; Lee Ann King, Director
Officers: Wanda Dawson, President; Kathleen Smith, Vice President; Debra Haas, Secretary; Wanda King, Treasurer
Volunteer Staff: 15
Non-Paid Artists: 25
Utilizes: Special Technical Talent; Guest Artists
Budget: $1,000 - $50,000
Income Sources: Private Foundations/Grants/Endowments; Business/Corporate Donations; Box Office; Individual Donations
Season: September - July   **Annual Attendance:** 2,500

DANCE GALLERY COMPANY
111 Third Street, Ann Arbor, MI 48103
(313) 761-2728
Founded: 1981
Arts Area: Modern; Ballet; Jazz
Status: Professional; Non-Profit
Type: Performing; Touring; Resident; Educational
Purpose: To bring quality modern dance to audiences; to promote and supply quality modern dance training
Management: Noonie Anderson, Studio Manager; Diane Black, Rental Coordinator
Officers: Linda Greene, President; Robin Cooper, Treasurer; Nancy Baker Fate Heers, Secretary; Stuart Tsubota, Jane Stanton, Harry Gable, Ron Miller, Board Members
Paid Staff: 2   **Volunteer Staff:** 2
Paid Artists: 8
Budget: $1,000 - $50,000
Income Sources: Private Foundations/Grants/Endowments; Business/Corporate Donations; Box Office; Government Grants; Individual Donations
Season: 52 Weeks   **Annual Attendance:** 2,000
Affiliations: Michigan Council for Arts and Cultural Affairs; Washtenaw Council of Arts

MALINI'S DANCES OF INDIA
1355 Wynnstone Drive, Ann Arbor, MI 48105
(313) 994-3167
Arts Area: Ethnic
Status: Non-Profit

Type: Performing; Touring; Resident; Educational; Sponsoring
Purpose: To promote East Indian classical and folk dances through performances, lecture demonstrations, workshops and residencies
Officers: Malini Srirama, Artistic Director; Vijaya Sarathy, President
Volunteer Staff: 30
Non-Paid Artists: 140
Utilizes: Special Technical Talent; Guest Artists
Budget: $1,000 - $50,000
Income Sources: Box Office; Government Grants; Individual Donations
Season: 52 Weeks **Annual Attendance:** 4,000

INSTRUMENTAL MUSIC

ANN ARBOR SYMPHONY ORCHESTRA
PO Box 1412, Ann Arbor, MI 48106
(313) 994-4801
FAX: (313) 994-3949
Founded: 1928
Arts Area: Symphony; Orchestra
Status: Professional
Type: Performing; Educational
Management: Anne Glendon, Executive Director; Kay Rowe, Personnel Manager; Kristin Reynolds, Librarian; Everett Armstrong, Operations Manager; Samuel Wong, Music Director
Officers: William W. Boddie, President; Roger Bookwalter, Vice President; Forrest Alter, Secretary; John Dale, Treasurer
Paid Staff: 4 **Volunteer Staff:** 10
Paid Artists: 75 **Non-Paid Artists:** 11
Utilizes: Guest Conductors; Guest Artists
Budget: $500,000 - $1,000,000
Income Sources: Private Foundations/Grants/Endowments; Business/Corporate Donations; Box Office; Government Grants; Individual Donations; Special Events
Season: September - May **Annual Attendance:** 6,000
Performance Facilities: Michigan Theater

VOCAL MUSIC

COMIC OPERA GUILD
PO Box 1922, Ann Arbor, MI 48106
(313) 973-3264
Founded: 1973
Arts Area: Operetta
Status: Professional; Semi-Professional; Non-Profit
Type: Performing; Touring; Resident
Purpose: The Comic Opera Guild was formed for the purpose of creating and developing interest in comic opera as a separate theatrical form. The touring approach is fundamental to this purpose because of the potential in reaching large numbers of people unacquainted with comic opera.
Management: Thomas Petiet, Managing Director
Officers: Nancy Kerner, President Board of Directors; Thomas Skylis, Secretary
Paid Staff: 8 **Volunteer Staff:** 10 ·
Paid Artists: 40 **Non-Paid Artists:** 40
Utilizes: Special Technical Talent; Guest Conductors; Guest Artists; Guest Directors
Budget: $1,000 - $50,000
Income Sources: Private Foundations/Grants/Endowments; Box Office; Government Grants; Individual Donations
Season: October - March **Annual Attendance:** 6,000
Affiliations: COS; Washtenaw Council for the Arts
Performance Facilities: Michigan Theater

UNIVERSITY OF MICHIGAN CHORAL UNION
University Musical Society, Burton Memorial Tower, Ann Arbor, MI 48109
(313) 764-2538
FAX: (313) 747-1171
Founded: 1879
Arts Area: Choral
Status: Non-Professional; Non-Profit
Type: Performing; Touring; Resident; Educational
Purpose: To provide an enterprise which offers the community a chance to be in an oratorio society
Management: Sara Billmann, Chorus Manager; Thomas Hilbish, Conductor
Officers: Norman G. Herbert, President, Board of Directors
Paid Staff: 2
Non-Paid Artists: 250

Utilizes: Guest Conductors; Guest Artists
Budget: $1,000 - $50,000
Income Sources: Box Office
Season: September - May   **Annual Attendance:** 18,000
Affiliations: University Musical Society
Performance Facilities: Hill Auditorium, University of Michigan

UNIVERSITY OF MICHIGAN GILBERT AND SULLIVAN SOCIETY
The Michigan League Building, 911 North University, Ann Arbor, MI 48109-1265
(313) 761-7855; (313) 764-0446
Founded: 1946
Arts Area: Operetta
Status: Non-Professional; Non-Profit
Type: Performing; Resident; Educational
Volunteer Staff: 20
Non-Paid Artists: 40
Budget: $50,000 - $100,000
Income Sources: Box Office; Individual Donations
Season: December - April   **Annual Attendance:** 12,000
Performance Facilities: Mendelssohn Theatre, University of Michigan

THEATRE

UNIVERSITY OF MICHIGAN, UNIVERSITY PRODUCTIONS
911 North University, Ann Arbor, MI 48109-1265
(313) 763-5213
FAX: (313) 747-2282
Founded: 1973
Arts Area: Professional; Musical; University
Status: Professional; Non-Profit; University
Type: Performing; Educational
Purpose: Producing unit for the University of Michigan departments of Dance, Musical Theatre, Opera and Theatre, creating 10 productions per year
Management: Jeffrey Kuras, Managing Director; Paul Boylan, Dean, School of Music
Paid Staff: 29
Non-Paid Artists: 200
Utilizes: Guest Directors;   Guest Designers
Budget: $1,000,000 - $5,000,000
Income Sources: Box Office; Government Grants
Season: September - April   **Annual Attendance:** 30,000
Performance Facilities: Power Center for Performing Arts; Trueblood Theatre; Mendelssohn Theatre

PERFORMING SERIES

ANN ARBOR SUMMER FESTIVAL
PO Box 4070, Ann Arbor, MI 48106
(313) 747-2278
FAX: (313) 936-3393
Founded: 1978
Arts Area: Dance; Theater; Festivals
Status: Professional; Non-Profit
Type: Performing; Sponsoring
Purpose: To present a wide variety of performing arts including free and ticketed events for a diverse audience
Management: Susan Pollay, Festival Director; Amy Harris, Develoment Director; Nancy Possley, Business Manager; Jamie Mistry, Program Assistant; Henry Reynolds, Production Manager
Officers: Ruth Whitaker, Chairman; Ronald Cresswell, President
Paid Staff: 34   **Volunteer Staff:** 20
Paid Artists: 50
Utilizes: Guest Artists
Budget: $500,000 - $1,000,000
Income Sources: Private Foundations/Grants/Endowments; Business/Corporate Donations; Box Office; Government Grants; Individual Donations
Season: June - July   **Annual Attendance:** 90,000
Affiliations: University of Michigan
Performance Facilities: Power Center; Lydia Mendelssohn; Top of the Park

UNIVERSITY MUSICAL SOCIETY OF THE UNIVERSITY OF MICHIGAN
Burton Memorial Tower, #100, Ann Arbor, MI 48109-1270
(313) 764-2538; (313) 747-1171
    Founded: 1879
    Arts Area: Dance; Vocal Music; Instrumental Music; Theater; Festivals; Grand Opera
    Status: Professional; Non-Profit
    Type: Performing; Educational
    Purpose: To present music, dance and theatre of high quality to the University and southeastern Michigan communities
    Management: Kenneth C. Fischer, Executive Director; John Kennard, Administrative Manager; Catherine Arcure, Director of Development; Robin Stephenson, Director of Marketing
    Officers: Norman Herbert, President; Lois Stegeman, Vice President; Rebecca McGowen, Secretary; Carl Braver, Treasurer
    Paid Staff: 16   **Volunteer Staff:** 300
    Paid Artists: 1,600   **Non-Paid Artists:** 250
    Budget: $1,000,000 - $5,000,000
    Income Sources: Private Foundations/Grants/Endowments; Business/Corporate Donations; Box Office; Government Grants; Individual Donations
    Season: September - May   **Annual Attendance:** 85,000
    Affiliations: APAP; CMA; ISPAA
    Performance Facilities: Hill Auditorium; Power Center; Rackham Auditorium

FACILITY

MICHIGAN THEATER
603 East Liberty, Ann Arbor, MI 48104
(313) 668-8397; (313) 668-8405
FAX: (313) 668-8397
    Founded: 1928
    Type of Facility: Concert Hall; Auditorium; Theatre House
    Facility Originally: Vaudeville; Movie House
    Type of Stage: Proscenium
    Stage Dimensions: 34'9"x25'8"; 24'6" proscenium opening   **Orchestra Pit**
    Seating Capacity: 1,710
    Year Built: 1928   **Architect:** Maurice Finkel   **Cost:** $600,000
    Year Remodeled: 1986   **Architect:** Osler/Milling and Quinn Evans   **Cost:** $1,500,000
    Contact for Rental: Debra Polich-Swain;   (313) 668-8397
    Resident Groups: Ann Arbor Symphony; Ann Arbor Film Festival; Ann Arbor Ballet Theatre

POWER CENTER FOR THE PERFORMING ARTS
Fletcher Street at East Huron, Ann Arbor, MI 48109
(313) 747-3327
FAX: (313) 747-2282
    Type of Facility: Theatre Complex; Concert Hall; Performance Center; Theatre House; Opera House
    Type of Stage: Flexible
    Stage Dimensions: 42'Dx28'Hx56'W   **Orchestra Pit**
    Seating Capacity: 1,412
    Year Built: 1971   **Architect:** John Dinkaloo & Kevin Roche
    Contact for Rental: Amanda Mengden;   (313) 747-3327
    Resident Groups: University Productions; University Musical Society; Office of Major Events

UNIVERSITY OF MICHIGAN - MENDELSSOHN THEATRE
911 North University, Ann Arbor, MI 48109
(313) 747-3327
FAX: (313) 747-2282
    Type of Facility: Theatre House
    Type of Stage: Proscenium
    Stage Dimensions: 30'Wx24'Dx17'6"   **Orchestra Pit**
    Seating Capacity: 658
    Year Built: 1928   **Cost:** $200,000
    Year Remodeled: 1976
    Contact for Rental: Amanda Mengden;   (313) 747-3327
    Manager: Jeffrey Kuras
    Resident Groups: University Productions, Office of Major Events

UNIVERSITY OF MICHIGAN - TRUEBLOOD THEATRE
State Street at Washington, Ann Arbor, MI 48109
(313) 763-0950
    Type of Facility: Theatre House

Facility Originally: School; High School Auditorium
Type of Stage: 3/4 Arena; Arena
Stage Dimensions: Arena - 35'Wx35'D; 3/4 arena - 35'Wx55'D
Seating Capacity: 200
Year Built: 1906
Year Remodeled: 1981   **Architect:** Engineering Services
Contact for Rental: Mark Sullivan;   (313) 763-0950
Resident Groups: University Players

Augusta

THEATRE

BARN THEATRE
13351 West Michigan 96, Augusta, MI 49012
(616) 731-4545
FAX: (616) 731-2306
Founded: 1946
Arts Area: Professional; Summer Stock; Musical
Status: Professional; Commercial
Type: Performing; Resident
Purpose: To produce high-quality commercial summer theatre for the southwestern Michigan region
Management: Jack P. Ragotzy, Founder/Producer; Betty Ebert Ragotzy, Dusty Reeds, Associate Producers; Howard McBride, General Manager; James B. Knox, Resident Manager; Brendan Ragotzy, Assistant to the Producer
Paid Staff: 25
Paid Artists: 25
Utilizes: Guest Artists; Equity Actors
Budget: $100,000 - $500,000
Income Sources: Box Office; Concessions
Season: June - September   **Annual Attendance:** 40,000
Affiliations: AEA

Battle Creek

INSTRUMENTAL MUSIC

BATTLE CREEK SYMPHONY ORCHESTRA
PO Box 1319, Battle Creek, MI 49016
(616) 962-2518
Founded: 1899
Arts Area: Symphony; Orchestra; Chamber
Status: Professional; Non-Profit
Type: Performing; Educational
Purpose: To perform classical and pops concerts
Management: Matthew Hazelwood, Music Director; Pamela Starrett, Executive Director
Officers: Arthur Learmonth, President
Paid Staff: 4   **Volunteer Staff:** 1
Paid Artists: 90
Utilizes: Guest Conductors; Guest Artists
Budget: $100,000 - $500,000
Income Sources: Private Foundations/Grants/Endowments; Business/Corporate Donations; Box Office; Government Grants; Individual Donations
Season: September - May   **Annual Attendance:** 10,000
Affiliations: MOA; ASOL
Performance Facilities: W.K. Kellogg Auditorium

FACILITY

BATTLE CREEK CIVIC THEATRE
PO Box 519, Battle Creek, MI 49106-0519
(616) 968-8131
Type of Facility: Theatre House
Type of Stage: 3/4 Arena
Seating Capacity: 160
Year Built: 1992
Contact for Rental: Kevin Schulz;   (616) 968-5752
Resident Groups: Battle Creek Civic Theatre; Battle Creek United Arts Council

KELLOGG CENTER ARENA
36 Hamblin Avenue, Battle Creek, MI 49017
(616) 963-4800
FAX: (616) 968-8840
>   **Type of Facility:** Concert Hall; Civic Center; Arena; Multi-Purpose
>   **Type of Stage:** Flexible; Platform; Arena
>   **Stage Dimensions:** 60'x40'
>   **Seating Capacity:** 6,083
>   **Year Built:** 1981   **Cost:** $6,000,000
>   **Contact for Rental:** Jim Walczak;   (616) 963-4800

Bay City

THEATRE

BAY CITY PLAYERS
1214 Columbus Avenue, Bay City, MI 48708
(517) 893-5555
>   **Mailing Address:** PO Box 1, Bay City, MI 48707
>   **Founded:** 1918
>   **Arts Area:** Musical; Community; Theatrical Group
>   **Status:** Non-Profit
>   **Type:** Performing
>   **Purpose:** To present quality theatrical productions to our area
>   **Management:** Kenneth Arnett, Manager
>   **Officers:** Tina Sills, President; Susan Craves, First Vice President; Dorothy Arnett, Second Vice President; Shari Neimann, Treasurer
>   **Paid Staff:** 1   **Volunteer Staff:** 200
>   **Non-Paid Artists:** 50
>   **Budget:** $100,000 - $500,000
>   **Income Sources:** Private Foundations/Grants/Endowments; Box Office; Individual Donations
>   **Season:** September - May   **Annual Attendance:** 13,000
>   **Affiliations:** Community Theatre Association of Michigan

Bay View

PERFORMING SERIES

BAY VIEW MUSIC FESITVAL
21 Encampment Drive, Bay View, MI 48801
(616) 347-4210
>   **Founded:** 1886
>   **Arts Area:** Vocal Music; Instrumental Music; Theater; Lyric Opera
>   **Status:** Professional; Non-Profit; Conservatory
>   **Type:** Performing; Educational
>   **Purpose:** To present musical concerts for the northern Michigan community
>   **Management:** Will Nichols, Director; Irving Prescott, Assistant Director; Rod Slocum, Executive Director
>   **Paid Staff:** 3   **Volunteer Staff:** 15
>   **Paid Artists:** 25
>   **Utilizes:** Guest Artists
>   **Budget:** $100,000 - $500,000
>   **Income Sources:** Private Foundations/Grants/Endowments; Box Office; Individual Donations
>   **Season:** June - August   **Annual Attendance:** 15,000
>   **Affiliations:** United Methodist Church
>   **Performance Facilities:** John M. Hall Auditorium

Birmingham

INSTRUMENTAL MUSIC

BIRMINGHAM-BLOOMFIELD SYMPHONY
1592 Buckingham, Birmingham, MI 48009
(313) 645-2276
>   **Founded:** 1975
>   **Arts Area:** Symphony; Orchestra; Ensemble
>   **Status:** Professional; Non-Profit

Type: Performing; Educational
Purpose: To promote an appreciation of the musical arts
Management: Carla Lamphere, Executive Director; Jon Boyd, Personnel Manager; Eldonna May, Librarian; Joe Labuta, Administrative Assistant
Officers: Barbara Diles-Zobl, Chairman of the Board; Ken Eaton, President; Ken Zorn, Vice President; Bill Estes, Treasurer; Lagratta Mitchell, Secretary
Paid Staff: 3   **Volunteer Staff:** 5
Paid Artists: 80
Utilizes: Guest Conductors; Guest Artists
Budget: $100,000 - $500,000
Income Sources: Private Foundations/Grants/Endowments; Business/Corporate Donations; Box Office; Government Grants; Individual Donations
Season: October - June   **Annual Attendance:** 5,000
Affiliations: ASCAP; MOA; Michigan Orchestra Volunteer Association
Performance Facilities: Temple Beth El

PERFORMING SERIES

MICHIGAN RENAISSANCE FESTIVAL
700 East Maple, Birmingham, MI 48011
(313) 645-9640
FAX: (313) 645-5351
Founded: 1980
Arts Area: Dance; Vocal Music; Instrumental Music; Theater; Festivals
Status: Professional; Commercial
Type: Performing
Purpose: To promote the Renaissance and bring the pageantry, excitement and romance of the 16th century to the southeastern Michigan area
Management: Mary Mann, General Manager
Paid Staff: 13
Paid Artists: 220   **Non-Paid Artists:** 30
Utilizes: Guest Artists
Season: August - September   **Annual Attendance:** 206,000
Performance Facilities: Hollygrove, Holly

Bloomfield Hills

PERFORMING SERIES

AMERICAN ARTISTS SERIES
435 Goodhue Road, Bloomfield Hills, MI 48304
(313) 547-2230
FAX: (313) 547-1525
Founded: 1970
Arts Area: Instrumental Music; Theater; Chamber Music
Status: Professional; Non-Profit
Type: Performing; Touring; Sponsoring
Purpose: To present a series of five diverse performing-arts events featuring native musicians and invited guest artists
Management: Joann Freeman, Artistic Director; Leonard Mazern, Executive Director; Morton Malitz, Business Manager
Volunteer Staff: 35
Paid Artists: 30
Utilizes: Guest Artists; Detroit Symphony Orchestra
Budget: $50,000 - $100,000
Income Sources: Private Foundations/Grants/Endowments; Business/Corporate Donations; Box Office; Government Grants; Individual Donations
Season: November - May   **Annual Attendance:** 2,000
Performance Facilities: Kingswood Auditorium

Cadillac

PERFORMING SERIES

GOPHERWOOD MUSIC SOCIETY
10212 East 48 Road, Cadillac, MI 49601
(616) 825-2113
Founded: 1984
Arts Area: Dance; Vocal Music; Instrumental Music

Status: Non-Profit
Type: Sponsoring
Purpose: To sponsor traditional music and dance concerts as well as children's concerts
Officers: Shelley Youngman, President; Janice Hever, Vice President; Rita Meech, Treasurer; Frank Youngman, Secretary
Utilizes: Guest Artists
Budget: $1,000 - $50,000
Income Sources: Box Office; Government Grants; Individual Donations
Season: September - April

Calumet

THEATRE

CALUMET THEATRE COMPANY
340 Sixth Street, Calumet, MI 49913
(906) 337-2610
    Founded: 1900
    Arts Area: Professional; Musical; Dinner; Community; Folk; Theatrical Group
    Status: Professional; Non-Profit
    Type: Educational; Sponsoring
    Purpose: A historic theatre and rural arts education center, the theatre both hosts and sponsors performing events
    Management: James F. O'Brien, III, Executive Director; James Jacobson, Technical Director
    Officers: Harry Cobb, Chairperson; Edward Burger, Vice Chairperson; Nancy Pintar, Secretary/Treasurer
    Paid Staff: 5   **Volunteer Staff:** 120
    Budget: $100,000 - $500,000
    Income Sources: Private Foundations/Grants/Endowments; Business/Corporate Donations; Box Office; Government Grants; Individual Donations
    Season: 52 Weeks   **Annual Attendance:** 26,000
    Affiliations: Michigan Association of Community Arts Agencies

Cass City

PERFORMING SERIES

VILLAGE BACH FESTIVAL
PO Box 27, Cass City, MI 48726
(517) 872-3465
FAX: (517) 872-2301
    Founded: 1979
    Arts Area: Vocal Music; Instrumental Music; Festivals
    Status: Professional; Non-Profit
    Type: Performing
    Purpose: To bring quality, professional musical performance to the Thumb Area of Michigan and to encourage the establishment of a tradition
    Officers: Holly Althaver, Chairman; Celia House, Treasurer; L. E. Althaver, Business Manager
    Volunteer Staff: 25
    Paid Artists: 30
    Utilizes: Guest Artists
    Budget: $1,000 - $50,000
    Income Sources: Private Foundations/Grants/Endowments; Business/Corporate Donations; Box Office; Government Grants; Individual Donations
    Season: November   **Annual Attendance:** 1,000

Cheboygan

PERFORMING SERIES

CHEBOYGAN AREA ARTS COUNCIL
PO Box 95, Cheboygan, MI 49721
(616) 627-5432
    Founded: 1972
    Arts Area: Dance; Vocal Music; Instrumental Music; Theater; Festivals; Lyric Opera
    Status: Non-Profit
    Type: Educational; Sponsoring
    Purpose: To operate with its facility, the Opera House, as a regional arts center with quality programming and arts education for the northern Michigan area

Management: Joann P. Leal, Executive Director; Jerry Bronson, Stage Technician
Officers: Jeannette Bronson, President; Michael Stack, Vice President; John Woodruff, Treasurer; Celeste Spencer, Secretary
Paid Staff: 4   **Volunteer Staff:** 160
Utilizes: Special Technical Talent; Guest Artists
Budget: $100,000 - $500,000
Income Sources: Private Foundations/Grants/Endowments; Business/Corporate Donations; Box Office; Government Grants; Individual Donations
Season: 52 Weeks   **Annual Attendance:** 10,000
Affiliations: Michigan Association of Community Arts Agencies; APAP
Performance Facilities: Opera House

FACILITY

CHEBOYGAN OPERA HOUSE - CITY HALL
403 North Huron, PO Box 95, Cheboygan, MI 49721
(616) 627-5432
Founded: 1877
Type of Facility: Performance Center; Theatre House; Opera House; Visual And Performing Arts Classrooms
Type of Stage: Proscenium
Stage Dimensions: 34'x20'; extended backstage - 40'D   **Orchestra Pit**
Seating Capacity: 581
Year Built: 1888   **Cost:** $35,000
Year Remodeled: 1984   **Architect:** Wolf & Nichols   **Cost:** $2,500,000
Contact for Rental: Joann P. Leal, Executive Director;   (616) 627-5432
Performing Arts and Arts Center, classes and performances

Coldwater

PERFORMING SERIES

TIBBITS OPERA AND ARTS COUNCIL
14 South Hanchett Street, Coldwater, MI 49036
(517) 278-6029
Founded: 1964
Arts Area: Dance; Vocal Music; Instrumental Music; Theater; Festivals; Lyric Opera
Status: Professional; Semi-Professional; Non-Professional; Non-Profit
Type: Performing; Touring; Resident; Educational; Sponsoring
Purpose: To restore and operate the historic Tibbits Opera House and provide facilities, programming classes, and arts service to a wide segment of the community
Management: Donald F Hebert, Executive Director
Officers: John Shea, President; Barry Case, Vice President; Kristina Gerlach, Correspondence Secretary; Rae Kleindirst, Recording Secretary; Caroline Lowe, Treasurer
Paid Staff: 6   **Volunteer Staff:** 35
Paid Artists: 40
Utilizes: Special Technical Talent; Guest Artists; Guest Directors
Budget: $100,000 - $500,000
Income Sources: Private Foundations/Grants/Endowments; Business/Corporate Donations; Box Office; Government Grants; Individual Donations
Season: 52 Weeks
Affiliations: APAP; Michigan Association of Community Arts Agencies
Performance Facilities: Tibbits Opera House

FACILITY

TIBBITS OPERA HOUSE
14 South Hanchett Street, Coldwater, MI 49036
(517) 278-6029; (800) 444-6029
Type of Facility: Theatre Complex; Concert Hall; Auditorium; Theatre House; Opera House; Civic Center; Multi-Purpose
Type of Stage: Proscenium
Orchestra Pit
Seating Capacity: 571
Year Built: 1882   **Architect:** Mortimer Smith   **Cost:** $25,000
Contact for Rental: John Shea;   (517) 278-6029
Manager: Donald F. Hebert
Resident Groups: Tibbits Summer Theatre; Coldwater Community Theatre; Tibbits Theatre for Young Audiences; Tibbtis Opera Foundation
To serve as a cultural center for our broadly-based constituency

---

Dearborn

PERFORMING SERIES

MICHIGAN BACH FESTIVAL
400 Town Center Drive, Suite 300, Dearborn, MI 48126
(313) 271-1939
FAX: (313) 593-5604
>**Founded:** 1982
>**Arts Area:** Vocal Music; Instrumental Music; Festivals
>**Status:** Professional; Non-Profit
>**Type:** Performing; Touring; Educational
>**Purpose:** To present a series of concerts
>**Officers:** Curtis J. Posuniak, General Director; Dr. Ronald Dobrzynski, Chairman of the Board; Dr. Shirley Harbin, Vice Chairman; V.C. Madias, Vice President; Carl Misiak, Treasurer; Judith Modelski, Secretary; Waltraud Prechter, Assistant Secretary
>**Paid Staff:** 3
>**Paid Artists:** 150
>**Utilizes:** Guest Conductors; Guest Artists
>**Budget:** $1,000 - $50,000
>**Income Sources:** Private Foundations/Grants/Endowments; Business/Corporate Donations; Government Grants; Individual Donations
>**Season:** March   **Annual Attendance:** 4,000

Detroit

DANCE

MADAME CADILLAC DANCE THEATRE
15 East Kirby, #903, Detroit, MI 48202
(313) 875-6354
FAX: (313) 832-4290
>**Founded:** 1982
>**Arts Area:** Ethnic; Folk; Historical
>**Status:** Semi-Professional; Non-Profit
>**Type:** Performing; Touring; Educational
>**Purpose:** To perform 18th-century dance and music of the court and country to tell the story of the American-French Colonial Period
>**Management:** Harriet Berg, Artistic Director; Matt Stockard, Business Manager; Callt Kypros, Booking Agent
>**Paid Staff:** 3   **Volunteer Staff:** 2
>**Paid Artists:** 10
>**Utilizes:** Special Technical Talent; Guest Artists
>**Budget:** $1,000 - $50,000
>**Income Sources:** Private Foundations/Grants/Endowments; Business/Corporate Donations; Box Office; Government Grants; Individual Donations
>**Season:** 52 Weeks

RENAISSANCE DANCE COMPANY OF DETROIT
15 East Kirby, #903, Detroit, MI 48202
(313) 875-6354
FAX: (313) 832-4290
>**Founded:** 1969
>**Arts Area:** Ethnic; Folk; Historical
>**Status:** Semi-Professional; Non-Profit
>**Type:** Performing; Touring; Educational
>**Purpose:** To perform 16th-century court and country dances of the Elizabethan age
>**Management:** Harriet Berg, Artistic Director; Matt Stockard, Business Manager
>**Paid Staff:** 2   **Volunteer Staff:** 2
>**Paid Artists:** 10
>**Utilizes:** Special Technical Talent; Guest Artists
>**Budget:** $1,000 - $50,000
>**Income Sources:** Private Foundations/Grants/Endowments; Business/Corporate Donations; Box Office; Government Grants; Individual Donations
>**Season:** 52 Weeks
>**Performance Facilities:** Detroit Institute of Arts

INSTRUMENTAL MUSIC

DETROIT JAZZ ORCHESTRA
1428 Broadway, #212, Detroit, MI 48226
(313) 393-5299
> **Founded:** 1981
> **Arts Area:** Orchestra; Ensemble; Ethnic; Instrumental Group
> **Status:** Professional; Non-Profit
> **Type:** Performing; Touring; Resident; Educational; Sponsoring
> **Purpose:** To preserve the history, evolve the art of, and improve the socio-economic conditions of jazz and its practitioners
> **Management:** Marsha Walden, Administrator; Linnette Phillips, Business Manager; Oliver Ragsdale, Administrative Assistant
> **Officers:** Donald Walden, Executive/Artistic Director; Reuben A. Munday, President; Marsha Walden, Vice President
> **Paid Staff:** 3 **Volunteer Staff:** 10
> **Paid Artists:** 35
> **Utilizes:** Guest Conductors; Guest Artists; Guest Directors
> **Budget:** $50,000 - $100,000
> **Income Sources:** Business/Corporate Donations; Box Office; Government Grants; Individual Donations
> **Season:** 52 Weeks **Annual Attendance:** 7,000
> **Performance Facilities:** New World Stage

DETROIT SYMPHONY ORCHESTRA
400 Buhl Building, Detroit, MI 48226
(313) 962-1000
FAX: (313) 962-9107
> **Founded:** 1914
> **Arts Area:** Symphony; Orchestra
> **Status:** Professional; Non-Profit
> **Type:** Performing; Touring; Resident; Educational; Sponsoring
> **Purpose:** To perform and educate
> **Management:** Neeme Jarvi, Music Director; Mark Volpe, Executive Director; Willa Rovder, Artistic Administrator
> **Officers:** Alfred R. Glancy III, Chairman of the Board of Directors
> **Paid Staff:** 59 **Volunteer Staff:** 600
> **Paid Artists:** 105
> **Utilizes:** Guest Conductors; Guest Artists
> **Budget:** Over 10,000,000
> **Income Sources:** Private Foundations/Grants/Endowments; Business/Corporate Donations; Box Office; Government Grants; Individual Donations
> **Season:** September - August **Annual Attendance:** 300,000
> **Performance Facilities:** Orchestra Hall; Meadow Brook Music Festival

VOCAL MUSIC

MICHIGAN OPERA THEATRE
6519 Second Avenue, Detroit, MI 48214
(313) 874-7850
> **Founded:** 1971
> **Arts Area:** Grand Opera; Operetta
> **Status:** Professional; Non-Profit
> **Type:** Performing; Touring
> **Purpose:** To present the highest quality opera possible in Michigan
> **Management:** Dr. David DiChiera, General Director
> **Officers:** Robert Dewar, Chairman
> **Paid Staff:** 28
> **Utilizes:** Special Technical Talent; Guest Conductors; Guest Artists; Guest Directors
> **Budget:** $1,000,000 - $5,000,000
> **Income Sources:** Private Foundations/Grants/Endowments; Business/Corporate Donations; Box Office; Government Grants; Individual Donations
> **Season:** Fall - Spring

OPERA LITE
PO Box 405, Dearborn, Detroit, MI 48121
(517) 482-3096
> **Founded:** 1986
> **Arts Area:** Light Opera
> **Type:** Performing; Touring; Resident
> **Management:** David Pulice, Managing Director; Amy Kutt, Assistant Director
> **Officers:** David Pulice, President

Paid Staff: 3   **Volunteer Staff:** 15
Paid Artists: 130
Utilizes: Guest Conductors; Guest Artists; Guest Directors
Income Sources: Business/Corporate Donations; Box Office; Individual Donations
Season: September - June

THEATRE

AFRO-AMERICAN STUDIO THEATRE
3944 Chalmers, Detroit, MI 48205
(313) 885-5222
Founded: 1982
Arts Area: Professional; Dinner; Community; Theatrical Group
Status: Professional; Semi-Professional; Non-Professional; Non-Profit
Type: Performing; Touring; Educational; Sponsoring
Purpose: To promote the development and exposure of dramatic works depicting and extolling the African-American experience while also giving Black artists a forum in which to perform and grow
Management: James Reed Faulkner, Artistic Director/Founder
Officers: Gail L. Faulkner, President of the Board; Carol Wilkerson, Secretary; Octavius Sapp, Treasurer; Nehemiah Pitts, Fundraising
Paid Staff: 6   **Volunteer Staff:** 7
Paid Artists: 9   **Non-Paid Artists:** 12
Utilizes: Special Technical Talent; Guest Artists; Guest Directors
Budget: $50,000 - $100,000
Income Sources: Private Foundations/Grants/Endowments; Business/Corporate Donations; Box Office; Individual Donations
Season: 52 Weeks   **Annual Attendance:** 8,000

ATTIC/NEW CENTER THEATRE
2990 West Grand Boulevard, Suite 308, Detroit, MI 48202-8285
(313) 875-8285
Founded: 1975
Arts Area: Professional; Musical; Theatrical Group
Status: Professional; Non-Profit
Type: Performing; Touring; Resident; Educational
Purpose: Attic/New Center Theatre is a resident, professional theatre company committed to the development of actors, directors, playwrights, and technicians as craftsmen in the art of theatre. It exists to create new works and to present new and challenging plays by contemporary playwrights.
Management: Lavinia Moyer, Artistic Director; Jim Moran, Managing Director
Officers: Andy Soffel, Chairman; Lavinia Moyer, President; Peter C. Gray, Treasurer; Paul R. Retenbach, Secretary
Paid Staff: 15   **Volunteer Staff:** 75
Paid Artists: 65
Utilizes: Special Technical Talent; Guest Artists; Guest Directors
Budget: $1,000,000 - $5,000,000
Income Sources: Private Foundations/Grants/Endowments; Business/Corporate Donations; Box Office; Government Grants; Individual Donations
Season: 52 Weeks
Annual Attendance: 36,000
Affiliations: TCG; FEDAPT
Performance Facilities: The New Center Theatre

CONCEPT EAST II
1144 Pengree, Detroit, MI 48202
(313) 972-1030
Founded: 1986
Arts Area: Professional; Theatrical Group
Status: Professional
Type: Performing; Touring; Educational; Sponsoring
Purpose: To preserve the art of Black cinema and theater
Management: James Wheeler, Founder/Artistic Director
Paid Staff: 4
Utilizes: Special Technical Talent; Guest Artists; Guest Directors
Budget: $1,000 - $50,000
Income Sources: Private Foundations/Grants/Endowments; Box Office; Government Grants; Individual Donations
Season: 52 Weeks
Performance Facilities: Concept East II

DETROIT REPERTORY THEATRE
13103 Woodrow Wilson, Detroit, MI 48238
(313) 868-1347
FAX: (313) 868-1705
Founded: 1956
Arts Area: Professional
Status: Professional; Non-Profit
Type: Performing
Management: Bruce E. Millan, Artistic Director/Managing Director
Officers: Hope Byrd, Chair, Advisory Board
Paid Staff: 7 **Volunteer Staff:** 4
Paid Artists: 12
Budget: $100,000 - $500,000
Income Sources: Private Foundations/Grants/Endowments; Business/Corporate Donations; Box Office; Government Grants; Individual Donations
Season: November - June **Annual Attendance:** 30,000
Performance Facilities: Detroit Repertory Theatre

PLOWSHARES THEATRE
PO Box 11399, Detroit, MI 48211
(313) 353-5591
Founded: 1989
Arts Area: Professional; Theatrical Group
Status: Professional; Non-Profit
Type: Performing; Touring
Purpose: To produce engaging theatre that reflects the cultural diversity of the Detroit area
Management: Gary Anderson, Micahel Garza, Artistic Directors
Officers: Gary Anderson, President; Michael Garza, Chairman; Addell Austin Anderson, Secretary/Treasurer
Paid Staff: 2 **Volunteer Staff:** 10
Utilizes: Guest Artists; Guest Directors
Budget: $1,000 - $50,000
Income Sources: Private Foundations/Grants/Endowments; Box Office; Individual Donations
Season: September - May
Annual Attendance: 6,600

THEATER GROTTESCO
PO Box 32658, Detroit, MI 48232
(313) 961-5880
Founded: 1983
Arts Area: Professional; Theatrical Group
Status: Professional; Non-Profit
Type: Performing; Touring; Educational
Purpose: To create modern original plays and conduct training workshops and master classes
Management: John Flax, Elizabeth Wiseman, Co-Artistic Directors
Officers: Mary A. Zatina, President; Eric Dueweke, Vice President; Sandra Abmrozy, Treasurer; Gerald Conway, Secretary
Paid Staff: 2
Paid Artists: 4
Budget: $100,000 - $500,000
Income Sources: Private Foundations/Grants/Endowments; Business/Corporate Donations; Box Office; Government Grants; Individual Donations
Season: 52 Weeks
Affiliations: APAP; TCG; Arts Midwest; NACA

WAYNE STATE UNIVERSITY HILBERRY AND BONSTELLE THEATRES
95 West Hancock, Detroit, MI 48092
(313) 577-3511
FAX: (313) 577-0935
Founded: 1963
Arts Area: Musical; Theatrical Group
Status: Non-Professional; Non-Profit
Type: Performing; Touring; Resident; Educational; Sponsoring
Purpose: The Bonstelle is the house of the undergraduate theatre program; the Hilberry houses our graduate repertory company
Management: Robert T. Hazzard, Chair/Director; Anthony B. Schmitt, Thomas Schraeder, Associate Directors; Robert E. McGill, Assistant Chair
Paid Staff: 20

Paid Artists: 48
Utilizes: Special Technical Talent; Guest Artists; Guest Directors
Budget: $1,000,000 - $5,000,000
Income Sources: Private Foundations/Grants/Endowments; Business/Corporate Donations; Box Office; Individual Donations; University Budget
Season: October - May   **Annual Attendance:** 90,000
Affiliations: ATHE; U/RTA; TCG; NAST
Performance Facilities: Bonstelle Theatre; Hilberry Theatre

PERFORMING SERIES

CASA DE UNIDAS
1920 Scotten, Detroit, MI 48209
(313) 843-9598
Founded: 1981
Arts Area: Dance; Vocal Music; Instrumental Music; Theater
Status: Non-Profit
Type: Performing; Touring; Educational; Sponsoring
Purpose: To present community-based, arts and media presentations serving predominantly Hispanic communities
Management: Marta Lagos, Program Coordinator/Community Relations
Officers: Delores Gonzalez, President; Violo Chakmakian, Vice President
Paid Staff: 4   **Volunteer Staff:** 10
Paid Artists: 15   **Non-Paid Artists:** 10
Utilizes: Special Technical Talent; Guest Artists; Guest Directors
Budget: $50,000 - $100,000
Income Sources: Private Foundations/Grants/Endowments; Business/Corporate Donations; Box Office; Government Grants; Individual Donations
Season: June - October
Performance Facilities: Clark Park Theatre

MONTREUX DETROIT JAZZ FESTIVAL - DETROIT RENAISSANCE FOUNDATION
100 Renaissance Center, Suite 1760, Detroit, MI 48243-1066
(313) 259-5400
FAX: (313) 567-8355
Founded: 1980
Arts Area: Vocal Music; Instrumental Music; Festivals
Status: Non-Profit
Type: Performing; Sponsoring
Purpose: To preseve, promote and maintain the understanding of jazz music
Management: Eric R. Dueweke, Director of Operations; Beryl J. Javery, Director of Administrative Services; Keith Kaminski, Director of Media Relations; Glenn Lapin, Director of Site Development; Kathleen M. McNamara, Managing Director; Michael D. Samueloff, Fireworks Director; Diane Taylor, Director of Event Services
Officers: Robert E. McCabe, President; Edward Fleischmann, Secretary/Treasurer
Paid Staff: 38   **Volunteer Staff:** 200
Income Sources: Private Foundations/Grants/Endowments
Season: September

UNITED BLACK ARTISTS, USA, INC.
7661 LaSalle Boulevard, Detroit, MI 48206
(313) 898-5574; (313) 363-0369
Founded: 1987
Arts Area: Instrumental Music; Theater
Status: Non-Profit
Type: Educational; Sponsoring
Purpose: To promote cultural and literary growth thereby stimulating the quality of life among blacks
Management: Dr. Daphne W. Ntiri, Management Staff
Officers: Roderick E. Warren, President/Treasurer; Verona Morton, Vice President
Paid Staff: 2   **Volunteer Staff:** 6
Paid Artists: 15   **Non-Paid Artists:** 20
Utilizes: Guest Artists
Budget: $1,000 - $50,000
Income Sources: Private Foundations/Grants/Endowments; Business/Corporate Donations; Government Grants; Individual Donations; City and Local Contributions
Season: 52 Weeks
Annual Attendance: 750
Affiliations: Harmony Park Playhouse

FACILITY

COBO ARENA
301 Civic Center Drive, Detroit, MI 48226
(313) 567-6000
     Type of Facility: Theatre House; Arena; Multi-Purpose
     Type of Stage: Flexible; Arena
     Seating Capacity: Arena - 12,191; 3/4 Arena - 7,000
     Year Built: 1960 **Architect:** Giffels & Rossetti **Cost:** $55,000,000
     Contact for Rental: Allan Vella; (313) 567-6000
     Cost reflects convention center construction

DETROIT CENTER FOR THE PERFORMING ARTS
8041 Harper, Detroit, MI 48213
(313) 925-7138
     Type of Facility: Theatre Complex; Concert Hall; Auditorium; Studio Performance; Performance Center; Off Broadway; Multi-Purpose
     Type of Stage: Proscenium
     Stage Dimensions: 36'x40'   **Orchestra Pit**
     Seating Capacity: 2,983
     Year Built: 1930
     Year Remodeled: 1980 **Architect:** Dietrich & Cassavaugh **Cost:** $200,000
     Contact for Rental: Bruce E. Nilsson; (313) 925-7138
     Manager: Nancy Engel
     Resident Groups: Detroit Center for the Performing Arts

DETROIT SYMPHONY ORCHESTRA HALL
3711 Woodward, Detroit, MI 48201
(313) 833-3362
     Type of Facility: Concert Hall
     Type of Stage: Proscenium
     Stage Dimensions: 40'x40'
     Seating Capacity: 2,038
     Year Built: 1919 **Architect:** C. Howard Crane **Cost:** $700,000
     Year Remodeled: 1990 **Architect:** Diohl and Diohl Architects **Cost:** $5,500,000
     Acoustical Consultant: Jaffe Acoustics
     Contact for Rental: Stanley Hobbs, Lori Boccia; (313) 833-3362
     Resident Groups: Detroit Symphony Orchestra; Chamber Music Society of Detroit; Detroit Symphony Chamber Orchestra

FOX THEATRE
2211 Woodward Avenue, Detroit, MI 48201
(313) 965-7100
     Type of Facility: Theatre House
     Facility Originally: Show Palace
     Seating Capacity: 5,600
     Year Built: 1928 **Architect:** C. Howard Crane **Cost:** $12,000,000
     Contact for Rental: Stu Mayer; (313) 965-7100
     Manager: Greg Bellamy

JOE LOUIS ARENA
600 Civic Center Drive, Detroit, MI 48226
(313) 567-6000
     Type of Facility: Theatre House; Arena; Multi-Purpose
     Type of Stage: Flexible; Arena
     Seating Capacity: End Stage - 19,868; Floor Stage - 20,666
     Year Built: 1979 **Architect:** Smith Hinchman & Grylls **Cost:** $29,700,000
     Year Remodeled: 1982 **Cost:** $4,000,000
     Contact for Rental: John Pettit, Operations Manager; (313) 567-7444

MUSIC HALL CENTER FOR THE PERFORMING ARTS
350 Madison Avenue, Detroit, MI 48226
(313) 963-7622
FAX: (313) 963-2466
     Type of Facility: Theatre House
     Type of Stage: Proscenium
     Stage Dimensions: 41'9"x44'x38; 40'x40' proscenium opening **Orchestra Pit**
     Seating Capacity: 1,790

Year Built: 1928   **Architect:** Smith Hinchman & Grylls
Contact for Rental: Karen Wright;   (313) 963-7622

Farmington Hills

FACILITY

THE COMMUNITY CENTER FARMINGTON - FARMINGTON HILLS
24705 Farmington, Farmington Hills, MI 48336
(313) 477-8404
   Founded: 1969
   Type of Facility: Outdoor (Concert); Amphitheater; Civic Center; Multi-Purpose; Room
   Facility Originally: Family Mansion
   Type of Stage: Proscenium; Platform
   Stage Dimensions: 40'x20'
   Seating Capacity: Indoor - 100; Outdoor - 300
   Year Built: 1869
   Year Remodeled: 1920   **Architect:** Marcus Burrowes
   Contact for Rental: Bobbi Gelman;   (313) 477-8404
   Resident Groups: Men's Club; Farmington Area Community Women; Ridge Writers

---

Ferndale

VOCAL MUSIC

CANTATA ACADEMY
2441 Pinecrest, Ferndale, MI 48220
(313) 546-0420
   Founded: 1961
   Arts Area: Choral
   Status: Semi-Professional; Non-Profit
   Type: Performing; Touring
   Purpose: To perform fine choral music
   Management: Phillip O'Jibway, Manager; Frederick Bellinger, Musical Director/Conductor
   Officers: Ellen Boyes, President; Robert Branch, Vice President; Jenny Meisel, Secretary; Bonnie Hart, Treasurer
   Paid Staff: 3
   Paid Artists: 50
   Budget: $1,000 - $50,000
   Income Sources: Private Foundations/Grants/Endowments; Business/Corporate Donations; Box Office; Government
   Grants; Individual Donations
   Season: September - June   **Annual Attendance:** 4,000
   Affiliations: CA

Flint

INSTRUMENTAL MUSIC

FLINT SYMPHONY ORCHESTRA
Flint Institute of Music, 1025 East Kearsley Street, Flint, MI 48503
(313) 238-9651
FAX: (313) 238-6385
   Founded: 1917
   Arts Area: Symphony; Orchestra
   Status: Professional; Non-Profit
   Type: Performing; Resident; Educational
   Management: Thomas Gerdon, Executive Director
   Utilizes: Guest Conductors; Guest Artists
   Income Sources: Private Foundations/Grants/Endowments; Business/Corporate Donations; Box Office; Government
   Grants; Individual Donations
   Performance Facilities: James H. Whiting Auditorium

PERFORMING SERIES

THE FLINT INSTITUTE OF MUSIC
1025 East Kearsley Street, Flint, MI 48503
(313) 238-9651
    Founded: 1966
    Arts Area: Dance; Vocal Music; Instrumental Music
    Status: Professional; Non-Profit
    Type: Performing; Touring; Educational; Sponsoring
    Purpose: To foster, promote and increase the musical knowledge and appreciation of the public through educational activities and the organization and presentation of performances of music and dance
    Management: Thomas Gerdom, Executive Director; Paul Torre, Director, Flint School of Performing Arts; Claudia J. Ferguson, Director of Development
    Officers: John D. Mott, Chairman; Gloria Van Duyne, Chairman-Elect; Edward P. Abbott, John R. Wilson, Vice Chairmen; Bruce J. Boss, Secretary; John E. Birky, Treasurer
    Paid Staff: 36
    Paid Artists: 87
    Utilizes: Special Technical Talent; Guest Conductors; Guest Artists
    Budget: $1,000,000 - $5,000,000
    Income Sources: Private Foundations/Grants/Endowments; Business/Corporate Donations; Box Office; Government Grants; Individual Donations
    Season: 52 Weeks
    Affiliations: ASOL; APAP; MOA; BOMI; NARB
    Performance Facilities: MacArthur Recital Hall; University of Michigan-Flint; Whiting Auditorium

FACILITY

THE FLINT INSTITUTE OF MUSIC
1025 East Kearsley Street, Flint, MI 48503
(313) 238-9651
    Type of Facility: Auditorium; Performance Center; Multi-Purpose
    Type of Stage: Proscenium
    Stage Dimensions: 45'x24'   **Seating Capacity:** 270
    Year Built: 1970 **Architect:** Ellis Arndt and Truesdale **Cost:** $1,500,000
    Contact for Rental: Paul Torre; (313) 238-9651
    Resident Groups: Ensembles of the Flint School of the Performing Arts; Ballet Michigan; Ensembles of the Flint Symphony Orchestra

JAMES H. WHITING AUDITORIUM
1241 East Kearsley Street, Flint, MI 48503
(313) 760-1138
    Type of Facility: Auditorium

Garden City

FACILITY

MAPLEWOOD COMMUNITY CENTER
31735 Maplewood, Garden City, MI 48135
(313) 525-8846
    Type of Facility: Multi-Purpose; Room
    Facility Originally: School
    Type of Stage: Platform
    Seating Capacity: 160
    Resident Groups: Ann Arbor Goodtime Players; Crossroads Productions
    Available for rent

Grand Haven

FACILITY

CITY OF GRAND HAVEN COMMUNITY CENTER
421 Columbus, Grand Haven, MI 49417
(616) 842-2550
FAX: (616) 842-0085
    Type of Facility: Auditorium
    Type of Stage: Proscenium

Stage Dimensions: 16'x22'x20'
Seating Capacity: 200
Year Built: 1967   **Architect:** Jickling & Lyman
Contact for Rental: Bill Kool;   (616) 842-2550
Resident Groups: Central Park Players Community Theater
Performing Arts events, conferences

Grand Rapids

DANCE

THE GRAND RAPIDS BALLET
233 East Fulton, Suite 8, Grand Rapids, MI 49503
(616) 454-4771
  Founded: 1973
  Arts Area: Ballet
  Status: Non-Professional; Non-Profit
  Type: Performing; Touring; Educational; Sponsoring
  Purpose: To present programs of professional and amateur dancers; to give ballet training to students of the area
  Management: Charthel Arthur, Artistic Director
  Officers: Susan Meyers, President; Judy Freeman, First Vice President; Deb Meadows, Second Vice President; Dale Iverson, Secretary; Mary Nell Baldwin, Treasurer
  Paid Staff: 3   **Volunteer Staff:** 50
  Non-Paid Artists: 55
  Utilizes: Special Technical Talent; Guest Conductors; Guest Artists; Guest Choreographers
  Budget: $100,000 - $500,000
  Income Sources: Private Foundations/Grants/Endowments; Business/Corporate Donations; Box Office; Government Grants; Individual Donations
  Season: December - June   **Annual Attendance:** 20,000
  Affiliations: Arts Council of Greater Grand Rapids; NARB
  Performance Facilities: DeVos Hall

INSTRUMENTAL MUSIC

THE CHAMBER MUSIC SOCIETY OF GRAND RAPIDS, INC.
c/o St. Cecilia Music Society, 24 Ransom Avenue Northeast, Grand Rapids, MI 49503
(616) 459-2224
  Founded: 1980
  Arts Area: Chamber
  Status: Non-Profit
  Type: Sponsoring
  Purpose: To promote and support chamber music performance in western Michigan, specifically Grand Rapids
  Management: LeAnn Arkema, Administrator of Saint Cecilia Music Society
  Officers: Mary Barr, President; Lance Jones and Kathy Bissell, Vice Presidents; Jan Candler, Secretary; Sue Meyer, Treasurer
  Paid Staff: 2   **Volunteer Staff:** 17
  Utilizes: Guest Artists
  Budget: $1,000 - $50,000
  Income Sources: Business/Corporate Donations; Box Office; Individual Donations
  Season: September - May   **Annual Attendance:** 250
  Performance Facilities: Royce Auditorium; Saint Cecilia Music Society

GRAND RAPIDS SYMPHONY ORCHESTRA
220 Lyon Street NW, Suite 415, Grand Rapids, MI 49503
(616) 454-9451
FAX: (616) 454-7477
  Founded: 1929
  Arts Area: Symphony; Orchestra; Chamber; Ensemble
  Status: Non-Profit
  Type: Performing; Touring; Resident; Educational
  Purpose: The purpose of the Grand Rapids Symphony Society is to provide concerts of orchestral and chamber music and educational programs of the highest quality to the widest possible audience.
  Management: Peter W. Smith, Executive Director/General Manager
  Paid Staff: 10   **Volunteer Staff:** 100
  Utilizes: Guest Conductors; Guest Artists; Guest Directors
  Budget: $1,000,000 - $5,000,000
  Income Sources: Private Foundations/Grants/Endowments; Business/Corporate Donations; Box Office; Government Grants; Individual Donations

Season: September - May   **Annual Attendance:** 65,000
Affiliations: ASOL; MOA
Performance Facilities: DeVos Hall

GRAND RAPIDS YOUTH SYMPHONY
220 Lyon Street NW, Suite 415, Grand Rapids, MI 49503
(616) 454-9451
Founded: 1959
Arts Area: Symphony; Orchestra
Status: Non-Professional; Non-Profit
Type: Performing; Educational
Purpose: The Grand Rapids Youth Symphony provides an opportunity for talented students to perform with other musicians of their caliber, to broaden their musical experience and to provide an invaluable training ground for the professional musicians of the future.
Management: John Varineau, Conductor; Pam French, Outreach Director
Paid Staff: 2
Non-Paid Artists: 80
Season: September - June   **Annual Attendance:** 1,000
Affiliations: ASOL (Youth Orchestra Division); Grand Rapids Symphony
Performance Facilities: Forest Hills Northern High School Auditorium

VOCAL MUSIC

OPERA GRAND RAPIDS
161 Ottawa NW, Suite 205B, Grand Rapids, MI 49503
(616) 451-2741
FAX: (616) 451-4587
Founded: 1967
Arts Area: Grand Opera; Musical Theatre
Status: Professional; Non-Profit
Type: Performing; Educational; Sponsoring
Purpose: To enhance the quality of life in the Grand Rapids area and western Michigan by providing professional-quality operatic/musical theater productions; to raise the level of appreciation and understanding of opera in all residents
Management: Robert Lyall, General Director; Andrea Creswick, Business Manager; Jody Parraguez, Public Relations/Marketing Director
Paid Staff: 6   **Volunteer Staff:** 4
Paid Artists: 100   **Non-Paid Artists:** 12
Utilizes: Special Technical Talent; Guest Conductors; Guest Artists; Guest Directors
Budget: $100,000 - $500,000
Income Sources: Private Foundations/Grants/Endowments; Business/Corporate Donations; Box Office; Government Grants; Individual Donations
Season: October - April   **Annual Attendance:** 8,500
Affiliations: OA
Performance Facilities: DeVos Hall

PERFORMING SERIES

FESTIVAL OF THE ARTS
207 Waters Building, Grand Rapids, MI 49503
(616) 459-2787
Founded: 1970
Arts Area: Dance; Vocal Music; Instrumental Music; Theater; Festivals
Status: Professional; Non-Profit
Type: Sponsoring
Purpose: To support the arts and artists of the Greater Grand Rapids Community; to promote and support the arts financially and through technical assistance to organizations or individuals; to promote experiences for participants and observers from within the general public
Management: Jacqueline Udell, Office Manager
Officers: Patricia Duthler, President; Norma Van Kuiken, Vice President; Johanne Neu, Secretary; Michael Julien, Treasurer
Paid Staff: 2   **Volunteer Staff:** 2,500
Non-Paid Artists: 3,000
Utilizes: Guest Artists
Budget: $50,000 - $100,000
Income Sources: Business/Corporate Donations; Individual Donations
Season: June   **Annual Attendance:** 600,000
Performance Facilities: Calder Plaza

FACILITY

CALVIN COLLEGE FINE ARTS CENTER
3201 Burton Street SE, Grand Rapids, MI 49546
(616) 957-6280
FAX: (616) 957-6469
    Type of Facility: Theatre Complex; Concert Hall; Auditorium; Performance Center; Multi-Purpose
    Type of Stage: Thrust; Proscenium
    Stage Dimensions: 60'Wx40'D
    Orchestra Pit
    Seating Capacity: 1,200
    Year Built: 1966 **Architect:** Daverman Associates **Cost:** $2,500,000
    Acoustical Consultant: Bolt, Beranek & Newman
    Contact for Rental: Jeff Stob; (616) 957-6280

FOUNTAIN STREET CHURCH
24 Fountain Street NE, Grand Rapids, MI 49503
(616) 459-8386
    Facility Originally: Church
    Type of Stage: Platform
    Stage Dimensions: 24'x24'
    Seating Capacity: 1,600
    Contact for Rental: Lisa Hill; (616) 459-8386
    Resident Groups: Fountain Street Church Choir
    Only rented to non-profit groups

GRAND CENTER - AUDITORIUM
245 Monroe Avenue NW, Grand Rapids, MI 49503
(616) 456-3922
    Type of Facility: Auditorium; Civic Center
    Type of Stage: Flexible; Proscenium
    Seating Capacity: 4,300
    Year Built: 1933 **Architect:** Robinson-Campau **Cost:** $1,500,000
    Year Remodeled: 1985 **Architect:** Daverman Associates **Cost:** $6,000,000
    Contact for Rental: Robert Hodge, Maryanne McIntyre; (616) 456-3922
    Manager: Robert Hodge
    Remodeling and additions done in 1985 to the Welsh Auditorium

GRAND CENTER - DEVOS HALL
245 Monroe Avenue NW, Grand Rapids, MI 49503
(616) 456-3922
FAX: (616) 456-3995
    Type of Facility: Performance Center; Off Broadway; Theatre House; Multi-Purpose
    Type of Stage: Proscenium
    Stage Dimensions: 58'Wx43'D; 58'Wx35'H proscenium opening **Orchestra Pit**
    Seating Capacity: 2,446
    Year Built: 1981
    Contact for Rental: Robert Hodge; (616) 456-3922
    Resident Groups: Grand Rapids Symphony; Grand Rapids Ballet; Opera Grand Rapids
    Part of the 1981 addition to Grand Center

Grosse Pointe Farms

VOCAL MUSIC

RACKHAM SYMPHONY CHOIR
165 Hillcrest Lane, Grosse Pointe Farms, MI 48236
(313) 882-1285; (313) 886-1821
    Founded: 1949
    Arts Area: Choral
    Status: Non-Profit
    Type: Performing; Educational
    Purpose: To provide the metropolitan Detroit area with choral symphonic performances of the classical masters
    Management: D. Frederic DeHaven, Music Director; Shari Fiori, Assistant Director
    Officers: Lance J. Kronzer, President of the Board; Anne Weston, Vice President; Luanne Offer, Treasurer; Janet Oakes, Secretary
    Paid Staff: 3 **Volunteer Staff:** 14

Non-Paid Artists: 60
Utilizes: Guest Artists
Budget: $50,000 - $100,000
Income Sources: Private Foundations/Grants/Endowments; Business/Corporate Donations; Box Office; Government Grants; Individual Donations
Season: September - June   **Annual Attendance:** 4,000

PERFORMING SERIES

GROSSE POINTE SUMMER FESTIVAL
181 Beaupre Avenue, Grosse Pointe Farms, MI 48236-3448
(313) 558-6370; (313) 885-0793
FAX: (313) 573-4806
Founded: 1957
Arts Area: Vocal Music; Instrumental Music; Theater; Festivals; Lyric Opera
Status: Professional; Non-Profit
Type: Performing; Touring; Resident
Purpose: To present outdoor concerts for community enrichment in summer
Management: Alexander C. Suczek, Founder/Artistic Director
Officers: Mrs. Barbara Denler, Program Director; Mrs. Johanna Gilber, General Chairman
Paid Staff: 10   **Volunteer Staff:** 20
Paid Artists: 5
Utilizes: Special Technical Talent; Guest Conductors; Guest Artists
Budget: $100,000 - $500,000•
Income Sources: Private Foundations/Grants/Endowments; Business/Corporate Donations; Box Office; Individual Donations
Annual Attendance: 5,000
Performance Facilities: Terrace of Alger House

PRO MUSICA, INC.
181 Beaupre Avenue, Grosse Pointe Farms, MI 48236-3448
(313) 558-6370; (313) 885-0793
FAX: (313) 573-4806
Founded: 1976
Arts Area: Vocal Music; Instrumental Music; Composers' New Works
Status: Professional; Non-Profit
Type: Performing
Purpose: To present emerging world-class artists in debut recitals in Detroit; to present composers in connection with performances of their music
Management: Alexander C. Suczek, President
Officers: Alice Haidostian, First Vice President; Dr. Hershel Sandberg, Second Vice President; Ann Kondak, Secretary; James Diamond, Treasurer
Paid Staff: 1
Paid Artists: 3
Utilizes: Guest Artists
Budget: $1,000 - $50,000
Income Sources: Private Foundations/Grants/Endowments; Business/Corporate Donations; Box Office; Individual Donations
Season: October - May   **Annual Attendance:** 1,000
Affiliations: Detroit Institute of the Arts
Performance Facilities: Recital Hall of the Detroit Institute of the Arts

Holland

INSTRUMENTAL MUSIC

HOPE COLLEGE ORCHESTRA AND SYMPHONETTE
Music Department, Holland, MI 49423
(616) 392-5111
Founded: 1949
Arts Area: Orchestra; Chamber
Status: Non-Professional; Non-Profit
Type: Performing; Touring; Resident; Educational
Purpose: To present concerts on campus and in other cities
Management: Robert Ritsema, Conductor
Paid Staff: 1
Non-Paid Artists: 60
Utilizes: Guest Conductors; Guest Artists; Guest Directors

Budget: $1,000 - $50,000
Season: September - May   Annual Attendance: 7,000
Affiliations: ASOL; MOA
Performance Facilities: Dimnent Chapel

FACILITY

HOPE COLLEGE THEATRE DEPARTMENT
Holland, MI 49423
(616) 392-5111
Founded: 1968
Type of Facility: Theatre Complex
Type of Stage: Thrust; Flexible; Proscenium
Stage Dimensions: 40'Wx20'Hx35'D   Orchestra Pit
Seating Capacity: 494
Year Built: 1971   Architect: Casler
Year Remodeled: 1983
Contact for Rental: Perry Landes;   (616) 394-7597

Interlochen

PERFORMING SERIES

INTERLOCHEN ARTS CAMP
Interlochen Center for the Arts, Interlochen, MI 49643
(616) 276-9221
FAX: (616) 276-6321
Founded: 1928
Arts Area: Dance; Vocal Music; Instrumental Music; Theater; Festivals; Visual Arts
Status: Non-Professional; Non-Profit
Type: Performing; Touring; Educational; Sponsoring
Purpose: To sponsor an eight-week summer program for talented boys and girls ages eight through college
Management: Edward J. Downing, Director of Arts Camp
Officers: Dean Boal, President
Paid Staff: 1
Utilizes: Guest Conductors; Guest Artists; Guest Directors
Budget: $5,000,000 - $10,000,000
Income Sources: Private Foundations/Grants/Endowments; Business/Corporate Donations; Box Office; Government Grants; Individual Donations
Season: June - August
Annual Attendance: 250,000
Performance Facilities: Corson Auditorium; Kresge Auditorium

INTERLOCHEN ARTS FESTIVAL
Interlochen Center for the Arts, Interlochen, MI 49643
(616) 276-9221
Founded: 1928
Arts Area: Dance; Vocal Music; Instrumental Music; Theater
Status: Semi-Professional; Non-Profit
Type: Performing; Educational
Purpose: To offer an eight-week extension of the National Music Camp
Officers: Edward Downing, Vice President
Paid Staff: 1,000
Utilizes: Special Technical Talent; Guest Artists; Guest Directors
Budget: $100,000 - $500,000
Income Sources: Private Foundations/Grants/Endowments; Business/Corporate Donations; Box Office; Government Grants; Individual Donations
Season: June - August
Performance Facilities: Kresge Auditorium; Corson Auditorium; Dendirnos Recital Hall

FACILITY

INTERLOCHEN CENTER FOR THE ARTS - CORSON AUDITORIUM
M-199, Interlochen, MI 49643
(616) 276-9221
Type of Facility: Concert Hall; Auditorium
Type of Stage: Proscenium
Stage Dimensions: 60'Wx28'Hx42'D   Orchestra Pit

Seating Capacity: 1,000
Year Built: 1975 **Architect:** Dow and Associates **Cost:** $2,100,000
Acoustical Consultant: Jaffe Acoustics
Resident Groups: All on-campus groups and guest artists
On-campus concerts

INTERLOCHEN CENTER FOR THE ARTS - DENDRINOS CHAPEL/RECITAL HALL
M-199, Interlochen, MI 49643
(616) 276-9221
Type of Facility: Concert Hall
Type of Stage: Platform
Stage Dimensions: 40'Wx40'Hx22'D
Seating Capacity: 230
Year Built: 1981 **Architect:** Dow, Howell, Gilmore & Associates **Cost:** $800,000
Acoustical Consultant: Jaffe Acoustics
Resident Groups: Selected on-campus groups and selected guest artists
On-campus concerts

INTERLOCHEN CENTER FOR THE ARTS - KRESGE AUDITORIUM
M-199, Interlochen, MI 49643
(616) 276-9221
Type of Facility: Concert Hall; Auditorium; Outdoor (Concert)
Type of Stage: Proscenium
Stage Dimensions: 60'Wx25'Hx40'D
Orchestra Pit
Seating Capacity: 4,000
Year Built: 1948
Year Remodeled: 1964 **Architect:** Dow and Associates
Acoustical Consultant: Bolt, Beranek & Newman
Resident Groups: All on-campus groups and guest artists
On-campus groups, primarily for music

Ironwood

FACILITY

HISTORIC IRONWOOD THEATRE
113 East Aurora, Ironwood, MI 49938
(906) 932-0618
FAX: (906) 932-4660
Founded: 1928
Type of Facility: Theatre Complex; Concert Hall; Performance Center; Off Broadway; Theatre House; Opera House; Multi-Purpose; Sponsorship
Facility Originally: Vaudeville; Movie House
Type of Stage: Proscenium
Stage Dimensions: 28'4"Wx30'H **Orchestra Pit**
Seating Capacity: Main Floor - 438
Year Built: 1928 **Architect:** Albert Nelson **Cost:** $160,000
Contact for Rental: Joan Borcherdt; (906) 932-0618
Resident Groups: Gogebic Range Players Productions
The theatre is available for art exhibitions, area school and college productions, second-run movies and as rental space for conventions and organizations.

Kalamazoo

DANCE

KALAMAZOO BALLET COMPANY
326 West Kalamazoo Avenue, Kalamazoo, MI 49007
(616) 343-3027
Founded: 1969
Arts Area: Modern; Ballet; Ethnic; Folk
Status: Semi-Professional; Non-Professional; Non-Profit
Type: Performing; Touring; Educational
Purpose: To give dancers the opportunity of experiencing professional rehearsals and performances while in Kalamazoo; to serve as a stepping stone to professional companies
Management: Birgitte Scheele, Business Manager; Therese Bullard, Artistic Director

Officers: Sherman Smith, President; Shirley Topp, Pat Middleton and Terry Bullard, Board Members
Paid Staff: 2 **Volunteer Staff:** 6
Paid Artists: 5 **Non-Paid Artists:** 50
Utilizes: Special Technical Talent; Guest Conductors; Guest Artists; Guest Choreographers
Budget: $1,000 - $50,000
Income Sources: Private Foundations/Grants/Endowments; Business/Corporate Donations; Box Office; Government Grants; Individual Donations
Season: September - June **Annual Attendance:** 40,000
Affiliations: NARB; Mid-State Regional Dance America
Performance Facilities: Civic Auditorium; Miller Auditorium

INSTRUMENTAL MUSIC

THE KALAMAZOO JUNIOR SYMPHONY SOCIETY
714 South Westnedge Avenue, Room 344, Kalamazoo, MI 49007
(616) 349-7557
Founded: 1939
Arts Area: Symphony; Orchestra
Status: Non-Profit
Type: Performing; Touring; Educational
Purpose: To encourage and develop artistic excellence among young musicians in the southwest area of Michigan by providing a diversity of quality orchestral experiences; to enhance the cultural environment of the families and communities we serve
Management: Lee Fletcher, Business Manager; Dr. Robert Ritsema, Conductor, Kalamazoo Junior Symphony Society; Mary Hinderliter, Conductor, Prep String
Officers: Andrew Tang, President; Sandra J. Zegerius, Vice President; Ruth Tomlinson, Secretary; Stuart Eddy, Treasurer
Paid Staff: 3
Paid Artists: 2 **Non-Paid Artists:** 1
Budget: $1,000 - $50,000
Income Sources: Private Foundations/Grants/Endowments; Business/Corporate Donations; Box Office; Individual Donations
Season: September - May **Annual Attendance:** 1,800
Performance Facilities: Chenery Auditorium

KALAMAZOO SYMPHONY ORCHESTRA
426 South Park Street, Kalamazoo, MI 49007
(616) 349-7759
FAX: (616) 349-9229
Founded: 1921
Arts Area: Symphony; Orchestra; Chamber; Ensemble
Status: Professional; Non-Profit
Type: Performing; Educational
Purpose: To support a professional symphony orchestra and staff; to present concerts of symphonic music and related programs of the highest possible artistic level; to support effective regional music education; to serve and involve the people of the greater Kalamazoo area in the Symphony Society
Management: Yoshimi Takeda, Music Director/Conductor; John Forsyte, General Manager; Paul Helfrich, Assistant Manager
Officers: Jacob Stucki, President
Paid Staff: 6 **Volunteer Staff:** 300
Paid Artists: 86
Utilizes: Guest Conductors; Guest Artists
Budget: $500,000 - $1,000,000
Income Sources: Private Foundations/Grants/Endowments; Business/Corporate Donations; Box Office; Government Grants; Individual Donations
Season: September - April **Annual Attendance:** 20,000
Affiliations: ASOL; MOA; Kalamazoo Chamber of Commerce
Performance Facilities: Miller Auditorium

THEATRE

KALAMAZOO CIVIC PLAYERS
329 South Park Street, Kalamazoo, MI 49007
(616) 343-1313
FAX: (616) 343-0532
Founded: 1929
Arts Area: Theatrical Group
Status: Non-Profit
Type: Performing
Purpose: To provide the area with the best possible dramatic experience

Management: James C. Carver, Managing Director
Officers: John Bernhard, President; Priscilla Cronley, Vice President; Gersteen Sherrod, Secretary; Richard Groh, Treasurer
Paid Staff: 19 **Volunteer Staff:** 800
Paid Artists: 25 **Non-Paid Artists:** 250
Utilizes: Guest Directors
Budget: $100,000 - $500,000
Income Sources: Private Foundations/Grants/Endowments; Business/Corporate Donations; Box Office; Government Grants; Individual Donations
Season: 52 Weeks **Annual Attendance:** 60,000
Affiliations: AACT; Community Theatre Association of Michigan
Performance Facilities: Civic Auditorium; Carver Center

THE MAD HATTERS EDUCATIONAL THEATRE
c/o Gilmore's, 143 South Kalamazoo Mall, Kalamazoo, MI 49007
(616) 385-5871
Founded: 1979
Status: Professional; Non-Profit
Type: Performing; Touring; Educational
Purpose: To foster full integration into society and greater understanding of people with special needs or disabilities
Management: Roberta Robinson, Executive Director; Kathleen McGookey, Fund and Program Manager/Program Facilitator; Timothy Hayden, Production Manager; Beatrice Olsen, Public Relations/Financial/Office Manager; Randy Seaman, Computer Manager
Officers: Harold H. Holland, President, Board of Trustees; James Avery Smith, Karl Sandelin, Vice Presidents; Donna Lambert, Secretary; Donald Vanderkooy, Treasurer
Paid Staff: 11
Paid Artists: 7
Utilizes: Contract Actors
Budget: $100,000 - $500,000
Income Sources: Private Foundations/Grants/Endowments; Business/Corporate Donations; Government Grants; Individual Donations
Season: 52 Weeks **Annual Attendance:** 10,000
Affiliations: Arts Council of Greater Kalamazoo

WHOLE ART THEATER
326 West Kalamazoo, Kalamazoo, MI 49007
(616) 344-0182
Founded: 1976
Arts Area: Professional; Theatrical Group
Status: Professional; Non-Profit
Type: Performing; Touring; Educational
Purpose: To provide experimental theater for all ages and tour such theater to schools, theaters and other locales in the Midwest
Management: Sniedze Rungis, Artistic Director; Daniel Runyan, Educational Director; Francis Bilancio, Managing Director; Matthew Clysdale, Office Manager
Officers: Dr. Irene S. Vasquez, President; Francis P. Bilancio, Vice President; Carol Manstrom, Secretary; John Hircsh, Treasurer
Paid Staff: 4
Paid Artists: 5
Utilizes: Guest Artists; Guest Directors
Budget: $50,000 - $100,000
Income Sources: Private Foundations/Grants/Endowments; Business/Corporate Donations; Box Office; Government Grants; Individual Donations
Season: 52 Weeks **Annual Attendance:** 15,000
Affiliations: Great Lakes Performing Arts Association

PERFORMING SERIES

FONTANA CONCERT SOCIETY
821 West South Street, Kalamazoo, MI 49007
(616) 382-0826
Founded: 1980
Arts Area: Vocal Music; Instrumental Music; Festivals
Status: Professional; Non-Profit
Type: Performing; Sponsoring
Purpose: To present high quality and diverse programs of chamber music in a rural and relaxed setting
Management: I Fu Wang, Robert Humiston, Interim Co-Directors; Janet Karpus, General Manager
Officers: Janlee Rothman, Ann Meade Sanders, Administrative Assistants
Paid Staff: 5 **Volunteer Staff:** 20

Paid Artists: 40
Utilizes: Guest Artists
Budget: $100,000 - $500,000
Income Sources: Private Foundations/Grants/Endowments; Business/Corporate Donations; Box Office; Individual Donations
Season: July - August   **Annual Attendance:** 5,000
Performance Facilities: The Art Emporium

IRVING S. GILMORE INTERNATIONAL KEYBOARD FESTIVAL
100 West Michigan Avenue, Kalamazoo, MI 49007
(616) 342-1166
FAX: (616) 342-0968
Founded: 1989
Arts Area: Festivals
Status: Non-Profit
Purpose: To identify and support concert pianists; to produce a biennial festival
Management: David Hook, Executive Director; David Pocock, Artistic Director; Sandra Wolfinbarger, Assistant Director; Julie Cook, Director of Public Relations and Marketing; Shannon Rininger, Box Office Manager/Secretary
Officers: Gayl Werme, President; James Westin, Vice President/Treasurer; Robert Luscombe, Secretary
Paid Staff: 5   **Volunteer Staff:** 500
Paid Artists: 185
Utilizes: Guest Artists
Budget: $1,000,000 - $5,000,000
Income Sources: Private Foundations/Grants/Endowments; Business/Corporate Donations; Box Office; Government Grants
Season: April - May   **Annual Attendance:** 45,000
Affiliations: APAP
Performance Facilities: Miller Auditorium; Dalton Center Recital Hall; State Theatre; Sturges-Young Auditorium

NEW YEAR'S FEST
128 North Kalamazoo Mall, Kalamazoo, MI 49002
(616) 381-4003
Founded: 1986
Arts Area: Dance; Vocal Music; Instrumental Music; Theater; Festivals; Lyric Opera
Status: Non-Profit
Type: Festival
Purpose: To present an annual New Year's Eve non-alcoholic celebration of performing arts in downtown Kalamazoo
Management: Jan Dancer, Executive Director
Officers: Jack Ullrey, President; Gordon Brown, Vice President; Marty Ream, Treasurer; Barb Chester, Secretary
Paid Staff: 1   **Volunteer Staff:** 13
Paid Artists: 40
Utilizes: Guest Artists
Budget: $100,000 - $500,000
Income Sources: Private Foundations/Grants/Endowments; Business/Corporate Donations; Box Office; Individual Donations
Season: New Year's Eve   **Annual Attendance:** 10,000

FACILITY

KALAMAZOO CIVIC AUDITORIUM
329 South Park Street, Kalamazoo, MI 49006
(616) 343-1313
FAX: (616) 343-0532
Type of Facility: Auditorium
Type of Stage: Proscenium   **Orchestra Pit**
Seating Capacity: 536
Year Built: 1931   **Architect:** Emery
Acoustical Consultant: Bolt, Beranek and Newman
Contact for Rental: Manager;   (616) 343-1313
Resident Groups: Kalamazoo Civic Players; Kalamazoo Chamber Orchestra

KALAMAZOO COLLEGE
1200 Academy Street, Kalamazoo, MI 49006
(616) 383-8511
Type of Facility: Theatre Complex; Concert Hall; Auditorium
Type of Stage: Thrust; Proscenium   **Orchestra Pit**
Seating Capacity: Thrust - 300; Proscenium - 400

Year Built: 1958
Contact for Rental: Carol Kennedy;   (616) 337-7047
Resident Groups: Festival Theatre Summer Company

WESTERN MICHIGAN UNIVERSITY - JAMES W. MILLER AUDITORIUM
Kalamazoo, MI 49008
(800) 228-9858; (616) 387-2300
Type of Facility: Auditorium
Type of Stage: Proscenium
Stage Dimensions: 150'x150'; 68' Proscenium
Seating Capacity: 3,527
Year Built: 1967   **Architect:** O'Dell, Hewlett & Luckenbach   **Cost:** $6,000,000
Acoustical Consultant: Bolt, Beranek & Newman
Contact for Rental: Ron Newhouse;   (616) 387-2311
Manager: Kenneth Farrance
Resident Groups: Kalamazoo Symphony Orchestra

WESTERN MICHIGAN UNIVERSITY - LAURA V. SHAW THEATRE
Kalamazoo, MI 49008
(616) 387-3224
Type of Facility: Theatre Complex
Type of Stage: Proscenium; Arena
Stage Dimensions: Arena - 40'x40"; 35'x30' proscenium opening   **Orchestra Pit**
Seating Capacity: 571
Year Built: 1968
Contact for Rental: Tery Williams;   (616) 387-3224

Lansing

INSTRUMENTAL MUSIC

GREATER LANSING SYMPHONY ORCHESTRA
230 North Washington Square, Suite 315, Lansing, MI 48933
(517) 487-5001
Founded: 1930
Arts Area: Symphony; Orchestra; Chamber; Ensemble
Status: Professional; Non-Profit
Type: Performing; Educational
Purpose: To provide the greater Lansing area with the finest quality symphonic music and educational services as is possible
Management: Sandra Sutton Gaffe', GeneralManager; Judith Kopeloff-Moore, Operations Manager; Bernie Geaham, Office Manager; Geoffrey Day, Personnel Manager
Officers: Ronald Pengescost, President; James Miller, President-Elect; Carol Fitzgerald, Treasurer
Paid Staff: 6   **Volunteer Staff:** 400
Paid Artists: 95
Utilizes: Guest Conductors; Guest Artists
Budget: $100,000 - $500,000
Income Sources: Private Foundations/Grants/Endowments; Business/Corporate Donations; Box Office; Government Grants; Individual Donations
Season: October - May   **Annual Attendance:** 60,000
Affiliations: ASOL; MOA; Arts Council of Greater Lansing
Performance Facilities: Wharton Center for Performing Arts

VOCAL MUSIC

OPERA COMPANY OF MID-MICHIGAN
300 South Washington, Suite 410, Lansing, MI 48933
(517) 482-1431
Founded: 1973
Arts Area: Grand Opera; Light Opera; Operetta
Status: Professional; Non-Profit
Type: Performing; Educational
Purpose: To bring to the mid-Michigan area operatic performances, augmented by an education program designed to enhance the understanding of opera and to aid in the development of future audiences
Management: Theresa Weller, Executive Director
Officers: Gina King, President; Sherwood Berman, President-Elect; Glenda Seiuphuis, Secretary; Kristina Arundel, Treasurer
Paid Staff: 1   **Volunteer Staff:** 6

Utilizes: Special Technical Talent; Guest Conductors; Guest Artists; Guest Directors
Budget: $100,000 - $500,000
Income Sources: Private Foundations/Grants/Endowments; Business/Corporate Donations; Box Office; Government Grants; Individual Donations
Annual Attendance: 2,100
Performance Facilities: Wharton Center for the Performing Arts

THEATRE

BOARSHEAD: MICHIGAN PUBLIC THEATER
425 South Grand Avenue, Lansing, MI 48933
(517) 484-7800
Founded: 1966
Arts Area: Professional
Status: Professional
Type: Performing; Touring; Resident; Educational; Sponsoring
Purpose: Top present a season featuring a collection of plays ranging from fresh productions of familiar theater works to the introduction of new and innovative plays and playwrights, as well as plays for children and families
Management: John Peakes, Founding Artistic Director; Judith Gentry, Managing Director; Romy Fitschen, Business Manager; Constance Peakes, Director of Public Relations/Marketing
Officers: Joseph Schwinger, Chairperson; Ute von der Heyden, Vice Chairperson; Doris Anderson, Secretary; William P. Weiner, Treasurer
Paid Staff: 18 **Volunteer Staff:** 100
Utilizes: Guest Artists; Guest Directors
Budget: $500,000 - $1,000,000
Income Sources: Private Foundations/Grants/Endowments; Business/Corporate Donations; Box Office; Government Grants; Individual Donations; Fund-raising
Season: October - May **Annual Attendance:** 24,000
Affiliations: TCG; AEA; IATSE; Lansing Chamber of Commerce
Performance Facilities: Lansing Center for the Arts

FACILITY

LANSING CIVIC ARENA
505 West Allegan Street, Lansing, MI 48933
(517) 483-7425
FAX: (517) 483-7440
Founded: 1956
Type of Facility: Auditorium; Civic Center; Arena; Multi-Purpose
Type of Stage: Proscenium
Stage Dimensions: 48'x48'
Seating Capacity: 5,400
Year Built: 1955 **Cost:** $3,500,000
Year Remodeled: 1977 **Architect:** Duncan Black **Cost:** $3,000,000
Contact for Rental: Executive Director; (517) 483-7425

Midland

INSTRUMENTAL MUSIC

MIDLAND SYMPHONY ORCHESTRA
1801 West St. Andrews Road, Midland, MI 48640
(517) 631-4234
FAX: (517) 631-7890
Founded: 1936
Arts Area: Symphony; Orchestra; Chamber; Ensemble; Instrumental Group
Status: Professional; Semi-Professional; Non-Professional; Non-Profit
Type: Performing; Touring; Educational; Sponsoring
Purpose: To encourage and support the Midland Symphony Orchestra in the pursuit of artistic excellence in its presentations
Management: Judyth L. Peterson, General Manager
Officers: James Kimball, Vice Chairman; Mary Van Cleve, Chairman
Paid Staff: 6 **Volunteer Staff:** 166
Paid Artists: 75
Utilizes: Guest Conductors; Guest Artists
Budget: $100,000 - $500,000
Income Sources: Private Foundations/Grants/Endowments; Business/Corporate Donations; Box Office; Government Grants; Individual Donations

Season: October - April   **Annual Attendance:** 7,000
Affiliations: MOA; ASOL
Performance Facilities: Midland Center for the Arts

MUSIC SOCIETY, MIDLAND CENTER FOR THE ARTS
1801 West St. Andrews, Midland, MI 48640
(517) 631-1072
    Founded: 1943
    Arts Area: Orchestra; Chamber; Ensemble; Folk; Instrumental Group; Band
    Status: Non-Profit
    Type: Performing; Educational; Sponsoring
    Purpose: To provide performing and educational opportunities that would not otherwise exist
    Management: Dr. Victor A. Klimash, Artistic Director
    Officers: George Callaghan, Chairman
    Paid Staff: 8   **Volunteer Staff:** 1,000
    Non-Paid Artists: 2,000
    Utilizes: Special Technical Talent; Guest Conductors; Guest Artists; Guest Directors
    Budget: $500,000 - $1,000,000
    Income Sources: Private Foundations/Grants/Endowments; Business/Corporate Donations; Box Office; Government Grants; Individual Donations
    Season: September - August   **Annual Attendance:** 52,254
    Performance Facilities: Midland Center for the Arts

NORTHWOOD ORCHESTRA
Northwood Institute, 3225 Cook Road, Midland, MI 48640-2398
(517) 837-4364
FAX: (517) 832-7744
    Founded: 1979
    Arts Area: Symphony; Orchestra; Chamber
    Status: Professional; Non-Profit
    Type: Performing; Touring; Resident
    Purpose: The Northwood Orchestra is a professional chamber ensemble which tours nationally, presents an annual summer festival in northern Michigan and performs on the campuses of Northwood as artists-in-residence.
    Management: Christine R. Goedert, Executive Director; Don T. Jaeger, Music Director/Conductor; Dana L. Zietz, Special Projects Coordinator
    Officers: Macauley Whiting, Chairman
    Paid Staff: 3
    Paid Artists: 48
    Utilizes: Special Technical Talent; Guest Artists
    Budget: $100,000 - $500,000
    Income Sources: Private Foundations/Grants/Endowments; Business/Corporate Donations; Box Office; Individual Donations
    Season: March; July - August   **Annual Attendance:** 10,000

PERFORMING SERIES

MIDLAND COMMUNITY CONCERT SOCIETY
1801 West St. Andrews Road, Midland, MI 48640
(517) 631-5930
    Arts Area: Vocal Music; Instrumental Music
    Status: Non-Profit
    Type: Educational; Sponsoring
    Purpose: To build and maintain a permanent concert audience on a membership basis; to provide opportunities for students to attend professional performances
    Officers: Mrs. James B. Arnold, Chairman
    Utilizes: Guest Artists; Guest Directors
    Income Sources: Box Office

FACILITY

MIDLAND CENTER FOR THE ARTS
1801 West St. Andrews Road, Midland, MI 48640
(517) 631-5930
    Type of Facility: Auditorium; Theatre House
    Type of Stage: Proscenium
    Stage Dimensions: 70'x50'; 40'x40'   **Orchestra Pit**
    Seating Capacity: Auditorium - 1,538; Theatre - 426; Lecture - 94
    Year Built: 1971   **Architect:** Alden B. Dow & Associates   **Cost:** $8,600,000
    Acoustical Consultant: Bolt, Beranek & Newman

Contact for Rental: Tina Siegmund; (517) 631-4573
Resident Groups: Midland Symphony Orchestra; Midland Theatre Guild; Midland Music Society; Midland Art Council; Midland County Historical Society; Hall of Ideas; Matrix: Midland Festival

---

Mt. Clemens

FACILITY

MACOMB CENTER FOR THE PERFORMING ARTS
44575 Garfield, Mt. Clemens, MI 48038
(313) 286-2141
FAX: (313) 286-2272
Founded: 1982
Type of Facility: Concert Hall; Auditorium; Performance Center; Theatre House; Opera House
Type of Stage: Proscenium
Stage Dimensions: 40'x40'   **Orchestra Pit**
Seating Capacity: 1,244
Year Built: 1982   **Architect:** TMP Associates   **Cost:** $8,000,000
Acoustical Consultant: Kirkegard and Associates
Contact for Rental: Operations Manager;   (313) 286-2183

Muskegon

INSTRUMENTAL MUSIC

WEST SHORE SYMPHONY
406 Frauenthal Center, Muskegon, MI 49440
(616) 726-3231
Founded: 1940
Arts Area: Symphony; Orchestra; Chamber
Status: Professional; Non-Profit
Type: Performing
Purpose: To bring fine live music to the west Michigan area
Management: Murray Gross, Music Director; Janet L. Smith, General Manager; Dr Lee Copenhaver, Youth Symphony Conductor
Officers: Thomas L. Jones, President; Meckie Tyson, Vice President; Stephan Patoprsty, Secretary; Timothy D. Arter, Treasurer
Paid Staff: 11
Paid Artists: 65
Utilizes: Guest Conductors; Guest Artists
Budget: $100,000 - $500,000
Income Sources: Private Foundations/Grants/Endowments; Business/Corporate Donations; Box Office; Government Grants; Individual Donations
Season: September - June   **Annual Attendance:** 18,000
Affiliations: MOA; ASOL; Concerned Citizens for the Arts in Michigan
Performance Facilities: Frauenthal Theater

WEST SHORE YOUTH SYMPHONY ORCHESTRA
425 West Western, Suite 406, Muskegon, MI 49440
(616) 726-3231
FAX: (616) 722-6913
Founded: 1966
Arts Area: Symphony; Orchestra
Status: Non-Professional; Non-Profit
Type: Performing; Educational; Sponsoring
Management: Susan Tindall, Manager; Dr. Lee Copenhaver, Conductor
Non-Paid Artists: 65
Utilizes: Guest Artists; Guest Directors
Season: September - May   **Annual Attendance:** 1,600
Affiliations: ASOL (Youth Orchestra Division); West Shore Symphony Orchestra
Performance Facilities: Frauenthal Center for the Performing Arts

THEATRE

CHERRY COUNTY PLAYHOUSE
411 West Western, Muskegon, MI 49440
(616) 727-8888
FAX: (616) 722-0549
> **Founded:** 1955
> **Arts Area:** Summer Stock
> **Status:** Professional; Commercial
> **Type:** Performing
> **Management:** Neil Rosen, Producer/Owner
> **Paid Staff:** 15   **Volunteer Staff:** 15
> **Paid Artists:** 50
> **Budget:** $100,000 - $500,000
> **Income Sources:** Box Office
> **Season:** July - September
> **Affiliations:** COST

COMMUNITY THEATRE ASSOCIATION OF MICHIGAN
3985 Grand Haven Road, 103A, Muskegon, MI 49441
(616) 798-7477
> **Founded:** 1952
> **Arts Area:** Community
> **Status:** Non-Profit
> **Type:** Service Organization
> **Purpose:** To promote communication and cooperation among community theatre groups in Michigan; to provide educational programs
> **Management:** Barbara L. Elliott, Executive Secretary; Barbara Beckers, Secretary
> **Officers:** Joanne Berry, President; Beverly Hellus, Vice-President; Mr. F. Merrill Wyble, Treasurer
> **Paid Staff:** 1
> **Budget:** $1,000 - $50,000
> **Income Sources:** Government Grants; Individual Donations

PERFORMING SERIES

FRAUENTHAL CENTER FOR THE PERFORMING ARTS
425 West Western Avenue, Suite 304, Muskegon, MI 49440
(616) 722-4538
FAX: (616) 722-4616
> **Founded:** 1976
> **Arts Area:** Dance; Vocal Music; Instrumental Music; Theater
> **Status:** Professional; Non-Professional; Non-Profit
> **Type:** Performing; Resident; Educational; Sponsoring; Presenter
> **Purpose:** To foster the growth, appreciation and development of the performing arts and film in western Michigan audiences
> **Management:** Tom Harryman, Managing Director
> **Officers:** Patricia B. Johnson, President
> **Paid Staff:** 13   **Volunteer Staff:** 200
> **Utilizes:** Guest Artists
> **Budget:** $100,000 - $500,000
> **Income Sources:** Private Foundations/Grants/Endowments; Business/Corporate Donations; Box Office; Government Grants; Individual Donations; Rental Income
> **Season:** 52 Weeks   **Annual Attendance:** 130,000
> **Affiliations:** League of Historic American Theatres
> **Performance Facilities:** Frauenthal Theatre; Beardsley Theatre

FACILITY

FRAUENTHAL FOUNDATION FINE ARTS CENTER
221 South Quarterline Road, Muskegon, MI 49442
(616) 777-0324
> **Type of Facility:** Theatre House; Multi-Purpose
> **Type of Stage:** Proscenium
> **Stage Dimensions:** 24'x59'x26'
> **Year Built:** 1968   **Architect:** Alden B. Dow & Associates   **Cost:** $1,000,000
> **Contact for Rental:** Lornella Faucher, MCC Business Office;   (616) 777-0319
> **Resident Groups:** Muskegon Community College Creative and Performing Arts Department

Omena

PERFORMING SERIES

CHAMBER ARTS NORTH
PO Box 2, Omena, MI 49674
(616) 386-5529
Founded: 1982
Arts Area: Dance; Instrumental Music; Theater; Lyric Opera
Status: Non-Profit
Type: Sponsoring
Purpose: To sponsor arts programs in Teelanan County
Officers: Daniel Viskochil, President; Jim Keeler, Vice President; Debbie Freed, Treasurer; Dick Sheppard, Tita Coleman
Budget: $1,000 - $50,000
Income Sources: Box Office; Individual Donations
Season: September - June   **Annual Attendance:** 1,500

Petoskey

PERFORMING SERIES

CROOKED TREE ARTS COUNCIL
461 East Mitchell Street, Petoskey, MI 49770
(616) 347-4337
Founded: 1972
Arts Area: Dance; Vocal Music; Instrumental Music; Festivals
Status: Non-Profit
Type: Performing; Educational; Sponsoring
Purpose: To sponsor and encourage cultural and educational activities in the fine arts for Charlevoix and Emmet Counties
Management: Sean Ley, Executive Director
Officers: Mary Fink, President; Valavra Nibblelink, Vice President for Volunteers; John Nicholson, Vice President for Finance; Otis Hardy, Secretary
Paid Staff: 5   **Volunteer Staff:** 42
Paid Artists: 3   **Non-Paid Artists:** 10
Utilizes: Guest Conductors; Guest Artists
Budget: $100,000 - $500,000
Income Sources: Private Foundations/Grants/Endowments; Business/Corporate Donations; Box Office; Government Grants; Individual Donations
Season: 52 Weeks   **Annual Attendance:** 22,000
Affiliations: NGCSA; Michigan Association of Community Arts Agencies; Michigan Council on the Arts
Performance Facilities: Virginia McCune Arts Center

Pontiac

INSTRUMENTAL MUSIC

PONTIAC-OAKLAND SYMPHONY
PO Box 431174, Pontiac, MI 48343
(313) 334-6024
Founded: 1954
Arts Area: Symphony; Orchestra; Chamber; Ensemble; Instrumental Group
Status: Semi-Professional; Non-Profit
Type: Performing; Touring; Educational; Sponsoring
Purpose: To present concerts of orchestral and chamber music
Management: Sheila Ashcraft, Consultant; David Daniels, Conductor; Peter Geiger, Personnel Manager
Officers: David Downing, President; Adrian Spinks, Vice President; Jan Roberts, Secretary
Paid Staff: 1   **Volunteer Staff:** 42
Paid Artists: 35   **Non-Paid Artists:** 25
Utilizes: Special Technical Talent; Guest Conductors; Guest Artists; Guest Directors
Budget: $50,000 - $100,000
Income Sources: Private Foundations/Grants/Endowments; Business/Corporate Donations; Box Office; Individual Donations
Season: September - April   **Annual Attendance:** 3,000
Affiliations: ASOL; MOA

THEATRE

ATTIC/STRAND THEATRE
12 North Saginaw, Pontiac, MI 48058
(313) 335-8100
    Arts Area: Professional; Musical; Theatrical Group
    Status: Professional; Non-Profit
    Type: Performing; Touring; Resident; Educational
    Purpose: To develop actors, directors, playwrights and technicians as craftsmen in the art of theatre; to create new works and to present new and challenging plays by contemporary playwrights
    Management: Lavinia Moyer, Artistic Director; Moran, Managing Director
    Officers: Andy Soffel, Chairman; Lavinia Moyer President; Peter C. Gray, Treasurer; Paul R. Rentenbach, Secretary
    Paid Staff: 15 **Volunteer Staff:** 75
    Paid Artists: 65
    Utilizes: Special Technical Talent; Guest Artists; Guest Directors
    Budget: $1,000,000 - $5,000,000
    Income Sources: Private Foundations/Grants/Endowments; Business/Corporate Donations; Box Office; Government Grants; Individual Donations
    Season: 52 Weeks
    Affiliations: TCG; FEDAPT
    Performance Facilities: Stand Theatre

Port Huron

INSTRUMENTAL MUSIC

INTERNATIONAL SYMPHONY ORCHESTRA OF SARNIA AND PORT HURON
PO Box 610242, Port Huron, MI 48060
(519) 337-7775; (313) 984-8857
    Alternate Address: 774 London Road, Sarnia, Ontario, Canada N7T 4Y1; (519) 337-7775
    Founded: 1956
    Arts Area: Symphony; Orchestra; Chamber
    Status: Non-Profit
    Type: Performing; Resident; Educational
    Purpose: To provide the communities of Port Huron, Michigan and Sarnia, Ontario with excellent symphonic and choral performances; to continue our committment to our "youth initiative" programs
    Management: Anne M. Brown, Executive Director; Zdzislaw Kopac, Music Director
    Officers: Bill Barill, President; Allan Peattie, Vice President; Nancy Corbett, Treasurer; Robert Fraser-Lee, Past President
    Paid Staff: 3
    Paid Artists: 5 **Non-Paid Artists:** 45
    Utilizes: Guest Conductors; Guest Artists
    Budget: $100,000 - $500,000
    Income Sources: Private Foundations/Grants/Endowments; Business/Corporate Donations; Box Office; Government Grants; Individual Donations; Fund-raising
    Season: September - May
    Annual Attendance: 16,000
    Affiliations: ASOL; MOA; Association of Canadian Orchestras; Ontario Federation of Symphony Orchestras
    Performance Facilities: McMorran Auditorium; SCITS Auditorium

THEATRE

PORT HURON CIVIC THEATRE
731 Griswold Street, PO Box 821, Port Huron, MI 48060
(313) 984-4014
    Founded: 1957
    Arts Area: Community; Theatrical Group
    Status: Semi-Professional; Non-Profit
    Type: Performing; Educational
    Purpose: To present a season of theatre each year; to educate and train; to further theatre arts
    Officers: Pamela Leslie, President; Nancy Osborn, Micki Lepla, Vice Presidents; Cindy Osgood, Treasurer; Viola Barr, Secretary
    Volunteer Staff: 150
    Paid Artists: 4 **Non-Paid Artists:** 200
    Utilizes: Guest Directors
    Budget: $50,000 - $100,000
    Income Sources: Private Foundations/Grants/Endowments; Business/Corporate Donations; Box Office; Government Grants; Individual Donations

Season: October - May
Annual Attendance: 12,000
Affiliations: Saint Clair County Community College
Performance Facilities: McMorran Place Theatre

FACILITY

MCMORRAN PLACE
701 McMorran Boulevard, Port Huron, MI 48060
(313) 985-6166
FAX: (313) 985-3358
Type of Facility: Theatre Complex; Arena; Multi-Purpose
Type of Stage: Thrust; Proscenium
Stage Dimensions: 50'Wx32'D
Orchestra Pit
Seating Capacity: 1,169
Year Built: 1959   **Architect:** Alden B. Dow & Associates
Contact for Rental: Morris Snider;   (313) 985-6166

Rochester

THEATRE

MEADOW BROOK THEATRE
Oakland University, Rochester, MI 48309-4401
(313) 370-3310
FAX: (313) 370-3108
Founded: 1967
Arts Area: Professional; Theatrical Group
Status: Professional; Non-Profit
Type: Performing; Touring
Purpose: To perform a wide variety of high-quality live theatre, from the classics to current works; to perform seven plays per season
Management: Terence Kilburn, Artistic Director; Gregg Bloomfield, Acting Managing Director; Jane Mosher, Director of Community Relations
Officers: Shirley Wells, President; Nancy Golick, Vice President; Brenda Hare, Recording Secretary; Kathie Eastman, Corresponding Secretary; Claudia Goss, Financial Secretary; Anne Parsons, Parliamentarian
Paid Staff: 42   **Volunteer Staff:** 120
Paid Artists: 70
Utilizes: Special Technical Talent; Guest Artists; Guest Directors
Budget: $1,000,000 - $5,000,000
Income Sources: Private Foundations/Grants/Endowments; Business/Corporate Donations; Box Office; Government Grants; Individual Donations
Season: October - May   **Annual Attendance:** 13,000
Affiliations: Oakland University; Concerned Citizens for the Arts in Michigan

PERFORMING SERIES

MEADOW BROOK MUSIC FESTIVAL
Oakland University, Rochester, MI 48309
(313) 370-3100
Founded: 1964
Arts Area: Dance; Vocal Music; Instrumental Music; Theater; Festivals
Status: Professional; Non-Profit
Type: Performing; Resident; Sponsoring
Purpose: To promote quality cultural and popular entertainment in the metropolitan Detroit area; summer home of the Detroit Symphony Orchestra
Paid Staff: 15   **Volunteer Staff:** 100
Paid Artists: 200
Utilizes: Special Technical Talent; Guest Conductors; Guest Artists
Budget: $1,000,000 - $5,000,000
Income Sources: Private Foundations/Grants/Endowments; Business/Corporate Donations; Box Office; Government Grants; Individual Donations
Season: June - September   **Annual Attendance:** 225,000
Performance Facilities: Howard C. Baldwin Memorial Pavilion

Rochester Hills

DANCE

OAKLAND FESTIVAL BALLET COMPANY
6841 North Rochester Road, Rochester Hills, MI 48309
(313) 652-3117
Arts Area: Ballet
Status: Professional; Non-Profit
Type: Performing; Resident
Income Sources: Box Office; Individual Donations

Saginaw

DANCE

BALLET CULTURAL AZTECA
2725 Brandon Place, Saginaw, MI 48603
(517) 793-6384
Founded: 1978
Arts Area: Ethnic; Folk
Status: Professional; Non-Profit
Type: Performing; Touring; Educational
Purpose: Our organization is dedicated to the research, preservation, presentation and education of our Mexican culture and heritage, through the realms of dance, music and art.
Management: Mary Lee Orozco, Artistic Director
Officers: Linda Banda, Bookkeeper; Ida Rocha, Secretary
Paid Staff: 3   **Volunteer Staff:** 15
Paid Artists: 16   **Non-Paid Artists:** 2
Utilizes: Special Technical Talent; Guest Artists; Guest Directors
Budget: $1,000 - $50,000
Income Sources: Box Office; Government Grants; Individual Donations
Season: 52 Weeks   **Annual Attendance:** 11,900

INSTRUMENTAL MUSIC

SAGINAW SYMPHONY ORCHESTRA
PO Box 415, Saginaw, MI 48606
(517) 755-6471
Founded: 1935
Arts Area: Symphony; Orchestra
Status: Professional; Non-Profit
Type: Performing; Educational
Purpose: Believing that great music can enrich the quality of life, the association will sustain an orchestra of the highest quality possible to serve audiences in the Saginaw and Bay counties. It will offer a full range of concerts and performances of music of artistic excellence.
Management: Leo Najar, Musical Director/Conductor; Horace T. Maddux, General Manager
Officers: Kristin Schmidt Maier, Administrative Assistant
Paid Staff: 5   **Volunteer Staff:** 200
Paid Artists: 80
Utilizes: Guest Conductors; Guest Artists; Guest Directors
Budget: $100,000 - $500,000
Income Sources: Private Foundations/Grants/Endowments; Business/Corporate Donations; Box Office; Government Grants; Individual Donations
Season: October - May   **Annual Attendance:** 10,000
Affiliations: ASOL; MOA
Performance Facilities: Heritage Theater, Saginaw Civic Center

SAGINAW SYMPHONY SCHOOL OF MUSIC AND YOUTH ORCHESTRA
PO Box 415, Saginaw, MI 48606
(517) 755-6471
Founded: 1978
Arts Area: Symphony; Orchestra; Chamber; Ensemble
Status: Non-Professional; Non-Profit
Type: Performing; Educational
Purpose: To help area young people grow in their musical development and to help them develop an appreciation for the arts
Management: Mrs. Toniann Amadio, Administrator

Paid Staff: 9
Non-Paid Artists: 35
Budget: $50,000 - $100,000
Income Sources: Private Foundations/Grants/Endowments; Business/Corporate Donations; Individual Donations
Season: September - May   **Annual Attendance:** 400
Affiliations: ASOL (Youth Orchestra Division); Saginaw Symphony Orchestra; Michigan School Band and Orchestra Association; National Guild of Community Schools of the Arts

THEATRE

TEMPLE THEATRE ORGAN CLUB
315 Court Street, Saginaw, MI 48602
(517) 793-8941; (517) 754-2575
FAX: (517) 793-7225
Founded: 1960
Status: Non-Profit
Type: Educational; Sponsoring; Historic Preservation
Purpose: To restore the Temple Theatre to its original splendor; to reestablish its prominence as a performing arts center
Management: Ken Wuepper, General Manager
Officers: Joanne Leach, President; Burt Castle, Vice President; Stanley Houser, Treasurer
Volunteer Staff: 300
Budget: $100,000 - $500,000
Income Sources: Private Foundations/Grants/Endowments; Business/Corporate Donations; Box Office; Individual Donations
Season: 52 Weeks   **Annual Attendance:** 100,000

FACILITY

SAGINAW CIVIC CENTER - HERITAGE THEATER
303 Johnson Street, Saginaw, MI 48607
(517) 759-1320
FAX: (517) 759-1322
Type of Facility: Theatre House
Type of Stage: Proscenium
Seating Capacity: 2,300
Year Built: 1972   **Architect:** Welton Becket & Associates   **Cost:** $11,500,000
Contact for Rental: A.C. Chapman;   (517) 759-1320
Manager: Clinton Walker;   (517) 759-1320
Resident Groups: Saginaw Symphony; Saginaw Choral Society; Town Hall

Saint Clair Shores

INSTRUMENTAL MUSIC

LAKE SAINT CLAIR SYMPHONY ORCHESTRA
21120 Benjamin, Saint Clair Shores, MI 48081
(313) 776-1012
Founded: 1961
Arts Area: Symphony; Orchestra
Status: Semi-Professional; Non-Profit
Type: Performing
Purpose: To provide the citizens of southeast Macomb County with live orchestral music programs designed to entertain our audience; to promote the artistic excellence of our constituents; to develop cultural awareness within the communities we serve
Management: Charlotte Zuraw, Executive Director
Paid Staff: 1   **Volunteer Staff:** 25
Paid Artists: 72
Utilizes: Guest Artists
Budget: $50,000 - $100,000
Income Sources: Private Foundations/Grants/Endowments; Business/Corporate Donations; Box Office; Government Grants; Individual Donations
Season: October - May   **Annual Attendance:** 6,500
Affiliations: ASOL; MOA

MACOMB CHAMBER MUSIC SOCIETY
28200 Ursuline, Saint Clair Shores, MI 48081
(313) 775-8138
Founded: 1984

Arts Area: Chamber
Status: Non-Professional; Non-Profit
Type: Sponsoring
Purpose: To present chamber music in an informal atmosphere; to provide an opportunity for musicians to perform
Officers: Thomas Ulrich, President; Jean Stanaitis, Secretary; Mae Dunn, Board Member
Utilizes: Guest Artists
Budget: $1,000 - $50,000
Income Sources: Business/Corporate Donations; Box Office; Government Grants; Individual Donations
Season: November - May   **Annual Attendance:** 200

Saint Joseph

INSTRUMENTAL MUSIC

SOUTHWEST MICHIGAN SYMPHONY ORCHESTRA
615 Broad Street, Saint Joseph, MI 49085
(616) 983-4334
    Founded: 1950
    Arts Area: Symphony; Orchestra
    Status: Professional
    Type: Performing; Educational
    Purpose: To present concerts; to sponsor an orchestra as well as music educational activities
    Management: Jeffrey G. White, General Manager; Robert Vodnoy, Music Director
    Officers: Albert E. Vossler, President
    Paid Staff: 6   **Volunteer Staff:** 1
    Paid Artists: 60
    Utilizes: Guest Artists
    Budget: $100,000 - $500,000
    Income Sources: Private Foundations/Grants/Endowments; Business/Corporate Donations; Box Office; Government Grants; Individual Donations
    Season: September - June
    Annual Attendance: 7,500
    Performance Facilities: Mendel Center, Lake Michigan College

Southfield

INSTRUMENTAL MUSIC

LYRIC CHAMBER ENSEMBLE
3000 Town Center, Suite 1335, Southfield, MI 48075
(313) 357-1111
FAX: (313) 357-3607
    Founded: 1980
    Arts Area: Chamber; Ensemble
    Status: Professional; Non-Profit
    Type: Performing; Touring; Resident
    Purpose: To provide innovative chamber music of the highest artistic quality that is accessible to all
    Management: Fedora Horowitz, Artistic Director; Valerie Youa, Administrator
    Officers: Tom Rhoads, Chairman; Sergio Sanchez, Vice Chairman
    Paid Staff: 2   **Volunteer Staff:** 10
    Paid Artists: 25
    Utilizes: Guest Conductors; Guest Artists
    Budget: $100,000 - $500,000
    Income Sources: Private Foundations/Grants/Endowments; Business/Corporate Donations; Box Office; Government Grants; Individual Donations
    Season: September - June
    Annual Attendance: 9,000
    Affiliations: CMA
    Performance Facilities: Orchestra Hall; Music Hall; Gem Theatre; Grosse Pointe War Memorial

THEATRE

ACTORS ALLIANCE THEATRE COMPANY
30800 Evergreen Road, Southfield, MI 48076
(313) 642-1326
    Founded: 1981
    Arts Area: Professional; Theatrical Group

Status: Professional; Non-Profit
Type: Performing; Touring; Resident; Educational
Purpose: To nuture the human creative spirit through educational and cultural programs that encourage excellence in art and individual expression, thereby enriching the community it serves
Management: Jeffrey M. Nahan, Artistic/Executive Director; Annette DePetris, Managing Director; Lorraine Walker, Educational Coordinator
Officers: Al Sasson, Chairman
Paid Staff: 3
Paid Artists: 85
Utilizes: Guest Artists; Guest Directors
Budget: $100,000 - $500,000
Income Sources: Private Foundations/Grants/Endowments; Business/Corporate Donations; Box Office; Government Grants; Individual Donations
Season: 52 Weeks
Affiliations: TCG; AEA; Michigan Council on the Arts

Tecumseh

FACILITY

TECUMSEH CIVIC AUDITORIUM
400 North Maumee, Tecumseh, MI 49286
(517) 423-6617
Founded: 1981
Type of Facility: Theatre Complex; Concert Hall; Auditorium; Performance Center; Theatre House; Room
Type of Stage: Proscenium
Stage Dimensions: 40'Wx30'D   **Orchestra Pit**
Seating Capacity: 572
Year Built: 1981   **Architect:** Tony Marino   **Cost:** $1,750,000
Year Remodeled: 1986   **Cost:** $500,000
Contact for Rental: John S. Raeburn;   (517) 423-6617
Resident Groups: Tecumseh Youth Theatre; Tecumseh Players; Tecumseh Pops

Traverse City

INSTRUMENTAL MUSIC

TRAVERSE SYMPHONY ORCHESTRA
123 1/2 East Front Street, PO Box 1247, Traverse City, MI 49685
(616) 947-7120
Founded: 1951
Arts Area: Symphony; Orchestra; Chamber
Status: Professional
Type: Performing; Touring; Sponsoring
Management: Timothy Gunsolley, General Manager
Officers: Cheryl Knight, President
Paid Staff: 3   **Volunteer Staff:** 80
Paid Artists: 75
Utilizes: Special Technical Talent; Guest Conductors; Guest Artists
Budget: $100,000 - $500,000
Income Sources: Private Foundations/Grants/Endowments

THEATRE

OLD TOWN PLAYHOUSE
148 East Eighth, Traverse City, MI 49684
(616) 947-2210
Founded: 1959
Arts Area: Community
Status: Non-Professional; Non-Profit
Type: Performing; Educational
Purpose: To assist, encourage, promote and improve the cultural and literary development of the community through entertainment and education in the dramatic arts
Management: Mary Cassaday Jone, Executive Director; Michael Kay, Technical Director; Mary Lou Iavco-Bewley, Marketing
Officers: Cinder Conlon, President; Pat Ganter, Vice President; Larry Hains, Secretary; George Beeby, Treasurer
Paid Staff: 4   **Volunteer Staff:** 1,060

Paid Artists: 10   **Non-Paid Artists:** 1,060
Utilizes: Special Technical Talent; Guest Artists
Budget: $100,000 - $500,000
Income Sources: Private Foundations/Grants/Endowments; Business/Corporate Donations; Box Office; Government
Grants; Individual Donations
Season: September - August   **Annual Attendance:** 17,000
Affiliations: Community Theatre Association of Michigan

FACILITY

DENNOS MUSEUM CENTER - MILLIKEN AUDITORIUM
1701 East Front Street, Traverse City, MI 49684
(616) 922-1055
FAX: (616) 922-1597
   Type of Facility: Auditorium
   Type of Stage: Open stage
   Stage Dimensions: 50'x28'
   Seating Capacity: 367
   Year Built: 1991   **Architect:** Robert Holdeman, AIA   **Cost:** $5,200,000
   Contact for Rental: Eugen Jenneman, Museum Director;   (616) 922-1572
   Resident Groups: Michigan Ensemble Theatre

PARK PLACE HOTEL
300 East State Street, Traverse City, MI 49684
(616) 946-5000
   Type of Facility: Multi-Purpose
   Type of Stage: Platform; Arena
   Seating Capacity: 729
   Year Built: 1964   **Architect:** Dow Chemical Company
   Resident Groups: Cherry County Playhouse
   Available for rent

Troy

INSTRUMENTAL MUSIC

DETROIT CHAMBER WINDS
755 West Big Beaver, Suite 1900, Troy, MI 48082
(313) 362-2622
FAX: (313) 362-2628
   Arts Area: Chamber
   Status: Professional; Non-Profit
   Type: Performing
   Purpose: To perform works featuring between six and 20 winds
   Management: H. Robert Reynolds, Artistic Advisor; Maury Okun, Executive Director
   Budget: $1,000 - $50,000
   Income Sources: Private Foundations/Grants/Endowments; Business/Corporate Donations; Box Office; Government
Grants; Individual Donations

VOCAL MUSIC

DETROIT SYMPHONY CHORALE
2696 English Drive, Troy, MI 48098
(313) 879-9362
   Arts Area: Choral
   Status: Professional; Non-Profit
   Type: Performing; Resident; Educational
   Purpose: To serve as the main choral group of the Detroit Symphony, formerly known as the Kenneth Jewell Chorale
   Management: Eric Freudigman, Director; Carol Petty, Personnel Manager
   Paid Staff: 4
   Paid Artists: 40
   Budget: $100,000 - $500,000
   Income Sources: Private Foundations/Grants/Endowments; Business/Corporate Donations; Box Office; Government
Grants; Individual Donations
   Season: 52 Weeks   **Annual Attendance:** 300,000
   Affiliations: CA; Detroit Symphony; Detroit Symphony Chorus
   Performance Facilities: Orchestra Hall

DETROIT SYMPHONY CHORUS
2696 English Drive, Troy, MI 48098
(313) 879-9362
    Arts Area: Choral
    Status: Professional; Non-Profit
    Type: Performing; Resident; Educational
    Purpose: The Detroit Symphony Chorus includes the 40-member Detroit Symphony Chorale
    Management: Eric Freudigman, Director; Carol Petty, Personnel Manager
    Paid Staff: 4
    Paid Artists: 100
    Budget: $100,000 - $500,000
    Income Sources: Private Foundations/Grants/Endowments; Business/Corporate Donations; Box Office; Government Grants; Individual Donations
    Season: 52 Weeks
    Affiliations: CA; Detroit Symphony
    Performance Facilities: Ford Auditorium; Orchestra Hall

Twin Lake

THEATRE

BLUE LAKE REPERTORY THEATRE
Route #2, Twin Lake, MI 49457
(616) 894-1966
FAX: (616) 893-5120
    Founded: 1966
    Arts Area: Summer Stock; Musical; Theatrical Group
    Status: Semi-Professional
    Type: Performing; Resident; Educational
    Purpose: To present quality summer-stock theatre for our community
    Management: Fritz Stansell, President; Reverend Walter Marek, Treasurer
    Paid Staff: 6
    Paid Artists: 14
    Budget: $50,000 - $100,000
    Income Sources: Business/Corporate Donations; Box Office; Individual Donations
    Season: July - August **Annual Attendance:** 5,000
    Affiliations: Blue Lake Fine Arts Camp
    Performance Facilities: Howmet Playhouse

Warren

INSTRUMENTAL MUSIC

WARREN SYMPHONY ORCHESTRA
4504 East Nine Mile Road, Warren, MI 48091
(313) 754-2950
FAX: (313) 755-5407
    Founded: 1972
    Arts Area: Symphony; Orchestra; Chamber; Ensemble
    Status: Semi-Professional
    Type: Performing; Resident; Educational
    Purpose: To present symphony concerts and chamber ensembles
    Management: David Daniels, Music Director
    Officers: Donald Chmura, President; Louise Anslow, Christine Bonkowski, Glen Musselman, Vice Presidents; John Ahern, Treasurer
    Paid Staff: 2 **Volunteer Staff:** 50
    Paid Artists: 45 **Non-Paid Artists:** 20
    Utilizes: Guest Artists
    Budget: $100,000 - $500,000
    Income Sources: Private Foundations/Grants/Endowments; Business/Corporate Donations; Box Office; Government Grants; Individual Donations
    Season: November - May **Annual Attendance:** 25,000
    Affiliations: ASOL; MOA
    Performance Facilities: Warren Woods Community Theater

Wyandotte

PERFORMING SERIES

DOWNRIVER COUNCIL FOR THE ARTS
2630 Biddle Avenue, Wyandotte, MI 48192
(313) 281-2787
FAX: (313) 281-0709
Founded: 1978
Arts Area: Dance; Vocal Music; Instrumental Music; Theater; Festivals
Status: Professional; Non-Profit
Type: Educational; Sponsoring
Purpose: To promote, stimulate and encourage the study and presentation of the performing and fine arts throughout the sixteen Downriver Communities
Management: Beth A. Stone, Executive Director
Officers: Raymond Lozano, Chairman of the Board; Dr. Donald F. Van Every, President
Paid Staff: 4 **Volunteer Staff:** 200
Paid Artists: 130 **Non-Paid Artists:** 35
Utilizes: Special Technical Talent; Guest Conductors; Guest Artists
Budget: $100,000 - $500,000
Income Sources: Private Foundations/Grants/Endowments; Business/Corporate Donations; Box Office; Government Grants; Individual Donations
Season: 52 Weeks

MINNESOTA

Albert Lea

FACILITY

ALBERT LEA CIVIC THEATER
147 North Broadway, Albert Lea, MN 56007
(507) 377-4371
FAX: (507) 377-4336
    Type of Facility: Concert Hall; Auditorium; Performance Center; Theatre House; Civic Center
    Facility Originally: Meeting Hall; Movie House
    Type of Stage: Proscenium
    Stage Dimensions: 28'x24'   **Orchestra Pit**
    Seating Capacity: 261
    Year Built: 1909
    Year Remodeled: 1981   **Architect:** Kilstofe   **Cost:** $650,000
    Contact for Rental: Anne Ehrhardt;   (507) 377-4372
    Resident Groups: Albert Lea Community Theatre; Minnesota Festival Theatre

Alexandria

INSTRUMENTAL MUSIC

ALEXANDRIA BIG BAND
Route 5, PO Box 92, Alexandria, MN 56308
(612) 762-2140; (612) 846-3273
    Founded: 1966
    Arts Area: Big Band; Swing
    Status: Non-Professional; Non-Profit; Commercial
    Type: Performing; Touring
    Purpose: Maintain the tradition of big band music of the past and present with an emphasis towards Glenn Miller and other big band leaders
    Officers: Bill Riggs, President; Rick Temple, Secretary; Bill Flaig, Treasurer
    Volunteer Staff: 17
    Non-Paid Artists: 17
    Budget: $1,000 - $50,000
    Income Sources: Individual Donations
    Annual Attendance: 2,000
    Affiliations: AFM

Austin

THEATRE

MATCHBOX CHILDREN'S THEATRE
PO Box 576, Austin, MN 55912
(507) 433-1931
    Arts Area: Musical; Community; Theatrical Group
    Status: Non-Profit
    Type: Performing; Resident
    Purpose: To provide quality theatre experiences for young audiences and families on a consistent basis
    Officers: Janet Anderson, President; Cynthia Dibble, Vice President; Cindy Bellrichard, Secretary; John Gray, Treasurer
    Volunteer Staff: 16
    Utilizes: Special Technical Talent; Guest Directors
    Budget: $1,000 - $50,000
    Income Sources: Private Foundations/Grants/Endowments; Business/Corporate Donations; Box Office; Government Grants; Individual Donations
    Season: September - April   **Annual Attendance:** 6,000
    Performance Facilities: Austin Community College Theatre

Bemidji

THEATRE

PAUL BUNYAN PLAYHOUSE
PO Box 752, Bemidji, MN 56601
(218) 751-7270
> **Founded:** 1951
> **Arts Area:** Professional; Summer Stock; Musical; Theatrical Group
> **Status:** Professional; Non-Profit
> **Type:** Performing; Educational
> **Purpose:** The oldest professional summer theatre running in Minnesota, our goal is to produce the best possible theatre utilizing local and regional talent as well as interns from Bemidji State University.
> **Management:** Jack Blanchard, Administrative Assistant Board of Directors; Michael Kissin, Artistic Director
> **Officers:** Becky Lueben, President; Kristine Cannon, Vice President; Karen Moe, Treasurer; Sandy Johnson, Secretary
> **Paid Staff:** 10   **Volunteer Staff:** 24
> **Paid Artists:** 30   **Non-Paid Artists:** 15
> **Utilizes:** Special Technical Talent; Guest Artists; Guest Directors
> **Budget:** $100,000 - $500,000
> **Income Sources:** Private Foundations/Grants/Endowments; Business/Corporate Donations; Box Office; Individual Donations
> **Season:** June - August   **Annual Attendance:** 13,250
> **Performance Facilities:** Paul Bunyan Playhouse, Old Chief Theatre

PERFORMING SERIES

HOBSON MEMORIAL UNION - PROGRAM BOARD
Bemidji State University, Bemidji, MN 56601
(218) 755-3760
FAX: (218) 755-4048
> **Arts Area:** Dance; Vocal Music; Instrumental Music
> **Status:** Non-Profit
> **Type:** Performing; Sponsoring
> **Purpose:** To provide social, cultural, and educational programs to Bemidji State University and the Bemidji Community
> **Paid Staff:** 1
> **Utilizes:** Guest Artists
> **Budget:** $1,000 - $50,000
> **Income Sources:** Private Foundations/Grants/Endowments; Student Fees
> **Season:** September - May

FACILITY

BEMIDJI STATE UNIVERSITY - BANGSBERG FINE ARTS BUILDING
1500 Birchmont Drive NE, Bemidji, MN 56601
(218) 755-3990
FAX: (218) 755-4048
> **Type of Facility:** Theatre Complex
> **Seating Capacity:** Recital Hall - 250; Theatre - 300
> **Year Built:** 1970   **Architect:** Grover Dimond   **Cost:** $3,000,000

Bloomington

FACILITY

ARTS IN THE PARKS - PORTABLE STAGE
2215 West Old Shakopee Road, Bloomington, MN 55431
(612) 887-9601, ext. 388
FAX: (612) 887-9695
> **Founded:** 1978
> **Type of Facility:** Auditorium; Outdoor (Concert)
> **Type of Stage:** Platform; Portable; Showmobile
> **Stage Dimensions:** 36'x36'
> **Seating Capacity:** 425 - see notation
> *Auditorium space at the community college is used for indoor performances as part of the Arts in the Parks concert series.*

Blue Earth

THEATRE

BLUE EARTH TOWN AND COUNTRY PLAYERS
PO Box 194, Blue Earth, MN 56013
(507) 526-2407
> **Founded:** 1976
> **Arts Area:** Musical; Community; Theatrical Group
> **Status:** Non-Professional; Non-Profit
> **Type:** Performing; Educational
> **Purpose:** Creative enrichment and leisure activity for members and area community members
> **Officers:** Mrs. Douglas Richards, President; Wayne Ankeny, Nancy Willette, Brian Roverud, Mike Ellingsen, Lil Robinson, Dr. Judith Edling
> **Volunteer Staff:** 50
> **Budget:** $1,000 - $50,000
> **Income Sources:** Box Office; Individual Donations
> **Season:** February - July **Annual Attendance:** 2,500
> **Performance Facilities:** Coleman Hall Auditorium

Brooklyn Center

FACILITY

BROOKLYN CENTER
6301 Shingle Creek Parkway, Brooklyn Center, MN 55430
(612) 561-5448
> **Type of Facility:** Multi-Purpose
> **Year Built:** 1986 **Cost:** $65,000
> *Summer concerts held on a weekly basis, free to the public*

Chanhassen

THEATRE

CHANHASSEN DINNER THEATRE
501 West 78th, Chanhassen, MN 55417
(612) 934-1500
> **Founded:** 1968
> **Arts Area:** Professional; Dinner; Theatrical Group
> **Status:** Professional
> **Type:** Performing
> **Purpose:** Present quality theatre and dining experience
> **Management:** Solveig Huseth, Managing Director; Michael Brindisi, Artistic Director
> **Officers:** Jim Jude, Chief Executive Officer; Marlin Schoep, Controller
> **Paid Staff:** 50
> **Paid Artists:** 40
> **Utilizes:** Special Technical Talent; Guest Artists; Guest Directors
> **Budget:** $5,000,000 - $10,000,000
> **Income Sources:** Box Office
> **Season:** 52 Weeks **Annual Attendance:** 300,000
> **Affiliations:** ADTI
> **Performance Facilities:** Chanhassen Dinner Theatres

Detroit Lakes

THEATRE

PLAYHOUSE 412
PO Box 1112, Detroit Lakes, MN 56502
(612) 459-1874
> **Arts Area:** Musical; Community; Theatrical Group
> **Status:** Non-Profit
> **Type:** Performing; Educational
> **Purpose:** A community theater for the local and surrounding area; a readers theater troupe; entertainment

Officers: Sharon Santwire, President; Lind Henderson, Vice President; Gladys Holt, Secretary; Rick Pechmann, Treasurer; Shirley Gunderson; Jim Pearson; Lorren Steinhaus; Dorothy Erickson; Joyce Wieners
Volunteer Staff: 40
Utilizes: Guest Directors
Budget: $1,000 - $50,000
Income Sources: Private Foundations/Grants/Endowments; Box Office; Government Grants; Individual Donations
Season: 52 Weeks   **Annual Attendance:** 1,000

Duluth

DANCE

THE DULUTH BALLET
506 West Michigan Street, Duluth, MN 55802
(218) 722-2314; (218) 722-2904
FAX: (218) 727-8025
   Founded: 1965
   Arts Area: Ballet; Jazz
   Status: Professional; Non-Profit
   Type: Performing; Touring; Resident; Educational; Sponsoring
   Purpose: To maintain a high-quality school of ballet and a company of professional dancers; to present a regular series of performances
   Management: Allen Fields, Artistic Director; Vicki Taruba, General Manager; Willy McManis, Secretary/Office Administration
   Officers: Mary Gummerson, President
   Paid Staff: 5   **Volunteer Staff:** 28
   Paid Artists: 8   **Non-Paid Artists:** 2
   Utilizes: Special Technical Talent; Guest Artists; Guest Directors
   Budget: $100,000 - $500,000
   Income Sources: Private Foundations/Grants/Endowments; Business/Corporate Donations; Box Office; Government Grants; Individual Donations
   Season: September - March   **Annual Attendance:** 6,500
   Affiliations: NARB
   Performance Facilities: Depot Theater; Marshall Performing Arts Center; The Deck Arena

INSTRUMENTAL MUSIC

DULUTH-SUPERIOR SYMPHONY ORCHESTRA
506 West Michigan Street, Duluth, MN 55802
(218) 727-7429
   Founded: 1934
   Arts Area: Symphony; Orchestra; Chamber; Ensemble
   Status: Professional; Non-Profit
   Type: Performing; Educational
   Purpose: To generate the requisite financial and artistic resources to maintain the finest possible symphony orchestra and related programs and services. The goals are to: 1) enhance the quality of life by providing audiences with symphonic music, 2) strengthen the artistic quality of the orchestra, 3) develop future musicians and audiences and 4) generate income necessary to fulfill program and service goals of the association.
   Management: Gerard Gibbs, Interim Manager; Taavo Virkhaus, Music Director/Conductor
   Paid Staff: 6
   Paid Artists: 88
   Utilizes: Guest Artists
   Budget: $100,000 - $500,000
   Income Sources: Private Foundations/Grants/Endowments; Box Office; Government Grants; Individual Donations
   Season: September - May   **Annual Attendance:** 20,000
   Affiliations: ASOL; Saint Louis County Heritage and Arts Center
   Performance Facilities: Duluth Auditorium

DULUTH-SUPERIOR YOUTH ORCHESTRA AND SINFONIA
506 West Michigan Street, Duluth, MN 55802
(218) 727-7429
FAX: (218) 722-0351
   Founded: 1940
   Arts Area: Symphony; Orchestra; Chamber; Ensemble
   Status: Non-Professional; Non-Profit
   Type: Performing; Educational
   Purpose: To offer a learning and performing experience for students in the Youth Orchestra (high school) and Sinfonia (junior and senior high school)

Management: Gerard Gibbs, Interim General Manager; Jeanne Doty, Director of Sinfonia; Kevin Hoeschen, Director Youth Orchestra
Non-Paid Artists: 100
Income Sources: Box Office
Season: September - May **Annual Attendance:** 3,000
Affiliations: ASOL (Youth Orchestra Division); Duluth-Superior Symphony Orchestra

THEATRE

COLDER BY THE LAKE
PO Box 452, Duluth, MN 55801
(218) 722-4192
> **Founded:** 1983
> **Arts Area:** Theatrical Group
> **Status:** Non-Profit
> **Type:** Performing; Touring
> **Purpose:** Colder by the Lake presents all original theater, specifically: satire, comedy and the offbeat.
> **Management:** Margaret Preus, Managing Director
> **Officers:** Harlan Quist, President; Mary Treuer, Vice President
> **Utilizes:** Guest Artists; Guest Directors
> **Budget:** $1,000 - $50,000
> **Income Sources:** Private Foundations/Grants/Endowments; Box Office
> **Season:** 52 Weeks **Annual Attendance:** 4,000

FACILITY

THE DEPOT, ST. LOUIS CO. HERITAGE AND ARTS CENTER
506 West Michigan Street, Duluth, MN 55802
(218) 727-8025
FAX: (218) 727-8025
> **Founded:** 1979
> **Type of Facility:** Theatre Complex; Auditorium; Theatre House
> **Type of Stage:** Thrust; Proscenium
> **Stage Dimensions:** 32'x24' **Orchestra Pit**
> **Seating Capacity:** 275
> **Year Built:** 1979
> **Contact for Rental:** Pat Shinn; (218) 727-8025
> **Resident Groups:** Duluth Playhouse

DULUTH ENTERTAINMENT CONVENTION CENTER
350 Harbor Drive, Duluth, MN 55802
(218) 722-5573
> **Type of Facility:** Auditorium; Arena
> **Seating Capacity:** Arena - 5,600; Auditorium - 2,403
> **Year Built:** 1966 **Cost:** $6,000,000
> **Contact for Rental:** Manager; (218) 722-5573
> **Manager:** Dan Russell, Executive Director
> **Resident Groups:** Duluth Ballet Company; Duluth-Superior Symphony Orchestra

Edina

THEATRE

CHILD'S PLAY THEATRE COMPANY
5701 Normandale Road, Room 343, Edina, MN 55424
(612) 925-5250
> **Founded:** 1984
> **Arts Area:** Musical; Theatrical Group
> **Status:** Semi-Professional; Non-Profit
> **Type:** Performing; Resident; Educational
> **Purpose:** To provide theatre education and entertainment for young people and families; premiere introductory theatre group for young people
> **Management:** Steve Barberio, Executive Director; Sandy Boren, Program Director; Bruce Wolen, Communications Director; Dave Hoaty, Production Manager; Alison Albrecht, Development Director
> **Officers:** Benjamin Auny, Chairman; Michelle Bergrud, Vice Chair; LeRona Redepenning, Secretary; David Mahler, Treasurer
> **Paid Staff:** 3 **Volunteer Staff:** 30
> **Paid Artists:** 8 **Non-Paid Artists:** 30

Utilizes: Special Technical Talent; Guest Directors
Budget: $50,000 - $100,000
Income Sources: Private Foundations/Grants/Endowments; Business/Corporate Donations; Box Office; Government Grants; Individual Donations
Season: August - July   **Annual Attendance:** 15,000
Performance Facilities: Eisenhower Community Center, Hopkins

Excelsior

THEATRE

OLD LOG THEATER
5175 Meadville Street, PO Box 250, Excelsior, MN 55331
(612) 474-5951
FAX: (612) 474-1290
Founded: 1940
Arts Area: Professional; Dinner; Theatrical Group
Status: Professional
Type: Performing; Touring; Resident
Purpose: To entertain the public
Management: Don Stolz, Manager
Paid Staff: 20
Paid Artists: 20
Budget: $1,000,000 - $5,000,000
Income Sources: Box Office
Season: 52 Weeks
Performance Facilities: Old Log Theatre

Fairmont

FACILITY

THE FAIRMONT OPERA HOUSE
45 Downtown Plaza, PO Box 226, Fairmont, MN 56031
(507) 238-4900
Type of Facility: Concert Hall; Auditorium; Theatre House; Opera House
Facility Originally: Vaudeville
Type of Stage: Proscenium
Stage Dimensions: 36'6"Wx25'D
Seating Capacity: 489
Year Built: 1901   **Architect:** C.S. Dunham
Contact for Rental: Janet Roth;   (507) 238-1448
Resident Groups: Fairmont Civic Summer Theatre; Fairmont Children's Theatre

Fergus Falls

INSTRUMENTAL MUSIC

OTTER TAIL VALLEY COMMUNITY ORCHESTRA
1324 Linwood Court, Fergus Falls, MN 56537
(218) 736-3694
Founded: 1947
Arts Area: Orchestra
Status: Non-Professional; Non-Profit
Type: Performing
Purpose: To give the community the opportunity to perform or listen to orchestral music
Management: Roger Solie, Director
Officers: Duane Larson, Treasurer
Paid Staff: 1   **Volunteer Staff:** 1
Non-Paid Artists: 50
Utilizes: Guest Artists
Budget: $1,000 - $50,000
Income Sources: Box Office

Season: October - March   **Annual Attendance:** 400
Performance Facilities: Fergus Falls Community College Auditorium

THEATRE

FERGUS FALLS SUMMER COMMUNITY THEATRE
1414 College Way, Fergus Falls, MN 56537
(218) 739-7509
FAX: (218) 739-7475
   Founded: 1972
   Arts Area: Musical; Community; Theatrical Group
   Status: Non-Professional; Non-Profit
   Type: Performing; Resident; Educational
   Purpose: Public-service project for local amateur performers and for area audiences
   Management: James J. McDonald, Director; Geneva Eschweiler, Music Director
   Paid Staff: 6   **Volunteer Staff:** 5
   Paid Artists: 6   **Non-Paid Artists:** 50
   Utilizes: Special Technical Talent; Guest Artists
   Budget: $1,000 - $50,000
   Income Sources: Business/Corporate Donations; Box Office; Government Grants; Individual Donations
   Season: June - August   **Annual Attendance:** 3,000
   Performance Facilities: Fergus Falls Community College Theatre

Grand Rapids

PERFORMING SERIES

THE REIF ARTS COUNCIL
800 Conifer Drive, PO Box 245, Grand Rapids, MN 55744
(218) 326-8215
   Founded: 1969
   Arts Area: Dance; Vocal Music; Instrumental Music; Theater
   Status: Non-Profit
   Type: Sponsoring
   Purpose: Main project: Center Series, annual seven concerts covering theater, music and dance
   Officers: Nancy Brierley, President; Caryl Kaler, Vice President; Mary Ives, Secretary; Dean Sing Sank, Treasurer
   Budget: $1,000 - $50,000
   Income Sources: Private Foundations/Grants/Endowments; Box Office; Government Grants
   Season: October - April   **Annual Attendance:** 3,000
   Performance Facilities: Reif Performing Arts Center

YOUNG ARTISTS SERIES
1851 East Highway 169, Grand Rapids, MN 55744
(218) 326-1639
   Founded: 1978
   Arts Area: Dance; Vocal Music; Instrumental Music
   Status: Professional; Non-Profit
   Type: Performing; Educational; Sponsoring
   Purpose: To serve as a showcase for the emerging professional performer
   Management: Ann Winberg, Director
   Paid Staff: 1   **Volunteer Staff:** 4
   Paid Artists: 5
   Utilizes: Guest Artists
   Budget: $1,000 - $50,000
   Income Sources: Private Foundations/Grants/Endowments; Box Office; Government Grants
   Season: September - April   **Annual Attendance:** 500
   Performance Facilities: Davies Theatre

Hibbing

INSTRUMENTAL MUSIC

HIBBING COLLEGE - COMMUNITY BAND
1515 East 25th Street, Hibbing, MN 55746
(218) 262-6729
   Founded: 1980
   Arts Area: Band

Status: Non-Professional; Non-Profit
Type: Performing; Touring; Resident; Educational
Purpose: To rehearse and perform contemporary works for wind ensemble as well as traditional literature; to provide a social function for musicians
Management: Thomas Palmersheim, Director
Volunteer Staff: 1
Non-Paid Artists: 30
Utilizes: Guest Conductors; Guest Artists; Guest Directors
Budget: $1,000 - $50,000
Season: October - May
Performance Facilities: Hibbing Community College Auditorium

Luverne

THEATRE

GREEN EARTH PLAYERS
216 West Main Street, Luverne, MN 56156
(507) 283-9891
Founded: 1978
Arts Area: Musical; Community; Theatrical Group
Status: Non-Profit
Type: Performing
Purpose: Provide live theatre for the area
Officers: Jim Jelken, President; Dee Korthal, Vice President; Sally McFadden, Secretary; Doug Eisma, Treasurer
Volunteer Staff: 75
Paid Artists: 2
Utilizes: Guest Directors
Budget: $1,000 - $50,000
Income Sources: Business/Corporate Donations; Box Office; Government Grants; Individual Donations
Season: October - June **Annual Attendance:** 2,500
Affiliations: ACT; Minnesota Arts Council; Southern Minnesota Arts and Humanities Council
Performance Facilities: Palace Theater

Mankato

INSTRUMENTAL MUSIC

MANKATO SYMPHONY ORCHESTRA
PO Box 645, Mankato, MN 56001
(507) 625-8880
Founded: 1952
Arts Area: Symphony; Orchestra
Status: Non-Professional; Non-Profit
Type: Performing; Resident; Educational
Purpose: To provide the regional Mankato area with fine public concerts at a minimal cost, expose students to high quality musical experiences and enrich the cultural climate of the area
Management: Mary Ann Holdrege, Executive Director
Officers: Kenneth Tate, President; Mary Ann Holdrege, Vice President/Executive Director; Jane Confer, Secretary; Dick Osborne, Treasurer
Paid Staff: 3 **Volunteer Staff:** 32
Paid Artists: 78
Utilizes: Special Technical Talent; Guest Artists
Budget: $100,000 - $500,000
Income Sources: Private Foundations/Grants/Endowments; Business/Corporate Donations; Box Office; Government Grants; Individual Donations
Season: October - May **Annual Attendance:** 8,500
Performance Facilities: Mankato West High School Auditorium

FACILITY

MANKATO STATE UNIVERSITY - ELIAS J. HALLING RECITAL HALL
Mankato, MN 56001
Type of Facility: Concert Hall
Type of Stage: Proscenium
Seating Capacity: 352

Year Built: 1967   **Architect:** Czerny Associates   **Cost:** $2,000,000
Contact for Rental: William Lecklider

Minneapolis

DANCE

THE ETHNIC DANCE THEATRE
1940 Hennepin Avenue South, Minneapolis, MN 55403
(612) 872-0024
> **Founded:** 1974
> **Arts Area:** Ethnic
> **Status:** Semi-Professional; Non-Profit
> **Type:** Performing; Touring; Resident; Educational
> **Purpose:** The Ethnic Dance Theatre is a regional performing arts company dedicated to the artistic and dynamic traditions of ethnic dance and music. The EDT performs concerts and conducts residencies and public workshops.
> **Management:** Donald LaCourse, Jonathan Frey, Artistic Directors; Gordy Abel, Orchestra Director; Deborah Ingebretsen, Vocal Director; Sara Oxton, Company Manager
> **Officers:** Graham Thatcher, Chairman; Cindy Geiger, Vice Chairman; Jeanette Anderson, Secretary; Richard Van Puyvelde, Treasurer
> **Paid Staff:** 5
> **Paid Artists:** 26   **Non-Paid Artists:** 20
> **Utilizes:** Guest Artists; Guest Choreographers
> **Budget:** $100,000 - $500,000
> **Income Sources:** Private Foundations/Grants/Endowments; Business/Corporate Donations; Box Office; Government Grants; Individual Donations
> **Season:** October - July   **Annual Attendance:** 25,000

MINNESOTA DANCE THEATRE AND SCHOOL
528 Hennepin Avenue, Studio 5B, Minneapolis, MN 55403
(612) 338-0627
> **Founded:** 1962
> **Arts Area:** Modern; Ballet
> **Status:** Professional; Non-Profit
> **Type:** Performing; Touring; Resident; Educational
> **Purpose:** To present classical and contemporary ballet and dance school training to career-oriented performers and teachers as well as the general public
> **Management:** Loyce Houlton, Artistic Director/Founder
> **Officers:** Dr. William Houlton, President
> **Paid Staff:** 18
> **Paid Artists:** 50
> **Utilizes:** Special Technical Talent; Guest Artists
> **Budget:** $1,000,000 - $5,000,000
> **Income Sources:** Private Foundations/Grants/Endowments; Business/Corporate Donations; Box Office; Government Grants; Individual Donations
> **Season:** September - May   **Annual Attendance:** 53,000
> **Affiliations:** NARB; NASD
> **Performance Facilities:** State Theatre

NANCY HAUSER DANCE COMPANY AND SCHOOL
1940 Hennepin Avenue, Minneapolis, MN 55403
(612) 871-9077
FAX: (612) 870-0764
> **Founded:** 1961
> **Arts Area:** Modern
> **Status:** Professional; Non-Profit
> **Type:** Performing; Touring; Educational; Sponsoring
> **Purpose:** The Nancy Hauser Dance Company and School fosters, performs and teaches the constantly evolving Mary Wiginan/Hanya Holm/Nancy Hauser aesthetic of modern dance in Minnesota, the Central United States and abroad.
> **Management:** Heidi Jasmin, Artistic Director
> **Officers:** Charles Zimmerman, Chairman; Michael Tezla, Treasurer
> **Paid Staff:** 2   **Volunteer Staff:** 25
> **Paid Artists:** 10   **Non-Paid Artists:** 9
> **Utilizes:** Special Technical Talent; Guest Artists
> **Budget:** $100,000 - $500,000

Income Sources: Private Foundations/Grants/Endowments; Business/Corporate Donations; Box Office; Government Grants; Individual Donations
Season: September - June   **Annual Attendance:** 1,000
Affiliations: Minnesota Dance Alliance
Performance Facilities: Nancy Hauser Memorial Theater

NEW DANCE PERFORMANCE LAB
528 Hennepin Avenue, #205, Minneapolis, MN 55404-3
(612) 341-3050
Founded: 1981
Arts Area: Modern
Status: Professional; Non-Profit
Type: Performing; Resident; Educational
Purpose: The lab is a national resource for choreographers and other artists to investigate new ideas and develop new material.
Management: Linda Shapiro, Artistic Director
Paid Staff: 4
Paid Artists: 8
Utilizes: Guest Choreographers
Budget: $100,000 - $500,000
Income Sources: Private Foundations/Grants/Endowments; Business/Corporate Donations; Box Office; Government Grants; Individual Donations
Season: September - May   **Annual Attendance:** 8,000
Affiliations: Dance USA; Minnesota Dance Alliance
Performance Facilities: Hennepin Center for the Arts

ZENON DANCE COMPANY AND SCHOOL, INC.
528 Hennepin Avenue, Suite 400, Minneapolis, MN 55403
(612) 338-1101
Founded: 1983
Arts Area: Modern; Ballet; Jazz
Status: Professional; Non-Profit
Type: Performing; Touring; Resident; Educational
Purpose: To sustain an artistically excellent, professional dance company in the Twin Cities
Management: Linda Z. Andrews, Artistic Director; Dawn Barrett, Executive Director; Mary Jo Peloquin, Operations Manager
Officers: Diane Fridley Norman, President; Mary J. Atmore, Vice President; Cynthia A. Pickard, Treasurer; Patricia A. Timpane, Secretary
Paid Staff: 3   **Volunteer Staff:** 20
Paid Artists: 11
Utilizes: Guest Choreographers
Budget: $100,000 - $500,000
Income Sources: Private Foundations/Grants/Endowments; Business/Corporate Donations; Box Office; Government Grants; Individual Donations; Proceeds from School
Season: September - June   **Annual Attendance:** 15,000
Performance Facilities: Ordway McKnight Theatre

INSTRUMENTAL MUSIC

CONCENTUS MUSICUS
1219 University Avenue SE, Minneapolis, MN 55414
(612) 379-4463
Founded: 1966
Arts Area: Ensemble
Status: Professional; Non-Professional; Non-Profit
Type: Performing; Touring; Educational
Purpose: Concentus Musicus seeks to recreate the best works of Medieval and Renaissance music and related arts and foster an appreciation of this heritage in the community.
Management: Arthur Maud, Artistic Director; Mark Ellenberger, Administrative Director; Carole Broad, Associate Administrator
Officers: Allen Siedle, Chairman/Board of Directors; Charles Bathke, Vice Chairman
Paid Staff: 3   **Volunteer Staff:** 5
Paid Artists: 20   **Non-Paid Artists:** 30
Utilizes: Special Technical Talent
Budget: $1,000 - $50,000
Income Sources: Private Foundations/Grants/Endowments; Business/Corporate Donations; Box Office; Individual Donations
Season: September - May   **Annual Attendance:** 2,700

GREATER TWIN CITIES YOUTH SYMPHONIES
430 Oak Grove, Suite B-5, Minneapolis, MN 55403
(612) 870-7611
Founded: 1972
Arts Area: Symphony; Chamber; Ensemble
Status: Non-Professional; Non-Profit
Type: Performing; Touring; Educational
Purpose: To provide the finest symphonic music experience to talented youth of the Greater Twin Cities Area in order that they might learn to grow artistically and socially, accomplished through the formation of ensembles that afford each student maximum opportunity commensurate with ability
Management: Dr. William L. Jones, Music Director/Administrator; Mary Mueller, Jane Anfinson, Shantel Nelson, Administrative Assistants
Officers: William Barber, Chairman of the Board; Fred Steiner, President; Kathy Cunningham, Vice President; Margaret Burchell, Treasurer
Paid Staff: 10
Utilizes: Special Technical Talent; Guest Artists
Budget: $100,000 - $500,000
Income Sources: Private Foundations/Grants/Endowments; Business/Corporate Donations; Box Office; Government Grants; Individual Donations
Season: 52 Weeks **Annual Attendance:** 25,000
Affiliations: ASOL; MENC
Performance Facilities: Orchestra Hall; O'Shaughnessy Auditorium

THE KENWOOD CHAMBER ORCHESTRA
2020 West Lake of Theisles Parkway, Minneapolis, MN 55406
(612) 377-5095
Founded: 1972
Arts Area: Orchestra; Chamber
Status: Non-Professional; Non-Profit
Type: Performing; Touring; Educational
Purpose: To give amateur musicians an opportunity to perform great music to serve the musical hunger of the Twin Cities Area
Officers: Kady Stauss, President; Sarah Headley, Secretary
Paid Staff: 1 **Volunteer Staff:** 8
Paid Artists: 1 **Non-Paid Artists:** 44
Utilizes: Guest Conductors; Guest Artists; Guest Directors
Budget: $1,000 - $50,000
Income Sources: Individual Donations
Season: September - July **Annual Attendance:** 4,000
Performance Facilities: Walker Art Center, Minneapolis Institute of Art

MINNEAPOLIS CHAMBER SYMPHONY
100 North Sixth Street, Suite 935C, Minneapolis, MN 55403
(612) 339-0235
Founded: 1978
Arts Area: Orchestra; Chamber
Status: Professional
Type: Performing; Touring; Resident; Educational
Purpose: To produce high quality, professional performances of music from the chamber orchestra repertoire
Management: Jere Lantz, Music Director; Peter Dross, Executive Director; John Coughlin, General Manager
Officers: John Schultz, Chair; Susan Finn, Vice Chair; Catherine Bernard, Treasurer; Angela Chicoine, Secretary
Paid Staff: 4
Paid Artists: 26
Utilizes: Guest Artists
Budget: $100,000 - $500,000
Income Sources: Private Foundations/Grants/Endowments; Business/Corporate Donations; Box Office; Government Grants; Individual Donations
Performance Facilities: World Theater; Walker Center

MINNEAPOLIS POPS ORCHESTRA
1611 West 32nd Street, Minneapolis, MN 55408
(612) 825-2922
Founded: 1950
Arts Area: Orchestra
Status: Professional; Non-Profit
Type: Performing
Purpose: To provide free, outdoor Pops concerts for the public
Management: Jere Lantz, Conductor; Cynthia Stokes, Manager; Marilyn Ford, Director of Development
Paid Staff: 3

Paid Artists: 44
Utilizes: Guest Artists
Budget: $50,000 - $100,000
Income Sources: Private Foundations/Grants/Endowments; Business/Corporate Donations; Government Grants; Individual Donations
Season: June 27 - July 26   **Annual Attendance:** 30,000
Affiliations: Minneapolis Park Board; People for Minneapolis Parks Fund
Performance Facilities: Bandstand, Lake Harriet

MINNESOTA ORCHESTRAL ASSOCIATION
1111 Nicollet Mall, Minneapolis, MN 55403
(612) 371-5600
FAX: (612) 371-0838
Founded: 1903
Arts Area: Symphony; Orchestra; Chamber
Status: Professional; Non-Profit
Type: Performing; Touring; Resident; Educational; Sponsoring
Purpose: To sponsor a symphony orchestra of world renown and devote its efforts to the cultural enrichment of citizens of this region as well as national and international audiences
Management: Steve Ovitsky, General Manager; Mary Ellen Kuhi, Director of Development
Officers: Nicky Carpenter, Chairman of the Board; David Hyslop, President
Paid Staff: 67
Paid Artists: 99
Utilizes: Special Technical Talent; Guest Conductors; Guest Artists; Guest Directors
Budget: Over 10,000,000
Income Sources: Private Foundations/Grants/Endowments; Business/Corporate Donations; Box Office; Government Grants; Individual Donations
Season: 52 Weeks   **Annual Attendance:** 750,000
Affiliations: ASOL; Minnesota Orchestra, Rochester; Women's Association of the Minnesota Symphony; Young People's Symphony Concert Association; Young Audiences
Performance Facilities: Orchestra Hall; Ordway Music Theatre

MINNESOTA YOUTH SYMPHONIES
2619 Coon Rapids Boulevard, Suite 205, Minneapolis, MN 55433
(612) 755-3277
Founded: 1972
Arts Area: Symphony; Orchestra
Status: Non-Professional; Non-Profit
Type: Performing; Touring; Educational; Sponsoring
Purpose: To provide the highest possible level of musical training and experience for talented students through study, rehearsal and performance of literature
Management: Vicki Krueger, Manager; Claudette and Manny Laureno, Music Directors
Officers: Kyung Park, President; Craig Runde, Vice President; Bill Hjerpe, Treasurer; Karen Newell, Secretary
Paid Staff: 7   **Volunteer Staff:** 200
Non-Paid Artists: 300
Utilizes: Guest Conductors; Guest Artists; Guest Directors
Budget: $50,000 - $100,000
Income Sources: Private Foundations/Grants/Endowments; Business/Corporate Donations; Box Office; Individual Donations
Season: September - May   **Annual Attendance:** 10,000
Affiliations: ASOL (Youth Orchestra Division); Minnesota Citizens For The Arts; ASCAP

VOCAL MUSIC

DALE WARLAND SINGERS
120 North Fourth Street, Minneapolis, MN 55401
(612) 339-9707
FAX: (612) 339-9826
Arts Area: Grand Opera; Light Opera; Folk; Jazz; New Music
Status: Professional
Type: Performing; Touring; Educational
Purpose: To strive for the highest standards of vocal perfection; to support music of the 20th century in live and media performances and educational programs within the context of choral music; to foster the creation of new music
Management: Dale Warland, Artistic Director; Russ Bursch, Manager
Officers: Michael McCarthy, President of the Board
Budget: $500,000 - $1,000,000
Income Sources: Private Foundations/Grants/Endowments; Business/Corporate Donations; Box Office; Government Grants; Individual Donations

THE MINNESOTA CHORALE
528 Hennepin Avenue, Suite 211, Minneapolis, MN 55408
(612) 333-4866
> **Founded:** 1972
> **Arts Area:** Choral
> **Status:** Semi-Professional; Non-Profit
> **Type:** Performing
> **Purpose:** To provide the orchestras of the Twin Cities with a symphonic chorus of the highest artistic calibre and to offer entertaining and educational concerts for area audiences
> **Management:** Rebecca Scheele, Executive Director; Carolann Haley, Operations/Management Assistant
> **Officers:** Joyce Gordon, President; Chris Trost, Vice President; Malcolm MacLean, Secretary; Ed Robinson, Treasurer
> **Paid Staff:** 2 **Volunteer Staff:** 25
> **Paid Artists:** 20 **Non-Paid Artists:** 130
> **Utilizes:** Guest Artists
> **Budget:** $100,000 - $500,000
> **Income Sources:** Private Foundations/Grants/Endowments; Business/Corporate Donations; Box Office; Government Grants; Individual Donations
> **Season:** September - June **Annual Attendance:** 27,000
> **Affiliations:** CA
> **Performance Facilities:** Orchestra Hall; Ordway Music Theatre

THE MINNESOTA OPERA
620 North First Street, Minneapolis, MN 55401
(612) 221-0122
> **Founded:** 1963
> **Arts Area:** Lyric Opera; Light Opera; Operetta
> **Status:** Professional; Non-Profit
> **Type:** Performing; Touring
> **Purpose:** The Minnesota Opera is a professional vocal/music/theater company dedicated to serving and developing audiences, artists, creators and, thus, providing the community with quality programs and creative productions of both standard and new works.
> **Management:** Kevin H. Smith, President/General Director; Dale Johnson, Director of Artistic Planning; George Manahan, Principal Conductor
> **Officers:** Karen Bachman, Chairperson of the Board; Philip G. Heasley, Vice President of the Board; Lucy Rosenberry Jones, Secretary; Timothy J. Admonius, Treasurer
> **Paid Staff:** 14
> **Paid Artists:** 50
> **Utilizes:** Special Technical Talent; Guest Conductors; Guest Artists; Guest Directors
> **Budget:** $1,000,000 - $5,000,000
> **Income Sources:** Private Foundations/Grants/Endowments; Business/Corporate Donations; Box Office; Government Grants; Individual Donations
> **Season:** October - July **Annual Attendance:** 63,550
> **Affiliations:** OA; Midwest Opera Theater; Minnesota Opera Association
> **Performance Facilities:** Ordway Music Theatre

NATIONAL LUTHERAN CHOIR
3355 Hiawatha Avenue South, PO Box 6450, Minneapolis, MN 55406
(612) 722-2301
> **Founded:** 1986
> **Arts Area:** Choral
> **Status:** Professional
> **Type:** Performing
> **Purpose:** To present sacred choral music
> **Management:** Mark Junkert, Executive Director/General Manager
> **Paid Staff:** 2
> **Paid Artists:** 55 **Non-Paid Artists:** 1
> **Utilizes:** Guest Conductors; Guest Artists
> **Budget:** $100,000 - $500,000
> **Income Sources:** Private Foundations/Grants/Endowments; Business/Corporate Donations; Box Office; Individual Donations
> **Season:** September - June
> **Affiliations:** ACA; American Lutheran Church Musicians; CA

TWIN CITIES GAY MEN'S CHORUS
528 Hennepin Avenue, Suite 701, Minneapolis, MN 55403
(612) 891-9130
> **Founded:** 1981
> **Arts Area:** Choral
> **Status:** Non-Profit

Type: Performing
Officers: James Wilson, President
Paid Staff: 2   **Volunteer Staff:** 94
Non-Paid Artists: 75
Utilizes: Guest Conductors; Guest Artists
Budget: $50,000 - $100,000
Income Sources: Business/Corporate Donations; Box Office; Individual Donations
Season: September - July
Annual Attendance: 5,200
Affiliations: Hennepin Center for the Arts

THEATRE

THE CHILDREN'S THEATER COMPANY
2400 Third Avenue South, Minneapolis, MN 55404
(612) 874-0500
FAX: (612) 874-8119
Founded: 1965
Arts Area: Professional; Musical; Theatrical Group
Status: Professional
Type: Performing; Touring; Educational
Purpose: To produce significant theatre experiences for young people and their families through nuturing a creative ensemble of the highest professional quality
Management: Jon Cranney, Artistic Director; Paula Gottschalk, Executive Director
Officers: Earl Klein, Chairman; Jeff Stiefler, Carol O'Toole, Co-Vice Chairs; Caroline Loken, Secretary; Robert Scott, Treasurer
Paid Staff: 280
Utilizes: Special Technical Talent; Guest Artists; Guest Directors
Budget: $5,000,000 - $10,000,000
Income Sources: Private Foundations/Grants/Endowments; Business/Corporate Donations; Box Office; Government Grants; Individual Donations
Season: September - June
Annual Attendance: 250,000
Affiliations: TCG; ASSITEJ; AEA

COMMEDIA THEATER COMPANY
3040 Tenth Avenue South, Minneapolis, MN 55407
(612) 788-2157
Founded: 1975
Arts Area: Professional; Theatrical Group
Status: Professional
Type: Performing; Touring; Educational
Purpose: To bring direct audience contact, improvisational comedy, to communities that don't usually see live theater
Management: Linda Bruning, General Manager; Rudd Rayfield, Office and Booking Manager
Volunteer Staff: 2
Paid Artists: 6
Budget: $1,000 - $50,000
Income Sources: Private Foundations/Grants/Endowments; Box Office; Sponsors
Season: 52 Weeks

THE CRICKET THEATRE
1407 Nicollet Avenue, Minneapolis, MN 55403
(612) 871-3763
FAX: (612) 871-0291
Founded: 1971
Arts Area: Professional; Theatrical Group
Status: Professional; Non-Profit
Type: Performing; Touring; Resident; Educational; Sponsoring
Purpose: The Cricket Theatre is a fully professional theatre dedicated to the production of works by emerging playwrights.
Management: William Partlan, Artistic Director
Officers: Don Arbour, Chairman; William Partlan, President
Paid Staff: 5   **Volunteer Staff:** 3
Paid Artists: 50
Utilizes: Guest Artists; Guest Directors
Budget: $500,000 - $1,000,000
Income Sources: Private Foundations/Grants/Endowments; Business/Corporate Donations; Box Office; Government Grants; Individual Donations
Season: September - June

Annual Attendance: 20,000
Affiliations: The Network; TCG
Performance Facilities: The Cricket Theatre

THE GUTHRIE THEATRE
725 Vineland Place, Minneapolis, MN 55403
(612) 377-2224; (612) 347-1100
FAX: (612) 347-1188
Founded: 1963
Arts Area: Professional
Status: Professional; Non-Profit
Type: Performing; Touring; Resident
Purpose: To present, in rotating repertory, classical plays—both ancient and modern—by a resident company of actors
Management: Garland Wright, Artistic Director; Edward Martenson, Executive Director
Officers: Ronald James, President; Mary Vaughan, Chairperson; DeWalt Ankeny Jr., Treasurer; Sarah Anderson, Secretary
Paid Staff: 115   **Volunteer Staff:** 225
Paid Artists: 231
Utilizes: Special Technical Talent; Guest Artists; Guest Directors
Budget: $5,000,000 - $10,000,000
Income Sources: Private Foundations/Grants/Endowments; Business/Corporate Donations; Box Office; Government Grants; Individual Donations
Season: June - March
Annual Attendance: 400,000
Affiliations: LORT
Performance Facilities: The Guthrie Theater

ILLUSION THEATER
528 Hennepin Avenue, Suite 704, Minneapolis, MN 55403
(612) 339-4944
Founded: 1974
Arts Area: Professional; Theatrical Group
Status: Professional; Non-Profit
Type: Performing; Touring; Resident; Educational; Sponsoring
Management: Michael Robins, Executive Director; Cordelia Anderson, Prevention Program Director; Bonnie Morris, Producing Director; John Montilino, Managing Director
Officers: Cecily Hines, Board President
Paid Staff: 5
Utilizes: Special Technical Talent; Guest Artists; Guest Directors
Income Sources: Private Foundations/Grants/Endowments; Business/Corporate Donations; Box Office; Government Grants; Individual Donations
Season: February - July
Affiliations: AEA; SPTA
Performance Facilities: Hennepin Center For The Arts

IN THE HEART OF THE BEAST PUPPET AND MASK THEATRE
1500 East Lake Street, Minneapolis, MN 55407
(612) 721-2535
Founded: 1973
Arts Area: Professional; Theatrical Group; Puppet
Status: Professional; Non-Profit
Type: Performing; Touring; Resident; Educational; Sponsoring
Purpose: To entertain and enrich audiences of all ages and cultures through puppetry and mask; to build a relationship between artist and audience; to be an active participant in the dialogue of our times
Management: Sandy Spieler, Artistic Director; Beth Peterson, Outreach Director; Nadya Reubenova, Executive Director; Heather Baum, Development Director
Officers: Judy Tilsen, Chair; Rosemary Williams, Vice Chair; Julie Stoneberg, Secretary; David Emerson, Treasurer
Paid Staff: 13   **Volunteer Staff:** 300
Paid Artists: 150
Utilizes: Special Technical Talent; Guest Artists; Guest Directors
Budget: $500,000 - $1,000,000
Income Sources: Private Foundations/Grants/Endowments; Business/Corporate Donations; Box Office; Government Grants; Individual Donations
Season: 52 Weeks
Annual Attendance: 50,000
Affiliations: Alliance for Cultural Democracy; Network; Minnesota Citizens for the Arts

JACKSON MARIONETTE PRODUCTIONS
2107 Perry Avenue North, Minneapolis, MN 55422
(612) 588-3629
    Arts Area: Professional; Puppet
    Status: Professional
    Type: Performing; Touring
    Management: Sara Jackson, Manager
    Volunteer Staff: 1
    Paid Artists: 1
    Utilizes: Special Technical Talent
    Budget: $1,000 - $50,000
    Income Sources: Box Office
    Season: 52 Weeks
    Affiliations: Puppeteers of America; UNIMA; Twin City Puppeteers

MIXED BLOOD THEATRE COMPANY
1501 South Fourth Street, Minneapolis, MN 55454
(612) 338-6131
    Founded: 1976
    Arts Area: Theatrical Group
    Status: Professional; Non-Profit
    Type: Performing; Touring; Educational
    Purpose: Professional, multiracial theatre ensemble utilizing "colorblind casting," dedicated to the spirit of Dr. King's dream
    Management: Jack Reuler, Managing Artistic Director; Charlie Moore, Marketing Director; Kim Walton, Director of Development; Christine Nelson, Associate Producer
    Paid Staff: 125
    Paid Artists: 125
    Utilizes: Guest Artists; Guest Directors
    Budget: $100,000 - $500,000
    Income Sources: Private Foundations/Grants/Endowments; Business/Corporate Donations; Box Office; Government Grants; Individual Donations
    Season: September - May   **Annual Attendance:** 80,000
    Affiliations: AEA; ASCAP

NEW MUSIC-THEATER ENSEMBLE
620 North First Street, Minneapolis, MN 55401
(612) 333-2700
FAX: (612) 333-0869
    Arts Area: Professional
    Status: Professional; Non-Profit
    Type: Performing; Educational
    Purpose: To develop and produce new musical theater works; to nurture the creative artist
    Management: Ben Krywosz, Karen Miller, Co-Artistic Directors; Marge Betley, Managing Director
    Budget: $100,000 - $500,000
    Income Sources: Private Foundations/Grants/Endowments; Box Office; Government Grants

THE PLAYWRIGHTS' CENTER
2301 Franklin Avenue East, Minneapolis, MN 55406
(612) 332-7481
FAX: (612) 332-6037
    Founded: 1971
    Arts Area: Playwright Service Organization
    Status: Non-Profit
    Type: Touring; Educational; Sponsoring; Developmental Workshops; Reading
    Purpose: To fuel the contemporary theatre by providing services that support the development and public appreciation of playwrights and playwriting
    The Playwrights' Center fuels the contemporary theater by providing services that support the development and public appreciation of playwrights and playwriting.
    Management: David Moore Jr., Executive Director
    Officers: Emily Ann Staples, President, Board of Directors
    Paid Staff: 8
    Paid Artists: 200
    Utilizes: Guest Artists; Guest Directors
    Budget: $100,000 - $500,000
    Income Sources: Private Foundations/Grants/Endowments; Business/Corporate Donations; Government Grants; Individual Donations

Season: 52 Weeks
Affiliations: AEA; TCG

RED EYE COLLABORATION
15 West 14th Street, Minneapolis, MN 55403
(612) 870-7531
Founded: 1983
Arts Area: Theatrical Group
Status: Professional; Non-Profit
Type: Performing; Touring; Resident; Educational
Purpose: An experimental theatre company committed to the development of multimedia theater productions
Management: Miriam Must, Managing Director; Steve Busa, Artistic Director; Karen Sauro, Marketing Director; Tim Heins, Production and Facility Manager
Officers: Peter Wold, President; David Kelley, Vice President; Terry Barczak, Secretary/Treasurer; Steve Busa, Andrea Fike, Lauren Marks, Miriam Must, Cheryl Rantala, Judy Thompson, Directors
Paid Staff: 4   **Volunteer Staff:** 2
Utilizes: Special Technical Talent; Guest Artists; Guest Directors
Budget: $100,000 - $500,000
Income Sources: Private Foundations/Grants/Endowments; Business/Corporate Donations; Box Office; Government Grants; Individual Donations
Season: January - November
Annual Attendance: 4,500
Affiliations: NEA; Dayton Hudson Foundation; Jerome Foundation; McKnight Foundation; United Artists; Metropolitan Regional Arts Council
Performance Facilities: Red Eye's 14th Street Theatre

THEATRE DE LA JEUNE LUNE
105 First Street North, Minneapolis, MN 55401
(612) 332-3968
Founded: 1978
Arts Area: Professional; Theatrical Group
Status: Non-Profit
Type: Performing; Touring
Purpose: To produce dynamic, energetic and immediate theatre through scripted material and company creations
Management: Robert Rosen, Barbra Berlovitz-Desbois, Dominique Serrand, Vincent Gracieux, Artistic Directors; Kit Waickman, Business Director; Jennifer Halcrow, Development Director; Steve Richardson, Marketing Director
Paid Staff: 3   **Volunteer Staff:** 4
Paid Artists: 7   **Non-Paid Artists:** 10
Budget: $500,000 - $1,000,000
Income Sources: Private Foundations/Grants/Endowments; Business/Corporate Donations; Box Office; Government Grants; Individual Donations
Season: September - May
Annual Attendance: 20,000
Affiliations: FEDAPT

THEATRE IN THE ROUND PLAYERS
245 Cedar Avenue, Minneapolis, MN 55454
(612) 333-3010
Founded: 1953
Arts Area: Community
Status: Non-Professional; Non-Profit
Type: Performing; Resident; Educational
Purpose: To serve as a bridge between amateur and professional theatre; to entertain and educate the community with quality drama
Management: Steve Antenucci, Managing Director
Officers: Jan Hilton, President; David Hancox, Vice President; Sheri Sheeks, Secretary; Lee Wilwerding, Treasurer
Paid Staff: 4   **Volunteer Staff:** 150
Paid Artists: 10   **Non-Paid Artists:** 250
Utilizes: Special Technical Talent; Guest Artists; Guest Directors
Budget: $100,000 - $500,000
Income Sources: Private Foundations/Grants/Endowments; Business/Corporate Donations; Box Office; Government Grants; Individual Donations
Season: 52 Weeks
Annual Attendance: 20,000
Affiliations: AACT; Minnesota Association of Community Theatres
Performance Facilities: Theatre-in-the-Round

TROUPE AMERICA INC.
528 Hennepin Avenue, Suite 206, Minneapolis, MN 55403
(612) 333-3302
FAX: (612) 333-4337
 Founded: 1987
 Arts Area: Professional; Musical; Theatrical Group
 Status: Professional; Commercial
 Type: Performing; Touring; Resident; Sponsoring
 Purpose: To provide top quality theatrical experiences for our audiences, on the road and in the Twin Cities
 Management: Curtis N. Wollan, Producing Director; John Tsafoxannis, Associate Producer; Thomas Hailey, Production
Manager; Jane Allen, Office Manager
 Officers: Curtis N. Wollan, President; Jane Wollan, Secretary/Treasurer
 Paid Staff: 7
 Paid Artists: 40
 Utilizes: Special Technical Talent; Guest Artists; Guest Directors
 Budget: $1,000,000 - $5,000,000
 Income Sources: Box Office; Producing Fees; Booking Agents
 Season: 52 Weeks **Annual Attendance:** 540,000
 Affiliations: SETC
 Performance Facilities: Plymouth Playhouse, Minneapolis; Venetian Playhouse, St. Paul

WALKER ART CENTER
Vineland Place, Minneapolis, MN 55403
(612) 375-7600
FAX: (612) 375-7618
 Arts Area: Professional
 Status: Non-Profit
 Type: Performing; Touring; Resident; Educational; Sponsoring; Exhibition
 Purpose: To serve as an international and regional catalyst for new forms of expression while engaging the audience in the
issues shaping the arts of our time
 Management: Kathy Halbreich, Director
 Officers: Gary Capen, President of the Board
 Income Sources: Private Foundations/Grants/Endowments; Business/Corporate Donations; Box Office; Government
Grants; Individual Donations
 Season: 52 Weeks
 Performance Facilities: Walker Art Center Auditorium

THE WORLD TREE PUPPET THEATER
3305 East Calhoun Parkway, Minneapolis, MN 55408
(612) 824-3112
 Founded: 1982
 Arts Area: Professional; Puppet
 Status: Professional
 Type: Performing; Touring; Resident
 Purpose: To use the traditions of puppetry and adaptations of folklore to entertain families and children; to employ experi-
mental uses of puppets, dolls and masks for adult theater
 Management: Joan Mickelson, Director
 Paid Staff: 1
 Paid Artists: 4
 Utilizes: Guest Artists
 Budget: $1,000 - $50,000
 Income Sources: Private Foundations/Grants/Endowments; Box Office; Government Grants; Individual Donations

PERFORMING SERIES

MACPHAIL CENTER FOR THE ARTS
1128 LaSalle Avenue, Minneapolis, MN 55403
(612) 627-4020
 Founded: 1907
 Arts Area: Vocal Music; Instrumental Music
 Status: Semi-Professional; Non-Profit
 Type: Educational
 Purpose: MacPhail Center, a part of the continuing education program of, and an extension of, the University of Minne-
sota, is one of the nation's oldest and largest community music schools, offering lessons and classes in music to both adults
and young people of all ages and levels.

Management: Joanna Cortright, Assistant Director
Paid Staff: 110   **Volunteer Staff:** 20
Utilizes: Guest Artists
Budget: $1,000,000 - $5,000,000
Income Sources: Private Foundations/Grants/Endowments; Business/Corporate Donations; Government Grants; Individual Donations
Season: 52 Weeks   **Annual Attendance:** 5,000
Affiliations: University of Minnesota; National Guild of Community Schools of Music

MINNESOTA ORCHESTRA
1111 Nicollet Mall, Minneapolis, MN 55403
(612) 371-5600
FAX: (612) 371-0838
Founded: 1903
Arts Area: Vocal Music; Instrumental Music; Festivals; Grand Opera
Status: Professional; Non-Profit
Type: Performing; Touring; Resident; Educational; Sponsoring
Purpose: To enrich and inspire the community through the highest quality performances of great music; provide the vision and leadership necessary to support, in a fiscally responsible manner a symphony orchestra internationally recognized for its artistic excellence and innovation
Management: David J. Hyslop, President; Steven A. Ovitsky, Vice President/General Manager; Mary Ellen Kuhi, Development Director; Edward Gill, Finance Director; Mary Loiselle, Director of Public Affairs; Helen Franczyk Roberts, Marketing Director; Asadour A. Santourian, Music Administrator
Officers: Nicky Carpenter, Chairman of the Board
Paid Staff: 800
Paid Artists: 250
Utilizes: Special Technical Talent; Guest Conductors; Guest Artists; Guest Directors
Budget: Over 10,000,000
Income Sources: Private Foundations/Grants/Endowments; Business/Corporate Donations; Box Office; Government Grants; Individual Donations
Season: 52 Weeks   **Annual Attendance:** 444,036

NORTHROP DANCE SERIES
84 Church Street SE, Minneapolis, MN 55455
(612) 625-6600
FAX: (612) 624-6369
Founded: 1919
Arts Area: Dance
Status: Professional
Type: Sponsoring
Purpose: To present a series of six to eight dance companies each year of the highest artistic quality
Management: Dale Schatzlein, Director
Paid Staff: 13   **Volunteer Staff:** 350
Utilizes: Touring Companies
Budget: $1,000,000 - $5,000,000
Income Sources: Private Foundations/Grants/Endowments; Business/Corporate Donations; Box Office; Government Grants; Individual Donations
Season: October - May
Affiliations: APAP; ISPAA
Performance Facilities: Northrop Memorial Auditorium

PLYMOUTH MUSIC SERIES OF MINNESOTA
1900 Nicollet Avenue, Minneapolis, MN 55403
(612) 870-0943
FAX: (612) 870-9962
Founded: 1969
Arts Area: Vocal Music
Status: Professional; Non-Profit
Type: Performing; Educational; Sponsoring
Purpose: To present choral/orchestral performances of newly commissioned and deserving but rarely heard works
Management: Philip Brunelle, Executive Director; Frank Stubbs, General Manager
Paid Staff: 8   **Volunteer Staff:** 3
Paid Artists: 80   **Non-Paid Artists:** 75
Utilizes: Guest Artists
Budget: $500,000 - $1,000,000
Income Sources: Private Foundations/Grants/Endowments; Business/Corporate Donations; Box Office; Government Grants; Individual Donations
Season: September - May   **Annual Attendance:** 15,000

FACILITY

THE CHILDREN'S THEATRE COMPANY
2400 Third Avenue South, Minneapolis, MN 55404
(612) 874-0500
FAX: (612) 874-8119
> **Founded:** 1965
> **Type of Facility:** Theatre House
> **Type of Stage:** Proscenium
> **Stage Dimensions:** 90'x90'x40'   **Orchestra Pit**
> **Seating Capacity:** 746
> **Year Built:** 1974   **Architect:** Kenzo Tange   **Cost:** $4,000,000
> **Acoustical Consultant:** Bolt, Beranek & Newman
> **Contact for Rental:** Donna Bachman;   (612) 874-0500
> **Manager:** Lynn Von Eschen
> **Resident Groups:** The Children's Theatre Company

THE GUTHRIE THEATER
725 Vineland Place, Minneapolis, MN 55403
(612) 347-1100
FAX: (612) 347-1188
> **Type of Facility:** Theatre Complex
> **Type of Stage:** Thrust; Flexible
> **Stage Dimensions:** 32'x36'
> **Seating Capacity:** 1,441
> **Year Built:** 1963   **Architect:** Ralph Rapson & Associates   **Cost:** $2,250,000
> **Acoustical Consultant:** Robert Lambert
> **Contact for Rental:** Sue McLean;   (612) 347-1161
> **Resident Groups:** Guthrie Theater Acting Company

HENNEPIN CENTER FOR THE ARTS
528 Hennepin Avenue, Minneapolis, MN 55403
(612) 332-4478
FAX: (612) 340-1255
> **Founded:** 1979
> **Type of Facility:** Theatre Complex; Auditorium; Studio Performance; Performance Center; Theatre House; Multi-Purpose; Room; Dance Studio
> **Facility Originally:** Ballroom; Mason Temple
> **Stage Dimensions:** 45'x35'
> **Year Built:** 1888   **Architect:** Long and Kees   **Cost:** $359,525
> **Year Remodeled:** 1979   **Architect:** Vern Svedberg   **Cost:** $5,500,000
> **Acoustical Consultant:** John Linnerson
> **Contact for Rental:** Doris Overby;   (612) 332-4478
> *Temporary and permanent space for performing artists, dancers and writers/publishers; Audition and rehearsal space available; Video and filming accommodated; Classes offered*

MACPHAIL CENTER FOR THE ARTS
1128 LaSalle Avenue, Minneapolis, MN 55403
(612) 627-4020
> **Founded:** 1907
> **Type of Facility:** Auditorium; No fixed seating
> **Facility Originally:** School
> **Type of Stage:** Proscenium
> **Stage Dimensions:** 32'Wx24'D
> **Seating Capacity:** 250
> **Year Built:** 1923   **Architect:** Magney & Associates
> *Educational*

ORCHESTRA HALL
1111 Nicollet Mall, Minneapolis, MN 55403
(612) 371-5600
> **Type of Facility:** Concert Hall
> **Type of Stage:** Proscenium
> **Stage Dimensions:** 45'x71'x32'
> **Seating Capacity:** 2,465
> **Year Built:** 1974   **Architect:** Hardy Holzman Pfeiffer Associates   **Cost:** $15,000,000
> **Acoustical Consultant:** Dr. Cyril Harris
> **Contact for Rental:** Susan Diffatte;   (612) 371-5633

Manager: Steven Ovitsky
Resident Groups: Minnesota Orchestra

THEATRE IN THE ROUND
245 Cedar Avenue, Minneapolis, MN 55454
(612) 333-3010
    Type of Facility: Theatre House; Arena
    Facility Originally: Warehouse
    Type of Stage: Arena
    Stage Dimensions: 20'x28'
    Seating Capacity: 261
    Year Remodeled: 1969 **Architect:** Ralph Rapson & Associates **Cost:** $75,000
    Contact for Rental: Steven Antenucci; (612) 333-3010
    Resident Groups: Theatre in the Round Players

Moorhead

PERFORMING SERIES

MOORHEAD STATE UNIVERSITY
1104 Seventh Avenue South, Moorhead, MN 56563
(218) 236-2764
FAX: (218) 236-2168
    Arts Area: Dance; Vocal Music; Instrumental Music; Theater
    Status: Professional; Non-Profit
    Type: Performing; Educational; Sponsoring
    Purpose: To provide cultural programming of the highest calibre to the community and campus audiences
    Management: Kathy Friese, Director, Performing Arts Series
    Paid Staff: 3
    Paid Artists: 75
    Utilizes: Guest Artists
    Budget: $50,000 - $100,000
    Income Sources: Private Foundations/Grants/Endowments; Box Office; Government Grants; Individual Donations
    Season: September - May **Annual Attendance:** 5,000
    Performance Facilities: Center for the Arts Auditorium

New Hope

THEATRE

OFF-BROADWAY MUSICAL THEATRE
3243 Flag Avenue North, New Hope, MN 55427
(612) 544-3810
    Founded: 1979
    Arts Area: Community
    Status: Non-Profit
    Type: Performing
    Purpose: To produce major musicals using local talent in varying degrees of proficiency at every age
    Officers: Barb Nordberg, President; Joan Hastings, Vice President; Keith Struck, Secretary; Dan Nordberg, Treasurer
    Volunteer Staff: 11
    Utilizes: Special Technical Talent; Guest Conductors; Guest Directors
    Budget: $1,000 - $50,000
    Income Sources: Box Office
    Season: 52 Weeks **Annual Attendance:** 5,000
    Affiliations: Minnesota State Arts Council
    Performance Facilities: New Hope Outdoor Theatre; Brooklyn Center Civic Center

FACILITY

NEW HOPE OUTDOOR THEATRE
4401 Xylon Avenue North, New Hope, MN 55428
(612) 531-5153
    Type of Facility: Outdoor (Concert)
    Type of Stage: Thrust
    Stage Dimensions: 36'x44'; Second Floor - 360 square feet **Orchestra Pit**
    Seating Capacity: 500
    Year Built: 1986 **Architect:** Bernard Herman **Cost:** $75,000

Resident Groups: Off-Broadway Musical Theatre
Performances of off-Broadway musical theatre; theatre classes

---

New Ulm

VOCAL MUSIC

THE CONCORD SINGERS OF NEW ULM
PO Box 492, New Ulm, MN 56073
(507) 354-8850
Founded: 1931
Arts Area: Choral; Ethnic
Status: Non-Professional; Non-Profit
Type: Performing; Sponsoring
Purpose: Good singing, fellowship and good will extended to the enjoyment and culture of the people and development of the musical art and promotion of community relations for the city of New Ulm; to keep alive the German language through the songs we sing
Management: Leo H. Berg, Manager; Bob Beusmann, Director
Officers: Gary Kliunek, President; Wally Ebert, Vice President; Fremont Franta, Secretary; Phil Vareuerk, Treasurer
Utilizes: Guest Artists
Budget: $1,000 - $50,000
Income Sources: Business/Corporate Donations; Box Office
Season: 52 Weeks

Northfield

INSTRUMENTAL MUSIC

BACH SOCIETY OF MINNESOTA
1114 Lia Court, Northfield, MN 55057
(507) 645-5209
FAX: (507) 663-3549
Founded: 1933
Arts Area: Orchestra; Chamber; Ensemble
Status: Semi-Professional; Non-Profit
Type: Performing; Educational
Purpose: The Bach Society of Minnesota is dedicated to studying and performing choral music with an emphasis on 18th century music and earlier; to pursue a committment to stylistic integrity and excellence as epitomized by Johanne Sebastian Bach
Management: Paul Oakley, Music Director
Officers: Pater Bolsted, Treasurer
Paid Staff: 3
Paid Artists: 7   **Non-Paid Artists:** 75
Utilizes: Guest Artists
Budget: $50,000 - $100,000
Income Sources: Private Foundations/Grants/Endowments; Business/Corporate Donations; Box Office; Government Grants; Individual Donations
Season: September - May   **Annual Attendance:** 5,000

PERFORMING SERIES

CARLETON COLLEGE CONCERT SERIES
One North College Street, Northfield, MN 55057
(507) 663-4354
FAX: (507) 633-4347
Founded: 1945
Arts Area: Vocal Music; Instrumental Music
Status: Professional; Non-Profit
Type: Educational; Sponsoring
Purpose: To provide music excellently performed, as an important part of our educational program
Management: Harry Nordstrom, Concert Manager
Paid Staff: 1
Paid Artists: 5
Utilizes: Guest Artists
Budget: $1,000 - $50,000
Season: September - May 15   **Annual Attendance:** 2,000
Performance Facilities: Carleton Concert Hall; Skinner Chapel

---

Owatonna

THEATRE

LITTLE THEATRE OF OWATONNA
Dunell Drive, PO Box 64, Owatonna, MN 55060
(507) 451-0764
> **Founded:** 1966
> **Arts Area:** Theatrical Group
> **Status:** Non-Professional; Non-Profit
> **Type:** Performing
> **Purpose:** Bring performing arts to the community, especially theatre
> **Management:** Sharon Stark, Executive Secretary
> **Officers:** Matt Kottke, President; Lois Vranesh, Vice President; Gail Plathe, Secretary & Treasurer
> **Utilizes:** Guest Directors
> **Budget:** $1,000 - $50,000
> **Income Sources:** Box Office; Individual Donations
> **Season:** September - July   **Annual Attendance:** 8,000

Rochester

INSTRUMENTAL MUSIC

ROCHESTER CIVIC MUSIC
City Hall, Room 109, Rochester, MN 55902
(507) 281-6005
FAX: (507) 285-8256
> **Founded:** 1869
> **Arts Area:** Symphony; Orchestra; Chamber; Ensemble; Ethnic; Folk; Instrumental Group; Band
> **Status:** Professional; Government Agency
> **Type:** Performing; Touring; Resident; Educational; Sponsoring
> **Purpose:** To provide a comprehensive and coordinated music program
> **Management:** Steven Schmidt, General Manager
> **Officers:** Richard Edwards, President; Ann Grooves, Vice President; Dan Kutzke, Treasurer; Martha Casey; Robert Pettit, Past President
> **Paid Staff:** 5   **Volunteer Staff:** 25
> **Paid Artists:** 150
> **Utilizes:** Special Technical Talent; Guest Conductors; Guest Artists
> **Budget:** $500,000 - $1,000,000
> **Income Sources:** Private Foundations/Grants/Endowments; Business/Corporate Donations; Box Office; Government Grants; Individual Donations; Government Tax Levy
> **Season:** 52 Weeks
> **Performance Facilities:** Mayo Civic Center

ROCHESTER SYMPHONY ORCHESTRA
City Hall, Room 109, Rochester, MN 55902
(507) 281-6005
FAX: (507) 285-8256
> **Founded:** 1869
> **Arts Area:** Symphony; Orchestra; Chamber; Ensemble; Band
> **Status:** Professional; Non-Professional; Non-Profit
> **Type:** Performing; Touring; Resident; Educational
> **Management:** Steven J. Schmidt, General Manager; Dr. Jere Lantz, Music Director
> **Officers:** Richard Edwards, President
> **Paid Staff:** 7   **Volunteer Staff:** 26
> **Paid Artists:** 80
> **Utilizes:** Special Technical Talent; Guest Conductors; Guest Artists; Guest Directors
> **Budget:** $100,000 - $500,000
> **Income Sources:** Private Foundations/Grants/Endowments; Business/Corporate Donations; Box Office; Government Grants; Individual Donations
> **Season:** September - May   **Annual Attendance:** 45,000
> **Performance Facilities:** Mayo Civic Auditorium

THEATRE

ROCHESTER CIVIC THEATRE
220 East Center Street, Rochester, MN 55904
(507) 282-8481
Founded: 1951
Arts Area: Community
Status: Non-Professional; Non-Profit
Type: Performing; Touring; Educational
Purpose: To promote interest in and enjoyment of the dramatic arts through educational and recreational programs and productions
Management: Russell Wiseman, Artistic/Executive Director
Officers: Glenna Wasko, President
Paid Staff: 6 **Volunteer Staff:** 300
Utilizes: Special Technical Talent; Guest Directors
Budget: $100,000 - $500,000
Income Sources: Private Foundations/Grants/Endowments; Business/Corporate Donations; Box Office; Government Grants; Individual Donations
Season: September - July **Annual Attendance:** 33,000
Affiliations: ACT; Minnesota Association of Community Theatres

FACILITY

MAYO CIVIC CENTER
30 Civic Center Drive SE, Rochester, MN 55904
(507) 281-6184
Type of Facility: Theatre Complex; Civic Center
Year Built: 1938 **Architect:** Ellerbe Architects **Cost:** $450,000
Year Remodeled: 1986 **Architect:** Ellerbe Architects **Cost:** $18,000,000
Acoustical Consultant: Bolt, Beranek & Newman
Contact for Rental: Director of Promotions; (507) 281-6184
Resident Groups: Rochester Symphony Orchestra; Minnesota Symphony
Mayo Civic Center contains the Arena, Auditorium and Theatre. See separate listings for additional information.

MAYO CIVIC CENTER - ARENA
30 Second Avenue SE, Rochester, MN 55904
(507) 281-6184
FAX: (507) 281-6277
Founded: 1938
Type of Facility: Auditorium
Type of Stage: Flexible
Orchestra Pit
Seating Capacity: 3,400
Year Built: 1938
Year Remodeled: 1986
Contact for Rental: Director of Promotions; (507) 281-6184
Resident Groups: Rochester Symphony Orchestra; Minnesota Orchestra

MAYO CIVIC CENTER - AUDITORIUM
30 Civic Center Drive SE, Rochester, MN 55904
(507) 281-6184
FAX: (507) 281-6277
Founded: 1938
Type of Facility: Auditorium
Type of Stage: Flexible; Hydraulic Lift Pit
Stage Dimensions: 80'Wx40'D **Orchestra Pit**
Seating Capacity: 3,400
Year Built: 1938
Year Remodeled: 1986
Contact for Rental: Director of Promotions; (507) 281-6184
Resident Groups: Rochester Symphony Orchestra; Minnesota Orchestra

MAYO CIVIC CENTER - THEATRE
30 Civic Center Drive SE, Rochester, MN 55904
(507) 281-6184
Type of Facility: Theatre House
Type of Stage: Proscenium
Stage Dimensions: 62'Wx25'D **Orchestra Pit**

Seating Capacity: 1,340
Year Built: 1938
Year Remodeled: 1986
Contact for Rental: Director of Promotions;   (507) 281-6184

Saint Cloud

INSTRUMENTAL MUSIC

CHAMBER MUSIC SOCIETY OF ST. CLOUD, INC.
PO Box 205, Saint Cloud, MN 56302
(612) 221-0382
Arts Area: Chamber
Status: Non-Profit
Type: Presenting
Purpose: To present high-quality chamber music concerts in central Minnesota
Management: Susan Dubin, Executive Director
Budget: $1,000 - $50,000
Income Sources: Private Foundations/Grants/Endowments; Business/Corporate Donations; Box Office; Government Grants; Individual Donations
Performance Facilities: Atonement Lutheran Church; First United Methodist Church

---

Saint Joseph

FACILITY

COLLEGE OF SAINT BENEDICT - BENEDICTA ARTS CENTER
Saint Joseph, MN 56374-2099
(612) 363-5777
Type of Facility: Theatre Complex; Multi-Purpose
Year Built: 1964   **Architect:** Hammel Green & Abrahamson   **Cost:** $2,750,000
Contact for Rental: Director of Fine Arts;   (612) 363-5777
The Arts Center hosts fine arts performances by regional presenting organizations

COLLEGE OF SAINT BENEDICT - BENEDICTA ARTS CENTER AUDITORIUM
Saint Joseph, MN 56374-2099
(612) 363-5777
Type of Facility: Auditorium
Type of Stage: Proscenium
Stage Dimensions: 50'Wx38'D   **Orchestra Pit**
Seating Capacity: 983
Year Built: 1964
Contact for Rental: Director of Fine Arts;   (612) 363-5777

COLLEGE OF SAINT BENEDICT - BENEDICTA ARTS CENTER FORUM
Saint Joseph, MN 56374-2099
(612) 363-5777
Type of Facility: Theatre House; Multi-Purpose
Type of Stage: Thrust; Flexible; 3/4 Arena
Stage Dimensions: 32'x8'
Seating Capacity: 292
Year Built: 1964
Contact for Rental: Director of Fine Arts;   (612) 363-5777

Saint Paul

DANCE

ANDAHAZY BALLET COMPANY
1680 Grand Avenue, Saint Paul, MN 55105
(612) 698-8786
Founded: 1937
Arts Area: Ballet
Status: Semi-Professional; Non-Profit
Type: Performing; Touring; Educational
Management: Marius Andahazy, Artistic Director; Lori Kartheiser, Business Manager

Paid Staff: 3
Utilizes: Special Technical Talent; Guest Artists
Budget: $1,000 - $50,000
Income Sources: Private Foundations/Grants/Endowments; Business/Corporate Donations; Box Office; Individual Donations

ESTYRE BRINDLE DANCE THEATRE
637 Ohio Street, Saint Paul, MN 55107
(612) 227-0027
Founded: 1930
Arts Area: Ballet; Jazz
Status: Non-Professional; Non-Profit; Commercial
Type: Performing; Educational
Purpose: Dance Education and Performance
Management: B.A. Brenny, Director

INSTRUMENTAL MUSIC

451ST ARMY BAND
Fort Snelling, Building 506, Saint Paul, MN 55111
(612) 725-5237
Founded: 1923
Arts Area: Ensemble; Ethnic; Folk; Band
Status: Professional; Non-Profit
Type: Performing; Touring; Educational
Purpose: To represent the 88th United States Army Reserve Command to the military and to the general public; to promote and encourage the performing arts
Management: CW4 Bruce J. Hedblom, Commander/Band Master; SSG Robert A. Lake, Assistant Conductor
Paid Staff: 45
Utilizes: Guest Conductors; Guest Artists; Guest Directors
Budget: $1,000 - $50,000
Income Sources: Government Grants
Season: 52 Weeks   **Annual Attendance:** 100,000

MINNESOTA STATE BAND
90 West Plato Boulevard, Saint Paul, MN 55107
(612) 296-1577
FAX: (612) 297-1056
Founded: 1898
Arts Area: Ensemble; Ethnic; Instrumental Group; Band
Status: Professional; Non-Profit
Type: Performing; Touring; Educational
Purpose: To continue the musical development and appreciation of America's concert band and wind ensemble movement and its appreciation by the public
Management: Joseph Komro, Conductor/Music Director; Neil Danielson, Public Relations; Adam Torres, Stage Manager; Helmut Kahlert, Concert Coordinator
Officers: Gordon Backlund, President
Paid Staff: 1   **Volunteer Staff:** 70
Non-Paid Artists: 70
Utilizes: Special Technical Talent; Guest Conductors; Guest Artists; Guest Directors
Budget: $100,000 - $500,000
Income Sources: Private Foundations/Grants/Endowments; Business/Corporate Donations; Box Office; Government Grants; Individual Donations
Season: 52 Weeks   **Annual Attendance:** 100,000
Affiliations: Association of Concert Bands

THE SAINT PAUL CHAMBER ORCHESTRA
Landmark Center, 75 West 5th Street, Saint Paul, MN 55102
(612) 292-3248
Founded: 1968
Arts Area: Orchestra; Chamber; Ensemble
Status: Professional; Non-Profit
Type: Performing; Touring; Resident; Educational
Purpose: To present a world-class professional chamber orchestra in the Twin Cities, dedicated to superior performance and artistic innovation, for the enrichment of community life and world audiences
Management: David Schillhammer, General Manager; David Feider, Public Relations Manager; William Vickery, President/Managing Director
Paid Staff: 29   **Volunteer Staff:** 15
Paid Artists: 36

Utilizes: Guest Conductors; Guest Artists
Budget: $1,000,000 - $5,000,000
Income Sources: Private Foundations/Grants/Endowments; Business/Corporate Donations; Box Office; Government Grants; Individual Donations
Season: September - June   **Annual Attendance:** 100,000
Affiliations: ASOL; APAP
Performance Facilities: Ordway Music Theater

VOCAL MUSIC

NORTH STAR OPERA
1863 Eleanor Avenue, Saint Paul, MN 55116
(612) 698-5386
Founded: 1980
Arts Area: Lyric Opera; Light Opera; Operetta
Status: Professional; Non-Profit
Type: Performing; Touring; Resident; Educational
Purpose: To develop and showcase highly-talented and well-qualified professional singers, musicians and stage personnel from the local and upper Midwest areas; to sponsor college internship programs
Management: Irma Wechtler, General Manager; Steven Stucki, Artistic Director
Officers: Irma Wechtler, President; Dr. Joyce Funke, Vice President; Don Machowicz, Treasurer; Florence Stephens, Secretary
Paid Staff: 1   **Volunteer Staff:** 8
Paid Artists: 65
Utilizes: Special Technical Talent; Guest Conductors; Guest Artists; Guest Directors
Budget: $100,000 - $500,000
Income Sources: Private Foundations/Grants/Endowments; Business/Corporate Donations; Box Office; Individual Donations
Season: October - July   **Annual Attendance:** 7,000
Performance Facilities: O'Shaughnessy Auditorium; Drew Fine Arts Theatre; Brady Auditorium

THEATRE

CLIMB THEATRE - CREATIVE LEARNING IDEAS FOR MIND AND BODY
500 North Robert Street, Suite 220, Saint Paul, MN 55101
(612) 227-9660; (800) 767-9660
FAX: (612) 227-9730
Founded: 1975
Arts Area: Professional; Theatrical Group
Status: Professional; Non-Profit
Type: Performing; Touring; Educational
Purpose: To harness and direct the creative power and artistic talents of its writers, directors, actors and educators to create and perform plays, classes and other creative works which communicate matters of social or educational significance to all citizens
Management: Peg Wetli, Executive Director; Peg Endres, Residency Company Manager; Susan Lund, Performance Company Sales Representative; Leigh Anne Adams, Performance Company Director
Officers: Peg Wetli, President; D. Joe Haller, Secretary; Greg Rybak, Treasurer
Paid Artists: 23
Utilizes: Special Technical Talent
Budget: $500,000 - $1,000,000
Income Sources: Private Foundations/Grants/Endowments; Business/Corporate Donations; Government Grants; Individual Donations; Performance Fees
Season: 52 Weeks   **Annual Attendance:** 200,000

GREAT AMERICAN HISTORY THEATRE
30 East Tenth Street, Saint Paul, MN 55101
(612) 292-4323
Founded: 1978
Arts Area: Professional; Musical; Folk; Theatrical Group
Status: Professional; Non-Profit
Type: Performing; Touring; Resident; Educational; Sponsoring
Purpose: To provide audiences with a mirror to the lives of the people of Minnesota and the Midwest and a window to other people and other times; to commission, produce and tour plays that dramatize the history, folklore and social issues of the region and other locales
Management: Lynn Lohr, Producer/Co-Artistic Director; Lance Belville, Co-Artistic Director/Playwright-in-Residence; Thomas H. Berger, General Manager/Tour Director; Carol Marget, Education/Group Director; Karen Kullman, Box Office Manager/Administrative Assistant
Paid Staff: 6
Utilizes: Special Technical Talent; Guest Artists; Guest Directors

Budget: $500,000 - $1,000,000
Income Sources: Private Foundations/Grants/Endowments; Business/Corporate Donations; Box Office; Government Grants; Individual Donations
Season: October - May
Affiliations: TCG
Performance Facilities: Crawford Livingston Theatre

GREAT NORTH AMERICAN HISTORY THEATRE
30 East Tenth Street, Saint Paul, MN 55101
(612) 227-1416
Founded: 1977
Arts Area: Professional; Theatrical Group
Status: Professional; Non-Profit
Type: Performing; Touring
Purpose: To develop and professionally produce new plays about the people, places, events of our home region and the great United States
Management: Lynnell M. Lohr, Producer; Thomas H. Berger, General Manager/Co-Artistic Director; Lance Belville, Playwright-in-Residence/Co-Artistic Director
Officers: David Byrd, President
Utilizes: Special Technical Talent
Budget: $100,000 - $500,000
Income Sources: Private Foundations/Grants/Endowments; Box Office; Individual Donations
Season: October - May   **Annual Attendance:** 20,000
Performance Facilities: Crawford Livingston Theater

PARK SQUARE THEATRE COMPANY
253 East Fourth Street, Saint Paul, MN 55101
(612) 291-7005
Founded: 1975
Arts Area: Theatrical Group
Status: Professional; Non-Profit
Type: Performing
Purpose: To entertain and enrich area audiences through the creation of high-quality productions of the classical repertory
Management: Richard G. Cook, Artistic Director; Steven Kent Lockwood, Managing Director
Officers: Melinda Urion, President; Mary E. Krell, Vice President; Brian J. Raney, Treasurer; Scott Peterson, Secretary
Paid Staff: 4
Paid Artists: 23
Budget: $100,000 - $500,000
Income Sources: Private Foundations/Grants/Endowments; Business/Corporate Donations; Box Office; Government Grants; Individual Donations
Season: September - June   **Annual Attendance:** 20,000
Affiliations: United Arts; TCG

PENUMBRA THEATRE COMPANY
270 North Kent, Saint Paul, MN 55102
(612) 224-4601
FAX: (612) 224-7074
Founded: 1976
Arts Area: Professional; Musical; Folk
Status: Professional; Non-Profit
Type: Performing; Touring; Educational
Purpose: To present artistically excellent theatre from the Pan African/American perspective
Management: Lou Bellamy, Artistic Director; Strider Hammer, Technical Director; Paula Sanders, Marketing Director
Paid Staff: 8   **Volunteer Staff:** 300
Utilizes: Guest Artists; Guest Directors
Budget: $500,000 - $1,000,000
Income Sources: Private Foundations/Grants/Endowments; Business/Corporate Donations; Box Office; Government Grants; Individual Donations
Season: August - May
Affiliations: AEA

RAINBO CHILDREN'S THEATRE COMPANY
688 Selby Avenue, Saint Paul, MN 55104
(612) 228-0854
Founded: 1979
Arts Area: Professional; Community; Folk; Theatrical Group
Status: Professional; Non-Profit
Type: Performing; Touring; Resident; Educational; Sponsoring

Purpose: Formed to bring children of different cultures together to learn about each other's cultures through the performing arts

Management: Merline Batiste Doty, Founder/Managing Artistic Director

Officers: Anne Waters, President; Fred B. Williams, First Vice President; Jonah Ogiamien, Treasurer; Denise LaBranch, Secretary

Paid Staff: 2   **Volunteer Staff:** 4

Paid Artists: 10   **Non-Paid Artists:** 10

Utilizes: Special Technical Talent; Guest Artists; Guest Directors

Budget: $50,000 - $100,000

Income Sources: Private Foundations/Grants/Endowments; Business/Corporate Donations; Box Office; Government Grants; Individual Donations

Season: 52 Weeks   **Annual Attendance:** 10,000

FACILITY

COLLEGE OF SAINT CATHERINE - O'SHAUGHNESSY AUDITORIUM
2004 Randolph, Saint Paul, MN 55105
(612) 690-6701
FAX: (612) 690-6769
  Founded: 1970
  Type of Facility: Performance Center
  Type of Stage: Flexible; Proscenium
  Orchestra Pit
  Seating Capacity: 1,900
  Year Built: 1970   **Architect:** Hammel Green & Abrahamson   **Cost:** $6,000,000
  Acoustical Consultant: George Izenour
  Contact for Rental: Susan Federbusch;   (612) 690-6701

ORDWAY MUSIC THEATRE
345 Washington Street, Saint Paul, MN 55102
(612) 282-3000
FAX: (612) 224-5319
  Type of Facility: Concert Hall; Theatre House
  Year Built: 1985   **Architect:** Benjamin Thompson & Associates   **Cost:** $45,000,000
  Acoustical Consultant: R. Lawrence Kirkegaard & Associates
  Contact for Rental: Marge Kazmierczak;   (612) 282-3000
  Manager: James C. Sheeley, General Manager
  Contains McKnight Theatre and The Main Hall. See separate listings for additional information.

ORDWAY MUSIC THEATRE - THE MAIN HALL
345 Washington Street, Saint Paul, MN 55102
(612) 282-3000
FAX: (612) 224-5319
  Type of Facility: Concert Hall; Theatre House; Opera House
  Type of Stage: Proscenium
  Stage Dimensions: 136'Wx49'6"D; 64'Wx34'6"H proscenium opening   **Orchestra Pit**
  Seating Capacity: 1,815
  Year Built: 1985
  Contact for Rental: Marge Kazmierczak;   (612) 282-3000
  Manager: James C. Sheeley
  Resident Groups: The Minnesota Opera; The Saint Paul Chamber Orchestra; The Shubert Club

ORDWAY MUSIC THEATRE - MCKNIGHT THEATRE
345 Washington Street, Saint Paul, MN 55102
(612) 282-3000
FAX: (612) 224-5319
  Type of Facility: Theatre House
  Type of Stage: Proscenium
  Stage Dimensions: 40'3"Wx33'6"D; 40'3"Wx22'H proscenium opening
  Seating Capacity: 315
  Year Built: 1985
  Contact for Rental: Marge Kazmierczak;   (612) 282-3000
  Manager: James C. Sheeeley, General Manager

SAINT PAUL CIVIC CENTER
143 West Fourth Street, Saint Paul, MN 55102
(612) 224-7361
  Type of Facility: Civic Center

Year Built: 1973   Architect: Convention Center Architects   Cost: $19,500,000
Year Remodeled: 1984   Architect: DWBR   Cost: $10,500,000
Contact for Rental: Barbara Chandler, Manager;   (612) 224-7361
Manager: Barbara Chandler
Saint Paul Civic Center contains the Arena and Auditorium. See separate listings for further information.

SAINT PAUL CIVIC CENTER - ARENA
143 West Fourth Street, Saint Paul, MN 55102
(612) 224-7361
FAX: (612) 224-1142
    Type of Facility: Concert Hall; Arena
    Type of Stage: Flexible; Platform
    Seating Capacity: 17,700
    Year Built: 1973
    Year Remodeled: 1984
    Contact for Rental: David Rosenwasser, Barbara Chandler;   (612) 224-7361
    Manager: David Rosenwasser, Executive Director;   (612) 224-7361

SAINT PAUL CIVIC CENTER - AUDITORIUM
143 West Fourth Street, Saint Paul, MN 55102
(612) 224-7361
FAX: (612) 224-1142
    Type of Facility: Concert Hall; Auditorium
    Type of Stage: Flexible; Platform
    Seating Capacity: 5,500
    Year Built: 1973
    Year Remodeled: 1984
    Contact for Rental: Barbara Chandler, David Rosenwasser;   (612) 224-7361
    Manager: Barbara Chandler, Managing Director;   (612) 224-7361

Saint Peter

FACILITY

GUSTAVUS ADOLPHUS COLLEGE - SCHAEFFER FINE ARTS COMPLEX
800 West College Avenue, Saint Peter, MN 56082
(507) 933-7363
    Founded: 1862
    Type of Facility: Performance Center
    Year Built: 1971   Architect: Hammel Green & Abrahamson   Cost: $3,500,000
    Acoustical Consultant: Hammel Green & Abrahamson
    Contact for Rental: Al Behrends;   (507) 933-7363
    Complex contains Evelyn E. Anderson Theatre and Jussi Bjorling Concert Hall. See separate listings for more information.

GUSTAVUS ADOLPHUS COLLEGE - SCHAEFFER FINE ARTS COMPLEX -
EVELYN E. ANDERSON THEATRE
800 West College Avenue, Saint Peter, MN 56082
(507) 933-7363
    Founded: 1862
    Type of Facility: Theatre House
    Type of Stage: Thrust
    Stage Dimensions: 30'Wx60'D
    Seating Capacity: 275
    Year Built: 1971
    Contact for Rental: Al Behrends;   (507) 933-7363

GUSTAVUS ADOLPHUS COLLEGE - SCHAEFFER FINE ARTS COMPLEX -
JUSSI BJORLING CONCERT HALL
800 West College Avenue, Saint Peter, MN 56082
(507) 933-7363
    Founded: 1862
    Type of Facility: Concert Hall
    Type of Stage: Concert Stage
    Stage Dimensions: 43'Wx34'D
    Seating Capacity: 510

Year Built: 1971
Contact for Rental: Al Behrends;   (507) 933-7363

White Bear Lake

THEATRE

LAKESHORE PLAYERS
4820 Stewart Avenue, PO Box 10562, White Bear Lake, MN 55110
(612) 426-3275
    Founded: 1953
    Arts Area: Musical; Theatrical Group
    Status: Non-Profit
    Type: Performing; Educational
    Purpose: To bring entertainment to the community
    Management: Sherrie Tarble, Business Manager
    Officers: Kevin Chandler, President; Bill Collins, Vice President; Sue Riedinger, Secretary; Danette Olsen, Treasurer
    Paid Staff: 4   **Volunteer Staff:** 14
    Non-Paid Artists: 25
    Utilizes: Special Technical Talent; Guest Directors
    Budget: $50,000 - $100,000
    Income Sources: Box Office; Individual Donations
    Season: August - May   **Annual Attendance:** 15,000
    Affiliations: ACT; Minnesota Association of Community Theatres
    Performance Facilities: Lakeshore Playhouse

FACILITY

LAKESHORE PLAYHOUSE
4820 Steward Avenue, PO Box 10562, White Bear Lake, MN 55110
(612) 429-5674
    Type of Facility: Theatre House
    Facility Originally: Church
    Seating Capacity: 210
    Year Remodeled: 1970
    Contact for Rental: Manager;   (612) 429-5674
    Manager: Sherrie Tarble, Business Manager
    Resident Groups: Lakeshore Players

Winona

INSTRUMENTAL MUSIC

JOHN PAULSON JAZZ QUARTET
725 37th Avenue, Winona, MN 55987
(507) 454-4948
    Founded: 1980
    Arts Area: Instrumental Group; Electronic & Live Electronic
    Status: Professional
    Type: Performing; Touring; Educational
    Purpose: To perform high quality creative jazz music and help advance the jazz idiom through education
    Management: Dr. John C. Paulson, Leader
    Paid Artists: 4
    Utilizes: Guest Artists
    Budget: $1,000 - $50,000

MISSISSIPPI

Belzoni

FACILITY

DEPOT THEATRE
110 Magnolia Street, Belzoni, MS 39038
(601) 247-1343
Type of Facility: Theatre House; Multi-Purpose
Type of Stage: Proscenium
Stage Dimensions: 26'Wx20'Dx8'H
Seating Capacity: 250
Year Remodeled: 1981
Contact for Rental: Tom Turner Jr.;   (601) 247-1343

Biloxi

VOCAL MUSIC

GULF COAST OPERA THEATRE
1279 Father Ryan, Biloxi, MS 39530
(601) 432-5956
Founded: 1973
Arts Area: Grand Opera; Operetta; Musical Theatre
Status: Semi-Professional; Non-Profit
Type: Performing; Resident
Purpose: To educate residents of the Mississippi Gulf Coast in the art forms of opera and musical theatre
Management: Dr. Laurence Oden, Director; Shirley Heitzman, Chairman of Opera Workshop
Officers: Charles Kremer, President, Board of Directors; Betty Kendall, President, Opera Salon
Paid Staff: 7
Paid Artists: 50   **Non-Paid Artists:** 40
Budget: $100,000 - $500,000
Income Sources: Box Office; Individual Donations
Season: November - May   **Annual Attendance:** 4,000
Performance Facilities: Saenger Theatre for the Performing Arts

FACILITY

SAENGER THEATRE FOR THE PERFORMING ARTS
416 Reynoir Street, PO Box 775, Biloxi, MS 39533
(601) 435-6291
Type of Facility: Performance Center; Theatre House
Facility Originally: Vaudeville
Type of Stage: Modified Apron Proscenium
Stage Dimensions: 58'Wx23'7"D, 36'Wx20'H proscenium opening   **Orchestra Pit**
Seating Capacity: 1,190
Year Built: 1929   **Architect:** Roy A. Benjamin   **Cost:** $200,000
Year Remodeled: 1984   **Architect:** Collins & Collins   **Cost:** $100,000
Contact for Rental: Tina Cowart;   (601) 435-6294
Manager: Benjamin Shelton;   (601) 435-6291
Resident Groups: Gulf Coast Opera Theatre; Gulf Coast Symphony; Riviera Productions; Kinetic Neoskeine; Walter Anderson Players
Opened January 15, 1929, with one of the first sound films, "Interference"

Cleveland

FACILITY

WHISTLE STOP PLAYHOUSE
Cleveland Community Theatre, PO Box 44, Cleveland, MS 38732
(601) 843-3096
Type of Facility: Theatre House
Facility Originally: Train Station
Type of Stage: Proscenium
Stage Dimensions: 40'Wx40'Dx40'H   **Orchestra Pit**

Seating Capacity: 150
Year Built: 1955
Contact for Rental: June McClendon; (601) 843-3096
Resident Groups: Cleveland Community Theatre

Columbus

FACILITY

COLUMBUS CONVENTION AND CIVIC CENTER
Second Avenue North, Columbus, MS 39701
(601) 328-4164
  Type of Facility: Auditorium
  Type of Stage: Proscenium
  Stage Dimensions: 33'Wx31'Dx12'H
  Seating Capacity: 1,900
  Year Remodeled: 1987   Architect: Virden & Alexander, Ltd.
  Contact for Rental: Property Manager; (601) 328-4164
  Manager: Frank Goodman

PRINCESS THEATER
Fifth Street South, Columbus, MS 39701
(601) 327-8665
  Type of Facility: Theatre House
  Facility Originally: Vaudeville
  Type of Stage: Proscenium
  Stage Dimensions: 75'Wx50'Dx30'H   Orchestra Pit
  Seating Capacity: 700
  Year Built: 1924
  Year Remodeled: 1986
  Contact for Rental: Mrs. Ed Kuykendall Sr.; (601) 327-8665

Corinth

THEATRE

CORINTH THEATRE-ARTS
Fulton Drive, PO Box 127, Corinth, MS 38834
(601) 287-2995
  Founded: 1967
  Arts Area: Community
  Status: Non-Profit
  Type: Resident
  Management: Murray Chase, Resident Director
  Paid Staff: 1   Volunteer Staff: 85
  Budget: $1,000 - $50,000
  Income Sources: Business/Corporate Donations; Box Office; Individual Donations
  Season: 52 Weeks   Annual Attendance: 9,000
  Performance Facilities: Crossroads Playhouse; Coliseum Civic Center

FACILITY

COLISEUM CIVIC CENTER
404 Taylor Street, PO Box 723, Corinth, MS 38834
(601) 287-1328
FAX: (601) 286-0903
  Type of Facility: Concert Hall; Auditorium; Theatre House; Opera House; Civic Center
  Facility Originally: Vaudeville; Movie House
  Type of Stage: Proscenium
  Stage Dimensions: 28'Wx20'Dx20'H   Orchestra Pit
  Seating Capacity: 900
  Year Built: 1924   Architect: Benjamin F. Liddon
  Year Remodeled: 1982   Architect: Ledbetter Associates   Cost: $250,000
  Contact for Rental: Mrs. H.L. Williams Jr.; (601) 287-1328
  Resident Groups: Northeast Mississippi Community Concert Association; Corinth Theatre-Arts; Corinth Symphony Orchestra

Greenwood

FACILITY

GREENWOOD LEFLORE CIVIC CENTER
Highway 7 North, Greenwood, MS 38930
(601) 453-4065
>**Type of Facility:** Civic Center; Arena
>**Type of Stage:** Proscenium
>**Stage Dimensions:** 60'Wx30'D
>**Seating Capacity:** 2,800
>**Year Built:** 1980   **Architect:** Bowman & Bowman, Ltd
>**Contact for Rental:** James Belk;   (601) 453-4065

Gulfport

INSTRUMENTAL MUSIC

GULF COAST SYMPHONY
PO Box 7294, Gulfport, MS 39506
(205) 666-9554
>**Founded:** 1963
>**Arts Area:** Symphony
>**Status:** Semi-Professional; Non-Profit
>**Type:** Performing; Touring; Educational
>**Purpose:** To present symphonic music to residents of the Gulf Coast
>**Officers:** Mrs. John Green, President of Board; Col. Sidney Lanier, Vice President; Elaine Martinolich, Publicity Chairman; Dr. Andrew Harper, Music Director
>**Volunteer Staff:** 25
>**Paid Artists:** 4
>**Utilizes:** Guest Artists
>**Budget:** $50,000 - $100,000
>**Income Sources:** Private Foundations/Grants/Endowments; Business/Corporate Donations; Box Office; Government Grants; Individual Donations
>**Season:** September - May   **Annual Attendance:** 4,000
>**Performance Facilities:** Saenger Theater, Hattiesburg

Hattiesburg

FACILITY

MANNONI PERFORMING ARTS CENTER
Southern Station, PO Box 5052, Hattiesburg, MS 39406-5052
(601) 266-4988
>**Type of Facility:** Performance Center; Theatre House
>**Type of Stage:** Proscenium
>**Stage Dimensions:** 43'6"Wx37'6"Dx29'H   **Orchestra Pit**
>**Seating Capacity:** 744
>**Year Built:** 1971
>**Contact for Rental:** Chris Zink;   (601) 266-4988
>**Resident Groups:** University of Southern Mississippi College of the Arts

SAENGER THEATRE
Forest & Front Streets, PO Box 1898, Hattiesburg, MS 39401
(601) 545-4580
>**Type of Facility:** Theatre House
>**Facility Originally:** Vaudeville
>**Type of Stage:** Proscenium
>**Stage Dimensions:** 32'Wx11'Dx22'H   **Orchestra Pit**
>**Seating Capacity:** 1,000
>**Year Built:** 1929
>**Year Remodeled:** 1976   **Architect:** David K. Hemeter
>**Contact for Rental:** Nan Wilson;   (601) 545-4580

Indianola

FACILITY

INDIANOLA LITTLE THEATRE
Main and Sunflower Avenue, Indianola, MS 38751
(601) 887-9920
    Type of Facility: Theatre House
    Facility Originally: Church
    Type of Stage: Proscenium
    Stage Dimensions: 30'Wx30'Dx20'H
    Seating Capacity: 160
    Year Remodeled: 1985
    Contact for Rental: D. Harold Manning;   (601) 887-1300

Jackson

DANCE

BALLET MISSISSIPPI
PO Box 1787, Jackson, MS 39215-1787
(601) 960-1560
    Founded: 1982
    Arts Area: Ballet
    Status: Professional; Non-Profit
    Type: Performing; Touring; Resident; Educational
    Purpose: To encourage and promote the study, understanding and appreciation of ballet and other forms of dance
    Management: Vladimir Juluhadze, Artistic Director; Joanna Hunt, Executive Director
    Officers: Dr. Michael Campbell, Chairman/President, Board of Directors
    Paid Staff: 11
    Paid Artists: 15
    Utilizes: Special Technical Talent; Guest Artists; Guest Choreographers
    Budget: $100,000 - $500,000
    Income Sources: Private Foundations/Grants/Endowments; Business/Corporate Donations; Box Office; Government Grants; Individual Donations
    Season: September - April   **Annual Attendance:** 8,500
    Performance Facilities: Jackson Municipal Auditorium

INSTRUMENTAL MUSIC

JACKSON SYMPHONY YOUTH ORCHESTRA
PO Box 2052, Jackson, MS 39225
(601) 960-1565
    Arts Area: Symphony; Orchestra
    Status: Non-Professional; Non-Profit
    Type: Performing; Touring; Educational
    Purpose: To promote education and appreciation of classical music through participation in the junior or senior youth orchestras
    Management: Philip Messner, Executive Director; Mark Hatchman, Assistant Manager; David Arnott, Conductor, Senior Youth Orchestra; Rebecca Ruttenberg, Conductor, Junior Youth Orchestra; Mark Hatch, Education Director
    Paid Staff: 3
    Non-Paid Artists: 70
    Budget: $1,000 - $50,000
    Income Sources: Fund-raising
    Season: September - May   **Annual Attendance:** 300
    Affiliations: ASOL(Youth Orchestra Division)
    Performance Facilities: Chastain Junior High School

MISSISSIPPI SYMPHONY ORCHESTRA
PO Box 2052, Jackson, MS 39225-2052
(601) 960-1565
    Founded: 1944
    Arts Area: Symphony; Orchestra; Chamber; Pops/Popular Selections
    Status: Professional; Non-Profit
    Type: Performing; Touring; Educational; Sponsoring
    Management: Phillip K. Messner, Executive Director; Guy Drake, Financial Director
    Officers: Jack Garner, Chairman/President, Board of Directors
    Paid Staff: 4   **Volunteer Staff:** 800

Paid Artists: 70
Budget: $500,000 - $1,000,000
Income Sources: Private Foundations/Grants/Endowments; Business/Corporate Donations; Box Office; Government Grants; Individual Donations
Season: September - May   **Annual Attendance:** 3,300
Affiliations: ASOL; Jackson Symphony Youth Orchestra
Performance Facilities: Jackson Municipal Auditorium; Briarwood Presbyterian Church

VOCAL MUSIC

MISSISSIPPI OPERA ASSOCIATION
PO Box 1551, Jackson, MS 39215
(601) 960-1528
FAX: (601) 960-1526
    Founded: 1945
    Arts Area: Grand Opera; Lyric Opera; Light Opera; Operetta; Musical Theatre
    Status: Professional; Non-Profit
    Type: Performing; Touring; Educational
    Purpose: To promote and encourage the study, understanding and appreciation of opera; to develop opera talent
    Management: Frank Marion Johnson, General Director
    Officers: Monroe Wright, President; Ovida Bass Holland, Guild President
    Paid Staff: 4   **Volunteer Staff:** 3
    Paid Artists: 100   **Non-Paid Artists:** 50
    Utilizes: Special Technical Talent; Guest Conductors; Guest Artists; Guest Directors
    Budget: $500,000 - $1,000,000
    Income Sources: Private Foundations/Grants/Endowments; Business/Corporate Donations; Box Office; Government Grants; Individual Donations
    Season: 52 Weeks   **Annual Attendance:** 10,000
    Affiliations: OA
    Performance Facilities: Jackson Municipal Auditorium

THEATRE

NEW STAGE THEATRE
PO Box 4792, Jackson, MS 39296
(601) 948-3533
FAX: (601) 948-3538
    Founded: 1965
    Arts Area: Professional
    Status: Professional; Non-Profit
    Type: Resident; Educational; Producing
    Management: Loyce Root, Business Manager; Janice Englehart, Managing Director
    Officers: Carol Daily, Board President
    Paid Staff: 7
    Utilizes: Special Technical Talent; Guest Artists; Guest Directors
    Budget: $100,000 - $500,000
    Income Sources: Private Foundations/Grants/Endowments; Business/Corporate Donations; Box Office; Government Grants; Individual Donations
    Season: September - May
    Affiliations: AEA
    Performance Facilities: New Stage Theatre

PUPPET ARTS THEATRE
1927 Springridge Drive, Jackson, MS 39211
(601) 956-3414
    Founded: 1968
    Arts Area: Puppet
    Status: Professional; Commercial
    Type: Performing; Touring
    Purpose: To provide entertaining and educational shows in the Southeast featuring classical music and puppets
    Management: Peter Zapletal, Artistic Director; Jarmila Zapletal, Business Manager
    Paid Staff: 2
    Paid Artists: 5
    Budget: $1,000 - $50,000
    Income Sources: Business/Corporate Donations; Box Office; Government Grants
    Season: 52 Weeks   **Annual Attendance:** 15,000

PERFORMING SERIES

USA INTERNATIONAL BALLET COMPETITION
PO Box 55791, Jackson, MS 39216
(601) 355-9853
FAX: (601) 355-5253
> **Founded:** 1979
> **Arts Area:** Dance
> **Status:** Semi-Professional; Non-Profit
> **Type:** Performing
> **Purpose:** The only world-class international dance event sanctioned by the ITT. This excellence-in-the-art competition is held every four years.
> **Management:** Sue Lobrano, Executive Director; Norma Barnett, Public Relations Director
> **Paid Staff:** 4
> **Utilizes:** Special Technical Talent; Guest Artists
> **Income Sources:** Private Foundations/Grants/Endowments; Business/Corporate Donations; Box Office; Government Grants; Individual Donations
> **Season:** June - July
> **Performance Facilities:** City Auditorium

FACILITY

GIRAULT AUDITORIUM
Belhaven College, 1500 Peachtree Street, Jackson, MS 39202-1789
(601) 968-8707
> **Founded:** 1883
> **Type of Facility:** Theatre Complex; Concert Hall; Auditorium; Performance Center; Theatre House; Opera House; Multi-Purpose
> **Type of Stage:** Platform
> **Stage Dimensions:** 36'Wx26'D   **Orchestra Pit**
> **Seating Capacity:** 600
> **Year Built:** 1949
> **Contact for Rental:** Office of Student Affairs;   (619) 968-5916

JACKSON MUNICIPAL AUDITORIUM
255 East Pacagoula Street, Jackson, MS 39205
(601) 960-1537
FAX: (601) 960-1583
> **Founded:** 1964
> **Type of Facility:** Concert Hall; Auditorium; Performance Center; Off Broadway; Theatre House; Opera House
> **Type of Stage:** Proscenium
> **Stage Dimensions:** 104'Wx45'D; 60'W proscenium opening   **Orchestra Pit**
> **Seating Capacity:** 2,510
> **Year Built:** 1964
> **Year Remodeled:** 1988
> **Contact for Rental:** Herb Anderson;   (601) 960-1537
> **Resident Groups:** Mississippi Symphony; Mississippi Ballet; Mississippi Opera

Mathiston

FACILITY

WOOD JUNIOR COLLEGE - THEATRE
Mathiston, MS 39752
(601) 263-5352
> **Type of Facility:** Auditorium
> **Type of Stage:** Proscenium
> **Stage Dimensions:** 20'x34'x28'
> **Seating Capacity:** 500
> **Year Built:** 1966   **Cost:** $180,000
> **Contact for Rental:** Shelby Oakes;   (601) 263-5352
> **Resident Groups:** Wood Players

McComb

FACILITY

STATE THEATRE
220 State Street, PO Box 1141, McComb, MS 39648
(601) 684-5229
    Type of Facility: Theatre House
    Type of Stage: Proscenium; Modified Thrust
    Stage Dimensions: 76'Wx36'D; 44'Wx18'H proscenium opening   **Orchestra Pit**
    Seating Capacity: 438
    Year Built: 1924
    Year Remodeled: 1982   **Architect:** Ragland Watkins
    Contact for Rental: Loretta Easley; (601) 684-5229
    Manager: Charles Schilling
    Resident Groups: Pike County Little Theatre; Pike County Arts Council, Inc.

Meridian

FACILITY

MERIDIAN COMMUNITY COLLEGE - THEATRE
5500 Highway 19 North, Meridian, MS 39301
(601) 483-8241
FAX: (601) 482-3936
    Type of Facility: Theatre Complex; Auditorium
    Type of Stage: Proscenium
    Stage Dimensions: 70'Wx35'D
    Seating Capacity: 600
    Year Built: 1964   **Architect:** Archer and Associates
    Year Remodeled: 1984
    Acoustical Consultant: Ronnie Miller
    Contact for Rental: Ronnie Miller; (601) 484-8666

Mississippi State

FACILITY

LEE HALL AUDITORIUM
Mississippi State Univeristy, Lee Boulevard, PO Box HY, Mississippi State, MS 39762
(601) 325-3228
    Type of Facility: Concert Hall; Auditorium
    Type of Stage: Thrust; Proscenium
    Stage Dimensions: 23'x35'1/2"
    Seating Capacity: 1,200
    Year Built: 1920

Oxford

FACILITY

UNIVERSITY OF MISSISSIPPI - FULTON CHAPEL
Oxford, MS 38677
(601) 232-7411
    Type of Facility: Theatre House
    Type of Stage: Modified Apron Proscenium
    Stage Dimensions: 60'Wx28'D, 36'4"x18'H proscenium opening
    Orchestra Pit
    Seating Capacity: 917
    Year Built: 1927
    Year Remodeled: 1982   **Cost:** $160,000
    Contact for Rental: Jerry Kellum; (601) 232-7411
    Originally built as a chapel with theatre capabilities

UNIVERSITY OF MISSISSIPPI - MEEK AUDITORIUM
Oxford, MS 38677
(601) 232-7411
Type of Facility: Auditorium
Type of Stage: Proscenium
Stage Dimensions: 72'Wx40'D, 32'W proscenium opening
Seating Capacity: 235
Year Built: 1955
Contact for Rental: Jerry Kellum;   (601) 232-7411

UNIVERSITY OF MISSISSIPPI - STUDIO THEATRE
Oxford, MS 38677
(601) 232-7411
Type of Facility: Studio Performance; Theatre House
Facility Originally: Library
Type of Stage: Proscenium
Stage Dimensions: 42'Wx25'D, 26'W proscenium opening
Seating Capacity: 100
Year Built: 1898
Year Remodeled: 1960

Sardis

FACILITY

PANOLA PLAYHOUSE
Main Street, PO Box 43, Sardis, MS 38666
(601) 487-3451
Type of Facility: Theatre House
Type of Stage: Proscenium
Stage Dimensions: 40'Wx30'Dx12'H
Seating Capacity: 180
Year Remodeled: 1964
Manager: Hugh Rhoads

Tupelo

INSTRUMENTAL MUSIC

TUPELO SYMPHONY
PO Box 474, Tupelo, MS 38802
(601) 842-8433
Founded: 1971
Arts Area: Symphony; Orchestra
Status: Professional
Type: Performing; Touring
Purpose: To perform symphonic works
Management: Eric Knight, Music Director
Officers: Doyce Deas, Chairman/Chief Executive Officer
Paid Staff: 1
Paid Artists: 80
Utilizes: Guest Artists
Budget: $50,000 - $100,000
Income Sources: Private Foundations/Grants/Endowments; Business/Corporate Donations; Box Office; Government Grants; Individual Donations
Season: October - April
Annual Attendance: 4,000
Affiliations: ASOL
Performance Facilities: Civic Auditorium

Yazoo City

FACILITY

TRIANGLE CULTURAL CENTER
322 North Main, Yazoo City, MS 39194
(601) 746-2273
Type of Facility: Theatre House
Facility Originally: School
Type of Stage: Proscenium
Stage Dimensions: 28'Wx22'Dx19'H
Seating Capacity: 250
Year Built: 1904
Year Remodeled: 1977   **Architect:** John E. De Cell   **Cost:** $220,000
Contact for Rental: Sandra Younger;   (601) 746-2273

MISSOURI

Arrow Rock

THEATRE

LYCEUM REPERTORY COMPANY
Main Street, Arrow Rock, MO 65320
(816) 837-3311
Founded: 1961
Arts Area: Professional
Status: Professional; Non-Profit
Type: Performing; Touring; Resident
Purpose: To touch, enrich and entertain human beings with live professional theatre
Management: Michael Bollinger, Artistic Producing
Officers: Janet Campbell, President; Eliz Kruse, Vice President; Winnie Davis, Secretary; Bob Bagby, Treasurer
Paid Staff: 35   **Volunteer Staff:** 40
Paid Artists: 20   **Non-Paid Artists:** 15
Utilizes: Special Technical Talent; Guest Artists; Guest Directors
Budget: $100,000 - $500,000
Income Sources: Private Foundations/Grants/Endowments; Business/Corporate Donations; Box Office; Government Grants; Individual Donations
Season: June - September   **Annual Attendance:** 16,000
Affiliations: AEA
Performance Facilities: Lyceum Theatre

FACILITY

LYCEUM THEATRE
Main Street, Arrow Rock, MO 65320
(816) 837-3311
Founded: 1961
Type of Facility: Theatre House
Facility Originally: Church
Type of Stage: Proscenium
Stage Dimensions: 23'9"Wx20'D; 23'9"Wx12'H proscenium opening
Seating Capacity: 300
Year Built: 1872
Year Remodeled: 1968   **Architect:** Henry Swanson   **Cost:** $37,000
Contact for Rental: Michael Bollinger;   (816) 837-3311
Resident Groups: Lyceum Repertory Company
Converted into a theater in 1961 for $10,000.

Boonville

PERFORMING SERIES

FRIENDS OF HISTORIC BOONVILLE
614 East Morgan, PO Box 1776, Boonville, MO 65233
(816) 882-7977
Founded: 1971
Arts Area: Dance; Vocal Music; Instrumental Music; Theater; Festivals; Lyric Opera; Grand Opera
Status: Non-Profit
Type: Performing; Educational; Sponsoring
Purpose: To provide community arts program in our historic theatre, Thespian Hall
Management: Judy Shields, Administrator
Officers: Julie Thacher, President; Paul Davis, Second Vice President; Maxine Hughes, First Vice President; Jerry Smith, Secretary; Paul Sombart, Treasurer
Paid Staff: 5   **Volunteer Staff:** 300
Budget: $100,000 - $500,000
Income Sources: Private Foundations/Grants/Endowments; Business/Corporate Donations; Box Office; Government Grants; Individual Donations
Season: March - December   **Annual Attendance:** 10,000
Performance Facilities: Thespian Hall

Branson

THEATRE

TRI LAKES COMMUNITY THEATRE
PO Box 1301, Branson, MO 65616
(417) 335-4241
Founded: 1983
Arts Area: Musical; Community; Theatrical Group
Status: Non-Profit
Type: Performing
Purpose: Promote the Performing Arts and to provide entertainment for our community
Officers: Mark Weisz, President; Magellen Shock, Vice President; Jean Cantwell, Secretary; Ted Reed, Treasurer
Volunteer Staff: 50
Paid Artists: 3   **Non-Paid Artists:** 30
Utilizes: Special Technical Talent
Budget: $1,000 - $50,000
Income Sources: Private Foundations/Grants/Endowments; Business/Corporate Donations; Box Office; Individual Donations
Season: November - March   **Annual Attendance:** 2,000
Affiliations: Missouri Arts Council

Cape Girardeau

PERFORMING SERIES

SOUTHEAST MISSOURI STATE UNIVERSITY - CULTURAL PROGRAMS
Southeast Missouri State University, Cape Girardeau, MO 63701
(314) 651-2154
FAX: (314) 651-2200
Founded: 1873
Arts Area: Dance; Vocal Music; Instrumental Music; Theater
Status: Non-Profit
Type: Educational; Sponsoring
Purpose: To bring in attractions of a professional quality in the arts; to sponsor workshops where students may learn from visiting professionals
Management: Dr. Martin Jones, Dean, College of Humanities; Dr. Ray G. Ewing, Chairperson, Speech Communications and Theatre Dept.
Volunteer Staff: 4
Utilizes: Guest Artists
Budget: $1,000 - $50,000
Income Sources: Box Office; Government Grants
Season: September - May   **Annual Attendance:** 1,000
Affiliations: Missouri Council on the Arts
Performance Facilities: Academic Hall Auditorium

FACILITY

SOUTHEAST MISSOURI STATE UNIVERSITY - ACADEMIC HALL AUDITORIUM
1 University Plaza, Cape Girardeau, MO 63701
(314) 651-2000
Type of Facility: Auditorium
Type of Stage: Proscenium
Stage Dimensions: 65'Wx40'H; 45'Wx20'H proscenium opening
Seating Capacity: 1,200
Year Built: 1906
Year Remodeled: 1986   **Architect:** Tom Holzhauser and Associates   **Cost:** $350,000
Contact for Rental: Facilities Scheduling;   (314) 651-2280

SOUTHEAST MISSOURI STATE UNIVERSITY - SHOW ME CENTER
1 University Plaza, Cape Girardeau, MO 63701
(314) 651-2297
Type of Facility: Multi-Purpose
Type of Stage: Flexible; 3/4 Arena; Arena
Seating Capacity: Arena - 6,778; 3/4 Arena - 7,400
Year Built: 1987   **Architect:** Hastings & Chivetta   **Cost:** $17,000,000

Contact for Rental: Facilities Scheduling;   (314) 651-2280
Manager: David Ross

Chesterfield

DANCE

ALEXANDRA BALLET COMPANY
68 East Four Seasons Center, Chesterfield, MO 63017
(314) 469-6222
Founded: 1984
Arts Area: Ballet
Status: Semi-Professional; Non-Profit
Type: Performing
Purpose: Training ground to produce dancers to go on to professional work
Management: Alexandra Zaharias, Artistic Director
Paid Artists: 1   **Non-Paid Artists:** 35
Utilizes: Guest Artists
Budget: $1,000 - $50,000
Income Sources: Private Foundations/Grants/Endowments; Business/Corporate Donations; Box Office; Government Grants; Individual Donations
Season: September - May   **Annual Attendance:** 2,000
Affiliations: NARB
Performance Facilities: Fontbonne College Theatre; Edison Theatre, Washington University

Columbia

INSTRUMENTAL MUSIC

MISSOURI SYMPHONY SOCIETY
203 South Ninth Street, PO Box 1121, Columbia, MO 65205
(314) 875-0600
Founded: 1971
Arts Area: Symphony; Orchestra; Chamber
Status: Professional; Non-Profit
Type: Performing; Touring; Educational; Sponsoring
Purpose: The Missouri Symphony Society is dedicated to the enhancement of the cultural environment through fine music, education and encouragment of young musicians.
Management: Hugo Vianello, Artistic Director/Conductor; Debra Sapp-Yarwood, General Manager
Officers: Arthur E. Rikli M.D., President; Kay Dinwiddie, Vice President-Membership; David Harrison, Vice President-Finance; Wiley Miller, Treasurer; Jackie Blanton, Secretary
Paid Staff: 4   **Volunteer Staff:** 65
Paid Artists: 45   **Non-Paid Artists:** 22
Utilizes: Guest Conductors; Guest Artists
Budget: $100,000 - $500,000
Income Sources: Private Foundations/Grants/Endowments; Business/Corporate Donations; Box Office; Government Grants; Individual Donations
Season: June - July   **Annual Attendance:** 12,000
Affiliations: Pops Orchestra; Chamber Orchestra Festival Symphony
Performance Facilities: Missouri Theatre

FACILITY

MISSOURI THEATRE
203 South Ninth Street, Columbia, MO 65205
(314) 875-0600
Founded: 1928
Type of Facility: Concert Hall; Auditorium; Historic
Facility Originally: Vaudeville; Movie House
Type of Stage: Proscenium
Stage Dimensions: 36'x24' proscenium opening; 9'x40' with apron
Seating Capacity: 1,184
Year Built: 1928
Year Remodeled: 1992   **Architect:** Luer and Associates

Contact for Rental: Debra Sapp-Yarnwood;   (314) 875-0600
Resident Groups: Missouri Symphony Society

UNIVERSITY OF MISSOURI- COLUMBIA - JESSE AUDITORIUM
311 Jesse Hall, Columbia, MO 65211
(314) 882-3753
    Type of Facility: Concert Hall; Auditorium; Performance Center; Theatre House; Opera House
    Type of Stage: Proscenium
    Stage Dimensions: 75'Wx35H' proscenium opening   **Orchestra Pit**
    Seating Capacity: 1,840
    Year Built: 1953   **Architect:** Jamieson, Spearl, Hammond & Grolock   **Cost:** $2,000,000
    Year Remodeled: 1986
    Contact for Rental: Pat Higgins;   (314) 882-7254

Fulton

FACILITY

WESTMINSTER COLLEGE - WESTMINSTER CHAMP AUDITORIUM
Fulton, MO 65251
(314) 642-3361
    Type of Facility: Auditorium
    Type of Stage: Proscenium
    Stage Dimensions: 20'x36'x28'   **Orchestra Pit**
    Seating Capacity: 1,400
    Year Built: 1967
    Contact for Rental: Kerry Farnham;   (314) 642-3361

WESTMINSTER COLLEGE - WINSTON CHURCHILL MEMORIAL AND LIBRARY IN THE UNITED STATES
Seventh and Westminster, Fulton, MO 65251
(314) 642-3361
    Type of Facility: Multi-Purpose
    Facility Originally: Church
    Type of Stage: Platform; Altar With Elevated Pulpit
    Seating Capacity: 280
    Year Built: 1676   **Architect:** Christopher Wren
    Year Remodeled: 1969   **Architect:** Marshall Sisson & Frederick C. Sternberg   **Cost:** $3,000,000
    Contact for Rental: Judith Pugh;   (314) 642-3361
    The Church of Saint Mary the Virgin, Aldermanbury, was dismantled in London in 1965, shipped to Fulton, reassembled in its original form and rehallowed on May 7, 1969.

WILLIAM WOODS COLLEGE - CAMPUS CENTER
200 West 12th Street, Fulton, MO 65251
(314) 642-2251
    Type of Facility: Auditorium
    Type of Stage: Proscenium
    Stage Dimensions: 100'Wx30'D; 46'Wx18'H proscenium opening
    Orchestra Pit
    Seating Capacity: 1,300
    Year Built: 1976
    Contact for Rental: Brenda Stafford;   (314) 642-2251

WILLIAM WOODS COLLEGE - DULANY AUDITORIUM
200 West 12th Street, Fulton, MO 65251
(314) 642-2251
    Type of Facility: Concert Hall; Theatre House
    Facility Originally: Church
    Type of Stage: Thrust
    Stage Dimensions: 40'Wx36'D
    Seating Capacity: 315
    Year Built: 1900

Year Remodeled: 1976
Contact for Rental: Brenda Stafford;   (314) 642-2251

Kansas City

DANCE

STATE BALLET OF MISSOURI
706 West 42nd Street, Kansas City, MO 64111
(816) 931-2232
Founded: 1980
Arts Area: Ballet
Status: Professional
Type: Performing; Touring
Purpose: To become the leading producer of world class ballet in the Midwest
Management: Todd Bolender, Artistic Director; Martin Cohen, General Manager
Officers: John Hunkele M.D., President; Randall Clark, Vice President/Finance; Roger Arwood, Vice President/Development; John Marvin, Secretary
Paid Staff: 11   **Volunteer Staff:** 40
Paid Artists: 26
Utilizes: Guest Conductors; Guest Choreographers
Budget: $1,000,000 - $5,000,000
Income Sources: Private Foundations/Grants/Endowments; Business/Corporate Donations; Box Office; Government Grants; Individual Donations
Season: September - May
Annual Attendance: 80,000
Performance Facilities: Midland Theatre

INSTRUMENTAL MUSIC

CHARLIE PARKER MEMORIAL FOUNDATION
4605 The Paseo, Kansas City, MO 64110
(816) 924-2200
FAX: (816) 924-8605
Arts Area: Instrumental Group; Voice; Dance; Theatre
Status: Non-Profit
Type: Performing; Educational; Sponsoring
Purpose: To foster the arts for underprivleged youth in the greater metropolitan area; to provide an opportunity for young people in humanizing programs
Management: Eddie Baker, Executive Director; Jack Lightfoot, Artistic Director
Officers: Kark J. Arterbery, Chairman
Budget: $50,000 - $100,000
Income Sources: Private Foundations/Grants/Endowments; Business/Corporate Donations; Box Office; Government Grants; Individual Donations
Performance Facilities: Charlie Parker

FRIENDS OF CHAMBER MUSIC KANSAS CITY
118 West 47th Street, Suite 201, Kansas City, MO 64112
(816) 561-9999
FAX: (816) 561-8810
Founded: 1976
Arts Area: Orchestra; Chamber; Ensemble; Ethnic
Status: Non-Profit
Type: Educational; Sponsoring
Purpose: To present the finest in chamber music possible
Management: Cynthia Siebert, Executive Director; Kathleen Markham, Marketing Director; Christy Peterson, Accountant
Officers: William Levi, President; Sally Rheinfrank, Vice President; David Steinhaus, Secretary; Betsey Hughes, Treasurer
Paid Staff: 5   **Volunteer Staff:** 30
Paid Artists: 112
Utilizes: Guest Artists
Budget: $500,000 - $1,000,000
Income Sources: Private Foundations/Grants/Endowments; Business/Corporate Donations; Box Office; Government Grants; Individual Donations; Fundraising; Merchandise Sales
Season: August - May

Annual Attendance: 15,000
Performance Facilities: Folly Theater

KANSAS CITY SYMPHONY
Lyric Theatre, 1020 Central, Kansas City, MO 64105-1672
(816) 471-1100
FAX: (816) 471-0976
Founded: 1982
Arts Area: Symphony; Orchestra
Status: Professional; Non-Profit
Type: Performing; Touring; Educational
Purpose: To present the widest range of symphonic music at the highest level with a special priority on its role as a major resource for the educational cultural development of citizens of all ages
Management: William McGlaughlin, Music Director/Conductor; Susan Franaho, Manager
Paid Staff: 11
Paid Artists: 79
Utilizes: Guest Conductors; Guest Artists
Budget: $1,000,000 - $5,000,000
Income Sources: Private Foundations/Grants/Endowments; Business/Corporate Donations; Box Office; Government Grants; Individual Donations
Season: August - May
Annual Attendance: 290,000
Affiliations: ASOL; Missouri Arts Council; Missouri Citizens for the Arts; MAAA
Performance Facilities: Lyric Theatre

VOCAL MUSIC

HEARTLAND MEN'S CHORUS
PO Box 32374, Kansas City, MO 64111
(816) 842-0399
Founded: 1986
Arts Area: Choral
Status: Non-Professional; Non-Profit
Type: Performing
Purpose: To maintain a chorus open to all men, age 18 and above, sensitive to community issues while serving the Kansas City community at large
Management: Reuben M. Reynolds, Artistic Director; Anthony Edwards, Accompanist
Officers: Randall L. Conradt, President/Treasurer; Brad Allen, Vice President; Lynn Reddick, Secretary
Paid Staff: 2   **Volunteer Staff:** 8
Non-Paid Artists: 46
Utilizes: Guest Artists
Budget: $1,000 - $50,000
Income Sources: Box Office; Government Grants; Individual Donations; Membership Dues
Season: 52 Weeks   **Annual Attendance:** 1,500
Affiliations: Gay and Lesbian Association of Choruses
Performance Facilities: The Granada Theater; The Folly Theater; St. Mark's Lutheran Church

LYRIC OPERA OF KANSAS CITY
Lyric Theatre, 1029 Central, Kansas City, MO 64105
(816) 471-4933
Founded: 1958
Arts Area: Grand Opera; Lyric Opera; Operetta
Status: Professional; Non-Profit
Type: Performing; Touring; Resident
Purpose: Opera theatre in English using American artists
Management: Russell Patterson, General Artistic Director; Evan R. Luskin, Managing Director
Officers: Richard Stern, Chairman; Stephen Hill, President
Paid Staff: 12
Paid Artists: 120
Utilizes: Special Technical Talent; Guest Conductors; Guest Artists; Guest Directors
Budget: $1,000,000 - $5,000,000
Income Sources: Private Foundations/Grants/Endowments; Business/Corporate Donations; Box Office; Government Grants; Individual Donations
Annual Attendance: 23,000
Affiliations: OA; AAA
Performance Facilities: Lyric Theatre

THEATRE

BLACK THEATER GUILD OF GREATER KANSAS CITY
411 East Armour Boulevard, Suite 206, Kansas City, MO 64109
(816) 531-4808
>**Founded:** 1991
>**Arts Area:** Professional; Community
>**Status:** Professional; Semi-Professional; Non-Profit
>**Type:** Performing; Educational; Sponsoring
>**Purpose:** To develop both theatre and audiences in the inner city and among youth
>**Management:** Elroy Reed, President; Demetrius Franklin, Vice President; Sammie Edwards, Legal Counsel
>**Officers:** Elroy Reed, Chairman of the Board; Yvonne Wilson, Joan Johnson, Donna Gray, Rick Peters, Lillie Evans, Dianne Crump, Board of Directors
>**Volunteer Staff:** 3
>**Paid Artists:** 10   **Non-Paid Artists:** 15
>**Utilizes:** Special Technical Talent; Guest Artists; Guest Directors
>**Budget:** $1,000 - $50,000
>**Income Sources:** Business/Corporate Donations; Box Office; Individual Donations
>**Season:** 52 Weeks   **Annual Attendance:** 15,000

THE COTERIE THEATRE
2450 Grand Avenue, Suite 144, Kansas City, MO 64108-2520
(816) 474-6785
>**Founded:** 1979
>**Arts Area:** Professional; Musical; Theatrical Group
>**Status:** Professional; Non-Profit
>**Type:** Performing; Touring; Resident; Educational
>**Purpose:** To produce theatre relevant to young audiences; expand the horizons of our audiences by offering the best theatrical works and literature for young people; to present work which challanges traditional views of the theatre, stereotypes of all kinds, and which opens lines of communication between races, sexes, and generations
>**Management:** Kim Ingels, Executive Director; Jeff Church, Artistic Director; Margaret Shelby, Marketing Manager; Daniel Epley, Office Manager; Joel Hoy, Box Office Manager; Laura Burkhart, Production Manager; Brad Shaw, Artist-in-Residence
>**Officers:** Greg Vranicar, President; Martha Crider, Vice President; John Carey, Secretary
>**Paid Staff:** 7
>**Paid Artists:** 45
>**Utilizes:** Guest Artists; Guest Directors
>**Budget:** $100,000 - $500,000
>**Income Sources:** Private Foundations/Grants/Endowments; Business/Corporate Donations; Box Office; Government Grants; Individual Donations
>**Season:** January - December   **Annual Attendance:** 47,239
>**Affiliations:** TCG; ASSITEJ

EAGLE-REED AMERICAN THEATER
411 East Armour Boulevard, Suite 206, Kansas City, MO 64106
(816) 531-4808
>**Founded:** 1987
>**Arts Area:** Professional; Community
>**Status:** Professional; Semi-Professional; Non-Profit
>**Type:** Performing; Educational; Sponsoring
>**Purpose:** To perform theatrical productions
>**Management:** Elroy Reed, President; Demetrius Franklin, Promotional Director; Sammy Edwards, Legal Counsel
>**Volunteer Staff:** 3
>**Utilizes:** Special Technical Talent; Guest Artists; Guest Directors
>**Budget:** $1,000 - $50,000
>**Income Sources:** Business/Corporate Donations; Box Office; Individual Donations
>**Season:** 52 Weeks   **Annual Attendance:** 5,000

MISSOURI REPERTORY THEATRE
4949 Cherry Street, Kansas City, MO 64110
(816) 235-2727
>**Founded:** 1964
>**Arts Area:** Professional
>**Status:** Professional; Non-Profit
>**Type:** Performing; Resident; Educational
>**Purpose:** To produce plays from classic and contemporary literature which have special significance to our company artists and our audiences
>**Management:** James D. Costin, Executive Director; George Keathley, Artistic Director

Officers: Mark S. Gilman, President; William L. Bruning, Vice President For Planning; Nancy M. Hatch, Vice President for Development; Thomas R. Brous, Vice President for Finance/Treasurer; Robert D. Firnhaber, Vice President for Marketing; Mrs. Richard Ballentine, Vice President for Volunteer Services; Mrs. William A. Fay, Secretary; Joseph Appelt, Assistant Secretary/Assistant Treasurer; Laurie Petring Jarrett, Business Manager
Paid Staff: 25
Paid Artists: 75   **Non-Paid Artists:** 15
Utilizes: Special Technical Talent; Guest Artists; Guest Directors
Budget: $1,000,000 - $5,000,000
Income Sources: Private Foundations/Grants/Endowments; Business/Corporate Donations; Box Office; Government Grants; Individual Donations
Season: September - May   **Annual Attendance:** 100,000
Affiliations: TCG; LORT
Performance Facilities: Helen F. Spencer Theatre

UNICORN THEATRE
3820 Main Street, Kansas City, MO 64111
(816) 531-7529
Founded: 1974
Arts Area: Professional; Musical; Theatrical Group
Status: Professional
Type: Performing
Purpose: Contemporary off-Broadway and original productions
Management: Cynthia Levin, Artistic Director
Officers: Daniel C. Hall, Board Chairman
Paid Staff: 5   **Volunteer Staff:** 2
Paid Artists: 96   **Non-Paid Artists:** 14
Utilizes: Special Technical Talent; Guest Artists; Guest Directors
Budget: $100,000 - $500,000
Income Sources: Private Foundations/Grants/Endowments; Business/Corporate Donations; Box Office; Government Grants; Individual Donations
Season: 52 Weeks   **Annual Attendance:** 12,000
Affiliations: AEA; TCG
Performance Facilities: Unicorn Theatre

PERFORMING SERIES

KANSAS CITY JAZZ FESTIVAL COMMITTEE
PO Box 26264, Kansas City, MO 64196
(913) 722-4258
FAX: (913) 722-3121
Founded: 1983
Arts Area: Festivals
Status: Non-Profit
Type: Educational; Producing
Purpose: To produce annual blues and jazz festival
Management: Kathe Kaul, Executive Director
Officers: Tim Swinney, President; Jack Davis, Vice President; Daphne Moore, Secretary; Michael Moore, Treasurer
Paid Staff: 1   **Volunteer Staff:** 400
Paid Artists: 300
Utilizes: Guest Artists
Budget: $100,000 - $500,000
Income Sources: Private Foundations/Grants/Endowments; Business/Corporate Donations; Government Grants; Individual Donations; Concessions; Novelties
Season: July   **Annual Attendance:** 110,000
Performance Facilities: Penn Valley Park

12TH STREET JAZZ SERIES
c/o Performing Arts Foundation of Kansas City, 300 West 12th Street, Kansas City, MO 64105
(816) 842-5500
Arts Area: Instrumental Music; Jazz
Status: Professional; Non-Profit
Type: Sponsoring
Purpose: To broaden community awareness, support and use of the Folly Theater; to encourage tourism in the Kansas City area; to provide educational services and programs in the performing arts
Management: Robert Dustman
Budget: $100,000 - $500,000
Income Sources: Business/Corporate Donations; Box Office; Government Grants; Individual Donations

Season: 52 Weeks
Performance Facilities: Folly Theater

FACILITY

AVILA COLLEGE - GOPPERT THEATRE
11901 Wornall Road, Kansas City, MO 64145
(816) 942-8400, ext. 289
FAX: (816) 942-3362
Founded: 1916
Type of Facility: Concert Hall; Auditorium; Performance Center; Theatre House
Type of Stage: Thrust; Modified Thrust
Stage Dimensions: 43'x34'x15' **Orchestra Pit**
Seating Capacity: 493
Year Built: 1974 **Architect:** Palmer & Kuehn **Cost:** $1,000,000
Acoustical Consultant: Coffeen Anderson & Associates
Contact for Rental: Dr. Daniel Paul Larson; (816) 942-8400, ext. 289
Resident Groups: Academic Theatre and Music Program

FOLLY
300 West 12th Street, Kansas City, MO 64105
(816) 842-5500
FAX: (816) 842-8709
Founded: 1900
Type of Facility: Concert Hall; Auditorium; Performance Center; Theatre House
Facility Originally: Burlesque Hall
Type of Stage: Proscenium
Stage Dimensions: 34'x21' proscenium opening; 4' apron edge; 10' pit lift; 27' back wall **Orchestra Pit**
Seating Capacity: 1,078
Year Built: 1900 **Architect:** Louis B. Curtiss
Year Remodeled: 1981 **Architect:** PENI **Cost:** $3,500,000
Acoustical Consultant: Wenger
Contact for Rental: Roselle Tyner; (816) 842-5500

KANSAS CITY MUNICIPAL AUDITORIUM
301 West 13th Street, Suite 100, Kansas City, MO 64105
(816) 871-3700
FAX: (816) 871-3710
Type of Facility: Civic Center
Year Built: 1936
Year Remodeled: 1981
Contact for Rental: Kathleen Lee; (816) 871-3700
Manager: Bill Langley; (816) 871-3700
Contains the Arena and Music Hall. See separate listings for additional information.

KANSAS CITY MUNICIPAL AUDITORIUM - ARENA
301 West 13th Street, Suite 100, Kansas City, MO 64105
(816) 871-3700
FAX: (816) 871-3710
Type of Facility: Concert Hall; Arena
Type of Stage: Flexible; Platform
Seating Capacity: 8,100 permanent; 10,500 concert seating
Year Built: 1936
Contact for Rental: Kathleen Lee; (816) 871-3700
Manager: Bill Langley; (816) 871-3700
Resident Groups: UMKC Basketball

KANSAS CITY MUNICIPAL AUDITORIUM - MUSIC HALL
301 West 13th Street, Suite 100, Kansas City, MO 64105
(816) 871-3700
FAX: (816) 871-3710
Type of Facility: Concert Hall
Type of Stage: Proscenium
Stage Dimensions: 85'6"Wx32'8"D; 46'Wx23'9"H proscenium opening **Orchestra Pit**
Seating Capacity: 2,402
Year Built: 1936
Year Remodeled: 1981 **Cost:** $26,000,000
Acoustical Consultant: Coffeen, Anderson & Associates

Contact for Rental: Kathleen Lee;   (816) 871-3700
Manager: Bill Langley;   (816) 871-3700
Resident Groups: State Ballet of Missouri; William Jewell College Fine Arts Series; Theatre League; Kansas City Symphony Pops Series

KEMPER ARENA
1800 Genessee, Kansas City, MO 64102
(816) 274-1900
FAX: (816) 274-0306
Type of Facility: Arena
Type of Stage: Platform
Seating Capacity: 17,500
Year Built: 1974
Contact for Rental: Carolyn Foxworthy;   (816) 274-6713
Resident Groups: Kansas City Blades Hockey Team; Kansas City Attack Soccer Club

LYRIC THEATRE
1029 Central, Kansas City, MO 64105
(816) 471-4933
Type of Facility: Theatre House
Facility Originally: Masonic Temple
Type of Stage: Proscenium
Stage Dimensions: 50'Wx45'Dx26'H   **Orchestra Pit**
Seating Capacity: 1,663
Year Built: 1930   **Architect:** Duncan Architects   **Cost:** $250,000
Year Remodeled: 1992   **Cost:** $300,000
Acoustical Consultant: Coffeen Anderson & Associates
Contact for Rental: Manager;   (816) 471-4933
Resident Groups: Lyric Opera of Kansas; Kansas City Symphony; State Ballet of Missouri

PARK COLLEGE - GRAHAM TYLER MEMORIAL CHAPEL
8700 River Park Drive, Kansas City, MO 64152
(816) 741-2000
Type of Facility: Concert Hall
Facility Originally: Church
Type of Stage: Platform
Stage Dimensions: 45'x35'
Seating Capacity: 600
Year Built: 1937
Year Remodeled: 1973   **Cost:** $20,000
Contact for Rental: Katy Goodwin;   (816) 741-2000, ext. 377
Resident Groups: Northland Symphony Orchestra; Parkville Chamber Players; Park College Band; Park College Choir
Rented on a very limited basis for serious musical events only

UNICORN THEATRE
3820 Main Street, Kansas City, MO 64111
(816) 531-7529
Type of Facility: Off Broadway
Facility Originally: Garage
Type of Stage: Thrust
Stage Dimensions: 30'x40'
Seating Capacity: 201
Year Built: 1926
Year Remodeled: 1986   **Architect:** Ralph Keyes   **Cost:** $200,000
Acoustical Consultant: Ralph Keyes
Contact for Rental: Jan Kohl;   (816) 531-7529
Manager: Cynthia Levin, Executive Artistic Dir.;   (816) 531-7529
Resident Groups: Unicorn Theatre

Marshall

INSTRUMENTAL MUSIC

MARSHALL PHILHARMONIC ORCHESTRA
1644 South Colby, Marshall, MO 65340
(816) 886-7044
Founded: 1963
Arts Area: Symphony

Status: Non-Professional; Non-Profit
Type: Performing; Educational
Purpose: To offer an opportunity to area amateur musicians to play
Management: Charles Ferguson, Conductor
Officers: Jane Huff, President; Buena Stolberg, Vice President; Marjorie Haggard, Secretary; Rodney Polson, Treasurer
Volunteer Staff: 4
Paid Artists: 3 **Non-Paid Artists:** 60
Utilizes: Guest Artists
Budget: $1,000 - $50,000
Income Sources: Business/Corporate Donations; Individual Donations
Season: October - April **Annual Attendance:** 2,800
Affiliations: Missouri Arts Council
Performance Facilities: Harold L. Lickey Auditorium

Maryville

PERFORMING SERIES

NORTHWEST MISSOURI STATE UNIVERSITY PERFORMING ARTS SERIES
800 University Drive, Maryville, MO 64468-6001
(816) 562-1212
    Arts Area: Vocal Music; Instrumental Music; Theater
    Status: Non-Profit
    Type: Educational; Sponsoring
    Purpose: To provide a variety of performing arts and lectures to the University and the community
    Management: David Gieseke, Chairman
    Volunteer Staff: 10
    Utilizes: Guest Artists
    Budget: $1,000 - $50,000
    Income Sources: Government Grants
    Season: September - May
    Affiliations: Missouri Arts Council
    Performance Facilities: Charles Johnson Theatre, Mary Linn Performing Arts Center

FACILITY

NORTHWEST MISSOURI STATE UNIVERSITY - CHARLES JOHNSON THEATRE
Maryville, MO 64468
(816) 582-4500
    Type of Facility: Auditorium
    Type of Stage: Proscenium
    Orchestra Pit
    Seating Capacity: 1,095
    Year Built: 1985
    Resident Groups: University Theatre Department

NORTHWEST MISSOURI STATE UNIVERSITY - MARY LINN PERFORMING ARTS CENTER
Maryville, MO 64468
(816) 562-1176
    Type of Facility: Auditorium; Studio Performance; Performance Center
    Type of Stage: Proscenium
    Stage Dimensions: 36'Wx30'D **Orchestra Pit**
    Seating Capacity: 1,100
    Year Built: 1984 **Architect:** Architect Design Collaborative **Cost:** $3,500,000
    Contact for Rental: Dean Robert Sunkel; (816) 562-1325
    Resident Groups: Northwest Missouri State University Department of Theatre

Memphis

THEATRE

MEMPHIS COMMUNITY PLAYERS
125 South Main, Memphis, MO 63555
(816) 465-7770
    Founded: 1974
    Arts Area: Musical; Community; Theatrical Group
    Status: Non-Professional; Non-Profit

Type: Performing; Resident; Educational
Purpose: To provide summer musical theatre for our area
Officers: Harlo L. Donelson, President; Rick Fischer, Vice President; Deb Seamster, Secretary; Ruth Kerr, Treasurer; Charles Harris, Board Member
Budget: $1,000 - $50,000
Income Sources: Box Office; Individual Donations
Season: June - August **Annual Attendance:** 1,000
Performance Facilities: Memphis Cinema

Moberly

THEATRE

MOBERLY COMMUNITY THEATRE
212 Crest Drive, Moberly, MO 65270
(816) 263-3345
Founded: 1979
Arts Area: Musical; Dinner; Community
Status: Non-Profit
Type: Performing; Sponsoring
Purpose: Promote the performing arts, community working together
Management: Carolee Hazlet, Producer/Director
Volunteer Staff: 15
Non-Paid Artists: 50
Utilizes: Special Technical Talent; Guest Directors
Budget: $1,000 - $50,000
Income Sources: Business/Corporate Donations; Box Office; Individual Donations
Season: 52 Weeks **Annual Attendance:** 1,500
Performance Facilities: Moberly Municipal Auditorium; Peppermint Loft

Parkville

FACILITY

PARK COLLEGE - ALUMNI HALL THEATRE
Park College, Parkville, MO 64152
(816) 741-2000
Type of Facility: Theatre Complex; Auditorium; Studio Performance; Theatre House; Black Box
Facility Originally: Movie House
Type of Stage: Proscenium
Stage Dimensions: 16'x22'x20'
Seating Capacity: 205
Year Built: 1950
Contact for Rental: S.L. Sartain, Dean of Students; (816) 741-2000, ext. 379
Manager: Marsha M. Morgan, Theatre Dept. Chairman; (816) 741-2000, ext. 450
Resident Groups: Park College Theatre Department

Point Lookout

FACILITY

COLLEGE OF THE OZARKS - JONES AUDITORIUM
Point Lookout, MO 65726
(417) 334-6411
Type of Facility: Auditorium
Type of Stage: Proscenium **Orchestra Pit**
Seating Capacity: 980
Year Built: 1968
Contact for Rental: Dr. William Todd, President; (417) 334-6411
Manager: Mark Young; (417) 334-6411

Saint Ann

DANCE

GATEWAY BALLET OF SAINT LOUIS
10674 Saint Charles Rock Road, Saint Ann, MO 63074
(314) 423-1600
Founded: 1970
Arts Area: Mime; Ballet; Jazz
Status: Non-Professional; Non-Profit
Type: Performing; Educational
Purpose: To give young dancers from the metropolitan St. Louis area the opportunity to dance in a professional atmosphere with guest artists and choreographers; to provide high-quality dance performances at reasonable prices
Management: Norma Beutell Van Sickle, Artistic Director
Officers: Paul Stuart, President; Dan Francis, Vice President; Carol Wofsey, Secretary; John Niemann, Treasurer
Paid Staff: 3   **Volunteer Staff:** 15
Paid Artists: 3   **Non-Paid Artists:** 30
Utilizes: Special Technical Talent; Guest Artists; Guest Directors; Guest Choreographers
Budget: $1,000 - $50,000
Income Sources: Private Foundations/Grants/Endowments; Business/Corporate Donations; Box Office; Individual Donations
Season: September - June   **Annual Attendance:** 6,000
Affiliations: Missouri Arts Council
Performance Facilities: Florissant Civic Center

Saint Joseph

INSTRUMENTAL MUSIC

THE SAINT JOSEPH SYMPHONY SOCIETY
120 South Eighth Street, Saint Joseph, MO 64501
(816) 233-7701
Founded: 1959
Arts Area: Symphony
Status: Professional; Non-Profit
Type: Performing; Educational
Purpose: To present symphonic concerts and educational activities for the citizens of northwest Missouri and eastern Kansas
Management: Judith A. McMurray, Managing Director
Officers: David W. Lewis Jr., President; Clay Whitehead M.D., Vice President; Pat Speiser, Treasurer; Dee Hurley, Secretary
Paid Staff: 6   **Volunteer Staff:** 200
Paid Artists: 61
Utilizes: Guest Artists
Budget: $100,000 - $500,000
Income Sources: Private Foundations/Grants/Endowments; Business/Corporate Donations; Box Office; Government Grants; Individual Donations
Season: September - May   **Annual Attendance:** 3,000
Affiliations: ASOL; Missouri Citizens for the Arts
Performance Facilities: Missouri Theater

FACILITY

SAINT JOSEPH CIVIC CENTER
100 North Fourth Street, Saint Joseph, MO 64501
(816) 271-4717
FAX: (816) 232-9213
Type of Facility: Theatre Complex; Arena
Year Built: 1980   **Cost:** $5,250,000
Contact for Rental: (816) 271-4717
Contains the Arena and the Missouri Theatre. See separate listings for additional information.

SAINT JOSEPH CIVIC CENTER - ARENA
100 North Fourth Street, Saint Joseph, MO 64501
(816) 271-4717
FAX: (816) 232-9213
Type of Facility: Arena

Type of Stage: Platform
Stage Dimensions: 36'x48'
Seating Capacity: 5,000
Year Built: 1980
Contact for Rental: Kathy Brock, Bill France;   (816) 271-4717
Manager: Bill France;   (816) 271-4717

SAINT JOSEPH CIVIC CENTER - MISSOURI THEATRE
100 North Fourth Street, Saint Joseph, MO 64501
(816) 271-4717
FAX: (816) 232-9213
Type of Facility: Concert Hall; Performance Center; Opera House; Multi-Purpose
Type of Stage: Proscenium
Stage Dimensions: 42'Wx30'D; 42'Wx25'H proscenium opening   **Orchestra Pit**
Seating Capacity: 1,217
Year Built: 1927   **Architect:** Boller Brothers   **Cost:** $1,000,000
Year Remodeled: 1979   **Architect:** Brunner & Brunner   **Cost:** $1,500,000
Contact for Rental: Kerry Strahm, Bill France;   (816) 271-4628
Manager: Bill France;   (816) 271-4717
Resident Groups: Allied Arts, Robidoux; St. Joseph Symphony; Performing Arts Association; Creative Arts Productions

Saint Louis

DANCE

DANCE ST. LOUIS
634 North Grand Boulevard, Suite 1102, Saint Louis, MO 63103
(314) 534-5000, ext. 6622
FAX: (314) 534-5001
Founded: 1966
Arts Area: Modern; Mime; Ballet; Jazz; Ethnic; Folk
Status: Non-Profit
Type: Resident; Educational; Sponsoring
Purpose: To promote an interest in dance by providing varied professional dance concerts and related programs
Management: Bill Eastman, General Manager; Adam A. Pinsker, Executive Director; Laura Burkhart, Operation Manager
Officers: Peter J. Genovese, President
Paid Staff: 4
Utilizes: Special Technical Talent; Guest Artists
Budget: $1,000,000 - $5,000,000
Income Sources: Private Foundations/Grants/Endowments; Business/Corporate Donations; Box Office; Government Grants; Individual Donations
Season: 52 Weeks   **Annual Attendance:** 65,000
Affiliations: Dance USA
Performance Facilities: Kiel Opera House; Edison Theatre, Washington University; J.C. Penney Auditorium, University of Missouri-Saint Louis; Fox Theatre

MID AMERICA DANCE COMPANY
4440 Lindell Boulevard, Suite 1104, Saint Louis, MO 63108
(314) 367-3620
Founded: 1976
Arts Area: Modern
Status: Professional; Non-Profit
Type: Performing; Touring; Educational
Purpose: To produce the highest level of modern dance through teaching, concerts and workshops
Management: Ross Winter, Executive Director; David Kruger, Booking Agent
Officers: Carolyn Maymon, President; Susan Fay, Vice President; Lynn Mutch, Secretary; Lois Ladd, Treasurer
Paid Staff: 2   **Volunteer Staff:** 12
Paid Artists: 7
Utilizes: Special Technical Talent; Guest Conductors; Guest Artists; Guest Choreographers
Budget: $100,000 - $500,000
Income Sources: Private Foundations/Grants/Endowments; Business/Corporate Donations; Box Office; Government Grants; Individual Donations
Season: September - June   **Annual Attendance:** 15,000
Affiliations: Mid-America Dance Network; Dance St, Louis; Arts & Education Council of Greater St. Louis
Performance Facilities: Edison Theatre

SAINT LOUIS BALLET
634 North Grand Boulevard, Suite 10E, Saint Louis, MO 63103
(314) 652-7711
FAX: (314) 533-3345
>**Founded:** 1985
>**Arts Area:** Ballet
>**Status:** Professional; Non-Profit
>**Type:** Performing; Touring; Resident; Educational
>**Purpose:** To provide St. Louis and surrounding areas with a permanent, professional resident ballet company capable of performing both classical and contemporary works in the Ballet Russe tradition
>**Management:** Betty L. Jehle, General Director; Cynthia S. Peak, Assistant to the General Director; Ludmila Dokoudovsky and Antoni Zalewski, Artistic Directors
>**Officers:** J. Kent McNeil, President; John M. Regan Jr., Vice President; Gwen Knight, Treasurer; James Whitener, Secretary
>**Paid Staff:** 3   **Volunteer Staff:** 1
>**Paid Artists:** 18
>**Utilizes:** Special Technical Talent; Guest Artists; Guest Choreographers
>**Budget:** $100,000 - $500,000
>**Income Sources:** Private Foundations/Grants/Endowments; Business/Corporate Donations; Box Office; Government Grants; Individual Donations; Interest; Product Sales
>**Season:** September - April   **Annual Attendance:** 25,000
>**Affiliations:** Grand Center
>**Performance Facilities:** Meramec Theatre; Edison Theatre; Orthwein Theatre

SAINT LOUIS CULTURAL FLAMENCO SOCIETY
PO Box 21818, Saint Louis, MO 63109
(314) 832-3911
>**Founded:** 1983
>**Arts Area:** Ballet
>**Status:** Non-Profit
>**Type:** Performing
>**Purpose:** To promote the Spanish culture through classical, regional and Flamenco dances
>**Management:** Marisel Weeks, Artistic Director; Alvaro Molano, Manager
>**Officers:** Rosa Schwarz, President; Roberto Alvarez, Vice President; Alvaro Molano, Treasurer; Irma Martinez, Secretary
>**Volunteer Staff:** 8
>**Non-Paid Artists:** 7
>**Utilizes:** Guest Artists; Guest Choreographers
>**Budget:** $1,000 - $50,000
>**Income Sources:** Private Foundations/Grants/Endowments; Business/Corporate Donations; Box Office; Government Grants
>**Season:** 52 Weeks   **Annual Attendance:** 7,000
>**Affiliations:** Dance St. Louis

INSTRUMENTAL MUSIC

METROPOLITAN ORCHESTRA OF SAINT LOUIS
8282 Big Ben Boulevard, Suite 206, Saint Louis, MO 63119
(314) 821-0119
>**Founded:** 1967
>**Arts Area:** Symphony; Orchestra; Ensemble
>**Status:** Semi-Professional; Non-Profit
>**Type:** Performing; Educational
>**Purpose:** To provide and present a high quality symphony orchestra in the Greater Saint Louis Area in order to expand the cultural resources of communities and audiences not readily served by other various orchestras
>**Management:** Allen Carl Larson, Music Director/Conductor; Jean Lovati, Executive Director; Carl Dettlebach, Director of Operations
>**Officers:** Jean Lovati, President, Board of Directors
>**Utilizes:** Guest Conductors; Guest Artists
>**Budget:** $100,000 - $500,000
>**Income Sources:** Private Foundations/Grants/Endowments; Business/Corporate Donations; Box Office; Government Grants; Individual Donations
>**Annual Attendance:** 6,000
>**Performance Facilities:** Loretto-Hilton Center for the Performing Arts, Webster University

NEW MUSIC CIRCLE
1110 Washington, 7th Floor, Saint Louis, MO 63101
(314) 567-5384
>**Arts Area:** Electronic & Live Electronic; New Music, Avant Garde

Status: Professional; Non-Profit
Type: Presenting
Purpose: To serve as an advocate for new music; to commission new works and promote promising composers and ensembles
Management: Rich O'Donnell, Music Director
Officers: Nancy Kranzberg, President
Budget: $1,000 - $50,000
Income Sources: Private Foundations/Grants/Endowments; Business/Corporate Donations; Box Office; Government Grants; Individual Donations

THE SAINT LOUIS CLASSICAL GUITAR SOCIETY
PO Box 24153, Saint Louis, MO 63130
(314) 725-0739
   Arts Area: Instrumental Group
   Status: Non-Profit
   Type: Sponsoring
   Purpose: To promote an appreciation of music for the classical guitar and related fretted instruments
   Management: Kathleen Ash, Program Director
   Officers: William B. Ash, President
   Budget: $50,000 - $100,000
   Income Sources: Private Foundations/Grants/Endowments; Business/Corporate Donations; Box Office; Government Grants; Individual Donations
   Performance Facilities: Ethical Society of Saint Louis

SAINT LOUIS PHILHARMONIC ORCHESTRA
PO Box 3858, Saint Louis, MO 63122
(314) 569-8520
   Founded: 1860
   Arts Area: Symphony
   Status: Non-Professional; Non-Profit
   Type: Performing
   Purpose: To provide an opportunity to play good music under an able conductor
   Officers: Marilyn K. Hamiston, President
   Utilizes: Guest Conductors
   Budget: $1,000 - $50,000
   Income Sources: Private Foundations/Grants/Endowments; Government Grants; Individual Donations
   Season: November - May
   Performance Facilities: Scottish Rite Cathedral

SAINT LOUIS SYMPHONY CHAMBER ORCHESTRA
Powell Symphony Hall, 718 North Grand Boulevard, Saint Louis, MO 63103
(314) 533-2500
   Founded: 1971
   Arts Area: Chamber
   Status: Professional; Non-Profit
   Type: Performing; Resident
   Utilizes: Guest Conductors; Guest Artists
   Income Sources: Individual Donations
   Season: October - May
   Affiliations: Saint Louis Symphony Orchestra
   Performance Facilities: Powell Symphony Hall at Grand Center

SAINT LOUIS SYMPHONY ORCHESTRA
Powell Symphony Hall, 718 North Grand Boulevard, Saint Louis, MO 63103
(314) 533-2500
   Founded: 1879
   Arts Area: Symphony
   Status: Professional; Non-Profit
   Type: Performing; Touring; Educational
   Management: Bruce Coppock, Executive Director
   Officers: Thomas H. Jacobsen, Chairman
   Paid Staff: 73   **Volunteer Staff:** 2,500
   Utilizes: Guest Conductors; Guest Artists
   Budget: Over 10,000,000
   Income Sources: Private Foundations/Grants/Endowments; Business/Corporate Donations; Box Office; Government Grants; Individual Donations
   Season: September - August
   Performance Facilities: Powell Symphony Hall at Grand Center

SAINT LOUIS SYMPHONY YOUTH ORCHESTRA
Powell Symphony Hall, 718 North Grand Boulevard, Saint Louis, MO 63103
(314) 533-2500
Founded: 1970
Arts Area: Symphony; Orchestra; Chamber
Status: Non-Professional; Non-Profit
Type: Performing; Touring; Educational; Sponsoring
Purpose: The Saint Louis Symphony Youth Orchestra was founded in 1970 by Leonard Slatkin to acquaint young instrumentalists with the atmosphere of a professional orchestra, to introduce them to the environment of the Saint Louis Symphony and to provide them with the opportunity of investigating and performing a wide spectrum of symphonic music.
Management: Margaret Neilson, Manager; David Loebel, Music Director; Leonard Slatkin, Music Advisor
Officers: Mrs. Matthew F. Mayer, Youth Orchestra Committee Chairman
Paid Staff: 2
Non-Paid Artists: 100
Utilizes: Guest Artists
Budget: $1,000 - $50,000
Income Sources: Private Foundations/Grants/Endowments; Business/Corporate Donations; Box Office; Individual Donations
Season: September - May   **Annual Attendance:** 3,500
Affiliations: ASOL (Youth Orchestra Division)
Performance Facilities: Powell Symphony Hall at Grand Center

SYNCHRONIA
PO Box 2937, Saint Louis, MO 63130
(314) 664-9313
Founded: 1985
Arts Area: Ensemble
Status: Professional; Non-Profit
Type: Performing; Touring; Educational
Purpose: To perform and promote recent art music with emphasis on the United States and living composers of the past 25 years
Officers: Timothy Vincent Clark, Music Director
Paid Staff: 1   **Volunteer Staff:** 1
Paid Artists: 6
Utilizes: Guest Artists
Budget: $50,000 - $100,000
Season: September - May   **Annual Attendance:** 1,000
Performance Facilities: Ethical Society

VOCAL MUSIC

OPERA THEATRE OF SAINT LOUIS
539 Garden Avenue, PO Box 19110, Saint Louis, MO 63119
(314) 961-0171
FAX: (314) 961-7463
Founded: 1964
Arts Area: Grand Opera; Lyric Opera; Light Opera; Operetta
Status: Non-Profit
Type: Performing; Touring; Educational
Purpose: To present opera in English affording career advancement of young American singers under direction of renowned directors and conductors
Management: Charles R. MacKay, General Director; Colin Graham, Artistic Director; Stephen Lord, Music Director; Jeff Thurston, Business Manager
Officers: Mrs. Monte Throdahl, Chairman; Donald Bryant Jr. and William B. McMillan Jr., Vice Chairmen; Robert L. Scharff Jr., Secretary; Reuben M. Morriss, III, Treasurer
Paid Staff: 15
Paid Artists: 90
Utilizes: Special Technical Talent; Guest Conductors; Guest Artists; Guest Directors
Budget: $1,000,000 - $5,000,000
Income Sources: Private Foundations/Grants/Endowments; Business/Corporate Donations; Box Office; Government Grants; Individual Donations
Season: May - June   **Annual Attendance:** 24,000
Performance Facilities: Loretto-Hilton Center for the Performing Arts; Webster University

SAINT LOUIS CHAMBER CHORUS
PO Box 11558, Saint Louis, MO 63105
(314) 458-4343
Founded: 1957

Arts Area: Choral
Status: Professional; Non-Profit
Type: Performing; Educational
Purpose: To present in concert choral works of unusual rarely performed music by outstanding composers, usually a cappela
Management: Board of Directors; Sally Jones, Executive Director; Philip Barnes, Music Director
Officers: Alfred O. Heitzmann, President; O.L. Lippard, Vice President; Barbara Boland, Secretary; M. Mark McCallum, Treasurer
Paid Staff: 2
Paid Artists: 40
Budget: $1,000 - $50,000
Income Sources: Private Foundations/Grants/Endowments; Business/Corporate Donations; Box Office; Government Grants; Individual Donations
Season: September - May   **Annual Attendance:** 1,500

SAINT LOUIS SYMPHONY CHORUS
718 North Grand Boulevard, Saint Louis, MO 63104
(314) 533-2500
FAX: (314) 533-6000
Founded: 1977
Arts Area: Choral
Status: Professional; Non-Professional; Non-Profit
Type: Performing; Touring; Educational
Purpose: To perform orchestral works involving chorus
Management: Richard Ashburner, Manager; Thomas Peck, Chorus Director; Alan Freed, Assistant Director; Barbara Liberman, Accompanist
Officers: Thomas H. Jacobsen, Chairman of the Board; Richard R. Hoffert, Acting Executive Director; Leon R. Strauss, Secretary; W.L. Hadley Griffin, Vice Chairman Development; Mrs. William W. Scott, Vice Chairman Affiliates and Artistic; Michale F. Neidorff, Vice Chairman Public Affairs
Paid Staff: 4
Paid Artists: 26   **Non-Paid Artists:** 114
Utilizes: Guest Conductors; Guest Artists
Budget: $100,000 - $500,000
Income Sources: Private Foundations/Grants/Endowments; Business/Corporate Donations; Box Office; Government Grants; Individual Donations
Season: September - May   **Annual Attendance:** 32,000
Affiliations: CA
Performance Facilities: Powell Symphony Hall
Income Sources: Private Foundations/Grants/Endowments; Business/Corporate Donations; Box Office; Government Grants; Individual Donations

THEATRE

CIRCUS ARTS FOUNDATION OF MISSOURI
634 North Grand Boulevard, Suite 1029, Saint Louis, MO 63103
(314) 531-6273
FAX: (314) 533-3345
Founded: 1988
Arts Area: Professional
Status: Non-Profit
Type: Performing; Touring; Educational
Purpose: To create and foster an artistic, enlightening and joyous circus
Management: Judy Pierson, Executive Director; Ivor David Balding, Artistic Director/Producer; Maria Atchison, Administrative Assistant; Jessica Hentoff, School Director
Officers: A.R. Naunheim, President; Harry Wuertenbaecher, Vice President; Eddie G. Davis, Treasurer; Judy C. Pierson, Secretary
Paid Staff: 3   **Volunteer Staff:** 3
Utilizes: Guest Artists
Budget: $500,000 - $1,000,000
Income Sources: Private Foundations/Grants/Endowments; Business/Corporate Donations; Box Office; Government Grants; Individual Donations
Season: May - October   **Annual Attendance:** 42,000
Performance Facilities: The Jewell Tent

METRO THEATER COMPANY/THE CENTER FOR CREATIVE ARTS
524 Trinity, Saint Louis, MO 63130
(314) 727-3552
Founded: 1973
Arts Area: Professional; Theatrical Group

Status: Professional; Non-Profit
Type: Performing; Touring; Resident; Educational
Purpose: To tour live theater for young people and families; to stimulate interest and participation in the creative arts
Management: Carol Evans, Producing Director; Kitty Daly, Marketing Director
Officers: Philip Moses, President; Mary Ellen Finch, Vice President; John Weil, Secretary/Treasurer
Paid Staff: 3
Paid Artists: 7
Utilizes: Guest Artists
Budget: $100,000 - $500,000
Income Sources: Private Foundations/Grants/Endowments; Business/Corporate Donations; Individual Donations
Season: October - June   **Annual Attendance:** 90,000
Affiliations: ASSITEJ; Missouri Citizens for the Arts

THE NEW THEATRE
634 North Grand Boulevard, Suite 10-C, Saint Louis, MO 63103
(314) 531-8330
FAX: (314) 533-3345
Founded: 1985
Arts Area: Professional; Theatrical Group
Status: Professional; Non-Profit
Type: Performing
Purpose: To provide innovative professional theatre in accessible locations for Saint Louis audiences
Management: Agnes Wilcox, Artistic Director; Amy Allen, Production Manager; Dean Minderman, Director of Public Relations and Marketing; Joan Duggan, Office Manager
Officers: DeLancey Smith, President; Suzanne Couch, Vice President; James F. O'Donnell, Treasurer; Agnes Wilcox, Secretary
Paid Staff: 4
Paid Artists: 75
Utilizes: Special Technical Talent; Guest Artists; Guest Directors
Budget: $100,000 - $500,000
Income Sources: Private Foundations/Grants/Endowments; Business/Corporate Donations; Box Office; Government Grants; Individual Donations
Season: October - July   **Annual Attendance:** 4,500
Affiliations: TCG; League of Saint Louis Theatres

THE REPERTORY THEATRE OF SAINT LOUIS
130 Edgar Road, Saint Louis, MO 63119
(314) 968-7340
Founded: 1966
Arts Area: Professional; Theatrical Group
Status: Professional
Type: Performing
Management: Steven Woolf, Artistic Director
Officers: Gretta Forrester, Board President
Paid Staff: 35
Paid Artists: 65
Utilizes: Special Technical Talent; Guest Artists; Guest Directors
Budget: $1,000,000 - $5,000,000
Income Sources: Private Foundations/Grants/Endowments; Business/Corporate Donations; Box Office; Government Grants; Individual Donations
Season: September - April   **Annual Attendance:** 100,000
Affiliations: AEA; SSDC; AFM; IATSE
Performance Facilities: Loretto-Hilton Center for the Performing Arts (Webster University)

SAINT LOUIS BLACK REPERTORY COMPANY
634 North Grand, Saint Louis, MO 63103
(314) 534-3807
FAX: (314) 533-3345
Founded: 1976
Arts Area: Professional; Musical; Community; Theatrical Group
Status: Professional; Non-Profit
Type: Performing; Touring; Educational; Sponsoring
Purpose: We are committed to providing quality Black Theatre to the Saint Louis area
Management: Ron Himes, Producing Director; Donna Adams, General Manager
Officers: Arthur D. Jordan, Chairman; Charles Polk, Vice Chairman; Stephen M. Coleman, Treasurer; Susan Corcoran, Secretary
Paid Staff: 9   **Volunteer Staff:** 5
Paid Artists: 55
Utilizes: Special Technical Talent; Guest Artists; Guest Directors

Budget: $500,000 - $1,000,000
Income Sources: Private Foundations/Grants/Endowments; Business/Corporate Donations; Box Office; Government Grants; Individual Donations
Season: September - June **Annual Attendance:** 15,000
Affiliations: TCG; AEA
Performance Facilities: Grandel Square Theatre

THEATER FACTORY SAINT LOUIS
4265 Shaw Avenue, Saint Louis, MO 63110
(314) 773-8880
Founded: 1982
Arts Area: Professional; Summer Stock; Theatrical Group
Status: Professional
Type: Performing; Educational
Management: Earl D. Weaver, Managing Director; Hope Wurdack, Artistic Director; Cindy Vahle, Business Manager
Officers: William Leith, President; Marie Brauer, Vice President; Cathy Coughlin, Secretary; Karen Herman, Treasurer; Mary Pat Blake, Marketing
Paid Staff: 3
Utilizes: Special Technical Talent; Guest Conductors; Guest Artists; Guest Directors; Musical Directors
Budget: $100,000 - $500,000
Income Sources: Private Foundations/Grants/Endowments; Business/Corporate Donations; Box Office; Government Grants; Individual Donations
Season: June - September **Annual Attendance:** 15,000
Affiliations: League of St. Louis Theatres

PERFORMING SERIES

BLACK MUSIC SOCIETY OF MISSOURI
3701 Grandel Square, Saint Louis, MO 63108
(314) 534-4344
Founded: 1984
Arts Area: Vocal Music; Instrumental Music; Festivals
Status: Professional; Semi-Professional; Non-Profit
Type: Performing; Touring; Resident; Educational; Sponsoring
Purpose: To preserve and promote Black America's musical heritage
Management: Prince A. Wells, Music Director
Officers: Prince A. Wells, III, President; Sheryl Jones, Vice President; Patricia Wilson, Secretary; Shirley Richardson, Treasurer
Paid Staff: 1 **Volunteer Staff:** 3
Paid Artists: 12
Utilizes: Guest Conductors; Guest Artists; Guest Directors
Budget: $1,000 - $50,000
Income Sources: Business/Corporate Donations; Box Office; Government Grants; Individual Donations
Season: 52 Weeks

CITICORP SUMMERFEST
Powell Symphony Hall, 718 North Grand Boulevard, Saint Louis, MO 63103
(314) 533-2500
Founded: 1984
Arts Area: Instrumental Music
Status: Professional; Non-Profit
Type: Performing
Management: Leonard Slatkin, Music Director/Conductor
Paid Staff: 15 **Volunteer Staff:** 50
Paid Artists: 101
Utilizes: Guest Conductors; Guest Artists
Income Sources: Business/Corporate Donations; Box Office; Government Grants; Individual Donations
Season: May - June **Annual Attendance:** 8,000
Affiliations: Saint Louis Symphony Orchestra
Performance Facilities: Powell Symphony Hall At Grand Center

EDISON THEATRE AT WASHINGTON UNIVERSITY
Campus Box 1119, One Brookings Drive, Saint Louis, MO 63130
(314) 935-6518
FAX: (314) 935-7362
Founded: 1973
Arts Area: Dance; Vocal Music; Instrumental Music; Theater
Status: Professional; Non-Profit
Type: Performing; Touring; Educational; Sponsoring; Presenting

Purpose: To present three annual series of national and international artists and companies in dance, theatre, music and other arts
Management: Evy Warshawski, Managing Director; Charles Robin, Operations Manager.
Paid Staff: 4   **Volunteer Staff:** 75
Utilizes: Guest Artists
Budget: $100,000 - $500,000
Income Sources: Private Foundations/Grants/Endowments; Business/Corporate Donations; Box Office; Government Grants; Individual Donations
Season: September - May
Annual Attendance: 45,000
Performance Facilities: Edison Theatre; Mallinckrodt Drama Studio

MUNICIPAL THEATER ASSOCIATION OF SAINT LOUIS
Forest Park, Saint Louis, MO 63112
(314) 361-1900
FAX: (314) 361-0009
    Founded: 1919
    Arts Area: Theater
    Status: Professional; Non-Profit
    Type: Performing; Educational
    Purpose: THE MUNY, 'Alone in its Greatness,' is the largest musical theatre in the country performing self-produced and touring shows 7 nights a week, run on the star system.
    Management: Dennis M. Reagan, General Manager/CEO
    Utilizes: Special Technical Talent; Guest Conductors; Guest Artists; Guest Directors
    Budget: $1,000,000 - $5,000,000
    Income Sources: Business/Corporate Donations; Box Office; Individual Donations
    Season: 52 Weeks
    Affiliations: NAMTP; Arts & Education Council of Greater Saint Louis
    Performance Facilities: THE MUNY, Forest Park

SAINT LOUIS SYMPHONY QUEENY POPS
Powell Symphony Hall, 718 North Grand Boulevard, Saint Louis, MO 63103
(314) 533-2500
FAX: (314) 533-6000
    Founded: 1975
    Arts Area: Vocal Music; Instrumental Music
    Status: Professional; Non-Profit
    Type: Performing
    Management: Richard Hayman, McDonnell Douglas Principal Pops Conductor; Sam Dixon, Director of Artistic Planning
    Paid Staff: 15   **Volunteer Staff:** 50
    Paid Artists: 101
    Utilizes: Guest Conductors; Guest Artists
    Income Sources: Business/Corporate Donations; Box Office; Government Grants
    Season: June - August
    Annual Attendance: 8,000
    Affiliations: Saint Louis Symphony Orchestra
    Performance Facilities: Greensfelder Recreation Center in Queeny Park

FACILITY

AMERICAN THEATRE
416 North Ninth Street, Saint Louis, MO 63101-1470
(314) 231-7000
    Type of Facility: Concert Hall; Theatre House
    Facility Originally: Vaudeville
    Type of Stage: Proscenium
    Seating Capacity: 1,853
    Year Built: 1918
    Year Remodeled: 1985   **Cost:** $175,000
    Contact for Rental: Karen McCrory;   (314) 231-7000
    Resident Groups: Municipal Theater Association of Saint Louis

ETHICAL SOCIETY AUDITORIUM
9001 Clayton Road, Saint Louis, MO 63117
(314) 991-0955
    Type of Facility: Auditorium
    Facility Originally: Lecture Hall
    Type of Stage: Platform

Seating Capacity: 450
Year Built: 1960   **Architect:** Harris Armstrong
Contact for Rental: John Hoad, Leader;   (314) 991-0955

THE FABULOUS FOX THEATRE
Grand Center, 527 North Grand Boulevard, Saint Louis, MO 63103
(314) 534-1678
Type of Facility: Performance Center; Theatre House
Facility Originally: Movie House
Type of Stage: Proscenium
Stage Dimensions: 125'Wx35'5"D; 78'Wx32'H proscenium opening   **Orchestra Pit**
Seating Capacity: 4,299
Year Built: 1929   **Architect:** C. Howard Crane   **Cost:** $6,000,000
Year Remodeled: 1982   **Cost:** $2,000,000
Contact for Rental: Fox Productions;   (314) 534-1678
Manager: David R. Fay
Resident Groups: Fox Productions; Dance St. Louis
Now listed on the National Register of Historic Places, the Fox Theatre was the second largest movie palace in the nation with 5,060 seats when it was built in 1929.

THE KIEL CENTER
100 North Broadway, Saint Louis, MO 63102
(314) 466-4649
FAX: (314) 466-4660
Type of Facility: Performance Center; Multi-Purpose
Year Built: 1932   **Cost:** $7,000,000
Contact for Rental: Christine Cool;   (314) 466-4649
Resident Groups: Dance Saint Louis; Saint Louis Philharmonic
Contains Arena and Opera House. See separate listings for additional information.

THE KIEL CENTER - ARENA
100 North Broadway, Suite 820, Saint Louis, MO 63102
(314) 466-4649
FAX: (314) 466-4660
Type of Facility: Concert Hall; Auditorium; Studio Performance; Arena; Multi-Purpose
Type of Stage: Proscenium; Hydraulic Lift Stage
Stage Dimensions: 95'Wx48'D; 67'W proscenium opening   **Orchestra Pit**
Seating Capacity: 10,500
Contact for Rental: Christine Cool;   (314) 466-4649
12'Dx80'W Hydraulic Lift Pit

THE KIEL CENTER - OPERA HOUSE
100 North Broadway, Suite 820, Saint Louis, MO 63102
(314) 466-4649
FAX: (314) 466-4660
Type of Facility: Concert Hall; Theatre House; Opera House
Type of Stage: Thrust; Proscenium; Hydraulic Lift Stage
Stage Dimensions: 63'Wx56'D; 63'W proscenium opening   **Orchestra Pit**
Seating Capacity: 3,500
Contact for Rental: Christine Cool;   (314) 466-4649
Resident Groups: Saint Louis Philharmonic; Dance Saint Louis
12'Dx63'W Hydraulic Lift Pit

THE MUNY
Forest Park, Saint Louis, MO 63112
(314) 361-1900
FAX: (314) 361-0009
Type of Facility: Outdoor (Concert); Amphitheater
Type of Stage: Proscenium; Environmental
Stage Dimensions: 90'Wx60'D with a 48' diameter turntable   **Orchestra Pit**
Seating Capacity: 12,000
Year Built: 1917
Resident Groups: Municipal Theater Association of Saint Louis

POWELL SYMPHONY HALL AT GRAND CENTER
718 North Grand Boulevard, Saint Louis, MO 63103
(314) 533-2500
Type of Facility: Concert Hall

Facility Originally: Vaudeville
Type of Stage: Proscenium; Concert Shell
Stage Dimensions: 65'6"Wx43'4"D
Seating Capacity: 2,777
Year Built: 1920   **Architect:** Rapp & Rapp
Year Remodeled: 1963   **Architect:** Angelo Corrubia   **Cost:** $2,000,000
Acoustical Consultant: Dr. Cyril Harris
Contact for Rental: Christine Wagnon;   (314) 533-2500
Resident Groups: Saint Louis Symphony Orchestra; Saint Louis Youth Orchestra

SHELDON CONCERT HALL AND BALLROOM
3648 Washington Avenue, Saint Louis, MO 63108
(314) 533-9900
FAX: (314) 533-2958
Founded: 1912
Type of Facility: Concert Hall; Performance Center; Multi-Purpose; Room; Loft
Facility Originally: Meeting Hall
Type of Stage: Thrust; Flexible; Platform
Stage Dimensions: Concert Hall - 13'x24' expandable; Ballroom - 19'x19' proscenium open
Seating Capacity: Main Hall - ,850; Ballroom - 414
Year Built: 1912   **Architect:** Louis C. Spiering   **Cost:** $300,000
Year Remodeled: 1986   **Architect:** Walter F. Gunn, Supervisor   **Cost:** $1,600,000
Acoustical Consultant: Walter F. Gunn
Contact for Rental: Jane Teichman;   (314) 533-9900
Resident Groups: Opera Theater of St. Louis; Premier Performances; Washington University; New Music Circle; River Styx; Endangered Arts Foundation

WASHINGTON UNIVERSITY - EDISON THEATRE
Mallinckrodt Center, Campus Box 1119, Saint Louis, MO 63130
(314) 935-6543
Type of Facility: Auditorium; Performance Center
Type of Stage: Flexible; Proscenium
Stage Dimensions: 32'Dx40'W upstage; 80'W downstage   **Orchestra Pit**
Seating Capacity: 656
Year Built: 1973   **Architect:** Robert Vickery; Smith & Entzeroth Architects
Acoustical Consultant: Ned Lustig, Theatre Consultant
Contact for Rental: Charlie Robin, Operations Director
Manager: Anne Yard
The Performing Arts Center of Washington University

WEBSTER UNIVERSITY-LORETTO - HILTON CENTER FOR THE PERFORMING ARTS
130 Edgar Road, Saint Louis, MO 63119
(314) 968-6933
Type of Facility: Theatre House
Type of Stage: Thrust
Orchestra Pit
Seating Capacity: 952
Year Built: 1965   **Architect:** Murphy & Mackey   **Cost:** $2,000,000
Acoustical Consultant: Bolt, Beranek & Newman; George C. Izenour Associates
Contact for Rental: Arthur L. Lueking, Director;   (314) 968-6933
Resident Groups: Repertory Theatre of Saint Louis; Opera Theatre of Saint Louis; Conservatory of Theatre Arts; Webster University; Metropolitan Orchestra of Saint Louis

Sedalia

INSTRUMENTAL MUSIC

SCOTT JOPLIN RAGTIME FESTIVAL
113 East Fourth Street, Sedalia, MO 65301
(816) 826-2271
Founded: 1974
Arts Area: Orchestra; Ensemble; Instrumental Group; Electronic & Live Electronic; Band
Status: Non-Profit
Type: Performing; Educational
Purpose: To bring the historical and aesthetic value of Scott Joplin and ragtime music to a greater variety of people and to enrich our understanding
Management: John Moore, Festival Coordinator; Julie Renberg, Executive Secretary
Officers: John Moore, President

Paid Staff: 2 **Volunteer Staff:** 30
Utilizes: Special Technical Talent; Guest Artists
Budget: $50,000 - $100,000
Income Sources: Private Foundations/Grants/Endowments; Business/Corporate Donations; Box Office; Individual Donations
Season: June 4 - June 7 **Annual Attendance:** 1,500

THEATRE

LIBERTY CENTER
111 West Fifth, Sedalia, MO 65301
(816) 827-3228
Founded: 1981
Arts Area: Professional; Musical; Dinner; Community; Folk; Theatrical Group; Puppet
Status: Professional; Non-Professional; Non-Profit
Type: Performing; Touring; Educational; Sponsoring
Purpose: To promote the Arts and activities which encourage the cultural growth of the community
Management: Patti McFatrich, Administrator
Officers: Don Buller, President; Carla Eding, Vice President; Debbie Klatt, Secretary; Chris Spangler, Treasurer
Paid Staff: 3 **Volunteer Staff:** 24
Paid Artists: 20 **Non-Paid Artists:** 100
Utilizes: Special Technical Talent; Guest Artists
Budget: $50,000 - $100,000
Income Sources: Business/Corporate Donations; Box Office; Government Grants; Individual Donations
Season: 52 Weeks **Annual Attendance:** 8,000
Performance Facilities: Liberty Center

Sikeston

THEATRE

SIKESTON LITTLE THEATRE
PO Box 126, Sikeston, MO 63801
(314) 471-6888
Founded: 1959
Arts Area: Musical; Community; Theatrical Group
Status: Non-Professional; Non-Profit
Type: Performing; Resident
Purpose: Promote theatrical arts for the Sikeston area and provide educational experience for students in theatre
Management: Lynn A. Colley, Administrator
Officers: Lynn A. Colley, President; Jim Wenneker, Vice President; Connie Thompson, Secretary; Electa O'Hara, Treasurer
Paid Staff: 1 **Volunteer Staff:** 15
Non-Paid Artists: 150
Budget: $1,000 - $50,000
Income Sources: Business/Corporate Donations; Box Office; Government Grants; Individual Donations
Season: July - June **Annual Attendance:** 3,000
Affiliations: Missouri Community Theatre Association
Performance Facilities: Chaney-Harris Cultural Center

Springfield

DANCE

SPRINGFIELD BALLET
305 East Walnut, Suite 301, Springfield, MO 65806-2300
(417) 862-1343
FAX: (417) 869-7815
Founded: 1976
Arts Area: Modern; Ballet; Jazz; Tap
Status: Non-Professional; Non-Profit
Type: Performing; Educational; Sponsoring
Purpose: To educate students and the public in techniques of dance; to perform at the highest possible level; to present guest dance companies
Management: Louis H. Schaeffer, Executive Director; Mark Rhodes, Artistic Director
Officers: J. Howard Schwartz, President; Brent Dunn, President Elect; Jack Weimer, Treasurer; Sherry Hopkins, Recording Secretary; Betty Luckie, Corresponding Secretary

Paid Staff: 9 **Volunteer Staff:** 8
Paid Artists: 43 **Non-Paid Artists:** 12
Utilizes: Special Technical Talent; Guest Artists; Guest Directors
Budget: $100,000 - $500,000
Income Sources: Private Foundations/Grants/Endowments; Business/Corporate Donations; Box Office; Government Grants; Individual Donations
Season: October - May **Annual Attendance:** 5,200
Performance Facilities: Landers Theatre, Vandivort Center; Hammons Hall for the Performing Arts

INSTRUMENTAL MUSIC

SPRINGFIELD SYMPHONY ASSOCIATION
1536 East Division, Springfield, MO 65803
(417) 864-6683
FAX: (417) 864-8967
    Founded: 1934
    Arts Area: Symphony
    Status: Semi-Professional
    Type: Performing
    Purpose: To recreate, with the highest possible degree of artistic and historical integrity, the body of orchestral literature from 1700 to present
    Management: Dana C. Randall, Executive Director; Charles Bontrager, Conductor
    Officers: Patricia LeFevre, President; Barbara Brian, Secretary; John Owens, Treasurer
    Paid Staff: 6 **Volunteer Staff:** 50
    Paid Artists: 80
    Utilizes: Special Technical Talent; Guest Conductors; Guest Artists; Guest Directors
    Budget: $100,000 - $500,000
    Income Sources: Private Foundations/Grants/Endowments; Business/Corporate Donations; Box Office; Government Grants; Individual Donations
    Season: September - May **Annual Attendance:** 16,000
    Affiliations: ASOL; Missouri Arts Council
    Performance Facilities: Juanita K. Hammons Hall for the Performing Arts

VOCAL MUSIC

SPRINGFIELD REGIONAL OPERA
305 East Walnut, Springfield, MO 65806
(417) 869-1960
FAX: (417) 869-7815
    Founded: 1979
    Arts Area: Grand Opera; Lyric Opera; Light Opera; Operetta
    Status: Professional; Non-Profit
    Type: Performing
    Purpose: To perform opera and musical theatre; to bring these performances to the southwest Missouri region; to offer young American singers an opportunity to perform and further their careers
    Management: James Billings, Managing Artistic/Administrative Director
    Paid Staff: 2
    Paid Artists: 8 **Non-Paid Artists:** 8
    Utilizes: Special Technical Talent; Guest Conductors; Guest Artists; Guest Directors
    Budget: $50,000 - $100,000
    Income Sources: Private Foundations/Grants/Endowments; Business/Corporate Donations; Box Office; Government Grants; Individual Donations
    Season: October - March
    Affiliations: OA

THEATRE

SPRINGFIELD LITTLE THEATRE
311 East Walnut, Springfield, MO 65806
(417) 869-3869
    Founded: 1934
    Arts Area: Musical; Dinner; Community; Theatrical Group; Puppet
    Status: Non-Professional; Non-Profit
    Type: Performing; Educational; Sponsoring
    Purpose: To bring live performances to Southwest Missourians
    Management: E. M. Denniston, Managing/Artistic Director; Kay Hamilton, Business Manager; Dorothy Lemmon, Education Director; Lisa Kristek, Development Director
    Officers: Art Luebke, President; Steve Sheppard, Vice President; Dan Busch, Secretary; David Hayes, Treasurer
    Paid Staff: 6 **Volunteer Staff:** 300

Paid Artists: 100 **Non-Paid Artists:** 200
Utilizes: Special Technical Talent; Guest Conductors; Guest Artists; Guest Directors
Budget: $100,000 - $500,000
Income Sources: Private Foundations/Grants/Endowments; Business/Corporate Donations; Box Office; Government Grants; Individual Donations
Season: September - July **Annual Attendance:** 50,000
Performance Facilities: Landers Theatre

FACILITY

LANDERS THEATRE
311 East Walnut, Springfield, MO 65806
(417) 869-3869
  Type of Facility: Auditorium; Theatre House; Opera House
  Facility Originally: Vaudeville
  Type of Stage: Proscenium
  Orchestra Pit
  Seating Capacity: 679
  Year Built: 1909 **Architect:** Carl Boller **Cost:** $100,000
  Year Remodeled: 1985 **Architect:** Galen Pellham **Cost:** $400,000
  Acoustical Consultant: Sounds Great
  Contact for Rental: E. M. Denniston; (417) 869-3869
  Resident Groups: Springfield Little Theatre

Tarkio

PERFORMING SERIES

MULE BARN THEATRE OF TARKIO COLLEGE
PO Box 114, 224 Main Street, Tarkio, MO 64491
(816) 736-4185
  Founded: 1967
  Arts Area: Theater
  Status: Professional; Non-Profit
  Type: Performing
  Purpose: To provide cultural and educational enrichment for the area featuring the American musical and children's theatre, theatre for the area residents and training for young professionals in theatre
  Paid Staff: 20
  Paid Artists: 30 **Non-Paid Artists:** 15
  Utilizes: Special Technical Talent; Guest Artists; Guest Directors
  Budget: $100,000 - $500,000
  Income Sources: Business/Corporate Donations; Box Office; Government Grants; Individual Donations
  Season: June - August **Annual Attendance:** 15,000
  Performance Facilities: Mule Barn Theatre

FACILITY

MULE BARN THEATRE
224 Main, Tarkio, MO 64491
(816) 736-4185
  Type of Facility: Theatre House
  Facility Originally: Barn
  Type of Stage: Thrust
  Seating Capacity: 212
  Year Built: 1892
  Year Remodeled: 1967 **Cost:** $30,000
  Manager: Wesley Van Tassel

Versailles

THEATRE

THE ROYAL ARTS COUNCIL
South Monroe Street, PO Box 273, Versailles, MO 65084
(314) 378-6226
  Founded: 1984
  Arts Area: Musical; Community; Theatrical Group

Status: Non-Professional; Non-Profit
Type: Performing; Educational; Sponsoring
Purpose: The performance, promotion, organization, and sponsorship of arts activities in the City of Versailles, Missouri
Management: Richard Elliott, Executive Director
Officers: Duane Miller, President; Emma Dornan, Vice President; David Baumgartner, Treasurer; Nancy Petersen, Secretary
Paid Staff: 1   **Volunteer Staff:** 5
Paid Artists: 3   **Non-Paid Artists:** 100
Utilizes: Special Technical Talent; Guest Artists; Guest Directors
Budget: $1,000 - $50,000
Income Sources: Private Foundations/Grants/Endowments; Business/Corporate Donations; Box Office; Government Grants; Individual Donations
Season: 52 Weeks   **Annual Attendance:** 4,000
Performance Facilities: Royal Theatre

MONTANA

Bigfork

FACILITY

BIGFORK CENTER FOR THE PERFORMING ARTS
PO Box 1230, Bigfork, MT 59911
(406) 837-4885
Type of Facility: Concert Hall; Auditorium; Performance Center; Theatre House
Type of Stage: Thrust; Proscenium
Stage Dimensions: 28'x32' **Orchestra Pit**
Seating Capacity: 435
Year Built: 1988 **Architect:** Wayne Whitney **Cost:** $750,000
Acoustical Consultant: Lee Irvine
Contact for Rental: General Manager; (406) 837-4885

Billings

INSTRUMENTAL MUSIC

BILLINGS SYMPHONY SOCIETY
PO Box 7055, Billings, MT 59103
(406) 252-3610
Founded: 1951
Arts Area: Symphony; Orchestra
Status: Semi-Professional; Non-Profit
Type: Performing
Purpose: To present live symphonic music to the community and the region
Management: Dr. Uri Barnea, Music Director; Lynn Jordan, Chorale Director; Maxine Pihlaja, General Manager
Officers: David Hummel, President
Paid Staff: 4 **Volunteer Staff:** 1
Paid Artists: 8
Utilizes: Guest Conductors; Guest Artists
Budget: $100,000 - $500,000
Income Sources: Private Foundations/Grants/Endowments; Business/Corporate Donations; Box Office; Government Grants; Individual Donations
Season: September - April **Annual Attendance:** 20,000
Affiliations: ASOL; Montana Association of Symphony Orchestras
Performance Facilities: The Alberta Bair Theater for the Performing Arts

YELLOWSTONE CHAMBER PLAYERS
1204 Rimhaven Way, Billings, MT 59102
(406) 248-2205
Founded: 1980
Arts Area: Chamber; Ensemble; Instrumental Group
Status: Professional; Non-Profit
Type: Performing; Touring; Resident
Purpose: To perform a wide variety of chamber music, from string quartets and piano quintets to small ensembles employing clarinet, flute and guitar
Management: Dr. Daniel Johnson, Publicity Manager; Elizabeth Adcock, Tour Director; Caron Schultz, Ticket Manager
Officers: Caron Schultz, President; Mary LaMonaca, Vice President; Joanne Solberg, Secretary; Ramona Turnbull, Treasurer; Janet Keating, Mike Peterson, Board Members
Volunteer Staff: 15
Paid Artists: 14
Budget: $1,000 - $50,000
Income Sources: Private Foundations/Grants/Endowments; Business/Corporate Donations; Box Office; Government Grants; Individual Donations
Season: 52 Weeks **Annual Attendance:** 2,000
Affiliations: Yellowstone Art Center

FACILITY

THE ALBERTA BAIR THEATER FOR THE PERFORMING ARTS
PO Box 1556, Billings, MT 59103
(406) 256-8915
    Type of Facility: Theatre House
    Facility Originally: Vaudeville
    Type of Stage: Proscenium
    Stage Dimensions: 54'Wx30'D   **Orchestra Pit**
    Seating Capacity: 1,416
    Year Built: 1931   **Architect:** Charles Renner
    Year Remodeled: 1986   **Architect:** Richard F. McCann   **Cost:** $5,300,000
    Contact for Rental: Barry Bonifas;   (406) 256-8915
    Resident Groups: Billings Symphony Orchestra

Bozeman

DANCE

MONTANA BALLET COMPANY
PO Box 6021, Bozeman, MT 59771-6021
(406) 587-7192
    Founded: 1983
    Arts Area: Modern; Ballet; Jazz
    Status: Professional; Non-Profit
    Type: Performing; Touring; Educational; Sponsoring
    Purpose: To provide affordable workshops and performance tours to rural communities throughout the western region; We offer New York Connection (NYCB dancers and teachers) and The Nutcracker annually.
    Management: Ann Bates, Artistic Director; Joan Chadwick, Business Manager
    Officers: Dianne Lorang, President; Susan Ledbetter, Vice President; Leslee Finck, Secretary
    Paid Staff: 2   **Volunteer Staff:** 100
    Paid Artists: 20   **Non-Paid Artists:** 6
    Utilizes: Guest Artists; Guest Choreographers; Guest Teachers
    Budget: $1,000 - $50,000
    Income Sources: Private Foundations/Grants/Endowments; Business/Corporate Donations; Box Office; Government Grants; Individual Donations
    Season: 52 Weeks   **Annual Attendance:** 6,000
    Affiliations: Montana Ballet Studio
    Performance Facilities: Willson Auditorium

INSTRUMENTAL MUSIC

BOZEMAN SYMPHONY ORCHESTRA
104 East Main, #101, Bozeman, MT 59715
(406) 585-9774
FAX: (406) 585-5293
    Founded: 1968
    Arts Area: Symphony; Orchestra
    Status: Non-Professional; Non-Profit
    Type: Performing; Resident; Sponsoring
    Purpose: To support performance of symphonic and choral music by a resident orchestra and choir
    Management: Elizabeth Sellers, Music Director/Conductor; Patricia McNamer, Business Manager; Lowell Hickman, Choir Director
    Officers: Sharon Tudor, President; Robyn Erlenbush, Vice President; John E. Taylor, Secretary
    Paid Staff: 3
    Paid Artists: 2   **Non-Paid Artists:** 55
    Utilizes: Guest Conductors; Guest Artists
    Budget: $50,000 - $100,000
    Income Sources: Private Foundations/Grants/Endowments; Business/Corporate Donations; Box Office; Government Grants; Individual Donations
    Season: September - April   **Annual Attendance:** 5,000
    Performance Facilities: Willson Auditorium

VOCAL MUSIC

INTERMOUNTAIN OPERA COMPANY
PO Box 37, Bozeman, MT 59715
(406) 587-1603; (406) 587-5589
> **Founded:** 1978
> **Arts Area:** Grand Opera; Light Opera
> **Status:** Professional; Non-Profit
> **Type:** Performing; Educational; Sponsoring
> **Purpose:** To introduce and involve young audiences of Montana in opera by producing operatic works and sponsoring education opportunities
> **Management:** Pablo Elvira, Artistic Director; Robert Stivanello, Producer
> **Officers:** Marilyn Hathaway, President
> **Volunteer Staff:** 12
> **Paid Artists:** 85
> **Utilizes:** Guest Artists
> **Budget:** $50,000 - $100,000
> **Income Sources:** Business/Corporate Donations; Box Office; Individual Donations
> **Season:** May   **Annual Attendance:** 2,000
> **Performance Facilities:** Willson Auditorium

THEATRE

VIGILANTE THEATRE COMPANY
PO Box 507, Bozeman, MT 59771-0507
(406) 994-5884
FAX: (406) 586-3732
> **Founded:** 1981
> **Arts Area:** Professional; Dinner; Theatrical Group
> **Status:** Professional; Non-Profit
> **Type:** Performing; Touring; Educational
> **Purpose:** To stimulate, cultivate and promote interest in theatre; to tour original, professional-quality theatre throughout the Northwest
> **Management:** John Hosking, Artistic Director; Joanne Eaton, Executive Director
> **Officers:** Jay Schuttler, President; Don McLaughlin, Vice President; Gwyn Ganjeau, Secretary/Treasurer
> **Paid Staff:** 2   **Volunteer Staff:** 10
> **Paid Artists:** 4
> **Utilizes:** Special Technical Talent
> **Budget:** $50,000 - $100,000
> **Income Sources:** Private Foundations/Grants/Endowments; Business/Corporate Donations; Box Office; Government Grants; Individual Donations
> **Season:** September - May   **Annual Attendance:** 10,000
> **Affiliations:** WESTAF; Montana State Theater Association; Pacific Northwest Arts Performers; Montana Performing Arts Council

Butte

INSTRUMENTAL MUSIC

BUTTE SYMPHONY ASSOCIATION
1009 Placer Street, Butte, MT 59701
(406) 782-2546
> **Founded:** 1950
> **Arts Area:** Symphony
> **Status:** Non-Profit
> **Type:** Performing
> **Purpose:** To provide fine concerts to the community and recreation for adults and teenagers in music
> **Officers:** Arthur Pascoe, President; Howard Wing, Vice President; Mrs. Warren Glover, Secretary; Dorothy Ann Honeychurch, Treasurer
> **Volunteer Staff:** 35
> **Non-Paid Artists:** 55
> **Utilizes:** Guest Artists
> **Budget:** $1,000 - $50,000
> **Income Sources:** Private Foundations/Grants/Endowments; Business/Corporate Donations; Box Office; Individual Donations
> **Season:** September - May   **Annual Attendance:** 2,400
> **Affiliations:** Montana Association of Symphonies
> **Performance Facilities:** Fox Theatre

Great Falls

INSTRUMENTAL MUSIC

GREAT FALLS SYMPHONY ASSOCIATION
Civic Center, PO Box 1078, Great Falls, MT 59403
(406) 453-4102
Founded: 1959
Arts Area: Symphony; Orchestra; Chamber; Ensemble
Status: Professional; Non-Profit
Type: Performing; Touring; Resident; Educational; Sponsoring
Purpose: To serve as the primary source of cultural and educational service to north central Montana. Performances include the symphony orchestra with guest artists, choir, musical theatre, ballet, opera and resident string quartet recitals as well as public school demonstrations.
Management: Carolyn Valacich, Executive Director; Gordon J. Johnson, Music Director/Conductor; Mary Moore, Choir Director
Paid Staff: 5   **Volunteer Staff:** 10
Paid Artists: 6   **Non-Paid Artists:** 135
Utilizes: Special Technical Talent; Guest Conductors; Guest Artists
Budget: $100,000 - $500,000
Income Sources: Private Foundations/Grants/Endowments; Business/Corporate Donations; Box Office; Government Grants; Individual Donations
Season: September - May   **Annual Attendance:** 25,000
Affiliations: ASOL; Montana Association of Symphony Orchestras
Performance Facilities: Great Falls Civic Center

VOCAL MUSIC

MONTANA CHORALE
PO Box 6083, Great Falls, MT 59406
(406) 771-7110
Founded: 1976
Arts Area: Choral
Status: Professional; Non-Profit
Type: Performing; Touring; Sponsoring
Purpose: To inspire and develop the choral arts in Montana, provide continuing education and employment for professional singers in Montana and develop an artistic climate with international reputation in Montana
Management: Linda Bottjer, General Manager
Officers: Ann Cogswell, President; Lorrin Darby, Vice President; Sharon Knowles, Treasurer
Paid Staff: 1
Paid Artists: 24
Utilizes: Guest Conductors; Guest Artists
Budget: $1,000 - $50,000
Income Sources: Private Foundations/Grants/Endowments; Business/Corporate Donations; Box Office; Government Grants; Individual Donations; Fund-raising
Season: 52 Weeks   **Annual Attendance:** 7,000
Affiliations: CA
Performance Facilities: Great Falls Civic Center

FACILITY

GREAT FALLS CENTER FOR THE PERFORMING ARTS
600 First Avenue SW, Great Falls, MT 59404
(406) 727-2974
Type of Facility: Theatre Complex; Auditorium; Studio Performance; Performance Center; Theatre House; Opera House; Multi-Purpose; Room
Facility Originally: Library; Business Facility; Meeting Hall; School; Ballroom
Type of Stage: Thrust; Flexible; Platform
Seating Capacity: 225
Year Built: 1940   **Architect:** Shanley and Van Teylingen
Year Remodeled: 1988
Contact for Rental: Great Falls Performing Arts Center;   (406) 727-2974
Resident Groups: Theatre Company; Costume Shop; Dance School; Music Department; Baton Instruction

GREAT FALLS CIVIC CENTER THEATER
PO Box 5021, Great Falls, MT 59403
(406) 727-5881
Type of Facility: Concert Hall; Theatre House; Civic Center

Type of Stage: Concert Shell
Stage Dimensions: 50'Wx33'D   **Orchestra Pit**
Seating Capacity: 1,857
Year Built: 1940   **Architect:** George H. Shanley & J. Van Teylingen   **Cost:** $665,000
Year Remodeled: 1987   **Architect:** Davidson & Cuhr
Acoustical Consultant: Towne Richards & Chaudiere
Contact for Rental: Parks & Recreation Department;   (406) 727-5881
Resident Groups: Great Falls Symphony Association; Community Concerts

Helena

INSTRUMENTAL MUSIC

HELENA SYMPHONY SOCIETY
Helena, MT 59601
(406) 442-1860
Founded: 1955
Arts Area: Symphony; Orchestra; Chamber; Ethnic
Status: Non-Profit
Type: Performing; Educational
Purpose: To present classical and popular symphony concerts, including choral and chamber concerts
Management: Sharon Nielsen, Business Manager; Dee Dawse, Development Director; Elizabeth Sellers, Music Director
Officers: Alton Hendrickson, President; Joe Schendel, Treasurer; Helen Ballinger, Secretary
Paid Staff: 3   **Volunteer Staff:** 22
Paid Artists: 12   **Non-Paid Artists:** 40
Utilizes: Guest Artists
Budget: $50,000 - $100,000
Income Sources: Private Foundations/Grants/Endowments; Business/Corporate Donations; Box Office; Individual Donations
Season: September - May   **Annual Attendance:** 5,000
Affiliations: ASCAP; BMI
Performance Facilities: Helena Civic Center

HOMEMADE JAM
526 Clarke Street, Helena, MT 59601
(406) 442-0535
Founded: 1980
Arts Area: Folk
Status: Professional
Type: Folk
Purpose: Performance of traditional Irish, American, and French-Canadian music in concert, in schools, and for dances
Officers: David Nimick, Angie Leprohon, Directors
Paid Artists: 4
Budget: $1,000 - $50,000
Income Sources: Box Office
Season: 52 Weeks

VOCAL MUSIC

HELENA YOUTH CHOIRS, INC.
PO Box 201, Helena, MT 59624
(406) 442-4877
Founded: 1982
Arts Area: Choral
Status: Non-Professional; Non-Profit
Type: Performing; Touring
Management: Dr. Melvin W. Roe, Choir Manager
Paid Staff: 4   **Volunteer Staff:** 20
Budget: $100,000 - $500,000
Income Sources: Private Foundations/Grants/Endowments; Business/Corporate Donations; Box Office; Individual Donations
Season: 52 Weeks

THEATRE

ALEPH MOVEMENT THEATRE
822 East Sixth Avenue, Helena, MT 59601
(406) 443-1274
Founded: 1985
Arts Area: Professional; Theatrical Group
Status: Professional; Non-Profit
Type: Performing; Touring; Educational
Purpose: Performance of movement theatre, to provide a vehicle for educational opportunities for individuals and organizations and cultural exchange between artists nationally and abroad
Management: Wally Bivins, Beck Newell
Officers: Peter Held, Vice President; Margaret Woo Showen, Secretary/Treasurer
Paid Staff: 2
Paid Artists: 2
Utilizes: Special Technical Talent; Guest Artists; Guest Directors
Budget: $1,000 - $50,000
Income Sources: Private Foundations/Grants/Endowments; Business/Corporate Donations; Box Office; Government Grants; Individual Donations
Season: 52 Weeks **Annual Attendance:** 5,000
Affiliations: National Mime Association

PERFORMING SERIES

HELENA PRESENTS
15 North Ewing, Helena, MT 59601
(406) 443-0287
FAX: (406) 443-6620
Arts Area: Dance; Vocal Music; Instrumental Music; Theater; Festivals; Lyric Opera
Status: Non-Profit
Type: Performing; Touring; Resident; Educational; Sponsoring
Purpose: To sponsor programs in performing, literary, media and visual arts; to provide educational activities, humanities programs and grants to artists
Management: Arnie Melina, Executive Director
Officers: Dr. Robert Shepard, Chairman of the Board
Income Sources: Private Foundations/Grants/Endowments; Business/Corporate Donations; Box Office; Government Grants; Individual Donations
Performance Facilities: Myrna Loy Center; Helena Middle School; Helena Civic Center Auditorium

FACILITY

CARROLL COLLEGE - THEATRE
North Benton Avenue, Helena, MT 59625
(406) 442-3450
FAX: (406) 447-4533
Type of Facility: Performance Center; Theatre House
Facility Originally: Library
Type of Stage: Flexible; Proscenium
Seating Capacity: 100
Year Remodeled: 1959
Contact for Rental: Kim DeLong;   (406) 442-3450
Resident Groups: Carroll Theatre
For touring production/lectures on a limited scale

HELENA CIVIC CENTER
Neill and Park Avenue, Helena, MT 59601
(406) 447-8481
Type of Facility: Civic Center
Facility Originally: Shrine Temple
Year Built: 1920
Contact for Rental: Gery Carpenter, Diane Stavnes;   (406) 447-8481
The Civic Center contains the Auditorium and Ballroom. See separate listings for additional information.

HELENA CIVIC CENTER - AUDITORIUM
Neill and Park Avenue, Helena, MT 59601
(406) 447-8481
Type of Facility: Concert Hall; Auditorium; Theatre House; Opera House
Facility Originally: Shrine Temple

Type of Stage: Proscenium
Stage Dimensions: 45'Wx38'Dx19'6"H
Seating Capacity: 2,000
Year Built: 1920
Contact for Rental: Diane Stavnes, Gery Carpenter;   (406) 447-8481

HELENA CIVIC CENTER - BALLROOM
Neill and Park Avenue, Helena, MT 59601
(406) 447-8481
 Type of Facility: Multi-Purpose; Room
 Facility Originally: Shrine Temple
 Type of Stage: Proscenium
 Stage Dimensions: 25'Wx15'Dx12'H
 Seating Capacity: 1,500
 Year Built: 1920
 Contact for Rental: Diane Stavnes, Gery Carpenter;   (406) 447-8481

Kalispell

DANCE

DANCE ART CENTER
1411 First Avenue West, Kalispell, MT 59901
(406) 755-0760
 Founded: 1977
 Arts Area: Modern; Ballet; Jazz; Tap
 Status: Non-Profit; Commercial
 Type: Performing; Touring; Resident; Educational; Sponsoring
 Purpose: To enhance and educate the dance world in our small town; to run a small touring company
 Management: Carol Jakes, Sole Proprietor; Kathy Barten, Kim Bristol, Janet Landon, Desiree Gravelle, Sherry Johns, Mary Jo Smith, Jazz Teachers
 Paid Staff: 7
 Non-Paid Artists: 5
 Utilizes: Special Technical Talent; Guest Artists
 Budget: $1,000 - $50,000
 Income Sources: Business/Corporate Donations; Box Office; Individual Donations
 Season: September - May; July   **Annual Attendance:** 1,000

INSTRUMENTAL MUSIC

GLACIER ORCHESTRA
140 First Avenue East, PO Box 2491, Kalispell, MT 59903
(406) 257-3241
FAX: (406) 257-3241
 Founded: 1982
 Arts Area: Symphony; Orchestra; Chamber; Chorus
 Status: Non-Professional; Non-Profit
 Type: Performing; Educational; Sponsoring
 Purpose: To bring quality classical music to area audiences and provide an opportunity for local musicians to perform
 Management: Robin Bailey, Executive Director; Gordon Johnson, Music Director; Shauneen Garner, Chorale Conductor/Children's Choir Conductor
 Officers: Steve Cummings, President; Eric Kaplan, Vice President; Sally Murdock, Secretary; Diane Thompson, Treasurer
 Paid Staff: 3   **Volunteer Staff:** 5
 Paid Artists: 1   **Non-Paid Artists:** 100
 Utilizes: Guest Conductors; Guest Artists
 Budget: $50,000 - $100,000
 Income Sources: Private Foundations/Grants/Endowments; Business/Corporate Donations; Box Office; Government Grants; Individual Donations
 Season: September - May
 Annual Attendance: 6,500
 Affiliations: ASOL; Montana Association of Symphony Orchestras; Flathead Arts Council
 Performance Facilities: Flathead High School Auditorium; Central School Auditorium

VOCAL MUSIC

GLACIER CHORALE
140 First Avenue East, Kalispell, MT 59901
(406) 257-3241
FAX: (406) 257-3241
Founded: 1982
Arts Area: Choral
Status: Non-Professional; Non-Profit
Type: Performing
Purpose: To bring classical choral works to area audiences; to provide local choral performers with the opportunity to perform
Management: Robin Bailey, Executive Director; Shauneen Garner, Chorale Conductor/Children's Choir Conductor; Gordon Johnson, Music Director
Officers: Steve Cummings, President; Eric Kaplan, Vice President; Sally Murdock, Secretary; Diane Thompson, Treasurer
Paid Staff: 3   **Volunteer Staff:** 5
Non-Paid Artists: 55
Utilizes: Guest Conductors; Guest Artists
Budget: $50,000 - $100,000
Income Sources: Private Foundations/Grants/Endowments; Business/Corporate Donations; Box Office; Government Grants; Individual Donations
Season: September - May   **Annual Attendance:** 6,500
Affiliations: ASOL; Montana Association of Symphony Orchestras; Glacier Orchestra
Performance Facilities: Flathead High School Auditorium; Central School Auditorium

Missoula

INSTRUMENTAL MUSIC

MISSOULA SYMPHONY ASSOCIATION
131 South Higgins Avenue, Missoula, MT 59802
(406) 721-3194
Founded: 1951
Arts Area: Symphony
Status: Non-Profit
Type: Performing; Sponsoring
Purpose: To present artistic programs of excellence to Missoula and the surrounding areas, provide an opportunity for young persons and develop an interest in the arts through concerts and master classes
Management: Caralee Blair, General Manager
Officers: Greg Davlin, President
Paid Staff: 2
Paid Artists: 18   **Non-Paid Artists:** 67
Utilizes: Guest Artists
Budget: $100,000 - $500,000
Income Sources: Private Foundations/Grants/Endowments; Business/Corporate Donations; Box Office; Individual Donations
Season: November - May   **Annual Attendance:** 6,000
Affiliations: ASOL
Performance Facilities: Wilma Theatre

STRING ORCHESTRA OF THE ROCKIES
PO Box 8265, Missoula, MT 59807
(406) 543-7803; (406) 549-0645
Founded: 1984
Arts Area: Symphony; Orchestra; Chamber; Ensemble
Status: Professional; Non-Profit
Type: Performing; Touring; Resident; Educational
Purpose: To provide high quality classical music performances and educational programs to audiences in Montana and beyond
Officers: Allison Justman, President; Fern Glassboyd, Orchestra Member
Paid Staff: 2   **Volunteer Staff:** 1
Paid Artists: 13
Utilizes: Special Technical Talent; Guest Artists
Budget: $1,000 - $50,000
Income Sources: Business/Corporate Donations; Box Office; Government Grants; Individual Donations
Season: 52 Weeks   **Annual Attendance:** 5,000

VOCAL MUSIC

MISSOULA MENDELSSOHN CLUB
University of Montana School of Music, Missoula, MT 59801
(406) 243-6880
> **Founded:** 1944
> **Arts Area:** Choral
> **Status:** Non-Professional
> **Type:** Performing; Touring; Sponsoring
> **Purpose:** To provide an opportunity to express music; to increase the public's enjoyment of music
> **Management:** Professor Donald Carey, Conductor
> **Officers:** Frank A. Carter, President; Walt Kaostra, Secretary/Treasurer
> **Non-Paid Artists:** 50
> **Budget:** $1,000 - $50,000
> **Income Sources:** Private Foundations/Grants/Endowments; Business/Corporate Donations; Box Office; Government Grants; Individual Donations
> **Season:** October - May   **Annual Attendance:** 500
> **Performance Facilities:** Music Recital Hall

THEATRE

THE MONTANA REP
Drama/Dance Department, University of Montana, Missoula, MT 59812
(406) 243-6809
> **Founded:** 1967
> **Arts Area:** Professional; Theatrical Group
> **Status:** Professional; Non-Profit
> **Type:** Performing; Touring; Resident; Educational
> **Purpose:** To bring quality theatre and educational outreach to the West
> **Management:** Arlynn Fishbaugh, Booking Manager
> **Officers:** Greg Johnson, Artistic Director; Steve Wing, Production Coordinator
> **Paid Artists:** 7   **Non-Paid Artists:** 8
> **Utilizes:** Special Technical Talent; Guest Artists; Guest Directors; Student Interns
> **Budget:** $100,000 - $500,000
> **Income Sources:** Private Foundations/Grants/Endowments; Business/Corporate Donations; Box Office; Government Grants; Individual Donations
> **Season:** September - June   **Annual Attendance:** 20,000
> **Affiliations:** AEA; Uiversity of Montana
> **Performance Facilities:** Montana Theatre, University of Montana

PERFORMING SERIES

YOUNG AUDIENCES OF WESTERN MONTANA
2920 Garfield, Missoula, MT 59801
(406) 721-5924
> **Founded:** 1966
> **Arts Area:** Dance; Vocal Music; Instrumental Music; Theater
> **Status:** Professional; Non-Profit
> **Type:** Performing; Touring; Educational
> **Purpose:** To introduce school-age children to the live performing arts
> **Management:** Dorothy Kinsley, Executive Director
> **Officers:** Mark Thane, President; Barney White, Vice President; Susan Carlson, Secretary; Margaret Langel, Treasurer
> **Paid Staff:** 1
> **Paid Artists:** 30
> **Budget:** $1,000 - $50,000
> **Income Sources:** Private Foundations/Grants/Endowments; Business/Corporate Donations; Box Office; Government Grants; Individual Donations; Program Fees
> **Season:** October - May   **Annual Attendance:** 21,000
> **Affiliations:** National Young Audiences

FACILITY

UNIVERSITY OF MONTANA - MONTANA THEATRE
Department of Drama and Dance, Missoula, MT 59812
(406) 243-4970
> **Type of Facility:** Theatre Complex
> **Type of Stage:** Proscenium   **Orchestra Pit**
> **Seating Capacity:** 499
> **Year Built:** 1985   **Architect:** CTA   **Cost:** $8,500,000

Contact for Rental: Bryan Spellman, School of Fine Arts;   (406) 243-4970
Resident Groups: University of Montana Department of Drama and Dance; Montana Repertory Theatre

Red Lodge

PERFORMING SERIES

SCANDINAVIAN DANCERS
PO Box 691, Red Lodge, MT 59068
(406) 446-2657
Founded: 1970
Arts Area: Dance; Festivals
Status: Non-Professional; Non-Profit
Type: Performing
Purpose: To plan and perform the Scandinavian Day program during the Red Lodge Festival of Nations
Management: Bob Holmen, Dance Coordinator
Officers: Greta Bummer, President; John McCampbell, Vice President; Ken Firebaugh, Secretary; Jim Guimont, Treasurer
Volunteer Staff: 1
Non-Paid Artists: 24
Budget: $1,000 - $50,000
Income Sources: Fundraisers
Season: 52 Weeks   **Annual Attendance:** 2,500
Affiliations: Member of the Red Lodge Festival of Nations
Performance Facilities: Red Lodge Civic Center

Sheridan

PERFORMING SERIES

OLD TIMERS CONCERT
Sheridan High School, Sheridan, MT 59749
(406) 842-5226
Founded: 1974
Arts Area: Dance; Vocal Music; Instrumental Music; Theater; Festivals
Status: Semi-Professional; Non-Professional
Type: Performing; Resident
Purpose: To provide an opportunity to share talent with the community; to promote the arts in all fields of music; to raise money for school music programs and scholarships
Management: Sue Nottingham, Manager
Officers: Sue Nottingham, Treasurer
Volunteer Staff: 12
Non-Paid Artists: 50
Utilizes: Special Technical Talent; Guest Conductors; Guest Artists; Guest Directors
Budget: $1,000 - $50,000
Income Sources: Box Office; Individual Donations
Performance Facilities: Sheridan School Gym

Sidney

VOCAL MUSIC

SUGAR VALLEY CHAPTER OF SWEET ADELINES
PO Box 384, Sidney, MT 59270
(406) 842-1194
Founded: 1976
Arts Area: Choral
Status: Semi-Professional; Non-Profit
Type: Performing; Resident
Purpose: Sugar Valley Chapter of Sweet Adelines is united by a common interest in singing four-part harmony, barbershop style; to bring the joy of music to our community
Paid Staff: 2
Utilizes: Special Technical Talent; Guest Artists; Guest Directors

Budget: $1,000 - $50,000
Income Sources: Business/Corporate Donations

Twin Bridges

VOCAL MUSIC

RUBY VALLEY CHORALE
248 Bayers Lane, Twin Bridges, MT 59754
(406) 684-5465
>**Founded:** 1976
>**Arts Area:** Choral
>**Status:** Non-Professional; Non-Profit
>**Type:** Performing
>**Purpose:** Entertainment for our small community; a means of expressing musically and vocally for those with talent in our community and an ecumenical effort of the churches
>**Management:** Pauline Bayers, Director
>**Officers:** Carolyn Carrol, Treasurer
>**Volunteer Staff:** 3
>**Income Sources:** Individual Donations
>**Season:** September - April   **Annual Attendance:** 1,200
>**Performance Facilities:** Church of the Valley; Bethel Methodist Church

Whitefish

PERFORMING SERIES

FLATHEAD FESTIVAL OF THE ARTS
PO Box 1780, Whitefish, MT 59937
(406) 862-1780
>**Founded:** 1986
>**Arts Area:** Vocal Music; Instrumental Music; Festivals; Lyric Opera
>**Status:** Non-Profit
>**Type:** Performing; Touring; Educational; Sponsoring
>**Management:** Charles Buchwalter, Executive Director; Gordon Johnson, Artistic Director; Rebecca Grouse, Administrative Director
>**Officers:** Carol Atkinson, President; Mike Bluk, Secretary; Rebecca Lyman, Treasurer
>**Paid Staff:** 6   **Volunteer Staff:** 200
>**Paid Artists:** 40
>**Utilizes:** Guest Artists
>**Budget:** $100,000 - $500,000
>**Income Sources:** Private Foundations/Grants/Endowments; Business/Corporate Donations; Box Office; Government Grants; Individual Donations
>**Season:** July   **Annual Attendance:** 2,000

NEBRASKA

Beatrice

FACILITY

COMMUNITY PLAYERS
412 Ella, PO Box 116, Beatrice, NE 68310
(402) 228-1801
Type of Facility: Studio Performance; Arena
Facility Originally: Garage; Warehouse
Type of Stage: Flexible; Platform; Arena
Stage Dimensions: 46'x63'
Seating Capacity: 280
Year Remodeled: 1982
Contact for Rental: Marya Lucca-Thyberg; (402) 228-1801
Resident Groups: Community Players
Performances; meetings; conventions

Bellevue

THEATRE

BELLEVUE LITTLE THEATRE
203 West Mission Avenue, PO Box 162, Bellevue, NE 68005
(402) 291-1554
Founded: 1968
Arts Area: Musical; Community; Theatrical Group; Puppet
Status: Non-Professional; Non-Profit
Type: Performing; Educational
Purpose: To provide a Performing Arts Center for the community and the surrounding area
Management: Board of Directors
Officers: Edward B. Roche, President; Cheryl Bailey, Vice President; Paula Darnell, Secretary; George Rice, Treasurer
Volunteer Staff: 100
Non-Paid Artists: 275
Utilizes: Special Technical Talent; Guest Artists; Guest Directors
Budget: $50,000 - $100,000
Income Sources: Private Foundations/Grants/Endowments; Business/Corporate Donations; Box Office; Government Grants; Individual Donations
Season: 52 Weeks   **Annual Attendance:** 5,000

FACILITY

BELLEVUE LITTLE THEATRE
203 West Mission, Bellevue, NE 68005
(402) 291-1554
Founded: 1968
Type of Facility: Auditorium; Theatre House
Type of Stage: Thrust; Platform
Stage Dimensions: 35'Wx33'D (10" rise at 25')
Seating Capacity: 244
Year Built: 1948
Year Remodeled: 1990   **Cost:** $32,000
Contact for Rental: Bette Swanson; (402) 292-1920
Educational activities

Bladen

FACILITY

BLADEN OPERA HOUSE
Main Street, Bladen, NE 68928
Type of Facility: Concert Hall; Studio Performance; Performance Center; Theatre House; Opera House
Facility Originally: Meeting Hall; Vaudeville; Movie House
Type of Stage: Thrust; Platform
Stage Dimensions: Main - 21'x18'; Thrust - 18'x12'   **Orchestra Pit**

Seating Capacity: 250
Year Built: 1913   Cost: $15,000
For local and surrounding community groups

Chadron

FACILITY

CHADRON STATE COLLEGE - MEMORIAL HALL
10th and Main, Chadron, NE 69337
(308) 432-6316
FAX: (308) 432-3561
    Type of Facility: Auditorium
    Type of Stage: Proscenium
    Orchestra Pit
    Seating Capacity: 764
    Year Built: 1953   Cost: $750,000
    Year Remodeled: 1984   Architect: Hindl and Harrison   Cost: $990,000
    Contact for Rental: Dr. Charles J. Harrington;   (308) 432-6316

Gothenburg

THEATRE

GOTHENBURG COMMUNITY PLAYHOUSE
10th and D Street, PO Box 15, Gothenburg, NE 69138
(308) 537-7596
    Founded: 1967
    Arts Area: Dinner; Community
    Status: Non-Professional; Non-Profit
    Type: Performing; Resident; Sponsoring
    Purpose: To provide cultural, educational and literary opportunities to the members of the community and the surrounding region
    Management: LaVon Pape, Manager
    Paid Staff: 1
    Utilizes: Special Technical Talent; Guest Artists; Guest Directors
    Budget: $1,000 - $50,000
    Income Sources: Box Office; Individual Donations
    Performance Facilities: Sun Theatre

FACILITY

GOTHENBURG COMMUNITY PLAYHOUSE - SUN THEATRE
10th and D Street, PO Box 15, Gothenburg, NE 69138
(308) 537-3235
    Type of Facility: Theatre House
    Type of Stage: Platform
    Seating Capacity: 324
    Contact for Rental: LaVon Pape;   (308) 537-7596
    Resident Groups: Gothenburg Community Playhouse
    To bring cultural and artistic entertainment to our community

Hastings

INSTRUMENTAL MUSIC

HASTINGS SYMPHONY ORCHESTRA
Fuhr Hall, Ninth and Ash, Hastings, NE 68901
(402) 463-2402
FAX: (402) 463-3002
    Founded: 1926
    Arts Area: Symphony; Orchestra; Chamber
    Status: Non-Professional; Non-Profit
    Type: Performing; Touring; Resident; Educational
    Purpose: To promote the best possible performance of symphonic music and to provide an educational and performance outlet for the citizens of south central Nebraska

Management: Dr. James Johnson, Conductor/Music Director; Becky Pitman, Executive Secretary
Officers: Karen Doer, President; Ann Martin, President Elect; Mary Wright, Treasurer
Paid Staff: 2   **Volunteer Staff:** 24
Paid Artists: 4   **Non-Paid Artists:** 70
Utilizes: Guest Artists
Budget: $1,000 - $50,000
Income Sources: Private Foundations/Grants/Endowments; Business/Corporate Donations; Box Office; Government Grants; Individual Donations
Season: September - May   **Annual Attendance:** 5,000
Affiliations: ASOL
Performance Facilities: Hastings Masonic Temple

Hyannis

THEATRE

VILLAGE PLAYERS
PO Box 81, Hyannis, NE 69350
(308) 458-2701
Founded: 1980
Arts Area: Professional; Summer Stock; Musical; Dinner; Community; Theatrical Group
Status: Semi-Professional; Non-Profit; Commercial
Type: Performing; Touring; Sponsoring
Purpose: Presenting and sponsoring organization
Management: Al Davis, Artistic Director
Officers: Les Schreurs, President; John Glenn, Treasurer; Erik Johnson, Vice President; Fayann Blaylock, Secretary
Volunteer Staff: 13
Paid Artists: 20
Utilizes: Special Technical Talent; Guest Artists; Guest Directors
Budget: $100,000 - $500,000
Income Sources: Private Foundations/Grants/Endowments; Business/Corporate Donations; Box Office; Government Grants; Individual Donations
Season: 52 Weeks   **Annual Attendance:** 1,000

Kearney

THEATRE

KEARNEY COMMUNITY THEATRE
83 Plaza Boulevard, Kearney, NE 68847
(308) 234-1529
Founded: 1977
Arts Area: Musical; Dinner; Community; Theatrical Group
Status: Non-Professional; Non-Profit
Type: Performing; Educational; Sponsoring
Purpose: Perform five shows yearly plus summer workshop for children who do their own show
Management: Bradley J. Driml, Executive Director
Paid Staff: 3   **Volunteer Staff:** 300
Utilizes: Guest Directors
Budget: $100,000 - $500,000
Income Sources: Private Foundations/Grants/Endowments; Business/Corporate Donations; Box Office; Government Grants; Individual Donations; Fundraising
Season: 52 Weeks   **Annual Attendance:** 11,000
Affiliations: Nebraska Arts Council; Nebraska Association of Community Theatres; AACT
Performance Facilities: Kearney Community Theatre

FACILITY

KEARNEY COMMUNITY THEATRE
83 Plaza Boulevard, Kearney, NE 68847
(308) 234-1529
Type of Facility: Theatre Complex
Facility Originally: Church
Type of Stage: Platform
Seating Capacity: Theater - 165; Dinner Theater - 115
Year Built: 1890
Year Remodeled: 1984   **Architect:** Theatre Board

Contact for Rental: (308) 234-1529
Manager: Bradley Driml, Administrator

UNIVERSITY OF NEBRASKA - UNIVERSITY THEATRE
905 West 25th Street, Kearney, NE 68849
(308) 234-8406
    Type of Facility: Theatre Complex; Studio Performance; Theatre House; Amphitheater
    Type of Stage: Flexible; Proscenium
    Stage Dimensions: 39'6"Wx25'D
    Orchestra Pit
    Seating Capacity: 334
    Year Built: 1970
    Architect: Helleberg
    Cost: $1,775,000
    Manager: Charles Davies
    The building also contains a 500-seat recital hall.

Lincoln

DANCE

LINCOLN CITY BALLET COMPANY
PO Box 2441, Lincoln, NE 68502
(402) 489-7218
    Founded: 1979
    Arts Area: Modern; Ballet; Jazz; Folk
    Status: Non-Professional; Non-Profit
    Type: Performing; Resident; Educational; Sponsoring
    Purpose: To give gifted young dancers of our community an additional performing outlet; to expose more community members to various forms of dance
    Management: Betsy Bobenhouse, Director
    Officers: Linda Haase, President; Dee Churchill, First Vice President; Debbie Guenzel, Second Vice President; Jan Budde, Treasurer
    Paid Staff: 1   **Volunteer Staff:** 17
    Non-Paid Artists: 32
    Utilizes: Special Technical Talent; Guest Artists
    Budget: $1,000 - $50,000
    Income Sources: Private Foundations/Grants/Endowments; Business/Corporate Donations; Box Office; Individual Donations
    Season: September - May

LINCOLN MIDWEST BALLET COMPANY
PO Box 30126, Lincoln, NE 68503-0126
(402) 464-7737
    Founded: 1985
    Arts Area: Ballet
    Status: Non-Profit
    Type: Performing; Touring; Educational
    Purpose: To contonue to foster, promote and expand classical ballet training and its expression in various dance forms; to develop an audience for ballet; to promote and expand education of dance and the arts in Nebraska
    Management: Shari Shell-True, Artistic Director
    Officers: Joann Reirden, President; Bill Ford, President Elect; Cindy Ketner, Secretary; Joan Chopp, Treasurer
    Paid Staff: 1   **Volunteer Staff:** 10
    Paid Artists: 1   **Non-Paid Artists:** 30
    Utilizes: Special Technical Talent; Guest Artists; Guest Directors
    Budget: $1,000 - $50,000
    Income Sources: Private Foundations/Grants/Endowments; Business/Corporate Donations; Box Office; Individual Donations
    Annual Attendance: 2,000
    Affiliations: Nebraska Arts Council
    Performance Facilities: Cotner Center; Pershing Auditorium

INSTRUMENTAL MUSIC

LINCOLN CIVIC EXPERIENCE/LINCOLN CIVIC ORCHESTRA
3800 South 48th Street, Lincoln, NE 68506
(402) 488-2331
    Arts Area: Orchestra

Status: Non-Profit
Type: Resident
Purpose: To provide community members a chance to perform serious music
Officers: Carol Rees, President; Beth Friedline, Secretary; Barbara Mercier, Treasurer
Paid Artists: 20 **Non-Paid Artists:** 130
Utilizes: Special Technical Talent; Guest Artists
Budget: $1,000 - $50,000
Income Sources: Private Foundations/Grants/Endowments; Individual Donations
Season: September - May **Annual Attendance:** 4,000
Performance Facilities: Union College

LINCOLN SYMPHONY
1200 North Street, Lincoln, NE 68508
(402) 474-5610
FAX: (402) 434-1163
Founded: 1925
Arts Area: Symphony; Orchestra
Status: Professional; Non-Profit
Type: Performing; Sponsoring
Management: Richard Frevert, Manager; Robert Emile, Music Director/Conductor
Paid Staff: 5 **Volunteer Staff:** 40
Paid Artists: 75
Utilizes: Guest Artists
Budget: $100,000 - $500,000
Income Sources: Private Foundations/Grants/Endowments; Business/Corporate Donations; Box Office; Government Grants; Individual Donations
Season: October - April **Annual Attendance:** 8,000
Affiliations: ASOL
Performance Facilities: Kimball Hall; Lied Center

LINCOLN YOUTH SYMPHONY ORCHESTRA
Public School Administration Building, 5901 O Street, Lincoln, NE 68501
(402) 475-1081
Founded: 1953
Arts Area: Symphony; Orchestra
Status: Non-Professional; Non-Profit
Type: Performing; Touring; Educational; Sponsoring
Purpose: The Lincoln Youth Symphony Orchestra was organized to perform symphonic literature unable to be played within regular school instruction through participation in the Youth Orchestra or the Junior Youth Orchestra.
Management: Richard Scott, Administrator; Michael Swartz, Business Manager; Dr. Brian Moore, Music Director/Conductor
Officers: Joyce Glaesemann, President; Linda Maack, Secretary; Carl Olson, Treasurer
Paid Staff: 5 **Volunteer Staff:** 80
Non-Paid Artists: 76
Budget: $1,000 - $50,000
Income Sources: Business/Corporate Donations; Individual Donations
Season: October - May
Annual Attendance: 1,500
Affiliations: ASOL (Youth Orchestra Division); Lincoln Public Schools
Performance Facilities: Kimball Recital Hall, University of Nebraska

NEBRASKA CHAMBER ORCHESTRA
749 NBC Center, Lincoln, NE 68512
(402) 477-0366
FAX: (402) 476-6368
Founded: 1976
Arts Area: Chamber
Status: Professional; Non-Profit
Type: Performing; Touring; Educational
Purpose: To offer a variety of entertaining, provocative and challenging chamber orchestra programs through a subscription series, touring concerts and chamber ensembles
Management: Sherrie Geier, General Manager
Officers: Carl Rohman, President; Tyler Sutton, Michael Letheby, Vice Presidents; Emily Zimmer, Secretary/Treasurer
Paid Staff: 2 **Volunteer Staff:** 50
Paid Artists: 50
Utilizes: Guest Conductors; Guest Artists
Budget: $100,000 - $500,000

Income Sources: Private Foundations/Grants/Endowments; Business/Corporate Donations; Box Office; Government Grants; Individual Donations
Season: September - April **Annual Attendance:** 3,000
Affiliations: ASOL

THEATRE

LINCOLN COMMUNITY PLAYHOUSE
2500 South 56th Street, Lincoln, NE 68506
(402) 489-9608
>   **Founded:** 1946
>   **Arts Area:** Community
>   **Status:** Non-Profit
>   **Type:** Performing
>   **Purpose:** The mission of the Lincoln Community Playhouse is to provide quality theatrical experiences offering education participation and entertainment opportunities to the community.
>   **Management:** Rod McCullough, Executive Director; Mark A. Adams, Artistic Director; Lenette Nelson Schwinn, Children's Theatre Director
>   **Officers:** Linda Hoff, President; Ginny Parker, Secretary; Mary Ann Kochler, Treasurer; Tom Larson, President-Elect
>   **Paid Staff:** 10
>   **Non-Paid Artists:** 400
>   **Utilizes:** Guest Artists; Guest Directors
>   **Budget:** $100,000 - $500,000
>   **Income Sources:** Private Foundations/Grants/Endowments; Business/Corporate Donations; Box Office; Government Grants; Individual Donations
>   **Season:** September - June **Annual Attendance:** 33,000
>   **Affiliations:** AACT; Nebraska Association of Community Theatres
>   **Performance Facilities:** Oliver T. Joy Mainstage; L.L. Coryell and Sons Children's Theatre; Lawrence A. Emerson Gallery Theatre

NEBRASKA REPERTORY THEATRE
215 Temple Building, 12th and R Streets, Lincoln, NE 68588-0201
(402) 472-2072
>   **Founded:** 1968
>   **Arts Area:** Professional; Theatrical Group
>   **Status:** Semi-Professional; Non-Profit
>   **Type:** Performing; Resident
>   **Management:** Tice Miller, Executive Director; Robert Hall, Artistic Director; Patricia Overton, Theatre Manager
>   **Paid Staff:** 10
>   **Utilizes:** Special Technical Talent; Guest Artists; Guest Directors
>   **Budget:** $100,000 - $500,000
>   **Income Sources:** Box Office; Government Grants; Individual Donations
>   **Season:** June - August **Annual Attendance:** 10,000
>   **Affiliations:** AEA; Guest Artist Contract
>   **Performance Facilities:** Howell Theatre; Studio Theatre; Carson Theatre

PERFORMING SERIES

THE LIED CENTER FOR PERFORMING ARTS
301 North 12th, Lincoln, NE 68588
(402) 472-4700
FAX: (402) 472-4730
>   **Founded:** 1972
>   **Arts Area:** Dance; Vocal Music; Instrumental Music; Theater
>   **Status:** Professional
>   **Type:** Performing
>   **Purpose:** To provide a top-quality series of performances during the school year; to provide the students with the opportunity to encounter these visiting artists in workshops and other learning situations
>   **Management:** Bob Chumbley, Director
>   **Paid Staff:** 7
>   **Utilizes:** Guest Artists
>   **Budget:** $100,000 - $500,000
>   **Income Sources:** Private Foundations/Grants/Endowments; Box Office; Government Grants; Individual Donations
>   **Season:** September - May **Annual Attendance:** 16,000
>   **Performance Facilities:** Lied Center

LINCOLN FRIENDS OF CHAMBER MUSIC
1935 A Street, Lincoln, NE 68502
(402) 475-0221
FAX: (402) 472-3574
> **Founded:** 1965
> **Arts Area:** Instrumental Music
> **Status:** Non-Profit
> **Type:** Sponsoring
> **Purpose:** To present chamber music; to promote community interest in chamber music; to aid local chamber music talent
> **Officers:** Bob Kuzelka, President
> **Volunteer Staff:** 10
> **Utilizes:** Guest Artists
> **Income Sources:** Private Foundations/Grants/Endowments; Business/Corporate Donations; Box Office; Government Grants; Individual Donations
> **Season:** October - April
> **Performance Facilities:** Sheldon Art Gallery Auditorium

FACILITY

LIED CENTER FOR THE PERFORMING ARTS
301 North 12th Street, Lincoln, NE 68588
(402) 472-4700
FAX: (402) 472-4730
> **Founded:** 1990
> **Type of Facility:** Theatre Complex
> **Type of Stage:** Flexible; Proscenium; Second Proscenium
> **Stage Dimensions:** Varied
> **Orchestra Pit**
> **Seating Capacity:** 2278; 850; 300
> **Year Built:** 1989   **Architect:** HDR and Associates   **Cost:** $30,000,000
> **Acoustical Consultant:** Paul Venaklausen
> **Contact for Rental:** Tim Bartholow;   (402) 472-4700
> **Resident Groups:** Lincoln Symphony; Nebraska Chamber Orchestra; Nebraska Repertory Theater

PERSHING AUDITORIUM
226 Centennial Mall South, PO Box 81126, Lincoln, NE 68501-1126
(402) 471-7500
> **Type of Facility:** Concert Hall; Auditorium; Theatre House; Arena; Multi-Purpose
> **Type of Stage:** Proscenium
> **Stage Dimensions:** 110'Wx40'D
> **Orchestra Pit**
> **Seating Capacity:** 7,691
> **Year Built:** 1957   **Architect:** Davis & Wilson   **Cost:** $2,500,000
> **Year Remodeled:** 1976   **Architect:** Morrow   **Cost:** $1,000,000
> **Contact for Rental:** Douglas Kuhnel;   (402) 471-7500
> **Resident Groups:** Lincoln Community Concert Association

UNIVERSITY OF NEBRASKA-LINCOLN - KIMBALL RECITAL HALL
11th & R Streets, Lincoln, NE 68588
(402) 472-2997
> **Type of Facility:** Concert Hall
> **Type of Stage:** Proscenium
> **Orchestra Pit**
> **Seating Capacity:** 849
> **Year Built:** 1970   **Architect:** Robinson   **Cost:** $1,000,000
> **Acoustical Consultant:** Bolt, Beranek & Newman
> **Manager:** Ron Bowlin;   (402) 472-2997
> **Resident Groups:** School of Music

McCook

PERFORMING SERIES

HERITAGE DAYS
PO Box 337, McCook, NE 69001
(308) 345-3200
> **Founded:** 1969

Arts Area: Dance; Vocal Music; Instrumental Music; Arts and Crafts
Status: Non-Professional; Non-Profit
Type: Sponsoring
Paid Staff: 2
Budget: $1,000 - $50,000
Income Sources: Private Foundations/Grants/Endowments; Business/Corporate Donations; Box Office; Government Grants; Individual Donations
Season: June - August

Omaha

DANCE

OMAHA BALLET COMPANY AND SCHOOL
2655 Farnham Street, Omaha, NE 68131
(402) 346-7332; (402) 346-7394
FAX: (402) 422-0148
Founded: 1968
Arts Area: Modern; Ballet
Status: Professional; Non-Profit
Type: Performing; Touring; Educational
Purpose: To provide high-quality, professional classical and contemporary ballet that responds to the region's cultural and educational needs and enriches the cultural fabric of the region
Management: Robert Vickrey, Artistic Director; Sharon McGill, Ballet Mistress; Robin Welch, Program Director/Associate Ballet Mistress; Kathleen Sullivan, Executive Director
Officers: Roger Lewis, President; Warren Whithed, Vice President/President-Elect
Paid Staff: 9   Volunteer Staff: 15
Paid Artists: 14   Non-Paid Artists: 5
Utilizes: Special Technical Talent; Guest Conductors; Guest Artists; Guest Directors
Budget: $1,000,000 - $5,000,000
Season: September - May   Annual Attendance: 25,000
Affiliations: Nebraska Arts Council
Performance Facilities: Orpheum Theater

OMAHA MODERN DANCE COLLECTIVE
PO Box 1084, Omaha, NE 68101
(402) 551-7473
Founded: 1981
Arts Area: Modern
Status: Non-Profit
Type: Educational; Sponsoring
Purpose: To serve the community of modern dancers and choreographers by providing educational and performance opportunities; to promote public awareness of modern dance
Officers: Amy Matthews, President; Carl Ogden, Vice President; Susan Dickson Matsunami, Secretary; Taffy Howard, Treasurer
Non-Paid Artists: 12
Utilizes: Special Technical Talent; Guest Artists; Guest Choreographers
Budget: $1,000 - $50,000
Income Sources: Private Foundations/Grants/Endowments; Box Office; Government Grants; Individual Donations
Season: 52 Weeks

INSTRUMENTAL MUSIC

NEBRASKA WIND SYMPHONY
PO Box 24114, Omaha, NE 68124
(402) 391-6329
Founded: 1977
Arts Area: Band
Status: Semi-Professional; Non-Profit
Type: Performing
Purpose: To provide wind and percussion players with a performance group; to encourage the composition of new literature for bands by awarding commissions and programming premiere performances; to entertain
Management: Darwyn Snyder, Music Director
Officers: Diana Bee, President; Mark Foster, Vice President; Geneviere Holtz, Secretary/Treasurer; Linda Ashley, Corresponding Secretary
Paid Staff: 3
Paid Artists: 10   Non-Paid Artists: 85
Utilizes: Guest Conductors; Guest Artists

Budget: $1,000 - $50,000
Income Sources: Private Foundations/Grants/Endowments; Business/Corporate Donations; Box Office; Government Grants; Individual Donations
Season: September - June   **Annual Attendance:** 3,500
Performance Facilities: Strauss Performing Arts Center, University of Nebraska at Omaha

OMAHA AREA YOUTH ORCHESTRAS
PO Box 24813, Omaha, NE 68124
(402) 553-7655
Founded: 1958
Arts Area: Symphony; Orchestra; Chamber; Ensemble
Status: Non-Professional; Non-Profit
Type: Performing; Educational; Sponsoring
Purpose: To enhance the musical education of aspiring and talented young musicians through the medium of orchestral performance; to help them become appreciative listeners; and to build discipline, cooperation, and other skills necessary for a group accomplishment
Management: Stephen G. Hobson, Music Director; Susan Bogden, General Manager
Officers: Mary Ellen Wychulis, Chairman of the Board; Patty Deckel, Associate Chairman; Robley Garrigan, Secretary; Richard Jorgenson, Treasurer
Paid Staff: 3   **Volunteer Staff:** 70
Non-Paid Artists: 300
Utilizes: Guest Artists
Budget: $50,000 - $100,000
Income Sources: Private Foundations/Grants/Endowments; Business/Corporate Donations; Box Office; Government Grants; Individual Donations
Season: September - May   **Annual Attendance:** 8,000
Affiliations: ASOL; Omaha Symphony Guild; ASTA; MENC
Performance Facilities: University Recital Hall

OMAHA SYMPHONY ASSOCIATION
1615 Howard Street, Suite 310, Omaha, NE 68102
(402) 342-3836
FAX: (402) 342-3819
Founded: 1921
Arts Area: Symphony; Orchestra; Chamber; Ensemble
Status: Professional; Non-Profit
Type: Performing; Touring; Resident; Educational; Sponsoring
Management: Bruce Hangen, Music Director
Paid Staff: 14
Paid Artists: 36
Utilizes: Guest Conductors; Guest Artists
Budget: $1,000,000 - $5,000,000
Income Sources: Private Foundations/Grants/Endowments; Business/Corporate Donations; Box Office; Government Grants; Individual Donations
Annual Attendance: 72,000
Affiliations: ASOL; NEA; Nebraska Arts Council; United Arts Omaha

VOCAL MUSIC

CLARION CHAMBER CHORALE
PO Box 31366, Omaha, NE 68131
(402) 597-1240; (402) 330-5505
Founded: 1982
Arts Area: Choral
Status: Semi-Professional; Non-Profit
Type: Performing; Touring
Purpose: To present concerts to the general public that focus on choral literature suitable for chamber ensembles; 80% performed is sung a cappella, 20% is sung with instrumental accompaniment
Management: Clarion Choral Foundation; Stanley Schmidt, Artistic Director
Officers: Morgan Holmes, President; Karen Weber, Publicist
Volunteer Staff: 32
Utilizes: Guest Artists
Budget: $1,000 - $50,000
Income Sources: Private Foundations/Grants/Endowments; Business/Corporate Donations; Box Office; Individual Donations
Season: September - April
Affiliations: Clarion Choral Foundations
Performance Facilities: First United Methodist Church

DIE MEISTERSINGERS
PO Box 241281, Omaha, NE 68124
(402) 453-3719
> **Founded:** 1964
> **Arts Area:** Choral; Ethnic; Folk; Jazz
> **Status:** Semi-Professional
> **Type:** Performing; Touring; Educational
> **Purpose:** Committed to the promotion of excellence in choral music in Nebraska
> **Management:** Jim Elsberry, Artistic Director
> **Officers:** Paul Rooker, President
> **Paid Staff:** 1   **Volunteer Staff:** 24
> **Utilizes:** Special Technical Talent; Guest Artists
> **Budget:** $1,000 - $50,000
> **Income Sources:** Private Foundations/Grants/Endowments; Box Office; Individual Donations
> **Season:** Fall - Spring   **Annual Attendance:** 3,000
> **Affiliations:** United Arts Council; Omaha Arts Council
> **Performance Facilities:** University of Nebraska Performing Arts Center

OPERA/OMAHA
PO Box 807 DTS, Omaha, NE 68101
(402) 346-4398
> **Founded:** 1958
> **Arts Area:** Grand Opera; Lyric Opera; Light Opera; Musical Theatre
> **Status:** Professional; Non-Profit
> **Type:** Performing; Touring; Resident; Educational; Sponsoring
> **Management:** Mary Robert, General/Artistic Director; Keith Warner, Associate Artistic Director; Hal France, Music Director
> **Paid Staff:** 12   **Volunteer Staff:** 250
> **Paid Artists:** 420   **Non-Paid Artists:** 260
> **Utilizes:** Special Technical Talent; Guest Conductors; Guest Artists; Guest Directors
> **Budget:** $1,000,000 - $5,000,000
> **Income Sources:** Private Foundations/Grants/Endowments; Business/Corporate Donations; Box Office; Government Grants; Individual Donations; Fundraising
> **Season:** September - March   **Annual Attendance:** 35,000
> **Affiliations:** OA
> **Performance Facilities:** Orpheum Theater; Witherspoon Hall

THEATRE

CENTER STAGE
3010 R Street, Omaha, NE 68107
(402) 733-5777
> **Founded:** 1980
> **Arts Area:** Community; Theatrical Group
> **Status:** Non-Professional; Non-Profit
> **Type:** Performing
> **Purpose:** The only theater in Omaha that attempts to present ethnic performances
> **Management:** Linda Runice, Executive Director
> **Officers:** Roger Sayers, President; Susan Murphy, Vice President; Mark Grieb, Treasurer
> **Paid Staff:** 2   **Volunteer Staff:** 2
> **Paid Artists:** 60
> **Utilizes:** Special Technical Talent; Guest Artists; Guest Directors
> **Budget:** $50,000 - $100,000
> **Income Sources:** Private Foundations/Grants/Endowments; Business/Corporate Donations; Box Office; Government Grants; Individual Donations
> **Season:** August - July   **Annual Attendance:** 6,000
> **Performance Facilities:** LaFerne Williams Center

CIRCLE THEATRE, INC.
2015 South 60th Street, Omaha, NE 68106
(402) 553-4715
> **Founded:** 1983
> **Arts Area:** Dinner; Theatrical Group
> **Status:** Semi-Professional; Non-Profit
> **Type:** Performing; Touring; Resident
> **Purpose:** To develop and produce new works by Nebraska playwrights utilizing Nebraska artists
> **Management:** Laura Marr, Executive Director; Peg Gibbs, Bookkeeper; Doug Marr, Artistic Director; Robyn Munger, Technical Director

Officers: Ward Peters, President; Jane Erdenberger, Vice President; Dave D'Elia, Treasurer; Doug Paterson, Secretary
Paid Staff: 4   **Volunteer Staff:** 5
Paid Artists: 75   **Non-Paid Artists:** 10
Utilizes: Guest Artists; Guest Directors
Budget: $50,000 - $100,000
Income Sources: Private Foundations/Grants/Endowments; Business/Corporate Donations; Box Office; Government Grants; Individual Donations
Season: 52 Weeks
Annual Attendance: 6,000
Performance Facilities: Vidlak's Cafe

EMMY GIFFORD CHILDREN'S THEATER
3504 Center Street, Omaha, NE 68105
(402) 345-4852
Founded: 1949
Arts Area: Theatrical Group
Status: Professional; Non-Profit
Type: Performing; Touring; Resident; Educational
Purpose: To provide a quality theater experience for the children of Omaha and their families
Management: Mark Hoeger, Executive Director; James Larson, Artistic Director; Roberta Larson, Associate Director; Lisa Winton, Marketing
Officers: Susy Buffet, Board President
Paid Staff: 10
Paid Artists: 9
Utilizes: Special Technical Talent; Guest Artists; Guest Directors
Budget: $500,000 - $1,000,000
Income Sources: Private Foundations/Grants/Endowments; Business/Corporate Donations; Box Office; Government Grants; Individual Donations
Season: September - June
Annual Attendance: 101,403
Affiliations: TCG; ASSITEJ

FIREHOUSE THEATRE/NOODLES COMEDY CLUB
11th & Jackson, Omaha, NE 68102
(402) 346-6009
Founded: 1972
Arts Area: Professional; Musical; Dinner; Theatrical Group
Status: Professional; Commercial
Type: Performing
Purpose: To provide good theatre commercially
Management: Keith Allerton, General Manager, Firehouse Theatre; Howard Koffin, General Manager, Noodles Comedy Club
Paid Staff: 20
Paid Artists: 10
Utilizes: Special Technical Talent; Guest Conductors; Guest Artists; Guest Directors
Budget: $1,000,000 - $5,000,000
Income Sources: Box Office
Season: 52 Weeks
Annual Attendance: 100,000
Affiliations: ADTI; NDTA; AEA
Performance Facilities: Firehouse Dinner Theatre

GRANDE OLDE PLAYERS
2339 North 90th, Omaha, NE 68134
(402) 397-5262
Founded: 1983
Arts Area: Musical; Community; Theatrical Group
Status: Non-Professional; Non-Profit
Type: Performing; Touring; Educational
Purpose: To provide an artistic outlet and education in the arts for people over fifty-five or those advocates of fifty-five and better
Management: Mark J. Manhart, Artistic Director; Bonnie Gill Kusleika, Administrative Director
Officers: Mark J. Manhart, President
Volunteer Staff: 50
Non-Paid Artists: 36
Utilizes: Guest Directors
Budget: $1,000 - $50,000

Income Sources: Private Foundations/Grants/Endowments; Business/Corporate Donations; Box Office; Government Grants; Individual Donations
Season: 52 Weeks   **Annual Attendance:** 3,000

NEBRASKA THEATRE CARAVAN
6915 Cass Street, Omaha, NE 68132
(402) 553-4890
FAX: (402) 553-6288
Founded: 1976
Arts Area: Professional; Theatrical Group
Status: Professional; Non-Profit
Type: Performing; Touring; Resident; Educational
Purpose: To bring quality entertainment and educational opportunities to communities where distance, financial limitations, or lack of appropriate resources has hindered or prevented such activities
Management: Charles Jones, Artistic Director; Carolyn Rutherford, Managing Director; Kathy Wheeldon, Public Relations Director
Officers: Redd Thomas, Board President
Paid Staff: 2
Utilizes: Special Technical Talent; Guest Artists; Guest Directors
Budget: $500,000 - $1,000,000
Income Sources: Private Foundations/Grants/Endowments; Business/Corporate Donations; Box Office; Government Grants; Individual Donations
Season: September - May
Affiliations: TCG
Performance Facilities: Omaha Playhouse

OMAHA COMMUNITY PLAYHOUSE
6915 Cass Street, Omaha, NE 68132
(402) 553-4890
FAX: (402) 553-6288
Founded: 1924
Arts Area: Theatrical Group
Status: Professional; Non-Professional; Non-Profit
Type: Performing; Touring
Purpose: To offer the best possible theatre for our audiences and to offer those people who choose to pursue theatre as an avocation a place to perform
Management: Charles Jones, Executive Director; Ginny Winsor, General Manager; Carolyn Rutherford, Managing Director; Nebraska Theatre Caravan; Susan Long, Comptroller
Officers: L.B. Thomas, President, Board of Trustees; Sue Fegler, Executive Vice President; Dee Owen, Secretary; John Hancock, Treasurer
Paid Staff: 24   **Volunteer Staff:** 3,000
Paid Artists: 15
Utilizes: Special Technical Talent; Guest Artists; Guest Directors
Budget: $1,000,000 - $5,000,000
Income Sources: Private Foundations/Grants/Endowments; Business/Corporate Donations; Box Office; Government Grants; Individual Donations
Season: September - July   **Annual Attendance:** 120,000
Affiliations: AACT; TCG
Performance Facilities: Omaha Community Playhouse

OMAHA MAGIC THEATRE
1417 Farnam, Omaha, NE 68102
(402) 346-1227
Founded: 1968
Arts Area: Professional; Musical; Theatrical Group
Status: Professional; Non-Profit
Type: Performing; Touring
Purpose: Research, development, production and touring of new plays with music; training of theatre artists
Management: JoAnn Schmidman, Artistic Director
Officers: JoAnn Schmidman, President; Bette Schmidman, Vice President
Paid Staff: 15   **Volunteer Staff:** 25
Paid Artists: 60   **Non-Paid Artists:** 12
Utilizes: Special Technical Talent; Guest Artists; Guest Directors
Budget: $100,000 - $500,000
Income Sources: Private Foundations/Grants/Endowments; Business/Corporate Donations; Box Office; Government Grants; Individual Donations
Season: 52 Weeks   **Annual Attendance:** 15,000

PERFORMING SERIES

TUESDAY MUSICAL CONCERT SERIES
8543 Hickory, Omaha, NE 68124
(402) 391-4661
FAX: (402) 397-9510
Founded: 1892
Arts Area: Present Classical Recitals
Status: Non-Professional; Non-Profit
Type: Sponsoring
Purpose: To present four or five concerts annually for the purpose of hearing fine performers play fine music
Officers: Mrs. Thomas P.K. Lim, President; Mrs. James Keene III, Vice President; Mrs. Julian Rips, Secretary; Mrs. David Shrader, Treasurer
Volunteer Staff: 36
Paid Artists: 5
Utilizes: Guest Artists
Budget: $50,000 - $100,000
Income Sources: Private Foundations/Grants/Endowments; Business/Corporate Donations; Box Office; Government Grants; Individual Donations
Season: September - May   **Annual Attendance:** 5,000
Performance Facilities: Josly Art Museum

FACILITY

FIREHOUSE DINNER THEATRE
11th & Jackson, Omaha, NE 68102
(402) 346-8833
Type of Facility: Theatre House
Facility Originally: Fire Station
Type of Stage: Thrust
Stage Dimensions: 26'x30'   **Orchestra Pit**
Seating Capacity: 289
Year Built: 1903
Year Remodeled: 1986   **Architect:** Mueller & Mueller   **Cost:** $200,000
Contact for Rental: Keith Allerton;   (402) 346-8833

OMAHA CIVIC AUDITORIUM - MUSIC HALL
1804 Capitol Avenue, Omaha, NE 68134
(402) 444-4750
Type of Facility: Theatre Complex; Auditorium; Arena
Facility Originally: Vaudeville
Type of Stage: Proscenium
Stage Dimensions: 114'Wx48'D   **Orchestra Pit**
Seating Capacity: Theater 2,608 **Cost:** $1,800,000
Acoustical Consultant: Coffeen and Associates
Contact for Rental: Susan Busskohl;   (402) 444-4750
Manager: Larry Foster;   (402) 444-4750
Resident Groups: Omaha Symphony Association; Opera Omaha; Omaha Ballet
The building also contains an 11,500-seat arena with flexible staging.

ORPHEUM THEATER
409 South 16th Street, Omaha, NE 68102
(402) 444-4750
Type of Facility: Theatre House
Facility Originally: Vaudeville
Type of Stage: Proscenium
Stage Dimensions: 54'Wx48'D
Orchestra Pit
Seating Capacity: 2,759
Year Built: 1927
Year Remodeled: 1975   **Architect:** Leo A. Daly   **Cost:** $2,000,000
Contact for Rental: Susan Busskohl;   (402) 444-4750
Manager: Larry Foster;   (402) 444-4750
Resident Groups: Omaha Symphony Association; Omaha Ballet; Opera/Omaha

Papillion

DANCE

OMAHA INTERNATIONAL FOLK DANCERS
525 Cordes Drive, Papillion, NE 68046
(402) 339-4660
Founded: 1979
Arts Area: Ethnic; Folk
Status: Non-Profit
Type: Performing; Educational
Purpose: To provide a cultural experience through folk dancing for both children and adults
Officers: Alice Morris, Chairman of the Board
Volunteer Staff: 20
Utilizes: Special Technical Talent; Guest Artists
Budget: $1,000 - $50,000
Income Sources: Individual Donations
Season: 52 Weeks

NEVADA

Carson City

THEATRE

BREWERY ARTS CENTER
449 West King, Carson City, NV 89703
(702) 883-1976
    Arts Area: Musical; Community; Folk; Theatrical Group
    Status: Non-Professional; Non-Profit
    Type: Performing; Sponsoring
    Purpose: To provide and promote arts and cultural opportunities in Carson City, Nevada
    Management: Carl Dahlen, Executive Director; Jean Murray, Program Director
    Paid Staff: 4   **Volunteer Staff:** 30
    Budget: $100,000 - $500,000
    Income Sources: Private Foundations/Grants/Endowments; Business/Corporate Donations; Box Office; Government Grants; Individual Donations
    Performance Facilities: Carson City Community Center; Brewery Arts Center

PROSCENIUM PLAYERS
PO Box 1165, Carson City, NV 89702
(702) 883-1976
    Arts Area: Community; Theatrical Group
    Status: Non-Professional; Non-Profit
    Type: Performing; Resident
    Purpose: To bring live theatre to the community; to give interested persons an opportunity to participate
    Officers: Carolyn Demar, President; Matt Rifley, Vice President; Carla Davis, Secretary; Jonni Moon, Treasurer; Pete Coates, Member-at-Large
    Volunteer Staff: 15
    Non-Paid Artists: 20
    Budget: $1,000 - $50,000
    Income Sources: Box Office; Individual Donations
    Season: September - June   **Annual Attendance:** 2,000
    Affiliations: Nevada Community Theatre Association; Brewery Arts Center; Carson City Chamber of Commerce
    Performance Facilities: Brewery Arts Center

Incline Village

INSTRUMENTAL MUSIC

NORTH LAKE TAHOE SYMPHONY ASSOCIATION
PO Box 4368, Incline Village, NV 89450
(702) 831-4024; (702) 831-4662
    Founded: 1972
    Arts Area: Symphony; Orchestra; Chamber; Instrumental Group
    Status: Professional; Non-Professional; Non-Profit
    Type: Resident; Sponsoring
    Purpose: To bring quality music to our community in an on-going series of free concerts
    Management: John Hays, President; Carl Robinson and Andrea Guthrie, Directors; Joy Miechel, Vice President
    Volunteer Staff: 25
    Paid Artists: 80
    Utilizes: Guest Conductors; Guest Artists; Guest Directors   **Budget:** $1,000 - $50,000
    Income Sources: Private Foundations/Grants/Endowments; Individual Donations; Membership Dues
    Season: 52 Weeks   **Annual Attendance:** 1,500
    Performance Facilities: The Chateau

Las Vegas

DANCE

BALLET COLBERT
4225 Spencer, #206, Las Vegas, NV 89119
(702) 893-9782
    Founded: 1980

Status: Semi-Professional; Non-Profit
Type: Performing; Educational
Officers: M.M. Colbert, Director
Utilizes: Visual Artists; Composers
Budget: $1,000 - $50,000
Income Sources: Business/Corporate Donations; Box Office; Government Grants; Individual Donations
Season: 52 Weeks

NEVADA DANCE THEATRE
4505 South Maryland Parkway, Las Vegas, NV 89154
(702) 739-3838
FAX: (702) 739-1355
Founded: 1972
Arts Area: Modern; Ballet; Ethnic
Status: Professional; Non-Profit
Type: Performing; Touring; Resident; Educational; Sponsoring
Purpose: To provide quality performance to the people of Nevada
Management: Norman Cain, Company Manager; Vassili Sulich, Artistic Director
Officers: Mrs. J.K. Houssels, Jr., Honorary Chairman of the Board
Paid Staff: 8   Volunteer Staff: 150
Paid Artists: 25   Non-Paid Artists: 12
Utilizes: Special Technical Talent; Guest Artists; Guest Choreographers
Budget: $500,000 - $1,000,000
Income Sources: Private Foundations/Grants/Endowments; Business/Corporate Donations; Box Office; Government Grants; Individual Donations
Season: 52 Weeks   Annual Attendance: 20,000
Affiliations: Academy of Nevada Dance Theatre; University of Nevada
Performance Facilities: Judy Bayley Theatre

INSTRUMENTAL MUSIC

CHAMBER MUSIC SOUTHWEST
UNLV Department of Music, 4505 Maryland Parkway, Las Vegas, NV 89154
(702) 739-3377
Founded: 1987
Arts Area: Chamber; Ensemble; Instrumental Group
Status: Professional; Non-Profit
Type: Performing; Touring; Educational
Purpose: To advance the cause of high quality chamber music in southern Nevada; to foster the growth of understanding of great music in Las Vegas
Officers: Richard L. Soule and Daniel Lewin, Directors
Volunteer Staff: 4
Paid Artists: 15   Non-Paid Artists: 8
Utilizes: Guest Artists
Budget: $1,000 - $50,000
Income Sources: Private Foundations/Grants/Endowments; Business/Corporate Donations; Box Office; Government Grants; Individual Donations
Season: October - May   Annual Attendance: 1,200
Affiliations: University of Nevada-Las Vegas; KNPR-FM
Performance Facilities: Artemus W. Ham Hall; Judy Bayley Theatre; Black Box Theatre

NEVADA SYMPHONY ORCHESTRA
4505 Maryland Parkway, Las Vegas, NV 89154
(702) 739-3420
FAX: (702) 739-3850
Founded: 1980
Arts Area: Symphony; Orchestra
Status: Professional; Non-Profit
Type: Performing; Educational
Management: Virko Baley, Music Director; Judith Markham, Executive Director; Timothy Bonenfant, Director of Operations
Officers: M. Rex Baird, President; Bruce B. Borgelt, Vice President; Colleen Schroeder, Secretary; B. Michl Lloyd, Treasurer/President Elect
Paid Staff: 4
Paid Artists: 60
Utilizes: Guest Conductors; Guest Artists
Budget: $500,000 - $1,000,000

Budget: $500,000 - $1,000,000
Income Sources: Private Foundations/Grants/Endowments; Business/Corporate Donations; Box Office; Government Grants; Individual Donations
Season: 52 Weeks **Annual Attendance:** 20,000
Affiliations: ASOL; Las Vegas Symphonic and Chamber Music Association
Performance Facilities: Artemus Ham Hall, University of Nevada-Las Vegas

SIERRA WIND QUINTET
4505 Maryland Parkway, Las Vegas, NV 89154
(702) 739-3738
FAX: (702) 597-4194
Arts Area: Chamber; Ensemble; Ethnic; Instrumental Group
Status: Professional; Non-Profit
Type: Performing; Touring; Resident; Educational; Sponsoring
Purpose: To promote the highest standards of chamber music and education nationally and internationally
Management: Stephen Caplan, Executive Director
Officers: Patrick Gaffey, President
Budget: $1,000 - $50,000
Income Sources: Private Foundations/Grants/Endowments; Business/Corporate Donations; Box Office; Government Grants; Individual Donations
Performance Facilities: Artemus W. Ham Concert Hall

THEATRE

LAS VEGAS LITTLE THEATRE
2026 Western Avenue, Las Vegas, NV 89102
(702) 383-0021
Founded: 1974
Arts Area: Musical; Community; Theatrical Group
Status: Semi-Professional; Non-Profit
Type: Performing; Educational
Purpose: To educate and entertain the community while providing an hands-on training ground for interested artists
Management: Jack Bell, Executive Producer; Paul A. Thornton, Managing Director
Officers: Paul A. Thornton, President; Erin Breen, Vice President; Karl Johnson, Secretary; Rae Fell, Treasurer
Volunteer Staff: 12
Paid Artists: 2
Utilizes: Special Technical Talent; Guest Directors
Budget: $1,000 - $50,000
Income Sources: Private Foundations/Grants/Endowments; Business/Corporate Donations; Box Office; Government Grants; Individual Donations
Season: September - June **Annual Attendance:** 5,000
Affiliations: Nevada Community Theatre Association; Allied Arts Council of Southern Nevada; AACT

PERFORMING SERIES

NEVADA SYMPHONY ORCHESTRA
4505 Maryland Parkway, Las Vegas, NV 89154
(702) 739-3420
FAX: (702) 736-6656
Founded: 1980
Arts Area: Vocal Music; Instrumental Music
Status: Professional; Non-Profit
Type: Performing; Educational; Sponsoring
Purpose: To offer performances, services and educational opportunities and add to the quality of life in Las Vegas through the Las Vegas Symphony Orchestra, Las Vegas Chamber Players and Las Vegas Opera Company
Management: Virko Baley, Artistic Director
Paid Staff: 2 **Volunteer Staff:** 100
Utilizes: Guest Artists
Budget: $100,000 - $500,000
Income Sources: Private Foundations/Grants/Endowments; Business/Corporate Donations; Box Office; Government Grants; Individual Donations

REED WHIPPLE CULTURAL ARTS CENTER
821 Las Vegas Boulevard North, Las Vegas, NV 89101
(702) 386-6211
Founded: 1961
Arts Area: Dance; Vocal Music; Instrumental Music; Theater
Status: Non-Profit

Type: Performing; Touring; Educational; Sponsoring
Purpose: Community arts developed through programming education, coordination and community involvement
Management: Patricia L. Harris, Center Coordinator; City of Las Vegas Department of Parks; And Leisure Activities; Cultural & Community Affairs Div.
Officers: David L.Kuiper, Department Director; Joanne L. Nivison, Division Chief; Jan L. Jones, Mayor; William Noonan, City Manager
Paid Staff: 5 **Volunteer Staff:** 10
Paid Artists: 20 **Non-Paid Artists:** 100
Utilizes: Special Technical Talent; Guest Artists; Guest Directors
Budget: $50,000 - $100,000
Income Sources: Private Foundations/Grants/Endowments; Business/Corporate Donations; Box Office; Government Grants; Individual Donations
Season: 52 Weeks
Affiliations: ACA; Nevada Recreation and Parks Society; Nevada Presenters Network

FACILITY

LAS VEGAS CONVENTION AND VISITORS AUTHORITY-CASHMAN'S FIELD CENTER
850 Las Vegas Boulevard North, Las Vegas, NV 89101
(702) 386-7100
   Type of Facility: Concert Hall; Auditorium; Theatre House; Multi-Purpose; Room; Loft
   Type of Stage: Proscenium
   Seating Capacity: 1,938
   Year Built: 1983
   Architect: SC3 Associates
   Cost: $26,000,000
   Contact for Rental: Thomas A. Smith, General Manager;   (702) 386-7100
   Manager: Thomas A. Smith

REED WHIPPLE CULTURAL ARTS CENTER
821 Las Vegas Boulevard North, Las Vegas, NV 89101
(702) 229-6211
FAX: (702) 383-6306
   Type of Facility: Theatre Complex; Studio Performance; Multi-Purpose; Room
   Facility Originally: LDS Church Stake Center
   Type of Stage: Proscenium
   Stage Dimensions: 18'x45'x24'   **Seating Capacity:** 300
   Year Built: 1961
   Year Remodeled: 1975
   Contact for Rental: Patricia Harris;   (702) 229-6211
   Resident Groups: Las Vegas Civic Symphony; The Rainbow Company; The Las Vegas Civic Ballet; Las Vegas Summer Orchestra; Las Vegas Youth Orchestra

UNIVERSITY OF NEVADA-LAS VEGAS - ARTEMUS HAM CONCERT HALL
4505 Maryland Parkway, Las Vegas, NV 89154
(702) 739-3737
   Type of Facility: Concert Hall; Opera House
   Type of Stage: End Stage
   Stage Dimensions: 60'Wx40'D; downstage 60'W; Hydraulic lift   **Orchestra Pit**
   Seating Capacity: 1,885
   Year Built: 1976
   Architect: James McDaniel
   Cost: $4,000,000
   Acoustical Consultant: Bolt, Beranek & Newman
   Contact for Rental: Facilities Manager;   (702) 739-3737
   Manager: Rick Romito
   Resident Groups: Las Vegas Chamber Players; Las Vegas Symphony; Las Vegas Opera; Nevada School of the Arts

Reno

INSTRUMENTAL MUSIC

RENO CHAMBER ORCHESTRA
1595 Skyline Boulevard, Reno, NV 89509
(702) 826-0880
   Founded: 1973
   Arts Area: Orchestra
   Status: Professional; Non-Profit

Type: Performing; Educational
Purpose: To present quality chamber orchestra music to the area
Management: Judith F. Simpson, Manager; Cathy Chapman, Assistant Manager
Officers: Doug Damon, President; Ralph Weiss, First Vice President; Neal Ferguson, Second Vice President; John Walker, Treasurer; Robbi Whipp, Secretary
Paid Staff: 3
Paid Artists: 45
Utilizes: Guest Conductors; Guest Artists; Guest Directors
Budget: $100,000 - $500,000
Income Sources: Private Foundations/Grants/Endowments; Business/Corporate Donations; Box Office; Government Grants; Individual Donations
Season: October - May
Annual Attendance: 3,500
Affiliations: ASOL
Performance Facilities: Nightingale Concert Hall

VOCAL MUSIC

NEVADA OPERA ASSOCIATION
150 South Virginia (rear), Reno, NV 89501
(702) 786-4046; (800) 992-2072
FAX: (702) 786-4063
Founded: 1968
Arts Area: Grand Opera; Lyric Opera; Light Opera; Operetta
Status: Professional; Non-Profit
Type: Performing; Resident
Purpose: To encourage and promote opera and musical theater in northern Nevada
Management: Ted Puffer, Artistic Director; Donna Picollo, Business Manager
Officers: Helen Buck, President
Paid Staff: 3 **Volunteer Staff:** 100
Paid Artists: 75
Utilizes: Special Technical Talent; Guest Conductors; Guest Artists
Budget: $500,000 - $1,000,000
Income Sources: Private Foundations/Grants/Endowments; Business/Corporate Donations; Box Office; Government Grants; Individual Donations
Season: October - April   **Annual Attendance:** 12,000
Affiliations: OA
Performance Facilities: Pioneer Theater

FACILITY

CENTENNIAL COLISEUM - RENO SPARKS CONVENTION AND VISITORS AUTHORITY
4590 South Virginia, Reno, NV 89502
(702) 827-7600
FAX: (702) 827-7646
Type of Facility: Auditorium
Type of Stage: Flexible
Seating Capacity: 7,500
Year Built: 1965   **Architect:** Richard J. Neutra   **Cost:** $5,000,000
Contact for Rental: Lindh Stednick;   (702) 827-7600

PIONEER CENTER FOR THE PERFROMING ARTS
100 South Virginia Street, Reno, NV 89501
(702) 786-5105
FAX: (702) 786-3086
Type of Facility: Auditorium; Theatre House; Multi-Purpose
Type of Stage: Proscenium
Stage Dimensions: 70'x100'x38'   **Orchestra Pit**
Seating Capacity: 1,434
Year Built: 1968   **Architect:** Bozalis, Dickinson, Roloff   **Cost:** $3,000,000
Contact for Rental: Kathi Baglin;   (702) 786-5105
Manager: John Shelton, Executive Director
Resident Groups: Nevada Opera Association; Reno Philharmonic Orchestra; UNR Performing Artists Series; Washoe County Community Concert Association; Nevada Festival Ballet

RENO LITTLE THEATER
690 North Sierra, PO Box 2088, Reno, NV 89505
(702) 329-0661
    Type of Facility: Theatre House
    Facility Originally: Meeting Hall; Movie House
    Type of Stage: Proscenium
    Seating Capacity: 289
    Year Remodeled: 1986   **Architect:** Graham Eskine   **Cost:** $260,000
    Acoustical Consultant: Phil Raglin
    Contact for Rental: Joan Long, Business Manager;   (702) 329-0661

UNIVERSITY OF NEVADA-RENO - CHURCH FINE ARTS CENTER
Reno, NV 89557
(702) 784-6659
    Type of Facility: Theatre Complex; Auditorium; Studio Performance; Performance Center; Theatre House
    Year Built: 1960   **Architect:** Richard J. Neutra   **Cost:** $1,250,000
    Year Remodeled: 1986   **Architect:** Vhay and Ferrari   **Cost:** $4,500,000
    Contact for Rental: Karren Garel;   (702) 784-6837
    Resident Groups: Nevada Repertory Company
    Church Fine Arts Center contains the Experimental Theatre, Fine Arts Theatre and Nightingale Hall. See separate listings for additional information.

UNIVERSITY OF NEVADA-RENO - CHURCH FINE ARTS CENTER - FINE ARTS THEATRE
Reno, NV 89557
(702) 784-6659
    Type of Facility: Theatre House
    Type of Stage: Proscenium
    Stage Dimensions: 30'x36'
    Seating Capacity: 270
    Year Built: 1960   **Architect:** Richard J. Neutra   **Cost:** $1,250,000
    Contact for Rental: Karren Garel;   (702) 784-6837
    Manager: James Bernardi

UNIVERSITY OF NEVADA-RENO - CHURCH FINE ARTS CENTER - NIGHTINGALE HALL
Reno, NV 89557
(702) 784-6659
    Type of Facility: Concert Hall
    Type of Stage: Proscenium
    Stage Dimensions: 48'x30'
    Seating Capacity: 650
    Year Built: 1986   **Architect:** Vhay and Ferrari   **Cost:** $3,000,000
    Contact for Rental: Karren Garel;   (702) 784-6837
    Manager: Music Department

UNIVERSITY OF NEVADA-RENO - CHURCH FINE ARTS CENTER, REDFIELD STUDIO THEATRE
Reno, NV 89557
(702) 784-6659
    Type of Facility: Studio Performance
    Type of Stage: Flexible
    Stage Dimensions: 50'x50'
    Seating Capacity: 200
    Year Built: 1986   **Architect:** Vhay and Ferrari   **Cost:** $1,000,000
    Contact for Rental: Karren Garel;   (702) 784-6837
    Manager: James Bernardi
    Resident Groups: The Nevada Repertory Company

UNIVERSITY OF NEVADA-RENO - LAWLOR EVENTS CENTER
Reno, NV 89557
(702) 784-4659
    Type of Facility: Arena; Multi-Purpose
    Type of Stage: Flexible
    Seating Capacity: 12,400
    Year Built: 1983   **Architect:** Crain Anderson   **Cost:** $26,000,000
    Acoustical Consultant: C.P. Boner & Associates
    Contact for Rental: Robert Stewart, Joseph Kerr;   (702) 784-4659
    Manager: Robert Stewart

Virginia City

FACILITY

PIPER'S OPERA HOUSE
Box 157, Virginia City, NV 89440
(702) 847-0433
    Type of Facility: Theatre House
    Type of Stage: Proscenium
    Stage Dimensions: 50'Wx35'D
    Seating Capacity: 500
    Year Built: 1867
    Year Remodeled: 1980
    Contact for Rental: Louise Driggs;   (702) 847-0433

NEW HAMPSHIRE

Centre Harbor

PERFORMING SERIES

NEW HAMPSHIRE MUSIC FESTIVAL
PO Box 147, Centre Harbor, NH 03226
(603) 253-4331
Founded: 1952
Arts Area: Festivals; Classical & Chamber music
Status: Professional; Non-Profit
Type: Performing; Touring; Educational
Purpose: To promote appreciation and dissemination of classical music in the Lakes Region of New Hampshire
Management: David H. Graham, Executive Director
Officers: T. Holmes Moore, President; Lewis A. Aldrich, Treasurer
Paid Staff: 3 **Volunteer Staff:** 1
Paid Artists: 48
Utilizes: Guest Conductors; Guest Artists
Budget: $100,000 - $500,000
Income Sources: Private Foundations/Grants/Endowments; Business/Corporate Donations; Box Office; Government Grants; Individual Donations
Season: July - August **Annual Attendance:** 9,000
Affiliations: ASOL
Performance Facilities: Plymouth's Silver Hall; Gilford's Middle High School Auditorium

Claremont

FACILITY

CLAREMONT OPERA HOUSE
PO Box 664, Claremont, NH 03755
(603) 542-4433
Founded: 1897
Type of Facility: Theatre Complex; Concert Hall; Multi-Purpose
Facility Originally: Opera House
Type of Stage: Proscenium
Stage Dimensions: 34'Wx30'D
Seating Capacity: 787
Year Built: 1897 **Architect:** Charles Rich **Cost:** $62,000
Year Remodeled: 1977 **Architect:** Paul Mirski **Cost:** $1,000,000
Contact for Rental: John Goyette; (603) 542-4433

Concord

INSTRUMENTAL MUSIC

NEVERS' 2ND REGIMENT BAND
110 South State Street, Concord, NH 03301
(603) 225-2684
Founded: 1861
Arts Area: Band
Status: Semi-Professional; Non-Profit
Type: Performing
Purpose: To provide live band music to the residents of the Concord area and other areas throughout New Hampshire at no charge to the public
Management: Maryanne Sisk, Director; George M. West, Business Manager
Officers: Deborah G. Lincoln, Secretary; Elizabeth Densmore, Treasurer; Paul T. Giles, Historian
Paid Artists: 25
Utilizes: Guest Conductors; Guest Artists
Budget: $1,000 - $50,000
Income Sources: Private Foundations/Grants/Endowments; Individual Donations
Annual Attendance: 2,000

THEATRE

COMMUNITY PLAYERS OF CONCORD
PO Box 681, Concord, NH 03302
(603) 224-4905
   Founded: 1927
   Arts Area: Community; Theatrical Group
   Status: Non-Profit
   Type: Performing
   Purpose: To promote interest in all phases of community theater
   Officers: Sharon LaJoie, President; Betsy Stebbins, Vice President; Jeanne Bailey, Secretary; Fritz Sabbow,
Treasurer
   Budget: $1,000 - $50,000
   Income Sources: Box Office; Individual Donations
   Season: November - May   **Annual Attendance:** 6,000
   Affiliations: New Hampshire Community Theater Association
   Performance Facilities: Concord City Auditorium

FACILITY

THE FRIENDS OF THE CONCORD CITY AUDITORIUM
PO Box 652, Concord, NH 03302-0652
(603) 225-8580
   Type of Facility: Concert Hall; Auditorium; Theatre House
   Type of Stage: Proscenium
   Stage Dimensions: 26'x26'   **Orchestra Pit**
   Seating Capacity: 792
   Year Built: 1904
   Architect: Barn Raising (Community Volunteers)
   Contact for Rental: Eugene Blake;   (603) 225-8580
   Resident Groups: Concord Community Players; Walker Lecture Series; Concord Community Concert Association
   Restoration and rehabilitation of building; Foster use of the facility to benefit community citizens

Durham

FACILITY

UNIVERSITY OF NEW HAMPSHIRE - DURHAM
Paul Creative Arts Center, Durham, NH 03824
(603) 862-3038
   Type of Facility: Theatre Complex; Multi-Purpose
   Year Built: 1960   **Architect:** Sheply Bulfinch Richardson Abbott   **Cost:** $2,100,000
   Year Remodeled: 1982   **Architect:** University Architects   **Cost:** $300,000
   *Paul Creative Arts Center contains Bratton Recital Hall, Hennessy Theater and Johnson Theater. See separate listings
   for additional information.*

UNIVERSITY OF NEW HAMPSHIRE-DURHAM - BRATTON RECITAL HALL
Paul Creative Arts Center, Durham, NH 03824
(603) 862-3038
   Type of Facility: Recital Hall
   Facility Originally: School
   Type of Stage: Flexible
   Seating Capacity: 150
   Year Built: 1960
   Year Remodeled: 1982
   Resident Groups: Music Department

UNIVERSITY OF NEW HAMPSHIRE-DURHAM - HENNESSY THEATER
Paul Creative Arts Center, Durham, NH 03824
(603) 862-3038
   Type of Facility: Studio Performance; Arena
   Type of Stage: Flexible; Arena
   Seating Capacity: 200
   Year Built: 1960
   Year Remodeled: 1982

UNIVERSITY OF NEW HAMPSHIRE-DURHAM - JOHNSON THEATER
Paul Creative Arts Center, Durham, NH 03824
(603) 862-3038
    Type of Facility: Concert Hall; Theatre House
    Type of Stage: Proscenium
    Stage Dimensions: 65'Wx60'D; 39'10"Wx20'H proscenium opening **Orchestra Pit**
    Seating Capacity: 716
    Year Built: 1960
    Year Remodeled: 1990 **Cost:** $300,000

East Sullivan

INSTRUMENTAL MUSIC

APPLE HILL CENTER FOR CHAMBER MUSIC
Apple Hill Road, East Sullivan, NH 03445
(603) 847-3371
FAX: (603) 847-9972
    Founded: 1971
    Arts Area: Chamber; Ensemble
    Status: Professional; Semi-Professional; Non-Professional; Non-Profit
    Type: Performing; Resident; Educational; Sponsoring
    Purpose: The Apple Hill Chamber Players, a full-time, professional concert ensemble, joined by a distinguished guest faculty, coach students of all ages and at different levels in the interpretation of chamber music of all periods.
    Management: Eric Stumacher, Executive Director; Kathy Stumacher, Director of Administration; Susan King, Fiscal Manager; Harriet Feinberg, Recruiter/Music Librarian
    Officers: Julie Albright, President; Arthur Cohen, Vice President; Jeremiah Dolan, Secretary; David Ross, Treasurer
    Paid Staff: 5
    Paid Artists: 6
    Utilizes: Guest Artists
    Budget: $100,000 - $500,000
    Income Sources: Private Foundations/Grants/Endowments; Business/Corporate Donations; Box Office; Government Grants; Individual Donations
    Season: June - October **Annual Attendance:** 1,500
    Performance Facilities: Louise Shonk Kelly Concert Barn

Franconia

DANCE

WHITE MOUNTAIN SUMMER DANCE FESTIVAL
PO Box 94, Franconia, NH 03580
(603) 444-2928
FAX: (603) 444-1258
    Winter Address: c/o Dance Base Inc., 162 West 21st Street, New York, NY 10011; (212) 929-5733;
    FAX: (203) 233-2941
    Founded: 1979
    Arts Area: Modern; Ballet
    Status: Professional; Semi-Professional; Non-Professional; Non-Profit
    Type: Performing; Educational; Resident
    Purpose: To provide dance training and movement-analysis education; to create performance opportunities for local and area communities through a three-week intensive summer program
    Management: Laura Glenn, Artistic Director; Rebecca Lazier, Festival Coordinator
    Officers: John Murphy, President; Jim Severyn, Vice President; Michael Valcourt, Secretary
    Paid Staff: 2 **Volunteer Staff:** 10
    Paid Artists: 13 **Non-Paid Artists:** 55
    Budget: $50,000 - $100,000
    Income Sources: Private Foundations/Grants/Endowments; Box Office; Individual Donations; Tuition
    Season: July - August (3 weeks) **Annual Attendance:** 355
    Performance Facilities: White Mountain School, Littleton

INSTRUMENTAL

NORTH COUNTRY CHAMBER PLAYERS
PO Box 94, Franconia, NH 03580
(603) 869-3154
FAX: (603) 869-2660
Arts Area: Chamber
Status: Professional; Non-Profit
Type: Performing; Touring; Resident; Educational
Purpose: To bring classical music to northern New England
Management: Bonnie Bauch, Artistic Director
Officers: Kate Walsh, Chairman of the Board
Budget: $100,000 - $500,000
Income Sources: Private Foundations/Grants/Endowments; Business/Corporate Donations; Box Office; Government Grants; Individual Donations
Performance Facilities: Governor Adams Lodge, Lincoln; Sugar Hill Meeting House, Sugar Hill

Hampton

THEATRE

HAMPTON PLAYHOUSE
Winnacunnet Road, Hampton, NH 03842
(603) 926-3076
Founded: 1948
Arts Area: Professional; Summer Stock; Musical
Status: Professional; Commercial
Type: Performing; Resident; Educational
Management: Alfred Christie, Producing/Artistic Director; John Vari, Producer
Paid Staff: 10
Paid Artists: 35
Utilizes: Special Technical Talent; Guest Artists; Guest Directors
Budget: $100,000 - $500,000
Income Sources: Business/Corporate Donations; Box Office; Individual Donations
Season: June - September   **Annual Attendance:** 30,000
Affiliations: AEA; SSDC; CORST
Performance Facilities: Hampton Playhouse Theatre Arts Workshop

FACILITY

HAMPTON PLAYHOUSE THEATRE ARTS WORKSHOP
357 Winnacunnet Road, Hampton, NH 03842
(603) 926-3073
Type of Facility: Auditorium
Facility Originally: Barn
Type of Stage: Proscenium
Seating Capacity: 500
Year Built: 1787
Manager: John Vari
Resident Groups: Hampton Playhouse Company

Hanover

PERFORMING SERIES

HOPKINS CENTER SUMMER
Hopkins Center, Dartmouth College, Hanover, NH 03755
(603) 646-2424
Founded: 1962
Arts Area: Dance; Vocal Music; Instrumental Music; Theater
Status: Professional; Non-Profit
Type: Educational; Sponsoring
Purpose: To present performing and visual arts as both a co-curricular component to the Dartmouth community and as a regional arts resource
Management: Lewis Crickard, Director
Utilizes: Guest Artists; Guest Directors
Budget: $1,000,000 - $5,000,000

Income Sources: Private Foundations/Grants/Endowments; Business/Corporate Donations; Box Office; Government Grants; Individual Donations
Season: July - August   **Annual Attendance:** 250,000
Affiliations: Dartmouth College
Performance Facilities: Hopkins Center

Keene
FACILITY

ARTS CENTER ON BRICKYARD POND - KEENE STATE COLLEGE
229 Main Street, Keene, NH 03431
(603) 358-2167
FAX: (603) 358-2257
Founded: 1909
Type of Facility: Theatre Complex
Type of Stage: Thrust; Flexible; Proscenium; 3/4 Arena
Stage Dimensions: 36'6"x35'
Seating Capacity: Main Theatre - 572; Recital Hall - 360; Studio Theatre - 100
Year Built: 1981
Architect: Sheplley, Bullfinch
Cost: $7,000,000
Contact for Rental: Events Coordinator;   (603) 358-2167

Lincoln
PERFORMING SERIES

NORTH COUNTRY CENTER FOR THE ARTS
PO Box 1060, Lincoln, NH 03251
(603) 745-6032
Founded: 1986
Arts Area: Theater; Festivals
Status: Professional; Non-Profit
Type: Performing; Touring; Educational
Purpose: To present both adult and childrens theatre, theatre education and special events
Management: Van McLeod, Producing Director; Lesley Parker, Managing Director
Officers: Peter E. Gould, Board Chairman
Paid Staff: 2   **Volunteer Staff:** 60
Paid Artists: 70   **Non-Paid Artists:** 30
Utilizes: Guest Artists; Guest Directors
Budget: $100,000 - $500,000
Income Sources: Private Foundations/Grants/Endowments; Business/Corporate Donations; Box Office; Government Grants; Individual Donations
Season: May - September   **Annual Attendance:** 17,000

Manchester
INSTRUMENTAL MUSIC

NEW HAMPSHIRE PHILHARMONIC ORCHESTRA
PO Box 4547, Manchester, NH 03108
(603) 666-9023
Founded: 1959
Arts Area: Symphony; Orchestra
Status: Professional; Non-Professional; Non-Profit
Type: Performing; Resident; Educational
Purpose: To present classical concerts, enhance music education, and give non-professionals the opportunity to work with music professionals
Management: Roxanne L. Turner, Executive Director; Darcy Scott, Director of Public Relations; Art Mirabile, Stage Manager
Officers: Gregg Cunningham, President; Gary Turner, Vice President; Pat Cunningham, Secretary; Robert Consaga, Treasurer
Paid Staff: 3   **Volunteer Staff:** 12
Paid Artists: 5   **Non-Paid Artists:** 65
Utilizes: Guest Artists

Budget: $100,000 - $500,000
Income Sources: Private Foundations/Grants/Endowments; Business/Corporate Donations; Box Office; Individual Donations
Season: September - May   **Annual Attendance:** 100,000
Affiliations: ASOL; Manchester Chamber of Commerce
Performance Facilities: Palace Theatre

NEW HAMPSHIRE SYMPHONY ORCHESTRA
PO Box 1298, Manchester, NH 03105-1298
(603) 669-3559
FAX: (603) 623-1195
Founded: 1973
Arts Area: Symphony; Orchestra
Status: Professional; Non-Profit
Type: Performing; Touring; Educational
Management: David A. Ball, Executive Director; Alan D. Jordan, Director of Operations; Marian Royal, Administrative Assistant; James Bolle, Music Director
Officers: Leonard Lacouture, President; Donald Gendron, Vice President, Development; Susan Monson, Vice President-Planning; John Graf, Secretary; Richard Hodgkinson, Treasurer
Paid Staff: 5
Utilizes: Guest Artists
Budget: $100,000 - $500,000
Income Sources: Private Foundations/Grants/Endowments; Business/Corporate Donations; Box Office; Government Grants; Individual Donations
Season: October - May   **Annual Attendance:** 7,954
Affiliations: ASOL
Performance Facilities: Palace Theatre

FACILITY

NEW HAMPSHIRE PERFORMING ARTS CENTER
80 Hanover Street, PO Box 3006, Manchester, NH 03105
(603) 669-8021
Type of Facility: Concert Hall; Performance Center; Theatre House; Opera House
Facility Originally: Vaudeville
Type of Stage: Proscenium
Stage Dimensions: 62'Wx33'D; 40'Wx26'H proscenium opening   **Orchestra Pit**
Seating Capacity: 893
Year Built: 1915   **Architect:** Leon Lempart
Year Remodeled: 1985   **Architect:** Fred Matuszewski   **Cost:** $650,000
Contact for Rental: Robert Shea;   (603) 669-8021
Resident Groups: New Hampshire Performing Arts Center; New Hampshire Symphony Orchestra; Opera League of New Hampshire

Milford

THEATRE

PEACOCK PLAYERS CHILDREN'S THEATRE
PO Box 225, Milford, NH 03055
(603) 673-4005
FAX: (603) 673-4792
Founded: 1980
Arts Area: Musical; Theatrical Group
Status: Non-Professional; Non-Profit
Type: Performing; Educational
Purpose: Education, Entertainment
Management: Lorraine Lanes, Managing Director; Blair Hundtertmark, Artistic Director
Paid Staff: 2
Utilizes: Guest Conductors; Guest Directors
Budget: $1,000 - $50,000
Income Sources: Private Foundations/Grants/Endowments; Business/Corporate Donations; Box Office; Individual Donations; Tuition - workshops
Season: September - August   **Annual Attendance:** 5,000

PERFORMING SERIES

AMERICAN STAGE FESTIVAL
PO Box 225, Milford, NH 03055
(603) 673-6896
FAX: (603) 673-4792
> **Founded:** 1971
> **Arts Area:** Theater; Festival
> **Status:** Professional; Non-Profit
> **Type:** Performing; Touring; Resident; Educational; Developmental
> **Purpose:** To expand the spectrum of theatre by presenting entertaining, rewarding and challenging theatrical material, paying particular attention to pieces that reflect the concerns of southern New Hampshire
> **Management:** Richard Rose, Producing Director; Robert Walsh, Associate Director; Blanche Risteen, Marketing/Education; Cynthia Marshall, Subscriptions; Blair Hundtermare, John Thichnor, Young Company
> **Officers:** Mark Roberts, President; Lionel Bourasa, Vice President of Finance; Dora Weiner, Secretary
> **Paid Staff:** 15
> **Paid Artists:** 70 **Non-Paid Artists:** 30
> **Utilizes:** Guest Conductors; Guest Artists; Guest Directors
> **Budget:** $500,000 - $1,000,000
> **Income Sources:** Private Foundations/Grants/Endowments; Business/Corporate Donations; Box Office; Government Grants; Individual Donations
> **Season:** May - August
> **Affiliations:** NETC; AEA; SSDC; TCG; New Hampshire Theatre Council; Souhegan Theatre Council
> **Performance Facilities:** Souhegan Valley Theatre

FACILITY

SOUHEGAN VALLEY THEATRE
Mount Vernon Street, Milford, NH 03055
(603) 673-4005
FAX: (603) 673-4792
> **Founded:** 1973
> **Type of Facility:** Theatre House
> **Type of Stage:** Proscenium
> **Orchestra Pit**
> **Seating Capacity:** 500
> **Year Built:** 1975 **Architect:** Thomas Johnson **Cost:** $250,000
> **Contact for Rental:** Richard Rose, Manager; (603) 673-4005
> **Manager:** Richard Rose
> **Resident Groups:** American Stage Festival

Nashua

PERFORMING SERIES

KIDS INTO DRAMA
14 Court Street, Nashua, NH 03060
(603) 883-1506
> **Founded:** 1981
> **Arts Area:** Theater
> **Status:** Non-Profit
> **Type:** Performing; Touring; Educational
> **Management:** Robert W. Haven, Director; Michele Laliberty, Music Director
> **Volunteer Staff:** 4
> **Budget:** $1,000 - $50,000
> **Income Sources:** Box Office; Individual Donations
> **Season:** 52 Weeks **Annual Attendance:** 1,800
> **Performance Facilities:** Arts and Science Center Theatre

FACILITY

ARTS AND SCIENCE CENTER THEATRE
14 Court Street, Nashua, NH 03060
(603) 883-1506
> **Type of Facility:** Auditorium; Performance Center; Exhibition Galleries
> **Type of Stage:** Proscenium
> **Stage Dimensions:** 80'Wx40'D
> **Seating Capacity:** 230

Year Built: 1974   **Architect:** Carter & Woodruff   **Cost:** $150,000
Contact for Rental: Debra Espersen;   (603) 883-1506
Manager: Robert Daniels
Resident Groups: Granite Statesmen

New London

THEATRE

NEW LONDON PLAYERS
Main Street, PO Box 285, New London, NH 03257
(603) 526-6710
Founded: 1933
Arts Area: Professional; Summer Stock; Musical; Theatrical Group
Status: Professional; Commercial
Type: Performing; Resident
Purpose: To provide theatrical entertainment for summer visitors and summer residents of the Lake Sunapee Area
Management: Norman M. Leger, Producer; Steve Mendelson, Associate Producer
Paid Staff: 15
Paid Artists: 25
Utilizes: Special Technical Talent; Guest Artists; Guest Directors
Budget: $100,000 - $500,000
Income Sources: Box Office
Season: June - Labor Day   **Annual Attendance:** 20,000
Affiliations: NETC
Performance Facilities: New London Barn Playhouse

PERFORMING SERIES

SUMMER MUSIC ASSOCIATES
PO Box 603, New London, NH 03257
(603) 526-2154
Founded: 1974
Arts Area: Vocal Music; Instrumental Music
Status: Non-Profit
Type: Sponsoring
Purpose: To present a series of summer concerts for our knowledgeable audience by a dedicated volunteer board
Management: Robert Fraley, Program Committee Chariman
Officers: Beverly Wolf, President; Barbara Chase, Vice President; Andrew Supplee, Treasurer
Volunteer Staff: 24
Utilizes: Guest Artists
Budget: $1,000 - $50,000
Income Sources: Private Foundations/Grants/Endowments; Business/Corporate Donations; Box Office; Individual Donations
Season: June - August   **Annual Attendance:** 2,500
Performance Facilities: King Ridge Ski Lodge; Colby-Sawyer College

FACILITY

NEW LONDON BARN PLAYHOUSE
Main Street, PO Box 285, New London, NH 03257
(603) 526-4631
Type of Facility: Theatre House
Facility Originally: Barn
Type of Stage: Proscenium
Stage Dimensions: 12'x24'x20'   **Orchestra Pit**
Seating Capacity: 325
Year Built: 1820
Year Remodeled: 1990   **Architect:** Mike English   **Cost:** $200,000
Manager: Norman W. Leger;   (603) 526-6570
Resident Groups: New London Players

North Conway

THEATRE

MOUNT WASHINGTON VALLEY THEATRE COMPANY
Main Street, North Conway, NH 03860
(603) 356-5776
Founded: 1972
Arts Area: Summer Stock; Musical
Status: Professional; Non-Profit
Type: Performing; Resident
Purpose: To fill the summer evenings with the joy and excitement of live theatre while offering a training ground to young professionals
Officers: Linda Pinkham, President; Olga Morrill, Vice President; Doris Levesgue, Secretary; Dorothy Lovering, Treasurer
Paid Staff: 15   **Volunteer Staff:** 5
Paid Artists: 20   **Non-Paid Artists:** 5
Utilizes: Special Technical Talent; Guest Artists
Budget: $50,000 - $100,000
Income Sources: Private Foundations/Grants/Endowments; Business/Corporate Donations; Box Office; Government Grants; Individual Donations
Season: June - September   **Annual Attendance:** 7,000
Performance Facilities: Eastern Slope Playhouse

FACILITY

EASTERN SLOPE PLAYHOUSE
Main Street, North Conway, NH 03860
(603) 356-5776 summer; (603) 356-5425
FAX: (603) 356-8357
Type of Facility: Auditorium; Performance Center; Theatre House; Multi-Purpose
Type of Stage: Thrust; Flexible; Proscenium
Stage Dimensions: 20'x20'x29'   **Orchestra Pit**
Seating Capacity: 183
Year Built: 1917
Year Remodeled: 1986
Contact for Rental: Linda Pinkham;   (603) 356-5425
Resident Groups: Mount Washington Valley Theatre Company

Peterborough

THEATRE

PETERBOROUGH PLAYERS
Middle Hancock Road, PO Box 1, Peterborough, NH 03458
(603) 924-7585
Founded: 1933
Arts Area: Professional; Theatrical Group
Status: Professional; Non-Profit
Type: Performing; Resident; Educational
Management: Ellen Dinerstein, Producing Director
Officers: Joan Brewster, Board President
Paid Staff: 6
Utilizes: Special Technical Talent; Guest Artists; Guest Directors
Budget: $100,000 - $500,000
Income Sources: Private Foundations/Grants/Endowments; Business/Corporate Donations; Box Office; Government Grants; Individual Donations
Season: June - September
Affiliations: AEA; CORST

PERFORMING SERIES

MONADNOCK MUSIC
PO Box 255, Peterborough, NH 03458
(603) 924-7610
FAX: (603) 924-9403
Founded: 1966
Arts Area: Vocal Music; Instrumental Music; Festivals; Lyric Opera

Status: Professional; Non-Profit
Type: Performing; Educational
Purpose: To present first-rate, professional performances of music representing as wide a repertory as possible; to maintain an atmosphere which is conducive to a close audience-performer relationship; to make these performances truly accessible to people in the Monadnock Region
Management: James Bolle, Director; Jocelyn Bolle, Executive Director
Officers: Edith Milton, President; Richard McAdoo, Vice President; Faith Hanson, Clerk; John Keefe, Treasurer
Paid Staff: 5   **Volunteer Staff:** 27
Paid Artists: 114
Utilizes: Guest Artists
Budget: $100,000 - $500,000
Income Sources: Private Foundations/Grants/Endowments; Business/Corporate Donations; Box Office; Government Grants; Individual Donations
Season: July - August   **Annual Attendance:** 7,500
Affiliations: Arts 1000; New Hampshire State Council on the Arts
Performance Facilities: Pine Hall Waldorf Auditorium; Old Meeting House

Plymouth

FACILITY

SILVER CULTURAL ARTS CENTER
Plymouth State College, Plymouth, NH 03264
(603) 536-5000
Type of Facility: Theatre Complex; Concert Hall; Auditorium; Studio Performance; Performance Center; Theatre House
Type of Stage: Thrust; Flexible; Proscenium; Three spaces
Stage Dimensions: 52'Wx32'Dx24'H proscenium opening   **Orchestra Pit**
Seating Capacity: Mainstage - 680; Recital Hall - 174; Studio Theatre - 150
Year Built: 1992   **Architect:** Koetter Kim Associates   **Cost:** $9,500,000
Acoustical Consultant: Carl Rosenberg, Accentech Inc.
Contact for Rental: John Clark, Assistant to the President;   (603) 536-1550
Resident Groups: Plymouth State College - Department of Music and Theatre; New Hampshire Music Festival; Plymouth Friends of the Arts

Portsmouth

THEATRE

PONTINE MOVEMENT THEATRE
135 McDonough Street, Portsmouth, NH 03801
(603) 436-6660
Founded: 1977
Arts Area: Professional
Status: Professional; Non-Profit
Type: Performing; Touring; Resident; Educational; Sponsoring
Purpose: Dedicated to the cultural enhancements of its various publics, its performances and educational programs are offered to inform the public in the art of corporeal mime and to the preservation and development of this exciting theatrical form
Management: Marguerite Mathews and Greg Gathers, Co-Artistic Directors
Paid Staff: 3   **Volunteer Staff:** 30
Paid Artists: 5
Utilizes: Guest Artists
Budget: $100,000 - $500,000
Income Sources: Private Foundations/Grants/Endowments; Business/Corporate Donations; Box Office; Government Grants; Individual Donations
Season: October - June   **Annual Attendance:** 6,500
Affiliations: Arts 1000, National Mime Association; New Hampshire State Council on the Arts
Performance Facilities: McDonough Street Theater

SEACOAST REPERTORY COMPANY
125 Bow Street, Portsmouth, NH 03801
(603) 433-4793
Founded: 1986
Arts Area: Professional; Summer Stock; Musical; Theatrical Group
Status: Professional; Non-Profit
Type: Performing; Resident; Educational
Purpose: To provide a safe haven for all performances and audiences

Management: Roy Rogosin, Artistic Director; Eileen Rogosin, Associate Director; Jean Benda, Administrative Director; Maurice Richards, Administrative Assistant
Officers: Sanford Roberts Esq, President; Irja Ciluffo, Vice President; John Colliander, Secretary; Van Sweat, Treasurer
Paid Staff: 12   **Volunteer Staff:** 20
Paid Artists: 100   **Non-Paid Artists:** 25
Utilizes: Special Technical Talent; Guest Artists; Guest Directors; Guest Designers
Budget: $100,000 - $500,000
Income Sources: Private Foundations/Grants/Endowments; Business/Corporate Donations; Box Office; Individual Donations
Season: 52 Weeks   **Annual Attendance:** 15,000
Affiliations: TCG
Performance Facilities: Bow Street Theater

PERFORMING SERIES

PRESCOTT PARK ARTS FESTIVAL
PO Box 4370, 105 Marcy Street, Portsmouth, NH 03802
(603) 436-2748
Founded: 1974
Arts Area: Dance; Vocal Music; Theater; Festivals
Status: Non-Profit
Type: Performing; Touring; Resident; Educational; Sponsoring
Purpose: To provide a financially accessible, quality mutli-arts festival to a diverse audience
Management: Michael Greenblatt, Executive Director; Sue Bolduc, Festival Coordinator; Mark Vadney, Program Director
Officers: Timothy Phoenix, President; Susan Anderson, Secretary; Anita Freedman, Treasurer
Paid Staff: 3
Paid Artists: 250
Utilizes: Special Technical Talent; Guest Artists
Budget: $500,000 - $1,000,000
Income Sources: Private Foundations/Grants/Endowments; Business/Corporate Donations; Individual Donations
Season: July - August   **Annual Attendance:** 100,000
Performance Facilities: Prescott Park

FACILITY

THE MUSIC HALL
28 Chestnut Street, Portsmouth, NH 03801
(603) 433-3100
Founded: 1986
Type of Facility: Theatre House
Facility Originally: Theater
Type of Stage: Proscenium
Stage Dimensions: 30'x32'
Seating Capacity: 900
Year Built: 1978   **Architect:** William A. Ashe
Contact for Rental: Executive Director;   (603) 433-3100

Tamworth

THEATRE

THE BARNSTORMERS
Tamworth, NH 03886
(603) 323-8500
Founded: 1931
Arts Area: Professional; Summer Stock
Status: Professional; Non-Profit
Type: Performing; Resident
Purpose: To provide a summer theatre program featuring old—and some new—plays
Officers: Helen Steele, Secretary; Bob Lloyd, Treasurer; Kate Thompson, Dana Steele, Co-Chairs
Paid Staff: 12
Paid Artists: 12
Budget: $50,000 - $100,000
Income Sources: Box Office
Season: July - September
Affiliations: AEA
Performance Facilities: The Barnstormers Theatre

Waterville Valley

PERFORMING SERIES

WATERVILLE VALLEY FOUNDATION
Town Square, Waterville Valley, NH 03215
(603) 236-8311
 Founded: 1985
 Arts Area: Vocal Music; Instrumental Music; Festivals; Concerts
 Status: Non-Profit
 Type: Performing; Educational
 Purpose: To present an annual summer festival of the arts
 Management: Peter Adams, Festival Director; Thomas A. Corcoran, Director
 Officers: Howard Grimes, Chairman; Henry Stebbins, Secretary; Robert Ashton, Treasurer
 Paid Staff: 3
 Paid Artists: 87
 Utilizes: Special Technical Talent; Guest Artists
 Budget: $100,000 - $500,000
 Income Sources: Private Foundations/Grants/Endowments; Business/Corporate Donations; Box Office; Government Grants; Membership; Sponsorship
 Season: July - August **Annual Attendance:** 25,000
 Performance Facilities: Town Square Concert Pavillion

Whitefield

THEATRE

WEATHERVANE THEATRE
55 Jefferson Road, Whitefield, NH 03598
(603) 837-9010
 Founded: 1965
 Arts Area: Professional; Summer Stock; Musical
 Status: Professional; Commercial
 Type: Performing
 Purpose: Resident alternating repertory theater company presenting 7-8 shows per season, including musicals
 Management: Gibbs Murray, Richard Portner, Producing Directors; Tom Barthel, Jacques Stewart, Associate Artists
 Paid Staff: 29 **Volunteer Staff:** 1
 Paid Artists: 15 **Non-Paid Artists:** 5
 Utilizes: Guest Artists; Guest Directors
 Budget: $100,000 - $500,000
 Income Sources: Private Foundations/Grants/Endowments; Box Office; Individual Donations
 Season: July - August **Annual Attendance:** 12,000
 Performance Facilities: Barn Theatre

NEW JERSEY

Aberdeen

THEATRE

CREATIVE PRODUCTIONS
2 Beaver Place, Aberdeen, NJ 07747
(908) 566-6985
Founded: 1975
Arts Area: Musical; Theatrical Group
Status: Non-Profit
Type: Performing; Educational
Purpose: Non-Equity musical-theater performing company that features folks with disabilities in leading roles
Management: Walter L. Born, Director
Officers: Mary Born, Treasurer
Volunteer Staff: 8
Non-Paid Artists: 10
Utilizes: Special Technical Talent; Guest Artists
Budget: $1,000 - $50,000
Income Sources: Box Office; Government Grants; Individual Donations
Season: 52 Weeks **Annual Attendance:** 2,000
Performance Facilities: Lloyd Road School, Aberdeen

Allenhurst

VOCAL MUSIC

METRO LYRIC OPERA
40 Ocean Avenue, PO Box 35, Allenhurst, NJ 07711
(908) 531-2378
Founded: 1959
Arts Area: Grand Opera; Operetta
Status: Professional
Type: Performing; Educational; Community Service
Purpose: To bring opera of a high standard to all people at popular prices; to create a professional outlet for deserving young artists as well as experienced professionals; to bring opera in English to public schools
Management: Mme. Fra Tognoli, Artistic/Executive Director; Vincent J. Rifici, Chairman of the Board/Business Advisor; Evelyn Axelrod, Vice President/Box Office Director; Lucious Zachary, Assistant Artistic Director
Officers: John Mullins, President; John Plunkett, Vice President; Joan Benoist, Secretary
Paid Staff: 2 **Volunteer Staff:** 6
Paid Artists: 20
Utilizes: Special Technical Talent; Guest Conductors; Guest Artists
Budget: $500,000 - $1,000,000
Income Sources: Private Foundations/Grants/Endowments; Business/Corporate Donations; Box Office; Government Grants; Individual Donations
Season: October - August **Annual Attendance:** 6,000
Affiliations: Monmouth Opera Guild
Performance Facilities: Paramount Theatre, Asbury Park

Alpine

DANCE

THE AMERICAN DANCE MACHINE
PO Box 647, Alpine, NJ 07620
(201) 784-1617
Founded: 1978
Arts Area: Modern; Ballet; Jazz; Ethnic
Status: Professional; Non-Profit
Type: Performing; Touring; Resident
Purpose: Reconstruct original Broadway pieces to keep the choreography alive
Management: Robert Tucker, Artistic Director
Paid Artists: 20 **Non-Paid Artists:** 10
Utilizes: Guest Artists; Guest Choreographers
Budget: $500,000 - $1,000,000

Income Sources: Private Foundations/Grants/Endowments; Box Office; Individual Donations
Season: 52 Weeks

Beach Haven

THEATRE

SURFLIGHT THEATRE
Beach and Engleside, PO Box 1155, Beach Haven, NJ 08008
(609) 492-9477
FAX: (609) 492-4469
    Founded: 1950
    Arts Area: Summer Stock; Musical
    Status: Semi-Professional
    Type: Performing; Resident
    Management: T. Scott Henderson, Executive Producer; Guil Fisher, Assistant Producer/Artistic Director
    Officers: T. Scott Henderson, President/CEO; Jane A. Henderson, Vice President/Secretary
    Paid Staff: 17   **Volunteer Staff:** 3
    Paid Artists: 20
    Utilizes: Guest Directors
    Budget: $100,000 - $500,000
    Income Sources: Box Office; Individual Donations
    Season: June - September   **Annual Attendance:** 25,000

FACILITY

SURFLIGHT SUMMER THEATRE
PO Box 1155, Beach Haven, NJ 08008
(609) 492-9477; (609) 492-2639
    Type of Facility: Theatre Complex; Theatre House
    Type of Stage: Proscenium
    Stage Dimensions: 40'Wx24'D
    Seating Capacity: 450
    Year Built: 1986   **Architect:** Tonge   **Cost:** $1,500,000
    Acoustical Consultant: Josh Weitzman
    Contact for Rental: T. Scott Henderson;   (609) 492-2639
    Available for rental only in winter

Bloomfield

INSTRUMENTAL MUSIC

BLOOMFIELD SYMPHONY ORCHESTRA
84 Broad Street, Bloomfield, NJ 07003
(201) 743-9074
    Founded: 1932
    Arts Area: Symphony
    Status: Non-Profit
    Type: Performing
    Purpose: A non-profit community orchestra sponsored by the Bloomfield Federation of Music
    Management: Edward J. Napiwocki, Conductor
    Officers: Stephen Lepp, President; Sig Harac, Vice President; Ruth Lepp, Corresponding Secretary; Phyllis Lax, Recording Secretary; Louis Cerrullo, Treasurer
    Paid Staff: 1   **Volunteer Staff:** 6
    Paid Artists: 8   **Non-Paid Artists:** 2
    Utilizes: Special Technical Talent; Guest Artists
    Income Sources: Private Foundations/Grants/Endowments; Business/Corporate Donations; Individual Donations
    Season: November - May   **Annual Attendance:** 3,000
    Affiliations: New Jersey Orchestra Association
    Performance Facilities: North Junior High School

Caldwell

FACILITY

CALDWELL COLLEGE - STUDENT UNION BUILDING
9 Ryerson Avenue, Caldwell, NJ 07006
(201) 228-4424
FAX: (201) 228-3851
    Type of Facility: Studio Performance
    Type of Stage: Proscenium
    Seating Capacity: 1,500
    Year Built: 1968
    Contact for Rental: Marianne Streleck; (201) 228-4424

Cape May

PERFORMING SERIES

MID-ATLANTIC CENTER FOR THE ARTS
1048 Washington Street, Cape May, NJ 08204-0340
(609) 884-5404
FAX: (609) 884-2006
    Founded: 1970
    Arts Area: Vocal Music; Instrumental Music; Theater
    Status: Professional; Non-Profit
    Type: Sponsoring
    Purpose: To promote awareness of the Victorian era and its customs; to promote the performing arts
    Management: B. Michael Zuckerman, Director; Mary Stewart, Sandra Allison, Assistant Directors; Stephen Rogers Radcliffe, Artistic Director Cape May Music Festival
    Officers: John Bailey, President; Tom Carroll, First Vice President; Fred Kuhner, Second Vice President; R. Norris Clark, Treasurer; Joan Wells, Secretary; R. Norris Clark, Cape May Music Festival Chairman
    Paid Staff: 35   **Volunteer Staff:** 200
    Paid Artists: 150
    Utilizes: Guest Conductors; Guest Artists; Guest Directors
    Budget: $1,000,000 - $5,000,000
    Income Sources: Private Foundations/Grants/Endowments; Business/Corporate Donations; Box Office; Government Grants; Individual Donations
    Season: May - June   **Annual Attendance:** 3,000
    Performance Facilities: Congress Hall Hotel

Chatham

INSTRUMENTAL MUSIC

SOLID BRASS
5 Sunset Drive, Chatham, NJ 07928
(201) 701-0674
FAX: (201) 701-0674
    Founded: 1982
    Arts Area: Chamber; Ensemble
    Status: Professional
    Type: Performing; Touring; Educational
    Purpose: To preserve and perpetuate brass chamber music through but not limited to performance, recording and composing
    Management: Paul Goldberg, Go Management
    Officers: Douglas Haislip, Carl Della Peruti, Managing Directors; Ted Wynant, President; Larry Hutton, Vice President; Linda Browner, Secretary
    Paid Staff: 2   **Volunteer Staff:** 10
    Paid Artists: 11
    Utilizes: Guest Composers; Arrangers
    Budget: $100,000 - $500,000
    Income Sources: Private Foundations/Grants/Endowments; Business/Corporate Donations; Box Office; Government Grants; Individual Donations; Touring Fees
    Season: 52 Weeks   **Annual Attendance:** 50,000

Cranford

THEATRE

CRANFORD DRAMATIC CLUB
78 Winans Avenue, PO Box 511, Cranford, NJ 07016
(908) 276-7611
Founded: 1919
Arts Area: Community
Status: Non-Professional; Non-Profit
Type: Performing
Purpose: To stimulate community interest in theatre
Officers: Kate Slavin, President; Carol Weltner, Business Vice President; Marilyn Court, Production Vice President; Barbara Heineman, Membership Vice President; Janet Peterson, Corresponding Secretary; Sue Chandler, Treasurer
Volunteer Staff: 175
Budget: $50,000 - $100,000
Income Sources: Box Office
Season: October - June   **Annual Attendance:** 9,000
Performance Facilities: Cranford Dramatic Club

FACILITY

CRANFORD DRAMATIC CLUB THEATRE
78 Winans Avenue, PO Box 511, Cranford, NJ 07016
(908) 276-7611
Type of Facility: Theatre House
Type of Stage: Proscenium
Stage Dimensions: 19'x30'x32'
Seating Capacity: 300
Year Built: 1957   **Cost:** $60,000
Year Remodeled: 1992   **Architect:** Maurice Moran   **Cost:** $25,000
Resident Groups: Cranford Dramatic Club

Dover

FACILITY

DOVER LITTLE THEATRE
Elliott Street, PO Box 82, Dover, NJ 07801
(201) 328-9202
Type of Facility: Theatre House
Facility Originally: Morgue
Type of Stage: Proscenium
Stage Dimensions: 8'6"x21'x17'
Seating Capacity: 115
Year Remodeled: 1933   **Cost:** $2,000
Manager: Dover Little Theatre

East Orange

FACILITY

UPSALA COLLEGE - WORKSHOP 90 THEATER
East Orange, NJ 07019
(201) 266-7202; (201) 266-7200
Type of Facility: Theatre House
Facility Originally: Carriage House
Type of Stage: Thrust
Stage Dimensions: 31'x18'
Seating Capacity: 140
Year Remodeled: 1984
Contact for Rental: Robert Marcazzo;   (201) 266-7202
Resident Groups: Workshop 90 Theater Group
Rarely available for rent

Elmer

PERFORMING SERIES

APPEL FARM ARTS AND MUSIC CENTER
PO Box 888, Elmer, NJ 08318
(609) 358-2472
FAX: (609) 358-6513
Founded: 1960
Arts Area: Dance; Vocal Music; Instrumental Music; Theater; Festivals
Status: Professional; Non-Profit
Type: Performing; Resident; Educational
Management: Mark E. Packer, Executive Director; Sean Timmons, Artistic Director; V. Susan Fisher, Development Director
Officers: Ronnie Cimprich VMD, President
Paid Staff: 14 **Volunteer Staff:** 200
Budget: $1,000,000 - $5,000,000
Income Sources: Private Foundations/Grants/Endowments; Business/Corporate Donations; Box Office; Government Grants; Individual Donations
Season: September - June **Annual Attendance:** 16,000

FACILITY

APPEL FARM ARTS AND MUSIC CENTER
PO Box 888, Elmer, NJ 08318
(609) 358-2472
FAX: (609) 358-6513
Type of Facility: Outdoor (Concert); Studio Performance; Performance Center; Theatre House; Multi-Purpose; Room
Facility Originally: Farm
Type of Stage: Proscenium
Stage Dimensions: 40'x40' **Orchestra Pit**
Seating Capacity: Theatre - 300; Outdoor Facility - 10,000
Year Built: 1960
Contact for Rental: Sean Timmons; (609) 358-2472
Summer camp program available

Englewood

FACILITY

JOHN HARMS CENTER FOR THE ARTS
30 North Van Brunt Street, Englewood, NJ 07631
(201) 567-5797
FAX: (201) 567-7357
Founded: 1976
Type of Facility: Performance Center
Facility Originally: Vaudeville; Movie House
Type of Stage: Thrust; Proscenium
Stage Dimensions: 40'x29' stage; 33'W proscenium **Orchestra Pit**
Seating Capacity: 1,246
Year Built: 1926
Year Remodeled: 1992 **Architect:** Ecoplan/Wells Associates **Cost:** $6,000,000
Contact for Rental: Allison Perrine; (201) 567-5797
Resident Groups: New Jersey Symphony

Fort Lee

VOCAL MUSIC

OPERA CLASSICS OF NEW JERSEY
One Bridge Plaza, Suite 400, Fort Lee, NJ 07024
(201) 592-5821; (212) 724-0989
Founded: 1963

Arts Area: Grand Opera
Status: Professional; Non-Profit
Type: Performing; Resident; Educational
Purpose: To present professional grand opera as well as build an audience from young people
Management: Giovanni Consiglio, Executive Director; Colin Ungaro, Assistant Director
Officers: Giovanni Consiglio, Presidnet; Colin Ungaro, Vice President; Marion Gambardella, Secretary; Peter Kerschhagel, Treasurer
Volunteer Staff: 50
Paid Artists: 100
Utilizes: Special Technical Talent; Guest Conductors; Guest Artists; Guest Directors
Budget: $100,000 - $500,000
Income Sources: Private Foundations/Grants/Endowments; Business/Corporate Donations; Box Office; Government Grants
Season: October - May
Annual Attendance: 7,000
Affiliations: AGMA; AFM
Performance Facilities: Orrie De Nooyer Auditorium, Hackensack

Glassboro

THEATRE

STAGEWORKS TOURING COMPANY
PO Box 922, Glassboro, NJ 08028
(609) 863-7150
FAX: (609) 863-6553
Arts Area: Professional; Folk; Theatrical Group
Status: Professional; Non-Equity
Type: Performing; Touring; Resident
Purpose: To create and tour plays based on regional history, folklore and oral history; to spotlight social issues and concerns of underserved segments of the local population
Management: Carolyn O'Donnell, Producing Artistic Director; Victoria Ford, Michael Sharp, Miles Thompson and Ray Verna, Artistic Corp
Officers: Carolyn O'Donnell, President; Bruce M. Bradway, Vice President; Carol N. Welsh, Treasurer; Polly K. Davis, Board Chairman
Paid Staff: 6 **Volunteer Staff:** 2
Paid Artists: 20
Budget: $50,000 - $100,000
Season: 52 Weeks **Annual Attendance:** 33,577
Affiliations: New Jersey Theater Association; Artpride, Inc.; Southern New Jersey Cultural Alliance; GPCA; Alternate ROOTS, Inc.
Performance Facilities: Rowan College (formerly Glassboro)

PERFORMING SERIES

GLASSBORO CENTER FOR THE ARTS
Rowan College of New Jersey, Wilson Music Building, Room 211, Glassboro, NJ 08028
(609) 863-5167
FAX: (603) 863-5021
Founded: 1989
Arts Area: Dance; Vocal Music; Instrumental Music; Theater; Festivals; Lyric Opera; Grand Opera; Jazz
Status: Professional
Type: Performing; Touring; Resident; Educational; Sponsoring
Purpose: To provide a variety of high-quality cultural events to the southern New Jersey general public
Management: Dr. Michael J. Rose, Executive Director; Mark Fields, Managing Director
Paid Staff: 6
Utilizes: Special Technical Talent; Guest Conductors; Guest Artists; Guest Directors
Budget: $100,000 - $500,000
Income Sources: Private Foundations/Grants/Endowments; Business/Corporate Donations; Box Office; Government Grants; Individual Donations
Season: October - May **Annual Attendance:** 35,000
Affiliations: APAP
Performance Facilities: Wilson Concert Hall

Hackensack

PERFORMING SERIES

FEDERATED ARTS
185 Prospect Avenue 12M, Hackensack, NJ 07601
(201) 646-1061
Arts Area: Instrumental Music; Festivals
Status: Professional; Non-Profit
Type: Performing
Purpose: To present free musical programs
Management: Isadore Freeman, Director
Utilizes: Guest Artists
Budget: $1,000 - $50,000
Income Sources: Business/Corporate Donations; Individual Donations
Season: July - September; December   **Annual Attendance:** 30,000

FACILITY

ORRIE DE NOOYER AUDITORIUM
200 Hackensack Avenue, Hackensack, NJ 07601
(201) 343-6000, ext. 308
Type of Facility: Concert Hall; Auditorium; Theatre House; Opera House
Type of Stage: Thrust; Proscenium
Stage Dimensions: 58'Wx45'D; 58'Wx20'H procenium opening   **Orchestra Pit**
Seating Capacity: 1201
Year Built: 1966   **Architect:** Frank E. Johnson   **Cost:** $3,000,000
Year Remodeled: 1987   **Cost:** $25,000
Contact for Rental: Steven Danieli, Technical Director;   (201) 343-6000, ext. 308
Resident Groups: The Fokine Ballet Company; Music, Music, Music Concert Productions

Haddonfield

INSTRUMENTAL MUSIC

HADDONFIELD SYMPHONY
30 Washington Avenue, PO Box 212, Haddonfield, NJ 08033
(609) 429-1880
FAX: (609) 428-5634
Founded: 1952
Arts Area: Symphony; Orchestra
Status: Professional; Non-Profit
Type: Performing; Educational
Purpose: To enrich the musical lives of the citizens and residents of the state of New Jersey
Management: Dorothy W. Rivers, Executive Director; Alan Gilbert, Music Director
Utilizes: Special Technical Talent; Guest Conductors; Guest Artists; Guest Directors
Budget: $100,000 - $500,000
Income Sources: Private Foundations/Grants/Endowments; Business/Corporate Donations; Box Office; Government Grants; Individual Donations

Holmdel

FACILITY

GARDEN STATE ARTS CENTER
PO Box 116, Holmdel, NJ 07733
(908) 442-9200
Type of Facility: Outdoor (Concert); Amphitheater
Type of Stage: Thrust; Proscenium
Stage Dimensions: 60'Wx30'H   **Orchestra Pit**
Seating Capacity: 5,163; addition lawn seating available
Year Built: 1968   **Architect:** Edward Durell Stone   **Cost:** $6,700,000
Year Remodeled: 1986   **Cost:** $3,400,000
Acoustical Consultant: Solstice Company
Contact for Rental: Linda P. Crane;   (908) 888-2030
Available for rent on a limited basis only

Jersey City

DANCE

AVODAH DANCE ENSEMBLE
243 Fifth Street, #9, Jersey City, NJ 07302
(201) 659-7072
Alternate Address: c/o HUC-JIR, One West Fourth Street, New York, NY 10012
Founded: 1974
Arts Area: Modern
Status: Professional
Type: Performing; Touring; Resident; Educational
Purpose: To develop a repertory based on Jewish ritual, history and culture; to present multicultural and interfaith pieces and projects
Management: JoAnne Tucker, Artistic Director
Officers: Stephen Bayer, President; Emily Gardner, Vice President; Marianne Mendelson, Treasurer; JoAnne Tucker, Executive Vice President
Volunteer Staff: 1
Paid Artists: 7
Utilizes: Special Technical Talent; Guest Artists; Guest Choreographers
Income Sources: Private Foundations/Grants/Endowments; Individual Donations; Booking Fees
Annual Attendance: 15,000

PERFORMING SERIES

FRIENDS OF MUSIC AND ART OF HUDSON COUNTY
880 Bergen Avenue, Jersey City, NJ 07306
(201) 963-4200
Founded: 1972
Arts Area: Vocal Music; Instrumental Music
Status: Non-Profit
Type: Performing
Purpose: To encourage young gifted students to continue their work; to promote interest and support of music and art in Hudson County
Officers: Jesse Moskowitz, President; Sol Seaith, Vice President; Hilda Feith, Recording Secretary; Sophie Filkner, Treasurer/Historian
Volunteer Staff: 9
Paid Artists: 7
Utilizes: Guest Artists   **Budget:** $1,000 - $50,000
Income Sources: Business/Corporate Donations; Individual Donations
Season: September - May   **Annual Attendance:** 1,000
Performance Facilities: Public Library Auditorium

FACILITY

MAJESTIC THEATRE
275 Grove Street, Jersey City, NJ 07303
(201) 433-7502
FAX: (201) 333-5948
Founded: 1907
Type of Facility: Concert Hall; Performance Center; Theatre House; Opera House; Multi-Purpose
Type of Stage: Flexible; Proscenium
Stage Dimensions: 85'Wx50'Dx90'H   **Orchestra Pit**
Seating Capacity: 1,546
Year Built: 1907   **Architect:** William McElfactrick   **Cost:** $700,000
Year Remodeled: 1992   **Cost:** $50,000,000
Contact for Rental: Albert Stinchcomb;   (201) 333-5948
Resident Groups: Liberty Center for the Performing Arts

Lakewood

FACILITY

OCEAN COUNTY CENTER FOR THE ARTS - STRAND THEATRE
PO Box 315, Lakewood, NJ 08701-0315
(908) 367-6688
Type of Facility: Concert Hall; Theatre House; Opera House

Facility Originally: Vaudeville
Type of Stage: Proscenium
Stage Dimensions: 40'Wx30'D
Seating Capacity: 1,000
Year Built: 1922   **Architect:** Thomas Lamb
Year Remodeled: 1987   **Architect:** Beyer Blinder & Belle   **Cost:** $3,000,000
Contact for Rental: Alan McCracken;   (201) 367-6688

Lawrenceville

FACILITY

RIDER COLLEGE - FINE ARTS THEATER
Rider College, PO Box 6400, Lawrenceville, NJ 08648
(609) 896-5168
  Type of Facility: Auditorium
  Type of Stage: Proscenium   **Orchestra Pit**
  Seating Capacity: 490
  Contact for Rental: Patrick Chmel;   (609) 896-5168

Madison

INSTRUMENTAL MUSIC

COLONIAL SYMPHONY
205 Madison Avenue, Madison, NJ 07940
(201) 377-1310
FAX: (201) 377-2337
  Arts Area: Symphony
  Status: Professional; Non-Profit
  Type: Performing; Educational
  Purpose: To nurture and sustain a superior orchestra emphasizing a balance of classical and contemporary music; to enhance the understanding of music through education
  Management: Yehuda Gilad, Artistic Director/Conductor; Elizabeth Stockly, Executive Director
  Officers: Myles J. Connor Jr., President
  Budget: $100,000 - $500,000
  Income Sources: Private Foundations/Grants/Endowments; Business/Corporate Donations; Box Office; Government Grants; Individual Donations
  Performance Facilities: Madison Junior School

VOCAL MUSIC

OPERA AT FLORHAM
295 Madison Avenue, Madison, NJ 07940
(201) 593-8622
FAX: (201) 593-8510
  Founded: 1982
  Arts Area: Grand Opera; Lyric Opera
  Status: Professional; Artists-In-Residence
  Type: Performing; Resident
  Purpose: To provide stage and music experience in productions for apprenticed young artists
  Management: Dr. Charles F. Del Rosso, General Manager
  Officers: German Bustos, Chairperson Board of Trustees; Edward Zamengo, First Vice Chair Board of Trustees
  Paid Staff: 2   **Volunteer Staff:** 10
  Paid Artists: 50
  Utilizes: Special Technical Talent; Guest Artists; Guest Directors
  Budget: $100,000 - $500,000
  Income Sources: Private Foundations/Grants/Endowments; Business/Corporate Donations; Box Office; Individual Donations
  Season: September - May   **Annual Attendance:** 2,000
  Affiliations: Fairleigh Dickinson University
  Performance Facilities: Dreyfuss Theater; Lengfell Hall

THEATRE

NEW JERSEY SHAKESPEARE FESTIVAL
Route 24, Madison, NJ 07940
(201) 408-3278
Founded: 1963
Arts Area: Professional; Theatrical Group
Status: Professional; Non-Profit
Type: Performing; Educational; Sponsoring
Purpose: To present professional productions of Shakespearean and other plays, including classics and modern
Management: Bonnie Jay Monte, Artistic Director; Michael Stotts, Managing Director
Paid Staff: 15   **Volunteer Staff:** 80
Paid Artists: 25   **Non-Paid Artists:** 80
Utilizes: Special Technical Talent; Guest Artists; Guest Directors
Budget: $500,000 - $1,000,000
Income Sources: Private Foundations/Grants/Endowments; Business/Corporate Donations; Box Office; Government Grants; Individual Donations
Season: June - October
Affiliations: AEA; SSDC
Performance Facilities: Bowne Theatre

FACILITY

DREW UNIVERSITY - BOWNE THEATRE
36 Madison Avenue, Madison, NJ 07940
(201) 408-3000
Type of Facility: Concert Hall; Theatre House
Facility Originally: Recreation Hall; Gymnasium
Type of Stage: Thrust
Seating Capacity: 238
Year Built: 1910
Year Remodeled: 1972
Resident Groups: New Jersey Shakespeare Festival; Drew University Theatre Arts Department

Maplewood

DANCE

NEW JERSEY DANCE THEATRE
202 Maplewood Avenue, Maplewood, NJ 07040
(201) 762-3033
Founded: 1982
Arts Area: Ballet
Status: Semi-Professional; Commercial
Type: Resident
Purpose: To acquaint the community with dance
Management: Anne Krohley, Artistic Director; Brian Gestring, Business Manager
Paid Artists: 15
Utilizes: Guest Artists
Budget: $1,000 - $50,000
Income Sources: Box Office
Season: September - June
Performance Facilities: New Jersey Dance Theatre

Millburn

THEATRE

PAPER MILL PLAYHOUSE
Brookside Drive, Millburn, NJ 07041
(201) 379-3636
Founded: 1934
Arts Area: Professional; Musical
Status: Professional; Non-Profit
Type: Performing; Touring; Resident; Educational; Sponsoring
Purpose: To produce and present a wide range of performing and visual arts, with emphasis on production, preservation and development of musical theatre work

Management: Angelo Del Rossi, Executive Producer; Robert Johanson, Artistic Director; Geoffrey Merrill Cohen, General Manager
Officers: C.E. Williams, Chairman; Maurice J. Ferris Jr., Vice-Chairman; Angelo Del Rossi, President
Paid Staff: 40
Paid Artists: 280
Utilizes: Special Technical Talent; Guest Conductors; Guest Artists; Guest Directors
Budget: Over 10,000,000
Income Sources: Private Foundations/Grants/Endowments; Business/Corporate Donations; Box Office; Government Grants; Individual Donations
Season: 52 Weeks **Annual Attendance:** 400,000
Affiliations: AEA; COST; SSDC; AFM; IATSE; USA; ARTPRIDE, NJ
Performance Facilities: Paper Mill Playhouse

FACILITY

PAPER MILL PLAYHOUSE
Brookside Drive, Millburn, NJ 07041
(201) 379-3636
Type of Facility: Theatre Complex; Performance Center; Theatre House; Multi-Purpose; Room
Facility Originally: Paper Mill
Type of Stage: Proscenium
Stage Dimensions: 100'Wx47'Dx56'H; 40'Wx24'H proscenium opening **Orchestra Pit**
Seating Capacity: 1,192
Year Built: 1795
Year Remodeled: 1982 **Architect:** Ashok Bhavnani **Cost:** $5,500,000
Acoustical Consultant: Peter George Associates
Resident Groups: New Jersey Ballet; Paper Mill Playhouse
Original structure was built in 1795 and converted to a theatre in 1934. Original structure was destroyed by fire in 1980 and was rebuilt in 1982.

Montclair

DANCE

DANMARI LTD./YASS HAKOSHIMA MIME THEATRE
239 Midland Avenue, Montclair, NJ 07042
(201) 783-9845
FAX: (201) 783-0001
Founded: 1976
Arts Area: Mime
Status: Professional; Non-Profit
Type: Performing; Touring; Resident; Educational
Purpose: To present the highest form of the art of mime through performances, master classes, lecture demonstrations and workshops worldwide
Management: Lynn K. Palmer, Business Manager; Danmari Ltd.
Officers: Yass Hakoshima, Artistic Director; Renate A. Boue, Assistant Director
Paid Staff: 3 **Volunteer Staff:** 8
Paid Artists: 4
Budget: $50,000 - $100,000
Income Sources: Private Foundations/Grants/Endowments; Business/Corporate Donations; Government Grants; Individual Donations
Season: 52 Weeks **Annual Attendance:** 35,000

RENATE BOUE DANCE COMPANY
239 Midland Avenue, Montclair, NJ 07042
(201) 783-9845
FAX: (201) 783-0001
Founded: 1972
Arts Area: Modern
Status: Professional; Semi-Professional
Type: Performing; Educational
Officers: Barbara Francett, Chairperson; Muriel Holub, Assistant Director; Renate Boue, Artistic Director
Paid Staff: 2 **Volunteer Staff:** 2
Paid Artists: 2 **Non-Paid Artists:** 4
Utilizes: Guest Artists
Income Sources: Box Office; Individual Donations

ST. JOHN'S RENAISSANCE DANCERS
239 Midland Avenue, Montclair, NJ 07042
(201) 783-9845
FAX: (201) 783-0001
Founded: 1979
Arts Area: Historic Dance
Status: Professional
Type: Performing; Touring; Educational
Purpose: To present high quality dance and music of the Renaissance, recreating the splendor of 15th and 16th-century Europe
Officers: Renate Boue, Artistic Director; Phyllis Workinger, Associate Director; Muriel Holub, Educational Director
Paid Staff: 1   **Volunteer Staff:** 1
Paid Artists: 10
Utilizes: Guest Musicians
Income Sources: Box Office; Individual Donations
Season: 52 Weeks

INSTRUMENTAL MUSIC

NEW JERSEY CHAMBER MUSIC SOCIETY
22 Valley Road, Montclair, NJ 07042
(201) 746-6068
FAX: (201) 746-0685
Founded: 1974
Arts Area: Chamber
Status: Professional; Non-Profit
Type: Performing; Touring; Resident; Educational
Management: Eileen Y. Sheldon, Executive Director; Peggy Scheeter and Bernice Silk, Artistic Directors; Jeremy V. Johnson, Director of Development
Officers: Richard Snyder, President; Martin McKerrow, Honey McGrath, Vice Presidents; Clarence Seniors, Secretary; Jack Nadler, Treasurer
Paid Staff: 3   **Volunteer Staff:** 4
Paid Artists: 19
Utilizes: Guest Artists
Budget: $100,000 - $500,000
Income Sources: Private Foundations/Grants/Endowments; Business/Corporate Donations; Box Office; Government Grants; Individual Donations
Season: October - May   **Annual Attendance:** 7,000
Performance Facilities: Union Congregational Church, Montclair

THEATRE

BLOOMING GROVE THEATER ENSEMBLE, LTD.
544 Bloomfield Avenue, Montclair, NJ 07042
(201) 744-3004
FAX: (201) 744-6208
Founded: 1985
Arts Area: Professional; Musical; Theatrical Group
Status: Professional; Non-Profit
Type: Performing; Resident; Educational
Purpose: To provide a wide range of theatrical performances and educational programs to northern New Jersey and the New York metropolitan area
Management: Michael Huseman, Managing Director; Alberta Huseman, Artistic Director
Officers: Alberta Huseman, President; Michael Huseman, Vice President
Utilizes: Special Technical Talent
Budget: $50,000 - $100,000
Income Sources: Private Foundations/Grants/Endowments; Business/Corporate Donations; Box Office; Government Grants; Individual Donations
Season: 52 Weeks   **Annual Attendance:** 32,000
Performance Facilities: Blooming Grove Theater

YASS HAKOSHIMA MIME THEATRE
239 Midland Avenue, Montclair, NJ 07042
(201) 783-9845
FAX: (201) 783-0001
Founded: 1976
Arts Area: Professional
Status: Professional; Non-Profit

Type: Performing; Touring; Resident; Educational
Purpose: To further the appreciation and understanding of the art of mime through performances, master classes and workshops
Management: Danmari Limited; Lynn K. Palmer, Business Manager; David VanZand, Assistant Manager
Officers: Yass Hakoshima, Artistic Director; Renate A. Boue, Assistant Director
Paid Staff: 3   **Volunteer Staff:** 5
Paid Artists: 3
Utilizes: Special Technical Talent; Guest Artists
Budget: $50,000 - $100,000
Income Sources: Private Foundations/Grants/Endowments; Business/Corporate Donations; Government Grants; Individual Donations; Performance Tours
Season: 52 Weeks   **Annual Attendance:** 30,000

PERFORMING SERIES

UNITY CONCERTS
22 Valley Road, Montclair, NJ 07042
(201) 744-6770
FAX: (201) 744-2169
Founded: 1920
Arts Area: Vocal Music; Instrumental Music; Classical
Status: Non-Profit
Type: Sponsoring
Purpose: To provide the finest classical music concerts to northern New Jersey
Management: Nancy P. Barry, Director; Kathy Schumacher, Assistant
Paid Staff: 4   **Volunteer Staff:** 24
Paid Artists: 100
Utilizes: Guest Conductors; Guest Artists
Budget: $100,000 - $500,000
Income Sources: Private Foundations/Grants/Endowments; Business/Corporate Donations; Box Office
Season: October - May   **Annual Attendance:** 11,700
Affiliations: APAP
Performance Facilities: Montclair Community Auditorium; Glenfield Auditorium

FACILITY

BLOOMING GROVE THEATRE
544 Bloomfield Avenue, Montclair, NJ 07042
(201) 744-3004
Type of Facility: Theatre House
Facility Originally: Bank
Type of Stage: Flexible
Stage Dimensions: 19'x44'x22'
Seating Capacity: 199
Year Remodeled: 1977
Cost: $156,000
Contact for Rental: Manager;   (201) 744-3004

Moorestown

INSTRUMENTAL MUSIC

WEST JERSEY CHAMBER MUSIC SOCIETY
PO Box 211, Moorestown, NJ 08057
(609) 778-1899
Founded: 1980
Arts Area: Orchestra; Chamber; Choral
Status: Professional; Non-Profit
Type: Performing; Touring
Utilizes: Guest Conductors; Guest Artists; Guest Directors
Season: October - June

Mount Laurel

DANCE

NATIONAL BALLET/NEW JERSEY
5113 Church Road, Mount Laurel, NJ 08054
(609) 235-5342
FAX: (609) 953-7212
Founded: 1974
Arts Area: Ballet; Contemporary
Status: Professional; Non-Profit
Type: Performing; Resident
Purpose: To foster quality dance in the state of New Jersey
Management: Kerina Connor, Assistant Director; Lorraine McAdams, Executive Artistic Director; Gayle Gardner, Manager
Paid Artists: 12
Utilizes: Guest Artists
Budget: $50,000 - $100,000
Income Sources: Private Foundations/Grants/Endowments; Business/Corporate Donations; Box Office; Government Grants
Season: October - May
Affiliations: NARB
Performance Facilities: The Grove

New Brunswick

DANCE

PRINCETON BALLET
80 Albany Street, New Brunswick, NJ 08901
(908) 249-1254
FAX: (908) 249-8475
Founded: 1978
Arts Area: Ballet
Status: Professional; Non-Profit
Type: Performing; Touring
Management: Judith Leviton, Director; Marjorie Nussman, Artistic Director
Paid Staff: 7
Paid Artists: 14
Utilizes: Guest Artists
Budget: $1,000,000 - $5,000,000
Income Sources: Private Foundations/Grants/Endowments; Business/Corporate Donations; Box Office; Government Grants; Individual Donations
Season: September - June
Affiliations: George Street Playhouse
Performance Facilities: McCarter Theatre, Princeton; State Theater, New Brunswick

THEATRE

CROSSROADS THEATRE COMPANY
7 Livingston Avenue, New Brunswick, NJ 08901
(908) 249-5581
FAX: (908) 249-1861
Founded: 1978
Arts Area: Professional; Theatrical Group; Afro-American Theatre Company
Status: Non-Profit
Type: Touring; Resident; Educational
Purpose: To provide a professional environment to encourage public interest of all backgrounds; to present honest portrayals and uphold the highest standard of artistic excellence of professional Black Theatre
Management: Rick Khan, Artistic Director/Producer; Paul Tetreault, General Manager; Marcia Wayand, Director of Development
Officers: Frank Bolden, Board President
Utilizes: Special Technical Talent; Guest Conductors; Guest Artists; Guest Directors
Budget: $500,000 - $1,000,000
Income Sources: Private Foundations/Grants/Endowments; Business/Corporate Donations; Box Office; Government Grants; Individual Donations

Season: September - May   **Annual Attendance:** 30,000
Affiliations: TCG; APAP

GEORGE STREET PLAYHOUSE
9 Livingston Avenue, New Brunswick, NJ 08901
(908) 846-2895
FAX: (908) 247-9151
Founded: 1974
Arts Area: Professional; Musical; Theatrical Group
Status: Professional; Non-Profit
Type: Performing; Touring; Resident; Producing
Purpose: To produce world premieres and new musicals; to revitalize contemporary classics
Management: Gregory Hurst, Production/Artistic Director; Diane Claussen, Managing Director; Wendy Liscow, Associate Artistic Director; Karen Price, Business Manager
Officers: Al D'Augusta, President, Board of Directors
Paid Staff: 35   **Volunteer Staff:** 70
Paid Artists: 75
Utilizes: Special Technical Talent; Guest Artists; Guest Directors
Budget: $1,000,000 - $5,000,000
Income Sources: Private Foundations/Grants/Endowments; Business/Corporate Donations; Box Office; Government Grants; Individual Donations
Season: October - May   **Annual Attendance:** 73,000
Affiliations: TCG
Performance Facilities: George Street Playhouse

PERFORMING SERIES

NEW BRUNSWICK CULTURAL CENTER, INC.
19 Livingston Avenue, New Brunswick, NJ 08901
(908) 247-7200
FAX: (908) 247-5004
Founded: 1983
Arts Area: Presenting
Status: Non-Profit
Type: Performing; Educational; Sponsoring
Purpose: To present the finest of the performing arts
Officers: William Wright, President; Doug Hosner, Vice President
Budget: $1,000,000 - $5,000,000
Income Sources: Private Foundations/Grants/Endowments; Business/Corporate Donations; Box Office; Government Grants; Individual Donations
Season: September - June   **Annual Attendance:** 150,000
Performance Facilities: State Theatre

RUTGERS SUMMERFEST
106 Walters Hall, Rutgers Art Center, New Brunswick, NJ 08901-5056
(908) 932-7591
FAX: (908) 932-6973
Arts Area: Dance; Vocal Music; Instrumental Music; Theater; Festivals
Status: Non-Profit
Type: Performing; Resident; Educational; Sponsoring
Purpose: To celebrate music, dance, theatre and visual art
Management: Lance Olson, Assistant Dean of Arts Programming; Charles Fessenden, Marketing Director; Ellen Saxon, Publicity Director; Kevin Coleman, Operations Manager; Jeanne Salzmann, Box Office Manager
Paid Staff: 27   **Volunteer Staff:** 3
Paid Artists: 250
Utilizes: Special Technical Talent; Guest Artists; Guest Directors
Budget: $100,000 - $500,000
Income Sources: Private Foundations/Grants/Endowments; Business/Corporate Donations; Box Office; Government Grants; Individual Donations
Season: June - August   **Annual Attendance:** 60,000
Performance Facilities: Rutgers Arts Center

RUTGERS UNIVERSITY CONCERT SERIES
106 Walters Hall, New Brunswick, NJ 08907-5056
(908) 932-7591
FAX: (908) 932-6973
Founded: 1917
Arts Area: Instrumental Music

Status: Professional
Type: Presenting
Purpose: To present artists who shape art music today
Management: Lance Olson, Assistant Dean for Arts Programming; Charles Fessenden, Marketing Director; Ellen Saxon, Publicity Director; Kevin Coleman, Operations Manager; Jeanne Salzman, Box Office Manager
Utilizes: Guest Artists
Budget: $100,000 - $500,000
Income Sources: Private Foundations/Grants/Endowments; Business/Corporate Donations; Box Office; Government Grants; Individual Donations
Season: September - May   **Annual Attendance:** 3,500
Performance Facilities: Rutgers Art Center

FACILITY

RUTGERS ARTS CENTER
George Street & Route 18, New Brunswick, NJ 08903-5056
(908) 932-7591
Founded: 1916
Type of Facility: Theatre Complex; Concert Hall; Studio Performance; Performance Center; Theatre House; Multi-Purpose
Type of Stage: Thrust; Flexible; Proscenium; Concert Hall
Stage Dimensions: four stages - various dimensions   **Orchestra Pit**

Newark

DANCE

GARDEN STATE BALLET
45 Academy Street, Newark, NJ 07102
(201) 623-0267
FAX: (201) 623-8269
Founded: 1960
Arts Area: Ballet
Status: Professional; Non-Profit
Type: Performing; Touring; Resident; Educational
Purpose: To present a varied repertory of quality classical ballets that will stimulate artistic growth for dancers and audiences alike
Management: Bonnie Hyslop, General Manager; Peter Anastos, Artistic Director
Officers: Joel Sobo, President; Barry H. Smith, Rosemary Alito, Vice Presidents; Paul Holte, Treasurer; Lois Van Deusen, Secretary
Paid Staff: 5   **Volunteer Staff:** 25
Paid Artists: 25
Budget: $100,000 - $500,000
Income Sources: Private Foundations/Grants/Endowments; Business/Corporate Donations; Box Office; Government Grants; Individual Donations
Season: October - May   **Annual Attendance:** 45,000

INSTRUMENTAL MUSIC

CATHEDRAL CONCERT SERIES
89 Ridge Street, Newark, NJ 07104
(201) 484-2400
FAX: (201) 484-8773
Founded: 1983
Arts Area: Symphony; Orchestra; Chamber; Ensemble
Status: Professional; Non-Profit
Type: Performing; Resident; Sponsoring
Purpose: To bring quality musical programs to the Newark community
Management: Keith Clark, Music Director; Gloria Christ, Executive Director; Susan Zeigler, Associate Director
Officers: Donald Caste, Board Chairman; Joseph Honle, Finance Chairman; James Blanchard, Development Chairman
Paid Staff: 3   **Volunteer Staff:** 20
Paid Artists: 100
Utilizes: Guest Conductors; Guest Artists
Budget: $100,000 - $500,000
Income Sources: Private Foundations/Grants/Endowments; Business/Corporate Donations; Box Office; Government Grants; Individual Donations

Season: October - May   **Annual Attendance:** 10,000
Performance Facilities: Cathedral of the Sacred Heart

NEW JERSEY SYMPHONY ORCHESTRA
50 Park Place, 11th Floor, Newark, NJ 07101
(201) 624-3713
FAX: (201) 624-2115
 Founded: 1922
 Arts Area: Symphony; Orchestra; Chamber; Ensemble
 Status: Professional; Non-Profit
 Type: Performing
 Purpose: To provide superior performances of music for symphonic orchestra and chamber orchestra and an exceptional educational program statewide
 Management: Lawrence J. Tamburri, Executive Director; Karen Swanson, Orchestra Manager
 Officers: Dr. Victor Parsonnet, Chairman of the Board; Robert C. Waggoner, Vice Chairman of the Board
 Paid Staff: 25   **Volunteer Staff:** 2
 Paid Artists: 85
 Utilizes: Guest Conductors; Guest Artists
 Budget: $5,000,000 - $10,000,000
 Income Sources: Private Foundations/Grants/Endowments; Business/Corporate Donations; Box Office; Government Grants; Individual Donations
 Season: October - August   **Annual Attendance:** 190,000
 Performance Facilities: Newark Symphony Hall; John Harms Center for the Performing Arts; Count Basie Theatre, Redbank; War Mem. Theatre, Trenton; New Brunswick State Theatre

VOCAL MUSIC

NEW JERSEY STATE OPERA
1020 Broad Street, Newark, NJ 07102
(201) 623-5757
FAX: (201) 623-5761
 Founded: 1966
 Arts Area: Grand Opera
 Status: Professional
 Type: Performing
 Management: Alfredo Silipigni, General Director; Gwen Hall, Executive Director; Brian Dallon, Director of Marketing
 Officers: Robert B. O'Brien, Chairman; Luna Kaufman, President; William Mikesell, Treasurer
 Paid Staff: 7   **Volunteer Staff:** 6
 Paid Artists: 210   **Non-Paid Artists:** 50
 Utilizes: Special Technical Talent; Guest Artists; Guest Directors
 Budget: $500,000 - $1,000,000
 Income Sources: Private Foundations/Grants/Endowments; Business/Corporate Donations; Box Office; Government Grants; Individual Donations
 Season: November - May   **Annual Attendance:** 18,000
 Affiliations: Essex County Arts Council; New Jersey State Arts Council
 Performance Facilities: Newark Symphony Hall

NEWARK BOYS CHORUS
1016 Broad Street, Newark, NJ 07102
(201) 621-8900
 Founded: 1967
 Arts Area: Choral; Ethnic
 Status: Professional; Non-Profit
 Type: Performing; Touring; Educational
 Budget: $100,000 - $500,000
 Income Sources: Private Foundations/Grants/Endowments; Business/Corporate Donations; Government Grants; Individual Donations
 Season: September - June

THEATRE

NEWARK PERFORMING ARTS CORPORATION/NEWARK SYMPHONY HALL
1030 Broad Street, Newark, NJ 07102
(201) 643-4550
FAX: (201) 643-6722
 Founded: 1986
 Arts Area: Professional; Musical; Community; Theatrical Group
 Status: Professional; Non-Profit

Type: Performing; Presenting
Purpose: To enrich the cultural, educational and community life of the citizens of the greater Newark area by developing a program of the highest quality emphasizing theatrical works which reflect contemporary urban culture
Management: Leon Denmark, Executive Director; Elisabeth Stewart, General Manager; Midge Guerrera, Director of Arts Education; Marshall Jones, Director of Events
Officers: Harold Lucas, Chair; Mamie Hale, Vice Chair; Marie Villani, Vice Chair; Walter Molineux, Treasurer/Secretary
Paid Staff: 320
Paid Artists: 200
Budget: $500,000 - $1,000,000
Income Sources: Private Foundations/Grants/Endowments; Business/Corporate Donations; Box Office; Government Grants; Individual Donations
Season: 52 Weeks   **Annual Attendance:** 180,000
Affiliations: IATSE; AEA
Performance Facilities: Newark Symphony Hall

THEATRE OF UNIVERSAL IMAGES
360 Central Avenue, Newark, NJ 07103
(201) 645-6930
FAX: (201) 642-6013
Founded: 1970
Arts Area: Professional
Status: Professional; Non-Profit
Type: Performing; Touring; Resident
Purpose: Providing education in the performing arts and telecommunications to the Greater Newark Community, the priority of TUI is to increase opportunities and cultural enrichment of African Americans in Greater Essex County.
Management: Clarence C. Lilley, Executive Producer
Paid Staff: 7   **Volunteer Staff:** 20
Utilizes: Special Technical Talent; Guest Artists; Guest Directors
Budget: $100,000 - $500,000
Income Sources: Private Foundations/Grants/Endowments; Business/Corporate Donations; Box Office; Government Grants; Individual Donations
Season: October - June   **Annual Attendance:** 108,000
Affiliations: NEA; Dodge Foundation; Victoria Foundation; Black United Foundation
Performance Facilities: Theatre of Universal Images

FACILITY

NEWARK SYMPHONY HALL
1020 Broad Street, Newark, NJ 07102-2410
(201) 643-4550
Type of Facility: Concert Hall
Type of Stage: Proscenium
Stage Dimensions: 87'Wx42'Dx60'H; 63'4"Wx28'H proscenium opening   **Orchestra Pit**
Seating Capacity: 2,821
Year Built: 1925
Contact for Rental: Marshal Jones;   (201) 643-4550
Resident Groups: New Jersey State Opera; New Jersey Symphony Orchestra; Newark Boys Chorus

Paramus

VOCAL MUSIC

ARS MUSICA CHORALE AND ORCHESTRA
PO Box 525, Paramus, NJ 07653
(201) 599-2732
Founded: 1967
Arts Area: Grand Opera; Lyric Opera; Choral
Status: Professional; Semi-Professional; Non-Profit
Type: Performing; Touring
Purpose: To present performances of rarely heard works by masters including national premieres
Management: Diane Montemurro, Administration; Italo Marchini, Artistic Director
Officers: Linda Glasgal, President
Paid Staff: 2   **Volunteer Staff:** 50
Paid Artists: 45   **Non-Paid Artists:** 60
Utilizes: Special Technical Talent; Guest Artists
Budget: $50,000 - $100,000

Income Sources: Private Foundations/Grants/Endowments; Business/Corporate Donations; Box Office; Government Grants; Individual Donations
Season: September - May   **Annual Attendance:** 2,600
Affiliations: American Institute Verdi Studies; OA; ACDA
Performance Facilities: John Harmes; First Presbyterian Church, Englewood; Alice Tully Hall, Lincoln Center, New York City

---

Pitman

INSTRUMENTAL MUSIC

SOUTH JERSEY SYMPHONY ORCHESTRA
27 Columbia Avenue, Pitman, NJ 08071
(609) 582-2374
    Arts Area: Symphony; Orchestra
    Status: Professional; Non-Profit
    Type: Performing
    Purpose: To perform symphony orchestra repertoire in southern New Jersey
    Management: Samuel Muni, Music/Artistic Director
    Officers: Sharon Kewish, President
    Budget: $100,000 - $500,000
    Income Sources: Private Foundations/Grants/Endowments; Business/Corporate Donations; Box Office; Government Grants; Individual Donations
    Season: 52 Weeks

Pomona

FACILITY

STOCKTON STATE COLLEGE - PERFORMING ARTS CENTER
Jim Leeds Road, Pomona, NJ 08240
(609) 652-9000
FAX: (609) 748-5523
    Type of Facility: Concert Hall; Theatre House
    Type of Stage: Thrust; Proscenium
    Stage Dimensions: 48'Wx28'H proscenium opening   **Orchestra Pit**
    Seating Capacity: 550
    Year Built: 1976
    Contact for Rental: Michael Cool;   (609) 652-4607
    Resident Groups: Professional Guest Artists Series
    The Center also contains a 100-seat black box theatre

Princeton

VOCAL MUSIC

THE AMERICAN BOYCHOIR
The American Boychoir School, Lambert Drive, Princeton, NJ 08540
(609) 924-5858
FAX: (609) 924-5812
    Founded: 1937
    Arts Area: Choral
    Status: Professional; Non-Profit
    Type: Performing; Touring; Educational
    Purpose: The Boychoir includes choristers from throughout North America, who are students at the internationally-renowned boarding and day choir school (which offers a full academic program)
    Management: James H. Litton, Music Director; Columbia Artists Management, Sheldon Division
    Officers: Herbert W. Hobler, Board Chairman; John Ellis, President; James H. Litton, Music Director; Thomas E. Thompson, Headmaster
    Paid Staff: 35
    Paid Artists: 72
    Utilizes: Guest Conductors; Guest Artists
    Budget: $1,000,000 - $5,000,000

Income Sources: Private Foundations/Grants/Endowments; Business/Corporate Donations; Box Office; Government Grants; Individual Donations; Touring Fees
Season: September - June   **Annual Attendance:** 150,000

PRINCETON PRO MUSICA
20 Nassau Street, Suite 241, Princeton, NJ 08542
(609) 683-5122; (609) 683-1154
FAX: (609) 683-9676
Founded: 1979
Arts Area: Choral
Status: Non-Profit
Type: Performing
Purpose: To perform masterpieces of the choral repertoire with a professional orchestra and soloists
Management: Lee Franklin Milhous, General Manager; Sandy Clark, Administrative Assistant
Officers: Robert Jones, President; Isabel Griffith, Vice President; Patricia Paynter, Secretary; Bruce Bedient, Treasurer; Frances Slade, Music Director
Paid Staff: 2
Paid Artists: 16   **Non-Paid Artists:** 120
Utilizes: Guest Conductors; Guest Artists
Budget: $100,000 - $500,000
Income Sources: Private Foundations/Grants/Endowments; Business/Corporate Donations; Box Office; Government Grants; Individual Donations; Fundraisers; Benefits
Season: September - June   **Annual Attendance:** 10,000
Affiliations: CA; Art Pride
Performance Facilities: Richardson Auditorium, Princeton University; Nicholas Music Center, Rutgers University

THEATRE

CREATIVE THEATRE
102 Witherspoon Street, Princeton, NJ 08540
(609) 924-3489
Founded: 1969
Arts Area: Professional; Children's Theatre
Status: Professional; Non-Profit
Type: Performing; Touring; Resident; Educational
Purpose: To offer creative drama and theatre for children through participatory experiences
Management: Carly Tilton, Executive Director; Eloise Bruce, Artistic Director; Jean Prall, Education Director
Officers: Deborah Gwajda, President; Margee Greenberg, Vice President; Robert Solomon, Treasurer
Paid Staff: 5   **Volunteer Staff:** 15
Paid Artists: 20
Budget: $100,000 - $500,000
Income Sources: Private Foundations/Grants/Endowments; Business/Corporate Donations; Box Office; Government Grants; Individual Donations
Season: September - May; July   **Annual Attendance:** 40,000

FACILITY

MCCARTER THEATRE
91 University Place, Princeton, NJ 08540
(609) 683-9100
FAX: (609) 497-0369
Type of Facility: Theatre House
Type of Stage: Proscenium
Stage Dimensions: 22'x41'x39'   **Orchestra Pit**
Seating Capacity: 1,078
Year Built: 1929   **Architect:** D.K. Este Fisher   **Cost:** $430,000
Year Remodeled: 1985   **Architect:** James R. Grieves Associates   **Cost:** $4,300,000
Acoustical Consultant: KMK Associates
Contact for Rental: Kathleen Nolan, General Manager;   (609) 683-9100
Resident Groups: McCarter Theatre Company
Extremely limited rental - performing-arts events only

RICHARDSON AUDITORIUM IN ALEXANDER HALL
Princeton University, Princeton, NJ 08544
(609) 258-4239
FAX: (609) 258-6793
Type of Facility: Concert Hall; Auditorium
Type of Stage: Platform

Stage Dimensions: 50'Wx30'D **Orchestra Pit**
Seating Capacity: 850
Year Built: 1894 **Architect:** William Appleton Potter
Year Remodeled: 1984 **Architect:** James R. Grieves Associates, Inc.
Acoustical Consultant: KMK Associates
Contact for Rental: Nathan A. Randall; (609) 250-4239

Princeton Junction

PERFORMING SERIES

OPERA FESTIVAL OF NEW JERSEY
55 Princeton-Hightstown Rd., Suite 202, Princeton Junction, NJ 08550
(609) 936-1505
FAX: (609) 936-0008
Founded: 1983
Arts Area: Vocal Music; Lyric Opera; Grand Opera
Status: Professional; Non-Profit
Type: Performing; Resident; Sponsoring
Purpose: To present opera in English of new and unusual works as well as classical works intended for an intimate theater setting
Management: Deborah Sandler, Executive Director; Michael Pratt, Artistic Director
Paid Staff: 5 **Volunteer Staff:** 50
Paid Artists: 85 **Non-Paid Artists:** 2
Utilizes: Special Technical Talent; Guest Conductors; Guest Artists; Guest Directors
Budget: $500,000 - $1,000,000
Income Sources: Private Foundations/Grants/Endowments; Business/Corporate Donations; Box Office; Government Grants; Individual Donations
Season: June - July; February - March **Annual Attendance:** 25,000
Affiliations: COS
Performance Facilities: Kirby Arts Center, Lawrenceville School

Rahway

FACILITY

UNION COUNTY ARTS CENTER
1601 Irving Street, Rahway, NJ 07065
(908) 499-0441
FAX: (908) 499-8227
Founded: 1928
Type of Facility: Concert Hall; Auditorium; Performance Center; Theatre House
Facility Originally: Vaudeville; Movie House
Type of Stage: Proscenium
Stage Dimensions: 48'Wx24'D **Orchestra Pit**
Seating Capacity: 1,300
Year Built: 1928 **Architect:** Oltarsh
Year Remodeled: 1986 **Cost:** $1,200,000
Acoustical Consultant: Ed O'Conner
Contact for Rental: Bruce A. Conway; (908) 499-0441

Red Bank

VOCAL MUSIC

MONMOUTH CIVIC CHORUS
PO Box 16, Red Bank, NJ 07701
(908) 747-0860
Founded: 1949
Arts Area: Light Opera; Choral
Status: Non-Professional; Non-Profit
Type: Performing; Touring
Purpose: To provide opportunities for community individuals to participate in the preparation and presentation of large choral works and staged musical productions all with orchestral accompaniment
Management: Mark Shapiro, Artistic Director/Conductor; Karin Moncrieff, Accompanist; Meredith Pennotti, Stage Director

Officers: Kathi Blinn, President; Laura Elliot, Vice President; Debbie Macock, Secretary; Tom Myers, Treasurer
Paid Staff: 3   **Volunteer Staff:** 60
Non-Paid Artists: 180
Utilizes: Special Technical Talent
Budget: $50,000 - $100,000
Income Sources: Private Foundations/Grants/Endowments; Business/Corporate Donations; Box Office; Government Grants; Individual Donations
Season: 52 Weeks   **Annual Attendance:** 7,000
Affiliations: Monmouth Arts Council
Performance Facilities: Count Basie Theatre

FACILITY

COUNT BASIE THEATRE
99 Monmouth Street, Red Bank, NJ 07701
(908) 842-9000
FAX: (908) 842-9323
Type of Facility: Theatre House
Facility Originally: Vaudeville
Type of Stage: Thrust; Proscenium
Stage Dimensions: 43'6"Wx27'Dx21'3"H
Orchestra Pit
Seating Capacity: 1,529
Year Built: 1926   **Architect:** William Lehman
Contact for Rental: Jerry Bakal;   (908) 842-9000
Resident Groups: New Jersey Symphony Orchestra; Monmouth Civic Chorus; Garden State Ballet; Monmouth Conservatory of Music; Monmouth Symphony; Dance East; Company of Dance Arts

Ridgewood

DANCE

IRINE FOKINE BALLET COMPANY
33 Chestnut Street, Ridgewood, NJ 07450
(201) 652-9653
Founded: 1956
Arts Area: Ballet
Status: Semi-Professional; Non-Profit
Type: Performing; Touring; Educational
Purpose: To bring ballet to young people in suburban communities and to give training to young dancers
Management: Irine Fokine, Director; Margaret Dunworth, Secretary
Paid Artists: 25
Utilizes: Special Technical Talent; Guest Artists
Season: 52 Weeks
Performance Facilities: Bergen County Technical High School, Hackensack

INSTRUMENTAL MUSIC

RIDGEWOOD SYMPHONY ORCHESTRA
PO Box 176, Ridgewood, NJ 07675
(201) 612-0118
Founded: 1939
Arts Area: Symphony; Orchestra
Status: Non-Profit
Type: Performing
Purpose: Performs orchestral concerts with playing opportunities for local musicians and provides music scholarships for high school and college students; to sponsor a childrens' series twice a year as well as the Ridgewood Symphony Orchestra Festival Strings for middle school youngsters
Management: Dr. Sandra Dackow, Musical Director; Donna Denniston, Personnel Manager
Officers: Jennifer McElrath, President
Paid Staff: 1   **Volunteer Staff:** 7
Paid Artists: 4   **Non-Paid Artists:** 75
Utilizes: Guest Artists
Budget: $1,000 - $50,000
Income Sources: Private Foundations/Grants/Endowments; Business/Corporate Donations; Box Office; Individual Donations
Season: September - May   **Annual Attendance:** 2,400
Performance Facilities: Benjamin Franklin Middle School

VOCAL MUSIC

RIDGEWOOD GILBERT AND SULLIVAN OPERA COMPANY
975 East Ridgewood Avenue, Ridgewood, NJ 07450
(201) 385-9314
>**Founded:** 1937
>**Arts Area:** Light Opera
>**Status:** Non-Professional; Non-Profit
>**Type:** Performing; Touring
>**Purpose:** To present the operas of Gilbert and Sullivan; to foster appreciation of music, drama, and production of the Gilbert and Sullivan operas
>**Management:** Wilbur Watkin Lewis, Stage Director; Chester Wolfson, Music Director; Jack Strangfeld, Business Manager
>**Officers:** Carol Ciancia, President; Welles Hotchkiss, Vice President; Phillip Sternenberg, Secretary; Rhonda Cooperstein, Treasurer
>**Paid Staff:** 2   **Volunteer Staff:** 50
>**Non-Paid Artists:** 50
>**Budget:** $1,000 - $50,000
>**Income Sources:** Box Office
>**Season:** April - June; November - December   **Annual Attendance:** 8,000
>**Affiliations:** AACT
>**Performance Facilities:** Ben Franklin Middle School

Rutherford

FACILITY

WILLIAMS CENTER FOR THE ARTS - THE RIVOLI
One Williams Plaza, Rutherford, NJ 07070
(201) 939-6969
FAX: (201) 939-0843
>**Founded:** 1979
>**Type of Facility:** Theatre Complex; Concert Hall; Environmental; Multi-Purpose; Movie Theatre
>**Facility Originally:** Vaudeville; Movie House
>**Type of Stage:** Flexible; Proscenium; Platform; Three stages
>**Stage Dimensions:** 12'x17'; 25'x40'; 30'D'x35'H proscenium opening
>**Seating Capacity:** George W. Newman Theatre - 640; Marcus Recital Hall - 147; Oscar Theatre - 325
>**Year Built:** 1922
>**Year Remodeled:** 1992   **Architect:** John Leyman, Designer; John Capazzi, Architect   **Cost:** $500,000
>**Acoustical Consultant:** Robert Hunsen Associates
>**Contact for Rental:** John Leyman, Director of Operations
>**Resident Groups:** Williams Center Repertory Theatre (WCRT); Dance Compass (modern dance); New Jersey Ballet; Vagabond Puppets
>*The Williams Center for the Arts contains the Marcus Recital Hall, the black box Oscar Theatre, and the mainstage George W. Newman Theatre.*

Somers Point

THEATRE

SOUTH JERSEY REGIONAL THEATRE
Bay Avenue & Higbee Avenue, Somers Point, NJ 08244
(609) 653-0553
>**Founded:** 1977
>**Arts Area:** Professional; Theatrical Group
>**Status:** Professional; Non-Profit
>**Type:** Performing; Educational
>**Purpose:** To produce the highest quality theatre entertainment for residents and visitors to this part of our state
>**Management:** Thom Maslow, Executive Director; Joanna Papada, Artistic Director
>**Officers:** George Kisby, Chairman
>**Paid Staff:** 15   **Volunteer Staff:** 100
>**Paid Artists:** 30
>**Utilizes:** Special Technical Talent; Guest Artists; Guest Directors
>**Budget:** $500,000 - $1,000,000
>**Income Sources:** Private Foundations/Grants/Endowments; Business/Corporate Donations; Box Office; Government Grants; Individual Donations
>**Season:** 52 Weeks   **Annual Attendance:** 40,000

Affiliations: LORT; AEA; GPCA; New Jersey Theatre Group
Performance Facilities: South Jersey Regional Theatre

Summit

INSTRUMENTAL MUSIC

SUMMIT SYMPHONY
5 Myrtle Avenue, Summit, NJ 07901
(908) 277-2932
    Founded: 1937
    Arts Area: Symphony
    Status: Non-Professional; Non-Profit
    Type: Performing
    Purpose: To provide orchestra music for Summit and surrounding communities; to provide an arena for non-professionals to perform major works
    Management: James Sadewhite, Music Director; Barry Davidson, Manager of Orchestra Personnel
    Officers: Carol Smith, President; Donald Hufnail, Vice President; Peter Boak, Treasurer
    Paid Staff: 1   **Volunteer Staff:** 16
    Paid Artists: 3
    Utilizes: Guest Artists
    Budget: $1,000 - $50,000
    Income Sources: Private Foundations/Grants/Endowments; Business/Corporate Donations; Individual Donations
    Season: September - May   **Annual Attendance:** 1,500
    Affiliations: Summit Board of Recreation; New Jersey Council on the Arts
    Performance Facilities: Summit Senior High School; Summit Middle School

VOCAL MUSIC

COMMUNITY OPERA, INCORPORATED
417 Morris Avenue #22, Summit, NJ 07901
(908) 277-1934
    Founded: 1981
    Arts Area: Grand Opera; Operetta
    Status: Professional
    Purpose: To provide a showcase for opera singers and composers of modern works
    Management: Edward Q. Watts, President
    Officers: Barbara Railo, Secretary/Treasurer
    Volunteer Staff: 2
    Paid Artists: 5
    Utilizes: Special Technical Talent; Guest Artists
    Income Sources: Private Foundations/Grants/Endowments; Business/Corporate Donations; Box Office; Individual Donations
    Season: September - June   **Annual Attendance:** 300
    Affiliations: Orpheus Society
    Performance Facilities: Hudson Guild; South Street Seaport - Fulton Center

Teaneck

THEATRE

AMERICAN STAGE COMPANY
892 River Road, Teaneck, NJ 07666
(201) 692-7744
    Founded: 1985
    Arts Area: Professional; Theatrical Group
    Status: Professional; Non-Profit
    Type: Performing; Resident; Educational
    Purpose: To present the best in dramatic art; to nurture recognizable talent in all aspects of theatre by providing a forum for established artists to hone their skills and for new artists to develop and expand their talents
    Management: James A. Vagias, Executive Producer
    Officers: Robert Lusko, President
    Paid Staff: 5   **Volunteer Staff:** 15
    Utilizes: Special Technical Talent; Guest Artists; Guest Directors
    Budget: $100,000 - $500,000
    Income Sources: Private Foundations/Grants/Endowments; Business/Corporate Donations; Box Office; Government Grants; Individual Donations

Season: October - May   **Annual Attendance:** 21,000
Affiliations: AEA; New Jersey Theatre Group; New Jersey Arts Council
Performance Facilities: Becton Theatre

Toms River

INSTRUMENTAL MUSIC

GARDEN STATE PHILHARMONIC SYMPHONY ORCHESTRA
PO Box 269, Toms River, NJ 08754
(908) 349-6277
Founded: 1956
Arts Area: Symphony; Orchestra
Status: Semi-Professional; Non-Profit
Type: Performing
Purpose: To maintain a community orchestra in Ocean County, NJ that will give concerts of the highest cultural and educational value for the community; to provide both educational and training programs; to foster activities that encourage an interest and appreciation of music
Management: Raymond Wojcik, Music Director/Conductor; JoAnn Montarelli, Administrator
Officers: Estelle Brodkey, President; Norman Olsen, Jack Lamping, Sylvia Davis, Vice Presidents; Winifred Ewart, Treasurer
Paid Staff: 2   **Volunteer Staff:** 150
Paid Artists: 125   **Non-Paid Artists:** 50
Utilizes: Guest Artists; New Jersey Composers
Budget: $100,000 - $500,000
Income Sources: Private Foundations/Grants/Endowments; Business/Corporate Donations; Box Office; Government Grants; Individual Donations
Season: November - May   **Annual Attendance:** 10,000
Affiliations: ASOL
Performance Facilities: Toms River High School North

GARDEN STATE PHILHARMONIC YOUTH ORCHESTRA
PO Box 269, Toms River, NJ 08754
(908) 349-6277
Founded: 1970
Arts Area: Symphony
Status: Non-Professional; Non-Profit
Type: Performing; Educational
Purpose: To provide musical training and orchestral performance experience for school-aged children
Management: Don Spaulding, Conductor
Officers: Morris Adler, Executive Vice President
Non-Paid Artists: 70
Budget: $1,000 - $50,000
Income Sources: Private Foundations/Grants/Endowments; Business/Corporate Donations; Box Office; Government Grants; Individual Donations
Season: September - May   **Annual Attendance:** 2,700
Affiliations: Garden State Philharmonic Symphony Orchestra

VOCAL MUSIC

GARDEN STATE PHILHARMONIC CHORUS
PO Box 269, Toms River, NJ 08754
(908) 349-6277
Founded: 1984
Arts Area: Choral
Status: Non-Professional; Non-Profit
Type: Performing
Management: Paul Chapin, Choral Director
Paid Artists: 3   **Non-Paid Artists:** 100
Utilizes: Guest Artists
Season: November - May   **Annual Attendance:** 2,000
Performance Facilities: Toms River High School North

Trenton

INSTRUMENTAL MUSIC

GREATER TRENTON SYMPHONY ORCHESTRA
28 West State Street, Trenton, NJ 08608
(609) 394-1338
> **Founded:** 1921
> **Arts Area:** Symphony; Orchestra
> **Status:** Professional; Non-Profit
> **Type:** Performing; Educational
> **Purpose:** To offer high-quality performances of classical music for orchestra to the residents of the greater Trenton area
> **Management:** John Peter Holly, Executive Director
> **Paid Staff:** 2   **Volunteer Staff:** 1
> **Paid Artists:** 100
> **Utilizes:** Local Artists   **Budget:** $100,000 - $500,000
> **Income Sources:** Private Foundations/Grants/Endowments; Business/Corporate Donations; Box Office; Government Grants; Individual Donations
> **Season:** October - May   **Annual Attendance:** 6,000
> **Performance Facilities:** War Memorial Theater

THEATRE

SHAKESPEARE '70
121 Grand Street, Trenton, NJ 08611
(609) 695-1955
> **Founded:** 1970
> **Arts Area:** Summer Stock; Musical; Theatrical Group
> **Status:** Semi-Professional; Non-Profit
> **Type:** Performing; Educational
> **Purpose:** To bring the works of William Shakespeare and other classical writers to the region; to perform musicals with a classical root and bring Shakespeare productions to New Jersey Cable TV and thus into the classrooms of schools and colleges
> **Management:** Gerald E. Guarnieri, Executive Director; John F. Erath, PhD, Director
> **Officers:** Gerald E. Guarnieri, Chief Executive Officer/President; John F. Erath, Vice President; Gail Erath, Secretary; Carol Rosenthal, Board Member; Bruce S. Bushman, Controller
> **Paid Staff:** 3   **Volunteer Staff:** 6
> **Paid Artists:** 4   **Non-Paid Artists:** 25
> **Utilizes:** Special Technical Talent; Guest Artists; Guest Directors
> **Budget:** $1,000 - $50,000
> **Income Sources:** Private Foundations/Grants/Endowments; Business/Corporate Donations; Box Office; Government Grants; Individual Donations
> **Season:** February - November   **Annual Attendance:** 10,000
> **Affiliations:** New Jersey Theatre League
> **Performance Facilities:** Washington Crossing Open Air Theatre; Artists Showcase Theatre

FACILITY

NEW JERSEY STATE MUSEUM AUDITORIUM
205 West State Street, Trenton, NJ 08625
(609) 292-6308
FAX: (609) 599-4098
> **Type of Facility:** Auditorium
> **Type of Stage:** Proscenium
> **Seating Capacity:** 416
> **Year Built:** 1964   **Architect:** Frank Grad

Union

FACILITY

KEAN COLLEGE OF NEW JERSEY - WILKENS THEATRE
Morris Avenue, Union, NJ 07083
(908) 527-2088
FAX: (908) 527-8345
> **Founded:** 1965
> **Type of Facility:** Theatre House

Type of Stage: Thrust
Stage Dimensions: 40'x30'   **Orchestra Pit**
Seating Capacity: 956
Year Built: 1965   **Architect:** S,S&P
Contact for Rental: Performing Arts Office;   (908) 527-2088
Resident Groups: New Jersey Ballet; Chaison Dance Theatre Company; Garden State Orchestra; Kean Dance Theatre

Union City

THEATRE

PARK PERFORMING ARTS CENTER
560 32nd Street, Union City, NJ 07087
(201) 865-6980
   Arts Area: Professional
   Status: Professional; Non-Profit
   Type: Performing
   Purpose: To provide cultural enrichment and quality entertainment to all residents of New Jersey and the surrounding area
   Management: Kevin P. Ashe, Executive Director; Eric Hafen, Artistic Director; Jorge Fernandez, Business Director; Pilar Suarez, Public Relations
   Paid Staff: 25   **Volunteer Staff:** 35
   Budget: $100,000 - $500,000
   Income Sources: Private Foundations/Grants/Endowments; Business/Corporate Donations; Box Office; Government Grants; Individual Donations
   Performance Facilities: Park Theatre Performing Arts Centre

FACILITY

PARK THEATRE PERFORMING ARTS CENTRE
560 32nd Street, Union City, NJ 07087
(201) 865-6980
   Type of Facility: Performance Center
   Type of Stage: Proscenium
   Orchestra Pit
   Year Built: 1931   **Architect:** Frank J. Ricker & Louis A. Axt
   Contact for Rental: Sixto Perez;   (201) 865-6980
   The Performing Arts Centre contains the Main Theatre. See separate listing for additional information.

PARK THEATRE PERFORMING ARTS CENTRE - MAIN THEATRE
560 32nd Street, Union City, NJ 07087
(201) 865-6980
FAX: (201) 865-5339
   Type of Facility: Concert Hall; Theatre House
   Facility Originally: Vaudeville
   Type of Stage: Proscenium
   Stage Dimensions: 44'Wx40'Dx70'H   **Orchestra Pit**
   Seating Capacity: 1,350
   Year Built: 1931
   Contact for Rental: Sixto Perez;   (201) 865-6980
   Resident Groups: Park Players

Upper Montclair.

FACILITY

MONTCLAIR STATE COLLEGE - MEMORIAL AUDITORIUM
Upper Montclair, NJ 07043
(201) 893-4351
   Type of Facility: Theatre Complex; Auditorium; Performance Center
   Type of Stage: Thrust; Proscenium
   Stage Dimensions: 40'x36'x18'   **Orchestra Pit**
   Seating Capacity: 1,009

Year Built: 1958   **Architect:** Rigolo Associates
Contact for Rental: Gene Lotito;   (201) 893-4351
Resident Groups: Cultural Progress Dance Series; SummerFest; Student Organizations; Theatre Series

Warren

INSTRUMENTAL MUSIC

PHILHARMONIC ORCHESTRA OF NEW JERSEY
PO Box 4064, Warren, NJ 07059
(908) 356-6165
FAX: (908) 560-0881
   Founded: 1987
   Arts Area: Symphony; Orchestra
   Status: Professional; Non-Profit
   Type: Performing
   Purpose: To present the highest quality symphonic concerts in Somerset and Hunterdon counties in New Jersey
   Management: Marcia Blackstone, Managing Director
   Officers: Judith-Ann Corrente, President; Patricia Hyer, Vice President; James Mersfelder, Treasurer
   Paid Staff: 1   **Volunteer Staff:** 5
   Paid Artists: 100
   Utilizes: Guest Artists
   Budget: $100,000 - $500,000
   Income Sources: Private Foundations/Grants/Endowments; Business/Corporate Donations; Box Office; Government
   Grants; Individual Donations
   Season: September - June   **Annual Attendance:** 3,000
   Affiliations: ASOL
   Performance Facilities: Pingry Auditorium, Pingry School, Martinsville

Waterloo

PERFORMING SERIES

WATERLOO MUSIC FESTIVAL
Waterloo Foundation for the Arts, Waterloo, NJ 07874
(201) 347-4700
FAX: (201) 347-0900
   Founded: 1967
   Arts Area: Dance; Vocal Music; Instrumental Music; Theater; Festivals; Grand Opera
   Status: Professional; Non-Profit
   Type: Performing; Sponsoring
   Purpose: To combine history, music, art and architecture; to educate all persons in the state of New Jersey with apprecia-
   tion of these arts forms; to aid in the rehabilitation of youth via the culinary arts, performing arts and
   maintenance—eventually leading to jobs in these fields
   Management: Carole Delaire, Administrative Director; Samuel Lipman, Art Director; Gerard Schwarz, Principal
   Conductor
   Officers: Percival Leach, President; Finn Casperson, Chariman
   Paid Staff: 15   **Volunteer Staff:** 10
   Paid Artists: 40
   Utilizes: Guest Conductors; Guest Artists; Guest Directors
   Budget: $1,000,000 - $5,000,000
   Income Sources: Private Foundations/Grants/Endowments; Business/Corporate Donations; Box Office; Government
   Grants; Individual Donations
   Season: May - October   **Annual Attendance:** 200,000
   Affiliations: New Jersey State Council of the Arts; New Jersey Tourism Council
   Performance Facilities: Waterloo Music Festival Tent

Wayne

INSTRUMENTAL MUSIC

FRIENDS OF MUSIC OF WAYNE, INC.
c/o Schuyler-Colfax JHS, 1500 Hamburg Turnpike, Wayne, NJ 07470
(201) 633-3021
FAX: (201) 628-8837
   Founded: 1981

Arts Area: Symphony; Orchestra; Chamber; Ensemble; Ethnic; Folk; Instrumental Group; Electronic & Live Electronic; Band
Status: Non-Profit
Type: Educational; Sponsoring
Purpose: To support a high quality music program in our schools as an integral part of a balanced curriculum; to foster the appreciation of music
Management: Dr. Jacques Rizzo, Fine Arts Supervisor
Officers: Dee Herrmann, Matthew Paterno, Co-Presidents; Beverly Sullivan, First Vice President; Larry Silano, Second Vice President; Gwen Eckstein, Cooresponding Secretary; Laura Macey, Recording Secretary; Ruth Kotik, Treasurer
Volunteer Staff: 25
Utilizes: Guest Conductors; Guest Artists
Budget: $1,000 - $50,000
Income Sources: Private Foundations/Grants/Endowments; Business/Corporate Donations; Government Grants; Individual Donations
Season: September - June   **Annual Attendance:** 5,000
Affiliations: MENC
Performance Facilities: Wayne Valley High School; Wayne Hills High School; George Washington Junior High School; Schuyler-Colfax Junior High School

WAYNE CHAMBER ORCHESTRA
William Paterson College, 300 Pompton Road, Wayne, NJ 07470
(201) 595-2674
FAX: (201) 595-2460
Founded: 1986
Arts Area: Orchestra
Status: Professional
Type: Performing
Purpose: To present American music; to present works that are not frequently performed by chamber orchestras
Management: Murry Colosimo, Conductor; Martin Krivin, Executive Director; Sheri Newberger, Business Manager
Officers: Fletcher Fish, President; Erwin Knauer, Vice President; Ronald Hinchman, Treasurer; Mae Fish, Secretary
Paid Staff: 7   **Volunteer Staff:** 15
Paid Artists: 40   **Non-Paid Artists:** 8
Utilizes: Guest Artists
Budget: $100,000 - $500,000
Income Sources: Private Foundations/Grants/Endowments; Business/Corporate Donations; Box Office; Government Grants; Individual Donations
Season: October - May   **Annual Attendance:** 2,600
Performance Facilities: Shea Center for the Performing Arts, William Paterson College

PERFORMING SERIES

WILLIAM PATERSON COLLEGE - THE JAZZ ROOM SERIES
300 Pompton Road, Wayne, NJ 07470
(201) 595-2268
FAX: (201) 595-2460
Founded: 1978
Arts Area: Instrumental Music
Status: Professional
Type: Performing
Purpose: To present a complete spectrum of jazz music
Management: Martin Krivin, Producer; Rufus Reid, Artistic Advisor
Paid Staff: 2
Paid Artists: 38
Utilizes: Guest Artists
Budget: $1,000 - $50,000
Income Sources: Box Office; Government Grants
Season: October - March   **Annual Attendance:** 2,700
Performance Facilities: Shea Center for the Performing Arts, William Paterson College

WILLOWBROOK JAZZ FESTIVAL
William Paterson College, 300 Pompton Road, Wayne, NJ 07470
(201) 595-2268
FAX: (201) 595-2460
Arts Area: Jazz
Status: Professional; Non-Profit
Type: Performing
Purpose: To make jazz music as accessible to the public as possible by making it free and by locating it at a convenient time and place

Management: Dr. Martin Krivin, Special Projects Assistant to the President; Rufus Reid, Director of Jazz Program at William Paterson College
Budget: $50,000 - $100,000
Income Sources: Business/Corporate Donations; Government Grants
Season: April
Performance Facilities: Willowbrook Mall

West Orange

DANCE

NEW JERSEY BALLET COMPANY
270 Pleasant Valley Way, West Orange, NJ 07940
(201) 736-5940
FAX: (201) 736-5582
Founded: 1958
Arts Area: Ballet; Jazz
Status: Professional; Non-Profit
Type: Performing; Touring; Educational
Purpose: To maintain a highly regarded reperatory of standard classical pieces and audience attracting contemporary classical and jazz pieces which can be programmed to meet the needs of all presenters; to retain a roster of highly qualified dancers to perform the reperatory for all audiences
Management: Carolyn Clark, Executive/Artistic Director; Eleanor D'Antuono, Leonid Kozlov and Edward Villella, Artistic Advisors; Paul Sutherland, Ballet Master
Officers: David Farris, Chairman; Francis Mastro, President; Carolyn Clark, Executive Vice President
Paid Staff: 7   **Volunteer Staff:** 6
Paid Artists: 20
Utilizes: Guest Conductors; Guest Artists; Guest Directors; Guest Choreographers
Budget: $500,000 - $1,000,000
Income Sources: Private Foundations/Grants/Endowments; Business/Corporate Donations; Box Office; Government Grants; Individual Donations
Season: 32 Weeks   **Annual Attendance:** 100,000
Performance Facilities: Paper Mill Playhouse; Newark Symphony Hall; John Harms Center for the Performing Arts; Kean College; Ocean City Music Pier

PERFORMING SERIES

JEWISH COMMUNITY CENTER OF METROPOLITAN NEW JERSEY
760 Northfield Avenue, West Orange, NJ 07052
(201) 736-3200
FAX: (201) 736-6871
Founded: 1877
Arts Area: Vocal Music; Instrumental Music; Theater; Festivals; Film Series
Status: Professional; Non-Professional; Non-Profit
Type: Performing; Educational; Sponsoring
Management: Jo Goldstien, Programming Supervisor; Marsha Fleisch, Program Assistant
Officers: Rhoda Goodman, Director YM-YWHA; Martha Cohen, Chairman of Committee of the Arts; Peter Leibman, Co-Chair of the Committee of the Arts
Paid Staff: 3   **Volunteer Staff:** 100
Paid Artists: 100
Utilizes: Special Technical Talent; Guest Artists
Budget: $100,000 - $500,000
Income Sources: Private Foundations/Grants/Endowments; Business/Corporate Donations; Box Office; Government Grants; Individual Donations
Season: September - May   **Annual Attendance:** 15,000
Performance Facilities: Maurice Levin Theater

FACILITY

MAURICE LEVIN THEATER
760 Northfield Avenue, West Orange, NJ 07052
(201) 736-3200
FAX: (201) 736-6871
Type of Facility: Concert Hall
Type of Stage: Proscenium
Stage Dimensions: 38'x50'   **Orchestra Pit**
Seating Capacity: 500
Year Built: 1966

Contact for Rental: Jo Goldstein;   (201) 736-3200
Resident Groups: Metropolitan Orchestra

Westfield

INSTRUMENTAL MUSIC

THE WESTFIELD SYMPHONY
321 Elm Street, PO Box 491, Westfield, NJ 07090
(908) 232-9400
FAX: (908) 232-2446
> **Founded:** 1983
> **Arts Area:** Symphony
> **Status:** Professional
> **Type:** Performing
> **Purpose:** To bring the highest quality professional music to the central New Jersey area; to provide education programs for grades 1-12 in the area
> **Management:** Kenneth W. Hopper, General Manager
> **Officers:** Nancy W. Priest, President; Robert J. Edelman, Treasurer; M.J. Vincentsen, Vice President; Ellen I. Albertson, Secretary
> **Paid Staff:** 3
> **Paid Artists:** 70
> **Utilizes:** Guest Artists
> **Budget:** $100,000 - $500,000
> **Income Sources:** Private Foundations/Grants/Endowments; Business/Corporate Donations; Box Office; Government Grants; Individual Donations
> **Season:** October - April   **Annual Attendance:** 4,500

VOCAL MUSIC

THE CHORAL ART SOCIETY OF NEW JERSEY
PO Box 2036, Westfield, NJ 07091
(908) 232-2173
> **Founded:** 1962
> **Arts Area:** Choral
> **Status:** Non-Professional
> **Type:** Performing
> **Purpose:** To study, perform and promote choral works
> **Management:** Evelyn Bleeke, Musical Director
> **Officers:** James Zgoda, President; Ted Schirm, Vice President; Linda Jacobey, Treasurer; Suzanne Beeny, Secretary
> **Paid Staff:** 2   **Volunteer Staff:** 21
> **Paid Artists:** 10
> **Utilizes:** Guest Artists
> **Budget:** $1,000 - $50,000
> **Income Sources:** Private Foundations/Grants/Endowments; Business/Corporate Donations; Box Office; Government Grants; Individual Donations
> **Season:** September - June   **Annual Attendance:** 1,000

Woodbridge

FACILITY

BARRON ARTS CENTER
582 Rahway Avenue, Woodbridge, NJ 07095
(908) 634-0413
> **Founded:** 1977
> **Type of Facility:** Concert Hall; Outdoor (Concert); Multi-Purpose
> **Facility Originally:** Library
> **Type of Stage:** Flexible
> **Seating Capacity:** 100
> **Year Built:** 1877   **Architect:** J. Cleveland Cadey   **Cost:** $19,000

NEW MEXICO

Alamogordo

FACILITY

FLICKINGER CENTER FOR THE PERFORMING ARTS
1110 New York Avenue, Alamogordo, NM 88310
(505) 437-2202
Founded: 1988
Type of Facility: Concert Hall; Auditorium; Performance Center; Theatre House; Multi-Purpose
Facility Originally: Movie House
Type of Stage: Proscenium
Stage Dimensions: 30'x40'
Orchestra Pit
Seating Capacity: 700
Year Built: 1956
Year Remodeled: 1992   **Architect:** Nolan and Associates   **Cost:** $380,000
Acoustical Consultant: Smith Electrical
Contact for Rental: Susie Hall;   (505) 437-2202
Resident Groups: Alamogordo Music Theater; Alamogordo Players Workshop

Albuquerque

DANCE

THE NEW MEXICO BALLET COMPANY
PO Box 21518, Albuquerque, NM 87154
(505) 292-4245
Founded: 1972
Arts Area: Ballet
Status: Non-Professional; Non-Profit
Type: Performing; Touring
Purpose: To promote the dance arts through education, training, and performances
Management: David Chavez, Artistic Director; Mildred Ness, Executive Director
Officers: June Leonard, Chairman
Paid Artists: 24   **Non-Paid Artists:** 40
Utilizes: Guest Artists; Guest Choreographers
Budget: $100,000 - $500,000
Income Sources: Private Foundations/Grants/Endowments; Business/Corporate Donations; Box Office; Individual Donations
Season: October - April
Performance Facilities: Popejoy Hall, University of New Mexico at Albuquerque

INSTRUMENTAL MUSIC

ALBUQUERQUE YOUTH SYMPHONY
220 Monroe SE, PO Box 25704, Albuquerque, NM 87104
(505) 345-5365, ext. 397
Founded: 1955
Arts Area: Symphony; Orchestra; Ensemble
Status: Non-Professional; Non-Profit
Type: Performing; Touring; Educational; Sponsoring
Purpose: To provide an outlet for talented students above and beyond their regular school musical programs through participation in one of four orchestras: Albuquerque Youth Symphony, Albuquerque Youth Orchestra, Albuquerque Junior Symphony or Albuquerque Junior Orchestra
Management: Dale E. Kempter, Conductor
Paid Staff: 4   **Volunteer Staff:** 200
Non-Paid Artists: 400
Income Sources: Fund-raising
Season: September - May   **Annual Attendance:** 15,000
Affiliations: ASOL (Youth Orchestra Division); ASCAP
Performance Facilities: Popejoy Hall, University of New Mexico

CHAMBER ORCHESTRA OF ALBUQUERQUE
PO Box 35081, Albuquerque, NM 87176-5081
(505) 881-0844
> **Founded:** 1976
> **Arts Area:** Orchestra
> **Status:** Professional; Non-Profit
> **Type:** Performing
> **Purpose:** To provide a broad range of listening and participatory musical opportunities to the State of New Mexico; to maintain a professional orchestra whose work enriches the quality of community life
> **Management:** David Oberg, Music Director/Conductor/General Manager; Diane V. Teare, Managing Assistant
> **Officers:** Michael H. Smith, President; John T. Duff, Treasurer; Julia Cohen, Secretary
> **Paid Staff:** 2 **Volunteer Staff:** 2
> **Paid Artists:** 37
> **Utilizes:** Guest Conductors; Guest Artists
> **Budget:** $100,000 - $500,000
> **Income Sources:** Private Foundations/Grants/Endowments; Business/Corporate Donations; Box Office; Government Grants; Individual Donations
> **Season:** October - June
> **Annual Attendance:** 9,000
> **Performance Facilities:** St. John's United Methodist Church

MUSICA ANTIGUA DE ALBUQUERQUE
1017 Roma NE, Albuquerque, NM 87106
(505) 842-9613
> **Founded:** 1978
> **Arts Area:** Ensemble
> **Status:** Professional; Non-Profit
> **Type:** Performing; Touring; Educational
> **Purpose:** To bring music of the Middle Ages, Renaissance and Baroque eras of music history to audiences through concert performances and lecture demonstrations
> **Officers:** Art Sheinberg, President of the Executive Board; Allison Edwards, Vice President; Colleen Sheinberg, Secretary/Treasurer
> **Paid Staff:** 1 **Volunteer Staff:** 1
> **Paid Artists:** 6
> **Utilizes:** Special Technical Talent; Guest Artists
> **Budget:** $1,000 - $50,000
> **Income Sources:** Business/Corporate Donations; Box Office; Government Grants; Individual Donations; Merchandise Sales
> **Season:** September - May
> **Annual Attendance:** 1,350
> **Affiliations:** Early Music America; Albuquerque Arts Alliance
> **Performance Facilities:** Central United Methodist Church; Loretto Chapel, Santa Fe

NEW MEXICO SYMPHONY ORCHESTRA
220 Gold Avenue SW, Albuquerque, NM 87102
(505) 843-7657
FAX: (505) 247-8422
> **Mailing Address:** PO Box 769, Albuquerque, NM 87103
> **Founded:** 1932
> **Arts Area:** Symphony; Orchestra; Chamber; Ensemble
> **Status:** Professional; Non-Profit
> **Type:** Performing; Educational
> **Purpose:** To present live concerts of music for small ensembles through full orchestra in both educational and concert settings
> **Management:** Paul Bunker, Executive Director; Carl Johnston, Finance Director; Geoge Sampson, Development Director; Marge Navarro, Marketing Director
> **Officers:** Herbert Koogle, President; Michael Bowlin, President-Elect; Derick Pasternak, Vice President; Michael Thompson, Vice President/Secretary; Mark Smith, Treasurer
> **Paid Staff:** 13 **Volunteer Staff:** 2
> **Paid Artists:** 78 **Non-Paid Artists:** 109
> **Utilizes:** Special Technical Talent; Guest Conductors; Guest Artists; Guest Directors
> **Budget:** $1,000,000 - $5,000,000
> **Income Sources:** Private Foundations/Grants/Endowments; Business/Corporate Donations; Box Office; Government Grants; Individual Donations
> **Season:** September - May
> **Annual Attendance:** 120,000
> **Affiliations:** ASOL; AAA
> **Performance Facilities:** Popejoy Hall

VOCAL MUSIC

ALBUQUERQUE CIVIC LIGHT OPERA
4201 Ellison NE, Albuquerque, NM 87109
(505) 345-6577
> **Founded:** 1968
> **Arts Area:** Light Opera; Musical Theatre
> **Status:** Non-Profit
> **Type:** Performing
> **Purpose:** To present musical theatre with community based performers, musicians and crews
> **Management:** Linda McVey, Executive Director
> **Officers:** Nickey Prokapiak, President; John Wright, Vice President; Karen Lynch, Secretary; E. John Caruso, Treasurer
> **Paid Staff:** 10   **Volunteer Staff:** 200
> **Paid Artists:** 3   **Non-Paid Artists:** 500
> **Utilizes:** Guest Directors
> **Budget:** $500,000 - $1,000,000
> **Income Sources:** Private Foundations/Grants/Endowments; Business/Corporate Donations; Box Office; Individual Donations
> **Season:** March - December   **Annual Attendance:** 12,000
> **Affiliations:** SWTC
> **Performance Facilities:** Popejoy Hall

ALBUQUERQUE OPERA THEATRE - OPERA SOUTHWEST
515 15th Street NW, Albuquerque, NM 87104
(505) 243-0591
> **Founded:** 1972
> **Arts Area:** Grand Opera; Lyric Opera; Light Opera; Operetta
> **Status:** Professional; Non-Profit
> **Type:** Performing; Educational
> **Purpose:** To present fully staged, costumed operas with accomplished musicians at the highest artistic level
> **Management:** Justine Tate-Opel, Production Manager/General Director
> **Officers:** Sheila Johnson, President, Board of Directors
> **Paid Staff:** 3   **Volunteer Staff:** 25
> **Paid Artists:** 20   **Non-Paid Artists:** 30
> **Utilizes:** Special Technical Talent; Guest Artists; Guest Directors
> **Budget:** $100,000 - $500,000
> **Income Sources:** Business/Corporate Donations; Box Office; Government Grants; Individual Donations
> **Season:** October - May   **Annual Attendance:** 8,000
> **Affiliations:** COS
> **Performance Facilities:** KiMo Theatre

NEW MEXICO GAY MEN'S CHORUS
8640 Horacio Place NE, Albuquerque, NM 87111
(505) 296-9215
> **Founded:** 1981
> **Arts Area:** Choral
> **Status:** Non-Professional; Non-Profit
> **Type:** Performing; Resident; Educational
> **Management:** David Arenallenes, Conductor
> **Officers:** Alan Stringer, Manager
> **Paid Staff:** 1   **Volunteer Staff:** 5
> **Paid Artists:** 1   **Non-Paid Artists:** 30
> **Budget:** $1,000 - $50,000
> **Income Sources:** Business/Corporate Donations; Box Office; Individual Donations
> **Season:** December - June   **Annual Attendance:** 500
> **Affiliations:** Common Bond
> **Performance Facilities:** First Unitarian Church

THEATRE

LA COMPANIA DE TEATRO DE ALBURQUERQUE
423 Central Avenue NE, PO Box 884, Albuquerque, NM 87103-0884
(505) 242-7929
> **Founded:** 1977
> **Arts Area:** Theatrical Group
> **Status:** Semi-Professional; Non-Profit
> **Type:** Performing; Touring; Resident; Educational
> **Purpose:** To reflect, preserve and empower the New Mexican society and culture through professional production; Southwest bilingual theatre

Management: Ramon A. Flores, Artistic Director; Jeannette Chavez, Administrative Aide
Officers: Dr. Joe Valles, President; Edward Benavidez Esq., Vice President; Patricia Romero CPA, Treasurer; Catherine Abeyta, Secretary
Paid Staff: 2   **Volunteer Staff:** 20
Paid Artists: 10   **Non-Paid Artists:** 30
Utilizes: Special Technical Talent
Budget: $100,000 - $500,000
Income Sources: Private Foundations/Grants/Endowments; Business/Corporate Donations; Box Office; Government Grants; Individual Donations; Touring Fees
Season: September - June   **Annual Attendance:** 7,000
Performance Facilities: KiMo Theatre; South Broadway Cutural Center

NEW MEXICO REPERTORY THEATRE
PO Box 789, Albuquerque, NM 87103-0789
(505) 243-4577
Founded: 1983
Arts Area: Professional; Theatrical Group
Status: Professional; Non-Profit
Type: Performing; Touring; Resident; Educational
Purpose: To present the finest in contemporary and classical theatre to the residents of New Mexico
Management: Martin L. Platt, Artistic Director; Bob MacDonald, Managing Director
Paid Staff: 12   **Volunteer Staff:** 200
Paid Artists: 45
Utilizes: Special Technical Talent; Guest Artists; Guest Directors
Budget: $1,000,000 - $5,000,000
Income Sources: Private Foundations/Grants/Endowments; Business/Corporate Donations; Box Office; Government Grants; Individual Donations
Season: October - June   **Annual Attendance:** 60,000
Affiliations: TCG
Performance Facilities: KiMo Theatre; New Mexico Repertory Theatre

PERFORMING SERIES

GUEST ARTIST SERIES
c/o New Mexico Jazz Workshop Inc., PO Box 1925, Albuquerque, NM 87103
(505) 255-9798
Arts Area: Jazz
Status: Professional; Non-Profit
Type: Performing; Touring
Purpose: To present major jazz artists January-May for performing and educational activities
Management: Jim Williams, Executive Director
Officers: George Sampson, President
Budget: $1,000 - $50,000
Income Sources: Private Foundations/Grants/Endowments; Business/Corporate Donations; Box Office; Government Grants; Individual Donations
Season: January - May
Performance Facilities: Albuquerque Little Theater; Kimo Theater; Sunshine Music Hall

FACILITY

ALBUQUERQUE CONVENTION CENTER
401 Second Street NW, Albuquerque, NM 87103
(505) 768-4575
FAX: (505) 768-3239
Type of Facility: Civic Center
Year Built: 1972   **Architect:** Flato Bryan and Moore   **Cost:** $12,000,000
Contact for Rental: Dale Scott;   (505) 768-4575
Albuquerque Convention Center contains the Ballroom and Kiva Auditorium. See separate listings for additional information.

ALBUQUERQUE CONVENTION CENTER - BALLROOM
401 Second Street NW, Albuquerque, NM 87103
(505) 768-4575
FAX: (505) 768-3239
Type of Facility: Multi-Purpose; Room
Type of Stage: Flexible; Platform

Seating Capacity: Banquet - 1,900; Theater - 2,400
Contact for Rental: Dale Scott;   (505) 768-4575

ALBUQUERQUE CONVENTION CENTER - KIVA AUDITORIUM
401 Second Street NW, Albuquerque, NM 87103
(505) 768-4575
FAX: (505) 768-3239
Type of Facility: Concert Hall; Auditorium
Type of Stage: Proscenium
Stage Dimensions: 36'Wx24'D
Seating Capacity: 2,300
Contact for Rental: Dale Scott;   (505) 768-4575
Resident Groups: Albuquerque Symphony

SOUTH BROADWAY CULTURAL CENTER
1025 Broadway SE, Albuquerque, NM 87102
(505) 848-1320
FAX: (505) 848-1329
Founded: 1970
Type of Facility: Multi-Purpose
Facility Originally: Library; Storefront
Type of Stage: Proscenium
Stage Dimensions: 20'x40'
Seating Capacity: 214
Year Built: 1985
Architect: City of Albuquerque
Cost: $60,000
Contact for Rental: Marge Armijo;   (505) 848-1320

UNIVERSITY OF NEW MEXICO - POPEJOY HALL
Albuquerque, NM 87131
(505) 277-3824
Type of Facility: Concert Hall
Type of Stage: Proscenium
Stage Dimensions: 120'Wx68'Dx38'H   **Orchestra Pit**
Seating Capacity: 2,002
Year Built: 1956
Architect: University of New Mexico
Cost: $3,000,000
Acoustical Consultant: Bolt, Beranek & Newman
Contact for Rental: William Martin, Director;   (505) 277-3824
Resident Groups: Albuquerque Civic Light Opera; New Mexico Symphony Orchestra; Albuquerque Children's Theatre

Angel Fire

INSTRUMENTAL MUSIC

MUSIC FROM ANGEL FIRE
PO Box 502, Angel Fire, NM 87710
(505) 989-4772
FAX: (505) 989-4773
Founded: 1984
Arts Area: Chamber
Status: Professional; Non-Profit
Type: Performing
Management: John W. Giovando, Executive Director; Ida Kavafian, Music Director
Paid Staff: 3   Volunteer Staff: 50
Paid Artists: 30
Budget: $100,000 - $500,000
Income Sources: Private Foundations/Grants/Endowments; Business/Corporate Donations; Box Office; Government Grants; Individual Donations
Season: August - September   Annual Attendance: 5,000
Performance Facilities: Taos; Angel Fire; Raton

Farmington

FACILITY

FARMINGTON CIVIC CENTER
200 West Arrington, Farmington, NM 87401
(505) 599-1150
FAX: (505) 599-1146
Founded: 1976
Type of Facility: Civic Center
Type of Stage: Modified Thrust   **Orchestra Pit**
Seating Capacity: 1,200
Year Built: 1976   **Architect:** Schermer & Schafer   **Cost:** $3,800,000
Contact for Rental: Civic Center;   (505) 599-1145

Las Cruces

THEATRE

LAS CRUCES COMMUNITY THEATRE
313 North Downtown Mall, Las Cruces, NM 88004
(505) 523-1200
Founded: 1963
Arts Area: Theatrical Group
Status: Non-Professional; Non-Profit
Type: Performing
Management: Yvette Lyannas, Box Office
Officers: Dick Rundell, President
Volunteer Staff: 20
Utilizes: Special Technical Talent; Guest Conductors; Guest Artists; Guest Directors
Budget: $1,000 - $50,000
Income Sources: Private Foundations/Grants/Endowments; Business/Corporate Donations; Box Office; Government Grants; Individual Donations
Season: October - July   **Annual Attendance:** 8,000

FACILITY

NEW MEXICO STATE UNIVERSITY - AMERICAN SOUTHWEST THEATRE
PO Box 3072, Las Cruces, NM 88003
(505) 646-4517
Type of Facility: Studio Performance; Theatre House
Type of Stage: Greek
Seating Capacity: 386
Year Built: 1962   **Architect:** Walgamood   **Cost:** $750,000
Year Remodeled: 1984   **Architect:** Len Auerbach   **Cost:** $1,500,000
Acoustical Consultant: Len Auerbach
Manager: Hilda Olivas
Resident Groups: American Southwest Theatre Company
Available for rent

PAN AMERICAN CENTER
PO Box 3SE, Las Cruces, NM 88003
(505) 646-4413
Type of Facility: Arena
Type of Stage: Flexible; Platform
Stage Dimensions: 72'Wx40'D
Seating Capacity: 13,500
Year Built: 1967
Contact for Rental: Barbara Hubbard;   (505) 646-4413

Los Alamos

FACILITY

LOS ALAMOS CIVIC AUDITORIUM
1400 Diamond Drive, Los Alamos, NM 87544
(505) 662-3683, ext. 53
FAX: (505) 662-4141
    Founded: 1950
    Type of Facility: Auditorium
    Type of Stage: Proscenium
    Stage Dimensions: 40'W   **Orchestra Pit**
    Seating Capacity: 965
    Year Built: 1950
    Contact for Rental: Carol Rodriguez; (505) 662-3683, ext. 53
    Resident Groups: Los Alamos Light Opera

Roswell

FACILITY

PEARSON AUDITORIUM
New Mexico Military Institute, College of Main, Roswell, NM 88201
(505) 622-6250
    Type of Facility: Auditorium
    Type of Stage: Proscenium   **Orchestra Pit**
    Seating Capacity: 1,300
    Year Built: 1940   **Cost:** $500,000
    Contact for Rental: Colonel Taylor; (505) 622-6250

Santa Fe

DANCE

MARIA BENITEZ SPANISH DANCE COMPANY
914 Rio Vista, Santa Fe, NM 87501
(505) 983-8477
    Founded: 1972
    Arts Area: Ethnic
    Status: Professional; Non-Profit
    Type: Performing; Touring; Educational
    Purpose: To foster the development of a high level of excellence in Spanish dancing through national and international touring, educational programs, concerts and television programs
    Management: Maria Benitez, Artistic Director
    Paid Staff: 4
    Paid Artists: 9
    Utilizes: Guest Artists
    Income Sources: Private Foundations/Grants/Endowments; Business/Corporate Donations; Box Office; Government Grants; Individual Donations
    Season: 52 Weeks   **Annual Attendance:** 12,000
    Performance Facilities: Sheraton of Sante Fe; Joyce Theatre, New York

INSTRUMENTAL MUSIC

THE ENSEMBLE OF SANTA FE
PO Box 8427, Santa Fe, NM 87504-8427
(505) 984-2501
    Founded: 1980
    Arts Area: Chamber
    Status: Professional; Non-Profit
    Type: Performing; Touring; Resident; Educational
    Purpose: To present chamber music and promote understanding
    Management: Santa Fe World Music Agency
    Officers: Thomas O'Connor, President; William Kirschke, Vice President; Carol Redman, Secretary/Treasurer
    Paid Staff: 2
    Paid Artists: 20
    Utilizes: Special Technical Talent; Guest Artists

Budget: $50,000 - $100,000
Income Sources: Private Foundations/Grants/Endowments; Business/Corporate Donations; Box Office; Government Grants; Individual Donations; Contracted Services
Season: 52 Weeks   **Annual Attendance:** 8,000
Performance Facilities: Loretto Chapel

ORCHESTRA OF SANTA FE
PO Box 2091, Santa Fe, NM 87504
(505) 988-4640
Founded: 1972
Arts Area: Symphony; Orchestra; Chamber
Status: Professional; Non-Profit
Type: Performing; Touring; Educational
Purpose: To provide the highest quality chamber music possible and make youth concerts and educational lectures available to the public
Management: Jennifer Martin, Business Manager; William Kirschke, Conductor; Anne Beeson, Development Director
Officers: Nancy Long Garcia, Roger Miller, Past Presidents
Paid Staff: 2   **Volunteer Staff:** 50
Paid Artists: 35
Utilizes: Guest Artists
Budget: $100,000 - $500,000
Income Sources: Private Foundations/Grants/Endowments; Business/Corporate Donations; Box Office; Government Grants; Individual Donations
Season: September - May   **Annual Attendance:** 12,000
Affiliations: ASOL
Performance Facilities: Lensic Theatre

SANTA FE SYMPHONY
PO Box 9692, Santa Fe, NM 87504
(505) 983-3530
FAX: (505) 982-3888
Founded: 1984
Arts Area: Symphony; Orchestra; Chamber; Folk
Status: Professional; Non-Profit
Type: Performing; Resident; Educational; Sponsoring
Management: Lynn Case, General Manager; Stewart Robertson, Music Director
Paid Staff: 2   **Volunteer Staff:** 110
Paid Artists: 80   **Non-Paid Artists:** 60
Utilizes: Guest Conductors; Guest Artists
Budget: $100,000 - $500,000
Income Sources: Private Foundations/Grants/Endowments; Business/Corporate Donations; Box Office; Government Grants; Individual Donations
Season: August - May   **Annual Attendance:** 8,000
Affiliations: ASOL; ASCAP
Performance Facilities: Sweeney Center

VOCAL MUSIC

THE SANTA FE DESERT CHORALE
PO Box 2813, Santa Fe, NM 87504-2813
(505) 988-7505
FAX: (505) 988-7522
Founded: 1982
Arts Area: Choral
Status: Professional; Non-Profit
Type: Performing; Educational
Purpose: To perform music from the choral repertoire within the last five centuries, especially baroque and modern
Management: Lawrence Bandfield, Music Director; Thomas Maguire, Executive Director
Officers: Mary Ann Nelson, President
Paid Staff: 4   **Volunteer Staff:** 100
Paid Artists: 45
Utilizes: Guest Conductors; Guest Artists
Budget: $100,000 - $500,000
Income Sources: Private Foundations/Grants/Endowments; Business/Corporate Donations; Box Office; Government Grants; Individual Donations
Season: June - September   **Annual Attendance:** 6,500

Affiliations: CA
Performance Facilities: Santuario de Guadalupe; Loretto Chapel; Sunshine Music Hall

THE SANTA FE OPERA
PO Box 2408, Santa Fe, NM 87504
(505) 982-3851
FAX: (505) 989-7012
　Arts Area: Lyric Opera; Light Opera; Operetta
　Status: Professional; Non-Profit
　Type: Performing; Educational; Sponsoring
　Purpose: To bring the finest opera productions to the American public with a varied repertoire, paying special attention to new works
　Management: John Crosby, Founder/General Director; Thomas Morris, Operations Manager
　Volunteer Staff: 25
　Paid Artists: 40
　Utilizes: Special Technical Talent; Guest Conductors; Guest Artists; Guest Directors
　Budget: $5,000,000 - $10,000,000
　Income Sources: Private Foundations/Grants/Endowments; Business/Corporate Donations; Box Office; Government Grants; Individual Donations
　Season: July - August
　Annual Attendance: 70,000
　Affiliations: OA
　Performance Facilities: Santa Fe Opera Theatre

THEATRE

SANTA FE COMMUNITY THEATRE
142 East DeVargas, Santa Fe, NM 87501
(505) 988-4262
　Founded: 1919
　Arts Area: Professional; Theatrical Group
　Status: Non-Professional; Non-Profit
　Type: Performing; Touring; Educational
　Officers: Robert Sinn, President; Carol Couch, Vice President; Ted Mclaughlin, Recording Secretary
　Volunteer Staff: 500
　Non-Paid Artists: 60
　Utilizes: Guest Artists; Guest Directors
　Income Sources: Private Foundations/Grants/Endowments; Business/Corporate Donations; Box Office; Government Grants; Individual Donations
　Season: 52 Weeks　**Annual Attendance:** 7,600
　Affiliations: AACT
　Performance Facilities: Santa Fe Community Theatre

PERFORMING SERIES

SANTA FE CHAMBER MUSIC FESTIVAL
640 Paseo de Peralta, Santa Fe, NM 87501
(505) 983-2075
FAX: (505) 986-0251
　Founded: 1973
　Arts Area: Chamber
　Status: Professional; Non-Profit
　Type: Performing; Touring; Resident; Educational
　Purpose: To produce innovative chamber music concerts and related educational programs of exceptional artistic quality; to serve as a chamber music center attracting American musicians, composers and audiences whose combined influence, stimulation and energy will benefit American culture
　Management: James E. McGarry, Executive Director; Heiichiro Ohyama, Artistic Director
　Officers: Gifford Phillips, Chairman, Board of Trustes; Jacqueline Hoefer, Vice-Chairman; Dode Kenney, Secretary; Terrence Melia, Treasurer
　Paid Staff: 12　**Volunteer Staff:** 150
　Paid Artists: 60
　Utilizes: Guest Conductors; Guest Artists
　Budget: $1,000,000 - $5,000,000
　Income Sources: Private Foundations/Grants/Endowments; Business/Corporate Donations; Box Office; Government Grants; Individual Donations
　Season: July - August　**Annual Attendance:** 20,000
　Performance Facilities: Saint Francis Auditorium: Museum of Fine Arts

FACILITY

CENTER FOR CONTEMPORARY ARTS
291 East Barcelona, Santa Fe, NM 87504
(505) 982-1338
FAX: (505) 982-9854
   Founded: 1979
   Type of Facility: Concert Hall; Multi-Purpose
   Type of Stage: Platform; Portable
   Stage Dimensions: 20'Wx12'D
   Seating Capacity: 140
   Year Remodeled: 1985   **Architect:** Mike Freeman

GREER GARSON THEATRE CENTER - COLLEGE OF SANTA FE
1600 St. Michael's Drive, Santa Fe, NM 87501
(505) 473-6439
   Type of Facility: Theatre House
   Type of Stage: Proscenium; Modified Apron Proscenium
   Stage Dimensions: 70'Wx32'Dx33'H; 40'Wx16'H proscenium opening   **Orchestra Pit**
   Seating Capacity: 514
   Year Built: 1965   **Architect:** Philippe Register   **Cost:** $1,000,000
   Year Remodeled: 1987   **Architect:** Davis & Associates
   Contact for Rental: Mary Ann Fellows;   (505) 473-6270
   Resident Groups: College of Santa Fe Performing Arts Department

NEW MEXICO REP
1050 Old Pecos Trail, Santa Fe, NM 87501
(505) 983-2382
FAX: (505) 984-1296
   Founded: 1984
   Type of Facility: Theatre House; Multi-Purpose
   Facility Originally: Armory
   Type of Stage: Modified Thrust Proscenium
   Stage Dimensions: 40'Wx30'D
   Seating Capacity: 340
   Year Built: 1971
   Year Remodeled: 1976
   Acoustical Consultant: Applied Acoustics Associates
   Contact for Rental: Bob McDonald;   (505) 983-2382
   Resident Groups: La Compania Working Classroom

SANTA FE CONVENTION AND VISITORS BUREAU AT SWEENEY CENTER
201 West Marcy, PO Box 909, Santa Fe, NM 87501-0909
(505) 984-6760; (800) 777-2489
FAX: (505) 984-6679
   Type of Facility: Concert Hall; Civic Center; Multi-Purpose
   Facility Originally: High School Gymnasium
   Type of Stage: Platform
   Stage Dimensions: 64'Wx38'D
   Seating Capacity: Theater - 1500; Banquet - 600
   Year Built: 1955
   Year Remodeled: 1979   **Architect:** Clark Aarison Germanas, AIA
   Contact for Rental: Roxanne Smyth;   (505) 984-6760
   Resident Groups: Santa Fe Symphony; New Mexico Symphony

SANTUARIO DE GUADALUPE
100 Guadalupe Street, Santa Fe, NM 87501
(505) 988-2027
   Type of Facility: Concert Hall; Theatre House
   Facility Originally: Church
   Type of Stage: Platform
   Stage Dimensions: 22'Wx13'W
   Seating Capacity: 250
   Year Built: 1776   **Architect:** Franciscan Missionaries
   Year Remodeled: 1976   **Architect:** Nathaniel Owings, Chairman, National Trust for Historic Preservation
   Contact for Rental: Emilio I. Ortiz;   (505) 988-2027

Resident Groups: Santa Fe Desert Chorale; Sangre de Cristo Chorale; Santa Fe Chamber Music Festival; Gamelan Encantada; Ars Nova Chamber Singers
State of New Mexico Bicentennial Project; National Register of Historic Places

SWEENEY CONVENTION CENTER
201 West Marcy Street, Santa Fe, NM 87501
(505) 984-6760
FAX: (505) 984-6679
    Founded: 1974
    Type of Facility: Concert Hall; Auditorium; Performance Center; Civic Center; Multi-Purpose
    Facility Originally: School
    Type of Stage: Flexible
    Stage Dimensions: 24'x64'
    Seating Capacity: 1,500
    Year Built: 1956
    Year Remodeled: 1972
    Contact for Rental: Kenny Tennyson;   (505) 984-6760

WECKESSER STUDIO THEATRE
Greer Garson Theatre Center, College of Santa Fe, 1600 St. Michael's Drive, Santa Fe, NM 87501
(505) 473-6439
    Type of Facility: Black Box
    Facility Originally: Lecture Hall
    Type of Stage: Flexible
    Stage Dimensions: 40'x39' with 40'x12' raised section at one end
    Seating Capacity: 100
    Year Built: 1965   **Architect:** Philippe Register
    Year Remodeled: 1987   **Architect:** Davis & Associates
    Contact for Rental: Mary Ann Fellows;   (505) 473-6270

Taos

PERFORMING SERIES

TAOS SCHOOL OF MUSIC, INC.
PO Box 1879, Taos, NM 87571
(505) 776-2388
    Founded: 1963
    Arts Area: Instrumental Music; Festivals
    Status: Non-Profit
    Type: Performing; Educational
    Purpose: To further the understanding, enjoyment and performance of chamber music through the school and festival
    Officers: Chilton Anderson, President/Treasurer; R. Jamesson Burns, Vice President; Grace M. Parr, Secretary
    Utilizes: Special Technical Talent; Guest Artists
    Budget: $50,000 - $100,000
    Income Sources: Private Foundations/Grants/Endowments; Business/Corporate Donations; Individual Donations
    Season: June - August   **Annual Attendance:** 2,500
    Performance Facilities: Taos Community Auditorium; Hotel St. Bernard

NEW YORK

Albany

INSTRUMENTAL MUSIC

ALBANY SYMPHONY ORCHESTRA
19 Clinton Avenue, Albany, NY 12207
(518) 465-4755
FAX: (518) 465-3711
Founded: 1931
Arts Area: Symphony
Status: Professional; Non-Profit
Type: Performing
Purpose: To give quality performances of classical music, with an emphasis on the establishment of an American symphonic repertoire, at the same time developing programs which bring new audiences to our concerts
Management: David Alan Miller, Music Director/Conductor; Susan Filipp, Executive Director
Officers: Peter R. Kermani, Chairman of the Board; Barry Richman, President; Anthony Esposito, Dennis L. Kemper, James E. Panton, Timothy D. White, Vice Presidents; E. Kristin Frederick, Secretary; John Lavaelle, Treasurer
Paid Staff: 4
Paid Artists: 76
Utilizes: Guest Conductors; Guest Artists
Budget: $500,000 - $1,000,000
Income Sources: Private Foundations/Grants/Endowments; Business/Corporate Donations; Box Office; Government Grants; Individual Donations
Season: September - May **Annual Attendance:** 18,000
Affiliations: ASOL
Performance Facilities: Palace Theatre; Troy Music Hall

CAPITOL CHAMBER ARTISTS, INC.
263 Manning Boulevard, Albany, NY 12206
(518) 458-9231
FAX: (518) 458-9231
Founded: 1969
Arts Area: Chamber
Status: Professional; Non-Profit
Type: Performing; Touring; Resident; Educational
Purpose: To perfrom the highest quality chamber music and to educate a new audience
Management: Mary Lou Saetta, Director
Officers: Mary Lou Saetta, President; Irvin E. Gilman, Vice President
Paid Staff: 2   **Volunteer Staff:** 8
Paid Artists: 21
Utilizes: Guest Artists
Budget: $50,000 - $100,000
Income Sources: Private Foundations/Grants/Endowments; Business/Corporate Donations; Box Office; Government Grants; Individual Donations
Season: 52 Weeks   **Annual Attendance:** 10,000

THEATRE

THE BLACK EXPERIENCE ENSEMBLE
5 Homestead Avenue, Albany, NY 12203
(518) 482-6683
Founded: 1968
Arts Area: Community; Theatrical Group
Status: Professional; Non-Profit
Type: Performing; Touring; Sponsoring
Purpose: To provide cultural exposure and enrichment to the minority community through the performing arts
Management: Mars Hill, President/Founder
Volunteer Staff: 7
Non-Paid Artists: 5
Utilizes: Special Technical Talent; Guest Conductors; Guest Artists; Guest Directors
Budget: $1,000 - $50,000
Income Sources: Private Foundations/Grants/Endowments; Business/Corporate Donations; Box Office; Individual Donations

Season: 52 Weeks **Annual Attendance:** 15,000
Affiliations: Albany League of Arts

CAPITAL REPERTORY COMPANY
111 North Pearl Street, Box 399, Albany, NY 12207
(518) 462-4531
Founded: 1980
Arts Area: Professional; Theatrical Group
Status: Professional; Non-Profit
Type: Performing; Resident
Purpose: Capital Repertory Company is a theater in which language is as vital as image or actions. The characters' survival of their immediate circumstances is framed by the playwright within a particular social, moral or political issue of concern to a section of the human community.
Management: Bruce Bouchard, Producing Director
Officers: Lynn Pauquette, President, Board of Trustees
Paid Staff: 10 **Volunteer Staff:** 75
Paid Artists: 44
Utilizes: Guest Artists; Guest Directors
Budget: $500,000 - $1,000,000
Income Sources: Private Foundations/Grants/Endowments; Business/Corporate Donations; Box Office; Government Grants; Individual Donations
Season: October - June
Annual Attendance: 41,000
Performance Facilities: The Market Theatre

THE NEW YORK STATE THEATER INSTITUTE
c/o State University of New York- Albany, 1400 Washington Avenue, Albany, NY 12222
(518) 442-3995
FAX: (518) 443-5782
Founded: 1975
Arts Area: Professional; Musical; Theatrical Group
Status: Professional; Non-Profit
Type: Performing; Touring; Resident; Educational; Sponsoring
Purpose: We utilize a great deal of talent from New York City to achieve our principal objectives: new play development; exceptional arts in education programming; the mounting of high-quality theatre for adult and family audiences; and international touring and exchange.
Management: Patricia Snyder, Producing Director/Founder
Paid Staff: 55 **Volunteer Staff:** 300
Paid Artists: 15
Utilizes: Special Technical Talent; Guest Artists; Guest Directors
Budget: $1,000,000 - $5,000,000
Income Sources: Private Foundations/Grants/Endowments; Business/Corporate Donations; Box Office; Government Grants; Individual Donations
Season: September - June **Annual Attendance:** 90,000
Affiliations: TCG; Albany League of Arts; Friends of the Kennedy Center

PERFORMING SERIES

L'ENSEMBLE
11 North Pearl Street, Suite 508, Albany, NY 12207
(518) 436-5321
Founded: 1972
Arts Area: Vocal Music; Instrumental Music; Festivals
Status: Professional; Non-Profit
Type: Performing; Touring; Resident; Educational
Purpose: To present the highest quality performance of chamber music as well as related workshops
Management: Ida Faiella, Executive Artistic Director; Kristine DeFord, Promotion and Publicity Assistant; Andrea Meldrum, Financial and Operations Assistant; Jennifer Chadwick, Music Assistant
Officers: Jonathan C. Mills, Chairman; Frank Gilmore, President; Timothy Smith, Vice President of Finance; Beverly Wittner, Vice President of Marketing; David Barnert, Treasurer; Timothy Meigher, Secretary
Paid Staff: 4 **Volunteer Staff:** 20
Utilizes: Special Technical Talent; Guest Artists
Budget: $50,000 - $100,000
Income Sources: Private Foundations/Grants/Endowments; Business/Corporate Donations; Box Office; Government Grants; Individual Donations
Season: July - September; October-April **Annual Attendance:** 10,000
Affiliations: CMA; Albany League of Arts; Minnesota Composers Forum
Performance Facilities: City Arts Building; L'Ensemble Chamber Music Center

FACILITY

THE EMPIRE STATE PERFORMING ARTS CENTER
PO Box 2065, Albany, NY 12220
(518) 473-1061
Type of Facility: Performance Center
Year Built: 1978 **Architect:** Harrison & Abramowitz **Cost:** $50,000,000
Contact for Rental: Paul Fontane; (518) 473-1061
Manager: Paul Fontane, House Manager
Resident Groups: Ellen Sinopoli Dance Company
The Empire State Performing Arts Center, also known as "The Egg" due to its elliptical shape, contains the Kitty Carlisle Hart Theater and the Lewis A. Swyer Theater. See separate listings for more information.

THE EMPIRE STATE PERFORMING ARTS CENTER - KITTY CARLISLE HART THEATER
PO Box 2065, Albany, NY 12220
(518) 473-1061
Type of Facility: Concert Hall; Theatre House
Type of Stage: Thrust; Flexible
Stage Dimensions: 39'2"Wx55'D **Orchestra Pit**
Seating Capacity: 956
Year Built: 1978
Contact for Rental: Paul Fontane, House Manager; (518) 473-1061

THE EMPIRE STATE PERFORMING ARTS CENTER- LEWIS A. SWYER THEATER
PO Box 2065, Albany, NY 12220
(518) 473-1061
Type of Facility: Theatre House; :
Type of Stage: Thrust
Stage Dimensions: 34'Wx23'D
Seating Capacity: 450
Year Built: 1978
Contact for Rental: Paul Fontane, House Manager; (518) 473-1061

PALACE THEATRE
19 Clinton Avenue, Albany, NY 12207
(518) 465-3334
Type of Facility: Concert Hall
Facility Originally: Vaudeville
Type of Stage: Proscenium
Stage Dimensions: 27'x64'x43' **Orchestra Pit**
Seating Capacity: 2,897
Year Built: 1931 **Architect:** John Eberson
Year Remodeled: 1960
Contact for Rental: Robert C. Goebfert; (518) 465-3334
Manager: Maureen Salkin
Resident Groups: Albany Symphony Orchestra

STATE UNIVERSITY OF NEW YORK-ALBANY - ALBANY PERFORMING ARTS CENTER
1400 Washington Avenue, Albany, NY 12222
(518) 442-3995
Type of Facility: Performance Center
Year Built: 1967 **Architect:** Edward Durell Stone
Acoustical Consultant: Jean Rosenthal
Contact for Rental: Alton McCloud; (518) 442-3996
Albany Performing Arts Center contains the Arena, Laboratory Theatre, Main Theatre, Recital Hall and Studio Theatre. See separate listings for additional information.

STATE UNIVERSITY OF NEW YORK-ALBANY - ARENA
Albany Performing Arts Center, 1400 Washington Avenue, Albany, NY 12222
(518) 442-3995
Type of Facility: Arena
Type of Stage: Arena; In-the-round Capability
Stage Dimensions: 25' diameter
Seating Capacity: 189
Year Built: 1967
Contact for Rental: Alton McCloud; (518) 442-3996

STATE UNIVERSITY OF NEW YORK-ALBANY - MAIN THEATRE
Albany Performing Arts Center, 1400 Washington Avenue, Albany, NY 12222
(518) 442-3995
    Type of Facility: Concert Hall; Auditorium; Theatre House
    Type of Stage: Proscenium; Hydraulic Lift Stage
    Stage Dimensions: 48'Wx37'Dx20'H; add 8'6"D for orchestra pit   **Orchestra Pit**
    Seating Capacity: 500
    Year Built: 1967
    Contact for Rental: Alton McCloud;   (518) 442-3996
    Resident Groups: State University of New York-Albany Department of Music and Theatre

STATE UNIVERSITY OF NEW YORK-ALBANY - RECITAL HALL
Albany Performing Arts Center, 1400 Washington Avenue, Albany, NY 12222
(518) 442-3995
    Type of Facility: Concert Hall; Recital Hall
    Type of Stage: Proscenium
    Stage Dimensions: 21'Wx24'D
    Seating Capacity: 242
    Year Built: 1967
    Contact for Rental: Alton McCloud;   (518) 442-3996
    Resident Groups: State Uiversity of New York-Albany Department of Music

Alfred

PERFORMING SERIES

ALFRED UNIVERSITY
PO Box 781, Alfred, NY 14802
(607) 871-2134
    Founded: 1836
    Arts Area: Dance; Instrumental Music; Theater
    Type: Performing; Educational; Sponsoring
    Purpose: To serve the southern tier of New York state by presenting quality professional performing artists
    Officers: Steven G. Johnson, Director of Arts Programming
    Paid Staff: 3
    Paid Artists: 10
    Utilizes: Guest Artists
    Budget: $50,000 - $100,000
    Income Sources: Private Foundations/Grants/Endowments; Government Grants
    Season: September - April

Amherst

FACILITY

DAEMEN COLLEGE - DAEMEN THEATRE
4380 Main Street, Amherst, NY 14226
(716) 839-3144
    Type of Facility: Theatre House
    Type of Stage: Flexible; Proscenium
    Stage Dimensions: 14'x32'x35'
    Seating Capacity: 120
    Year Built: 1949
    Year Remodeled: 1986   **Cost:** $200,000
    Contact for Rental: Rosalynd Cramer;   (716) 839-3144
    Resident Groups: The New Ensemble

Astoria

INSTRUMENTAL MUSIC

GOLIARD CHAMBER SOLOISTS
c/o Goliard Concerts Inc., 21-65 41st Street, Astoria, NY 11105
(718) 728-8927
    Arts Area: Chamber
    Status: Professional; Non-Profit

Type: Performing; Touring; Presenting
Purpose: To perform eclectic chamber music in various vocal and instrumental combinations
Management: Patricia Handy, Artistic Director; Limor Tomer, Executive Director
Officers: Suzanne Gimbrere, President of the Board; Jacqueline Taylor, Vice President
Budget: $50,000 - $100,000
Income Sources: Private Foundations/Grants/Endowments; Business/Corporate Donations; Box Office; Government Grants; Individual Donations
Performance Facilities: Merkin Concert Hall at the Abrahman Goodman House; Steinway Reformed Church, Astoria

Auburn

THEATRE

THE AUBURN PLAYERS COMMUNITY THEATRE
PO Box 543, Auburn, NY 13021
(315) 252-6310
Founded: 1961
Arts Area: Community
Status: Non-Profit
Type: Performing
Purpose: To be a non-profit, educational and cultural organization; to present dramatic productions; to increase appreciation for the theatre
Management: Joseph and Eileen Daloia, Directors
Officers: Cindy Nangle, President
Volunteer Staff: 17
Non-Paid Artists: 100
Budget: $1,000 - $50,000
Income Sources: Private Foundations/Grants/Endowments; Box Office; Individual Donations
Season: July - June   **Annual Attendance:** 3,500

MERRY-GO-ROUND PLAYHOUSE
17 Williams Street, Box 506, Auburn, NY 13021
(315) 255-1305
Founded: 1958
Arts Area: Professional; Musical; Theatrical Group
Status: Professional; Non-Profit
Type: Performing; Touring; Educational
Purpose: To provide quality musical summer stock, experimental contemporary theater and alternative youth theater
Management: Edward Sayles, Producing Director; Karen Buttaro, Business Manager
Paid Staff: 12
Paid Artists: 50
Utilizes: Special Technical Talent; Guest Artists; Guest Directors
Budget: $100,000 - $500,000
Income Sources: Private Foundations/Grants/Endowments; Business/Corporate Donations; Box Office; Government Grants; Individual Donations
Season: June - April   **Annual Attendance:** 120,000
Affiliations: TCG
Performance Facilities: Merry-Go-Round Playhouse

Babylon

THEATRE

MOHAWK PLAYERS
PO Box 382, Babylon, NY 11702
(516) 669-7605
Founded: 1954
Arts Area: Community
Status: Non-Profit
Type: Performing; Touring
Purpose: To bring live theatre to various groups at library locations
Officers: Kathleen Ryerson, President
Paid Artists: 1   **Non-Paid Artists:** 10
Budget: $1,000 - $50,000
Income Sources: Box Office; Government Grants; Individual Donations

Season: 52 Weeks   Annual Attendance: 3,000
Affiliations: NYSCA

Bayside

VOCAL MUSIC

THE QUEENSBOROUGH CHORUS
c/o Music Department, Queensborough Community College, Bayside, NY 11364
(718) 631-6394
FAX: (718) 423-9620
   Founded: 1970
   Arts Area: Choral
   Status: Non-Professional; Non-Profit
   Type: Performing; Educational
   Purpose: To provide opportunities for performance of choral works of all eras to students and the community; to bring artistic performances to the community
   Management: R. John Specht, Director
   Paid Staff: 2   **Volunteer Staff:** 1
   Utilizes: Guest Artists
   Budget: $1,000 - $50,000
   Income Sources: Private Foundations/Grants/Endowments; Business/Corporate Donations; Box Office; Individual Donations
   Season: September - June   **Annual Attendance:** 1,200
   Performance Facilities: Queensborough Community College Theater

FACILITY

QUEENSBOROUGH COMMUNITY COLLEGE THEATER
222-05 56th Avenue near Springfield Boulevard, Bayside, NY 11364-1497
(718) 631-6311; (718) 631-6321
FAX: (718) 428-0802
   Type of Facility: Concert Hall; Auditorium; Studio Performance; Off-Broadway; Theatre House; Opera House; Multi-Purpose
   Type of Stage: Proscenium   **Orchestra Pit**
   Seating Capacity: 875
   Year Built: 1967
   Contact for Rental: Anthony Carobine;   (718) 631-6321

Bearsville

THEATRE

RIVER ARTS REPERTORY
Route 212, Bearsville, NY 12409
(914) 679-2100
FAX: (914) 679-9239
   Founded: 1979
   Arts Area: Professional; Summer Stock; Theatrical Group; Puppet
   Status: Professional; Non-Profit
   Type: Performing; Sponsoring
   Purpose: To present fresh interpretations of classic plays; to develop innovative new plays
   Management: Lawrence Sacharow, Michael Cristofer, Co-Artistic Directors; Albert Idhe, Managing Director
   Officers: Carol Ricken, Chairman of Board
   Paid Staff: 5   **Volunteer Staff:** 25
   Utilizes: Special Technical Talent; Guest Artists; Guest Directors
   Budget: $100,000 - $500,000
   Income Sources: Private Foundations/Grants/Endowments; Business/Corporate Donations; Box Office; Government Grants; Individual Donations
   Season: June - September   **Annual Attendance:** 5,000
   Affiliations: AEA; TCG
   Performance Facilities: Bearsville Theatre

Binghamton

INSTRUMENTAL MUSIC

B.C. POPS
1 Marine Midland Plaza, 6th Floor, West Tower, Binghamton, NY 13901
(607) 724-0007
FAX: (607) 777-0902
Founded: 1976
Arts Area: Orchestra; Pops/Popular Selections
Status: Professional; Non-Profit
Type: Performing
Management: W. Mack Richardson, Executive Director; David L. Agard, Conductor/Artistic Director
Officers: Edwin C. Gent, President, Board of Directors
Paid Staff: 5 **Volunteer Staff:** 5
Paid Artists: 65
Utilizes: Guest Artists
Income Sources: Private Foundations/Grants/Endowments; Business/Corporate Donations; Box Office; Government Grants; Individual Donations
Season: October - July
Affiliations: B.C. Pops Chorus
Performance Facilities: Forum Theatre

BINGHAMTON SYMPHONY ORCHESTRA AND CHORAL SOCIETY
315 Clinton Street, Binghamton, NY 13905
(607) 729-3444
FAX: (607) 797-6344
Founded: 1954
Arts Area: Symphony; Orchestra
Status: Professional; Semi-Professional; Non-Profit
Type: Performing; Touring; Educational
Purpose: To bring high quality symphonic orchestral music to this community and the surrounding area
Management: Nancy Marshall, Executive Director; John Covelli, Music Director/Conductor; Rosemary Henkle, Director of Subscriptions; Marilyn Sall, Director of Publicity; Susan Stanhope, Office Manager; Betty Warner, Director of Marketing
Officers: Lillian Levy Esq., President; Louise Akel, David Howard, Vice Presidents; Joseph Nishimura, Treasurer
Paid Staff: 7 **Volunteer Staff:** 200
Paid Artists: 80
Utilizes: Guest Artists
Budget: $100,000 - $500,000
Income Sources: Private Foundations/Grants/Endowments; Business/Corporate Donations; Box Office; Government Grants; Individual Donations
Season: September - May **Annual Attendance:** 15,000
Affiliations: ASOL
Performance Facilities: The Forum Theatre

BINGHAMTON YOUTH SYMPHONY
26 Murray, Binghamton, NY 13905
(607) 722-7150
Founded: 1962
Arts Area: Symphony
Status: Non-Professional; Non-Profit
Type: Performing; Touring; Educational
Purpose: Offering music and performance opportunities not found in the regular music curriculum of Binghamton area schools, membership in the Senior and Junior Orchestras is determined by auditions held three times annually and draws musicians from 20 area schools.
Management: Bernard J, Shifrin, Music Director/Conductor; Russell Colton, Junior Orchestra Music Director
Officers: Leonard Hoover, President; Philip Westcott, Vice President; Dana Thurston, Treasurer
Paid Staff: 2 **Volunteer Staff:** 13
Non-Paid Artists: 160
Budget: $1,000 - $50,000
Income Sources: Private Foundations/Grants/Endowments; Business/Corporate Donations; Box Office; Individual Donations
Season: September - June **Annual Attendance:** 10,000
Affiliations: Binghamton Symphony; Broome County Arts Council; B.C. Pops; Tri-Cities Opera; Binghampton Symphony
Performance Facilities: West Middle School

VOCAL MUSIC

TRI-CITIES OPERA COMPANY
315 Clinton Street, Binghamton, NY 13905
(607) 729-3444
FAX: (607) 797-6344
> **Founded:** 1949
> **Arts Area:** Grand Opera
> **Status:** Professional; Non-Profit
> **Type:** Performing; Resident; Educational
> **Management:** Carmen Savoca, Peyton Hibbitt, Artistic Directors; Richard Hook, Interim Director
> **Officers:** Chuck Ungraham, President; George Akel, First Vice President; Sandra Perkins, Second First President; John Westcott, Treasurer; Stephanie Franck, Secretary
> **Paid Staff:** 13   **Volunteer Staff:** 25
> **Paid Artists:** 30   **Non-Paid Artists:** 50
> **Utilizes:** Guest Artists
> **Budget:** $500,000 - $1,000,000
> **Income Sources:** Private Foundations/Grants/Endowments; Business/Corporate Donations; Box Office; Government Grants; Individual Donations
> **Season:** September - May   **Annual Attendance:** 13,500
> **Affiliations:** AGMA; AFM; IATSE
> **Performance Facilities:** Broome County Forum

PERFORMING SERIES

BINGHAMTON SUMMER MUSIC FESTIVAL, INC.
PO Box 112 SVS, Binghamton, NY 13903
(607) 777-4777
FAX: (607) 777-4000
> **Founded:** 1984
> **Arts Area:** Dance; Vocal Music; Instrumental Music; Festivals
> **Status:** Non-Profit
> **Type:** Performing; Educational
> **Purpose:** To provide an annual summer performing arts program for audiences in New York's Southern Tier
> **Management:** David K. Patterson, Executive Director; Ethan Lercher, Assistant Director
> **Officers:** Gary E. Lind, President; Thomas E. Bell, Vice President; Peter C. Cronk, Secretary; Donald H. Weber, Treasurer
> **Paid Staff:** 2   **Volunteer Staff:** 30
> **Utilizes:** Guest Conductors; Guest Artists
> **Budget:** $100,000 - $500,000
> **Income Sources:** Private Foundations/Grants/Endowments; Business/Corporate Donations; Box Office; Government Grants; Individual Donations
> **Season:** July - August   **Annual Attendance:** 12,000
> **Performance Facilities:** Anderson Center for Performing Arts, SUNY Binghamton

FACILITY

BROOME CENTER FOR THE PRFORMING ARTS - THE FORUM
236 Washington Street, Binghamton, NY 13901
(607) 778-2480
FAX: (607) 778-6041
> **Founded:** 1975
> **Type of Facility:** Concert Hall; Theatre House; Opera House
> **Facility Originally:** Vaudeville
> **Type of Stage:** Proscenium
> **Stage Dimensions:** 38'6"Wx24'6"H proscenium opening; 36'D includes 4" apron   **Orchestra Pit**
> **Seating Capacity:** 1,519
> **Year Built:** 1919
> **Year Remodeled:** 1974   **Architect:** Cummings and Pash
> **Contact for Rental:** Christine A. Springer;   (607) 778-2480
> **Resident Groups:** Binghamton Symphony Orchestra; BC Pops Orchestra; Tri-Cities Opera; Broadway Theatre League of Binghampton

STATE UNIVERSITY OF NEW YORK-BINGHAMPTON - CHAMBER HALL
Anderson Center for the Arts, PO Box 6000, Binghamton, NY 13902-6000
(607) 777-6802
> **Type of Facility:** Concert Hall; Theatre House
> **Type of Stage:** Proscenium
> **Stage Dimensions:** 62'Wx27'D   **Orchestra Pit**

Seating Capacity: 430
Year Built: 1985 **Architect:** Hutchins Evans & Lefferts
Acoustical Consultant: Paul S. Veneklasen & Associates
Contact for Rental: Floyd Herzog; (607) 777-6802

STATE UNIVERSITY OF NEW YORK-BINGHAMPTON - CONCERT THEATRE
Anderson Center for the Arts, PO Box 6000, Binghamton, NY 13902-6000
(607) 777-6802
   Type of Facility: Theatre House; Amphitheater
   Type of Stage: Proscenium
   Stage Dimensions: 92'Wx38'6"D **Orchestra Pit**
   Seating Capacity: 1,200 with 24 wheelchair spaces
   Year Built: 1985 **Architect:** Hutchins Evans & Lefferts
   Acoustical Consultant: Paul S. Veneklasen & Associates
   Contact for Rental: Floyd Herzog; (607) 777-6802
   Rear wall opens to provide outdoor audience space

Blue Mountain Lake

FACILITY

ADIRONDACK LAKES CENTER FOR THE ARTS
PO Box 101, Blue Mountain Lake, NY 12812
(518) 352-7715
   Type of Facility: Concert Hall; Performance Center; Theatre House; Multi-Purpose; Room
   Facility Originally: Garage
   Type of Stage: Platform
   Stage Dimensions: 25'x30'
   Seating Capacity: 200
   Year Built: 1936
   Year Remodeled: 1967

Brentwood

FACILITY

SUFFOLK COUNTY COMMUNITY COLLEGE - SAQTIKOS THEATRE
Crooked Hill Road, Brentwood, NY 11717
(516) 451-4163
   Type of Facility: Theatre House
   Type of Stage: Proscenium
   Stage Dimensions: 36'x40' **Orchestra Pit**
   Seating Capacity: 474
   Year Built: 1989

Brockport

INSTRUMENTAL MUSIC

BROCKPORT SYMPHONY ORCHESTRA
PO Box 344, Brockport, NY 14420
(716) 637-2115
   Founded: 1966
   Arts Area: Symphony
   Status: Semi-Professional; Non-Profit
   Type: Performing
   Purpose: To provide fine music for the Western Monroe County Area, at times in joint performances with the Greece Symphony and the Geneseo Chamber Symphony
   Management: James Walker, Music Director; Mary Edwards, Business Manager
   Paid Staff: 2 **Volunteer Staff:** 17
   Paid Artists: 6 **Non-Paid Artists:** 45
   Utilizes: Guest Artists
   Budget: $1,000 - $50,000
   Income Sources: Private Foundations/Grants/Endowments; Business/Corporate Donations; Box Office; Individual Donations
   Season: September - May **Annual Attendance:** 1,000

Affiliations: Arts For Greater Rochester
Performance Facilities: Tower Fine Arts Center, State University of New York-Brockport

FACILITY

STATE UNIVERSITY OF NEW YORK COLLEGE-BROCKPORT - TOWER FINE ARTS CENTER
Department of Dance, Brockport, NY 14420
(716) 395-2153
Type of Facility: Theatre House
Type of Stage: Proscenium
Stage Dimensions: 30'Wx35'L
Seating Capacity: 450
Year Remodeled: 1972
Contact for Rental: Chairman, Department of Dance;   (716) 395-2153
Resident Groups: Danscore; Brockport Dance Department; Brockport Symphony Orchestra

Bronx

INSTRUMENTAL MUSIC

BRONX ARTS ENSEMBLE INC.
c/o Golf House, Van Cortland Park, Bronx, NY 10471
(212) 601-7399
FAX: (212) 549-4008
Arts Area: Symphony; Chamber
Status: Professional; Non-Profit
Type: Performing; Resident; Educational
Purpose: To bring chamber music programs and chamber orchestras to a variety of locations in the Bronx at affordable prices
Management: William Scribner, Artistic Director
Officers: Gail McMillan, Chairman of the Board
Budget: $100,000 - $500,000
Income Sources: Private Foundations/Grants/Endowments; Business/Corporate Donations; Box Office; Government Grants; Individual Donations
Performance Facilities: Fordham University

VOCAL MUSIC

BRONX OPERA COMPANY
5 Minerva Place, Apt 2J, Bronx, NY 10468
(212) 365-4209
Founded: 1967
Arts Area: Grand Opera; Lyric Opera; Light Opera; Operetta
Status: Semi-Professional; Non-Profit
Type: Performing
Purpose: To bring high-quality, full opera productions, in English with an orchestra, to the community; to give excellent young performers the opportunity for experience and exposure
Management: Michael Spierman, Artistic Director
Non-Paid Artists: 120
Budget: $100,000 - $500,000
Income Sources: Private Foundations/Grants/Endowments; Business/Corporate Donations; Government Grants; Individual Donations
Season: September - June   **Annual Attendance:** 10,000
Performance Facilities: Lehman College Theatre; John Jay College Theatre

THEATRE

PREGONES THEATER
295 St. Ann's Avenue, Bronx, NY 10454
(212) 585-1202
FAX: (212) 585-1608
Founded: 1979
Arts Area: Theatrical Group
Status: Professional; Non-Profit
Type: Performing; Touring

Purpose: To provide bilingual theatre programming primarily for Latino audiences; to present a wide range of professional artists at the theatre
Management: Rosalba Rolon, Executive Director; Aluan Colon, Judith Rivera, Jorge Merced, Associate Directors
Officers: Harold A. Stella, Chairman of the Board; Ada Brinas, Treasurer; Sistuido Benitez, Vice Chairman; Elmer Sanchez, Secretary
Paid Staff: 7 **Volunteer Staff:** 9
Paid Artists: 11
Utilizes: Guest Artists; Guest Directors; Resident Artists
Budget: $100,000 - $500,000
Income Sources: Private Foundations/Grants/Endowments; Business/Corporate Donations; Box Office; Government Grants; Individual Donations; Contracted Tours
Season: September - May

Bronxville

DANCE

ELLEN KOGAN SOLO DANCE
14 McIntyre Street, Bronxville, NY 10708
(914) 337-6063
Status: Professional; Non-Profit
Type: Performing; Touring; Resident; Educational
Purpose: To promote and preserve solo dance as an integral part of the art of contemporary dance; to contribute to the heritage of modern dance by adding reconstructions of modern dance classics to the repertoire; to bring historic dances to life for contemporary audiences
Management: Kathryn Wolf, Manager; Mark Mongold, Technical Director
Budget: $1,000 - $50,000
Income Sources: Private Foundations/Grants/Endowments; Government Grants; Booking Fees

Brooklyn

DANCE

BEVERLY BLOSSOM AND COMPANY
311 Ocean Parkway, #125, Brooklyn, NY 11235
(718) 266-1286
Founded: 1981
Arts Area: Modern; Theater Dance
Status: Professional
Type: Performing; Touring
Management: Circum-Arts, Inc.
Officers: Beverly Blossom, Director
Paid Artists: 5
Budget: $1,000 - $50,000
Income Sources: Private Foundations/Grants/Endowments; Box Office; Government Grants; Individual Donations
Season: September - May
Affiliations: Circum-Arts, Inc.
Performance Facilities: Dance Theatre Workshop

BROOKLYN CENTER FOR THE PERFORMING ARTS AT BROOKLYN COLLEGE
c/o College Community Services Inc., PO Box 163, Brooklyn, NY 11210
(718) 258-5291
FAX: (718) 258-3475
Arts Area: Modern; Mime; Ballet; Jazz; Ethnic; Folk
Status: Non-Profit
Type: Educational; Sponsoring
Purpose: To provide world-famous artists and ensembles at affordable prices
Management: David Levenson, Managing Director; Richard Grossberg, General Manager
Officers: William Slapin, President of the Board
Budget: $1,000,000 - $5,000,000
Income Sources: Private Foundations/Grants/Endowments; Business/Corporate Donations; Box Office; Government Grants; Individual Donations

Season: 52 Weeks
Performance Facilities: Whitman Hall

CHARLES MOORE - DANCES AND DRUMS OF AFRICA
1043 President Street, Brooklyn, NY 11225
(718) 467-7127
   Arts Area: Modern; Jazz; Ethnic
   Status: Professional; Non-Profit
   Type: Performing; Touring; Educational
   Purpose: To promote the spiritual, social and physical welfare of individuals pursuing research and studies in the field of African and Afro-American dance and music
   Management: Ella Thompson-Moore, Artistic Director; Pam Mitchell-Yarber, Executive Director; Marina Lynk, Company Director
   Paid Staff: 3
   Paid Artists: 20
   Utilizes: Special Technical Talent; Guest Artists
   Income Sources: Box Office; Government Grants
   Affiliations: NEA; Brooklyn Arts and Culture Association; New York Division of the Humanities, Education Department
   Performance Facilities: Charles Moore Center for Ethnic Studies

DANCEWAVE, INC. (THE DIANE JACOBOWITZ DANCE THEATER)
72 Seventh Avenue, Brooklyn, NY 11217
(718) 622-1810
   Founded: 1979
   Arts Area: Modern
   Status: Professional
   Type: Performing; Touring; Resident; Educational; Sponsoring
   Paid Artists: 6
   Utilizes: Special Technical Talent; Guest Artists; Guest Choreographers
   Budget: $1,000 - $50,000
   Income Sources: Private Foundations/Grants/Endowments; Business/Corporate Donations; Box Office; Government Grants; Individual Donations
   Performance Facilities: Long Island University-Triangle Theater

JUBILATION DANCE COMPANY
PO Box 401804, Brooklyn, NY 11240-1804
(718) 237-0634
   Founded: 1982
   Arts Area: Modern; Ballet; Jazz; Ethnic
   Status: Professional; Non-Profit
   Type: Performing; Touring
   Purpose: To support individuals in realizing their creative potential
   Management: Laverne Jeff, Managing Director
   Paid Staff: 2   **Volunteer Staff:** 5
   Paid Artists: 11
   Utilizes: Special Technical Talent; Guest Conductors; Guest Artists; Guest Directors
   Budget: $100,000 - $500,000
   Income Sources: Private Foundations/Grants/Endowments; Business/Corporate Donations; Box Office; Government Grants; Individual Donations
   Season: October - November

MARTHA BOWERS' DANCE THEATRE
143 Bond Street, Brooklyn, NY 11217
(718) 858-0841
   Founded: 1976
   Arts Area: Modern
   Status: Professional; Non-Profit
   Type: Performing; Touring; Resident
   Purpose: To perform contemporary dance theatre works
   Management: Martha Bowers, Artistic Director
   Paid Staff: 1
   Paid Artists: 12
   Utilizes: Guest Artists
   Budget: $1,000 - $50,000
   Income Sources: Private Foundations/Grants/Endowments; Box Office; Government Grants; Individual Donations
   Season: 52 Weeks
   Affiliations: Dancing in the Streets; Mayfair

INSTRUMENTAL MUSIC

THE BROOKLYN PHILHARMONIC
30 Lafayette Avenue, Brooklyn, NY 11217
(718) 622-1000
FAX: (718) 857-2021
  Founded: 1954
  Arts Area: Symphony; Orchestra; Chamber; Ensemble; Ethnic
  Status: Professional; Non-Profit
  Type: Performing; Educational
  Purpose: To bring the best in standard and modern repertoire at the lowest possible prices and best performance level to the borough of Brooklyn and Greater New York, as well as free concerts to the general public in the parks and in the schools
  Management: Vicki Margulies, Executive Director; Maurice Edwards, Artistic Director; Jana Strauss, Director of Development; Eric Klein, Operations Manager/Education Director
  Officers: Stanley H. Kaplan, Chairman of the Board; Robert C. Rosenberg, President; I. Stanley Kriegel, Honorary Chairman; Richard Kane, Treasurer; Craig Matthews and John Tamberlane, Executive Vice Presidents
  Paid Staff: 7   **Volunteer Staff:** 3
  Paid Artists: 100
  Utilizes: Guest Conductors; Guest Artists
  Budget: $1,000,000 - $5,000,000
  Income Sources: Private Foundations/Grants/Endowments; Business/Corporate Donations; Box Office; Government Grants; Individual Donations
  Annual Attendance: 125,000
  Affiliations: Brooklyn Academy of Music
  Performance Facilities: Brooklyn Academy of Music

MANHATTAN MARIMBA QUARTET
160 North Fourth Street, Brooklyn, NY 11211
(201) 567-8108
  Arts Area: Chamber; Ensemble
  Status: Professional; Non-Profit
  Type: Performing; Touring; Resident; Educational
  Purpose: To perform music that spans eight centuries and many different styles, spotlighting the beauty, individuality and versatility of the marimba as a concert instrument
  Management: Sheila Rizzo, Manager
  Budget: $1,000 - $50,000
  Income Sources: Private Foundations/Grants/Endowments; Business/Corporate Donations; Box Office; Government Grants; Individual Donations

S.E.M. ENSEMBLE
25 Columbia Place, Brooklyn, NY 11201
(718) 243-0964
FAX: (718) 243-0964
  Arts Area: Orchestra; Chamber
  Status: Professional
  Type: Performing; Touring; Resident; Educational
  Purpose: To perform new music; education in new music
  Officers: William J. Buckley, President; John Maggiotto, Secretary; Petr Kotik, Artistic Director
  Paid Staff: 2   **Volunteer Staff:** 3
  Paid Artists: 30
  Budget: $50,000 - $100,000
  Income Sources: Private Foundations/Grants/Endowments; Business/Corporate Donations; Box Office; Government Grants; Individual Donations
  Season: September - June   **Annual Attendance:** 1,500
  Performance Facilities: Willow Place Auditorium

VOCAL MUSIC

IL PICCOLO TEATRO DELL'OPERA, INC.
118 Pierrepont Street, Brooklyn, NY 11201-2768
(718) 643-7775
FAX: (718) 855-4751
  Founded: 1984
  Arts Area: Grand Opera; Lyric Opera; Light Opera; Piccolo Teatro
  Status: Professional
  Type: Performing; Educational
  Purpose: To develop new audiences for opera/theatre and nurture emerging careers

Management: Barbara Elliot, General Director/Artistic Director
Officers: Stephen Zelnick, Chairman; Barbara Elliot, President; Nancy Lowendahl, Secretary
Paid Staff: 3 **Volunteer Staff:** 10
Paid Artists: 100
Utilizes: Special Technical Talent; Guest Conductors; Guest Artists; Guest Directors
Budget: $100,000 - $500,000
Income Sources: Private Foundations/Grants/Endowments; Business/Corporate Donations; Box Office; Government Grants; Individual Donations
Season: 52 Weeks **Annual Attendance:** 25,000
Performance Facilities: Brooklyn Academy of Music

QUEENS OPERA ASSOCIATION
313 Bay 14th Street, Brooklyn, NY 11214
(718) 256-6045
FAX: (718) 837-8726
Founded: 1961
Arts Area: Grand Opera
Status: Professional; Non-Profit
Type: Performing; Touring; Resident
Purpose: To present opera and concerts to communities where it is not available; to discover new voices
Management: Joseph Messina, General Director
Officers: Jerry Cannon, President; Michael Callaghan, Vice President; Fran Callaghan, Secretary
Paid Staff: 2 **Volunteer Staff:** 10
Paid Artists: 60
Utilizes: Guest Conductors; Guest Artists
Budget: $100,000 - $500,000
Income Sources: Private Foundations/Grants/Endowments; Business/Corporate Donations; Box Office; Government Grants; Individual Donations
Season: October - July **Annual Attendance:** 14,000
Performance Facilities: Saint John's University Auditorium

REGINA OPERA COMPANY
1251 Tabor Court, Brooklyn, NY 11219
(718) 232-3555
FAX: (718) 232-3555
Founded: 1971
Arts Area: Grand Opera; Lyric Opera; Light Opera; Operetta
Status: Semi-Professional; Non-Profit
Type: Performing
Purpose: To provide a training ground for young porfessionals and showcase more experienced performers and directors
Officers: Marie Cantoni, President; Francine Garber-Cohen, Executive Vice President; Linda Cantoni, Vice President/Legal Advisor; Selma Tepper, Secretary
Utilizes: Guest Conductors; Guest Artists; Guest Directors
Budget: $1,000 - $50,000
Income Sources: Business/Corporate Donations; Box Office; Individual Donations; Brooklyn Arts Council
Season: September - June **Annual Attendance:** 4,000
Performance Facilities: Regina Hall

THEATRE

ADELPHIAN PLAYERS
8515 Ridge Boulevard, Brooklyn, NY 11209
(718) 238-3308
FAX: (718) 238-2894
Founded: 1964
Arts Area: Summer Stock; Theatrical Group
Status: Non-Professional
Type: Performing; Educational
Purpose: To bring theatre to the people of Brooklyn
Management: Russel Bonanno, Artistic Director; Philip Stone, Business Manager
Volunteer Staff: 10
Non-Paid Artists: 25
Utilizes: Guest Artists; Guest Directors
Budget: $1,000 - $50,000
Income Sources: Private Foundations/Grants/Endowments; Business/Corporate Donations; Box Office; Government Grants; Individual Donations
Season: June - August
Performance Facilities: Adelphi Academy

BILLIE HOLIDAY THEATRE
1368 Fulton Street, Brooklyn, NY 11216
(718) 636-0919
FAX: (718) 636-6956
>**Founded:** 1972
>**Arts Area:** Theatrical Group
>**Status:** Professional; Non-Profit
>**Type:** Performing; Resident
>**Purpose:** To provide trained Black artists with a professional environment; to present theatre that educates and enlightens the community
>**Management:** Marjorie Moon, Executive Director
>**Utilizes:** Special Technical Talent; Guest Artists; Guest Directors
>**Budget:** $100,000 - $500,000
>**Income Sources:** Box Office; Government Grants; Individual Donations
>**Season:** 52 Weeks

CONEY ISLAND, USA
1205-11 Boardwalk at West 12th Street, Brooklyn, NY 11224
(718) 372-5159
>**Founded:** 1980
>**Arts Area:** Professional; Musical; Theatrical Group
>**Status:** Professional; Non-Profit
>**Type:** Performing; Educational; Sponsoring
>**Purpose:** To champion the honor of American popular art forms through innovative exhibitions and performances
>**Management:** Dick D. Zigun, Artistic Director; Valerie Haller, Design Director
>**Officers:** Dick D. Zigun, President
>**Paid Staff:** 4   **Volunteer Staff:** 6
>**Paid Artists:** 50   **Non-Paid Artists:** 100
>**Utilizes:** Special Technical Talent; Guest Artists
>**Budget:** $100,000 - $500,000
>**Income Sources:** Private Foundations/Grants/Endowments; Business/Corporate Donations; Box Office; Government Grants; Individual Donations
>**Season:** March - Decemer   **Annual Attendance:** 100,000
>**Affiliations:** ART/NY; TCG

INTERBOROUGH REPERTORY THEATER (IRT)
467 Pacific Street, #6, Brooklyn, NY 11217
(718) 522-2858
>**Founded:** 1986
>**Arts Area:** Musical; Theatrical Group
>**Status:** Semi-Professional; Non-Profit; Non-AEA
>**Type:** Performing; Touring; Educational
>**Purpose:** To present issues of current interest or adaptions of literature/history to the disenfranchised audience; to show-case standard repertory to general audiences
>**Management:** Luane Davis, Artistic Director; Jonathan Fluck, General Manager; Stephanie Trudeau, Publicity; Suan Mondzak, Fund-raising
>**Paid Staff:** 2   **Volunteer Staff:** 3
>**Paid Artists:** 30
>**Utilizes:** Special Technical Talent; Guest Artists; Guest Directors
>**Budget:** $100,000 - $500,000
>**Income Sources:** Private Foundations/Grants/Endowments; Business/Corporate Donations; Box Office; Government Grants; Individual Donations; Performance Fees
>**Season:** August - June   **Annual Attendance:** 200,000
>**Affiliations:** Brooklyn Arts and Cultural Association; AEA; Encore; Saturaday Theater for Children, Division of American Theater Wing

MARGOLIS BROWN ADAPTORS
397 Bridge Street, 2nd Floor, Brooklyn, NY 11201
(718) 797-3930
>**Founded:** 1983
>**Arts Area:** Professional; Theatrical Group; Multimedia Movement Theatre
>**Status:** Professional; Non-Profit
>**Type:** Performing; Touring; Resident; Educational; Sponsoring; Dramatic Movement School
>**Purpose:** To create original multimedia movement theatre productions; to share video editing studio and facility with other artists at low cost
>**Management:** Beverly Perlman, Touring/Performance Manager; Tony Brown, Artistic/Executive Director; Kari Margolis, Artistic/Executive Director
>**Officers:** Olympia Dukakis; Ted Killmer; Lauren Farber; Anna Salmi; Luke Gordon

Paid Staff: 3 **Volunteer Staff:** 5
Paid Artists: 10
Utilizes: Special Technical Talent; Guest Artists
Budget: $100,000 - $500,000
Income Sources: Private Foundations/Grants/Endowments; Business/Corporate Donations; Box Office; Government Grants; Individual Donations; School; Video/Recording Studio
Season: 52 Weeks **Annual Attendance:** 2,000
Affiliations: NMTA

RYAN REPERTORY COMPANY AT HARRY WARREN THEATRE
2445 Bath Avenue, Brooklyn, NY 11214
(718) 996-4800
Founded: 1972
Arts Area: Professional; Musical; Theatrical Group
Status: Professional; Non-Profit
Type: Performing; Resident
Purpose: To develop new musicals, and to work on new plays for playwrights' purposes
Management: Barbara Parisi, Executive Director; Jonathan Rosenblum, Producing Director; John Sannuto, Artistic Director
Volunteer Staff: 15
Paid Artists: 50 **Non-Paid Artists:** 150
Utilizes: Guest Artists; Guest Directors
Budget: $1,000 - $50,000
Income Sources: Private Foundations/Grants/Endowments; Business/Corporate Donations; Box Office; Government Grants; Individual Donations
Season: 52 Weeks **Annual Attendance:** 5,000
Performance Facilities: Harry Warren Theatre

PERFORMING SERIES

BARGEMUSIC LTD.
Fulton Ferry Landing, Brooklyn, NY 11201
(718) 624-4061
FAX: (718) 596-7137
Founded: 1977
Arts Area: Instrumental Music
Status: Non-Profit
Type: Performing
Purpose: To present chamber music concerts throughout the year in concert space in a barge permantly moored in New York Harbor
Management: Olga Bloom, President; Ik-Hwan Bae, Artistic Director; Margaret Barclay, Executive Director
Paid Staff: 8
Paid Artists: 100
Budget: $500,000 - $1,000,000
Income Sources: Private Foundations/Grants/Endowments; Business/Corporate Donations; Box Office; Government Grants; Individual Donations
Season: 52 Weeks **Annual Attendance:** 10,000
Affiliations: CMA

BROOKLYN ACADEMY OF MUSIC
30 Lafayette Avenue, Brooklyn, NY 11217-1486
(718) 636-4100
Founded: 1861
Arts Area: Dance; Vocal Music; Instrumental Music; Theater; Festivals
Status: Professional; Non-Profit
Type: Performing; Touring; Educational; Sponsoring
Purpose: BAM's programming policy involves a commitment to provide our audiences with quality performing arts, new and innovative theatre, and dance and music, both foreign and domestic, as well as diversified choices in all areas at affordable and accessible prices.
Management: Harvey Lichtenstein, Executive Producer; Judith E. Daykin, Managing Director; Karen Hopkins, Planning/Development; Richard Balzano, Finance; Doug Allan, Promotion/Marketing
Officers: Neil Chrisman, Chairman of the Board; Rita Hillman, Franklin Weissberg, I. Stanley Kriegel, Vice Chairmen; Harvey Lichtenstein, President; David Kleiser, Vice President; Judith E. Daykin, Executive Vice President; Richard Balzano, Treasurer
Paid Staff: 100
Paid Artists: 500
Utilizes: Special Technical Talent; Guest Conductors; Guest Artists; Guest Directors
Budget: $5,000,000 - $10,000,000

Income Sources: Private Foundations/Grants/Endowments; Business/Corporate Donations; Box Office; Government Grants; Individual Donations
Season: October - June   **Annual Attendance:** 250,000
Affiliations: New York Department of Cultural Affairs
Performance Facilities: Brooklyn Academy of Music

CELEBRATE BROOKLYN FESTIVAL
16 Court Street, Suite 1400W, Brooklyn, NY 11241
(718) 855-7882
 Founded: 1979
 Arts Area: Dance; Vocal Music; Instrumental Music; Theater; Festivals
 Status: Professional; Non-Profit
 Type: Performing
 Purpose: To identify and present professional music, theater and dance reflecting the international community of Brooklyn, and produce original music, dance and theatre
 Management: Stacey Temple, Producer
 Officers: Ninetta Rain, President
 Paid Staff: 15
 Paid Artists: 300
 Budget: $100,000 - $500,000
 Income Sources: Private Foundations/Grants/Endowments; Business/Corporate Donations; Box Office; Government Grants; Individual Donations
 Annual Attendance: 100,000
 Performance Facilities: Prospect Park Bandshell and Picnic House

FACILITY

BROOKLYN ACADEMY OF MUSIC
30 Lafayette Avenue, Brooklyn, NY 11217-1486
(718) 636-4100
FAX: (718) 857-2021
 Type of Facility: Theatre Complex; School
 Year Built: 1907   **Architect:** Herts & Tallant   **Cost:** $1,500,000
 Year Remodeled: 1975   **Architect:** Hardy Holzman Pfeiffer
 Acoustical Consultant: Peter George; Christopher Jaffe
 Contact for Rental: Lynn Moffat;   (718) 636-4195
 Manager: Laurie Sackler
 Resident Groups: Brooklyn Philharmonic
Brooklyn Academy of Music contains Carey Playhouse, Lepercq Space and the Opera House. See separate listings for additional information.

BROOKLYN ACADEMY OF MUSIC - CAREY PLAYHOUSE
30 Lafayette Avenue, Brooklyn, NY 11217-1486
(718) 636-4100
FAX: (718) 857-2021
 Type of Facility: Concert Hall; Theatre House
 Type of Stage: Thrust; Proscenium
 Stage Dimensions: 38'Wx31'D
 Seating Capacity: 1,011
 Year Built: 1907
 Year Remodeled: 1975   **Architect:** Hardy Holzman Pfeiffer
 Acoustical Consultant: Peter George; Christopher Jaffe
 Contact for Rental: Lynn Moffat;   (718) 636-4195
 Manager: Laurie Sackler
 Resident Groups: Brooklyn Philharmonic

BROOKLYN ACADEMY OF MUSIC - LEPERCQ SPACE
30 Lafayette Avenue, Brooklyn, NY 11217-1486
(718) 636-4100
FAX: (718) 857-2021
 Type of Facility: Theatre House; Multi-Purpose
 Facility Originally: Ballroom
 Type of Stage: Flexible
 Stage Dimensions: 125'Wx42'Dx35'H
 Seating Capacity: 550
 Year Built: 1907
 Year Remodeled: 1973   **Architect:** Edward Knoles
 Acoustical Consultant: Peter George

Contact for Rental: Lynn Moffat;   (718) 636-4195
Manager: Laurie Sackler

BROOKLYN ACADEMY OF MUSIC - OPERA HOUSE
30 Lafayette Avenue, Brooklyn, NY 11217-1486
(718) 636-4100
FAX: (718) 857-2021
    Type of Facility: Opera House
    Type of Stage: Proscenium
    Stage Dimensions: 47'Wx47'D   **Orchestra Pit**
    Seating Capacity: 2,086
    Year Built: 1907
    Contact for Rental: Lynn Moffat;   (718) 636-4195
    Manager: Laurie Sackler
    Resident Groups: Brooklyn Philharmonic

PRATT INSTITUTE - AUDITORIUM
200 Willoughby Avenue, Brooklyn, NY 11205
(718) 636-3422
    Type of Facility: Auditorium
    Type of Stage: Proscenium
    Seating Capacity: 555
    Contact for Rental: Jeff Kessler;   (718) 636-3422

Buffalo

INSTRUMENTAL MUSIC

AMHERST SAXOPHONE QUARTET
PO Box 101, Buffalo, NY 14207-0101
(716) 832-7411
FAX: (716) 832-7411
    Founded: 1978
    Arts Area: Chamber; Ensemble; Instrumental Group
    Status: Professional; Non-Profit
    Type: Performing; Touring; Resident; Educational
    Purpose: To maintain an international touring quartet; to promote new music
    Management: Ethel Siegel, Siegel Artists Management; Stephen Rosenthal, Executive Director Amherst Saxophone Society, Inc.; Tom Gallant, Director
    Officers: Eleanor Millonzi, President; Harry R. Stainrook, Vice President; Michael Swart, Secretary; Felix Gramza, Treasurer
    Paid Staff: 1   **Volunteer Staff:** 18
    Paid Artists: 4
    Utilizes: Guest Artists
    Budget: $100,000 - $500,000
    Income Sources: Private Foundations/Grants/Endowments; Business/Corporate Donations; Box Office; Government Grants; Individual Donations; Touring Fees
    Season: 52 Weeks   **Annual Attendance:** 50,000
    Performance Facilities: Rockwell Hall

ARS NOVA MUSICIANS CHAMBER ORCHESTRA
136 Goethe Street, Buffalo, NY 14206
    Founded: 1974
    Status: Professional
    Type: Performing
    Purpose: To provide a 16-member chamber orchestra, most members belonging to the Buffalo Philharmonic
    Management: Marylouise Nanna, Music Director; Susan Willet, Managing Director

BUFFALO PHILHARMONIC ORCHESTRA
71 Symphony Circle, PO Box 905, Buffalo, NY 14222
(716) 885-0331
FAX: (716) 885-9372
    Founded: 1936
    Arts Area: Symphony; Orchestra; Chamber; Ethnic
    Status: Professional; Non-Profit
    Type: Performing; Touring; Educational

Purpose: To provide a resident, professional, major symphony orchestra of artistic excellence and integrity to enrich the quality of life in western New York through the presentation of live symphonic music and other music events which will educate and entertain the broadest audiences possible
Management: Michael Tiknis, Excutive Director; Maximiano Valdes, Music Director; Lynn Osmond, General Manager; Doc Severinsen, Principal Pops Conductor
Officers: Andrew Rudnick, Chairman
Paid Staff: 21   **Volunteer Staff:** 600
Paid Artists: 300
Utilizes: Special Technical Talent; Guest Conductors; Guest Artists; Guest Directors
Budget: $5,000,000 - $10,000,000
Income Sources: Private Foundations/Grants/Endowments; Business/Corporate Donations; Box Office; Government Grants; Individual Donations
Season: September - May   **Annual Attendance:** 500,000
Affiliations: ASOL
Performance Facilities: Kleinhaus Music Hall

MAELSTROM PERCUSSION ENSEMBLE, LTD.
PO Box 841, Buffalo, NY 14213-0841
(716) 668-4729
Founded: 1982
Arts Area: Chamber; Ensemble; Ethnic; Instrumental Group; Electronic & Live Electronic
Status: Professional; Non-Profit
Type: Performing; Touring; Resident; Educational
Purpose: To perform existing works for percussion, original compositions and pieces written for or commissioned by the ensemble
Management: Robert D. Accurso, Executive Director
Officers: Robert B. Fleming Jr., President; Paul Musilli, Treasurer; Allan Hebeler, Secretary
Paid Staff: 2
Paid Artists: 4
Utilizes: Guest Artists
Budget: $50,000 - $100,000
Income Sources: Private Foundations/Grants/Endowments; Business/Corporate Donations; Box Office; Government Grants
Season: 52 Weeks   **Annual Attendance:** 30,000
Affiliations: Artists-in-Residence, State University College at Buffalo

VOCAL MUSIC

GREATER BUFFALO OPERA COMPANY
24 Linwood Avenue, Buffalo, NY 14215
Founded: 1987
Arts Area: Grand Opera; Light Opera; Operetta; Ethnic
Status: Professional
Type: Performing; Resident; Educational
Purpose: To produce and present grand and light opera at its finest and accessible to people of all backgrounds
Management: Gary Burgess, Artistic Director; Dr. Judith G. Wolf, Executive Director
Officers: Harry R. Stainrook, Chairman of Board of Trustees; Eugene M. Setel, President; Albert J. Meaney CPA, Treasurer
Paid Staff: 5   **Volunteer Staff:** 10
Utilizes: Special Technical Talent; Guest Conductors; Guest Artists; Guest Directors
Budget: $500,000 - $1,000,000
Income Sources: Private Foundations/Grants/Endowments; Business/Corporate Donations; Box Office; Government Grants; Individual Donations
Season: September - April   **Annual Attendance:** 15,200
Performance Facilities: Shea's Buffalo Theater

THEATRE

PAUL ROBESON THEATRE
350 Masten Avenue, Buffalo, NY 14209
(716) 884-2013
Founded: 1958
Arts Area: Theatrical Group
Status: Semi-Professional; Non-Profit
Type: Performing; Educational
Purpose: To promote, sponsor, foster and develop in the Black community, particularly among Black youth, a taste and love of Black theatre
Management: Agnes M. Bain, Executive Director

Officers: Darlene Badgett, Chairman; Emma Bassett, Vice Chairman; Paulette S. Counts, Treasurer; Gwendolyn Neal, Secretary
Paid Staff: 10 **Volunteer Staff:** 22
Utilizes: Special Technical Talent; Guest Artists; Guest Directors
Budget: $50,000 - $100,000
Income Sources: Private Foundations/Grants/Endowments; Box Office; Government Grants; Individual Donations
Season: 52 Weeks
Performance Facilities: Paul Robeson Theatre

STUDIO ARENA THEATRE
710 Main Street, Buffalo, NY 14202
(716) 856-8025
FAX: (716) 845-4123
Arts Area: Professional
Status: Professional; Non-Profit
Type: Performing; Educational
Purpose: To provide a varied season of plays, produced at the highest possible quality, for the western New York area
Management: Gavin Cameron-Webb, Artistic Director; Raymond Bonnard, Executive Director; Anne E. Hayes, Director of Development; Courtney Walsh, Director of Marketing
Officers: Frank J. Colantuono, President, Board of Trustees
Paid Staff: 73 **Volunteer Staff:** 7
Utilizes: Special Technical Talent; Guest Artists; Guest Directors
Budget: $1,000,000 - $5,000,000
Income Sources: Private Foundations/Grants/Endowments; Business/Corporate Donations; Box Office; Government Grants; Individual Donations
Season: October - June **Annual Attendance:** 128,000
Affiliations: LORT; TCG; AEA

THEATRE OF YOUTH CO.
282 Franklin Street, Buffalo, NY 14202
Founded: 1972
Arts Area: Professional; Children's Theatre
Status: Professional; Non-Profit
Type: Performing; Touring; Educational
Management: Collen Maroney Fahey, Managing Director; Cathy Block, Business Manager; Sonya Swain, Box Office Manager/Bookkeeper; Cathy Schultz, Development Director; Meg Quinn, Marketing Director
Officers: Meg Rosters, Artistic Director; Pat Gorman, Technical Director; Greg Rapp, Stage Manager; David Bathrich, Costume Designer
Paid Staff: 5 **Volunteer Staff:** 2
Paid Artists: 7
Utilizes: Special Technical Talent; Guest Artists; Guest Directors
Budget: $50,000 - $100,000
Income Sources: Private Foundations/Grants/Endowments; Business/Corporate Donations; Box Office; Government Grants; Individual Donations
Season: September - May **Annual Attendance:** 60,000

PERFORMING SERIES

AFRICAN-AMERICAN CULTURAL CENTER
350 Masten Avenue, Buffalo, NY 14209
(716) 884-2013
Founded: 1958
Arts Area: Dance; Theater
Status: Non-Profit
Type: Performing; Sponsoring
Purpose: To cultivate, promote, sponsor, foster and develop an appreciation, understanding, taste and love of the traditions of the arts of Africa through social and cultural activities
Management: Agnes M. Bain, Executive Director
Officers: Darlene Badgett, Chairman; Emma Bassett, Vice Chairman; Gwendolyn Neal, Secretary; Paulett S. Counts, Treasurer
Paid Staff: 9 **Volunteer Staff:** 8
Paid Artists: 8 **Non-Paid Artists:** 35
Utilizes: Guest Artists
Budget: $100,000 - $500,000
Income Sources: Private Foundations/Grants/Endowments; Box Office; Government Grants; Individual Donations
Season: January - December **Annual Attendance:** 15,000
Performance Facilities: Paul Robeson Theatre

NORTH AMERICAN NEW MUSIC FESTIVAL
c/o State University of New York at Buffalo, Department of Music, 222 Baird Hall, Buffalo, NY 14260
(716) 636-2765
FAX: (716) 636-3821
Arts Area: Instrumental Music; Festivals
Status: Professional; Non-Profit
Type: Performing
Purpose: To promote the understanding and awareness of new music
Management: Yvar Mikashoff, Artistic Director; Donald Metz, Assistant Artistic Director
Budget: $1,000 - $50,000
Income Sources: Private Foundations/Grants/Endowments; Box Office; Government Grants
Performance Facilities: Slee Concert Hall; Albright-Knox Art Gallery; Hallwalls Art Gallery

QRS ARTS FOUNDATION
1026 Niagara Street, Buffalo, NY 14213
(716) 886-0067
FAX: (716) 885-7510
Founded: 1973
Arts Area: Dance; Vocal Music; Instrumental Music
Status: Professional
Type: Sponsoring
Purpose: To present the highest quality artists in recital; to present a variety of dance from ballet to modern
Management: Arlette Rosen, Director
Officers: Mary Collins Demske, President; Ramsi P. Tick, Chairman
Paid Staff: 3
Paid Artists: 15
Utilizes: Guest Artists
Budget: $100,000 - $500,000
Income Sources: Private Foundations/Grants/Endowments; Business/Corporate Donations; Box Office; Government Grants; Individual Donations
Season: August - May   **Annual Attendance:** 15,000
Affiliations: APAP
Performance Facilities: Kleinhans Music Hall; Shea's Buffalo; Rockwell Hall Auditorium; Slee Hall

FACILITY

AFRICAN-AMERICAN CULTURAL CENTER - PAUL ROBESON THEATRE
350 Masten Avenue, Buffalo, NY 14209
(716) 884-2013
Founded: 1958
Type of Facility: Multi-Purpose
Facility Originally: Welding Shop
Type of Stage: Platform
Stage Dimensions: 28'6"x16'3"
Seating Capacity: 100
Year Remodeled: 1958
Contact for Rental: Agnes M. Bain;   (716) 884-2013

BUFFALO MEMORIAL AUDITORIUM
140 Main Street, Buffalo, NY 14202
(716) 851-5663
FAX: (716) 851-4269
Type of Facility: Auditorium
Type of Stage: Proscenium   **Orchestra Pit**
Contact for Rental: Manager;   (716) 851-5663

BUFFALO STATE COLLEGE-PERFORMING ARTS CENTER - ROCKWELL HALL
1300 Elmwood Avenue, Buffalo, NY 14222
(716) 878-3032
FAX: (716) 878-6914
Founded: 1987
Type of Facility: Auditorium; Performance Center
Type of Stage: Proscenium
Stage Dimensions: 40'Wx20'H   **Orchestra Pit**
Seating Capacity: 856
Year Built: 1932
Year Remodeled: 1987   **Cost:** $15,000,000
Contact for Rental: J.V. Flanagan;   (716) 878-3032

KLEINHANS MUSIC HALL
Symphony Circle, Buffalo, NY 14201
(716) 883-3560
Type of Facility: Concert Hall; Auditorium
Type of Stage: Proscenium
Stage Dimensions: 33'x68'x44'   **Orchestra Pit**
Seating Capacity: 2,839
Year Built: 1940
Architect: Eliel & Eero Saarinen
Cost: $1,000,000
Contact for Rental: Douglas J. Lengyel, Director;   (716) 883-3560
Resident Groups: Buffalo Philharmonic; QRS Arts Foundation; Buffalo Chamber Music Society

STATE UNIVERSITY OF NEW YORK-BUFFALO - DEPARTMENT OF THEATRE AND DANCE
201 Harriman Hall, Buffalo, NY 14214
(716) 829-3742
Type of Facility: Studio Performance; Theatre House
Facility Originally: Library; Vaudeville
Type of Stage: Thrust; Flexible
Seating Capacity: Thrust - 350; Flex - 150
Year Built: 1920
Year Remodeled: 1986   **Cost:** $250,000
Contact for Rental: Jerry Kegler;   (716) 645-2038
Manager: Gary Casarella
Resident Groups: State University of New York-Buffalo Department of Theatre and Dance

Cambridge

INSTRUMENTAL MUSIC

L'ENSEMBLE DU MUSIQUE
Content Farm Road, Cambridge, NY 12816
(518) 677-5455
Arts Area: Chamber; Ensemble
Status: Professional; Non-Profit
Type: Performing; Touring; Resident; Educational
Purpose: Dedicated to the performance of rarely heard works as well as works of living American composers
Management: Ida Faiella, Artistic Director; Kristine DeFord, Assistant Artistic Director
Officers: Jonathan C. Mills, Chairman; Frank Gilmore, President; Timothy D. Smith, Vice President Finance
Budget: $100,000 - $500,000
Income Sources: Private Foundations/Grants/Endowments; Business/Corporate Donations; Box Office; Government Grants; Individual Donations
Performance Facilities: Albany City Arts Building

PERFORMING SERIES

MUSIC FROM SALEM
25 East Main Street, Cambridge, NY 12816
(518) 677-2495
Founded: 1986
Arts Area: Vocal Music; Instrumental Music
Status: Professional
Type: Performing; Resident
Purpose: To provide a summer residency for European and American musicians presenting chamber music in a rural setting as a member of the larger community
Officers: Judith Eissenberg, Lila Brown, Co-Directors
Paid Staff: 1   **Volunteer Staff:** 8
Paid Artists: 12
Budget: $1,000 - $50,000
Income Sources: Private Foundations/Grants/Endowments; Business/Corporate Donations; Government Grants; Individual Donations
Season: July - August   **Annual Attendance:** 600
Performance Facilities: Hubbard Hall

Chautauqua

INSTRUMENTAL MUSIC

CHAUTAUQUA SYMPHONY ORCHESTRA
Chautauqua Institution, Chautauqua, NY 14722
(716) 357-6200
FAX: (716) 357-9014
    Founded: 1874
    Arts Area: Symphony; Orchestra
    Status: Professional; Non-Profit
    Type: Performing; Resident; Educational
    Management: Daniel L. Bration, President; Marty Merkley, Program Director; James Stubbs, Personnel Manager
    Paid Staff: 6
    Paid Artists: 200
    Utilizes: Guest Conductors; Guest Artists
    Budget: $500,000 - $1,000,000
    Income Sources: Private Foundations/Grants/Endowments; Business/Corporate Donations; Box Office; Government Grants; Individual Donations
    Season: July - August   **Annual Attendance:** 80,000
    Affiliations: ASOL
    Performance Facilities: Amphitheater, Chautauqua Institution

VOCAL MUSIC

CHAUTAUQUA OPERA
Chautauqua, NY 14722
(716) 357-6200
FAX: (716) 357-9014
    Founded: 1929
    Arts Area: Grand Opera; Lyric Opera; Light Opera; Operetta
    Status: Professional
    Type: Performing; Resident; Educational
    Purpose: To present opera sung in English by young, up-and-coming artists as well as run a training program for young singers
    Management: Daniel Bratton, President; Linda Jackson, General Director
    Paid Staff: 30
    Paid Artists: 50
    Utilizes: Special Technical Talent; Guest Conductors; Guest Artists; Guest Directors
    Budget: $500,000 - $1,000,000
    Income Sources: Private Foundations/Grants/Endowments; Business/Corporate Donations; Box Office; Government Grants; Individual Donations
    Season: July - August   **Annual Attendance:** 12,500
    Affiliations: OA
    Performance Facilities: Norton Hall; Chautauqua Institution

PERFORMING SERIES

CHAUTAUQUA INSTITUTION
Chautauqua, NY 14722
(716) 357-6200
    Founded: 1874
    Arts Area: Dance; Vocal Music; Instrumental Music; Theater; Grand Opera
    Status: Professional; Semi-Professional; Non-Professional; Non-Profit
    Type: Performing; Resident; Educational; Sponsoring
    Purpose: A superb interplay of the arts, education, religion and recreation, all available on a self-selecting basis within a Victorian community
    Management: Marty Merkley, Program Director
    Officers: Dr. Daniel L. Bratton, President
    Paid Staff: 52   **Volunteer Staff:** 700
    Paid Artists: 400   **Non-Paid Artists:** 300
    Utilizes: Special Technical Talent; Guest Conductors; Guest Artists; Guest Directors
    Budget: $5,000,000 - $10,000,000
    Income Sources: Private Foundations/Grants/Endowments; Business/Corporate Donations; Box Office; Government Grants; Individual Donations
    Season: June - August   **Annual Attendance:** 200,000
    Affiliations: OA; ASOL; APAP; MENC; AAA
    Performance Facilities: Amphitheater; Norton Hall

FACILITY

CHAUTAUQUA INSTITUTION - AMPHITHEATER
Chautauqua, NY 14722
(716) 357-6200
FAX: (716) 357-9014
    Type of Facility: Concert Hall; Auditorium; Outdoor (Concert); Performance Center; Amphitheater; Arena; Multi-Purpose
    Facility Originally: Meeting Hall; Movie House
    Type of Stage: Thrust; Platform; 3/4 Arena; Arena
    Stage Dimensions: 40'x60'
    Seating Capacity: 6,000
    Year Built: 1874
    Year Remodeled: 1979 **Architect:** Lawson Pulver Knapp **Cost:** $2,900,000
    Acoustical Consultant: Farrell Becker
    Contact for Rental: Ed Keating; (716) 357-6264
    Resident Groups: Chautauqua Symphony Orchestra; Chautauqua Dance Festival Company; Chautauqua Music Festival Orchestra; Chautauqua Lecture Series; Chautauqua Youth Orchestra

CHAUTAUQUA INSTITUTION - NORTON HALL
Chautauqua, NY 14722
(716) 357-6000
    Type of Facility: Concert Hall; Theatre House; Opera House
    Type of Stage: Proscenium
    Stage Dimensions: 40'Wx30'D **Orchestra Pit**
    Seating Capacity: 1,367
    Year Built: 1929
    Year Remodeled: 1984 **Architect:** W. Thomas Smith **Cost:** $500,000
    Contact for Rental: Ed Keating; (716) 357-6264
    Resident Groups: Chautauqua Opera

Clinton

INSTRUMENTAL MUSIC

CHAMBER MUSIC SOCIETY OF UTICA INC.
Rural Route 4, PO Box 396, Clinton, NY 13323
(315) 330-4664
    Arts Area: Chamber
    Status: Non-Profit
    Type: Presenting
    Purpose: To present an annual series of high-quality chamber music concerts
    Management: James Taylor, Trustee; Dr. Jon Magendanz, Head of Music Selection
    Officers: Dorothy Deimel, President
    Budget: $1,000 - $50,000
    Income Sources: Private Foundations/Grants/Endowments; Business/Corporate Donations; Box Office; Government Grants; Individual Donations
    Performance Facilities: Munson-Williams-Proctor Museum of Art Auditorium

FACILITY

HAMILTON COLLEGE - MINOR THEATRE
198 College Hill Road, Clinton, NY 13323
(315) 859-4205
    Type of Facility: Theatre House
    Facility Originally: Library
    Type of Stage: Flexible
    Stage Dimensions: 50'x26'x34'
    Seating Capacity: 250
    Year Built: 1890
    Year Remodeled: 1963 **Architect:** Edward Durell Stone
    Contact for Rental: Bill Burd; (315) 859-4205
    Resident Groups: Hamilton College Departments of Theatre and Dance

KIRKLAND ART CENTER
East Park Row, PO Box 213, Clinton, NY 13323
(315) 853-8871
    Founded: 1960

Type of Facility: Multi-Purpose
Facility Originally: Church
Type of Stage: Platform
Stage Dimensions: 22'x14'
Seating Capacity: 130
Year Built: 1842
Year Remodeled: 1965
Contact for Rental: Dare Thompson;   (315) 853-8871

Cohoes

THEATRE

HERITAGE ARTISTS
PO Box 586, Cohoes, NY 12047
(518) 235-7909
    Founded: 1982
    Arts Area: Theatrical Group; Musical Theatre
    Status: Professional; Non-Profit
    Type: Performing
    Purpose: To produce musical theatre works
    Management: Robert Tolan, Producing Director; Sarah S. Burke, Public Relations Director; Joseph Abaldo, Casting Director
    Officers: John P. Ryan, Board President
    Paid Staff: 12
    Utilizes: Special Technical Talent; Guest Artists; Guest Directors
    Budget: $100,000 - $500,000
    Income Sources: Private Foundations/Grants/Endowments; Business/Corporate Donations; Box Office; Government Grants; Individual Donations
    Season: October - May
    Affiliations: TCG

Cooperstown

PERFORMING SERIES

COOPERSTOWN CONCERT SERIES, INC.
PO Box 624, Cooperstown, NY 13326
(607) 293-6124
FAX: (617) 293-6130
    Founded: 1970
    Arts Area: Dance; Vocal Music; Instrumental Music; Theater
    Status: Non-Profit
    Type: Sponsoring
    Purpose: To promote the cultural growth of our community by presenting live performances of high quality
    Officers: Jane Johngren and Donna Thomson, Co-Directors; Lois Hopper, Treasurer; Dottie Leslie, Secretary
    Volunteer Staff: 40
    Paid Artists: 25
    Budget: $1,000 - $50,000
    Income Sources: Private Foundations/Grants/Endowments; Business/Corporate Donations; Box Office; Government Grants; Individual Donations; In-Kind; Program Advertising
    Season: September - May   **Annual Attendance:** 1,500
    Performance Facilities: Sterling Auditorium

GLIMMERGLASS OPERA
PO Box 191, Cooperstown, NY 13326
(607) 547-5704
    Founded: 1975
    Arts Area: Vocal Music; Lyric Opera; Grand Opera
    Status: Professional; Non-Profit
    Type: Performing
    Purpose: To present opera with gifted young American professional talent and to introduce opera to new audiences
    Management: Paul Kellogg, General Director; Stewart Robertson, Music Director
    Paid Staff: 8   **Volunteer Staff:** 8
    Paid Artists: 70   **Non-Paid Artists:** 32
    Utilizes: Special Technical Talent; Guest Conductors; Guest Artists; Guest Directors
    Budget: $500,000 - $1,000,000

Income Sources: Private Foundations/Grants/Endowments; Business/Corporate Donations; Box Office; Government Grants; Individual Donations
Season: July - August   **Annual Attendance:** 20,000
Affiliations: OA
Performance Facilities: Alice Busch Opera Theater

Corning

INSTRUMENTAL MUSIC

CORNING PHILHARMONIC SOCIETY
PO Box 113, Corning, NY 14830
(607) 962-8582
 Founded: 1933
 Arts Area: Symphony; Orchestra
 Status: Professional; Non-Profit
 Type: Performing; Educational; Sponsoring
 Purpose: To provide high quality musical experiences at an affordable price
 Management: Marietta Cheng, Music Director/Conductor; Fitzray Stewart, Conductor, Youth Orchestra; David Thurkins, Business Manager
 Officers: Jane Fenn, President; John Jay, Vice President
 Paid Staff: 3   **Volunteer Staff:** 30
 Paid Artists: 45   **Non-Paid Artists:** 5
 Utilizes: Guest Artists
 Budget: $50,000 - $100,000
 Income Sources: Private Foundations/Grants/Endowments; Business/Corporate Donations; Box Office; Government Grants; Individual Donations
 Season: October - April   **Annual Attendance:** 3,500
 Performance Facilities: Corning Glass Center Auditorium

PERFORMING SERIES

CORNING-PAINTED POST CIVIC MUSIC ASSOCIATION
PO Box 1402, Corning, NY 14830
(607) 962-5713
 Founded: 1928
 Arts Area: Dance; Vocal Music; Instrumental Music; Jazz; Classical Presentation
 Status: Professional
 Type: Performing
 Purpose: To present the finest artists and talent at the lowest possible cost; subscription series
 Officers: David Schirmer, President; Nancy Martin, First Vice President; Ginger Schirmer, Second Vice President; Evelyn Baum, Corresponding Secretary; Gaile Felli, Membersip Secretary; Virginia Wrench, Treasurer
 Volunteer Staff: 36
 Paid Artists: 5
 Utilizes: Five Seasonal Concerts
 Budget: $1,000 - $50,000
 Income Sources: Private Foundations/Grants/Endowments; Business/Corporate Donations; Box Office; Government Grants; Individual Donations
 Season: October - May   **Annual Attendance:** 5,000
 Performance Facilities: Corning Glass Center Auditorium

FACILITY

CORNING GLASS CENTER
Centerway, Corning, NY 14831
(607) 974-8276
FAX: (607) 974-8310
 Type of Facility: Concert Hall; Auditorium; Theatre House; Multi-Purpose
 Type of Stage: Proscenium
 Seating Capacity: 1,000
 Year Built: 1951   **Architect:** Harrison & Abramovitz
 Year Remodeled: 1972

Cortland

THEATRE

CORTLAND REPERTORY THEATRE
PO Box 783, Cortland, NY 13045
(607) 753-6161
Founded: 1971
Arts Area: Professional; Summer Stock; Musical
Status: Non-Profit
Type: Performing
Purpose: To provide live theater for the region
Management: Jana Mack, Managing Director; Marie Alyn King, Artistic Director
Officers: Karl Blixt, President; Richard Fox, Vice President; Nancy Mann, Secretary; Edward Karsch, Treasurer
Paid Staff: 6 **Volunteer Staff:** 30
Paid Artists: 35 **Non-Paid Artists:** 30
Utilizes: Special Technical Talent; Guest Artists; Guest Directors
Budget: $100,000 - $500,000
Income Sources: Private Foundations/Grants/Endowments; Business/Corporate Donations; Box Office; Individual Donations
Season: June - August **Annual Attendance:** 11,000
Performance Facilities: Pavilion Theatre

PERFORMING SERIES

STATE UNIVERSITY OF NEW YORK - CORTLAND CAMPUS ARTIST AND LECTURE SERIES
PO Box 2000, Cortland, NY 13045
(607) 753-2321
FAX: (607) 753-2807
Founded: 1984
Arts Area: Dance; Instrumental Music; Theater; Festivals
Status: Professional; Non-Profit
Type: Presenting
Purpose: To enhance the cultural awareness of the Cortland College and general community
Management: Donna Margine, Coordinator of Performing Arts Programs
Paid Staff: 1
Paid Artists: 7
Budget: $1,000 - $50,000
Income Sources: Private Foundations/Grants/Endowments
Season: September - May
Affiliations: APAP; Upstate New York Presenters
Performance Facilities: Dowd Fine Arts Theatre

Craryville

PERFORMING SERIES

TOURING CONCERT OPERA CO. INC. - BERKSHIRE-HUDSON VALLEY FESTIVAL OF OPERA AND BALLET
PO Box 156A, Craryville, NY 12521
(518) 851-6778
Founded: 1971
Arts Area: Dance; Vocal Music; Instrumental Music; Theater; Lyric Opera; Grand Opera
Status: Professional; Non-Profit
Type: Performing; Touring
Purpose: To bring live professional opera and dance to people who would not normally have access to productions on a regular basis; primarily serving Massachusetts, the Southern Berkshires and the Hudson Valley
Management: Ramon Alsina, Artist Representative
Officers: Alberto Figols, President; Glenn Wilder, Vice President; Priscilla Gordon, Secretary/Treasurer
Paid Staff: 1 **Volunteer Staff:** 15
Paid Artists: 8 **Non-Paid Artists:** 30
Utilizes: Guest Conductors; Guest Artists; Guest Directors
Budget: $1,000 - $50,000
Income Sources: Private Foundations/Grants/Endowments; Business/Corporate Donations; Box Office; Government Grants; Individual Donations
Season: 52 Weeks **Annual Attendance:** 6,000

Crompond
FACILITY

MARTHA GUINSBERG PAVILION
Baron De Hirsh Road, Crompond, NY 10517
(914) 528-1835
    Type of Stage: Proscenium
    Stage Dimensions: 22'x28'x20'
    Seating Capacity: 800
    Year Built: 1956
    Contact for Rental: Manager; (914) 528-1835

Delhi
FACILITY

STATE UNIVERSITY AGRICULTURAL AND TECHNICAL COLLEGE - LITTLE THEATRE
Delhi, NY 13753
(607) 746-4222
    Type of Facility: Theatre Complex; Auditorium; Theatre House; Film & Lecture Hall
    Type of Stage: Proscenium
    Stage Dimensions: 36'Wx24'D   **Orchestra Pit**
    Seating Capacity: 356
    Year Built: 1967
    Contact for Rental: William Campbell; (607) 746-4222
    Resident Groups: Delhi College Players

Dobbs Ferry
INSTRUMENTAL MUSIC

PHILHARMONIA VIRTUOSI CORPORATION
145 Palisade Street, Dobbs Ferry, NY 10522
(914) 693-5595
FAX: (914) 693-7040
    Founded: 1974
    Arts Area: Orchestra; Chamber
    Status: Professional; Non-Profit
    Type: Performing; Touring; Educational; Recording
    Purpose: To perform an exceptionally broad spectrum of music from the 1600s to the present; to remain a flexible ensemble that performs orchestra concerts with up to 45 players and chamber music programs with as few as three
    Management: Richard Kapp, Music Director
    Budget: $500,000 - $1,000,000
    Season: 52 Weeks

FACILITY

MERCY COLLEGE - LECTURE HALL
555 Broadway, Dobbs Ferry, NY 10566
(914) 693-4500
    Type of Facility: Theatre House
    Type of Stage: Proscenium
    Seating Capacity: 230
    Year Built: 1968
    Contact for Rental: Anne Grow; (914) 693-4500, ext. 228
    Manager: Anthony Ivancich

Earlville
FACILITY

EARLVILLE OPERA HOUSE
West Main Street, Earlville, NY 13332
(315) 691-3500
    Type of Facility: Auditorium; Opera House

Facility Originally: Vaudeville
Type of Stage: Proscenium
Stage Dimensions: 13'x19'x19'
Seating Capacity: 300
Year Built: 1892
Year Remodeled: 1975   **Architect:** A.H. Arnold
Contact for Rental: Director;   (315) 691-3550

East Farmingdale

THEATRE

ARENA PLAYERS REPERTORY COMPANY OF LONG ISLAND
296 Route 109, East Farmingdale, NY 11735
(516) 293-0674
Founded: 1955
Arts Area: Theatrical Group
Status: Professional; Non-Profit
Type: Performing; Touring
Purpose: To develop and encourage appreciation of arena theatre, and to assist new playwrights in the development of original scripts.
Management: Frederic De Feis, Artistic Director; Joanne Gobrick, Production Coordinator; George Snow, Administrative Assistant
Officers: Frederic De Feis, President; Joanne Gobrick, Vice President; Frank Zummo, Secretary; George Anderson, Treasurer
Paid Staff: 3   **Volunteer Staff:** 4
Paid Artists: 7
Utilizes: Guest Directors
Budget: $100,000 - $500,000
Income Sources: Private Foundations/Grants/Endowments; Business/Corporate Donations; Box Office; Government Grants; Individual Donations
Season: 52 Weeks
Annual Attendance: 55,000
Affiliations: TCG
Performance Facilities: Arena Players Repertory Theater

East Hampton

PERFORMING SERIES

THE JOHN DREW THEATER OF GUILD HALL
158 Main Street, East Hampton, NY 11937
(516) 324-4051
FAX: (516) 324-2722
Founded: 1931
Arts Area: Dance; Instrumental Music; Theater
Status: Professional; Non-Profit
Type: Performing; Educational
Purpose: The John Drew Theater of Guild Hall operates under an educational/arts charter; dedicated to the presentation of the finest in the performing arts.
Management: Joy Gordon, Executive Director; Pamela Calvert, Program Director
Officers: Jo Raymond, Chairman of the Board
Paid Staff: 15   **Volunteer Staff:** 10
Paid Artists: 130   **Non-Paid Artists:** 50
Utilizes: Special Technical Talent; Guest Artists; Guest Directors
Budget: $100,000 - $500,000
Income Sources: Private Foundations/Grants/Endowments; Business/Corporate Donations; Box Office; Government Grants; Individual Donations
Season: 52 Weeks   **Annual Attendance:** 25,000
Affiliations: AEA
Performance Facilities: John Drew Theater

East Islip

PERFORMING SERIES

ISLIP ARTS COUNCIL
40 Irish Lane, East Islip, NY 11730
(516) 224-5420
FAX: (516) 224-5440
Founded: 1974
Arts Area: Vocal Music; Instrumental Music
Status: Professional; Non-Profit
Type: Performing
Purpose: To present a variety of disciplines ranging from fine classical music to young persons' programs to avant garde performance art; to enable exsisting and emerging art organizations to gain information and assistance from the Arts Council library and staff in applying for not-for-profit status, funding, computer services, publicity, mailing lists, etc; to publicize the activities of the arts organization around Long Island
Management: Lillian Barbash, Executive Director; Jodi Gianni, Dorothy Kalson, Co-Directors of Operations; Angela Wallace, Clerk Typist; Barbara Kreisler, Director of Marketing and Development
Officers: Helene Katz, President; Nicholas Wartella, Vice President; Jean Lipshie, Secretary; Edward E. Wankel, Treasurer
Paid Staff: 5   **Volunteer Staff:** 2
Paid Artists: 35
Utilizes: Special Technical Talent; Guest Artists
Budget: $100,000 - $500,000
Income Sources: Private Foundations/Grants/Endowments; Business/Corporate Donations; Box Office; Government Grants; Individual Donations
Season: January - December   **Annual Attendance:** 60,000
Affiliations: Township of Islip; Suffolk County
Performance Facilities: Sayville Schools; Dowling College; Bayard Cutting Arboretum; Heckscher State Park

---

Elmira

INSTRUMENTAL MUSIC

ELMIRA SYMPHONY AND CHORAL SOCIETY
PO Box 22, Elmira, NY 14902
(607) 732-3011
Founded: 1903
Arts Area: Symphony; Chamber
Status: Professional
Type: Performing; Sponsoring
Purpose: To perform standard classical orchestral and choral music, with occasional popular concerts
Officers: Anita Kimball, President; Mark Fleisher, Vice President; Carol Balmer, Secretary; Donald Peterson, Treasurer
Paid Staff: 62   **Volunteer Staff:** 30
Paid Artists: 3
Utilizes: Guest Artists
Budget: $50,000 - $100,000
Income Sources: Private Foundations/Grants/Endowments; Business/Corporate Donations; Box Office; Individual Donations
Season: September - April   **Annual Attendance:** 11,000

FACILITY

CLEMENS CENTER
Clemens Center Parkway and Gray Street, PO Box 1046, Elmira, NY 14902
(607) 733-5639
FAX: (607) 737-1162
Type of Facility: Performance Center
Facility Originally: Vaudeville
Type of Stage: Proscenium
Stage Dimensions: 48'Wx28'H   **Orchestra Pit**
Seating Capacity: 1,615
Year Built: 1925
Year Remodeled: 1976   **Architect:** Haskell, Conner & Frost
Contact for Rental: Michael Kenna;   (607) 733-5639
Manager: Thomas Weidemann;   (607) 733-5639
Resident Groups: Elmira Little Theatre; Elmira Symphony and Choral Society

Elmsford

FACILITY

WESTCHESTER BROADWAY THEATRE
1 Broadway Plaza, Elmsford, NY 10523
(914) 592-2222
    Type of Facility: Theatre House
    Type of Stage: Thrust; Proscenium
    Stage Dimensions: 20'x20'   **Orchestra Pit**
    Seating Capacity: 449
    Year Built: 1991   **Architect:** Judith Chafee
    Cost: $4,500,000
    Contact for Rental: Robert Funking; (914) 592-2268

Fishkill

DANCE

MID HUDSON BALLET COMPANY
Route 9 North, Fishkill, NY 12524
(914) 897-2667
    Founded: 1959
    Arts Area: Ballet
    Status: Non-Profit
    Type: Performing; Educational
    Management: Shirley Sedore, Company Manager; Estelle and Alfonso, Artistic Directors
    Officers: Cheryl Kroll, President; Pat Holt, Secretary; Sue Maio, Treasurer
    Paid Staff: 3 **Volunteer Staff:** 23
    Utilizes: Guest Artists; Guest Directors
    Budget: $50,000 - $100,000
    Income Sources: Business/Corporate Donations; Box Office; Government Grants; Individual Donations
    Season: September - August
    Affiliations: Northeast Regional Ballet; Dutchess County Arts Council
    Performance Facilities: Mid Hudson Civic Center

Flushing

FACILITY

COLDEN CENTER FOR THE PERFORMING ARTS
Queens College, Flushing, NY 11367
(718) 544-2996
FAX: (718) 261-7063
    Founded: 1961
    Type of Facility: Theatre Complex; Concert Hall; Auditorium
    Type of Stage: Proscenium
    Stage Dimensions: 76'Wx37'Dx20'H proscenium opening   **Orchestra Pit**
    Seating Capacity: 2,143
    Year Built: 1961
    Acoustical Consultant: Peterheorge Associates
    Contact for Rental: Stephen Mallalieu; (718) 544-2996
    Resident Groups: Queens Symphony Orchestra; Queen's College: Choral Society; Drama Department

QUEENS COLLEGE - COLDEN CENTER FOR THE PERFORMING ARTS
Flushing, NY 11367
(718) 544-2996
FAX: (718) 261-7063
    Type of Facility: Concert Hall; Auditorium; Theatre House
    Type of Stage: Proscenium
    Stage Dimensions: 76'x37'   **Orchestra Pit**
    Seating Capacity: 2,143
    Year Built: 1961   **Architect:** Felheimer & Wagner
    Contact for Rental: Steve Mallalieu; (718) 544-2996
    Resident Groups: Queens Symphony

Fredonia

INSTRUMENTAL MUSIC

FREDONIA CHAMBER PLAYERS
Mason Hall, State University College, Fredonia, NY 14063
(716) 673-3463
FAX: (716) 673-3397
> **Founded:** 1981
> **Arts Area:** Orchestra; Chamber
> **Status:** Professional; Non-Profit
> **Type:** Performing; Touring; Resident; Educational; Sponsoring
> **Purpose:** To present concerts throughout western New York, Pennsylvania and on tour; to sponsor a chamber orchestra and chamber music series; to sponsor an ensemble-in-residence at the State University of New York, Fredonia School of Music
> **Management:** James East, Executive Director; Grant Cooper, Music Director
> **Officers:** Gary Woodbury, President; Sue Evans, Vice President; Catherine Kilpatrick, Secretary; Hal Kwasniewski, Treasurer
> **Paid Staff:** 2   **Volunteer Staff:** 8
> **Paid Artists:** 45   **Non-Paid Artists:** 45
> **Utilizes:** Guest Conductors; Guest Artists
> **Budget:** $50,000 - $100,000
> **Income Sources:** Private Foundations/Grants/Endowments; Business/Corporate Donations; Box Office; Government Grants; Individual Donations
> **Season:** September - June   **Annual Attendance:** 15,000
> **Affiliations:** Arts Council for Chautauqua County; Fund for the Arts in Chautauqua County
> **Performance Facilities:** King Concert Hall, State University of New York-Fredonia

FACILITY

STATE UNIVERSITY OF NEW YORK-FREDONIA - MICHAEL C. ROCKEFELLER ARTS CENTER
Michael C. Rockefeller Arts Center, Fredonia, NY 14063
(716) 673-3217
> **Type of Facility:** Theatre Complex; Concert Hall
> **Type of Stage:** Flexible; Proscenium
> **Year Built:** 1969   **Architect:** I. M. Pei
> **Acoustical Consultant:** Bolt, Beranek & Newman
> **Contact for Rental:** Jefferson Westwood;   (716) 673-3217
> **Resident Groups:** Fredonia Chamber Players
> *The Michael C. Rockefeller Arts Center contains the Concert Hall, Experimental Theatre and Proscenium Theatre. See separate listings for additional information.*

STATE UNIVERSITY OF NEW YORK-FREDONIA - MICHAEL C. ROCKEFELLER ARTS CENTER - CONCERT HALL
Michael C. Rockefeller Arts Center, Fredonia, NY 14063
(716) 673-3217
> **Type of Facility:** Concert Hall
> **Type of Stage:** Proscenium
> **Stage Dimensions:** 60'x45'
> **Seating Capacity:** 1,200
> **Year Built:** 1969
> **Contact for Rental:** Jefferson Westwood;   (716) 673-3217

STATE UNIVERSITY OF NEW YORK-FREDONIA - MICHAEL C. ROCKEFELLER ARTS CENTER - EXPERIMENTAL THEATRE
Michael C. Rockefeller Arts Center, Fredonia, NY 14063
(716) 673-3217
> **Type of Facility:** Multi-Purpose; Black Box
> **Type of Stage:** Flexible
> **Seating Capacity:** 150
> **Year Built:** 1969
> **Contact for Rental:** Jurgen Banse-Fay;   (716) 673-3217

STATE UNIVERSITY OF NEW YORK-FREDONIA - MICHAEL C. ROCKEFELLER ARTS CENTER - THEATRE
Michael C. Rockefeller Arts Center, Fredonia, NY 14063
(716) 673-3217
> **Type of Facility:** Theatre House

Type of Stage: Proscenium
Seating Capacity: 400
Year Built: 1969
Contact for Rental: Jurgen Banse-Fay;   (716) 673-3217

Freeport

INSTRUMENTAL MUSIC

AMERICAN MUSICAL ROOTS ASSOCIATION
101 North Bergen Place, Freeport, NY 11520
(212) 850-6423
  Founded: 1984
  Arts Area: Ethnic; Folk
  Status: Professional; Semi-Professional; Non-Profit
  Type: Sponsoring
  Purpose: Provide local musicians work opportunities, provide area residents with traditional culture, and expose both to the best national traditional groups
  Officers: Larry Brittain, President; Billy Clockel, Treasurer
  Paid Staff: 2   **Volunteer Staff:** 15
  Utilizes: Guest Artists
  Budget: $1,000 - $50,000
  Income Sources: Private Foundations/Grants/Endowments; Business/Corporate Donations; Box Office; Government Grants; Individual Donations
  Season: 52 Weeks   **Annual Attendance:** 10,000

Garden City

VOCAL MUSIC

NATIONAL GRAND OPERA
231 Washington Avenue, Garden City, NY 11530-1707
(516) 248-1040
  Founded: 1983
  Arts Area: Grand Opera
  Status: Professional; Non-Profit
  Type: Performing; Resident
  Purpose: To bring the highest quality operatic entertainment to the residents of our area
  Management: Linda Holgers, General Director; Eugene Brister, Artistic Director
  Paid Staff: 2   **Volunteer Staff:** 20
  Paid Artists: 175
  Utilizes: Special Technical Talent; Guest Conductors; Guest Artists; Guest Directors
  Budget: $100,000 - $500,000
  Income Sources: Private Foundations/Grants/Endowments; Business/Corporate Donations; Box Office; Government Grants; Individual Donations
  Season: October - July   **Annual Attendance:** 28,000
  Affiliations: Long Island University
  Performance Facilities: Tilles Center for the Performing Arts

Geneseo

INSTRUMENTAL MUSIC

FRIENDS OF MUSIC ORCHESTRA AT SAINT MICHAEL'S
Brodie Fine Arts Building, State University of New York - Geneseo, Geneseo, NY 14454
(716) 243-2958
  Founded: 1970
  Arts Area: Orchestra
  Status: Professional; Profit
  Type: Performing; Educational; Sponsoring
  Purpose: To provide on a professional level a wide range of repertoire including emphasis on new music for chamber orchestra to the Geneseo Valley region
  Management: James Walker, Musical Director
  Officers: Dr. James Willey, President
  Volunteer Staff: 6
  Paid Artists: 27

Utilizes: Guest Artists
Budget: $1,000 - $50,000
Income Sources: Private Foundations/Grants/Endowments; Business/Corporate Donations; Box Office; Government Grants; Individual Donations
Season: September - May   **Annual Attendance:** 6,000
Performance Facilities: Saint Michael's Church

GENESEO CHAMBER SYMPHONY
Brodie Fine Arts Building, State University of New York-Geneseo, Geneseo, NY 14454
(716) 245-5824
Founded: 1970
Arts Area: Chamber
Status: Semi-Professional; Non-Profit
Type: Performing; Educational; Sponsoring
Purpose: To give younger performers an opportunity to interact with respected, established artists in both performance and educational environments
Management: James Walker, Musical Director
Paid Staff: 3
Paid Artists: 12   **Non-Paid Artists:** 39
Budget: $50,000 - $100,000
Income Sources: Private Foundations/Grants/Endowments; Government Grants
Season: September - May   **Annual Attendance:** 3,600
Performance Facilities: Wadsworth Auditorium

TREMONT STRING QUARTET, INC.
PO Box 396, Geneseo, NY 14454
(716) 243-4429
FAX: (716) 245-5005
Arts Area: Chamber
Status: Professional; Non-Profit
Type: Performing; Touring; Resident; Educational; Sponsoring
Purpose: To perform the best contemporary and standard chamber music repertory for venues throughout the world
Management: Richard Balkin, Artistic Director; James Kirkwood, Executive Director
Officers: James Walker, Mark Congdon, Board Members
Budget: $100,000 - $500,000
Income Sources: Private Foundations/Grants/Endowments; Business/Corporate Donations; Box Office; Government Grants; Individual Donations

FACILITY

WADSWORTH AUDITORIUM
State University of New York-Geneseo, 1 College Circle, Geneseo, NY 14454
(716) 245-5855
FAX: (716) 245-5400
Type of Facility: Concert Hall; Auditorium
Facility Originally: School
Type of Stage: Proscenium
Stage Dimensions: 46'Wx26'Dx32'8"H proscenium opening   **Orchestra Pit**
Seating Capacity: 942
Year Built: 1930

Geneva

PERFORMING SERIES

GENEVA CONCERTS, INC.
PO Box 709, Geneva, NY 14456
(315) 789-2310
FAX: (315) 787-2326
Founded: 1946
Arts Area: Dance; Vocal Music; Instrumental Music; Theater; Lyric Opera; Grand Opera
Status: Professional; Non-Profit
Type: Educational; Sponsoring
Purpose: To promote the arts in Geneva and the surrounding Finger Lakes community by presenting music, dance and vocal
Officers: Tony Shelton, President; Kim Hardy, First Vice President; Lee Thomas, Second Vice President; Ford Weiskittel, Secretary; Addie Heosler, Treasurer
Volunteer Staff: 21

Utilizes: Guest Conductors; Guest Artists; Guest Directors
Budget: $50,000 - $100,000
Income Sources: Private Foundations/Grants/Endowments; Business/Corporate Donations; Box Office; Government Grants; Individual Donations
Season: September - April   **Annual Attendance:** 3,500
Performance Facilities: Smith Opera House

FACILITY

SMITH OPERA HOUSE FOR THE PERFORMING ARTS
Finger Lakes Regional Arts Council, Inc., PO Box 58, Geneva, NY 14456
(315) 789-2221
Type of Facility: Performance Center; Theatre House; Opera House; Multi-Purpose; Film & Lecture Hall
Facility Originally: Vaudeville
Type of Stage: Thrust; Proscenium
Stage Dimensions: 43'10"Wx37'D, 43'10"Wx28'H proscenium opening   **Orchestra Pit**
Seating Capacity: 1,500
Year Built: 1892   **Architect:** Pierce & Bickford
Year Remodeled: 1927   **Architect:** Victor Ridgemont & Associates   **Cost:** $600,000
Contact for Rental: Richard Erwin, Executive Director;   (315) 789-2221
Resident Groups: Geneva Theatre Guild; Finger Lakes Symphony; Geneva Concerts

Glen Falls

PERFORMING SERIES

LAKE GEORGE OPERA FESTIVAL
13 South Street, PO Box 425, Glen Falls, NY 12801
(518) 793-3858
Founded: 1961
Arts Area: Vocal Music; Instrumental Music
Status: Professional; Non-Profit
Type: Performing
Purpose: To present opera in English with professional young American singers, and to perform a fully-staged season of opera and musical theater work repertory
Management: Brian Lingham, General Director; John Clark, Business Manager; Christopher Minnes, Director of Marketing; Theresa Riddell, Company Administrator; William Wyatt, Production Manager
Officers: Ross Masterman, President; Captain John K. Ryder, Treasurer
Paid Staff: 6   **Volunteer Staff:** 200
Paid Artists: 200   **Non-Paid Artists:** 25
Utilizes: Guest Conductors; Guest Artists; Guest Directors
Budget: $500,000 - $1,000,000
Income Sources: Private Foundations/Grants/Endowments; Business/Corporate Donations; Box Office; Government Grants; Individual Donations
Season: July - August
Affiliations: OA; Albany League of Arts
Performance Facilities: Queensbury High School

FACILITY

OPERA FESTIVAL AUDITORIUM
PO Box 2172, Glen Falls, NY 12801
(518) 793-3858
Type of Facility: Auditorium
Type of Stage: Thrust   **Orchestra Pit**
Seating Capacity: 876
Year Built: 1962

Greenfield Center

PERFORMING SERIES

FOUNDATION FOR BAROQUE MUSIC
165 Wilton Road, Greenfield Center, NY 12833
(518) 893-7527
Founded: 1959
Arts Area: Dance; Vocal Music; Instrumental Music; Festivals

Status: Professional; Non-Profit
Type: Performing; Resident; Educational
Purpose: To promote the music of the 17th and 18th centuries using historical instruments and performance practices
Management: Robert Conant, Artistic Director; Mark E. Baker, Administrative Director
Officers: Robert Conant, President; Eugene M. Krader, Vice President/Secretary
Paid Staff: 1   **Volunteer Staff:** 3
Paid Artists: 30
Utilizes: Guest Artists
Budget: $1,000 - $50,000
Income Sources: Private Foundations/Grants/Endowments; Business/Corporate Donations; Box Office; Government Grants; Individual Donations
Season: July - August   **Annual Attendance:** 1,000
Affiliations: Albany League of Arts; Saratoga County Arts Council; CMA; EMA
Performance Facilities: Baroque Festival Studio

FACILITY

BAROQUE FESTIVAL STUDIO
165 Wilton Road, Greenfield Center, NY 12833
(518) 893-7527
Type of Facility: Concert Hall; Recording Studio
Type of Stage: Flexible
Stage Dimensions: 25'x30'
Seating Capacity: 110
Year Built: 1973   **Architect:** Michael Curtis   **Cost:** $30,000
Acoustical Consultant: Michael Curtis
Contact for Rental: Robert Conant;   (518) 893-7527
Resident Groups: Festival of Baroque Music

Hamilton

PERFORMING SERIES

COLGATE UNIVERSITY CONCERT SERIES
Colgate University, Hamilton, NY 13346-1398
(315) 824-7642
FAX: (315) 824-7787
Arts Area: Dance; Vocal Music; Instrumental Music; Theater
Status: Non-Professional; Non-Profit
Type: Educational; Sponsoring
Purpose: To present concerts to the Colgate University student body and others
Officers: Joseph Swain, Chairperson; Roberta Healey, Concert Manager
Utilizes: Guest Artists
Budget: $1,000 - $50,000
Income Sources: Box Office; Government Grants
Season: 52 Weeks
Performance Facilities: Colgate Memorial Chapel

FACILITY

COLGATE UNIVERSITY - BREHMER THEATER
Dana Arts Center, 13 Oak Drive, Hamilton, NY 13346
(315) 824-1000
Type of Facility: Auditorium
Type of Stage: Proscenium
Stage Dimensions: 20'x30'x40'
Seating Capacity: 400
Year Built: 1966
Architect: Paul Rudolph
Manager: Garda M. Parker
Resident Groups: Colgate University Theater; Colgate Dance Theater

COLGATE UNIVERSITY - UNIVERSITY THEATER
Dana Arts Center, 13 Oak Drive, Hamilton, NY 13346
(315) 824-1000
Type of Facility: Auditorium
Type of Stage: Proscenium
Stage Dimensions: 20'x30'x40'

Seating Capacity: 400
Year Built: 1966 **Architect:** Paul Rudolph
Acoustical Consultant: W. G. Brown Sound

Hartsdale

INSTRUMENTAL MUSIC

THE NEW ORCHESTRA OF WESTCHESTER
111 North Central Avenue, Hartsdale, NY 10530
(914) 682-3707
FAX: (914) 682-3716
Founded: 1983
Arts Area: Symphony
Status: Professional; Non-Profit
Type: Performing; Educational
Purpose: The New Orchestra of Westchester is committed to bringing the highest quality music to the Westchester area with a goal of featuring music by living American composers as part of annual programming
Management: Mary Luehrsen-Young, Executive Director; Paul Lustig Dunkel, Music Director; Jonathan Taylor, Personnel Manager; Susan Hackel, Assistant Director; Peggy Levin, Development Director; Dan Johnsen, Box Office Manager; Karen Castopoulos, Administrative Manager
Officers: Michael Baun, Chairman; Tom Bezanson, Music Chair; Neal Gantchen, Secretary/Counsel
Paid Staff: 5 **Volunteer Staff:** 30
Paid Artists: 75
Utilizes: Guest Artists
Budget: $500,000 - $1,000,000
Income Sources: Private Foundations/Grants/Endowments; Business/Corporate Donations; Box Office; Government Grants; Individual Donations
Season: September - May **Annual Attendance:** 9,000
Affiliations: Council for Arts Westchester
Performance Facilities: Performing Arts Center, State University of New York-Purchase

Hawthorne

INSTRUMENTAL MUSIC

WESTCHESTER ELEMENTARY ORCHESTRA
Westchester County Dept. of Parks and Recreation, 19 Bradhurst Avenue, Hawthorne, NY 10532
(914) 593-2626
Founded: 1983
Arts Area: Orchestra
Status: Non-Profit
Type: Performing; Educational
Purpose: To provide educational and performing experience for gifted young musicians, grades 4-6, from throughout Westchester County
Management: Arnold Gamson, Supervisor; Jacqueline Stern, Music Director
Officers: Park Allen, Chairman of the Board
Volunteer Staff: 3
Non-Paid Artists: 30
Utilizes: Special Technical Talent; Guest Artists
Budget: $1,000 - $50,000
Income Sources: Private Foundations/Grants/Endowments; Business/Corporate Donations; Government Grants; Individual Donations
Season: September - May **Annual Attendance:** 1,500
Performance Facilities: Westchester Community College

WESTCHESTER JUNIOR STRING ORCHESTRA
Westchester County Dept. of Parks and Recreation, 19 Bradhurst Avenue, Hawthorne, NY 10532
(914) 593-2626
Founded: 1959
Arts Area: Orchestra
Status: Non-Professional; Non-Profit
Type: Performing; Touring; Educational
Purpose: To provide educational and performing experience for gifted young musicians, grades 7-9, from throughout Westchester County
Management: Arnold Gamson, Supervisor; Dale Lewis, Music Department
Officers: Park Allen, Chairman of the Board

Volunteer Staff: 6
Non-Paid Artists: 46
Utilizes: Special Technical Talent; Guest Artists
Budget: $1,000 - $50,000
Income Sources: Private Foundations/Grants/Endowments; Business/Corporate Donations; Government Grants; Individual Donations
Season: September - May
Annual Attendance: 4,000
Performance Facilities: Westchester Community College

WESTCHESTER YOUTH SYMPHONY
Westchester County Dept. of Parks and Recreation, 19 Bradhurst Avenue, Hawthorne, NY 10532
(914) 593-2626
Founded: 1959
Arts Area: Orchestra
Status: Non-Professional; Non-Profit
Type: Performing; Educational
Purpose: To provide educational and performing experience for gifted young musicians, grades 10-12, from throughout Westchester County
Management: Arnold Gamson, Supervisor; C. Vincent Lionti, Music Director
Officers: Park Allen, Chairman of the Board
Volunteer Staff: 6
Paid Artists: 3   Non-Paid Artists: 96
Utilizes: Special Technical Talent; Guest Artists
Budget: $1,000 - $50,000
Income Sources: Private Foundations/Grants/Endowments; Business/Corporate Donations; Government Grants; Individual Donations
Season: September - May
Annual Attendance: 8,500
Performance Facilities: Westchester Community College

PERFORMING SERIES

COUNTY OF WESTCHESTER - PARKS, RECREATION AND CONSERVATION - PERFORMING ARTS
19 Bradhurst Avenue, Hawthorne, NY 10532
(914) 593-2626
Arts Area: Dance; Instrumental Music; Theater
Status: Non-Profit
Type: Performing
Purpose: Production and presentation of concerts, ethnic events in parks and county facilities; and provision of training in performing arts to talented young people and amateurs
Management: Arnold Gamson, Supervisor Performing Arts
Officers: Andrew O'Rourke, County Executive; Barry C. Samuel, Commissioner of Parks Recreation and Conservation
Paid Staff: 60
Paid Artists: 50
Utilizes: Special Technical Talent; Guest Artists; Guest Directors
Budget: $100,000 - $500,000
Income Sources: Business/Corporate Donations; Box Office; Government Grants
Season: 52 Weeks
Annual Attendance: 40,000
Affiliations: Westchester County Department of Parks, Recreation and Conservation
Performance Facilities: Kensico Dam Plaza; Westchester County Center

Houghton

PERFORMING SERIES

HOUGHTON COLLEGE ARTIST SERIES
Houghton College, Houghton, NY 14744
(716) 567-2211
Founded: 1930
Arts Area: Vocal Music; Instrumental Music; Theater; Grand Opera
Status: Non-Profit
Type: Performing; Educational; Sponsoring
Purpose: Serious concert presentations
Management: Dr. Bruce Brown, Director
Paid Staff: 2   Volunteer Staff: 5
Paid Artists: 5

Utilizes: Guest Conductors; Guest Artists
Budget: $1,000 - $50,000
Income Sources: Private Foundations/Grants/Endowments; Box Office; Individual Donations
Season: September - May   **Annual Attendance:** 4,000
Affiliations: APAP
Performance Facilities: Wesley Chapel

FACILITY

HOUGHTON COLLEGE - WESLEY CHAPEL
Houghton College, Houghton, NY 14744
(716) 567-2211
Type of Facility: Concert Hall; Auditorium
Type of Stage: Concert Stage
Stage Dimensions: 57'x35'
Seating Capacity: 1,200

Ithaca

DANCE

ITHACA BALLET (BALLET GUILD OF ITHACA, INC.)
105 Sheldon Road, Ithaca, NY 14850
(607) 257-1967
Founded: 1959
Arts Area: Modern; Ballet
Status: Semi-Professional; Non-Profit
Type: Performing; Touring
Purpose: To bring classical and contemporary ballet to areas of upstate New York and Pennsylvania
Management: Lawrence Brantley, General Manager
Officers: Elisabeth Thorn, President; Charlotte Fogel, Vice President; Elizabeth Schermerhorn, Secretary; Helene Wilmarth, Treasurer
Paid Staff: 2   **Volunteer Staff:** 20
Utilizes: Special Technical Talent
Budget: $50,000 - $100,000
Income Sources: Private Foundations/Grants/Endowments; Business/Corporate Donations; Box Office; Individual Donations
Season: 52 Weeks   **Annual Attendance:** 6,000
Performance Facilities: Statler Auditorium, Cornell University

VOCAL MUSIC

ITHACA OPERA ASSOCIATION
109 East Seneca Street, Ithaca, NY 14850
(607) 272-0168
Founded: 1949
Arts Area: Grand Opera; Lyric Opera; Light Opera; Operetta; Musical Theatre
Status: Professional; Non-Profit
Type: Performing; Touring; Educational
Purpose: To bring quality entertainment to the Finger Lakes community through the use of local and regional talent
Management: Edward Murray, Musical Director
Officers: James P. Cassaro, President, Board of Directors
Paid Staff: 1   **Volunteer Staff:** 75
Paid Artists: 45   **Non-Paid Artists:** 20
Utilizes: Special Technical Talent; Guest Conductors; Guest Artists; Guest Directors
Budget: $50,000 - $100,000
Income Sources: Private Foundations/Grants/Endowments; Business/Corporate Donations; Box Office; Government Grants; Individual Donations
Affiliations: NYSCA
Performance Facilities: Hangar Theatre; Statler Auditorium, Cornell University

THEATRE

THE HANGAR THEATRE
DeWitt Mall, PO Box 205, Ithaca, NY 14851
(607) 273-8588
Founded: 1970
Arts Area: Professional

Status: Professional; Non-Profit
Type: Performing; Educational
Purpose: To produce outstanding professional theatre for the benefit of our region and to provide hands-on educational opportunities for theatre artists through our directing fellowship, acting internship and acting training programs
Management: Robert Moss, Producing Director; Lynn Fitzpatrick, Managing Director
Officers: Andrea Fleck Clardy, President; John Alexander, Vice President; Susan Kaplan, Secretary; John A. Elliott, Treasurer
Paid Staff: 100   **Volunteer Staff:** 20
Paid Artists: 35   **Non-Paid Artists:** 15
Utilizes: Special Technical Talent; Guest Artists; Guest Directors
Budget: $100,000 - $500,000
Income Sources: Private Foundations/Grants/Endowments; Business/Corporate Donations; Box Office; Government Grants; Individual Donations
Season: June - September   **Annual Attendance:** 23,000
Affiliations: Finger Lakes Chamber of Commerce; Tompkins City Chamber of Commerce
Performance Facilities: Hangar Theatre, Cass Park

FACILITY

CORNELL UNIVERSITY - ALICE STATLER AUDITORIUM
Statler Hotel, Ithaca, NY 14853-7001
(607) 254-2604
FAX: (607) 257-6432
   Founded: 1989
   Type of Facility: Auditorium
   Type of Stage: Proscenium
   Stage Dimensions: 30'x36'   **Orchestra Pit**
   Seating Capacity: 921
   Contact for Rental: Carol Markwardt;   (607) 255-2331
   Resident Groups: Cornell Concert Series; Cornell Cinema; Cornell Lecture Series; Cornell Dance Club; Cornell Savoyards

HANGAR THEATRE
Cass Park, PO Box 205, Ithaca, NY 14851
(607) 273-8588
   Type of Facility: Performance Center; Theatre House
   Facility Originally: Airplane Hangar
   Type of Stage: Thrust; Platform; In-the-Round Capability
   Stage Dimensions: 28'x26'
   Seating Capacity: 380
   Year Built: 1934
   Year Remodeled: 1974   **Architect:** Robert Mueller   **Cost:** $125,000
   Contact for Rental: Lynn Fitzpatrick, Managing Director;   (607) 273-8588
   Resident Groups: Hangar Theatre Company; North Lobby Company
   Available for rent May and September only

ITHACA COLLEGE - DILLINGHAM CENTER FOR THE PERFORMING ARTS
Dillingham Center for the Performing Arts, Ithaca, NY 14850
(607) 274-3345
   Type of Facility: Theatre Complex; Performance Center
   Year Built: 1968   **Architect:** T.A. Canfield
   Contact for Rental: Special Events Office;   (607) 274-3313
   Resident Groups: Ithaca College Department of Theatre Arts
   The Performing Arts Center contains the Arena and Hoerner Auditorium. See separate listings for additional information.

ITHACA COLLEGE - DILLINGHAM CENTER FOR THE PERFORMING ARTS - ARENA
Dillingham Center for the Performing Arts, Ithaca, NY 14850
(607) 274-3345
   Type of Facility: Arena
   Type of Stage: Flexible; Arena
   Seating Capacity: 312
   Year Built: 1968
   Contact for Rental: Special Events Office;   (607) 274-3313

ITHACA COLLEGE - DILLINGHAM CENTER FOR THE PERFORMING ARTS - HOERNER AUDITORIUM
Dillingham Center for the Performing Arts, Ithaca, NY 14850
(607) 274-3345
   Type of Facility: Auditorium

Type of Stage: Proscenium
Stage Dimensions: 56'Wx39'D; 56'Wx22'H proscenium opening   **Orchestra Pit**
Seating Capacity: 535
Year Built: 1968
Contact for Rental: Special Events Office;   (607) 274-3313

Jackson Heights

THEATRE

YUEH LUNG SHADOW THEATRE
34-41 74th Street, Jackson Heights, NY 11372
(718) 478-6246
Founded: 1976
Arts Area: Professional; Folk; Puppet
Status: Professional; Non-Profit
Type: Performing; Touring; Educational
Purpose: To preserve and perpetuate the 2000-year-old Chinese art of shadow theatre
Management: Mrs. Joe Humphrey, Executive/Artistic Director; Sarah Jonker-Burke, Assistant Director
Officers: Samuel Magdoff, Chairman; Katharine McKelligott, Treasurer; David Sterling, Vice Chairman
Paid Staff: 3   **Volunteer Staff:** 5
Paid Artists: 9
Budget: $1,000 - $50,000
Income Sources: Private Foundations/Grants/Endowments; Business/Corporate Donations; Government Grants; Individual Donations; Performance Fees
Season: 52 Weeks   **Annual Attendance:** 10,000
Affiliations: ART/NY; UNIMA; Queens Council on Arts; Puppeteers of America; UNIMA

Jamaica

DANCE

DINIZULU AFRICAN DANCERS, DRUMMERS AND SINGERS
c/o Aims of Modzawe, 115-62 Sutphin Boulevard, Jamaica, NY 11434
(718) 843-6213
Arts Area: Ethnic
Status: Professional; Non-Profit
Type: Performing; Touring; Resident; Educational; Sponsoring
Purpose: To present the beauty and majesty of African culture through dance
Management: Alice Dinizulu, Executive Director; Esi-Ayisi Dinizulu, Artistic Director
Income Sources: Private Foundations/Grants/Endowments; Business/Corporate Donations; Box Office; Government Grants; Individual Donations

THEATRE

AFRIKAN POETRY THEATRE
176-03 Jamaica Avenue, Jamaica, NY 11432
(718) 523-3312
Founded: 1976
Arts Area: Professional; Musical; Community; Folk
Status: Professional; Non-Profit
Type: Performing; Touring; Educational; Sponsoring
Purpose: To provide cultural and educational classes and workshops, performances, exhibits and cultural reference sources for the benefit of the community
Management: John Watusi Branch, Executive Director; Byron W. Perry, Ronald Burwell, Administrative Assistants; Shadiyah Waliyaya, Program Director
Officers: Fred Abramson, President; Roger Burwell, Vice President; Willie E. Cooper, Secretary; Louise Adelokiki, Treasurer
Paid Staff: 3   **Volunteer Staff:** 12
Paid Artists: 5   **Non-Paid Artists:** 20
Utilizes: Guest Artists
Budget: $100,000 - $500,000
Income Sources: Private Foundations/Grants/Endowments; Business/Corporate Donations; Box Office; Government Grants; Individual Donations
Season: 52 Weeks   **Annual Attendance:** 15,000
Performance Facilities: Afrikan Poetry Theatre

FACILITY

JAMAICA ARTS CENTER
161-04 Jamaica Avenue, Jamaica, NY 11432
(718) 658-7400
Type of Facility: Studio Performance; Performance Center; Multi-Purpose; Room
Facility Originally: Business Facility
Type of Stage: Platform
Seating Capacity: 50
Year Built: 1898   **Architect:** Geoffrey Freeman & Associates   **Cost:** $1,000,000
Contact for Rental: Vevonique LeMelle, Executive Director
Resident Groups: The Tribe Ensemble; New York Street Theater Caravan; Mimestrals; Jamaica Arts Center Jazz Ensemble; Jamaica Arts Center Co-Op
Continuous renovations done on the New York City landmark; formerly Queens Hall of Records

SAINT JOHN'S UNIVERSITY
Grand Central and Utopia Parkways, Jamaica, NY 11439
(718) 990-6452
FAX: (718) 380-0353
Type of Facility: Auditorium; Theatre House
Type of Stage: Proscenium
Stage Dimensions: 29'x35'x30'
Seating Capacity: 400
Manager: Ed Guinan;   (718) 990-6452

Jamaica Estates

THEATRE

NEW YORK STREET THEATRE CARAVAN
8705 Chelsea Street, Jamaica Estates, NY 11432
(718) 657-8070
Founded: 1968
Arts Area: Theatrical Group
Status: Professional
Type: Performing
Management: Marketa Kimbrell, Artistic Director of the Collective
Paid Staff: 4
Budget: $50,000 - $100,000
Income Sources: Private Foundations/Grants/Endowments; Box Office

---

Jamestown

INSTRUMENTAL MUSIC

JAMESTOWN CONCERT ASSOCIATION
PO Box 747, Jamestown, NY 14702-0747
(716) 487-1522
FAX: (716) 484-2300
Founded: 1932
Arts Area: Symphony; Orchestra; Chamber; Ensemble; Ethnic; Instrumental Group; Band
Status: Non-Profit
Type: Educational; Sponsoring
Purpose: To sponsor professional musicians in concert for our membership
Management: Shirlea Roman, Executive Secretary
Officers: R. Richard Corbin, President; Clayton Berlinghoff, Vice President; Katherine Kotsi, Treasurer
Volunteer Staff: 30
Utilizes: Guest Conductors; Guest Artists
Budget: $1,000 - $50,000
Income Sources: Private Foundations/Grants/Endowments; Business/Corporate Donations; Box Office; Government Grants; Individual Donations
Season: 52 Weeks   **Annual Attendance:** 9,500
Affiliations: Arts Association Chautauqua County
Performance Facilities: Civic Center

FACILITY

LUCILLE BALL LITTLE THEATRE BUILDING
18-24 East Second Street, Jamestown, NY 14701
(716) 483-1095
 Type of Facility: Auditorium
 Type of Stage: Proscenium
 Stage Dimensions: 80'x40'x24' **Orchestra Pit**
 Seating Capacity: 440
 Year Built: 1900
 Year Remodeled: 1969 **Cost:** $250,000
 Contact for Rental: (716) 483-1095

Katonah

PERFORMING SERIES

CARAMOOR CENTER FOR MUSIC AND THE ARTS
Katonah, NY 10536
(914) 232-4206
 Founded: 1945
 Arts Area: Vocal Music; Instrumental Music; Festivals
 Status: Professional; Non-Profit
 Type: Performing; Educational; Sponsoring
 Purpose: To provide a center for music and the arts for the town of Bedford and the state of New York
 Management: Howard Herring, Executive Director
 Officers: Peter M. Gottsegen, Chairman
 Paid Staff: 35 **Volunteer Staff:** 90
 Paid Artists: 100
 Utilizes: Guest Conductors; Guest Artists; Guest Directors
 Budget: $1,000,000 - $5,000,000
 Income Sources: Private Foundations/Grants/Endowments; Business/Corporate Donations; Box Office; Government Grants; Individual Donations
 Performance Facilities: Museum Music Room Venetian Theatre; Spanish Courtyard

FACILITY

CARAMOOR CENTER FOR MUSIC AND THE ARTS
Girdle Ridge Road, Katonah, NY 10536
(914) 232-5035
FAX: (914) 232-5521
 Founded: 1945
 Type of Facility: Concert Hall; Outdoor (Concert); Multi-Purpose
 Type of Stage: Proscenium; Platform; Environmental
 Stage Dimensions: 35'x35'; 20'x24'
 Contact for Rental: Paul Rosenblum; (914) 232-5035
 Resident Groups: Orchestra and Ensemble of St. Luke's; Cassatt String Quartet

VENETIAN THEATRE
Caramoor, Girdle Ridge Road, Katonah, NY 10536
(914) 232-5035
FAX: (914) 232-5521
 Founded: 1946
 Type of Facility: Concert Hall; Outdoor (Concert); Performance Center; Theatre House
 Type of Stage: Proscenium
 Orchestra Pit
 Seating Capacity: 1,650
 Year Built: 1957 **Architect:** Frederick Kiesler
 Contact for Rental: Paul Rosenblum; (914) 232-5035
 Resident Groups: Orchestra of St. Luke's; Cossott String Quartet
 Off-season (before mid-June and after mid-August)

Kingston

THEATRE

COACH HOUSE PLAYERS
12 Augusta Street, PO Box 3481, Kingston, NY 12401
(914) 338-7097
    Founded: 1950
    Arts Area: Musical; Community; Theatrical Group
    Status: Non-Profit
    Type: Performing; Educational
    Purpose: To present the best possible productions in all phases of theatre
    Management: Kay Finn, Business Manager
    Officers: Tom Tierney, President; Cate Tomlinson, Vice President; Pat Tonzi, Treasurer
    Utilizes: Guest Directors
    Budget: $1,000 - $50,000
    Income Sources: Box Office; Individual Donations
    Season: September - June   **Annual Attendance:** 5,000
    Performance Facilities: J. Watson Bailey School

FACILITY

ULSTER PERFORMING ARTS CENTER
601 Broadway, Kingston, NY 12401
(914) 331-1613
FAX: (914) 339-3814
    Founded: 1978
    Type of Facility: Theatre Complex; Concert Hall; Studio Performance; Performance Center; Civic Center; Teaching Facility
    Facility Originally: Vaudeville; Movie House
    Type of Stage: Proscenium
    Stage Dimensions: 37'Wx28'D   **Orchestra Pit**
    Seating Capacity: 1,538
    Year Built: 1927   **Architect:** Douglas Hall
    Acoustical Consultant: Jaffe
    Contact for Rental: Joan Roberts;   (914) 331-1613

Lafayette

THEATRE

CONTEMPORARY THEATRE OF SYRACUSE
2888 Eager Road, Lafayette, NY 13084
    Founded: 1980
    Arts Area: Theatrical Group
    Status: Semi-Professional
    Type: Performing
    Purpose: To present contemporary drama, stage readings of works-in-progress, and programs in schools
    Management: Kristi McKay, Producer; Jo Lynn Stressing, Summer Producer; David Feldman, New Plays Artistic Director; Shirley Myrls, New Plays Production Director
    Officers: Mary Earle, President; Kitty McCarthy, Secretary
    Paid Staff: 4   **Volunteer Staff:** 20
    Paid Artists: 20   **Non-Paid Artists:** 35
    Budget: $50,000 - $100,000
    Income Sources: Private Foundations/Grants/Endowments; Business/Corporate Donations; Box Office; Government Grants; Individual Donations
    Season: 52 Weeks   **Annual Attendance:** 1,500

Lake George

THEATRE

LAKE GEORGE DINNER THEATRE
Canada Street, Lake George, NY 12845
(518) 761-1092
FAX: (518) 798-0735
    Mailing Address: PO Box 4623, Queensbury, NY 12804

Founded: 1967
Arts Area: Professional; Dinner; Theatrical Group
Status: Professional
Type: Performing
Management: Sharon Reynolds, General Manager
Officers: David Eastwood, Producer
Paid Staff: 2
Non-Paid Artists: 8
Budget: $50,000 - $100,000
Income Sources: Box Office
Season: June - October   **Annual Attendance:** 15,000

PERFORMING SERIES

LAKE GEORGE JAZZ WEEKEND
c/o Lake George Arts Project Inc., Canada Street, Lake George, NY 12845
(518) 668-2616
FAX: (518) 668-3788
Arts Area: Instrumental Music; Jazz
Status: Professional; Non-Profit
Type: Performing; Touring
Purpose: To sponsor a two-day festival held each September that features nationally acclaimed and emerging jazz artists
Management: John Strong, Executive Director; Paul Pines, Music Director
Officers: Theodore Zoli Jr., President of the Board
Budget: $1,000 - $50,000
Income Sources: Private Foundations/Grants/Endowments; Business/Corporate Donations; Government Grants; Individual Donations
Performance Facilities: Shepard Park Bandstand

FACILITY

LAKE GEORGE DINNER THEATRE
PO Box 4623, Lake George, NY 12845
(518) 761-1092
Type of Facility: Theatre House
Facility Originally: Ballroom
Type of Stage: 3/4 Arena
Stage Dimensions: 14'x24'
Seating Capacity: 166
Manager: Sharon Reynolds

Lake Placid

PERFORMING SERIES

LAKE PLACID CENTER FOR THE ARTS
Saranac Avenue, Lake Placid, NY 12946
(518) 523-2512
Founded: 1972
Arts Area: Dance; Vocal Music; Theater; Festivals
Status: Non-Profit
Type: Performing; Resident; Sponsoring
Purpose: To disseminate arts in a rural, sports-oriented community
Management: Nadine Duhaime, Director
Officers: Lesly Handler, President
Paid Staff: 4   **Volunteer Staff:** 20
Utilizes: Guest Artists; Guest Directors
Income Sources: Private Foundations/Grants/Endowments; Business/Corporate Donations; Box Office; Government Grants; Individual Donations
Season: 52 Weeks   **Annual Attendance:** 25,000
Affiliations: Lyceum/Sinfonietta CTP Players

FACILITY

LAKE PLACID CENTER FOR THE ARTS - THEATER
Saranac Avenue, Lake Placid, NY 12946
(518) 523-2512
Type of Facility: Concert Hall; Performance Center; Theatre House

Type of Stage: Proscenium
Stage Dimensions: 66'Wx35'D; 48'Wx15'H proscenium opening **Orchestra Pit**
Seating Capacity: 353
Year Built: 1972
Architect: Frost/McConnell
Cost: $3,000,000
Contact for Rental: Robin Pell; (518) 523-2512
The Center also contains an art gallery and studios.

Lancaster

FACILITY

LANCASTER NEW YORK OPERA HOUSE
21 Central Avenue, Lancaster, NY 14086
(716) 683-1776
Type of Facility: Theatre House; Multi-Purpose
Type of Stage: Proscenium
Stage Dimensions: 18'Dx24'W
Seating Capacity: 350
Year Built: 1897   Architect: George J. Metzger
Year Remodeled: 1981   Architect: William Shelgren   Cost: $700,000
Contact for Rental: Executive Director; (716) 683-1776

Lewiston

PERFORMING SERIES

ARTPARK
PO Box 371, Lewiston, NY 14092
(716) 754-9000
Founded: 1974
Arts Area: Dance; Vocal Music; Instrumental Music; Festivals; Grand Opera
Status: Professional; Non-Profit
Type: Performing; Resident; Sponsoring
Purpose: Publicly-funded state park devoted to the visual and performing arts, intended to bridge the gap between the public and the arts
Management: David Midland, Executive Director; Jennifer McDonough, Director of Development; Tracy Gibbons, Director of Finance; Dean Cohan, Director of Operations; Katherine Rooney, Director of Marketing
Officers: David Midland, President
Paid Staff: 18   Volunteer Staff: 500
Paid Artists: 200
Utilizes: Special Technical Talent; Guest Conductors; Guest Artists; Guest Directors
Budget: $1,000,000 - $5,000,000
Income Sources: Private Foundations/Grants/Endowments; Business/Corporate Donations; Box Office; Government Grants; Individual Donations
Season: June - September   Annual Attendance: 840,000
Affiliations: AEA; IATSE; AGMA; AFM

FACILITY

ARTPARK THEATER
PO Box 371, Lewiston, NY 14092
(716) 754-9000
FAX: (716) 754-2741
Founded: 1974
Type of Facility: Concert Hall; Auditorium; Outdoor (Concert); Performance Center; Theatre House; Opera House
Type of Stage: Proscenium
Stage Dimensions: 38'-50'Wx20'-30'H adjustable proscenium; 48'x39'x79'   **Orchestra Pit**
Seating Capacity: Inside - 2,324; Outside - 1,500
Year Built: 1972   Architect: Volmer Associates   Cost: $7,500,000

Lindenhurst

FACILITY

STUDIO THEATRE
141 South Wellwood Avenue, Lindenhurst, NY 11757
(516) 226-1833
Type of Facility: Theatre House
Facility Originally: Upstairs Loft
Type of Stage: Thrust
Stage Dimensions: 10'x60'x40'
Seating Capacity: 175
Converted into a theatre in 1972 for $5,000

Little Falls

FACILITY

MOHAWK VALLEY CENTER FOR THE ARTS
401 South Ann Street, Little Falls, NY 13365-0611
(315) 823-0808
Type of Facility: Room
Facility Originally: Meeting Hall; Movie House
Type of Stage: Proscenium
Stage Dimensions: 40'x32'
Seating Capacity: 300
Year Built: 1914 **Architect:** Smith **Cost:** $40,000
Contact for Rental: Matt Mielnick; (315) 823-0808

Locust Valley

INSTRUMENTAL MUSIC

LONG ISLAND BAROQUE ENSEMBLE
PO Box 7, Locust Valley, NY 11560
(516) 724-7386
Founded: 1970
Arts Area: Chamber; Ensemble
Status: Professional; Non-Profit
Type: Performing; Touring; Educational
Purpose: To perform early music on period instruments with vocal specialists
Officers: Edward Pressman, President; Michael Pressman, Treasurer; Dominic Buonanno, Secretary; Victor Fetter, Vice President
Paid Staff: 2 **Volunteer Staff:** 15
Paid Artists: 14
Utilizes: Guest Artists
Budget: $50,000 - $100,000
Income Sources: Private Foundations/Grants/Endowments; Business/Corporate Donations; Box Office; Government Grants; Individual Donations; Subscriptions
Season: September - April **Annual Attendance:** 2,100
Performance Facilities: Coe Hall; Planting Fields Arboretum, Oyster Bay

PERFORMING SERIES

BEETHOVEN FESTIVAL
c/o Friends of the Arts Inc., PO Box 702, Locust Valley, NY 11560
(516) 922-0061
FAX: (516) 922-0770
Arts Area: Instrumental Music
Status: Professional; Non-Profit
Type: Performing
Purpose: To present Beethoven's lifetime of work in one spectacular weekend
Management: Theodora Bookman, Executive Director
Officers: Morton Weber Esq., Chairman of the Board
Budget: $1,000 - $50,000
Income Sources: Box Office; Government Grants; Individual Donations
Performance Facilities: Planting Fields Arboretum

Mamaroneck

FACILITY

THE EMELIN THEATRE FOR THE PERFORMING ARTS
Library Lane, Mamaroneck, NY 10543
(914) 698-3045; (914) 698-0098
FAX: (914) 698-1404
   Type of Facility: Performance Center
   Stage Dimensions: 22'x40'x18'
   Seating Capacity: 280
   Year Built: 1972   **Cost:** $350,000
   Contact for Rental: Norman Kline;   (914) 698-3045
   Resident Groups: Emelin Trio
   To present high-quality performing arts to Westchester County and the New York area

---
Melville

INSTRUMENTAL MUSIC

LONG ISLAND PHILHARMONIC
One Huntington Quadrangle, #LL-09, Melville, NY 11747
(516) 293-2222
FAX: (516) 293-2655
   Founded: 1979
   Arts Area: Symphony; Orchestra; Chamber
   Status: Professional
   Type: Performing; Resident; Educational
   Management: Daniel C. Brown, General Manager; Kevin Barnes, Orchestra Manager; Robin Postiglione, Accounting Manager
   Officers: Barry R. Shapio, Chairman; John J. Rusell, Robert M. Johnson, Vice Chairmen
   Paid Staff: 8
   Utilizes: Guest Artists
   Budget: $1,000,000 - $5,000,000
   Income Sources: Private Foundations/Grants/Endowments; Business/Corporate Donations; Box Office; Government Grants; Individual Donations
   Season: October - May
   Performance Facilities: Tilles Center; Staller Center

Monticello

THEATRE

PERIWINKLE NATIONAL THEATRE
19 Clinton Avenue, Monticello, NY 12701
(914) 794-1666
FAX: (914) 794-0304
   Founded: 1963
   Arts Area: Professional; Theatrical Group
   Status: Professional; Non-Profit
   Type: Performing; Touring; Educational
   Purpose: To provide quality programming with a unique blend of preliminary materials, original productions and workshops designed to challenge students intellectually, imaginatively and artistically
   Management: Sunna Rasch, Executive Director; Kathy Sharpe, Business Manager
   Officers: Robert S. Kapito, President; Dr. Nellie McCaslin, Vice President; Alfred Christie, Secretary/Treasurer
   Paid Staff: 4
   Paid Artists: 15
   Utilizes: Special Technical Talent
   Budget: $100,000 - $500,000
   Income Sources: Private Foundations/Grants/Endowments; Business/Corporate Donations; Government Grants; Individual Donations; Program Fees
   Season: September-December; - January-May   **Annual Attendance:** 100,000

Mount Vernon

INSTRUMENTAL MUSIC

BOWDOIN SUMMER MUSIC FESTIVAL
141 Rich Avenue, Mount Vernon, NY 10550
(207) 725-3322, ext. June-Aug; (914) 664-5957
Arts Area: Chamber
Status: Non-Profit
Type: Educational; Presenting
Purpose: To provide intensive training to pre-professional music students and professional concert presentations
Management: Lewis Kaplan, Artistic Director; Mary Klibonoff, Administrator
Officers: George S. Isaacson, President
Budget: $100,000 - $500,000
Income Sources: Private Foundations/Grants/Endowments; Business/Corporate Donations; Box Office; Government Grants; Individual Donations
Performance Facilities: First Parish Church

Narrowsburg

VOCAL MUSIC

DELAWARE VALLEY OPERA
PO Box 188, Narrowsburg, NY 12764
(914) 252-3910
Founded: 1986
Arts Area: Light Opera; Operetta
Status: Semi-Professional; Non-Profit
Type: Performing; Educational
Management: Gloria Krause, General Manager
Officers: Sheldon Soffer, President; Lester Wallman, Vice President; Elizabeth Brown, Finance; Sharon Schroeder, Secretary; Gloria Krause, Treasurer
Paid Staff: 2   **Volunteer Staff:** 15
Non-Paid Artists: 40
Utilizes: Special Technical Talent; Guest Artists
Budget: $1,000 - $50,000
Income Sources: Box Office; Government Grants; Individual Donations
Season: May - December   **Annual Attendance:** 2,000
Performance Facilities: Tusten Theatre; Sullivan County Community College

New Berlin

INSTRUMENTAL MUSIC

DEL-SE-NANGO OLDE TYME FIDDLERS ASSOCIATION, INC.
RD #3, PO Box 233, New Berlin, NY 13411
(607) 847-8501
Founded: 1978
Arts Area: Folk
Status: Non-Profit
Type: Performing; Educational; Sponsoring
Purpose: To preserve, promote and perpetuate the art of olde tyme fiddling, its music and dances
Officers: Marjorie T. Crawford, President; Paul Krum, Vice President; Catherine Whitbeck, Secretary; Margaret Sherwood, Treasurer
Volunteer Staff: 250
Non-Paid Artists: 40
Utilizes: Guest Artists
Budget: $1,000 - $50,000
Income Sources: Box Office; Individual Donations
Season: April - December

New Paltz
THEATRE

NINETY MILES OFF BROADWAY
PO Box 565, New Paltz, NY 12651
  Founded: 1963
  Arts Area: Theatrical Group
  Status: Non-Profit
  Type: Performing
  Officers: Judy Eliott, President
  Volunteer Staff: 50
  Budget: $1,000 - $50,000
  Income Sources: Box Office; Individual Donations

New Windsor
DANCE

ORANGE COUNTY BALLET THEATRE
170 Windsor Highway, New Windsor, NY 12553
(914) 562-6750
  Founded: 1963
  Arts Area: Ballet
  Status: Non-Professional; Non-Profit
  Type: Resident
  Management: Regis Powers, Artistic Director
  Non-Paid Artists: 30
  Utilizes: Guest Choreographers
  Budget: $1,000 - $50,000
  Income Sources: Private Foundations/Grants/Endowments; Business/Corporate Donations; Box Office; Individual Donations
  Season: September - August

New York
DANCE

AGNES DE MILLE DANCE THEATER
25 East 9th Street, New York, NY 10003
(212) 473-3024
  Founded: 1953
  Arts Area: Ballet; Folk
  Status: Professional; Non-Profit
  Type: Performing; Touring; Educational
  Purpose: A ballet repertoire based on and stemming from the American Heritage
  Management: Agnes De Mille, Artistic Director
  Officers: Robert Whitehead, President; Beatrio Renfield, Vice President; Charles Hallerith, Secretary/Treasurer
  Paid Staff: 12 **Volunteer Staff:** 2
  Paid Artists: 28
  Utilizes: Guest Artists; Guest Directors
  Budget: $100,000 - $500,000
  Income Sources: Private Foundations/Grants/Endowments; Business/Corporate Donations; Box Office; Government Grants
  Season: October - November; March - April

ALLNATIONS DANCE COMPANY
Performing Arts Foundation, 500 Riverside Drive, New York, NY 10027
(212) 316-8430
  Founded: 1967
  Arts Area: Ethnic
  Status: Professional; Non-Profit
  Type: Performing; Touring; Educational
  Purpose: Different people from different parts of the world, can dance in harmony and peace and with mutual respect. "That Brotherhood May Prevail"
  Management: Chuck Golden, Artistic Director; Herman Rottenberg, Founder/Executive Director
  Paid Artists: 9

Utilizes: Special Technical Talent; Guest Choreographers
Budget: $100,000 - $500,000
Income Sources: Private Foundations/Grants/Endowments; Box Office
Season: September - June   **Annual Attendance:** 100,000
Performance Facilities: International House

ALPHA-OMEGA THEATRICAL DANCE COMPANY
c/o Dolores Vanison-Blakely, 711 Amsterdam Avenue, #4E, New York, NY 10025
(212) 749-0095
Founded: 1972
Arts Area: Modern; Jazz
Status: Professional; Non-Profit
Type: Performing
Purpose: To promote knowledge and appreciation of artistic activities related to dance through schools, repertory emsembles and a professional company
Management: Dolores Vanison-Blakely, Executive Director; Martial Roumain, Artistic Director; Ettie Cooper, Fiscal/Bookings
Officers: Migdalia Rodriguez, President; Minnie Richardson, Secretary/Treasurer
Paid Staff: 4   **Volunteer Staff:** 6
Utilizes: Special Technical Talent; Guest Artists; Guest Choreographers
Budget: $1,000 - $50,000
Income Sources: Private Foundations/Grants/Endowments; Business/Corporate Donations; Box Office; Government Grants; Individual Donations
Annual Attendance: 2,000

ALVIN AILEY AMERICAN DANCE THEATER
211 West 61st Street, 3rd Floor, New York, NY 10023
(212) 767-0590
FAX: (212) 767-0625
Founded: 1958
Arts Area: Modern; Ballet; Jazz; Ethnic
Status: Professional; Non-Profit
Type: Performing; Touring; Educational
Purpose: A repertory company dedicated to the presentation and enrichment of the American modern dance heritage and the uniqueness of Black cultural expression; administered by Dance Theater Foundation; affiliated with the Alvin Ailey Repertory Ensemble, a junior company comprised of outstanding scholarship students and the Alvin Ailey American Dance Center, the official school
Management: Judith Jamison, Artistic Director; Masazumi Chaya, Associate Artistic Director; Bill Ferry, General Manager; Michael Kaiser, Executive Director; Sharon Luckman, Director of Development; Laura Beaumont, Director of Marketing; Paul Carlson, Finance Director; Kathleen Rose, Assistant Finance Director/Personnel Director; Sylvia Waters, Artistic Director/Alvin Ailey Dance Ensemble; Denise Jefferson, Director of the Ailey School; Donald Washington, Alvin Company Manager
Officers: Kenneth D. Brody, President; Eleanor Appleharte, Esq., Allan S. Gray, Alex J. Plinio, Vice Chairmen
Paid Staff: 50
Paid Artists: 30
Utilizes: Special Technical Talent; Guest Artists; Guest Choreographers
Budget: $5,000,000 - $10,000,000
Income Sources: Private Foundations/Grants/Endowments; Business/Corporate Donations; Box Office; Government Grants; Individual Donations
Season: 52 Weeks
Affiliations: AGMA; Dance USA
Performance Facilities: City Center Theatre

ALVIN AILEY REPERTORY ENSEMBLE
211 West 61st Street, New York, NY 10023
(212) 767-0590
FAX: (212) 767-0625
Founded: 1974
Arts Area: Modern; Ballet; Jazz; Ethnic
Status: Professional; Non-Profit
Type: Performing; Touring; Educational
Management: Sylvia Waters, Artistic Director; Judith Schray, Business Manager
Officers: Harold Levine, Chairman; Kenneth D. Brody, President
Paid Staff: 18
Paid Artists: 32
Utilizes: Special Technical Talent; Guest Artists; Guest Choreographers
Budget: $5,000,000 - $10,000,000
Income Sources: Private Foundations/Grants/Endowments; Business/Corporate Donations; Box Office; Government Grants; Individual Donations

Season: 52 Weeks
Affiliations: National Corporate Funds For Dance; Dance USA

AMERICAN AUTHENTIC JAZZ DANCE THEATRE
554 West 53rd Street, Suite 8-24, New York, NY 10019
(212) 265-4412
Founded: 1972
Arts Area: Jazz
Status: Non-Profit
Type: Resident; Educational
Management: Ludwig Sheppard, Administrator
Officers: Pepsi Bethel, Artistic Director
Paid Artists: 2
Utilizes: Special Technical Talent; Guest Artists; Guest Choreographers
Budget: $100,000 - $500,000
Income Sources: Private Foundations/Grants/Endowments; Business/Corporate Donations; Box Office; Government Grants; Individual Donations
Season: 52 Weeks

AMERICAN BALLET THEATRE
890 Broadway, 3rd Floor, New York, NY 10003
(212) 477-3030
FAX: (212) 254-5938
Founded: 1940
Arts Area: Ballet
Status: Professional
Type: Performing; Touring
Purpose: National touring annually, international bookings
Management: Les Schoof, General Manager
Paid Artists: 90
Budget: Over 10,000,000
Income Sources: Private Foundations/Grants/Endowments; Business/Corporate Donations; Box Office; Government Grants; Individual Donations
Season: 52 Weeks
Performance Facilities: The Metropolitan Opera House

AMERICAN BALLROOM THEATER COMPANY INC.
305 East 24th Street, #7T, New York, NY 10010
(212) 532-8091
FAX: (212) 532-8091
Arts Area: Ballroom
Status: Professional; Non-Profit
Type: Performing; Educational
Purpose: To preserve, develop and further the tradition of American ballroom dancing; to present it in a choreographed and theatrical form on the stage
Management: Pierre Dulaine, Yvonne Marceau, Co-Artistic Directors; Otto Cappel, Executive Director
Officers: Edward J. Ross, President of the Board
Budget: $500,000 - $1,000,000
Income Sources: Private Foundations/Grants/Endowments; Business/Corporate Donations; Box Office; Government Grants; Individual Donations; Performance Fees
Performance Facilities: St. Paul the Apostle Church, Manhattan

AMERICAN INTERNATIONAL DANCE THEATRE, INC.
375 Riverside Drive, Suite 13A, New York, NY 10025-2170
(212) 662-3468
FAX: (212) 489-9727
Founded: 1981
Arts Area: Ballet; Ethnic; Folk
Status: Professional
Type: Performing; Touring; Educational
Purpose: To present dance shows and concerts for theatres, colleges, municipalities and hotels
Management: Paulette Singer, Managing Director; Russell Miller, Art Director; Max Block, Musical Director
Officers: Paulette Singer, President; Andrew Miller, Secretary; Russell Miller, Treasurer
Paid Staff: 3
Paid Artists: 50
Utilizes: Special Technical Talent; Guest Conductors; Guest Artists; Guest Directors; Guest Choreographers
Budget: $100,000 - $500,000
Income Sources: Box Office

Season: 52 Weeks
Annual Attendance: 100,000
Affiliations: American International Lyric Theatre, Inc.

THE AMERICAN MIME THEATRE
123-40 83rd Avenue, New York, NY 10003
(212) 777-1710
Founded: 1952
Arts Area: Mime; American Mime
Status: Professional; Non-Profit
Type: Performing; Educational
Purpose: To perform and train artists in "American Mime, " a form created by Paul J. Curtis, Director of the American Mime Theatre
Management: Paul J. Curtis, Founder/Director; Jean Barbour, Managing Director
Paid Staff: 1   **Volunteer Staff:** 4
Paid Artists: 10
Budget: $1,000 - $50,000
Income Sources: Private Foundations/Grants/Endowments; Business/Corporate Donations; Individual Donations
Season: September - July

ANNABELLA GONZALEZ DANCE THEATER, INC.
4 East 89th Street, #PH-C, New York, NY 10128
(212) 722-4128
Founded: 1976
Arts Area: Modern; Ethnic
Status: Non-Profit
Type: Performing; Touring; Educational
Purpose: To create excellent and original dances; to educate through art
Management: Sonia Miller, Management Consultant
Officers: Annabella Gonzalez, Director; Richard Grimm, Board Chairman; Claude M. Scales, Board Secretary; George Budabin, Carolyn Sanchez, Board Members
Paid Staff: 1   **Volunteer Staff:** 1
Paid Artists: 5   **Non-Paid Artists:** 2
Utilizes: Special Technical Talent; Guest Artists; Guest Choreographers
Budget: $1,000 - $50,000
Income Sources: Private Foundations/Grants/Endowments; Business/Corporate Donations; Box Office; Government Grants; Individual Donations; Class Fees
Season: 52 Weeks
Annual Attendance: 10,000
Affiliations: DTW; The American Dance Guild; The Association of Hispanic Arts

ART BRIDGMAN/MYRNA PACKER
c/o Foundation for Independent Artists, 104 Franklin, New York, NY 10013
(914) 268-9008
Arts Area: Contempory
Status: Professional; Non-Profit
Type: Performing; Touring; Resident; Educational
Purpose: To perform the works and choreography of Myrna Packer and Art Bridgman
Management: Art Bridgman, Myrna Packer, Co-Managers/Choreographers
Budget: $50,000 - $100,000
Income Sources: Business/Corporate Donations; Government Grants; Individual Donations; Touring Fees

ASIAN AMERICAN DANCE THEATRE
26 Bowery, New York, NY 10013
(212) 233-2154
Founded: 1974
Arts Area: Modern; Ethnic; Folk
Status: Professional; Non-Profit
Type: Performing; Touring; Educational
Purpose: Promote traditional Asian dance and its synthesis with traditional dance by performing and visual art programs, concerts, exhibitions, research center and a forum for critical exchange
Management: Eleanor Yung, Artistic Director; Ananya Chatterjea, Manager
Paid Staff: 3
Paid Artists: 25
Utilizes: Guest Artists; Guest Choreographers
Budget: $50,000 - $100,000
Income Sources: Box Office; Government Grants
Season: September - August

BALLET HISPANICO OF NEW YORK
167 West 89th Street, New York, NY 10024
(212) 362-6710
   Founded: 1970
   Arts Area: Modern; Ballet; Ethnic
   Status: Professional; Non-Profit
   Type: Performing; Touring; Educational
   Purpose: To provide performances and training in contemporary and traditional Hispanic-American dance
   Management: Tina Ramirez, Artistic Director; Verdery Roosevelt, Executive Director
   Officers: Dhuanne Tansill, President
   Paid Staff: 55   **Volunteer Staff:** 15
   Paid Artists: 33
   Utilizes: Guest Choreographers
   Budget: $1,000,000 - $5,000,000
   Income Sources: Private Foundations/Grants/Endowments; Business/Corporate Donations; Box Office; Government Grants; Individual Donations
   Season: 52 Weeks   **Annual Attendance:** 60,000
   Affiliations: Dance USA
   Performance Facilities: The Joyce Theater

BALLET MANHATTAN FOUNDATION, INC.
61 West 62nd Street, Suite 17M, New York, NY 10023
(212) 315-4478
FAX: (212) 272-6527
   Founded: 1985
   Arts Area: Modern; Ballet
   Status: Non-Profit
   Type: Performing; Touring
   Purpose: To perform eclectic works by contemporary choreographers to a wide audience throughout the world
   Management: Paul Croitoroo, Executive Director; Charla Genn, Artistic Director; Carollyn Philip, Development Director
   Officers: Charla Genn, Vice President; Lawrence C. Manson III; Paul Croitoroo
   Paid Staff: 1   **Volunteer Staff:** 2
   Paid Artists: 20
   Utilizes: Guest Choreographers
   Budget: $100,000 - $500,000
   Income Sources: Private Foundations/Grants/Endowments; Box Office; Individual Donations; Performance Fees
   Annual Attendance: 100,000

BATTERY DANCE COMPANY
380 Broadway, Fifth Floor, New York, NY 10013
(212) 219-3910
FAX: (212) 219-3911
   Founded: 1976
   Arts Area: Modern
   Status: Professional
   Type: Performing; Touring; Resident; Educational; Sponsoring
   Management: Jonathan Hollander, Artistic Director; Catherine Iannone, Company Manager; Audrey Ross, Press Representative
   Officers: Steven Field, Chairman; Robert Brodeegaard, Vice Chairman; Jonathan Hollander, President
   Paid Staff: 3   **Volunteer Staff:** 4
   Paid Artists: 15
   Utilizes: Guest Conductors
   Budget: $100,000 - $500,000
   Income Sources: Private Foundations/Grants/Endowments; Business/Corporate Donations; Box Office; Government Grants; Individual Donations
   Season: 52 Weeks   **Annual Attendance:** 25,000
   Affiliations: Pace University
   Performance Facilities: French Alliance; Florence Gould Hall

BEBE MILLER COMPANY
c/o Gotham Dance Inc., 54 West 21st Street, Suite 502, New York, NY 10010
(212) 242-6433
FAX: (212) 645-6317
   Arts Area: Modern
   Status: Professional; Non-Profit
   Type: Performing; Touring; Resident
   Purpose: To perform the works of Bebe Miller throughout the United States and abroad
   Management: Bebe Miller, Artistic Director; Tricia Pierson, Managing Director

Budget: $100,000 - $500,000
Income Sources: Private Foundations/Grants/Endowments; Business/Corporate Donations; Box Office; Government Grants; Individual Donations

BILL T. JONES/ARNIE ZANE AND COMPANY
853 Broadway, Suite 1706, New York, NY 10003
(212) 477-1850
   Founded: 1979
   Arts Area: Modern
   Status: Professional; Non-Profit
   Type: Performing; Touring
   Purpose: To promote the works of choreographers Bill T. Jones and Arnie Zane
   Management: Billena Briggs, Executive Director; Jodi Krizer, Associate Director; Bill T. Jones, Artistic Director
   Paid Staff: 5
   Paid Artists: 11
   Budget: $500,000 - $1,000,000
   Income Sources: Private Foundations/Grants/Endowments; Business/Corporate Donations; Box Office; Government Grants; Individual Donations
   Season: 52 Weeks

BRUCE KING FOUNDATION FOR AMERICAN DANCE
160 West 73rd Street, New York, NY 10023
(212) 877-6700
   Founded: 1959
   Arts Area: Modern
   Status: Professional; Non-Profit
   Type: Performing; Educational
   Management: Bruce King Foundation
   Officers: Bruce King, President; R.E. Townsend, Secretary; Ron Rader, Treasurer
   Volunteer Staff: 3
   Paid Artists: 1
   Utilizes: Special Technical Talent
   Budget: $1,000 - $50,000
   Income Sources: Box Office; Individual Donations
   Affiliations: AEA; AFTRA

CARLOTA SANTANA SPANISH DANCE COMPANY
One University Place, New York, NY 10003
(212) 473-4605
   Founded: 1983
   Arts Area: Ethnic
   Status: Professional; Non-Profit
   Type: Performing; Touring; Resident; Educational
   Purpose: To create new ways to work within the traditional Spanish dance vocabulary; to develop new Spanish dance music
   Management: Cliff Scott, Downtown Art Company
   Officers: Carlota Santana, Artistic Director; Alexandra Teaff, Administrative Assistant
   Paid Staff: 3
   Paid Artists: 12
   Utilizes: Guest Artists; Guest Choreographers
   Budget: $50,000 - $100,000
   Income Sources: Private Foundations/Grants/Endowments; Business/Corporate Donations; Box Office; Government Grants; Individual Donations
   Season: 52 Weeks

CAROL FONDA AND COMPANY/DANCE FORUM, INC.
111 Sullivan Street, Suite B, New York, NY 10012
(212) 431-3364
   Founded: 1978
   Arts Area: Modern
   Status: Professional; Non-Profit
   Type: Performing; Touring; Resident; Educational
   Purpose: Performing arts series; Arts-in-Education projects; health and wellness projects
   Management: Carol Fonda, Acting Managing Director
   Officers: Dominick Attanasio, President/Phizer; Russ O'Haver, Vice President/Ernst & Young; Carol Fonda, Vice President/Artistic Director; Denise Mason, Finance Officer/Ernst & Young; Pat Lewis, Vice President/Citibank
   Paid Staff: 1   **Volunteer Staff:** 3
   Paid Artists: 6
   Budget: $50,000 - $100,000

Income Sources: Private Foundations/Grants/Endowments; Business/Corporate Donations; Box Office; Individual Donations; Health & Education products
Annual Attendance: 3,000
Performance Facilities: Triplex; DIA Arts Center

CHARLES MOULTON DANCE COMPANY
285 Mott Street, #18A, New York, NY 10012
(212) 226-3616
Arts Area: Modern; Tap
Status: Professional; Non-Profit
Type: Performing; Touring
Purpose: To make art
Paid Staff: 3   Volunteer Staff: 1
Paid Artists: 7
Budget: $50,000 - $100,000
Income Sources: Private Foundations/Grants/Endowments; Business/Corporate Donations; Box Office; Government Grants; Individual Donations
Season: 52 Weeks   Annual Attendance: 2,000
Performance Facilities: Performance Space 122

CHEN AND DANCERS
70 Mulberry Street, 2nd Floor, New York, NY 10013
(212) 349-0126
Founded: 1978
Arts Area: Modern
Status: Professional; Non-Profit
Type: Performing; Touring; Resident; Educational
Purpose: Chen and Dancers is a professional touring dance company performing contemporary works rooted in an Asian-American heritage.
Management: H.T. Chen, Artistic Director; Dian Dong, Associate Director; Osamu Uehara, Company Associate; David B. Cheng, Business Manager; Catherine M. Vaucher, Development Coordinator; Sumon Chin, School Administrator, AGC
Officers: Chris Wu, President/Chairman
Paid Staff: 14   Volunteer Staff: 2
Paid Artists: 12
Utilizes: Guest Choreographers
Budget: $100,000 - $500,000
Income Sources: Private Foundations/Grants/Endowments; Business/Corporate Donations; Box Office; Government Grants; Individual Donations
Season: 52 Weeks   Annual Attendance: 20,000
Affiliations: APAP

CHINESE FOLK DANCE COMPANY
c/o NY Chinese Cultural Center, 90 West Broadway, #5A, New York, NY 10007
(212) 964-7903
FAX: (212) 732-2482
Founded: 1973
Arts Area: Ethnic; Folk
Status: Professional; Non-Profit
Type: Performing; Touring; Educational
Purpose: To perform, present and commission traditional and contemporary dances in the Chinese idiom
Management: Amy Chin, Executive Director
Paid Staff: 2   Volunteer Staff: 1
Paid Artists: 20
Utilizes: Guest Artists
Budget: $50,000 - $100,000
Income Sources: Private Foundations/Grants/Endowments; Business/Corporate Donations; Box Office; Government Grants; Individual Donations; Tuition; Fees
Season: 52 Weeks   Annual Attendance: 22,000
Performance Facilities: Triplex Performing Arts Center/Borough of Manhattan Community College

CODANCECO
47 West 73rd Street, New York, NY 10023
(516) 286-7939
Founded: 1983
Arts Area: Modern
Status: Professional; Non-Profit
Type: Performing; Touring; Resident
Management: Nancy Duncan, Producing Director
Paid Staff: 2

Paid Artists: 12
Utilizes: Guest Artists
Budget: $50,000 - $100,000
Income Sources: Private Foundations/Grants/Endowments; Business/Corporate Donations; Box Office; Government Grants; Individual Donations

COURANTE DANCE COMPANY
335 West 35th Street, 12th Floor, New York, NY 10001
(212) 695-3943
Founded: 1981
Arts Area: Historical
Status: Professional
Type: Performing; Touring; Educational
Purpose: To recreate dance from the 16th to 19th centuries; to provide a resource for theater and dance performance practice in historical dance style
Management: Janis Pforsich, Director
Officers: Janis Pforsich, President; Larry Gillaspie, Treasurer; Eleanor Siebold, Secretary
Utilizes: Special Technical Talent; Guest Conductors; Guest Musicians
Budget: $1,000 - $50,000
Income Sources: Private Foundations/Grants/Endowments; Box Office; Individual Donations
Affiliations: Society of Dance History Scholars

DAN WAGONER AND DANCERS
476 Broadway, New York, NY 10013
(212) 334-1880
FAX: (212) 941-1071
Founded: 1969
Arts Area: Modern
Status: Professional; Non-Profit
Type: Performing; Touring; Resident; Educational
Purpose: To maintain Dan Wagoner's dance company; to facilitate the making of new works and the performance of the repertory of Dan Wagoner
Management: Dan Wagoner, Artistic Director; Renee Aarons, Administrative Director; Karen Kloster, Company Manager; Laura Marlow, Development Associate
Officers: Russell Piccione, President; Grace Goodman, Vice President; Edward Henry, Treasurer; Essie Borden, Secretary
Paid Staff: 4 **Volunteer Staff:** 12
Paid Artists: 9
Utilizes: Special Technical Talent; Guest Artists; Guest Accompanists
Budget: $100,000 - $500,000
Income Sources: Private Foundations/Grants/Endowments; Business/Corporate Donations; Box Office; Government Grants; Individual Donations
Season: 52 Weeks **Annual Attendance:** 15,000

DANCE - JUNE LEWIS AND COMPANY
48 West 21st Street, New York, NY 10010
(212) 741-3044
Founded: 1968
Arts Area: Modern
Status: Professional
Type: Performing; Touring; Resident; Educational
Management: Mel Leifer, Publicity Manager; June Lewis, Artistic Director
Paid Artists: 11

DANCE COLLECTIVE
463 West Street, 512A, New York, NY 10014
(212) 624-4275
FAX: (718) 398-9898
Founded: 1974
Arts Area: Modern
Status: Professional; Non-Profit
Type: Performing; Touring
Management: Carol Nolte, Artistic Director; Deborah Demast, Assistant Director
Officers: Allyn Freeman, Chairman, Board of Directors; Stanley Alpert, Attorney
Paid Staff: 1 **Volunteer Staff:** 4
Paid Artists: 6
Budget: $1,000 - $50,000
Income Sources: Private Foundations/Grants/Endowments; Box Office; Individual Donations
Season: September - June

DANCE THEATRE OF HARLEM
466 West 152nd Street, New York, NY 10031
(212) 690-2800
> **Founded:** 1969
> **Arts Area:** Ballet
> **Status:** Professional; Non-Profit
> **Type:** Performing; Touring; Educational
> **Purpose:** To provide creative and educational opportunities for youngsters while maintaining a professional dance company
> **Management:** Arthur Mitchell, Artistic Director; Robert Taylor, Executive Director; Amy Wynn, Director of Administration
> **Officers:** Shahara Ahmad-Llewellyn, Chair; Della Baeza, Gordon Davis, Vice Chairs; Arthur Mitchell, President; Kenneth Ross, Treasurer; Ponchita Pierce, Secretary
> **Paid Staff:** 51 **Volunteer Staff:** 1
> **Paid Artists:** 52
> **Utilizes:** Special Technical Talent; Guest Conductors; Guest Choreographers
> **Budget:** $5,000,000 - $10,000,000
> **Income Sources:** Private Foundations/Grants/Endowments; Business/Corporate Donations; Box Office; Government Grants; Individual Donations; Performance Fees; Tuition
> **Season:** March - April
> **Annual Attendance:** 21,000

DANCE THEATRE WORKSHOP
219 West 19th Street, New York, NY 10011
(212) 691-0173
> **Founded:** 1965
> **Arts Area:** Modern
> **Status:** Professional; Non-Profit
> **Type:** Performing
> **Purpose:** To identify and nurture the most provocative and visionary independent artists at work in the contemporary arena of dance, performance, theatre, music and allied arts
> **Management:** David R. White, Artistic Director/Producer; Laura Shandlemyer, Associate Producer; Gail Goldstein, Assistant Producer
> **Officers:** Bessie Schoenberg, Chairman; Carol Brice Buchanan, Secretary of Development
> **Paid Staff:** 25 **Volunteer Staff:** 5
> **Budget:** $1,000,000 - $5,000,000
> **Income Sources:** Private Foundations/Grants/Endowments; Business/Corporate Donations; Box Office; Government Grants; Individual Donations
> **Season:** August - June **Annual Attendance:** 25,000
> **Performance Facilities:** Bessie Schoenberg Theater

DANCE 2000: THE FELICE LESSER DANCE THEATER
484 West 43rd Street, #4J, New York, NY 10036
(212) 594-3388
> **Founded:** 1975
> **Arts Area:** Modern; Ballet
> **Status:** Professional; Non-Profit
> **Type:** Performing; Touring; Resident; Educational
> **Purpose:** To engage in the creation of new dance works; To perform, teach and tour
> **Management:** Felice Lesser, Artistic Director
> **Utilizes:** Special Technical Talent; Guest Artists; Composers; Fine Artists
> **Budget:** $1,000 - $50,000
> **Income Sources:** Private Foundations/Grants/Endowments; Business/Corporate Donations; Box Office; Individual Donations

DANCEBRAZIL
c/o Capoeira Foundation Inc., 104 Franklin Street, New York, NY 10013
(212) 274-9737
FAX: (212) 925-0369
> **Arts Area:** Modern; Ethnic; Folk
> **Status:** Professional; Non-Profit
> **Type:** Performing; Touring; Resident; Educational; Sponsoring
> **Purpose:** To produce, perform and preserve traditional and contemporary Brazilian and Afro-Brazilian dance and music; to explore, educate and innovate within the context of a culturally specific art form so that an African-based tradition is renewed and maintained, new audiences are created and linkages among differing communities are built
> **Management:** Jelon Viera, Artistic Director; Nem Brito, Associate Artistic Director
> **Budget:** $100,000 - $500,000

Income Sources: Private Foundations/Grants/Endowments; Business/Corporate Donations; Box Office; Government Grants; Individual Donations

DANCELLINGTON, INC.
PO Box 20346, Parkwest Finance Station, New York, NY 10025
(212) 724-5562
Founded: 1982
Arts Area: Modern; Ballet; Jazz; Ethnic; Tap
Status: Professional; Non-Profit; Commercial
Type: Performing; Touring; Educational
Purpose: To preserve tap dance heritage and its place in American history; to present the development of tap dance combining other dance forms
Management: Mercedes Ellington, Artistic Director; Ilona Copen, Advisory Coimmittee Chair; Florio Roettger, Financial Advisor; Rosemary Joyce, Public Relations/Grant Producer
Officers: Mercedes Ellington, President; Ruth B. Boatwright, Vice President; Denise Batts, Secretary
Volunteer Staff: 4
Non-Paid Artists: 16
Utilizes: Special Technical Talent; Guest Artists; Guest Choreographers; Grant Writers
Budget: $1,000 - $50,000
Income Sources: Private Foundations/Grants/Endowments; Business/Corporate Donations; Box Office; Government Grants; Individual Donations
Season: 52 Weeks

DANCING IN THE KITCHEN SERIES
c/o Haleakala Inc., 512 West 19th Street, New York, NY 10011
(212) 255-5793
FAX: (212) 645-4258
Arts Area: Modern
Status: Professional; Non-Profit
Type: Performing; Resident; Educational; Sponsoring
Purpose: To identify and nurture artists whose distinguished voices contribute to the development of the field; to reflect a diversity of artists from a vast landscape of cultural perspectives, exploring their own issues of personal and cultural identity through their work
Management: Lauren Amazeen, Executive Director; JoAnn Jansen, Dance Curator
Officers: Paula Cooper, Chairman of the Board
Income Sources: Private Foundations/Grants/Endowments; Business/Corporate Donations; Box Office; Government Grants; Individual Donations
Performance Facilities: The Kitchen

DANCING IN THE STREETS, INC.
131 Varick Street, Suite 903, New York, NY 10013
(212) 989-6830
FAX: (212) 727-2535
Arts Area: Modern; Ethnic; Folk
Status: Professional; Non-Profit
Type: Producing
Purpose: To make performing arts recognized as a public art form, drawing attention to unusual architecture and natural settings; to bring the work of innovative artists to new audiences
Management: Elise Bernhardt, Executive Director/Producer
Budget: $100,000 - $500,000
Income Sources: Private Foundations/Grants/Endowments; Business/Corporate Donations; Government Grants; Individual Donations

DANSE MIRAGE, INC./ELINOR COLEMAN DANCE EMSEMBLE
153 Mercer Street, 2nd Floor, New York, NY 10012-3239
(212) 226-5767
FAX: (212) 219-0601
Founded: 1982
Arts Area: Modern; Jazz
Status: Professional
Type: Performing; Touring; Educational; Sponsoring
Management: Donna M. Bost, Managing Director
Officers: Elinor Coleman, President/Artistic Director
Paid Staff: 3　**Volunteer Staff:** 2
Paid Artists: 10
Budget: $100,000 - $500,000
Income Sources: Private Foundations/Grants/Endowments; Business/Corporate Donations; Individual Donations
Season: September - July

THE DANSPACE PROJECT, INC.
St. Mark's Church, Second Avenue and Tenth Street, New York, NY 10003
(212) 674-8112
FAX: (212) 529-2318
  Founded: 1974
  Arts Area: Modern; Experimental; Postmodern
  Status: Professional; Non-Profit
  Type: Performing; Artists Services
  Purpose: To present new choreography by emerging and seasoned artists
  Management: Laurie Uprichard, Executive Director
  Officers: Penelope Dannenberg, President; Elizabeth Berger, Vice President; Elizabeth Rectanus, Bebe Miller, Co-Treasurers; Pamela Auchincloss, Secretary
  Paid Staff: 7   **Volunteer Staff:** 20
  Paid Artists: 50
  Utilizes: Guest Artists; Guest Choreographers
  Budget: $100,000 - $500,000
  Income Sources: Private Foundations/Grants/Endowments; Business/Corporate Donations; Box Office; Government Grants; Individual Donations
  Season: September - June   **Annual Attendance:** 9,000
  Performance Facilities: Sanctuary Performace Space at St. Mark's Church

DAVID GORDON/PICK UP COMPANY
104 Franklin, New York, NY 10013
(212) 431-0447
FAX: (212) 431-0425
  Founded: 1978
  Arts Area: Modern; Theater
  Status: Professional; Non-Profit
  Type: Performing; Touring; Resident
  Purpose: To produce and promote the work of David Gordon
  Management: June Poster, Managing Director
  Officers: Arlene Shuler, Chairperson; Michael Brill, Vice Chairperson; Michael Remer, Secretary
  Paid Staff: 2   **Volunteer Staff:** 1
  Paid Artists: 15
  Budget: $100,000 - $500,000
  Income Sources: Private Foundations/Grants/Endowments; Business/Corporate Donations; Box Office; Government Grants; Individual Donations
  Affiliations: Dance USA; APAP; WAAA

DAVID PARSONS DANCE COMPANY
476 Broadway, New York, NY 10013
(212) 941-1038
FAX: (212) 941-1071
  Founded: 1985
  Arts Area: Modern; Ballet
  Status: Professional
  Type: Performing; Touring; Resident; Educational
  Purpose: To create and perform modern dance; to educate and experiment
  Management: Sheldon Soffer, Management; David Parsons, Artistic Director; Gray Montague, Executive Director
  Paid Staff: 3
  Paid Artists: 8
  Utilizes: Guest Artists
  Budget: $500,000 - $1,000,000
  Income Sources: Private Foundations/Grants/Endowments; Business/Corporate Donations; Box Office; Government Grants; Individual Donations
  Season: 52 Weeks   **Annual Attendance:** 180,000

DINOSAUR DANCE COMPANY
211 West 61st Street, 4th Floor, New York, NY 10023
(212) 315-3616
  Founded: 1968
  Arts Area: Modern
  Status: Professional; Non-Profit
  Type: Performing; Touring
  Purpose: Modern dance performances, self-produced, and touring
  Management: Michael Mao, Artistic Director; Joseph Richards, Manager Director
  Officers: Elizabeth Mallinckroot, President; Michael Klein, Treasurer

Paid Staff: 4   **Volunteer Staff:** 15
Paid Artists: 15
Utilizes: Special Technical Talent; Guest Artists
Budget: $100,000 - $500,000
Income Sources: Private Foundations/Grants/Endowments; Box Office; Government Grants; Individual Donations
Season: March - May - September - November
Performance Facilities: Studio Workshop

THE DONALD BYRD DANCE FOUNDATION, INC.
59 Franklin Street, New York, NY 10013
(212) 431-7362
FAX: (212) 431-3025
Founded: 1984
Arts Area: Modern; Ballet; Jazz
Status: Professional
Type: Performing; Touring; Resident; Educational
Purpose: To introduce dance to as wide an audience as possible
Management: Donald Byrd, Artistic Director; Dee Warfield, Administrative Director; Fabio Pacciucci, Development Director
Officers: Donald Byrd, President; Andrea Reese, Treasurer; Clarence Clark, Secretary
Paid Staff: 3   **Volunteer Staff:** 2
Paid Artists: 14
Utilizes: Special Technical Talent; Guest Artists; Guest Choreographers
Budget: $100,000 - $500,000
Income Sources: Private Foundations/Grants/Endowments; Business/Corporate Donations; Box Office; Government Grants; Individual Donations
Season: September - March
Annual Attendance: 20,000

DOUG ELKINS DANCE COMPANY
PO Box 951, New York, NY 10011
(212) 228-2071
Founded: 1987
Arts Area: Modern; Street Styles; House Styles
Status: Professional; Non-Profit
Type: Performing; Educational
Purpose: To create and present the work of Doug Elkins; to teach all levels and ages
Management: Doug Elkins, Artistic Director; Jane Weiner, Company Manager; Lisa Nicks, Financial Director; Cathy Zimmerman, Booking
Paid Staff: 4
Paid Artists: 9
Utilizes: Guest Artists
Budget: $50,000 - $100,000
Income Sources: Private Foundations/Grants/Endowments; Box Office; Government Grants; Individual Donations
Season: September - August
Annual Attendance: 10,000

DOUGLAS DUNN AND DANCERS
c/o Rio Grande Union, Inc., 541 Broadway, New York, NY 10012
(212) 966-6999
FAX: (212) 274-1804
Founded: 1976
Arts Area: Modern
Status: Professional; Non-Profit
Type: Performing; Touring; Educational
Purpose: To produce and promote the works of contemporary choreographer Douglas Dunn
Management: Elizabeth Powers, Manager; Jessica Baker, Booking Representative-Pentacle
Officers: Christopher Sweet, Amy Lamphere, Anne Bradner, Douglas Dunn, Directors
Paid Staff: 2
Paid Artists: 8
Utilizes: Special Technical Talent
Budget: $100,000 - $500,000
Income Sources: Private Foundations/Grants/Endowments; Business/Corporate Donations; Box Office; Government Grants; Individual Donations; Presenter Commissions
Season: 52 Weeks
Annual Attendance: 10,000
Affiliations: Pentacle/Danceworks, Inc.

EDITH STEPHEN ELECTRIC CURRENTS
55 Bethune Street, 630 A, New York, NY 10014
(212) 989-2250
> **Founded:** 1980
> **Arts Area:** Modern
> **Status:** Professional
> **Type:** Performing; Touring
> **Purpose:** To perform throughout the United States and Europe giving multimedia programs combining dance with film, sculpture, new music and visuals
> **Management:** Ben Jennings, Company Manager
> **Officers:** Lee Wallace, President Board of Directors; Lucille Jason, Treasurer; Elaine Shipman, Secretary
> **Paid Staff:** 3
> **Paid Artists:** 6   **Non-Paid Artists:** 1
> **Utilizes:** Special Technical Talent
> **Budget:** $50,000 - $100,000
> **Income Sources:** Private Foundations/Grants/Endowments; Box Office; Government Grants; Individual Donations
> **Season:** 52 Weeks
> **Annual Attendance:** 5,000
> **Affiliations:** American Dance Guild; Foundation for the Advancement of Dance; American Dance Guild
> **Performance Facilities:** Dance Connection

EDWARD VILLELLA AND DANCERS
316 West 82nd Street, 1R, New York, NY 10024
(914) 462-7384
FAX: (914) 462-1858
> **Founded:** 1976
> **Arts Area:** Ballet
> **Status:** Professional
> **Type:** Performing; Touring; Resident; Educational
> **Purpose:** To illuminate the art of ballet
> **Management:** Marcia Preiss, Management
> **Paid Artists:** 5
> **Budget:** $1,000 - $50,000
> **Income Sources:** Fees
> **Season:** 52 Weeks

EIKO AND KOMA
c/o Foundation for Independent Artists, 104 Franklin Street, New York, NY 10013
(212) 226-2000
FAX: (212) 925-0369
> **Arts Area:** Contemporary
> **Status:** Professional; Non-Profit
> **Type:** Performing; Touring; Resident; Educational
> **Purpose:** To perform the theater choreography of Eiko and Koma
> **Management:** Eiko and Koma Otake, Artistic Directors/Choreographers
> **Budget:** $100,000 - $500,000
> **Income Sources:** Business/Corporate Donations; Government Grants; Touring Income; Fees

ELEO POMARE DANCE COMPANY
325 West 16th Street, New York, NY 10011
(212) 924-4628
> **Founded:** 1958
> **Arts Area:** Modern
> **Status:** Professional; Non-Profit
> **Type:** Performing; Touring; Resident; Educational
> **Management:** Eleo Pomare, Company Manager
> **Paid Staff:** 3
> **Paid Artists:** 20
> **Season:** 52 Weeks

ELISA MONTE DANCE COMPANY
39 Great Jones Street, New York, NY 10012
(212) 533-2226
FAX: (212) 254-4071
> **Founded:** 1981
> **Arts Area:** Modern
> **Status:** Professional; Non-Profit
> **Type:** Performing; Touring; Educational

Purpose: To advance and enrich the art of dance through the presentation of the innovative choreography and outreach activities of Elisa Monte
Management: Bernard G. Schmidt, Managing Director
Officers: Elisa Monte, President; David Brown, Treasurer; Nathalie Berliet, Chair
Paid Staff: 2   **Volunteer Staff:** 2
Paid Artists: 9
Budget: $100,000 - $500,000
Income Sources: Private Foundations/Grants/Endowments; Business/Corporate Donations; Box Office; Government Grants; Individual Donations
Season: 52 Weeks   **Annual Attendance:** 30,000
Affiliations: Dance USA
Performance Facilities: The Joyce Theater

ERICK HAWKINS DANCE COMPANY
38 East 19th Street, 8th Floor, New York, NY 10003
(212) 777-7355
Founded: 1952
Arts Area: Modern
Status: Professional; Non-Profit
Type: Performing; Touring; Educational
Purpose: To perform the choreography of Erick Hawkins with an annual home season in New York City; to tour
Management: Erick Hawkins, Artistic Director; Robert Engstrom, President; Michael Wright, Executive Director; Beverly Wright, Booking Management
Officers: Michael Levin, Chairman of the Board
Paid Staff: 5   **Volunteer Staff:** 1
Paid Artists: 24
Utilizes: Special Technical Talent; Commissioned Music
Budget: $500,000 - $1,000,000
Income Sources: Private Foundations/Grants/Endowments; Business/Corporate Donations; Box Office; Government Grants; Individual Donations; Touring Fees; School Tuition
Season: 52 Weeks   **Annual Attendance:** 40,000
Affiliations: APAP

ERNESTA CORVINO'S DANCE CIRCLE COMPANY
c/o DanceCor, Inc., 451 West 50th Street, New York, NY 10019
(212) 582-0571
Founded: 1981
Arts Area: Ballet
Status: Professional; Non-Profit
Type: Performing
Purpose: To provide the public with high quality and affordable dance performances as well as workshops and lecture demonstrations
Management: Ernesta Corvino, Director; Andra Corvino, Ballet Mistress; Gail S. Block, Manager
Officers: Ernesta Corvino, President; Andra Corvino, Vice President; Robert E. Lynn, Treasurer/Secretary
Budget: $1,000 - $50,000
Income Sources: Box Office; Individual Donations
Performance Facilities: Marymount Manhattan Theatre

EUGENE JAMES DANCE COMPANY
GPO 2504, New York, NY 10116
(212) 564-1026
Founded: 1967
Arts Area: Modern; Ethnic
Status: Professional; Non-Profit
Type: Performing; Touring; Resident
Purpose: To extend the contributions of Afro-American rhythms in dance
Management: Richard Williams, Manager; Eugene James, Artistic Director
Volunteer Staff: 3
Paid Artists: 8
Budget: $1,000 - $50,000
Income Sources: Box Office; Individual Donations
Season: September - May

FELD BALLETS/NY
The Lawrence A. Wien Center for Dance & Theatre, 890 Broadway, New York, NY 10003
(212) 777-7710
FAX: (212) 353-0936
Founded: 1974

Arts Area: Ballet
Status: Professional; Non-Profit
Type: Performing; Touring; Resident; Educational
Purpose: To perform the works of Eliot Feld that span his twenty-five years of choreography; the company tours both domestically and abroad and performs at the Joyce Theatre approximately six weeks a year and tours for approximately 10 weeks a year
Management: Eliot Feld, Director/Choreographer; Susan Spier, Director of Media and Public Relations; Eugene Lowery, Booking Manager; Susan J. Kirschner, Director of Finance; Roz Black, Director of Development; Zetta Zaka, Company Manager; Patrice Thomas, Production Manager
Officers: Eliot Feld, President; Cora Cahan, Vice President; Bernard Gersten, Treasurer; Peter L. Felcher Esq., Secretary
Paid Staff: 12   **Volunteer Staff:** 1
Paid Artists: 22
Budget: $1,000,000 - $5,000,000
Income Sources: Private Foundations/Grants/Endowments; Business/Corporate Donations; Box Office; Government Grants; Individual Donations; Sponsor Fees
Season: 52 Weeks
Annual Attendance: 21,000
Affiliations: AGMA
Performance Facilities: Joyce Theater

14TH STREET DANCE CENTER AT EDUCATIONAL ALLIANCE
197 East Broadway, New York, NY 10002
(212) 673-2207
Arts Area: Modern; Mime; Ballet; Jazz; Ethnic; Folk
Status: Non-Profit
Type: Sponsoring; Presenting
Purpose: To present contemporary music and dance at affordable prices
Management: Oceola Bragg, Executive/Artistic Director
Officers: Bradley Nance, Chairman of the Board
Budget: $100,000 - $500,000
Income Sources: Private Foundations/Grants/Endowments; Business/Corporate Donations; Box Office; Government Grants; Individual Donations
Performance Facilities: Theater at Educational Alliance

ICE THEATER OF NEW YORK, INC.
Sky Rink, 450 West 33rd Street, 16th Floor, New York, NY 10001
(212) 239-4320
FAX: (212) 239-4327
Arts Area: Modern
Status: Professional; Non-Profit
Type: Performing; Touring; Educational
Purpose: To build an artistic repertory of ice skating performance pieces; to provide an environment in which professional skaters from various backgrounds can collaborate with choreographers, musicians and visual artists to create and perform new works
Management: Moira North, Director; Rob McBrien, Artistic Director
Officers: William Candee III, Chairman
Budget: $100,000 - $500,000
Income Sources: Private Foundations/Grants/Endowments; Business/Corporate Donations; Box Office; Government Grants; Individual Donations
Performance Facilities: Sky Rink

JANIS BRENNER AND DANCERS
356 East 89th Street, 5A, New York, NY 10128
(212) 534-3227
Founded: 1987
Arts Area: Modern
Status: Professional; Non-Profit
Type: Performing; Touring; Educational
Purpose: To perform the work of Janis Brenner; to conduct teaching workshops in technique, improvisation, composition, repertory and voice
Management: Brenda Sale Artists Managment
Paid Artists: 6
Utilizes: Special Technical Talent; Guest Composers; Designers
Budget: $1,000 - $50,000
Income Sources: Private Foundations/Grants/Endowments; Business/Corporate Donations; Box Office; Individual Donations

JENNIFER MULLER-THE WORKS
131 West 24th Street, New York, NY 10011
(212) 691-3803
FAX: (212) 206-6630
Founded: 1970
Arts Area: Modern
Status: Professional; Non-Profit
Type: Performing; Touring; Resident
Management: Lauren Barnes, Executive Director; Jennifer Muller, Artistic Director
Paid Staff: 2 **Volunteer Staff:** 1
Paid Artists: 10
Utilizes: Guest Artists
Budget: $100,000 - $500,000
Income Sources: Private Foundations/Grants/Endowments; Business/Corporate Donations; Box Office; Government Grants; Individual Donations
Season: 52 Weeks

JOAN MILLER'S DANCE PLAYERS
1380 Riverside Drive, New York, NY 10033
(212) 568-8854
Founded: 1969
Arts Area: Modern; Ballet; Jazz; Ethnic
Status: Professional
Type: Performing; Touring
Purpose: Joan Miller's Dance Players are primarily a multi-ethnic performing company but are excellently qualified to teach a wide range of dance-related activities.
Management: Joan Miller, Artistic Director/Choreographer; Margaret Hanks, Company Manager
Officers: Samuel Coleman, President of the Board; Susan Skovronek, Vice President; Michael Flanigan, Treasurer; Davis Roberts, Secretary
Paid Staff: 3 **Volunteer Staff:** 5
Paid Artists: 15 **Non-Paid Artists:** 5
Utilizes: Special Technical Talent; Guest Artists
Budget: $1,000 - $50,000
Income Sources: Private Foundations/Grants/Endowments; Business/Corporate Donations; Box Office; Government Grants; Individual Donations
Season: October - June **Annual Attendance:** 9,000
Affiliations: DTW

JOFFREY BALLET
130 West 56th Street, New York, NY 10019
(212) 265-7300
FAX: (212) 397-1786
West Coast Operations Office: 14819 Magnolia Boulevard, Suite 202, Sherman Oaks, CA 91403; (818) 986-4503
Founded: 1956
Arts Area: Ballet
Status: Professional; Non-Profit
Type: Performing; Touring; Resident; Educational; Sponsoring
Management: Gerald Arpino, Artistic Director; C.C. Conner, Acting Executive Director; Roberta Stewart, West Coast Representative
Officers: Michael Tennebaum, Chairman
Paid Staff: 39 **Volunteer Staff:** 10
Paid Artists: 51
Utilizes: Special Technical Talent; Guest Choreographers
Budget: $5,000,000 - $10,000,000
Income Sources: Private Foundations/Grants/Endowments; Business/Corporate Donations; Box Office; Government Grants; Individual Donations
Annual Attendance: 250,000
Performance Facilities: City Center

THE JOFFREY II DANCERS
130 West 56th Street, New York, NY 10019
(212) 265-7300
Arts Area: Ballet
Status: Professional; Non-Profit
Type: Performing; Educational
Management: Jeremy Blanton, Artistic Director
Paid Artists: 10
Budget: $100,000 - $500,000

Income Sources: Private Foundations/Grants/Endowments; Business/Corporate Donations; Individual Donations
Season: September - May
Affiliations: Joffrey Ballet

JOSE LIMON DANCE COMPANY
622 Broadway, 5th Floor, New York, NY 10012
(212) 777-3353
FAX: (212) 777-4764
Founded: 1968
Arts Area: Modern
Status: Professional; Non-Profit
Type: Performing; Touring; Resident
Management: Carla Maxwell, Artistic Director
Paid Staff: 3
Paid Artists: 14
Utilizes: Special Technical Talent; Guest Artists; Guest Choreographers
Budget: $100,000 - $500,000
Income Sources: Private Foundations/Grants/Endowments; Business/Corporate Donations; Box Office; Government Grants; Individual Donations
Season: 52 Weeks

JUILLIARD DANCE ENSEMBLE
The Juilliard School, 60 Lincoln Center Plaza, New York, NY 10023
(212) 799-5000
Founded: 1951
Arts Area: Modern; Ballet; Jazz; Ethnic; Tap
Status: Non-Professional; Non-Profit
Type: Performing; Resident
Purpose: Training company
Management: Benjamin Jarkarvy, Artistic Director; Martha Hill, Artistic Director Emeritus
Non-Paid Artists: 30
Utilizes: Guest Artists
Season: November - March
Performance Facilities: Juilliard Theater

K2 DANCE AND ARTS COMPANY, INC.
336 East 5th Street, New York, NY 10003
(718) 852-5944
Founded: 1981
Arts Area: Modern
Status: Professional
Type: Performing; Educational
Purpose: To develop cultural awareness in the community through dance performances
Officers: Diane Roberts, Publicist; Penny Ward, Board Director; Kay Nishikawa, Artistic Director
Paid Staff: 2   **Volunteer Staff:** 2
Paid Artists: 8
Utilizes: Guest Artists
Budget: $1,000 - $50,000
Income Sources: Box Office; Individual Donations
Season: Fall; Winter   **Annual Attendance:** 1,000

KAZUKO HIRABAYASHI DANCE THEATRE
330 Broome Street, New York, NY 10002
(212) 966-6414
Founded: 1971
Arts Area: Modern
Status: Professional; Non-Profit
Type: Performing; Touring; Educational
Purpose: Combining her Japanese heritage, Eastern philosophy and artistic grounding, with a firm base in classical and modern dance, Kazuko Hirabayashi creates her own strikingly beautiful dance pieces. Performances to the public are offered, as well as educational programs.
Officers: Kazuko Hirabayashi, President; Robert Swinton, Vice President
Non-Paid Artists: 10
Budget: $1,000 - $50,000
Annual Attendance: 1,500
Performance Facilities: Kazuko Hirabayashi Dance Theatre

KEI TAKEI'S MOVING EARTH (MOVING EARTH INC.)
28 Vesey Street, #2200, New York, NY 10007
(212) 459-4383
FAX: (212) 732-3926
Founded: 1969
Arts Area: Modern
Status: Professional
Type: Performing; Touring
Purpose: To perform the internationally acclaimed, award-winning choreography of Kei Takei
Management: Laz Brezer, Executive Director
Officers: Kei Takei, Chairwoman; Louise Roberts, President; Maldwyn Pate, Vice President; Lawrence Brezer, Secretary/Treasurer
Paid Staff: 3   **Volunteer Staff:** 12
Paid Artists: 18   **Non-Paid Artists:** 8
Budget: $100,000 - $500,000
Income Sources: Private Foundations/Grants/Endowments; Business/Corporate Donations; Box Office; Government Grants; Individual Donations
Season: 52 Weeks   **Annual Attendance:** 100,000

KENNETH KING AND DANCERS
c/o Transmedia Kinetrics Coalition Inc., 104 Franklin, New York, NY 10013
(212) 226-2000; (212) 925-6917
FAX: (212) 925-0369
Arts Area: Contemporary
Status: Professional; Non-Profit
Type: Performing; Touring; Resident; Educational
Purpose: To perform the work and choreography of Kenneth King
Management: Kenneth King, Manager/Choreographer
Budget: $50,000 - $100,000
Income Sources: Business/Corporate Donations; Government Grants; Individual Donations; Touring Fees

LABAN/BARTENIEFF INSTITUTE OF MOVEMENT STUDIES
11 East Fourth Street, 3rd Floor, New York, NY 10003-6902
(212) 477-4299
FAX: (212) 477-3702
Founded: 1978
Arts Area: Modern; Mime; Ballet; Body Therapy; Movement Analysis
Status: Professional; Non-Professional; Non-Profit
Type: Performing; Educational; Sponsoring
Purpose: To teach Labon movement analysis, Bartenieff fundamentals and movement dance theatre and health
Management: Martha Eddy, Executive Director; Janis Pforsich, Certificate Director; Cheryl Clark, Programming Director
Officers: Frank Didero, Chair; Riccardo Gondolfo, Treasurer; Dorit Dyke, Vice President of Promotion; Karen Bradley, Vice President of Education
Paid Staff: 3
Utilizes: Guest Artists
Budget: $100,000 - $500,000
Income Sources: Private Foundations/Grants/Endowments; Business/Corporate Donations; Box Office; Government Grants; Individual Donations; Tuition
Season: September - July
Affiliations: NASD; Emergency Fund for Student Dancers; DTW: ADTA; International Movement Therapists Association; National Dance Association; International Association for Dance Medicine and Science

LAR LUBOVITCH DANCE COMPANY
15-17 West 18th Street, 5th Floor, New York, NY 10011-4601
(212) 242-0633
FAX: (212) 691-8315
Founded: 1968
Arts Area: Modern
Status: Professional; Non-Profit
Type: Performing; Touring; Educational
Purpose: The creation, performance and teaching of contemporary dance throughout the United States and the world
Management: Dick Caples, Executive Director; Lar Lubovitch, Artistic Director
Paid Staff: 5
Paid Artists: 16
Utilizes: Guest Artists
Budget: $1,000,000 - $5,000,000
Income Sources: Private Foundations/Grants/Endowments; Business/Corporate Donations; Box Office; Government Grants; Individual Donations

Season: 52 Weeks   **Annual Attendance:** 100,000
Affiliations: Dance USA; APAP
Performance Facilities: City Center Theater

LARRY RICHARDSON DANCE FOUNDATION
40 Park Avenue, New York, NY 10016
(212) 685-5972
> **Founded:** 1967
> **Arts Area:** Modern; Mime; Ballet; Jazz; Ethnic
> **Status:** Professional; Non-Profit
> **Type:** Performing; Resident; Educational; Sponsoring
> **Purpose:** To foster interest in and create a new audience for dance and the allied performing arts in the community
> **Management:** Larry Richardson, Artistic Director; J. Antony Siciliano, Administrative Director
> **Officers:** John Afton, Counsel
> **Paid Staff:** 4
> **Paid Artists:** 8
> **Utilizes:** Special Technical Talent; Guest Artists
> **Income Sources:** Box Office
> **Season:** 52 Weeks
> **Performance Facilities:** Larry Richardson's Dance Gallery

LAURA DEAN DANCERS AND MUSICIANS
260 West Broadway, New York, NY 10013
(212) 941-7746
> **Founded:** 1976
> **Arts Area:** Modern
> **Status:** Professional; Non-Profit
> **Type:** Performing; Touring; Educational
> **Purpose:** This internationally acclaimed company presents the works of choreographer/composer Laura Dean.
> **Management:** Laura Dean, Artistic Director; Michael Feibish, Managing Director; Mary Rindfleisch, Company Manager
> **Officers:** Charles Burger, Laura Dean, Fran Kaufman, W. McNeil Lowry, Elaine Malsin
> **Paid Staff:** 3   **Volunteer Staff:** 1
> **Paid Artists:** 17
> **Utilizes:** Special Technical Talent
> **Budget:** $500,000 - $1,000,000
> **Income Sources:** Private Foundations/Grants/Endowments; Business/Corporate Donations; Box Office; Government
> Grants; Individual Donations
> **Season:** 52 Weeks

LES BALLETS TROCKADERO DE MONTE CARLO
130 West 56 Street, New York, NY 10019
(212) 757-8060
> **Founded:** 1973
> **Arts Area:** Ballet
> **Status:** Professional; Non-Profit
> **Type:** Performing; Touring
> **Purpose:** Ballet parody
> **Management:** Sheldon Soffer Management
> **Paid Artists:** 12
> **Utilizes:** Guest Artists
> **Budget:** $500,000 - $1,000,000
> **Income Sources:** Box Office; Individual Donations
> **Season:** 52 Weeks

LUCINDA CHILDS DANCE COMPANY
541 Broadway, New York, NY 10012
(212) 431-7599
> **Founded:** 1973
> **Arts Area:** Modern
> **Status:** Professional; Non-Profit
> **Type:** Performing; Touring; Resident; Educational
> **Purpose:** To create and perform works by Lucinda Childs
> **Management:** Lucinda Childs, Artistic Director
> **Officers:** Lucinda Childs, President
> **Paid Staff:** 3
> **Paid Artists:** 10
> **Utilizes:** Special Technical Talent
> **Budget:** $100,000 - $500,000

Income Sources: Private Foundations/Grants/Endowments; Business/Corporate Donations; Government Grants; Individual Donations
Season: July - June **Annual Attendance:** 5,000
Affiliations: Dance USA; APAP; WAAA

LUIS RIVERA SPANISH DANCE COMPANY
232 East 26th Street, New York, NY 10010
(212) 689-0921
Founded: 1970
Arts Area: Ethnic; Folk
Status: Professional; Non-Profit; Commercial
Type: Performing; Touring; Educational
Purpose: To further the knowledge and appreciation of Spanish dance
Management: Luis Rivera, Artistic Director
Officers: Robert P. Luzell, President; Maura G. Luzell, Secretary/Treasurer; Ruth Ontiveros, Dale Goodwin, Directors
Paid Artists: 6
Utilizes: Special Technical Talent; Guest Artists
Income Sources: Box Office; Government Grants; Individual Donations

MANHATTAN BALLET FOUNDATION
61 West 62nd Street, New York, NY 10023
(212) 315-4478
Founded: 1985
Arts Area: Ballet; Contemporary
Status: Professional; Non-Profit
Type: Performing; Touring
Management: Charla Genn, Artistic Director; Paul Croitoroo, Executive Director; Karollyn Philip, Director of Development
Paid Staff: 3
Paid Artists: 16
Utilizes: Guest Artists
Budget: $100,000 - $500,000
Income Sources: Box Office; Individual Donations
Season: 52 Weeks

MARK DE GARMO AND DANCERS
179 East Third Street, #24, New York, NY 10009-7754
(212) 353-1351
FAX: (212) 353-1351
Founded: 1982
Arts Area: Modern
Status: Professional
Type: Performing; Touring; Resident; Educational
Purpose: To develop and perform the original choreography of Mark DeGarmo
Management: Jan Michael Hanvik, Manager
Paid Staff: 1 **Volunteer Staff:** 2
Paid Artists: 6
Budget: $50,000 - $100,000
Income Sources: Private Foundations/Grants/Endowments; Business/Corporate Donations; Box Office; Government Grants; Individual Donations
Season: 52 Weeks
Affiliations: Dance USA

MARK MORRIS DANCE GROUP
225 Lafayette Street, Suite 504, New York, NY 10012
(212) 219-3660
FAX: (212) 219-3960
Founded: 1980
Arts Area: Modern
Status: Professional; Non-Profit
Type: Performing; Touring
Purpose: To create and perform the works of Mark Morris
Management: Mark Morris, Artistic Director; Barry Alterman, General Director; Nancy Umanoff, Managing Director
Paid Staff: 9 **Volunteer Staff:** 2
Paid Artists: 17
Utilizes: Special Technical Talent; Guest Conductors; Guest Artists
Budget: $1,000,000 - $5,000,000

Income Sources: Private Foundations/Grants/Endowments; Business/Corporate Donations; Box Office; Government Grants; Individual Donations

MARTHA GRAHAM DANCE COMPANY
316 East 63rd Street, New York, NY 10021
(212) 832-9166
FAX: (212) 223-0351
Founded: 1926
Arts Area: Modern
Status: Professional; Non-Profit
Type: Performing; Touring; Educational
Purpose: To perform the original works of Martha Graham
Management: Ron Protas and Linda Hooks, Artistic Directors; Russ Alley, Executive Director; James M. Johnson, Director of Operations
Paid Staff: 12
Paid Artists: 30
Utilizes: Guest Conductors
Budget: $1,000,000 - $5,000,000
Income Sources: Private Foundations/Grants/Endowments; Business/Corporate Donations; Box Office; Government Grants; Individual Donations
Season: 52 Weeks

MARY ANTHONY DANCE THEATRE-PHOENIX
736 Broadway, New York, NY 10003
(212) 674-8191
Founded: 1956
Arts Area: Modern
Status: Professional; Non-Profit
Type: Performing; Touring; Educational
Purpose: To present modern dance through performances, lecture-demonstrations and technique classes
Management: Mary Anthony, Artistic Director
Officers: Mary Anthony, President
Paid Staff: 6   **Volunteer Staff:** 15
Paid Artists: 12
Budget: $50,000 - $100,000
Income Sources: Private Foundations/Grants/Endowments; Business/Corporate Donations; Box Office; Government Grants; Individual Donations

MERCE CUNNINGHAM DANCE COMPANY
55 Bethune Street, New York, NY 10014
(212) 255-8240
FAX: (212) 633-2453
Founded: 1964
Arts Area: Modern
Status: Professional; Non-Profit
Type: Performing; Touring; Educational
Purpose: To develop understanding and public interest in the field of dance through performances, dance instruction and videotapes
Management: Merce Cunningham, Artistic Director; Art Becofsky, Executive Director
Officers: Daniel Wolf, Chairman; Allan G. Sperling, Vice Chairman; Candace Krugman Beinecke, Treasurer; David Vaughan, Secretary/Archivist
Paid Staff: 36
Paid Artists: 27
Utilizes: Special Technical Talent; Guest Artists
Budget: $1,000,000 - $5,000,000
Income Sources: Private Foundations/Grants/Endowments; Business/Corporate Donations; Box Office; Government Grants; Individual Donations
Season: 52 Weeks
Affiliations: AGMA; NASD; Dance USA
Performance Facilities: Merce Cunningham Studio

MEREDITH MONK - THE HOUSE FOUNDATION FOR THE ARTS
131 Varick Street, Suite 901, New York, NY 10013
(212) 206-1440
Founded: 1968
Arts Area: Modern
Status: Professional; Non-Profit
Type: Performing; Touring; Educational

Purpose: Meredith Monk is an internationally renowned composer, director, singer, choreographer and filmmaker. The House Foundation for the Arts administrates her companies and activities.
Management: Meredith Monk, Artistic Director; Barbara Dufty, Managing Director; Sue Latham, Company Manager
Officers: Micki Wesson, President
Paid Staff: 4
Budget: $500,000 - $1,000,000
Income Sources: Private Foundations/Grants/Endowments; Business/Corporate Donations; Box Office; Government Grants; Individual Donations
Season: 52 Weeks
Affiliations: APAP; MAAA

MIMI GARRARD DANCE COMPANY
155 Wooster Street, New York, NY 10012
(212) 674-6868
Founded: 1972
Arts Area: Modern
Status: Professional; Non-Profit
Type: Performing; Touring; Resident
Purpose: To present original, professional dance theatre productions to the public and offer classes, and workshops for participants of all ages
Management: Liz Rodgers, Booking Manager
Officers: James Seawright, Secretary/Treasurer
Paid Staff: 1
Paid Artists: 8
Utilizes: Guest Artists
Budget: $1,000 - $50,000
Income Sources: Private Foundations/Grants/Endowments; Business/Corporate Donations; Box Office; Government Grants; Individual Donations
Season: September - June
Affiliations: DTW
Performance Facilities: Mimi Garrard Dance Company

MOMIX
130 West 56th Street, New York, NY 10019
(203) 868-7454
FAX: (203) 868-2317
Founded: 1980
Arts Area: Modern; Dancer Illusionists
Status: Professional; Commercial
Type: Performing; Touring
Purpose: Dance theatre
Management: Scheldon-Soffer Management; Moses Pendleton, Artistic Director
Paid Staff: 3
Paid Artists: 10
Utilizes: Guest Artists
Budget: $100,000 - $500,000
Income Sources: Box Office
Season: September - July

MULTIGRAVITATIONAL AERODANCE GROUP
234 East 23rd Street, New York, NY 10010
(212) 696-5274; (212) 255-8166
FAX: (212) 633-1128
Founded: 1971
Arts Area: Modern
Status: Professional; Non-Profit
Type: Performing; Touring
Purpose: The Multigravitational Aerodance Group is involved in the choreographic exploration of aerial dance/theatre. Aerodance performs on various suspended sculptural sets allowing the dancers to move through 360 degrees in space.
Management: Barbara Salz, Administrative Director
Officers: Dr. Kenneth L. Mathis, President; Catherine L. Woodman, Secretary
Paid Staff: 1   **Volunteer Staff:** 4
Paid Artists: 4
Utilizes: Special Technical Talent; Guest Artists
Budget: $1,000 - $50,000
Income Sources: Private Foundations/Grants/Endowments; Business/Corporate Donations; Box Office; Government Grants; Individual Donations
Season: 52 Weeks   **Annual Attendance:** 50,000
Performance Facilities: The Sirovich Center

THE NANETTE BEARDEN CONTEMPORARY DANCE THEATRE
357 Canal Street, New York, NY 10013
(212) 966-6828
>**Founded:** 1976
>**Arts Area:** Modern; Ballet; Jazz
>**Status:** Professional; Non-Profit
>**Type:** Performing; Resident
>**Purpose:** A choreographers collective, founded in 1976, their works are examined and performed, uniting modern and ballet
>**Management:** Nanette Bearden, Artistic Director; Walter Rutledge, Assistant Artistic Director
>**Paid Staff:** 4
>**Paid Artists:** 12
>**Utilizes:** Guest Artists; Guest Choreographers
>**Budget:** $100,000 - $500,000
>**Income Sources:** Private Foundations/Grants/Endowments; Business/Corporate Donations; Box Office; Government Grants; Individual Donations
>**Season:** 52 Weeks

NATIONAL DANCE INSTITUTE
594 Broadway, Room 805, New York, NY 10012
(212) 226-0083
FAX: (212) 226-0761
>**Founded:** 1976
>**Arts Area:** Modern; Jazz
>**Status:** Non-Profit
>**Type:** Performing; Educational
>**Purpose:** To make the arts, through the media of dance, a foundation of children's education; to reach children who otherwise would not have the opportunity to be involved in the arts
>**Management:** Jacques d'Amboise, Artistic Director/Choreographer; Barbara Vogdes, Executive Director
>**Officers:** Robert D. Krinsky, Acting Chairman
>**Paid Staff:** 15
>**Utilizes:** Special Technical Talent; Guest Conductors; Guest Artists; Guest Choreographers
>**Budget:** $1,000,000 - $5,000,000
>**Income Sources:** Private Foundations/Grants/Endowments; Business/Corporate Donations; Box Office; Government Grants; Individual Donations
>**Season:** September - June
>**Annual Attendance:** 10,000

NETA PULVERMACHER AND DANCERS
39 Claremont Avenue, #41, New York, NY 10027
(212) 316-3888
>**Founded:** 1987
>**Arts Area:** Modern; Ballet
>**Status:** Professional
>**Type:** Performing; Touring; Resident; Educational; Sponsoring
>**Purpose:** To bring contemporary performance arts to the public through performances
>**Management:** Circum Arts Foundation
>**Officers:** Neta Pulvermacher, President; Kate Foley, Treasurer/Secretary; Paul Hendrix, Vice President
>**Paid Staff:** 1   **Volunteer Staff:** 2
>**Paid Artists:** 12   **Non-Paid Artists:** 2
>**Utilizes:** Guest Choreographers
>**Budget:** $1,000 - $50,000
>**Income Sources:** Private Foundations/Grants/Endowments; Business/Corporate Donations; Box Office; Government Grants; Individual Donations
>**Annual Attendance:** 15,000
>**Affiliations:** DTW; Circum Arts

THE NEW BALLET SCHOOL
The Lawrence A. Wien Center for Dance and Theatre, 890 Broadway, New York, NY 10003
(212) 777-7710
FAX: (212) 353-0936
>**Founded:** 1978
>**Arts Area:** Ballet
>**Status:** Professional; Non-Profit
>**Type:** Educational
>**Purpose:** To provide tuition-free professional ballet training to gifted New York City Public School children; to reflect the variety of NYC's racial and ethnic population long absent from ballet schools and stages

Management: Eliot Feld, Founder and Director; Katherine Moore, Administrative Director; Elizabeth Barrow, Faculty Co-ordinator; Lynn Muller, Administrative Coordinator
Officers: Feld Ballets/NY
Paid Staff: 14   **Volunteer Staff:** 1
Utilizes: Special Technical Talent
Budget: $1,000,000 - $5,000,000
Income Sources: Private Foundations/Grants/Endowments; Business/Corporate Donations; Government Grants; Individual Donations
Affiliations: New York City Board of Education

NEW DANCE GROUP STUDIO INC.
254 West 47th Street, New York, NY 10036
(212) 719-2733
Founded: 1932
Arts Area: Modern; Ballet; Jazz; Ethnic
Status: Professional; Non-Profit
Type: Performing; Educational
Purpose: To foster the art of dance through a wide range of classes, scholarships, rehearsal space and performance
Management: Rick Schussel, Artistic/Executive Director
Paid Staff: 6
Budget: $100,000 - $500,000
Income Sources: Private Foundations/Grants/Endowments; Business/Corporate Donations; Government Grants
Season: 52 Weeks

THE NEW YORK BAROQUE DANCE COMPANY
280 Riverside Drive, #5H, New York, NY 10025
(212) 662-8829
Founded: 1976
Arts Area: Historical
Status: Professional
Type: Performing; Touring; Resident; Educational
Purpose: To revive the dances of the 18th century with a sense of spontaneity and scholarship and educate the public and the dance field
Officers: Catherine Turocy, Artistic Director; James Richman, Music Director
Paid Staff: 2   **Volunteer Staff:** 2
Paid Artists: 14   **Non-Paid Artists:** 2
Utilizes: Special Technical Talent; Guest Directors; Guest Choreographers
Budget: $100,000 - $500,000
Income Sources: Private Foundations/Grants/Endowments; Business/Corporate Donations; Box Office; Government Grants; Individual Donations

NEW YORK CITY BALLET
20 Lincoln Center, New York, NY 10023
(212) 877-4700
Founded: 1948
Arts Area: Ballet
Status: Professional; Non-Profit
Type: Performing; Touring; Resident; Educational
Management: Patricia Turk, General Director; Jerome Robbins, Ballet Master-In-Chief; Peter Martins, Ballet Master-in-Chief/Artistic Director; Lincoln Kirstein, Director Emeritus
Officers: Orville H. Schell, Paul A. Allaire, Co-Chairmans; Gillian Attfield, President/Chief Executive Officer; Marvin A. Asnes, Treasurer
Paid Staff: 45   **Volunteer Staff:** 400
Paid Artists: 185
Utilizes: Special Technical Talent
Budget: Over 10,000,000
Income Sources: Private Foundations/Grants/Endowments; Business/Corporate Donations; Box Office; Government Grants
Season: November - April - February - June   **Annual Attendance:** 420,000
Affiliations: School of American Ballet
Performance Facilities: New York State Theater

NIKOLAIS AND MURRAY LOUIS DANCE COMPANY
375 West Broadway, New York, NY 10012
(212) 226-7700
FAX: (212) 226-0442
Founded: 1953
Arts Area: Modern
Status: Professional; Non-Profit

Type: Performing; Touring; Resident; Educational
Purpose: To present the choreographic work of Murray Louis and Alwin Nikolais and to display their aesthetics of dance
Management: Ian McColl, Director of Development/Company Manager
Officers: Murray Louis, Alwin Nikolais, Co-Artistic Directors
Paid Staff: 4
Paid Artists: 11
Budget: $500,000 - $1,000,000
Income Sources: Private Foundations/Grants/Endowments; Business/Corporate Donations; Box Office; Government Grants; Individual Donations
Season: 52 Weeks
Affiliations: APAP; Dance USA; AAA

PAUL TAYLOR DANCE COMPANY
552 Broadway, New York, NY 10012
(212) 431-5562
FAX: (212) 966-5673
Founded: 1966
Arts Area: Modern
Status: Professional; Non-Profit
Type: Performing; Touring; Resident
Purpose: To promote interest in dance, allow creation of new dance works and present them to broad audiences
Management: Paul Taylor, Director; Ross Kramberg, Executive Director
Paid Staff: 8
Paid Artists: 20
Utilizes: Special Technical Talent
Budget: $1,000,000 - $5,000,000
Income Sources: Private Foundations/Grants/Endowments; Business/Corporate Donations; Box Office; Government Grants; Individual Donations
Season: 42 weeks
Performance Facilities: City Center Theatre

PEARL LANG DANCE COMPANY AND FOUNDATION
382 Central Park West, New York, NY 10025
(212) 866-2680
Founded: 1954
Arts Area: Modern; Ethnic
Status: Professional; Non-Profit
Type: Performing; Touring; Educational
Management: Pearl Lang, Artistic Director; Lois Schaffer, General Manager
Paid Artists: 12
Utilizes: Guest Artists
Budget: $100,000 - $500,000
Income Sources: Private Foundations/Grants/Endowments

PERFORMANCE SPACE 122 INC.
150 First Avenue, New York, NY 10009
(212) 477-5829
FAX: (212) 353-1315
Arts Area: Modern; Mime; Ballet; Jazz; Ethnic; Folk
Status: Professional; Non-Profit
Type: Sponsoring
Purpose: To be a not-for-profit arts center serving the New York City dance and performing community
Management: Mark Russell, Director; Dominick Balletta, Managing Director
Budget: $500,000 - $1,000,000
Income Sources: Private Foundations/Grants/Endowments; Business/Corporate Donations; Box Office; Government Grants; Individual Donations
Performance Facilities: Performing Space 122

PERIDANCE ENSEMBLE
132 Fourth Avenue, 2nd Floor, New York, NY 10003
(212) 505-0886
Founded: 1985
Arts Area: Modern; Ballet
Status: Professional; Non-Profit
Type: Performing; Touring
Management: Igal Perry, Artistic Director

Paid Artists: 15
Budget: $1,000 - $50,000
Income Sources: Private Foundations/Grants/Endowments; Business/Corporate Donations; Box Office; Government Grants; Individual Donations
Season: November - Ferbruary

PHYLLIS LAMHUT DANCE COMPANY
225 West 71st Street, #31, New York, NY 10023
(212) 799-9048
Founded: 1970
Arts Area: Modern
Status: Professional
Type: Performing; Touring; Resident; Educational
Purpose: To present the work of Phyllis Lamhut, Choreographer
Management: Mrs. A.M. Sutton, Manager
Officers: Jon Garness, President; Ruth Scherer, Vice President; Ruth Gravert, Secretary/Treasurer
Volunteer Staff: 1
Paid Artists: 3
Utilizes: Special Technical Talent; Guest Conductors; Guest Artists
Budget: $1,000 - $50,000
Income Sources: Private Foundations/Grants/Endowments; Business/Corporate Donations; Box Office; Government Grants; Individual Donations
Annual Attendance: 2,000

POLISH AMERICAN FOLK DANCE COMPANY
58 West 58th Street, New York, NY 10019
(212) 753-0450
FAX: (212) 935-3706
Founded: 1948
Arts Area: Folk
Status: Non-Professional; Non-Profit
Type: Performing; Touring
Purpose: To preserve and present the culture of Poland
Management: Stanley Pelc, Artistic Director
Paid Staff: 1
Paid Artists: 48
Budget: $1,000 - $50,000
Income Sources: Private Foundations/Grants/Endowments; Business/Corporate Donations; Box Office; Government Grants; Individual Donations
Season: 52 Weeks

POOH KAYE/ECCENTRIC MOTIONS INC.
99 Vandam Street, New York, NY 10013
(212) 691-9522
Arts Area: Experimental Dance
Status: Professional; Non-Profit
Type: Performing; Touring; Educational
Purpose: To produce dance and films for public performance and distribution; to conduct educational seminars on movement and film language
Management: Pooh Kaye, Artistic Director
Budget: $50,000 - $100,000
Income Sources: Government Grants; Fees

RALPH LEMON COMPANY
PO Box 143, New York, NY 10011
(212) 675-8394
Arts Area: Modern
Status: Professional; Non-Profit
Type: Performing; Touring; Resident; Educational
Purpose: To present the work of choreographer Ralph Lemon through performances, workshops and lecture demonstrations
Management: Ralph Lemon, Artistic Director; Heide Sackerlotzky, Management
Officers: Norton Owen, Chairman of the Board
Budget: $100,000 - $500,000
Income Sources: Private Foundations/Grants/Endowments; Business/Corporate Donations; Box Office; Government Grants; Individual Donations

RISA JAROSLOW AND DANCERS
65 Greene Street, New York, NY 10012
(212) 941-9358
FAX: (212) 475-3278
 Arts Area: Modern
 Status: Professional; Non-Profit
 Type: Performing; Touring; Resident; Educational
 Purpose: To bring new dance and music to as wide an audience as possible; to reveal the essence of human relationships through dance
 Management: Risa Jaroslow, Artistic Director; Beverly Wright and Associates, Booking Agents
 Budget: $50,000 - $100,000
 Income Sources: Private Foundations/Grants/Endowments; Business/Corporate Donations; Box Office; Government Grants; Individual Donations
 Performance Facilities: University Settlement

ROSALIND NEWMAN AND DANCERS
124 Chambers Street, New York, NY 10007
(212) 962-1327
 Founded: 1977
 Arts Area: Modern
 Status: Professional; Non-Profit
 Type: Performing; Touring; Educational
 Purpose: To perform the choreography of Rosalind Newman
 Paid Artists: 8 **Non-Paid Artists:** 4
 Income Sources: Private Foundations/Grants/Endowments; Business/Corporate Donations; Box Office; Government Grants; Individual Donations

SAEKO OCHINOHE AND COMPANY, INC.
159 West 53rd Street, New York, NY 10019
(212) 757-2531
FAX: (212) 757-3614
 Founded: 1970
 Arts Area: Modern; Ethnic
 Status: Professional; Non-Profit
 Type: Performing; Touring; Educational
 Purpose: To present multicultural dance programs of the highest quality to all walks of life while showing inter-ethnic harmony
 Management: Saeko Ichinohe, Executive Director; Mariko Hirata, Assistant to Director
 Officers: Miki Tatum, Chairman of the Board; Saeko Ichinohe, President; Jane Berenbeim, Treasurer; Elizabeth Massey, Secretary
 Paid Staff: 1 **Volunteer Staff:** 5
 Paid Artists: 7
 Utilizes: Special Technical Talent; Guest Artists
 Budget: $1,000 - $50,000
 Income Sources: Private Foundations/Grants/Endowments; Business/Corporate Donations; Box Office; Government Grants; Individual Donations
 Annual Attendance: 10,000

SCHOOL OF HARD KNOCKS
201 East Fourth Street, New York, NY 10009
(212) 533-9473
FAX: (212) 260-5382
 Arts Area: Post-Modern
 Status: Non-Profit
 Type: Performing; Touring
 Purpose: To produce the works of Yoshiko Chuma and other members of the School of Hard Knocks
 Management: Yoshiko Chuma, Artistic Director; Carolyn Palmer, Manager
 Budget: $1,000 - $50,000
 Income Sources: Private Foundations/Grants/Endowments; Business/Corporate Donations; Box Office; Government Grants; Individual Donations

SOLARIS DANCE THEATRE
264 West 19th Street, Room 53, New York, NY 10011
(212) 741-0778
FAX: (212) 242-2201
 Founded: 1976
 Arts Area: Modern; Ethnic; Folk
 Status: Professional; Non-Profit

Type: Performing; Touring; Resident; Educational
Purpose: To create experimental dance theatre through the workshop process and through cross-cultural performance; to create bonds with people otherwise unrecognized in our society
Paid Staff: 5   **Volunteer Staff:** 10
Paid Artists: 15
Utilizes: Special Technical Talent; Guest Artists
Budget: $100,000 - $500,000
Income Sources: Private Foundations/Grants/Endowments; Business/Corporate Donations; Box Office; Government Grants; Individual Donations
Season: September - June   **Annual Attendance:** 15,000

THE SOLOMONS COMPANY-DANCE
889 Broadway, New York, NY 10003
(212) 477-1321
Founded: 1972
Arts Area: Modern
Status: Non-Profit
Type: Performing; Touring; Educational
Purpose: Presentation of experimental pure-motion dances and environmental dance events accessible to public audiences
Management: Gus Solomons, Jr., Artistic Director; Toby Twining, Musical Director; Pentacle, Fiscal Management CircumArts Administrative Representation
Paid Staff: 2
Paid Artists: 8
Budget: $50,000 - $100,000
Income Sources: Box Office; Government Grants; Individual Donations
Season: 52 Weeks

SPANISH THEATRE REPERTORY CO., LTD.
138 East 27th Street, New York, NY 10016
(212) 889-2850
FAX: (212) 686-3732
Founded: 1968
Arts Area: Spanish Classical
Status: Professional; Non-Profit
Type: Performing; Touring; Resident; Educational; Sponsoring
Purpose: To create and showcase the best of Hispanic theatre forms, including dance
Management: Rene Buch, Artistic Director; Gilberto Zaldivar, Producer; Robert Weber Federico, Associate Producer
Officers: Gilberto Zaldivar, President; Rene Buch, Vice President; Robert Weber Federico, Secretary/Treasurer
Paid Staff: 12
Paid Artists: 25
Utilizes: Special Technical Talent; Guest Artists; Guest Directors; Guest Choreographers
Budget: $1,000,000 - $5,000,000
Income Sources: Private Foundations/Grants/Endowments; Business/Corporate Donations; Box Office; Government Grants; Individual Donations
Annual Attendance: 40,000
Performance Facilities: Gramercy Arts Theatre

STEPHEN PETRONIO DANCE COMPANY
95 St. Mark's Place, Suite 10, New York, NY 10009
(212) 473-1660
FAX: (212) 477-3471
Arts Area: Modern
Status: Professional; Non-Profit
Type: Performing; Touring
Management: Stephen Petronio, Artistic Director; Janet Stapleton, Managing Director
Budget: $100,000 - $500,000
Income Sources: Private Foundations/Grants/Endowments; Business/Corporate Donations; Government Grants; Individual Donations

SUSAN MARSHALL & COMPANY
c/o Downtown Art Co., 280 Broadway, Room 412, New York, NY 10007-1896
(212) 732-1201
FAX: (212) 732-1297
Founded: 1983
Arts Area: Modern
Status: Professional; Non-Profit
Type: Performing; Touring
Purpose: To support the creation, development and performance of the works of choreographer Susan Marshall

Management: Downtown Art Co., Ryan Gilliam, Management Services; Rena Shagen Associates, Booking Services
Paid Staff: 8
Paid Artists: 8
Budget: $100,000 - $500,000
Income Sources: Private Foundations/Grants/Endowments; Business/Corporate Donations; Government Grants; Individual Donations
Season: 52 Weeks
Affiliations: Dance USA

THEATRE OF THE RIVERSIDE CHURCH
490 River Drive, New York, NY 10027
(212) 864-2929
Founded: 1978
Status: Professional; Non-Profit
Type: Performing; Educational
Purpose: To present a yearly dance festival
Management: Shellie Bransford, General Manager
Budget: $50,000 - $100,000
Income Sources: Business/Corporate Donations; Box Office; Government Grants; Individual Donations
Season: 52 Weeks
Performance Facilities: Theatre of the Riverside Church

TOKUNAGA DANCE COMPANY
1 Sheridan Square, New York, NY 10014
(212) 929-8937
Founded: 1974
Arts Area: Modern; Ballet; Ethnic
Status: Professional; Non-Profit
Type: Performing; Touring; Educational
Purpose: To educate and entertain audiences through various cultural and historical aspects of dance
Officers: Robert Asahina, Chairman; Emiko Tokunaga, President; Elaine Tokunaga, Treasurer; Donna Quon, Secretary
Paid Staff: 3 **Volunteer Staff:** 4
Paid Artists: 7
Utilizes: Special Technical Talent
Budget: $50,000 - $100,000
Income Sources: Private Foundations/Grants/Endowments; Business/Corporate Donations; Box Office; Government Grants; Individual Donations
Season: 52 Weeks **Annual Attendance:** 50,000

TRISHA BROWN COMPANY
225 Lafayette Street, New York, NY 10012
(212) 334-9374
Founded: 1964
Arts Area: Modern
Status: Professional; Non-Profit
Type: Performing; Touring; Resident; Educational
Purpose: Trisha Brown has been recognized as seminal in contemporary dance and for the past 16 years has created a repertory known for its structural rigor and supple kineticism.
Management: Lawrence C. Zucker, Executive Director; Johanna C. Foley, Company Administrator
Officers: Robert Rauschenberg, Chairman; Sylvia Mazzola, Vice Chairman; Trisha Brown, President; Fredericka Hunter, Secretary
Paid Staff: 5
Paid Artists: 13
Utilizes: Guest Artists
Budget: $500,000 - $1,000,000
Income Sources: Private Foundations/Grants/Endowments; Business/Corporate Donations; Box Office; Government Grants; Individual Donations
Annual Attendance: 1,000,000
Performance Facilities: City Center Theatre

TWYLA THARP DANCE FOUNDATION
c/o MPL Productions 170 West 74th Street, New York, NY 10023
(212) 874-3990
FAX: (212) 874-8605
Founded: 1970
Arts Area: Modern; Ballet; Jazz
Status: Professional; Non-Profit
Type: Performing; Touring
Purpose: The making and performance of dance works

Management: Pam Strahl, Office Manager; Penny Curry, Manager for Twyla Tharp and TTDF; Diana Estigarribia, Office Assistant; Shelley Washington, Ballet Mistress
Paid Staff: 4
Income Sources: Private Foundations/Grants/Endowments; Business/Corporate Donations; Box Office; Government Grants; Individual Donations

URBAN BUSH WOMEN
c/o St. Marks Church, Tenth Street and Second Avenue, New York, NY 10003
(212) 777-4425
FAX: (212) 529-2318
Arts Area: Modern; Ethnic
Status: Non-Professional
Type: Performing; Touring
Purpose: To realize a creative vision continuously enriched by the folklore and religious traditions of Africans throughout the diaspora; through movement, live music, a cappella vocalizations, and the drama and wit of the spoken word, Urban Bush Women explores the struggle, growth, transformation, and survival of the human spirit
Management: Laurie Uprichard, Managing Director; Jawole Willa Jo Zollar, Artistic Director; Rhoda Cerritelli, Administrative Director
Officers: Jawole Willa Jo Zollar, Chairman of the Board
Budget: $500,000 - $1,000,000
Income Sources: Private Foundations/Grants/Endowments; Business/Corporate Donations; Government Grants; Individual Donations; Earned Income; Fees
Season: 52 Weeks

VICTORIA MARKS PERFORMANCE COMPANY
c/o Terra Moto Inc., 47-49 King Street, Suite 10, New York, NY 10014
(212) 255-7738
Arts Area: Modern
Status: Professional; Non-Profit
Type: Performing; Touring; Resident; Educational
Purpose: To provide a creative vehicle for the choreography of Victoria Marks; to bring the arts to diverse communities and educational situations
Management: Victoria Marks
Budget: $50,000 - $100,000
Income Sources: Private Foundations/Grants/Endowments; Box Office; Government Grants; Individual Donations

WORLD MUSIC INSTITUTE INC.
49 West 27th Street, Ste 810, New York, NY 10001
(212) 545-7536
FAX: (212) 889-2771
Arts Area: Ethnic; Folk
Status: Non-Profit
Type: Touring
Purpose: To present traditional & contemporary music and dance from around the world
Management: Robert H. Browning, Executive and Artistic Director; Eileen Macholl, Administrative Director
Officers: Daisy Paradis, Chair
Budget: $500,000 - $1,000,000
Income Sources: Private Foundations/Grants/Endowments; Business/Corporate Donations; Box Office; Government Grants; Individual Donations
Season: 52 Weeks

ZE'EVA COHEN AND DANCERS
c/o Pentacle Management, 104 Franklin Street, New York, NY 10013
(212) 226-2000
FAX: (212) 925-0369
Founded: 1972
Arts Area: Modern
Status: Professional; Non-Profit
Type: Performing; Touring; Resident
Management: Ze'Eva Cohen, Artistic Director
Paid Staff: 4
Paid Artists: 15
Utilizes: Guest Artists
Budget: $1,000 - $50,000
Income Sources: Private Foundations/Grants/Endowments; Business/Corporate Donations; Box Office; Government Grants; Individual Donations
Season: 52 Weeks

INSTRUMENTAL MUSIC

AEOLIAN CHAMBER PLAYERS
173 Riverside Drive, New York, NY 10024
(212) 595-4688
FAX: (212) 724-5283
Founded: 1961
Arts Area: Chamber
Status: Professional
Type: Performing; Touring; Resident
Purpose: The performance of a broad repertoire with music from the classical to the contemporary
Management: Joanne Rile Artists Management
Officers: Lewis Kaplan, President
Paid Staff: 2   **Volunteer Staff:** 2
Paid Artists: 4
Utilizes: Guest Artists
Budget: $1,000 - $50,000
Income Sources: Private Foundations/Grants/Endowments; Business/Corporate Donations; Box Office; Government Grants; Individual Donations
Season: 52 Weeks   **Annual Attendance:** 15,000
Affiliations: NEA; NYSCA; Bowdoin Summer Music Festival

AFFILIATE ARTISTS INC.
37 West 65th Street, New York, NY 10023
(212) 580-2000
Arts Area: Soloists
Status: Professional; Non-Profit
Type: Resident; Educational; Sponsoring
Purpose: To help develop the careers of the nation's most promising young performing artists; to help develop audiences for the arts throughout the country; to develop corporate and foundational support for the arts
Management: Richard C. Clark, President/Artistic Director; Joseph Chart, Director of Programs/and Development
Budget: $1,000,000 - $5,000,000
Income Sources: Private Foundations/Grants/Endowments; Business/Corporate Donations; Government Grants

AMERICAN COMPOSERS ORCHESTRA
37 West 65th Street, New York, NY 10023
(212) 496-5330
FAX: (212) 580-1356
Founded: 1976
Arts Area: Symphony; Orchestra
Status: Professional; Non-Profit
Type: Performing
Purpose: The ACO's purpose is to discover, produce and present the widest possible spectrum of American repertoire, past and present, in performances of the highest quality, thereby focusing national awareness and support of American composers and their music.
Management: Jesse Rosen, Executive Director; Dennis Russell Davies, Music Director
Officers: Francis Thorne, President
Paid Staff: 4
Paid Artists: 80
Utilizes: Guest Conductors; Guest Artists
Budget: $500,000 - $1,000,000
Income Sources: Private Foundations/Grants/Endowments; Business/Corporate Donations; Box Office; Government Grants; Individual Donations
Season: September - June
Affiliations: ASOL
Performance Facilities: Carnegie Hall

AMERICAN SYMPHONY ORCHESTRA
850 Seventh Avenue, Suite 1106, New York, NY 10019
(212) 581-1365
Founded: 1962
Arts Area: Symphony; Orchestra; Ensemble
Status: Professional; Non-Profit
Type: Performing
Purpose: American Symphony Orchestra is the only self-governing orchestra in the United States with a subscription series at Carnegie Hall. It is also a resource organization providing musical service to communities nurturing young artists.
Management: Eugene Carr, Executive Director
Paid Staff: 2

Non-Paid Artists: 8
Utilizes: Guest Conductors; Guest Artists
Budget: $1,000,000 - $5,000,000
Income Sources: Private Foundations/Grants/Endowments; Business/Corporate Donations; Box Office; Government Grants; Individual Donations
Season: October - July
Performance Facilities: Carnegie Hall

AMERICAN TAP DANCE ORCHESTRA
170 Mercer Street, New York, NY 10012
(212) 925-3980
Founded: 1986
Arts Area: Rhythm, Jazz and Tap Dance
Status: Professional; Non-Profit
Type: Performing; Touring; Educational
Purpose: To celebrate, preserve and perpetuate one of America's few indigenous art forms, tap dance
Management: Siegel Artist Management; Liz Silverstein, Ethel Siegel, Jane Lawrence Curtiss
Officers: Brenda Bufalino, Founder/Artistic Director; Tony Waag, Executive Director; Barbara Duffy, Dance Captain; Lurea Herman, Company Manager
Paid Staff: 3   **Volunteer Staff:** 10
Utilizes: Special Technical Talent; Guest Artists
Budget: $100,000 - $500,000
Income Sources: Private Foundations/Grants/Endowments; Business/Corporate Donations; Box Office; Government Grants; Individual Donations
Performance Facilities: Woodpeckers Tap Dance Center

THE ASSOCIATION FOR THE ADVANCEMENT OF CREATIVE MUSICIANS, NEW YORK CHAPTER
PO Box 187, Times Square Station, New York, NY 10108
(212) 594-7121
Arts Area: Ensemble
Status: Professional; Non-Profit
Type: Performing
Purpose: To provide a forum for composers and performers to perform their own original music
Management: Richard Abrams
Income Sources: Government Grants

THE BLOOMINGDALE HOUSE OF MUSIC
323 West 108th Street, New York, NY 10025
(212) 663-6021
Founded: 1964
Arts Area: Orchestra; Chamber; Ensemble; Ethnic; Folk; Electronic & Live Electronic
Status: Professional; Non-Profit
Type: Performing; Educational; Sponsoring
Purpose: To promote, foster and develop the love of and interest for the musical arts
Management: Lawrence Davis, Executive Director
Paid Staff: 8
Paid Artists: 50
Budget: $500,000 - $1,000,000
Income Sources: Private Foundations/Grants/Endowments; Business/Corporate Donations; Government Grants; Individual Donations
Season: 52 Weeks
Affiliations: NGCSA

CARNEGIE CHAMBER PLAYERS
514 West 110th Street, Suite 41, New York, NY 10025
(212) 666-6740
Arts Area: Chamber; Ensemble
Status: Professional; Non-Profit
Type: Performing; Touring; Resident; Educational
Purpose: To promote chamber music in a mixed string and woodwind ensemble, commissioning new works as well as performing a traditional chamber music repertoire
Management: Richard Goldsmith, Yari Bond, Artistic Directors
Budget: $1,000 - $50,000
Income Sources: Private Foundations/Grants/Endowments; Business/Corporate Donations; Box Office; Government Grants; Individual Donations
Performance Facilities: Montshire Science Museum, Norwich VT; Therneaur School, Tenafly NJ

CHAMBER MUSIC AMERICA
545 Eighth Avenue, New York, NY 10018
(212) 244-2772
FAX: (212) 244-2776
Founded: 1977
Arts Area: Chamber
Status: Professional; Non-Profit
Type: Educational; Service Organization
Purpose: To promote professional chamber music and to make chamber music a vital part of American cultural life
Management: Dean K. Stein, Executive Director
Officers: Richard Bogomolny, Chairman; Paul Katz, President
Paid Staff: 8
Budget: $500,000 - $1,000,000
Income Sources: Private Foundations/Grants/Endowments; Business/Corporate Donations; Government Grants; Individual Donations

THE CHAMBER MUSIC SOCIETY OF LINCOLN CENTER
70 Lincoln Center Plaza, New York, NY 10023
(212) 875-5775
FAX: (212) 875-5799
Founded: 1969
Arts Area: Chamber; Ensemble; Instrumental Group
Status: Professional; Non-Profit
Type: Performing; Touring; Resident; Educational
Purpose: To present chamber music concerts
Management: David Shifrin, Artistic Director; Charles Kargacos, Executive Director
Officers: Laurence Dow Lorett, Chairman; Henry S. Ziegler, Vice Chairman; Mrs. John D. Coffin, President; Donaldson C. Pillsbury, Secretary; Donald Schnabel, Treasurer
Paid Staff: 11   **Volunteer Staff:** 8
Paid Artists: 18
Utilizes: Guest Artists
Budget: $1,000,000 - $5,000,000
Income Sources: Private Foundations/Grants/Endowments; Business/Corporate Donations; Box Office; Government Grants; Individual Donations
Season: October - May
Annual Attendance: 80,000
Performance Facilities: Alice Tully Hall

CHELSEA CHAMBER ENSEMBLE
c/o Timothy Malosh, 69 West End Avenue, Apt. 1-F, New York, NY 10025
(212) 222-3472
Arts Area: Chamber; Ensemble
Status: Professional; Non-Profit
Type: Performing; Touring; Resident; Educational
Purpose: To present unusual music from the past; to commission new works by American composers
Management: Timothy Malosh, Marc Goldberg, David Jolley, Artistic Directors
Officers: Theodore W. Volck, Chairman of the Board
Budget: $1,000 - $50,000
Income Sources: Private Foundations/Grants/Endowments; Business/Corporate Donations; Box Office; Government Grants; Individual Donations
Performance Facilities: Weill Recital Hall, Carnegie Hall

THE CHINESE MUSIC ENSEMBLE OF NEW YORK, INC.
149 Canal Street, New York, NY 10002
(212) 925-6110
Founded: 1961
Arts Area: Ensemble; Ethnic; Folk
Status: Semi-Professional; Non-Profit
Type: Performing; Touring; Educational
Purpose: To promote Chinese music in the United States
Officers: Yu-chiung Teng, Director; Terence Yeh and Oiman Chan, Associate Directors
Paid Staff: 3   **Volunteer Staff:** 12
Paid Artists: 45
Budget: $50,000 - $100,000
Income Sources: Private Foundations/Grants/Endowments; Business/Corporate Donations; Box Office; Government Grants; Individual Donations
Season: 52 Weeks
Annual Attendance: 9,000

CITY SYMPHONY ORCHESTRA OF NEW YORK, INC.
311 West 34th Street, New York, NY 10001
(212) 947-3362
FAX: (212) 465-2367
>**Arts Area:** Symphony; Chamber
>**Status:** Professional; Non-Profit
>**Type:** Performing
>**Purpose:** To present young performers at the major concert halls in New York City; to present performances and music by artists of different ethnic backgrounds
>**Management:** David Eaton, Artistic Director; Leonid Fleishaker, Personnel Contractor
>**Officers:** Chung Hwan Kwak, Chairman of the Board; David Eaton, President
>**Budget:** $100,000 - $500,000
>**Income Sources:** Private Foundations/Grants/Endowments; Business/Corporate Donations; Box Office; Government Grants; Individual Donations
>**Performance Facilities:** Carnegie Hall; Alice Tully Hall

THE CLASSICAL QUARTET
225 West 99th Street, New York, NY 10025
(212) 222-2700
>**Founded:** 1979
>**Arts Area:** Chamber; Ensemble
>**Status:** Professional
>**Type:** Performing; Touring; Resident; Educational
>**Purpose:** The Classical Quartet was founded to present masterpieces of the Classic Era, string quartets of Haydn, Mozart, Beethoven and their contemporaries, on period instruments.
>**Management:** Beverly Simmons, Artist Representative
>**Officers:** Nancy Wilson, President; David Miller, Treasurer
>**Volunteer Staff:** 2
>**Paid Artists:** 4
>**Utilizes:** Guest Artists
>**Budget:** $1,000 - $50,000
>**Income Sources:** Box Office; Government Grants; Individual Donations
>**Season:** 52 Weeks
>**Performance Facilities:** Saint Michael's Church

CONCORDIA
330 Seventh Avenue, 21st Floor, New York, NY 10001
(212) 967-1290
FAX: (212) 629-0508
>**Founded:** 1984
>**Arts Area:** Orchestra; Chamber
>**Status:** Professional; Non-Profit
>**Type:** Performing; Educational
>**Purpose:** A unique and adventurous fifty piece orchestra dedicated to breaking down the barriers between jazz and classical music by presenting innovative concerts combining American Symphonic masterpieces, orchestral jazz, and commissioned premieres
>**Management:** Maria Alsop, Artistic Director/Conductor; Leslie Stifelman, Executive Director
>**Officers:** Tomio Taki, Chairman/Board of Directors; Joel Hirschtritt, President/Board of Directors
>**Paid Staff:** 4   **Volunteer Staff:** 15
>**Utilizes:** Guest Artists
>**Budget:** $100,000 - $500,000
>**Income Sources:** Private Foundations/Grants/Endowments; Business/Corporate Donations; Box Office; Government Grants; Individual Donations
>**Season:** October - June
>**Annual Attendance:** 4,000
>**Performance Facilities:** Alice Tully Hall, Lincoln Center

CONTINUUM (THE PERFORMERS' COMMITTEE INC.)
333 West End Avenue, 16C, New York, NY 10023
(212) 873-3258
>**Founded:** 1966
>**Arts Area:** Orchestra; Chamber; Ensemble; Instrumental Group; Vocal
>**Status:** Professional
>**Type:** Performing; Touring; Educational
>**Purpose:** To promote 20th century music through annual concert series in New York; to tour in the U.S. and abroad; to educate through mini-residences and recordings
>**Management:** Cheryl Seltzer and Joel Sachs, Co-Directors

Officers: Cheryl Seltzer, President; Joel Sachs, Vice President
Paid Staff: 1
Paid Artists: 50
Budget: $100,000 - $500,000
Income Sources: Private Foundations/Grants/Endowments; Business/Corporate Donations; Box Office; Government Grants; Individual Donations; Performance Fees
Season: September - June
Performance Facilities: Alice Tully Hall

COSMOPOLITAN SYMPHONY ORCHESTRA
PO Box 1045, Ansonia Station, New York, NY 10023
(212) 873-7784
Founded: 1964
Arts Area: Symphony
Status: Non-Profit
Type: Performing; Educational
Purpose: To give young professional conductors, instrumentalists and soloists an opportunity to make New York appearances; to create a new audience
Management: Rita Asen, Managing Director; Simon Asen, Founder
Officers: Martin Snyder, Vice President
Volunteer Staff: 4
Paid Artists: 8   **Non-Paid Artists:** 45
Utilizes: Guest Conductors; Guest Artists
Budget: $1,000 - $50,000
Income Sources: Private Foundations/Grants/Endowments; Business/Corporate Donations; Individual Donations
Season: November - May
Performance Facilities: Town Hall

DA CAPO CHAMBER PLAYERS, INCORPORATED
215 West 90th Street, New York, NY 10024
(212) 873-1065
FAX: (212) 873-1065
Arts Area: Chamber
Status: Professional
Type: Performing; Touring; Resident; Educational
Purpose: To perform a repertoire of the music of today, including scores of commissioned works, often featured with traditional repertoire selections
Management: John Gingrich Management, Inc.
Paid Artists: 5
Utilizes: Guest Artists
Budget: $50,000 - $100,000
Income Sources: Private Foundations/Grants/Endowments; Business/Corporate Donations; Box Office; Government Grants; Individual Donations
Annual Attendance: 2,765
Performance Facilities: Merkin Concert Hall; Kathryn Bache Miller Theatre; 92nd Street Y

THE DOCTORS' ORCHESTRAL SOCIETY OF NEW YORK
201 East 19th Street, New York, NY 10003
(212) 477-1660
FAX: (212) 477-1888
Founded: 1938
Arts Area: Symphony; Orchestra
Status: Non-Professional; Non-Profit
Type: Performing; Educational
Purpose: To perform the great music of the world for our own education and enjoyment and to bring this music to our community for their enjoyment and education; the group also works with the public school system of New York City
Management: Philip Traugott, Music Director
Officers: Dr. Harvey Salomon, President; Dr. Pauline Hecht, Vice President; Dr. Edward Bowe; Dr. David Tiersten, Treasurers
Volunteer Staff: 5
Non-Paid Artists: 5
Utilizes: Guest Artists
Budget: $1,000 - $50,000
Income Sources: Business/Corporate Donations; Individual Donations
Season: September - June
Annual Attendance: 2,000
Performance Facilities: Stuyvesant High School Auditorium

DOWNTOWN MUSIC PRODUCTIONS
310 East 12th Street, New York, NY 10003
(212) 477-1594
FAX: (212) 477-5567
Arts Area: Orchestra; Chamber; Instrumental Group; Adult/Children's Operatic
Status: Professional; Non-Profit
Type: Performing; Educational
Purpose: To produce music programs that heighten our consciousness on the possibility of meaningful communication through art; the organization has been a recipient of the 1992 Mayor's Special Arts Award in music, the American Composer's Alliance Laurel Leaf Award for fostering and encouraging American music and the 1990 ASCAP/Chamber Music America Award for adventuresome programming.
Management: Mimi Stern-Wolfe, Artistic Director/Conductor/Pianist
Budget: $100,000 - $500,000
Income Sources: Private Foundations/Grants/Endowments; Business/Corporate Donations; Government Grants; Individual Donations

EARLY MUSIC AMERICA, INC.
30 West 26th Street, Suite 1001, New York, NY 10015
(212) 366-5643
FAX: (212) 366-5265
Arts Area: Early Music
Status: Non-Profit
Type: Service Organization
Purpose: To expand the audiences for early music in North America; to foster an appreciation for early American music among our listeners
Management: Daniel Nimetz, Executive Director; Thomas F. Kelly, President
Budget: $100,000 - $500,000
Income Sources: Private Foundations/Grants/Endowments; Business/Corporate Donations; Government Grants; Membership Dues

EXPERIMENTAL INTERMEDIA FOUNDATION
224 Centre Street, New York, NY 10013
(212) 431-5127
FAX: (212) 431-4486
Founded: 1968
Arts Area: Chamber; Ensemble; Instrumental Group; Electronic & Live Electronic; Video; Film
Status: Non-Profit
Type: Performing; Educational; Sponsoring
Purpose: To provide a forum for experimental music and intermedia
Management: Phill Niblock, Director; Mary Jane Leach, Associate Director
Officers: Arthur Stidfole, President; Mary Jane Leach, Treasurer
Paid Staff: 4   **Volunteer Staff:** 5
Paid Artists: 30
Utilizes: Special Technical Talent; Guest Artists
Budget: $100,000 - $500,000
Income Sources: Private Foundations/Grants/Endowments; Business/Corporate Donations; Box Office; Government Grants; Individual Donations
Season: 52 Weeks
Annual Attendance: 2,000

FLUTE FORCE
124 West 72 Street, Suite #5C, New York, NY 10023
(212) 873-0272
Founded: 1981
Arts Area: Chamber; Ensemble; Instrumental Group
Status: Professional
Type: Performing; Touring; Educational
Purpose: To further the knowledge of the flute and its repertiore through performance and lectures
Management: Simonds Management
Officers: Rie Schmidt, Artistic Director; Gretchen Pusch, Executive Director
Volunteer Staff: 4
Paid Artists: 4
Utilizes: Guest Artists
Budget: $1,000 - $50,000
Income Sources: Private Foundations/Grants/Endowments; Business/Corporate Donations; Box Office; Government Grants; Individual Donations
Season: 52 Weeks

HIGHLIGHTS IN JAZZ
7 Peter Copper Road, New York, NY 10010
(212) 982-3697
Founded: 1973
Arts Area: Jazz
Status: Professional
Type: Performing
Purpose: To perform in an 8-concert series at Pace University, NY, with all-star assemblages
Management: Jack Kleinsinger, Producer; Sid Trommer, Development Director
Officers: Jack Kleinsinger, President; Arnold Jay Smith, James Bartow, Harriet Wasser and Sid Trommer, Board Members; Richard Kalty, Treasurer
Paid Staff: 2   **Volunteer Staff:** 5
Paid Artists: 100
Utilizes: Guest Artists
Budget: $50,000 - $100,000
Income Sources: Private Foundations/Grants/Endowments; Business/Corporate Donations; Box Office; Government Grants; Individual Donations; Fundraising
Season: October - May   **Annual Attendance:** 5,700
Affiliations: New Jersey Symphony Orchestra
Performance Facilities: Pace University Theatre

HORIZON CONCERTS INC.
475 Riverside Drive, Suite 249, New York, NY 10115
(212) 563-6885
FAX: (212) 563-6885
Arts Area: Ensemble; Instrumental Group
Status: Professional; Non-Profit
Type: Performing; Educational
Purpose: To bring free, classical-music concerts to people deprived of the opportunity to hear live performances including the elderly, AIDS hospices, homeless shelters, Alzheimer clinics and underprivileged youth
Management: Clive Lythgoe, Executive Director/Music Director
Officers: Joan T. Ades, President of the Board
Budget: $100,000 - $500,000
Income Sources: Private Foundations/Grants/Endowments; Business/Corporate Donations; Government Grants; Individual Donations

JUPITER SYMPHONY
155 West 68th Street, New York, NY 10023
(212) 799-1259
Founded: 1979
Arts Area: Symphony; Orchestra; Chamber; Instrumental Group
Status: Professional; Non-Profit
Type: Performing; Touring; Resident; Educational; Sponsoring
Purpose: To interest young people in music at a most crucial time of their lives
Management: Harry Beall Management
Officers: Jens Nygaard, Conductor/Artistic Director; Carole Mertz, Director of Development
Budget: $100,000 - $500,000
Income Sources: Private Foundations/Grants/Endowments; Business/Corporate Donations; Box Office; Government Grants; Individual Donations
Season: 52 Weeks

THE LITTLE ORCHESTRA SOCIETY OF NEW YORK
220 West 42nd Street, 18th Floor, New York, NY 10036
(212) 704-2100
FAX: (212) 704-4037
Founded: 1947
Arts Area: Orchestra
Status: Non-Profit
Type: Performing
Purpose: To provide unique adventures in the world's finest music for concert-goers of all ages
Officers: John Kordel, Managing Director
Paid Staff: 5
Utilizes: Special Technical Talent; Guest Conductors; Guest Artists; Guest Directors
Budget: $500,000 - $1,000,000
Income Sources: Private Foundations/Grants/Endowments; Business/Corporate Donations; Box Office; Government Grants; Individual Donations
Season: September - August
Affiliations: ASOL

Performance Facilities: Avery Fisher Hall; Alice Tully Hall; Bruno Walter Auditorium; Greek Orthodox Cathedral of the Holy Trinity

MEET THE COMPOSER INC.
2112 Broadway, Suite 505, New York, NY 10023
(212) 787-3601
FAX: (212) 787-3745
    Arts Area: Symphony; Orchestra; Chamber; Ensemble; Ethnic; Folk; Instrumental Group; Electronic & Live Electronic; Band
    Status: Non-Profit
    Type: Grant-giving
    Purpose: To foster the creation, performance and recording of music by American composers; to expand audience fields
    Management: John Duffy, Director/President
    Budget: $1,000,000 - $5,000,000
    Income Sources: Private Foundations/Grants/Endowments; Business/Corporate Donations; Box Office; Government Grants; Individual Donations
    Performance Facilities: Springfield Symphony Hall

MOZART FESTIVAL ORCHESTRA
33 Greenwich Avenue, New York, NY 10014
(212) 675-9127
    Founded: 1960
    Arts Area: Symphony; Orchestra
    Status: Professional; Non-Profit
    Type: Performing
    Purpose: To present idiomatic performances of music of all styles and periods emphasizing the 18th century; to enlarge repertory; to sponsor lectures, publications, exhibitions, and young artists
    Management: Baird Hastings, Conductor
    Officers: Baird Hastings, Treasurer; Louise Hastings, Secretary
    Paid Artists: 20
    Utilizes: Guest Directors
    Budget: $1,000 - $50,000
    Income Sources: Private Foundations/Grants/Endowments; Box Office; Individual Donations
    Season: February - May   **Annual Attendance:** 1,200
    Performance Facilities: Main Hall, First Presbyterian Church

MUSIC BEFORE 1800, INC.
Corpus Christi Church, 529 West 121st Street, New York, NY 10027
(212) 666-0675
    Founded: 1975
    Arts Area: Chamber
    Status: Professional
    Type: Performing; Sponsoring
    Purpose: To present performances of vocal and instrumental chamber music before 1800
    Officers: Louise Basbas, President/Executive Director
    Paid Staff: 3   **Volunteer Staff:** 10
    Paid Artists: 60
    Budget: $50,000 - $100,000
    Income Sources: Private Foundations/Grants/Endowments; Business/Corporate Donations; Box Office; Government Grants; Individual Donations
    Season: September - May   **Annual Attendance:** 2,500
    Affiliations: CMA; EMA
    Performance Facilities: Corpus Christi Church

MUSICA DE CAMARA, INC.
1215 Fifth Avenue, Apt. 1-B, New York, NY 10029
(212) 410-5612
    Arts Area: Orchestra; Chamber; Ensemble; Solo; Baroque Orchestra
    Status: Professional; Non-Profit
    Type: Performing; Touring; Educational
    Purpose: To promote classical instrumental singers and composers of Puerto Rican and Hispanic background
    Management: Eva de la O, Executive Director
    Officers: Tonio Burgos, Chairman; Carlotta Madura, Anita Soto, Myrna Riveria, Michael Nieves, Board Members
    Budget: $1,000 - $50,000
    Income Sources: Private Foundations/Grants/Endowments; Business/Corporate Donations; Government Grants
    Performance Facilities: Merkin Concert Hall

NATIONAL ORCHESTRAL ASSOCIATION INC.
475 Riverside Drive, Suite 249, New York, NY 10115
(212) 870-2009
FAX: (212) 870-2129
Arts Area: Orchestra; Chamber
Status: Non-Profit
Type: Educational
Officers: Frances Kennedy, President
Performance Facilities: Carnegie Hall

NEW MUSIC CONSORT, INC.
498 West End Avenue, #1B, New York, NY 10024
(212) 362-0962
Arts Area: Chamber; 20th Century
Status: Professional; Non-Profit
Type: Performing; Touring; Educational
Purpose: To present a wide variety of music of 20th century performers on the highest interpretive level; to encourage audience awareness of 20th century chamber music through performances and lecture demonstrations
Management: Madeline Shapiro and Claire Heldrich, Artistic Directors
Budget: $50,000 - $100,000

THE NEW SONG QUINTET (PROJECT)
New Song Foundation Inc., 510 West 112th Street, New York, NY 10025
(212) 866-3827
Founded: 1979
Arts Area: Ethnic; Folk; Instrumental Group; Children's Music
Status: Professional; Non-Profit
Type: Performing; Touring; Educational; Workshops
Purpose: To promote multi-cultural understanding through music performances and workshops for all ages and communities; to give children insight into, and to elicit their participation in, songwriting and creativity; to provide musical experiences for special communities including seniors, intergenerational groups, the psychiatric community and the developmentally and physically disabled community
Management: Mike Glick, Artistic Director; The New Music Foundation
Officers: Alan Diamond, Treasurer
Volunteer Staff: 1
Paid Artists: 6
Budget: $50,000 - $100,000
Income Sources: Private Foundations/Grants/Endowments; Box Office
Season: 52 Weeks
Affiliations: New York Foundation for the Arts

NEW YORK CHAMBER ENSEMBLE
475 Riverside Drive, Suite 621, New York, NY 10115-0621
(212) 870-2439
FAX: (212) 870-2192
Founded: 1987
Arts Area: Ensemble
Status: Professional; Non-Profit
Type: Performing; Touring
Purpose: To perform a 15-member, mixed ensemble repertoire, usually requiring a conductor
Management: Donna Zajonc Management, Ann Arbor, MI
Officers: Peter Morris Dixon, President; Kathleen Byrum, Vice President; Charles L. Marshall Jr., Secretary; Howard W. Connaughton, Treasurer
Paid Staff: 1
Paid Artists: 40
Utilizes: Guest Artists
Budget: $50,000 - $100,000
Income Sources: Private Foundations/Grants/Endowments; Business/Corporate Donations; Box Office; Government Grants; Individual Donations
Season: Fall - Spring   **Annual Attendance:** 6,000
Performance Facilities: Florence Gould Hall

NEW YORK CONSORT OF VIOLS
201 West 86th Street, New York, NY 10024
(212) 580-9787
Arts Area: Chamber
Status: Professional; Non-Profit

Type: Performing; Touring; Educational
Purpose: To perform the vast repertoire of music for viols from the Renaissance and baroque periods; to encourage the composition of new works for viols
Management: Judith Davidoff, Artistic Director
Budget: $1,000 - $50,000
Income Sources: Private Foundations/Grants/Endowments; Business/Corporate Donations; Box Office; Government Grants; Individual Donations
Season: 52 Weeks

NEW YORK HARP ENSEMBLE
140 West End Avenue, Suite 3K, New York, NY 10023
(212) 799-5989
FAX: (212) 799-5989
Founded: 1970
Arts Area: Chamber
Status: Professional; Non-Profit
Type: Performing; Touring; Resident; Educational
Purpose: To play concerts worldwide; to perform new contemporary compositions for four harps; to provide master classes and participate in recordings and television
Management: Dr. Aristid von Wurtzler, Music Director; Metropolitan Artists Management
Officers: Dr. Aristid von Wurtzler, President
Paid Staff: 2 **Volunteer Staff:** 6
Paid Artists: 5
Budget: $1,000 - $50,000
Income Sources: Private Foundations/Grants/Endowments; Individual Donations
Season: 52 Weeks

NEW YORK NEW MUSIC ENSEMBLE
48 Horatio Street, New York, NY 10014
(212) 633-6260
Founded: 1976
Arts Area: Chamber; Ensemble; Instrumental Group; Electronic & Live Electronic; Contemporary; 20th Century
Status: Professional
Type: Performing; Touring; Educational
Purpose: To crusade for contemporary music; to support new composers by performing significant contemporary works; to play experimental avant garde mixtures of music, electronics, theatre and music
Officers: Jayn Rosenfeld, Executive Director/Flutist; Daniel Druckman, Treasurer/Percussionist/Tour Manager; Jean Kopperud, Tour Manager/Clarinetist; Christopher Finckel, Repertory Research/Cellist/Conductor; James Winn, Composer Liaison/Pianist; Linda Quan, Schedule Coordinator/Violinist; Robert Black, Tour Research/Conductor
Paid Staff: 2 **Volunteer Staff:** 7
Paid Artists: 7
Utilizes: Special Technical Talent; Guest Conductors; Guest Artists; Guest Directors
Budget: $50,000 - $100,000
Income Sources: Private Foundations/Grants/Endowments; Business/Corporate Donations; Box Office; Government Grants; Individual Donations
Season: October - May **Annual Attendance:** 2,500

NEW YORK PHILHARMONIC
65th Street at Broadway, New York, NY 10023
(212) 875-5700
FAX: (212) 875-5929
Founded: 1842
Arts Area: Symphony; Orchestra; Chamber
Status: Professional
Type: Performing; Touring; Resident; Educational
Management: Deborah Borda, Managing Director; Edward Sermier, Controller; Allison Vulgamore, General Manager; Elizabeth Ostrow, Music Administrator
Officers: Stephen Stamas, Chairman; H. Frederick Krimendahl II, President
Paid Staff: 60 **Volunteer Staff:** 375
Paid Artists: 106
Utilizes: Guest Conductors; Guest Artists
Budget: Over 10,000,000
Income Sources: Private Foundations/Grants/Endowments; Business/Corporate Donations; Box Office; Government Grants; Individual Donations
Season: 52 Weeks
Affiliations: ASOL
Performance Facilities: Avery Fisher Hall

NEW YORK PHILOMUSICA CHAMBER ENSEMBLE
105 West 73rd Street, #4C, New York, NY 10023
(212) 580-9933
> **Arts Area:** Chamber; Ensemble
> **Status:** Professional; Non-Profit
> **Type:** Performing; Recording
> **Purpose:** To perform and record the music written from 1750 to the present for wind, strings and piano, with guest soloists
> **Management:** Robert Johnson, Artistic Director
> **Officers:** George Plimpton, President of the Board
> **Utilizes:** Guest Artists
> **Budget:** $100,000 - $500,000
> **Income Sources:** Private Foundations/Grants/Endowments; Business/Corporate Donations; Box Office; Government Grants; Individual Donations
> **Performance Facilities:** American Concert Hall; Alice Tully Hall

NEW YORK POPS ORCHESTRA
ICM Artists, Ltd., 40 West 57th Street, 16th Floor, New York, NY 10019
(212) 556-6871
FAX: (212) 556-6877
> **Founded:** 1983
> **Arts Area:** Symphony
> **Status:** Professional; Non-Profit
> **Type:** Performing; Touring
> **Purpose:** The New York Pops was founded to fill the void that has existed between highbrow classical tastes and top-10 rock with emphasis on light classical selections as well as contemporary works of merit.
> **Management:** Skitch Henderson, Founder/Music Director; Peter Lane, Executive Director; Dick Corrado, Agent
> **Paid Artists:** 95
> **Utilizes:** Guest Conductors; Guest Artists
> **Income Sources:** Business/Corporate Donations; Box Office; Individual Donations
> **Season:** October - May   **Annual Attendance:** 30,000
> **Performance Facilities:** Carnegie Hall

NEW YORK YOUTH SYMPHONY
Carnegie Hall, Suite 504, 881 Seventh Avenue, New York, NY 10019
(212) 581-5933
> **Founded:** 1963
> **Arts Area:** Symphony; Chamber
> **Status:** Non-Professional; Non-Profit
> **Type:** Performing; Educational; Sponsoring
> **Purpose:** New York Youth Symphony is established as the premier orchestra in metropolitan New York offering a unique learning experience and musical showcase for the gifted, young orchestral musician, conductor, soloist and composer. Composed of 135 of the most talented musicians aged 12 to 22 from the Tri-State Area, representing every racial, ethnic and economic background.
> **Management:** Barry Goldberg, Executive Director; Samuel Wong, Music Director; Jonathan David, Manager of Operations
> **Officers:** Leslie J. Garfield, Chairman; Theodore L. Kesselman, President; Robert L. Poster, Vice President; Benson J. Chapman, Treasurer
> **Paid Staff:** 3
> **Non-Paid Artists:** 135
> **Utilizes:** Guest Artists
> **Budget:** $100,000 - $500,000
> **Income Sources:** Private Foundations/Grants/Endowments; Business/Corporate Donations; Government Grants; Individual Donations; Fund-raising
> **Season:** September - May   **Annual Attendance:** 10,000
> **Performance Facilities:** Carnegie Hall

NEW YORK'S ENSEMBLE FOR EARLY MUSIC
217 West 71 Street, New York, NY 10023
(212) 749-6600
FAX: (212) 316-7404
> **Founded:** 1974
> **Arts Area:** Ensemble; Medieval Music; Drama
> **Status:** Professional; Non-Profit
> **Type:** Performing; Touring; Resident
> **Purpose:** To present authentic performances of medieval music and music drama
> **Management:** Fredrick Renz, Director; Carl K. Steffes, Managing Director; Kerby Lovallo, Hillyer International Tour Management

Officers: Lawrence M. Addington, Treasurer; Myles Astor, Diane Cochrane, Janice Haggerty and Edwin David Robertson, Board Members
Paid Staff: 2
Paid Artists: 30
Budget: $100,000 - $500,000
Income Sources: Private Foundations/Grants/Endowments; Business/Corporate Donations; Box Office; Government Grants; Individual Donations
Season: October - May
Annual Attendance: 10,000
Affiliations: Early Music America
Performance Facilities: Cathedral of Saint John the Divine

NORTH/SOUTH CONSONANCE, INC.
PO Box 698, Cathedral Station, New York, NY 10025-0698
(518) 274-4956
FAX: (518) 274-4956
Founded: 1980
Arts Area: Chamber; Ensemble; Instrumental Group; Electronic & Live Electronic; New Music
Status: Professional; Non-Profit
Type: Performing; Touring; Resident; Educational
Purpose: To promote and perform the music of living composers with emphasis placed on music from the Americas
Officers: Max Lifchitz, Director; Laura Ellis, President
Volunteer Staff: 2
Paid Artists: 12
Utilizes: Special Technical Talent; Guest Conductors; Guest Artists
Budget: $1,000 - $50,000
Income Sources: Private Foundations/Grants/Endowments; Business/Corporate Donations; Box Office; Government Grants; Individual Donations
Season: October - June
Annual Attendance: 2,000
Affiliations: CMA
Performance Facilities: Merkin Hall; Weil Recital Hall

ODYSSEY CHAMBER PLAYERS, INC.
PO Box 1607, Cathedral Station, New York, NY 10025
(212) 496-7071
FAX: (508) 291-0087
Arts Area: Chamber
Status: Professional; Non-Profit
Type: Performing
Purpose: To perform works featuring between six and 20 winds
Management: H. Robert Reynolds, Artistic Advisor; Maury Okun, Executive Director
Budget: $1,000 - $50,000
Income Sources: Private Foundations/Grants/Endowments; Business/Corporate Donations; Box Office; Government Grants; Individual Donations
Performance Facilities: Brooklyn Music School; Madison Avenue Presbyterian Church

ORCHESTRA OF ST. LUKE'S
130 West 42nd Street, New York, NY 10036
(212) 840-7470
FAX: (212) 840-7585
Founded: 1974
Arts Area: Orchestra; Chamber; Ensemble
Status: Professional; Non-Profit
Type: Performing
Management: Michael Feldman, Artistic Director; Marianne C. Lockwood, Executive Director; Curt Sharp, General Manager; Susannah Halston, Director of Marketing and Development; Rosalyn Bindman, Education Director
Officers: M. Bernard Aidinoff, Chairman; Michael Feldman, President; Marianne C. Lockwood, Vice President/Secretary; Steven Leifer, Treasurer
Paid Staff: 10   **Volunteer Staff:** 15
Paid Artists: 300
Utilizes: Guest Conductors; Guest Artists; Guest Directors
Budget: $1,000,000 - $5,000,000
Income Sources: Private Foundations/Grants/Endowments; Business/Corporate Donations; Box Office; Government Grants; Individual Donations
Season: October - May
Annual Attendance: 100,000

Affiliations: St. Luke's Chamber Ensemble
Performance Facilities: Merkin Concert Hall; Carnegie Hall; Caramoor Music Festival; Avery Fisher Hall

ORPHEUS CHAMBER ORCHESTRA, INC.
490 Riverside Drive, New York, NY 10027
(212) 678-1700
FAX: (212) 678-1717
   Arts Area: Orchestra; Chamber
   Status: Professional; Non-Profit
   Type: Performing; Touring
   Purpose: To allow members to work in collaboration on the selection and interpretation of pieces
   Management: Julian Fifer, Executive Director/President; Norma Hurlburt, Vice President/General Manager
   Officers: Fred Rubenstein, Chairman of the Board
   Budget: $1,000,000 - $5,000,000
   Income Sources: Private Foundations/Grants/Endowments; Business/Corporate Donations; Box Office; Government Grants; Individual Donations
   Performance Facilities: Carnegie Hall

QUINTET OF THE AMERICAS
134 Bowery, New York, NY 10013
(212) 431-8786
FAX: (212) 966-0954
   Founded: 1976
   Arts Area: Chamber; Ethnic
   Status: Professional; Non-Profit
   Type: Performing; Touring; Resident; Educational
   Purpose: To present chamber music and contemporary music especially from North and South America
   Officers: Barbara Oldham, President; Matt Sullivan, Vice President; Tom Novak, Treasurer; Christopher Jepperson, Secretary
   Paid Artists: 5
   Utilizes: Guest Artists
   Budget: $1,000 - $50,000
   Income Sources: Private Foundations/Grants/Endowments; Business/Corporate Donations; Box Office; Government Grants; Individual Donations
   Season: 52 Weeks
   Performance Facilities: Center for Inter-American Relations

THE RIVERSIDE SYMPHONY
258 Riverside Drive, #7C, New York, NY 10025
(212) 864-4197
FAX: (212) 864-9795
   Arts Area: Symphony; Orchestra
   Status: Professional; Non-Profit
   Type: Performing; Resident; Educational
   Purpose: To present new and less-familiar work; to present emerging artists; to produce American music
   Management: Anthony Korf, Artistic Director; George Rothman, Conductor/Music Director; Elaine Carroll, Administrative Director
   Budget: $100,000 - $500,000
   Income Sources: Private Foundations/Grants/Endowments; Business/Corporate Donations; Box Office; Government Grants; Individual Donations
   Performance Facilities: Kathyrn Bache Miller Theatre, Columbia University; Alice Tully Hall

ROULETTE INTERMEDIUM, INC.
228 West Broadway, New York, NY 10013
(212) 219-8242
FAX: (212) 219-8773
   Arts Area: Chamber; Ensemble; Ethnic; Folk; Instrumental Group; Electronic & Live Electronic; Band
   Status: Non-Profit
   Type: Presenting
   Purpose: To be a presenting organization and facility for innovative composers and musicians through its concert series, commissions and recording distribution services; to support a broad range of new music by young established artists
   Management: Jim Staley, Program Director; David Weinstein, Projects Director; Suzanne Youngerman, Managing Director
   Officers: Jim Staley, President
   Budget: $100,000 - $500,000
   Income Sources: Private Foundations/Grants/Endowments; Business/Corporate Donations; Box Office; Government Grants; Individual Donations
   Performance Facilities: Roul

SAINT LUKES CHAMBER ENSEMBLE, INC.
130 West 42nd Street, Suite 804, New York, NY 10036
(212) 840-7470
FAX: (212) 840-7585
    Arts Area: Orchestra; Chamber
    Status: Non-Profit
    Type: Performing; Touring; Educational; Sponsoring
    Purpose: Encompasses three performing divisions; St. Luke's Chamber Ensemble; Orchestra of St. Luke's; Children's Free Opera and Dance of New York
    Management: Michael Feldman, Artistic Director; Marriane C. Lockwood, Executive Director
    Officers: M. Bernard Aidinoff, Chairman of the Board
    Budget: $1,000,000 - $5,000,000
    Income Sources: Private Foundations/Grants/Endowments; Business/Corporate Donations; Box Office; Government Grants; Individual Donations
    Performance Facilities: Avery Fisher Hall; Merkin Concert Hall; Brooklyn Academy of Music; Triplex Theatre; Town Hall

SATURDAY BRASS QUNITET
c/o St. Michael's Episcopal Church, 225 West 99th Street, New York, NY 10025
(212) 222-2700
    Arts Area: Chamber
    Status: Professional; Non-Profit
    Type: Performing; Touring; Resident; Educational
    Purpose: To present classics of the brass chamber genre; to solicit and perform new selections for brass
    Budget: $50,000 - $100,000
    Income Sources: Private Foundations/Grants/Endowments; Business/Corporate Donations; Box Office; Government Grants; Individual Donations

SPECULUM MUSICAE, INC.
127 West 96th Street, #16H, New York, NY 10025
(212) 865-9028
    Arts Area: Chamber; Ensemble
    Status: Professional; Non-Profit
    Type: Performing; Touring; Resident; Educational; Sponsoring
    Purpose: To devote its performances and recordings to high quality interpretations of a broad range of new music and older "classics" of the 20th century
    Management: Amy Frawley, Adminstrative Director; Eric Bartlett, President
    Budget: $50,000 - $100,000
    Income Sources: Private Foundations/Grants/Endowments; Business/Corporate Donations; Box Office; Government Grants; Individual Donations
    Performance Facilities: Merkin Concert Hall

SYLVAN WINDS, INCORPORATED
246 West 38th Street, New York, NY 10018
FAX: (212) 944-9082
    Arts Area: Chamber; Ensemble; Instrumental Group
    Status: Professional; Non-Profit
    Type: Performing; Touring; Educational
    Purpose: Since its formation in 1976, Sylvan Winds has devoted itself exclusively to the performance of chamber music for wind instruments.
    Management: Steve Elmer, Executive Director; Svjetlana Kabalin, Artistic Director
    Officers: Florence Reif Richman, President of the Board
    Budget: $50,000 - $100,000
    Income Sources: Private Foundations/Grants/Endowments; Business/Corporate Donations; Box Office; Government Grants; Individual Donations
    Performance Facilities: Weill Recital Hall at Carnegie Hall; Merkin Concert Hall at Abraham Goodman House

SYMPHONY FOR UNITED NATIONS
205 West End Avenue, Suite 21C, New York, NY 10023
(212) 873-2872
FAX: (212) 874-7720
    Founded: 1974
    Arts Area: Symphony; Chamber; Ensemble; Ethnic; Folk
    Status: Professional; Semi-Professional; Non-Profit
    Type: Performing; Touring; Educational; Sponsoring
    Purpose: To produce concerts and festivals around issues of human and global concern
    Management: Joseph Eger, Conductor
    Officers: Joseph Eger, President; Dr. Ruth Mack, Vice President; Diane Siewering, Secretary

Paid Staff: 4   **Volunteer Staff:** 22
Utilizes: Special Technical Talent; Guest Conductors; Guest Artists; Guest Directors
Budget: $100,000 - $500,000
Income Sources: Private Foundations/Grants/Endowments; Business/Corporate Donations; Box Office; Government Grants; Individual Donations
Season: 52 Weeks

TISCH CENTER FOR THE ARTS
1395 Lexington Avenue, New York, NY 10128
(212) 415-5740
FAX: (212) 415-5738
Arts Area: Orchestra; Chamber; Ensemble; Pops; Theatre; Jazz
Status: Non-Profit
Type: Performing; Educational
Management: Omus Hirshbein, Vice Chairman; Raymond Grant, Director; Jacqueline Taylor, Managing Director
Paid Staff: 8
Utilizes: Special Technical Talent; Guest Conductors; Guest Artists; Guest Directors
Budget: $1,000,000 - $5,000,000
Income Sources: Private Foundations/Grants/Endowments; Business/Corporate Donations; Box Office; Government Grants; Individual Donations
Season: September - July
Performance Facilities: Kaufmann Concert Hall

WAVERLY CONSORT, INC.
305 Riverside Drive, 5#, New York, NY 10025
(212) 666-1260
FAX: (212) 666-1559
Arts Area: Ensemble
Status: Professional; Non-Profit
Type: Performing; Touring
Purpose: To present early music to the public in NY and throughout the country
Management: Michael Jaffee, Artistic Director
Budget: $50,000 - $100,000
Income Sources: Private Foundations/Grants/Endowments; Business/Corporate Donations; Box Office; Government Grants; Individual Donations

VOCAL MUSIC

AFTER DINNER OPERA COMPANY
23 Stuyvesant Street, New York, NY 10003
(212) 477-6212
Founded: 1949
Arts Area: Lyric Opera
Status: Professional; Non-Profit
Type: Performing; Touring; Educational
Purpose: To perform opera, promote American composers and performers and educate the public in opera
Management: Richard Flusser, Administrative Director; Beth Flusser, Production Manager; Elizabeth Mozza, Producer; Conrad Strausser, Musical Director
Officers: Roslyn Borkow, President
Paid Staff: 4   **Volunteer Staff:** 6
Paid Artists: 20
Utilizes: Special Technical Talent; Guest Artists; Guest Directors
Budget: $50,000 - $100,000
Income Sources: Private Foundations/Grants/Endowments; Business/Corporate Donations; Box Office; Government Grants
Season: September - June
Annual Attendance: 10,000
Performance Facilities: Lincoln Center for the Performing Arts; Queensborough Community College

AMATO OPERA THEATRE
319 Bowery, New York, NY 10003
(212) 228-8200
Founded: 1948
Arts Area: Grand Opera; Light Opera
Status: Professional; Semi-Professional; Non-Profit
Type: Performing
Officers: Anthony Amato, President; Sally Amato, Treasurer
Volunteer Staff: 10

Non-Paid Artists: 100
Utilizes: Special Technical Talent; Guest Conductors; Guest Artists
Budget: $50,000 - $100,000
Income Sources: Private Foundations/Grants/Endowments; Business/Corporate Donations; Box Office; Government Grants; Individual Donations
Season: September - May
Annual Attendance: 8,500

AMERICAN CHAMBER OPERA COMPANY, INC.
657 West 161st Street, #3F, New York, NY 10032
(212) 781-0857
Founded: 1983
Arts Area: Chamber Opera
Status: Professional; Non-Profit
Type: Performing
Purpose: To present American and other chamber operas in full productions emphasizing musical and dramatic values
Management: Raquel Rossman, Production Manager; George Zarr, Stage Manager
Officers: Douglas Anderson, Executive Director; Laura Greenberg, Artistic Director; Giboney Whyte, Managing Director
Paid Staff: 5   **Volunteer Staff:** 15
Paid Artists: 95
Utilizes: Special Technical Talent; Guest Conductors; Guest Artists; Guest Directors
Budget: $1,000 - $50,000
Income Sources: Private Foundations/Grants/Endowments; Business/Corporate Donations; Box Office; Government Grants; Individual Donations
Season: October - May   **Annual Attendance:** 1,500
Performance Facilities: Marymount Manhattan Theatre

ASSOCIATION FOR THE FURTHERMENT OF BEL CANTO
11 Riverside Drive, New York, NY 10023
(212) 877-1595
Founded: 1968
Status: Professional; Non-Profit
Type: Performing; Resident
Purpose: To present productions of Bel Canto, Italian and French Opera pieces
Management: Stefan Zucker, General Manager/Artistic Director
Paid Staff: 3   **Volunteer Staff:** 5
Paid Artists: 100   **Non-Paid Artists:** 5
Utilizes: Special Technical Talent; Guest Conductors; Guest Artists; Guest Directors
Budget: $50,000 - $100,000
Income Sources: Business/Corporate Donations; Box Office; Individual Donations
Season: 52 Weeks
Performance Facilities: Merkin Concert Hall; Casa Italiana, Columbia University

CENTER FOR CONTEMPORARY OPERA
Gracie Station, PO Box 1350, New York, NY 10028-0010
(212) 308-6728
FAX: (212) 308-6744
Founded: 1982
Arts Area: Lyric Opera
Status: Professional; Non-Profit
Type: Performing
Management: Richard Marshall, Director
Paid Staff: 1
Utilizes: Special Technical Talent; Guest Artists; Guest Directors
Budget: $50,000 - $100,000
Income Sources: Private Foundations/Grants/Endowments; Business/Corporate Donations; Box Office; Government Grants; Individual Donations
Season: October - June
Affiliations: NOA; Operaliner

CONCERT ROYAL, INC.
280 Riverside Drive, Suite 5H, New York, NY 10025
(212) 662-8829
FAX: (212) 662-8829
Arts Area: Baroque Opera; Ballet; Orchestra
Status: Professional; Non-Profit
Type: Performing; Touring
Purpose: To perform baroque and classical music on original instruments with a strong vocal and dance component

Management: James Richman, Artistic Director/Conductor; Suzanne Konowitz, General Manager
Budget: $100,000 - $500,000
Income Sources: Private Foundations/Grants/Endowments; Business/Corporate Donations; Box Office; Government Grants; Individual Donations
Performance Facilities: Merkin Concert Hall; Florence Gould Hall

GOODMAN CHAMBER CHOIR
145 Fourth Avenue, New York, NY 10003
(212) 254-1717
Founded: 1984
Arts Area: Choral
Status: Professional; Non-Profit
Type: Performing; Touring
Purpose: To employ American and Russian emigres for performances of choral music
Budget: $1,000 - $50,000
Income Sources: Private Foundations/Grants/Endowments; Business/Corporate Donations; Box Office; Government Grants; Individual Donations
Season: September - June   **Annual Attendance:** 10,000

GREGG SMITH SINGERS, INC.
171 West 71st Street, New York, NY 10023
(212) 874-2990
Arts Area: Choral
Status: Professional; Non-Profit
Type: Performing; Touring; Resident; Educational
Purpose: To lead the way in establishing the rightful place of American choral music
Management: Gregg Smith, Music Director; Walter Gould, Booking Manager
Budget: $100,000 - $500,000
Income Sources: Private Foundations/Grants/Endowments; Business/Corporate Donations; Box Office; Government Grants; Individual Donations

I CANTORI DI NEW YORK
PO Box 4156, New York, NY 10185-0035
Founded: 1983
Arts Area: Choral
Status: Semi-Professional
Type: Performing
Purpose: To present a wide variety of choral music, juxtaposing contemporary and the past
Utilizes: Guest Artists
Budget: $1,000 - $50,000
Income Sources: Private Foundations/Grants/Endowments; Business/Corporate Donations; Box Office; Individual Donations
Season: September - May   **Annual Attendance:** 1,500

JUILLIARD OPERA CENTER
The Juilliard School, 60 Lincoln Center Plaza, New York, NY 10023-6588
(212) 799-5000
FAX: (212) 724-0263
Founded: 1969
Arts Area: Grand Opera; Lyric Opera; Light Opera
Status: Non-Professional; Non-Profit; Training
Type: Performing; Educational
Purpose: To provide training for post-graduate, pre-professional opera singers
Management: Frank Corsaro, Artistic Director
Officers: Joseph W. Polisi, President, The Juilliard School
Paid Staff: 20
Non-Paid Artists: 20
Utilizes: Special Technical Talent; Guest Conductors; Guest Directors
Budget: $100,000 - $500,000
Income Sources: The Juilliard School
Season: December - April   **Annual Attendance:** 8,000
Affiliations: The Juilliard School
Performance Facilities: Juilliard Theater

L'OPERA FRANCAIS DE NEW YORK
515 West 111th Street, Suite 3F, New York, NY 10025
(212) 678-0548
Founded: 1988

Arts Area: Lyric Opera
Status: Professional
Type: Performing
Purpose: To bring French lyric opera to American audiences
Management: Yves Abel, Susan Mebroin, Artistic Directors; Melanie Smith, General Manager; Ron Jamini, Administrative Assistant; Caroline Criscuolo, Development
Officers: Yves Abel, President; Susan Melvora, Vice President; Melanie Smith, Secretary
Paid Staff: 4   **Volunteer Staff:** 2
Paid Artists: 120
Utilizes: Special Technical Talent; Guest Artists; Guest Directors
Budget: $100,000 - $500,000
Income Sources: Private Foundations/Grants/Endowments; Business/Corporate Donations; Box Office; Individual Donations
Season: February - June   **Annual Attendance:** 3,000
Affiliations: French Institute; Alliance Francaise
Performance Facilities: Florence Gould Hall

LIEDERKRANZ OPERA THEATRE
6 East 87th, New York, NY 10128
(212) 534-0880
Founded: 1960
Arts Area: Grand Opera; Lyric Opera; Light Opera; Operetta
Status: Professional
Type: Performing
Purpose: To foster a performance outlet for young singers
Management: John Balme, Music Director
Officers: Hans Hachmann, President
Paid Staff: 1
Paid Artists: 40
Utilizes: Guest Artists; Guest Directors
Budget: $1,000 - $50,000
Income Sources: Private Foundations/Grants/Endowments; Box Office
Season: September - May   **Annual Attendance:** 2,500
Performance Facilities: Liederkranz Building

LIGHT OPERA OF MANHATTAN
316 East 91st Street, New York, NY 10028
(212) 831-2000; (212) 222-9192
FAX: (212) 864-6682
Founded: 1969
Arts Area: Light Opera; Operetta; Musical Theatre
Status: Professional; Non-Profit
Type: Performing
Purpose: To promote the continued performance and appreciation of a nearly-forgotten art form, the operetta
Management: Steven M. Levy, Producer; Elaine Malbin, Artistic Director
Officers: Patricia Greenwald, Chairman; Jean Dairymple, President; Steven Levy, Secretary; Reed Simmons, Treasurer
Paid Staff: 3   **Volunteer Staff:** 12
Paid Artists: 33
Utilizes: Guest Conductors; Guest Directors
Budget: $500,000 - $1,000,000
Income Sources: Private Foundations/Grants/Endowments; Business/Corporate Donations; Box Office; Government Grants; Individual Donations
Season: 52 Weeks   **Annual Attendance:** 30,000
Performance Facilities: Playhouse 91

MEASURED BREATHS THEATRE COMPANY
193 Spring Street, #3R, New York, NY 10012
(212) 334-8402
Founded: 1989
Arts Area: Lyric Opera; Theatre
Status: Professional; Commercial
Type: Performing
Purpose: To create and revive all forms of operatic musical theatre in order to strengthen the dramatic basis of museum theatre
Management: Robert Press, Artistic Director
Utilizes: Special Technical Talent; Guest Conductors; Guest Artists
Budget: $1,000 - $50,000
Income Sources: Box Office; Individual Donations
Season: 52 Weeks   **Annual Attendance:** 600

THE METROPOLITAN GREEK CHORALE
PO Box 2690, New York, NY 10185
(212) 475-3394; (212) 874-4482
Founded: 1965
Arts Area: Choral; Ethnic
Status: Semi-Professional; Non-Professional; Non-Profit
Type: Performing
Purpose: To present fine performances of traditional Greek music, as well as contemporary Greek and Greek-American composers
Officers: George Haikalis, President; Elaine Scurtis, Vice President; Frances Bishop, Secretary; Jerry Kolaitis, Treasurer
Volunteer Staff: 12
Non-Paid Artists: 35
Utilizes: Guest Artists
Budget: $1,000 - $50,000
Income Sources: Private Foundations/Grants/Endowments; Business/Corporate Donations; Box Office; Government Grants; Individual Donations
Season: October.- June   **Annual Attendance:** 700
Performance Facilities: Merkin Hall; Alice Tully Hall

METROPOLITAN OPERA
Lincoln Center, New York, NY 10023
(212) 799-3100
Founded: 1883
Arts Area: Grand Opera
Status: Professional; Non-Profit
Type: Performing; Touring; Resident
Purpose: To produce and present opera performances in New York, on tour and through broadcasts of live performances throughout the United States and Canada
Management: Joseph Volpe, General Director; James Levine, Artistic Director
Officers: Mrs. Gilbert W. Humphrey, Honorary Chairman of the Board; James S. Marcus, Chairman; Bruce Crawford, President; Wilbur Daniels, Chairman, Executive Committee; Alton E. Peters, Robert L.B. Tobin, Vice Presidents; Ray J. Groves, Treasurer/Secretary
Utilizes: Special Technical Talent; Guest Conductors; Guest Artists; Guest Directors
Budget: Over 10,000,000
Income Sources: Private Foundations/Grants/Endowments; Business/Corporate Donations; Box Office; Government Grants; Individual Donations
Season: September - April
Affiliations: OA
Performance Facilities: Metropolitan Opera House

MUSIC-THEATRE GROUP, INC.
29 Bethune Street, New York, NY 10014
(212) 924-3108
FAX: (212) 255-1981
Founded: 1971
Arts Area: Music Theatre
Status: Professional; Non-Profit
Type: Performing; Touring
Purpose: To commission, develop and produce innovative music theatre
Management: Diane Wondisford, Managing Director; Lyn Austin, CEO/Producing Director
Officers: Lyn Austin, President; Lynda Sturner Traum, Vice President; Charles Houerith Jr., Secretary; Bernard Rosenberg, Treasurer; Rosita Sarnoff, Chair
Paid Staff: 4   **Volunteer Staff:** 2
Paid Artists: 75
Utilizes: Special Technical Talent; Guest Conductors; Guest Artists; Guest Directors
Budget: $500,000 - $1,000,000
Income Sources: Private Foundations/Grants/Endowments; Business/Corporate Donations; Box Office; Government Grants; Individual Donations; Touring
Season: September - May   **Annual Attendance:** 15,000
Affiliations: OA; TCG; ART/NY

MUSICA SACRA
165 West 86th Street, New York, NY 10024
(212) 874-3104
FAX: (212) 874-7815
Founded: 1973
Arts Area: Choral
Status: Professional

Type: Performing
Purpose: To perform choral works spanning the ages
Management: Elizabeth Bond, General Manager
Officers: Jonathan Prinz, President; Jen T. Farrah, Robert F. Langley, Robert Brauer, Vice Presidents; Barbara G. Landau, Secretary; Gerald W. Richman, Treasurer
Paid Staff: 2
Paid Artists: 120
Utilizes: Guest Artists
Budget: $500,000 - $1,000,000
Income Sources: Private Foundations/Grants/Endowments; Business/Corporate Donations; Box Office; Government Grants; Individual Donations
Season: September - April
Performance Facilities: Lincoln Center; Carnegie Hall

NEW AMSTERDAM SINGERS
PO Box 373, Cathedral Station, New York, NY 10025
(212) 662-6523
 Founded: 1968
 Arts Area: Choral
 Status: Non-Professional
 Type: Performing
 Purpose: To perform and promote choral music
 Management: Clara Longstreth, Music Director; Wendy S. Fay, Manager
 Officers: Joanne Cossa, President; Carol O' Connor, Vice President; Paul Pausekian, Treasurer; Paula Franklin, Secretary
 Paid Staff: 4   **Volunteer Staff:** 10
 Non-Paid Artists: 70
 Utilizes: Guest Artists
 Budget: $50,000 - $100,000
 Income Sources: Private Foundations/Grants/Endowments; Business/Corporate Donations; Box Office; Government Grants; Individual Donations
 Season: October - June   **Annual Attendance:** 800

NEW YORK CHORAL SOCIETY
165 West 57th Street, New York, NY 10019
(212) 624-0027
 Founded: 1958
 Arts Area: Choral
 Status: Non-Professional; Non-Profit
 Type: Performing; Touring
 Purpose: To present choral masterpieces and lesser-known works in Carnegie Hall
 Officers: David Nickols, President; Joanne Lawson, Treasurer; Pam Reich, Vice President; Lisa Guida, President Elect
 Volunteer Staff: 14
 Paid Artists: 2   **Non-Paid Artists:** 180
 Utilizes: Special Technical Talent; Guest Conductors; Guest Artists; Contract Orchestras
 Budget: $100,000 - $500,000
 Income Sources: Private Foundations/Grants/Endowments; Business/Corporate Donations; Box Office; Government Grants; Individual Donations; Perfomance Fees
 Season: September - May   **Annual Attendance:** 10,000
 Performance Facilities: Carnegie Hall; Lincoln Center

NEW YORK CITY OPERA
20 Lincoln Center, New York, NY 10023
(212) 870-5600
FAX: (212) 724-1120
 Founded: 1944
 Arts Area: Grand Opera; Musical Theatre
 Status: Professional
 Type: Performing; Touring; Resident; Educational
 Purpose: To produce grand opera; to develop and present young American singers; to present opera as theater
 Management: Christopher A. Keene, General Director
 Officers: Robert W. Wilson, Chairman; Martin J. Oppenheimer, Vice Chairman
 Paid Staff: 70   **Volunteer Staff:** 50
 Paid Artists: 450
 Utilizes: Special Technical Talent; Guest Conductors; Guest Artists; Guest Directors
 Budget: Over 10,000,000
 Income Sources: Private Foundations/Grants/Endowments; Business/Corporate Donations; Box Office; Government Grants; Individual Donations
 Season: July - November   **Annual Attendance:** 350,000

Affiliations: OA
Performance Facilities: New York State Theater

NEW YORK CITY OPERA NATIONAL COMPANY
211 West 61st Street, 6th Floor, New York, NY 10023
(212) 399-6409
FAX: (212) 399-6414
Founded: 1979
Arts Area: Grand Opera; Lyric Opera
Status: Professional; Non-Profit
Type: Performing; Touring
Purpose: To take top-quality, fully-staged orchestra performances of standard repertory operas to relatively isolated areas; to provide young singers with valuable performing experience
Management: Christopher Keene, General Director; Nancy Kelly, Administrative Director; Joseph Colaneri, Music Director
Officers: Robert W. Wilson, Chairman; Martin J. Oppenheimer, Vice Chairman
Paid Staff: 3   **Volunteer Staff:** 2
Paid Artists: 70
Utilizes: Special Technical Talent; Guest Artists; Guest Directors
Budget: $1,000,000 - $5,000,000
Income Sources: Private Foundations/Grants/Endowments; Business/Corporate Donations; Government Grants; Performance Fees
Season: January - April   **Annual Attendance:** 100,000

THE NEW YORK CONCERT SINGERS
401 East 80th Street, New York, NY 10021
(212) 879-4412
Founded: 1988
Arts Area: Choral; Vocal Chamber Music
Status: Professional
Type: Performing; Educational
Purpose: To present choral and vocal chamber programs
Officers: Judith Clurman, Chair; Marcia Klugman, Vice Chair/Treasurer; Lola Terch Gold, Secretary
Paid Staff: 1   **Volunteer Staff:** 3
Utilizes: Guest Artists
Budget: $1,000 - $50,000
Income Sources: Private Foundations/Grants/Endowments; Box Office; Individual Donations
Season: 52 Weeks   **Annual Attendance:** 600
Performance Facilities: Mertan Hall; Lincoln Center

NEW YORK GILBERT AND SULLIVAN PLAYERS
251 West 91st Street #4C, New York, NY 10024
(212) 769-1000
Founded: 1974
Arts Area: Operetta; Musical Theatre
Status: Professional
Type: Performing; Touring; Resident; Educational
Purpose: To promote and produce works of Gilbert and Sullivan, as well as related works using orchestras and small ensembles
Management: Albert Bergeret, Artistic Director/General Manager
Officers: Charles Pye, President; Albert Bergeret, Vice President; Ivy Reale, Secretary; John Behonet, Treasurer
Paid Staff: 1   **Volunteer Staff:** 1
Paid Artists: 80
Utilizes: Guest Artists
Budget: $100,000 - $500,000
Income Sources: Private Foundations/Grants/Endowments; Business/Corporate Donations; Box Office; Government Grants; Individual Donations
Season: 52 Weeks   **Annual Attendance:** 20,000
Affiliations: AEA; AFM

OPERA EBONY
2109 Broadway, New York, NY 10023
(212) 874-7245
FAX: (212) 580-2920
Founded: 1973
Arts Area: Grand Opera; Ethnic; Folk; 20th Century Works
Status: Professional; Non-Profit

Type: Performing; Touring; Educational
Purpose: To promote and discover singers, directors, composers, technicians and choreographers
Management: Wayne Sanders, Music Director; Benjamin Matthews, Artistic Director; Mohammed Hatim, Special Projects Director
Officers: Ibraham Abdul-Malek, Chairman; Garnald King, Vice President; Clarie Stanton, Secretary
Paid Staff: 6   **Volunteer Staff:** 15
Utilizes: Special Technical Talent; Guest Conductors; Guest Artists; Guest Directors
Budget: $1,000,000 - $5,000,000
Income Sources: Private Foundations/Grants/Endowments; Business/Corporate Donations; Box Office; Government Grants; Individual Donations
Season: September - July   **Annual Attendance:** 8,000
Affiliations: The American Music Center; OA
Performance Facilities: Aaron Davis Hall

OPERA NORTHEAST
530 East 89th Street, New York, NY 10128
(212) 472-2168
Founded: 1972
Arts Area: Grand Opera; Operetta
Status: Professional; Non-Profit
Type: Performing; Touring; Educational
Purpose: Build a first-class touring organization to produce and present authentic classical lyric theatre
Management: Donald Westwood, Artistic Director; Ronald Forsmo, David Seatter, Managing Directors
Paid Staff: 5
Paid Artists: 200
Utilizes: Special Technical Talent; Guest Conductors; Guest Artists; Guest Directors
Budget: $500,000 - $1,000,000
Income Sources: Private Foundations/Grants/Endowments; Business/Corporate Donations; Box Office; Government Grants; Individual Donations
Season: 52 Weeks   **Annual Attendance:** 150,000

OPERA ORCHESTRA OF NEW YORK
239 West 72nd Street, Suite 2R, New York, NY 10023-2734
(212) 799-1982
Founded: 1971
Arts Area: Grand Opera; Lyric Opera
Status: Professional; Non-Profit
Type: Performing; Sponsoring
Purpose: To bring rarely heard or little-known operas to the public
Management: Eve Queler, Music Director; Yvonne Altmann, Director of Development; Alix Barthelmes, Manager
Paid Staff: 3   **Volunteer Staff:** 4
Paid Artists: 140
Utilizes: Guest Artists
Budget: $500,000 - $1,000,000
Income Sources: Private Foundations/Grants/Endowments; Business/Corporate Donations; Box Office; Government Grants; Individual Donations
Season: November - May   **Annual Attendance:** 15,000
Performance Facilities: Carnegie Hall

ORATORIO SOCIETY OF NEW YORK
881 Seventh Avenue, Carnegie Hall, #504, New York, NY 10019
(212) 247-4199
Founded: 1873
Arts Area: Choral
Status: Non-Professional; Non-Profit
Type: Performing; Touring; Resident; Educational
Purpose: To bring the people of Greater New York seldom-done, good oratorio music and to offer a platform for promising young artists
Officers: Joseph W. Brinkley, Chairman; Ellen L. Blair, President; Evelyn Arcudi and Janet Plucknett, Vice Presidents
Paid Staff: 2   **Volunteer Staff:** 3
Non-Paid Artists: 200
Utilizes: Guest Conductors; Guest Artists
Budget: $100,000 - $500,000
Income Sources: Private Foundations/Grants/Endowments; Business/Corporate Donations; Box Office; Government Grants; Individual Donations
Season: September - June   **Annual Attendance:** 10,000
Performance Facilities: Carnegie Hall

PALA OPERA ASSOCIATION
7 West 81st Street, New York, NY 10024
(212) 769-8760
FAX: (212) 769-8760
Founded: 1989
Arts Area: Grand Opera; Opera/Theater Combinations
Status: Professional
Type: Performing
Purpose: To present high-calibre, ascendent-star artists in an elegant, professional situation, with full orchestra and chorus, where they will be heard by critics and discerning, paying audiences
Management: Elizabeth Moxley Falk, Producer/Artistic Director; Timothy Lindberg, Music Director; Richard Woitach, Chief Music Consultant; Phillip Gossett, Bel Canto Enbellishments
Officers: Lee Falk, President of Parent Organization: Provincetown Academy of the Living Arts; Elizabeth Moxley Falk, Richard Woitach, Vice Presidents P.A.L.A.
Utilizes: Guest Artists
Budget: $100,000 - $500,000
Income Sources: Private Foundations/Grants/Endowments; Business/Corporate Donations; Box Office; Individual Donations
Season: October - June   **Annual Attendance:** 2,000
Affiliations: OA; NOA

POMERIUM MUSICES, INCORPORATED
945 West End Avenue, #1C, New York, NY 10025
(212) 316-3953
FAX: (215) 247-4323
Arts Area: Choral; Renaissance
Status: Professional; Non-Profit
Type: Performing; Touring
Purpose: A 13-member a cappella ensemble dedicated to performing the music written for virtuoso chapel choirs in the 15th and 16th centuries
Management: Alexander Blachly, Artistic Director
Budget: $50,000 - $100,000
Income Sources: Private Foundations/Grants/Endowments; Box Office; Government Grants; Individual Donations

PRO MUSICIS FOUNDATION, INC.
140 West 79th Street, Suite 9F, New York, NY 10024
(212) 787-0993
FAX: (212) 362-0352
Founded: 1965
Arts Area: Recital
Status: Professional; Non-Profit; Community Service
Type: Performing; Sponsoring
Purpose: To encourgage career development for emerging recitalists through recitals in major concert halls; to perform community service through recitals in various institutions
Officers: Fr. Eugene Merlet, President; John E. Haag, Executive Director
Paid Staff: 1   **Volunteer Staff:** 3
Budget: $100,000 - $500,000
Income Sources: Private Foundations/Grants/Endowments; Business/Corporate Donations; Box Office; Government Grants; Individual Donations
Season: January - May   **Annual Attendance:** 3,000
Performance Facilities: Weill Hall, New York; Jordan Hall, Boston

THE SAINT THOMAS CHOIR OF MEN AND BOYS
Saint Thomas Church, Fifth Avenue, 1 West 53rd Street, New York, NY 10019
(212) 757-7013
Founded: 1919
Arts Area: Choral
Status: Professional; Non-Profit
Type: Performing; Touring; Resident
Purpose: To provide Anglican music of the highest standards for Saint Thomas Church Fifth Avenue; to give a concert series each season and to record; to tour domestically and overseas
Management: Saint Thomas Church Fifth Avenue; Karen Mc Farlane Artists, Inc.
Officers: Gerre Hancock, Director; Phelicia Wingfield, Music Administrator; Lee Whitley, Marketing Consultant
Paid Staff: 3   **Volunteer Staff:** 50
Paid Artists: 32
Utilizes: Special Technical Talent; Guest Artists; Guest Directors
Budget: $50,000 - $100,000

Income Sources: Private Foundations/Grants/Endowments; Business/Corporate Donations; Box Office; Individual Donations

Season: September - June   **Annual Attendance:** 6,000

Performance Facilities: Saint Thomas Church

THEATRE ROCOCO

Empire State Building, Suite 3304, New York, NY 10118

(212) 971-9702

> **Founded:** 1969
> **Arts Area:** 18th Century Opera
> **Status:** Professional
> **Type:** Performing; Touring; Educational
> **Purpose:** To perform opera of the 18th century
> **Management:** Jeannette Ferrell, General Manager; Janet Poland, Producer
> **Officers:** Fritz Maraffi, Musical Director
> **Paid Staff:** 2   **Volunteer Staff:** 3
> **Paid Artists:** 29
> **Utilizes:** Guest Artists; Guest Musicians
> **Budget:** $50,000 - $100,000
> **Income Sources:** Box Office; Touring Fees Worldwide
> **Season:** October - April

TOURING CONCERT OPERA COMPANY

228 East 80th Street, New York, NY 10021

(212) 988-2542

> **Founded:** 1971
> **Arts Area:** Grand Opera
> **Status:** Professional; Non-Profit
> **Type:** Performing; Touring; Educational
> **Purpose:** To bring live, fully professional grand opera to areas where it is less frequently seen and heard; to give young professional artists another outlet for their talents
> **Management:** Ramon Alsina, Company Representative
> **Officers:** Ramon Alsina, President/Treasurer; Anne de Figols, Vice President/Secretary
> **Paid Staff:** 3   **Volunteer Staff:** 7
> **Paid Artists:** 20
> **Utilizes:** Special Technical Talent; Guest Conductors; Guest Artists; Guest Directors; Guest Choreographers
> **Budget:** $1,000 - $50,000
> **Income Sources:** Private Foundations/Grants/Endowments; Business/Corporate Donations; Box Office; Government Grants; Individual Donations
> **Season:** 52 Weeks

VILLAGE LIGHT OPERA GROUP

PO Box 143, Village Station, New York, NY 10014

(212) 243-6281

> **Founded:** 1934
> **Arts Area:** Light Opera; Operetta; Musical Theatre
> **Status:** Non-Professional; Non-Profit
> **Type:** Performing; Educational
> **Purpose:** To provide high-quality lyric theatre experiences in all phases of production and performance for interested amateurs at the lowest possible ticket prices
> **Volunteer Staff:** 50
> **Paid Artists:** 24
> **Budget:** $50,000 - $100,000
> **Income Sources:** Business/Corporate Donations; Box Office; Individual Donations; Rentals
> **Season:** November - and April
> **Annual Attendance:** 5,000
> **Performance Facilities:** Haft Theatre, Fashion Institute of Technology

WESTERN WIND VOCAL ENSEMBLE, INC.

263 West 86th Street, New York, NY 10024

(212) 873-2848

FAX: (212) 873-2849

> **Founded:** 1969
> **Arts Area:** Ensemble
> **Status:** Professional
> **Type:** Performing; Touring; Resident; Educational
> **Purpose:** To bring to the public the beauty of vocal music through performance, recording, radio and workshops
> **Management:** William Zukof, Executive Director; Margaret O'Brien, Administrator
> **Officers:** Hazel Toennies, Treasurer; David Freund, Chairman; Diane Cochrane, President

Paid Staff: 2
Paid Artists: 6
Utilizes: Guest Artists
Budget: $100,000 - $500,000
Income Sources: Private Foundations/Grants/Endowments; Business/Corporate Donations; Box Office; Government Grants; Individual Donations
Season: 52 Weeks
Affiliations: AFTRA; CMA; ACDA

THEATRE

ABOUTFACE THEATRE COMPANY
442 West 42nd Street, New York, NY 10036
(212) 268-9638
Founded: 1984
Arts Area: Professional; Musical; Theatrical Group
Status: Professional; Non-Profit
Type: Resident; Sponsoring
Purpose: To generate, develop and produce original new plays exploring American mythology and idealogy
Management: Sean Burke, Artistic Director; Allison Jones, Managing Director; Martin Fluger, Resident Director; Michael Herz, General Manager; Ron O'Conner, Barry Rowell, Ralph Lewis, Development
Officers: Julie Tibbetts, Chair; Kerry Mackenzie, Michael Mejias, April Cowin, Cheryl Davis-Counsel, Thomas G. Dunn
Volunteer Staff: 40
Utilizes: Special Technical Talent
Budget: $50,000 - $100,000
Income Sources: Private Foundations/Grants/Endowments; Business/Corporate Donations; Box Office; Government Grants; Individual Donations
Season: September - June
Annual Attendance: 5,000
Affiliations: ART/NY; New York Foundation for the Arts
Performance Facilities: Nat Horne Theatre and Studios

THE ACTING COMPANY
PO Box 898, Times Square Station, New York, NY 10108
(212) 564-3510
FAX: (212) 714-2643
Founded: 1972
Arts Area: Professional
Status: Professional; Non-Profit
Type: Performing; Touring; Resident; Educational
Purpose: The Company is dedicated to the development of classical repertory actors and a national audience for the theatre.
Management: Margot Harley, Executive Producer; Zelda Fichandler, Artistic Director
Officers: Edgar Lansbury, Chairman/President; Margot Harley, Carol Crowley, Vice Presidents; John McDonald, Earl Weiner, Secretaries; Martha L. Jay, Secretary/Treasurer
Paid Staff: 22   **Volunteer Staff:** 3
Paid Artists: 29
Utilizes: Special Technical Talent; Guest Directors
Budget: $1,000,000 - $5,000,000
Income Sources: Private Foundations/Grants/Endowments; Business/Corporate Donations; Box Office; Government Grants; Individual Donations
Season: July - May   **Annual Attendance:** 150,000

THE ACTING STUDIO, INC./NEW THEATRE ALLIANCE/CHELSEA REPERTORY COMPANY
29 East 19th Street, 4th Floor, New York, NY 10003
(212) 228-2700
Founded: 1983
Arts Area: Theatrical Group; School
Status: Professional; Semi-Professional
Type: Performing; Resident; Educational
Purpose: To serve as a training institution; to develop new scripts; to provide a resident theatre company
Management: James Price, Artistic Director; John Grabowski, Associate Director
Paid Staff: 3   **Volunteer Staff:** 30
Budget: $50,000 - $100,000
Income Sources: Box Office; Tuition
Season: 52 Weeks
Annual Attendance: 1,500

ACTORS' ALLIANCE INC. (AAI)
JAF PO Box 7370, New York, NY 10116-4630
(718) 768-6110
Founded: 1976
Arts Area: Professional
Status: Professional; Non-Profit
Type: Performing; Touring; Resident
Purpose: To produce classical, contemporary and new plays explored and developed by a resident company of theatre artists
Management: Melanie Sutherland, Artistic Director
Volunteer Staff: 9
Non-Paid Artists: 8
Utilizes: Special Technical Talent; Guest Artists; Guest Directors
Budget: $1,000 - $50,000
Income Sources: Private Foundations/Grants/Endowments; Business/Corporate Donations; Box Office; Government Grants; Individual Donations
Season: September - June

ACTORS STUDIO
432 West 44th Street, New York, NY 1947
(212) 757-0870
Founded: 1947
Arts Area: Professional
Status: Professional; Non-Profit
Type: Resident
Purpose: Theater workshop of professional actors
Management: Ellen Burstyn, Artistic Director; Frank Corsaro, Artistic Director
Officers: Paul Newman, President
Paid Staff: 5   **Volunteer Staff:** 100
Budget: $100,000 - $500,000
Income Sources: Private Foundations/Grants/Endowments; Business/Corporate Donations; Government Grants; Individual Donations
Season: October - May
Performance Facilities: Actors Studio

AMAS REPERTORY THEATRE
450 West 42nd Street, New York, NY 10036
(212) 563-2565
Founded: 1967
Arts Area: Professional; Summer Stock; Musical; Folk
Status: Professional; Non-Profit
Type: Performing; Touring; Resident; Educational; Sponsoring
Purpose: To provide a starting place for new American theatrical pieces in a multi-racial environment which instills creative professionalism
Management: Rosetta LeNoire, Founder/Artistic Director; Gary Halcott, Business Manager/Administrator; Stephen Schaffer, Administrator
Officers: Don Ellwood, Chairman; Rosetta LeNoire, President; Catherine McDonald, Secretary; Daisy Haynes, Treasurer
Paid Staff: 3   **Volunteer Staff:** 20
Paid Artists: 10   **Non-Paid Artists:** 5
Utilizes: Special Technical Talent; Guest Artists; Guest Directors
Income Sources: Private Foundations/Grants/Endowments; Business/Corporate Donations; Box Office; Government Grants; Individual Donations
Season: 52 Weeks
Annual Attendance: 10,000

AMERICAN CENTER FOR STANISLAVSKI THEATRE ART, INC.
485 Park Avenue, New York, NY 10022
(212) 755-5120
Founded: 1964
Arts Area: Professional
Status: Professional; Non-Profit
Type: Performing; Touring; Educational
Purpose: To bring Stanislavski's method of Physical Actions, his ultimate acting technique, solution to spontaneity to the American theatre
Management: Sonia Moore, Artistic Director; Thalia White, Executive Director; Marie Lou Catalano, Development Consultant
Officers: Sonia Moore, President; Edward Katz, Acting Chairman
Paid Staff: 4   **Volunteer Staff:** 1
Non-Paid Artists: 15

Utilizes: Special Technical Talent; Guest Directors
Budget: $50,000 - $100,000
Income Sources: Business/Corporate Donations; Box Office; Individual Donations; Student Tuition
Season: 52 Weeks
Annual Attendance: 1,000
Affiliations: ART/NY
Performance Facilities: Trinity Presbyterian Church

THE AMERICAN ENSEMBLE COMPANY
PO Box 972, Peck Slip Station, New York, NY 10272
(212) 571-7594
Founded: 1967
Arts Area: Professional; Musical; Theatrical Group
Status: Professional; Non-Profit
Type: Performing; Touring; Resident; Educational
Purpose: Production of plays and musicals of literary merit and development of a working ensemble of actors, directors, designers, and writers
Management: Robert Petito, Artistic Director; Robert Dominguez, General Manager
Paid Staff: 1 **Volunteer Staff:** 8
Utilizes: Special Technical Talent; Guest Directors
Budget: $1,000 - $50,000
Income Sources: Business/Corporate Donations; Box Office; Individual Donations
Season: September - June **Annual Attendance:** 8,000

THE AMERICAN PLACE THEATRE
111 West 46th Street, New York, NY 10036
(212) 840-2960
FAX: (212) 391-4019
Founded: 1963
Arts Area: Theatrical Group
Status: Professional; Non-Profit
Type: Performing
Purpose: To produce new plays by living American writers
Management: Wynn Handman, Director; Dara Hershman, General Manager
Officers: Wynn Handman, Acting Board Chairman
Paid Staff: 6
Utilizes: Special Technical Talent; Guest Artists; Guest Directors
Budget: $500,000 - $1,000,000
Income Sources: Private Foundations/Grants/Endowments; Business/Corporate Donations; Box Office; Government Grants; Individual Donations
Season: September - June **Affiliations:** AEA
Performance Facilities: Main Stage; Subplot Theatre; First Floor Theatre

AMERICAN THEATRE OF ACTORS
314 West 54th Street, New York, NY 10019
(212) 581-3044
Founded: 1977
Arts Area: Theatrical Group
Status: Professional; Non-Profit
Type: Performing
Purpose: To help develop new playwrights, actors and directors; to produce new plays
Management: James Jennings, Artistic Director; James Lynn, Technical Director; David Lipsky, Press Agent
Officers: James Jennings, President; Jane Culley, Vice President; William Kirksey, Treasurer; James Bernet, Secretary
Paid Staff: 1 **Volunteer Staff:** 3
Utilizes: Guest Artists; Guest Directors
Income Sources: Private Foundations/Grants/Endowments; Business/Corporate Donations; Box Office; Individual Donations; Rentals; Rehearsals
Season: 52 Weeks

BLACK SPECTRUM
119-07 Merrick Boulevard, New York, NY 11434
(718) 723-1800
FAX: (718) 723-1806
Founded: 1970
Arts Area: Professional; Musical; Dinner; Theatrical Group
Status: Professional; Non-Profit
Type: Performing; Touring; Educational
Purpose: To present Black classical and contemporary works of social significance

Management: Carl Clay, Founder/Producer
Paid Staff: 6   **Volunteer Staff:** 50
Utilizes: Special Technical Talent; Guest Artists; Guest Directors
Budget: $100,000 - $500,000
Income Sources: Private Foundations/Grants/Endowments; Business/Corporate Donations; Box Office; Government Grants
Season: October - June   **Annual Attendance:** 4,000

BOND STREET THEATRE COALITION
2 Bond Street, New York, NY 10012
(212) 254-4614; (518) 678-3332
FAX: (212) 254-4614; (212) 678-3332
Founded: 1975
Arts Area: Professional; Theatrical Group; Artists' Colony
Status: Professional; Non-Profit
Type: Performing; Touring; Sponsoring; Artists' Colony
Purpose: To create new theatre works using a physical and imagistic vocabulary, illuminating politically relevant themes to a broad range of audiences
Management: Joanna Sherman, Artistic Director; Patrick Sciarratta, Producing Director; Mariella Bisson, Director of Development; Michael McGuigan, Associate Director; Brad Beckman, Marketing Director
Officers: Patrick Sciarratta, President; Joanna Sherman, Vice President; Linda Sweet, Secretary; Lisa Brill, Treasurer
Paid Staff: 5   **Volunteer Staff:** 6
Paid Artists: 8
Utilizes: Special Technical Talent; Guest Artists; Guest Directors; Guest Choreographers, Composers
Budget: $100,000 - $500,000
Income Sources: Private Foundations/Grants/Endowments; Business/Corporate Donations; Box Office; Government Grants; Individual Donations; Performance Fees
Season: 52 Weeks   **Annual Attendance:** 15,000
Affiliations: ART/NY
Performance Facilities: Interarts Theatre

BROADWAY TOMORROW, INC.
191 Claremont Avenue, Suite 53, New York, NY 10027
(212) 864-4736
Founded: 1983
Arts Area: Musical
Status: Professional; Non-Profit
Type: Performing
Purpose: To nurture new musicals
Management: Elyse Curtis, Artistic Director; Ellie Serena, Literary Manager; Norman Curtis, Musical Director
Officers: Elyse Curtis, President; Gene Liberty, Vice President; Norman Curtis, Secretary/Treasurer
Volunteer Staff: 6
Paid Artists: 10
Utilizes: Special Technical Talent; Guest Conductors; Guest Artists; Guest Directors
Budget: $1,000 - $50,000
Income Sources: Private Foundations/Grants/Endowments; Business/Corporate Donations; Box Office; Government Grants; Individual Donations
Season: Fall; Spring
Performance Facilities: Phipps Plaza Theatre

CHICAGO CITY LIMITS
351 East 74th Street, New York, NY 10021
(212) 772-8707
Founded: 1977
Arts Area: Professional
Status: Professional; Commercial
Type: Performing; Touring; Resident; Educational
Purpose: Chicago City Limits presents satirical comedy revues which incorporate audience suggestions into an evening of comedy, improvisation and song.
Management: Paul Zuckerman, Artistic Director; Andrea Olin-Gomes, Touring Manager
Paid Staff: 4
Paid Artists: 12
Utilizes: Guest Artists
Budget: $100,000 - $500,000
Income Sources: Box Office; Touring Fees
Season: 52 Weeks   **Annual Attendance:** 20,000
Performance Facilities: Jan Hus Theatre

CIRCLE IN THE SQUARE
1633 Broadway, New York, NY 10019
(212) 307-2700
FAX: (212) 581-6371
Founded: 1951
Arts Area: Professional
Status: Professional; Non-Profit
Type: Performing
Purpose: To produce classics, rarely-done works that deserve a second look, and new plays
Management: Theodore Mann, Artistic Director; Robert A. Buckley, Managing Director
Officers: John C. Russell, Chairman of the Board
Paid Staff: 14
Paid Artists: 80
Utilizes: Special Technical Talent; Guest Artists; Guest Directors
Budget: $1,000,000 - $5,000,000
Income Sources: Private Foundations/Grants/Endowments; Business/Corporate Donations; Box Office; Government Grants; Individual Donations
Season: 52 Weeks
Affiliations: LORT; TCG; League of American Theatres and Producers
Performance Facilities: Circle In The Square

CIRCLE REPERTORY THEATRE COMPANY
161 Avenue of the Americas, 4th Floor, New York, NY 10013
(212) 691-3210
FAX: (212) 675-8098
Founded: 1969
Arts Area: Professional
Status: Professional; Non-Profit
Type: Performing; Resident
Purpose: A resident theatre company producing professional theatre with an emphasis on new American plays
Management: Tanya Berezin, Artistic Director; Abigail Evans, Managing Director; Meredith Freeman, General Manager; Mark S. Romant, Associate Artistic Director
Officers: John Lack, Chairman; Priscilla Morgan, Secretary; Duane Wilder, Treasurer; Elaine Bond
Paid Staff: 18
Utilizes: Special Technical Talent; Guest Artists; Guest Directors
Budget: $1,000,000 - $5,000,000
Income Sources: Private Foundations/Grants/Endowments; Business/Corporate Donations; Box Office; Government Grants; Individual Donations
Season: September - May
Annual Attendance: 50,000
Performance Facilities: Circle Repertory Theatre

CREATION PRODUCTION COMPANY
127 Greene Street, New York, NY 10012
(212) 674-5593
Founded: 1977
Arts Area: Theatrical Group
Status: Professional; Non-Profit
Type: Performing; Touring; Educational
Purpose: Experimental theatre
Management: Anne Hemenway, Director; Jennifer McDowall, Managing Director; Susan Mosakowski, Matthew Maguire, Co-Artistic Directors
Paid Staff: 3
Paid Artists: 30
Budget: $100,000 - $500,000
Income Sources: Private Foundations/Grants/Endowments; Business/Corporate Donations; Box Office; Government Grants; Individual Donations
Season: 52 Weeks
Annual Attendance: 3,500

CREATIVE ARTS TEAM
715 Broadway, 5th Floor, New York University, New York, NY 10003
(212) 998-7380
FAX: (212) 995-4151
Founded: 1974
Arts Area: Professional; Theatrical Group
Status: Professional; Non-Profit
Type: Performing; Touring; Resident; Educational

Management: Lynda Zimmerman, Executive Director; Jim Mirrione, Playwright-in-Residence; Dr. Leslie White, Managing Director; Mark Riherd, Program Director
Paid Staff: 70
Paid Artists: 50
Budget: $500,000 - $1,000,000
Income Sources: Private Foundations/Grants/Endowments; Business/Corporate Donations; Government Grants; Individual Donations
Season: September - July
Annual Attendance: 40,000
Affiliations: NYSCA; TCG; New York University

CSC REPERTORY
136 East 13th Street, New York, NY 10003
(212) 677-4210
FAX: (212) 477-7504
Founded: 1967
Arts Area: Professional; Theatrical Group
Status: Professional; Non-Profit
Type: Performing; Resident
Purpose: To produce classics with a relevance to today's audience
Management: David Esbjornson, Artistic Director; Patricia Taylor, Managing Director; Kelley Voorhees, Company Manager; Jeffrey Berzon, Production Manager
Officers: Turner P. Smith, President; Donald S. Donovan, Vice President
Paid Staff: 5   **Volunteer Staff:** 4
Utilizes: Special Technical Talent; Guest Directors
Budget: $500,000 - $1,000,000
Income Sources: Private Foundations/Grants/Endowments; Business/Corporate Donations; Box Office; Government Grants; Individual Donations
Season: October - March
Affiliations: AEA
Performance Facilities: CSC Repertory

DON QUIJOTE CHILDREN'S THEATRE
250 West 65th Street, New York, NY 10023
(212) 496-8009
Founded: 1972
Arts Area: Professional; Musical; Theatrical Group; Puppet
Status: Professional; Non-Profit
Type: Performing; Touring; Resident; Educational
Purpose: To provide inspirational, entertaining, educational theatre for children
Management: Oswaldo Pradere, Artistic Director; Stefanie Scott, Resident Director; Jim Finn, Administrator; Wendy Samuel, Administrative Assistant
Officers: Martha Bograd, President; Estrellita Brodsky, Vice President; Oswaldo Pradere, Treasurer; Karen Cooke, Secretary
Paid Staff: 3   **Volunteer Staff:** 2
Paid Artists: 25
Budget: $50,000 - $100,000
Income Sources: Private Foundations/Grants/Endowments; Business/Corporate Donations; Box Office; Government Grants; Individual Donations
Season: 52 Weeks
Annual Attendance: 45,000

DOWLING ENTERTAINMENT CORPORATION
226 West 47th Street, Suite 700, New York, NY 10036
(212) 719-3090
FAX: (212) 719-2987
Founded: 1984
Arts Area: Professional
Status: Professional; Commercial
Type: Performing
Purpose: Business management
Management: Doreen Chila, Office Manager
Officers: Kevin Dowling, President; Carol Prugh, Vice President
Paid Staff: 3
Income Sources: Box Office
Season: 52 Weeks
Performance Facilities: The Cherry Lane Theatre

DOWNTOWN ART CO., INC.
280 Broadway, Room 412, New York, NY 10007-1896
(212) 732-1201
FAX: (212) 732-1297
Founded: 1987
Arts Area: Professional; Theatrical Group
Status: Professional; Non-Profit
Type: Performing; Touring; Sponsoring
Purpose: To support the creation, development and presentation of comtemporary performance works
Management: Ryan Gilliam, Artistic Director; Cliff Scott, Producing Director; Dan Hurlin, Dan Froot, Artistic Associates
Officers: Cliff Scott, President; Ryan Gilliam, Vice President/Treasurer; Dan Hurlin, Secretary
Paid Staff: 6   **Volunteer Staff:** 1
Paid Artists: 25
Utilizes: Special Technical Talent; Guest Artists
Budget: $100,000 - $500,000
Income Sources: Private Foundations/Grants/Endowments; Box Office; Government Grants; Individual Donations
Season: September - June   **Annual Attendance:** 5,000
Affiliations: National Association of Artists; ART/NY

ECCENTRIC CIRCLES THEATRE
400 West 43rd Street, Suite 4N, New York, NY 10036
(212) 564-3798
Founded: 1979
Arts Area: Professional; Theatrical Group
Status: Non-Profit
Type: Performing
Purpose: To produce original works, one-act and full-length plays
Management: Rosemary Hopkins, Paula Kay Pierce, Artistic Directors; Maryanne Mongoni, Production Manager
Paid Staff: 3   **Volunteer Staff:** 5
Budget: $1,000 - $50,000
Income Sources: Private Foundations/Grants/Endowments; Business/Corporate Donations; Box Office; Individual Donations
Season: 52 Weeks   **Annual Attendance:** 2,500
Affiliations: ART/NY

EN GARDE ARTS, INC.
225 Rector Place, Suite 3A, New York, NY 10280
(212) 941-9793
FAX: (212) 274-8123
Arts Area: Professional
Status: Professional; Non-Profit
Type: Performing
Purpose: To commission artists to create theatrical productions inspired by architecturally, historically or socially significant sites; the only site specific theatre in the country
Management: Anne Hamburger, Producer; Ron Aja, Managing Director; Mary McBride, Director of Development
Budget: $100,000 - $500,000
Income Sources: Private Foundations/Grants/Endowments; Business/Corporate Donations; Box Office; Government Grants; Individual Donations
Season: 52 Weeks

THE ENSEMBLE STUDIO THEATRE
549 West 52nd Street, New York, NY 10019
(212) 247-4982
FAX: (212) 664-0041
Arts Area: Professional; Theatrical Group
Status: Non-Profit
Type: Performing
Purpose: To nurture and develop the American theatre artist
Management: Curt Dempster, Artistic Director
Budget: $500,000 - $1,000,000
Income Sources: Private Foundations/Grants/Endowments; Business/Corporate Donations; Box Office; Government Grants; Individual Donations
Performance Facilities: The Ensemble Studio Theatre

THE FIJI COMPANY
47 Great Jones Street, New York, NY 10012
(212) 966-0284
Founded: 1972

Arts Area: Professional; Theatrical Group
Status: Professional; Non-Profit
Type: Performing; Touring; Resident; Educational
Purpose: Created out of a desire to incorporate the visual arts (dance, film, video and theater) into a multimedia show questioning the syntax of global theater
Management: Ping Chong, Artistic Director; Joe Jeffcoat, Managing Director
Paid Staff: 4 **Volunteer Staff:** 3
Paid Artists: 55
Utilizes: Special Technical Talent; Guest Artists
Budget: $100,000 - $500,000
Income Sources: Private Foundations/Grants/Endowments; Business/Corporate Donations; Box Office; Government Grants; Individual Donations
Season: July - July **Annual Attendance:** 25,000
Affiliations: TCG; ART/NY

FREDERICK DOUGLASS CREATIVE ARTS CENTER, INC.
168 West 46th Street, New York, NY 10036
(212) 944-9870
Founded: 1971
Arts Area: Theatrical Group; Literary
Status: Professional; Non-Profit
Type: Resident
Purpose: A writers development group with a performance component
Management: Fred Hudson, Artistic Director; Yvonne Hudson, Executive Administrator
Utilizes: Special Technical Talent; Guest Artists; Guest Directors
Budget: $100,000 - $500,000
Income Sources: Private Foundations/Grants/Endowments; Business/Corporate Donations; Box Office; Government Grants; Individual Donations
Season: September - June

GAY PERFORMANCES COMPANY
PO Box 1647, Old Chelsea Station, New York, NY 10011
(212) 595-1445
Founded: 1987
Arts Area: Professional; Theatrical Group
Status: Professional; Non-Profit
Type: Performing
Purpose: To present positive images of gay people and to counteract the negative stereotypes of gay people prevalent in society at large; to represent the lives and experiences of women and all the minorities in the gay community
Management: Don Barrington, Founder
Utilizes: Special Technical Talent; Volunteer Artists
Budget: $1,000 - $50,000
Income Sources: Government Grants; Individual Donations
Season: May - October
Performance Facilities: Gay Community Center

THE GLINES
240 West 44th Street, New York, NY 10036
(212) 354-8899
Founded: 1976
Arts Area: Theatrical Group
Status: Non-Profit
Type: Performing; Resident
Purpose: To promote positive gay images and dispel negative stereotyping
Management: John Glines, Artistic Director
Officers: John Glines, President/Treasurer; Steve Carpenter, Vice President; Ralph DeMarco, Secretary; Tom Cannon, Kathleen Mary, Mark Hostetter, Richard Glatfelter, Dr. Harry Clarke Noyes, Board of Directors
Paid Staff: 3 **Volunteer Staff:** 20
Paid Artists: 12
Budget: $100,000 - $500,000
Income Sources: Box Office; Individual Donations
Annual Attendance: 12,000
Performance Facilities: Courtyard Playhouse

HARLEM ARTISTS' DEVELOPMENT LEAGUE ESPECIALLY FOR YOU (HADLEY PLAYERS)
207 West 133rd Street, New York, NY 10030
(212) 368-9314
Arts Area: Professional; Community; Theatrical Group
Status: Professional; Semi-Professional; Non-Profit

Type: Performing; Resident; Educational
Purpose: To present professional theatre in the Harlem community at affordable prices; to train aspiring artists in acting, speech, and dance
Management: Gertrude Jeannette, Artistic Director; Ajene Washington, Business/Company Manager; Murphree Johnson, Secretary/Treasurer; Louise Mike, Training Supervisor; Dr. Nathan A. Wright, Chairman of the Board
Volunteer Staff: 15
Non-Paid Artists: 25
Utilizes: Special Technical Talent; Guest Artists; Guest Directors
Budget: $1,000 - $50,000
Income Sources: Private Foundations/Grants/Endowments; Box Office; Individual Donations
Season: September 15 - June 30   **Annual Attendance:** 4,026
Affiliations: Community Service Council of Greater Harlem
Performance Facilities: Saint Philips Church

HISPANIC ORGANIZATION OF LATIN ACTORS (HOLA)
250 West 65th Street, New York, NY 10023
(212) 595-8286
FAX: (212) 799-6718
Founded: 1977
Arts Area: Professional; Community; Theatrical Group
Status: Non-Profit
Type: Arts Service Organization
Purpose: Advocacy-training, workshops and referrals
Management: Francisco G. Rivela, Executive Director; Manny Alfaro, Managing Director
Officers: Elsie C. Stark, President/Chairman of the Board; Arnaldo Melendez, Arnold E. Rivera, Board Members
Paid Staff: 3   **Volunteer Staff:** 4
Utilizes: Special Technical Talent; Guest Directors
Budget: $50,000 - $100,000
Income Sources: Private Foundations/Grants/Endowments; Business/Corporate Donations; Government Grants; Individual Donations

HUDSON GUILD THEATRE
441 West 26th Street, New York, NY 10001
(212) 760-9816; (212) 760-9800
Founded: 1973
Arts Area: Professional; Theatrical Group
Status: Professional; Non-Profit
Type: Performing
Management: Geoffrey Sherman, Producing Director; James Abar, Associate Director; Steve Ramay, Literary Manager; Laura Fowler, Business Manager
Officers: Emily Meschter, Board Chairperson
Paid Staff: 59   **Volunteer Staff:** 5
Paid Artists: 50
Utilizes: Special Technical Talent; Guest Artists; Guest Directors
Budget: $100,000 - $500,000
Income Sources: Private Foundations/Grants/Endowments; Business/Corporate Donations; Box Office; Government Grants; Individual Donations
Season: September - June
Annual Attendance: 22,000
Performance Facilities: Strasser Auditorium

IGLOO, THE THEATRICAL GROUP
225 East Fourth Street, Apt. 6, New York, NY 10009
(212) 460-9055
Founded: 1985
Arts Area: Professional; Musical; Theatrical Group
Status: Professional; Non-Profit
Type: Performing; Resident
Purpose: Based on ensemble participation in the acting design, direction and choice of productions, Igloo is dedicated to new and rarely done works.
Management: Maria Taribassi, Chris Peditto and Paul Peditto, Artistic Directors
Officers: Chris Peditto, President; Maria Tirabassi, Treasurer; Dan Piburn, Secretary
Paid Staff: 2
Non-Paid Artists: 10
Utilizes: Guest Artists; Guest Directors
Budget: $1,000 - $50,000
Income Sources: Private Foundations/Grants/Endowments; Business/Corporate Donations; Box Office; Individual Donations

Season: May - April
Annual Attendance: 12,000

INTERNATIONAL ARTS RELATIONS DBA INTAR HISPANIC AMERICAN ARTS CENTER
420 West 42nd Street, New York, NY 10036
(212) 695-6135
FAX: (212) 268-0102
    Founded: 1966
    Arts Area: Professional
    Status: Professional; Non-Profit
    Type: Performing
    Purpose: To identify, develop and present the work of Hispanic-American theatre artists and multi-cultural visual artists, as well as to introduce outstanding works by internationally respected Latin artists to American audiences
    Management: May Ferra, Artistic Director; Eva Brune, Managing Director
    Officers: Stanley Stairs, Chairman; Richard Ramirez, Tony Bechara, Co-Vice Presidents; Paul Vidich, Treasurer; Jane Stanicki, Secretary
    Paid Staff: 13 **Volunteer Staff:** 8
    Paid Artists: 32
    Utilizes: Special Technical Talent; Guest Artists; Guest Directors
    Budget: $100,000 - $500,000
    Income Sources: Private Foundations/Grants/Endowments; Business/Corporate Donations; Box Office; Government Grants; Individual Donations
    Season: October - June **Annual Attendance:** 10,000
    Affiliations: TCG; ART/NY

INTERNATIONAL FESTIVAL OF PUPPETRY
c/o Jim Henson Foundation, 117 East 69th Street, New York, NY 10021
(212) 794-2400
FAX: (212) 570-1147
    Arts Area: Puppet
    Status: Non-Profit
    Type: Sponsoring
    Purpose: To bring a sampling of the best of international puppetry performers to American audiences
    Management: Leslee Asch, Executive Director
    Budget: $500,000 - $1,000,000
    Income Sources: Private Foundations/Grants/Endowments; Business/Corporate Donations; Box Office; Government Grants; Individual Donations
    Performance Facilities: Joseph Papp Public

IRISH ARTS CENTRE THEATRE
553 West 51st Street, New York, NY 10019
(212) 757-3318
    Founded: 1972
    Arts Area: Professional
    Status: Professional; Non-Profit
    Type: Performing; Resident
    Purpose: To preserve, celebrate and develop Irish culture in America by producing Classic Irish, New Irish and Irish-American plays
    Management: Nye Heron, Artistic Director; Marianne Delaney, Executive Director
    Officers: Jim Sheridan, Chairman of the Board
    Paid Staff: 3 **Volunteer Staff:** 6
    Paid Artists: 200 **Non-Paid Artists:** 30
    Utilizes: Guest Artists
    Budget: $500,000 - $1,000,000
    Income Sources: Private Foundations/Grants/Endowments; Business/Corporate Donations; Box Office; Government Grants; Individual Donations
    Season: 52 Weeks **Annual Attendance:** 20,000
    Performance Facilities: Irish Arts Center Theatre

JAM AND COMPANY
331 West 38th Street, #5, New York, NY 10018
(212) 714-2263
    Founded: 1985
    Arts Area: Theatrical Group
    Status: Semi-Professional
    Type: Performing
    Management: John Amudd, Artistic Director
    Paid Staff: 13 **Volunteer Staff:** 1

Budget: $1,000 - $50,000
Income Sources: Private Foundations/Grants/Endowments; Box Office; Individual Donations

JEAN COCTEAU REPERTORY
330 Bowery, New York, NY 10012
(212) 677-0060
Founded: 1971
Arts Area: Professional; Theatrical Group
Status: Professional; Non-Profit
Type: Performing; Resident; Educational
Purpose: Cocteau Repertory is committed to presenting the classics of world literature in an innovative light. We are also dedicated to a resident company working rotating repertory.
Management: Robert Hupp, Artistic Director; Scott Shattuck, Managing Director
Officers: Albert Podell, President; Robert Berend, Alan Goldman, Co-Chairmans; Barbara Udell, Treasurer; Susan Fawcett, Secretary
Paid Staff: 7   **Volunteer Staff:** 4
Paid Artists: 16   **Non-Paid Artists:** 10
Utilizes: Guest Directors; Guest Designers
Budget: $100,000 - $500,000
Income Sources: Private Foundations/Grants/Endowments; Business/Corporate Donations; Box Office; Government Grants; Individual Donations
Season: August - May   **Annual Attendance:** 21,000
Affiliations: TCG; ART/NY
Performance Facilities: Bouwerie Lane Theatre

JEWISH REPERTORY THEATRE
344 East 14th Street, New York, NY 10003
(212) 674-7200
Arts Area: Professional
Status: Professional; Non-Profit
Type: Performing
Purpose: To present plays, in English, relating to the Jewish experience
Management: Rau Avni, Artistic Director
Paid Staff: 6
Paid Artists: 50
Budget: $100,000 - $500,000
Income Sources: Private Foundations/Grants/Endowments; Business/Corporate Donations; Box Office; Government Grants; Individual Donations
Season: September - July   **Annual Attendance:** 14,000
Affiliations: AEA
Performance Facilities: Jewish Repertory Theatre

LA MAMA EXPERIMENTAL THEATRE CLUB
74A East Fourth Street, New York, NY 10003
(212) 475-7710
FAX: (212) 254-7597
Founded: 1961
Arts Area: Theatrical Group; Multi-Art
Status: Professional; Non-Profit
Type: Performing; Producing
Purpose: To further the playwright and all aspects of the theater
Management: Ellen Stewart, Founder/Artistic Director; Meryl Vladimer, Executive Director
Utilizes: Special Technical Talent; Guest Artists; Guest Directors
Budget: $500,000 - $1,000,000
Income Sources: Private Foundations/Grants/Endowments; Business/Corporate Donations; Box Office; Government Grants; Individual Donations
Season: September - July
Performance Facilities: La Mama Experimental Theatre

THE LAMB'S THEATRE COMPANY LTD.
130 West 44th Street, New York, NY 10036
(212) 997-0210
Founded: 1980
Arts Area: Professional
Status: Professional; Non-Profit
Type: Performing; Touring; Educational
Purpose: To develop and present the work of new American theatre artists hoping to offer positive solutions to modern ethical problems

Management: Carolyn Rossi-Copeland, Producing Director; Clark Cameron, Production Manager; Carl H. Jaynes, Administrative Coordinator; Larry Staroff, Box Office Treasurer
Officers: Kendyl K. Monroe, Chairman; Patricia McCorkle, Secretary; Reverend David Best
Paid Staff: 11
Paid Artists: 45
Utilizes: Guest Directors
Budget: $100,000 - $500,000
Income Sources: Private Foundations/Grants/Endowments; Business/Corporate Donations; Box Office; Government Grants; Individual Donations
Season: August - June   **Annual Attendance:** 67,500
Affiliations: TCG, ART/NY
Performance Facilities: Lamb's Theatre; Lamb's Little Theatre

LATIN AMERICAN THEATRE ENSEMBLE
PO Box 18, Radio City Station, New York, NY 10019
(212) 246-7478
Founded: 1970
Arts Area: Professional; Theatrical Group
Status: Professional; Non-Profit
Type: Performing; Touring; Resident; Educational
Purpose: Our purpose is to expand the theatre movement to the Spanish and English communities.
Management: Margarita Toirac, Executive Director; Mario Pena, Founder
Officers: Mario Pena, President; Tania Robles-Pena, Secretary; Guillermo Fernandez, Treaurer
Paid Staff: 2   **Volunteer Staff:** 10
Paid Artists: 20
Utilizes: Guest Artists; Guest Directors
Budget: $1,000 - $50,000
Income Sources: Business/Corporate Donations; Box Office; Government Grants; Individual Donations
Season: 52 Weeks
Annual Attendance: 4,000

LINCOLN CENTER THEATER
150 West 65th Street, New York, NY 10023
(212) 362-7600
FAX: (212) 873-0761
Founded: 1985
Arts Area: Professional; Theatrical Group
Status: Professional; Non-Profit
Type: Performing
Management: Hattie Jutagin, Director of Development; Jeffrey Hamlin, Production Manager; Stephen Callahan, General Manager; Bernard Gernstein, Executive Producer
Paid Staff: 33
Utilizes: Special Technical Talent; Guest Artists; Guest Directors
Budget: Over 10,000,000
Income Sources: Private Foundations/Grants/Endowments; Business/Corporate Donations; Box Office; Government Grants; Individual Donations
Season: September - June
Performance Facilities: Vivian Beaumont Theater; Mitzi E. Newhouse Theater

THE LIVING THEATRE, INC.
272 East Third Street, New York, NY 10009
(212) 979-0601
FAX: (212) 865-3234
Founded: 1947
Arts Area: Theatrical Group
Status: Non-Profit
Type: Performing; Touring; Resident; Educational
Purpose: To create socially relevant theatre to be performed by an artistic ensemble of the highest calibre
Management: Hanon Reznikov, Executive Director; Judith Malina, Artistic Director; Joanie Fritz, Managing Director; Isha Manna Beck, Managing Associate
Officers: Hanon Reznikov, President, Board of Directors
Paid Staff: 4
Paid Artists: 20
Utilizes: Guest Conductors; Guest Artists; Guest Directors
Budget: $100,000 - $500,000
Income Sources: Private Foundations/Grants/Endowments; Business/Corporate Donations; Box Office; Government Grants; Individual Donations
Season: September - June   **Annual Attendance:** 16,000
Affiliations: ART/NY; TCG

MABOU MINES
150 First Avenue, New York, NY 10009
(212) 473-0559
FAX: (212) 473-2410
Founded: 1969
Arts Area: Professional; Theatrical Group
Status: Professional; Non-Profit
Type: Performing; Touring; Educational
Purpose: This is a four-member, producing collective dedicated to the creation of original work.
Management: Allison Astor, Company Manager
Officers: Terry O'Reilly, President
Paid Staff: 4   **Volunteer Staff:** 3
Paid Artists: 10
Utilizes: Special Technical Talent; Guest Artists; Guest Directors
Budget: $500,000 - $1,000,000
Income Sources: Private Foundations/Grants/Endowments; Business/Corporate Donations; Box Office; Government Grants; Individual Donations
Season: September - June
Annual Attendance: 20,000
Affiliations: TCG; ART/NY
Performance Facilities: Mabou Mines/Suite

MANHATTAN THEATRE CLUB
453 West 16th Street, New York, NY 10011
(212) 645-5590
Founded: 1970
Arts Area: Professional
Status: Non-Profit
Type: Performing
Purpose: To encourage, develop, and present important new theatrical work providing insights to life, culture, and conflict by American and international writers
Management: Lynne Meadow, Artistic Director; Barry Grove, Managing Director; Victoria B. Bailey, General Manager
Paid Staff: 25   **Volunteer Staff:** 12
Paid Artists: 46
Utilizes: Guest Artists; Guest Directors
Budget: $1,000,000 - $5,000,000
Income Sources: Private Foundations/Grants/Endowments; Business/Corporate Donations; Box Office; Government Grants; Individual Donations
Season: September - July   **Annual Attendance:** 60,000
Affiliations: TCG; ART/NY; FEDAPT

MIRROR REPERTORY COMPANY
50 East 96th Street, New York, NY 10028
(212) 427-7393
Founded: 1982
Arts Area: Professional; Theatrical Group
Status: Professional; Non-Profit
Type: Performing; Resident; Educational
Management: Sabra Jones, Artistic Director; Weiler/Miller Associates, Managing Directors; Shirley Herz Associates, Press Representative
Officers: Robert Treat, Chairman of the Board
Paid Staff: 5
Utilizes: Guest Artists; Guest Directors
Budget: $1,000,000 - $5,000,000
Income Sources: Private Foundations/Grants/Endowments; Business/Corporate Donations; Box Office; Government Grants; Individual Donations
Season: January - May
Affiliations: AEA
Performance Facilities: Mirror Repertory Theater

MUSIC THEATRE GROUP AT LENOX ARTS CENTER
29 Bethune Street, New York, NY 10014
(413) 298-5122
Founded: 1970
Arts Area: Professional; Theatrical Group; Musical Theatre
Status: Professional; Non-Profit
Type: Performing; Touring

Purpose: Exclusively engaged in and dedicated to the creation of new musical theatre works with distinctive focus on developing new forms and artists through unique combinations of music, theatre, dance and visual arts
Management: Lyn Austin, Producing Director; Diane Wondisford, General Director; Jessica Balboni, Development
Officers: Rosita Sarnoff, Chairman; Lynda Sturher-Traum, Vice Chairman; Lyn Austin, President; Charles Hollerith, Jr., Secretary; Bernard Rosenberg, Treasurer
Paid Staff: 9   **Volunteer Staff:** 10
Paid Artists: 150
Utilizes: Special Technical Talent; Guest Conductors; Guest Artists
Budget: $1,000,000 - $5,000,000
Income Sources: Private Foundations/Grants/Endowments; Business/Corporate Donations; Box Office; Government Grants; Individual Donations
Season: November - May   **Annual Attendance:** 52,000
Affiliations: AEA; TCG; ART/NY

MUSICAL THEATRE WORKS
440 Lafayette Street, New York, NY 10003
(212) 677-0040
Founded: 1983
Arts Area: Professional; Musical; Theatrical Group
Status: Professional; Non-Profit
Type: Performing; Resident
Purpose: To develop and produce new works for the American musical theatre
Management: Anthony Stimack, Artistic Director; Marilyn Stimack, General Manager; Mike Teel, Managing Director
Paid Staff: 6
Utilizes: Special Technical Talent; Guest Artists; Guest Directors
Budget: $100,000 - $500,000
Income Sources: Private Foundations/Grants/Endowments; Business/Corporate Donations; Box Office; Government Grants; Individual Donations
Season: 52 Weeks
Affiliations: AEA; TCG; ART/NY

NAT HORNE MUSICAL THEATRE
440 West 42nd Street, New York, NY 10036
(212) 268-4125
Founded: 1973
Arts Area: Professional; Musical
Status: Professional; Non-Profit
Type: Performing
Purpose: To provide actors with training in the American musical theater
Management: Rick Pool, Artistic Director
Budget: $100,000 - $500,000
Income Sources: Private Foundations/Grants/Endowments; Business/Corporate Donations; Box Office; Government Grants; Individual Donations
Season: 52 Weeks   **Annual Attendance:** 20,000
Affiliations: AEA; ART/NY; Theater Development Fund
Performance Facilities: Nat Horne Musical Theatre

NATIONAL BLACK THEATRE
2033 Fifth Avenue, New York, NY 10035
(212) 427-5615; (212) 722-3800
FAX: (212) 926-1571
Founded: 1968
Arts Area: Theatrical Group
Status: Professional; Non-Profit
Type: Performing; Touring; Resident
Purpose: To instill human dignity and respect by broadening the availability, appreciation and unity of Black Theatre and workshops
Management: Barbara Ann Teer, Founder/CEO; Shirley Faison, Executive Director; Tunde Samuel, Performing Program Director; Ade Faison, Action Arts Director; Nabi Faison, Rental Program Director
Officers: Dr. Eugene Callender, Chairman; Julietta Velma Banks, Secretary/Treasurer; Jim Haughton, Martin Leaf, Jerry Lewis, Basil Patterson, William Strickland, Barbara Ann Teer
Paid Staff: 9
Paid Artists: 50
Utilizes: Guest Artists; Guest Directors
Budget: $100,000 - $500,000
Income Sources: Private Foundations/Grants/Endowments; Business/Corporate Donations; Box Office; Government Grants; Individual Donations
Season: November - October
Performance Facilities: National Black Institute of Communication Through Theatre Arts

NATIONAL BLACK TOURING CIRCUIT
466 Grand Street, New York, NY 10002
(212) 598-0400
> **Founded:** 1974
> **Arts Area:** Professional; Theatrical Group
> **Status:** Professional; Non-Profit
> **Type:** Performing; Touring; Resident; Educational
> **Purpose:** To make existing Black theatre productions available to a larger audience by touring to colleges, Black art centers, community organizations and resident professional theatres
> **Management:** Woodie King, Jr., Producer; Herman LeVern Jones, Gloria Mitchell, Associate Producers
> **Officers:** Majorie Moon, Chair; Shaneille Perry, Vantile Whitfield, Gloria Mitchell, Board Members
> **Paid Staff:** 3 **Volunteer Staff:** 3
> **Utilizes:** Special Technical Talent; Guest Artists; Guest Directors
> **Budget:** $50,000 - $100,000
> **Income Sources:** Private Foundations/Grants/Endowments; Business/Corporate Donations; Box Office; Government Grants
> **Season:** 52 Weeks **Annual Attendance:** 10,000
> **Affiliations:** New Federal Theatre
> **Performance Facilities:** Henry Street Settlement

NATIONAL IMPROVISATIONAL THEATRE
223 Eighth Avenue, New York, NY 10011
(212) 243-7224
FAX: (212) 366-4312
> **Founded:** 1984
> **Arts Area:** Professional; Theatrical Group
> **Status:** Non-Profit
> **Type:** Performing; Educational
> **Purpose:** To take art improvisation to it highest potential
> **Management:** Christopher Smith, Executive Director; Tamara Wilcox-Smith, Artistic Director; Robert Martin, Vice President of Public Relations; Eva Mahoney, Vice President of Operations
> **Paid Staff:** 6 **Volunteer Staff:** 20
> **Non-Paid Artists:** 30
> **Budget:** $100,000 - $500,000
> **Income Sources:** Business/Corporate Donations; Box Office; Individual Donations; Sale of Services
> **Season:** September - July

NATIONAL SHAKESPEARE COMPANY
414 West 51st Street, New York, NY 10019
(212) 265-1340
> **Founded:** 1963
> **Arts Area:** Professional
> **Status:** Professional
> **Type:** Performing; Touring
> **Purpose:** To nurture and develop the performing arts in America by bringing professional, live theatre to its communities
> **Management:** Elaine Sulka, Artistic Director; Michael Cooper, Executive Director; Tom Rice, General Manager
> **Paid Staff:** 5
> **Paid Artists:** 15
> **Budget:** $500,000 - $1,000,000
> **Income Sources:** Business/Corporate Donations; Box Office; Individual Donations
> **Season:** 52 Weeks **Annual Attendance:** 100,000
> **Performance Facilities:** The Cubiculo

NEGRO ENSEMBLE COMPANY
155 West 46th Street, Suite 409, New York, NY 10036
(212) 575-5860
> **Founded:** 1967
> **Arts Area:** Theatrical Group
> **Status:** Professional; Non-Profit
> **Type:** Performing; Touring
> **Purpose:** To perform plays that are about Black people and their experiences
> **Management:** Douglas Turner Ward, Artistic Director; Leon B. Denmark, Managing Director
> **Utilizes:** Special Technical Talent; Guest Artists; Guest Directors
> **Budget:** $50,000 - $100,000
> **Income Sources:** Private Foundations/Grants/Endowments; Business/Corporate Donations; Box Office; Government Grants; Individual Donations
> **Season:** September - May
> **Performance Facilities:** Theatre Four

NEW DRAMATISTS
424 West 44th Street, New York, NY 10036
(212) 757-6960
> **Founded:** 1949
> **Arts Area:** Theatrical Group
> **Status:** Semi-Professional; Non-Profit
> **Type:** Resident; Educational
> **Purpose:** To the development of playwrights and plays
> **Management:** Elana Greenfield, Director of Artistic; Jana Jevnikar, Director of Finance; Paul Slee, Director of Development
> **Officers:** Isabelle Robins-Konecky, Board Chairman
> **Paid Staff:** 3
> **Budget:** $100,000 - $500,000
> **Income Sources:** Private Foundations/Grants/Endowments; Business/Corporate Donations; Government Grants; Individual Donations
> **Season:** 52 Weeks
> **Affiliations:** AEA
> **Performance Facilities:** New Dramatists Theater

NEW FEDERAL THEATRE
466 Grand Street, New York, NY 10002
(212) 598-0400
> **Founded:** 1970
> **Arts Area:** Theatrical Group
> **Status:** Professional; Non-Profit
> **Type:** Performing; Resident
> **Purpose:** To present new works and unknown works while allowing known and unknown actors and directors the chance to work together
> **Management:** Woodie King Jr., Producing Director; Linda Herring, Managing Director
> **Officers:** Woodie King Jr., President; Linda Herring, Treasurer; Maritza Myers, Secretary; Leon Gildin, Chairman of the Board
> **Paid Staff:** 8   **Volunteer Staff:** 2
> **Utilizes:** Special Technical Talent; Guest Artists; Guest Directors
> **Budget:** $100,000 - $500,000
> **Income Sources:** Private Foundations/Grants/Endowments; Business/Corporate Donations; Box Office; Government Grants; Individual Donations
> **Season:** September - June   **Annual Attendance:** 10,000
> **Affiliations:** AEA; ART/NY; TCG
> **Performance Facilities:** Henry Street Settlement; New Federal Theater

THE NEW RAFT THEATER COMPANY
450 West 42nd Street, Suite 2J, New York, NY 10036
(212) 967-7079
FAX: (212) 268-5501
> **Founded:** 1976
> **Arts Area:** Professional; Musical; Theatrical Group
> **Status:** Professional; Non-Profit
> **Type:** Performing
> **Purpose:** To find and develop original plays and musicals
> **Management:** Avi Ber Hoffman, Artistic Director; Mary Ellen Ashley, Associate Producer
> **Officers:** Eric Krebs, Executive Director; Avi Ber Hoffman, Artistic Director
> **Volunteer Staff:** 10
> **Budget:** $1,000 - $50,000
> **Income Sources:** Private Foundations/Grants/Endowments; Business/Corporate Donations; Box Office; Government Grants; Individual Donations
> **Season:** 52 Weeks
> **Performance Facilities:** Houseman Theatre Complex

NEW YORK SHAKESPEARE FESTIVAL
425 Lafayette Street, Joseph Papp Public Theater, New York, NY 10003
(212) 598-7150
> **Founded:** 1954
> **Arts Area:** Professional
> **Status:** Professional; Non-Profit
> **Type:** Performing
> **Purpose:** Operated in the belief that a theater with the highest professional standards can attract and should be made available to a broadly based public. From this guiding principal has emerged a contemporary theater of extraordinary range and quality, rooted in the classics with more American plays as its primary focus.

Management: Joseph Papp, Founder; JoAnne Akalaitis, Artistic Director; Jason Steven Cohen, Producing Director; Rosemarie Tichler, Associate Artistic Director; Bruce Campbell, Press Representative
Officers: Robert W. Pittman, Chairman; Larry F. Condon, Joan K. Davidson, H. Scott Higgins, Judith Peabody, Vice Presidents; Stanley H. Lowell, Secretary/Treasurer
Paid Staff: 150
Paid Artists: 450
Utilizes: Special Technical Talent; Guest Conductors; Guest Artists; Guest Directors
Budget: Over 10,000,000
Income Sources: Private Foundations/Grants/Endowments; Business/Corporate Donations; Box Office; Government Grants; Individual Donations
Season: 52 Weeks
Performance Facilities: Joseph Papp Public Theater; Delacorte Theater

NEW YORK THEATRE WORKSHOP
220 West 42nd Street, 18th Floor, New York, NY 10036
(212) 302-7737
Founded: 1983
Arts Area: Professional
Status: Professional; Non-Profit
Type: Performing
Purpose: To present new plays that are inventive in style and form, and to present new directors
Management: Nancy Kassak-Diekmann, Managing Director; James C. Nicola, Artistic Director
Officers: Stephen Graham, Founding Trustee; Elizabeth Williams, Chairman; Alison Clarkson, Vice Chairman; Dena M. Steele, Treasurer; Elliot Brown, Secretary
Paid Staff: 10   **Volunteer Staff:** 4
Paid Artists: 35
Utilizes: Guest Artists; Guest Directors
Budget: $500,000 - $1,000,000
Income Sources: Private Foundations/Grants/Endowments; Business/Corporate Donations; Box Office; Government Grants; Individual Donations
Season: October - May   **Annual Attendance:** 5,000
Affiliations: AEA; TCG; ART/NY
Performance Facilities: New York Theatre Workshop

OHIO THEATRE
66 Wooster, New York, NY 10012
(212) 966-4844
Founded: 1977
Arts Area: Professional; Theatrical Group
Status: Professional
Type: Performing; Sponsoring
Purpose: To present experimental theatre
Management: Robert Lyons, Artistic Director
Paid Staff: 1   **Volunteer Staff:** 4
Utilizes: Guest Artists; Guest Directors; Resident Company
Budget: $1,000 - $50,000
Income Sources: Box Office; Rentals
Season: September - July
Affiliations: Downtown Theatre Coalition
Performance Facilities: Ohio Theatre

ONTOLOGICAL-HYSTERIC THEATRE, INC.
260 West Broadway, New York, NY 10013
(212) 941-8911
FAX: (212) 334-5149
Arts Area: Professional
Status: Professional; Non-Profit
Type: Performing
Purpose: To produce and present the works of playwright/director/designer Richard Foreman
Management: Richard Foreman, Artistic Director; Susan Latham, Administrator
Budget: $100,000 - $500,000
Income Sources: Private Foundations/Grants/Endowments; Business/Corporate Donations; Box Office; Government Grants; Individual Donations
Performance Facilities: Ontological at St. Mark's Theater

THE OPEN BOOK
525 West End Avenue, 12E, New York, NY 10024-3207
(212) 362-0329
Founded: 1975

Arts Area: Professional; Theatrical Group; Authors Reading Series
Status: Professional; Non-Profit
Type: Performing; Touring; Resident
Purpose: To present the best of all genres of literature—prose, poetry, drama and nonfiction—in readers theatre format with emphasis on work bypassed by commercial theatre
Management: Marvin Kaye, Artistic Director; Nancy Temple, Public Relations Director; Pat Costello, Director of Development
Officers: Bill Bonham, Chief Executive Officer; Saralee Kaye, Chief Financial Officer; Jay Broad, Mary Higgins Clark, Mario Fratti, Rev. Kathleen La Camera, Marc Lewis, Beverly Penberthy, Eugenia Rawls, Board
Volunteer Staff: 3
Utilizes: Guest Artists
Budget: $1,000 - $50,000
Income Sources: Private Foundations/Grants/Endowments; Business/Corporate Donations; Box Office; Government Grants; Individual Donations
Season: Spring; Fall   **Annual Attendance:** 400
Affiliations: AEA
Performance Facilities: Bruno Walter Auditorium; Lincoln Center 2; The Amsterdam Room

THE OPEN EYE: NEW STAGINGS
270 West 89th Street, New York, NY 10024
(212) 769-4141
FAX: (212) 595-0336
Founded: 1972
Arts Area: Professional; Theatrical Group
Status: Professional; Non-Profit
Type: Performing; Touring; Educational
Purpose: Presents productions of new and rare plays, plays geared for family audiences and provides playwrights the opportunity to develop new works through the New Stagings Lab
Management: Jean Erdman, Founding Director; Amie Brockway, Artistic Director; Adrienne Brockway, Production Manager/Business Manager
Officers: Stephen Graham, Chairman; Joan Stein, Vice President; Elliot Brown, Secretary
Paid Staff: 3   **Volunteer Staff:** 5
Paid Artists: 35
Utilizes: Special Technical Talent; Guest Artists; Guest Directors
Budget: $100,000 - $500,000
Income Sources: Private Foundations/Grants/Endowments; Business/Corporate Donations; Box Office; Government Grants; Individual Donations
Season: September - June   **Annual Attendance:** 65,000
Affiliations: TCG; ART/NY; ASSITEJ
Performance Facilities: The Open Eye: New Stagings

OTRABANDA COMPANY
345 East Fifth Street, New York, NY 10003
(212) 420-9090
Arts Area: Experimental Theatre Dance
Status: Professional; Non-Profit
Type: Performing; Touring
Purpose: To create works which attempt to blur the distinction between theater and dance
Management: Roger Barb, Artistic Director; Rachelle Bornstein, Manager
Budget: $1,000 - $50,000
Income Sources: Private Foundations/Grants/Endowments; Government Grants
Season: 52 Weeks
Performance Facilities: Downtown Arts; Public School 122

PAN ASIAN REPERTORY THEATRE
423 West 46th Street, New York, NY 10036
(212) 245-2660
Mailing Address: 47 Great Jones Street, New York, NY 10012
Founded: 1977
Arts Area: Professional; Theatrical Group
Status: Professional; Non-Profit
Type: Performing; Touring; Resident; Educational
Purpose: To produce, under the highest artistic standards, new plays from the Asian-American experience, adaptations of world classics and American premieres of Asian masterworks
Management: Tisa Chang, Artistic/Producing Manager; Russell Murphy, Business Manager; Marjorie Hebard, Development Associate
Officers: Tisa Chang, President; Jeff Chin, Chairman; Muzaffar Chishti, Vice Chairman; Bonnie Crown, Secretary; Thomas Ruppel, Treasurer
Paid Staff: 4   **Volunteer Staff:** 50

       Paid Artists: 150
       Utilizes: Guest Artists; Guest Directors
       Budget: $100,000 - $500,000
       Income Sources: Private Foundations/Grants/Endowments; Business/Corporate Donations; Box Office; Government
       Grants; Individual Donations
       Season: October - June
       Annual Attendance: 14,000
       Affiliations: TCG: ART/NY
       Performance Facilities: Playhouse 46

THE PAPER BAG PLAYERS
50 Riverside Drive, New York, NY 10024
(212) 362-0431
       Founded: 1958
       Arts Area: Professional; Theatrical Group
       Status: Professional; Non-Profit
       Type: Performing; Touring; Resident; Educational
       Purpose: To create a contemporary theatre for children with shows based on a child's everyday experiences and percep-
       tions of the world
       Management: Judith Liss, Administrator; Judith Martin, Director
       Officers: Susan Patricof, President; Marjorie Federbush, Vice President
       Paid Staff: 4   **Volunteer Staff:** 1
       Paid Artists: 9
       Budget: $500,000 - $1,000,000
       Income Sources: Private Foundations/Grants/Endowments; Business/Corporate Donations; Box Office; Government
       Grants; Individual Donations
       Season: 52 Weeks
       Annual Attendance: 150,000

THE PEARL THEATRE COMPANY
125 West 22nd Street, New York, NY 10011
(212) 645-7708
FAX: (212) 645-7709
       Founded: 1982
       Arts Area: Professional; Theatrical Group
       Status: Professional; Non-Profit
       Type: Performing; Resident; Educational
       Purpose: To present a full-range repertory strongly rooted in the classics with a resident acting company, guest artists and
       theatre staff
       Management: Shepard Sobel, Artistic Director; Mary Harpster, General Manager; Joanne Camp, Artistic Associate; Larry
       Auld, Director of Development
       Officers: Kenneth J. Rotman, President; Alice Teirstein, Secretary; Walter Fekula, Treasurer
       Paid Staff: 3   **Volunteer Staff:** 1
       Utilizes: Guest Artists; Guest Directors
       Budget: $100,000 - $500,000
       Income Sources: Private Foundations/Grants/Endowments; Business/Corporate Donations; Box Office; Government
       Grants; Individual Donations
       Season: November - April   **Annual Attendance:** 5,000
       Affiliations: ART/NY; TCG; AEA

PLAYWRIGHTS HORIZONS
416 West 42nd Street, New York, NY 10036
(212) 564-1235
       Founded: 1971
       Arts Area: Professional
       Status: Professional; Non-Profit
       Type: Performing; Educational
       Purpose: Dedicated to the development of American playwrights, composers and lyricists, Playwrights Horizons also of-
       fers internship opportunities and training programs.
       Management: Don Scardino, Artistic Director; Paul S. Daniels, Executive Director
       Paid Staff: 30
       Paid Artists: 150
       Utilizes: Special Technical Talent; Guest Artists; Guest Directors
       Budget: $1,000,000 - $5,000,000
       Income Sources: Private Foundations/Grants/Endowments; Business/Corporate Donations; Box Office; Government
       Grants; Individual Donations
       Season: October - June   **Annual Attendance:** 25,000

Affiliations: AEA; ART/NY; New York University
Performance Facilities: Mainstage Theatre; Studio Theatre

PRIMARY STAGES COMPANY
584 Ninth Avenue, New York, NY 10036
(212) 333-7471
Founded: 1983
Arts Area: Professional; Theatrical Group
Status: Professional; Non-Profit
Type: Performing
Purpose: To identify and produce the best new American plays
Management: Casey Childs, Artistic Director; Janet Reed, Associate Artistic Director; Anne Binhorn, Director of Public Relations; Seth Gordon, Literary Manager; Gina Gionfriddo, Casting Director
Utilizes: Special Technical Talent; Guest Artists; Guest Directors
Budget: $100,000 - $500,000
Income Sources: Private Foundations/Grants/Endowments; Business/Corporate Donations; Box Office; Individual Donations
Season: September - June
Performance Facilities: 45th Street Theatre; William Redfield Theatre

PROCESS STUDIO THEATRE
257 Church Street, New York, NY 10007
(212) 226-1124
Founded: 1977
Arts Area: Professional; Musical; Theatrical Group
Status: Professional; Non-Profit
Type: Performing; Touring; Resident; Educational; Sponsoring; Outreach
Purpose: To promote new works and artists; home for professional artists
Management: Bonnie Loren, Artistic Director; Anthony Sandkamp, Technical Director
Utilizes: Special Technical Talent; Guest Conductors; Guest Artists; Guest Directors
Income Sources: Private Foundations/Grants/Endowments; Box Office; Individual Donations
Season: 52 Weeks

PUERTO RICAN TRAVELING THEATRE COMPANY
141 West 94th Street, New York, NY 10025
(212) 354-1293
Founded: 1967
Arts Area: Professional
Status: Professional; Non-Profit
Type: Performing; Touring; Educational
Purpose: To present bilingual plays; to conduct workshops for financially underprivileged youth; to provide training for new playwrights
Management: Miriam Colon, Artistic Director; Michael Palma, Managing Director
Utilizes: Special Technical Talent; Guest Artists; Guest Directors
Budget: $500,000 - $1,000,000
Income Sources: Private Foundations/Grants/Endowments; Business/Corporate Donations; Box Office; Government Grants; Individual Donations
Season: January - August
Annual Attendance: 25,000
Performance Facilities: Puerto Rican Travelling Theatre

QUAIGH THEATRE
205 West 89th Street, New York, NY 10024
(212) 787-0862
Founded: 1971
Arts Area: Theatrical Group
Status: Professional; Non-Profit
Type: Performing; Resident
Purpose: Quaigh is a playwrights theatre presenting four new, full-length plays and, roughly, 60 one-act plays each season.
Management: Will Liebenson, Artistic Director; Judith Robin, Executive Director
Officers: Albert Brower, Chairman; Jane Wolf, Secretary
Paid Staff: 2 **Volunteer Staff:** 10
Paid Artists: 50 **Non-Paid Artists:** 100
Budget: $100,000 - $500,000
Income Sources: Private Foundations/Grants/Endowments; Business/Corporate Donations; Box Office; Government Grants; Individual Donations
Season: October - June
Affiliations: TCG; ART/NY

RIDGE THEATER
141 Ridge Street, Suite 8, New York, NY 10002
(212) 674-5485
   Arts Area: Professional
   Status: Non-Profit
   Type: Performing
   Purpose: To explore the boundaries of opera and theater
   Management: Bob McGrath, Artistic Director
   Officers: Laurie Olinder, President of the Board
   Budget: $50,000 - $100,000
   Income Sources: Private Foundations/Grants/Endowments; Business/Corporate Donations; Box Office; Government
   Grants; Individual Donations

THE RIDICULOUS THEATRICAL COMPANY
1 Sheridan Square, New York, NY 10014-3505
(212) 989-6524
   Founded: 1967
   Arts Area: Professional
   Status: Professional; Non-Profit
   Type: Performing; Resident
   Purpose: With Everett Quinton as artistic director, the company synthesizes wit, parody, vaudeville, farce, melodrama and
   satire, giving reckless immediacy to classical stagecraft.
   Management: Everett Quinton, Artistic Director; Steven Asher, General Manager
   Officers: Elaine Friedman, Bruce Donnell, Nancy Scerbo, Ross Anesin, Board of Directors; Walter Gidaly, Attorney
   Paid Staff: 7
   Paid Artists: 12
   Budget: $500,000 - $1,000,000
   Income Sources: Private Foundations/Grants/Endowments; Business/Corporate Donations; Box Office; Government
   Grants; Individual Donations
   Annual Attendance: 25,000
   Performance Facilities: The Theatre at 1 Sheridan Square

RIVERSIDE SHAKESPEARE COMPANY
Shakespeare Center, 165 West 86th Street, New York, NY 10024
(212) 369-2273
FAX: (212) 410-6663
   Founded: 1976
   Arts Area: Professional; Theatrical Group
   Status: Professional
   Type: Performing; Touring; Resident; Educational
   Purpose: To bring the classics to life making them accessible to the public in a way unique to the demands of the context
   of modern theater
   Management: Gus Kaikkonen, Artistic Director; Ann Harvey, Executive Director; Robert Mooney, Academy Director
   Officers: Judith C. Radash, Chairman; John Pfisterer, Treasurer
   Paid Staff: 5   **Volunteer Staff:** 10
   Paid Artists: 36
   Utilizes: Special Technical Talent; Guest Artists; Guest Directors
   Budget: $100,000 - $500,000
   Income Sources: Private Foundations/Grants/Endowments; Business/Corporate Donations; Box Office; Government
   Grants; Individual Donations
   Season: 52 Weeks
   Annual Attendance: 7,000

ROGER FURMAN THEATRE
60 East 42nd Street, Suite 1336, New York, NY 10017
(212) 599-1922
FAX: (212) 599-2414
   Founded: 1964
   Arts Area: Professional; Theatrical Group
   Status: Professional; Non-Profit
   Type: Performing; Touring; Resident; Educational
   Purpose: Roger Furman Theatre has established a fine reputation for contributing to the cultural pluralism of New York
   City by presenting quality and professional Black theatrical productions.
   Management: Voza Rivers, Executive Director
   Paid Staff: 3   **Volunteer Staff:** 10
   Paid Artists: 30   **Non-Paid Artists:** 5
   Utilizes: Special Technical Talent; Guest Artists; Guest Directors
   Budget: $1,000 - $50,000

Income Sources: Business/Corporate Donations; Box Office; Government Grants; Individual Donations
Season: September - June
Affiliations: NEA; Department of Cultural Affairs
Performance Facilities: Roger Furman Theater; B Smiths Rooftop Cafe

ROUNDABOUT THEATRE COMPANY
1530 Broadway, New York, NY 10036
(212) 719-9393; (212) 869-8400
FAX: (212) 869-8817
Founded: 1965
Arts Area: Professional; Theatrical Group
Status: Professional; Non-Profit
Type: Performing; Resident
Purpose: Resident theatre institution emphasizing the production of revivals of ancient and modern classics
Management: Todd Haimes, Producing Director; Ellen Richard, General Manager
Officers: Christian C. Yegen, Chairman of the Board
Paid Staff: 75 **Volunteer Staff:** 15
Paid Artists: 80
Utilizes: Special Technical Talent; Guest Artists; Guest Directors
Budget: $1,000,000 - $5,000,000
Income Sources: Private Foundations/Grants/Endowments; Business/Corporate Donations; Box Office; Government Grants; Individual Donations
Season: 52 Weeks **Annual Attendance:** 150,000
Affiliations: AEA; LORT; SSDC

SAINT BART'S PLAYHOUSE
109 East 50th Street, New York, NY 10022
(212) 751-1616
Founded: 1927
Arts Area: Musical; Theatrical Group; Revival
Status: Semi-Professional; Non-Profit
Type: Performing; Resident; Educational
Paid Staff: 5 **Volunteer Staff:** 16
Paid Artists: 5 **Non-Paid Artists:** 75
Utilizes: Special Technical Talent; Guest Directors
Budget: $100,000 - $500,000
Income Sources: Business/Corporate Donations; Box Office; Individual Donations
Season: September - May **Annual Attendance:** 10,000
Affiliations: TCG
Performance Facilities: Saint Bartholomew's Community House

SALT AND PEPPER MIME COMPANY, INC.
320 East 90th, #1B, New York, NY 10128
(212) 262-4989
Founded: 1978
Arts Area: Professional; Musical; Community; Theatrical Group; Drama; Variety; Children's
Status: Professional; Non-Profit
Type: Performing; Touring; Educational
Purpose: To preserve the art of mime and vaudeville through performing, exhibitions and workshops
Management: Scottie Davis, Artistic Manager/Producer; Chuck Wise, Director; Mark Pearce, Resident Playwright
Officers: Houston Brummit, President; Marian Straw, Secretary; Tim Taylor, Treasurer
Paid Staff: 1 **Volunteer Staff:** 2
Paid Artists: 6
Utilizes: Special Technical Talent; Guest Artists; Guest Directors
Budget: $1,000 - $50,000
Income Sources: Private Foundations/Grants/Endowments; Box Office; Government Grants; Individual Donations
Season: January - October **Annual Attendance:** 4,000
Affiliations: ART/NY; Westside Arts Coalition
Performance Facilities: Lincoln Square Theatre; Studio Theatre

THE SECOND STAGE THEATRE
2162 Broadway, New York, NY 10022
(212) 787-8302; (212) 873-6103
FAX: (212) 877-9886
Mailing Address: PO Box 1807, Ansonia Station, NY 10023
Founded: 1979
Arts Area: Professional; Theatrical Group
Status: Professional; Non-Profit

Type: Performing
Purpose: To produce plays of the recent past which we feel deserve a second production; to produce world and New York premieres by emerging authors, with emphasis on women authors and authors of color
Management: Carole Rothman, Artistic Director; Carol Fishman, Associate Producer; Suzanne Davidson, Producing Director
Paid Staff: 16
Utilizes: Guest Artists; Guest Directors
Budget: $500,000 - $1,000,000
Income Sources: Private Foundations/Grants/Endowments; Business/Corporate Donations; Box Office; Government Grants; Individual Donations
Season: October - June   **Annual Attendance:** 16,000

SEVENTH SIGN THEATRE COMPANY, INC.
PO Box 20467, Park West Finance, New York, NY 10025
(212) 666-3955
Founded: 1979
Arts Area: Theatrical Group
Status: Professional; Non-Profit
Type: Performing; Educational
Purpose: To produce theatre of quality at low box office prices; to present literate plays, both classical and contemporary
Management: Donna Niemann, Artistic Director; Emma Nicole, Producing Director; Kim T. Sharp, Artistic Associate; Lila Gaynes Vornchuck, Treasurer
Officers: Donna Niemann, President; Emma Nicole, Vice President; Lila Vornchuck, Treasurer/Secretary
Volunteer Staff: 6
Non-Paid Artists: 20
Utilizes: Special Technical Talent; Guest Artists; Guest Directors
Budget: $1,000 - $50,000
Income Sources: Box Office; Government Grants; Individual Donations
Season: September - May   **Annual Attendance:** 1,000
Performance Facilities: Good Shepherd Church

THE SHADOW BOX THEATRE
325 West End Avenue, New York, NY 10023
(212) 877-7356
FAX: (212) 724-0767
Arts Area: Musical; Folk; Puppet
Status: Professional; Non-Profit
Type: Performing; Touring; Resident; Educational; Sponsoring
Purpose: To serve inner city disadvantaged children with a high quality art-in-education program
Management: Sandra Robbins, Executive Director; Michael Royce, Managing Director
Paid Staff: 3   **Volunteer Staff:** 5
Paid Artists: 10
Budget: $100,000 - $500,000
Income Sources: Private Foundations/Grants/Endowments; Business/Corporate Donations; Box Office; Government Grants; Individual Donations
Season: September - May   **Annual Attendance:** 40,000

SKYSAVER PRODUCTIONS
5 East Third Street, New York, NY 10003
(212) 677-3190
Season: 52 Weeks

SOUPSTONE PROJECT
309 East Fifth Street, Suite 19, New York, NY 10003
(212) 473-7584
Founded: 1985
Arts Area: Professional; Theatrical Group
Status: Professional
Type: Performing
Purpose: To expand the constituency of theatergoers through free, trilingually-accessible productions of new American works
Management: Neile Weissman, Director/Literary Manager
Paid Staff: 1
Paid Artists: 45
Budget: $1,000 - $50,000
Income Sources: Private Foundations/Grants/Endowments; Business/Corporate Donations; Government Grants; Individual Donations
Season: 52 Weeks   **Annual Attendance:** 2,400
Performance Facilities: Henry Street Settlement; Louis Abrons Art Center

SPANISH THEATRE REPERTORY COMPANY
138 East 27th Street, New York, NY 10016
(212) 889-2850
FAX: (212) 686-3732
Founded: 1969
Arts Area: Professional; Musical; Community; Theatrical Group
Status: Professional
Type: Performing
Purpose: To fulfill the need for professional Spanish-language theatre and to promote the rich heritage of the Hispanic culture
Management: Gilbert Zaldivar, Producer; Robert Federico, Associate Producer; Ellen Jacobs, Press Agent
Officers: Gilbert Zaldivar, President; Rene Buch, Vice President; Robert Federico, Financial Secretary
Paid Staff: 25
Utilizes: Guest Artists; Guest Directors
Budget: $1,000,000 - $5,000,000
Income Sources: Private Foundations/Grants/Endowments; Business/Corporate Donations; Box Office; Government Grants; Individual Donations
Season: 52 Weeks   **Annual Attendance:** 40,000
Affiliations: TCG; AAA; ART/NY
Performance Facilities: Gramercy Arts Theatre; Equitable Tower Auditorium

STAGEWRIGHTS, INC.
PO Box 4745, Rockefeller Center Station, New York, NY 10185-0041
(212) 768-8964
Founded: 1983
Arts Area: Theatrical Group
Status: Semi-Professional; Non-Profit
Type: Writer's Theatre
Purpose: Script development
Officers: Tom Ross; Uwe Taubert; John Albanese
Volunteer Staff: 25
Non-Paid Artists: 100
Utilizes: Guest Directors
Budget: $1,000 - $50,000
Income Sources: Private Foundations/Grants/Endowments; Business/Corporate Donations; Individual Donations
Season: 52 Weeks

TALKING BAND
PO Box 293, Prince Street Station, New York, NY 10012
(212) 295-0371
Arts Area: Professional; Theatrical Group
Status: Professional; Non-Profit
Type: Performing; Touring
Purpose: To create and perform n ew works for the theater
Management: Paul Zinet, Artistic Director
Officers: J. Anthony Sheldon, President of the Board
Budget: $50,000 - $100,000
Income Sources: Private Foundations/Grants/Endowments; Business/Corporate Donations; Box Office; Government Grants; Individual Donations

THEATER FOR THE NEW CITY
155-57 First Avenue, New York, NY 10003
(212) 254-1109
Founded: 1970
Arts Area: Professional; Theatrical Group
Status: Professional; Non-Profit
Type: Performing; Touring
Purpose: Dedicated to the creation and performance of new theater of new writers; to produce 30 to 40 new works each year with our annual free summer street-theater tour
Management: George Bartenieff, Executive Director; Crystal Field, Artistic Directors
Paid Staff: 9
Paid Artists: 700
Utilizes: Special Technical Talent; Guest Artists; Guest Directors
Budget: $500,000 - $1,000,000
Income Sources: Private Foundations/Grants/Endowments; Business/Corporate Donations; Box Office; Government Grants; Individual Donations
Season: August - July   **Annual Attendance:** 50,000
Affiliations: ART/NY; TCG; AAA

THEATRE DU GRAND-GUIGNOL® DE PARIS (GRAND-GUIGNOL® THEATRE OF PARIS)
310 East 70th Street, New York, NY 10021
(212) 861-1813
> **Founded:** 1896
> **Arts Area:** Professional
> **Status:** Professional; National Theatre of Montmartre
> **Type:** Performing; Touring; Resident
> **Purpose:** World's largest theatre specializing in grotesquery, the macabre, shock, terror, and earthy laughter
> **Management:** Ministry of Culture
> **Officers:** Barry Alan Richmond, Director-General
> **Paid Artists:** 15
> **Utilizes:** Special Technical Talent; Guest Artists; Guest Directors
> **Budget:** $1,000,000 - $5,000,000
> **Income Sources:** Private Foundations/Grants/Endowments; Box Office; Government Grants; Other State Entities
> **Season:** 52 Weeks
> **Affiliations:** State Theatre of the Republic of Montmartre

THEATRE FOR A NEW AUDIENCE
154 Christopher Street, Suite 36, New York, NY 10014-2839
(212) 229-2819
> **Founded:** 1979
> **Arts Area:** Professional; Theatrical Group
> **Status:** Professional; Non-Profit
> **Type:** Performing; Educational
> **Purpose:** To produce plays of poetic imagination; to build a diverse theatre audience
> **Management:** Jeffrey Horowitz, Artistic/Production Director; Lisa A. Lacroce, General Manager; Margie Salvante, Education Director; Kristin Ebbert, Development Associate; Patrick Scully, Production Manager
> **Officers:** Daryl D. Smith, Chairman; Jeffrey Horowitz, President; Adelaide Kent, Treasurer; Larry Loeb, Secretary
> **Paid Staff:** 15
> **Paid Artists:** 35
> **Budget:** $500,000 - $1,000,000
> **Income Sources:** Private Foundations/Grants/Endowments; Business/Corporate Donations; Box Office; Government Grants; Individual Donations
> **Season:** January - April   **Annual Attendance:** 12,000
> **Affiliations:** TCG
> **Performance Facilities:** Theatre at Saint Clement's Church

THEATRE OFF PARK
224 Waverly Place, New York, NY 10014
(212) 627-2556
> **Founded:** 1975
> **Arts Area:** Professional; Musical; Theatrical Group
> **Status:** Professional; Non-Profit
> **Type:** Educational
> **Purpose:** To produce new works as well as focus on neglected or unproduced works by established writers
> **Management:** Albert Harris, Artistic Director
> **Paid Staff:** 3   **Volunteer Staff:** 10
> **Paid Artists:** 75
> **Utilizes:** Special Technical Talent; Guest Artists; Guest Directors
> **Budget:** $100,000 - $500,000
> **Income Sources:** Private Foundations/Grants/Endowments; Business/Corporate Donations; Box Office; Government Grants; Individual Donations
> **Season:** October - June   **Annual Attendance:** 12,000
> **Affiliations:** AEA; ART/NY
> **Performance Facilities:** Theatre Off Park

THEATREMOVES, INC./RAJECKAS AND INTRAUB MOVEMENT THEATER
PO Box 1333, New York, NY 10009
(212) 529-8068
> **Arts Area:** Professional; Community; Theatrical Group; Movement Theatre
> **Status:** Professional; Non-Profit
> **Type:** Performing; Touring; Educational
> **Purpose:** To increase public exposure to movement theatre as a viable art form
> **Management:** Neil Intraub, Paul Rajeckas, Co-Artistic Directors
> **Budget:** $50,000 - $100,000
> **Income Sources:** Private Foundations/Grants/Endowments; Business/Corporate Donations; Government Grants; Individual Donations; Performance Fees

THEATREWORKS/USA
890 Broadway, New York, NY 10003
(212) 926-4100
FAX: (212) 353-1632
>**Founded:** 1961
>**Arts Area:** Professional; Musical; Folk; Theatrical Group; Puppet
>**Status:** Professional; Non-Profit
>**Type:** Performing; Touring; Resident; Educational; Sponsoring
>**Purpose:** Theatreworks/USA, a nonprofit organization and America's largest theatre creating, producing, and touring plays for young audiences, has presented more than 27,000 performances to well over 22 million young people in schools, art centers, museums and theatres, in 49 states.
>**Management:** Charles Hull, Managing Director; Jay Harnick, Artistic Director
>**Officers:** Robert Wood, Chairman of the Board; Jay Harnick, President; Charles Hull, Vice President/Treasurer; David Dretzin, Secretary
>**Paid Staff:** 15
>**Paid Artists:** 145
>**Utilizes:** Guest Artists; Guest Directors; Composers; Lyricists; Writers
>**Budget:** $1,000,000 - $5,000,000
>**Income Sources:** Private Foundations/Grants/Endowments; Business/Corporate Donations; Box Office; Government Grants; Individual Donations
>**Season:** September - August   **Annual Attendance:** 2,000,000
>**Performance Facilities:** Town Hall; Promenade Theatre; Variety Arts Theatre

THUNDER BAY ENSEMBLE
350 Central Park West, Apt. 14H, New York, NY 10025
(212) 749-2262
>**Season:** 52 Weeks

UBU REPERTORY THEATER
15 West 28th Street, New York, NY 10001
(212) 679-7540
FAX: (212) 679-2033
>**Founded:** 1982
>**Arts Area:** Professional
>**Status:** Professional; Non-Profit
>**Type:** Performing
>**Purpose:** To present French language playwrights in translation to American audiences
>**Management:** Francoise Kourilsky, Artistic Director; Kevin Duffy, Acting Literary Manager; Ingrid Nyeboe, Administrator; Anna Morrone, Marketing Director
>**Officers:** Jacques Bouhet, Chairman
>**Paid Staff:** 5   **Volunteer Staff:** 2
>**Paid Artists:** 100
>**Utilizes:** Special Technical Talent; Guest Conductors; Guest Artists; Guest Directors
>**Budget:** $500,000 - $1,000,000
>**Income Sources:** Private Foundations/Grants/Endowments; Business/Corporate Donations; Box Office; Government Grants; Individual Donations
>**Season:** September - June   **Annual Attendance:** 10,000
>**Affiliations:** TCG

VINEYARD THEATRE
108 East 15th Street, New York, NY 10003-9689
(212) 353-3366
FAX: (212) 353-3803
>**Founded:** 1981
>**Arts Area:** Professional; Musical; Theatrical Group
>**Status:** Professional; Non-Profit
>**Type:** Performing
>**Purpose:** To develop new plays and musical theatre
>**Management:** Douglas Aibel, Artistic Director; Barbara Zinn Krieger, Executive Director; Jon Nakagawa, Managing Director
>**Paid Staff:** 3   **Volunteer Staff:** 2
>**Utilizes:** Guest Artists; Guest Directors
>**Budget:** $500,000 - $1,000,000
>**Income Sources:** Private Foundations/Grants/Endowments; Business/Corporate Donations; Box Office; Government Grants; Individual Donations
>**Season:** 52 Weeks   **Annual Attendance:** 10,000
>**Affiliations:** TCG, OA

WESTBETH THEATRE CENTER
151 Bank Street, New York, NY 10014
(212) 691-2272
FAX: (212) 924-7185
Founded: 1977
Arts Area: Professional
Status: Professional; Non-Profit
Purpose: To develop new plays and musicals
Management: Arnold Engelman, Producing Director; Anne Rothschild, Administrative Assistant; Steven Bloom, Literary Manager
Paid Staff: 4   **Volunteer Staff:** 2
Budget: $100,000 - $500,000
Income Sources: Private Foundations/Grants/Endowments; Business/Corporate Donations; Box Office; Government Grants; Individual Donations
Season: 52 Weeks

WESTSIDE COMMUNITY REPERTORY
252 West 81st Street, New York, NY 10024
(212) 874-7290
Founded: 1969
Arts Area: Professional; Theatrical Group
Status: Semi-Professional; Non-Profit
Type: Performing; Resident
Purpose: To perform classics and provide a less expensive alternative to Broadway in the process
Management: Allen Schroeter, Artistic Director
Paid Staff: 5   **Volunteer Staff:** 5
Paid Artists: 5   **Non-Paid Artists:** 20
Budget: $1,000 - $50,000
Income Sources: Private Foundations/Grants/Endowments; Box Office; Government Grants; Individual Donations
Season: 52 Weeks
Annual Attendance: 3,500
Affiliations: ART/NY; Westside Arts Coalition

WHITE BIRD PRODUCTIONS, INC.
PO Box 20233, Columbus Circle Station, New York, NY 10023
(718) 788-5984
Founded: 1989
Arts Area: Professional; Theatrical Group
Status: Professional; Non-Profit
Type: Performing; Touring; Educational
Purpose: To assist in the development of theatrical pieces that generally or specifically address an environmental theme
Management: Kathryn Dickinson, Artistic Director; Liz Loftus, Associate Artistic Director; John Istel, Dramaturge; Christina Denzinger, Literary Manager
Volunteer Staff: 4
Utilizes: Guest Artists; Guest Directors
Budget: $1,000 - $50,000
Income Sources: Box Office; Government Grants; Individual Donations
Season: 52 Weeks

WOMEN'S INTERART CENTER
549 West 52nd Street, New York, NY 10019
(212) 246-1050
Founded: 1971
Arts Area: Professional; Theatrical Group
Status: Professional; Non-Profit
Type: Performing
Purpose: Committed to exploring all areas of theatrical expression while emphasizing the presentation of new playwrights
Management: Margot Lewitin, Artistic Director; Jean Rowan, Dramaturge; Susan Waring Morris, Development Director
Officers: Bill Perlman, Board Chairman
Paid Staff: 3
Utilizes: Special Technical Talent; Guest Artists; Guest Directors
Budget: $100,000 - $500,000
Income Sources: Private Foundations/Grants/Endowments; Business/Corporate Donations; Box Office; Government Grants; Individual Donations
Season: 52 Weeks
Affiliations: AEA
Performance Facilities: Interart Theater

WOMEN'S PROJECT AND PRODUCTIONS
7 West 63rd Street, New York, NY 10023
(212) 873-3040
FAX: (212) 873-3788
Founded: 1978
Arts Area: Professional; Theatrical Group
Status: Professional; Non-Profit
Type: Performing; Resident; Educational; Sponsoring
Purpose: To promote and develop the work of women playwrights and directors in the theatre by creating opportunities for them to work
Management: Julia Miles, Artistic Director; Liz Diamond, Artistic Associate; Jennifer Greenfield, Managing Director
Officers: Julia Miles, President; Pat Schoenfeld, Chairperson; Billie Allen, Treasurer; Helene Kaplan, Secretary
Paid Staff: 9
Utilizes: Special Technical Talent; Guest Artists; Guest Directors; Playwrights
Budget: $500,000 - $1,000,000
Income Sources: Private Foundations/Grants/Endowments; Business/Corporate Donations; Box Office; Government Grants; Individual Donations
Season: October - June **Annual Attendance:** 5,000
Affiliations: TCG; ART/NY

THE WOOSTER GROUP
PO Box 654, Canal Street Station, New York, NY 10013
(212) 966-9796; (212) 966-3651
FAX: (212) 226-6576
Founded: 1967
Arts Area: Theatrical Group
Status: Non-Profit
Type: Performing; Touring; Resident; Sponsoring
Purpose: A collective of artists working together on collaborative projects over long periods of time
Management: Elizabeth LeCompte, Artistic Director; Andrea Most, Administrative Director
Officers: Peyton Smith, President; Kate Valk, Secretary
Paid Staff: 8 **Volunteer Staff:** 4
Paid Artists: 17
Budget: $500,000 - $1,000,000
Income Sources: Private Foundations/Grants/Endowments; Business/Corporate Donations; Box Office; Government Grants; Individual Donations
Season: 52 Weeks
Affiliations: TCG
Performance Facilities: The Performing Garage

THE WORKING THEATRE COMPANY, INC.
400 West 40th Street, New York, NY 10018
(212) 967-5464
Arts Area: Professional
Status: Professional; Non-Profit
Type: Performing; Educational
Purpose: America's only professional theatre company dedicated to producing new plays of cultural diversities that reflect the issues and concerns that working people face in the modern world
Management: Bill Mitchelson, Artistic Director; Honour Molloy, Development Director
Officers: Larry Beers, Chairman
Budget: $100,000 - $500,000
Income Sources: Private Foundations/Grants/Endowments; Business/Corporate Donations; Box Office; Government Grants; Individual Donations

WPA THEATRE
519 West 23rd Street, New York, NY 10011
(212) 206-0523
FAX: (212) 637-7154
Founded: 1977
Arts Area: Professional
Status: Professional; Non-Profit
Type: Performing
Purpose: The WPA Theatre is dedicated to the creation of a new American repertory theatre based on realistic writing, acting and design.
Management: Kyle Renick, Artistic Director; Donna Lieberman, Managing Director
Paid Staff: 6
Paid Artists: 60
Budget: $500,000 - $1,000,000

Income Sources: Private Foundations/Grants/Endowments; Business/Corporate Donations; Box Office; Government Grants; Individual Donations
Season: October - June
Annual Attendance: 13,000
Affiliations: ART/NY; TCG
Performance Facilities: Chelsea Playhouse

THE YORK THEATRE COMPANY
2 East 90th Street, New York, NY 10128
(212) 534-5366
FAX: (212) 222-9458
Founded: 1969
Arts Area: Professional; Musical; Theatrical Group
Status: Professional; Non-Profit
Type: Performing
Purpose: A professional equity off-off-Broadway company dedicated to presenting great classical works as well as revivals and/or premieres of unusual, avant-garde musicals
Management: Janet Hayes Walker, Producing Director; Molly Pickering Grose, Managing Director; Charles Dodsley Walker, Business Manager; Sarah Tod Smith, Technical Director
Officers: W. David McCoy, Chairman of the Board
Paid Staff: 8 **Volunteer Staff:** 6
Paid Artists: 36
Utilizes: Special Technical Talent; Guest Conductors; Guest Artists; Guest Directors
Budget: $100,000 - $500,000
Income Sources: Private Foundations/Grants/Endowments; Business/Corporate Donations; Box Office; Individual Donations
Season: October - June **Annual Attendance:** 7,500
Affiliations: AEA

PERFORMING SERIES

AMERICAN LANDMARK FESTIVALS
26 Wall Street, Federal Hall National Monmument, New York, NY 10005
(212) 866-2086
FAX: (212) 264-3186
Founded: 1973
Arts Area: Dance; Vocal Music; Instrumental Music; Theater; Festivals; Lyric Opera; Grand Opera
Status: Professional
Type: Performing
Purpose: To combine performances with exceptional historic settings
Officers: Francis L. Heilbut, President
Utilizes: Special Technical Talent; Guest Conductors; Guest Artists; Guest Directors
Income Sources: Individual Donations
Season: 52 Weeks **Annual Attendance:** 100,000

BANG ON A CAN, INC.
222 East Fifth Street, #16, New York, NY 10003
(212) 777-8442
FAX: (212) 777-8442
Founded: 1987
Arts Area: Festivals
Status: Professional; Non-Profit
Type: Performing
Purpose: To present new music by young and emerging composers
Management: Rebecca A. Sayles, Executive Director
Officers: Michael Gordon, David Lang, Julia Wolfe, Artistic Directors
Paid Staff: 1
Budget: $100,000 - $500,000
Income Sources: Private Foundations/Grants/Endowments; Business/Corporate Donations; Box Office; Government Grants; Individual Donations
Season: May **Annual Attendance:** 3,000

CHILDREN'S FREE OPERA AND DANCE
130 West 42nd Street, New York, NY 10036
(212) 840-7470
FAX: (212) 840-7585
Founded: 1976
Arts Area: Dance; Theater; Opera; Music

Status: Professional; Non-Profit
Type: Performing; Educational
Purpose: Educational
Management: Michael Feldman, Artistic Director; Marianne C. Lockwood, Executive Director; Curt Sharp, General Manager; Susannah Halston, Director of Marketing/Development; Rosalyn Bindman, Education Director
Officers: M. Bernar Aidinoff, Chairman; Michael Feldman, President; Marianne C. Lockwood, Vice President; Steven Leifer, Treasurer
Paid Staff: 10   **Volunteer Staff:** 15
Paid Artists: 60
Utilizes: Special Technical Talent; Guest Conductors; Guest Artists; Guest Directors
Budget: $100,000 - $500,000
Income Sources: Private Foundations/Grants/Endowments; Business/Corporate Donations; Government Grants; Individual Donations
Season: October - May   **Annual Attendance:** 60,000
Affiliations: Orchestra of Saint Luke's
Performance Facilities: Town Hall; Brooklyn Academy of Music; State University of New York at Purchase; Lehman Center Triplex Theatre

CITY CENTER OF MUSIC AND DRAMA
70 Lincoln Central Plaza, 4th Floor, New York, NY 10023-6580
(212) 870-4266
Founded: 1943
Arts Area: Dance; Vocal Music; Instrumental Music; Theater
Status: Professional; Non-Profit
Type: Performing; Touring; Educational
Purpose: To provide opera, ballet and drama so that everyone, regardless of income, can see and hear great works
Management: Carla Hunter, Controller
Officers: Martin J. Oppenheimer, Chairman; Gillian Attfield, Vice Chairman
Paid Staff: 12   **Volunteer Staff:** 2
Utilizes: Guest Conductors; Guest Artists; Guest Directors
Budget: Over 10,000,000
Income Sources: Private Foundations/Grants/Endowments; Business/Corporate Donations; Box Office; Government Grants; Individual Donations
Season: 52 Weeks   **Annual Attendance:** 801,000
Performance Facilities: New York State Theater

FOOLS COMPANY, INC.: THE INTERNATIONAL OFFESTIVAL
358 West 44th Street, New York, NY 10036-5426
(212) 307-6000
Founded: 1970
Arts Area: Theater; Festivals
Status: Professional; Non-Profit
Type: Performing; Educational
Purpose: To produce a theatre arts festival and other works and workshops in the performing arts
Management: Jill Russell, Executive Director; Martin Russell, Associate Executive Director; Susan Cline, Executive Administrator
Officers: James Wertheim, President; Marcus Bicknell, Vice President; Joseph Benitez, Secretary/Treasurer
Paid Staff: 5   **Volunteer Staff:** 12
Utilizes: Guest Artists
Budget: $1,000 - $50,000
Income Sources: Private Foundations/Grants/Endowments; Business/Corporate Donations; Box Office; Government Grants; Individual Donations
Season: April - June   **Annual Attendance:** 3,000
Performance Facilities: John Houseman Theatre Studio

JAZZMOBILE INCORPORATED
154 West 127th Street, New York, NY 10027
(212) 866-4900
FAX: (212) 866-3613
Arts Area: Instrumental Music; Jazz
Status: Professional; Non-Profit
Type: Performing; Touring; Resident; Educational
Purpose: To preserve, propogate and present jazz--America's classical music--by all means possible
Management: David Bailey, Executive Director; Dr. Anita Batisti, Development Director
Officers: Dr. George Butler, Chairman of the Board
Budget: $500,000 - $1,000,000
Income Sources: Private Foundations/Grants/Endowments; Business/Corporate Donations; Box Office; Government Grants; Individual Donations; Earned Income

KOHAV THEATRE FOUNDATION
118 Riverside Drive, New York, NY 10024
(212) 877-1667
> **Founded:** 1959
> **Arts Area:** Theater
> **Status:** Professional; Non-Profit
> **Type:** Performing
> **Management:** Hava Kohav Beller, Director; Kathleen Greene, Production Assistant; Herbert C. Kantor, Counsel
> **Paid Staff:** 1   **Volunteer Staff:** 1
> **Utilizes:** Special Technical Talent; Guest Artists
> **Income Sources:** Private Foundations/Grants/Endowments; Government Grants; Individual Donations

LINCOLN CENTER OUT-OF-DOORS
c/o Lincoln Center for the Performing Arts, 70 Lincoln Center Plza., New York, NY 10023
(212) 875-5000
FAX: (212) 875-5145
> **Arts Area:** Dance; Vocal Music; Instrumental Music; Theater
> **Status:** Professional; Non-Profit
> **Type:** Sponsoring
> **Management:** Jenneth Webster, Associate Director - Programming
> **Paid Staff:** 24
> **Paid Artists:** 600
> **Utilizes:** Guest Artists
> **Budget:** $100,000 - $500,000
> **Income Sources:** Private Foundations/Grants/Endowments; Business/Corporate Donations; Box Office; Government Grants; Individual Donations
> **Season:** August - September
> **Annual Attendance:** 300,000
> **Performance Facilities:** Lincoln Center North Plaza, Damrosch Park Bandshell

LINCOLN CENTER'S MOSTLY MOZART FESTIVAL
70 Lincoln Center Plaza, 9th Floor, New York, NY 10023
(212) 875-5000
> **Founded:** 1966
> **Arts Area:** Instrumental Music
> **Status:** Professional; Non-Profit
> **Type:** Sponsoring
> **Purpose:** A major summer festival in New York where the focus of the programing is on Mozart and music of that period
> **Management:** Gerard Schwarz, Music Director; W.W. Lockwood Jr., Festival Director; Frederick W. Noonan, Associate Director; Michele A. Balm, Production Coordinator
> **Paid Staff:** 6
> **Paid Artists:** 150
> **Utilizes:** Guest Conductors; Guest Artists
> **Budget:** $1,000,000 - $5,000,000
> **Income Sources:** Private Foundations/Grants/Endowments; Business/Corporate Donations; Box Office; Government Grants; Individual Donations
> **Season:** July - August   **Annual Attendance:** 105,000
> **Performance Facilities:** Avery Fisher Hall

METROPOLITAN MUSEUM CONCERTS AND LECTURES
1000 5th Avenue and 82nd Street, New York, NY 10028
(212) 879-5500
FAX: (212) 570-3973
> **Founded:** 1954
> **Arts Area:** Vocal Music; Instrumental Music; Festivals
> **Status:** Professional
> **Type:** Sponsoring
> **Purpose:** To sense a vital function as one of the major presenting organizations in New York City and reflect the museum's charter in promoting education and cultural events which reflect the museum's holdings
> **Management:** Hilde Annik Limondjian, Program Administrator
> **Paid Staff:** 50
> **Budget:** $1,000,000 - $5,000,000
> **Income Sources:** Box Office; Government Grants
> **Season:** October - May
> **Annual Attendance:** 200,000
> **Affiliations:** AAM
> **Performance Facilities:** Grace Rainey Rogers Auditorium; Velez Blanco Patio

THE NEW YORK INTERNATIONAL FESTIVAL OF THE ARTS
386 Park Avenue South, Suite 2000, New York, NY 10016
(212) 679-5200
FAX: (212) 679-5677
      Founded: 1986
      Arts Area: Festivals
      Status: Professional; Non-Profit
      Type: Sponsoring
      Purpose: To encourage international friendships; to demonstrate why New York City is considered to be the cultural capital; to promote tourism and its positive economic role
      Management: Claudia E. Keenan, Director of Public Affairs
      Officers: Martin E. Segal, Chairman; Frank A. Bennack, George B. Munroe, Vice Chairmen; Gordon J. Davis, Treasurer; Diane M. Coffey, Secretary
      Paid Staff: 5
      Utilizes: Music, Dance, Theatre Companies
      Budget: $500,000 - $1,000,000
      Income Sources: Private Foundations/Grants/Endowments; Business/Corporate Donations; Individual Donations
      Season: June   **Annual Attendance:** 95,000

PRESENTATIONS OF THE ELAINE KAUFMAN CULTURAL CENTER
129 West 67th Street, New York, NY 10023
(212) 362-8060; (212) 362-8719
FAX: (212) 874-7865
      Arts Area: Vocal Music; Instrumental Music; Festivals
      Status: Professional
      Type: Educational; Sponsoring
      Management: Andrew Berger, Concert Director
      Officers: Lewis Kruger, Chairman
      Utilizes: Guest Artists
      Income Sources: Private Foundations/Grants/Endowments; Business/Corporate Donations; Box Office; Government Grants; Individual Donations
      Season: September - May
      Performance Facilities: Merkin Concert Hall

THE YARD
890 Broadway, New York, NY 10003
(212) 228-0911; (508) 645-9662
      Founded: 1973
      Arts Area: Dance; Instrumental Music; Theater
      Status: Professional; Non-Profit
      Type: Performing; Touring; Resident; Educational
      Purpose: To support the growth and development of professional choreographers through residency programs and other services
      Management: Patricia N. Nanon, Director
      Officers: Patricia N. Nanon, President; Polly Siwek, Vice President; David Washburn, Secretary; Joseph S. Iseman, Treasurer
      Paid Staff: 4   **Volunteer Staff:** 2
      Paid Artists: 25
      Utilizes: Guest Artists
      Budget: $100,000 - $500,000
      Income Sources: Private Foundations/Grants/Endowments; Business/Corporate Donations; Box Office; Government Grants; Individual Donations
      Season: May - September   **Annual Attendance:** 2,000
      Performance Facilities: Barn Theater, Chilmark, MA

FACILITY

AMBASSADOR THEATRE
215 West 49th Street, New York, NY 10019
(212) 239-6200
FAX: (212) 944-4136
      Type of Facility: Theatre House
      Type of Stage: Proscenium   **Orchestra Pit**
      Seating Capacity: 1,125
      Year Built: 1921   **Architect:** Herbert J. Krapp
      Year Remodeled: 1956

Contact for Rental: Peter Entin;   (212) 944-3700
Manager: Shubert Organization

AMERICAN PLACE THEATRE
111 West 46th Street, New York, NY 10036
(212) 840-2960
FAX: (212) 391-4019
   Type of Facility: Theatre House
   Type of Stage: Flexible
   Seating Capacity: 299
   Year Built: 1971   **Architect:** Richard D. Kaplan
   Manager: Sara Hershman
   Resident Groups: The American Place Theatre

APOLLO THEATRE
253 West 125th Street, New York, NY 10027
(212) 661-3344
FAX: (212) 749-2743
   Type of Facility: Concert Hall; Theatre House
   Facility Originally: Vaudeville
   Type of Stage: Modified Apron Proscenium
   Stage Dimensions: 68'6"Wx37'6"D; 37'6"Wx28'2"H proscenium opening
   Seating Capacity: 1,500
   Year Built: 1914   **Architect:** George Kiester
   Year Remodeled: 1987   **Architect:** LeGendre Johnson McNeil   **Cost:** $16,900,000
   Contact for Rental: Oliver Sutton;   (212) 661-3344

BELASCO THEATRE
111 West 44th Street, New York, NY 10036
(212) 239-6200
   Type of Facility: Theatre House
   Type of Stage: Proscenium
   Seating Capacity: 1,018
   Year Built: 1907   **Architect:** George Kiester
   Year Remodeled: 1953
   Contact for Rental: Peter Entin;   (212) 239-6200
   Manager: Shubert Organization

BMCC/TRIPLEX PERFORMING ARTS CENTER
199 Chambers Street, New York, NY 10007
(212) 618-1900
FAX: (212) 732-2482
   Type of Facility: Theatre Complex; Concert Hall; Auditorium; Studio Performance; Environmental; Performance Center;
   Off Broadway; Theatre House; Multi-Purpose
   Facility Originally: School
   Type of Stage: Proscenium; 3/4 Arena; Environmental
   Stage Dimensions: 3 spaces: A - 46'x37'x19'; B - 28'x39'x18'; C - 24'x26'x18'   **Orchestra Pit**
   Seating Capacity: A - 930; B - 280; C - 99
   Contact for Rental: Joel Bassin;   (212) 618-1900

BOOTH THEATRE
222 West 45th Street, New York, NY 10036
(212) 239-6200
   Type of Facility: Theatre House
   Type of Stage: Proscenium   **Orchestra Pit**
   Seating Capacity: 783
   Year Remodeled: 1913   **Architect:** Henry B. Herts
   Contact for Rental: Philip Smith;   (212) 239-6200
   Manager: Shubert Organization
   Orchestra pit available upon request

BROADHURST THEATRE
235 West 44th Street, New York, NY 10035
(212) 239-6200
   Type of Facility: Theatre House
   Type of Stage: Proscenium   **Orchestra Pit**
   Seating Capacity: 1,157
   Year Built: 1917   **Architect:** Herbert J. Krapp

Contact for Rental: Peter Entin or Philip Smith; (212) 239-6200
Manager: Shubert Organization

BROADWAY THEATRE
1681 Broadway, New York, NY 10019
(212) 239-6200
    Type of Facility: Theatre House
    Type of Stage: Proscenium   **Orchestra Pit**
    Seating Capacity: 1,765
    Year Built: 1924   **Architect:** Eugene DeRosa
    Year Remodeled: 1942
    Contact for Rental: Peter Entin;   (212) 239-6200
    Manager: Shubert Organization

BROOKS ATKINSON THEATRE
256 West 47th Street, New York, NY 10036
(212) 719-4099
    Type of Facility: Theatre House
    Type of Stage: Proscenium
    Seating Capacity: 1,086
    Year Built: 1926
    Contact for Rental: Peter Russell;   (212) 730-8200
    Manager: The Nederlander Organization

CARNEGIE HALL
154 West 57th Street, New York, NY 10019
(212) 903-9600
FAX: (212) 581-6539
    Type of Facility: Concert Hall
    Type of Stage: Proscenium
    Seating Capacity: Main Hall - 2,804, Recital Hall - 268
    Year Built: 1891   **Architect:** William Burnett Tuthill   **Cost:** $1,000,000
    Year Remodeled: 1986   **Architect:** James S. Polshek & Partners   **Cost:** $60,000,000
    Contact for Rental: Gilda Weissberger;   (212) 903-9710

CIRCLE IN THE SQUARE INC.
1633 Broadway, New York, NY 10019
(212) 307-2700
FAX: (212) 581-6371
    Type of Facility: Theatre House
    Type of Stage: 3/4 Arena
    Seating Capacity: 750
    Year Built: 1951
    Contact for Rental: Robert Buckley;   (212) 307-2700

CITY CENTER
131 West 55th Street, New York, NY 10019-5390
(212) 247-0430
FAX: (212) 246-9778
    Founded: 1943
    Type of Facility: Theatre Complex; Concert Hall; Auditorium; Studio Performance; Performance Center; Office Space
    Facility Originally: Masonic Hall; Shriner's "Mecca Temple"
    Type of Stage: Proscenium
    Stage Dimensions: 38'H proscenium; 45'Wx43'Dx60' to grid stage   **Orchestra Pit**
    Seating Capacity: 2,684
    Year Built: 1923
    Year Remodeled: 1988   **Architect:** Rothzeid, Kaiserman, Thompson & Bee
    Acoustical Consultant: Sound Associates
    Contact for Rental: Peter Clark, Theater Manager;   (212) 247-0430
    Resident Groups: Joffrey Ballet; Alvin Ailey Dance Theater; Paul Taylor Dance Company; Merce Cunningham Dance Company; Lar Lubovitch Dance Company; Martha Graham Dance; Trisha Brown Dance
    City Center contains Stage I, Stage II and City Center Theater.

CITY CENTER - CITY CENTER STAGE I
131 West 55th Street, New York, NY 10019-5390
(212) 247-0430
FAX: (212) 246-9778
    Type of Facility: Black Box

Type of Stage: Flexible
Stage Dimensions: 40'x50'
Seating Capacity: 299
Contact for Rental: Peter Clark

CITY CENTER - CITY CENTER STAGE II
131 West 55th Street, New York, NY 10019-5390
(212) 247-0430
FAX: (212) 246-9778
    Type of Facility: Black Box
    Type of Stage: Flexible
    Stage Dimensions: 45'x60'
    Seating Capacity: 150
    Contact for Rental: Peter Clark

CITY CENTER - CITY CENTER THEATRE
131 West 55th Street, New York, NY 10019-5390
(212) 247-0430
FAX: (212) 246-9778
    Type of Facility: Theatre House
    Facility Originally: Meeting Hall; Movie House
    Type of Stage: Proscenium
    Stage Dimensions: 45'Wx60'D   **Orchestra Pit**
    Seating Capacity: 2,731
    Year Built: 1923
    Year Remodeled: 1986   **Architect:** Fred Lebensohl, Bernard Rothzeid
    Contact for Rental: Peter Clark

CORT THEATRE
138 West 48th Street, New York, NY 10036
(212) 239-6200
FAX: (212) 239-5134
    Type of Facility: Theatre House
    Type of Stage: Proscenium   **Orchestra Pit**
    Seating Capacity: 1,089
    Year Built: 1912   **Architect:** Edward B. Corey
    Contact for Rental: Philip Smith;   (212) 944-3710
    Manager: Shubert Organization

CSC REPERTORY LTD.
136 East 13th Street, New York, NY 10003
(212) 677-4210
FAX: (212) 477-7504
    Founded: 1967
    Type of Facility: Theatre House
    Facility Originally: Movie House
    Type of Stage: 3/4 Arena
    Stage Dimensions: 30'x30'
    Seating Capacity: 180
    Year Built: 1890
    Year Remodeled: 1974
    Contact for Rental: Patricia Taylor, Manager;   (212) 677-4210
    Resident Groups: CSC Repertory Ltd.
    For resident company to perform classics

DANCE THEATER WORKSHOP'S BESSIE SCHONBERG THEATRE
219 West 19th Street, New York, NY 10011
(212) 691-6500
FAX: (212) 633-1974
    Founded: 1960
    Type of Facility: Loft; Black Box Proscenium Style
    Facility Originally: Business Facility
    Type of Stage: Proscenium; Black Box Proscenium style
    Stage Dimensions: 26'x32' with wings; 26'x48' without wings
    Seating Capacity: 100
    Contact for Rental: Laura Schandelmeier, Phil Sandstrom, Production Managers;   (212) 691-6500
    Manager: David R. White, Executive Director;   (212) 691-6500
    31'x35' rehearsal studio is available for rent.

DELACORTE THEATRE IN CENTRAL PARK
81st Street at Central Park West, New York, NY 10003
(212) 861-7277
Type of Facility: Amphitheater
Type of Stage: Thrust
Seating Capacity: 1,936
Year Built: 1962   **Architect:** Eldon Elder
Year Remodeled: 1977   **Architect:** Giorgio Cavaglieri
Performance facility of the New York Shakespeare Festival. Contact address is: 425 Lafayette Street, New York, NY 10003

EDEN'S EXPRESSWAY
537 Broadway, New York, NY 10012
(212) 925-0880
Type of Facility: Studio Performance; Multi-Purpose; Loft
Facility Originally: Business Facility
Type of Stage: Flexible
Stage Dimensions: 35'x45'x11'
Seating Capacity: 100
Year Built: 1974   **Architect:** Jorge Abrosini   **Cost:** $50,000
Year Remodeled: 1977   **Architect:** Tod Miller   **Cost:** $16,000
Contact for Rental: Frances Alenikoff, Director;   (516) 324-1833
Resident Groups: Frances Alenikoff Dance Theater; T'ai Chi (Maggie Newman)
Ongoing renovations; available for rehearsals and workshops

EISNER-LUBIN AUDITORIUM
566 LaGuardia Place, New York, NY 10012
(212) 998-4909
FAX: (212) 995-4094
Type of Facility: Theatre Complex; Concert Hall; Auditorium; Multi-Purpose
Type of Stage: Platform
Stage Dimensions: 17'x27'6"x13'6"
Seating Capacity: 726
Year Built: 1959
Acoustical Consultant: Steve Freytag
Contact for Rental: Jonathan Ross, Operations Scheduling;   (212) 998-4909
Located at Loeb Student Center, New York University; groups renting must be non-profit organizations

ENSEMBLE STUDIO THEATRE
549 West 52nd Street, New York, NY 10019
(212) 247-4982
Type of Facility: Studio Performance
Facility Originally: Warehouse
Type of Stage: Flexible
Seating Capacity: 100
Acoustical Consultant: Kert Lundell

ETHEL BARRYMORE THEATRE
243 West 47th Street, New York, NY 10036
(212) 239-6200
Type of Facility: Theatre House
Type of Stage: Proscenium
Orchestra Pit
Seating Capacity: 1,096
Year Built: 1928
Architect: Herbert J. Krapp
Contact for Rental: Philip Smith;   (212) 944-3710
Manager: Shubert Organization

EUGENE O'NEILL THEATER
230 West 49th Street, New York, NY 10019
(212) 239-6200
Type of Facility: Theatre House
Type of Stage: Proscenium
Orchestra Pit
Seating Capacity: 1,101

Year Built: 1925   **Architect:** Herbert J. Krapp
Contact for Rental: Jujamcyn Theaters;   (212) 840-8181

46TH STREET THEATRE
226 West 46th Street, New York, NY 10036
(212) 221-1211
Type of Facility: Theatre House
Type of Stage: Proscenium
Seating Capacity: 1,338
Year Built: 1924   **Architect:** Herbert J. Krapp
Contact for Rental: Peter Russell;   (212) 730-8200
Manager: The Nederlander Organization

GERSHWIN THEATRE
222 West 51st Street, New York, NY 10019
(212) 586-6510
Type of Facility: Theatre House
Type of Stage: Proscenium
Seating Capacity: 1,933
Year Built: 1972
Architect: Ralph Alswang   **Cost:** $9,000,000
Contact for Rental: Leo Cohen;   (212) 262-2400
Manager: The Nederlander Organization;   (212) 262-2400

GRAMERCY ARTS THEATER
138 East 27th Street, New York, NY 10016
(212) 889-2850
Type of Facility: Off Broadway; Theatre House
Facility Originally: Private Residence
Type of Stage: Proscenium; Platform
Stage Dimensions: 20'x25'
Seating Capacity: 153
Year Built: 1850
Year Remodeled: 1972   **Architect:** Leslie Cortese   **Cost:** $20,000
Manager: Gilberto Zaldivar
Resident Groups: Spanish Theater Repertory Company

H.B. PLAYWRIGHTS FOUNDATION THEATRE HOUSE
124 South Bank Street, New York, NY 10014
(212) 989-6540
Type of Facility: Auditorium; Theatre House
Facility Originally: Garage
Type of Stage: Flexible
Stage Dimensions: 18'x32'
Seating Capacity: 100
Year Remodeled: 1964   **Architect:** V. Gruen
Acoustical Consultant: V. Gruen
Manager: Glen Paris, Artistic Director;   (212) 989-6540
Resident Groups: H.B. Playwrights Foundation

HELEN HAYES THEATRE
240 West 44th Street, New York, NY 10036
(212) 944-9450; (212) 944-9457
FAX: (212) 302-3584
Type of Facility: Theatre House
Type of Stage: Proscenium
Stage Dimensions: 28'Wx28'D; 28'Wx17'10"H proscenium opening
Seating Capacity: 565
Year Built: 1912
Year Remodeled: 1980
Contact for Rental: Susan Myerberg;   (212) 944-9457
Built in 1912 by Winthrop Ames as the Little Theatre, it became the Helen Hayes Theatre in 1983. It is the smallest theatre on Broadway and is independently owned by the Little Theatre Company.

IMPERIAL THEATRE
249 West 45th Street, New York, NY 10036
(212) 944-3700
Type of Facility: Theatre House

Type of Stage: Proscenium   **Orchestra Pit**
Seating Capacity: 1,452
Year Built: 1923   **Architect:** Herbert J. Krapp
Contact for Rental: Philip Smith;   (212) 944-3710
Manager: Shubert Organization

JOHN GOLDEN THEATRE
252 West 45th Street, New York, NY 10036
(212) 944-3700
Type of Facility: Theatre House
Type of Stage: Proscenium
Orchestra Pit
Seating Capacity: 805
Year Built: 1927   **Architect:** Herbert J. Krapp
Contact for Rental: ;   (212) 944-3710
Manager: Shubert Organization

THE JOSEPH PAPP PUBLIC THEATER
425 Lafayette Street, New York, NY 10003
(212) 598-7100
FAX: (212) 598-7199
Type of Facility: Performance Center
Year Built: 1860
Year Remodeled: 1970   **Architect:** Giorgio Caraglieri   **Cost:** $700,000
Acoustical Consultant: Christopher Jaffe
Resident Groups: New York Shakespeare Festival
Converted into a theater in 1970 Seating Capacity: Anspacher Theater - 275; Little Film Theater - 91; LuEsther Hall - 240; Martinson Hall - 240; Shiva Theater - 90

THE JOYCE THEATER
175 Eighth Avenue, New York, NY 10011
(212) 691-9740
FAX: (212) 727-3658
Founded: 1981
Type of Facility: Performance Center; Theatre House; Dance Theater
Type of Stage: Proscenium
Stage Dimensions: 43'x35'x21'
Seating Capacity: 472
Year Built: 1981   **Architect:** Hugh Hardy of Hardy, Holzman, Pfeiffer   **Cost:** $4,000,000
Acoustical Consultant: Chris Jaffe, Jaffe Acoustics
Contact for Rental: Martin Wechsler;   (212) 691-9740
Resident Groups: Feld Ballets/NY; Pilobolus

KAUFMANN CONCERT HALL
1395 Lexington Avenue, New York, NY 10028
(212) 415-5740
FAX: (212) 415-5738
Type of Facility: Concert Hall; Auditorium; Theatre House
Type of Stage: Proscenium
Stage Dimensions: 35'x30'x23'6"
Seating Capacity: 916
Year Built: 1929
Year Remodeled: 1977
Contact for Rental: Valerie Simmons;   (212) 415-5740
Manager: Raymond T. Grant;   (212) 415-5740
Resident Groups: New York Chamber Symphony

KAZUKO HIRABAYASHI DANCE THEATRE
330 Broome Street, New York, NY 10002
(212) 966-6414
Type of Facility: Studio Performance; Loft
Facility Originally: School
Type of Stage: Flexible
Stage Dimensions: 32'x38'
Seating Capacity: 100
Year Built: 1979   **Cost:** $10,000
Contact for Rental: Robert Swinston;   (212) 966-6414

THE LAMB'S THEATRE
130 West 44th Street, New York, NY 10036
(212) 997-0210
FAX: (212) 997-1082
Type of Facility: Studio Performance; Off Broadway; Theatre House; Room
Facility Originally: Lamb's Club, Men's Theatre Organization
Type of Stage: Flexible; Proscenium
Stage Dimensions: Mainstage 26'x23'x27'6"; Little Theatre 23'x23'x12'
Seating Capacity: Main Theatre - 349, Little Theatre - 99
Year Built: 1902   **Architect:** Stanford White
Year Remodeled: 1974
Contact for Rental: Carl H. Jaynes, Facilities Manager;   (212) 997-0210
Resident Groups: Lamb's Theatre Company

LEHMAN CENTER FOR THE PERFORMING ARTS
Bedford Park Boulevard, West, New York, NY 10468
(212) 960-8232
FAX: (212) 960-8935
Type of Facility: Theatre Complex; Concert Hall; Auditorium; Outdoor (Concert); Theatre House; Amphitheater
Type of Stage: Proscenium
Stage Dimensions: Concert Hall - 60'x30'; Theatre - 35'4"x26'6"   **Orchestra Pit**
Seating Capacity: Concert Hall - 2,300; Theatre - 500
Year Built: 1980   **Architect:** David Todd/Jan Pokorny
Contact for Rental: Jack Globenfelt;   (212) 960-8232
Resident Groups: Aeolian Chamber Players

LINCOLN CENTER FOR THE PERFORMING ARTS
140 West 65th Street, New York, NY 10023
(212) 877-1800
FAX: (212) 874-2659
Type of Facility: Theatre Complex; Performance Center
Lincoln Center contains Alice Tully Hall, Avery Fisher Hall, Juilliard Opera Theatre, Juillard School Drama Workshop, Metropolitan Opera House, Mitzi E. Newhouse Theater, New York Public Library   Auditorium, New York State Theater, Paul Recital Hall and Vivian Beaumont Theater. See separate listings for additional information.

LINCOLN CENTER FOR THE PERFORMING ARTS - ALICE TULLY HALL
1941 Broadway, New York, NY 10023
(212) 875-5000
Type of Facility: Concert Hall
Type of Stage: Proscenium
Stage Dimensions: 50'Wx21'6"D   **Orchestra Pit**
Seating Capacity: 1,096
Year Built: 1969   **Architect:** Pietro Belluschi, Helge Westermann
Acoustical Consultant: Heinrich Keilholz
Contact for Rental: Delmar Hendricks;   (212) 580-8700
Manager: John Fleming
Resident Groups: Chamber Music Society of Lincoln Center; Film Society of Lincoln Center

LINCOLN CENTER FOR THE PERFORMING ARTS - AVERY FISHER HALL
Broadway and 65th Street, New York, NY 10023
(212) 875-5000
FAX: (212) 875-5011
Type of Facility: Concert Hall
Type of Stage: Concert Shell
Stage Dimensions: 45'x68'x40'4"
Seating Capacity: 2,738
Year Built: 1962   **Architect:** Harrison & Abramovitz
Contact for Rental: Delmar Hendricks;   (212) 580-8700
Manager: John Fleming
Resident Groups: New York Philharmonic

LINCOLN CENTER FOR THE PERFORMING ARTS - THE JUILLIARD OPERA CENTER
60 Lincoln Center Plaza, New York, NY 10023
(212) 799-5000
FAX: (212) 724-0263
Type of Facility: Theatre House
Type of Stage: Proscenium
Orchestra Pit

Seating Capacity: 1,026
Year Built: 1969   **Architect:** Pietro Belluschi
Acoustical Consultant: Heinrich Keilholz
Manager: Rick Harold

LINCOLN CENTER FOR THE PERFORMING ARTS - THE JUILLIARD SCHOOL DRAMA WORKSHOP
60 Lincoln Center Plaza, New York, NY 10023
(212) 799-5000
FAX: (212) 875-8437
   Type of Facility: Theatre House
   Type of Stage: Flexible
   Seating Capacity: 206
   Year Built: 1969   **Architect:** Pietro Belluschi
   Acoustical Consultant: Heinrich Keilholz
   Manager: Katherine Hood

LINCOLN CENTER FOR THE PERFORMING ARTS - METROPOLITAN OPERA HOUSE
30 Lincoln Center Plaza, New York, NY 10023
(212) 799-3100
FAX: (212) 874-2659
   Type of Facility: Opera House
   Seating Capacity: Auditorium - 3,788; Liszt Hall - 144
   Year Built: 1966   **Architect:** Wallace K. Harrison   **Cost:** $46,900,000
   Acoustical Consultant: Vilhelm L. Jordan and Dr. Cyril Harris
   Contact for Rental: Bruce Crawford;   (212) 799-3100
   Resident Groups: Metropolitan Opera

LINCOLN CENTER FOR THE PERFORMING ARTS - MITZI E. NEWHOUSE THEATER
150 West 65th Street, New York, NY 10023
(212) 362-7600
FAX: (212) 873-0761
   Type of Facility: Theatre House
   Type of Stage: Thrust
   Stage Dimensions: 25'x35'
   Seating Capacity: 280
   Year Built: 1965   **Architect:** Eero Saarinen

LINCOLN CENTER FOR THE PERFORMING ARTS - NEW YORK PUBLIC LIBRARY AUDITORIUM
40 Lincoln Center Plaza, New York, NY 10023
(212) 870-5500
   Type of Facility: Auditorium
   Type of Stage: Platform
   Stage Dimensions: 14'x36'
   Seating Capacity: 212
   Year Built: 1965
   Architect: Skidmore, Owings & Merrill
   Cost: $8,000,000
   Contact for Rental: Richard M. Buck;   (212) 870-1613
   Free concerts and events daily. The Heckscher Oval Theater is in the children's section.

LINCOLN CENTER FOR THE PERFORMING ARTS - NEW YORK STATE THEATER
20 Lincoln Center Plaza, New York, NY 10023
(212) 870-5500
FAX: (212) 870-4285
   Type of Facility: Theatre House
   Type of Stage: Proscenium   **Orchestra Pit**
   Seating Capacity: 2,737
   Year Built: 1964
   Architect: Philip Johnson
   Manager: Mitchell Brower;   (212) 870-5505
   Resident Groups: New York City Ballet; New York City Opera

LINCOLN CENTER FOR THE PERFORMING ARTS - PAUL RECITAL HALL
60 Lincoln Center Plaza, New York, NY 10023
(212) 799-5000
FAX: (212) 724-0263
   Type of Facility: Concert Hall
   Seating Capacity: 278

Year Built: 1969
Architect: Pietro Belluschi
Acoustical Consultant: Heinrich Keilholz
Manager: Ed Fleischman

LINCOLN CENTER FOR THE PERFORMING ARTS - VIVIAN BEAUMONT THEATER
150 West 65th Street, New York, NY 10023
(212) 362-7600
Type of Facility: Theatre House
Type of Stage: Thrust
Stage Dimensions: 40'x90'
Seating Capacity: 1,089
Year Built: 1965   **Architect:** Eero Saarinen
Contact for Rental: Steve Callahan;   (212) 362-7600

LONGACRE THEATRE
220 West 48th Street, New York, NY 10036
(212) 239-6200
Type of Facility: Theatre House
Type of Stage: Proscenium   **Orchestra Pit**
Seating Capacity: 1,096
Year Built: 1913   **Architect:** Henry B. Herts
Contact for Rental: Philip Smith;   (212) 944-3710
Manager: Shubert Organization

LUCILLE LORTEL THEATRE
121 Christopher Street, New York, NY 10014
(212) 924-2817
Type of Facility: Off Broadway
Type of Stage: Thrust; Proscenium
Stage Dimensions: 28'x30'
Seating Capacity: 299
Year Built: 1950
Contact for Rental: Ben Sprecher;   (212) 924-2817

LUNT-FONTANNE THEATRE
205 West 46th Street, New York, NY 10036
(212) 575-9200
Type of Facility: Theatre House
Type of Stage: Proscenium
Seating Capacity: 1,478
Year Built: 1910   **Architect:** Carrere & Hastings
Contact for Rental:
Manager: The Nederlander Organization

LYCEUM THEATRE
149 West 45th Street, New York, NY 10036
(212) 239-6200
Type of Facility: Theatre House
Type of Stage: Proscenium   **Orchestra Pit**
Seating Capacity: 924
Year Built: 1903   **Architect:** Herts & Tallent
Contact for Rental: Philip Smith;   (212) 944-3710
Manager: Shubert Organization

MADISON SQUARE GARDEN
Pennsylvania Plaza, New York, NY 10001
(212) 456-6000
Type of Facility: Concert Hall; Auditorium; Performance Center; Theatre House; Arena; Multi-Purpose
Type of Stage: Thrust; Flexible; 3/4 Arena; Arena
Seating Capacity: Arena - 20,000; The Paramount - 5,000
Year Built: 1968   **Architect:** Charles Luckman Associates   **Cost:** $50,000,000
Contact for Rental: Booking Department;   (212) 563-8000
Resident Groups: New York Knicks; New York Rangers

MAJESTIC THEATRE
245 West 44th Street, New York, NY 10036
(212) 239-6200
   Type of Facility: Theatre House
   Type of Stage: Proscenium   **Orchestra Pit**
   Seating Capacity: 1,655
   Year Built: 1927   **Architect:** Herbert J. Krapp
   Contact for Rental: Philip Smith;   (212) 944-3710
   Manager: Shubert Organization

MANHATTAN THEATRE CLUB
453 West 16th Street, New York, NY 10011
(212) 645-5590
FAX: (212) 691-9106
   Type of Facility: Multi-Purpose; Room
   Facility Originally: Meeting Hall; Movie House
   Type of Stage: Experimental Space
   Year Remodeled: 1986   **Architect:** Superstructures
   Contact for Rental: Production Office;   (212) 645-5590
   Resident Groups: Manhattan Theatre Club

MARQUIS
211 West 45th Street, New York, NY 10036
(212) 382-0100
   Type of Facility: Theatre House
   Type of Stage: Proscenium
   Seating Capacity: 1,617
   Year Built: 1986
   Contact for Rental: Peter Russell;   (212) 730-8200
   Manager: The Nederlander Organization

MARTIN BECK THEATER
302 West 45th Street, New York, NY 10036
(212) 239-6200
   Type of Facility: Theatre House
   Type of Stage: Proscenium   **Orchestra Pit**
   Seating Capacity: 1,302
   Year Built: 1924   **Architect:** G. Albert Lansburg
   Contact for Rental: Jujamcyn Theaters;   (212) 840-8181

MARYMOUNT MANHATTAN COLLEGE - MARYMOUNT MANHATTAN THEATRE
221 East 71st Street, New York, NY 10021
(212) 517-0475
FAX: (212) 517-0413
   Type of Facility: Off Broadway; Theatre House
   Type of Stage: Proscenium
   Stage Dimensions: 30'x30' unmasked and 12' apron   **Orchestra Pit**
   Seating Capacity: 249
   Year Built: 1975   **Architect:** Evans & Delehanty
   Acoustical Consultant: Steven Wolf
   Contact for Rental: Mary Fleischer, Managing Director;   (212) 517-0475
   Resident Groups: Dramatists Guild; American Chamber Opera; Martha Graham Ensemble

MERCE CUNNINGHAM DANCE STUDIO
55 Bethune Street, New York, NY 10014
(212) 691-9751
FAX: (212) 633-2453
   Type of Facility: Studio Performance
   Stage Dimensions: 52'x45'
   Seating Capacity: 150
   Year Remodeled: 1971   **Architect:** Justin Hanshell   **Cost:** $25,000
   Acoustical Consultant: Nicole Werner
   Contact for Rental: Alice Hepern;   (212) 691-9751
   Resident Groups: Merce Cunningham Dance Company

MERKIN CONCERT HALL AT ELAINE KAUFMAN CONCERT CENTER
129 West 67th Street, New York, NY 10023
(212) 362-8060
FAX: (212) 874-7865
    Type of Facility: Performance Center
    Facility Originally: School
    Type of Stage: Proscenium
    Stage Dimensions: 57'Wx22'D, stage 35'W at back
    Seating Capacity: 457
    Year Built: 1978   **Architect:** Ashok M. Bhavnani
    Acoustical Consultant: Peter George
    Contact for Rental: Linda Gel; (212) 362-8060
    Resident Groups: Mendelssohn String Quartet; Music Today
    Contains the Ann Goodman Recital Hall, which has a seating capacity of 125

MINETTA LANE THEATRE
18 Minetta Lane, New York, NY 10012-1207
(212) 420-8000
    Type of Facility: Off Broadway; Theatre House
    Facility Originally: Factory
    Type of Stage: Platform
    Seating Capacity: 399
    Year Built: 1984   **Cost:** $2,000,000
    Contact for Rental: Alan Schuster, Managing Director; (212) 460-0990

MINSKOFF THEATRE
200 West 45th Street, New York, NY 10036
(212) 869-0550
    Type of Facility: Theatre House
    Type of Stage: Proscenium   **Orchestra Pit**
    Seating Capacity: 1,621
    Year Built: 1972
    Architect: Kahn & Jacobs
    Contact for Rental: Peter Russell; (212) 730-8200
    Manager: The Nederlander Organization

MUSIC BOX
239 West 45th Street, New York, NY 10036
(212) 239-6200
    Type of Facility: Theatre House
    Type of Stage: Proscenium   **Orchestra Pit**
    Seating Capacity: 1,010
    Year Built: 1921   **Architect:** C. Howard Crane
    Contact for Rental: Sherman Gross; (212) 239-6200
    Manager: Shubert Organization

NEDERLANDER THEATRE
208 West 41st Street, New York, NY 10036
(212) 921-8000; (212) 262-2400
    Type of Facility: Theatre House
    Type of Stage: Proscenium   **Orchestra Pit**
    Seating Capacity: 1,206
    Year Built: 1921   **Architect:** William N. Smith
    Contact for Rental: Leo Cohen
    Manager: The Nederlander Organization

NEIL SIMON THEATRE
250 West 52nd Street, New York, NY 10019
(212) 757-8646
    Type of Facility: Theatre House
    Type of Stage: Proscenium
    Orchestra Pit
    Seating Capacity: 1,334
    Year Built: 1927   **Architect:** Herbert J. Krapp   **Cost:** $800,000
    Contact for Rental:
    Manager: The Nederlander Organization

NEW DRAMATISTS
424 West 44th Street, New York, NY 10036
(212) 757-6960
FAX: (212) 265-4738
Founded: 1949
Type of Facility: Studio Performance; Multi-Purpose; Black Box
Facility Originally: Church
Seating Capacity: Theatre 1 - 90; Theatre 2 - 60
Contact for Rental: (212) 757-6960
Resident Groups: New Dramatists

THE OPEN EYE: NEW STAGINGS
270 West 89th Street, New York, NY 10024
(212) 769-4141
Founded: 1972
Type of Facility: Theatre House
Facility Originally: Bowling Alley
Type of Stage: Modified Apron Proscenium
Stage Dimensions: 25'Wx30'D
Seating Capacity: 105
Year Built: 1927
Year Remodeled: 1987 **Architect:** Mitchell Kurtz **Cost:** $350,000
Contact for Rental: Adrienne Brockway; (212) 769-4141
Resident Groups: The Open Eye: New Stagings

ORPHEUM THEATRE
126 Second Avenue, New York, NY 10003
(212) 477-2477
Type of Facility: Off Broadway; Theatre House
Facility Originally: Orpheum Concert Gardens
Type of Stage: Proscenium
Stage Dimensions: 26'Dx24'W
Seating Capacity: 349
Year Built: 1902
Year Remodeled: 1979
Contact for Rental: Alan Schuster; (212) 420-8000

PACE DOWNTOWN THEATER
1 Pace Plaza, New York, NY 10038
(212) 346-1715
FAX: (212) 346-1933
Type of Facility: Theatre Complex; Concert Hall; Performance Center; Theatre House; Multi-Purpose
Type of Stage: Proscenium
Stage Dimensions: 60'x40'
Seating Capacity: 659
Year Built: 1970
Contact for Rental: Jillian Panfel; (212) 346-1398
Resident Groups: Eiko & Koma

PALACE THEATRE
1564 Broadway, New York, NY 10036
(212) 730-8200
Type of Facility: Theatre House
Facility Originally: Vaudeville
Type of Stage: Proscenium **Orchestra Pit**
Seating Capacity: 1,723
Year Built: 1913 **Architect:** Kirchoff & Rose
Year Remodeled: 1966 **Architect:** McNamara **Cost:** $288,000
Contact for Rental: Leo Cohen; (212) 730-8200
Manager: The Nederlander Organization; (212) 242-2400

PERFORMING GARAGE
33 Wooster Street, New York, NY 10013
(212) 966-3651
FAX: (212) 226-6576
Founded: 1972
Type of Facility: Multi-Purpose; Room
Facility Originally: Machine Shop

      Type of Stage: Flexible
      Seating Capacity: 220
      Year Built: 1958
      Year Remodeled: 1962   **Architect:** Jerry N. Rojo   **Cost:** $45,000
      Manager: Andrea Most;   (212) 966-9796
      Resident Groups: The Wooster Group

PLYMOUTH THEATRE
236 West 45th Street, New York, NY 10036
(212) 239-6200
      Type of Facility: Theatre House
      Type of Stage: Proscenium   **Orchestra Pit**
      Seating Capacity: 1,082
      Year Built: 1917
      Architect: Herbert J. Krapp
      Contact for Rental: Philip Smith;   (212) 944-3710
      Manager: Shubert Organization;   (212) 944-3700

PROMENADE THEATRE
2162 Broadway, New York, NY 10023
(212) 924-2817
      Type of Facility: Theatre House
      Type of Stage: Proscenium
      Stage Dimensions: 40'W proscenium opening
      Seating Capacity: 299
      Contact for Rental: Ben Sprecher;   (212) 580-3777

PROVINCETOWN PLAYHOUSE
133 McDougal, New York, NY 10014
(212) 477-5048
      Type of Facility: Theatre House
      Type of Stage: Proscenium
      Seating Capacity: 175
      Contact for Rental: Arthur Cantor, Inc.;   (212) 496-5710

RADIO CITY MUSIC HALL
1260 Avenue of the Americas, New York, NY 10020
(212) 632-4000
      Type of Facility: Theatre Complex; Concert Hall; Auditorium; Studio Performance; Theatre House; Opera House
      Type of Stage: Proscenium
      Stage Dimensions: 144'Wx80'D   **Orchestra Pit**
      Seating Capacity: 6,000
      Year Built: 1932   **Architect:** Raymond Hood   **Cost:** $250,000,000
      Year Remodeled: 1980
      Acoustical Consultant: Donald Deskey
      Contact for Rental: Nancy De Sotto;   (212) 632-4000
      Resident Groups: The Rockettes; Radio City Music Hall Orchestra
      Radio City Music Hall has been designated a National Historic Landmark. The indicated original construction cost shown above constitutes the original construction cost of the Music Hall plus the cost for construction of the remaining buildings in the complex built concurrently. These buildings, along with subsequent additions over the years, are now known as Rockefeller Center.

ROYALE THEATRE
242 West 45th Street, New York, NY 10036
(212) 239-6200
      Type of Facility: Theatre House
      Type of Stage: Proscenium   **Orchestra Pit**
      Seating Capacity: 1,058
      Year Built: 1927   **Architect:** Herbert J. Krapp
      Contact for Rental: Philip Smith;   (212) 944-3710

SAINT CLEMENT'S CHURCH
423 West 46th Street, New York, NY 10036
(212) 246-7277
FAX: (212) 246-7278
      Type of Facility: Concert Hall; Auditorium; Off Broadway; Theatre House; Church Sanctuary
      Facility Originally: Church
      Type of Stage: Thrust; Flexible

Stage Dimensions: 45'x45'
Seating Capacity: 151
Year Built: 1830
Year Remodeled: 1989
Contact for Rental: Douglas Williams;　(212) 246-7277
Resident Groups: Theatre for a New Audience; Pan-Asian Repertory

SAINT JAMES THEATER
246 West 44th Street, New York, NY 10036
(212) 239-6200
Type of Facility: Theatre House
Type of Stage: Proscenium　**Orchestra Pit**
Seating Capacity: 1,644
Year Built: 1927　**Architect:** Warren and Wetmore
Contact for Rental: Jujamcyn Theaters;　(212) 840-8181

SHUBERT THEATRE
225 West 45th Street, New York, NY 10036
(212) 239-6200
Type of Facility: Theatre House
Type of Stage: Proscenium　**Orchestra Pit**
Seating Capacity: 1,483
Year Built: 1913　**Architect:** Henry B. Harris
Contact for Rental: Philip Smith;　(212) 944-3710
Manager: Shubert Organization;　(212) 944-3700

SOHO REP
524 West 57th Street, Building 533/1, New York, NY 10019
(212) 977-5955
Founded: 1974
Type of Facility: Theatre House; Off-Broadway
Type of Stage: Flexible
Stage Dimensions: 22'x28'
Seating Capacity: 75
Year Remodeled: 1991　**Architect:** Martin Holub
Contact for Rental: Julian Webber

STEVE MCGRAW'S
158 West 72nd Street, New York, NY 10023
(212) 595-7400
Founded: 1989
Type of Facility: Cabaret Theatre
Facility Originally: Small Supper Club
Type of Stage: Proscenium; Platform
Stage Dimensions: 19'Wx10'D
Seating Capacity: 135
Year Built: 1980
Year Remodeled: 1988　**Architect:** Al D'Avanzo　**Cost:** $400,000
Contact for Rental: Nancy McGraw;　(212) 595-7400
Resident Groups: Forever Plaid
Available for rental on a limited basis

SULLIVAN STREET PLAYHOUSE
181 Sullivan Street, New York, NY 10012
(212) 674-3838
Type of Facility: Off Broadway; Theatre House
Facility Originally: Nightclub
Type of Stage: 3/4 Arena
Seating Capacity: 155
Year Built: 1895
Year Remodeled: 1922
Contact for Rental: Jules Field;　(212) 674-3838
Resident Groups: The Fantasticks

THE SUPPER CLUB
240 West 47th Street, New York, NY 10036
(212) 921-1940
Type of Facility: Supper Club

Facility Originally: Edison Hotel Ballroom
Type of Stage: Flexible
Stage Dimensions: 44'x56'
Seating Capacity: 450
Year Built: 1960   **Architect:** Gehron & Seltzer
Year Remodeled: 1991   **Architect:** Robert Couturier
Contact for Rental: Lionel Casseroux, Armando Rivera;   (212) 921-1940
Manager: Rick Wahlstedt, General Manager

UNIVERSITY SETTLEMENT
184 Eldridge Street, New York, NY 10002
(212) 674-9120, ext. 183
FAX: (212) 475-3278
Type of Facility: Studio Performance; Multi-Purpose; Room
Type of Stage: Flexible
Stage Dimensions: 1,900 square feet studio space (no obstructions)
Seating Capacity: 120
Contact for Rental: Jeff Lependorf;   (212) 674-9120, ext. 183

VILLAGE GATE
160 Bleecker Street, New York, NY 10012
(212) 475-5120
FAX: (212) 982-3490
Type of Facility: Theatre Complex; Concert Hall; Performance Center; Off Broadway; Theatre House; Multi-Purpose;
Room
Facility Originally: Hotel & Meeting Rooms
Type of Stage: Thrust; Flexible; 3/4 Arena
Seating Capacity: 855
Year Built: 1898
Year Remodeled: 1972   **Architect:** Max Vogel
Manager: Arthur D'Lugoff
Available for rent

VIRGINIA THEATER
245 West 52nd Street, New York, NY 10019
(212) 840-8181
Type of Facility: Theatre House
Type of Stage: Proscenium
Orchestra Pit
Seating Capacity: 1,260
Year Built: 1925   **Architect:** Crane, Franzheim & Bettis
Contact for Rental: Jujamcyn Theaters;   (212) 840-8181

WALTER KERR THEATRE
219 West 48th Street, New York, NY 10036
Type of Facility: Theatre House
Type of Stage: Proscenium   **Orchestra Pit**
Seating Capacity: 954
Year Built: 1921   **Architect:** Herbert J. Krapp
Contact for Rental: Jujamcyn Theaters;   (212) 840-8181

WESTBETH THEATRE CENTER
151 Bank Street, New York, NY 10014
(212) 691-2272
Type of Facility: Theatre Complex; Performance Center; Off Broadway; Theatre House
Facility Originally: Bell Labs Sound Stage
Year Built: 1900
Year Remodeled: 1977   **Architect:** David Chapman   **Cost:** $150,000
Contact for Rental: Arnold Engelman;   (212) 691-2272
*The Theatre Center contains the Big Room, Second Floor Theatre and Studio Theatre. See separate listings for additional
information.*

WESTBETH THEATRE CENTER - BIG ROOM
151 Bank Street, New York, NY 10014
(212) 691-2272
Type of Facility: Theatre House
Type of Stage: Proscenium
Stage Dimensions: 32'x48'

Seating Capacity: 125
Contact for Rental: Arnold Engelman;   (212) 691-2272

WESTBETH THEATRE CENTER - SECOND FLOOR THEATRE
151 Bank Street, New York, NY 10014
(212) 691-2272
 Type of Facility: Theatre House
 Type of Stage: Proscenium
 Stage Dimensions: 22'x30'
 Seating Capacity: 70
 Contact for Rental: Arnold Engelman;   (212) 691-2272

WESTBETH THEATRE CENTER - STUDIO THEATRE
151 Bank Street, New York, NY 10014
(212) 691-2272
 Type of Facility: Theatre House
 Type of Stage: Proscenium
 Stage Dimensions: 25'x30'
 Seating Capacity: 90
 Contact for Rental: Arnold Engelman;   (212) 691-2272

WESTSIDE ARTS THEATRE
407 West 43rd Street, New York, NY 10036
(212) 315-2302; (212) 315-2244
FAX: (212) 315-2307
 Founded: 1991
 Type of Facility: Theatre Complex; Performance Center; Off-Broadway; Two-Stage Theatre Complex
 Facility Originally: Church
 Type of Stage: Thrust; Proscenium
 Stage Dimensions: Stage 1 (modified thrust) - 40'x18'; Stage 2 - 40'x26'6"
 Seating Capacity: 299; 250
 Year Built: 1889   **Architect:** Henry F. Kilburn   **Cost:** $25,000
 Year Remodeled: 1991   **Architect:** Roger Morgan Studios, Designer   **Cost:** $1,200,000
 Acoustical Consultant: Masque Sound; Jaffe Acoustics
 Contact for Rental: Terry Byrne;   (212) 315-2302
 Manager: Peter Askin, Director;   (212) 315-2302
 Built originally as the Second Baptist Church, the building, remodeled as a theatre in 1973, became the Westside Theatre in 1991 after extensive restoration.

WINTER GARDEN THEATRE
1634 Broadway, New York, NY 10019
(212) 239-6200
 Type of Facility: Theatre House
 Type of Stage: Proscenium   **Orchestra Pit**
 Seating Capacity: 1,503
 Year Built: 1911
 Architect: William A. Swasey
 Contact for Rental: Philip Smith;   (212) 944-3710
 Manager: Shubert Organization

North Greece

PERFORMING SERIES

GREECE PERFORMING ARTS SOCIETY
PO Box 300, North Greece, NY 14515
(716) 227-5953
 Founded: 1972
 Arts Area: Vocal Music; Instrumental Music; Theater
 Status: Non-Profit
 Type: Sponsoring
 Purpose: To foster the development, in the community of Greece, of an appreciation for artistic and cultural activities, GPAS sponsors the Greece Symphony Orchestra, Greece Community Orchestra and Greece Choral Society & GPAS Summer Theatre
 Management: William Coons, Program Coordinator
 Officers: Joanne Dennstedt, President; William Coons, Treasurer; Carol Coons, Secretary
 Paid Staff: 2   **Volunteer Staff:** 25
 Paid Artists: 7

Utilizes: Guest Artists
Budget: $1,000 - $50,000
Income Sources: Business/Corporate Donations; Box Office; Government Grants; Individual Donations

---

North Tonawanda

PERFORMING SERIES

HERSHELL CARROUSEL FACTORY MUSEUM
180 Thompson Street, PO Box 672, North Tonawanda, NY 14120
(716) 693-1885
Founded: 1983
Arts Area: Dance; Vocal Music; Instrumental Music; Theater; Festivals
Status: Professional; Semi-Professional; Non-Profit
Type: Sponsoring; Museum
Purpose: Family-oriented entertainment in a carousel museum setting
Management: Elizabeth Brick, Director; Trent Turlock, Education Coordinator
Officers: Raphaelle A. Proefrock, President; Douglas A. Bathke, Vice President; Albert Baked, Secretary; Philip Lockman, Treasurer
Paid Staff: 4   **Volunteer Staff:** 70
Paid Artists: 12   **Non-Paid Artists:** 10
Budget: $1,000 - $50,000
Income Sources: Private Foundations/Grants/Endowments; Box Office
Season: June - September   **Annual Attendance:** 2,000
Affiliations: New York State Council of Arts

Northport

DANCE

POSEY DANCE EDUCATION SERVICE
PO Box 254, Northport, NY 11768
(516) 757-2700; (212) 966-8658
Founded: 1953
Arts Area: Modern; Ballet; Jazz
Status: Professional; Non-Profit
Type: Performing; Touring; Educational
Purpose: Education
Management: Elsa Posey, Artistic Director; Donna Brady, Managing Director
Paid Artists: 12
Utilizes: Guest Artists; Guest Choreographers
Budget: $50,000 - $100,000
Income Sources: Private Foundations/Grants/Endowments; Business/Corporate Donations; Box Office; Government Grants; Individual Donations
Season: September - June   **Annual Attendance:** 1,400
Affiliations: American Dance Guild

FACILITY

POSEY SCHOOL OF DANCE
57 Main Street, PO Box 254, Northport, NY 11768
(516) 757-2700
Founded: 1953
Type of Facility: Studio Performance
Facility Originally: Meeting Hall; Ballroom
Type of Stage: 3/4 Arena
Stage Dimensions: 20'x25'
Seating Capacity: 125
Year Built: 1891
Year Remodeled: 1992   **Architect:** Bob Ruege   **Cost:** $4,000
Contact for Rental: Elsa Posey, Director;   (516) 757-2700
Resident Groups: Posey Dance Company; Posey School of Dance

Nyack

DANCE

DEBRA WEISS DANCE COMPANY
51 Summit Street, Nyack, NY 10960
(914) 353-3860
Founded: 1983
Arts Area: Modern; Ethnic; Historical Dance Drama
Status: Professional; Non-Profit
Type: Performing; Touring; Resident; Educational
Management: Debra Weiss, Artistic Director/President
Officers: Eric Bender, Treasurer
Paid Staff: 1 **Volunteer Staff:** 4
Paid Artists: 4
Utilizes: Guest Artists
Budget: $1,000 - $50,000
Income Sources: Private Foundations/Grants/Endowments; Business/Corporate Donations; Box Office; Government Grants; Individual Donations
Season: 52 Weeks **Annual Attendance:** 8,000

THEATRE

ELMWOOD PLAYHOUSE
16 Park Street, Nyack, NY 10960
(914) 353-1313
Founded: 1946
Arts Area: Community
Status: Non-Professional; Non-Profit
Type: Performing; Educational
Officers: Maggie Klappas, President; Candy Pittari, Vice President
Budget: $50,000 - $100,000
Income Sources: Box Office; Individual Donations
Season: September - June **Annual Attendance:** 8,000
Affiliations: Art Council of Rockland County
Performance Facilities: Elmwood Playhouse

Ogdensburg

THEATRE

OGDENSBURG COMMAND PERFORMANCES
PO Box 322, Ogdensburg, NY 13669
(315) 393-2323
Founded: 1962
Arts Area: Professional; Musical
Status: Non-Profit
Type: Sponsoring
Purpose: To present drama, music, and other theatrical productions for the stimulation, inspiration, and enjoyment of the citizens of Ogdensburg and the surrounding North Country Area
Officers: Sally Palao, President; Mary Jane Wilson, Executive Vice President; Cynthia Wilson, Administrative Vice President; Terry Rhinehold, Recording Secretary; Nancy Siegel, Corresponding Secretary; Betty Simms, Treasurer
Volunteer Staff: 60
Utilizes: Guest Artists
Budget: $50,000 - $100,000
Income Sources: Private Foundations/Grants/Endowments; Business/Corporate Donations; Box Office; Government Grants; Individual Donations
Season: October - May **Annual Attendance:** 4,000
Performance Facilities: George Hall Auditorium, Ogdensburg Free Academy

---

Old Forge

FACILITY

ARTS CENTER/OLD FORGE
Route 28, Old Forge, NY 13420
Founded: 1952

Type of Facility: Multi-Purpose
Facility Originally: Warehouse
Type of Stage: No stage-concrete floor
Seating Capacity: 250
Year Remodeled: 1974

Oneonta

INSTRUMENTAL MUSIC

CATSKILL SYMPHONY ORCHESTRA
PO Box 14, Oneonta, NY 13820
(607) 432-6670
Founded: 1972
Arts Area: Symphony; Orchestra
Status: Professional; Non-Profit
Type: Performing; Educational
Purpose: To bring quality music to the immediate and outlying areas of central New York State
Management: Deborah Wolfanger, General Manager; Charles England, Personnel Manager
Officers: Ciara Markuson, President; Rita Brown, Vice President; Allan Cleinman, Treasurer; Mary Ann Mazarak, Secretary
Paid Staff: 4
Paid Artists: 75 **Non-Paid Artists:** 7
Utilizes: Guest Artists
Budget: $100,000 - $500,000
Income Sources: Private Foundations/Grants/Endowments; Business/Corporate Donations; Box Office; Government Grants; Individual Donations
Season: September - April **Annual Attendance:** 2,000
Performance Facilities: Hunt Union, State University of New York-Oneonta

PERFORMING SERIES

FESTIVAL OF THE ARTS
248 Main Street, Upper Catskill Community Council of the Arts, Oneonta, NY 13820
(607) 432-2070
Founded: 1969
Arts Area: Dance; Vocal Music; Instrumental Music; Theater; Festivals
Status: Professional; Non-Profit
Type: Educational; Sponsoring
Management: Pamela Cooley, Director
Paid Staff: 5 **Volunteer Staff:** 125
Paid Artists: 300
Utilizes: Guest Conductors; Guest Artists
Budget: $50,000 - $100,000
Income Sources: Private Foundations/Grants/Endowments; Business/Corporate Donations; Box Office; Government Grants; Individual Donations
Season: September - July **Annual Attendance:** 10,000
Affiliations: State University of New York-Oneonta
Performance Facilities: Slade Auditorium; Anderson Theater

UPPER CATSKILL COMMUNITY COUNCIL OF THE ARTS
248 Main Street, Oneonta, NY 13820
(607) 432-2070
Founded: 1970
Arts Area: Dance; Vocal Music; Theater
Status: Professional; Non-Professional; Non-Profit
Type: Educational; Sponsoring
Purpose: As a community service arts agency, we sponsor community performances and coordinate elementary and secondary school performances
Management: Pamela Cooley, Executive Director; Elissa Kane, Associate Director
Officers: Katherine Dailey, President; Margaret Hathaway, Vice President
Paid Staff: 4 **Volunteer Staff:** 75
Utilizes: Guest Artists
Budget: $100,000 - $500,000
Income Sources: Private Foundations/Grants/Endowments; Business/Corporate Donations; Box Office; Government Grants; Individual Donations
Season: 52 Weeks

Ossining

DANCE

WESTCHESTER BALLET COMPANY
2 Dale Avenue, Ossining, NY 10562
(914) 941-4532
Founded: 1954
Arts Area: Ballet
Status: Professional; Semi-Professional; Non-Professional; Non-Profit
Type: Performing; Educational
Purpose: To provide high-quality ballet training; to be an integral part of the community
Management: Jean Logrea, Artistic Director
Officers: Beth Fritz Logrea, President; Dennis Cole, Vice President; Jane Truebig, Secretary; Jaime Rich, Treasurer
Volunteer Staff: 20
Paid Artists: 8 **Non-Paid Artists:** 70
Utilizes: Special Technical Talent; Guest Artists
Budget: $1,000 - $50,000
Income Sources: Private Foundations/Grants/Endowments; Business/Corporate Donations; Box Office; Individual Donations
Season: September - May **Annual Attendance:** 2,000
Performance Facilities: Marymount College, Tarrytown

Oyster Bay

DANCE

OYSTER BAY CONTEMPORARY BALLET
PO Box 374, Oyster Bay, NY 11771
(516) 549-0025
Founded: 1981
Arts Area: Ballet; Jazz
Status: Professional; Non-Profit
Type: Performing
Purpose: Contemporary Ballet Company was formed by a group of dedicated dance professionals motivated by the strong belief in dance as a creative performing art. Its primary goal is to communicate this interest in dance and to widen appreciation among the audiences of Long Island.
Management: Regina Collins, Artistic Director; Diane Bellas, General Manager
Officers: Regina Collins, President; Diane Bellas, Secretary
Paid Artists: 9
Budget: $1,000 - $50,000
Income Sources: Box Office; Government Grants; Individual Donations
Season: May - August **Annual Attendance:** 3,000

Pawling

DANCE

JOSE MOLINA BAILES ESPANOLES
Arthur Shafman International Limited, PO Box 352, Pawling, NY 12564
(914) 855-3005
FAX: (914) 855-3167
Founded: 1962
Arts Area: Ethnic
Status: Professional; Commercial
Type: Performing; Touring
Purpose: To present American audiences with the best of all styles of Spanish dance
Management: Arthur Shafman, International Limited; Jose Molina, Artistic Director
Paid Staff: 1
Paid Artists: 8
Utilizes: Guest Artists
Budget: $100,000 - $500,000
Income Sources: Box Office
Season: September - June

THEATRE FANTASTIQUE
c/o Arthur Shafman International Ltd., PO Box 352, Pawling, NY 12564
(914) 855-3005
FAX: (914) 855-3167
Founded: 1984
Arts Area: Mime
Status: Professional; Commercial
Type: Performing; Touring; Resident; Educational; Sponsoring
Management: Richard Zachary, Director
Officers: Arthur Shafman, President
Paid Staff: 4
Paid Artists: 5
Utilizes: Special Technical Talent
Budget: $100,000 - $500,000
Income Sources: Box Office; Performance Fees
Season: September - April   **Annual Attendance:** 125,000

THEATRE

IMAGO, THE THEATRE MASK ENSEMBLE
PO Box 352, Pawling, NY 12564
(914) 855-3005
FAX: (914) 855-3167
Founded: 1981
Arts Area: Professional; Summer Stock; Community; Theatrical Group
Status: Professional
Type: Performing; Touring; Resident; Educational
Purpose: To present their special art form to audiences
Management: Carol Uselman, Jerry Mouwad, Artistic Directors
Officers: Arthur Shafman, President
Utilizes: Special Technical Talent
Budget: $100,000 - $500,000
Income Sources: Private Foundations/Grants/Endowments; Business/Corporate Donations; Box Office; Government Grants; Individual Donations; Earned Fees
Annual Attendance: 200,000
Affiliations: Westaff Touring Program; North Carolina Touring Program; Arts Midwest; Performing Arts Touring Program of Oregon

PERFORMING SERIES

PAWLING CONCERT SERIES
300 Route 22, Pawling, NY 12564
(914) 855-3100
Founded: 1973
Arts Area: Vocal Music; Instrumental Music
Status: Non-Profit
Type: Sponsoring; Presenting
Purpose: To bring excellent quality live classical, folk and jazz music to the area
Budget: $1,000 - $50,000
Income Sources: Private Foundations/Grants/Endowments; Individual Donations
Season: October - May   **Annual Attendance:** 1,200

Pearl River

DANCE

PAT CANNON FOOT AND FIDDLE DANCE COMPANY
164 Prospect Place, Pearl River, NY 10965
(914) 735-8951
FAX: (914) 735-1431
Founded: 1981
Arts Area: Tap; Clogging
Status: Professional; Non-Profit
Type: Performing; Touring; Resident; Educational
Purpose: To present a blend of clogging, square dance and tap dance; to perform folk material with tap technique
Officers: Pat Cannon, Artistic Director
Volunteer Staff: 2

Non-Paid Artists: 12
Budget: $100,000 - $500,000
Income Sources: Private Foundations/Grants/Endowments; Contracted Services
Season: 52 Weeks

Peekskill

FACILITY

PARAMOUNT CENTER FOR THE ARTS
1008 Brown Street, Peekskill, NY 10990
(914) 739-2333
Founded: 1980
Type of Facility: Performance Center
Facility Originally: Movie House
Type of Stage: Proscenium
Stage Dimensions: 40'Wx36'D
Seating Capacity: 1,025
Year Built: 1930   **Architect:** Rapp & Rapp
Year Remodeled: 1986   **Architect:** Battaglia & Seckler   **Cost:** $100,000
Contact for Rental: Mark Hough;   (914) 739-2333
Resident Groups: Orpheus Chamber Orchestra; Taghkanic Chorale; Philharmonia Virtuosi

Penn Yan

PERFORMING SERIES

YATES PERFORMING ARTS SERIES
PO Box 503, Penn Yan, NY 14527
(315) 536-2095
Founded: 1972
Arts Area: Dance; Vocal Music; Instrumental Music; Festivals; Lyric Opera
Status: Professional; Non-Professional; Non-Profit
Type: Performing; Touring
Purpose: To supply entertainment to the residents of Yates County
Officers: Sylvia Eisenhart, President; Emily Seager, Vice President; Linda Dofy, Secretary; Engelke Heggis, Treasurer
Volunteer Staff: 25
Paid Artists: 5
Budget: $1,000 - $50,000
Income Sources: Business/Corporate Donations; Box Office; Government Grants; Individual Donations; Season Tickets
Season: September - May   **Annual Attendance:** 2,000
Performance Facilities: Penn Yan Academy

Plainview

PERFORMING SERIES

UNITED JEWISH YS OF LONG ISLAND
55 Manetto Hill Road, Plainview, NY 11803
(516) 938-4600
FAX: (516) 938-3006
Founded: 1973
Arts Area: Dance; Vocal Music; Instrumental Music; Theater; Festivals; Lyric Opera
Status: Professional; Non-Profit
Type: Performing; Sponsoring
Purpose: International Jewish Arts Festival of Long Island and the Grand Performance Series provide unique cultural experiences unattainable elsewhere on Long Island
Management: Rea Jacobs, Director, Cultural Arts
Officers: Arthur M. Katz, President; Sidney N. Soloman, Chairman of the Board; Alfred W. Levy, Chairman of the Executive Board; Kenneth J. Gabel, Executive Vice President; Martin Eglow, Vice President
Paid Staff: 12   **Volunteer Staff:** 500
Paid Artists: 105
Utilizes: Special Technical Talent; Guest Conductors; Guest Artists
Budget: $500,000 - $1,000,000
Income Sources: Private Foundations/Grants/Endowments; Business/Corporate Donations; Box Office; Government Grants; Individual Donations; Rentals

Season: September - April   **Annual Attendance:** 45,000
Affiliations: ISPAA; APAP

Port Jefferson

THEATRE

THEATRE THREE PRODUCTIONS
412 Main Street, PO Box 512, Port Jefferson, NY 11777
(516) 928-9202
    Founded: 1969
    Arts Area: Professional; Musical; Theatrical Group
    Status: Professional; Non-Profit
    Type: Performing; Touring; Resident; Educational
    Purpose: To produce the finest in professional theatre on central Long Island and Suffolk County in Port Jefferson
    Management: Bradlee Bing, Executive Artistic Director; Jeffrey Sanzel, Associate Artistic Director
    Paid Staff: 9   **Volunteer Staff:** 4
    Paid Artists: 100
    Utilizes: Special Technical Talent; Guest Artists; Guest Directors
    Budget: $500,000 - $1,000,000
    Income Sources: Private Foundations/Grants/Endowments; Business/Corporate Donations; Box Office; Government Grants; Individual Donations
    Season: July - June   **Annual Attendance:** 70,000
    Affiliations: Port Jefferson Arts Council

FACILITY

THEATRE THREE PRODUCTIONS - MAINSTAGE
412 Main Street, PO Box 512, Port Jefferson, NY 11777
(516) 928-9202
    Type of Facility: Theatre House
    Facility Originally: Vaudeville
    Type of Stage: Thrust
    Seating Capacity: 473
    Year Built: 1875
    Contact for Rental: Sharon Greenstone;   (516) 928-9202
    A $3,000,000 renovation beginning in 1992.

THEATRE THREE PRODUCTIONS - SECOND STAGE
412 Main Street, PO Box 512, Port Jefferson, NY 11777
(516) 928-9202
    Type of Facility: Theatre House
    Type of Stage: 3/4 Arena
    Seating Capacity: 154
    Year Remodeled: 1987   **Cost:** $100,000
    Contact for Rental: Sharon Greenstone;   (516) 928-9202
    A $3,000,000 renovation beginning in 1992

Poughkeepsie

DANCE

POUGHKEEPSIE CIVIC BALLET
6 Raymond Avenue, Poughkeepsie, NY 12603
(914) 452-3055
    Founded: 1968
    Arts Area: Ballet; Jazz
    Status: Non-Profit
    Type: Resident
    Management: Roya Curie, Artistic Director
    Paid Artists: 10
    Income Sources: Box Office; Individual Donations
    Season: 52 Weeks
    Performance Facilities: Marist College Theater

INSTRUMENTAL MUSIC

HUDSON VALLEY PHILHARMONIC
129 North Water Street, PO Box 191, Poughkeepsie, NY 12602
(914) 454-1222
 Founded: 1959
 Arts Area: Symphony; Orchestra; Chamber
 Status: Professional
 Type: Performing; Resident; Sponsoring
 Purpose: To sponsor and support a professional symphony orchestra which will present performances of the highest artistic quality and promote the musical growth of the region
 Management: Randall Fleischer, Musical Director; Babette Schmidt, General Manager
 Officers: Hamilton Meserve, President; Henry Peters, Vice President; Andrea Simon, Treasurer; Ziva Dahl, Secretary
 Paid Staff: 8 **Volunteer Staff:** 2
 Paid Artists: 80
 Utilizes: Guest Artists
 Budget: $500,000 - $1,000,000
 Income Sources: Private Foundations/Grants/Endowments; Business/Corporate Donations; Box Office; Government Grants; Individual Donations
 Season: September - May **Annual Attendance:** 200,000
 Affiliations: ASOL; ASCAP; BMI
 Performance Facilities: Ulster Performing Arts Center; Bardavon 1869 Opera House; Paramount Theatre, Vassar College

THEATRE

NEW DAY REPERTORY COMPANY, INC.
12 Vassar Street, PO Box 269, Poughkeepsie, NY 12601
(914) 485-7399
 Founded: 1963
 Arts Area: Professional; Community
 Status: Professional; Non-Profit
 Type: Performing; Touring; Resident; Educational
 Purpose: To promote the arts and culture through theatre; to enhance the quality of life and leisure for all within our sphere, regardless of race or creed
 Management: Rodney K. Douglas, Producer/Artistic Director
 Officers: Noel Tepper, Chairman; Janet Nicodemus, Treasurer; Rodney K. Douglas, President; Olive Douglas, Vice President
 Paid Staff: 3 **Volunteer Staff:** 3
 Utilizes: Guest Artists; Guest Directors
 Budget: $100,000 - $500,000
 Income Sources: Private Foundations/Grants/Endowments; Business/Corporate Donations; Box Office; Government Grants; Individual Donations; Fund-raising
 Season: 52 Weeks **Annual Attendance:** 15,000
 Performance Facilities: Vassar Institute Theatre

FACILITY

BARDAVON 1869 OPERA HOUSE
35 Market Street, Poughkeepsie, NY 12601
(914) 473-5288
FAX: (914) 473-4259
 Founded: 1976
 Type of Facility: Concert Hall; Auditorium; Performance Center; Theatre House; Opera House
 Type of Stage: Proscenium
 Stage Dimensions: 34'Wx24'D and thrust **Orchestra Pit**
 Seating Capacity: 944
 Year Built: 1869 **Architect:** James S. Post **Cost:** $50,000
 Year Remodeled: 1976 **Cost:** $1,600,000
 Contact for Rental: Lucia S. Edgcomb, Managing Director, Theatre Operations; (914) 473-5288
 Manager: Barbara Hauptman, Executive Director; (914) 473-5288
 Resident Groups: Hudson Valley Philharmonic
 Box Office (914) 473-2072

MID-HUDSON CIVIC CENTER
14 Civic Center Plaza, Poughkeepsie, NY 12601
(914) 454-9800
FAX: (914) 454-5877
 Type of Facility: Concert Hall; Auditorium; Civic Center; Multi-Purpose

Type of Stage: Proscenium
Stage Dimensions: 70'x32'
Seating Capacity: 3,050
Year Built: 1976
Contact for Rental: Cathy Vodrazka;   (914) 454-9800

Purchase

FACILITY

STATE UNIVERSITY OF NEW YORK-PURCHASE - PERFORMING ARTS CENTER
735 Anderson Hill Road, Purchase, NY 10577
(914) 251-6222
  Type of Facility: Performance Center
  Year Built: 1978   **Architect:** Edward Larabee Barnes   **Cost:** $35,000,000
  Acoustical Consultant: Bolt, Beranek & Newman
  Contact for Rental: Steve Grober;   (914) 253-5949
  Resident Groups: State University of New York-Purchase Music, Theater and Dance Departments
  The Performing Arts Center contains Theaters A, B, C and D. See separate listings for additional information.

STATE UNIVERSITY OF NEW YORK-PURCHASE - THEATER A
735 Anderson Hill Road, Purchase, NY 10577
(914) 251-6222
  Type of Facility: Concert Hall; Theatre House
  Type of Stage: Thrust; Flexible; Proscenium; Hydraulic Lift Stage
  Stage Dimensions: 9"Dx76'3"H; 53'10"H proscenium opening
  Orchestra Pit
  Seating Capacity: 1,372
  Year Built: 1978
  Contact for Rental: Steve Grober;   (914) 253-5949

STATE UNIVERSITY OF NEW YORK-PURCHASE - THEATRE B
735 Anderson Hill Road, Purchase, NY 10577
(914) 251-6222
  Type of Facility: Concert Hall; Theatre House
  Type of Stage: Proscenium; Hydraulic Lift Stage
  Stage Dimensions: 95'7"Wx43'10"Dx68'H; 54'9"Wx28'H proscenium opening
  Orchestra Pit
  Seating Capacity: 673
  Year Built: 1978
  Contact for Rental: Steve Grober;   (914) 253-5949

STATE UNIVERSITY OF NEW YORK-PURCHASE - THEATRE C
735 Anderson Hill Road, Purchase, NY 10577
(914) 251-6222
  Type of Facility: Concert Hall; Theatre House
  Type of Stage: Proscenium
  Stage Dimensions: 3'11"Dx67'6"H; 44'8"Wx30'H proscenium opening
  Seating Capacity: 476
  Year Built: 1978
  Contact for Rental: Steve Grober;   (914) 253-5949

STATE UNIVERSITY OF NEW YORK-PURCHASE - THEATRE D
735 Anderson Hill Road, Purchase, NY 10577
(914) 251-6222
  Type of Facility: Theatre House
  Type of Stage: Flexible
  Stage Dimensions: 82'8"Dx34'H
  Seating Capacity: 500
  Year Built: 1978
  Contact for Rental: Steve Grober;   (914) 253-5949

Rego Park

INSTRUMENTAL MUSIC

QUEENS SYMPHONY ORCHESTRA
99-11 Queens Boulevard, Rego Park, NY 11374
(718) 275-5000
FAX: (718) 261-5224
Founded: 1953
Arts Area: Symphony
Status: Professional; Non-Profit
Type: Performing
Management: Ellen Young, Executive Director; John Harmon, Box Office Manager
Paid Staff: 7   **Volunteer Staff:** 7
Paid Artists: 78
Utilizes: Guest Conductors; Guest Artists; Guest Directors
Budget: $500,000 - $1,000,000
Income Sources: Private Foundations/Grants/Endowments; Business/Corporate Donations; Box Office; Government Grants; Individual Donations
Season: October - August   **Annual Attendance:** 125,000
Affiliations: ASOL
Performance Facilities: Colden Center for the Arts, Queens College

Rochester

DANCE

GARTH FAGAN DANCE
50 Chestnut Street, Rochester, NY 14604
(716) 454-3260
FAX: (716) 454-6191
Founded: 1970
Arts Area: Modern; Ethnic
Status: Professional; Non-Profit
Type: Performing; Touring; Resident; Educational
Purpose: A modern dance company that is highly competitive on a national level. The original choreography by Garth Fagan offers a blend of modern dance and Black culture.
Management: Garth Fagan, Founder/Artistic Director; Cynthia C. Wassell, General Manager
Officers: Garth Fagan, President; Nancy D. Peck Esq., Chair of the Board; Deborah Runner Esq., Vice Chair of the Board; Jesse Dudley, Joseph Bonvissoto, Vice Chairs; Patricia D. Baker, Treasurer; Philip Silver, Secretary
Paid Staff: 6
Paid Artists: 17
Budget: $1,000,000 - $5,000,000
Income Sources: Private Foundations/Grants/Endowments; Business/Corporate Donations; Box Office; Government Grants; Individual Donations
Annual Attendance: 5,000
Performance Facilities: Nazareth Arts Center

INSTRUMENTAL MUSIC

GREECE SYMPHONY ORCHESTRA
950 East Avenue, Rochester, NY 14607
(716) 473-6711
Founded: 1968
Arts Area: Orchestra
Status: Semi-Professional; Non-Profit
Type: Performing; Sponsoring
Purpose: To enhance the cultural life of Greece and the surrounding area through free concerts and other performances; to sponsor young artists competition through local schools
Management: David Fetler, Director
Non-Paid Artists: 65
Utilizes: Guest Artists
Budget: $1,000 - $50,000
Income Sources: Government Grants; Individual Donations
Season: October - May   **Annual Attendance:** 1,000
Affiliations: Greece (NY) Performing Arts Society

ROCHESTER CHAMBER ORCHESTRA
950 East Avenue, Rochester, NY 14607
(716) 473-6711
> **Founded:** 1964
> **Arts Area:** Orchestra
> **Status:** Professional; Non-Profit
> **Type:** Performing; Sponsoring
> **Purpose:** To offer the Rochester community an outstanding music repertoire from the 17th century to the present for chamber orchestra; to present newly commissioned works
> **Management:** David Fetler, Director
> **Officers:** Betty Allman, President
> **Volunteer Staff:** 16
> **Paid Artists:** 40
> **Utilizes:** Guest Artists
> **Budget:** $1,000 - $50,000
> **Income Sources:** Business/Corporate Donations; Box Office; Government Grants; Individual Donations
> **Season:** October - May   **Annual Attendance:** 44,000
> **Performance Facilities:** Asbury First Methodist Church

ROCHESTER PHILHARMONIC ORCHESTRA
108 East Avenue, Rochester, NY 14604
(716) 454-2620
> **Founded:** 1922
> **Arts Area:** Symphony
> **Status:** Professional; Non-Profit
> **Type:** Performing; Sponsoring
> **Purpose:** Presentation of Rochester Philharmonic Orchestra and other events for the area community
> **Officers:** Carl J. Atkins, President/Chief Executive Officer
> **Paid Staff:** 30   **Volunteer Staff:** 1,000
> **Utilizes:** Guest Conductors; Guest Artists
> **Budget:** $5,000,000 - $10,000,000
> **Income Sources:** Private Foundations/Grants/Endowments; Business/Corporate Donations; Box Office; Government Grants; Individual Donations
> **Season:** 52 Weeks   **Annual Attendance:** 250,000
> **Performance Facilities:** Eastman Theatre; Finger Lakes Performing Arts Center

THEATRE

GEVA THEATRE
75 Woodbury Boulevard, Rochester, NY 14607
(716) 232-1366
FAX: (716) 232-4031
> **Founded:** 1973
> **Arts Area:** Professional; Musical; Theatrical Group
> **Status:** Professional; Non-Profit
> **Type:** Performing; Resident; Educational
> **Management:** Howard Millman, Producing Director; Anthony Zerbe, Artistic Director; Ann Patrice Carrigan, Literary Director; Timothy Shields, Managing Director
> **Officers:** Linda Cornell Weinstein, Chairman
> **Paid Staff:** 50
> **Paid Artists:** 70
> **Utilizes:** Special Technical Talent; Guest Artists; Guest Directors
> **Budget:** $1,000,000 - $5,000,000
> **Income Sources:** Private Foundations/Grants/Endowments; Business/Corporate Donations; Box Office; Government Grants; Individual Donations
> **Season:** September - July   **Annual Attendance:** 120,000
> **Affiliations:** TCG; AAA; LORT
> **Performance Facilities:** Richard Pine Theatre; Elaine Wilson Theatre

THEATRE ON THE RIDGE
200 Ridge Road West, Building 28, Rochester, NY 14652-3211
(716) 477-7519
FAX: (716) 477-8041
> **Arts Area:** Professional; Musical; Dinner; Community
> **Status:** Professional; Commercial
> **Type:** Performing; Resident; Sponsoring
> **Purpose:** To provide entertainment to Eastman Kodak Company and the local community
> **Management:** David R. Dunn, Manager

Paid Staff: 7   **Volunteer Staff:** 1,000
Utilizes: Guest Artists
Income Sources: Business/Corporate Donations; Box Office
Season: 52 Weeks

PERFORMING SERIES

KODACTORS
200 Ridge Road West, Rochester, NY 14652-3211
(716) 722-2402
FAX: (716) 477-8041
Founded: 1956
Arts Area: Dance; Vocal Music; Instrumental Music; Theater
Status: Non-Professional
Type: Performing
Purpose: To provide cultural outlet for members of Eastman Kodak Company, their families and friends
Management: Philip E. Roy, Artistic Director; Mary Agnes Alrutz-Roy, Musical Director; Kimm Leuhm Wesley, Dance Director
Volunteer Staff: 5
Non-Paid Artists: 25
Utilizes: Special Technical Talent
Budget: $1,000 - $50,000
Income Sources: Business/Corporate Donations; Box Office
Season: September - June   **Annual Attendance:** 10,000
Performance Facilities: Eastman Kodak Recreation Center Auditorium

NAZARETH COLLEGE ARTS CENTER
Nazareth College, 4245 East Avenue, Rochester, NY 14618-3790
(716) 586-2483
FAX: (716) 586-1284
Founded: 1967
Arts Area: Dance; Vocal Music; Instrumental Music; Theater
Status: Professional; Non-Profit
Type: Performing; Sponsoring
Purpose: To present a subscription series of professional performing artists and organizations for the benefit of Nazareth students and the community of Rochester
Management: Joseph F. Baranowski, Director of Programs; Dr. David M. Ferrell, Director
Officers: Fred E. Strauss, Chairman of the Board; Dr. Rose Marie Beston, President of the College
Paid Staff: 7   **Volunteer Staff:** 50
Utilizes: Guest Artists
Budget: $100,000 - $500,000
Income Sources: Box Office; Government Grants
Season: September - May   **Annual Attendance:** 15,000
Affiliations: APAP
Performance Facilities: Nazareth College Arts Center

THE QUARTET PROGRAM
1163 East Avenue, Rochester, NY 14607
(716) 274-1592
Founded: 1970
Arts Area: Instrumental Music
Status: Professional; Non-Profit
Type: Performing; Resident; Educational; Sponsoring
Officers: Charles Castleman, Artistic Director; Joseph Cunningham, Board Chairman
Paid Staff: 2
Non-Paid Artists: 42
Utilizes: Guest Artists
Budget: $100,000 - $500,000
Income Sources: Private Foundations/Grants/Endowments; Business/Corporate Donations; Box Office; Government Grants; Individual Donations
Season: June - August   **Annual Attendance:** 1,500
Performance Facilities: Fireman Performance Arts Center

UNIVERSITY OF ROCHESTER THEATRE PROGRAM
107 Todd Union, Rochester, NY 14627
(716) 275-4088
Founded: 1968
Arts Area: Theater

Status: Semi-Professional; Non-Profit
Type: Performing; Resident; Educational
Purpose: To provide a classical, contemporary and modern series of plays combined with a professional training program taught by the members of our company
Management: Maxim Kunin, Production Manager; Mervyn Willis, Artistic Director
Paid Staff: 4   **Volunteer Staff:** 160
Paid Artists: 16   **Non-Paid Artists:** 4
Utilizes: Special Technical Talent; Guest Artists; Guest Directors
Budget: $100,000 - $500,000
Income Sources: Box Office; Government Grants; Individual Donations
Season: September - May   **Annual Attendance:** 5,500
Performance Facilities: Black Box Theatre

FACILITY

AUDITORIUM CENTER
875 East Main Street, Rochester, NY 14605-2789
(716) 271-3250
FAX: (716) 423-9539
Founded: 1989
Type of Facility: Theatre Complex; Concert Hall; Auditorium; Performance Center; Off Broadway; Theatre House; Opera House
Type of Stage: Proscenium
Stage Dimensions: 96'Wx42'D   **Orchestra Pit**
Seating Capacity: 2,541
Year Built: 1929
Contact for Rental: Daniel Black;   (716) 271-3250

EASTMAN SCHOOL OF MUSIC - KILBOURN HALL
26 Gibbs Street, Rochester, NY 14604
(716) 274-1110
Type of Facility: Concert Hall
Type of Stage: Proscenium   **Orchestra Pit**
Seating Capacity: 459
Year Built: 1921
Year Remodeled: 1976
Manager: Andrew E. Green
Resident Groups: Eastman School of Music

NAZARETH COLLEGE - NAZARETH ARTS CENTER
4245 East Avenue, Rochester, NY 14618
(716) 586-2483
Type of Facility: Theatre Complex; Concert Hall; Auditorium; Performance Center
Type of Stage: Thrust
Seating Capacity: 1,153
Year Built: 1967   **Architect:** Giffels & Rossetti   **Cost:** $4,000,000
Contact for Rental: Terry Meyer, Assistant Director;   (716) 586-2483
Resident Groups: Nazareth College Theatre League

PYRAMID ARTS CENTER
274 North Goodman Street, Rochester, NY 14607
(716) 461-2222
FAX: (716) 442-2870
Type of Facility: Theatre Complex; Auditorium; Studio Performance; Multi-Purpose
Facility Originally: Warehouse
Type of Stage: Flexible
Seating Capacity: 200
Year Remodeled: 1989
Contact for Rental: Fredric Wagner;   (716) 461-2222

UNIVERSITY OF ROCHESTER-RIVER CAMPUS - STRONG AUDITORIUM
Rochester, NY 14627
(716) 275-2330
Type of Facility: Auditorium
Type of Stage: Proscenium   **Orchestra Pit**
Seating Capacity: 1,100
Year Built: 1921
Manager: Brian Sickels

Resident Groups: University Music Groups
Limited availability

Rockaway Park

DANCE

THE PHYLLIS ROSE DANCE COMPANY
102-00 Shore Front Parkway, Suite 10P, Rockaway Park, NY 11694
(718) 474-1672; (914) 245-7163
Founded: 1969
Arts Area: Modern; Jazz; Ethnic; Folk; Novelty; Theatre
Status: Professional; Non-Profit
Type: Performing; Resident; Educational; Sponsoring
Purpose: To bring high quality multi-cultural dance and movement programs to audiences of all ages, with a special focus on young audiences
Management: Dance Vectors, Inc.; Phyllis Rose, Company Director; Phyllis Cohn, Agent/Program Coordinator
Officers: Phyllis Rose, President; Ivy Rosen, Secretary; Susan Cherniak, Treasurer
Paid Staff: 20   **Volunteer Staff:** 2
Paid Artists: 13
Utilizes: Special Technical Talent; Guest Artists; Guest Choreographers
Budget: $1,000 - $50,000
Income Sources: Business/Corporate Donations; Box Office; Government Grants; Individual Donations; Touring
Season: September 1 - June 30   **Annual Attendance:** 200
Performance Facilities: The Intimate Space Dance Theater

Rome

FACILITY

CAPITOL CIVIC CENTER
218 Liberty Plaza, Rome, NY 13440
(315) 337-6277
Type of Facility: Theatre House
Type of Stage: Proscenium
Stage Dimensions: 22'x4'   **Orchestra Pit**
Seating Capacity: 1,750
Year Built: 1928   **Architect:** Lempert
Contact for Rental: Joseph Ferlo
Resident Groups: Summerstock Theatre

Rosendale

DANCE

THE VANAVER CARAVAN
140A Mountain Road, Rosendale, NY 12472
(914) 658-9748
FAX: (914) 255-3202
Founded: 1972
Arts Area: Modern; Ethnic; Folk
Status: Professional; Non-Profit
Type: Performing; Touring; Educational
Management: Arthur Shafman International Ltd., Tour Direction
Officers: Livia Vanaver; Julien Studley; Eileen Channer; Elizabeth Murphy; Joseph Esposito
Paid Staff: 3   **Volunteer Staff:** 10
Paid Artists: 14
Utilizes: Special Technical Talent; Guest Artists
Budget: $100,000 - $500,000
Income Sources: Private Foundations/Grants/Endowments; Business/Corporate Donations; Box Office; Government Grants; Individual Donations; Performance Fees
Annual Attendance: 50,000

Rye Brook

DANCE

DANCE SOLOS, INC.
Hillandale Road, Rye Brook, NY 10573
    Arts Area: Modern
    Status: Professional; Non-Profit
    Type: Performing; Touring; Resident; Educational
    Purpose: To educate and disseminate the art of solo dancing; to keep alive the art of the great solo dancers
    Management: Annabelle Gamson, Artistic Director; Sheldon Soffer, Booking Manager
    Officers: Annabelle Gamson, President; Arnold Gamson, Secretary
    Budget: $50,000 - $100,000
    Income Sources: Private Foundations/Grants/Endowments; Box Office; Government Grants; Individual Donations
    Performance Facilities: St. Mark's Church; Joyce Theater; Dance Theater Workshop

Salem

THEATRE

METTAWEE THEATRE COMPANY
RD #3, Salem, NY 12865
(518) 854-9357
    Arts Area: Professional
    Status: Professional; Non-Profit
    Type: Performing; Touring
    Purpose: To present original theatre works which incorporate masks, larger than life figures and live music in adaptions of myths and legends from many different cultures
    Management: Ralph Lee, Artistic Director; Casey Compton, Managing Director
    Officers: Stephanie Gallas, President
    Budget: $50,000 - $100,000
    Income Sources: Private Foundations/Grants/Endowments; Business/Corporate Donations; Box Office; Government Grants; Individual Donations

Saranac Lake

PERFORMING SERIES

ADIRONDACK FESTIVAL OF AMERICAN MUSIC
c/o Gregg Smith Singers, PO Box 562, Saranac Lake, NY 12983
(518) 891-1057
    Arts Area: Vocal Music; Instrumental Music; Choral
    Status: Professional; Non-Profit
    Type: Performing; Educational
    Purpose: To present a program focusing on American music--past and present, as well as some traditional repertoire
    Management: Gregg Smith, Artistic Director; Linda Ferriera, Director of Vocal Workshop
    Officers: Frank Manley, Chairman of the Board
    Budget: $50,000 - $100,000
    Income Sources: Private Foundations/Grants/Endowments; Business/Corporate Donations; Box Office; Government Grants; Individual Donations
    Season: 52 Weeks
    Performance Facilities: Town Hall

Saratoga Springs

PERFORMING SERIES

SARATOGA PERFORMING ARTS CENTER
Saratoga Spa State Park, Saratoga Springs, NY 12866
(518) 584-9330
FAX: (518) 584-0809
    Founded: 1966
    Arts Area: Dance; Vocal Music; Instrumental Music; Theater; Grand Opera
    Status: Professional; Non-Profit
    Type: Performing; Educational; Sponsoring

Officers: Mrs. Cornelius Vanderbilt Whitney, Honorary Chairman; Charles V. Wait, Chairman; Herbert A. Chesbrough, President; Mrs. Walter M. Jeffords Jr., Secretary; Harold N. Langlitz, Treasurer
Paid Staff: 14   **Volunteer Staff:** 600
Paid Artists: 625
Utilizes: Special Technical Talent; Guest Conductors; Guest Artists; Guest Directors
Budget: $5,000,000 - $10,000,000
Income Sources: Private Foundations/Grants/Endowments; Business/Corporate Donations; Box Office; Government Grants; Individual Donations
Season: June - September
Affiliations: IAAM; New York Performing Arts Association

FACILITY

SARATOGA PERFORMING ARTS CENTER
Saratoga Springs, NY 12866
(518) 584-9330
    Type of Facility: Performance Center
    Year Built: 1966   **Architect:** Vollmer Associates   **Cost:** $4,000,000
    Acoustical Consultant: Paul S. Veneklasen
    Resident Groups: Summer only: New York City Ballet; Philadelphia Orchestra
    The Performing Arts Center contains the Amphitheatre and the Little Theatre. See separate listings for additional information.

SARATOGA PERFORMING ARTS CENTER - AMPHITHEATRE
Saratoga Springs, NY 12866
(518) 584-9330
FAX: (518) 584-0809
    Founded: 1966
    Type of Facility: Amphitheater
    Type of Stage: Proscenium
    Stage Dimensions: 80'Wx60'D   **Orchestra Pit**
    Seating Capacity: 5,100 indoor; Additional lawn seating
    Year Built: 1965   **Architect:** Vollmer Associates   **Cost:** $4,000,000

SARATOGA PERFORMING ARTS CENTER - LITTLE THEATRE
Saratoga Springs, NY 12866
(518) 584-9330
    Type of Facility: Theatre House
    Facility Originally: Lecture Hall
    Type of Stage: Proscenium
    Stage Dimensions: 40'Wx30'D
    Seating Capacity: 500
    Year Built: 1930

Scarsdale

THEATRE

GREENVILLE COMMUNITY THEATER
PO Box 291, Scarsdale, NY 10583
(914) 472-0389
    Founded: 1964
    Arts Area: Community
    Status: Non-Profit
    Type: Performing
    Purpose: To provide quality theatrical entertainment through two major productions each year and approximately eight one-act workshops
    Management: Board of Directors
    Officers: Valerie Gehn, President; Barbara Evans, Vice-President; Marie Lee, Corresponding Secretary; Nancy Smith, Recording Secretary; Al Gehn, Treasurer
    Volunteer Staff: 110
    Utilizes: Special Technical Talent
    Budget: $1,000 - $50,000
    Income Sources: Business/Corporate Donations; Box Office; Individual Donations
    Season: September - June   **Annual Attendance:** 2,000
    Affiliations: NYSCA
    Performance Facilities: Edgemont High School Auditorium

Schenectady

VOCAL MUSIC

SCHENECTADY LIGHT OPERA COMPANY
PO Box 1006, Schenectady, NY 12301
(518) 393-5732; (518) 374-9566
> **Founded:** 1926
> **Arts Area:** Light Opera; Broadway Musicals
> **Status:** Non-Profit
> **Type:** Performing
> **Purpose:** To present Light Opera and Broadway Musicals
> **Management:** Peter Codella, Business Manager
> **Officers:** Joseph Agostine, President; Della Gilman, Secretary; Michael Jegabbi, Treasurer
> **Volunteer Staff:** 200
> **Budget:** $50,000 - $100,000
> **Income Sources:** Box Office; Individual Donations
> **Season:** October - May   **Annual Attendance:** 9,000
> **Affiliations:** NYSCA

THEATRE

THE SCHENECTADY CIVIC PLAYERS
12 South Church Street, Schenectady, NY 12305
(518) 382-2081
> **Founded:** 1928
> **Arts Area:** Community
> **Status:** Non-Professional; Non-Profit
> **Type:** Performing; Resident
> **Purpose:** Continuation of long tradition of providing non-profit community theatre
> **Volunteer Staff:** 131
> **Budget:** $1,000 - $50,000
> **Income Sources:** Business/Corporate Donations; Box Office; Government Grants
> **Season:** September - June
> **Annual Attendance:** 6,000
> **Affiliations:** New York State Community Theatre Association, New York State Theater Festival Association

FACILITY

PROCTOR'S THEATRE
432 State Street, Schenectady, NY 12305
(518) 382-3884
> **Type of Facility:** Concert Hall; Auditorium; Off Broadway; Theatre House; Opera House
> **Facility Originally:** Vaudeville
> **Type of Stage:** Proscenium
> **Stage Dimensions:** 35'x47'   **Orchestra Pit**
> **Seating Capacity:** 2,700
> **Year Built:** 1926   **Architect:** Thomas Lamb   **Cost:** $1,500,000
> **Year Remodeled:** 1979
> **Acoustical Consultant:** Jaffe Acoustics
> **Contact for Rental:** Jacqueline E. Mosher;   (518) 382-3884

THE SCHENECTADY CIVIC PLAYERS, INC.
12 South Church Street, Schenectady, NY 12305
(518) 382-2081
> **Founded:** 1928
> **Type of Facility:** Theatre House
> **Facility Originally:** Shrine Temple
> **Type of Stage:** Proscenium
> **Stage Dimensions:** 19'Wx26'Dx60'H
> **Seating Capacity:** 267
> **Year Built:** 1868
> **Year Remodeled:** 1961   **Architect:** Sarkis Parkell

Sea Cliff

INSTRUMENTAL MUSIC

THE SEA CLIFF CHAMBER PLAYERS
PO Box 311, Sea Cliff, NY 11579
(516) 671-6263
FAX: (561) 671-6514
  Founded: 1970
  Arts Area: Orchestra; Chamber
  Status: Professional; Non-Profit
  Type: Performing; Touring
  Purpose: To produce quality chamber music concerts on Long Island featuring a chamber ensemble, chamber orchestra, and the Long Island Mozart Festival
  Management: Herbert Sucoff, Executive Director; Barbara Speer, Musical Director
  Officers: David Sterling, President; Sam Goldman, Vice President; Harry F. Lavo, Treasurer; David A. Black, Treasurer
  Paid Staff: 6   **Volunteer Staff:** 80
  Paid Artists: 62
  Utilizes: Guest Artists
  Budget: $100,000 - $500,000
  Income Sources: Private Foundations/Grants/Endowments; Business/Corporate Donations; Box Office; Government Grants; Individual Donations
  Season: October - May
  Annual Attendance: 30,000
  Performance Facilities: The Sea Cliff School; Tilles Center; Planting Fields Arboretum; Northport School; Rockville Center School; Staller Center

Skaneateles

PERFORMING SERIES

SKANEATELES FESTIVAL
PO Box 385, Skaneateles, NY 13152
(315) 685-7418
FAX: (315) 685-0744
  Founded: 1980
  Arts Area: Festivals
  Status: Professional; Non-Profit
  Type: Performing; Educational
  Purpose: To present live chamber music concerts featuring nationally recognized musicians during the last four weeks of summer
  Management: Claire Howard, General Manager; Robert Weirich, Music Director
  Officers: Andrea Latchem, President; Judith Lauerons, Vice President; Karen Pardee, Treasurer; Mary Ellen Casey, Secretary
  Paid Staff: 2
  Paid Artists: 80
  Utilizes: Guest Conductors; Guest Artists
  Budget: $50,000 - $100,000
  Income Sources: Private Foundations/Grants/Endowments; Business/Corporate Donations; Box Office; Government Grants; Individual Donations
  Season: August - September   **Annual Attendance:** 5,000

South Nyack

DANCE

HUMAN ARMS
19 Division Avenue, South Nyack, NY 10960
(914) 358-0489
  Founded: 1985
  Arts Area: Modern; Jazz
  Status: Professional; Non-Profit
  Type: Performing; Touring; Educational
  Purpose: To present dramatic works that examine contradictions that appear in our most intimate thoughts and in the society that surrounds these thoughts, and to encourage and guide children to express themselves creatively through dance
  Management: Harry Streep, Artistic Director; Frank Ferrucci, Cyro Baptista, Pentacle Management
  Officers: John Rothman, Chairman

Paid Artists: 7
Utilizes: Guest Artists
Budget: $1,000 - $50,000
Income Sources: Business/Corporate Donations; Box Office; Individual Donations
Season: 52 Weeks

South Salem

VOCAL MUSIC

THE NEW YORK VIRTUOSO SINGERS
Cove Road, South Salem, NY 10590
(914) 763-3453
Founded: 1988
Arts Area: Choral
Status: Professional; Non-Profit
Type: Performing
Purpose: To perform chamber choral works from all periods with a special emphasis on 20th century repertoire; to commission, perform and record premieres
Paid Staff: 2
Paid Artists: 16
Utilizes: Guest Artists
Budget: $1,000 - $50,000
Income Sources: Private Foundations/Grants/Endowments; Business/Corporate Donations; Box Office; Government Grants; Individual Donations
Season: September - June   Annual Attendance: 550
Performance Facilities: Merkin Concert Hall

Southampton

FACILITY

LONG ISLAND UNIVERSITY - FINE ARTS THEATRE
Southampton Campus, Montauk Highway, Southampton, NY 11968
(516) 283-4000
Type of Facility: Concert Hall; Auditorium; Theatre House
Type of Stage: Thrust; Proscenium
Stage Dimensions: 50'Wx48'D, 18' of depth beyond proscenium
Seating Capacity: 440
Year Built: 1966   Architect: A. Alverez
Contact for Rental: Tim Bishop, Provost;   (516) 283-4000
Manager: Jon Fraser, Associate Dean

Staten Island

FACILITY

SNUG HARBOR CULTURAL CENTER
1000 Richmond Terrace, Staten Island, NY 10301
(718) 448-2500
FAX: (718) 442-8534
Type of Facility: Concert Hall; Outdoor (Concert)
Facility Originally: Church
Type of Stage: Platform
Stage Dimensions: Platform - 30'x50'; Chapel - 10'x40'
Seating Capacity: 210
Year Built: 1856   Architect: James Salmon
Year Remodeled: 1984   Architect: Gibson-Bauer Associates
Contact for Rental: Brian Rehr, Performing Arts Director;   (718) 448-2500

VETERANS MEMORIAL HALL
1000 Richmond Terrace, Staten Island, NY 10301
(718) 448-2500
FAX: (718) 442-8534
Type of Facility: Concert Hall
Facility Originally: Church

Type of Stage: Platform
Stage Dimensions: 35'Wx12'D
Seating Capacity: 200
Year Built: 1856
Year Remodeled: 1985
Acoustical Consultant: Jaffe
Contact for Rental: Kim D. Sio;   (718) 448-2500

WILLIAMSON THEATRE
715 Ocean Terrace, Staten Island, NY 10301
(718) 390-7725
Founded: 1968
Type of Facility: Auditorium; Performance Center; Theatre House; Multi-Purpose
Type of Stage: Proscenium   **Orchestra Pit**
Seating Capacity: 900
Contact for Rental: D. Zarrilli or C. Brandifino;   (718) 390-7948

Stony Brook

DANCE

LONG ISLAND DANCE COMPANY
1320 Stony Brook Road, Stony Brook, NY 11790
(516) 751-2195
Founded: 1969
Arts Area: Modern; Ballet; Jazz
Status: Professional; Non-Profit
Type: Performing; Touring; Resident
Purpose: To promote the awareness of dance and its varied styles
Management: Sandra Jemal, Artistic Director
Paid Artists: 16
Utilizes: Guest Artists
Budget: $1,000 - $50,000
Income Sources: Private Foundations/Grants/Endowments; Business/Corporate Donations; Box Office; Government Grants; Individual Donations
Season: 52 Weeks

PERFORMING SERIES

BACH ARIA FESTIVAL AND INSTITUTE
PO Box 997, Stony Brook, NY 11790
(516) 632-7239
FAX: (516) 632-6252
Founded: 1981
Arts Area: Vocal Music; Instrumental Music; Festivals; Baroque Opera
Status: Professional; Non-Profit
Type: Performing; Educational
Purpose: To provide professional training and concertizing based on cantata literature of J.S. Bach; to study and present other literature
Management: Carol K. Baron, Executive Director
Paid Staff: 2   **Volunteer Staff:** 30
Paid Artists: 50
Utilizes: Guest Artists; Fellows of Insitute
Budget: $100,000 - $500,000
Income Sources: Private Foundations/Grants/Endowments; Business/Corporate Donations; Box Office; Government Grants; Individual Donations
Season: June   **Annual Attendance:** 3,000
Affiliations: SUNY Stony Brook
Performance Facilities: Staller Center for the Arts; Chelsea Mansion; Cathedral of Saint John the Divine

Stony Point

THEATRE

PENGUIN REPERTORY COMPANY
Crickettown Road, Stony Point, NY 10980
Founded: 1977

Arts Area: Professional
Status: Professional; Non-Profit
Type: Performing
Purpose: To mount new plays, giving new playwrights opportunities; to stage "tried and true" works
Management: Joe Brancato, Artistic Director; Andrew Horn, Executive Director
Officers: Annabelle Goldschmidt, President; Francine Newman McCarthy, Vice President; Catherine Grassi, Secretary/Treasurer
Paid Staff: 4   **Volunteer Staff:** 2
Utilizes: Guest Artists; Guest Directors
Budget: $100,000 - $500,000
Income Sources: Private Foundations/Grants/Endowments; Business/Corporate Donations; Box Office; Government Grants; Individual Donations
Season: October - August
Affiliations: AEA; SSDC

Sunnyside

INSTRUMENTAL MUSIC

ROSEWOOD CHAMBER ENSEMBLE, INC.
43-31 39th Street, Sunnyside, NY 11104
(718) 729-4614
Founded: 1980
Arts Area: Chamber; Ensemble
Status: Professional; Non-Profit
Type: Performing; Educational
Purpose: To bring good classical music to the community; to provide musical education for the young
Officers: Ruth Javna, Chairman; Bridie Race, Secretary; Al Friedman, Treasurer; Karla Moc and David Moore, Co-Artistic Directors; Chris Bianchi, Vice Chair
Paid Staff: 1   **Volunteer Staff:** 10
Paid Artists: 20
Utilizes: Guest Artists
Budget: $1,000 - $50,000
Income Sources: Business/Corporate Donations; Box Office; Government Grants; Individual Donations
Season: November - April
Annual Attendance: 700

THEATRE

THALIA SPANISH THEATRE
41-17 Greenpoint Avenue, Sunnyside, NY 11104
(718) 729-3880
Founded: 1969
Arts Area: Professional; Musical; Community; Theatrical Group
Status: Professional; Non-Profit
Type: Performing; Touring; Resident
Purpose: To present to the Hispanic communities of New York City, productions of the highest artistic quality and professionalism
Management: Silvia Brito, Artistic/Executive Director; Kathryn A. Giaimo, Administrative Director; Felix Arocho, Marketing Director; Guillermo Escudero, Technical Director
Officers: Anna Harrsch, Chairperson/Treasurer; Silvia Brito, President; Emilio C. Cueto, Vice President; Ruth Diez, Secretary
Paid Staff: 4   **Volunteer Staff:** 4
Paid Artists: 40
Utilizes: Special Technical Talent; Guest Artists; Guest Directors
Budget: $100,000 - $500,000
Income Sources: Private Foundations/Grants/Endowments; Business/Corporate Donations; Box Office; Government Grants; Individual Donations
Season: 52 Weeks
Annual Attendance: 9,000
Affiliations: ART/NY; AHA; TCG; Flushing Council on Culture and the Arts; Arts and Business Council; Queens Council on the Arts
Performance Facilities: Thalia Theatre

Syracuse

INSTRUMENTAL MUSIC

SYRACUSE SOCIETY FOR NEW MUSIC
312 Crawford Avenue, Syracuse, NY 13224
(315) 446-5733
    Founded: 1971
    Arts Area: Chamber; Electronic & Live Electronic; Chamber Opera; Jazz; New Music
    Status: Professional; Non-Profit
    Type: Performing; Touring; Resident; Educational; Sponsoring
    Purpose: To present new music, commission new works and take new music into the public schools
    Officers: Harris Lindenfield, President; Ann Sitsbee and Daniel Godfrey, Vice Presidents; Steven Stuckey and Neva Pilgrim, Program Advisor
    Volunteer Staff: 6
    Paid Artists: 175
    Utilizes: Guest Artists
    Budget: $50,000 - $100,000
    Income Sources: Private Foundations/Grants/Endowments; Business/Corporate Donations; Box Office; Government Grants; Individual Donations; Benefits
    Season: September - April; July-August   **Annual Attendance:** 10,000
    Performance Facilities: Syracuse University; Crouse College; Everson Muesum

SYRACUSE SYMPHONY ORCHESTRA
411 Montgomery Street, Syracuse, NY 13203
(315) 424-8222
FAX: (315) 424-1131
    Founded: 1960
    Arts Area: Symphony; Orchestra; Chamber
    Status: Professional; Non-Profit
    Type: Performing; Touring; Resident; Educational
    Purpose: To maintain and further develop a resident, professional symphony orchestra; to produce musical performances of the highest artistic quality; to fulfill the cultural, educational and entertainment needs of the central and northern New York communities we serve
    Management: Melvin A. Eggers, President/Executive Director; Kazuyoshi Akiyama, Music Director/Conductor; Fabio Mechetti, Associate Conductor; Richard Decker, Orchestra Manager; Susan Schwartz, Director of Marketing/Public Relations
    Paid Staff: 25   **Volunteer Staff:** 700
    Paid Artists: 86
    Utilizes: Special Technical Talent; Guest Conductors; Guest Artists
    Budget: $1,000,000 - $5,000,000
    Income Sources: Private Foundations/Grants/Endowments; Business/Corporate Donations; Box Office; Government Grants; Individual Donations
    Season: 52 Weeks   **Annual Attendance:** 210,000
    Affiliations: ASOL; APAP
    Performance Facilities: John H. Mulroy Civic Center

SYRACUSE SYMPHONY YOUTH ORCHESTRA
411 Montogomery Street, Syracuse, NY 13203
(315) 424-8222
FAX: (315) 424-1131
    Founded: 1961
    Arts Area: Symphony; Orchestra
    Status: Non-Professional; Non-Profit
    Type: Performing; Touring; Resident; Educational
    Management: Ernest Muzquiz, Conductor
    Officers: Dr. Arthur Rosenbaum, Chairman
    Paid Staff: 1   **Volunteer Staff:** 10
    Non-Paid Artists: 80
    Utilizes: Guest Artists
    Budget: $1,000 - $50,000
    Income Sources: Private Foundations/Grants/Endowments; Box Office; Individual Donations
    Season: September - May   **Annual Attendance:** 5,000
    Affiliations: ASOL (Youth Orchestra Division); Syracuse Symphony Orchestra
    Performance Facilities: H.W. Smith Elementary School

VOCAL MUSIC

SYRACUSE OPERA COMPANY
100 East Washington Street, PO Box 6904, Syracuse, NY 13217-6904
(315) 475-5915
> **Founded:** 1973
> **Arts Area:** Grand Opera; Lyric Opera; Light Opera; Operetta
> **Status:** Professional; Non-Profit
> **Type:** Performing; Touring; Resident; Educational
> **Purpose:** To produce high-quality opera productions using talented, young American artists from the central New York region; to provide quality opera productions outside the central New York region
> **Management:** Julie Richards, General Director; Richard McKee, Artistic Director
> **Paid Staff:** 11   **Volunteer Staff:** 4
> **Paid Artists:** 75   **Non-Paid Artists:** 20
> **Utilizes:** Special Technical Talent; Guest Conductors; Guest Artists; Guest Directors
> **Budget:** $500,000 - $1,000,000
> **Income Sources:** Private Foundations/Grants/Endowments; Business/Corporate Donations; Box Office; Government Grants; Individual Donations
> **Season:** October - May   **Annual Attendance:** 33,500
> **Affiliations:** OA; NYSCA
> **Performance Facilities:** Crouse-Hinds Concert Theater

THEATRE

SYRACUSE STAGE
820 East Genesee, Syracuse, NY 13210
(315) 443-4008
FAX: (315) 443-9846
> **Founded:** 1974
> **Arts Area:** Professional; Theatrical Group
> **Status:** Professional; Non-Profit
> **Type:** Performing; Touring; Educational
> **Purpose:** Through the artistry of the playwrights, directors, designers and actors, Syracuse Stage seeks to enrich the lives of Central New York theater-goers and to challenge their perceptions of the world.
> **Management:** James A. Clark, Producing Director; Tazewell Thompson, Artistic Director; Diana C. Coles, Administrative Director; Don Buschmann, Production Manager
> **Officers:** Joan Green, Chairman; Lucius Kempton, President; Louis Marcoccia, Treasurer; Sandra Townes, Secretary
> **Paid Staff:** 40
> **Paid Artists:** 75
> **Utilizes:** Guest Artists; Guest Directors
> **Budget:** $1,000,000 - $5,000,000
> **Income Sources:** Private Foundations/Grants/Endowments; Business/Corporate Donations; Box Office; Government Grants; Individual Donations
> **Season:** October - May   **Annual Attendance:** 100,000
> **Affiliations:** TCG; LORT; AEA
> **Performance Facilities:** The John D. Archbold Theatre

PERFORMING SERIES

CULTURAL RESOURCES COUNCIL OF SYRACUSE AND ONONDAGA COUNTY
411 Montgomery Street, Syracuse, NY 13202
(315) 435-2155
> **Founded:** 1968
> **Arts Area:** Dance; Theater; Festivals
> **Status:** Professional; Non-Profit
> **Type:** Performing
> **Purpose:** To identify, coordinate, promote and present all the performing arts to serve a 10-county central New York area
> **Management:** Jerold Reichard, Executive Directorn
> **Officers:** Wallace Conkling, President; Susan Connelly, Vice President; Jay Jackler CPA, Treasurer
> **Paid Staff:** 22   **Volunteer Staff:** 150
> **Paid Artists:** 250   **Non-Paid Artists:** 2
> **Utilizes:** Special Technical Talent; Guest Artists; Guest Directors
> **Income Sources:** Private Foundations/Grants/Endowments; Business/Corporate Donations; Box Office; Government Grants; Individual Donations
> **Annual Attendance:** 350,000
> **Affiliations:** ISPAA
> **Performance Facilities:** Civic Center of Ononadaga County

FACILITY

CIVIC CENTER OF ONONDAGA COUNTY
411 Montgomery Street, Syracuse, NY 13202
(315) 425-2155
Type of Facility: Performance Center; Civic Center
Year Built: 1976   **Architect:** McAfee Malo Afflect Lebensold Nichol   **Cost:** $23,000,000
Acoustical Consultant: ARTEC
Contact for Rental: Robert Oliver;   (315) 425-2155
Resident Groups: Syracuse Symphony Orchestra; Opera Theater of Syracuse; Syracuse Ballet Theater
The Civic Center contains Bevard Community Room, Carrier Theater and Crouse-Hinds Concert Theater. See separate listings for additional information.

CIVIC CENTER OF ONONDAGA COUNTY - BEVARD COMMUNITY ROOM
411 Montgomery Street, Syracuse, NY 13202
(315) 425-2155
Type of Facility: Black Box
Type of Stage: Flexible
Stage Dimensions: 60'Wx40'Dx24'H
Seating Capacity: 200
Year Built: 1976
Contact for Rental: Robert Oliver;   (315) 425-2155

CIVIC CENTER OF ONONDAGA COUNTY - CARRIER THEATER
411 Montgomery Street, Syracuse, NY 13202
(315) 425-2155
Type of Facility: Studio Performance
Type of Stage: Flexible
Stage Dimensions: 27'x57'x25'
Seating Capacity: 463
Year Built: 1976
Contact for Rental: Robert Oliver;   (315) 425-2155

CIVIC CENTER OF ONONDAGA COUNTY - CROUSE-HINDS CONCERT THEATER
411 Montgomery Street, Syracuse, NY 13202
(315) 425-2155
Type of Facility: Concert Hall; Theatre House
Type of Stage: Proscenium
Stage Dimensions: 110'Wx50'Dx85'H; 60'Wx40'H proscenium opening   **Orchestra Pit**
Seating Capacity: 2,117
Year Built: 1976
Contact for Rental: Robert Oliver;   (315) 425-2155
Two separate lifts - 60'Wx14'D and 60'Wx10'D

SYRACUSE AREA LANDMARK THEATRE
362 South Salina Street, Syracuse, NY 13202
(315) 475-7979
FAX: (315) 475-7993
Founded: 1975
Type of Facility: Theatre Complex; Concert Hall; Auditorium; Off Broadway; Theatre House; Opera House; Multi-Purpose; Movie House
Facility Originally: Movie House
Type of Stage: Proscenium
Stage Dimensions: 30'x50'   **Orchestra Pit**
Seating Capacity: 2,922
Year Built: 1928   **Architect:** Thomas Lamb   **Cost:** $2,000,000
Year Remodeled: 1975   **Cost:** $1,000,000
Contact for Rental: Frank M. Malfitano;   (315) 475-7979

Tarrytown

DANCE

BALLET THEATRE OF WESTCHESTER
62 Main Street, Tarrytown, NY 10591
(914) 631-6878
Arts Area: Ballet

Status: Professional
Type: Performing; Touring; Resident
Management: Claire Kelley, Artistic Director; Carmen Williams, Administrative Director
Income Sources: Box Office; Individual Donations
Performance Facilities: Master School Auditorium

FACILITY

LYNDHURST
635 South Broadway, Tarrytown, NY 10591
(914) 631-0046
FAX: (914) 631-6825
Type of Facility: Outdoor (Concert)
Type of Stage: Proscenium
Seating Capacity: Tent - 1,000; Outdoors - 4,000
Manager: Susanne Pandrich, Director
Resident Groups: Sunset Serenades

Ticonderoga

PERFORMING SERIES

TICONDEROGA FESTIVAL GUILD, INC.
PO Box 125, 324 Champlain Avenue, Ticonderoga, NY 12883
(518) 545-6716
Founded: 1980
Arts Area: Festivals
Status: Non-Profit
Type: Performing
Purpose: To bring cultural events to an area rural in nature, where the performing arts are at a premium
Management: Sharon P. Ofner, Executive Director
Officers: Mark Johnson, President; Thomas Latrell, First Vice President; Richard Cunningham, Second Vice President; Michael Corsi, Treasurer; Carolyn Malaney, Secretary
Paid Staff: 1   **Volunteer Staff:** 20
Income Sources: Private Foundations/Grants/Endowments; Business/Corporate Donations; Box Office; Government Grants; Individual Donations
Season: July - August   **Annual Attendance:** 3,500

Troy

INSTRUMENTAL MUSIC

TROY CHROMATICS CONCERTS, INC.
PO Box 1574, Troy, NY 12181
(518) 235-3000
Founded: 1895
Arts Area: Symphony; Chamber; Ensemble; Soloists
Status: Non-Profit
Type: Sponsoring
Purpose: To provide world class artists and programs to the capital region of New York state
Officers: Michael A. Nofac, President
Budget: $50,000 - $100,000
Income Sources: Private Foundations/Grants/Endowments; Business/Corporate Donations; Box Office; Government Grants; Individual Donations
Season: October - May   **Annual Attendance:** 5,000
Performance Facilities: Troy Savings Bank Music Hall

FACILITY

RENSSELAER NEWMAN FOUNDATION CHAPEL AND CULTURAL CENTER
2125 Burdett Avenue, Troy, NY 12180
(518) 274-7793
Type of Facility: Theatre Complex; Concert Hall; Auditorium; Outdoor (Concert); Performance Center; Multi-Purpose
Type of Stage: Thrust; Flexible; Platform
Stage Dimensions: 80'x80'

Seating Capacity: 400
Year Built: 1967   Architect: Peter Levatich   Cost: $500,000
Contact for Rental: William McQuiston, Director;   (518) 274-7793
Resident Groups: Rensselaer Theater Company; Electronic-Video Arts At RPI; RPI Ensembles; Religion and the Arts Festival; Literary Arts At RPI; Visiting Artists Series; RPI Youth Theater Workshop

TROY ARENA
689 Burden Avenue, PO Box 97, Troy, NY 12181
(518) 273-8400
    Type of Facility: Civic Center; Arena; Multi-Purpose
    Type of Stage: Arena
    Stage Dimensions: 40'Wx60'D
    Seating Capacity: 4,000
    Year Built: 1945
    Contact for Rental: Ted Bayly;   (518) 273-8400

TROY - HAYNER CULTURAL CENTER
301 West Main Street, Troy, NY 45373
(513) 339-0457
    Founded: 1976
    Type of Facility: Outdoor (Concert); Community Cultural Center
    Facility Originally: Historic Mansion
    Type of Stage: Ballroom
    Stage Dimensions: 20'x20' floor space
    Seating Capacity: 115
    Year Built: 1914
    Architect: Leonard B. Willeke
    Contact for Rental: Martha Stone;   (513) 339-0457

TROY SAVINGS BANK MUSIC HALL
State and Second Streets, Troy, NY 12180
(518) 273-0038
FAX: (518) 274-7762
    Mailing Address: 88 Fourth Street, Troy, NY 12180
    Founded: 1875
    Type of Facility: Concert Hall
    Facility Originally: Concert Hall
    Type of Stage: Thrust; Apron is curved; stage is slighty raised
    Stage Dimensions: 68'Wx21'D
    Seating Capacity: 1,200
    Year Built: 1875
    Architect: George Brown Post   Cost: $500,000
    Contact for Rental: Mitchell A. Gordon;   (518) 273-0038

Uniondale

INSTRUMENTAL MUSIC

NASSAU SYMPHONY SOCIETY, INC.
185 California Avenue, Uniondale, NY 11553-1131
(516) 481-3196
FAX: (516) 481-3382
    Arts Area: Symphony
    Status: Professional; Non-Profit
    Type: Performing; Educational
    Purpose: To perform symphonic music of the highest quality for residents of all ages on Long Island
    Management: Sherry Smolev, Executive Director
    Officers: Robert Buescher, Chairman of the Board
    Budget: $500,000 - $1,000,000
    Income Sources: Private Foundations/Grants/Endowments; Business/Corporate Donations; Box Office; Government Grants; Individual Donations
    Performance Facilities: John Cranford Adams Playhouse, Hofstra University

---

Utica

PERFORMING SERIES

MUNSON-WILLIAMS-PROCTOR INSTITUTE PERFORMING ARTS DIVISION
310 Genesee Street, Utica, NY 13502
(315) 797-0055
FAX: (315) 797-5608
Founded: 1932
Arts Area: Dance; Vocal Music; Instrumental Music; Theater; Festivals; Lyric Opera; Grand Opera; Jazz; Folk; Children's; Film
Status: Professional; Non-Profit
Type: Performing; Educational; Sponsoring
Purpose: To provide exemplary programs and educational opportunites in the performing and cinematic arts, setting a national standard for artistic achievement.
Officers: Milton J. Bloch, President; George J. Trudeau, Director of Performing Arts
Paid Staff: 5 **Volunteer Staff:** 30
Paid Artists: 200
Utilizes: Guest Artists
Budget: $500,000 - $1,000,000
Income Sources: Private Foundations/Grants/Endowments; Business/Corporate Donations; Box Office; Government Grants; Individual Donations; Program Advertising
Annual Attendance: 30,000
Affiliations: ISPAA; BOMI; ASOL; NEP; APAP
Performance Facilities: Stanley Performing Arts Center; Museum of Art Auditorium and Sculpture Court; Festival Tent

FACILITY

STANLEY PERFORMING ARTS CENTER
259 Genesee Street, Utica, NY 13501
(315) 724-5919
FAX: (315) 732-8468
Type of Facility: Concert Hall; Auditorium; Theatre House
Facility Originally: Movie House
Type of Stage: Proscenium
Stage Dimensions: 57'Wx30'D **Orchestra Pit**
Seating Capacity: 2,945
Year Built: 1928 **Architect:** Thomas Lamb **Cost:** $1,500,000
Year Remodeled: 1992 **Architect:** Alesia and Crewell **Cost:** $4,000,000
Acoustical Consultant: Jacek Figwer
Contact for Rental: John Faust; (315) 724-5919
Resident Groups: Broadway Theatre League (touring shows); Great Artists Series; Utica Symphony Orchestra

UTICA MEMORIAL AUDITORIUM
400 Oriskany Street, Utica, NY 13502
(315) 738-0164
Type of Facility: Auditorium; Multi-Purpose
Type of Stage: Flexible
Stage Dimensions: 44'x56'
Seating Capacity: 6,000
Year Built: 1960 **Architect:** Gehron and Seltzer
Year Remodeled: 1986
Contact for Rental: Murray Sislen
Resident Groups: Utica Devils Hockey Team

Watertown

DANCE

1000 ISLANDS FESTIVAL BALLET COMPANY, INC.
PO Box 513, Watertown, NY 13601
(315) 782-2566
Founded: 1985
Arts Area: Ballet
Status: Semi-Professional; Non-Profit
Type: Performing; Touring; Educational; Sponsoring
Purpose: To provide educational and performance opportunities for students and the community

Management: Jean Spear, Artistic Director
Officers: Mark Gebo, Attorney; Charles Hamlin, Comptroller; Patricia Johnson, Secretary/Treasurer; Beverly Youngs, Public Relations
Paid Staff: 1   **Volunteer Staff:** 15
Utilizes: Special Technical Talent; Guest Artists
Budget: $1,000 - $50,000
Income Sources: Private Foundations/Grants/Endowments; Box Office; Individual Donations
Season: September - May   **Annual Attendance:** 8,000
Performance Facilities: Dulles State Office Building

THEATRE

WATERTOWN LYRIC THEATER PRODUCTIONS
1333 Holcomb Street, Watertown, NY 13601
(315) 788-6492
Founded: 1972
Arts Area: Musical; Community; Theatrical Group
Status: Non-Professional; Non-Profit
Type: Performing; Educational
Purpose: To present live theatre to the community using local talent and provide the youth of the community an education in musical theatre
Officers: Michael Bajjaly, President; William Boulter, Vice President; Barbara Flynn, Secretary; Daniel Davis, Treasurer
Volunteer Staff: 75
Non-Paid Artists: 300
Utilizes: Special Technical Talent
Budget: $1,000 - $50,000
Income Sources: Box Office; Individual Donations
Season: 52 Weeks   **Annual Attendance:** 3,000
Performance Facilities: State Office Building Auditorium

FACILITY

NEW YORK STATE OFFICE OF GENERAL SERVICES
317 Washington Street, Dulles State Building, Watertown, NY 13601
(315) 785-2451
Type of Facility: Theatre Complex; Concert Hall; Auditorium; Performance Center; Theatre House; Multi-Purpose
Type of Stage: Proscenium
Stage Dimensions: 20'x60'x30'   **Orchestra Pit**
Seating Capacity: 795
Year Built: 1972   **Architect:** Sargeant, Webster Cronshaw and Folley
Contact for Rental: Gerald F. Casey;   (315) 785-2451
Resident Groups: Watertown Lyric Theater; Watertown Little Theater; Third Wave Productions

Westbury

PERFORMING SERIES

WESTBURY MUSIC FAIR
960 Brush Hollow Road, Westbury, NY 11590
(516) 333-7228
FAX: (516) 333-7991
Founded: 1956
Arts Area: Dance; Vocal Music; Instrumental Music; Theater
Status: Professional; Commercial
Type: Performing
Purpose: To provide the best entertainment in all areas of entertaiment to metropolitan New York
Management: Dana F.X. Amendola, General Manager
Paid Staff: 100
Utilizes: Special Technical Talent; Guest Conductors; Guest Artists
Budget: $100,000 - $500,000
Income Sources: Box Office
Season: February - December

FACILITY

WESTBURY MUSIC FAIR
960 Brush Hollow Road, Westbury, NY 11590
(516) 333-7228
Type of Facility: Performance Center; Theatre House; Arena
Type of Stage: Arena; In-the-round Capability
Stage Dimensions: 30' diameter   **Orchestra Pit**
Seating Capacity: 2,932
Year Built: 1965   **Architect:** Hassinger & Schwamm   **Cost:** $1,500,000
Acoustical Consultant: Kevin Hickson
Contact for Rental: Laurel Kramer;   (516) 333-2101
Management reserves the right to permit rentals for specific purposes.

Westfield

THEATRE

DAS PUPPENSPIEL PUPPET THEATER, INC.
1 1/2 East Main Street, Westfield, NY 14787-1319
(716) 326-2611
FAX: (716) 326-6625
Founded: 1974
Arts Area: Professional; Theatrical Group; Puppet
Status: Professional; Non-Profit
Type: Performing; Touring; Educational
Management: Kevin Kuhlman, Managing Director
Paid Staff: 2   **Volunteer Staff:** 1
Paid Artists: 6   **Non-Paid Artists:** 1
Utilizes: Guest Directors
Budget: $100,000 - $500,000
Income Sources: Private Foundations/Grants/Endowments; Business/Corporate Donations; Box Office; Government Grants; Individual Donations
Season: October - August   **Annual Attendance:** 65,000
Affiliations: UNIMA; Puppeteers of America; Children's Theatre Association of America

White Plains

VOCAL MUSIC

WESTCHESTER CHORAL SOCIETY, INC.
Box 94, White Plains, NY 10604
(914) 693-2453
Founded: 1942
Arts Area: Choral
Status: Non-Professional; Non-Profit
Type: Performing; Resident
Purpose: To promote appreciation of fine music in the community
Management: Lyndon Woodside, Music Director; David Ralph, Accompanist; Shirley Rubenstein, Administration
Officers: David Issacs, President; Irving Shepard, Treasurer
Paid Staff: 3   **Volunteer Staff:** 20
Utilizes: Guest Artists
Budget: $1,000 - $50,000
Income Sources: Private Foundations/Grants/Endowments; Business/Corporate Donations; Box Office; Government Grants; Individual Donations
Season: August   **Annual Attendance:** 1,000
Performance Facilities: SUNY Purchase

THEATRE

THE STREET THEATER
228 Fisher Avenue, White Plains, NY 10606
(914) 761-3307
FAX: (914) 422-2340
Founded: 1970
Arts Area: Professional; Theatrical Group
Status: Semi-Professional; Non-Profit

Type: Performing; Touring; Educational
Purpose: Committed to educational programs dealing with social issues; to support a touring youth company
Management: Gray Smith, Artistic Director
Paid Staff: 2
Utilizes: Special Technical Talent; Guest Artists; Guest Directors
Budget: $100,000 - $500,000
Income Sources: Private Foundations/Grants/Endowments; Business/Corporate Donations; Box Office; Government Grants; Individual Donations
Season: 52 Weeks
Affiliations: AEA

TRAVELING PLAYHOUSE
104 Northampton Drive, White Plains, NY 10603
(914) 946-5289
Founded: 1948
Arts Area: Professional; Summer Stock
Status: Professional; Non-Profit
Type: Performing; Touring; Resident; Educational
Purpose: To present a repertory of plays for children 6-12 years of age by adult professional actors
Management: Kay Rockefeller, Director; Ken Rockefeller, Producer; Franklin Birt, Production Manager; Richard Kinter, Resident Author/Composer
Paid Staff: 6
Paid Artists: 30
Budget: $100,000 - $500,000
Income Sources: Box Office
Season: 52 Weeks
Affiliations: AATA; AEA
Performance Facilities: Kaufmann Auditorium; Symphony Space

Woodside

DANCE

TOMOV FOLK DANCE ENSEMBLE
66-12 48th Street, Woodside, NY 11377
Founded: 1974
Arts Area: Folk
Status: Semi-Professional; Non-Profit
Type: Performing; Touring; Educational
Purpose: To showcase the folk music, dance and songs of the Balkans
Management: Folkdance Foundation, Inc. (Parent Organization)
Officers: George Tomov, President/Artistic Director
Volunteer Staff: 20
Paid Artists: 40
Utilizes: Guest Artists; Guest Choreographers
Budget: $1,000 - $50,000
Income Sources: Private Foundations/Grants/Endowments; Business/Corporate Donations; Box Office; Government Grants; Individual Donations
Season: 52 Weeks

Woodstock

INSTRUMENTAL MUSIC

MAVERICK CONCERTS, INC.
PO Box 102, Woodstock, NY 12498
(914) 679-8217
Arts Area: Chamber
Status: Professional; Non-Profit
Type: Performing
Purpose: To provide Sunday afternoon chamber-music concerts during the summer; Maverick Concerts is the oldest chamber music session in the United States and is about to celebrate its 78th season
Management: Vincent Wagner, Artistic Director
Officers: Gerald Widoff, Chairman of the Board
Budget: $1,000 - $50,000

Income Sources: Private Foundations/Grants/Endowments; Business/Corporate Donations; Box Office; Government Grants; Individual Donations
Performance Facilities: Maverick Concert Hall

THEATRE

COMMON STAGE THEATRE COMPANY, INC.
PO Box 1028, Woodstock, NY 12498
(914) 679-9256
Founded: 1989
Arts Area: Theatrical Group; Women Playwrights Only
Status: Semi-Professional; Non-Profit
Purpose: To develop and produce plays by women
Officers: Gloria Dickler, Kathi Wood, Co-Artistic Directors; Joseph Schwarz, Managing Director
Volunteer Staff: 15
Paid Artists: 10   **Non-Paid Artists:** 10
Utilizes: Special Technical Talent; Guest Artists
Budget: $1,000 - $50,000
Income Sources: Private Foundations/Grants/Endowments; Business/Corporate Donations; Box Office; Individual Donations
Season: May - June; September-October   **Annual Attendance:** 800

FACILITY

MAVERICK CONCERT HALL
PO Box 102, Woodstock, NY 12498
(914) 679-8217
Founded: 1915
Type of Facility: Concert Hall; Outdoor (Concert)
Type of Stage: Platform
Stage Dimensions: 20'x12'
Seating Capacity: Inside-270; Outside-150
Year Built: 1916
Year Remodeled: 1977   **Architect:** Leonhard T. Hartman   **Cost:** $59,000
Acoustical Consultant: Edgar Villchiure
Contact for Rental: Vincent Wagner;   (914) 338-3074

Yonkers

PERFORMING SERIES

MANCHESTER MUSIC FESTIVAL
93 Franklin Avenue, Yonkers, NY 10705
(914) 965-5533
Founded: 1974
Arts Area: Vocal Music; Instrumental Music; Festivals
Status: Non-Profit
Type: Performing; Educational
Purpose: School for gifted instrumentalists; festival concerts
Management: Michael Rudiakov, Director; Ariel Rudiakov, Assistant
Paid Staff: 10   **Volunteer Staff:** 16
Paid Artists: 10
Utilizes: Guest Artists
Budget: $100,000 - $500,000
Income Sources: Private Foundations/Grants/Endowments; Business/Corporate Donations; Box Office; Government Grants; Individual Donations
Season: July - August   **Annual Attendance:** 1,000
Performance Facilities: Southern Vermont Arts Center

Yorktown Heights

DANCE

DANCE THEATRE IN WESTCHESTER
1974 Commerce Street, Yorktown Heights, NY 10598
(914) 245-2940
Founded: 1979

Arts Area: Modern; Ballet; Jazz
Status: Professional; Non-Profit
Type: Performing; Touring; Resident
Purpose: Regional Dance Company
Management: Rose-Marie Menes, Artistic Director
Officers: Bernard Werner, President Board of Directors
Paid Staff: 4   **Volunteer Staff:** 10
Paid Artists: 11   **Non-Paid Artists:** 6
Utilizes: Guest Artists; Guest Choreographers
Budget: $50,000 - $100,000
Income Sources: Private Foundations/Grants/Endowments; Business/Corporate Donations; Box Office; Individual Donations
Season: September - May   **Annual Attendance:** 10,000

VOCAL MUSIC

THE TAGHKANIC CHORALE
PO Box 144, Yorktown Heights, NY 10598
(914) 621-1240
Founded: 1967
Arts Area: Choral
Status: Semi-Professional; Non-Profit
Type: Performing; Educational
Purpose: Preparation and performance of choral works with emphasis on quality and authenticity
Management: Johannes Somary, Music Director
Officers: Sallye Adams, President; Virgina Perunko, Vice President; Ed Falcone, Secretary; Eileen Donnelly, Treasurer
Paid Staff: 2   **Volunteer Staff:** 40
Paid Artists: 75   **Non-Paid Artists:** 100
Utilizes: Special Technical Talent; Guest Artists
Budget: $1,000 - $50,000
Income Sources: Private Foundations/Grants/Endowments; Business/Corporate Donations; Box Office; Government Grants; Individual Donations
Season: September - June   **Annual Attendance:** 2,000
Affiliations: CA

NORTH CAROLINA

Asheville

INSTRUMENTAL MUSIC

HOWARD HANGER JAZZ FANTASY
31 Park Avenue, Asheville, NC 28801
(704) 254-6265
Founded: 1966
Arts Area: Ensemble; Electronic & Live Electronic
Status: Professional
Type: Performing; Touring; Educational
Purpose: To perform new age and traditional jazz and to introduce jazz to children ages 6-12
Management: Howard Hanger, Musical Director
Budget: $50,000 - $100,000

THEATRE

PISGAH PLAYERS
One University Heights, Asheville, NC 28804
(704) 251-6580
Founded: 1988
Arts Area: Theatrical Group
Status: Non-Professional; Non-Profit
Type: Performing; Touring; Sponsoring
Purpose: To produce original contemporary scripts and reinterpret the classics
Management: David B. Hopes, Jade Parsons, Directors
Volunteer Staff: 8
Non-Paid Artists: 70
Utilizes: Special Technical Talent; Guest Artists; Guest Directors
Budget: $1,000 - $50,000
Income Sources: Private Foundations/Grants/Endowments; Box Office; Individual Donations
Season: 52 Weeks   **Annual Attendance:** 1,000
Affiliations: University of North Carolina at Asheville Creative Writing Department

SMOKY MOUNTAIN REPERTORY THEATRE
26 South Lexington Street, Asheville, NC 28801
(704) 252-9661
Founded: 1981
Arts Area: Professional; Folk; Theatrical Group
Status: Semi-Professional; Non-Profit
Type: Performing; Touring; Resident; Educational
Purpose: To produce new works and new adaptations with a particular focus on works of regional significance
Management: H. Byron Ballard, Managing Director; Joe Fioccola, Business Manager; M. Michael Hyatt, Technical Director; Vivienne Conjura, Youth Director
Officers: M. Michael Hyatt, President; Anne Monteath Hyatt, Vice President; H. Byron Ballard, Secretary
Paid Staff: 1   **Volunteer Staff:** 3
Paid Artists: 25   **Non-Paid Artists:** 10
Utilizes: Special Technical Talent
Budget: $1,000 - $50,000
Income Sources: Private Foundations/Grants/Endowments; Business/Corporate Donations; Box Office; Individual Donations
Season: 52 Weeks
Performance Facilities: First Artists Studio-Theater

PERFORMING SERIES

ASHEVILLE CHAMBER MUSIC SERIES
PO Box 1003, Asheville, NC 28802
(704) 669-6141
Founded: 1952
Arts Area: Instrumental Music
Status: Non-Professional; Non-Profit
Type: Performing
Purpose: To provide chamber music concerts
Officers: Dr. Harold Rotman, President; Philip Walker, Vice President; Perien Gray, Secretary; J. H. Wynn, Treasurer

Volunteer Staff: 15
Utilizes: Guest Artists
Budget: $1,000 - $50,000
Income Sources: Private Foundations/Grants/Endowments; Box Office; Individual Donations
Season: October - March   **Annual Attendance:** 720
Affiliations: CMA

FACILITY

ASHEVILLE CIVIC CENTER
87 Haywood Street, Asheville, NC 28801
(704) 259-5736
    Type of Facility: Auditorium
    Type of Stage: Proscenium
    Stage Dimensions: 40'x70'; working stage - 32'x50'   **Orchestra Pit**
    Seating Capacity: 2,357
    Year Built: 1936
    Year Remodeled: 1974   **Architect:** Wood & Cort, PA   **Cost:** $125,000
    Contact for Rental: William J. Murphy;   (704) 259-5736

Banner Elk

FACILITY

LEES MCRAE COLLEGE - HAYES AUDITORIUM
Main Street, Banner Elk, NC 28604
(704) 898-8748
FAX: (704) 898-8711
    Type of Facility: Concert Hall; Auditorium
    Type of Stage: Thrust; Proscenium
    Seating Capacity: 815
    Year Built: 1973
    Contact for Rental: Roy D. Krege;   (704) 898-8748
    Resident Groups: Lees McRae College Summer Theatre Forum

Boone

PERFORMING SERIES

AN APPALACHIAN SUMMER
c/o Office of Cultural Affairs, ASU, 801 Rivers Street, Boone, NC 28608
(704) 262-6084
FAX: (704) 262-2848
    Arts Area: Dance; Vocal Music; Instrumental Music; Theater
    Status: Professional; Non-Profit
    Type: Performing; Touring; Resident; Educational; Sponsoring
    Purpose: To enrich the lives of people in northwestern North Carolina and the surrounding region through music, theater, dance and art
    Management: Gil Morgenstern, Artistic Director; H. Perry Mixter, Director of Cultural Affairs
    Officers: Arnold and Muriel Rosen, Broyhill Family Foundation, Martin and Doris Rosen, Contributors
    Budget: $100,000 - $500,000
    Income Sources: Private Foundations/Grants/Endowments; Business/Corporate Donations; Box Office; Government Grants; Individual Donations
    Season: 52 Weeks
    Performance Facilities: Farthing Auditorium

HORN IN THE WEST
PO Box 295, Boone, NC 28607
(704) 264-2120
    Founded: 1952
    Arts Area: Dance; Vocal Music; Theater; Festivals
    Status: Professional; Non-Profit
    Type: Performing; Educational
    Purpose: To relive the past, focusing mainly on the revolutionary war period and the early settlers' struggles with the Indians
    Management: Curtis Smalling, General Manager/ Museum Director; Sharon Fairweather, Public Relations
    Paid Staff: 80   **Volunteer Staff:** 12

Paid Artists: 50
Income Sources: Private Foundations/Grants/Endowments; Business/Corporate Donations; Box Office; Government Grants; Individual Donations
Season: June - August
Affiliations: Southern Appalachian Historical Association
Performance Facilities: Horn In The West

FACILITY

FARTHING AUDITORIUM
Rivers Street, ASU, Boone, NC 28608
(704) 262-6372
FAX: (704) 262-2848
    Founded: 1975
    Type of Facility: Auditorium
    Type of Stage: Proscenium
    Stage Dimensions: 56'x44' **Orchestra Pit**
    Seating Capacity: 1,800
    Year Built: 1975 **Architect:** Fred W. Butner and Associates **Cost:** $2,300,000
    Contact for Rental: Gregory Williams; (704) 262-6372

Brevard

FACILITY

BREVARD MUSIC CENTER - STRAUS AUDITORIUM
Probart Street, PO Box 592, Brevard, NC 28712
(704) 884-2011
FAX: (704) 884-2036
    Type of Facility: Concert Hall; Auditorium
    Facility Originally: Recreation Hall; Gymnasium
    Type of Stage: Proscenium
    Stage Dimensions: 25'Wx15'D
    Seating Capacity: 300
    Year Built: 1927
    Contact for Rental: Bill Boggs; (704) 884-2011

BREVARD MUSIC CENTER - WHITTINGTON-PFOHL AUDITORIUM
Probart Street, PO Box 592, Brevard, NC 28712
(704) 884-2011
FAX: (704) 884-2036
    Type of Facility: Concert Hall; Auditorium; Opera House
    Type of Stage: Proscenium
    Stage Dimensions: 50'Wx35'D **Orchestra Pit**
    Seating Capacity: 1,647
    Year Built: 1964 **Architect:** Six Associates **Cost:** $225,000
    Year Remodeled: 1983 **Architect:** Alfred F. Platt **Cost:** $220,000
    Contact for Rental: Bill Boggs; (704) 884-2011
    Resident Groups: Brevard Music Center Orchestra; Transylvania Symphony Orchestra; Transylvania Youth Orchestra; Wind Ensemble; Brevard Music Center Opera Workshop

Cameron

INSTRUMENTAL MUSIC

MOORE COMMUNITY BAND
Route 1, PO Box 98, Cameron, NC 28326
(919) 245-7267
    Founded: 1984
    Arts Area: Band
    Status: Non-Profit
    Type: Performing; Resident
    Purpose: Provide opportunity to play and perform good band literature; to support local civic and community programs
    Management: David Sieberling, Director
    Officers: Jay Phillips, President; Elouise Whitesell, Secretary; Dorothy Verney, Treasurer
    Volunteer Staff: 8
    Paid Artists: 6 **Non-Paid Artists:** 35

Utilizes: Guest Conductors; Guest Artists; Guest Directors
Budget: $1,000 - $50,000
Income Sources: Business/Corporate Donations; Box Office; Individual Donations
Season: 52 Weeks   **Annual Attendance:** 1,200
Affiliations: Sandhills Arts Council
Performance Facilities: Performing Arts Center

***

Camp Lejeune

FACILITY

CAMP THEATER
Building 19, Camp Lejeune, NC 28542
(919) 451-1759
FAX: (919) 451-1879
    Type of Facility: Theatre House
    Type of Stage: Proscenium
    Stage Dimensions: 45'x45'   **Orchestra Pit**
    Seating Capacity: 1,585
    Year Built: 1942   **Architect:** Carr & J.E. Greiner Company
    Contact for Rental: Ray Herbert

***

Carrboro

THEATRE

ARTSCENTER
300-G East Main Street, Carrboro, NC 27510
(919) 942-2041
    Founded: 1973
    Arts Area: Professional; Musical; Community; Theatrical Group
    Status: Professional; Non-Professional; Non-Profit
    Type: Performing; Touring; Resident; Educational; Sponsoring
    Purpose: To produce and present a balanced selection of community and professional performing arts groups, offering opportunities for participation in all aspects of theatre art; Visual arts gallery and art school are included
    Management: Mary H. Ruth, Operations Manager; Eileen Helton, General Manager
    Officers: Fred Good, Chairman; Hank Straus, Chairman-Elect; Tyler Vermylia, Secretary; Gina DeVine, Treasurer
    Paid Staff: 10   **Volunteer Staff:** 2
    Utilizes: Special Technical Talent; Guest Artists; Guest Directors
    Budget: $100,000 - $500,000
    Income Sources: Private Foundations/Grants/Endowments; Business/Corporate Donations; Box Office; Government Grants; Individual Donations
    Season: 52 Weeks   **Annual Attendance:** 15,000
    Performance Facilities: Earl Wynn Theatre

TOUCH
PO Box 631, Carrboro, NC 27510
(919) 968-1721
    Founded: 1976
    Arts Area: Professional; Theatrical Group
    Status: Professional; Non-Profit
    Type: Performing; Touring; Educational
    Purpose: Tour, perform original mime theatre for adults and children: "It's all right to laugh out loud."
    Management: Patricia Towne, Secretary
    Officers: Jef, President; Patricia Towne, Secretary; Laurie Wolf, Sheila Kerrigan, Jef, Co-Artistic Directors
    Paid Staff: 1
    Paid Artists: 6
    Utilizes: Special Technical Talent; Guest Artists; Guest Directors
    Budget: $100,000 - $500,000
    Income Sources: Private Foundations/Grants/Endowments; Business/Corporate Donations; Box Office; Government Grants; Individual Donations
    Season: September - May
    Affiliations: North Carolina Theatre Conference; SETC; ROOTS; NMTA

FACILITY

THE ARTSCENTER
300-G East Main Street, Carrboro, NC 27510
(919) 929-2787
>**Founded:** 1974
>**Type of Facility:** Theatre Complex; Concert Hall; Auditorium; Studio Performance; Performance Center; Theatre House; Multi-Purpose; Visual And Performing Arts Classrooms
>**Facility Originally:** Grocery Store
>**Type of Stage:** Greek; 3/4 Arena
>**Stage Dimensions:** 16'x24'
>**Seating Capacity:** 350
>**Year Built:** 1968
>**Year Remodeled:** 1986   **Architect:** Lucy Carol Davis Associates   **Cost:** $1,000,000
>**Contact for Rental:** Mary Ruth;   (919) 929-2787
>**Manager:** Eileen Helton;   (919) 929-2787
>**Resident Groups:** Transactors Improv Company; New Plays Rising; The Children's Tap Compnay
>*The facility is available for non-arts events only*

Chapel Hill

THEATRE

PLAYMAKERS REPERTORY COMPANY
Graham Memorial Building, CB# 3235, Chapel Hill, NC 27599
(919) 962-1122
FAX: (919) 962-4069
>**Founded:** 1976
>**Arts Area:** Professional; Theatrical Group
>**Status:** Professional
>**Type:** Performing; Educational
>**Purpose:** Provide professional training for promising actors who work with a LORT professional company
>**Management:** Milly S. Barranger, Executive Producer; David Hammond, Artistic Director; Mary Robin Wells, Administrative Director
>**Paid Staff:** 42   **Volunteer Staff:** 82
>**Paid Artists:** 35   **Non-Paid Artists:** 7
>**Utilizes:** Special Technical Talent; Guest Artists; Guest Directors
>**Budget:** $500,000 - $1,000,000
>**Income Sources:** Private Foundations/Grants/Endowments; Business/Corporate Donations; Box Office; Government Grants; Individual Donations
>**Season:** September - May   **Annual Attendance:** 50,000
>**Affiliations:** LORT; TCG
>**Performance Facilities:** Paul Green Theatre

PERFORMING SERIES

INSTITUTE OF OUTDOOR DRAMA
CB 32-40 Nations Bank Plaza, UNC, Chapel Hill, NC 27599-3240
(919) 962-1328
>**Founded:** 1963
>**Arts Area:** Theater; Outdoor
>**Status:** Non-Profit
>**Type:** Educational; Sponsoring
>**Purpose:** Research and advisory agency of University of North Carolina, sponsors regional auditions annually for performers and technicians in outdoor dramas; hosts management conference annually; conducts feasibility studies; assists established dramas
>**Management:** Scott J. Parker, Director
>**Paid Staff:** 5
>**Utilizes:** Special Technical Talent; Guest Artists
>**Budget:** $50,000 - $100,000
>**Income Sources:** Government Grants; Individual Donations; Fees

---
Charlotte

DANCE

CHARLOTTE CITY BALLET
8612 Monroe Road, Charlotte, NC 28212
(704) 536-0615
> **Founded:** 1986
> **Arts Area:** Ballet
> **Status:** Semi-Professional; Non-Profit
> **Type:** Performing; Resident
> **Purpose:** To give professionals and pre-professionals an outlet and bring the art of ballet to the community
> **Management:** Claudia Folts-Mercure, Artistic Director
> **Paid Artists:** 4   **Non-Paid Artists:** 16
> **Utilizes:** Guest Artists; Guest Choreographers
> **Budget:** $1,000 - $50,000
> **Income Sources:** Private Foundations/Grants/Endowments; Business/Corporate Donations; Box Office; Government Grants; Individual Donations
> **Season:** October - March
> **Affiliations:** Charlotte Ballet Association

NORTH CAROLINA DANCE THEATER
800 North College Street, Charlotte, NC 28202
(704) 372-0101
FAX: (704) 375-0260
> **Founded:** 1970
> **Arts Area:** Modern; Ballet
> **Status:** Professional; Non-Profit
> **Type:** Performing; Touring
> **Purpose:** To present the art of dance and dancers doing choreographers' work
> **Management:** Nyrna Saturn Gatty, Executive Director
> **Officers:** Guy A. Wilson, President; Elisabeth Hair, Vice President
> **Paid Staff:** 9
> **Paid Artists:** 16
> **Utilizes:** Guest Artists; Guest Choreographers
> **Budget:** $1,000,000 - $5,000,000
> **Income Sources:** Private Foundations/Grants/Endowments; Business/Corporate Donations; Box Office; Government Grants; Individual Donations
> **Season:** September - June   **Annual Attendance:** 70,000
> **Affiliations:** North Carolina School of the Arts
> **Performance Facilities:** North Carolina Blumenthal Performing Arts Center

INSTRUMENTAL MUSIC

CAROLINA PRO MUSICA
PO Box 32022, Charlotte, NC 28232
(704) 334-3468
> **Founded:** 1977
> **Arts Area:** Chamber; Ensemble; Choral
> **Status:** Professional; Non-Profit
> **Type:** Performing; Touring; Educational; Sponsoring
> **Purpose:** To perform music primarily written before 1800 in an historically-correct style, using period instruments
> **Management:** Karen Hite Jacob, Artistic Director; Edward Ferrell, Research; Susan Shoemaker, Technician
> **Paid Staff:** 3   **Volunteer Staff:** 10
> **Paid Artists:** 10
> **Utilizes:** Special Technical Talent; Guest Artists
> **Budget:** $1,000 - $50,000
> **Income Sources:** Private Foundations/Grants/Endowments; Business/Corporate Donations; Box Office; Individual Donations
> **Season:** October - March   **Annual Attendance:** 450
> **Affiliations:** Early Music America
> **Performance Facilities:** Historic 1892 Chapel

CHAMBER MUSIC OF CHARLOTTE
2114 Amboy Court, Charlotte, NC 28205
(704) 535-3024
> **Founded:** 1977
> **Arts Area:** Chamber

Status: Professional; Semi-Professional; Non-Profit
Type: Performing; Educational
Purpose: To encourage composition, performance and enjoyment of chamber music
Officers: Lisa Spring, President; Jeff Bernard, Vice President; Linda Whitener, Secretary; Linda Hess, Treasurer
Volunteer Staff: 5
Paid Artists: 60 **Non-Paid Artists:** 15
Budget: $1,000 - $50,000
Income Sources: Private Foundations/Grants/Endowments; Business/Corporate Donations; Box Office; Government Grants; Individual Donations
Season: 52 Weeks **Annual Attendance:** 17,000

CHARLOTTE SYMPHONY ORCHESTRA SOCIETY
1415 South Church Street, Suite S, Charlotte, NC 28203
(704) 332-6136
FAX: (704) 332-1963
Founded: 1932
Arts Area: Symphony; Orchestra; Chamber; Ensemble
Status: Professional; Non-Profit
Type: Performing; Touring; Resident; Educational
Purpose: To bring the rewards of great music to the citizens of Charlotte and the surrounding region by presenting a professional symphony orchestra and its ensembles in a full range of musical performances of artistic excellence
Management: Sally Meanor, Interim Executive Director; Leo B. Driehuys, Music Director
Officers: James Worrell, President; Fred Figge, Secretary/Treasurer
Paid Staff: 12 **Volunteer Staff:** 700
Paid Artists: 90
Utilizes: Guest Conductors; Guest Artists
Budget: $1,000,000 - $5,000,000
Income Sources: Private Foundations/Grants/Endowments; Business/Corporate Donations; Box Office; Government Grants; Individual Donations
Season: September - July **Annual Attendance:** 190,000
Affiliations: ASOL; Association of Symphony Orchestras of North Carolina; Arts Advocates of North Carolina
Performance Facilities: Ovens Auditorium; Dana Auditorium

VOCAL MUSIC

CHARLOTTE CHORAL SOCIETY
345 North College Street, #407, Charlotte, NC 28202
(704) 374-1564
Founded: 1953
Arts Area: Choral
Status: Non-Profit
Type: Performing
Purpose: To provide a wide range of quality productions to a varied audience
Management: Vince DeLap, Executive Director; Keri Blocker, Development Director; Lynda Shuler, Administrative Assistant
Officers: Thomas Schaumburg, Chairman; Pam Summey, President
Paid Staff: 7
Utilizes: Special Technical Talent; Guest Conductors; Guest Artists; Guest Directors
Budget: $100,000 - $500,000
Income Sources: Private Foundations/Grants/Endowments; Business/Corporate Donations; Box Office; Individual Donations
Season: 52 Weeks **Annual Attendance:** 30,000
Affiliations: Arts and Science Council
Performance Facilities: Ovens Auditorium; Spirit Square

OPERA CAROLINA
345 North College Street, Charlotte, NC 28202
(704) 332-7177
Founded: 1948
Arts Area: Grand Opera; Lyric Opera; Light Opera; Operetta
Status: Professional; Non-Profit
Type: Performing; Touring; Resident; Educational
Purpose: To provide the highest quality of professional opera, in season and touring form; to provide educational and community programs throughout the region; to encourage and develop talent
Management: James W. Wright, Chief Executive Officer
Officers: Woodrow E. Nail, Chairman
Paid Staff: 11 **Volunteer Staff:** 100
Paid Artists: 115 **Non-Paid Artists:** 20
Utilizes: Special Technical Talent; Guest Conductors; Guest Artists; Guest Directors

Budget: $1,000,000 - $5,000,000
Income Sources: Private Foundations/Grants/Endowments; Business/Corporate Donations; Box Office; Government Grants; Individual Donations
Season: October - May
Affiliations: OA; COS; NOA
Performance Facilities: Ovens Auditorium

ORATORIO SINGERS OF CHARLOTTE
345 North College Street, Suite 408, Charlotte, NC 28202
(704) 332-8151
FAX: (704) 332-3627
Founded: 1951
Arts Area: Choral
Status: Semi-Professional; Non-Profit
Type: Performing; Touring; Educational
Purpose: To provide choral training for church directors and provide excellent choral (classical) music for the Piedmont area
Management: Gregory A. Siberman, Executive Director
Officers: Kathryn C. Preyer, President; Carol F. Innes, Vice President; Sally Pierce Hall, President-Elect; Lynn Seals De-Jaco, Treasurer; Carolyn Wells Kibler, Secretary
Paid Staff: 2
Paid Artists: 3
Utilizes: Guest Artists
Budget: $100,000 - $500,000
Income Sources: Private Foundations/Grants/Endowments; Business/Corporate Donations; Box Office; Government Grants; Individual Donations
Season: September - May   **Annual Attendance:** 10,000
Affiliations: CA; Arts and Science Council
Performance Facilities: Calvary Church; Performing Arts Center

THEATRE

CENTRAL PIEDMONT COMMUNITY THEATRE
Kings Drive at Elizabeth Avenue, Charlotte, NC 28212
(704) 342-6568
FAX: (704) 342-5934
Founded: 1974
Arts Area: Musical; Theatrical Group
Status: Semi-Professional
Type: Performing; Educational
Purpose: To provide training to students entering professional theatre and provide quality community entertainment
Management: Tom Vance, Producer/Director; Tom Hollis, Director
Officers: Gene Bryant, Chairman
Paid Staff: 6
Paid Artists: 40   **Non-Paid Artists:** 40
Utilizes: Special Technical Talent; Guest Artists; Guest Directors
Budget: $100,000 - $500,000
Income Sources: Box Office
Season: June - August   **Annual Attendance:** 27,000
Affiliations: North Carolina Theatre Conference; SETC
Performance Facilities: Pease Auditorium

CHARLOTTE REPERTORY THEATRE
345 North College Street, Charlotte, NC 28202
(704) 375-4796
FAX: (704) 375-9462
Founded: 1976
Arts Area: Professional; Theatrical Group
Status: Professional; Non-Profit
Type: Performing; Resident
Purpose: To present contemporary plays, to develop and present new works, and revive the classics of modern drama
Management: Keith T. Martin, Managing Director
Officers: Muriel W. Helms, President; Buddy LeTourneau, President-Elect; Tate K. Sterrett, Secretary; Rick Fujita, Treasurer
Paid Staff: 8   **Volunteer Staff:** 2
Paid Artists: 86
Utilizes: Special Technical Talent; Guest Artists; Guest Directors
Budget: $500,000 - $1,000,000

Income Sources: Private Foundations/Grants/Endowments; Business/Corporate Donations; Box Office; Government Grants; Individual Donations
Season: September - June   **Annual Attendance:** 32,500
Affiliations: AEA
Performance Facilities: Spirit Square Center for the arts; North Carolina Blumenthal Performing Arts Center; Jewish Community Center

THEATRE CHARLOTTE
501 Queens Road, Charlotte, NC 28207
(704) 376-3777; (704) 334-9128
FAX: (704) 347-5216
   Founded: 1927
   Arts Area: Community; Theatrical Group
   Status: Non-Profit
   Type: Performing; Educational
   Purpose: To provide an opportunity to community members to attend or participate in an avocational theatre experience
   Management: Denise Malloy Hubbard, Executive Director
   Officers: Terry Shook, President
   Paid Staff: 4
   Utilizes: Special Technical Talent; Guest Directors
   Budget: $100,000 - $500,000
   Income Sources: Private Foundations/Grants/Endowments; Business/Corporate Donations; Box Office; Individual Donations
   Season: 52 Weeks   **Annual Attendance:** 12,465
   Affiliations: Auxiliary and First Nighters

FACILITY

CENTRAL PIEDMONT COMMUNITY COLLEGE - SUMMER THEATRE
Box 35009, Charlotte, NC 28235
(704) 342-6568
   Type of Facility: Theatre Complex; Auditorium
   Type of Stage: Proscenium
   Stage Dimensions: 40'Wx29'D   **Orchestra Pit**
   Seating Capacity: 439
   Year Built: 1969   **Architect:** J.N. Pease   **Cost:** $1,500,000
   Contact for Rental: Central Piedmont Community College;   (704) 342-6950
   Resident Groups: Central Piedmont Community College Theatre; Central Piedmont Community College Summer Theatre

NORTH CAROLINA BLUMENTHAL PERFORMING ARTS CENTER
130 North Tryon Street, Charlotte, NC 28202
(704) 333-4686
FAX: (704) 376-2289
   Founded: 1992
   Type of Facility: Theatre Complex; Performance Center
   Type of Stage: Proscenium
   Stage Dimensions: Belk Theatre - 55'x54'; Booth Playhouse - 40'x37'
   Orchestra Pit
   Seating Capacity: Belk - 2,100; Booth - 440
   Year Built: 1992   **Architect:** Cesar Pelli & Associates
   Contact for Rental: Drew Murphy;   (704) 333-4686
   Resident Groups: Charlotte Symphony; Opera Carolina; Community Concerts; North Carolina Dance Theater; Charlotte Repertory Theater; Charollotte Choral Society; Oratorio Singers of Charlotte

OVENS AUDITORIUM
2700 East Independence Boulevard, Charlotte, NC 28205
(704) 372-3600
FAX: (704) 372-3620
   Type of Facility: Auditorium
   Type of Stage: Proscenium
   Stage Dimensions: 100'Wx50'D   **Orchestra Pit**
   Seating Capacity: 2,603
   Acoustical Consultant: Carey Heintz
   Contact for Rental: Hubert J. McLendon;   (704) 372-3600

SPIRIT SQUARE CENTER FOR THE ARTS
345 North College Street, Charlotte, NC 28202
(704) 372-9664
FAX: (704) 377-9808
>**Founded:** 1976
>**Type of Facility:** Concert Hall; Studio Performance; Theatre House; Multi-Purpose; Visual Art Galleries; Studio Spaces
>**Facility Originally:** Church; Education Building; Print Shop
>**Type of Stage:** Thrust; Proscenium
>**Seating Capacity:** Hall 1 - 692; Hall 2 - 180; Hall 3 - 110 (Flexible)
>**Year Built:** 1909 **Architect:** J.M. McMichael
>**Year Remodeled:** 1989 **Architect:** Middleton-McMillan **Cost:** $6,500,000
>**Contact for Rental:** Lesa Delahunty; (704) 372-9664
>**Resident Groups:** Charlotte Repertory Theatre; Opera Carolina; Oratorio Singers Choral Society

---

Cullowhee

INSTRUMENTAL MUSIC

SMOKY MOUNTAIN BRITISH BRASS
PO Box 2438, Cullowhee, NC 28723
(704) 293-9312
>**Founded:** 1981
>**Arts Area:** Chamber; Band
>**Status:** Semi-Professional
>**Type:** Performing; Touring; Educational
>**Purpose:** To perform quality brass band music of all eras and artists
>**Management:** Bert Wiley, General Manager
>**Paid Staff:** 2 **Volunteer Staff:** 28
>**Utilizes:** Guest Conductors
>**Budget:** $1,000 - $50,000
>**Income Sources:** Private Foundations/Grants/Endowments; Business/Corporate Donations; Box Office; Government Grants; Individual Donations
>**Season:** 52 Weeks **Annual Attendance:** 15,000

Durham

DANCE

THE AFRICAN-AMERICAN DANCE ENSEMBLE
804 Berkeley Street, Durham, NC 27701
(919) 560-2720
>**Founded:** 1983
>**Arts Area:** Ethnic
>**Status:** Semi-Professional; Non-Profit
>**Type:** Performing; Touring; Resident; Educational
>**Purpose:** The African-American Dance Ensemble is dedicated to sharing and preserving the finest dance and music of the African and Afro-American tradition as a cultural resource for all people.
>**Management:** Pamela D. Martin, Company Manager; Chuck Davis, Artistic Director; Khalid Saleem, Musical Director
>**Officers:** Joseph T. Hughes Jr., Board Chairman
>**Paid Staff:** 1 **Volunteer Staff:** 10
>**Paid Artists:** 18
>**Utilizes:** Special Technical Talent; Guest Artists
>**Budget:** $100,000 - $500,000
>**Income Sources:** Private Foundations/Grants/Endowments
>**Season:** 52 Weeks
>**Affiliations:** American Dance Festival

AMERICAN DANCE FESTIVAL
PO Box 6097, College Station, Durham, NC 27708
(919) 684-6402
FAX: (919) 684-5459
>**Founded:** 1934
>**Arts Area:** Modern
>**Status:** Professional; Non-Profit
>**Type:** Educational; Sponsoring

Purpose: To encourage and support the creation of our dance heritage by established and emerging choreographers; to provide a sound scientific/aesthetic professional education; to assist in the enlargement of a national and international American modern dance audience

Management: Charles Reinhart, Director; Stephanie Reinhart, Associate Director; Art Waber, Operations Manager
Officers: Carlton Midytte, Chairperson; Judith Sagan, Secretary
Paid Staff: 75 **Volunteer Staff:** 350
Paid Artists: 150
Utilizes: Guest Artists
Budget: $1,000,000 - $5,000,000
Income Sources: Private Foundations/Grants/Endowments; Business/Corporate Donations; Box Office; Government Grants; Individual Donations
Season: June - July **Annual Attendance:** 25,000
Affiliations: Duke University
Performance Facilities: Page Auditorium; Reynolds Industries Theatre

NEW PERFORMING DANCE COMPANY
120 Morris Street, Durham, NC 27701
(919) 560-2732
> **Founded:** 1975
> **Arts Area:** Modern
> **Status:** Professional; Non-Profit
> **Type:** Performing; Touring
> **Purpose:** To promote the art form of modern dance by regular production and performance of original choreography
> **Management:** Linda Stier, Administrative Director; Lee Wenger, Artistic Director
> **Officers:** Mary Ellen Taylor, President Board of Directors
> **Paid Staff:** 6 **Volunteer Staff:** 1
> **Paid Artists:** 5 **Non-Paid Artists:** 1
> **Utilizes:** Special Technical Talent
> **Budget:** $1,000 - $50,000
> **Income Sources:** Box Office; Government Grants; Individual Donations
> **Season:** September - June **Annual Attendance:** 2,000
> **Affiliations:** Durham Arts Council

INSTRUMENTAL MUSIC

CHAMBER ARTS SOCIETY
PO Box 22146, Duke Station, Durham, NC 27706
(919) 684-5578
FAX: (919) 684-3200
> **Founded:** 1945
> **Arts Area:** Chamber
> **Status:** Non-Profit
> **Type:** Sponsoring
> **Purpose:** To provide five or six chamber music concerts a year of the highest possible quality, with an emphasis on string quartet
> **Management:** Ruth M. Blum, Director; Susan Coon, Ex Officio, Director of Office of Cultural Affairs
> **Paid Staff:** 3 **Volunteer Staff:** 8
> **Paid Artists:** 20
> **Utilizes:** Guest Artists
> **Budget:** $1,000 - $50,000
> **Income Sources:** Private Foundations/Grants/Endowments; Box Office; Individual Donations
> **Season:** September - April
> **Affiliations:** Duke University, Office of Cultural Affairs
> **Performance Facilities:** Bryan Center

VOCAL MUSIC

DURHAM CIVIC CHORAL SOCIETY
120 Morris Street, Durham, NC 27701
(919) 560-2733
> **Arts Area:** Choral
> **Status:** Non-Professional; Non-Profit
> **Type:** Performing
> **Management:** Susan L. Van Wyck, Membership Chair
> **Officers:** Judy Via, President; Ken Hoover, Vice President; Kate Goldstucker, Secretary; Mary Ann Dotson, Treasurer; Barbara NamKoong, Librarian; Joan Wall, Historian
> **Paid Staff:** 1
> **Paid Artists:** 2 **Non-Paid Artists:** 154
> **Utilizes:** Guest Artists

Budget: $50,000 - $100,000
Income Sources: Private Foundations/Grants/Endowments; Business/Corporate Donations; Box Office; Individual Donations
Season: September - May   **Annual Attendance:** 2,100
Performance Facilities: Duke University Chapel; Baldwin Auditorium, Duke University

TRIANGLE OPERA THEATER
120 Morris Street, Durham, NC 27701
(919) 560-2741
FAX: (919) 560-2704
Founded: 1985
Arts Area: Grand Opera; Lyric Opera; Light Opera
Status: Non-Profit
Type: Performing
Purpose: To present and perform opera in the Raleigh-Durham-Chapel Hill area
Management: Sara Elizabeth J. Hyre, Manager; Scott Tilley, Music Director
Officers: Kenneth Susiska, Chair; Wes Neuman, Vice Chair; Sara Armentrout, Secretary; Steven Largent, Treasurer
Paid Staff: 2   **Volunteer Staff:** 20
Paid Artists: 75   **Non-Paid Artists:** 20
Utilizes: Special Technical Talent; Guest Artists
Budget: $100,000 - $500,000
Income Sources: Private Foundations/Grants/Endowments; Business/Corporate Donations; Box Office; Individual Donations
Season: October - June   **Annual Attendance:** 7,500
Affiliations: OA
Performance Facilities: Pace Auditorium/Duke University; Brighthead Square

Eden

THEATRE

CHILDREN'S THEATRE OF EDEN
PO Box 547, Eden, NC 27288
(919) 342-2536
Founded: 1971
Arts Area: Professional; Musical; Folk; Theatrical Group; Puppet
Status: Non-Profit
Type: Sponsoring
Purpose: Provide professional plays to all Eden city school children free of charge
Officers: Susan Pace, President; Clayton Nations, Treasurer
Volunteer Staff: 15
Paid Artists: 35
Budget: $1,000 - $50,000
Income Sources: Private Foundations/Grants/Endowments; Business/Corporate Donations
Season: September - May   **Annual Attendance:** 2,500
Performance Facilities: High School Auditorium

Elkin

INSTRUMENTAL MUSIC

ELKIN BIG BAND
116 East Main Street, Elkin, NC 28621
(919) 835-2621
Founded: 1982
Arts Area: Band
Status: Non-Profit
Type: Performing
Purpose: To present the big band sounds for both public and private functions
Management: Larry Irwin, Organizer/Leader
Volunteer Staff: 16
Income Sources: Private Foundations/Grants/Endowments

Season: 52 Weeks   **Annual Attendance:** 700
Affiliations: Foot Hills Arts Council

Fayetteville

INSTRUMENTAL MUSIC

CUMBERLAND COUNTY FRIENDS OF THE ORCHESTRA
1624 Ireland Drive, Fayetteville, NC 28304
(919) 484-8121
Founded: 1980
Arts Area: Orchestra
Status: Non-Profit
Type: Educational; Sponsoring
Purpose: To maintain a community support group for the Cumberland County School Orchestra Program, lending volunteer hours and financial aid where needed to maintain excellence in the program
Management: Janice Swoope, Orchestra Coordinator
Officers: Mrs. David J. Phleeger, President; Rita Warren, Secretary; Lynn Gloyeski, Treasurer
Utilizes: Guest Artists; Guest Directors
Budget: $1,000 - $50,000
Income Sources: Private Foundations/Grants/Endowments; Business/Corporate Donations; Individual Donations
Season: 52 Weeks   **Annual Attendance:** 5,000

HIGHLAND BRITISH BRASS BAND ASSOCIATION
2405 Morganton Road, Fayetteville, NC 28303
(919) 484-0281
Founded: 1980
Arts Area: Band
Status: Semi-Professional; Non-Profit
Type: Performing
Purpose: To provide a suitable outlet for musically talented adults who are interested in promoting good band music in the British Brass Band format for the instruction and edification of the general public
Officers: Robert Downing, Chairman, Board of Directors
Utilizes: Guest Conductors; Guest Artists
Budget: $1,000 - $50,000
Income Sources: Private Foundations/Grants/Endowments; Business/Corporate Donations; Box Office; Government Grants; Individual Donations
Season: 52 Weeks
Affiliations: Arts Council of Fayetteville and Cumberland County
Performance Facilities: Methodist College

THEATRE

CAPE FEAR REGIONAL THEATRE
1209 Hay Street, Fayetteville, NC 28305
(919) 323-4234
FAX: (919) 323-0898
Founded: 1962
Arts Area: Professional; Musical; Community; Puppet; Drama
Status: Semi-Professional; Non-Profit
Type: Performing
Purpose: To present a regional theatre program that incorporates a diverse selection of plays which will appeal to a wide selection of potential theatre-goers in the Cape Fear Region
Management: Bo Thorp, Artistic Director; Deborah Martin-Mintz, Associate Director
Officers: Steven Tussey, President of the Board; Bill Bowman, Vice President; Gina Keel, Secretary; Charlie Johnson, Treasurer
Paid Staff: 9   **Volunteer Staff:** 100
Paid Artists: 1
Utilizes: Special Technical Talent; Guest Conductors; Guest Artists; Guest Directors; Choreographers; Designers
Budget: $100,000 - $500,000
Income Sources: Private Foundations/Grants/Endowments; Business/Corporate Donations; Box Office; Government Grants; Individual Donations
Season: September - June   **Annual Attendance:** 1,156,500
Affiliations: North Carolina Theatre Conference; SETC; Arts Council

FACILITY

CUMBERLAND COUNTY CIVIC CENTER
Highway 301 South, Fayetteville, NC 28306
(919) 323-5088
FAX: (919) 323-2742
Type of Facility: Theatre Complex; Auditorium; Arena; Multi-Purpose
Type of Stage: Flexible; Proscenium; Platform
Stage Dimensions: 64'x40'
Orchestra Pit
Seating Capacity: Arena - 6,300; Auditorium - 2,439
Contact for Rental: Kendall Wall, Danny Lucas; (919) 323-5088
Manager: Wilson Roger

Flat Rock

THEATRE

FLAT ROCK PLAYHOUSE
Thomas Wolfe Drive, Flat Rock, NC 28731
(704) 693-0731
FAX: (704) 693-6795
Founded: 1937
Arts Area: Professional; Summer Stock; Musical; Theatrical Group
Status: Professional; Non-Profit; Commercial
Type: Performing; Touring; Resident; Educational; Sponsoring
Purpose: To present a 16-week summer stock season in conjunction with The Vagabond School of Drama Workshops; to tour North Carolina schools throughout the year
Management: Robin R. Farquhar, Executive/Artistic Director
Officers: Albert Gooch, President of Board of Trustees
Paid Staff: 60   **Volunteer Staff:** 4
Paid Artists: 25   **Non-Paid Artists:** 20
Utilizes: Special Technical Talent; Guest Artists; Guest Directors
Budget: $500,000 - $1,000,000
Income Sources: Private Foundations/Grants/Endowments; Business/Corporate Donations; Box Office; Government Grants; Individual Donations
Season: May - September   **Annual Attendance:** 60,000
Affiliations: AEA; SETC
Performance Facilities: Flat Rock Playhouse

Gastonia

THEATRE

LITTLE THEATRE OF GASTONIA
238 South Clay Street, Gastonia, NC 28052
(704) 865-0160
Founded: 1950
Arts Area: Musical; Community
Status: Non-Professional; Non-Profit
Type: Performing; Educational
Purpose: To provide entertainment and instruction in theatre arts and sciences
Management: Carolyn E. Sanders, Administrator
Officers: Locke Bell, President; Sherry Abernathy, Vice President; Eleanor Wixson, Secretary; Betty C. Blume, Treasurer
Paid Staff: 1   **Volunteer Staff:** 20
Non-Paid Artists: 50
Utilizes: Special Technical Talent
Budget: $50,000 - $100,000
Income Sources: Private Foundations/Grants/Endowments; Business/Corporate Donations; Box Office; Government Grants; Individual Donations
Season: September - July   **Annual Attendance:** 9,000
Affiliations: United Arts & Science Council of Gastonia; North Carolina Theatre Conference; SETC
Performance Facilities: The Little Theatre of Gastonia

Greensboro

DANCE

JOHN GAMBLE/JAN VAN DYKE DANCE COMPANY
306 Aberdeen Terrace, Greensboro, NC 27403
(919) 370-4819
Founded: 1989
Arts Area: Modern
Status: Professional; Non-Profit
Type: Performing; Touring
Management: Darlene Errett, Administrative Assistant
Officers: John Gamble, Jan Van Dyke, Artistic Directors
Paid Staff: 1 **Volunteer Staff:** 2
Paid Artists: 12
Budget: $1,000 - $50,000
Income Sources: Private Foundations/Grants/Endowments; Box Office; Government Grants; Individual Donations
Season: 52 Weeks **Annual Attendance:** 2,500
Affiliations: University of North Carolina-Greensboro
Performance Facilities: University of North Carolina-Greensboro Dance Theatre

INSTRUMENTAL MUSIC

BEL CANTO COMPANY
PO Box 10752, Greensboro, NC 27404
Founded: 1983
Arts Area: Ensemble
Status: Semi-Professional
Type: Performing
Purpose: Dedicated to the highest performance standards of choral literature of all historical periods
Management: David Pegg, Music Director/Conductor
Officers: Alice Isaacson, Chairman; Sarah Warmath, Vice Chairman; Linda Shaban, Secretary; Lauren Search, Treasurer
Paid Staff: 2 **Volunteer Staff:** 18
Paid Artists: 2 **Non-Paid Artists:** 18
Utilizes: Special Technical Talent; Guest Artists
Budget: $1,000 - $50,000
Income Sources: Private Foundations/Grants/Endowments; Business/Corporate Donations; Box Office; Individual Donations
Season: September - May
Annual Attendance: 1,200
Affiliations: Greensboro Parks and Recreation
Performance Facilities: Dana Auditorium

GREENSBORO CONCERT BAND
200 North Davie Street, Greensboro, NC 27401
(919) 373-2549
FAX: (919) 373-2060
Founded: 1977
Arts Area: Band
Status: Non-Professional
Type: Performing
Purpose: To share musical understanding through serious practice and the real enthusiasm, pleasure, and sense of accomplishment in public performance
Management: Lynn H. Donovan, Executive Director; Charles Murph, Conductor
Officers: Stuart Fitzpatrick, President; Gary Anderson, Vice President; Ninette Humbler, Recording Secretary; Shirley Vann, Correspondence Secretary; John Morck, Treasurer; Linda Deese, Librarian
Paid Staff: 2 **Volunteer Staff:** 20
Paid Artists: 2 **Non-Paid Artists:** 75
Utilizes: Guest Conductors; Guest Artists
Budget: $1,000 - $50,000
Income Sources: Private Foundations/Grants/Endowments; Business/Corporate Donations; Box Office; Individual Donations
Season: September - July
Annual Attendance: 6,500

Affiliations: City of Greensboro; The Music Center
Performance Facilities: Dana Auditorium

GREENSBORO SYMPHONY ORCHESTRA
200 North Davie Street, PO Box 20303, Greensboro, NC 27420
(919) 333-7490
Founded: 1977
Arts Area: Orchestra
Status: Professional
Type: Performing
Purpose: To strive seriously for the highest quality of performance, with the ultimate goal of attaining a truly professional sound, the love of playing orchestral literature remaining the prime factor for participation
Management: Barry Auman, Music Director
Officers: Robert Lavietas, President; Erik Salzwedel, Librarian
Utilizes: Guest Conductors; Guest Artists
Budget: $500,000 - $1,000,000
Income Sources: Private Foundations/Grants/Endowments; Business/Corporate Donations; Box Office; Government Grants; Individual Donations
Season: September - May
Annual Attendance: 2,900
Affiliations: City of Greensboro
Performance Facilities: War Memorial Auditorium

VOCAL MUSIC

CHORAL SOCIETY OF GREENSBORO
200 North Davie Street, Greensboro, NC 27401
(919) 373-2549
FAX: (919) 373-2060
Founded: 1984
Arts Area: Choral
Status: Non-Professional
Type: Performing
Purpose: To share musical understanding through serious practice and the real pleasure, enthusiasm, sense of accomplishment and quality musicianship in public performance
Management: William Carroll, Conductor; Lynn H. Donovan, Executive Director
Officers: Peggy Clapper, President; Tom Wright, Vice President; Jennifer Blevins, Recording Secretary; Kathy Riffe, Correspondence Secretary; Lucy Amaxopulus, Treasurer; Sandra Schaller, Librarian
Paid Staff: 2 **Volunteer Staff:** 25
Paid Artists: 2 **Non-Paid Artists:** 200
Utilizes: Guest Conductors; Guest Artists
Budget: $1,000 - $50,000
Income Sources: Private Foundations/Grants/Endowments; Business/Corporate Donations; Box Office; Individual Donations
Season: September - May
Annual Attendance: 6,500
Affiliations: City of Greensboro; The Music Center
Performance Facilities: Dana Auditorium

GREENSBORO OPERA COMPANY
1828 Banking Street, Greensboro, NC 27408
(919) 273-9472
Founded: 1981
Arts Area: Grand Opera
Status: Professional; Non-Profit
Type: Performing; Educational; Sponsoring
Purpose: To serve and enrich the cultural life of Greensboro and the surrounding area through the development and promotion of a program of quality operas and opera education
Management: Mary C. Eubanks, Administrator
Officers: Ann Snyder, President
Paid Staff: 1 **Volunteer Staff:** 50
Utilizes: Special Technical Talent; Guest Artists
Budget: $100,000 - $500,000
Income Sources: Private Foundations/Grants/Endowments; Business/Corporate Donations; Box Office; Individual Donations
Season: November
Annual Attendance: 4,500
Affiliations: OA; COS
Performance Facilities: War Memorial Auditorium; Carolina Theatre

THEATRE

COMMUNITY THEATRE OF GREENSBORO
200 North Davie Street, Greensboro, NC 27401
(919) 333-7470; (919) 333-7445
   Arts Area: Musical; Dinner; Community; Theatrical Group
   Status: Non-Professional; Non-Profit
   Type: Performing; Resident; Educational
   Purpose: To provide an outlet in the community whereby persons may participate avocationally in a live theatrical experience of high calibre, both as talent and audience under professional guidance
   Management: Mitchel Sommers, Executive Director; Pauline Cobrda, Business Manager; Darleen Callaghan, Administrative Assistant
   Officers: Pamela Murphy, President Board of Trustees; Doug Anderson, Vice President; Stephen Wilkowski, Secretary; Dennis Duquette, Treasurer
   Paid Staff: 3   **Volunteer Staff:** 10
   Paid Artists: 50   **Non-Paid Artists:** 200
   Utilizes: Special Technical Talent; Guest Artists; Guest Directors
   Budget: $100,000 - $500,000
   Income Sources: Private Foundations/Grants/Endowments; Business/Corporate Donations; Box Office; Government Grants; Individual Donations
   Season: October - June   **Annual Attendance:** 15,000
   Affiliations: United Arts Council of Greensboro; SETC; North Carolina State Arts Council
   Performance Facilities: Carolina Theatre; Town Hall; Coliseum; Weaver Education Center

GREENSBORO CHILDREN'S THEATRE
200 North Davie Street, Greensboro, NC 27401
(919) 373-2026
   Founded: 1971
   Arts Area: Musical; Community; Theatrical Group
   Status: Non-Professional; Non-Profit
   Type: Performing
   Purpose: To perform three shows throughout the year by and for children
   Management: Barbara Britton, Director
   Paid Staff: 3   **Volunteer Staff:** 20
   Non-Paid Artists: 100
   Utilizes: Guest Directors
   Budget: $1,000 - $50,000
   Income Sources: Box Office; Government Grants; Individual Donations
   Season: November - May   **Annual Attendance:** 3,000
   Affiliations: SETC
   Performance Facilities: Town Hall; Greensboro Coliseum Complex

LIVESTOCK PLAYERS MUSICAL THEATRE
200 North Davie Street, Greensboro, NC 27401
(919) 373-2026
   Founded: 1971
   Arts Area: Musical; Dinner; Community; Theatrical Group
   Status: Non-Professional; Non-Profit
   Type: Performing
   Purpose: To perform six musicals throughout the year
   Management: Barbara Britton, Director
   Paid Staff: 10
   Non-Paid Artists: 200
   Utilizes: Guest Conductors; Guest Directors
   Budget: $1,000 - $50,000
   Income Sources: Box Office; Government Grants; Individual Donations
   Season: 52 Weeks   **Annual Attendance:** 10,000
   Affiliations: SETC
   Performance Facilities: Carolina Theatre

PERFORMING SERIES

EASTERN MUSIC FESTIVAL
200 North Davie Street, Greensboro, NC 27401
(919) 333-7450
FAX: (919) 333-7454
   Founded: 1961
   Arts Area: Symphony; Orchestra; Chamber

Status: Professional; Non-Profit
Type: Performing; Educational
Purpose: To provide six weeks of intensive music study to 200 gifted young musicians from the U.S. and abroad; to provide a high-level music series for the southeast region
Management: Walter W. Heid, Executive Director; Sheldon Morgenstern, Music Director; Juanita Lawson-Haith, Development/Marketing; Dianne Lyle, Business Manager; Janis Nilsen, Admissions Director; Renee Ward, Artistic Administrator
Officers: Dr. Gerald Truesdale, President; William Bearding, James Bethel, Pamela Allen, Thorns Craven and Sue Starr, Vice Presidents; Nancye Tothill, Secretary; Kenneth Dimmock, Treasurer; Howard Covington, Past President
Paid Staff: 10 **Volunteer Staff:** 120
Paid Artists: 100
Utilizes: Guest Conductors; Guest Artists
Budget: $1,000,000 - $5,000,000
Income Sources: Private Foundations/Grants/Endowments; Business/Corporate Donations; Box Office; Government Grants; Individual Donations; Tuition
Season: June - August **Annual Attendance:** 60,000
Affiliations: BMI; ASCAP

FACILITY

AYCOCK AUDITORIUM
University of North Carolina at Greensboro, Greensboro, NC 27412
(919) 334-5800
FAX: (919) 334-3008
   Type of Facility: Auditorium
   Type of Stage: Proscenium
   Orchestra Pit
   Seating Capacity: 2,300

THE CAROLINA THEATRE
310 South Greene Street, Greensboro, NC 27401
(919) 333-2605; (919) 333-2600
   Type of Facility: Concert Hall; Auditorium; Performance Center; Theatre House
   Facility Originally: Vaudeville
   Type of Stage: Flexible; Proscenium
   Stage Dimensions: 30'x40'x35'
   Orchestra Pit
   Seating Capacity: 1,139
   Year Built: 1927 **Architect:** J.H. DeSibour **Cost:** $500,000
   Year Remodeled: 1981 **Architect:** Ken Bell **Cost:** $200,000
   Contact for Rental: Brian Gray; (919) 333-2600
   Manager: Kathy Worrell
   Resident Groups: Livestock Players Musical Theatre; Community Theatre of Greensboro; Greensboro Civic Ballet; Greensboro Symphony Orchestra

GREENSBORO WAR MEMORIAL AUDITORIUM
1921 West Lee Street, Greensboro, NC 27403
(919) 373-7400
   Type of Facility: Auditorium
   Type of Stage: Proscenium
   Stage Dimensions: 95'Wx46'D
   Orchestra Pit
   Seating Capacity: 2,414
   Year Built: 1959
   Architect: McMinn, Norfleet & Wicker
   Cost: $3,000,000
   Contact for Rental: Andrea Turner; (919) 373-7400
   Manager: James Evans; (918) 373-7400

Greenville

INSTRUMENTAL MUSIC

SUMMER STRINGS ON THE MEHERRIN
303 South Elm Street, Greenville, NC 27858
(919) 752-2542
   Founded: 1972

Arts Area: Chamber; Ensemble
Status: Non-Profit
Type: Performing; Resident; Educational
Purpose: Summer Strings On The Meherrin offers a three-week program for 12 to 18-year-old bowed string players to improve their musicianship and techniques and to present chamber music concerts
Management: Paul Topper, Musical Director; James Chamblee, Chowan College Officer
Officers: John R. Kernodle Jr., President; Thaddeus A. Adams III, Howard E. Covington Jr., Robert C. Ketner, Rollin J. McCrory; Angela Seawell, Secretary
Paid Staff: 4
Paid Artists: 4
Utilizes: Guest Artists
Budget: $1,000 - $50,000
Income Sources: Private Foundations/Grants/Endowments; Tuition
Season: July - August   **Annual Attendance:** 500
Affiliations: Chowan College
Performance Facilities: Daniels Hall, Chowan College

FACILITY

HENDRIX THEATRE
c/o Mendenhall Student Center, Greenville, NC 27858-4353
(919) 757-4702
FAX: (919) 757-4778
Founded: 1973
Type of Facility: Concert Hall; Auditorium; Performance Center; Theatre House
Type of Stage: Proscenium
Stage Dimensions: 22'Dx50'W
Seating Capacity: 760
Year Built: 1974   **Architect:** Carter Williams
Contact for Rental: Central Reservations Office;   (919) 757-4731

WRIGHT AUDITORIUM
East Carolina University, Campus Circle, Greenville, NC 27858-4353
(919) 757-6269; (919) 757-6290
FAX: (919) 757-4778
Founded: 1927
Type of Facility: Concert Hall; Auditorium; Performance Center; Theatre House
Type of Stage: Proscenium
Stage Dimensions: 70'x18' apron; 40'Wx25'D stage   **Orchestra Pit**
Seating Capacity: 1,510
Year Remodeled: 1986   **Architect:** J.N. Pease   **Cost:** $4,000,000
Acoustical Consultant: Rein Pirn
Contact for Rental: Central Reservations Office;   (919) 757-4731

Hickory

THEATRE

HICKORY COMMUNITY THEATRE
30 Third Street, NW, Hickory, NC 28601
(704) 327-3855
Founded: 1949
Arts Area: Musical; Community; Dramatic
Status: Non-Professional; Non-Profit
Type: Performing; Touring; Resident; Educational
Purpose: To provide quality theatre performances for the benefit of the community and for the involvement of local talent
Management: Pamela Sinclair, Executive Director; Dana Biehler, Executive Secretary; Aaron Lewis, Technical Director; John Coffey, Musical Director; Charles E. Jeffers, Artistic Director
Officers: Vivienne Stafford, President; Allen Finley, Vice President; Rae Hunsucker, Secretary; G. Rudy Wright, Treasurer
Paid Staff: 4   **Volunteer Staff:** 650
Non-Paid Artists: 250
Utilizes: Special Technical Talent; Guest Artists; Guest Directors
Budget: $100,000 - $500,000
Income Sources: Private Foundations/Grants/Endowments; Business/Corporate Donations; Box Office; Government Grants; Individual Donations
Season: September - July   **Annual Attendance:** 16,000
Affiliations: Catawba County Council for the Arts; North Carolina Theatre Conference; SETC
Performance Facilities: Old City Hall

YOUTHEATRE
810 8th Street NE, Hickory, NC 28601
(704) 327-8081
> **Founded:** 1976
> **Arts Area:** Community; Theatrical Group
> **Status:** Professional; Semi-Professional; Commercial
> **Type:** Performing; Touring; Educational; Sponsoring
> **Purpose:** To provide a forum for young people's creative expression through study and performance
> **Management:** Sylvia B. Hoffmire, Owner/Executive Director
> **Paid Staff:** 3
> **Utilizes:** Special Technical Talent; Guest Artists; Guest Directors
> **Budget:** $1,000 - $50,000
> **Income Sources:** Private Foundations/Grants/Endowments; Business/Corporate Donations; Box Office; Government Grants
> **Season:** September - May
> **Affiliations:** Catawba County Council for the Arts

High Point

THEATRE

HIGH POINT COMMUNITY THEATRE
305 North Main Street, Suite 205, High Point, NC 27260
(919) 882-2542
FAX: (919) 889-2298
> **Founded:** 1976
> **Arts Area:** Community; Theatrical Group
> **Status:** Non-Professional; Non-Profit
> **Type:** Performing
> **Purpose:** To foster community involvement in the performing arts and provide quality entertainment to the citizens of our area
> **Management:** Jennifer Blevins, Executive Director
> **Officers:** Elizabeth Koonce, President; Katherine Grigg, Vice President; Carol Traen, Secretary; Sharon Janesick, Treasurer
> **Paid Staff:** 9   **Volunteer Staff:** 100
> **Non-Paid Artists:** 100
> **Utilizes:** Special Technical Talent; Guest Conductors; Guest Directors
> **Budget:** $50,000 - $100,000
> **Income Sources:** Private Foundations/Grants/Endowments; Business/Corporate Donations; Box Office; Individual Donations
> **Season:** September - May   **Annual Attendance:** 5,000
> **Affiliations:** High Point Arts Council
> **Performance Facilities:** High Point Theatre and Exhibition Center

PERFORMING SERIES

HIGH POINT THEATRE AND EXHIBITION CENTER
220 East Commerce Street, High Point, NC 27260
(919) 883-3401
> **Founded:** 1975
> **Arts Area:** Dance; Vocal Music; Theater; Festivals
> **Status:** Professional; Non-Profit
> **Type:** Performing; Touring; Resident; Educational; Sponsoring
> **Purpose:** To provide quality experiences in the performing arts for the community as entertainment and as education
> **Management:** Steve Willis, Theatre Director
> **Paid Staff:** 5   **Volunteer Staff:** 300
> **Utilizes:** Special Technical Talent; Guest Artists
> **Budget:** $100,000 - $500,000
> **Income Sources:** Private Foundations/Grants/Endowments; Box Office; Government Grants
> **Season:** September - May   **Annual Attendance:** 68,000
> **Affiliations:** APAP; SAF

THE NORTH CAROLINA SHAKESPEARE FESTIVAL
305 North Main Street, PO Box 6066, High Point, NC 27262
(919) 841-2273
> **Founded:** 1977
> **Arts Area:** Theater
> **Status:** Professional; Non-Profit

Type: Performing; Touring; Resident; Educational
Purpose: NCSF seeks to serve the cultural and educational needs of North Carolina audiences through traditional and non-traditional staging of the plays of Shakespeare and other classic playwrights.
Management: Lou Rackoff, Artistic Director; Gian Paul Morelli, Marketing/Public Relatons Director; Pedro Silva, Producer
Officers: William DiPaolo, Chairman of the Board; Kay Philipps, Vice Chairman
Paid Staff: 9
Paid Artists: 60
Utilizes: Guest Artists; Guest Directors
Budget: $500,000 - $1,000,000
Income Sources: Private Foundations/Grants/Endowments; Business/Corporate Donations; Box Office; Government Grants; Individual Donations; Booking Fees
Season: July - September **Annual Attendance:** 1,300
Affiliations: The North Carolina School of the Arts; The Arts Councils of High Point
Performance Facilities: High Point Theatre

FACILITY

HIGH POINT THEATRE AND EXHIBITION CENTER
220 East Commerce Avenue, High Point, NC 27260
(919) 883-3401
FAX: (919) 883-3419
Founded: 1975
Type of Facility: Theatre Complex; Concert Hall; Auditorium; Performance Center; Civic Center; Multi-Purpose
Type of Stage: Proscenium
Stage Dimensions: 65'x40'x35' **Orchestra Pit**
Seating Capacity: 967
Year Built: 1975 **Architect:** Six Associates **Cost:** $2,000,000
Contact for Rental: Steve Willis; (919) 887-3109
Resident Groups: North Carolina Shakespeare Festival

Highlands

PERFORMING SERIES

HIGHLANDS CHAMBER MUSIC FESTIVAL
PO Box 1702, Highlands, NC 28741
(704) 526-4904
Founded: 1982
Arts Area: Vocal Music; Instrumental Music; Festivals
Status: Professional
Type: Performing; Touring; Resident; Educational; Sponsoring
Purpose: To promote the performance and appreciation of chamber music
Management: Dean F. Zuch, Festival Manager; Lucas Drew, Artistic Director
Officers: Alanson G. Charles, President & CEO; Joanna Rainey, Vice President/Artistic Affairs; Dr. Louis Reynaud, Vice President/Administrative Affairs; Dr. Thomas A. Garman, Secretary; Stephen L. Lucas, Treasurer; Dr. Lucas Drew, Artistic Director
Paid Staff: 2 **Volunteer Staff:** 15
Paid Artists: 22
Utilizes: Guest Artists
Budget: $50,000 - $100,000
Income Sources: Private Foundations/Grants/Endowments; Business/Corporate Donations; Box Office; Government Grants; Individual Donations
Season: July - August **Annual Attendance:** 1,550
Affiliations: CMA; Macon County Cultural Arts Council
Performance Facilities: Great Hall, Episcopal Church of the Incarnation

FACILITY

HIGHLANDS PLAYHOUSE
PO Box 896, Highlands, NC 28741
(704) 526-2695
Type of Facility: Theatre House
Facility Originally: School
Type of Stage: Proscenium
Seating Capacity: 200
Year Built: 1932
Manager: A.W. Staub, Producer

Resident Groups: Highlands Playhouse
Converted into a theater in 1960

Lincolnton

PERFORMING SERIES

LINCOLN ARTS COUNCIL
PO Box 45, Lincolnton, NC 28093
(704) 732-9044
Founded: 1973
Arts Area: Instrumental Music; Festivals
Status: Non-Profit
Type: Performing; Educational; Sponsoring
Purpose: To develop, promote and foster all forms of art by arranging and offering exhibits, lectures, demonstrations, classes and performances, etc. in the field of creative arts
Management: Lea Evelyn Tatich, Director; Amy Crump, Office Asssistant
Officers: Madeline Elmore, President; Kenneth Brown, First Vice President; beverly McAdams, Second Vice President
Paid Staff: 2   **Volunteer Staff:** 100
Budget: $50,000 - $100,000
Income Sources: Business/Corporate Donations; Box Office; Government Grants; Individual Donations
Annual Attendance: 1,200
Affiliations: North Carolina Association of Arts Councils; North Carolina Arts Council
Performance Facilities: Lincoln Citizens Center; Lincoln Cultural Center

---

Lumberton

INSTRUMENTAL MUSIC

TRINKLE BRASS WORKS
803 West 24th Street, Lumberton, NC 28358
(919) 671-4556
Founded: 1977
Arts Area: Chamber; Ensemble; Instrumental Group
Status: Professional; Non-Profit
Type: Performing; Touring; Resident; Educational
Purpose: Established in 1977 to provide art centers, universities and schools with concerts and lecture-recitals in brass and percussion chamber music. Concerts include performances on Renaissance, Baroque and modern instruments.
Officers: Steven Trinkle, President; Genie Burkett, Vice President; Dr. Alan Kalkor, Secretary; Joel Gordon, Treasurer
Volunteer Staff: 4
Paid Artists: 4
Utilizes: Special Technical Talent; Guest Artists
Budget: $1,000 - $50,000
Income Sources: Private Foundations/Grants/Endowments; Business/Corporate Donations; Government Grants; Individual Donations
Season: 52 Weeks
Annual Attendance: 5,000
Affiliations: Wisconsin Arts Board

Manteo

PERFORMING SERIES

ROANOKE ISLAND HISTORICAL ASSOCIATION INC.
PO Box 40, Manteo, NC 27954
(919) 473-2127
FAX: (919) 473-6000
Founded: 1932
Arts Area: Dance; Theater
Status: Professional; Non-Profit
Type: Performing
Purpose: Non-profit, educational and historical corporation dedicated to commemorating Sir Walter Raleigh, Virginia Dare and English colonists from 1584-1587
Management: Robert Knowles, General Manager
Officers: Thomas L. White Jr., Chairman; Casher Evans, Vice Chairman; Mollie A. Fearing, Secretary; Ellen Newbold, Treasurer

Paid Staff: 50   **Volunteer Staff:** 25
Paid Artists: 125
Budget: $500,000 - $1,000,000
Income Sources: Business/Corporate Donations; Box Office; Government Grants; Individual Donations
Season: June - August   **Annual Attendance:** 75,000
Affiliations: Institute of Outdoor Drama; SETC
Performance Facilities: Waterside Theatre

Marion

THEATRE

FOOTHILLS COMMUNITY THEATRE
24 South Main, PO Box 1387, Marion, NC 28752
(704) 652-8610
Founded: 1972
Arts Area: Community
Status: Non-Professional; Non-Profit
Type: Performing
Purpose: Provide opportunity for participation in performing arts and to help in advancement of culture plus entertainment of our community
Management: Sandra Epperson, Artistic Director
Officers: Sandi McCarter, President; Pat Reel, Vice President; Bebe Ragaz, Secretary; Nancy Greenlee, Treasurer
Paid Staff: 2   **Volunteer Staff:** 3
Utilizes: Special Technical Talent; Guest Conductors; Guest Artists; Guest Directors
Budget: $1,000 - $50,000
Income Sources: Private Foundations/Grants/Endowments; Business/Corporate Donations; Box Office; Government Grants
Season: October - May   **Annual Attendance:** 3,570
Affiliations: McDowell Arts and Craft Association
Performance Facilities: McDowell East Junior High; McDowell Technical College

Mars Hill

THEATRE

SOUTHERN APPALACHIAN REPERTORY THEATRE
PO Box 620, Mars Hill, NC 28754
(704) 689-1384
FAX: (704) 689-1474
Founded: 1975
Arts Area: Professional; Summer Stock; Musical; Community
Status: Professional; Non-Profit
Type: Performing; Touring; Resident
Purpose: To present quality theatre, including drama that portrays the life and traditions of the Appalachian region and to encourage the writing and production of new plays; We invite new scripts each year and choose five for the annual Southern Applachian Playwrights Conference in January. One of the five is produced in the summer season with 29 premieres produced in an 18 year history.
Management: James W. Thomas, Artistic Director; Jan W. Blalock, Assistant Managing Director/Business Manager; John T. Oertling, Managing Director
Paid Staff: 6   **Volunteer Staff:** 5
Paid Artists: 45   **Non-Paid Artists:** 25
Utilizes: Special Technical Talent; Guest Artists; Guest Directors
Budget: $50,000 - $100,000
Income Sources: Private Foundations/Grants/Endowments; Box Office; Government Grants; Individual Donations
Season: June - August
Annual Attendance: 8,000
Affiliations: Mars Hill College
Performance Facilities: Owen Theatre

FACILITY

MOORE AUDITORIUM
Mars Hill College, Marshall Highway, Mars Hill, NC 28754
(704) 689-1260
FAX: (704) 689-1474
Founded: 1856

Type of Facility: Concert Hall; Auditorium; Performance Center; Theatre House; Multi-Purpose
Type of Stage: Proscenium
Stage Dimensions: 80'x35'
Orchestra Pit
Seating Capacity: 1,750
Year Built: 1965
Year Remodeled: 1987
Contact for Rental: David Hartley;   (704) 689-1260

Marshville

INSTRUMENTAL MUSIC

UNION SYMPHONY ORCHESTRA
Route 2, Box 248A, Marshville, NC 28103
(800) 438-4129
Founded: 1986
Arts Area: Symphony; Orchestra; Chamber; Ensemble; Instrumental Group
Status: Non-Profit
Type: Performing; Touring; Educational
Purpose: USO is a Union County civic and educational organization which practices and performs music in central North Carolina and South Carolina.
Management: David Lowry, Conductor
Non-Paid Artists: 35
Budget: $1,000 - $50,000
Income Sources: Private Foundations/Grants/Endowments; Individual Donations
Season: September - April
Performance Facilities: Austin Auditorium

Mooresville

THEATRE

MOORESVILLE COMMUNITY THEATRE
PO Box 194, Mooresville, NC 28115
(704) 664-5254
Founded: 1973
Arts Area: Community; Theatrical Group
Status: Non-Professional; Non-Profit
Type: Performing
Purpose: To bring the opportunity of live theatre to the Mooresville area
Officers: Clayton Miller, President; Larry Gambill, Vice President; Clayton Miller, Secretary/Treasurer; Agnes Neel, Finance Chairman
Volunteer Staff: 2
Non-Paid Artists: 12
Budget: $1,000 - $50,000
Income Sources: Business/Corporate Donations; Box Office; Individual Donations
Season: October - May   Annual Attendance: 800
Affiliations: Kedell Arts Council

Mount Airy

PERFORMING SERIES

SURRY ARTS COUNCIL
PO Box 141, Mount Airy, NC 27030
(919) 786-7998
FAX: (919) 786-9822
Founded: 1968
Arts Area: Musical
Status: Non-Profit
Type: Educational; Sponsoring
Purpose: To give encouragement and direction in the arts through classroom instruction, workshops and performances to the children and adults of Surry County
Management: Tanya Reese, Executive Director
Paid Staff: 2

Utilizes: Guest Conductors; Guest Artists; Guest Directors
Budget: $50,000 - $100,000
Income Sources: Business/Corporate Donations; Box Office; Government Grants; Individual Donations
Season: September - May   **Annual Attendance:** 1,650
Performance Facilities: Andy Griffith Playhouse; Mount Airy Fine Arts Center

FACILITY

MOUNT AIRY FINE ARTS CENTER/ANDY GRIFFITH PLAYHOUSE
218 Rockford Street, Mount Airy, NC 27030
(919) 786-7998
FAX: (919) 986-9822
   Type of Facility: Auditorium
   Facility Originally: School
   Type of Stage: Proscenium
   Seating Capacity: 300
   Contact for Rental: Tanya Rees;   (919) 786-7998
   Converted into an auditorium in 1967

Murfreesboro

FACILITY

CHOWAN COLLEGE - MCDOWELL COLUMNS AUDITORIUM
Jones Drive, Murfreesboro, NC 27855
(919) 398-4101
FAX: (919) 398-1190
   Type of Facility: Auditorium
   Facility Originally: School
   Type of Stage: Thrust
   Stage Dimensions: 60'x40'
   Seating Capacity: 600
   Year Built: 1912
   Year Remodeled: 1983   **Cost:** $40,000
   Contact for Rental: Director of Special Programs;   (919) 398-4101

New Bern

DANCE

ATLANTIC DANCE THEATRE
262 Shoreline Drive, New Bern, NC 28562
(919) 636-1760
   Founded: 1985
   Arts Area: Modern; Ballet
   Status: Non-Profit
   Type: Performing; Touring; Resident
   Utilizes: Guest Artists
   Budget: $1,000 - $50,000
   Income Sources: Business/Corporate Donations; Box Office; Government Grants

Pembroke

FACILITY

PEMBROKE STATE UNIVERSITY - GIVENS PERFORMING ARTS CENTER
Pembroke, NC 28372
(919) 521-4214
   Type of Facility: Concert Hall; Auditorium; Performance Center; Theatre House
   Type of Stage: Thrust; Proscenium
   Stage Dimensions: 64'Wx35'D
   Orchestra Pit
   Seating Capacity: 1,688
   Year Built: 1975   **Architect:** Hayes & Howell   **Cost:** $1,800,000
   Acoustical Consultant: Jaffe Acoustics
   Contact for Rental: William Biddle;   (919) 521-6287

Resident Groups: Pembroke State University Performing Arts Groups
Only non-profit organizations may use the facility

Pittsboro

VOCAL MUSIC

CHAPEL HILL-CARRBORO COMMUNITY CHORUS
164 Fearrington Post, Pittsboro, NC 27312
(919) 542-1602
    Founded: 1980
    Arts Area: Choral
    Status: Non-Professional; Non-Profit
    Type: Performing; Educational
    Purpose: To develop arts appreciation in the area, and to provide a cultural resource for all citizens in the area
    Officers: Henry Castner, President; Steve Lockwood, Vice-President; Judy Purvis, Treasurer; Carl L. Stam, Conductor; Bonnie Olsen, Secretary; Cornelia Johnson, Librarian
    Volunteer Staff: 2
    Paid Artists: 5 **Non-Paid Artists:** 70
    Budget: $1,000 - $50,000
    Income Sources: Business/Corporate Donations; Government Grants; Individual Donations; Contributions at Concerts
    Season: September - April
    Annual Attendance: 750

Raleigh

INSTRUMENTAL MUSIC

NORTH CAROLINA SYMPHONY
2 South Street, Raleigh, NC 27601
(919) 733-2750
FAX: (919) 733-9920
    Founded: 1932
    Arts Area: Symphony; Orchestra; Chamber; Ensemble
    Status: Professional; Non-Profit
    Type: Performing; Touring; Resident; Educational; Sponsoring
    Purpose: To bring live orchestral music to the citizens of North Carolina; to provide music education to the school children of the state
    Management: Banks C. Talley, Jr., Executive Director; Gerhardt Zimmermann, Music Director/Conductor; Hiram B. Black, General Manager
    Officers: R. Horace Johnson, Chairman; William Kress, Vice Chairman; Mrs. Johnny Bryant, Secretary; J. Richard Futrell Jr., Treasurer
    Paid Staff: 20
    Paid Artists: 68
    Utilizes: Guest Conductors; Guest Artists
    Budget: $1,000,000 - $5,000,000
    Income Sources: Private Foundations/Grants/Endowments; Business/Corporate Donations; Box Office; Government Grants; Individual Donations
    Season: September - June
    Affiliations: ASOL

VOCAL MUSIC

NATIONAL OPERA COMPANY
Box 12800, Raleigh, NC 27605
(919) 890-6082
FAX: (919) 890-6095
    Founded: 1948
    Arts Area: Lyric Opera; Light Opera; Operetta
    Status: Professional; Non-Profit
    Type: Performing; Touring; Educational
    Purpose: To introduce art form to students; to give experience to young singers; to perform in a language the audience understands
    Management: Don Wilder, Artistic Director/Conductor
    Officers: J.A. Goodmon, President; David Witherspoon, Vice President; Louise Stephenson, Secretary; John Brennan, Treasurer
    Paid Staff: 4

Paid Artists: 12
Utilizes: Special Technical Talent; Guest Artists; Guest Directors
Budget: $100,000 - $500,000
Income Sources: Private Foundations/Grants/Endowments
Season: September - May

RALEIGH BOYCHOIR
1329 Ridge Road, Raleigh, NC 27607
(919) 881-9259
Mailing Address: PO Box 12481, Raleigh, NC 27605
Founded: 1968
Arts Area: Choral
Status: Semi-Professional
Type: Performing; Touring; Resident; Educational
Purpose: To give 8 to 15-year-old boys an opportunity to perform some of the world's great choral music
Management: Thomas E. Sibley, Founder/Director; Terry L. Poe, Associate Director/Accompanist; Betsy Hood, Pat Simms, Administrative Coordinators
Officers: Gene Brown, President; Donald and Candy Teeter, Vice Presidents; Betty Warren, Secretary; Dwight Davis, Treasurer; Gail Black, President Elect
Paid Staff: 3   **Volunteer Staff:** 40
Utilizes: Special Technical Talent; Guest Artists
Budget: $50,000 - $100,000
Income Sources: Private Foundations/Grants/Endowments; Business/Corporate Donations; Individual Donations
Season: July - June   **Annual Attendance:** 9,000

THEATRE

THE NORTH CAROLINA THEATRE
One East South Street, Raleigh, NC 27601
(919) 755-6916
Founded: 1983
Arts Area: Professional; Musical; Theatrical Group
Status: Professional
Type: Performing
Purpose: To provide Broadway-quality professional theatre at an affordable price as well as provide available employment to theatre artists and craftsmen
Management: De Ann S. Jones, Executive Director
Officers: Dianne Davidian, Chairman, Board of Directors; K.D. Kennedy Jr., Vice Chairman
Paid Staff: 7   **Volunteer Staff:** 65
Paid Artists: 215
Utilizes: Guest Artists; Guest Directors
Budget: $500,000 - $1,000,000
Income Sources: Private Foundations/Grants/Endowments; Business/Corporate Donations; Box Office; Government Grants; Individual Donations
Season: April - November   **Annual Attendance:** 75,000

SIDE BY SIDE
PO Box 19416, Raleigh, NC 27619
(919) 829-2003
Founded: 1981
Arts Area: Musical; Dinner; Community; Folk
Status: Semi-Professional; Non-Profit
Type: Performing
Purpose: To entertain
Management: Paul B. Conway, Director
Paid Artists: 5
Budget: $1,000 - $50,000
Income Sources: Box Office; Individual Donations
Season: 52 Weeks   **Annual Attendance:** 1,600

THEATRE IN THE PARK
107 Pullen Road, Raleigh, NC 27605
(919) 831-6936
FAX: (919) 831-9475
Founded: 1972
Arts Area: Musical; Community; Theatrical Group
Status: Non-Professional; Non-Profit
Type: Performing; Touring; Resident; Educational; Sponsoring

Purpose: Theatre In The Park is a non-profit community theatre established to provide the Greater Raleigh community with the very best in live theatre, and to provide a training ground for young actors and actresses.
Management: Ira David Wood, III, Executive Director; Alan Reet, General Manager; Bruce Laks, Office Manager; Peter Girvin, Technical Director
Officers: Bill Parmelee, President; G. Troy Page, Vice President; Camille Patterson, Secretary; Johy Taylor, Treasurer
Paid Staff: 6
Utilizes: Guest Directors
Budget: $100,000 - $500,000
Income Sources: Private Foundations/Grants/Endowments; Business/Corporate Donations; Box Office; Government Grants; Individual Donations
Season: 52 Weeks **Annual Attendance:** 30,000
Affiliations: AATA; North Carolina Community Theatre
Performance Facilities: Theatre In The Park

PERFORMING SERIES

ARTSPLOSURE
300/200 Parham Street, Raleigh, NC 27312
(919) 831-6221
Founded: 1980
Arts Area: Dance; Vocal Music; Instrumental Music; Theater; Festivals
Status: Non-Profit
Type: Performing; Festivals
Purpose: To produce annual arts festivals for Raleigh and Walce Communities
Management: Debra Karp, Executive Director
Officers: Miller Sigmon, President
Paid Staff: 3 **Volunteer Staff:** 150
Paid Artists: 200
Budget: $100,000 - $500,000
Income Sources: Private Foundations/Grants/Endowments; Business/Corporate Donations; Box Office; Government Grants; Individual Donations
Season: September - June **Annual Attendance:** 100,000

UNITED ARTISTS OF RALEIGH AND WAKE COUNTY
201 East Dazie Street, Raleigh, NC 27605
(919) 839-1498
FAX: (919) 839-6002
Founded: 1962
Status: Non-Profit
Type: Educational; Sponsoring
Purpose: Develops and supports cultural programs for all Wake County citizens
Management: Robert Bush, Executive Director
Officers: Michael Lowder, President; Travis Tracy, President-Elect; Joy Cook, Secretary; Mike Whitley, Treasurer
Paid Staff: 3 **Volunteer Staff:** 40
Paid Artists: 75
Utilizes: Guest Conductors; Guest Artists
Budget: $100,000 - $500,000
Income Sources: Private Foundations/Grants/Endowments; Business/Corporate Donations; Government Grants; Individual Donations
Season: 52 Weeks

FACILITY

RALEIGH CIVIC CENTER
500 Fayetteville Street Mall, Raleigh, NC 27601
(919) 831-6011
FAX: (919) 831-6013
Type of Facility: Civic Center
Year Built: 1977 **Architect:** Haskins Rice Savage & Pierce; A.G. Odell **Cost:** $19,000,000
Contact for Rental: Holly Kreuz; (919) 831-6011
Raleigh Civic Center contains the Arena and Theatre. See separate listings for further information.

RALEIGH CIVIC CENTER - ARENA
500 Fayetteville Street Mall, Raleigh, NC 27601
(919) 831-6011
FAX: (919) 831-6013
Type of Facility: Concert Hall; Civic Center; Arena
Type of Stage: Platform

Seating Capacity: 4,000
Year Built: 1977   **Architect:** Haskins Rice Savage & Pierce; A.G. Odell   **Cost:** $18,000,000
Contact for Rental: Holly Kreuz;   (919) 831-6011

RALEIGH CIVIC CENTER - THEATRE
500 Fayetteville Street Mall, Raleigh, NC 27601
(919) 831-6011
FAX: (919) 831-6013
Type of Facility: Concert Hall; Theatre House
Type of Stage: Proscenium
Stage Dimensions: 0'Wx30'H proscenium opening
Orchestra Pit
Seating Capacity: 2,300
Year Built: 1932
Year Remodeled: 1977   **Architect:** Haskins Rice Savage & Pierce; A.G. Odell   **Cost:** $1,000,000
Contact for Rental: Holly Kreuz;   (919) 831-6011
Resident Groups: North Carolina Symphony; North Carolina Theatre
The Theatre was remodeled at the time of the Arena construction.

RALEIGH LITTLE THEATRE
301 Pogue Street, PO Box 5637, Raleigh, NC 27650
(919) 821-4579
FAX: (919) 821-7961
Type of Facility: Studio Performance; Theatre House; Amphitheater
Type of Stage: Proscenium
Stage Dimensions: 46'x36'
Orchestra Pit
Seating Capacity: Main Stage - 268; Studio Stage - 150
Year Built: 1938
Contact for Rental: Managing Director;   (919) 821-4579
Resident Groups: Raleigh Little Theatre

THEATRE IN THE PARK
107 Pullen Road, Raleigh, NC 27605
(919) 831-6936
FAX: (919) 831-9475
Founded: 1973
Type of Facility: Theatre House
Facility Originally: National Guard Armory
Type of Stage: Flexible
Stage Dimensions: 30'x60'
Seating Capacity: 300
Year Built: 1937
Year Remodeled: 1985   **Architect:** Envirotech, Phillip Safriet   **Cost:** $163,000
Acoustical Consultant: Gene Brantley
Contact for Rental: Allen Reep;   (919) 831-6936
Manager: Allen Reep, General Manager;   (919) 831-6936

Roanoke Rapids

THEATRE

ROANOKE VALLEY PLAYERS
PO Box 729, Roanoke Rapids, NC 27870
(919) 535-4161
Founded: 1965
Arts Area: Community; Theatrical Group
Status: Non-Profit
Type: Performing; Educational
Purpose: As the Drama Division of the Roanoke Valley Arts Council, to promote the theatrical arts in Roanoke Valley.
Management: Jim Ivey, Manager
Paid Staff: 1   **Volunteer Staff:** 150
Paid Artists: 5   **Non-Paid Artists:** 150
Utilizes: Special Technical Talent; Guest Artists; Guest Directors
Budget: $1,000 - $50,000
Income Sources: Private Foundations/Grants/Endowments; Business/Corporate Donations; Box Office; Government Grants; Individual Donations
Season: 52 Weeks

Annual Attendance: 3,500
Affiliations: Roanoke Valley Arts Council; North Carolina Theatre Conference
Performance Facilities: Canal Arts Center

Salisbury

INSTRUMENTAL MUSIC

SALISBURY SYMPHONY ORCHESTRA
PO Box 4264, Salisbury, NC 28144
(704) 637-4314
Founded: 1966
Arts Area: Symphony; Orchestra
Status: Professional; Non-Profit
Type: Performing; Educational
Purpose: To perform symphonic music and to increase the musical knowledge and appreciation in the area; to present four full concerts a year, including a free concert for young people
Management: Missy Shives, General Manager; David Hagy, Conductor/Music Director
Officers: Jim Norman, President; Richard Harris, Vice President; Laura Rusher, Secretary; Chester zumBrunnen, Treasurer
Paid Staff: 2
Paid Artists: 67   **Non-Paid Artists:** 4
Utilizes: Guest Artists
Budget: $100,000 - $500,000
Income Sources: Private Foundations/Grants/Endowments; Business/Corporate Donations; Box Office; Government Grants; Individual Donations
Season: 52 Weeks
Annual Attendance: 2,500
Affiliations: The United Arts Council of Rowan; ASOL; Association of Symphony Orchestras of North Carolina; Arts Advocates of North Carolina
Performance Facilities: Keppel Auditorium, Catawba College

THEATRE

PIEDMONT PLAYERS THEATRE
PO Box 762, Salisbury, NC 28145-0762
(704) 633-5471
Founded: 1961
Arts Area: Community; Theatrical Group
Status: Non-Professional; Non-Profit
Type: Performing
Purpose: To entertain the community
Management: Brenda C. Bouser, Executive Assistant
Officers: Kevin Eddinger, President; B. Douglas Robinson, Vice President; Kay Weden, Secretary; Gunnar Fromen, Treasurer
Paid Staff: 1   **Volunteer Staff:** 100
Utilizes: Special Technical Talent; Guest Conductors; Guest Artists
Budget: $100,000 - $500,000
Income Sources: Business/Corporate Donations; Box Office; Government Grants; Individual Donations
Season: September - July
Annual Attendance: 10,000
Performance Facilities: Catawba College's Hendrick Theatre

PERFORMING SERIES

ROWAN COMMUNITY CONCERT ASSOCIATION
PO Box 4234, Salisbury, NC 28145-4234
(704) 636-5861
Founded: 1981
Arts Area: Dance; Vocal Music; Instrumental Music
Status: Professional
Type: Sponsoring
Purpose: To bring the best music to the area by means of a non-profit organization; to foster and encourage public appreciation of music
Officers: Richard Miller, President; Susan Eldridge, Vice President
Utilizes: Guest Artists
Budget: $1,000 - $50,000

Income Sources: Box Office; Government Grants
Season: Fall - Spring
Affiliations: Community Concerts, New York
Performance Facilities: Keppel Auditorium

FACILITY

COLLEGE COMMUNITY CENTER
Catawba College, Salisbury, NC 28144
(704) 637-4417
FAX: (704) 637-4304
Founded: 1925
Type of Facility: Theatre Complex; Auditorium; Theatre House
Type of Stage: Thrust; Proscenium
Stage Dimensions: Keppel Auditorium - 42'x60'; Hedrick Theatre - 45'x40'
Orchestra Pit
Seating Capacity: Keppel Auditorium - 1,500; Hedrick Theatre - 251
Year Built: 1966   **Architect:** John Ramsay
Contact for Rental: Hoyt McCachren;   (704) 637-4417
Resident Groups: School of Performing Arts

Sanford

THEATRE

TEMPLE THEATRE COMPANY
120 Carthage Street, PO Box 1391, Sanford, NC 27330
(919) 774-4512
Founded: 1925
Arts Area: Professional; Musical; Community
Status: Semi-Professional; Non-Profit
Type: Performing; Educational; Sponsoring
Purpose: To provide experiences in live theatre and performing arts for our audiences' entertainment; to provide the opportunity for artistic involvement in live theatre and performing arts for anyone wishing to participate
Management: Tim Morrissey, Artistic Director; Bill Freeman, Technical Director; Sheila Brewer, Office Manager; Corinna Wicker, Box Office Manager
Officers: Jim Stevens, President; Joe Raulerson, Vice President; Mary Ellen Bowen, Secretary; Ted Havens, Treasurer
Paid Staff: 4   **Volunteer Staff:** 25
Paid Artists: 20   **Non-Paid Artists:** 60
Utilizes: Special Technical Talent; Guest Artists; Guest Directors
Budget: $100,000 - $500,000
Income Sources: Private Foundations/Grants/Endowments; Business/Corporate Donations; Box Office; Government Grants; Individual Donations
Season: 52 Weeks
Annual Attendance: 19,000
Affiliations: SETC; North Carolina Theatre Conference
Performance Facilities: Temple Theatre

FACILITY

TEMPLE THEATRE COMPANY INC.
PO Box 1391, 120 Carthage Street, Sanford, NC 27331-1391
(919) 774-4512
Founded: 1981
Type of Facility: Auditorium; Performance Center; Theatre House
Facility Originally: Vaudeville
Type of Stage: Proscenium
Stage Dimensions: 27'x42'   **Orchestra Pit**
Seating Capacity: 339
Year Built: 1925   **Cost:** $40,000
Year Remodeled: 1984   **Architect:** Frank DeStefano   **Cost:** $500,000
Contact for Rental: Tim Morrissey;   (919) 774-4512

Southern Pines

THEATRE

SANDHILLS LITTLE THEATRE
250 NW Broad Street, Southern Pines, NC 28387
(919) 692-3799
Founded: 1981
Arts Area: Community
Status: Non-Professional; Non-Profit
Type: Performing; Resident; Sponsoring
Purpose: To please our audiences
Management: Paula Reeder, Administrator
Officers: Sandy Tuten, President; Edd Sechrist, Vice President; Bernice Vernon, Secretary; Howard Stevens, Treasurer
Paid Staff: 1
Non-Paid Artists: 200
Utilizes: Special Technical Talent; Guest Directors
Budget: $1,000 - $50,000
Income Sources: Box Office; Individual Donations
Season: September - June   **Annual Attendance:** 10,000
Affiliations: NETC; SETC
Performance Facilities: Performing Arts Center

FACILITY

PERFORMING ARTS CENTER
250 NW Broad Street, PO Box 405, Southern Pines, NC 28388
(919) 692-4356; (919) 692-3611
Type of Facility: Multi-Purpose
Type of Stage: Platform
Stage Dimensions: 20'x40'
Seating Capacity: 369
Year Built: 1898
Year Remodeled: 1985   **Cost:** $280,000
Contact for Rental: Stuart Fulghum

Statesville

THEATRE

STATESVILLE COMMUNITY THEATRE
PO Box 1702, Statesville, NC 28677
(704) 871-2743
Founded: 1958
Arts Area: Community
Status: Non-Profit
Type: Performing; Educational
Purpose: To provide entertainment; to encourage public appreciation of drama, experimental theatre, and individual artistic expression; to present music theatre productions
Officers: David Farris, President; Nathan Sisk, Vice President
Volunteer Staff: 8
Non-Paid Artists: 30
Budget: $1,000 - $50,000
Income Sources: Box Office; Individual Donations
Season: 52 Weeks   **Annual Attendance:** 1,800
Performance Facilities: Landmark Theater

Tryon

INSTRUMENTAL MUSIC

PADDYWHACK
Route 2, PO Box 60, Tryon, NC 28782
(704) 894-8091
Founded: 1978
Arts Area: Ensemble; Ethnic; Folk; Band
Status: Semi-Professional

Type: Performing; Touring; Educational
Purpose: To play and promote the popular music of the 16th-19th centuries
Officers: Claude Graves, Owner/Booking; Richard Beard, Historian/Arranger
Volunteer Staff: 6
Paid Artists: 6
Utilizes: Guest Artists
Budget: $1,000 - $50,000
Income Sources: Box Office
Season: 52 Weeks
Affiliations: Schiele Museum

FACILITY

TRYON FINE ARTS CENTER
208 Melrose Avenue, Tryon, NC 28782
(704) 859-8322
Type of Facility: Theatre Complex; Concert Hall; Auditorium; Multi-Purpose
Type of Stage: Proscenium
Stage Dimensions: 31'x26'
Seating Capacity: 315
Year Built: 1968 **Architect:** Benkert **Cost:** $300,000
Acoustical Consultant: Robert Cook
Contact for Rental: Sylvia Brink; (704) 859-8322
Resident Groups: Tryon Little Theatre; Tryon Concert Association; Tryon Community Chorus; Tryon Youth Center; Tryon Painter and Sculptors; Tryon Film Club; Tryon Crafts; Carolina Camera Club

Valdese

THEATRE

OLD COLONY PLAYERS
PO Box 112, Valdese, NC 28690
(704) 874-0176
Founded: 1967
Arts Area: Professional; Musical; Dinner; Community; Theatrical Group; Choral Society
Status: Professional; Non-Profit
Type: Performing; Touring; Resident; Educational
Purpose: To produce the historical outdoor drama "From This Day Forward" annually; to produce Dicken's "A Christmas Carol" annually; to produce other dramas, engage in outreach activities, and sponser workshops and cultural events.
Management: Martin R. Rice, General Manager
Officers: Kenneth Newcomb, President Board of Directors; Doug Setzer, Vice President Board of Directors; Charles Moseley, Treasurer; Louise Barrett, Secretary
Paid Staff: 2
Paid Artists: 54
Utilizes: Special Technical Talent; Guest Conductors; Guest Directors
Budget: $50,000 - $100,000
Income Sources: Private Foundations/Grants/Endowments; Business/Corporate Donations; Box Office; Government Grants; Individual Donations
Season: 52 Weeks **Annual Attendance:** 3,500
Affiliations: SETC; North Carolina Theatre Conference; North Carolina Association of Professional Theatres; Burke County Chamber of Commerce; Burke Arts Council
Performance Facilities: Old Colony Players Amphitheater; Old Rock School, Valdese

Wilkesboro

PERFORMING SERIES

JOHN A. WALKER EVENTS, INC.
Collegiate Drive, PO Box 120, Wilkesboro, NC 28697
(919) 651-8666
FAX: (919) 651-8749
Founded: 1985
Arts Area: Dance; Vocal Music; Instrumental Music; Theater; Festivals
Status: Non-Profit
Type: Performing; Touring; Resident; Educational; Sponsoring
Officers: Arnold Lakey, President
Paid Staff: 7 **Volunteer Staff:** 20

Budget: $100,000 - $500,000
Income Sources: Business/Corporate Donations; Box Office; Government Grants; Individual Donations
Season: 52 Weeks
Annual Attendance: 32,000
Affiliations: APAP; North Carolina Arts Council
Performance Facilities: John A. Walker Community Center

FACILITY

JOHN A. WALKER COMMUNITY CENTER
Wilkes Community College, Collegiate Drive, Wilkesboro, NC 28697
(919) 651-8666
FAX: (919) 651-8749
Founded: 1985
Type of Facility: Auditorium; Outdoor (Concert); Civic Center
Type of Stage: Proscenium
Stage Dimensions: 33'Dx80'W add 16' from curtain; 21Hx42'W proscenium opening
Orchestra Pit
Seating Capacity: 1,131
Year Built: 1985 **Cost:** $2,000,000
Contact for Rental: Kathy Thomas;   (919) 651-8666

Williamston

THEATRE

MARTIN COMMUNITY PLAYERS
Watts Street, Williamston, NC 27892
(919) 792-6104
Founded: 1974
Arts Area: Musical; Community; Theatrical Group
Status: Non-Professional; Non-Profit
Type: Performing; Resident
Purpose: To bring theatre to all the citizens in the county, mainly through the schools, with one selected offering per year
Management: Allan Osborne, Artistic Director
Officers: Cynthia Veneris, President; Stan Crowe, Vice President; Janie Griffin, Treasurer; Lucy Weaver, Secretary
Paid Staff: 1   **Volunteer Staff:** 100
Paid Artists: 10
Budget: $1,000 - $50,000
Income Sources: Private Foundations/Grants/Endowments; Business/Corporate Donations; Box Office; Government Grants; Individual Donations
Season: September - June
Annual Attendance: 3,000
Performance Facilities: Martin County Auditorium

Wilmington

INSTRUMENTAL MUSIC

WILMINGTON SYMPHONY ORCHESTRA
601 South College Road, Wilmington, NC 28403
(919) 791-9262
Founded: 1970
Arts Area: Symphony
Status: Non-Professional; Non-Profit
Type: Performing; Educational
Purpose: To act as a local cultural resource and educational institution
Management: Joanne Riesz, General Manager
Officers: Dr. Clayton Callaway, President, Board of Directors; Dr. Ruth Funk, Vice President, Board of Directors
Paid Staff: 2   **Volunteer Staff:** 20
Paid Artists: 5   **Non-Paid Artists:** 60
Utilizes: Guest Artists
Budget: $50,000 - $100,000
Income Sources: Private Foundations/Grants/Endowments; Business/Corporate Donations; Box Office; Government Grants; Individual Donations
Season: September - May   **Annual Attendance:** 4,000

Affiliations: ASOL; Association of Symphony Orchestras of North Carolina
Performance Facilities: Kenan Auditorium

THEATRE

OPERA HOUSE THEATRE COMPANY
306 Nun Street, Wilmington, NC 28401
(919) 762-4234
Founded: 1985
Arts Area: Professional; Summer Stock; Musical; Theatrical Group
Status: Professional
Type: Performing; Educational
Purpose: To produce and promote high quality, professional theatre and to make theatre available for all audiences; to train and develop the talents of actors, technicians amd musicians
Management: Lou Criscuolo, Executive Director/Founder; Mary James Morgan, Company Manager; Beverly S. Skinner, Assistant Company Manager
Officers: Diane F. Green, President; Guy Ferreri, Vice President; Rebecca Rhine, Secretary/Treasurer
Paid Staff: 4 **Volunteer Staff:** 1
Paid Artists: 15 **Non-Paid Artists:** 20
Utilizes: Special Technical Talent; Guest Conductors; Guest Artists; Guest Directors
Budget: $100,000 - $500,000
Income Sources: Private Foundations/Grants/Endowments; Business/Corporate Donations; Box Office; Government Grants; Individual Donations
Season: 52 Weeks **Annual Attendance:** 7,500
Performance Facilities: Thalian Hall Center for the Performing Arts

PERFORMING SERIES

NORTH CAROLINA JAZZ FESTIVAL
1924 South 16th Street, Wilmington, NC 28401
(919) 762-5207
Founded: 1980
Arts Area: Festivals
Status: Non-Profit
Type: Sponsoring
Purpose: To promote traditional jazz to the general public
Officers: Dr. Harry Van Velsor, President; A.R. Harold, Vice President; Ren Williamson, Treasurer
Volunteer Staff: 20
Paid Artists: 12
Utilizes: Guest Artists
Budget: $1,000 - $50,000
Income Sources: Box Office
Annual Attendance: 1,000
Affiliations: American Federation of Jazz Societies
Performance Facilities: Wilmington Hilton

FACILITY

THALIAN HALL - THALIAN HALL CENTER FOR THE PERFORMING ARTS
310 Chestnut Street, PO Box 371, Wilmington, NC 28402
(919) 343-3660
Founded: 1963
Type of Facility: Theatre Complex; Concert Hall; Auditorium; Studio Performance; Performance Center; Theatre House; Arena; Multi-Purpose
Facility Originally: Opera House
Type of Stage: Flexible; Proscenium; Mainstage; Studio Theater; Ballroom
Stage Dimensions: 32'Wx30'D; 32Wx20'H proscenium opening **Orchestra Pit**
Seating Capacity: Mainstage - 750; Studio Theatre - 140; Ballroom - 250
Year Built: 1858 **Architect:** John Montague Trimble **Cost:** $17,000
Year Remodeled: 1990 **Architect:** Hanbury Evans/Ligon Flynn; Peter George Theatre Consultant
Cost: $5,000,000
Acoustical Consultant: Peter George Theatre Consultants
Contact for Rental: Tony Rivenbark, Executive Director; (919) 343-3660
Resident Groups: Opera House Theatre Company; Thalian Association Community Theatre; Tapestry Theatre Company; Willis Richarim Players; Playwrights Producing Company

UNIVERSITY OF NORTH CAROLINA-WILMINGTON - SARAH GRAHAM KENAN MEMORIAL AUDITORIUM
PO Box 3725, Wilmington, NC 28401
(919) 791-9695; (800) 732-3643
Type of Facility: Theatre House
Type of Stage: Proscenium
Stage Dimensions: 16'x40'x30' **Orchestra Pit**
Seating Capacity: 982
Year Built: 1970
Contact for Rental: Don Hawley

Wilson

INSTRUMENTAL MUSIC

WILSON SYMPHONY
West Lee Street, Wilson, NC 27893
(919) 399-6300
Founded: 1985
Arts Area: Symphony
Status: Non-Profit
Type: Performing
Purpose: Community orchestra for non-professionals
Management: Virginia Whitehurst, Director
Officers: Dr. Harold Ladwig, President; Harlee Lyon, Vice President
Utilizes: Guest Artists
Budget: $1,000 - $50,000
Income Sources: Box Office; Government Grants
Season: August - May
Affiliations: Arts Council of Wilson

Winston-Salem

INSTRUMENTAL MUSIC

WINSTON-SALEM SYMPHONY ASSOCIATION
610 Coliseum Drive, Winston-Salem, NC 27106
(919) 725-1035
Founded: 1947
Arts Area: Symphony; Orchestra; Chamber; Ensemble
Status: Professional; Non-Profit
Type: Performing; Resident; Educational
Purpose: To present the finest in symphonic and choral literature; to provide the best in music education for the children of Winston-Salem and Forsythe County
Management: Christine Belcik-Griffith, Executive Director; Peter Perret, Music Director
Officers: Angela Peterson, Guild President
Paid Staff: 9 **Volunteer Staff:** 250
Paid Artists: 81
Utilizes: Guest Conductors; Guest Artists
Budget: $500,000 - $1,000,000
Income Sources: Private Foundations/Grants/Endowments; Business/Corporate Donations; Box Office; Government Grants; Individual Donations
Season: September - July
Annual Attendance: 70,000
Affiliations: ASOL; BMI; ASCAP; Association of Symphony Orchestras of North Carolina
Performance Facilities: Roger L. Stevens Center for the Performing Arts

VOCAL MUSIC

PIEDMONT OPERA THEATRE
610 Coliseum Drive, Winston-Salem, NC 27106
(919) 725-2022
Founded: 1978
Arts Area: Grand Opera; Lyric Opera; Light Opera; Operetta
Status: Professional; Non-Profit
Type: Performing; Resident; Educational
Purpose: To increase knowledge of the opera art form, produce high quality opera and provide educational opportunities for the furtherance of opera

Management: Norman Johnson, General Director; Carollee Harman, Administrator
Officers: Clyde W. Fitzgerald Jr., President; Lynne Hart, Executive Vice President; Vicky Auchincloss, Vice President of Patronage; Loy McGill, Vice President of Marketing; Dr. William McCall Jr., Vice President of Corporate Sponsorship; Sharon Reed, Vice President of Special Projects; Margaret Kolb, Vice President of Education; Timothy K. Cahill, Secretary; N. Broughton Correll III, Treasurer
Paid Staff: 2 **Volunteer Staff:** 30
Paid Artists: 100
Utilizes: Special Technical Talent; Guest Artists; Guest Directors
Budget: $100,000 - $500,000
Income Sources: Private Foundations/Grants/Endowments; Business/Corporate Donations; Box Office; Government Grants; Individual Donations
Season: September; - April **Annual Attendance:** 6,500
Affiliations: OA; COS; NOA; Arts Council, Inc./Winston-Salem
Performance Facilities: Roger L. Stevens Center for the Performing Arts

THEATRE

CHILDREN'S THEATRE BOARD, INC.
610 Coliseum Drive, Winston-Salem, NC 27106
(919) 725-4531
Founded: 1940
Arts Area: Theatrical Group
Status: Professional; Non-Profit
Type: Performing; Educational; Sponsoring
Purpose: Children's Theatre Board (CTB) provides opportunities for students, educators and families to experience and participate in the performing arts. CTB offers multidisciplinary, culturally diverse programs to foster sensitivity and acceptance of others. Our programs are accessible and entertaining, our vision is to reach young people through experimental learning.
Management: Pat Land, Executive Director; Jennifer Lewis, Director of Marketing and Development
Officers: Mary Harper, President; Libby Noah, President-Elect; Leslie Madigan, Treasurer; Ernestine Worley, Treasurer-Elect; Janet Bondurant, Immediate Past President
Paid Staff: 2 **Volunteer Staff:** 60
Paid Artists: 120
Utilizes: Special Technical Talent
Budget: $100,000 - $500,000
Income Sources: Private Foundations/Grants/Endowments; Business/Corporate Donations; Box Office; Government Grants; Individual Donations
Season: September - May **Annual Attendance:** 45,000
Performance Facilities: The Arts Council Theatre; W-S/FC Schools; Reynolds Auditorium

THE LITTLE THEATRE OF WINSTON-SALEM
610 Coliseum Drive, Winston-Salem, NC 27106
(919) 725-4001·
Founded: 1935
Arts Area: Community
Status: Non-Professional; Non-Profit
Type: Performing; Educational
Purpose: To provide for all within the community an avenue for education and development in all aspects of theatrical arts and to provide entertainment for the community by offering a series of well-staged performances of live theatre
Management: Roger A. Richardson, Managing Producer
Officers: Eva Wu, President of the Board
Paid Staff: 7 **Volunteer Staff:** 200
Non-Paid Artists: 100
Utilizes: Special Technical Talent; Guest Directors
Budget: $100,000 - $500,000
Income Sources: Business/Corporate Donations; Box Office; Individual Donations
Season: 52 Weeks **Annual Attendance:** 20,000
Affiliations: Winston-Salem Arts Council
Performance Facilities: Hanes Community Center; Arts Council Theatre

NORTH CAROLINA BLACK REPERTORY COMPANY
610 Coliseum Drive, PO Box 2793, Winston-Salem, NC 27102
(919) 723-7907
Founded: 1979
Arts Area: Professional; Musical; Theatrical Group
Status: Professional; Non-Profit
Type: Performing; Touring; Resident; Educational; Sponsoring
Purpose: The professional production of plays and musicals with a repertoire of renowned and original works having universal and ethnic (African-American) themes

Management: Larry Leon Hamlin, Founder/Executive/Artistic Director; Nathan Ross Freeman, Resident Playwright; Chena Sulley, Administrative Assistant
Officers: Will T. Jenkins, President; Irvin Hodges, Vice President; Warren Leggett, Treasurer
Paid Staff: 3 **Volunteer Staff:** 500
Paid Artists: 70
Utilizes: Special Technical Talent; Guest Artists; Guest Directors
Budget: $100,000 - $500,000
Income Sources: Private Foundations/Grants/Endowments; Business/Corporate Donations; Box Office; Government Grants; Individual Donations
Season: September - June
Annual Attendance: 8,000
Performance Facilities: Winston-Salem Arts Council Theatre

FACILITY

THE ARTS COUNCIL THEATRE
610 Coliseum Drive, Winston-Salem, NC 27106
(919) 724-6776
FAX: (919) 724-0490
Founded: 1958
Type of Facility: Auditorium; Theatre House; Multi-Purpose
Type of Stage: Proscenium
Stage Dimensions: 32'x28' **Orchestra Pit**
Seating Capacity: 541
Year Built: 1958 **Architect:** Larson & Larson **Cost:** $1,000,000
Year Remodeled: 1980 **Architect:** Arthur Cotton Moore Associates **Cost:** $1,000,000
Contact for Rental: Russell J. Wicker, Manager; (919) 724-6776
Manager: Russell J. Wicker; (919) 724-6776
Resident Groups: The Little Theatre of Winston-Salem; Children's Theatre; North Carolina Black Repertory Company
Live theatre; films; assemblies

THE NORTH CAROLINA SCHOOL OF THE ARTS - ROGER L. STEVENS CENTER FOR THE PERFORMING ARTS
405 West Fourth Street, Winston-Salem, NC 27101
(919) 721-1654
Type of Facility: Concert Hall; Theatre House; Opera House
Facility Originally: Movie House
Type of Stage: Proscenium
Stage Dimensions: 82'Wx44'D; 42'Wx30'H proscenium opening **Orchestra Pit**
Seating Capacity: 1,380
Year Built: 1929 **Architect:** Johnson & Brannan Architects **Cost:** $1,000,000
Year Remodeled: 1983 **Architect:** Newman Calloway Johnson Winfree **Cost:** $10,300,000
Acoustical Consultant: Peter George and Glenn White
Contact for Rental: Steve Davis, Executive Director; (919) 726-6320
Resident Groups: North Carolina School of the Arts; Winston-Salem Symphony; Piedmont Opera Company

REYNOLDS MEMORIAL AUDITORIUM
301 North Hawthorne Road, Winston-Salem, NC 27104
(919) 727-2180
Type of Facility: Concert Hall; Auditorium; Theatre House; Opera House
Type of Stage: Proscenium
Stage Dimensions: 66'Wx36'Dx27'H
Orchestra Pit
Seating Capacity: 1,922
Year Built: 1923
Year Remodeled: 1963
Contact for Rental: Terry Hicks, Manager; (919) 727-2260
Manager: Terry Hicks; (919) 727-2260
Resident Groups: Winston-Salem Symphony Society

Yadkinville

THEATRE

YADKIN PLAYERS/YADKIN YOUTH THEATRE
108 East Elm Street, PO Box 667, Yadkinville, NC 27055
(919) 679-2941
Founded: 1974
Arts Area: Community

Status: Non-Profit
Type: Performing; Touring; Educational
Management: Nancy Davis, Executive Director
Officers: Gray Renegar, Chairman
Paid Staff: 1
Non-Paid Artists: 80
Utilizes: Guest Artists; Guest Directors
Budget: $1,000 - $50,000
Income Sources: Private Foundations/Grants/Endowments; Business/Corporate Donations; Box Office; Government Grants; Individual Donations
Season: October - May
Annual Attendance: 3,000

Yanceyville

FACILITY

CASWELL COUNTY CIVIC CENTER
Intersection of Highway 158 & Highway 62, PO Box 609, Yanceyville, NC 27379
(919) 694-4591
FAX: (919) 694-5154
Type of Facility: Auditorium; Civic Center; Multi-Purpose
Type of Stage: Thrust; Proscenium
Stage Dimensions: 45'Wx30'D and a 14' apron
Seating Capacity: 1,000
Year Built: 1979 **Architect:** Smart & Isley **Cost:** $1,200,000
Contact for Rental: H. Lee Fowlkes, Director; (919) 694-4591

NORTH DAKOTA

Bismarck

INSTRUMENTAL MUSIC

BISMARCK-MANDAN ORCHESTRAL ASSOCIATION
216 North Sixth Street, Bismarck, ND 58501
(701) 258-8345
Founded: 1975
Arts Area: Symphony; Orchestra; Instrumental Group
Status: Non-Profit
Type: Performing
Purpose: To present an ensemble chamber-music series
Management: Susan Lundberg-Dehoff, Executive Director; Thomas Wellin, Music Director
Officers: Troy Vredanburg, President; Joanne Pearson, Secretary; James Collins, Vice President/Treasurer
Paid Staff: 2   **Volunteer Staff:** 1
Paid Artists: 3   **Non-Paid Artists:** 60
Utilizes: Guest Artists
Budget: $100,000 - $500,000
Income Sources: Private Foundations/Grants/Endowments; Business/Corporate Donations; Box Office; Government Grants; Individual Donations
Season: September - April   **Annual Attendance:** 3,500
Performance Facilities: Bismarck City Auditorium

FACILITY

BISMARCK CIVIC CENTER - ARENA
201 North Sixth Street, PO Box 1075, Bismarck, ND 58502
(701) 222-6487
FAX: (701) 222-6599
Type of Facility: Civic Center; Arena; Multi-Purpose
Type of Stage: Arena
Seating Capacity: 8,500
Year Built: 1969   **Cost:** $2,500,000
Contact for Rental: Paul Johnson;   (701) 222-6487

BISMARCK CIVIC CENTER - BISMARCK CITY AUDITORIUM
201 North Sixth Street, Bismarck, ND 58502
(701) 222-6487
FAX: (701) 222-6599
Type of Facility: Concert Hall; Auditorium; Theatre House; Opera House
Type of Stage: Proscenium
Stage Dimensions: 54'Wx29'7"D   **Orchestra Pit**
Seating Capacity: 1,074
Year Built: 1914   **Cost:** $46,000
Year Remodeled: 1987   **Architect:** Jiran
Contact for Rental: Paul Johnson;   (701) 222-6487
Resident Groups: Bismarck-Mandan Orchestra; Bismarck-Mandan Concerts; Dakota Stage Limited; University of Mary Theater Department

Devils Lake

INSTRUMENTAL MUSIC

DEVILS LAKE COMMUNITY ORCHESTRA
828 Fifth Street, PO Box 151, Devils Lake, ND 58301
(701) 662-8353
Founded: 1980
Arts Area: Orchestra; Chamber
Status: Non-Profit
Type: Performing; Educational
Purpose: To provide orchestral music for the Devils Lake area
Management: Russell Pearson, Music Director
Officers: Curtis Sinness, President; Agnes Christianson, Secretary; Reuben Schnaidt, Treasurer
Volunteer Staff: 6

Non-Paid Artists: 48
Budget: $1,000 - $50,000
Income Sources: Business/Corporate Donations; Box Office; Government Grants; Individual Donations
Season: November - March   **Annual Attendance:** 1,200
Affiliations: NEA; Lake Region Arts Council
Performance Facilities: Ramsey County Memorial Building

Fargo

DANCE

RED RIVER DANCE AND PERFORMING COMPANY
824 Main Avenue PO Box 283, Fargo, ND 58107
(701) 280-2289; (701) 280-0004
    Founded: 1979
    Arts Area: Ballet; Jazz; Tap
    Status: Professional; Non-Profit
    Type: Performing; Touring; Resident; Educational
    Purpose: A non-profit tax exempt arts and educational organization as well as a professional, regional dance company with an established season and educational programming and touring history
    Management: Kathryn and Eddie Gasper, Co-Artistic Directors; Sandra Lee, Business Manager; Linda Christman, Director of Touring; Lois Neys, Business Assistant
    Officers: Ellen Cromwell-Cecrle, President; Katie Oppegard, Treasurer; Joel Charon, Secretary
    Paid Staff: 3
    Paid Artists: 8   **Non-Paid Artists:** 7
    Utilizes: Special Technical Talent; Guest Conductors; Guest Artists; Guest Choreographers
    Budget: $100,000 - $500,000
    Income Sources: Private Foundations/Grants/Endowments; Business/Corporate Donations; Box Office; Government Grants; Individual Donations
    Season: September - May   **Annual Attendance:** 20,000
    Performance Facilities: North Dakota State University; Reineke Fine Arts Council

INSTRUMENTAL MUSIC

FARGO-MOORHEAD ORCHESTRAL ASSOCIATION
PO Box 1753, Fargo, ND 58107
(218) 233-8397
FAX: (218) 236-1845
    Founded: 1931
    Arts Area: Symphony; Orchestra; Chamber; Ensemble; Instrumental Group
    Status: Semi-Professional; Non-Profit
    Type: Performing; Resident
    Purpose: To provide quality symphonic music to the Fargo-Moorhead area
    Management: Mark D. Madson, Manager; Joel N. Revzen, Music Director
    Officers: Howard Dahl, President; Mary Stahl, Vice President; Gen Eidem, Secretary; Allan Severson, Treasurer
    Paid Staff: 6
    Paid Artists: 85
    Utilizes: Special Technical Talent; Guest Conductors; Guest Artists
    Budget: $1,000,000 - $5,000,000
    Income Sources: Private Foundations/Grants/Endowments; Business/Corporate Donations; Box Office; Government Grants; Individual Donations
    Season: September - April   **Annual Attendance:** 11,500
    Affiliations: ASOL
    Performance Facilities: Concordia College Memorial Auditorium

FARGO-MOORHEAD SYMPHONY ORCHESTRA
PO Box 1753, Fargo, ND 58107
(218) 233-8397
FAX: (218) 236-1846
    Founded: 1931
    Arts Area: Symphony; Orchestra; Chamber; Ensemble; Instrumental Group
    Status: Semi-Professional; Non-Profit
    Type: Performing; Resident
    Purpose: To provide quality symphonic music to the Fargo-Moorhead area
    Management: Mark D. Madson, Manager; Joel Revzen, Music Director
    Officers: Howard Dahl, President; Mary Staahl, Vice President; Gen Eidem, Secretary; Allan Severson, Treasurer
    Paid Staff: 3
    Paid Artists: 95

Utilizes: Special Technical Talent; Guest Conductors; Guest Artists
Budget: $100,000 - $500,000
Income Sources: Private Foundations/Grants/Endowments; Business/Corporate Donations; Box Office; Government Grants; Individual Donations
Season: September - April   **Annual Attendance:** 11,500
Affiliations: ASOL
Performance Facilities: Concordia Memorial Auditorium

VOCAL MUSIC

FARGO-MOORHEAD CIVIC OPERA COMPANY
806 NP Avenue, Fargo, ND 58102
(701) 239-4558
Founded: 1968
Arts Area: Grand Opera; Lyric Opera; Light Opera; Operetta
Status: Professional; Non-Profit
Type: Performing; Touring; Educational
Purpose: To produce three different operas a year, performing each usually three times
Management: David Martin, Artistic Director; Jill M. Johnson-Danielson, Exective Director
Officers: Winnie Stadter, President; Dr. George O'Neill, Vice President; Ruth Swenson, Secretary; Dr. Grey McCarthy, Treasurer
Paid Staff: 4   **Volunteer Staff:** 12
Paid Artists: 50   **Non-Paid Artists:** 45
Utilizes: Special Technical Talent; Guest Artists; Guest Directors
Budget: $100,000 - $500,000
Income Sources: Private Foundations/Grants/Endowments; Business/Corporate Donations; Box Office; Government Grants; Individual Donations; Fundraising
Season: October - May   **Annual Attendance:** 5,000
Affiliations: OA

THEATRE

FARGO-MOORHEAD COMMUNITY THEATRE
333 South Fourth Street, Fargo, ND 58107
(701) 235-1901
Founded: 1946
Arts Area: Community
Status: Non-Profit
Type: Resident
Purpose: To provide quality avocational theatre opportunities to the cities of Fargo and Moorhead, as well as the region
Management: Bruce E. Tinker, Artistic Director; Richard J. Jordan, Finance Director
Officers: Pamela Anderson, President; Timothy Hill, Vice President; Perry Score, Treasurer; Gerry Emery, Secretary; Richard Burns, Member at Large
Paid Staff: 9   **Volunteer Staff:** 300
Paid Artists: 6   **Non-Paid Artists:** 175
Utilizes: Special Technical Talent; Guest Conductors; Guest Artists; Guest Directors
Budget: $100,000 - $500,000
Income Sources: Private Foundations/Grants/Endowments; Business/Corporate Donations; Box Office; Individual Donations; Charitable Gaming
Season: September - June   **Annual Attendance:** 20,000
Affiliations: NACT; NDAA; ACT; Lake Agassiz Arts Council; North Dakota Community Theatre Association; Minnesota Association of Community Theaters; Fargo Chamber of Commerce; Minnesota Citizens for the Arts
Performance Facilities: Emma K. Herbst Playhouse

LITTLE COUNTRY THEATRE
12th Avenue North and West College Street, Fargo, ND 58105
(701) 237-7784
Founded: 1914
Arts Area: Theatrical Group
Status: Non-Profit
Type: Educational
Purpose: To produce theatrical productions reflecting a high degree of professionalism; to develop artists in the theatre as well as responsive audiences
Management: Don Stowell Jr., Director, Division of Fine Arts; Don Larew, Artistic Director; M. Joy Erickson, Managing Director
Paid Staff: 11
Non-Paid Artists: 50
Utilizes: Special Technical Talent; Guest Artists
Budget: $1,000 - $50,000

Income Sources: Box Office; Individual Donations; Student Government Fees
Season: September - May   Annual Attendance: 4,000
Affiliations: ACTF; USITT
Performance Facilities: Askanase Auditorium; Walsh Studio Theatre

FACILITY

FESTIVAL CONCERT HALL
North Dakota State University, Fargo, ND 58105
(701) 237-8241
FAX: (701) 237-8043
Founded: 1982
Type of Facility: Concert Hall
Type of Stage: Proscenium
Stage Dimensions: 50'x40'   Orchestra Pit
Seating Capacity: 997
Year Built: 1982   Architect: Foss Associates
Contact for Rental: William Blain;   (701) 237-8241

Fort Totten

THEATRE

FORT TOTTEN LITTLE THEATRE
PO Box 97, Fort Totten, ND 58335
(701) 766-4473
Founded: 1962
Arts Area: Musical; Community; Theatrical Group
Status: Semi-Professional; Non-Professional; Non-Profit
Type: Performing; Resident
Purpose: Provide an opportunity for talented people to have theatre experience; attract tourists to a state historic site; entertainment for the citizens of rural areas
Management: Carol Leevers, Jane Traynor, Community Relations; John Traynor, Attorney; Chuck Jerome, Advanced Ticket Drive; Armin Hanson, Publicity
Officers: Carol Leevers, President; Jane Traynor, Vice President; Dean Petska, Treasurer/Secretary; Judy Ryan, Artistic Director
Paid Staff: 12   Volunteer Staff: 60
Non-Paid Artists: 20
Utilizes: Special Technical Talent
Budget: $1,000 - $50,000
Income Sources: Private Foundations/Grants/Endowments; Box Office
Season: July - August   Annual Attendance: 6,000
Affiliations: North Dakota Council of Arts; Council of Lake Region
Performance Facilities: Cavalry Square, Historic Site

Grafton

DANCE

POLISH NATIONAL ALLIANCE DANCERS
c/o Sandy Schuster, Rural Route 3, PO Box 107, Grafton, ND 58237
(701) 352-3483
Founded: 1940
Arts Area: Ethnic; Folk
Status: Non-Professional; Non-Profit
Type: Performing
Purpose: To preserve authentic Polish folk dances which are native to residents of Northeast North Dakota
Management: Sandy Schuster, Dance Director
Utilizes: Guest Artists; Guest Directors; Guest Choreographers
Budget: $1,000 - $50,000
Income Sources: Individual Donations
Season: April - November

Grand Forks

FACILITY

UNIVERSITY OF NORTH DAKOTA - CHESTER FRITZ AUDITORIUM
University Station, PO Box 8282, Grand Forks, ND 58202
(701) 777-3076
Type of Facility: Concert Hall; Auditorium
Type of Stage: Thrust; Proscenium
Stage Dimensions: 90'Wx35'D; 90'Wx35'H proscenium opening **Orchestra Pit**
Seating Capacity: 2,386
Year Built: 1972 **Architect:** Wells Denbrook Adams **Cost:** $3,500,000
Acoustical Consultant: Coffeen & Associates
Contact for Rental: Truman Reed; (701) 777-3076
Resident Groups: Grand Fork Symphony

Milton

THEATRE

THE LITTLE STAR THEATRE ASSOCIATION
PO Box 47, Milton, ND 58260
(701) 496-3353
Founded: 1985
Arts Area: Community
Status: Non-Profit
Type: Touring; Resident; Sponsoring
Purpose: To make available theatre arts (acting, directing and so forth) to the people of a rural community
Management: Peggy Gross, Director
Officers: Harlan Hanson, President; Carol Goodman, Secretary/Treasurer
Volunteer Staff: 25
Paid Artists: 2
Budget: $1,000 - $50,000
Income Sources: Private Foundations/Grants/Endowments; Box Office; Individual Donations
Season: April - November **Annual Attendance:** 1,500
Affiliations: Milton Community Betterment Organization
Performance Facilities: The Little Star Theatre

Minot

INSTRUMENTAL MUSIC

INTERNATIONAL MUSIC CAMP
1725 11th Street, SW, Minot, ND 58701
(701) 838-8472
FAX: (701) 838-8472
Founded: 1956
Arts Area: Symphony; Orchestra; Chamber; Ensemble; Instrumental Group; Electronic & Live Electronic; Band
Status: Professional; Semi-Professional; Non-Professional; Non-Profit
Type: Performing; Resident; Educational
Purpose: To develop a greater appreciation among students of all nations through their mutual interest in the arts
Management: Joseph T. Alme, Camp Director
Officers: Vernon Gerig, President; Clifford Grubb, Vice President; Roy Johnson, Secretary; Carter Lehmann, Treasurer
Paid Staff: 50
Paid Artists: 150
Utilizes: Special Technical Talent; Guest Conductors; Guest Artists
Budget: $100,000 - $500,000
Income Sources: Private Foundations/Grants/Endowments; Business/Corporate Donations; Government Grants; Individual Donations
Season: June - July **Annual Attendance:** 3,000

MINOT SYMPHONY ASSOCIATION
PO Box 461, Minot, ND 58702
(701) 839-8844
Founded: 1965
Arts Area: Symphony; Orchestra
Status: Professional; Non-Profit

Type: Performing; Resident
Purpose: To foster and perpetuate the Minot Symphony Orchestra, a college-community orchestra
Management: Sylvia Kerian, Manager; Dr. Daniel Hornstein, Conductor
Officers: Richard White, President; Dr. Selmer Moen, Treasurer
Paid Staff: 1   **Volunteer Staff:** 4
Paid Artists: 65
Utilizes: Guest Artists
Budget: $50,000 - $100,000
Income Sources: Private Foundations/Grants/Endowments; Business/Corporate Donations; Box Office; Government Grants; Individual Donations
Season: September - May
Annual Attendance: 3,000
Affiliations: North Dakota Council of Arts; Minot Area Council of Arts; North Dakota Arts Alliance; ASOL; NEA
Performance Facilities: McFarland Auditorium

VOCAL MUSIC

MINOT CHAMBER CHORALE
PO Box 1855, Minot, ND 58701
(701) 857-3837
Founded: 1973
Arts Area: Choral
Status: Semi-Professional; Non-Professional; Non-Profit
Type: Performing; Touring; Educational
Purpose: To bring the finest in choral literature to the north central area of North Dakota
Management: Sandra Starr, Executive Director/Conductor
Officers: Charles Weiser, President; Kenneth Starr, Vice President; Mary Muhlbradt, Secretary; Doug Freeman, Treasurer
Paid Staff: 4   **Volunteer Staff:** 42
Paid Artists: 2   **Non-Paid Artists:** 42
Utilizes: Special Technical Talent; Guest Artists; Guest Composers
Budget: $1,000 - $50,000
Income Sources: Private Foundations/Grants/Endowments; Business/Corporate Donations; Box Office; Government Grants; Individual Donations
Season: September - May
Annual Attendance: 1,200
Affiliations: Minot Area Council of the Arts

MINOT COMMUNITY OPERA
PO Box 2012, Minot, ND 58702
(701) 839-5341; (701) 857-3269
Founded: 1976
Arts Area: Grand Opera; Lyric Opera; Light Opera
Status: Non-Profit
Type: Performing; Resident; Educational
Purpose: To bring the highest quality opera to Minot; to educate, develop and encourage regional talent
Management: Julianne Walling, General Director
Officers: Linda Luedke, President; Jan Clark, Public Relations
Paid Staff: 1   **Volunteer Staff:** 20
Paid Artists: 5
Utilizes: Guest Artists; Guest Directors
Budget: $1,000 - $50,000
Income Sources: Business/Corporate Donations; Box Office; Government Grants; Individual Donations
Annual Attendance: 900
Affiliations: Minot State University
Performance Facilities: Minot State Auditorium; McFarland Auditorium, Minot State University

THEATRE

MOUSE RIVER PLAYERS
PO Box 1101, Minot, ND 58702
(701) 838-3939
Founded: 1972
Arts Area: Musical; Dinner; Community; Theatrical Group; Puppet
Status: Non-Professional; Non-Profit
Type: Performing; Touring; Educational

Purpose: Community theatre to promote adult education and provide theatre arts to surrounding communities children's educational performing arts
Management: Sandra Karnack, Resident Director
Officers: Ken Haarstad, President; Shirley Olson, Vice President; Lori Garnes, Secretary; Jerry Jorgenson, Treasurer
Paid Staff: 4   **Volunteer Staff:** 1
Non-Paid Artists: 187
Utilizes: Special Technical Talent; Guest Artists
Budget: $50,000 - $100,000
Income Sources: Private Foundations/Grants/Endowments; Business/Corporate Donations; Box Office; Government Grants; Individual Donations
Season: 52 Weeks
Annual Attendance: 11,400
Affiliations: Minot Area Council on the Arts; North Dakota Community Theatre Association
Performance Facilities: Minot Holiday Inn

Moorhead

THEATRE

GOOSEBERRY PARK PLAYERS
500 Center Avenue, POP Box 779, Moorhead, ND 56560
(701) 235-3534; (218) 299-5340
   Founded: 1984
   Arts Area: Theatrical Group
   Status: Non-Profit
   Type: Performing
   Purpose: Provide a summer outdoor theatre for and by children for family entertainment providing a fun, educational experience for young people
   Management: Ann and John Vandermaten, Directors
   Officers: Ann Vandermaten, President
   Paid Staff: 6   **Volunteer Staff:** 20
   Utilizes: Special Technical Talent
   Budget: $1,000 - $50,000
   Income Sources: Private Foundations/Grants/Endowments; Business/Corporate Donations; Box Office; Individual Donations
   Season: May - August
   Annual Attendance: 1,000
   Affiliations: Moorhead Parks and Recreational Department

Park River

THEATRE

PARK RIVER COMMUNITY THEATRE
PO Box 4, Park River, ND 58270
(701) 284-7221, ext. X285
   Founded: 1984
   Arts Area: Musical; Dinner; Community; Theatrical Group
   Status: Non-Professional; Non-Profit
   Type: Performing; Educational; Sponsoring
   Purpose: Provide community theatre productions for the citizens of Park River and arts involvement for the youth of the city and surrounding area
   Officers: Ray Alkofer, President; Darla Sheldon, Vice President; Tony Klienjan, Secretary; Peggy Seboe, Treasurer
   Volunteer Staff: 10
   Utilizes: Special Technical Talent; Guest Directors
   Budget: $1,000 - $50,000
   Income Sources: Private Foundations/Grants/Endowments; Business/Corporate Donations; Box Office; Government Grants; Individual Donations
   Season: 52 Weeks   **Annual Attendance:** 1,000
   Affiliations: North Dakota Community Theatre Association
   Performance Facilities: Park River City Hall

OHIO

Akron

DANCE

OHIO BALLET
354 East Market Street, Akron, OH 44325
(216) 375-7900
> **Founded:** 1968
> **Arts Area:** Ballet
> **Status:** Professional; Non-Profit
> **Type:** Performing; Touring
> **Purpose:** To produce and perform the ballets of Heinz Poll, master works of major and emerging choreographers of our time
> **Management:** Jack R. Lemmon, General Manager; Heinz Poll, Artistic Director; Thomas R. Skelton, Barbara S. Schubert, Associate Directors
> **Officers:** Jon R. Kelly, President
> **Paid Staff:** 15   **Volunteer Staff:** 4
> **Paid Artists:** 18
> **Utilizes:** Guest Choreographers
> **Budget:** $1,000,000 - $5,000,000
> **Income Sources:** Private Foundations/Grants/Endowments; Business/Corporate Donations; Box Office; Government Grants; Individual Donations
> **Season:** July - June   **Annual Attendance:** 120,000
> **Affiliations:** Dance USA
> **Performance Facilities:** E.J. Thomas Hall; Akron Ohio Theater, Playhouse Square Center

INSTRUMENTAL MUSIC

AKRON SYMPHONY ORCHESTRA
17 North Broadway, Akron, OH 44308
(216) 535-8131
FAX: (216) 535-7302
> **Founded:** 1951
> **Arts Area:** Symphony; Orchestra; Chamber; Ensemble
> **Status:** Professional; Non-Profit
> **Type:** Performing; Educational
> **Purpose:** To provide the community with the finest quality symphonic and choral music; to educate the local public with respect to classical and contemporary music; and to extend special support to worthy local individual artists and projects
> **Management:** Connie F. Linsler, General Manager; Maureen Horrigan, Director of Marketing and Public Relations
> **Paid Staff:** 7   **Volunteer Staff:** 160
> **Paid Artists:** 95
> **Utilizes:** Guest Conductors; Guest Artists
> **Budget:** $500,000 - $1,000,000
> **Income Sources:** Private Foundations/Grants/Endowments; Business/Corporate Donations; Box Office; Government Grants; Individual Donations
> **Season:** September - May   **Annual Attendance:** 60,000
> **Affiliations:** ASOL; OOOO
> **Performance Facilities:** E.J. Thomas Hall

AKRON YOUTH SYMPHONY
17 North Broadway, Akron, OH 44308
(216) 535-8131
FAX: (216) 535-7302
> **Founded:** 1954
> **Arts Area:** Symphony; Orchestra; Chamber; Ensemble
> **Status:** Non-Professional; Non-Profit
> **Type:** Performing; Educational; Sponsoring
> **Management:** Eric Benjamin, Music Director/Conductor
> **Non-Paid Artists:** 75
> **Season:** September - May   **Annual Attendance:** 2,700
> **Affiliations:** Akron Symphony Orchestra; ASOL (Youth Orchestra Division)
> **Performance Facilities:** E.J. Thomas Hall

MUSIC FROM STAN HYWET
714 North Portage Path, Akron, OH 44303
(216) 836-5533; (216) 672-3114
Founded: 1982
Arts Area: Chamber
Status: Non-Profit
Type: Sponsoring
Purpose: To showcase the great wealth of musical talent in northeast Ohio; to promote Stan Hywet Hall, a manor house and its tradition of music
Management: Lola Rothmann, Concert Chair
Officers: Bruce F. Rothmann MD, President; John E. Perry, Vice President; Robert L. Henke, Treasurer; Duane L. Isham Esq., Secretary; Diana Truyell, Recording Secretary
Volunteer Staff: 17
Utilizes: Guest Artists
Budget: $1,000 - $50,000
Income Sources: Private Foundations/Grants/Endowments; Business/Corporate Donations; Box Office; Government Grants; Individual Donations
Season: September - May   **Annual Attendance:** 900
Performance Facilities: Music Room at Stan Hywet Hall

THEATRE

CAROUSEL DINNER THEATRE
1275 East Waterloo, Akron, OH 44306
(216) 724-9855; (800) 362-4100
Founded: 1973
Arts Area: Professional; Musical; Dinner
Status: Professional
Type: Performing
Purpose: To provide professional musical theatre and Las Vegas entertainers to guests of America's largest professional dinner theatre
Management: Scott Griffith, Executive Producer/Owner; Marc A. Resnik, Associate Producer
Paid Staff: 26
Paid Artists: 25
Utilizes: Special Technical Talent; Guest Artists; Guest Directors
Budget: $1,000,000 - $5,000,000
Income Sources: Box Office
Season: 52 Weeks   **Annual Attendance:** 175,000
Affiliations: ADTA; AEA
Performance Facilities: Carousel Dinner Theatre

PERFORMING SERIES

E.J. THOMAS HALL
198 Hill Street, Akron, OH 44325
(216) 972-7595
Founded: 1973
Arts Area: Dance; Vocal Music; Instrumental Music; Theater; Festivals; Lyric Opera; Grand Opera
Status: Professional; Non-Profit
Type: Performing; Educational; Sponsoring
Purpose: To present a varied program to community
Management: Dan Dahl, Managing Director
Paid Staff: 11   **Volunteer Staff:** 120
Utilizes: Guest Conductors; Guest Artists; Guest Directors
Budget: $1,000,000 - $5,000,000
Income Sources: Private Foundations/Grants/Endowments; Business/Corporate Donations; Box Office; Government Grants; Individual Donations
Season: 52 Weeks
Affiliations: IAAM; ISPAA; APAP
Performance Facilities: E.J. Thomas Hall

GREATER AKRON MUSICAL ASSOCIATION
17 North Broadway, Akron, OH 44308
(216) 535-8131
FAX: (216) 535-7302
Founded: 1950
Arts Area: Vocal Music; Instrumental Music
Status: Professional; Non-Profit

Type: Performing; Educational
Purpose: To provide the Greater Akron Area with the finest quality symphonic and choral music and related fine arts; to educate the local public with respect to classical and contemporary music
Management: Alan Balter, Music Director/Conductor; Eric Benjamin, Conductor/Youth Symphony; Connie F. Linsler, General Manager
Officers: Wayne Knabel, President; Ellen Otto, Executive Vice President
Paid Staff: 10
Paid Artists: 95
Utilizes: Guest Conductors; Guest Artists
Budget: $500,000 - $1,000,000
Income Sources: Private Foundations/Grants/Endowments; Business/Corporate Donations; Box Office; Government Grants; Individual Donations
Season: September - May   **Annual Attendance:** 140,000
Performance Facilities: E.J. Thomas Hall

FACILITY

AKRON CIVIC THEATRE
182 South Main Street, Akron, OH 44308
(216) 535-3179
   Type of Facility: Auditorium; Performance Center; Theatre House; Opera House
   Facility Originally: Movie House
   Type of Stage: Proscenium
   Orchestra Pit
   Seating Capacity: 2,668
   Year Built: 1929   **Architect:** John Eberson   **Cost:** $2,000,000
   Year Remodeled: 1982   **Architect:** John Eberson
   Acoustical Consultant: Ronald Rasmussen
   Contact for Rental: Tammy Kaylor;   (216) 535-3179
   Manager: Lynn Dudnick;   (216) 535-3179

CAROUSEL DINNER THEATRE
1275 East Waterloo, PO Box 7530, Akron, OH 44306
(216) 724-9855
FAX: (216) 724-9855
   Type of Facility: Theatre House; Arena; Dinner Theatre
   Facility Originally: Supermarket
   Type of Stage: Arena
   Stage Dimensions: 20'x24'   **Orchestra Pit**
   Seating Capacity: 518
   Year Remodeled: 1973   **Cost:** $100,000
   Contact for Rental: Virginia Kancler;   (216) 272-9855
   Resident Groups: Carousel Dinner Theatre

E.J. THOMAS PERFORMING ARTS HALL
University Avenue and Hill Streets, The University of Akron, Akron, OH 44325-0501
(216) 972-7595
FAX: (216) 972-6571
   Founded: 1973
   Type of Facility: Concert Hall; Auditorium; Performance Center; Theatre House; Opera House; Multi-Purpose
   Type of Stage: Proscenium
   Stage Dimensions: 60'x55'   **Orchestra Pit**
   Seating Capacity: 2,969
   Year Built: 1973   **Architect:** Caudill Rowlett Scott   **Cost:** $13,900,000
   Acoustical Consultant: Vern Knudsen
   Contact for Rental: Cynthia Hollis;   (216) 972-7595
   Manager: Dan Dahl, Managing Director;   (216) 972-7595
   Resident Groups: Akron Symphony; Ohio Ballet; Tuesday Musical Society; Children's Concert Society

Ashland

INSTRUMENTAL MUSIC

ASHLAND SYMPHONY ORCHESTRA
PO Box 13, Ashland, OH 44805
(419) 289-5115
   Founded: 1970
   Arts Area: Symphony; Orchestra

Status: Semi-Professional; Non-Profit
Type: Performing; Educational
Purpose: To provide symphonic orchestra programs for people of all ages in Ashland and the surrounding area
Management: James E. Thomas, General Manager; Albert George Schram, Music Director/Conductor
Officers: Dr. John W. Fraas, President, Board of Directors
Paid Staff: 3   **Volunteer Staff:** 350
Paid Artists: 87   **Non-Paid Artists:** 35
Utilizes: Guest Artists
Budget: $50,000 - $100,000
Income Sources: Private Foundations/Grants/Endowments; Business/Corporate Donations; Box Office; Individual Donations
Season: September - June   **Annual Attendance:** 4,500
Affiliations: OOOO
Performance Facilities: Hugo Young Theatre

Ashtabula

INSTRUMENTAL MUSIC

THE ASHTABULA CHAMBER ORCHESTRA
3325 West 13th Street, Ashtabula, OH 44004
(216) 964-3322
Founded: 1982
Arts Area: Orchestra; Chamber
Status: Non-Professional; Non-Profit
Type: Performing; Resident
Purpose: To educate the people of the area in all types of stringed music; to provide string ensemble music for public enjoyment; to encourage young people on strings
Management: Michael Gelfand, Music Director
Officers: Brad Stevenson, President; Carol Quirke, Vice President; Eleanor Stevenson, Secretary/Treasurer
Paid Staff: 1
Non-Paid Artists: 35
Utilizes: Special Technical Talent; Guest Conductors; Guest Artists; Guest Directors
Budget: $1,000 - $50,000
Income Sources: Private Foundations/Grants/Endowments; Business/Corporate Donations; Box Office; Individual Donations
Season: 52 Weeks   **Annual Attendance:** 850
Affiliations: Kent State University, Ashtabula Campus
Performance Facilities: Kent State University Auditorium, Ashtabula Campus

FACILITY

ASHTABULA ARTS CENTER
2928 West 13th Street, Ashtabula, OH 44004
(216) 964-3396
Founded: 1953
Type of Facility: Outdoor (Concert); Environmental; Performance Center; Theatre House; Multi-Purpose
Facility Originally: Private Residence
Type of Stage: Proscenium
Stage Dimensions: 70'x30'
Seating Capacity: 235
Year Built: 1975   **Architect:** Fred Toguchi   **Cost:** $167,000
Year Remodeled: 1987   **Architect:** John George   **Cost:** $367,000
Resident Groups: GB Repertory

Athens

FACILITY

ATHENS MEMORIAL AUDITORIUM
Athens, OH 45701
(614) 593-1761
FAX: (614) 593-0047
Type of Facility: Auditorium
Type of Stage: Proscenium   **Orchestra Pit**
Seating Capacity: 2,200
Year Built: 1928   **Architect:** Howell & Thomas   **Cost:** $349,000

Year Remodeled: 1974 **Architect:** Gronsow & Guss **Cost:** $90,000
Contact for Rental: Gretchen Stephens; (614) 593-1761
Resident Groups: Ohio University Symphony Orchestra

OHIO UNIVERSITY - PATIO THEATER
307 Kantner Hall, School of Theater, Athens, OH 45701
(614) 593-4818
Type of Facility: Theatre House
Type of Stage: Proscenium
Seating Capacity: 300
Contact for Rental: Lonny Fraze; (614) 593-4850
Manager: William F. Condee
Resident Groups: Ohio University Theater; Ohio Valley Summer Theater

OHIO UNIVERSITY - SCHOOL OF MUSIC
Athens, OH 45701
(614) 593-4244
Type of Facility: Auditorium
Seating Capacity: 198
Year Built: 1970
Architect: Joe Baker
Contact for Rental: Harold Robinson; (614) 593-4246
Resident Groups: Music School Organizations

Barberton

THEATRE

MAGICAL THEATRE COMPANY
565 West Tuscarawas Avenue, Barberton, OH 44203
(216) 848-3708
Founded: 1973
Arts Area: Theatrical Group
Status: Professional; Non-Profit
Type: Performing; Touring; Resident; Educational; Sponsoring
Management: Graham Whitehead, Ph.D., Artistic Director; Nancy Steimel-Sistek, Executive Director
Officers: JeriLynn Ferguson, President; Kevin McQuaide, Vice President; Frank Heckel, Treasurer; Donna Early, Secretary
Paid Staff: 6 **Volunteer Staff:** 30
Paid Artists: 9 **Non-Paid Artists:** 15
Utilizes: Special Technical Talent; Guest Artists; Guest Directors
Budget: $100,000 - $500,000
Income Sources: Private Foundations/Grants/Endowments; Business/Corporate Donations; Box Office; Individual Donations
Season: 52 Weeks **Annual Attendance:** 63,000
Affiliations: OTA

FACILITY

MAGICAL THEATRE COMPANY
565 West Tuscarawas Avenue, Barberton, OH 44203
(216) 848-3708
Type of Facility: Auditorium; Theatre House
Facility Originally: Movie House
Type of Stage: Proscenium
Stage Dimensions: 28'x26'
Seating Capacity: 380
Year Built: 1919
Year Remodeled: 1985 **Architect:** Curtis & Rassmussen
Cost: $120,000
Acoustical Consultant: Reid Woodbury
Resident Groups: Magical Theatre Company
Phase II of remodeling plan underway

Bay Village
THEATRE

HUNTINGTON THEATRE
28601 Lake Road, Bay Village, OH 44140
(216) 871-8333
    Founded: 1958
    Arts Area: Musical; Community; Theatrical Group
    Status: Non-Professional; Non-Profit
    Type: Performing; Educational
    Purpose: Community theatre
    Officers: J.B. Binns, President; T. Meyrose, Vice President; A. Clark, Secretary/Treasurer
    Volunteer Staff: 100
    Paid Artists: 3 **Non-Paid Artists:** 100
    Utilizes: Special Technical Talent; Guest Directors
    Budget: $1,000 - $50,000
    Income Sources: Business/Corporate Donations; Box Office; Individual Donations
    Season: May - January
    Performance Facilities: Huntington Playhouse

FACILITY

HUNTINGTON PLAYHOUSE
28601 Lake Road, Bay Village, OH 44140
(216) 871-8333
    Type of Facility: Theatre Complex; Auditorium
    Type of Stage: Proscenium **Seating Capacity:** 248
    Year Built: 1971 **Cost:** $250,000
    Contact for Rental: Mr. Melrose or Mr. Clark; (216) 521-1525
    Manager: Mr. Melrose; (216) 344-7700
    Resident Groups: Huntington Theatre

Beachwood
INSTRUMENTAL MUSIC

SUBURBAN SYMPHONY ORCHESTRA
PO Box 22653, Beachwood, OH 44122
(216) 449-2389
    Founded: 1954
    Arts Area: Symphony; Orchestra
    Status: Professional; Semi-Professional; Non-Professional; Non-Profit
    Type: Performing
    Purpose: To provide accomplished professional and non-professional musicians with the opportunity to perform in a symphony orchestra, and to perform five free symphonic concerts per season
    Management: Martin Kessler, Music Director; Paul Pride, General Manager
    Officers: Ethel Epstein, President; Allan Scherl, Vice President; Connie West, Secretary; Harlan Meinwald, Treasurer
    Paid Staff: 2 **Volunteer Staff:** 10
    Paid Artists: 15 **Non-Paid Artists:** 70
    Utilizes: Guest Conductors; Guest Artists
    Budget: $1,000 - $50,000
    Income Sources: Private Foundations/Grants/Endowments; Business/Corporate Donations; Government Grants; Individual Donations
    Season: September - May **Annual Attendance:** 4,000
    Performance Facilities: Beachwood High School Auditorium

Berea
FACILITY

BALDWIN WALLACE COLLEGE - KULAS MUSICAL ARTS CONCERT HALL
96 Front Street, Berea, OH 44017
(216) 826-2375
    Type of Facility: Concert Hall
    Facility Originally: School

Type of Stage: Platform
Orchestra Pit
Seating Capacity: 650
Year Built: 1912
Year Remodeled: 1958
Manager: William R. Carlson;   (216) 826-2376
Resident Groups: Conservatory-Ohio Chamber Orchestra

Bowling Green

INSTRUMENTAL

VENTI DA CAMERA
Bowling Green State University, Bowling Green, OH 43403
(419) 372-2955
Founded: 1965
Arts Area: Chamber; Woodwind Quintet
Status: Professional
Type: Performing; Touring; Resident; Educational
Purpose: To perform works for wind quintet and other ensembles using these instruments in various combinations, offering a wide range of repertoire for a wide range of audiences
Management: College of Musical Arts, Bowling Green State University Ensemble Members - John Bently, Oboe/Correspondent; Judith Bentley, Flute; Edward Marks, Clarinet; Robert Moore, Bassoon; Herbert Spencer, Horn
Paid Artists: 5
Budget: $1,000 - $50,000
Season: September - May
Affiliations: Bowling Green State University College of Music
Performance Facilities: Bryan Recital Hall

THEATRE

THE HURON PLAYHOUSE
Bowling Green State University, Theatre Department, Bowling Green, OH 43403
(419) 372-2523
Founded: 1949
Arts Area: Summer Stock; Musical
Status: Non-Professional; Non-Profit
Type: Performing; Educational
Purpose: To provide a unique educational theatre experience for company members; to extend services of Bowling Green State University; to provide live theatre to a large area
Management: Dr. Allen Kepke, Chairman, Theatre Department
Officers: Dr. P.J. Olscamp, President; Dr. E. Clark, Vice President; Dr. Ralph Townsend, Interim Dean, Arts and Sciences
Paid Staff: 20
Paid Artists: 30
Utilizes: Special Technical Talent; Guest Conductors; Guest Directors
Budget: $100,000 - $500,000
Income Sources: Box Office; University Subsidies
Season: June - August   **Annual Attendance:** 15,000
Affiliations: North Central Ohio Arts Council
Performance Facilities: McCormick Junior High School Auditorium, Huron

Brecksville

THEATRE

BRECKSVILLE LITTLE THEATRE
PO Box 41131, Brecksville, OH 44141
(216) 526-4477
Founded: 1941
Arts Area: Musical; Community; Theatrical Group
Status: Non-Professional; Non-Profit
Type: Performing; Resident; Educational
Purpose: To present good theatre; to provide an opportunity to perform
Officers: Georgia Maresh, President; Ruth Wheaton, Vice President; Jan Futhey, Secretary; Ann Leopold, Treasurer
Volunteer Staff: 45
Non-Paid Artists: 100

Utilizes: Special Technical Talent; Guest Conductors; Guest Artists; Guest Directors
Budget: $1,000 - $50,000
Income Sources: Business/Corporate Donations; Box Office; Individual Donations
Season: September - June   **Annual Attendance:** 2,500
Performance Facilities: Old Towne Hall, Brecksville Square

THEATER ON THE SQUARE
47 Public Square, PO Box 41002, Brecksville, OH 44141
(216) 526-6245
Founded: 1975
Arts Area: Community
Status: Semi-Professional; Non-Profit
Type: Performing; Educational
Purpose: To mount a variety of shows as a community theater and to educate area youth
Management: Marlene Kalnitzky, Managing Director
Paid Staff: 3   **Volunteer Staff:** 18
Utilizes: Guest Directors
Budget: $1,000 - $50,000
Income Sources: Private Foundations/Grants/Endowments; Business/Corporate Donations; Box Office; Government Grants; Individual Donations
Season: April - September   **Annual Attendance:** 2,500
Affiliations: OAC
Performance Facilities: Old Towne Hall

FACILITY

BRECKSVILLE LITTLE THEATRE
49 Public Square, Brecksville, OH 44141
(216) 526-4477
Type of Facility: Auditorium; Theatre House; Civic Center; Multi-Purpose
Facility Originally: Meeting Hall; Movie House
Type of Stage: Proscenium
Stage Dimensions: 16'x31'
Seating Capacity: 144
Contact for Rental: City of Brecksville;   (216) 526-4351
Resident Groups: Brecksville Little Theatre; Brecksville Senior Citizens; Theatre On The Square

Cambridge

PERFORMING SERIES

CAMBRIDGE CONCERT ASSOCIATION
63041 Ridgewood Drive, Cambridge, OH 43725
(614) 432-7371; (614) 439-7735
Founded: 1936
Arts Area: Dance; Vocal Music; Instrumental Music; Lyric Opera
Status: Non-Profit
Type: Sponsoring
Purpose: To make available to the community, on a membership basis, high quality artistic talents and entertainment
Officers: David Carroll, Chairman
Volunteer Staff: 37
Paid Artists: 4
Utilizes: Guest Artists
Budget: $1,000 - $50,000
Income Sources: Private Foundations/Grants/Endowments; Business/Corporate Donations; Box Office; Government Grants; Individual Donations
Season: September - May   **Annual Attendance:** 2,600
Affiliations: ORACLE
Performance Facilities: Vergari's State Theater

FACILITY

SCOTTISH RITE AUDITORIUM
941 Wheeling Avenue, Cambridge, OH 43725
(614) 432-4346
Type of Facility: Theatre House
Type of Stage: Flexible; Proscenium

Stage Dimensions: 39'x26'
Orchestra Pit
Seating Capacity: 955
Year Built: 1937   **Cost:** $900,000
Year Remodeled: 1975   **Architect:** Higgins Construction Company   **Cost:** $100,000
Available for rent

Canton

DANCE

CANTON BALLET
1001 North Market Avenue, Canton, OH 44702
(216) 455-7220
    Founded: 1965
    Arts Area: Ballet
    Status: Non-Professional; Non-Profit
    Type: Performing; Touring; Resident; Educational
    Purpose: To offer progressive levels of dance training of the highest quality and provide performance opportunities for dancers
    Management: Cassandra Crowley, Artistic Director; Kris Furlan, General Manager; Deborah Sherrod, Administrative Assistant
    Officers: Christine Wilkof, President; Catherine Di Maio, Past President; Christine Trudeau, Vice President; Paul Stolic, Treasurer
    Paid Staff: 12   **Volunteer Staff:** 3
    Non-Paid Artists: 17
    Utilizes: Special Technical Talent; Guest Artists
    Budget: $100,000 - $500,000
    Income Sources: Private Foundations/Grants/Endowments; Business/Corporate Donations; Box Office; Government Grants; Individual Donations
    Season: September - June   **Annual Attendance:** 22,000
    Affiliations: Regional Dance America; Ohio Citizens Committee for the Arts; NARB; Ohio Dance
    Performance Facilities: Palace Theatre

INSTRUMENTAL MUSIC

CANTON SYMPHONY ORCHESTRA
1001 North Market Avenue, Canton, OH 44702
(216) 452-3434
FAX: (216) 452-4429
    Founded: 1937
    Arts Area: Symphony; Orchestra; Chamber; Ensemble
    Status: Professional; Non-Profit
    Type: Performing
    Purpose: To maintain an orchestra of the highest quality as a cultural and educational resource and to bring the enjoyment and enrichment of great music to increasing numbers of citizens in northeastern Ohio
    Management: Linda V. Moorhouse, Executive Director
    Officers: Sheila M. Markley, President
    Paid Staff: 4
    Paid Artists: 80
    Utilizes: Guest Conductors; Guest Artists
    Budget: $500,000 - $1,000,000
    Income Sources: Private Foundations/Grants/Endowments; Business/Corporate Donations; Box Office; Government Grants; Individual Donations
    Season: October - May   **Annual Attendance:** 101,000
    Affiliations: ASOL
    Performance Facilities: William E. Umstattd Performing Arts Hall

CANTON YOUTH SYMPHONY
1001 North Market Avenue, Canton, OH 44702
(216) 452-3434
FAX: (216) 452-4429
    Founded: 1962
    Arts Area: Symphony; Orchestra
    Status: Non-Professional; Non-Profit
    Type: Performing; Educational; Sponsoring
    Management: Linda V. Moorhouse, Manager; Janna Hymes, Conductor
    Volunteer Staff: 6

Non-Paid Artists: 60
Budget: $1,000 - $50,000
Season: September - May   **Annual Attendance:** 1,000
Affiliations: ASOL (Youth Orchestra Division); Canton Symphony Orchestra
Performance Facilities: Fine and Professional Arts Building, Kent State University

THEATRE

PLAYERS GUILD OF CANTON
1001 North Market Street, Canton, OH 44702
(216) 453-7619
Founded: 1932
Arts Area: Community
Status: Non-Professional; Non-Profit
Type: Performing
Purpose: A charitable and educational institution which produces and exhibits plays and provides instruction of the theatre arts for the purpose of fostering and advancing education in and appreciation of the theatre by and among the people of the Greater Canton Area
Management: Lisa Alter, General Manager; Rick Lombardo, Artistic Director; Donald E. Keith, Technical Director/Designer; Deanna Kuebel, Administrative Associate; William Fry, Youth Theatre Director
Officers: Beve Carver, President; William Strohmenger, First Vice President; Frank Ianni, Second Vice President; Janet Barry, Secretary; Carolyn Brothers, Treasurer
Paid Staff: 6
Utilizes: Guest Artists; Guest Directors
Budget: $500,000 - $1,000,000
Income Sources: Box Office
Season: August - June   **Annual Attendance:** 39,000
Affiliations: ATA; Ohio Community Theatre Alliance

FACILITY

PALACE THEATRE
605 Market Avenue North, Canton, OH 44702-1016
(216) 454-8172
Type of Facility: Multi-Purpose
Facility Originally: Vaudeville
Type of Stage: Proscenium
Stage Dimensions: 52'Wx27'D
Orchestra Pit
Seating Capacity: 1,500
Year Built: 1926   **Architect:** John Eberson   **Cost:** $1,000,000
Year Remodeled: 1987   **Architect:** Lawrence Dykes Bower & Clancy   **Cost:** $1,200,000
Contact for Rental: Bea W. Constantino;   (216) 454-8172
Resident Groups: Canton Ballet Company; North Canton Theatre Guild
The Palace is a member of the League of Historic American Theatres

PLAYERS GUILD OF CANTON
1001 North Market Street, Canton, OH 44702
(216) 453-7619
Type of Facility: Cultural Center
Type of Stage: Proscenium
Stage Dimensions: 56'6"Wx22'Hx40'D   **Orchestra Pit**
Seating Capacity: 496
Year Built: 1971   **Architect:** Lawrence Dykes Bower & Clancy   **Cost:** $9,000,000
Contact for Rental: (216) 453-7619
Manager: Lisa Atler

Chagrin Falls

THEATRE

CHAGRIN VALLEY LITTLE THEATRE
40 River Street, Chagrin Falls, OH 44022
(216) 247-8955
Founded: 1930
Arts Area: Theatrical Group
Status: Non-Professional; Non-Profit
Type: Performing

Purpose: Community theater
Management: Rollin DeVere, Business Manager
Officers: Craig Kasper, President
Paid Staff: 3   **Volunteer Staff:** 30
Non-Paid Artists: 150
Budget: $50,000 - $100,000
Income Sources: Private Foundations/Grants/Endowments; Box Office; Individual Donations
Season: 52 Weeks   **Annual Attendance:** 22,000

Cincinnati

DANCE

CINCINNATI BALLET
1216 Central Parkway, Cincinnati, OH 45210
(513) 621-5219
FAX: (513) 621-4844
Founded: 1966
Arts Area: Ballet
Status: Professional
Type: Performing; Touring; Resident; Educational
Purpose: To perform an extensive ballet repertoire in both Cincinnati and Knoxville
Management: Paul Stuhlreyer, Executive Producer; Nigel Burgoine, Artistic Director; Michael Dennison, Operations Director
Officers: Blanche Maier, Chairman; Charles MacDonell, President
Paid Staff: 16   **Volunteer Staff:** 500
Paid Artists: 51
Utilizes: Guest Directors; Guest Choreographers
Budget: $1,000,000 - $5,000,000
Income Sources: Private Foundations/Grants/Endowments; Business/Corporate Donations; Box Office; Government Grants; Individual Donations
Season: August - May   **Annual Attendance:** 45,000
Affiliations: Dance USA; Ohio Dance; NAA
Performance Facilities: Music Hall

CONTEMPORARY DANCE THEATER
2728 Vine Street, PO Box 19220, Cincinnati, OH 45219
(513) 751-2800
Founded: 1972
Arts Area: Modern; Mime; Jazz; Ethnic
Status: Professional; Non-Profit
Type: Performing; Touring; Resident; Educational; Sponsoring
Purpose: To promote the art of dance; provide educational demonstrations and performances for the community and provide dance instruction; to present and produce dance
Management: Jefferson James, Artistic Director; Kathy Valin, Publicity Director; Dennis Reed, Technical Director
Officers: Janelle Montgomery, President; Bea Rose, Vice President; Edna Rosenberg, Secretary; Steve Schwartz, Treasurer
Paid Staff: 4   **Volunteer Staff:** 15
Paid Artists: 20
Utilizes: Guest Artists; Guest Choreographers
Budget: $100,000 - $500,000
Income Sources: Private Foundations/Grants/Endowments; Business/Corporate Donations; Box Office; Government Grants; Individual Donations; Benefits
Season: September - July   **Annual Attendance:** 30,000
Affiliations: Ohio Dance; Cincinnati Commission of the Arts; Dance Action
Performance Facilities: The Dance Hall

INSTRUMENTAL MUSIC

CINCINNATI POPS ORCHESTRA
1241 Elm Street, Cincinnati, OH 45210
(513) 621-1919
Founded: 1977
Arts Area: Pops
Status: Professional; Non-Profit
Type: Performing; Touring
Management: Erich Kunzel, Conductor; Steven Monder, Executive Director
Paid Artists: 98
Utilizes: Guest Artists

Season: 52 Weeks
Affiliations: Cincinnati Symphony Orchestra
Performance Facilities: Music Hall

CINCINNATI SYMPHONY
1241 Elm Street, Cincinnati, OH 45210
(513) 621-1919
FAX: (513) 621-2132
> **Founded:** 1895
> **Arts Area:** Symphony; Orchestra; Chamber; Ensemble
> **Status:** Professional; Non-Profit
> **Type:** Performing; Touring; Resident; Educational
> **Purpose:** To provide an orchestra of such high quality that it is an aesthetic joy, is patronized to the capacity of our facility, is a source of civic pride and community reputation and is tailored to the character of our city
> **Management:** Steven Monder, Executive Director; Jesus Lopez-Cobos, Music Director; Jeffrey Alexander, Manager; Dianne Cooper, Marketing Director; Donald Auberger, Financial Director; Kenneth Goode, Development Director
> **Officers:** Clement L. Buenger, President; Stephen P. Donovan, Vice-President; Harold Poe, Treasurer; Patricia Bryan, Secretary
> **Paid Staff:** 43   **Volunteer Staff:** 600
> **Paid Artists:** 98
> **Utilizes:** Guest Conductors; Guest Artists
> **Budget:** Over 10,000,000
> **Income Sources:** Private Foundations/Grants/Endowments; Business/Corporate Donations; Box Office; Government Grants; Individual Donations; Fund-raising
> **Season:** 52 Weeks
> **Affiliations:** ASOL; OOOO; AFM; Cincinnati Fine Arts Fund
> **Performance Facilities:** Music Hall; Riverbend

CINCINNATI YOUTH SYMPHONY ORCHESTRA
8529 Morning Calm Drive, Cincinnati, OH 45221
(513) 474-9719
> **Founded:** 1965
> **Arts Area:** Symphony; Orchestra; Chamber
> **Status:** Non-Professional; Non-Profit
> **Type:** Performing; Educational; Sponsoring
> **Purpose:** To provide an experience that augments the educational opportunities available in public school programs, afford an opportunity to perform with other talented student musicians as well as performing in concert with the Cincinnati Symphony, and to provide knowledge that students can take with them to their respective school programs
> **Management:** H. Teri Murai, Music Director/Conductor; Mack Richardson, Manager/Assistant Conductor
> **Paid Staff:** 2   **Volunteer Staff:** 16
> **Non-Paid Artists:** 85
> **Budget:** $1,000 - $50,000
> **Income Sources:** Business/Corporate Donations; Box Office; Individual Donations
> **Season:** September - May   **Annual Attendance:** 5,000
> **Affiliations:** ASOL (Youth Orchestra Division)
> **Performance Facilities:** Corbett Auditorium, University of Cincinnati

VOCAL MUSIC

CINCINNATI BOYCHOIR
8315 Firshade Terrace, Cincinnati, OH 45239
(513) 385-7276
> **Founded:** 1965
> **Arts Area:** Choral
> **Status:** Non-Profit
> **Type:** Performing; Touring; Resident; Educational
> **Purpose:** The Cincinnati Boychoir was formed in 1965 to give boys with unchanged voices an educational and performing experience and to encourage singing through the voice change.
> **Management:** Randall Wolfe, Director; Barry Mersmann, Program Manager
> **Officers:** Randall Wolfe, President
> **Paid Staff:** 2   **Volunteer Staff:** 8
> **Paid Artists:** 3   **Non-Paid Artists:** 110
> **Utilizes:** Guest Conductors
> **Budget:** $50,000 - $100,000
> **Income Sources:** Private Foundations/Grants/Endowments; Business/Corporate Donations; Box Office; Individual Donations
> **Season:** September - June

CINCINNATI OPERA
1241 Elm Street, Cincinnati, OH 45220
(513) 621-1919
    Founded: 1920
    Arts Area: Grand Opera; Lyric Opera; Operetta
    Status: Professional; Non-Profit
    Type: Performing
    Purpose: To present opera to Cincinnati and the Tri-State Area
    Management: James de Blasis, Artistic Director; Paul A. Stuhlreyer III, Managing Director
    Officers: Kingston Fletcher, Chairman; Ellen G. van der Horst, President
    Paid Staff: 11   **Volunteer Staff:** 22
    Paid Artists: 247
    Utilizes: Special Technical Talent; Guest Conductors; Guest Artists; Guest Directors
    Budget: $1,000,000 - $5,000,000
    Income Sources: Private Foundations/Grants/Endowments; Business/Corporate Donations; Box Office; Government Grants; Individual Donations
    Season: June - July   **Annual Attendance:** 30,000
    Affiliations: OA
    Performance Facilities: Music Hall

VOCAL ARTS ENSEMBLE OF CINCINNATI
PO Box 8904, Cincinnati, OH 45208
(513) 483-5888
FAX: (513) 556-2698
    Founded: 1979
    Arts Area: Choral
    Status: Professional; Non-Profit
    Type: Performing; Touring; Educational
    Purpose: To present choral music
    Management: Lindsay Zierolf, Manager; Kathy Wall, Box Office/Ticket Sales; Nancy Nolan, Marketing; Vicki Ross, Publicity; Richard Weinberg, Development; Earl Rivers, Music Director/Conductor; Mary Bramlage, Librarian
    Officers: James R. Cumming, President; Lisa Vorst, Treasurer; Amy Hill, Secretary
    Paid Staff: 4   **Volunteer Staff:** 6
    Paid Artists: 26
    Utilizes: Guest Conductors; Guest Artists; Guest Composers
    Budget: $50,000 - $100,000
    Income Sources: Private Foundations/Grants/Endowments; Business/Corporate Donations; Box Office; Government Grants; Individual Donations
    Season: October - June   **Annual Attendance:** 18,000
    Affiliations: CA

THEATRE

ARTREACH TOURING THEATRE
3074 Madison Road, Cincinnati, OH 45209
(513) 871-2300
FAX: (513) 871-2501
    Founded: 1976
    Purpose: To provide quality, theatrical presentations to family audiences in schools and theatres across the nation
    Management: Kathryn Schultz Miller, Artistic Director; Dahns Schwarz, Production Manager; Andi Guess, Business Manager; Selley Weisheit, Tour Coordinator
    Officers: Barry Miller, President; Bob Bonini, Chairman; Cindy Piccano, Treasurer; Janis Flanagan, Secretary
    Paid Staff: 5   **Volunteer Staff:** 1
    Paid Artists: 13
    Utilizes: Special Technical Talent; Guest Artists; Guest Directors
    Budget: $100,000 - $500,000
    Income Sources: Private Foundations/Grants/Endowments; Government Grants
    Season: September - May   **Annual Attendance:** 300,000
    Affiliations: TCG; APAP; AATE; Arts Midwest

CINCINNATI PLAYHOUSE IN THE PARK
962 Mount Adams Circle, Cincinnati, OH 45202
(513) 345-2242
FAX: (513) 345-2254
    Founded: 1960
    Arts Area: Professional
    Status: Professional; Non-Profit

Type: Performing; Resident
Purpose: To bring the highest quality of professional theatre to the Greater Cincinnati Area and to contribute to the growth and development of American theatre
Management: Edward Stern, Producing Artistic Director; Buzz Ward, Executive Director
Officers: James M. Edwards, President; Howard Tomb, Vice President; Alberta Marsh, Secretary; Martin Wade, Treasurer
Paid Staff: 60
Paid Artists: 150
Utilizes: Special Technical Talent; Guest Artists; Guest Directors
Budget: $1,000,000 - $5,000,000
Income Sources: Private Foundations/Grants/Endowments; Business/Corporate Donations; Box Office; Government Grants; Individual Donations
Season: September - August   **Annual Attendance:** 240,000
Affiliations: LORT; TCG
Performance Facilities: Cincinnati Playhouse, Thompson Shelterhouse; Robert S. Marx

INTUITION THEATRE COMPANY
4735 Winton Road, Cincinnati, OH 45232
(513) 541-1257
FAX: (513) 542-7858
Founded: 1981
Arts Area: Theatrical Group; MIME
Status: Professional; Non-Profit
Type: Performing; Touring; Resident
Purpose: To perform original theatre for children and adults using mime, movement, clown, improvisation and music
Management: The Talent Center; Connie Gregory
Paid Staff: 4   **Volunteer Staff:** 2
Paid Artists: 3
Utilizes: Special Technical Talent
Budget: $1,000 - $50,000
Income Sources: Private Foundations/Grants/Endowments; Business/Corporate Donations; Box Office; Government Grants; Individual Donations
Season: September - July
Annual Attendance: 100,000
Affiliations: National Mime Association

MADCAP PRODUCTIONS
1630 First Avenue, Cincinnati, OH 45205
(513) 921-5965
Founded: 1984
Arts Area: Puppet
Status: Professional; Non-Profit
Type: Performing; Touring; Educational
Purpose: To present educational theatre experiences and further the art of puppet theatre
Management: Jerry Handorf, Art Director
Officers: Jerry Handorf, President; Lisa Hall, Vice President
Paid Staff: 4
Paid Artists: 6
Utilizes: Special Technical Talent
Budget: $1,000 - $50,000
Income Sources: Private Foundations/Grants/Endowments; Business/Corporate Donations; Box Office
Season: 52 Weeks

MARIEMONT PLAYERS
4101 Walton Creek Road, Cincinnati, OH 45227
(513) 561-9775
Founded: 1937
Arts Area: Community; Theatrical Group
Status: Non-Professional; Non-Profit
Type: Performing
Purpose: To produce plays for the enjoyment of area audiences
Officers: Kathy Biel-Morgan, President; Pam Lux, Secretary; Rick Pender, Treasurer
Budget: $1,000 - $50,000
Income Sources: Private Foundations/Grants/Endowments; Business/Corporate Donations; Box Office; Individual Donations
Season: 52 Weeks
Affiliations: AACT-Cincinnati; Ohio Community Theatre Alliance
Performance Facilities: Walton Creek Playhouse

STAGECRAFTERS
1580 Summit Road, Cincinnati, OH 45237
(513) 761-7500
Founded: 1952
Arts Area: Community
Status: Non-Professional
Type: Performing; Resident
Purpose: For people who are interested in theatre and perform for the community
Management: Board of Directors
Officers: Bernard Berg, Chairperson; Marcella Valin, Vice President/Production; Saranne Funk, Secretary; Ethel Younger-man, Treasurer; Gittee Bortz, Vice President/Administration
Volunteer Staff: 50
Non-Paid Artists: 25
Utilizes: Special Technical Talent; Guest Directors
Budget: $1,000 - $50,000
Income Sources: Box Office; Individual Donations
Season: September - April   **Annual Attendance:** 2,400
Affiliations: AACT; Ohio Community Theatre Alliance
Performance Facilities: Jewish Community Center

PERFORMING SERIES

ARTS CONSORTIUM STUDIO THEATRE
1515 Linn Street, Cincinnati, OH 45214
(513) 381-0645
Founded: 1980
Arts Area: Dance; Vocal Music; Instrumental Music; Theater; Festivals; Photography; Visual Arts
Status: Non-Profit
Type: Performing; Resident; Educational
Purpose: To celebrate, advance and preserve African-American culture and achievment through art, history and education
Management: Candace Roseman, Arts and Education Director; Ernest Britton, Executive Director; Jerry Denges, Administrative Director
Paid Staff: 1   **Volunteer Staff:** 10
Non-Paid Artists: 75
Utilizes: Special Technical Talent; Guest Artists; Guest Directors
Budget: $1,000 - $50,000
Income Sources: Private Foundations/Grants/Endowments; Box Office; Individual Donations
Season: September - June   **Annual Attendance:** 3,000
Performance Facilities: Arts Consortium Studio Theatre

CINCINNATI MAY FESTIVAL
1241 Elm Street, Cincinnati, OH 45210
(513) 621-1919
Founded: 1873
Arts Area: Vocal Music; Instrumental Music; Festivals
Status: Professional; Non-Profit
Type: Performing; Resident; Sponsoring
Purpose: Cincinnati May Festival presents, as the oldest continuing choral festival in the Western Hemisphere, an exciting repertoire of choral and orchestral music featuring the May Festival Chorus, world-renowned guest soloists and conductors and the Cincinnati Symphony Orchestra.
Management: James Conlon, May Festival Music Director; Robert Porco, May Festival Chorus Director; Steven Monder, Executive Director; Jeffrey Alexander, Manager; Vera Menner, Director of Marketing/Development
Officers: Mary Margret Rochford, Chairman; Alice Sweet, Vice Chairman; Ruthy Korelitz, Secretary
Paid Staff: 3   **Volunteer Staff:** 100
Paid Artists: 20   **Non-Paid Artists:** 200
Utilizes: Guest Conductors; Guest Artists
Budget: $500,000 - $1,000,000
Income Sources: Private Foundations/Grants/Endowments; Business/Corporate Donations; Box Office; Government Grants; Individual Donations
Season: May   **Annual Attendance:** 13,000
Affiliations: Cincinnati Symphony Orchestra
Performance Facilities: Music Hall; Cathedral Basillica of the Assumption

CINCINNATI MUSIC HALL ASSOCIATION
1243 Elm Street, Cincinnati, OH 45210
(513) 621-1919
FAX: (513) 621-5390
Founded: 1878

Arts Area: Dance; Vocal Music; Instrumental Music; Theater; Festivals; Lyric Opera; Grand Opera
Status: Non-Profit
Type: Performing; Touring; Resident; Educational
Purpose: Concert and performance hall
Management: David Curry, General Manager; Joe Dopkins, Manager; Tom Bockenstette, Manager
Officers: Dudley S. Taft, President
Paid Staff: 15   **Volunteer Staff:** 20
Budget: $1,000,000 - $5,000,000
Income Sources: Private Foundations/Grants/Endowments; Business/Corporate Donations; Government Grants; Individual Donations; Rentals
Season: 52 Weeks   **Annual Attendance:** 700,000
Performance Facilities: Music Hall

RIVERBEND-CINCINNATI SYMPHONY AND POPS ORCHESTRA CONCERTS
1241 Elm Street, Cincinnati, OH 45210
(513) 621-1919
FAX: (513) 621-2132
Founded: 1984
Arts Area: Vocal Music; Instrumental Music
Status: Professional; Non-Profit
Type: Sponsoring
Management: Jesus Lopez-Cobos, CSO Music Director; Erich Kunzel, POPS Conductor; Cincinnati Symphony Orchestra
Utilizes: Guest Conductors; Guest Artists
Income Sources: Business/Corporate Donations; Box Office
Season: June - August   **Annual Attendance:** 100,000
Performance Facilities: Riverbend Music Center

FACILITY

CINCINNATI JEWISH COMMUNITY CENTER
1580 Summit Road, Cincinnati, OH 45237-1999
(513) 761-7500
FAX: (513) 761-0084
Type of Facility: Civic Center
Type of Stage: Proscenium
Seating Capacity: 800
Year Built: 1958
Year Remodeled: 1986   **Architect:** Richard Lemker   **Cost:** $100,000
Acoustical Consultant: Richard Lemker & Associates
Contact for Rental: Anna Geottleman;   (513) 761-7500
Manager: Marie Wolfson
Resident Groups: Center Stage; Just Us Kids; Spotlight; Stagecrafters; Senior Adult Theater

CINCINNATI MUSIC HALL
1243 Elm Street, Cincinnati, OH 45210
(513) 621-1919
Founded: 1878
Type of Facility: Concert Hall; Auditorium; Multi-Purpose
Type of Stage: Proscenium
Stage Dimensions: 50'Wx48'D; 50'Wx39'H proscenium opening   **Orchestra Pit**
Seating Capacity: 3,357
Year Built: 1878   **Architect:** Hannaford & Proctor   **Cost:** $325,000
Year Remodeled: 1970   **Architect:** Schatz Associates   **Cost:** $10,000,000
Contact for Rental: David Curry;   (513) 621-1919
Resident Groups: Cincinnati Symphony Orchestra; Cincinnati Opera; Cincinnati Ballet Company; Cincinnati May Festival; Cincinnati Pops Orchestra
Music Hall was designated a National Historic Landmark in 1975.

CINCINNATI PLAYHOUSE - ROBERT S. MARX THEATRE
962 Mount Adams Circle, Eden Park, Cincinnati, OH 45202
(513) 345-2242
FAX: (513) 345-2254
Founded: 1960
Type of Facility: Theatre House
Type of Stage: Thrust; Symmetrical Thrust
Stage Dimensions: 35'Wx60'D
Seating Capacity: 629

Year Built: 1968   **Architect:** Hardy Holzman Pfeiffer Associates   **Cost:** $1,000,000
Acoustical Consultant: Robert A. Hansen Associates

CINCINNATI PLAYHOUSE - THOMPSON SHELTERHOUSE
962 Mount Adams Circle, Eden Park, Cincinnati, OH 45202
(513) 345-2242
FAX: (513) 345-2254
        Founded: 1960
        Type of Facility: Theatre House
        Facility Originally: Meeting Hall
        Type of Stage: Thrust
        Stage Dimensions: 18'Wx24'D
        Seating Capacity: 219
        Year Built: 1874
        Year Remodeled: 1980   **Architect:** Architects Team Associates   **Cost:** $100,000

RIVERBEND MUSIC CENTER
6295 Kellogg Avenue, Cincinnati, OH 45230
(513) 232-5882
FAX: (513) 232-7577
        Founded: 1983
        Type of Facility: Outdoor (Concert); Performance Center; Amphitheater
        Type of Stage: Proscenium
        Stage Dimensions: 70'x62'   **Orchestra Pit**
        Seating Capacity: Pavilion-6,000; On Lawn-12,000
        Year Built: 1983   **Architect:** Michael Graves   **Cost:** $15,000,000
        Acoustical Consultant: Jaffe Acoustics
        Resident Groups: Cincinnati Symphony Orchestra

SHOWBOAT MAJESTIC
Foot of Broadway at the Public Landing, Cincinnati, OH 45203
(513) 475-5803
        Mailing Address: c/o Cincinnati Recreation Commission, 644 Linn Street, Cincinnati, OH 45203
        Founded: 1923
        Type of Facility: Showboat
        Type of Stage: Proscenium
        Stage Dimensions: 17'9"Wx14'5"Dx12'H; 6'D apron
        Seating Capacity: 233
        Year Built: 1923   **Architect:** Tom Reynolds
        Year Remodeled: 1967
        Manager: Tim Perrino;   (513) 241-6550
        The Showboat is on the National Register of Historic Places.

UNIVERSITY OF CINCINNATI - CORBETT AUDITORIUM
Corbett Center for the Performing Arts, College Conservatory of Music, Cincinnati, OH 45221-0003
(513) 556-9430
        Type of Facility: Concert Hall; Theatre House
        Type of Stage: Modified Apron Proscenium
        Stage Dimensions: 53'8"Wx30'D with 16'8" apron; hydraulic orchestra pit lift   **Orchestra Pit**
        Seating Capacity: 743
        Year Built: 1967
        Contact for Rental: Martha Crabtree

UNIVERSITY OF CINCINNATI - CORBETT CENTER FOR THE PERFORMING ARTS
College Conservatory of Music, Cincinnati, OH 45221-0003
(513) 556-9430
        Type of Facility: Theatre Complex
        Year Built: 1967   **Architect:** Edward Schulte
        Year Remodeled: 1972   **Architect:** Pistler Brown Architection   **Cost:** $4,000,000
        Contact for Rental: Martha Crabtree
        Manager: John Mcdonagh
        Resident Groups: Philharmonia Orchestra; Concert Orchestra; Opera and Musical Theater & Drama Series; Hot Summer
Nights
        *Corbett Center for the Performing Arts contains Corbett Auditorium, Patricia Corbett Theater and Watson Hall. See
separate listings for further information. Limited availability.*

UNIVERSITY OF CINCINNATI - PATRICIA CORBETT THEATER
Corbett Center for the Performing Arts, College Conservatory of Music, Cincinnati, OH 45221-0003
(513) 556-9430
  Type of Facility: Concert Hall; Theatre House
  Type of Stage: Proscenium
  Stage Dimensions: 44'1"Wx34'2"D   **Orchestra Pit**
  Seating Capacity: 400
  Year Built: 1967
  Contact for Rental: Martha Crabtree

UNIVERSITY OF CINCINNATI - WATSON HALL
Corbett Center for the Performing Arts, College Conservatory of Music, Cincinnati, OH 45221-0003
(513) 556-9430
  Type of Facility: Recital Hall
  Type of Stage: Platform
  Seating Capacity: 140
  Year Built: 1967
  Contact for Rental: Martha Crabtree

WALTON CREEK PLAYHOUSE
4101 Walton Creek Road, Cincinnati, OH 45227
(513) 561-9775
  Type of Facility: Auditorium; Theatre House; Room
  Facility Originally: School
  Type of Stage: Proscenium
  Seating Capacity: 120
  Year Built: 1861
  Year Remodeled: 1960
  Contact for Rental: Elemor Shepard;   (513) 561-7688
  Resident Groups: Mariemont Players

WESTWOOD TOWN HALL
3017 Harrison Avenue, Cincinnati, OH 45213
(513) 662-9109
  Type of Facility: Theatre Complex; Auditorium; Civic Center; Multi-Purpose
  Facility Originally: Town Hall
  Type of Stage: Proscenium; 3/4 Arena
  Stage Dimensions: 53'Wx25'Dx30'H
  Seating Capacity: 250
  Year Built: 1888   **Architect:** Charles Crapsey/William Brown
  Contact for Rental: Director;   (513) 662-9109
  Manager: Mike Thomas
  Resident Groups: Cincinnati Civic Orchestra; The Drama Workshop; The Footlighters; Cincinnati Young People's Theatre; Womens Theatre of Cincinnati; Continental Round Dancers

Cleveland

DANCE

CLEVELAND SAN JOSE BALLET
One Playhouse Square, #330, Cleveland, OH 44115
(216) 621-2260
FAX: (216) 566-0752
  Founded: 1976
  Arts Area: Ballet
  Status: Professional; Non-Profit
  Type: Performing; Touring; Resident; Educational; Sponsoring
  Purpose: Dedicated to creating quality ballet
  Management: Dennis Nahat, Artistic Director; David Oakland, General Manager
  Paid Staff: 25
  Paid Artists: 37
  Utilizes: Special Technical Talent; Guest Artists; Guest Choreographers
  Budget: $5,000,000 - $10,000,000
  Income Sources: Private Foundations/Grants/Endowments; Business/Corporate Donations; Box Office; Government Grants; Individual Donations
  Season: October - May   **Annual Attendance:** 120,000

Affiliations: Dance USA; USITT; BOMI
Performance Facilities: State Theatre; Playhouse Square Center

DANCECLEVELAND
1148 Euclid Avenue, 3rd Floor, Cleveland, OH 44115
(216) 861-2213
Founded: 1956
Arts Area: Modern; Mime; Ballet; Jazz; Folk
Status: Non-Profit
Type: Educational; Sponsoring
Purpose: DANCECLEVELAND was formed to foster an appreciation of and interest in dance in the Greater Cleveland Area through education and concert programming, the presentation of an annual concert series, dance education and dance/movement therapy programs.
Management: Stephanie Brown, Executive Director; Craig Rich, Marketing Director
Officers: Jeffrey S. Glazer, President; Lucinda Lavelli, Vice President, Programming; Ann Sethness, Vice President, Contributed Revenues; Jeffrey Linton, Vice President, Earned Revenues; Tom Leib, Secretary/Treasurer; Sheila Fox, Vice President, Trustees
Paid Staff: 5   **Volunteer Staff:** 35
Paid Artists: 124
Utilizes: Guest Artists
Budget: $100,000 - $500,000
Income Sources: Private Foundations/Grants/Endowments; Business/Corporate Donations; Box Office; Government Grants; Individual Donations
Season: October - July   **Annual Attendance:** 22,500
Affiliations: OAC; NEA; ORACLE; APAP; ISPAA; Arts Midwest; Dance USA; Arts Presenters; Ohio Dance
Performance Facilities: Ohio Theatre; Playhouse Square Center; Beck Center for the Cultural Arts

SAINT SAVA FREE SERBIAN ORTHODOX CHURCH
2151 West Wallings, Cleveland, OH 44147
(216) 524-5991
Founded: 1982
Arts Area: Ethnic; Folk
Status: Non-Professional; Non-Profit
Type: Performing; Touring; Resident; Educational
Purpose: To encourage and perpetuate our Serbian music, dance, language, culture and heritage, and to have fun doing it
Management: Dragica Zamiska, Director
Volunteer Staff: 4
Budget: $1,000 - $50,000
Income Sources: Individual Donations
Season: September - July
Affiliations: Saint Sava Free Serbian Orthodox Church; School Congregation; Cleveland Area Arts Council

INSTRUMENTAL MUSIC

THE CHINA MUSIC PROJECT
334 Claymore Boulevard, Cleveland, OH 44143-1730
(216) 531-2188
Founded: 1980
Arts Area: Orchestra; Chamber; Ensemble; Ethnic; Instrumental Group
Status: Professional; Non-Profit
Type: Performing; Touring; Resident; Educational; Sponsoring
Purpose: To bring traditional Chinese music and information about it to the American public through performances, lectures, demonstrations, radio and TV broadcasts
Management: Marjorie Ann Ciarlillo, Director
Officers: Dr. K. Laurence Chang, Chairman of the Board
Utilizes: Guest Artists
Budget: $1,000 - $50,000
Income Sources: Private Foundations/Grants/Endowments; Business/Corporate Donations
Season: 52 Weeks

CLEVELAND CHAMBER MUSIC SOCIETY
2316 Belvoir Boulevard, Cleveland, OH 44121
(216) 531-7094
Founded: 1950
Arts Area: Chamber; Ensemble
Status: Non-Profit
Type: Sponsoring
Purpose: To promote chamber music through presentation of the best available works and through the commissioning of new works

Officers: Toni Miller, President; David A. Richardson, First Vice President; John Boatright, Second Vice President; Lois Rose, Third Vice President
Paid Staff: 1   **Volunteer Staff:** 18
Paid Artists: 45
Utilizes: Guest Artists
Budget: $50,000 - $100,000
Income Sources: Private Foundations/Grants/Endowments; Box Office; Individual Donations
Season: September - May   **Annual Attendance:** 3,500

CLEVELAND JAZZ ORCHESTRA
PO Box 360140, Cleveland, OH 44136
(216) 572-2562
Founded: 1985
Arts Area: Ensemble; Instrumental Group; Band
Status: Professional; Non-Profit
Type: Performing; Resident; Educational; Sponsoring
Purpose: To establish Cleveland Jazz Orchestra in Northeast Ohio; to enhance availability and quality of jazz; to assist in educating young musicians; to encourage involvement and training of minority musicians
Officers: Gary Scott, President; Kris Lutz, Secretary; Joseph Mikelonis, Treasurer
Volunteer Staff: 10
Paid Artists: 18
Utilizes: Guest Artists
Budget: $1,000 - $50,000
Income Sources: Private Foundations/Grants/Endowments; Business/Corporate Donations; Box Office; Government Grants; Individual Donations
Season: 52 Weeks
Affiliations: Cuyahoga Community College; Northeast Ohio Jazz Society; Cleveland Playhouse

CLEVELAND ORCHESTRA
11001 Euclid Avenue, Cleveland, OH 44106
(216) 231-7300
FAX: (216) 231-0202
Founded: 1918
Arts Area: Symphony; Orchestra; Ensemble
Status: Professional; Non-Profit
Type: Performing; Touring; Resident; Educational; Sponsoring
Management: Thomas W. Morris, Executive Director; Christoph von Dohnanyi, Music Director; Nancy Bell Cue, Manager
Paid Staff: 60
Paid Artists: 110
Utilizes: Guest Conductors; Guest Artists
Budget: Over 10,000,000
Income Sources: Private Foundations/Grants/Endowments; Business/Corporate Donations; Box Office; Individual Donations
Season: September - May
Affiliations: ASOL; OOOO
Performance Facilities: Severance Hall; Blossom Music Center

CLEVELAND PHILHARMONIC ORCHESTRA
8702 Bessemer Avenue, PO Box 16251, Cleveland, OH 44116
(216) 341-7474
Founded: 1938
Arts Area: Symphony; Orchestra
Status: Semi-Professional; Non-Profit
Type: Performing; Resident; Sponsoring
Purpose: To provide quality performances at modest ticket prices; to be a training orchestra for aspiring musicians; and to provide technical education for musicians
Management: Martha Hamilton, General Manager; William B. Slocum, Music Director/Conductor
Officers: James Roosa, President; Stanley Lasky and Kris Pasternak, Vice Presidents; Susan Reusser, Secretary; Philip Melaragno, Treasurer
Paid Staff: 2   **Volunteer Staff:** 3
Non-Paid Artists: 60
Utilizes: Guest Conductors; Guest Artists
Budget: $1,000 - $50,000
Income Sources: Private Foundations/Grants/Endowments; Business/Corporate Donations; Box Office; Government Grants; Individual Donations
Season: September - May   **Annual Attendance:** 3,000

Affiliations: ASOL; Saint Vincent Quadrangle Association
Performance Facilities: Cuyahoga Community College

OHIO CHAMBER ORCHESTRA
PO Box 14886, Cleveland, OH 44114
(216) 781-4466
> **Founded:** 1972
> **Arts Area:** Symphony; Orchestra; Chamber; Ensemble
> **Status:** Professional
> **Type:** Performing; Touring; Resident
> **Purpose:** To perform at the highest artistic level possible programs specialiozing in literatire written specifically for chamber orchestra in appropriate (intimate) settings, featuring soloists of local and international standing
> **Management:** Eugenia L. Epperson, Executive Director
> **Officers:** Paul R. Bunker, President; William Steffee MD, Chairman Executive Committee; Robert H. Jackson, Executive Vice Chairman; James E. Wilcosky, Treasurer; Martha Vail, Secretary; Norma Glazer, President of Ohio Chamber Orchestra Council
> **Paid Staff:** 7
> **Paid Artists:** 75
> **Utilizes:** Guest Conductors; Guest Artists
> **Budget:** $500,000 - $1,000,000
> **Income Sources:** Private Foundations/Grants/Endowments; Business/Corporate Donations; Box Office; Government Grants; Individual Donations
> **Season:** October - May   **Annual Attendance:** 14,000
> **Performance Facilities:** The Cleveland Play House

UNIVERSITY CIRCLE CHAMBER ORCHESTRA
Music Department, Case Western Reserve University, Cleveland, OH 44106
(216) 368-2400
> **Arts Area:** Symphony; Orchestra; Chamber; Ensemble; Instrumental Group
> **Status:** Non-Professional; Non-Profit
> **Type:** Performing; Resident; Educational
> **Purpose:** A community orchestra open to both university students and interested amateurs, performing stimulating repertoire in an enjoyable yet intense atmosphere
> **Management:** Music Department, Case Western Reserve University
> **Officers:** Rando Laycock, Music Director
> **Paid Staff:** 2
> **Non-Paid Artists:** 18
> **Utilizes:** Guest Artists
> **Budget:** $1,000 - $50,000
> **Income Sources:** Private Foundations/Grants/Endowments; Individual Donations
> **Season:** August - May
> **Affiliations:** Case Western Reserve University
> **Performance Facilities:** Harkness Chapel

VOCAL MUSIC

CLEVELAND OPERA
1422 Euclid Avenue, Suite 1052, Cleveland, OH 44115-2001
(216) 575-0903
FAX: (216) 575-1918
> **Founded:** 1976
> **Arts Area:** Grand Opera; Lyric Opera; Light Opera
> **Status:** Professional; Non-Profit
> **Type:** Performing; Touring; Resident; Educational
> **Purpose:** To bring outstanding presentations of opera to the people of Northern Ohio; create the opportunity to develop operatic and dramatic skills of local artists; to make opera accessible to the broadest possible spectrum of the community and region
> **Management:** David Bamberger, General Manager/Artistic Director
> **Paid Staff:** 55   **Volunteer Staff:** 250
> **Paid Artists:** 300   **Non-Paid Artists:** 6
> **Utilizes:** Special Technical Talent; Guest Conductors; Guest Artists; Guest Directors
> **Budget:** $1,000,000 - $5,000,000
> **Income Sources:** Private Foundations/Grants/Endowments; Business/Corporate Donations; Box Office; Government Grants; Individual Donations
> **Season:** October - May   **Annual Attendance:** 62,000
> **Affiliations:** OA
> **Performance Facilities:** State Theatre, Playhouse Square Center

THE CLEVELAND ORCHESTRA CHORUS
11001 Euclid Avenue, Cleveland, OH 44106
(216) 231-7300
FAX: (216) 231-0202
> **Founded:** 1952
> **Arts Area:** Choral; Concert Opera; Pops
> **Status:** Non-Professional; Non-Profit
> **Type:** Performing; Touring; Resident
> **Purpose:** To assist the Cleveland Orchestra in performing choral-orchestral works
> **Management:** Gareth Morrell, Director of Choruses; Nancy Gage, Coordinator of Choruses; Eleanor Kushnick, Librarian; Joela Jones, Accompanist/Soloist; Betty Meyers, Donald Shelhorn, Assitant Accompanists
> **Officers:** Margaret B. Robinson, Chair; The Cleveland Orchestra Chorus Operating Committee
> **Paid Staff:** 6
> **Non-Paid Artists:** 170
> **Utilizes:** Guest Conductors; Guest Artists
> **Income Sources:** Private Foundations/Grants/Endowments
> **Season:** September - August   **Annual Attendance:** 100,000
> **Performance Facilities:** Severence Hall; Blossom Music Center

LYRIC OPERA CLEVELAND
PO Box 06198, Cleveland, OH 44106
(216) 231-2484
> **Founded:** 1973
> **Arts Area:** Lyric Opera; Light Opera; Operetta; Musical Theatre
> **Status:** Professional; Non-Profit
> **Type:** Performing; Resident; Educational; Sponsoring
> **Purpose:** To utilize talented artists from the North in music theatre productions
> **Management:** Michael McConnell, Executive Director; Kristen Manthey, Artistic Administrator; Joe Wochna, Marketing/Development Assistant; Amy Capwell, Administrative Assistant; Stephen Szabo, Business Manager
> **Officers:** Richard C. Gordon, President Board of Trustees; Becky Elliot, President Guild
> **Utilizes:** Special Technical Talent; Guest Conductors; Guest Directors
> **Budget:** $100,000 - $500,000
> **Income Sources:** Private Foundations/Grants/Endowments; Business/Corporate Donations; Box Office; Government Grants; Individual Donations
> **Season:** July - August   **Annual Attendance:** 5,000
> **Affiliations:** OA
> **Performance Facilities:** Cleveland Institute Of Music

NEW CLEVELAND OPERA COMPANY
1422 Euclid Avenue, #1052, Cleveland, OH 44115-2001
(216) 575-0903
> **Founded:** 1976
> **Arts Area:** Grand Opera; Lyric Opera; Light Opera; Operetta
> **Status:** Professional; Non-Profit
> **Type:** Resident
> **Management:** David Bamberger, General Director; Carola Bamberger, Associate Director
> **Officers:** Dr. Clyde L. Nash Jr. MD, President; Oliver F. Emerson, Chairman; John N. Lauer, Derek R. Mumford and Frederick C. Tyler Jr., Vice Presidents; Ronald H. Bell DDS, Secretary; Charles W. Hall, Treasurer
> **Paid Staff:** 15   **Volunteer Staff:** 1
> **Utilizes:** Special Technical Talent; Guest Conductors; Guest Artists; Guest Directors
> **Budget:** $1,000,000 - $5,000,000
> **Income Sources:** Private Foundations/Grants/Endowments; Business/Corporate Donations; Box Office; Government Grants; Individual Donations
> **Season:** October - May
> **Affiliations:** OA
> **Performance Facilities:** State Theatre; Playhouse Square Center

THEATRE

THE CLEVELAND PLAY HOUSE
8500 Euclid Avenue, Cleveland, OH 44106
(216) 795-7010
FAX: (216) 795-7005
> **Founded:** 1916
> **Arts Area:** Professional
> **Status:** Professional; Non-Profit
> **Type:** Performing; Educational

Purpose: To provide the experience of a complete performing arts environment through its varied repertoire of classical and contemporary theatre, facilities and the continuance of young people's theatre training
Management: Dean R. Gladden, Managing Director; Will Rhys, Artistic Director
Officers: George D. Kirkham, Chairman; Richard H. Hahn, President; Harold Fallon, Joseph Gorman, William Jones, Frances Pendleton, Claiborne Rankin, Vice Presidents
Paid Staff: 80
Utilizes: Special Technical Talent; Guest Artists; Guest Directors
Budget: $5,000,000 - $10,000,000
Income Sources: Private Foundations/Grants/Endowments; Business/Corporate Donations; Box Office; Government Grants; Individual Donations
Season: September - May   **Annual Attendance:** 165,000
Affiliations: LORT; TCG; OAC
Performance Facilities: Bolton Theatre; Drury Theatre; Brooks Theatre

CLEVELAND PUBLIC THEATRE
6415 Detroit Avenue, Cleveland, OH 44102
(216) 631-2727
FAX: (216) 523-1440
Founded: 1981
Arts Area: Musical; Community; Folk; Theatrical Group; Puppet; Performance Art
Status: Semi-Professional; Non-Profit
Type: Performing; Touring; Resident; Educational; Sponsoring
Purpose: To provide access to theatre to nontraditional audiences and provide opportunities for artists in the Greater Cleveland Area
Management: James A. Levin, Executive Director; Linda Eisenstein, Development Director; Kevin Beaney, Administrative Director
Officers: William Grulich, President, Board of Trustees; Beverly Wykoff, Secretary; David Ellison, Treasurer
Paid Staff: 10   **Volunteer Staff:** 40
Paid Artists: 50   **Non-Paid Artists:** 80
Utilizes: Special Technical Talent; Guest Artists; Guest Directors
Budget: $100,000 - $500,000
Income Sources: Private Foundations/Grants/Endowments; Business/Corporate Donations; Box Office; Government Grants; Individual Donations
Season: 52 Weeks   **Annual Attendance:** 12,000
Affiliations: OTA; TCG

FAIRMOUNT THEATRE OF THE DEAF
8500 Euclid Avenue, Cleveland, OH 44106
(216) 229-2838
Founded: 1975
Arts Area: Theatrical Group; Sign Language Translators
Status: Professional; Non-Profit
Type: Performing; Touring; Resident; Educational
Purpose: FTD accepts the unique responsibility for providing theatrical and educational performances and workshops for deaf, hearing impaired and hearing people.
Management: Michael G. Regnier, Acting Executive Director; Shanny Mow, Artistic Director
Officers: Jonathan K. Wise, President
Paid Staff: 4   **Volunteer Staff:** 6
Paid Artists: 10
Utilizes: Special Technical Talent; Guest Artists; Guest Directors; SIGN LANGUAGE TRANSLATORS
Budget: $100,000 - $500,000
Income Sources: Private Foundations/Grants/Endowments; Business/Corporate Donations; Box Office; Government Grants; Individual Donations
Season: September - May   **Annual Attendance:** 40,000
Performance Facilities: Cleveland Play House

KARAMU HOUSE
2355 East 89th Street, Cleveland, OH 44106-9990
(216) 795-7070
Founded: 1915
Arts Area: Community
Status: Semi-Professional; Non-Profit
Type: Performing; Touring; Resident
Purpose: To continue the history of rich commitment and dedication to the arts community which has made Karamu House a very important resource in the arts
Management: Margaret Ford-Taylor, Executive Director; Jeff Gruszewski, Program Director
Officers: Lyman Phillips, President; William Robertson, First Vice President; Rev. Marvin McMikle, Second Vice President; Andrew Jackson, Third Vice President; Helen Forbes, Secretary; David Richards, Treasurer
Paid Staff: 7   **Volunteer Staff:** 100

Paid Artists: 12
Utilizes: Special Technical Talent; Guest Artists; Guest Directors
Budget: $100,000 - $500,000
Income Sources: Private Foundations/Grants/Endowments; Business/Corporate Donations; Box Office; Government Grants; Individual Donations
Season: September - June   **Annual Attendance:** 30,000
Affiliations: AATA
Performance Facilities: Karamu House Performing Arts Theatre

PLAYHOUSE SQUARE FOUNDATION
1501 Euclid Avenue, Cleveland, OH 44115
(216) 771-4444
FAX: (216) 771-0217
Founded: 1970
Arts Area: Professional; Musical; Community; Theatrical Group
Status: Professional; Non-Profit
Type: Performing; Touring; Resident; Educational
Purpose: Renovate and operate the three theatres of the Playhouse Square Center
Management: John H. Hemsath, Director of Theatre Operations; Robert J. Rody, Technical Director; Gina Vernaci, Director of Programming; Richard Hyer, Director of Marketing; William Hilyard, Director of Development
Officers: Art J. Falco, President
Paid Staff: 150   **Volunteer Staff:** 1,200
Utilizes: Special Technical Talent; Guest Conductors; Guest Artists; Guest Directors
Budget: $5,000,000 - $10,000,000
Income Sources: Private Foundations/Grants/Endowments; Business/Corporate Donations; Box Office; Government Grants; Individual Donations
Season: 52 Weeks   **Annual Attendance:** 700,000
Affiliations: League of Historic American Theatres; APAP; IAAM; APAC
Performance Facilities: Palace, State and Ohio theatres

PERFORMING SERIES

ART SONG FESTIVAL
c/o The Cleveland Insitute of Music, 11021 East Boulevard, Cleveland, OH 44106
(216) 791-5000, ext. 299
FAX: (216) 791-3063
Founded: 1985
Arts Area: Vocal Music; Instrumental Music; Festivals
Status: Professional; Non-Profit
Type: Performing; Resident; Educational
Purpose: To further collaborative aspects of art song; two singer/pianist master teams offer master classes to participant teams; master recitals and team finale recitals at culmination of festival week
Management: George Vassos, Artistic Director; Karen Knowlton, Executive Director; Sara Smith, Assistant Administrator
Officers: Ralph Drake, Beverly Page and Enid Politzer, Committee Members
Paid Staff: 3   **Volunteer Staff:** 3
Paid Artists: 4   **Non-Paid Artists:** 20
Utilizes: Guest Artists
Budget: $50,000 - $100,000
Income Sources: Private Foundations/Grants/Endowments; Business/Corporate Donations; Box Office; Government Grants; Individual Donations
Season: May   **Annual Attendance:** 1,500
Affiliations: The Cleveland Institute of Music
Performance Facilities: Kulas Recital Hall; Le Pavillon at CIM

THE CLEVELAND MUSEUM OF ART CONCERTS
11150 East Boulevard, Cleveland, OH 44106
(216) 421-7340
FAX: (216) 421-0411
Founded: 1916
Arts Area: Vocal Music; Instrumental Music
Status: Non-Profit
Type: Educational; Sponsoring
Management: Karel Paukert, Chief Curator of Musical Arts; Bruce Shewitz, Associate Curator of Musical Arts
Paid Staff: 3   **Volunteer Staff:** 10
Utilizes: Guest Artists
Income Sources: Private Foundations/Grants/Endowments; Box Office; Individual Donations
Season: 52 Weeks   **Annual Attendance:** 15,000
Performance Facilities: Gartner Auditorium

GREAT LAKES THEATER FESTIVAL
1501 Euclid Avenue, Suite 250, Cleveland, OH 44115
(216) 241-5490
>**Founded:** 1962
Arts Area: Professional
Status: Professional; Non-Profit
Type: Performing; Educational
Purpose: Produce theater with the emphasis on world classics, especially Shakespeare and nonclassical works that contribute significantly to the American theater
Management: Gerald Freedman, Artistic Director; Mary Bill, Managing Director; Phil Crosby, Marketing Director; Bill Rudman, Special Projects Directors; Ann Gardbler, Development Director
Officers: William MacDonald III, Chairman; Mary Ann Jorgenson, Co-Chair; John E. Katzenmeyer, President
Paid Staff: 13 **Volunteer Staff:** 100
Paid Artists: 100
Utilizes: Special Technical Talent; Guest Artists; Guest Directors
Budget: $1,000,000 - $5,000,000
Income Sources: Private Foundations/Grants/Endowments; Business/Corporate Donations; Box Office; Government Grants; Individual Donations
Season: MayandJune - September **Annual Attendance:** 50,000
Affiliations: LORT; AAA
Performance Facilities: Ohio Theatre, Playhouse Square Center

TRI-C JAZZFEST
2900 Community College Avenue, Theatre 11, Cleveland, OH 44115
(216) 987-4444
FAX: (216) 987-4404
>**Founded:** 1980
Arts Area: Vocal Music; Festivals
Status: Non-Profit
Type: Performing; Educational
Purpose: To provide a major event in jazz education for high school and college students, permitting aspiring high school and college jazz musicians to improve their skills and techniques in jazz through instruction by leading jazz educators and artists; to bring together outstanding jazz artists, educators and high school and college students in planned and shared educational and musical experiences
Management: Dr. Thomas Horning, Director; Susan Stone, Education Events Coordinator; Max Dehn, Booking Coordinator; Terri Pontremolli, Special Projects; Cliffie Jones, Office Manager
Paid Staff: 5 **Volunteer Staff:** 50
Paid Artists: 20 **Non-Paid Artists:** 20
Utilizes: Special Technical Talent; Guest Conductors; Guest Artists; Guest Directors
Budget: $100,000 - $500,000
Income Sources: Private Foundations/Grants/Endowments; Business/Corporate Donations; Box Office; Government Grants; Individual Donations
Season: April **Annual Attendance:** 15,000
Affiliations: IAJE
Performance Facilities: College Campus Auditorium; Severance Hall; State Theatre at Playhouse Square

FACILITY

CASE WESTERN RESERVE UNIVERSITY - ELDRED HALL
219099 Euclid Avenue, Cleveland, OH 44106-7077
(216) 368-2858
FAX: (216) 368-5184
>**Type of Facility:** Theatre House
Type of Stage: Proscenium
Stage Dimensions: 17'x27'x31'
Seating Capacity: 152
Year Built: 1897
Year Remodeled: 1938 **Cost:** $35,000
Manager: John M. Orlock, Artistic Director
Originally converted in 1920 at a cost of $11,000

THE CLEVELAND INSTITUTE OF MUSIC - KULAS HALL
11021 East Boulevard, Cleveland, OH 44106
(216) 791-5165
FAX: (216) 791-3063
>**Type of Facility:** Concert Hall; Auditorium; Opera House
Type of Stage: Proscenium

Stage Dimensions: 45'Wx26'D; add 10'D with pit cover in place
Orchestra Pit
Seating Capacity: 540
Year Built: 1960   **Architect:** Shaffer, Flynn, Williams   **Cost:** $3,000,000
Contact for Rental: Laurie Wright;   (216) 791-5165
Resident Groups: Cleveland Baroque Soloists; Canterbury Trio; Cleveland Institute of Music Symphony Orchestra; Chamber Orchestra; Opera Ensemble; Case Western Reserve University Wind Ensemble; Jazz Ensemble; University Chorale and Chamber Choir
Available for rent on a very limited basis

THE CLEVELAND MUSEUM OF ART - GARTNER AUDITORIUM
11150 East Boulevard, Cleveland, OH 44106
(216) 421-7340, ext. 284
FAX: (216) 421-0411
Type of Facility: Concert Hall; Auditorium
Type of Stage: Platform
Stage Dimensions: 67'Wx18'D
Seating Capacity: 765
Year Built: 1971   **Architect:** Marcel Breuer
Resident Groups: Department of Musical Arts: Karel Paukert, Chief Curator/Organist-in-Residence; Bruce Shewitz, Associate Curator
Presents a performing-arts series of 80 concerts each season

THE CLEVELAND PLAY HOUSE
8500 Euclid Avenue, Cleveland, OH 44106
(216) 795-7010
FAX: (216) 795-7005
Type of Facility: Theatre Complex; Performance Center
Year Built: 1927   **Architect:** Francis Draz   **Cost:** $250,000
Year Remodeled: 1984   **Architect:** Philip Johnson   **Cost:** $15,000,000
Contact for Rental: Carl Ritenour, Facilities Coordinator;   (216) 795-7010
The Cleveland Play House contains the Boulton, Brooks and Drury Theatres. See separate listings for further information. 1984 addition added the Boulton Theatre & support facilities for the Center.

THE CLEVELAND PLAY HOUSE - BOULTON THEATRE
8500 Euclid Avenue, Cleveland, OH 44106
(216) 795-7010
FAX: (216) 795-7005
Type of Facility: Theatre House
Type of Stage: Proscenium
Stage Dimensions: 42'Wx40'D; 42'Wx28'H proscenium opening   **Orchestra Pit**
Seating Capacity: 612
Year Built: 1984   **Architect:** Philip Johnson
Contact for Rental: Carl Ritenour, Facilities Coordinator;   (216) 795-7010

THE CLEVELAND PLAY HOUSE - BROOKS THEATRE
8500 Euclid Avenue, Cleveland, OH 44106
(216) 795-7010
FAX: (216) 795-7005
Type of Facility: Theatre House
Type of Stage: Proscenium
Stage Dimensions: 20'Wx26'D; 20'Wx14'H proscenium opening
Seating Capacity: 160
Year Built: 1927
Contact for Rental: Carl Ritenour, Facilities Coordinator;   (216) 795-7010

THE CLEVELAND PLAY HOUSE - DRURY THEATRE
8500 Euclid Avenue, Cleveland, OH 44106
(216) 795-7010
FAX: (216) 795-7005
Type of Facility: Theatre House
Type of Stage: Proscenium
Stage Dimensions: 30'Wx40'D; 30'Wx28'H proscenium opening   **Orchestra Pit**
Seating Capacity: 499
Year Built: 1927
Contact for Rental: Carl Ritenour, Facilities Coordinator;   (216) 795-7010

CLEVELAND PUBLIC THEATRE
6415 Detroit Avenue, Cleveland, OH 44102
(216) 631-2727
FAX: (216) 523-1440
> **Founded:** 1982
> **Type of Facility:** Studio Performance; Environmental; Theatre House; Arena; Multi-Purpose; Loft
> **Facility Originally:** Ballroom; Warehouse
> **Type of Stage:** Flexible; Environmental; Arena
> **Seating Capacity:** 171
> **Year Built:** 1910
> **Year Remodeled:** 1986
> **Contact for Rental:** James A. Levin;   (216) 523-1600;   (216) 631-2727
> **Resident Groups:** Cleveland Public Theatre
> *Theatre, performance art, music and mixed-media events*

KARAMU HOUSE PERFORMING ARTS THEATRE
2355 East 89th Street, Cleveland, OH 44106
(216) 795-7070
> **Type of Facility:** Outdoor (Concert); Theatre House; Amphitheater
> **Year Built:** 1949   **Architect:** Francis Draz   **Cost:** $600,000
> **Contact for Rental:** Thelma McKinley, Registrar;   (216) 795-7070
> **Manager:** Jeff Gruszewski

KARAMU HOUSE PERFORMING ARTS THEATRE - AMPHITHEATRE
2355 East 89th Street, Cleveland, OH 44106
(216) 795-7070
FAX: (216) 795-7070
> **Type of Facility:** Outdoor (Concert); Amphitheater
> **Type of Stage:** Proscenium; Environmental
> **Stage Dimensions:** 17'9"x32'x32'
> **Seating Capacity:** 400
> **Year Built:** 1949
> **Contact for Rental:** Thelma McKinley, Registrar;   (216) 795-7070
> **Manager:** Jeff Gruszewski

KARAMU HOUSE PERFORMING ARTS THEATRE - ARENA
2355 East 89th Street, Cleveland, OH 44106
(216) 795-7070
> **Type of Facility:** Arena
> **Type of Stage:** Arena
> **Stage Dimensions:** 13'6"x45'
> **Seating Capacity:** 125
> **Year Built:** 1949
> **Contact for Rental:** Thelma McKinley, Registrar;   (216) 795-7070
> **Manager:** Jeff Gruszewski

KARAMU HOUSE PERFORMING ARTS THEATRE - PROSCENIUM
2355 East 89th Street, Cleveland, OH 44106
(216) 795-7070
FAX: (216) 795-7070
> **Type of Facility:** Theatre House
> **Type of Stage:** Proscenium
> **Stage Dimensions:** 40'x60'
> **Seating Capacity:** 200
> **Year Built:** 1949
> **Contact for Rental:** Thelma McKinley, Registrar;   (216) 795-7070
> **Manager:** Jeff Gruszewski

PLAYHOUSE SQUARE CENTER
1501 Euclid Avenue, Cleveland, OH 44115
(216) 771-4444
> **Type of Facility:** Theatre Complex; Performance Center
> **Acoustical Consultant:** Jaffe Acoustics
> **Contact for Rental:** John Hemsath;   (216) 771-4444
> **Resident Groups:** Cleveland Ballet; Cleveland Opera; Great Lakes Theatre Festival; Dance Cleveland; Ohio Ballet; Playhouse Square Center Productions
> *Playhouse Square Center contains the Ohio, Palace and State Theatres. See separate listings for further information.*

PLAYHOUSE SQUARE CENTER - OHIO THEATRE
1519 Euclid Avenue, Cleveland, OH 44115
(216) 771-4444
    Type of Facility: Concert Hall; Auditorium; Studio Performance; Theatre House; Opera House
    Facility Originally: Vaudeville
    Type of Stage: Proscenium
    Stage Dimensions: 70'Wx40'D; 41'Wx28'H proscenium opening **Orchestra Pit**
    Seating Capacity: 1,035
    Year Built: 1921 **Architect:** Thomas Lamb
    Year Remodeled: 1982 **Architect:** van Dijk Johnson & Partners **Cost:** $4,000,000
    Acoustical Consultant: Jaffe Acoustics
    Contact for Rental: John Hemsath
    Resident Groups: Great Lakes Theatre Festival; DANCECLEVELAND
    The Theatre is a National Historic Landmark.

PLAYHOUSE SQUARE CENTER - PALACE THEATRE
1519 Euclid Avenue, Cleveland, OH 44115
(216) 771-4444
    Type of Facility: Concert Hall; Auditorium; Studio Performance; Theatre House; Opera House
    Facility Originally: Vaudeville
    Type of Stage: Proscenium; Hydraulic Lift Stage
    Stage Dimensions: 90'Wx38'D; 55'Wx35'H proscenium opening **Orchestra Pit**
    Seating Capacity: 2,800
    Year Built: 1922 **Architect:** Rapp & Rapp
    Architect: van Dijk Johnson & Partners **Cost:** $8,000,000
    Acoustical Consultant: Jaffe Acoustics
    The Theatre is a National Historic Landmark.

PLAYHOUSE SQUARE CENTER - STATE THEATRE
1519 Euclid Avenue, Cleveland, OH 44115
(216) 771-4444
    Type of Facility: Concert Hall; Auditorium; Studio Performance; Theatre House; Opera House
    Facility Originally: Vaudeville
    Type of Stage: Proscenium
    Stage Dimensions: 110'Wx65'D; 55'Wx34'H proscenium opening **Orchestra Pit**
    Seating Capacity: 3,098
    Year Built: 1921 **Architect:** Thomas Lamb
    Year Remodeled: 1984 **Architect:** van Dijk Johnson & Partners **Cost:** $12,000,000
    Acoustical Consultant: Jaffe Acoustics
    Contact for Rental: John Hemsath
    Resident Groups: Cleveland Opera; San Jose Cleveland Ballet
    The Theatre is a National Historic Landmark.

SEVERANCE HALL
11001 Euclid, Cleveland, OH 44106
(216) 231-7300
FAX: (216) 231-0202
    Type of Facility: Auditorium
    Type of Stage: Proscenium **Orchestra Pit**
    Seating Capacity: 2,046
    Year Built: 1931
    Contact for Rental: Cherilyn Byers; (216) 231-7300
    Manager: Peter Karas; (216) 231-7300
    Resident Groups: Cleveland Orchestra

Cleveland Heights

DANCE

SHALHEVET INTERNATIONAL FOLK ENSEMBLE
2140 Lee Road, Suite 218, Cleveland Heights, OH 44118
(216) 932-3455
    Founded: 1968
    Arts Area: Ethnic; Folk
    Status: Professional
    Type: Performing; Touring; Resident; Educational

Purpose: To preserve and promote folklore dance and music from around the world in which the Jewish people have lived; to foster an appreciation of all people; to promote an understanding of our nation's cultural diversity
Management: Clara A. Amster, Executive Director; Daniel M. Ducoff, Artistic Director
Officers: Daniel Ducoff, President; Paul Kantor, Vice President; Stuart Meyer, Treasurer; Clara Amster, Secretary
Paid Staff: 1 **Volunteer Staff:** 20
Paid Artists: 20
Utilizes: Special Technical Talent; Guest Artists; Guest Choreographers
Budget: $1,000 - $50,000
Income Sources: Private Foundations/Grants/Endowments; Business/Corporate Donations; Box Office; Individual Donations
Season: 52 Weeks **Annual Attendance:** 10,000
Performance Facilities: Blance R. Halle Theatre

INSTRUMENTAL MUSIC

THE CLEVELAND OCTET
1510 Crest Road, Cleveland Heights, OH 44121
(216) 381-9031
FAX: (216) 291-0502
Founded: 1977
Arts Area: Chamber; Ensemble
Status: Professional; Non-Profit
Type: Performing; Touring
Purpose: To present and perform rarely performed masterpieces for ensembles of six to eight players
Management: Columbia Artist Management, NY Sheldon Division
Officers: Erich Eichhorn, Founder and Director
Volunteer Staff: 1
Paid Artists: 8
Utilizes: Guest Artists
Income Sources: Private Foundations/Grants/Endowments; Box Office; Individual Donations
Season: September - May
Affiliations: ORACLE; Cleveland Museum of Art; Cleveland Orchestra
Performance Facilities: Cleveland Museum of Art

HEIGHTS CHAMBER ORCHESTRA
3165 Monmouth Road, Cleveland Heights, OH 44118
(216) 321-4259
Founded: 1983
Arts Area: Symphony; Orchestra
Status: Non-Profit
Type: Performing
Purpose: Community orchestra and extension of music education in the public and private schools
Management: Gino Raffaeli, Concert Master; John Fioritto, Conductor
Volunteer Staff: 1
Paid Artists: 4 **Non-Paid Artists:** 52
Budget: $1,000 - $50,000
Income Sources: Government Grants; Individual Donations
Season: September - May **Annual Attendance:** 1,500
Affiliations: Cleveland Heights Board of Education; Cleveland Heights Parks and Recreation Department
Performance Facilities: Performing Arts Center, Cleveland Heights High School

SHAKER SYMPHONY ORCHESTRA
2843 Edgehill Road, Cleveland Heights, OH 44118
(216) 321-3704
Founded: 1938
Arts Area: Symphony; Orchestra
Status: Non-Professional; Non-Profit
Type: Performing
Purpose: Opportunity for amateurs to perform 5-6 times in concert
Management: Dr. Henry Schackne, Manager
Budget: $1,000 - $50,000
Income Sources: Private Foundations/Grants/Endowments; Individual Donations

THEATRE

DOBAMA THEATRE
1846 Coventry Road, Cleveland Heights, OH 44118
(216) 932-6838
Founded: 1959

Arts Area: Theatrical Group
Status: Non-Professional; Non-Profit
Type: Performing; Resident; Educational
Purpose: Produce five plays not yet available to Cleveland Heights audiences; encourage new American playwrights by offering staged readings and full world premiere productions of their work; encourage creative expression in children through annual Marilyn Biarchi Kids Playwriting Festival
Management: Jean Cummins, Literary Manager; Owen Kelly, Public Relations Director; Joyce Casey, Artistic and Managing Director; Deborah Bradlin, Development Director; Ron Newell, Technical Director; Dave Morris, House Manager
Officers: Jewish Community Center of Cleveland Board of Directors
Volunteer Staff: 10
Non-Paid Artists: 70
Budget: $50,000 - $100,000
Income Sources: Private Foundations/Grants/Endowments; Business/Corporate Donations; Box Office; Government Grants; Individual Donations
Season: September - June   **Annual Attendance:** 7,000
Affiliations: OTA

PERFORMING SERIES

JEWISH COMMUNITY CENTER OF CLEVELAND
3505 Mayfield Road, Cleveland Heights, OH 44118
(216) 382-4000
FAX: (216) 382-5401
    Arts Area: Dance; Theater; Visual Arts
    Status: Professional; Non-Professional; Non-Profit
    Type: Performing; Resident; Educational
    Purpose: To provide opportunities through the arts for persons of all ages to explore and strengthen Jewish identity, arts expertise, and human-relation skills toward more effective living in our diverse, democratic society
    Management: David Kleinman, Executive Director; Michael J. Peterman, President
    Utilizes: Guest Conductors; Guest Artists; Guest Directors
    Income Sources: Box Office; Individual Donations
    Affiliations: National Jewish Welfare Board; United Torch; Jewish Community Center
    Performance Facilities: Blanche R. Halle Theater

PARK ARTS FESTIVAL - SUMMER SEASON
Lee and Superior Roads, Cleveland Heights, OH 44118
(216) 291-5796
FAX: (216) 291-2064
    Founded: 1938
    Arts Area: Dance; Vocal Music; Instrumental Music; Theater; Festivals; Visual Arts
    Status: Professional; Non-Profit
    Type: Sponsoring
    Management: Janet Herman-Barlow, General Manager; B.D. Thomas, Operations Manager
    Paid Staff: 50
    Paid Artists: 200
    Utilizes: Guest Conductors; Guest Artists; Guest Directors
    Budget: $100,000 - $500,000
    Income Sources: Private Foundations/Grants/Endowments; Business/Corporate Donations; Box Office; Government Grants; Individual Donations
    Season: June - September   **Annual Attendance:** 100,000
    Affiliations: OAC
    Performance Facilities: Evans Amphitheatre; Evans Alma Theater

SHALHAVET
2140 Lee Road, Suite 218, Cleveland Heights, OH 44118
(216) 932-3455
    Management: Clara Amster, Executive Director
    Budget: $1,000 - $50,000

FACILITY

DOBAMA THEATRE
1846 Coventry Road, Cleveland Heights, OH 44118
(216) 932-6838
    Type of Facility: Theatre House
    Facility Originally: Bowling Alley
    Type of Stage: Thrust
    Stage Dimensions: 13'x24'x16'

Seating Capacity: 200
Year Built: 1920
Year Remodeled: 1968
Converted into a theatre in 1968

Columbus

DANCE

BALLET METROPOLITAN
322 Mount Vernon Avenue, Columbus, OH 43215
(614) 224-1672
Founded: 1974
Arts Area: Ballet
Status: Professional; Non-Profit
Type: Performing; Touring; Resident; Educational; Sponsoring
Purpose: To maintain a resident professional ballet company; to develop a repertoire encompassing a range of classical and contemporary work; to provide educational audience development services to the community; to build a dance academy which provides professional training and vocational instruction
Management: John McFall, Artistic Director; Xandra Auderhalt, Dance Academy Administrator; Mary K. Bailey, Executive Director
Officers: Nancy Strause, Chairman of the Board; Jeff Rich, Executive Officer
Paid Staff: 20   **Volunteer Staff:** 5
Paid Artists: 25
Utilizes: Special Technical Talent; Guest Artists
Budget: $1,000,000 - $5,000,000
Income Sources: Private Foundations/Grants/Endowments; Business/Corporate Donations; Box Office; Government Grants; Individual Donations
Season: August - April   **Annual Attendance:** 100,000
Affiliations: NARB; Dance USA
Performance Facilities: Ohio Theatre

PERFORMING ARTS PROGRAMS IN DANCE
Wexner Center for the Arts, North High Street at 15th Avenue, Columbus, OH 43210
(614) 292-0330
FAX: (614) 292-3369
Arts Area: Modern; Mime; Ballet; Jazz; Ethnic; Folk
Status: Professional; Non-Profit
Type: Performing; Touring; Resident; Educational; Sponsoring
Purpose: To present the best in contemporary arts
Management: William Cook, Acting Director; Adrienne Bosworth, Director of Communications
Budget: $100,000 - $500,000
Income Sources: Private Foundations/Grants/Endowments; Business/Corporate Donations; Box Office; Government Grants; Individual Donations
Performance Facilities: Mershon Auditorium

STUART PIMSLER DANCE & THEATER
61 Jefferson Avenue, Columbus, OH 43215
(614) 461-0132
Founded: 1978
Arts Area: Modern
Status: Professional
Type: Performing
Purpose: To present performance work that comments on contemporary issues
Management: William Powell, Company Administrator; Stuart Pimsler
Officers: Elizabeth Bank, President; Katherine Burman, Secretary; Sue Haidle, Treasurer
Paid Staff: 1   **Volunteer Staff:** 3
Paid Artists: 6
Utilizes: Special Technical Talent; Guest Artists; Guest Directors
Budget: $100,000 - $500,000
Income Sources: Private Foundations/Grants/Endowments; Business/Corporate Donations; Individual Donations
Season: September - June
Affiliations: Ohio Dance; APAP; Alliance for Dance and Movement Arts

UNIVERSITY DANCE COMPANY
Dance Dept., Ohio State University, 1813 North High Street, Columbus, OH 43210
(614) 292-7977
Founded: 1968

Arts Area: Modern
Status: Semi-Professional; Non-Profit
Type: Performing; Touring; Resident; Educational
Purpose: University Dance Company functions as a professional training ground for selected dance majors working towards a professional career in dance and performance.
Management: Rosalind Pierson, Director; Vera Blaine, Chair, Department of Dance
Paid Staff: 4
Paid Artists: 7 **Non-Paid Artists:** 20
Utilizes: Special Technical Talent; Guest Conductors; Guest Artists
Budget: $1,000 - $50,000
Income Sources: Private Foundations/Grants/Endowments; Business/Corporate Donations; Box Office
Season: September - June **Annual Attendance:** 12,000
Affiliations: National Association of School of Dance; American College Dance Festival Association
Performance Facilities: Sullivan Theatre

WORTHINGTON CIVIC BALLET AND JAZZ NORTH DANCE COMPANIES
7029 Huntley Road, Suite G, Columbus, OH 43229
(614) 888-7471
Founded: 1963
Arts Area: Ballet; Jazz
Status: Professional; Semi-Professional; Non-Profit
Type: Performing; Touring; Educational
Purpose: Worthington Civic Ballet, a student-civic company, presents yearly performances of "The Nutcracker" as well as spring concerts and "Jazz North" artists-in-schools tours throughout central Ohio.
Management: Barbara Burrows, Director/Choreographer
Officers: Barbara Burrows, President; Duard Farquhar, Vice President; Robert Albright, Secretary
Paid Staff: 12 **Volunteer Staff:** 15
Paid Artists: 6 **Non-Paid Artists:** 20
Utilizes: Special Technical Talent; Guest Artists; Guest Directors
Budget: $100,000 - $500,000
Income Sources: Private Foundations/Grants/Endowments; Business/Corporate Donations; Box Office; Individual Donations
Season: 52 Weeks **Annual Attendance:** 24,000
Performance Facilities: Battelle Auditorium; Ohio Theatre; Worthington High School

INSTRUMENTAL MUSIC

COLUMBUS SYMPHONY ORCHESTRA
55 East State Street, Columbus, OH 43215
(614) 224-5281
FAX: (614) 224-7273
Founded: 1952
Arts Area: Symphony; Orchestra; Chamber; Ensemble
Status: Professional
Type: Performing; Educational; Sponsoring
Purpose: To foster, promote, and increase musical knowledge of the public by educational activities and presenting performances of music
Management: Stephen Vann, Executive Director; Susan Rosenstock, Orchestra Manager
Officers: John Kane, Chairman; Ronald Pizzuti, First Vice Chairman; Peter Frenzer and Paula B. Brothers, Vice Chairmen; John Josephson, Secretary; David Lauer, Treasurer
Paid Staff: 24 **Volunteer Staff:** 1,500
Paid Artists: 125
Utilizes: Special Technical Talent; Guest Conductors; Guest Artists
Budget: $5,000,000 - $10,000,000
Income Sources: Private Foundations/Grants/Endowments; Business/Corporate Donations; Box Office; Government Grants; Individual Donations
Season: September - August **Annual Attendance:** 250,000
Affiliations: ASOL
Performance Facilities: Ohio Theatre; Mershon Auditorium

COLUMBUS SYMPHONY YOUTH ORCHESTRA
55 East State Street, Columbus, OH 43215
(614) 224-5281
FAX: (614) 234-7273
Founded: 1955
Arts Area: Symphony; Orchestra; Chamber
Status: Non-Professional; Non-Profit
Type: Performing; Touring; Educational

Purpose: To provide the highest quality educational and performance experiences for central Ohio's most gifted instrumentalists
Management: Peter Stafford Wilson, Music Director/Conductor
Officers: Linda Odronic, Chairman; Harold Scharp, Vice Chairman; Linda Hampton, Secretary; Becky Stains, Treasurer
Paid Staff: 4   **Volunteer Staff:** 15
Non-Paid Artists: 250
Utilizes: Guest Artists
Budget: $50,000 - $100,000
Income Sources: Box Office
Season: November - May   **Annual Attendance:** 5,000
Affiliations: ASOL (Youth Orchestra Division); Columbus Symphony Orchestra
Performance Facilities: Weigel Hall, Ohio State University

THE JAZZ ARTS GROUP OF COLUMBUS
709 College Avenue, Columbus, OH 43209
(614) 231-7836
FAX: (614) 235-9744
   Founded: 1972
   Arts Area: Orchestra; Jazz
   Status: Professional; Non-Profit
   Type: Performing; Touring; Resident; Educational
   Purpose: To present and perform America's only indigenous art form
   Management: Ray Eubanks, General Manager/Artistic Director; Margaret Barr, Operations; Mitch Swain, Marketing/Development; Andy Houser, Box Office
   Officers: Jim Brock, President; Bob Ackerman, Vice President; Mark Shary, Treasurer; Ethel Shapiro, Secretary
   Volunteer Staff: 25
   Utilizes: Guest Artists
   Budget: $1,000,000 - $5,000,000
   Income Sources: Private Foundations/Grants/Endowments; Business/Corporate Donations; Box Office; Government Grants; Individual Donations
   Season: 52 Weeks   **Annual Attendance:** 305,000
   Affiliations: City of Columbus Music in the Air
   Performance Facilities: Batelle Auditorium; Palace Theatre

PRO MUSICA CHAMBER ORCHESTRA OF COLUMBUS
444 East Broad Street, Columbus, OH 43215
(614) 464-0066
FAX: (614) 464-4141
   Arts Area: Symphony; Orchestra; Chamber
   Status: Professional; Non-Profit
   Type: Performing; Touring
   Purpose: To establish a partnership with the audience in order to understand and fulfill audience needs for a variety of entertaining and enlightening musical performances as well as educational experiences
   Management: Francis Little, General Manager; Dr. Timothy Russell, Music Director/Conductor
   Paid Staff: 5   **Volunteer Staff:** 15
   Utilizes: Guest Conductors; Guest Artists
   Income Sources: Private Foundations/Grants/Endowments; Business/Corporate Donations; Box Office; Individual Donations
   Season: October - July
   Performance Facilities: Weigel Hall; Riverfront Amphitheatre

VOCAL MUSIC

COLUMBUS SYMPHONY CHORUS
c/o Columbus Symphony Orchestra Inc., 55 East State Street, Columbus, OH 43215
(614) 224-5281
FAX: (614) 224-7273
   Arts Area: Choral
   Status: Non-Professional; Non-Profit
   Type: Performing; Resident; Educational
   Purpose: To educate and inform the public about great music
   Management: Ron Jenkins, Conductor; Lois Zook, Assistant to Conductor
   Officers: John Kane, Chairman of the Board
   Budget: $1,000 - $50,000
   Income Sources: Private Foundations/Grants/Endowments; Business/Corporate Donations; Box Office; Government Grants; Individual Donations
   Season: 52 Weeks
   Performance Facilities: Ohio Theatre

OPERA/COLUMBUS
177 Naghten Street, Columbus, OH 43215
(614) 461-8101
FAX: (614) 461-0806
Founded: 1980
Arts Area: Grand Opera
Status: Professional; Non-Profit
Type: Performing; Educational
Purpose: Opera/Columbus shall produce high-quality, professional opera and make it easily accessible to the diverse audience in the central Ohio area while also providing educational and audience-building outreach programs, growing into a regional producing company of national stature. Opera/Columbus shall engage established artists of national and international prominence, all the while maintaining the fiscal stability necessary to achieve its artistic goals.
Management: William F. Russell, General Director; Barb Seckler, Director of Marketing; Michael Ranney, Director of Development; Ned Snyder, Business Manager; Alice Hunt, Office Manager
Officers: Sheldon Taft, President; Walt Holway and Irma Cooper, Vice Presidents; Lois Chope, Secretary; Molly Morris, Past President
Paid Staff: 10   **Volunteer Staff:** 2
Paid Artists: 100
Utilizes: Special Technical Talent; Guest Conductors; Guest Artists; Guest Directors
Budget: $1,000,000 - $5,000,000
Income Sources: Private Foundations/Grants/Endowments; Business/Corporate Donations; Box Office; Government Grants; Individual Donations
Season: October - May   **Annual Attendance:** 25,000
Affiliations: OA
Performance Facilities: Palace Theatre

THEATRE

ACTORS' SUMMER THEATRE COMPANY
1000 City Park, Columbus, OH 43206
(614) 444-6888
Founded: 1982
Arts Area: Summer Stock; Musical; Community; Theatrical Group
Status: Semi-Professional; Non-Profit
Type: Performing; Touring; Resident; Educational
Purpose: Free, outdoor, public theatre company which aims to make quality theatre with an emphasis on entertaining productions of Shakespeare, accessible to the entire area
Management: Patricia B. Ellson, Artistic Director; Scott Skiles, Designer/Technical Director
Officers: Howard Hamilton, President
Paid Staff: 3   **Volunteer Staff:** 2
Paid Artists: 35   **Non-Paid Artists:** 100
Utilizes: Special Technical Talent; Guest Conductors; Guest Artists; Guest Directors
Budget: $100,000 - $500,000
Income Sources: Private Foundations/Grants/Endowments; Business/Corporate Donations; Box Office; Government Grants; Individual Donations
Season: June - September   **Annual Attendance:** 30,000
Performance Facilities: Schiller Park Amphitheatre

PLAYERS THEATRE COLUMBUS
77 South High Street, Columbus, OH 43215
(614) 644-5300
FAX: (614) 621-2338
Mailing Address: PO Box 18185, Columbus, OH 43218-0185
Founded: 1923
Arts Area: Professional
Status: Professional; Non-Profit
Type: Performing; Touring; Resident; Educational
Purpose: Committed to providing a wide range of high quality theatrical productions and programs to Central Ohio audiences, young and old
Management: Ed Graczyk, Artistic Director; Jean Ann Klaus, Managing Director; Steven C. Anderson, Associate Artistic Director; Lenore P. Kaler, Marketing Director; P. Susan Sharrock, Public Relations Manager; John York, Carol Dultigg, Production Managers
Officers: Charles R. Martin, President-Board of Directors; Kenneth Warren, Executive Vice President; Tanny Crane, Secretary; Robert G. Jones, Treasurer; Joel Teaford, Vice President
Paid Staff: 45   **Volunteer Staff:** 1,800
Paid Artists: 120

Utilizes: Special Technical Talent; Guest Conductors; Guest Artists; Guest Directors
Budget: Over 10,000,000
Income Sources: Private Foundations/Grants/Endowments; Business/Corporate Donations; Box Office; Government Grants; Individual Donations
Season: September - June
Annual Attendance: 125,000
Affiliations: LORT; OTA; AEA; USA; TCG; Cols Area Chamber of Commerce; Greater Columbus Commercial Visitor Bureau
Performance Facilities: Vern Riffe Center for Government and the Arts; Capitol Theatre; Studio One Theatre; Studio Two Theatre

THE REALITY THEATRE
736 North Pearl Street, Columbus, OH 43215
(614) 294-7541
Founded: 1985
Arts Area: Theatrical Group
Status: Semi-Professional; Non-Profit
Type: Performing; Resident
Purpose: Primarily dedicated to the development of experimental plays and also the presentation of original scripts written by Ohio playwrights
Management: Frank A. Barnhart, Producer/Artistic Director; Daneta Shepherd, Producer/Artistic Director
Paid Staff: 16   **Volunteer Staff:** 10
Paid Artists: 16
Utilizes: Guest Artists; Guest Directors
Budget: $50,000 - $100,000
Income Sources: Private Foundations/Grants/Endowments; Business/Corporate Donations; Box Office; Government Grants; Individual Donations
Season: 52 Weeks
Annual Attendance: 6,000

STROLLERS STUDENT THEATRICS
1739 North High Street, Ohio Union, Box 36, Columbus, OH 43201
(614) 292-6061
Founded: 1892
Arts Area: Musical; Community; Theatrical Group
Status: Non-Professional; Non-Profit
Type: Performing
Purpose: To provide the students of Ohio State University and members of the community with the opportunity to participate in all aspects of the performing arts
Officers: Kyle Grube, President; Sandy Hugill, Vice President; Stacey Feldman, Recording Secretary; Keith Davis, Corresponding Secretary; Katy Beachy, Treasurer
Budget: $1,000 - $50,000
Income Sources: Box Office
Season: September - May

PERFORMING SERIES

COLUMBUS ARTS FESTIVAL
55 East State Street, Columbus, OH 43215
(614) 224-2606
Founded: 1961
Arts Area: Dance; Vocal Music; Instrumental Music; Festivals
Status: Professional; Non-Professional; Non-Profit
Type: Performing; Festival
Purpose: To present an annual arts festival
Management: Rod Reiner, General Manager; Vikki Shultz, Fesitval Assistant
Officers: Ray Hanley, President
Paid Staff: 2   **Volunteer Staff:** 35
Budget: $500,000 - $1,000,000
Income Sources: Business/Corporate Donations; Earned Income
Season: June   **Annual Attendance:** 500,000
Affiliations: Greater Columbus Arts Council

FACILITY

DAVIS DISCOVERY CENTER - AGNES JEFFREY SHEDD THEATRE
549 Franklin Avenue, Columbus, OH 43215
(614) 645-7469
Type of Facility: Theatre House

> **Type of Stage:** Proscenium
> **Stage Dimensions:** 42'Wx30'Dx30'H; 42'Wx12'H proscenium opening   **Orchestra Pit**
> **Seating Capacity:** 350
> **Year Built:** 1976   **Architect:** Feinknoff, Maclore & Shappa
> **Contact for Rental:** Jack Zimmerman;   (614) 645-6639
> *Limited availability on theatre rental*

DAVIS DISCOVERY CENTER - HENRY VAN FLEET THEATRE
549 Franklin Avenue, Columbus, OH 43215
(614) 645-7469
> **Type of Facility:** Black Box
> **Type of Stage:** Flexible
> **Stage Dimensions:** 28'Wx21'Dx16'H
> **Seating Capacity:** 199
> **Year Remodeled:** 1976   **Architect:** Feinknoff, Maclore & Shappa
> **Contact for Rental:** Jack Zimmerman;   (614) 645-6639

JEWISH COMMUNITY CENTER OF CLEVELAND - BLANCHE R. HALLE THEATER
3505 Mayfield Road, Columbus, OH 44118
(216) 382-4000
> **Type of Facility:** Cultural Center
> **Orchestra Pit**
> **Seating Capacity:** 275
> **Year Built:** 1960
> **Manager:** Dorothy Silver

MARTIN LUTHER KING JR. PERFORMING AND CULTURAL ARTS COMPLEX
867 Mt. Vernon Avenue, Columbus, OH 43203
(614) 252-5464
FAX: (614) 252-3807
> **Founded:** 1985
> **Type of Facility:** Performance Center; Multi-Purpose
> **Facility Originally:** Vaudeville; Ballroom
> **Type of Stage:** Proscenium
> **Stage Dimensions:** 19'11"Dx50'10"W apron to proscenium
> **Seating Capacity:** 444
> **Year Built:** 1926   **Architect:** Samuel Plato   **Cost:** $125,000
> **Year Remodeled:** 1986   **Architect:** Moody Nolan and Associates
> **Acoustical Consultant:** Howard Newman
> **Contact for Rental:** Joe Barrett;   (614) 252-5464
> **Resident Groups:** Center Stage Theatre; Imani Theatre Folk

OHIO STATE UNIVERSITY - STADIUM II THEATRE
1089 Drake Union, 1849 Cannon Drive, Columbus, OH 43210
(614) 292-5821
> **Type of Facility:** Theatre Complex; Studio Performance; Theatre House
> **Type of Stage:** Thrust; Platform; 3/4 Arena
> **Stage Dimensions:** 29'x24'
> **Seating Capacity:** 250
> **Year Built:** 1972
> **Year Remodeled:** 1987
> **Contact for Rental:**   (614) 252-5821
> **Resident Groups:** Ohio State University Theatre Company

OHIO STATE UNIVERSITY - THURBER THEATRE
1089 Drake Union, 1849 Cannon Drive, Columbus, OH 43210
(614) 292-5821
> **Type of Facility:** Theatre Complex; Auditorium; Theatre House
> **Type of Stage:** Proscenium
> **Stage Dimensions:** 36'x30'
> **Orchestra Pit**
> **Seating Capacity:** 600
> **Year Built:** 1972
> **Year Remodeled:** 1986
> *Available for rent*

OHIO THEATRE
55 East State Street, Columbus, OH 43215-4264
(614) 469-1045
FAX: (614) 224-7461
Founded: 1927
Type of Facility: Concert Hall; Auditorium; Studio Performance; Performance Center; Theatre House; Multi-Purpose
Facility Originally: Movie House
Type of Stage: Proscenium
Stage Dimensions: 47'4x62'
Orchestra Pit
Seating Capacity: 2,897
Year Built: 1927   **Architect:** Thomas W. Lamb   **Cost:** $865,000
Year Remodeled: 1984   **Architect:** Hardy Holzman Pfeiffer Associates   **Cost:** $6,000,000
Acoustical Consultant: Peter George Associates
Contact for Rental: Douglas F. Kridler or Debra Rosental;   (614) 469-1045
Resident Groups: Columbus Symphony Orchestra; BalletMet; Columbus Theatrical Association; Columbus Association for the Performing Arts (CAPA)

PALACE THEATRE
34 West Broad Street, Columbus, OH 43215-4264
(614) 469-1045
FAX: (614) 224-7461
Founded: 1926
Type of Facility: Concert Hall; Auditorium; Performance Center; Theatre House; Opera House; Multi-Purpose
Facility Originally: Vaudeville; Movie House
Type of Stage: Proscenium
Stage Dimensions: 47'8"x35'
Orchestra Pit
Seating Capacity: 2,827
Year Built: 1926   **Architect:** Thomas W. Lamb   **Cost:** $3,000,000
Year Remodeled: 1980   **Architect:** Bohm-NBBJ   **Cost:** $2,000,000
Contact for Rental: Douglas F. Kridler or Debra Rosenthal;   (614) 469-1045
Resident Groups: Opera/Columbus; Jazz Arts Group; Columbus Theatrical Association (producer of Broadway plays); CAPA

PLAYERS THEATRE COLUMBUS
Vern Riffe Center for Government & the Arts, 77 High Street South, Columbus, OH 43215
(614) 644-5300
Type of Facility: Theatre Complex
Facility Originally: Private Residence
Year Remodeled: 1976   **Architect:** Feinknoff Maclore & Shappa   **Cost:** $1,000,000
Contact for Rental: John H. York;   (614) 644-5300
Resident Groups: Players Theatre Columbus
The Players Theatre contains the Agnes Jeffrey Shedd Theatre and the Henry Van Fleet Theatre. Limited availability on theatre rental

VETERANS MEMORIAL
300 West Broad Street, Columbus, OH 43215
(614) 221-4341
FAX: (614) 221-8422
Type of Facility: Multi-Purpose
Type of Stage: Proscenium
Stage Dimensions: 182'Wx32'D; 72'Wx27'H proscenium opening
Orchestra Pit
Seating Capacity: 3,944
Year Built: 1955   **Architect:** Associate Architects   **Cost:** $6,000,000
Contact for Rental: Richard P. Nolan, Melody A. Stevens;   (614) 221-4341

WEXNER CENTER FOR THE ARTS/MERSHON AUDITORIUM
30 West 15th Avenue, Columbus, OH 43210
(614) 292-5785
Type of Facility: Concert Hall; Auditorium
Type of Stage: Proscenium
Stage Dimensions: 42'x100'x63'9"
Orchestra Pit

Seating Capacity: 3,058
Year Built: 1957
Acoustical Consultant: Jeff McMahon
Contact for Rental: Claudia Bonham;   (614) 292-5785
Manager: Charles Helm, Director, Performing Arts;   (614) 292-5785

Cuyahoga Falls

DANCE

CUYAHOGA VALLEY YOUTH BALLET
1853 Joan of Arc Circle, PO Box 3131, Cuyahoga Falls, OH 44223
(216) 928-4027
Founded: 1975
Arts Area: Modern; Ballet
Status: Non-Professional; Non-Profit
Type: Performing; Resident; Educational
Purpose: To provide performing experience for talented young dancers, educating them in the realities of professional ballet; to educate area children and families in the appreciation of ballet as an art form at affordable prices
Management: Nan Klinger, Artistic Director
Officers: Tom Hardy, President; Andrea Kok, Vice President; Gail Noble, Recording Secretary; Bernadette Harris, Corresponding Secretary; David Sarver, Treasurer
Volunteer Staff: 33
Non-Paid Artists: 33
Utilizes: Guest Artists; Guest Choreographers
Budget: $1,000 - $50,000
Income Sources: Private Foundations/Grants/Endowments; Business/Corporate Donations; Box Office; Individual Donations
Affiliations: OAC
Performance Facilities: Akron Civic Theatre; E.J. Thomas Hall

FACILITY

BLOSSOM MUSIC CENTER
1145 West Steels Corners Road, Cuyahoga Falls, OH 44223
(216) 231-7300
Type of Facility: Outdoor (Concert); Amphitheater
Type of Stage: Proscenium
Stage Dimensions: 71'x49'   **Orchestra Pit**
Seating Capacity: Pavilion - 5,281; Lawn - 13,500
Year Built: 1968   **Architect:** Peter van Dijk   **Cost:** $9,113,230
Acoustical Consultant: Jaffe Acoustics
Contact for Rental: Alan J. DeZon;   (216) 920-8040
Resident Groups: Cleveland Orchestra
To promote and present approximately 60 events during an 18-week summer season ranging from classical to rock 'n roll

Dayton

DANCE

DANCE THEATRE DAYTON
1306 East Fifth Street, Dayton, OH 45402
(513) 223-9228
Arts Area: Ballet
Status: Professional; Non-Profit
Type: Performing
Management: Deborah DeRado, Artistic Director
Paid Artists: 17
Income Sources: Box Office; Individual Donations
Performance Facilities: Victory Theater

DAYTON BALLET
140 North Main Street, Dayton, OH 45402
(513) 449-5060
FAX: (513) 461-8353
Founded: 1937
Arts Area: Ballet; Contemporary

Status: Non-Profit
Type: Performing
Purpose: To present professional dance; to train professional dancers; to aid the growth and development of dance
Management: James R. Albright, General Manager; James Clouser, Artistic Director/Choreographer; Dermot Burke, Executive Director
Officers: R. Daniel Sadlier, President; Daniel W. Duval, Chairman of the Board
Paid Staff: 19　**Volunteer Staff:** 10
Paid Artists: 17　**Non-Paid Artists:** 25
Utilizes: Special Technical Talent; Guest Choreographers
Budget: $100,000 - $500,000
Income Sources: Private Foundations/Grants/Endowments; Business/Corporate Donations; Box Office; Government Grants; Individual Donations
Season: October - April　**Annual Attendance:** 48,000
Affiliations: APAP; Ohio Dance; ORACLE
Performance Facilities: Victoria Theatre

DAYTON CONTEMPORARY DANCE COMPANY
126 North Main Street, Suite 200, Dayton, OH 45402
(513) 223-3232
FAX: (513) 223-6156
Founded: 1968
Arts Area: Modern; Ballet; Jazz; Ethnic; Folk; Contemporary
Status: Professional; Non-Profit
Type: Performing; Touring; Resident
Management: Jeraldyne Blunden, Artistic Director; Hal Andress, Managing Director; Kevin Ward, Associate Artistic Director; Debbie Blunden-Diggs, Director, 2nd Company; Mark Coldiron, Production Manager; Karen Clark, Stage Manager; Lowell Mathwich, Tour Manager; Dawn Wood, Rehearsal Mistress
Officers: Stanley Earley, Chairman of the Board of Trustees
Paid Staff: 11　**Volunteer Staff:** 10
Paid Artists: 15　**Non-Paid Artists:** 12
Utilizes: Special Technical Talent; Guest Artists; Guest Choreographers
Budget: $100,000 - $500,000
Income Sources: Private Foundations/Grants/Endowments; Business/Corporate Donations; Box Office; Government Grants; Individual Donations; Performance Fees
Season: August - May　**Annual Attendance:** 32,000
Affiliations: American Dance Festival
Performance Facilities: The Victory Theatre

INSTRUMENTAL MUSIC

DAYTON PHILHARMONIC ORCHESTRA ASSOCIATION
Memorial Hall, 125 East First Street, Dayton, OH 45422
(513) 224-3521
FAX: (513) 223-9189
Founded: 1933
Arts Area: Symphony; Orchestra; Chamber
Status: Professional; Non-Profit
Type: Performing; Resident; Educational; Sponsoring
Purpose: To maintain and foster a professional symphonic orchestra of the highest possible quality and provide live concerts for pleasure and cultural enhancement
Management: John E. Bauser, Executive Director; Isaiah Jackson, Music Director
Officers: James Vanvleck, President; Mrs. Steve Mason, Vice President; Mrs. William McCormick, Secretary; John Hazelton, Treasurer
Paid Staff: 7　**Volunteer Staff:** 1
Paid Artists: 102
Utilizes: Guest Conductors; Guest Artists
Budget: $1,000,000 - $5,000,000
Income Sources: Private Foundations/Grants/Endowments; Business/Corporate Donations; Box Office; Government Grants; Individual Donations
Season: September - May
Affiliations: ASOL; AAA; ACA; OOOO; OCCA
Performance Facilities: Montgomery County's Memorial Hall; Dayton Convention and Exhibition Center

DAYTON PHILHARMONIC YOUTH ORCHESTRA
Memorial Hall, 125 East First Street, Dayton, OH 45402
(513) 224-3521
FAX: (513) 223-9189
Founded: 1982
Arts Area: Symphony; Orchestra

Status: Non-Professional; Non-Profit
Type: Performing; Educational
Purpose: To give aspiring young musicians of the Dayton area an opportunity to work together studying challenging orchestral music; to attempt to strengthen and expand the musical skills, knowledge, talent and experience through the study of the symphonic orchestral literature
Management: Dr. William J. Steinhort, Conductor/Music Director; Sonia Goldfarb, Operations Manager, Dayton Philharmonic Orchestra; Xiao-Guang Zhu, Conductor, Junior String Orchestra
Paid Staff: 1   **Volunteer Staff:** 180
Non-Paid Artists: 90
Utilizes: Guest Artists
Budget: $1,000 - $50,000
Season: September - July   **Annual Attendance:** 16,000
Affiliations: ASOL (Youth Orchestra Division); Ohio Music Club; Dayton Philharmonic Orchestra
Performance Facilities: Concert Hall, Wright State University

THE TOP BRASS QUARTET
PO Box 9327, Dayton, OH 45409
(513) 253-5812
Founded: 1979
Arts Area: Chamber; Instrumental Group
Status: Professional
Type: Performing; Touring; Recording
Purpose: Nationwide performance in a wide variety of settings
Management: Scott Bridges, Management Director; David Coleman, Internal Manager; Norlan Bewley, Artistic Manager
Paid Staff: 3
Paid Artists: 5
Utilizes: Guest Artists
Season: 52 Weeks
Annual Attendance: 50,000

VOCAL MUSIC

DAYTON OPERA ASSOCIATION
Memorial Hall, 125 East First Street, Dayton, OH 45402
(513) 228-0662; (513) 228-0287
FAX: (513) 228-9612
Founded: 1960
Arts Area: Grand Opera; Operetta; Musical Theatre
Status: Professional; Non-Profit
Type: Performing; Resident; Educational
Purpose: To increase appreciation for opera through education; to present and promote opera of high quality to the Dayton region as well as present balanced programs; to utilize international artists; to encourage local and regional artistic development
Management: Jane Nelson, General Director
Paid Staff: 4   **Volunteer Staff:** 325
Paid Artists: 150   **Non-Paid Artists:** 30
Utilizes: Special Technical Talent; Guest Conductors; Guest Artists; Guest Directors
Budget: $1,000,000 - $5,000,000
Income Sources: Private Foundations/Grants/Endowments; Business/Corporate Donations; Box Office; Government Grants; Individual Donations
Season: October - May
Annual Attendance: 20,000
Affiliations: OA; AAA; Dayton Performing Arts Fund
Performance Facilities: Montgomery County's Memorial Hall

THEATRE

THE CREEKSIDE PLAYERS
636 Superior Avenue, Dayton, OH 45407
(513) 228-2012
Founded: 1978
Arts Area: Community
Status: Non-Professional; Non-Profit
Type: Performing

Purpose: To develop, present, and promote Black Theatre as an important art form, using dramatic art as the medium to convey the African and African-American experience
Management: Ray Alexander, Artistic Director; Nancy Gibson, Administrative Assistant
Officers: Leo A. Lucas, Treasurer
Volunteer Staff: 7
Non-Paid Artists: 10
Utilizes: Guest Directors
Budget: $1,000 - $50,000
Income Sources: Private Foundations/Grants/Endowments; Box Office; Individual Donations
Season: October - July
Annual Attendance: 3,000

DAYTON PLAYHOUSE
1301 East Siebenthaler Avenue, Dayton, OH 45414
(513) 277-0144
Founded: 1959
Arts Area: Musical; Community; Theatrical Group
Status: Non-Professional; Non-Profit
Type: Performing
Management: Jim Payne, Managing Director
Officers: Noel Vaughn, Chairman; John Riley, Treasurer
Paid Staff: 7 **Volunteer Staff:** 650
Utilizes: Special Technical Talent; Guest Artists; Guest Directors
Budget: $100,000 - $500,000
Income Sources: Private Foundations/Grants/Endowments; Business/Corporate Donations; Box Office; Government Grants; Individual Donations
Season: 52 Weeks **Annual Attendance:** 13,500
Affiliations: ACT; OCTA
Performance Facilities: Dayton Playhouse

PERFORMING SERIES

THE UNIVERSITY OF DAYTON ARTS SERIES
Dayton, OH 45469-0619
(513) 229-2787
FAX: (513) 229-4000
Founded: 1961
Arts Area: Dance; Vocal Music; Instrumental Music; Theater
Status: Professional; Non-Profit
Type: Performing; Sponsoring
Purpose: To provide a performing arts series presenting the variety of the arts to campus and community
Management: Maureen Cronin Masters, Directors
Paid Staff: 2 **Volunteer Staff:** 18
Paid Artists: 10
Utilizes: Special Technical Talent; Guest Artists
Budget: $1,000 - $50,000
Income Sources: Private Foundations/Grants/Endowments; Box Office; Government Grants; Individual Donations
Season: September - April **Annual Attendance:** 5,000
Affiliations: APAP
Performance Facilities: Boll Theatre

FACILITY

DAYTON CONVENTION AND EXHIBITION CENTER
22 Dave Hall Plaza, East 5th Street, Dayton, OH 45402
(513) 443-4700
FAX: (513) 443-4711
Type of Facility: Civic Center
Type of Stage: In-the-round Capability
Seating Capacity: 674
Year Built: 1973 **Architect:** DeVeau-Kleski **Cost:** $6,000,000
Contact for Rental: Manager; (513) 443-4700

DAYTON PLAYHOUSE
1301 East Siebenthaler Avenue, Dayton, OH 45414
(513) 222-7000
FAX: (513) 277-9539
Type of Facility: Auditorium; Theatre House

Type of Stage: Thrust; Flexible; Proscenium; 3/4 Arena; Arena
Stage Dimensions: 39'x28'
Seating Capacity: 210
Year Built: 1988

MONTGOMERY COUNTY'S MEMORIAL HALL
125 East First Street, Dayton, OH 45422
(513) 225-5898
FAX: (513) 225-4922
   Type of Facility: Concert Hall; Auditorium; Theatre House; Opera House
   Facility Originally: Meeting Hall; Veteran's Memorial
   Type of Stage: Proscenium
   Stage Dimensions: 73'6"Wx36'71/2"D; 58'Wx26'H proscenium opening   **Orchestra Pit**
   Seating Capacity: 2,501 **Year Built:** 1910
   Year Remodeled: 1990
   Acoustical Consultant: Sound Force
   Contact for Rental: Betty Rice;   (513) 225-5898
   Manager: Carol Cleavenger, Director of Cultural Facilities and Affairs
   Resident Groups: Dayton Philharmonic Orchestra; Dayton Opera

Euclid

DANCE

THE TOM EVERT DANCE COMPANY
Shore Cultural Centre, 291 East 222 Street, Euclid, OH 44123
(216) 261-3654
   Founded: 1986
   Arts Area: Modern
   Status: Professional; Non-Profit
   Type: Performing; Touring; Resident; Educational; Special Events
   Purpose: To create choreography and perform it in concerts; to serve as an educational resource
   Management: Tom Evert, Artistic Director; Marcia Unger, Administrative Assistant; Susana Evert, Marketing Director; Lawrence L. Evert Jr., Bookings
   Officers: Dennis Sutcliff, Chairman; Timothy Evert, President; Thomas R. Hawn, Treasurer; Hugh McKay, Secretary
   Paid Staff: 3   **Volunteer Staff:** 2
   Paid Artists: 6   **Non-Paid Artists:** 1
   Utilizes: Special Technical Talent; Guest Artists; Original Music Scores
   Budget: $100,000 - $500,000
   Income Sources: Private Foundations/Grants/Endowments; Business/Corporate Donations; Box Office; Government Grants; Individual Donations; Benefits and Fundraisers
   Season: 52 Weeks   **Annual Attendance:** 20,000
   Affiliations: APAP; Arts Midwest; Arts Presenters Network; Ohio Dance; Ohio Citizens Committee for the Arts
   Performance Facilities: Cleveland Playhouse

Fostoria

THEATRE

FOSTORIA FOOTLIGHTERS
PO Box 542, Fostoria, OH 44830
(419) 435-7501
   Founded: 1959
   Arts Area: Musical; Community; Theatrical Group
   Status: Non-Professional; Non-Profit
   Type: Performing; Resident; Educational
   Officers: Ann Duffield, President; Jackie Bodart, Vice President; Douglas F. Bland, Secretary; C. Browning Payne, Treasurer
   Volunteer Staff: 12
   Non-Paid Artists: 100
   Utilizes: Guest Artists; Guest Directors
   Budget: $1,000 - $50,000
   Income Sources: Business/Corporate Donations; Box Office; Individual Donations

Season: September - May   **Annual Attendance:** 4,000
Affiliations: Ohio Community Theatre Alliance
Performance Facilities: Fostoria Footlighters

FACILITY

FOSTORIA FOOTLIGHTERS, INC.
PO Box 542, Fostoria, OH 44830
(419) 435-7501
    Type of Facility: Theatre House
    Facility Originally: Church
    Type of Stage: Thrust; Proscenium
    Stage Dimensions: 30'x30'
    Seating Capacity: 180
    Year Built: 1885   **Cost:** $18,000
    Year Remodeled: 1972   **Cost:** $8,000
    Contact for Rental: Donald Shoub;   (419) 435-1063
    Manager: Joanne Love;   (419) 435-0337
    Resident Groups: Fostoria Footlighters

Gates Mills

INSTRUMENTAL MUSIC

CROATIAN TAMBURITZA ORCHESTRA OF CLEVELAND
6974 Gates Road, Gates Mills, OH 44040-9646
(216) 442-0231
    Founded: 1953
    Arts Area: Orchestra; Ethnic; Folk; Instrumental Group
    Status: Semi-Professional; Non-Profit
    Type: Performing; Touring; Educational
    Purpose: To preserve and perpetuate the art of playing the national folk instrument of Croatia (the tamburitza) as well as Croatia's classical/semi-classical and folk music
    Management: Nick S. Babic, Manager/Musical Director
    Officers: Rudy Ujcich, President; Linda Fuduric, Treasurer
    Volunteer Staff: 20
    Non-Paid Artists: 20
    Utilizes: Special Technical Talent
    Budget: $1,000 - $50,000
    Income Sources: Private Foundations/Grants/Endowments; Business/Corporate Donations; Individual Donations
    Season: 52 Weeks
    Annual Attendance: 10,000

Granville

DANCE

ZIVILI: DANCES AND MUSIC OF THE SOUTH SLAVS
1753 Loudon Street, Granville, OH 43023
(614) 855-7805
FAX: (614) 587-1690
    Founded: 1973
    Arts Area: Ethnic
    Status: Professional; Non-Profit
    Type: Performing; Touring; Educational
    Purpose: To preserve the dance, music and song of the Croations, Slovenians, Serbs, Bosnians and Montenegrins
    Management: Robert M. Gewald, Booking Agent; Melissa P. Obenauf, Executive Director
    Officers: Sue P. Glander, President; Diane M. Lease, President-Elect; Constance Leal, Treasurer

Paid Staff: 9   **Volunteer Staff:** 1
Paid Artists: 28
Utilizes: Special Technical Talent; Guest Choreographers
Budget: $100,000 - $500,000
Income Sources: Private Foundations/Grants/Endowments; Business/Corporate Donations; Box Office; Government Grants; Individual Donations
Season: September - May   **Annual Attendance:** 50,000
Performance Facilities: Palace Theatre

Kent

THEATRE

PORTHOUSE THEATRE COMPANY
PO Box 5190, Kent, OH 44242-0001
(216) 672-3884
Founded: 1968
Arts Area: Professional; Summer Stock; Musical; Theatrical Group
Status: Professional; Semi-Professional; Non-Profit
Type: Performing; Educational
Management: Raynette Halvorsen Smith, Producing Director; David Colwell, Managing Director; Eric Barr, Interim Artistic Director
Officers: Jay Thomas, President; Bryan Williams, Secretary; Maria Mastromatteo, Treasurer
Paid Staff: 3
Paid Artists: 50
Utilizes: Special Technical Talent; Guest Conductors; Guest Artists; Guest Directors
Budget: $100,000 - $500,000
Income Sources: Private Foundations/Grants/Endowments; Business/Corporate Donations; Box Office; Government Grants; Individual Donations; Kent State University
Season: June 19 - August 16   **Annual Attendance:** 8,000
Affiliations: Kent State University
Performance Facilities: Porthouse Theatre of Blossom Music Center

Lakeside

INSTRUMENTAL MUSIC

LAKESIDE SYMPHONY
236 Walnut Avenue, Lakeside, OH 43440
(419) 798-4461
Founded: 1925
Arts Area: Symphony; Orchestra; Chamber
Status: Professional; Non-Profit
Type: Performing; Resident; Educational
Purpose: To provide a resident orchestra at Lakeside on a professional level for part of the summer season
Management: Philip L. Zimmerman, Executive Director; Robert L. Conquist, Musical Director; Barbara J. Sauvey, Manager
Officers: Lary L. Faris, President; Kenneth J. Erb, Vice President; Lucille Smith, Secretary; Neil L. Allen, Treasurer
Paid Staff: 3   **Volunteer Staff:** 20
Paid Artists: 60
Utilizes: Guest Artists
Budget: $50,000 - $100,000
Income Sources: Individual Donations
Season: August 1 - August 28   **Annual Attendance:** 10,000
Performance Facilities: Hoover Auditorium

PERFORMING SERIES

THE LAKESIDE ASSOCIATION
236 Walnut Avenue, Lakeside, OH 43440
(419) 798-4461
FAX: (419) 798-5033
Founded: 1873
Arts Area: Dance; Vocal Music; Instrumental Music; Theater

Status: Professional; Non-Profit; Commercial
Type: Sponsoring
Purpose: To establish and maintain schools, conferences, institutes, lecture courses and other means of aesthetic culture
Management: Philip Zimmerman, Executive Director
Paid Staff: 100   **Volunteer Staff:** 1
Utilizes: Guest Conductors; Guest Artists
Budget: $1,000,000 - $5,000,000
Income Sources: Individual Donations
Season: June - September   **Annual Attendance:** 44,000
Performance Facilities: Auditorium

Lakewood

THEATRE

THE BECK CENTER FOR THE CULTURAL ARTS
17801 Detroit Avenue, Lakewood, OH 44107
(216) 521-2540
Founded: 1930
Arts Area: Musical; Community
Status: Non-Professional
Type: Performing; Touring; Resident; Educational
Purpose: The Beck Center is one of only two comprehensive cultural arts organizations in the state.
Management: Scott Spencer, Acting Artistic Director; Andrea Krist, Managing Director; Stuart Mendel, Director of Development; Linda Sackett, Director of Education; Don McBride, Production and Design
Officers: Rosemary Corcoran, President; Brian King, Vice President; Marjorie Wiess, Treasurer
Paid Staff: 78   **Volunteer Staff:** 300
Non-Paid Artists: 200
Utilizes: Special Technical Talent; Guest Conductors; Guest Artists; Guest Directors
Budget: $1,000,000 - $5,000,000
Income Sources: Private Foundations/Grants/Endowments; Business/Corporate Donations; Box Office; Government Grants; Individual Donations
Season: September - June
Annual Attendance: 60,000

FACILITY

KENNETH C. BECK CENTER FOR THE PERFORMING ARTS
17801 Detroit Avenue, Lakewood, OH 44107
(216) 521-2540
Type of Facility: Auditorium
Type of Stage: Proscenium
Seating Capacity: 500
Year Built: 1976   **Architect:** Fred Toguchi   **Cost:** $1,500,000
Contact for Rental: Manager;   (216) 521-2540

Lancaster

VOCAL MUSIC

THE LANCASTER CHORALE
PO Box 251, Lancaster, OH 43130
(614) 569-4306
Founded: 1985
Arts Area: Choral
Status: Professional
Type: Performing; Touring
Purpose: To bring the highest quality choral art to Lancaster in a subscription series and to record and tour

Officers: Cathy Tolbert, President Board of Directors
Paid Staff: 3
Paid Artists: 32
Utilizes: Guest Artists
Budget: $1,000 - $50,000
Income Sources: Private Foundations/Grants/Endowments; Business/Corporate Donations; Box Office; Government Grants; Individual Donations
Season: November - July
Affiliations: CA

PERFORMING SERIES

CAMEO CONCERTS, INC.
127 West Wheeling Street, PO Box 1452, Lancaster, OH 43130
(614) 687-4808
FAX: (614) 654-4626
Founded: 1980
Status: Non-Profit
Type: Educational; Sponsoring
Purpose: To promote and foster an appreciation of classical musicl; to organize concerts and other programs in the community which feature classical music; to sponsor dramas and other theatrical productions, films, lectures, art exhibits, choreographic presentations and other events which serve to enrich the cultural climate of the community
Management: Eleanor Hood and Barbara Hunzicker, Co-Directors; Jim Bletzacker, Site Manager; Gary Sheldon, Music Director; Steve Rosenberg, Orchestra Manager
Officers: Don Wendel Jr, President; Jim Carpenter, Vice President; Connie Leitnaker, Secretary; Bob Wolfinger, Financial Director
Paid Staff: 1   **Volunteer Staff:** 30
Paid Artists: 473
Utilizes: Special Technical Talent; Guest Conductors; Guest Artists; Guest Directors
Budget: $100,000 - $500,000
Income Sources: Private Foundations/Grants/Endowments; Business/Corporate Donations; Box Office; Government Grants; Individual Donations
Season: July - August   **Annual Attendance:** 45,000

Lima

INSTRUMENTAL MUSIC

LIMA SYMPHONY ORCHESTRA
PO Box 1651, Lima, OH 45802
(419) 222-5701
Founded: 1953
Arts Area: Symphony; Orchestra; Chamber
Status: Semi-Professional; Non-Profit
Type: Performing; Educational; Sponsoring
Purpose: To promote the musical knowledge and appreciation of the public by organizing and presenting performances of live music (symphonic, chamber, opera and others)
Management: Leslie Vining, Executive Director; Joseph Firszt, Music Director/Conductor; Anita Sims Skinner, Personnel Manager
Officers: Victor Marone, President; James Chiles, First Vice President; Anita Hayes, Treasurer
Paid Staff: 4
Paid Artists: 80
Utilizes: Guest Conductors; Guest Artists; Guest Directors
Budget: $100,000 - $500,000
Income Sources: Private Foundations/Grants/Endowments; Business/Corporate Donations; Box Office; Government Grants; Individual Donations
Season: September - April   **Annual Attendance:** 20,000
Affiliations: ASOL
Performance Facilities: Veterans Memorial Civic and Convention Center

PERFORMING SERIES

COUNCIL FOR THE ARTS OF GREATER LIMA
120 East Elm Street, Lima, OH 45801
(419) 222-1096
Founded: 1966
Arts Area: Dance; Vocal Music; Instrumental Music; Theater; Festivals; Lyric Opera
Status: Non-Profit

Type: Educational; Sponsoring
Purpose: To promote, encourage, foster, develop, increase, advance, and diffuse knowledge, respect, understanding, taste, and public appreciation in the fields of literature, science, and the arts to benefit the people of Lima
Management: Diane Peterson, Executive Director; Cheryl Krouse, Assistant Director; Rebecca Elberfeld-Hoge, Development Director; Nora Davis, Office Manager
Officers: Richard Seitz, President; Neil Winget, Vice President; Starr Cook, Financial Officer; Mary Ann Sadlier, Secretary
Paid Staff: 4
Paid Artists: 250
Budget: $100,000 - $500,000
Income Sources: Private Foundations/Grants/Endowments; Business/Corporate Donations; Box Office; Government Grants; Individual Donations
Season: 52 Weeks   **Annual Attendance:** 125,000
Performance Facilities: Civic Center

FACILITY

VETERANS MEMORIAL CIVIC AND CONVENTION CENTER
7 Public Square, Lima, OH 45801
(419) 224-5222
Founded: 1984
Type of Facility: Theatre Complex; Multi-Purpose
Type of Stage: Proscenium
Stage Dimensions: 60'x40'   **Orchestra Pit**
Seating Capacity: 1,767
Year Built: 1984   **Architect:** Sasaki Associates, Inc.   **Cost:** $10,000,000
Acoustical Consultant: Bolt, Beranek & Newman
Contact for Rental: Jane L. Riggs or Roger Lammers;   (419) 224-5222
Manager: Florian Smith
Veterans Memorial Convention and Civic Center contains the Crouse Performance Hall, Exhibition Hall and meeting rooms. See separate listing for further information on Crouse Performance Hall.

VETERANS MEMORIAL CIVIC AND CONVENTION CENTER - CROUSE PERFORMANCE HALL
7 Public Square, Lima, OH 45801
(419) 224-5222
Type of Facility: Concert Hall; Theatre House
Type of Stage: Proscenium
Stage Dimensions: 60'Wx40'D   **Orchestra Pit**
Seating Capacity: 1,771
Year Built: 1984
Contact for Rental: Florian Smith;   (419) 224-5222
Resident Groups: Lima Symphony Orchestra; Lima Area Concert Band; Lima Civic Chorus

Lorain

FACILITY

PALACE CIVIC CENTER
Broadway at 6th Street, Lorain, OH 44052
(216) 245-2323
Type of Facility: Performance Center; Multi-Purpose
Facility Originally: Vaudeville; Movie House
Type of Stage: Proscenium
Stage Dimensions: 40'x50'x26'   **Orchestra Pit**
Seating Capacity: 1,399
Year Built: 1928
Year Remodeled: 1977   **Cost:** $500,000
Contact for Rental: John R. Handyside;   (216) 245-2323

Loveland

INSTRUMENTAL MUSIC

OHIO VALLEY BRASS QUINTET
156 Buckboard Lane, Loveland, OH 45140
(513) 722-1855
Founded: 1982

Arts Area: Chamber; Instrumental Group
Status: Professional
Type: Performing; Educational
Purpose: To provide a fine musical experience as part of any occasion for which brass ensemble music is appropriate
Management: Stephen E. Heimlich, Managing Director
Volunteer Staff: 2
Paid Artists: 5
Budget: $1,000 - $50,000
Income Sources: Private Foundations/Grants/Endowments; Business/Corporate Donations
Season: 52 Weeks

Lyndhurst

DANCE

GRANDINELE LITHUANIAN FOLK DANCERS
1620 Curry Drive, Lyndhurst, OH 44124
(216) 442-8674
Founded: 1953
Arts Area: Ethnic
Status: Non-Professional; Non-Profit
Type: Performing; Touring
Purpose: To promote folk art
Volunteer Staff: 3
Non-Paid Artists: 43
Budget: $1,000 - $50,000
Income Sources: Private Foundations/Grants/Endowments; Business/Corporate Donations; Box Office; Individual Donations
Season: September 15 - June 15 **Annual Attendance:** 5,000

Mansfield

INSTRUMENTAL MUSIC

MANSFIELD SYMPHONY SOCIETY, INC.
142 Park Avenue West, Mansfield, OH 44902
(419) 524-5927
Founded: 1930
Arts Area: Symphony; Orchestra; Ensemble
Status: Professional; Non-Profit
Type: Performing; Touring; Educational
Purpose: To present symphony concerts mainly from symphony repertoire including educational and pops programming
Management: Dr. Thomas J. Carto, General Manager; Jeff Holland Cook, Music Director/Conductor; Janet E. Keeler, Development Director
Officers: William McIntyre, President; Jeanne Alexander, Vice President; J. Brad Preston, Secretary; Dan Scurci, Treasurer
Paid Staff: 8 **Volunteer Staff:** 15
Paid Artists: 120
Utilizes: Guest Conductors; Guest Artists
Budget: $100,000 - $500,000
Income Sources: Private Foundations/Grants/Endowments; Business/Corporate Donations; Box Office; Government Grants; Individual Donations
Season: September - May **Annual Attendance:** 18,000
Affiliations: ASOL; ORACLE; OCCA
Performance Facilities: Renaissance Theater

THEATRE

MANSFIELD PLAYHOUSE
95 East Third Street, Mansfield, OH 44902
(419) 522-8140
Founded: 1929
Arts Area: Musical; Community; Theatrical Group
Status: Non-Professional
Type: Performing; Touring; Resident; Educational
Purpose: To provide entertainment and to encourage the advancement of theatre art in all its branches

Management: Lisa Plant, Artistic Director; Cliff Mears, Business Manager; Gary Simmons, Building Manager; Kathy Maxwell, Secretary/Box Office Manager
Officers: Sondra Asher, President; Lynda Smith, Treasurer; Cliff Mears, Business Manager; Doug Wertz, First Vice President; Maggie Paul, Second Vice President; Gene White, Secretary; Steve Zigmund, Assistant Secretary
Paid Staff: 30 **Volunteer Staff:** 70
Paid Artists: 7
Utilizes: Special Technical Talent; Guest Conductors; Guest Artists; Guest Directors; Guest Musicians
Budget: $100,000 - $500,000
Income Sources: Private Foundations/Grants/Endowments; Business/Corporate Donations; Box Office; Government Grants; Individual Donations
Season: September - June **Annual Attendance:** 12,000
Affiliations: OTA; OAC; Ohio Community Theatre Alliance

THE RENAISSANCE THEATRE
138 Park Avenue West, Mansfield, OH 44902
(419) 522-2726
Founded: 1979
Arts Area: Professional; Community
Status: Professional; Semi-Professional; Non-Profit; Commercial
Type: Performing; Educational; Sponsoring
Purpose: To operate a community and regional entertainment, cultural, educational and civic center; to preserve and restore the Renaissance Theatre
Management: Tony Miller, Executive Director; Joan Gemzer, Operations Manager; Aaron Ferguson, Technical Director
Paid Staff: 9 **Volunteer Staff:** 350
Utilizes: Special Technical Talent; Guest Conductors; Guest Artists; Guest Directors
Budget: $500,000 - $1,000,000
Income Sources: Private Foundations/Grants/Endowments; Business/Corporate Donations; Box Office; Government Grants; Individual Donations
Season: 52 Weeks **Annual Attendance:** 125,000
Affiliations: APAP; ORACLE; OTA
Performance Facilities: Renaissance Theatre

FACILITY

CENTRAL PARK BANDSHELL
Mansfield City Square, Mansfield, OH 44902
(419) 755-9819
Type of Facility: Outdoor (Concert); Amphitheater
Type of Stage: Concert Shell
Stage Dimensions: 20'x20'
Seating Capacity: 100
Year Built: 1977 **Architect:** Tim Alexander
Contact for Rental: Park Office
Rental available at no charge

Marietta

INSTRUMENTAL MUSIC

MARIETTA COLLEGE/CIVIC SYMPHONETTE
Department of Music, Marietta College, Marietta, OH 45750
(614) 374-4688
Founded: 1963
Arts Area: Symphony; Orchestra
Status: Non-Professional; Non-Profit
Type: Performing
Purpose: To provide playing experience for students, faculty, and community; to provide the community with an opportunity to hear symphonic music
Management: H. Dean Cummings, Conductor/Manager
Paid Staff: 3
Paid Artists: 8
Utilizes: Guest Artists
Budget: $1,000 - $50,000
Income Sources: Private Foundations/Grants/Endowments
Season: August - May **Annual Attendance:** 2,000
Affiliations: ASOL; OOOO

Marion

THEATRE

MARION COMMUNITY THEATER
PO Box 981, Marion, OH 43302
(614) 383-2101
    Founded: 1963
    Arts Area: Musical; Theatrical Group
    Status: Non-Professional; Non-Profit
    Type: Performing; Educational
    Purpose: To stimulate, promote and develop interest in the dramatic arts by operation of a permanent theatre
    Management: Val Freeman, Tim McGhee, Kevin Orth, Directors
    Officers: Tim McGhee, President; Kathy Heberding, Secretary
    Volunteer Staff: 25
    Non-Paid Artists: 90
    Budget: $50,000 - $100,000
    Income Sources: Private Foundations/Grants/Endowments; Business/Corporate Donations; Box Office;
    Individual Donations
    Season: September - June   **Annual Attendance:** 8,000
    Affiliations: Ohio Concerned Citizens for the Arts; FACT
    Performance Facilities: Palace Theatre

FACILITY

PALACE THEATRE
276 West Center Street, Marion, OH 43302
(614) 383-2101
    Type of Facility: Performance Center
    Type of Stage: Thrust; Flexible; Proscenium
    Stage Dimensions: 49'8"Wx30'D   **Orchestra Pit**
    Seating Capacity: 1,431
    Year Built: 1928   **Architect:** John Eberson   **Cost:** $500,000
    Year Remodeled: 1976   **Architect:** Burris Edwards Lockwood   **Cost:** $550,000
    Contact for Rental: Errol Selsby, Managing Director;   (614) 383-2101
    Resident Groups: Marion Community Theatre; Marion Concert Association; Marion Travel & Adventure Series; Marion
    Community Band
    The Palace Cultural Arts Association manages the theatre

Mayfield Heights

INSTRUMENTAL MUSIC

THE SHAKER SYMPHONY ORCHESTRA
5910 Mayflower Avenue, Mayfield Heights, OH 44124
(216) 461-7149
    Founded: 1938
    Arts Area: Symphony; Orchestra
    Status: Non-Professional; Non-Profit
    Type: Performing; Resident
    Purpose: For the weekly meeting and classical music playing by non-professionals of all ages and backgrounds for public
    free concerts
    Management: Henry Schakne, Business Manager
    Officers: Dr. J. Werner Kiwi, President; Debbie Horn, Secretary; Bernard Biederman, Treasurer
    Paid Staff: 1   **Volunteer Staff:** 9
    Non-Paid Artists: 2
    Utilizes: Guest Artists
    Budget: $1,000 - $50,000
    Income Sources: Business/Corporate Donations; Individual Donations
    Season: September - May   **Annual Attendance:** 1,500
    Performance Facilities: Orange High School Auditorium

Mentor

INSTRUMENTAL MUSIC

THE HERITAGE BRASS QUINTET
6231 Dawson Boulevard, Mentor, OH 44060
(216) 257-4678
Founded: 1981
Arts Area: Ensemble
Status: Professional; Non-Profit
Type: Performing; Touring; Resident; Educational
Purpose: To develop awareness and to give performances of brass quintet literature at the highest level
Management: Erik S. Svoboda, Manager
Paid Staff: 1
Paid Artists: 5
Budget: $1,000 - $50,000
Income Sources: Private Foundations/Grants/Endowments; Business/Corporate Donations; Box Office; Individual Donations

---
New Philadelphia

INSTRUMENTAL MUSIC

TUSCARAWAS PHILHARMONIC
PO Box 406, New Philadelphia, OH 44663
(216) 477-6153
Founded: 1935
Arts Area: Symphony; Orchestra
Status: Semi-Professional; Non-Profit
Type: Performing
Purpose: To bring musical enjoyment to young and old, and improve cultural aspects of the community
Management: Margery Kent Henke, Music Director/Conductor; Robert L. Henke, General Manager
Officers: Melanie Winn, President; Paul Hurd, Vice President; Janice Cosenza, Secretary; Peggy Bears, Treasurer
Paid Staff: 2
Paid Artists: 25 **Non-Paid Artists:** 35
Utilizes: Guest Artists
Budget: $1,000 - $50,000
Income Sources: Private Foundations/Grants/Endowments; Business/Corporate Donations; Box Office; Government Grants; Individual Donations
Season: October - May **Annual Attendance:** 3,500
Performance Facilities: Dover High School

PERFORMING SERIES

OHIO OUTDOOR HISTORICAL DRAMA ASSOCIATION
PO Box 450, New Philadelphia, OH 44633
(216) 364-5111
Founded: 1967
Arts Area: Musical
Status: Non-Profit
Type: Educational; Sponsoring
Purpose: To produce Paul Green's original outdoor drama, "Trumpet in the Land"
Management: Margaret M. Bonamico, Producer
Officers: Jim Stoll, President; James E. King, Vice President; Rhonda Leeper, Secretary; Todd Turner, Treasurer
Paid Staff: 3 **Volunteer Staff:** 1
Paid Artists: 70
Utilizes: Special Technical Talent; Guest Directors
Budget: $100,000 - $500,000
Income Sources: Private Foundations/Grants/Endowments; Business/Corporate Donations; Box Office; Government Grants; Individual Donations
Season: June - September **Annual Attendance:** 30,000
Affiliations: AEA
Performance Facilities: Schoenbrunn Amphitheatre

FACILITY

SCHOENBRUNN AMPHITHEATRE
PO Box 450, New Philadelphia, OH 44663
(216) 339-1132; (216) 364-5111
Type of Facility: Amphitheater
Type of Stage: Proscenium
Stage Dimensions: 60'Wx30'D
Seating Capacity: 1,600
Year Built: 1969   **Architect:** Don M. Hisaka   **Cost:** $725,000
Contact for Rental: Manager;   (216) 339-1132

TUSCARAWAS CAMPUS OF KENT STATE UNIVERSITY - AUDITORIUM
University Drive, NE, New Philadelphia, OH 44663
(216) 339-3391
Type of Facility: Auditorium; Film & Lecture Hall
Type of Stage: Proscenium
Seating Capacity: 300
Year Built: 1968   **Architect:** Marr Knapp Crawfis
Year Remodeled: 1971   **Architect:** Marr Knapp Crawfis
Contact for Rental: Tuscarawas Campus of Kent State University;   (216) 339-3391

Niles

FACILITY

TRUMBULL NEW THEATRE
5883 Youngstown-Warren Road, Niles, OH 44446
(216) 652-1103
Type of Facility: Theatre House
Type of Stage: Thrust
Stage Dimensions: 38'Wx30'D
Seating Capacity: 186
Year Built: 1957   **Architect:** Thomas A. Schroth   **Cost:** $50,000
Year Remodeled: 1977   **Cost:** $100,000
Contact for Rental: Manager;   (216) 652-1103

Norwalk

THEATRE

TOWNE AND COUNTRY PLAYERS
55 East Main Street, PO Box 551, Norwalk, OH 44857
(419) 668-1641
Founded: 1966
Arts Area: Musical; Dinner; Community; Theatrical Group
Status: Semi-Professional; Non-Profit
Type: Performing
Purpose: Clean family programs
Management: Ronn Koerper, Executive Director
Officers: Cheryl Gfell, President
Paid Staff: 15   **Volunteer Staff:** 75
Paid Artists: 3   **Non-Paid Artists:** 2
Utilizes: Special Technical Talent; Guest Artists
Budget: $100,000 - $500,000
Income Sources: Private Foundations/Grants/Endowments; Business/Corporate Donations; Box Office;
Individual Donations
Season: 52 Weeks   **Annual Attendance:** 50,000

FACILITY

TOWNE AND COUNTRY PLAYERS
55 East Main Street, PO Box 551, Norwalk, OH 44857
(419) 668-1641
Type of Facility: Theatre House
Type of Stage: Proscenium
Stage Dimensions: 30'x25'   **Orchestra Pit**

Seating Capacity: 900
Year Built: 1941
Year Remodeled: 1986
Contact for Rental: Ronn Koerper;   (419) 668-1641

Novelty

FACILITY

FAIRMOUNT FINE ARTS CENTER
8400 Fairmount Road, PO Box 80, Novelty, OH 44072
(216) 338-3171
    Type of Facility: Film & Lecture Hall
    Type of Stage: Rehearsal Studio
    Year Built: 1970   **Cost:** $150,000
    Contact for Rental: Marsha Carl;   (216) 338-3171
    Resident Groups: Fairmount Spanish Dancers; Fairmount Dancin' Jazz Company; Fairmount Junior Spanish Dancers
    Studio rental and meetings

Oberlin

INSTRUMENTAL MUSIC

OBERLIN BAROQUE ENSEMBLE
Conservatory of Music, Oberlin College, Oberlin, OH 44074
(216) 338-3171
    Founded: 1973
    Arts Area: Chamber; Ensemble; Instrumental Group
    Status: Professional
    Type: Performing; Touring; Resident; Educational
    Purpose: An ensemble dedicated to performing 17th and 18th-century music on original instruments
    Management: Kathie Stewart
    Paid Staff: 1
    Paid Artists: 4
    Utilizes: Guest Artists
    Budget: $1,000 - $50,000
    Income Sources: Private Foundations/Grants/Endowments; Box Office
    Season: September - July   **Annual Attendance:** 2,000
    Affiliations: Oberlin College Conservatory of Music
    Performance Facilities: Oberlin Conservatory

VOCAL MUSIC

OBERLIN COMMUNITY CHAMBER SINGERS
PO Box 0354, Oberlin, OH 44074
(216) 774-2226
    Founded: 1966
    Arts Area: Choral
    Status: Non-Profit
    Type: Performing; Touring; Educational
    Purpose: To bring together excellent musicians to learn and perform a wide variety of quality choral repertoire; to specialize in music by female or black composers; to provide staged programs as well as others
    Management: Fran Baumann, Concert Manager; Carol Longsworth, Music Director
    Officers: Sharon Morgan, President; Brian Schieferstein, Vice President; Doug Fox, Secretary; Marion Drummond, Treasurer
    Paid Staff: 2   **Volunteer Staff:** 20
    Paid Artists: 2   **Non-Paid Artists:** 22
    Utilizes: Guest Artists; Guest Directors
    Budget: $1,000 - $50,000
    Income Sources: Private Foundations/Grants/Endowments; Business/Corporate Donations; Box Office; Government Grants; Individual Donations
    Season: September - June   **Annual Attendance:** 1,000

Oxford

INSTRUMENTAL MUSIC

MIAMI WIND QUINTET
Department of Music, Miami University, Oxford, OH 45056
(513) 529-1809, ext. 3014
FAX: (513) 529-3841
Founded: 1985
Arts Area: Chamber; Instrumental Group
Status: Professional
Type: Performing; Touring; Resident; Educational
Purpose: Perform chamber music for winds and assist young wind players
Management: Cathy McVey, Director of Audience Development
Paid Staff: 1
Paid Artists: 5
Utilizes: Guest Artists
Budget: $1,000 - $50,000
Income Sources: Private Foundations/Grants/Endowments
Season: August - May   **Annual Attendance:** 7,000
Affiliations: Miami University
Performance Facilities: Souers Recital Hall, Miami University

---

Parma Heights

FACILITY

CUYAHOGA COMMUNITY COLLEGE - WESTERN CAMPUS THEATRE
11000 Pleasant Valley, Parma Heights, OH 44130
(216) 842-7773
Type of Facility: Theatre Complex
Type of Stage: Proscenium
Stage Dimensions: 20'x40'x40'
Orchestra Pit
Seating Capacity: 476
Year Built: 1975
Architect: Caudill Rowlett Scott; Lipaj Woyer & Tomsick
Cost: $2,000,000
Contact for Rental: Kathy Moskin;   (216) 987-5051
Manager: Michael Stone
Resident Groups: Western Campus Theatre; Cleveland Philharmonic

---

Shaker Heights

INSTRUMENTAL MUSIC

CLEVELAND BAROQUE SOLOISTS
268 Bratemahl Place, Shaker Heights, OH 44120
(216) 751-5327; (216) 268-1729
Founded: 1972
Arts Area: Chamber; VOCAL
Status: Professional; Non-Profit
Type: Performing; Touring; Resident; Educational
Purpose: To present a wide variety of vocal works and instrumental works on historically appropriate instruments
Management: Beverly Simmons, Artists Manager; Doris Ornstein, Director
Paid Staff: 1
Paid Artists: 5
Utilizes: Guest Artists
Budget: $1,000 - $50,000
Income Sources: Box Office
Season: 52 Weeks   **Annual Attendance:** 8,000
Affiliations: Cleveland Institute of Music; Case Western Reserve University
Performance Facilities: Cleveland Institute of Music Concert Hall; Harkness Chapel

HOTFOOT QUARTET
3712 Traynham Road, Shaker Heights, OH 44122
(216) 991-4911
Founded: 1978
Arts Area: Ensemble; Folk; Band
Status: Professional
Type: Performing, Touring; Educational
Purpose: To perform modern and traditional Bluegrass music
Management: Robert Frank, Business Manager
Officers: Quartet members - Robert Frank, Guitarist; Roland Kausen, Mandolin; Ron Jarvis, Bass; John Saunders, Banjo
Paid Artists: 4
Budget: $1,000 - $50,000
Income Sources: Box Office
Season: 52 Weeks

THEATRE

UNITARIAN PLAYERS
21600 Shaker Boulevard, Shaker Heights, OH 44122
(216) 751-0715
Founded: 1955
Arts Area: Community
Status: Non-Professional; Non-Profit
Type: Performing
Purpose: To provide a vehicle of expression for cast and crew as well as entertainment for a thoughtful audience
Management: Board of Directors
Officers: Benham Bates, President; Dale Clark, Secretary; Carol Bates, Treasurer
Volunteer Staff: 50
Budget: $1,000 - $50,000
Income Sources: Box Office
Season: September - June **Annual Attendance:** 800

FACILITY

UNITARIAN PLAYERS
21600 Shaker Boulevard, Shaker Heights, OH 44122
(216) 751-2320
Type of Facility: Auditorium; Multi-Purpose
Facility Originally: Church; Meeting Hall; Movie House
Type of Stage: Proscenium
Stage Dimensions: 30'Wx24'D
Seating Capacity: 120
Year Built: 1955 **Architect:** Philip Small
Year Remodeled: 1985
Contact for Rental: Carol Gibson; (216) 751-2320
Resident Groups: Unitarian Players

Springfield

INSTRUMENTAL MUSIC

SPRINGFIELD SYMPHONY ORCHESTRA
PO Box 1374, Springfield, OH 45501
(513) 325-8100
Founded: 1944
Arts Area: Symphony; Chamber
Status: Professional; Non-Profit
Type: Performing; Sponsoring
Purpose: To provide the best in symphonic music to the entire community and music education to young people
Management: Gregory Anthes, Executive Director
Officers: Maxine E. Harris, President
Paid Staff: 2
Paid Artists: 86
Utilizes: Guest Conductors; Guest Artists
Budget: $100,000 - $500,000
Income Sources: Private Foundations/Grants/Endowments; Business/Corporate Donations; Box Office; Government Grants; Individual Donations

Season: October - April   Annual Attendance: 6,800
Affiliations: ASOL
Performance Facilities: North Auditorium

VOCAL MUSIC

OHIO LYRIC THEATRE
PO Box 432, Springfield, OH 45501
(513) 323-7755
Founded: 1962
Arts Area: Lyric Opera; Light Opera; Choral; Musical Theatre
Status: Semi-Professional; Non-Profit
Type: Performing; Touring; Educational; Sponsoring
Purpose: To produce and promote quality vocal music/musical theatre experiences in order to progress cultural enrichment and the appreciation of lyric theater and vocal music presentations
Management: Cindy Needles, General Manager
Officers: Kathleen Wilkins, President; Trudi Byrd, Vice President; Marilyn Engle, Secretary; Linda Berger, Treasurer
Paid Staff: 1
Utilizes: Special Technical Talent; Guest Conductors; Guest Artists; Guest Directors
Budget: $1,000 - $50,000
Income Sources: Private Foundations/Grants/Endowments; Business/Corporate Donations; Box Office; Government Grants; Individual Donations
Season: 52 Weeks   Annual Attendance: 10,000
Affiliations: Springfield Arts Council; OAC; NOA; COS
Performance Facilities: Veteran's Park Amphitheater; Kuss Auditorium

PERFORMING SERIES

WITTENBERG UNIVERSITY - WITTENBERG SERIES
PO Box 720, Springfield, OH 45501
(513) 327-6231
FAX: (513) 327-6340
Founded: 1845
Arts Area: Dance; Vocal Music; Instrumental Music; Theater; Grand Opera
Status: Non-Profit
Type: Educational; Sponsoring
Purpose: To enrich the cultural life of the Springfield and Wittenberg and to fulfill the University's mission
Management: Gwen Scheffel, Series Coordinator
Paid Staff: 1   Volunteer Staff: 9
Utilizes: Guest Artists
Budget: $50,000 - $100,000
Income Sources: Private Foundations/Grants/Endowments; Business/Corporate Donations; Individual Donations; University Funding
Season: September - June
Performance Facilities: Weaver Chapel; Student Center; HPERC-Gym 2

Sylvania

FACILITY

FRANCISCAN LIFE CENTER
6832 Convent Boulevard, Sylvania, OH 43560
(419) 885-1547
FAX: (419) 882-2981
Founded: 1981
Type of Facility: Theatre Complex; Auditorium; Multi-Purpose
Type of Stage: Flexible; Proscenium
Seating Capacity: 872
Year Built: 1981   Architect: Angel, Mull and Associates   Cost: $8,000,000
Contact for Rental: Patricia Zajac;   (419) 885-1547
Resident Groups: Toledo Repertoire Theatre; Toledo Symphony Mainly Mozart Series

Toledo

DANCE

THE TOLEDO BALLET SCHOOL
Franklin Park Mall Shopping Center, Toledo, OH 43623
(419) 471-0049
Founded: 1958
Arts Area: Ballet; Jazz
Status: Professional; Semi-Professional; Non-Professional; Non-Profit
Type: Performing; Touring; Resident; Educational; Sponsoring
Purpose: To provide performing opportunities for area dancers, quality dance to the community, dance scholarships and dance education
Management: Marie Bollinger Vogt, Artistic Director/Founder; Jack Jones Jr., Business Manager; Roger L. Benham Jr., Assistant Business Manager
Officers: James Bugert, President; Dan Jenks, III, Mrs. D.L. Schwartz, Mrs. John P. Stockwell, Vice Presidents; Mrs. Duane Schooley, Mrs. W.E. Willie, Secretaries; Michael L. DeBacker, Treasurer
Volunteer Staff: 50
Paid Artists: 41   **Non-Paid Artists:** 23
Utilizes: Guest Conductors; Guest Artists
Budget: $100,000 - $500,000
Income Sources: Private Foundations/Grants/Endowments; Business/Corporate Donations; Box Office; Government Grants; Individual Donations
Season: September - June   **Annual Attendance:** 15,000
Affiliations: Ohio Dance
Performance Facilities: Lourdes Auditorium; Masonic Auditorium

INSTRUMENTAL MUSIC

BRAVADO STRING QUARTET
2619 Sherbrooke Road, Toledo, OH 43606
(419) 471-9751
Founded: 1980
Arts Area: Chamber; Ensemble; Instrumental Group
Status: Semi-Professional
Type: Performing; Resident
Purpose: To perform at various public and private functions throughout northwest Ohio and southeast Michigan
Management: Risa Sindel, Manager
Budget: $1,000 - $50,000
Income Sources: Business/Corporate Donations
Season: 52 Weeks

TOLEDO JAZZ SOCIETY
1700 North Reynolds Road, Toledo, OH 43615
(419) 531-9935
Founded: 1980
Arts Area: Orchestra; Ensemble; Band
Status: Professional; Non-Profit
Type: Performing; Resident; Educational; Sponsoring
Purpose: To promote the performance and preservation of the jazz art form through educational programs, concerts, lectures, and the fostering of the Toledo Jazz Orchestra
Officers: Bart Polot, President; Richard Shell, Vice President; Joan DiRondo, Secretary; Susan Gilmore, Treasurer
Volunteer Staff: 10
Paid Artists: 82
Utilizes: Guest Artists
Budget: $50,000 - $100,000
Income Sources: Private Foundations/Grants/Endowments; Business/Corporate Donations; Box Office; Government Grants; Individual Donations
Season: 52 Weeks   **Annual Attendance:** 37,400
Affiliations: APAP; Arts Midwest
Performance Facilities: The Embers

THE TOLEDO SYMPHONY
One Stranahan Square, Toledo, OH 43604
(419) 241-1272
FAX: (419) 321-6890
Founded: 1943
Arts Area: Symphony; Orchestra; Chamber; Ensemble; Instrumental Group

Status: Professional; Non-Profit
Type: Performing; Touring; Educational
Purpose: To furnish performances of the highest artistic caliber to the widest possible audience; to conduct public service and education functions
Management: Robert Bell, Managing Director; Andrew Massey, Music Director; John Hancock, Orchestra Manager
Officers: Robert Lanigan, President, Board of Trustees
Paid Staff: 13
Paid Artists: 17
Utilizes: Guest Conductors; Guest Artists
Budget: $1,000,000 - $5,000,000
Income Sources: Private Foundations/Grants/Endowments; Business/Corporate Donations; Box Office; Government Grants; Individual Donations
Season: September - May
Performance Facilities: Toledo Museum of Art Peristyle

VOCAL MUSIC

TOLEDO OPERA
1700 North Reynolds Road, Toledo, OH 43615
(419) 531-5511
FAX: (419) 531-7196
Founded: 1959
Arts Area: Grand Opera; Lyric Opera; Light Opera
Status: Professional; Non-Profit
Type: Performing; Touring; Educational
Purpose: To present opera and works of an operatic nature to the communities of northwestern Ohio and southern Michigan; to conduct widespread community outreach programs and offer educational apprenticeship programs through the schools
Management: James Meena, Artistic Director; Joan Eckermann, Company/Education Coordinator
Officers: Marina Lury, President; Jon W. Klotz, First Vice President; Joseph M. Colturi, Eugene R. Wos, Sam Boteck Jr., Worth W. Wilson, Vice Presidents; Orval Seydlitz, Mark K. Hemsatch, Treasurers; Lyman F. Spitzer, Secretary
Paid Staff: 4
Paid Artists: 75   **Non-Paid Artists:** 50
Utilizes: Special Technical Talent; Guest Conductors; Guest Artists; Guest Directors
Budget: $100,000 - $500,000
Income Sources: Private Foundations/Grants/Endowments; Business/Corporate Donations; Box Office; Government Grants; Individual Donations
Season: October - May   **Annual Attendance:** 7,500
Affiliations: OA; AGMA; IATSE; AFM
Performance Facilities: Toledo Masonic Auditorium

THEATRE

THE TOLEDO REP
16 Tenth Street, Toledo, OH 43624
(419) 243-7335
Founded: 1933
Arts Area: Theatrical Group
Status: Semi-Professional; Non-Profit
Type: Performing; Educational
Purpose: To entertain, educate, and provide services to the Greater Toledo Area and surrounding communities
Management: Matthew Parent, Producing Artistic Director
Officers: Douglas Braun, Chairman of the Board; Michael Calabrese, President; Carlane Miller, Second Vice President
Paid Staff: 8   **Volunteer Staff:** 25
Utilizes: Special Technical Talent; Guest Conductors; Guest Artists; Guest Directors
Budget: $100,000 - $500,000
Income Sources: Private Foundations/Grants/Endowments; Business/Corporate Donations; Box Office; Government Grants; Individual Donations
Season: September - June   **Annual Attendance:** 35,000
Affiliations: Ohio Concerned Citizens for the Arts

PERFORMING SERIES

THE TOLEDO MUSEUM OF ART
2445 Monroe Street, Box 1013, Toledo, OH 43697
(419) 255-8000
Founded: 1901
Arts Area: Dance; Vocal Music; Instrumental Music; Theater; Lyric Opera

Status: Non-Profit
Type: Performing; Educational; Sponsoring
Purpose: To present the finest local, national and international performing artists
Management: Joyce E. Smar, Manager of Performing Arts; Annette Baker, Performing Arts Assistant; Ann Mather, Coordinator of Ticketing Services
Paid Staff: 8   **Volunteer Staff:** 80
Paid Artists: 5   **Non-Paid Artists:** 40
Utilizes: Guest Artists
Budget: $100,000 - $500,000
Income Sources: Private Foundations/Grants/Endowments; Business/Corporate Donations; Box Office; Government Grants; Individual Donations
Season: September - May   **Annual Attendance:** 60,000
Affiliations: APAP; BOMI; ISPAA; League of Historical American Theaters
Performance Facilities: Peristyle; Great Gallery; Little Theatre

FACILITY

OHIO THEATRE
3114 Lagrange Street, Toledo, OH 43608
(419) 241-6785
Founded: 1976
Type of Facility: Concert Hall; Auditorium; Theatre House; Multi-Purpose
Facility Originally: Vaudeville; Movie House
Type of Stage: Thrust
Stage Dimensions: 40'x60'
Seating Capacity: 975
Year Built: 1921
Contact for Rental: Roxanne Stone;   (419) 241-6785

TOLEDO MASONIC AUDITORIUM
4645 Heather Downs Boulevard, Toledo, OH 43614
(419) 381-8851
Type of Facility: Concert Hall; Auditorium; Theatre House; Opera House
Type of Stage: Proscenium; Hydraulic Lift Stage
Stage Dimensions: 48'x60'   **Orchestra Pit**
Seating Capacity: 2,520
Year Built: 1969
Contact for Rental: Penny Marks;   (419) 381-8851

THE TOLEDO MUSEUM OF ART - PERISTYLE
2445 Monroe Street, Box 1013, Toledo, OH 43697
(419) 255-8000
FAX: (419) 255-8534
Type of Facility: Museum
Type of Stage: Proscenium
Stage Dimensions: 45'Wx35'D   **Orchestra Pit**
Seating Capacity: 1,752
Year Built: 1933   **Architect:** E.B. Green & Son   **Cost:** $1,000,000
Acoustical Consultant: Clifford Swan
Contact for Rental: Manager of Performing Arts;   (419) 255-8000
Resident Groups: Toledo Symphony; Toledo Choral Society
Available for rental to non-profit groups only

Upper Arlington

PERFORMING SERIES

UPPER ARLINGTON CULTURAL ARTS COMMISSION
3600 Tremont Road, Upper Arlington, OH 43220
(614) 457-5080, ext. 324
FAX: (614) 457-6620
Founded: 1972
Arts Area: Dance; Vocal Music; Instrumental Music; Theater; Festivals; Lyric Opera
Status: Non-Profit
Type: Sponsoring
Purpose: To encourage, promote and provide cultural activities and opportunities for the enrichment of the lives of the community
Management: Doris T. Nelson, Arts Manager

Officers: Jan Schmidt, Chairman; William C. Lamneck, Vice Chairman
Paid Staff: 1   **Volunteer Staff:** 16
Paid Artists: 300
Utilizes: Guest Conductors; Guest Artists
Budget: $50,000 - $100,000
Income Sources: Private Foundations/Grants/Endowments; Business/Corporate Donations; Box Office; Government Grants
Annual Attendance: 7,000
Performance Facilities: Upper Arlington Municipal Center

Warren

INSTRUMENTAL MUSIC

THE JAZZ REVIVAL ORCHESTRA
2252 Wilson NE, Warren, OH 44483
(216) 372-1933
Founded: 1985
Arts Area: Ensemble; Instrumental Group
Status: Semi-Professional; Non-Profit
Type: Performing; Educational
Purpose: To educate and entertain
Officers: Dennis Reynolds, Chairman; Rich Rollo, President; Mike Kamuf, Vice President; John Veneskey, Secretary/Treasurer
Volunteer Staff: 4
Paid Artists: 17
Utilizes: Guest Artists
Budget: $1,000 - $50,000
Income Sources: Box Office; Government Grants; Individual Donations
Season: 52 Weeks

PERFORMING SERIES

WARREN CIVIC MUSIC ASSOCIATION
PO Box 1052, 837 Trumbull SE, Warren, OH 44484
(216) 369-5670
Founded: 1937
Arts Area: Dance; Vocal Music; Instrumental Music; Theater; Lyric Opera; Grand Opera
Status: Professional; Semi-Professional; Non-Profit
Type: Performing; Educational; Sponsoring
Purpose: To build and maintain a permanent concert audience in Warren and surrounding areas; to cultivate interest in music and encourage the performance of music by qualified artists
Officers: Robert I. Lowry, President; Mrs. Kenneth C. Gibson, George F. Gilbert, K. Robert Matheny and William E. Mottice, Vice Presidents; Phillip R. Meigs, Treasurer; David R. Vogt, Assistant Treasurer; Carole Menelle, Secretary; Jeannette Dietz, Membership
Volunteer Staff: 15
Budget: $50,000 - $100,000
Income Sources: Private Foundations/Grants/Endowments; Business/Corporate Donations; Box Office; Government Grants; Individual Donations
Season: September - April   **Annual Attendance:** 10,000
Affiliations: Ohio Arts Council
Performance Facilities: W.D. Packard Music Hall and Convention Center

West Liberty

THEATRE

MAD RIVER THEATER WORKS
105 1/2 North Detroit Street, West Liberty, OH 43357
(513) 465-6751
Founded: 1978
Arts Area: Professional; Musical; Theatrical Group
Status: Professional; Non-Profit
Type: Performing; Touring; Resident; Educational
Purpose: To preserve the rich heritage of the Midwest by collecting stories and crafting them into plays that depict life around the turn of the century, all adapted from true stories
Management: Jeff Hooper, Producing Director; Margaret A. Heinlen, Administrative Director

Officers: Shelley Wammes, Chair; Joyce Woodruff, Vice Chair; Bill Montgomey, Secretary
Paid Staff: 3   **Volunteer Staff:** 60
Paid Artists: 20
Utilizes: Special Technical Talent; Guest Artists; Guest Directors
Budget: $100,000 - $500,000
Income Sources: Private Foundations/Grants/Endowments; Business/Corporate Donations; Box Office; Government Grants; Individual Donations
Season: 52 Weeks   **Annual Attendance:** 65,000
Affiliations: TCG

Westerville

INSTRUMENTAL MUSIC

WESTERVILLE CIVIC SYMPHONY
170 West Park Street, Westerville, OH 43081
(614) 895-1102
Founded: 1982
Arts Area: Symphony; Orchestra; Ensemble
Status: Non-Professional; Non-Profit
Type: Performing; Educational
Purpose: A non-profit, charitable corporation functioning as an aesthetic, educational and cultural resource, presenting performances primarily of symphonic music; an artistic outlet for amateur and semi-professional musicians
Management: Jeanne Earhart, Business Manager
Officers: Donna Kerr, President, Board of Trustees; John Gale, Vice President; Lyle Barkhymer, Secretary; Michael Howard, Treasurer
Paid Staff: 2
Paid Artists: 20   **Non-Paid Artists:** 50
Utilizes: Guest Artists
Budget: $1,000 - $50,000
Income Sources: Private Foundations/Grants/Endowments; Business/Corporate Donations; Box Office; Government Grants; Individual Donations
Season: September - July   **Annual Attendance:** 2,400
Performance Facilities: Cowan Hall, Otterbein College

FACILITY

COWAN HALL
30 Grove Street, Westerville, OH 43081
(614) 898-1657
FAX: (614) 898-1898
Founded: 1959
Type of Facility: Theatre Complex; Concert Hall; Auditorium; Theatre House; Multi-Purpose
Type of Stage: Proscenium
Stage Dimensions: 44'2"Wx30'Dx20'H
Seating Capacity: 1,120
Year Built: 1959
Contact for Rental: Jeanne Augustus;   (614) 898-1657
Resident Groups: Otterbein College - various groups

Wooster

INSTRUMENTAL MUSIC

WOOSTER SYMPHONY ORCHESTRA
College of Wooster, Music Department, Wooster, OH 44691
(216) 263-2047
Founded: 1915
Arts Area: Symphony; Orchestra
Status: Non-Professional
Type: Performing; Resident
Purpose: To bring live orchestral repertoire to the community
Paid Staff: 2
Paid Artists: 12   **Non-Paid Artists:** 48
Utilizes: Guest Artists
Budget: $1,000 - $50,000
Income Sources: Box Office; Individual Donations

Season: November - April   **Annual Attendance:** 3,800
Affiliations: College of Wooster
Performance Facilities: McGaw Chapel

Yellow Springs

INSTRUMENTAL MUSIC

CHAMBER MUSIC IN YELLOW SPRINGS, INC.
Box 448, Yellow Springs, OH 45387
(513) 767-1458
FAX: (513) 767-9350
     Founded: 1983
     Arts Area: Chamber
     Status: Professional; Non-Profit
     Type: Sponsoring
     Purpose: To present high quality professional chamber music performances
     Officers: Bruce Bradtmiller, President; Ruth Bunt, Vice President; Barbara Mann, Secretary; Kenneth Tregillus, Treasurer
     Paid Artists: 6
     Utilizes: Guest Artists
     Budget: $1,000 - $50,000
     Income Sources: Private Foundations/Grants/Endowments; Business/Corporate Donations; Box Office; Government Grants; Individual Donations
     Season: October - April   **Annual Attendance:** 900
     Performance Facilities: First Presbyterian Church

THE EARLY MUSIC CENTER
242 Northwood Drive, Yellow Springs, OH 45387
(513) 767-8181
     Founded: 1979
     Arts Area: Chamber; Instrumental Group
     Status: Professional; Non-Profit
     Type: Performing; Touring; Resident; Educational; Sponsoring
     Purpose: To perform and encourage the performance of music written before 1750
     Management: Patricia Olds, Director
     Paid Staff: 1   **Volunteer Staff:** 1
     Paid Artists: 4
     Utilizes: Guest Artists   **Budget:** $1,000 - $50,000
     Income Sources: Private Foundations/Grants/Endowments; Business/Corporate Donations; Box Office; Government Grants; Individual Donations
     Season: 52 Weeks   **Annual Attendance:** 10,000

Youngstown

DANCE

BALLET WESTERN RESERVE
1361 Fifth Avenue, Youngstown, OH 44504
(216) 744-1934
     Founded: 1962
     Arts Area: Modern; Ballet; Jazz
     Status: Non-Professional; Non-Profit
     Type: Performing; Educational
     Purpose: To promote interest in ballet, modern dance and jazz, arrange performances and prepare students for performance and professional dance careers
     Management: Anita Lin O'Donnell, Director; Kathy DuBois, Office Manager
     Officers: Alan Goldberg and Sara Kennedy, Co-Presidents; James Kennedy, First Vice President; Charlene Pastoro, Second Vice President; Patti Keenan, Secretary; Kathy DuBois, Treasurer
     Paid Staff: 7   **Volunteer Staff:** 25
     Utilizes: Special Technical Talent; Guest Artists; Guest Choreographers
     Budget: $100,000 - $500,000
     Income Sources: Private Foundations/Grants/Endowments; Business/Corporate Donations; Box Office; Individual Donations
     Season: September - July   **Annual Attendance:** 15,000
     Performance Facilities: Youngstown State University; Powers Auditorium; Stambaugh Auditorium; Penn State University

INSTRUMENTAL MUSIC

YOUNGSTOWN SYMPHONY ORCHESTRA
260 Federal Plaza West, Youngstown, OH 44503
(216) 744-4269
> **Founded:** 1931
> **Arts Area:** Symphony
> **Status:** Professional; Non-Profit
> **Type:** Performing; Resident; Educational
> **Management:** Patricia C. Syak, General Manager
> **Paid Staff:** 10
> **Paid Artists:** 85   **Non-Paid Artists:** 150
> **Utilizes:** Special Technical Talent; Guest Conductors; Guest Artists; Guest Directors
> **Budget:** $1,000,000 - $5,000,000
> **Income Sources:** Private Foundations/Grants/Endowments; Business/Corporate Donations; Box Office; Government Grants; Individual Donations
> **Season:** September - May   **Annual Attendance:** 50,000
> **Affiliations:** ASOL; OOOO
> **Performance Facilities:** Youngstown Symphony Center, Edward W. Powers Auditorium

VOCAL MUSIC

YOUNGSTOWN MUSICA SACRA
323 Wick Avenue, Youngstown, OH 44503
(216) 743-3175
> **Founded:** 1980
> **Arts Area:** Choral
> **Status:** Semi-Professional
> **Type:** Performing; Resident
> **Purpose:** To perform masterpieces of sacred choral literature in liturgical and concert settings
> **Management:** Dr. Ronald L. Gould, Daniel W. Laginua, Co-Conductors
> **Utilizes:** Guest Artists
> **Budget:** $1,000 - $50,000
> **Income Sources:** Private Foundations/Grants/Endowments; Individual Donations
> **Season:** October - May

FACILITY

STAMBAUGH AUDITORIUM
Monday Musical Club Inc., 1000 Fifth Avenue, Youngstown, OH 44504-1603
(216) 743-2617
> **Founded:** 1896
> **Type of Facility:** Concert Hall; Auditorium; Lecture Room; Ballroom
> **Type of Stage:** Proscenium
> **Stage Dimensions:** 60'Wx27'   **Orchestra Pit**
> **Seating Capacity:** 2,535
> **Year Built:** 1925   **Architect:** Harvey Wiley Corbett   **Cost:** $1,500,000
> **Contact for Rental:** Barbara J. Armstrong;   (216) 747-5175
> *For the enjoyment, pleasure, entertainment, and education of the community of Youngstown and the contigous area.*

THE YOUNGSTOWN PLAYHOUSE
600 Playhouse Lane, Youngstown, OH 44511
(216) 788-8739
FAX: (216) 788-1208
> **Type of Facility:** Theatre Complex; Auditorium; Studio Performance; Environmental; Performance Center; Arena; Multi-Purpose; Room; Loft
> **Type of Stage:** Flexible; Proscenium; Arena
> **Stage Dimensions:** 34'Wx36'D; 34'Wx18'H proscenium opening   **Orchestra Pit**
> **Seating Capacity:** Auditorium - 624; Arena - 120
> **Year Built:** 1959   **Architect:** Jones & Buchanon
> **Contact for Rental:** Charles H. Reed;   (216) 788-8739
> **Resident Groups:** Youngstown Community Theatre; Youngstown Youth Theatre

YOUNGSTOWN STATE UNIVERSITY - BLISS RECITAL HALL
410 Wick Avenue, Youngstown, OH 44555
(216) 742-3636
> **Type of Facility:** Concert Hall; Multi-Purpose
> **Type of Stage:** Greek

Stage Dimensions: 60'Wx35'D
Seating Capacity: 250
Year Built: 1977   **Architect:** Caudill Rowlett Scott   **Cost:** $2,600,000
Acoustical Consultant: Caudill Rowlett Scott
Contact for Rental: Rocco Mediate;   (216) 742-3115

YOUNGSTOWN STATE UNIVERSITY - FORD THEATRE
410 Wick Avenue, Youngstown, OH 44555
(216) 742-3625
FAX: (216) 742-3499
Type of Facility: Auditorium; Performance Center; Theatre House
Type of Stage: Proscenium
Stage Dimensions: 36'Wx28'D
Orchestra Pit
Seating Capacity: 425
Year Built: 1973   **Architect:** Caudill Rowlett Scott   **Cost:** $6,000,000
Contact for Rental: Rocco A. Mediate;   (216) 742-3115
Resident Groups: Youngstown State University Theatre

YOUNGSTOWN STATE UNIVERSITY - SPOTLIGHT ARENA THEATRE
410 Wick Avenue, Youngstown, OH 44555
(216) 742-3625
Type of Facility: Studio Performance; Arena
Type of Stage: Flexible; 3/4 Arena; Arena
Stage Dimensions: 16'x21'
Seating Capacity: 200
Year Built: 1973   **Architect:** Caudill Rowlett Scott   **Cost:** $6,000,000
Contact for Rental: Rocco A. Mediate;   (216) 742-3115
Resident Groups: Youngstown State University Theatre

YOUNGSTOWN SYMPHONY CENTER - POWERS AUDITORIUM
260 Federal Plaza West, Youngstown, OH 44503
(216) 744-4269
FAX: (216) 744-1441
Type of Facility: Auditorium
Type of Stage: Proscenium
Orchestra Pit
Seating Capacity: 2,351
Year Built: 1930   **Cost:** $1,500,000
Year Remodeled: 1969   **Architect:** Damon, Worley, Cady, Kirk   **Cost:** $1,000,000
Acoustical Consultant: Christopher Jaffe
Contact for Rental: Patricia Syak
Resident Groups: Youngstown Symphony Orchestra; Youngstown Symphony Chorus; Youngstown Symphony Youth Orchestra; Junior League Town Hall Lecture Series; Youngstown State University Lectures

Zanesville

INSTRUMENTAL MUSIC

ZANESVILLE CHAMBER ORCHESTRA
1102 South Slope Bay, Zanesville, OH 43761
(614) 453-4925
Founded: 1982
Arts Area: Chamber
Status: Semi-Professional; Non-Profit
Type: Performing; Educational; Sponsoring
Purpose: To promote music for string orchestra and string chamber ensemble
Management: Renee Shaw, Executive Director
Paid Staff: 1   **Volunteer Staff:** 3
Non-Paid Artists: 15
Utilizes: Guest Artists
Budget: $1,000 - $50,000
Income Sources: Private Foundations/Grants/Endowments; Business/Corporate Donations; Box Office; Individual Donations
Season: 52 Weeks   **Annual Attendance:** 400
Performance Facilities: Zanesville Art Center

FACILITY

ZANESVILLE ART CENTER
620 Military Road, Zanesville, OH 43701
(614) 452-0741
Type of Facility: Auditorium
Facility Originally: Private Residence
Type of Stage: Platform
Stage Dimensions: 18'x22'
Seating Capacity: 125
Year Remodeled: 1985   **Architect:** Richard Dittmar & Associates   **Cost:** $400,000
Contact for Rental: Mrs. Joseph Howell;   (614) 452-0741
Resident Groups: Thursday Music Club; Junior Music Club; Beaux Arts Club

OKLAHOMA

Ada

FACILITY

EAST CENTRAL UNIVERSITY - DOROTHY I. SUMMERS THEATER
Ada, OK 74820-6899
(405) 332-8000
> **Type of Facility:** Theatre Complex; Concert Hall; Auditorium; Performance Center; Theatre House; Multi-Purpose
> **Type of Stage:** Proscenium
> **Seating Capacity:** 600
> **Contact for Rental:** Dr. Bob Payne;   (405) 332-8000

Alva

FACILITY

ALVA MEMORIAL AUDITORIUM
14th and Flynn, Alva, OK 73717
(405) 327-4823
> **Type of Facility:** Auditorium
> **Type of Stage:** Platform
> **Seating Capacity:** 900
> **Year Built:** 1956   **Architect:** Dow Gumerson   **Cost:** $200,000
> **Contact for Rental:** Lynn Hoskins;   (405) 327-4823

ALVA PUBLIC LIBRARY AUDITORIUM
504 Seventh, Alva, OK 73717
(405) 327-1833
> **Type of Facility:** Auditorium
> **Facility Originally:** Library
> **Seating Capacity:** 150
> **Year Remodeled:** 1963   **Architect:** Lawrence & Fletcher   **Cost:** $350,000
> **Contact for Rental:** Larry Thorne;   (405) 327-1833
> *Promotion of the arts*

Ardmore

THEATRE

ARDMORE LITTLE THEATRE
PO Box 245, Ardmore, OK 73402
(405) 223-6387
> **Founded:** 1955
> **Arts Area:** Community
> **Status:** Non-Profit
> **Type:** Performing
> **Purpose:** To provide live theatre to Ardmore and the surrounding communities and act as a local showcase for talent
> **Management:** Board of Directors elected by membership
> **Officers:** Charles Tate, President; Lil Williams, Vice President; Carla Reasoner, Secretary; Joel Wellnitz, Treasurer
> **Volunteer Staff:** 20
> **Non-Paid Artists:** 150
> **Utilizes:** Special Technical Talent; Guest Directors
> **Budget:** $1,000 - $50,000
> **Income Sources:** Business/Corporate Donations; Box Office; Government Grants; Individual Donations
> **Season:** September - April
> **Annual Attendance:** 4,000
> **Affiliations:** Oklahoma Community Theatre Association; SWTC
> **Performance Facilities:** Charles B. Goddard Center

FACILITY

CHARLES B. GODDARD CENTER
First Avenue and D Street SW, Ardmore, OK 73401
(405) 226-0909
> **Type of Facility:** Theatre Complex; Concert Hall; Performance Center; Civic Center
> **Type of Stage:** Proscenium
> **Stage Dimensions:** 50'x54'x36'
> **Seating Capacity:** 350
> **Year Built:** 1970 **Architect:** Flood-Isenberg-Hann **Cost:** $1,040,000
> **Year Remodeled:** 1986 **Architect:** Isenberg-Hann **Cost:** $290,000
> **Contact for Rental:** Mort Halmilton; Becky Jones; (405) 226-0909
> **Resident Groups:** Ardmore Little Theatre

Bartlesville

DANCE

BARTLESVILLE CIVIC BALLET
PO Box 921, Bartlesville, OK 74005
(918) 336-4746
> **Founded:** 1970
> **Arts Area:** Ballet
> **Status:** Non-Professional; Non-Profit
> **Type:** Performing; Resident
> **Purpose:** To offer youngsters the opportunity to perform ballet for the community
> **Management:** Charlotte Lyke, Artistic Director
> **Officers:** Glenn E. Davis, President; William J. Carter, Executive Vice President; Phil Blender, Treasurer
> **Non-Paid Artists:** 25
> **Utilizes:** Guest Artists; Guest Choreographers
> **Budget:** $50,000 - $100,000
> **Income Sources:** Private Foundations/Grants/Endowments; Business/Corporate Donations; Box Office; Individual Donations
> **Season:** Fall - Spring **Annual Attendance:** 4,000
> **Performance Facilities:** Bartlesville Community Center

INSTRUMENTAL MUSIC

BARTLESVILLE SYMPHONY ORCHESTRA
PO Box 263, Bartlesville, OK 74005
(918) 333-8287
> **Founded:** 1957
> **Arts Area:** Symphony; Orchestra
> **Status:** Non-Professional; Non-Profit
> **Type:** Resident
> **Purpose:** To provide symphonic musical experiences both for community musicians and community audiences
> **Management:** Lauren Green, Music Director/Conductor/Manager
> **Officers:** Mark Roberts, President; Beverly Taverner, David Laurin, Vice Presidents
> **Paid Staff:** 2 **Volunteer Staff:** 30
> **Paid Artists:** 1 **Non-Paid Artists:** 50
> **Utilizes:** Special Technical Talent; Guest Conductors; Guest Artists
> **Budget:** $100,000 - $500,000
> **Income Sources:** Private Foundations/Grants/Endowments; Business/Corporate Donations; Box Office; Government Grants; Individual Donations
> **Season:** September - May **Annual Attendance:** 7,000
> **Performance Facilities:** Bartlesville Community Center

PERFORMING SERIES

OK MOZART INTERNATIONAL FESTIVAL
500 Southeast Dewey, Bartlesville, OK 74003
(918) 336-9900
FAX: (918) 662-1527
> **Mailing Address:** PO Box 2344, Bartlesville, OK 74005
> **Founded:** 1985
> **Arts Area:** Dance; Vocal Music; Instrumental Music; Festivals; Grand Opera
> **Status:** Professional; Non-Profit
> **Type:** Sponsoring

Management: Nan Buhlinger, Artistic Administrator; Ransom Wilson, Artistic Director; Linda Cubbage, General Manager
Paid Staff: 3 **Volunteer Staff:** 400
Paid Artists: 40
Utilizes: Guest Conductors; Guest Artists
Budget: $100,000 - $500,000
Income Sources: Private Foundations/Grants/Endowments; Business/Corporate Donations; Box Office; Government Grants; Individual Donations
Season: June - July **Annual Attendance:** 8,000
Affiliations: APAP; Oklahoma State Arts Council
Performance Facilities: Bartlesville Community Center

FACILITY

BARTLESVILLE COMMUNITY CENTER
300 East Adams Boulevard, Bartlesville, OK 74003
(918) 337-2787
    Type of Facility: Theatre Complex; Concert Hall; Studio Performance; Performance Center; Civic Center; Multi-Purpose
    Type of Stage: Proscenium
    Stage Dimensions: 60'Wx46'D; 18' and 30' wing space   **Orchestra Pit**
    Seating Capacity: 1,735
    Year Built: 1982   **Architect:** William Wesley Peters; Taliesin Associated Architects   **Cost:** $13,500,000
    Acoustical Consultant: Vern C. Plane
    Contact for Rental: Pat Johnson;   (918) 337-2787
    Manager: Allan Longacre
    Resident Groups: Bartlesville Theater Guild; Bartlesville Symphony Orchestra; Bartlesville Civic Ballet

Bristow

FACILITY

AMERICAN LEGION
121 West Eighth Street, Bristow, OK 74010
    Type of Facility: Concert Hall; Auditorium; Performance Center; Multi-Purpose
    Facility Originally: Meeting Hall; Ballroom; Movie House
    Type of Stage: Proscenium
    Stage Dimensions: 49'Dx24'6"D
    Seating Capacity: 5,000
    Contact for Rental: Bobbie Lloyd, Bob Burris;   (918) 367-9767
    Resident Groups: Bristow Arts and Humanities
    Performing arts; dance; concerts; banquets

KLINGENSMITH PARK AMPHITHEATRE
110 West Seventh Street, Bristow, OK 74010
(918) 367-2237
    Type of Facility: Outdoor (Concert); Amphitheater
    Type of Stage: Proscenium
    Seating Capacity: 5,000
    Year Built: 1934
    Year Remodeled: 1987
    Contact for Rental: Tony Elias, Mayor;   (918) 367-2237
    Resident Groups: Bristow Community Players

Clinton

DANCE

WESTERN OKLAHOMA BALLET THEATRE
700 Avant, Clinton, OK 73601
(405) 323-5954
    Founded: 1977
    Arts Area: Modern; Ballet
    Status: Non-Professional; Non-Profit
    Type: Performing; Educational
    Purpose: To foster and promote dance in western Oklahoma
    Management: Penny Askew, Artistic Director
    Officers: Marian Tisdal, President; Susie Simon, Vice President; Cindi Delay, Secretary; Don Askew, Treasurer
    Volunteer Staff: 2

Non-Paid Artists: 9
Utilizes: Guest Artists; Guest Choreographers
Budget: $1,000 - $50,000
Income Sources: Business/Corporate Donations; Box Office; Government Grants; Individual Donations
Season: 52 Weeks   **Annual Attendance:** 2,500
Affiliations: Regional Dance America; Southwestern Regional Ballet Association
Performance Facilities: Southwestern Oklahoma State University Fine Arts Center

---

Enid

INSTRUMENTAL MUSIC

ENID-PHILLIPS SYMPHONY ORCHESTRA
301 West Maine, Suite 15, Enid, OK 73701
(405) 237-9646
Founded: 1906
Arts Area: Symphony; Orchestra
Status: Professional; Non-Profit
Type: Performing; Educational
Management: Douglas Newell, Artostic Director; Eleanor Hornbaker, Administrative Associate
Officers: Maye Adele Kirtley, President, Enid Phillips Symphony Association
Paid Staff: 1   **Volunteer Staff:** 4
Paid Artists: 65
Utilizes: Guest Conductors; Guest Artists
Budget: $50,000 - $100,000
Income Sources: Private Foundations/Grants/Endowments; Business/Corporate Donations; Box Office; Government Grants; Individual Donations
Season: September - May   **Annual Attendance:** 9,500
Affiliations: ASOL
Performance Facilities: Eugene S. Briggs Auditorium

Lawton

INSTRUMENTAL MUSIC

LAWTON PHILHARMONIC ORCHESTRA
PO Box 1473, Lawton, OK 73502
(405) 248-2001
Founded: 1962
Arts Area: Symphony; Orchestra
Status: Professional; Non-Profit
Type: Performing; Touring; Resident; Educational; Sponsoring
Purpose: To educate the public and provide entertainment for the Lawton community
Management: Carlana N. Sitch, General Manager; Whittie Rainwater, Assistant Manager
Paid Staff: 3   **Volunteer Staff:** 250
Paid Artists: 75
Utilizes: Guest Conductors; Guest Artists
Budget: $100,000 - $500,000
Income Sources: Private Foundations/Grants/Endowments; Business/Corporate Donations; Box Office; Government Grants; Individual Donations; Fund-raising
Season: October - June   **Annual Attendance:** 15,000
Affiliations: ASOL
Performance Facilities: McMahon Memorial Auditorium

VOCAL MUSIC

AMERICAN CHORAL DIRECTORS ASSOCIATION
PO Box 6310, Lawton, OK 73506
(405) 355-8161
FAX: (405) 248-1465
Arts Area: Choral
Status: Non-Profit
Type: Educational
Purpose: To provide information to members
Management: Dr. Gene Brooks, Executive Director; John Haberlen, President
Income Sources: Government Grants
Season: 52 Weeks

FACILITY

CAMERON UNIVERSITY, THEATRE ARTS DEPARTMENT
2800 West Gore Boulevard, Lawton, OK 73505
(405) 536-2346
  Type of Facility: Auditorium; Studio Performance; Theatre House
  Type of Stage: Flexible; Proscenium
  Seating Capacity: 432
  Acoustical Consultant: Scott Hofmann
  Contact for Rental: Scott Hofmann;   (405) 581-2428

MCMAHON MEMORIAL AUDITORIUM
801 Ferris, PO Box 522, Lawton, OK 73502
(405) 581-3470
FAX: (405) 248-0243
  Founded: 1954
  Type of Facility: Auditorium
  Type of Stage: Proscenium
  Stage Dimensions: 92'Wx40'D   **Orchestra Pit**
  Seating Capacity: 1,525
  Year Built: 1954   **Architect:** Paul Harris
  Year Remodeled: 1991   **Architect:** Philip Burk   **Cost:** $900,000
  Acoustical Consultant: C.P. Boner & Associates
  Contact for Rental: Jim McCarthy;   (405) 581-3470
  Manager: Ann Weisman;   (405) 581-3470
  Resident Groups: Lawton Philharmonic Society; Lawton Community Concerts; Lawton Arts and Humanities Council; Miss Lawton Pageant

---

Muskogee

THEATRE

MUSKOGEE LITTLE THEATRE
329 East Cincinnati, PO Box 964, Muskogee, OK 74402
(918) 683-5332
  Founded: 1972
  Arts Area: Community
  Status: Non-Profit
  Type: Performing
  Purpose: To foster interest and support of dramatic arts in the community; to design programs and activities to encourage involvement of community members in the study of dramatic arts; to produce and perform plays benefiting the community and surroundings
  Officers: Bob Crandell, President; Janice Ward, Vice President; Nancy Williams, Secretary; David King, Treasurer
  Volunteer Staff: 200
  Non-Paid Artists: 75
  Budget: $1,000 - $50,000
  Income Sources: Business/Corporate Donations; Box Office; Individual Donations
  Season: September - July   **Annual Attendance:** 2,500
  Affiliations: Oklahoma Community Theatre Association
  Performance Facilities: Muskogee Little Theatre

FACILITY

MUSKOGEE LITTLE THEATRE
Cincinnati and D, Muskogee, OK 74402-0964
(918) 683-5332
  Type of Facility: Concert Hall; Auditorium; Performance Center; Theatre House
  Type of Stage: Proscenium
  Stage Dimensions: 36'Wx12'D
  Seating Capacity: 114
  Year Built: 1962
  Year Remodeled: 1972
  Contact for Rental: Marjorie Szabo, Treasurer;   (918) 682-3257

Norman

DANCE

OKLAHOMA FESTIVAL BALLET
563 Elm Avenue, Room 209, Norman, OK 73019
(405) 325-4021
FAX: (405) 325-5322
    Arts Area: Ballet
    Status: Semi-Professional
    Type: Performing; Touring; Resident; Educational
    Purpose: To perform an eclectic repertoire using a classical ballet of young dancers
    Officers: Mary Margaret Holt, Director; Dennis Poole, Ballet Master; Kathleen Burnett, Rehearsal Assistant; Max Burnett, Manager; Scott Simmons, Technical Director
    Paid Staff: 5   **Volunteer Staff:** 2
    Paid Artists: 16
    Budget: $50,000 - $100,000
    Income Sources: Private Foundations/Grants/Endowments; Box Office; Government Grants; Individual Donations
    Season: August - May
    Annual Attendance: 20,000
    Affiliations: University of Oklahoma
    Performance Facilities: Rupel Jones Theatre

VOCAL MUSIC

CIMARRON CIRCUIT OPERA COMPANY
PO Box 1085, Norman, OK 73070
(405) 364-8962
    Founded: 1975
    Arts Area: Grand Opera; Lyric Opera; Light Opera; Children's Opera
    Status: Professional; Non-Profit
    Type: Performing; Touring; Sponsoring
    Purpose: To provide training and experience for young singers in Oklahoma and take opera to areas of Oklahoma where residents would not normally have access to opera performances
    Management: Thomas Carey, Artistic Director; Lisa Anderson, Musical Director; Alan Parker, Technical Director
    Officers: Stan Williams, President; Mike Abraham, Vice President; Mary McCord, Secretary; Rodney Evans, Treasurer
    Paid Staff: 6   **Volunteer Staff:** 15
    Paid Artists: 30   **Non-Paid Artists:** 5
    Utilizes: Guest Artists; Guest Directors
    Budget: $50,000 - $100,000
    Income Sources: Private Foundations/Grants/Endowments; Business/Corporate Donations; Box Office; Government Grants; Individual Donations; Fundraising
    Season: September - April   **Annual Attendance:** 25,000
    Affiliations: COS; MAAA

PERFORMING SERIES

JAZZ IN JUNE, INC.
PO Box 2405, Norman, OK 73070
(405) 325-3388
    Founded: 1985
    Arts Area: Vocal Music; Instrumental Music
    Status: Professional; Semi-Professional
    Type: Performing
    Purpose: To present a jazz festival for Oklahoma residents
    Management: Phoebe Morales, Executive Director of the Norman Arts and Humanities Council
    Volunteer Staff: 20
    Paid Artists: 25
    Utilizes: Special Technical Talent; Guest Conductors; Guest Artists; Guest Directors
    Budget: $1,000 - $50,000
    Income Sources: Business/Corporate Donations; Box Office; Government Grants; Individual Donations
    Season: June   **Annual Attendance:** 5,000
    Affiliations: AFM

FACILITY

THE SOONER THEATRE OF NORMAN, INC.
PO Box 6565, 101 East Main, Norman, OK 73070
(405) 321-9600
> **Founded:** 1976
> **Type of Facility:** Concert Hall; Auditorium; Performance Center; Theatre House; Opera House; Civic Center
> **Facility Originally:** Vaudeville; Movie House
> **Type of Stage:** Proscenium
> **Stage Dimensions:** 29'Dx45'W; 25'5"Dx25'W playing area **Orchestra Pit**
> **Seating Capacity:** 687
> **Year Built:** 1929 **Architect:** Harold Gimeno **Cost:** $200,000
> **Year Remodeled:** 1982 **Cost:** $150,000
> **Contact for Rental:** Kym E. Bracken; (405) 321-9600
> **Resident Groups:** Stone Soup Theatre; Cimarron Circuit Opera Company; Norman Ballet Company

UNIVERSITY OF OKLAHOMA THEATRE
563 Elm Street, Norman, OK 73019
(405) 325-4021
> **Type of Facility:** Theatre Complex; Studio Performance; Performance Center
> **Type of Stage:** Thrust; Flexible; Proscenium; Arena
> **Stage Dimensions:** 40'Wx20'Hx47'D with a 45' deep thrust **Orchestra Pit**
> **Seating Capacity:** 668
> **Year Built:** 1965 **Architect:** A. Blaine Imel **Cost:** $1,500,000
> **Contact for Rental:** Dr. Gregory Kunesh, Director; (405) 325-4021
> **Resident Groups:** Oklahoma Festival Ballet; Modern Dance Repertory; University Theatre; Southwest Repertory Theatre

---

Oklahoma City

DANCE

BALLET OKLAHOMA
7421 North Classen, Oklahoma City, OK 73116
(405) 843-9898
FAX: (405) 843-9894
> **Founded:** 1972
> **Arts Area:** Ballet; Jazz
> **Status:** Professional
> **Type:** Performing; Touring; Resident; Educational; Sponsoring
> **Purpose:** Professional resident ballet company and ballet school
> **Management:** Bryan Pitts, Artistic Director; Gail Beals, General Manager
> **Officers:** Michael Laird, President, Board of Trustees
> **Paid Staff:** 10
> **Paid Artists:** 21
> **Utilizes:** Special Technical Talent; Guest Artists; Guest Choreographers
> **Budget:** $1,000,000 - $5,000,000
> **Income Sources:** Private Foundations/Grants/Endowments; Business/Corporate Donations; Box Office; Government Grants; Individual Donations
> **Season:** September - April **Annual Attendance:** 40,000
> **Performance Facilities:** Civic Center

PRAIRIE DANCE THEATRE
2100 NE 52nd, Oklahoma City, OK 73111
(405) 842-5235
> **Founded:** 1978
> **Arts Area:** Modern; Ethnic; Folk
> **Status:** Professional; Non-Profit
> **Type:** Performing; Touring; Resident; Educational
> **Purpose:** To present modern dance performances with Southwestern USA themes
> **Management:** Peter Shumway, Manager; Beth Shumway, Artistic Director; Cynthia Longley, Public Relations
> **Officers:** Vicky Galloway, President; Pat Hughes, Vice President; Keesa Crouch, Secretary/Treasurer
> **Paid Staff:** 1 **Volunteer Staff:** 10
> **Paid Artists:** 6
> **Utilizes:** Special Technical Talent; Guest Artists; Guest Directors; Guest Choreographers
> **Budget:** $50,000 - $100,000
> **Income Sources:** Private Foundations/Grants/Endowments; Business/Corporate Donations; Box Office; Individual Donations
> **Season:** September - May **Annual Attendance:** 2,000

Affiliations: Kirpatrick Center Museum; MidAmerica Dance Network
Performance Facilities: Kirpatrick Centre

INSTRUMENTAL MUSIC

GO FOR BAROQUE
PO Box 20178, Oklahoma City, OK 73120
(405) 840-0278
   Founded: 1982
   Arts Area: Chamber; Ensemble
   Status: Professional
   Type: Performing; Touring; Educational
   Purpose: Formal Baroque Concerts, Young People's Concerts
   Management: Peggy Green Payne
   Paid Artists: 8
   Budget: $1,000 - $50,000
   Income Sources: Private Foundations/Grants/Endowments; Business/Corporate Donations
   Season: 52 Weeks

OKLAHOMA CITY PHILHARMONIC ORCHESTRA
428 West California, Suite 210, Oklahoma City, OK 73102
(405) 232-7575
FAX: (405) 232-4353
   Founded: 1988
   Arts Area: Symphony; Orchestra
   Status: Professional; Non-Profit
   Type: Performing; Resident
   Purpose: To perform orchestral, classical and popular music; to entertain and educate; to enhance cultural environment of the city and the state
   Management: Joel Levine, Music Director/Conductor; Alan D. Valentine, General Manager; Eddie Walker, Operations Manager
   Officers: Paul Reed, President of Board of Directors; Jane Harlow, President-Elect; Al Dearmon, Vice President; Harrison Levy, Treasurer; Priscilla Braun, Secretary
   Paid Staff: 11
   Paid Artists: 85
   Utilizes: Special Technical Talent; Guest Conductors; Guest Artists
   Budget: $1,000,000 - $5,000,000
   Income Sources: Private Foundations/Grants/Endowments; Business/Corporate Donations; Box Office; Government Grants; Individual Donations; Fee Engagements
   Season: September - May   **Annual Attendance:** 105,000
   Affiliations: ASOL; Allied Arts of Oklahoma City
   Performance Facilities: Civic Center Music Hall

VOCAL MUSIC

OKLAHOMA OPERA AND MUSIC THEATER COMPANY
Oklahoma City University, 2501 North Blackwelder, Oklahoma City, OK 73106
(405) 521-5315
FAX: (405) 521-5264
   Founded: 1904
   Arts Area: Grand Opera; Lyric Opera; Light Opera; Operetta; Choral
   Status: Non-Professional; Non-Profit
   Type: Performing; Educational
   Purpose: To provide high quality performances for the general public; to provide a professional forum in which students can develop their talents
   Management: Cheryl L. Zrnic, General Director
   Paid Staff: 5   **Volunteer Staff:** 50
   Paid Artists: 4
   Utilizes: Special Technical Talent; Guest Directors
   Budget: $50,000 - $100,000
   Income Sources: Private Foundations/Grants/Endowments; Business/Corporate Donations; Box Office; Government Grants; Individual Donations
   Season: October - April   **Annual Attendance:** 10,000
   Affiliations: Oklahoma City University
   Performance Facilities: Kirpatrick Theater

THEATRE

JEWEL BOX THEATRE
3700 North Walker, Oklahoma City, OK 73118
(405) 521-1786
Founded: 1957
Arts Area: Community
Status: Non-Professional
Type: Performing
Purpose: Continuing excellence in theatre
Management: Charles Tweed, Production Director
Officers: Pat Tweed, Chairman of Board of Advisors; Neta Unger, Co-Chairman
Paid Staff: 1   **Volunteer Staff:** 50
Budget: $50,000 - $100,000
Income Sources: Business/Corporate Donations; Box Office; Individual Donations
Season: August - May
Affiliations: ACTA; Oklahoma Community Theatre Association; Southwest Repertory Theatre Association
Performance Facilities: Jewel Box Theatre

LYRIC THEATRE OF OKLAHOMA
2501 North Blackwelder, Oklahoma City, OK 73106
(405) 528-3636
Founded: 1962
Arts Area: Musical
Status: Professional; Non-Profit
Type: Performing; Resident
Purpose: To provide a professional atmosphere for trained young artists; an extension of the University of Oklahoma Drama Department
Management: Gayle Pearson, Producing Manager
Paid Staff: 3
Utilizes: Special Technical Talent; Guest Artists; Guest Directors
Budget: $500,000 - $1,000,000
Income Sources: Private Foundations/Grants/Endowments; Business/Corporate Donations; Box Office; Government Grants; Individual Donations
Season: June - August
Affiliations: U/RTA
Performance Facilities: Kirkpatrick Auditorium, Oklahoma City University

OKLAHOMA COMMUNITY THEATRE ASSOCIATION
200 North Harvey, Suite 902, Oklahoma City, OK 73102
(405) 235-9508
Founded: 1969
Arts Area: Community
Status: Non-Professional; Non-Profit
Type: State Theatre Association
Purpose: To encourage excellence in community theatre throughout the state of Oklahoma
Management: Anthony Klatt, Administrative Coordinator
Officers: Mary S. Patterson, President; Charles Hair, President-Elect
Paid Staff: 1   **Volunteer Staff:** 18
Utilizes: Special Technical Talent; Guest Conductors; Guest Artists; Guest Directors
Budget: $100,000 - $500,000
Income Sources: Private Foundations/Grants/Endowments; Business/Corporate Donations; Box Office; Government Grants; Individual Donations
Affiliations: SWTC; AACT

FACILITY

CIVIC CENTER MUSIC HALL
201 Channing Square, Suite 100, Oklahoma City, OK 73102
(405) 297-2584
Founded: 1937
Type of Facility: Theatre Complex; Concert Hall; Auditorium; Performance Center; Civic Center; Multi-Purpose
Facility Originally: Arena   **Type of Stage:** Proscenium
Stage Dimensions: 69'10"Wx48'D   **Orchestra Pit**
Seating Capacity: 3,200
Year Built: 1937   **Architect:** J.O. Parr
Year Remodeled: 1967   **Architect:** Turnbull & Mills
Contact for Rental: Tom Anderson;   (405) 297-2584
Resident Groups: Oklahoma City Philharmonic Orchestra; Ballet Oklahoma; Canterbury Choral Society

OKLAHOMA CITY UNIVERSITY
2501 North Blackwelder, Oklahoma City, OK 73106
(405) 521-5315
    Type of Facility: Performance Center
    Year Built: 1929 **Architect:** Seminoff-Bowman-Bowdie **Cost:** $1,000,000
    Year Remodeled: 1969 **Architect:** Seminoff-Bowman-Bowdie **Cost:** $250,000
    Contact for Rental: Nina Anderson; (405) 521-5316
    Resident Groups: Sinfonia of Mid-America Lyric Theater; American Spirit Dancers; Civic Music Association
    Oklahoma City University contains Burg Theatre and Kirkpatrick Auditorium. See separate listings for additional information.

OKLAHOMA CITY UNIVERSITY - BURG THEATRE
2501 North Blackwelder, Oklahoma City, OK 73106
(405) 521-5315
    Type of Facility: Theatre House
    Type of Stage: Proscenium **Orchestra Pit**
    Seating Capacity: 300
    Year Built: 1929
    Year Remodeled: 1969
    Contact for Rental: Nina Anderson; (405) 521-5316

OKLAHOMA CITY UNIVERSITY - KIRKPATRICK AUDITORIUM
2501 North Blackwelder, Oklahoma City, OK 73106
(405) 521-5315
    Type of Facility: Auditorium
    Type of Stage: 3/4 Arena
    Seating Capacity: 1,119
    Year Built: 1929
    Year Remodeled: 1969
    Contact for Rental: Nina Anderson; (405) 521-5316

OKLAHOMA CITY ZOO AMPHITHEATRE
2101 NE 50th, Oklahoma City, OK 73111
(405) 424-3344
    Type of Facility: Concert Hall; Outdoor (Concert); Environmental; Amphitheater; Multi-Purpose
    Type of Stage: Greek; Proscenium
    Stage Dimensions: 60'Wx40'D
    Seating Capacity: 9,000
    Year Built: 1936
    Architect: Civilian Conservation Corps
    Contact for Rental: Donna Chain; (405) 424-3344
    Updating facility yearly

Ponca City

THEATRE

PONCA PLAYHOUSE
516 East Grand, Ponca City, OK 74601
(405) 765-7786; (405) 765-5360
    Mailing Address: PO Box 1414, Ponca City, OK 74602
    Founded: 1959
    Arts Area: Musical; Community; Theatrical Group
    Status: Non-Professional; Non-Profit; Commercial
    Type: Performing; Touring; Resident
    Purpose: To provide the interested area amateur with the opportunity to participate in the process of producing live theatre for a discriminating audience
    Officers: Jerry Hughes, President; Iris Ballou, Secretary; Tom Cawley, Vice President
    Paid Staff: 4 **Volunteer Staff:** 20
    Paid Artists: 2
    Utilizes: Special Technical Talent; Guest Artists; Guest Directors
    Budget: $50,000 - $100,000
    Income Sources: Business/Corporate Donations; Box Office; Individual Donations
    Season: September - May **Annual Attendance:** 10,000
    Affiliations: AACT; Oklahoma Community Theatre Association; SWTC

FACILITY

PONCA PLAYHOUSE
516 East Grand, Ponca City, OK 74601
(508) 765-7786
   Type of Facility: Theatre House
   Type of Stage: Proscenium
   Stage Dimensions: 30'Wx20'H proscenium opening   **Orchestra Pit**
   Seating Capacity: 412
   Year Built: 1927
   Contact for Rental: John A. Robinson;   (405) 765-7786
   Resident Groups: Ponca Playhouse

Tahlequah

THEATRE

CHEROKEE NATIONAL HISTORICAL SOCIETY
PO Box 515, Tahlequah, OK 74465
(918) 456-6007
   Founded: 1964
   Arts Area: Theatrical Group
   Status: Professional; Non-Profit
   Type: Resident; Educational
   Purpose: The Cherokee National Historical Society seeks to preserve the history and traditions of the Cherokee Indian tribe and to educate the public concerning the Cherokee story through the presentation of the "Trail of Tears" drama and other endeavors.
   Management: Tom Mooney, Acting Executive Director
   Officers: Gary Chapman, President; Wilma Mankiller, Vice President
   Paid Staff: 10
   Paid Artists: 80
   Utilizes: Special Technical Talent
   Budget: $100,000 - $500,000
   Income Sources: Private Foundations/Grants/Endowments; Business/Corporate Donations; Box Office; Government Grants; Individual Donations
   Season: June - August   **Annual Attendance:** 30,000
   Affiliations: Outdoor Drama Association
   Performance Facilities: Cherokee Heritage Center Amphitheater

FACILITY

CHEROKEE HERITAGE CENTER AMPHITHEATER
Willis Road, PO Box 515, Tahlequah, OK 74465
(918) 456-6007
   Type of Facility: Amphitheater
   Type of Stage: Greek
   Seating Capacity: 1,800
   Year Built: 1969   **Architect:** Charles Chief Boyd   **Cost:** $400,000
   Contact for Rental: Lisa Finley, Director of Marketing;   (918) 456-6007
   Resident Groups: Trail of Tears

Tulsa

DANCE

TULSA BALLET THEATRE
4512 South Peoria, Tulsa, OK 74105
(918) 749-6030
FAX: (918) 749-0532
   Founded: 1956
   Arts Area: Ballet
   Status: Professional; Non-Profit
   Type: Performing; Touring
   Purpose: The understanding of ballet and its related arts through the establishment of a ballet company which is part of the cultural life of Tulsa and its environs
   Management: Roman Jasinski, Artistic Director; Connie Cronley, General Manager

Officers: Hannah Robson, President; Donald F. Marlar, Chairman of the Board; Larry Chambers, Executive Vice President; Jack Kelley, Vice President/ Long Range Planning; Bob Morgan, Vice President/ Finance and Budget; Mary Barnes, Edward Taylor, Vice Presidents at Large; Ginny Creveling, Vice President/ Development; Aubyn Howe, Vice President/ Research and Development of Fundraising; Bonnie Henke, Parliamentarian; Elizabeth Rainey, Corresponding Secretary; Jim Burdett, Treasurer; Patty Floyd, Recording Secretary
Paid Staff: 11
Paid Artists: 28
Utilizes: Special Technical Talent; Guest Conductors; Guest Artists; Guest Directors; Guest Choreographers
Budget: $1,000,000 - $5,000,000
Income Sources: Private Foundations/Grants/Endowments; Business/Corporate Donations; Box Office; Government Grants; Individual Donations
Season: September - May   **Annual Attendance:** 101,000
Affiliations: NARB; Dance USA
Performance Facilities: Chapman Music Hall; Tulsa Performing Arts Center

INSTRUMENTAL MUSIC

CONCERTIME
3936 East 38th, Tulsa, OK 74135-2406
(918) 742-4087
Founded: 1954
Arts Area: Chamber
Status: Professional; Non-Profit
Type: Performing; Educational
Purpose: We introduced chamber music to Tulsa and, because of our efforts, interest has been increased. Our continuing purpose is to cultivate future audiences for chamber music.
Management: Robert Heckman, Manager
Officers: Deborah Pinkerton, President; Dr. John K. Major, Vice President; Bathany Kolmar, Secretary; Dr. Richard W. Ekdahl, Treasurer
Paid Staff: 1   **Volunteer Staff:** 27
Paid Artists: 4
Utilizes: Guest Artists
Budget: $1,000 - $50,000
Income Sources: Private Foundations/Grants/Endowments; Box Office; Government Grants; Individual Donations
Season: October - April   **Annual Attendance:** 1,600
Affiliations: CMA
Performance Facilities: John H. Williams Theater, Tulsa Performing Arts Center

TULSA PHILHARMONIC
2901 South Harvard Avenue, Suite A, Tulsa, OK 74114-6100
(918) 584-2533
FAX: (918) 747-7496
Founded: 1947
Arts Area: Symphony; Orchestra; Chamber; Ensemble
Status: Professional; Non-Profit
Type: Performing; Touring; Resident; Educational; Sponsoring
Purpose: Live symphony music
Management: Stepehen Boyd, Executive Director; William Schmieding, Orchestra Manager; Virginia Will, Business Manager
Officers: Henry Will, Chairman; Sally Minshall, Vice Chairman; Betty Clark, President
Paid Staff: 15   **Volunteer Staff:** 1
Paid Artists: 80
Utilizes: Guest Conductors; Guest Artists
Budget: $1,000,000 - $5,000,000
Income Sources: Private Foundations/Grants/Endowments; Business/Corporate Donations; Box Office; Government Grants; Individual Donations
Season: September - May   **Annual Attendance:** 100,000
Affiliations: ASOL
Performance Facilities: Tulsa Performing Arts Center

TULSA YOUTH SYMPHONY ORCHESTRA
2901 South Harvard, Tulsa, OK 74114
(918) 747-7473
FAX: (918) 747-7496
Founded: 1963
Arts Area: Symphony; Orchestra; Chamber
Status: Non-Professional; Non-Profit
Type: Performing; Touring; Educational

Purpose: Tulsa Youth Symphony Orchestra aims to encourage and develop students' musical abilities through rehearsal, concert performance and regular contact with professional musicians, offering training and performance opportunities unavailable at any single educational institution.
Management: Ronald Wheeler, Conductor/Administrator; Catherine Venable, Administrative Assistant; Christopher Henry, Librarian
Officers: Rebecca Robinson, President; Neema Drew, Treasurer
Paid Staff: 3
Non-Paid Artists: 85
Utilizes: Guest Conductors; Guest Artists
Budget: $1,000 - $50,000
Income Sources: Business/Corporate Donations; Individual Donations; Fundraising
Season: September - May   **Annual Attendance:** 4,000
Affiliations: ASOL (Youth Orchestra Division); Tulsa Philharmonic; Junior Division of the Tulsa Philharmonic Society, Inc.
Performance Facilities: Union High School Performing Arts Center; Tulsa Performing Arts Center

VOCAL MUSIC

TULSA OPERA
1610 South Boulder, Tulsa, OK 74119
(918) 582-4035
Founded: 1948
Arts Area: Grand Opera
Status: Professional; Non-Profit
Type: Performing; Sponsoring
Purpose: To present music/opera theater of the finest quality for a diverse audience drawn from a four-state region (OK, KS, AR, MI); to encourage musical talents, composers, lyricists and related artists through scholarships and opportunities; to develop an awareness of, and appreciation for opera through extensive educational programs
Management: Myrna Smart Ruffner, Executive Director; Cheryl L. Zrnic, Managing Director; Nicholas Muni, Artistic Director
Officers: Hilliary Kito, President; Scott Graham, Chairman of the Board; Jim Dodd, Vice President; Marilyn Strange, Secretary; Edgar Sandeton, Treasurer
Paid Staff: 10   **Volunteer Staff:** 25
Paid Artists: 40   **Non-Paid Artists:** 75
Utilizes: Special Technical Talent; Guest Conductors; Guest Artists; Guest Directors
Budget: $1,000,000 - $5,000,000
Income Sources: Private Foundations/Grants/Endowments; Business/Corporate Donations; Box Office; Government Grants; Individual Donations
Season: November - May   **Annual Attendance:** 20,000
Affiliations: OA; AAA; Arts and Humanities Council of Tulsa
Performance Facilities: Chapman Music Hall

THEATRE

AMERICAN THEATRE COMPANY
1820 South Boulder Place, Tulsa, OK 74119
(918) 747-9494
Founded: 1970
Arts Area: Theatrical Group
Status: Professional; Non-Profit
Type: Performing
Management: Kitty Roberts, Producing Artistic Director; Laurie Bryant, Education Director
Paid Staff: 4   **Volunteer Staff:** 30
Paid Artists: 20
Utilizes: Special Technical Talent
Budget: $100,000 - $500,000
Income Sources: Private Foundations/Grants/Endowments; Business/Corporate Donations; Box Office; Government Grants; Individual Donations
Season: 52 Weeks   **Annual Attendance:** 22,000
Affiliations: TCG; Arts and Humanities Council of Tulsa
Performance Facilities: The Williams Theatre

THEATRE TULSA
207 North Main, Tulsa, OK 74103
(918) 587-8402
Founded: 1922
Arts Area: Community; Theatrical Group
Status: Non-Professional; Non-Profit
Type: Performing; Touring; Resident; Educational; Sponsoring

Purpose: To provide entertainment, education, and enrichment to any and all sections of the community through participation in and enjoyment of the theatre arts
Management: Wayne G. Campbell, President/Chief Operating Officer; Kelly Jackson, Office Manager
Officers: Wayne Campbell, President/Chief Operating Officer; Jim Holloman, Chairman of the Board; Brent Curry, Treasurer; Ed Behnken, Vice President of Fund-raising; Pat Hanford, Vice President of Production; Kirby Lehman, Secretary
Paid Staff: 3 **Volunteer Staff:** 300
Paid Artists: 20 **Non-Paid Artists:** 100
Utilizes: Special Technical Talent; Guest Conductors; Guest Artists; Guest Directors
Budget: $100,000 - $500,000
Income Sources: Private Foundations/Grants/Endowments; Business/Corporate Donations; Box Office; Government Grants; Individual Donations
Season: July - June **Annual Attendance:** 40,000
Affiliations: Oklahoma Community Theatre Association; State Arts Council of Oklahoma
Performance Facilities: Performing Arts Center

FACILITY

A.D.A.M.S. THEATRE
1511 South Delaware, Tulsa, OK 74104
(918) 835-5843
    Type of Facility: Performance Center; Off Broadway
    Type of Stage: Proscenium
    Stage Dimensions: 24'x30'
    Seating Capacity: 383
    Year Built: 1932
    Year Remodeled: 1992 **Architect:** John Morrison
    Contact for Rental: Ruth Davis; (918) 742-3267
    Resident Groups: Actors, Dancers and Musicians Society

BRADY THEATRE
105 West Brady, Tulsa, OK 74103
(918) 582-5239
FAX: (918) 587-9531
    Type of Facility: Concert Hall; Theatre House
    Facility Originally: Vaudeville
    Type of Stage: Proscenium
    Stage Dimensions: 65'Wx37'D; 50'Wx20'H proscenium opening **Orchestra Pit**
    Seating Capacity: 2,800
    Year Built: 1914
    Year Remodeled: 1985
    Acoustical Consultant: Peking Sound
    Contact for Rental: Joe Trotter; (918) 582-5239
    Resident Groups: Oklahoma Symphony; Tulsa Pops Orchestra

TULSA PERFORMING ARTS CENTER
110 East Second Street, Tulsa, OK 74103-3212
(918) 596-7122
FAX: (918) 596-7144
    Founded: 1977
    Type of Facility: Theatre Complex; Concert Hall; Studio Performance; Performance Center; Multi-Purpose
    Type of Stage: Proscenium
    Stage Dimensions: 94'Wx51'Dx85'H **Orchestra Pit**
    Seating Capacity: 2,345
    Year Built: 1977 **Architect:** Minoru Yamasaki & Associates **Cost:** $19,000,000
    Acoustical Consultant: Bolt, Beranek & Newman
    Contact for Rental: John E. Scott; (918) 596-7122
    Resident Groups: Tulsa Opera; Tulsa Philharmonic Orchestra; Tulsa Ballet Theatre; Theatre Tulsa; American Theatre Company; Tulsa Town Hall Lecture Series; Tulsa Summer Stage
    The Tulsa Performing Arts Center also contains the Chapman Music Hall, John H. Williams Theatre, Studio I and Studio II. See separate listings for additional information.

TULSA PERFORMING ARTS CENTER - CHAPMAN MUSIC HALL
110 East Second Street, Tulsa, OK 74103-3204
(918) 596-7122
FAX: (918) 596-7144
    Founded: 1977
    Type of Facility: Concert Hall
    Type of Stage: Proscenium

Stage Dimensions: 60'W'x34"H   **Orchestra Pit**
Seating Capacity: 2,450
Year Built: 1977   **Architect:** Minoru Yamasaki   **Cost:** $22,000,000
Acoustical Consultant: Warren Houtz
Contact for Rental: John E. Scott;   (918) 596-7122

TULSA PERFORMING ARTS CENTER - JOHN H. WILLIAMS THEATRE
110 East Second Street, Tulsa, OK 74103-3212
(918) 596-7122
FAX: (918) 596-7144
   Type of Facility: Theatre Complex
   Type of Stage: Proscenium
   Stage Dimensions: 38'Wx22'H   **Orchestra Pit**
   Seating Capacity: 429
   Year Built: 1977   **Architect:** Minoru Yamasaki   **Cost:** $22,000,000
   Acoustical Consultant: Warren Houtz
   Contact for Rental: John E. Scott;   (918) 596-7122

TULSA PERFORMING ARTS CENTER - STUDIO I
110 East Second Street, Tulsa, OK 74103-3212
(918) 596-7122
FAX: (918) 596-7144
   Founded: 1977
   Type of Facility: Studio Performance
   Type of Stage: Flexible
   Stage Dimensions: 60'x36'
   Seating Capacity: 288
   Year Built: 1977   **Architect:** Minoru Yamasaki   **Cost:** $22,000,000
   Acoustical Consultant: Warren Houtz
   Contact for Rental: John E. Scott;   (918) 596-7122

TULSA PERFORMING ARTS CENTER - STUDIO II
110 East Second Street, Tulsa, OK 74103-3212
(918) 596-7122
FAX: (918) 596-7144
   Founded: 1977
   Type of Facility: Studio Performance
   Type of Stage: Flexible
   Stage Dimensions: 52'x52'
   Seating Capacity: 200
   Year Built: 1977   **Architect:** Minoru Yamasaki   **Cost:** $22,000,000
   Acoustical Consultant: Warren Houtz
   Contact for Rental: John E. Scott;   (918) 596-7122

UNIVERSITY OF TULSA - KENDALL HALL
600 South College, Tulsa, OK 74104
(918) 592-6000
   Founded: 1884
   Type of Facility: Multi-Purpose
   Type of Stage: Flexible
   Orchestra Pit
   Seating Capacity: 400
   Year Built: 1975   **Architect:** McCune McCune & Associates   **Cost:** $3,500,000
   Acoustical Consultant: C.P. Boner & Associates
   Contact for Rental: David Cook;   (918) 631-2566
   Resident Groups: Tulsa University Theatre Department

UNIVERSITY OF TULSA - TYRRELL HALL
600 South College, Tulsa, OK 74114
(918) 631-2000
   Type of Facility: Concert Hall
   Facility Originally: Meeting Hall; Movie House
   Type of Stage: Proscenium
   Seating Capacity: 131
   Year Remodeled: 1974   **Architect:** McCune McCune & Associates   **Cost:** $400,000
   Manager: Ronald Predl

Weatherford

FACILITY

SOUTHWESTERN OKLAHOMA STATE UNIVERSITY - FINE ARTS CENTER
Department of Music, 100 Campus Drive, Weatherford, OK 73096
(405) 772-6611
FAX: (405) 774-3795
Type of Facility: Concert Hall; Auditorium; Multi-Purpose
Type of Stage: Proscenium
Stage Dimensions: 64'Wx40'D, 49'10"Wx22'H proscenium opening   **Orchestra Pit**
Seating Capacity: 1,465
Year Built: 1984   **Architect:** RGDG   **Cost:** $2,500,000
Contact for Rental: Joe B. Thompson;   (405) 774-3705

Woodward

THEATRE

WOODWARD ARTS AND THEATRE COUNCIL
818 Main, Woodward, OK 73802
(405) 256-7120
Founded: 1981
Arts Area: Musical; Community; Theatrical Group
Status: Non-Profit
Type: Performing; Sponsoring
Purpose: To encourage and correlate activities dedicated to the promotion of the cultural arts of Woodward and neighboring areas and to own, manage, and operate the Woodward Arts Theatre
Management: E.J. Mann, Manager
Officers: Laverne Phillips, President; Larry Kelley, Vice President; Leonard Hart, Secretary/Treasurer
Paid Staff: 1   **Volunteer Staff:** 1
Utilizes: Special Technical Talent; Guest Artists
Budget: $1,000 - $50,000
Income Sources: Private Foundations/Grants/Endowments; Business/Corporate Donations; Box Office; Government Grants; Individual Donations
Season: July - June   **Annual Attendance:** 5,000
Affiliations: State Arts Council of Oklahoma

OREGON

Albany

PERFORMING SERIES

CITY OF ALBANY PARKS AND RECREATION DEPARTMENT
433 SW Fourth Avenue, Albany, OR 97321
   Founded: 1983
   Arts Area: Vocal Music; Instrumental Music; Festivals
   Status: Non-Profit
   Type: Sponsoring
   Purpose: To present a free summer outdoor concert series "River Rhythms", plus a six concert childrens performing arts series
   Management: Dave Clark, Director; Sherry Halligan, Program Coordinator
   Paid Staff: 6
   Utilizes: Special Technical Talent; Guest Artists
   Budget: $50,000 - $100,000
   Income Sources: Private Foundations/Grants/Endowments; Business/Corporate Donations
   Season: July - August; September-May   **Annual Attendance:** 53,200

Ashland

INSTRUMENTAL MUSIC

CHAMBER MUSIC CONCERTS
SOSC, 1250 Siskiyou Boulevard, Ashland, OR 97520
(503) 552-6333
FAX: (503) 552-6380
   Founded: 1984
   Arts Area: Chamber
   Status: Professional; Non-Profit
   Type: Performing
   Purpose: To bring excellence in chamber music performances to the southern Oregon community
   Management: Dr. Gregory Fowler, Founder/Director; Lesley Pohl, Assistant
   Paid Staff: 1   **Volunteer Staff:** 12
   Paid Artists: 20
   Utilizes: Guest Artists
   Budget: $1,000 - $50,000
   Income Sources: Private Foundations/Grants/Endowments; Business/Corporate Donations; Box Office; Individual Donations
   Season: October - May   **Annual Attendance:** 2,500
   Performance Facilities: SOSC Music Building Recital Hall

VOCAL MUSIC

ROQUE OPERA
1250 Siskiyou Boulevard, Music Hall 107, Ashland, OR 97520
(508) 552-6400
   Founded: 1978
   Arts Area: Grand Opera; Light Opera; Operetta
   Status: Non-Profit
   Type: Performing; Touring
   Management: Marcia Von Furstenberg, Managing Director
   Officers: Judith Audley, President; Ron Kramer, Vice President; Tim Cusick, Treasurer
   Paid Staff: 1   **Volunteer Staff:** 60
   Paid Artists: 100
   Utilizes: Special Technical Talent; Guest Conductors; Guest Artists; Guest Directors
   Budget: $50,000 - $100,000
   Income Sources: Private Foundations/Grants/Endowments; Business/Corporate Donations; Box Office; Individual Donations
   Season: August - January   **Annual Attendance:** 10,000
   Performance Facilities: Oregon Shakespeare Festival Theatres; Cabaret Theatre; Dorothy Stolp Theatre

THEATRE

ACTORS' THEATER OF ASHLAND
295 East Main, Suite 5, Ashland, OR 97520
(503) 482-9659
>**Founded:** 1982
>**Arts Area:** Professional; Musical; Community; Folk; Theatrical Group; Puppet
>**Status:** Semi-Professional; Non-Profit
>**Type:** Performing; Touring; Educational
>**Purpose:** To encourage local playwrights and composers through production of their works; to challenge the status quo through public demonstration of freedom of the imagination; to strive to increase awareness of the ecology, politics and social issues; to entertain
>**Management:** Michael O'Rourke, Artistic Director, Actors' Workshop; Alison Grant, Artistic Director, Young Actors' Workshop
>**Officers:** Elliot Reinert, President
>**Paid Staff:** 2   **Volunteer Staff:** 3
>**Paid Artists:** 10   **Non-Paid Artists:** 20
>**Utilizes:** Special Technical Talent; Guest Artists; Guest Directors
>**Budget:** $1,000 - $50,000
>**Income Sources:** Business/Corporate Donations; Box Office; Individual Donations
>**Season:** 52 Weeks   **Annual Attendance:** 4,000
>**Affiliations:** Oregon Theatre Association

OREGON SHAKESPEAREAN FESTIVAL ASSOCIATION
15 South Pioneer, Ashland, OR 97520
(503) 482-2111
>**Founded:** 1935
>**Arts Area:** Professional
>**Status:** Professional; Non-Profit
>**Type:** Performing; Touring; Resident; Educational
>**Purpose:** Production of professional performances of the plays of Shakespeare and other works of high literary quality in a rotating repertory system
>**Management:** Henry Woronicz, Artistic Director; William Patton, Executive Director; Paul Nicholson, General Manager
>**Officers:** William R. Moffat, President; John Hassen, Vice President; Patricia Romeo, Secretary; Robert Rasmussen, Treasurer
>**Paid Staff:** 281   **Volunteer Staff:** 800
>**Paid Artists:** 84
>**Utilizes:** Special Technical Talent; Guest Directors
>**Budget:** $5,000,000 - $10,000,000
>**Income Sources:** Private Foundations/Grants/Endowments; Business/Corporate Donations; Box Office; Government Grants; Individual Donations
>**Season:** February - October   **Annual Attendance:** 360,000
>**Affiliations:** AEA; ATA; U/RTA; TCG
>**Performance Facilities:** Angus Bowmer Theatre; Black Swan Theatre; Elizabethan Stage

QUARTZ THEATRE
392 Taylor, Ashland, OR 97520
(513) 482-8119
>**Founded:** 1976
>**Arts Area:** Theatrical Group
>**Status:** Non-Profit
>**Type:** Performing
>**Purpose:** Playwright development
>**Management:** Robert Spira, Artistic Director
>**Budget:** $1,000 - $50,000
>**Income Sources:** Box Office
>**Season:** 52 Weeks

STUDIO X PLAYHOUSE
208 Oak Street, Ashland, OR 89502
(503) 488-2011
>**Founded:** 1988
>**Arts Area:** Theatrical Group
>**Status:** Semi-Professional; Non-Profit
>**Type:** Performing; Resident
>**Purpose:** To produce all types of theatre--classic, contemporary and new

Management: Jim Funk, Artistic Director
Paid Staff: 1   **Volunteer Staff:** 10
Non-Paid Artists: 10
Utilizes: Guest Directors
Budget: $1,000 - $50,000
Income Sources: Private Foundations/Grants/Endowments; Box Office; Government Grants; Individual Donations
Season: 52 Weeks   **Annual Attendance:** 6,000

PERFORMING SERIES

ASHLAND FOLK MUSIC CLUB
PO Box 63, Ashland, OR 97520
(503) 488-1561
  Founded: 1984
  Arts Area: Dance; Vocal Music; Instrumental Music
  Status: Non-Profit
  Type: Performing; Sponsoring
  Purpose: To perpetuate folk traditions; to bring the best in folk music to the area
  Management: Nancy Spencer, Coordinator
  Volunteer Staff: 4
  Utilizes: Guest Artists
  Budget: $1,000 - $50,000
  Income Sources: Box Office; Individual Donations
  Season: 52 Weeks   **Annual Attendance:** 600
  Performance Facilities: Carpenter Hall

FACILITY

OREGON SHAKESPEARE FESTIVAL - ANGUS BOWMER THEATRE
15 South Pioneer, Ashland, OR 97520
(503) 482-2111
  Type of Facility: Theatre Complex; Theatre House
  Type of Stage: Open-end Modified Thrust
  Orchestra Pit
  Seating Capacity: 601
  Year Built: 1970   **Architect:** Kirk Wallace McKinley   **Cost:** $2,500,000
  Acoustical Consultant: Robin M. Towne Associates
  Contact for Rental: Paul Nicholson;   (503) 482-2111
  Resident Groups: Oregon Shakespeare Festival
  Shares backstage space with Elizabethan Stage

OREGON SHAKESPEARE FESTIVAL - BLACK SWAN THEATRE
15 South Pioneer, Ashland, OR 97520
(503) 482-2111
  Type of Facility: Theatre Complex; Theatre House
  Facility Originally: Garage
  Type of Stage: 3/4 Arena
  Seating Capacity: 140
  Year Remodeled: 1977   **Cost:** $127,000
  Contact for Rental: Paul Nicholson;   (503) 482-2111
  Resident Groups: Oregon Shakespeare Festival

OREGON SHAKESPEARE FESTIVAL - ELIZABETHAN STAGE
15 South Pioneer, Ashland, OR 97520
(503) 482-2111
  Type of Facility: Theatre Complex; Outdoor (Concert); Amphitheater
  Type of Stage: Environmental; Elizabethan-style with Modified Thrust
  Seating Capacity: 1,194
  Year Built: 1959   **Architect:** Jack Edson   **Cost:** $425,000
  Year Remodeled: 1992   **Architect:** Treffinger, Walz & MacLeod   **Cost:** $7,500,000
  Contact for Rental: Paul Nicholson;   (503) 482-2111
  Resident Groups: Oregon Shakespeare Festival
  America's first Elizabethan Stage, it shares backstage space with the Angus Bowmer Theatre.

Astoria

DANCE

LITTLE BALLET THEATRE
3432 Franklin, Astoria, OR 97103
(503) 325-3961
Founded: 1978
Arts Area: Ballet
Status: Non-Professional; Non-Profit
Type: Performing; Educational
Purpose: To provide exposure to ballet to all people in the North Coast area of Oregon
Management: Jeanne Maddox Fastabend, Artistic Director
Officers: Terri Johnson, President; Wendy Page, Vice President; Tina Ames, Secretary; Linda Dugan, Treasurer
Volunteer Staff: 55
Paid Artists: 2   **Non-Paid Artists:** 100
Utilizes: Guest Artists
Budget: $1,000 - $50,000
Income Sources: Private Foundations/Grants/Endowments; Business/Corporate Donations; Box Office; Individual Donations
Season: October - December   **Annual Attendance:** 1,800
Performance Facilities: Astoria High School Auditorium

Bend

THEATRE

COMMUNITY THEATRE OF THE CASCADES
148 NW Greenwood, Bend, OR 97701
(503) 389-0803
Founded: 1978
Arts Area: Musical; Community; Theatrical Group
Status: Non-Professional; Non-Profit
Type: Performing
Purpose: To provide quality live theatre for the community
Management: Barbara Matlick, Business Manager
Officers: Zelia Nauer, Chairman; Barbara Jordan, Secretary
Paid Staff: 1   **Volunteer Staff:** 100
Non-Paid Artists: 50
Utilizes: Special Technical Talent
Budget: $1,000 - $50,000
Income Sources: Business/Corporate Donations; Box Office; Individual Donations
Season: July - June   **Annual Attendance:** 10,000
Affiliations: Oregon Theatre Association

Cannon Beach

FACILITY

COASTER THEATER
108 North Hemlock, PO Box 643, Cannon Beach, OR 97110
(503) 436-1242
Type of Facility: Concert Hall; Auditorium; Studio Performance; Performance Center; Off Broadway; Theatre House; Multi-Purpose
Facility Originally: Skating Rink
Type of Stage: Flexible; Proscenium; Platform
Stage Dimensions: 30'x35'
Seating Capacity: 200
Year Built: 1920
Year Remodeled: 1972   **Architect:** Ray Watkins
Contact for Rental: Stephen A. Diehl;   (503) 436-1242
Resident Groups: Coaster Theater Players

Cave Junction

INSTRUMENTAL MUSIC

SISKIYOU BAROQUE ENSEMBLE
9345 Takilma Road, Cave Junction, OR 97523
(503) 592-2681
>**Founded:** 1982
>**Arts Area:** Ensemble
>**Status:** Professional
>**Type:** Performing
>**Purpose:** To offer original instrument performances of 17th and 18th-century vocal and instrumental chamber music to residents of the Siskiyou Bioregion
>**Management:** James Rich, Musical Director
>**Volunteer Staff:** 1
>**Paid Artists:** 7
>**Utilizes:** Guest Artists
>**Budget:** $1,000 - $50,000
>**Income Sources:** Box Office; Individual Donations
>**Season:** Fall - Spring   **Annual Attendance:** 700
>**Performance Facilities:** Barnstormers' Theater, Grants Pass; Carpenter Hall, Ashland

---
Coos Bay

PERFORMING SERIES

OREGON COAST MUSIC ASSOCIATION
PO Box 663, Coos Bay, OR 97420
(503) 267-0938
>**Founded:** 1988
>**Arts Area:** Instrumental Music; Festivals
>**Status:** Non-Profit
>**Type:** Educational; Sponsoring
>**Purpose:** To present an annual classical music festival and year round musical and educational activities
>**Management:** Crystal Landucci, General Manager; Linda Kissinger, Office Manager
>**Officers:** Kim Thompson, Board President; Kay Snelgrove, Treasurer
>**Paid Staff:** 2   **Volunteer Staff:** 20
>**Paid Artists:** 120   **Non-Paid Artists:** 5
>**Utilizes:** Guest Artists
>**Budget:** $50,000 - $100,000
>**Income Sources:** Private Foundations/Grants/Endowments; Business/Corporate Donations; Box Office; Government Grants; Individual Donations
>**Season:** October - July   **Annual Attendance:** 8,000
>**Performance Facilities:** Marshfield Auditorium

Corvallis

INSTRUMENTAL MUSIC

FRIENDS OF CHAMBER MUSIC
3904 NW Clarence Circus, Corvallis, OR 97330
(503) 757-0086
FAX: (503) 967-8902
>**Founded:** 1958
>**Arts Area:** Chamber
>**Status:** Non-Professional; Non-Profit
>**Type:** Sponsoring
>**Purpose:** To present the highest quality chamber music
>**Officers:** Carole Orloff, Chair; John Morris, Vice Chair; Jean Nath, Secretary; Stefan Bloomfield, Treasurer
>**Paid Artists:** 6
>**Utilizes:** Guest Artists
>**Budget:** $1,000 - $50,000
>**Income Sources:** Business/Corporate Donations; Box Office; Individual Donations
>**Season:** September - May   **Annual Attendance:** 3,000
>**Performance Facilities:** Laseus Stewart Center

FACILITY

LA SELLS STEWART CENTER
Oregon State University, Corvallis, OR 97331-3102
(503) 737-2402
FAX: (503) 737-3187
 Founded: 1981
 Type of Facility: Concert Hall
 Type of Stage: Flexible
 Stage Dimensions: 53'8"x43'4"x26' **Orchestra Pit**
 Seating Capacity: 1,200
 Year Built: 1981 **Cost:** $4,500,000
 Contact for Rental: Sylvia Moore; (503) 737-2402

OREGON STATE UNIVERSITY - GILL COLISEUM
15th and Jefferson, Corvallis, OR 97331
(503) 737-2547
 Type of Facility: Basketball Gymnasium
 Type of Stage: Proscenium
 Stage Dimensions: 4'x8' up to 24'x44', can be made larger if needed
 Seating Capacity: 15,000
 Year Built: 1949
 Year Remodeled: 1986 **Cost:** $1,700,000
 Contact for Rental: Sylvia Moore; (503) 737-2402
 Manager: Bob Herndon

OREGON STATE UNIVERSITY - MILAN AUDITORIUM
26th and Campus Way, Corvallis, OR 97331
(503) 737-0123
 Type of Facility: Auditorium
 Type of Stage: Platform
 Seating Capacity: 750
 Year Built: 1952
 Contact for Rental: Beth Dyer; (503) 737-2181

Eugene

DANCE

EUGENE BALLET COMPANY
PO Box 11200, Eugene, OR 97440
(503) 485-3992
 Founded: 1978
 Arts Area: Ballet
 Status: Professional; Non-Profit
 Type: Performing; Touring; Resident; Sponsoring
 Management: Toni Pimble, Artistic Director; Riley Grannan, Managing Director; Robert Dwan, Development Director; Eloise Zenger, Financial Manager; Tamara Richey, Marketing Director
 Officers: Janet Reed, President; Larry Hedberg, Vice President; Margaret Leonard, Secretary; Kenneth Kohnen, Treasurer
 Paid Staff: 5 **Volunteer Staff:** 5
 Paid Artists: 20 **Non-Paid Artists:** 3
 Utilizes: Guest Conductors
 Budget: $100,000 - $500,000
 Income Sources: Private Foundations/Grants/Endowments; Business/Corporate Donations; Box Office; Government Grants; Individual Donations
 Season: September - April **Annual Attendance:** 40,000
 Performance Facilities: Hult Center for the Performing Arts

INSTRUMENTAL MUSIC

EMERALD CHAMBER PLAYERS
3080 Potter, Eugene, OR 97405
(503) 344-0483
 Founded: 1962
 Arts Area: Orchestra; Chamber; Ensemble; Instrumental Group
 Status: Non-Professional; Non-Profit
 Type: Performing

Purpose: To afford amateurs opportunities to play chamber music for themselves and for others
Management: Orval Etter, Convener
Income Sources: Private Foundations/Grants/Endowments; Government Grants; Individual Donations
Season: 52 Weeks   **Annual Attendance:** 2,000

EUGENE SYMPHONY
45 West Broadway, #201, Eugene, OR 97401
(503) 687-9487
FAX: (503) 687-0527
  Founded: 1966
  Arts Area: Symphony; Orchestra
  Status: Semi-Professional; Non-Profit
  Type: Performing; Resident
  Purpose: To produce music of the highest professional quality for the enjoyment of a diverse public
  Management: Michael Anderson, Interim Executive Director
  Officers: John C. Watkinson, President; Georgianne Beaudet, Vice President; Ted Scherer, Secretary; Robert Fenstermacher, Treasurer
  Paid Staff: 10   **Volunteer Staff:** 15
  Paid Artists: 85
  Utilizes: Guest Conductors; Guest Artists
  Budget: $100,000 - $500,000
  Income Sources: Private Foundations/Grants/Endowments; Business/Corporate Donations; Box Office; Government Grants; Individual Donations
  Season: September - May   **Annual Attendance:** 40,150
  Affiliations: ASCAP; ASOL
  Performance Facilities: Hult Center for the Performing Arts

OREGON MOZART PLAYERS
541 Willametta Street, Suite 308, Eugene, OR 97401
(503) 345-6648
  Founded: 1982
  Arts Area: Orchestra; Chamber
  Status: Professional; Non-Profit
  Type: Performing; Touring; Resident; Educational
  Purpose: To play chamber orchestra music and provide an opportunity for talented, local musicians to perform as soloists as members of the orchestra, and in chamber ensembles
  Management: Jeffrey Eaton, General Manager
  Officers: Jim Dotson, President; Sharon Schuman, Vice President; Russell Donnelly, Secretary/Treasurer
  Paid Staff: 1   **Volunteer Staff:** 2
  Paid Artists: 35
  Utilizes: Special Technical Talent; Guest Conductors; Guest Artists
  Budget: $100,000 - $500,000
  Income Sources: Private Foundations/Grants/Endowments; Business/Corporate Donations; Box Office; Government Grants; Individual Donations; Special Events
  Season: September - May   **Annual Attendance:** 6,000
  Performance Facilities: Hult Center For The Performing Arts; Beall Concert Hall, University of Oregon

VOCAL MUSIC

EUGENE OPERA
PO Box 11200, Eugene, OR 97440
(503) 485-3985
FAX: (503) 683-3783
  Founded: 1976
  Arts Area: Grand Opera; Lyric Opera; Light Opera; Operetta
  Status: Professional; Non-Profit
  Type: Performing; Educational
  Purpose: To produce opera
  Management: James Toland, Artistic Director
  Officers: Alan Evans, Board President
  Paid Staff: 5   **Volunteer Staff:** 4
  Utilizes: Special Technical Talent; Guest Conductors; Guest Artists; Guest Directors
  Budget: $100,000 - $500,000
  Income Sources: Private Foundations/Grants/Endowments; Business/Corporate Donations; Box Office; Government Grants; Individual Donations
  Season: December - April   **Annual Attendance:** 14,000
  Affiliations: OA; COS
  Performance Facilities: Hult Center for the Performing Arts

THEATRE

MAINSTAGE THEATRE COMPANY
996 Willamette Street, Eugene, OR 97401
(503) 683-4368
> **Founded:** 1979
> **Arts Area:** Professional; Musical; Dinner; Community; Theatrical Group
> **Status:** Semi-Professional; Non-Professional; Non-Profit
> **Type:** Performing
> **Purpose:** To offer a wide range of experiences for participants and audiences both in a community theatre and in a professional theater atmosphere
> **Management:** Jim Roberts, Producer/Executive Director; Joe Zingo, Artistic Director
> **Officers:** Joe Zingo, Chairperson
> **Paid Staff:** 2   **Volunteer Staff:** 12
> **Paid Artists:** 24   **Non-Paid Artists:** 100
> **Budget:** $50,000 - $100,000
> **Income Sources:** Business/Corporate Donations; Box Office; Individual Donations
> **Season:** 52 Weeks   **Annual Attendance:** 15,200
> **Performance Facilities:** Downtown Cabaret; Eugene Downtown Mall

OREGON FANTASY THEATRE
820 East 36th Street, Eugene, OR 97405
(503) 686-1574
> **Founded:** 1978
> **Arts Area:** Musical; Community; Theatrical Group; Puppet
> **Status:** Professional; Non-Professional; Commercial
> **Type:** Performing; Touring; Educational
> **Purpose:** Produce and perform puppet shows with combination live actors, marionettes, hand puppets, shadows and masks
> **Management:** Celeste Rose, Director
> **Paid Staff:** 1   **Volunteer Staff:** 10
> **Paid Artists:** 3   **Non-Paid Artists:** 3
> **Utilizes:** Special Technical Talent; Guest Artists
> **Budget:** $1,000 - $50,000
> **Income Sources:** Box Office
> **Season:** 52 Weeks   **Annual Attendance:** 2,000
> **Affiliations:** Puppeteers of America
> **Performance Facilities:** Hult Center for the Performing Arts

PERFORMING SERIES

CHAMBER MUSIC SERIES
University of Oregon, Eugene, OR 97403
(503) 346-5678
FAX: (503) 346-5669
> **Founded:** 1968
> **Arts Area:** Dance; Vocal Music; Instrumental Music; Festivals
> **Status:** Non-Profit
> **Type:** Performing; Touring; Educational
> **Purpose:** To present classical chamber music concerts
> **Management:** Stephen Stone, Manager
> **Paid Staff:** 2
> **Budget:** $1,000 - $50,000
> **Income Sources:** Private Foundations/Grants/Endowments; Business/Corporate Donations; Box Office; Individual Donations
> **Season:** October - May   **Annual Attendance:** 3,800
> **Performance Facilities:** Beall Concert Hall

OREGON BACH FESTIVAL
University of Oregon, School of Music, Eugene, OR 97403
(503) 346-5666
FAX: (503) 346-5669
> **Founded:** 1970
> **Arts Area:** Vocal Music; Instrumental Music; Festivals
> **Status:** Professional; Non-Profit
> **Type:** Performing; Resident; Educational
> **Purpose:** To create for performers, audience and the community at large an artistic experience that elevates the human spirit through excellence in performance
> **Utilizes:** Special Technical Talent; Guest Conductors; Guest Artists

Budget: $1,000,000 - $5,000,000
Income Sources: Private Foundations/Grants/Endowments; Business/Corporate Donations; Box Office; Government Grants; Individual Donations
Season: June - July   **Annual Attendance:** 31,000
Performance Facilities: University of Oregon School of Music; Beall Concert Hall; Hult Center for Performing Arts; Silva Concert Hall; Soreng Theatre

FACILITY

HULT CENTER FOR THE PERFORMING ARTS
One Eugene Centre, Eugene, OR 97401
(503) 687-5087
Type of Facility: Theatre Complex; Performance Center
Year Built: 1982   **Architect:** Hardy Holzman Pfeiffer Associates
Acoustical Consultant: Jaffe Acoustics
Contact for Rental: Karm Hagedorn;   (503) 687-5087
Hult Center for the Performing Arts contains Silva Concert Hall and Soreng Theatre. See separate listings for further information.

HULT CENTER FOR THE PERFORMING ARTS - SILVA CONCERT HALL
One Eugene Centre, Eugene, OR 97401
(503) 687-5087
Type of Facility: Concert Hall; Performance Center; Opera House; Multi-Purpose
Type of Stage: Proscenium
Stage Dimensions: 113'Wx50'D; 57'10"W proscenium opening   **Orchestra Pit**
Seating Capacity: 2,504
Year Built: 1982
Contact for Rental: Karm Hagedorn;   (503) 687-5087
Resident Groups: Eugene Symphony; Eugene Ballet; Eugene Festival of Musical Theater; Oregon Bach Festival

HULT CENTER FOR THE PERFORMING ARTS - SORENG THEATRE
One Eugene Centre, Eugene, OR 97401
(503) 687-5087
Type of Facility: Concert Hall; Theatre House
Type of Stage: Proscenium
Stage Dimensions: 55'Wx30'D; 55'W proscenium opening   **Orchestra Pit**
Seating Capacity: 500
Year Built: 1982
Contact for Rental: Karm Hagedorn;   (503) 687-5087
Resident Groups: Oregon Mozart Players; Hult Children's Series

UNIVERSITY OF OREGON - BEALL CONCERT HALL
Eugene, OR 97403
(503) 686-5678
Type of Facility: Concert Hall; Auditorium
Type of Stage: Platform
Stage Dimensions: 50'Wx35'D
Seating Capacity: 550
Year Built: 1921   **Architect:** Ellis Lawrence
Year Remodeled: 1973   **Architect:** John Amundsen   **Cost:** $100,000
Contact for Rental: Manager;   (503) 686-5678

Forest Grove

INSTRUMENTAL MUSIC

PACIFIC UNIVERSITY COMMUNITY ORCHESTRA
Pacific University, Music Department, Forest Grove, OR 97116
(503) 357-6151
Founded: 1849
Arts Area: Orchestra; Chamber
Status: Non-Professional; Non-Profit
Type: Performing; Resident; Educational
Purpose: Educational training for music students and music outlet for members of the community
Management: Craig Gibson, Conductor
Paid Staff: 1
Paid Artists: 50
Utilizes: Guest Artists

Budget: $1,000 - $50,000
Season: September - May   **Annual Attendance:** 1,000
Performance Facilities: University Center

FACILITY

PACIFIC UNIVERSITY - TOM MILES THEATRE
2043 College Way, Forest Grove, OR 97116
(503) 359-2200
    Type of Facility: Multi-Purpose; Room
    Facility Originally: Meeting Hall; Movie House
    Type of Stage: Proscenium
    Stage Dimensions: 10'x20'x20'
    Seating Capacity: 350
    Year Built: 1962
    Contact for Rental: Ed Collier;   (503) 359-2200

THEATRE IN THE GROVE
2028 Pacific Avenue, PO Box 263, Forest Grove, OR 97116
(503) 359-5349
    Founded: 1970
    Type of Facility: Auditorium; Theatre House
    Facility Originally: Movie House
    Type of Stage: Thrust; Flexible; Proscenium; revolving center stage
    Stage Dimensions: 20'x30'x30'   **Orchestra Pit**
    Seating Capacity: 350
    Year Built: 1910
    Year Remodeled: 1992   **Architect:** Dave Giulletti   **Cost:** $200,000
    Contact for Rental: Jeff Zimmerman, Manager;   (503) 359-5349
    Manager: Jeff Zimmerman
    Resident Groups: Theatre in the Grove

Lake Oswego

INSTRUMENTAL MUSIC

PORTLAND FESTIVAL SYMPHONY
PO Box 359, Lake Oswego, OR 97034
(503) 636-8769
    Founded: 1986
    Arts Area: Symphony
    Status: Professional
    Type: Performing
    Purpose: To provide free concerts (to promote symphonic music) to large audiences in cooperation with the City Park Bureau
    Management: Lajos Balogh, Music Director/Conductor
    Volunteer Staff: 15
    Paid Artists: 72
    Utilizes: Guest Conductors; Guest Artists
    Budget: $1,000 - $50,000
    Income Sources: Private Foundations/Grants/Endowments; Business/Corporate Donations; Government Grants; Individual Donations
    Annual Attendance: 20,000
    Performance Facilities: Washington Park

THEATRE

LAKEWOOD THEATRE COMPANY
368 South State Street, PO Box 274, Lake Oswego, OR 97034
(503) 635-3901
    Founded: 1952
    Arts Area: Musical; Community; Theatrical Group
    Status: Non-Professional; Non-Profit
    Type: Performing; Resident; Educational; Sponsoring
    Purpose: Training for actors, actresses, directors and technical people for personal and/or professional enjoyment
    Management: Andrew Edwards, Executive Director; Kay Vega, Executive Producer
    Officers: Paul Graham, President
    Paid Staff: 5   **Volunteer Staff:** 2

Paid Artists: 100 **Non-Paid Artists:** 50
Utilizes: Special Technical Talent; Guest Conductors; Guest Artists; Guest Directors
Budget: $100,000 - $500,000
Income Sources: Private Foundations/Grants/Endowments; Business/Corporate Donations; Box Office; Individual Donations
Season: 52 Weeks **Annual Attendance:** 25,000
Affiliations: Oregon Theatre Association; Oregon Advocates for the Arts; Portland Area Theatre Alliance

McMinnville

THEATRE

GALLERY THEATRE OF OREGON
Second and Ford Streets, McMinnville, OR 97128
(503) 472-2227
Founded: 1968
Arts Area: Musical; Community
Status: Non-Profit
Type: Performing; Educational
Purpose: Provide center for the performing arts in Yamhill County
Management: Corby Wright, Managing Director
Officers: Chris Browne, President of the Board; Carol Burnett, Vice President; Barbara Knutson, Secretary; Jim Capps, Treasurer
Volunteer Staff: 20
Non-Paid Artists: 150
Utilizes: Special Technical Talent; Guest Artists; Guest Directors
Budget: $100,000 - $500,000
Income Sources: Private Foundations/Grants/Endowments; Business/Corporate Donations; Box Office; Government Grants; Individual Donations
Season: 52 Weeks **Annual Attendance:** 30,000

Medford

DANCE

MEDFORD CIVIC BALLET
9 Hawthorne Street, Medford, OR 97502
(503) 772-1362
Founded: 1982
Arts Area: Ballet
Status: Non-Profit
Type: Performing
Purpose: To excel in dance and dance education
Management: Mary Cowden Snyder, Artistic Director
Officers: Bonnie McKinley, Chairperson
Paid Staff: 3 **Volunteer Staff:** 20
Paid Artists: 3 **Non-Paid Artists:** 20
Utilizes: Guest Artists
Budget: $1,000 - $50,000
Income Sources: Private Foundations/Grants/Endowments; Business/Corporate Donations; Box Office; Individual Donations
Season: September - July **Annual Attendance:** 10,000

PERFORMING SERIES

BRITT FESTIVALS
PO Box 1124, Medford, OR 97501
(503) 779-0847
FAX: (503) 776-3712
Founded: 1963
Arts Area: Dance; Vocal Music; Instrumental Music; Theater; Festivals
Status: Professional; Non-Profit
Type: Performing; Touring; Resident; Educational; Sponsoring
Management: Ron Mellne, General Manager; Chris Sackett, Productions Manager; Stacey Stover, Marketing; Debbie Whipple, Financial Manager; Barbara Frenna, Box Office Manager
Officers: Diane Christopher, President; Gary Lovre, Vice President; Diane Somers, Vice President; Lois Thorson, Treasurer; Margaret Cutler, Secretary

Paid Staff: 15   Volunteer Staff: 500
Paid Artists: 240
Utilizes: Guest Conductors; Guest Artists; Guest Directors
Budget: $500,000 - $1,000,000
Income Sources: Private Foundations/Grants/Endowments; Business/Corporate Donations; Box Office; Government Grants; Individual Donations
Season: June - September   Annual Attendance: 51,000
Performance Facilities: The Britt Gardens

FACILITY

CRATERIAN THEATRE
23 South Central Avenue, Medford, OR 97501
(503) 779-8195
Founded: 1924
Type of Facility: Performance Center; Theatre House; Multi-Purpose
Facility Originally: Vaudeville; Movie House
Type of Stage: Thrust; Proscenium; Stage is elevated 4' from main floor
Stage Dimensions: 32'x35'   Orchestra Pit
Seating Capacity: 650
Year Built: 1924   Architect: Frank Clark   Cost: $176,000
Contact for Rental: Teresa Collins Ley;   (503) 779-8195

Monmouth
FACILITY

WESTERN OREGON STATE COLLEGE
345 Monmouth Avenue, Monmouth, OR 97361
(503) 838-8462
Type of Facility: Theatre Complex; Auditorium; Studio Performance; Recital Hall
Type of Stage: Flexible; Proscenium; Platform; Environmental; 3/4 Arena with on-stage seating
Stage Dimensions: 52'x30'   Orchestra Pit
Seating Capacity: 619
Year Built: 1976   Architect: Payne and Setticase   Cost: $2,000,000
Contact for Rental: (503) 838-8462
Resident Groups: Western Oregon State College Theatre

North Bend
THEATRE

DOLPHIN PLAYERS
2540 Union, North Bend, OR 97459
(503) 756-7088
Founded: 1980
Arts Area: Musical; Dinner; Community; Theatrical Group
Status: Non-Professional; Non-Profit
Type: Performing; Resident; Educational; Sponsoring
Purpose: To present quality theater productions in an intimate setting
Officers: Alice Carlson, President; Mark Thimm, Vice President; Clara Radcliffe, Secretary; Mable Hayes, Treasurer
Volunteer Staff: 3
Non-Paid Artists: 50
Budget: $1,000 - $50,000
Income Sources: Business/Corporate Donations; Box Office; Individual Donations
Season: 52 Weeks

Portland
DANCE

THE CONTEMPORARY DANCE SEASON
c/o Portland State University, PO Box 751, Portland, OR 90207
(503) 725-3131
FAX: (503) 725-4882
Arts Area: Modern

Status: Professional; Non-Profit
Type: Educational; Presenting
Purpose: To present contemporary dance and dance education of the highest quality
Management: Carolyn Altman, Managing Director
Budget: $100,000 - $500,000
Income Sources: Private Foundations/Grants/Endowments; Business/Corporate Donations; Box Office; Government Grants; Individual Donations
Performance Facilities: Lincoln Hall

METRO DANCERS
6433 NE Tillamook, Portland, OR 97213
(503) 282-5061
Founded: 1979
Arts Area: Modern; Ballet
Status: Non-Professional; Non-Profit
Type: Performing
Purpose: Arts should be accessible to everyone.
Management: Nancy Y. Thompson, Artistic Director
Non-Paid Artists: 20
Utilizes: Guest Artists
Budget: $1,000 - $50,000
Income Sources: Government Grants
Season: April - October
Affiliations: Regional Dance Association/Pacific

OREGON BALLET THEATRE
1120 SW Tenth Avenue, Portland, OR 97205
(503) 227-0977
FAX: (503) 227-4186
Founded: 1989
Arts Area: Modern; Ballet; Jazz
Status: Professional; Non-Profit
Type: Performing; Touring; Resident; Educational; Sponsoring
Purpose: To offer the highest quality professional ballet to the people of Oregon, the Pacific Northwest and the U.S.; to entertain and educate audiences, and to encourage the creative talents of dancers, choreographers, composers and musicians
Management: James Canfield, Artistic Director; Dennis Spaight, Associate Director/Resident Choreographer; Niel De Ponte, Music Director
Officers: Ken Lewis, Chairman; Scott Howard, Secretary; Tracy Montgomery, Treasurer
Paid Staff: 67   **Volunteer Staff:** 135
Paid Artists: 25
Utilizes: Guest Artists; Guest Choreographers
Budget: $1,000,000 - $5,000,000
Income Sources: Private Foundations/Grants/Endowments; Business/Corporate Donations; Box Office; Government Grants; Individual Donations
Season: October - May   **Annual Attendance:** 76,000
Affiliations: WESTAF; WAA; Dance USA; Portland Arts Alliance
Performance Facilities: Portland Civic Auditorium

INSTRUMENTAL MUSIC

CHAMBER MUSIC NORTHWEST
522 SW Fifth Avenue, Suite 725, Portland, OR 97204
(503) 233-3202
Founded: 1971
Arts Area: Chamber; Ensemble
Status: Professional; Non-Profit
Type: Performing
Purpose: To present an annual summer music festival (five weeks/25 concerts) with world renowned performers in residence
Management: Linda Magee, Executive Director; David Shifrin, Music Director; Marte Lamb, Operations Director; Katherine King, Business Manager
Officers: Anne Munch, President; Sharon Van Sickle, Vice President; Jeffrey Grayson, Secretary; Robert Steinberg, Treasurer
Paid Staff: 14
Paid Artists: 43
Utilizes: Guest Artists
Budget: $100,000 - $500,000
Income Sources: Private Foundations/Grants/Endowments; Business/Corporate Donations; Box Office; Government Grants; Individual Donations

Season: June - July   **Annual Attendance:** 14,000
Affiliations: CMA
Performance Facilities: Reed College Commons; Catlin Gabel School's Cabell Center

THE CHAMBER MUSIC SOCIETY OF OREGON
1935 NE 59th Avenue, Portland, OR 97213
(503) 287-2175
Founded: 1973
Arts Area: Orchestra; Chamber; Ensemble; Instrumental Group
Status: Non-Professional; Non-Profit
Type: Performing; Resident; Educational
Purpose: To promote music in our schools for its value in teaching children how to learn
Officers: Patricia Ann Haim, President; Dr. Floyd Grant Jackson, Vice President; Beatrice Matin, Secretary; John B. Gould, Treasurer; Hazel M. DeLorenzo, Executive Director
Volunteer Staff: 25
Utilizes: Special Technical Talent; Guest Artists
Budget: $1,000 - $50,000
Income Sources: Private Foundations/Grants/Endowments; Business/Corporate Donations; Individual Donations; Fees from Summer Music Day Camp
Season: 52 Weeks   **Annual Attendance:** 12,000
Performance Facilities: St. Philip Neri Church; Hood River Middle School

OREGON SYMPHONY ORCHESTRA
711 SW Alder, Suite 200, Portland, OR 97205
(503) 228-4294
Founded: 1896
Arts Area: Symphony; Orchestra
Status: Non-Profit
Type: Performing; Sponsoring
Purpose: To provide concerts of the highest quality orchestral music for the people of Oregon and the Northwest
Management: Don Roth, Managing Director
Officers: William Scott, Chairman of the Board
Paid Staff: 23   **Volunteer Staff:** 1
Paid Artists: 88
Utilizes: Special Technical Talent; Guest Conductors; Guest Artists
Budget: $5,000,000 - $10,000,000
Income Sources: Private Foundations/Grants/Endowments; Business/Corporate Donations; Box Office; Government Grants; Individual Donations
Season: August - June   **Annual Attendance:** 300,000
Affiliations: ASOL; AFM
Performance Facilities: Arlene Schnitzer Concert Hall

PORTLAND YOUTH PHILHARMONIC ASSOCIATION
1119 SW Park Avenue, Portland, OR 97205
(503) 223-5939
FAX: (503) 223-5003
Founded: 1924
Arts Area: Symphony; Orchestra; Ensemble
Status: Non-Professional; Non-Profit
Type: Performing; Touring; Resident; Educational
Purpose: It is the purpose of the Portland Youth Philharmonic to maintain the finest possible resident youth orchestra in order to inspire, train and educate young people in the performance and appreciation of symphonic music and to provide a cultural asset to the community.
Management: Jacob Avshalomov, Conductor/Musical Director; Janet Fry, General Manager; Maria Yolz, Secretary/Receptionist
Officers: Ernestine Oringdulph, President; Kathy Froom, Wayne Landsreck, Doug McCaslin, Richard Wouldridge, Vice Presidents; Charles Kobin, Corporate Secretary; Catherine Freedman, Recording Secretary; Kathy Whilteman Johnson, Treasurer
Paid Staff: 3   **Volunteer Staff:** 400
Paid Artists: 2   **Non-Paid Artists:** 206
Utilizes: Guest Artists
Budget: $100,000 - $500,000
Income Sources: Private Foundations/Grants/Endowments; Business/Corporate Donations; Box Office; Government Grants; Individual Donations
Season: September - June   **Annual Attendance:** 43,000
Affiliations: ASOL (Youth Orchestra Division)
Performance Facilities: Arlene Schnitzer Concert Hall; Civic Auditorium

VIRTUOSI DELLA ROSA, INC.
1501 SE Holly Street, Portland, OR 97214
(503) 236-8678
  Founded: 1985
  Arts Area: Chamber; Contemporary; Multimedia
  Status: Professional; Non-Profit
  Type: Performing; Touring; Educational; Sponsoring
  Purpose: To perform new music with excellence and with particular attention to women, minorities and Northwest composers
  Management: Judith Bokor, Founder/Director; Scott Kritzer, Co-Director; George Anne Ries, Assistant Director
  Officers: Elizabeth Booker, President; Brian Wagner, Vice President; Ronald Kogen, Treasurer; Sara Mahler, Steve Prince
  Volunteer Staff: 3
  Paid Artists: 15
  Utilizes: Guest Artists
  Budget: $1,000 - $50,000
  Income Sources: Private Foundations/Grants/Endowments; Business/Corporate Donations; Box Office; Government Grants; Individual Donations; Fundraising
  Season: September - June   **Annual Attendance:** 1,500

VOCAL MUSIC

OREGON REPERTORY SINGERS
PO Box 894, Portland, OR 97207
(503) 227-3929
  Founded: 1974
  Arts Area: Choral
  Status: Non-Profit
  Type: Performing
  Purpose: ORS contributes to the cultural community through performances in Portland, tours outside the metropolitan area, educational programs and special projects of an edifying nature.
  Management: Richard Seeley, Artistic Director; Richard Brown, Administration
  Paid Staff: 1   **Volunteer Staff:** 3
  Paid Artists: 30   **Non-Paid Artists:** 50
  Utilizes: Guest Artists
  Budget: $1,000 - $50,000
  Income Sources: Private Foundations/Grants/Endowments; Business/Corporate Donations; Box Office; Government Grants; Individual Donations
  Season: September - June   **Annual Attendance:** 4,000
  Performance Facilities: Agnes Flanagan Chapel, Lewis and Clark College

PORTLAND OPERA
1516 SW Alder, Portland, OR 97201
(503) 241-1407
FAX: (503) 241-4212
  Founded: 1964
  Arts Area: Grand Opera; Lyric Opera; Light Opera; Operetta
  Status: Professional; Non-Profit
  Type: Performing; Touring; Resident
  Management: Robert Bailey, General Director
  Paid Staff: 22   **Volunteer Staff:** 100
  Paid Artists: 200   **Non-Paid Artists:** 50
  Utilizes: Special Technical Talent; Guest Conductors; Guest Artists; Guest Directors; Guest Designers; Guest Soloists
  Budget: $1,000,000 - $5,000,000
  Income Sources: Private Foundations/Grants/Endowments; Business/Corporate Donations; Box Office; Government Grants; Individual Donations; Set & Costume Rentals
  Season: September - June   **Annual Attendance:** 55,000
  Affiliations: OA
  Performance Facilities: Portland Civic Auditorium

PORTLAND SYMPHONIC CHOIR
PO Box 1517, Portland, OR 97207
(503) 223-1217
  Founded: 1946
  Arts Area: Choral
  Status: Non-Professional; Non-Profit
  Type: Performing
  Purpose: To provide an opportunity for talented singers to perform music representing the widest spectrum of choral literature

Management: Board of Directors
Officers: Ralph Nelson, President; Robert Morrison, Vice President; Jan Sapinski, Secretary; Karen Shepard, Treasurer
Paid Staff: 3   **Volunteer Staff:** 30
Paid Artists: 45
Utilizes: Guest Conductors; Guest Artists
Budget: $50,000 - $100,000
Income Sources: Private Foundations/Grants/Endowments; Business/Corporate Donations; Box Office; Government Grants; Individual Donations
Season: September - May   **Annual Attendance:** 5,500
Affiliations: Oregon Symphony
Performance Facilities: First United Methodist Church

THEATRE

PORTLAND BLACK REPERTORY
PO Box 8655, Portland, OR 97207-8655
(503) 287-3959
Founded: 1978
Arts Area: Community; Theatrical Group
Status: Semi-Professional; Non-Profit
Type: Performing; Touring; Resident; Educational; Sponsoring; Equity Company
Purpose: To produce excellent quality live theatre utilizing the skills and talents of local artists and to present and preserve the rich culture of African-Americans; Its aim is to produce an annual season of classic and superior contemporary plays acted, directed and designed at a standard of excellence comparable to that of the nation's leading professional companies.
Management: Rosemary Allen, Producing Artistic Director; Patrick Stewart, Resident Designer; Eugene Hughes, Manager
Officers: Rosemary Allen, President; Lonnie Nettles, Secretary; LeCheryl Cooper, Treasurer
Utilizes: Special Technical Talent; Guest Directors
Budget: $50,000 - $100,000
Income Sources: Private Foundations/Grants/Endowments; Business/Corporate Donations; Box Office; Individual Donations
Season: September - May   **Annual Attendance:** 7,000
Affiliations: Oregon Advocates for the Arts; Portland Theater Alliance; Oregon Association of Minority Entrepreneurs

PERFORMING SERIES

ARTS CELEBRATION/ARTQUAKE FESTIVAL
720 SW Washington, Suite 100, Portland, OR 97205
(503) 227-2787
Founded: 1977
Arts Area: Dance; Vocal Music; Instrumental Music; Theater; Festivals
Status: Professional; Non-Profit
Type: Sponsoring
Purpose: Annual arts showcase of local, regional companies, artists and performers
Management: Keri Hoops, Executive Director
Officers: Stuart Tiecher, President; Don Vallaster, Vice President; Patsy Ferman, Secretary; Trudy Thatcher, Treasurer
Paid Staff: 2
Paid Artists: 600
Utilizes: Special Technical Talent; Guest Conductors; Guest Artists; Guest Directors
Budget: $100,000 - $500,000
Income Sources: Private Foundations/Grants/Endowments; Business/Corporate Donations; Box Office; Government Grants; Individual Donations
Season: May - September   **Annual Attendance:** 300,000
Performance Facilities: Portland Performing Arts Center; Outdoor Festival

FACILITY

ARLENE SCHNITZER CONCERT HALL
SW Broadway at Main Street, Portland, OR 97201
(503) 248-4335
FAX: (503) 274-7490
Type of Facility: Concert Hall
Type of Stage: Proscenium
Stage Dimensions: 54'x32'x34'   **Orchestra Pit**
Seating Capacity: 2,776
Year Built: 1928   **Architect:** Rapp & Rapp
Year Remodeled: 1984   **Architect:** Broome Oringdulph O'Toole Rudolph & Associates; ELS Design Group
Cost: $10,000,000
Acoustical Consultant: R. Lawrence Kirkegaard & Associates

Contact for Rental: Booking Manager;   (503) 248-4335
Resident Groups: Oregon Symphony Orchestra; Portland Youth Philharmonic

COMMUNITY MUSIC CENTER - DAVID CAMPBELL RECITAL HALL
3350 SE Francis, Portland, OR 97202
(530) 823-3177
Type of Facility: Auditorium
Facility Originally: Fire Station
Type of Stage: Thrust; Platform
Stage Dimensions: 16'x26'
Seating Capacity: 110
Year Built: 1912
Year Remodeled: 1969   **Architect:** Robert Oringdulph   **Cost:** $80,000
Contact for Rental: Charles Farmer;   (530) 823-3177

ECHO THEATRE
1515 SE 37th Avenue, Portland, OR 97214
(503) 231-1232
Founded: 1983
Type of Facility: Concert Hall; Studio Performance; Environmental; Performance Center; Theatre House; Multi-Purpose; Room
Facility Originally: Movie House
Type of Stage: Flexible; Proscenium; Dance Theatre
Stage Dimensions: 42'Wx36'D
Seating Capacity: 185
Year Built: 1910
Year Remodeled: 1983   **Architect:** Aaron Faegre   **Cost:** $24,000
Acoustical Consultant: Aron Faegre
Contact for Rental: Office Manager;   (503) 231-1232
Resident Groups: Do Jump Movement Theatre

NEW ROSE THEATRE
904 SW Main Street, Portland, OR 97205
(503) 222-2487
Type of Facility: Theatre House
Facility Originally: Business Facility
Type of Stage: 3/4 Arena
Stage Dimensions: 22'x25'
Seating Capacity: 119
Resident Groups: New Rose Theatre Company

PORTLAND CENTER FOR THE PERFORMING ARTS - PORTLAND CIVIC AUDITORIUM
222 SW Clay Street, Portland, OR 97201
(503) 248-4335
Type of Facility: Auditorium
Type of Stage: Proscenium
Stage Dimensions: 30'x60'x42'   **Orchestra Pit**
Seating Capacity: 3,000
Year Built: 1917   **Architect:** A.J. Doyle
Year Remodeled: 1968   **Architect:** Stanton Boles Maguire & Church   **Cost:** $3,900,000
Contact for Rental: Lori Leyba, Booking Manager;   (503) 248-4335
Resident Groups: Portland Opera; Oregon Symphony

REED COLLEGE - REED THEATRE
Portland, OR 97202
(503) 771-1112, ext. X357
Type of Facility: Theatre House
Facility Originally: Warehouse
Type of Stage: Flexible
Stage Dimensions: 40'x80'
Seating Capacity: 150
Year Built: 1972   **Architect:** Robert Oringdulph   **Cost:** $140,000
Year Remodeled: 1979

WILSON CENTER FOR THE PERFORMING ARTS
1111 SW 10th, Portland, OR 97205
(503) 223-6281
Type of Facility: Performance Center

Facility Originally: Business Facility
Type of Stage: Arena
Stage Dimensions: 20'x40'
Seating Capacity: 110
Year Built: 1973   **Architect:** Stanton Boles Maguire & Church   **Cost:** $56,231
Year Remodeled: 1977   **Architect:** Stanton Boles Maguire & Church   **Cost:** $2,693
Contact for Rental: YWCA;   (503) 223-6281
Manager: Artists Repertory Theatre;   (503) 242-2420
Resident Groups: Artists Repertory Theatre

Roseburg

INSTRUMENTAL MUSIC

UMPQUA SYMPHONY ASSOCIATION
PO Box 241, Roseburg, OR 97470
(503) 672-6104
   Founded: 1955
   Arts Area: Symphony; Orchestra; Chamber; Ensemble; Instrumental Group
   Status: Non-Profit
   Type: Sponsoring
   Purpose: To bring classical music and dance to the local community
   Management: Bob Robbins, Production Director
   Officers: David Jones, President; Anita Daily, Vice President
   Volunteer Staff: 15
   Utilizes: Guest Artists
   Budget: $1,000 - $50,000
   Income Sources: Private Foundations/Grants/Endowments; Business/Corporate Donations; Box Office; Individual Donations
   Season: October - May   **Annual Attendance:** 2,400
   Performance Facilities: Umpqua Community College Auditorium

Saint Benedict

PERFORMING SERIES

ABBEY BACH FESTIVAL
Mount Angel Abbey, Saint Benedict, OR 97373
(503) 845-3321
FAX: (503) 845-3594
   Founded: 1972
   Arts Area: Vocal Music; Instrumental Music
   Status: Professional; Semi-Professional
   Type: Performing
   Officers: Abbot Peter Ebere OSB, President; Father Bruno Becker OSB, Executive Director
   Volunteer Staff: 20
   Paid Artists: 15
   Utilizes: Guest Artists
   Budget: $1,000 - $50,000
   Income Sources: Box Office; Individual Donations
   Season: July   **Annual Attendance:** 1,500
   Performance Facilities: Damian Center

Salem

INSTRUMENTAL MUSIC

CAMERATA MUSICA
714 Tillman Avenue SE, Salem, OR 97302
(503) 364-8263
   Founded: 1976
   Arts Area: Chamber; Instrumental Group
   Status: Professional; Non-Professional; Non-Profit
   Type: Performing; Sponsoring
   Purpose: Camerata Musica presents a series of six chamber music concerts each season at the Salem Public Library. All of the concerts are open to the public without charge.

Management: Lydia Woods, Program Coordinator
Officers: Miriam Bednarz, President; Lydia Woods, Vice President; Dorothy Boardman, Secretary; Kelly Woods, Treasurer
Volunteer Staff: 10
Paid Artists: 12   **Non-Paid Artists:** 12
Utilizes: Special Technical Talent
Budget: $1,000 - $50,000
Income Sources: Private Foundations/Grants/Endowments; Business/Corporate Donations; Individual Donations
Season: October - May   **Annual Attendance:** 1,600
Performance Facilities: Salem Public Library Lecture Hall

OREGON SYMPHONY ASSOCIATION
161 High Street SE, Suite 230, Salem, OR 97301
(503) 364-0149
Founded: 1955
Arts Area: Symphony; Orchestra
Status: Non-Profit
Type: Sponsoring
Purpose: To use corporate funds exclusively for literary, benevolent, educational and cultural purposes by one or more of the following means: sponsor and promote public orchestral group or individual performances in the city of Salem and promote community interest
Management: N. Andrew Toney, Executive Director
Officers: Elaine K. Young, President; Gregor Strum MD, Vice President; Charles Weyant, Secretary; Jack Donovan, Treasurer; Ron Kelemen, Member-at-Large
Paid Staff: 1
Budget: $100,000 - $500,000
Income Sources: Business/Corporate Donations; Box Office; Individual Donations; Fund-raising
Season: September - May   **Annual Attendance:** 10,000
Affiliations: ASOL; Mid-Valley Arts Council
Performance Facilities: Smith Auditorium, Willamette University

WHEATLAND CHAMBER PLAYERS
7390 Wheatland Road, Salem, OR 97303-3451
(503) 393-6950
Founded: 1980
Arts Area: Chamber; Ethnic; Folk; Instrumental Group
Status: Professional; Non-Profit
Type: Performing; Resident; Educational
Purpose: To exhibit good classical and folk music
Management: Ralph Cater, Director
Officers: E. Bengingheim, Judith Dwyer, Norvada Smedley, Victor Palmerson, Del Giglio, Ralph Cater
Budget: $1,000 - $50,000
Income Sources: Individual Donations
Season: October - May
Annual Attendance: 2,000
Affiliations: American String Teachers Association

THEATRE

SALEM THEATER OF PERFORMING ARTS
191 High Street NE, Salem, OR 97301
(503) 588-7002
Founded: 1980
Arts Area: Musical; Community; Theatrical Group
Status: Non-Professional; Non-Profit
Type: Performing; Educational
Purpose: We present a variety of entertainment events and allow participation by all persons, whether experienced or not. We are incorporated as a non-profit educational group, and present productions, classes and manage a theatre facility which is open to other organizations.
Management: Dorothy Gahlsdorf, Theatre Manager; Bill Smith, Technical Director
Officers: Gary Esgate, President; Dan Nelson, Vice President; Diane Fredricks, Secretary; Eloise Smith, Treasurer
Volunteer Staff: 3
Utilizes: Guest Directors
Budget: $1,000 - $50,000
Income Sources: Private Foundations/Grants/Endowments; Business/Corporate Donations; Box Office; Individual Donations
Affiliations: Oregon Theatre Association
Performance Facilities: Grand Theatre

Seaside

FACILITY

SEASIDE CIVIC AND CONVENTION CENTER
415 First Avenue, Seaside, OR 97138
(503) 738-8585
FAX: (503) 738-0198
    Type of Facility: Civic Center
    Type of Stage: Proscenium
    Seating Capacity: 1,350
    Year Built: 1971   **Architect:** Brown Brown & Grider   **Cost:** $500,000
    Year Remodeled: 1992   **Architect:** HDN   **Cost:** $2,000,000
    Contact for Rental: Betty Wilson;   (503) 738-8585
    Manager: Les McNary;   (503) 738-8585

The Dalles

THEATRE

THE MASQUERADERS
7440 Mill Creek Road, The Dalles, OR 97058
(503) 298-4644
    Founded: 1965
    Arts Area: Musical; Dinner; Community; Theatrical Group
    Status: Non-Profit
    Type: Performing; Educational; Sponsoring
    Purpose: To provide the community with various performing arts presentations using a variety of formats; to provide community services and scholarships
    Officers: Paula Richmond, President; Robert Carsner, Vice President; Adrienne Stacher, Secretary
    Volunteer Staff: 10
    Non-Paid Artists: 50
    Utilizes: Special Technical Talent
    Budget: $1,000 - $50,000
    Income Sources: Box Office
    Season: September - May   **Annual Attendance:** 2,000

PENNSYLVANIA

Allentown

INSTRUMENTAL MUSIC

ALLENTOWN SYMPHONY ASSOCIATION
Symphony Hall, 23 North Sixth Street, Allentown, PA 18101
(215) 432-7961
FAX: (215) 432-6009
Founded: 1950
Arts Area: Symphony; Orchestra; Performing Arts; Comedians
Status: Non-Profit
Type: Performing; Educational
Purpose: To promote cultural values by providing high quality symphonic music and performing arts events, with broad community appeal, and education concerning them, in Allentown's historic Symphony Hall
Management: Anna Maria Marzullo, Music Director
Officers: Lona Farr, President; Judge James Knoll Gardner, First Vice President; Julian Lewis, Third Vice President; Reed Steele, Secretary; Barbara McGovern, Treasurer; Boyd Kreglow, Assistant Treasurer
Paid Staff: 6
Paid Artists: 80
Utilizes: Special Technical Talent; Guest Artists
Budget: $500,000 - $1,000,000
Income Sources: Private Foundations/Grants/Endowments; Business/Corporate Donations; Box Office; Government Grants; Individual Donations
Season: September - May
Annual Attendance: 100,000
Affiliations: ASOL; Association of Pennsylvania Orchestras; Lehigh Valley Arts Council; ASCAP; Preservation Pennsylvania; Allentown Chamber of Commerce; Allentown Cultural Alliance; Allentown Arts Commission
Performance Facilities: Symphony Hall

IMPROVISATIONALMUSICCO, INC.
908 North Penn Street, Allentown, PA 18102
(215) 820-9017
FAX: (215) 820-9017
Arts Area: Ethnic; Instrumental Group; New Music
Status: Professional; Non-Profit
Type: Educational; Presenting
Purpose: To expose people in eastern Pennsylvania to new music; to support the performers of that music, both American and foreign
Management: Pamela Fearing-Hassey, Executive Director
Officers: Gary Hassay, President; Donald Lehr, Hope Carr, Vice Presidents
Budget: $1,000 - $50,000
Income Sources: Private Foundations/Grants/Endowments; Business/Corporate Donations; Box Office; Government Grants; Individual Donations
Performance Facilities: Open Space Gallery

THEATRE

PENNSYLVANIA STAGE COMPANY
837 Linden Street, Allentown, PA 18101
(215) 434-6110
Founded: 1979
Arts Area: Professional; Theatrical Group
Status: Professional; Non-Profit
Type: Performing; Touring; Resident; Educational
Management: Ellen Baker-Baltz, Managing Director; Charles Richter, Artistic Director; Rosanne Damico, Marketing/Public Relations
Officers: Nancy Orr, Board President
Paid Staff: 14
Utilizes: Special Technical Talent; Guest Artists; Guest Directors
Income Sources: Private Foundations/Grants/Endowments; Business/Corporate Donations; Box Office; Government Grants; Individual Donations
Season: October - June
Affiliations: AEA; LORT
Performance Facilities: Pennsylvania Stage Company Theater

PERFORMING SERIES

ALLENTOWN COMMUNITY CONCERT ASSOCIATION
3736 Broadway, Allentown, PA 18104
(215) 432-9143
Founded: 1927
Arts Area: Dance; Vocal Music; Instrumental Music
Status: Non-Profit
Type: Educational; Sponsoring
Purpose: To present four annual concerts with varied programs; membership is open to the public during the annual campaign
Management: Agnus Balluit, Executive Director
Officers: William Lazenberg, President
Volunteer Staff: 2
Paid Artists: 4
Utilizes: Guest Artists
Affiliations: Community Concerts

FACILITY

SYMPHONY HALL
23 North Sixth Street, Allentown, PA 18103
(215) 432-7961
Type of Facility: Concert Hall
Facility Originally: Vaudeville
Type of Stage: Proscenium
Stage Dimensions: 70'Wx45'D; 36'Wx38'H proscenium opening   **Orchestra Pit**
Seating Capacity: 1,465
Year Built: 1890
Contact for Rental: Charles Kalan;   (215) 770-1932
Resident Groups: Allentown Symphony
Major renovation planned with Benjamin Walbert, Architect. Check for availability.

Altoona

DANCE

ALLEGHENY BALLET COMPANY
PO Box 369, Altoona, PA 16603
(814) 941-9944
Arts Area: Ballet
Status: Semi-Professional; Non-Profit
Type: Performing; Resident
Management: Deborah Anthony, Artistic Director; Marjorie Lantz, Business Manager
Paid Artists: 8
Income Sources: Box Office; Individual Donations
Performance Facilities: Mishler Theatre

PERFORMING SERIES

BLAIR COUNTY CIVIC MUSIC ASSOCIATION
PO Box 6Q, Altoona, PA 16602
(814) 943-9951
Founded: 1944
Arts Area: Dance; Vocal Music; Instrumental Music; Theater; Grand Opera
Status: Professional; Non-Profit
Type: Presenting
Purpose: To bring the best of the performing arts to Blair County at an affordable fee for our league of subscribers
Officers: Patricia Gilder, President; Charlotte Morris, First Vice President; Richard Russell, Second Vice President; Estrida McLaughlin, Third Vice President; Pauline Hoover, Recording Secretary; Jane Gable, Membership Secretary
Volunteer Staff: 38
Budget: $50,000 - $100,000
Income Sources: Box Office
Season: October - April   **Annual Attendance:** 7,500
Performance Facilities: Roosevelt Junior High School Auditorium

FACILITY

MISHLER THEATRE
1208 12th Avenue, Altoona, PA 16601
(814) 944-9434
> **Type of Facility:** Theatre House
> **Type of Stage:** Proscenium   **Orchestra Pit**
> **Seating Capacity:** 910
> **Year Built:** 1906
> **Architect:** Pietrolungo and Kimbell
> **Cost:** $118,000
> **Contact for Rental:** William B. Malloy;   (814) 944-9434

Avoca

INSTRUMENTAL MUSIC

NORTHEASTERN PENNSYLVANIA PHILHARMONIC
PO Box 71, Avoca, PA 18641
(717) 342-0920
FAX: (717) 457-5901
> **Founded:** 1972
> **Arts Area:** Symphony; Orchestra
> **Status:** Professional; Non-Profit
> **Type:** Performing; Touring; Educational
> **Purpose:** To produce the highest quality symphony orchestra and chamber ensemble performances possible; to provide musical services; to maintain an organizational environment in which local and national talent serve as a cultural resource and source of pride
> **Management:** Jeth Mill, Executive Director; Hugh Keelan, Music Director/Conductor; Mary Walsh, Director of Operations; John Jablowski, Director of Development
> **Officers:** Larry Stetler, President; George Ginader, Wallace Stettler, Kathleen Graff, Vice Presidents; Jay Niskey, Treasurer; Otto Robinson, Assistant Treasurer; Joyce Lomma, Secretary
> **Paid Staff:** 6   **Volunteer Staff:** 3
> **Paid Artists:** 80
> **Utilizes:** Guest Conductors; Guest Artists
> **Budget:** $1,000,000 - $5,000,000
> **Income Sources:** Private Foundations/Grants/Endowments; Business/Corporate Donations; Box Office; Government Grants; Individual Donations
> **Season:** September - May   **Annual Attendance:** 350,000
> **Affiliations:** ASOL; Citizens for the Arts in Pennsylvania
> **Performance Facilities:** Masonic Temple; Kirby Center for the Performing Arts

Bethlehem

DANCE

BALLET GUILD OF LEHIGH VALLEY
556 Main Street, Bethlehem, PA 18018
(215) 865-0353
> **Founded:** 1958
> **Arts Area:** Ballet
> **Status:** Semi-Professional; Non-Profit
> **Type:** Performing; Educational
> **Management:** Pat McAndrew, General Manager; Alexi Ramov, Artistic Director
> **Officers:** John L. Cleveland, President; Charlotte M. Fretz, Treasurer; Marjorie Heiberger, Secretary
> **Paid Staff:** 6   **Volunteer Staff:** 2
> **Paid Artists:** 3   **Non-Paid Artists:** 18
> **Utilizes:** Guest Artists; Guest Choreographers
> **Budget:** $100,000 - $500,000

Income Sources: Private Foundations/Grants/Endowments; Business/Corporate Donations; Box Office; Government Grants; Individual Donations
Season: 52 Weeks
Affiliations: Northeast Regional Association

INSTRUMENTAL MUSIC

CHAMBER MUSIC SOCIETY OF BETHLEHEM
PO Box 4208, Bethlehem, PA 18018
(215) 868-8702
Founded: 1951
Arts Area: Chamber
Status: Non-Profit
Type: Performing; Sponsoring
Purpose: To provide chamber music and promote educational activities
Management: H.F. Dienel, President; J.P. Allen, Vice President; E. Walakovits, Treasurer; M.J. Van DePutte, Secretary
Volunteer Staff: 13
Utilizes: Guest Artists
Budget: $1,000 - $50,000
Income Sources: Private Foundations/Grants/Endowments; Business/Corporate Donations; Box Office; Individual Donations
Season: September - May   **Annual Attendance:** 2,000

THEATRE

TOUCHSTONE THEATRE
321-323 East Fourth Street, Bethlehem, PA 18015
(215) 867-1689
Founded: 1981
Arts Area: Professional; Musical; Folk; Theatrical Group
Status: Professional; Non-Profit
Type: Performing; Touring; Resident; Educational; Sponsoring
Purpose: Dedicated to the creation and performance of original movement-inspired drama that enriches our diverse audiences with a voice at once personal and universal; Non-profit regional theatre dedicated to the creation and presentation of orignal and esemble drama; Serving our community and audiences of all ages and cultures, at home and on tour, by entertaining, illuminating, challenging and fostering international and intercultural collaborations
Management: Bridget George, Producing Director; Eric Beatty, Esemble Manager; Billie P. Lindo, Marketing Director; Christina Lankay, Office Manager
Officers: Richard E. Thulin, President Board of Trustees; Robert Davidson, Treasurer; Harold G. Black, Secretary
Paid Staff: 8   **Volunteer Staff:** 30
Paid Artists: 36
Utilizes: Special Technical Talent; Guest Artists; Guest Directors
Budget: $100,000 - $500,000
Income Sources: Private Foundations/Grants/Endowments; Business/Corporate Donations; Box Office; Government Grants; Individual Donations; Touring
Season: September - August   **Annual Attendance:** 60,000
Affiliations: TCG; Theatre Association of Pennsylvania; National Mime Association
Performance Facilities: Touchstone Theatre

FACILITY

TOUCHSTONE THEATRE
321-323 East Fourth Street, Bethlehem, PA 18015
(215) 867-1689; (215) 866-5279
Type of Facility: Performance Center; Black Box
Facility Originally: Fire Station
Type of Stage: Platform
Stage Dimensions: 18'1"Wx18'6"D
Seating Capacity: 72
Year Built: 1875
Year Remodeled: 1987   **Architect:** Christine Uffler-Trumbell   **Cost:** $203,750
Contact for Rental: Billie Lindo;   (215) 867-1689
Resident Groups: Touchstone Ensemble

Bloomsburg

THEATRE

BLOOMSBURG THEATRE ENSEMBLE
226 Center Street, PO Box 66, Bloomsburg, PA 17815
(717) 784-5530
    Founded: 1978
    Arts Area: Professional; Theatrical Group
    Status: Professional; Non-Profit
    Type: Performing; Touring; Resident; Educational; Sponsoring
    Purpose: The resident professional ensemble lives and works in this rural region because, in the face of world events, we feel we need to be in a place where dialogue with an audience is possible, and the impact of our theatre on a community is positive and demonstrable.
    Management: Leigh Strimbeck, Ensemble Director; Stephen Loppick, Administrative Director
    Officers: Joe Petruncio, President; Shirley Alters, Secretary; Bill Frost, Treasurer
    Paid Staff: 10   **Volunteer Staff:** 1
    Paid Artists: 23
    Utilizes: Guest Artists; Guest Directors
    Budget: $100,000 - $500,000
    Income Sources: Private Foundations/Grants/Endowments; Business/Corporate Donations; Box Office; Government Grants; Individual Donations
    Season: September - May   **Annual Attendance:** 32,925
    Affiliations: TCG; Theatre Association of Pennsylvania
    Performance Facilities: Alvina Krause Theatre

FACILITY

BLOOMSBURG UNIVERSITY - CARVER HALL
Bloomsburg, PA 17815
(717) 389-4291
    Type of Facility: Auditorium
    Type of Stage: Proscenium
    Seating Capacity: 900
    Year Built: 1869
    Year Remodeled: 1900   **Architect:** Price Dickey
    Acoustical Consultant: Boyd Buckingham
    Contact for Rental: Tom Wright;   (717) 389-4291
    Resident Groups: Bloomsburg Players; Music Department groups
    Small groups (comedians, simple plays, speakers)

BLOOMSBURG UNIVERSITY - HAAS CENTER FOR THE ARTS
Bloomsburg, PA 17815
(717) 389-4291
    Type of Facility: Concert Hall; Auditorium; Theatre House; Road House
    Type of Stage: Proscenium
    Stage Dimensions: 60'Wx30'D   **Orchestra Pit**
    Seating Capacity: 1,900
    Year Built: 1968   **Architect:** Price Dickey   **Cost:** $1,500,000
    Acoustical Consultant: Dr. Jiri Tishi
    Contact for Rental: Tom Wright;   (717) 389-4291
    Resident Groups: Bloomsburg Players
    Remodeling currently in progress

Boiling Springs

THEATRE

ALLENBERRY PLAYHOUSE
PO Box 7, Boiling Springs, PA 17007
(717) 258-3211
FAX: (717) 258-1464
    Founded: 1949
    Arts Area: Professional; Theatrical Group
    Status: Professional; Commercial
    Type: Performing; Resident
    Purpose: Legitimate repertory equity theatre presenting shows April-November

Management: John J. Heinze, Producer
Paid Artists: 14
Budget: $100,000 - $500,000
Income Sources: Box Office
Season: April - November
Affiliations: AEA; SSDC
Performance Facilities: Allenberry Playhouse

Bradford

PERFORMING SERIES

BRADFORD CREATIVE AND PERFORMING ARTS CENTER, INC.
PO Box 153, Bradford, PA 16701
(814) 362-2522; (814) 362-1025
FAX: (814) 368-7040
Founded: 1984
Arts Area: Dance; Instrumental Music; Theater; Grand Opera
Status: Non-Profit
Type: Sponsoring
Purpose: To foster and promote the creative and performing arts
Officers: James D. Guelfi, President; Rosemary, Morici, Vice President; Patricia D. Vecellio, Treasurer; Sandra Lyter, Secretary; Olie Lowry, Corresponding Secretary
Volunteer Staff: 15
Paid Artists: 8
Utilizes: Guest Conductors; Guest Artists; Guest Directors
Budget: $100,000 - $500,000
Income Sources: Private Foundations/Grants/Endowments; Business/Corporate Donations; Box Office; Government Grants; Individual Donations
Season: 52 Weeks   **Annual Attendance:** 5,000
Affiliations: Pennsylvania Presenters; Citizens for the Arts in Pennsylvania; Pennsylvania Rural Association

Broomall

PERFORMING SERIES

CRS NATIONAL FESTIVAL FOR THE PERFORMING ARTS
724 Winchester Road, Broomall, PA 19008
(215) 544-5920
FAX: (215) 544-5921
Founded: 1981
Arts Area: Dance; Vocal Music; Instrumental Music; Festivals
Status: Professional; Semi-Professional; Non-Profit
Type: Performing; Touring; Resident; Educational
Purpose: To offer performers, composers, teachers, libraries, educational institutions, amateurs, devotees of music and prosepective sponsors cultural enrichment through vast musical sources
Management: Contemporary Record Society Artists Management
Volunteer Staff: 30
Utilizes: Special Technical Talent; Guest Conductors; Guest Artists; Guest Directors; Soloist; Composers
Budget: $1,000 - $50,000
Income Sources: Private Foundations/Grants/Endowments; Business/Corporate Donations; Government Grants; Individual Donations; Membership
Season: July
Affiliations: Contemporary Record Society

Chester

FACILITY

WIDENER UNIVERSITY-ALUMNI AUDITORIUM - BERT MUSTIN THEATRE
1 University Place, Chester, PA 19013
(215) 499-4000
Type of Facility: Concert Hall; Auditorium; Theatre House; Amphitheater; Multi-Purpose
Type of Stage: Proscenium
Stage Dimensions: 20'x36'x26'   **Orchestra Pit**
Seating Capacity: 425

Year Built: 1962
Acoustical Consultant: John Vanore, Widener University Music Director
Contact for Rental: Kristin McJunkins;   (215) 499-4400
Limited availability due to extensive use by university groups

Clarion

FACILITY

MARWICK - BOYD AUDITORIUM
Clarion University, Clarion, PA 16214
(814) 226-2449
FAX: (814) 226-2037
Founded: 1812
Type of Facility: Auditorium; Performance Center; Theatre House
Type of Stage: Proscenium
Stage Dimensions: 51'Wx30'Dx17'H   **Orchestra Pit**
Seating Capacity: 1,500
Year Built: 1972
Contact for Rental: Carl Callenburg;   (814) 226-4167

Coraopolis

THEATRE

ROBERT MORRIS COLONIAL THEATER
Narrows Run Road, Coraopolis, PA 15108
(412) 262-8336
Founded: 1967
Arts Area: Community
Status: Non-Professional; Non-Profit
Type: Performing; Educational
Purpose: To provide our Western Pennsylvania Community with a high standard of community theater in light summer fare and winter classics
Management: Tom Gaydos, Managing Director
Paid Staff: 3
Utilizes: Special Technical Talent; Guest Directors
Budget: $50,000 - $100,000
Income Sources: Box Office; Individual Donations
Season: February - November   **Annual Attendance:** 6,000
Affiliations: TAP; ATHE; East Coast Theatre Conference

Devon

THEATRE

VALLEY FORGE MUSIC FAIR PRODUCTIONS, INC.
176 Swedesford Road, Devon, PA 19333
(215) 644-5004
FAX: (215) 647-6860
Founded: 1955
Arts Area: Professional
Status: Professional
Type: Touring; Sponsoring
Purpose: One of a number of professional, commercial theatres operated and owned by Music Fair Group, Incorporated
Management: James McCormick, Vice President/General Manager
Officers: Rick Gross, President
Paid Staff: 150
Paid Artists: 250
Utilizes: Special Technical Talent; Guest Conductors; Guest Artists; Guest Directors
Budget: $5,000,000 - $10,000,000
Income Sources: Box Office
Season: March - December   **Annual Attendance:** 700,000
Affiliations: Music Fair Group
Performance Facilities: Valley Forge Music Fair

FACILITY

VALLEY FORGE MUSIC FAIR
7 Route 202, Devon, PA 19333
(215) 644-5004
    Type of Facility: Performance Center; Theatre House; Arena
    Type of Stage: Arena; In-the-round Capability
    Stage Dimensions: 30' diameter   **Orchestra Pit**
    Seating Capacity: 2932
    Year Built: 1972   **Architect:** Hassinger & Schwamm   **Cost:** $2,500,000
    Acoustical Consultant: Donald Pacitti
    Contact for Rental: Barbara Abrahams;   (215) 644-5004
    Manager: James McCormick
    Management reserves the right to permit rentals only for specific purposes

---

Ephrata

VOCAL MUSIC

EPHRATA CLOISTER CHORUS
632 West Main Street, Ephrata, PA 17522
(717) 733-4811
FAX: (717) 733-4811
    Founded: 1959
    Arts Area: Choral
    Status: Non-Profit
    Type: Performing; Educational
    Purpose: To interpret the Ephrata Cloister through music
    Management: Barry L. Sawyer, Director
    Officers: Betty Weidman, President; Janer Colodonato, Vice President; George Andrews, Secretary; Susan Miller, Treasurer
    Paid Staff: 1   **Volunteer Staff:** 35
    Utilizes: Guest Conductors; Guest Artists
    Budget: $1,000 - $50,000
    Income Sources: Private Foundations/Grants/Endowments; Box Office; Individual Donations
    Season: 52 Weeks   **Annual Attendance:** 2,000
    Performance Facilities: Ephrata Cloister

PERFORMING SERIES

VORSPIEL DRAMA EPHRATA CLOISTER ASSOCIATES
632 West Main Street, Ephrata, PA 17522
(717) 733-4811
FAX: (717) 733-4811
    Founded: 1958
    Arts Area: Musical
    Status: Non-Profit
    Type: Performing; Educational
    Purpose: To interpret the Ephrata Cloister through musical, historical drama
    Management: Board of Directors
    Officers: Becky Weidman, President; Janet Colodonato, Vice President; George Andrews, Secretary; Susan Miller, Treasurer
    Paid Staff: 8   **Volunteer Staff:** 75
    Utilizes: Guest Artists
    Budget: $100,000 - $500,000
    Income Sources: Box Office; Individual Donations
    Season: July - August   **Annual Attendance:** 2,200
    Performance Facilities: Amphitheater, Ephrata Cloister

FACILITY

EPHRATA PERFORMING ARTS CENTER - EPHRATA COMMUNITY PARK
Cocalico Street, PO Box 173, Ephrata, PA 17522
(717) 738-0664; (717) 733-7966
    Type of Facility: Theatre House; Amphitheater
    Facility Originally: Barn
    Type of Stage: 3/4 Arena
    Stage Dimensions: 50'x25'   **Orchestra Pit**

Seating Capacity: 203
Year Built: 1913
Resident Groups: Summer Stock; Ephrata Performing Arts Center - Mainstage; Children's Theatre;
Monday Series
Modified barn used in the summer for theatrical productions

Erie

INSTRUMENTAL MUSIC

ERIE PHILHARMONIC
1001 State Street, Suite 924, Erie, PA 16501-1878
(814) 455-1375
FAX: (814) 455-1377
    Founded: 1913
    Arts Area: Symphony; Orchestra
    Status: Non-Profit
    Type: Performing
    Purpose: To provide symphonic, pops and youth orchestra concerts, quality educational experiences for all ages, as well
as leadership in the cultural life of Erie and the tri-state area
    Management: Eiji Oue, Music Director; Tony Beadle, Executive Director
    Officers: Wallace J. Knox, President; J. Gary Ramy, Executive Vice President; Charles Harris, Vice President of Marketing; M. Peter Scibetta, Vice President of Music; Douglas Murphy, Treasurer
    Paid Staff: 5
    Utilizes: Guest Conductors; Guest Artists
    Budget: $500,000 - $1,000,000
    Income Sources: Private Foundations/Grants/Endowments; Business/Corporate Donations; Box Office; Government
Grants; Individual Donations
    Season: September - May   **Annual Attendance:** 20,869
    Performance Facilities: Warner Theatre

PERFORMING SERIES

ERIE CIVIC MUSIC ASSOCIATION
PO Box 143, Erie, PA 16512
(814) 864-0875
    Founded: 1928
    Arts Area: Vocal Music; Instrumental Music
    Status: Non-Profit
    Type: Sponsoring
    Purpose: We present the greatest international talent available at the most reasonable costs.
    Officers: Rodney Blystone Jr., President; John Brauns, Naomi Purchase, Vice Presidents; Beatrice Hansen, Secretary;
Lois Blystone, Corresponding Secretary; Jerome Neidinger, Treasurer
    Volunteer Staff: 40
    Utilizes: Guest Artists
    Budget: $50,000 - $100,000
    Income Sources: Private Foundations/Grants/Endowments
    Season: September - May   **Annual Attendance:** 7,500
    Affiliations: Erie Area Fund for the Arts
    Performance Facilities: Warner Theatre

FACILITY

ERIE CIVIC CENTER
811 State Street, PO Box 6140, Erie, PA 16512
(814) 452-4857
    Type of Facility: Civic Center
    Contact for Rental: John "Casey" Wells; (814) 452-4857
    *The Civic Center contains the L.J. Tullio Convention Hall and the Warner Theatre. See separate listings for
additional information.*

ERIE CIVIC CENTER - L.J. TULLIO CONVENTION HALL
811 State Street, PO Box 6140, Erie, PA 16512
(814) 452-4857
    Type of Facility: Concert Hall; Auditorium; Arena
    Type of Stage: Flexible; Platform
    Seating Capacity: 7,500
    Year Built: 1983   **Architect:** Heidt Evans Salata   **Cost:** $13,000,000

Contact for Rental: John "Casey" Wells;   (814) 452-4857
Resident Groups: East Coast Hockey League - Erie Panthers

ERIE CIVIC CENTER - WARNER THEATRE
811 State Street, PO Box 6140, Erie, PA 16512
(814) 452-4857
Type of Facility: Concert Hall; Theatre House
Facility Originally: Movie House
Type of Stage: Proscenium
Stage Dimensions: 42'Wx28'D   **Orchestra Pit**
Seating Capacity: 2,506
Year Built: 1931   **Architect:** Rapp & Rapp
Contact for Rental: John "Casey" Wells;   (814) 452-4857
Resident Groups: Erie Philharmonic Orchestra; Erie Civic Ballet; Erie Civic Music Association

Fayetteville

THEATRE

TOTEM POLE PLAYHOUSE
9555 Golf Course Road, PO Box 603, Fayetteville, PA 17222-0603
(717) 352-2164
Founded: 1954
Arts Area: Professional; Summer Stock
Status: Professional; Commercial
Type: Performing; Resident
Purpose: To provide the best in professional theater in our local area
Management: Sue Kocek, Managing Director; Carl Schurr, Producing Artistic Director
Officers: Carl Schurr, President/Treasurer; Sue Kocek, Secretary
Paid Staff: 75
Paid Artists: 14
Utilizes: Special Technical Talent; Guest Artists; Guest Directors
Budget: $100,000 - $500,000
Income Sources: Box Office
Season: May - September   **Annual Attendance:** 40,000
Affiliations: AEA
Performance Facilities: Totem Pole Playhouse

FACILITY

TOTEM POLE PLAYHOUSE
9555 Golf Course Road, Fayetteville, PA 17222
(717) 352-2164
Type of Facility: Theatre House
Type of Stage: Proscenium
Stage Dimensions: 28'Wx24'D
Seating Capacity: 453
Year Built: 1970   **Architect:** Noelker and Hull
Manager: Sue Kocek;   (717) 352-2164
Resident Groups: Totem Pole Playhouse; Thunder Bird Ltd, Inc.

Glenside

DANCE

BODY LANGUAGE DANCE COMPANY
230 Clivedon Avenue, Glenside, PA 19128
(215) 886-9227
Founded: 1974
Arts Area: Modern
Status: Professional
Type: Performing; Touring; Resident; Educational
Purpose: To create and perform new forms of dance-theater
Officers: Ellen Forman, Director; Hettie Drummond, Secretary; Ellen Foody, Treasurer
Paid Staff: 1
Paid Artists: 8
Utilizes: Guest Artists; Guest Directors

Budget: $50,000 - $100,000
Income Sources: Private Foundations/Grants/Endowments; Business/Corporate Donations; Box Office; Government Grants; Individual Donations
Affiliations: Philadelphia Dance Alliance; Greater Philadelphia Clutural Alliance

Grantham

VOCAL MUSIC

GRANTHAM ORATORIO SOCIETY
Messiah College, Grantham, PA 17027
(717) 766-2511
> **Founded:** 1948
> **Arts Area:** Choral
> **Status:** Non-Professional; Non-Profit
> **Type:** Performing; Resident; Educational
> **Purpose:** To present choral works with orchestra
> **Management:** Dr. Ronald Sider, Conductor
> **Officers:** Rebecca Probst, President; Nancy Travitz, Secretary; Kenneth Stoessel, Treasurer
> **Paid Staff:** 1   **Volunteer Staff:** 5
> **Paid Artists:** 30   **Non-Paid Artists:** 150
> **Utilizes:** Guest Artists
> **Budget:** $1,000 - $50,000
> **Income Sources:** Business/Corporate Donations; Box Office; Individual Donations
> **Season:** January - April   **Annual Attendance:** 1,000
> **Affiliations:** Messiah College
> **Performance Facilities:** Eisenhower Auditorium

Greensburg

INSTRUMENTAL MUSIC

WESTMORELAND SYMPHONY ORCHESTRA
PO Box 1025, Greensburg, PA 15601
(412) 837-1850
FAX: (412) 836-6126
> **Arts Area:** Symphony; Orchestra; Ensemble
> **Status:** Semi-Professional; Non-Profit
> **Type:** Performing; Educational
> **Purpose:** To bring cultural enrichment through music to an ever-expanding segment of the community; to provide an enjoyable, inspirational and motivating experience
> **Management:** Kypros Markov, Music Director; Christel Horner, Manager
> **Officers:** Hugh M. Dempsey, President; John Foreman, Treaurer
> **Budget:** $100,000 - $500,000
> **Income Sources:** Private Foundations/Grants/Endowments; Business/Corporate Donations; Box Office; Government Grants
> **Performance Facilities:** Palace Theatre

Greenville

INSTRUMENTAL MUSIC

GREENVILLE SYMPHONY SOCIETY
PO Box 364, Greenville, PA 16125
(412) 588-2911
> **Founded:** 1927
> **Arts Area:** Symphony; Orchestra
> **Status:** Non-Profit
> **Type:** Performing
> **Purpose:** To educate in the field of music through performances
> **Management:** John H. Evans, Manager; Vicki Poe, Jamie Scott, Personnel Directors; Jean Sankey, Librarian
> **Officers:** Richard Szymkowski, President; Mark McGrath, Vice President/Grants Officer; Robert E. Davis, Treasurer
> **Paid Staff:** 1   **Volunteer Staff:** 20
> **Paid Artists:** 3
> **Utilizes:** Guest Artists
> **Budget:** $1,000 - $50,000

Income Sources: Private Foundations/Grants/Endowments; Business/Corporate Donations; Box Office; Government Grants; Individual Donations
Season: September - June   Annual Attendance: 7,700
Affiliations: Pennsylvania Council on the Arts
Performance Facilities: Passavant Memorial Center, Thiel College

FACILITY

THIEL COLLEGE - PASSAVANT MEMORIAL CENTER
Greenville, PA 16125
(412) 589-2125
Type of Facility: Auditorium
Type of Stage: Proscenium
Stage Dimensions: 70'Wx50'D
Seating Capacity: 2,000
Year Built: 1971
Architect: Brooks & Redfoot
Cost: $1,500,000
Contact for Rental: Susan Richards;   (412) 589-2125
Resident Groups: Greenville Symphony Orchestra; Thiel College Performing Arts; Greenville Community Performing Arts
Concerts; plays; ballet; community events

Harrisburg

INSTRUMENTAL MUSIC

HARRISBURG SYMPHONY ASSOCIATION
128 Locust Street, Harrisburg, PA 17101
(717) 232-8751
FAX: (717) 232-2921
Founded: 1930
Arts Area: Symphony; Orchestra
Status: Professional; Non-Profit
Type: Performing
Purpose: To bring symphonic music to central Pennsylvania
Management: Larry Newland, Music Director; Kathleen D. Ebner, Executive Director
Paid Staff: 5   Volunteer Staff: 3
Paid Artists: 80
Utilizes: Guest Artists
Budget: $500,000 - $1,000,000
Income Sources: Private Foundations/Grants/Endowments; Business/Corporate Donations; Box Office; Government Grants; Individual Donations; Fund-raising
Season: October - May   Annual Attendance: 12,000
Affiliations: ASOL; ASCAP
Performance Facilities: The Forum

HARRISBURG YOUTH SYMPHONY ORCHESTRA
128 Locust Street, Harrisburg, PA 17101
(717) 232-8751
FAX: (717) 232-2921
Arts Area: Symphony; Orchestra
Status: Non-Professional; Non-Profit
Type: Performing; Touring; Educational; Sponsoring
Purpose: To give young people an opportunity to play in an orchestra
Management: Dr. Ronald E. Schafer, Music Director/Conductor
Paid Staff: 3
Non-Paid Artists: 70
Budget: $1,000 - $50,000
Income Sources: Private Foundations/Grants/Endowments; Box Office; Government Grants
Season: October - May
Affiliations: ASOL (Youth Orchestra Division)
Performance Facilities: Susquehanna Township Middle School

THEATRE

HARRISBURG COMMUNITY THEATRE
513 Hurlock Street, Harrisburg, PA 17110
(717) 232-5501
>**Founded:** 1926
>**Arts Area:** Musical; Community; Theatrical Group
>**Status:** Non-Professional; Non-Profit
>**Type:** Performing; Educational
>**Purpose:** To provide quality theatrical experiences, opportunities and education to the Capital Region
>**Management:** Thomas G. Hostetter, Artistic Director; Kathy Lemke, Managing Director
>**Officers:** David A. Schankweiler, President; George F. Grode, Vice President of Grants and Gifts; Michael L. Greenwald, Vice President of Audience Development; Sheri L. Phillips, Secretary; Michael S. Cover, Treasurer
>**Paid Staff:** 8   **Volunteer Staff:** 400
>**Paid Artists:** 5
>**Utilizes:** Guest Artists; Guest Directors
>**Budget:** $100,000 - $500,000
>**Income Sources:** Private Foundations/Grants/Endowments; Business/Corporate Donations; Box Office; Government Grants; Individual Donations
>**Season:** September - June   **Annual Attendance:** 21,000
>**Affiliations:** Theatre Association of Pennsylvania; AACT

OPEN STAGE OF HARRISBURG
PO Box 3805, Harrisburg, PA 17105
(717) 652-7529
>**Founded:** 1983
>**Arts Area:** Professional
>**Status:** Professional; Non-Profit
>**Type:** Performing; Touring; Resident; Educational; Sponsoring
>**Purpose:** To develop and support an ensemble of theatre artists for the purpose of presenting modern, contemporary and original dramatic literature in close relationship with its audiences; to provide educational opportunites through a school and outreach program
>**Management:** Donald L. Alsedek, Artistic Director/Chief Executive Officer; Marianne M. Fischer, Managing Director; Anne L. Alsedek, Studio/School Director
>**Officers:** Dennis W. Felty, President; Ruth Leventhal, Vice President; Jonathan Vipond III Esq., Treasurer; Dolly Holtzman, Secretary
>**Paid Staff:** 2   **Volunteer Staff:** 10
>**Paid Artists:** 30
>**Utilizes:** Special Technical Talent; Guest Artists; Guest Directors
>**Budget:** $50,000 - $100,000
>**Income Sources:** Private Foundations/Grants/Endowments; Business/Corporate Donations; Box Office; Government Grants; Individual Donations
>**Season:** October - June   **Annual Attendance:** 3,000
>**Affiliations:** TCG; Citizens for the Arts in Pennsylvania; Theatre Association of Pennsylvania

PERFORMING SERIES

CENTRAL PENNSYLVANIA FRIENDS OF JAZZ, INC.
PO Box 10738, Harrisburg, PA 17105
(717) 540-1010
FAX: (717) 540-7735
>**Founded:** 1980
>**Arts Area:** Instrumental Music; Festivals
>**Status:** Non-Profit
>**Type:** Performing; Educational; Sponsoring
>**Purpose:** To present, promote and preserve America's unique art form, jazz
>**Management:** Steve Rudolph, Executive Director
>**Officers:** Lee Swartz, President; Robert Hendershot, First Vice President; Keith Thomas, Second Vice President; Rosemary Barrett, Third Vice President; Don Senoi, Treasurer; John Bottonari, Secretary
>**Paid Staff:** 1   **Volunteer Staff:** 25
>**Paid Artists:** 90   **Non-Paid Artists:** 30
>**Utilizes:** Guest Artists
>**Budget:** $100,000 - $500,000
>**Income Sources:** Private Foundations/Grants/Endowments; Business/Corporate Donations; Box Office; Government Grants; Individual Donations
>**Season:** 52 Weeks   **Annual Attendance:** 5,000
>**Affiliations:** Allied Arts Fund; Metro Arts of Central Pennsylvania

MARKET SQUARE CONCERTS
PO Box 1292, Harrisburg, PA 17108
(717) 697-6224
FAX: (717) 697-6430
    Arts Area: Chamber Music
    Status: Professional; Non-Profit
    Type: Educational; Presenting
    Purpose: To present a wide representation of solo and chamber music by distinguished artists, both established and emerging
    Management: Lucy Miller, Director
    Officers: Jason J. Litton, President
    Budget: $100,000 - $500,000
    Income Sources: Private Foundations/Grants/Endowments; Business/Corporate Donations; Box Office; Government Grants; Individual Donations
    Season: 52 Weeks
    Performance Facilities: Market Square Church; Rose Lehrman Art Center

FACILITY

FARM SHOW ARENA
2301 North Cameron Street, Harrisburg, PA 17110-9408
(717) 787-5373
    Type of Facility: Arena; Multi-Purpose
    Facility Originally: Business Facility
    Type of Stage: Flexible
    Stage Dimensions: 36'x72'
    Seating Capacity: 7,600
    Year Built: 1939
    Architect: Laurie & Green   **Cost:** $1,250,000
    Contact for Rental: Victoria Ritter;   (717) 787-5373

Hershey

PERFORMING SERIES

HERSHEY THEATRE
15 East Caracas Avenue, Hershey, PA 17033
(717) 534-3411
FAX: (717) 533-2882
    Founded: 1965
    Arts Area: Dance; Vocal Music; Instrumental Music; Theater; Grand Opera
    Status: Professional; Non-Profit
    Type: Touring; Sponsoring
    Purpose: To provide a variety of high quality live entertainment with emphasis on enhancing the cultural and educational opportunities in Central Pennsylvania
    Management: Susan R. Fowler, Executive Director
    Paid Staff: 35
    Paid Artists: 100
    Utilizes: Guest Artists
    Budget: $500,000 - $1,000,000
    Income Sources: Private Foundations/Grants/Endowments; Box Office
    Season: September - April   **Annual Attendance:** 50,000
    Performance Facilities: Hershey Theatre

FACILITY

HERSHEY THEATRE
15 East Caracas Avenue, Hershey, PA 17033
(717) 534-3411
    Type of Facility: Concert Hall; Auditorium; Theatre House
    Facility Originally: Vaudeville
    Type of Stage: Proscenium
    Stage Dimensions: 70'Wx44'6"D   **Orchestra Pit**
    Seating Capacity: 1,904
    Year Built: 1933
    Manager: Susan R. Fowler, Executive Director

Huntingdon Valley

VOCAL MUSIC

THE MARY GREEN SINGERS
990 Old Huntingdon Pike, Huntingdon Valley, PA 19006
(215) 572-5063
> **Founded:** 1986
> **Arts Area:** Choral
> **Status:** Semi-Professional
> **Type:** Performing; Touring; Educational
> **Officers:** Mary Woodmansee Green, Music Director/Conductor
> **Paid Staff:** 1
> **Budget:** $100,000 - $500,000
> **Income Sources:** Box Office; Individual Donations

Jennerstown

THEATRE

MOUNTAIN PLAYHOUSE
PO Box 54, Jennerstown, PA 15547
(814) 629-9201
> **Founded:** 1939
> **Arts Area:** Professional; Musical
> **Status:** Professional; Commercial
> **Type:** Resident; Educational
> **Management:** Teresa M. Stoughton, Teresa A. Stoughton, Mary Louise Stoughton, Producing Directors
> **Paid Staff:** 18
> **Paid Artists:** 40
> **Utilizes:** Guest Directors
> **Budget:** $100,000 - $500,000
> **Income Sources:** Box Office
> **Season:** May - October   **Annual Attendance:** 35,000
> **Performance Facilities:** Mountain Playhouse

FACILITY

MOUNTAIN PLAYHOUSE
PO Box 205, Jennerstown, PA 15547
(814) 629-9201
FAX: (814) 629-6221
> **Type of Facility:** Theatre House
> **Type of Stage:** Proscenium
> **Seating Capacity:** 444
> **Year Built:** 1939   **Architect:** James Stoughton   **Cost:** $4,000
> **Acoustical Consultant:** R.A. Stoughton, Sr.
> *Original structure was converted to a theater in 1939.*

Jim Thorpe

PERFORMING SERIES

LAUREL FESTIVAL OF THE ARTS
PO Box 206, Jim Thorpe, PA 18229
(717) 325-4439
> **Founded:** 1990
> **Arts Area:** Dance; Vocal Music; Instrumental Music; Festivals; Poetry
> **Status:** Professional; Non-Profit
> **Type:** Performing; Resident; Educational
> **Purpose:** To bring together the finest performers to work together and present events to the public
> **Management:** Marc Mostaroy, Artistic Director; Randall Perry, Weeknight Concerts; Herbert Thompson, Publicity; Barbara Loeffler, Marketing
> **Officers:** Harry Hintz, Chairman; Peter Kern, Vice Chairman; Shirley Stermer, Treasurer
> **Paid Staff:** 2   **Volunteer Staff:** 30
> **Paid Artists:** 30
> **Utilizes:** Guest Artists

Budget: $1,000 - $50,000
Income Sources: Private Foundations/Grants/Endowments; Business/Corporate Donations; Box Office; Government Grants; Individual Donations
Season: June   **Annual Attendance:** 1,500
Performance Facilities: Mauch Chunk Opera House

Johnstown

INSTRUMENTAL MUSIC

JOHNSTOWN SYMPHONY ORCHESTRA
215 Main Street, Johnstown, PA 15901
(814) 535-6738
Founded: 1929
Arts Area: Symphony; Orchestra; Chamber
Status: Professional
Type: Performing
Purpose: To perform classical music to the greater Johnstown area
Management: Anthony M. Blackner, Executive Director; Lawrence R. Samay, Business Manager; Helen Chiclot, Administrative Assistant; Istvan Jaray, Music Director
Officers: James Richey, President; Mary DiFrancesco, Past President; Mary Borkow, President Elect; Carmela Bagistro, Secretary; Orlando Hanselman, Treasurer
Paid Staff: 4   **Volunteer Staff:** 5
Paid Artists: 75
Utilizes: Guest Artists
Budget: $100,000 - $500,000
Income Sources: Private Foundations/Grants/Endowments; Business/Corporate Donations; Box Office; Government Grants; Individual Donations
Season: October - May   **Annual Attendance:** 5,500
Performance Facilities: Pasquerilla Performing Arts Center

Kennett Square

PERFORMING SERIES

LONGWOOD GARDENS
PO Box 501, Kennett Square, PA 19348
(215) 388-6741
Founded: 1929
Arts Area: Instrumental Music; Theater; Festivals
Status: Non-Profit
Type: Performing; Educational
Management: Priscilla Johnson, Performing Arts Coordinator
Paid Artists: 250   **Non-Paid Artists:** 50
Budget: $1,000 - $50,000
Income Sources: Private Foundations/Grants/Endowments; Box Office
Season: 52 Weeks

FACILITY

OPEN AIR THEATRE
Longwood Gardens, PO Box 501, Kennett Square, PA 19348
(215) 388-6741
FAX: (215) 388-2078
Type of Facility: Amphitheater
Type of Stage: Trapezoidal
Stage Dimensions: 75'Wx35'D
Seating Capacity: 2,080
Year Built: 1912   **Architect:** Pierre S. du Pont
Year Remodeled: 1927
Contact for Rental: Priscilla Johnson;   (215) 388-6741, ext. 451
Resident Groups: The Savoy Company; Brandywiners; Kennett Symphony
Dressing rooms and water curtain added in 1927 renovation

Kingston

DANCE

BALLET THEATRE PENNSYLVANIA
239 Schuyler Avenue, Kingston, PA 18704
(717) 283-9682
> **Founded:** 1983
> **Arts Area:** Modern; Ballet
> **Status:** Professional; Non-Profit
> **Type:** Performing; Touring; Resident; Educational
> **Management:** Mary Hepner, Artistic/Executive Director
> **Paid Staff:** 6   **Volunteer Staff:** 6
> **Paid Artists:** 16   **Non-Paid Artists:** 12
> **Utilizes:** Guest Artists; Guest Choreographers
> **Budget:** $100,000 - $500,000
> **Income Sources:** Private Foundations/Grants/Endowments; Business/Corporate Donations; Box Office; Government Grants; Individual Donations
> **Season:** October - June
> **Performance Facilities:** F.M. Kirby Center for the Performing Arts

---

Kutztown

PERFORMING SERIES

NEW ARTS PROGRAM
173 West Main Street, PO Box 82, Kutztown, PA 19530
(215) 683-6440
> **Founded:** 1974
> **Arts Area:** Dance; Literary; Visual; Performing
> **Status:** Professional; Non-Profit
> **Type:** Performing; Resident
> **Purpose:** To present individual artists from the literary, performing and visual arts for two days of one-to-one consultations plus a collective consultation in a presentation/performance setting
> **Management:** James F.L. Carroll, Director
> **Officers:** James F.L. Carroll, President; Michael Kessler, Vice President; James F.L. Carroll, Treasurer; Joanne P. Carroll, Secretary
> **Paid Staff:** 1   **Volunteer Staff:** 3
> **Budget:** $50,000 - $100,000
> **Income Sources:** Private Foundations/Grants/Endowments; Business/Corporate Donations; Box Office; Government Grants; Individual Donations
> **Season:** September - July   **Annual Attendance:** 975
> **Performance Facilities:** Saint Johns UCC

FACILITY

KUTZTOWN UNIVERSITY - SCHAEFFER AUDITORIUM
College Hill, Kutztown, PA 19530
(215) 683-4000
FAX: (215) 683-4671
> **Founded:** 1867
> **Type of Facility:** Concert Hall; Auditorium; Outdoor (Concert); Studio Performance; Theatre House; Opera House; Arena; Multi-Purpose; Room
> **Type of Stage:** Proscenium; Arena
> **Stage Dimensions:** 54'Wx40'D
> **Seating Capacity:** 800
> **Contact for Rental:** Kutztown University Foundation;   (215) 683-4118
> **Resident Groups:** Theatre Department

Lancaster

THEATRE

FULTON OPERA HOUSE
12 North Prince Street, PO Box 1865, Lancaster, PA 17603
(717) 394-7133
> **Founded:** 1963

Arts Area: Professional; Musical; Theatrical Group
Status: Professional; Non-Profit
Type: Performing; Touring; Educational
Management: Deidre W. Simmons, Executive Director; Kathleen A. Collins, Artistic Director; Barry Kornhauser, Education Director; Lettie Herbert, General Manager
Officers: L. Thomas Gemmil Jr., President; John W. Espenshade, M. Waldron Vail, Vice Presidents; John A. Church, Treasurer; Patricia J. Otto, Secretary
Paid Staff: 13   Volunteer Staff: 300
Paid Artists: 200
Utilizes: Special Technical Talent; Guest Artists; Guest Directors
Budget: $500,000 - $1,000,000
Income Sources: Private Foundations/Grants/Endowments; Business/Corporate Donations; Box Office; Government Grants; Individual Donations
Season: October - June   Annual Attendance: 130,000
Affiliations: TCG; AEA; League of Historic American Theaters; National Historic Theatres
Performance Facilities: Fulton Opera House

THE INDEPENDENT EYE
PO Box 8, Lancaster, PA 17603
(717) 393-9088
Founded: 1974
Arts Area: Professional; Theatrical Group
Status: Professional; Non-Profit
Type: Performing; Touring; Resident; Educational
Purpose: Avant-garde and experimental theatre showcasing new works
Management: Conrad Bishop, Producing Director; Elizabeth Fuller, Associate Producing Director
Officers: Robert Webber, Chair, Board of Trustees
Paid Staff: 2
Paid Artists: 8
Utilizes: Special Technical Talent; Guest Artists
Budget: $50,000 - $100,000
Income Sources: Private Foundations/Grants/Endowments; Business/Corporate Donations; Box Office; Government Grants; Individual Donations
Season: September - May   Annual Attendance: 10,000
Affiliations: TCG

FACILITY

FULTON OPERA HOUSE FOUNDATION
12 North Prince Street, Lancaster, PA 17603
(717) 394-7133
FAX: (717) 397-3780
Founded: 1963
Type of Facility: Theatre House; Opera House
Facility Originally: Meeting Hall; Built on foundations of historic jail
Type of Stage: Proscenium
Stage Dimensions: 33'Wx39'Dx28'H proscenium opening   Orchestra Pit
Seating Capacity: 909
Year Built: 1852   Architect: Samuel Sloane
Year Remodeled: 1904   Architect: C. Emlen Urban
Contact for Rental: Lettie Herbert;   (717) 394-7133
Resident Groups: Fulton Opera House Professional Theatre; Lancaster Opera Company; Lancaster Symphony Orchestra; Actors' Company of Pennsylvania

Lehigh Valley

INSTRUMENTAL MUSIC

LEHIGH VALLEY CHAMBER ORCHESTRA
PO Box 20641, Lehigh Valley, PA 18002-0641
(215) 770-9666
Founded: 1980
Arts Area: Orchestra
Status: Professional; Non-Profit
Type: Performing; Touring; Educational; Recording

Purpose: To nurture interest, support, and appreciation for classical music through performances of the highest standard of excellence; to enhance the quality of life in our community by fostering musical heritage by promoting contemporary American music, providing educational programming and presenting virtuoso performers of international stature; create and seek opportunities to enhance our reputation in the community, region and world of performing arts
Management: Llyena Boylan, Executive Director; Donald Spieth, Music Director
Officers: Clifford G. Vernick M.D., President; Michael Miller, Treasurer; John Rumsey, V.P. Development; Glenn Ossiander, V.P. Marketing; Robert Stanton, Secretary
Paid Staff: 4   **Volunteer Staff:** 40
Paid Artists: 50
Utilizes: Guest Artists
Budget: $100,000 - $500,000
Income Sources: Private Foundations/Grants/Endowments; Business/Corporate Donations; Box Office; Government Grants; Individual Donations
Season: September - June   **Annual Attendance:** 30,000
Affiliations: ASOL; Citizens for the Arts in Pennsylvania; The Association of Pennsylvania Orchestras
Performance Facilities: Dorothy & Dexter Baker Center for the Arts, Muhlenberg College, Allentown

Malvern

THEATRE

THE PEOPLE'S LIGHT AND THEATRE COMPANY
39 Conestoga Road, Malvern, PA 19355
(215) 647-1900
FAX: (215) 640-9521
   Founded: 1974
   Arts Area: Professional; Theatrical Group
   Status: Professional; Non-Profit
   Type: Performing; Resident; Educational
   Purpose: To help unify a culturally diverse society by giving the community barrier-free access to drama that celebrates our joys, terrors and dreams as we struggle to live together in difficult times
   Management: Danny S. Fruchter, Producing Director; Greg Rowe, Managing Director; Alda Cortese, Literary Manager; Mary Bashaw, Public Information Director; Abigail Adams, Associate Artistic Director; Wendy E. Worthington, Marketing Director
   Officers: William F. Drake Jr., Board President; Carole Haas, Vice President; L. Frederick Sutherland, Treasurer; Paul H. Rohrkemper, Secretary
   Paid Staff: 16
   Paid Artists: 24
   Utilizes: Special Technical Talent; Guest Artists; Guest Directors
   Budget: $1,000,000 - $5,000,000
   Income Sources: Private Foundations/Grants/Endowments; Business/Corporate Donations; Box Office; Government Grants; Individual Donations
   Season: 52 Weeks   **Annual Attendance:** 60,000
   Affiliations: AEA; LORT
   Performance Facilities: The People's Light Theater - Mainstage and Steinbright Stage

Meadville

INSTRUMENTAL MUSIC

ALLEGHENY CIVIC SYMPHONY
Music Department, Allegheny College, Meadville, PA 16335
(814) 332-3356
   Founded: 1957
   Arts Area: Symphony
   Status: Semi-Professional; Non-Profit
   Type: Performing; Educational
   Purpose: To give an opportunity for student artists to perform with area musicians; to present high quality performances to local audiences
   Management: Robert Bond, Conductor
   Non-Paid Artists: 60
   Utilizes: Guest Artists
   Season: September - June   **Annual Attendance:** 2,000
   Affiliations: Allegheny College
   Performance Facilities: Raymond P. Shafer Auditorium

Merion Station

PERFORMING SERIES

MOZART ON THE SQUARE
PO Box 237, Merion Station, PA 19066
(215) 668-1799
Founded: 1980
Arts Area: Festivals
Status: Non-Profit
Type: Performing
Purpose: To present chamber music concerts, mainly of music from the Classic and early Romantic eras
Officers: Carole F. Haas, President; David Crownover, Vice President; William H. Roberts, Treasurer; F. Otto Haas, Acting Secretary
Paid Staff: 2 **Volunteer Staff:** 15
Paid Artists: 80
Utilizes: Guest Artists
Budget: $50,000 - $100,000
Income Sources: Private Foundations/Grants/Endowments; Business/Corporate Donations; Box Office; Government Grants; Individual Donations
Season: May - June **Annual Attendance:** 5,000
Performance Facilities: The Church of the Holy Trinity; Curtis Hall; BZ-BI Synagog

Mill Hall

FACILITY

MILLBROOK PLAYHOUSE
Country Club Lane, Mill Hall, PA 17751
(717) 748-8083
Type of Facility: Theatre House
Facility Originally: Barn
Type of Stage: Arena
Stage Dimensions: 12'x30'x20'
Seating Capacity: 300
Year Remodeled: 1963 **Architect:** Richard Swietzer **Cost:** $15,000

Mount Gretna

THEATRE

GRETNA PRODUCTIONS
Mt. Gretna Playhouse, PO Box 578, Mount Gretna, PA 17064
(717) 964-3322
Founded: 1978
Arts Area: Professional; Theatrical Group
Status: Professional; Non-Profit
Type: Performing; Touring
Management: Robin Wray, Managing Director; Al Franklin, Producing Director
Officers: Wendy DiMatteo, President
Paid Staff: 7 **Volunteer Staff:** 40
Paid Artists: 20 **Non-Paid Artists:** 3
Utilizes: Special Technical Talent; Guest Artists; Guest Directors
Budget: $100,000 - $500,000
Income Sources: Private Foundations/Grants/Endowments; Business/Corporate Donations; Box Office; Government Grants; Individual Donations
Season: June - August **Annual Attendance:** 20,000
Affiliations: LORT; AEA; Theatre Association of Pennsylvania; Metro Arts of Harrisburg
Performance Facilities: Mt. Gretna Playhouse

TIMBERS DINNER THEATER
Timber Road, Mount Gretna, PA 17064
(717) 964-3601
Arts Area: Musical; Dinner
Status: Professional; Commercial
Type: Performing
Management: John Briody, Owner

Paid Staff: 20
Paid Artists: 11
Income Sources: Box Office

PERFORMING SERIES

MUSIC AT GRETNA
PO Box 519, Mount Gretna, PA 17064
(717) 964-3836
Founded: 1975
Arts Area: Festivals
Status: Professional; Non-Profit
Type: Educational; Sponsoring; Producing
Management: Kathy Judd, Executive Director; Gail Nourse, Assistant Director
Officers: Carl Ellenberger Jr., Founder/Artistic Director; Charles V. Henry III, President
Paid Staff: 3 **Volunteer Staff:** 30
Paid Artists: 35
Utilizes: Guest Artists
Budget: $100,000 - $500,000
Income Sources: Private Foundations/Grants/Endowments; Business/Corporate Donations; Box Office; Government Grants; Individual Donations
Season: 52 Weeks **Annual Attendance:** 15,000
Affiliations: Chautauqua Playhouse; Strand-Capitol Performance Hall

FACILITY

TIMBERS DINNER THEATER
Timber Road, Mount Gretna, PA 17064
(717) 964-3601
Type of Facility: Theatre House
Facility Originally: Restaurant
Type of Stage: Proscenium **Orchestra Pit**
Seating Capacity: 500
Year Built: 1960 **Architect:** John Briody
Year Remodeled: 1976
Acoustical Consultant: John Briody
Manager: John Briody

Mountainhome

THEATRE

POCONO PLAYHOUSE
Playhouse Lane, Mountainhome, PA 18342
(717) 595-7456
Founded: 1947
Arts Area: Professional; Musical; Theatrical Group
Status: Professional; Commercial
Type: Performing; Educational
Management: Hubert Fryman, Owner/Producer; Donna McMicken, General Manager
Paid Staff: 5 **Volunteer Staff:** 30
Paid Artists: 250
Utilizes: Guest Directors
Income Sources: Box Office
Season: June - October
Performance Facilities: Pocono Playhouse

FACILITY

POCONO PLAYHOUSE
Playhouse Lane, Mountainhome, PA 18342
(717) 595-7456
FAX: (717) 595-7465
Founded: 1947
Type of Facility: Theatre House
Type of Stage: Proscenium
Seating Capacity: 497

Year Built: 1947
Resident Groups: Pocono Playhouse

Narberth

VOCAL MUSIC

SPRUCE STREET SINGERS
244 Woodbine Avenue, Narberth, PA 19072
(215) 667-1532
Founded: 1985
Arts Area: Choral
Status: Non-Professional
Type: Performing
Purpose: To have fun; to make music; to raise monies for community causes in the Philadelphia area
Management: David Hall, Musical Director
Officers: John Simpson, President; Jim Rinier, Vice President; Ed Zacks, Treasurer
Paid Staff: 1   **Volunteer Staff:** 7
Non-Paid Artists: 32
Utilizes: Guest Artists
Budget: $1,000 - $50,000
Income Sources: Business/Corporate Donations; Individual Donations; Fundraising
Season: 52 Weeks
Annual Attendance: 500
Performance Facilities: Saint Luke and the Epiphany Episcopal Church

---

New Hope

THEATRE

BUCKS COUNTY PLAYHOUSE
70 South Main, PO Box 313, New Hope, PA 18938
(215) 862-2046
Founded: 1939
Arts Area: Professional; Musical; Theatrical Group
Status: Professional; Commercial
Type: Performing; Educational; Partial-Equity Season
Management: Jade Curtain Ltd.: Hubert Fryman Jr., Associate Producer
Paid Staff: 5   **Volunteer Staff:** 30
Paid Artists: 250
Utilizes: Guest Directors
Income Sources: Box Office
Season: June - October
Performance Facilities: Bucks County Playhouse

FACILITY

BUCKS COUNTY PLAYHOUSE
70 South Main, PO Box 313, New Hope, PA 18938
(215) 862-2046
Type of Facility: Theatre House
Facility Originally: Paper Mill
Type of Stage: Proscenium
Stage Dimensions: 59'6"Wx27'D; 29'6"Wx18'H proscenium opening
Seating Capacity: 453
Year Remodeled: 1939
Contact for Rental: Nancy Pflaumer, General Manager;   (215) 862-2046
Resident Groups: Bucks County Playhouse

New Wilmington

PERFORMING SERIES

CELEBRITY SERIES
Westminster College, Market Street, New Wilmington, PA 16172
(412) 946-7371
Founded: 1852
Arts Area: Dance; Instrumental Music; Theater; Grand Opera
Status: Non-Profit
Type: Educational; Sponsoring
Purpose: To present a variety of the Performing Arts for the campus and community
Management: Eugene Decaprio, Assistant Dean of the College, Director of the Celebrity Series; Maria McKee, Box Office Manager
Paid Staff: 11
Paid Artists: 7
Utilizes: Guest Artists
Budget: $50,000 - $100,000
Income Sources: Private Foundations/Grants/Endowments; Box Office; Government Grants
Season: September - May   **Annual Attendance:** 6,000
Affiliations: APAP
Performance Facilities: Will W. Orr Auditorium

FACILITY

WESTMINSTER COLLEGE - BEEGHLY THEATER
New Wilmington, PA 16172-0001
(412) 946-7241
Type of Facility: Auditorium; Theatre House
Type of Stage: Proscenium
Stage Dimensions: 36'Wx28'Dx16'H   **Orchestra Pit**
Seating Capacity: 300
Year Built: 1966   **Architect:** W.G. Eckles Company
Contact for Rental: Business Manager;   (412) 946-7140
Limited availability due to theatre department activities. Shallow orchestra pit

WESTMINSTER COLLEGE - WILL W. ORR AUDITORIUM
Market Street, New Wilmington, PA 16172
(412) 946-7371
Type of Facility: Concert Hall; Auditorium
Type of Stage: Proscenium
Stage Dimensions: 50'Wx38'Dx30'H
Seating Capacity: 1,756
Year Built: 1962   **Architect:** W.G. Eckels Company
Acoustical Consultant: Ed Simons & Company
Contact for Rental: Business Manager;   (412) 946-7140
Manager: Gene De Caprio;   (412) 946-7271

Philadelphia

DANCE

BALLET DES JEUNES
1447 Manoa Road, Philadelphia, PA 19151
(215) 473-2253
Founded: 1958
Arts Area: Modern; Ballet; Jazz
Status: Non-Professional; Non-Profit
Type: Performing; Touring
Purpose: To give gifted young performers the opportunity to develop talent
Management: Ursula Maleta, Artistic Director; Donna Tambussi, Co-Director
Non-Paid Artists: 30
Utilizes: Guest Artists; Guest Choreographers
Budget: $1,000 - $50,000
Income Sources: Private Foundations/Grants/Endowments; Box Office
Season: September - July

CONVERGENCE DANCERS & MUSICIANS
32 Strawberry Street, Philadelphia, PA 19106
(215) 627-3374
    Founded: 1989
    Arts Area: Modern
    Status: Professional
    Type: Performing; Touring; Educational
    Purpose: To develop and present collaborative contemporary dance and music
    Management: Janaea Rose Lyn, Anthony Scafide, Artistic Directors
    Volunteer Staff: 4
    Paid Artists: 14   **Non-Paid Artists:** 2
    Utilizes: Guest Artists; Guest Choreographers; Guest Composers
    Budget: $1,000 - $50,000
    Income Sources: Private Foundations/Grants/Endowments; Business/Corporate Donations; Box Office; Government Grants; Individual Donations
    Season: Fall; Spring   **Annual Attendance:** 1,000

DANCE AFFILIATES OF AMERICAN BALLET COMPETITION
910 Cherry Street, 4th Floor, Philadelphia, PA 19107
(215) 829-9800
FAX: (215) 829-0508
    Arts Area: Modern; Ballet; Jazz; Ethnic; Folk
    Status: Non-Profit
    Type: Sponsoring
    Purpose: To create an environment where the arts are a necessary and integral part of our lives so they may illuminate, enrich and civilize the human spirit
    Management: F. Randolph Swartz, Artistic Director; Virginia Villalon, Director of Development
    Officers: F. Randolph Swartz, President; Cheryl V. Shepherd, Chairman of the Board; Mikhail Korogodsky, Lolly LaGreca, Ira Lefton Esq., Marietta Nettl, Barbara Sandonato, Board Members
    Paid Staff: 4   **Volunteer Staff:** 1
    Utilizes: Guest Artists; Guest Choreographers
    Budget: $500,000 - $1,000,000
    Income Sources: Private Foundations/Grants/Endowments; Business/Corporate Donations; Box Office; Government Grants; Individual Donations
    Season: November - May   **Annual Attendance:** 20,000
    Affiliations: University of the Arts; Annenberg Center; Philadelphia Dance Alliance
    Performance Facilities: Annenberg Center; Drake Theatre

GROUP MOTION MULTI MEDIA DANCE THEATER
624 South Fourth Street, 3rd Floor, Philadelphia, PA 19147
(215) 928-1495
    Founded: 1971
    Arts Area: Modern
    Status: Professional; Semi-Professional; Non-Professional; Non-Profit
    Type: Performing; Resident; Educational; Sponsoring
    Purpose: To provide artistic and educational services in all phases of multimedia dance theatre in the forms of teaching and instructing, production and presentation of performances
    Officers: Brigitta Herrmann, President; Manfred Fischbeck, Secretary
    Paid Staff: 3   **Volunteer Staff:** 8
    Paid Artists: 8
    Utilizes: Special Technical Talent; Guest Artists
    Budget: $1,000 - $50,000
    Income Sources: Private Foundations/Grants/Endowments; Business/Corporate Donations; Box Office; Government Grants; Individual Donations
    Season: September - June
    Affiliations: Philadelphia Dance Alliance; Greater Philadelphia Cultural Alliance

PENNSYLVANIA BALLET
1101 South Broad Street, Philadelphia, PA 19147
(215) 551-7000
FAX: (215) 551-7224
    Founded: 1961
    Arts Area: Ballet
    Status: Professional; Non-Profit
    Type: Performing; Touring; Resident
    Management: Christopher D'Ambose, Artistic Director
    Paid Staff: 35
    Paid Artists: 36

Utilizes: Guest Artists; Guest Choreographers
Budget: $100,000 - $500,000
Income Sources: Private Foundations/Grants/Endowments; Business/Corporate Donations; Box Office; Government Grants; Individual Donations
Season: September - August
Affiliations: Milwaukee Ballet
Performance Facilities: Academy of Music; Merriam Theatre

PHILDANCE/PHILADELPHIA DANCE COMPANY
9 North Preston Street, Philadelphia, PA 19104
(215) 387-8200
    Founded: 1970
    Arts Area: Modern; Ballet; Jazz
    Status: Professional; Non-Profit
    Type: Performing; Touring; Resident; Educational
    Purpose: A professional dance company that also has instruction and training programs annually offering tuition-free instruction and performing opportunities to young dancers
    Management: Joan Myers Brown, Artistic/Executive Director; Blondell Reynolds, Managing Director; Gwen Coleman, General Manager; Shaw Concerts, Tour Representative
    Officers: Spencer Werthemier, Chairman; Beverly Harper, President; Don Haskin, Alton Knight, Vice Presidents; Geri Packman, Secretary
    Paid Staff: 7   **Volunteer Staff:** 4
    Paid Artists: 17
    Utilizes: Special Technical Talent; Guest Artists; Guest Choreographers
    Budget: $500,000 - $1,000,000
    Income Sources: Private Foundations/Grants/Endowments; Business/Corporate Donations; Box Office; Government Grants; Individual Donations; Fundraising Efforts
    Season: Fall - Spring   **Annual Attendance:** 50,000
    Affiliations: Dance USA; International Association for Blacks in Dance; Coalition of Afro-American Cultural Organizations; American Dance Guild; Greater Philadelphia Cultural Alliance; PDA; TAAC

ZERO MOVING DANCE COMPANY
3500 Lancaster Avenue, Philadelphia, PA 19104
(215) 243-0260
FAX: (215) 222-4038
    Founded: 1974
    Arts Area: Modern
    Status: Professional; Non-Profit
    Type: Performing; Touring; Educational
    Purpose: To present original works by founding artist Hellmut Gottschild and Artistic Director Karen Bamonte
    Management: Karen Bamonte, Artistic Director; Jane E. Brown, Executive Director
    Officers: Hellmut Gottschild, President
    Budget: $100,000 - $500,000
    Income Sources: Private Foundations/Grants/Endowments; Business/Corporate Donations; Box Office; Government Grants; Individual Donations
    Affiliations: Philadelphia Dance Alliance; Dance Theatre Worker; Greater Phildelphia Cultural Alliance; Dance USA
    Performance Facilities: Community Education Center

INSTRUMENTAL MUSIC

BALTIMORE CONSORT
8871 Norwood Avenue, Philadelphia, PA 19118-2710
(410) 889-5123; (215) 247-4323
FAX: (215) 247-4323
    Founded: 1980
    Arts Area: Chamber; Ensemble; Folk; Instrumental Group
    Status: Professional; Non-Profit
    Type: Performing; Touring; Resident; Educational
    Purpose: Performance of popular music from the 16th and 17th centuries
    Management: Joane Rile, Artist Management
    Officers: Franklin T. Caudill, Chairman
    Paid Staff: 2
    Paid Artists: 7
    Utilizes: Guest Artists
    Budget: $50,000 - $100,000
    Income Sources: Private Foundations/Grants/Endowments; Business/Corporate Donations; Box Office; Government Grants; Individual Donations

Season: September - May   Annual Attendance: 5,000
Affiliations: Walters Art Gallery

CHESTNUT BRASS COMPANY
PO Box 30165, Philadelphia, PA 19103
(215) 787-6792
Founded: 1977
Arts Area: Chamber; Ensemble; Instrumental Group
Status: Professional; Non-Profit
Type: Performing; Touring; Resident; Educational
Purpose: To present to the public a historical view of brass instruments
Management: Joanne Rile Management Company
Officers: Marian Hesse, President; Jay Krush, Vice President; Bruce Barrie, Treasurer
Budget: $100,000 - $500,000
Income Sources: Private Foundations/Grants/Endowments; Government Grants; Individual Donations
Season: 52 Weeks
Affiliations: Greater Philadelphia Cultural Alliance; Temple University, Esther Boyle School

CONCERTO SOLOISTS
Walnut Street Theatre Building, Ninth and Walnut Streets, Philadelphia, PA 19107
(215) 574-3550
FAX: (215) 574-3598
Founded: 1964
Arts Area: Orchestra; Chamber; Ensemble; Instrumental Group
Status: Non-Profit
Type: Performing; Touring; Resident; Educational; Sponsor Produced
Purpose: To be a part of the Philadelphia community and cultural institutions
Management: Marc Mostovoy, Artistic/Music Director; Ken Wesler, General Manager; Kelli Marshall, Artistic Administrator
Officers: Kenneth Jarin, President of Board; Otto Haas, Chairman of Board
Utilizes: Guest Conductors; Guest Artists
Budget: $1,000,000 - $5,000,000
Income Sources: Private Foundations/Grants/Endowments; Business/Corporate Donations; Box Office; Government Grants; Individual Donations
Season: October - May
Affiliations: Greater Philadelphia Arts Council; Performing Arts League of Philadelphia; ASOL
Performance Facilities: Walnut Street Theatre; Church of the Holy Trinity

MARLBORO SCHOOL OF MUSIC
135 South 18th Street, Philadelphia, PA 19103
(215) 569-4690
Founded: 1951
Arts Area: Chamber
Status: Professional; Non-Profit
Type: Performing; Educational
Purpose: Professional school for advanced training in chamber music
Management: Anthony P. Checchia, Manager
Officers: Irving Moskovitz, Chairman; James H. Heineman, Phyllis J. Mills, Paul N. Olson, Vice Presidents;
M. Todd Cooke, Treasurer
Paid Staff: 7
Non-Paid Artists: 70
Budget: $500,000 - $1,000,000
Income Sources: Private Foundations/Grants/Endowments; Business/Corporate Donations; Box Office; Government Grants; Individual Donations
Season: June - August
Performance Facilities: Marlboro College Concert Hall

PHILADELPHIA CHAMBER MUSIC SOCIETY
135 South 18th Street, Philadelphia, PA 19103
(215) 569-8587
FAX: (215) 569-9497
Arts Area: Chamber
Status: Professional; Non-Profit
Type: Educational; Sponsoring; Presenting
Purpose: To present a diverse roster of acclaimed artists and ensembles featuring both highly experienced and emerging performers

Management: Philip Maneval, Manager; Anthony P. Checchia, Museum Director
Officers: Jerry G. Rubenstein, Chairman of the Board; Anthony P. Checchia, President of the Board
Budget: $100,000 - $500,000
Income Sources: Private Foundations/Grants/Endowments; Business/Corporate Donations; Box Office; Government
Grants; Individual Donations
Performance Facilities: Port of History Museum

PHILADELPHIA ORCHESTRA ASSOCIATION
1420 Locust Street, Philadelphia, PA 19102
(215) 893-1900
FAX: (215) 893-1948
Founded: 1900
Arts Area: Symphony; Orchestra
Status: Professional; Non-Profit
Type: Performing
Purpose: To maintain the preeminence of the Philadelphia Orchestra as one of Philadelphia's outstanding cultural assets
and as one of the world's greatest orchestras
Management: Joseph H. Kluger, President/Chief Operating Officer; Joseph A. Horgan, Director of Finance;
Judith Frankfurt, General Manager; Cathy Barbash, Orchestra Manager; Jean E. Brubaker, Director of Marketing;
Diana Burgwyn, Director of Public Relations; Maria T. Giliotto, Director of Development; Phyllis Susen, Director of
Education; Elizabeth Walker, Director of Volunteer Activities; Hugh F. Walsh Jr., Manager of the Academy of Music
Officers: Joseph Neubauer, Chairman of the Board/CEO
Paid Staff: 40
Paid Artists: 106
Utilizes: Guest Conductors; Guest Artists
Budget: Over 10,000,000
Income Sources: Private Foundations/Grants/Endowments; Business/Corporate Donations; Box Office; Government
Grants; Individual Donations
Season: 52 Weeks   **Annual Attendance:** 775,000
Affiliations: ASOL
Performance Facilities: Academy of Music

PHILADELPHIA RENAISSANCE WIND BAND
739 North 25th Street, Philadelphia, PA 19130
(215) 235-8469
Founded: 1980
Arts Area: Chamber; Ensemble; Early Music
Status: Professional; Non-Profit
Type: Performing; Touring; Educational
Purpose: To perform Renaissance and early Baroque music on period instruments
Management: Siegel Artist Management; Ethel Siegel, Joan Kimball, Co-Directors; Liz Silverstein, Associate Director
Officers: William Gross, Chairman of the Board
Utilizes: Guest Artists
Budget: $50,000 - $100,000
Income Sources: Private Foundations/Grants/Endowments; Business/Corporate Donations; Box Office; Government
Grants; Individual Donations
Season: September - April   **Annual Attendance:** 1,600
Affiliations: CMA; EMA

PHILADELPHIA YOUTH ORCHESTRA
PO Box 41810, Philadelphia, PA 19101
(215) 765-8485
Founded: 1939
Arts Area: Symphony; Orchestra; Chamber; Ensemble
Status: Non-Professional; Non-Profit
Type: Performing; Touring; Educational
Purpose: To promote, encourage and foster the study and practice of music by making available to deserving and talented
youth opportunities for orchestra instruction and supervision of their work and to provide concerts for promoting musical
art and its appreciation
Management: Joseph Primavera, Music Director/Conductor; Troy Peters, Assistant Conductor
Officers: Barbara Noseworthy, President
Paid Staff: 1   **Volunteer Staff:** 30
Non-Paid Artists: 105
Budget: $50,000 - $100,000
Income Sources: Private Foundations/Grants/Endowments; Business/Corporate Donations; Box Office; Government
Grants; Individual Donations; Fund-raising
Season: September - May   **Annual Attendance:** 15,000

Affiliations: ASOL (Youth Orchestra Division); Greater Philadelphia Cultural Alliance
Performance Facilities: Academy of Music

RELACHE ENSEMBLE
c/o Relache, Inc., 11 South Strawberry Street, Philadelphia, PA 19106
(215) 574-8246
FAX: (215) 574-0253
Arts Area: Chamber; Ensemble; Instrumental Group; Electronic & Live Electronic; Contemporary Music
Status: Professional; Non-Profit
Type: Performing; Touring; Resident; Educational; Sponsoring
Purpose: To develop, produce and present works by living composers
Management: Joseph Franklin, Executive Artistic Director; Arthur Stidfole, Director of Planning and Development; Laurel Wyckoff, Director of Educational Projects
Budget: $100,000 - $500,000
Income Sources: Private Foundations/Grants/Endowments; Business/Corporate Donations; Box Office; Government Grants; Individual Donations
Performance Facilities: Mandell Theater

VOCAL MUSIC

CHORAL ARTS SOCIETY OF PHILADELPHIA
1420 Locust Street, Suite 220, Philadelphia, PA 19102
(215) 545-8634
Founded: 1982
Arts Area: Choral
Status: Semi-Professional; Non-Profit
Type: Performing; Touring; Educational
Purpose: To present a choral/symphonic repertoire from all periods of music
Management: Sean Deibler, Artistic Director; Michael Scolamiero, Executive Director
Paid Artists: 10   **Non-Paid Artists:** 140
Utilizes: Guest Artists
Budget: $100,000 - $500,000
Income Sources: Private Foundations/Grants/Endowments; Business/Corporate Donations; Box Office; Government Grants; Individual Donations; Special Events
Season: December - May   **Annual Attendance:** 20,000
Performance Facilities: Mann Music Center; Academy of Music

CHORUS AMERICA
2111 Sansom Street, Philadelphia, PA 19103
(215) 563-2430
FAX: (215) 563-2431
Founded: 1977
Arts Area: Choral
Status: Non-Profit
Purpose: To promote the high quality and artistic growth of vocal ensembles; to stimulate further development of remuneration for singers; to encourage greater understanding, appreciation and enjoyment of choral music by all segments of society
Officers: Robert Page, President; Marshall A. Rutter Esq., Vice President
Paid Staff: 5
Income Sources: Private Foundations/Grants/Endowments; Business/Corporate Donations; Government Grants; Individual Donations

LITTLE LYRIC OPERA THEATRE
608 South Broad Street, Philadelphia, PA 19145
(215) 755-1288
Founded: 1987
Arts Area: Grand Opera; Lyric Opera
Status: Non-Profit
Type: Performing; Educational
Purpose: To provide repertoire experience for deserving amateur, professional and semi-professional singers
Management: A.C. Pugliese, President; Margaret Kastle, Vice President/Secretary; Maestro Carl Suppa, Musical Director
Utilizes: Guest Artists
Budget: $1,000 - $50,000
Income Sources: Box Office; Individual Donations
Season: September - May   **Annual Attendance:** 2,000

OPERA COMPANY OF PHILADELPHIA
Graham Building, 20th Floor, One Penn Square West, Philadelphia, PA 19102
(215) 981-1450; (215) 981-1454
FAX: (215) 981-1455
Founded: 1975
Arts Area: Grand Opera
Status: Professional; Non-Profit
Type: Performing
Purpose: OCP presents original productions of classical opera literature featuring renowned artists and promising young singers. OCP also sponsors the world's largest voice competition--the Opera Company of Philadelphia/Luciano Pavarotti International Voice Competition.
Management: Robert B. Driver, General Director; Catherine Welborn, Director of Marketing and Public Relations; Danielle Orlando, Artistic Administrator; Grey Nemeth, Competition Director
Officers: John P. Mulroney, President; Mrs. H. Douglas Paxson, Chairman of the Board
Paid Staff: 18   **Volunteer Staff:** 10
Paid Artists: 163
Utilizes: Special Technical Talent; Guest Conductors; Guest Artists; Guest Directors
Budget: $1,000,000 - $5,000,000
Income Sources: Private Foundations/Grants/Endowments; Business/Corporate Donations; Box Office; Government Grants; Individual Donations
Season: October - May   **Annual Attendance:** 39,000
Affiliations: OA; Greater Philadelphia Cultural Alliance
Performance Facilities: Academy of Music

OPERA NORTH
6933 Ardley Street, Philadelphia, PA 19119
(215) 472-3111
Founded: 1978
Arts Area: Grand Opera; Light Opera
Status: Professional; Non-Profit
Type: Performing; Educational
Purpose: Opera North was formed to provide additional opportunities in grand opera for previously unheralded minority talent, among others, in the Delaware Valley.
Management: Darryl Hobson-Reynolds, Artistic Director
Officers: Samuel R. Crosby, President
Paid Staff: 2
Paid Artists: 50
Utilizes: Special Technical Talent; Guest Conductors; Guest Artists; Guest Directors
Budget: $100,000 - $500,000
Income Sources: Private Foundations/Grants/Endowments; Business/Corporate Donations; Box Office; Government Grants; Individual Donations; Fund-raising
Season: 52 Weeks
Annual Attendance: 15,000
Affiliations: OA; Greater Philadelphia Cultural Alliance
Performance Facilities: Academy of Music

THE PENNSYLVANIA OPERA THEATER
1217 Sanson Street, Philadelphia, PA 19107
(215) 440-9797
Founded: 1975
Arts Area: Lyric Opera
Status: Professional; Non-Profit
Type: Performing; Touring; Educational
Purpose: To present high-quality productions which emphasize the theatrical as much as the musical elements; to present operas from all eras, sung in English; to commission new works of America opera; to broaden opera audiences through education and outreach
Management: Barbara Silverstein, Artistic Director; Scott Kessler, Acting General Manager; Tonia Kimbrough, Director of Development and Marketing
Officers: William L. Leonard, Chairman; Joyce S. Sando, Vice Chairman
Paid Staff: 9   **Volunteer Staff:** 50
Paid Artists: 75   **Non-Paid Artists:** 5
Utilizes: Special Technical Talent; Guest Conductors; Guest Artists; Guest Directors
Budget: $1,000,000 - $5,000,000
Income Sources: Private Foundations/Grants/Endowments; Business/Corporate Donations; Box Office; Government Grants; Individual Donations; Fund-raising
Season: October - May   **Annual Attendance:** 10,000
Affiliations: OA; COS
Performance Facilities: Merriam Theatre

THE PHILADELPHIA SINGERS
1700 Walnut Street, Suite 510, Philadelphia, PA 19103
(215) 732-3370
FAX: (215) 732-8288
Founded: 1972
Arts Area: Choral
Status: Professional
Type: Performing
Management: Oliver Bass, Executive Director; David Hayes, Artistic Director; Janice Bryson, Director of Development; Deborah Fleischman, Director of Marketing; Kenneth Landis, Administrative Director
Officers: Edith Reinhardt, Chairman of the Board; Alexis Barron, President of Board; Samuel Rudofker, Vice President; F. Hastings Griffin Esq., Secretary; James K. Abel, Treasurer
Paid Staff: 6 **Volunteer Staff:** 3
Paid Artists: 75
Utilizes: Guest Artists
Budget: $500,000 - $1,000,000
Income Sources: Private Foundations/Grants/Endowments; Business/Corporate Donations; Box Office; Government Grants; Individual Donations
Season: October - April **Annual Attendance:** 30,000
Performance Facilities: Academy of Music; Church of the Holy Trinity; St. Clement's Church

THEATRE

BUSHFIRE THEATRE OF PERFORMING ARTS
228 South 52nd Street & Locust, Philadelphia, PA 19139
(215) 747-9230
Founded: 1976
Arts Area: Professional; Musical; Theatrical Group
Status: Professional; Non-Profit
Type: Performing; Educational
Management: Al Simpkins, Artistic Director; Verlina Dawson, Executive Director
Paid Staff: 5 **Volunteer Staff:** 4
Paid Artists: 50
Utilizes: Special Technical Talent; Guest Artists; Guest Directors
Budget: $100,000 - $500,000
Income Sources: Private Foundations/Grants/Endowments; Business/Corporate Donations; Box Office; Government Grants; Individual Donations
Season: October - May
Affiliations: AEA
Performance Facilities: Bushfire Theatre of Performing Arts; Writers Workshop; Sassy's Salt Peanut Cafe; Artists' Hut

GERMANTOWN THEATRE GUILD
4821 Germantown Avenue, Philadelphia, PA 19144
(215) 842-0658
Founded: 1933
Arts Area: Professional; Theatrical Group
Status: Professional; Non-Profit
Type: Performing; Touring; Educational; Sponsoring
Management: Katherine Minehart, Artistic Director; Darla Max, Executive Assistant
Officers: Michael Carr, President; John Jordan, Secretary/Treasurer
Paid Staff: 2 **Volunteer Staff:** 10
Paid Artists: 15
Utilizes: Guest Artists; Guest Directors
Budget: $50,000 - $100,000
Income Sources: Private Foundations/Grants/Endowments; Business/Corporate Donations; Box Office; Individual Donations; Touring
Season: Fall - Spring **Annual Attendance:** 30,000
Affiliations: Theatre Alliance of Pennsylvania; Greater Philadelphia Cultural Alliance; Citizens for the Performing Arts in Pennsylvania; Performing Arts League of Philadelphia

MOVEMENT THEATRE INTERNATIONAL
3700 Chestnut Street, Philadelphia, PA 19104
(215) 382-0600
FAX: (215) 382-0627
Arts Area: Professional; Mime; Clown
Status: Non-Profit
Type: Performing; Educational; Sponsoring

Purpose: To support and increase awareness and understanding of performing artists who originate and perform their own work
Management: Michael A. Pedretti, Director; Sylvia Purnell, Development Officer; Beth Case, Administrative Assistant
Officers: Bob Krutsick, Chair; Judy Wicks, Prentice Cole, Vice Chairs; Oliver Franklin, Secretary
Paid Staff: 8
Paid Artists: 100
Budget: $500,000 - $1,000,000
Income Sources: Private Foundations/Grants/Endowments; Business/Corporate Donations; Box Office; Government Grants; Individual Donations; Tours
Season: January - August   **Annual Attendance:** 18,000
Affiliations: NMTA; PALP; Greater Philadelphia Cultural Alliance; Dance USA
Performance Facilities: MTI Tabernacle Theatre

NEW FREEDOM THEATRE
1346 North Broad Street, Philadelphia, PA 19121
(215) 765-2793
Management: John E. Allen, Founder; Robert E. Leslie, General Manager; A. Warren Merrick, Development Director
Officers: Lorenna Marshall, Chairman of the Board; Robert E. Baker and H. Theodore Roudford, Vice Chairmen; Steven Sanders, Secretary

PHILADELPHIA DRAMA GUILD
100 North 17th Street, Robert Morris Building, Philadelphia, PA 19103
(215) 563-7530
Founded: 1970
Arts Area: Professional; Theatrical Group
Status: Professional; Non-Profit
Type: Performing; Educational
Purpose: To deliver an ongoing program of professional theatre employing the highest standards in acting, directing and design; to make the theatre-going experience integral in the lives of our young people; to provide an alternative to the mass media's homogenization of our culture
Management: Mary B. Robinson, Artistic Director; Daniel L. Schay, Executive Director; Scott Robinson, Marketing Director
Officers: Carl A. Posse, Chairman of the Board
Paid Staff: 20
Utilizes: Special Technical Talent; Guest Artists; Guest Directors
Budget: $1,000,000 - $5,000,000
Income Sources: Private Foundations/Grants/Endowments; Business/Corporate Donations; Box Office; Government Grants; Individual Donations
Season: October - May
Affiliations: AEA; LORT
Performance Facilities: Zellerbach Theater

PHILADELPHIA FESTIVAL THEATRE FOR NEW PLAYS
3900 Chestnut Street, Philadelphia, PA 19104
(215) 222-5000
Founded: 1981
Arts Area: Professional; Theatrical Group
Status: Professional; Non-Profit
Type: Performing
Purpose: To produce only new plays by contemporary playwrights
Management: Carol Rocamora, Artistic/Producing Director; Michael Hollinger, Literary Manager; Hilary Missan, Casting Director
Officers: Eleanor Tarbox, Board President
Paid Staff: 5
Utilizes: Special Technical Talent; Guest Artists; Guest Directors
Budget: $500,000 - $1,000,000
Income Sources: Private Foundations/Grants/Endowments; Business/Corporate Donations; Box Office; Government Grants; Individual Donations
Season: October - June
Affiliations: AEA; LORT
Performance Facilities: Harold Prince Theater

THE PHILADELPHIA THEATRE COMPANY
The Bourse Building, 21 South Fifth Street, Philadelphia, PA 19106
(215) 592-8333
Founded: 1981
Arts Area: Professional; Theatrical Group
Status: Professional; Non-Profit
Type: Performing; Resident

Management: Sarah Garonzik, Producing Artistic Director; Ada Coppock, General Manager
Officers: Monika Krug, Board President
Paid Staff: 12
Income Sources: Private Foundations/Grants/Endowments; Business/Corporate Donations; Box Office; Government Grants; Individual Donations
Season: September - June
Affiliations: AEA
Performance Facilities: Plays and Players Theater

SOCIETY HILL PLAYHOUSE
507 South Eighth Street, Philadelphia, PA 19147
(215) 923-0210
Founded: 1959
Arts Area: Professional; Theatrical Group
Status: Professional; Non-Profit
Type: Performing; Touring; Educational
Purpose: Dedicated to sharing the magic of theater with its audience, presenting the best of contemporary European and American writers
Management: Jay Kogan, Artistic Director; Deen Kogan, Managing Director; Walter Vail, Director of Play Development
Paid Staff: 6
Utilizes: Special Technical Talent; Guest Artists; Guest Directors
Budget: $100,000 - $500,000
Income Sources: Private Foundations/Grants/Endowments; Business/Corporate Donations; Box Office; Government Grants; Individual Donations
Season: 52 Weeks
Affiliations: AEA; SPT; TCG; Theatre Association of Pennsylvania; AAA
Performance Facilities: Society Hill Playhouse

WALNUT STREET THEATRE COMPANY
Ninth and Walnut Streets, Philadelphia, PA 19107
(215) 574-3550
FAX: (215) 574-3598
Founded: 1982
Arts Area: Professional; Musical; Theatrical Group
Status: Professional; Non-Profit
Type: Performing; Resident; Educational
Purpose: Committed to developing the art form of theatre in the Delaware Valley, developing audiences for the theatre and sponsoring and training local artists and technicians, Walnut Street Theatre Company believes that as the art form prospers and grows in Philadelphia, it creates an exciting environment which builds on its own successes.
Management: Bernard Havard, Executive Director; Ken Wesler, General Manager
Officers: John D. Graham, Board President
Paid Staff: 110   **Volunteer Staff:** 210
Paid Artists: 144
Utilizes: Special Technical Talent; Guest Artists; Guest Directors
Budget: $1,000,000 - $5,000,000
Income Sources: Private Foundations/Grants/Endowments; Business/Corporate Donations; Box Office; Government Grants; Individual Donations
Season: October - April   **Annual Attendance:** 195,000
Affiliations: Greater Philadelphia Cultural Alliance; Philadelphia Chamber of Commerce
Performance Facilities: The Walnut Street Theatre

THE WILMA THEATER
2030 Sansom Street, Philadelphia, PA 19103-4417
(215) 963-0249
FAX: (215) 963-0377
Founded: 1973
Arts Area: Professional
Status: Professional
Type: Performing
Purpose: To produce innovative theatre of the highest artistic quality from international and contemporary American repertoires
Management: W. Courtenay Wilson, Managing Director; Florence Zeller, Director of Development; Frank Wood, Director of Marketing; Larry Kenney, Business Manager; Ian Goldstein, Audience Services Manager; Blanka Zizka, Jiri Zizka, Co-Artistic/Producing Directors; Roy Gray, Technical Director; Janet E. Finegar, Literary Manager
Paid Staff: 13
Paid Artists: 6
Utilizes: Special Technical Talent; Guest Directors
Budget: $500,000 - $1,000,000

Income Sources: Private Foundations/Grants/Endowments; Business/Corporate Donations; Box Office; Government Grants; Individual Donations
Season: September - June **Annual Attendance:** 23,000
Affiliations: TCG

PERFORMING SERIES

AMERICAN MUSIC THEATER FESTIVAL
2005 Market Street-1 Commerce Square, 18th Floor, Philadelphia, PA 19103
(215) 851-6450
Founded: 1983
Arts Area: Festivals; Musical Theater
Status: Non-Profit
Type: Sponsoring
Purpose: A national festival exclusively dedicated to the development of music theatre in all its forms: contemporary, drama, comedy
Management: Donna Powell, General Manager; Marjorie Samoff, Producing Director; Eric Salzman, Artistic Director
Officers: Nichand Sherman, President
Paid Staff: 60 **Volunteer Staff:** 50
Paid Artists: 100
Utilizes: Special Technical Talent; Guest Conductors; Guest Artists; Guest Directors
Budget: $1,000,000 - $5,000,000
Income Sources: Private Foundations/Grants/Endowments; Business/Corporate Donations; Box Office; Government Grants; Individual Donations
Season: September - October **Annual Attendance:** 30,000

BACH FESTIVAL OF PHILADELPHIA
8419 Germantown Road, Philadelphia, PA 19118
(215) 247-4070
FAX: (215) 247-4070
Founded: 1976
Arts Area: Vocal Music; Instrumental Music; Festivals
Status: Professional; Non-Profit
Type: Educational; Presenting
Purpose: The Bach Festival of Philadelphia is dedicated to enriching the community through concerts and educational programs presented by some of the best Baroque interpreters in the world.
Management: Janice Fiore, Director; Robert Mikrut, Development Administrator
Officers: Allen Model, President; Edna Phillips, Chairman; George Reath, Vice President; Dr. Margaret Rappaport, Secretary
Paid Staff: 5 **Volunteer Staff:** 1
Utilizes: Special Technical Talent; Guest Conductors; Guest Artists; Guest Directors
Budget: $100,000 - $500,000
Income Sources: Private Foundations/Grants/Endowments; Business/Corporate Donations; Box Office; Government Grants; Individual Donations
Season: 52 Weeks
Affiliations: Greater Philadelphia Cultural Alliance
Performance Facilities: St. Paul's Episcopal Church; Unitarian Society of Germantown; Mother of Consolation Church; Bryn Mawr Church; Springside School

MANN MUSIC CENTER, INC.
52nd Street & Parkside Avenue, Fairmount Park, Philadelphia, PA
(215) 567-0707
FAX: (215) 567-0734
Executive Offices: 1617 John F. Kennedy Boulevard, Philadelphia, PA 19103
Founded: 1930 (as Robin Hood Dell)
Arts Area: Dance; Instrumental Music; Orchestra; Special Events
Status: Professional
Type: Performing
Purpose: To present the Philadelphia Orchestra in an 18-concert summer series--providing 10,000 free general-admission tickets for each concert; supported by individual and corporate memberships as well as government agencies
Management: Charles Dutoit, Artistic Director/Principal Conductor; Helen W. Martin, President/Chief Executive Officer
Officers: Bernard M. Guth, Chairman of the Board; Helen W. Martin, President
Paid Staff: 6
Utilizes: Guest Conductors; Guest Artists
Budget: $1,000,000 - $5,000,000
Income Sources: Private Foundations/Grants/Endowments; Business/Corporate Donations; Box Office; Government Grants; Individual Donations
Season: June - September

PRESIDENTIAL JAZZ WEEKEND
c/o African-American History Museum, 701 Arch Street, Philadelphia, PA 19106
(215) 574-0380
FAX: (215) 574-3110
    Founded: 1989
    Arts Area: Vocal Music; Instrumental Music; Festivals; Ethnic
    Status: Professional; Semi-Professional; Non-Profit
    Type: Performing; Educational; Sponsoring
    Purpose: To celebrate African-American classical music
    Management: Rhoda Blount, Jazz Live Director; Dr. Rowena Stewart, Museum Director
    Officers: Clarence Farmer, Chairman of the Board; Leslie Willis, Head of Public Relations
    Utilizes: Special Technical Talent; Guest Artists; Guest Directors
    Income Sources: Private Foundations/Grants/Endowments; Business/Corporate Donations; Box Office; Government Grants; Individual Donations
    Season: 52 Weeks
    Affiliations: Greater Philadelphia Cultural Alliance; AAM; Coalition of Afro-American Organizations

FACILITY

ACADEMY OF MUSIC
Broad and Locust Streets, Philadelphia, PA 19102
(215) 893-1935
FAX: (215) 545-4588
    Type of Facility: Concert Hall; Performance Center; Opera House
    Year Built: 1857
    Year Remodeled: 1987
    Contact for Rental: Hugh Walsh, Jr.; (215) 893-1935
    A National Historic Landmark, the Academy of Music is the oldest operating opera house in the United States. The building contains the Hall and Main Auditorium. See separate listings for additional information.

ACADEMY OF MUSIC - HALL
Broad and Locust Streets, Philadelphia, PA 19102
(215) 893-1935
FAX: (215) 545-4588
    Type of Facility: Ballroom
    Type of Stage: Platform
    Seating Capacity: 480
    Contact for Rental: Hugh Walsh, Jr.; (215) 893-1935

ACADEMY OF MUSIC - MAIN AUDITORIUM
Broad and Locust Streets, Philadelphia, PA 19102
(215) 893-1935
FAX: (215) 545-4588
    Type of Facility: Concert Hall; Theatre House; Opera House
    Type of Stage: Proscenium
    Stage Dimensions: 48'Wx70'D; 48'Wx34'H proscenium opening   **Orchestra Pit**
    Seating Capacity: 2,929
    Contact for Rental: Hugh Walsh, Jr.; (215) 893-1935
    Resident Groups: Philadelphia Orchestra

CURTIS INSTITUTE - CURTIS HALL
1724 Locust Street, Philadelphia, PA 19103
(215) 893-5252
    Type of Facility: Auditorium
    Type of Stage: Proscenium
    Stage Dimensions: 15'x15'
    Seating Capacity: 235
    Year Built: 1927   **Architect:** E. Pederson   **Cost:** $305,000
    Manager: Dr. V. Sokoloff

FORREST THEATRE
1114 Walnut Street, Philadelphia, PA 19107
(212) 923-1515
    Type of Facility: Theatre House
    Type of Stage: Proscenium
    Stage Dimensions: 94'Wx39'D; 43'Wx30'H proscenium opening   **Orchestra Pit**
    Seating Capacity: 1,847

Contact for Rental: Peter Entin;   (212) 944-3700
Manager: Shubert Organization
Limited availability for rental

MANN MUSIC CENTER
1617 John F. Kennedy Boulevard, #850, Philadelphia, PA 19103
(215) 567-0707
FAX: (215) 567-0734
Type of Facility: Outdoor (Concert); Amphitheater; Multi-Purpose
Type of Stage: Proscenium
Stage Dimensions: 71'Wx60'D   **Orchestra Pit**
Seating Capacity: 4,639
Year Built: 1976   **Architect:** MacFadyen and DeVido   **Cost:** $7,500,000
Acoustical Consultant: Avram Melzer
Resident Groups: Philadelphia Orchestra

MERRIAM THEATER
250 South Broad Street, Philadelphia, PA 19102
(215) 732-5997
FAX: (215) 732-1396
Founded: 1918
Type of Facility: Theatre House
Facility Originally: Horticulture Center
Type of Stage: Proscenium
Stage Dimensions: 45'Wx25'H'42'7"D   **Orchestra Pit**
Seating Capacity: 1,668
Year Remodeled: 1987   **Architect:** Raphael Vilamil
Contact for Rental: Mary Bensel;   (215) 732-5997
Resident Groups: Pennsylvania Ballet; The Pennsylvania Opera Theater

PAINTED BRIDE
230 Vine Street, Philadelphia, PA 19104
(215) 925-9914
FAX: (215) 925-7402
Founded: 1969
Type of Facility: Performance Center; Theatre House; Visual Arts Gallery
Facility Originally: Factory
Type of Stage: Flexible
Stage Dimensions: 30'x50'
Seating Capacity: 300
Year Remodeled: 1982
Acoustical Consultant: Dan Araco
Contact for Rental: Lenny Seidman;   (215) 925-9914
Manager: Patricia Robinson;   (215) 925-9914

PHILADELPHIA CIVIC CENTER
34th Street and Civic Centre Boulevard, Philadelphia, PA 19104
(215) 823-5601
Type of Facility: Civic Center
Contact for Rental: James Reardon
Philadelphia Civic Center contains the Convention Hall, Exhibition Halls and Pennsylvania Hall. See separate listings for additional information.

PHILADELPHIA CIVIC CENTER - CONVENTION HALL
34th Street and Civic Centre Boulevard, Philadelphia, PA 19104
(215) 823-5601
Type of Facility: Auditorium
Type of Stage: Flexible
Seating Capacity: 11,000
Year Built: 1930
Year Remodeled: 1955
Contact for Rental: James Reardon

PHILADELPHIA CIVIC CENTER - EXHIBITION HALLS
34th Street and Civic Centre Boulevard, Philadelphia, PA 19104
(215) 823-5601
Type of Facility: Exhibition Hall
Type of Stage: Flexible

Year Built: 1967
Contact for Rental: James Reardon
The five Exhibition Halls total 283,000 square feet.

PHILADELPHIA CIVIC CENTER - PENNSYLVANIA HALL
34th Street and Civic Centre Boulevard, Philadelphia, PA 19104
(215) 823-5601
Type of Facility: Concert Hall; Auditorium
Type of Stage: End Stage
Stage Dimensions: 56'6"Wx45'Dx21'H
Seating Capacity: 4,000
Year Built: 1978
Contact for Rental: James Reardon

SOCIETY HILL PLAYHOUSE
507 South Eighth Street, Philadelphia, PA 19147
(215) 923-0210
FAX: (215) 923-1789
Founded: 1959
Type of Facility: Studio Performance; Theatre House
Facility Originally: Meeting Hall; Movie House
Type of Stage: Proscenium
Stage Dimensions: 24'Wx20'D
Seating Capacity: 250
Year Built: 1902
Year Remodeled: 1984
Contact for Rental: Deen Kogan;   (215) 923-0210
Resident Groups: Society Hill Playhouse Company; Philadelphia Youth Theatre
The Playhouse also contains a 90-seat, black box theatre.

THE SPECTRUM
Pattison Place, Philadelphia, PA 19148
(215) 336-3600
Type of Facility: Concert Hall; Auditorium; Arena; Multi-Purpose
Type of Stage: Flexible
Stage Dimensions: 60'x40'
Seating Capacity: 19,500
Year Built: 1967
Contact for Rental: Roger Dixon, General Manager;   (215) 389-9530
Resident Groups: Philadelphia Flyers ; Philadelphia '76ers

WALNUT STREET THEATRE
Ninth and Walnut Streets, Philadelphia, PA 19107
(215) 574-3550
FAX: (215) 574-3598
Type of Facility: Theatre Complex; Concert Hall; Studio Performance; Performance Center; Theatre House
Facility Originally: "New Circus" Equestrian Theatre
Type of Stage: Flexible; Proscenium
Seating Capacity: 1,052
Year Built: 1809
Year Remodeled: 1971   **Architect:** F. Brian Loving   **Cost:** $4,000,000
Contact for Rental: Ken Wesler;   (215) 923-2055
Resident Groups: Walnut Street Theatre Company; Concerto Soloists Chamber Orchestra
America's oldest theater, the building became Walnut Street Theatre—a legitimate theater—in 1812. Designated a National Historic Landmark in 1964, the building contains Mainstage, Studio Five and Studio Three. See separate listings for additional information.

WALNUT STREET THEATRE - MAINSTAGE
Ninth and Walnut Streets, Philadelphia, PA 19107
(215) 574-3550
Type of Facility: Theatre House
Type of Stage: Proscenium
Stage Dimensions: 60'6"Wx41'D; 38'Wx24'H proscenium opening   **Orchestra Pit**
Seating Capacity: 1,052
Contact for Rental: Ken Wesler;   (215) 923-2055
Resident Groups: Walnut Street Theatre Company

WALNUT STREET THEATRE - STUDIO 3
Ninth and Walnut Streets, Philadelphia, PA 19107.
(215) 574-3550
    Type of Facility: Studio Performance; Multi-Purpose
    Type of Stage: Flexible
    Stage Dimensions: 22'2"Wx43'D
    Seating Capacity: 85
    Contact for Rental: Ken Wesler;   (215) 923-2055

WALNUT STREET THEATRE - STUDIO 5
Ninth and Walnut Streets, Philadelphia, PA 19107
(215) 574-3550
    Type of Facility: Theatre House
    Type of Stage: Proscenium
    Stage Dimensions: 21'11"Wx15'10"D; 10'5"H grid
    Seating Capacity: 99
    Contact for Rental: Ken Wesler;   (215) 923-2055

WILMA THEATER
2030 Sansom Street, Philadelphia, PA 19103
(215) 963-0249
    Type of Facility: Black Box
    Facility Originally: Factory
    Type of Stage: Flexible
    Stage Dimensions: 50'9"Dx37'W
    Seating Capacity: 106
    Year Remodeled: 1972
    Resident Groups: The Wilma Theater

Pittsburgh

DANCE

DANCE ALLOY
4400 Forbes Avenue, Pittsburgh, PA 15213
(412) 621-6670
FAX: (412) 621-6671
    Founded: 1976
    Arts Area: Modern
    Status: Professional; Non-Profit
    Type: Performing; Touring; Educational
    Purpose: To perform; to provide educational services
    Management: Mark Taylor, Artistic Director; Marilyn M. Coleman, Managing Director
    Paid Staff: 3
    Non-Paid Artists: 6
    Utilizes: Special Technical Talent; Guest Artists; Guest Choreographers
    Budget: $1,000 - $50,000
    Income Sources: Private Foundations/Grants/Endowments; Business/Corporate Donations; Box Office; Government Grants; Individual Donations
    Season: October - March
    Performance Facilities: Fulton Theatre

PITTSBURGH BALLET THEATRE
2900 Liberty Avenue, Pittsburgh, PA 15201
(412) 281-0360
FAX: (412) 281-9901
    Founded: 1969
    Arts Area: Ballet
    Status: Professional; Non-Profit
    Type: Performing; Touring; Resident; Educational
    Purpose: To present quality professional ballet performances in Pittsburgh, regionally and nationally
    Management: Steven B. Libman, Managing Director; Patricia Wilde, Artistic Director; Nancy Hrynkiw, Director of Marketing; Mary Ellen Miller, Director of Development
    Officers: Eugene Barone, Chairman; Harry Weil, President
    Paid Staff: 25   **Volunteer Staff:** 109

Paid Artists: 35
Utilizes: Guest Conductors; Guest Artists; Guest Choreographers
Budget: $5,000,000 - $10,000,000
Income Sources: Private Foundations/Grants/Endowments; Business/Corporate Donations; Box Office; Government Grants; Individual Donations
Season: October - April   **Annual Attendance:** 125,000
Affiliations: NEA; Dance USA
Performance Facilities: Benedum Center for the Performing Arts

PITTSBURGH DANCE COUNCIL INC.
719 Liberty Avenue, Pittsburgh, PA 15222
FAX: (412) 355-0413
Founded: 1969
Arts Area: Modern; Ballet; Ethnic; Folk
Status: Non-Profit
Type: Sponsoring; Presenting
Purpose: To invest in the research and development of new artists and educational projects
Management: Carolelinda Dickey, Executive Director
Officers: William Wycoff, President, Board of Directors
Paid Staff: 5
Utilizes: Special Technical Talent
Budget: $50,000 - $100,000
Income Sources: Private Foundations/Grants/Endowments; Business/Corporate Donations; Box Office; Government Grants; Individual Donations
Affiliations: Pittsburgh Cultural Trust
Performance Facilities: Benedum Center; Eddy Theater at Chatham College; Fulton Theater

INSTRUMENTAL MUSIC

DUQUESNE UNIVERSITY TAMBURITZANS
1801 Boulevard of the Allies, Pittsburgh, PA 15219
(412) 434-5185
FAX: (412) 434-5583
Founded: 1937
Arts Area: Ensemble; Ethnic; Folk
Status: Non-Professional; Non-Profit
Type: Performing; Touring
Purpose: To preserve and perpetuate Eastern European cultural heritage in the United States
Management: Paul G. Stafura, Managing Director
Paid Staff: 11
Non-Paid Artists: 40
Utilizes: Special Technical Talent
Budget: $100,000 - $500,000
Income Sources: Private Foundations/Grants/Endowments; Business/Corporate Donations; Box Office; Government Grants; Individual Donations
Season: September - June
Annual Attendance: 200,000
Affiliations: Duquesne University

PITTSBURGH CHAMBER MUSIC SOCIETY
4200 Fifth Avenue, Pittsburgh, PA 15260
(412) 624-4129
Founded: 1961
Arts Area: Chamber
Status: Professional; Non-Profit
Type: Sponsoring
Purpose: To present chamber music; to commission new works; outreach
Management: Joan Sher, Executive Director
Officers: Michael Kumer, President; Dale Hershey, Vice President; Jane MacLeod, Secretary; Marlee S. Myers, Treasurer
Paid Staff: 2
Utilizes: Guest Artists
Budget: $100,000 - $500,000
Income Sources: Private Foundations/Grants/Endowments; Business/Corporate Donations; Box Office; Government Grants; Individual Donations
Season: October - May
Annual Attendance: 5,000

Affiliations: CMA; PA Presenters
Performance Facilities: The Carnegie Music Hall

THE PITTSBURGH NEW MUSIC ENSEMBLE
Duquesne University School of Music, 600 Forbes Avenue, Pittsburgh, PA 15282
(412) 261-0554
FAX: (412) 434-5479
Founded: 1975
Arts Area: Chamber; Instrumental Group; Contemporary Chamber Ensemble
Status: Professional; Non-Profit
Type: Performing; Touring; Resident; Educational; Sponsoring
Purpose: The Pittsburgh New Music Ensemble performs 20th century music, mostly American, providing a showcase for many live composers. Many of the works were written for the ensemble or commissioned.
Management: Eva Tumiel-Kozak, Executive Director; David Stock, Conductor
Officers: Michael Kumer, President; Joan Humphrey, Vice President; John C. Juback, Secretary; Jaime Brown, Treasurer
Paid Staff: 1   **Volunteer Staff:** 5
Paid Artists: 20
Utilizes: Guest Conductors; Guest Artists
Budget: $100,000 - $500,000
Income Sources: Private Foundations/Grants/Endowments; Business/Corporate Donations; Box Office; Government Grants; Individual Donations
Season: October - May   **Annual Attendance:** 8,400
Affiliations: CMA
Performance Facilities: Levy Hall at The Fulton Theatres

PITTSBURGH SYMPHONY ORCHESTRA
Heinz Hall, 600 Penn Avenue, Pittsburgh, PA 15222
(412) 392-4800
Founded: 1926
Arts Area: Symphony; Orchestra; Chamber
Status: Non-Profit
Type: Performing; Touring; Educational; Presenting
Purpose: To strive for and attain the highest standards of artistic achievement
Management: Gideon Toeplitz, Executive Vice President/Managing Director
Officers: David W. Christopher, President; Gideon Toeplitz, Executive Vice President/Managing Director
Paid Staff: 51
Paid Artists: 102
Utilizes: Guest Conductors; Guest Artists
Budget: Over 10,000,000
Income Sources: Private Foundations/Grants/Endowments; Business/Corporate Donations; Box Office; Government Grants; Individual Donations
Season: 52 Weeks
Annual Attendance: 500,000
Affiliations: Pittsburgh Symphony Society
Performance Facilities: Heinz Hall for the Performing Arts

PITTSBURGH YOUTH SYMPHONY ORCHESTRA ASSOCIATION, INC.
Heinz Hall, 600 Penn Avenue, Pittsburgh, PA 15222
(412) 392-4872
Founded: 1954
Arts Area: Symphony; Orchestra; Chamber; Ensemble
Status: Non-Professional; Non-Profit
Type: Performing; Touring; Resident; Educational; Sponsoring
Purpose: To maintain a music and educational program designed to aid young people to attain solid positions in the music profession, be it in performance, symphony orchestra, or teaching
Management: Barbara Yahr, Music Director; Willa Moriarity, Managing Director; Gina Zeglinski, Personnel Manager/Librarian; Cecelia Klaphake, Administrative Assistant
Officers: Suzanne C. Ross, President; Mrs. William H. George, Executive Vice President; Evelyn B. Pearson, Secretary; John McElroy, Treasurer
Paid Staff: 5   **Volunteer Staff:** 2
Paid Artists: 6
Utilizes: Guest Artists
Budget: $100,000 - $500,000
Income Sources: Private Foundations/Grants/Endowments; Business/Corporate Donations; Box Office; Individual Donations
Season: September - June
Annual Attendance: 10,000
Affiliations: Pittsburgh Symphony Society
Performance Facilities: Heinz Hall for the Performing Arts

RENAISSANCE AND BAROQUE SOCIETY OF PITTSBURGH
PO Box 10156, Pittsburgh, PA 15232
(412) 682-5253
   Founded: 1969
   Arts Area: Orchestra; Chamber; Early Music Presenter
   Status: Professional
   Type: Sponsoring
   Purpose: To sponsor touring ensembles from the US and abroad who perform early music on period instruments
   Officers: Russell W. Ayers III, President; Cynthia Elm, Vice President; Abigail McGuire, Secretary; Tod Pike, Treasurer
   Utilizes: Guest Artists
   Budget: $100,000 - $500,000
   Income Sources: Private Foundations/Grants/Endowments; Business/Corporate Donations; Box Office; Government Grants; Individual Donations
   Season: September - May   **Annual Attendance:** 7,000
   Performance Facilities: Synod Hall; Fulton Theatre; Carnegie Music Hall

RIVER CITY BRASS BAND
PO Box 6436, Pittsburgh, PA 15212
(412) 322-7222
FAX: (412) 322-6821
   Founded: 1980
   Arts Area: Band
   Status: Professional; Non-Profit
   Type: Performing; Touring; Resident
   Purpose: To produce superior quality performances of brass band and brass ensemble music that appeals to a broad spectrum of the community
   Management: Robert Bernat, President/Music Director; William Schlageter, Regional Concert Sales Manager; Milton Orkin, Contracted Performances Representative; Joseph Zuback, Personnel/Production Manager; Carl Jackson, Recording Manager
   Officers: W. Keith Smith, Chairman; John C. Marous Jr., Vice Chairman; Robert Bernat, President; R. Daniel McMichael, Vice President; Richard M. Hays, Secretary; Jay C. Juliussen, Treasurer
   Paid Staff: 10   **Volunteer Staff:** 95
   Paid Artists: 29
   Utilizes: Guest Conductors; Guest Artists
   Budget: $1,000,000 - $5,000,000
   Income Sources: Private Foundations/Grants/Endowments; Business/Corporate Donations; Box Office; Government Grants; Individual Donations; Sponsors
   Season: September - April   **Annual Attendance:** 125,000
   Affiliations: APAP; American Concert Band
   Performance Facilities: Carnegie Music Hall

VOCAL MUSIC

OPERA THEATER OF PITTSBURGH, INC.
PO Box 110108, Pittsburgh, PA 15232
(412) 521-5209; (412) 683-1967
   Arts Area: Grand Opera; Children's Opera; Chamber Opera
   Status: Professional; Non-Profit
   Type: Performing; Touring; Educational
   Purpose: To provide professional opera to areas outside the metropolitan centers; to introduce children to opera; to develop emerging professionals
   Management: Gary Race, Artistic Director
   Officers: Mildred Miller Posvar, President/Co-Founder; Henry Hoffstot, Chairman of the Board
   Budget: $50,000 - $100,000
   Income Sources: Private Foundations/Grants/Endowments; Business/Corporate Donations; Box Office; Government Grants; Individual Donations
   Performance Facilities: The Carnegie Music Hall

PITTSBURGH BOYCHOIR, INC.
300 Mt. Lebanon Boulevard, Suite 315, Pittsburgh, PA 15234
(412) 343-7464
FAX: (412) 343-9281
   Founded: 1986
   Arts Area: Choral; Musical Theatre
   Status: Semi-Professional; Non-Profit
   Type: Performing; Touring; Educational
   Purpose: To provide a choral training program for Pittsburgh youth with a goal of music excellence; to tour abroad
   Management: J. Scot Franklin, Managing Director; Judith Phelps, Administrator

Officers: Roy L. Franklin, President; John Ferguson, Secretary; Thomas Funk, Treasurer; William S. Smith, Esquire; Mark Stahl, CPA
Paid Staff: 5 **Volunteer Staff:** 200
Paid Artists: 4 **Non-Paid Artists:** 105
Utilizes: Special Technical Talent; Guest Conductors; Guest Artists
Budget: $100,000 - $500,000
Income Sources: Private Foundations/Grants/Endowments; Business/Corporate Donations; Box Office; Individual Donations; Fundraisers; Sales
Season: August - June **Annual Attendance:** 600
Affiliations: CA; ACDA; MENC; American Guild of Organists
Performance Facilities: Fulton Theatre; Heinz Chapel-University of Pittsburgh

PITTSBURGH CIVIC LIGHT OPERA
719 Liberty Avenue, Benedum Center, Pittsburgh, PA 15222
(412) 281-3973
FAX: (412) 281-5339
Founded: 1946
Arts Area: Light Opera; Operetta
Status: Professional; Non-Profit
Type: Performing; Educational
Purpose: To perpetuate, preserve and create musical, light opera and drama productions for the cultural and educational enrichment of our audiences, primarily in western Pennsylvania and, secondarily, the United States; ticket prices are set to enable maximum community participation
Management: Charles Gray, Executive Director/General Manager; Corinne Imbach, Director of Development
Paid Staff: 200 **Volunteer Staff:** 20
Paid Artists: 60
Utilizes: Special Technical Talent; Guest Artists; Guest Directors
Budget: $5,000,000 - $10,000,000
Income Sources: Private Foundations/Grants/Endowments; Business/Corporate Donations; Box Office; Government Grants; Individual Donations
Season: May - August **Annual Attendance:** 165,000
Affiliations: Musical Theater Works; National Musical Theater Network

PITTSBURGH OPERA
711 Penn Avenue, 8th Floor, Pittsburgh, PA 15222
(412) 281-0912
FAX: (412) 281-4324
Founded: 1940
Arts Area: Grand Opera
Status: Professional; Non-Profit
Type: Performing
Purpose: To present grand operas
Management: Tito Capobianco, General Director
Officers: Vincent A. Sarni, Chairman; Thomas H. O'Brien, President; Tito Capobianco, Vice President
Paid Staff: 22
Utilizes: Special Technical Talent; Guest Conductors; Guest Artists; Guest Directors
Budget: $1,000,000 - $5,000,000
Income Sources: Private Foundations/Grants/Endowments; Business/Corporate Donations; Box Office; Government Grants; Individual Donations
Season: October - May **Annual Attendance:** 55,400
Affiliations: OA
Performance Facilities: Benedum Center for the Performing Arts

RENAISSANCE CITY CHOIR
1432 Summit Street, Pittsburgh, PA 15221
(412) 242-5539
Founded: 1985
Arts Area: Choral
Status: Non-Professional; Non-Profit
Type: Performing
Management: Ed Burau, General Manager
Paid Staff: 1 **Volunteer Staff:** 4
Non-Paid Artists: 30
Utilizes: Guest Conductors; Guest Artists
Budget: $1,000 - $50,000
Income Sources: Private Foundations/Grants/Endowments; Business/Corporate Donations; Box Office; Individual Donations
Season: May - December **Annual Attendance:** 1,000
Performance Facilities: Campbell Chapel/Chatham College

THEATRE

CITY THEATRE COMPANY
57 South 13th Street, Pittsburgh, PA 15203
(412) 431-4400
FAX: (412) 431-5535
    Founded: 1974
    Arts Area: Professional; Theatrical Group
    Status: Professional; Non-Profit
    Type: Performing; Resident; Educational
    Purpose: To bring the richness and excitement of live theatre to a diverse public through the production of plays of relevant to contemporary American values and culture
    Management: Marc Masterson, Producing Director
    Officers: Robert M. Frankel, President; Thomas Hollander, Vice President; Jane Arkus, Secretary; Libby G. Fishman, Treasurer
    Paid Staff: 20   **Volunteer Staff:** 2
    Paid Artists: 50
    Utilizes: Special Technical Talent; Guest Artists; Guest Directors
    Budget: $500,000 - $1,000,000
    Income Sources: Private Foundations/Grants/Endowments; Business/Corporate Donations; Box Office; Government Grants; Individual Donations
    Season: October - May   **Annual Attendance:** 24,000
    Affiliations: TCG
    Performance Facilities: City Theatre

PITTSBURGH PUBLIC THEATER
Allegheny Square, Pittsburgh, PA 15212-5362
(412) 323-8200
    Founded: 1974
    Arts Area: Professional; Theatrical Group
    Status: Professional; Non-Profit
    Type: Performing; Educational
    Purpose: To present the highest quality of professional theater in classical and modern genres to the Pittsburgh community
    Management: William T. Gardner, Producing Director; Dan Fallon, Managing Director
    Officers: Richard H. Daniel, Chairman
    Paid Staff: 25
    Utilizes: Special Technical Talent; Guest Artists; Guest Directors
    Budget: $1,000,000 - $5,000,000
    Income Sources: Private Foundations/Grants/Endowments; Business/Corporate Donations; Box Office; Government Grants; Individual Donations
    Season: September - June
    Affiliations: AEA; LORT
    Performance Facilities: Theodore Hazlett Theatre

SALTWORKS
5001 Baum Boulevard, Pittsburgh, PA 15213
    Founded: 1982
    Arts Area: Professional; Theatrical Group
    Status: Semi-Professional; Non-Profit
    Type: Performing; Touring; Educational
    Purpose: To perform plays for youth and families that address social issues
    Management: Lynn George, Executive Director
    Paid Staff: 6
    Paid Artists: 5
    Utilizes: Special Technical Talent; Guest Directors
    Budget: $100,000 - $500,000
    Income Sources: Private Foundations/Grants/Endowments; Business/Corporate Donations; Box Office; Individual Donations; Performance Fees
    Season: 52 Weeks   **Annual Attendance:** 250

PERFORMING SERIES

LIVING MASTERS SUBSCRIPTION SERIES
c/o Manchester Craftsmen's Guild, 1815 Metropolitan Street, Pittsburgh, PA 15233
(412) 322-1773
FAX: (412) 321-2120
    Arts Area: Jazz

Status: Professional; Non-Profit
Type: Educational; Presenting
Purpose: To present jazz as an art form and include educational and community activities
Management: Martin Jay Ashby, Director of Performing Arts; Jay Ashby, Music Educational Director
Officers: William Strickland Jr., Director
Budget: $100,000 - $500,000
Income Sources: Private Foundations/Grants/Endowments; Business/Corporate Donations; Box Office; Government Grants; Individual Donations
Performance Facilities: Manchester Craftmen's Guild Music Hall

THREE RIVERS SHAKESPEARE FESTIVAL
1617 Cathedral of Learning, University of Pittsburgh, Pittsburgh, PA 15260
(412) 624-1953
FAX: (412) 624-6338
Founded: 1980
Arts Area: Vocal Music; Theater
Status: Professional; Non-Profit
Type: Performing; Touring; Resident; Educational
Purpose: To produce works of William Shakespeare and other classical dramatists in a manner accessible to the general public while maintaining high artistic standards
Management: Attilio Favorini, Producing Director; Susan O'Connell, Publicity Director; Christine Frezza, Planning Administrator; Sharyn Redpath, Director of Outreach; Eileen Davin, Director of Finance; Cathy Focareta, Director of Group Sales; Ellen Kelson, Literay Manager
Officers: Joseph Coogle Jr., Board President; Eric Springer, Vice Chairman/Board of Advisors
Paid Staff: 20   **Volunteer Staff:** 10
Paid Artists: 60   **Non-Paid Artists:** 10
Utilizes: Special Technical Talent; Guest Artists; Guest Directors
Budget: $5,000,000 - $10,000,000
Income Sources: Private Foundations/Grants/Endowments; Business/Corporate Donations; Box Office; Government Grants; Individual Donations; University of Pittsburgh
Season: May - August
Annual Attendance: 40,000
Affiliations: AEA; U/RTA
Performance Facilities: Stephen Foster Memorial

FACILITY

BENEDUM CENTER
719 Liberty Avenue, Pittsburgh, PA 15222
(412) 456-2600
FAX: (412) 456-2645
Founded: 1987
Type of Facility: Concert Hall; Theatre House; Opera House
Facility Originally: Movie Palace
Type of Stage: Proscenium
Stage Dimensions: 144'Wx78'D; 56'Wx36'6" proscenium opening   **Orchestra Pit**
Seating Capacity: 2,887
Year Built: 1928
Year Remodeled: 1987   **Architect:** MacLachlin Cornelius & Filoni   **Cost:** $42,000,000
Acoustical Consultant: Schultz
Contact for Rental: Gene Ciavarra;   (412) 456-2600
Manager: Michael Taormina;   (412) 456-2600
Resident Groups: Pittsburgh Opera; Pittsburgh Ballet Theatre; Pittsburgh Civic Light Opera; Pittsburgh Dance Council
Formerly the Stanley Theater, Benedum Center has the third-largest stage in the country.

THE CARNEGIE - LECTURE HALL
4400 Forbes Avenue, Pittsburgh, PA 15213
(412) 622-3360
FAX: (412) 622-3274
Type of Facility: Film & Lecture Hall
Type of Stage: Platform
Stage Dimensions: 30'Wx11'D
Seating Capacity: 617
Year Built: 1895   **Architect:** Longfellow Alden & Harlow
Contact for Rental: Eilene Dewalt, Special Events Coordinator;   (412) 622-3360
Resident Groups: International Poetry Forum

THE CARNEGIE - MUSEUM OF ART THEATRE
4400 Forbes Avenue, Pittsburgh, PA 15213
(412) 622-3360
   Type of Facility: Visual And Performing Arts Classrooms
   Type of Stage: Platform
   Stage Dimensions: 33'Wx9'D
   Seating Capacity: 198
   Year Built: 1974   **Architect:** Edward Larabee Barnes
   Contact for Rental: Eilene Dewalt;   (412) 622-3360
   Resident Groups: The Carnegie Film and Video Series

THE CARNEGIE - MUSIC HALL
4400 Forbes Avenue, Pittsburgh, PA 15213
(412) 622-3360
   Type of Facility: Concert Hall; Civic Center
   Type of Stage: Concert Shell
   Stage Dimensions: 66'3"Wx34'Dx51'H
   Seating Capacity: 1,950
   Year Built: 1895   **Architect:** Longfellow Alden & Harlow
   Year Remodeled: 1907
   Contact for Rental: Eilene Dewalt;   (412) 622-3360
   Resident Groups: River City Brass Band; Pittsburgh Chamber Music; Mendelssohn Choir; Bach Choir;
   Travel & Adventure Series; Man & Ideas Series; Carnegie Music Hall Philharmonic

HEINZ HALL FOR THE PERFORMING ARTS
600 Penn Avenue, Pittsburgh, PA 15222
(412) 392-4800
   Type of Facility: Concert Hall; Studio Performance; Performance Center; Theatre House; Opera House; Multi-Purpose
   Facility Originally: Vaudeville
   Type of Stage: Proscenium
   Stage Dimensions: 32'x54'x60'
   Orchestra Pit
   Seating Capacity: 2,847
   Year Built: 1927   **Architect:** Rapp & Rapp
   Year Remodeled: 1971   **Architect:** Stotz Hess McLachlin & Fosner   **Cost:** $13,000,000
   Acoustical Consultant: Dr. Heinrich Keilholz
   Contact for Rental: Don Craig;   (412) 392-4843
   Resident Groups: Pittsburgh Symphony Orchestra; Pittsburgh Symphony Youth Orchestra; Mendelssohn Choir;
   Diet Coke Broadway Series

PITTSBURGH CIVIC ARENA
300 Auditorium Place, Pittsburgh, PA 15219
(412) 642-1800
   Type of Facility: Civic Center
   Type of Stage: Proscenium
   Orchestra Pit
   Seating Capacity: 15,000
   Year Built: 1961   **Architect:** Deeter, Ritchey, Sippel   **Cost:** $22,000,000
   Contact for Rental: Booking Director;   (412) 642-1800
   Manager: Tim Murphy

Reading

INSTRUMENTAL MUSIC

READING SYMPHONY ORCHESTRA
147 North Fifth Street, Reading, PA 19601
(215) 373-7557
   Founded: 1912
   Arts Area: Symphony
   Status: Professional
   Type: Performing; Educational; Sponsoring
   Purpose: To present the highest quality orchestral concerts possible in Berks County and the city of Reading
   Management: Stuart B. Weiser, Executive Director
   Officers: Robert S. Pollack, President; Thomas B. Souders, Vice President; Alice F. Friedman, Treasurer
   Paid Staff: 2   **Volunteer Staff:** 1

Utilizes: Guest Conductors; Guest Artists
Budget: $100,000 - $500,000
Income Sources: Private Foundations/Grants/Endowments; Business/Corporate Donations; Box Office; Government Grants; Individual Donations
Season: October - April   **Annual Attendance:** 15,000
Affiliations: ASOL
Performance Facilities: Rajah Theatre

THEATRE

READING COMMUNITY PLAYERS
11th and Buttonwood Street, PO Box 1032, Reading, PA 19604
(215) 375-9106
    Founded: 1920
    Arts Area: Community; Theatrical Group
    Status: Non-Professional; Non-Profit
    Type: Performing; Educational
    Purpose: To create and develop interest in the theatrical arts of the community
    Management: Terry Fullmer, Business Manager
    Officers: Hal Kremser, Treasurer
    Volunteer Staff: 114
    Non-Paid Artists: 114
    Budget: $1,000 - $50,000
    Income Sources: Private Foundations/Grants/Endowments; Business/Corporate Donations; Box Office; Government Grants
    Season: 52 Weeks

PERFORMING SERIES

HAAGE CONCERTS/HARRIS PRESENTS
435 Walnut Street, Reading, PA 19611
(215) 374-3161
    Founded: 1907
    Arts Area: Dance; Vocal Music; Instrumental Music; Theater
    Status: Professional
    Type: Sponsoring
    Purpose: To present classical and pops attractions of high quality featuring new and innovative groups, dance, mime, Renaissance and others
    Management: Louise M. Harris, Manager
    Utilizes: Guest Artists
    Budget: $50,000 - $100,000
    Income Sources: Box Office; Individual Donations
    Season: October - April
    Performance Facilities: Rajah Theatre

STAR SERIES OF READING
147 North Fifth Street, Reading, PA 19601
(215) 376-3395
FAX: (215) 376-3336
    Founded: 1970
    Arts Area: Dance; Vocal Music; Instrumental Music
    Status: Non-Profit
    Type: Sponsoring
    Purpose: Presentation of music and music-related performances of cultural value to the community, in the areas of classical music, jazz, dance, ethnic music, and others
    Management: Lawrence H. Passmore, Executive Director
    Officers: James A. Williamson, Jr., Chairman; Louise Dreisbach, Secretary; Patricia Moulton, Treasurer; Nicole Backenstoss, Artist Selection Chairman
    Utilizes: Guest Artists
    Budget: $50,000 - $100,000
    Income Sources: Private Foundations/Grants/Endowments; Box Office; Government Grants; Individual Donations
    Season: September - May
    Affiliations: Reading Musical Foundation
    Performance Facilities: Rajah Theatre; Albright Theatre

FACILITY

RAJAH THEATRE
136 North Sixth Street, Reading, PA 19601
(215) 375-0185
FAX: (215) 376-7821
   Type of Facility: Theatre Complex; Concert Hall; Auditorium; Theatre House
   Type of Stage: Proscenium   **Orchestra Pit**
   Seating Capacity: 2,040
   Year Remodeled: 1922
   Contact for Rental: Diane L. Lewis;   (215) 372-8936

Rose Valley

THEATRE

HEDGEROW THEATRE
64 West Rose Valley Road, Rose Valley, PA 19065
(215) 565-4211
   Founded: 1923
   Arts Area: Theatre Group
   Status: Professional; Non-Equity
   Type: Performing; Touring; Resident; Educational
   Purpose: To build an ensemble capable of presenting all types of theatre in repertory
   Management: Penelope Reed, Artistic Director; John Gallagher, General Manager; Gay Kuhn, Fiscal Director
   Officers: Patrick Horrigan, President; Janet Kelsey, Secretary/Treasurer
   Paid Staff: 15   **Volunteer Staff:** 70
   Paid Artists: 15   **Non-Paid Artists:** 70
   Utilizes: Special Technical Talent; Guest Artists; Guest Directors
   Budget: $100,000 - $500,000
   Income Sources: Private Foundations/Grants/Endowments; Business/Corporate Donations; Box Office; Government Grants; Individual Donations; Touring
   Season: 52 Weeks
   Performance Facilities: Hedgerow Theatre

Scranton

FACILITY

SCRANTON CULTURAL CENTER AT THE MASONIC TEMPLE
420 North Washington Avenue, Scranton, PA 18503
(717) 346-7369
FAX: (717) 346-7365
   Founded: 1927
   Type of Facility: Theatre Complex; Civic Center
   Type of Stage: Proscenium
   Stage Dimensions: 50'x31'
   Orchestra Pit
   Seating Capacity: 1,836
   Year Built: 1927   **Architect:** Raymond Hood   **Cost:** $3,000,000
   Contact for Rental: Colin Bissett;   (717) 346-7369
   Resident Groups: Northeastern Philharmonic Orchestra; Community Concerts; Broadway Theatre League

Slippery Rock

FACILITY

MILLER AUDITORIUM
Slippery Rock Unversity, Slippery Rock, PA 16057
(412) 738-2090
FAX: (412) 738-2098
   Founded: 1960
   Type of Facility: Auditorium
   Type of Stage: Proscenium
   Stage Dimensions: 65'x37' stage floor; 45'x13'9" proscenium opening
   Seating Capacity: 896

Year Built: 1960
Architect: Altenhof and Bown
Contact for Rental: Laurel Dagnon;   (412) 738-2027
Resident Groups: Slippery Rock University Department of Theatre

Somerset

PERFORMING SERIES

LAUREL ARTS, INC./THE PHILIP DRESSLER CENTER FOR THE ARTS
214 South Harrison Avenue, PO Box 414, Somerset, PA 15501-0414
(814) 443-2433
  Founded: 1975
  Arts Area: Dance; Vocal Music; Instrumental Music; Theater; Festivals; Multidisciplinary
  Status: Professional; Non-Profit
  Type: Performing; Touring; Resident; Educational; Sponsoring
  Purpose: To promote, exhibit and preserve multidisciplinary art; to foster the creative process of individuals and groups; to provide cultural diversity an accessibility to a broad scope of arts for people of all ages in Someset County
  Management: Robert B. Locklin Jr., Executive Director; Lori M. Troy, Office Manager; Carol L. Ogle, Public Relations Director; Stephanie Williams, Dance Administrator; Terri Klink, Financial Recordkeeper
  Officers: Lana Miller, President; Robert Spochart, Vice President; Bonne Gurzenda, Secretary; Eugene Hankinson, Treasurer; Dorothy Dressler, Director Emeritus
  Paid Staff: 7   **Volunteer Staff:** 300
  Paid Artists: 500
  Utilizes: Special Technical Talent; Guest Artists
  Budget: $100,000 - $500,000
  Income Sources: Private Foundations/Grants/Endowments; Business/Corporate Donations; Box Office; Government Grants; Individual Donations
  Season: 52 Weeks   **Annual Attendance:** 75,000

State College

DANCE

PENNSYLVANIA DANCE THEATRE
101 South Fraser Street, State College, PA 16801
(814) 237-2188
  Founded: 1979
  Arts Area: Modern
  Status: Professional; Non-Profit
  Type: Performing; Touring; Educational
  Purpose: To offer audiences an overview of the mainstream as well as the cutting edge in modern dance
  Management: Michael Casper, Managing Director; Annunciata Marino, Company Manager
  Officers: Ann Van Kuren, Artistic Director
  Paid Staff: 2   **Volunteer Staff:** 2
  Paid Artists: 8   **Non-Paid Artists:** 1
  Utilizes: Special Technical Talent; Guest Artists; Guest Choreographers
  Budget: $100,000 - $500,000
  Income Sources: Private Foundations/Grants/Endowments; Business/Corporate Donations; Box Office; Government Grants; Individual Donations
  Season: September - July

PERFORMING SERIES

CENTRAL PENNSYLVANIA FESTIVAL OF THE ARTS
PO Box 1023, State College, PA 16804
(814) 237-3682
FAX: (814) 237-0708
  Founded: 1967
  Arts Area: Festivals
  Status: Non-Profit
  Type: Performing
  Purpose: To produce an annual arts festival celebrating all the arts: performing, visual and literary
  Management: Philip L. Walz, Executive Director; Katherine Talcott, Assistant Director
  Officers: Linda J. Gall, President; Kenneth Thigpen, Vice President; Grace Pilato, Secretary; John Black, Treasurer
  Paid Staff: 2   **Volunteer Staff:** 200

Paid Artists: 200   Non-Paid Artists: 400
Utilizes: Guest Artists
Budget: $100,000 - $500,000
Income Sources: Business/Corporate Donations; Government Grants; Individual Donations
Season: July   Annual Attendance: 250,000
Affiliations: APAP

Swarthmore

PERFORMING SERIES

SWARTHMORE MUSIC AND DANCE FESTIVAL
Swarthmore College, Swarthmore, PA 19081
(215) 328-8239
Founded: 1982
Arts Area: Dance; Vocal Music; Instrumental Music; Festivals
Status: Professional; Non-Professional; Non-Profit
Type: Resident; Educational; Sponsoring
Purpose: To present and interrelate top quality music and dance events to a wide audience
Management: Allison Herz, Executive Director; James Freeman, Artistic Director; Sharon Friedler, Artistic Director; Judy Lord, Administrative Assistant
Paid Staff: 4   Volunteer Staff: 3
Paid Artists: 30   Non-Paid Artists: 15
Utilizes: Guest Conductors; Guest Artists
Budget: $50,000 - $100,000
Income Sources: Private Foundations/Grants/Endowments; Business/Corporate Donations; Box Office; Government Grants; Individual Donations; Advertising
Season: September - November   Annual Attendance: 6,000
Affiliations: Pennsylvania Presenters
Performance Facilities: Lang Hall; Pearson Hall Theatre

Uniontown

FACILITY

STATE THEATRE CENTER FOR THE ARTS
27 East Main Street, Uniontown, PA 15401
(412) 439-1360
Founded: 1989
Facility Originally: Vaudeville; Movie House
Type of Stage: Proscenium
Stage Dimensions: 36'6"x28'   Orchestra Pit
Seating Capacity: 1,650
Year Built: 1921
Architect: Lamb
Contact for Rental: Kelly Johnson;   (412) 439-1360

University Park

THEATRE

PENNSYLVANIA CENTRE STAGE
213 Arts Building, University Park, PA 16802
(814) 863-0255
Founded: 1985
Arts Area: Professional; Theatrical Group
Status: Professional
Type: Performing; Educational
Purpose: Professional regional theatre on the Pennsylvania State University campus
Management: Travis DeCastro, Producing Director
Paid Staff: 10
Paid Artists: 75

Utilizes: Special Technical Talent; Guest Artists; Guest Directors
Budget: $500,000 - $1,000,000
Income Sources: Private Foundations/Grants/Endowments; Business/Corporate Donations; Box Office;
Individual Donations
Season: June - October
Annual Attendance: 30,000
Affiliations: TCG; U/RTA; Theatre Association of Pennsylvania
Performance Facilities: Playhouse Theatre; Pavilion Theatre

FACILITY

PENNSYLVANIA STATE UNIVERSITY - EISENHOWER AUDITORIUM
University Park, PA 16802
(814) 863-0388
> **Type of Facility:** Concert Hall; Auditorium; Performance Center; Theatre House
> **Type of Stage:** Proscenium
> **Stage Dimensions:** 104'Wx52'D   **Orchestra Pit**
> **Seating Capacity:** 2,599
> **Year Built:** 1974   **Architect:** Sanders and Bicksler   **Cost:** $6,700,000
> **Acoustical Consultant:** Bolt, Beranek & Newman
> **Contact for Rental:** Lisa Faust;   (814) 863-0388
> **Resident Groups:** Center for the Performing Arts/Artist Series; University Performing Ensembles; Independent Presenters

PENNSYLVANIA STATE UNIVERSITY - PAVILION THEATRE
137 Arts Building, University Park, PA 16802
(814) 863-0381
FAX: (814) 863-7327
> **Type of Facility:** Theatre House
> **Facility Originally:** Livestock Judging Facility
> **Type of Stage:** 3/4 Arena; Arena
> **Stage Dimensions:** 20'x32'
> **Seating Capacity:** 5318
> **Year Built:** 1914   **Architect:** Day & Klauder   **Cost:** $76,152
> **Year Remodeled:** 1992   **Architect:** Peno & Associates   **Cost:** $1,500,000
> **Acoustical Consultant:** Bolt, Beranek & Newman
> **Manager:** Lee Byron;   (814) 863-0381
> **Resident Groups:** Penn State University Resident Theatre Company; Department of Theatre Arts;
> Pennsylvania Centre Stage

PENNSYLVANIA STATE UNIVERSITY - PLAYHOUSE THEATRE
137 Arts Building, University Park, PA 16802
(814) 863-0381
FAX: (814) 863-7327
> **Type of Facility:** Theatre House
> **Type of Stage:** Thrust; Proscenium
> **Stage Dimensions:** 90'x62'   **Orchestra Pit**
> **Seating Capacity:** 515
> **Year Built:** 1963   **Architect:** Eschbach Pullinger Stevens & Bruder   **Cost:** $1,835,030
> **Acoustical Consultant:** Bolt, Beranek & Newman
> **Manager:** Lee Byron;   (814) 863-0381
> **Resident Groups:** Penn State University Resident Theatre Company; Department of Theatre Arts;
> Pennsylvania Centre Stage

PENNSYLVANIA STATE UNIVERSITY - SCHWAB AUDITORIUM
University Park, PA 16802
(814) 863-0388
> **Type of Facility:** Concert Hall; Auditorium; Performance Center; Theatre House
> **Type of Stage:** Proscenium
> **Stage Dimensions:** 42'Wx20'D
> **Seating Capacity:** 972
> **Year Built:** 1902   **Cost:** $155,863
> **Year Remodeled:** 1978   **Architect:** Office of Physical Plant   **Cost:** $1,305,811
> **Acoustical Consultant:** Howard Kingsbury
> **Contact for Rental:** Lisa Faust;   (814) 863-0388
> **Resident Groups:** Center for the Performing Arts/Artist Series; University Performing Ensembles; Independent Presenters

Wilkes-Barre

DANCE

WILKES-BARRE BALLET THEATRE
102-104 South Main Street, Wilkes-Barre, PA 18701
(717) 824-8602
Arts Area: Modern; Ballet
Status: Professional; Non-Profit
Type: Resident
Management: Mary Hepner, Artistic Director
Paid Staff: 6
Paid Artists: 9 **Non-Paid Artists:** 3
Utilizes: Special Technical Talent; Guest Artists
Budget: $100,000 - $500,000
Income Sources: Private Foundations/Grants/Endowments; Business/Corporate Donations; Box Office;
Individual Donations
Season: October - June
Performance Facilities: F.M. Kirby Center for the Performing Arts

FACILITY

F.M. KIRBY CENTER FOR THE PERFORMING ARTS
71 Public Square, Wilkes-Barre, PA 18701
(717) 823-4599
FAX: (717) 823-4890
Founded: 1986
Type of Facility: Performance Center
Facility Originally: Movie House
Type of Stage: Proscenium
Stage Dimensions: 47'Wx26'6"D **Orchestra Pit**
Seating Capacity: 1,800
Year Built: 1938
Year Remodeled: 1986 **Architect:** Eugene Ogozolet; Pyros & Sanderson **Cost:** $3,500,000
Contact for Rental: Dennis Madden; (717) 823-4599
Resident Groups: Wilkes-Barre Ballet Theatre; Northeastern Philharmonic Orchestra
*Kirby Center, designated a National Historic Landmark, is a member theatre of the League of Historic
American Theatres.*

WILKES UNIVERSITY - DOROTHY DICKSON DARTE CENTER FOR THE PERFORMING ARTS
South Street, Wilkes-Barre, PA 18766
(717) 824-4651
Type of Facility: Theatre Complex; Concert Hall; Performance Center; Amphitheater
Type of Stage: Proscenium
Stage Dimensions: 30'x38' **Orchestra Pit**
Seating Capacity: 500
Year Built: 1965
Architect: Lacy Atherton & Davis **Cost:** $980,000
Contact for Rental: Bruce Phair; (717) 824-4651
Resident Groups: Wilkes University Department of Music, Theatre and Dance
Community cultural events

Wind Gap

VOCAL MUSIC

SINGING BOYS OF PENNSYLVANIA
PO Box 206, Wind Gap, PA 18091
(215) 759-6002
FAX: (215) 759-6042
Arts Area: Choral; Ethnic; Folk
Status: Non-Professional; Non-Profit
Type: Performing; Touring; Resident; Educational; Sponsoring
Purpose: To provide audiences with a wide spectrum of repertoire covering five centuries of classical, sacred
and secular music
Officers: Dr. K. Bernard Schade, Director
Paid Staff: 2 **Volunteer Staff:** 2

Non-Paid Artists: 26
Utilizes: Special Technical Talent; Guest Artists
Budget: $100,000 - $500,000
Income Sources: Private Foundations/Grants/Endowments; Business/Corporate Donations; Box Office; Government Grants; Individual Donations; Tuition
Season: 52 Weeks   **Annual Attendance:** 72,000

York

FACILITY

STRAND-CAPITOL PERFORMING ARTS CENTER - CAPITOL THEATRE
50 North George Street, York, PA 17401
(717) 846-1155
FAX: (717) 843-1208
   Type of Facility: Theatre House; Film & Lecture Hall
   Facility Originally: Vaudeville
   Type of Stage: Proscenium
   Seating Capacity: 718
   Year Built: 1917   **Architect:** Demp Wolf
   Year Remodeled: 1982   **Architect:** Hardy Holzman & Pfeiffer; Hamme Associates
   Contact for Rental: Clyde Lindsley;   (717) 846-1155
   Resident Groups: York Flicks (fine films)
   Stage being remodeled

STRAND-CAPITOL PERFORMING ARTS CENTER - STRAND THEATRE
50 North George Street, York, PA 17401
(717) 846-1155; (717) 846-1111
FAX: (717) 843-1208
   Type of Facility: Concert Hall; Theatre House; Opera House
   Facility Originally: Vaudeville
   Type of Stage: Proscenium
   Stage Dimensions: 61'Wx24'6"D; 37'4"Wx19'9"H proscenium opening   **Orchestra Pit**
   Seating Capacity: 1,214
   Year Built: 1925   **Architect:** Demp Wolf   **Cost:** $1,000,000
   Year Remodeled: 1980   **Architect:** Hardy Holzman & Pfeiffer   **Cost:** $1,600,000
   Contact for Rental: Clyde Lindsley;   (717) 846-1155
   Resident Groups: York Symphony Orchestra; Spring Garden Band; Performing Arts for Children; Dance A Story; Strand-Capitol Performing Arts Series

RHODE ISLAND

Barrington

DANCE

SHODA MOVING THEATRE (M.O.V.E. CO.)
110 Highland Anvenue, Barrington, RI 02806
(401) 245-6956
Founded: 1974
Arts Area: Modern; Mime; Movement Theatre
Status: Professional; Non-Profit
Type: Performing; Touring
Officers: Kelli Wicke Davis, Artistic Director
Paid Artists: 6
Budget: $1,000 - $50,000
Income Sources: Private Foundations/Grants/Endowments; Business/Corporate Donations; Box Office; Individual Donations

Bristol

PERFORMING SERIES

BLITHEWOLD GARDENS AND ARBORETUM "CONCERTS BY THE BAY"
101 Ferry Road, Route 114, Bristol, RI 02809-0716
(401) 253-2707
Founded: 1978
Arts Area: Vocal Music; Instrumental Music
Status: Non-Profit
Type: Performing
Purpose: To carry on the tradition of live musical performances in this gracious home along the shores of the Narragansett Bay
Management: Mark Zelonis, Executive Director; Harriet Linn, Special Events Coordinator; Joan Roth, Series Coordinator
Paid Staff: 2   **Volunteer Staff:** 5
Utilizes: Guest Artists
Budget: $1,000 - $50,000
Income Sources: Private Foundations/Grants/Endowments; Box Office
Season: June - September   **Annual Attendance:** 1,000

Kingston

FACILITY

UNIVERSITY OF RHODE ISLAND FINE ARTS CENTER
Kingston, RI 02881
(401) 792-5921
Type of Facility: Theatre Complex; Performance Center
Year Built: 1970   **Architect:** Lester Millman
Contact for Rental: Paula McGlasson;   (401) 792-2705
Resident Groups: University of Rhode Island Department of Theatre
University of Rhode Island Fine Arts Center contains J Studio and Robert E. Will Theatre. See separate listings for further information.

UNIVERSITY OF RHODE ISLAND FINE ARTS CENTER - J STUDIO
Kingston, RI 02881
(401) 792-5921
Type of Facility: Studio Performance; Environmental; Black Box
Type of Stage: Flexible; Environmental
Stage Dimensions: 66'Wx88'Dx32'H
Seating Capacity: 250
Year Built: 1970
Contact for Rental: Paula McGlasson;   (401) 792-2705

UNIVERSITY OF RHODE ISLAND FINE ARTS CENTER - ROBERT E. WILL THEATRE
Kingston, RI 02881
(401) 792-5921
FAX: (401) 792-5618
> **Type of Facility:** Theatre Complex; Concert Hall; Theatre House
> **Type of Stage:** Thrust; Proscenium
> **Stage Dimensions:** 50'Wx24'Hx45'D proscenium opening   **Orchestra Pit**
> **Seating Capacity:** 550
> **Year Built:** 1970
> **Year Remodeled:** 1992
> **Contact for Rental:** Paula McGlasson;   (401) 792-2705

Lincoln

DANCE

STATE BALLET OF RHODE ISLAND
Sherman Avenue, PO Box 155, Lincoln, RI 02865
(401) 334-2560
> **Founded:** 1960
> **Arts Area:** Ballet
> **Status:** Semi-Professional; Non-Profit
> **Type:** Performing; Touring; Resident; Educational
> **Purpose:** A training ground for future professional dancers as well as for future teachers and ballet lovers
> **Management:** Herci Marsden, Artistic Director; Ana Marsden Fox, General Manager
> **Officers:** Herci Marsden, Chairperson; Ana Mardsen Fox, Vice Chairperson/Treasurer; Marion Fattore, Recording Secretary
> **Paid Staff:** 2   **Volunteer Staff:** 50
> **Paid Artists:** 8   **Non-Paid Artists:** 50
> **Utilizes:** Special Technical Talent; Guest Artists; Guest Choreographers
> **Budget:** $1,000 - $50,000
> **Income Sources:** Private Foundations/Grants/Endowments; Business/Corporate Donations; Box Office; Individual Donations
> **Season:** 52 Weeks   **Annual Attendance:** 5,000
> **Performance Facilities:** Roberts Hall Theatre; Rhode Island College

Matunuck

THEATRE

THEATRE-BY-THE-SEA
364 Cards Pond Road, Matunuck, RI 02879
(401) 782-8587
FAX: (401) 783-9452
> **Founded:** 1933
> **Arts Area:** Professional; Summer Stock; Musical
> **Status:** Commercial
> **Type:** Performing; Resident
> **Purpose:** Summer theatre entertainment
> **Management:** Richard Ericson, Laura Harris, Lawrence Serre, Rolt Smith, Producers
> **Paid Staff:** 20
> **Paid Artists:** 40
> **Utilizes:** Special Technical Talent; Guest Conductors; Guest Artists; Guest Directors
> **Income Sources:** Box Office
> **Season:** June - September
> **Performance Facilities:** Theatre-by-the-Sea

Newport

DANCE

ISLAND MOVING COMPANY
3 Charles Street, Newport, RI 02840
(401) 847-4470
FAX: (401) 849-7718
> **Founded:** 1982

Arts Area: Modern; Ballet
Status: Professional; Non-Profit
Type: Performing; Touring; Resident; Educational
Purpose: To present new choreography; to educate a dance audience; to act as a training ground for dance
Management: Dominique Alfandre, Managing Director; Miki Ohlsen, Artistic Director
Officers: R. William Ohlsen, President; Jean Sanders, Treasurer; Teresa Ritter, Secretary
Paid Staff: 3   **Volunteer Staff:** 4
Paid Artists: 10   **Non-Paid Artists:** 2
Utilizes: Guest Artists; Guest Choreographers; Guest Musicians
Budget: $50,000 - $100,000
Income Sources: Private Foundations/Grants/Endowments; Business/Corporate Donations; Box Office; Government Grants; Individual Donations; Contracted Services
Season: October - August   **Annual Attendance:** 7,500
Affiliations: ACA
Performance Facilities: Rogers Auditorium; Bristol Community College; St. Georges School

THEATRE

THE RHODE ISLAND SHAKESPEARE THEATRE
PO Box 1126, Newport, RI 02840
(401) 849-7892
Founded: 1971
Arts Area: Theatrical Group
Status: Semi-Professional; Non-Profit
Type: Performing; Educational
Purpose: TRIST serves as a pre-professional training ground for those with community theater experience who wish to increase their skills by working with an artistic director with professional experience.
Management: Bob Colonna, Artistic Director; Maureen Collura, General Manager
Officers: Mardi Sayer, Board President; Jan Prager, Vice President; Gloria Dunn, Secretary; Rick Meffert, Treasurer
Paid Staff: 1
Utilizes: Guest Artists; Guest Directors
Budget: $50,000 - $100,000
Income Sources: Private Foundations/Grants/Endowments; Business/Corporate Donations; Box Office; Individual Donations
Season: January - August

PERFORMING SERIES

NEWPORT MUSIC FESTIVAL
PO Box 3300, Newport, RI 02840
(401) 846-1133
FAX: (401) 849-1857
Founded: 1969
Arts Area: Dance; Vocal Music; Instrumental Music; Festivals
Status: Non-Profit
Type: Performing; Sponsoring
Purpose: The world-renowned Newport Music Festival performs little-known music of the Romantic era and sponsors the North American debuts of international artists.
Management: Mark P. Malkovich, III, General Director
Officers: Herbert B. Swope Jr., President
Paid Staff: 5   **Volunteer Staff:** 150
Paid Artists: 60
Utilizes: Guest Artists
Budget: $500,000 - $1,000,000
Income Sources: Private Foundations/Grants/Endowments; Business/Corporate Donations; Box Office; Government Grants; Individual Donations
Season: July   **Annual Attendance:** 20,000
Performance Facilities: Fabled Mansions of Newport

North Providence

DANCE

FESTIVAL BALLET
5 Hennessey Avenue, North Providence, RI 02911
(401) 353-1129
Founded: 1977

Arts Area: Ballet
Status: Professional; Non-Profit
Type: Performing; Touring; Resident
Purpose: To present the best works from the classical and contemporary repertoire
Management: Christine Hennessy, Artistic Director
Officers: Joan Abrams, President; Kerry Altman, Vice President; Henry Barney, Treasurer; Gail Higgins Fogarty, Secretary
Paid Staff: 2 **Volunteer Staff:** 5
Paid Artists: 8 **Non-Paid Artists:** 20
Utilizes: Special Technical Talent; Guest Artists; Guest Directors
Budget: $100,000 - $500,000
Income Sources: Private Foundations/Grants/Endowments; Business/Corporate Donations; Box Office; Government Grants; Individual Donations
Season: September - May **Annual Attendance:** 25,000
Performance Facilities: Providence Performing Arts Center

Pascoag

DANCE

AMERICAN BALLET
86 Main Street, Pascoag, RI 02859
(401) 568-0015; (401) 568-1680
Founded: 1984
Arts Area: Ballet
Status: Semi-Professional; Non-Profit
Type: Performing; Touring; Educational
Purpose: Non-profit educational and performance institution devoted to the highest standard in the art of classical ballet
Management: Patricia A. Christiansen, Artistic Director
Paid Staff: 4 **Volunteer Staff:** 6
Paid Artists: 10 **Non-Paid Artists:** 20
Utilizes: Special Technical Talent; Guest Artists
Budget: $50,000 - $100,000
Income Sources: Private Foundations/Grants/Endowments; Business/Corporate Donations; Box Office; Government Grants; Individual Donations
Season: September - August **Annual Attendance:** 4,000
Affiliations: NARB
Performance Facilities: Assembly Theatre

Providence

INSTRUMENTAL MUSIC

RHODE ISLAND PHILHARMONIC ORCHESTRA
222 Richmond Street, Providence, RI 02903
(401) 831-3123
Founded: 1945
Arts Area: Symphony
Status: Professional; Non-Profit
Type: Performing; Resident; Educational
Management: Karen R. Dobbs, Executive Director
Paid Staff: 6
Paid Artists: 80
Utilizes: Guest Conductors; Guest Artists
Budget: $1,000,000 - $5,000,000
Income Sources: Private Foundations/Grants/Endowments; Business/Corporate Donations; Box Office; Government Grants; Individual Donations
Season: October - May **Annual Attendance:** 150,000
Performance Facilities: Veterans Memorial Auditorium

YOUNG PEOPLES SYMPHONY OF RHODE ISLAND
131 Washington Street, Providence, RI 02903
(401) 421-0460
Founded: 1970
Arts Area: Symphony; Orchestra; Chamber
Status: Non-Profit
Type: Performing; Educational

Purpose: To provide music study and performance opportunity for all talented youngsters from an early age through college
Management: Dr. Joseph Conte, Music Director; Rose Tragar, Manager
Officers: Joseph Puleo, President
Paid Staff: 10   **Volunteer Staff:** 25
Utilizes: Guest Conductors; Guest Artists
Budget: $1,000 - $50,000
Income Sources: Private Foundations/Grants/Endowments; Business/Corporate Donations; Box Office; Individual Donations
Season: September - June   **Annual Attendance:** 5,000
Performance Facilities: Veterans Memorial Auditorium

VOCAL MUSIC

RHODE ISLAND CIVIC CHORALE AND ORCHESTRA
334 Westminster Mall, Room #300, Providence, RI 02903
(401) 521-5670
Founded: 1958
Arts Area: Choral; Chamber
Status: Non-Profit
Type: Performing
Purpose: To present choral music at concerts and public performances; to promote musical concerts; to perform all other acts necessary and incidental to the maintenance, furtherance and encouragement of the musical and artistic knowledge, spirit and appreciation of the community
Management: Diana Cerwonka, Manager; Edward Markward, Music Director
Officers: Chester S. Labedz Jr., President; Roberta Padula, First Vice President; Margaret Gidley, Second Vice President; Herman Eschentacher, Third Vice President; David T. Riedel, Secretary; Walter Hope Jr., Treasurer; Joseph A. Goldkamp, Assistant Treasurer
Paid Staff: 2   **Volunteer Staff:** 130
Paid Artists: 45   **Non-Paid Artists:** 70
Utilizes: Guest Conductors; Guest Artists; Guest Directors
Budget: $50,000 - $100,000
Income Sources: Private Foundations/Grants/Endowments; Business/Corporate Donations; Box Office; Government Grants; Individual Donations
Season: September - May   **Annual Attendance:** 1,200
Performance Facilities: Veterans Memorial Auditorium; Grace Church

THEATRE

ALIAS STAGE
120 Manton Avenue, Providence, RI 02909
(401) 831-2919
Founded: 1984
Arts Area: Professional
Status: Semi-Professional; Non-Profit
Type: Performing
Purpose: To develop new works which focus on a true expression of the world in which we live
Officers: Kate Stone, Chairperson; George Marcincavage, President; Daniel Welch, Treasurer; Steve Sookikian; Dan Devine, Ann Powers, Lucinda Powers, Board Members
Volunteer Staff: 26
Paid Artists: 30
Utilizes: Guest Artists; Guest Directors
Budget: $1,000 - $50,000
Income Sources: Business/Corporate Donations; Box Office; Fund-raising
Season: 52 Weeks   **Annual Attendance:** 2,500
Performance Facilities: Building 1-A

BRIGHT LIGHTS THEATRE COMPANY
PO Box 3277, Providence, RI 02906
(401) 273-8982
FAX: (401) 273-8987
Founded: 1983
Arts Area: Theatrical Group
Status: Non-Profit
Type: Performing
Purpose: To present little-known works, classics and new plays while remaining an "open-shop" for artists in Rhode Island
Management: Elaine Raka, Artistic Director
Volunteer Staff: 20
Non-Paid Artists: 20

Utilizes: Guest Artists; Guest Directors
Budget: $1,000 - $50,000
Income Sources: Box Office; Government Grants; Individual Donations
Annual Attendance: 5,000

BROWN UNIVERSITY THEATRE
77 Waterman Street, Providence, RI 02912
(401) 863-2838
Founded: 1901
Arts Area: Summer Stock; Theatrical Group
Status: Non-Professional; Non-Profit
Type: Performing; Resident; Educational; Sponsoring
Purpose: To provide a balanced theatrical season (academic year and summer) for the university community and the Providence community, and to provide training for students
Management: John R. Lucas, Managing Director; John Emigh, Chairman
Paid Staff: 4
Non-Paid Artists: 200
Utilizes: Guest Directors
Budget: $1,000 - $50,000
Income Sources: Private Foundations/Grants/Endowments; Business/Corporate Donations; Box Office
Season: September - August **Annual Attendance:** 20,000
Performance Facilities: Faunce House Theatre; Leeds Theatre

LOOKING GLASS THEATRE
50 Orchard Avenue, Providence, RI 02906
(401) 331-9080
Founded: 1965
Arts Area: Professional
Status: Professional; Non-Profit
Type: Touring; Educational; Sponsoring
Purpose: Looking Glass Theatre strives to enlighten and educate children and their families through audience participation, theater and follow-up workshops. LGT presents four new productions annually focusing on the classics and topical issues.
Management: Pat Clark, Managing Director; Diane Postoian, Artistic Director
Paid Staff: 3 **Volunteer Staff:** 25
Paid Artists: 30
Utilizes: Guest Artists; Guest Directors
Budget: $50,000 - $100,000
Income Sources: Private Foundations/Grants/Endowments; Business/Corporate Donations; Box Office; Government Grants; Individual Donations
Season: September - June **Annual Attendance:** 50,000
Affiliations: TCG
Performance Facilities: Looking Glass Theatre

NEWGATE THEATER
134 Mathewson Street, Providence, RI 02903
(401) 421-9680
Founded: 1982
Status: Semi-Professional; Non-Profit
Type: Performing; Resident; Producing
Purpose: To create a theatrical community of social substance, important ideas and significant language; to produce theatre of visual beauty and power with a sense of excitement and spiritual renewal
Management: Alan Hawkridge, Artistic Director; Crista Crewdson, General Manager
Paid Staff: 1 **Volunteer Staff:** 25
Paid Artists: 22
Utilizes: Guest Artists; Guest Directors
Budget: $50,000 - $100,000
Income Sources: Box Office; Government Grants; Individual Donations
Season: September - June **Annual Attendance:** 2,000
Affiliations: NETC

RITES AND REASON
Brown University, PO Box 1148, Providence, RI 02912
(401) 863-3558
Founded: 1970
Arts Area: Professional; Theatrical Group
Status: Professional; Non-Profit

Type: Performing; Touring; Resident; Educational
Purpose: Rites and Reasons is a developmental research theatre dedicated to producing new plays that celebrate and explore Afro-American history and culture.
Management: Elmo Terry-Morgan, Artistic Director; Karen Baxter, Managing Director; Rhett Jones, Research Director; Donna Mitchell, Administrative Director
Paid Staff: 5
Utilizes: Guest Artists; Guest Directors
Budget: $500,000 - $1,000,000
Income Sources: Private Foundations/Grants/Endowments; Box Office; Government Grants; Individual Donations
Season: February - May
Affiliations: AEA; U/RTA
Performance Facilities: Churchill House

TRINITY REPERTORY COMPANY
201 Washington Street, Providence, RI 02903
(401) 521-1100
Founded: 1964
Arts Area: Professional; Theatrical Group
Status: Professional; Non-Profit
Type: Performing; Touring; Educational
Purpose: To provide theatrical performances and educational services to Rhode Island and nearby New England audiences
Management: Richard Jenkins, Artistic Director; Dennis Conway, General Manager; Pamela Messore, Audience Development Director; Neal Baron, Assistant to Richard Jenkins; Kibbe Reilly, Director of Development
Officers: Sally T. Dowling, Chairman; Edward P. Grace, III, Vice Chairman; John M. Harpootian, Secretary; Harry A. Schult, Treasurer
Paid Staff: 50   **Volunteer Staff:** 600
Paid Artists: 50
Utilizes: Guest Artists; Guest Directors
Budget: $1,000,000 - $5,000,000
Income Sources: Private Foundations/Grants/Endowments; Business/Corporate Donations; Box Office; Government Grants; Individual Donations
Season: 52 Weeks   **Annual Attendance:** 170,000
Affiliations: LORT   **Performance Facilities:** Trinity Repertory Company

PERFORMING SERIES

FIRST NIGHT PROVIDENCE
c/o Shanon Tise Stormer & Assoc., 10 Donnace Street, Suite 1205, Providence, RI 02903
(401) 521-1166
FAX: (401) 273-5630
Arts Area: Dance; Vocal Music; Instrumental Music; Theater; Festivals
Status: Non-Profit
Type: Performing; Educational; Sponsoring
Management: Shanon Stormer, Director; Doris Stephens, Community Relations; Carolyn Ticil, Associate Director; Jan Matthews, Administrative Director
Paid Staff: 4   **Volunteer Staff:** 8
Paid Artists: 200
Budget: $100,000 - $500,000
Income Sources: Private Foundations/Grants/Endowments; Business/Corporate Donations; Box Office; Government Grants; Individual Donations
Season: New Years Eve   **Annual Attendance:** 50,000

PERFORMING ARTS ASSOCIATION
338 Rochambeau Avenue, Providence, RI 02906
(401) 331-0061
FAX: (401) 751-3227
Founded: 1954
Arts Area: Dance; Theater
Status: Professional; Non-Profit
Type: Sponsoring
Purpose: To present professional concerts
Management: Board of Directors
Officers: Mrs. Frederic W. Schwartz, President
Volunteer Staff: 5
Utilizes: Guest Artists
Income Sources: Box Office

Season: October - May
Performance Facilities: Veterans Memorial Auditorium: Providence Civic Center

FACILITY

PROVIDENCE CIVIC CENTER
One LaSalle Square, Providence, RI 02903
(401) 331-0700
Type of Facility: Civic Center
Seating Capacity: 13,000
Year Built: 1971 **Architect:** Ellerbe Architects **Cost:** $13,000,000
Contact for Rental: Stephen M. Lombardi, Executive Director; (401) 331-0700

PROVIDENCE PERFORMING ARTS CENTER
220 Weybosset Street, Providence, RI 02903
(401) 421-2997
Type of Facility: Concert Hall; Performance Center; Theatre House; Opera House
Type of Stage: Proscenium
Stage Dimensions: 86'Wx28'6"D(left); 31'6"D(right); 52'Wx33'6"H proscenium opening **Orchestra Pit**
Seating Capacity: 3,198
Year Built: 1928 **Architect:** Rapp & Rapp **Cost:** $2,500,000
Acoustical Consultant: P.M.A. Engineering
Contact for Rental: Norbertt Mongeon; (401) 421-2997
Manager: Alan Chille
Resident Groups: Rhode Island Philharmonic Orchestra; Festival Ballet

TRINITY ARTS CENTER
55 Locust Street, Providence, RI 02906
(401) 751-6480
Type of Facility: Auditorium
Facility Originally: Church; School
Type of Stage: Proscenium
Stage Dimensions: 35'Wx22'D **Orchestra Pit**
Seating Capacity: 400

VETERANS MEMORIAL AUDITORIUM
Brownell Street and Park Streets, Providence, RI 02903
(401) 277-1467; (401) 277-3150
FAX: (401) 277-1466
Mailing Address: PO Box 28345, Providence, RI 02908
Founded: 1950
Type of Facility: Concert Hall
Type of Stage: Proscenium
Stage Dimensions: 85'Wx40'D **Orchestra Pit**
Seating Capacity: 2,118
Year Built: 1928 **Architect:** Osgood & Osgood **Cost:** $1,800,000
Year Remodeled: 1990 **Architect:** Robert Haig Associates **Cost:** $5,500,000
Acoustical Consultant: Chris Blair
Contact for Rental: Jack Lafond, Director; (401) 277-1467
Resident Groups: Rhode Island Philharmonic Orchestra

Warwick

THEATRE

WARWICK PLAYERS
PO Box 545, Warwick, RI 02889
(401) 738-2000, ext. 372
Founded: 1974
Arts Area: Theatrical Group
Status: Non-Professional; Non-Profit
Type: Performing
Purpose: To provide the community with quality comedies, dramas and musicals
Officers: Armand Leroux, Vice President; Maria Toxi, Recording Secretary; Patricia Renaud, Correspondence Secretary; Diana Addessi, Treasurer
Paid Staff: 1
Budget: $1,000 - $50,000
Income Sources: Private Foundations/Grants/Endowments; Business/Corporate Donations; Box Office

Season: October - May   **Annual Attendance:** 1,500
Affiliations: Warwick Consortium For The Arts and Humanities; AACT, Rhode Island
Performance Facilities: Warwick City Hall

Westerly

VOCAL MUSIC

CHORUS OF WESTERLY
16 High Street, PO Box 132, Westerly, RI 02891
(401) 596-8663
Founded: 1959
Arts Area: Choral
Status: Non-Professional; Non-Profit
Type: Performing; Educational; Sponsoring
Purpose: To present fine choral and orchestral music; to promote interest in choral singing and choral music appreciation
Management: Susan Bosworth, Manager
Officers: Dr. Douglas Rayner, President; Jill Blanchette, Katie Utter and Jane Gencarelli, Vice Presidents; Bailey Blandette, Treasurer; Dr. Nora Spens, Recording Secretary; Anne Utter, Cooresponding Secretary
Paid Staff: 2   **Volunteer Staff:** 10
Paid Artists: 101   **Non-Paid Artists:** 180
Utilizes: Special Technical Talent; Guest Artists; Guest Directors
Budget: $100,000 - $500,000
Income Sources: Private Foundations/Grants/Endowments; Business/Corporate Donations; Box Office; Government Grants; Individual Donations; Fundraising Events
Season: November - June   **Annual Attendance:** 36,000
Affiliations: CA
Performance Facilities: Chorus of Westerly Performance Hall

SOUTH CAROLINA

Abbeville

FACILITY

THE ABBEVILLE OPERA HOUSE
Court Square, PO Box 247, Abbeville, SC 29620
(803) 459-2157
FAX: (803) 459-9266
 Founded: 1908
 Type of Facility: Theatre House; Opera House
 Type of Stage: Proscenium **Orchestra Pit**
 Seating Capacity: 300
 Year Built: 1908
 Year Remodeled: 1968
 Contact for Rental: Kathy Genevie; (803) 459-2157
 Manager: Michael Genevie; (803) 459-5338
 Resident Groups: Summer Stock

Aiken

DANCE

AIKEN CIVIC BALLET COMPANY
142 Greenville Street, Aiken, SC 29801
(803) 648-5771
 Founded: 1972
 Arts Area: Modern; Ballet; Jazz
 Status: Semi-Professional; Non-Professional; Non-Profit
 Type: Touring; Resident; Educational
 Purpose: To further dance in the immediate area
 Management: Carl Crosby, Artistic Director
 Officers: Mary Lou Wallace, President; Mary Jo Wilson, Secretary; Helen Kelly, Costume Chairman
 Volunteer Staff: 12
 Paid Artists: 3
 Utilizes: Guest Artists; Guest Directors; Guest Choreographers
 Budget: $1,000 - $50,000
 Income Sources: Box Office; Individual Donations
 Season: September - May **Annual Attendance:** 500
 Performance Facilities: Etherredge Center, University of South Carolina

THEATRE

AIKEN COMMUNITY PLAYHOUSE
PO Box 125, Aiken, SC 29802
(803) 648-1438
 Founded: 1953
 Arts Area: Community
 Status: Non-Profit
 Type: Performing
 Purpose: To allow people of the community to act in and produce plays of the legitimate theatre and to encourage public appreciation of the theatre arts
 Management: Board of Directors
 Officers: David Howard, President; Marcia Harris, First Vice President; Elaine Schmidt, Second Vice President
 Budget: $1,000 - $50,000
 Income Sources: Business/Corporate Donations; Box Office; Individual Donations
 Season: 52 Weeks **Annual Attendance:** 3,500
 Affiliations: South Carolina Theatre Association
 Performance Facilities: Aiken Community Playhouse

FACILITY

ETHERREDGE CENTER - UNIVERSITY OF SOUTH CAROLINA AT AIKEN
171 University Parkway, Aiken, SC 29803
(803) 641-3328
    Founded: 1986
    Type of Facility: Theatre Complex; Concert Hall; Auditorium; Studio Performance; Performance Center; Multi-Purpose
    Type of Stage: Thrust; Proscenium
    Stage Dimensions: 38'x24'   **Orchestra Pit**
    Seating Capacity: 687
    Year Built: 1985   **Architect:** Alexander Moorman   **Cost:** $3,000,000
    Acoustical Consultant: George Izenhaur
    Contact for Rental: Marti Costantino; (803) 641-3328
    Resident Groups: University of South Carolina, Aiken: Players; Band; Choral Society; Faculty

Anderson

THEATRE

THE SOUTH CAROLINA THEATRE COMPANY
PO Box 331, Anderson, SC 29622-0331
(803) 224-7648
    Founded: 1965
    Arts Area: Professional; Theatrical Group
    Status: Professional
    Type: Performing; Touring; Resident; Educational
    Purpose: To provide continued employment for actors; to bring Shakespeare and classics to students at colleges, universities and high schools in 30 states
    Management: Milton A. Dickson, Producer/Director; A. Alexander, Casting Director/New York, NY
    Paid Staff: 2
    Paid Artists: 43
    Utilizes: Guest Artists
    Budget: $100,000 - $500,000
    Income Sources: Box Office
    Season: 52 Weeks
    Performance Facilities: Play Box Theatre

Beaufort

PERFORMING SERIES

THE BYRNE MILLER DANCE THEATRE, INC.
2400 Wilson Drive, PO Box 1667, Beaufort, SC 29901
(803) 524-9148
    Founded: 1971
    Arts Area: Dance; Mime; Movement Theatre
    Status: Professional; Non-Profit
    Type: Educational; Sponsoring
    Purpose: To present a wide variety of excellent dance and related movement, both to our concert audience and to students in our schools
    Management: Byrne Miller, Director; Mary Whisonant, Assistant Director
    Officers: Lillian Nilsson, President; William Cochrane, Vice President; Byrne Miller, Secretary; David Harper, Treasurer
    Volunteer Staff: 15
    Paid Artists: 4
    Utilizes: Special Technical Talent; Guest Artists
    Budget: $1,000 - $50,000
    Income Sources: Private Foundations/Grants/Endowments; Business/Corporate Donations; Box Office; Government Grants; Individual Donations; Fundraising
    Season: October - May   **Annual Attendance:** 3,500
    Affiliations: APAP
    Performance Facilities: Lasseter Theatre; Marine Corps Air Station

FACILITY

UNIVERSITY OF SOUTH CAROLINA BEAUFORT ARTS CENTER
800 Carteret, Beaufort, SC 29902
(803) 521-4156
FAX: (803) 521-4199; (803) 521-4198
  Facility Originally: School
  Type of Stage: Proscenium
  Seating Capacity: 472
  Year Remodeled: 1991   **Architect:** Denziger
  Contact for Rental: John P. Blair Jr.;   (803) 521-4156
  Resident Groups: Rafael Sabatini Players; Beaufort Little Theatre; Beaufort Chamber Orchestra

Charleston

DANCE

THE CHARLESTON BALLET
354 1/2 King Street, PO Box 262, Charleston, SC 29401
(803) 722-8779
  Founded: 1959
  Arts Area: Modern; Ballet; Jazz
  Status: Professional; Non-Profit
  Type: Performing; Touring; Educational; Sponsoring
  Purpose: To present dance of the highest quality to the Charleston Area and to provide training and performance opportunities for talented area dancers
  Management: Don and Patricia Cantwell, Artistic Directors; Jill Eathorne Bahr, Resident Choreographer; Kim Brantingham, Company Manager
  Officers: Courtney Quattlebaum, President; Linda Helmly, Vice President; Andrea Crappa-Hurley, Treasurer; Bradford Marshall, Secretary
  Paid Staff: 4   **Volunteer Staff:** 25
  Paid Artists: 18   **Non-Paid Artists:** 10
  Utilizes: Guest Artists; Guest Choreographers
  Budget: $100,000 - $500,000
  Income Sources: Private Foundations/Grants/Endowments; Business/Corporate Donations; Box Office; Government Grants; Individual Donations
  Season: September - June   **Annual Attendance:** 25,000
  Affiliations: NARB; SERBA
  Performance Facilities: Gaillard Municipal Auditorium

ROBERT IVEY BALLET
1632 Ashley Hall Road, Charleston, SC 29407
(803) 556-1343
  Founded: 1977
  Arts Area: Modern; Ballet; Jazz; Guest Choreographers
  Status: Semi-Professional; Non-Profit
  Type: Resident
  Management: Robert Ivey, Artistic Director
  Officers: Sandra Cook, Assistant to Director; Nancy Barnwell, President of Board
  Non-Paid Artists: 30
  Utilizes: Guest Artists; Guest Choreographers
  Budget: $50,000 - $100,000
  Income Sources: Private Foundations/Grants/Endowments; Business/Corporate Donations; Box Office; Government Grants; Individual Donations
  Season: September - May   **Annual Attendance:** 20,000
  Affiliations: College of Charleston
  Performance Facilities: Emmett Robinson Theatre; School of the Arts; College of Charleston

INSTRUMENTAL MUSIC

CHARLESTON SYMPHONY ORCHESTRA
14 George Street, Charleston, SC 29401
(803) 723-7528
FAX: (803) 722-3463
  Founded: 1936
  Arts Area: Symphony; Orchestra; Chamber; Ensemble
  Status: Professional; Non-Profit

Type: Performing; Touring; Resident; Educational
Purpose: To provide quality musical performances to the citizens of our state and to educate children using smaller orchestra and ensembles
Management: Darrell G. Edwards, Executive Director; David Stahl, Music Director/Conductor
Officers: Marianne P. Mead, President; Burton Schools, Vice President of Development; Edward H. Sparkman, Treasurer; Laura Hewitt, Secretary
Paid Staff: 7   **Volunteer Staff:** 20
Paid Artists: 89
Utilizes: Guest Conductors; Guest Artists
Budget: $1,000,000 - $5,000,000
Income Sources: Private Foundations/Grants/Endowments; Business/Corporate Donations; Box Office; Government Grants; Individual Donations
Season: September - May   **Annual Attendance:** 30,000
Affiliations: Charleston Symphony League; Singers Guild
Performance Facilities: Gaillard Municipal Auditorium

THEATRE

FOOTLIGHT PLAYERS
20 Queen Street, PO Box 62, Charleston, SC 29402
(803) 722-7521
Founded: 1931
Arts Area: Musical; Community; Theatrical Group
Status: Non-Professional; Non-Profit
Type: Performing; Resident
Purpose: As a community theatre, to produce plays, to be a means of self-expression for the community through amateur theatre, and to hold classes in drama and allied subjects
Management: Mrs. Kit Lyons, General Manager; Richard Heffner, Designer/Technical Director; Dorothy D'Anna, Artistic Director
Officers: Vic Brandt, President; Dr. A. Bert Pruitt, First Vice President; Edward DiResta, Second Vice President; Ms. Suzanne Kaiser, Secretary; Mr. Hasell Barton, Treasurer
Paid Staff: 2   **Volunteer Staff:** 150
Non-Paid Artists: 100
Utilizes: Guest Directors
Budget: $100,000 - $500,000
Income Sources: Private Foundations/Grants/Endowments; Business/Corporate Donations; Box Office; Government Grants; Individual Donations
Season: September - May   **Annual Attendance:** 12,000
Affiliations: South Carolina Theatre Association; Charleston Area Arts Council; Southeastern Theatre Conference; American Association of Community Theatres
Performance Facilities: Footlight Players Theatre

PERFORMING SERIES

SPOLETO FESTIVAL USA
PO Box 157, Charleston, SC 29402
(803) 722-2764
Founded: 1976
Arts Area: Dance; Vocal Music; Instrumental Music; Theater; Festivals; Lyric Opera; Grand Opera
Status: Professional; Semi-Professional; Non-Profit
Type: Performing; Educational; Sponsoring
Purpose: The Festival presents opera, dance, theater, symphonic and chamber music, jazz and visual arts exhibits of the highest quality. It also serves as an educational environment for young artists and arts administrators.
Management: Gian Carlo Menotti, Artistic Director; Marcus L. Overton, Executive Director; Carmen Kovens, Director of Operations; Betty Kunreuther, Director of Finance; Constance M. Baldwin, Acting Director of Development
Officers: Homer C. Burrows, Chairman; Giancarla Berti, President; Charles S. Way, Chairman Emeritus
Paid Staff: 16   **Volunteer Staff:** 300
Paid Artists: 350
Utilizes: Special Technical Talent; Guest Conductors; Guest Artists; Guest Directors
Budget: $1,000,000 - $5,000,000
Income Sources: Private Foundations/Grants/Endowments; Business/Corporate Donations; Box Office; Government Grants; Individual Donations
Season: May - June
Annual Attendance: 80,000
Affiliations: OA; Dance USA; TCG; NIMT; AAA
Performance Facilities: Gaillard Municipal Auditorium; Dock Street Theater; Garden Theater

FACILITY

DOCK STREET THEATRE
135 Church Street, Charleston, SC 29401
(803) 720-3968
    Type of Facility: Theatre House
    Facility Originally: Hotel & Meeting Rooms
    Type of Stage: Proscenium
    Stage Dimensions: 33'8"Wx33'3"D; 33'8"Wx17'6"H proscenium opening   **Orchestra Pit**
    Seating Capacity: 463
    Year Built: 1736
    Year Remodeled: 1937 **Architect:** Albert Simons **Cost:** $400,000
    Contact for Rental: Lorraine Adrahamfon, Curator; (803) 724-7308
    Resident Groups: Spoleto Festival USA; Charleston Symphony; Events, Inc.; Amazing Stage; Moja Arts Festival; Department of Special Facilities, Charleston; Piccolo Spoleto Festival; Sherry Grace Productions; Charleston Theatre Works; Chopstick Theatre; Professional Theatre
    The original 1736 structure is no longer standing. Using various documentation, a conjectural reconstruction was completed in 1937.

FOOTLIGHT PLAYERS THEATRE
20 Queen Street, PO Box 62, Charleston, SC 29401
(803) 722-7521
    Founded: 1931
    Type of Facility: Theatre House
    Facility Originally: Warehouse
    Type of Stage: Proscenium
    Stage Dimensions: 40'Wx33'D
    Seating Capacity: 285
    Year Built: 1840
    Year Remodeled: 1941
    Contact for Rental: Kit Lyons, General Manager; (803) 722-7521
    Resident Groups: Footlight Players

GAILLARD MUNICIPAL AUDITORIUM
77 Calhoun Street, Charleston, SC 29403
(803) 577-7400
    Type of Facility: Theatre Complex; Concert Hall; Auditorium; Multi-Purpose
    Type of Stage: Proscenium
    Stage Dimensions: 80'Wx50'Dx65'H **Orchestra Pit**
    Seating Capacity: 2,734
    Year Built: 1968 **Architect:** Lucas & Stubbs **Cost:** $6,000,000
    Contact for Rental: Cam Patterson; (803) 577-7400

Columbia

DANCE

COLUMBIA CITY BALLET
PO Box 11898, Columbia, SC 29211
(803) 799-7605
FAX: (803) 799-7928
    Founded: 1960
    Arts Area: Ballet
    Status: Semi-Professional; Non-Profit
    Type: Performing; Touring; Resident; Educational
    Purpose: To present the art of dance to Columbia and its surrounding communities; to contribute to the cultural and educational lives of audiences, dancers, and students
    Management: William Starrett, Artistic Director
    Officers: Lyles Glenn, President; Bill Timmerman, Treasurer; Karen Schulze, Secretary
    Paid Staff: 5
    Paid Artists: 12 **Non-Paid Artists:** 35
    Utilizes: Special Technical Talent; Guest Artists; Guest Choreographers; Guest Instructors
    Budget: $100,000 - $500,000
    Income Sources: Private Foundations/Grants/Endowments; Business/Corporate Donations; Box Office; Government Grants; Individual Donations
    Season: September - April **Annual Attendance:** 35,000
    Performance Facilities: Koger Center for the Arts

INSTRUMENTAL MUSIC

COLUMBIA YOUTH ORCHESTRA
PO Box 5703, Columbia, SC 29250
(803) 771-7937
> **Arts Area:** Symphony; Orchestra
> **Status:** Non-Professional; Non-Profit
> **Type:** Performing; Educational
> **Management:** Judith Lawrence, General Manager; Robert Kemsley, Resident Conductor
> **Paid Staff:** 2 **Volunteer Staff:** 50
> **Non-Paid Artists:** 100
> **Season:** September - April **Annual Attendance:** 2,000
> **Affiliations:** ASOL(Youth Orchestra Division); South Carolina Philharmonic
> **Performance Facilities:** Booker T. Washington Hall; Frazier Hall, University of South Carolina

SOUTH CAROLINA PHILHARMONIC AND CHAMBER ORCHESTRAS
PO Box 5703, Columbia, SC 29250
(803) 771-7937
> **Founded:** 1964
> **Arts Area:** Symphony; Orchestra; Chamber
> **Status:** Professional; Non-Profit
> **Type:** Performing; Touring; Educational; Sponsoring
> **Purpose:** To present symphony orchestra performances; sponsOr educational programs
> **Management:** Mark Huber, Executive Director; Catherine Comet, Artistic Advisor
> **Officers:** Frank Brown, President
> **Paid Staff:** 9 **Volunteer Staff:** 200
> **Paid Artists:** 90
> **Utilizes:** Special Technical Talent; Guest Conductors; Guest Artists
> **Budget:** $500,000 - $1,000,000
> **Income Sources:** Private Foundations/Grants/Endowments; Business/Corporate Donations; Box Office; Government Grants; Individual Donations
> **Season:** November - April **Annual Attendance:** 15,000
> **Affiliations:** ASOL
> **Performance Facilities:** Richland Township Auditorium; Keenan Theatre; Koger Center

THEATRE

COLUMBIA STAGE SOCIETY AT TOWN THEATRE
1012 Sumter Street, Columbia, SC 29201
(803) 799-2510
> **Founded:** 1919
> **Arts Area:** Community; Theatrical Group
> **Status:** Non-Professional; Non-Profit
> **Type:** Performing; Educational
> **Purpose:** The advancement in the community, both city and state, of the experimental arts of the little theatre, including spoken drama, pantomime, music, musical drama, and promotion of such literary and artistic objects as will foster and develop the cultural aspects of our community life
> **Management:** W. J. Arvay, Manager; Emmalee E. Robbins, Director; John W.K. Young, Technical Director; Ann B. Fogle, Assistant Manager
> **Officers:** Robert R. Russell Jr., President; E. Warner Wells, Vice President; Thomas P. Monahan, Treasurer; David M. Dunlap, Secretary
> **Paid Staff:** 4 **Volunteer Staff:** 500
> **Utilizes:** Guest Conductors; Guest Artists
> **Budget:** $100,000 - $500,000
> **Income Sources:** Private Foundations/Grants/Endowments; Business/Corporate Donations; Box Office; Government Grants; Individual Donations
> **Season:** August - June **Annual Attendance:** 26,000
> **Affiliations:** South Carolina Theatre Association
> **Performance Facilities:** The Town Theatre

TRUSTUS
529 Lady Street, PO Box 11721, Columbia, SC 29211
(803) 254-9732
> **Founded:** 1985
> **Arts Area:** Professional
> **Status:** Professional; Non-Profit
> **Type:** Performing; Resident; Educational
> **Purpose:** To bring to the area a professional theatre dedicated to new works, plays of literary and artistic merit, and quality mainstream theatre in an environment that allows us to reach a broad spectrum of patrons

Management: Jim Thigpen, Artistic Director; Kay Thigpen, Producing Director; Steve Levine, Box Office Manager; Brian Riley, Technical Director
Officers: Robert Howard, President; Len Marini, Vice President; Sam Wilkins, Secretary; Kay Thigpen, Treasurer
Paid Staff: 9   **Volunteer Staff:** 25
Paid Artists: 65
Utilizes: Special Technical Talent; Guest Artists; Guest Directors
Budget: $100,000 - $500,000
Income Sources: Private Foundations/Grants/Endowments; Business/Corporate Donations; Box Office; Government Grants; Individual Donations
Season: 52 Weeks   **Annual Attendance:** 11,000
Affiliations: TCG; South Carolina Theatre Association

FACILITY

KOGER CENTER FOR THE ARTS
University of South Carolina, Columbia, SC 29208
(803) 777-7500
FAX: (803) 777-5774
Founded: 1989
Type of Facility: Concert Hall; Auditorium; Theatre House; Opera House; Multi-Purpose
Type of Stage: Proscenium   **Orchestra Pit**
Seating Capacity: 2,236
Year Built: 1989   **Architect:** GMH and Associates   **Cost:** $15,000,000
Acoustical Consultant: Chris Jaffe
Contact for Rental: Ron Pearson;   (803) 777-7500
Resident Groups: South Carolina Philharmonic; Columbia City Ballet; University of South Carolina: Symphony; Chamber; Orchestra; Opera; Mastersingers

UNIVERSITY OF SOUTH CAROLINA - DRAYTON HALL THEATRE
Green and Sumter Streets, Columbia, SC 29208
(803) 777-4288
Type of Facility: Theatre Complex; Concert Hall; Auditorium; Theatre House
Type of Stage: Proscenium
Stage Dimensions: 36'Wx22'D   **Orchestra Pit**
Seating Capacity: 400
Year Built: 1890
Year Remodeled: 1987
Acoustical Consultant: Elbin Cleveland
Contact for Rental: Carol DuPree, Business Manager;   (803) 777-5863
Resident Groups: University Mainstage Productions; University of South Carolina Departments of Music, Theatre and Speech; University of South Carolina Dance Company; The Puppet Regime
For theatrical or musical productions

UNIVERSITY OF SOUTH CAROLINA - LONGSTREET THEATRE
Green and Sumter Streets, Columbia, SC 29208
(803) 777-4288
Type of Facility: Theatre Complex; Theatre House; Arena; Multi-Purpose
Facility Originally: Church
Type of Stage: Thrust; Arena
Stage Dimensions: 28' Diameter Circle
Seating Capacity: 312
Year Built: 1855
Year Remodeled: 1972   **Architect:** George Izenour
Acoustical Consultant: George Izenour
Contact for Rental: Carol DuPree, Business Manager;   (803) 777-5863
Resident Groups: University of South Carolina Department of Theatre and Speech; University of South Carolina Dance Company; The Puppet Regime

Conway

FACILITY

UNIVERSITY OF SOUTH CAROLINA-COASTAL CAROLINA COLLEGE - LITTLE THEATRE
Conway, SC 29526
(803) 347-3161
Type of Facility: Concert Hall; Auditorium; Studio Performance; Theatre House; Multi-Purpose; Room
Type of Stage: Proscenium; Environmental; Arena

Stage Dimensions: 20'x30'
Seating Capacity: 125
Contact for Rental: Thomas E. Jones, Director;   (803) 349-2510
Manager: Dr. Mallard, Chairman of Theatre Dept.;   (803) 349-2442
Resident Groups: Upstage Company

UNIVERSITY OF SOUTH CAROLINA-COASTAL CAROLINA COLLEGE -
WHEELWRIGHT PERFORMING ARTS CENTER
Conway, SC 29526
(803) 347-3161
Type of Facility: Concert Hall; Auditorium; Studio Performance; Performance Center; Theatre House
Type of Stage: Proscenium
Stage Dimensions: 40'x40'   Orchestra Pit
Seating Capacity: 817
Year Built: 1981   Architect: Riddle & Wilkes   Cost: $3,500,000
Contact for Rental: Thomas E. Jones, Director;   (803) 349-2510
Manager: Dr. Mallard, Chairman of Theatre Dept.;   (803) 349-2442
Resident Groups: Coastal Carolina Theatre; Coastal Carolina Choir

Georgetown

THEATRE

SWAMP FOX PLAYERS
PO Box 911, Georgetown, SC 29442
(803) 527-2924
Founded: 1971
Arts Area: Community
Status: Non-Professional; Non-Profit
Type: Performing; Resident
Purpose: To develop a cultural center for the area; to bring dramatic presentations to the citizens of this region
Officers: Ruth Buck, President; Mark Brown, Vice President; Lyn Going-Smith, Secretary; Nina Morris, Treasurer
Volunteer Staff: 11
Non-Paid Artists: 60
Utilizes: Guest Artists
Budget: $1,000 - $50,000
Income Sources: Box Office
Performance Facilities: The Strand Theatre

FACILITY

THE STRAND THEATRE
710 Front Street, PO Box 911, Georgetown, SC 29442
(803) 527-2297
Type of Facility: Theatre House
Type of Stage: Platform
Seating Capacity: 200
Year Built: 1937
Contact for Rental: Abe Fogel;   (803) 546-7800
Resident Groups: Swamp Fox Players
Member, League of Historic American Theatres; National Register of Historic Places

Greenville

DANCE

CAROLINA BALLET THEATRE
872 Woodruff Road, Greenville, SC 29607
(803) 297-1635
Founded: 1974
Arts Area: Ballet
Status: Non-Professional; Non-Profit
Type: Performing
Management: Barbara Selvey, Artistic Director
Officers: Cindy DeLoache, Chairman
Paid Artists: 3   Non-Paid Artists: 20

Utilizes: Guest Artists; Guest Choreographers
Budget: $50,000 - $100,000
Income Sources: Private Foundations/Grants/Endowments; Business/Corporate Donations; Box Office; Individual Donations
Season: October - June
Performance Facilities: Peace Center

INSTRUMENTAL MUSIC

GREENVILLE SYMPHONY ASSOCIATION
Magill Music Hall, PO Box 10002, Greenville, SC 29603
(803) 232-0344
FAX: (803) 240-3113
Founded: 1948
Arts Area: Symphony; Chamber; Ensemble; Pops
Status: Semi-Professional; Non-Profit
Type: Performing; Resident; Educational
Purpose: To provide the community with the finest possible musical education and entertainment
Management: Patricia G. Quarles, Office Manager; Julie Greer, Operations Manager; David Sz. Pollitt, Conductor; Joel E. Keller, General Manager; Edith K. Diver, Ticket Manager; Susan Bocook, Librarian
Officers: Edward H. Stall Jr., President; Mrs. David E. Mills, First Vice President; Robert T. Thompson Sr., Second Vice President; Mrs. R. J. Stephenson III, Secretary; William J. Rothfuss, Treasurer
Paid Staff: 6   **Volunteer Staff:** 304
Paid Artists: 90
Utilizes: Guest Artists
Budget: $1,000,000 - $5,000,000
Income Sources: Private Foundations/Grants/Endowments; Business/Corporate Donations; Box Office; Government Grants; Individual Donations
Season: September - April   **Annual Attendance:** 23,000
Affiliations: ASOL; ASCAP; BMI
Performance Facilities: Peace Center for the Performing Arts

VOCAL MUSIC

THE GREENVILLE CHORALE
c/o Dr. Bingham Vick Jr., Furman University, Greenville, SC 29613
(803) 294-2161; (803) 242-0890
Founded: 1961
Arts Area: Choral
Status: Semi-Professional; Non-Profit
Type: Performing; Resident
Purpose: To provide opportunities for professional and amateur singers to study and perform choral/orchestral literature by classical and contemporary composers; to continue to add challenging choral/orchestral works to the repertoire; to provide the community with opportunities to hear professional performances of great music
Management: Bingham Vick, Jr., Director/Primary Administrator
Officers: Maurice Brown, President; M. Gordon Howle, Martha A. Vaughn, Shirley L. Duncan, Vice Presidents; Ann Keith, Secretary; L.W. Brummer, Treasurer
Paid Staff: 4   **Volunteer Staff:** 15
Paid Artists: 12   **Non-Paid Artists:** 190
Utilizes: Special Technical Talent; Guest Conductors; Guest Artists
Budget: $50,000 - $100,000
Income Sources: Private Foundations/Grants/Endowments; Business/Corporate Donations; Box Office; Government Grants; Individual Donations
Season: September - May   **Annual Attendance:** 6,000
Affiliations: ASCAP; ACDA; CA
Performance Facilities: Peace Center for the Performing Arts; McAlister Auditorium-Furman University

FACILITY

FURMAN UNIVERSITY - MCALISTER AUDITORIUM
Greenville, SC 29613
(803) 294-2124
Type of Facility: Concert Hall; Auditorium; Opera House; Multi-Purpose
Type of Stage: Proscenium
Stage Dimensions: 80'x65'x60'   **Orchestra Pit**
Seating Capacity: 1,922
Year Built: 1962   **Architect:** Perry, Dean & Stewart
Contact for Rental: Eric R. Harrell;   (803) 294-2124
Resident Groups: Furman University Music Department; Furman Presents; Greenville Civic Chorale

GREENVILLE MEMORIAL AUDITORIUM
401 East North Street, Greenville, SC 29601
(803) 241-3800
>   **Type of Facility:** Concert Hall; Theatre House; Arena; Multi-Purpose
>   **Type of Stage:** Flexible
>   **Seating Capacity:** 6,200
>   **Year Built:** 1959 **Architect:** Cunningham and Walker   **Cost:** $2,100,000
>   **Contact for Rental:** Clifford Gray
>   *Contains a 25,000 square foot exhibit hall*

Greenwood

FACILITY

GREENWOOD CIVIC CENTER
PO Box 3008, Greenwood, SC 29648
(803) 223-3395
>   **Type of Facility:** Concert Hall; Theatre House; Arena; Multi-Purpose
>   **Type of Stage:** Flexible
>   **Seating Capacity:** 4,800
>   **Year Built:** 1979 **Architect:** Greenwood Associates   **Cost:** $4,000,000
>   **Contact for Rental:** Gary Craigo;   (803) 223-3395

Hartsville

THEATRE

HARTSVILLE COMMUNITY PLAYERS
PO Box 1192, Hartsville, SC 29550
(803) 332-5721
>   **Founded:** 1970
>   **Arts Area:** Musical; Community
>   **Status:** Non-Profit
>   **Type:** Performing
>   **Officers:** Vicki Price, President; Harry Wallace Sr., Vice President; Liz Taylor, Secretary; Cliff McBride, Treasurer
>   **Volunteer Staff:** 12
>   **Non-Paid Artists:** 100
>   **Utilizes:** Guest Artists; Guest Directors
>   **Budget:** $1,000 - $50,000
>   **Income Sources:** Business/Corporate Donations; Box Office; Individual Donations
>   **Season:** October - March   **Annual Attendance:** 125
>   **Performance Facilities:** Center Theater

FACILITY

CENTER THEATER
212 North Fifth Street, Hartsville, SC 29550
(803) 332-5721
>   **Founded:** 1936
>   **Type of Facility:** Concert Hall; Auditorium; Performance Center; Off Broadway; Opera House
>   **Facility Originally:** Movie House/Civic Auditorium
>   **Type of Stage:** Proscenium
>   **Stage Dimensions:** 34'Wx20'3"H proscenium opening; 34'Hx64/74'Wx29'7"D stage   **Orchestra Pit**
>   **Seating Capacity:** 861
>   **Year Built:** 1936 **Architect:** Lafaye and Lafaye
>   **Year Remodeled:** 1969 **Architect:** Clark and McCall, AIA   **Cost:** $175,000
>   **Contact for Rental:** J. Lamar Caldwell Jr.;   (803) 332-5721
>   **Resident Groups:** Hartsville Community Players

Myrtle Beach

FACILITY

CONVENTION CENTER
21st Avenue North and Oak Street, Myrtle Beach, SC 29577
(803) 448-7166
FAX: (803) 448-7448
  Type of Facility: Auditorium; Arena
  Year Built: 1967   **Architect:** Riddle & Wilkes
  Contact for Rental: Steve Jones;   (803) 448-7166
  Manager: Mani Costa
  Convention Center contains the Auditorium and Exhibit Hall. See separate listings for further information.

CONVENTION CENTER - AUDITORIUM
21st Avenue North and Oak Street, Myrtle Beach, SC 29577
(803) 448-7166
FAX: (803) 448-7448
  Type of Stage: Proscenium
  Stage Dimensions: 65'Wx65'D; 48'Wx20'H proscenium opening
  Seating Capacity: 2,100
  Year Built: 1967
  Contact for Rental: Steve Jones;   (803) 448-7166
  Manager: Mani Costa

CONVENTION CENTER - EXHIBIT HALL
21st Avenue North and Oak Street, Myrtle Beach, SC 29577
(803) 448-7166
FAX: (803) 448-7448
  Type of Facility: Exhibition Hall
  Type of Stage: Arena
  Stage Dimensions: 42'Wx20'D
  Seating Capacity: 2,550
  Year Built: 1977
  Contact for Rental: Steve Jones;   (803) 448-7166
  Manager: Mani Costa

Newberry

THEATRE

NEWBERRY COLLEGE THEATRE
Newberry College, Newberry, SC 29108
(803) 276-5010
  Founded: 1856
  Arts Area: Musical; Dinner; Theatrical Group
  Status: College
  Type: Performing; Educational
  Purpose: To provide a quality performing arts program in a liberal arts college environment
  Officers: Sidney C. Pitts, Director of Theatre/Coordinator of Performing Arts/Chair, Department of Theatre; Rupert Gaddy, Technical Director
  Paid Staff: 3   **Volunteer Staff:** 45
  Utilizes: Special Technical Talent; Guest Artists; Guest Directors
  Budget: $1,000 - $50,000
  Income Sources: Business/Corporate Donations; Box Office; Individual Donations
  Season: September - May   **Annual Attendance:** 1,500
  Affiliations: SETC

Rock Hill

FACILITY

WINTHROP COLLEGE - JAMES F. BYRNES AUDITORIUM
Rock Hill, SC 29733
(803) 323-2196
  Type of Facility: Auditorium

Type of Stage: Proscenium   **Orchestra Pit**
Seating Capacity: 3,496
Year Built: 1939   **Architect:** James B. Urquhart   **Cost:** $1,000,000
Contact for Rental: Joynes Center;   (803) 323-2196
Under renovation; not available for use

Spartanburg

FACILITY

SPARTANBURG MEMORIAL AUDITORIUM
385 North Church Street, PO Box 1410, Spartanburg, SC 29304
(803) 582-8107
FAX: (803) 583-9850
   Type of Facility: Civic Center
   Year Built: 1951
   Year Remodeled: 1986   **Architect:** Ned Lustig   **Cost:** $3,000,000
   Acoustical Consultant: Atlee Pettit
   Contact for Rental: Steve Jones;   (803) 582-8107
   Spartanburg Memorial Auditorium contains the Arena and Theatre. See separate listings for additional information.

SPARTANBURG MEMORIAL AUDITORIUM - ARENA
385 North Church Road, PO Box 1410, Spartanburg, SC 29304
(803) 582-8107
   Type of Facility: Arena
   Type of Stage: Platform
   Stage Dimensions: 100'Wx100'D
   Seating Capacity: 3,500
   Year Built: 1951
   Year Remodeled: 1986
   Acoustical Consultant: Atlee Pettit
   Contact for Rental: Steve Jones;   (803) 582-8107

SPARTANBURG MEMORIAL AUDITORIUM - THEATRE
385 North Church Street, PO Box 1410, Spartanburg, SC 29304
(803) 582-8107
FAX: (803) 583-9850
   Type of Facility: Auditorium
   Type of Stage: Proscenium
   Stage Dimensions: 55'Wx35'D; 55'Wx28'H proscenium opening; add 18'D with pit inserts   **Orchestra Pit**
   Seating Capacity: 3,406
   Year Built: 1951
   Year Remodeled: 1986
   Acoustical Consultant: Atlee Pettit
   Contact for Rental: Steve Jones;   (803) 582-8107

Sumter

FACILITY

SUMTER COUNTY CULTURAL CENTER
135 Haynsworth, Sumter, SC 29150
(803) 775-1455
   Founded: 1987
   Type of Facility: Concert Hall; Auditorium; Theatre House; Multi-Purpose; Gallery
   Facility Originally: School
   Type of Stage: Proscenium
   Stage Dimensions: 47'x26'   **Orchestra Pit**
   Seating Capacity: 1,017
   Year Built: 1929   **Architect:** James, DuRant, Mathews and Shelley
   Year Remodeled: 1986   **Architect:** James, DuRant, Matthews and Shelley   **Cost:** $3,700,000
   Contact for Rental: Director;   (803) 775-1455

SOUTH DAKOTA

Aberdeen

INSTRUMENTAL MUSIC

ABERDEEN UNIVERSITY CIVIC SYMPHONY
Northern State College, Aberdeen, SD 57401
(605) 622-2519
Founded: 1920
Arts Area: Symphony; Orchestra; Ensemble
Status: Non-Professional; Non-Profit
Type: Performing; Resident; Educational
Purpose: To study and perform literature for orchestra; to provide opportunity for music students to become acquainted with standard literature
Management: Joseph E. Koob, II, Conductor
Paid Staff: 1
Paid Artists: 20   **Non-Paid Artists:** 50
Utilizes: Guest Artists
Budget: $1,000 - $50,000
Income Sources: Private Foundations/Grants/Endowments; Government Grants; Individual Donations
Season: September - June   **Annual Attendance:** 3,000
Performance Facilities: Johnson Fine Arts Center

THEATRE

ABERDEEN COMMUNITY THEATRE (ACT 2)
PO Box 813, Aberdeen, SD 57401
(605) 225-6273
Founded: 1979
Arts Area: Musical; Dinner; Community; Theatrical Group
Status: Non-Professional; Non-Profit
Type: Performing; Educational; Sponsoring
Purpose: To educate, entertain and further the performing arts through local involvement
Management: James L. Walker, Artistic/Managing Director
Officers: Rory King, President; Merry Coleman, Vice President; Sherri Rawstern, Secretary; Rosemary Walker, Treasurer
Paid Staff: 1   **Volunteer Staff:** 1
Non-Paid Artists: 50
Utilizes: Guest Directors
Budget: $50,000 - $100,000
Income Sources: Private Foundations/Grants/Endowments; Business/Corporate Donations; Box Office; Government Grants; Individual Donations
Season: April - November   **Annual Attendance:** 8,000
Affiliations: AACT; South Dakota Theatre Association

Armour

THEATRE

ARMOUR STAR HAM PLAYERS
921 Main, Armour, SD 57313
(605) 724-2370
Founded: 1976
Arts Area: Community
Status: Non-Professional; Non-Profit
Type: Resident; Educational; Sponsoring
Purpose: Provide live theatre for the community and sponsor art groups
Officers: Carter Wiese, President; Kim Krull, Vice President; Cheri Altenburg, Secretary; Marjory Hartman, Treasurer
Utilizes: Special Technical Talent
Budget: $1,000 - $50,000
Income Sources: Box Office
Season: June - September   **Annual Attendance:** 700

Brookings

INSTRUMENTAL MUSIC

BROOKINGS CHAMBER MUSIC SOCIETY
Music Department, South Dakota State University, Brookings, Brookings, SD 57007
(605) 688-5187
 Founded: 1982
 Arts Area: Orchestra; Chamber; Ensemble; Instrumental Group
 Status: Non-Profit
 Type: Performing; Educational; Sponsoring
 Purpose: To bring outstanding artists and ensembles to the Brookings area and South Dakota State University
 Management: John F. Colson, Program Coordinator
 Officers: Barbara Fishback, President; Warren Hatfield, Vice President; Joan Tabor, Secretary; Norma Linn, Treasurer
 Volunteer Staff: 15
 Paid Artists: 35
 Utilizes: Guest Artists
 Budget: $1,000 - $50,000
 Income Sources: Private Foundations/Grants/Endowments; Business/Corporate Donations; Box Office; Government Grants; Individual Donations
 Season: October - April **Annual Attendance:** 2,000
 Affiliations: South Dakota State University
 Performance Facilities: Peterson Recital Hall

SOUTH DAKOTA STATE UNIVERSITY CIVIC SYMPHONY
Music Department, South Dakota State University, Brookings, SD 57007
(605) 688-5187
 Founded: 1966
 Arts Area: Symphony; Orchestra
 Status: Non-Professional; Non-Profit
 Type: Performing; Educational
 Purpose: To perform symphonic literature from the Baroque through contemporary periods; to highlight outstanding soloists
 Management: John F. Colson, Music Director/Conductor
 Paid Staff: 1
 Paid Artists: 20 **Non-Paid Artists:** 50
 Utilizes: Guest Artists
 Budget: $1,000 - $50,000
 Income Sources: Private Foundations/Grants/Endowments; Business/Corporate Donations; Government Grants; Individual Donations
 Season: October - April **Annual Attendance:** 6,000
 Affiliations: South Dakota State University
 Performance Facilities: Peterson Recital Hall

FACILITY

SOUTH DAKOTA ART MUSEUM
PO Box 2250, Brookings, SD 57007
(605) 688-5423
 Type of Facility: Multi-Purpose
 Type of Stage: Thrust
 Seating Capacity: 147
 Year Built: 1969 **Architect:** Howard Parezo **Cost:** $500,000
 Manager: Joseph M. Stuart
 Resident Groups: University Theatre

De Smet

PERFORMING SERIES

LAURA INGALLS WILDER PAGEANT SOCIETY
PO Box 154, De Smet, SD 57231
(605) 688-5423
 Founded: 1971
 Arts Area: Theater
 Status: Non-Profit
 Type: Performing

Purpose: An outdoor pageant that depicts The Little Town on the Prairie books by Laura Ingalls Wilder, the site of the pageant is across the road from the Ingalls homestead site
Management: Portia Potvin, Managing Director
Officers: Arnold Poppen, President; Norma Dannenbring, Secretary/Treasurer
Volunteer Staff: 12
Budget: $1,000 - $50,000
Income Sources: Box Office; Individual Donations
Season: June - July   **Annual Attendance:** 10,000

Dell Rapids

THEATRE

OLD OPERA HOUSE PLAYERS
PO Box 163, Dell Rapids, SD 57022
(605) 428-3260
Founded: 1976
Arts Area: Community
Status: Non-Professional; Non-Profit
Type: Performing; Resident
Purpose: To support community theatre; to train young actors
Officers: Phyllis Rydberg, President; Richard Fitzgerald, Vice President; Dale Nighbert, Treasurer; Angie Sward, Secretary
Volunteer Staff: 15
Budget: $1,000 - $50,000
Income Sources: Box Office
Season: June - August   **Annual Attendance:** 600
Performance Facilities: The Hayloft Theater

Huron

INSTRUMENTAL MUSIC

HURON MUNICIPAL BAND
PO Box 1387, Huron, SD 57350
(605) 352-8561
Founded: 1885
Arts Area: Band
Status: Semi-Professional
Type: Performing
Purpose: To provide the community with live band music for patriotic and civic functions and summer concerts
Officers: Clarke Christiansen, President; Ted Peterman, Secretary; Randall Lampe, Treasurer
Paid Artists: 32
Budget: $1,000 - $50,000
Income Sources: Government Grants
Season: Memorial Day - August   **Annual Attendance:** 10,000
Performance Facilities: Band Shell, City Park

Lennox

INSTRUMENTAL MUSIC

LENNOX MUNICIPAL BAND
c/o Lennox Independent Newspaper, Lennox, SD 57039
(605) 647-2284
Founded: 1883
Arts Area: Band
Status: Non-Professional; Non-Profit
Type: Performing
Purpose: To provide band music for civic and municipal events in and around Lennox; to provide weekly concerts in the park during the summer season
Management: William Hoffman, Director
Officers: Sharla West, President; Marion Smith, Vice President; Betty Barnett, Secretary; Nancy Straatmeyer, Treasurer
Paid Staff: 1
Non-Paid Artists: 35
Utilizes: Guest Artists

Budget: $1,000 - $50,000
Season: June - August   **Annual Attendance:** 1,000
Performance Facilities: Jacobs Memorial Band Shell, City Park

Madison

PERFORMING SERIES

MADISON AREA ARTS COUNCIL
PO Box 147, Madison, SD 57042
(605) 256-5270
Founded: 1968
Arts Area: Dance; Vocal Music; Instrumental Music; Theater; Festivals
Status: Non-Profit
Type: Educational; Sponsoring
Purpose: Promote an appreciation of the arts; sponsor activities in the arts; and provide opportunities for instruction in the arts for members of the community
Management: Eve Fisher, Arts Coordinator
Officers: Katherine Presuhn, President; Mollie Freier, Vice President; Nancy Sabbe, Secretary; Keith Knutson, Treasurer
Paid Staff: 1   **Volunteer Staff:** 17
Utilizes: Guest Artists; Guest Directors
Budget: $1,000 - $50,000
Income Sources: Private Foundations/Grants/Endowments; Business/Corporate Donations; Box Office; Government Grants; Individual Donations
Season: September - May   **Annual Attendance:** 2,000
Affiliations: South Dakota Arts Council; Community Arts Council Network; South Dakota Alliance
Performance Facilities: Dakota Prairie Playhouse

Mitchell

INSTRUMENTAL MUSIC

MITCHELL MUNICIPAL BAND
1509 Bridle Drive, Mitchell, SD 57301
(605) 996-5467
Founded: 1900
Arts Area: Band
Status: Professional
Type: Performing
Purpose: Free summer family entertainment and city affairs
Management: Joseph F. Pekas, Director
Officers: Arnold Braught, President; Bernice Sellars, Secretary/Treasurer
Paid Staff: 2
Paid Artists: 35
Budget: $1,000 - $50,000
Season: May - August   **Annual Attendance:** 50,000
Affiliations: AFM
Performance Facilities: Band Shell

Pierre

INSTRUMENTAL MUSIC

CAPITAL CITY BAND
1005 West Elizabeth, Pierre, SD 57501
(605) 224-1343
FAX: (605) 224-1343
Founded: 1900
Arts Area: Band
Status: Non-Professional; Non-Profit
Type: Performing; Touring
Purpose: Provide weekly summer band concerts in city parks and make special appearances
Management: Terry C. Anderson, Director
Paid Staff: 1
Non-Paid Artists: 53
Utilizes: Guest Directors

Budget: $1,000 - $50,000
Income Sources: Government Grants
Season: June - August   **Annual Attendance:** 10,000
Affiliations: American Association of Concert Bands

THEATRE

PIERRE PLAYERS
109 South Pierre Street, PO Box 933, Pierre, SD 57501
(605) 224-9709
Founded: 1968
Arts Area: Community
Status: Non-Professional; Non-Profit
Type: Performing
Purpose: Providing quality theatre to the people of Central South Dakota; Pierre Players gives them an appreciation of legitimate theatre and provides an opportunity to take part in the active production
Management: Don Boyd, Manager
Officers: Bob Brancel, President; Kathy Valnes, Vice President; Darlene Gage, Secretary; John Clauson, Treasurer
Paid Staff: 1   **Volunteer Staff:** 100
Non-Paid Artists: 100
Utilizes: Special Technical Talent; Guest Directors
Budget: $50,000 - $100,000
Income Sources: Business/Corporate Donations; Box Office; Individual Donations
Season: 52 Weeks   **Annual Attendance:** 8,000

Rapid City

INSTRUMENTAL MUSIC

BLACK HILLS SYMPHONY ORCHESTRA
PO Box 2246, Rapid City, SD 57709
(605) 348-4676
Founded: 1931
Arts Area: Symphony; Orchestra
Status: Non-Profit
Type: Performing; Resident; Educational
Purpose: To encourage understanding and appreciation of music in the area and to provide opportunities to area musicians to develop and express talent through performance and training
Management: Lowell Holmgren, Executive Director; Jack Knowles, Conductor; Coral White, Concert Master
Officers: Jo Anne Messerli, President, Board of Directors; Steve Montgomery, First Vice President; Linda Zazula, Secretary; Craig Grotenhouse, Treasurer
Paid Staff: 3
Paid Artists: 75   **Non-Paid Artists:** 10
Utilizes: Guest Artists
Budget: $100,000 - $500,000
Income Sources: Private Foundations/Grants/Endowments; Business/Corporate Donations; Box Office; Government Grants; Individual Donations
Season: October - April   **Annual Attendance:** 5,500
Performance Facilities: Rushmore Plaza Civic Center Theater

THEATRE

BLACK HILLS COMMUNITY THEATRE
713 Seventh Street, Rapid City, SD 57701
(605) 394-1786
Founded: 1968
Arts Area: Community
Status: Non-Profit
Type: Performing
Purpose: To provide quality theatrical entertainment utilizing talent from the community
Management: Merritt Olsen, Manager
Officers: Angie McKie, President; Tim Pittman, Treasurer; Wayne Gilbert, Secretary
Paid Staff: 2   **Volunteer Staff:** 25
Paid Artists: 15   **Non-Paid Artists:** 150
Budget: $50,000 - $100,000
Income Sources: Business/Corporate Donations; Box Office; Government Grants; Individual Donations
Season: September - May   **Annual Attendance:** 6,000
Affiliations: South Dakota Arts Council; Allied Arts Fund

BLACK HILLS PLAYHOUSE
PO Box 2513, Rapid City, SD 57709
(605) 255-4242
> **Founded:** 1946
> **Arts Area:** Summer Stock; Theatrical Group
> **Status:** Professional; Semi-Professional; Non-Profit
> **Type:** Performing; Resident; Educational
> **Purpose:** To provide high quality performances for its theater audience and to provide intensive professional training for theater students
> **Management:** Jan D. Swank, Managing Artistic Director; Jill Swank, Business Manager
> **Officers:** Kay Snyder, President; Tim Case, Vice President; Clara Clay, Secretary; Patrick Burchill, Treasurer
> **Paid Staff:** 65
> **Utilizes:** Special Technical Talent; Guest Artists; Guest Directors; Students
> **Budget:** $100,000 - $500,000
> **Income Sources:** Private Foundations/Grants/Endowments; Business/Corporate Donations; Box Office; Government Grants; Individual Donations
> **Season:** June - August   **Annual Attendance:** 20,000
> **Performance Facilities:** Black Hills Playhouse (Custer State Park)

FACILITY

RUSHMORE PLAZA CIVIC CENTER
444 Mount Rushmore Road North, Rapid City, SD 57701
(605) 394-4115
FAX: (605) 394-4119
> **Founded:** 1977
> **Type of Facility:** Concert Hall; Theatre House; Civic Center; Arena; Multi-Purpose
> **Type of Stage:** Proscenium
> **Stage Dimensions:** 43'Dx55' proscenium opening; 68' to grid   **Orchestra Pit**
> **Seating Capacity:** 1,774
> **Year Built:** 1977   **Architect:** Spitznagel   **Cost:** $10,000,000
> **Contact for Rental:**   (605) 394-4119
> **Manager:** Kevin Buntrock;   (605) 394-4115
> **Resident Groups:** Black Hills Symphony; Rapid City Concert Association; Black Hills Dance Theatre
> *Rushmore Plaza Civic Center also contains an 11,200 seat Arena and 150,000 square foot Convention Auditorium.*

Sioux Falls

DANCE

CIVIC DANCE ASSOCIATION
PO Box 646, Sioux Falls, SD 57101
(605) 335-8913
> **Founded:** 1970
> **Arts Area:** Modern; Ballet; Jazz
> **Status:** Non-Profit
> **Type:** Performing; Touring; Resident; Educational; Sponsoring
> **Purpose:** To bring professional dance to our city
> **Officers:** Terri Bowden, President; Gary Wirt, Vice President; Karen Johnson, Secretary; J.D. Thompson, Treasurer
> **Volunteer Staff:** 8
> **Budget:** $1,000 - $50,000
> **Income Sources:** Private Foundations/Grants/Endowments; Business/Corporate Donations; Box Office; Government Grants; Individual Donations
> **Season:** Spring - Fall

INSTRUMENTAL MUSIC

SIOUX FALLS MUNICIPAL BAND
City Hall, Sioux Falls, SD 57102
(605) 339-7290
> **Founded:** 1919
> **Arts Area:** Instrumental Group; Band
> **Status:** Semi-Professional; Non-Profit
> **Type:** Performing
> **Purpose:** To provide free concerts of band music to the citizens of our community

Management: Dr. Bruce T. Ammann, Conductor
Officers: Craig Alberty, President
Paid Staff: 3
Paid Artists: 50
Utilizes: Guest Conductors; Guest Artists
Budget: $50,000 - $100,000
Income Sources: Private Foundations/Grants/Endowments; Business/Corporate Donations; Individual Donations
Season: October - August   **Annual Attendance:** 40,000

SOUTH DAKOTA SYMPHONY
300 Norh Dakota, Suite 405, Sioux Falls, SD 57102
(605) 335-7933
Founded: 1922
Arts Area: Symphony; Orchestra; Chamber; Ensemble
Status: Professional; Non-Profit
Type: Performing; Touring; Resident; Educational
Purpose: Providing the highest quality orchestral music to the people of the Northern Plains, the South Dakota Symphony takes leadership in enhancing the cultural environment of the region, developing an understanding and interest in the people of the state for fine artistic expression.
Management: Marti A. Baumert, Executive Director; Henry Charles Smith, Music Director
Officers: Ron Williamson, President
Paid Staff: 5   **Volunteer Staff:** 150
Paid Artists: 85
Utilizes: Guest Artists; Guest Directors
Budget: $500,000 - $1,000,000
Income Sources: Private Foundations/Grants/Endowments; Business/Corporate Donations; Box Office; Government Grants; Individual Donations
Season: September - May   **Annual Attendance:** 67,000
Affiliations: ASOL
Performance Facilities: Sioux Falls Coliseum

VOCAL MUSIC

SIOUX FALLS MASTER SINGERS
PO Box 1753, Sioux Falls, SD 57101
(605) 368-2390
Founded: 1984
Arts Area: Light Opera; Choral; Ethnic; Folk
Status: Non-Profit
Type: Performing; Educational
Purpose: To perform quality choral literature to a regional audience of all ages
Management: Jamesina McLeod, Business Manager; Alan Stanza, Music Director
Officers: Diane Hohn, President; Elmer Tursan, Secretary/Treasurer
Paid Staff: 1   **Volunteer Staff:** 25
Non-Paid Artists: 30
Utilizes: Guest Artists
Budget: $1,000 - $50,000
Income Sources: Private Foundations/Grants/Endowments; Business/Corporate Donations; Box Office; Government Grants; Individual Donations
Season: October - April   **Annual Attendance:** 2,500

THEATRE

THE BARN THEATER
Rural Route 3, PO Box 126, Sioux Falls, SD 57106
(605) 339-1263
Founded: 1978
Arts Area: Summer Stock; Theatrical Group
Status: Semi-Professional
Type: Performing; Resident
Purpose: To provide wholesome summer entertainment and an outlet for actors who wish to perform
Management: Delores Cullen, Owner/Producer; James Connor, Director
Paid Staff: 2
Utilizes: Special Technical Talent; Guest Directors
Budget: $1,000 - $50,000

Income Sources: Box Office
Season: June - August   Annual Attendance: 2,200

SIOUX FALLS COMMUNITY PLAYHOUSE
315 North Phillips, PO Box 600, Sioux Falls, SD 57101
(605) 336-7418
Founded: 1931
Arts Area: Community
Status: Non-Profit
Type: Performing; Touring; Resident; Educational; Sponsoring
Purpose: To provide the community and area with an opportunity to experience live theatre at a variety of participatory
levels
Management: Ron Ziegler, Managing Director
Paid Staff: 5   Volunteer Staff: 500
Paid Artists: 5   Non-Paid Artists: 150
Budget: $100,000 - $500,000
Income Sources: Private Foundations/Grants/Endowments; Business/Corporate Donations; Box Office; Government
Grants; Individual Donations
Season: 52 Weeks   Annual Attendance: 25,000
Affiliations: AACT; South Dakota Arts Council
Performance Facilities: Sioux Falls Community Playhouse

FACILITY

SIOUX FALLS COLISEUM
600 East Seventh Street, Sioux Falls, SD 57102
(605) 339-7196
Type of Facility: Theatre Complex; Auditorium; Theatre House
Type of Stage: Proscenium
Stage Dimensions: 60'x40'x35'   Orchestra Pit
Seating Capacity: 1,933
Year Built: 1917
Year Remodeled: 1972   Architect: Kock   Cost: $168,000
Contact for Rental: Kenn Friesen;   (605) 339-7060
Resident Groups: Sioux Falls Symphony; Community Concerts Association

SIOUX FALLS COMMUNITY PLAYHOUSE
315 North Phillips, PO Box 600, Sioux Falls, SD 57101
(605) 336-7418
FAX: (605) 336-2243
Type of Facility: Theatre Complex
Facility Originally: Vaudeville
Type of Stage: Proscenium
Stage Dimensions: 53'Wx32'D   Orchestra Pit
Seating Capacity: 692
Year Built: 1913   Architect: Solari Brothers
Year Remodeled: 1984   Architect: Spitznagel Partners   Cost: $800,000
Contact for Rental: Bob Wyant, Business Manager;   (605) 336-7418
Manager: Ron Ziegler;   (605) 336-7418
Resident Groups: Sioux Falls Community Playhouse

Spearfish

THEATRE

MATTHEWS OPERA HOUSE SOCIETY
PO Box 874, Spearfish, SD 57783-0874
(605) 642-7973
Founded: 1987
Arts Area: Musical; Community; Theatrical Group
Status: Non-Professional; Non-Profit
Type: Performing; Educational
Purpose: To provide opportunities for people with talent and interest in theatre to work together; to continue Opera House
restoration efforts
Management: Julie Bulat, Arts Coordinator
Officers: Sandy Sorlie, President; Brian McNeill, Treasurer
Paid Staff: 1
Utilizes: Special Technical Talent

Budget: $1,000 - $50,000
Income Sources: Box Office; Government Grants; Individual Donations
Performance Facilities: Senior High Theatre; Matthews Opera House

FACILITY

MATTHEWS OPERA HOUSE
PO Box 874, Spearfish, SD 57783
(605) 642-7973
Founded: 1910
Type of Facility: Performance Center; Theatre House; Opera House
Facility Originally: Vaudeville; Movie House
Type of Stage: Proscenium; Platform
Stage Dimensions: 16'x26'
Seating Capacity: 250
Year Built: 1910
Year Remodeled: 1989   **Architect:** James McDonald; Herb AsLesen   **Cost:** $500,000
Contact for Rental: Julie Bulat;   (605) 642-7973

Vermillion

FACILITY

UNIVERSITY OF SOUTH DAKOTA - SLAGLE AUDITORIUM
414 East Clark, Vermillion, SD 57069
(605) 677-5481
Type of Facility: Concert Hall
Facility Originally: School
Type of Stage: Proscenium   **Orchestra Pit**
Seating Capacity: 2,400
Year Built: 1924
Contact for Rental: College of Fine Arts;   (605) 677-5481
Manager: Wayne S. Knutsen

UNIVERSITY OF SOUTH DAKOTA - WARREN M. LEE CENTER FOR THE FINE ARTS
414 East Clark, Vermillion, SD 57069
(605) 677-5481
Type of Facility: Theatre Complex; Performance Center; Multi-Purpose
Seating Capacity: Theatre I - 470
Year Built: 1974   **Architect:** The Spitznagel Partners   **Cost:** $3,500,000
Acoustical Consultant: Richard Borgen
Contact for Rental: Cheryl Feight;   (605) 677-5481
Manager: Wayne S. Knutsen
Resident Groups: University of South Dakota Departments of Music, Art and Theater

Wagner

INSTRUMENTAL MUSIC

YANKTON AREA SUMMER BAND
Rural Route 1, PO Box 133, Wagner, SD 57380-9627
(605) 384-3355
FAX: (605) 384-3156
Founded: 1982
Arts Area: Band
Status: Semi-Professional; Non-Profit
Type: Performing
Purpose: Providing summer band concerts, each concert is directed by a member of the band who is an area band director.
Management: Chuck Stastny, Band Manager
Paid Staff: 11
Non-Paid Artists: 80
Utilizes: Special Technical Talent
Budget: $1,000 - $50,000
Income Sources: Private Foundations/Grants/Endowments; Business/Corporate Donations; Individual Donations
Season: June - July   **Annual Attendance:** 3,000

Affiliations: Yankton Department of Parks and Recreation; Yankton Area Arts Association
Performance Facilities: Riverside Park

Watertown

INSTRUMENTAL MUSIC

WATERTOWN MUNICIPAL BAND
1015 North Park, Watertown, SD 57201
(605) 886-3216
>**Founded:** 1930
>**Arts Area:** Band
>**Status:** Semi-Professional; Non-Profit
>**Type:** Performing
>**Purpose:** To provide summer concerts in the park for area residents
>**Management:** Douglas R. Carpenter, Director
>**Officers:** Leonard Timmerman, Treasurer
>**Paid Staff:** 2
>**Paid Artists:** 45
>**Utilizes:** Guest Directors
>**Budget:** $1,000 - $50,000
>**Income Sources:** Government Grants
>**Season:** May - August   **Annual Attendance:** 8,000
>**Performance Facilities:** Wenger Showmobile

THEATRE

TOWN PLAYERS
5 South Broadway, Watertown, SD 57201
(605) 882-2076
>**Founded:** 1940
>**Arts Area:** Musical; Community; Theatrical Group
>**Status:** Non-Professional; Non-Profit
>**Type:** Performing; Touring; Resident
>**Purpose:** To promote interest in and appreciation of the dramatic arts
>**Management:** Renee Carey, Manager
>**Paid Staff:** 1   **Volunteer Staff:** 20
>**Paid Artists:** 14   **Non-Paid Artists:** 45
>**Utilizes:** Special Technical Talent; Guest Conductors; Guest Artists; Guest Directors
>**Budget:** $1,000 - $50,000
>**Income Sources:** Private Foundations/Grants/Endowments; Box Office; Individual Donations
>**Season:** September - April   **Annual Attendance:** 5,000

Webster

INSTRUMENTAL MUSIC

WEBSTER COMMUNITY EDUCATION
102 East Ninth Avenue, Webster, SD 57274
(605) 345-4653
>**Founded:** 1983
>**Arts Area:** Ensemble; Band
>**Status:** Non-Professional; Non-Profit
>**Type:** Performing; Resident; Educational
>**Purpose:** To provide an opportunity for members of the community (youth and adult) to gather to present performances in various mediums of the performing arts
>**Management:** Barbara Ohleen, Community Education Director
>**Volunteer Staff:** 3
>**Non-Paid Artists:** 50
>**Budget:** $1,000 - $50,000
>**Annual Attendance:** 300

TENNESSEE

Alcoa

FACILITY

SMOKY MOUNTAIN PASSION PLAY
366 Glascock Street, Alcoa, TN 37701-2439
(615) 448-2244
Type of Facility: Amphitheater
Type of Stage: Greek
Stage Dimensions: 80'x45'
Seating Capacity: 2,000
Year Built: 1973
Architect: Lindsay-Maples
Cost: $350,000
Contact for Rental: Charles Reese;   (615) 984-4111
Resident Groups: Smoky Mountain Passion Play Company

Austin

INSTRUMENTAL MUSIC

CREATIVE OPPORTUNITY ORCHESTRA
PO Box 3215, Austin, TN 78764
(512) 448-3485
Arts Area: Ensemble; Jazz; New Music
Status: Professional; Non-Profit
Type: Performing; Touring; Resident; Educational
Purpose: To create a performing composers' forum for the evolution of new jazz music
Management: Tina Marsh, Artistic Director
Budget: $100,000 - $500,000
Income Sources: Private Foundations/Grants/Endowments; Business/Corporate Donations; Box Office; Government Grants; Individual Donations

Bristol

THEATRE

THEATER BRISTOL
512 State Street, Bristol, TN 37620
(615) 968-4977
Founded: 1965
Arts Area: Musical; Community; Theatrical Group
Status: Non-Professional; Non-Profit
Type: Performing; Resident; Educational; Sponsoring
Purpose: To provide quality entertainment and educational programs for children and adults, offering complete seasons for both
Management: Cathy De Caterina, Executive Director; Libby Everett, Business Manager; Robert Dean, Producing Director
Officers: Debbie Curry, President, Board of Directors; William H. Thompson, First Vice President; Michael E. Riley, Second Vice President; Lettie Jackson, Treasurer
Paid Staff: 6   **Volunteer Staff:** 400
Paid Artists: 25   **Non-Paid Artists:** 300
Utilizes: Special Technical Talent; Guest Conductors; Guest Directors
Budget: $100,000 - $500,000
Income Sources: Business/Corporate Donations; Box Office; Government Grants; Individual Donations
Season: February - November
Annual Attendance: 35,000
Performance Facilities: The Paramount Center for the Arts

Chattanooga

DANCE

CHATTANOOGA BALLET
PO Box 6175, Chattanooga, TN 37401
(615) 755-4672
    Founded: 1976
    Arts Area: Modern; Ballet; Jazz
    Status: Non-Profit
    Type: Performing; Touring; Resident; Educational; Sponsoring
    Purpose: We are a producing and presenting ballet company and school
    Management: Robert Willie, Artistic Director; Karen Smith, School Director; Frank Hay, Ballet Master
    Officers: William Montague, Board President; John Phillips, Vice President; Sally Wall, Secretary;
Lynn Pfannkuche, Treasurer
    Paid Staff: 4 **Volunteer Staff:** 11
    Paid Artists: 3 **Non-Paid Artists:** 11
    Utilizes: Special Technical Talent; Guest Artists; Guest Directors
    Budget: $50,000 - $100,000
    Income Sources: Private Foundations/Grants/Endowments; Business/Corporate Donations; Box Office; Government
Grants; Individual Donations
    Season: December - June
    Affiliations: SERBA; Allied Arts of Greater Chattanooga
    Performance Facilities: Fine Arts Center, University of Tennessee-Chattanooga; Tivoli Theater

VOCAL MUSIC

CHATTANOOGA BOYS CHOIR
1206 Market Street, #27 Freight Depot, Chattanooga, TN 37402
(615) 265-3030
FAX: (615) 265-3030
    Founded: 1954
    Arts Area: Choral
    Status: Professional; Non-Profit
    Type: Performing; Touring
    Purpose: To teach boys the love and appreciation of good music through a comprehensive training program
    Management: Alkahest Agency
    Officers: Phyllis Brewer, Administrator; Everett O'Neal, Conductor
    Paid Staff: 1 **Volunteer Staff:** 30
    Paid Artists: 7 **Non-Paid Artists:** 45
    Utilizes: Guest Artists
    Budget: $100,000 - $500,000
    Income Sources: Private Foundations/Grants/Endowments; Business/Corporate Donations; Box Office; Government
Grants; Individual Donations
    Season: September - June **Annual Attendance:** 25,000

CHATTANOOGA SYMPHONY AND OPERA ASSOCIATION
630 Chestnut Street, Chattanooga, TN 37402
(615) 267-8583
    Founded: Symphony - 1933; Opera - 1944
    Arts Area: Grand Opera; Lyric Opera; Light Opera; Operetta; Symphony
    Status: Professional; Non-Profit
    Type: Performing; Touring; Educational
    Management: Donald L. Andrews, Managing Director
    Officers: Thomas C. Hardy, President
    Paid Staff: 7 **Volunteer Staff:** 1
    Paid Artists: 95 **Non-Paid Artists:** 40
    Utilizes: Special Technical Talent; Guest Conductors; Guest Artists; Guest Directors
    Budget: $1,000,000 - $5,000,000
    Income Sources: Private Foundations/Grants/Endowments; Business/Corporate Donations; Box Office; Government
Grants; Individual Donations
    Season: September - May **Annual Attendance:** 100,000
    Affiliations: Tennesseans for the Arts; OA; ASOL
    Performance Facilities: Tivoli Theatre

FACILITY

ROLAND HAYES CONCERT HALL
University of Tennessee, 615 McCallie Avenue/ FAC #324, Chattanooga, TN 37403
(615) 755-4371
FAX: (615) 755-5249
> **Founded:** 1980
> **Type of Facility:** Theatre Complex; Concert Hall; Studio Performance; Performance Center
> **Type of Stage:** Thrust; Proscenium
> **Stage Dimensions:** 45'x42'; 17'x2' wings   **Orchestra Pit**
> **Seating Capacity:** 505
> **Year Built:** 1980   **Architect:** Derthick & Henley, Architects   **Cost:** $7,000,000
> **Acoustical Consultant:** Stephen M. Sessler, Newcomb & Boyd
> **Contact for Rental:** Ken Kapelinski;   (615) 755-4371
> **Resident Groups:** University of Tennessee: Theatre Department; Music Department; Visual Arts Department

TIVOLI THEATRE
709 Broad Street, Chattanooga, TN 37402
(615) 757-5042
FAX: (615) 757-5326
> **Founded:** 1921
> **Type of Facility:** Concert Hall; Performance Center; Theatre House
> **Facility Originally:** Vaudeville
> **Type of Stage:** Proscenium
> **Stage Dimensions:** 43'Dx46'Wx26'H   **Orchestra Pit**
> **Seating Capacity:** 1,700
> **Year Built:** 1921   **Architect:** Rapp & Rapp   **Cost:** $700,000
> **Year Remodeled:** 1989   **Architect:** Selmon T. Franklin   **Cost:** $6,500,000
> **Contact for Rental:** David E. Johnson;   (615) 757-5050
> *The Tivoli Theatre is a National Historic Landmark.*

Clarksville

THEATRE

ROXY THEATER
100 Franklin Street, Clarksville, TN 37040
(615) 645-7699
> **Founded:** 1983
> **Arts Area:** Professional; Musical; Community; Theatrical Group
> **Status:** Non-Profit
> **Type:** Performing; Educational
> **Purpose:** To promote and produce the visual and performing arts
> **Management:** Tom Thayer, General Manager; John McDonald, Artistic Director
> **Officers:** Tom Thayer, President; Cinders Murdock-Vaughan, Vice President; Linda Ellis, Secretary;
> Jean J. Faust, Treasurer
> **Paid Staff:** 3   **Volunteer Staff:** 5
> **Non-Paid Artists:** 2
> **Utilizes:** Guest Artists; Guest Directors
> **Budget:** $50,000 - $100,000
> **Income Sources:** Private Foundations/Grants/Endowments; Business/Corporate Donations; Box Office; Government
> Grants; Individual Donations
> **Season:** 52 Weeks   **Annual Attendance:** 7,500

Cleveland

THEATRE

CLEVELAND CREATIVE ARTS GUILD
PO Box 395, Cleveland, TN 37364
(615) 478-3114
> **Founded:** 1965
> **Arts Area:** Dinner; Community
> **Status:** Non-Profit
> **Type:** Performing; Educational
> **Purpose:** Working to provide creative opportunity and to enrich the cultural life of the community

Officers: Gaye Ogle, President; Julia Penney, First Vice President; Dale Dotson, Second Vice President; Pat McCracken, Secretary; Gaye Ogle, Treasurer
Volunteer Staff: 50
Utilizes: Guest Artists
Budget: $1,000 - $50,000
Income Sources: Box Office; Individual Donations
Season: 52 Weeks **Annual Attendance:** 1,600
Affiliations: Tennesseans for the Arts

Crossville

THEATRE

CUMBERLAND COUNTY PLAYHOUSE
Highway 70, PO Box 484, Crossville, TN 38557
(615) 484-5000
Founded: 1965
Arts Area: Professional; Theatrical Group
Status: Professional; Non-Profit
Type: Performing; Touring; Resident; Educational; Sponsoring
Purpose: To provide cultural enrichment for the area
Management: Jim Crabtree, Producing Director; Mary Crabtree, Consulting Producer
Officers: Steven Douglas, Chairman; Bill Startup, First Vice Chairman; L.A. Ezell, Second Vice Chairman; Stan Bise, Secretary
Paid Staff: 14 **Volunteer Staff:** 10
Paid Artists: 13 **Non-Paid Artists:** 65
Utilizes: Guest Artists; Guest Directors
Budget: $500,000 - $1,000,000
Income Sources: Private Foundations/Grants/Endowments; Business/Corporate Donations; Box Office; Government Grants; Individual Donations
Season: March - November **Annual Attendance:** 70,000
Affiliations: TCG
Performance Facilities: Cumberland County Playhouse

Franklin

THEATRE

PULL-TIGHT PLAYERS
Second Avenue South, PO Box 105, Franklin, TN 37064
(615) 790-6782
Founded: 1968
Arts Area: Community; Theatrical Group
Status: Non-Professional; Non-Profit
Type: Performing; Resident
Purpose: To bring quality community theatre to the Williamson County Area
Officers: Iain MacPherson, President; Roz Highfill, Vice President; Steve Evans, Secretary; John Emberton, Treasurer
Non-Paid Artists: 60
Utilizes: Guest Artists; Guest Directors
Budget: $1,000 - $50,000
Income Sources: Private Foundations/Grants/Endowments; Business/Corporate Donations; Box Office
Season: 52 Weeks **Annual Attendance:** 3,000

Germantown

THEATRE

POPLAR PIKE PLAYHOUSE
7653 Old Poplar Pike, Germantown, TN 38138
(901) 755-7775
FAX: (901) 756-2356
Founded: 1976
Arts Area: Musical; Community; Theatrical Group
Status: Non-Profit
Type: Performing; Educational
Purpose: Basically an educational theatre housed at Germantown High School

Management: Frank Bluestein, Managing Director; Robin McDurmott, Assistant Managing Director/Musical Director; Almeda Zent, Scenic Artist; Norma Early and Brenda Bluestein, Costumes; Staci Martin, Box Office
Paid Staff: 5   **Volunteer Staff:** 20
Non-Paid Artists: 20
Utilizes: Special Technical Talent; Guest Conductors; Guest Artists; Guest Directors
Budget: $50,000 - $100,000
Income Sources: Private Foundations/Grants/Endowments; Business/Corporate Donations; Box Office; Government Grants; Individual Donations
Season: September - May   **Annual Attendance:** 5,000
Affiliations: Tennessee Theater Association

Jackson

INSTRUMENTAL MUSIC

JACKSON SYMPHONY ASSOCIATION
1903 North Highland, Suite 4, Jackson, TN 38303-3429
(901) 427-6440
Mailing Address: PO Box 3429, Jackson, TN 38303
Founded: 1961
Arts Area: Symphony; Orchestra
Status: Semi-Professional
Type: Performing; Touring; Resident; Educational
Purpose: To support a performing orchestra of increasing quality for Jackson and its surrounding area; to promote the preservation of our musical heritage and audience exposure to the finer aspects of that heritage by providing programs that are attractive and entertaining
Management: Dr. Jordan Tang, Music Director; Karen Lenard, Administrative Assistant
Officers: Larry Dooley, President; Mary Jane McWherter, Secretary
Paid Staff: 3
Paid Artists: 70   **Non-Paid Artists:** 1
Utilizes: Guest Artists
Budget: $100,000 - $500,000
Income Sources: Private Foundations/Grants/Endowments; Business/Corporate Donations; Box Office; Government Grants; Individual Donations
Season: September - May   **Annual Attendance:** 25,000
Affiliations: ASOL
Performance Facilities: The Jackson Civic Center

THEATRE

JACKSON RECREATION CHILDREN'S THEATRE
400 South Highland, Jackson, TN 38301
(901) 423-0075
Founded: 1974
Arts Area: Musical; Dinner; Community
Status: Non-Professional
Type: Performing
Purpose: Provide training to young people interested in the performing arts; provide entertainment to children and adults and encourage them to be patrons of the arts
Management: Pat Gilliland-Alford, Director
Volunteer Staff: 2
Non-Paid Artists: 100
Budget: $1,000 - $50,000
Income Sources: Box Office
Annual Attendance: 3,000
Affiliations: Jackson Recreation and Parks; Jackson Theatre Guild
Performance Facilities: Jackson Civic Center, Little Theatre

JACKSON THEATRE GUILD
PO Box 7041, Jackson, TN 38308
(901) 422-2484
Founded: 1966
Arts Area: Musical; Community; Theatrical Group
Status: Non-Profit
Type: Performing; Resident; Educational
Purpose: To provide live theatre and performance education in the area
Management: Scott Conley, Artistic Director; Melody Pierce, Business Manager
Officers: Emily Canter, President; Phillip Collins, Vice President; Brian Kurt, Secretary; Roxanne Rhoads, Treasurer

Paid Staff: 1
Paid Artists: 1
Utilizes: Special Technical Talent; Guest Artists; Guest Directors
Budget: $50,000 - $100,000
Income Sources: Private Foundations/Grants/Endowments; Business/Corporate Donations; Box Office; Government Grants; Individual Donations
Season: 52 Weeks
Affiliations: Jackson Arts Council

FACILITY

JACKSON CIVIC CENTER
400 South Highland Avenue, Jackson, TN 38301
(901) 423-9404
Type of Facility: Concert Hall; Civic Center; Multi-Purpose
Type of Stage: Proscenium
Stage Dimensions: 150'Wx50'D   Orchestra Pit
Seating Capacity: 2,200
Year Built: 1973   Architect: W.C. Harris   Cost: $5,000,000
Acoustical Consultant: Burris-Meyer
Contact for Rental: Jerry Gist, Executive Director;   (901) 423-9404

LAMBUTH COLLEGE - LAMBUTH THEATRE
Department of Theatre, 705 Lamburth Boulevard, Jackson, TN 38301
(901) 425-2500, ext. 235
FAX: (901) 423-1990
Type of Facility: Theatre Complex
Facility Originally: Recreation Hall; Gymnasium
Type of Stage: Proscenium
Stage Dimensions: 35'Wx28'D
Seating Capacity: 250
Year Built: 1945
Year Remodeled: 1972
Contact for Rental: Jesse Byron

Johnson City

DANCE

TENNESSEE ASSOCIATION OF DANCE
PO Box 2432, Johnson City, TN 37605
(615) 929-1129
Founded: 1971
Arts Area: Modern; Ballet; Jazz; Tap
Status: Professional; Non-Professional; Non-Profit
Type: Educational
Purpose: To unite people in the state of Tennessee with interest in the advancement of dance in all its forms; to upgrade training programs; to promote dance opportunities and appreciation
Management: Judith Woodruff, Executive Coordinator
Officers: Jane Fabian, President
Volunteer Staff: 13
Utilizes: Guest Artists
Budget: $1,000 - $50,000
Income Sources: Private Foundations/Grants/Endowments; Box Office; Government Grants; Individual Donations
Annual Attendance: 200
Performance Facilities: Middle Tennessee State University

VOCAL MUSIC

JOHNSON CITY CIVIC CHORALE
Eastern Tennessee State University, PO Box 24427, Johnson City, TN 37614
(615) 753-2722
Founded: 1975
Arts Area: Choral
Status: Non-Professional; Non-Profit
Type: Performing; Touring; Resident
Purpose: To enhance the musical life of the community; to provide a musical outlet for talented area singers through performance of great choral music

Management: Robert LaPella, Musical Director/Conductor
Officers: Dr. James Odum, President
Volunteer Staff: 5
Non-Paid Artists: 3
Budget: $1,000 - $50,000
Income Sources: Private Foundations/Grants/Endowments; Business/Corporate Donations; Individual Donations
Season: September - May   **Annual Attendance:** 1,600
Performance Facilities: Munsey Memorial Methodist Church; Gilbreath Auditorium

THEATRE

THE ROAD COMPANY
PO Box 5278 EKS, Johnson City, TN 37603
(615) 926-7726
Founded: 1976
Arts Area: Professional; Theatrical Group
Status: Professional; Non-Profit
Type: Performing; Touring; Resident
Purpose: Dedicated to the production of new theatre which reflects the concerns and interests of the community in which we live and work, TRC is a touring theatre based in Johnson City serving the Upper Tennessee Valley, the southern mountains from the East Coast to the Mississippi River.
Management: Robert H. Leonard, Artistic Director; Nancy Fischman, Development Director; Eugene Wolf, Christine Murdock, Laurene Scalf, Senior Ensemble Members; Emily Green, Projects Director; Ailene Watterson, Administrative Assistant
Officers: Constance Douglas, President; Ignacy Fonberg, Vice President; Nancy Fischman, Treasurer
Paid Staff: 4   **Volunteer Staff:** 25
Paid Artists: 6
Utilizes: Guest Artists; Guest Directors
Budget: $100,000 - $500,000
Income Sources: Private Foundations/Grants/Endowments; Business/Corporate Donations; Box Office; Government Grants; Individual Donations
Season: September - June   **Annual Attendance:** 6,000
Affiliations: TCG; Johnson City Arts Council; Alternate ROOTS
Performance Facilities: Beeson Hall/Johnson City

Jonesborough

THEATRE

JONESBOROUGH REPERTORY THEATRE
125 1/2 Main Street, Jonesborough, TN 37659
(615) 282-2876
Founded: 1970
Arts Area: Community; Theatrical Group
Status: Non-Professional; Non-Profit
Type: Performing; Resident
Purpose: To bring live theatre to the area
Officers: Mylene Starr, President; Fred Bechelhimer, Treasurer
Volunteer Staff: 12
Non-Paid Artists: 25
Budget: $1,000 - $50,000
Income Sources: Box Office; Individual Donations
Season: April - November   **Annual Attendance:** 4,000
Affiliations: Arts Council

Kingsport

INSTRUMENTAL MUSIC

KINGSPORT SYMPHONY ORCHESTRA
1200 East Center Street, Kingsport, TN 37660
(615) 372-8423
Founded: 1947
Arts Area: Symphony; Orchestra; Chamber; Ensemble; Instrumental Group
Status: Semi-Professional; Non-Professional; Non-Profit
Type: Performing; Resident; Educational; Sponsoring
Purpose: To provide orchestral concerts to the public and educational and entertainment-oriented programs

Management: Mr. David Itkin, Music Director; Barbara Gerwe, General Manager; Mrs. Jolly Hill, Librarian
Officers: Alice Barlow, President; Charles Norrell, First Vice President; Louise Ammons, Second Vice President; Ann Bacon, Secretary; Mrs. Charles Eberhart, Treasurer
Paid Staff: 4   **Volunteer Staff:** 2
Paid Artists: 13   **Non-Paid Artists:** 60
Utilizes: Special Technical Talent; Guest Conductors; Guest Artists
Budget: $100,000 - $500,000
Income Sources: Private Foundations/Grants/Endowments; Business/Corporate Donations; Box Office; Government Grants; Individual Donations
Season: September - May   **Annual Attendance:** 8,500
Affiliations: ASOL; Kingsport Fine Arts Center
Performance Facilities: Eastmen Employee Center

Knoxville

DANCE

THE KNOXVILLE BALLET COMPANY
PO Box 10305, Knoxville, TN 37939-0305
(615) 966-7654
   Founded: 1973
   Arts Area: Modern; Ballet; Jazz
   Status: Semi-Professional; Non-Profit
   Type: Educational; Sponsoring
   Purpose: To raise the calibre of dance in this area through public performances; to build technically proficient dancers through the use of professional teachers, choreographers, and performers brought in by the company
   Management: Irma Witt O'Fallon, Artistic Director
   Officers: Samuel A. Shipman, President
   Volunteer Staff: 13
   Paid Artists: 3   **Non-Paid Artists:** 24
   Utilizes: Special Technical Talent; Guest Conductors; Guest Artists; Guest Choreographers
   Budget: $1,000 - $50,000
   Income Sources: Private Foundations/Grants/Endowments; Business/Corporate Donations; Box Office; Government Grants; Individual Donations
   Season: September - May   **Annual Attendance:** 1,500

KNOXVILLE METROPOLITAN DANCE THEATRE
201 Sherway Road, Knoxville, TN 37922
(615) 691-2671
   Founded: 1982
   Arts Area: Modern; Ballet; Jazz
   Status: Non-Professional; Non-Profit
   Type: Performing
   Purpose: To promote an appreciation of dance in many forms
   Management: Sondra Nanney, Administrative Director
   Volunteer Staff: 5
   Non-Paid Artists: 30
   Budget: $1,000 - $50,000
   Income Sources: Box Office; Individual Donations
   Season: September - May
   Affiliations: Tennessee Association of Dance

NEW REPERTORY DANCE COMPANY
Alumni Gym Dance Program, Knoxville, TN 37996
(615) 974-2169
   Founded: 1973
   Arts Area: Modern; Ballet; Jazz
   Status: Semi-Professional
   Type: Performing; Educational
   Purpose: To train college dancers in the art of performing; to provide quality dance concerts to the university community
   Management: Barbara B. Mason, Director
   Paid Staff: 4
   Utilizes: Special Technical Talent; Guest Artists
   Budget: $1,000 - $50,000
   Income Sources: Business/Corporate Donations; Box Office; Individual Donations
   Season: September - May   **Annual Attendance:** 1,800
   Affiliations: University of Tennessee-Knoxville
   Performance Facilities: Clarence Brown Theatre

TENNESSEE CHILDREN'S DANCE ENSEMBLE
4216 Sutherland Avenue, Knoxville, TN 37919
(615) 588-8842
Founded: 1981
Arts Area: Modern
Status: Professional; Non-Profit
Type: Performing; Touring; Resident; Educational
Purpose: To perform professionally using the medium of modern dance and, in so doing, show that children can achieve the same artistic excellence as a professional adult company
Management: Judy Robinson, Administrative Coordinator
Officers: Laura Kress, President; Fran Shea, Vice President; Deborah Wallace, Secretary; Louise Josephson, Treasurer
Paid Staff: 4   **Volunteer Staff:** 24
Paid Artists: 26
Utilizes: Special Technical Talent; Guest Artists; Guest Choreographers
Budget: $100,000 - $500,000
Income Sources: Private Foundations/Grants/Endowments; Business/Corporate Donations; Box Office; Government Grants; Individual Donations
Season: 52 Weeks   **Annual Attendance:** 200,000
Performance Facilities: Concert Stage

INSTRUMENTAL MUSIC

KNOXVILLE SYMPHONY ORCHESTRA
708 Gay Street, Knoxville, TN 37902
(615) 523-1178
FAX: (615) 546-3766
Founded: 1935
Arts Area: Symphony; Orchestra
Status: Professional; Non-Profit
Type: Performing; Touring; Educational
Purpose: To maintain a symphony orchestra for the entertainment and education of the east Tennessee region
Management: Constance Harrison, Executive Director; Martha Weaver, Director of Development
Officers: Jame L. Clayton, President; Mrs. E.E. Duncan, Vice President
Paid Staff: 9
Paid Artists: 85
Utilizes: Guest Conductors; Guest Artists
Budget: $1,000,000 - $5,000,000
Income Sources: Private Foundations/Grants/Endowments; Business/Corporate Donations; Box Office; Government Grants; Individual Donations
Season: September - May   **Annual Attendance:** 50,000
Performance Facilities: Tennessee Theatre

KNOXVILLE SYMPHONY YOUTH ORCHESTRA
708 Gay Street, Knoxville, TN 37902
(615) 523-1178
Founded: 1974
Arts Area: Symphony; Orchestra
Status: Non-Professional; Non-Profit
Type: Performing; Educational
Purpose: To give young people a chance to learn symphonic music, to rehearse in an organized setting and to perform in a symphony orchestra
Management: Barbara Adamick, Manager; Sande MacMorran, Music Director/Conductor
Paid Staff: 1   **Volunteer Staff:** 3
Non-Paid Artists: 60
Budget: $1,000 - $50,000
Income Sources: Box Office; Individual Donations
Season: September - April   **Annual Attendance:** 1,000
Affiliations: ASOL (Youth Orchestra Division); Knoxville Symphony
Performance Facilities: University of Tennessee Music Hall

VOCAL MUSIC

KNOXVILLE OPERA COMPANY
602 South Gay Street, Suite 700, Knoxville, TN 37902
(615) 524-0795
Founded: 1976
Arts Area: Grand Opera; Lyric Opera; Light Opera; Musical Theatre
Status: Professional; Non-Profit

Type: Performing; Sponsoring
Purpose: To produce opera and musical theatre performances on with current standards; to provide performance opportunities for developing American artists; to develop an appreciation for the art form through a program of opera education
Management: Robert Lyall, General Director; Ann Broadhead, Business Manager; Don Townsend, Production Manager
Officers: Joseph De Leese, President; Sammie Lynn Puett, President-Elect; Fuad Mishu, Secretary; Ruth Love, Treasurer
Paid Staff: 6
Paid Artists: 150 **Non-Paid Artists:** 160
Utilizes: Special Technical Talent; Guest Artists; Guest Directors
Budget: $500,000 - $1,000,000
Income Sources: Private Foundations/Grants/Endowments; Business/Corporate Donations; Box Office; Government Grants; Individual Donations
Season: 52 Weeks **Annual Attendance:** 15,000
Affiliations: OA
Performance Facilities: Civic Auditorium

THEATRE

CARPET BAG THEATRE
3018 East Fifth Avenue, Knoxville, TN 37914
(615) 522-2801
Founded: 1970
Arts Area: Professional
Status: Professional; Non-Profit
Type: Touring
Purpose: Dedicated to the production of new work, the ensemble creates new scripts through improvisation and collaboration. CBT is comprised of writers, actors, dancers, musicians and is known for its performances, workshops and other activities.
Management: Linda Parris-Bailey, Executive Director/Producer; Jeff Cody, Business Director/Technical Director
Paid Staff: 1 **Volunteer Staff:** 3
Paid Artists: 5
Utilizes: Special Technical Talent; Guest Artists; Guest Directors
Budget: $1,000 - $50,000
Income Sources: Government Grants; Individual Donations
Season: September - February; November-June **Annual Attendance:** 150,000
Affiliations: Alternate ROOTS; Black Theatre Alliance

CLARENCE BROWN THEATRE COMPANY
University of Tennessee, 1714 Andy Holt Avenue, PO Box 8450, Knoxville, TN 37996
(615) 974-3447
Founded: 1974
Arts Area: Professional; Theatrical Group
Status: Professional; Non-Profit
Type: Performing; Touring; Resident
Management: Margaret Ferguson, General Manager; Dennis E. Perkins, Company Manager
Paid Staff: 18
Paid Artists: 35
Utilizes: Guest Artists; Guest Directors
Budget: $100,000 - $500,000
Income Sources: Business/Corporate Donations; Box Office; Individual Donations
Season: October - April **Annual Attendance:** 20,000
Affiliations: LORT; TCG; Knoxville Arts Council; University of Tennessee
Performance Facilities: Clarence Brown Theatre

THEATER KNOXVILLE
c/o The Bijou Theater, PO Box 1746, Knoxville, TN 37901
(615) 523-4211
Founded: 1976
Arts Area: Community
Status: Non-Professional; Non-Profit
Type: Performing; Touring; Educational
Purpose: To provide quality shows using actors and technical persons from the community
Officers: Rusty Young, President; Gerry Diftler, Vice President; Debbie Feldman, Secretary; Wendie Wilson, Treasurer
Volunteer Staff: 15
Utilizes: Special Technical Talent
Budget: $1,000 - $50,000
Income Sources: Private Foundations/Grants/Endowments; Box Office; Individual Donations
Season: September - August **Annual Attendance:** 6,000
Performance Facilities: The Bijou Theater

PERFORMING SERIES

THE ARTS COUNCIL OF GREATER KNOXVILLE
PO Box 2506, Knoxville, TN 37901
(615) 523-7543
FAX: (615) 523-7312
Founded: 1976
Arts Area: Festivals
Status: Non-Profit
Type: Educational
Purpose: To promote the importance of a rich cultural life to the vitality and economic well-being of the Knoxville region; this is accomplished through public advocacy, programs and the support of the cultural institution
Management: Sandy Garber, Executive Director
Officers: Jerry Becker, President; Mary Lynn Majors, President Elect/Vice President; Donald Wright, Treasurer; Linda Underwood, Secretary; Bill Hays, Vice President Special Projects; Katherine Bell, Vice President Community Service
Paid Staff: 7   **Volunteer Staff:** 3
Budget: $100,000 - $500,000
Income Sources: Private Foundations/Grants/Endowments; Business/Corporate Donations; Box Office; Government Grants; Individual Donations; Fundraising

FACILITY

BIJOU THEATRE CENTER
803 South Gay Street, Knoxville, TN 37901
(615) 523-4211
FAX: (615) 524-0821
Founded: 1980
Type of Facility: Theatre House
Facility Originally: Vaudeville
Type of Stage: Proscenium
Stage Dimensions: 35'x30'
Seating Capacity: 750
Year Built: 1908
Year Remodeled: 1980
Contact for Rental: Stephen F. Krempasky;   (615) 523-4211
Resident Groups: Knoxville Chamber Orchestra; Appalachian Ballet; Young Pianist Series

KNOXVILLE CIVIC AUDITORIUM AND COLISEUM - AUDITORIUM
500 East Church Avenue, Knoxville, TN 37901
(615) 544-5399
FAX: (615) 544-5386
Type of Facility: Auditorium
Type of Stage: Proscenium
Stage Dimensions: 108'Wx54'D; 60'Wx27'H proscenium opening   **Orchestra Pit**
Seating Capacity: 2,534
Year Built: 1961   **Architect:** McCarty Holsaple   **Cost:** $5,400,000
Year Remodeled: 1987   **Architect:** McCarty Holsaple   **Cost:** $1,500,000
Contact for Rental: Paul C. Sherbakoff, Manager;   (615) 544-5399
Manager: Paul C. Sherbakoff;   (615) 544-5399

TENNESSEE THEATER
604 South Gay Street, Knoxville, TN 37902
(615) 525-2250
FAX: (615) 523-3954
Type of Facility: Performance Center; Theatre House; Opera House
Type of Stage: Proscenium
Stage Dimensions: 54'Dx26'H   **Orchestra Pit**
Seating Capacity: 1,515
Year Built: 1928   **Architect:** Graven & Mayger   **Cost:** $1,200,000
Year Remodeled: 1982   **Architect:** Ron Childrif & Associates   **Cost:** $1,500,000
Acoustical Consultant: Coffeen & Associates
Contact for Rental: Robert Frost;   (615) 525-2250

UNIVERSITY OF TENNESSEE MUSIC HALL
1741 Volunteer Boulevard, Knoxville, TN 37996-2600
(615) 974-5110
Founded: 1965
Type of Facility: Concert Hall; Auditorium; Multi-Purpose

Type of Stage: Proscenium
Stage Dimensions: 43'x33'   **Orchestra Pit**
Seating Capacity: 573
Year Built: 1965
Architect: Barber & McMurray
Contact for Rental: W. Harvey Smeltzer;   (615) 974-5110
Resident Groups: Knoxville Symphony Orchestra; Knoxville Opera Company
The Tennessee Theater is on the National Register of Historic Places.

Lebanon

FACILITY

CUMBERLAND UNIVERSITY AUDITORIUM
South Greenwood Street, Lebanon, TN 37087
(615) 444-2562
FAX: (615) 444-2569
  Type of Facility: Auditorium
  Year Built: 1920
  Architect: Beaty Gresham
  Manager: Mike Wiggington

Maryville

DANCE

APPALACHIAN BALLET COMPANY
215 West Broadway, Maryville, TN 37801
(615) 982-8463
  Founded: 1972
  Arts Area: Ballet
  Status: Semi-Professional; Non-Profit
  Type: Performing; Touring; Resident; Educational
  Purpose: To promote excellence in dance
  Management: Cheryl Van Metre, Artistic Director; Katharine Dorner, Company Manager
  Officers: Aleta Ledendecker, Chairman; Greg Walters, Vice Chairman; Jane Tolhurst, Fundraising Chairman;
  Tanya Prine, Special Events Chairman
  Paid Staff: 7
  Paid Artists: 6   **Non-Paid Artists:** 32
  Utilizes: Special Technical Talent; Guest Artists
  Budget: $50,000 - $100,000
  Income Sources: Private Foundations/Grants/Endowments; Business/Corporate Donations; Box Office; Government
  Grants; Individual Donations
  Season: September - May   **Annual Attendance:** 20,000
  Performance Facilities: Knoxville Civic Auditorium; Tennessee Theater

FACILITY

MARYVILLE COLLEGE
Maryville, TN 37801
(615) 981-8000
FAX: (615) 983-0581
  Type of Facility: Concert Hall; Auditorium; Theatre House
  Type of Stage: Thrust; Proscenium; Platform   **Orchestra Pit**
  Seating Capacity: Auditorium - 1,200; Theatre - 450; Recital Hall - 250
  Year Built: 1950   **Architect:** Schweiken and Elting
  Year Remodeled: 1956
  Contact for Rental: Office of Conferences and Special Programs;   (615) 981-8117
  Resident Groups: Maryville College: Community Wind Ensemble; Community Chorus; Theatre; Concert Choir; Jazz
  Band; Maryville-Alcoa College Community Orchestra

Memphis

INSTRUMENTAL MUSIC

MEMPHIS SYMPHONY
3100 Walnut Grove Road, Suite 501, Memphis, TN 38111
(901) 324-3627
FAX: (901) 324-3698
  Founded: 1952
  Arts Area: Symphony; Orchestra; Chamber
  Status: Professional; Non-Profit
  Type: Performing; Educational; Sponsoring
  Management: Alan Balter, Music Director/Conductor; Michael Maxwell, Executive Director; Mark Salvage, Director of Operations; Ron Jewell, Marketing Director
  Paid Staff: 14
  Paid Artists: 80
  Utilizes: Guest Conductors; Guest Artists
  Budget: $1,000,000 - $5,000,000
  Income Sources: Private Foundations/Grants/Endowments; Business/Corporate Donations; Box Office; Government Grants; Individual Donations
  Season: October - May **Annual Attendance:** 300,000
  Affiliations: ASOL; Memphis Arts Council
  Performance Facilities: Vincent deFrank Hall, Memphis Convention Center Complex

MEMPHIS YOUTH SYMPHONY ORCHESTRA
3100 Walnut Grove Road, Suite 402, Memphis, TN 38111
(901) 324-3627
  Arts Area: Symphony; Orchestra
  Status: Non-Professional; Non-Profit
  Type: Performing; Educational
  Management: Rita Garrigan, Manager
  Non-Paid Artists: 60
  Income Sources: Business/Corporate Donations; Box Office; Government Grants; Individual Donations
  Season: October - May
  Affiliations: ASOL (Youth Orchestra Division)
  Performance Facilities: Harding Academy; Ridgeway High School

ROSCOE'S SURPRISE ORCHESTRA
PO Box 41824, Memphis, TN 38174
(901) 725-4147
  Founded: 1981
  Arts Area: Orchestra; Chamber; Ensemble; Ethnic; Instrumental Group; Electronic & Live Electronic
  Status: Professional; Non-Profit
  Type: Performing; Touring; Educational; Sponsoring
  Purpose: To perform and promote music of the 20th century and, whenever possible, the music of living composers and produce concerts
  Management: John Boatner, Executive Director
  Officers: Karin English, Chairman; Floyd Deal, Secretary; Alfred Rudd, Treasurer
  Paid Staff: 1 **Volunteer Staff:** 5
  Paid Artists: 95
  Utilizes: Special Technical Talent; Guest Conductors; Guest Artists; Guest Directors
  Budget: $1,000 - $50,000
  Income Sources: Private Foundations/Grants/Endowments; Business/Corporate Donations; Box Office; Government Grants; Individual Donations
  Season: 52 Weeks **Annual Attendance:** 2,095
  Affiliations: Memphis Arts Council; CMA

VOCAL MUSIC

THE GARY BEARD CHORALE
40 East Parkway South, Memphis, TN 38104
(901) 458-1652
FAX: (901) 458-0145
  Arts Area: Grand Opera; Lyric Opera; Operetta; Choral
  Status: Professional
  Type: Performing; Touring; Resident
  Purpose: To return the professional chorale to prominence, excelling in the great choral literature and quality performances
  Officers: Gary Beard, Director/Conductor; Chris Nemec, Associate Director/Conductor/Accompanist

Paid Staff: 2
Paid Artists: 23
Utilizes: Guest Artists
Budget: $1,000 - $50,000
Income Sources: Private Foundations/Grants/Endowments; Box Office; Individual Donations
Season: 52 Weeks   Annual Attendance: 30,000
Affiliations: Community Concerts
Performance Facilities: Lindenwood Christian Church Sanctuary

OPERA MEMPHIS
Memphis State University, South Campus, Memphis, TN 38152
(901) 678-2706
FAX: (901) 678-3506
Founded: 1956
Arts Area: Grand Opera; Music; Theatre
Status: Professional; Non-Profit
Type: Performing; Touring
Purpose: To present high-quality opera performances for regional audiences
Management: Robert Driver, General/Artistic Director; Bert Adler-Wolss, Executive Director; Michael Ching, Artistic Director
Officers: Willis H. Willie, Chairman, Board of Trustees; James P. Gates, First Vice President; Hugh M. Stephens Jr., Treasurer; Martin H. Hawssenberg, Secretary; Sheila Zancor, Opera Guild President
Paid Staff: 8
Utilizes: Special Technical Talent; Guest Artists; Guest Directors
Budget: $500,000 - $1,000,000
Income Sources: Private Foundations/Grants/Endowments; Business/Corporate Donations; Box Office; Government Grants; Individual Donations
Season: October - February   Annual Attendance: 37,000
Affiliations: OA; COS; AAA; Tennesseans for the Arts
Performance Facilities: Orpheum Theatre

THEATRE

CIRCUIT PLAYHOUSE
51 South Cooper, Memphis, TN 38104
(901) 725-0776
FAX: (901) 272-7530
Founded: 1969
Arts Area: Professional; Theatrical Group
Status: Professional
Type: Performing; Resident
Purpose: To produce live theatrical productions in a two-theater complex, as well as new plays, off-Broadway and Broadway offerings
Management: Jackie Nichols, Executive Director; Elizabeth Howard, Administrative Director; Kay Zimmerman, Artistic Director; Chuck Britt, Technical Director
Officers: William Clark, President; Nino Shipp, Past President/First Vice President; Gene Katz, Second Vice President; David Williams, Secretary; Pat Bogan, Treasurer
Paid Staff: 20   Volunteer Staff: 6
Paid Artists: 15   Non-Paid Artists: 80
Utilizes: Special Technical Talent; Guest Artists; Guest Directors
Budget: $100,000 - $500,000
Income Sources: Private Foundations/Grants/Endowments; Business/Corporate Donations; Box Office; Government Grants; Individual Donations
Season: 52 Weeks   Annual Attendance: 40,000
Affiliations: SETC; TCG; Tennessee Theatre Association; Playhouse on the Square
Performance Facilities: Circuit Playhouse

MEMPHIS CHILDREN'S THEATRE
2599 Avery Avenue, Memphis, TN 38112
(901) 452-3968
Founded: 1948
Arts Area: Community
Status: Non-Profit
Type: Performing; Educational
Purpose: Memphis Children's Theatre uses children, ages 5-18, and involves them in all aspects of theatre
Management: Lisa M. Sikes, Theatre Director; Ken Lightfoot, Theatre Coordinator
Officers: Brian Ford, Chairman of Support Group; Ashley Bugg, Children Committee President
Paid Staff: 5   Volunteer Staff: 27
Paid Artists: 7   Non-Paid Artists: 6

Utilizes: Special Technical Talent; Guest Artists; Guest Directors
Budget: $100,000 - $500,000
Income Sources: Private Foundations/Grants/Endowments; Business/Corporate Donations; Government Grants; Individual Donations
Season: 52 Weeks   **Annual Attendance:** 10,000
Affiliations: American Children's Theatre Association; Tennessee Theatre Association; Southeastern Theatre Conference

PLAYHOUSE ON THE SQUARE
51 South Cooper Street, Memphis, TN 38104
(901) 725-0776
  Founded: 1968
  Arts Area: Professional; Theatrical Group
  Status: Professional; Non-Profit
  Type: Performing; Touring; Resident; Educational
  Purpose: To produce live theatrical productions in a two-theatre complex, as well as new plays, off-Broadway and Broadway productions
  Management: Jackie Nichols, Executive Director; Elizabeth Howard, Administrative Director; Patty McNaulty, Public Relations Director
  Officers: William Clark, President; Randall Reagan, Vice President; Pat Bogan, Secretary; Gene Katz, Treasurer
  Paid Staff: 10   **Volunteer Staff:** 6
  Paid Artists: 12
  Utilizes: Special Technical Talent; Guest Artists; Guest Directors
  Income Sources: Private Foundations/Grants/Endowments; Business/Corporate Donations; Box Office; Government Grants; Individual Donations
  Season: September - July
  Affiliations: TCG; Circuit Playhouse
  Performance Facilities: Playhouse On The Square

THEATRE MEMPHIS
630 Perkins Extended, Memphis, TN 38117-4799
(901) 682-8323
  Mailing: PO Box 240117, Memphis, TN 38124
  Founded: 1919
  Arts Area: Community; Theatrical Group
  Status: Non-Professional; Non-Profit
  Type: Performing
  Purpose: To provide interested persons with the opportunity to see theatrical productions and provide the opportunity to act in and/or assist with the production of plays
  Management: Brad Watson, Director of Marketing; Diane M. Jahnke, Subscription and Ticketing Director; Dr. Jim Seemann, Scenic Designer/Production Manager
  Officers: Sherwood Lohrey, President; Jim Cairns, General Manager
  Paid Staff: 14   **Volunteer Staff:** 500
  Paid Artists: 5   **Non-Paid Artists:** 200
  Utilizes: Guest Artists; Guest Directors
  Budget: $500,000 - $1,000,000
  Income Sources: Private Foundations/Grants/Endowments; Business/Corporate Donations; Box Office; Government Grants; Individual Donations
  Season: September - June   **Annual Attendance:** 80,000
  Affiliations: ACT; SETC; Tennessee Theatre Association; Memphis Arts Council; Tennessee Arts Commission
  Performance Facilities: Theatre Memphis

PERFORMING SERIES

MEMPHIS IN MAY INTERNATIONAL FESTIVAL
245 Wagner Place, Suite 220, Memphis, TN 38103
(901) 525-4611
  Founded: 1976
  Arts Area: Dance; Vocal Music; Instrumental Music; Theater; Festivals
  Status: Non-Profit
  Type: Educational; Sponsoring
  Management: Cynthia Ham, Executive Director; Davis Tillman, Artistic Director; Deanie Parker, Marketing Director
  Officers: Harry Miller, President; Joyce Blackmon, President-Elect; Tom Jones, Secretary; John Presley, Treasurer
  Paid Staff: 12   **Volunteer Staff:** 2,200
  Utilizes: Guest Artists
  Budget: $1,000,000 - $5,000,000
  Income Sources: Business/Corporate Donations; Box Office; Government Grants; Individual Donations
  Season: May - June   **Annual Attendance:** 1,000,000

FACILITY

MEMPHIS CHILDREN'S THEATRE
2599 Avery Avenue, Memphis, TN 38112
(901) 452-3968
Type of Facility: Theatre House
Type of Stage: Proscenium
Seating Capacity: 200
Year Built: 1982　**Architect:** Awsumb Waye Watson　**Cost:** $250,000
Acoustical Consultant: Gott
Contact for Rental: Lisa Sikes;　(901) 452-3968

MEMPHIS COOK CONVENTION CENTER COMPLEX
255 North Main Street, Memphis, TN 38103
(901) 576-1200
FAX: (901) 576-1212
Type of Facility: Auditorium; Civic Center
Year Built: 1924　**Architect:** George Awsumb　**Cost:** $800,000
Year Remodeled: 1958　**Architect:** Haglund & Venable　**Cost:** $4,500,000
Contact for Rental: Betty Ball;　(901) 576-1200
Manager: David E. Greer
Resident Groups: Memphis Orchestral Society; Memphis Symphony Orchestra; Beethoven Club
Memphis Convention Center Complex contains Dixon-Myers Hall and Vincent DeFrank Hall. See separate listings for further information.

MEMPHIS COOK CONVENTION CENTER COMPLEX - DIXON-MYERS HALL
255 North Main Street, Memphis, TN 38103
(901) 576-1200
Type of Facility: Auditorium
Type of Stage: Proscenium; Hydraulic Lift Stage
Stage Dimensions: 72'9"Wx32'D; add 8'D with pit at stage level　**Orchestra Pit**
Seating Capacity: 4,361
Year Remodeled: 1974　**Architect:** Haglund & Venable
Contact for Rental: Betty Ball;　(901) 576-1200
Manager: David E. Greer
Shares stage with Vincent DeFrank Hall, spaces cannot be used concurrently

MEMPHIS COOK CONVENTION CENTER COMPLEX - VINCENT DEFRANK HALL
255 North Main Street, Memphis, TN 38103
(901) 576-1200
Type of Facility: Concert Hall
Type of Stage: Proscenium
Stage Dimensions: 69'Wx32'Hx32'D　**Orchestra Pit**
Seating Capacity: 2,424
Year Remodeled: 1974　**Architect:** Haglund & Venable
Contact for Rental: Betty Ball;　(901) 576-1200
Manager: David E. Greer
Shares stage with Dixon-Meyers Hall, spaces cannot be used concurrently

ORPHEUM THEATRE
203 South Main Street, PO Box 3370, Memphis, TN 38173
(901) 525-7800
FAX: (901) 526-0829
Founded: 1928
Type of Facility: Concert Hall; Performance Center; Off Broadway; Theatre House; Opera House
Facility Originally: Vaudeville
Type of Stage: Proscenium　**Orchestra Pit**
Seating Capacity: 2,300
Year Built: 1928　**Architect:** Rapp & Rapp　**Cost:** $1,600,000
Year Remodeled: 1982　**Architect:** Awsumb & Williamson　**Cost:** $4,500,000
Contact for Rental: Donna Darwin;　(901) 525-7800
Resident Groups: Opera Memphis; Memphis Concert Band

THEATRE MEMPHIS
630 Perkins Extended, Memphis, TN 38117-4799
(901) 682-8323
FAX: (901) 763-4096
Type of Facility: Studio Performance; Theatre House

Type of Stage: Flexible; Proscenium
Stage Dimensions: Mainstage - 65'x50'x25'   **Orchestra Pit**
Seating Capacity: Mainstage - 435; Little Theatre - 100
Year Built: 1975   **Architect:** Wells Awsumb   **Cost:** $1,500,000
Acoustical Consultant: Bolt, Beranek & Newman
Contact for Rental: James Cairns;   (901) 682-8323
Resident Groups: Show Wagon Troop
Theatrical performances; meetings; shows

Milligan College

FACILITY

MILLIGAN COLLEGE - DERTHICK THEATRE
Milligan College, TN 37682
(615) 461-8705
   Type of Facility: Theatre House
   Type of Stage: Thrust; Proscenium
   Seating Capacity: 150
   Year Remodeled: 1975
   Contact for Rental: (615) 461-8705

MILLIGAN COLLEGE - SEEGER CHAPEL CONCERT HALL
Milligan College, TN 37682
(615) 929-0116
   Type of Facility: Concert Hall
   Type of Stage: Proscenium
   Stage Dimensions: 25'x50'x30'   **Orchestra Pit**
   Seating Capacity: 1,196
   Year Built: 1966   **Architect:** E. Rawls   **Cost:** $1,800,000
   Contact for Rental: Ruth Loving;   (615) 561-8720
   Resident Groups: Milligan College Concert Choir; Milligan College Chorale; Milligan College Chamber Singers

---

Morristown

THEATRE

MORRISTOWN THEATRE GUILD
314 South Hill Street, Morristown, TN 37814
(615) 586-9260
   Founded: 1934
   Arts Area: Musical; Dinner; Community
   Status: Non-Professional; Non-Profit
   Type: Performing; Educational
   Purpose: Exposure to and participation in live theatre; educational training for school-age children
   Management: David Horton, Artistic Director
   Officers: Linda Dietrich, Chairman; Randy Turner, Vice Chairman; Sue Carey, Secretary; George Haggard, Treasurer
   Paid Staff: 1   **Volunteer Staff:** 30
   Non-Paid Artists: 50
   Budget: $1,000 - $50,000
   Income Sources: Business/Corporate Donations; Box Office; Individual Donations
   Season: September - May   **Annual Attendance:** 3,000
   Affiliations: Tennessee Theatre Association
   Performance Facilities: Theatre Guild

FACILITY

THEATRE GUILD
314 South Hill Street, Morristown, TN 37814
(615) 586-9260
   Type of Facility: Theatre House
   Facility Originally: Church
   Type of Stage: Thrust
   Stage Dimensions: 40'x140'
   Seating Capacity: 125
   Year Built: 1881

Year Remodeled: 1981   Cost: $6,000
Contact for Rental: Linda Dietrich, Chairman;   (615) 587-2164

Nashville

DANCE

NASHVILLE BALLET
2976 Sidco Drive, Nashville, TN 37204-3715
(615) 244-7233
FAX: (615) 242-1741
Founded: 1986
Arts Area: Ballet
Status: Professional; Non-Profit
Type: Performing; Touring; Educational
Purpose: To present both classical and modern ballet in a manner that entertains and educates our audiences; to foster a love of dance in the community through education of both pre-professionals and the general audience
Management: Edward Myers, Artistic Director; Terrance L. Demas, Managing Director; Jane Fabian, School Administrator
Officers: Dudley Richter, President; Elizabeth Nichols, Vice President; Don Shriver, Treasurer; John Stein, Secretary
Paid Staff: 14
Paid Artists: 28   **Non-Paid Artists:** 8
Utilizes: Special Technical Talent; Guest Conductors; Guest Choreographers; Composers; Designers; Educators
Budget: $1,000,000 - $5,000,000
Income Sources: Private Foundations/Grants/Endowments; Business/Corporate Donations; Box Office; Government Grants; Individual Donations; Concessions; Touring; Video
Season: September - June   **Annual Attendance:** 18,322
Performance Facilities: Tennessee Performing Arts Center

NASHVILLE CONTEMPORARY BALLET COMPANY
PO Box 50580, Nashville, TN 37205
(615) 352-8078
Founded: 1984
Arts Area: Ballet; Jazz
Status: Semi-Professional; Non-Profit
Type: Performing
Purpose: To provide a performing outlet for Middle Tennessee young people/artists with professional/semi-professional quality
Management: Jan Brooks, Artistic Director
Officers: Wanda Lenk Walters, President; Michael Childers, Daryle Tallent, Treasurers; Marci Fairhead, Secretary
Paid Staff: 1   **Volunteer Staff:** 3
Non-Paid Artists: 12
Utilizes: Guest Artists
Budget: $1,000 - $50,000
Income Sources: Private Foundations/Grants/Endowments; Business/Corporate Donations; Government Grants; Individual Donations
Season: September - July   **Annual Attendance:** 2,000
Affiliations: Dance Alliance

TENNESSEE DANCE THEATRE
PO Box 121884, Nashville, TN 37212
(615) 255-9533; (615) 248-3262
Founded: 1983
Arts Area: Modern
Status: Professional; Non-Profit
Type: Performing; Touring; Resident
Purpose: To cultivate, promote, foster and develop the love, understanding and appreciation of the art of dance in Tennessee
Management: Linda Mason, Executive Director; Susan Sanders, Managing Director
Officers: Lind Mason, President; Suzanne Shambaugh, Secretary
Paid Staff: 1   **Volunteer Staff:** 2
Paid Artists: 6
Utilizes: Special Technical Talent; Guest Artists
Budget: $100,000 - $500,000
Income Sources: Private Foundations/Grants/Endowments; Business/Corporate Donations; Box Office; Government Grants; Individual Donations

Season: October - June **Annual Attendance:** 4,000
Affiliations: Metro Division of Parks and Recreation

INSTRUMENTAL MUSIC

NASHVILLE SYMPHONY ASSOCIATION
208 23rd Avenue North, Nashville, TN 37203
(615) 329-3033
FAX: (615) 329-2304
Founded: 1946
Arts Area: Symphony; Orchestra; Chamber
Status: Professional
Type: Performing
Purpose: Dedicated to enhancing the quality of life in Nashville and the surrounding communities by providing opportunities for all citizens to enjoy live performances of symphonic music in its various forms
Management: Steven Greil, Executive Director; Beth Zeitlin, Director of Public Relations; Laura Lonergan, Controller/Financial Director; Kim Carpenter, Director of Development
Officers: Susan R. Russell, Chairman; Larry Larkin, Vice Chairman; Mary Neil Price, Secretary; Bill Hawkins, Treasurer
Paid Staff: 28
Paid Artists: 82
Utilizes: Special Technical Talent; Guest Conductors; Guest Artists
Budget: $1,000,000 - $5,000,000
Income Sources: Private Foundations/Grants/Endowments; Business/Corporate Donations; Box Office; Government Grants; Individual Donations
Season: September - August **Annual Attendance:** 250,000
Affiliations: ASOL; AAA; ASCAP; BMI
Performance Facilities: Tennessee Performing Arts Center; War Memorial Auditorium

NASHVILLE YOUTH SYMPHONY
2400 Blakemore Avenue, Nashville, TN 37212
(615) 322-7651
Founded: 1947
Arts Area: Symphony; Orchestra
Status: Non-Professional; Non-Profit
Type: Performing; Touring; Educational; Sponsoring
Management: Emelyne Bingham, Manager/Conductor
Paid Staff: 4 **Volunteer Staff:** 20
Non-Paid Artists: 160
Utilizes: Guest Artists
Budget: $50,000 - $100,000
Income Sources: Private Foundations/Grants/Endowments; Box Office; Individual Donations
Season: August - May **Annual Attendance:** 2,500
Affiliations: ASOL (Youth Orchestra Division)
Performance Facilities: War Memorial Auditorium; Cohn High School Auditorium; Blair School of Music Recital Hall

VOCAL MUSIC

NASHVILLE OPERA
1900 Belmont Boulevard, Fidelity Hall 402, Nashville, TN 37212
(615) 292-5710
FAX: (615) 292-0549
Founded: 1981
Arts Area: Grand Opera; Lyric Opera; Light Opera
Status: Professional; Non-Profit
Type: Performing; Educational
Purpose: To present operatic productions to middle Tennesseeans
Management: Kyle Ridout, General Director; Leanne Porter, Executive Assistant
Paid Staff: 2 **Volunteer Staff:** 10
Paid Artists: 120
Utilizes: Special Technical Talent; Guest Conductors; Guest Artists; Guest Directors
Budget: $500,000 - $1,000,000
Income Sources: Private Foundations/Grants/Endowments; Business/Corporate Donations; Box Office; Government Grants; Individual Donations
Season: 52 Weeks **Annual Attendance:** 7,500
Affiliations: OA
Performance Facilities: Tennessee Performing Arts Center

THEATRE

ACTORS PLAYHOUSE OF NASHVILLE
2318 West End Avenue, Nashville, TN 37203
(615) 327-0049
Arts Area: Professional; Theatrical Group
Status: Semi-Professional; Non-Profit
Type: Performing
Purpose: Specializes in off-Broadway plays to contemporary playwrights to present plays not routinely seen in the Nashville area
Management: Dennis Ewing, Artistic Director/Co-Founder; Janet Claire, Producing Director/Co-Founder
Officers: Janet Claire, President of Board; Dennis Ewing, Vice President of Board
Paid Staff: 4
Utilizes: Special Technical Talent; Guest Directors
Budget: $1,000 - $50,000
Income Sources: Box Office
Season: 52 Weeks   **Annual Attendance:** 10,000
Performance Facilities: Actors Playhouse of Nashville

CHAFFIN'S BARN - A DINNER THEATRE
8204 Highway 100, Nashville, TN 37221
(615) 646-9977
Founded: 1967
Arts Area: Professional; Musical; Dinner
Status: Professional
Type: Performing
Purpose: Package price for buffet dining and professional theatre productions produced by staff directors utilizing professional, non-equity performers
Management: John P. Chaffin and Dianne Chaffin, Managers
Officers: John P. Chaffin, President; Dianne Chaffin, Secretary
Paid Staff: 15
Paid Artists: 120
Utilizes: Guest Directors
Budget: $100,000 - $500,000
Income Sources: Box Office
Season: 52 Weeks   **Annual Attendance:** 32,000
Performance Facilities: Chaffin's Barn

NASHVILLE ACADEMY THEATRE
724 Second Avenue South, Nashville, TN 37210
(615) 254-9103
Founded: 1931
Arts Area: Professional; Theatrical Group
Status: Professional; Non-Profit
Type: Performing; Resident; Educational
Purpose: To contribute to the cultural development of young people by providing them with the finest in professional theatre for young audiences
Management: Scot Copeland, Artistic Director; Jean Johnson, Financial Administration
Officers: Dr. Helen Brown, Chair; Dorothy Wright, Vice Chair; Beth Alexander, Secretary; Mary Jones, Treasurer; John Lehman, Chair-Elect
Paid Staff: 9   **Volunteer Staff:** 30
Paid Artists: 24
Utilizes: Special Technical Talent; Guest Artists; Guest Directors
Budget: $100,000 - $500,000
Income Sources: Private Foundations/Grants/Endowments; Business/Corporate Donations; Box Office; Government Grants; Individual Donations
Season: September - May   **Annual Attendance:** 72,050

TENNESSEE REPERTORY THEATRE
427 Chestnut Street, Nashville, TN 37203
(615) 244-4878
FAX: (615) 244-1232
Founded: 1985
Arts Area: Professional; Theatrical Group
Status: Professional
Type: Performing; Resident
Purpose: To present quality, professional theatre in a full season of plays as a resident company at the Tennessee Performing Arts Center

Management: Brian J. Laczko, Managing Director; Mac Pirkle, Artistic Director; Jennifer Orth, Company Manager; Edie Crane, Director of Public Relations/Marketing; Sherry R. Ridlon, Director of Audience Development; Don Jones, Associate Artistic Director; Donna J. Gillroy, Director of Development
Officers: Nicky Weaver, President, Board of Trustees; John O. Bovender Jr., President-Elect; Mac Pirkle, Trustee
Paid Staff: 5 **Volunteer Staff:** 12
Utilizes: Guest Conductors; Guest Artists; Guest Directors
Budget: $1,000,000 - $5,000,000
Income Sources: Private Foundations/Grants/Endowments; Business/Corporate Donations; Box Office; Government Grants; Individual Donations
Season: October - June **Annual Attendance:** 35,000
Affiliations: AEA; LORT
Performance Facilities: James K. Polk Theater, Tennessee Performing Arts Center

WEST END DRAMA MINISTRIES
2200 West End Avenue, Nashville, TN 37203
(615) 321-8500
Founded: 1976
Arts Area: Theatrical Group
Status: Non-Profit
Type: Resident; Educational
Purpose: To develop community through dramatic projects that not only enhance performance skills but tell the Gospel through dramatic media
Management: Ken Nelson, Chairman; Alice Swason, Assistant Director; Don Marler, Director of Music
Paid Staff: 1 **Volunteer Staff:** 30
Paid Artists: 4 **Non-Paid Artists:** 50
Utilizes: Special Technical Talent; Guest Directors
Budget: $1,000 - $50,000
Income Sources: Private Foundations/Grants/Endowments; Individual Donations
Season: 52 Weeks **Annual Attendance:** 2,000

PERFORMING SERIES

TENNESSEE PERFORMING ARTS CENTER MANAGEMENT CORPORATION
505 Deaderick Street, Nashville, TN 32719
(615) 741-7985
FAX: (615) 741-1266
Founded: 1977
Arts Area: Dance; Vocal Music; Instrumental Music; Theater
Status: Non-Profit
Type: Educational; Sponsoring
Purpose: To present touring groups; to operate educational programs; to coordinate constituent programs
Officers: James Randolph, President
Paid Staff: 47 **Volunteer Staff:** 30
Utilizes: Guest Artists
Budget: $1,000,000 - $5,000,000
Income Sources: Private Foundations/Grants/Endowments; Business/Corporate Donations; Box Office; Government Grants; Individual Donations
Season: 52 Weeks **Annual Attendance:** 500,000
Affiliations: APAP; IAAM
Performance Facilities: Tennessee Performing Arts Center

FACILITY

CHAFFIN'S BARN
8204 Highway 100, Nashville, TN 37221
(615) 646-9977
Founded: 1967
Type of Facility: Dinner Theatre
Type of Stage: Arena; Arena has in-the-round capability
Stage Dimensions: 16'x16'
Seating Capacity: 300
Year Built: 1966 **Cost:** $100,000
Year Remodeled: 1986 **Cost:** $250,000
Contact for Rental: John P. Chaffin; (615) 646-9977
Resident Groups: Chaffin's Barn - A Dinner Theatre
Conventions; groups; private functions

GRAND OLE OPRY HOUSE
2804 Opryland Drive, Nashville, TN 37214
(615) 889-7502
Type of Facility: Opera House
Type of Stage: Thrust
Stage Dimensions: 75'Wx80'D   **Orchestra Pit**
Seating Capacity: 4,424
Year Built: 1974   **Architect:** Welton Becket   **Cost:** $25,000,000
Contact for Rental: Jerry Stobel;   (615) 889-7502
Manager: Hal Derm, General Manager

LANGFORD AUDITORIUM
Garland Avenue, Nashville, TN 37232
(615) 322-2170
Founded: 1978
Type of Facility: Auditorium
Type of Stage: Platform
Stage Dimensions: 30'x50'W curved lip
Seating Capacity: 1,200
Year Built: 1978
Acoustical Consultant: Steven Durr
Contact for Rental: Betty King;   (615) 343-3365

NASHVILLE CONVENTION CENTER
601 Commerce Street, Nashville, TN 37203
(615) 259-7900
Type of Facility: Civic Center; Multi-Purpose; Room; Exhibition Hall
Type of Stage: Flexible
Seating Capacity: 5,300
Year Built: 1987   **Architect:** Yearwood Johnson & Crabtree   **Cost:** $45,500,000
Contact for Rental: Judy McCoy, Acting Managing Director;   (615) 742-2000
Nashville Convention Center also contains 22 meeting rooms

TENNESSEE PERFORMING ARTS CENTER
505 Deaderick Street, Nashville, TN 37219
(615) 741-7975
Type of Facility: Theatre Complex; Concert Hall; Theatre House; Multi-Purpose
Year Built: 1980   **Architect:** Taylor & Crabtree   **Cost:** $42,000,000
Acoustical Consultant: Bolt, Beranek & Newman
Contact for Rental: Tom Baker;   (615) 741-7975
Resident Groups: Nashville Symphony Orchestra; Tennessee Repertory Theatre; Nashville City Ballet; Circle Players;
Nashville Opera Association; Friends of Music Chamber Music Series
Tennessee Performing Arts Center contains Andrew Jackson Hall, Andrew Johnson Theatre and James K. Polk Theatre.
See individual listings for additional information. TPAC is a mixed-use development encompassing three performing-arts
halls, a museum and an office tower.

TENNESSEE PERFORMING ARTS CENTER - ANDREW JACKSON HALL
505 Deaderick Street, Nashville, TN 37219
(615) 741-7975
FAX: (615) 741-1266
Type of Facility: Concert Hall; Performance Center
Type of Stage: Proscenium
Stage Dimensions: 130'6"Wx53'D; 57'x35' proscenium opening   **Orchestra Pit**
Seating Capacity: 2,398
Year Built: 1980   **Architect:** Taylor and Crabtree
Acoustical Consultant: Bolt Beranek & Newman - original; Jaffe Acoustics - current
Contact for Rental: Sherri Rheinhardt, Sales Manager;   (615) 741-7975
Manager: James L. Randolph, President/Chief Executive Officer;   (615) 741-7975
Resident Groups: Nashville Symphony; Nashville Opera Association; Tennessee Performing Arts Center's
Broadway Series
A museum and office tower are included in the building as well as the three theaters.

TENNESSEE PERFORMING ARTS CENTER - ANDREW JOHNSON THEATER
505 Deaderick Street, Nashville, TN 37219
(615) 741-7975
FAX: (615) 741-1266
Type of Facility: Studio Performance; Performance Center; Multi-Purpose
Type of Stage: Flexible

Stage Dimensions: 59'6"Wx52'D
Seating Capacity: 300
Year Built: 1980   **Architect:** Taylor and Crabtree
Contact for Rental: Sherri Rheinhardt, Sales Manager;   (615) 741-7975
Manager: James L. Randolph, President/Chief Executive Officer;   (615) 741-7975
Resident Groups: Circle Players

TENNESSEE PERFORMING ARTS CENTER - JAMES K. POLK THEATER
505 Deaderick Street, Nashville, TN 37219
(615) 741-7975
FAX: (615) 741-1266
Type of Facility: Performance Center; Theatre House
Type of Stage: Thrust; Proscenium
Stage Dimensions: 90'Wx50'D; 47'x27'6" proscenium opening   **Orchestra Pit**
Seating Capacity: 1,010
Year Built: 1980   **Architect:** Taylor and Crabtree
Contact for Rental: Sherri Rheinhardt, Sales Manager;   (615) 741-7975
Manager: James L. Randolph, President/Chief Executive Officer;   (615) 741-7975
Resident Groups: Tennessee Repertory Theatre; Nashville Ballet; Friends of Music Chamber Music Series
The Polk Theater includes two vomitories

Oak Ridge

INSTRUMENTAL MUSIC

OAK RIDGE SYMPHONY ORCHESTRA
PO Box 4271, Oak Ridge, TN 37831
(615) 483-5569
Founded: 1942
Arts Area: Symphony; Orchestra
Status: Semi-Professional; Non-Profit
Type: Performing; Educational
Purpose: To provide quality music to the community and serve as an outlet for gifted performers
Management: John D. Welsh, Music Director/Conductor; Rosemary Ahmad, Choral Director; C. Anne Brackins, Office Administrator; Robert Adamcik, Operations Manager
Officers: Sydney Ball, President; Ernest Silver, Secretary; Amy Hagemeyer, Treasurer
Paid Staff: 4
Paid Artists: 40   **Non-Paid Artists:** 35
Utilizes: Special Technical Talent; Guest Conductors; Guest Artists
Budget: $100,000 - $500,000
Income Sources: Private Foundations/Grants/Endowments; Business/Corporate Donations; Box Office; Government Grants; Individual Donations
Season: October - May   **Annual Attendance:** 8,000
Affiliations: ASOL; Tennesseans for the Arts
Performance Facilities: Oak Ridge High School Auditorium

THEATRE

OAK RIDGE COMMUNITY PLAYHOUSE
PO Box 5705, Oak Ridge, TN 37831-5705
(615) 482-9999
Founded: 1943
Arts Area: Community
Status: Non-Profit
Type: Performing
Purpose: To offer quality, varied theatre to the community and maintain volunteer status
Management: Ron McIntyre, Founder/Artistic Director; Patti Rogers-Copeland, General Manager; Bradley E. Brown, Public Relations Director
Officers: Nathan E. Way, President, Board of Directors; Reeva Abraham, Vice President; Harold Clark, Secretary; Jeff Backus, Treasurer
Paid Staff: 5
Paid Artists: 6   **Non-Paid Artists:** 300
Utilizes: Special Technical Talent; Guest Directors

Budget: $100,000 - $500,000
Income Sources: Private Foundations/Grants/Endowments; Business/Corporate Donations; Box Office;
Individual Donations
Season: 52 Weeks **Annual Attendance:** 20,000
Affiliations: ACT; SETC; TTA; Knoxville Area Theatre Coalition, Arts Council of Oak Ridge, Greater Knoxville Area
Arts Council
Performance Facilities: Oak Ridge Playhouse in Jackson Square

PERFORMING SERIES

OAK RIDGE CIVIC MUSIC ASSOCIATION
PO Box 4271, Oak Ridge, TN 37831-4271
(615) 483-5569
Founded: 1944
Arts Area: Vocal Music; Instrumental Music; Chamber Series
Status: Professional; Non-Professional; Non-Profit
Type: Performing; Educational; Sponsoring
Purpose: To bring quality music to the community and to encourage the youth of the community to appreciate good music
Management: Robert Adamcik, Operations Manager; John Welsh, Orchestra Conductor; Rosemary Ahmad,
Chorus Conductor
Officers: Sidney Boll, President
Paid Staff: 3
Paid Artists: 16 **Non-Paid Artists:** 50
Utilizes: Guest Artists
Budget: $100,000 - $500,000
Income Sources: Private Foundations/Grants/Endowments; Business/Corporate Donations; Box Office; Government
Grants; Individual Donations
Season: October - June
Annual Attendance: 7,000
Performance Facilities: Oak Ridge High School Auditorium

FACILITY

OAK RIDGE COMMUNITY PLAYHOUSE
PO Box 5705, Oak Ridge, TN 37831
(615) 482-9999
Founded: 1942
Type of Facility: Theatre House
Facility Originally: Movie House
Type of Stage: Proscenium
Stage Dimensions: 32'x40'
Seating Capacity: 344
Contact for Rental: Patti Lynn Rogers-Copeland; (615) 482-9999
Resident Groups: Oak Ridge Community Playhouse; Oak Ridge Junior Playhouse

Sewanee

INSTRUMENTAL MUSIC

SEWANEE SUMMER MUSIC CENTER
University of the South, Sewanee, TN 37375
(615) 598-5931
Founded: 1957
Arts Area: Symphony; Chamber; Ensemble
Status: Non-Profit
Type: Performing; Educational
Management: Martha McCrory, Director
Volunteer Staff: 6
Utilizes: Guest Conductors; Guest Artists
Budget: $100,000 - $500,000
Income Sources: Box Office; Government Grants; Individual Donations
Season: June 27 - August 2
Performance Facilities: Guerry Auditorium

Tullahoma

FACILITY

SOUTH JACKSON CIVIC CENTER
Corner of South Jackson and Decherd Streets, Tullahoma, TN 37388
(615) 455-5321
Founded: 1978
Type of Facility: Concert Hall; Auditorium; Performance Center; Theatre House; Civic Center; Multi-Purpose; Room; Rehearsal Hall
Facility Originally: School
Type of Stage: Proscenium
Stage Dimensions: 48'x36'
Seating Capacity: 450
Year Built: 1922
Year Remodeled: 1978
Contact for Rental: Emma Lee Cowan;   (615) 455-3991
Resident Groups: Community Playhouse

Woodbury

THEATRE

CANNON COMMUNITY PLAYHOUSE
PO Box 404, Woodbury, TN 37190
(615) 563-5206
Founded: 1979
Arts Area: Community
Status: Non-Professional; Non-Profit
Type: Performing; Educational; Sponsoring
Purpose: Theatre productions and theatre arts education
Officers: Darryl T. Deason, President; Drunell Higgins, Vice President; E.L. Richards, Secretary/Treasurer
Volunteer Staff: 200
Non-Paid Artists: 65
Utilizes: Special Technical Talent; Guest Artists
Budget: $1,000 - $50,000
Income Sources: Private Foundations/Grants/Endowments; Business/Corporate Donations; Box Office; Government Grants; Individual Donations
Season: March - November   **Annual Attendance:** 3,000
Affiliations: Tennessee Theatre Association

TEXAS

Abilene

INSTRUMENTAL MUSIC

ABILENE PHILHARMONIC ASSOCIATION
310 North Willis, Suite 108, Abilene, TX 79603
(915) 677-6710
Founded: 1950
Arts Area: Symphony; Orchestra
Status: Professional; Non-Profit
Type: Performing; Educational
Purpose: To present to the people of Abilene and the surrounding area the opportunity to hear the best in symphonic literature
Management: George Yaeger, Music Director/Conductor; Ed Allcorn, Manager/Librarian; Susan Saver, Executive Secretary
Officers: Tom Boecking, President; Dick Tarpley, First Vice President; David Watson, Second Vice President; Susan King, Third Vice President; Harriet Connor, Fourth Vice President; Jane Bell, Secretary
Paid Staff: 3   **Volunteer Staff:** 180
Paid Artists: 70
Utilizes: Guest Conductors; Guest Artists
Budget: $100,000 - $500,000
Income Sources: Private Foundations/Grants/Endowments; Business/Corporate Donations; Box Office; Government Grants; Individual Donations
Season: September - April   **Annual Attendance:** 18,000
Affiliations: ASOL
Performance Facilities: Abilene Civic Center

FACILITY

ABILENE CIVIC CENTER
1100 North Sixth Street, PO Box 60, Abilene, TX 79604
(915) 676-6211
FAX: (915) 676-6343
Type of Facility: Theatre Complex; Concert Hall; Auditorium; Performance Center; Theatre House; Civic Center; Multi-Purpose
Type of Stage: Proscenium   **Orchestra Pit**
Year Built: 1970
Contact for Rental: Tim Stephens;   (915) 676-6211
The Civic Center contains the Exhibit Hall and Theater. See separate listings for additional information.

ABILENE CIVIC CENTER - EXHIBIT HALL
1100 North Sixth Street, PO Box 60, Abilene, TX 79604
(915) 676-6211
FAX: (915) 676-6343
Founded: 1970
Type of Facility: Concert Hall; Civic Center; Multi-Purpose
Type of Stage: Flexible; Portable
Stage Dimensions: Flexible
Year Built: 1970
Contact for Rental: Tim Stephens;   (915) 676-6211
Contains 20,000 square feet of exhibit space

ABILENE CIVIC CENTER - THEATER
1100 North Sixth Street, PO Box 60, Abilene, TX 79604
(915) 676-6211
FAX: (915) 676-6343
Type of Facility: Concert Hall; Auditorium; Theatre House; Civic Center
Type of Stage: Proscenium
Stage Dimensions: 60'Wx72'D   **Orchestra Pit**
Seating Capacity: 2,150
Year Built: 1970
Contact for Rental: Tim Stephens;   (915) 676-6211
Resident Groups: Abilene Philharmonic Orchestra

Addison

THEATRE

ADDISON CENTRE THEATRE
15650 Addison Road, Addison, TX 75248
(214) 934-3913
Founded: 1976
Arts Area: Theatrical Group
Status: Professional; Non-Profit
Type: Performing; Touring; Educational; Sponsoring
Management: David Minton, Executive Director; Kelly Cotten, Artistic Director
Paid Staff: 3
Paid Artists: 200
Utilizes: Guest Directors
Budget: $100,000 - $500,000
Income Sources: Private Foundations/Grants/Endowments; Business/Corporate Donations; Box Office; Government Grants; Individual Donations
Season: 52 Weeks   **Annual Attendance:** 6,000
Performance Facilities: Addison Centre Theatre

Albany

THEATRE

FORT GRIFFIN FANDANGLE ASSOCIATION
PO Box 185, Albany, TX 76430
(817) 762-2525
Founded: 1938
Arts Area: Theatrical Group
Status: Non-Professional; Non-Profit
Type: Performing
Purpose: Historical narration accompanied by song and dance
Management: Board of Directors
Officers: Watt R. Matthews, President; John Matthews, Vice President; K.C. Jones, Vice President/Treasurer; Louann George, Executive Secretary
Paid Staff: 6
Non-Paid Artists: 250
Utilizes: Special Technical Talent
Budget: $50,000 - $100,000
Income Sources: Box Office; Individual Donations
Season: June   **Annual Attendance:** 10,000
Performance Facilities: Fort Griffin Fandangle Outdoor Theatre

FACILITY

THE AZTEC
c/o Albany Chamber of Commerce, PO Box 185, Albany, TX 76430
(915) 762-2525
Type of Facility: Theatre House
Facility Originally: Movie House
Type of Stage: Thrust
Stage Dimensions: 30'x30'   **Orchestra Pit**
Seating Capacity: 250
Year Built: 1927
Year Remodeled: 1991   **Architect:** Bill Booziotis & Associates
Contact for Rental: Sally Stapp;   (915) 762-2525
Musical theatre, organizational performances and meetings; due to open in summer 1993

FORT GRIFFIN FANDANGLE OUTDOOR THEATRE
PO Box 155, Albany, TX 76430
(915) 762-2525; (915) 762-3642
Type of Facility: Amphitheater
Type of Stage: Greek
Seating Capacity: 1,650
Year Built: 1955   **Architect:** Robert Nail
Manager: Marge Bray
Hosts annual original song and dance contest during last two weekends in June, since 1937.

OLD JAIL ART CENTER
Route 1, PO Box 1, Albany, TX 76430
(915) 762-2269
>**Type of Facility:** Studio Performance; Civic Center; Room; Art Museum; Research Library
>**Type of Stage:** Platform
>**Stage Dimensions:** 28'x28'
>**Seating Capacity:** 150
>**Year Built:** 1877   **Architect:** John Thomas   **Cost:** $9,500
>**Year Remodeled:** 1979   **Architect:** Arthur Weinman, AIA   **Cost:** $700,000
>**Acoustical Consultant:** Arthur Weinman
>**Contact for Rental:** Joan Farmer;   (915) 762-2269

Amarillo

DANCE

LONE STAR BALLET, INC.
1,000 South Polk, Amarillo, TX 79101
(806) 372-2463
FAX: (806) 373-3909
>**Founded:** 1976
>**Arts Area:** Ballet
>**Status:** Non-Profit
>**Type:** Performing; Touring; Resident; Educational; Sponsoring
>**Purpose:** To present ballet both as a sponsoring and performing company to citizens of this area which includes five states
>**Management:** Neil Hess, Artistic Director; Juana Ree Forrester, Administrative Secretary; Kathy McAfee, Wardrobe Mistress
>**Officers:** C. Mac Douglas, President; R. Michael Isley, Vice President; Jayne Brainard, Secretary; A. Dale Williams, Treasurer
>**Paid Staff:** 3
>**Paid Artists:** 24
>**Utilizes:** Special Technical Talent; Guest Artists
>**Budget:** $100,000 - $500,000
>**Income Sources:** Private Foundations/Grants/Endowments; Business/Corporate Donations; Box Office; Government Grants; Individual Donations
>**Season:** October - April   **Annual Attendance:** 17,200
>**Affiliations:** MAAA
>**Performance Facilities:** Amarillo Civic Center

INSTRUMENTAL MUSIC

AMARILLO SYMPHONY
PO Box 2552, Amarillo, TX 79105
(806) 376-8782
>**Founded:** 1924
>**Arts Area:** Symphony; Orchestra; Chamber; Ensemble
>**Status:** Professional; Non-Profit
>**Type:** Performing; Educational
>**Purpose:** To educate and stimulate appreciation of music in the Texas Panhandle
>**Management:** Cheryl C. Cox, Executive Director; James Setapen, Music Director
>**Officers:** Don Patterson, President; C.C. Burgess, Vice President; Celine Freeman, Secretary; Joe Street, Treasurer
>**Paid Staff:** 11
>**Paid Artists:** 85
>**Utilizes:** Guest Conductors; Guest Artists
>**Budget:** $500,000 - $1,000,000
>**Income Sources:** Private Foundations/Grants/Endowments; Business/Corporate Donations; Box Office; Government Grants; Individual Donations; Fund-raising; Guild Support
>**Season:** September - May
>**Annual Attendance:** 19,000
>**Affiliations:** ASOL
>**Performance Facilities:** Amarillo Civic Center

FACILITY

AMARILLO CIVIC CENTER
401 South Buchanan, Amarillo, TX 79101
(806) 378-4297
>**Type of Facility:** Civic Center

Year Built: 1969
Year Remodeled: 1978
Contact for Rental: Operations Manager;   (806) 378-4297
Resident Groups: Amarillo Symphony
The Civic Center contains the Arena and Music Hall. See separate listings for additional information.

AMARILLO CIVIC CENTER - ARENA
401 South Buchanan, Amarillo, TX 79101
(806) 378-4297
FAX: (806) 378-4234
Type of Facility: Arena
Type of Stage: Flexible; Arena
Seating Capacity: 7,600
Year Built: 1969
Year Remodeled: 1978
Contact for Rental: Operations Manager;   (806) 378-4297

AMARILLO CIVIC CENTER - MUSIC HALL
401 South Buchanan, Amarillo, TX 79101
(806) 378-4297
FAX: (806) 378-4234
Type of Facility: Auditorium
Type of Stage: Proscenium   **Orchestra Pit**
Seating Capacity: 2,400
Year Built: 1969
Year Remodeled: 1978
Contact for Rental: Operations Manager;   (806) 378-4297
Resident Groups: Amarillo Symphony

Arlington

VOCAL MUSIC

ARLINGTON OPERA ASSOCIATION
6103 Cool Springs Drive, Arlington, TX 76017
(817) 483-5022
FAX: (817) 277-7126
Founded: 1985
Arts Area: Lyric Opera; Light Opera; Operetta
Status: Professional; Non-Profit
Type: Performing; Resident; Educational
Purpose: To produce at least two operas per year and to promote interest in and appreciation of opera
Management: Karen Earnest, General Director; Gehlin Menti, Artistic Director
Officers: Dr. Frank Bendiks, President; Mike Yaw, Vice President; Rosemary Biel, Secretary; Dr. Dorothy Brooks, Treasurer
Paid Staff: 2   Volunteer Staff: 10
Paid Artists: 37   Non-Paid Artists: 20
Utilizes: Special Technical Talent; Guest Artists; Guest Directors
Budget: $1,000 - $50,000
Income Sources: Private Foundations/Grants/Endowments; Business/Corporate Donations; Box Office; Individual Donations
Season: April - July   Annual Attendance: 750
Affiliations: Arts Council of Fort Worth and Tarrant County; Arlington Arts Council
Performance Facilities: Arlington Community Center

THEATRE

THEATRE ARLINGTON
305 West Main Street, Arlington, TX 76010
(817) 275-7661
Founded: 1973
Arts Area: Community; Theatrical Group
Status: Semi-Professional; Non-Profit
Type: Performing; Resident; Educational
Management: Penny Patrick, Managing/Producing Director; J. Kathryn "Judy" Rehders, Assistant Director
Paid Staff: 8   Volunteer Staff: 95
Paid Artists: 10   Non-Paid Artists: 400
Utilizes: Special Technical Talent; Guest Artists; Guest Directors

Budget: $100,000 - $500,000
Income Sources: Private Foundations/Grants/Endowments; Business/Corporate Donations; Box Office; Individual Donations
Season: September - August   **Annual Attendance:** 25,000
Affiliations: Texas Nonprofit Theatre
Performance Facilities: Theatre Arlington

FACILITY

THEATRE ARLINGTON
305 West Main Street, Arlington, TX 76010
(817) 275-7661
    Type of Facility: Performance Center
    Facility Originally: Church
    Type of Stage: Proscenium
    Stage Dimensions: 28'Wx26'D; 28'Wx27'H proscenium opening
    Seating Capacity: 134
    Year Built: 1951
    Year Remodeled: 1980   **Architect:** Mike Smith   **Cost:** $200,000
    Contact for Rental: Judy Rehder;   (817) 275-7661
    Resident Groups: Theatre Arlington; Creative Arts Theatre
    Theatre has limited availability for rental

UNIVERSITY OF TEXAS AT ARLINGTON - MAINSTAGE THEATER
Arlington, TX 76019
(817) 273-2011
    Type of Facility: Theatre House
    Type of Stage: Flexible; Proscenium   **Orchestra Pit**
    Seating Capacity: 450
    Year Built: 1970
    Contact for Rental: Dennis Maher;   (817) 273-2650

UNIVERSITY OF TEXAS AT ARLINGTON - STUDIO THEATER
Arlington, TX 76019
(817) 273-2011
    Type of Facility: Studio Performance; Black Box
    Type of Stage: Flexible; Arena
    Seating Capacity: 250
    Year Built: 1970
    Contact for Rental: Dennis Maher;   (817) 273-2650

Austin

DANCE

BALLET AUSTIN
3002 Guadalupe, Austin, TX 78705
(512) 476-9051
FAX: (512) 472-3073
    Founded: 1956
    Arts Area: Ballet
    Status: Professional; Non-Profit
    Type: Performing; Touring
    Management: Lambros Lambrou, Artistic Director; Mitchell Gordon, General Manager
    Paid Artists: 14
    Utilizes: Guest Artists; Guest Choreographers
    Budget: $100,000 - $500,000
    Income Sources: Private Foundations/Grants/Endowments; Box Office; Individual Donations
    Season: September - March
    Performance Facilities: Performing Arts Center, University of Texas at Austin; Paramount Theatre for the Performing Arts

DANCE UMBRELLA
PO Box 1352, Austin, TX 78701
(512) 322-0227
    Founded: 1977
    Arts Area: Modern; Mime; Ballet; Jazz; Ethnic; Folk; New Dance; Performance
    Status: Professional; Semi-Professional; Non-Professional; Non-Profit

Type: Educational; Sponsoring; Producing
Purpose: To foster the growth of the dance community of Austin and surrounding areas
Management: Phyllis Slattery, Executive Director
Officers: Sharon Vasquez, President; Livia Baskin, Vice President/Treasurer; Robin Coiley, Secretary
Paid Staff: 1   **Volunteer Staff:** 5
Paid Artists: 35
Utilizes: Special Technical Talent; Guest Artists
Budget: $100,000 - $500,000
Income Sources: Private Foundations/Grants/Endowments; Business/Corporate Donations; Box Office; Government Grants; Individual Donations; Member Dues
Season: 52 Weeks   **Annual Attendance:** 12,000
Affiliations: National Performance Network
Performance Facilities: Synergy Studio

DEBORAH HAY DANCE COMPANY
1007 Lorrain, Austin, TX 78703
(512) 472-0763
Founded: 1980
Arts Area: Modern; New Dance
Status: Professional; Non-Profit
Type: Performing; Touring
Purpose: To foster, support and preserve the creation and performance of the highest quality contemporary dance works by Deborah Hay
Officers: Johanna Smith, President; Claudia Boles, Treasurer
Paid Artists: 1
Utilizes: Guest Composers
Budget: $1,000 - $50,000
Income Sources: Government Grants; Individual Donations
Season: January - May

SHARIR DANCE COMPANY
PO Box 339, Austin, TX 78767
(512) 458-8158
Founded: 1982
Arts Area: Modern; Post-Modern
Status: Professional
Type: Performing; Touring; Resident; Sponsoring
Purpose: To produce, promote and present new dance, art and music
Management: Carol Smith Adams, Managing Director; Amarante Lucero, Production Manager; Yacov Sharir, Founder/Artistic Director
Officers: Margaret Perry, President; Beverly Reeve, Vice President; Kim Weidman, Secretary; Chris Adams, Treasurer
Paid Staff: 4   **Volunteer Staff:** 3
Paid Artists: 13
Utilizes: Guest Artists
Budget: $100,000 - $500,000
Income Sources: Private Foundations/Grants/Endowments; Business/Corporate Donations; Box Office; Government Grants; Individual Donations
Season: September - May   **Annual Attendance:** 7,500
Affiliations: University of Texas

INSTRUMENTAL MUSIC

AUSTIN CHAMBER MUSIC CENTER
4925 Strass Drive, Austin, TX 78731
(512) 454-7562
Founded: 1981
Arts Area: Chamber
Status: Professional; Non-Profit
Type: Performing; Educational; Sponsoring
Purpose: To foster the love and knowledge of chamber music through education and performance
Officers: Felicity Coltman, Director; Fiona Otten, President; Hugh Sparks, Vice President of Programs; Kathy Thatcher, Secretary; Ora Shay, Treasurer
Volunteer Staff: 3
Paid Artists: 20
Utilizes: Guest Artists
Budget: $1,000 - $50,000
Income Sources: Private Foundations/Grants/Endowments; Business/Corporate Donations; Box Office; Government Grants; Individual Donations
Season: September - June   **Annual Attendance:** 1,000

THE AUSTIN SYMPHONY ORCHESTRA SOCIETY
1101 Red River, Austin, TX 78701
(512) 476-6064
FAX: (512) 476-6242
>**Founded:** 1911
>**Arts Area:** Symphony; Orchestra; Chamber; Ensemble; Ethnic; Folk; Band
>**Status:** Professional
>**Type:** Performing; Touring; Resident; Educational; Sponsoring
>**Purpose:** To provide live symphonic music for the citizens of Austin and central Texas
>**Management:** Kenneth Caswell, Executive Director; Rusty Buckner, Technical Director; Diana Eblen, Director of Educational Programs; Barbara Uhlaender, Assistant to Executive Director; David Ray, Production Manager
>**Officers:** Mrs. D.J. Shibley Jr., President; George More, Executive Vice President
>**Paid Staff:** 8
>**Paid Artists:** 120
>**Utilizes:** Guest Conductors; Guest Artists
>**Budget:** $1,000,000 - $5,000,000
>**Income Sources:** Private Foundations/Grants/Endowments; Business/Corporate Donations; Box Office; Government Grants; Individual Donations
>**Affiliations:** ASOL
>**Performance Facilities:** University of Texas Theater for the Performing Arts

VOCAL MUSIC

THE AUSTIN LYRIC OPERA
PO Box 984, Austin, TX 78767
(512) 472-5927
FAX: (512) 472-4143
>**Founded:** 1985
>**Arts Area:** Grand Opera; Lyric Opera
>**Status:** Professional; Non-Profit
>**Type:** Performing; Educational
>**Purpose:** To promote and support opera; to foster public awareness of opera as a fine art; to provide opportunities
>**Management:** Joseph McClain, General Director; Jeannie Lynch, Business Manager; Molly Brownie, Marketing/Development; Sam Smith, Administrative Assistant
>**Officers:** Bryce Jordan, Chairman; Joanne Christian, President
>**Paid Staff:** 4   **Volunteer Staff:** 20
>**Utilizes:** Special Technical Talent; Guest Conductors; Guest Artists; Guest Directors
>**Budget:** $500,000 - $1,000,000
>**Income Sources:** Private Foundations/Grants/Endowments; Business/Corporate Donations; Box Office; Individual Donations
>**Season:** October - May
>**Affiliations:** COS

THEATRE

GENESIUS PLAYERS
6307 Wild Street, Austin, TX 78757
(512) 452-1775
>**Founded:** 1976
>**Arts Area:** Theatrical Group
>**Status:** Non-Profit
>**Type:** Performing; Touring; Educational
>**Management:** Wanda Van Stone-Pierce, Executive Producer
>**Officers:** Wanda Van Stone-Pierce, President; April Hayner, Vice President; Cary Smith, Secretary/Treasurer
>**Volunteer Staff:** 4
>**Utilizes:** Special Technical Talent; Guest Artists; Guest Directors
>**Budget:** $1,000 - $50,000
>**Income Sources:** Private Foundations/Grants/Endowments; Business/Corporate Donations; Box Office; Government Grants; Individual Donations
>**Affiliations:** Austin Circle of Theatres

PROJECT INTERACT - ZACHARY SCOTT THEATRE CENTER
1510 Toomey Road, Austin, TX 78704
(512) 476-0594
FAX: (512) 476-0314
>**Founded:** 1977
>**Arts Area:** Professional; Theatrical Group
>**Status:** Professional

Type: Performing; Touring; Educational
Purpose: To present the best of classical and contemporary scripts as well as original works for youth using a multicultural company
Management: Jeff Frank, Artistic Director; Alex B. Alford, Business Manager
Officers: Karen R. Campbell, President; John Whisenhunt, Vice President; Kit Webster. Treasurer; Wade Porter, Secretary
Paid Staff: 2
Paid Artists: 18
Utilizes: Special Technical Talent; Guest Artists
Budget: $100,000 - $500,000
Income Sources: Private Foundations/Grants/Endowments; Business/Corporate Donations; Box Office; Government Grants; Individual Donations; Support Organization
Season: September - May   **Annual Attendance:** 75,000
Affiliations: TCG; AATE; Theatre in Disability; Austin Circle of Theatres
Performance Facilities: ZSTC Arena; ZSTC Kleberg

VORTEX REPERTORY COMPANY
1921 East Ben White, Austin, TX 78741
(512) 448-2299
Founded: 1988
Arts Area: Professional; Theatrical Group
Status: Professional; Non-Profit
Type: Performing; Touring; Resident; Educational; Sponsoring
Purpose: To produce and present cutting-edge theatre and performance art
Management: Steve Bacher, Managing Director; Bonnie Cullum, Artistic Director
Paid Staff: 2   **Volunteer Staff:** 2
Paid Artists: 100   **Non-Paid Artists:** 200
Utilizes: Special Technical Talent; Guest Artists; Guest Directors
Budget: $100,000 - $500,000
Income Sources: Private Foundations/Grants/Endowments; Business/Corporate Donations; Box Office; Government Grants; Individual Donations
Season: October - September   **Annual Attendance:** 6,000
Performance Facilities: Vortex Performance Cafe

PERFORMING SERIES

BLACK ARTS ALLIANCE
1157 Navasota, Austin, TX 78702
(512) 477-9660
Founded: 1981
Arts Area: Dance; Vocal Music; Theater
Status: Professional; Non-Profit; Commercial Art
Type: Performing; Educational; Sponsoring
Purpose: Featuring the Black artist of Central Texas and touring artist from around the nation, we are a multi-disciplinary arts organization dedicated to the promotion of artists in the Central Texas Region.
Management: Michele Bocknite, Director; Trina McKenzie, Publicist; Karol McMary, Clerical Assistant
Officers: Pam Hart, President; Rudy Greene, Vice President
Paid Staff: 3   **Volunteer Staff:** 2
Paid Artists: 50   **Non-Paid Artists:** 20
Utilizes: Special Technical Talent; Guest Conductors; Guest Artists; Guest Directors
Budget: $50,000 - $100,000
Income Sources: Private Foundations/Grants/Endowments; Business/Corporate Donations; Box Office; Government Grants; Individual Donations
Season: 52 Weeks
Affiliations: ISPAA; Texas Performing Network

FACILITY

LESTER E. PALMER AUDITORIUM
400 South First Street, Austin, TX 78704
(512) 476-5461
FAX: (512) 404-4416
Founded: 1958
Type of Facility: Auditorium
Type of Stage: Modified Apron Proscenium
Stage Dimensions: 100'Wx50'D; 68'Wx26'H proscenium opening   **Orchestra Pit**
Seating Capacity: Configurations of 3,000, 4,300 or 6,000 seats
Year Built: 1958   **Architect:** Wolf Jesson & Associates   **Cost:** $3,200,000
Year Remodeled: 1986   **Architect:** Walker Doty Freeman   **Cost:** $3,000,000
Acoustical Consultant: C.P. Boner & Associates

Contact for Rental: Raylene Brookshire;   (512) 476-5461
Includes City Coliseum, a 2000-seat arena with 40'x60' maximum size portable stage

PARAMOUNT THEATER FOR THE PERFORMING ARTS
713 Congress Avenue, Austin, TX 78767
(512) 472-2901
    Type of Facility: Theatre House
    Facility Originally: Vaudeville
    Type of Stage: Proscenium
    Stage Dimensions: 30'x33'   **Orchestra Pit**
    Seating Capacity: 1,332
    Year Built: 1915   **Architect:** Eberson Fugard & Knapp
    Year Remodeled: 1979   **Architect:** Bell Klein & Hoffman
    Contact for Rental: Paul Beutel;   (512) 472-2901
    Presenting and producing performing arts including dance, music, theatre

UNIVERSITY OF TEXAS AT AUSTIN - B. IDEN PAYNE THEATRE
Winship Drama Building, Austin, TX 78712
(512) 471-5793
    Type of Facility: Performance Center
    Type of Stage: Proscenium   **Orchestra Pit**
    Seating Capacity: 500
    Year Built: 1963
    Year Remodeled: 1976
    Contact for Rental: Sharon Vasquez
    Resident Groups: Dance Repertory
    Rarely available for rent

UNIVERSITY OF TEXAS AT AUSTIN - THEATRE ROOM
Winship Drama Building, Austin, TX 78712
(512) 471-5793
    Type of Facility: Performance Center; Room
    Type of Stage: Flexible; In-the-round Capability
    Stage Dimensions: 60'x60'
    Seating Capacity: 250
    Year Built: 1963
    Year Remodeled: 1976
    Contact for Rental: Sharon Vasquez
    Rarely available for rent

UNIVERSITY OF TEXAS AT AUSTIN PERFORMING ARTS CENTER
23rd and East Campus Drive, PO Box 7818, Austin, TX 78713
(512) 471-2787
    Type of Facility: Theatre Complex; Performance Center
    Year Built: 1981   **Architect:** Fisher & Spillman   **Cost:** $44,000,000
    Acoustical Consultant: C.P. Boner & Associates
    Contact for Rental: Pebbles Wadsworth
    The Performing Arts Center contains the Bass Concert Hall, Bates Recital Hall and the McCullough Theatre . See separate listings for additional information.

UNIVERSITY OF TEXAS AT AUSTIN PERFORMING ARTS CENTER - THE BASS CONCERT HALL
23rd and East Campus Drive, PO Box 7818, Austin, TX 78713
(512) 471-2787
    Type of Facility: Concert Hall; Performance Center; Off Broadway; Opera House
    Type of Stage: Proscenium
    Stage Dimensions: 52'Wx32'H proscenium opening   **Orchestra Pit**
    Seating Capacity: 3,000
    Contact for Rental: Pebbles Wadsworth

UNIVERSITY OF TEXAS AT AUSTIN PERFORMING ARTS CENTER - BATES RECITAL HALL
23rd and East Campus Drive, PO Box 7818, Austin, TX 78713
(512) 471-2787
    Type of Facility: Auditorium; Performance Center; Organ Concert Hall
    Type of Stage: Platform
    Stage Dimensions: 25'Wx8'D
    Seating Capacity: 700
    Contact for Rental: Pebbles Wadsworth;   (512) 471-2787
    Contains a Viser-Rowland Tracker Organ

UNIVERSITY OF TEXAS AT AUSTIN PERFORMING ARTS CENTER - THE MCCULLOUGH THEATRE
23rd and East Campus Drive, PO Box 7818, Austin, TX 78713
(512) 471-2787
    Type of Facility: Performance Center; Opera House
    Type of Stage: Proscenium
    Stage Dimensions: 30'Wx36'D; 30'Wx18'H proscenium opening   **Orchestra Pit**
    Seating Capacity: 400
    Contact for Rental: Pebbles Wadsworth; (512) 471-2787

Bastrop

THEATRE

OLD BASTROP OPERA HOUSE
711 Spring, PO Box 691, Bastrop, TX 78602
(512) 321-6283
    Founded: 1889
    Arts Area: Summer Stock; Musical; Dinner; Community; Theatrical Group
    Status: Semi-Professional; Non-Professional; Non-Profit
    Type: Performing; Sponsoring
    Purpose: To use the restored opera house as a performing arts center for theatre, dance and music
    Management: Chester Eitze, Executive Director
    Officers: Henry Gideon, President
    Paid Staff: 1 **Volunteer Staff:** 15
    Paid Artists: 10
    Utilizes: Special Technical Talent; Guest Artists; Guest Directors
    Budget: $50,000 - $100,000
    Income Sources: Private Foundations/Grants/Endowments; Business/Corporate Donations; Box Office;
    Individual Donations
    Season: May - January   **Annual Attendance:** 8,000
    Performance Facilities: Old Bastrop Opera House

FACILITY

OLD BASTROP OPERA HOUSE
711 Spring, PO Box 691, Bastrop, TX 78602
(512) 321-6283
    Type of Facility: Concert Hall; Auditorium; Performance Center; Theatre House; Opera House; Reception/Party Hall
    Facility Originally: Meeting Hall; Vaudeville; Movie House
    Type of Stage: Thrust; Proscenium
    Stage Dimensions: 24'Wx28'Dx14'H
    Seating Capacity: 300
    Year Built: 1889 **Architect:** Dave Green & P.O. Elzner **Cost:** $15,000
    Year Remodeled: 1979 **Cost:** $50,000
    Contact for Rental: Chester Eitze; (512) 321-6283
    Resident Groups: Bastrop Community Chorus; Bastrop Chamber Singers; Bastrop Community Orchestra;
    Bastrop Children's Chorus; Bastrop Children's Theatre Program

Beaumont

DANCE

BEAUMONT BALLET THEATRE
4555 Calder, Beaumont, TX 77706
(409) 892-4441
    Founded: 1978
    Arts Area: Ballet; Jazz
    Status: Non-Professional; Non-Profit
    Type: Performing; Educational
    Purpose: Educate and train qualified students in the art of dance; encourage and develop public appreciation of dance and
    ballet
    Management: Bonnie Cokinos, Artistic Director
    Officers: Jimmie P. Cokinos, President; Pat Walker, Vice President; Mildred Sohlinger, Secretary/Treasurer
    Volunteer Staff: 12
    Paid Artists: 2 **Non-Paid Artists:** 50
    Utilizes: Guest Artists; Guest Directors
    Budget: $1,000 - $50,000

Income Sources: Private Foundations/Grants/Endowments; Box Office; Individual Donations
Season: 52 Weeks   **Annual Attendance:** 3,000
Affiliations: SWRBA
Performance Facilities: Julie Rogers Theatre

BEAUMONT CIVIC BALLET
c/o Marsha Woody Academy of Dance, 3717 Calder, Beaumont, TX 77706
(409) 838-4397; (409) 892-2605
    Founded: 1971
    Arts Area: Ballet
    Status: Non-Profit
    Type: Performing
    Purpose: To provide high-quality dance to our area; to develop dance-arts educational programs for all ages
    Management: Marsha Woody, Founder/Director
    Officers: Ron Cole, President; N. Edwards, Vice President
    Paid Staff: 2   **Volunteer Staff:** 75
    Utilizes: Guest Artists
    Budget: $50,000 - $100,000
    Income Sources: Private Foundations/Grants/Endowments; Business/Corporate Donations; Box Office; Government Grants; Individual Donations
    Season: August - May   **Annual Attendance:** 13,000
    Affiliations: Marsha Woody Academy
    Performance Facilities: Julie Rogers Theatre

INSTRUMENTAL MUSIC

SYMPHONY OF SOUTHEAST TEXAS
PO Box 1047, Beaumont, TX 77704
(409) 835-7100
    Founded: 1953
    Arts Area: Symphony; Orchestra
    Status: Semi-Professional; Non-Profit
    Type: Performing; Resident
    Purpose: Provide quality musical entertainment of all types for the people of Southeast Texas
    Management: Kathy Clark, Business Manager
    Officers: Brian Alter, President; Allison Golias, President-Elect; Jan Allred, First Vice President; Martha Hicks, Second Vice President; Elaine Verret, Secretary; Ed Aromi, Treasurer
    Paid Staff: 1
    Paid Artists: 5
    Utilizes: Guest Artists
    Budget: $100,000 - $500,000
    Income Sources: Private Foundations/Grants/Endowments; Business/Corporate Donations; Box Office; Government Grants; Individual Donations
    Season: September - March   **Annual Attendance:** 16,100
    Affiliations: ASOL; ASCAP; BMI
    Performance Facilities: Julie Rogers Theatre

VOCAL MUSIC

BEAUMONT CIVIC OPERA
1030 Harriott, Beaumont, TX 77705
(409) 833-2120
    Founded: 1962
    Arts Area: Grand Opera; Light Opera; Operetta; Musical Comedy
    Status: Non-Profit
    Type: Resident
    Purpose: To bring quality musical productions to Southwest Texas and to give young artists performing opportunities
    Officers: Matthew White, President; Delores Black, Business Manager; Charlene Kiker, BM Emeritus; Irma Silvernail, Treasurer
    Volunteer Staff: 20
    Utilizes: Special Technical Talent; Guest Artists; Guest Directors
    Budget: $50,000 - $100,000
    Income Sources: Private Foundations/Grants/Endowments; Business/Corporate Donations; Box Office; Government Grants; Individual Donations; Fundraising
    Season: March
    Annual Attendance: 24,000
    Affiliations: OA
    Performance Facilities: Julie Rogers Theatre

PERFORMING SERIES

BEAUMONT MUSIC COMMISSION
PO Box 3926, Beaumont, TX 77704
(409) 833-7832
> **Founded:** 1923
> **Arts Area:** Dance; Vocal Music; Instrumental Music
> **Status:** Non-Profit
> **Type:** Educational; Sponsoring
> **Purpose:** To present vocal and instrumental artists in recitals/concerts, small ensembles, small orchestras, dance groups, operas and musicals
> **Officers:** Mrs. Russell R. Phels, President; Naaman J. Woodland Jr., First Vice President/Chairman; Charlene Kiker, Second Vice President; J. Robert Madden, Third Vice President; Mrs. Irving Eisen, Fourth Vice President; Mary Frances Roach, Recording Secretary; Mrs. Edwin Gale, Assistant Recording Secretary; Murray Anderson, Treasurer
> **Utilizes:** Guest Artists
> **Budget:** $50,000 - $100,000
> **Income Sources:** Private Foundations/Grants/Endowments; Business/Corporate Donations; Box Office; Individual Donations
> **Season:** September - May
> **Annual Attendance:** 5,000
> **Performance Facilities:** Julie Rogers Theatre for the Performing Arts

YOUNG AUDIENCES OF BEAUMONT
PO Box 5346, Beaumont, TX 77726-5346
(409) 835-3884
> **Founded:** 1963
> **Arts Area:** Dance; Instrumental Music; Theater; Drama
> **Status:** Non-Profit
> **Type:** Performing; Educational
> **Purpose:** To provide school students an opportunity to listen to, and participate in, live performances by professional artists; To promote the arts in education
> **Management:** Helen Smith, Executive Assistant
> **Officers:** Carolyn Whaley, President; Becky Moss, Betsy Boyd, Vice Presidents; Cathy Ingraham, Secretary; Don Tantzen, Treasurer
> **Paid Staff:** 1
> **Paid Artists:** 6
> **Utilizes:** Guest Artists
> **Budget:** $1,000 - $50,000
> **Income Sources:** Private Foundations/Grants/Endowments; Business/Corporate Donations; Individual Donations
> **Season:** September - May

FACILITY

CIVIC CENTER COMPLEX - EXHIBIT HALL
701 Main Street, Beaumont, TX 77701
(409) 838-3435
FAX: (409) 838-3715
> **Type of Facility:** Exhibition Hall
> **Type of Stage:** Flexible
> **Stage Dimensions:** 130'x225'
> **Seating Capacity:** 6,500
> **Year Built:** 1979   **Architect:** Gruen & Associates
> **Contact for Rental:** Claudie Hawkins;   (409) 838-3435

CIVIC CENTER COMPLEX - THE JEFFERSON THEATRE
345 Fannin Street, Beaumont, TX 77701
(409) 838-3435
FAX: (409) 838-3715
> **Type of Facility:** Theatre House
> **Facility Originally:** Vaudeville
> **Type of Stage:** Proscenium
> **Stage Dimensions:** 40'Wx31'D   **Orchestra Pit**
> **Seating Capacity:** 1,500
> **Year Built:** 1927   **Architect:** Emil Weil
> **Year Remodeled:** 1987   **Architect:** David Hoffman
> **Contact for Rental:** Claudie Hawkins;   (409) 838-3435

Resident Groups: Beaumont Community Players
Restoration/remodeling is in progress

CIVIC CENTER COMPLEX - JULIE ROGERS THEATRE FOR THE PERFORMING ARTS
701 Main Street, Beaumont, TX 77701
(800) 782-3081
FAX: (409) 838-3715
    Type of Facility: Theatre Complex; Concert Hall; Auditorium; Performance Center; Theatre House
    Facility Originally: City Hall
    Type of Stage: Proscenium
    Stage Dimensions: 50'Wx34'9"D   **Orchestra Pit**
    Seating Capacity: 1,695
    Year Built: 1922
    Year Remodeled: 1982   **Architect:** Milton Bell, Rex Goode   **Cost:** $4,600,000
    Acoustical Consultant: Variable Acoustics
    Contact for Rental: Claudie Hawkins;   (800) 782-3081
    Resident Groups: Beaumont Symphony Orchestra; Beaumont Civic Ballet; Beaumont Music Commission; Beaumont Ballet Theatre; Beaumont Civic Opera

LAMAR UNIVERSITY - LAMAR UNIVERSITY PROSCENIUM THEATRE
Beaumont, TX 77710
(409) 880-8037
    Type of Facility: Theatre House
    Type of Stage: Proscenium
    Stage Dimensions: 21'x48'x56'   **Orchestra Pit**
    Seating Capacity: 520
    Year Built: 1960   **Architect:** Miller Mebane Pitts & Phelps
    Year Remodeled: 1982   **Architect:** Miller Mebane Pitts & Phelps
    Acoustical Consultant: James Miller
    Manager: Dr. Adonia Placette
    Resident Groups: Lamar Theatre

LAMAR UNIVERSITY - LAMAR UNIVERSITY STUDIO THEATRE
Beaumont, TX 77710
(409) 880-8037
    Type of Facility: Studio Performance
    Type of Stage: Flexible
    Stage Dimensions: 60'x60'
    Seating Capacity: 200
    Year Built: 1960   **Architect:** Miller Mebane Pitts & Phelps
    Year Remodeled: 1982   **Architect:** Miller Mebane Pitts & Phelps
    Acoustical Consultant: James Miller
    Manager: Dr. Adonia Placette
    Resident Groups: Lamar Theatre

Big Spring

PERFORMING SERIES

BIG SPRING CULTURAL AFFAIRS COUNCIL
215 West Third, Big Spring, TX 79720
(915) 263-7641
    Arts Area: Dance; Vocal Music; Instrumental Music; Theater
    Status: Non-Profit
    Type: Touring
    Purpose: To provide a balance of cultural activities for the community; to enrich our natural cultural resources locally, regionally, statewide, and nationally
    Management: Marae Brooks, Director
    Officers: Gloria Hopkins, Volunteer Chairman
    Paid Staff: 1
    Utilizes: Special Technical Talent; Guest Conductors; Guest Artists
    Budget: $1,000 - $50,000
    Income Sources: Private Foundations/Grants/Endowments; Business/Corporate Donations; Box Office; Government Grants; Individual Donations

FACILITY

HOWARD COLLEGE AT BIG SPRING - HOWARD COLLEGE AUDITORIUM
1001 Birdwell Lane, Big Spring, TX 79720
(915) 264-5000
    Type of Facility: Auditorium
    Type of Stage: Proscenium **Orchestra Pit**
    Seating Capacity: 475
    Year Built: 1956
    Contact for Rental: President's Office; (915) 264-5027

HOWARD COLLEGE AT BIG SPRING - HOWARD COLLEGE COLISEUM
1001 Birdwell Lane, Big Spring, TX 79720
(915) 264-5000
    Type of Facility: Multi-Purpose
    Type of Stage: Arena
    Seating Capacity: 5,000
    Contact for Rental: Auxiliary Services Director; (915) 264-5051

Brenham

PERFORMING SERIES

ARTS COUNCIL OF WASHINGTON COUNTY
701 Milroy Drive, Brenham, TX 77833
(409) 836-3120
    Founded: 1981
    Arts Area: Vocal Music; Instrumental Music; Theater
    Status: Professional; Semi-Professional; Non-Professional; Non-Profit
    Type: Touring; Resident; Educational; Sponsoring
    Purpose: To promote the local arts in the community and to bring things to the community that cannot be locally provided
    Officers: Dr. Wilfred D. Dietrich, President; Ann Horton, Vice President; Linda Patterson, Secretary; Helen Harris, Treasurer
    Volunteer Staff: 21
    Utilizes: Special Technical Talent; Guest Conductors; Guest Artists; Guest Directors
    Budget: $1,000 - $50,000
    Income Sources: Private Foundations/Grants/Endowments; Business/Corporate Donations; Box Office; Individual Donations
    Season: 52 Weeks **Annual Attendance:** 750
    Affiliations: TCA

Brownsville

THEATRE

CAMILLE PLAYERS
1 Dean Porter Park, Brownsville, TX 78520
(210) 542-8900
    Founded: 1964
    Arts Area: Musical; Community; CHILDREN'S THEATRE
    Status: Non-Professional; Non-Profit
    Type: Performing
    Purpose: To stimulate an interest in drama by the presentation of plays and the application of the arts necessary to such presentations using the talents of interested persons to accomplish this
    Management: Laurence Siegle, Artistic Director; Richard Moore, Executive Director
    Officers: Henri De Stefano, President; Nina Fisher, Operating Advertising Vice President; Thelma Taylor, Secretary; Nena Roser, Treasurer
    Paid Staff: 2 **Volunteer Staff:** 6
    Budget: $50,000 - $100,000
    Income Sources: Private Foundations/Grants/Endowments; Business/Corporate Donations; Box Office; Individual Donations
    Season: September - June **Annual Attendance:** 9,000
    Performance Facilities: Camille Lightner Playhouse

FACILITY

CAMILLE LIGHTNER PLAYHOUSE
1 Dean Porter Park, Brownsville, TX 78520
(210) 542-8900
    Type of Facility: Theatre House
    Type of Stage: Thrust; Proscenium
    Stage Dimensions: 20'x48'x28' **Orchestra Pit**
    Seating Capacity: 301
    Year Built: 1964 **Architect:** Robert E. Velten
    Contact for Rental: Dr. Laurence Siegle; (512) 542-8900
    Resident Groups: Camille Players

Brownwood

FACILITY

BROWNWOOD COLISEUM
500 East Baker, Brownwood, TX 76804
(915) 646-3586
FAX: (915) 646-0938
    Founded: 1963
    Type of Facility: Theatre Complex; Civic Center; Arena; Multi-Purpose
    Type of Stage: Flexible; 3/4 Arena; Arena
    Stage Dimensions: 64'Wx32'D
    Seating Capacity: 3,500
    Year Built: 1963
    Architect: Frank C. Dill, AIA **Cost:** $821,784
    Contact for Rental: David Withers; (915) 646-3586

Bryan

INSTRUMENTAL MUSIC

BRAZOS VALLEY SYMPHONY ORCHESTRA
PO Box 3524, Bryan, TX 77805
(409) 774-2877
    Arts Area: Symphony; Orchestra; Chamber
    Status: Non-Professional
    Type: Performing
    Purpose: Provide an outlet for musicians in the area and entertainment for residents of the Brazos Valley
    Management: Jennifer Nelson, Manager; Franz Anton Krager, Music Director
    Paid Staff: 2
    Paid Artists: 3
    Utilizes: Guest Artists
    Budget: $100,000 - $500,000
    Income Sources: Private Foundations/Grants/Endowments; Business/Corporate Donations; Box Office; Individual Donations
    Season: August - May

PERFORMING SERIES

CITY OF BRYAN PARKS AND RECREATION
PO Box 1000, Bryan, TX 77805
(409) 361-3656
FAX: (409) 361-3885
    Arts Area: Dance; Vocal Music; Theater; Festivals
    Status: Non-Profit
    Type: Performing; Touring; Resident; Educational; Sponsoring
    Purpose: Provide quality entertainment to area residents
    Management: Sarah Cliver, Recreation Programmer
    Paid Staff: 2 **Volunteer Staff:** 20
    Paid Artists: 20 **Non-Paid Artists:** 10
    Utilizes: Special Technical Talent
    Budget: $1,000 - $50,000
    Income Sources: Government Grants
    Season: 52 Weeks

Canyon

PERFORMING SERIES

TEXAS - THE MUSICAL DRAMA
Palo Duro Canyon State Park, PO Box 268, Canyon, TX 79015
(806) 655-2181
FAX: (806) 655-7425
>**Founded:** 1966
>**Arts Area:** Dance; Vocal Music; Instrumental Music; Theater
>**Status:** Professional; Non-Profit
>**Type:** Performing; Educational
>**Purpose:** To perpetuate the heritage of the area by presenting a historical drama about the 1880's settling of the Texas Panhandle
>**Management:** Patty Bryant, Assistant Manager; Neil Hess, Director; Raymond Raillard, Manager; Monette Merriman, Office Manager; Joan Castleman, Bookkeeper; Katie Greer, Publicist
>**Officers:** Lois Rice, President; Raymond Raillard, Executive Vice President; Mrs. Ralph Randel, Vice President; Carolyn Blackburn, Secretary; Don Maxvars, Treasurer
>**Paid Staff:** 12
>**Paid Artists:** 140
>**Utilizes:** Special Technical Talent
>**Budget:** $1,000,000 - $5,000,000
>**Income Sources:** Private Foundations/Grants/Endowments; Business/Corporate Donations; Box Office; Individual Donations
>**Season:** June - August   **Annual Attendance:** 100,000
>**Affiliations:** Texas Panhandle Heritage Foundation, Inc.
>**Performance Facilities:** Pioneer Amphitheatre

FACILITY

PIONEER AMPHITHEATRE
Palo Duro Canyon State Park, PO Box 268, Canyon, TX 79015
(806) 488-2421
>**Type of Facility:** Amphitheater
>**Type of Stage:** Thrust; Proscenium
>**Seating Capacity:** 1,744
>**Year Built:** 1964   **Architect:** Earl Parge   **Cost:** $500,000
>**Contact for Rental:** Manager;   (806) 488-2421
>**Resident Groups:** Texas - The Musical Drama

WEST TEXAS STATE UNIVERSITY - BRANDING IRON THEATER
Canyon, TX 79016
(806) 656-2000
>**Type of Facility:** Theatre House
>**Type of Stage:** Proscenium
>**Stage Dimensions:** 16'x40'x28'   **Orchestra Pit**
>**Seating Capacity:** 305
>**Year Built:** 1959   **Architect:** Macon O. Carden   **Cost:** $180,000
>**Contact for Rental:** Royal R. Brantley;   (806) 656-2811

Cisco

FACILITY

KENDRICK AMPHITHEATER
Route 2, PO Box 46, Cisco, TX 76437
(817) 629-8672
>**Type of Facility:** Outdoor (Concert); Amphitheater; Multi-Purpose
>**Type of Stage:** Flexible; Greek
>**Stage Dimensions:** 365'W
>**Seating Capacity:** 100,000
>**Year Built:** 1965   **Architect:** J.H. Kendrick Family
>**Contact for Rental:** Mrs. J.H. Kendrick or Phil Kendrick;   (817) 629-8672
>**Manager:** J.H. Kendrick
>*The Amphitheater was specially constructed for the outdoor religious production of "The Life of Christ."*

College Station

THEATRE

STAGECENTER
PO Box 9475, College Station, TX 77842
(409) 846-0287
  Founded: 1966
  Arts Area: Community
  Status: Non-Profit
  Type: Performing; Educational
  Purpose: To provide the community with an outlet for direct participation in theatre as actors/technicians and audience members
  Management: Winnie Nelson, Business Manager
  Officers: Sandy Siddall, President
  Non-Paid Artists: 50
  Utilizes: Special Technical Talent; Guest Directors
  Budget: $1,000 - $50,000
  Income Sources: Private Foundations/Grants/Endowments; Business/Corporate Donations; Box Office; Individual Donations
  Season: September - June **Annual Attendance:** 3,000
  Affiliations: Arts Council of Brazos Valley

FACILITY

UNIVERSITY CENTER THEATRE COMPLEX AND CONFERENCE TOWER
Texas A&M University, College Station, TX 77840
(409) 845-8903
  Type of Facility: Theatre Complex; Auditorium; Performance Center; Theatre House; Multi-Purpose
  Year Built: 1973 **Architect:** JPJ Architects **Cost:** $20,000,000
  Contact for Rental: Tom Baxter; (409) 845-8903
  The University Center contains the Theatre Complex in which the performance spaces of Rudder Auditorium, Rudder Forum and Rudder Theatre are found as well as the Conference Tower. See individual listings for additional information.

UNIVERSITY CENTER THEATRE COMPLEX AND CONFERENCE TOWER - RUDDER AUDITORIUM
Texas A&M University, College Station, TX 77840
(409) 845-8903
  Type of Facility: Auditorium
  Type of Stage: Proscenium; Hydraulic Lift Stage
  Stage Dimensions: 126'Wx48'D; 60'Wx28'H proscenium opening   **Orchestra Pit**
  Seating Capacity: 2,500
  Year Built: 1973
  Contact for Rental: Tom Baxter; (409) 845-8903

UNIVERSITY CENTER THEATRE COMPLEX AND CONFERENCE TOWER - RUDDER FORUM
Texas A&M University, College Station, TX 77840
(409) 845-8903
  Type of Facility: Studio Performance
  Type of Stage: Flexible; Platform
  Seating Capacity: 245
  Year Built: 1973
  Contact for Rental: Tom Baxter; (409) 845-8903

UNIVERSITY CENTER THEATRE COMPLEX AND CONFERENCE TOWER - RUDDER THEATRE
Texas A&M University, College Station, TX 77840
(409) 845-8903
  Type of Facility: Theatre House
  Type of Stage: Proscenium
  Stage Dimensions: 77'Wx18'8"D; 47'Wx25'H proscenium opening
  Seating Capacity: 750
  Year Built: 1973
  Contact for Rental: Tom Baxter; (409) 845-8903

Commerce

FACILITY

EAST TEXAS STATE UNIVERSITY - UNIVERSITY PLAYHOUSE STAGE
Performing Arts Center, Commerce, TX 75429
(903) 886-5337
Type of Facility: Theatre House
Type of Stage: Modified Apron Proscenium
Stage Dimensions: 36'Wx40'D;36'Wx20'H proscenium opening;28' diameter turntable
Seating Capacity: 304
Year Built: 1976   **Architect:** Harper Kemp Clutts & Parker   **Cost:** $2,105,602
Resident Groups: East Texas State University Theater Department
Additionally, within the building is located a 40' square, Black Box theatre seating 110.

Coppell

VOCAL MUSIC

COPPELL COMMUNITY CHORUS
524 Leavalley Circle, Coppell, TX 75019
(214) 462-1090
Founded: 1986
Arts Area: Choral
Status: Non-Professional; Non-Profit
Type: Performing; Resident
Purpose: Enjoyment of singing together in a group
Management: Peggy Waldschmidt, Music Director
Officers: Donna Knox, President
Volunteer Staff: 6
Paid Artists: 2
Utilizes: Guest Directors
Budget: $1,000 - $50,000
Income Sources: Business/Corporate Donations; Box Office; Government Grants; Individual Donations
Season: Fall - Spring   **Annual Attendance:** 200

Corpus Christi

DANCE

CORPUS CHRISTI BALLET
5610 Everhart, Corpus Christi, TX 78411
(512) 991-8521
FAX: (512) 991-8521
Founded: 1972
Arts Area: Ballet
Status: Non-Professional; Non-Profit
Type: Performing; Touring; Resident; Educational; Sponsoring
Management: Cristina Stirling Munro, Director
Paid Staff: 3   **Volunteer Staff:** 10
Paid Artists: 15
Utilizes: Guest Conductors; Guest Artists; Guest Choreographers
Budget: $100,000 - $500,000
Income Sources: Private Foundations/Grants/Endowments; Business/Corporate Donations; Box Office; Individual Donations
Season: September - May
Affiliations: Munro Ballet Studios
Performance Facilities: Bayfront Plaza Auditorium

INSTRUMENTAL MUSIC

CORPUS CHRISTI CHAMBER MUSIC SOCIETY, INC.
4709 Curtis Clark, Corpus Christi, TX 78411
(512) 855-0264; (512) 886-1614
Founded: 1982
Arts Area: Chamber
Status: Non-Profit

Type: Performing
Purpose: To bring world-class chamber music groups to our city
Management: Joan Allison, Vice President/Program Director
Officers: Michael Evans, President; Joan Allison, David Parker, Vice Presidents; Betty Allen, Secretary; Gretchen Perrin, Treasurer
Volunteer Staff: 25
Paid Artists: 15
Budget: $1,000 - $50,000
Income Sources: Private Foundations/Grants/Endowments; Business/Corporate Donations; Box Office; Government Grants; Individual Donations
Season: September - May   **Annual Attendance:** 2,500
Performance Facilities: Richardson Auditorium

CORPUS CHRISTI SYMPHONY
PO Box 495, Corpus Christi, TX 78403
(512) 882-4091
 Founded: 1945
 Arts Area: Symphony; Orchestra; Chamber; Ensemble
 Status: Semi-Professional; Non-Profit
 Type: Performing
 Management: Litta R. Kline, Executive Director/Manager
 Officers: Harold Gillispie, Chairman of the Board; Dr. Herbert Madalin, President; George Hodges, President Elect; Jace Hoffman, Vice President; Maxine Somers, Secretary
 Paid Staff: 3
 Utilizes: Special Technical Talent; Guest Conductors; Guest Artists; Guest Directors
 Budget: $100,000 - $500,000
 Income Sources: Private Foundations/Grants/Endowments; Business/Corporate Donations; Box Office; Government Grants; Individual Donations
 Season: October - April   **Annual Attendance:** 15,000
 Affiliations: ASOL
 Performance Facilities: Bayfront Plaza Auditorium

THEATRE

BILINGUAL THEATER COMPANY/SOUTH TEXAS PERFORMANCE CO.
4722 Everhart, Corpus Christi, TX 78411
(512) 993-8898
 Founded: 1980
 Arts Area: Theatrical Group
 Status: Professional; Non-Profit
 Type: Performing; Touring; Resident; Educational
 Purpose: To present bilingual/bicultural performances
 Management: Dr. Graciela P. Rosenberg, Managing Director; Dr. Joe Rosenberg, Artistic Director; Larry Bogus, Executive Director; John Daniels Jr., Theatre Manager; Jose Gayton, Financial Director; Christopher Lawrence, Publicity Director
 Officers: George Dunson, Chairman; Dr. Joe Rosenberg, President; Dr. Graciela P. Rosenberg, Vice President
 Paid Artists: 15
 Utilizes: Special Technical Talent; Guest Artists
 Budget: $100,000 - $500,000
 Income Sources: Private Foundations/Grants/Endowments; Business/Corporate Donations; Box Office; Government Grants; Individual Donations
 Season: July - June   **Annual Attendance:** 35,000

PERFORMING SERIES

CATHEDRAL CONCERT SERIES
620 Lipan, Corpus Christi, TX 78401
(512) 888-6520
FAX: (512) 882-9018
 Founded: 1985
 Arts Area: Vocal Music; Instrumental Music; Festivals
 Status: Professional; Semi-Professional; Non-Professional; Non-Profit
 Type: Performing; Touring; Resident
 Utilizes: Guest Conductors; Guest Artists; Guest Directors
 Budget: $1,000 - $50,000
 Income Sources: Private Foundations/Grants/Endowments; Business/Corporate Donations; Government Grants; Individual Donations
 Season: October - June   **Annual Attendance:** 5,000

TEXAS JAZZ FESTIVAL SOCIETY
403 North Shoreline Boulevard, Corpus Christi, TX 78403
(512) 883-4500
    Founded: 1969
    Arts Area: Vocal Music; Instrumental Music; Festivals
    Status: Professional; Non-Profit
    Type: Performing
    Purpose: Now in its 28th year of producing the annual Texas Jazz Festival, free of charge to the public, the Society promotes and preserves American jazz as a fine art.
    Management: Al Beto Garcia, Festival Originator
    Officers: Wanda Gregory, President; Eddie Olivares, Vice President; Kate Trevino, Secretary; Herb Hicks, Treasurer
    Volunteer Staff: 15
    Utilizes: Special Technical Talent; Guest Conductors; Guest Artists; Guest Directors
    Budget: $1,000 - $50,000
    Income Sources: Private Foundations/Grants/Endowments; Business/Corporate Donations; Government Grants; Individual Donations
    Season: 52 Weeks   **Annual Attendance:** 8,000
    Performance Facilities: Bayfront Plaza Convention Center

FACILITY

BAYFRONT PLAZA CONVENTION CENTER - AUDITORIUM
1901 North Shoreline Drive, Corpus Christi, TX 78401
(512) 883-8543
FAX: (512) 883-0788
    Type of Facility: Auditorium
    Type of Stage: Proscenium
    Stage Dimensions: 48'Wx40'D; 48'Wx25'H proscenium opening   **Orchestra Pit**
    Seating Capacity: 2,526
    Year Built: 1978   **Architect:** SHWC Architects; CRS Architects
    Contact for Rental: Terri Cardona;   (512) 883-8543
    Resident Groups: Corpus Christi Symphony; Munro Ballet

RICHARDSON AUDITORIUM
101 Baldwin Avenue, Corpus Christi, TX 78404
(512) 886-1243
FAX: (512) 886-1276
    Type of Facility: Auditorium; Theatre House
    Type of Stage: Proscenium
    Stage Dimensions: 55'Wx37'Dx24'H   **Orchestra Pit**
    Seating Capacity: 1,780
    Year Built: 1951   **Architect:** Brock & Anderson
    Acoustical Consultant: Boner & Associates
    Contact for Rental: Brad Gallaway;   (512) 886-1243
    Resident Groups: Corpus Christi Chamber Music Society; Corpus Christi Chorale; Corpus Christi Creative Arts Center

Corsicana

THEATRE

CORSICANA COMMUNITY PLAYHOUSE
119 West Sixth, Corsicana, TX 75110
(903) 872-5421
    Founded: 1971
    Arts Area: Community; Theatrical Group
    Status: Semi-Professional; Non-Profit
    Type: Performing; Touring
    Purpose: To provide quality theatrical performances to Corsicana and north and east Texas cities
    Management: Cranston Dodds, Resident Director
    Officers: Tom Hecker, President; David Ralston, Vice President; Mary Burson, Secretary; Steve Johnson, Treasurer
    Paid Staff: 5
    Utilizes: Guest Artists
    Budget: $100,000 - $500,000
    Income Sources: Private Foundations/Grants/Endowments; Business/Corporate Donations; Box Office; Government Grants; Individual Donations
    Season: February - December   **Annual Attendance:** 10,000

Affiliations: Texas Nonprofit Theatre
Performance Facilities: Warehouse Living Arts Center

FACILITY

WAREHOUSE LIVING ARTS CENTER
119 West Sixth, Corsicana, TX 75110
(903) 872-5421
Founded: 1971
Type of Facility: Theatre Complex; Theatre House
Facility Originally: Warehouse
Type of Stage: Thrust
Stage Dimensions: 31'x41'
Seating Capacity: 127
Year Built: 1900
Year Remodeled: 1980   **Architect:** Cranston Dodds   **Cost:** $250,000
Manager: Cranston Dodds;   (903) 872-5421
Resident Groups: Corsicana Community Playhouse

Crockett

FACILITY

DISCOVER HOUSTON COUNTY VISITORS CENTER - MUSEUM
303 South First, Crockett, TX 75835
(409) 544-9520
Mailing Address: 629 North Fourth, Crockett, TX 75835
Founded: 1983
Type of Facility: Theatre Complex; Auditorium; Outdoor (Concert); Environmental; Civic Center; Arena; Multi-Purpose; Room
Facility Originally: Business Facility; Railroad Depot
Type of Stage: Platform; Environmental
Seating Capacity: 250
Year Built: 1909   **Architect:** International & Great Northern Railroad Company
Year Remodeled: 1987   **Architect:** David Woodcock, AIA, RIBA   **Cost:** $75,000
Contact for Rental: Eliza H. Bishop;   (409) 544-5304
Resident Groups: Piney Woods Fine Arts Association
Restoration is expected to be completed in 1995.

Dallas

DANCE

DALLAS BLACK DANCE THEATRE
2627 Flora Street, Dallas, TX 75201
(214) 871-2387
FAX: (214) 871-2842
Founded: 1976
Arts Area: Modern; Jazz; Ethnic
Status: Non-Profit
Type: Performing; Touring; Educational
Purpose: To present ethnic dance as a truly meaningful art form
Management: Ann M. Williams, Founder/Artistic Director; Venetta Drew, Executive Director
Officers: Marvin Robinson, President
Paid Staff: 4
Utilizes: Guest Artists
Budget: $50,000 - $100,000
Income Sources: Private Foundations/Grants/Endowments; Business/Corporate Donations; Box Office; Government Grants; Individual Donations
Season: August - May

DALLAS DANCE COUNCIL
PO Box 740511, Dallas, TX 75374-0511
(214) 713-2795
Founded: 1974
Arts Area: Modern; Ballet; Jazz; Ethnic; Folk
Status: Semi-Professional; Non-Profit

Type: Educational; Sponsoring
Purpose: To support the art of dance, including ballet, modern, jazz, ethnic, post-modern, experimental and theatre dance; to represent the dance community, serving as a central information agency for all aspects of dance
Officers: Taura Hunter, President; JoAnn Robertson, Board Chairman
Budget: $1,000 - $50,000
Income Sources: Private Foundations/Grants/Endowments; Business/Corporate Donations; Government Grants; Individual Donations

DALLAS METROPOLITAN BALLET
6815 Hillcrest Avenue, Dallas, TX 75205
(214) 361-0278
> **Founded:** 1964
> **Arts Area:** Ballet
> **Status:** Semi-Professional; Non-Profit
> **Type:** Performing; Touring; Resident; Educational
> **Purpose:** To develop an audience for dance; to develop dancers in the Dallas area and the Southwest
> **Management:** Ann Etgen, Bill Atkinson, Artistic Directors; Board of Directors
> **Paid Staff:** 3
> **Paid Artists:** 4 **Non-Paid Artists:** 18
> **Utilizes:** Special Technical Talent; Guest Artists; Guest Choreographers
> **Budget:** $1,000 - $50,000
> **Income Sources:** Private Foundations/Grants/Endowments; Business/Corporate Donations; Box Office; Government Grants; Individual Donations
> **Season:** August - June **Annual Attendance:** 15,000
> **Affiliations:** NARB
> **Performance Facilities:** McFarlin Auditorium; Southern Methodist University

INSTRUMENTAL MUSIC

DALLAS BACH SOCIETY
PO Box 140201, Dallas, TX 75214
(214) 827-2224
> **Founded:** 1982
> **Arts Area:** Orchestra; Chamber; Choral
> **Status:** Professional; Semi-Professional; Non-Profit
> **Type:** Performing; Sponsoring
> **Purpose:** To produce and present Baroque music: to perform choral, instrumental, chamber and keyboard selections; to operate the Dallas Bach Orchestra and the Dallas Bach Choir
> **Management:** Paul Riedo, Artistic Director; Angeline Churchill, General Manager
> **Officers:** Mary Glerum, President; Betty Nadalini, Vice President
> **Volunteer Staff:** 2
> **Paid Artists:** 50 **Non-Paid Artists:** 20
> **Utilizes:** Guest Artists
> **Budget:** $100,000 - $500,000
> **Income Sources:** Private Foundations/Grants/Endowments; Business/Corporate Donations; Box Office; Individual Donations
> **Season:** September - May **Annual Attendance:** 5,000
> **Affiliations:** CA; International Bach Society
> **Performance Facilities:** Dallas Museum of Art; Saint Thomas Aquinas Church

DALLAS CHAMBER ORCHESTRA
Sammons Center for the Arts, 3630 Harry Hines Boulevard, Suite 302, Dallas, TX 75219-3201
(214) 520-3121
FAX: (214) 522-9174
> **Founded:** 1979
> **Arts Area:** Orchestra; Chamber; Ensemble
> **Status:** Professional; Non-Profit; Commercial
> **Type:** Performing; Touring; Resident; Educational
> **Management:** Jack Bunning, Executive Director; Ronald Neal, Music Director
> **Officers:** Dan Chesnut, President; John Fesperman, Lyla O'Driscoll, Vice Presidents; Gordon Lindsey, Secretary; Bob Melvin, Treasurer
> **Paid Staff:** 2 **Volunteer Staff:** 20
> **Paid Artists:** 15
> **Utilizes:** Guest Artists
> **Budget:** $100,000 - $500,000
> **Income Sources:** Private Foundations/Grants/Endowments; Business/Corporate Donations; Box Office; Government Grants; Individual Donations
> **Season:** September - May **Annual Attendance:** 15,000
> **Performance Facilities:** Caruth Auditorium, Southern Methodist University

DALLAS CLASSIC GUITAR SOCIETY
PO Box 140724, Dallas, TX 75214
(214) 528-3733
> **Founded:** 1979
> **Arts Area:** Chamber; Ensemble; Ethnic; Folk
> **Status:** Non-Profit
> **Type:** Performing; Resident; Educational; Sponsoring
> **Purpose:** To promote appreciation and understanding of classical guitar by increasing exposure to the instrument and its music
> **Management:** Suzanne Davidson, General Manager
> **Officers:** James R. Shaw, President; Christopher McGuire, Chairman, Advisory Board
> **Paid Staff:** 2
> **Paid Artists:** 50
> **Utilizes:** Guest Artists
> **Budget:** $100,000 - $500,000
> **Income Sources:** Private Foundations/Grants/Endowments; Business/Corporate Donations; Box Office; Government Grants; Individual Donations
> **Season:** September - April   **Annual Attendance:** 10,000
> **Affiliations:** APAP; GFA
> **Performance Facilities:** Majestic Theatre; Meyerson Symphony Center; Caruth Hall, Southern Methodist University; Music Hall at Fair Park

DALLAS SYMPHONY ASSOCIATION, INC.
2301 Flora Street, Suite 300, Dallas, TX 75201
(214) 871-4000
FAX: (214) 953-1218
> **Founded:** 1900
> **Arts Area:** Symphony
> **Status:** Professional; Non-Profit
> **Type:** Performing; Resident; Educational
> **Purpose:** To manage the Dallas Symphony Orchestra; to secure additional funding as necessary over and above revenue
> **Management:** Leonard D. Stone, Executive Director; Fred W. Hoster, General Manager; Victor Marshall, Music Administrator; Mark Melson, Director of Orchestra Operations
> **Officers:** R.A. Freling, Chairman; Howard Haflam, President; Donald G. Reynolds, Vice President of Marketing; Darryl D. Pounds, Treasurer
> **Paid Staff:** 50   **Volunteer Staff:** 5
> **Paid Artists:** 45
> **Utilizes:** Guest Conductors; Guest Artists
> **Budget:** Over 10,000,000
> **Income Sources:** Private Foundations/Grants/Endowments; Business/Corporate Donations; Box Office; Government Grants; Individual Donations
> **Season:** 52 Weeks
> **Annual Attendance:** 425,000
> **Affiliations:** ASOL
> **Performance Facilities:** Morton H. Meyerson Symphony Center

DALLAS SYMPHONY ORCHESTRA
2301 Flora Street, Dallas, TX 75201
(214) 871-4000
FAX: (214) 953-1218
> **Founded:** 1900
> **Arts Area:** Symphony; Orchestra
> **Status:** Professional; Non-Profit
> **Type:** Performing; Touring; Resident; Educational; Sponsoring
> **Purpose:** DSO provides the Dallas community with the very best in musical performances and education as recognized by national and international standards, audience acclaim, and critical appraisal
> **Management:** Leonard Stone, Executive Director; Eduardo Mata, Director of Music/Conductor; Douglas Kinzey, Director of Marketing; Warren Gould, Director of Development; Fred Hoster, General Manager; Mark Melson, Director of Orchestra Operations; Amy Groff, Director of Finance; Sydney Reid-Hedge, Director of Volunteers
> **Officers:** Liener Temerlin, Chairman; William Schilling, President; Nancy Nelson, Secretary; Seymour Thum, Treasurer
> **Paid Staff:** 34
> **Paid Artists:** 93
> **Utilizes:** Guest Conductors; Guest Artists
> **Budget:** Over 10,000,000
> **Income Sources:** Private Foundations/Grants/Endowments; Business/Corporate Donations; Box Office; Government Grants; Individual Donations
> **Season:** 52 Weeks
> **Performance Facilities:** Morton H. Meyerson Symphony Center

EARTHLY PLEASURES
9215 Forest Hills Boulevard, Dallas, TX 75218
(214) 327-6823
Founded: 1978
Arts Area: Instrumental Group
Status: Semi-Professional
Type: Performing
Purpose: Performance of Renaissance and Medieval music on period instruments
Management: David G. Barton, Director; Susan Barton, Assistant Director
Paid Artists: 5
Budget: $1,000 - $50,000
Income Sources: Box Office   **Season:** 52 Weeks

FINE ARTS CHAMBER PLAYERS
3630 Harry Hines Boulevard, Dallas, TX 75219
(214) 520-2219
FAX: (214) 522-9174
Founded: 1980
Arts Area: Chamber; Ensemble
Status: Professional; Non-Profit
Type: Performing; Educational
Purpose: To provide high-quality, professional chamber ensemble concerts to Dallas citizens free of charge
Management: Rogene Russell, Artistic Director
Officers: David S. Nafziger, Board President; Natalie Nielson, Vice President; Fred Sims, Treasurer; Rebecca Hamilton, Secretary
Paid Staff: 1   **Volunteer Staff:** 3
Paid Artists: 34
Budget: $50,000 - $100,000
Income Sources: Private Foundations/Grants/Endowments; Business/Corporate Donations; Government Grants; Individual Donations
Season: September - August   **Annual Attendance:** 14,000
Performance Facilities: Dallas Civic Garden Center; Dallas Museum of Art

GREATER DALLAS YOUTH ORCHESTRA ASSOCIATION
3630 Harry Hines, Dallas, TX 75219
(214) 528-7747
FAX: (214) 522-9174
Founded: 1972
Arts Area: Symphony; Orchestra; Ensemble
Status: Non-Professional; Non-Profit
Type: Performing; Resident; Educational
Purpose: To provide ensemble training for serious student musicians in the Dallas Area
Management: Carol Cobb, Executive Director
Officers: Kevin Wiggins, President
Paid Staff: 3
Paid Artists: 4
Utilizes: Guest Conductors; Guest Artists; Guest Directors
Budget: $100,000 - $500,000
Income Sources: Private Foundations/Grants/Endowments; Business/Corporate Donations; Box Office; Government Grants; Individual Donations; Tuition
Season: September - May
Annual Attendance: 14,200
Affiliations: ASOL
Performance Facilities: Morton H. Meyerson Symphony Center

VOICES OF CHANGE
310 Meadows Building, 5646 Milton, Dallas, TX 75206
(214) 987-0889
Founded: 1975
Arts Area: Chamber; Ensemble
Status: Professional; Non-Profit
Type: Performing; Touring; Resident; Educational
Purpose: To present music of living composers and 20th-century "classics"; to present work through a seasonal series, monthly radio broadcasts, tours, recordings, commissionings and special-event concerts
Management: Jo Boatright, Artistic Director
Officers: Lydia Scheer, President; Ken Long, Vice President; John Lumsford, Secretary; Sylvia Elton, Treasurer
Paid Staff: 2   **Volunteer Staff:** 25
Paid Artists: 15

Utilizes: Special Technical Talent; Guest Conductors; Guest Artists
Budget: $100,000 - $500,000
Income Sources: Private Foundations/Grants/Endowments; Business/Corporate Donations; Box Office; Government Grants; Individual Donations; Benefit Promotions
Season: September - August
Annual Attendance: 5,000
Affiliations: CMA; Southern Methodist University; American Music Center; Meet the Composers; Texas Composers Forum
Performance Facilities: Caruth Auditorium, Southern Methodist University; Dallas Museum of Art; Greiner Middle School Academy; Morton Meyerson Center

VOCAL MUSIC

THE DALLAS OPERA
3102 Oak Lawn Avenue, Suite 430, Dallas, TX 75210
(214) 443-1043
FAX: (214) 443-1060
Founded: 1957
Arts Area: Grand Opera
Status: Professional; Non-Profit
Type: Performing; Educational; Sponsoring
Purpose: The Dallas Opera is an opera company committed to the presentation of opera at the international level. It enriches the community through performances of grand and chamber opera, operatic concerts, recitals and attendant education and community service programs.
Management: Plato Karayanis, General Director; Jonathon Pell, Artistic Administrator
Officers: Jim Erwin, President
Paid Staff: 28   **Volunteer Staff:** 800
Paid Artists: 262
Utilizes: Special Technical Talent; Guest Conductors; Guest Artists; Guest Directors
Budget: $5,000,000 - $10,000,000
Income Sources: Private Foundations/Grants/Endowments; Business/Corporate Donations; Box Office; Government Grants; Individual Donations
Season: October - May   **Annual Attendance:** 116,400
Affiliations: OA; AAA; Texas Arts Alliance
Performance Facilities: Music Hall at Fair Park

DALLAS SYMPHONY CHORUS
c/o Dallas Symphony Association, 2301 Flora Street, Suite 300, Dallas, TX 75201
(214) 871-4000
FAX: (214) 953-1218
Arts Area: Lyric Opera; Light Opera; Operetta; Choral; Ethnic; Folk
Status: Non-Professional; Non-Profit
Type: Performing; Touring; Resident
Purpose: To support the Dallas Symphony Association by performing major choral works with the symphony
Management: Leann Binford, Chorus Representative
Officers: Paul Talbot, President
Budget: $1,000 - $50,000
Income Sources: Private Foundations/Grants/Endowments; Business/Corporate Donations; Government Grants; Individual Donations
Performance Facilities: Meyerson Symphony Center

THE LYRIC OPERA OF DALLAS
PO Box 12656, Dallas, TX 75225-0656
(214) 368-2183
Founded: 1982
Arts Area: Grand Opera; Lyric Opera; Light Opera; Operetta
Status: Professional; Non-Profit
Type: Performing; Resident; Educational
Purpose: To produce music theatre that is accessible and appealing to a wide audience and gives opportunities to new American talent
Management: Terry Hicklin, General Director; John Burrows, Artistic Director; LeAnn Binford, Managing Director; Elizabeth Daggerhart, Director of Box Office; Robert Hull, Development Counsel; Steven Friedlander, Producing Director/Lighting Designer
Officers: Donald G. Williamson, President; Robert M. Dickson, Eugene Coker, Vice Presidents; Mrs. Charles Blaylock, Secretary; Alice Worham Austin, Treasurer
Paid Staff: 5   **Volunteer Staff:** 65
Paid Artists: 118
Utilizes: Guest Conductors; Guest Artists; Guest Directors
Budget: $500,000 - $1,000,000

Income Sources: Private Foundations/Grants/Endowments; Business/Corporate Donations; Box Office; Government Grants; Individual Donations
Season: May - August
Annual Attendance: 12,000
Affiliations: OA
Performance Facilities: Plaza Theatre

TURTLE CREEK CHORALE
PO Box 190806, Dallas, TX 75219-0806
(214) 526-3214
FAX: (214) 522-9174
Founded: 1980
Arts Area: Choral
Status: Non-Professional; Non-Profit
Type: Performing
Purpose: To enhance the musical, educational and cultural life in Dallas and the state of Texas through the presentation of chorale music for men's voices
Management: Dr. Timothy Seelig, Artistic Director; Ann Albritton, Principal Accompanist; Antoine Spener, Assistant Accompanist; Jeannette Teel, Business Manager
Officers: Chet Flake, Chairman of the Board; A.G. Black, President; Dennis Plemmons, Vice President; Gary Williams, Secretary; Franklin Reed, Treasurer
Paid Staff: 2   **Volunteer Staff:** 10
Paid Artists: 10
Utilizes: Special Technical Talent; Guest Artists
Budget: $100,000 - $500,000
Income Sources: Private Foundations/Grants/Endowments; Business/Corporate Donations; Box Office; Government Grants; Individual Donations; Fund-raising
Season: October - August
Annual Attendance: 1,500
Performance Facilities: Meyerson Symphony Center

THEATRE

AFRO-AMERICAN PLAYERS
PO Box 36309, Dallas, TX 75235
(214) 399-0161
FAX: (214) 506-9030
Founded: 1971
Arts Area: Professional; Theatrical Group; Children's Theatre
Status: Professional; Non-Profit
Type: Performing; Touring; Resident; Educational
Purpose: To educate, entertain, and enlighten through theatre so that cross-cultural communication and interaction can occur
Management: Glodean Baker, Executive Director; Fred Gardner, Executive Producer
Paid Staff: 3   **Volunteer Staff:** 13
Paid Artists: 8
Utilizes: Special Technical Talent; Guest Artists; Guest Directors
Budget: $100,000 - $500,000
Income Sources: Private Foundations/Grants/Endowments; Business/Corporate Donations; Box Office; Government Grants; Individual Donations
Season: 52 Weeks
Annual Attendance: 100,000
Affiliations: STAGE; Black Theatre Network
Performance Facilities: Cultural Arts Center

CABBAGES AND KINGS
7732 Forest Lane, #224, Dallas, TX 75230
(214) 363-7292
FAX: (214) 867-7615
Founded: 1984
Arts Area: Professional; Theatrical Group
Status: Professional; Non-Profit
Type: Performing; Touring
Purpose: To entertain and enlighten children and their families; to present original plays based on stories and mythology and to relate them to present day situations
Management: Linda Comess, Founder/Artistic Director; Tricia Avery, Business Manager
Officers: Linda Comess, President; Hal Harris, Vice President; Leonard Comess, Secretary; Miriam Harris, Treasurer
Paid Staff: 2   **Volunteer Staff:** 2
Paid Artists: 28

Utilizes: Special Technical Talent; Guest Artists; Guest Directors
Budget: $50,000 - $100,000
Income Sources: Private Foundations/Grants/Endowments; Business/Corporate Donations; Box Office; Government Grants; Individual Donations
Season: 52 Weeks
Affiliations: AEA
Performance Facilities: Addison Centre Theatre

DALLAS CHILDREN'S THEATER
2215 Cedar Springs, Dallas, TX 75201
(214) 978-0110
> **Founded:** 1984
> **Arts Area:** Professional; Theatrical Group
> **Status:** Non-Profit
> **Type:** Performing; Touring; Educational
> **Purpose:** To enrich the lives of children through the art of theater
> **Management:** Robin Baker Flatt, Executive Director; Dennis Vincent; Executive Producer
> **Officers:** Laurie Harrison, President; Melissa Deakins, Chairman of Executive Committee
> **Paid Staff:** 4
> **Utilizes:** Special Technical Talent; Guest Artists; Guest Directors
> **Budget:** $100,000 - $500,000
> **Income Sources:** Private Foundations/Grants/Endowments; Business/Corporate Donations; Box Office; Government Grants; Individual Donations
> **Season:** September - July
> **Annual Attendance:** 35,000
> **Affiliations:** ASSITEJ
> **Performance Facilities:** El Centro College, Crescent Theatre

DALLAS PUPPET THEATER
3018 Commerce, Dallas, TX 75229
(214) 939-0004
> **Founded:** 1982
> **Arts Area:** Professional; Puppet
> **Status:** Professional; Non-Profit
> **Type:** Performing; Touring; Resident; Educational; Sponsoring
> **Purpose:** To provide a greater awareness of the art of puppetry in construction and performance
> **Management:** James Smith, Founding Artistic Director; Michael Robinson, Technical Director
> **Paid Staff:** 3 **Volunteer Staff:** 7
> **Utilizes:** Special Technical Talent; Guest Artists; Guest Directors
> **Budget:** $1,000 - $50,000
> **Income Sources:** Private Foundations/Grants/Endowments; Business/Corporate Donations; Box Office; Government Grants; Individual Donations
> **Season:** 52 Weeks **Annual Attendance:** 60,000

DALLAS REPERTORY THEATRE
PO Box 12208, Dallas, TX 75225
(214) 692-5611
> **Founded:** 1969
> **Arts Area:** Professional; Theatrical Group
> **Status:** Professional; Non-Profit
> **Type:** Performing
> **Purpose:** To promote, encourage and advance the performing arts in Dallas through the production of fine-quality, current Broadway plays and musicals
> **Management:** Ed DeLatte, Founder
> **Officers:** Charles McMullen, President; Jay MacAuley, Secretary/Treasurer
> **Paid Staff:** 8 **Volunteer Staff:** 20
> **Paid Artists:** 75 **Non-Paid Artists:** 250
> **Utilizes:** Special Technical Talent; Guest Conductors
> **Budget:** $500,000 - $1,000,000
> **Income Sources:** Private Foundations/Grants/Endowments; Business/Corporate Donations; Box Office; Government Grants; Individual Donations
> **Season:** September - August **Annual Attendance:** 40,000
> **Affiliations:** AEA; Texas Nonprofit Theatre
> **Performance Facilities:** Crescent Theatre

DALLAS SUMMER MUSICALS
Music Hall at Fair Park, 909 First Avenue Parry, Dallas, TX 75210
(214) 565-1116
> **Arts Area:** Professional; Musical

Status: Professional; Non-Profit
Type: Performing; Sponsoring
Purpose: To arouse public interest in good music; to educate the public in music appreciation and in one phase of the performing arts
Management: Tom Hughes, Producer/Manager
Utilizes: Special Technical Talent; Guest Artists; Guest Directors
Income Sources: Box Office
Performance Facilities: Music Hall at Fair Park

DALLAS THEATER CENTER
3636 Turtle Creek Boulevard, Dallas, TX 75219
(214) 526-8210
FAX: (214) 521-7666
  Founded: 1959
  Arts Area: Professional; Theatrical Group
  Status: Professional; Non-Profit
  Type: Performing; Resident; Educational
  Purpose: To provide a variety of artistically excellent professional theatre experiences representing a wide range of styles and periods
  Management: Richard Hamburger, Artistic Director; Jeff West, Managing Director
  Officers: Bess Enloe, Chairman; Richard Boysen, President
  Paid Staff: 78   **Volunteer Staff:** 14
  Paid Artists: 104
  Utilizes: Special Technical Talent; Guest Artists; Guest Directors
  Budget: $1,000,000 - $5,000,000
  Income Sources: Private Foundations/Grants/Endowments; Business/Corporate Donations; Box Office; Government Grants; Individual Donations
  Season: October - May   **Annual Attendance:** 136,229
  Affiliations: TCG; LORT; AAA
  Performance Facilities: Kalita Humphreys Theater; Arts District Theater

DRAMA CIRCLE THEATRE
2929 Mayhew, Dallas, TX 75228
(214) 270-9255
  Founded: 1971
  Arts Area: Theatrical Group
  Status: Semi-Professional; Non-Profit
  Type: Performing; Touring; Educational
  Purpose: To promote the theatre arts
  Management: Linda Boatman, Managing Director; Bill Green, Founder; Nan Truax, Co-Founder
  Volunteer Staff: 4
  Non-Paid Artists: 30
  Budget: $1,000 - $50,000
  Income Sources: Private Foundations/Grants/Endowments; Business/Corporate Donations; Box Office; Individual Donations
  Season: December - October
  Annual Attendance: 4,500

KATHY BURKS MARIONETTES
2979 Ladybird Lane, Dallas, TX 75229
(214) 353-9277
  Founded: 1971
  Arts Area: Professional; Theatrical Group; Puppet
  Status: Professional; Non-Profit
  Type: Performing; Resident; Educational
  Purpose: We do this for the perpetuation of the art of puppetry. We cover the spectrum of the art itself.
  Management: Kathy Burks, Artistic Director; Sarah Jayne Fiorello, Managing Director; Douglas Burks, Master Puppeteer/Co-Artistic Director; Beatrice Wolf, Composer/Lyricist
  Paid Staff: 7
  Paid Artists: 5
  Utilizes: Guest Artists
  Budget: $50,000 - $100,000
  Income Sources: Box Office
  Season: September - August
  Annual Attendance: 100,000
  Affiliations: Puppeteers of America; Lone Star Puppet Guild
  Performance Facilities: The Loft Puppet Theatre at Fairview Farms, Plano, TX

PEGASUS THEATRE
3916 Main Street, Dallas, TX 75226
(214) 821-6005
> **Founded:** 1985
> **Arts Area:** Professional; Musical; Theatrical Group
> **Status:** Professional; Non-Profit
> **Type:** Performing; Touring
> **Purpose:** To produce new and original comedies
> **Management:** Kurt Kleinmann, Artistic Director; Barbara Weinberger, General Manager
> **Officers:** Pat Hadley, President; Becky Chavarria Chairez, Vice President; Billy Stone, Secretary; Jay Marshall, Treasurer
> **Paid Staff:** 3   **Volunteer Staff:** 1
> **Paid Artists:** 100
> **Utilizes:** Special Technical Talent; Guest Artists; Guest Directors
> **Budget:** $100,000 - $500,000
> **Income Sources:** Private Foundations/Grants/Endowments; Business/Corporate Donations; Box Office; Government Grants; Individual Donations
> **Season:** 52 Weeks   **Annual Attendance:** 16,500
> **Affiliations:** STAGE
> **Performance Facilities:** Pegasus Theatre

POCKET SANDWICH THEATRE
5400 East Mockingbird, #119, Dallas, TX 75206
(214) 821-1860
> **Founded:** 1980
> **Arts Area:** Professional; Musical; Dinner
> **Status:** Professional; Commercial
> **Type:** Performing
> **Purpose:** To present a variety of live theatre performances
> **Management:** Rodney Dobbs, Owner/Technical Director; Joe Dickinson, Owner/Artistic Director
> **Paid Staff:** 9
> **Paid Artists:** 73
> **Utilizes:** Special Technical Talent; Guest Artists; Guest Directors
> **Budget:** $1,000 - $50,000
> **Income Sources:** Box Office; Food Sales
> **Season:** 52 Weeks   **Annual Attendance:** 24,000
> **Performance Facilities:** Pocket Sandwich Theatre

TEATRO HISPANO DE DALLAS
2204 Commerce, Dallas, TX 75201
(214) 741-6833
FAX: (214) 946-5820
> **Founded:** 1985
> **Arts Area:** Professional; Community; Theatrical Group
> **Status:** Professional; Semi-Professional; Non-Profit
> **Type:** Performing
> **Management:** Cora Cardona, Artistic Director/Producer; Christie Hernandez, Executive Director
> **Officers:** Vicki Meek, President; Donna Miller, Vice President
> **Paid Staff:** 2   **Volunteer Staff:** 25
> **Paid Artists:** 20
> **Utilizes:** Special Technical Talent; Guest Artists; Guest Directors
> **Budget:** $100,000 - $500,000
> **Income Sources:** Private Foundations/Grants/Endowments; Business/Corporate Donations; Box Office; Government Grants; Individual Donations
> **Season:** February - November   **Annual Attendance:** 3,000
> **Performance Facilities:** Teatro Dallas

THEATRE GEMINI
PO Box 191225, Dallas, TX 75219
(214) 521-6331
> **Founded:** 1984
> **Arts Area:** Community; Theatrical Group
> **Status:** Non-Professional; Non-Profit
> **Type:** Performing; Educational
> **Management:** Craig Hess, General Manager
> **Volunteer Staff:** 50
> **Non-Paid Artists:** 60
> **Budget:** $50,000 - $100,000

Income Sources: Private Foundations/Grants/Endowments; Business/Corporate Donations; Box Office; Individual Donations
Season: 52 Weeks   **Annual Attendance:** 2,500

THEATRE THREE
2800 Routh, Dallas, TX 75201
(214) 871-2933
FAX: (214) 871-3139
    Founded: 1961
    Arts Area: Professional; Musical
    Status: Professional; Non-Profit
    Type: Performing; Touring; Resident; Educational; Sponsoring
    Purpose: To provide professional theatre and related activities for the Dallas community
    Management: Jac Alder, Executive Producer; Norma Young, Artistic Director; Larry O'Dwyer, Associate Director
    Officers: David Wells, President; Greg Balew, Treasurer
    Paid Staff: 30   **Volunteer Staff:** 60
    Paid Artists: 60   **Non-Paid Artists:** 20
    Utilizes: Special Technical Talent; Guest Conductors; Guest Artists; Guest Directors
    Budget: $1,000,000 - $5,000,000
    Income Sources: Private Foundations/Grants/Endowments; Business/Corporate Donations; Box Office; Government Grants; Individual Donations
    Season: 52 Weeks   **Annual Attendance:** 61,600
    Affiliations: AEA; TCG

UNDERMAIN THEATRE
3202 Elm, Dallas, TX 75226
(214) 748-3082
    Founded: 1983
    Arts Area: Professional
    Status: Non-Profit
    Type: Performing
    Purpose: To focus on regional and national premieres of emotionally, intellectually and philosphically challanging work
    Management: Katherine Owens, Raphael Perry, Artistic Directors; Robert McVay, Technical Director; Sheila L. Sullivan, Marketing
    Utilizes: Special Technical Talent; Guest Directors
    Budget: $100,000 - $500,000
    Income Sources: Private Foundations/Grants/Endowments; Business/Corporate Donations; Box Office; Government Grants; Individual Donations
    Season: August - June   **Annual Attendance:** 5,000
    Affiliations: TCG; Texas Association of Performing Arts; AEA
    Performance Facilities: Undermain Theatre Basement

PERFORMING SERIES

CHAUTAUQUA SERIES
1928 Ross Avenue, Dallas, TX 75201
(214) 220-2727
    Founded: 1948
    Arts Area: Vocal Music; Instrumental Music; Theater
    Status: Non-Professional; Non-Profit
    Type: Performing; Sponsoring
    Purpose: To provide entertainment to the community Sunday evenings in summer
    Management: Ronald Kauffmann, Director of Music and Arts
    Paid Staff: 2
    Utilizes: Special Technical Talent; Guest Artists; Guest Directors
    Budget: $1,000 - $50,000
    Income Sources: Private Foundations/Grants/Endowments; Individual Donations
    Season: July - August   **Annual Attendance:** 4,500
    Performance Facilities: First United Methodist Church

DALLAS CHAMBER MUSIC SOCIETY
4808 Drexel Drive, Dallas, TX 75205
(214) 526-7301
    Founded: 1954
    Arts Area: Instrumental Music
    Status: Professional; Non-Profit
    Type: Performing; Sponsoring
    Purpose: To give chamber music concerts on the highest professional level at minimum cost to Dallas audiences
    Management: Dorothea Kelley, Manager; Celia Bingham, Assistant

Officers: Walter Brudno, President; Masha Porte, Vice President; Margaret Stevenson, Secretary; Mrs. Martin Anastasi, Membership Secretary; Mrs. Ray Entenman, Entertainment Secretary; Mrs. Karl Kahn, Treasurer
Paid Staff: 1 **Volunteer Staff:** 10
Paid Artists: 21
Utilizes: Guest Artists
Budget: $1,000 - $50,000
Income Sources: Private Foundations/Grants/Endowments; Box Office; Individual Donations
Season: October - April **Annual Attendance:** 2,800
Performance Facilities: Caruth Auditorium, Southern Methodist University

JUNIOR BLACK ACADEMY OF ARTS AND LETTERS
650 South Griffin, Dallas, TX 75202
(214) 658-7144; (214) 658-7147
FAX: (214) 658-7163
Founded: 1977
Arts Area: Dance; Vocal Music; Instrumental Music; Theater; Festivals
Status: Professional; Non-Profit
Type: Performing; Educational
Purpose: Designed to promote, foster, cultivate, perpetuate and preserve the arts and letters of Black Americans in the fine, literary and performing arts
Management: Curtis King, Founder and President; Gwen Hargrove, Facility Operations Manager; Ken Rowe, Developmental Manager; Gail Johnson, Membership Developer; Marilyn Clark, Publicist
Officers: Brooks Fitch, Chairman of the Board
Paid Staff: 7 **Volunteer Staff:** 150
Paid Artists: 100 **Non-Paid Artists:** 100
Utilizes: Special Technical Talent; Guest Conductors; Guest Artists; Guest Directors
Budget: $100,000 - $500,000
Income Sources: Private Foundations/Grants/Endowments; Business/Corporate Donations; Box Office; Government Grants; Individual Donations
Season: September - August

SHAKESPEARE FESTIVAL OF DALLAS
3630 Harry Hine Boulevard, Dallas, TX 75219
(214) 807-4046
Founded: 1972
Arts Area: Professional
Status: Professional; Non-Profit
Type: Performing; Educational
Management: Jeff West, Managing Director; Dale A.J. Rose, Artistic Director; Robert Glenn, Founder/Consulting Producer
Officers: Otto K. Wetzel, Chairman of the Board; Sherry Patterson, Secretary; Catherine Z. Smith, Treasurer
Paid Staff: 4 **Volunteer Staff:** 20
Paid Artists: 30 **Non-Paid Artists:** 10
Utilizes: Special Technical Talent; Guest Artists; Guest Directors
Budget: $100,000 - $500,000
Income Sources: Private Foundations/Grants/Endowments; Business/Corporate Donations; Government Grants; Individual Donations
Season: June - July **Annual Attendance:** 36,000
Performance Facilities: Fair Park Band Shell

TITAS - THE INTERNATIONAL THEATRICAL ARTS SOCIETY
3900 Lemmon Avenue, Suite 20, Dallas, TX 75219
(214) 528-5576
FAX: (214) 528-2617
Founded: 1982
Arts Area: Dance; Instrumental Music
Status: Non-Profit
Type: Sponsoring
Purpose: To present international cultural and educational programs
Management: Tom Adams, Executive Producer
Officers: Margie Reese, President
Paid Staff: 3 **Volunteer Staff:** 2
Utilizes: Guest Artists
Budget: $100,000 - $500,000
Income Sources: Private Foundations/Grants/Endowments; Business/Corporate Donations; Box Office; Government Grants; Individual Donations
Season: September - May
Annual Attendance: 69,000

Affiliations: ISPAA
Performance Facilities: McFarlin Auditorium, Southern Methodist University

FACILITY

BATH HOUSE CULTURAL CENTER
521 East Lawther Drive, Dallas, TX 75218
(214) 670-8749
Type of Facility: Theatre House
Facility Originally: Bathhouse
Type of Stage: 3/4 Arena; In-the-round Capability
Seating Capacity: 130
Year Built: 1930
Year Remodeled: 1981
Contact for Rental: Teri Aguilar;　(214) 328-8428
Resident Groups: The Gryphon Players; Actors Theatre of Dallas; Irregular Pearl; Actors Stock Company; New Horizon Theatre; Moving Collaborations; Dance Fusion
To foster the growth, development and quality of multi-cultural arts within the City of Dallas

BIBLICAL ARTS CENTER
7500 Park Lane, Dallas, TX 75225
(214) 691-4661
FAX: (214) 691-4752
Type of Facility: Auditorium; Multi-Purpose
Facility Originally: Museum
Type of Stage: Proscenium
Stage Dimensions: 25'Wx25'6"D
Seating Capacity: 350
Year Built: 1981　**Architect:** Burson Hendricks & Wall　**Cost:** $1,200,000
Acoustical Consultant: Variable Acoustics
Contact for Rental: Ronnie L. Roese;　(214) 691-4661

DALLAS CONVENTION CENTER
650 South Griffin, Dallas, TX 75202
(214) 939-2700
Type of Facility: Civic Center; Multi-Purpose
Architect: George Dahl
Contact for Rental: Gloria Medrano;　(214) 939-2700
The Convention Center contains the Arena and Theater. See separate listings for additional information.

DALLAS CONVENTION CENTER - ARENA
650 South Griffin, Dallas, TX 75202
(214) 939-2700
Type of Facility: Arena; Multi-Purpose
Type of Stage: Flexible; Arena
Seating Capacity: 9,816
Year Built: 1958
Acoustical Consultant: Jim Moxley
Contact for Rental: Gloria Medrano;　(214) 939-2700

DALLAS CONVENTION CENTER - THEATER
650 South Griffin, Dallas, TX 75202
(214) 393-2700
Type of Facility: Concert Hall; Auditorium; Theatre House; Multi-Purpose
Type of Stage: Proscenium
Stage Dimensions: 80'Wx45'5"D
Orchestra Pit
Seating Capacity: 1,770
Year Built: 1957
Contact for Rental: Gloria Medrano;　(214) 939-2700

DALLAS REPERTORY THEATRE
PO Box 12208, Dallas, TX 75225
(214) 358-3997
Founded: 1969
Type of Facility: Auditorium; Theatre House
Facility Originally: Business Facility
Type of Stage: Thrust

Stage Dimensions: 20'x30'
Seating Capacity: 215
Year Built: 1966   **Architect:** Harrell & Hamilton, OmniPlan Architects
Year Remodeled: 1984   **Architect:** Art Rogers   **Cost:** $650,000
Resident Groups: Dallas Repertory Theatre
Ed DeLatte, Founder/Artistic Director

DALLAS THEATER CENTER - ARTS DISTRICT
2401 Flora Street, Dallas, TX 75204
(214) 922-0422
Type of Facility: Theatre House; Arena; Multi-Purpose
Type of Stage: Flexible
Seating Capacity: 500
Year Built: 1984
Contact for Rental: Donna Flippin;   (214) 526-8210
Resident Groups: Dallas Theater Center

DALLAS THEATER CENTER - KALITA HUMPHREYS THEATER
3636 Turtle Creek Boulevard, Dallas, TX 75219
(214) 526-8210
Type of Facility: Theatre House
Type of Stage: Thrust
Seating Capacity: 466
Year Built: 1959   **Architect:** Frank Lloyd Wright   **Cost:** $1,000,000
Contact for Rental: Donna Flippin;   (214) 526-8210
Resident Groups: Dallas Theater Center

FAIR PARK BANDSHELL
Cullum Boulevard and Martin Luther King Drive, Dallas, TX 75226
(214) 421-8702
Type of Facility: Amphitheater
Type of Stage: Elizabethan
Seating Capacity: 3,792
Year Built: 1936   **Architect:** George Dahl
Year Remodeled: 1986   **Architect:** City of Dallas
Contact for Rental: Frank Wyatt;   (214) 670-8402
Manager: Eddie Hueston, Executive General Manager;   (214) 670-8463

MAJESTIC THEATRE
1925 Elm, Dallas, TX 75201-4516
(214) 880-0137
FAX: (214) 880-0097
Founded: 1921
Type of Facility: Concert Hall; Auditorium; Performance Center; Off Broadway; Theatre House; Opera House; Multi-Purpose
Facility Originally: Vaudeville
Type of Stage: Proscenium; Includes 12' apron
Stage Dimensions: 39'Wx28'D   **Orchestra Pit**
Seating Capacity: 1,648
Year Built: 1921   **Architect:** John Eberson   **Cost:** $2,000,000
Year Remodeled: 1983   **Architect:** The Oglesby Group   **Cost:** $5,000,000
Acoustical Consultant: Jaffe Acoustics
Contact for Rental: David Boddie;   (214) 880-0137
Resident Groups: Dallas Broadway Series (touring shows); Dallas Black Dance Theatre; Anita N. Martinez Ballet Folk-lorico; Dallas Classic Guitar Society; Ballet Dallas
Performances, meetings, conferences, banquet/party facilities

THE MORTON H. MEYERSON SYMPHONY CENTER - EUGENE MCDERMOTT CONCERT HALL
2301 Flora Street, PO Box 26207, Dallas, TX 75226
(214) 565-9100
Founded: 1989
Type of Facility: Concert Hall; Performance Center
Type of Stage: Platform
Stage Dimensions: 36'D; 60'W downstage, 41'W upstage
Seating Capacity: 2,200
Architect: I.M. Pei and Partners   **Cost:** $85,000,000

Acoustical Consultant: ARTEC
Contact for Rental: City of Dallas; (214) 565-9100
Resident Groups: Dallas Symphony Association

MUSIC HALL AT FAIR PARK
PO Box 150188, Dallas, TX 75315
(214) 565-1116
FAX: (214) 428-4526
    Type of Facility: Theatre House
    Type of Stage: Proscenium; Modified Apron Proscenium
    Stage Dimensions: 52'Wx42'D; 52'Wx30'H proscenium opening   Orchestra Pit
    Seating Capacity: 3,420
    Year Built: 1925
    Year Remodeled: 1972   Architect: JPJ Architects   Cost: $5,500,000
    Contact for Rental: Nancy Marshall; (214) 565-1116
    Manager: Gary Surratt
    Resident Groups: The Dallas Opera; Dallas Summer Musicals

REUNION ARENA
777 Sports Street, Dallas, TX 75207
(214) 939-2770
    Type of Facility: Concert Hall; Performance Center; Arena
    Type of Stage: Arena
    Seating Capacity: 9,500
    Year Built: 1980   Architect: Harwood K. Smith & Partners   Cost: $27,000,000
    Acoustical Consultant: Don Moxley
    Contact for Rental: Will Caudell; (214) 939-2770

SOUTH DALLAS CULTURAL CENTER
3400 South Fitzhugh, Dallas, TX 75210
(214) 670-0314
    Type of Facility: Auditorium; Theatre House; Multi-Purpose
    Type of Stage: In-the-round Capability
    Seating Capacity: 160
    Year Built: 1986   Cost: $1,500,000
    Contact for Rental: Sydney Davis, Technical Director;   (214) 670-0314
    Manager: Mittie Jordan, Director;   (214) 670-0314

SOUTHERN METHODIST UNIVERSITY - BOB HOPE THEATRE
Owen Fine Arts Center, Dallas, TX 75275
(214) 692-3383
FAX: (214) 692-4138
    Type of Facility: Theatre Complex; Theatre House
    Type of Stage: Proscenium
    Stage Dimensions: 42'Wx38'D   Orchestra Pit
    Seating Capacity: 392
    Year Built: 1968   Architect: George Dahl
    Acoustical Consultant: C.P. Boner & Associates
    Contact for Rental: Jim D'Asaro; (214) 692-3383
    Resident Groups: SMU Theatre; SMU Dance; SMU Opera

SOUTHERN METHODIST UNIVERSITY - CARUTH AUDITORIUM
Owen Fine Arts Center, Dallas, TX 75275
(214) 692-2713
FAX: (214) 692-4138
    Type of Facility: Concert Hall
    Type of Stage: Arena
    Stage Dimensions: 63'Wx24'D
    Seating Capacity: 521
    Year Built: 1968   Architect: George Dahl
    Acoustical Consultant: C.P. Boner & Associates
    Contact for Rental: John Gibson; (214) 692-2713
    Resident Groups: SMU Symphony; SMU Wind Ensemble; SMU Jazz Ensemble; Dallas Chamber Music Society; Voices
    of Change; Dallas Chamber Orchestra
    Recitals, instrumental concerts

SOUTHERN METHODIST UNIVERSITY - MARGO JONES THEATRE
Owen Fine Arts Center, Dallas, TX 75275
(214) 692-3383
FAX: (214) 692-4138
    Type of Facility: Arena
    Type of Stage: Flexible; Arena
    Stage Dimensions: 60'x60'
    Seating Capacity: 132
    Year Built: 1968   **Architect:** George Dahl
    Acoustical Consultant: C.P. Boner & Associates
    Contact for Rental: Jim D'Asaro; (214) 692-3383
    Resident Groups: SMU Theatre; SMU Dance

SOUTHERN METHODIST UNIVERSITY - MCFARLIN MEMORIAL AUDITORIUM
6400 Hillcrest Avenue, PO Box 152, Dallas, TX 75275
(214) 692-3129
FAX: (214) 692-4138
    Type of Facility: Auditorium
    Facility Originally: Convocation Hall
    Type of Stage: Proscenium
    Stage Dimensions: 47'6"Wx33'D; 46'6"Wx32'H proscenium opening **Orchestra Pit**
    Seating Capacity: 2,404
    Year Built: 1926 **Cost:** $500,000
    Year Remodeled: 1961 **Cost:** $900,000
    Contact for Rental: Jane Lane; (214) 692-3129

THANKS-GIVING SQUARE
Intresection of Bryan, Pacific and Ervay, PO Box 1777, Dallas, TX 75221
(214) 969-1977
    Type of Facility: Environmental; Performance Center
    Year Built: 1977 **Architect:** Philip Johnson **Cost:** $6,000,000
    Contact for Rental: Elizabeth Espersen, Executive Director; (214) 969-1977
    Thanks-Giving Square, built to express gratitude and praise to God, contains the Chapel of Thanksgiving, Courtyard and Hall of World Thanksgiving. See separate listings for additional information.

THANKS-GIVING SQUARE - CHAPEL OF THANKSGIVING
Intersection of Bryan, Pacific and Ervay, PO Box 1777, Dallas, TX 75221
(214) 969-1977
    Type of Facility: Chapel
    Type of Stage: Curved Ramp
    Stage Dimensions: 4'Wx100'L
    Seating Capacity: 100
    Year Built: 1977
    Contact for Rental: Elizabeth Espersen, Executive Director; (214) 969-1977

THANKS-GIVING SQUARE - COURTYARD AT THANKS-GIVING SQUARE
Intersection of Bryan, Pacific and Ervay, PO Box 1777, Dallas, TX 75221
(214) 969-1977
    Type of Facility: Outdoor Garden Courtyard
    Type of Stage: Patio & Elevated Bridge
    Stage Dimensions: Patio - 20'x24'; Bridge - 5'Wx80'L
    Seating Capacity: 500
    Year Built: 1977
    Contact for Rental: Elizabeth Espersen, Executive Director; (214) 969-1977

THANKS-GIVING SQUARE - HALL OF WORLD THANKSGIVING
Intersection of Byran, Pacific and Ervay, PO Box 1777, Dallas, TX 75221
(214) 969-1977
    Type of Facility: Multi-Purpose; Room
    Type of Stage: Flexible
    Seating Capacity: 125
    Year Built: 1977
    Contact for Rental: Elizabeth Espersen, Executive Director; (214) 969-1977

THEATRE THREE
2800 Routh, Dallas, TX 75201
(214) 871-2933; (214) 871-3139
    Type of Facility: Theatre House

Facility Originally: Meeting Hall; Movie House
Type of Stage: Arena
Stage Dimensions: 20'x26' plus alcove stages
Seating Capacity: 243
Year Built: 1969   Architect: Jac Alder   Cost: $60,000
Year Remodeled: 1986   Architect: RTKL; The Oglesby Group   Cost: $650,000
Acoustical Consultant: Jac Alder
Contact for Rental: Jack Alder;   (214) 871-2933

Denton

INSTRUMENTAL MUSIC

ONE O'CLOCK LAB BAND
North Texas State University Lab Bands, PO Box 5038, Denton, TX 76203
(817) 565-3743
Founded: 1947
Arts Area: Ensemble
Status: Non-Profit
Type: Performing; Touring; Educational
Management: Neil Slater, Director/Professor of Music
Non-Paid Artists: 21
Income Sources: Box Office
Season: 52 Weeks
Affiliations: North Texas State University

THEATRE

BREAD AND CIRCUS THEATRE
1009 Bull Run, Denton, TX 76201
(817) 387-2408
Founded: 1982
Arts Area: Professional; Theatrical Group; Summer Stock; Community; Musical
Status: Professional; Semi-Professional
Type: Performing; Touring
Purpose: To provide a fun theatrical experience for audiences of all ages through audience participation
Management: Connie Whitt-Lambert, Managing Director
Officers: Artistic Board - Jeannene Abney, Jim Wilson, John Evarts, Dennis Welch, Melinda Milstead, Kyla Haynes, Marth Kirkpatrick
Paid Staff: 1   Paid Artists: 8
Utilize: Special Technical Talent; Guest Artists
Budget: $1,000 - $50,000
Income Sources: Box Office
Season: June - August   Annual Attendance: 3,500

DENTON COMMUNITY THEATRE
400 East Hickory, PO Box 1931, Denton, TX 76202
(817) 382-7014
Founded: 1969
Arts Area: Community; Theatrical Group
Status: Non-Professional; Non-Profit
Type: Performing; Educational
Purpose: To provide artistic, educational experiences for participants and quality theatre for audiences
Management: Julie Crawford Angelo, Executive Director
Officers: Lindsay Keffer, President; Jeff Springer, Vice President; Terry Widmer, Development Secretary; Phil Diebel, Treasurer; Gayland Howell, Vice President of Membership; Michael Flanagan, Vice President of Production
Paid Staff: 5   Volunteer Staff: 12
Paid Artists: 4   Non-Paid Artists: 250
Utilizes: Special Technical Talent; Guest Artists; Guest Directors
Budget: $100,000 - $500,000
Income Sources: Private Foundations/Grants/Endowments; Business/Corporate Donations; Box Office; Government Grants; Individual Donations; Membership; Special Events
Season: 52 Weeks   Annual Attendance: 7,500
Affiliations: ACT; SWTC; Texas Nonprofit Theatre
Performance Facilities: Center for the Visual Arts

FACILITY

TEXAS WOMAN'S UNIVERSITY - REDBUD THEATRE
PO Box 23865, TWU Station, Denton, TX 76204
(817) 898-2500
FAX: (817) 898-3198
>**Type of Facility:** Theatre Complex
>**Type of Stage:** Proscenium
>**Stage Dimensions:** 32'Wx16'H   **Orchestra Pit**
>**Seating Capacity:** 332
>**Year Built:** 1952
>**Year Remodeled:** 1985   **Architect:** Glenn McFaddin   **Cost:** $150,000
>**Contact for Rental:** Vice President for Academic Affairs;   (817) 898-3301
>**Manager:** Charles Harrill
>**Resident Groups:** TWU Theatre

UNIVERSITY OF NORTH TEXAS - CONCERT HALL
College of Music, Denton, TX 76203
(817) 565-2791
FAX: (817) 565-4919
>**Founded:** 1890
>**Type of Facility:** Concert Hall
>**Type of Stage:** Proscenium
>**Seating Capacity:** 714
>**Year Built:** 1961   **Cost:** $1,000,000
>**Contact for Rental:** Conference Management;   (817) 565-3628
>**Manager:** M. Wade Kelley, Assistant to the Dean;   (817) 565-3707
>**Resident Groups:** University Symphony; Symphonic Wind Ensemble; Chamber Orchestra; Concert Band; Chamber Winds; A Cappella Choir; Grand Chorus; Men's and Women's Chorus Brass Choir

UNIVERSITY OF NORTH TEXAS - DEPARTMENT OF DANCE AND DRAMA
PO Box 13126, Denton, TX 76203-3126
(817) 565-2211
>**Type of Facility:** Theatre Complex; Concert Hall; Auditorium; Studio Performance
>**Type of Stage:** Flexible; Proscenium
>**Stage Dimensions:** 44'x40'   **Orchestra Pit**
>**Seating Capacity:** 500
>**Year Built:** 1968   **Architect:** CRS Architects
>**Year Remodeled:** 1987   **Cost:** $225,000
>**Acoustical Consultant:** C.P. Boner & Associates
>**Contact for Rental:** Ralph B. Culp, Chairman;   (817) 565-2211
>**Resident Groups:** University of North Texas Department of Dance and Drama; School of Music
>*Total cost of Speech and Drama Building - $2,053,000*

Edinburg

INSTRUMENTAL MUSIC

SOUTH TEXAS SYMPHONY ASSOCIATION
PO Box 2832, First City Tower 1305, Edinburg, TX 78502
(512) 630-5355
FAX: (512) 632-2352
>**Founded:** 1976
>**Arts Area:** Symphony; Chamber
>**Status:** Semi-Professional; Non-Profit
>**Type:** Performing; Resident; Educational
>**Purpose:** The purpose of South Texas Symphony Association is to promote, encourage and support the performance of symphonic music in South Texas.
>**Management:** John Daugherty, Executive Director
>**Officers:** Walter Passmore, President; Kathy Didieu, Vice President; Billy Joe Day, Treasurer; Marilyn Meyer, Parliamentarian
>**Paid Staff:** 2
>**Paid Artists:** 70   **Non-Paid Artists:** 60
>**Utilizes:** Special Technical Talent; Guest Artists
>**Budget:** $100,000 - $500,000
>**Income Sources:** Private Foundations/Grants/Endowments; Business/Corporate Donations; Box Office; Government Grants; Individual Donations

Season: October - May   **Annual Attendance:** 6,500
Affiliations: ASOL; Pan American University
Performance Facilities: Pan American University Fine Arts Auditorium

FACILITY

UNIVERSITY OF TEXAS-PAN AMERICAN - FINE ARTS AUDITORIUM
Pan American University, Edinburg, TX 78539
(512) 381-3471
   Type of Facility: Auditorium
   Type of Stage: Proscenium   **Orchestra Pit**
   Seating Capacity: 1,000
   Year Built: 1967   **Architect:** Kenneth Bentsen
   Contact for Rental: Manager;   (512) 381-3471
   Resident Groups: University faculty and groups

UNIVERSITY OF TEXAS-PAN AMERICAN - THEATER
1201 West University Drive, Edinburg, TX 78539
(512) 381-3581
   Type of Facility: Theatre Complex; Studio Performance; Environmental; Theatre House; Multi-Purpose; Black Box
   Type of Stage: Thrust; Flexible
   Seating Capacity: Thrust - 296; Black Box - 200
   Year Built: 1984   **Architect:** SHSC   **Cost:** $8,000,000
   Contact for Rental: Tom Grabowski;   (512) 381-3588
   Manager: Linda Donahue, Managing Director;   (512) 381-3581
   Resident Groups: Pan American University Theater

El Paso

DANCE

BALLET OF THE AMERICAS
PO Box 335, El Paso, TX 79968
(915) 533-2200
   Founded: 1970
   Arts Area: Ballet
   Status: Professional; Non-Profit
   Type: Performing; Touring; Resident
   Purpose: Binational and bicultural ballet company
   Management: Ingeborg Heuser, Artistic Director; James R. Osborne, Executive Director; Susan Merrill, Development Director
   Officers: Marlene Stewart, Chairman of the Board; Manuel Vargas, President of the Board
   Paid Staff: 4
   Utilizes: Guest Artists; Guest Choreographers
   Budget: $500,000 - $1,000,000
   Income Sources: Private Foundations/Grants/Endowments; Business/Corporate Donations; Box Office; Individual Donations
   Season: September - May

INTERNATIONAL BALLET FOLKLORICO
PO Box 3777, El Paso, TX 79923
(915) 566-5084
   Arts Area: Modern; Jazz; Ethnic; Folk
   Status: Semi-Professional; Non-Profit
   Type: Performing; Educational
   Purpose: To provide cultural entertainment to the community and surrounding areas; to preserve the cultural heritage of the Southwest through dance
   Management: Rosa Guerrico, Artistic Director; Oscar Hernandez, Jessica Bravo, Assistant Directors
   Officers: Yolanda Delgado, President
   Volunteer Staff: 28
   Paid Artists: 18   **Non-Paid Artists:** 35
   Budget: $1,000 - $50,000
   Income Sources: Private Foundations/Grants/Endowments; Business/Corporate Donations; Box Office; Individual Donations
   Season: 52 Weeks   **Annual Attendance:** 400,000
   Performance Facilities: Lower Valley YWCA

INSTRUMENTAL MUSIC

EL PASO PRO-MUSICA
1330 East Yandell, El Paso, TX 79902
(915) 532-9139
FAX: (915) 532-9199
Founded: 1977
Arts Area: Orchestra; Chamber; Ensemble
Status: Professional; Non-Profit
Type: Performing; Educational
Purpose: To promote musical and cultural development in El Pasoand environs by presenting choral and instrumental performances ranging from the Renaissance to the contemporary
Management: C.C. Leeper, Executive Director; Michelle Chapa, Office Manager; Dr. Jerry Forderhase, Artistic Director; Jana Tippen, Publicity Coordinator
Officers: Bryan McVeigh, Chairman of the Board/President; Lonnie Busby, President Elect; Russell Blanchard, Mary Ann Gum, Lynn Jacobson, Robert Rosen MD, Marlene Stewart, Nancy Wacker, Bobbie Young, Vice Presidents; Marion S. Becker MD, Secretary; William D. Tippin Jr., Treasurer
Paid Staff: 7 **Volunteer Staff:** 1
Paid Artists: 81
Utilizes: Guest Conductors; Guest Artists; Guest Directors
Budget: $100,000 - $500,000
Income Sources: Private Foundations/Grants/Endowments; Business/Corporate Donations; Box Office; Government Grants; Individual Donations
Season: October - May **Annual Attendance:** 15,000
Affiliations: CA

EL PASO SYMPHONY ORCHESTRA
PO Box 180, El Paso, TX 79942
(915) 532-3776
Founded: 1930
Arts Area: Symphony; Orchestra
Status: Professional; Non-Profit
Type: Performing; Educational; Sponsoring
Purpose: To promote symphonic music in the El Paso community
Management: Gay Brown, General Manager; Abraham Chavez Jr., Music Director/Conductor
Officers: Ann C. Brown, Chairman of the Board
Paid Staff: 4 **Volunteer Staff:** 400
Paid Artists: 85
Utilizes: Guest Conductors; Guest Artists
Budget: $500,000 - $1,000,000
Income Sources: Private Foundations/Grants/Endowments; Business/Corporate Donations; Box Office; Government Grants; Individual Donations
Season: September - April **Annual Attendance:** 35,000
Affiliations: ASOL; El Paso Arts Alliance; El Paso Arts Resource Board
Performance Facilities: El Paso Civic Center Theater

THEATRE

SOUTHWEST REPERTORY ORGANIZATION
1301 Texas Avenue, El Paso, TX 79901
(915) 533-1671
Founded: 1978
Arts Area: Musical; Community; Theatrical Group
Status: Non-Professional; Non-Profit
Type: Performing; Touring
Purpose: A community theatre providing a main season of contemporary dramas, musicals, comedies, a summer repertory of contemporary plays, and acting, directing and technical classes
Management: Ed Hamilton, Interim Executive/Artistic Director; Glen O. Brooks, Technical Director; Glenda Nevarez, Office Manager
Officers: Maryanne Phinney, President; Sarah Griffin, President of the Board; Mike Williams, Vice President
Paid Staff: 3 **Volunteer Staff:** 28
Paid Artists: 6
Utilizes: Guest Directors
Budget: $50,000 - $100,000
Income Sources: Private Foundations/Grants/Endowments; Business/Corporate Donations; Box Office; Government Grants; Individual Donations
Season: 52 Weeks **Annual Attendance:** 6,000

PERFORMING SERIES

VIVA EL PASO!
PO Box 31340, El Paso, TX 79931
(915) 565-6900
FAX: (915) 565-6999
> **Founded:** 1978
> **Arts Area:** Dance; Vocal Music; Theater; Ballet; FOLK
> **Status:** Professional; Non-Profit
> **Type:** Performing; Resident
> **Purpose:** VIVA EL PASO! is an outdoor drama with heavy dance emphasis which celebrates the Indian, Spanish, Mexican and Western American cultures that have blended during El Paso's history.
> **Management:** David D. Mills, Managing Director; Hector M. Serrano, Artistic Director
> **Officers:** Barbara Daughtry, President; Jan Drehr, Ruly Armendariz, Madge Zuloaga, Vice Presidents; Consuelo Forti, Secretary; Sheila Loudner, Treasurer
> **Paid Staff:** 12
> **Paid Artists:** 50   **Non-Paid Artists:** 7
> **Budget:** $500,000 - $1,000,000
> **Income Sources:** Private Foundations/Grants/Endowments; Business/Corporate Donations; Box Office; Government Grants; Individual Donations
> **Season:** June - September   **Annual Attendance:** 40,000
> **Affiliations:** Institute of Outdoor Drama
> **Performance Facilities:** McKelligon Canyon Amphitheater

FACILITY

CHAMIZAL NATIONAL MEMORIAL - THEATER
800 South San Marcial, PO Box 722, El Paso, TX 79905
(915) 532-7273
FAX: (915) 532-7240
> **Type of Facility:** Concert Hall; Auditorium; Outdoor (Concert); Theatre House; Amphitheater; Multi-Purpose
> **Type of Stage:** Flexible; Modified Thrust Proscenium
> **Stage Dimensions:** 60'Wx38'D; 60'Wx48'D with pit cover in place   **Orchestra Pit**
> **Seating Capacity:** 502; 446 in thrust configuration
> **Year Built:** 1973   **Architect:** George Izenour   **Cost:** $1,200,000
> **Acoustical Consultant:** George Izenour
> **Contact for Rental:** Manager
> **Resident Groups:** Siglo de Oro Drama Festival; Zarzuela Festival; Borden Folk Festival; Music Theatre El Paso; On Stage
> *Rentals are restricted to non-profit groups only*

EL PASO CIVIC CENTER - EXHIBITION HALL
1 Civic Center Plaza, El Paso, TX 79901-1187
(915) 534-0600
> **Type of Facility:** Auditorium; Performance Center; Theatre House; Civic Center; Arena
> **Type of Stage:** Proscenium; Platform
> **Stage Dimensions:** Platform - 60'Wx40'D; Proscenium - 30'x56'   **Orchestra Pit**
> **Seating Capacity:** Concert Hall - 6,000; Performance Theatre - 2,400
> **Year Built:** 1972
> **Contact for Rental:** Joyce Trujillo, Booking Manager;   (915) 534-0609

EL PASO CIVIC CENTER - THEATRE
1 Civic Center Plaza, El Paso, TX 79901
(915) 541-4920
> **Type of Facility:** Concert Hall; Performance Center; Theatre House
> **Type of Stage:** Proscenium
> **Stage Dimensions:** 56'Wx56'D   **Orchestra Pit**
> **Seating Capacity:** 2,548
> **Year Built:** 1974
> **Contact for Rental:** Manager;   (915) 541-4920

UNIVERSITY OF TEXAS AT EL PASO - MAIN PLAYHOUSE
500 West University, El Paso, TX 79968-0549
(915) 747-5146
> **Type of Facility:** Theatre House; University Playhouse
> **Type of Stage:** Thrust; Flexible; Proscenium
> **Stage Dimensions:** 80'Wx32'D, 46'W proscenium opening   **Orchestra Pit**
> **Seating Capacity:** 430

Year Built: 1974   **Architect:** Marmon & Mok Associates
Acoustical Consultant: Bolt, Beranek & Newman

Fort Hood

PERFORMING SERIES

FORT HOOD COMMUNITY MUSIC AND THEATER - FORT HOOD COMMUNITY PLAYERS
Building 2803, Fort Hood, TX 76544
(817) 287-6116
> **Founded:** 1950
> **Arts Area:** Dance; Vocal Music; Instrumental Music; Theater; Festivals
> **Status:** Non-Professional
> **Type:** Performing; Touring
> **Purpose:** To afford the opportunity to the military man, his family and the area residents to perform in shows, musicals and talent competitions (variety shows)
> **Management:** Jean Zavoina, Director Music/Theater; Roland Gagne, Music Director; Fred Baker, Technical Director; Tom Ross, Costumer
> **Paid Staff:** 11   **Volunteer Staff:** 25
> **Utilizes:** Guest Conductors; Guest Directors
> **Budget:** $1,000 - $50,000
> **Season:** 52 Weeks   **Annual Attendance:** 3,000

FACILITY

FORT HOOD MUSIC AND THEATER - THEATER #1
Building 134, Fort Hood, TX 76544-5056
(817) 287-6116
> **Type of Facility:** Concert Hall; Auditorium; Performance Center; Theatre House; Multi-Purpose
> **Facility Originally:** Movie House
> **Type of Stage:** Thrust; Proscenium
> **Stage Dimensions:** 34'Wx20'Dx18'H (flexible)
> **Seating Capacity:** 320
> **Year Built:** 1951
> **Architect:** United States Government
> **Contact for Rental:** Brent D. Pierson;   (817) 287-6116
> **Resident Groups:** Fort Hood Community Players; Fort Hood Silver Singers; Fort Hood Community Singers

Fort Worth

DANCE

BALLET CONCERTO
3803 Camp Bowie, Fort Worth, TX 76107
(817) 738-7915
> **Founded:** 1969
> **Arts Area:** Ballet
> **Status:** Non-Profit
> **Type:** Performing
> **Purpose:** Free and paid exposure to ballet through performances in public schools and concerts in other locations
> **Management:** Margo Dean, Artistic Director
> **Officers:** John Merrifield, President
> **Paid Staff:** 1   **Volunteer Staff:** 20
> **Paid Artists:** 3   **Non-Paid Artists:** 10
> **Utilizes:** Special Technical Talent; Guest Conductors; Guest Artists; Guest Directors
> **Budget:** $1,000 - $50,000
> **Income Sources:** Private Foundations/Grants/Endowments; Business/Corporate Donations; Box Office; Government Grants; Individual Donations
> **Season:** 52 Weeks   **Annual Attendance:** 5,000
> **Affiliations:** SWRBA

FORT WORTH BALLET COMPANY
6845 Green Oaks Road, Fort Worth, TX 76116
(817) 763-0207
FAX: (817) 763-0624
> **Founded:** 1964
> **Arts Area:** Ballet

Status: Professional; Non-Profit
Type: Performing; Touring; Resident; Educational
Purpose: High quality ballet
Management: Paul Mejia, Artistic Director; David Mallette, Executive Director
Paid Staff: 5
Paid Artists: 23
Utilizes: Special Technical Talent; Guest Artists
Budget: $1,000,000 - $5,000,000
Income Sources: Private Foundations/Grants/Endowments; Business/Corporate Donations; Box Office
Season: September - April
Performance Facilities: Tarrant County Convention Center

INSTRUMENTAL MUSIC

FORT WORTH SYMPHONY
4401 Trail Lake Drive, Fort Worth, TX 76109
(817) 921-2676
FAX: (817) 921-9795
Founded: 1925
Arts Area: Symphony; Orchestra; Chamber
Status: Professional; Non-Profit
Type: Performing; Touring
Purpose: To provide the leadership and financial support required to maintain a symphony orchestra of the first rank and to build an internationally-recognized chamber orchestra, both dedicated to artistic development and performances of superior quality
Management: Ann Koonsman, Executive Director; John Giordano, Music Director
Paid Staff: 16
Paid Artists: 90
Utilizes: Guest Conductors; Guest Artists
Budget: $500,000 - $1,000,000
Income Sources: Private Foundations/Grants/Endowments; Business/Corporate Donations; Box Office; Government Grants; Individual Donations
Season: September - May   **Annual Attendance:** 54,000
Affiliations: ASOL
Performance Facilities: Tarrant County Convention Center; Ed Landreth Auditorium, Texas Christian University

YOUTH ORCHESTRA OF GREATER FORT WORTH
Orchestra Hall, 4401 Trail Lake Drive, Fort Worth, TX 76109
(817) 923-3121
FAX: (817) 923-3174
Founded: 1965
Arts Area: Orchestra
Status: Non-Profit
Type: Performing; Touring; Educational
Purpose: To educate young musicians, ages 3 to 22
Management: Freda Wise, General Manager
Officers: Betty Landy, President; Jonathan Suder, Executive Vice President; Nancy Mitchell, June Wolff, Vice Presidents
Paid Staff: 4   **Volunteer Staff:** 3
Paid Artists: 22   **Non-Paid Artists:** 1
Utilizes: Guest Artists
Budget: $100,000 - $500,000
Income Sources: Private Foundations/Grants/Endowments; Business/Corporate Donations; Individual Donations; Tuition
Season: September - May   **Annual Attendance:** 5,000
Affiliations: ASOL
Performance Facilities: Orchestra Hall

VOCAL MUSIC

FORT WORTH OPERA ASSOCIATION
3505 West Lancaster, Fort Worth, TX 76107
(817) 731-0833; (817) 731-0200
FAX: (817) 731-0835
Founded: 1946
Arts Area: Grand Opera; Lyric Opera
Status: Professional; Non-Profit
Type: Performing; Resident; Educational
Purpose: To cultivate and promote understanding and love of opera
Management: William Walker, General Director; Leeanne Parma, Development Assistant
Officers: Dr. Jack S. Hardwick, President; Dr. Adelia Hale-Stanley, President, Opera Guild of Fort Worth

Paid Staff: 5 **Volunteer Staff:** 2
Paid Artists: 392
Utilizes: Special Technical Talent; Guest Conductors; Guest Artists; Guest Directors
Budget: $500,000 - $1,000,000
Income Sources: Private Foundations/Grants/Endowments; Business/Corporate Donations; Box Office; Government Grants; Individual Donations
Season: November - May **Annual Attendance:** 22,000
Affiliations: OA; Arts Council of Fort Worth and Tarrant County
Performance Facilities: Tarrant County Convention Center

SCHOLA CANTORUM OF TEXAS
3505 West Lancaster, Fort Worth, TX 76107
(817) 737-5788
Founded: 1962
Arts Area: Choral
Status: Semi-Professional; Non-Profit
Type: Performing
Purpose: To provide top quality choral music to the Metroplex; to provide a musical outlet for our singers
Management: Gary Ebensberger, Director; Pamela Wood, Executive Director
Officers: Shelby L. Adams, Board President; Steven O'Kelley, President-Elect
Paid Staff: 3
Non-Paid Artists: 60
Utilizes: Special Technical Talent; Guest Artists
Budget: $50,000 - $100,000
Income Sources: Private Foundations/Grants/Endowments; Business/Corporate Donations; Box Office; Individual Donations
Season: October - May **Annual Attendance:** 3,800
Performance Facilities: Kimbell Art Museum; Irons Recital Hall, University of Texas-Arlington; Ed Landreth Auditorium, Texas Christian University

THE TEXAS BOYS CHOIR
PO Box 100219, Fort Worth, TX 76185-0219
(817) 924-1482
FAX: (817) 926-9932
Founded: 1946
Arts Area: Choral; Folk
Status: Professional; Non-Profit
Type: Performing; Touring; Resident; Educational
Purpose: To establish, create, organize, and manage a boys' choir and related educational activities and provide for the education and training of boys in the art of music and scholastic achievement
Management: Jack Noble White, Executive Director; A.Z. Rowland, Jr., Business Manager
Officers: Jeffrey B. King, Assistant Treasurer; A.Z. Rowland Jr., Ex-Officio/Business Manager; Jack Noble White, Ex-Officio/Executive Director; Michael D. Palmer, Immediate Past President; Billy B. Hill Jr., President; Michael C. Mason, President of Parents Club; Mrs. S. Keith Jackson Jr., Vice President of Administration; Derrell H. Boggs, Vice President of Dallas Affairs; Bruce A. Rockett, Vice President of Finance/Treasurer; John M. Thompson Jr., Vice President of Marketing/Public Relations; T. Pollard Rogers, Vice President of Program & President/"Friends"; Terry McGrath, Vice President of Property
Paid Staff: 6
Utilizes: Special Technical Talent; Guest Conductors; Guest Artists
Budget: $500,000 - $1,000,000
Income Sources: Private Foundations/Grants/Endowments; Business/Corporate Donations; Box Office; Individual Donations
Season: August - June **Annual Attendance:** 100,000
Affiliations: Arts Council of Fort Worth

THE TEXAS GIRLS CHOIR
4449 Camp Bowie Boulevard, Fort Worth, TX 76107
(817) 732-8161
Founded: 1962
Arts Area: Choral; Ethnic; Folk
Status: Non-Professional; Non-Profit
Type: Performing; Touring; Educational
Purpose: To develop little girls' lives through excellence in music; girls, ages 8-14, come from 30 different north Texas cities and participate in music and leadership training throughout the year
Management: Shirley Carter, Founder/Executive Director; Debi Weir, Administrative Assistant/Handbell Director
Paid Staff: 11 **Volunteer Staff:** 100
Non-Paid Artists: 200
Utilizes: Guest Artists

Budget: $100,000 - $500,000
Income Sources: Private Foundations/Grants/Endowments; Business/Corporate Donations; Box Office;
Individual Donations
Season: October - May
Annual Attendance: 30,000

THEATRE

CASA MANANA MUSICALS INC.
3101 West Lancaster, Fort Worth, TX 76107
(817) 332-2272
FAX: (817) 332-5711
> **Founded:** 1958
> **Arts Area:** Professional; Summer Stock; Musical
> **Status:** Non-Profit
> **Type:** Performing; Touring; Resident; Educational
> **Purpose:** To bring Broadway musicals to Fort Worth, with special appearances by stars; to produce plays for
> children and adults
> **Management:** Van Kaplan, Producer/General Manager; Deborah Brown, Assistant Producer/Executive Director of
> Children's Playhouse
> **Officers:** Kay Granger, Chairman of the Board; Michael Hyatt, President
> **Paid Staff:** 24   **Volunteer Staff:** 82
> **Paid Artists:** 100
> **Utilizes:** Special Technical Talent; Guest Artists; Guest Directors
> **Budget:** $1,000,000 - $5,000,000
> **Income Sources:** Private Foundations/Grants/Endowments; Box Office; Individual Donations
> **Season:** 52 Weeks   **Annual Attendance:** 250,000
> **Performance Facilities:** Casa Manana Theatre

CASA MANANA PLAYHOUSE
3101 West Lancaster, Fort Worth, TX 76107
(817) 332-9319
> **Founded:** 1962
> **Arts Area:** Professional; Musical
> **Status:** Professional; Non-Profit
> **Type:** Performing; Resident; Educational
> **Purpose:** To present plays for children Fridays and Saturday with special weekday performances for local schools;
> to present Casa Kids, 15 children who provide free performances for area civic and non-profit organizations
> **Management:** Van Kaplan, Executive Producer; Deborah Brown, Director of the Playhouse
> **Officers:** Bob Bolen, Chairman; Ted B. Bevan, President; David Walker, Vice President, Finance and Budget; D'Ann
> Reed Dagen, Secretary
> **Paid Staff:** 35
> **Paid Artists:** 15
> **Utilizes:** Guest Artists; Guest Directors
> **Budget:** $100,000 - $500,000
> **Income Sources:** Private Foundations/Grants/Endowments; Business/Corporate Donations; Box Office; Government
> Grants; Individual Donations
> **Season:** September - May   **Annual Attendance:** 130,000
> **Affiliations:** ASSITEJ; AEA; AFM
> **Performance Facilities:** Casa Manana Theatre

CIRCLE THEATRE, INC.
1227 West Magnolia Avenue, #520, Fort Worth, TX 76104
(817) 921-3040
FAX: (817) 923-6087
> **Founded:** 1981
> **Arts Area:** Theatrical Group
> **Status:** Semi-Professional; Non-Profit
> **Type:** Performing; Resident
> **Purpose:** To produce original and contemporary theatre scripts not yet seen in Fort Worth
> **Management:** Rose Pearson, Executive Director; Bill Newberry, Managing Director; Carlo Cuesta, Director of
> Public Relations/Marketing
> **Officers:** Joan Kline, President; Robert I. Fenandez, Tom Gaffney, Vice Presidents; Kim Kirk, Sherry Jackson,
> Corresponding and Recording Secretaries; Marilyn Austin, Treasurer
> **Paid Staff:** 4   **Volunteer Staff:** 50
> **Paid Artists:** 75

Utilizes: Special Technical Talent; Guest Directors
Budget: $100,000 - $500,000
Income Sources: Private Foundations/Grants/Endowments; Business/Corporate Donations; Box Office; Government Grants; Individual Donations
Season: 52 Weeks   **Annual Attendance:** 10,000

FORT WORTH THEATRE
3505 West Lancaster, Fort Worth, TX 76107
(817) 738-7491
Founded: 1955
Arts Area: Theatrical Group
Status: Non-Professional; Non-Profit
Type: Performing; Resident
Purpose: To present quality theatre for Fort Worth; to provide an avocation for talented amateurs in all phases of production
Management: William Garber, Artistic Director; Brynn Bristol, Administrative Director
Officers: Gaylord Lummis, President
Paid Staff: 5   **Volunteer Staff:** 30
Utilizes: Guest Artists; Guest Directors
Budget: $50,000 - $100,000
Income Sources: Private Foundations/Grants/Endowments; Business/Corporate Donations; Box Office; Government Grants; Individual Donations
Season: 52 Weeks   **Annual Attendance:** 22,500
Performance Facilities: William Edrington Scott Theatre

HIP POCKET THEATRE
1627 Fairmount Avenue, Fort Worth, TX 76104
(817) 927-2833
Founded: 1977
Arts Area: Professional; Musical; Folk; Theatrical Group; Puppet
Status: Professional; Non-Profit
Type: Performing; Touring; Resident; Educational
Purpose: Showcase original works by regional playwrights and composers, as well as other works rarely performed in this area
Management: Diane Simons, Producer; Johnny Simons, Artistic Director; Holly Nelson Leach, General Manager
Officers: D. Lee Thomas, President; Carlela K. Vogel, President-Elect; Mary Kaye Juran, Secretary; Richard W. Chowning, Treasurer
Paid Staff: 3   **Volunteer Staff:** 3
Paid Artists: 23
Utilizes: Special Technical Talent; Guest Artists; Guest Directors
Budget: $100,000 - $500,000
Income Sources: Private Foundations/Grants/Endowments; Business/Corporate Donations; Box Office; Government Grants; Individual Donations
Season: June - November   **Annual Attendance:** 11,000
Affiliations: TCG
Performance Facilities: Oak Acres Amphitheatre

SOJOURNER TRUTH PLAYERS
6619 Forest Hill Drive, Fort Worth, TX 76140
(817) 483-7111
Founded: 1972
Arts Area: Theatrical Group
Status: Non-Professional; Non-Profit
Type: Performing; Touring; Educational; Sponsoring
Purpose: To provide arts entertainment to the community and provide training classes and quality instruction to children and adults
Management: Charlece Thomas-James, Producer
Officers: Mattie Peterson Compton, Chairperson
Paid Staff: 3   **Volunteer Staff:** 5
Paid Artists: 2   **Non-Paid Artists:** 25
Utilizes: Special Technical Talent; Guest Artists; Guest Directors
Budget: $50,000 - $100,000
Income Sources: Private Foundations/Grants/Endowments; Business/Corporate Donations; Box Office; Government Grants; Individual Donations
Season: August - June   **Annual Attendance:** 10,000
Affiliations: Texas Nonprofit Theatre; SWTC; Texas Assembly Arts Agency
Performance Facilities: Sojourner Truth Players Cultural Arts Center

STAGE WEST
312 Houston Street, PO Box 2587, Fort Worth, TX 76113
(817) 332-6265
Founded: 1979
Arts Area: Professional; Theatrical Group
Status: Professional; Non-Profit
Type: Performing
Purpose: To produce a variety of works with at least eight major productions a year including some musicals; to present theater works ranging from new to classical and contemporary.
Management: Jerry Russell, Artistic/Managing Director; James Covault, Associate Director; Sam Hatcher, Technical Director; Lu Ann Adamson, Business Manager; Buckley Sachs, Box Office Manager; Diane Anglim, Marketing Director
Officers: Jack L. Johnson, Board President; Jeff Davis, Vice President; Carol Stanford, Treasurer
Paid Staff: 7 **Volunteer Staff:** 1
Paid Artists: 60
Utilizes: Special Technical Talent; Guest Artists; Guest Directors
Budget: $100,000 - $500,000
Income Sources: Private Foundations/Grants/Endowments; Business/Corporate Donations; Box Office; Government Grants; Individual Donations
Season: October - September **Annual Attendance:** 30,000
Affiliations: AEA; SPT; TCG; Texas Nonprofit Theatre; Live Theatre League of Tarrant County; Arts Council of Fort Worth and Tarrant County
Performance Facilities: Stage West at the Caravan of Dreams Performing Arts Center

PERFORMING SERIES

CARAVAN OF DREAMS
312 Houston Street, Fort Worth, TX 76102
(817) 877-3000
Mailing Address: PO Box 886, Fort Worth, TX 76101
Founded: 1983
Arts Area: Dance; Vocal Music; Instrumental Music; Theater
Status: Professional; Commercial
Type: Sponsoring
Management: Mike Dunagan, Booking Manager; Ken Bergle, Technical Director
Utilizes: Guest Artists
Budget: $500,000 - $1,000,000
Income Sources: Box Office
Season: 52 Weeks
Performance Facilities: Caravan of Dreams

SHAKESPEARE-IN-THE-PARK
3113 South University, Suite 310, Fort Worth, TX 76109
(817) 923-6698
Founded: 1977
Arts Area: Theater; Festivals
Status: Professional; Non-Profit
Type: Performing; Touring
Purpose: To provide free Shakespeare-in-the-Park to the people of Fort Worth
Management: Michael Muller, Producing Director
Officers: Judy Harmon, President
Paid Staff: 2 **Volunteer Staff:** 1,500
Paid Artists: 60
Utilizes: Guest Directors
Budget: $100,000 - $500,000
Income Sources: Private Foundations/Grants/Endowments; Business/Corporate Donations; Box Office; Government Grants; Individual Donations
Season: June - July; November - December **Annual Attendance:** 43,000
Affiliations: Texas Christian University; City of Fort Worth
Performance Facilities: The Trinity Park Playhouse; Southwest United States Tour

VAN CLIBURN FOUNDATION
2525 Ridgmar Boulevard, Fort Worth, TX 76116
(817) 738-6536
FAX: (817) 738-6534
Founded: 1961
Arts Area: Vocal Music; Instrumental Music
Status: Professional; Non-Profit
Type: Performing; Touring; Educational; Sponsoring

Purpose: To produce the Van Cliburn International Piano Competition and to produce the Cliburn Concert Series
Management: Richard Rodzinski, Executive Director
Officers: Susan Tilley, Chairman
Paid Staff: 9
Paid Artists: 12
Utilizes: Guest Artists
Budget: $100,000 - $500,000
Income Sources: Private Foundations/Grants/Endowments; Business/Corporate Donations; Box Office; Government Grants; Individual Donations
Season: September - May **Annual Attendance:** 5,000
Affiliations: Texas Arts Council; ASOL; APAP; ISPAA
Performance Facilities: Kimbell Art Museum; Ed Landreth Auditorium, Texas Christian University

FACILITY

CARAVAN OF DREAMS
312 Houston Street, Fort Worth, TX 76102
(817) 877-3000
FAX: (817) 877-3752
   Type of Facility: Performance Center; Multi-Purpose
   Type of Stage: Thrust; Proscenium; 3/4 Arena
   Seating Capacity: Theater - 212; Jazz Club - 300
   Year Built: 1983 **Architect:** Margaret Augustine
   Contact for Rental: Rob Hansen;   (817) 877-3000
   Manager: Jerry Thompson
   Resident Groups: Theatre of All Possibilities Stage West
   Also used a a jazz recording studio; live radio broadcasts Tuesdays

CASA MANANA THEATRE
3101 West Lancaster, Fort Worth, TX 76107
(817) 332-9319
FAX: (817) 332-5711
   Type of Facility: Theatre House
   Type of Stage: In-the-round Capability
   Stage Dimensions: 28'x34' **Orchestra Pit**
   Seating Capacity: 1,816
   Year Built: 1958 **Architect:** R. Buckminster Fuller **Cost:** $500,000
   Acoustical Consultant: Ricky Pratt
   Contact for Rental: Candice Nickelson, Assistant General Manager;   (817) 332-9319
   Manager: Bud Franks
   Resident Groups: Casa Manana Musicals, Inc.
   Only limited rental possible

FORT WORTH/TARRANT COUNTY CONVENTION CENTER - CONVENTION CENTER THEATER
1111 Houston Street, Fort Worth, TX 76102
(817) 884-2222
FAX: (817) 884-2323
   Type of Facility: Auditorium
   Type of Stage: Proscenium
   Stage Dimensions: 30'x65'x50' **Orchestra Pit**
   Seating Capacity: 3,054
   Year Built: 1968 **Architect:** The Associated Convention Center Architects
   Acoustical Consultant: Tracor
   Contact for Rental: Helen Crawford, Booking Manager;   (817) 884-2222
   Manager: Jimmy Earl
   Resident Groups: Fort Worth Symphony; Fort Worth Ballet; Texas Boys Choir; Fort Worth Opera Association
   Total construction cost of Tarrant County Convention Center was $20,000,000 in 1968.

OAK ACRES AMPHITHEATRE
1627 Fairmont Avenue, Fort Worth, TX 76104
(817) 927-2833
   Type of Facility: Amphitheater
   Type of Stage: Environmental
   Seating Capacity: 200
   Year Built: 1979 **Cost:** $500
   Contact for Rental: James Quave;   (817) 927-2833
   Resident Groups: Hip Pocket Theater
   Available for rental November through April

SOUTHWESTERN BAPTIST THEOLOGICAL SEMINARY - REYNOLDS AUDITORIUM
PO Box 22000, Fort Worth, TX 76122
(817) 923-1921
    Type of Facility: Concert Hall; Auditorium; Studio Performance
    Type of Stage: Proscenium
    Seating Capacity: 500
    Year Built: 1926   **Architect:** Preston Geren   **Cost:** $150,000
    Year Remodeled: 1961   **Cost:** $500,000
    Contact for Rental: Dr. David Music;   (817) 923-1921

TEXAS CHRISTIAN UNIVERSITY - ED LANDRETH AUDITORIUM
School of Fine Arts, PO Box 32928, Fort Worth, TX 76129
(817) 921-7625
FAX: (817) 921-7333
    Type of Facility: Theatre House
    Type of Stage: Proscenium
    Stage Dimensions: 35'x40'
    Seating Capacity: 218
    Year Built: 1949   **Architect:** Hedrick Geren Peblich
    Manager: Vince Pankey

TEXAS WESLEYAN COLLEGE - TEXAS WESLEYAN FINE ARTS AUDITORIUM
Rosedale and Wesleyan, PO Box 50010, Fort Worth, TX 76105
(817) 531-4443
    Type of Facility: Auditorium
    Facility Originally: Church
    Type of Stage: Proscenium; Modified Thrust
    Stage Dimensions: 20'x30'   **Orchestra Pit**
    Seating Capacity: 750
    Year Built: 1923
    Year Remodeled: 1962
    Contact for Rental: J. Allen Brown;   (817) 531-4443
    Resident Groups: Texas Wesleyan College Theatre Department

WILLIAM EDRINGTON SCOTT THEATRE
3505 West Lancaster, Fort Worth, TX 76107
(817) 738-1938
    Type of Facility: Theatre House
    Type of Stage: Thrust; Proscenium   **Orchestra Pit**
    Seating Capacity: 493
    Year Built: 1966   **Architect:** Joseph Pelich   **Cost:** $1,250,000
    Contact for Rental: William Garber;   (817) 738-1938
    Resident Groups: Fort Worth Theatre

Galveston

PERFORMING SERIES

THE GRAND 1894 OPERA HOUSE
2020 Post Office Street, Galveston, TX 77550
(409) 763-7173
FAX: (409) 763-1068
    Founded: 1974
    Arts Area: Dance; Vocal Music; Instrumental Music; Theater; Lyric Opera; Grand Opera; Meetings; Parties; Workshops
    Status: Professional; Non-Professional; Non-Profit
    Type: Performing; Touring; Resident; Educational; Sponsoring; Presenting
    Purpose: To present professional performing arts in a restored, historic structure and to maintain that structure; to serve the Galveston and the Greater Houston areas
    Management: Maureen M. Patton, Executive Director; William C. Lindstrom, Stage Manager
    Paid Staff: 9   **Volunteer Staff:** 350
    Utilizes: Guest Artists
    Budget: $500,000 - $1,000,000
    Income Sources: Private Foundations/Grants/Endowments; Business/Corporate Donations; Box Office; Government Grants; Individual Donations; Rentals
    Season: September - May   **Annual Attendance:** 29,000
    Affiliations: APAP; League of Historic American Theatres; Southwest Performing Arts Presenters
    Performance Facilities: The Grand 1894 Opera House

FACILITY

GRAND 1894 OPERA HOUSE
2020 Postoffice Street, Galveston, TX 77550
(409) 763-7173
FAX: (409) 763-1068
    Type of Facility: Concert Hall; Performance Center; Theatre House; Opera House; Multi-Purpose
    Type of Stage: Proscenium
    Stage Dimensions: 27'Hx38'Wx36'D   **Orchestra Pit**
    Seating Capacity: 1,000
    Year Built: 1894   **Architect:** Frank Cox   **Cost:** $100,000
    Year Remodeled: 1986   **Architect:** Killis P. Almond, AIA   **Cost:** $7,000,000
    Contact for Rental: Maureen M. Patton, Director;   (409) 763-7173
    Resident Groups: Galveston Symphony Orchestra; Galveston Ballet

MOODY CIVIC CENTER - EXHIBITION HALL
2100 Seawall Boulevard, Galveston, TX 77550
(409) 762-9608
FAX: (406) 762-8911
    Type of Facility: Multi-Purpose
    Type of Stage: Platform
    Stage Dimensions: 90'Wx200'D
    Seating Capacity: 2,000
    Year Built: 1956
    Year Remodeled: 1981   **Architect:** Louis Oliver
    Contact for Rental: Anthony Martinez, Joe Romero;   (409) 762-9608

Garland

INSTRUMENTAL MUSIC

DALLAS BRASS
4321 Clemson Drive, Garland, TX 75042
(214) 276-7114
    Founded: 1982
    Arts Area: Ensemble; Instrumental Group
    Status: Professional; Commercial
    Type: Performing; Touring; Resident; Educational
    Purpose: To strive to bridge the musical gaps from classical to pop
    Management: Michael Levin, Director; Wiss Rudd, Booking Coordinator
    Paid Staff: 3   **Volunteer Staff:** 25
    Paid Artists: 8
    Utilizes: Guest Artists
    Income Sources: Box Office
    Season: 52 Weeks

GARLAND SYMPHONY ORCHESTRA
1721 Reserve, Garland, TX 75042
(214) 553-1223
FAX: (214) 533-0081
    Founded: 1978
    Arts Area: Symphony; Orchestra
    Status: Professional; Non-Profit
    Type: Performing; Educational
    Purpose: To present the finest concerts possible consistent with financial integrity
    Management: Robert Carter Austin, Music Director; Richard Stieber, Assistant General Manager
    Officers: George and Lee Ann Christ, Co-Presidents; Tom and Peggy Jenkins, Co-Presidents Elect; Duane Blakely, Secretary; Douglas Taylor, Treasurer
    Paid Staff: 2
    Paid Artists: 75
    Utilizes: Guest Conductors; Guest Artists
    Budget: $100,000 - $500,000
    Income Sources: Private Foundations/Grants/Endowments; Business/Corporate Donations; Box Office; Individual Donations
    Season: October - April   **Annual Attendance:** 9,000
    Performance Facilities: Garland Performing Arts Center

TEXAS BAROQUE ENSEMBLE
2221 Royal Crest Drive, Garland, TX 75043
(214) 278-2458
FAX: (214) 278-2458
Founded: 1980
Arts Area: Chamber; Ensemble; Choir
Status: Professional; Non-Profit
Type: Performing; Touring; Resident; Educational
Purpose: The Texas Baroque Ensemble focuses on performing music written before 1800 with the music being played on the original instruments for which the music was written.
Management: Susan Ferre, Musical Director/Administrator; Rosemary Heffley, Development Director; Eileen Rees, Membership
Officers: Brooks Morris II; Eileen Rees; Charles Lang; Susan Ferre; Rosemary Heffley; Ed Rodriguez; Jean Rodriguez
Volunteer Staff: 3
Paid Artists: 50
Utilizes: Special Technical Talent
Budget: $1,000 - $50,000
Income Sources: Private Foundations/Grants/Endowments; Business/Corporate Donations; Box Office; Government Grants; Individual Donations
Season: 52 Weeks   **Annual Attendance:** 3,000
Affiliations: Early Music at Round Top
Performance Facilities: Perkins Chapel, Southern Methodist University; Saint Stephen Presbyterian Church; Round Top Festival Institute; San Fernando Cathedral, San Antonio; Catholic Cathedral, Guadalupe

THEATRE

GARLAND CIVIC THEATRE
PO Box 461252, Garland, TX 75046
(214) 349-1331
FAX: (214) 553-0081
Founded: 1967
Arts Area: Musical; Theatrical Group
Status: Semi-Professional; Non-Profit
Type: Performing; Resident
Purpose: To provide quality entertainment for our audiences, provide a space for performers in the community, and to advance theatre in general
Management: James Weir, Producing Director; Linda White, Administrative Assistant; Dwight Swanson, Technical Director
Officers: Holt Irby, President; Steve Chaffin, Vice President; Marilyn Schwartz, Secretary; Anne Bond, Treasurer; Michelle Tucker, Vice President of Development
Paid Staff: 2   **Volunteer Staff:** 3
Budget: $100,000 - $500,000
Income Sources: Private Foundations/Grants/Endowments; Business/Corporate Donations; Box Office; Government Grants; Individual Donations
Season: September - June   **Annual Attendance:** 10,000
Affiliations: Texas Nonprofit Theatre; TCG
Performance Facilities: Garland Center For the Performing Arts

PERFORMING SERIES

GARLAND SUMMER MUSICALS
P.O. Box 462049, Garland, TX 75046-2049
(214) 205-2780
Founded: 1983
Arts Area: Dance; Vocal Music; Instrumental Music
Status: Semi-Professional; Non-Profit
Type: Sponsoring
Purpose: Committed to the community to present the highest quality productions and continue a tradition of excellence in family entertainment
Management: Patty Granville, Producer; Buff Shurr, Director
Paid Staff: 6
Utilizes: Special Technical Talent; Guest Artists
Budget: $50,000 - $100,000
Income Sources: Business/Corporate Donations; Box Office
Season: June - July
Affiliations: AEA
Performance Facilities: Garland Center for the Performing Arts

FACILITY

GARLAND CENTER FOR THE PERFORMING ARTS
PO Box 469002, Garland, TX 75046-9002
(214) 205-2780
    Type of Facility: Theatre Complex
    Year Built: 1982   **Architect:** Harper, Kemp, Clutts & Parker   **Cost:** $3,500,000
    Contact for Rental: Patty Granville; (214) 205-2780
    Resident Groups: Garland Civic Theater; Garland Symphony Orchestra; Garland Summer Musicals

GARLAND CENTER FOR THE PERFORMING ARTS - THEATER #1
PO Box 469002, Garland, TX 75046-9002
(214) 205-2780
    Type of Facility: Theatre House
    Type of Stage: Proscenium
    Seating Capacity: 195
    Year Built: 1982
    Contact for Rental: Patty Granville; (214) 205-2780

GARLAND CENTER FOR THE PERFORMING ARTS - THEATER #2
PO Box 469002, Garland, TX 75046-9002
(214) 205-2780
    Type of Facility: Theatre House
    Type of Stage: Proscenium
    Stage Dimensions: 40'x35'   **Orchestra Pit**
    Seating Capacity: 719
    Year Built: 1982
    Contact for Rental: Patty Granville; (214) 205-2780

Granbury

THEATRE

GRANBURY OPERA HOUSE
116 East Pearl Street, PO Box 297, Granbury, TX 76048
(817) 573-9191
    Founded: 1974
    Arts Area: Year-round Stock
    Status: Non-Profit
    Type: Performing; Educational
    Management: Joann Miller, Manager
    Paid Staff: 15
    Utilizes: Guest Artists
    Budget: $50,000 - $100,000
    Income Sources: Box Office; Individual Donations
    Season: 52 Weeks
    Performance Facilities: Granbury Opera House

FACILITY

GRANBURY OPERA HOUSE
116 East Pearl Street, PO Box 297, Granbury, TX 76048
(817) 573-9191
    Type of Facility: Opera House
    Type of Stage: Proscenium
    Stage Dimensions: 26'x18'   **Orchestra Pit**
    Seating Capacity: 303
    Year Built: 1886 **Cost:** $2,500
    Year Remodeled: 1974   **Architect:** Ed Beran **Cost:** $250,000
    Manager: Joanne Miller, Managing Director
    Resident Groups: Granbury Opera House Company

Harlingen

FACILITY

HARLINGEN CULTURAL ARTS CENTER - AUDITORIUM
576 '76 Drive, PO Box 609, Harlingen, TX 78551
(210) 423-9736
  Type of Facility: Multi-Purpose
  Type of Stage: Proscenium
  Stage Dimensions: 30'Wx16'D
  Seating Capacity: 150
  Year Built: 1986   **Cost:** $260,000
  Contact for Rental: Cultural Arts Center Office;   (512) 423-9736
  The Cultural Arts Center also contains a 50-seat Studio Theatre and a 30-seat Studio Theatre. Cost referenced above is the total construction cost for the Center.

Houston

DANCE

ALLEGRO BALLET OF HOUSTON
1801 Dairy Ashford, Suite 130, Houston, TX 77077
(713) 496-4670
  Arts Area: Modern; Ballet; Jazz; Ethnic
  Status: Semi-Professional; Non-Profit
  Type: Performing; Resident; Educational
  Purpose: To offer a performing outlet for gifted dancers by presenting them in concerts both at home and abroad in a classical and contemporary repertoire
  Management: Peggy Girouard, Glenda Brown, Directors; Vanessa Brown, Associate Director/Manager
  Officers: Ray Cashman, President; Jeff Love, Vice President; Pamela Penny, Secretary; John Niemann, Treasurer; James Crownover, Chairman of the Board
  Paid Staff: 3   **Volunteer Staff:** 4
  Paid Artists: 2   **Non-Paid Artists:** 15
  Utilizes: Special Technical Talent; Guest Artists; Guest Choreographers
  Budget: $1,000 - $50,000
  Income Sources: Private Foundations/Grants/Endowments; Business/Corporate Donations; Box Office; Individual Donations; Fund-raising
  Season: September - June   **Annual Attendance:** 10,000
  Affiliations: SWRBA; Regional Dance America
  Performance Facilities: Jones Hall, Wortham; Mitchell Pavillion, Woodland; Episcopal High School Auditorium

CHRYSALIS REPERTORY DANCE COMPANY
10006 Briar Rose, Houston, TX 77042
(713) 522-6557
  Founded: 1983
  Arts Area: Modern; Post-Modern; Performance Art
  Status: Professional; Non-Profit
  Type: Performing; Touring; Resident; Educational; Sponsoring
  Purpose: To present innovative, quality dance to enhance Houston and other communities where we perfrom
  Management: Christine Lidvall, Linda Phenix, Co-Directors
  Officers: Elizabeth Jones-Boswell, President; Daniel Platt, Vice President/Treasurer; Flora Yeh, Secretary
  Paid Staff: 2
  Paid Artists: 7
  Utilizes: Special Technical Talent; Guest Artists; Guest Choreographers
  Budget: $50,000 - $100,000
  Income Sources: Private Foundations/Grants/Endowments; Business/Corporate Donations; Box Office; Government Grants; Individual Donations
  Season: September - May   **Annual Attendance:** 10,000
  Affiliations: Texas Arts Council; Houston Dance Coalition
  Performance Facilities: Heinen Theatre, Houston Community College; Kaplan Theatre; Jewish Community Center

CITY BALLET OF HOUSTON
9902 Long Point, Houston, TX 77055
(713) 468-8708
FAX: (713) 468-8708
  Founded: 1958
  Arts Area: Ballet

Status: Non-Profit
Type: Performing
Purpose: To serve as a training ground for young dancers and as a showcase for choreographers, both local and well-established; to offer presentations of high-quality performances at low ticket cost
Management: Margo and Dennis Marshall, Co-Artistic Directors; Victoria Vittum, Resident Choreographer; Frederic Franklin, Artistic Advisor; Jennifer Mettar, Stage Director
Officers: James DeVault, President, Board of Directors; Tom Shoffner, Vice President
Paid Staff: 2   **Volunteer Staff:** 2
Paid Artists: 4   **Non-Paid Artists:** 30
Utilizes: Guest Artists; Guest Choreographers
Budget: $100,000 - $500,000
Income Sources: Private Foundations/Grants/Endowments; Business/Corporate Donations; Box Office; Individual Donations
Season: September - May   **Annual Attendance:** 5,000
Affiliations: NARB; SWRBA
Performance Facilities: Galveston Grand Opera House; Music Hall; Scottish Rite Temple

CLEAR LAKE METROPOLITAN BALLET
PO Box 580466, Houston, TX 77258
(713) 338-1615
Founded: 1976
Arts Area: Ballet
Status: Semi-Professional; Non-Profit
Type: Performing
Management: Lynette Mason-Hale, Artistic Director
Paid Staff: 1   **Volunteer Staff:** 25
Paid Artists: 6   **Non-Paid Artists:** 20
Utilizes: Guest Artists
Budget: $1,000 - $50,000
Income Sources: Private Foundations/Grants/Endowments; Box Office; Individual Donations
Season: September - May   **Annual Attendance:** 8,000
Affiliations: Southwest Regional Ballet Association
Performance Facilities: University of Houston at CLear Lake

THE DELIA STEWART DANCE COMPANY
1202 Calumet Street, Houston, TX 77004
(713) 522-6375
Founded: 1981
Arts Area: Jazz
Status: Semi-Professional; Non-Profit
Type: Performing; Touring; Resident; Educational
Purpose: To foster the art of musical theater concert jazz dance; to provide an opportunity to educate the community about this art form and establish in Houston an internationally-recognized concert jazz dance company
Management: Delia Stewart, Director; Julie Stewart, Associate Director; Michelle Smith, Administrator
Officers: John Burris, President; Floyd Robinson Jr., Secretary
Paid Staff: 4
Paid Artists: 4   **Non-Paid Artists:** 8
Utilizes: Guest Artists
Budget: $100,000 - $500,000
Income Sources: Private Foundations/Grants/Endowments; Business/Corporate Donations; Individual Donations
Season: 52 Weeks   **Annual Attendance:** 10,000
Affiliations: CACH; Houston Coalition

DISCOVERY DANCE GROUP AND TRAINING CENTER
6427 Atwell, Houston, TX 77006
(713) 667-3416
Founded: 1963
Arts Area: Modern; Ballet; Jazz; Ethnic
Status: Professional; Non-Profit
Type: Performing; Touring; Educational
Purpose: To provide an outlet for talented dancers and further educate them in performance techniques and to perpetuate the unique Camille Long Hill technique and method
Management: Camille Long Hill, Artistic Director/Managing Director; Pam Stockman, Associate Artistic/Managing Director
Officers: Alice Lanza, President; Martha Owen, First Vice President; Shelley Johnson, Secretary; Gary Lynn McGregor, Treasurer
Paid Staff: 4   **Volunteer Staff:** 4
Paid Artists: 10   **Non-Paid Artists:** 6
Utilizes: Guest Artists

Budget: $50,000 - $100,000
Income Sources: Private Foundations/Grants/Endowments; Business/Corporate Donations; Box Office; Individual Donations
Season: September - August

HOUSTON BALLET
1916 West Gray, PO Box 130487, Houston, TX 77219-0487
(713) 523-6300
    Arts Area: Ballet
    Status: Professional; Non-Profit
    Type: Performing; Touring; Resident; Educational
    Paid Staff: 35
    Paid Artists: 46
    Budget: $5,000,000 - $10,000,000
    Income Sources: Private Foundations/Grants/Endowments; Business/Corporate Donations; Box Office; Government Grants; Individual Donations
    Season: September - June
    Affiliations: Dance USA; National Corporate Fund for Dance
    Performance Facilities: Jesse H. Jones Hall for the Performing Arts

JOAN KARFF'S NEW DANCE
5443 Parsley Group, Houston, TX 77096
(713) 721-2316
    Founded: 1979
    Arts Area: Modern
    Status: Semi-Professional; Non-Profit
    Type: Performing; Educational
    Purpose: To provide modern dance works of quality and to collaborate with other local artists
    Management: Joan Karff, Director
    Officers: Paula Friedlander, President
    Paid Staff: 1
    Paid Artists: 8
    Utilizes: Special Technical Talent; Guest Artists
    Budget: $1,000 - $50,000
    Income Sources: Private Foundations/Grants/Endowments; Business/Corporate Donations; Box Office; Government Grants; Individual Donations
    Season: September - May   **Annual Attendance:** 1,500
    Performance Facilities: Saint John's School Theatre; Jewish Center Theatre

SEVERAL DANCERS CORE
2332 Bissonnet, Houston, TX 77005
(713) 520-5530
FAX: (713) 524-4036
    Founded: 1980
    Arts Area: Modern
    Status: Professional; Non-Profit
    Type: Performing; Touring; Presenting
    Purpose: To provide quality dance to the public and to provide an outlet for choreographers and dancers to present their work
    Management: Sue Schroeder, Kathy Russell, Co-Artistic/Executive Directors; Rebecca Leary Safon, Development Coordinator/Community Liason; Deborah Schultz , Erica Yoder, Projects Coordinators
    Officers: Sue Schroeder, President; Kathy Russell, Secretary/Treasurer
    Paid Staff: 2   **Volunteer Staff:** 5
    Paid Artists: 4
    Utilizes: Special Technical Talent; Guest Artists; Guest Choreographers
    Budget: $100,000 - $500,000
    Income Sources: Private Foundations/Grants/Endowments; Business/Corporate Donations; Box Office; Government Grants; Individual Donations
    Season: September - May   **Annual Attendance:** 5,000
    Affiliations: Several Dancers Core of Atlanta

SOCIETY FOR THE PERFORMING ARTS
615 Louisiana, Houston, TX 77002
(713) 227-5134
FAX: (713) 223-8301
    Arts Area: Modern; Mime; Ballet; Jazz; Ethnic; Folk
    Status: Professional; Non-Profit
    Type: Sponsoring

Purpose: To present the world's greatest in performing arts, whether dance, music or theatre
Management: Toby Mattox, Executive Director
Officers: John M. Kirksey, Chairman of the Board
Income Sources: Private Foundations/Grants/Endowments; Business/Corporate Donations; Box Office; Government Grants; Individual Donations
Performance Facilities: Jones Hall; Wortham Theatre Center

SOUTHWEST JAZZ BALLET COMPANY
720 1/2 Pinemont, Houston, TX 77018
(713) 694-6114
FAX: (713) 686-4868
    Founded: 1979
    Arts Area: Ballet; Jazz
    Status: Professional; Non-Profit; Commercial
    Type: Performing; Touring; Educational
    Purpose: America through song and dance
    Management: Rita Brosh, Artistic Director; Pamela Eden, Musical Coordinator
    Officers: G. R. DeFillipe, President/Chief Executive Officer
    Paid Staff: 16   **Volunteer Staff:** 40
    Paid Artists: 14   **Non-Paid Artists:** 25
    Utilizes: Special Technical Talent; Guest Conductors; Guest Artists; Guest Directors
    Budget: $500,000 - $1,000,000
    Income Sources: Private Foundations/Grants/Endowments; Business/Corporate Donations; Box Office; Government Grants; Individual Donations
    Season: 52 Weeks   **Annual Attendance:** 400,000

INSTRUMENTAL MUSIC

CLEAR LAKE SYMPHONY
PO Box 890582, Houston, TX 77289-0582
(713) 534-7610; (713) 251-9210
    Founded: 1976
    Arts Area: Symphony; Orchestra
    Status: Non-Professional; Non-Profit
    Type: Performing
    Purpose: To provide the community with a source of live symphonic music and provide the performers with an outlet for their talents
    Officers: Roje Yap, President; Melodie Cunningham, Secretary
    Paid Staff: 1   **Volunteer Staff:** 55
    Paid Artists: 2   **Non-Paid Artists:** 6
    Utilizes: Guest Artists
    Budget: $1,000 - $50,000
    Income Sources: Private Foundations/Grants/Endowments; Business/Corporate Donations; Box Office; Individual Donations
    Season: October - June   **Annual Attendance:** 2,500
    Affiliations: NSOL
    Performance Facilities: Bayou Auditorium

HOUSTON CIVIC SYMPHONY ORCHESTRA
University of Houston School of Music, Houston, TX 77204-4893
(713) 747-0018
    Founded: 1967
    Arts Area: Symphony; Orchestra; Chamber
    Status: Semi-Professional; Non-Profit
    Type: Performing
    Purpose: To provide a playing and performance opportunity for professional and non-professional musicians who earn the major portion of their livelihood outside full-time, professional music performances
    Management: Oscar Wehmanen, Director of Performances; Marlene Ballard, Manager of Personnel; Bruce Leon, Librarian; Joe Munsteri, Director of Funding; Dan Sloan, Director of Sound Recording
    Officers: Kathy Hannah, President; Nancy Francis, Vice President; John Snyder, Secretary; Greg Nelson, Treasurer
    Volunteer Staff: 13
    Non-Paid Artists: 65
    Utilizes: Guest Directors
    Budget: $1,000 - $50,000
    Income Sources: Private Foundations/Grants/Endowments; Business/Corporate Donations; Individual Donations
    Season: September - May   **Annual Attendance:** 2,000
    Affiliations: University of Houston
    Performance Facilities: Cullen Hall, University of Houston

HOUSTON FRIENDS OF MUSIC

c/o Shepperd School of Music, Rice University, PO Box 1892, Houston, TX 77251
(713) 285-5400

Founded: 1959
Arts Area: Chamber; Ensemble; Instrumental Group
Status: Professional; Non-Profit
Type: Performing; Sponsoring
Purpose: The Houston Friends of Music is a non-profit organization dedicated to the presentation of chamber ensembles with national and international reputations and development of new audiences.
Management: Alicia D. Less, Administrative Director
Volunteer Staff: 25
Utilizes: Guest Artists
Budget: $50,000 - $100,000
Income Sources: Private Foundations/Grants/Endowments; Business/Corporate Donations; Box Office; Government Grants; Individual Donations
Season: September - May   **Annual Attendance:** 5,000
Affiliations: Shepherd School of Music
Performance Facilities: Seude Concert Hall

HOUSTON HARPSICHORD SOCIETY

PO Box 271193, Houston, TX 77277
(713) 977-4581

Founded: 1968
Arts Area: Chamber; Ensemble; Ethnic; Folk; Dance
Status: Professional; Non-Profit
Type: Educational; Sponsoring
Purpose: To perform early music, especially works arranged for harpsichord
Management: Becky Lao, President/Executive Director
Officers: Becky Lao, President; Dr. Maritza Mascarenhas, Vice President; Lola Norton, Secretary; Robert Thomas, Treasurer
Paid Artists: 50   **Non-Paid Artists:** 8
Utilizes: Guest Artists
Budget: $1,000 - $50,000
Income Sources: Private Foundations/Grants/Endowments; Business/Corporate Donations; Box Office; Government Grants; Individual Donations
Season: September - June   **Annual Attendance:** 2,000

HOUSTON SYMPHONY

615 Louisiana, Houston, TX 77002
(713) 224-4240

Founded: 1913
Arts Area: Orchestra; Chamber; Ensemble; Ethnic; Folk
Status: Professional; Non-Profit
Type: Performing; Touring; Resident; Educational
Purpose: To provide a musical organization committed to fulfilling Houston's need for outstanding cultural entertainment and music education; to present works consistently at the highest level of performance quality
Management: David Wax, Executive Director
Officers: Jane McDavid, Chairman
Paid Staff: 32   **Volunteer Staff:** 2
Paid Artists: 150
Utilizes: Special Technical Talent; Guest Conductors; Guest Artists; Guest Directors
Budget: $5,000,000 - $10,000,000
Income Sources: Private Foundations/Grants/Endowments; Business/Corporate Donations; Box Office; Government Grants; Individual Donations
Season: June - May
Performance Facilities: Jesse H. Jones Hall for the Performing Arts

VOCAL MUSIC

HOUSTON GRAND OPERA

510 Preston, Houston, TX 77002-1594
(713) 546-0200
FAX: (713) 247-0906

Founded: 1955
Arts Area: Grand Opera; Lyric Opera; Light Opera; Operetta; Musical Theatre
Status: Professional; Non-Profit
Type: Performing; Touring; Resident; Educational

Purpose: To produce opera of consistent excellence offering nontraditional and innovative works; to develop new forms, new artists and new audiences; In addition, Houston Grand Opera must direct itself toward becoming accessible to all segments of the greater community.
Management: David Gockley, General Director; John DeMain, Music Director; Dolores Johnson, Managing Director; James Ireland, Producing Director; Krista Rimple, Community Programs Director
Officers: Constantine S. Nicandros, President; Harris Masterson III, Honorary Chairman; John M. Seidl, Chairman of the Board; Mrs. Oscar S. Wyatt Jr., Vice Chairman; David Gockley, Executive Vice President
Paid Staff: 110
Paid Artists: 600
Utilizes: Special Technical Talent; Guest Conductors; Guest Artists; Guest Directors
Budget: Over 10,000,000
Income Sources: Private Foundations/Grants/Endowments; Business/Corporate Donations; Box Office; Government Grants; Individual Donations
Season: October - July
Annual Attendance: 200,000
Affiliations: OA
Performance Facilities: Wortham Theater Center

HOUSTON SYMPHONY CHORUS
615 Louisiana, Houston, TX 77002
(713) 224-4240
FAX: (713) 222-7024
Founded: 1946
Arts Area: Choral
Status: Non-Professional; Non-Profit
Type: Performing; Resident
Management: Dr. Charles Hausmann, Director; Marilyn Dyess, Chorus Manager; Scott Holshouser, Accompanist; Betsy Weber, Assistant Director
Paid Staff: 5 **Volunteer Staff:** 1
Non-Paid Artists: 170
Utilizes: Guest Conductors; Guest Artists
Budget: $50,000 - $100,000
Season: 52 Weeks
Affiliations: CA
Performance Facilities: Jesse H. Jones Hall for the Performing Arts

THE RUMBLE SEAT FOUR QUARTET
PO Box 25348, Houston, TX 77265
(713) 522-3805
Founded: 1984
Arts Area: Barbershop Quartet
Status: Semi-Professional
Type: Performing
Purpose: Preserve and encourage barbershop quartet singing
Management: Richard A. Mills, Agent
Paid Staff: 1
Paid Artists: 4
Budget: $1,000 - $50,000
Income Sources: Box Office
Season: 52 Weeks
Affiliations: SPEBSQSA

TEXAS OPERA THEATER
510 Preston, Suite 500, Houston, TX 77002
(713) 546-0290
FAX: (713) 247-0906
Founded: 1973
Arts Area: Grand Opera; Lyric Opera; Light Opera; Operetta
Status: Non-Profit
Type: Performing; Touring; Resident; Educational
Purpose: To nurture the careers of young American artists
Management: David Gockley, General Director
Paid Staff: 9
Paid Artists: 7
Utilizes: Special Technical Talent; Guest Conductors; Guest Artists; Guest Directors
Budget: $500,000 - $1,000,000
Income Sources: Private Foundations/Grants/Endowments; Business/Corporate Donations; Box Office; Government Grants; Individual Donations

Season: September - May
Annual Attendance: 75,000

THEATRE

A.D. PLAYERS
2710 West Alabama, Houston, TX 77098
(713) 526-2721
   Founded: 1967
   Arts Area: Professional; Theatrical Group
   Status: Semi-Professional; Non-Profit
   Type: Performing; Touring; Resident; Educational
   Purpose: To provide a full season of Christian theatrical productions to the Houston audience; to send touring repertory and concert productions nationally and internationally
   Management: Jeannette Clift George, Artistic Director/Co-Manager; Doug Gettyl, Production Manager
   Officers: Jim Hunt, Chairman, Board of Directors
   Paid Staff: 4
   Paid Artists: 19
   Utilizes: Special Technical Talent; Guest Artists; Guest Directors
   Budget: $100,000 - $500,000
   Income Sources: Private Foundations/Grants/Endowments; Business/Corporate Donations; Box Office; Individual Donations
   Season: 52 Weeks
   Annual Attendance: 15,000
   Affiliations: Texas Nonprofit Theatre; TCG; Houston Theatre Association; Cultural Arts Council of Houston
   Performance Facilities: Grace Theatre

ALLEY THEATRE
615 Texas Avenue, Houston, TX 77002
(713) 228-9341
FAX: (713) 222-6542
   Founded: 1947
   Arts Area: Professional; Theatrical Group
   Status: Professional; Non-Profit
   Type: Performing; Touring; Resident; Educational; Sponsoring
   Purpose: To promote the performance of theatrical literature
   Management: Gregory Boyd, Artistic Director; Stephen J. Albert, Executive Director
   Officers: Meredith J. Long, Chairman; T. William Porter, President
   Paid Staff: 140   **Volunteer Staff:** 1,000
   Paid Artists: 100
   Utilizes: Special Technical Talent; Guest Artists; Guest Directors
   Budget: $5,000,000 - $10,000,000
   Income Sources: Private Foundations/Grants/Endowments; Business/Corporate Donations; Box Office; Government Grants; Individual Donations
   Season: September - August
   Annual Attendance: 500,000
   Affiliations: LORT; AEA; USA; SSDC
   Performance Facilities: Alley Theatre

CHANNING PLAYERS
PO Box 631363, Houston, TX 77263
(713) 785-9492
   Founded: 1955
   Arts Area: Community
   Status: Non-Profit
   Type: Performing; Educational
   Purpose: To produce quality plays
   Management: Janis Halliday, Artistic Director; Donald Williams, Technical Director
   Officers: Martha Raymond, President; Janis Halliday, Vice President; Anthony Addison, Secretary; Linda Stern, Treasurer
   Volunteer Staff: 50
   Non-Paid Artists: 50
   Utilizes: Special Technical Talent
   Budget: $1,000 - $50,000
   Income Sources: Private Foundations/Grants/Endowments; Business/Corporate Donations; Box Office; Individual Donations
   Season: October - June   **Annual Attendance:** 1,500
   Affiliations: Cultural Arts Council of Houston; Texas Nonprofit Theatre

THE ENSEMBLE
3535 Main, Houston, TX 77002
(713) 520-0055; (713) 520-0063
>**Founded:** 1976
>**Arts Area:** Theatrical Group
>**Status:** Professional; Non-Profit
>**Type:** Performing; Touring; Resident; Educational
>**Purpose:** To provide professional Black theatre to the city of Houston
>**Management:** Eileen Morris, Artistic Director
>**Paid Staff:** 10 **Volunteer Staff:** 25
>**Paid Artists:** 50
>**Utilizes:** Special Technical Talent; Guest Artists; Guest Directors
>**Budget:** $100,000 - $500,000
>**Income Sources:** Private Foundations/Grants/Endowments; Business/Corporate Donations; Box Office;
>Individual Donations
>**Season:** September - August **Annual Attendance:** 25,000
>**Performance Facilities:** The Ensemble Theatre

MAIN STREET THEATER
2540 Times Boulevard, Houston, TX 77005
(713) 524-6706
>**Founded:** 1975
>**Arts Area:** Theatrical Group
>**Status:** Professional; Semi-Professional; Non-Professional
>**Type:** Performing; Touring; Resident
>**Management:** Rebecca Greene Udden, Artistic Director; Patti Bean, Production Manager
>**Officers:** Susan Imle, President; David Cooney Jr., Vice President; Victoria Benson, Secretary; Jack S. Blanton, Jr.,
>Treasurer
>**Paid Staff:** 5 **Volunteer Staff:** 15
>**Paid Artists:** 45
>**Budget:** $100,000 - $500,000
>**Income Sources:** Private Foundations/Grants/Endowments; Business/Corporate Donations; Box Office;
>Individual Donations
>**Season:** 52 Weeks

STAGES REPERTORY THEATRE
3201 Allen Parkway, #101, Houston, TX 77019
(713) 527-0240
FAX: (713) 527-8669
>**Founded:** 1978
>**Arts Area:** Professional; Theatrical Group
>**Status:** Professional; Non-Profit
>**Type:** Performing; Touring; Resident; Educational; Sponsoring
>**Purpose:** To produce plays that challenge a developing artistic company, being of social value to the community and set-
>ting a standard of excellence deserving of audience and critical acclaim
>**Management:** Peter Bennett, Artistic Director
>**Officers:** Anne Wright, President; Mimi Kilgore, Chair
>**Paid Staff:** 18 **Volunteer Staff:** 250
>**Paid Artists:** 65
>**Utilizes:** Special Technical Talent; Guest Artists; Guest Directors
>**Budget:** $500,000 - $1,000,000
>**Income Sources:** Private Foundations/Grants/Endowments; Business/Corporate Donations; Box Office; Government
>Grants; Individual Donations
>**Season:** 52 Weeks **Annual Attendance:** 65,000
>**Affiliations:** TCG

TALENTO BILINGUE DE HOUSTON
PO Box 230326, Houston, TX 77223-0326
(713) 921-5093
>**Founded:** 1976
>**Arts Area:** Musical; Community; Theatrical Group
>**Status:** Non-Profit
>**Type:** Performing; Touring; Educational; Sponsoring
>**Purpose:** Non-profit educational and cultural organization
>**Management:** Richard E. Reyes, Artistic/Project Director; Fernando Gonzales, Manager; Rodney Becerra,
>Technical Director; Jim Bratton, Publicity
>**Officers:** Peter Garcia, President; Jim Bratton, Vice President; Manuel Barrera, Secretary/Treasurer
>**Paid Staff:** 3 **Volunteer Staff:** 2

Paid Artists: 10 **Non-Paid Artists:** 40
Utilizes: Guest Artists; Guest Directors
Budget: $50,000 - $100,000
Income Sources: Private Foundations/Grants/Endowments; Business/Corporate Donations; Box Office; Government Grants; Individual Donations
Season: 52 Weeks
Annual Attendance: 12,000

THEATRE ON WHEELS
PO Box 440056, Houston, TX 77244
(713) 493-5500
Founded: 1979
Arts Area: Theater
Status: Semi-Professional; Non-Profit
Type: Performing; Touring; Resident; Educational; Sponsoring
Purpose: To reach as many school age students with our quality children's theatre repertoire and after-school dramatic instruction for kids in grades K - 12
Management: Ellen Baltz, Founder/Executive Director; Cari Skain, Events Coordinator; Cindy Wigginton, Public Relations and Education Director; Terry McManigle, Associate Administrator
Officers: Jan Norris, Chairman; Ellen B. Baltz, President; Dow Heard, Vice President; Diane Sturgess, Treasurer
Paid Staff: 4 **Volunteer Staff:** 2
Paid Artists: 9 **Non-Paid Artists:** 15
Utilizes: Special Technical Talent; Guest Artists; Guest Directors
Budget: $100,000 - $500,000
Income Sources: Private Foundations/Grants/Endowments; Business/Corporate Donations; Box Office; Government Grants; Individual Donations
Season: 52 Weeks
Affiliations: AATY; Cultural Arts Council of Houston; SWTC

THEATRE SUBURBIA
1410 West 43rd, Houston, TX 77018
(713) 682-3525
Founded: 1960
Arts Area: Theatrical Group
Status: Non-Professional; Non-Profit
Type: Performing
Purpose: To provide quality entertainment for the general public with a wide variety of plays ranging from light comedy to heavy drama, being noted for producing top quality original scripts
Management: C.R. Glover, Box Office; Keith Ross, Technical Director; Melissa Merten, Back Stage Coordinator
Officers: Doris Merten, President; Sherah Bates, Vice President; Bette Ann Ross, Secretary; Carolyn Montgomery, Treasurer
Paid Staff: 1 **Volunteer Staff:** 30
Paid Artists: 20
Utilizes: Guest Directors
Budget: $1,000 - $50,000
Income Sources: Private Foundations/Grants/Endowments; Business/Corporate Donations; Box Office; Individual Donations
Season: 52 Weeks
Annual Attendance: 12,000
Performance Facilities: Theatre Suburbia

THEATRE UNDER THE STARS
4235 San Felipe, Houston, TX 77002
(713) 622-1626
FAX: (713) 622-0025
Arts Area: Professional; Musical; Theatrical Group
Status: Professional; Non-Profit
Type: Performing; Touring; Educational
Purpose: To present light opera regionally and on tour; to operate a school for future artists; to foster the creation of new works of musical theatre
Management: Frank M. Young, Executive Director/Founder; John Holly, Producing Director; Cissy Segall, Managing Director; Vivian Flynn, General Manager
Officers: Dennis Irvine, President of the Board
Budget: Over 10,000,000
Income Sources: Private Foundations/Grants/Endowments; Business/Corporate Donations; Box Office; Government Grants; Individual Donations
Performance Facilities: The Music Hall

PERFORMING SERIES

THE HOUSTON INTERNATIONAL FESTIVAL
1100 Louisania, Suite 1275, Houston, TX 77002
(713) 654-8808
FAX: (713) 654-1719
   Founded: 1966
   Arts Area: Dance; Vocal Music; Instrumental Music; Festivals
   Status: Professional; Non-Profit
   Type: Educational; Sponsoring
   Purpose: To sponsor a 10-day cultural celebration in an urban setting, focusing on a different country every year
   Management: Dr. James Austin, President and COO
   Paid Staff: 10   **Volunteer Staff:** 4
   Paid Artists: 2
   Utilizes: Guest Artists
   Budget: $1,000,000 - $5,000,000
   Income Sources: Private Foundations/Grants/Endowments; Business/Corporate Donations; Box Office
   Season: Spring
   Annual Attendance: 1,000,000
   Affiliations: Cultural Arts Council of Houston; Houston Convention and Visitors Center

HOUSTON SHAKESPEARE FESTIVAL
University of Houston, Drama Department, Houston, TX 77204-5071
(713) 743-3003
   Founded: 1975
   Arts Area: Theater; Festivals
   Status: Professional; Non-Profit
   Type: Performing
   Purpose: To provide free classical theater to the citizens of Houston and the surrounding area
   Management: Sidney L. Berger, Producing Director; Suzanne Phillips, Associate Producer; Roxanne Collins, Business Manager
   Paid Staff: 4   **Volunteer Staff:** 100
   Paid Artists: 35
   Utilizes: Guest Artists; Guest Directors
   Budget: $100,000 - $500,000
   Income Sources: Private Foundations/Grants/Endowments; Business/Corporate Donations; Government Grants; Individual Donations
   Season: July - September
   Annual Attendance: 25,000
   Affiliations: University of Houston
   Performance Facilities: Miller Outdoor Theatre

JEWISH COMMUNITY CENTER OF HOUSTON
5601 South Braeswood, Houston, TX 77096
(713) 729-3200
FAX: (713) 551-7223
   Founded: 1935
   Arts Area: Dance; Vocal Music; Instrumental Music; Theater; Festivals
   Status: Non-Profit
   Type: Performing; Educational; Sponsoring
   Purpose: To provide education and leisure time activities, and recreational services to the southwest Houston community; to promote an appreciation of theatre
   Management: Jerry Wische, Executive Director; Gerry Buncher, Assistant Executive Director; David J. Marco, Director of Performing Arts
   Officers: Linda Walters, President
   Paid Staff: 120   **Volunteer Staff:** 100
   Paid Artists: 125   **Non-Paid Artists:** 50
   Utilizes: Special Technical Talent; Guest Artists; Guest Directors
   Budget: $100,000 - $500,000
   Income Sources: Private Foundations/Grants/Endowments; Business/Corporate Donations; Box Office; Government Grants; Individual Donations
   Season: 52 Weeks
   Annual Attendance: 35,000
   Affiliations: Texas Nonprofit Theatre; National Council of Jewish Theatres
   Performance Facilities: Jewish Community Center - Kaplan Theatre, Joe Frank Theater of the Arts

FACILITY

ALLEY THEATRE
615 Texas Avenue, Houston, TX 77002
(713) 228-9341
FAX: (713) 222-6542
    Founded: 1947
    Type of Facility: Theatre Complex
    Type of Stage: Arena; Modified Thrust
    Seating Capacity: Large Stage - 824; Arena Stage - 296
    Year Built: 1968   **Architect:** Ulrich Franzen   **Cost:** $6,500,000
    Contact for Rental: Zannie Voss;   (713) 228-9341
    Manager: Stephen J. Albert;   (713) 228-9341
    Resident Groups: Alley Theatre
    The Alley Theatre contains the Hugo V. Neuhaus Arena Stage and Large Stage. See separate listings for additional information.

ALLEY THEATRE - HUGO V. NEUHAUS ARENA STAGE
615 Texas Avenue, Houston, TX 77002
(713) 228-9341
FAX: (713) 222-6542
    Founded: 1947
    Type of Facility: Theatre House; Arena
    Type of Stage: Arena
    Stage Dimensions: 30'x30'
    Seating Capacity: 296
    Year Built: 1968   **Architect:** Ulrich Franzen   **Cost:** $6,500,000
    Contact for Rental: Zannie Voss;   (713) 228-9341
    Manager: Stephen J. Albert;   (713) 228-9341

ALLEY THEATRE - LARGE STAGE
615 Texas Avenue, Houston, TX 77002
(713) 228-9341
FAX: (713) 222-6542
    Founded: 1947
    Type of Facility: Theatre House
    Type of Stage: Modified Thrust
    Stage Dimensions: 36'Dx20'W, widening to 38'W upstage
    Seating Capacity: 824
    Year Built: 1968   **Architect:** Ulrich Franzen   **Cost:** $6,500,000
    Contact for Rental: Zannie Voss;   (713) 228-9341
    Manager: Stephen J. Albert;   (713) 228-9341

HOUSTON CIVIC CENTER
PO Box 61649, Houston, TX 77208
(713) 247-1000
    Type of Facility: Theatre Complex; Performance Center; Civic Center
    Year Built: 1938
    George R. Brown Convention Center, Gus Wortham Theater Center, Jesse H. Jones Hall for the Performing Arts, The Music Hall and Sam Houston Coliseum comprise Houston Civic Center. See separate listings for further information.

HOUSTON CIVIC CENTER-GEORGE R. BROWN CONVENTION CENTER
1001 Convention Center Boulevard, Houston, TX 77010
(713) 853-8000
FAX: (713) 853-8090
    Type of Facility: Convention Center
    Year Built: 1987   **Architect:** Convention Center Architects   **Cost:** $175,000,000
    Manager: Melanie Meeks;   (713) 853-8039
    George R. Brown Convention Center is part of Houston Civic Center and contains a Ballroom, Exhibition Hall and General Assembly Hall. See separate listings for further information. Rental purpose and contacts are as follows: Public Show Rentals, Melvina Chapman (713) 853-8020; Corporate Meetings, Jennifer Hanson (713) 855-8042; Conventions, Melanie Meeks, (713) 853-8039. This center is rarely used for performance, musical or theatrical events.

HOUSTON CIVIC CENTER-GEORGE R. BROWN CONVENTION CENTER - BALLROOM
1001 Convention Center Boulevard, Houston, TX 77010
(713) 853-8000
    Type of Facility: Multi-Purpose; Room; Chamber Hall
    Type of Stage: Flexible

Seating Capacity: 4,500
Manager: Melanie Meeks;   (713) 853-8039

HOUSTON CIVIC CENTER-GEORGE R. BROWN CONVENTION CENTER - EXHIBITION HALL
1001 Convention Center Boulevard, Houston, TX 77010
(713) 853-8000
    Type of Facility: Multi-Purpose; Room
    Type of Stage: Flexible
    Stage Dimensions: 87 sections, 6'x8' each
    Year Built: 1987
    Manager: Melanie Meeks;   (713) 853-8039
    The Exhibition Hall contains 470,500 square feet of usable floor area.

HOUSTON CIVIC CENTER-GEORGE R. BROWN CONVENTION CENTER - GENERAL ASSEMBLY HALL
1001 Convention Center Boulevard, Houston, TX 77010
(713) 853-8000
    Type of Facility: Concert Hall; Auditorium; Theatre House; Multi-Purpose
    Type of Stage: Flexible
    Stage Dimensions: 76'Wx70'D
    Seating Capacity: 3,600 - 3 sections of 1,200 seats each
    Manager: Melanie Meeks;   (713) 853-8039

HOUSTON CIVIC CENTER-GUS WORTHAM THEATER CENTER
510 Preston, Houston, TX 77002
(713) 237-1439
FAX: (713) 237-9313
    Founded: 1987
    Type of Facility: Theatre Complex; Concert Hall; Performance Center; Opera House
    Type of Stage: Proscenium   **Orchestra Pit**
    Seating Capacity: 2,174; 1,066
    Year Built: 1987   **Architect:** Morris-Aubrey Architects   **Cost:** $74,000,000
    Acoustical Consultant: Jaffe Acoustics
    Contact for Rental: Leslie Watson;   (713) 237-1439
    Manager: Robyn Williams
    Resident Groups: Houston Grand Opera; Houston Ballet
    The Gus Wortham Theater Center, part of Houston Civic Center, contains Alice & George Brown Theater and Lilly &
    Roy Cullen Theater. See separate listings for additional information.

HOUSTON CIVIC CENTER-GUS WORTHAM THEATER CENTER - ALICE AND GEORGE BROWN THEATER
510 Preston, Houston, TX 77002
(713) 237-1439
FAX: (713) 237-9313
    Type of Facility: Concert Hall; Theatre House; Opera House
    Type of Stage: Proscenium; Hydraulic Lift Stage
    Stage Dimensions: 52'Wx65'6"D
    Orchestra Pit
    Seating Capacity: 2,176
    Year Built: 1987
    Acoustical Consultant: Jaffe Acoustics
    Contact for Rental: Leslie Watson;   (713) 237-1439
    Manager: Robyn Williams;   (713) 237-1439
    Resident Groups: Houston Grand Opera; Houston Ballet

HOUSTON CIVIC CENTER-GUS WORTHAM THEATER CENTER - LILLY AND ROY CULLEN THEATER
510 Preston, Houston, TX 77002
(713) 237-1439
FAX: (713) 237-9313
    Type of Facility: Concert Hall; Theatre House
    Type of Stage: Proscenium; Hydraulic Lift Stage
    Stage Dimensions: 38'Wx51'D
    Orchestra Pit
    Seating Capacity: 1,101
    Year Built: 1987
    Acoustical Consultant: Jaffe Acoustics
    Contact for Rental: Leslie Watson;   (713) 237-1439
    Manager: Robyn Williams;   (713) 237-1439

HOUSTON CIVIC CENTER - JESSE H. JONES HALL FOR THE PERFORMING ARTS
615 Louisiana, PO Box 61469, Houston, TX 77208
(713) 227-3974
>**Type of Facility:** Concert Hall; Auditorium; Theatre House
>**Type of Stage:** Proscenium
>**Stage Dimensions:** 60'Wx36'D; 60'Wx32'H proscenium opening
>**Orchestra Pit**
>**Seating Capacity:** 3,001
>**Year Built:** 1966   **Architect:** CRS Architects   **Cost:** $9,000,000
>**Contact for Rental:** Donna Barrett;   (713) 227-3974
>**Manager:** Vivian Montejano;   (713) 227-3974
>*Jones Hall is part of the Houston Civic Center.*

HOUSTON CIVIC CENTER - THE MUSIC HALL
810 Bagby, PO Box 61649, Houston, TX 77208
(713) 247-2592
>**Type of Facility:** Auditorium; Theatre House
>**Type of Stage:** Proscenium
>**Stage Dimensions:** 50'Wx36'Dx27'H
>**Seating Capacity:** 3,010
>**Year Built:** 1938
>**Contact for Rental:** John Thomas;   (713) 247-2697
>**Resident Groups:** Theatre Under the Stars

HOUSTON CIVIC CENTER - SAM HOUSTON COLISEUM
810 Bagby, PO Box 61649, Houston, TX 77208
(713) 237-1439
>**Type of Facility:** Performance Center; Arena; Multi-Purpose
>**Type of Stage:** Arena
>**Stage Dimensions:** 230'x91'
>**Seating Capacity:** Permanent - 8,806; Portable - add 2,400
>**Year Built:** 1938
>**Contact for Rental:** Tracy Johnson;   (713) 237-1439
>*Part of Houston Civic Center*

JEWISH COMMUNITY CENTER - JOE FRANK THEATRE
5601 South Braeswood, Houston, TX 77096
(713) 729-3200
FAX: (713) 551-7223
>**Founded:** 1984
>**Type of Facility:** Environmental; Multi-Purpose; Room
>**Facility Originally:** Meeting Hall; Movie House
>**Type of Stage:** Flexible
>**Stage Dimensions:** 27'Wx45'D
>**Seating Capacity:** 125
>**Year Built:** 1984   **Cost:** $150,000
>**Contact for Rental:** David J. Marco;   (713) 729-3200, ext. 275
>*Performances, lectures, meetings, demonstrations*

JEWISH COMMUNITY CENTER - KAPLAN THEATRE
5601 South Braeswood, Houston, TX 77096
(713) 729-3200
FAX: (713) 551-7223
>**Founded:** 1970
>**Type of Facility:** Theatre Complex; Performance Center; Theatre House
>**Type of Stage:** Thrust; Proscenium
>**Stage Dimensions:** 40'Wx32'D
>**Seating Capacity:** 318
>**Year Built:** 1970   **Cost:** $400,000
>**Contact for Rental:** David J. Marco;   (713) 729-3200, ext. 275
>*Performances, lectures, demonstrations*

MILLER OUTDOOR THEATRE
Hermann Park, PO Box 1562, Houston, TX 77251
(713) 520-3291
>**Type of Facility:** Outdoor (Concert); Performance Center
>**Type of Stage:** Proscenium
>**Stage Dimensions:** 58'Wx40'D

Orchestra Pit
Seating Capacity: Permanent - 1,583; Hillside - 12,000
Year Built: 1968   **Architect:** Eugene Werlin & Associates   **Cost:** $1,300,000
Year Remodeled: 1986   **Architect:** 3D/International   **Cost:** $1,700,000
Contact for Rental: Robert Forshaw;   (713) 520-1391

RICE UNIVERSITY - HAMMAN HALL
PO Box 1892, Houston, TX 77251
(713) 527-4027
Type of Facility: Theatre House
Type of Stage: Proscenium
Stage Dimensions: 42'Wx45'D
Seating Capacity: 506
Year Built: 1957   **Architect:** Harvin C. Moore
Year Remodeled: 1967
Contact for Rental: Neil Haven;   (713) 527-4027
Resident Groups: Rice Players; Rice Chorales

STAGES REPERTORY THEATRE
3201 Allen Parkway, #101, Houston, TX 77019
(713) 527-0240
Type of Facility: Theatre Complex; Studio Performance; Performance Center; Off Broadway; Theatre House; Arena; Multi-Purpose; Room
Facility Originally: Engraving Plant
Type of Stage: Thrust; Flexible; Platform; 3/4 Arena; Arena
Stage Dimensions: Arena - 20'x30'; Thrust - 20'x20'
Seating Capacity: Arena - 248; Thrust - 191
Year Built: 1929
Year Remodeled: 1984   **Architect:** W.O. Neuhaus & Associates   **Cost:** $660,000
Acoustical Consultant: John F. Bos
Contact for Rental: James Gladwin;   (713) 527-0240
Manager: Peter Bennett, Artistic Director;   (713) 527-0240
Resident Groups: Stages Repertory Theatre

THEATRE SUBURBIA
1410 West 43rd, Houston, TX 77018
(713) 682-3525
Founded: 1961
Type of Facility: Theatre House
Facility Originally: Business Facility
Type of Stage: Flexible
Seating Capacity: 110
Year Remodeled: 1986   **Architect:** Brian Wycoff   **Cost:** $2,000
Resident Groups: Theatre Suburbia

Huntsville

FACILITY

SAM HOUSTON STATE UNIVERSITY THEATRE AND DANCE DIVISION
Theatre and Dance Division, Avenue H at 17th Street, Huntsville, TX 77341
(409) 294-1329
FAX: (409) 294-1598
Type of Facility: Theatre Complex; Auditorium; Performance Center
Year Built: 1976   **Architect:** Calhoun Tungate & Jackson   **Cost:** $3,500,000
Acoustical Consultant: Variable Acoustics
Manager: Dr. James R. Miller;   (409) 294-1329
Resident Groups: Drama Department
The facility contains the Main Stage Theatre and Studio Theatre. See separate listings for further information.

SAM HOUSTON STATE UNIVERSITY THEATRE AND DANCE DIVISION - MAIN STAGE THEATRE
Drama Center, Avenue I at 17th Street, Huntsville, TX 77341
(409) 294-1329
Type of Facility: Auditorium; Theatre House
Type of Stage: Proscenium
Stage Dimensions: 20'x54'4"x38'8"   **Orchestra Pit**
Seating Capacity: 495
Year Built: 1976

SAM HOUSTON STATE UNIVERSITY THEATRE AND DANCE DIVISION - STUDIO THEATRE
Theatre and Dance Division, Avenue H at 17th Street, Huntsville, TX 77341
(409) 294-1329
FAX: (409) 294-1598
>   **Type of Facility:** Black Box
>   **Type of Stage:** Flexible
>   **Seating Capacity:** 120
>   **Year Built:** 1976
>   **Manager:** Dr. James R. Miller;   (409) 294-1329

Ingram

THEATRE

SMITH-RITCH POINT THEATRE
PO Box 176, Highway 39, Ingram, TX 78025
(210) 367-5121
>   **Founded:** 1959
>   **Arts Area:** Community
>   **Status:** Non-Professional; Non-Profit
>   **Type:** Performing; Touring; Educational
>   **Purpose:** Dedicated to the visual and performing arts
>   **Management:** Susan Balentine, Theatre Director; Lane Tait, Executive Director; Douglas Balentine, Technical Director
>   **Paid Staff:** 20
>   **Paid Artists:** 3
>   **Utilizes:** Guest Conductors; Guest Artists; Guest Directors
>   **Budget:** $50,000 - $100,000
>   **Income Sources:** Private Foundations/Grants/Endowments; Business/Corporate Donations; Box Office; Government Grants; Individual Donations
>   **Season:** June - August
>   **Affiliations:** Texas Nonprofit Theatre; Texas Educators Theatre Association
>   **Performance Facilities:** Smith-Ritch Point Theater

PERFORMING SERIES

HILL COUNTRY ARTS FOUNDATION
Highway 39, PO Box 176, Ingram, TX 78025
(210) 367-5121
>   **Founded:** 1958
>   **Arts Area:** Dance; Vocal Music; Instrumental Music; Theater
>   **Status:** Non-Profit
>   **Type:** Performing; Educational
>   **Purpose:** To promote the visual and performing arts
>   **Management:** Lane Tait, Executive Director; Susan Balentine, Theatre Director
>   **Officers:** J. Tom Graham, President of Board of Directors
>   **Paid Staff:** 5   **Volunteer Staff:** 150
>   **Paid Artists:** 30   **Non-Paid Artists:** 75
>   **Utilizes:** Special Technical Talent; Guest Conductors; Guest Directors
>   **Budget:** $100,000 - $500,000
>   **Income Sources:** Private Foundations/Grants/Endowments; Business/Corporate Donations; Box Office; Government Grants; Individual Donations
>   **Season:** 52 Weeks   **Annual Attendance:** 23,000
>   **Affiliations:** AACT; Texas Nonprofit Theatre
>   **Performance Facilities:** Outdoor Amphitheatre

Irving

DANCE

IRVING BALLET COMPANY
3900 Acapulco, Irving, TX 75062
(214) 717-3926
>   **Founded:** 1982
>   **Arts Area:** Ballet; Jazz
>   **Status:** Semi-Professional
>   **Type:** Performing
>   **Purpose:** To expand ballet audiences in the Irving area and establish a permanent base for future dance audiences

Management: Dale Riley, Artistic Director
Officers: Laurita Wilkinson, President; Bud Tatum, Vice President; Janine Philips, Secretary; Barbara Cardwell, Treasurer
Volunteer Staff: 20
Paid Artists: 6   **Non-Paid Artists:** 25
Utilizes: Guest Artists; Guest Directors; Guest Choreographers
Budget: $1,000 - $50,000
Income Sources: Private Foundations/Grants/Endowments; Business/Corporate Donations; Box Office
Season: December - May   **Annual Attendance:** 4,000
Affiliations: Irving Symphony; Cultural Affairs Council
Performance Facilities: Irving Arts Center

INSTRUMENTAL MUSIC

IRVING SYMPHONY ORCHESTRA
3501 North MacArthur Boulevard, Suite 406, Irving, TX 75062
(214) 257-1210
Founded: 1962
Arts Area: Symphony; Orchestra
Status: Non-Profit
Type: Performing
Purpose: To provide outstanding music to Irving and surrounding communities
Management: Hector Guzman, Music Director/Conductor; Marguerite Korkmas, Executive Director
Officers: Donald J. Schiller, President; Ron Drew, President-Elect; Norman McMurray, Vice President of Administration; Nelda Bailey, Secretary; Pam Carroll, Treasurer
Paid Staff: 1
Paid Artists: 5
Utilizes: Guest Artists
Budget: $100,000 - $500,000
Income Sources: Private Foundations/Grants/Endowments; Business/Corporate Donations; Box Office; Individual Donations
Season: October - May
Performance Facilities: Irving Arts Center; Carpenter Hall

THEATRE

IRVING COMMUNITY THEATER
3333 North MacArthur Boulevard, Suite 300, Irving, TX 75060
(214) 252-7558
Arts Area: Musical; Community; Theatrical Group
Status: Non-Professional; Non-Profit
Type: Performing; Resident
Purpose: For the literary, educational, and cultural advancement of the citizens of Irving and outlying areas
Officers: Mary Bongfeldt, President; Steve Crozier, Treasurer
Utilizes: Guest Directors
Budget: $1,000 - $50,000
Income Sources: Private Foundations/Grants/Endowments; Business/Corporate Donations; Box Office; Individual Donations
Season: 52 Weeks   **Annual Attendance:** 5,000
Affiliations: Cultural Affairs Council
Performance Facilities: Irving Center for Cultural Arts

PERFORMING SERIES

IRVING COMMUNITY CONCERT ASSOCIATION
PO Box 154336, Irving, TX 75015
(214) 252-3838
Founded: 1956
Arts Area: Dance; Vocal Music; Instrumental Music; Theater
Status: Non-Profit
Type: Sponsoring
Officers: Dotty Verett, President; Mary Higbie, Vice President
Volunteer Staff: 30
Utilizes: Guest Artists
Budget: $1,000 - $50,000
Income Sources: Business/Corporate Donations; Box Office; Government Grants; Individual Donations
Season: October - April
Affiliations: Community Concerts

FACILITY

IRVING ARTS CENTER
3333 North MacArthur Boulevard, Suite 300, Irving, TX 75062
(214) 252-7558
FAX: (214) 570-4962
   Type of Facility: Theatre Complex; Concert Hall; Performance Center; Theatre House
   Type of Stage: Proscenium   **Orchestra Pit**
   Seating Capacity: Dupree Theatre - 256; Carpenter Theatre - 712
   Year Built: 1990   **Architect:** F & S Partners   **Cost:** $7,200,000
   Contact for Rental: George Cook;   (214) 252-7558
   Manager: Robert O. Cloutier;   (214) 252-7558
   The Irving Arts Center contains two theatres.

Kerrville

PERFORMING SERIES

KERRVILLE FESTIVALS
Quiet Valley Ranch, PO Box 1466, Kerrville, TX 78029
(210) 257-3600
   Founded: 1972
   Arts Area: Dance; Vocal Music; Instrumental Music; Theater; Festivals
   Status: Professional; Commercial
   Type: Performing
   Purpose: To provide music festivals, workshops and recordings presenting regional and national performers with an emphasis on song writers and acoustic musicians
   Management: Rod Kennedy, Producer
   Officers: Rod Kennedy, President
   Paid Staff: 3   **Volunteer Staff:** 350
   Paid Artists: 150   **Non-Paid Artists:** 40
   Utilizes: Special Technical Talent; Guest Artists
   Budget: $100,000 - $500,000
   Income Sources: Box Office; Advertising; Commercial Sponsors
   Season: May - September   **Annual Attendance:** 30,000
   Affiliations: Texas Festivals Association; Texas Music Association
   Performance Facilities: Festival Outdoor Theater

KERRVILLE PERFORMING ARTS SOCIETY
PO Box 1884, Kerrville, TX 78029
(210) 257-4600
   Founded: 1983
   Arts Area: Vocal Music; Instrumental Music; Festivals; Lyric Opera; Grand Opera
   Status: Non-Profit
   Type: Performing
   Purpose: Provide classical and popular music
   Officers: Arney Davis, President; Hubert Palmer, President-Elect; Nancy Neal, Treasurer
   Volunteer Staff: 25
   Non-Paid Artists: 12
   Utilizes: Special Technical Talent; Guest Conductors; Guest Artists; Guest Directors
   Budget: $50,000 - $100,000
   Income Sources: Private Foundations/Grants/Endowments; Business/Corporate Donations; Box Office; Government Grants; Individual Donations
   Season: 52 Weeks   **Annual Attendance:** 6,000
   Performance Facilities: City Auditorium

FACILITY

FESTIVAL OUTDOOR THEATER
Quiet Valley Ranch, PO Box 1466, Kerrville, TX 78029
(210) 257-3600
   Type of Facility: Outdoor (Concert); Amphitheater
   Type of Stage: Proscenium; Environmental
   Stage Dimensions: 26'x46'
   Seating Capacity: 5,000
   Year Built: 1974   **Architect:** Rod Kennedy   **Cost:** $26,000
   Year Remodeled: 1981   **Architect:** Rod Kennedy   **Cost:** $21,000
   Acoustical Consultant: Spectratech

Contact for Rental: Rod Kennedy;   (512) 257-3600
Resident Groups: Kerrville Folk Festival; Kerrville Wine and Music Festival

Killeen

THEATRE

VIVE LES ARTS THEATRE
3401 South W.S. Young Drive, Killeen, TX 76547
(817) 526-9090
    Founded: 1976
    Arts Area: Professional; Musical; Community; Theatrical Group
    Status: Professional; Non-Professional; Non-Profit
    Type: Performing; Touring; Sponsoring
    Purpose: To develop and maintain cultural and artistic activities in the Killeen, Harker Heights, Fort Hood and Copperas Cove areas
    Management: Ron Hannemann, Managing/Artistic Director
    Officers: Jetty and Grady Monaghan, Chairmen
    Paid Staff: 1   **Volunteer Staff:** 150
    Utilizes: Special Technical Talent; Guest Conductors; Guest Artists
    Budget: $50,000 - $100,000
    Income Sources: Private Foundations/Grants/Endowments; Business/Corporate Donations; Box Office; Government Grants; Individual Donations
    Season: 52 Weeks   **Annual Attendance:** 6,500
    Affiliations: Texas Commission on the Arts; NALAA
    Performance Facilities: Vive Les Arts Center for the Arts

FACILITY

VIVE LES ARTS SOCIETE AND THEATRE
2501 SW Young Drive, PO Box 3401, Killeen, TX 76547
(817) 526-4599
    Type of Facility: Theatre Complex; Concert Hall; Auditorium; Performance Center; Theatre House; Multi-Purpose
    Type of Stage: Thrust; Proscenium
    Stage Dimensions: 30'Wx32'D
    Orchestra Pit
    Seating Capacity: 400
    Year Built: 1987   **Architect:** Paul E. Burns & Associates   **Cost:** $1,500,000
    Acoustical Consultant: Variable Acoustics
    Contact for Rental: Ron Hannemann;   (817) 526-9090

Laredo

INSTRUMENTAL MUSIC

LAREDO PHILHARMONIC ORCHESTRA
518 Flightline, Laredo, TX 78040
(210) 727-8886
    Founded: 1980
    Arts Area: Symphony; Orchestra; Chamber
    Status: Professional; Non-Profit
    Type: Performing; Touring; Resident; Educational
    Purpose: Cultural enrichment of the Laredo Area
    Management: Robert W. Muir, General Manager
    Officers: Julia Watson Jones, President; James E. Moore, Vice President; Amber Yeary, Secretary; Tanya K. Rose, Treasurer
    Paid Staff: 4   **Volunteer Staff:** 75
    Paid Artists: 75
    Budget: $100,000 - $500,000
    Income Sources: Private Foundations/Grants/Endowments; Business/Corporate Donations; Box Office; Individual Donations
    Season: September - May   **Annual Attendance:** 15,000
    Performance Facilities: Laredo Civic Center

Longview

INSTRUMENTAL MUSIC

LONGVIEW SYMPHONY ORCHESTRA
PO Box 1825, Longview, TX 75606
(903) 236-9739
>**Founded:** 1968
>**Arts Area:** Symphony; Orchestra
>**Status:** Semi-Professional; Non-Profit
>**Type:** Performing; Resident; Educational
>**Purpose:** To present orchestral music of the highest calibre, performed in the most capable manner, as an alternative music medium to the citizens of east Texas
>**Management:** Tonu Kalam, Conductor/Music Director; Sally Bommarito, Business Manager
>**Officers:** W.H. Throckmorton, President; Richard Miller, Vice President; Mrs. Robert Rigby, Secretary; Richard Wade, Treasurer
>**Paid Staff:** 1 **Volunteer Staff:** 33
>**Paid Artists:** 65
>**Utilizes:** Guest Conductors; Guest Artists
>**Budget:** $100,000 - $500,000
>**Income Sources:** Private Foundations/Grants/Endowments; Business/Corporate Donations; Box Office; Government Grants; Individual Donations
>**Season:** September - April **Annual Attendance:** 4,500
>**Performance Facilities:** T.G. Field Auditorium

Lubbock

INSTRUMENTAL MUSIC

LUBBOCK SYMPHONY ORCHESTRA
916 Main Street, Suite 442, Lubbock, TX 79401
(806) 762-4707
FAX: (806) 762-5776
>**Founded:** 1942
>**Arts Area:** Symphony; Orchestra; Chamber; Ensemble
>**Status:** Professional; Non-Profit
>**Type:** Performing; Educational
>**Purpose:** To bring symphonic music to Lubbock and to enrich the quality of life and music of the Lubbock Area
>**Management:** Jim Regan, Executive Director; Gurer Aykal, Music Director/Conductor
>**Paid Staff:** 3 **Volunteer Staff:** 400
>**Paid Artists:** 76
>**Utilizes:** Guest Conductors; Guest Artists
>**Budget:** $100,000 - $500,000
>**Income Sources:** Private Foundations/Grants/Endowments; Business/Corporate Donations; Box Office; Individual Donations
>**Season:** September - June **Annual Attendance:** 22,000
>**Affiliations:** ASOL; ASCAP
>**Performance Facilities:** Lubbock Memorial Civic Center; Lubbock Municipal Auditorium

PERFORMING SERIES

UNIVERSITY CENTER CULTURAL EVENTS
University Center, Texas Tech University, Lubbock, TX 79409
(806) 742-3621
>**Founded:** 1925
>**Arts Area:** Dance; Vocal Music; Instrumental Music; Theater; Lyric Opera
>**Status:** Professional; Non-Profit
>**Type:** Educational; Sponsoring
>**Purpose:** To add to the educational experience of Texas Tech students and the quality of life in the Lubbock area
>**Management:** Jennifer Lampe, Activites Spec. I; Mary Donahue, Activities Spec. IV
>**Paid Staff:** 3
>**Utilizes:** Guest Artists
>**Budget:** $100,000 - $500,000
>**Income Sources:** Box Office; Government Grants; Student Service Fees
>**Season:** September - April
>**Affiliations:** NACA; APAP
>**Performance Facilities:** Allen Theatre

FACILITY

LUBBOCK MEMORIAL CIVIC CENTER
1501 Sixth Street, Lubbock, TX 79401
(806) 762-6411
FAX: (806) 765-5803
 Type of Facility: Civic Center
 Type of Stage: Platform
 Year Built: 1977 **Architect:** The Architect Group
 Contact for Rental: (806) 762-6411
 Manager: Sandy Baker
 Lubbock Memorial Civic Center contains the Banquet Hall, Coliseum, Exhibit Hall, Municipal Auditorium and Theater.
 See separate listings for further information.

LUBBOCK MEMORIAL CIVIC CENTER - BANQUET HALL
1501 Sixth Street, Lubbock, TX 79401
(806) 762-6411
 Type of Facility: Performance Center; Multi-Purpose; Reception/party Hall
 Type of Stage: Proscenium
 Stage Dimensions: 30'Wx16'D
 Seating Capacity: 1,300
 Year Built: 1977
 Contact for Rental: (806) 762-6411
 Manager: Sandy Baker
 The entire Hall covers 14,105 square feet.

LUBBOCK MEMORIAL CIVIC CENTER - COLISEUM
Fourth and Boston, Lubbock, TX 79457
(806) 762-6411
FAX: (806) 765-5803
 Type of Facility: Performance Center; Arena; Multi-Purpose
 Type of Stage: Arena
 Seating Capacity: Reserved-7,510; Festival-10,500
 Year Built: 1977
 Contact for Rental: Sandy Baker; (806) 762-6411

LUBBOCK MEMORIAL CIVIC CENTER - EXHIBIT HALL
1501 Sixth Street, Lubbock, TX 79457
(806) 762-6411
FAX: (806) 765-5803
 Type of Facility: Multi-Purpose; Exhibition Hall
 Type of Stage: Platform
 Seating Capacity: 400
 Year Built: 1977
 Contact for Rental: (806) 762-6411
 Manager: Sandy Baker
 The Exhibit Hall contains 30,000 square feet

LUBBOCK MEMORIAL CIVIC CENTER - MUNICIPAL AUDITORIUM
Fourth and Boston, Lubbock, TX 79457
(806) 762-6411
FAX: (806) 765-5803
 Type of Facility: Auditorium; Performance Center; Multi-Purpose
 Type of Stage: Proscenium
 Stage Dimensions: 100'Wx50'D **Orchestra Pit**
 Seating Capacity: 3,015
 Year Built: 1977
 Contact for Rental: (806) 762-6411
 Manager: Sandy Baker

LUBBOCK MEMORIAL CIVIC CENTER - THEATER
1501 Sixth Street, Lubbock, TX 79457
(806) 762-6411
 Type of Facility: Theatre House
 Type of Stage: Proscenium
 Stage Dimensions: 80'Wx40'D **Orchestra Pit**
 Seating Capacity: 1,422
 Year Built: 1977

Contact for Rental: (806) 762-6411
Manager: Vick Barker
Resident Groups: Lubbock Symphony Orchestra; Ballet Lubbock; Lubbock Summer Repertory

TEXAS TECH UNIVERSITY CENTER - ALLEN THEATRE
15th and Boston, Box 42031, Lubbock, TX 79409
(806) 742-3636
FAX: (806) 742-1974
Type of Facility: Theatre House; Multi-Purpose
Type of Stage: Proscenium
Stage Dimensions: 102'Wx60'D **Orchestra Pit**
Seating Capacity: 1,006
Year Built: 1951 **Architect:** Atcheson & Atkinson
Year Remodeled: 1974 **Architect:** Atcheson & Atkinson
Contact for Rental: Bill Branan, Theatre Coordinator

TEXAS TECH UNIVERSITY CENTER - MUSIC BUILDING
15th and Boston, Box 42033, Lubbock, TX 79409
(806) 742-2270
Type of Facility: Concert Hall; Auditorium
Type of Stage: Proscenium; Platform
Orchestra Pit
Seating Capacity: Hall I - 1,000; Hall II - 600
Year Built: 1976 **Architect:** Architects III **Cost:** $5,500,000
Acoustical Consultant: C.P. Boner & Associates
Contact for Rental: Wayne Hobbs

Marshall

INSTRUMENTAL MUSIC

MARSHALL SYMPHONY ORCHESTRA
PO Box 421, Marshall, TX 75671
(903) 935-4484
Founded: 1952
Arts Area: Symphony; Orchestra
Status: Semi-Professional; Non-Profit
Type: Performing
Purpose: To allow local musicians to perform with a core of professional musicians for an audience composed of local and area lovers of symphonic music
Management: Leonard Kacenjar, Artistic Director/Conductor; Jim Bob McMillan, Management Consultant; Mona Collins, Bookkeeper
Officers: Mrs. Sam B. Hall Jr., President, Marshall Symphony Society
Paid Staff: 3 **Volunteer Staff:** 35
Paid Artists: 50 **Non-Paid Artists:** 15
Utilizes: Special Technical Talent; Guest Conductors; Guest Artists
Budget: $50,000 - $100,000
Income Sources: Private Foundations/Grants/Endowments; Business/Corporate Donations; Box Office; Individual Donations
Season: October - May **Annual Attendance:** 2,000
Affiliations: Marshall Regional Arts Council; Texas Association of Symphony Orchestras
Performance Facilities: Marshall Theater at the Civic Center

PERFORMING SERIES

MARSHALL REGIONAL ARTS COUNCIL
2501 East End Boulevard, PO Box C, Marshall, TX 75670
(903) 935-4484
FAX: (903) 938-3531
Founded: 1979
Arts Area: Dance; Vocal Music; Instrumental Music; Theater; Festivals; Grand Opera
Status: Professional; Non-Profit
Type: Educational; Sponsoring
Purpose: To encourage and support the arts in East Texas
Management: Jim Bob McMillan, Executive Director
Officers: Sandy Toussaint, President
Paid Staff: 2 **Volunteer Staff:** 10
Paid Artists: 300

Utilizes: Special Technical Talent; Guest Artists
Budget: $100,000 - $500,000
Income Sources: Private Foundations/Grants/Endowments; Business/Corporate Donations; Box Office; Government Grants; Individual Donations
Season: October - May   **Annual Attendance:** 6,000
Affiliations: APAP; NALAA; Texas Arts Council; Country Music Association
Performance Facilities: Marshall Theater at the Civic Center

FACILITY

MARSHALL CIVIC CENTER
2501 East End Boulevard South, Marshall, TX 75670
(903) 935-4472
    Type of Facility: Civic Center
    Year Built: 1984   **Architect:** George Rodgers   **Cost:** $3,700,000
    Acoustical Consultant: C.P. Boner & Associates
    Contact for Rental: Manager;   (903) 935-4472
    Resident Groups: Marshall Parks and Recreation Department; Marshall Regional Arts Council
    Marshall Civic Center contains the Marshall Theater at the Civic Center. See separate listing for further information.

MARSHALL THEATER AT THE CIVIC CENTER
2501 East End Boulevard South, Marshall, TX 75670
(903) 935-4472
    Type of Facility: Concert Hall; Auditorium; Performance Center; Theatre House; Opera House
    Type of Stage: Proscenium
    Stage Dimensions: 62'Wx58'D   **Orchestra Pit**
    Seating Capacity: 1,608
    Year Built: 1984
    Contact for Rental: Manager;   (903) 935-4472

McAllen

DANCE

RIO GRANDE VALLEY BALLET
205 Pecan Boulevard, McAllen, TX 78501
(210) 682-2721
    Founded: 1973
    Arts Area: Ballet; Jazz; Ethnic; Folk
    Status: Semi-Professional; Non-Profit
    Type: Performing; Touring; Resident; Educational; Sponsoring
    Purpose: To present top-quality Mexican Folkloric, Spanish and Flamenco; to produce the "Nutcracker" and other classic ballets to paying audiences in Rio Grande Valley; to hold "Nutcracker" matinees for schools in the Valley; to present 16 one-hour concerts at the Texas State Fair in Dallas each October
    Management: Mr. Doria Avila, Artistic Director/Executive Director; Rosemary Tatum, Executive Secretary; Deborah Martin, Director of Development and Community Support/Public School Coordinator
    Officers: Rosemary Tatum, President/Treasurer; Mr. Doria Avila, Vice President
    Paid Staff: 1   **Volunteer Staff:** 15
    Paid Artists: 12   **Non-Paid Artists:** 60
    Utilizes: Special Technical Talent; Guest Artists; Guest Choreographers
    Budget: $100,000 - $500,000
    Income Sources: Private Foundations/Grants/Endowments; Business/Corporate Donations; Box Office; Government Grants; Individual Donations
    Season: September - May   **Annual Attendance:** 38,000
    Performance Facilities: Mc Allen Civic Center; Harlingen Municipal Auditorium

INSTRUMENTAL MUSIC

VALLEY SYMPHONY ORCHESTRA & CHORALE AND VALLEY SINFONETTE
PO Box 2832, McAllen, TX 78502
(210) 381-8682
FAX: (210) 632-2352
    Founded: 1952
    Arts Area: Symphony; Orchestra; Chamber
    Status: Non-Profit
    Type: Educational
    Management: John D. Daugherty, Executive Director
    Officers: Walter Passmore, President

Paid Staff: 2
Paid Artists: 70
Utilizes: Guest Artists
Budget: $100,000 - $500,000
Income Sources: Private Foundations/Grants/Endowments; Business/Corporate Donations; Box Office; Government Grants; Individual Donations; Runout Concert Contracts
Season: September - May   **Annual Attendance:** 5,000
Affiliations: University of Texas-Pan American
Performance Facilities: UTPA Fine Arts Auditorium; McAllen Civic Center

PERFORMING SERIES

MCALLEN PERFORMING ARTS, INC.
10 North Broadway, McAllen, TX 78501
(210) 631-2545
FAX: (210) 631-8571
Arts Area: Vocal Music; Theater; Broadway Musicals
Status: Professional; Non-Profit
Type: Performing; Touring
Purpose: To provide the public with professional touring theatre productions and entertainment not available through local agencies
Management: Genevia Crow, Executive Director
Paid Staff: 1   **Volunteer Staff:** 12
Paid Artists: 5
Budget: $100,000 - $500,000
Income Sources: Box Office
Season: November - March   **Annual Attendance:** 1,300
Performance Facilities: McAllen Civic Center

RIO GRANDE VALLEY INTERNATIONAL MUSIC FESTIVAL
PO Box 2315, McAllen, TX 78502
(210) 686-1456
Founded: 1960
Arts Area: Dance; Vocal Music; Instrumental Music; Festivals; Grand Opera
Status: Non-Profit
Type: Performing; Touring; Educational; Presenting
Purpose: To present a major symphony orchestra annually, in varied concerts for students and adults, with emphasis on education of young listeners; by experiencing highly artistic musical performances, lives of area residents are culturally enriched
Officers: Dean R. Canty PhD, Chairman; Joy Judin, Vice Chairman; Carol Edrington, Secretary/Treasurer; Mildred Erhart, Financial Secretary
Volunteer Staff: 93
Paid Artists: 55   **Non-Paid Artists:** 14
Utilizes: Special Technical Talent; Guest Artists
Budget: $100,000 - $500,000
Income Sources: Private Foundations/Grants/Endowments; Business/Corporate Donations; Box Office; Government Grants; Individual Donations
Season: February   **Annual Attendance:** 12,669
Performance Facilities: McAllen International Civic Center; Rowe School Auditorium; SPI Convention Center

Mesquite

INSTRUMENTAL MUSIC

MESQUITE COMMUNITY BAND
1525 Springbrook Drive, Mesquite, TX 75149
(214) 289-6365
Founded: 1986
Arts Area: Band
Status: Non-Professional; Non-Profit
Type: Performing
Purpose: The purpose of the Mesquite Community Band is to contribute to the musical environment of the areas it serves.
Management: Elton Polk, Conductor
Volunteer Staff: 10
Non-Paid Artists: 70
Budget: $1,000 - $50,000
Income Sources: Private Foundations/Grants/Endowments; Business/Corporate Donations; Individual Donations
Season: 52 Weeks

THEATRE

MESQUITE COMMUNITY THEATRE
PO Box 850-918, Mesquite, TX 75185-0918
(214) 270-3309
Founded: 1983
Arts Area: Professional; Community; Theatrical Group
Status: Semi-Professional; Non-Profit
Type: Performing
Purpose: To have good, live theatre for the Mesquite Community
Officers: John Nichols, Chairperson
Volunteer Staff: 10
Utilizes: Special Technical Talent; Guest Artists; Guest Directors
Budget: $1,000 - $50,000
Income Sources: Private Foundations/Grants/Endowments; Business/Corporate Donations; Box Office; Government Grants; Individual Donations
Season: February - October
Performance Facilities: East Ridge Park Christian Church

Midland

INSTRUMENTAL MUSIC

MIDLAND-ODESSA SYMPHONY AND CHORALE, INC.
3100 LaForce Boulevard, PO Box 6266, Midland, TX 79711
(915) 563-0921
Founded: 1962
Arts Area: Symphony; Orchestra; Chamber; Ensemble
Status: Non-Profit
Type: Performing; Educational
Purpose: To provide symphonic, choral and chamber music for the people of the Permian Basin
Management: Don Th. Jaeger, Music Director; Philip D. West, General Manager
Officers: Jerry Caddel, President
Paid Staff: 6
Paid Artists: 80   **Non-Paid Artists:** 100
Utilizes: Guest Conductors; Guest Artists
Budget: $500,000 - $1,000,000
Income Sources: Private Foundations/Grants/Endowments; Business/Corporate Donations; Box Office; Government Grants; Individual Donations
Season: August - June
Affiliations: ASOL
Performance Facilities: Lee Auditorium; Barham Junior High School Auditorium

Nacogdoches

THEATRE

LAMP-LITE THEATER
PO Box 630466, Nacogdoches, TX 75936
(409) 564-8300
Founded: 1971
Arts Area: Musical; Community
Status: Non-Professional; Non-Profit
Type: Performing; Touring; Educational
Purpose: To bring high-quality live theatre to the east Texas area; to offer a vital creative experience to actors and other artists
Officers: Dr. Tom Nall, President; Hazel Abernathy, Vice President; Diana Haney, Treasurer; Anne Hurst, Secretary
Volunteer Staff: 60
Non-Paid Artists: 120
Budget: $1,000 - $50,000
Income Sources: Private Foundations/Grants/Endowments; Business/Corporate Donations; Box Office; Individual Donations
Season: 52 Weeks
Affiliations: Texas Nonprofit Theatre
Performance Facilities: Lamp-Lite Theater

Odessa

THEATRE

GLOBE OF THE GREAT SOUTHWEST
2308 Shakespeare Road, Odessa, TX 79761
(915) 332-1586
Founded: 1958
Arts Area: Professional; Community; Theatrical Group
Status: Non-Profit
Type: Performing; Educational
Purpose: To provide Shakespearean and classical plays that are educational; to present contemporary and religious plays and musicals; to sponsor a touring program for schools and universities; to present an annual Shakespeare Festival; to advance the enjoyment, appreciation and study of great literature; to make available the Globe Building and grounds to the community for all the arts and a convention center for the cultural and business affairs of the area
Management: Clay Francell, Executive Director; Myrtle Crane, Box Office Manager
Officers: Sue McLelland, Chairman; Mike Gieb, Vice Chairman; Shawn Watson, Secretary; Frances Dunn, Treasurer
Paid Staff: 3   **Volunteer Staff:** 5
Paid Artists: 5   **Non-Paid Artists:** 15
Utilizes: Special Technical Talent; Guest Artists; Guest Directors
Budget: $100,000 - $500,000
Income Sources: Private Foundations/Grants/Endowments; Business/Corporate Donations; Box Office; Government Grants; Individual Donations
Season: 52 Weeks   **Annual Attendance:** 11,000
Affiliations: Fine Arts Society of Texas; Texas Arts Council; Odessa Cultural Council
Performance Facilities: Globe of the Great Southwest

PERMIAN PLAYHOUSE OF ODESSA INC.
310 West 42nd, PO Box 13374, Odessa, TX 79768
(915) 362-2329
Founded: 1939
Arts Area: Community; Theatrical Group
Status: Non-Professional; Non-Profit
Type: Performing; Touring; Educational
Management: Coy L. Sharp, Artistic Director; Carla Bryant, Business Manager
Paid Staff: 6   **Volunteer Staff:** 442
Non-Paid Artists: 157
Utilizes: Special Technical Talent; Guest Conductors; Guest Artists; Guest Directors
Budget: $100,000 - $500,000
Income Sources: Private Foundations/Grants/Endowments; Business/Corporate Donations; Box Office; Government Grants; Individual Donations
Season: September - June   **Annual Attendance:** 12,280
Affiliations: AACT; SWTC; Texas Nonprofit Theater

FACILITY

GLOBE OF THE GREAT SOUTHWEST
2308 Shakespeare Road, Odessa, TX 79761
(915) 332-1586
Type of Facility: Theatre House
Type of Stage: Elizabethan
Stage Dimensions: 36'x60'
Orchestra Pit
Seating Capacity: 410
Year Built: 1958   **Architect:** J. Ellsworth Powell
Acoustical Consultant: J. Ellsworth Powell
Contact for Rental: Clay Francell;   (915) 332-1586

Orange

FACILITY

LUTCHER THEATER
707 West Main Street, Orange, TX 77630
(409) 886-5535
FAX: (409) 886-5537
Founded: 1980

Type of Facility: Theatre Complex; Concert Hall; Auditorium; Performance Center; Theatre House
Facility Originally: Nightclub
Type of Stage: Proscenium
Stage Dimensions: 45'Wx35'D   **Orchestra Pit**
Seating Capacity: 1,494
Year Built: 1979   **Architect:** Page Southerland Page   **Cost:** $8,000,000
Acoustical Consultant: Charles Boner, Boner Associates, Inc.
Contact for Rental: James Clark;   (409) 886-5535

Palestine

FACILITY

PALESTINE CIVIC CENTER COMPLEX
Highway 287-19N, Palestine, TX 75801
(903) 723-3014; (903) 729-6066
FAX: (903) 729-2083
   Type of Facility: Auditorium; Civic Center; Multi-Purpose
   Type of Stage: Proscenium
   Stage Dimensions: 52'Wx19'10"D
   Seating Capacity: 1,375
   Year Built: 1981   **Architect:** Ted Moffitt   **Cost:** $1,500,000
   Contact for Rental: Palestine Chamber of Commerce;   (903) 723-3014
   Manager: Susan Mervish

Pampa

DANCE

PAMPA CIVIC BALLET
315 North Nelson, Pampa, TX 79065
(806) 669-6361
   Founded: 1972
   Arts Area: Ballet
   Status: Non-Professional; Non-Profit
   Type: Performing; Resident; Educational; Sponsoring
   Purpose: To encourage the more gifted and dedicated dancers in the area and to offer them a performance opportunity
   Management: Jeanne M. Willingham, Artistic Director
   Officers: Mary Wilson, President; Iris Day, Vice President; Linda Holt, Secretary; Michael Epps, Treasurer; Ruth Riehart, Company Representative
   Volunteer Staff: 1
   Non-Paid Artists: 20
   Utilizes: Special Technical Talent; Guest Artists; Guest Directors; Guest Choreographers
   Budget: $1,000 - $50,000
   Income Sources: Business/Corporate Donations; Box Office; Individual Donations
   Season: September - June   **Annual Attendance:** 1,600
   Affiliations: Texas Arts Alliance
   Performance Facilities: M.K. Brown Auditorium

FACILITY

M.K. BROWN AUDITORIUM
1100 West Coronado Drive, Pampa, TX 79065
(806) 669-5790
FAX: (806) 669-5712
   Type of Facility: Civic Center
   Seating Capacity: 700
   Year Built: 1972
   Architect: Brasher, Gayetter & Repier
   Cost: $1,200,000
   Contact for Rental: Seleta Chance;   (806) 669-5790

Paris

FACILITY

PARIS JUNIOR COLLEGE
2400 Clarksville, Paris, TX 75460
(903) 785-7661
FAX: (903) 784-9370
    Founded: 1924
    Type of Facility: Auditorium
    Type of Stage: Proscenium
    Seating Capacity: 350
    Year Built: 1939   **Architect:** Bill Lightfoot
    Year Remodeled: 1975   **Architect:** B.P. Denney   **Cost:** $140,000
    Contact for Rental: Kenneth Webb; (903) 784-9433
    Manager: Ray E. Karrer
    Resident Groups: Le Troupe

Pasadena

FACILITY

SLOCOMB AUDITORIUM
8060 Spencer Highway, Pasadena, TX 77501
(713) 476-1829
    Founded: 1965
    Type of Facility: Theatre Complex; Concert Hall; Auditorium; Theatre House
    Type of Stage: Proscenium
    Stage Dimensions: 47'10" at arch; 22'Hx37'D
    Seating Capacity: 1,003
    Year Built: 1965   **Architect:** Burleson and Associates
    Year Remodeled: 1992   **Architect:** P.B.R. Architects   **Cost:** $1,000,000
    Contact for Rental: Debbie Wade; (713) 476-1863
    Resident Groups: Theatre San Jacinto; San Jacinto College School of Music

Plano

THEATRE

PLANO REPERTORY THEATRE
1028 East 15th Place, Plano, TX 75074
(214) 422-7460
    Founded: 1975
    Arts Area: Musical; Community; Theatrical Group
    Status: Non-Professional; Non-Profit
    Type: Performing; Educational
    Volunteer Staff: 30
    Non-Paid Artists: 100
    Utilizes: Guest Directors
    Budget: $50,000 - $100,000
    Income Sources: Private Foundations/Grants/Endowments; Business/Corporate Donations; Box Office; Government Grants; Individual Donations
    Season: 52 Weeks   **Annual Attendance:** 9,000
    Affiliations: Cultural Arts Council of Plano
    Performance Facilities: PRT Art Centre Theatre

Rockport

THEATRE

REPERTORY THEATER OF AMERICA
PO Box 1296, Rockport, TX 78382
(512) 729-6274
    Founded: 1967
    Arts Area: Professional; Dinner
    Status: Professional

Type: Performing; Touring
Purpose: To provide quality professional theatre to schools, colleges, clubs, and community organizations
Management: Drexel H. Riley, Director
Paid Staff: 4
Paid Artists: 12
Utilizes: Guest Directors
Budget: $100,000 - $500,000
Income Sources: Sponser Fees
Season: September - May
Affiliations: NACA

Round Top

PERFORMING SERIES

FESTIVAL AT ROUND TOP/INTERNATIONAL FESTIVAL-INSTITUTE AT ROUND TOP
Festival Institute, PO Drawer 89, Round Top, TX 78954
(409) 249-3129
FAX: (409) 249-3100
 Founded: 1971
 Arts Area: Instrumental Music; Festivals
 Status: Professional; Non-Profit
 Type: Performing; Educational
 Purpose: To conduct an intensive educational institute for young artists of demonstrated ability in the performaing arts, with particular emphasis on music; to conduct festivals, workshops, and symposia; to commission the composition and production of new music and works of art for the education of the public and the training of young artists
 Management: James Dick, Founder/Artistic Director; Richard Royall, Managing Director; Alain Declert, Director of Information; Lamar Lentz, Curator; Charles Reeves, Office Manager
 Paid Staff: 6 **Volunteer Staff:** 20
 Paid Artists: 25
 Utilizes: Guest Conductors; Guest Artists
 Budget: $100,000 - $500,000
 Income Sources: Private Foundations/Grants/Endowments; Business/Corporate Donations; Box Office; Government Grants; Individual Donations
 Season: May - August **Annual Attendance:** 12,000
 Performance Facilities: Festival Concert Hall; Menke Conference Center; W.L. Clayton House

FACILITY

INTERNATIONAL FESTIVAL-INSTITUTE AT ROUND TOP - FESTIVAL CONCERT HALL
State Highway 237 and Jaster Road, Round Top, TX 78954
(409) 249-3129
FAX: (409) 249-3100
 Founded: 1981
 Type of Facility: Concert Hall; Auditorium; Performance Center
 Type of Stage: Flexible; Proscenium; Platform
 Stage Dimensions: 70'x50'
 Orchestra Pit
 Seating Capacity: 1,200
 Year Built: 1981 **Architect:** Edward Mattingly, Dale Norton and James Dick **Cost:** $3,000,000
 Acoustical Consultant: Boner Associates
 Contact for Rental: Alain G. Declert; (409) 249-3086
 Festival-Institute is a center for intensive studies in classical music May-August. It is a conference center and site of monthly benefit concerts during the rest of the year.

San Angelo

INSTRUMENTAL MUSIC

SAN ANGELO SYMPHONY ORCHESTRA AND CHORALE
PO Box 5922, San Angelo, TX 76902
(915) 658-5877
 Founded: 1948
 Arts Area: Symphony
 Status: Professional; Non-Professional; Non-Profit
 Type: Performing
 Purpose: To promote cultural advancement and interest in the field of symphonic music in San Angelo and the vicinity

Management: Gene Chartier Smith, Music Director/Conductor; Tim Young, Manager
Officers: Tom Ridgway, President; Juanita Baker, Secretary; George Randall, Treasurer
Paid Staff: 3 **Volunteer Staff:** 45
Paid Artists: 100 **Non-Paid Artists:** 140
Utilizes: Special Technical Talent; Guest Artists
Budget: $100,000 - $500,000
Income Sources: Private Foundations/Grants/Endowments; Business/Corporate Donations; Box Office; Government Grants; Individual Donations
Season: October - July **Annual Attendance:** 25,000
Affiliations: BMI; ASCAP; ASOL
Performance Facilities: City Auditorium

VOCAL MUSIC

TWIN MOUNTAIN TONESMEN
PO Box 2711, San Angelo, TX 76902
(915) 949-0608
Founded: 1979
Arts Area: Barbershop Quartet
Status: Non-Professional; Non-Profit
Type: Performing; Resident
Purpose: As members of the National Society of Barbershop Singing, we perform this type of music around our area and in contests
Management: Mark E. Clark, Assistant Director
Officers: Laylan Bratcher, President; Nolen Mears, Executive Vice Presidents; John Parker, Secretary; Bob Gordon, Treasurer; Lanny Kiest, Program Director
Volunteer Staff: 10
Non-Paid Artists: 38
Utilizes: Guest Artists
Budget: $1,000 - $50,000
Income Sources: Private Foundations/Grants/Endowments; Box Office
Season: 52 Weeks **Annual Attendance:** 1,500
Affiliations: Cultural Affairs Council; SPEBSQSA
Performance Facilities: City Auditorium

FACILITY

ANGELO STATE UNIVERSITY - AUDITORIUM
2601 West Avenue North, San Angelo, TX 76909
(915) 942-2021
Type of Facility: Auditorium
Type of Stage: Proscenium
Orchestra Pit
Seating Capacity: 450
Year Built: 1950 **Architect:** Lovett & Sellars
Year Remodeled: 1974 **Architect:** Lovett & Sellars **Cost:** $300,000
Manager: Dr. Raymond E. Carver

ANGELO STATE UNIVERSITY - MODULAR THEATRE
2601 West Avenue North, San Angelo, TX 76909
(915) 942-2021
Type of Facility: Modular Theatre
Type of Stage: Flexible
Seating Capacity: 300
Year Built: 1975 **Architect:** Chakos Zentner Marks
Acoustical Consultant: Jules Fisher
Manager: Dr. Raymond E. Carver; (915) 942-2146

SAN ANGELO CITY AUDITORIUM
500 Rio Concho Drive, San Angelo, TX 76903
(915) 653-9577
FAX: (915) 658-1110
Type of Facility: Auditorium
Type of Stage: Proscenium
Stage Dimensions: 35'x40' **Orchestra Pit**
Seating Capacity: 1,577
Year Built: 1929
Year Remodeled: 1982 **Architect:** Barbutti **Cost:** $1,200,000
Acoustical Consultant: C.P. Boner & Associates

Contact for Rental: John L. Braswell;   (915) 653-9577
Manager: Michael McEnrue;   (915) 653-9577
Resident Groups: San Angelo Symphony; San Angelo Civic Ballet

---

San Antonio

DANCE

GUADALUPE FOLK DANCE COMPANY
c/o Guadalupe Cultural Arts Center, 1300 Guadalupe Street, San Antonio, TX 78207
(210) 271-3151
FAX: (210) 271-3480
>**Arts Area:** Modern; Folk
>**Status:** Non-Profit
>**Type:** Resident
>**Purpose:** To perform two major theatrical dance productions per year with functions interspersed throughout the year
>**Management:** Pedro Rodriguez, Executive Director
>**Officers:** Maria Elena Torralva, Chairman of the Board
>**Income Sources:** Private Foundations/Grants/Endowments; Business/Corporate Donations; Box Office; Government Grants; Individual Donations
>**Season:** 52 Weeks
>**Performance Facilities:** Guadalupe Theater

SAN ANTONIO BALLET
212 East Mulberry, San Antonio, TX 78212
(210) 736-5144
>**Founded:** 1970
>**Arts Area:** Ballet
>**Status:** Professional; Non-Profit
>**Type:** Performing; Educational
>**Purpose:** To promote the art of dance through performances and educational programs and provide for the professional development of gifted dancers
>**Management:** Vladimir Marek, Artistic Director; Nancy Smith, Administration Director
>**Officers:** Dr. D. Ford Nielsen, President; Nancy Smith, Vice President/Treasurer; Vladimir Marek, Secretary
>**Paid Staff:** 2
>**Non-Paid Artists:** 20
>**Budget:** $50,000 - $100,000
>**Income Sources:** Private Foundations/Grants/Endowments; Business/Corporate Donations; Individual Donations
>**Season:** 52 Weeks

INSTRUMENTAL MUSIC

SAN ANTONIO CHAMBER MUSIC SOCIETY
PO Box 12702, San Antonio, TX 78212
>**Founded:** 1938
>**Arts Area:** Orchestra; Chamber; Ensemble; Instrumental Group
>**Status:** Non-Profit
>**Type:** Sponsoring
>**Purpose:** To present five to six chamber music concerts per year
>**Officers:** Lyle Donaldson, President; Robert Persellin, Artists Committee
>**Volunteer Staff:** 25
>**Utilizes:** Guest Artists
>**Budget:** $1,000 - $50,000
>**Income Sources:** Private Foundations/Grants/Endowments; Business/Corporate Donations; Box Office; Individual Donations
>**Season:** September - May   **Annual Attendance:** 4,200

SAN ANTONIO SYMPHONY
222 East Houstin Street, Suite 200, San Antonio, TX 78205
(210) 225-6161
FAX: (210) 554-1008
>**Founded:** 1939
>**Arts Area:** Symphony; Orchestra
>**Status:** Professional; Non-Profit
>**Type:** Performing; Educational
>**Purpose:** To meet selected cultural, educational and entertainment needs of the South Texas Community by providing the highest possible quality professional symphony presenting orchestral music

Management: Christopher Wilkins, Music Director Designate; David Mairs, Resident Conductor; Jorge Ramirez, Director of Marketing/Public Relations; Stephanie Cavanaugh, Finance Director
Officers: Rick Lester, President
Paid Staff: 10
Paid Artists: 81
Utilizes: Guest Conductors; Guest Artists
Budget: $1,000,000 - $5,000,000
Income Sources: Private Foundations/Grants/Endowments; Business/Corporate Donations; Box Office; Government Grants; Individual Donations
Season: September - June   **Annual Attendance:** 156,000
Affiliations: ASOL
Performance Facilities: Lila Cockrell Theatre, San Antonio Convention Center; Laurie Auditorium, Trinity University

VOCAL MUSIC

TEXAS BACH CHOIR
504 Avenue E, San Antonio, TX 78215
(210) 824-6597
Founded: 1976
Arts Area: Choral
Status: Semi-Professional; Non-Profit
Type: Performing; Touring; Resident
Purpose: To perform classical sacred choral music from all periods, specializing in Baroque
Management: Daniel Long, Musical Director; John Moore, Accompanist; Samantha A. Beer, Administrator
Officers: Loula Gregg, President
Paid Staff: 3
Paid Artists: 12   **Non-Paid Artists:** 36
Utilizes: Special Technical Talent; Guest Artists
Budget: $1,000 - $50,000
Income Sources: Private Foundations/Grants/Endowments; Business/Corporate Donations; Box Office; Government Grants; Individual Donations
Season: September - May   **Annual Attendance:** 2,500
Affiliations: CA

THEATRE

GUADALUPE CULTURAL ARTS CENTER
1300 Guadalupe Street, San Antonio, TX 78207
(210) 271-3151
FAX: (210) 271-3480
Arts Area: Professional; Musical; Community; Folk; Puppet; Multi-Cultural Events
Status: Non-Profit
Type: Performing; Touring; Resident; Educational; Sponsoring; Presenting
Purpose: To present and promote Mexican-American arts; to facilitate a deeper understanding and appreciation of Latino and Native American cultures and their respective artistic expressions
Management: Pedro Rodriguez, Executive Director
Officers: Maria Elena Torralva, Chairman of the Board
Budget: $1,000,000 - $5,000,000
Income Sources: Private Foundations/Grants/Endowments; Business/Corporate Donations; Box Office; Government Grants; Individual Donations
Performance Facilities: Guadalupe Theater

JUMP-START PERFORMANCE COMPANY
1035 South Alamo, San Antonio, TX 78210
(210) 227-5867
Founded: 1985
Arts Area: Professional; Community; Theatrical Group
Status: Semi-Professional
Type: Performing; Touring; Resident; Educational; Sponsoring; Commissioning
Purpose: Jump-Start Performance Company (JSPC) was founded by a group of diverse artists to encourage and promote new ideas in performance
Management: Steve Bailey, Artistic Director; Sterling Houston, Administrator; Max Parrilla, Technical Director
Officers: Dennis Poplin, President; Cathy Pollock, Secretary
Paid Staff: 3   **Volunteer Staff:** 10
Paid Artists: 200
Utilizes: Guest Artists; Guest Directors
Budget: $50,000 - $100,000

Income Sources: Private Foundations/Grants/Endowments; Box Office; Government Grants; Individual Donations; Tuition; Sponsor Fees
Season: September - June   **Annual Attendance:** 6,000
Affiliations: AACT; ROOTS
Performance Facilities: Jump-Start Theater

SAN ANTONIO LITTLE THEATRE
800 West Ashby, San Antonio, TX 78212
(210) 735-6922
FAX: (210) 734-2651
>   **Founded:** 1912
>   **Arts Area:** Community
>   **Status:** Non-Profit
>   **Type:** Performing; Educational
>   **Purpose:** Literary and educational community theatre
>   **Management:** Francis Elborne, Managing Artistic Director; Steve Hernandez, Office Manager
>   **Officers:** Dora Hauser, President, Board of Directors; John Thuman, Vice President; Richard Taylor, Treasurer
>   **Paid Staff:** 6
>   **Utilizes:** Guest Directors
>   **Budget:** $100,000 - $500,000
>   **Income Sources:** Private Foundations/Grants/Endowments; Business/Corporate Donations; Box Office; Individual Donations
>   **Season:** September - August
>   **Affiliations:** Texas Nonprofit Theatre

24TH STREET EXPERIMENT
411 SW 24th Street, San Antonio, TX 78207
(210) 435-2103
>   **Founded:** 1981
>   **Arts Area:** Professional; Musical; Community
>   **Status:** Professional; Non-Profit
>   **Type:** Performing; Touring; Resident; Educational
>   **Purpose:** To provide professional, quality, experimental, musical and children's theatre to San Antonio and Texas, and to provide jobs for local theatre artists
>   **Management:** Richard Slocum, Artistic Director; Kevin Lechler, General Manager
>   **Officers:** Anna Hoelting, President, Board of Directors; Tina Cantu-Navarro, Vice President; Charles A. Schmidt, Secretary/Treasurer
>   **Paid Staff:** 4
>   **Paid Artists:** 20
>   **Budget:** $50,000 - $100,000
>   **Income Sources:** Private Foundations/Grants/Endowments; Business/Corporate Donations; Box Office; Government Grants; Individual Donations
>   **Season:** October - September   **Annual Attendance:** 40,000
>   **Affiliations:** Our Lady of the Lake University
>   **Performance Facilities:** Theatre West Thiry Auditorium

PERFORMING SERIES

ARTS SAN ANTONIO!
217 East Travis, San Antonio, TX 78205
(210) 226-2891
FAX: (210) 226-1981
>   **Founded:** 1981
>   **Arts Area:** Dance; Vocal Music; Instrumental Music; Theater; Festivals; Lyric Opera; Grand Opera
>   **Status:** Professional; Non-Profit
>   **Type:** Performing
>   **Purpose:** To provide a versatile program of the performing arts, including local, regional, national and international talent
>   **Management:** Frank Villani, Acting General Manager
>   **Officers:** Jon Wood, President; Elaine Dagen Bela, Chairman; Bobby Duncan, Treasurer
>   **Paid Staff:** 4   **Volunteer Staff:** 3
>   **Paid Artists:** 120
>   **Utilizes:** Special Technical Talent; Guest Conductors; Guest Artists; Guest Directors
>   **Budget:** $1,000,000 - $5,000,000
>   **Income Sources:** Private Foundations/Grants/Endowments; Business/Corporate Donations; Box Office; Government Grants; Individual Donations
>   **Season:** 52 Weeks   **Annual Attendance:** 30,000

SAN ANTONIO PERFORMING ARTS ASSOCIATION
110 Broadway, Suite 320, San Antonio, TX 78205
(210) 224-8187
>   **Founded:** 1978
>   **Arts Area:** Dance; Vocal Music; Instrumental Music; Theater; Festivals
>   **Status:** Non-Profit
>   **Type:** Sponsoring
>   **Purpose:** To present the most outstanding national and international music, dance and theatre year-round in San Antonio
>   **Management:** Margaret K. Stanley, Executive Director
>   **Officers:** Timothy L. Austin, Chairman; Woody York, President
>   **Paid Staff:** 8
>   **Utilizes:** Guest Artists
>   **Budget:** $1,000,000 - $5,000,000
>   **Income Sources:** Private Foundations/Grants/Endowments; Business/Corporate Donations; Box Office; Government Grants; Individual Donations
>   **Season:** 52 Weeks   **Annual Attendance:** 30,000
>   **Affiliations:** TCA; NEA; City of San Antonio

FACILITY

ARNESON RIVER THEATRE
418 Villita Street, San Antonio, TX 78205
(210) 299-8610
FAX: (210) 299-8444
>   **Founded:** 1940
>   **Type of Facility:** Outdoor (Concert)
>   **Type of Stage:** Greek
>   **Stage Dimensions:** 630 square feet
>   **Seating Capacity:** 800
>   **Year Built:** 1939   **Architect:** Robert Hugmann
>   **Year Remodeled:** 1988   **Architect:** Milton Babbitt   **Cost:** $290,000
>   **Acoustical Consultant:** Variable Acoustics
>   **Contact for Rental:** ;   (210) 299-8610
>   **Resident Groups:** Fiesta Noche Del Rio; Fiesta Flamenca

BEETHOVEN HALL - SAN JOSE CONVENTION CENTER
200 East Market, San Antonio, TX 78205
(210) 299-8500
FAX: (210) 223-1495
>   **Type of Facility:** Concert Hall
>   **Type of Stage:** Proscenium
>   **Stage Dimensions:** 32'Wx41'6"D; 32'Wx21'H proscenium opening
>   **Seating Capacity:** 640
>   **Year Built:** 1895
>   **Year Remodeled:** 1981
>   **Contact for Rental:** Martha Wood;   (210) 299-8500
>   *Originally built by Mannerchor, a German immigrants' vocal group*

MUNICIPAL AUDITORIUM
100 Auditorium Circle, San Antonio, TX 78205
(210) 299-8500
>   **Type of Facility:** Auditorium
>   **Type of Stage:** Proscenium
>   **Stage Dimensions:** 120'Wx54'D; 76'Wx37'H proscenium opening   **Orchestra Pit**
>   **Seating Capacity:** 5,000
>   **Year Built:** 1926
>   **Year Remodeled:** 1985   **Architect:** Phelps Garza Simmons & Baumberger   **Cost:** $13,500,000
>   **Contact for Rental:** Martha Wood;   (210) 299-8500
>   *Original Auditorium burned in 1979. It was rebuilt on the same site and was reopened in 1985.*

SAN ANTONIO CONVENTION CENTER
200 East Market Street, San Antonio, TX 78205
(210) 299-8500
>   **Type of Facility:** Theatre Complex; Theatre House; Civic Center; Arena; Multi-Purpose
>   **Type of Stage:** Proscenium; Arena
>   **Seating Capacity:** Theatre - 2,540; Arena - 15,500

Year Built: 1968
Year Remodeled: 1986   **Cost:** $32,000,000
Contact for Rental: Martha Wood, Charlotte Winans;   (210) 299-8500
Manager: Yolanda Jensen, Facilities Manager
The San Antonio Convention Center contains the Lila Cockrell Theatre. See separate listing for further information.

SAN ANTONIO CONVENTION CENTER - LILA COCKRELL THEATRE
200 East Market Street, San Antonio, TX 78205
(210) 299-8500
    Type of Facility: Theatre Complex; Concert Hall; Performance Center; Off Broadway; Theatre House; Opera House; Multi-Purpose; Room; Loft
    Type of Stage: Proscenium
    Stage Dimensions: 55'5"Wx60'D; 55'5"Wx30'H proscenium opening   **Orchestra Pit**
    Seating Capacity: 2,541
    Year Built: 1968
    Year Remodeled: 1986
    Contact for Rental: Martha Wood or Charlotte Winans;   (210) 299-8500

TRINITY UNIVERSITY - DEPARTMENT OF SPEECH AND DRAMA
715 Stadium Drive, San Antonio, TX 78284
(210) 736-8511
FAX: (210) 736-7305
    Type of Facility: Theatre Complex
    Type of Stage: Thrust; Flexible; Proscenium; Black Box
    Seating Capacity: Theater I - 235; Attic II - 110; Cafe - 80
    Year Built: 1966   **Architect:** O'Neil Ford   **Cost:** $1,250,000
    Acoustical Consultant: O'Neil Ford

TRINITY UNIVERSITY - LAURIE AUDITORIUM
San Antonio, TX 78212
(210) 736-8119
FAX: (210) 736-8100
    Type of Facility: Concert Hall; Auditorium
    Type of Stage: Flexible; Proscenium
    Stage Dimensions: 78'Wx24'D   **Orchestra Pit**
    Seating Capacity: 2,965
    Year Built: 1971   **Architect:** Ford, Powell & Carson   **Cost:** $7,000,000
    Acoustical Consultant: Jaffe Acoustics
    Contact for Rental: John McFadden;   (210) 736-8119
    No rock or rap shows

San Benito

THEATRE

DAWSON THEATRE GUILD
925 East Stenger, San Benito, TX 78586
(210) 399-5321
    Founded: 1984
    Arts Area: Dinner; Community
    Status: Non-Professional; Non-Profit
    Type: Performing; Touring; Educational
    Purpose: Enhance cultural and theatrical offerings in the Lower Rio Grande Valley
    Officers: Ivan Baker, President; Arlene Hushen, Velma de los Santon, Vice Presidents; Mickey Boland, Treasurer
    Volunteer Staff: 3
    Non-Paid Artists: 50
    Utilizes: Guest Artists; Guest Directors
    Budget: $1,000 - $50,000
    Income Sources: Private Foundations/Grants/Endowments; Business/Corporate Donations; Box Office; Individual Donations
    Season: 52 Weeks   **Annual Attendance:** 4,000
    Affiliations: Texas Nonprofit Theater
    Performance Facilities: South Padre Island Hilton; San Benito Auditorium

Seguin

FACILITY

JACKSON AUDITORIUM
1000 West Court, Seguin, TX 78155
(210) 372-8180
FAX: (210) 372-8096
> **Founded:** 1986
> **Type of Facility:** Auditorium
> **Type of Stage:** Proscenium
> **Stage Dimensions:** 45'x22' proscenium opening **Orchestra Pit**
> **Seating Capacity:** 1,050
> **Year Built:** 1986 **Architect:** Marmon Mok **Cost:** $3,000,000
> **Contact for Rental:** Susan Rinn; (210) 372-8180

Sherman

INSTRUMENTAL MUSIC

SHERMAN SYMPHONY ORCHESTRA
Austin College, Suite 61592, Sherman, TX 75091
(903) 813-2251
> **Founded:** 1966
> **Arts Area:** Symphony; Orchestra
> **Status:** Non-Professional; Non-Profit
> **Type:** Performing; Educational; Sponsoring
> **Purpose:** To provide concert performances of standard orchestral repertoire for area audiences, with guest appearances of nationally-known concert soloists
> **Management:** Dan Dominick, Conductor
> **Paid Staff:** 5 **Volunteer Staff:** 9
> **Paid Artists:** 4 **Non-Paid Artists:** 2
> **Utilizes:** Guest Artists
> **Budget:** $1,000 - $50,000
> **Income Sources:** Private Foundations/Grants/Endowments; Business/Corporate Donations; Government Grants; Individual Donations
> **Season:** September - May **Annual Attendance:** 4,000
> **Performance Facilities:** Wynne Chapel

PERFORMING SERIES

COMMUNITY SERIES, INC.
61602 Austin College, PO Box 1177, Sherman, TX 75091-1177
(903) 813-2472
FAX: (903) 813-3199
> **Founded:** 1967
> **Arts Area:** Dance; Vocal Music; Instrumental Music; Theater; Lyric Opera; Grand Opera
> **Status:** Professional
> **Type:** Educational; Sponsoring
> **Purpose:** To bring to the Sherman-Denison area the best of a diversity of music, dance and drama and to offer some events in residency and in the schools
> **Management:** Bruce G. Lunkley, Manager; Susan Brown, Assistant Manager
> **Officers:** Dr. A.J. Carlson, President; Janie Whitten, Vice President
> **Paid Staff:** 2 **Volunteer Staff:** 34
> **Paid Artists:** 60
> **Utilizes:** Guest Conductors; Guest Artists
> **Budget:** $50,000 - $100,000
> **Income Sources:** Private Foundations/Grants/Endowments; Business/Corporate Donations; Box Office; Individual Donations
> **Season:** September - May **Annual Attendance:** 7,000
> **Affiliations:** APAP; Southwest Arts Presenters Association
> **Performance Facilities:** Wynne Chapel; Richardson Center; Ida Green Theatre

Sonora

PERFORMING SERIES

THE OUTDOOR DRAMA GROUP ASSOCIATION
PO Box 1196, Sonora, TX 76950
(915) 387-3105
Founded: 1987
Arts Area: Folk
Status: Non-Profit
Type: Performing; Educational
Purpose: To plan for and create an outdoor drama depicting the heritage of Sutton County as a means of promoting tourism in order to enhance the economy
Management: Jimmy Cahill, Coordinator
Volunteer Staff: 10
Non-Paid Artists: 100
Utilizes: Guest Artists
Budget: $1,000 - $50,000
Income Sources: Business/Corporate Donations; Box Office; Individual Donations
Season: June - August **Annual Attendance:** 2,000
Performance Facilities: Caverns of Sonora

Temple

THEATRE

TEMPLE CIVIC THEATRE
2413 South 13th Street, Temple, TX 76504
(817) 778-4751
Founded: 1965
Arts Area: Community; Theatrical Group
Status: Non-Professional; Non-Profit
Type: Performing; Educational
Purpose: To promote the development of theatre arts in the community and to offer a creative outlet for the talents of the community
Management: C. Suzanne Hudson-Smith, Artistic/Managing Director; Roger Daniels, Technical Director
Officers: Dick Sweeden, President; Jody Donaldson, Vice President; Deborah Ellis, Secretary; Bill Stokes, Treasurer
Paid Staff: 3 **Volunteer Staff:** 200
Utilizes: Guest Directors
Budget: $100,000 - $500,000
Income Sources: Private Foundations/Grants/Endowments; Business/Corporate Donations; Box Office; Individual Donations
Season: 52 Weeks **Annual Attendance:** 17,000
Affiliations: TNT; SWTC

PERFORMING SERIES

CULTURAL ACTIVITIES CENTER
3011 North Third Street, Temple, TX 76501
(817) 773-9926
Founded: 1958
Arts Area: Dance; Vocal Music; Theater; Festivals; Grand Opera
Status: Professional; Semi-Professional; Non-Professional; Non-Profit
Type: Performing; Touring; Resident; Educational; Sponsoring
Purpose: The Cultural Activities Center is a creative and performing arts center that also serves as the community arts council for Temple and the surrounding area.
Management: Larry Scottfield, Executive Director; Deloris Rosen, Business Manager; Richard Phillips, Operations Manager/Technical Director; Helen Kwiatkowski, Visual Arts Director
Officers: Robert Mason, President; Marilyn Hoster, President-Elect; Marianne String Fellow, Vice President; Allan Walters, Treasurer
Paid Staff: 7
Utilizes: Guest Conductors; Guest Artists
Budget: $100,000 - $500,000
Income Sources: Private Foundations/Grants/Endowments; Business/Corporate Donations; Box Office; Government Grants; Individual Donations
Season: September - May **Annual Attendance:** 30,000
Affiliations: APAP; NALAA; ACA; Texas Arts Council

FACILITY

CULTURAL ACTIVITIES CENTER
3011 North Third Street, Temple, TX 76501
(817) 773-9926
    Type of Facility: Theatre House; Multi-Purpose; Room
    Type of Stage: Proscenium
    Stage Dimensions: 40'Wx30'D   **Orchestra Pit**
    Seating Capacity: 489
    Year Built: 1978   **Architect:** Rucker & Chamlee   **Cost:** $1,200,000
    Year Remodeled: 1984   **Architect:** Bill Chamlee   **Cost:** $300,000
    Contact for Rental: Richard Phillips, Technical Director;   (817) 773-9926
    Manager: Larry Scofield, Executive Director

TEMPLE CIVIC THEATRE
2413 South 13th Street, PO Box 3732, Temple, TX 76501
(817) 778-4751
    Type of Facility: Theatre House; Loft
    Type of Stage: Thrust; 3/4 Arena
    Stage Dimensions: 24'x18'   **Orchestra Pit**
    Seating Capacity: 249
    Year Built: 1977   **Architect:** Charles Voelter   **Cost:** $235,000
    Acoustical Consultant: C.P. Boner & Associates
    Contact for Rental: C. Suzanne Hudson-Smith;   (817) 778-4751

Texarkana

FACILITY

PEROT THEATRE
221 Main Street, Texarkana, TX 75501
(903) 792-8681
    Type of Facility: Performance Center
    Facility Originally: Vaudeville
    Type of Stage: Proscenium
    Stage Dimensions: 68'9"Wx30'D; 43'3"Wx25"H proscenium opening   **Orchestra Pit**
    Seating Capacity: 1,606
    Year Built: 1924   **Architect:** Emil Weil   **Cost:** $300,000
    Year Remodeled: 1981   **Architect:** Bell Klein Hoffman   **Cost:** $1,900,000
    Acoustical Consultant: David McCandless, Jr.
    Contact for Rental: Texarkana Regional Arts and Humanities Council;   (214) 792-8681
    Manager: Charles R. Rogers
    Resident Groups: Perot Theatre Series
The Perot Theatre, originally the Saenger Theatre, has been designated a National Historic Landmark. Cary Grant's last appearance was on the stage at the Perot Theatre.

Tyler

INSTRUMENTAL MUSIC

EAST TEXAS SYMPHONY ORCHESTRA
911 South Broadway, Tyler, TX 75701
(903) 592-1427
    Founded: 1936
    Arts Area: Symphony; Orchestra
    Status: Professional; Semi-Professional
    Type: Performing
    Purpose: To bring quality orchestral music to the East Texas area
    Management: Lloyd Roesch, Executive Director
    Officers: Andrew Morawski, President
    Paid Staff: 3
    Paid Artists: 70
    Utilizes: Guest Conductors; Guest Artists
    Budget: $100,000 - $500,000
    Income Sources: Private Foundations/Grants/Endowments; Business/Corporate Donations; Box Office; Government Grants; Individual Donations
    Season: October - April   **Annual Attendance:** 15,000

Affiliations: ASOL
Performance Facilities: Caldwell Auditorium

Victoria

PERFORMING SERIES

VICTORIA BACH FESTIVAL ASSOCIATION
PO Box 3522, Victoria, TX 77903
(512) 575-1375
Founded: 1976
Arts Area: Vocal Music; Instrumental Music; Festivals
Status: Professional; Semi-Professional; Non-Professional; Non-Profit
Type: Performing; Educational; Sponsoring
Purpose: To sponsor and promote a three to five-day festival featuring symphonic, chamber and choral works, with strong emphasis on the Baroque period
Management: Craig Johnson, Artistic Director/Conductor
Officers: Dorothy L. Welton, President; Ann V. Herbst, First Vice President; James Reinhardt, Second Vice President; Myrna L. Wallace, Secretary; E.P. Mixon, Treasurer
Volunteer Staff: 18
Paid Artists: 39
Utilizes: Guest Artists
Budget: $1,000 - $50,000
Income Sources: Private Foundations/Grants/Endowments; Business/Corporate Donations; Box Office; Government Grants; Individual Donations; Auctions; Benefit Concerts
Season: May   **Annual Attendance:** 700
Performance Facilities: First United Methodist Church

Waco

THEATRE

HIPPODROME THEATRE
724 Austin Avenue, Waco, TX 76701
(817) 752-9797
Founded: 1980
Arts Area: Professional; Musical; Theatrical Group; Puppet
Status: Non-Profit
Type: Performing; Touring; Sponsoring
Purpose: To present professional touring theatre, dance, and music groups to the Waco area and to provide a fully-equipped performing arts center for use by local performing groups
Management: Mary L. Isham, Managing Director
Officers: Brenda Marwitz, Chairman; Don Mayfield Jr., Vice Chairman; Susan Diebolt, Secretary; Derral Parks, Treasurer
Paid Staff: 3
Utilizes: Special Technical Talent; Guest Artists
Budget: $100,000 - $500,000
Income Sources: Private Foundations/Grants/Endowments; Business/Corporate Donations; Box Office; Government Grants; Individual Donations
Season: September - May
Performance Facilities: Hippodrome

FACILITY

HIPPODROME
724 Austin Avenue, Waco, TX 76701
(817) 752-9797
Founded: 1981
Type of Facility: Theatre House
Facility Originally: Vaudeville
Type of Stage: Proscenium
Stage Dimensions: 30'Wx25'D   **Orchestra Pit**
Seating Capacity: 955
Year Built: 1914
Year Remodeled: 1986   **Architect:** Bell & Hoffman   **Cost:** $2,200,000
Contact for Rental: Shelli Wright, Interim Managing Director;   (817) 752-9797

WACO CONVENTION CENTER
100 Washington Avenue, PO Box 2570, Waco, TX 76703
(817) 750-5810
    Type of Facility: Multi-Purpose; Room
    Year Built: 1971 **Architect:** Bennett Carnahan **Cost:** $3,000,000
    Year Remodeled: 1988 **Architect:** Dudley Bailey Jezek & Rose **Cost:** $2,500,000
    Contact for Rental: Emory Oney
    Waco Convention Center contains Chisholm Hall and 12 other rooms. See separate listing for further information.

WACO CONVENTION CENTER - CHISHOLM HALL
100 Washington Avenue, PO Box 2570, Waco, TX 76703
(817) 750-5810
FAX: (817) 750-5801
    Type of Facility: Multi-Purpose
    Type of Stage: Flexible; Platform
    Stage Dimensions: 60'Wx24'D
    Seating Capacity: 4,000
    Contact for Rental: Emory Oney

Wichita Falls

DANCE

WICHITA FALLS BALLET THEATRE
3412 Buchanan, Wichita Falls, TX 76308-1825
(817) 322-2552; (817) 322-5538
    Founded: 1963
    Arts Area: Modern; Ballet
    Status: Semi-Professional; Non-Profit
    Type: Performing; Touring; Resident
    Purpose: To foster the art of dance through ballet
    Management: Gari Boehm, Patricia Thornton, Co-Artistic Directors
    Officers: Joy Williams, President of the Board
    Paid Artists: 2 **Non-Paid Artists:** 18
    Utilizes: Special Technical Talent; Guest Artists
    Budget: $50,000 - $100,000
    Income Sources: Private Foundations/Grants/Endowments; Business/Corporate Donations; Box Office;
    Individual Donations
    Season: September - May
    Affiliations: SWRBA
    Performance Facilities: Memorial Auditorium

INSTRUMENTAL MUSIC

WICHITA FALLS SYMPHONY ORCHESTRA
30005 Garnett, Parker Square, Wichita Falls, TX 76308
(817) 322-4489
FAX: (817) 322-4480
    Founded: 1946
    Arts Area: Symphony; Orchestra
    Status: Non-Profit
    Type: Performing
    Purpose: To provide for our community symphonic music of the highest quality, serving as an educational organization
    for the youth of our area
    Management: Alex Rouggieri, Manager; Theodore Plute, Music Director/Conductor
    Officers: Dr. Grant Huse Wagner M.D., President
    Paid Staff: 2
    Utilizes: Guest Artists
    Budget: $100,000 - $500,000
    Income Sources: Business/Corporate Donations; Box Office; Individual Donations
    Season: October - May **Annual Attendance:** 8,000
    Performance Facilities: Memorial Auditorium

THEATRE

WICHITA FALLS BACKDOOR PLAYERS
501 Indiana, PO Box 896, Wichita Falls, TX 76307
(817) 322-5000
Founded: 1971
Arts Area: Musical; Dinner; Community; Theatrical Group
Status: Non-Profit
Type: Performing
Purpose: Producing theatre group that encourages participation from anyone interested in any aspect of theatre regardless of experience
Management: Gare Brundidge, Managing Director; Linda Bates, Business Manager
Officers: Linda Frischer, President; Rick Taylor, First Vice President; Jeanne Meharg, Second Vice President; Suzanne Russell, Secretary; Nona Bailey, Treasurer
Paid Staff: 4
Non-Paid Artists: 250
Utilizes: Special Technical Talent; Guest Artists; Guest Directors
Budget: $100,000 - $500,000
Income Sources: Private Foundations/Grants/Endowments; Box Office; Individual Donations
Season: 52 Weeks   **Annual Attendance:** 16,000

FACILITY

MEMORIAL AUDITORIUM
1300 Seventh Street, Wichita Falls, TX 76307
(817) 761-7974
Founded: 1927
Type of Facility: Auditorium
Type of Stage: Proscenium
Stage Dimensions: 60'Wx42'D   **Orchestra Pit**
Seating Capacity: 2,717
Year Built: 1927   **Architect:** Voelker & Dixon   **Cost:** $700,000
Year Remodeled: 1963   **Architect:** Pardue Reed & Dice
Acoustical Consultant: C.P. Boner & Associates
Contact for Rental: Donald M. Burkman;   (817) 761-7974
Resident Groups: Wichita Falls Ballet Theatre; Wichita Falls Symphony Orchestra

The Woodlands

FACILITY

CYNTHIA WOODS MITCHELL PAVILION
2005 Lake Robbins Drive, The Woodlands, TX 77380
(713) 363-3300
FAX: (713) 364-3011
Founded: 1990
Type of Facility: Amphitheater
Type of Stage: Proscenium
Stage Dimensions: 50'x60'   **Orchestra Pit**
Seating Capacity: 10,000
Year Built: 1990   **Architect:** Abe Sustaita   **Cost:** $9,000,000
Resident Groups: Houston Symphony

UTAH

American Fork

DANCE

UTAH REGIONAL BALLET
88 North, 350 West, PO Box 321, American Fork, UT 84003
(801) 768-8859; (801) 756-8091
    Arts Area: Ballet
    Status: Professional; Non-Profit
    Type: Performing; Touring
    Management: Jacqueline Coolidge, Artistic Director; Stoh Harston, Executive Director
    Officers: Carol Clarke, Chairman of the Board
    Paid Artists: 20
    Budget: $100,000 - $500,000
    Income Sources: Box Office; Individual Donations
    Season: September - May
    Performance Facilities: De Jong Concert Hall, BYU

Cedar City

PERFORMING SERIES

UTAH SHAKESPEAREAN FESTIVAL
351 West Center, Cedar City, UT 84720
(801) 596-7880; (801) 586-7878
    Founded: 1961
    Arts Area: Theater
    Status: Semi-Professional; Non-Profit
    Type: Performing; Resident; Educational
    Purpose: Repertory performance of six Shakespearean and classic works each summer
    Management: Fred C. Adams, Executive Producer; R. Scott Phillips, Managing Director; Cameron Harvey, Producing Artistic Director; Douglas N. Cook, Producing Artistic Director; Roger Bean, Marketing Director
    Paid Staff: 52   **Volunteer Staff:** 100
    Paid Artists: 200
    Utilizes: Special Technical Talent; Guest Artists; Guest Directors
    Budget: $1,000,000 - $5,000,000
    Income Sources: Private Foundations/Grants/Endowments; Business/Corporate Donations; Box Office; Government Grants; Individual Donations
    Season: June - September   **Annual Attendance:** 125,000
    Affiliations: ATA; URTA; TCG
    Performance Facilities: Adams Memorial Shakespearean Theatre; Randall L. Jones Theatre

Farmington

FACILITY

LAGOON OPERA HOUSE
375 North Highway 91, Farmington, UT 84025
(801) 451-0101
    Type of Facility: Theatre House
    Type of Stage: Proscenium
    Stage Dimensions: 25'Wx35'D   **Orchestra Pit**
    Seating Capacity: 300
    Year Built: 1968   **Cost:** $375,000
    Acoustical Consultant: Tim Leishman
    Contact for Rental: Ron Van Woerden; (801) 451-0101
    Meetings; small theatrical offerings. Opera House is only open during summer months, June-August.

Logan

INSTRUMENTAL MUSIC

THE CHAMBER MUSIC SOCIETY OF LOGAN, INC.
PO Box 3620, Logan, UT 84321
(801) 752-5867
> **Founded:** 1981
> **Arts Area:** Chamber
> **Status:** Non-Profit
> **Type:** Sponsoring
> **Purpose:** To present chamber music concerts
> **Officers:** Howard Carlisle, Chair; L. Grant Reese, Past Chair; Andrew Keller, Treasurer; Melva Wiebe, Secretary
> **Volunteer Staff:** 12
> **Paid Artists:** 34
> **Budget:** $1,000 - $50,000
> **Income Sources:** Private Foundations/Grants/Endowments; Business/Corporate Donations; Box Office; Government Grants; Individual Donations
> **Season:** October - April **Annual Attendance:** 1,100
> **Performance Facilities:** Harrison Auditorium

FACILITY

LYRIC THEATRE
28 West Center, Logan, UT 84321
(801) 750-1500
> **Type of Facility:** Theatre House
> **Type of Stage:** Proscenium
> **Stage Dimensions:** 21'Wx25'D; 21'Wx25'H proscenium opening
> **Seating Capacity:** 388
> **Year Built:** 1913
> **Contact for Rental:** Arlene Hoggan; (801) 750-3040
> **Resident Groups:** Old Repertory Company

UTAH STATE UNIVERSITY - CHASE FINE ARTS CENTER
Logan, UT 84322
(801) 750-3040
> **Type of Facility:** Theatre Complex; Concert Hall; Theatre House
> **Year Built:** 1966 **Architect:** Burtch W. Beall **Cost:** $2,500,000
> **Acoustical Consultant:** L.K. Levine
> **Contact for Rental:** Arlene Hoggan, Scheduling Clerk; (801) 750-3040
> *Chase Fine Arts Center contains Kent Concert Hall and Morgan Theatre. See separate listings for further information.*

UTAH STATE UNIVERSITY - KENT CONCERT HALL
Chase Fine Arts Center, Logan, UT 84322
(801) 750-3040
> **Type of Facility:** Concert Hall
> **Type of Stage:** Proscenium
> **Stage Dimensions:** 72'Wx33'D; 72'Wx20'H proscenium opening **Orchestra Pit**
> **Seating Capacity:** 2,183
> **Year Built:** 1966
> **Contact for Rental:** Arlene Hoggan, Scheduling Clerk; (801) 750-3040

UTAH STATE UNIVERSITY - MORGAN THEATRE
Chase Fine Arts Center, Logan, UT 84322
(801) 750-3040
> **Type of Facility:** Theatre House
> **Type of Stage:** Modified Thrust
> **Stage Dimensions:** 63'Wx26'D; 63'Wx25'H proscenium opening; 25'D thrust **Orchestra Pit**
> **Seating Capacity:** 711
> **Year Built:** 1966
> **Contact for Rental:** Arlene Hoggan, Scheduling Clerk; (801) 750-3040

Manti

PERFORMING SERIES

MORMON MIRACLE PAGEANT
PO Box O, Manti, UT 84642
(801) 835-2333
    Founded: 1967
    Arts Area: Theater
    Status: Non-Professional; Non-Profit
    Type: Performing; Resident
    Purpose: Portrayal of Latter-Day Saints' religious history as it relates to national events
    Management: Macksene Rux, Artistic Director
    Officers: Lee R. Barton, Chairman
    Utilizes: Guest Directors
    Income Sources: Individual Donations
    Season: July
    Performance Facilities: Manti Temple Grounds Amphitheatre

FACILITY

MANTI TEMPLE GROUNDS AMPHITHEATRE
Manti, UT 84642
(801) 835-3000
    Type of Facility: Amphitheatre
    Stage Dimensions: 300'x100'
    Seating Capacity: 18,000
    Year Built: 1885
    Manager: Lee R. Barton
    Resident Groups: Mormon Miracle Pageant

Ogden

FACILITY

DEE EVENTS CENTER
4450 Harrison Boulevard, Ogden, UT 84408
(801) 626-6666
    Type of Facility: Arena; Multi-Purpose
    Type of Stage: Flexible; Arena
    Seating Capacity: 11,615 permanent; 500 portable
    Year Built: 1977   **Cost:** $13,500,000
    Contact for Rental: Lou Johnson, Manager/Director;   (801) 626-7001

VAL A. BROWNING CENTER FOR THE PERFORMING ARTS
Weber State University, Ogden, UT 84408-1901
(801) 626-7000
FAX: (801) 626-6811
    Founded: 1965
    Type of Facility: Theatre Complex; Concert Hall; Auditorium; Outdoor (Concert); Studio Performance; Performance Center; Amphitheater; Civic Center; Multi-Purpose
    Type of Stage: Flexible; Proscenium; Amphitheatre
    Stage Dimensions: 60'x50'; 35'x45; 40'x40'flexible   **Orchestra Pit**
    Seating Capacity: 1800; 330; 200; 200
    Year Built: 1964
    Contact for Rental: Scott Jensen;   (801) 626-7000
    Resident Groups: Utah Musical Theatre; Webster State University Performing Arts Department

---
Orem

DANCE

CLOG AMERICA
PO Box 903, Orem, UT 84057
(801) 225-6450
    Founded: 1970

Arts Area: Folk
Status: Semi-Professional; Commercial
Type: Performing; Touring; Educational
Purpose: To promote clogging workshops, festivals, tours and performances throughout the USA and abroad
Management: Dennis H. Cobia, Director; D. Bryan Steele, Co-Director
Paid Staff: 1   **Volunteer Staff:** 20
Paid Artists: 150   **Non-Paid Artists:** 1,500
Budget: $1,000 - $50,000
Income Sources: Individual Donations
Season: 52 Weeks   **Annual Attendance:** 7,000
Affiliations: Utah Arts Council; National Clogging Leaders Organization
Performance Facilities: Scera Shell Amphitheatre

Payson

THEATRE

PLAYMAKERS CHILDREN'S ACADEMY OF THEATRE ARTS
PO Box 182, Payson, UT 84651
(801) 465-2752
   Founded: 1984
   Arts Area: Musical; Community; Theatrical Group; Children's
   Status: Non-Professional; Non-Profit
   Type: Performing; Resident; Educational
   Purpose: To give children a hands-on experience with as many aspects of theatre as possible
   Officers: Marilyn Crawford, President; Rose Cope, Vice President; Coco Hardle, Secretary; Valerie Massey, Treasurer; Delcia Hill, Publicity
   Paid Staff: 4
   Paid Artists: 2
   Utilizes: Special Technical Talent; Guest Directors
   Budget: $1,000 - $50,000
   Income Sources: Private Foundations/Grants/Endowments; Business/Corporate Donations; Box Office; Government Grants
   Season: June - August   **Annual Attendance:** 800

Provo

INSTRUMENTAL MUSIC

UTAH CLASSICAL GUITAR SOCIETY
1466 East 920 South, Provo, UT 84606
   Founded: 1984
   Arts Area: Chamber
   Status: Non-Profit
   Type: Performing
   Purpose: To promote the study and performance of classical guitar music in Utah
   Management: James Mahood, President; David Norton, Program Director; Stephen Hanka, Secretary
   Volunteer Staff: 5
   Paid Artists: 2   **Non-Paid Artists:** 5
   Utilizes: Guest Artists
   Budget: $1,000 - $50,000
   Income Sources: Government Grants; Individual Donations
   Season: September - June   **Annual Attendance:** 500
   Performance Facilities: First Presbyterian Church, Salt Lake City

UTAH VALLEY SYMPHONY
461 East 2875 North, Provo, UT 84604
(801) 377-6995
   Founded: 1958
   Arts Area: Symphony
   Status: Non-Professional; Non-Profit
   Type: Performing; Resident; Educational
   Purpose: To bring fine music to the Utah Valley and afford a musical outlet for the musicians of Utah County
   Management: Beverly D. Dunford, Business Manager
   Officers: Dr. Willard V. Loveridge, Board President; Dr. Duane Davis, Cornelia Madsen, Rhoda Vaun Young, Vice Presidents; Helen Robinson, Treasurer; Joyce Hooker, Secretary
   Volunteer Staff: 23

Utilizes: Guest Conductors; Guest Artists
Budget: $1,000 - $50,000
Income Sources: Box Office; Individual Donations
Season: September - April   **Annual Attendance:** 7,200
Performance Facilities: Provo LDS Tabernacle

UTAH VALLEY YOUTH SYMPHONY
PO Box 1235, Provo, UT 84603
(708) 244-2258
FAX: (708) 244-8283
Founded: 1958
Arts Area: Symphony; Orchestra; Chamber
Status: Non-Profit
Type: Performing; Touring; Educational
Purpose: To educate
Management: Brent E. Taylor, Executive Director; Britton E. Davis, Music Director
Officers: A. Harold Goodman, President
Paid Staff: 10
Utilizes: Guest Conductors; Guest Artists
Budget: $1,000 - $50,000
Income Sources: Private Foundations/Grants/Endowments; Business/Corporate Donations; Government Grants
Season: September - May   **Annual Attendance:** 5,000
Affiliations: ASOL
Performance Facilities: Symphony Hall

THEATRE

PROVO THEATRE COMPANY
3319 North University Avenue, Suite 200, Provo, UT 84604
(801) 224-3543
FAX: (801) 375-3865
Founded: 1986
Arts Area: Theatrical Group
Status: Semi-Professional; Non-Profit
Type: Performing
Purpose: High quality community theatre, focused on education, exposure and audience entertainment
Management: Charles L. Frost, Artistic Director; Richard L. Hill, Business Manager
Officers: Charles L. Frost, President; Shawn Moon, Vice President
Paid Staff: 10   **Volunteer Staff:** 65
Paid Artists: 20   **Non-Paid Artists:** 60
Utilizes: Special Technical Talent; Guest Conductors; Guest Artists; Guest Directors
Budget: $50,000 - $100,000
Income Sources: Private Foundations/Grants/Endowments; Business/Corporate Donations; Box Office; Government Grants; Individual Donations
Season: July - March   **Annual Attendance:** 15,000
Affiliations: ACTA; ATA

PERFORMING SERIES

BRIGHAM YOUNG UNIVERSITY - UNIVERSITY CONCERTS
Harris Fine Arts Center, E316, Provo, UT 84602
(801) 378-6340
FAX: (801) 378-5973
Founded: 1875
Arts Area: Dance; Vocal Music; Instrumental Music; Theater; Grand Opera
Status: Professional; Semi-Professional; Non-Profit
Type: Performing; Touring; Educational; Sponsoring
Purpose: A varied production and concert season in support of academic programs in music, dance and theatre
Management: Paul Duerden, Concert Manager
Officers: K. Newell Dayley, Chairman
Paid Staff: 8   **Volunteer Staff:** 15
Paid Artists: 15
Utilizes: Special Technical Talent; Guest Conductors; Guest Artists; Guest Directors
Budget: $100,000 - $500,000
Income Sources: Private Foundations/Grants/Endowments; Box Office; Individual Donations
Season: 52 Weeks   **Annual Attendance:** 150,000
Affiliations: APAP; WAAA
Performance Facilities: Harris Fine Arts Center, Brigham Young University

FACILITY

BRIGHAM YOUNG UNIVERSITY - HARRIS FINE ARTS CENTER
Provo, UT 84602
(801) 378-2818
FAX: (801) 378-4730
Type of Facility: Cultural Center
Type of Stage: Flexible; Proscenium; Arena
Year Built: 1964   **Architect:** William Pereira & James Langenheim
Seating Capacity: Concert Hall - 1,450; Drama Theatre - 600; Recital Hall - 425; Experimental Theatre - 325; Music Theatre - 200; Arena Theatre - 150

Saint George

INSTRUMENTAL MUSIC

SOUTHWEST SYMPHONY ORCHESTRA
2961 Jacob Hamblin Drive, Saint George, UT 84770
(801) 673-6290
Founded: 1980
Arts Area: Symphony; Orchestra
Status: Non-Professional; Non-Profit
Type: Performing; Resident; Educational
Purpose: To provide symphony concerts in the community, offer youth instruction programs and foster and develop a youth symphony
Management: Linda Sappington, General Manager
Volunteer Staff: 16
Paid Artists: 1   **Non-Paid Artists:** 65
Utilizes: Guest Artists
Budget: $1,000 - $50,000
Income Sources: Business/Corporate Donations; Box Office; Government Grants; Individual Donations
Season: September1 - June1   **Annual Attendance:** 6,000
Performance Facilities: Dixie Center Proscenium Stage

FACILITY

DIXIE COLLEGE - DIXIE CENTER
425 South 700 East, Saint George, UT 84770
(801) 628-3121
Type of Facility: Concert Hall; Auditorium; Performance Center; Theatre House; Civic Center; Arena; Room; Basketball Arena
Type of Stage: Proscenium; Arena
Stage Dimensions: 56'x45' - play area   **Orchestra Pit**
Seating Capacity: 1,200
Year Built: 1986   **Architect:** Les Stoker
Acoustical Consultant: Milo Hughes
Contact for Rental: Pam Hilton;   (801) 628-7003
Manager: Randy Lowell;   (801) 628-7003
Resident Groups: Southwest Symphony; College Band; Jazz Ensemble; Southern Utah Dance Theatre
Dixie Center contains the Proscenium Stage. See separate listing for additional information regarding Theatre/Auditorium; Convention Hall.

DIXIE COLLEGE - DIXIE CENTER PROSCENIUM STAGE
225 South 700 East, Saint George, UT 84770
(801) 628-3121
Type of Facility: Theatre House
Type of Stage: Proscenium
Seating Capacity: 1,200
Year Built: 1986
Contact for Rental: Sherm Bennett;   (801) 628-3121

DIXIE COLLEGE FINE ARTS CENTER
225 South 700 East, Saint George, UT 84770
(801) 628-3121
Type of Facility: Performance Center
Year Built: 1963   **Architect:** Rowe Smith
Contact for Rental: C. Paul Andersen;   (801) 673-4811

Resident Groups: Pioneer Courthouse Players; Southwest Symphony; Dixie College Theatre Productions; Jazz Ensemble; Southern Utah Dance Theatre; Dixie College Band
The Fine Arts Center contains the Arena Theatre and Proscenium Theatre. See separate listings for additional information.

DIXIE COLLEGE FINE ARTS CENTER - ARENA THEATRE
225 South 700 East, Saint George, UT 84770
(801) 628-3121
>**Type of Facility:** Theatre House
>**Type of Stage:** Arena
>**Seating Capacity:** 200
>**Year Built:** 1963
>**Contact for Rental:** C. Paul Andersen; (801) 673-4811

DIXIE COLLEGE FINE ARTS CENTER - PROSCENIUM THEATRE
225 South 700 East, Saint George, UT 84770
(801) 628-3121
>**Type of Facility:** Theatre House
>**Type of Stage:** Proscenium
>**Seating Capacity:** 512
>**Year Built:** 1963
>**Contact for Rental:** C. Paul Andersen; (801) 673-4811

Salt Lake City

DANCE

BALLET WEST
50 West 200 South, Salt Lake City, UT 84101
(801) 524-8300
>**Founded:** 1963
>**Arts Area:** Ballet
>**Status:** Professional
>**Type:** Performing; Touring; Resident; Educational
>**Purpose:** To present ballet performances of high quality
>**Management:** John Hart, CBE, Artistic Director; Susan Barrell, Executive Director; Kenneth O. Hill, President
>**Officers:** Richard Kieffer, Chairman; Fredric Reed, Vice Chairman; Kevin Bischoff, Secretary; Lynne Wilhelmsen, Treasurer
>**Paid Staff:** 28
>**Paid Artists:** 39   **Non-Paid Artists:** 6
>**Utilizes:** Special Technical Talent; Guest Conductors; Guest Artists; Guest Choreographers
>**Budget:** $1,000,000 - $5,000,000
>**Income Sources:** Private Foundations/Grants/Endowments; Business/Corporate Donations; Box Office; Government Grants; Individual Donations
>**Season:** June - April   **Annual Attendance:** 130,000
>**Affiliations:** Dance USA; WAAA; APAP
>**Performance Facilities:** Capitol Theatre

EASTERN ARTS ETHNIC DANCE COMPANY
PO Box 526362, Salt Lake City, UT 84152
(801) 487-9208; (801) 485-5824
>**Founded:** 1977
>**Arts Area:** Ethnic
>**Status:** Professional; Non-Profit
>**Type:** Performing; Educational; Sponsoring
>**Purpose:** To present the highest quality of authentic Eastern ethnic dance and dance masters
>**Officers:** Katherine St. John, Dance Director; Lloyd Miller, Music Director
>**Paid Staff:** 2   **Volunteer Staff:** 2
>**Paid Artists:** 8   **Non-Paid Artists:** 10
>**Utilizes:** Guest Artists
>**Budget:** $1,000 - $50,000
>**Income Sources:** Private Foundations/Grants/Endowments; Business/Corporate Donations; Government Grants; Individual Donations; Workshops; Arts Products Sales
>**Season:** October - August   **Annual Attendance:** 250,000
>**Affiliations:** WAAA; Society for Ethno-Musicology; Middle East Studies Association; Society for Dance Ethnology

REPERTORY DANCE THEATRE
PO Box 510427, Salt Lake City, UT 84151-0427
(801) 534-6345
FAX: (801) 534-6344
    Founded: 1966
    Arts Area: Modern
    Status: Professional
    Type: Performing; Touring; Resident; Educational; Sponsoring
    Purpose: To preserve old choreographies; nurturing new works and commissioning dances committed to presenting works from the full spectrum of modern dance
    Management: Kathy Johnson, General Manager; Linda C. Smith, Artistic Director; Amy Sawyer, Director of Development; Liz McClane, Booking Director; Vickie Hutter, Publicist
    Officers: Ralph Sawyer, President; B. Murphy, Vice President; John Harrington, Secretary; Carol Horton, Treasurer
    Paid Staff: 5 **Volunteer Staff:** 10
    Paid Artists: 11
    Utilizes: Guest Artists
    Budget: $100,000 - $500,000
    Income Sources: Private Foundations/Grants/Endowments; Business/Corporate Donations; Box Office; Government Grants; Individual Donations
    Season: September - August **Annual Attendance:** 10,000
    Performance Facilities: Capitol Theatre; Local Festival Auditorium

RIRIE-WOODBURY DANCE COMPANY
200 South 50 West, Salt Lake City, UT 84101
(801) 328-1062
FAX: (801) 359-3504
    Founded: 1963
    Arts Area: Modern
    Status: Professional; Non-Profit
    Type: Performing; Touring; Resident; Educational; Sponsoring
    Management: Joan Woodbury, Shirley Ririe, Artistic and Co-Directors; Francis McGovern, Executive Director
    Officers: Kathy Black, Office Manager; Jena Thompson, Outreach/Marketing Director; Greg Gielmann, Company Manager
    Paid Staff: 6 **Volunteer Staff:** 20
    Paid Artists: 9
    Utilizes: Special Technical Talent; Guest Conductors; Guest Artists; Guest Directors; Guest Choreographers
    Income Sources: Private Foundations/Grants/Endowments; Business/Corporate Donations; Box Office; Government Grants; Individual Donations
    Season: Fall - Spring **Annual Attendance:** 2,000
    Performance Facilities: Capital Theatre

INSTRUMENTAL MUSIC

CHAMBER MUSIC SOCIETY OF SALT LAKE CITY
PO Box 58825, Salt Lake City, TN
(801) 583-9264
    Founded: 1966
    Arts Area: Chamber
    Status: Non-Profit
    Type: Sponsoring
    Purpose: To present an annual series of recitals by world-class chamber music ensembles
    Officers: Gwen Hovey, President; Carter Foss, Vice President; Paul Griffin, Treasurer; Kathleen Rice, Secretary
    Volunteer Staff: 20
    Utilizes: Guest Artists
    Income Sources: Private Foundations/Grants/Endowments; Individual Donations; Membership Fees
    Season: November - May
    Performance Facilities: Museum of Fine Arts, University of Utah

GRANITE YOUTH SYMPHONY
340 East 3545 South, Salt Lake City, UT 84115
(801) 268-8542
FAX: (801) 263-6128
    Founded: 1957
    Arts Area: Symphony; Orchestra; Instrumental Group
    Status: Non-Profit
    Type: Performing; Touring; Educational
    Purpose: Study and performance of standard symphonic literature

Management: Ellis C. Worthen, PhD Staff Associate, Music Education, Granite School District
Paid Staff: 4
Paid Artists: 1
Utilizes: Guest Conductors; Guest Artists
Budget: $1,000 - $50,000
Season: September - July   **Annual Attendance:** 10,000
Affiliations: Granite School District

UTAH SYMPHONY
123 West South Temple, Salt Lake City, UT 84101
(801) 533-5626
FAX: (801) 521-6634
Founded: 1940
Arts Area: Symphony
Status: Professional; Non-Profit
Type: Performing; Educational
Purpose: To maintain a symphony orchestra capable of providing performances of the highest possible quality; to provide performance opportunities for skilled professional musicians; to foster musical education for persons of all ages
Management: Joseph Silverstein, Music Director; Robert Henderson, Associate Conductor; Paul L. Chummers, Executive Director
Officers: Ken Knight, Chairman of the Board
Paid Staff: 20
Paid Artists: 85
Utilizes: Guest Conductors; Guest Artists; Guest Directors
Budget: $5,000,000 - $10,000,000
Income Sources: Private Foundations/Grants/Endowments; Business/Corporate Donations; Box Office; Government Grants; Individual Donations
Season: 52 Weeks   **Annual Attendance:** 450,000
Affiliations: ASOL; AAA
Performance Facilities: Symphony Hall

UTAH YOUTH SYMPHONY
204 Gardner Hall, University Of Utah, Salt Lake City, UT 84112
(801) 485-5252
Founded: 1959
Arts Area: Symphony
Status: Non-Professional; Non-Profit
Type: Performing
Purpose: To rehearse and perform original master works from the orchestral repertoire under professional leadership
Management: Barbara Ann Scowcroft, Music Director
Officers: Lynn Larson, President
Paid Staff: 1   **Volunteer Staff:** 10
Non-Paid Artists: 85
Utilizes: Guest Artists
Budget: $1,000 - $50,000
Income Sources: Business/Corporate Donations; Individual Donations
Season: September - June   **Annual Attendance:** 1,500
Performance Facilities: 200 Gardner Hall

VOCAL MUSIC

MORMON TABERNACLE CHOIR
50 East North Temple Street, Salt Lake City, UT 84150
(801) 531-3221
Founded: 1847
Arts Area: Choral
Status: Non-Professional; Non-Profit
Type: Performing; Touring; Resident
Purpose: To serve as a public relations organization of The Church of Jesus Christ of Latter-day Saints performing in Salt Lake City and on tours, both national and international; to represent the Latter-day Saints Church and, at times, the United States of America
Management: Jerold D. Ottley, Director; Donald Ripplinger, Associate Director; Richard Elliott, John Longhurst, Clay Christiansen, Organists
Officers: Wendell M. Smoot, President; Udell Poulsen, Manager; Herold Gregory, Adminisrative Assistant
Paid Staff: 5   **Volunteer Staff:** 15
Non-Paid Artists: 325
Utilizes: Guest Conductors; Guest Artists
Income Sources: Private Foundations/Grants/Endowments; Business/Corporate Donations; Individual Donations
Season: 52 Weeks

Affiliations: Utah Symphony; Church of Jesus Christ of Latter-day Saints
Performance Facilities: Mormon Tabernacle

ORATORIO SOCIETY OF UTAH
PO Box 11714, Salt Lake City, UT 84147
(801) 943-3416
Founded: 1915
Arts Area: Choral
Status: Semi-Professional; Non-Profit
Type: Performing; Touring
Purpose: Oratorio music and cultural exchanges to other countries
Officers: Richard G. Horak, President
Volunteer Staff: 20
Paid Artists: 20 **Non-Paid Artists:** 250
Utilizes: Guest Conductors; Guest Artists
Budget: $50,000 - $100,000
Income Sources: Private Foundations/Grants/Endowments; Business/Corporate Donations; Box Office; Government Grants; Individual Donations
Season: 52 Weeks **Annual Attendance:** 10,000

SALT LAKE OPERA THEATRE
44 West Broadway, Suite 807-S, Salt Lake City, UT 84101
(801) 965-4147
Arts Area: Grand Opera; Lyric Opera; Light Opera; Operetta; Choral
Status: Semi-Professional; Non-Profit
Type: Performing; Touring
Purpose: To serve the community with quality opera and light opera at reasonable prices; to provide a launching opportunity for aspiring artists
Management: Robert Zabriskie, General Director; Robert Van Wagenen, Assistant; Columb Robinson, Artistic Director
Officers: Guy Curtis, Orchestra Manager; Brian Johnson, Orchestra Contract Manager; Beverly Zabriskie, Secretary
Volunteer Staff: 6
Non-Paid Artists: 90
Utilizes: Special Technical Talent; Guest Artists; Guest Directors
Budget: $1,000 - $50,000
Income Sources: Private Foundations/Grants/Endowments; Business/Corporate Donations; Box Office; Government Grants; Individual Donations
Season: September - June **Annual Attendance:** 3,000
Performance Facilities: Kingbury Hall; Judge Memorial Auditorium

SALT LAKE SYMPHONIC CHOIR
PO Box 45, Salt Lake City, UT 84110
(801) 466-8701
Founded: 1959
Arts Area: Choral
Status: Professional; Non-Profit
Type: Performing; Touring
Purpose: To present choral concerts throughout the world, "a choral adventure from Bach to rock"
Management: Richard M. Taggart, Manager; George Welch, Choral Director
Officers: Richard M. Taggart, President; Greg Bettinson, Vice President; Bethne Hickcox, Secretary
Budget: $1,000 - $50,000
Income Sources: Private Foundations/Grants/Endowments; Business/Corporate Donations; Box Office; Government Grants; Individual Donations
Season: September - May

UTAH OPERA COMPANY
50 West 200 South, Salt Lake City, UT 84101
(801) 534-0842
FAX: (801) 359-3504
Founded: 1978
Arts Area: Grand Opera; Light Opera
Status: Professional; Non-Profit
Type: Performing; Resident; Educational
Purpose: To present quality productions of standard opera repertoire for the community and as an educational enterprise
Management: Leslie Peterson, Director of Operations; Anne Ewers, General Director; Lynn Jemison-Renner, Music Administration
Officers: David T. Mortensen, Chairman
Paid Staff: 10 **Volunteer Staff:** 2
Paid Artists: 100 **Non-Paid Artists:** 30
Utilizes: Special Technical Talent; Guest Conductors; Guest Artists; Guest Directors

Budget: $1,000,000 - $5,000,000
Income Sources: Private Foundations/Grants/Endowments; Business/Corporate Donations; Box Office; Government Grants; Individual Donations
Season: October - May   **Annual Attendance:** 30,000
Affiliations: OA; AAA; Utah Arts Council; Salt Lake City Arts Council
Performance Facilities: Capitol Theatre

THEATRE

PIONEER THEATRE COMPANY
University of Utah, Salt Lake City, UT 84112
(801) 581-7118
FAX: (801) 581-5472
Founded: 1962
Arts Area: Professional; Theatrical Group
Status: Professional; Non-Profit
Type: Performing; Educational
Purpose: Committed to quality professional theater for Utah and the northwestern United States
Management: Charles Morey, Artistic Director; Christopher Lino, Managing Director; Susan Koles, Audience Development Director
Paid Staff: 20
Utilizes: Special Technical Talent; Guest Artists; Guest Directors
Budget: $1,000,000 - $5,000,000
Income Sources: Private Foundations/Grants/Endowments; Business/Corporate Donations; Box Office; Government Grants; Individual Donations
Season: September - May
Affiliations: AEA; LORT
Performance Facilities: Pioneer Memorial Theater

THE SALT LAKE ACTING COMPANY
168 West 500 North, Salt Lake City, UT 84103
(801) 363-0526
FAX: (801) 363-8681
Founded: 1977
Arts Area: Professional; Theatrical Group
Status: Professional; Non-Profit
Type: Performing
Purpose: To present a unique and innovative repertoire of plays and regional premieres to the city; to support new works and develop a community of artists; to make a contribution to the American professional theater
Management: Edward J. Gryska, Producing Artistic Director; Victoria Panella, Managing Director
Paid Staff: 8
Paid Artists: 70
Utilizes: Guest Artists; Guest Directors
Budget: $500,000 - $1,000,000
Income Sources: Private Foundations/Grants/Endowments; Business/Corporate Donations; Box Office; Government Grants; Individual Donations
Season: September - July
Annual Attendance: 25,000
Affiliations: TCG
Performance Facilities: The Salt Lake Acting Company Theater

SUNDANCE INSTITUTE
PO Box 16450, Salt Lake City, UT 84116
(801) 328-3456
FAX: (801) 575-5175
Founded: 1981
Arts Area: Professional; Film
Status: Professional; Non-Profit
Type: Educational
Purpose: To support the development of emerging filmmakers; to exhibit new, independent dramatic and documentary films
Management: Nicole Guillemet, Director of Administration; Geoff Gilmore, Program Director; Michelle Satter, Director of Feature Film Programming
Officers: Robert Redford, President; Gary Beer, Executive Vice President
Paid Staff: 7   **Volunteer Staff:** 50
Budget: $1,000,000 - $5,000,000

Income Sources: Private Foundations/Grants/Endowments; Business/Corporate Donations; Box Office; Government Grants; Individual Donations
Season: 52 Weeks

PERFORMING SERIES

THE GINA BACHAUER INTERNATIONAL PIANO FOUNDATION
PO Box 11664, #5 Triad Center, Suite 515, Salt Lake City, UT 84147
(801) 521-9200
FAX: (801) 521-9202
Founded: 1976
Arts Area: Instrumental Music; Festivals
Status: Non-Profit
Type: Performing; Educational; Sponsoring
Purpose: To further the pianistic art by holding international piano competitions, solo recitals and educational sessions; to enrich the community and build an artistic and educational environment for musicians and non-musicians alike
Management: Andrea Barnes, General Manager; Paul Pollei, Artistic Director/Founder
Officers: Robert W. Mendenhall, Chairman; Arlene Darger, Vice Chairman; Kent M. Acomb, Treasurer; Linda Babcock, Secretary; Andrea Barnes, Ex-Officio Member
Paid Staff: 3 **Volunteer Staff:** 3
Utilizes: Guest Artists
Budget: $100,000 - $500,000
Income Sources: Private Foundations/Grants/Endowments; Business/Corporate Donations; Box Office; Government Grants; Individual Donations
Performance Facilities: Symphony Hall; Salt Lake City Assembly Hall; Temple Square

FACILITY

CAPITOL THEATRE
48 West Second South, Salt Lake City, UT 84101
(801) 534-6660
FAX: (801) 538-2272
Type of Facility: Theatre House; Opera House
Type of Stage: Proscenium
Stage Dimensions: 100'Wx48'D; 43'6"Wx40'3"H proscenium opening **Orchestra Pit**
Seating Capacity: 1927
Year Built: 1913 **Architect:** G. Albert Lansburg
Year Remodeled: 1978 **Architect:** Steven T. Baird **Cost:** $5,000,000
Contact for Rental: Marion Iwasaki; (801) 534-6364
Resident Groups: Ballet West; Utah Opera Company; Ririe-Woodbury Company

SYMPHONY HALL
123 West South Temple, Salt Lake City, UT 84101
(801) 534-6660
Type of Facility: Concert Hall
Type of Stage: Proscenium
Stage Dimensions: 72'Wx36'D; 72'Wx36'H proscenium opening
Seating Capacity: 2,801
Year Built: 1976 **Architect:** FFKR/Architects **Cost:** $12,000,000
Acoustical Consultant: Dr. Cyril Harris
Contact for Rental: Marion Vigio; (801) 534-6364
Manager: Samuel Driggs
Resident Groups: Utah Symphony Orchestra

UNIVERSITY OF UTAH - KINGSBURY HALL
Salt Lake City, Salt Lake City, UT 84112
(801) 581-6261
Type of Facility: Concert Hall; Auditorium; Theatre House; Opera House
Type of Stage: Greek; Proscenium; Platform
Stage Dimensions: 46'x59'x29' **Orchestra Pit**
Seating Capacity: 1,917
Year Built: 1929 **Architect:** Raymond Evans
Contact for Rental: Linda Christenson; (801) 581-6261
Resident Groups: University of Utah Music Department Ensembles; University of Utah Ballet and Modern Dance Companies

Sundance

THEATRE

THE SUNDANCE CHILDREN'S THEATRE
Rural Route 3, PO Box 624-D, Sundance, UT 84604
(801) 225-4107
FAX: (801) 225-3096
Founded: 1990
Arts Area: Professional; Theatrical Group
Status: Professional; Semi-Professional; Non-Profit
Type: Performing; Touring
Purpose: To develop and produce new plays for young audiences
Management: David Kirk Chambers, Managing Director; Jerry Parch, Artistic Director
Paid Staff: 2
Utilizes: Guest Artists; Guest Directors
Budget: $100,000 - $500,000
Income Sources: Private Foundations/Grants/Endowments; Business/Corporate Donations; Box Office; Government Grants; Individual Donations
Season: June - October   **Annual Attendance:** 30,000

VERMONT

Barre

VOCAL MUSIC

VERMONT OPERA THEATER
PO Box 1030, Barre, VT 05641
(802) 223-5801
>**Arts Area:** Lyric Opera; Light Opera; Operetta
>**Status:** Semi-Professional; Non-Profit
>**Type:** Performing; Educational
>**Officers:** Naomi Flanders, President; Ken Carter, Vice President; Ellen Pitkin, Treasurer; Debbie Quick, Secretary; Mark W. Hall, Artistic Director
>**Budget:** $1,000 - $50,000
>**Income Sources:** Business/Corporate Donations; Box Office; Government Grants; Individual Donations

FACILITY

BARRE OPERA HOUSE
12 North Main Street, PO Box 583, Barre, VT 05641
(802) 476-8188
>**Type of Facility:** Concert Hall; Theatre House; Opera House
>**Type of Stage:** Proscenium
>**Stage Dimensions:** 59'Wx34'D; 35'Wx22'H proscenium opening   **Orchestra Pit**
>**Seating Capacity:** 434
>**Year Built:** 1899   **Architect:** Charles Adams
>**Year Remodeled:** 1984   **Architect:** Robert Burley   **Cost:** $500,000
>**Contact for Rental:** Don Hirsch;   (802) 476-8188
>**Resident Groups:** Vermont Opera Theatre; Vermont Philharmonic Orchestra; Vermont Symphony Orchestra; Barre Players; Centerstage Company
>*The Opera House has been designated a National Historic Landmark and is a member theatre of the League of Historic American Theatres.*

Bennington

THEATRE

OLDCASTLE THEATRE COMPANY
PO Box 1555, Bennington, VT 05201
(802) 447-0564
>**Founded:** 1972
>**Arts Area:** Professional; Musical; Theatrical Group
>**Status:** Professional; Non-Profit
>**Type:** Performing; Touring; Resident; Educational; Sponsoring
>**Purpose:** Full-time professional theatre currently in residence at Southern Vermont College in Bennington
>**Management:** Eric Peterson, Producing Director; Shelli DuBoff, Richard Howe, Associate Artistic Directors; Deborah Woodward, General Manager
>**Officers:** Thomas Steffen, Board President
>**Paid Staff:** 6   **Volunteer Staff:** 30
>**Utilizes:** Guest Artists; Guest Directors
>**Budget:** $100,000 - $500,000
>**Income Sources:** Private Foundations/Grants/Endowments; Business/Corporate Donations; Box Office; Government Grants; Individual Donations
>**Season:** 52 Weeks   **Annual Attendance:** 10,000
>**Performance Facilities:** Southern Vermont College Theatre

Brattleboro

VOCAL MUSIC

BLANCHE MOYSE CHORALE
15 Walnut Street, Brattleboro, VT 05301
(802) 257-4523
>**Founded:** 1976
>**Arts Area:** Choral

Status: Non-Professional; Non-Profit
Type: Performing; Touring; Resident
Purpose: To perform the music of J.S. Bach as the resident choral ensemble of the New England Bach Festival; to tour with programs of a cappella works from all periods
Management: Blanche Honegger Moyse, Conductor; Zon Eastes, Manager
Officers: Beth-Ann Betz, President
Paid Staff: 1 **Volunteer Staff:** 2
Non-Paid Artists: 36
Budget: $1,000 - $50,000
Income Sources: Private Foundations/Grants/Endowments; Business/Corporate Donations; Box Office; Individual Donations
Season: 52 Weeks **Annual Attendance:** 5,000
Performance Facilities: Persons Auditorium, Marlboro College; First Baptist Church

THEATRE

NATIONAL MARIONETTE THEATRE
82 Putney Road, Bratleboro, VT 05301
(802) 257-3090
> **Founded:** 1968
> **Arts Area:** Professional; Theatrical Group; Puppet
> **Status:** Professional; Non-Profit
> **Type:** Performing; Touring
> **Management:** David Syrotiak, Artistic Director
> **Paid Staff:** 6 **Volunteer Staff:** 15
> **Paid Artists:** 6
> **Utilizes:** Special Technical Talent
> **Budget:** $100,000 - $500,000
> **Income Sources:** Private Foundations/Grants/Endowments; Business/Corporate Donations; Box Office
> **Season:** September - May
> **Affiliations:** APAP; NECA; New England Arts Foundation

PERFORMING SERIES

BRATTLEBORO MUSIC CENTER
15 Walnut Street, Brattleboro, VT 05301
(802) 257-4523
> **Founded:** 1952
> **Arts Area:** Vocal Music; Instrumental Music; Festivals
> **Status:** Non-Profit
> **Type:** Performing; Sponsoring
> **Management:** Zon Eastes, Managing Director
> **Paid Staff:** 4 **Volunteer Staff:** 10
> **Paid Artists:** 100 **Non-Paid Artists:** 100
> **Utilizes:** Guest Artists
> **Budget:** $100,000 - $500,000
> **Income Sources:** Private Foundations/Grants/Endowments; Box Office; Government Grants; Individual Donations
> **Season:** September - June **Annual Attendance:** 12,000

Burlington

DANCE

VERMONT BALLET THEATRE
PO Box 5069, Burlington, VT 05402
(802) 862-6466
> **Founded:** 1985
> **Arts Area:** Ballet
> **Status:** Professional; Non-Profit
> **Type:** Performing; Touring; Educational
> **Purpose:** A company of ten professional dancers performing classical and contemporary repertory in concerts with lecture demonstrations throughout the Northeast
> **Management:** Angela Whitehill, Artistic Director; James Whitehill, Technical Director; William Noble, Director, Public Relations; Arthur Leeth, Ballet Master
> **Officers:** Ralph Carbo, President; Rena Chernick, Vice President; Carolyn Singer, Secretary; Kathy Brunovski, Treasurer
> **Paid Staff:** 2 **Volunteer Staff:** 2
> **Paid Artists:** 10
> **Utilizes:** Guest Choreographers

Budget: $1,000 - $50,000
Income Sources: Private Foundations/Grants/Endowments; Business/Corporate Donations; Box Office; Government Grants; Individual Donations
Season: April - November

INSTRUMENTAL MUSIC

HEXAGON
c/o Melvin Kaplan Inc., 115 College Street, Burlington, VT 05401
FAX: (802) 658-6089
    Arts Area: Chamber; Ensemble
    Status: Professional
    Type: Performing
    Purpose: An ensemble of five winds and piano that performs masterworks from Mozart to Poulenc as well as new compositions for wind and piano combinations
    Management: Melvin Kaplan, Manager
    Income Sources: Box Office; Government Grants
    Season: 52 Weeks

LA FAMILLE BEAUDOIN - FAMILY GROUP
14 Lyman Avenue, Burlington, VT 05401
(802) 862-5076
    Founded: 1972
    Arts Area: Ethnic
    Status: Non-Professional
    Type: Performing
    Purpose: To promote and perpetuate French Canadian folklore music
    Management: Wilfred J. Beaudoin, Leader
    Paid Artists: 5
    Income Sources: Private Foundations/Grants/Endowments
    Season: April - October
    Affiliations: Vermont Council of the Arts

VERMONT SYMPHONY ORCHESTRA
2 Church Street, Burlington, VT 05401
(802) 864-5741
    Founded: 1934
    Arts Area: Symphony; Ensemble
    Status: Professional; Non-Profit
    Type: Performing; Touring; Educational
    Purpose: To provide high quality live classical music to all the areas of the state
    Management: Thomas Philion, General Manager; Frances Combs, Office Manager; Natalie Nevert, Marketing and Production Coordinator; Kate Tamarkin, Music Director
    Officers: Wayne Granquist, President
    Paid Staff: 4
    Paid Artists: 65
    Utilizes: Guest Artists
    Budget: $500,000 - $1,000,000
    Income Sources: Private Foundations/Grants/Endowments; Business/Corporate Donations; Box Office; Government Grants; Individual Donations
    Season: 52 Weeks   **Annual Attendance:** 60,000
    Affiliations: ASCAP; BMI
    Performance Facilities: Flynn Theatre

VERMONT YOUTH ORCHESTRA
PO Box 905, Burlington, VT 05402
(802) 862-6732
    Founded: 1964
    Arts Area: Symphony; Orchestra
    Status: Non-Professional; Non-Profit
    Type: Performing; Educational
    Purpose: To bring music to young people, especially classical
    Management: Carolyn Long, Manager; David Dworkin, Music Director/Conductor
    Officers: Burlington Friends of Music
    Paid Staff: 2   **Volunteer Staff:** 10
    Non-Paid Artists: 85
    Utilizes: Guest Conductors
    Budget: $1,000 - $50,000

Income Sources: Private Foundations/Grants/Endowments; Business/Corporate Donations; Box Office; Government Grants; Individual Donations
Season: August - May   **Annual Attendance:** 4,000
Affiliations: ASOL (Youth Orchestra Division)
Performance Facilities: Flynn Theatre

PERFORMING SERIES

DISCOVER JAZZ FESTIVAL
153 Main Street, Burlington, VT 05401
(802) 863-7992
Founded: 1983
Arts Area: Vocal Music; Instrumental Music; Festivals
Status: Non-Profit
Type: Performing; Educational; Sponsoring
Purpose: To offer the widest possible diversity of jazz
Management: James P. Swift, Director
Officers: Andrea Rogers, Director Flynn Theatre for the Performing Arts; Susan Green, Burlington City Arts
Budget: $50,000 - $100,000
Income Sources: Private Foundations/Grants/Endowments; Business/Corporate Donations; Box Office; Government Grants; Individual Donations
Season: June   **Annual Attendance:** 25,000
Affiliations: Burlington City Arts; Flynn Theatre

VERMONT MOZART FESTIVAL
PO Box 512, Burlington, VT 05402
(802) 862-7352
Founded: 1973
Arts Area: Vocal Music; Instrumental Music; Festivals
Status: Professional; Non-Profit
Type: Performing
Purpose: To provide high-quality chamber music to Vermont in various picturesque settings
Management: Joy Facos, Manager; Mary Madigan, General Manager; Rhoda Rowell, Assistant Manager
Paid Staff: 2   **Volunteer Staff:** 400
Paid Artists: 75
Utilizes: Special Technical Talent; Guest Conductors; Guest Artists; Guest Directors
Budget: $100,000 - $500,000
Income Sources: Private Foundations/Grants/Endowments; Business/Corporate Donations; Box Office; Government Grants; Individual Donations
Season: July - March   **Annual Attendance:** 16,000
Affiliations: Greater Burlington Performing Arts Council

FACILITY

BURLINGTON MEMORIAL AUDITORIUM
250 Main Street, Burlington, VT 05401
(802) 864-6044
Type of Facility: Concert Hall; Auditorium; Studio Performance; Performance Center; Multi-Purpose; Loft; Multi-Purpose Building
Type of Stage: Proscenium; Gymnasium
Seating Capacity: 2,500
Year Built: 1928
Contact for Rental: (802) 864-6044

FLYNN THEATRE FOR THE PERFORMING ARTS
153 Main Street, Burlington, VT 05401-8402
(802) 863-8778
Type of Facility: Concert Hall; Performance Center; Theatre House; Multi-Purpose
Facility Originally: Vaudeville; Movie House
Type of Stage: Proscenium
Stage Dimensions: 85'Wx24'D; 48'Wx29'H proscenium opening   **Orchestra Pit**
Seating Capacity: 1,454
Year Built: 1930   **Architect:** Mowll & Rand
Year Remodeled: 1989   **Architect:** Wiemann & Camphere, Ashok Bhaunani, Roland Batten   **Cost:** $2,000,000
Contact for Rental: Philip Bither;   (802) 863-8778
Manager: Andrea Rogers, Executive Director;   (802) 863-8778
Resident Groups: Lyric Theatre; Vermont Symphony Orchestra; Vermont Youth Orchestra; Flynn Theatre Presentations

UNIVERSITY OF VERMONT - RECITAL HALL
Music Building, Redstone Campus - South Prospect Street, Burlington, VT 05405
(802) 656-3040
   Type of Facility: Concert Hall
   Type of Stage: Concert Stage
   Stage Dimensions: 40'x36'x26'
   Seating Capacity: 300
   Year Built: 1974   **Architect:** Burlington Associates   **Cost:** $1,400,000
   Acoustical Consultant: Bolt, Beranek & Newman
   Manager: Jane Ambrose
   Resident Groups: University Music Department student and faculty ensembles; Lane Series

Craftsbury

INSTRUMENTAL MUSIC

CRAFTSBURY CHAMBER PLAYERS
PO Box 37, Craftsbury, VT 05826
(802) 586-2822
   Founded: 1966
   Arts Area: Chamber
   Status: Non-Profit
   Type: Performing; Touring; Educational
   Purpose: To present a variety of chamber music to a wide section of audiences in northern Vermont
   Management: Mary Anthony Cox, Executive Director
   Officers: Morrow Decker, President; Andrea Brightenback, Secretary
   Paid Staff: 3   **Volunteer Staff:** 50
   Utilizes: Guest Artists
   Budget: $1,000 - $50,000
   Income Sources: Private Foundations/Grants/Endowments; Business/Corporate Donations; Box Office;
   Individual Donations
   Season: July - August   **Annual Attendance:** 2,550
   Affiliations: Vermont Council on the Arts; Vermont Touring Artists Registry
   Performance Facilities: Hardwick Town House; Alumni Auditorium, Champlain College, Burlington; Recital Hall,
   Redstone Campus, University of Vermont, Burlington

Dorset

THEATRE

AMERICAN THEATRE WORKS, INC.
PO Box 519, Dorset, VT 05251
(802) 867-2223
FAX: (802) 867-0144
   Founded: 1976
   Arts Area: Professional; Summer Stock
   Status: Professional; Non-Profit
   Type: Performing; Resident; Educational; Publishing
   Purpose: Summer production season of five plays; writers' colony; youth theatre program; publisher of national
   theatre directories
   Management: Jill Charles, Artistic Director; John Nassivera, Producing Director; C. Barrack Evans, Managing Director;
   Gene Sirotof, Publications Manager
   Officers: Sally Brown, President of Board of Trustees; Paul Wheeler Jr., Vice President; Michael Scelsi, Treasurer;
   Dr. Maxine Bernstein, Secretary
   Paid Staff: 15
   Paid Artists: 30
   Utilizes: Special Technical Talent; Guest Artists
   Budget: $100,000 - $500,000
   Income Sources: Private Foundations/Grants/Endowments; Business/Corporate Donations; Box Office; Government
   Grants; Individual Donations; Publications Sales
   Season: June - September   **Annual Attendance:** 14,000
   Affiliations: TCG
   Performance Facilities: Dorset Playhouse

PERFORMING SERIES

DORSET THEATRE FESTIVAL
PO Box 519, Dorset, VT 05251
(802) 867-2223
      Founded: 1960
      Arts Area: Theater
      Status: Professional; Non-Profit
      Type: Performing
      Management: Jill Charles, Artistic Director; John Nassicera, Producing Director
      Paid Staff: 6   **Volunteer Staff:** 21
      Paid Artists: 50
      Utilizes: Guest Artists; Guest Directors
      Budget: $100.000 - $500,000
      Income Sources: Private Foundations/Grants/Endowments; Business/Corporate Donations; Box Office; Government Grants; Individual Donations
      Season: June - September   **Annual Attendance:** 14,000
      Affiliations: TCG
      Performance Facilities: Dorset Playhouse

Manchester

PERFORMING SERIES

FESTIVAL OF THE ARTS
Southern Vermont Arts Center/West Coast, Manchester, VT 05254
(802) 362-1405
      Founded: 1929
      Arts Area: Vocal Music; Instrumental Music; Festivals
      Status: Professional; Non-Profit
      Type: Sponsoring
      Management: Christopher Madkour, Executive Director
      Paid Staff: 9   **Volunteer Staff:** 150
      Paid Artists: 5
      Utilizes: Guest Artists
      Budget: $50,000 - $100,000
      Income Sources: Private Foundations/Grants/Endowments; Business/Corporate Donations; Box Office; Government Grants; Individual Donations
      Season: August
      Performance Facilities: Southern Vermont Arts Center

MANCHESTER MUSIC FESTIVAL
PO Box 735, Manchester, VT 05254
(802) 362-1956
      Founded: 1975
      Arts Area: Instrumental Music; Grand Opera; Classical; Chamber
      Status: Non-Professional; Non-Profit
      Type: Performing; Touring; Educational
      Purpose: To educate young artists toward a professional career
      Management: Carol Glenn, Eugene List, Founders; Michael Rudiakov, Director
      Paid Staff: 20
      Non-Paid Artists: 6
      Utilizes: Guest Conductors; Guest Artists
      Budget: $1,000 - $50,000
      Income Sources: Government Grants; Individual Donations
      Season: June - August   **Annual Attendance:** 2,000
      Performance Facilities: The Louise Arkell Pavilion

Marlboro

PERFORMING SERIES

MARLBORO MUSIC FESTIVAL
Marlboro, VT 05344
(802) 254-2394
FAX: (802) 254-4307
      Founded: 1951

Arts Area: Instrumental Music
Status: Professional; Non-Profit
Type: Performing; Touring; Resident; Educational; Sponsoring
Purpose: Artistic development of younger musicians with older, more experienced musicians
Management: Frank Saloman, Anthony Checchia, Administrators
Paid Staff: 20   **Volunteer Staff:** 5
Non-Paid Artists: 75
Utilizes: Guest Artists; Guest Directors
Budget: $500,000 - $1,000,000
Income Sources: Private Foundations/Grants/Endowments; Business/Corporate Donations; Box Office; Government Grants; Individual Donations
Season: July - August   **Annual Attendance:** 11,000
Performance Facilities: Persons Auditorium

Middlebury

THEATRE

POTOMAC THEATRE PROJECT
4 Nedde Lane, Middlebury, VT 05753
(802) 388-3318
Founded: 1977
Arts Area: Professional; Theatrical Group
Status: Professional; Non-Profit
Type: Performing; Resident; Educational
Purpose: To produce new works of a highly theatrical nature; to have a substantial involvement with professional theatre training
Management: Cheryl Faraone, James Petosa, Richard Romagnoli, Directors
Officers: Ellen Schaplowsky, Board Chairperson
Paid Staff: 3   **Volunteer Staff:** 10
Paid Artists: 12   **Non-Paid Artists:** 15
Utilizes: Guest Artists
Budget: $50,000 - $100,000
Income Sources: Private Foundations/Grants/Endowments; Business/Corporate Donations; Box Office; Government Grants; Individual Donations
Affiliations: ART/NY; Vermont Council on the Arts
Performance Facilities: Hall of Nations

FACILITY

MIDDLEBURY COLLEGE - WRIGHT THEATRE
Middlebury, VT 05753
(802) 388-3711, ext. 5601
Founded: 1800
Type of Facility: Theatre House
Type of Stage: Proscenium With Forestage
Stage Dimensions: 28'Wx14'H; 48'D from forestage to upstage wall   **Orchestra Pit**
Seating Capacity: 375
Year Built: 1958   **Architect:** Edward Cole   **Cost:** $700,000
Acoustical Consultant: Bolt, Beranek & Newman

Montpelier

INSTRUMENTAL MUSIC

BANJO DAN AND THE MID-NITE PLOWBOYS
25 Kent Street, Montpelier, VT 05602
(802) 229-5733
Founded: 1972
Arts Area: Folk
Status: Professional   **Type:** Performing
Purpose: We are a professional band, 4 or 5 pieces, playing bluegrass music in concerts, festivals and schools.
Management: Dan Lindner, Band Leader/Booking Agent

THEATRE

MONTPELIER THEATRE GUILD
33 Clarendon Avenue, Montpelier, VT 05602
(802) 223-5392
Founded: 1922
Arts Area: Musical; Community
Status: Non-Professional; Non-Profit
Type: Performing
Purpose: To advance the appreciation of theatrical arts by providing good theatre in all its forms
Management: Board of Directors
Officers: George Kleine, President; Brian Stone, Vice President; James Catone, Corresponding Secretary; Ann Monte, Recording Secretary; Olga Wackerman, Treasurer
Volunteer Staff: 100
Non-Paid Artists: 100
Budget: $1,000 - $50,000
Income Sources: Box Office
Season: November - April   **Annual Attendance:** 1,500
Performance Facilities: Union School Auditorium

Norwich

VOCAL MUSIC

OPERA NORTH
PO Box 83, Norwich, VT 05055
(802) 649-3750
Founded: 1980
Arts Area: Grand Opera; Lyric Opera; Light Opera; Operetta
Status: Professional; Non-Professional; Non-Profit
Type: Performing; Touring; Educational
Purpose: To create opera and musical theatre productions of professional orientation and quality, primarily in northern New England; to develop the artistic resources of the region through training and performance; to work in and with related arts disciplines
Management: Board of Directors
Officers: Nancy Saccani, President; Flo Klausner, Producer; Louis Burkot, Artistic Director; George Klausner, Treasurer
Paid Artists: 40   **Non-Paid Artists:** 25
Utilizes: Special Technical Talent; Guest Artists
Budget: $50,000 - $100,000
Income Sources: Private Foundations/Grants/Endowments; Business/Corporate Donations; Box Office; Individual Donations
Season: July - January   **Annual Attendance:** 3,000
Performance Facilities: Lebanon Opera House

Pittsfield

THEATRE

GREEN MOUNTAIN GUILD
PO Box 659, Pittsfield, VT 05762
(802) 746-8320
Founded: 1971
Arts Area: Professional; Summer Stock; Musical; Theatre for Children
Status: Professional
Type: Performing; Touring; Resident
Purpose: To develop and promote excellence in the performing arts in Northern New England
Management: Marjorie O'Neill-Butler, Program Coordinator/Managing Director; Robert O'Neill-Butler, Artistic Director; Jay Berkow, Associate Artistic Director
Officers: Robert O'Neill-Butler, President; Jonathan Huberth, Vice President; Marjorie O'Neill-Butler, Secretary/Treasurer
Paid Staff: 3   **Volunteer Staff:** 2
Paid Artists: 30   **Non-Paid Artists:** 3
Utilizes: Guest Directors
Income Sources: Box Office; Individual Donations
Season: March - December   **Annual Attendance:** 10,000
Affiliations: NETC; Vermont Council on the Arts; New England Touring Foundation
Performance Facilities: Killington Playhouse, Killington

Putney

PERFORMING SERIES

YELLOW BARN MUSIC FESTIVAL
Rural Delivery 2, Box 371, Putney, VT 05346
(802) 387-6637
Founded: 1969
Arts Area: Instrumental Music; Festivals
Status: Non-Profit
Type: Performing; Educational
Purpose: To provide a professional training institute and performance festival for gifted young chamber artists
Management: Tova Malin, Executive Director; David Wells and Janet Wells, Artistic Directors; Maury McNaughton, Administrator
Officers: Hanz Vitzthum, Chair
Paid Staff: 10
Paid Artists: 20   **Non-Paid Artists:** 50
Utilizes: Guest Conductors; Guest Artists
Budget: $100,000 - $500,000
Income Sources: Private Foundations/Grants/Endowments; Business/Corporate Donations; Box Office; Government Grants; Individual Donations; Fundraising
Season: July - August   **Annual Attendance:** 4,000

FACILITY

YELLOW BARN
Rural Delivery 2, Box 371, Putney, VT 05346
(802) 387-6637
Type of Facility: Barn
Type of Stage: Platform
Seating Capacity: 150

Randolph

FACILITY

CHANDLER MUSIC HALL AND CULTURAL CENTER
71-73 Main Street, Randolph, VT 05060
(802) 728-9878
Founded: 1907
Type of Facility: Theatre Complex; Concert Hall; Performance Center; Theatre House; Opera House; Civic Center; Art Gallery; Cultural Center
Facility Originally: Music Hall
Type of Stage: Proscenium
Stage Dimensions: 31'6"x19'4" proscenium opening   **Orchestra Pit**
Seating Capacity: 625
Year Built: 1907   **Architect:** Ernest H. Boyden   **Cost:** $31,500
Year Remodeled: 1972   **Cost:** $250,000
Contact for Rental: Francis Hartigan;   (802) 728-3849
Resident Groups: Chandler Players; Randolph Singers

Rutland

PERFORMING SERIES

KILLINGTON MUSIC FESTIVAL
PO Box 386, Rutland, VT 05702
(802) 773-4003
Founded: 1982
Arts Area: Instrumental Music
Status: Non-Profit
Type: Performing; Educational
Purpose: To present summer chamber concert series and operate a summer school for aspiring musicians
Paid Staff: 1
Paid Artists: 10
Utilizes: Guest Directors
Budget: $100,000 - $500,000

Income Sources: Private Foundations/Grants/Endowments; Business/Corporate Donations; Box Office; Government Grants; Individual Donations
Season: July - August   **Annual Attendance:** 2,000

Saint Johnsbury

DANCE

CATAMOUNT FILM AND ARTS COMPANY
PO Box 324, Saint Johnsbury, VT 05819
(802) 748-2600
    Founded: 1975
    Arts Area: Modern; Mime; Ballet; Jazz; Ethnic; Folk
    Status: Professional; Non-Profit
    Type: Performing; Educational
    Purpose: Catamount is a community-based multidisciplinary presenter
    Management: Phil Reynolds, Executive Director
    Paid Staff: 9   **Volunteer Staff:** 20
    Budget: $100,000 - $500,000
    Income Sources: Private Foundations/Grants/Endowments; Business/Corporate Donations; Box Office; Government Grants; Individual Donations; Concessions; Rental Income
    Season: 52 Weeks   **Annual Attendance:** 25,000

Thetford Center

VOCAL MUSIC

THROUGH THE OPERA GLASS
Rural Route 1, Box 7, Tucker Hill Road, Thetford Center, VT 05075
(802) 785-4559; (800) 932-7396
    Founded: 1987
    Arts Area: Grand Opera; Lyric Opera; Light Opera; Operetta; Musical Theatre
    Status: Professional
    Type: Performing; Touring; Resident; Educational; Produce-it-Yourself Programs
    Purpose: To tour thematic excerpted opera programs, including collaborations; to make these unique thematic programs available to other performing groups in "produce-it-yourself" packages
    Management: Caren Calafati Showerman, Managing Director
    Paid Staff: 2
    Paid Artists: 12
    Utilizes: Guest Artists; Collaborations
    Budget: $50,000 - $100,000
    Income Sources: Private Foundations/Grants/Endowments; Box Office; Individual Presenters; Budget
    Season: 52 Weeks
    Affiliations: Vermont Council on the Arts; New Hampshire Council on the Arts; Massachusetts Cultural Council

---

Tunbridge

DANCE

ED LARKIN OLD-TIME CONTRA DANCERS
c/o Swayze, RFD, PO Box 131B, Tunbridge, VT 05077
(802) 889-5584
    Founded: 1956
    Arts Area: Ethnic
    Status: Semi-Professional; Non-Professional; Non-Profit
    Type: Performing; Touring; Educational
    Purpose: To perform authentic Vermont-style contradances and quadrilles as they were done in the 1930s and earlier with traditional music and antique costumes
    Officers: Carl Martin, President; George Cushman, Vice President; Dorothy Swayze, Secretary; Wayne Martin, Treasurer
    Volunteer Staff: 25
    Non-Paid Artists: 37
    Income Sources: Individual Donations
    Season: 52 Weeks
    Affiliations: Vermont Council on the Arts

Wells River

VOCAL MUSIC

NORTH COUNTRY CHORUS
65 Main Street, Wells River, VT 05081
(802) 757-2325
     Founded: 1948
     Arts Area: Choral
     Status: Semi-Professional; Non-Profit
     Type: Performing; Touring; Resident
     Purpose: The enriching of the musical life of residents of the North Country Area through participation in a singing group whose membership is open to all who love to sing
     Management: Mary Whitney Rowe, Conductor; Jean Anderson, Pianist
     Officers: Joan M. Blankinship, President; Edith Emery, Vice President; Margaret Eastman, Secretary; Amy Jarrell, Treasurer
     Paid Staff: 1
     Paid Artists: 6
     Utilizes: Special Technical Talent; Guest Artists; Guest Directors
     Budget: $1,000 - $50,000
     Income Sources: Private Foundations/Grants/Endowments; Business/Corporate Donations; Box Office; Government Grants; Individual Donations
     Season: 52 Weeks

VIRGINIA

Abingdon

THEATRE

BARTER THEATRE - STATE THEATRE OF VIRGINIA
Main Street, PO Box 867, Abingdon, VA 24210
(703) 628-2281
FAX: (703) 628-4551
   Founded: 1933
   Arts Area: Professional
   Status: Professional; Non-Profit
   Type: Performing; Touring; Resident; Educational
   Purpose: To perform the best in classical and contemporary theatre for residents and visitors to our region
   Management: Rex Partington, Artistic Director/Producer
   Officers: Fillmore McPherson, President; Frank Defrience Jr., Vice President/Treasurer; James P. Jones, Secretary
   Paid Staff: 25
   Paid Artists: 50
   Utilizes: Guest Artists; Guest Directors
   Budget: $1,000,000 - $5,000,000
   Income Sources: Private Foundations/Grants/Endowments; Business/Corporate Donations; Box Office; Government Grants; Individual Donations
   Season: April - October   **Annual Attendance:** 75,000
   Affiliations: AEA; LORT; TCG
   Performance Facilities: Barter Playhouse; Barter Theatre House

FACILITY

BARTER PLAYHOUSE
Main Street, PO Box 867, Abingdon, VA 24210
(703) 628-2281
   Type of Facility: Theatre House
   Facility Originally: Church
   Type of Stage: 3/4 Arena
   Seating Capacity: 138
   Year Built: 1833
   Year Remodeled: 1978
   Contact for Rental: (703) 628-2281
   Resident Groups: Barter Theatre

BARTER THEATRE HOUSE
Main Street, PO Box 867, Abingdon, VA 24210
(703) 628-3991
   Type of Facility: Theatre House
   Facility Originally: Church
   Type of Stage: Proscenium   **Orchestra Pit**
   Seating Capacity: 394
   Year Built: 1833
   Contact for Rental: Pearl Hayter;   (703) 628-2281
   Resident Groups: Barter Theatre
   Converted into a theatre in 1933

Alexandria

THEATRE

AMERICAN SHOWCASE THEATRE COMPANY
1822 Duke Street, Alexandria, VA 22314
(703) 548-9044
FAX: (703) 548-9089
   Founded: 1984
   Arts Area: Professional; Theatrical Group
   Status: Professional; Non-Profit
   Type: Performing; Touring; Educational
   Purpose: To offer a season of mainstage productions, staged readings and new-play development, as well as acting classes

Management: Sherry Brown, Director of Management Resources; Carolyn Griffin, Producing Director
Officers: Trudy B. Levy Esq., President; Thomas P. Hartnett Esq., Vice President; Barbara Berschler Esq., Treasurer; Louise Rosenbaum, Secretary
Paid Staff: 2   **Volunteer Staff:** 3
Utilizes: Guest Directors
Budget: $100,000 - $500,000
Income Sources: Private Foundations/Grants/Endowments; Business/Corporate Donations; Box Office; Government Grants; Individual Donations
Season: September - June   **Annual Attendance:** 4,000
Affiliations: TGC; League of Washington Theatres; Alexandria Chamber of Commerce; Cultural Alliance of Greater Washington; King Street Metro Enterprise Team

Annandale

INSTRUMENTAL MUSIC

FAIRFAX SYMPHONY ORCHESTRA
PO Box 1300, Annandale, VA 22003
(703) 642-7200
FAX: (703) 642-7205
Founded: 1957
Arts Area: Symphony; Orchestra; Chamber; Ensemble; Instrumental Group
Status: Professional; Non-Profit
Type: Performing; Touring; Resident; Educational
Management: Mark W. Ohnmacht, Executive Director
Officers: Fredrick G. Hutchinson Jr., President; Paul H. Geithner Jr., Immediate Past President
Paid Staff: 4   **Volunteer Staff:** 10
Paid Artists: 90
Utilizes: Guest Artists
Budget: $500,000 - $1,000,000
Income Sources: Private Foundations/Grants/Endowments; Business/Corporate Donations; Box Office; Government Grants; Individual Donations
Season: October - July   **Annual Attendance:** 75,000
Performance Facilities: George Mason University

PERFORMING SERIES

INTERNATIONAL CHILDREN'S FESTIVAL
4022 Hummer Road, Annandale, VA 22003
(703) 642-0862
FAX: (703) 642-1773
Founded: 1971
Arts Area: Dance; Vocal Music; Instrumental Music; Theater; Festivals
Status: Professional; Non-Profit
Type: Performing; Resident; Sponsoring
Management: Toni Winters McMahon, President/Chief Operating Officer; Kathy Sears, Program Director
Officers: John P. Stenbit, Chairman
Paid Staff: 6   **Volunteer Staff:** 1,250
Paid Artists: 40
Utilizes: Special Technical Talent; Guest Artists
Budget: $100,000 - $500,000
Income Sources: Private Foundations/Grants/Endowments; Business/Corporate Donations; Box Office; Government Grants; Individual Donations
Annual Attendance: 35,000
Affiliations: Fairfax County Council of the Arts
Performance Facilities: Wolf Trap Farm Park for the Performing Arts

Arlington

DANCE

ARLINGTON DANCE THEATRE
2700 South Lang Street, Arlington, VA 22204
(703) 548-1017
Founded: 1956
Arts Area: Modern; Ballet; Jazz
Status: Semi-Professional; Non-Profit

Type: Performing; Educational
Purpose: Dedicated to excellence in the performance and teaching of dance
Management: Robens Siegel, Artistic Director; Judy Rhodes, Director, Children's Program and Apprentice Company
Officers: M.J. Boster, President; Robin Shallant, Vice President; Kathy Cagel, Secretary; Julia Blackburn, Treasurer
Volunteer Staff: 21
Non-Paid Artists: 16
Utilizes: Special Technical Talent; Guest Artists
Budget: $50,000 - $100,000
Income Sources: Private Foundations/Grants/Endowments; Business/Corporate Donations; Box Office; Government Grants; Individual Donations
Season: September - July **Annual Attendance:** 2,000
Affiliations: Arlington County Cultural Affairs Office
Performance Facilities: Thomas Jefferson Community Theatre

INSTRUMENTAL MUSIC

HESPERUS
3706 North 17th Street, Arlington, VA 22207
(703) 525-7550
    Arts Area: Chamber; Folk; Early Music; Classical
    Status: Professional; Non-Profit
    Type: Touring; Resident
    Purpose: To trace the cultural parallels between the Old World and the New World
    Management: Scott Reiss, Artistic Director; Tina Chancey, Producing Director
    Budget: $100,000 - $500,000
    Income Sources: Private Foundations/Grants/Endowments; Business/Corporate Donations; Box Office; Government Grants; Individual Donations; Fees
    Performance Facilities: Smithsonian Institute - National Museum of American History

TWENTIETH CENTURY CONSORI
828 South Wakefield Street, Arlington, VA 22204
(703) 920-9727
    Arts Area: Chamber
    Status: Professional; Non-Profit
    Type: Performing; Touring; Resident; Educational
    Purpose: To provide the best in 20th-century classical music
    Management: Christopher Kendall, Artistic Director
    Budget: $1,000 - $50,000
    Income Sources: Private Foundations/Grants/Endowments; Business/Corporate Donations; Box Office; Government Grants; Individual Donations
    Performance Facilities: Hirshorn Museum

VOCAL MUSIC

OPERA THEATRE OF NORTHERN VIRGINIA
2700 South Lang Street, Arlington, VA 22206
(703) 739-2918
    Founded: 1961
    Arts Area: Grand Opera; Light Opera
    Status: Professional; Non-Profit
    Type: Performing; Resident
    Purpose: To provide affordable opera in English to the northern Virginia and Greater Metropolitan Washington Area; to sponsor educational programs and performances geared to young audiences; to provide stage experience emphasizing utilization of local talent
    Management: John Edward Niles, Artistic Director/Conductor
    Officers: Virginia D. Marrin, Vice President, Production
    Paid Staff: 1 **Volunteer Staff:** 25
    Paid Artists: 100
    Utilizes: Special Technical Talent; Guest Artists; Guest Directors
    Budget: $50,000 - $100,000
    Income Sources: Private Foundations/Grants/Endowments; Business/Corporate Donations; Box Office; Government Grants; Individual Donations; Fundraising
    Season: December - April **Annual Attendance:** 7,000
    Affiliations: OA; Cultural Alliance of Greater Washington
    Performance Facilities: Thomas Jefferson Community Theatre

PERFORMING SERIES

OFFICE OF CULTURAL AFFAIRS
2700 South Lang Street, Arlington, VA 22206
(703) 358-6960
Arts Area: Dance; Vocal Music; Instrumental Music; Theater; Festivals; Grand Opera
Status: Non-Profit
Type: Performing; Educational; Sponsoring
Purpose: To create and maintain an environment within Arlington County that is conducive to the development of the arts
Management: Norma Kaplan, Supervisor
Paid Staff: 14
Paid Artists: 100 **Non-Paid Artists:** 100
Utilizes: Special Technical Talent; Guest Conductors; Guest Artists; Guest Directors
Budget: $100,000 - $500,000
Income Sources: Private Foundations/Grants/Endowments; Government Grants
Season: 52 Weeks
Affiliations: NALAA

Blacksburg

FACILITY

BURRUSS AUDITORIUM
Virginia Technical Campus, 225 Squires Center, Blacksburg, VA 24061-0138
(703) 231-5431
FAX: (703) 231-5430
Founded: 1936
Type of Facility: Auditorium
Facility Originally: Meeting Hall; School
Type of Stage: Proscenium
Stage Dimensions: 58'Wx17'6"H **Orchestra Pit**
Seating Capacity: 2,960
Year Built: 1936
Year Remodeled: 1985 **Cost:** $1,200,000
Acoustical Consultant: Acentech
Contact for Rental: UUSA Events Planning; (703) 231-5005

Bristol

DANCE

BRISTOL BALLET COMPANY
628 Cumberland Street, Bristol, VA 24201
(703) 466-2401
Founded: 1959
Arts Area: Ballet
Status: Non-Profit
Type: Performing
Purpose: To promote, encourage and sustain community interest in the art of ballet; to contribute to the cultural progress and entertainment of the community and the larger Tri-cities Area
Management: Mary Anne Snyder-Sowers, Artistic Director; Nancy Peoples, Production Director
Officers: Sam Crockett, President; Rita Hairston, Vice President; Lee Duncan, Recording Secretary; Nancy Peoples, Treasurer
Paid Staff: 4 **Volunteer Staff:** 27
Non-Paid Artists: 15
Utilizes: Guest Artists; Guest Choreographers
Budget: $50,000 - $100,000
Income Sources: Private Foundations/Grants/Endowments; Business/Corporate Donations; Box Office; Government Grants; Individual Donations
Season: September - August **Annual Attendance:** 6,000
Affiliations: SERBA; Tennessee Arts Commission; Virginia Commission for the Arts
Performance Facilities: Paramount Center

Charlottesville

INSTRUMENTAL MUSIC

TUESDAY EVENING CONCERT SERIES
112 Old Cabell Hall, University of Virginia, Charlottesville, VA 22903
(804) 924-3600
FAX: (804) 982-2002
> **Founded:** 1948
> **Arts Area:** Chamber; Ensemble; Soloists
> **Status:** Professional; Non-Profit
> **Type:** Sponsoring
> **Purpose:** To sponsor an annual series of six chamber concerts
> **Management:** Karen Pellon, Manager
> **Officers:** Lilli Meier, President; Collins Beagle, Vice President; Jean Minehart, Treasurer
> **Paid Staff:** 1   **Volunteer Staff:** 25
> **Utilizes:** Guest Artists
> **Budget:** $50,000 - $100,000
> **Income Sources:** Private Foundations/Grants/Endowments; Business/Corporate Donations; Box Office; Government Grants; Individual Donations
> **Season:** September - April   **Annual Attendance:** 4,000
> **Affiliations:** University of Virginia
> **Performance Facilities:** Cabell Hall Auditorium, University of Virginia

THEATRE

OFFSTAGE THEATRE
PO Box 131, Charlottesville, VA 22902
(804) 295-7249
> **Founded:** 1989
> **Arts Area:** Professional; Theatrical Group; Independent Theatre
> **Status:** Semi-Professional; Non-Profit
> **Type:** Performing; Touring; Resident; Educational
> **Purpose:** Dedicated to producing high-quality, new plays in low-cost, nontraditional theatre environments
> **Management:** Tom Coash, Doug Grissom, Co-Artistic Directors; John Quinn, Resident Director; Amy Lowenstein, Public Relations Director
> **Officers:** Tom Coash, President; Doug Grissom, Vice President; John Quinn, Treasurer; Amy Lowenstein, Secretary
> **Paid Staff:** 2   **Volunteer Staff:** 20
> **Paid Artists:** 15
> **Utilizes:** Guest Artists; Guest Directors
> **Budget:** $1,000 - $50,000
> **Income Sources:** Business/Corporate Donations; Box Office; Individual Donations
> **Season:** 52 Weeks   **Annual Attendance:** 10,000

Fairfax

DANCE

JANE FRANKLIN AND DANCERS
10723 West Drive, #304, Fairfax, VA 22030
(703) 591-1893
> **Founded:** 1983
> **Arts Area:** Modern
> **Status:** Professional; Non-Profit
> **Type:** Performing; Touring; Educational
> **Purpose:** To present dance and live music with pieces featuring voice and text
> **Management:** Jane Franklin, Artistic Director; Carol Coteus, Administrative Assistant
> **Paid Staff:** 1   **Volunteer Staff:** 8
> **Paid Artists:** 5   **Non-Paid Artists:** 3
> **Utilizes:** Guest Artists
> **Budget:** $1,000 - $50,000
> **Income Sources:** Private Foundations/Grants/Endowments; Box Office
> **Season:** 52 Weeks

FACILITY

GEORGE MASON UNIVERSITY CENTER FOR THE ARTS
4400 University Drive, Fairfax, VA 22030
(703) 993-8877
FAX: (703) 993-8883
    Founded: 1990
    Type of Facility: Theatre Complex; Concert Hall; Studio Performance; Theatre House; Opera House; Multi-Purpose
    Type of Stage: Thrust; Flexible; Proscenium
    Stage Dimensions: Concert Hall - 52'x40'   **Orchestra Pit**
    Seating Capacity: Concert Hall - 1,935
    Year Built: 1990   **Architect:** General - McGuire Group; Concert Hall - Izenour Associates   **Cost:** $12,000,000
    Acoustical Consultant: Izenour Associates
    Contact for Rental: Director of Operations;   (703) 993-8877

Fort Eustis

FACILITY

FORT EUSTIS MUSIC AND VIDEO CENTER
ATZF-PRC-MT BUILDING 224, Fort Eustis, VA 23604-5109
(804) 878-5031
    Type of Facility: Studio Performance; Environmental; Performance Center; Civic Center; Multi-Purpose
    Facility Originally: Library; Recreation Hall/gymnasium
    Year Built: 1950   **Architect:** U.S. Army Corps of Engineers
    Year Remodeled: 1976   **Architect:** U.S. Army Corps of Engineers
    Manager: Mike Hassell
    Resident Groups: Soldier Theatre
    Fort Eustis Music and Video Center contains the Jacobs Theatre and Soldier Theatre. See separate listings for further information.

FORT EUSTIS MUSIC AND VIDEO CENTER - JACOBS THEATRE
ATZF-PRC-MT BUILDING 224, Fort Eustis, VA 23604-5109
(804) 878-5031
    Type of Facility: Studio Performance
    Type of Stage: Modified Apron Proscenium
    Stage Dimensions: 48'Wx48'D, includes 12'D apron past proscenium
    Seating Capacity: 1,000
    Contact for Rental: Mike Hassell;   (804) 878-5031

FORT EUSTIS MUSIC AND VIDEO CENTER - SOLDIER THEATRE
ATZF-PRC-MT BUILDING 224, Fort Eustis, VA 23604-5109
(804) 878-5031
    Type of Facility: Studio Performance; Multi-Purpose
    Type of Stage: Platform
    Stage Dimensions: 36'Wx28'Dx16'H
    Seating Capacity: 800
    Contact for Rental: Mike Hassell;   (804) 878-5031

Fredericksburg

PERFORMING SERIES

FREDERICKSBURG CHAMBER MUSIC FESTIVAL
PO Box 7816, Fredericksburg, VA 22404
(703) 371-4805
    Founded: 1988
    Arts Area: Vocal Music; Instrumental Music
    Status: Non-Profit
    Type: Performing; Educational
    Purpose: To present the finest in performing arts to Fredericksburg and the surrounding area at reasonable prices
    Management: David R. Freeman, Chairman; Edward Bennan, President of the Board; Mary Triola, Festival Coordinator; Heidi Lehwalder, Artistic Director
    Volunteer Staff: 50
    Paid Artists: 13

Utilizes: Guest Conductors; Guest Artists
Budget: $50,000 - $100,000
Income Sources: Private Foundations/Grants/Endowments; Business/Corporate Donations; Box Office; Individual Donations
Season: June
Performance Facilities: Dodd Auditorium, Mary Washington College; St. George Episcopal Church

Hampton

DANCE

HAMPTON ROADS CIVIC BALLET
4607 Victoria Boulevard, Hampton, VA 23669
(804) 722-8216
    Founded: 1959
    Arts Area: Ballet
    Status: Non-Profit
    Type: Performing; Resident; Educational
    Purpose: To bring live ballet to our area at affordable prices; to provide training for young dancers hoping to become professionals
    Management: Muriel Evans, Director; Lisa Schultz, Ballet Mistress
    Officers: Mark Watson, President; Melissa Berry, Vice President; Diane Nusbaum, Secretary; Debbie Scott, Treasurer
    Utilizes: Guest Artists
    Budget: $1,000 - $50,000
    Income Sources: Box Office; Individual Donations
    Annual Attendance: 2,000

PERFORMING SERIES

HAMPTON ARTS COMMISSION
4205 Victoria Boulevard, Hampton, VA 23669
(804) 722-2787
FAX: (804) 727-1152
    Founded: 1987
    Arts Area: Dance; Vocal Music; Instrumental Music; Theater
    Status: Professional
    Type: Performing; Educational; Sponsoring
    Purpose: To present and promote the finest in the performing and visual arts
    Management: Michael P. Curry, Director
    Officers: Nancy B. Adams, Chair
    Paid Staff: 3 **Volunteer Staff:** 12
    Paid Artists: 8
    Utilizes: Guest Artists
    Budget: $100,000 - $500,000
    Income Sources: Box Office; Government Grants
    Season: September - May **Annual Attendance:** 30,000
    Affiliations: APAP
    Performance Facilities: Ogden Hall

FACILITY

HAMPTON COLISEUM
PO Box 7309, Hampton, VA 23666
(804) 838-5650
FAX: (804) 838-2595
    Type of Facility: Arena
    Type of Stage: Proscenium
    Stage Dimensions: 80'Wx40'H
    Seating Capacity: 10,953; 13,800
    Year Built: 1969 **Architect:** A.G. Odell **Cost:** $8,500,000
    Contact for Rental: Andrew G. Greenwell; (804) 838-5650
    Manager: Andrew D. Greenwell; (804) 838-5650

Hanover

THEATRE

BARKSDALE THEATRE
PO Box 7, Hanover, VA 23069
(804) 730-4860
Founded: 1953
Arts Area: Professional; Musical; Dinner; Theatrical Group
Status: Professional; Non-Profit
Type: Performing; Touring
Purpose: To offer excellent theatre
Management: David Kilgore, Muriel McAvley, Artistic Directors/Co-Owners; Nancy Kilgore, Co-Owner; Katherine Tracy, General Manager; Cynthia Theaksto, Director of Audience Relations and Group Sales; Jacqueline O'Conner, Box Office Manager
Paid Staff: 5   **Volunteer Staff:** 15
Utilizes: Special Technical Talent; Guest Artists; Guest Directors
Budget: $50,000 - $100,000
Income Sources: Private Foundations/Grants/Endowments; Business/Corporate Donations; Box Office; Government Grants; Individual Donations
Season: 52 Weeks   **Annual Attendance:** 30,000
Affiliations: Actor's Studio

Harrisonburg

FACILITY

WILSON HALL AUDITORIUM
James Madison University, Harrisonburg, VA 22807
(703) 568-6754
FAX: (703) 568-6920
Founded: 1930
Type of Facility: Auditorium; Theatre House
Type of Stage: Thrust; Proscenium
Stage Dimensions: 34'x35' proscenium opening   **Orchestra Pit**
Seating Capacity: 1,347
Year Built: 1930   **Architect:** Charles M. Robinson   **Cost:** $250,000
Year Remodeled: 1987   **Architect:** McClintock and Associates   **Cost:** $900,000
Contact for Rental: Connie Kerlin, Programming;   (703) 568-6330

Hot Springs

PERFORMING SERIES

GARTH NEWEL MUSIC CENTER
Route 220, Hot Springs, VA 24445
(703) 839-5018
FAX: (703) 839-3154
Founded: 1975
Arts Area: Vocal Music; Instrumental Music; Festivals
Status: Professional; Non-Profit; Student Program
Type: Performing; Touring; Resident; Educational
Purpose: To promote and perform chamber music
Management: Luca and Arlene Di Cecco, Directors
Officers: H.H. Ingalls, President; Luca Di Cecco, Executive Vice President; Thomas Roberts, Treasurer; Arlene Di Cecco, Secretary
Paid Staff: 6   **Volunteer Staff:** 10
Paid Artists: 12
Utilizes: Guest Conductors; Guest Artists
Budget: $100,000 - $500,000
Income Sources: Private Foundations/Grants/Endowments; Business/Corporate Donations; Box Office; Government Grants; Individual Donations
Season: July - September   **Annual Attendance:** 5,000
Performance Facilities: Herter Hall

Leesburg

PERFORMING SERIES

BLUEMONT CONCERT SERIES
PO Box 208, Leesburg, VA 22075-0208
    Arts Area: Festivals; Traditional; Variety
    Status: Non-Profit
    Type: Educational; Sponsoring
    Purpose: To provide a wide variety of high-quality events for the community
    Management: Pete H. Dunning, President
    Paid Staff: 3 **Volunteer Staff:** 400
    Paid Artists: 400
    Utilizes: Special Technical Talent
    Budget: $100,000 - $500,000
    Income Sources: Private Foundations/Grants/Endowments; Business/Corporate Donations; Box Office; Government Grants; Individual Donations
    Season: 52 Weeks **Annual Attendance:** 150,000

Lexington

INSTRUMENTAL MUSIC

WASHINGTON AND LEE UNIVERSITY CONCERT GUILD
Washington and Lee University, Lexington, VA 24450
(703) 463-8855
    Arts Area: Chamber
    Status: Professional; Non-Profit
    Type: Educational; Sponsoring
    Management: Timothy Gaylord, Music Department
    Budget: $1,000 - $50,000
    Season: October - March
    Performance Facilities: Lenfest Centre

THEATRE

LIME KILN ARTS INCORPORATED
PO Box 663, Lexington, VA 24450
(703) 463-7088
    Arts Area: Professional; Summer Stock; Musical; Folk; Theatrical Group
    Status: Professional; Non-Profit
    Type: Performing; Touring; Resident; Educational; Sponsoring
    Purpose: To promote and preserve the tradition of the southern Appalachian Mountains and explore their myths and potential
    Management: Don Baker, Artistic Director; Ken Sheck, Manager
    Officers: Bob Martis, President
    Budget: $500,000 - $1,000,000
    Income Sources: Private Foundations/Grants/Endowments; Business/Corporate Donations; Box Office; Government Grants; Individual Donations
    Performance Facilities: Lime Kiln Theater

Lynchburg

FACILITY

LYNCHBURG FINE ARTS CENTER
1815 Thomson Drive, Lynchburg, VA 24501
(804) 846-8451
    Type of Facility: Concert Hall; Theatre House
    Type of Stage: Proscenium
    Orchestra Pit
    Seating Capacity: 510
    Year Built: 1962 **Architect:** Carl Cress
    Contact for Rental: (804) 846-8451
    Manager: Kathleen Bowne, Contact Person
    Resident Groups: Women's Group
    Also contains the Dillard and Lounge Visual Arts Galleries

Martinsville

VOCAL MUSIC

MARTINSVILLE-HENRY COUNTY FESTIVAL OF OPERA
South College Street, PO Box 406, Martinsville, VA 24112
(703) 632-5861
Founded: 1977
Arts Area: Grand Opera; Lyric Opera; Light Opera; Operetta; Choral
Status: Professional; Non-Profit
Type: Performing; Touring; Resident; Educational
Purpose: To bring live professional opera to the region on a regular basis
Management: Priscilla Gordon, Artistic Director; Alberto Figols, Managing Director; Floyd Sharp,
Musical Director
Volunteer Staff: 6
Paid Artists: 12
Utilizes: Special Technical Talent; Guest Conductors; Guest Artists; Guest Directors
Budget: $1,000 - $50,000
Income Sources: Private Foundations/Grants/Endowments; Business/Corporate Donations; Box Office; Government
Grants; Individual Donations
Season: April - December
Affiliations: Touring Concert Opera Company

McLean

FACILITY

ALDEN THEATRE
1234 Ingleside Avenue, McLean, VA 22101
(703) 790-0123
FAX: (703) 556-0547
Founded: 1975
Type of Facility: Theatre Complex
Type of Stage: Proscenium
Stage Dimensions: 28'x35'   **Orchestra Pit**
Seating Capacity: 424
Year Built: 1975
Year Remodeled: 1988   **Architect:** Cooper-Lecky
Contact for Rental: Clare Kiley;   (703) 790-0123

Middletown

THEATRE

WAYSIDE THEATRE
7853 Main Street, Middletown, VA 22645
(703) 869-1776
FAX: (703) 869-1782
Founded: 1962
Arts Area: Professional
Status: Professional; Non-Profit
Type: Performing; Touring; Resident
Purpose: To produce the best contemporary English-American theatre for the entertainment and education of the citizens
of northern Virginia
Management: Christopher Owens, Artistic Director; Donna Johnson, General Manager; Kay Parker, Box Office Manager;
Sharon Gochenauer, Administrative Assistant; John Ervin, Technical Director
Officers: Nick Nerangis, President of the Board; Ian Williams, Vice President; Richard Helm, Treasurer; Diane Collis,
Secretary
Paid Staff: 8   **Volunteer Staff:** 3
Paid Artists: 30
Utilizes: Special Technical Talent; Guest Directors; Organization Contracts
Budget: $100,000 - $500,000
Income Sources: Private Foundations/Grants/Endowments; Business/Corporate Donations; Box Office; Government
Grants; Individual Donations
Season: May - December   **Annual Attendance:** 22,000

Newport News

VOCAL MUSIC

VIRGINIA CHORAL SOCIETY
Warwick Station, PO Box 1131, Newport News, VA 23601
(804) 851-9114
>**Founded:** 1931
>**Arts Area:** Choral
>**Status:** Non-Profit
>**Type:** Performing
>**Purpose:** To bring to the community an appreciation and enjoyment of fine music
>**Management:** Gary Lewis, Artistic Director; Oliver Douberly, Assistant Artistic Director; Constance J. O'Sullivan, Marketing Director
>**Officers:** Jean Putnam, President; Barbara Sardella, Vice President; Kay Stewart, Corresponding Secretary; Katherine Bradshaw, Recording Secretary; Michael Martin, Treasurer; Phyllis Wharton, Archivist
>**Paid Staff:** 1   **Volunteer Staff:** 23
>**Paid Artists:** 2   **Non-Paid Artists:** 90
>**Utilizes:** Guest Artists
>**Budget:** $1,000 - $50,000
>**Income Sources:** Private Foundations/Grants/Endowments; Business/Corporate Donations; Box Office; Government Grants; Individual Donations
>**Season:** December - May   **Annual Attendance:** 4,600

Norfolk

DANCE

VIRGINIA BALLET THEATRE
134-136 West Onley Road, Norfolk, VA 23510
(804) 622-4822
>**Founded:** 1961
>**Arts Area:** Ballet
>**Status:** Non-Professional; Non-Profit
>**Type:** Performing; Resident
>**Management:** Frank and Janina Bove, Artistic Directors
>**Non-Paid Artists:** 40
>**Utilizes:** Guest Artists
>**Budget:** $1,000 - $50,000
>**Income Sources:** Private Foundations/Grants/Endowments; Business/Corporate Donations; Box Office; Government Grants; Individual Donations
>**Season:** May - December

INSTRUMENTAL MUSIC

NORFOLK CHAMBER CONSORT
5511 Willow Grove Court, Norfolk, VA 23505
(804) 440-1803
FAX: (804) 440-0080
>**Founded:** 1969
>**Arts Area:** Chamber
>**Status:** Professional
>**Type:** Performing
>**Purpose:** To present known and unknown works from the vast repertoire of chamber music from 1600 to the present, with a concentration on chamber music for mixed winds, strings, and voice
>**Management:** Allen Shaffer, F. Gerard Errante, Co-Directors
>**Utilizes:** Special Technical Talent; Guest Conductors; Guest Artists
>**Budget:** $1,000 - $50,000
>**Income Sources:** Business/Corporate Donations; Box Office; Government Grants; Individual Donations
>**Annual Attendance:** 1,000
>**Performance Facilities:** Chrysler Museum Theater; Chandler Recital Hall, Old Dominion University

THE VIRGINIA SYMPHONY
PO Box 26, Norfolk, VA 23501
(804) 623-8590
FAX: (804) 623-7068
>**Founded:** 1920

Arts Area: Symphony; Orchestra; Chamber
Status: Professional; Non-Profit
Type: Performing; Touring; Educational
Purpose: To support an orchestra of the highest artistic excellence and reputation; to provide enjoyment, education, enrichment, inspiration and pride for the citizens of Hampton Roads and the Commonwealth of Virginia; to bring recognition and credit to the entire region
Management: Benjamin Greene, Executive Director; Joann Falletta, Music Director; Skitch Henderson, Principal Pops Conductor
Officers: Asa Shield Jr., President of Board of Directors
Paid Staff: 12   **Volunteer Staff:** 500
Paid Artists: 81
Utilizes: Guest Conductors; Guest Artists
Budget: $1,000,000 - $5,000,000
Income Sources: Private Foundations/Grants/Endowments; Business/Corporate Donations; Box Office; Government Grants; Individual Donations
Season: September - June   **Annual Attendance:** 100,000
Affiliations: ASOL
Performance Facilities: Chrysler Hall; Pavilion Theatre; Ogden Hall

VOCAL MUSIC

CANTATA CHORUS OF NORFOLK
560 West Olney Road, Norfolk, VA 23507
(804) 627-5665
Founded: 1960
Arts Area: Choral
Status: Semi-Professional; Non-Profit
Type: Performing
Purpose: To present major choral works as near to the composer's concept and instrumentation as possible
Management: Grover J. Oberle, Director; Dr. Allen Shaffer, Assistant Director
Paid Staff: 1   **Volunteer Staff:** 6
Paid Artists: 40   **Non-Paid Artists:** 60
Utilizes: Special Technical Talent; Guest Conductors; Guest Artists
Budget: $1,000 - $50,000
Income Sources: Business/Corporate Donations; Individual Donations
Season: September - May   **Annual Attendance:** 2,000

I. SHERMAN GREENE CHORALE, INC.
PO Box 1071, Norfolk, VA 23501
(804) 467-8971
Arts Area: Choral
Status: Semi-Professional
Type: Performing; Touring; Resident; Educational
Purpose: To promote and render quality performances of choral works of the great masters and music by black composers
Officers: Harry Scott, President; Lynn Briley, Vice President; Emogene Mc Artis, Secretary; Zenobia Pendleton, Treasurer; Carl Haywood, Conductor
Paid Staff: 4   **Volunteer Staff:** 14
Paid Artists: 1   **Non-Paid Artists:** 45
Utilizes: Guest Artists; Guest Directors
Budget: $1,000 - $50,000
Income Sources: Private Foundations/Grants/Endowments; Business/Corporate Donations; Box Office; Government Grants; Individual Donations
Season: October - May   **Annual Attendance:** 1,900
Affiliations: Cultural Alliance
Performance Facilities: Booker T. Washington High School Auditorium; Grace Episcopal Church

VIRGINIA OPERA
PO Box 2580, Norfolk, VA 23501
(804) 853-7567; (804) 623-1223
FAX: (804) 853-9162
Founded: 1974
Arts Area: Grand Opera
Status: Professional; Non-Profit
Type: Performing; Touring; Educational
Management: Peter Mark, General/Artistic Director; Ken Freeman, General Manager; George Glander, Production Manager; Virginia Thumm, Developing Director; Lisa Jardanhazy, Marketing Director

Paid Staff: 36 **Volunteer Staff:** 24
Paid Artists: 105 **Non-Paid Artists:** 12
Utilizes: Special Technical Talent; Guest Conductors; Guest Artists; Guest Directors
Budget: $1,000,000 - $5,000,000
Income Sources: Private Foundations/Grants/Endowments; Business/Corporate Donations; Box Office; Government Grants; Individual Donations; Fund-raising
Season: September - April **Annual Attendance:** 40,000
Affiliations: Cultural Arts Alliance of Greater Hampton Roads; OA; AAA

THEATRE

GENERIC THEATRE
912 West 21st Street, Norfolk, VA 23517
(804) 441-2160
Founded: 1982
Arts Area: Community; Theatrical Group
Status: Non-Profit
Type: Performing; Producing
Purpose: To produce new plays; to produce adult-orientated black-box theatre at dirt-cheap prices
Management: Elmwood Robinson, Technical Director; Bob Nelson, Artistic Director
Paid Staff: 4 **Volunteer Staff:** 4
Non-Paid Artists: 36
Utilizes: Special Technical Talent; Guest Directors
Budget: $50,000 - $100,000
Season: September - May **Annual Attendance:** 5,000
Affiliations: City of Norfolk Parks and Recreation Department
Performance Facilities: Generic Theatre

LITTLE THEATRE OF NORFOLK
801 Claremont Avenue, Norfolk, VA 23507
(804) 627-8551
Founded: 1926
Arts Area: Community
Status: Non-Profit
Type: Performing
Purpose: To provide excellent amateur theatre with commercial box office attractions, giving all non-professional artists a chance to use their talents
Officers: E.H. Strawbridge, Past President; Marguerite Burgess, Secretary; Eunice Pittman, Treasurer
Budget: $1,000 - $50,000
Income Sources: Box Office
Season: September - June **Annual Attendance:** 4,000
Performance Facilities: Little Theatre of Norfolk

VIRGINIA STAGE COMPANY
PO Box 3770, Norfolk, VA 23514
(804) 627-6988; (804) 627-1234
FAX: (804) 628-5958
Founded: 1980
Arts Area: Professional; Theatrical Group
Status: Professional; Non-Profit
Type: Performing; Resident; Educational; Sponsoring
Purpose: To serve Hampton Roads through the production of theatrical art of the highest quality; to produce plays of language and literacy; to reaffirm the theatre's place in the age of electronic media and choose work which is uniquely stage-worthy
Management: Tom Gardner, Artistic Director; Kathleen Bateson-Glass, Executive Director
Officers: Sidney N. Askew Jr., President, Board of Trustees; Patrick M. Barberrich, Vice President/Treasurer; Van Van der Meer, Vice President of Administration; Denver Hicks, Vice President of Development
Paid Staff: 35 **Volunteer Staff:** 100
Paid Artists: 40
Utilizes: Special Technical Talent; Guest Artists; Guest Directors
Budget: $1,000,000 - $5,000,000
Income Sources: Private Foundations/Grants/Endowments; Business/Corporate Donations; Box Office; Government Grants; Individual Donations
Season: October - March **Annual Attendance:** 45,000
Affiliations: LORT; TCG
Performance Facilities: Wells Theatre

FACILITY

GENERIE THEATER
912 West 21st Street, Norfolk, VA 23517
(804) 441-2160
Type of Facility: Studio Performance; Multi-Purpose
Facility Originally: Warehouse
Type of Stage: Flexible
Stage Dimensions: 28'x56'
Seating Capacity: 120
Contact for Rental: Bob Nelson;   (804) 441-2160
Resident Groups: Generic Theatre
The original warehouse was converted into a theatre space by the city of Norfolk in 1983.

LITTLE THEATRE OF NORFOLK
801 Claremont Avenue, Norfolk, VA 23508
(804) 627-8551
Founded: 1926
Type of Facility: Theatre House
Type of Stage: Proscenium
Seating Capacity: 224
Year Built: 1950

NORFOLK SCOPE CULTURAL AND CONVENTION CENTER
Scope Plaza, 201 East Brambleton Avenue, Norfolk, VA 23501
(804) 441-2764
Type of Facility: Civic Center
Seating Capacity: 11,584
Year Built: 1971   **Architect:** Williams, Tazewell & Associates   **Cost:** $35,000,000
Acoustical Consultant: Bolt, Beranek and Newman
SCOPE contains the Arena and Chrysler Hall. See separate listings for additional information.

NORFOLK SCOPE CULTURAL AND CONVENTION CENTER - ARENA
Scope Plaza, 201 East Brambleton Avenue, Norfolk, VA 23501
(804) 441-2764
Type of Facility: Arena
Type of Stage: Platform; Arena
Stage Dimensions: 36'x60'x48'
Seating Capacity: 11500
Year Built: 1971   **Architect:** Williams, Tazewell & Associates   **Cost:** $35,000,000
Contact for Rental: John Rhamstine, Cynthia Carter West;   (804) 441-2764
Manager: W.H. "Bill" Luther;   (804) 441-2764
Resident Groups: Hampton Roads Admirals - ECHL Hockey Team

NORFOLK SCOPE CULTURAL AND CONVENTION CENTER - CHRYSLER HALL
Scope Plaza, 201 East Brambleton Avenue, Norfolk, VA 23501
(804) 441-2764
Founded: 1971
Type of Facility: Theatre House
Type of Stage: Proscenium
Stage Dimensions: 31'x159'x43'   **Orchestra Pit**
Seating Capacity: 2,461
Year Built: 1971
Contact for Rental: John Ramstine, Cynthia Carter West;   (804) 441-2764
Manager: W.H. "Bill" Carter;   (804) 441-2764
Resident Groups: The Virginia Symphony

WELLS THEATRE
Monticello Avenue and Tazewell Street, Norfolk, VA 23514
(804) 627-6988
Type of Facility: Theatre House
Facility Originally: Vaudeville
Type of Stage: Proscenium
Seating Capacity: 677
Year Built: 1913
Year Remodeled: 1987   **Architect:** Hanbury Evans Newill & Vlattas   **Cost:** $3,850,000
Contact for Rental: Cynthia Carter;   (804) 444-2764, ext. 253

Resident Groups: Virginia Stage Company
The Wells Theatre has been designated a National Historic Landmark.

Petersburg

DANCE

PETERSBURG BALLET
44 Goodwich Avenue, Petersburg, VA 23805
(804) 733-9998
Founded: 1984
Arts Area: Ballet; Jazz
Status: Semi-Professional; Non-Profit
Type: Performing; Touring; Resident
Purpose: To allow area students the opportunity to perform and dance with the company
Management: Gloria F. Dance, Artistic Director; Evelia Emiliani, President; Ann Taylor, Vice President; Donna Yeatts, Secretary; Dr. Christopher Egan, Treasurer
Non-Paid Artists: 24
Utilizes: Guest Artists
Budget: $1,000 - $50,000
Income Sources: Private Foundations/Grants/Endowments; Business/Corporate Donations; Box Office; Government Grants; Individual Donations
Season: 52 Weeks

Radford

FACILITY

RADFORD UNIVERSITY THEATRE
Norwood Street, PO Box 6969, Radford, VA 24142
(703) 831-5207
FAX: (703) 831-6313
Type of Facility: Theatre Complex; Performance Center
Type of Stage: Thrust; Proscenium
Stage Dimensions: 58'Wx30'Dx21'H   **Orchestra Pit**
Seating Capacity: 483
Year Built: 1972   **Architect:** Thompson & Payne   **Cost:** $1,000,000
Resident Groups: Radford University Theatre Department

Reston

FACILITY

RESTON COMMUNITY CENTER THEATRE
2310 Colts Neck Road, Reston, VA 22091
(703) 476-4500; (703) 476-1111
FAX: (703) 476-8617
Type of Facility: Theatre House
Type of Stage: Proscenium
Stage Dimensions: 32'Wx28'D   **Orchestra Pit**
Seating Capacity: 300
Year Built: 1979
Year Remodeled: 1986   **Architect:** Kinetic Artistry   **Cost:** $25,000
Contact for Rental: Leila H. El-Bisi;   (703) 476-4500
Resident Groups: Community organizations; regularly-scheduled children's theatre; international film series

Richmond

DANCE

THE CONCERT BALLET OF VIRGINIA
103 East Main Street, Richmond, VA 23219
(804) 780-1279; (804) 644-5991
Founded: 1976

Arts Area: Modern; Ballet; Jazz
Status: Non-Professional; Non-Profit; Commercial
Type: Performing; Touring; Educational
Purpose: To provide a regular season of classical and contemporary innovative dance programming for the Richmond area along with statewide performances for the public as well as civic, educational and social organizations
Management: Robert Watkins, Director; Scott Boyer, Associate Director; Mrs. Thomas C. Rennie, Executive Assistant; deVeaux Riddick, Technical Director
Officers: Mrs. James St. Germain, President; Pat Morris, Vice President; Jill Melichar, Public Relations
Volunteer Staff: 40
Paid Artists: 5   **Non-Paid Artists:** 15
Utilizes: Guest Conductors; Guest Artists; Guest Choreographers
Budget: $50,000 - $100,000
Income Sources: Private Foundations/Grants/Endowments; Business/Corporate Donations; Box Office; Individual Donations
Season: 52 Weeks   **Annual Attendance:** 15,000
Affiliations: Sacred Dance Guild
Performance Facilities: The Woman's Club Auditorium; Blackwell Auditorium, Randolph Macon College; Alberarle High School Auditorium; Dogwood Dell Amphitheatre

EZIBU MUNTU AFRICAN DANCE COMPANY
PO Box 62, Richmond, VA 23201
(804) 264-3965
Founded: 1973
Arts Area: Ethnic; Folk
Status: Professional
Type: Performing; Touring; Educational
Purpose: To communicate the richness of a variety of African cultures and customs through dance, rhythm, and song in an exciting, energetic and colorful manner
Management: Janine Bell, General Manager; C. Rene Taylor, Business Manager; Faye Walker, Artistic Director; Kurt Patterson, Drum Captain
Officers: Janine Bell, President; Faye Walker, Secretary; C. Rene Taylor, Treasurer
Paid Staff: 4   **Volunteer Staff:** 2
Paid Artists: 12
Utilizes: Guest Artists; Guest Directors
Budget: $1,000 - $50,000
Income Sources: Private Foundations/Grants/Endowments; Business/Corporate Donations; Individual Donations
Season: 52 Weeks
Annual Attendance: 13,000

RICHMOND BALLET - THE STATE BALLET OF VIRGINIA
614 North Lombardy Street, Richmond, VA 23220
(804) 359-0906
FAX: (804) 355-4640
Founded: 1957
Arts Area: Ballet
Status: Professional; Non-Profit
Type: Performing; Touring; Resident; Educational
Purpose: To preserve the tradition of classical ballet; to perform works of this century and to create new works
Management: Stoner Winslett, Artistic Director; Dwight Bowes, Managing Director
Paid Staff: 31   **Volunteer Staff:** 5
Paid Artists: 22
Utilizes: Guest Conductors; Guest Artists; Guest Choreographers
Budget: $1,000,000 - $5,000,000
Income Sources: Private Foundations/Grants/Endowments; Business/Corporate Donations; Box Office; Government Grants; Individual Donations
Season: November - April
Annual Attendance: 55,000
Performance Facilities: The Mosque; Carpenter Center for the Performing Arts

INSTRUMENTAL MUSIC

RICHMOND SYMPHONY
The Berkshire, 300 West Franklin Street, Richmond, VA 23220
(804) 788-4717
FAX: (804) 788-1541
Founded: 1956

Arts Area: Symphony; Orchestra; Chamber
Status: Professional; Non-Profit
Type: Performing; Touring; Educational
Management: Catherine Wichterman, Executive Director; George Manahan, Music Director/Conductor
Paid Staff: 19
Paid Artists: 90
Utilizes: Guest Conductors; Guest Artists
Budget: $1,000,000 - $5,000,000
Income Sources: Private Foundations/Grants/Endowments; Business/Corporate Donations; Box Office; Government Grants; Individual Donations; Fund-raising
Season: September - June
Annual Attendance: 140,000
Affiliations: ASOL
Performance Facilities: The Mosque; Carpenter Center for the Performing Arts; Virginia Commonwealth University Performing Arts Center

ROXBURY CHAMBER PLAYERS
6207 Dustin Drive, Richmond, VA 23226
(804) 288-5935
Arts Area: Chamber
Status: Professional; Non-Profit
Type: Performing; Touring
Purpose: To perform repertory from baroque to modern utilizing visiting composers, guest artists, lecture concerts and student concerts
Management: David Niethamer, Artistic Director
Budget: $1,000 - $50,000
Income Sources: Private Foundations/Grants/Endowments; Business/Corporate Donations; Box Office; Government Grants; Individual Donations

THEATRE

THEATRE IV
114 West Broad Street, Richmond, VA 23220
(804) 783-1688
FAX: (804) 775-2325
Founded: 1975
Arts Area: Professional; Theatrical Group
Status: Professional; Non-Profit
Type: Performing; Touring; Resident; Educational
Purpose: To create professional, exciting and innovative theatrical productions of the highest calibre
Management: Bruce C. Miller, Artistic Director; Phil Whiteway, Managing Director
Paid Staff: 16
Utilizes: Special Technical Talent; Guest Artists; Guest Directors
Budget: $1,000,000 - $5,000,000
Income Sources: Private Foundations/Grants/Endowments; Business/Corporate Donations; Box Office; Government Grants; Individual Donations
Season: October - May
Affiliations: TCG
Performance Facilities: The Empire Theatre; The Little Theatre

THEATRE VIRGINIA
2800 Grove Avenue, Richmond, VA 23221
(804) 367-0840
Founded: 1955
Arts Area: Professional
Status: Professional; Non-Profit
Type: Performing; Resident
Management: William Gregg, Artistic Director; Paul Tyler, General Manager
Paid Staff: 25   **Volunteer Staff:** 250
Paid Artists: 75
Utilizes: Special Technical Talent; Guest Artists; Guest Directors
Budget: $1,000,000 - $5,000,000
Income Sources: Private Foundations/Grants/Endowments; Business/Corporate Donations; Box Office; Government Grants; Individual Donations
Season: September - May
Annual Attendance: 90,000
Affiliations: LORT; AEA; SSDC

FACILITY

CARPENTER CENTER FOR THE PERFORMING ARTS
600 East Grace Street, Richmond, VA 23219
(804) 782-3930
FAX: (804) 649-7402
    Type of Facility: Concert Hall; Performance Center; Theatre House; Room
    Type of Stage: Proscenium
    Stage Dimensions: 46'Wx35'D
    Orchestra Pit
    Seating Capacity: 2,033
    Year Built: 1928   **Architect:** John Eberson   **Cost:** $1,000,000
    Year Remodeled: 1983   **Cost:** $7,000,000
    Contact for Rental: Sue Bahen
    Resident Groups: Richmond Ballet; Richmond Symphony; Virginia Opera Association

THE EMPIRE THEATRE COMPLEX
114 West Broad Street, Richmond, VA 23220
(804) 344-8040
FAX: (804) 775-2325
    Type of Facility: Theatre Complex
    Year Built: 1911
    Contact for Rental: Phil Whiteway;   (804) 783-1688
    Resident Groups: Theater IV
    The Empire Theatre Complex contains the Empire Stage and the Litte Theatre Stage. See separate listings for additional information.

THE EMPIRE THEATRE COMPLEX - EMPIRE STAGE
118 West Broad Street, Richmond, VA 23220
(804) 344-8040
FAX: (804) 775-2325
    Type of Facility: Theatre House
    Type of Stage: Proscenium
    Stage Dimensions: 58'Wx31'6"D
    Seating Capacity: 604
    Year Built: 1911
    Contact for Rental: Phil Whiteway;   (804) 783-1688
    Resident Groups: Theater IV

THE EMPIRE THEATRE COMPLEX - LITTLE THEATRE STAGE
114 West Broad Street, Richmond, VA 23220
(804) 783-1688
FAX: (804) 775-2325
    Type of Facility: Studio Performance
    Facility Originally: Vaudeville
    Type of Stage: Proscenium
    Stage Dimensions: 25'x14'
    Orchestra Pit
    Seating Capacity: 80
    Year Built: 1911
    Year Remodeled: 1990   **Architect:** Bond, Comet, Westmoreland & Galusha
    Cost: $2,300,000
    Contact for Rental: Mr. L. Moore;   (804) 344-8048
    Manager: Phil Whiteway;   (804) 783-1688
    Resident Groups: Theatre IV; Gilpin Stage Company

UNIVERSITY OF RICHMOND - JAMES L. CAMP MEMORIAL THEATRE
Richmond, VA 23173
(804) 289-8263
    Type of Facility: Auditorium; Theatre House
    Type of Stage: Proscenium
    Stage Dimensions: 34'3"Wx25'H
    Orchestra Pit
    Seating Capacity: 686
    Year Built: 1967
    Resident Groups: University Players

Roanoke

INSTRUMENTAL MUSIC

ROANOKE SYMPHONY SOCIETY
PO Box 2433, Roanoke, VA 24010
(703) 343-6221
FAX: (703) 343-3954
>**Arts Area:** Symphony
>**Status:** Professional; Non-Profit
>**Type:** Performing; Touring; Educational
>**Purpose:** To perform the highest quality symphonic music for the largest possible audiences throughout the region
>**Management:** Victoria Bond, Music Director; Margarite Fourcoy, Executive Director
>**Officers:** Heidi Krisch, President
>**Budget:** $1,000,000 - $5,000,000
>**Income Sources:** Private Foundations/Grants/Endowments; Business/Corporate Donations; Box Office; Government Grants; Individual Donations
>**Performance Facilities:** Roanoke Civic Center

ROANOKE VALLEY CHAMBER MUSIC SOCIETY
PO Box 8041, Roanoke, VA 24014
(703) 774-2899
>**Founded:** 1980
>**Arts Area:** Chamber
>**Status:** Professional; Non-Profit
>**Type:** Educational; Sponsoring
>**Purpose:** To present professionally-performed chamber-music concerts; to sponsor educational functions; to create an awareness of music and especially chamber music
>**Management:** Ann-Marie W. Horner, President/Executive Director
>**Paid Staff:** 1
>**Utilizes:** Guest Artists
>**Budget:** $1,000 - $50,000
>**Income Sources:** Private Foundations/Grants/Endowments; Business/Corporate Donations; Box Office; Individual Donations
>**Season:** Fall - Spring   **Annual Attendance:** 1,500
>**Affiliations:** CMA
>**Performance Facilities:** Olin Theater, Roanoke College

VOCAL MUSIC

OPERA ROANOKE
111 West Campbell Avenue, Roanoke, VA 24011
(703) 982-2742
FAX: (703) 343-3954
>**Founded:** 1977
>**Arts Area:** Grand Opera; Light Opera; Operetta
>**Status:** Professional
>**Type:** Performing; Resident
>**Purpose:** To produce professional opera in southwestern Virginia
>**Management:** Judith Clark, Executive Director; Victoria Band, Artistic Director
>**Officers:** J. Tyler Pugh, President; Joseph Logan III, Vice President; Michael Quinn, Treasurer; Carol Danielsen, Secretary; Cynthia Dillon, Vice President Friends of the Opera
>**Paid Staff:** 5
>**Utilizes:** Guest Artists; Guest Directors
>**Budget:** $100,000 - $500,000
>**Income Sources:** Business/Corporate Donations; Box Office; Government Grants; Individual Donations
>**Season:** 52 Weeks   **Annual Attendance:** 1,600
>**Affiliations:** OA
>**Performance Facilities:** Mill Mountain Theatre; Olin Theatre

THEATRE

MILL MOUNTAIN THEATRE COMPANY
One Market Square SE, Second Floor, Roanoke, VA 24011-1437
(703) 342-5730
FAX: (703) 224-1238
>**Founded:** 1964
>**Arts Area:** Professional; Musical; Theatrical Group

Status: Professional; Non-Profit
Type: Performing; Resident; Educational
Purpose: Professional production of musicals, dramas and comedies with particular emphasis on the production and development of original works
Management: Jere Lee Hodgin, Executive/Artistic Director; James L. Ayers, Business Manager; Judy Graham, Director of Marketing/Development
Officers: Michael Warner, President; E.R. Feinour, Vice President; Robert Fishburn, Senior Vice President; Ann Hammersley, Secretary; Sandra Light, Treasurer
Paid Staff: 24   **Volunteer Staff:** 1
Paid Artists: 95   **Non-Paid Artists:** 50
Utilizes: Guest Artists; Guest Directors
Budget: $1,000,000 - $5,000,000
Income Sources: Private Foundations/Grants/Endowments; Business/Corporate Donations; Box Office; Government Grants; Individual Donations
Season: 52 Weeks   **Annual Attendance:** 50,000
Affiliations: TCG; New Dramatists; SETC; Theatre Council of Virginia
Performance Facilities: Mill Mountain Theatre; Mainstage; Theatre B

FACILITY

MILL MOUNTAIN THEATRE
One Market Square, Second Floor, Roanoke, VA 24011-1437
(703) 342-5730
FAX: (703) 224-1238
   Founded: 1964
   Type of Facility: Theatre Complex
   Type of Stage: Greek; Proscenium; Alternate stage - Black Box
   Stage Dimensions: 35'Wx35'D
   Orchestra Pit
   Seating Capacity: Main Stage - 411; Alternate Stage - 125
   Year Built: 1983   **Architect:** Hayes, Seay, Mattern & Mattern   **Cost:** $1,400,000
   Acoustical Consultant: Systems Design
   Contact for Rental: Mona Black;   (703) 345-5730
   Resident Groups: Mill Mountain Theatre Company
   Primarily for the in-house production of live, professional theatre

ROANOKE CIVIC CENTER
710 Williamson Road, NE, Roanoke, VA 24016
(703) 981-2241
FAX: (703) 981-2748
   Type of Facility: Theatre House; Civic Center; Arena; Multi-Purpose
   Type of Stage: Proscenium
   Stage Dimensions: 66'x105'x55'
   Orchestra Pit
   Seating Capacity: 2,475
   Year Built: 1971   **Architect:** Associated Architects & Engineers   **Cost:** $14,800,000
   Acoustical Consultant: Bolt, Beranek & Newman
   Contact for Rental: B.E. Chapman;   (703) 981-2241
   Resident Groups: Roanoke Symphony Orchestra

Salem

FACILITY

SALEM CIVIC CENTER
PO Box 886, Salem, VA 24153
(703) 981-2241
   Type of Facility: Concert Hall; Civic Center; Arena
   Type of Stage: Flexible
   Seating Capacity: 8,000
   Year Built: 1967   **Architect:** Wells and Meagher
   Contact for Rental: Manager;   (703) 375-3004

Sweet Briar

FACILITY

SWEET BRIAR COLLEGE - BABCOCK AUDITORIUM
Sweet Briar, VA 24595
(804) 381-6123
    Type of Facility: Concert Hall; Auditorium
    Type of Stage: Proscenium
    Stage Dimensions: 55'x50'x28'   **Orchestra Pit**
    Seating Capacity: 652
    Year Built: 1961   **Architect:** Clark, Nexson and Owen
    Acoustical Consultant: Harold Burris-Meyer
    Contact for Rental: Thomas N. Connors;   (804) 381-6200
    Resident Groups: Student theatre and dance groups
    In addition to Babcock Auditorium, the building also contains a small, black box theatre.

Vienna

PERFORMING SERIES

WOLF TRAP FARM FOUNDATION
1624 Trap Road, Vienna, VA 22182
(703) 255-1900
    Founded: 1971
    Arts Area: Dance; Vocal Music; Instrumental Music; Theater; Lyric Opera
    Status: Professional; Non-Profit
    Type: Educational; Sponsoring
    Purpose: To expose people of all ages to every aspect of the performing arts; to increase understanding and appreciation of the role the performing arts has in community life
    Management: Matthew Hessburg, Director, Public Affairs and Communications; Paulann Doane, Director of Special Events
    Officers: Charles A. Walters Jr., Vice President/Finance Officer; Ann McPherson McKee, Vice President of Program and Production
    Paid Staff: 40
    Utilizes: Special Technical Talent; Guest Conductors; Guest Artists; Guest Directors
    Budget: $5,000,000 - $10,000,000
    Income Sources: Private Foundations/Grants/Endowments; Business/Corporate Donations; Box Office; Government Grants; Individual Donations
    Season: June - August; October - May   **Annual Attendance:** 420,000
    Performance Facilities: Filene Center; The Barns

FACILITY

WOLF TRAP FARM PARK FOR THE PERFORMING ARTS
1624 Trap Road, Vienna, VA 22180
(703) 255-1900
    Type of Facility: Outdoor Theatre
    Type of Stage: Proscenium
    Seating Capacity: 900
    Year Built: 1977   **Architect:** Thomas J. Madigan   **Cost:** $71,000
    Manager: Vistoria Rapaport;   (703) 938-8463

Virginia Beach

FACILITY

VIRGINIA BEACH PAVILION CONVENTION CENTER
1000 19th Street, Virginia Beach, VA 23458
(804) 428-8000
FAX: (804) 422-8860
    Type of Facility: Civic Center; Convention Center
    Year Built: 1980   **Architect:** Walsh Ashet Dill   **Cost:** $20,000,000
    Acoustical Consultant: Coffeen & Anderson
    Contact for Rental: Bill Holland;   (804) 428-8000
    The Convention Center contains the Exhibit Hall and Pavilion Theater. See separate listings for additional information.

VIRGINIA BEACH PAVILION CONVENTION CENTER - EXHIBIT HALL
1000 19th Street, Virginia Beach, VA 23458
(804) 428-8000
FAX: (804) 422-8860
> **Type of Facility:** Exhibition Hall
> **Type of Stage:** Flexible
> **Year Built:** 1980
> **Contact for Rental:** Bill Holland;   (804) 428-8000
> *The Exhibit Hall contains 57,200 square feet of usable floor area.*

VIRGINIA BEACH PAVILION CONVENTION CENTER - PAVILION THEATER
1000 19th Street, Virginia Beach, VA 23458
(804) 428-8000
FAX: (804) 422-8860
> **Type of Facility:** Concert Hall; Theatre House; Opera House
> **Type of Stage:** Proscenium
> **Stage Dimensions:** 55'Wx47'6"D; 46'7"Wx24'H proscenium opening   **Orchestra Pit**
> **Seating Capacity:** 1,000
> **Year Built:** 1980
> **Contact for Rental:** Bill Holland;   (804) 428-8000

Williamsburg

DANCE

THE INSTITUTE FOR DANCE, INC.
PO Box 1568, Williamsburg, VA 23187
(804) 229-1717
> **Founded:** 1978
> **Arts Area:** Ballet; Jazz; Ethnic; Folk; Tap
> **Status:** Non-Profit
> **Type:** Performing; Educational
> **Purpose:** To promote the art of dance
> **Management:** Heidi S. Robitshek, Director
> **Officers:** Anne Hamrick, President; Paul Kershner, Vice President; Irving H. Robitshek, Secretary/Treasurer
> **Paid Staff:** 7   **Volunteer Staff:** 100
> **Utilizes:** Special Technical Talent; Guest Artists; Guest Choreographers
> **Budget:** $100,000 - $500,000
> **Income Sources:** Business/Corporate Donations; Box Office; Government Grants; Individual Donations
> **Season:** 52 Weeks   **Annual Attendance:** 7,000
> **Performance Facilities:** Phi Beta Kappa Memorial Hall, The College of William and Mary

PERFORMING SERIES

VIRGINIA SHAKESPEARE FESTIVAL
College of William and Mary, PO Box 8795, Williamsburg, VA 23187-8795
(804) 221-2660
FAX: (804) 221-1773
> **Founded:** 1978
> **Arts Area:** Theater; Festivals
> **Status:** Professional; Non-Profit
> **Type:** Performing; Educational
> **Purpose:** To perform quality Shakespeare in a classical manner
> **Management:** Jerry H. Bledsoe, Executive Director
> **Volunteer Staff:** 10
> **Paid Artists:** 50   **Non-Paid Artists:** 20
> **Utilizes:** Special Technical Talent; Guest Artists; Guest Directors
> **Budget:** $50,000 - $100,000
> **Income Sources:** Private Foundations/Grants/Endowments; Business/Corporate Donations; Box Office; Government Grants; Individual Donations
> **Season:** July - August   **Annual Attendance:** 10,000
> **Affiliations:** The College of William and Mary
> **Performance Facilities:** Phi Beta Kappa Memorial Hall, The College of William and Mary

---
Woodstock

PERFORMING SERIES

SHENANDOAH VALLEY MUSIC FESTIVAL
PO Box 12, Woodstock, VA 22664
(703) 459-3396
    Founded: 1963
    Arts Area: Dance; Vocal Music; Instrumental Music; Festivals; Lyric Opera; Grand Opera
    Status: Non-Profit
    Type: Sponsoring
    Purpose: To foster, promote, and increase the musical knowledge of the public by organizing and presenting programs chosen primarily from the literature of symphonic music, and incidentally from chamber music, opera, solo recitals, vocal chorus and dance; to present jazz, folk and others forms
    Management: Melissa S. Deibert, Executive Director
    Paid Staff: 3   **Volunteer Staff:** 50
    Paid Artists: 125
    Budget: $100,000 - $500,000
    Income Sources: Private Foundations/Grants/Endowments; Business/Corporate Donations; Box Office; Government Grants; Individual Donations
    Season: April - September   **Annual Attendance:** 7,500
    Affiliations: Shenandoah Arts Council
    Performance Facilities: Orkney Springs Pavilion

WASHINGTON

Aberdeen

FACILITY

BISHOP CENTER FOR PERFORMING ARTS
1610 E.P. Smith Drive, Aberdeen, WA 98520
(206) 533-0177
FAX: (206) 532-6716
  Founded: 1974
  Type of Facility: Concert Hall; Performance Center
  Type of Stage: Thrust; Proscenium
  Stage Dimensions: 40'x60'   **Orchestra Pit**
  Seating Capacity: 500
  Year Built: 1974
  Architect: Sneet & Lundgren
  Cost: $1,000,000
  Contact for Rental: C. Wellington;   (206) 532-9020
  Resident Groups: Grays Harbor Symphony; Elks National Band; Hume Street Jazz Band

---

Bellevue

PERFORMING SERIES

BELLEVUE PARKS AND RECREATION DEPARTMENT - BELLEVUE JAZZ FESTIVAL
PO Box 90012, Bellevue, WA 98009-9012
(206) 451-4106
FAX: (206) 451-7259
  Founded: 1976
  Arts Area: Vocal Music; Instrumental Music; Festivals
  Status: Professional; Non-Profit
  Type: Performing; Sponsoring
  Purpose: To present the oldest jazz festival in the Pacific Northwest featuring 100 professionals, Northwest-resident jazz musicians and vocalists performing all aspects of jazz
  Management: Mick Mellor, Festival Director
  Paid Staff: 2   **Volunteer Staff:** 30
  Paid Artists: 100
  Utilizes: Guest Artists
  Budget: $1,000 - $50,000
  Income Sources: Private Foundations/Grants/Endowments; Box Office; Government Grants; City of Bellevue
  Season: July   **Annual Attendance:** 8,000
  Affiliations: BMI
  Performance Facilities: Bellevue Community College

Bellingham

FACILITY

MORCA FOUNDATION OF THE DANCE
1349 Franklin, Bellingham, WA 98225
(206) 676-1864
  Type of Facility: Studio Performance
  Facility Originally: Church
  Type of Stage: Greek; 3/4 Arena
  Stage Dimensions: 18'x20'
  Seating Capacity: 65
  Year Built: 1902
  Year Remodeled: 1979
  Contact for Rental: Ted Morca;   (206) 676-1864

Resident Groups: Morca Dance Theatre
Concerts, Lectures, Music Recitals

MOUNT BAKER THEATRE
106 North Commercial, Bellingham, WA 98225
(206) 734-6080
FAX: (206) 671-0114
Founded: 1927
Type of Facility: Performance Center; Film House
Facility Originally: Vaudeville; Movie House
Type of Stage: Proscenium
Stage Dimensions: 26'Dx42'W   **Orchestra Pit**
Seating Capacity: 1,500
Year Built: 1927
Architect: R.C. Reamer
Contact for Rental: Ruth Shaw, General Manager;   (206) 734-6080
Resident Groups: Whatcom Symphony Orchestra

WESTERN WASHINGTON UNIVERSITY - CONCERT HALL
Performing Arts Center, Bellingham, WA 98225
(206) 676-3866
FAX: (206) 676-3028
Type of Facility: Concert Hall
Type of Stage: Concert Stage
Seating Capacity: 711
Year Built: 1973
Architect: Henry Klein & Associates
Cost: $2,053,321
Acoustical Consultant: Jaffe Acoustics
Contact for Rental:
Manager: Robert Sylvester

WESTERN WASHINGTON UNIVERSITY - EXPERIMENTAL THEATER
Performing Arts Center, Bellingham, WA 98225
(206) 676-3876
Type of Facility: Performance Center
Type of Stage: Flexible
Stage Dimensions: 16'x38'x25'
Year Built: 1978   **Architect:** Henry Klein & Associates
Manager: Tom Ward

WESTERN WASHINGTON UNIVERSITY - MAIN STAGE
Performing Arts Center, Bellingham, WA 98225
(206) 676-3866
FAX: (206) 676-3028
Type of Facility: Auditorium
Facility Originally: School
Type of Stage: Proscenium
Stage Dimensions: 40'Wx35'D   **Orchestra Pit**
Seating Capacity: 1,130
Year Built: 1952   **Cost:** $1,250,000
Year Remodeled: 1973
Contact for Rental: Robert Sylvester, Dean, College of Fine and Performing Arts;   (206) 676-3866

WESTERN WASHINGTON UNIVERSITY - OLD MAIN THEATER
High Street, Bellingham, WA 98225
(206) 676-3866
Type of Facility: Auditorium
Facility Originally: Recreation Hall; Gymnasium
Type of Stage: Thrust
Stage Dimensions: 11'6"x32'x31'
Seating Capacity: 300
Year Built: 1960
Year Remodeled: 1974
Architect: Henry Klein & Associates
Contact for Rental: Robert Sylvester, Manager;   (206) 676-3866

Bremerton

DANCE

PENINSULA DANCE THEATRE
515 Chester Avenue, Bremerton, WA 98310
(206) 377-6214
Arts Area: Ballet
Status: Professional; Non-Profit
Type: Performing; Resident
Management: Lawan Morrison, Artistic Director
Paid Artists: 15
Income Sources: Box Office; Individual Donations
Performance Facilities: Win Graulund Performing Arts Center

INSTRUMENTAL MUSIC

BREMERTON SYMPHONY ASSOCIATION
PO Box 996, Bremerton, WA 98310
(206) 373-1722
Founded: 1942
Arts Area: Symphony; Orchestra; Ensemble
Status: Non-Professional; Non-Profit
Type: Performing; Resident; Educational
Purpose: To provide musical outlets for qualified performers and quality performances for interested audiences
Officers: Al Dillan, President; Fran Reh, First Vice President; Jan Cisler, Second Vice President; Stephen Chertok, Secretary; Jeffrey Smith, Treasurer
Volunteer Staff: 8
Paid Artists: 5   **Non-Paid Artists:** 60
Utilizes: Special Technical Talent; Guest Artists
Budget: $50,000 - $100,000
Income Sources: Business/Corporate Donations; Box Office; Government Grants; Individual Donations
Season: September - June   **Annual Attendance:** 5,000
Affiliations: ASOL
Performance Facilities: Sylvan Way Baptist Church

THEATRE

COMMUNITY THEATRE
599 Lebo Boulevard, Bremerton, WA 98310
(206) 373-5152
Founded: 1945
Arts Area: Musical; Community; Theatrical Group
Status: Non-Professional; Non-Profit
Type: Performing
Management: Robert Montgomery, Business Manager
Officers: Bruce Hankins, President; Betty Bell, Secretary; Robert Montgomery, Treasurer
Volunteer Staff: 10
Non-Paid Artists: 35
Utilizes: Special Technical Talent; Guest Conductors; Guest Artists; Guest Directors
Budget: $1,000 - $50,000
Income Sources: Business/Corporate Donations; Box Office; Individual Donations
Season: September - June   **Annual Attendance:** 10,000

FACILITY

COMMUNITY THEATRE
599 Lebo Boulevard, Bremerton, WA 98310
(206) 373-5152
Founded: 1947
Type of Facility: Auditorium; Theatre House
Type of Stage: Proscenium
Stage Dimensions: 65'Wx25'D, 30'Wx15'H proscenium opening   **Orchestra Pit**
Seating Capacity: 192
Year Built: 1976   **Architect:** Anderson Associates   **Cost:** $350,000
Contact for Rental: Shirley Chase, Office Manager;   (206) 373-5152
Availability limited

Centralia

FACILITY

CENTRALIA COLLEGE - CORBET THEATRE
600 West Locust, Centralia, WA 98531
(206) 723-9391
FAX: (206) 753-3404
   Type of Facility: Performance Center
   Type of Stage: Thrust; Proscenium
   Stage Dimensions: 40'x28'   **Orchestra Pit**
   Seating Capacity: 170
   Year Built: 1972   **Cost:** $600,000
   Contact for Rental: Helen Lucier;   (206) 736-9391, ext. 218
   Manager: Philip R. Wickstrom

Chelan

PERFORMING SERIES

LAKE CHELAN BACH FESTIVAL
PO Box 554, Chelan, WA 98816
(509) 687-3918
   Founded: 1982
   Arts Area: Vocal Music; Instrumental Music; Lyric Opera
   Status: Professional; Non-Professional; Non-Profit
   Type: Performing; Educational
   Purpose: To foster the classical arts
   Volunteer Staff: 42
   Paid Artists: 8   **Non-Paid Artists:** 40
   Utilizes: Guest Artists
   Budget: $1,000 - $50,000
   Income Sources: Private Foundations/Grants/Endowments; Business/Corporate Donations; Box Office;
Individual Donations
   Season: July   **Annual Attendance:** 5,000

Edmonds

DANCE

OLYMPIC BALLET THEATRE
700 Main Street, Anderson Cultural Center, Edmonds, WA 98020
(206) 774-7570
   Founded: 1981
   Arts Area: Ballet
   Status: Semi-Professional; Non-Profit
   Type: Resident
   Purpose: To create high-quality dance; to provide training and performance opportunities for pre-professional dancers
   Management: John and Helena Wilkins, Artistic Directors
   Officers: Dave Railsback
   Paid Staff: 12
   Non-Paid Artists: 21
   Utilizes: Special Technical Talent; Guest Artists
   Budget: $50,000 - $100,000
   Income Sources: Private Foundations/Grants/Endowments; Business/Corporate Donations; Box Office; Government
Grants; Individual Donations
   Season: September - June
   Affiliations: PRBA
   Performance Facilities: Puget Sound Theatre

INSTRUMENTAL MUSIC

CASCADE SYMPHONY ORCHESTRA
PO Box 550, Edmonds, WA 98026
(206) 778-4737
   Founded: 1962
   Arts Area: Symphony; Orchestra; Chamber; Ensemble

Status: Semi-Professional; Non-Professional
Type: Performing; Resident; Sponsoring
Purpose: To perform symphonic literature ranging from baroque to contemporary
Management: Ropen Shakarian, Conductor
Officers: David Earling, President; Philip Elvrum, Vice President; Alice Dawson, Recording Secretary; Judith Bogataj, Corresponding Secretary; Gail Hankinson, Treasurer
Paid Staff: 1   **Volunteer Staff:** 19
Utilizes: Guest Conductors; Guest Artists
Budget: $1,000 - $50,000
Income Sources: Private Foundations/Grants/Endowments; Business/Corporate Donations; Box Office; Individual Donations
Season: October - April   **Annual Attendance:** 3,000
Affiliations: ASOL; BMI; ASCAP; AFM
Performance Facilities: Puget Sound Christian College

Everett

FACILITY

EVERETT CIVIC AUDITORIUM
2415 Colby Avenue, Everett, WA 98201
(206) 339-4298
Type of Facility: Auditorium
Type of Stage: Thrust
Stage Dimensions: 50'Wx58'D   **Orchestra Pit**
Seating Capacity: 1,565; 1,506 with orchestra pit
Year Built: 1939   **Architect:** Earl W. Morrison
Year Remodeled: 1979   **Architect:** Bryant Butterfield & Frets   **Cost:** $1,300,000
Acoustical Consultant: Towne Richards and Chaudibre
Contact for Rental: Nola Deierling;   (206) 339-4280
Manager: W.D. Williamson, Technical Manager;   (206) 339-4280

Fort Lewis

PERFORMING SERIES

ENTERTAINMENT BRANCH, CRD
Building 2410, Fort Lewis, WA 98433
(206) 967-3044
Founded: 1950
Arts Area: Dance; Vocal Music; Instrumental Music; Theater
Status: Semi-Professional; Non-Profit
Type: Performing; Educational
Purpose: To provide diverse and comprehensive performing arts-related activities for the soldier, his family, the Fort Lewis community and for interested individuals in the surrounding civilian community
Management: Howard A. Hoadley, Entertainment Director; William C. Strock, David V. Wright, Theatre Specialists; Leona M. Hay, Administrative Assistant
Paid Staff: 4   **Volunteer Staff:** 12
Utilizes: Special Technical Talent; Guest Artists; Guest Directors
Income Sources: Box Office; Government Grants
Season: October - June   **Annual Attendance:** 5,000
Performance Facilities: Chinook Center for the Performing Arts

FACILITY

CENTURION PLAYHOUSE
Building 5300, Music & Theatre Branch, Fort Lewis, WA 98433
(206) 968-3402
Type of Facility: Theatre House
Type of Stage: Flexible
Stage Dimensions: 60'x100'   **Orchestra Pit**
Seating Capacity: 200

THE CHINOOK THEATRE FOR THE PERFORMING ARTS
F Street, Fort Lewis, WA 98433-5000
(206) 967-5636
Type of Facility: Performance Center; Theatre House

Facility Originally: Recreation Hall; Gymnasium
Type of Stage: Thrust; Proscenium
Stage Dimensions: 36'x17'6"x28'; 36'W proscenium opening   **Orchestra Pit**
Seating Capacity: 100
Year Built: 1940
Year Remodeled: 1977
Contact for Rental: Howard Hoadley;   (206) 967-3044

Friday Harbor

THEATRE

SAN JUAN COMMUNITY THEATRE AND ARTS CENTER
100 Second Street, Friday Harbor, WA 98250
(206) 378-3210
Founded: 1989
Arts Area: Community
Status: Non-Professional; Non-Profit
Type: Performing; Educational; Sponsoring
Purpose: To maintain a center for performing and visual arts for the island community
Management: Douglas Scott, Executive Director
Officers: Shirley Neilson, President of the Board
Paid Staff: 3 **Volunteer Staff:** 70
Income Sources: Box Office; Individual Donations
Season: 52 Weeks   **Annual Attendance:** 16,000

Gig Harbor

THEATRE

THE PERFORMANCE CIRCLE
6615 38th Avenue NW, Gig Harbor, WA 98335
(206) 851-7529
Founded: 1976
Arts Area: Musical; Theatrical Group
Status: Semi-Professional; Non-Profit
Type: Performing; Touring; Educational
Purpose: To promote theatre arts and cultural enrichment through performances as well as educational workshops and classes
Management: Kathleen L. McGilliard, Artistic Director/Founder; Shirley M. Coffin, Managing Director; Milt Boyd, Technical Director
Officers: Jill Johnson, President; Kris Quinn, Vice President; Ruth Peacock, Treasurer; Melinda Wilson, Secretary; John O'Melveny, Immediate Past President
Paid Staff: 3 **Volunteer Staff:** 50
Utilizes: Special Technical Talent; Guest Artists; Guest Directors
Budget: $100,000 - $500,000
Income Sources: Private Foundations/Grants/Endowments; Business/Corporate Donations; Box Office; Individual Donations
Season: 52 Weeks

Hoquiam

FACILITY

7TH STREET THEATRE
313 Seventh Street, Hoquiam, WA 98550
(206) 532-0302; (206) 532-6058
Founded: 1928
Type of Facility: Auditorium; Theatre House
Facility Originally: Vaudeville; Movie House
Type of Stage: Proscenium   **Orchestra Pit**
Seating Capacity: 1,106
Year Built: 1928   **Cost:** $175,000
Year Remodeled: 1992   **Architect:** Andring and Gozart   **Cost:** $2,000,000
Contact for Rental: Patricia C. Stevenson;   (206) 532-6058

Longview

THEATRE

COLUMBIA THEATRE FOR THE PERFORMING ARTS
1231 Vandercook Way, Longview, WA 98632
(206) 423-1011
Arts Area: Musical; Community; Theatrical Group
Status: Non-Profit
Type: Performing; Sponsoring
Purpose: Facility is used by a variety of groups to present and produce events
Management: James Murphy, General Manager
Paid Staff: 2   **Volunteer Staff:** 6
Budget: $100,000 - $500,000
Income Sources: Private Foundations/Grants/Endowments; Business/Corporate Donations; Box Office; Government Grants; Individual Donations
Season: September - July   **Annual Attendance:** 30,000

FACILITY

MCCLELLAND ARTS CENTER
951 Delaware, Longview, WA 98632
(206) 577-3356
Founded: 1974
Type of Facility: Theatre Complex; Concert Hall; Auditorium; Outdoor (Concert); Multi-Purpose
Type of Stage: Flexible
Seating Capacity: 515
Year Built: 1974   **Architect:** Robert and Shaw   **Cost:** $200,000
Contact for Rental: Phyllis L. Sayles;   (206) 577-3356

Lynnwood

DANCE

ANACRUSIS MODERN TAP DANCE
c/o The FAME Agency, 19003 52nd Avenue West, Lynnwood, WA 98036
(206) 670-3890
FAX: (206) 670-3890
Founded: 1986
Arts Area: Tap
Status: Professional; Non-Profit
Type: Performing; Touring; Educational
Purpose: To create tap dance that is strikingly visual, in which movement in space and percussive footwork are equal partners
Management: Thomas M. Ries, Owner, The FAME Agency
Officers: Cheryl Johnson, Anthony Peters, Artistic Directors
Paid Staff: 1
Paid Artists: 6   **Non-Paid Artists:** 2
Utilizes: Special Technical Talent; Guest Artists; Guest Choreographers
Budget: $50,000 - $100,000
Income Sources: Private Foundations/Grants/Endowments; Business/Corporate Donations; Box Office; Government Grants; Individual Donations
Season: September - June
Affiliations: National Tap Dance Association

Mt. Vernon

FACILITY

LINCOLN THEATRE CENTRE
712 South First Street, Mt. Vernon, WA 98273
(206) 336-2858
FAX: (206) 336-2929
Founded: 1987
Type of Facility: Concert Hall; Auditorium; Performance Center; Theatre House
Facility Originally: Vaudeville; Movie House
Type of Stage: Flexible; Proscenium; Platform

Stage Dimensions: Main - 13'x24'; Platform - 16'x20'   **Orchestra Pit**
Year Built: 1926   **Cost:** $2,000,000

Oak Harbor

FACILITY

WHIDBEY PLAYHOUSE
1094 Midway Boulevard, Oak Harbor, WA 98277
(206) 679-2237
Founded: 1966
Type of Facility: Theatre House
Facility Originally: Church
Type of Stage: Proscenium
Stage Dimensions: 15'x40'
Seating Capacity: 138

Olympia

INSTRUMENTAL MUSIC

OLYMPIA SYMPHONY ORCHESTRA
PO Box 7635, Olympia, WA 98507
(206) 753-0074
Founded: 1970
Arts Area: Symphony; Orchestra
Status: Professional; Non-Profit
Type: Performing; Educational
Purpose: To encourage the growth and development of the symphony orchestra and maintain the orchestra; to promote musical and cultural entertainment in diverse forms; to provide the musicians of Thurston County and its surrounding areas with the opportunity to play in a symphony
Management: Cynthia Morrison, General Manager; Ian Edlund, Music Director/Conductor
Paid Staff: 1
Paid Artists: 80
Budget: $50,000 - $100,000
Income Sources: Private Foundations/Grants/Endowments; Business/Corporate Donations; Box Office; Government Grants; Individual Donations
Season: October - March   **Annual Attendance:** 3,500
Affiliations: ASOL
Performance Facilities: Washington Center for the Performing Arts

FACILITY

WASHINGTON CENTER FOR THE PERFORMING ARTS
512 Washington Street SE, Olympia, WA 98501
(206) 753-8585
FAX: (206) 754-1177
Founded: 1985
Type of Facility: Performance Center
Facility Originally: Movie House
Type of Stage: Proscenium; Black Box
Stage Dimensions: Black Box - 54'x48'; 45'Wx35'6"Hx35'1"D proscenium opening   **Orchestra Pit**
Seating Capacity: Proscenium - 982; Black Box - 125
Year Built: 1924
Year Remodeled: 1985   **Cost:** $5,000,000
Contact for Rental: Ruth Palmerlee, Operations Manager;   (206) 753-8585

Richland

INSTRUMENTAL MUSIC

MID-COLUMBIA SYMPHONY
PO Box 65, Richland, WA 99352
(509) 735-7356
Founded: 1945
Arts Area: Symphony; Orchestra

Status: Non-Professional; Non-Profit
Type: Performing; Resident; Educational
Purpose: To promote music education, interest and appreciation through the presentation of concerts, lectures, and other activities
Officers: Richard Romanelli, President; Kathy Dempsey, Vice President; Jim O'Brien, Secretary; Sid Gire, Treasurer
Paid Staff: 6 **Volunteer Staff:** 2
Paid Artists: 5
Utilizes: Guest Artists
Budget: $100,000 - $500,000
Income Sources: Private Foundations/Grants/Endowments; Business/Corporate Donations; Box Office; Individual Donations
Season: October - May **Annual Attendance:** 5,000
Affiliations: ASOL
Performance Facilities: Richland High School Auditorium

Seattle

DANCE

CO-MOTION DANCE
PO Box 20025, Seattle, WA 98102
(206) 382-0626
Founded: 1979
Arts Area: Modern
Status: Professional; Non-Profit
Type: Performing; Touring; Educational; Sponsoring
Purpose: To develop a diverse and informed audience for professional modern dance
Management: Jane Hyde Walsh, Executive Director
Officers: Paula Swenson, President; Jesse Jaramillo, Vice President; Barron Aoyama, Treasurer; Mary Lou McCollum, Secretary
Paid Staff: 1 **Volunteer Staff:** 2
Paid Artists: 12
Utilizes: Special Technical Talent; Guest Artists; Guest Choreographers
Budget: $50,000 - $100,000
Income Sources: Private Foundations/Grants/Endowments; Business/Corporate Donations; Box Office; Government Grants; Individual Donations
Season: July - March **Annual Attendance:** 35,000

FILIPINIANA ARTS AND CULTURAL CENTER
569 North 166th Street, Seattle, WA 98133
(206) 542-7245
Founded: 1970
Arts Area: Ethnic
Status: Semi-Professional; Non-Profit
Type: Performing; Touring; Resident; Educational; Sponsoring
Purpose: To preserve, promote and enhance the Filipino people's cultural heritage
Management: Roger Del Rosario, Director
Officers: Roger Del Rosario, President; Mencho Santos, Vice President; Marilyn Sanchez, Secretary/Treasurer; John Urrotia, Auditor
Utilizes: Special Technical Talent; Guest Artists; Guest Choreographers
Budget: $1,000 - $50,000
Income Sources: Private Foundations/Grants/Endowments; Business/Corporate Donations; Box Office; Government Grants; Individual Donations
Season: 52 Weeks
Annual Attendance: 5,000

MEANY HALL FOR THE PERFORMING ARTS
University of Washington, AB-10, Seattle, WA 98195
(206) 543-4882
FAX: (206) 685-2759
Arts Area: Modern; Mime; Ballet; Jazz; Ethnic
Status: Non-Profit
Type: Sponsoring; Presenting
Management: Matthew Krashan, Director; Deborah Fishler, Director of Business and Finance; John Idstrom, Director of Development; Jan Steadman, Director of Marketing and Public Relations
Officers: Robert Frayn Jr., Board Chair; John Nesholm, Vice Chair; Jo Allen Patton, Secretary/Treasurer; Frances J. Carr; Professor Ernest Henley

Paid Staff: 15
Utilizes: Guest Conductors; Guest Artists; Guest Directors; Guest Choreographers
Budget: $1,000,000 - $5,000,000
Income Sources: Private Foundations/Grants/Endowments; Business/Corporate Donations; Box Office; Government Grants; Individual Donations
Season: 52 Weeks **Annual Attendance:** 130,000
Affiliations: University of Washington
Performance Facilities: Meany Hall

NEW PERFORMANCE SERIES/NORTHWEST NEW WORKS
c/o On the Boards, 153 14th Avenue, Seattle, WA 98122
(206) 325-7901
FAX: (206) 325-7903
Arts Area: Modern
Status: Professional; Non-Profit
Type: Commissioning; Presenting
Purpose: To intoduce audiences and artists to a wide variety of performances from around the world; to support the development of contemporary artists in the Northwest
Management: Mark Murphy, Programming Director; Andrea Wagner, Managing Director
Budget: $100,000 - $500,000
Income Sources: Private Foundations/Grants/Endowments; Business/Corporate Donations; Box Office; Government Grants; Individual Donations
Affiliations: Washington Hall Performance Gallery

OCHEAMI
PO Box 31635, Seattle, WA 98103-1635
(206) 329-8876
Founded: 1978
Arts Area: Ethnic
Status: Professional; Non-Profit
Type: Performing; Touring; Educational
Purpose: To promote cultural enrichment in the form of traditional African music and dance
Management: Kofi Anang, Artistic Director; Cecilia Anang, Manager
Paid Staff: 2 **Volunteer Staff:** 4
Paid Artists: 4
Utilizes: Guest Artists; Guest Choreographers
Budget: $1,000 - $50,000
Income Sources: Private Foundations/Grants/Endowments; Business/Corporate Donations; Box Office; Government Grants; Individual Donations
Season: 52 Weeks

PACIFIC NORTHWEST BALLET
4649 Sunnyside Avenue North, Seattle, WA 98103
(206) 547-5900
Founded: 1972
Arts Area: Ballet
Status: Professional; Non-Profit
Type: Performing; Touring; Resident
Purpose: To maintain a professional ballet company and school
Management: Kent Stowell, Francia Russell, Artistic Directors
Officers: Arthur Jacobus, President/Chief Executive Officer; Susan Brotman, Chairperson
Paid Staff: 300 **Volunteer Staff:** 200
Paid Artists: 81
Utilizes: Special Technical Talent; Guest Choreographers
Budget: $5,000,000 - $10,000,000
Income Sources: Private Foundations/Grants/Endowments; Business/Corporate Donations; Box Office; Government Grants; Individual Donations
Season: October - June **Annual Attendance:** 200,000
Affiliations: Dance USA; AAA; Washington State Arts Alliance
Performance Facilities: Seattle Center Opera House

RADOST FOLK EMSEMBLE
PO Box 31295, Seattle, WA 98103
Founded: 1975
Arts Area: Ethnic
Status: Semi-Professional; Non-Profit
Type: Performing; Touring; Educational; Sponsoring
Purpose: To present and preserve the ethnic dance and music of Eastern Europe and America
Management: Glenn Nielsen, Artistic Director; Karen Powell, Producing Director; Scott Nagel, General Manager

Officers: Karen Powell; Mario Isely; Jill Lole; Scott Nagel; Glenn Nielsen; Jill Johnson
Paid Staff: 1   **Volunteer Staff:** 4
Utilizes: Special Technical Talent; Guest Artists; Guest Choreographers
Budget: $50,000 - $100,000
Income Sources: Private Foundations/Grants/Endowments; Business/Corporate Donations; Box Office; Government Grants; Individual Donations
Season: October - July   **Annual Attendance:** 30,000

WORLD DANCE SERIES
c/o University of Washington, AB-10, Seattle, WA 98195
(206) 543-4880
FAX: (206) 685-2759
Arts Area: Modern; Ballet; Jazz; Ethnic
Status: Professional; Non-Profit
Type: Performing; Touring; Educational
Purpose: To bring world-class performers to the Seattle community via the University of Washington
Management: Matt Krashan, Director; Jan Steadman, Director of Marketing and Public Relations
Budget: $100,000 - $500,000
Income Sources: Private Foundations/Grants/Endowments; Business/Corporate Donations; Box Office; Government Grants; Individual Donations
Performance Facilities: Meany Theater

INSTRUMENTAL MUSIC

EARLY MUSIC GUILD OF SEATTLE
1605 12th Avenue, Suite 19, Seattle, WA 98122
(206) 325-7066
Founded: 1977
Arts Area: Chamber; Early Music
Status: Professional; Non-Profit
Type: Educational; Sponsoring
Purpose: To present an international series of six concerts by touring ensembles each year
Management: Maria Caldwell, Executive Director
Paid Staff: 1   **Volunteer Staff:** 2
Utilizes: Guest Artists
Budget: $100,000 - $500,000
Income Sources: Private Foundations/Grants/Endowments; Business/Corporate Donations; Box Office; Government Grants; Individual Donations
Season: October - May   **Annual Attendance:** 5,000

NORTHWEST CHAMBER ORCHESTRA
1305 Fourth Avenue, #522, Seattle, WA 98101
(206) 343-0445
Founded: 1973
Arts Area: Orchestra; Chamber
Status: Professional; Non-Profit
Type: Performing; Touring; Resident; Educational
Purpose: To bring chamber repertoire to our community and provide employment opportunities for professional musicians; to present educational programs through young people's concerts and workshops
Management: Sandra Schwab, Managing Director; Sidney Harth, Principal Director
Officers: Jeannette Privat, President; Corinne Campbell, Vice President; Phillip LeDuc, Vice President; Kathryn Battuello, Secretary; Pamela Hughes, Treasurer
Paid Staff: 4   **Volunteer Staff:** 20
Paid Artists: 15
Utilizes: Guest Conductors; Guest Artists
Budget: $100,000 - $500,000
Income Sources: Private Foundations/Grants/Endowments; Business/Corporate Donations; Box Office; Government Grants; Individual Donations
Season: September - May   **Annual Attendance:** 8,000
Affiliations: AFM
Performance Facilities: Kane Hall, University of Washington

PHILADELPHIA STRING QUARTET
PO Box 45776, Seattle, WA 98145
(206) 527-8839
Founded: 1960
Arts Area: Chamber
Status: Professional; Non-Profit
Type: Performing; Touring; Educational; Sponsoring

Purpose: To perform string quartets; to produce the Olympic Music Festival
Management: Alan Iglitzin, Executive Director
Paid Staff: 3 **Volunteer Staff:** 60
Paid Artists: 4
Utilizes: Guest Artists
Budget: $100,000 - $500,000
Income Sources: Private Foundations/Grants/Endowments; Business/Corporate Donations; Box Office; Government Grants; Individual Donations
Season: 52 Weeks **Annual Attendance:** 25,000

PUGET SOUND CHAMBER MUSIC SOCIETY
93 Pike Street, #315, Seattle, WA 98101
(206) 622-1393
Arts Area: Chamber
Status: Non-Profit
Type: Presenting
Purpose: To present a chamber music festival of the highest quality
Management: Kyle Siebrecht, Executive Director
Officers: Stuart Rolfe, President of the Board
Budget: $100,000 - $500,000
Income Sources: Private Foundations/Grants/Endowments; Business/Corporate Donations; Box Office; Government Grants; Individual Donations

SEATTLE CHAMBER MUSIC FESTIVAL
2618 Eastlake Avenue East, Seattle, WA 98102
(206) 328-5606
Founded: 1982
Arts Area: Chamber
Status: Professional; Non-Profit
Type: Performing
Purpose: To present twelve chamber-music concerts of the highest artistry during a four-week summer series
Management: Toby Saks, Artistic Director; Cheryl Swab, Executive Director
Officers: Alan Morgan, President; Bill Cohn, Ruth Gerberding, Vice Presidents; Helen Gurvich, Secretary; Bill Cobb, Treasurer
Paid Staff: 4 **Volunteer Staff:** 50
Paid Artists: 31
Utilizes: Guest Artists
Budget: $100,000 - $500,000
Income Sources: Private Foundations/Grants/Endowments; Business/Corporate Donations; Box Office; Government Grants; Individual Donations
Season: June - July **Annual Attendance:** 4,800
Performance Facilities: Lakeside School; Saint Nicholas Hall

SEATTLE SYMPHONY ORCHESTRA
305 Harrison Street, Seattle, WA 98109
(206) 443-4740
Founded: 1903
Arts Area: Symphony; Orchestra; Chamber; Ensemble; Instrumental Group
Status: Professional; Non-Profit
Type: Performing; Resident; Educational
Purpose: To present classical music concerts and special events throughout the Puget Sound region for people of all ages
Management: Gerard Schwarz, Music Director/Conductor
Officers: Ron Woodard, Chairman of the Board; Mary Ann Champion, President
Paid Staff: 34 **Volunteer Staff:** 5
Paid Artists: 84
Utilizes: Special Technical Talent; Guest Conductors; Guest Artists
Budget: $5,000,000 - $10,000,000
Income Sources: Private Foundations/Grants/Endowments; Business/Corporate Donations; Box Office; Government Grants; Individual Donations
Season: September - July **Annual Attendance:** 180,000
Affiliations: ASOL; Corporate Council for the Arts
Performance Facilities: Seattle Center Opera House; Moore Theatre

SEATTLE YOUTH SYMPHONY ORCHESTRA
11065 Fifth NE, Suite E, Seattle, WA 98125
(206) 362-2300
Founded: 1942
Arts Area: Symphony; Orchestra
Status: Non-Profit

Type: Performing; Educational
Purpose: To perform and promote an appreciation of good music
Management: Ruben Gurevich, Conductor/Musical Director; Davis B. Fox, Executive Director
Officers: Joyce Brewster, President
Paid Staff: 20
Paid Artists: 3
Utilizes: Guest Artists
Budget: $100,000 - $500,000
Income Sources: Private Foundations/Grants/Endowments; Business/Corporate Donations; Box Office; Government Grants; Individual Donations
Season: September - May   **Annual Attendance:** 6,700
Affiliations: ASCAP; BMI
Performance Facilities: Seattle Center Opera House

VOCAL MUSIC

CIVIC LIGHT OPERA
PO Box 75672, Northgate Station, Seattle, WA 98125
(206) 363-2809
Founded: 1978
Arts Area: Light Opera; Musical Theatre
Status: Semi-Professional; Non-Profit
Type: Performing; Resident
Purpose: To introduce the community to musical productions; to give actors, directors, and other artists practical experience and exposure
Management: Susan Jensen, Publicity; Elma Badten, Finance
Officers: Julia Quinton, President; Wadad Saba, Vice President; Stella Warnick, Secretary; Alma Badten, Treasurer
Paid Staff: 2   **Volunteer Staff:** 50
Utilizes: Guest Conductors; Guest Artists; Guest Directors
Budget: $100,000 - $500,000
Income Sources: Box Office; Individual Donations
Season: October - June   **Annual Attendance:** 14,000
Performance Facilities: Jane Addams Auditorium

ORCHESTRA SEATTLE/SEATTLE CHAMBER SINGERS
1305 Fourth Avenue, Suite 402, Seattle, WA 98101
(206) 682-5208
Founded: 1969
Arts Area: Choral; Folk; Baroque Opera; Symphonic Works
Status: Semi-Professional; Non-Profit
Type: Performing; Resident
Purpose: To enrich the quality of life in the Pacific Northwest by musical performance; to introduce audiences to rarely-heard works and to perform new works by Northwest composers
Management: Daniel Peterson, Managing Director; Ron Haight, Production Manager; George Shangrow, Music Director
Officers: Paula Rimmer, President; Dennis Purvine, Treasurer
Paid Staff: 8   **Volunteer Staff:** 3
Paid Artists: 80   **Non-Paid Artists:** 120
Utilizes: Special Technical Talent; Guest Conductors; Guest Artists; Guest Directors
Budget: $100,000 - $500,000
Income Sources: Private Foundations/Grants/Endowments; Business/Corporate Donations; Box Office; Government Grants; Individual Donations
Season: August - May   **Annual Attendance:** 8,000
Affiliations: KING-FM; Western Pianos; University Unitarian Church
Performance Facilities: University Unitarian Church; Kane and Meany Halls, University of Washington

SEATTLE MEN'S CHORUS
PO Box 20146, Seattle, WA 98102
(206) 323-0750
FAX: (206) 323-9425
Founded: 1979
Arts Area: Choral
Status: Non-Professional; Non-Profit
Type: Performing; Touring
Management: Dennis Coleman, Conductor; Debra Berend, Executive Director
Officers: John Rochford, President
Paid Staff: 8   **Volunteer Staff:** 7
Non-Paid Artists: 125
Utilizes: Guest Artists

Budget: $500,000 - $1,000,000
Income Sources: Private Foundations/Grants/Endowments; Business/Corporate Donations; Box Office; Government Grants; Individual Donations
Season: September - June   **Annual Attendance:** 12,000
Performance Facilities: Meany Hall, University of Washington; Seattle Opera House

SEATTLE OPERA ASSOCIATION
1020 John Street, Seattle, WA 98109
(206) 389-7600
FAX: (206) 389-7651
Founded: 1964
Arts Area: Grand Opera
Status: Non-Profit
Type: Performing; Educational
Purpose: To promote and present grand opera
Management: Speight Jenkins, General Director; Gary Tribble, Finance Director; Kathy Magiera, Administrative Director; Melanie Ross, Production Director; Linda Prather, Marketing Director
Officers: Richard S. Twiss, President; Beverly Brazeau, Assistant President; Sylvia Black, Secretary; Jack Irwin, Treasurer; Lawrence W. Clarkson, Chairman
Paid Staff: 75   **Volunteer Staff:** 150
Paid Artists: 300
Utilizes: Special Technical Talent; Guest Conductors; Guest Artists; Guest Directors
Budget: Over 10,000,000
Income Sources: Private Foundations/Grants/Endowments; Business/Corporate Donations; Box Office; Government Grants; Individual Donations
Season: 52 Weeks   **Annual Attendance:** 100,000
Affiliations: OA
Performance Facilities: Seattle Opera House

THEATRE

ALICE B THEATRE
1100 East Pike, Third Floor, Seattle, WA 98122
(206) 322-5742
Arts Area: Professional
Status: Professional; Non-Profit
Type: Performing; Touring; Educational
Purpose: To present professional-quality theatrical and cultural events that are racially and culturally diverse and have gender parity; to offer the productions in a spirit of creativity, integrity, social responsiblity, adventure and excellence
Management: Christopher, Managing Director; Susan Finque, Rick Ranklin, Artistic Directors
Officers: Mark Miller, President of the Board
Budget: $100,000 - $500,000
Income Sources: Private Foundations/Grants/Endowments; Business/Corporate Donations; Box Office; Government Grants; Individual Donations
Performance Facilities: Pioneer Square Theater; Broadway Performance Hall; Theater Off Jackson

BATHHOUSE THEATRE
7312 West Greenlake Drive North, Seattle, WA 98103
(206) 524-3608
FAX: (206) 527-1942
Founded: 1970
Arts Area: Professional; Theatrical Group
Status: Professional; Non-Profit
Type: Performing; Touring; Resident
Purpose: To develop the full potential of a permanent resident theatre company; to make excellent theatre accessible to the broadest possible public
Management: Arne Zaslove, Artistic Director; Steven Lerian, Managing Director
Officers: Kathleen Southwick, Board President; Donald W. Rowe, Vice President; Joy Jackson, Secretary; Bob Kaplan, Treasurer
Paid Staff: 16
Paid Artists: 30
Utilizes: Guest Directors
Budget: $1,000,000 - $5,000,000
Income Sources: Private Foundations/Grants/Endowments; Business/Corporate Donations; Box Office; Government Grants; Individual Donations
Season: January - December   **Annual Attendance:** 74,000
Affiliations: TCG; AEA; SPTA
Performance Facilities: Bathhouse Theatre

A CONTEMPORARY THEATRE
100 West Roy Street, Seattle, WA 98119
(206) 285-3220
Founded: 1965
Arts Area: Theatrical Group
Status: Professional; Non-Profit
Type: Resident
Purpose: To present the best contemporary theater and the most important plays
Management: Jeff Steitzer, Artistic Director; Susan Trapnell Moritz, Managing Director; Philip G. Schermer, Producing Manager; Gregory A. Falls, Founding Director; Barry Allar, Public Relations Director
Officers: Douglass E. Norberg, President Board of Directors
Paid Staff: 30
Utilizes: Special Technical Talent; Guest Artists; Guest Directors
Budget: $1,000,000 - $5,000,000
Income Sources: Private Foundations/Grants/Endowments; Business/Corporate Donations; Box Office; Government Grants; Individual Donations
Season: May - January   **Annual Attendance:** 100,000
Affiliations: AEA; LORT; AAA; Washington State Arts Alliance
Performance Facilities: A Contemporary Theatre

THE EMPTY SPACE THEATRE
PO Box 1748, Seattle, WA 98111-1748
(206) 587-3737
Founded: 1970
Arts Area: Professional; Musical; Theatrical Group
Status: Professional; Non-Profit
Type: Performing; Resident; Educational
Management: Kurt Beattie, Artistic Director; Melissa Hines, Managing Director
Paid Staff: 20
Utilizes: Special Technical Talent; Guest Artists; Guest Directors
Income Sources: Business/Corporate Donations; Box Office; Individual Donations
Season: September - May
Affiliations: AEA
Performance Facilities: Empty Space Theatre

THE GROUP THEATRE COMPANY
3940 Brooklyn Avenue NE, Seattle, WA 98105
(206) 545-4969
Founded: 1978
Arts Area: Professional; Musical; Theatrical Group
Status: Professional; Non-Profit
Type: Performing; Touring
Management: Ruben Sierra, Founding Artistic Director; Tim Bond, Artistic Director; Paul O'Connell, Producing Director
Paid Staff: 14
Paid Artists: 150
Utilizes: Guest Artists; Guest Directors
Budget: $500,000 - $1,000,000
Income Sources: Private Foundations/Grants/Endowments; Business/Corporate Donations; Box Office; Government Grants; Individual Donations
Season: September - July   **Annual Attendance:** 45,000
Affiliations: TCG; AEA
Performance Facilities: The Ethnic Theatre

INTIMAN THEATRE COMPANY
PO Box 19760, Seattle, WA 98109
(206) 626-0775
FAX: (206) 626-0778
Arts Area: Theatrical Group
Season: 52 Weeks

THE NEW CITY THEATER
1634 11th Avenue, Seattle, WA 98122
(206) 323-6801
FAX: (206) 328-4683
Founded: 1982
Arts Area: Professional; Theatrical Group
Status: Professional; Non-Profit
Type: Performing; Resident

Purpose: Dedicated to research and development in the contemporary arts
Management: John Kazanjian, Artistic Director; Alan Horton, Theater Manager
Paid Staff: 3   **Volunteer Staff:** 6
Paid Artists: 85
Utilizes: Guest Directors
Budget: $100,000 - $500,000
Income Sources: Private Foundations/Grants/Endowments; Business/Corporate Donations; Box Office; Government Grants; Individual Donations
Season: September - May
Affiliations: TCG
Performance Facilities: The New City Theatre

NW PUPPET CENTER
6615 Dayton Avenue North, Seattle, WA 98103
(206) 782-3955
FAX: (206) 783-0851
   Founded: 1985
   Arts Area: Puppet
   Status: Professional; Non-Profit
   Type: Performing; Touring; Resident; Educational; Sponsoring
   Purpose: To present and produce quality professional puppet theatre
   Management: Stephen Carter, Chris Carter, Executive Co-Directors
   Officers: Barbara Sand, Joan Weiss, Board Co-Chairs; Iris Okimoto-Nielson, Secretary; Jim Thwing, Treasurer
   Paid Staff: 5   **Volunteer Staff:** 65
   Paid Artists: 15   **Non-Paid Artists:** 2
   Utilizes: Guest Artists
   Budget: $100,000 - $500,000
   Income Sources: Private Foundations/Grants/Endowments; Business/Corporate Donations; Box Office; Government Grants; Individual Donations
   Season: October - June   **Annual Attendance:** 65,000
   Affiliations: Puppeteers of America; UNIMA

SEATTLE CHILDREN'S THEATRE
305 Harrison, Seattle, WA 98109
(206) 443-0807
FAX: (206) 443-0442
   Founded: 1975
   Arts Area: Professional; Theatrical Group
   Status: Professional; Non-Profit
   Type: Performing; Touring; Resident; Educational
   Purpose: To produce professional theater for the young with appeal to people of all ages; to provide theater education and theater arts training; to develop scripts and musical scores for new theater works and young audiences
   Management: Linda Hartzell, Artistic Director; Thomas Pechar, Managing Director
   Officers: Craig Schuman, Board President; Roberta Katz, First Vice President; Diane Kuenster, Second Vice President; Eve Alvord, Secretary; Jim Williams, Treasurer
   Paid Staff: 36
   Paid Artists: 120
   Utilizes: Special Technical Talent; Guest Artists; Guest Directors
   Budget: $1,000,000 - $5,000,000
   Income Sources: Private Foundations/Grants/Endowments; Business/Corporate Donations; Box Office; Government Grants; Individual Donations
   Season: September - July   **Annual Attendance:** 160,000
   Affiliations: TCG; AATE; AAA; Equity
   Performance Facilities: PONCHO Theatre; Charlotte Martin Theatre (opening Fall, 1993)

SEATTLE MIME THEATRE
915 East Pine Street, #419, Seattle, WA 98122
(206) 324-8788
   Founded: 1977
   Arts Area: Theatrical Group
   Status: Non-Profit
   Type: Performing; Touring; Educational
   Purpose: To present physical/visual theatre
   Management: Beth Amsbany, General Manager; David Lieberman, Artists' Representative
   Officers: Bruce L. Wylie, President; Richard L. Davidson, Secretary; Elizabeth Roth, Treasurer
   Paid Staff: 1
   Paid Artists: 3
   Utilizes: Guest Artists; Guest Directors
   Budget: $100,000 - $500,000

Income Sources: Private Foundations/Grants/Endowments; Business/Corporate Donations; Box Office; Government Grants; Individual Donations
Season: 52 Weeks

SEATTLE REPERTORY THEATRE
155 Mercer Street, Seattle, WA 98109
(206) 443-2210
FAX: (206) 443-2379
Founded: 1963
Arts Area: Professional; Theatrical Group
Status: Professional; Non-Profit
Type: Performing; Resident
Purpose: To provide professional live theatre productions and educational services for the Pacific Northwest community
Management: Daniel Sullivan, Artistic Director; Benjamin Moore, Managing Director; Douglas Hughes, Associate Artistic Director
Officers: Stanley D. Savage, Chairman of the Board; Ann Ramsay-Jenkins, President of the Board
Paid Staff: 350
Paid Artists: 200
Utilizes: Special Technical Talent; Guest Conductors; Guest Artists; Guest Directors
Budget: $5,000,000 - $10,000,000
Income Sources: Private Foundations/Grants/Endowments; Business/Corporate Donations; Box Office; Government Grants; Individual Donations
Season: October - May
Annual Attendance: 242,000
Affiliations: AEA; LORT
Performance Facilities: Bagley Wright Theatre

TAPROOT THEATRE COMPANY
204 North 85th Street, Seattle, WA 98103
(206) 781-9705
Founded: 1976
Arts Area: Professional; Dinner; Theatrical Group
Status: Semi-Professional; Non-Profit
Type: Performing; Touring; Resident
Purpose: To preserve the integrity of Christian values and perspectives, maintaining excellence through diverse production activities
Management: Scott Nolte, Producing Artistic Director
Officers: M.B. Jewell, Board President; Scott Nolte, Vice President; Daniel Ichinaga, Secretary; Sharon Morrison, Treasurer
Paid Staff: 14   **Volunteer Staff:** 30
Paid Artists: 25   **Non-Paid Artists:** 10
Utilizes: Guest Artists; Guest Directors
Budget: $100,000 - $500,000
Income Sources: Private Foundations/Grants/Endowments; Business/Corporate Donations; Box Office; Individual Donations
Season: 52 Weeks
Annual Attendance: 110,000
Affiliations: Seattle Chamber of Commerce; TCG; USITT

PERFORMING SERIES

BUMBERSHOOT, THE SEATTLE ARTS FESTIVAL
PO Box 9750, Seattle, WA 98109-0750
(206) 622-5123
FAX: (206) 622-5154
Founded: 1971
Arts Area: Dance; Vocal Music; Instrumental Music; Theater; Festival; Literary; Visual
Status: Non-Profit
Type: Performing
Purpose: To produce a four-day art festival featuring all genres of the arts; to produce an affordable, high-quality festival
Management: One Reel, Producer
Paid Staff: 20   **Volunteer Staff:** 300
Utilizes: Guest Artists
Budget: $1,000,000 - $5,000,000
Income Sources: Private Foundations/Grants/Endowments; Business/Corporate Donations; Box Office
Season: September   **Annual Attendance:** 250,000
Performance Facilities: Seattle Center

LADIES MUSICAL CLUB (LMC)
Cobb Building, 1305 Fourth Avenue, Suite 500, Seattle, WA 98101
(206) 622-6882
> **Founded:** 1891
> **Arts Area:** Vocal Music; Instrumental Music
> **Status:** Professional; Semi-Professional; Non-Profit
> **Type:** Performing; Resident; Educational; Sponsoring
> **Purpose:** To grant scholarships to deserving music students; to sponsor a yearly International Artists Series; to foster music among its members and the community
> **Officers:** Helen Holtzclaw, President; Peggy Bardarson, Vice President; Leone Turner, Recording Secretary; Eleanor Gozinsky, Corresponding Secretary; Kathleen Dow, Treasurer; Phyllis Mines, Concert Manager
> **Utilizes:** Special Technical Talent; Guest Artists
> **Budget:** $100,000 - $500,000
> **Income Sources:** Private Foundations/Grants/Endowments; Business/Corporate Donations; Box Office; Government Grants; Individual Donations
> **Season:** September - May   **Annual Attendance:** 10,000
> **Performance Facilities:** Meany Hall, University of Washington; Seattle Public Library; Museum of History and Industry

NORTHWEST FOLKLIFE
305 Harrison Street, Seattle, WA 98109-4695
(206) 684-7300
FAX: (206) 684-7190
> **Founded:** 1971
> **Arts Area:** Festivals
> **Status:** Professional; Semi-Professional; Non-Professional; Non-Profit
> **Type:** Performing; Touring; Educational; Sponsoring
> **Purpose:** To preserve and present ethnic and traditional arts; to foster understanding of different cultures
> **Management:** Scott Nagel, Executive Director; Paul de Barros, Program Director; Annie Jamison, Producing Director; Dana Giddings, Public Affairs Director
> **Officers:** Vivian Williams, President; Anthony Butler, Vice President; Frank Hungate, Treasurer
> **Paid Staff:** 8   **Volunteer Staff:** 800
> **Paid Artists:** 100   **Non-Paid Artists:** 6,000
> **Budget:** $500,000 - $1,000,000
> **Income Sources:** Private Foundations/Grants/Endowments; Business/Corporate Donations; Box Office; Government Grants; Individual Donations
> **Season:** Memorial Day Weekend   **Annual Attendance:** 200,000
> **Performance Facilities:** Seattle Center

PACIFIC NORTHWEST FESTIVAL
Seattle Opera, 1020 John Street, PO Box 9248, Seattle, WA 98109
(206) 389-7699
FAX: (206) 389-7651
> **Founded:** 1975
> **Arts Area:** Grand Opera
> **Status:** Professional; Non-Profit
> **Type:** Performing; Resident; Sponsoring
> **Management:** Speight Jenkins, General Director
> **Officers:** Richard Twiss, President
> **Paid Staff:** 60   **Volunteer Staff:** 150
> **Paid Artists:** 30
> **Utilizes:** Guest Conductors; Guest Artists
> **Budget:** $1,000,000 - $5,000,000
> **Income Sources:** Private Foundations/Grants/Endowments; Business/Corporate Donations; Box Office; Government Grants; Individual Donations
> **Season:** August   **Annual Attendance:** 20,000
> **Affiliations:** Seattle Symphony; Seattle Opera
> **Performance Facilities:** Seattle Opera House

SEATTLE INTERNATIONAL CHILDREN'S FESTIVAL
305 Harrison Street, Seattle, WA 98109
(206) 684-7338
FAX: (206) 684-7342
> **Founded:** 1987
> **Arts Area:** Festivals
> **Status:** Professional; Non-Profit
> **Type:** Performing; Educational
> **Purpose:** To provide an international performing-arts festival for children

Management: Marilyn Raichle, Festival Director; Mary Machala, Projects Director; Cathy Palmer, Director of Education
Officers: Karla Steel, President of the Board; Gerald Hendin, Marcia Garrett, Vice Presidents; Susan Vergara, Secretary; Timothy Dawes, Treasurer
Paid Staff: 8   **Volunteer Staff:** 230
Paid Artists: 160
Utilizes: Guest Artists
Budget: $100,000 - $500,000
Income Sources: Private Foundations/Grants/Endowments; Business/Corporate Donations; Box Office; Government Grants; Individual Donations
Season: May
Annual Attendance: 70,000
Affiliations: WAAA; ASSITEJ; USA
Performance Facilities: Seattle Center

UPSTAGE!
PO Box 7094, Seattle, WA 98133
(206) 743-4240; (206) 363-3306
Founded: 1991
Arts Area: Theater
Status: Semi-Professional; Non-Profit
Type: Touring; Educational
Purpose: Upstage! is dedicated to engaging the mind, emotions, and conscience through artistically and culturally diverse productions for youths and adults.
Officers: Richard Reuther, President; Robert Sibson, Vice President; Gayle Record, Secretary; Ralph Eatom, Treasurer
Utilizes: Special Technical Talent; Guest Conductors; Guest Artists; Guest Directors
Budget: $1,000 - $50,000
Season: September - May
Affiliations: Washington Community Theatre Association; Snohomish County Arts Community

FACILITY

A CONTEMPORARY THEATRE
100 West Roy Street, Seattle, WA 98119
(206) 285-3220
FAX: (206) 298-3100
Founded: 1965
Type of Facility: Theatre House
Facility Originally: Meeting Hall; Movie House
Type of Stage: Thrust
Stage Dimensions: 16'x20'x36'
Seating Capacity: 423
Year Built: 1913
Year Remodeled: 1965   **Architect:** Hewitt-Daly   **Cost:** $100,000
Contact for Rental: Jim Verdery;   (206) 285-3220

ALICE B THEATRE
1100 East Pike, Third Floor, Seattle, WA 98122
(206) 322-5742
Type of Facility: Studio
Type of Stage: Thrust
Seating Capacity: 150
Year Built: 1991
Contact for Rental: Christopher Malarkey;   (206) 322-5742

BAGLEY WRIGHT THEATRE
305 Harrison, Seattle, WA 98109
(206) 625-4254
Type of Facility: Theatre House
Type of Stage: Proscenium
Stage Dimensions: 90'Wx45'D, 44'Wx24'H proscenium opening   **Orchestra Pit**
Seating Capacity: 864
Year Built: 1983   **Architect:** The NBBJ Group   **Cost:** $10,000,000
Acoustical Consultant: Purcell Noppe & Associates
Contact for Rental: Margaret Wetter;   (206) 625-4254
Resident Groups: The Seattle Repertory Theatre

BATHHOUSE THEATRE
7312 West Greenlake Drive North, Seattle, WA 98103
(206) 524-3608
FAX: (206) 527-1942
    Founded: 1970
    Type of Facility: Theatre House
    Facility Originally: Bathhouse
    Type of Stage: Thrust
    Stage Dimensions: 13'x29'x20'
    Seating Capacity: 174
    Year Built: 1927   **Cost:** $26,000
    Year Remodeled: 1970   **Architect:** Arne Bystrom   **Cost:** $20,000
    Resident Groups: Bathhouse Theatre Company

MEANY HALL
University of Washington, Seattle, WA 98195
(206) 543-4882
FAX: (206) 685-2759
    Founded: 1974
    Type of Facility: Concert Hall; Performance Center; Theatre House; Opera House
    Type of Stage: Proscenium
    Stage Dimensions: 130'Wx55'D   **Orchestra Pit**
    Seating Capacity: 1,210
    Year Built: 1974   **Architect:** Kirk Wallace and Hatch   **Cost:** $10,000,000
    Acoustical Consultant: Paul Vaneklausen
    Contact for Rental: Sue Stark;   (206) 543-4882

SEATTLE CENTER ARENA
305 Harrison, Seattle, WA 98109
(206) 684-7202
FAX: (206) 684-7234
    Type of Facility: Arena
    Facility Originally: Ice Arena
    Type of Stage: Flexible
    Seating Capacity: 6,100
    Year Built: 1927
    Year Remodeled: 1976   **Cost:** $500,000
    Contact for Rental: Margaret Wetter;   (206) 684-7202
    Manager: Virginia Anderson;   (206) 684-7342
    Resident Groups: Seattle Thunderbirds - WHL Hockey Team

SEATTLE CENTER COLISEUM
305 Harrison, Seattle, WA 98109
(206) 684-7202
FAX: (206) 684-7342
    Founded: 1962
    Type of Facility: Arena
    Type of Stage: Flexible
    Seating Capacity: 15,000
    Year Built: 1962
    Year Remodeled: 1976   **Cost:** $750,000
    Contact for Rental: Margaret Wetter;   (206) 684-7202
    Manager: Virginia Anderson, Director;   (206) 684-7330
    Resident Groups: Seattle Super Sonics - NBA Basketball Team; Seattle Thunderbirds - WHL Hockey Team

SEATTLE CENTER OPERA HOUSE
305 Harrison, Seattle, WA 98109
(206) 625-4254
    Type of Facility: Opera House
    Facility Originally: Vaudeville
    Type of Stage: Proscenium
    Stage Dimensions: 70'x108'   **Orchestra Pit**
    Seating Capacity: 3,099
    Year Built: 1927   **Cost:** $4,000,000
    Year Remodeled: 1976   **Cost:** $1,500,000
    Contact for Rental: Margaret Wetter;   (206) 684-7202
    Manager: Virginia Anderson, Director;   (206) 684-7330

Resident Groups: Seattle Opera Association; Seattle Symphony Orchestra; Pacific Northwest Ballet; Seattle Youth Symphony; World Cavalcade (Film Travelogues)

SEATTLE PUBLIC LIBRARY-DOWNTOWN LIBRARY
1000 Fourth Avenue, Seattle, WA 98104
(206) 386-4636
FAX: (206) 386-4685
 Type of Facility: Auditorium; Multi-Purpose
 Type of Stage: Proscenium
 Seating Capacity: 200
 Contact for Rental: Ray Serebrin; (206) 386-4660
 Rental is free of charge.

Sedro-Woolley

INSTRUMENTAL MUSIC

WESTWOOD WIND QUARTET
2235 Willida Lane, Sedro-Woolley, WA 98284
(206) 856-4779
FAX: (206) 856-4989
 Founded: 1959
 Arts Area: Chamber; Ensemble; Instrumental Group
 Status: Professional
 Type: Performing; Touring; Educational; Recording
 Management: Artists' Alliance Management
 Officers: Peter Christ, Leader
 Volunteer Staff: 2
 Budget: $1,000 - $50,000
 Income Sources: Private Foundations/Grants/Endowments; Business/Corporate Donations; Box Office; Individual Donations
 Season: 52 Weeks

Sequim

DANCE

PERFORMING COMPANY OF PIONEER DANCE ARTS
503 North Sequim Avenue, PO Box 238, Sequim, WA 98382
(206) 683-3693
 Founded: 1976
 Arts Area: Modern; Ballet; Jazz; Ethnic; Tap
 Status: Non-Professional; Non-Profit
 Type: Performing; Resident; Educational; Sponsoring
 Purpose: To raise dance-art awareness in the north Olympic Peninsula
 Management: Kathleen H. Moore, Director; Gloria Price, Secretary; Judy Lynn, Treasurer
 Officers: Judy Reandeau, President; Beverly Hendrickson, Vice President; Gloria Price, Secretary; Judy Lynn, Treasurer
 Paid Staff: 3 **Volunteer Staff:** 12
 Paid Artists: 2 **Non-Paid Artists:** 100
 Utilizes: Guest Artists; Guest Choreographers
 Budget: $1,000 - $50,000
 Income Sources: Business/Corporate Donations; Box Office; Government Grants; Individual Donations
 Annual Attendance: 1,600
 Performance Facilities: Port Angeles High School Auditorium

Spokane

DANCE

SPOKANE BALLET
1427 West Dean, Spokane, WA 99201
(509) 327-4049
 Founded: 1980
 Arts Area: Ballet
 Status: Professional; Non-Profit
 Type: Performing; Touring; Resident; Educational

Purpose: To maintain and further a professional ballet company and school in eastern Washington, providing home seasons, educational programs and concert touring
Management: Robert C. Herold PhD, Executive Director; Susan Hales, Assistant Executive Director; Jane Grovijahn, General Manager; Julie E. Stocker, Company Manager
Officers: Diane Kane, President of Board of Directors; Maryann Sanger, President-Elect; David Mattson, Vice President; Judi Kyle, Secretary
Paid Staff: 17 **Volunteer Staff:** 45
Paid Artists: 10
Utilizes: Special Technical Talent; Guest Artists; Guest Choreographers
Budget: $100,000 - $500,000
Income Sources: Private Foundations/Grants/Endowments; Business/Corporate Donations; Box Office; Government Grants; Individual Donations
Season: August - May   **Annual Attendance:** 38,100
Affiliations: Eastern Washington University
Performance Facilities: Spokane Opera House

INSTRUMENTAL MUSIC

SPOKANE SYMPHONY ORCHESTRA
621 West Mallon, Suite 203, Spokane, WA 99201
(509) 326-3136
Arts Area: Symphony; Orchestra; Chamber
Status: Professional; Non-Profit
Type: Performing; Touring; Resident; Educational; Sponsoring
Purpose: The Spokane Symphony Orchestra exists to provide orchestral music in its many forms to meet the cultural needs of Spokane and the inland northwest region. It seeks to provide the highest quality musical product of which it is able within a sound economic framework that ensures its continuance.
Management: Richard Early, Executive Director; Vakhpang Jordania, Music Director
Officers: Donald Hart, President
Paid Staff: 15 **Volunteer Staff:** 4
Paid Artists: 75
Utilizes: Special Technical Talent; Guest Conductors; Guest Artists; Guest Directors
Budget: $1,000,000 - $5,000,000
Income Sources: Private Foundations/Grants/Endowments; Business/Corporate Donations; Box Office; Government Grants; Individual Donations
Season: September - May   **Annual Attendance:** 122,000
Performance Facilities: Spokane Opera House

THEATRE

SPOKANE CIVIC THEATRE
1020 Howard, PO Box 5222, Spokane, WA 99205
(509) 325-1413
Founded: 1947
Arts Area: Community; Theatrical Group
Status: Non-Professional; Non-Profit
Type: Performing; Educational
Purpose: To offer residents the opportunity to participate (on-stage, backstage and as members of the audience) in the art of theatre; to promote the development of new plays
Management: John (Jack) G. Phillips, Executive Producer
Paid Staff: 9 **Volunteer Staff:** 2,000
Paid Artists: 20 **Non-Paid Artists:** 150
Utilizes: Special Technical Talent; Guest Conductors; Guest Artists; Guest Directors
Budget: $100,000 - $500,000
Income Sources: Private Foundations/Grants/Endowments; Business/Corporate Donations; Box Office; Government Grants; Individual Donations
Season: October - June   **Annual Attendance:** 45,000
Affiliations: ACT; Washington State Arts Commission; Washington Arts Alliance
Performance Facilities: Spokane Civic Theatres

SPOKANE INTERPLAYERS ENSEMBLE
174 South Howard Street, Spokane, WA 99204
(509) 455-7529
Founded: 1980
Arts Area: Professional; Theatrical Group
Status: Professional; Non-Profit
Type: Performing; Resident; Educational
Purpose: To establish, maintain and nurture a non-profit, resident, professional theatre company performing an annual season of plays chosen from contemporary, classic and original works

Management: Robert A. Welch, Producing Artistic Director; Joan Welch, Artistic Director; Mary Cravens, Office Manager; Dave Zack, Clark-White & Associates, Marketing/Public Relations
Officers: Geoff Praeger, President; Don Moeller, Vice President; Robert Clausen, Secretary; Shirley Cornelius, Treasurer
Paid Staff: 8   **Volunteer Staff:** 250
Paid Artists: 52
Utilizes: Guest Directors
Budget: $100,000 - $500,000
Income Sources: Private Foundations/Grants/Endowments; Business/Corporate Donations; Box Office; Government Grants; Individual Donations
Season: October - June   **Annual Attendance:** 34,000
Affiliations: TCG; Arts Alliance of Washington
Performance Facilities: Spokane Interplayers Ensemble Theatre

PERFORMING SERIES

PINESONG/SPOKANE FALLS COMMUNITY COLLEGE
3410 West Fort George Wright Drive, MS 3020, Spokane, WA 99204-2052
(509) 533-3800
FAX: (509) 533-3433
Founded: 1986
Arts Area: Festivals
Status: Non-Profit
Type: Sponsoring
Purpose: To present a multi-cultural festival featuring arts, music and hands-on participation
Management: Nancy Lindberg, Festival Manager; John Thompson, Festival Director
Paid Staff: 2   **Volunteer Staff:** 100
Paid Artists: 50
Utilizes: Special Technical Talent; Guest Artists
Budget: $1,000 - $50,000
Income Sources: Private Foundations/Grants/Endowments; Business/Corporate Donations; Box Office; Government Grants
Season: June   **Annual Attendance:** 12,000

FACILITY

GONZAGA UNIVERSITY - GENE RUSSELL THEATRE
Spokane, WA 99258-0001
(509) 328-4220, ext. 3257
Type of Facility: Theatre House
Facility Originally: Recreation Hall; Gymnasium
Type of Stage: Thrust; Flexible
Stage Dimensions: 50'x60'
Seating Capacity: 225
Year Remodeled: 1968   **Cost:** $25,000
Contact for Rental: Dr. Tim Soulis, Director;   (509) 328-4220, ext. 3257

THE METROPOLITAN PERFORMING ARTS CENTER
901 West Sprague, Spokane, WA 99204
(509) 455-6500
FAX: (509) 459-0898
Founded: 1988
Type of Facility: Concert Hall; Auditorium; Studio Performance; Performance Center; Theatre House; Opera House
Facility Originally: Vaudeville; Movie House
Type of Stage: Thrust
Stage Dimensions: 32'Wx24'D   **Orchestra Pit**
Seating Capacity: 760
Year Built: 1915
Year Remodeled: 1988   **Architect:** Bill Arsenault   **Cost:** $2,000,000
Contact for Rental: Michael Smith;   (509) 455-7811
Resident Groups: Uptown Opera; Spokane Symphony; Spokane String Quartet; Allegro Theatre Ballet

SPOKANE COLISEUM
1101 North Howard, Spokane, WA 99201
(509) 353-6500
FAX: (509) 353-6511
Type of Facility: Arena; Multi-Purpose
Type of Stage: Arena
Seating Capacity: 7,200 reserved; 8,500 festival seating

Year Built: 1953   **Cost:** $3,000,000
Contact for Rental: Events Supervisor;   (509) 353-6500

SPOKANE CONVENTION CENTER
1101 North Howard, Spokane, WA 99201
(509) 353-6500
FAX: (509) 353-6511
Seating Capacity: Concert - 5,000; Theatre - 4,000; Banquet - 3,200
Contact for Rental: Events Supervisor;   (509) 353-6500

SPOKANE OPERA HOUSE
334 West Spokane Falls Boulevard, Spokane, WA 99201
(509) 353-6500
FAX: (509) 353-6511
Type of Facility: Concert Hall; Auditorium; Opera House
Facility Originally: Auditorium
Type of Stage: Proscenium
Stage Dimensions: 150'Wx59"D; 67'Wx27'H proscenium opening   **Orchestra Pit**
Seating Capacity: 2,700
Year Built: 1974   **Architect:** WMFL   **Cost:** $9,000,000
Acoustical Consultant: Purcell-Noppe
Contact for Rental: Kevin Twohig;   (509) 353-6500
Resident Groups: Spokane Symphony; G & B Presents
Curved-edge pit lift adds 16'D at center line raised to stage level

---

Tacoma

DANCE

BALLETACOMA
508 Sixth Avenue, Tacoma, WA 98402
(206) 272-9631
Founded: 1955
Arts Area: Ballet
Status: Semi-Professional
Type: Performing
Purpose: To provide quality, fully-staged classical ballets for the southern Puget Sound area
Management: Nikki Smith, Executive Director
Officers: John Hodder, Chairman
Paid Staff: 4   **Volunteer Staff:** 2
Paid Artists: 3   **Non-Paid Artists:** 20
Utilizes: Guest Artists; Guest Choreographers
Budget: $100,000 - $500,000
Income Sources: Private Foundations/Grants/Endowments; Business/Corporate Donations; Box Office; Government Grants; Individual Donations
Season: October - May   **Annual Attendance:** 12,000
Affiliations: NARB; PRBA
Performance Facilities: Pantages Theater

JO EMERY DANCE COMPANY
2315 Sixth Avenue, Tacoma, WA 98403
(206) 627-8272
Arts Area: Jazz
Status: Professional; Non-Profit
Type: Performing
Management: Jo Emery, Artistic Director
Paid Artists: 8
Utilizes: Guest Choreographers
Budget: $1,000 - $50,000
Income Sources: Private Foundations/Grants/Endowments; Business/Corporate Donations; Box Office; Government Grants; Individual Donations
Season: 52 Weeks

TACOMA PERFORMING DANCE COMPANY
2315 Sixth Avenue, Tacoma, WA 98407
(206) 759-0782
Founded: 1967

Arts Area: Modern; Ballet; Jazz
Status: Semi-Professional; Non-Profit
Type: Performing; Touring; Resident
Management: Jo Emery, Director
Utilizes: Guest Artists; Guest Directors
Budget: $1,000 - $50,000
Income Sources: Private Foundations/Grants/Endowments; Box Office; Government Grants
Season: September - June
Performance Facilities: Pantages Centre

INSTRUMENTAL MUSIC

TACOMA CONCERT BAND
717 San Juan Avenue, Tacoma, WA 98466
(206) 564-4954
Founded: 1981
Arts Area: Band
Status: Non-Profit
Type: Performing
Purpose: To present band concerts throughout the year in Tacoma and the surrounding area
Management: Robert C. Musser, Conductor/Musical Director
Volunteer Staff: 1
Non-Paid Artists: 60
Utilizes: Guest Conductors; Guest Artists
Budget: $1,000 - $50,000
Income Sources: Box Office; Individual Donations
Season: September - April   **Annual Attendance:** 5,000
Affiliations: University of Puget Sound
Performance Facilities: Pantages Centre

TACOMA PHILHARMONIC
901 Broadway, Tacoma, WA 98402
Founded: 1936
Arts Area: Symphony; Chamber; Soloists of Classical Music
Status: Professional; Non-Profit
Type: Presenting
Purpose: To present classical music concerts, offering the community a six-series season
Management: Kathryn O. Galbraith, Executive Director
Paid Staff: 2
Utilizes: Guest Artists
Budget: $100,000 - $500,000
Income Sources: Private Foundations/Grants/Endowments; Business/Corporate Donations; Box Office; Government Grants; Individual Donations
Season: August - May   **Annual Attendance:** 6,000
Performance Facilities: Pantages Theatre

TACOMA SYMPHONY ORCHESTRA
PO Box 19, Tacoma, WA 98401
(206) 272-7264
Founded: 1959
Arts Area: Symphony; Orchestra
Status: Professional; Non-Profit
Type: Performing
Purpose: To provide affordable classical music to the community
Management: Carlene Garner, Executive Director; Edward Seferian, Musical Director; Hollie Seibert, Office Manager
Officers: Thomas Park, President; Parker Geesen, Vice President; Landon Brazier, Treasurer
Paid Staff: 3
Paid Artists: 75   **Non-Paid Artists:** 10
Utilizes: Guest Conductors; Guest Artists
Budget: $100,000 - $500,000
Income Sources: Private Foundations/Grants/Endowments; Business/Corporate Donations; Box Office; Government Grants; Individual Donations
Season: October - April
Annual Attendance: 20,000
Affiliations: ASOL
Performance Facilities: Pantages Theatre

TACOMA YOUTH SYMPHONY
PO Box 660, Tacoma, WA 98401
(206) 627-2792
FAX: (206) 591-2013
   Founded: 1962
   Arts Area: Symphony; Orchestra; Chamber; Ensemble
   Status: Non-Professional; Non-Profit
   Type: Performing; Educational
   Purpose: To provide leadership by competent conductors and coaches; to educate and inspire youth musicians from seven to 21 years of age; to work for excellence in the performance of symphonic literature
   Management: Shirley M. Getzin, Executive Director
   Officers: James Billingsley MD, President; Patricia Borgen, First Vice President; George Fong, Second Vice President; Kaye Adkins, Third Vice President; Dagny Sollie, Treasurer; Rodney Ray, Past President
   Paid Staff: 4
   Non-Paid Artists: 285
   Utilizes: Guest Artists
   Budget: $100,000 - $500,000
   Income Sources: Private Foundations/Grants/Endowments; Business/Corporate Donations; Box Office; Government Grants; Individual Donations; Fund-raising
   Season: September - May   **Annual Attendance:** 21,000
   Affiliations: ASOL (Youth Orchestra Division)
   Performance Facilities: Pantages Centre

VOCAL MUSIC

ORPHEUS MALE CHORUS OF TACOMA
PO Box 1222, Tacoma, WA 98401
(206) 582-4435
   Founded: 1903
   Arts Area: Choral
   Status: Non-Professional; Non-Profit
   Type: Performing
   Purpose: To cultivate and develop refined musical numbers and present them to our audiences; to further music appreciation
   Management: Peter Herpst, Conductor; Vern Anderson, Assistant Conductor; David Abbott, Financial Secretary; Frank O. Boers, Auditor; Vicki Lynn Day, Accompanist
   Officers: Bill Zimmerman, President; David Abbott, Financial; Larry Palbert, Recording Secretary; Hal Mortland, Treasurer; Ray Wall, Assistant Financial Secretary
   Paid Staff: 2   **Volunteer Staff:** 15
   Paid Artists: 2   **Non-Paid Artists:** 40
   Utilizes: Special Technical Talent; Guest Artists
   Budget: $1,000 - $50,000
   Income Sources: Business/Corporate Donations; Box Office; Individual Donations
   Season: February - May; September - December
   Annual Attendance: 600
   Performance Facilities: First United Methodist Church

TACOMA OPERA ASSOCIATION
PO Box 7468, Tacoma, WA 98407
(206) 627-7789
   Founded: 1968
   Arts Area: Light Opera
   Status: Professional
   Type: Performing
   Purpose: To produce light opera in English for patrons in the South Puget Sound region
   Management: Anne W. Farrell, Executive Director; Hans Wolf, Artistic Director
   Officers: Bob Slaton, President; William Ryberg, Priscilla Bosch, Vice Presidents; John Hodder, Treasurer; Mickey Kramer, Secretary
   Paid Staff: 3   **Volunteer Staff:** 2
   Paid Artists: 100   **Non-Paid Artists:** 100
   Utilizes: Special Technical Talent; Guest Conductors; Guest Artists; Guest Directors
   Budget: $100,000 - $500,000
   Income Sources: Private Foundations/Grants/Endowments; Business/Corporate Donations; Box Office; Government Grants; Individual Donations; Opera Guilds
   Season: October - March
   Annual Attendance: 7,000
   Performance Facilities: Pantages Theater; Railto Theater

THEATRE

TACOMA ACTORS GUILD
1323 South Yakima, Tacoma, WA 98405
(206) 272-3107
Founded: 1978
Arts Area: Professional; Theatrical Group
Status: Professional; Non-Profit
Type: Performing; Resident
Purpose: To provide quality theatre that entertains and enriches the south Puget Sound community and engages that community in a dynamic partnership that explores challenging dramatic literature
Management: Kate Haas, Managing Director; Bruce K. Sevy, Artistic Director
Paid Staff: 20 **Volunteer Staff:** 100
Paid Artists: 85
Utilizes: Special Technical Talent; Guest Artists; Guest Directors
Budget: $1,000,000 - $5,000,000
Income Sources: Private Foundations/Grants/Endowments; Business/Corporate Donations; Box Office; Government Grants; Individual Donations; Benefit Events
Season: October - May **Annual Attendance:** 37,000
Affiliations: TCG
Performance Facilities: Tacoma Actors Guild

Toledo

INSTRUMENTAL MUSIC

WASHINGTON BLUEGRASS ASSOCIATION
PO Box 490, Toledo, WA 98591
(206) 864-2074
Founded: 1982
Arts Area: Ethnic; Folk; Instrumental Group; Band; Acoustic Bluegrass
Status: Non-Profit
Type: Educational; Sponsoring
Purpose: To perform at concerts throughout the year
Officers: Earla Harding, President; Sue Murphy, Secretary/Treasurer
Volunteer Staff: 100
Utilizes: Special Technical Talent; Guest Artists
Budget: $1,000 - $50,000
Income Sources: Individual Donations; Dues
Season: 52 Weeks **Annual Attendance:** 5,000
Affiliations: BMI
Performance Facilities: Toledo High School Grounds

Vancouver

THEATRE

OLD SLOCUM HOUSE THEATRE COMPANY
605 Esther Street, Vancouver, WA 98660
Founded: 1969
Arts Area: Musical; Community
Status: Non-Profit
Type: Resident
Purpose: To restore the Slocum House Theatre; to produce 19th-century plays
Management: Board of Directors
Officers: Hermine Guthie Decker, President; Mike Heywood, Vice President; Ruby Lloyd, Secretary
Budget: $1,000 - $50,000
Season: 52 Weeks

FACILITY

COLUMBIA ARTS CENTER
400 West Evergreen Boulevard, Vancouver, WA 98660
(206) 693-0351
FAX: (206) 643-0794
Type of Facility: Cultural Center
Facility Originally: Church

Type of Stage: Platform
Stage Dimensions: 26'6"Wx33'D
Seating Capacity: 220
Year Built: 1912 **Architect:** William Tobey
Year Remodeled: 1983 **Architect:** Dolle/Swatash **Cost:** $350,000
Contact for Rental: Ralph Welsh; (206) 693-0351

Walla Walla

INSTRUMENTAL MUSIC

WALLA WALLA SYMPHONY
PO Box 92, Walla Walla, WA 99362
(509) 529-8020
Founded: 1906
Arts Area: Symphony; Orchestra
Status: Non-Professional; Non-Profit
Type: Performing
Purpose: To promote the tradition of great symphonic music; to bring high-quality performances to all segments of the community, including children
Management: Sharon Thompson, Manager; Linda Desmond, Assistant Manager
Officers: Michael de Grasse, President; Dina Baker, Vice President; Jane Drabeck, Secretary; Albert Marshall, Treasurer
Paid Staff: 4
Paid Artists: 13 **Non-Paid Artists:** 40
Utilizes: Guest Conductors; Guest Artists
Budget: $100,000 - $500,000
Income Sources: Private Foundations/Grants/Endowments; Business/Corporate Donations; Box Office; Government Grants; Individual Donations
Season: October - May **Annual Attendance:** 6,000
Performance Facilities: Cordiner Hall

FACILITY

WHITMAN COLLEGE - CORDINER HALL
Walla Walla, WA 99362
(509) 527-5111
Type of Facility: Concert Hall
Type of Stage: Proscenium
Year Built: 1968 **Cost:** $1,600,000
Contact for Rental: Gayle Worthington; (509) 527-5111
Resident Groups: Walla Walla Symphony Orchestra; Community Concerts; Walla Walla School District

Wenatchee

DANCE

CHILDREN'S BALLET THEATRE
PO Box 2053, Wenatchee, WA 98801
(509) 663-4056
Founded: 1985
Arts Area: Ballet; Multi-Media Productions
Status: Semi-Professional; Non-Profit
Type: Performing; Touring; Resident
Purpose: Children's Ballet Theatre is an outgrowth of Wenatchee Civic Ballet, which was the first company of its kind to be incorporated in the Pacific Northwest. It has brought the finest professional artists to north-central Washington for the past fifteen years.
Management: Joan Shelton-Mason, Director
Officers: Betty Jean Gibson, Chairman of the Board; Lillian Auwerter, Secretary; Joan Shelton-Mason, Founder/Director
Volunteer Staff: 50
Utilizes: Special Technical Talent; Guest Artists; Guest Choreographers; 0
Budget: $1,000 - $50,000
Income Sources: Private Foundations/Grants/Endowments; Business/Corporate Donations; Box Office; Government Grants; Individual Donations
Season: September - June **Annual Attendance:** 5,000

Yakima

INSTRUMENTAL MUSIC

YAKIMA SYMPHONY ORCHESTRA
PO Box 307, Yakima, WA 98907
(509) 248-1414
FAX: (509) 457-0980
Founded: 1971
Arts Area: Symphony; Orchestra
Status: Professional; Non-Profit
Type: Performing; Educational
Purpose: To perform and promote symphonic music
Management: Sarah S. Marley, Manager; Brooke Creswell, Music Director
Officers: John Bloxom Jr., President; Carmela Newstead, First Vice President; Bruce Willis, Second Vice President; Darrell Blue, Treasurer; Priscilla Wyckoff, Secretary; Gayle Scholl, Member at Large
Paid Staff: 4
Paid Artists: 60
Utilizes: Guest Conductors; Guest Artists
Budget: $100,000 - $500,000
Income Sources: Private Foundations/Grants/Endowments; Business/Corporate Donations; Box Office; Government Grants; Individual Donations
Season: October - April   **Annual Attendance:** 4,500
Affiliations: ASOL
Performance Facilities: Capitol Theatre

YAKIMA YOUTH ORCHESTRA
PO Box 307, Yakima, WA 98907
(509) 248-1414
Arts Area: Symphony; Orchestra; Chamber
Status: Non-Professional; Non-Profit
Type: Performing; Educational
Management: Dennis Clauss, Conductor
Non-Paid Artists: 20
Season: September - May   **Annual Attendance:** 300
Affiliations: Yakima Symphony Orchestra

FACILITY

CAPITAL THEATRE
19 South Third Street, PO Box 102, Yakima, WA 98907
(509) 575-6267
Type of Facility: Theatre House
Facility Originally: Vaudeville
Type of Stage: Proscenium
Stage Dimensions: 90'Wx38'D; 30'Hx30'W proscenium opening   **Orchestra Pit**
Seating Capacity: 1,505
Year Built: 1920   **Architect:** B. Marcus Priteca
Year Remodeled: 1978   **Architect:** William Paddock   **Cost:** $4,200,000
Contact for Rental: Steven J. Caffery;   (509) 575-6267
The Capital Theatre is a National Historic Landmark.

WEST VIRGINIA

Beckley

THEATRE

THEATRE WEST VIRGINIA, INC.
PO Box 1205, Beckley, WV 25801
(304) 256-6800; (800) 666-9142
FAX: (304) 256-6807
Founded: 1955
Arts Area: Professional; Theatrical Group; Puppet
Status: Professional
Type: Performing; Touring; Educational; Sponsoring
Purpose: To provide theatre of the highest quality to community and state residents as well as tourists
Management: Susan Landis, Acting General Manager; John Arnold, Artistic Director; Carrie Sandersturner, Development Director; Marina Hunley, Sales Director; Gayle Bowling, Administrative Assistant
Officers: Susan Landis, President; Blair Friar, President-Elect; John Rust, Vice President; Judy Harrah, Secretary; Arnold Graybeat, Treasurer
Paid Staff: 5 **Volunteer Staff:** 50
Paid Artists: 50
Utilizes: Guest Artists; Guest Directors
Budget: $500,000 - $1,000,000
Income Sources: Private Foundations/Grants/Endowments; Business/Corporate Donations; Box Office; Government Grants; Individual Donations
Season: 52 Weeks **Annual Attendance:** 140,000

FACILITY

CLIFFSIDE AMPHITHEATRE OF WEST VIRGINIA
PO Box 1205, Beckley, WV 25801
(304) 253-8131
FAX: (304) 256-6807
Type of Facility: Outdoor (Concert); Amphitheater
Type of Stage: Proscenium
Stage Dimensions: 60'x45'
Orchestra Pit
Seating Capacity: 1,200
Year Built: 1961 **Cost:** $250,000
Year Remodeled: 1991
Contact for Rental: Robert Shreue, Executive Director; (304) 256-6803
Resident Groups: Hatfields & McCoys; Broadway Musical Repertory; Stonewall - Old Blue Light

Buckhannon

FACILITY

WEST VIRGINIA WESLEYAN COLLEGE - ATKINSON AUDITORIUM
59 College Avenue, Buckhannon, WV 26201
(304) 473-8000, ext. 8044
Type of Facility: Auditorium
Facility Originally: Chapel
Type of Stage: Proscenium
Stage Dimensions: 32'Wx24'D
Seating Capacity: 500
Year Built: 1920
Year Remodeled: 1977
Contact for Rental: (304) 473-8258
Resident Groups: West Virginia Wesleyan College Theatre

Charles Town

FACILITY

THE OLD OPERA HOUSE COMPANY
204 North George Street, Charles Town, WV 25414
(304) 725-4420
    Founded: 1973
    Type of Facility: Opera House
    Type of Stage: Proscenium
    Stage Dimensions: 42'Wx24'D   **Orchestra Pit**
    Seating Capacity: 336
    Year Built: 1910   **Architect:** T.A. Mullett   **Cost:** $50,000
    Year Remodeled: 1979   **Cost:** $400,000
    Contact for Rental: Hubert Rolling, Manager;   (304) 725-4420
    Manager: Hubert Rolling;   (304) 725-4420
    Resident Groups: Old Opera House Theatre Company
Available for concerts or two-night runs. We also do a full season consisting of three plays, two musicals and a children's show.

Charleston

DANCE

APPALACHIAN YOUTH JAZZ-BALLET COMPANY
PO Box 575, Charleston, WV 25301
(304) 343-1076
    Founded: 1982
    Arts Area: Ballet; Jazz
    Status: Non-Profit
    Type: Performing; Touring; Educational
    Purpose: To provide talented aspiring dancers liaisons between classroom and the professional stage; to enrich the community through concerts and lecture demonstrations; to provide inspiration to youngsters in the audience
    Management: Nina Denton, Artistic Director
    Officers: Ricklin Brown, President; John Breed, Vice President; Catherine Halloran, Secretary; Carol Velasquez, Treasurer
    Volunteer Staff: 2
    Non-Paid Artists: 2
    Utilizes: Guest Artists; Guest Choreographers
    Budget: $1,000 - $50,000
    Income Sources: Private Foundations/Grants/Endowments; Business/Corporate Donations; Box Office; Individual Donations
    Season: September - June   **Annual Attendance:** 15,000
    Affiliations: Washington Community Education
    Performance Facilities: Charleston Civic Center; Municipal Auditorium

CHARLESTON BALLET
822 Virginia Street East, Charleston, WV 25301
(304) 342-6541
    Founded: 1956
    Arts Area: Modern; Ballet; Folk
    Status: Semi-Professional; Non-Profit
    Type: Performing; Touring
    Purpose: To present ballet concerts for professional and talented young dancers
    Management: Kim R. Pauley, Director/Choreographer
    Officers: Mary Lou Lewis, MD, President; Jerry Howard, Vice President; Jean McCune, Secretary; Kim R. Pauley, Treasurer
    Paid Staff: 2   **Volunteer Staff:** 10
    Paid Artists: 15   **Non-Paid Artists:** 20
    Utilizes: Special Technical Talent; Guest Artists; Guest Choreographers
    Budget: $50,000 - $100,000
    Income Sources: Private Foundations/Grants/Endowments; Business/Corporate Donations; Box Office; Government Grants; Individual Donations
    Season: 52 Weeks

INSTRUMENTAL MUSIC

CHARLESTON CHAMBER MUSIC SOCIETY
PO Box 641, Charleston, WV 25323
(304) 344-5389
>**Founded:** 1941
>**Arts Area:** Chamber; Ensemble
>**Status:** Non-Profit
>**Type:** Performing; Sponsoring
>**Purpose:** To bring outstanding chamber-music ensembles to Charleston
>**Management:** N. David Stern, Executive Director
>**Paid Staff:** 1   **Volunteer Staff:** 25
>**Paid Artists:** 6
>**Utilizes:** Guest Artists
>**Budget:** $1,000 - $50,000
>**Income Sources:** Private Foundations/Grants/Endowments; Business/Corporate Donations; Box Office; Government Grants; Individual Donations
>**Season:** October - May   **Annual Attendance:** 2,500
>**Affiliations:** APAP; CMA
>**Performance Facilities:** Christ Church United Methodist

LILLIPUT ORCHESTRA
16 Terrace Road, Charleston, WV 25314
(304) 346-6095
>**Founded:** 1979
>**Arts Area:** Symphony; Orchestra; Chamber; Opera
>**Status:** Professional
>**Type:** Performing; Touring; Educational
>**Purpose:** To bring symphonic music and opera to West Virginians and others
>**Management:** Suzanne Riggio, General Manager
>**Officers:** Robert Bobst, President
>**Volunteer Staff:** 1
>**Paid Artists:** 40
>**Utilizes:** Guest Artists
>**Budget:** $1,000 - $50,000
>**Income Sources:** Private Foundations/Grants/Endowments; Business/Corporate Donations; Box Office; Government Grants; Individual Donations
>**Season:** August - June   **Annual Attendance:** 10,000

MONTCLAIRE STRING QUARTET
c/o West Virginia Symphony Orchestra, PO Box 2292, Charleston, WV 25328
(304) 342-0151
FAX: (304) 342-0152
>**Founded:** 1982
>**Arts Area:** Symphony; Chamber; Ensemble; Instrumental Group
>**Status:** Professional
>**Type:** Performing; Touring; Resident; Educational; Sponsoring
>**Purpose:** To present the highest quality string quartet repertoire throughout the state of West Virginia; to provide leadership in the West Virginia Symphony Orchestra; to present educational programs in West Virginia schools
>**Management:** Shirley Furry, Executive Director; Thomas Conlin, Artistic Director; Emily Papadopoulos, Director of Development
>**Officers:** John L. McClaugherty, President; Patrick Bond, Vice President of Development
>**Utilizes:** Guest Artists
>**Budget:** $1,000,000 - $5,000,000
>**Income Sources:** Private Foundations/Grants/Endowments; Business/Corporate Donations; Box Office; Government Grants; Individual Donations
>**Season:** September - May
>**Performance Facilities:** St. Matthew's Episcopal Church

WEST VIRGINIA SYMPHONY
1210 Virginia Street East, Charleston, WV 25301
(304) 342-0151
FAX: (304) 342-0152
>**Arts Area:** Symphony; Ensemble
>**Status:** Professional
>**Type:** Performing

Purpose: To present classical music concerts and education throughout the state of West Virginia
Management: Shirley A. Furry, Executive Director
Officers: John L. McClaugherty, President
Volunteer Staff: 7
Non-Paid Artists: 85
Utilizes: Special Technical Talent; Guest Artists
Budget: $1,000,000 - $5,000,000
Income Sources: Private Foundations/Grants/Endowments; Business/Corporate Donations; Box Office; Government Grants; Individual Donations
Season: September - May   **Annual Attendance:** 42,500
Affiliations: ASOL
Performance Facilities: Municipal Auditorium

VOCAL MUSIC

CHARLESTON AREA COMMUNITY CHOIR
PO Box 20253, Charleston, WV 25302
(304) 342-3183
Founded: 1976
Arts Area: Choral; Ethnic; Folk
Status: Professional; Semi-Professional; Non-Professional; Non-Profit
Type: Performing; Touring; Resident; Educational; Sponsoring
Purpose: To stimulate composition of original works; to illustrate meaningful application of various musical instruments in accompanying vocal groups; to identify and analyze Black religious music
Management: Ethel Caffie-Austin, Director; Barbara Rowell, Executive Secretary/Business Manager
Officers: Elston Canada, President
Volunteer Staff: 75
Non-Paid Artists: 8
Utilizes: Special Technical Talent; Guest Artists; Guest Directors
Budget: $1,000 - $50,000
Income Sources: Private Foundations/Grants/Endowments; Box Office; Government Grants; Individual Donations
Season: 52 Weeks
Performance Facilities: Charleston Cultural Center

CHARLESTON CIVIC CHORUS
PO Box 2014, Charleston, WV 25327-2014
(304) 747-4944
Founded: 1952
Arts Area: Choral
Status: Non-Professional; Non-Profit
Type: Performing; Resident
Purpose: To perform high-quality choral classics as well as some lighter fare
Management: J. Truman Dalton, Music Director
Officers: Judith Arnold, President; Thomas Llewellyn, Vice President; Evan Buck, Treasurer
Paid Staff: 2
Utilizes: Guest Artists
Budget: $1,000 - $50,000
Income Sources: Business/Corporate Donations; Government Grants; Individual Donations
Season: September - May   **Annual Attendance:** 600
Performance Facilities: The Baptist Temple

CHARLESTON LIGHT OPERA GUILD
PO Box 1762, Charleston, WV 25326
(304) 342-9312
Founded: 1949
Arts Area: Light Opera
Status: Non-Profit
Type: Performing
Purpose: To present musical comedy
Officers: Horace Emery, President; Tim Harper, Vice President; Emma Jean Thomas, Secretary; Bill Rogers, Treasurer
Paid Artists: 3
Utilizes: Special Technical Talent
Budget: $50,000 - $100,000
Income Sources: Private Foundations/Grants/Endowments; Business/Corporate Donations; Box Office; Government Grants; Individual Donations
Season: 52 Weeks   **Annual Attendance:** 10,000
Performance Facilities: Charleston Civic Center - Little Theater

THEATRE

KANAWHA PLAYERS
5315 MacCorkle Avenue, SE, Charleston, WV 25304
(304) 925-5051
    Founded: 1922
    Arts Area: Dinner; Community; Theatrical Group
    Status: Non-Professional; Non-Profit
    Type: Performing; Touring; Educational
    Management: Kathie M. Frank, Company Administrator; Betsy Stuart, Historian
    Officers: Stephen E. Kawash, President
    Paid Staff: 1 **Volunteer Staff:** 30
    Paid Artists: 5 **Non-Paid Artists:** 175
    Utilizes: Special Technical Talent; Guest Artists; Guest Directors
    Budget: $50,000 - $100,000
    Income Sources: Private Foundations/Grants/Endowments; Business/Corporate Donations; Box Office;
    Individual Donations
    Season: September - June **Annual Attendance:** 6,500
    Affiliations: Arts Advocacy of West Virginia
    Performance Facilities: Charleston Civic Center - Little Theatre

FACILITY

CHARLESTON CIVIC CENTER
200 Civic Center Drive, Charleston, WV 25301
(304) 345-1500
FAX: (304) 357-7432
    Type of Facility: Civic Center
    Type of Stage: Proscenium
    Stage Dimensions: 38'Wx30'D
    Seating Capacity: 750
    Year Built: 1959
    Contact for Rental: John Robertson; (304) 345-1500
    The Charleston Civic Center contains the Coliseum, Little Theater and Municipal Auditorium. See separate listings for
    further information.

CHARLESTON CIVIC CENTER - COLISEUM
200 Civic Center Drive, Charleston, WV 25301
(304) 345-1500
FAX: (304) 357-7435
    Type of Facility: Concert Hall; Performance Center; Multi-Purpose
    Type of Stage: Flexible
    Seating Capacity: 3,500
    Contact for Rental: John Robertson; (304) 345-1500

CHARLESTON CIVIC CENTER - LITTLE THEATER
200 Civic Center Drive, Charleston, WV 25301
(304) 345-1500
FAX: (304) 357-7435
    Type of Facility: Auditorium; Multi-Purpose
    Type of Stage: Proscenium
    Stage Dimensions: 34'Wx30'D; 50'H to grid **Orchestra Pit**
    Seating Capacity: 750
    Year Built: 1959
    Contact for Rental: John Robertson; (304) 345-1500

CHARLESTON CIVIC CENTER - MUNICIPAL AUDITORIUM
200 Civic Center Drive, Charleston, WV 25301
(304) 345-1500
FAX: (304) 357-7432
    Type of Facility: Auditorium
    Type of Stage: Proscenium
    Stage Dimensions: 62'Wx35'D; 50'H to grid; 40 fly lines
    Orchestra Pit
    Seating Capacity: 3,483
    Contact for Rental: John Robertson; (304) 345-1500

GEARY AUDITORIUM
2300 MacCorkle Avenue, SE, Charleston, WV 25304-1099
(304) 357-4807
FAX: (304) 357-4915
    Type of Facility: Auditorium
    Type of Stage: Proscenium
    Stage Dimensions: 38'4"Wx25'4"D
    Seating Capacity: 1,000
    Year Built: 1947
    Contact for Rental: Diane Stockholm;   (304) 357-4807
    Resident Groups: Capital Events; University of Charleston Conservatory

WEST VIRGINIA STATE COLLEGE CAPITOL CENTER
123 Summers Street, Charleston, WV 25301
(304) 342-6522
    Type of Facility: Theatre House
    Facility Originally: Vaudeville
    Type of Stage: Modified Apron Proscenium
    Stage Dimensions: 48'Wx24'D; 30'Wx22'H proscenium opening   **Orchestra Pit**
    Seating Capacity: 1,132
    Year Built: 1912
    Year Remodeled: 1984 **Architect:** Paul D. Marshall & Associates **Cost:** $650,000
    Contact for Rental: Laura McCullough; (304) 342-6522
    The Theater is a National Historic Landmark constantly undergoing renovation.

Fairmont

INSTRUMENTAL MUSIC

FAIRMONT CHAMBER MUSIC SOCIETY, INC.
1109 Alexander Place, Fairmont, WV 26554
(304) 363-1326
    Arts Area: Chamber
    Status: Professional; Non-Profit
    Type: Sponsoring
    Purpose: To present classical chamber music in northern West Virginia
    Officers: John Ashton, President; D.J. Romino II, Vice President; Ruth Brooks, Secretary; Nancy Hussey, Treasurer
    Volunteer Staff: 15
    Paid Artists: 13
    Utilizes: Guest Artists
    Budget: $1,000 - $50,000
    Income Sources: Private Foundations/Grants/Endowments; Box Office; Government Grants; Individual Donations
    Season: September - May **Annual Attendance:** 600
    Performance Facilities: Christ Episcopal Church

Huntington

INSTRUMENTAL MUSIC

HUNTINGTON CHAMBER ORCHESTRA
800 Fifth Avenue, Huntington, WV 25701
(304) 525-0670
    Founded: 1970
    Arts Area: Orchestra; Chamber
    Status: Professional; Non-Profit
    Type: Performing; Resident
    Purpose: To perform the finest music written for chamber orchestras
    Management: George Beter, Manager; Paul W. Whear, Music Director
    Officers: Leland Thornburg, President; Kay Wildman, Secretary; Morris Kuntz, Treasurer
    Paid Staff: 2 **Volunteer Staff:** 50
    Paid Artists: 42
    Utilizes: Guest Artists
    Budget: $1,000 - $50,000
    Income Sources: Private Foundations/Grants/Endowments; Business/Corporate Donations; Box Office; Government Grants; Individual Donations
    Season: October - May **Annual Attendance:** 2,400

Affiliations: ASOL
Performance Facilities: Huntington Galleries

PERFORMING SERIES

MARSHALL ARTISTS SERIES
Marshall University, 400 Hal Greek Boulevard, Huntington, WV 25701
(304) 696-6656
Founded: 1936
Arts Area: Dance; Vocal Music; Instrumental Music; Theater; Lyric Opera; Grand Opera
Status: Non-Profit
Type: Educational; Sponsoring
Purpose: To aid, promote and contribute to the educational and cultural life of Marshall University and the surrounding area
Management: Celeste Winters-Nunley, Manager; Anne S. Moncer, Administrative Assistant
Officers: J. Wade Gilley, President
Paid Staff: 2   **Volunteer Staff:** 30
Budget: $100,000 - $500,000
Income Sources: Private Foundations/Grants/Endowments; Business/Corporate Donations; Box Office; Government Grants; Individual Donations
Season: September - May   **Annual Attendance:** 14,000
Affiliations: Marshall University
Performance Facilities: Keith-Albee Theatre

FACILITY

THE HUNTINGTON CIVIC CENTRE
1 Civic Center Plaza, Huntington, WV 25727
Type of Facility: Civic Center
Type of Stage: Wenger
Stage Dimensions: 60'x40'x4'
Seating Capacity: 8,500
Year Built: 1976
Contact for Rental: Maria DiGabriele;   (304) 696-5990

HUNTINGTON MUSEUM OF ART - AMPHITHEATRE
Park Hills, Huntington, WV 25701
(304) 529-2701
Type of Facility: Amphitheater
Type of Stage: Environmental
Stage Dimensions: 60'Wx30'D
Seating Capacity: 750
Year Built: 1976   **Architect:** Dean
Contact for Rental: James Lawhorn;   (304) 529-2701

HUNTINGTON MUSEUM OF ART - AUDITORIUM
Park Hills, Huntington, WV 25701
(304) 529-2701
Type of Facility: Auditorium
Type of Stage: Proscenium
Stage Dimensions: 34'Wx19'D
Seating Capacity: 300
Year Built: 1972   **Architect:** Walter Gropius
Contact for Rental: James Lawhorn;   (304) 529-2701
Resident Groups: Community Players

KEITH-ALBEE THEATRE
925 Fourth Avenue, Huntington, WV 25720
(304) 525-8311
Type of Facility: Theatre House
Type of Stage: Proscenium
Stage Dimensions: 47'Wx27'D   **Orchestra Pit**
Seating Capacity: 1,800
Year Built: 1928   **Architect:** Thomas W. Lamb   **Cost:** $2,000,000
Year Remodeled: 1976   **Architect:** Mel Glatz   **Cost:** $250,000
Contact for Rental: Manager;   (304) 525-8311

MARSHALL UNIVERSITY - JOAN C. EDWARDS PLAYHOUSE
400 Halgreer Boulevard, Huntington, WV 25755-2242
(304) 696-2787
    Type of Facility: Auditorium
    Type of Stage: Proscenium
    Stage Dimensions: 52'Wx27'D
    Seating Capacity: 650
    Year Built: 1907
    Year Remodeled: 1964
    Contact for Rental: James Morris Smith;   (304) 696-7514
    Resident Groups: Marshall University Performing Arts groups

MARSHALL UNIVERSITY - SMITH RECITAL HALL
400 Halgreer, Huntington, WV 25755-2242
(304) 696-3117
    Type of Facility: Concert Hall
    Type of Stage: Proscenium
    Stage Dimensions: 57'Wx30'D
    Seating Capacity: 650
    Year Built: 1907
    Year Remodeled: 1964
    Contact for Rental: James Morris Smith;   (304) 696-2514
    Resident Groups: Marshall University Performing Arts groups

Institute

FACILITY

WEST VIRGINIA STATE COLLEGE - F.S. BELCHER THEATRE
Fine Arts Building, Institute, WV 25112
(304) 766-3186
    Type of Facility: Auditorium; Studio Performance; Theatre House
    Type of Stage: Proscenium
    Stage Dimensions: 30'x32'x35'   **Orchestra Pit**
    Seating Capacity: 355
    Year Built: 1965   **Architect:** C.E. Sillings   **Cost:** $1,700,000
    Contact for Rental: David Wohl;   (304) 766-3186
    Resident Groups: West Virginia State College Players

Keyser

THEATRE

APPLE ALLEY PLAYERS
PO Box 144, Keyser, WV 26726
(304) 788-1105
    Founded: 1980
    Arts Area: Community
    Status: Non-Profit
    Type: Resident; Sponsoring
    Purpose: To provide quality theatre for the surrounding area
    Officers: Annette Favara, President; Bob Shadler, Vice President; Alexa Fazenbaker, Secretary; Sandy Shadler, Treasurer
    Volunteer Staff: 20
    Paid Artists: 6
    Utilizes: Special Technical Talent
    Budget: $1,000 - $50,000
    Income Sources: Business/Corporate Donations; Box Office; Government Grants; Individual Donations
    Annual Attendance: 25,000
    Performance Facilities: McKee Art Center, Potomac State College

---
Lewisburg

THEATRE

THE GREENBRIER VALLEY THEATRE
PO Box 494, Lewisburg, WV 24901
(304) 645-3838; (304) 645-1354
    Founded: 1966
    Arts Area: Summer Stock; Musical
    Status: Non-Professional
    Type: Performing; Touring; Educational
    Purpose: To provide a vehicle for bringing live, professional-quality theatre experiences to our community; to explore all practical means of encouraging the performing arts and artists in our area
    Management: Cathey Crowell Sawyer, Artistic Director; Kit Stauton, Managing Producer
    Officers: Greg Johnson, President; Rita Hassen, Secretary; Jack Hewitt, Treasurer
    Volunteer Staff: 40
    Utilizes: Guest Directors
    Budget: $50,000 - $100,000
    Income Sources: Private Foundations/Grants/Endowments; Business/Corporate Donations; Box Office; Individual Donations
    Season: 52 Weeks   **Annual Attendance:** 4,000
    Performance Facilities: The Barn

FACILITY

CARNEGIE HALL, INC.
105 Church Street, Lewisburg, WV 24901
(304) 645-7917
    Founded: 1983
    Type of Facility: Concert Hall; Auditorium; Performance Center; Multi-Purpose; Cultural/Educational Center
    Facility Originally: School
    Type of Stage: Proscenium
    Stage Dimensions: 31'x23'3"
    Seating Capacity: 500
    Year Built: 1902   **Architect:** W.G. McDowell   **Cost:** $33,000
    Year Remodeled: 1992   **Architect:** Paul Marshall
    Acoustical Consultant: Mary Leb
    Contact for Rental: Lynn Creamer; (304) 645-7917

Morgantown

FACILITY

WEST VIRGINIA UNIVERSITY CREATIVE ARTS CENTER
PO Box 6111, Morgantown, WV 26505-6111
(304) 293-4841
    Type of Facility: Performance Center
    Architect: Alex Manhood
    Acoustical Consultant: Bolt, Beranek & Newman
    Contact for Rental: Mark Oreskovich; (304) 293-4642, ext. 105
    Resident Groups: West Virginia University Divisions of Music and Theater; University Symphony Orchestra; University Jazz, Percussion and Wind Ensembles; University Concert Band; University Chorus
    West Virginia University Creative Arts Center contains the Choral Recital Hall, Classroom Theatre, Concert Theatre, Opera Theatre and Studio Theater. See separate listings for additional information.

WEST VIRGINIA UNIVERSITY CREATIVE ARTS CENTER - CHORAL RECITAL HALL
PO Box 6111, Morgantown, WV 26505-6111
(304) 293-4841
    Type of Facility: Concert Hall
    Type of Stage: Platform

Stage Dimensions: 40'Wx20'D
Seating Capacity: 150
Contact for Rental: Mark Oreskovich;   (304) 293-4642, ext. 105

WEST VIRGINIA UNIVERSITY CREATIVE ARTS CENTER - CLASSROOM THEATRE
PO Box 6111, Morgantown, WV 26505-6111
(304) 293-4841
Type of Facility: Theatre House; Room
Type of Stage: Proscenium
Stage Dimensions: 40'Wx25'D
Seating Capacity: 50
Contact for Rental: Mark Oreskovich;   (304) 293-4642, ext. 105
Used as a laboratory and experimental theater for students

WEST VIRGINIA UNIVERSITY CREATIVE ARTS CENTER - CONCERT THEATRE
PO Box 6111, Morgantown, WV 26505-6111
(304) 293-4841
Type of Facility: Concert Hall; Theatre House; Opera House
Type of Stage: Proscenium
Stage Dimensions: 58'Wx40'D
Orchestra Pit
Seating Capacity: 1,500
Contact for Rental: Mark Oreskovich;   (304) 293-4642, ext. 105

WEST VIRGINIA UNIVERSITY CREATIVE ARTS CENTER - OPERA THEATRE
PO Box 6111, Morgantown, WV 26505-6111
(304) 293-4841
Type of Facility: Theatre House; Opera House; Black Box
Type of Stage: Flexible
Seating Capacity: 150
Contact for Rental: Mark Oreskovich;   (304) 293-4642, ext. 105

WEST VIRGINIA UNIVERSITY CREATIVE ARTS CENTER - STUDIO THEATER
PO Box 6111, Morgantown, WV 26505-6111
(304) 293-4841
Type of Facility: Theatre House; Black Box
Type of Stage: Flexible
Seating Capacity: 250
Contact for Rental: Mark Oreskovich;   (304) 293-4642, ext. 105

Oak Hill

PERFORMING SERIES

FAYETTE COUNTY FINE ARTS COUNCIL
1147 Country Club Road, Oak Hill, WV 25901
(304) 469-6517
Founded: 1974
Arts Area: Dance; Vocal Music; Theater
Status: Non-Profit
Type: Sponsoring
Purpose: To provide fine-arts programs to an area which is culturally and economically deprived
Officers: Betty M. Steen, Guy O. Baker, Co-Chairmen; Nancy Boyd, Secretary; Nancy Hannabass, Treasurer; Carolyn Hill, Historian
Volunteer Staff: 10
Utilizes: Special Technical Talent; Guest Artists
Budget: $1,000 - $50,000
Income Sources: Business/Corporate Donations; Box Office; Government Grants; Individual Donations
Season: September - May
Annual Attendance: 1,000
Performance Facilities: Fayette High School; Oak Hill High School

Parkersburg

DANCE

PARKERSBURG WHEELING BALLET COMPANY
PO Box 4204, Parkersburg, WV 26104
(304) 428-2010
> **Founded:** 1982
> **Arts Area:** Ballet
> **Status:** Professional; Non-Profit
> **Type:** Performing; Touring; Educational; Sponsoring
> **Management:** N. Gunter, Artistic Director; S. Gunter, Choreographer; D. Dix, Marketing Director; T. Forster, Development Director
> **Officers:** Tom Wiseman, President; D. Dix, Vice President; S. LeMasters, Secretary; S. Stout, Treasurer
> **Paid Staff:** 2   **Volunteer Staff:** 9
> **Paid Artists:** 2   **Non-Paid Artists:** 40
> **Utilizes:** Special Technical Talent; Guest Artists
> **Budget:** $1,000 - $50,000
> **Income Sources:** Business/Corporate Donations; Box Office; Government Grants; Individual Donations
> **Season:** 52 Weeks
> **Annual Attendance:** 40,000

Wheeling

INSTRUMENTAL MUSIC

WHEELING SYMPHONY
Hawley Building, Wheeling, WV 26003
(304) 232-6191
FAX: (304) 233-2679
> **Founded:** 1929
> **Arts Area:** Symphony; Orchestra
> **Status:** Professional; Non-Profit
> **Type:** Performing; Touring; Resident; Educational
> **Purpose:** To provide balanced and diversified musical programs which broaden audience appreciation and improve the quality of life in our area
> **Management:** Laura Willumsen, Executive Director
> **Officers:** Joan C. Stamp, President
> **Paid Staff:** 8
> **Paid Artists:** 78
> **Utilizes:** Guest Artists
> **Budget:** $500,000 - $1,000,000
> **Income Sources:** Private Foundations/Grants/Endowments; Business/Corporate Donations; Box Office; Government Grants; Individual Donations; Special Projects; Fund-raising
> **Season:** 52 Weeks   **Annual Attendance:** 40,000
> **Affiliations:** ASOL; ASCAP; BMI
> **Performance Facilities:** Capitol Music Hall

PERFORMING SERIES

OGLEBAY INSTITUTE
Oglebay Park, Wheeling, WV 26003
> **Founded:** 1930
> **Arts Area:** Dance; Instrumental Music; Theater; Lyric Opera
> **Status:** Professional; Non-Profit
> **Type:** Performing; Touring; Educational
> **Utilizes:** Guest Artists
> **Budget:** $1,000 - $50,000
> **Income Sources:** Private Foundations/Grants/Endowments; Business/Corporate Donations; Box Office; Government Grants; Individual Donations
> **Season:** October - May

FACILITY

CAPITOL MUSIC HALL
1015 Main Street, Wheeling, WV 26003
(304) 232-1170
FAX: (304) 234-0067
    Type of Facility: Concert Hall; Theatre House; Opera House
    Type of Stage: Proscenium
    Stage Dimensions: 72'Wx35'D; 44'W proscenium opening   **Orchestra Pit**
    Seating Capacity: 2,500
    Year Built: 1928
    Year Remodeled: 1977
    Contact for Rental: Paula Anderson
    Resident Groups: Wheeling Symphony; Music Hall Players; Jamboree USA

WHEELING CIVIC CENTER
14th Street, #2, Wheeling, WV 26003
(304) 233-7000
    Type of Facility: Arena; Multi-Purpose
    Type of Stage: Flexible
    Seating Capacity: Concert - 7,700; Festival - 9,800
    Year Built: 1977
    Contact for Rental: Dennis Magruder;   (304) 233-7000

WISCONSIN

Appleton

THEATRE

APPLETON WEST THEATRE
610 North Badger Avenue, Appleton, WI 54912
(414) 832-6259
Arts Area: Theatrical Group
Status: Non-Profit
Type: Educational
Management: Roger Danielson, Manager
Paid Staff: 4
Utilizes: Special Technical Talent; Guest Conductors; Guest Artists; Guest Directors
Budget: $1,000 - $50,000
Income Sources: Private Foundations/Grants/Endowments; Business/Corporate Donations; Box Office; Government Grants
Season: September - June   **Annual Attendance:** 50,000
Performance Facilities: Appleton West Community Auditorium

FACILITY

LAWRENCE UNIVERSITY - MUSIC-DRAMA CENTER
420 East College Avenue, Appleton, WI 54912
(414) 832-7000
Type of Facility: Concert Hall
Facility Originally: School
Type of Stage: Flexible   **Orchestra Pit**
Seating Capacity: 250
Year Built: 1958   **Architect:** Frank C. Shattuck Associates   **Cost:** $1,250,000
Acoustical Consultant: Bolt, Beranek & Newman
Contact for Rental: Conservatory Business Office, Lawrence University

Beloit

PERFORMING SERIES

BELOIT COLLEGE PERFORMING ARTS SERIES
700 College Street, Beloit, WI 53511
(608) 363-2577
FAX: (608) 363-2718
Arts Area: Dance; Vocal Music; Instrumental Music; Theater; Jazz
Status: Professional; Non-Profit
Management: William F. Faust, Events Coordinator
Paid Staff: 1
Utilizes: Guest Artists
Budget: $1,000 - $50,000
Income Sources: Private Foundations/Grants/Endowments; Box Office; Government Grants
Season: September - April   **Annual Attendance:** 650
Affiliations: Beloit College
Performance Facilities: Eaton Chapel

Eagle River

PERFORMING SERIES

HEADWATERS COUNCIL, PERFORMING ARTS
Box 1481, Eagle River, WI 54521
(715) 479-3131
FAX: (715) 479-1015
Founded: 1982
Arts Area: Dance; Vocal Music; Instrumental Music; Theater
Status: Non-Profit
Type: Performing

Purpose: To bring quality entertainment to our community, located in a rather remote area of Wisconsin
Officers: Sharon Nielsen, President; Robert Schroeter, Vice President; Deborah Heehn, Secretary; Mary Schwaiger, Treasurer
Volunteer Staff: 20
Utilizes: Guest Artists
Budget: $1,000 - $50,000
Income Sources: Business/Corporate Donations; Government Grants; Individual Donations
Season: October - May   **Annual Attendance:** 2,400
Performance Facilities: Northland Pines High School

FACILITY

NORTHLAND PINES HIGH SCHOOL
Eagle River, PO Box 1269, Eagle River, WI 54521
(715) 479-4473
Type of Facility: Auditorium
Type of Stage: Proscenium
Stage Dimensions: 40'Wx28'D
Seating Capacity: 500
Contact for Rental: Northland Pines High School;   (715) 479-4473
Resident Groups: Headwaters Council Performing Arts

Eau Claire

THEATRE

CHIPPEWA VALLEY THEATRE GUILD
316 Eau Claire Street, Eau Claire, WI 54701
(715) 832-7529
Founded: 1982
Arts Area: Community
Status: Non-Profit
Type: Performing; Educational
Purpose: To bring quality theatre productions to our area, as well as allowing community members to perform in a theatrical production
Officers: Susan Frederick, President; Lynn Weber, Vice President
Volunteer Staff: 50
Paid Artists: 3
Utilizes: Special Technical Talent; Guest Conductors; Guest Directors
Budget: $1,000 - $50,000
Income Sources: Private Foundations/Grants/Endowments; Business/Corporate Donations; Box Office; Individual Donations
Season: September - May   **Annual Attendance:** 5,000
Affiliations: Eau Claire Parks and Recreation
Performance Facilities: The State Regional Arts Center

PERFORMING SERIES

UNIVERSITY ARTISTS SERIES
Davies Center 133, University of Wisconsin, Eau Claire, WI 54702
(715) 836-4805
Arts Area: Dance; Vocal Music; Instrumental Music; Theater
Status: Non-Profit
Type: Performing; Educational
Purpose: To provide students and area citizens with opportunities to see and hear professional orchestras, solo artists, dance and opera
Management: Beatrice Foley, Performing Arts Director
Paid Staff: 8
Utilizes: Guest Conductors; Guest Artists; Guest Directors
Budget: $50,000 - $100,000
Income Sources: Box Office; Government Grants
Season: September - April   **Annual Attendance:** 9,400
Affiliations: APAP; NACA
Performance Facilities: University Arena, Fine Arts Center

FACILITY

W.L. ZORN ARENA
Garfield Avenue, Eau Claire, WI 54702-4004
(715) 836-4805
FAX: (715) 836-5030
Type of Facility: Arena
Type of Stage: Platform
Stage Dimensions: 44'x48'
Seating Capacity: 3,307
Year Built: 1953
Contact for Rental: Karen Stuber;   (715) 836-3881

Egg Harbor

PERFORMING SERIES

BIRCH CREEK MUSIC CENTER
PO Box 230, Egg Harbor, WI 54209
(414) 868-3763
Founded: 1976
Arts Area: Instrumental Music; Festivals
Status: Professional; Non-Professional; Non-Profit
Type: Performing; Resident; Educational
Purpose: To present a summer concert series; to train young professionals and music students
Management: James Dutton, Executive Director; Fran Dutton, Manager
Officers: James Dutton, President; Duane Feurer, Vice President; Fran Dutton, Treasurer; Paul Dickinson, Secretary; Lois Deanne, Richard Stolley, and Bill White
Paid Staff: 21   **Volunteer Staff:** 10
Paid Artists: 35   **Non-Paid Artists:** 60
Utilizes: Guest Artists
Budget: $100,000 - $500,000
Income Sources: Private Foundations/Grants/Endowments; Business/Corporate Donations; Box Office; Individual Donations
Season: June - August   **Annual Attendance:** 7,500

FACILITY

BIRCH CREEK MUSIC CENTER
PO Box 230, Egg Harbor, WI 54209
(414) 868-3763
Founded: 1976
Type of Facility: Concert Hall; Performance Center
Facility Originally: Barn
Type of Stage: Thrust
Stage Dimensions: 30'x30'
Seating Capacity: 375
Summer music workshops

Elm Grove

THEATRE

SUNSET PLAYHOUSE
800 Elm Grove Road, Elm Grove, WI 53122
(414) 782-4430
Founded: 1953
Arts Area: Community; Theatrical Group
Status: Non-Professional; Non-Profit
Type: Performing; Open Auditions
Purpose: To introduce as many new people as possible to live entertainment
Management: Tom Somerville, Artistic Director; John Kleis, Technical Director
Income Sources: Box Office
Performance Facilities: Sunset Playhouse

Ephraim

PERFORMING SERIES

PENINSULA FESTIVAL
PO Box 340, Ephraim, WI 54211
(414) 854-4060
> **Founded:** 1953
> **Arts Area:** Instrumental Music; Festivals
> **Status:** Professional; Non-Profit
> **Type:** Performing; Educational
> **Purpose:** To perform quality music in a casual atmosphere and promote young, new artists
> **Management:** Sharon Grutzmacher, General Manager
> **Officers:** Virginia Terhune, Chairman
> **Paid Staff:** 1   **Volunteer Staff:** 100
> **Paid Artists:** 55
> **Utilizes:** Guest Conductors; Guest Artists
> **Budget:** $100,000 - $500,000
> **Income Sources:** Private Foundations/Grants/Endowments; Business/Corporate Donations; Box Office; Government Grants; Individual Donations
> **Season:** August   **Annual Attendance:** 7,500
> **Affiliations:** ASOL
> **Performance Facilities:** Door Community Auditorium

Fish Creek

THEATRE

THE PENINSULA PLAYERS
W4351 Peninsula Players Road, Fish Creek, WI 54212-9799
(414) 868-3287
FAX: (414) 868-3288
> **Founded:** 1935
> **Arts Area:** Professional; Summer Stock; Theatrical Group
> **Status:** Professional; Non-Profit
> **Type:** Performing; Resident; Educational
> **Purpose:** As America's oldest professional resident summer theatre, our purpose is to present the latest of Broadway fare.
> **Management:** Tom Birmingham, General Manager; James B. McKenzie, Executive Producer
> **Budget:** $100,000 - $500,000
> **Income Sources:** Private Foundations/Grants/Endowments; Business/Corporate Donations; Box Office; Individual Donations
> **Season:** June - October   **Annual Attendance:** 33,000
> **Affiliations:** CORST; AEA
> **Performance Facilities:** Theatre in a Garden; Open Air Pavilion

Fond du Lac

INSTRUMENTAL MUSIC

FOND DU LAC SYMPHONIC BAND
536 East Tenth Street, PO Box 1779, Fond du Lac, WI 54916-1779
(414) 922-5703
> **Founded:** 1898
> **Arts Area:** Band
> **Status:** Semi-Professional; Non-Profit
> **Type:** Performing; Touring
> **Purpose:** To provide quality musical entertainment for our area and beyond; to enhance the image of the concert band as a performing medium; to provide a sophisticated performing opportunity for adult instrumentalists
> **Management:** Raymond C. Wifler, Music Director; Mary A. Arthur, Manager; Mary Liz Julka, Treasurer; Bruce Zabel, Equipment Manager; Joan Perry, Librarian
> **Officers:** Kathy Nachtwey, President; James Neujahr, Vice President; Tess Flaherty, Secretary
> **Paid Staff:** 5
> **Paid Artists:** 50   **Non-Paid Artists:** 20
> **Utilizes:** Guest Conductors; Guest Artists
> **Budget:** $1,000 - $50,000
> **Income Sources:** Private Foundations/Grants/Endowments; Business/Corporate Donations; Box Office; Government Grants; Individual Donations

Season: 52 Weeks   **Annual Attendance:** 10,000
Affiliations: Association of Concert Bands; AFM

Green Bay

INSTRUMENTAL MUSIC

GREEN BAY SYMPHONY ORCHESTRA
115 South Jefferson Street, Green Bay, WI 54301
(414) 435-3465
FAX: (414) 435-3465
  Founded: 1914
  Arts Area: Symphony; Orchestra; Chamber
  Status: Non-Profit
  Type: Performing; Educational
  Purpose: To maintain an orchestra of the highest quality possible within our means to enhance the cultural reputation of the area; to provide the youth of the community the opportunity to develop their musical abilities
  Management: Dr. James Bankhead, Executive Director
  Officers: Frederick L. Schmidt, President; David Schanke, Vice President; Rick Nuetzel, Treasurer
  Paid Staff: 4
  Paid Artists: 8   **Non-Paid Artists:** 75
  Utilizes: Guest Artists
  Budget: $500,000 - $1,000,000
  Income Sources: Private Foundations/Grants/Endowments; Business/Corporate Donations; Box Office; Government Grants; Individual Donations
  Season: October - May   **Annual Attendance:** 1,522
  Affiliations: ASOL; AWSO
  Performance Facilities: Weidner Center for The Performing Arts

FACILITY

WEIDNER CENTER FOR THE PERFORMING ARTS
2420 Nicolet Drive, Green Bay, WI 54311
(414) 465-2726
FAX: (414) 465-2619
  Founded: 1992
  Type of Facility: Theatre Complex; Concert Hall; Multi-Purpose
  Type of Stage: Flexible; Proscenium
  Orchestra Pit
  Seating Capacity: 2,040; 220; 90
  Year Built: 1992   **Architect:** Beckley Myers   **Cost:** $16,000,000
  Acoustical Consultant: Chris Jaffe and Associates
  Contact for Rental: Sid McQueen, Director;   (414) 465-2726

Green Lake

PERFORMING SERIES

GREEN LAKE FESTIVAL OF MUSIC
PO Box 569, Green Lake, WI 54941
(414) 748-9398
  Founded: 1979
  Arts Area: Vocal Music; Instrumental Music; Festivals
  Status: Professional; Semi-Professional; Non-Professional; Non-Profit
  Type: Performing; Touring; Resident; Educational; Sponsoring
  Purpose: The Green Lake Festival of Music is a non-profit corporation founded for cultural enrichment through the creation, promotion and public performance of the musical arts
  Management: Douglas Morris, Executive/Artistic Director; Marie Deitrich, Administrative Director
  Paid Staff: 2
  Paid Artists: 50   **Non-Paid Artists:** 130
  Utilizes: Guest Conductors; Guest Artists
  Budget: $50,000 - $100,000

Income Sources: Private Foundations/Grants/Endowments; Business/Corporate Donations; Box Office; Government Grants; Individual Donations
Season: June - August   Annual Attendance: 2,500

Hudson

FACILITY

PHIPPS CENTER FOR THE ARTS
109 Locust Street, Hudson, WI 54016
(715) 386-2305
Founded: 1980
Type of Facility: Concert Hall; Studio Performance; Performance Center; Theatre House; Multi-Purpose; Art Galleries & Studios
Facility Originally: Meeting Hall; Movie House
Type of Stage: Proscenium; Black Box
Stage Dimensions: 87'Wx34'D; 17'Hx36'W proscenium opening   **Orchestra Pit**
Seating Capacity: Proscenium - 241; Black Box - 125
Year Built: 1983   **Architect:** BWBR Architects   **Cost:** $2,500,000
Year Remodeled: 1992   **Architect:** KKE Architects   **Cost:** $4,000,000
Acoustical Consultant: William H.O. Kroll
Contact for Rental: General Manager;   (715) 386-2305
Manager: John H. Potter;   (715) 386-2305
Resident Groups: The Phipps Center for the Arts Drama Council; Children's Theatre Council; Music Council; Visual Arts Council; The Phipps Center Oratorio Society; The Western Wisconsin Photographic Club; The Phipps Festival Chorus

Kenosha

INSTRUMENTAL MUSIC

KENOSHA SYMPHONY ASSOCIATION, INC.
4917 68th Street, Kenosha, WI 53142
(414) 654-9080
FAX: (414) 654-9080
Founded: 1941
Arts Area: Symphony; Orchestra; Chamber
Status: Professional; Semi-Professional; Non-Professional; Non-Profit
Type: Performing; Educational
Purpose: To provide a symphony orchestra in a community setting
Management: Deborah Dunlap Ruffolo, General Manager
Officers: Kathleen Braun, President; John Mongreig, First Vice President; Bill Kuessow, Second Vice President; Sharon Bailey, Secretary; Keith Bell, Treasurer
Paid Staff: 1
Paid Artists: 4
Utilizes: Guest Artists
Budget: $100,000 - $500,000
Income Sources: Private Foundations/Grants/Endowments; Business/Corporate Donations; Box Office; Individual Donations
Season: October - May
Annual Attendance: 7,000
Affiliations: Kenosha Unified Schools
Performance Facilities: Reuther Auditorium

Kohler

PERFORMING SERIES

KOHLER FOUNDATION, INC.
104 Orchard Road, Kohler, WI 53044
(414) 458-1972
Founded: 1940
Arts Area: Dance; Vocal Music; Instrumental Music; Theater
Status: Non-Profit
Type: Performing
Purpose: To provide cultural opportunities for the benefit of the community
Management: Eleaner A. Jung, Executive Director

Paid Staff: 3
Paid Artists: 4
Budget: $1,000 - $50,000
Income Sources: Private Foundations/Grants/Endowments; Box Office
Season: September - April   **Annual Attendance:** 3,200
Performance Facilities: Kohler Memorial Theater

La Crosse

INSTRUMENTAL MUSIC

LA CROSSE SYMPHONY ORCHESTRA
815 South Ninth Street, La Crosse, WI 54601
(608) 791-0491
FAX: (608) 791-0367
Founded: 1938
Arts Area: Symphony; Orchestra; Ensemble; Instrumental Group
Status: Semi-Professional; Non-Profit
Type: Performing
Management: Marcee H. Peplinski, Manager
Officers: Kim Kress, President; Bill Schrum, Vice President; Brian Elder, Treasurer
Paid Staff: 3
Paid Artists: 53   **Non-Paid Artists:** 8
Utilizes: Special Technical Talent; Guest Artists
Budget: $100,000 - $500,000
Income Sources: Private Foundations/Grants/Endowments; Business/Corporate Donations; Box Office; Government Grants; Individual Donations
Season: October - May   **Annual Attendance:** 15,000
Affiliations: ASOL; AWSO
Performance Facilities: Viterbo College Fine Arts Center

VOCAL MUSIC

THE LA CROSSE BOYCHOIR
PO Box 186, 815 South Ninth Street, La Crosse, WI 54602
(608) 784-0040, ext. 476
Founded: 1974
Arts Area: Choral
Status: Professional; Non-Profit
Type: Performing; Touring
Purpose: To encourage, select and train boys from the La Crosse area in choral activities; to develop an appreciation for music and teach self-discipline and social responsibility; to develop a boychoir as a cultural asset; to arrange, sponsor and support musical engagements and other events
Management: Daniel Johnson-Wilmot, Founder/Director; Judy Stafslien, Accompanist
Officers: Ann Arlt, President; Roger Grant, First Vice President; Lynn Blakeley, Second Vice President; Ronald Pugh, Treasurer; Cynthia Vileth, Secretary
Paid Staff: 3   **Volunteer Staff:** 13
Utilizes: Guest Artists
Budget: $50,000 - $100,000
Income Sources: Private Foundations/Grants/Endowments; Business/Corporate Donations; Box Office; Government Grants; Individual Donations
Season: August - May   **Annual Attendance:** 5,000
Performance Facilities: Viterbo College Fine Arts Center

PERFORMING SERIES

GREAT RIVER FESTIVAL OF ARTS
119 King Street, La Crosse, WI 54601
(608) 785-1434
Founded: 1960
Arts Area: Dance; Vocal Music; Instrumental Music; Festivals
Status: Professional; Non-Profit
Type: Sponsoring
Management: Kathy Fitchuk, Administrator
Paid Staff: 1   **Volunteer Staff:** 1,500
Paid Artists: 100
Utilizes: Guest Artists
Budget: $50,000 - $100,000

Income Sources: Private Foundations/Grants/Endowments; Box Office; Individual Donations
Season: July - August   **Annual Attendance:** 28,500
Performance Facilities: Great River Festival of Arts

FACILITY

LA CROSSE CENTER
300 Harborview Plaza, La Crosse, WI 54601
(608) 789-7400
   Type of Facility: Auditorium; Civic Center; Arena
   Type of Stage: Flexible; Proscenium
   Stage Dimensions: 40'x60'
   Seating Capacity: 8,000
   Year Built: 1980   **Architect:** HRS Associates   **Cost:** $10,000,000
   Contact for Rental: (608) 782-4500
   Manager: Glen Walinski

Ladysmith

DANCE

LYNN DANCE COMPANY
W8555 Deertail Road, Ladysmith, WI 54848
(715) 532-6863
   Founded: 1976
   Arts Area: Modern
   Status: Professional
   Type: Performing; Resident; Educational
   Purpose: Development of the Chalicestream Dance Center for dance performance and teaching; dance development
   Management: Barry Lynn, Michael Doran
   Paid Staff: 2
   Paid Artists: 2
   Utilizes: Guest Artists
   Budget: $1,000 - $50,000
   Income Sources: Box Office; Individual Donations; Teaching
   Season: February - August
   Performance Facilities: Chalicestream Dance Center

Madison

DANCE

KANOPY DANCE THEATRE
315 North Henry Street, Madison, WI 53703
(608) 255-2211
   Founded: 1978
   Arts Area: Modern; Jazz
   Status: Professional
   Type: Performing; Touring; Resident; Educational; Sponsoring
   Purpose: To maintain a full-time dance company and teaching studio, present concerts, conduct residencies and teach classes
   Management: Elizabeth Ogden, Associate Director; Christine Stevens, Artistic Director; Mary Beth Heydt, General Clerical
   Officers: Deirdre Wilson Garton, President; David Egger, Secretary; Colin Jefcoate, Treasurer
   Paid Staff: 3   **Volunteer Staff:** 1
   Paid Artists: 10
   Utilizes: Special Technical Talent; Guest Conductors; Guest Artists; Guest Directors
   Budget: $50,000 - $100,000
   Income Sources: Private Foundations/Grants/Endowments; Business/Corporate Donations; Box Office; Government Grants; Individual Donations
   Season: September - May   **Annual Attendance:** 5,000
   Affiliations: Wisconsin Dance Council
   Performance Facilities: Kanopy Studio; Wisconsin Union Theatre

M.M. COLBERT
1321 East Johnson Street, Madison, WI 53703
(608) 257-9807
> **Founded:** 1980
> **Arts Area:** Modern; Ballet; Jazz
> **Status:** Non-Profit
> **Type:** Performing
> **Purpose:** To present original modern ballets in collaboration with other living artists
> **Management:** M. M. Colbert, Director/Choreographer
> **Officers:** Nancy Idaka Sheran, Chairperson, Board of Directors
> **Utilizes:** Special Technical Talent; Guest Artists
> **Budget:** $1,000 - $50,000
> **Income Sources:** Private Foundations/Grants/Endowments; Business/Corporate Donations; Box Office; Government Grants; Individual Donations
> **Annual Attendance:** 2,000

MADISON SCOTTISH COUNTRY DANCERS
2404 Fox Avenue, Madison, WI 53711
(608) 238-1227
> **Founded:** 1977
> **Arts Area:** Ethnic
> **Status:** Non-Professional; Non-Profit
> **Type:** Performing; Educational
> **Purpose:** To perform, teach, and promote Scottish country dancing and its music
> **Management:** Norma Briggs and Chuck Snowdon, Teachers
> **Officers:** Priscilla Arsove, Chair; Nancy McClements, Secretary
> **Volunteer Staff:** 2
> **Non-Paid Artists:** 60
> **Utilizes:** Guest Artists
> **Budget:** $1,000 - $50,000
> **Income Sources:** Business/Corporate Donations; Box Office; Government Grants; Individual Donations
> **Season:** 52 Weeks   **Annual Attendance:** 3,000
> **Affiliations:** Royal Scottish Country Dance Society (Scotland)
> **Performance Facilities:** University of Wisconsin; Memorial Union

MELROSE MOTION COMPANY
1050 University Avenue, Madison, WI 53706
(608) 262-0382
> **Founded:** 1985
> **Arts Area:** Modern
> **Status:** Professional; Non-Profit
> **Type:** Performing; Touring
> **Purpose:** To present works by Claudia Melrose and selected guest artists; to create and maintain high standards for dance in the Midwest; to educate and build audiences; to create a strong reputation for dance in the Midwest; to bring quality modern dance to the largest public eye possible
> **Management:** Claudia Melrose, Director; Tim Glenn, Assistant
> **Paid Staff:** 1   **Volunteer Staff:** 10
> **Paid Artists:** 10   **Non-Paid Artists:** 1
> **Utilizes:** Special Technical Talent; Guest Artists
> **Budget:** $1,000 - $50,000
> **Income Sources:** Private Foundations/Grants/Endowments; Business/Corporate Donations; Box Office; Government Grants; Individual Donations
> **Season:** October - April   **Annual Attendance:** 5,000
> **Affiliations:** University of Wisconsin-Madison

TAP-IT DANCING AND THEATRICAL COMPANY, LTD.
1957 Winnebago Street, Madison, WI 53704
(608) 244-2938
> **Founded:** 1985
> **Arts Area:** Jazz; Tap; Theater
> **Status:** Professional; Non-Profit
> **Type:** Performing; Touring; Educational; Sponsoring
> **Purpose:** To promote professional tap dance; to bring quality tap artists to the Midwest; to sponsor educational workshops and tap dance demonstrations; Tap-It creates and produces new theatre works; all productions speak to all socioeconomic backrounds
> **Management:** Donna Peckett, Danielle Dresden, Associate Directors
> **Officers:** Felicia Roberts, President; Valerie Hodgson, Vice President; Jane Denny, Secretary; Bob Queen, Treasurer
> **Paid Staff:** 2   **Volunteer Staff:** 3

Paid Artists: 10   Non-Paid Artists: 4
Utilizes: Special Technical Talent; Guest Artists
Budget: $1,000 - $50,000
Income Sources: Private Foundations/Grants/Endowments; Business/Corporate Donations; Box Office; Government Grants; Individual Donations
Season: 52 Weeks

WILLOW...A DANCE CONCERN
122 State Street, Lower Level, Madison, WI 53703
(608) 251-5233
Founded: 1975
Arts Area: Modern
Status: Non-Profit
Type: Performing
Purpose: To promote dance as a performing art and form of personal expression
Management: Phyllis Sanfilippo, Director
Volunteer Staff: 2
Non-Paid Artists: 5
Utilizes: Special Technical Talent; Guest Artists
Budget: $1,000 - $50,000
Income Sources: Private Foundations/Grants/Endowments; Business/Corporate Donations; Box Office; Government Grants; Individual Donations
Season: 52 Weeks   Annual Attendance: 1,000

INSTRUMENTAL MUSIC

MADISON JAZZ SOCIETY
PO Box 8866, Madison, WI 53708-8866
(608) 233-2702
Founded: 1984
Arts Area: Instrumental Group
Status: Non-Profit
Type: Sponsoring
Purpose: To promote the performance and education of jazz in the Madison area
Utilizes: Guest Artists
Budget: $1,000 - $50,000
Income Sources: Private Foundations/Grants/Endowments; Box Office; Individual Donations
Annual Attendance: 1,300

MADISON MUSIC COLLECTIVE
PO Box 2096, Madison, WI 53701-2096
(608) 241-4631
Founded: 1985
Arts Area: Ensemble; Instrumental Group; Electronic & Live Electronic; Improvised Music
Status: Non-Profit
Type: Educational; Sponsoring
Purpose: To support improvised music in the Madison Dane County Wisconsin area.
Officers: Joan Wildman, President; Dave Stoler, Vice President; Bill Grahm, Secretary; Don Breitenbach, Treasurer; Marilyn Fisher, Member at Large
Volunteer Staff: 10
Paid Artists: 50
Utilizes: Local and Regional Artists   Budget: $1,000 - $50,000
Income Sources: Private Foundations/Grants/Endowments; Business/Corporate Donations; Government Grants; Individual Donations
Season: 52 Weeks   Annual Attendance: 1,000
Affiliations: IAJE

MADISON SYMPHONY ORCHESTRA
211 North Carroll Street, Madison, WI 53703
(608) 257-3734
FAX: (608) 258-2315
Founded: 1926
Arts Area: Symphony
Status: Semi-Professional
Type: Performing; Educational
Management: Robert R. Palmer, General Manager
Officers: Marian Bolz, President
Paid Staff: 4
Paid Artists: 80

Utilizes: Guest Conductors; Guest Artists
Budget: $500,000 - $1,000,000
Income Sources: Private Foundations/Grants/Endowments; Business/Corporate Donations; Box Office; Government Grants; Individual Donations
Season: September - May   **Annual Attendance:** 16,000
Performance Facilities: Oscar Mayer Theatre

WISCONSIN CHAMBER ORCHESTRA
22 North Carroll Street, Suite 104, Madison, WI 53703
(608) 257-0638
FAX: (608) 257-0611
Founded: 1962
Arts Area: Orchestra; Chamber
Status: Professional; Non-Profit
Type: Performing
Purpose: To perform musical works
Management: Samuel Woodward, Executive Director; David Lewis Crosby, Artistic Director
Officers: Bob Mohelnitzky, President of Board; Susan Schmitz, Vice President; Joe Boucher, Treasurer; Stuart Sears, Secretary
Paid Staff: 4
Paid Artists: 40
Utilizes: Guest Conductors; Guest Artists
Budget: $100,000 - $500,000
Income Sources: Private Foundations/Grants/Endowments; Business/Corporate Donations; Box Office; Government Grants; Individual Donations
Season: 52 Weeks   **Annual Attendance:** 127,000
Performance Facilities: Capitol Square; First Congregational Church; Oscar Mayer Theatre

WISCONSIN YOUTH SYMPHONY ORCHESTRAS
1621 C Humanities Building, 455 North Park Street, Madison, WI 53706
(608) 263-3320
FAX: (608) 262-2150
Founded: 1966
Arts Area: Orchestra
Status: Non-Profit
Type: Performing; Touring; Educational
Purpose: To meet the symphonic needs of the musically-talented youth of southern Wisconsin
Management: James R. Smith, Music Director; Kenneth Strmiska, Manager
Officers: Steve Rosing, President
Paid Staff: 10
Utilizes: Special Technical Talent
Budget: $50,000 - $100,000
Income Sources: Private Foundations/Grants/Endowments; Business/Corporate Donations; Government Grants; Individual Donations
Season: September - May   **Annual Attendance:** 10,000
Performance Facilities: Mills Concert Hall, University of Wisconsin

VOCAL MUSIC

THE FESTIVAL CHOIR
PO Box 44634, Madison, WI 53744
(608) 849-9672
Founded: 1972
Arts Area: Operetta; Choral; Folk; A Cappella; Instrumental
Status: Semi-Professional; Non-Profit
Type: Performing; Touring
Purpose: To perform an ever-growing repertoire of choral works, drawn from classical literature, traditional carols, madrigals and contemporary compositions, for audiences worldwide
Management: David Lewis Crosby, Music Director/Conductor; Becky C. Olson, General Manager
Officers: Paul Cleven, President; Sarah Stoltz, Vice President/Secretary; June Johnson, Treasurer
Paid Staff: 2
Non-Paid Artists: 45
Utilizes: Guest Artists
Budget: $1,000 - $50,000
Income Sources: Private Foundations/Grants/Endowments; Business/Corporate Donations; Individual Donations
Season: September - April   **Annual Attendance:** 3,000
Performance Facilities: Madison Civic Center

THE MADISON BOYCHOIR
PO Box 326, Madison, WI 53701
(608) 256-5709
> **Founded:** 1971
> **Arts Area:** Choral
> **Status:** Professional; Non-Profit
> **Type:** Performing; Touring; Resident; Educational
> **Purpose:** To encourage, select and train boys from the Madison area in choral activities; to develop an appreciation for music and to teach self-discipline and social responsibility; to be a cultural asset to the community, cooperating with other music groups in performances
> **Management:** Gregory Dennis, Director; Margaret hadley, Accompanist; Ellen Seuferer, General Manager
> **Paid Staff:** 4
> **Utilizes:** Guest Artists
> **Budget:** $100,000 - $500,000
> **Income Sources:** Private Foundations/Grants/Endowments; Business/Corporate Donations; Box Office; Government Grants; Individual Donations
> **Season:** June - May **Annual Attendance:** 12,000

MADISON OPERA
458 Charles Lane, Madison, WI 53711
(608) 238-8085
> **Founded:** 1962
> **Arts Area:** Grand Opera; Light Opera
> **Status:** Semi-Professional; Non-Profit
> **Type:** Performing; Educational
> **Purpose:** To bring quality opera, locally produced, to the city of Madison with sponsorship and support of the Madison Opera Guild
> **Management:** Ann Stanke, Opera Manager; Robert Palmer, Manager, Madison Civic Music Association
> **Officers:** Jack Poulson, President; Thomas Travers, Vice President; Mary Jane Woerpel, Secretary; C. George Extrom, Treasurer
> **Paid Staff:** 1 **Volunteer Staff:** 38
> **Paid Artists:** 75 **Non-Paid Artists:** 75
> **Utilizes:** Special Technical Talent; Guest Artists; Guest Directors
> **Budget:** $100,000 - $500,000
> **Income Sources:** Private Foundations/Grants/Endowments; Business/Corporate Donations; Box Office; Government Grants; Individual Donations
> **Season:** September - April **Annual Attendance:** 5,000
> **Affiliations:** OA; OGI
> **Performance Facilities:** Oscar Mayer Theatre

OPERA FOR THE YOUNG
c/o James Tucker, 2914 Robin Court, Madison, WI 53711
(608) 274-3138
> **Founded:** 1965
> **Arts Area:** Lyric Opera; Light Opera
> **Status:** Semi-Professional; Non-Profit
> **Type:** Performing; Touring; Educational
> **Purpose:** Touring of abridged opera productions (fully staged and performed in English) to schools throughout Wisconsin and northern Illinois
> **Management:** James Tucker, Executive Director
> **Officers:** Rachelle Richards, President; Susanna Herro, Vice President; Jane Ferris, Secretary; Mary Stroud, Treasurer
> **Volunteer Staff:** 3
> **Paid Artists:** 9
> **Budget:** $50,000 - $100,000
> **Income Sources:** Business/Corporate Donations; Box Office; Government Grants; Individual Donations
> **Season:** September - May **Annual Attendance:** 12,000

THEATRE

BROOM STREET THEATER
1119 Williamson Street, Madison, WI 53703
(608) 244-8338
> **Founded:** 1969
> **Arts Area:** Professional; Theatrical Group
> **Status:** Professional; Non-Profit
> **Type:** Performing

Purpose: Produces eight original plays by Madison playwrights per year. The shows are directed or supervised by the playwrights. Our work is highly visual and physical. We are one of the oldest experimental theaters in the United States, and occasionally tour.
Management: Joel Gersmann, Artistic Director; Gary Cleven, Technical Director
Officers: Rod Clark, Chairperson; Kurt Meyer, Acting Chairperson/Vice Chairperson; Tracy Will, Treasurer
Paid Staff: 3   **Volunteer Staff:** 25
Paid Artists: 64   **Non-Paid Artists:** 150
Budget: $50,000 - $100,000
Income Sources: Private Foundations/Grants/Endowments; Business/Corporate Donations; Box Office; Government Grants; Individual Donations
Season: 52 Weeks   **Annual Attendance:** 6,000

MADISON REPERTORY THEATRE
122 State Street, Suite 201, Madison, WI 53703
(608) 256-0029
Founded: 1969
Arts Area: Professional
Status: Professional
Type: Performing; Resident
Management: Joseph Hanreddy, Artistic Director; Vick Stewart, Managing Director
Officers: Beth Korth, President
Paid Staff: 8   **Volunteer Staff:** 20
Utilizes: Guest Artists; Guest Directors
Budget: $1,000,000 - $5,000,000
Income Sources: Private Foundations/Grants/Endowments; Business/Corporate Donations; Box Office; Government Grants; Individual Donations
Season: July - May   **Annual Attendance:** 33,000
Affiliations: TCG
Performance Facilities: Madison Civic Center

MADISON THEATRE GUILD
2410 Monroe Street, Madison, WI 53711
(608) 238-9322
Founded: 1946
Arts Area: Community; Theatrical Group
Status: Non-Profit
Type: Performing; Educational
Purpose: To provide education and recreation through theatrical production
Management: Robby Sonzogi, Costume Shop Manager
Officers: Jay Rath, President; Carol Pierick, Treasurer
Paid Staff: 4   **Volunteer Staff:** 15
Non-Paid Artists: 150
Utilizes: Special Technical Talent; Guest Directors
Budget: $50,000 - $100,000
Income Sources: Private Foundations/Grants/Endowments; Business/Corporate Donations; Box Office; Government Grants; Individual Donations
Season: September - May   **Annual Attendance:** 8,000
Affiliations: Wisconsin Theatre Association
Performance Facilities: McDaniels Auditorium

WISCONSIN UNION THEATER
800 Langdon Street, Madison, WI 53706-1495
(608) 262-2202
FAX: (608) 262-5487
Founded: 1939
Arts Area: Professional; Musical; Community; Folk; Theatrical Group
Status: Non-Profit
Type: Sponsoring
Purpose: Cultural, entertainment and educational programming for university and community audiences
Management: Michael Goldberg, Director; Rauel LaBreche, Operations Manager
Paid Staff: 10   **Volunteer Staff:** 40
Paid Artists: 60
Utilizes: Special Technical Talent; Guest Artists
Budget: $100,000 - $500,000
Income Sources: Box Office; Government Grants
Season: September - May   **Annual Attendance:** 200,000
Affiliations: APAP
Performance Facilities: Wisconsin Union Theater

FACILITY

MADISON CIVIC CENTER
211 State Street, Madison, WI 53703
(608) 266-6550
    Type of Facility: Theatre Complex; Civic Center; Multi-Purpose
    Year Built: 1980
    Architect: Hardy, Holtzman & Pfeiffer
    Contact for Rental: Rudy Lienau; (608) 266-6550
    Resident Groups: Madison Art Center; Madison Symphony Orchestra; CTM, Inc.; The Rep
    Madison Civic Center contains the Isthmus Playhouse and Oscar Mayer Theatre. See separate listings for further information.

MADISON CIVIC CENTER - ISTHMUS PLAYHOUSE
211 State Street, Madison, WI 53703
(608) 266-6550
    Type of Facility: Auditorium; Performance Center; Theatre House
    Type of Stage: Thrust
    Stage Dimensions: 30'x18'; 20'x24' proscenium opening
    Seating Capacity: 343
    Year Built: 1979   **Architect:** Hardy Holzman & Pfeiffer
    Acoustical Consultant: Jaffe Acoustics
    Contact for Rental: Rudy Lienau; (608) 266-6550
    Resident Groups: CTM, Inc.; Madison Repertory Theater

MADISON CIVIC CENTER - OSCAR MAYER THEATRE
211 State Street, Madison, WI 53703
(608) 266-6550
    Type of Facility: Auditorium; Theatre House; Multi-Purpose
    Facility Originally: Vaudeville; Movie House
    Type of Stage: Proscenium
    Stage Dimensions: 42'Dx80'W; 56' proscenium opening   **Orchestra Pit**
    Seating Capacity: 2,225
    Year Built: 1928   **Architect:** Rapp & Rapp
    Year Remodeled: 1980   **Architect:** Hardy Holzman & Pfeiffer   **Cost:** $9,000,000
    Acoustical Consultant: Jaffe Acoustics
    Contact for Rental: Rudy Lienau; (608) 266-6550
    Resident Groups: Madison Civic Music Association

Manitowoc

FACILITY

SILVER LAKE COLLEGE
2406 South Alverno Road, Manitowoc, WI 54220
(414) 684-6691
    Type of Facility: Concert Hall; Performance Center; Theatre House
    Facility Originally: Church
    Type of Stage: Proscenium; Platform
    Seating Capacity: 380
    Year Built: 1960
    Acoustical Consultant: L. Brey
    Resident Groups: Silver Lake College Concert Band; Jazz Band; Madrigal Singers; Concert Choir; Recorder Ensemble; String Ensemble; Women's Choir
    Concerts; Recitals; Lectures

Marshfield

INSTRUMENTAL MUSIC

MARSHFIELD-WOOD COMMUNITY SYMPHONY
2000 West Fifth Street, Marshfield, WI 54449
(715) 387-1147
FAX: (715) 389-6539
    Founded: 1965
    Arts Area: Symphony; Orchestra
    Status: Non-Profit

Type: Performing; Educational
Purpose: To present the best music possible for the least possible cost
Management: Robert I. Biederwolf, Conductor
Officers: Sarah Hanson, President, Friends of the Orchestra
Paid Staff: 1   **Volunteer Staff:** 20
Utilizes: Guest Artists
Budget: $1,000 - $50,000
Income Sources: Private Foundations/Grants/Endowments; Business/Corporate Donations; Box Office; Government Grants; Individual Donations
Season: October - May   **Annual Attendance:** 1,800
Affiliations: ASOL
Performance Facilities: Fine Arts Building Theatre

PERFORMING SERIES

UNIVERSITY OF WISCONSIN LECTURES AND FINE ARTS SERIES
200 West 5th Street, Marshfield, WI 54449
(715) 387-1147
Founded: 1962
Arts Area: Dance; Vocal Music; Instrumental Music; Theater
Status: Non-Profit
Type: Educational; Sponsoring
Purpose: Provide performances and lectures for the University and the community
Management: Robert I. Biederwolf, Professor of Music
Paid Staff: 1
Paid Artists: 20
Utilizes: Guest Artists
Budget: $1,000 - $50,000
Income Sources: Private Foundations/Grants/Endowments; Business/Corporate Donations; Box Office; Government Grants; Individual Donations
Season: August - May
Performance Facilities: University of Wisconsin Center Theater

Menasha

INSTRUMENTAL MUSIC

FOX VALLEY SYMPHONY
1800 Appleton Road, Menasha, WI 54952
(414) 731-3385
Founded: 1966
Arts Area: Symphony
Status: Non-Profit
Type: Performing; Resident; Educational; Sponsoring
Purpose: To provide symphonic music for all; to sponsor youth orchestras
Management: Patricia D. Rodgers, General Manager
Officers: Robert Young, President, Fox Valley Symphony Association; Jeanette Kranzusch, President, Symphony League
Paid Staff: 2
Paid Artists: 2
Utilizes: Guest Conductors; Guest Artists
Budget: $100,000 - $500,000
Income Sources: Private Foundations/Grants/Endowments; Business/Corporate Donations; Box Office; Government Grants; Individual Donations
Season: September - May   **Annual Attendance:** 8,000
Affiliations: ASOL; AWSO; Fox Valley Arts Alliance
Performance Facilities: Pickard Auditorium; Lawrence University Chapel

PERFORMING SERIES

UNIVERSITY OF WISCONSIN CENTER - FOX VALLEY
1478 Midway Road, Menasha, WI 54952
(414) 832-2600
Arts Area: Dance; Vocal Music; Instrumental Music; Theater
Status: Non-Profit
Type: Performing; Educational
Paid Staff: 1
Budget: $1,000 - $50,000

Income Sources: Private Foundations/Grants/Endowments; Box Office; Student Fees
Season: September - May
Annual Attendance: 1,500
Performance Facilities: Fine Arts Theatre

Menomonie

THEATRE

GREENWOOD PLAYERS CHILDREN'S THEATER
314 11th Street, Menomonie, WI 54751
(715) 235-6650
> **Founded:** 1981
> **Arts Area:** THEATRE
> **Status:** Semi-Professional; Non-Profit
> **Type:** Performing; Touring; Resident; Educational
> **Purpose:** To create original plays based on folk tales using improvisation
> **Management:** Marion Lang, Artistic Director; Nancy Blake, Program Coordinator
> **Officers:** William O'Neill, President; Jane B. Hoyt, Treasurer
> **Paid Staff:** 4
> **Paid Artists:** 10
> **Budget:** $50,000 - $100,000
> **Income Sources:** Private Foundations/Grants/Endowments; Business/Corporate Donations; Box Office; Government Grants; Individual Donations
> **Season:** 52 Weeks
> **Annual Attendance:** 4,000
> **Affiliations:** Educational Outreach
> **Performance Facilities:** Mabel Tainter Theater

MABEL TAINTER MEMORIAL THEATER
205 Main Street, Menomonie, WI 54751
(715) 235-9726
> **Founded:** 1890
> **Arts Area:** Professional; Musical; Community; Folk
> **Status:** Non-Profit
> **Type:** Sponsoring
> **Purpose:** Historic 1890's theater with a performing arts season
> **Management:** Maggie Foote, Executive Director
> **Paid Staff:** 8   **Volunteer Staff:** 15
> **Utilizes:** Guest Artists
> **Budget:** $100,000 - $500,000
> **Income Sources:** Private Foundations/Grants/Endowments; Business/Corporate Donations; Box Office; Government Grants; Individual Donations
> **Season:** 52 Weeks   **Annual Attendance:** 10,800
> **Affiliations:** League of Historic American Theaters
> **Performance Facilities:** Mabel Tainter Memorial Theater

FACILITY

MABEL TAINTER MEMORIAL THEATER BUILDING
205 Main Street, PO Box 250, Menomonie, WI 54751
(715) 235-9726, ext. 0001
> **Type of Facility:** Concert Hall; Auditorium; Performance Center; Theatre House; Opera House; Civic Center; Multi-Purpose
> **Facility Originally:** Library; Church; Meeting Hall; Movie House
> **Type of Stage:** Thrust; Proscenium
> **Stage Dimensions:** 26'1/2"x20'x14'H   **Orchestra Pit**
> **Seating Capacity:** 313
> **Year Built:** 1889   **Architect:** Harvey Ellis, L. S. Buffington Company   **Cost:** $125,000
> **Year Remodeled:** 1966   **Architect:** DeNardo Studios   **Cost:** $80,000
> **Contact for Rental:** Maggie Foote, Executive Director;   (715) 235-9726
> **Resident Groups:** Greenwood Players Children's Theater

Middleton

DANCE

MESOGHIOS DANCE TROUP
3813 South Meadow Drive, Middleton, WI 53562
(608) 831-4485
Founded: 1978
Arts Area: Ethnic; Folk
Status: Semi-Professional; Non-Profit
Type: Performing; Educational
Purpose: Performance of Greek, Turkish and Russian ethnic and folk dances, and presentation and description of Greek and Turkish ethnic dress, decoration and custom
Management: Vicky Knoedler, Artistic Director
Officers: Craig Schreiner, President; Vicky Knoedler, President-Elect; William Knoedler, Secretary/Treasurer
Volunteer Staff: 1
Non-Paid Artists: 15
Utilizes: Guest Artists; Guest Choreographers
Budget: $1,000 - $50,000
Income Sources: Private Foundations/Grants/Endowments; Box Office; Government Grants; Individual Donations
Season: 52 Weeks   **Annual Attendance:** 5,000

Milwaukee

DANCE

BAUER CONTEMPORARY BALLET
727 North Milwaukee Street, Milwaukee, WI 53202
(414) 276-3180
Founded: 1974
Arts Area: Modern; Ballet; Jazz; Tap
Status: Professional; Non-Profit
Type: Performing; Touring; Resident; Educational
Purpose: To move toward becoming a repertory company performing new works from various choreographers
Management: Susie Bauer, Artistic Director; Richard Rovito, Executive Director
Officers: Polly Morris, President; Ray Vogel, Vice President; Michael Williams, Treasurer; Eddie Jackson; Sally Ann Mesich
Paid Staff: 2   **Volunteer Staff:** 2
Paid Artists: 8
Utilizes: Guest Choreographers
Budget: $100,000 - $500,000
Income Sources: Private Foundations/Grants/Endowments; Business/Corporate Donations; Box Office; Government Grants; Individual Donations
Season: 52 Weeks   **Annual Attendance:** 1,000
Affiliations: United Performing Arts Fund
Performance Facilities: Bauer Contemporary Ballet Studio Theatre

BETTY SALAMUN'S DANCECIRCUS
404 South Seventh Street, 2nd Floor, Milwaukee, WI 53204
(414) 272-6683
Founded: 1975
Arts Area: Modern; Folk
Status: Professional; Non-Profit
Type: Performing; Touring; Educational
Purpose: To encourage advancement of the fine arts
Management: Betty Salamun, Artistic Director; Gordon Reistad, Compny Manager
Officers: Susan Mingesz, Board President; David H.B. Drake, Controller
Paid Staff: 3
Utilizes: Guest Artists; Guest Choreographers
Budget: $50,000 - $100,000
Income Sources: Private Foundations/Grants/Endowments; Business/Corporate Donations; Box Office; Government Grants; Individual Donations; Classes
Season: 52 Weeks   **Annual Attendance:** 30,000

DANCECIRCUS LIMITED
404 South Seventh Street, 2nd Floor, Milwaukee, WI 53204
(414) 272-6683
Founded: 1975

Arts Area: Modern; Arts/Environment
Status: Professional
Type: Performing; Touring; Resident; Educational; Sponsoring
Purpose: Professional touring modern dance company emphasizing environmental programs in concert and outreach programs and a diverse modern dance repertoire concert
Management: Betty Salamun, Artistic Director; Gordon Reistad, Company Manager
Officers: Susan Mingesz, President; Terry Rice, Treasurer; Becky Skulrolsky, Secretary
Paid Staff: 3   **Volunteer Staff:** 1
Paid Artists: 6
Utilizes: Special Technical Talent; Guest Artists; Guest Choreographers; Poets, Visual Artists, Composers
Budget: $50,000 - $100,000
Income Sources: Private Foundations/Grants/Endowments; Business/Corporate Donations; Box Office; Government Grants; Individual Donations
Season: 52 Weeks   **Annual Attendance:** 30,000

MILWAUKEE BALLET
504 West National Avenue, Milwaukee, WI 53204
(414) 643-7677
FAX: (414) 649-4066
Founded: 1970
Arts Area: Ballet
Status: Professional; Non-Profit
Type: Performing; Touring; Resident; Educational
Purpose: To blend volunteer support, artistic direction, and professional management to create, nurture, and preserve a nationally recognized, resident ballet company performing classical, contemporary and new works on a scale which evokes support sufficient to endure
Management: Dane LaFontsee, Artistic Director; Basil Thompson, Ballet Master Regisseur
Officers: Gary Keller, President/Chief Executive Officer
Paid Staff: 29   **Volunteer Staff:** 650
Paid Artists: 60
Utilizes: Special Technical Talent; Guest Artists
Budget: $1,000,000 - $5,000,000
Income Sources: Private Foundations/Grants/Endowments; Business/Corporate Donations; Box Office; Government Grants; Individual Donations
Season: September - May   **Annual Attendance:** 86,000
Affiliations: Arts Midwest, Wisconsin Citizens for the Arts
Performance Facilities: Uihlein Hall; Milwaukee Performing Arts Center

INSTRUMENTAL MUSIC

EARLY MUSIC NOW
PO Box 71303, Milwaukee, WI 53211-1303
(414) 225-3113
FAX: (414) 278-0335
Founded: 1986
Arts Area: Early Music
Status: Non-Profit
Type: Educational; Sponsoring
Purpose: To enrich and expand Milwaukee's musical offerings by presenting historically informed performances and educational experiences by recognized artists and ensembles who specialize in music before 1800
Officers: Ralph Bielenberg, President; Eric Duncan, Vice President; Jean Neal, Secretary; JoAnn Husslein, Treasurer; Thallis Hoyt Drake, Founder
Volunteer Staff: 25
Utilizes: Guest Artists
Budget: $1,000 - $50,000
Income Sources: Private Foundations/Grants/Endowments; Box Office; Individual Donations
Season: September - May   **Annual Attendance:** 1,500
Performance Facilities: Public Library Hall

MILWAUKEE CHAMBER ORCHESTRA
929 North Water Street, Milwaukee, WI 53202
(414) 347-1564
Founded: 1974
Arts Area: Orchestra; Chamber
Status: Professional
Type: Performing

Purpose: To present six to ten concerts annually, encompassing chamber orchestra repertoire from Baroque to 20th century
Management: Lisa A. Froemming, Managing Director; Stephen Colburn, Music Director
Officers: Herbert M. Swick, MD, President; Joseph F. Ahern, Marlene Stocking, Vice Presidents; Thomas Wakefield, Treasurer
Paid Staff: 2 **Volunteer Staff:** 4
Paid Artists: 60
Utilizes: Guest Conductors; Guest Artists
Budget: $100,000 - $500,000
Income Sources: Private Foundations/Grants/Endowments; Business/Corporate Donations; Box Office; Government Grants; Individual Donations
Season: September - June **Annual Attendance:** 4,000
Performance Facilities: Vogel Hall, Milwaukee County Performing Arts Center

MILWAUKEE SYMPHONY ORCHESTRA
330 East Kilbourn Avenue, Suite 900, Milwaukee, WI 53202
(414) 291-6010
FAX: (414) 291-7610
Founded: 1959
Arts Area: Symphony; Orchestra
Status: Professional; Non-Profit
Type: Performing; Touring; Educational
Management: Gary L. Good, Executive Director
Officers: Michael J. Schmitz, President
Paid Artists: 95
Budget: Over 10,000,000
Income Sources: Private Foundations/Grants/Endowments; Business/Corporate Donations; Box Office; Government Grants; Individual Donations
Season: September - July
Performance Facilities: Performing Arts Center; Uihlein Hall

MILWAUKEE YOUTH SYMPHONY ORCHESTRA
929 North Water Street, Milwaukee, WI 53202
(414) 272-8540
Founded: 1956
Arts Area: Symphony; Orchestra; Chamber; Ensemble
Status: Non-Professional; Non-Profit; Youth Orchestra
Type: Performing; Educational
Management: Frances S. Richman, Managing Director; Susan M. Chandler, Music Coordinator; Margery Deutsch, Music Director/Senior Symphony
Officers: Wilson D. Perry, President
Paid Staff: 15
Utilizes: Guest Conductors; Guest Artists
Budget: $100,000 - $500,000
Income Sources: Private Foundations/Grants/Endowments; Business/Corporate Donations; Box Office; Government Grants; Individual Donations; Student Fees
Season: September - May
Annual Attendance: 10,000
Affiliations: ASOL
Performance Facilities: Uihlein Hall

PRESENT MUSIC, INCORPORATED
1840 North Farwell, Suite 301, Milwaukee, WI 53202
(414) 271-0711
Founded: 1983
Arts Area: Chamber; Ensemble; Instrumental Group
Status: Professional; Non-Profit
Type: Performing; Touring; Resident; Educational; Recording
Purpose: To broaden public appreciation of music with an emphasis on small ensemble productions of contemporary concert music in a manner that is engaging, provocative and fun
Management: Kevin Stalheim, Artistic Director; Daniel Petry, Managing Director
Officers: Timothy C. Frautschi, President; James Chenevert, Secretary
Utilizes: Guest Artists
Budget: $100,000 - $500,000
Income Sources: Private Foundations/Grants/Endowments; Business/Corporate Donations; Box Office; Government Grants; Individual Donations
Season: September - May
Affiliations: NPN; Art Reach Milwaukee

VOCAL MUSIC

THE BACH CHAMBER CHOIR AND ORCHESTRA
PO Box 14503, Milwaukee, WI 53214
(414) 228-7468
>   **Founded:** 1970
>   **Arts Area:** Choral
>   **Status:** Semi-Professional; Non-Profit
>   **Type:** Performing
>   **Purpose:** To promote chamber music and choral music to the public through performance
>   **Management:** Steven L. Joyal, Music Director; Liz Joyal, General Manager
>   **Officers:** Carol Kennedy, President; Ed Eurich, Vice President; Patricia P. Radzin, Secretary; Ellen Chesak Ball, Treasurer
>   **Paid Staff:** 2   **Volunteer Staff:** 11
>   **Non-Paid Artists:** 45
>   **Utilizes:** Guest Artists
>   **Budget:** $1,000 - $50,000
>   **Income Sources:** Private Foundations/Grants/Endowments; Business/Corporate Donations; Box Office; Individual Donations
>   **Season:** 52 Weeks   **Annual Attendance:** 1,000

BEL CANTO CHORUS OF MILWAUKEE
828 North Broadway, #510, Milwaukee, WI 53202
(414) 272-7950
>   **Founded:** 1945
>   **Arts Area:** Choral
>   **Status:** Semi-Professional; Non-Profit
>   **Type:** Performing; Touring
>   **Purpose:** To present to the citizens of Milwaukee and Southeastern Wisconsin the great choral literature for chorus and orchestra
>   **Management:** Kathleen Asta, General Manager; Richard Hynson, Musical Director
>   **Paid Staff:** 2
>   **Paid Artists:** 10   **Non-Paid Artists:** 150
>   **Utilizes:** Guest Conductors; Guest Artists
>   **Budget:** $100,000 - $500,000
>   **Income Sources:** Private Foundations/Grants/Endowments; Business/Corporate Donations; Box Office; Government Grants; Individual Donations
>   **Season:** September - June   **Annual Attendance:** 10,000
>   **Affiliations:** CA; United Performing Arts Fund
>   **Performance Facilities:** Performing Arts Center; Pabst Theater

FLORENTINE OPERA COMPANY
750 North Lincoln Memorial Drive, Milwaukee, WI 53202
(414) 273-1474
FAX: (414) 273-2480
>   **Founded:** 1933
>   **Arts Area:** Grand Opera
>   **Status:** Professional; Non-Profit
>   **Type:** Performing; Touring; Educational
>   **Purpose:** Production of Grand Opera in the state of Wisconsin
>   **Management:** Dennis Hanthorn, General Manager; Joseph Rescigno, Artistic Director
>   **Officers:** George T. Jacobi, President
>   **Paid Staff:** 8
>   **Paid Artists:** 285
>   **Utilizes:** Special Technical Talent; Guest Conductors; Guest Artists; Guest Directors
>   **Budget:** $1,000,000 - $5,000,000
>   **Income Sources:** Private Foundations/Grants/Endowments; Business/Corporate Donations; Box Office; Government Grants; Individual Donations
>   **Season:** November - May   **Annual Attendance:** 32,000
>   **Affiliations:** OA; United Performing Arts Foundation
>   **Performance Facilities:** Milwaukee Performing Arts Center; Pabst Theater

MILWAUKEE OPERA COMPANY
820 East Knapp Street, Milwaukee, WI 53202
(414) 276-2244; (414) 961-1474
>   **Founded:** 1966
>   **Arts Area:** Grand Opera; Light Opera; Operetta
>   **Status:** Professional; Non-Profit
>   **Type:** Performing; Educational

Purpose: To develop and showcase local and regional artists; to develop audiences for Milwaukee arts groups; to present opera and musical theatre at moderate prices
Management: Josephine Busalacchi, Executive Director/Founder
Paid Staff: 4 **Volunteer Staff:** 4
Paid Artists: 100
Utilizes: Guest Artists
Budget: $50,000 - $100,000
Income Sources: Private Foundations/Grants/Endowments; Business/Corporate Donations; Box Office; Government Grants; Individual Donations
Season: 52 Weeks **Annual Attendance:** 25,000
Performance Facilities: Pabst Theatre; Milwaukee Performing Arts Center; Lincoln Center for the Arts

SKYLIGHT COMIC OPERA LIMITED
813 North Jefferson Street, Milwaukee, WI 53202
(414) 271-9580
FAX: (414) 271-8896
Founded: 1959
Arts Area: Grand Opera; Lyric Opera; Light Opera; Operetta; Musical Theatre
Status: Professional; Non-Profit
Type: Performing; Resident; Educational; Sponsoring
Purpose: To present musical theater in southeastern Wisconsin; to make the productions the best possible
Management: Chas Rader-Shieber, Artistic Director; Richard Carsey, Music Director
Officers: Byron Foster, President; Linda Rieke, Vice President of Finance
Paid Staff: 9
Paid Artists: 230
Utilizes: Special Technical Talent; Guest Conductors; Guest Artists; Guest Directors
Budget: $1,000,000 - $5,000,000
Income Sources: Private Foundations/Grants/Endowments; Business/Corporate Donations; Box Office; Government Grants; Individual Donations; Fund-raising
Season: September - May; July; August **Annual Attendance:** 42,000
Affiliations: OA; Arts, Inc; AAA
Performance Facilities: Skylight Theatre

THEATRE

ACACIA THEATRE
924 East Juneau Avenue, Suite 227, Milwaukee, WI 53202-2748
(414) 223-4996
Founded: 1980
Arts Area: Theatrical Group
Status: Semi-Professional; Non-Profit
Type: Touring; Resident; Educational
Purpose: To produce plays of various kinds on a regular basis with a Christian world view
Management: Jon Layton, Artistic Director; Jeffrey Bohmann, Marketing Director
Officers: David Stubbs, President; Jane Domach, Secretary; Randy Peterson, Treasurer
Paid Staff: 2 **Volunteer Staff:** 90
Paid Artists: 5 **Non-Paid Artists:** 10
Utilizes: Special Technical Talent; Guest Artists; Guest Directors
Budget: $100,000 - $500,000
Income Sources: Private Foundations/Grants/Endowments; Business/Corporate Donations; Box Office; Individual Donations
Season: October - August **Annual Attendance:** 43,000

THE GREAT AMERICAN CHILDREN'S THEATRE COMPANY
PO Box 92123, Milwaukee, WI 53202
(414) 276-4230
FAX: (414) 276-2214
Founded: 1975
Arts Area: Professional
Status: Professional; Non-Profit
Type: Performing; Touring; Educational; Sponsoring
Purpose: To provide quality theatre for young audiences
Management: Teri Solomon Mitze, Producer; Annie Jurczyk, Managing Director
Officers: Paul Medved, President; Danita Medved, Vice President of Development; Thomas Balgeman, Secretary/Treasurer
Paid Staff: 3 **Volunteer Staff:** 100
Paid Artists: 1
Utilizes: Special Technical Talent; Guest Artists
Budget: $1,000,000 - $5,000,000

Income Sources: Private Foundations/Grants/Endowments; Business/Corporate Donations; Box Office;
Individual Donations
Season: September - May   **Annual Attendance:** 70,000
Performance Facilities: Pabst Theatre

MILWAUKEE CHAMBER THEATRE
152 West Wisconsin Avenue, Suite 731, Milwaukee, WI 53203
(414) 276-8842
FAX: (414) 276-8842
Founded: 1979
Arts Area: Theatrical Group
Status: Professional; Non-Profit
Type: Performing; Touring; Resident
Purpose: To produce professional quality shows of a classical and neoclassical nature, highlighting the season with an
annual Shaw Festival (George Bernard) in May and June
Management: Carla Slawson, General Manager; Montgomery Davis, Artistic Director; Sharon Middleton, Subscription
Manager
Officers: Richard Moake, President; Mary Ann Gerlack, Vice President; Richard Meadows, Secretary; Philip Crump,
Treasurer
Paid Staff: 3   **Volunteer Staff:** 4
Paid Artists: 35   **Non-Paid Artists:** 10
Utilizes: Guest Artists; Guest Directors
Budget: $100,000 - $500,000
Income Sources: Private Foundations/Grants/Endowments; Business/Corporate Donations; Box Office; Government
Grants; Individual Donations
Season: October - June   **Annual Attendance:** 12,500
Affiliations: TCG
Performance Facilities: Stiemke Theatre; Helfaer Theatre

MILWAUKEE PUBLIC THEATRE
PO Box 07147, Milwaukee, WI 53207
(414) 271-8484
Founded: 1973
Arts Area: Professional; Musical; Theatrical Group; Puppet
Status: Professional
Type: Performing; Touring; Resident; Educational; Sponsoring
Purpose: Creation and presentation of theatre, performance, video, and celebrations/festivals
Management: Mike Moynihan, Barbara Leigh, Co-Founders; Melinda Boyd, Production Manager
Officers: Paul Sardry, President; Win Quirmbach, Keith Roberts, Vice Presidents; Lon Frederick, Treasurer
Paid Staff: 20   **Volunteer Staff:** 30
Paid Artists: 15   **Non-Paid Artists:** 5
Utilizes: Special Technical Talent; Guest Artists; Guest Directors
Budget: $100,000 - $500,000
Income Sources: Private Foundations/Grants/Endowments; Business/Corporate Donations; Box Office; Government
Grants; Individual Donations
Season: February - December
Annual Attendance: 49,000
Affiliations: TCG; WTA; MACA

MILWAUKEE REPERTORY THEATER
108 East Wells, Milwaukee, WI 53202
(414) 273-7121
Founded: 1954
Arts Area: Professional; Theatrical Group
Status: Professional; Non-Profit
Type: Performing; Resident; Educational
Purpose: Devoted to the creation of theatrical experiences that explore and illuminate the human condition
Management: John Dillon, Artistic Director; Sarah O'Conner, Managing Director; Cindy Moran, Public Relations
Officers: Vincent L. Martin, Board President
Paid Staff: 15
Utilizes: Special Technical Talent; Guest Artists; Guest Directors
Budget: $1,000,000 - $5,000,000
Income Sources: Private Foundations/Grants/Endowments; Business/Corporate Donations; Box Office; Government
Grants; Individual Donations
Season: October - June
Affiliations: AEA; LORT
Performance Facilities: Milwaukee Repertory Theater

NEXT ACT THEATRE
PO Box 394, Milwaukee, WI 53201
(414) 278-7780
Founded: 1990
Arts Area: Professional; Theatrical Group
Status: Professional; Non-Profit
Type: Performing
Purpose: Professional equity company producing engaging intimate and exciting adventures in theatrical presentation of classical and contemporary drama
Management: David Cecsarini, Producing Director; Charles Kakuk, General Manager
Officers: Catherine Anderson, Acting President
Paid Staff: 3
Utilizes: Guest Artists; Guest Directors
Budget: $100,000 - $500,000
Income Sources: Private Foundations/Grants/Endowments; Business/Corporate Donations; Box Office; Government Grants; Individual Donations
Season: September - May   **Annual Attendance:** 8,000
Affiliations: Wisconsin Professional Community Theatre Association
Performance Facilities: Milwaukee Repertory Theater; Stimeke theater

THEATRE X
PO Box 92206, Milwaukee, WI 53202
(414) 278-0555
FAX: (414) 278-8233
Founded: 1969
Arts Area: Professional; Theatrical Group
Status: Professional; Non-Profit
Type: Performing; Touring; Sponsoring
Purpose: Theatre X is an ensemble devoted to theatrical research and development
Management: John Schneider, Wes Savick, Co-Artistic Directors; Pam Percy, Managing Director
Officers: Leonard Sobczak, President; John Ogden, Vice President; William Fox, Secretary
Paid Staff: 1
Paid Artists: 7
Utilizes: Special Technical Talent; Guest Artists; Guest Directors
Budget: $100,000 - $500,000
Income Sources: Private Foundations/Grants/Endowments; Business/Corporate Donations; Box Office; Government Grants; Individual Donations
Season: September - June   **Annual Attendance:** 5,000
Affiliations: TCG

PERFORMING SERIES

ARTIST SERIES AT THE PABST
144 East Wells Street, Milwaukee, WI 53202
(414) 226-8802
FAX: (414) 286-2793
Arts Area: Instrumental Music; Classical Music
Status: Non-Profit
Type: Performing
Purpose: To present fine chamber music to the city of Milwaukee
Management: Joan Lounsbery, Executive Director; Lynn Lucius, General Manager
Officers: Dennis Conta, President of the Board
Budget: $100,000 - $500,000
Income Sources: Private Foundations/Grants/Endowments; Business/Corporate Donations; Box Office; Government Grants; Individual Donations
Performance Facilities: Pabst Theatre

FACILITY

ALVERNO COLLEGE
Pitman Theatre, 3401 South 39th Street, PO Box 343922, Milwaukee, WI 53234-3922
(414) 382-6151
Founded: 1944
Type of Facility: Auditorium; Theatre House; Recital Hall (three facilities)
Type of Stage: Proscenium
Stage Dimensions: 39'x42'   **Orchestra Pit**
Seating Capacity: 930; 360; 175
Contact for Rental: Erick Hoffman;   (414) 382-6151

BLATZ TEMPLE OF MUSIC - WASHINGTON PARK BANDSHELL
4420 West Vliet Street, Milwaukee, WI 53208
(414) 278-4389
FAX: (414) 933-4104
   Type of Facility: Outdoor (Concert); Video Studio
   Type of Stage: Concert Shell
   Seating Capacity: 12,000
   Year Built: 1938
   Resident Groups: Washington Park Temple of Music
   Available for rent

MILWAUKEE AREA TECHNICAL COLLEGE - COOLEY AUDITORIUM
700 West State Street, Milwaukee, WI 53233-1443
(414) 278-6600
FAX: (414) 271-2195
   Type of Facility: Auditorium; Loft
   Type of Stage: Proscenium
   Stage Dimensions: 40'Wx35'D   **Orchestra Pit**
   Seating Capacity: 1,800
   Year Built: 1918
   Year Remodeled: 1977   **Cost:** $90,000
   Contact for Rental: Ruby Collier;   (414) 278-6223
   Manager: Dale S. Shively;   (414) 278-6310
   Resident Groups: Milwaukee Civic Band; Milwaukee Civic Orchestra; M & W Productions
   Theatre, Dance, Audio Visual Presentations

MILWAUKEE PERFORMING ARTS CENTER
929 North Water Street, Milwaukee, WI 53202
(414) 273-7121
FAX: (414) 273-5480
   Type of Facility: Theatre Complex; Concert Hall; Performance Center; Amphitheater; Multi-Purpose
   Type of Stage: Proscenium; Platform; 3/4 Arena; Environmental   **Orchestra Pit**
   Seating Capacity: Uihleen - 2,301; Vogel- 486; Wehr - 500
   Year Built: 1969   **Architect:** Harry Weese & Associates   **Cost:** $12,500,000
   Acoustical Consultant: Bolt, Beranek & Newman
   Contact for Rental: Joe Ahern;   (414) 273-7121
   Manager: Michael T. Stirdivant;   (414) 273-7121
   Resident Groups: Milwaukee Symphony Orchestra; Milwaukee Ballet; Florentine Opera; Bel Canto Chorus; First Stage
   Milwaukee Theater for Children; Milwaukee Youth Symphony Orchestra
   Milwaukee Performing Arts Center contains The Uihleen, Vogel and Wehr Theatres.

PABST THEATER
144 East Wells Street, Milwaukee, WI 53202
(414) 278-3665
FAX: (414) 278-2154
   Founded: 1895
   Type of Facility: Concert Hall; Theatre House; Opera House
   Type of Stage: Proscenium
   Stage Dimensions: 72'Wx38'D; 35' proscenium opening   **Orchestra Pit**
   Seating Capacity: 1,400
   Year Built: 1895   **Architect:** Otto Strack   **Cost:** $600,000
   Year Remodeled: 1976   **Architect:** Mark F. Pfaller II   **Cost:** $2,500,000
   Contact for Rental: Charlane O'Rourke;   (414) 278-3665
   Manager: Philip Proctor;   (414) 278-3665
   Resident Groups: Bel Canto Chorus; Artist Series at the Pabst; Great Artists Series; Milwaukee Theater Festival; Kennan
   Forum on International Affairs

SKYLIGHT OPERA THEATRE
813 North Jefferson Street, Milwaukee, WI 53202
(414) 271-9580
FAX: (414) 271-8896
   Type of Facility: Theatre House; Opera House; Room
   Facility Originally: Garage
   Type of Stage: Flexible; Platform; 3/4 Arena
   Stage Dimensions: 12'x24' Expandable   **Orchestra Pit**
   Seating Capacity: 249
   Year Built: 1918
   Year Remodeled: 1981   **Architect:** Wenzler & Associates   **Cost:** $250,000

Contact for Rental: John VandeWalle, Artistic Administrator;   (414) 271-9580
Resident Groups: Skylight Opera Theatre

Monona

DANCE

WISCONSIN DANCE ENSEMBLE
6332 Monona Drive, Monona, WI 53716
(608) 221-4535
Founded: 1977
Arts Area: Ballet
Status: Semi-Professional; Non-Profit
Type: Performing; Resident; Educational
Purpose: To perform and teach the art of ballet for young dancers and young audiences
Management: Jo Jean Retrum, Director
Paid Staff: 3   **Volunteer Staff:** 4
Paid Artists: 6   **Non-Paid Artists:** 200
Utilizes: Guest Artists
Budget: $1,000 - $50,000
Income Sources: Private Foundations/Grants/Endowments; Business/Corporate Donations; Box Office; Government Grants; Individual Donations
Season: 52 Weeks   **Annual Attendance:** 25,000
Affiliations: Regional Dance America
Performance Facilities: Madison Civic Center; Wisconsin Union Theatre

---

Mount Horeb

VOCAL MUSIC

SONG OF NORWAY FESTIVAL
PO Box 132, Mount Horeb, WI 53572
(608) 437-4600
Founded: 1966
Arts Area: Operetta
Status: Non-Professional; Non-Profit
Type: Performing; Educational
Purpose: To present Forrest and Wright's operetta "Song of Norway" and other Norwegian/American-related material as an annual summer educational and entertainment offering in south central Wisconsin
Officers: Michael Mudrey, President; Orville Phillips, Vice President; Joanne Hall, Secretary; Valonne Eckel, Treasurer
Paid Staff: 7   **Volunteer Staff:** 20
Paid Artists: 45   **Non-Paid Artists:** 70
Utilizes: Special Technical Talent
Budget: $1,000 - $50,000
Income Sources: Private Foundations/Grants/Endowments; Business/Corporate Donations; Box Office; Government Grants; Individual Donations
Season: June - July   **Annual Attendance:** 3,000

Oshkosh

INSTRUMENTAL MUSIC

OSHKOSH SYMPHONY ORCHESTRA
PO Box 522, Oshkosh, WI 54902
(414) 233-7510
Founded: 1940
Arts Area: Symphony; Orchestra
Status: Semi-Professional
Type: Performing
Management: Rebecca Spurlock, Business Manager
Officers: David Hayford, President
Paid Staff: 2
Paid Artists: 4
Utilizes: Guest Artists

Budget: $100,000 - $500,000
Income Sources: Private Foundations/Grants/Endowments; Business/Corporate Donations; Box Office;
Individual Donations
Season: October - May
Annual Attendance: 5,000
Affiliations: AWSO; ASOL
Performance Facilities: Osh Kosh Civic Auditorium

FACILITY

GRAND OPERA HOUSE
100 High Avenue, PO Box 1004, Oshkosh, WI 54902
(414) 424-2355
    Type of Facility: Opera House
    Type of Stage: Proscenium
    Stage Dimensions: 30'x30' **Orchestra Pit**
    Seating Capacity: 730
    Year Built: 1883 **Architect:** William Waters
    Year Remodeled: 1986 **Architect:** Robert Yarbro **Cost:** $3,400,000
    Contact for Rental: Mark A. Nerenhausen; (414) 424-2355

Platteville

PERFORMING SERIES

UNIVERSITY OF WISCONSIN - PLATTEVILLE PERFORMING ARTS SERIES
One University Plaza, Platteville, WI 53818
(608) 342-1495
FAX: (608) 342-1478
    Founded: 1959
    Arts Area: Dance; Vocal Music; Instrumental Music; Theater; Festivals; Lyric Opera; Grand Opera
    Status: Non-Profit
    Type: Educational; Sponsoring
    Purpose: To provide a well balanced performing arts series to our students and our community
    Management: John Mominee, Director; Jim Waite, Coordinator/Programming; Susan Berggren, Coordinator/Fine Arts
    Paid Staff: 3 **Volunteer Staff:** 10
    Utilizes: Guest Artists
    Budget: $50,000 - $100,000
    Income Sources: Private Foundations/Grants/Endowments; Box Office; Government Grants; Individual Donations
    Season: September - May
    Annual Attendance: 4,200
    Affiliations: University of Wisconsin
    Performance Facilities: Center for the Arts Concert Hall

FACILITY

CENTER FOR THE ARTS - UNIVERSITY OF WISCONSIN, PLATTEVILLE
One University Plaza, Platteville, WI 53818
(608) 342-1398
FAX: (608) 342-1478
    Founded: 1866
    Type of Facility: Concert Hall; Theatre House
    Type of Stage: Flexible; Proscenium
    Stage Dimensions: Concert Hall - 55'4"x48'6"; Theatre - 24'x36' **Orchestra Pit**
    Seating Capacity: Concert Hall - 600; Theatre - 300
    Year Built: 1983
    Architect: Bill Wenzler
    Cost: $5,200,000
    Acoustical Consultant: Artel
    Contact for Rental: Director, Center for the Arts; (608) 342-1398
    Resident Groups: Theatre Department; Music Department; SAB Performing Arts Series

Portage

THEATRE

PORTAGE AREA COMMUNITY THEATRE
PO Box 263, Portage, WI 53901
(608) 742-6942
      Founded: 1971
      Arts Area: Community; Theatrical Group
      Status: Non-Professional; Non-Profit
      Type: Performing
      Purpose: To promote, encourage and increase the public's knowledge and appreciation of the arts, especially theatre, and to provide an outlet for the above
      Management: Board of Directors
      Officers: Pat Madoni, President; Lisa Piekarski, Vice President; Fran Malone, Secretary/Registered Agent; Hans Jensen, Treasurer
      Volunteer Staff: 100
      Non-Paid Artists: 300
      Budget: $1,000 - $50,000
      Income Sources: Box Office; Individual Donations
      Season: September - June   **Annual Attendance:** 4,500
      Affiliations: Wisconsin Theatre Association; Wisconsin Council on the Arts

Racine

INSTRUMENTAL MUSIC

RACINE SYMPHONY ORCHESTRA
PO Box 1751, Racine, WI 53401
(414) 636-9285
      Founded: 1931
      Arts Area: Symphony; Orchestra
      Status: Semi-Professional; Non-Professional
      Type: Performing
      Purpose: To supply the community of Racine with its own symphony orchestra and provide an outlet for good local talent, non-professional and semi-professional
      Management: Mildred Schroth, Executive Secretary/Administrative Coordinator; Carol Wallace, General Manager
      Officers: Janet Tidwell, President; Charlene Melzer, Vice President; James Cook, Past President; Barbara Namowicz, Treasurer
      Paid Staff: 3   **Volunteer Staff:** 21
      Paid Artists: 70
      Utilizes: Special Technical Talent; Guest Conductors; Guest Artists; Guest Directors
      Budget: $100,000 - $500,000
      Income Sources: Private Foundations/Grants/Endowments; Business/Corporate Donations; Box Office; Individual Donations
      Season: 52 Weeks   **Annual Attendance:** 40,000
      Affiliations: Racine Arts Council   **Performance Facilities:** Racine-on-the-Lake Festival Hall

Ripon

PERFORMING SERIES

RIPON COLLEGE/CAESTECKER FINE ARTS SERIES
300 Seward Street, PO Box 248, Ripon, WI 54971
(414) 748-8112
FAX: (414) 748-9262
      Arts Area: Dance; Vocal Music; Instrumental Music; Theater
      Status: Non-Profit
      Type: Sponsoring
      Purpose: To present four to five performing and visual artists, representing diverse backgrounds and arts areas each season for the college and surrounding Ripon community
      Management: Stacy Shrode, Director of Student Activities
      Budget: $1,000 - $50,000
      Income Sources: Private Foundations/Grants/Endowments; Box Office
      Season: September - April   **Annual Attendance:** 1,200
      Performance Facilities: Memorial Hall Gym; Benstead Theater; Demmer Recital Hall

FACILITY

RIPON COLLEGE - DEMMER RECITAL HALL
Rodman Arts Center, 300 Seward Street, Box 248, Ripon, WI 54971
(414) 748-8120
   Type of Facility: Performance Center
   Type of Stage: Platform
   Stage Dimensions: 65'x40'
   Seating Capacity: 286
   Year Built: 1972   **Architect:** Shattuck & Stewart   **Cost:** $2,500,000
   Acoustical Consultant: Bolt, Beranek & Neumann
   Contact for Rental: Cal Wolff, Director of Conferences;   (414) 748-8137
   Manager: Raymond Stahura
   Resident Groups: Ripon College Music Department (Demmer); Ripon College Drama Department; Ripon College Dance
Company (Benstead Theater)

Shawano

THEATRE

SHAWANO COUNTY ARTS COUNCIL
PO Box 213, Shawano, WI 54166
(715) 526-2525
   Founded: 1967
   Arts Area: Musical; Community; Folk; Theatrical Group
   Status: Non-Profit
   Type: Resident; Sponsoring
   Officers: Dolly Danbury, President; Deb Lonick, Vice President; Jaquee Salzman, Treasurer
   Paid Staff: 1   **Volunteer Staff:** 50
   Budget: $50,000 - $100,000
   Income Sources: Private Foundations/Grants/Endowments; Business/Corporate Donations; Box Office; Government
Grants; Individual Donations
   Season: 52 Weeks   **Annual Attendance:** 10,000
   Performance Facilities: Mielke Theatre

Sheboygan

INSTRUMENTAL MUSIC

SHEBOYGAN SYMPHONY ORCHESTRA
901 Superior Avenue, Room 344, Sheboygan, WI 53081
(414) 452-1985
   Founded: 1918
   Arts Area: Symphony; Orchestra
   Status: Semi-Professional; Non-Profit
   Type: Performing; Educational
   Management: Arnold W. Gesch, General Manager
   Officers: Barbara G. Bossewitz, President; Karl Grube, Vice President; Lee Robinson, Treasurer
   Paid Staff: 2   **Volunteer Staff:** 6
   Paid Artists: 4   **Non-Paid Artists:** 70
   Utilizes: Guest Conductors; Guest Artists
   Budget: $50,000 - $100,000
   Income Sources: Private Foundations/Grants/Endowments; Business/Corporate Donations; Box Office;
Individual Donations
   Season: September - May   **Annual Attendance:** 5,000
   Performance Facilities: Kohler Memorial Auditorium

THEATRE

SHEBOYGAN COMMUNITY PLAYERS
607 South Water Street, Sheboygan, WI 53081
(414) 459-3779
   Founded: 1934
   Arts Area: Community; Theatrical Group
   Status: Non-Professional; Non-Profit
   Type: Performing; Resident; Educational

Purpose: The advancement of and involvement in quality community theatre from the classical to contemporary, that afford entertainment and education for both audience and participants
Management: Ralph Maffongelli, Director of Theatre; Steven Stauber, Business Manager; Marty Kooi, Technical Director
Officers: Liz Kohlbeck, President; Wally Waldhart, First Vice President; Valerie Black, Second Vice President; Harold Lang, Secretary; Bob Travis, Treasurer
Paid Staff: 2   **Volunteer Staff:** 300
Budget: $100,000 - $500,000
Income Sources: Business/Corporate Donations; Box Office; Individual Donations; Concessions/Program Advertising
Season: September - May   **Annual Attendance:** 18,000
Performance Facilities: Leslie W. Johnson Theatre; Horace Mann Middle School

FACILITY

FINE ARTS THEATRE
One University Drive, Sheboygan, WI 53081
(414) 459-6600
> **Type of Facility:** Auditorium; Theatre House
> **Type of Stage:** Thrust
> **Stage Dimensions:** 40'x36'   **Orchestra Pit**
> **Seating Capacity:** 400
> **Year Built:** 1970   **Architect:** Bray   **Cost:** $700,000
> **Year Remodeled:** 1986   **Architect:** Bray   **Cost:** $556,000
> **Contact for Rental:** Tom Mortenson;   (414) 459-6600
> **Manager:** Bruce Browne
> **Resident Groups:** UWS Players

JOHN MICHAEL KOHLER ARTS CENTER
608 New York Avenue, Sheboygan, WI 53081
(414) 458-6144
> **Type of Facility:** Theatre Complex; Concert Hall; Performance Center; Multi-Purpose
> **Type of Stage:** Thrust
> **Stage Dimensions:** 22'x38'   **Seating Capacity:** 162
> **Year Built:** 1970   **Architect:** Eugene Wasserman   **Cost:** $750,000
> **Contact for Rental:** Mary Jo Ballschmider;   (414) 458-6144

Spring Green

THEATRE

AMERICAN PLAYERS THEATRE
Route 3, Spring Green, WI 53588
(608) 588-7401
> **Founded:** 1980
> **Arts Area:** Professional; Theatrical Group
> **Status:** Professional; Non-Profit
> **Type:** Performing; Touring; Resident; Educational
> **Management:** Sheldon Wilner, Managing Director; David Frank, Associate Director; Kathryn Long, Artistic Director
> **Utilizes:** Special Technical Talent; Guest Artists; Guest Directors
> **Budget:** $1,000,000 - $5,000,000
> **Income Sources:** Private Foundations/Grants/Endowments; Business/Corporate Donations; Box Office; Government Grants; Individual Donations
> **Season:** June - October
> **Affiliations:** TCG; AEA
> **Performance Facilities:** American Players Theater

Stevens Point

INSTRUMENTAL MUSIC

CENTRAL WISCONSIN SYMPHONY ORCHESTRA
PO Box 65, Stevens Point, WI 54481
(715) 344-1420
> **Founded:** 1947
> **Arts Area:** Symphony; Orchestra
> **Status:** Non-Professional; Non-Profit
> **Type:** Performing; Resident
> **Purpose:** To promote the appreciation and enjoyment of orchestral literature through live performance

Management: Jodi Engum Kryshak, Manager
Officers: Ed Wotruba, President; Jennifer Burton, Vice President; Jeff Peterson, Treasurer; Nancy Mattowitz, Secretary
Paid Staff: 3   **Volunteer Staff:** 1
Paid Artists: 75
Utilizes: Special Technical Talent; Guest Conductors; Guest Artists; Community Members; Students
Budget: $100,000 - $500,000
Income Sources: Private Foundations/Grants/Endowments; Business/Corporate Donations; Box Office; Government Grants; Individual Donations
Season: October - May   **Annual Attendance:** 7,000
Performance Facilities: Sentry Theater

Superior

FACILITY

UNIVERSITY OF WISCONSIN-SUPERIOR - PAUL E. HOLDEN FINE AND APPLIED ARTS CENTER
Superior, WI 54880
(715) 394-8369
    Type of Facility: Theatre Complex; Multi-Purpose
    Type of Stage: Flexible
    Stage Dimensions: 50'x85'   **Orchestra Pit**
    Seating Capacity: 350
    Year Built: 1973   **Architect:** Larson, Playter & Smith   **Cost:** $5,000,000
    Contact for Rental: William Stock;   (715) 394-8269

Wales

THEATRE

REED MARIONETTES, INC.
700 Llambaris Pass, Wales, WI 53183
(414) 968-3277
    Founded: 1950
    Arts Area: Professional; Puppet
    Status: Professional
    Type: Performing; Touring
    Purpose: A professional touring company presenting colorful, entertaining and faithful versions of children's classics, combining the best of the arts of puppetry and theatre
    Management: Robin Reed, Managing Director
    Officers: Robin Reed, President
    Paid Staff: 3
    Paid Artists: 3
    Utilizes: Special Technical Talent
    Budget: $1,000 - $50,000
    Income Sources: Box Office
    Season: 52 Weeks   **Annual Attendance:** 80,000
    Affiliations: Puppeteers of America; Wisconsin Puppetry Guild

Waukesha

INSTRUMENTAL MUSIC

WAUKESHA SYMPHONY
PO Box 531, Waukesha, WI 53187
(414) 547-1858
    Founded: 1947
    Arts Area: Symphony; Orchestra
    Status: Semi-Professional; Non-Profit
    Type: Performing; Resident
    Purpose: To play classical music for the Waukesha area
    Management: Diane M. Bennett, General Manager
    Officers: Tom Derse, President; Sandy Stuckmann, Executive Vice President; Jane Darling, Senior Vice President; Jeannine Gabel, Secretary; Jim Wilkie, Treasurer
    Paid Staff: 1
    Paid Artists: 85
    Utilizes: Guest Artists

Budget: $100,000 - $500,000
Income Sources: Private Foundations/Grants/Endowments; Business/Corporate Donations; Box Office; Individual Donations
Season: October - May **Annual Attendance:** 5,000
Affiliations: ASOL; AWSO
Performance Facilities: Shattuck Auditorium

THEATRE

WAUKESHA CIVIC THEATRE
506 North Washington, Waukesha, WI 53188
(414) 547-4911
Founded: 1957
Arts Area: Musical; Community; Theatrical Group
Status: Semi-Professional; Non-Professional; Non-Profit
Type: Performing; Educational
Purpose: To stimulate an interest in drama, offer theatre opportunities and promote theatre as an educational tool
Management: Betsey Folsom, Managing Director; Pat Trecker, Development Director
Officers: Tim Hawley, President; Robb Moodie, Vice President; Debra Zibrel, Secretary; Brad Sebena, Treasurer
Paid Staff: 2 **Volunteer Staff:** 200
Paid Artists: 1 **Non-Paid Artists:** 80
Utilizes: Guest Directors
Budget: $50,000 - $100,000
Income Sources: Private Foundations/Grants/Endowments; Business/Corporate Donations; Box Office; Government Grants; Individual Donations
Season: 52 Weeks **Annual Attendance:** 7,000
Affiliations: ATA; AACT

FACILITY

WAUKESHA CIVIC THEATRE
506 North Washington, Waukesha, WI 53188
(414) 547-4911
Type of Facility: Theatre House
Facility Originally: Church
Type of Stage: Thrust
Stage Dimensions: 17'x38'
Seating Capacity: 136
Year Built: 1950
Year Remodeled: 1964
Resident Groups: Waukesha Civic Theatre

Waupacu

PERFORMING SERIES

WAUPACA FINE ARTS FESTIVAL
Box 55, Waupacu, WI 54981
(715) 258-3054
Founded: 1962
Arts Area: Dance; Vocal Music; Instrumental Music; Theater
Status: Non-Profit
Type: Performing
Purpose: Encouragement of active participation of musicians, artists and listeners/viewers of all the fine arts
Officers: Gerald Knoepfel, Chairman; Charles Spanhauer, Co-Chairman; Blanche Fanik, Treasurer
Volunteer Staff: 50
Paid Artists: 50 **Non-Paid Artists:** 300
Utilizes: Guest Artists
Budget: $1,000 - $50,000
Income Sources: Business/Corporate Donations; Box Office; Individual Donations
Season: October - June
Affiliations: Wisconsin Art Council
Performance Facilities: High School Auditorium

WYOMING

Casper

INSTRUMENTAL MUSIC

CASPER CHAMBER MUSIC SOCIETY
PO Box 2899, Casper, WY 82602
(307) 234-7127
Founded: 1983
Arts Area: Chamber
Status: Semi-Professional; Non-Profit
Type: Performing
Purpose: To provide high-calibre performing opportunities to local and regional chamber ensembles
Officers: Inge N. Kutchins, President; Judy Vernon, Vice President; Adrienne Bonnet, Secretary; Louis C. Rognstad, Treasurer; Janet Ahlquist, Jo Jackson and Albert V. Metz, Board-at-Large
Paid Artists: 17
Utilizes: Guest Artists
Budget: $1,000 - $50,000
Income Sources: Private Foundations/Grants/Endowments; Business/Corporate Donations; Box Office; Individual Donations
Season: October - April   **Annual Attendance:** 550
Performance Facilities: Aley Fine Arts Hall, Casper College

CASPER SYMPHONY ORCHESTRA
PO Box 667, Casper, WY 82602
(307) 266-1478
Founded: 1950
Arts Area: Symphony; Orchestra
Status: Professional; Non-Profit
Type: Performing; Touring; Educational
Purpose: To enrich the cultural lives of audiences; to expand the musical horizons of children; to provide an outlet for the creative talents of area musicians and for an expanding audience
Management: Christopher Boor, General Adminstrator; Curtis Peacock, Music Director/Conductor
Paid Staff: 4   **Volunteer Staff:** 10
Paid Artists: 72   **Non-Paid Artists:** 2
Utilizes: Guest Artists
Budget: $100,000 - $500,000
Income Sources: Private Foundations/Grants/Endowments; Business/Corporate Donations; Box Office; Government Grants; Individual Donations; Fund-raising
Season: September - May   **Annual Attendance:** 10,000
Affiliations: Casper Chamber of Commerce; Wyoming Council on the Arts; NEA; ASOL; Wyoming Advocates for Cultural Development
Performance Facilities: John F. Welsh Auditorium; Natrona County High School

FACILITY

CASPER COLLEGE - DURHAM HALL
125 College Drive, Casper, WY 82601
(307) 268-2606
Type of Facility: Concert Hall; Studio Performance; Performance Center
Type of Stage: Platform
Seating Capacity: 309
Year Built: 1968   **Architect:** Henry Therkildson   **Cost:** $600,000
Contact for Rental: Jan Delgarno;   (307) 268-2606
Resident Groups: Casper College - Jazz Ensemble; Percussion Ensemble; Concert Band; Chamber Orchestra; String Ensemble
Also hosts student recitals, jazz combos and contemporary singers

CASPER EVENTS CENTER
1 Events Center Drive, PO Box K10, Casper, WY 82602
(307) 235-8441
FAX: (307) 235-8445
Type of Facility: Concert Hall; Theatre House; Arena; Multi-Purpose
Type of Stage: Flexible; Platform
Seating Capacity: 10,452

Year Built: 1982 **Architect:** Gorder South Group **Cost:** $22,000,000
Contact for Rental: Max L. Torbert, General Manager; (307) 235-8441

Cheyenne

INSTRUMENTAL MUSIC

CHEYENNE SYMPHONY ORCHESTRA
PO Box 851, Cheyenne, WY 82003
(307) 778-8561
Founded: 1954
Arts Area: Symphony; Orchestra; Chamber
Status: Professional; Non-Profit
Type: Performing; Educational
Purpose: To present high-quality professional symphonic music to the widest possible audience with emphasis on educational outreach
Management: Betty Flood, Executive Director
Officers: Renee Middleton, President; Larry Wolfe, President-Elect
Paid Staff: 3
Paid Artists: 110
Utilizes: Guest Conductors; Guest Artists
Budget: $100,000 - $500,000
Income Sources: Private Foundations/Grants/Endowments; Business/Corporate Donations; Box Office; Government Grants; Individual Donations
Season: September - May **Annual Attendance:** 9,028
Affiliations: ASOL; Symphony and Choral Society of Cheyenne
Performance Facilities: Cheyenne Civic Center

THEATRE

CHEYENNE LITTLE THEATRE PLAYERS
2706 East Pershing Boulevard, PO Box 1086, Cheyenne, WY 82001
(307) 638-6543
Founded: 1930
Arts Area: Musical; Dinner; Community
Status: Non-Professional; Non-Profit
Type: Performing; Educational
Purpose: To provide entertainment and education through theatre to residents of southeastern Wyoming; to promote creativity and excellence among volunteers
Management: Patrick Brien, Managing Director
Officers: Rick Flood, President; Barbara Dorr, President-Elect; Marlyn Salley, Secretary; Vicki Lewis, Treasurer
Paid Staff: 2 **Volunteer Staff:** 250
Paid Artists: 2 **Non-Paid Artists:** 100
Utilizes: Guest Artists; Guest Directors
Budget: $100,000 - $500,000
Income Sources: Private Foundations/Grants/Endowments; Business/Corporate Donations; Box Office; Government Grants; Individual Donations
Season: 52 Weeks **Annual Attendance:** 12,000
Affiliations: AACT
Performance Facilities: Mary Godfrey Playhouse; Atlas Theatre

PERFORMING SERIES

WYOMING ARTS COUNCIL
2320 Capitol Avenue, Cheyenne, WY 82002
(307) 777-7742
FAX: (307) 777-5499
Founded: 1967
Arts Area: Dance; Vocal Music; Instrumental Music; Theater; Festivals; Lyric Opera; Grand Opera
Status: Non-Profit
Type: Educational; Sponsoring
Purpose: To promote visual, literary and performing arts in Wyoming
Management: Rita Moxey, Acting Director of Community Services; Renee Bovee, Performing Arts Coordinator; Wendy Bredehoft, AIE Coordinator
Officers: Jo Campbell, Chairman
Paid Staff: 7 **Volunteer Staff:** 2
Budget: $100,000 - $500,000

Income Sources: Private Foundations/Grants/Endowments; Government Grants
Affiliations: WSAF; NASSA; NALAA; WAAA

FACILITY

CHEYENNE CIVIC CENTER
2101 O'Neil Avenue, Cheyenne, WY 82001
(307) 637-6364
FAX: (307) 637-6454
Founded: 1981
Type of Facility: Concert Hall; Auditorium; Performance Center; Off Broadway; Theatre House; Civic Center
Type of Stage: Proscenium
Stage Dimensions: 60'Wx40'D   **Orchestra Pit**
Seating Capacity: 1,496
Year Built: 1981   **Architect:** Ira Blackwell Architects   **Cost:** $4,200,000
Contact for Rental: Dru Rohla;   (307) 637-6364
Resident Groups: Cheyenne Symphony Orchestra

Laramie

PERFORMING SERIES

WESTERN ARTS MUSIC FESTIVAL
University of Wyoming, Department of Music, PO Box 3037, Laramie, WY 82071-3037
(307) 766-5242
Founded: 1972
Arts Area: Vocal Music; Instrumental Music; Festivals; Lyric Opera
Status: Professional; Non-Profit
Type: Performing; Touring; Resident; Educational
Purpose: To bring quality music to the public during the summer months
Management: Fredrick Gersten, Chairman of the Music Department
Paid Staff: 1   **Volunteer Staff:** 10
Paid Artists: 15
Utilizes: Guest Artists
Budget: $1,000 - $50,000
Income Sources: Private Foundations/Grants/Endowments; Business/Corporate Donations; Government Grants; Individual Donations
Season: June - July   **Annual Attendance:** 4,850
Affiliations: Wyoming Council of the Arts
Performance Facilities: The Fine Arts Council Hall, University of Wyoming; Saint Mary's Cathedral

FACILITY

UNIVERSITY OF WYOMING - ARENA AUDITORIUM
PO Box 3254, Laramie, WY 82071
(307) 766-1121
Type of Facility: Auditorium; Arena
Type of Stage: Flexible; Platform   **Stage Dimensions:** 60'Wx40'D
Seating Capacity: 15,000
Year Built: 1982
Contact for Rental: Terri Howes;   (307) 766-4091

UNIVERSITY OF WYOMING - ARTS AND SCIENCES AUDITORIUM
PO Box 3254, Laramie, WY 82071
(307) 766-1121
Type of Facility: Concert Hall; Auditorium; Theatre House
Type of Stage: Proscenium   **Stage Dimensions:** 48'Wx32'D
Seating Capacity: 1,996
Year Built: 1945
Contact for Rental: Violet Baker;   (307) 766-4388
Resident Groups: University of Wyoming Music and Theater Departments

UNIVERSITY OF WYOMING - FINE ARTS CONCERT HALL
PO Box 3037, Laramie, WY 82071
(307) 766-6250
Type of Facility: Concert Hall
Type of Stage: Proscenium
Seating Capacity: 700

Year Built: 1976
Contact for Rental: Frederick Gersten;   (307) 766-5242
Resident Groups: University of Wyoming Music Department

Moose

DANCE

THE LAUBINS
PO Box 4, Moose, WY 83012
(307) 733-2690
Founded: 1948
Arts Area: Ethnic
Status: Professional
Type: Performing; Touring; Resident; Educational
Purpose: To introduce Native American dancing (Plains and Woodlands) as a fine art; to bring about a better understanding of Indian dancing
Management: Reginald K. and Gladys Laubin, Directors
Paid Artists: 2
Income Sources: Box Office
Annual Attendance: 10,000

Sheridan

THEATRE

SHERIDAN CIVIC THEATRE GUILD
PO Box 1, Sheridan, WY 82801
(307) 672-9886
Founded: 1953
Arts Area: Musical; Community; Theatrical Group
Status: Non-Profit
Type: Performing; Resident
Purpose: To foster community theatre in the area; to involve community members in all aspects of theatre; to entertain
Management: Judi O'Neal, Manager
Officers: Tim Lervick, President; Sam Yorks, Vice President; Sarah Olson, Secretary; Marilyn Palmer, Treasurer
Paid Staff: 1
Utilizes: Special Technical Talent; Guest Conductors
Budget: $1,000 - $50,000
Income Sources: Private Foundations/Grants/Endowments; Business/Corporate Donations; Box Office; Government Grants; Individual Donations
Season: September - May   **Annual Attendance:** 2,000
Performance Facilities: Carriage House Theatre

FACILITY

WYO THEATER, INC.
42 North Main Street, Sheridan, WY 82801
(307) 672-9083
Founded: 1923
Type of Facility: Concert Hall; Auditorium; Performance Center; Theatre House; Multi-Purpose
Facility Originally: Vaudeville
Type of Stage: Thrust; Proscenium
Stage Dimensions: 33'x20'; 6'thrust
Seating Capacity: 487
Year Built: 1923
Year Remodeled: 1989   **Architect:** Tim Belton, Malone, Belton Architects   **Cost:** $1,400,000
Acoustical Consultant: David Adams Associates
Contact for Rental: Sophie S. Pelissier;   (307) 672-9083
Resident Groups: WYO Theater, Inc.

Teton Village

PERFORMING SERIES

GRAND TETON MUSIC FESTIVAL
PO Box 490, Teton Village, WY 83025
(307) 733-1128
Founded: 1962
Arts Area: Vocal Music; Instrumental Music; Festivals
Status: Professional; Non-Profit
Type: Performing; Sponsoring
Purpose: To establish a resident ensemble of like-minded artists to perform in small ensembles in a superb symphony orchestra; to bring the musical resources of a great metropolis to the northern Rocky Mountain region for the summer season
Management: Ling Tung, Music Director
Officers: William D. Weiss, President
Paid Staff: 15   **Volunteer Staff:** 45
Paid Artists: 175
Utilizes: Guest Conductors
Budget: $1,000,000 - $5,000,000
Income Sources: Private Foundations/Grants/Endowments; Business/Corporate Donations; Box Office; Government Grants; Individual Donations
Season: June - August   **Annual Attendance:** 17,000
Performance Facilities: Walk Festival Hall

PUERTO RICO

Corozal

DANCE

GUATEQUE FOLKLORIC BALLET OF PUERTO RICO
HC-01, PO Box 6894, Corozal, PR 00783
(809) 859-8601; (809) 787-3837
   Arts Area: Ethnic; Folk
   Status: Non-Professional; Non-Profit
   Type: Performing; Educational; Touring
   Purpose: To promote and preserve the culture of Puerto Rico and to expose other people to its culture
   Management: Joachim Nieres; Luz Esther Ortiz, Secretary; Orlando Gonzalez, Public Relations
   Budget: $1,000 - $50,000
   Income Sources: Box Office; Government Grants; Individual Donations; Touring Fees

San Juan

DANCE

BALLETS DE SAN JUAN
PO Box S-5713, San Juan, PR 00901
(809) 725-9140; (809) 721-3257
FAX: (809) 721-3257
   Arts Area: Ballet
   Status: Professional; Non-Profit
   Type: Performing; Touring
   Purpose: To develop professional ballet dancers and choreographers in Puerto Rico
   Management: Ana Garcia, Director; Nydia Fernandez, Administrative Assistant
   Officers: Ana Garcia, Director; Jaime Suarez, President, Friends of Ballets de San Juan
   Paid Staff: 6   **Volunteer Staff:** 3
   Paid Artists: 12   **Non-Paid Artists:** 12
   Utilizes: Special Technical Talent; Guest Artists; Guest Conductors; Guest Choreographers
   Income Sources: Private Foundations/Grants/Endowments; Business/Corporate Donations; Box Office; Government Grants; Individual Donations
   Budget: $100,000 - $500,000
   Season: August-June   **Annual Attendance:** 12,000
   Performance Facilities: Bellas Artes Center

THEATRE

TEATRO DEL SERENTA INC.
PO Box 5122, Puerta de Tierra Station, San Juan, PR 00906
(809) 723-1403; (809) 725-9494
FAX: (809) 723-1403
   Founded: 1963
   Arts Area: Professional; Theatrical Group
   Status: Professional; Non-Profit
   Type: Performing; Educational; Touring
   Purpose: To perform and develop national and international theater of the highest quality for Puerto Rico
   Management: Alexis Gueits, General Manager; Belein Rios, Public Relations; Idalia Perez-Garay, Artistic Director; Jose Felix Gomez, Associate Artistic Director
   Officers: Jaime S. Ramirez, President; Israel Rodriguez, Director; Flora Perez-Garay, Director; Mamel Portela, Treasurer
   Utilizes: Special Technical Talent; Guest Artists; Guest Directors
   Budget: $100,000 - $500,000
   Income Sources: Private Foundations/Grants/Endowments; Business/Corporate Donations; Box Office; Government Grants; Individual Donations
   Season: 52 Weeks   **Annual Attendance:** 30,000
   Performance Facilities: Center for Performing Arts-Theater Hall, University of Puerto Rico

---
Santurce
DANCE

BALLET CONCIERTO DE PUERTO RICO
PO Box 13245, Santurce, PR 00908-3245
(809) 724-7023
FAX: (809) 725-5642
    Arts Area: Modern; Ballet
    Status: Professional; Non-Profit
    Type: Performing; Educational; Touring; Resident; Sponsoring
    Purpose: To teach the people of Puerto Rico about ballet and dancing
    Management: Lolita San Miguel, Artistic Director; Julie Montes, Administration
    Officers: Carlos Ivan Berrios, Chairman of the Board
    Income Sources: Private Foundations/Grants/Endowments; Business/Corporate Donations; Box Office; Government Grants; Individual Donations
    Performance Facilities: Centro de Bellas Artes

VIRGIN ISLANDS

Charlotte Amalie

FACILITY

REICHHOLD CENTER FOR THE ARTS
2 John Brews Bay, Charlotte Amalie, VI 00802-9990
(809) 774-8475
FAX: (809) 774-4482
    Type of Facility: Performance Center; Multi-Purpose
    Type of Stage: Proscenium
    Stage Dimensions: 48'Wx26'Dx38'6"H; 48'Wx26'H proscenium opening
    Seating Capacity: 1,196
    Year Built: 1978
    Contact for Rental: Maysen Gore;   (809) 774-8475
    Resident Groups: Caribbean Dance Company

DANCE INDEX

ABHINAYA DANCE COMPANY, 75
ACADEMY OF CREATIVE DANCE AND ELIZABETH
    MANDEVILLE DANCE COMPANY, 234
AFRICAN-AMERICAN DANCE ENSEMBLE, THE, 1052
AFRICAN DANCE FESTIVAL FOR KANKOURAN WEST
    AFRICAN DANCE CO., 297
AGNES DE MILLE DANCE THEATER, 908
AIKEN CIVIC BALLET COMPANY, 1255
AJDE! FOLK DANCE ENSEMBLE, 270
AKASHA AND COMPANY, 422
ALBANO BALLET COMPANY, 262
ALEXANDRA BALLET COMPANY, 743
ALLEGHENY BALLET COMPANY, 1194
ALLEGRO BALLET OF HOUSTON, 1354
ALLNATIONS DANCE COMPANY, 908
ALPHA-OMEGA THEATRICAL DANCE COMPANY, 909
ALVIN AILEY AMERICAN DANCE THEATER, 909
ALVIN AILEY REPERTORY ENSEMBLE, 909
AMAN INTERNATIONAL MUSIC AND DANCE COMPANY, 100
AMERICAN AUTHENTIC JAZZ DANCE THEATRE, 910
AMERICAN BALLET, 1248
AMERICAN BALLET THEATRE, 910
AMERICAN BALLROOM THEATER COMPANY INC., 910
AMERICAN DANCE FESTIVAL, 1052
AMERICAN DANCE MACHINE, THE, 815
AMERICAN FESTIVAL BALLET, 411
AMERICAN INTERNATIONAL DANCE THEATRE, INC., 910
AMERICAN MIME THEATRE, THE, 911
AMERICAN YOUTH BALLET, 531
AMERICAN YOUTH BALLET COMPANY, 597
AMHERST BALLET THEATRE COMPANY, 601
ANACRUSIS MODERN TAP DANCE, 1451
ANCHORAGE CONCERT ASSOCIATION INC., 13
ANCHORAGE FOLK DANCE CONSORTIUM, 13
ANDAHAZY BALLET COMPANY, 723
ANJANI'S KATHAK DANCE OF INDIA, 215
ANN ARBOR BALLET THEATRE, 657
ANN ARBOR CIVIC BALLET, 657
ANNABELLA GONZALEZ DANCE THEATER, INC., 911
APPALACHIAN BALLET COMPANY, 1288
APPALACHIAN YOUTH JAZZ-BALLET COMPANY, 1476
ARLINGTON DANCE THEATRE, 1422
ART BRIDGMAN/MYRNA PACKER, 911
ART OF BLACK DANCE AND MUSIC, 643
ASIAN AMERICAN DANCE PERFORMANCES, 161
ASIAN AMERICAN DANCE THEATRE, 911
ATLANTA BALLET, THE, 377
ATHENS BALLET, 376
ATLANTIC DANCE THEATRE, 1067
AUGUSTA BALLET COMPANY, 387
AURORA DANCE ARTS, 223
AVAZ INTERNATIONAL DANCE THEATRE, 203
AVODAH DANCE ENSEMBLE, 822
BAILES FLAMENCOS, 162
BALLET ALASKA, 13
BALLET ARIZONA, 28
BALLET ARKANSAS, 48
BALLET AUSTIN, 1307
BALLET CHICAGO, 422
BALLET COLBERT, 795
BALLET CONCERTO, 1343
BALLET CONCERTO COMPANY OF MIAMI, 339
BALLET CONCIERTO DE PUERTO RICO, 1526
BALLET CULTURAL AZTECA, 691
BALLET DENVER, 234
BALLET DES JEUNES, 1215
BALLET ETUDES, 329
BALLET FLORIDA, 372
BALLET FOLKLORICO OF EAST CHICAGO, INDIANA, 487
BALLET GUILD OF LEHIGH VALLEY, 1195
BALLET HISPANICO OF NEW YORK, 912
BALLET IOWA, 522
BALLET IOWA ASSOCIATION, 522
BALLET MANHATTAN FOUNDATION, INC., 912
BALLET METROPOLITAN, 1121

BALLET MISSISSIPPI, 734
BALLET MONTMARTRE, THE, 72
BALLET OF THE AMERICAS, 1340
BALLET OKLAHOMA, 1163
BALLET PACIFICA, 95,
BALLET SPECTACULAR/INTERNATIONAL CULTURAL
    EXCHANGE, INC., 340
BALLET THEATRE OF ANNAPOLIS, 585
BALLET THEATRE OF WESTCHESTER, 1033
BALLET THEATRE PENNSYLVANIA, 1209
BALLET WEST, 1401
BALLET WESTERN RESERVE, 1152
BALLETACOMA, 1468
BALLETS DE SAN JUAN, 1525
BALTIMORE DANCE THEATRE, 586
BARBARA FELDMAN AND DANCERS, 270
BARTLESVILLE CIVIC BALLET, 1158
BATON ROUGE BALLET THEATRE, 555
BATTERY DANCE COMPANY, 912
BAUER CONTEMPORARY BALLET, 1503
BAY AREA REPERTORY DANCE THEATRE (BARD), 59
BEACON DANCE COMPANY, 391
BEAUMONT BALLET THEATRE, 1312
BEAUMONT CIVIC BALLET, 1313
BEBE MILLER COMPANY, 912
BERKELEY CITY BALLET, 59
BETHUNE THEATREDANSE, 100
BETTY SALAMUN'S DANCECIRCUS, 1503
BEVERLY BLOSSOM AND COMPANY, 869
BILL T. JONES/ARNIE ZANE AND COMPANY, 913
BODY LANGUAGE DANCE COMPANY, 1202
BOSTON BALLET COMPANY, 604
BOSTON BALLET II, 605
BOSTON FLAMENCO BALLET, 617
BRISTOL BALLET COMPANY, 1424
BROOKLYN CENTER FOR THE PERFORMING ARTS AT
    BROOKLYN COLLEGE, 869
BRUCE KING FOUNDATION FOR AMERICAN DANCE, 913
CALIFORNIA BALLET COMPANY, 152
CANTON BALLET, 1099
CAPITOL BALLET COMPANY, 297
CARLOTA SANTANA SPANISH DANCE COMPANY, 913
CAROL FONDA AND COMPANY/DANCE FORUM, INC., 913
CAROLINA BALLET THEATRE, 1262
CATAMOUNT FILM AND ARTS COMPANY, 1418
CHARLES MOORE - DANCES AND DRUMS OF AFRICA, 870
CHARLES MOULTON DANCE COMPANY, 914
CHARLESTON BALLET, 1476
CHARLESTON BALLET, THE, 1257
CHARLOTTE CITY BALLET, 1048
CHATTANOOGA BALLET, 1278
CHEN AND DANCERS, 914
CHHANDAM CHITRESH DAS DANCE COMPANY, 151
CHICAGO DANCE COALITION, 422
CHICAGO MOVING COMPANY, 423
CHILDREN'S BALLET THEATRE, 1472
CHILDREN'S DANCE THEATRE OF NEW MILFORD, 275
CINCINNATI BALLET, 1101
CITY BALLET OF HOUSTON, 1354
CITY CELEBRATION, INC., 162
CIVIC DANCE ASSOCIATION, 1272
CHINESE FOLK DANCE COMPANY, 914
CHRYSALIS REPERTORY DANCE COMPANY, 1354
CLEAR LAKE METROPOLITAN BALLET, 1355
CLEO PARKER ROBINSON DANCE ENSEMBLE, 234
CLEVELAND SAN JOSE BALLET, 1108
CLOG AMERICA, 1397
CODANCECO, 914
COLORADO BALLET, 234
COLORADO SPRINGS DANCE THEATRE, 229
COLUMBIA CITY BALLET, 1259
CO-MOTION DANCE, 1453
CO'MOTION DANCE THEATER, 507
CONCERT BALLET OF VIRGINIA, THE, 1435
CONCERT DANCE THEATRE, 211

CONNECTICUT BALLET THEATRE, 279
CONNECTICUT CONCERT BALLET, 265
CONTEMPORARY DANCE SEASON, THE, 1184
CONTEMPORARY DANCE THEATER, 1101
CONTRABAND, 162
CONVERGENCE DANCERS & MUSICIANS, 1216
CORPUS CHRISTI BALLET, 1320
COURANTE DANCE COMPANY, 915
CRASH, BURN AND DIE DANCE COMPANY, 56
CRESCENT BALLET COMPANY, 561
CUYAHOGA VALLEY YOUTH BALLET, 1128
DALE SCHOLL DANCE ART, 147
DALLAS BLACK DANCE THEATRE, 1323
DALLAS DANCE COUNCIL, 1323
DALLAS METROPOLITAN BALLET, 1324
DAN WAGONER AND DANCERS, 915
DANCE AFFILIATES OF AMERICAN BALLET
    COMPETITION, 1216
DANCE ALIVE!, 328
DANCE ALLOY, 1229
DANCE ART CENTER, 775
DANCE ASPEN, 221
DANCE ASSOCIATION/RUTH LANGRIDGE DANCE
    COMPANY, THE, 58
DANCE BRIGADE, 130
DANCE CENTER OF COLUMBIA COLLEGE, THE, 423
DANCE COLLECTIVE, 915
DANCE CONNECTION, THE, 245
DANCE EXCHANGE, 297
DANCE GALLERY COMPANY, 657
DANCE - JUNE LEWIS AND COMPANY, 915
DANCE KALEIDOSCOPE, 494
DANCE NETWORK, THE, 292
DANCE ON THE EDGE, 598
DANCE PLACE, 298
DANCE PROJECTS INC./BETH SOLL AND COMPANY, 605
DANCE REPERTORY THEATRE, 83
DANCE ST. LOUIS, 754
DANCE SOLOS, INC., 1024
DANCE THEATRE DAYTON, 1128
DANCE THEATRE IN WESTCHESTER, 1040
DANCE THEATRE OF HARLEM, 916
DANCE THEATRE WORKSHOP, 916
DANCE 2000: THE FELICE LESSER DANCE THEATER, 915
DANCE UMBRELLA, 1307
DANCE UMBRELLA, BOSTON, INC., 618
DANCEBRAZIL, 916
DANCECIRCUS LIMITED, 1503
DANCECLEVELAND, 1109
DANCELLINGTON, INC., 917
DANCERS' GROUP, 162
DANCES FOR 2, 266
DANCES WE DANCE, 402
DANCEWAVE, INC. (THE DIANE JACOBOWITZ DANCE
    THEATER), 870
DANCING IN THE KITCHEN SERIES, 917
DANCING IN THE STREETS, INC., 917
DANMARI LTD./YASS HAKOSHIMA MIME THEATRE, 825
DANSE MIRAGE, INC./ELINOR COLEMAN DANCE
    EMSEMBLE, 917
DANSPACE PROJECT, INC., THE, 918
DANSWINTER/DANSUMMER, 232
DAVID GORDON/PICK UP COMPANY, 918
DAVID PARSONS DANCE COMPANY, 918
DAVID TAYLOR DANCE THEATRE, 250
DAYTON BALLET, 1128
DAYTON CONTEMPORARY DANCE COMPANY, 1129
D.C. CONTEMPORARY DANCE THEATRE, 297
DEBORAH HAY DANCE COMPANY, 1308
DEBORAH SLATER AND COMPANY, 163
DEBRA WEISS DANCE COMPANY, 1011
DELAWARE DANCE COMPANY, 292
DELAWARE REGIONAL BALLET, 291
DELIA STEWART DANCE COMPANY, THE, 1355
DELLA DAVIDSON DANCE COMPANY, 163
DELTA FESTIVAL BALLET, 561
DESERT DANCE THEATRE, 35
DIMENSIONS DANCE THEATER, 130

DINIZULU AFRICAN DANCERS, DRUMMERS
    AND SINGERS, 899
DINOSAUR DANCE COMPANY, 918
DISCOVERY DANCE GROUP AND TRAINING CENTER, 1355
DONALD BYRD DANCE FOUNDATION, INC., THE, 919
DOUG ELKINS DANCE COMPANY, 919
DOUGLAS DUNN AND DANCERS, 919
DOWNTOWN DANCE COMPANY, 586
DULUTH BALLET, THE, 702
EASTERN ARTS ETHNIC DANCE COMPANY, 1401
ED LARKIN OLD-TIME CONTRA DANCERS, 1418
EDITH STEPHEN ELECTRIC CURRENTS, 920
EDWARD VILLELLA AND DANCERS, 920
EIKO AND KOMA, 920
ELEO POMARE DANCE COMPANY, 920
ELISA MONTE DANCE COMPANY, 920
ELLEN KOGAN SOLO DANCE, 869
ELLEN WEBB DANCE FOUNDATION, 131
EMERGENCE DANCE THEATRE, 449
ERICK HAWKINS DANCE COMPANY, 921
ERNESTA CORVINO'S DANCE CIRCLE COMPANY, 921
ESTYRE BRINDLE DANCE THEATRE, 724
ETHNIC DANCE THEATRE, THE, 707
EUGENE BALLET COMPANY, 1178
EUGENE JAMES DANCE COMPANY, 921
EVA ANDERSON DANCERS LTD., 593
EVANSVILLE DANCE THEATRE, 488
EZIBU MUNTU AFRICAN DANCE COMPANY, 1436
FELD BALLETS/NY, 921
FESTIVAL BALLET, 1247
FIDDLE PUPPET DANCERS, THE, 596
FILIPINIANA ARTS AND CULTURAL CENTER, 1453
FLAMENCO FANTASY DANCE THEATRE/GYPSY
    PRODUCTIONS INC., 235
FLORIDA BALLET AT JACKSONVILLE, 331
FLORIDA DANCE ASSOCIATION INC., 340
FORT WAYNE BALLET, 489
FORT WAYNE DANCE COLLECTIVE, 489
FORT WORTH BALLET COMPANY, 1343
14TH STREET DANCE CENTER AT EDUCATIONAL
    ALLIANCE, 908
FRANCISCO MARTINEZ DANCE THEATRE, THE, 212
FREDDICK BRATCHER AND COMPANY, 319
FRESNO BALLET, 80
GAINESVILLE BALLET, THE, 392
GARDEN STATE BALLET, 830
GATEWAY BALLET OF SAINT LOUIS, 753
GENESIS ARTS/KENTUCKY INC., 546
GRAND RAPIDS BALLET, THE, 674
GRANDINELE LITHUANIAN FOLK DANCERS, 1138
GROUP MOTION MULTI MEDIA DANCE THEATER, 1216
GUADALUPE FOLK DANCE COMPANY, 1383
GUATEQUE FOLKLORIC BALLET OF PUERTO RICO, 1525
GRUPO FOLKLORICO MEXICANA, 364
GULFCOAST DANCE, 326
GUS GIORDANO JAZZ DANCE CHICAGO, 453
HAMPTON ROADS CIVIC BALLET, 1427
HANNAH KAHN DANCE COMPANY, 79
HARTFORD BALLET, 262
HARVARD SUMMER DANCE CENTER, 618
HAWAII STATE BALLET, 402
HIS IMAGE, SACRED DANCE, 317
HOUSTON BALLET, 1356
HUBBARD STREET DANCE COMPANY, 423
HUMAN ARMS, 1027
HUNTSVILLE CIVIC BALLET, 5
ICE THEATER OF NEW YORK, INC., 922
INDIANAPOLIS BALLET THEATRE, 494
INSTITUTE FOR DANCE, INC., THE, 1442
INTERNATIONAL BALLET FOLKLORICO, 1340
IOWA DANCE THEATRE, 514
IRINE FOKINE BALLET COMPANY, 836
IRVING BALLET COMPANY, 1368
ISADORA DUNCAN DANCE CENTER, 163
ISLAND MOVING COMPANY, 1246
ITHACA BALLET (BALLET GUILD OF ITHACA, INC.), 897
JACKSONVILLE BALLET THEATRE, 331
JACOB'S PILLOW DANCE FESTIVAL, 603

JAN ERKERT AND COMPANY, 423
JAN JUSTIS DANCE COMPANY, 223
JANE FRANKLIN AND DANCERS, 1425
JANIS BRENNER AND DANCERS, 922
JAZZ DANCE THEATRE SOUTH, 394
JAZZ DANCERS, INC., 68
JAZZ TAP ENSEMBLE, 100
JENNIFER MULLER-THE WORKS, 923
JO EMERY DANCE COMPANY, 1468
JOAN KARFF'S NEW DANCE, 1356
JOAN MILLER'S DANCE PLAYERS, 923
JOEL HALL DANCERS, 424
JOFFREY BALLET, 923
JOFFREY II DANCERS, THE, 923
JOHN CHOOKASIAN FOLK ENSEMBLE-KING TUT REVUE
    BELLY DANCE, 81
JOHN GAMBLE/JAN VAN DYKE DANCE COMPANY, 1057
JOPPA JAZZ DANCE COMPANY, 635
JOSE LIMON DANCE COMPANY, 924
JOSE MOLINA BAILES ESPANOLES, 1013
JOSEPH HOLMES CHICAGO DANCE THEATRE, 424
JUBILATION DANCE COMPANY, 870
JUILLIARD DANCE ENSEMBLE, 924
JUNEAU FOLK ENSEMBLE, 17
KALAMAZOO BALLET COMPANY, 679
KALEIDOSCOPE DANCE THEATRE BALLET, 352
KANOPY DANCE THEATRE, 1494
KARPATOK HUNGARIAN FOLK ENSEMBLE, 67
KAST AND COMPANY, 424
KAZUKO HIRABAYASHI DANCE THEATRE, 924
KEI TAKEI'S MOVING EARTH (MOVING EARTH INC.), 925
KENNETH KING AND DANCERS, 925
KETCHIKAN THEATRE BALLET SCHOOL, 22
KHADRA INTERNATIONAL FOLK BALLET, 163
KNOXVILLE BALLET COMPANY, THE, 1284
KNOXVILLE METROPOLITAN DANCE THEATRE, 1284
K2 DANCE AND ARTS COMPANY, INC., 924
LABAN/BARTENIEFF INSTITUTE OF MOVEMENT
    STUDIES, 925
LACE/LOS ANGELES CONTEMPORARY EXHIBITIONS, 100
LAKE CHARLES BALLET SOCIETY, 559
LAKE CHARLES SOCIETY FOR BALLET JOYEUX, 559
LAR LUBOVITCH DANCE COMPANY, 925
LARRY RICHARDSON DANCE FOUNDATION, 926
LAUBINS, THE, 1522
LAURA DEAN DANCERS AND MUSICIANS, 926
LE BALLET PETIT GUILD, 424
LES BALLETS TROCKADERO DE MONTE CARLO, 926
LEWITZKY DANCE COMPANY, 101
LEXINGTON BALLET, 544
LINCOLN CITY BALLET COMPANY, 784
LINCOLN MIDWEST BALLET COMPANY, 784
LITHUANIAN FOLK DANCE GROUP OF BOSTON, 629
LITTLE BALLET THEATRE, 1176
LIZ LERMAN EXCHANGE, 298
LOLA MONTES AND HER SPANISH DANCERS, 101
LONE STAR BALLET, 1305
LONG ISLAND DANCE COMPANY, 1029
LORETTA LIVINGSTON AND DANCERS, 101
LOS ANGELES CHAMBER BALLET, 101
LOS ANGELES CHOREOGRAPHERS AND DANCERS, 102
LOS ANGELES CLASSICAL BALLET, 96
LOTTE GOSLAR AND COMPANY, 286
LOUISVILLE BALLET, 546
LUCINDA CHILDS DANCE COMPANY, 926
LUIS RIVERA SPANISH DANCE COMPANY, 927
LULA WASHINGTON CONTEMPORARY DANCE
    FOUNDATION, 102
LYNN DANCE COMPANY, 1494
MADAME CADILLAC DANCE THEATRE, 666
MADISON SCOTTISH COUNTRY DANCERS, 1495
MALASHOCK DANCE AND COMPANY, 152
MALINI'S DANCES OF INDIA, 657
MANDALA FOLK DANCE ENSEMBLE, 618
MANHATTAN BALLET FOUNDATION, 927
MARCUS SCHULKIND DANCE COMPANY, 605
MARGARET JENKINS DANCE COMPANY, 164
MARGOT GRIMMER AMERICAN DANCE COMPANY, 458

MARIA BENITEZ SPANISH DANCE COMPANY, 853
MARIN BALLET, THE, 190
MARK DE GARMO AND DANCERS, 927
MARK MORRIS DANCE GROUP, 927
MARTHA BOWERS' DANCE THEATRE, 870
MARTHA GRAHAM DANCE COMPANY, 928
MARY ANTHONY DANCE THEATRE-PHOENIX, 928
MARYLAND BALLET, THE, 587
MEANY HALL FOR THE PERFORMING ARTS, 1453
MEDFORD CIVIC BALLET, 1183
MELROSE MOTION COMPANY, 1495
MENDOCINO DANCE SERIES, 122
MERCE CUNNINGHAM DANCE COMPANY, 928
MEREDITH MONK - THE HOUSE FOUNDATION FOR THE
    ARTS, 928
MESOGHIOS DANCE TROUP, 1503
METRO DANCERS, 1185
MIAMI BALLET COMPANY, 364
MIAMI CITY BALLET, 344
MIAMI DANCE THEATRE, 340
MICHELLE AVA AND COMPANY, 298
MID AMERICA DANCE COMPANY, 754
MID HUDSON BALLET COMPANY, 889
MILWAUKEE BALLET, 1504
MIMI GARRARD DANCE COMPANY, 929
MINNESOTA DANCE THEATRE AND SCHOOL, 707
MIRANA MIDDLE EASTERN DANCE COMPANY, 51
MJT DANCE COMPANY, 605
M.M. COLBERT, 1495
MODESTO CIVIC BALLET THEATRE, 124
MOMENTUM DANCE COMPANY, 340
MOMIX, 929
MONTANA BALLET COMPANY, 770
MONTGOMERY BALLET, 9
MORDINE AND COMPANY DANCE THEATRE, 425
MULTIGRAVITATIONAL AERODANCE GROUP, 929
MUNTU DANCE THEATRE, 425
NAJWA DANCE CORPS, 425
NANCY HAUSER DANCE COMPANY AND SCHOOL, 707
NANCY KARP AND DANCERS, 78
NANETTE BEARDEN CONTEMPORARY DANCE THEATRE,
    THE, 930
NASHVILLE BALLET, 1294
NASHVILLE CITY BALLET, 1294
NASHVILLE CONTEMPORARY BALLET COMPANY, 1294
NATIONAL BALLET/NEW JERSEY, 828
NATIONAL DANCE INSTITUTE, 930
NETA PULVERMACHER AND DANCERS, 930
NEVA RUSSIAN DANCE ENSEMBLE, 164
NEVADA DANCE THEATRE, 796
NEW BALLET SCHOOL, THE, 930
NEW DANCE GROUP STUDIO INC., 931
NEW DANCE PERFORMANCE LAB, 708
NEW JERSEY BALLET COMPANY, 844
NEW JERSEY DANCE THEATRE, 824
NEW MEXICO BALLET COMPANY, THE, 847
NEW ORLEANS BALLET ASSOCIATION, 563
NEW PERFORMANCE SERIES/NORTHWEST NEW
    WORKS, 1454
NEW PERFORMING DANCE COMPANY, 1053
NEW REPERTORY DANCE COMPANY, 1284
NEW YORK BAROQUE DANCE COMPANY, THE, 931
NEW YORK CITY BALLET, 931
NIKOLAIS AND MURRAY LOUIS DANCE COMPANY, 931
NORTH CAROLINA DANCE THEATER, 1048
NORTH STAR DANCE FOUNDATION, 17
NORTHWEST FLORIDA BALLET, 327
NUTMEG BALLET COMPANY, 283
OAK PARK CIVIC BALLET COMPANY, 465
OAKLAND BALLET, 131
OAKLAND FESTIVAL BALLET COMPANY, 691
OCHEAMI, 1454
ODC/SAN FRANCISCO, 164
OHIO BALLET, 1091
OINKARI BASQUE DANCERS, 411
OKLAHOMA FESTIVAL BALLET, 1162
OLGA DUNN DANCE COMPANY, 628
OLYMPIC BALLET THEATRE, 1448

OMAHA BALLET COMPANY AND SCHOOL, 788
OMAHA INTERNATIONAL FOLK DANCERS, 794
OMAHA MODERN DANCE COLLECTIVE, 788
1000 ISLANDS FESTIVAL BALLET COMPANY, INC., 1036
ORANGE COUNTY BALLET THEATRE, 908
OREGON BALLET THEATRE, 1185
OYSTER BAY CONTEMPORARY BALLET, 1013
PACIFIC NORTHWEST BALLET, 1454
PAMPA CIVIC BALLET, 1379
PARKERSBURG WHEELING BALLET COMPANY, 1484
PASADENA CIVIC BALLET, 139
PASADENA DANCE THEATRE, 204
PASCUAL OLIVERA AND ANGELA DEL MORAL'S
     CELEBRATION OF SPANISH DANCE, 473
PAT CANNON FOOT AND FIDDLE DANCE COMPANY, 1014
PAUL TAYLOR DANCE COMPANY, 932
PEARL LANG DANCE COMPANY AND FOUNDATION, 932
PENINSULA BALLET THEATRE, 190
PENINSULA DANCE THEATRE, 1447
PENNSYLVANIA BALLET, 1216
PENNSYLVANIA DANCE THEATRE, 1239
PEORIA CIVIC BALLET, 467
PERFORMANCE SPACE 122 INC., 932
PERFORMING ARTS PROGRAMS IN DANCE, 1121
PERFORMING COMPANY OF PIONEER DANCE ARTS, 1465
PERIDANCE ENSEMBLE, 932
PETERSBURG BALLET, 1435
PHILDANCE/PHILADELPHIA DANCE COMPANY, 1217
PHOENIX DANCE THEATRE, 28
PHYLLIS LAMHUT DANCE COMPANY, 933
PHYLLIS ROSE DANCE COMPANY, THE, 1023
PILOBOLUS DANCE THEATRE, 285
PITTSBURGH BALLET THEATRE, 1229
PITTSBURGH DANCE COUNCIL INC., 1230
POLISH AMERICAN FOLK DANCE COMPANY, 933
POLISH NATIONAL ALLIANCE DANCERS, 1086
POOH KAYE/ECCENTRIC MOTIONS INC., 933
POSEY DANCE EDUCATION SERVICE, 1010
POUGHKEEPSIE CIVIC BALLET, 1016
PRAIRIE DANCE THEATRE, 1163
PRINCETON BALLET, 828
PUEBLO BALLET, 250
RADOST FOLK EMSEMBLE, 1454
RALPH LEMON COMPANY, 933
RAM ISLAND DANCE, 581
RED RIVER DANCE AND PERFORMING COMPANY, 1084
RENAISSANCE DANCE COMPANY OF DETROIT, 666
RENATE BOUE DANCE COMPANY, 825
REPERTORY DANCE THEATRE, 1402
RHAPSODY IN TAPS, 102
RICHMOND BALLET - THE STATE BALLET OF
     VIRGINIA, 1436
RIO GRANDE VALLEY BALLET, 1375
RIRIE-WOODBURY DANCE COMPANY, 1402
RISA JAROSLOW AND DANCERS, 934
RIVERSIDE BALLET THEATRE, 145
ROBERT IVEY BALLET, 1257
ROCKFORD DANCE COMPANY, 471
ROSALIND NEWMAN AND DANCERS, 934
RUDY PEREZ PERFORMANCE ENSEMBLE, 102
RUTH MITCHELL DANCE COMPANY, THE, 377
RUTH ST. DENIS FOUNDATION, 103
SACRAMENTO BALLET, 147
SAEKO OCHINOHE AND COMPANY, INC., 934
ST. JOHN'S RENAISSANCE DANCERS, 826
SAINT LOUIS CULTURAL FLAMENCO SOCIETY, 755
SAINT SAVA FREE SERBIAN ORTHODOX CHURCH, 1109
SAMAHAN PHILIPPINE DANCE COMPANY, 77
SAN ANTONIO BALLET, 1383
SAN DIEGO FOUNDATION FOR THE PERFORMING ARTS, 153
SAN FRANCISCO BALLET ASSOCIATION, 164
SAN FRANCISCO JAZZ DANCE COMPANY, 165
SAN FRANCISCO PERFORMANCES, 165
SAN FRANCISCO'S BALLET CELESTE-INTERNATIONAL, 165
SAN JOSE CLEVELAND BALLET, 184
SAN JOSE DANCE THEATRE, 185
SANTA CLARA BALLET, 196

SCHOOL OF HARD KNOCKS, 934
SEVERAL DANCERS CORE, 1356
SHALHEVET INTERNATIONAL FOLK ENSEMBLE, 1118
SHARIR DANCE COMPANY, 1308
SHODA MOVING THEATRE (M.O.V.E. CO.), 1245
SHREVEPORT METROPOLITAN BALLET, 569
SILO CONCERT DANCERS, 256
SIOUXLAND CIVIC DANCE ASSOCIATION, 519
SOCIETY FOR THE PERFORMING ARTS, 1356
SOLARIS DANCE THEATRE, 934
SOLOMONS COMPANY-DANCE, THE, 935
SOUTHERN BALLET THEATRE, 348
SOUTHERN DANCEWORKS, 1
SOUTHWEST JAZZ BALLET COMPANY, 1357
SPANISH DANCE THEATRE, 606
SPANISH THEATRE REPERTORY CO., LTD., 935
SPOKANE BALLET, 1465
SPRINGFIELD BALLET, 764
SPRINGFIELD BALLET COMPANY, 474
STATE BALLET OF MISSOURI, 745
STATE BALLET OF RHODE ISLAND, 1246
STATE OF ALABAMA BALLET/BALLET SOUTH, THE, 2
STEPHEN PETRONIO DANCE COMPANY, 935
STUART PIMSLER DANCE & THEATER, 1121
SUSAN MARSHALL & COMPANY, 935
SUSHI PERFORMANCE AND VISUAL ART, 153
TACOMA PERFORMING DANCE COMPANY, 1468
TALLAHASSEE BALLET COMPANY, 365
TANCE DANZ, 166
TANDY BEAL AND COMPANY, 196
TAP-IT DANCING AND THEATRICAL COMPANY, LTD., 1495
TENNESSEE ASSOCIATION OF DANCE, 1282
TENNESSEE CHILDREN'S DANCE ENSEMBLE, 1285
TENNESSEE DANCE THEATRE, 1294
TERRI LEWIS DANCE ENSEMBLE, 139
THEATER ARTAUD, 166
THEATRE BALLET OF SAN FRANCISCO, 166
THEATRE FANTASTIQUE, 1014
THEATRE OF THE RIVERSIDE CHURCH, 936
TNR-MOEBIUS, 103
TOKUNAGA DANCE COMPANY, 936
TOLEDO BALLET SCHOOL, THE, 1147
TOM EVERT DANCE COMPANY, THE, 1132
TOMOV FOLK DANCE ENSEMBLE, 1039
TRISHA BROWN COMPANY, 936
TULSA BALLET THEATRE, 1167
TWYLA THARP DANCE FOUNDATION, 936
UNIVERSITY DANCE COMPANY, 1121
URBAN BUSH WOMEN, 937
USA INTERNATIONAL BALLET COMPETITION, 734
UTAH REGIONAL BALLET, 1395
VALENTINA OUMANSKY DRAMATIC DANCE
     FOUNDATION, 103
VANAVER CARAVAN, THE, 1023
VERMONT BALLET THEATRE, 1410
VICTORIA MARKS PERFORMANCE COMPANY, 937
VIRGINIA BALLET THEATRE, 1431
WASHINGTON BALLET, THE, 298
WENDY ROGERS/CHOREOGRAPHICS, 59
WESTCHESTER BALLET COMPANY, 1013
WESTERN OKLAHOMA BALLET THEATRE, 1159
WHITE MOUNTAIN SUMMER DANCE FESTIVAL, 805
WICHITA FALLS BALLET THEATRE, 1392
WILKES-BARRE BALLET THEATRE, 1242
WILLOW...A DANCE CONCERN, 1496
WISCONSIN DANCE ENSEMBLE, 1511
WORLD DANCE SERIES, 1455
WORLD MUSIC INSTITUTE INC., 937
WORTHINGTON CIVIC BALLET AND JAZZ NORTH DANCE
     COMPANIES, 1122
XIPE TOTEC AZTEC DANCERS/VIRGINIA CARMELO, 55
YUMA BALLET THEATRE, 41
ZAPPED TAPS/ALFRED DESIO, 103
ZE'EVA COHEN AND DANCERS, 937
ZENON DANCE COMPANY AND SCHOOL, INC., 708
ZERO MOVING DANCE COMPANY, 1217
ZIVILI: DANCES AND MUSIC OF THE SOUTH SLAVS, 1133

INSTRUMENTAL MUSIC

ABERDEEN UNIVERSITY CIVIC SYMPHONY, 1267
ABILENE PHILHARMONIC ASSOCIATION, 1303
ADRIAN SYMPHONY ORCHESTRA, 655
AEOLIAN CHAMBER PLAYERS, 938
AFFILIATE ARTISTS INC., 938
AKRON SYMPHONY ORCHESTRA, 1091
AKRON YOUTH SYMPHONY, 1091
ALABAMA SYMPHONY ORCHESTRA, 2
ALBANY SYMPHONY ASSOCIATION, INC., 375
ALBANY SYMPHONY ORCHESTRA, 859
ALBUQUERQUE YOUTH SYMPHONY, 847
ALEA III, 606
ALEXANDRIA BIG BAND, 699
ALLEGHENY CIVIC SYMPHONY, 1211
ALLENTOWN SYMPHONY ASSOCIATION, 1193
ALTON SYMPHONY ORCHESTRA, 419
AMARILLO SYMPHONY, 1305
AMERICAN COMPOSERS ORCHESTRA, 938
AMERICAN MUSICAL ROOTS ASSOCIATION, 891
AMERICAN SYMPHONY ORCHESTRA, 938
AMERICAN SYMPHONY ORCHESTRA LEAGUE, 299
AMERICAN TAP DANCE ORCHESTRA, 939
AMERICAN YOUTH SYMPHONY, 217
AMES TOWN AND GOWN CHAMBER MUSIC
    ASSOCIATION, 507
AMHERST SAXOPHONE QUARTET, 876
ANCHORAGE SYMPHONY ORCHESTRA, 13
ANCHORAGE YOUTH SYMPHONY, 14
ANDERSON SYMPHONY ORCHESTRA, 483
ANN ARBOR SYMPHONY ORCHESTRA, 658
APPLE HILL CENTER FOR CHAMBER MUSIC, 805
ARIOSO WIND QUARTET, 153
ARKANSAS SYMPHONY ORCHESTRA SOCIETY, 48
ARS NOVA MUSICIANS CHAMBER ORCHESTRA, 876
ASHLAND SYMPHONY ORCHESTRA, 1093
ASHMONT HILL CHAMBER MUSIC, 625
ASHTABULA CHAMBER ORCHESTRA, THE, 1094
ASSOCIATION FOR THE ADVANCEMENT OF CREATIVE
    MUSICIANS, NEW YORK CHAPTER, THE, 939
ASTON MAGNA FOUNDATION FOR MUSIC AND THE
    HUMANITIES, INC., 258
ATLANTA CHAMBER PLAYERS, 378
ATLANTA POPS ORCHESTRA, 378
ATLANTA SYMPHONY ORCHESTRA, 378
ATLANTA SYMPHONY YOUTH ORCHESTRA, 378
AUGUSTA SYMPHONY, 573
AUGUSTA SYMPHONY, 388
AURORA SYMPHONY, 223
AUSTIN CHAMBER MUSIC CENTER, 1308
AUSTIN SYMPHONY ORCHESTRA SOCIETY, THE, 1309
BACH SOCIETY OF MINNESOTA, 720
BAKERSFIELD SYMPHONY ORCHESTRA, 57
BALTIMORE CONSORT, 1217
BALTIMORE SYMPHONY ORCHESTRA, 587
BANGOR SYMPHONY ORCHESTRA, 574
BANJO DAN AND THE MID-NITE PLOWBOYS, 1415
BARTLESVILLE SYMPHONY ORCHESTRA, 1158
BATON ROUGE SYMPHONY ORCHESTRA, 555
BATTLE CREEK SYMPHONY ORCHESTRA, 661
B.C. POPS, 865
BEACH CITIES SYMPHONY, 144
BEL CANTO COMPANY, 1057
BELLEVILLE PHILHARMONIC, 420
BERKELEY SYMPHONY ORCHESTRA, 59
BERKSHIRE SYMPHONY, 650
BEVERLY HILLS SYMPHONY, 64
BILLINGS SYMPHONY SOCIETY, 769
BINGHAMTON SYMPHONY ORCHESTRA AND CHORAL
    SOCIETY, 865
BINGHAMTON YOUTH SYMPHONY, 865
BIRMINGHAM-BLOOMFIELD SYMPHONY, 662
BISMARCK-MANDAN ORCHESTRAL ASSOCIATION, 1083
BLACK HILLS SYMPHONY ORCHESTRA, 1271
BLACK MUSIC REPERTORY ENSEMBLE, 426
BLOOMFIELD SYMPHONY ORCHESTRA, 816

BLOOMINGDALE HOUSE OF MUSIC, THE, 939
BLOOMINGTON SYMPHONY ORCHESTRA, 484
BLOOMINGTON-NORMAL SYMPHONY SOCIETY, 420
BOISE PHILHARMONIC, 411
BOSTON BAROQUE, 619
BOSTON CLASSICAL ORCHESTRA, 606
BOSTON MUSICA VIVA, 606
BOSTON PHILHARMONIC, 619
BOSTON POPS, 607
BOSTON SYMPHONY CHAMBER PLAYERS, 607
BOSTON SYMPHONY ORCHESTRA, 607
BOULDER PHILHARMONIC ORCHESTRA, 225
BOWDOIN SUMMER MUSIC FESTIVAL, 907
BOWLING GREEN-WESTERN SYMPHONY ORCHESTRA, 540
BOZEMAN SYMPHONY ORCHESTRA, 770
BRANDEIS UNIVERSITY DEPARTMENT OF MUSIC, 648
BRASS CHAMBER MUSIC SOCIETY OF ANNAPOLIS, 586
BRASS RING, 270
BRAVADO STRING QUARTET, 1147
BRAVO! COLORADO MUSIC FESTIVAL AT VAIL-BEAVER
    CREEK, 253
BRAZOS VALLEY SYMPHONY ORCHESTRA, 1317
BREMERTON SYMPHONY ASSOCIATION, 1447
BRIDGEPORT CIVIC ORCHESTRA, 255
BROCKPORT SYMPHONY ORCHESTRA, 867
BRONX ARTS ENSEMBLE INC., 868
BROOKINGS CHAMBER MUSIC SOCIETY, 1268
BROOKLYN PHILHARMONIC, THE, 871
BROWARD SYMPHONY ORCHESTRA, 344
BROWARD'S FRIENDS OF CHAMBER MUSIC, INC., 354
BUFFALO PHILHARMONIC ORCHESTRA, 876
BURBANK SYMPHONY ASSOCIATION, 66
BUTTE SYMPHONY ASSOCIATION, 771
CALIFORNIA E.A.R. UNIT FOUNDATION, 104
CALIFORNIA YOUTH SYMPHONY, 137
CAMBRIDGE FOLK ORCHESTRA, 617
CAMELLIA SYMPHONY, 148
CAMERATA MUSICA, 1190
CANTON SYMPHONY ORCHESTRA, 1099
CANTON YOUTH SYMPHONY, 1099
CAPE COD SYMPHONY ORCHESTRA, 639
CAPITAL CITY BAND, 1270
CAPITOL CHAMBER ARTISTS, INC., 859
CARNEGIE CHAMBER PLAYERS, 939
CAROLINA PRO MUSICA, 1048
CASCADE SYMPHONY ORCHESTRA, 1448
CASPER CHAMBER MUSIC SOCIETY, 1519
CASPER SYMPHONY ORCHESTRA, 1519
CATHEDRAL CONCERT SERIES, 830
CATSKILL SYMPHONY ORCHESTRA, 1012
CEDAR RAPIDS SYMPHONY ORCHESTRA, 510
CEDARHURST CHAMBER MUSIC, 463
CENTRAL WISCONSIN SYMPHONY ORCHESTRA, 1515
CHAMBER ARTS SOCIETY, 1053
CHAMBER MUSIC AMERICA, 940
CHAMBER MUSIC CONCERTS, 1173
CHAMBER MUSIC HAWAII, 402
CHAMBER MUSIC IN YELLOW SPRINGS, INC., 1152
CHAMBER MUSIC NORTHWEST, 1185
CHAMBER MUSIC OF CHARLOTTE, 1048
CHAMBER MUSIC SOCIETY OF BALTIMORE, 587
CHAMBER MUSIC SOCIETY OF BETHLEHEM, 1196
CHAMBER MUSIC SOCIETY OF GRAND RAPIDS,
    INC., THE, 674
CHAMBER MUSIC SOCIETY OF LINCOLN CENTER, THE, 940
CHAMBER MUSIC SOCIETY OF LOGAN, INC., THE, 1396
CHAMBER MUSIC SOCIETY OF OREGON, THE, 1186
CHAMBER MUSIC SOCIETY OF SAINT CLOUD, INC., 723
CHAMBER MUSIC SOCIETY OF SALT LAKE CITY, 1402
CHAMBER MUSIC SOCIETY OF THE MONTEREY
    PENISULA, 68
CHAMBER MUSIC SOCIETY OF UTICA INC., 882
CHAMBER MUSIC SOUTHWEST, 796
CHAMBER MUSIC WEST FESTIVAL, 167
CHAMBER ORCHESTRA OF ALBUQUERQUE, 848

CHAMPAIGN-URBANA SYMPHONY, 421
CHANTICLEER STRING QUARTET, 501
CHARLESTON CHAMBER MUSIC SOCIETY, 1477
CHARLESTON SYMPHONY ORCHESTRA, 1257
CHARLIE PARKER MEMORIAL FOUNDATION, 745
CHARLIN JAZZ SOCIETY, INC., 299
CHARLOTTE SYMPHONY ORCHESTRA SOCIETY, 1049
CHAUTAUQUA SYMPHONY ORCHESTRA, 881
CHELSEA CHAMBER ENSEMBLE, 940
CHESTNUT BRASS COMPANY, 1218
CHEYENNE SYMPHONY ORCHESTRA, 1520
CHICAGO BAR ASSOCIATION SYMPHONY ORCHESTRA, 426
CHICAGO BRASS QUINTET, 426
CHICAGO CHAMBER ORCHESTRA, THE, 426
CHICAGO PHILHARMONIA, 427
CHICAGO SINFONIETTA, 470
CHICAGO STRING ENSEMBLE, 427
CHICAGO SYMPHONY ORCHESTRA, 427
CHICAGO YOUTH SYMPHONY, 428
CHINA MUSIC PROJECT, THE, 1109
CHINESE CLASSICAL ORCHESTRA, THE, 479
CHINESE MUSIC EDUCATIONAL PROGRAM, 479
CHINESE MUSIC ENSEMBLE OF NEW YORK, INC., THE, 940
CHINESE MUSIC SOCIETY OF NORTH AMERICA, 479
CINCINNATI POPS ORCHESTRA, 1101
CINCINNATI SYMPHONY, 1102
CINCINNATI YOUTH SYMPHONY ORCHESTRA, 1102
CITY SYMPHONY ORCHESTRA OF NEW YORK, INC., 941
CIVIC ORCHESTRA OF CHICAGO, 428
CLARION BRASS QUINTET, THE, 283
CLASSICAL QUARTET, THE, 941
CLEAR LAKE SYMPHONY, 1357
CLEVELAND BAROQUE SOLOISTS, 1144
CLEVELAND CHAMBER MUSIC SOCIETY, 1109
CLEVELAND JAZZ ORCHESTRA, 1110
CLEVELAND OCTET, THE, 1119
CLEVELAND ORCHESTRA, 1110
CLEVELAND PHILHARMONIC ORCHESTRA, 1110
COLEMAN CHAMBER MUSIC ASSOCIATION, 140
COLONIAL SYMPHONY, 823
COLORADO SPRINGS SYMPHONY ORCHESTRA, 229
COLORADO SYMPHONY ORCHESTRA, 235
COLUMBIA YOUTH ORCHESTRA, 1260
COLUMBUS PRO MUSICA, 486
COLUMBUS SYMPHONY ORCHESTRA, 389, 1122
COLUMBUS SYMPHONY YOUTH ORCHESTRA, 1122
CONCENTUS MUSICUS, 708
CONCERTIME, 1168
CONCERTO AMABILE, 60
CONCERTO SOLOISTS, 1218
CONCORD BAND, THE, 623
CONCORD ORCHESTRA, 623
CONCORDIA, 941
CONEJO SYMPHONY ORCHESTRA, 208
CONNECTICUT STRING ORCHESTRA, INC., 287
CONTEMPORARY MUSIC FORUM, 299
CONTINUUM (THE PERFORMERS' COMMITTEE INC.), 941
CORNING PHILHARMONIC SOCIETY, 884
CORPUS CHRISTI CHAMBER MUSIC SOCIETY, INC., 1320
CORPUS CHRISTI SYMPHONY, 1321
COSMOPOLITAN SYMPHONY ORCHESTRA, 942
CRAFTSBURY CHAMBER PLAYERS, 1413
CREATIVE OPPORTUNITY ORCHESTRA, 1277
CROATIAN TAMBURITZA ORCHESTRA OF
    CLEVELAND, 1133
CUMBERLAND COUNTY FRIENDS OF THE ORCHESTRA, 1055
DA CAPO CHAMBER PLAYERS, INCORPORATED, 942
DA VINCI QUARTET, 229
DALLAS BACH SOCIETY, 1324
DALLAS BRASS, 1351
DALLAS CHAMBER ORCHESTRA, 1324
DALLAS CLASSIC GUITAR SOCIETY, 1325
DALLAS SYMPHONY ASSOCIATION, INC., 1325
DALLAS SYMPHONY ORCHESTRA, 1325
DANBURY MUSIC CENTRE, INC., 258
DANVILLE SYMPHONY ORCHESTRA, 448
DAYTON PHILHARMONIC ORCHESTRA ASSOCIATION, 1129
DAYTON PHILHARMONIC YOUTH ORCHESTRA, 1129

DAYTONA BEACH SYMPHONY SOCIETY, 320
D.C. YOUTH ORCHESTRA PROGRAM, INC., 300
DEL-SE-NANGO OLDE TYME FIDDLERS ASSOCIATION,
    INC., 907
DELAWARE SYMPHONY ASSOCIATION, 293
DENVER CHAMBER ORCHESTRA, 235
DENVER MUNICIPAL BAND, 236
DES MOINES SYMPHONY, 514
DETROIT CHAMBER WINDS, 695
DETROIT JAZZ ORCHESTRA, 667
DETROIT SYMPHONY ORCHESTRA, 667
DEVILS LAKE COMMUNITY ORCHESTRA, 1083
DIABLO SYMPHONY ORCHESTRA, THE, 215
DICKINSON THEATRE ORGAN SOCIETY, 293
DINOSAUR ANNEX MUSIC ENSEMBLE, 607
DOCTORS' ORCHESTRAL SOCIETY OF NEW YORK, THE, 942
DOWNEY SYMPHONIC SOCIETY, 77
DOWNTOWN MUSIC PRODUCTIONS, 943
DUBUQUE SYMPHONY ORCHESTRA, 515
DULUTH-SUPERIOR SYMPHONY ORCHESTRA, 702
DULUTH-SUPERIOR YOUTH ORCHESTRA AND
    SINFONIA, 702
DUPAGE SYMPHONY, 456
DUQUESNE UNIVERSITY TAMBURITZANS, 1230
EARLY MUSIC AMERICA, INC., 943
EARLY MUSIC CENTER, THE, 1152
EARLY MUSIC GUILD OF SEATTLE, 1455
EARLY MUSIC NOW, 1504
EARPLAY, 135
EARTHLY PLEASURES, 1326
EAST TEXAS SYMPHONY ORCHESTRA, 1390
EASTERN BRASS QUINTET, 261
EASTERN CONNECTICUT SYMPHONY, 273
EL CAMINO COLLEGE - COMMUNITY ORCHESTRA, 209
EL PASO PRO-MUSICA, 1341
EL PASO SYMPHONY ORCHESTRA, 1341
ELGIN AREA YOUTH ORCHESTRA, 452
ELGIN SYMPHONY ORCHESTRA, 452
ELKIN BIG BAND, 1054
ELMIRA SYMPHONY AND CHORAL SOCIETY, 888
EMERALD CHAMBER PLAYERS, 1178
ENID-PHILLIPS SYMPHONY ORCHESTRA, 1160
ENSEMBLE MUSIC SOCIETY, THE, 494
ENSEMBLE OF SANTA FE, THE, 853
ERIE PHILHARMONIC, 1201
EUGENE SYMPHONY, 1179
EVANSVILLE PHILHARMONIC ORCHESTRA, 488
EXPERIMENTAL INTERMEDIA FOUNDATION, 943
FAIRBANKS SYMPHONY ASSOCIATION, 18
FAIRFAX SYMPHONY ORCHESTRA, 1422
FAIRFIELD ORCHESTRA, THE, 269
FAIRMONT CHAMBER MUSIC SOCIETY, INC., 1480
FARGO-MOORHEAD ORCHESTRAL ASSOCIATION, 1084
FARGO-MOORHEAD SYMPHONY ORCHESTRA, 1084
FINE ARTS CHAMBER PLAYERS, 1326
FLAGSTAFF SYMPHONY ORCHESTRA, 26
FLINT SYMPHONY ORCHESTRA, 672
FLORIDA BRASS QUINTET, 358
FLORIDA ORCHESTRA, THE, 367
FLORIDA SYMPHONY ORCHESTRA, 349
FLORIDA WEST COAST CHAMBER ORCHESTRA, 359
FLORIDA WEST COAST SYMPHONY ORCHESTRA, 359
FLORIDA WEST COAST YOUTH ORCHESTRAS, 359
FLORIDA WIND QUINTET, 360
FLUTE FORCE, 943
FOND DU LAC SYMPHONIC BAND, 1490
FORT COLLINS SYMPHONY ORCHESTRA, 245
FORT DODGE AREA SYMPHONY ORCHESTRA, 517
FORT SMITH SYMPHONY, 46
FORT WAYNE PHILHARMONIC ORCHESTRA, 490
FORT WORTH SYMPHONY, 1344
451ST ARMY BAND, 724
FOX VALLEY SYMPHONY, 1501
FREDONIA CHAMBER PLAYERS, 890
FREMONT-NEWARK PHILHARMONIC, 80
FRESNO PHILHARMONIC ASSOCIATION, 81
FRESNO PHILHARMONIC ORCHESTRA, 81
FRIENDS OF CHAMBER MUSIC, 236, 1177

FRIENDS OF CHAMBER MUSIC KANSAS CITY, 745
FRIENDS OF MUSIC OF WAYNE, INC., 842
FRIENDS OF MUSIC ORCHESTRA AT SAINT MICHAEL'S, 891
GAINESVILLE SYMPHONY ORCHESTRA, THE, 393
GARDEN STATE PHILHARMONIC SYMPHONY
    ORCHESTRA, 839
GARDEN STATE PHILHARMONIC YOUTH ORCHESTRA, 839
GARLAND SYMPHONY ORCHESTRA, 1351
GENESEO CHAMBER SYMPHONY, 892
GETTYSBURG SYMPHONY ORCHESTRA, 587
GLACIER ORCHESTRA, 775
GLENDALE SYMPHONY, 85
GO FOR BAROQUE, 1164
GOLIARD CHAMBER SOLOISTS, 862
GRAND CANYON CHAMBER MUSIC FESTIVAL, 27
GRAND JUNCTION MUSICAL ARTS ASSOCIATION, 247
GRAND RAPIDS SYMPHONY ORCHESTRA, 674
GRAND RAPIDS YOUTH SYMPHONY, 675
GRANITE YOUTH SYMPHONY, 1402
GREAT FALLS SYMPHONY ASSOCIATION, 772
GREATER BOSTON YOUTH SYMPHONY ORCHESTRAS, 608
GREATER BRIDGEPORT SYMPHONY, 256
GREATER BRIDGEPORT SYMPHONY YOUTH
    ORCHESTRA, 260
GREATER DALLAS YOUTH ORCHESTRA ASSOCIATION, 1326
GREATER FALL RIVER SYMPHONY SOCIETY, 626
GREATER LANSING SYMPHONY ORCHESTRA, 683
GREATER MIAMI MERRY MUMMERS STRING BAND, 341
GREATER PALM BEACH SYMPHONY, 351
GREATER TRENTON SYMPHONY ORCHESTRA, 840
GREATER TWIN CITIES YOUTH SYMPHONIES, 709
GREECE SYMPHONY ORCHESTRA, 1019
GREEN BAY SYMPHONY ORCHESTRA, 1491
GREENSBORO CONCERT BAND, 1057
GREENSBORO SYMPHONY ORCHESTRA, 1058
GREENVILLE SYMPHONY ASSOCIATION, 1263
GREENVILLE SYMPHONY SOCIETY, 1203
GREENWICH SYMPHONY ORCHESTRA, 260
GULF COAST SYMPHONY, 733
HADDONFIELD SYMPHONY, 821
HANDEL AND HAYDN SOCIETY, 608
HARRISBURG SYMPHONY ASSOCIATION, 1204
HARRISBURG YOUTH SYMPHONY ORCHESTRA, 1204
HARTFORD JAZZ SOCIETY, 255
HARTFORD SYMPHONY ORCHESTRA INC., THE, 262
HASTINGS SYMPHONY ORCHESTRA, 782
HAWAII CHAMBER ORCHESTRA, 403
HAWAII CONCERT SOCIETY, 401
HAWAII YOUTH SYMPHONY ASSOCIATION, 403
HAYS SYMPHONY ORCHESTRA, 527
HEIGHTS CHAMBER ORCHESTRA, 1119
HELENA SYMPHONY SOCIETY, 773
HERITAGE BRASS QUINTET, THE, 1141
HESPERUS, 1423
HEXAGON, 1411
HIBBING COLLEGE - COMMUNITY BAND, 705
HIGHLAND BRITISH BRASS BAND ASSOCIATION, 1055
HIGHLIGHTS IN JAZZ, 944
HOMEMADE JAM, 773
HONOLULU SYMPHONY SOCIETY, 403
HOPE COLLEGE ORCHESTRA AND SYMPHONETTE, 677
HORIZON CONCERTS INC., 944
HOTFOOT QUARTET, 1145
HOUSTON CIVIC SYMPHONY ORCHESTRA, 1357
HOUSTON FRIENDS OF MUSIC, 1358
HOUSTON HARPSICHORD SOCIETY, 1358
HOUSTON SYMPHONY, 1358
HOWARD HANGER JAZZ FANTASY, 1043
HUDSON VALLEY PHILHARMONIC, 1017
HUNTINGTON CHAMBER ORCHESTRA, 1480
HUNTSVILLE SYMPHONY ORCHESTRA, 6
HUNTSVILLE YOUTH ORCHESTRA, 6
HURON MUNICIPAL BAND, 1269
HUTCHINSON SYMPHONY, 528
IDAHO FALLS SYMPHONY, 413
ILLINOIS CHAMBER SYMPHONY, 473
ILLINOIS PHILHARMONIC ORCHESTRA ASSOCIATION, 466
IMPERIAL SYMPHONY, 335

IMPROVISATIONALMUSICCO, INC., 1193
INDIANA JAZZ, 495
INDIANAPOLIS SYMPHONY ORCHESTRA, 495
INLAND EMPIRE SYMPHONY ASSOCIATION, 151
INTERNATIONAL ASSOCIATION OF JAZZ
    APPRECIATION, THE, 104
INTERNATIONAL CREATIVE MUSIC ORCHESTRA, 167
INTERNATIONAL MUSIC CAMP, 1087
INTERNATIONAL SYMPHONY ORCHESTRA OF SARNIA
    AND PORT HURON, 689
IRVING SYMPHONY ORCHESTRA, 1369
JACKSON SYMPHONY ASSOCIATION, 1281
JACKSON SYMPHONY YOUTH ORCHESTRA, 734
JACKSONVILLE SYMPHONY ORCHESTRA, 331
JAMES E. BUFFAN GOLD COAST BAND, THE, 316
JAMESTOWN CONCERT ASSOCIATION, 900
JAZZ ARTS GROUP OF COLUMBUS, THE, 1123
JAZZ COMPOSERS ALLIANCE, 617
JAZZ REVIVAL ORCHESTRA, THE, 1150
JEFFERSON SYMPHONY ORCHESTRA, 247
JOHN PAULSON JAZZ QUARTET, 729
JOHNSTOWN SYMPHONY ORCHESTRA, 1208
JUPITER SYMPHONY, 944
KALAMAZOO JUNIOR SYMPHONY SOCIETY, THE, 680
KALAMAZOO SYMPHONY ORCHESTRA, 680
KANSAS CITY SYMPHONY, 746
KANSAS UNIVERSITY SYMPHONY ORCHESTRA, 529
KENOSHA SYMPHONY ASSOCIATION, INC., 1492
KENTUCKY CENTER CHAMBER PLAYERS, 547
KENWOOD CHAMBER ORCHESTRA, THE, 709
KINGSPORT SYMPHONY ORCHESTRA, 1283
KLEZMER CONSERVATORY BAND, 619
KNOX GALESBURG SYMPHONY, 456
KNOXVILLE SYMPHONY ORCHESTRA, 1285
KNOXVILLE SYMPHONY YOUTH ORCHESTRA, 1285
KOKOMO SYMPHONY, 498
"KOROYAR" FOLKLORE ENSEMBLE, 104
KRONOS QUARTET, 167
LA CROSSE SYMPHONY ORCHESTRA, 1493
LA FAMILLE BEAUDOIN - FAMILY GROUP, 1411
LA JOLLA CHAMBER MUSIC SOCIETY, 93
LAFAYETTE CONCERT BAND, 558
LAFAYETTE SYMPHONY, 499
LAGUNA CHAMBER MUSIC SOCIETY, 96
LAKE FOREST SYMPHONY ASSOCIATION, INC., 460
LAKE SAINT CLAIR SYMPHONY ORCHESTRA, 692
LAKESIDE SYMPHONY, 1134
LAREDO PHILHARMONIC ORCHESTRA, 1371
LARK SOCIETY FOR CHAMBER MUSIC, 581
LAWTON PHILHARMONIC ORCHESTRA, 1160
LEHIGH VALLEY CHAMBER ORCHESTRA, 1210
LENNOX MUNICIPAL BAND, 1269
L'ENSEMBLE DU MUSIQUE, 880
LEXINGTON PHILHARMONIC SOCIETY, 544
LILLIPUT ORCHESTRA, 1477
LIMA SYMPHONY ORCHESTRA, 1136
LINCOLN CIVIC EXPERIENCE/LINCOLN CIVIC
    ORCHESTRA, 784
LINCOLN SYMPHONY, 785
LINCOLN YOUTH SYMPHONY ORCHESTRA, 785
LITTLE ORCHESTRA SOCIETY OF NEW YORK, THE, 944
LONG BEACH SYMPHONY ORCHESTRA, 97
LONG ISLAND BAROQUE ENSEMBLE, 905
LONG ISLAND PHILHARMONIC, 906
LONGVIEW SYMPHONY ORCHESTRA, 1372
LOS ANGELES CHAMBER ORCHESTRA, 105
LOS ANGELES DOCTORS SYMPHONY, 64
LOS ANGELES PHILHARMONIC ASSOCIATION, 105
LOUISIANA JAZZ FEDERATION, 563
LOUISVILLE BACH SOCIETY, 547
LOUISVILLE ORCHESTRA, THE, 547
LOUISVILLE YOUTH ORCHESTRA, 547
LUBBOCK SYMPHONY ORCHESTRA, 1372
LYRIC CHAMBER ENSEMBLE, 693
MACON SYMPHONY ORCHESTRA, INCORPORATED, 393
MADISON JAZZ SOCIETY, 1496
MADISON MUSIC COLLECTIVE, 1496
MADISON SYMPHONY ORCHESTRA, 1496

MAELSTROM PERCUSSION ENSEMBLE, LTD., 877
MAGIC VALLEY SYMPHONY, 418
MANCHESTER PIPE BAND, 279
MANCHESTER SYMPHONY ORCHESTRA/CHORALE, 266
MANHATTAN MARIMBA QUARTET, 871
MANKATO SYMPHONY ORCHESTRA, 706
MANSFIELD SYMPHONY SOCIETY, INC., 1138
MARIETTA COLLEGE/CIVIC SYMPHONETTE, 1139
MARIN COMMUNITY COLLEGE SYMPHONY, 92
MARIN SYMPHONY ASSOCIATION, 191
MARIN SYMPHONY YOUTH ORCHESTRA, 191
MARION PHILHARMONIC ORCHESTRA, 500
MARLBORO SCHOOL OF MUSIC, 1218
MARSHALL PHILHARMONIC ORCHESTRA, 750
MARSHALL SYMPHONY ORCHESTRA, 1374
MARSHFIELD-WOOD COMMUNITY SYMPHONY, 1500
MARYLAND SYMPHONY ORCHESTRA, 595
MASSACHUSETTS YOUTH WIND ENSEMBLE, 608
MAUI SYMPHONY ORCHESTRA, 408
MAVERICK CONCERTS, INC., 1039
MCHENRY COUNTY YOUTH ORCHESTRA, 448
MEET THE COMPOSER INC., 945
MELBOURNE CHAMBER MUSIC SOCIETY, 330
MELROSE ORCHESTRAL ASSOCIATION, 633
MEMPHIS SYMPHONY, 1289
MEMPHIS YOUTH SYMPHONY ORCHESTRA, 1289
MESQUITE COMMUNITY BAND, 1376
METROPOLITAN ORCHESTRA OF SAINT LOUIS, 755
MIAMI CHAMBER SYMPHONY, 341
MIAMI WIND QUINTET, 1144
MID-COLUMBIA SYMPHONY, 1452
MIDLAND SYMPHONY ORCHESTRA, 684
MIDLAND-ODESSA SYMPHONY AND CHORALE, INC., 1377
MILL VALLEY CHAMBER MUSIC SOCIETY, 123
MILWAUKEE CHAMBER ORCHESTRA, 1504
MILWAUKEE SYMPHONY ORCHESTRA, 1505
MILWAUKEE YOUTH SYMPHONY ORCHESTRA, 1505
MINNEAPOLIS CHAMBER SYMPHONY, 709
MINNEAPOLIS POPS ORCHESTRA, 709
MINNESOTA ORCHESTRAL ASSOCIATION, 710
MINNESOTA STATE BAND, 724
MINNESOTA YOUTH SYMPHONIES, 710
MINOT SYMPHONY ASSOCIATION, 1087
MISSISSIPPI SYMPHONY ORCHESTRA, 734
MISSOULA SYMPHONY ASSOCIATION, 776
MISSOURI SYMPHONY SOCIETY, 743
MITCHELL MUNICIPAL BAND, 1270
MODESTO SYMPHONY, 124
MONROE SYMPHONY ORCHESTRA, 562
MONTCLAIRE STRING QUARTET, 1477
MONTEREY COUNTY SYMPHONY, 69
MONTGOMERY SYMPHONY ORCHESTRA, 10
MOORE COMMUNITY BAND, 1045
MOZART FESTIVAL ORCHESTRA, 945
MUNCIE SYMPHONY ORCHESTRA, 500
MUSIC ACADEMY OF THE WEST, 193
MUSIC BEFORE 1800, INC., 945
MUSIC FROM ANGEL FIRE, 851
MUSIC FROM STAN HYWET, 1092
MUSIC IN DEERFIELD, 624
MUSIC OF THE BAROQUE, 428
MUSIC PROJECTS HONOLULU, 403
MUSIC SOCIETY, MIDLAND CENTER FOR THE ARTS, 685
MUSICA ANTIGUA DE ALBUQUERQUE, 848
MUSICA DE CAMARA, INC., 945
NAPA VALLEY SYMPHONY, 126
NASHVILLE SYMPHONY ASSOCIATION, 1295
NASHVILLE YOUTH SYMPHONY, 1295
NASSAU SYMPHONY SOCIETY, INC., 1035
NATIONAL CHAMBER ORCHESTRA SOCIETY, INC., 597
NATIONAL GALLERY ORCHESTRA, 300
NATIONAL MUSICAL ARTS, 300
NATIONAL ORCHESTRAL ASSOCIATION INC., 946
NATIONAL REPERTORY ORCHESTRA, 236
NATIONAL SYMPHONY ORCHESTRA ASSOCIATION, 300
NEBRASKA CHAMBER ORCHESTRA, 785
NEBRASKA WIND SYMPHONY, 788
NEVADA SYMPHONY ORCHESTRA, 796

NEVERS' 2ND REGIMENT BAND, 803
NEW ARTISTS PIANO QUARTET, 360
NEW ARTISTS STRING QUARTET, 360
NEW BRITAIN SYMPHONY ORCHESTRA, 268
NEW CENTURY PLAYERS, 211
NEW ENGLAND PHILHARMONIC, 619
NEW HAMPSHIRE PHILHARMONIC ORCHESTRA, 807
NEW HAMPSHIRE SYMPHONY ORCHESTRA, 808
NEW HAVEN CIVIC ORCHESTRA, 270
NEW HAVEN SYMPHONY ORCHESTRA, 271
NEW JERSEY CHAMBER MUSIC SOCIETY, 826
NEW JERSEY SYMPHONY ORCHESTRA, 831
NEW MEXICO SYMPHONY ORCHESTRA, 848
NEW MUSIC CONSORT, INC., 946
NEW ORCHESTRA OF WESTCHESTER, THE, 895
NEW ORLEANS CONCERT BAND, 564
NEW ORLEANS FRIENDS OF MUSIC, 564
NEW SONG QUINTET (PROJECT), THE, 946
NEW WORLD SYMPHONY, 344
NEW YORK CHAMBER ENSEMBLE, 946
NEW YORK CONSORT OF VIOLS, 946
NEW YORK HARP ENSEMBLE, 947
NEW YORK NEW MUSIC ENSEMBLE, 947
NEW YORK PHILHARMONIC, 947
NEW YORK PHILOMUSICA CHAMBER ENSEMBLE, 948
NEW YORK POPS ORCHESTRA, 948
NEW YORK YOUTH SYMPHONY, 948
NEW YORK'S ENSEMBLE FOR EARLY MUSIC, 948
NEWARK SYMPHONY ORCHESTRA, 292
NEWTON SYMPHONY ORCHESTRA, 636
NORFOLK CHAMBER CONSORT, 1431
NORTH CAROLINA SYMPHONY, 1068
NORTH COUNTRY CHAMBER PLAYERS, 805
NORTH LAKE TAHOE SYMPHONY ASSOCIATION, 795
NORTH SHORE PHILHARMONIC ORCHESTRA, 632
NORTH/SOUTH CONSONANCE, INC., 949
NORTHEASTERN PENNSYLVANIA PHILHARMONIC, 1195
NORTHWEST CHAMBER ORCHESTRA, 1455
NORTHWEST INDIANA SYMPHONY SOCIETY, 500
NORTHWEST SYMPHONIC POPS ORCHESTRA, 338
NORTHWEST SYMPHONY ORCHESTRA, 451
NORTHWOOD ORCHESTRA, 685
NORWALK SYMPHONY SOCIETY, 276
NORWALK YOUTH SYMPHONY, 276
OAK RIDGE SYMPHONY ORCHESTRA, 1299
OBERLIN BAROQUE ENSEMBLE, 1143
ODYSSEY CHAMBER PLAYERS, INC., 949
OHIO CHAMBER ORCHESTRA, 1111
OHIO VALLEY BRASS QUINTET, 1137
OKLAHOMA CITY PHILHARMONIC ORCHESTRA, 1164
OLYMPIA SYMPHONY ORCHESTRA, 1452
OMAHA AREA YOUTH ORCHESTRAS, 789
OMAHA SYMPHONY ASSOCIATION, 789
ONE O'CLOCK LAB BAND, 1338
ORANGE COUNTY PHILHARMONIC SOCIETY, 91
ORANGE COUNTY SYMPHONY, 84
ORCHESTRA NEW ENGLAND, 271
ORCHESTRA OF SAINT LUKE'S, 949
ORCHESTRA OF SANTA FE, 854
OREGON MOZART PLAYERS, 1179
OREGON SYMPHONY ASSOCIATION, 1191
OREGON SYMPHONY ORCHESTRA, 1186
ORPHEUS CHAMBER ORCHESTRA, INC., 950
OSHKOSH SYMPHONY ORCHESTRA, 1511
OTTER TAIL VALLEY COMMUNITY ORCHESTRA, 704
OWENSBORO SYMPHONY ORCHESTRA, 551
PACIFIC SYMPHONY ASSOCIATION, 91
PACIFIC UNIVERSITY COMMUNITY ORCHESTRA, 1181
PADDYWHACK, 1074
PALISADES SYMPHONY ORCHESTRA, 135
PASADENA SYMPHONY, 140
PENSACOLA SYMPHONY ORCHESTRA, 352
PEORIA SYMPHONY ORCHESTRA, 467
PERFORMING ARTS CHICAGO, 429
PHILADELPHIA CHAMBER MUSIC SOCIETY, 1218
PHILADELPHIA ORCHESTRA ASSOCIATION, 1219
PHILADELPHIA RENAISSANCE WIND BAND, 1219
PHILADELPHIA STRING QUARTET, 1455

PHILADELPHIA YOUTH ORCHESTRA, 1219
PHILADELPHOIA RENAISSANCE WIND BAND, 1220
PHILHARMONIA BAROQUE ORCHESTRA, 167
PHILHARMONIA VIRTUOSI CORPORATION, 886
PHILHARMONIC ORCHESTRA OF FLORIDA, 323
PHILHARMONIC ORCHESTRA OF INDIANAPOLIS, 495
PHILHARMONIC ORCHESTRA OF NEW JERSEY, 842
PHOENIX CHAMBER MUSIC SOCIETY, 29
PHOENIX SYMPHONY, 29
PHOENIX SYMPHONY YOUTH ORCHESTRA, 29
PITTSBURGH CHAMBER MUSIC SOCIETY, 1230
PITTSBURGH NEW MUSIC ENSEMBLE, THE, 1231
PITTSBURGH SYMPHONY ORCHESTRA, 1231
PITTSBURGH YOUTH SYMPHONY ORCHESTRA
    ASSOCIATION, INC., 1231
PLYMOUTH PHILHARMONIC ORCHESTRA, 640
PONTIAC-OAKLAND SYMPHONY, 688
PORTLAND FESTIVAL SYMPHONY, 1182
PORTLAND SYMPHONY ORCHESTRA, 582
PORTLAND YOUTH PHILHARMONIC ASSOCIATION, 1186
PRESENT MUSIC, INCORPORATED, 1505
PRO ARTE CHAMBER ORCHESTRA, 620
PRO MUSICA CHAMBER ORCHESTRA OF COLUMBUS, 1123
PUEBLO SYMPHONY ORCHESTRA, 251
PUGET SOUND CHAMBER MUSIC SOCIETY, 1456
QUAD CITY SYMPHONY ORCHESTRA, 511
QUAD CITY YOUTH SYMPHONY ORCHESTRA, 512
QUEENS SYMPHONY ORCHESTRA, 1019
QUINCY SYMPHONY ORCHESTRA, 469
QUINTET OF THE AMERICAS, 950
RACINE SYMPHONY ORCHESTRA, 1513
READING SYMPHONY ORCHESTRA, 1236
RED HACKLE PIPE BAND, 18
RELACHE ENSEMBLE, 1220
RENAISSANCE AND BAROQUE SOCIETY OF
    PITTSBURGH, 1232
RENO CHAMBER ORCHESTRA, 798
RHODE ISLAND PHILHARMONIC ORCHESTRA, 1248
RICHMOND SYMPHONY, 1436
RICHMOND SYMPHONY ORCHESTRA, 502
RIDGEFIELD SYMPHONY ORCHESTRA, 277
RIDGEWOOD SYMPHONY ORCHESTRA, 836
RIO HONDO SYMPHONY ASSOCIATION, 217
RIVER CITY BRASS BAND, 1232
RIVERSIDE COUNTY PHILHARMONIC, 145
RIVERSIDE SYMPHONY, THE, 950
ROANOKE SYMPHONY SOCIETY, 1439
ROANOKE VALLEY CHAMBER MUSIC SOCIETY, 1438 - 1439
ROCHESTER CHAMBER ORCHESTRA, 1020
ROCHESTER CIVIC MUSIC, 721
ROCHESTER PHILHARMONIC ORCHESTRA, 1020
ROCHESTER SYMPHONY ORCHESTRA, 721
ROCKFORD SYMPHONY ORCHESTRA, 472
ROCKPORT CHAMBER MUSIC FESTIVAL, 641
ROCKY MOUNTAIN BRASSWORKS, 221
ROSALIE GERUT AND FRIENDS, 633
ROSCOE'S SURPRISE ORCHESTRA, 1289
ROSEWOOD CHAMBER ENSEMBLE, INC., 1030
ROULETTE INTERMEDIUM, INC., 950
ROXBURY CHAMBER PLAYERS, 1437
SACRAMENTO SYMPHONY ASSOCIATION, 148
SAGINAW SYMPHONY ORCHESTRA, 691
SAGINAW SYMPHONY SCHOOL OF MUSIC AND YOUTH
    ORCHESTRA, 691
SAINT JOSEPH SYMPHONY SOCIETY, THE, 753
SAINT LOUIS PHILHARMONIC ORCHESTRA, 756
SAINT LOUIS SYMPHONY CHAMBER ORCHESTRA, 756
SAINT LOUIS SYMPHONY ORCHESTRA, 756
SAINT LOUIS SYMPHONY YOUTH ORCHESTRA, 757
SAINT LUKES CHAMBER ENSEMBLE, INC., 951
SAINT PAUL CHAMBER ORCHESTRA, THE, 724
SALISBURY SYMPHONY ORCHESTRA, 1072
SAN ANGELO SYMPHONY ORCHESTRA AND CHORALE, 1381
SAN ANTONIO CHAMBER MUSIC SOCIETY, 1383
SAN ANTONIO SYMPHONY, 1383
SAN DIEGO CHAMBER ORCHESTRA, 142
SAN DIEGO SYMPHONY ORCHESTRA, 154
SAN DIEGO YOUTH SYMPHONY, 154

SAN FRANCISCO CONSERVATORY OF MUSIC, 168
SAN FRANCISCO CONTEMPORARY MUSIC PLAYERS, 168
SAN FRANCISCO EARLY MUSIC SOCIETY, 60
SAN FRANCISCO SYMPHONY ORCHESTRA, 168
SAN FRANCISCO SYMPHONY YOUTH ORCHESTRA, 168
SAN JOSE SYMPHONY, 185
SAN JOSE TAIKO GROUP, 185
SAN LUIS OBISPO COUNTY SYMPHONY, 189
SANTA BARBARA SYMPHONY ORCHESTRA, 193
SANTA CRUZ BRASS QUINTET, 196
SANTA CRUZ COUNTY SYMPHONY, 197
SANTA FE SYMPHONY, 854
SANTA MARIA SYMPHONY SOCIETY, 198
SANTA ROSA SYMPHONY, 200
SARASOTA-MANATEE COMMUNITY ORCHESTRA, 337
SATURDAY BRASS QUNITET, 951
SAVANNAH SYMPHONY, 396
SCOTT HARRIS BIG BAND, THE, 197
SCOTT JOPLIN RAGTIME FESTIVAL, 763
SCOTTSDALE SYMPHONY ORCHESTRA, 33
SEA CLIFF CHAMBER PLAYERS, THE, 1027
SEATTLE CHAMBER MUSIC FESTIVAL, 1456
SEATTLE SYMPHONY ORCHESTRA, 1456
SEATTLE YOUTH SYMPHONY ORCHESTRA, 1456
SEAVER COLLEGE COMMUNITY SYMPHONY, 121
S.E.M. ENSEMBLE, 871
SEWANEE SUMMER MUSIC CENTER, 1300
SHAKER SYMPHONY ORCHESTRA, 1119
SHAKER SYMPHONY ORCHESTRA, THE, 1140
SHASTA SYMPHONY, 142
SHEBOYGAN SYMPHONY ORCHESTRA, 1514
SHERMAN SYMPHONY ORCHESTRA, 1388
SHIRIM KLEZMER ORCHESTRA, 608
SHREVEPORT SYMPHONY ORCHESTRA, 569
SIERRA WIND QUINTET, 797
SILK AND BAMBOO ENSEMBLE, THE, 480
SIOUX CITY SYMPHONY ORCHESTRA, 520
SIOUX FALLS MUNICIPAL BAND, 1272
SISKIYOU BAROQUE ENSEMBLE, 1177
SMOKY MOUNTAIN BRITISH BRASS, 1052
SOLID BRASS, 817
SOUNDSCAPES, 230
SOUTH ARKANSAS SYMPHONY, 43
SOUTH BEND SYMPHONY, 503
SOUTH CAROLINA PHILHARMONIC AND CHAMBER
    ORCHESTRAS, 1260
SOUTH COAST SYMPHONY, 192
SOUTH DAKOTA STATE UNIVERSITY CIVIC
    SYMPHONY, 1268
SOUTH DAKOTA SYMPHONY, 1273
SOUTH FLORIDA YOUTH SYMPHONY, 341
SOUTH JERSEY SYMPHONY ORCHESTRA, 833
SOUTH TEXAS SYMPHONY ASSOCIATION, 1339
SOUTHEAST IOWA SYMPHONY ORCHESTRA, 519
SOUTHWEST MICHIGAN SYMPHONY ORCHESTRA, 693
SOUTHWEST SYMPHONY ORCHESTRA, 1400
SPECULUM MUSICAE, INC., 951
SPOKANE SYMPHONY ORCHESTRA, 1466
SPRING WIND QUARTET, 404
SPRINGFIELD ORCHESTRA ASSOCIATION, 645
SPRINGFIELD SYMPHONY ASSOCIATION, 765
SPRINGFIELD SYMPHONY ORCHESTRA, 475, 1145
STAMFORD SYMPHONY ORCHESTRA, 280
STAN MCDONALD'S BLUE HORIZON JAZZ BAND, 643
STOCKTON SYMPHONY ASSOCIATION, 205
STREET MINSTRELS JAZZ SOCIETY, 429
STRING ORCHESTRA OF THE ROCKIES, 776
SUBURBAN SYMPHONY ORCHESTRA, 1096
SUMMER STRINGS ON THE MEHERRIN, 1060
SUMMIT SYMPHONY, 838
SUN CITIES CHAMBER MUSIC SOCIETY, 35
SYLVAN WINDS, INCORPORATED, 951
SYMPHONY FOR UNITED NATIONS, 951
SYMPHONY OF SOUTHEAST TEXAS, 1313
SYMPHONY SOCIETY OF NORTH ARKANSAS, 45
SYNCHRONIA, 757
SYRACUSE SOCIETY FOR NEW MUSIC, 1031
SYRACUSE SYMPHONY ORCHESTRA, 1031

SYRACUSE SYMPHONY YOUTH ORCHESTRA, 1031
TACOMA CONCERT BAND, 1469
TACOMA PHILHARMONIC, 1469
TACOMA SYMPHONY ORCHESTRA, 1469
TACOMA YOUTH SYMPHONY, 1470
TALLAHASSEE SYMPHONY ORCHESTRA, 365
TAMPA BAY CHAMBER ORCHESTRA, 367
TERRE HAUTE SYMPHONY ORCHESTRA, 504
TEXAS BAROQUE ENSEMBLE, 1352
THAYER SYMPHONY ORCHESTRA, 644
TOLEDO SYMPHONY, THE, 1147
TOP BRASS QUARTET, THE, 1130
THE. ART. RE. GRUP, INC./THE LAB, 169
THEATER CHAMBER PLAYERS OF THE KENNEDY
    CENTER, 301
THEATRE CHAMBER PLAYERS OF THE KENNEDY
    CENTER, 301
TISCH CENTER FOR THE ARTS, 952
TOCCOA SYMPHONY ORCHESTRA GUILD, 399
TOLEDO JAZZ SOCIETY, 1147
TOPEKA JAZZ WORKSHOP, 534
TRAVERSE SYMPHONY ORCHESTRA, 694
TREMONT STRING QUARTET, INC., 892
TRINKLE BRASS WORKS, 1064
TROY CHROMATICS CONCERTS, INC., 1034
TUCSON JAZZ SOCIETY, INC., 36
TUCSON SYMPHONY ORCHESTRA, 36
TUESDAY EVENING CONCERT SERIES, 1425
TULARE COUNTY SYMPHONY ORCHESTRA, 214
TULSA PHILHARMONIC, 1168
TULSA YOUTH SYMPHONY ORCHESTRA, 1168
TUPELO SYMPHONY, 738
TUSCARAWAS PHILHARMONIC, 1141
TWENTIETH CENTURY CONSORI, 1423
UMPQUA SYMPHONY ASSOCIATION, 1190
UNION SYMPHONY ORCHESTRA, 1066
UNITED STATES AIR FORCE BAND, THE, 301
UNIVERSITY CIRCLE CHAMBER ORCHESTRA, 1111
UNIVERSITY OF HAWAII AT MANOA, COLLEGE OF
    CONTINUING EDUCATION AND COMMUNITY
    SERVICE, 404
UTAH CLASSICAL GUITAR SOCIETY, 1398
UTAH SYMPHONY, 1403
UTAH VALLEY SYMPHONY, 1398
UTAH VALLEY YOUTH SYMPHONY, 1399
UTAH YOUTH SYMPHONY, 1403
VALLEY SYMPHONY ORCHESTRA & CHORALE AND
    VALLEY SINFONETTE, 1375
VENTI DA CAMERA, 1097
VENTURA COUNTY SYMPHONY ASSOCIATION, 213
VERMONT SYMPHONY ORCHESTRA, 1411
VERMONT YOUTH ORCHESTRA, 1411
VIKLARBO CHAMBER EMSEMBLE, 105
VIRGINIA SYMPHONY, THE, 1431
VIRTUOSI DELLA ROSA, INC., 1187
VOICES OF CHANGE, 1326
WALLA WALLA SYMPHONY, 1472
WALLINGFORD SYMPHONY ORCHESTRA, 284
WARREN SYMPHONY ORCHESTRA, 696

WASHINGTON AND LEE UNIVERSITY CONCERT
    GUILD, 1429
WASHINGTON BLUEGRASS ASSOCIATION, 1471
WASHINGTON CHAMBER SYMPHONY, 301
WASHINGTON IDAHO SYMPHONY, 414
WATER MUSIC, 620
WATERBURY SYMPHONY ORCHESTRA, 286
WATERLOO-CEDAR FALLS SYMPHONY ORCHESTRA, 521
WATERTOWN MUNICIPAL BAND, 1276
WAUKESHA SYMPHONY, 1516
WAVERLY CONSORT, INC., 952
WAYNE CHAMBER ORCHESTRA, 843
WEBSTER COMMUNITY EDUCATION, 1276
WEST COAST CHAMBER ORCHESTRA, 194
WEST COAST SYMPHONY, 194
WEST JERSEY CHAMBER MUSIC SOCIETY, 827
WEST SHORE SYMPHONY, 686
WEST SHORE YOUTH SYMPHONY ORCHESTRA, 686
WEST VALLEY CHAMBER ORCHESTRA, THE, 218
WEST VALLEY SYMPHONY, DIVISION OF THE LOS
    ANGELES CIVIC ORCHESTRA, 68
WEST VIRGINIA SYMPHONY, 1477
WESTCHESTER ELEMENTARY ORCHESTRA, 895
WESTCHESTER JUNIOR STRING ORCHESTRA, 895
WESTCHESTER YOUTH SYMPHONY, 896
WESTERN MASSACHUSETTS YOUNG PEOPLE'S
    SYMPHONY/PHILHARMONIA, 645
WESTERVILLE CIVIC SYMPHONY, 1151
WESTFIELD SYMPHONY, THE, 845
WESTMORELAND SYMPHONY ORCHESTRA, 1203
WESTWOOD WIND QUARTET, 1465
WHEATLAND CHAMBER PLAYERS, 1191
WHEATON SYMPHONY ORCHESTRA, 477
WHEELING SYMPHONY, 1485
WICHITA FALLS SYMPHONY ORCHESTRA, 1392
WICHITA SYMPHONY, 535
WICHITA YOUTH ORCHESTRA, 536
WILLIAMS TRIO, THE, 651
WILMINGTON SYMPHONY ORCHESTRA, 1076
WILSON SYMPHONY, 1078
WINSTON-SALEM SYMPHONY ASSOCIATION, 1078
WISCONSIN CHAMBER ORCHESTRA, 1497
WISCONSIN YOUTH SYMPHONY ORCHESTRAS, 1497
WOMEN'S PHILHARMONIC, 169
WOOSTER SYMPHONY ORCHESTRA, 1151
YAKIMA SYMPHONY ORCHESTRA, 1473
YAKIMA YOUTH ORCHESTRA, 1473
YALE SYMPHONY ORCHESTRA, 271
YANKTON AREA SUMMER BAND, 1275
YAVAPI SYMPHONY ASSOCIATION, 32
YELLOWSTONE CHAMBER PLAYERS, 769
YOUNG ARTISTS PHILHARMONIC, THE, 280
YOUNG ARTISTS SYMPHONY ORCHESTRA, 215
YOUNG PEOPLES SYMPHONY OF RHODE ISLAND, 1248
YOUNGSTOWN SYMPHONY ORCHESTRA, 1153
YOUTH ORCHESTRA OF GREATER FORT WORTH, 1344
YOUTH SYMPHONY OF KANSAS CITY, 532
YOUTH SYMPHONY WEST, 77
ZANESVILLE CHAMBER ORCHESTRA, 1154

VOCAL MUSIC

AFTER DINNER OPERA COMPANY, 952
ALASKA LIGHT OPERA THEATRE, 14
ALBUQUERQUE CIVIC LIGHT OPERA, 849
ALBUQUERQUE OPERA THEATRE - OPERA SOUTHWEST, 849
AMATO OPERA THEATRE, 952
AMERICAN BOYCHOIR SCHOOL, 833
AMERICAN CHAMBER OPERA COMPANY, INC., 953
AMERICAN CHORAL DIRECTORS ASSOCIATION, 1160
ANCHORAGE CONCERT CHORUS, 14
ANCHORAGE OPERA COMPANY, 15
ANNAPOLIS OPERA, 585
ARIZONA OPERA COMPANY, 37
ARLINGTON OPERA ASSOCIATION, 1306
ARS MUSICA CHORALE AND ORCHESTRA, 832
ASSOCIATION FOR THE FURTHERMENT OF BEL CANTO, 953
ATLANTA BACH CHOIR, 379
ATLANTA OPERA, THE, 379
ATLANTA SYMPHONY CHORUS, 379
AUGUSTA OPERA ASSOCIATION, 388
AURORA SINGERS, 224
AUSTIN LYRIC OPERA, THE, 1309
B SHARP MUSIC CLUB OF NEW ORLEANS, THE, 564
BACH CHAMBER CHOIR AND ORCHESTRA, THE, 1506
BALTIMORE CHORAL ARTS SOCIETY, 588
BALTIMORE MEN'S CHORUS, 588
BALTIMORE OPERA COMPANY, 588
BALTIMORE SYMPHONY CHORUS, 589
BATON ROUGE GILBERT AND SULLIVAN SOCIETY, 555
BATON ROUGE OPERA, 555
BEAUMONT CIVIC OPERA, 1313
BEL CANTO CHORUS OF MILWAUKEE, 1506
BERKELEY OPERA, 60
BERKSHIRE CHORAL INSTITUTE, 642
BERKSHIRE LYRIC THEATRE, 639
BERKSHIRE OPERA COMPANY, INC., 630
BIRMINGHAM OPERA THEATER, 2
BLANCHE MOYSE CHORALE, 1409
BOISE MASTER CHORALE, 412
BOISE OPERA, 412
BOSTON LYRIC OPERA COMPANY, 609
BOSTON OPERA ASSOCIATION, 609
BRAINTREE CHORAL SOCIETY, 616
BRONX OPERA COMPANY, 868
CANTATA ACADEMY, 672
CANTATA CHORUS OF NORFOLK, 1432
CENTER FOR CONTEMPORARY OPERA, 953
CENTRAL CITY OPERA, 236
CHAMBER OPERA CHICAGO, 429
CHAPEL HILL-CARRBORO COMMUNITY CHORUS, 1068
CHARLESTON AREA COMMUNITY CHOIR, 1478
CHARLESTON CIVIC CHORUS, 1478
CHARLESTON LIGHT OPERA GUILD, 1478
CHARLOTTE CHORAL SOCIETY, 1049
CHATTANOOGA BOYS CHOIR, 1278
CHATTANOOGA OPERA ASSOCIATION, 1278
CHATTANOOGA SYMPHONY AND OPERA ASSOCIATION, 1278
CHAUTAUQUA OPERA, 881
CHERRY CREEK CHORALE, 243
CHICAGO CHILDREN'S CHOIR, 429
CHICAGO OPERA THEATER, 430
CHICAGO SYMPHONY CHORUS, 430
CHILDREN'S OPERA THEATER, 592
CHORAL ART SOCIETY OF NEW JERSEY, THE, 845
CHORAL ARTS SOCIETY OF PHILADELPHIA, 1220
CHORAL ARTS SOCIETY OF WASHINGTON, 302
CHORAL GUILD OF ATLANTA, 379
CHORAL SOCIETY OF GREENSBORO, 1058
CHORAL SOCIETY OF PENSACOLA, 353
CHORAL SOCIETY OF THE PALM BEACHES, INC., THE, 352
CHORUS AMERICA, 1220
CHORUS OF WESTERLY, 1253
CIMARRON CIRCUIT OPERA COMPANY, 1162
CINCINNATI BOYCHOIR, 1102
CINCINNATI OPERA, 1103

CIVIC LIGHT OPERA, 1457
CLARION CHAMBER CHORALE, 789
CLEVELAND OPERA, 1111
CLEVELAND ORCHESTRA CHORUS, THE, 1112
COLLEGE LIGHT OPERA COMPANY, 627
COLORADO CHILDREN'S CHORALE, 237
COLORADO SPRINGS CHORALE, 230
COLUMBUS SYMPHONY CHORUS, 1123
COMIC OPERA GUILD, 658
COMMONWEALTH OPERA, 637
COMMUNITY OPERA, INCORPORATED, 838
CONCERT ROYAL, INC., 953
CONCORD SINGERS OF NEW ULM, THE, 720
CONNECTICUT CHORAL ARTISTS, INC., 268
CONNECTICUT GRAND OPERA, 280
CONNECTICUT OPERA, 263
COPPELL COMMUNITY CHORUS, 1320
DALE WARLAND SINGERS, 710
DALLAS OPERA, THE, 1327
DALLAS SYMPHONY CHORUS, 1327
DAYTON OPERA ASSOCIATION, 1130
DELAWARE SINGERS, THE, 293
DELAWARE VALLEY OPERA, 907
DENVER CHAMBER CHOIR, THE, 237
DES MOINES METRO OPERA, 518
DESERT OPERA THEATRE, 137
DETROIT SYMPHONY CHORALE, 695
DETROIT SYMPHONY CHORUS, 696
DIABLO LIGHT OPERA COMPANY, 216
DIAMOND STATE CHORUS OF SWEET ADELINES INTERNATIONAL, 291
DIE MEISTERSINGERS, 790
DISTRICT CURATORS, INC., 302
DORIAN OPERA THEATRE, 513
DURANGO CHORAL SOCIETY, 243
DURHAM CIVIC CHORAL SOCIETY, 1053
EPHRATA CLOISTER CHORUS, 1200
EUGENE OPERA, 1179
FAIRBANKS CHORAL SOCIETY, CHILDREN'S CHOIR AND CHORUS!, 18
FAIRBANKS LIGHT OPERA THEATRE, 19
FARGO-MOORHEAD CIVIC OPERA COMPANY, 1085
FESTIVAL CHOIR, THE, 1497
FINE ARTS CHORALE, 645
FLORENTINE OPERA COMPANY, 1506
FLORIDA LYRIC OPERA, 357
FLORIDA STATE OPERA AT FLORIDA STATE UNIVERSITY, 365
FORT LAUDERDALE OPERA, 323
FORT WORTH OPERA ASSOCIATION, 1344
FRIEDRICH SCHORR MEMORIAL PERFORMANCE PRIZE IN VOICE, 655
FULLERTON CIVIC LIGHT OPERA, 83
GARDEN STATE PHILHARMONIC CHORUS, 839
GARY BEARD CHORALE, THE, 1289
GLACIER CHORALE, 776
GLEN ELLYN CHILDREN'S CHORUS, 457
GOLD COAST OPERA, 355
GOODMAN CHAMBER CHOIR, 954
GRANTHAM ORATORIO SOCIETY, 1203
GREATER BUFFALO OPERA COMPANY, 877
GREATER MIAMI OPERA ASSOCIATION, THE, 342
GREATER NEW BRITAIN OPERA ASSOCIATION, 268
GREELEY CHORALE, THE, 248
GREENSBORO OPERA COMPANY, 1058
GREENVILLE CHORALE, THE, 1263
GREENWICH CHORAL SOCIETY, 261
GREGG SMITH SINGERS, INC., 954
GUILD OPERA COMPANY, INC., 106
GULF COAST OPERA THEATRE, 731
HARTFORD CHORALE, INC., THE, 255
HAWAII ECUMENICAL CHORALE, 404
HAWAII OPERA THEATRE, 405
HEARTLAND MEN'S CHORUS, 746
HELENA YOUTH CHOIRS, INC., 773

HIS MAJESTIE'S CLERKES, 453
HONOLULU CHILDREN'S OPERA CHORUS, 405
HOUSTON GRAND OPERA, 1358
HOUSTON SYMPHONY CHORUS, 1359
HUNGARIAN OPERA WORKSHOP, 430
HUNTSVILLE OPERA THEATER, 6
I CANTORI DI NEW YORK, 954
I. SHERMAN GREENE CHORALE, INC., 1432
IL PICCOLO TEATRO DELL'OPERA, INC., 871
INDIANAPOLIS OPERA, 496
INTERMOUNTAIN OPERA COMPANY, 771
ITHACA OPERA ASSOCIATION, 897
JOHNSON CITY CIVIC CHORALE, 1282
JUBILLEE MENS CHORUS, 346
JUILLIARD OPERA CENTER, 954
KENTUCKY OPERA, 548
KITKA, 131
KNOXVILLE OPERA COMPANY, 1285
LA CROSSE BOYCHOIR, THE, 1493
LA MARCA AMERICAN VARIETY SINGERS, 209
LAMPLIGHTERS/OPERA WEST FOUNDATION, 169
LANCASTER CHORALE, THE, 1135
LARIMER CHORAL SOCIETY, THE, 245
LIBERTY FREMONT CHAMBER SINGERS, 459
LIEDERKRANZ OPERA THEATRE, 955
LIGHT OPERA OF MANHATTAN, 955
LIGHT OPERA WORKS, 453
LINCOLN OPERA, 431
LITTLE LYRIC OPERA THEATRE, 1220
LONG BEACH CIVIC LIGHT OPERA, 97
LONG BEACH OPERA, 97
L'OPERA FRANCAIS DE NEW YORK, 954
LOS ANGELES CONCERT OPERA ASSOCIATION, 64
LOS ANGELES MASTER CHORALE ASSOCIATION, 106
LOS ANGELES MUSIC CENTER OPERA, 106
LOUISVILLE CHORUS, THE, 548
LYRIC OPERA CENTER FOR AMERICAN ARTISTS, 431
LYRIC OPERA CLEVELAND, 1112
LYRIC OPERA OF CHICAGO, 431
LYRIC OPERA OF DALLAS, THE, 1327
LYRIC OPERA OF KANSAS CITY, 746
MACALLISTER, 496
MADISON BOYCHOIR, THE, 1498
MADISON OPERA, 1498
MADRIGAL SINGERS OF WILMINGTON, 294
MARTINSVILLE-HENRY COUNTY FESTIVAL OF OPERA, 1430
MARY GREEN SINGERS, THE, 1207
MASTER CHORALE OF ORANGE COUNTY, 72
MASTER SINGERS, THE, 630
MASTERWORKS CHORALE, 636
MEASURED BREATHS THEATRE COMPANY, 955
MEROLA OPERA PROGRAM, 170
METRO LYRIC OPERA, 815
METROPOLITAN GREEK CHORALE, THE, 956
METROPOLITAN OPERA, 956
MICHIGAN OPERA THEATRE, 667
MILLIKIN UNIVERSITY OPERA THEATRE, 450
MILWAUKEE OPERA COMPANY, 1506
MINNESOTA CHORALE, THE, 711
MINNESOTA OPERA, THE, 711
MINOT CHAMBER CHORALE, 1088
MINOT COMMUNITY OPERA, 1088
MISSISSIPPI OPERA ASSOCIATION, 735
MISSOULA MENDELSSOHN CLUB, 777
MOBILE OPERA, 8
MOLINE BOYS CHOIR, THE, 463
MONMOUTH CIVIC CHORUS, 835
MONTANA CHORALE, 772
MORMON TABERNACLE CHOIR, 1403
MOSAIC, 230
MUSICA SACRA, 956
MUSICAL AMERICA, 127
MUSIC-THEATRE GROUP, INC., 956
NASHVILLE OPERA, 1295
NATIONAL GRAND OPERA, 891
NATIONAL LUTHERAN CHOIR, 711
NATIONAL LYRIC OPERA COMPANY, 302
NATIONAL OPERA COMPANY, 1068

NEVADA OPERA ASSOCIATION, 799
NEW AMSTERDAM SINGERS, 957
NEW CLEVELAND OPERA COMPANY, 1112
NEW ENGLAND LYRIC OPERETTA, 281
NEW JERSEY STATE OPERA, 831
NEW MEXICO GAY MEN'S CHORUS, 849
NEW ORLEANS OPERA ASSOCIATION, 565
NEW YORK CHORAL SOCIETY, 957
NEW YORK CITY OPERA, 957
NEW YORK CITY OPERA NATIONAL COMPANY, 958
NEW YORK CONCERT SINGERS, THE, 958
NEW YORK GILBERT AND SULLIVAN PLAYERS, 958
NEW YORK VIRTUOSO SINGERS, THE, 1028
NEWARK BOYS CHORUS, 831
NORTH COUNTRY CHORUS, 1419
NORTH STAR OPERA, 725
NORTHERN DELAWARE ORATORIO SOCIETY, 294
OAKLAND YOUTH CHORUS, 131
OBERLIN COMMUNITY CHAMBER SINGERS, 1143
OHIO LYRIC THEATRE, 1146
OKLAHOMA OPERA AND MUSIC THEATER COMPANY, 1164
OPERA AT FLORHAM, 823
OPERA CAROLINA, 1049
OPERA CLASSICS OF NEW JERSEY, 819
OPERA COLORADO, 237
OPERA/COLUMBUS, 1124
OPERA COMPANY OF BOSTON, 609
OPERA COMPANY OF MID-MICHIGAN, 683
OPERA COMPANY OF PHILADELPHIA, 1221
OPERA DELAWARE, 294
OPERA EBONY, 958
OPERA FACTORY, THE, 432
OPERA FOR THE YOUNG, 1498
OPERA GRAND RAPIDS, 675
OPERA GUILD, 324
OPERA! LEWANEE, 655
OPERA LITE, 667
OPERA MEMPHIS, 1290
OPERA NEW ENGLAND, 610, 620
OPERA NORTH, 1221, 1416
OPERA NORTHEAST, 959
OPERA ORCHESTRA OF NEW YORK, 959
OPERA/OMAHA, 790
OPERA PACIFIC, 72
OPERA ROANOKE, 1439
OPERA SAN JOSE, 186
OPERA THEATER OF PITTSBURGH, INC., 1232
OPERA THEATRE AT WILDWOOD PARK FOR THE
    PERFORMING ARTS, 49
OPERA THEATRE OF NORTHERN VIRGINIA, 1423
OPERA THEATRE OF SAINT LOUIS, 757
ORATORIO SINGERS OF CHARLOTTE, 1050
ORATORIO SOCIETY OF NEW YORK, 959
ORATORIO SOCIETY OF UTAH, 1404
ORCHESTRA SEATTLE/ SEATTLE CHAMBER SINGERS, 1457
OREGON REPERTORY SINGERS, 1187
ORLANDO OPERA, 349
ORPHEUS MALE CHORUS OF PHOENIX, 30
ORPHEUS MALE CHORUS OF TACOMA, 1470
PACIFIC CHORALE, 91
PALA OPERA ASSOCIATION, 960
PALM BEACH OPERA, 372
PALM SPRINGS OPERA GUILD OF THE DESERT, 136
PAN-AMERICAN SOCIETY OF ARTISTS INC., 345
PAUL DRESHER ENSEMBLE, 170
PAUL HILL CHORALE/THE WASHINGTON SINGERS, THE, 302
PAUL MADORE CHORALE, 642
PENNSYLVANIA OPERA THEATER, THE, 1221
PEORIA CIVIC OPERA, 468
PHILADELPHIA SINGERS, THE, 1222
PHOENIX BOYS CHOIR ASSOCIATION, 30
PICCOLO OPERA COMPANY, 315
PIEDMONT OPERA THEATRE, 1078
PITTSBURGH BOYCHOIR, INC., 1232
PITTSBURGH CIVIC LIGHT OPERA, 1233
PITTSBURGH OPERA, 1233
POMERIUM MUSICES, INCORPORATED, 960
PORTLAND OPERA, 1187

PORTLAND SYMPHONIC CHOIR, 1187
PRINCETON PRO MUSICA, 834
PRO ARTE CHAMBER SINGERS OF CONNECTICUT, 281
PRO MUSICIS FOUNDATION, INC., 960
QUEENS OPERA ASSOCIATION, 872
QUEENSBOROUGH CHORUS, THE, 864
RACKHAM SYMPHONY CHOIR, 676
RALEIGH BOYCHOIR, 1069
REGINA OPERA COMPANY, 872
RENAISSANCE CITY CHOIR, 1233
REVELS INC., 621
RHODE ISLAND CIVIC CHORALE AND ORCHESTRA, 1249
RIDGEWOOD GILBERT AND SULLIVAN OPERA
    COMPANY, 837
ROQUE OPERA, 1173
RUBY VALLEY CHORALE, 779
RUMBLE SEAT FOUR QUARTET, THE, 1359
SACRAMENTO MEN'S CHORUS, 148
SACRAMENTO OPERA, 148
SAINT LOUIS CHAMBER CHORUS, 757
SAINT LOUIS SYMPHONY CHORUS, 758
SAINT THOMAS CHOIR OF MEN AND BOYS, THE, 960
SALT LAKE OPERA THEATRE, 1404
SALT LAKE SYMPHONIC CHOIR, 1404
SAN BERNARDINO CIVIC LIGHT OPERA ASSOCIATION, 151
SAN DIEGO COMIC OPERA, 154
SAN DIEGO MEN'S CHORUS, 155
SAN DIEGO OPERA ASSOCIATION, 155
SAN FRANCISCO CHANTICLEER, INC., 170
SAN FRANCISCO CHILDREN'S OPERA ASSOCIATION, 171
SAN FRANCISCO CHORAL ARTISTS, 171
SAN FRANCISCO GIRLS CHORAL ASSOCIATION, 171
SAN FRANCISCO OPERA ASSOCIATION, 171
SAN FRANCISCO OPERA CENTER, 172
SAN FRANCISCO POCKET OPERA, 172
SAN FRANCISCO SYMPHONY CHORUS, 172
SAN JOSE CIVIC LIGHT OPERA ASSOCIATION INC., 186
SANTA FE DESERT CHORALE, THE, 854
SANTA FE OPERA, THE, 855
SARASOTA OPERA ASSOCIATION, 361
SCHENECTADY LIGHT OPERA COMPANY, 1026
SCHOLA CANTORUM OF TEXAS, 1345
SEATTLE MEN'S CHORUS, 1457
SEATTLE OPERA ASSOCIATION, 1458
SHREVEPORT OPERA, 569
SILICON VALLEY GAY MEN'S CHORUS OF SAN JOSE, 208
SINGING BOYS OF PENNSYLVANIA, 1242
SIOUX FALLS MASTER SINGERS, 1273
SKYLIGHT COMIC OPERA LIMITED, 1507
SONG OF NORWAY FESTIVAL, 1511
SPRINGFIELD REGIONAL OPERA, 765

SPRUCE STREET SINGERS, 1214
STARLIGHT MUSICAL THEATRE/SAN DIEGO CIVIC LIGHT
    OPERA ASSOCIATION, 155
SUGAR VALLEY CHAPTER OF SWEET ADELINES, 778
SUMMER OPERA THEATRE COMPANY, 303
SYRACUSE OPERA COMPANY, 1032
TACOMA OPERA ASSOCIATION, 1470
TAGHKANIC CHORALE, THE, 1041
TEXAS BACH CHOIR, 1384
TEXAS BOYS CHOIR, THE, 1345
TEXAS GIRLS CHOIR, THE, 1345
TEXAS OPERA THEATER, 1359
THEATRE ROCOCO, 961
THROUGH THE OPERA GLASS, 1418
THURSDAY MUSICALE, THE, 346
TOLEDO OPERA, 1148
TOURING CONCERT OPERA COMPANY, 961
TOWNSEND OPERA PLAYERS, 125
TRIANGLE OPERA THEATER, 1054
TRI-CITIES OPERA COMPANY, 866
TUCSON ARIZONA BOYS CHORUS, 37
TULSA OPERA, 1169
TURTLE CREEK CHORALE, 1328
TWIN CITIES GAY MEN'S CHORUS, 711
TWIN MOUNTAIN TONESMEN, 1382
UNIVERSITY OF MICHIGAN CHORAL UNION, 658
UNIVERSITY OF MICHIGAN GILBERT AND SULLIVAN
    SOCIETY, 659
UNIVERSITY OF SOUTHERN CALIFORNIA OPERA, 107
UP WITH PEOPLE, 37
UTAH OPERA COMPANY, 1404
VALLEY LIGHT OPERA, 601
VERMONT OPERA THEATER, 1409
VILLAGE LIGHT OPERA GROUP, 961
VIRGINIA CHORAL SOCIETY, 1431
VIRGINIA OPERA, 1432
VOCAL ARTS ENSEMBLE OF CINCINNATI, 1103
WASHINGTON BACH CONSORT, 303
WASHINGTON OPERA, 303
WASHINGTON SINGERS, 304
WEST BAY OPERA, 138
WEST COAST OPERA THEATRE, 136
WESTCHESTER CHORAL SOCIETY, INC., 1038
WESTERN WIND VOCAL ENSEMBLE, 952
WHITEWATER OPERA COMPANY, 502
WOMEN'S GUILD OF THE NEW ORLEANS OPERA
    ASSOCIATION, 565
YOUNG SINGERS OF CALLANWOLDE, INC., 391
YOUNGSTOWN MUSICA SACRA, 1153
YOUTH PRO MUSICA, 649
ZAMIR CHORALE OF BOSTON, 636

THEATRE

ABERDEEN COMMUNITY THEATRE (ACT 2), 1267
ABOUTFACE THEATRE COMPANY, 962
ACACIA THEATRE, 1507
ACADEMY OF PERFORMING ARTS, INC., 638
ACADEMY THEATRE, 380
ACME PERFORMANCE GROUP, INC., 67
ACTING COMPANY, THE, 962
ACTING COMPANY OF RIVERSIDE THEATRE, THE, 371
ACTING STUDIO, INC./NEW THEATRE ALLIANCE/CHELSEA
      REPERTORY COMPANY, THE, 962
ACTORS ALLEY REPERTORY THEATER, 128
ACTORS' ALLIANCE INC. (AAI), 963
ACTORS ALLIANCE THEATRE COMPANY, 693
ACTORS COMMUNITY THEATRE SHOWCASE, 330
ACTORS FOR THEMSELVES, 107
ACTORS LAB ARIZONA, 33
ACTORS PLAYHOUSE OF NASHVILLE, 1296
ACTORS REPERTORY THEATRE & SANTA MONICA GROUP
      THEATRE, 199
ACTORS STUDIO, 963
ACTORS' SUMMER THEATRE COMPANY, 1124
ACTORS' THEATER OF ASHLAND, 1174
ACTORS THEATRE OF LOUISVILLE, 548
ACTORS THEATRE OF NANTUCKET, 634
ACTORS THEATRE OF PHOENIX, 30
A.D. PLAYERS, 1360
ADDISON CENTRE THEATRE, 1304
ADELPHIAN PLAYERS, 872
AFRICAN AMERICAN DRAMA COMPANY, 173
AFRIKAN POETRY THEATRE, 899
AFRO-AMERICAN PLAYERS, 1328
AFRO-AMERICAN STUDIO THEATRE, 668
AIKEN COMMUNITY PLAYHOUSE, 1255
ALBUNDEGUS ALL-STARS, 248
ALEPH MOVEMENT THEATRE, 774
ALHAMBRA DINNER THEATRE, 332
ALIAS STAGE, 1249
ALICE B THEATRE, 1458
ALLENBERRY PLAYHOUSE, 1197
ALLEY THEATRE, 1360
ALLIANCE THEATRE COMPANY, 380
AMAS REPERTORY THEATRE, 963
AMERICAN BLUES THEATRE, 432
AMERICAN CENTER FOR STANISLAVSKI THEATRE
      ART, INC., 963
AMERICAN CONSERVATORY THEATRE, 173
AMERICAN ENSEMBLE COMPANY, THE, 964
AMERICAN LIVING HISTORY THEATER, 87
AMERICAN PLACE THEATRE, THE, 964
AMERICAN PLAYERS THEATRE, 1515
AMERICAN REPERTORY THEATRE, 621
AMERICAN SHOWCASE THEATRE COMPANY, 1421
AMERICAN STAGE COMPANY, 357, 838
AMERICAN THEATRE COMPANY, 1169
AMERICAN THEATRE OF ACTORS, 964
AMERICAN THEATRE WORKS, INC., 1413
ANCHOR THEATRE, 539
ANNIE RUSSELL THEATRE, 374
ANNISTON COMMUNITY THEATER, 1
ANTENNA THEATER, 203
APOLLO THEATER CENTER, 432
APPLE ALLEY PLAYERS, 1482
APPLE TREE THEATRE COMPANY, THE, 459
APPLETON WEST THEATRE, 1487
ARDMORE LITTLE THEATRE, 1157
ARENA CIVIC THEATRE, 628
ARENA DINNER THEATRE, 490
ARENA PLAYERS, 589
ARENA PLAYERS REPERTORY COMPANY OF LONG
      ISLAND, 887
ARENA STAGE, 304
ARIZONA THEATRE COMPANY, 38
ARKANSAS ARTS CENTER CHILDREN'S THEATER, THE, 49
ARKANSAS REPERTORY THEATRE, 49
ARMOUR STAR HAM PLAYERS, 1267

ARMY ENTERTAINMENT PROGRAM, 401
ARTISTS CIVIC THEATRE AND STUDIO, 559
ARTISTS COLLECTIVE, 263
ARTISTS THEATRE ASSOCIATION, 294
ARTREACH TOURING THEATRE, 1103
ARTS PROGRAM, GARDEN CITY RECREATION
      COMMISSION, THE, 526
ARTSCENTER, 1046
ASOLO CENTER FOR THE PERFORMING ARTS, 361
ATHENS PUPPET THEATRE COMPANY, 376
ATLANTA SHAKESPEARE COMPANY, 380
ATLANTA STREET THEATRE, 381
ATTIC/NEW CENTER THEATRE, 668
ATTIC/STRAND THEATRE, 689
ATTIC THEATRE, 107
AUBURN PLAYERS COMMUNITY THEATRE, THE, 863
AUGUSTA PLAYERS, 388
AURORA CHILDREN'S THEATRE COMPANY, 224
AURORA THEATRE COMPANY, 224
AVERY POINT PLAYERS, THE, 261
BACKSTAGE THEATRE COMPANY, 228
BAILIWICK REPERTORY, 432
BALTIMORE ACTORS' THEATRE, INC., 589
BARKSDALE THEATRE, 1428
BARN COMMUNITY THEATRE, 515
BARN PLAYERS THEATRE, THE, 533
BARN THEATRE, 661
BARN THEATER, THE, 1273
BARNSTORMERS, THE, 813
BARRIO PLAYERS - ACTORES DEL BARRIO, 128
BARTER THEATRE-STATE THEATRE OF VIRGINIA, 1421
BATHHOUSE THEATRE, 1458
BATON ROUGE LITTLE THEATRE, 556
BAY CITY PLAYERS, 662
BAY STREET PLAYERS, 323
BECK CENTER FOR THE CULTURAL ARTS, THE, 1135
BEDFORD LITTLE THEATRE, 483
BEEF AND BOARDS DINNER THEATRE, 496
BELLEVUE LITTLE THEATRE, 781
BELMONT CHILDREN'S THEATRE, 603
BELMONT DRAMATIC CLUB, 603
BERKELEY COMMUNITY THEATRE, 61
BERKELEY REPERTORY THEATRE, 61
BERKSHIRE PUBLIC THEATRE COMPANY, THE, 639
BILINGUAL FOUNDATION OF THE ARTS, 107
BILINGUAL THEATER COMPANY/SOUTH TEXAS
      PERFORMANCE CO., 1321
BILLIE HOLIDAY THEATRE, 873
BIRMINGHAM CHILDREN'S THEATRE, 3
BITS 'N PIECES GIANT PUPPET THEATRE, 367
BLACK ENSEMBLE THEATER, 433
BLACK EXPERIENCE ENSEMBLE, THE, 859
BLACK HILLS COMMUNITY THEATRE, 1271
BLACK HILLS PLAYHOUSE, 1272
BLACK REPERTORY GROUP INC., 61
BLACK SPECTRUM, 964
BLACK THEATER GUILD OF GREATER KANSAS CITY, 747
BLACK THEATRE TROUPE, 31
BLACKFRIARS THEATRE, 155
BLAKE STREET HAWKEYES, 191
BLIND PARROT PRODUCTIONS, 433
BLOOMING GROVE THEATER ENSEMBLE, LTD., 826
BLOOMSBURG THEATRE ENSEMBLE, 1197
BLUE EARTH TOWN AND COUNTRY PLAYERS, 701
BLUE LAKE REPERTORY THEATRE, 696
BMT THEATER, THE, 78
BOARSHEAD: MICHIGAN PUBLIC THEATER, 684
BOB BAKER PRODUCTIONS, 108
BODY POLITIC THEATRE, 433
BOND STREET THEATRE COALITION, 965
BORDERLANDS THEATER/TEATRO FRONTERIZO, 38
BOULDER REPERTORY COMPANY, THE, 225
BOSTON CHILDREN'S THEATRE, 610
BOSTON THEATER GROUP, 625
BRECKSVILLE LITTLE THEATRE, 1097

BREWERY ARTS CENTER, 795
BRIDGEWORK THEATER, THE, 492
BRIGHT LIGHTS THEATRE COMPANY, 1249
BROADWAY THEATRE LEAGUE OF PUEBLO, 251
BROADWAY TOMORROW, INC., 965
BROOM STREET THEATER, 1498
BROWN GRAND THEATRE, 526
BROWN UNIVERSITY THEATRE, 1250
BUCKS COUNTY PLAYHOUSE, 1214
BURBAGE THEATRE ENSEMBLE, 108
BURT REYNOLDS INSTITUTE FOR THEATRE TRAINING, 370
BUSHFIRE THEATRE OF PERFORMING ARTS, 1222
CABBAGES AND KINGS, 1328
CALDWELL THEATRE COMPANY, 316
CALIFORNIA THEATRE CENTER, 208
CALUMET THEATRE COMPANY, 664
CAMILLE PLAYERS, 1316
CANDLELIGHT DINNER PLAYHOUSE AND FORUM
    THEATRE, 475
CANDLEWOOD PLAYHOUSE, 269
CANNON COMMUNITY PLAYHOUSE, 1301
CAPE FEAR REGIONAL THEATRE, 1055
CAPE PLAYHOUSE OF THE RAYMOND MOORE
    FOUNDATION, 624
CAPITAL REPERTORY COMPANY, 860
CAROUSEL DINNER THEATRE, 1092
CARPET BAG THEATRE, 1286
CASA MANANA MUSICALS INC., 1346
CASA MANANA PLAYHOUSE, 1346
CAST THEATRE/THE CAST-AT-THE-CIRCLE, THE, 87
CELEBRATION THEATRE, 108
CENTER FOR PUPPETRY ARTS, 381
CENTER STAGE, 589, 790
CENTER THEATER AND THE TRAINING CENTER, 434
CENTRAL PIEDMONT COMMUNITY THEATRE, 1050
CENTRE EAST, 474
CHAFFIN'S BARN - A DINNER THEATRE, 1296
CHAGRIN VALLEY LITTLE THEATRE, 1100
CHANGING SCENE THEATER, 238
CHANHASSEN DINNER THEATRE, 701
CHANNING PLAYERS, 1360
CHANTICLEER, 511
CHANUTE COMMUNITY THEATRE, 525
CHARLESTOWN WORKING THEATER, 622
CHARLOTTE PLAYERS, 356
CHARLOTTE REPERTORY THEATRE, 1050
CHEROKEE NATIONAL HISTORICAL SOCIETY, 1167
CHERRY COUNTY PLAYHOUSE, 687
CHESHIRE COMMUNITY THEATRE, 257
CHEYENNE LITTLE THEATRE PLAYERS, 1520
CHICAGO ACTORS ENSEMBLE, 434
CHICAGO CITY LIMITS, 965
CHICAGO CITY THEATRE COMPANY, 434
CHICAGO DRAMATISTS WORKSHOP, 434
CHICAGO MEDIEVAL PLAYERS, THE, 435
CHICAGO THEATRE COMPANY, THE, 435
CHILD'S PLAY THEATRE COMPANY, 703
CHILD'S PLAY TOURING THEATRE, 435
CHILDREN'S THEATER ASSOCIATION, 590
CHILDREN'S THEATRE BOARD, INC., 1079
CHILDREN'S THEATER COMPANY, THE, 712
CHILDREN'S THEATRE OF EDEN, 1054
CHIPPEWA VALLEY THEATRE GUILD, 1488
CINCINNATI PLAYHOUSE IN THE PARK, 1103
CIRCA '21 DINNER PLAYHOUSE, 470
CIRCLE IN THE SQUARE, 966
CIRCLE REPERTORY THEATRE COMPANY, 966
CIRCLE THEATRE, INC., 790, 1346
CIRCUIT PLAYHOUSE, 1290
CIRCUS ARTS FOUNDATION OF MISSOURI, 758
CITIARTS THEATRE, 71
CITY LIT THEATER COMPANY, 436
CITY PLAYERS, 317
CITY STAGE COMPANY, 610
CITY THEATRE COMPANY, 1234
CIVIC THEATRE OF CENTRAL FLORIDA, 349
CLARENCE BROWN THEATRE COMPANY, 1286
CLASSICS ON STAGE! LTD, 436

CLEVELAND CREATIVE ARTS GUILD, 1279
CLEVELAND PLAY HOUSE, TEH, 1112
CLEVELAND PUBLIC THEATRE, 1113
CLIMB THEATRE - CREATIVE LEARNING IDEAS FOR MIND
    AND BODY, 725
CLOCKWORK REPERTORY THEATRE, 277
COACH HOUSE PLAYERS, 902
COACHLIGHT DINNER THEATRE, 260
COASTAL PLAYERS/JUPITER CIVIC THEATRE, 333
COCONUT GROVE PLAYHOUSE, 342
COFFEYVILLE COMMUNITY THEATRE, 525
COLDER BY THE LAKE, 703
COLEMAN PUPPET THEATRE, 462
COLONY THEATRE COMPANY, 109
COLUMBIA STAGE SOCIETY AT TOWN THEATRE, 1260
COLUMBIA THEATRE FOR THE PERFORMING ARTS, 1451
COMMEDIA THEATER COMPANY, 712
COMMON STAGE THEATRE COMPANY, INC., 1040
COMMUNITY PLAYERS, 543
COMMUNITY PLAYERS OF CONCORD, 804
COMMUNITY THEATRE, 1447
COMMUNITY THEATRE ASSOCIATION OF MICHIGAN, 687
COMMUNITY THEATRE OF CLAY COUNTY, 485
COMMUNITY THEATRE OF GREENSBORO, 1059
COMMUNITY THEATRE OF THE CASCADES, 1176
COMPANY ONE, 263
COMPLEX, THE, 109
CONCEPT EAST II, 668
CONEY ISLAND, USA, 873
CONKLIN PLAYERS DINNER THEATRE, 458
CONNECTICUT'S BROADWAY THEATRE, DARIEN, 259
CONTEMPORARY ART CENTER, 565
CONTEMPORARY THEATRE, A, 1459
CONTEMPORARY THEATRE OF SYRACUSE, 902
CO-REAL ARTISTS, 108
CORINTH THEATRE-ARTS, 732
CORSICANA COMMUNITY PLAYHOUSE, 1322
CORTLAND REPERTORY THEATRE, 885
COTERIE THEATRE, THE, 747
COUNTRY DINNER PLAYHOUSE, 244
COURT THEATRE, 436
CRANFORD DRAMATIC CLUB, 818
CREATION PRODUCTION COMPANY, 966
CREATIVE ARTS TEAM, 966
CREATIVE PRODUCTIONS, 815
CREATIVE THEATRE, 834
CREEDE REPERTORY THEATRE, 232
CREEKSIDE PLAYERS, THE, 1130
CRICKET THEATRE, THE, 712
CROSSROADS THEATRE COMPANY, 828
CSC REPERTORY, 967
CUMBERLAND COUNTY PLAYHOUSE, 1280
DALLAS CHILDREN'S THEATER, 1329
DALLAS PUPPET THEATER, 1329
DALLAS REPERTORY THEATRE, 1329
DALLAS SUMMER MUSICALS, 1329
DALLAS THEATER CENTER, 1330
DAS PUPPENSPIEL PUPPET THEATER, INC., 1038
DAWSON THEATRE GUILD, 1387
DAYTON PLAYHOUSE, 1131
DAYTONA PLAYHOUSE, 320
DELAWARE THEATRE COMPANY, 295
DELL' ARTE PLAYERS COMPANY, 66
DELRAY BEACH PLAYHOUSE, 322
DENTON COMMUNITY THEATRE, 1338
DENVER CENTER THEATER COMPANY, 238
DERBY DINNER PLAYHOUSE, 486
DES PLAINES THEATRE GUILD, 451
DETROIT REPERTORY THEATRE, 669
DIAMOND HEAD THEATRE, 405
DILLON STREET PLAYERS, 109
DOBAMA THEATRE, 1119
DOLPHIN PLAYERS, 1184
DON QUIJOTE CHILDREN'S THEATRE, 967
DOUBLE EDGE THEATRE PRODUCTIONS INC., 601
DOWLING ENTERTAINMENT CORPORATION, 967
DOWNTOWN ART CO., INC., 968
DRAMA CIRCLE THEATRE, 1330

DRAMALITES, 285
DREISKE PERFORMANCE COMPANY, 436
DRURY LANE OAKBROOK TERRACE, 466
DUMAS AREA ARTS COUNCIL, INC., 43
EAGLE-REED AMERICAN THEATER, 747
EAST WEST PLAYERS, 109
EAST-WEST FUSION THEATRE, 278
EBONY SHOWCASE THEATRE, 110
ECCENTRIC CIRCLES THEATRE, 968
EL CENTRO SU TEATRO, 238
EL TEATRO CAMPESINO, 188
EL TEATRO DE LA ESPERANZA, 173
ELKHART CIVIC THEATRE, 485
ELMWOOD PLAYHOUSE, 1011
ELNA M. SMITH FOUNDATION, 44
EMMY GIFFORD CHILDREN'S THEATER, 791
EMPTY SPACE THEATRE, THE, 1459
EN GARDE ARTS, INC., 968
ENCHANTED HILLS PLAYHOUSE, 487
ENCORE PLAYERS, 461
ENSEMBLE, THE, 1361
ENSEMBLE ESPANOL, 437
ENSEMBLE STUDIO THEATRE, THE, 968
ETA CREATIVE ARTS FOUNDATION, 437
EUNICE PLAYERS THEATRE, 557
EUREKA THEATRE COMPANY, 173
FAIRFIELD COUNTY STAGE COMPANY, THE, 288
FAIRMOUNT THEATRE OF THE DEAF, 1113
FALMOUTH PLAYHOUSE, 637
FARGO-MOORHEAD COMMUNITY THEATRE, 1085
FAR-OFF BROADWAY PLAYERS, THE, 542
FERGUS FALLS SUMMER COMMUNITY THEATRE, 705
FERNDALE REPERTORY THEATRE, 79
FIGURES OF SPEECH THEATRE, 577
FIJI COMPANY, THE, 968
FIREHOUSE THEATRE/NOODLES COMEDY CLUB, 791
FIRST PRESBYTERIAN THEATER, 490
FLAT ROCK PLAYHOUSE, 1056
FLORENCE SCHWIMLEY LITTLE THEATRE, 61
FLORIDA STUDIO THEATRE, 361
FLORIDA SUNCOAST PUPPET GUILD, 368
FLS ENTERTAINMENT, 492
FOOTHILLS COMMUNITY THEATRE, 1065
FOOTLIGHT CLUB, THE, 630
FOOTLIGHT PLAYERS, 1258
FORD'S THEATRE SOCIETY, 304
FORT GRIFFIN FANDANGLE ASSOCIATION, 1304
FORT LAUDERDALE CHILDREN'S THEATRE, 324
FORT SMITH LITTLE THEATRE, 46
FORT TOTTEN LITTLE THEATRE, 1086
FORT WAYNE CIVIC THEATRE, 490
FORT WORTH THEATRE, 1347
FOSTORIA FOOTLIGHTERS, 1132
FOUND THEATRE, THE, 98
FOUNTAIN SQUARE PLAYERS, 540
FREDERICK DOUGLASS CREATIVE ARTS CENTER, INC., 969
FREE STREET THEATER, 438
FRIENDS AND ARTISTS THEATRE ENSEMBLE, 87
FULTON OPERA HOUSE, 1209
GABBIES PUPPETS, 377
GALA HISPANIC THEATRE, 304
GALLERY THEATRE OF OREGON, 1183
GARLAND CIVIC THEATRE, 1352
GARTH FAGAN DANCE, 1020
GASLAMP QUARTER THEATRE, 156
GAS LIGHT PLAYERS, THE, 570
GATEWAY PERFORMANCE PRODUCTIONS, 381
GATEWAY PLAYERS, THE, 626
GAY PERFORMANCES COMPANY, 969
GENE DYNARSKI THEATER ENSEMBLE, 110
GENERIC THEATRE, 1433
GENESIUS PLAYERS, 1309
GEORGE COATES PERFORMANCE WORKS, 174
GEORGE STREET PLAYHOUSE, 829
GEORGETOWN CHILDREN'S THEATRE, 542
GERMANTOWN THEATRE GUILD, 1222
GERMINAL STAGE DENVER, 238
GEVA THEATRE, 1020

GLINES, THE, 969
GLOBE OF THE GREAT SOUTHWEST, 1378
GLOUCESTER STAGE COMPANY, 627
GOLD COAST MIME COMPANY, 345
GOLDEN APPLE DINNER THEATRE, 362
GOLDEN THESPIANS, THE, 329
GOOD COMPANY PLAYERS, 81
GOODMAN THEATRE, 438
GOODSPEED OPERA HOUSE, 259
GOODSPEED-AT-CHESTER/THE NORMA TERRIS THEATRE, 257
GOOSEBERRY PARK PLAYERS, 1089
GOTHENBURG COMMUNITY PLAYHOUSE, 782
GRANBURY OPERA HOUSE, 1353
GRANDE OLDE PLAYERS, 791
GREAT AMERICAN CHILDREN'S THEATRE COMPANY, THE, 1507
GREAT AMERICAN HISTORY THEATRE, 725
GREAT NORTH AMERICAN HISTORY THEATRE, 726
GREEN EARTH PLAYERS, 706
GREEN MOUNTAIN GUILD, 1416
GREENBRIER VALLEY THEATRE, THE, 1483
GREENSBORO CHILDREN'S THEATRE, 1059
GREENVILLE COMMUNITY THEATER, 1025
GREENWOOD PLAYERS CHILDREN'S THEATER, 1502
GRETNA PRODUCTIONS, 1214
GROUNDLING THEATRE, THE, 110
GROUP REPERTORY THEATRE, 128
GROUP THEATRE COMPANY, THE, 1459
GROVE SHAKESPEARE, 84
GUADALUPE CULTURAL ARTS CENTER, 1384
GUTHRIE THEATRE, THE, 713
HAMPTON PLAYHOUSE, 806
HANGAR THEATRE, THE, 897
HARDIN COUNTY PLAYHOUSE, 552
HARLEM ARTISTS' DEVELOPMENT LEAGUE ESPECIALLY FOR YOU (HADLEY PLAYERS), 969
HARRISBURG COMMUNITY THEATRE, 1205
HARTFORD STAGE COMPANY, 264
HARTSVILLE COMMUNITY PLAYERS, 1264
HEDGEROW THEATRE, 1238
HERITAGE ARTISTS, 883
HERITAGE SQUARE MUSIC HALL, 247
HICKORY COMMUNITY THEATRE, 1061
HIGH POINT COMMUNITY THEATRE, 1062
HILO COMMUNITY PLAYERS, 401
HINGHAM CIVIC MUSIC THEATRE, 629
HIP POCKET THEATRE, 1347
HIPPODROME STATE THEATRE, 328
HIPPODROME THEATRE, 1391
HISPANIC ORGANIZATION OF LATIN ACTORS (HOLA), 970
HISTORY MAKING PRODUCTIONS, 649
HOLE IN THE WALL THEATRE, 269
HOLLYWOOD PLAYHOUSE, 329
HOLLYWOOD THEATER COMPANY, 207
HONOLULU THEATRE FOR YOUTH, 405
HORIZONS THEATRE, 305
HORSE CAVE THEATRE, 544
HUDSON GUILD THEATRE, 970
HUDSON THEATRE, 213
HUNTINGTON BEACH PLAYHOUSE, 89
HUNTINGTON PARK CIVIC THEATRE, 90
HUNTINGTON THEATRE, 1096
HUNTINGTON THEATRE COMPANY, 611
HUNTSVILLE LITTLE THEATRE, 7
HURON PLAYHOUSE, THE, 1097
IDAHO REPERTORY THEATRE COMPANY, 414
IDAHO THEATER FOR YOUTH, 412
IGLOO, THE THEATRICAL GROUP, 970
ILLINOIS THEATRE CENTER, 466
ILLUSION THEATER, 713
ILLUSTRATED STAGE COMPANY, 174
IMAGINATION THEATER, 438
IMAGO, THE THEATRE MASK ENSEMBLE, 1014
IMPERIAL PLAYERS, 233
IMPOSSIBLE PLAYERS, THE, 251
IN THE HEART OF THE BEAST PUPPET AND MASK THEATRE, 713

INDEPENDENT EYE, THE, 1210
INDIANA REPERTORY THEATRE, 496
INSTITUTE FOR READERS THEATRE, 156
INTERBOROUGH REPERTORY THEATER (IRT), 873
INTERNATIONAL ARTS RELATIONS DBA INTAR HISPANIC
    AMERICAN ARTS CENTER, 971
INTERNATIONAL FESTIVAL OF PUPPETRY, 971
INTIMAN THEATRE COMPANY, 1459
INTUITION THEATRE COMPANY, 1104
INVISIBLE THEATRE, 38
IRISH ARTS CENTRE THEATRE, 971
IRVING COMMUNITY THEATER, 1369
ISLAND PLAYERS, 315
IVY GREEN THEATER, 12
JACKSON COUNTY COMMUNITY THEATRE, 486
JACKSON MARIONETTE PRODUCTIONS, 714
JACKSON RECREATION CHILDREN'S THEATRE, 1281
JACKSON THEATRE GUILD, 1281
JAM AND COMPANY, 971
JEAN COCTEAU REPERTORY, 972
JEKYLL ISLAND MUSICAL THEATRE FESTIVAL, 399
JEWEL BOX THEATRE, 1165
JEWISH REPERTORY THEATRE, 972
JOMANDI PRODUCTIONS, 381
JONESBOROUGH REPERTORY THEATRE, 1283
JULIAN THEATRE, THE, 174
JUMP-START PERFORMANCE COMPANY, 1384
JUNEBUG PRODUCTIONS INC., 566
JUNIOR THEATRE, 512
JUST US THEATER COMPANY, 382
KAHILU THEATRE, 408
KALAMAZOO CIVIC PLAYERS, 680
KALEIDOSCOPE THEATRE, 337
KANAWHA PLAYERS, 1479
KARAMU HOUSE, 1113
KATHY BURKS MARIONETTES, 1330
KEARNEY COMMUNITY THEATRE, 783
KEY WEST PLAYERS, 333
KINCAID REGIONAL THEATRE, 542
LA COMPANIA DE TEATRO DE ALBURQUERQUE, 849
LA JOLLA PLAYHOUSE, 93
LA MAMA EXPERIMENTAL THEATRE CLUB, 972
LA MIRADA THEATRE FOR THE PERFORMING ARTS, 95
LAFAYETTE COMMUNITY THEATRE, 558
LAGUNA PLAYHOUSE, 96
LAKE GEORGE DINNER THEATRE, 902
LAKESHORE PLAYERS, 729
LAKEWOOD THEATRE COMPANY, 1182
LAMB'S PLAYERS THEATRE, THE, 127
LAMB'S THEATRE COMPANY LTD., THE, 972
LAMP-LITE THEATER, 1377
LAS CRUCES COMMUNITY THEATRE, 852
LAS MASCARAS THEATRE, 342
LAS VEGAS LITTLE THEATRE, 797
LATIN AMERICAN THEATRE ENSEMBLE, 973
LAWRENCE WELK RESORT THEATRE, 79
LEXINGTON CHILDREN'S THEATRE, 545
LIBERTY CENTER, 764
LIFELINE THEATRE, 438
LIME KILN ARTS INCORPORATED, 1429
LIMELIGHT DINNER THEATRE, 356
LINCOLN CENTER THEATER, 973
LINCOLN COMMUNITY PLAYHOUSE, 786
LITTLE BROADWAY PRODUCTIONS, INC., 124
LITTLE COUNTRY THEATRE, 1085
LITTLE STAR THEATRE ASSOCIATION, THE, 1087
LITTLE THEATRE OF GASTONIA, 1056
LITTLE THEATRE OF NORFOLK, 1433
LITTLE THEATRE OF OWATONNA, 721
LITTLE THEATRE OF WINSTON-SALEM, THE, 1079
LIVE THEATRE, 454
LIVESTOCK PLAYERS MUSICAL THEATRE, 1059
LIVING STAGE, 305
LIVING THEATRE, INC., THE, 973
LONG BEACH JEWISH COMMUNITY CENTER YOUTH
    SUMMER STOCK, 98
LONG WHARF THEATRE, 272
LOOKING GLASS THEATRE, 1250
LORRAINE HANSBERRY THEATER, 175
LOS ANGELES CIVIC LIGHT OPERA, 110
LOS ANGELES THEATRE ACADEMY, THE, 111
LOS ANGELES THEATRE CENTER, 111
LOS ANGELES THEATRE WORKS, 213
LYCEUM REPERTORY COMPANY, 741
LYNN CANAL COMMUNITY PLAYERS, 20
LYNWOOD PERFORMING ARTS, 71
LYRIC STAGE, 611
LYRIC THEATRE OF OKLAHOMA, 1165
MABEL TAINTER MEMORIAL THEATER, 1502
MABOU MINES, 974
MAD HATTERS EDUCATIONAL THEATRE, THE, 681
MAD RIVER THEATER WORKS, 1150 - 1151
MADCAP PRODUCTIONS, 1104
MADISON REPERTORY THEATRE, 1499
MADISON THEATRE GUILD, 1499
MAGIC CIRCLE THEATER, THE, 633
MAGIC THEATRE, 175
MAGICAL THEATRE COMPANY, 1095
MAIN SQUARE PLAYERS, 493
MAIN STREET THEATER, 1361
MAINE STATE MUSIC THEATER, 575
MAINSTAGE THEATRE COMPANY, 1180
MAKE A CIRCUS, 175
MANATEE PLAYERS/RIVERFRONT THEATRE, 317
MANCHESTER MUSICAL PLAYERS, 266
MANHATTAN THEATRE CLUB, 974
MANSFIELD PLAYHOUSE, 1138
MARATHON COMMUNITY THEATRE, 338
MARGOLIS BROWN ADAPTORS, 873
MARIEMONT PLAYERS, 1104
MARIN THEATRE COMPANY, 123
MARION COMMUNITY THEATER, 1140
MARK TWO DINNER THEATER, 350
MARKET HOUSE THEATRE, 552
MARLBORO CULTURAL AFFAIRS, 632
MARRIOTT'S LINCOLNSHIRE THEATRE, 460
MARSH ISLAND STAGE, 580
MARTIN COMMUNITY PLAYERS, 1076
MARYLAND THEATRE, 595
MASQUERADERS, THE, 1192
MATCHBOX CHILDREN'S THEATRE, 699
MATTHEWS OPERA HOUSE SOCIETY, 1274
MAUI ACADEMY OF PERFORMING ARTS, 407
MAYFAIR THEATRE/"SHEAR MADNESS", 439
MCCADDEN PLACE THEATRE, 88
MEADOW BROOK THEATRE, 690
MELBOURNE CIVIC THEATRE, 339
MELROSE THEATRE ASSOCIATION, 111
MEMPHIS CHILDREN'S THEATRE, 1290
MEMPHIS COMMUNITY PLAYERS, 751
MENDOTA COMMUNITY THEATRE, 463
MERRIMACK REPERTORY THEATRE, 631
MERRY-GO-ROUND PLAYHOUSE, 863
MESQUITE COMMUNITY THEATRE, 1377
METRO THEATER COMPANY/THE CENTER FOR CREATIVE
    ARTS, 758
METTAWEE THEATRE COMPANY, 1024
MILL MOUNTAIN THEATRE COMPANY, 1439
MILWAUKEE CHAMBER THEATRE, 1508
MILWAUKEE PUBLIC THEATRE, 1508
MILWAUKEE REPERTORY THEATER, 1508
MIRROR REPERTORY COMPANY, 974
MISSOURI REPERTORY THEATRE, 747
MITKOF MUMMERS, 23
MIXED BLOOD THEATRE COMPANY, 714
MOBERLY COMMUNITY THEATRE, 752
MOBILE THEATRE GUILD, 8
MOHAWK PLAYERS, 863
MOLE END PUPPETRY PRODUCTIONS INC., 602
MONTANA REP, THE, 777
MONTPELIER THEATRE GUILD, 1416
MOORESVILLE COMMUNITY THEATRE, 1066
MORRISTOWN THEATRE GUILD, 1293
MOUNT WASHINGTON VALLEY THEATRE COMPANY, 811
MOUNTAIN PLAYHOUSE, 1207
MOUSE RIVER PLAYERS, 1088

MOVEMENT THEATRE INTERNATIONAL, 1222
MUHLENBERG COMMUNITY THEATRE, 543
MUSIC THEATRE GROUP AT LENOX ARTS CENTER, 974
MUSICAL THEATRE WORKS, 975
MUSICAL TRADITIONS INC., 175
MUSKOGEE LITTLE THEATRE, 1161
NASHVILLE ACADEMY THEATRE, 1296
NAT HORNE MUSICAL THEATRE, 975
NATIONAL BLACK THEATRE, 975
NATIONAL BLACK TOURING CIRCUIT, 976
NATIONAL IMPROVISATIONAL THEATRE, 976
NATIONAL MARIONETTE THEATRE, 1410
NATIONAL SHAKESPEARE COMPANY, 976
NATIONAL THEATRE, 305
NATIONAL THEATRE OF THE DEAF, THE, 257
NEBRASKA REPERTORY THEATRE, 786
NEBRASKA THEATRE CARAVAN, 792
NEGRO ENSEMBLE COMPANY, 976
NEIGHBORHOOD PLAYHOUSE, 391
NETTLE CREEK PLAYERS, 493
NEW AMERICAN THEATER, 472
NEW CITY THEATER, THE, 1459
NEW CONSERVATORY CHILDRENS THEATRE COMPANY
    AND SCHOOL, THE, 175
NEW DAY REPERTORY COMPANY, INC., 1017
NEW DRAMATISTS, 977
NEW FEDERAL THEATRE, 977
NEW FREEDOM THEATRE, 1223
NEW JERSEY SHAKESPEARE FESTIVAL, 824
NEW LONDON PLAYERS, 810
NEW MEXICO REPERTORY THEATRE, 850
NEW MUSIC-THEATER ENSEMBLE, 714
NEW PHOENIX, THE, 651
NEW PLAYWRIGHTS' PROGRAM - UNIVERSITY OF
    ALABAMA, 11
NEW RAFT THEATER COMPANY, THE, 977
NEW STAGE THEATRE, 735
NEW THEATRE, 319, 611
NEW THEATRE, THE, 759
NEW THEATER COMPANY, THE, 532
NEW TUNERS THEATRE, 439
NEW YORK SHAKESPEARE FESTIVAL, 977
NEW YORK STATE THEATER INSTITUTE, THE, 860
NEW YORK STREET THEATRE CARAVAN, 900
NEW YORK THEATRE WORKSHOP, 978
NEWARK PERFORMING ARTS CORPORATION/NEWARK
    SYMPHONY HALL, 831
NEWBERRY COLLEGE THEATRE, 1265
NEWGATE THEATER, 1250
NEWINGTON CHILDREN'S THEATRE, 275
NEXT ACT THEATRE, 1509
NEXT THEATRE COMPANY, 454
NINE O'CLOCK PLAYERS, 111
NINETY MILES OFF BROADWAY, 908
NKYIMKYIM STORY THEATRE, 39
NO THEATRE, 637
NORTH CAROLINA BLACK REPERTORY COMPANY, 1079
NORTH CAROLINA THEATRE, THE, 1069
NORTH COAST REPERTORY THEATRE, 203
NORTH SHORE MUSIC THEATRE, 604
NORTHLIGHT THEATRE AT THE CORONET, 454
NORTHSIDE THEATRE COMPANY, THE, 186
NW PUPPET CENTER, 1460
OAK PARK FESTIVAL THEATRE, 465
OAK RIDGE COMMUNITY PLAYHOUSE, 1299
OAKLAND CIVIC THEATRE, 132
OAKLAND ENSEMBLE THEATRE, 132
OAKLAND SUMMER THEATRE, 132
ODYSSEY THEATRE ENSEMBLE, 112
OFF-BROADWAY MUSICAL THEATRE, 719
OFFSTAGE THEATRE, 1425
OGDENSBURG COMMAND PERFORMANCES, 1011
OGUNQUIT PLAYHOUSE, 580
OHIO THEATRE, 978
OKLAHOMA COMMUNITY THEATRE ASSOCIATION, 1165
OLD BASTROP OPERA HOUSE, 1312
OLD COLONY PLAYERS, 1075
OLD CREAMERY THEATRE COMPANY, THE, 517

OLD GLOBE THEATRE, 156
OLD LOG THEATER, 704
OLD OPERA HOUSE PLAYERS, 1269
OLD SLOCUM HOUSE THEATRE COMPANY, 1471
OLD TOWN PLAYHOUSE, 694
OLDCASTLE THEATRE COMPANY, 1409
OLE OLSEN MEMORIAL THEATRE, 501
OLNEY THEATRE/NATIONAL PLAYERS, 596
OMAHA COMMUNITY PLAYHOUSE, 792
OMAHA MAGIC THEATRE, 792
OMILAMI PRODUCTIONS/PEOPLE'S SURVIVAL
    THEATRE, 382
ONE WAY PUPPETS, 324
O'NEILL THEATER CENTER, 286
ONTOLOGICAL-HYSTERIC THEATRE, INC., 978
OPEN BOOK, THE, 978
OPEN EYE: NEW STAGINGS, THE, 979
OPEN STAGE OF HARRISBURG, 1205
OPENSTAGE THEATRE AND COMPANY, INC., 246
OPERA HOUSE THEATRE COMPANY, 1077
ORANGE PARK COMMUNITY THEATRE, 348
OREGON FANTASY THEATRE, 1180
OREGON SHAKESPEAREAN FESTIVAL ASSOCIATION, 1174
ORGANIC THEATER COMPANY, 439
OSCEOLA PLAYERS, 335
OTRABANDA COMPANY, 979
OUACHITA LITTLE THEATRE, 50
OUT NORTH THEATRE COMPANY, 15
PACIFIC AMPHITHEATRE, 73
PADUA HILLS PLAYWRIGHTS WORKSHOP, 112
PALACE THEATRE OF THE ARTS, 281
PALO ALTO CHILDREN'S THEATRE, 138
PAN ASIAN REPERTORY THEATRE, 979
PANIDA THEATER, 416
PAPER BAG PLAYERS, THE, 980
PAPER MILL PLAYHOUSE, 824
PARENTHESIS THEATRE CLUB, 394
PARK PERFORMING ARTS CENTER, 841
PARK RIVER COMMUNITY THEATRE, 1089
PARK SQUARE THEATRE COMPANY, 726
PASSAGE THEATRE, 212
PAUL BUNYAN PLAYHOUSE, 700
PAUL ROBESON THEATRE, 877
PCPA THEATERFEST, 198
PEACOCK PLAYERS CHILDREN'S THEATRE, 808
PEARL THEATRE COMPANY, THE, 980
PEGASUS PLAYERS, 439
PEGASUS THEATRE, 1331
PENGUIN REPERTORY COMPANY, 1029
PENINSULA PLAYERS, 326
PENINSULA PLAYERS, THE, 1490
PENNSYLVANIA CENTRE STAGE, 1240
PENNSYLVANIA STAGE COMPANY, 1193
PENNYRILE PLAYERS, 543
PENOBSCOT THEATRE COMPANY, 574
PENSACOLA LITTLE THEATRE, 353
PENUMBRA THEATRE COMPANY, 726
PEOPLE'S LIGHT AND THEATRE COMPANY, THE, 1211
PEORIA PLAYERS THEATRE, 468
PERFORMANCE CIRCLE, THE, 1450
PERIWINKLE NATIONAL THEATRE, 906
PERMIAN PLAYHOUSE OF ODESSA INC., 1378
PERRY PLAYERS, INC., 396
PERSEVERANCE THEATRE, 17
PERSONA GRATA PRODUCTIONS, INC., 176
PETERBOROUGH PLAYERS, 811
PETRUCCI'S DINNER THEATRE, 596
PHEASANT RUN THEATRE, 473
PHILADELPHIA DRAMA GUILD, 1223
PHILADELPHIA FESTIVAL THEATRE FOR NEW PLAYS, 1223
PHILADELPHIA THEATRE COMPANY, THE, 1223
PHOENIX LITTLE THEATRE, 31
PHOENIX THEATRE, 497
PICCADILLY PUPPETS COMPANY, THE, 392
PICKETWIRE PLAYERS, 249
PICKLE FAMILY CIRCUS AND PICKLE FAMILY CIRCUS
    SCHOOL, 176
PIEDMONT PLAYERS THEATRE, 1072

PIER ONE THEATRE, 21
PIERRE PLAYERS, 1271
PIONEER PLAYHOUSE OF KENTUCKY, 541
PIONEER THEATRE COMPANY, 1405
PIPELINE, INC., 112
PIRATE PLAYHOUSE, 358
PISGAH PLAYERS, 1043
PITTSBURGH PUBLIC THEATER, 1234
PIVEN THEATRE WORKSHOP, 455
PLANO REPERTORY THEATRE, 1380
PLANTATION THEATRE COMPANY, 355
PLAYERS GUILD OF CANTON, 1100
PLAYERS OF SARASOTA, THE, 362
PLAYERS THEATRE COLUMBUS, 1124
PLAYHOUSE 412, 701
PLAYHOUSE ON THE SQUARE, 1291
PLAYHOUSE SQUARE FOUNDATION, 1114
PLAYMAKERS, 368
PLAYMAKERS CHILDREN'S ACADEMY OF
    THEATRE ARTS, 1398
PLAYMAKERS REPERTORY COMPANY, 1047
PLAYWRIGHTS' CENTER, 440
PLAYWRIGHTS' CENTER, THE, 714
PLAYWRIGHTS HORIZONS, 980
PLOWSHARES THEATRE, 669
POCKET SANDWICH THEATRE, 1331
POCONO PLAYHOUSE, 1213
POMPANO PLAYERS, INC., 355
PONCA PLAYHOUSE, 1166
PONTINE MOVEMENT THEATRE, 812
POOBLEY GREEGY PUPPET THEATRE, 641
POPLAR PIKE PLAYHOUSE, 1280
PORT HURON CIVIC THEATRE, 689
PORTAGE AREA COMMUNITY THEATRE, 1513
PORTHOUSE THEATRE COMPANY, 1134
PORTLAND BLACK REPERTORY, 1188
PORTLAND STAGE COMPANY, 582
POSSUM POINT PLAYERS, 291
POTOMAC THEATRE PROJECT, 1415
PRAIRIE PLAYERS CIVIC THEATRE, 456
PRAIRIE PLAYERS, INC., 528
PREGONES THEATER, 868
PRIMARY STAGES COMPANY, 981
PROCESS STUDIO THEATRE, 981
PROJECT INTERACT - ZACHARY SCOTT
    THEATRE CENTER, 1309
PROSCENIUM PLAYERS, 795
PROVO THEATRE COMPANY, 1399
PUBLICK THEATRE, THE, 611
PUERTO RICAN TRAVELING THEATRE COMPANY, 981
PULL-TIGHT PLAYERS, 1280
PUPPET ARTS THEATRE, 735
PUPPET HOUSE THEATRE, 282
PUPPET SHOWPLACE THEATRE, 616
PURDUE PROFESSIONAL SUMMER THEATRE, 505
QUAIGH THEATRE, 981
QUARTZ THEATRE, 1174
RAINBO CHILDREN'S THEATRE COMPANY, 726
RAVEN THEATRE COMPANY, 440
READING COMMUNITY PLAYERS, 1237
REALITY THEATRE, THE, 1125
RED BARN THEATRE, 334
RED EYE COLLABORATION, 715
REED MARIONETTES, INC., 1516
REMAINS THEATRE, 440
RENAISSANCE THEATRE, THE, 1139
RENAISSANCE THEATER COMPANY, 272
REPERTORY PEOPLE OF EVANSVILLE, 488
REPERTORY THEATER OF AMERICA, 1380
REPERTORY THEATRE OF SAINT LOUIS, THE, 759
RHODE ISLAND SHAKESPEARE THEATRE, THE, 1247
RICHMOND CHILDREN'S THEATRE, 553
RIDGE THEATER, 982
RIDICULOUS THEATRICAL COMPANY, THE, 982
RITES AND REASON, 1250
RIVER ARTS REPERTORY, 864
RIVERSIDE SHAKESPEARE COMPANY, 982
RIVERSIDE THEATRE, 518

RIVERTOWN PLAYERS, 499
ROAD COMPANY, THE, 1283
ROADSIDE THEATER, 553
ROANOKE VALLEY PLAYERS, 1071
ROBBINS - ZUST FAMILY MARIONETTES, 641
ROBERT MORRIS COLONIAL THEATER, 1199
ROCHESTER CIVIC THEATRE, 722
ROGER FURMAN THEATRE, 982
ROUND HOUSE THEATRE, 598
ROUNDABOUT THEATRE COMPANY, 983
ROXY THEATER, 1279
ROYAL ARTS COUNCIL, THE, 766
RYAN REPERTORY COMPANY AT HARRY WARREN
    THEATRE, 874
SACRAMENTO MUSIC CIRCUS, 149
SACRAMENTO THEATRE COMPANY, 149
SAINT BART'S PLAYHOUSE, 983
SAINT JOHN THEATRE, 568
SAINT LOUIS BLACK REPERTORY COMPANY, 759
SAINT SEBASTIAN PLAYERS, 441
SALEM THEATER OF PERFORMING ARTS, 1191
SALINA COMMUNITY THEATRE, 533
SALT AND PEPPER MIME COMPANY, INC., 983
SALT LAKE ACTING COMPANY, THE, 1405
SALTWORKS, 1234
SAN ANTONIO LITTLE THEATRE, 1385
SAN DIEGO GUILD OF PUPPETRY, 204
SAN DIEGO JUNIOR THEATRE, 157
SAN DIEGO REPERTORY THEATRE, 157
SAN FRANCISCO MIME TROUPE, 176
SAN JOSE REPERTORY THEATRE, 186
SAN JUAN COMMUNITY THEATRE AND ARTS CENTER, 1450
SANDHILLS LITTLE THEATRE, 1074
SANTA BARBARA CHILDREN'S THEATRE, 194
SANTA FE COMMUNITY THEATRE, 855
SANTA MONICA PLAYHOUSE AND GROUP THEATRE, 199
SCHENECTADY CIVIC PLAYERS, THE, 1026
SEACOAST REPERTORY COMPANY, 812
SEASIDE MUSIC THEATER, 320
SEATTLE CHILDREN'S THEATRE, 1460
SEATTLE MIME THEATRE, 1460
SEATTLE REPERTORY THEATRE, 1461
SECOND CITY, THE, 441
SECOND STAGE THEATRE, THE, 983
SENIOR BARN PLAYERS, THE, 534
SEVEN STAGES, 382
SEVENTH SIGN THEATRE COMPANY, INC. 984
SHADOW BOX THEATRE, THE, 984
SHADY LANE THEATER, 462
SHAKESPEARE REPERTORY, 441
SHAKESPEARE '70, 840
SHAKESPEARE THEATRE, THE, 305
SHARON COMMUNITY THEATRE, INC., 642
SHATTERED GLOBE THEATER, 441
SHAWANO COUNTY ARTS COUNCIL, 1514
SHEBOYGAN COMMUNITY PLAYERS, 1514
SHERIDAN CIVIC THEATRE GUILD, 1522
SHERMAN PLAYERS, 278
SHOESTRING PRODUCTIONS, LIMITED, 295
SHOWBOAT DINNER THEATRE, 318
SHOWBOAT TROUPE, 218
SHREVEPORT LITTLE THEATRE, 570
SIDE BY SIDE, 1069
SIKESTON LITTLE THEATRE, 764
SIOUX CITY COMMUNITY THEATRE, 520
SIOUX FALLS COMMUNITY PLAYHOUSE, 1274
SKYSAVER PRODUCTIONS, 984
SMITH-RITCH POINT THEATRE, 1368
SMOKY MOUNTAIN REPERTORY THEATRE, 1043
SOCIETY HILL PLAYHOUSE, 1224
SOJOURNER TRUTH PLAYERS, 1347
SOLVANG THEATERFEST, 199
SOON 3 THEATER, 177
SOUPSTONE PROJECT, 984
SOURCE THEATRE COMPANY, 306
SOUTH CAROLINA THEATRE COMPANY, THE, 1256
SOUTH COAST REPERTORY, 73
SOUTH JERSEY REGIONAL THEATRE, 837

SOUTHEAST ALABAMA COMMUNITY THEATRE, 5
SOUTHEAST COMMUNITY THEATRE, 157
SOUTHEASTERN SAVOYARDS, THE, 383
SOUTHERN APPALACHIAN REPERTORY THEATRE, 1065
SOUTHWEST REPERTORY ORGANIZATION, 1341
SPANISH LYRIC THEATRE, 368
SPANISH THEATRE REPERTORY COMPANY, 985
SPOKANE CIVIC THEATRE, 1466
SPOKANE INTERPLAYERS ENSEMBLE, 1466
SPRINGER OPERA HOUSE/THE STATE THEATER OF
    GEORGIA, 390
SPRINGFIELD LITTLE THEATRE, 765
STAGE LEFT THEATRE, 442
STAGE ONE THE LOUISVILLE CHILDREN'S THEATRE, 549
STAGE WEST, 1348
STAGECENTER, 1319
STAGECRAFTERS, 1105
STAGES REPERTORY THEATRE, 1361
STAGES THEATRE, 88
STAGES THEATRE CENTER, 113
STAGEWEST, 646
STAGEWORKS TOURING COMPANY, 820
STAGEWRIGHTS, INC., 985
STAMFORD THEATRE WORKS, 281
STATESVILLE COMMUNITY THEATRE, 1074
STEPPENWOLF THEATRE COMPANY, 442
STEVE SILVER PRODUCTIONS, 177
STOCKTON CIVIC THEATRE, 206
STOP-GAP, 193
STREET THEATER, THE, 1038
STROLLERS STUDENT THEATRICS, 1125
STUDEBAKER MOVEMENT THEATER COMPANY, 644
STUDIO ARENA THEATRE, 878
STUDIO E THEATRE ENSEMBLE, 239
STUDIO THEATRE, THE, 306
STUDIO X PLAYHOUSE, 1174
SU TEATRO, INC., 239
SUMMER MUSIC THEATRE, 461
SUNDANCE CHILDREN'S THEATRE, THE, 1407
SUNDANCE INSTITUTE, 1405
SUNSET PLAYHOUSE, 1489
SURFLIGHT THEATRE, 816
SWAMP FOX PLAYERS, 1262
SYNTHAXIS THEATRE COMPANY, 128
SYRACUSE STAGE, 1032
T. DANIEL MIME/MOVEMENT THEATRE, 478
TACOMA ACTORS GUILD, 1471
TALENTO BILINGUE DE HOUSTON, 1361
TALKING BAND, 985
TAMPA PLAYERS, THE, 368
TAPROOT THEATRE COMPANY, 1461
TEATRO AVANTE, 343
TEATRO DEL SERENTA INC., 1525
TEATRO HISPANO DE DALLAS, 1331
TEATRO VISION, 187
TEMPLE CIVIC THEATRE, 1389
TEMPLE THEATRE COMPANY, 1073
TEMPLE THEATRE ORGAN CLUB, 692
TENNESSEE REPERTORY THEATRE, 1296
THALIA SPANISH THEATRE, 1030
THEATER AT MONMOUTH, THE, 579
THEATER BRISTOL, 1277
THEATER FACTORY SAINT LOUIS, 760
THEATER FOR THE NEW CITY, 985
THEATER GROTTESCO, 669
THEATER KNOXVILLE, 1286
THEATER ON THE SQUARE, 1098
THEATER RHINOCERUS, INC., 177
THEATRE ALBANY, 375
THEATRE ARLINGTON, 1306
THEATRE-BY-THE-SEA, 1246
THEATRE CHARLOTTE, 1051
THEATRE CLUB OF THE PALM BEACHES, 338
THEATRE DE LA JEUNE LUNE, 715
THEATRE DU GRAND-GUIGNOL DE PARIS
    (GRAND-GUIGNOL THEATRE OF PARIS), 986
THEATRE EAST, 207
THEATRE EXCHANGE, 129
THEATRE FIRST, 442
THEATRE FOR A NEW AUDIENCE, 986
THEATRE IV, 1437
THEATRE 40, 65
THEATRE GAEL, 383
THEATRE GEMINI, 1331
THEATRE IN THE PARK, 1069
THEATRE IN THE ROUND PLAYERS, 715
THEATRE IN THE SQUARE, 395
THEATRE-IN-THE-WORKS, 350
THEATRE MEMPHIS, 1291
THEATRE OF THE ENCHANTED FOREST, 580
THEATRE OF UNIVERSAL IMAGES, 832
THEATRE OF WESTERN SPRINGS, 477
THEATRE OF YOUTH CO., 878
THEATRE OFF PARK, 986
THEATRE ON THE RIDGE, 1020
THEATRE ON THE SQUARE, 177
THEATRE ON WHEELS, 1362
THEATRE PROJECT, 590
THEATRE RAPPORT/HOLLYWOOD THEATRE CLUB, 88
THEATRE SUBURBIA, 1362
THEATRE THREE, 1332
THEATRE THREE PRODUCTIONS, 1016
THEATRE TULSA, 1169
THEATRE II COMPANY, 443
THEATRE UNDER THE STARS, 1362
THEATRE VIRGINIA, 1437
THEATRE WEST, 113
THEATRE WEST VIRGINIA, INC., 1475
THEATRE WINTER HAVEN, 373
THEATRE WORKSHOP OF NANTUCKET, INC., THE, 634
THEATRE WORKSHOP OF OWENSBORO, 552
THEATRE X, 1509
THEATREMOVES, INC./RAJECKAS AND INTRAUB
    MOVEMENT THEATER, 986
THEATREWORKS, 138
THEATREWORKS/USA, 987
THEATRICAL OUTFIT, 383
THESPIAN THEATRICAL CLUB, THE, 178
THUNDER BAY ENSEMBLE, 987
THUNDER BAY THEATRE, 656
TIMBERS DINNER THEATER, 1212
TOLEDO REP, THE, 1148
TOPEKA CIVIC THEATRE, 534
TORRANCE COMMUNITY THEATRE, 210
TORRINGTON CIVIC THEATRE, 283
TOTEM POLE PLAYHOUSE, 1202
TOUCH, 1046
TOUCHSTONE THEATRE, 1196
TOWN AND GOWN THEATER, 3
TOWN PLAYERS, 1276
TOWNE AND COUNTRY PLAYERS, 1142
TRAVELING JEWISH THEATRE, A, 173
TRAVELING PLAYHOUSE, 1039
TRI LAKES COMMUNITY THEATRE, 742
TRINITY REPERTORY COMPANY, 1251
TRINITY SQUARE ENSEMBLE, 455
TROUPE AMERICA INC., 716
TRUSTUS, 1260
24TH STREET EXPERIMENT, 1384
TWIN LAKES PLAYHOUSE, 51
UBU REPERTORY THEATER, 987
UKIAH PLAYERS THEATRE, 211
UNDERGROUND RAILWAY THEATER, 602
UNDERMAIN THEATRE, 1332
UNICORN PLAYERS INC., 88
UNICORN THEATRE, 748
UNITARIAN PLAYERS, 1145
UNIVERSITY OF MICHIGAN, UNIVERSITY
    PRODUCTIONS, 659
UNIVERSITY OF NEW ORLEANS RESIDENT ACTING
    COMPANY, 566
VALLEY COMMUNITY THEATER, 418
VALLEY FORGE MUSIC FAIR PRODUCTIONS, INC., 1199
VAUDEVILLE PALACE, 358
VEERA WIBAUX MIME THEATRE, 178
VENICE LITTLE THEATRE, THE, 370

VERO BEACH THEATRE GUILD, 371
VICTORIAN THEATRE, 239
VICTORY GARDENS THEATER, 443
VICTORY THEATRE, 67
VIGILANTE THEATRE COMPANY, 771
VILLAGE PLAYERS, 783
VILLAGE PLAYERS, THE, 347
VILLAGE PLAYERS (OAK PARK-RIVER FOREST CIVIC
    THEATRE, INC.), 465
VINCENNES UNIVERSITY SUMMER THEATRE, 505
VINEYARD THEATRE, 987
VIRGINIA STAGE COMPANY, 1433
VIVE LES ARTS THEATRE, 1371
VORTEX REPERTORY COMPANY, 1310
WAIMEA COMMUNITY THEATRE, 408
WALKER ART CENTER, 716
WALNUT STREET THEATRE COMPANY, 1224
WARWICK PLAYERS, 1252
WASHINGTON STAGE GUILD, THE, 306
WATERLOO COMMUNITY PLAYHOUSE/BLACK HAWK
    CHILDREN'S THEATRE, 521
WATERTOWN LYRIC THEATER PRODUCTIONS, 1037
WATERVILLE SUMMER THEATRE CORPORATION, 535
WAUKESHA CIVIC THEATRE, 1517
WAYNE STATE UNIVERSITY HILBERRY AND BONSTELLE
    THEATRES, 669
WAYSIDE THEATRE, 1430
WEATHERVANE THEATRE, 814
WEST END DRAMA MINISTRIES, 1297
WESTBETH THEATRE CENTER, 988
WESTPORT COMMUNITY THEATRE, 288
WESTPORT COUNTRY PLAYHOUSE, 288
WESTSIDE COMMUNITY REPERTORY, 988
WESTWOOD PLAYHOUSE, THE, 113

WHITE BIRD PRODUCTIONS, INC., 988
WHITTIER JUNIOR THEATRE, 217
WHOLE ART THEATER, 681
WICHITA COMMUNITY THEATRE, 536
WICHITA FALLS BACKDOOR PLAYERS, 1393
WILL GEER THEATRICUM BOTANICUM, THE, 209
WILLIAMSTOWN THEATRE FESTIVAL, 651
WILMA THEATER, THE, 1224
WILMINGTON DRAMA LEAGUE, 295
WILTON PLAYSHOP, THE, 289
WINDWARD THEATRE GUILD, 407
WISCONSIN UNION THEATER, 1499
WISDOM BRIDGE THEATRE, 443
WOMEN'S INTERART CENTER, 988
WOMEN'S PROJECT AND PRODUCTIONS, 989
WOODWARD ARTS AND THEATRE COUNCIL, 1172
WOOLLY MAMMOTH THEATRE COMPANY, 307
WOOSTER GROUP, THE, 989
WORCESTER CHILDREN'S THEATRE, 652
WORCESTER FOOTHILLS THEATRE COMPANY, 652
WORKING THEATRE COMPANY, INC., THE, 989
WORLD TREE PUPPET THEATER, THE, 716
WORLD'S FIRST INNER-MUSICAL THEATRE, THE, 113
WPA THEATRE, 989
YADKIN PLAYERS/YADKIN YOUTH THEATRE, 1080
YALE REPERTORY THEATRE, 272
YASS HAKOSHIMA MIME THEATRE, 826
YORK THEATRE COMPANY, THE, 990
YOUNG ACTORS THEATRE, 366
YOUTHEATRE, 1062
YUEH LUNG SHADOW THEATRE, 899
ZEITERION THEATRE, 634
ZEPHYR THEATRE, 114
ZION PASSION PLAY, 481

PERFORMING SERIES

ABBEY BACH FESTIVAL, 1190
ADIRONDACK FESTIVAL OF AMERICAN MUSIC, 1024
AFRICAN-AMERICAN CULTURAL CENTER, 878
ALABAMA SHAKESPEARE FESTIVAL, 10
ALFRED UNIVERSITY, 862
ALLENTOWN COMMUNITY CONCERT ASSOCIATION, 1194
AMATEUR MUSICAL CLUB OF PEORIA, INC., 468
AMERICAN ARTISTS SERIES, 663
AMERICAN LANDMARK FESTIVALS, 990
AMERICAN MUSIC THEATER FESTIVAL, 1225
AMERICAN MUSIC THEATRE GROUP, 264
AMERICAN STAGE FESTIVAL, 809
AMES INTERNATIONAL ORCHESTRA FESTIVAL
    ASSOCIATION, 507
ANCHORAGE FESTIVAL OF MUSIC, 15
ANN ARBOR SUMMER FESTIVAL, 659
APPALACHIAN SUMMER, AN, 1044
APPEL FARM ARTS AND MUSIC CENTER, 819
ARCADY MUSIC SOCIETY, 575
ARIZONA MINI-CONCERTS, 39
ARMSTRONG CHAMBER CONCERTS, INC., 285
ART SONG FESTIVAL, 1114
ARTIST SERIES AT THE PABST, 1509
ARTPARK, 904
ARTS AT ARGONNE, 419
ARTS CELEBRATION/ARTQUAKE FESTIVAL, 1188
ARTS CONSORTIUM STUDIO THEATRE, 1105
ARTS COUNCIL OF GREATER KNOXVILLE, THE, 1287
ARTS COUNCIL OF WASHINGTON COUNTY, 1316
ARTS SAN ANTONIO!, 1385
ARTSPLOSURE, 1070
ASHEVILLE CHAMBER MUSIC SERIES, 1043
ASHLAND FOLK MUSIC CLUB, 1175
ASPEN MUSIC FESTIVAL AND SCHOOL, 221
ASSEMBLY HALL, 421
ATLANTA JAZZ FESTIVAL, 383
ATLANTIC CENTER FOR THE ARTS, 346
AUDITORIUM THEATRE COUNCIL, 443
BACH ARIA FESTIVAL AND INSTITUTE, 1029
BACH DANCING AND DYNAMITE SOCIETY GROUP, 78
BACH FESTIVAL OF PHILADELPHIA, 1225
BANG ON A CAN, INC., 990
BAR HARBOR MUSIC FESTIVAL, 575
BARGEMUSIC LTD., 874
BATES DANCE FESTIVAL, 577
BAY CHAMBER CONCERTS, 576
BAY VIEW MUSIC FESITVAL, 662
BEAUMONT MUSIC COMMISSION, 1314
BEETHOVEN FESTIVAL, 905
BELLEVUE PARKS AND RECREATION DEPARTMENT -
    BELLEVUE JAZZ FESTIVAL, 1445
BELOIT COLLEGE PERFORMING ARTS SERIES, 1487
BERKELEY SHAKESPEARE FESTIVAL, 62
BERKSHIRE HILLS MUSIC AND DANCE ASSOCIATION, 278
BERKSHIRE THEATRE FESTIVAL, 647
BG-WC ARTS COMMISSION, 540
BIG SPRING CULTURAL AFFAIRS COUNCIL, 1315
BING CONCERTS, 114
BINGHAMTON SUMMER MUSIC FESTIVAL, INC., 866
BIRCH CREEK MUSIC CENTER, 1489
BIRMINGHAM FESTIVAL OF ARTS ASSOCIATION, 3
BLACK ARTS ALLIANCE, 1310
BLACK MUSIC SOCIETY OF MISSOURI, 760
BLAIR COUNTY CIVIC MUSIC ASSOCIATION, 1194
BLITHEWOLD GARDENS AND ARBORETUM "CONCERTS BY
    THE BAY", 1245
BLUEMONT CONCERT SERIES, 1429
BOSTON EARLY MUSIC FESTIVAL AND
    EXHIBITION, INC., 612
BOULDER FOLK AND BLUEGRASS ASSOCIATION, 226
BRADFORD CREATIVE AND PERFORMING ARTS
    CENTER, INC., 1198
BRANDEIS SUMMER MUSIC FESTIVAL, 648
BRATTLEBORO MUSIC CENTER, 1410
BRECKENRIDGE MUSIC INSTITUTE, 228

BRIGHAM YOUNG UNIVERSITY - UNIVERSITY
    CONCERTS, 1399
BRITT FESTIVALS, 1183
BROADWAY THEATRE LEAGUE OF THE QUAD-CITIES, 512
BROOKLYN ACADEMY OF MUSIC, 874
BUMBERSHOOT, THE SEATTLE ARTS FESTIVAL, 1461
BYRNE MILLER DANCE THEATRE, INC., THE, 12
CABRILLO MUSIC FESTIVAL, 56
CALDWELL FINE ARTS SERIES, 413
CAMBRIDGE CONCERT ASSOCIATION, 1098
CAMEO CONCERTS, INC., 1136
CANDLELIGHT CONCERT SOCIETY, INC., 593
CAPE AND ISLANDS CHAMBER MUSIC FESTIVAL, THE, 638
CARAMOOR CENTER FOR MUSIC AND THE ARTS, 901
CARAVAN OF DREAMS, 1348
CARLETON COLLEGE CONCERT SERIES, 720
CARMEL BACH FESTIVAL, 69
CASA DE UNIDAS, 670
CASTLE HILL FESTIVAL, 629
CATHEDRAL CONCERT SERIES, 1321
CELEBRATE BROOKLYN FESTIVAL, 875
CELEBRITY SERIES, 1215
CELEBRITY SERIES OF BOSTON, INC., 612
CENTRAL FLORIDA CULTURAL ENDEAVORS, 321
CENTRAL PENNSYLVANIA FESTIVAL OF THE ARTS, 1239
CENTRAL PENNSYLVANIA FRIENDS OF JAZZ, INC., 1205
CHAMBER ARTS NORTH, 688
CHAMBER MUSIC/LA FESTIVAL, 114
CHAMBER MUSIC SERIES, 1180
CHARLES RIVER CREATIVE ARTS PROGRAM, 625
CHAUTAUQUA INSTITUTION, 881
CHAUTAUQUA SERIES, 1332
CHEBOYGAN AREA ARTS COUNCIL, 664
CHILDREN'S FREE OPERA AND DANCE, 990
CINCINNATI MAY FESTIVAL, 1105
CINCINNATI MUSIC HALL ASSOCIATION, 1105
CITICORP SUMMERFEST, 760
CITY CELEBRATION ARTS, 178
CITY CENTER OF MUSIC AND DRAMA, 991
CITY OF ALBANY PARKS AND RECREATION
    DEPARTMENT, 1173
CITY OF BRYAN PARKS AND RECREATION, 1317
CITY OF LOS ANGELES CULTURAL AFFAIRS
    DEPARTMENT, 115
CLEVELAND MUSEUM OF ART CONCERTS, THE, 1114
CLOWES MEMORIAL HALL, 497
COLGATE UNIVERSITY CONCERT SERIES, 894
COLORADO COUNCIL ON THE ARTS, 239
COLORADO DANCE FESTIVAL, 226
COLORADO MUSIC FESTIVAL, 226
COLORADO OPERA FESTIVAL, 230
COLORADO SHAKESPEARE FESTIVAL, 227
COLORADO STATE UNIVERSITY - OFFICE OF CULTURAL
    PROGRAMS, 246
COLUMBIA FESTIVAL, INC., 594
COLUMBUS ARTS FESTIVAL, 1125
COMMUNITY ARTS AND MUSIC ASSOCIATION OF SANTA
    BARBARA, 195
COMMUNITY PLAYERS, INC., 1388
COMMUNITY SERIES, INC., 1388
CONCERTS-AT-THE-COMMON (HARVARD UNITARIAN
    CHURCH), 650
CONNECTICUT EARLY MUSIC FESTIVAL, 274
CONNETICUT COLLEGE CONCERT AND ARTIST SERIES, 274
COOPERSTOWN CONCERT SERIES, INC., 883
CORNING-PAINTED POST CIVIC MUSIC ASSOCIATION, 884
COUNCIL FOR THE ARTS OF GREATER LIMA, 1136
COUNTY OF WESTCHESTER - PARKS, RECREATION AND
    CONSERVATION - PERFORMING ARTS, 896
CROCKER ART MUSEUM, 149
CROOKED TREE ARTS COUNCIL, 688
CRS NATIONAL FESTIVAL FOR THE
    PERFORMING ARTS, 1198
CRYSTAL BALLROOM CONCERT ASSOCIATION, 444
CULTURAL ACTIVITIES CENTER, 1389

CULTURAL RESOURCES COUNCIL OF SYRACUSE AND ONONDAGA COUNTY, 1032
DALLAS CHAMBER MUSIC SOCIETY, 1332
DANCE ASPEN FESTIVAL, THE, 222
DECORAH COMMUNITY CONCERT ASSOCIATION, 513
DESERT FOOTHILLS MUSIC FEST, 25
DETROIT CONCERT BAND, INC., 33
DISCOVER JAZZ FESTIVAL, 1412
DORSET THEATRE FESTIVAL, 1414
DOWNERS GROVE CONCERT ASSOCIATION, 451
DOWNRIVER COUNCIL FOR THE ARTS, 697
DRAWING LEGION, THE, 510
DUMBARTON CONCERT SERIES, 307
EASTERN MUSIC FESTIVAL, 1059
EDISON THEATRE AT WASHINGTON UNIVERSITY, 760
E.J. THOMAS HALL, 1092
ELKHART CONCERT CLUB, 487
ELKHORN MUSIC FESTIVAL, INC., 417
ENTERTAINMENT BRANCH, CRD, 1449
ERIE CIVIC MUSIC ASSOCIATION, 1201
EVANSVILLE ARTIST EDUCATION COUNCIL, 488
FAIRBANKS SUMMER ARTS FESTIVAL, 19
FAYETTE COUNTY FINE ARTS COUNCIL, 1484
FEDERATED ARTS, 821
FERMILAB ARTS SERIES, 420
FESTIVAL AT ROUND TOP/INTERNATIONAL FESTIVAL-INSTITUTE AT ROUND TOP, 1381
FESTIVAL AT SANDPOINT, 417
FESTIVAL DANCE AND PERFORMING ARTS, 415
FESTIVAL OF NEW AMERICAN MUSIC, 150
FESTIVAL OF THE ARTS, 675, 1012, 1414
FESTIVAL PLAYERS OF CALIFORNIA, 115
FINEST ASIAN PERFORMING ARTS, INC., 150
FIREFLY FESTIVAL FOR THE PERFORMING ARTS, 503
FIRST NIGHT HARTFORD, INC., 264
FIRST NIGHT, INC., 612
FIRST NIGHT PROVIDENCE, 1251
FLAGSTAFF FESTIVAL OF THE ARTS, 26
FLATHEAD FESTIVAL OF THE ARTS, 779
FLINT CENTER FOR THE PERFORMING ARTS, 75
FLINT INSTITUTE OF MUSIC, THE, 673
FLORIDA INTERNATIONAL FESITVAL, 321
FLORIDA SHAKESPEARE FESTIVAL, 319
FLORIDA WEST COAST SYMPHONY, 362
FLORIDA'S CROSS AND SWORD, 356
FONTANA CONCERT SOCIETY, 681
FOOLS COMPANY, INC.: THE INTERNATIONAL OFFESTIVAL, 991
FORT HOOD COMMUNITY MUSIC AND THEATER - FORT HOOD COMMUNITY PLAYERS, 1343
FOUNDATION FOR BAROQUE MUSIC, 893
14TH ANNUAL CHICAGO JAZZ FESTIVAL, 444
FRAUENTHAL CENTER FOR THE PERFORMING ARTS, 687
FREDERICKSBURG CHAMBER MUSIC FESTIVAL, 1426
FRIENDS OF HISTORIC BOONVILLE, 741
FRIENDS OF MUSIC AND ART OF HUDSON COUNTY, 822
GARLAND SUMMER MUSICALS, 1352
GARTH NEWEL MUSIC CENTER, 1428
GENEVA CONCERTS, INC., 892
GEORGIA SHAKESPEARE FESTIVAL, 384
GINA BACHAUER INTERNATIONAL PIANO FOUNDATION, THE, 1406
GLASSBORO CENTER FOR THE ARTS, 820
GLIMMERGLASS OPERA, 883
GOLDEN ISLES CHAMBER MUSIC FESTIVAL, INC., 398
GOPHERWOOD MUSIC SOCIETY, 663
GRAND 1894 OPERA HOUSE, THE, 1350
GRAND OPERA HOUSE, 296
GRAND PRAIRIE FESTIVAL OF THE ARTS, 53
GRAND TETON MUSIC FESTIVAL, 1523
GRANT PARK MUSIC FESTIVAL, 444
GREAT AMERICAN PEOPLE SHOW, THE, 421
GREAT LAKES THEATER FESTIVAL, 1115
GREAT RIVER FESTIVAL OF ARTS, 1493
GREATER AKRON MUSICAL ASSOCIATION, 1092
GREECE PERFORMING ARTS SOCIETY, 1009
GREEK THEATRE, 115
GREEN LAKE FESTIVAL OF MUSIC, 1491

GROSSE POINTE SUMMER FESTIVAL, 677
GROSSMONT COMMUNITY CONCERTS, 94
GROVE SHAKESPEARE FESTIVAL, THE, 84
GUEST ARTIST SERIES, 850
HAAGE CONCERTS/HARRIS PRESENTS, 1237
HAINES ARTS COUNCIL, 20
HAMPTON ARTS COMMISSION, 1427
HARTT SUMMER YOUTH MUSIC FESTIVAL, 287
HEADWATERS COUNCIL, PERFORMING ARTS, 1487
HELENA PRESENTS, 774
HERITAGE DAYS, 787
HERSHELL CARROUSEL FACTORY MUSEUM, 1010
HERSHEY THEATRE, 1206
HESSTON PERFORMING ARTS SERIES, 527
HIGH POINT THEATRE AND EXHIBITION CENTER, 1062
HIGHLANDS CHAMBER MUSIC FESTIVAL, 1063
HILL COUNTRY ARTS FOUNDATION, 1368
HOBSON MEMORIAL UNION - PROGRAM BOARD, 700
HOLLYWOOD BOWL SUMMER FESTIVAL, 115
HOPKINS CENTER SUMMER, 806
HORN IN THE WEST, 1044
HOUGHTON COLLEGE ARTIST SERIES, 896
HOUSTON INTERNATIONAL FESTIVAL, THE, 1363
HOUSTON SHAKESPEARE FESTIVAL, 1363
IDAHO SHAKESPEARE FESTIVAL, 412
IDYLLWILD SCHOOL OF MUSIC AND THE ARTS, 90
ILLINOIS SHAKESPEARE FESTIVAL, 464
INDIANA UNIVERSITY PERFORMING ARTS SERIES, 484
INNER CITY CULTURAL CENTER, 116
INSPIRATION POINT FINE ARTS COLONY, 44
INSTITUTE OF OUTDOOR DRAMA, 1047
INTERLOCHEN ARTS CAMP, 678
INTERLOCHEN ARTS FESTIVAL, 678
INTERNATIONAL CHILDREN'S FESTIVAL, 1422
INTERNATIONAL CONCERTS EXCHANGE, 65
IRVING COMMUNITY CONCERT ASSOCIATION, 1369
IRVING S. GILMORE INTERNATIONAL KEYBOARD FESTIVAL, 682
ISABELLA STEWART GARDNER MUSEUM, 613
ISLIP ARTS COUNCIL, 888
I.U. DONS, INC., 492
JAZZ IN JUNE, INC., 1162
JAZZMOBILE INCORPORATED, 991
JEFFERSON PERFORMING ARTS SOCIETY, 562
JEWISH COMMUNITY CENTER OF CLEVELAND, 1120
JEWISH COMMUNITY CENTER OF HOUSTON, 1363
JEWISH COMMUNITY CENTER OF METROPOLITAN NEW JERSEY, 844
JOHN A. WALKER EVENTS, INC., 1075
JOHN F. KENNEDY CENTER FOR THE PERFORMING ARTS, 307
JOHN DREW THEATER OF GUILD HALL, THE, 887
JUNEAU JAZZ AND CLASSICS, 21
JUNIOR BLACK ACADEMY OF ARTS AND LETTERS, 1333
KANSAS CITY JAZZ FESTIVAL COMMITTEE, 748
KERRVILLE FESTIVALS, 1370
KERRVILLE PERFORMING ARTS SOCIETY, 1370
KIDS INTO DRAMA, 809
KILLINGTON MUSIC FESTIVAL, 1417
KING'S CHAPEL CONCERT SERIES, 613
KODACTORS, 1021
KOHAV THEATRE FOUNDATION, 992
KOHLER FOUNDATION, INC., 1492
LA ARTS, 577
LA PENA CULTURAL CENTER, 62
LADIES MUSICAL CLUB (LMC), 1462
LAKE CHARLES LITTLE THEATRE, 560
LAKE CHELAN BACH FESTIVAL, 1448
LAKE GEORGE JAZZ WEEKEND, 903
LAKE GEORGE OPERA FESTIVAL, 893
LAKE PLACID CENTER FOR THE ARTS, 903
LAKESIDE ASSOCIATION, THE, 1134
LAURA INGALLS WILDER PAGEANT SOCIETY, 1268
LAUREL ARTS, INC./THE PHILIP DRESSLER CENTER FOR THE ARTS, 1239
LAUREL FESTIVAL OF THE ARTS, 1207
LEAGUE OF OFF-BROADWAY THEATRES AND PRODUCERS, 992

L'ENSEMBLE, 860
LEVITT PAVILION FOR THE PERFOMING ARTS, 289
LIED CENTER FOR PERFORMING ARTS, THE, 786
LINCOLN ARTS COUNCIL, 1064
LINCOLN CENTER OUT-OF-DOORS, 992
LINCOLN CENTER'S MOSTLY MOZART FESTIVAL, 992
LINCOLN FRIENDS OF CHAMBER MUSIC, 787
LIONEL HAMPTON, CHEVRON JAZZ FESTIVAL, 415
LIVELY ARTS AT STANFORD UNIVERSITY, THE, 204
LIVING MASTERS SUBSCRIPTION SERIES, 1234
LONGWOOD GARDENS, 1208
LOS ANGELES COUNTY MUSEUM OF ART: MUSIC
     PROGRAMS, 116
LOS ANGELES FESTIVAL, 116
MACHIAS BAY CHAMBER CONCERTS, INC., 578
MACPHAIL CENTER FOR THE ARTS, 716
MADISON AREA ARTS COUNCIL, 1270
MAINE FESTIVAL, THE, 582
MAMOU CAJUN MUSIC FESTIVAL ASSOCIATION, 561
MANCHESTER MUSIC FESTIVAL, 1040, 1414
MANHATTAN ARTS COUNCIL, 530
MANN MUSIC CENTER, INC., 1225
MARKET SQUARE CONCERTS, 1206
MARLBORO MUSIC FESTIVAL, 1414
MARSHALL ARTISTS SERIES, 1481
MARSHALL REGIONAL ARTS COUNCIL, 1374
MARYLAND HANDEL FESTIVAL, 593
MATEEL COMMUNITY CENTER, INC., 144
MCALLEN PERFORMING ARTS, INC., 1376
MEADOW BROOK MUSIC FESTIVAL, 690
MEMPHIS IN MAY INTERNATIONAL FESTIVAL, 1291
MENDOCINO MUSIC FESTIVAL ASSOCIATION, 122
MESSIAH FESTIVAL OF MUSIC, 529
METROPOLITAN MUSEUM CONCERTS AND LECTURES, 992
MICHIGAN BACH FESTIVAL, 666
MICHIGAN RENAISSANCE FESTIVAL, 663
MID-ATLANTIC CENTER FOR THE ARTS, 817
MIDLAND COMMUNITY CONCERT SOCIETY, 685
MIDSUMMER MOZART, 179
MINNESOTA ORCHESTRA, 717
MOHAWK TRAIL CONCERTS, 643
MONADNOCK MUSIC, 811
MONTEREY JAZZ FESTIVAL, 126
MONTREUX ATLANTA MUSIC FESTIVAL, 384
MONTREUX DETROIT JAZZ FESTIVAL - DETROIT
     RENAISSANCE FOUNDATION, 670
MOORHEAD STATE UNIVERSITY, 719
MORMON MIRACLE PAGEANT, 177
MOUNT DESERT FESTIVAL OF CHAMBER MUSIC, 579
MOZART ON THE SQUARE, 1212
MULE BARN THEATRE OF TARKIO COLLEGE, 766
MULTI-CULTURAL MUSIC AND ART FOUNDATION OF
     NORTHRIDGE, 129
MUNICIPAL THEATER ASSOCIATION OF SAINT LOUIS, 761
MUNSON-WILLIAMS-PROCTOR INSTITUTE PERFORMING
     ARTS DIVISION, 1036
MURRAY CIVIC MUSIC ASSOCIATION, 551
MUSIC AT GRETNA, 1213
MUSIC CENTER OF LOS ANGELES COUNTY, THE, 116
MUSIC FESTIVAL OF ARKANSAS, 45
MUSIC FROM BEAR VALLEY, 58
MUSIC FROM SALEM, 880
MUSIC HALL ARTIST SERIES, 353
MUSIC IN THE MOUNTAINS, 127
MUSIC IN THE MOUNTAINS, FESTIVAL OF MUSIC AT
     PURGATORY, 243
MUSIC MOUNTAIN, 260
MUSIC THEATRE OF WICHITA, 536
MUSICORDA SUMMER STRING PROGRAM AND
     FESTIVAL, THE, 644
NAPERVILLE-NORTH CENTRAL COLLEGE PERFORMING
     ARTS ASSOCIATION, 464
NATIONAL BLACK ARTS FESTIVAL, 384
NATIONAL GALLERY OF ART/CONCERT SERIES, 308
NAZARETH COLLEGE ARTS CENTER, 1021
NEVADA SYMPHONY ORCHESTRA, 797
NEW ARTS PROGRAM, 1209
NEW BRUNSWICK CULTURAL CENTER, INC., 829

NEW HAMPSHIRE MUSIC FESTIVAL, 803
NEW MUSIK DIRECTIONS, 573
NEW ORLEANS JAZZ AND HERITAGE FESTIVAL, 566
NEW YEAR'S FEST, 682
NEW YORK INTERNATIONAL FESTIVAL OF THE
     ARTS, THE, 993
NEWBURYPORT FAMILY YMCA, 635
NEWPORT MUSIC FESTIVAL, 1247
NORFOLK CHAMBER MUSIC FESTIVAL - YALE SUMMER
     SCHOOL OF MUSIC, 276
NORTH AMERICAN NEW MUSIC FESTIVAL, 879
NORTH CAROLINA JAZZ FESTIVAL, 1077
NORTH CAROLINA SHAKESPEARE FESTIVAL, THE, 1062
NORTH CENTRAL ARKANSAS CONCERT ASSOCIATION, 47
NORTH COUNTRY CENTER FOR THE ARTS, 807
NORTHEAST LOUISIANA UNIVERSITY CONCERTS, 562
NORTHROP DANCE SERIES, 717
NORTHWEST FOLKLIFE, 1462
NORTHWEST MISSOURI STATE UNIVERSITY PERFORMING
     ARTS SERIES, 751
OAK RIDGE CIVIC MUSIC ASSOCIATION, 1300
OAKLAND JAZZ ALLIANCE, 133
OCCIDENTAL COLLEGE ARTIST SERIES, 117
OFFICE OF CULTURAL AFFAIRS, 1424
OFFICE OF PUBLIC EVENTS, 140
OGLEBAY INSTITUTE, 1485
OHIO OUTDOOR HISTORICAL DRAMA ASSOCIATION, 1141
OJAI FESTIVALS, 134
OK MOZART INTERNATIONAL FESTIVAL, 1158
OLD TIMERS CONCERT, 778
OPERA FESTIVAL OF NEW JERSEY, 835
ORANGE COAST COLLEGE, 73
OREGON BACH FESTIVAL, 1180
OREGON COAST MUSIC ASSOCIATION, 1177
OUTDOOR DRAMA GROUP ASSOCIATION, THE, 1389
PACIFIC NORTHWEST FESTIVAL, 1462
PACT-RUTH ECKERD HALL AT THE BAUMGARDNER
     PERFORMING ARTS CENTER, 318
PARADISE AREA ARTS COUNCIL, 139
PARK ARTS FESTIVAL - SUMMER SEASON, 1120
PAUL MASSON SUMMER SERIES, 201
PAWLING CONCERT SERIES, 1014
PENINSULA FESTIVAL, 1490
PERFORMING ARTS ASSOCIATION, 1251
PERFORMING ARTS PRESENTATIONS, 146
PERFORMING ARTS SERIES OF MOUNTAIN HOME, 415
PIERRE MONTEUX SCHOOL, THE, 577
PINESONG/SPOKANE FALLS COMMUNITY COLLEGE, 1467
PLAYBOY JAZZ FESTIVAL, 65
PLYMOUTH MUSIC SERIES OF MINNESOTA, 717
PORTLAND PERFORMING ARTS CENTER, INC., 583
PRESCOTT PARK ARTS FESTIVAL, 813
PRESENTATIONS OF THE ELAINE KAUFMAN CULTURAL
     CENTER, 993
PRESIDENTIAL JAZZ WEEKEND, 1226
PRINCESS THEATRE, 25
PRO MUSICA, INC., 677
PTG-FLORIDA, INC./PARKER PLAYHOUSE, 324
QUAD CITY ARTS, 471
QUARTET PROGRAM, THE, 1021
QRS ARTS FOUNDATION, 879
RAMONA HILLSIDE PLAYERS, 86
RAMONA PAGEANT ASSOCIATION, 86
RAVINIA FESTIVAL, 459
REDLANDS BOWL SUMMER MUSIC FESTIVAL, 143
REDLANDS SYMPHONY ASSOCIATION, 143
REED WHIPPLE CULTURAL ARTS CENTER, 797
REGIONAL CENTER FOR THE ARTS, 216
REIF ARTS COUNCIL, THE, 705
RIO GRANDE VALLEY INTERNATIONAL MUSIC
     FESTIVAL, 1376
RIPON COLLEGE/CAESTECKER FINE ARTS SERIES, 1513
RIVERBEND-CINCINNATI SYMPHONY AND POPS
     ORCHESTRA CONCERTS, 1106
ROANOKE ISLAND HISTORICAL ASSOCIATION INC., 1064
ROCKY RIDGE MUSIC CENTER, 787
ROWAN COMMUNITY CONCERT ASSOCIATION, 1072
RUSSIAN RIVER JAZZ FESTIVAL, INC., 85

RUTGERS SUMMERFEST, 829
RUTGERS UNIVERSITY CONCERT SERIES, 829
SAINT AMBROSE COLLEGE - GALVIN FINE ARTS
    CENTER, 512
SAINT LOUIS SYMPHONY QUEENY POPS, 761
SAN ANTONIO PERFORMING ARTS ASSOCIATION, 1386
SAN FRANCISCO ARTS COMMISSION, 179
SAN FRANCISCO JAZZ FESTIVAL, 179
SAN LUIS OBISPO MOZART FESITVAL, 189
SANGRE DE CRISTO ARTS AND CONFERENCE CENTER, 251
SANTA CRUZ BAROQUE FESTIVAL, 197
SANTA FE CHAMBER MUSIC FESTIVAL, 855
SARASOTA MUSIC FESTIVAL, 363
SARATOGA PERFORMING ARTS CENTER, 1024
SCANDINAVIAN DANCERS, 778
SEATTLE INTERNATIONAL CHILDREN'S FESTIVAL, 1462
SEDONA JAZZ ON THE ROCKS, 34
SEVENARS CONCERTS, 653
SHAKESPEARE FESTIVAL OF DALLAS, 1333
SHAKESPEARE IN CENTRAL PARK - KENTUCKY
    SHAKESPEARE FESTIVAL, 549
SHAKESPEARE-IN-THE-PARK, 1348
SHALHAVET, 1120
SHENANDOAH VALLEY MUSIC FESTIVAL, 1443
SITKA SUMMER MUSIC FESTIVAL, 16
SKANEATELES FESTIVAL, 1027
SMITHSONIAN INSTITUTION RESIDENT ASSOCIATE
    PROGRAM, 308
SONO ARTS CELEBRATION, INC., 277
SOUTH MOUNTAIN ASSOCIATION, 640
SOUTHEAST MISSOURI STATE UNIVERSITY - CULTURAL
    PROGRAMS, 742
SOUTHEASTERN MUSIC CENTER, 390
SOUTHERN ILLINOIS UNIVERSITY-EDWARDSVILLE, 452
SPINGOLD THEATER CENTER, 648
SPOLETO FESTIVAL USA, 1258
SPRING MUSIC FESTIVAL, 212
STAGE FRONT: THE ARTS DOWNEAST, 578
STAR SERIES OF READING, 1237
STARLIGHT-SAN DIEGO CIVIC LIGHT OPERA
    ASSOCIATION, 158
STARLITE PATIO THEATER SUMMER SERIES, 125
STATE UNIVERSITY OF NEW YORK - CORTLAND CAMPUS
    ARTIST AND LECTURE SERIES, 885
STEPHEN FOSTER DRAMA ASSOCIATION, 539
STERN GROVE FESTIVAL ASSOCIATION, 180
STOCKBRIDGE CHAMBER CONCERTS, 647
STRINGS IN THE MOUNTAINS, 252
SUE BENNETT COLLEGE, APPALACHIAN FOLK
    FESTIVAL, 546
SUMMER MUSIC ASSOCIATES, 810
SUMMER MUSIC, INC., 274
SUN VALLEY CENTER FOR THE ARTS AND
    HUMANITIES, 417
SUNFEST OF PALM BEACH COUNTY, INC., 372
SURRY ARTS COUNCIL, 1066
SWARTHMORE MUSIC AND DANCE FESTIVAL, 1240
TANGLEWOOD FESTIVAL, 613
TAOS SCHOOL OF MUSIC, INC., 857
TELLURIDE JAZZ CELEBRATION, 253
TENNESSEE PERFORMING ARTS CENTER MANAGEMENT
    CORPORATION, 1297
TENNESSEE WILLIAMS FINE ARTS CENTER, 334
TEXAS JAZZ FESTIVAL SOCIETY, 1322
TEXAS - THE MUSICAL DRAMA, 1318
THEATER OF THE STARS, 384
THEATRE OF THE PERFORMING ARTS, 570
THOMASTON-UPSON ARTS COUNCIL, 398
THREE RIVERS SHAKESPEARE FESTIVAL, 1235
THUNDER BAY ARTS COUNCIL, 656
TIBBITS OPERA AND ARTS COUNCIL, 665
TICONDEROGA FESTIVAL GUILD, INC., 1034
TITAS - THE INTERNATIONAL THEATRICAL ARTS
    SOCIETY, 1333
TOLEDO MUSEUM OF ART, THE, 1148

TORRANCE CULTURAL ARTS CENTER, 210
TOURING CONCERT OPERA CO. INC. - BERKSHIRE-HUDSON
    VALLEY FESTIVAL OF OPERA AND BALLET, 885
TRI-C JAZZFEST, 1115
TUCSON FESTIVAL SOCIETY, 39
TUESDAY MUSICAL CONCERT SERIES, 793
12TH STREET JAZZ SERIES, 748
UCI CULTURAL EVENTS, 92
UNITED ARTISTS OF RALEIGH AND WAKE COUNTY, 1070
UNITED BLACK ARTISTS, USA, INC., 670
UNITED JEWISH YS OF LONG ISLAND, 1015
UNITY CONCERTS, 827
UNIVERSITY ARTISTS SERIES, 1488
UNIVERSITY CENTER CULTURAL EVENTS, 1372
UNIVERSITY MUSICAL SOCIETY OF THE UNIVERSITY OF
    MICHIGAN, 660
UNIVERSITY OF CALIFORNIA-BERKELEY - CALIFORNIA
    PERFORMANCES, 62
UNIVERSITY OF CALIFORNIA-DAVIS - UC DAVIS
    PRESENTS, 76
UNIVERSITY OF CALIFORNIA-SAN DIEGO UNIVERSITY
    EVENTS OFFICE, 93
UNIVERSITY OF CALIFORNIA-SANTA BARBARA - ARTS &
    LECTURES, 195
UNIVERSITY OF DAYTON ARTS SERIES, THE, 1131
UNIVERSITY OF MARYLAND INTERNATIONAL PIANO
    FESTIVAL AND WILLIAM KAPELL COMPETITION, 593
UNIVERSITY OF ROCHESTER THEATRE PROGRAM, 1021
UNIVERSITY OF WISCONSIN CENTER - FOX VALLEY, 1501
UNIVERSITY OF WISCONSIN LECTURES AND FINE ARTS
    SERIES, 1501
UNIVERSITY OF WISCONSIN-PLATTEVILLE - PERFORMING
    ARTS SERIES, 1512
UPPER ARLINGTON CULTURAL ARTS COMMISSION, 1149
UPPER CATSKILL COMMUNITY COUNCIL OF THE
    ARTS, 1012
UPSTAGE!, 1463
U.S.A. INTERNATIONAL BALLET COMPETITION, 736
UTAH SHAKESPEAREAN FESTIVAL, 1395
VALLEY PERFORMING ARTS, 22
VAN CLIBURN FOUNDATION, 1348
VERMONT MOZART FESTIVAL, 1412
VICTORIA BACH FESTIVAL ASSOCIATION, 1391
VILLA MONTALVO CENTER FOR THE ARTS, 202
VILLAGE BACH FESTIVAL, 664
VIRGINIA SHAKESPEARE FESTIVAL, 1442
VIVA EL PASO!, 1342
VORSPIEL DRAMA EPHRATA CLOISTER
    ASSOCIATES, 1200
WALDORF COMMUNITY ARTISTS SERIES, 516
WARREN CIVIC MUSIC ASSOCIATION, 1150
WARTBURG COLLEGE ARTISTS SERIES, 522
WASHINGTON PERFORMING ARTS SOCIETY, 309
WATERLOO MUSIC FESTIVAL, 842
WATERVILLE VALLEY FOUNDATION, 814
WAUPACA FINE ARTS FESTIVAL, 1517
WESLEYAN UNIVERSITY CENTER FOR THE ARTS, 267
WESTBURY MUSIC FAIR, 1037
WESTERN ARTS MUSIC FESTIVAL, 1521
WESTMINSTER COMMUNITY ARTIST SERIES, 254
WHEELER OPERA HOUSE ASSOCIATION, 222
WILLIAM PATERSON COLLEGE - THE JAZZ ROOM
    SERIES, 843
WILLOWBROOK JAZZ FESTIVAL, 843
WITTENBERG UNIVERSITY - WITTENBERG SERIES, 1146
WOLF TRAP FARM FOUNDATION, 1441
WOODSTOCK OPERA HOUSE, 480
WYOMING ARTS COUNCIL, 1520
YARD, THE, 993
YATES PERFORMING ARTS SERIES, 1015
YELLOW BARN MUSIC FESTIVAL, 1417
YOUNG ARTISTS SERIES, 705
YOUNG AUDIENCES OF BEAUMONT, 1314
YOUNG AUDIENCES OF MARYLAND, 590
YOUNG AUDIENCES OF WESTERN MONTANA, 777

FACILITY INDEX

ABBEVILLE OPERA HOUSE, THE, 1255
ABILENE CIVIC CENTER, 1303
ABILENE CIVIC CENTER - EXHIBIT HALL, 1303
ABILENE CIVIC CENTER - THEATER, 1303
ACADEMY OF MUSIC, 1226
ACADEMY OF MUSIC - HALL, 1226
ACADEMY OF MUSIC - MAIN AUDITORIUM, 1226
ACADEMY PLAYHOUSE, 638
ACADEMY THEATRE - LAB, 385
ACADEMY THEATRE - PHOEBE THEATRE, 385
A.D.A.M.S. THEATRE, 1170
ADIRONDACK LAKES CENTER FOR THE ARTS, 867
ADRIAN COLLEGE, 656
AFRICAN-AMERICAN CULTURAL CENTER - PAUL
    ROBESON THEATRE, 879
AKRON CIVIC THEATRE, 1093
ALABAMA SHAKESPEARE FESTIVAL, 10
ALABAMA SHAKESPEARE FESTIVAL - FESTIVAL STAGE, 11
ALABAMA SHAKESPEARE FESTIVAL - OCTAGON, 11
ALASKA CENTER FOR THE PERFORMING ARTS, 16
ALASKALAND CIVIC CENTER, 19
ALBANO BALLET AND PERFORMING ARTS CENTER, 264
ALBANY JAMES H. GRAY, SR., CIVIC CENTER, 375
ALBANY JAMES H. GRAY, SR., CIVIC CENTER - ARENA, 376
ALBANY JAMES H. GRAY, SR., CIVIC CENTER -
    BALLROOM, 376
ALBERT LEA CIVIC THEATER, 699
ALBERTA BAIR THEATER FOR THE PERFORMING
    ARTS, THE, 770
ALBUQUERQUE CONVENTION CENTER, 850
ALBUQUERQUE CONVENTION CENTER - BALLROOM, 850
ALBUQUERQUE CONVENTION CENTER - KIVA
    AUDITORIUM, 851
ALCAZAR THEATRE, THE, 180
ALDEN THEATRE, 1430
ALHAMBRA DINNER THEATRE, 332
ALICE B THEATRE, 1463
ALLEY THEATRE, 1364
ALLEY THEATRE - HUGO V. NEUHAUS ARENA STAGE, 1364
ALLEY THEATRE - LARGE STAGE, 1364
ALVA MEMORIAL AUDITORIUM, 1157
ALVA PUBLIC LIBRARY AUDITORIUM, 1157
ALVERNO COLLEGE, 1509
AMARILLO CIVIC CENTER, 1305
AMARILLO CIVIC CENTER - ARENA, 1306
AMARILLO CIVIC CENTER - MUSIC HALL, 1306
AMBASSADOR THEATRE, 993
AMERICAN LEGION, 1159
AMERICAN PLACE THEATRE, 994
AMERICAN THEATRE, 761
AMERICAN UNIVERSITY - MCDONALD RECITAL
    HALL, THE, 309
AMERICAN UNIVERSITY - NEW LECTURE HALL
    THEATRE, THE, 309
ANAHEIM CONVENTION CENTER, 55
ANAHEIM CONVENTION CENTER - ANAHEIM ROOM, 55
ANAHEIM CONVENTION CENTER - ARENA, 55
ANAHEIM CULTURAL ARTS CENTER, 55
ANGELO STATE UNIVERSITY - AUDITORIUM, 1382
ANGELO STATE UNIVERSITY - MODULAR THEATRE, 1382
ANGELS GATE CULTURAL CENTER, 190
APOLLO THEATRE, 994
APPEL FARM ARTS AND MUSIC CENTER, 819
APPLE TREE THEATRE, 459
ARENA PLAYERS, 591
ARENA STAGE - FICHANDLER THEATER, 309
ARENA STAGE - KREEGER THEATER, 309
ARENA STAGE - OLD VAT THEATER, 310
ARIE CROWN THEATRE, 444
ARIZONA STATE UNIVERSITY - GAMMAGE CENTER, 36
ARIZONA STATE UNIVERSITY - SUNDOME CENTER FOR
    THE PERFORMING ARTS, 35
ARIZONA STATE UNIVERSITY - UNIVERSITY ACTIVITY
    CENTER, 36
ARKANSAS ARTS CENTER, 49

ARKANSAS REPERTORY THEATRE, 50
ARKANSAS RIVER VALLEY ARTS CENTER, 52
ARKANSAS TECH UNIVERSITY - WITHERSPOON ARTS AND
    HUMANITIES BUILDING, 52
ARLENE SCHNITZER CONCERT HALL, 1188
ARLINGTON CENTER FOR THE PERFORMING ARTS, 195
ARMSTRONG STATE COLLEGE FINE ARTS
    AUDITORIUM, 397
ARNESON RIVER THEATRE, 1386
ARNOLD HALL THEATER - UNITED STATES AIR FORCE
    ACADEMY, 231
ARTPARK THEATER, 904
ARTS AND SCIENCE CENTER OF SOUTHEAST ARKANSAS, 51
ARTS AND SCIENCE CENTER THEATRE, 809
ARTS CENTER OF THE OZARKS, 52
ARTS CENTER ON BRICKYARD POND - KEENE STATE
    COLLEGE, 807
ARTS CENTER/OLD FORGE, 1011
ARTS COUNCIL THEATRE, THE, 1080
ARTS IN THE PARKS - PORTABLE STAGE, 700
ARTSCENTER, THE, 1047
ARVADA CENTER FOR THE ARTS AND HUMANITIES, 221
ASHEVILLE CIVIC CENTER, 1044
ASHTABULA ARTS CENTER, 1094
ATHENAEUM THEATRE, 445
ATHENS MEMORIAL AUDITORIUM, 1094
ATHERTON AUDITORIUM, 206
ATLANTA CIVIC CENTER, 385
ATLANTA CIVIC CENTER - ROOM 104, 385
ATLANTA CIVIC CENTER - THEATER AUDITORIUM, 385
AUDITORIUM CENTER, 1022
AUDITORIUM THEATER - DENVER PERFORMING ARTS
    COMPLEX, 240
AUDITORIUM THEATRE, 445
AUGUSTA CIVIC CENTER, 573
AUGUSTA CIVIC CENTER - ARENA, 573
AUGUSTA CIVIC CENTER - NORTH HALL, 574
AUGUSTA/RICHMOND COUNTY CIVIC CENTER COMPLEX -
    ARENA, 389
AUGUSTANA COLLEGE - CENTENNIAL HALL, 471
AURORA FOX ARTS CENTER, 225
AVILA COLLEGE - GOPPERT THEATRE, 749
AYCOCK AUDITORIUM, 1060
AZTEC, THE, 1304
BACKSTAGE THEATRE, 228
BAGLEY WRIGHT THEATRE, 1463
BAILEY HALL, 325
BAKERSFIELD CIVIC AUDITORIUM, 58
BALDWIN WALLACE COLLEGE - KULAS MUSICAL ARTS
    CONCERT HALL, 1096
BALTIMORE MUSEUM OF ART - AUDITORIUM, 591
BAMA THEATRE PERFORMING ARTS CENTER, 11
BANGOR AUDITORIUM, 574
BANGOR CIVIC CENTER, 575
BARBARA B. MANN PERFORMING ARTS HALL, 326
BARDAVON 1869 OPERA HOUSE, 1017
BARN THEATRE, 623
BAROQUE FESTIVAL STUDIO, 894
BARRE OPERA HOUSE, 1409
BARRON ARTS CENTER, 845
BARTER PLAYHOUSE, 1421
BARTER THEATRE HOUSE, 1421
BARTLESVILLE COMMUNITY CENTER, 1159
BATES COLLEGE - CONCERT HALL, 578
BATES COLLEGE - OLIN ARTS CENTER, 578
BATH HOUSE CULTURAL CENTER, 1334
BATHHOUSE THEATRE, 1464
BATTLE CREEK CIVIC THEATRE, 661
BAYFRONT CENTER COMPLEX, 358
BAYFRONT PLAZA CONVENTION CENTER -
    AUDITORIUM, 1322
BAYVIEW OPERA HOUSE, 180
BEACH THEATRE UNDER THE STARS, 330
BEETHOVEN HALL - SAN JOSE CONVENTION CENTER, 1386
BELASCO THEATRE, 994

BELLEVUE LITTLE THEATRE, 781
BEMIDJI STATE UNIVERSITY - BANGSBERG FINE ARTS
    BUILDING, 700
BENEDUM CENTER, 1235
BENSON AUDITORIUM, 52
BERKELEY COMMUNITY THEATRE, 63
BERKELEY REPERTORY THEATRE, 63
BERKSHIRE COMMUNITY COLLEGE - KOUSSEVITZKY
    ARTS CENTER, 640
BERKSHIRE THEATRE FESTIVAL, 647
BETHANY COLLEGE - BURNETT CENTER FOR
    PERFORMING ARTS, 530
BEVERLY ART CENTER, 445
BEVERLY HILLS PLAYHOUSE, 65
BIBLICAL ARTS CENTER, 1334
BICENTENNIAL ART CENTER, 225
BIG BEAR LAKE PERFORMING ARTS CENTER, 66
BIGFORK CENTER FOR THE PERFORMING ARTS, 769
BIRCH CREEK MUSIC CENTER, 1489
BIRMINGHAM-JEFFERSON CIVIC CENTER, 4
BIRMINGHAM-JEFFERSON CIVIC CENTER - COLISEUM, 4
BIRMINGHAM-JEFFERSON CIVIC CENTER -
    CONCERT HALL, 4
BIRMINGHAM-JEFFERSON CIVIC CENTER -
    EXHIBITION HALL, 4
BIRMINGHAM-JEFFERSON CIVIC CENTER - THEATRE, 4
BIRMINGHAM-SOUTHERN COLLEGE THEATRE, 4
BISHOP CENTER FOR PERFORMING ARTS, 1445
BISMARCK CIVIC CENTER - ARENA, 1083
BISMARCK CIVIC CENTER - BISMARCK CITY
    AUDITORIUM, 1083
BLACKFRIARS THEATRE, 158
BLADEN OPERA HOUSE, 781
BLATZ TEMPLE OF MUSIC - WASHINGTON PARK
    BANDSHELL, 1510
BLOOMING GROVE THEATRE, 827
BLOOMSBURG UNIVERSITY - CARVER HALL, 1197
BLOOMSBURG UNIVERSITY - HAAS CENTER FOR
    THE ARTS, 1197
BLOSSOM MUSIC CENTER, 1128
BMCC/TRIPLEX PERFORMING ARTS CENTER, 994
BOB BAKER MARIONETTE THEATER, 117
BOB CARR PERFORMING ARTS CENTER, 350
BOB HOPE CULTURAL CENTER - MCALLUM THEATRE, 136
BOETTCHER CONCERT HALL - DENVER PERFORMING
    ARTS COMPLEX, 240
BOISE STATE UNIVERSITY - MORRISON CENTER FOR THE
    PERFORMING ARTS, 413
BOOTH THEATRE, 994
BOSTON CENTER FOR THE ARTS - CYCLORAMA, 614
BOSTON CENTER FOR THE ARTS - THE NATIONAL
    THEATRE, 614
BOSTON OPERA HOUSE, 614
BOSTON UNIVERSITY SCHOOL FOR THE ARTS -
    CONCERT HALL, 614
BOSTON UNIVERSITY THEATRE, 614
BOSTON UNIVERSITY THEATRE - MAIN STAGE, 614
BOSTON UNIVERSITY THEATRE - STUDIO 210, 615
BOULDER ART CENTER, 227
BOWIE STATE COLLEGE - MARTIN LUTHER KING, JR.,
    COMMUNICATION ARTS CENTER, 592
BOWLUS FINE ARTS CENTER, 528
BRADY THEATRE, 1170
BRANDEIS UNIVERSITY - SPINGOLD THEATER CENTER, 649
BRANSCOMB MEMORIAL AUDITORIUM, 336
BRECKSVILLE LITTLE THEATRE, 1098
BREN EVENTS CENTER, 92
BREVARD MUSIC CENTER - STRAUS AUDITORIUM, 1045
BREVARD MUSIC CENTER - WHITTINGTON-PFOHL
    AUDITORIUM, 1045
BRIGHAM YOUNG UNIVERSITY - HARRIS FINE ARTS
    CENTER, 1400
BROADHURST THEATRE, 994
BROADWAY THEATRE, 995
BROOKLYN ACADEMY OF MUSIC, 875
BROOKLYN ACADEMY OF MUSIC - CAREY PLAYHOUSE, 875
BROOKLYN ACADEMY OF MUSIC - LEPERCQ SPACE, 875
BROOKLYN ACADEMY OF MUSIC - OPERA HOUSE, 876
BROOKLYN CENTER, 701
BROOKS ATKINSON THEATRE, 995
BROOME CENTER FOR THE PRFORMING ARTS -
    THE FORUM, 866
BROWARD CENTER FOR THE PERFORMING ARTS, 325
BROWNWOOD COLISEUM, 1317
BUCKS COUNTY PLAYHOUSE, 1214
BUFFALO MEMORIAL AUDITORIUM, 879
BUFFALO STATE COLLEGE-PERFORMING ARTS CENTER -
    ROCKWELL HALL, 879
BURLINGTON MEMORIAL AUDITORIUM, 1412
BURRUSS AUDITORIUM, 1424
CABRILLO COLLEGE THEATER, 56
CAFE DEL REY MORO, 158
CALDWELL COLLEGE - STUDENT UNION BUILDING, 817
CALIFORNIA INSTITUTE OF TECHNOLOGY - BECKMAN
    AUDITORIUM, 141
CALIFORNIA INSTITUTE OF TECHNOLOGY -
    RAMO AUDITORIUM, 141
CALIFORNIA LUTHERAN UNIVERSITY - PREUS-BRANDT
    FORUM, 209
CALIFORNIA PLAZA, 117
CALIFORNIA POLYTECHNIC UNIVERSITY-POMONA -
    THEATRE, 142
CALIFORNIA STATE UNIVERSITY - CREATIVE ARTS
    BUILDING, 152
CALIFORNIA STATE UNIVERSITY-DOMINGUEZ HILLS -
    CONCERT HALL, 70
CALIFORNIA STATE UNIVERSITY-DOMINGUEZ HILLS -
    UNIVERSITY THEATRE, 70
CALIFORNIA STATE UNIVERSITY-FRESNO -
    JOHN WRIGHT THEATRE, 82
CALIFORNIA STATE UNIVERSITY-FRESNO -
    WAHLBERG RECITAL HALL, 82
CALIFORNIA STATE UNIVERSITY-HAYWARD -
    MAIN THEATRE, 86
CALIFORNIA STATE UNIVERSITY-LOS ANGELES -
    MUSIC HALL, 117
CALIFORNIA STATE UNIVERSITY-LOS ANGELES -
    PLAYHOUSE, 117
CALIFORNIA STATE UNIVERSITY-NORTHRIDGE -
    CAMPUS THEATRE, 129
CALIFORNIA STATE UNIVERSITY-NORTHRIDGE -
    LITTLE THEATRE, 130
CALIFORNIA STATE UNIVERSITY-NORTHRIDGE -
    STUDIO THEATRE, 130
CALIFORNIA STATE UNIVERSITY-STANISLAUS -
    MAINSTAGE THEATRE, 210
CALIFORNIA THEATRE OF PERFORMING ARTS, THE, 152
CALVIN COLLEGE FINE ARTS CENTER, 676
CAMDEN OPERA HOUSE, 576
CAMERON UNIVERSITY, THEATRE ARTS
    DEPARTMENT, 1161
CAMILLE LIGHTNER PLAYHOUSE, 1317
CAMP THEATER, 1046
CAPE PLAYHOUSE, 624
CAPITAL THEATRE, 1473
CAPITOL ARTS CENTER, 541
CAPITOL CIVIC CENTER, 1023
CAPITOL MUSIC HALL, 1485
CAPITOL THEATRE, 1406
CARAMOOR CENTER FOR MUSIC AND THE ARTS, 901
CARAVAN OF DREAMS, 1349
CARNEGIE HALL, 995
CARNEGIE HALL, INC., 1483
CARNEGIE - LECTURE HALL, THE, 1235
CARNEGIE - MUSEUM OF ART THEATRE, THE, 1236
CARNEGIE - MUSIC HALL, THE, 1236
CAROLINA THEATRE, THE, 1060
CAROUSEL DINNER THEATRE, 1093
CARPENTER CENTER FOR THE PERFORMING ARTS, 1438
CARROLL COLLEGE - THEATRE, 774
CASA DEL PRADO THEATRE, 158
CASA MANANA THEATRE, 1349
CASE WESTERN RESERVE UNIVERSITY -
    ELDRED HALL, 1115
CASPER COLLEGE - DURHAM HALL, 1519
CASPER EVENTS CENTER, 1519

CASWELL COUNTY CIVIC CENTER, 1081
CEDARTOWN CIVIC AUDITORIUM, 389
CELEBRATION BARN THEATER, 584
CELEBRATION THEATRE, 118
CENTENARY COLLEGE - RECITAL HALL, 570
CENTENNIAL COLISEUM - RENO SPARKS CONVENTION
    AND VISITORS AUTHORITY, 799
CENTENNIAL HALL CONVENTION CENTER, 21
CENTER FOR AFRICAN AND AFRICAN AMERICAN ART AND
    CULTURE, 180
CENTER FOR CONTEMPORARY ARTS, 856
CENTER FOR THE ARTS - UNIVERSITY OF WISCONSIN,
    PLATTEVILLE, 1512
CENTER STAGE, 591
CENTER STAGE AT EVERGREEN, 244
CENTER THEATER, 1264
CENTRAL CITY OPERA HOUSE, 228
CENTRAL FLORIDA COMMUNITY COLLEGE - FINE ARTS
    AUDITORIUM, 348
CENTRAL PARK BANDSHELL, 1139
CENTRAL PIEDMONT COMMUNITY COLLEGE - SUMMER
    THEATRE, 1051
CENTRALIA COLLEGE - CORBET THEATRE, 1448
CENTRE EAST, 474
CENTURION PLAYHOUSE, 1449
CENTURY CENTER, 503
CENTURY CENTER - BENDIX THEATRE, 503
CENTURY CENTER - CONVENTION HALL, 504
CENTURY CENTER - RECITAL HALL, 504
CENTURY II CIVIC CENTER, 537
CENTURY II CIVIC CENTER - CONCERT HALL, 537
CENTURY II CIVIC CENTER - CONVENTION HALL, 537
CENTURY II CIVIC CENTER - EXHIBITION HALL, 537
CENTURY II CIVIC CENTER - THEATRE, 537
CHABOT COLLEGE PERFORMING ARTS CENTER, 86
CHADRON STATE COLLEGE - MEMORIAL HALL, 782
CHAFFIN'S BARN, 1297
CHAMIZAL NATIONAL MEMORIAL - THEATER, 1342
CHANDLER CENTER FOR THE ARTS, 25
CHANDLER MUSIC HALL AND CULTURAL CENTER, 1417
CHANGING SCENE THEATER, 240
CHARLES B. GODDARD CENTER, 1158
CHARLES IVES CENTER - PAVILION, 258
CHARLESTON CIVIC CENTER, 1479
CHARLESTON CIVIC CENTER - COLISEUM, 1479
CHARLESTON CIVIC CENTER - LITTLE THEATER, 1479
CHARLESTON CIVIC CENTER - MUNICIPAL
    AUDITORIUM, 1479
CHARLOTTE COUNTY MEMORIAL AUDITORIUM, 356
CHAUTAUQUA INSTITUTION - AMPHITHEATER, 882
CHAUTAUQUA INSTITUTION - NORTON HALL, 882
CHEBOYGAN OPERA HOUSE - CITY HALL, 665
CHEROKEE HERITAGE CENTER AMPHITHEATER, 1167
CHEYENNE CIVIC CENTER, 1521
CHILDREN'S THEATRE COMPANY, THE, 718
CHILKAT CENTER FOR THE ARTS, 20
CHINOOK THEATRE FOR THE PERFORMING ARTS, THE, 1449
CHOWAN COLLEGE - MCDOWELL COLUMNS
    AUDITORIUM, 1067
CHRISTIAN ARTS AUDITORIUM, 481
CINCINNATI JEWISH COMMUNITY CENTER, 1106
CINCINNATI MUSIC HALL, 1106
CINCINNATI PLAYHOUSE - ROBERT S. MARX
    THEATRE, 1106
CINCINNATI PLAYHOUSE - THOMPSON
    SHELTERHOUSE, 1107
CIRCLE IN THE SQUARE INC., 995
CITY AUDITORIUM, 231
CITY CENTER, 995
CITY CENTER - CITY CENTER STAGE I, 995
CITY CENTER - CITY CENTER STAGE II, 996
CITY CENTER - CITY CENTER THEATRE, 996
CITY OF GRAND HAVEN COMMUNITY CENTER, 673
CIVIC AUDITORIUM, 414
CIVIC CENTER COMPLEX - EXHIBIT HALL, 1314
CIVIC CENTER COMPLEX - THE JEFFERSON THEATRE, 1314
CIVIC CENTER COMPLEX - JULIE ROGERS THEATRE, 1315
CIVIC CENTER MUSIC HALL, 1165

CIVIC CENTER OF GREATER DES MOINES, 514
CIVIC CENTER OF ONONDAGA COUNTY, 1033
CIVIC CENTER OF ONONDAGA COUNTY - BEVARD
    COMMUNITY ROOM, 1033
CIVIC CENTER OF ONONDAGA COUNTY - CARRIER
    THEATER, 1033
CIVIC CENTER OF ONONDAGA COUNTY - CROUSE-HINDS
    CONCERT THEATER, 1033
CIVIC STAGES CHICAGO, 445
CIVIC STAGES CHICAGO - CIVIC THEATRE, 445
CIVIC STAGES CHICAGO - OPERA HOUSE, 446
CLAREMONT COLLEGES - GARRISON THEATRE, THE, 70
CLAREMONT COLLEGES - MABEL SHAW BRIDGES
    AUDITORIUM, THE, 70
CLAREMONT OPERA HOUSE, 803
CLEMENS CENTER, 888
CLEVELAND INSTITUTE OF MUSIC -
    KULAS HALL, THE, 1115
CLEVELAND MUSEUM OF ART - GARTNER
    AUDITORIUM, THE, 1116
CLEVELAND PLAY HOUSE, THE, 1116
CLEVELAND PLAY HOUSE - BOULTON THEATRE, THE, 1116
CLEVELAND PLAY HOUSE - BROOKS THEATRE, THE, 1116
CLEVELAND PLAY HOUSE - DRURY THEATRE, THE, 1116
CLEVELAND PUBLIC THEATRE, 1117
CLIFFSIDE AMPHITHEATRE OF WEST VIRGINIA, 1475
CLOWES MEMORIAL HALL OF BUTLER UNIVERSITY, 497
COASTER THEATER, 1176
COBB COUNTY CIVIC CENTER, 395
COBB COUNTY CIVIC CENTER - JENNIE T. ANDERSON
    THEATER, 395
COBB COUNTY CIVIC CENTER - ROMEO HUDGINS
    MEMORIAL HALL, 395
COBO ARENA, 671
COCONINO CENTER FOR THE ARTS, 26
COE PARK CIVIC CENTER, 284
COLBY COLLEGE - GIVEN AUDITORIUM, 584
COLDEN CENTER FOR THE PERFORMING ARTS, 889
COLGATE UNIVERSITY - BREHMER THEATER, 894
COLGATE UNIVERSITY - UNIVERSITY THEATER, 894
COLISEUM CIVIC CENTER, 732
COLLEGE COMMUNITY CENTER, 1073
COLLEGE OF DUPAGE ARTS CENTER, 457
COLLEGE OF DUPAGE ARTS CENTER - AUDITORIUM, 457
COLLEGE OF DUPAGE ARTS CENTER - MAINSTAGE, 457
COLLEGE OF DUPAGE ARTS CENTER - STUDIO
    THEATRE, 458
COLLEGE OF DUPAGE ARTS CENTER - THEATRE 2, 458
COLLEGE OF SAINT BENEDICT - BENEDICTA ARTS
    CENTER, 723
COLLEGE OF SAINT BENEDICT - BENEDICTA ARTS CENTER
    AUDITORIUM, 723
COLLEGE OF SAINT BENEDICT - BENEDICTA ARTS CENTER
    FORUM, 723
COLLEGE OF SAINT CATHERINE - O'SHAUGHNESSY
    AUDITORIUM, 727
COLLEGE OF THE OZARKS - JONES AUDITORIUM, 752
COLLEGE OF THE SISKIYOUS - THEATRE, 216
COLORADO COLLEGE - PACKARD HALL, 231
COLORADO SPRINGS FINE ARTS CENTER THEATRE, 231
COLORADO STATE UNIVERSITY - UNIVERSITY
    THEATRE, 246
COLUMBIA ARTS CENTER, 1471
COLUMBUS CONVENTION AND CIVIC CENTER, 732
COLUMBUS MUNICIPAL AUDITORIUM, 390
COMMUNITY CENTER FARMINGTON - FARMINGTON
    HILLS, THE, 672
COMMUNITY MUSIC CENTER, 181
COMMUNITY MUSIC CENTER - DAVID CAMPBELL RECITAL
    HALL, 1189
COMMUNITY PLAYERS, 781
COMMUNITY THEATRE, 1447
COMMUNITY THEATRE OF TERRE HAUTE, 505
COMPLEX, THE, 89
CONCORD PAVILION, 71
CONNECTICUT COLLEGE - PALMER AUDITORIUM, 275
CONSTITUTION HALL, 310
CONVENTION CENTER, 1265

CONVENTION CENTER - AUDITORIUM, 1265
CONVENTION CENTER - EXHIBIT HALL, 1265
COPLEY SYMPHONY HALL, 159
CORNELL UNIVERSITY - ALICE STATLER AUDITORIUM, 898
CORNING GLASS CENTER, 884
CORT THEATRE, 996
COUNT BASIE THEATRE, 836
COWAN HALL, 1151
CRANFORD DRAMATIC CLUB THEATRE, 818
CRATERIAN THEATRE, 1184
CREEDE REPERTORY THEATRE, 232
CRESTED BUTTE MOUNTAIN THEATRE, 233
CROSS AND SWORD AMPHITHEATRE, 357
CSC REPERTORY LTD., 996
CUESTA COLLEGE AUDITORIUM, 189
CULTURAL ACTIVITIES CENTER, 1390
CUMBERLAND COUNTY CIVIC CENTER, 583, 1056
CUMBERLAND UNIVERSITY AUDITORIUM, 1288
CUMSTON HALL, 579
CURRAN THEATRE, 181
CURTIS INSTITUTE - CURTIS HALL, 1226
CURTIS THEATRE, 66
CURTISS HALL, 446
CUYAHOGA COMMUNITY COLLEGE - WESTERN CAMPUS
    THEATRE, 1144
CYNTHIA WOODS MITCHELL PAVILION, 1393
DADE COUNTY AUDITORIUM, 343
DAEMEN COLLEGE - DAEMEN THEATRE, 862
DALLAS CONVENTION CENTER, 1334
DALLAS CONVENTION CENTER - ARENA, 1334
DALLAS CONVENTION CENTER - THEATER, 1334
DALLAS REPERTORY THEATRE, 1334
DALLAS THEATER CENTER - ARTS DISTRICT, 1335
DALLAS THEATER CENTER - KALITA HUMPHREYS
    THEATER, 1335
DANCE THEATER WORKSHOP'S BESSIE SCHONBERG
    THEATRE, 996
DAVID ADLER CULTURAL CENTER, 460
DAVIS ART CENTER, 76
DAVIS DISCOVERY CENTER - AGNES JEFFREY SHEDD
    THEATRE, 1125
DAVIS DISCOVERY CENTER - HENRY VAN FLEET
    THEATRE, 1126
DAYTON CONVENTION AND EXHIBITION CENTER, 1131
DAYTON PLAYHOUSE, 1131
DAYTONA BEACH COMMUNITY COLLEGE - THEATRE
    CENTER, 321
DAYTONA PLAYHOUSE, 321
DE ANZA COLLEGE - FLINT CENTER FOR THE
    PERFORMING ARTS, 76
DE PAUL UNIVERSITY - BLACKSTONE THEATRE, 446
DECATUR CIVIC CENTER, 450
DECATUR CIVIC CENTER - ARENA, 450
DECATUR CIVIC CENTER - THEATER, 450
DEE EVENTS CENTER, 1397
DELACORTE THEATRE IN CENTRAL PARK, 997
DELRAY BEACH PLAYHOUSE, 322
DENNOS MUSEUM CENTER - MILLIKEN AUDITORIUM, 695
DENVER AUDITORIUM - ARENA, 240
DENVER AUDITORIUM - CURRIGAN EXHIBITION HALL, 240
DENVER AUDITORIUM - MCNICHOLS SPORTS ARENA, 241
DENVER AUDITORIUM - THEATRE, 241
DENVER COLISEUM, 241
DENVER PERFORMING ARTS COMPLEX - BUELL
    THEATRE, 241
DEPOT, SAINT LOUIS COUNTY HERITAGE AND ARTS
    CENTER, THE, 703
DEPOT THEATRE, 731
DES MOINES WOMEN'S CLUB, 514
DETROIT CENTER FOR THE PERFORMING ARTS, 671
DETROIT SYMPHONY ORCHESTRA HALL, 671
DICKENS OPERA HOUSE, 250
DILLER STREET THEATER, 478
DISCOVER HOUSTON COUNTY VISITORS CENTER -
    MUSEUM, 1323
DIXIE COLLEGE - DIXIE CENTER, 1400
DIXIE COLLEGE - DIXIE CENTER PROSCENIUM STAGE, 1400
DIXIE COLLEGE FINE ARTS CENTER, 1400

DIXIE COLLEGE FINE ARTS CENTER - ARENA
    THEATRE, 1401
DIXIE COLLEGE FINE ARTS CENTER - PROSCENIUM
    THEATRE, 1401
DIXON CENTER FOR THE PERFORMING ARTS, 1
DOBAMA THEATRE, 1120
DOCK STREET THEATRE, 1259
DODGE CITY CIVIC CENTER, 526
DOLLY HAND CULTURAL ARTS CENTER, 315
DOMINICAN COLLEGE - AUDITORIUM, 192
DORE THEATRE - CALIFORNIA STATE UNIVERSITY,
    BAKERSFIELD, 58
DOTHAN CIVIC CENTER, 5
DOVER LITTLE THEATRE, 818
DOWNTOWN CABARET THEATRE, 256
DRAKE UNIVERISTY - OLD MAIN AUDITORIUM, 515
DRAKE UNIVERSITY - HALL OF PERFORMING ARTS,
    HARMON FINE ARTS CENTER, 515
DREW UNIVERSITY - BOWNE THEATRE, 824
DULUTH ENTERTAINMENT CONVENTION CENTER, 703
DUMAS AREA ARTS COUNCIL, INC., 43
DUNBAR PERFORMING ARTS CENTER, 591
EARLVILLE OPERA HOUSE, 886
EAST CENTRAL UNIVERSITY - DOROTHY I. SUMMERS
    THEATER, 1157
EAST COUNTY PERFORMING ARTS CENTER - THEATRE
    EAST, 78
EAST TEXAS STATE UNIVERSITY - UNIVERSITY
    PLAYHOUSE STAGE, 1320
EAST WEST PLAYERS, 118
EASTERN SLOPE PLAYHOUSE, 811
EASTMAN SCHOOL OF MUSIC - KILBOURN HALL, 1022
ECHO THEATRE, 1189
EDEN'S EXPRESSWAY, 997
EGYPTIAN THEATRE, 449
EISNER-LUBIN AUDITORIUM, 997
E.J. THOMAS PERFORMING ARTS HALL, 1093
EL CAMINO COLLEGE - SOUTH BAY CENTER FOR THE
    ARTS, 210
EL DORADO MUNICIPAL AUDITORIUM, 44
EL PASO CIVIC CENTER - EXHIBITION HALL, 1342
EL PASO CIVIC CENTER - THEATER, 1342
ELIZA R. SNOW PERFORMING ARTS CENTER, 416
ELLIOTT HALL OF MUSIC, 505
EMBASSY THEATRE, 491
EMELIN THEATRE FOR THE PERFORMING ARTS, THE, 906
EMPIRE STATE PERFORMING ARTS CENTER, THE, 861
EMPIRE STATE PERFORMING ARTS CENTER - KITTY
    CARLISLE HART THEATER, THE, 861
EMPIRE STATE PERFORMING ARTS CENTER- LEWIS A.
    SWYER THEATER, THE, 861
EMPIRE THEATRE COMPLEX, THE, 1438
EMPIRE THEATRE COMPLEX - EMPIRE STAGE, THE, 1438
EMPIRE THEATRE COMPLEX - LITTLE THEATRE
    STAGE, THE, 1438
EMERSON MAJESTIC THEATRE, 615
ENSEMBLE STUDIO THEATRE, 997
EPHRATA PERFORMING ARTS CENTER - EPHRATA
    COMMUNITY PARK, 1200
ERIE CIVIC CENTER, 1201
ERIE CIVIC CENTER - L.J. TULLIO CONVENTION HALL, 1201
ERIE CIVIC CENTER - WARNER THEATRE, 1202
ETHEL BARRYMORE THEATRE, 997
ETHERREDGE CENTER - UNIVERSITY OF SOUTH
    CAROLINA AT AIKEN, 1256
ETHICAL SOCIETY AUDITORIUM, 761
EUGENE O'NEILL THEATER, 997
EUNICE PLAYERS THEATRE, 557
EVERETT CIVIC AUDITORIUM, 1449
FABULOUS FOX THEATRE, THE, 762
FAIR PARK BANDSHELL, 1335
FAIRMOUNT FINE ARTS CENTER, 1143
FAIRMONT OPERA HOUSE, THE, 704
FALLON HOUSE THEATRE, 70
FALMOUTH PLAYHOUSE, 637
FARM SHOW ARENA, 1206
FARMINGTON CIVIC CENTER, 852
FARTHING AUDITORIUM, 1045

FESTIVAL CONCERT HALL, 1086
FESTIVAL OUTDOOR THEATER, 1370
FESTIVAL THEATRE, 626
FINE ARTS CONCERT HALL, 45
FINE ARTS THEATRE, 1515
FIREHOUSE DINNER THEATRE, 793
FIVE FLAGS CENTER, 516
FIVE FLAGS CENTER - ARENA, 516
FIVE FLAGS CENTER - THEATRE, 516
FIVE SEASONS CENTER ARENA, 510
FLICKINGER CENTER FOR THE PERFORMING ARTS, 847
FLINT INSTITUTE OF MUSIC, THE, 673
FLORAL HALL, 525
FLORENCE GOULD THEATRE IN THE CALIFORNIA PALACE
    OF THE LEGION OF HONOR, 181
FLORIDA A & M UNIVERSITY - CHARLES WINTER WOOD
    THEATRE, 366
FLORIDA KEYS COMMUNITY COLLEGE - TENNESSEE
    WILLIAMS THEATRE, 334
FLORIDA NATIONAL PAVILION, 332
FLORIDA SOUTHERN COLLEGE - BUCKNER THEATRE, 336
FLORIDA STUDIO THEATRE, 363
FLORIDA THEATRE PERFORMING ARTS CENTER, 332
FLYNN THEATRE FOR THE PERFORMING ARTS, 1412
F.M. KIRBY CENTER FOR THE PERFORMING ARTS, 1242
FOELLINGER THEATER IN FRANKE PARK, 491
FOLLY, 749
FONTANA PERFORMING ARTS CENTER, 80
FOOTLIGHT PLAYERS THEATRE, 1259
FORD'S THEATRE, 310
FORREST THEATRE, 1226
FORT EUSTIS MUSIC AND VIDEO CENTER, 1426
FORT EUSTIS MUSIC AND VIDEO CENTER - JACOBS
    THEATRE, 1426
FORT EUSTIS MUSIC AND VIDEO CENTER - SOLDIER
    THEATRE, 1426
FORT GRIFFIN FANDANGLE OUTDOOR THEATRE, 1304
FORT HAYS STATE UNIVERSITY-FELTON - START
    THEATRE, 527
FORT HOOD MUSIC AND THEATER - THEATER #1, 1343
FORT MASON CENTER - COWELL THEATRE, 181
FORT MYERS HARBORSIDE 3 BUILDINGS, 326
FORT SMITH CIVIC CENTER, 46
FORT SMITH CIVIC CENTER - EXHIBITION HALL, 46
FORT SMITH CIVIC CENTER - THEATER, 47
FORT SMITH LITTLE THEATRE, 47
FORT WORTH/TARRANT COUNTY CONVENTION CENTER -
    CONVENTION CENTER THEATER, 1349
46TH STREET THEATRE, 993
14TH STREET PLAYHOUSE, 386
FORUM, THE, 48
FOSTORIA FOOTLIGHTERS, INC., 1133
FOUNTAIN STREET CHURCH, 676
FOX THEATRE, 386, 671
FRANCIS SCOTT KEY AUDITORIUM, 585
FRANCISCAN LIFE CENTER, 1146
FRAUENTHAL FOUNDATION FINE ARTS CENTER, 687
FREEDOM HALL, NATHAN MANILOW THEATRE, 467
FRESNO CONVENTION CENTER THEATRE, 82
FRIENDS OF THE CONCORD CITY AUDITORIUM, THE, 804
FRIENDS OF THE PERFORMING ARTS IN CONCORD -
    51 WALDEN, THE, 623
FULTON OPERA HOUSE FOUNDATION, 1210
FURMAN UNIVERSITY - MCALISTER AUDITORIUM, 1263
GAILLARD MUNICIPAL AUDITORIUM, 1259
GAINES CHAPEL, AGNES SCOTT COLLEGE, 392
GARDE ARTS CENTER, 275
GARDEN STATE ARTS CENTER, 821
GARLAND CENTER FOR THE PERFORMING ARTS, 1353
GARLAND CENTER FOR THE PERFORMING ARTS -
    THEATER #1, 1353
GARLAND CENTER FOR THE PERFORMING ARTS -
    THEATER #2, 1353
GASLAMP QUARTER THEATRE, 159
GASTON HALL, 310
GEARY AUDITORIUM, 1480
GENERIE THEATER, 1434
GEORGE MASON UNIVERSITY CENTER FOR THE ARTS, 1426

GEORGE WASHINGTON UNIVERSITY - LISNER
    AUDITORIUM, 310
GEORGIA SOUTHERN UNIVERSITY - FOY FINE ARTS
    RECITAL HALL, 398
GEORGIA SOUTHERN UNIVERSITY - PUPPET THEATRE, 398
GERMINAL STAGE DENVER, 241
GERSHWIN THEATRE, 998
GILL COLISEUM, 1178
GIRAULT AUDITORIUM, 736
GLENDALE COMMUNITY COLLEGE PERFORMING ARTS
    CENTER, 27
GLENN MEMORIAL AUDITORIUM, 386
GLOBE OF THE GREAT SOUTHWEST, 1378
GOLD BAR ROOM THEATRE, IMPERIAL HOTEL, 233
GOLDEN GATE THEATRE, 181
GOLDEN WEST COLLEGE - MAINSTAGE THEATRE, 90
GONZAGA UNIVERSITY - GENE RUSSELL THEATRE, 1467
GOODFELLOW HALL (JACK BENNY CENTER FOR THE
    ARTS), 477
GOODSPEED-AT-CHESTER/THE NORMA TERRIS
    THEATRE, 258
GOODSPEED OPERA HOUSE, 259
GOSHEN COLLEGE - JOHN S. UMBLE CENTER, 493
GOTHENBURG COMMUNITY PLAYHOUSE - SUN
    THEATRE, 782
GRAMERCY ARTS THEATER, 998
GRANBURY OPERA HOUSE, 1353
GRAND 1894 OPERA HOUSE, 1351
GRAND CENTER - AUDITORIUM, 676
GRAND CENTER - DEVOS HALL, 676
GRAND OLE OPRY HOUSE, 1298
GRAND OPERA HOUSE, 296, 393, 1512
GRAND PRAIRIE WAR MEMORIAL AUDITORIUM, 53
GREAT FALLS CENTER FOR THE PERFORMING ARTS, 772
GREAT FALLS CIVIC CENTER THEATER, 772
GREAT WESTERN FORUM, THE, 91
GREAT WOODS CENTER FOR THE PERFORMING ARTS, 632
GREEK THEATRE, 118
GREENSBORO WAR MEMORIAL AUDITORIUM, 1060
GREENVILLE MEMORIAL AUDITORIUM, 1264
GREENWOOD CIVIC CENTER, 1264
GREENWOOD LEFLORE CIVIC CENTER, 733
GREER GARSON THEATRE CENTER - COLLEGE OF
    SANTA FE, 856
GUNN HIGH SCHOOL - SPANGENBERG THEATRE, 139
GUSMAN CENTER FOR THE PERFORMING ARTS, 343
GUSTAVUS ADOLPHUS COLLEGE - SCHAEFFER FINE ARTS
    COMPLEX, 728
GUSTAVUS ADOLPHUS COLLEGE - SCHAEFFER FINE ARTS
    COMPLEX - EVELYN E. ANDERSON THEATRE, 728
GUSTAVUS ADOLPHUS COLLEGE - SCHAEFFER FINE ARTS
    COMPLEX - JUSSI BJORLING CONCERT HALL, 728
GUTHRIE THEATER, THE, 718
HALL OF NATIONS BLACK BOX THEATRE, 311
HAMILTON COLLEGE - MINOR THEATRE, 882
HAMPTON COLISEUM, 1427
HAMPTON PLAYHOUSE THEATRE ARTS WORKSHOP, 806
HANGAR THEATRE, 898
HARLINGEN CULTURAL ARTS CENTER - AUDITORIUM, 1354
HARTFORD CIVIC CENTER, 265
HARTFORD STAGE COMPANY, 265
HAUGH PERFORMING ARTS CENTER, 85
H.B. PLAYWRIGHTS FOUNDATION THEATRE HOUSE, 998
HEINZ HALL FOR THE PERFORMING ARTS, 1236
HELEN HAYES THEATRE, 998
HELENA CIVIC CENTER, 774
HELENA CIVIC CENTER - AUDITORIUM, 774
HELENA CIVIC CENTER - BALLROOM, 775
HENDRIX THEATRE, 1061
HENNEPIN CENTER FOR THE ARTS, 718
HENRY J. KAISER CONVENTION CENTER, 133
HENRY J. KAISER CONVENTION CENTER - ARENA, 133
HENRY J. KAISER CONVENTION CENTER - CALVIN
    SIMMONS THEATRE, 133
HERSHEY THEATRE, 1206
HEYMANN PERFORMING ARTS AND CONVENTION
    CENTER, 558
HIGH POINT THEATRE AND EXHIBITION CENTER, 1063

HIGHFIELD THEATRE, 627
HIGHLANDS PLAYHOUSE, 1063
HINGHAM HIGH SCHOOL - AUDITORIUM, 629
HIPPODROME, 328, 1391
HIRSCH MEMORIAL COLISEUM, 571
HISTORIC IRONWOOD THEATRE, 679
HOLLYWOOD BOWL, 89
HOLLYWOOD PALLADIUM, 89
HOPE COLLEGE THEATRE DEPARTMENT, 678
HOPE MARTIN THEATRE, 521
HORACE A. MOSES BUILDING, 650
HORACE BUSHNELL MEMORIAL HALL, 265
HOT SPRINGS CONVENTION AND VISITORS' BUREAU, 47
HOUGHTON COLLEGE - WESLEY CHAPEL, 897
HOUSTON CIVIC CENTER, 1364
HOUSTON CIVIC CENTER-GEORGE R. BROWN
    CONVENTION CENTER, 1364
HOUSTON CIVIC CENTER-GEORGE R. BROWN
    CONVENTION CENTER - BALLROOM, 1364
HOUSTON CIVIC CENTER-GEORGE R. BROWN
    CONVENTION CENTER - EXHIBITION HALL, 1365
HOUSTON CIVIC CENTER-GEORGE R. BROWN
    CONVENTION CENTER - GENERAL ASSEMBLY
    HALL, 1365
HOUSTON CIVIC CENTER-GUS WORTHAM THEATER
    CENTER, 1365
HOUSTON CIVIC CENTER-GUS WORTHAM THEATER
    CENTER - ALICE AND GEORGE BROWN THEATER, 1365
HOUSTON CIVIC CENTER-GUS WORTHAM THEATER
    CENTER - LILLY AND ROY CULLEN THEATER, 1365
HOUSTON CIVIC CENTER - JESSE H. JONES HALL FOR THE
    PERFORMING ARTS, 1366
HOUSTON CIVIC CENTER - THE MUSIC HALL, 1366
HOUSTON CIVIC CENTER - SAM HOUSTON COLISEUM, 1366
HOUSTON FINE ARTS CENTER, 241
HOWARD COLLEGE AT BIG SPRING - HOWARD COLLEGE
    AUDITORIUM, 1316
HOWARD COLLEGE AT BIG SPRING - HOWARD COLLEGE
    COLISEUM, 1316
HULT CENTER FOR THE PERFORMING ARTS, 1181
HULT CENTER FOR THE PERFORMING ARTS - SILVA
    CONCERT HALL, 1181
HULT CENTER FOR THE PERFORMING ARTS - SORENG
    THEATRE, 1181
HUMBOLDT STATE UNIVERSITY, 56
HUMBOLDT STATE UNIVERSITY - EAST GYMNASIUM, 57
HUMBOLDT STATE UNIVERSITY - FULKERSON RECITAL
    HALL, 57
HUMBOLDT STATE UNIVERSITY - JOHN VAN DUZER
    THEATRE, 57
HUMBOLDT STATE UNIVERSITY - KATE BUCHANAN
    ROOM, 57
HUNTINGTON CIVIC CENTRE, THE, 1481
HUNTINGTON MUSEUM OF ART - AMPHITHEATRE, 1481
HUNTINGTON MUSEUM OF ART - AUDITORIUM, 1481
HUNTINGTON PLAYHOUSE, 1096
IDAHO STATE UNIVERSITY - FRAZIER AUDITORIUM, 416
IDAHO STATE UNIVERSITY - GORANSON HALL, 416
IDAHO STATE UNIVERSITY - POWELL LITTLE THEATRE, 416
ILLINOIS THEATRE CENTER, 467
ILLINOIS WESLEYAN SCHOOL OF DRAMA - MCPHERSON
    HALL, 421
ILLINOIS WESLEYAN UNIVERSITY - WESTBROOK
    AUDITORIUM, 421
IMPERIAL THEATRE, 389, 998
INDIANA UNIVERSITY AUDITORIUM, 484
INDIANA UNIVERSITY MUSICAL ARTS CENTER, 484
INDIANA UNIVERSITY THEATRE, 485
INDIANOLA LITTLE THEATRE, 734
INTERLOCHEN CENTER FOR THE ARTS - CORSON
    AUDITORIUM, 678
INTERLOCHEN CENTER FOR THE ARTS - DENDRINOS
    CHAPEL/RECITAL HALL, 679
INTERLOCHEN CENTER FOR THE ARTS - KRESGE
    AUDITORIUM, 679
INTERMOUNTAIN CULTURAL CENTER AND MUSEUM, 418
INTERNATIONAL FESTIVAL-INSTITUTE AT ROUND TOP -
    FESTIVAL CONCERT HALL, 1381

IOWA STATE UNIVERSITY - BENTON AUDITORIUM, 508
IOWA STATE UNIVERSITY - C.Y. STEPHENS
    AUDITORIUM, 508
IOWA STATE UNIVERSITY - HILTON COLISEUM, 508
IOWA STATE UNIVERSITY - IOWA STATE CENTER, 508
IOWA STATE UNIVERSITY - J.W. FISHER AUDITORIUM, 508
IRVING ARTS CENTER, 1370
ISABELLA STEWART GARDNER MUSEUM, 615
ISLAND PLAYERS THEATRE, 315
ITHACA COLLEGE - DILLINGHAM CENTER FOR THE
    PERFORMING ARTS, 898
ITHACA COLLEGE - DILLINGHAM CENTER FOR THE
    PERFORMING ARTS - ARENA, 898
ITHACA COLLEGE - DILLINGHAM CENTER FOR THE
    PERFORMING ARTS - HOERNER AUDITORIUM, 898
JACKIE GLEASON THEATER, 345
JACKSON AUDITORIUM, 1388
JACKSON CIVIC CENTER, 1282
JACKSON MUNICIPAL AUDITORIUM, 736
JACKSONVILLE CIVIC AUDITORIUM, 332
JACKSONVILLE CIVIC AUDITORIUM - EXHIBITION
    HALL, 333
JACKSONVILLE CIVIC AUDITORIUM - LITTLE THEATER, 333
JAMAICA ARTS CENTER, 900
JAMES A. DOOLITTLE THEATRE, 89
JAMES C. PETRILLO MUSIC SHELL, 446
JAMES H. WHITING AUDITORIUM, 673
JAMES L. KNIGHT CENTER, 343
JAPAN AMERICA THEATER, 118
JASPER CIVIC AUDITORIUM, 498
JEKYLL ISLAND AMPHITHEATER, 393
JEWISH COMMUNITY CENTER - JOE FRANK THEATRE, 1366
JEWISH COMMUNITY CENTER - KAPLAN THEATRE, 1366
JEWISH COMMUNITY CENTER OF CLEVELAND - BLANCHE
    R. HALLE THEATER, 1126
JOE LOUIS ARENA, 671
JOHN A. WALKER COMMUNITY CENTER, 1076
JOHN ADDISON CONCERT HALL, 594
JOHN F. KENNEDY CENTER FOR THE PERFORMING
    ARTS, 311
JOHN F. KENNEDY CENTER FOR THE PERFORMING ARTS -
    AMERICAN FILM INSTITUTE THEATER, 311
JOHN F. KENNEDY CENTER FOR THE PERFORMING ARTS -
    CONCERT HALL, 311
JOHN F. KENNEDY CENTER FOR THE PERFORMING ARTS -
    EISENHOWER THEATER, 311
JOHN F. KENNEDY CENTER FOR THE PERFORMING ARTS -
    OPERA HOUSE, 311
JOHN F. KENNEDY CENTER FOR THE PERFORMING ARTS -
    TERRACE THEATER, 312
JOHN F. KENNEDY CENTER FOR THE PERFORMING ARTS -
    THEATER LAB, 312
JOHN GOLDEN THEATRE, 999
JOHN HARMS CENTER FOR THE ARTS, 819
JOHN MICHAEL KOHLER ARTS CENTER, 1515
JOHN PAUL THEATRE, 31
JOHNS HOPKINS UNIVERSITY - THE MERRICK
    BARN, THE, 591
JOSEPH PAPP PUBLIC THEATER, THE, 999
JORDAN HALL AT NEW ENGLAND CONSERVATORY, 615
JORDAN THEATRE, 98
JOYCE THEATER, THE, 999
JULIE ROGERS THEATRE FOR THE PERFORMING ARTS, 1315
KALAMAZOO CIVIC AUDITORIUM, 682
KALAMAZOO COLLEGE, 682
KANSAS CITY MUNICIPAL AUDITORIUM, 749
KANSAS CITY MUNICIPAL AUDITORIUM - ARENA, 749
KANSAS CITY MUNICIPAL AUDITORIUM - MUSIC HALL, 749
KANSAS STATE FAIR - GRANDSTAND, 528
KANSAS STATE UNIVERSITY - MCCAIN AUDITORIUM, 530
KARAMU HOUSE PERFORMING ARTS THEATRE, 1117
KARAMU HOUSE PERFORMING ARTS THEATRE -
    AMPHITHEATRE, 1117
KARAMU HOUSE PERFORMING ARTS THEATRE -
    ARENA, 1117
KARAMU HOUSE PERFORMING ARTS THEATRE -
    PROSCENIUM, 1117
KATHARINE CORNELL MEMORIAL THEATRE, 647

KAUFMANN CONCERT HALL, 999
KAZUKO HIRABAYASHI DANCE THEATRE, 999
KEAN COLLEGE OF NEW JERSEY - WILKINS THEATRE, 840
KEARNEY COMMUNITY THEATRE, 783
KEITH-ALBEE THEATRE, 1481
KELLOGG CENTER ARENA, 662
KEMPER ARENA, 750
KENDRICK AMPHITHEATER, 1318
KENNETH C. BECK CENTER FOR THE PERFORMING ARTS, 1135
KENTUCKY CENTER FOR THE ARTS, 549
KENTUCKY CENTER FOR THE ARTS - BOMHARD THEATER, 550
KENTUCKY CENTER FOR THE ARTS - BOYD MARTIN EXPERIMENTAL THEATER, 550
KENTUCKY CENTER FOR THE ARTS - WHITNEY HALL, 550
KIEL CENTER, THE, 762
KIEL CENTER - ARENA, THE, 762
KIEL CENTER - OPERA HOUSE, THE, 762
KIRKLAND ART CENTER, 882
KIRKLAND FINE ARTS CENTER, 450
KLEIN MEMORIAL AUDITORIUM, 256
KLEINHANS MUSIC HALL, 880
KLINGENSMITH PARK AMPHITHEATRE, 1159
KNOX COLLEGE - ELEANOR ABBOTT FORD CENTER FOR THE FINE ARTS, 456
KNOXVILLE CIVIC AUDITORIUM AND COLISEUM - AUDITORIUM, 1287
KODIAK ARTS COUNCIL, 22
KRANNERT CENTER FOR THE PERFORMING ARTS, 476
KRANNERT CENTER FOR THE PERFORMING ARTS - COLWELL PLAYHOUSE, 476
KRANNERT CENTER FOR THE PERFORMING ARTS - FESTIVAL THEATRE, 476
KRANNERT CENTER FOR THE PERFORMING ARTS - FOELLINGER GREAT HALL, 477
KRANNERT CENTER FOR THE PERFORMING ARTS - STUDIO THEATRE, 476
KREEGER FINE ARTS AUDITORIUM, 597
KUTZTOWN UNIVERSITY - SCHAEFFER AUDITORIUM, 1209
KUUMBWA JAZZ CENTER, 197
LA CROSSE CENTER, 1494
LA MIRADA THEATRE FOR THE PERFORMING ARTS, 95
LA SELLS STEWART CENTER, 1178
LAFAYETTE COMMUNITY THEATRE, 558
LAGOON OPERA HOUSE, 1395
LAGUNA PLAYHOUSE, 96
LAKE CHARLES CIVIC CENTER, 560
LAKE CHARLES CIVIC CENTER - COLISEUM, 560
LAKE CHARLES CIVIC CENTER - EXHIBITION HALL, 560
LAKE CHARLES CIVIC CENTER - ROSA HART THEATRE, 560
LAKE GEORGE DINNER THEATRE, 903
LAKE PLACID CENTER FOR THE ARTS - THEATER, 903
LAKELAND CIVIC CENTER, 336
LAKELAND CIVIC CENTER - ARENA, 336
LAKELAND CIVIC CENTER - EXHIBITION HALL, 337
LAKELAND CIVIC CENTER - THEATER, 337
LAKESHORE PLAYHOUSE, 729
LAMAR UNIVERSITY - LAMAR UNIVERSITY PROSCENIUM THEATRE, 1315
LAMAR UNIVERSITY - LAMAR UNIVERSITY STUDIO THEATRE, 1315
LAMB'S THEATRE, THE, 1000
LAMBUTH COLLEGE - LAMBUTH THEATRE, 1282
LANCASTER NEW YORK OPERA HOUSE, 904
LANDERS THEATRE, 766
LANEY COLLEGE THEATRE, 133
LANGFORD AUDITORIUM, 1298
LANSING CIVIC ARENA, 684
LAS VEGAS CONVENTION AND VISITORS AUTHORITY-CASHMAN'S FIELD CENTER, 798
LAWRENCE ACADEMY THEATRE, 628
LAWRENCE UNIVERSITY - MUSIC-DRAMA CENTER, 1487
LE PETIT THEATRE DU VIEUX CARRE, 566
LEE CIVIC CENTER, 347
LEE CIVIC CENTER - ARENA, 347
LEE CIVIC CENTER - SMALL THEATER, 347
LEE HALL AUDITORIUM, 737
LEES MCRAE COLLEGE - HAYES AUDITORIUM, 1044
LEHMAN CENTER FOR THE PERFORMING ARTS, 1000
LESTER E. PALMER AUDITORIUM, 1310
LEVITT PAVILION FOR THE PERFORMING ARTS, 289
LEXINGTON OPERA HOUSE, 545
LIBRARY OF CONGRESS, 312
LIED CENTER FOR THE PERFORMING ARTS, 787
LINCOLN CENTER, 246
LINCOLN CENTER FOR THE CULTURAL ARTS, 509
LINCOLN CENTER FOR THE PERFORMING ARTS, 1000
LINCOLN CENTER FOR THE PERFORMING ARTS - ALICE TULLY HALL, 1000
LINCOLN CENTER FOR THE PERFORMING ARTS - AVERY FISHER HALL, 1000
LINCOLN CENTER FOR THE PERFORMING ARTS - THE JUILLIARD OPERA CENTER, 1000
LINCOLN CENTER FOR THE PERFORMING ARTS - THE JUILLIARD SCHOOL DRAMA WORKSHOP, 1001
LINCOLN CENTER FOR THE PERFORMING ARTS - METROPOLITAN OPERA HOUSE, 1001
LINCOLN CENTER FOR THE PERFORMING ARTS - MITZI E. NEWHOUSE THEATER, 1001
LINCOLN CENTER FOR THE PERFORMING ARTS - NEW YORK PUBLIC LIBRARY AUDITORIUM, 1001
LINCOLN CENTER FOR THE PERFORMING ARTS - NEW YORK STATE THEATER, 1001
LINCOLN CENTER FOR THE PERFORMING ARTS - PAUL RECITAL HALL, 1001
LINCOLN CENTER FOR THE PERFORMING ARTS - VIVIAN BEAUMONT THEATER, 1002
LINCOLN THEATER, 287
LINCOLN THEATRE CENTRE, 1451
LITTLE THEATRE OF NORFOLK, 1434
LOBERO THEATRE, 195
LOEB DRAMA CENTER, 621
LONG BEACH COMMUNITY PLAYHOUSE - STAGE, 98
LONG BEACH CONVENTION AND ENTERTAINMENT CENTER, 99
LONG BEACH PLAYHOUSE - MAINSTAGE THEATRE, 99
LONG BEACH PLAYHOUSE - STUDIO THEATRE, 99
LONG CENTER FOR THE PERFORMING ARTS, 499
LONG ISLAND UNIVERSITY - FINE ARTS THEATRE, 1028
LONG WHARF THEATRE, 272
LONG WHARF THEATRE - STAGE II, 273
LONGACRE THEATRE, 1002
LOS ALAMOS CIVIC AUDITORIUM, 853
LOS ANGELES COUNTY MUSEUM OF ART - LEO S. BING THEATER, 118
LOS ANGELES THEATRE CENTER, 118
LOS ANGELES THEATRE CENTER - THEATRE 2, 119
LOS ANGELES THEATRE CENTER - THEATRE 3, 119
LOS ANGELES THEATRE CENTER - THEATRE 4, 119
LOS ANGELES THEATRE CENTER - TOM BRADLEY THEATRE, 119
LOUISIANA TECH - HOWARD AUDITORIUM CENTER FOR THE PERFORMING ARTS, 568
LOUISVILLE MEMORIAL AUDITORIUM, 550
LOYOLA UNIVERSITY - LOUIS J. ROUSSEL PERFORMANCE HALL, 567
LOYOLA UNIVERSITY - MARQUETTE THEATRE, 567
LSU UNION THEATER, 556
LUBBOCK MEMORIAL CIVIC CENTER, 1373
LUBBOCK MEMORIAL CIVIC CENTER - BANQUET HALL, 1373
LUBBOCK MEMORIAL CIVIC CENTER - COLISEUM, 1373
LUBBOCK MEMORIAL CIVIC CENTER - EXHIBIT HALL, 1373
LUBBOCK MEMORIAL CIVIC CENTER - MUNICIPAL AUDITORIUM, 1373
LUBBOCK MEMORIAL CIVIC CENTER - THEATER, 1373
LUCILLE BALL LITTLE THEATRE BUILDING, 901
LUCILLE LORTEL THEATRE, 1002
LUNT-FONTANNE THEATRE, 1002
LUTCHER THEATER, 1378
LUTHER BURBANK CENTER FOR THE ARTS, 200
LUTHER BURBANK CENTER FOR THE ARTS - CONCERT CHAMBER, 201
LUTHER BURBANK CENTER FOR THE ARTS - EAST AUDITORIUM, 201

LUTHER BURBANK CENTER FOR THE ARTS - GOLD
    ROOM, 201
LUTHER BURBANK CENTER FOR THE ARTS - RUTH FINLEY
    PERSON MEMORIAL THEATRE, 201
LYCEUM THEATRE, 741, 1002
LYNCHBURG FINE ARTS CENTER, 1429
LYNDHURST, 1034
LYNN CITY HALL MEMORIAL AUDITORIUM, 631
LYRIC INC./LYRIC OPERA HOUSE, 592
LYRIC THEATRE, 750, 1396
MABEL TAINTER MEMORIAL THEATER BUILDING, 1502
MACAULEY THEATRE, 550
MACOMB CENTER FOR THE PERFORMING ARTS, 686
MACPHAIL CENTER FOR THE ARTS, 718
MADISON CIVIC CENTER, 1500
MADISON CIVIC CENTER - ISTHMUS PLAYHOUSE, 1500
MADISON CIVIC CENTER - OSCAR MAYER THEATRE, 1500
MADISON - MORGAN CULTURAL CENTER, 394
MADISON SQUARE GARDEN, 1002
MAGICAL THEATRE COMPANY, 1095
MAJESTIC THEATRE, 822, 1003, 1335
MANCHESTER COLLEGE - CORDIER AUDITORIUM, 501
MANDELL WEISS PERFORMING ARTS CENTER, 94
MANHATTAN THEATRE CLUB, 1003
MANKATO STATE UNIVERSITY - ELIAS J. HALLING
    RECITAL HALL, 706
MANN MUSIC CENTER, 1227
MANNONI PERFORMING ARTS CENTER, 733
MANTI TEMPLE GROUNDS AMPHITHEATRE, 1397
MAPLEWOOD COMMUNITY CENTER, 673
MARIE HITCHCOCK PUPPET THEATRE IN
    BALBOA PARK, THE, 159
MARIN CENTER, 192
MARIN CENTER - SHOWCASE THEATRE, 192
MARIN CENTER - VETERANS MEMORIAL AUDITORIUM, 192
MARION CULTURAL AND CIVIC CENTER, 462
MARQUIS, 1003
MARSHALL CIVIC CENTER, 1375
MARSHALL THEATER AT THE CIVIC CENTER, 1375
MARSHALL UNIVERSITY - JOAN C. EDWARDS
    PLAYHOUSE, 1482
MARSHALL UNIVERSITY - SMITH RECITAL HALL, 1482
MARTHA GUINSBERG PAVILION, 886
MARTIN BECK THEATER, 1003
MARTIN LUTHER KING JR. PERFORMING AND CULTURAL
    ARTS COMPLEX, 1126
MARWICK - BOYD AUDITORIUM, 1199
MARYCREST COLLEGE - UPHAM AUDITORIUM, 513
MARYLAND HALL FOR THE CREATIVE ARTS, 585
MARYLAND THEATRE, 595
MARYMOUNT MANHATTAN COLLEGE - MARYMOUNT
    MANHATTAN THEATRE, 1003
MARYVILLE COLLEGE, 1288
MASK AND BAUBLE DRAMATIC SOCIETY THEATER, 312
MATTHEWS OPERA HOUSE, 1275
MAURICE LEVIN THEATER, 844
MAVERICK CONCERT HALL, 1040
MAXWELL C. KING CENTER FOR THE PERFORMING
    ARTS, 339
MAY BONFILS STANTON CENTER FOR THE PERFORMING
    ARTS, 242
MAY BONFILS STANTON CENTER FOR THE PERFORMING
    ARTS - LITTLE AUDITORIUM, 242
MAY BONFILS STANTON CENTER FOR THE PERFORMING
    ARTS - PROSCENIUM THEATRE, 242
MAY BONFILS STANTON CENTER FOR THE PERFORMING
    ARTS - STAGE 2, 242
MAYO CIVIC CENTER, 722
MAYO CIVIC CENTER - ARENA, 722
MAYO CIVIC CENTER - AUDITORIUM, 722
MAYO CIVIC CENTER - THEATRE, 722
MCCARTER THEATRE, 834
MCCLELLAND ARTS CENTER, 1451
MCKAY AUDITORIUM AT BRIGHAM YOUNG UNIVERSITY
    HAWAII, 408
MCMAHON MEMORIAL AUDITORIUM, 1161
MCMORRAN PLACE, 690
MCPHERSON COLLEGE - BROWN AUDITORIUM, 531

MEANY HALL, 1464
MECHANICS HALL, 652
MELBOURNE AUDITORIUM, 339
MEMORIAL AUDITORIUM, 525, 1393
MEMORIAL AUDITORIUM AND CONVENTION CENTER, 532
MEMPHIS CHILDREN'S THEATRE, 1292
MEMPHIS COOK CONVENTION CENTER COMPLEX, 1292
MEMPHIS COOK CONVENTION CENTER COMPLEX -
    DIXON-MYERS HALL, 1292
MEMPHIS COOK CONVENTION CENTER COMPLEX -
    VINCENT DEFRANK HALL, 1292
MENDOCINO ART CENTER - HELEN SCHOENI THEATER, 123
MERCE CUNNINGHAM DANCE STUDIO, 1003
MERCY COLLEGE - LECTURE HALL, 886
MERIDIAN COMMUNITY COLLEGE - THEATRE, 737
MERKIN CONCERT HALL AT ELAINE KAUFMAN CONCERT
    CENTER, 1004
MERRIAM THEATER, 1227
MESA COLLEGE - WALTER WALKER AUDITORIUM, 248
MESA COMMUNITY CENTER, 27
MESA COMMUNITY CENTER - AMPHITHEATRE, 28
MESA COMMUNITY CENTER - CENTENNIAL HALL, 28
MESA COMMUNITY CENTER - CONFERENCE CENTER, 28
METROPOLITAN PERFORMING ARTS CENTER, THE, 1467
MORTON H. MEYERSON SYMPHONY CENTER - EUGENE
    MCDERMOTT CONCERT HALL, THE, 1335
MICHIGAN THEATER, 660
MIDDLEBURY COLLEGE - WRIGHT THEATRE, 1415
MID-HUDSON CIVIC CENTER, 1017
MIDLAND CENTER FOR THE ARTS, 685
MIDWAY THEATRE, 472
MILL MOUNTAIN THEATRE, 1440
MILLBROOK PLAYHOUSE, 1212
MILLER AUDITORIUM, 1238
MILLER OUTDOOR THEATRE, 1366
MILLIGAN COLLEGE - DERTHICK THEATRE, 1293
MILLIGAN COLLEGE - SEEGER CHAPEL CONCERT
    HALL, 1293
MILLS COLLEGE CONCERT HALL, 134
MILWAUKEE AREA TECHNICAL COLLEGE - COOLEY
    AUDITORIUM, 1510
MILWAUKEE PERFORMING ARTS CENTER, 1510
MINETTA LANE THEATRE, 1004
MINSKOFF THEATRE, 1004
MISHLER THEATRE, 1195
MISSOURI THEATRE, 743
M.K. BROWN AUDITORIUM, 1379
MOBILE CIVIC CENTER, 9
MOBILE CIVIC CENTER - ARENA, 9
MOBILE CIVIC CENTER - EXPOSITION HALL, 9
MOBILE CIVIC CENTER - THEATRE, 9
MOBILE THEATRE GUILD, 9
MODESTO JUNIOR COLLEGE CABARET, 125
MOHAWK VALLEY CENTER FOR THE ARTS, 905
MONROE CIVIC CENTER, 563
MONROE CIVIC CENTER - ARENA, 563
MONROE CIVIC CENTER - THEATER, 563
MONTCLAIR CIVIC CENTER - STARLITE PATIO
    THEATRE, 125
MONTCLAIR STATE COLLEGE - MEMORIAL
    AUDITORIUM, 841
MONTGOMERY COUNTY'S MEMORIAL HALL, 1132
MONTICELLO OPERA HOUSE, 345
MOODY CIVIC CENTER - EXHIBITION HALL, 1351
MOORE AUDITORIUM, 1065
MORCA FOUNDATION OF THE DANCE, 1445
MORGAN-WIXSON THEATRE, 200
MORRIS CIVIC AUDITORIUM, 504
MOUNT AIRY FINE ARTS CENTER/ANDY GRIFFITH
    PLAYHOUSE, 1067
MOUNT BAKER THEATRE, 1446
MOUNTAIN PLAYHOUSE, 1207
MUCKENTHALER CULTURAL CENTER, 83
MULE BARN THEATRE, 766
MUNICIPAL ART GALLERY - GALLERY THEATER, 119
MUNICIPAL AUDITORIUM, 1386
MUNY, THE, 762
MURRAY STATE UNIVERSITY - LOVETT AUDITORIUM, 551

MUSIC AND ARTS INSTITUTE, 181
MUSIC BOX, 1004
MUSIC CENTER OF LOS ANGELES COUNTY, THE, 119
MUSIC CENTER OF LOS ANGELES COUNTY - AHMANSON THEATER, THE, 120
MUSIC CENTER OF LOS ANGELES COUNTY - DOROTHY CHANDLER PAVILION, THE, 120
MUSIC CENTER OF LOS ANGELES COUNTY - MARK TAPER FORUM, THE, 120
MUSIC HALL, 1367
MUSIC HALL, THE, 813
MUSIC HALL AT FAIR PARK, 1336
MUSIC HALL CENTER FOR THE PERFORMING ARTS, 671
MUSIC TENT, 222
MUSKOGEE LITTLE THEATRE, 1161
NAPA VALLEY OPERA HOUSE, 126
NAROPA INSTITUTE, THE, 227
NASHVILLE CONVENTION CENTER, 1298
NATIONAL - LOUIS UNIVERSITY'S WEINSTEIN CENTER FOR THE PERFORMING ARTS, 455
NATIONAL THEATRE, 312
NAZARETH COLLEGE - NAZARETH ARTS CENTER, 1022
NEAL S. BLAISDELL CENTER, 406
NEAL S. BLAISDELL CENTER - ARENA, 406
NEAL S. BLAISDELL CENTER - CONCERT HALL, 406
NEAL S. BLAISDELL CENTER - WAIKIKI SHELL, 406
NEDERLANDER THEATRE, 1004
NEIL SIMON THEATRE, 1004
NEODESHA ARTS ASSOCIATION, 531
NEW DRAMATISTS, 1005
NEW HAMPSHIRE PERFORMING ARTS CENTER, 808
NEW HOPE OUTDOOR THEATRE, 719
NEW JERSEY STATE MUSEUM AUDITORIUM, 840
NEW LONDON BARN PLAYHOUSE, 810
NEW MEXICO REP, 856
NEW MEXICO STATE UNIVERSITY - AMERICAN SOUTHWEST THEATRE, 852
NEW ORLEANS MUNICIPAL AUDITORIUM, 567
NEW ORLEANS THEATRE OF THE PERFORMING ARTS, 567
NEW PERFORMANCE GALLERY OF SAN FRANCISCO, 182
NEW ROSE THEATRE, 1189
NEW YORK STATE OFFICE OF GENERAL SERVICES, 1037
NEWARK SYMPHONY HALL, 832
NOB HILL MASONIC CENTER, 182
NORFOLK SCOPE CULTURAL AND CONVENTION CENTER, 1434
NORFOLK SCOPE CULTURAL AND CONVENTION CENTER - ARENA, 1434
NORFOLK SCOPE CULTURAL AND CONVENTION CENTER - CHRYSLER HALL, 1434
NORRIS CULTURAL ARTS CENTER, 473
NORRIS THEATRE FOR THE PERFORMING ARTS, 147
NORTH CAROLINA BLUMENTHAL PERFORMING ARTS CENTER, 1051
NORTH CAROLINA SCHOOL OF THE ARTS - ROGER L. STEVENS CENTER FOR THE PERFORMING ARTS, THE, 1080
NORTH IOWA COMMUNITY AUDITORIUM, 519
NORTH SHORE MUSIC THEATRE, 604
NORTHEASTERN JUNIOR COLLEGE THEATRE, 252
NORTHERN ARIZONA AUDITORIUM - ARDREY MEMORIAL AUDITORIUM, 26
NORTHLAND PINES HIGH SCHOOL, 1488
NORTHWEST MISSOURI STATE UNIVERSITY - CHARLES JOHNSON THEATRE, 751
NORTHWEST MISSOURI STATE UNIVERSITY - MARY LINN PERFORMING ARTS CENTER, 751
NORTHWESTERN COLLEGE, 519
NORTON CENTER FOR THE ARTS, 541
OAK ACRES AMPHITHEATRE, 1349
OAK RIDGE COMMUNITY PLAYHOUSE, 1300
OAKDALE THEATRE, 284
OCCIDENTAL COLLEGE - THORNE HALL, 120
OCEAN CENTER, 321
OCEAN CENTER - ARENA, 322
OCEAN CENTER - CONFERENCE CENTER, 322
OCEAN CITY CONVENTION CENTER, 596

OCEAN COUNTY CENTER FOR THE ARTS - STRAND THEATRE, 822
OGUNQUIT PLAYHOUSE, 580
OHIO STATE UNIVERSITY - STADIUM II THEATRE, 1126
OHIO STATE UNIVERSITY - THURBER THEATRE, 1126
OHIO THEATRE, 1127, 1149
OHIO UNIVERSITY - PATIO THEATER, 1095
OHIO UNIVERSITY - SCHOOL OF MUSIC, 1095
OJAI FESTIVAL BOWL, 134
OKLAHOMA CITY UNIVERSITY, 1166
OKLAHOMA CITY UNIVERSITY - BURG THEATRE, 1166
OKLAHOMA CITY UNIVERSITY - KIRKPATRICK AUDITORIUM, 1166
OKLAHOMA CITY ZOO AMPHITHEATRE, 1166
OKOBOJI SUMMER THEATRE, 520
OLD AUDITORIUM, 509
OLD BASTROP OPERA HOUSE, 1312
OLD CREAMERY THEATRE, THE, 517
OLD FORT RUGER THEATRE, 406
OLD JAIL ART CENTER, 1305
OLD OPERA HOUSE COMPANY, THE, 1476
OMAHA CIVIC AUDITORIUM - MUSIC HALL, 793
OMNI AUDITORIUM - BROWARD COMMUNITY COLLEGE, 318
ONE REID STREET THEATRE, 560
OPEN AIR THEATRE, 1208
OPEN EYE: NEW STAGINGS, 1005
OPERA FESTIVAL AUDITORIUM, 893
ORANGE COUNTY CIVIC CENTER, 351
ORANGE COUNTY PERFORMING ARTS CENTER, 74
ORANGE COUNTY PERFORMING ARTS CENTER - FOUNDERS HALL, 74
ORANGE COUNTY PERFORMING ARTS CENTER - SEGERSTROM HALL, 74
ORCHESTRA HALL, 446, 718
ORDWAY MUSIC THEATRE, 727
ORDWAY MUSIC THEATRE - MCKNIGHT THEATRE, 727
ORDWAY MUSIC THEATRE - THE MAIN HALL, 727
OREGON SHAKESPEARE FESTIVAL - ANGUS BOWMER THEATRE, 1175
OREGON SHAKESPEARE FESTIVAL - BLACK SWAN THEATRE, 1175
OREGON SHAKESPEARE FESTIVAL - ELIZABETHAN STAGE, 1175
OREGON STATE UNIVERSITY - GILL COLISEUM, 1178
OREGON STATE UNIVERSITY - MILAN AUDITORIUM, 1178
OROVILLE STATE THEATER, 135
ORPHEUM THEATER, 182, 567, 793
ORPHEUM THEATRE, 615, 1005, 1292
ORRIE DE NOOYER AUDITORIUM, 821
OSCEOLA CENTER FOR THE ARTS, 335
OTERO JUNIOR COLLEGE - HUMANITIES CENTER THEATRE, 249
OTIS A. SINGLETARY CENTER FOR THE ARTS, 545
OTTAWA MUNICIPAL AUDITORIUM, 531
OUACHITA BAPTIST UNIVERSITY - DEPARTMENT OF THEATRE & ARTS, 43
OVENS AUDITORIUM, 1051
OXNARD CIVIC AUDITORIUM, 135
PABST THEATER, 1510
PACE DOWNTOWN THEATER, 1005
PACIFIC CONSERVATORY OF THE PERFORMING ARTS, 199
PACIFIC UNIVERSITY - TOM MILES THEATRE, 1182
PAINTED BRIDE, 1227
PALACE CIVIC CENTER, 1137
PALACE OF FINE ARTS, 182
PALACE OF FINE ARTS THEATRE, 182
PALACE THEATRE, 273, 861, 1005, 1100, 1127, 1140
PALACE THEATRE - STAMFORD CENTER FOR THE ARTS, 282
PALESTINE CIVIC CENTER COMPLEX, 1379
PALM BEACH COMMUNITY COLLEGE - WATSON B. DUNCAN, III, THEATRE, 335
PALM SPRINGS DESERT MUSEUM/ANNENBERG THEATER, 137
PAN AMERICAN CENTER, 852
PANOLA PLAYHOUSE, 738
PAPER MILL PLAYHOUSE, 825
PARAMOUNT ARTS CENTER, 539

PARAMOUNT ARTS CENTRE, 419
PARAMOUNT CENTER FOR THE ARTS, 1015
PARAMOUNT THEATER FOR THE PERFORMING ARTS, 1311
PARAMOUNT THEATRE, 134
PARAMOUNT THEATRE FOR THE PERFORMING ARTS, 511
PARIS JUNIOR COLLEGE, 1380
PARK COLLEGE - ALUMNI HALL THEATRE, 752
PARK COLLEGE - GRAHAM TYLER MEMORIAL CHAPEL, 750
PARK PLACE HOTEL, 695
PARK THEATRE PERFORMING ARTS CENTRE, 841
PARK THEATRE PERFORMING ARTS CENTRE - MAIN
    THEATRE, 841
PARKER PLAYHOUSE, 325
PARKWAY PLAYHOUSE, 446
PASADENA CIVIC AUDITORIUM, 141
PASADENA PLAYHOUSE - BALCONY THEATRE, 141
PASADENA PLAYHOUSE - MAINSTAGE THEATRE, 141
PAUL MELLON ARTS CENTER, 284
PEABODY AUDITORIUM, 322
PEARSON AUDITORIUM, 853
PEMBROKE STATE UNIVERSITY - GIVENS PERFORMING
    ARTS CENTER, 1067
PENNSYLVANIA STATE UNIVERSITY - EISENHOWER
    AUDITORIUM, 1241
PENNSYLVANIA STATE UNIVERSITY - PAVILION
    THEATRE, 1241
PENNSYLVANIA STATE UNIVERSITY - PLAYHOUSE
    THEATRE, 1241
PENNSYLVANIA STATE UNIVERSITY - SCHWAB
    AUDITORIUM, 1241
PENSACOLA CIVIC CENTER, 354
PENSACOLA JUNIOR COLLEGE, MUSIC AND DRAMA
    DEPARTMENT, 354
PEORIA CIVIC CENTER, 468
PEORIA CIVIC CENTER - ARENA, 469
PEORIA CIVIC CENTER - EXHIBITION HALL, 469
PEORIA CIVIC CENTER - THEATRE, 469
PEORIA PLAYERS THEATRE, 469
PEPPERDINE UNIVERSITY - AMPHITHEATRE, FINE ARTS
    DIVISION, 122
PEPPERDINE UNIVERSITY - MINI-THEATRE, FINE ARTS
    DIVISION, 122
PEPPERDINE UNIVERSITY - SMOTHERS THEATRE, 122
PERFORMING ARTS CENTER, 491, 1074
PERFORMING GARAGE, 1005
PEROT THEATRE, 1390
PERSHING AUDITORIUM, 787
PETRILLO MUSIC SHELL, 447
PHELPS - STOKES AUDITORIUM, 540
PHILADELPHIA CIVIC CENTER, 1227
PHILADELPHIA CIVIC CENTER - CONVENTION HALL, 1227
PHILADELPHIA CIVIC CENTER - EXHIBITION HALLS, 1227
PHILADELPHIA CIVIC CENTER - PENNSYLVANIA
    HALL, 1228
PHIPPS CENTER FOR THE ARTS, 1492
PHOENIX CIVIC PLAZA, 31
PHOENIX CIVIC PLAZA - CONVENTION CENTER AND
    SYMPHONY HALL, 32
PHOENIX CIVIC PLAZA - EXHIBITION HALLS, 32
PHOENIX CIVIC PLAZA - GRAND BALLROOM, 32
PICKARD THEATRE, 576
PICKETWIRE PLAYERS AND COMMUNITY THEATRE, 249
PICK - STAIGER CONCERT HALL, 455
PIER ONE THEATRE, 21
PIKES PEAK CENTER, 232
PINE BLUFF CONVENTION CENTER, 51
PINE BLUFF CONVENTION CENTER - ARENA, 51
PINE BLUFF CONVENTION CENTER - AUDITORIUM, 52
PIONEER AMPHITHEATRE, 1318
PIONEER CENTER FOR THE PERFROMING ARTS, 799
PIPER'S OPERA HOUSE, 801
PITTSBURGH CIVIC ARENA, 1236
PLAYERS GUILD OF CANTON, 1100
PLAYERS OF SARASOTA THEATRE, THE, 363
PLAYERS THEATRE COLUMBUS, 1127
PLAYHOUSE SQUARE CENTER, 1117
PLAYHOUSE SQUARE CENTER - OHIO THEATRE, 1118
PLAYHOUSE SQUARE CENTER - PALACE THEATRE, 1118

PLAYHOUSE SQUARE CENTER - STATE THEATRE, 1118
PLAYHOUSE THEATRE, THE, 296
PLAYWRIGHTS' CENTER OF CHICAGO, 447
PLUMMER AUDITORIUM, 83
PLYMOUTH THEATRE, 1006
POCONO PLAYHOUSE, 1213
PONCA PLAYHOUSE, 1167
PORTLAND CENTER FOR THE PERFORMING ARTS -
    PORTLAND CIVIC AUDITORIUM, 1189
PORTLAND EXPOSITION BUILDING, 583
PORTLAND PERFORMING ARTS CENTER, 583
POSEY SCHOOL OF DANCE, 1010
POWELL SYMPHONY HALL AT GRAND CENTER, 762
POWER CENTER FOR THE PERFORMING ARTS, 660
PRATT INSTITUTE - AUDITORIUM, 876
PRINCESS THEATER, 732
PRINCESS THEATRE, 5
PRISCILLA BEACH THEATER SCHOOL, 650
PROCTOR'S THEATRE, 1026
PROMENADE THEATRE, 1006
PROVIDENCE CIVIC CENTER, 1252
PROVIDENCE PERFORMING ARTS CENTER, 1252
PROVINCETOWN PLAYHOUSE, 1006
PYRAMID ARTS CENTER, 1022
QUEENS COLLEGE - COLDEN CENTER FOR THE
    PERFORMING ARTS, 889
QUEENSBOROUGH COMMUNITY COLLEGE
    THEATER, 864
RADCLIFFE COLLEGE - AGASSIZ THEATER, 622
RADCLIFFE COLLEGE - LYMAN COMMON ROOM, 622
RADFORD UNIVERSITY THEATRE, 1435
RADIO CITY MUSIC HALL, 1006
RAJAH THEATRE, 1238
RALEIGH CIVIC CENTER, 1070
RALEIGH CIVIC CENTER - ARENA, 1070
RALEIGH CIVIC CENTER - THEATRE, 1071
RALEIGH LITTLE THEATRE, 1071
RAMONA BOWL, 87
REARDON AUDITORIUM, 483
RECITAL HALL-BALBOA PARK, THE, 159
RED BARN THEATRE, 334
RED ROCKS AMPHITHEATRE - MORRISON COLORADO, 242
REDDING CIVIC AUDITORIUM - TRADE AND CONVENTION
    CENTER, 143
REDLANDS COMMUNITY MUSIC ASSOCIATION, INC., 144
REED COLLEGE - REED THEATRE, 1189
REED WHIPPLE CULTURAL ARTS CENTER, 798
REICHHOLD CENTER FOR THE ARTS, 1527
RENO LITTLE THEATER, 799
RENSSELAER NEWMAN FOUNDATION CHAPEL AND
    CULTURAL CENTER, 1034
RESTON COMMUNITY CENTER THEATRE, 1435
REUNION ARENA, 1336
REYNOLDS MEMORIAL AUDITORIUM, 1080
RIALTO SQUARE THEATRE, 460
RICE UNIVERSITY - HAMMAN HALL, 1367
RICHARD BURTON PERFORMING ARTS CENTER TRITON
    COLLEGE, 470
RICHARDSON AUDITORIUM, 1322
RICHARDSON AUDITORIUM IN ALEXANDER HALL, 834
RICHMOND CIVIC THEATRE, 502
RICHMOND MEMORIAL CONVENTION CENTER, 145
RIDER COLLEGE - FINE ARTS THEATER, 823
RIO HONDO COLLEGE - MERTON WRAY THEATRE, 218
RIPON COLLEGE - DEMMER RECITAL HALL, 1514
RIVERBEND MUSIC CENTER, 1107
RIVERSIDE CENTROPLEX, 556
RIVERSIDE CENTROPLEX - ARENA, 556
RIVERSIDE CENTROPLEX - EXHIBITION HALL, 556
RIVERSIDE CENTROPLEX - THEATRE FOR PERFORMING
    ARTS, 557
RIVERSIDE CONVENTION CENTER AT RAINCROSS
    SQUARE, 146
RIVERSIDE MUNICIPAL AUDITORIUM, 146
RIVERSIDE THEATRE, 372
ROANOKE CIVIC CENTER, 1440
ROBERT C. SMITHWICK THEATRE, 99
ROBERT W. WOODRUFF ARTS CENTER, 386

ROBERT W. WOODRUFF ARTS CENTER - ALLIANCE
THEATRE, 386
ROBERT W. WOODRUFF ARTS CENTER - ALLIANCE
THEATRE-STUDIO THEATRE, 387
ROBERT W. WOODRUFF ARTS CENTER - RICHARD H. RICH
AUDITORIUM, 387
ROBERT W. WOODRUFF ARTS CENTER -
SYMPHONY HALL, 387
ROBERTS CENTER THEATRE, 287
ROBINSON CENTER MUSIC HALL, 50
ROCKPORT OPERA HOUSE - TOWN OF ROCKPORT, 583
ROLAND HAYES CONCERT HALL, 1279
ROLLINS COLLEGE - ANNIE RUSSELL THEATRE, 374
ROME CITY AUDITORIUM, 396
ROOSEVELT UNIVERSITY - PATRICK L. O'MALLEY
THEATRE, 447
ROYALE THEATRE, 1006
RUSHMORE PLAZA CIVIC CENTER, 1272
RUTGERS ARTS CENTER, 830
SACRAMENTO COMMUNITY CENTER EXHIBITION
HALL, 150
SACRAMENTO COMMUNITY CENTER THEATER, 150
SACRAMENTO COMMUNITY CONVENTION
CENTER, 151
SAENGER PERFORMING ARTS CENTER, 567
SAENGER THEATRE, 354, 733
SAENGER THEATRE FOR THE PERFORMING ARTS, 731
SAGINAW CIVIC CENTER - HERITAGE THEATER, 692
SAINT AMBROSE COLLEGE - ALLAERT HALL, 513
SAINT CLEMENT'S CHURCH, 1006
SAINT JAMES THEATER, 1007
SAINT JOHN'S UNIVERSITY, 900
SAINT JOSEPH CIVIC CENTER, 753
SAINT JOSEPH CIVIC CENTER - ARENA, 753
SAINT JOSEPH CIVIC CENTER - MISSOURI THEATRE, 754
SAINT LOUIS CENTER FOR THE PERFORMING ARTS - THE
MAMIYA THEATRE, 407
SAINT LUCIE COUNTY CIVIC CENTER, 327
SAINT LUCIE COUNTY CIVIC CENTER - AUDITORIUM, 327
SAINT LUCIE COUNTY CIVIC CENTER - THEATER, 327
SAINT MARY COLLEGE - XAVIER HALL THEATRE, 529
SAINT PAUL CIVIC CENTER, 727
SAINT PAUL CIVIC CENTER - ARENA, 728
SAINT PAUL CIVIC CENTER - AUDITORIUM, 728
SALEM CIVIC CENTER, 1440
SALINA BICENTENNIAL CENTER, 533
SAM HOUSTON STATE UNIVERSITY-THEATRE AND DANCE
DIVISION, 1368
SAM HOUSTON STATE UNIVERSITY-THEATRE AND DANCE
DIVISION - MAIN STAGE THEATRE, 1367
SAM HOUSTON STATE UNIVERSITY-THEATRE AND DANCE
DIVISION - STUDIO THEATRE, 1368
SAN ANGELO CITY AUDITORIUM, 1382
SAN ANTONIO CONVENTION CENTER, 1386
SAN ANTONIO CONVENTION CENTER - LILA COCKRELL
THEATRE, 1387
SAN DIEGO CONCOURSE, 159
SAN DIEGO CONCOURSE - CIVIC THEATRE, 160
SAN DIEGO CONCOURSE - GOLDEN HALL, 160
SAN FRANCISCO CIVIC AUDITORIUM, 182
SAN FRANCISCO COUNTY FAIR BUILDING, 183
SAN FRANCISCO WAR MEMORIAL AND PERFORMING ARTS
CENTER, 183
SAN FRANCISCO WAR MEMORIAL AND PERFORMING ARTS
CENTER - GREEN ROOM, 183
SAN FRANCISCO WAR MEMORIAL AND PERFORMING ARTS
CENTER - HERBST THEATRE, 183
SAN FRANCISCO WAR MEMORIAL AND PERFORMING ARTS
CENTER - LOUISE M. DAVIES SYMPHONY HALL, 183
SAN FRANCISCO WAR MEMORIAL AND PERFORMING ARTS
CENTER - WAR MEMORIAL OPERA HOUSE, 184
SAN GABRIEL CIVIC AUDITORIUM, 184
SAN JOSE CITY COLLEGE, 187
SAN JOSE CONVENTION AND CULTURAL FACILITIES, 187
SAN JOSE CONVENTION AND CULTURAL FACILITIES -
CENTER FOR THE PERFORMING ARTS, 187
SAN JOSE CONVENTION AND CULTURAL FACILITIES -
CIVIC AUDITORIUM, 188

SAN JOSE CONVENTION AND CULTURAL FACILITIES -
MONTGOMERY THEATER, 188
SAN JOSE STATE UNIVERSITY - CONCERT HALL, 188
SAN JOSE STATE UNIVERSITY - UNIVERSITY THEATRE, 188
SAN MATEO PERFORMING ARTS CENTER, 190
SANDERS THEATRE, 622
SANGAMON STATE UNIVERSITY AUDITORIUM, 475
SANGRE DE CRISTO ARTS AND CONFERENCE CENTER, 252
SANTA CRUZ CIVIC AUDITORIUM, 198
SANTA FE CONVENTION AND VISITORS BUREAU AT
SWEENEY CENTER, 856
SANTA MONICA CIVIC AUDITORIUM, 200
SANTUARIO DE GUADALUPE, 856
SARASOTA OPERA HOUSE, 363
SARATOGA PERFORMING ARTS CENTER, 1025
SARATOGA PERFORMING ARTS CENTER -
AMPHITHEATRE, 1025
SARATOGA PERFORMING ARTS CENTER - LITTLE
THEATRE, 1025
SAVANNAH CIVIC CENTER, 397
SAVANNAH CIVIC CENTER - ARENA, 397
SAVANNAH CIVIC CENTER - THEATRE, 397
SCHENECTADY CIVIC PLAYERS, INC., THE, 1026
SCHOENBRUNN AMPHITHEATRE, 1142
SCOTTISH RITE AUDITORIUM, 491, 1098
SCOTTSDALE CENTER FOR THE ARTS, 34
SCOTTSDALE CENTER FOR THE ARTS - CINEMA, 34
SCOTTSDALE CENTER FOR THE ARTS - THEATER, 34
SCRANTON CULTURAL CENTER AT THE MASONIC
TEMPLE, 1238
SEASIDE CIVIC AND CONVENTION CENTER, 1192
SEATTLE CENTER ARENA, 1464
SEATTLE CENTER COLISEUM, 1464
SEATTLE CENTER OPERA HOUSE, 1464
SEATTLE PUBLIC LIBRARY-DOWNTOWN LIBRARY, 1465
SEVEN STAGES, 387
7TH STREET THEATRE, 1450
SEVERANCE HALL, 1118
SHAKESPEARE THEATRE, THE, 312
SHASTA COLLEGE - FINE ARTS THEATRE, 143
SHEELY CENTER FOR THE PERFORMING ARTS, 464
SHERIDAN OPERA HOUSE, 253
SHERMAN PLAYHOUSE, 279
SHERWOOD AUDITORIUM, 94
SHOWBOAT MAJESTIC, 1107
SHREVEPORT CIVIC THEATRE, 571
SHREVEPORT MUNICIPAL AUDITORIUM, 571
SHRINE AUDITORIUM AND EXPOSITION CENTER, 120
SHUBERT PERFORMING ARTS CENTER, 273
SHUBERT THEATRE, 120, 447, 616, 1007
SILVER CULTURAL ARTS CENTER, 812
SILVER LAKE COLLEGE, 1500
SIMON EDISON CENTER FOR THE PERFORMING ARTS, 160
SIMON EDISON CENTER FOR THE PERFORMING ARTS -
CASSIUS CARTER CENTRE STAGE, 160
SIMON EDISON CENTER FOR THE PERFORMING ARTS -
LOWELL DAVIES FESTIVAL THEATRE, 160
SIMON EDISON CENTER FOR THE PERFORMING ARTS - OLD
GLOBE THEATRE, 161
SIOUX FALLS COLISEUM, 1274
SIOUX FALLS COMMUNITY PLAYHOUSE, 1274
SITKA CENTENNIAL BUILDING, 23
SKYLIGHT OPERA THEATRE, 1510
SLOCOMB AUDITORIUM, 1380
SMITH OPERA HOUSE FOR THE PERFORMING ARTS, 893
SMITHSONIAN INSTITUTION - BAIRD AUDITORIUM, 313
SMITHSONIAN INSTITUTION - CARMICHAEL
AUDITORIUM, 313
SMOKY MOUNTAIN PASSION PLAY, 1277
SNUG HARBOR CULTURAL CENTER, 1028
SOCIETY HILL PLAYHOUSE, 1228
SOCIETY OF THE FOUR ARTS GALLERY -
THEATER, THE, 351
SOHO REP, 1007
SOONER THEATRE OF NORMAN, INC., THE, 1163
SOUHEGAN VALLEY THEATRE, 809
SOUTH ARKANSAS ARTS CENTER, 44
SOUTH BROADWAY CULTURAL CENTER, 851

SOUTH COAST REPERTORY, 74
SOUTH COAST REPERTORY - SECOND STAGE, 74
SOUTH COAST REPERTORY - SEGERSTROM AUDITORIUM,
MAINSTAGE, 75
SOUTH DAKOTA ART MUSEUM, 1268
SOUTH DALLAS CULTURAL CENTER, 1336
SOUTH JACKSON CIVIC CENTER, 1301
SOUTHEAST MISSOURI STATE UNIVERSITY - ACADEMIC
HALL AUDITORIUM, 742
SOUTHEAST MISSOURI STATE UNIVERSITY - SHOW ME
CENTER, 742
SOUTHEASTERN LOUISIANA UNIVERSITY - VONNIE
BORDEN THEATRE, 557
SOUTHERN BAPTIST THEOLOGICAL SEMINARY - ALUMNI
MEMORIAL CHAPEL, 550
SOUTHERN BAPTIST THEOLOGICAL SEMINARY - HEEREN
RECITAL HALL, 551
SOUTHERN METHODIST UNIVERSITY - BOB HOPE
THEATRE, 1336
SOUTHERN METHODIST UNIVERSITY - CARUTH
AUDITORIUM, 1336
SOUTHERN METHODIST UNIVERSITY - MARGO JONES
THEATRE, 1337
SOUTHERN METHODIST UNIVERSITY - MCFARLIN
MEMORIAL AUDITORIUM, 1337
SOUTHINGTON COMMUNITY THEATRE, 279
SOUTHWESTERN BAPTIST THEOLOGICAL SEMINARY -
REYNOLDS AUDITORIUM, 1350
SOUTHWESTERN OKLAHOMA STATE UNIVERSITY - FINE
ARTS CENTER, 1172
SPARTANBURG MEMORIAL AUDITORIUM, 1266
SPARTANBURG MEMORIAL AUDITORIUM - ARENA, 1266
SPARTANBURG MEMORIAL AUDITORIUM - THEATRE, 1266
SPECTRUM, THE, 1228
SPIRIT SQUARE CENTER FOR THE ARTS, 1052
SPOKANE COLISEUM, 1467
SPOKANE CONVENTION CENTER, 1468
SPOKANE OPERA HOUSE, 1468
SPRAGUE - GRISWOLD CULTURAL ART CENTER, 646
SPRECKELS ORGAN PAVILION, 161
SPRINGER OPERA HOUSE - THE STATE THEATRE OF
GEORGIA, 390
SPRiNGFIELD CIVIC CENTER, 646
SPRINGFIELD COLLEGE - MUSIC HALL, 475
SPRINGFIELD SYMPHONY HALL, 646
SPRINGSTEAD THEATRE, THE, 364
STAGES REPERTORY THEATRE, 1367
STAMBAUGH AUDITORIUM, 1153
STANFORD UNIVERSITY - ANNENBURG AUDITORIUM, 205
STANFORD UNIVERSITY - BRAUN RECITAL HALL, 205
STANFORD UNIVERSITY - CAMBLE RECITAL HALL, 205
STANFORD UNIVERSITY - COVERLY AUDITORIUM, 205
STANFORD UNIVERSITY - DINKELSPIEL
AUDITORIUM, 205
STANFORD UNIVERSITY - MEMORIAL AUDITORIUM, 205
STANLEY PERFORMING ARTS CENTER, 1036
STARLIGHT BOWL, 161
STATE THEATRE, 737
STATE THEATRE CENTER FOR THE ARTS, 1240
STATE UNIVERSITY AGRICULTURAL AND TECHNICAL
COLLEGE - LITTLE THEATRE, 886
STATE UNIVERSITY OF NEW YORK COLLEGE-BROCKPORT-
TOWER FINE ARTS CENTER, 868
STATE UNIVERSITY OF NEW YORK-ALBANY - ALBANY
PERFORMING ARTS CENTER, 861
STATE UNIVERSITY OF NEW YORK-ALBANY - ARENA, 861
STATE UNIVERSITY OF NEW YORK-ALBANY - MAIN
THEATRE, 862
STATE UNIVERSITY OF NEW YORK-ALBANY - RECITAL
HALL, 862
STATE UNIVERSITY OF NEW YORK-BINGHAMPTON -
CHAMBER HALL, 866
STATE UNIVERSITY OF NEW YORK-BINGHAMPTON -
CONCERT THEATRE, 867
STATE UNIVERSITY OF NEW YORK-BUFFALO -
DEPARTMENT OF THEATRE AND DANCE, 880
STATE UNIVERSITY OF NEW YORK-FREDONIA - MICHAEL
C. ROCKEFELLER ARTS CENTER, 890
STATE UNIVERSITY OF NEW YORK-FREDONIA - MICHAEL
C. ROCKEFELLER ARTS CENTER - CONCERT HALL, 890
STATE UNIVERSITY OF NEW YORK-FREDONIA - MICHAEL
C. ROCKEFELLER ARTS CENTER - EXPERIMENTAL
THEATRE, 890
STATE UNIVERSITY OF NEW YORK-FREDONIA - MICHAEL
C. ROCKEFELLER ARTS CENTER - THEATRE, 890
STATE UNIVERSITY OF NEW YORK-PURCHASE -
PERFORMING ARTS CENTER, 1018
STATE UNIVERSITY OF NEW YORK-PURCHASE -
THEATER A, 1018
STATE UNIVERSITY OF NEW YORK-PURCHASE -
THEATRE B, 1018
STATE UNIVERSITY OF NEW YORK-PURCHASE -
THEATRE C, 1018
STATE UNIVERSITY OF NEW YORK-PURCHASE -
THEATRE D, 1018
STEPHEN FOSTER STATE FOLK CULTURE CENTER -
AMPHITHEATRE, 373
STEVE MCGRAW'S, 1007
STOCKTON STATE COLLEGE - PERFORMING ARTS
CENTER, 833
STRAND THEATRE, 571
STRAND THEATRE, THE, 1262
STRAND-CAPITOL PERFORMING ARTS CENTER - CAPITOL
THEATRE, 1243
STRAND-CAPITOL PERFORMING ARTS CENTER - STRAND
THEATRE, 1243
STUDIO THEATRE, 905
SUFFOLK COUNTY COMMUNITY COLLEGE - SAQTIKOS
THEATRE, 867
SULLIVAN STREET PLAYHOUSE, 1007
SUMTER COUNTY CULTURAL CENTER, 1266
SUNSET CENTER THEATRE, 69
SUPPER CLUB, THE, 1007
SURFLIGHT SUMMER THEATRE, 816
SWEENEY CONVENTION CENTER, 857
SWEET BRIAR COLLEGE - BABCOCK AUDITORIUM, 1441
SYMPHONY HALL, 616, 1194, 1406
SYRACUSE AREA LANDMARK THEATRE, 1033
TALLAHASSEE-LEON COUNTY CIVIC CENTER, 366
TAMPA BAY PERFORMING ARTS CENTER, 369
TAMPA BAY PERFORMING ARTS CENTER - FESTIVAL
HALL, 369
TAMPA BAY PERFORMING ARTS CENTER - JAEB
THEATER, 369
TAMPA BAY PERFORMING ARTS CENTER - PLAYHOUSE, 369
TAMPA THEATRE, 369
TECUMSEH CIVIC AUDITORIUM, 694
TEMPLE CIVIC THEATRE, 1390
TEMPLE THEATRE COMPANY INC., 1073
TENNESSEE PERFORMING ARTS CENTER, 1298
TENNESSEE PERFORMING ARTS CENTER - ANDREW
JACKSON HALL, 1298
TENNESSEE PERFORMING ARTS CENTER - ANDREW
JOHNSON THEATER, 1298
TENNESSEE PERFORMING ARTS CENTER - JAMES K. POLK
THEATER, 1299
TENNESSEE THEATER, 1287
TEXAS CHRISTIAN UNIVERSITY - ED LANDRETH
AUDITORIUM, 1350
TEXAS TECH UNIVERSITY CENTER - ALLEN THEATRE, 1374
TEXAS TECH UNIVERSITY CENTER - MUSIC BUILDING, 1374
TEXAS WESLEYAN COLLEGE - TEXAS WESLEYAN FINE
ARTS AUDITORIUM, 1350
TEXAS WOMAN'S UNIVERSITY - REDBUD THEATRE, 1339
THALIAN HALL - THALIAN HALL CENTER FOR THE
PERFORMING ARTS, 1077
THANKS-GIVING SQUARE, 1337
THANKS-GIVING SQUARE - CHAPEL OF
THANKSGIVING, 1337
THANKS-GIVING SQUARE - COURTYARD AT
THANKS-GIVING SQUARE, 1337
THANKS-GIVING SQUARE - HALL OF WORLD
THANKSGIVING, 1337
THEATRE ALBANY, 376
THEATRE ARLINGTON, 1307
THEATRE BUILDING, 447

THEATRE EAST, 207
THEATRE GUILD, 1293
THEATRE IN THE GROVE, 1182
THEATRE IN THE PARK, 1071
THEATRE IN THE ROUND, 719
THEATRE IN THE SQUARE, 396
THEATRE MEMPHIS, 1292
THEATRE PROJECT, 592
THEATRE SUBURBIA, 1367
THEATRE THREE, 1337
THEATRE THREE PRODUCTIONS - MAINSTAGE, 1016
THEATRE THREE PRODUCTIONS - SECOND STAGE, 1016
THIEL COLLEGE - PASSAVANT MEMORIAL
     CENTER, 1204
THOMASVILLE CULTURAL CENTER AUDITORIUM, 399
THREE ARTS THEATRE, 391
TIBBITS OPERA HOUSE, 665
TIMBERS DINNER THEATER, 1213
TIVOLI THEATRE, 1279
TOBY'S DINNER THEATRE, 594
TOLEDO MASONIC AUDITORIUM, 1149
TOLEDO MUSEUM OF ART - PERISTYLE, THE, 1149
TOPEKA PERFORMING ARTS CENTER, 535
TOTEM POLE PLAYHOUSE, 1202
TOUCHSTONE THEATRE, 1196
TOWER THEATRE FOR THE PERFORMING ARTS, 82
TOWNE AND COUNTRY PLAYERS, 1142
TOWSON STATE UNIVERSITY FINE ARTS CENTER, 599
TOWSON STATE UNIVERSITY FINE ARTS CENTER -
     CONCERT HALL, 599
TOWSON STATE UNIVERSITY FINE ARTS CENTER - MAIN
     STAGE, 599
TOWSON STATE UNIVERSITY FINE ARTS CENTER - STUDIO
     THEATRE, 599
TOWSON STATE UNIVERSITY - STEPHENS
     AUDITORIUM, 599
TRANSYLVANIA UNIVERSITY, 545
TRIANGLE CULTURAL CENTER, 739
TRINITY ARTS CENTER, 1252
TRINITY UNIVERSITY - DEPARTMENT OF SPEECH AND
     DRAMA, 1387
TRINITY UNIVERSITY - LAURIE AUDITORIUM, 1387
TROY ARENA, 1035
TROY - HAYNER CULTURAL CENTER, 1035
TROY SAVINGS BANK MUSIC HALL, 1035
TRUMAN COLLEGE - O'ROURKE CENTER FOR THE
     PERFORMING ARTS, 448
TRUMBULL NEW THEATRE, 1142
TRUSTEES AUDITORIUM - ASIAN ART MUSEUM, 184
TRYON FINE ARTS CENTER, 1075
TUCSON CONVENTION CENTER, 39
TUCSON CONVENTION CENTER - ARENA, 40
TUCSON CONVENTION CENTER - EXHIBITION HALL, 40
TUCSON CONVENTION CENTER - LITTLE THEATRE, 40
TUCSON CONVENTION CENTER - MUSIC HALL, 40
TUCSON CONVENTION CENTER - THEATRE, 40
TUFTS UNIVERSITY - BALCH ARENA THEATER, 633
TULANE UNIVERSITY - ALBERT I. LUPIN MEMORIAL
     EXPERIMENTAL THEATRE, 568
TULSA PERFORMING ARTS CENTER, 1170
TULSA PERFORMING ARTS CENTER - CHAPMAN MUSIC
     HALL, 1170
TULSA PERFORMING ARTS CENTER - JOHN H. WILLIAMS
     THEATRE, 1171
TULSA PERFORMING ARTS CENTER - STUDIO I, 1171
TULSA PERFORMING ARTS CENTER - STUDIO II, 1171
TUSCARAWAS CAMPUS OF KENT STATE UNIVERSITY -
     AUDITORIUM, 1142
ULSTER PERFORMING ARTS CENTER, 902
UNICORN THEATRE, 750
UNION COLONY CIVIC CENTER, 248
UNION COUNTY ARTS CENTER, 835
UNITARIAN PLAYERS, 1145
UNIVERSITY CENTER AUDITORIUM, 316
UNIVERSITY CENTER THEATRE COMPLEX AND
     CONFERENCE TOWER, 1319
UNIVERSITY CENTER THEATRE COMPLEX AND
     CONFERENCE TOWER - RUDDER AUDITORIUM, 1319

UNIVERSITY CENTER THEATRE COMPLEX AND
     CONFERENCE TOWER - RUDDER FORUM, 1319
UNIVERSITY CENTER THEATRE COMPLEX AND
     CONFERENCE TOWER - RUDDER THEATRE, 1319
UNIVERSITY OF ALABAMA - CONCERT HALL, 12
UNIVERSITY OF ALABAMA - GALLAWAY THEATRE, 12
UNIVERSITY OF ALABAMA - HUEY RECITAL HALL, 12
UNIVERSITY OF ALABAMA - MORGAN AUDITORIUM, 12
UNIVERSITY OF ALASKA - CHARLES W. DAVIS CONCERT
     HALL, 19
UNIVERSITY OF ARIZONA - CENTENNIAL HALL, 40
UNIVERSITY OF ARIZONA - CROWDER HALL, 41
UNIVERSITY OF ARKANSAS-LITTLE ROCK - STELLA BOYLE
     SMITH CONCERT HALL, 50
UNIVERSITY OF BRIDGEPORT - BERNHARD CENTER, 256
UNIVERSITY OF CALIFORNIA-BERKELEY - ALFRED HERTZ
     MEMORIAL HALL, 63
UNIVERSITY OF CALIFORNIA-BERKELEY - HEARST GREEK
     THEATRE, 63
UNIVERSITY OF CALIFORNIA-BERKELEY - ZELLERBACH
     HALL, 63
UNIVERSITY OF CALIFORNIA-BERKELEY - ZELLERBACH
     PLAYHOUSE, 63
UNIVERSITY OF CALIFORNIA-IRVINE - VILLAGE
     THEATRE, 92
UNIVERSITY OF CALIFORNIA-LOS ANGELES - ROYCE
     HALL, 121
UNIVERSITY OF CALIFORNIA-LOS ANGELES -
     WADSWORTH THEATER, 121
UNIVERSITY OF CALIFORNIA-RIVERSIDE - UNIVERSITY
     THEATRE, 146
UNIVERSITY OF CALIFORNIA-SAN DIEGO - MANDEVILLE
     AUDITORIUM, 94
UNIVERSITY OF CALIFORNIA-SANTA CRUZ - PERFORMING
     ARTS CENTER, 198
UNIVERSITY OF CINCINNATI - CORBETT AUDITORIUM, 1107
UNIVERSITY OF CINCINNATI - CORBETT CENTER FOR THE
     PERFORMING ARTS, 1107
UNIVERSITY OF CINCINNATI - PATRICIA CORBETT
     THEATER, 1108
UNIVERSITY OF CINCINNATI - WATSON HALL, 1108
UNIVERSITY OF COLORADO - MACKY AUDITORIUM
     CONCERT HALL, 227
UNIVERSITY OF CONNECTICUT - HARRIET S. JORGENSEN
     THEATRE, 282
UNIVERSITY OF CONNECTICUT - STUDIO THEATRE, 283
UNIVERSITY OF HAWAII - HILO THEATRE, 402
UNIVERSITY OF IOWA - HANCHER AUDITORIUM, THE, 518
UNIVERSITY OF KANSAS - CRAFTON-PREYER
     THEATRE, 529
UNIVERSITY OF LOWELL - CENTER FOR THE ARTS, 631
UNIVERSITY OF MAINE - MAINE CENTER FOR
     THE ARTS, 581
UNIVERSITY OF MAINE AT MACHIAS - STAGE FRONT, 579
UNIVERSITY OF MASSACHUSETTS - BOWKER
     AUDITORIUM, 602
UNIVERSITY OF MASSACHUSETTS - CONCERT HALL, 602
UNIVERSITY OF MICHIGAN - MENDELSSOHN THEATRE, 660
UNIVERSITY OF MICHIGAN - TRUEBLOOD THEATRE, 660
UNIVERSITY OF MISSISSIPPI - FULTON CHAPEL, 737
UNIVERSITY OF MISSISSIPPI - MEEK AUDITORIUM, 738
UNIVERSITY OF MISSISSIPPI - STUDIO THEATRE, 738
UNIVERSITY OF MISSOURI- COLUMBIA - JESSE
     AUDITORIUM, 744
UNIVERSITY OF MONTANA - MONTANA THEATRE, 777
UNIVERSITY OF NEBRASKA - UNIVERSITY THEATRE, 784
UNIVERSITY OF NEBRASKA-LINCOLN - KIMBALL RECITAL
     HALL, 787
UNIVERSITY OF NEVADA-LAS VEGAS - ARTEMUS HAM
     CONCERT HALL, 798
UNIVERSITY OF NEVADA-RENO - CHURCH FINE ARTS
     CENTER, 800
UNIVERSITY OF NEVADA-RENO - CHURCH FINE ARTS
     CENTER - FINE ARTS THEATRE, 800
UNIVERSITY OF NEVADA-RENO - CHURCH FINE ARTS
     CENTER - NIGHTINGALE HALL, 800
UNIVERSITY OF NEVADA-RENO - CHURCH FINE ARTS
     CENTER, REDFIELD STUDIO THEATRE, 800

UNIVERSITY OF NEVADA-RENO - LAWLOR EVENTS
    CENTER, 800
UNIVERSITY OF NEW HAMPSHIRE-DURHAM, 804
UNIVERSITY OF NEW HAMPSHIRE-DURHAM - BRATTON
    RECITAL HALL, 804
UNIVERSITY OF NEW HAMPSHIRE-DURHAM - HENNESSY
    THEATER, 804
UNIVERSITY OF NEW HAMPSHIRE-DURHAM - JOHNSON
    THEATER, 805
UNIVERSITY OF NEW MEXICO - POPEJOY HALL, 851
UNIVERSITY OF NEW ORLEANS PERFORMING ARTS
    CENTER, 568
UNIVERSITY OF NORTH CAROLINA-WILMINGTON - SARAH
    GRAHAM KENAN MEMORIAL AUDITORIUM, 1078
UNIVERSITY OF NORTH DAKOTA - CHESTER FRITZ
    AUDITORIUM, 1087
UNIVERSITY OF NORTH TEXAS - CONCERT HALL, 1339
UNIVERSITY OF NORTH TEXAS - DEPARTMENT OF DANCE
    AND DRAMA, 1339
UNIVERSITY OF NORTHERN COLORADO - HELEN
    LANGWORTHY THEATRE, 249
UNIVERSITY OF NORTHERN IOWA - RUSSELL
    HALL, 509
UNIVERSITY OF NORTHERN IOWA - STRAYER-WOOD
    THEATRE, 509
UNIVERSITY OF NORTHERN IOWA - STRAYER-WOOD
    THEATRE-BLACK BOX, 509
UNIVERSITY OF NORTHERN IOWA - STRAYER-WOOD
    THEATRE-MAIN STAGE, 510
UNIVERSITY OF OKLAHOMA THEATRE, 1163
UNIVERSITY OF OREGON - BEALL CONCERT HALL, 1181
UNIVERSITY OF THE PACIFIC - DE MARCUS BROWN
    STUDIO THEATRE, 206
UNIVERSITY OF THE PACIFIC - FAYE SPANOS CONCERT
    HALL, 206
UNIVERSITY OF THE PACIFIC - LONG THEATRE, 207
UNIVERSITY OF THE PACIFIC - RECITAL HALL, 207
UNIVERSITY OF RHODE ISLAND FINE ARTS CENTER, 1245
UNIVERSITY OF RHODE ISLAND FINE ARTS CENTER -
    J STUDIO, 1245
UNIVERSITY OF RHODE ISLAND FINE ARTS CENTER -
    ROBERT E. WILL THEATRE, 1246
UNIVERSITY OF RICHMOND - JAMES L. CAMP MEMORIAL
    THEATRE, 1438
UNIVERSITY OF ROCHESTER-RIVER CAMPUS - STRONG
    AUDITORIUM, 1022
UNIVERSITY OF SOUTH CAROLINA - DRAYTON HALL
    THEATRE, 1261
UNIVERSITY OF SOUTH CAROLINA - LONGSTREET
    THEATRE, 1261
UNIVERSITY OF SOUTH CAROLINA BEAUFORT ARTS
    CENTER, 1257
UNIVERSITY OF SOUTH CAROLINA-COASTAL CAROLINA
    COLLEGE - LITTLE THEATRE, 1261
UNIVERSITY OF SOUTH CAROLINA-COASTAL CAROLINA
    COLLEGE - WHEELWRIGHT PERFORMING ARTS
    CENTER, 1262
UNIVERSITY OF SOUTH DAKOTA - SLAGLE
    AUDITORIUM, 1275
UNIVERSITY OF SOUTH DAKOTA - WARREN M. LEE
    CENTER FOR THE FINE ARTS, 1275
UNIVERSITY OF SOUTH FLORIDA - STUDIO THEATRE, 370
UNIVERSITY OF SOUTH FLORIDA - THEATRE I, 370
UNIVERSITY OF SOUTH FLORIDA - THEATRE II, 370´
UNIVERSITY OF SOUTHERN CALIFORNIA - BOVARD
    AUDITORIUM, 121
UNIVERSITY OF TENNESSEE MUSIC HALL, 1287
UNIVERSITY OF TEXAS AT ARLINGTON - MAINSTAGE
    THEATER, 1307
UNIVERSITY OF TEXAS AT ARLINGTON - STUDIO
    THEATER, 1307
UNIVERSITY OF TEXAS AT AUSTIN - B. IDEN PAYNE
    THEATRE, 1311
UNIVERSITY OF TEXAS AT AUSTIN - THEATRE ROOM, 1311
UNIVERSITY OF TEXAS AT AUSTIN PERFORMING ARTS
    CENTER, 1311
UNIVERSITY OF TEXAS AT AUSTIN PERFORMING ARTS
    CENTER - THE BASS CONCERT HALL, 1311
UNIVERSITY OF TEXAS AT AUSTIN PERFORMING ARTS
    CENTER - BATES RECITAL HALL, 1311
UNIVERSITY OF TEXAS AT AUSTIN PERFORMING ARTS
    CENTER - THE MCCULLOUGH THEATRE, 1312
UNIVERSITY OF TEXAS AT EL PASO - MAIN
    PLAYHOUSE, 1342
UNIVERSITY OF TEXAS-PAN AMERICAN - FINE ARTS
    AUDITORIUM, 1340
UNIVERSITY OF TEXAS-PAN AMERICAN - THEATER, 1340
UNIVERSITY OF TULSA - KENDALL HALL, 1171
UNIVERSITY OF TULSA - TYRRELL HALL, 1171
UNIVERSITY OF UTAH - KINGSBURY HALL, 1406
UNIVERSITY OF VERMONT - RECITAL HALL, 1413
UNIVERSITY OF WEST FLORIDA CENTER FOR THE
    PERFORMING ARTS, 354
UNIVERSITY OF WISCONSIN-SUPERIOR - PAUL E. HOLDEN
    FINE AND APPLIED ARTS CENTER, 1516
UNIVERSITY OF WYOMING - ARENA AUDITORIUM, 1521
UNIVERSITY OF WYOMING - ARTS AND SCIENCES
    AUDITORIUM, 1521
UNIVERSITY OF WYOMING - FINE ARTS
    CONCERT HALL, 1521
UNIVERSITY SETTLEMENT, 1008
UPSALA COLLEGE - WORKSHOP 90 THEATER, 818
UTAH STATE UNIVERSITY - CHASE FINE ARTS
    CENTER, 1396
UTAH STATE UNIVERSITY - KENT CONCERT HALL, 1396
UTAH STATE UNIVERSITY - MORGAN THEATRE, 1396
UTICA MEMORIAL AUDITORIUM, 1036
VAL A. BROWNING CENTER FOR THE PERFORMING
    ARTS, 1397
VALDOSTA STATE COLLEGE - SAWYER THEATRE, 400
VALDOSTA STATE COLLEGE - WHITEHEAD
    AUDITORIUM, 400
VALENCIA COMMUNITY COLLEGE - BLACK BOX
    THEATRE, 351
VALENCIA COMMUNITY COLLEGE - PERFORMING ARTS
    CENTER, 351
VALLEY FORGE MUSIC FAIR, 1200
VAN WEZEL AUDITORIUM, 364
VANDERBURGH AUDITORIUM CONVENTION CENTER, 489
VENETIAN THEATRE, 901
VENICE COMMUNITY CENTER, 371
VETERANS MEMORIAL, 1127
VETERAN'S MEMORIAL AUDITORIUM, 75
VETERANS MEMORIAL AUDITORIUM, 1252
VETERANS MEMORIAL CIVIC AND CONVENTION
    CENTER, 1137
VETERANS MEMORIAL CIVIC AND CONVENTION CENTER -
    CROUSE PERFORMANCE HALL, 1137
VETERANS MEMORIAL HALL, 1028
VETERANS' MEMORIAL THEATRE, 76
VICTOR VALLEY COLLEGE PERFORMING ARTS
    CENTER, 214
VICTORIAN THEATRE, 242
VICTORY GARDENS THEATER, 448
VICTORY PARK AUDITORIUM, 347
VILLA JULIA COLLEGE - INSCAPE THEATRE, 598
VILLA MONTALVO CENTER FOR THE ARTS, 202
VILLA MONTALVO CENTER FOR THE ARTS - CARRIAGE
    HOUSE THEATRE, 202
VILLA MONTALVO CENTER FOR THE ARTS - LILIAN
    FONTAINE GARDEN THEATRE, 202
VILLAGE GATE, 1008
VIRGINIA BEACH PAVILION CONVENTION CENTER, 1441
VIRGINIA BEACH PAVILION CONVENTION CENTER -
    EXHIBIT HALL, 1442
VIRGINIA BEACH PAVILION CONVENTION CENTER -
    PAVILION THEATER, 1442
VIRGINIA THEATER, 1008
VISALIA CONVENTION CENTER - EXHIBIT HALL, 214
VISALIA CONVENTION CENTER - L.J. WILLIAMS
    THEATRE, 214
VISALIA CONVENTION CENTER - ROTARY THEATRE, 215
VIVE LES ARTS SOCIETE AND THEATRE, 1371
VON BRAUN CIVIC CENTER, 7
VON BRAUN CIVIC CENTER - ARENA, 7
VON BRAUN CIVIC CENTER - CONCERT HALL, 7

VON BRAUN CIVIC CENTER - EXHIBIT HALL, 7
VON BRAUN CIVIC CENTER - PLAYHOUSE, 8
WACO CONVENTION CENTER, 1392
WACO CONVENTION CENTER - CHISHOLM HALL, 1392
WADSWORTH AUDITORIUM, 892
WALNUT STREET THEATRE, 1228
WALNUT STREET THEATRE - MAINSTAGE, 1228
WALNUT STREET THEATRE - STUDIO FIVE, 1229
WALNUT STREET THEATRE - STUDIO THREE, 1229
WALTER KERR THEATRE, 1008
WALTON CREEK PLAYHOUSE, 1108
WANG CENTER FOR THE PERFORMING ARTS, THE, 616
WAR MEMORIAL AUDITORIUM, 325
WAREHOUSE LIVING ARTS CENTER, 1323
WARNER THEATRE, 313
WARNOR'S THEATER, 82
WARREN PERFORMING ARTS CENTER, 498
WARREN PERFORMING ARTS CENTER - ESCH
    AUDITORIUM, 498
WARREN PERFORMING ARTS CENTER - STUDIO
    THEATER, 498
WARTBURG COLLEGE - NEUMANN AUDITORIUM, 522
WASHINGTON CENTER FOR THE PERFORMING ARTS, 1452
WASHINGTON UNIVERSITY - EDISON THEATRE, 763
WATERVILLE OPERA HOUSE, 535
WAUKESHA CIVIC THEATRE, 1517
WEBSTER UNIVERSITY-LORETTO - HILTON CENTER FOR
    THE PERFORMING ARTS, 763
WECKESSER STUDIO THEATRE, 857
WEIDNER CENTER FOR THE PERFORMING ARTS, 1491
WEIDNER CENTER FOR THE PERFROMING ARTS, 1491
WELLS THEATRE, 1434
WESLEYAN COLLEGE - PORTER AUDITORIUM, 394
WESLEYAN UNIVERSITY CENTER FOR THE ARTS, 267
WESLEYAN UNIVERSITY CENTER FOR THE ARTS -
    CINEMA, 267
WESLEYAN UNIVERSITY CENTER FOR THE ARTS -
    CROWELL CONCERT HALL, 267
WESLEYAN UNIVERSITY CENTER FOR THE ARTS -
    THEATER, 267
WESLEYAN UNIVERSITY CENTER FOR THE ARTS - WORLD
    MUSIC HALL, 268
WEST PALM BEACH AUDITORIUM, 373
WEST TEXAS STATE UNIVERSITY - BRANDING IRON
    THEATER, 1318
WEST VIRGINIA STATE COLLEGE - CAPITOL CENTER, 1480
WEST VIRGINIA STATE COLLEGE - F.S. BELCHER
    THEATRE, 1482
WEST VIRGINIA UNIVERSITY CREATIVE ARTS
    CENTER, 1483
WEST VIRGINIA UNIVERSITY CREATIVE ARTS CENTER -
    CHORAL RECITAL HALL, 1483
WEST VIRGINIA UNIVERSITY CREATIVE ARTS CENTER -
    CLASSROOM THEATRE, 1484
WEST VIRGINIA UNIVERSITY CREATIVE ARTS CENTER -
    CONCERT THEATRE, 1484
WEST VIRGINIA UNIVERSITY CREATIVE ARTS CENTER -
    OPERA THEATRE, 1484
WEST VIRGINIA UNIVERSITY CREATIVE ARTS CENTER -
    STUDIO THEATER, 1484
WEST VIRGINIA WESLEYAN COLLEGE - ATKINSON
    AUDITORIUM, 1475
WESTARK COMMUNITY COLLEGE - BREEDLOVE
    AUDITORIUM, 47
WESTBETH THEATRE CENTER, 1008
WESTBETH THEATRE CENTER - BIG ROOM, 1008
WESTBETH THEATRE CENTER - SECOND FLOOR
    THEATRE, 1009
WESTBETH THEATRE CENTER - STUDIO THEATRE, 1009
WESTBURY MUSIC FAIR, 1038
WESTCHESTER BROADWAY THEATRE, 889
WESTERN ILLINOIS UNIVERSITY - HAINLINE THEATRE, 461
WESTERN MICHIGAN UNIVERSITY - JAMES W. MILLER
    AUDITORIUM, 683
WESTERN MICHIGAN UNIVERSITY - LAURA V. SHAW
    THEATRE, 683

WESTERN OREGON STATE COLLEGE, 1184
WESTERN WASHINGTON UNIVERSITY - CONCERT
    HALL, 1446
WESTERN WASHINGTON UNIVERSITY - EXPERIMENTAL
    THEATER, 1446
WESTERN WASHINGTON UNIVERSITY - MAIN STAGE, 1446
WESTERN WASHINGTON UNIVERSITY - OLD MAIN
    THEATER, 1446
WESTMINSTER COLLEGE - BEEGHLY THEATER, 1215
WESTMINSTER COLLEGE - WESTMINSTER CHAMP
    AUDITORIUM, 744
WESTMINSTER COLLEGE - WILL W. ORR
    AUDITORIUM, 1215
WESTMINSTER COLLEGE - WINSTON CHURCHILL
    MEMORIAL AND LIBRARY IN THE UNITED STATES, 744
WESTPORT COMMUNITY THEATRE, 289
WESTPORT COUNTRY PLAYHOUSE, 289
WESTSIDE ARTS THEATRE, 1009
WESTWOOD TOWN HALL, 1108
WEXNER CENTER FOR THE ARTS/MERSHON
    AUDITORIUM, 1127
WHEATON COLLEGE - ARENA THEATER, 478
WHEATON COLLEGE - EDMAN CHAPEL, 478
WHEELER OPERA HOUSE, 223
WHEELING CIVIC CENTER, 1486
WHIDBEY PLAYHOUSE, 1452
WHISTLE STOP PLAYHOUSE, 731
WHITMAN COLLEGE - CORDINER HALL, 1472
WICOMICO YOUTH AND CIVIC CENTER, 597
WIDENER UNIVERSITY-ALUMNI AUDITORIUM - BERT
    MUSTIN THEATRE, 1198
WILKES UNIVERSITY - DOROTHY DICKSON DARTE
    CENTER FOR THE PERFORMING ARTS, 1242
WILLIAM A. EGAN CIVIC AND CONVENTION CENTER, 16
WILLIAM A. EGAN CIVIC AND CONVENTION CENTER -
    EXPLORERS HALL, 16
WILLIAM A. EGAN CIVIC AND CONVENTION CENTER -
    SUMMIT HALL, 16
WILLIAM EDRINGTON SCOTT THEATRE, 1350
WILLIAM WOODS COLLEGE - CAMPUS CENTER, 744
WILLIAM WOODS COLLEGE - DULANY AUDITORIUM, 744
WILLIAMS CENTER FOR THE ARTS - THE RIVOLI, 837
WILLIAMS COLLEGE - CHAPIN HALL, 652
WILLIAMSON THEATRE, 1029
WILLOWS THEATRE, 72
WILMA THEATER, 1229
WILSON CENTER FOR THE PERFORMING ARTS, 1189
WILSON HALL AUDITORIUM, 1428
WINTER GARDEN THEATRE, 1009
WINTHROP COLLEGE - JAMES F. BYRNES
    AUDITORIUM, 1265
W.L. ZORN ARENA, 1489
WOLF TRAP FARM PARK FOR THE PERFORMING ARTS, 1441
WOOD JUNIOR COLLEGE - THEATRE, 736
WOODLAND OPERA HOUSE, 218
WOODROW WILSON HIGH SCHOOL, 99
WOODSTOCK OPERA HOUSE, 480
WORCESTER MEMORIAL AUDITORIUM, 653
WRIGHT AUDITORIUM, 1061
WYNMOOR RECITAL HALL, 318
WYO THEATER, INC., 1522
YALE REPERTORY THEATRE, 273
YELLOW BARN, 1417
YOUNG CIRCLE PARK AND BANDSHELL, 330
YOUNGSTOWN PLAYHOUSE, THE, 1153
YOUNGSTOWN STATE UNIVERSITY - BLISS RECITAL
    HALL, 1153
YOUNGSTOWN STATE UNIVERSITY - FORD THEATRE, 1154
YOUNGSTOWN STATE UNIVERSITY - SPOTLIGHT ARENA
    THEATRE, 1154
YOUNGSTOWN SYMPHONY CENTER - POWERS
    AUDITORIUM, 1154
YREKA COMMUNITY THEATRE CENTER, 219
YUMA CIVIC AND CONVENTION CENTER - YUMA ROOM, 41
ZANESVILLE ART CENTER, 1155
ZEITERION THEATRE, 635

GENERAL INDEX

ABBEVILLE OPERA HOUSE, THE, 1255
ABBEY BACH FESTIVAL, 1190
ABERDEEN COMMUNITY THEATRE (ACT 2), 1267
ABERDEEN UNIVERSITY CIVIC SYMPHONY, 1267
ABHINAYA DANCE COMPANY, 75
ABILENE CIVIC CENTER, 1303
ABILENE CIVIC CENTER - EXHIBIT HALL, 1303
ABILENE CIVIC CENTER - THEATER, 1303
ABILENE PHILHARMONIC ASSOCIATION, 1303
ABOUTFACE THEATRE COMPANY, 962
ACACIA THEATRE, 1507
ACADEMY OF CREATIVE DANCE AND ELIZABETH
    MANDEVILLE DANCE COMPANY, 234
ACADEMY OF MUSIC, 1226
ACADEMY OF MUSIC - HALL, 1226
ACADEMY OF MUSIC - MAIN AUDITORIUM, 1226
ACADEMY OF PERFORMING ARTS, INC., 638
ACADEMY PLAYHOUSE, 638
ACADEMY THEATRE, 380
ACADEMY THEATRE - LAB, 385
ACADEMY THEATRE - PHOEBE THEATRE, 385
ACME PERFORMANCE GROUP, INC., 67
ACTING COMPANY, THE, 962
ACTING COMPANY OF RIVERSIDE THEATRE, THE, 371
ACTING STUDIO, INC./NEW THEATRE ALLIANCE/CHELSEA
    REPERTORY COMPANY, THE, 962
ACTORS ALLEY REPERTORY THEATER, 128
ACTORS' ALLIANCE INC. (AAI), 963
ACTORS ALLIANCE THEATRE COMPANY, 693
ACTORS COMMUNITY THEATRE SHOWCASE, 330
ACTORS FOR THEMSELVES, 107
ACTORS LAB ARIZONA, 33
ACTORS PLAYHOUSE OF NASHVILLE, 1296
ACTORS REPERTORY THEATRE & SANTA MONICA GROUP
    THEATRE, 199
ACTORS STUDIO, 963
ACTORS' SUMMER THEATRE COMPANY, 1124
ACTORS' THEATER OF ASHLAND, 1174
ACTORS THEATRE OF LOUISVILLE, 548
ACTORS THEATRE OF NANTUCKET, 634
ACTORS THEATRE OF PHOENIX, 30
A.D. PLAYERS, 1360
A.D.A.M.S. THEATRE, 1170
ADDISON CENTRE THEATRE, 1304
ADELPHIAN PLAYERS, 872
ADIRONDACK FESTIVAL OF AMERICAN MUSIC, 1024
ADIRONDACK LAKES CENTER FOR THE ARTS, 867
ADRIAN COLLEGE, 656
ADRIAN SYMPHONY ORCHESTRA, 655
AEOLIAN CHAMBER PLAYERS, 938
AFFILIATE ARTISTS INC., 938
AFRICAN-AMERICAN CULTURAL CENTER, 878
AFRICAN-AMERICAN CULTURAL CENTER - PAUL
    ROBESON THEATRE, 879
AFRICAN-AMERICAN DANCE ENSEMBLE, THE, 1052
AFRICAN AMERICAN DRAMA COMPANY, 173
AFRICAN DANCE FESTIVAL FOR KANKOURAN WEST
    AFRICAN DANCE CO., 297
AFRIKAN POETRY THEATRE, 899
AFRO-AMERICAN PLAYERS, 1328
AFRO-AMERICAN STUDIO THEATRE, 668
AFTER DINNER OPERA COMPANY, 952
AGNES DE MILLE DANCE THEATER, 908
AIKEN CIVIC BALLET COMPANY, 1255
AIKEN COMMUNITY PLAYHOUSE, 1255
AJDE! FOLK DANCE ENSEMBLE, 270
AKASHA AND COMPANY, 422
AKRON CIVIC THEATRE, 1093
AKRON SYMPHONY ORCHESTRA, 1091
AKRON YOUTH SYMPHONY, 1091
ALABAMA SHAKESPEARE FESTIVAL, 10
ALABAMA SHAKESPEARE FESTIVAL - FESTIVAL STAGE, 11
ALABAMA SHAKESPEARE FESTIVAL - OCTAGON, 11
ALABAMA SYMPHONY ORCHESTRA, 2
ALASKA CENTER FOR THE PERFORMING ARTS, 16

ALASKA LIGHT OPERA THEATRE, 14
ALASKALAND CIVIC CENTER, 19
ALBANO BALLET AND PERFORMING ARTS CENTER, 264
ALBANO BALLET COMPANY, 262
ALBANY JAMES H. GRAY, SR., CIVIC CENTER, 375
ALBANY JAMES H. GRAY, SR., CIVIC CENTER -
    ARENA, 376
ALBANY JAMES H. GRAY, SR., CIVIC CENTER -
    BALLROOM, 376
ALBANY SYMPHONY ASSOCIATION, INC., 375
ALBANY SYMPHONY ORCHESTRA, 859
ALBERT LEA CIVIC THEATER, 699
ALBERTA BAIR THEATER FOR THE PERFORMING ARTS,
    THE, 770
ALBUNDEGUS ALL-STARS, 248
ALBUQUERQUE CIVIC LIGHT OPERA, 849
ALBUQUERQUE CONVENTION CENTER, 850
ALBUQUERQUE CONVENTION CENTER - BALLROOM, 850
ALBUQUERQUE CONVENTION CENTER - KIVA
    AUDITORIUM, 851
ALBUQUERQUE OPERA THEATRE - OPERA SOUTHWEST, 849
ALBUQUERQUE YOUTH SYMPHONY, 847
ALCAZAR THEATRE, THE, 180
ALDEN THEATRE, 1430
ALEA III, 606
ALEPH MOVEMENT THEATRE, 774
ALEXANDRA BALLET COMPANY, 743
ALEXANDRIA BIG BAND, 699
ALFRED UNIVERSITY, 862
ALHAMBRA DINNER THEATRE, 332
ALIAS STAGE, 1249
ALICE B THEATRE, 1458, 1463
ALLEGHENY BALLET COMPANY, 1194
ALLEGHENY CIVIC SYMPHONY, 1211
ALLEGRO BALLET OF HOUSTON, 1354
ALLENBERRY PLAYHOUSE, 1197
ALLENTOWN COMMUNITY CONCERT ASSOCIATION, 1194
ALLENTOWN SYMPHONY ASSOCIATION, 1193
ALLEY THEATRE, 1360, 1364
ALLEY THEATRE - HUGO V. NEUHAUS ARENA STAGE, 1364
ALLEY THEATRE - LARGE STAGE, 1364
ALLIANCE THEATRE COMPANY, 380
ALLNATIONS DANCE COMPANY, 908
ALPHA-OMEGA THEATRICAL DANCE COMPANY, 909
ALTON SYMPHONY ORCHESTRA, 419
ALVA MEMORIAL AUDITORIUM, 1157
ALVA PUBLIC LIBRARY AUDITORIUM, 1157
ALVERNO COLLEGE, 1509
ALVIN AILEY AMERICAN DANCE THEATER, 909
ALVIN AILEY REPERTORY ENSEMBLE, 909
AMAN INTERNATIONAL MUSIC AND DANCE COMPANY, 100
AMARILLO CIVIC CENTER, 1305
AMARILLO CIVIC CENTER - ARENA, 1306
AMARILLO CIVIC CENTER - MUSIC HALL, 1306
AMARILLO SYMPHONY, 1305
AMAS REPERTORY THEATRE, 963
AMATEUR MUSICAL CLUB OF PEORIA, INC., 468
AMATO OPERA THEATRE, 952
AMBASSADOR THEATRE, 993
AMERICAN ARTISTS SERIES, 663
AMERICAN AUTHENTIC JAZZ DANCE THEATRE, 910
AMERICAN BALLET, 1248
AMERICAN BALLET THEATRE, 910
AMERICAN BALLROOM THEATER COMPANY INC., 910
AMERICAN BLUES THEATRE, 432
AMERICAN BOYCHOIR SCHOOL, 833
AMERICAN CENTER FOR STANISLAVSKI THEATRE ART,
    INC., 963
AMERICAN CHAMBER OPERA COMPANY, INC., 953
AMERICAN CHORAL DIRECTORS ASSOCIATION, 1160
AMERICAN COMPOSERS ORCHESTRA, 938
AMERICAN CONSERVATORY THEATRE, 173
AMERICAN DANCE FESTIVAL, 1052
AMERICAN DANCE MACHINE, THE, 815
AMERICAN ENSEMBLE COMPANY, THE, 964

AMERICAN FESTIVAL BALLET, 411
AMERICAN INTERNATIONAL DANCE THEATRE, INC., 910
AMERICAN LANDMARK FESTIVALS, 990
AMERICAN LEGION, 1159
AMERICAN LIVING HISTORY THEATER, 87
AMERICAN MIME THEATRE, THE, 911
AMERICAN MUSIC THEATER FESTIVAL, 1225
AMERICAN MUSIC THEATRE GROUP, 264
AMERICAN MUSICAL ROOTS ASSOCIATION, 891
AMERICAN PLACE THEATRE, 994
AMERICAN PLACE THEATRE, THE, 964
AMERICAN PLAYERS THEATRE, 1515
AMERICAN REPERTORY THEATRE, 621
AMERICAN SHOWCASE THEATRE COMPANY, 1421
AMERICAN STAGE COMPANY, 357, 838
AMERICAN STAGE FESTIVAL, 809
AMERICAN SYMPHONY ORCHESTRA, 938
AMERICAN SYMPHONY ORCHESTRA LEAGUE, 299
AMERICAN TAP DANCE ORCHESTRA, 939
AMERICAN THEATRE, 761
AMERICAN THEATRE COMPANY, 1169
AMERICAN THEATRE OF ACTORS, 964
AMERICAN THEATRE WORKS, INC., 1413
AMERICAN UNIVERSITY - MCDONALD RECITAL HALL,
   THE, 309
AMERICAN UNIVERSITY - NEW LECTURE HALL THEATRE,
   THE, 309
AMERICAN YOUTH BALLET, 531
AMERICAN YOUTH BALLET COMPANY, 597
AMERICAN YOUTH SYMPHONY, 217
AMES INTERNATIONAL ORCHESTRA FESTIVAL
   ASSOCIATION, 507
AMES TOWN AND GOWN CHAMBER MUSIC
   ASSOCIATION, 507
AMHERST BALLET THEATRE COMPANY, 601
AMHERST SAXOPHONE QUARTET, 876
ANACRUSIS MODERN TAP DANCE, 1451
ANAHEIM CONVENTION CENTER, 55
ANAHEIM CONVENTION CENTER - ANAHEIM ROOM, 55
ANAHEIM CONVENTION CENTER - ARENA, 55
ANAHEIM CULTURAL ARTS CENTER, 55
ANCHOR THEATRE, 539
ANCHORAGE CONCERT ASSOCIATION INC., 13
ANCHORAGE CONCERT CHORUS, 14
ANCHORAGE FESTIVAL OF MUSIC, 15
ANCHORAGE FOLK DANCE CONSORTIUM, 13
ANCHORAGE OPERA COMPANY, 15
ANCHORAGE SYMPHONY ORCHESTRA, 13
ANCHORAGE YOUTH SYMPHONY, 14
ANDAHAZY BALLET COMPANY, 723
ANDERSON SYMPHONY ORCHESTRA, 483
ANGELO STATE UNIVERSITY - AUDITORIUM, 1382
ANGELO STATE UNIVERSITY - MODULAR THEATRE, 1382
ANGELS GATE CULTURAL CENTER, 190
ANJANI'S KATHAK DANCE OF INDIA, 215
ANN ARBOR BALLET THEATRE, 657
ANN ARBOR CIVIC BALLET, 657
ANN ARBOR SUMMER FESTIVAL, 659
ANN ARBOR SYMPHONY ORCHESTRA, 658
ANNABELLA GONZALEZ DANCE THEATER, INC., 911
ANNAPOLIS OPERA, 585
ANNIE RUSSELL THEATRE, 374
ANNISTON COMMUNITY THEATER, 1
ANTENNA THEATER, 203
APOLLO THEATER CENTER, 432
APOLLO THEATRE, 994
APPALACHIAN BALLET COMPANY, 1288
APPALACHIAN SUMMER, AN, 1044
APPALACHIAN YOUTH JAZZ-BALLET COMPANY, 1476
APPEL FARM ARTS AND MUSIC CENTER, 819
APPLE ALLEY PLAYERS, 1482
APPLE HILL CENTER FOR CHAMBER MUSIC, 805
APPLE TREE THEATRE, 459
APPLE TREE THEATRE COMPANY, THE, 459
APPLETON WEST THEATRE, 1487
ARCADY MUSIC SOCIETY, 575
ARDMORE LITTLE THEATRE, 1157
ARENA CIVIC THEATRE, 628

ARENA DINNER THEATRE, 490
ARENA PLAYERS, 589, 591
ARENA PLAYERS REPERTORY COMPANY OF LONG
   ISLAND, 887
ARENA STAGE, 304
ARENA STAGE - FICHANDLER THEATER, 309
ARENA STAGE - KREEGER THEATER, 309
ARENA STAGE - OLD VAT THEATER, 310
ARIE CROWN THEATRE, 444
ARIOSO WIND QUARTET, 153
ARIZONA MINI-CONCERTS, 39
ARIZONA OPERA COMPANY, 37
ARIZONA STATE UNIVERSITY - GAMMAGE CENTER, 36
ARIZONA STATE UNIVERSITY - SUNDOME CENTER FOR
   THE PERFORMING ARTS, 35
ARIZONA STATE UNIVERSITY - UNIVERSITY ACTIVITY
   CENTER, 36
ARIZONA THEATRE COMPANY, 38
ARKANSAS ARTS CENTER, 49
ARKANSAS ARTS CENTER CHILDREN'S THEATER, THE, 49
ARKANSAS REPERTORY THEATRE, 49, 50
ARKANSAS RIVER VALLEY ARTS CENTER, 52
ARKANSAS SYMPHONY ORCHESTRA SOCIETY, 48
ARKANSAS TECH UNIVERSITY - WITHERSPOON ARTS AND
   HUMANITIES BUILDING, 52
ARLENE SCHNITZER CONCERT HALL, 1188
ARLINGTON CENTER FOR THE PERFORMING ARTS, 195
ARLINGTON DANCE THEATRE, 1422
ARLINGTON OPERA ASSOCIATION, 1306
ARMOUR STAR HAM PLAYERS, 1267
ARMSTRONG CHAMBER CONCERTS, INC., 285
ARMSTRONG STATE COLLEGE FINE ARTS
   AUDITORIUM, 397
ARMY ENTERTAINMENT PROGRAM, 401
ARNESON RIVER THEATRE, 1386
ARNOLD HALL THEATER - UNITED STATES AIR FORCE
   ACADEMY, 231
ARS MUSICA CHORALE AND ORCHESTRA, 832
ARS NOVA MUSICIANS CHAMBER ORCHESTRA, 876
ART BRIDGMAN/MYRNA PACKER, 911
ART OF BLACK DANCE AND MUSIC, 643
ART SONG FESTIVAL, 1114
ARTIST SERIES AT THE PABST, 1509
ARTISTS CIVIC THEATRE AND STUDIO, 559
ARTISTS COLLECTIVE, 263
ARTISTS THEATRE ASSOCIATION, 294
ARTPARK, 904
ARTPARK THEATER, 904
ARTREACH TOURING THEATRE, 1103
ARTS AND SCIENCE CENTER OF SOUTHEAST
   ARKANSAS, 51
ARTS AND SCIENCE CENTER THEATRE, 809
ARTS AT ARGONNE, 419
ARTS CELEBRATION/ARTQUAKE FESTIVAL, 1188
ARTS CENTER OF THE OZARKS, 52
ARTS CENTER/OLD FORGE, 1011
ARTS CENTER ON BRICKYARD POND - KEENE STATE
   COLLEGE, 807
ARTS CONSORTIUM STUDIO THEATRE, 1105
ARTS COUNCIL OF GREATER KNOXVILLE, THE, 1287
ARTS COUNCIL OF WASHINGTON COUNTY, 1316
ARTS COUNCIL THEATRE, THE, 1080
ARTS IN THE PARKS - PORTABLE STAGE, 700
ARTS PROGRAM, GARDEN CITY RECREATION
   COMMISSION, THE, 526
ARTS SAN ANTONIO!, 1385
ARTSCENTER, 1046
ARTSCENTER, THE, 1047
ARTSPLOSURE, 1070
ARVADA CENTER FOR THE ARTS AND HUMANITIES, 221
ASHEVILLE CHAMBER MUSIC SERIES, 1043
ASHEVILLE CIVIC CENTER, 1044
ASHLAND FOLK MUSIC CLUB, 1175
ASHLAND SYMPHONY ORCHESTRA, 1093
ASHMONT HILL CHAMBER MUSIC, 625
ASHTABULA ARTS CENTER, 1094
ASHTABULA CHAMBER ORCHESTRA, THE, 1094
ASIAN AMERICAN DANCE PERFORMANCES, 161

ASIAN AMERICAN DANCE THEATRE, 911
ASOLO CENTER FOR THE PERFORMING ARTS, 361
ASPEN MUSIC FESTIVAL AND SCHOOL, 221
ASSEMBLY HALL, 421
ASSOCIATION FOR THE ADVANCEMENT OF CREATIVE
     MUSICIANS, NEW YORK CHAPTER, THE, 939
ASSOCIATION FOR THE FURTHERMENT OF BEL CANTO, 953
ASTON MAGNA FOUNDATION FOR MUSIC AND THE
     HUMANITIES, INC., 258
ATHENAEUM THEATRE, 445
ATHENS BALLET, 376
ATHENS MEMORIAL AUDITORIUM, 1094
ATHENS PUPPET THEATRE COMPANY, 376
ATHERTON AUDITORIUM, 206
ATLANTA BACH CHOIR, 379
ATLANTA BALLET, THE, 377
ATLANTA CHAMBER PLAYERS, 378
ATLANTA CIVIC CENTER, 385
ATLANTA CIVIC CENTER - ROOM 104, 385
ATLANTA CIVIC CENTER - THEATER AUDITORIUM, 385
ATLANTA JAZZ FESTIVAL, 383
ATLANTA OPERA, THE, 379
ATLANTA POPS ORCHESTRA, 378
ATLANTA SHAKESPEARE COMPANY, 380
ATLANTA STREET THEATRE, 381
ATLANTA SYMPHONY CHORUS, 379
ATLANTA SYMPHONY ORCHESTRA, 378
ATLANTA SYMPHONY YOUTH ORCHESTRA, 378
ATLANTIC CENTER FOR THE ARTS, 346
ATLANTIC DANCE THEATRE, 1067
ATTIC/NEW CENTER THEATRE, 668
ATTIC/STRAND THEATRE, 689
ATTIC THEATRE, 107
AUBURN PLAYERS COMMUNITY THEATRE, THE, 863
AUDITORIUM CENTER, 1022
AUDITORIUM THEATER - DENVER PERFORMING ARTS
     COMPLEX, 240
AUDITORIUM THEATRE, 445
AUDITORIUM THEATRE COUNCIL, 443
AUGUSTA BALLET COMPANY, 387
AUGUSTA CIVIC CENTER, 573
AUGUSTA CIVIC CENTER - ARENA, 573
AUGUSTA CIVIC CENTER - NORTH HALL, 574
AUGUSTA OPERA ASSOCIATION, 388
AUGUSTA PLAYERS, 388
AUGUSTA/RICHMOND COUNTY CIVIC CENTER COMPLEX -
     ARENA, 389
AUGUSTA SYMPHONY, 573
AUGUSTA SYMPHONY ORCHESTRA, 388
AUGUSTANA COLLEGE - CENTENNIAL HALL, 471
AURORA CHILDREN'S THEATRE COMPANY, 224
AURORA DANCE ARTS, 223
AURORA FOX ARTS CENTER, 225
AURORA SINGERS, 224
AURORA SYMPHONY, 223
AURORA THEATRE COMPANY, 224
AUSTIN CHAMBER MUSIC CENTER, 1308
AUSTIN LYRIC OPERA, THE, 1309
AUSTIN SYMPHONY ORCHESTRA SOCIETY, THE, 1309
AVAZ INTERNATIONAL DANCE THEATRE, 203
AVERY POINT PLAYERS, THE, 261
AVILA COLLEGE - GOPPERT THEATRE, 749
AVODAH DANCE ENSEMBLE, 822
AYCOCK AUDITORIUM, 1060
AZTEC, THE, 1304
B SHARP MUSIC CLUB OF NEW ORLEANS, THE, 564
BACH ARIA FESTIVAL AND INSTITUTE, 1029
BACH CHAMBER CHOIR AND ORCHESTRA, THE, 1506
BACH DANCING AND DYNAMITE SOCIETY GROUP, 78
BACH FESTIVAL OF PHILADELPHIA, 1225
BACH SOCIETY OF MINNESOTA, 720
BACKSTAGE THEATRE, 228
BACKSTAGE THEATRE COMPANY, 228
BAGLEY WRIGHT THEATRE, 1463
BAILES FLAMENCOS, 162
BAILEY HALL, 325
BAILIWICK REPERTORY, 432
BAKERSFIELD CIVIC AUDITORIUM, 58

BAKERSFIELD SYMPHONY ORCHESTRA, 57
BALDWIN WALLACE COLLEGE - KULAS MUSICAL ARTS
     CONCERT HALL, 1096
BALLET ALASKA, 13
BALLET ARIZONA, 28
BALLET ARKANSAS, 48
BALLET AUSTIN, 1307
BALLET CHICAGO, 422
BALLET COLBERT, 795
BALLET CONCERTO, 1343
BALLET CONCERTO COMPANY OF MIAMI, 339
BALLET CONCIERTO DE PUERTO RICO, 1526
BALLET CULTURAL AZTECA, 691
BALLET DENVER, 234
BALLET DES JEUNES, 1215
BALLET ETUDES, 329
BALLET FLORIDA, 372
BALLET FOLKLORICO OF EAST CHICAGO, INDIANA, 487
BALLET GUILD OF LEHIGH VALLEY, 1195
BALLET HISPANICO OF NEW YORK, 912
BALLET IOWA, 522
BALLET IOWA ASSOCIATION, 522
BALLET MANHATTAN FOUNDATION, INC., 912
BALLET METROPOLITAN, 1121
BALLET MISSISSIPPI, 734
BALLET MONTMARTRE, THE, 72
BALLET OF THE AMERICAS, 1340
BALLET OKLAHOMA, 1163
BALLET PACIFICA, 95,
BALLET SPECTACULAR/INTERNATIONAL CULTURAL
     EXCHANGE, INC., 340
BALLET THEATRE OF ANNAPOLIS, 585
BALLET THEATRE OF WESTCHESTER, 1033
BALLET THEATRE PENNSYLVANIA, 1209
BALLET WEST, 1401
BALLET WESTERN RESERVE, 1152
BALLETACOMA, 1468
BALLETS DE SAN JUAN, 1525
BALTIMORE ACTORS' THEATRE, INC., 589
BALTIMORE CHORAL ARTS SOCIETY, 588
BALTIMORE CONSORT, 1217
BALTIMORE DANCE THEATRE, 586
BALTIMORE MEN'S CHORUS, 588
BALTIMORE MUSEUM OF ART - AUDITORIUM, 591
BALTIMORE OPERA COMPANY, 588
BALTIMORE SYMPHONY CHORUS, 589
BALTIMORE SYMPHONY ORCHESTRA, 587
BAMA THEATRE PERFORMING ARTS CENTER, 11
BANG ON A CAN, INC., 990
BANGOR AUDITORIUM, 574
BANGOR CIVIC CENTER, 575
BANGOR SYMPHONY ORCHESTRA, 574
BANJO DAN AND THE MID-NITE PLOWBOYS, 1415
BAR HARBOR MUSIC FESTIVAL, 575
BARBARA B. MANN PERFORMING ARTS HALL, 326
BARBARA FELDMAN AND DANCERS, 270
BARDAVON 1869 OPERA HOUSE, 1017
BARGEMUSIC LTD., 874
BARKSDALE THEATRE, 1428
BARN COMMUNITY THEATRE, 515
BARN PLAYERS THEATRE, THE, 533
BARN THEATER, THE, 1273
BARN THEATRE, 623, 661
BARNSTORMERS, THE, 813
BAROQUE FESTIVAL STUDIO, 894
BARRE OPERA HOUSE, 1409
BARRIO PLAYERS - ACTORES DEL BARRIO, 128
BARRON ARTS CENTER, 845
BARTER PLAYHOUSE, 1421
BARTER THEATRE HOUSE, 1421
BARTER THEATRE-STATE THEATRE OF VIRGINIA, 1421
BARTLESVILLE CIVIC BALLET, 1158
BARTLESVILLE COMMUNITY CENTER, 1159
BARTLESVILLE SYMPHONY ORCHESTRA, 1158
BATES COLLEGE - CONCERT HALL, 578
BATES COLLEGE - OLIN ARTS CENTER, 578
BATES DANCE FESTIVAL, 577
BATH HOUSE CULTURAL CENTER, 1334

BATHHOUSE THEATRE, 1458, 1464
BATON ROUGE BALLET THEATRE, 555
BATON ROUGE GILBERT AND SULLIVAN SOCIETY, 555
BATON ROUGE LITTLE THEATRE, 556
BATON ROUGE OPERA, 555
BATON ROUGE SYMPHONY ORCHESTRA, 555
BATTERY DANCE COMPANY, 912
BATTLE CREEK CIVIC THEATRE, 661
BATTLE CREEK SYMPHONY ORCHESTRA, 661
BAUER CONTEMPORARY BALLET, 1503
BAY AREA REPERTORY DANCE THEATRE (BARD), 59
BAY CHAMBER CONCERTS, 576
BAY CITY PLAYERS, 662
BAY STREET PLAYERS, 323
BAY VIEW MUSIC FESITVAL, 662
BAYFRONT CENTER COMPLEX, 358
BAYFRONT PLAZA CONVENTION CENTER -
    AUDITORIUM, 1322
BAYVIEW OPERA HOUSE, 180
B.C. POPS, 865
BEACH CITIES SYMPHONY, 144
BEACH THEATRE UNDER THE STARS, 330
BEACON DANCE COMPANY, 391
BEAUMONT BALLET THEATRE, 1312
BEAUMONT CIVIC BALLET, 1313
BEAUMONT CIVIC OPERA, 1313
BEAUMONT MUSIC COMMISSION, 1314
BEBE MILLER COMPANY, 912
BECK CENTER FOR THE CULTURAL ARTS, THE, 1135
BEDFORD LITTLE THEATRE, 483
BEEF AND BOARDS DINNER THEATRE, 496
BEETHOVEN FESTIVAL, 905
BEETHOVEN HALL - SAN JOSE CONVENTION
    CENTER, 1386
BEL CANTO CHORUS OF MILWAUKEE, 1506
BEL CANTO COMPANY, 1057
BELASCO THEATRE, 994
BELLEVILLE PHILHARMONIC, 420
BELLEVUE LITTLE THEATRE, 781
BELLEVUE PARKS AND RECREATION DEPARTMENT -
    BELLEVUE JAZZ FESTIVAL, 1445
BELMONT CHILDREN'S THEATRE, 603
BELMONT DRAMATIC CLUB, 603
BELOIT COLLEGE PERFORMING ARTS SERIES, 1487
BEMIDJI STATE UNIVERSITY - BANGSBERG FINE ARTS
    BUILDING, 700
BENEDUM CENTER, 1235
BENSON AUDITORIUM, 52
BERKELEY CITY BALLET, 59
BERKELEY COMMUNITY THEATRE, 61, 63
BERKELEY OPERA, 60
BERKELEY REPERTORY THEATRE, 61, 63
BERKELEY SHAKESPEARE FESTIVAL, 62
BERKELEY SYMPHONY ORCHESTRA, 59
BERKSHIRE CHORAL INSTITUTE, 642
BERKSHIRE COMMUNITY COLLEGE - KOUSSEVITZKY
    ARTS CENTER, 640
BERKSHIRE HILLS MUSIC AND DANCE ASSOCIATION, 278
BERKSHIRE LYRIC THEATRE, 639
BERKSHIRE OPERA COMPANY, INC., 630
BERKSHIRE PUBLIC THEATRE COMPANY, THE, 639
BERKSHIRE SYMPHONY, 650
BERKSHIRE THEATRE FESTIVAL, 647
BETHANY COLLEGE - BURNETT CENTER FOR
    PERFORMING ARTS, 530
BETHUNE THEATREDANSE, 100
BETTY SALAMUN'S DANCECIRCUS, 1503
BEVERLY ART CENTER, 445
BEVERLY BLOSSOM AND COMPANY, 869
BEVERLY HILLS PLAYHOUSE, 65
BEVERLY HILLS SYMPHONY, 64
BG-WC ARTS COMMISSION, 540
BIBLICAL ARTS CENTER, 1334
BICENTENNIAL ART CENTER, 225
BIG BEAR LAKE PERFORMING ARTS CENTER, 66
BIG SPRING CULTURAL AFFAIRS COUNCIL, 1315
BIGFORK CENTER FOR THE PERFORMING ARTS, 769
BILINGUAL FOUNDATION OF THE ARTS, 107

BILINGUAL THEATER COMPANY/SOUTH TEXAS
    PERFORMANCE CO., 1321
BILL T. JONES/ARNIE ZANE AND COMPANY, 913
BILLIE HOLIDAY THEATRE, 873
BILLINGS SYMPHONY SOCIETY, 769
BING CONCERTS, 114
BINGHAMTON SUMMER MUSIC FESTIVAL, INC., 866
BINGHAMTON SYMPHONY ORCHESTRA AND CHORAL
    SOCIETY, 865
BINGHAMTON YOUTH SYMPHONY, 865
BIRCH CREEK MUSIC CENTER, 1489
BIRMINGHAM CHILDREN'S THEATRE, 3
BIRMINGHAM FESTIVAL OF ARTS ASSOCIATION, 3
BIRMINGHAM OPERA THEATER, 2
BIRMINGHAM-BLOOMFIELD SYMPHONY, 662
BIRMINGHAM-JEFFERSON CIVIC CENTER, 4
BIRMINGHAM-JEFFERSON CIVIC CENTER - COLISEUM, 4
BIRMINGHAM-JEFFERSON CIVIC CENTER - CONCERT
    HALL, 4
BIRMINGHAM-JEFFERSON CIVIC CENTER - EXHIBITION
    HALL, 4
BIRMINGHAM-JEFFERSON CIVIC CENTER - THEATRE, 4
BIRMINGHAM-SOUTHERN COLLEGE THEATRE, 4
BISHOP CENTER FOR PERFORMING ARTS, 1445
BISMARCK CIVIC CENTER - ARENA, 1083
BISMARCK CIVIC CENTER - BISMARCK CITY
    AUDITORIUM, 1083
BISMARCK-MANDAN ORCHESTRAL ASSOCIATION, 1083
BITS 'N PIECES GIANT PUPPET THEATRE, 367
BLACK ARTS ALLIANCE, 1310
BLACK ENSEMBLE THEATER, 433
BLACK EXPERIENCE ENSEMBLE, THE, 859
BLACK HILLS COMMUNITY THEATRE, 1271
BLACK HILLS PLAYHOUSE, 1272
BLACK HILLS SYMPHONY ORCHESTRA, 1271
BLACK MUSIC REPERTORY ENSEMBLE, 426
BLACK MUSIC SOCIETY OF MISSOURI, 760
BLACK REPERTORY GROUP INC., 61
BLACK SPECTRUM, 964
BLACK THEATER GUILD OF GREATER KANSAS CITY, 747
BLACK THEATRE TROUPE, 31
BLACKFRIARS THEATRE, 155, 158
BLADEN OPERA HOUSE, 781
BLAIR COUNTY CIVIC MUSIC ASSOCIATION, 1194
BLAKE STREET HAWKEYES, 191
BLANCHE MOYSE CHORALE, 1409
BLATZ TEMPLE OF MUSIC - WASHINGTON PARK
    BANDSHELL, 1510
BLIND PARROT PRODUCTIONS, 433
BLITHEWOLD GARDENS AND ARBORETUM "CONCERTS BY
    THE BAY", 1245
BLOOMFIELD SYMPHONY ORCHESTRA, 816
BLOOMING GROVE THEATER ENSEMBLE, LTD., 826
BLOOMING GROVE THEATRE, 827
BLOOMINGDALE HOUSE OF MUSIC, THE, 939
BLOOMINGTON-NORMAL SYMPHONY SOCIETY, 420
BLOOMINGTON SYMPHONY ORCHESTRA, 484
BLOOMSBURG THEATRE ENSEMBLE, 1197
BLOOMSBURG UNIVERSITY - CARVER HALL, 1197
BLOOMSBURG UNIVERSITY - HAAS CENTER FOR THE
    ARTS, 1197
BLOSSOM MUSIC CENTER, 1128
BLUE EARTH TOWN AND COUNTRY PLAYERS, 701
BLUE LAKE REPERTORY THEATRE, 696
BLUEMONT CONCERT SERIES, 1429
BMCC/TRIPLEX PERFORMING ARTS CENTER, 994
BMT THEATER, THE, 78
BOARSHEAD: MICHIGAN PUBLIC THEATER, 684
BOB BAKER MARIONETTE THEATER, 117
BOB BAKER PRODUCTIONS, 108
BOB CARR PERFORMING ARTS CENTER, 350
BOB HOPE CULTURAL CENTER - MCALLUM THEATRE, 136
BODY LANGUAGE DANCE COMPANY, 1202
BODY POLITIC THEATRE, 433
BOETTCHER CONCERT HALL - DENVER PERFORMING
    ARTS COMPLEX, 240
BOISE MASTER CHORALE, 412
BOISE OPERA, 412

BOISE PHILHARMONIC, 411
BOISE STATE UNIVERSITY - MORRISON CENTER FOR THE
    PERFORMING ARTS, 413
BOND STREET THEATRE COALITION, 965
BOOTH THEATRE, 994
BORDERLANDS THEATER/TEATRO FRONTERIZO, 38
BOSTON BALLET COMPANY, 604
BOSTON BALLET II, 605
BOSTON BAROQUE, 619
BOSTON CENTER FOR THE ARTS - CYCLORAMA, 614
BOSTON CENTER FOR THE ARTS - THE NATIONAL
    THEATRE, 614
BOSTON CHILDREN'S THEATRE, 610
BOSTON CLASSICAL ORCHESTRA, 606
BOSTON EARLY MUSIC FESTIVAL AND EXHIBITION,
    INC., 612
BOSTON FLAMENCO BALLET, 617
BOSTON LYRIC OPERA COMPANY, 609
BOSTON MUSICA VIVA, 606
BOSTON OPERA ASSOCIATION, 609
BOSTON OPERA HOUSE, 614
BOSTON PHILHARMONIC, 619
BOSTON POPS, 607
BOSTON SYMPHONY CHAMBER PLAYERS, 607
BOSTON SYMPHONY ORCHESTRA, 607
BOSTON THEATER GROUP, 625
BOSTON UNIVERSITY SCHOOL FOR THE ARTS - CONCERT
    HALL, 614
BOSTON UNIVERSITY THEATRE, 614
BOSTON UNIVERSITY THEATRE - MAIN STAGE, 614
BOSTON UNIVERSITY THEATRE - STUDIO 210, 615
BOULDER ART CENTER, 227
BOULDER FOLK AND BLUEGRASS ASSOCIATION, 226
BOULDER PHILHARMONIC ORCHESTRA, 225
BOULDER REPERTORY COMPANY, THE, 225
BOWDOIN SUMMER MUSIC FESTIVAL, 907
BOWIE STATE COLLEGE - MARTIN LUTHER KING, JR.,
    COMMUNICATION ARTS CENTER, 592
BOWLING GREEN-WESTERN SYMPHONY ORCHESTRA, 540
BOWLUS FINE ARTS CENTER, 528
BOZEMAN SYMPHONY ORCHESTRA, 770
BRADFORD CREATIVE AND PERFORMING ARTS CENTER,
    INC., 1198
BRADY THEATRE, 1170
BRAINTREE CHORAL SOCIETY, 616
BRANDEIS SUMMER MUSIC FESTIVAL, 648
BRANDEIS UNIVERSITY - SPINGOLD THEATER CENTER, 649
BRANDEIS UNIVERSITY DEPARTMENT OF MUSIC, 648
BRANSCOMB MEMORIAL AUDITORIUM, 336
BRASS CHAMBER MUSIC SOCIETY OF ANNAPOLIS, 586
BRASS RING, 270
BRATTLEBORO MUSIC CENTER, 1410
BRAVADO STRING QUARTET, 1147
BRAVO! COLORADO MUSIC FESTIVAL AT VAIL-BEAVER
    CREEK, 253
BRAZOS VALLEY SYMPHONY ORCHESTRA, 1317
BRECKENRIDGE MUSIC INSTITUTE, 228
BRECKSVILLE LITTLE THEATRE, 1097, 1098
BREMERTON SYMPHONY ASSOCIATION, 1447
BREN EVENTS CENTER, 92
BREVARD MUSIC CENTER - STRAUS AUDITORIUM, 1045
BREVARD MUSIC CENTER - WHITTINGTON-PFOHL
    AUDITORIUM, 1045
BREWERY ARTS CENTER, 795
BRIDGEPORT CIVIC ORCHESTRA, 255
BRIDGEWORK THEATER, THE, 492
BRIGHAM YOUNG UNIVERSITY - HARRIS FINE ARTS
    CENTER, 1400
BRIGHAM YOUNG UNIVERSITY - UNIVERSITY
    CONCERTS, 1399
BRIGHT LIGHTS THEATRE COMPANY, 1249
BRISTOL BALLET COMPANY, 1424
BRITT FESTIVALS, 1183
BROADHURST THEATRE, 994
BROADWAY THEATRE, 995
BROADWAY THEATRE LEAGUE OF PUEBLO, 251
BROADWAY THEATRE LEAGUE OF THE QUAD-CITIES, 512
BROADWAY TOMORROW, INC., 965

BROCKPORT SYMPHONY ORCHESTRA, 867
BRONX ARTS ENSEMBLE INC., 868
BRONX OPERA COMPANY, 868
BROOKINGS CHAMBER MUSIC SOCIETY, 1268
BROOKLYN ACADEMY OF MUSIC, 874, 875
BROOKLYN ACADEMY OF MUSIC - CAREY
    PLAYHOUSE, 875
BROOKLYN ACADEMY OF MUSIC - LEPERCQ SPACE, 875
BROOKLYN ACADEMY OF MUSIC - OPERA HOUSE, 876
BROOKLYN CENTER, 701
BROOKLYN CENTER FOR THE PERFORMING ARTS AT
    BROOKLYN COLLEGE, 869
BROOKLYN PHILHARMONIC, THE, 871
BROOKS ATKINSON THEATRE, 995
BROOM STREET THEATER, 1498
BROOME CENTER FOR THE PRFORMING ARTS - THE
    FORUM, 866
BROWARD CENTER FOR THE PERFORMING ARTS, 325
BROWARD SYMPHONY ORCHESTRA, 344
BROWARD'S FRIENDS OF CHAMBER MUSIC, INC., 354
BROWN GRAND THEATRE, 526
BROWN UNIVERSITY THEATRE, 1250
BROWNWOOD COLISEUM, 1317
BRUCE KING FOUNDATION FOR AMERICAN DANCE, 913
BUCKS COUNTY PLAYHOUSE, 1214
BUFFALO MEMORIAL AUDITORIUM, 879
BUFFALO PHILHARMONIC ORCHESTRA, 876
BUFFALO STATE COLLEGE-PERFORMING ARTS CENTER -
    ROCKWELL HALL, 879
BUMBERSHOOT, THE SEATTLE ARTS FESTIVAL, 1461
BURBAGE THEATRE ENSEMBLE, 108
BURBANK SYMPHONY ASSOCIATION, 66
BURLINGTON MEMORIAL AUDITORIUM, 1412
BURRUSS AUDITORIUM, 1424
BURT REYNOLDS INSTITUTE FOR THEATRE TRAINING, 370
BUSHFIRE THEATRE OF PERFORMING ARTS, 1222
BUTTE SYMPHONY ASSOCIATION, 771
BYRNE MILLER DANCE THEATRE, INC., THE, 12
CABBAGES AND KINGS, 1328
CABRILLO COLLEGE THEATER, 56
CABRILLO MUSIC FESTIVAL, 56
CAFE DEL REY MORO, 158
CALDWELL COLLEGE - STUDENT UNION BUILDING, 817
CALDWELL FINE ARTS SERIES, 413
CALDWELL THEATRE COMPANY, 316
CALIFORNIA BALLET COMPANY, 152
CALIFORNIA E.A.R. UNIT FOUNDATION, 104
CALIFORNIA INSTITUTE OF TECHNOLOGY - BECKMAN
    AUDITORIUM, 141
CALIFORNIA INSTITUTE OF TECHNOLOGY - RAMO
    AUDITORIUM, 141
CALIFORNIA LUTHERAN UNIVERSITY - PREUS-BRANDT
    FORUM, 209
CALIFORNIA PLAZA, 117
CALIFORNIA POLYTECHNIC UNIVERSITY-POMONA -
    THEATRE, 142
CALIFORNIA STATE UNIVERSITY - CREATIVE ARTS
    BUILDING, 152
CALIFORNIA STATE UNIVERSITY-DOMINGUEZ HILLS -
    CONCERT HALL, 70
CALIFORNIA STATE UNIVERSITY-DOMINGUEZ HILLS -
    UNIVERSITY THEATRE, 70
CALIFORNIA STATE UNIVERSITY-FRESNO - JOHN WRIGHT
    THEATRE, 82
CALIFORNIA STATE UNIVERSITY-FRESNO - WAHLBERG
    RECITAL HALL, 82
CALIFORNIA STATE UNIVERSITY-HAYWARD - MAIN
    THEATRE, 86
CALIFORNIA STATE UNIVERSITY-LOS ANGELES - MUSIC
    HALL, 117
CALIFORNIA STATE UNIVERSITY-LOS ANGELES -
    PLAYHOUSE, 117
CALIFORNIA STATE UNIVERSITY-NORTHRIDGE - CAMPUS
    THEATRE, 129
CALIFORNIA STATE UNIVERSITY-NORTHRIDGE - LITTLE
    THEATRE, 130
CALIFORNIA STATE UNIVERSITY-NORTHRIDGE - STUDIO
    THEATRE, 130

CALIFORNIA STATE UNIVERSITY-STANISLAUS - MAINSTAGE THEATRE, 210
CALIFORNIA THEATRE CENTER, 208
CALIFORNIA THEATRE OF PERFORMING ARTS, THE, 152
CALIFORNIA YOUTH SYMPHONY, 137
CALUMET THEATRE COMPANY, 664
CALVIN COLLEGE FINE ARTS CENTER, 676
CAMBRIDGE CONCERT ASSOCIATION, 1098
CAMBRIDGE FOLK ORCHESTRA, 617
CAMDEN OPERA HOUSE, 576
CAMELLIA SYMPHONY, 148
CAMEO CONCERTS, INC., 1136
CAMERATA MUSICA, 1190
CAMERON UNIVERSITY, THEATRE ARTS DEPARTMENT, 1161
CAMILLE LIGHTNER PLAYHOUSE, 1317
CAMILLE PLAYERS, 1316
CAMP THEATER, 1046
CANDLELIGHT CONCERT SOCIETY, INC., 593
CANDLELIGHT DINNER PLAYHOUSE AND FORUM THEATRE, 475
CANDLEWOOD PLAYHOUSE, 269
CANNON COMMUNITY PLAYHOUSE, 1301
CANTATA ACADEMY, 672
CANTATA CHORUS OF NORFOLK, 1432
CANTON BALLET, 1099
CANTON SYMPHONY ORCHESTRA, 1099
CANTON YOUTH SYMPHONY, 1099
CAPE AND ISLANDS CHAMBER MUSIC FESTIVAL, THE, 638
CAPE COD SYMPHONY ORCHESTRA, 639
CAPE FEAR REGIONAL THEATRE, 1055
CAPE PLAYHOUSE, 624
CAPE PLAYHOUSE OF THE RAYMOND MOORE FOUNDATION, 624
CAPITAL CITY BAND, 1270
CAPITAL REPERTORY COMPANY, 860
CAPITAL THEATRE, 1473
CAPITOL ARTS CENTER, 541
CAPITOL BALLET COMPANY, 297
CAPITOL CHAMBER ARTISTS, INC., 859
CAPITOL CIVIC CENTER, 1023
CAPITOL MUSIC HALL, 1485
CAPITOL THEATRE, 1406
CARAMOOR CENTER FOR MUSIC AND THE ARTS, 901
CARAVAN OF DREAMS, 1348, 1349
CARLETON COLLEGE CONCERT SERIES, 720
CARLOTA SANTANA SPANISH DANCE COMPANY, 913
CARMEL BACH FESTIVAL, 69
CARNEGIE HALL, 995
CARNEGIE HALL, INC., 1483
CARNEGIE - LECTURE HALL, THE, 1235
CARNEGIE - MUSEUM OF ART THEATRE, THE, 1236
CARNEGIE - MUSIC HALL, THE, 1236
CARNEGIE CHAMBER PLAYERS, 939
CAROL FONDA AND COMPANY/DANCE FORUM, INC., 913
CAROLINA BALLET THEATRE, 1262
CAROLINA PRO MUSICA, 1048
CAROLINA THEATRE, THE, 1060
CAROUSEL DINNER THEATRE, 1092, 1093
CARPENTER CENTER FOR THE PERFORMING ARTS, 1438
CARPET BAG THEATRE, 1286
CARROLL COLLEGE - THEATRE, 774
CASA DE UNIDAS, 670
CASA DEL PRADO THEATRE, 158
CASA MANANA MUSICALS INC., 1346
CASA MANANA PLAYHOUSE, 1346
CASA MANANA THEATRE, 1349
CASCADE SYMPHONY ORCHESTRA, 1448
CASE WESTERN RESERVE UNIVERSITY - ELDRED HALL, 1115
CASPER CHAMBER MUSIC SOCIETY, 1519
CASPER COLLEGE - DURHAM HALL, 1519
CASPER EVENTS CENTER, 1519
CASPER SYMPHONY ORCHESTRA, 1519
CAST THEATRE/THE CAST-AT-THE-CIRCLE, THE, 87
CASTLE HILL FESTIVAL, 629
CASWELL COUNTY CIVIC CENTER, 1081
CATAMOUNT FILM AND ARTS COMPANY, 1418

CATHEDRAL CONCERT SERIES, 830, 1321
CATSKILL SYMPHONY ORCHESTRA, 1012
CEDAR RAPIDS SYMPHONY ORCHESTRA, 510
CEDARHURST CHAMBER MUSIC, 463
CEDARTOWN CIVIC AUDITORIUM, 389
CELEBRATE BROOKLYN FESTIVAL, 875
CELEBRATION BARN THEATER, 584
CELEBRATION THEATRE, 108, 118
CELEBRITY SERIES, 1215
CELEBRITY SERIES OF BOSTON, INC., 612
CENTENARY COLLEGE - RECITAL HALL, 570
CENTENNIAL COLISEUM - RENO SPARKS CONVENTION AND VISITORS AUTHORITY, 799
CENTENNIAL HALL CONVENTION CENTER, 21
CENTER FOR AFRICAN AND AFRICAN AMERICAN ART AND CULTURE, 180
CENTER FOR CONTEMPORARY ARTS, 856
CENTER FOR CONTEMPORARY OPERA, 953
CENTER FOR PUPPETRY ARTS, 381
CENTER FOR THE ARTS - UNIVERSITY OF WISCONSIN, PLATTEVILLE, 1512
CENTER STAGE, 589, 591, 790
CENTER STAGE AT EVERGREEN, 244
CENTER THEATER, 1264
CENTER THEATER AND THE TRAINING CENTER, 434
CENTRAL CITY OPERA, 236
CENTRAL CITY OPERA HOUSE, 228
CENTRAL FLORIDA COMMUNITY COLLEGE - FINE ARTS AUDITORIUM, 348
CENTRAL FLORIDA CULTURAL ENDEAVORS, 321
CENTRAL PARK BANDSHELL, 1139
CENTRAL PENNSYLVANIA FESTIVAL OF THE ARTS, 1239
CENTRAL PENNSYLVANIA FRIENDS OF JAZZ, INC., 1205
CENTRAL PIEDMONT COMMUNITY COLLEGE - SUMMER THEATRE, 1051
CENTRAL PIEDMONT COMMUNITY THEATRE, 1050
CENTRAL WISCONSIN SYMPHONY ORCHESTRA, 1515
CENTRALIA COLLEGE - CORBET THEATRE, 1448
CENTRE EAST, 474
CENTURION PLAYHOUSE, 1449
CENTURY CENTER, 503
CENTURY CENTER - BENDIX THEATRE, 503
CENTURY CENTER - CONVENTION HALL, 504
CENTURY CENTER - RECITAL HALL, 504
CENTURY II CIVIC CENTER, 537
CENTURY II CIVIC CENTER - CONCERT HALL, 537
CENTURY II CIVIC CENTER - CONVENTION HALL, 537
CENTURY II CIVIC CENTER - EXHIBITION HALL, 537
CENTURY II CIVIC CENTER - THEATRE, 537
CHABOT COLLEGE PERFORMING ARTS CENTER, 86
CHADRON STATE COLLEGE - MEMORIAL HALL, 782
CHAFFIN'S BARN, 1297
CHAFFIN'S BARN - A DINNER THEATRE, 1296
CHAGRIN VALLEY LITTLE THEATRE, 1100
CHAMBER ARTS NORTH, 688
CHAMBER ARTS SOCIETY, 1053
CHAMBER MUSIC AMERICA, 940
CHAMBER MUSIC CONCERTS, 1173
CHAMBER MUSIC HAWAII, 402
CHAMBER MUSIC IN YELLOW SPRINGS, INC., 1152
CHAMBER MUSIC NORTHWEST, 1185
CHAMBER MUSIC OF CHARLOTTE, 1048
CHAMBER MUSIC SERIES, 1180
CHAMBER MUSIC SOCIETY OF BALTIMORE, 587
CHAMBER MUSIC SOCIETY OF BETHLEHEM, 1196
CHAMBER MUSIC SOCIETY OF GRAND RAPIDS, INC.,THE, 674
CHAMBER MUSIC SOCIETY OF LINCOLN CENTER, THE, 940
CHAMBER MUSIC SOCIETY OF LOGAN, INC., THE, 1396
CHAMBER MUSIC SOCIETY OF OREGON, THE, 1186
CHAMBER MUSIC SOCIETY OF SAINT CLOUD, INC., 723
CHAMBER MUSIC SOCIETY OF SALT LAKE CITY, 1402
CHAMBER MUSIC SOCIETY OF THE MONTEREY PENINSULA, 68
CHAMBER MUSIC SOCIETY OF UTICA INC., 882
CHAMBER MUSIC SOUTHWEST, 796
CHAMBER MUSIC WEST FESTIVAL, 167
CHAMBER MUSIC/LA FESTIVAL, 114

CHAMBER OPERA CHICAGO, 429
CHAMBER ORCHESTRA OF ALBUQUERQUE, 848
CHAMIZAL NATIONAL MEMORIAL - THEATER, 1342
CHAMPAIGN-URBANA SYMPHONY, 421
CHANDLER CENTER FOR THE ARTS, 25
CHANDLER MUSIC HALL AND CULTURAL CENTER, 1417
CHANGING SCENE THEATER, 238, 240
CHANHASSEN DINNER THEATRE, 701
CHANNING PLAYERS, 1360
CHANTICLEER, 511
CHANTICLEER STRING QUARTET, 501
CHANUTE COMMUNITY THEATRE, 525
CHAPEL HILL-CARRBORO COMMUNITY CHORUS, 1068
CHARLES B. GODDARD CENTER, 1158
CHARLES IVES CENTER - PAVILION, 258
CHARLES MOORE - DANCES AND DRUMS OF AFRICA, 870
CHARLES MOULTON DANCE COMPANY, 914
CHARLES RIVER CREATIVE ARTS PROGRAM, 625
CHARLESTON AREA COMMUNITY CHOIR, 1478
CHARLESTON BALLET, 1476
CHARLESTON BALLET, THE, 1257
CHARLESTON CHAMBER MUSIC SOCIETY, 1477
CHARLESTON CIVIC CENTER, 1479
CHARLESTON CIVIC CENTER - COLISEUM, 1479
CHARLESTON CIVIC CENTER - LITTLE THEATER, 1479
CHARLESTON CIVIC CENTER - MUNICIPAL
    AUDITORIUM, 1479
CHARLESTON CIVIC CHORUS, 1478
CHARLESTON LIGHT OPERA GUILD, 1478
CHARLESTON SYMPHONY ORCHESTRA, 1257
CHARLESTOWN WORKING THEATER, 622
CHARLIE PARKER MEMORIAL FOUNDATION, 745
CHARLIN JAZZ SOCIETY, INC., 299
CHARLOTTE CHORAL SOCIETY, 1049
CHARLOTTE CITY BALLET, 1048
CHARLOTTE COUNTY MEMORIAL AUDITORIUM, 356
CHARLOTTE PLAYERS, 356
CHARLOTTE REPERTORY THEATRE, 1050
CHARLOTTE SYMPHONY ORCHESTRA SOCIETY, 1049
CHATTANOOGA BALLET, 1278
CHATTANOOGA BOYS CHOIR, 1278
CHATTANOOGA OPERA ASSOCIATION, 1278
CHATTANOOGA SYMPHONY AND OPERA
    ASSOCIATION, 1278
CHAUTAUQUA INSTITUTION, 881
CHAUTAUQUA INSTITUTION - AMPHITHEATER, 882
CHAUTAUQUA INSTITUTION - NORTON HALL, 882
CHAUTAUQUA OPERA, 881
CHAUTAUQUA SERIES, 1332
CHAUTAUQUA SYMPHONY ORCHESTRA, 881
CHEBOYGAN AREA ARTS COUNCIL, 664
CHEBOYGAN OPERA HOUSE - CITY HALL, 665
CHELSEA CHAMBER ENSEMBLE, 940
CHEN AND DANCERS, 914
CHEROKEE HERITAGE CENTER AMPHITHEATER, 1167
CHEROKEE NATIONAL HISTORICAL SOCIETY, 1167
CHERRY COUNTY PLAYHOUSE, 687
CHERRY CREEK CHORALE, 243
CHESHIRE COMMUNITY THEATRE, 257
CHESTNUT BRASS COMPANY, 1218
CHEYENNE CIVIC CENTER, 1521
CHEYENNE LITTLE THEATRE PLAYERS, 1520
CHEYENNE SYMPHONY ORCHESTRA, 1520
CHHANDAM CHITRESH DAS DANCE COMPANY, 151
CHICAGO ACTORS ENSEMBLE, 434
CHICAGO BAR ASSOCIATION SYMPHONY ORCHESTRA, 426
CHICAGO BRASS QUINTET, 426
CHICAGO CHAMBER ORCHESTRA, THE, 426
CHICAGO CHILDREN'S CHOIR, 429
CHICAGO CITY LIMITS, 965
CHICAGO CITY THEATRE COMPANY, 434
CHICAGO DANCE COALITION, 422
CHICAGO DRAMATISTS WORKSHOP, 434
CHICAGO MEDIEVAL PLAYERS, THE, 435
CHICAGO MOVING COMPANY, 423
CHICAGO OPERA THEATER, 430
CHICAGO PHILHARMONIA, 427
CHICAGO SINFONIETTA, 470

CHICAGO STRING ENSEMBLE, 427
CHICAGO SYMPHONY CHORUS, 430
CHICAGO SYMPHONY ORCHESTRA, 427
CHICAGO THEATRE COMPANY, THE, 435
CHICAGO YOUTH SYMPHONY, 428
CHILD'S PLAY THEATRE COMPANY, 703
CHILD'S PLAY TOURING THEATRE, 435
CHILDREN'S BALLET THEATRE, 1472
CHILDREN'S DANCE THEATRE OF NEW MILFORD, 275
CHILDREN'S FREE OPERA AND DANCE, 990
CHILDREN'S OPERA THEATER, 592
CHILDREN'S THEATER ASSOCIATION, 590
CHILDREN'S THEATER COMPANY, THE, 712
CHILDREN'S THEATRE BOARD, INC., 1079
CHILDREN'S THEATRE COMPANY, THE, 718
CHILDREN'S THEATRE OF EDEN, 1054
CHILKAT CENTER FOR THE ARTS, 20
CHINA MUSIC PROJECT, THE, 1109
CHINESE CLASSICAL ORCHESTRA, THE, 479
CHINESE FOLK DANCE COMPANY, 914
CHINESE MUSIC EDUCATIONAL PROGRAM, 479
CHINESE MUSIC ENSEMBLE OF NEW YORK, INC., THE, 940
CHINESE MUSIC SOCIETY OF NORTH AMERICA, 479
CHINOOK THEATRE FOR THE PERFORMING
    ARTS, THE, 1449
CHIPPEWA VALLEY THEATRE GUILD, 1488
CHORAL ART SOCIETY OF NEW JERSEY, THE, 845
CHORAL ARTS SOCIETY OF PHILADELPHIA, 1220
CHORAL ARTS SOCIETY OF WASHINGTON, 302
CHORAL GUILD OF ATLANTA, 379
CHORAL SOCIETY OF GREENSBORO, 1058
CHORAL SOCIETY OF PENSACOLA, 353
CHORAL SOCIETY OF THE PALM BEACHES, INC., THE, 352
CHORUS AMERICA, 1220
CHORUS OF WESTERLY, 1253
CHOWAN COLLEGE - MCDOWELL COLUMNS
    AUDITORIUM, 1067
CHRISTIAN ARTS AUDITORIUM, 481
CHRYSALIS REPERTORY DANCE COMPANY, 1354
CIMARRON CIRCUIT OPERA COMPANY, 1162
CINCINNATI BALLET, 1101
CINCINNATI BOYCHOIR, 1102
CINCINNATI JEWISH COMMUNITY CENTER, 1106
CINCINNATI MAY FESTIVAL, 1105
CINCINNATI MUSIC HALL, 1106
CINCINNATI MUSIC HALL ASSOCIATION, 1105
CINCINNATI OPERA, 1103
CINCINNATI PLAYHOUSE - ROBERT S. MARX
    THEATRE, 1106
CINCINNATI PLAYHOUSE - THOMPSON
    SHELTERHOUSE, 1107
CINCINNATI PLAYHOUSE IN THE PARK, 1103
CINCINNATI POPS ORCHESTRA, 1101
CINCINNATI SYMPHONY, 1102
CINCINNATI YOUTH SYMPHONY ORCHESTRA, 1102
CIRCA '21 DINNER PLAYHOUSE, 470
CIRCLE IN THE SQUARE, 966
CIRCLE IN THE SQUARE INC., 995
CIRCLE REPERTORY THEATRE COMPANY, 966
CIRCLE THEATRE, INC., 790, 1346
CIRCUIT PLAYHOUSE, 1290
CIRCUS ARTS FOUNDATION OF MISSOURI, 758
CITIARTS THEATRE, 71
CITICORP SUMMERFEST, 760
CITY AUDITORIUM, 231
CITY BALLET OF HOUSTON, 1354
CITY CELEBRATION, INC., 162
CITY CELEBRATION ARTS, 178
CITY CENTER, 995
CITY CENTER - CITY CENTER STAGE I, 995
CITY CENTER - CITY CENTER STAGE II, 996
CITY CENTER - CITY CENTER THEATRE, 996
CITY CENTER OF MUSIC AND DRAMA, 991
CITY LIT THEATER COMPANY, 436
CITY OF ALBANY PARKS AND RECREATION
    DEPARTMENT, 1173
CITY OF BRYAN PARKS AND RECREATION, 1317
CITY OF GRAND HAVEN COMMUNITY CENTER, 673

CITY OF LOS ANGELES CULTURAL AFFAIRS
    DEPARTMENT, 115
CITY PLAYERS, 317
CITY STAGE COMPANY, 610
CITY SYMPHONY ORCHESTRA OF NEW YORK, INC., 941
CITY THEATRE COMPANY, 1234
CIVIC AUDITORIUM, 414
CIVIC CENTER COMPLEX - EXHIBIT HALL, 1314
CIVIC CENTER COMPLEX - JULIE ROGERS THEATRE, 1315
CIVIC CENTER COMPLEX - THE JEFFERSON THEATRE, 1314
CIVIC CENTER MUSIC HALL, 1165
CIVIC CENTER OF GREATER DES MOINES, 514
CIVIC CENTER OF ONONDAGA COUNTY, 1033
CIVIC CENTER OF ONONDAGA COUNTY - BEVARD
    COMMUNITY ROOM, 1033
CIVIC CENTER OF ONONDAGA COUNTY - CARRIER
    THEATER, 1033
CIVIC CENTER OF ONONDAGA COUNTY - CROUSE-HINDS
    CONCERT THEATER, 1033
CIVIC DANCE ASSOCIATION, 1272
CIVIC LIGHT OPERA, 1457
CIVIC ORCHESTRA OF CHICAGO, 428
CIVIC STAGES CHICAGO, 445
CIVIC STAGES CHICAGO - CIVIC THEATRE, 445
CIVIC STAGES CHICAGO - OPERA HOUSE, 446
CIVIC THEATRE OF CENTRAL FLORIDA, 349
CLAREMONT COLLEGES - GARRISON THEATRE, THE, 70
CLAREMONT COLLEGES - MABEL SHAW BRIDGES
    AUDITORIUM, THE, 70
CLAREMONT OPERA HOUSE, 803
CLARENCE BROWN THEATRE COMPANY, 1286
CLARION BRASS QUINTET, THE, 283
CLARION CHAMBER CHORALE, 789
CLASSICAL QUARTET, THE, 941
CLASSICS ON STAGE! LTD, 436
CLEAR LAKE METROPOLITAN BALLET, 1355
CLEAR LAKE SYMPHONY, 1357
CLEMENS CENTER, 888
CLEO PARKER ROBINSON DANCE ENSEMBLE, 234
CLEVELAND BAROQUE SOLOISTS, 1144
CLEVELAND CHAMBER MUSIC SOCIETY, 1109
CLEVELAND CREATIVE ARTS GUILD, 1279
CLEVELAND INSTITUTE OF MUSIC - KULAS HALL,
    THE, 1115
CLEVELAND JAZZ ORCHESTRA, 1110
CLEVELAND MUSEUM OF ART - GARTNER AUDITORIUM,
    THE, 1116
CLEVELAND MUSEUM OF ART CONCERTS, THE, 1114
CLEVELAND OCTET, THE, 1119
CLEVELAND OPERA, 1111
CLEVELAND ORCHESTRA, 1110
CLEVELAND ORCHESTRA CHORUS, THE, 1112
CLEVELAND PHILHARMONIC ORCHESTRA, 1110
CLEVELAND PLAY HOUSE, THE, 1112, 1116
CLEVELAND PLAY HOUSE - BOULTON THEATRE, THE, 1116
CLEVELAND PLAY HOUSE - BROOKS THEATRE, THE, 1116
CLEVELAND PLAY HOUSE - DRURY THEATRE, THE, 1116
CLEVELAND PUBLIC THEATRE, 1117
CLEVELAND PUBLIC THEATRE, 1113
CLEVELAND SAN JOSE BALLET, 1108
CLIFFSIDE AMPHITHEATRE OF WEST VIRGINIA, 1475
CLIMB THEATRE - CREATIVE LEARNING IDEAS FOR MIND
    AND BODY, 725
CLOCKWORK REPERTORY THEATRE, 277
CLOG AMERICA, 1397
CLOWES MEMORIAL HALL, 497
CLOWES MEMORIAL HALL OF BUTLER UNIVERSITY, 497
COACH HOUSE PLAYERS, 902
COACHLIGHT DINNER THEATRE, 260
COASTAL PLAYERS/JUPITER CIVIC THEATRE, 333
COASTER THEATER, 1176
COBB COUNTY CIVIC CENTER, 395
COBB COUNTY CIVIC CENTER - JENNIE T. ANDERSON
    THEATER, 395
COBB COUNTY CIVIC CENTER - ROMEO HUDGINS
    MEMORIAL HALL, 395
COBO ARENA, 671
COCONINO CENTER FOR THE ARTS, 26

COCONUT GROVE PLAYHOUSE, 342
CODANCECO, 914
COE PARK CIVIC CENTER, 284
COFFEYVILLE COMMUNITY THEATRE, 525
COLBY COLLEGE - GIVEN AUDITORIUM, 584
COLDEN CENTER FOR THE PERFORMING ARTS, 889
COLDER BY THE LAKE, 703
COLEMAN CHAMBER MUSIC ASSOCIATION, 140
COLEMAN PUPPET THEATRE, 462
COLGATE UNIVERSITY - BREHMER THEATER, 894
COLGATE UNIVERSITY - UNIVERSITY THEATER, 894
COLGATE UNIVERSITY CONCERT SERIES, 894
COLISEUM CIVIC CENTER, 732
COLLEGE COMMUNITY CENTER, 1073
COLLEGE LIGHT OPERA COMPANY, 627
COLLEGE OF DUPAGE ARTS CENTER, 457
COLLEGE OF DUPAGE ARTS CENTER - AUDITORIUM, 457
COLLEGE OF DUPAGE ARTS CENTER - MAINSTAGE, 457
COLLEGE OF DUPAGE ARTS CENTER - STUDIO
    THEATRE, 458
COLLEGE OF DUPAGE ARTS CENTER - THEATRE 2, 458
COLLEGE OF SAINT BENEDICT - BENEDICTA ARTS
    CENTER, 723
COLLEGE OF SAINT BENEDICT - BENEDICTA ARTS CENTER
    AUDITORIUM, 723
COLLEGE OF SAINT BENEDICT - BENEDICTA ARTS CENTER
    FORUM, 723
COLLEGE OF SAINT CATHERINE - O'SHAUGHNESSY
    AUDITORIUM, 727
COLLEGE OF THE OZARKS - JONES AUDITORIUM, 752
COLLEGE OF THE SISKIYOUS - THEATRE, 216
COLONIAL SYMPHONY, 823
COLONY THEATRE COMPANY, 109
COLORADO BALLET, 234
COLORADO CHILDREN'S CHORALE, 237
COLORADO COLLEGE - PACKARD HALL, 231
COLORADO COUNCIL ON THE ARTS, 239
COLORADO DANCE FESTIVAL, 226
COLORADO MUSIC FESTIVAL, 226
COLORADO OPERA FESTIVAL, 230
COLORADO SHAKESPEARE FESTIVAL, 227
COLORADO SPRINGS CHORALE, 230
COLORADO SPRINGS DANCE THEATRE, 229
COLORADO SPRINGS FINE ARTS CENTER THEATRE, 231
COLORADO SPRINGS SYMPHONY ORCHESTRA, 229
COLORADO STATE UNIVERSITY - OFFICE OF CULTURAL
    PROGRAMS, 246
COLORADO STATE UNIVERSITY - UNIVERSITY
    THEATRE, 246
COLORADO SYMPHONY ORCHESTRA, 235
COLUMBIA ARTS CENTER, 1471
COLUMBIA CITY BALLET, 1259
COLUMBIA FESTIVAL, INC., 594
COLUMBIA STAGE SOCIETY AT TOWN THEATRE, 1260
COLUMBIA THEATRE FOR THE PERFORMING ARTS, 1451
COLUMBIA YOUTH ORCHESTRA, 1260
COLUMBUS ARTS FESTIVAL, 1125
COLUMBUS CONVENTION AND CIVIC CENTER, 732
COLUMBUS MUNICIPAL AUDITORIUM, 390
COLUMBUS PRO MUSICA, 486
COLUMBUS SYMPHONY CHORUS, 1123
COLUMBUS SYMPHONY ORCHESTRA, 389, 1122
COLUMBUS SYMPHONY YOUTH ORCHESTRA, 1122
COMIC OPERA GUILD, 658
COMMEDIA THEATER COMPANY, 712
COMMON STAGE THEATRE COMPANY, INC., 1040
COMMONWEALTH OPERA, 637
COMMUNITY ARTS AND MUSIC ASSOCIATION OF SANTA
    BARBARA, 195
COMMUNITY CENTER FARMINGTON - FARMINGTON
    HILLS, THE, 672
COMMUNITY MUSIC CENTER, 181
COMMUNITY MUSIC CENTER - DAVID CAMPBELL RECITAL
    HALL, 1189
COMMUNITY OPERA, INCORPORATED, 838
COMMUNITY PLAYERS, 543, 781
COMMUNITY PLAYERS, INC., 1388
COMMUNITY PLAYERS OF CONCORD, 804

COMMUNITY SERIES, INC., 1388
COMMUNITY THEATRE, 1447
COMMUNITY THEATRE ASSOCIATION OF MICHIGAN, 687
COMMUNITY THEATRE OF CLAY COUNTY, 485
COMMUNITY THEATRE OF GREENSBORO, 1059
COMMUNITY THEATRE OF TERRE HAUTE, 505
COMMUNITY THEATRE OF THE CASCADES, 1176
CO-MOTION DANCE, 1453
CO'MOTION DANCE THEATER, 507
COMPANY ONE, 263
COMPLEX, THE, 89, 109
CONCENTUS MUSICUS, 708
CONCEPT EAST II, 668
CONCERT BALLET OF VIRGINIA, THE, 1435
CONCERT DANCE THEATRE, 211
CONCERT ROYAL, INC., 953
CONCERTIME, 1168
CONCERTO AMABILE, 60
CONCERTO SOLOISTS, 1218
CONCERTS-AT-THE-COMMON (HARVARD UNITARIAN
    CHURCH), 650
CONCORD BAND, THE, 623
CONCORD ORCHESTRA, 623
CONCORD PAVILION, 71
CONCORD SINGERS OF NEW ULM, THE, 720
CONCORDIA, 941
CONEJO SYMPHONY ORCHESTRA, 208
CONEY ISLAND, USA, 873
CONKLIN PLAYERS DINNER THEATRE, 458
CONNECTICUT BALLET THEATRE, 279
CONNECTICUT CHORAL ARTISTS, INC., 268
CONNECTICUT COLLEGE - PALMER AUDITORIUM, 275
CONNECTICUT CONCERT BALLET, 265
CONNECTICUT EARLY MUSIC FESTIVAL, 274
CONNECTICUT GRAND OPERA, 280
CONNECTICUT OPERA, 263
CONNECTICUT STRING ORCHESTRA, INC., 287
CONNECTICUT'S BROADWAY THEATRE, DARIEN, 259
CONNETICUT COLLEGE CONCERT AND ARTIST SERIES, 274
CONSTITUTION HALL, 310
CONTEMPORARY ART CENTER, 565
CONTEMPORARY DANCE SEASON, THE, 1184
CONTEMPORARY DANCE THEATER, 1101
CONTEMPORARY MUSIC FORUM, 299
CONTEMPORARY THEATRE, A, 1459
CONTEMPORARY THEATRE OF SYRACUSE, 902
CONTINUUM (THE PERFORMERS' COMMITTEE INC.), 941
CONTRABAND, 162
CONVENTION CENTER, 1265
CONVENTION CENTER - AUDITORIUM, 1265
CONVENTION CENTER - EXHIBIT HALL, 1265
CONVERGENCE DANCERS & MUSICIANS, 1216
COOPERSTOWN CONCERT SERIES, INC., 883
COPLEY SYMPHONY HALL, 159
COPPELL COMMUNITY CHORUS, 1320
CO-REAL ARTISTS, 108
CORINTH THEATRE-ARTS, 732
CORNELL UNIVERSITY - ALICE STATLER AUDITORIUM, 898
CORNING GLASS CENTER, 884
CORNING PHILHARMONIC SOCIETY, 884
CORNING-PAINTED POST CIVIC MUSIC ASSOCIATION, 884
CORPUS CHRISTI BALLET, 1320
CORPUS CHRISTI CHAMBER MUSIC SOCIETY, INC., 1320
CORPUS CHRISTI SYMPHONY, 1321
CORSICANA COMMUNITY PLAYHOUSE, 1322
CORT THEATRE, 996
CORTLAND REPERTORY THEATRE, 885
COSMOPOLITAN SYMPHONY ORCHESTRA, 942
COTERIE THEATRE, THE, 747
COUNCIL FOR THE ARTS OF GREATER LIMA, 1136
COUNT BASIE THEATRE, 836
COUNTRY DINNER PLAYHOUSE, 244
COUNTY OF WESTCHESTER - PARKS, RECREATION AND
    CONSERVATION - PERFORMING ARTS, 896
COURANTE DANCE COMPANY, 915
COURT THEATRE, 436
COWAN HALL, 1151
CRAFTSBURY CHAMBER PLAYERS, 1413

CRANFORD DRAMATIC CLUB, 818
CRANFORD DRAMATIC CLUB THEATRE, 818
CRASH, BURN AND DIE DANCE COMPANY, 56
CRATERIAN THEATRE, 1184
CREATION PRODUCTION COMPANY, 966
CREATIVE ARTS TEAM, 966
CREATIVE OPPORTUNITY ORCHESTRA, 1277
CREATIVE PRODUCTIONS, 815
CREATIVE THEATRE, 834
CREEDE REPERTORY THEATRE, 232
CREEKSIDE PLAYERS, THE, 1130
CRESCENT BALLET COMPANY, 561
CRESTED BUTTE MOUNTAIN THEATRE, 233
CRICKET THEATRE, THE, 712
CROATIAN TAMBURITZA ORCHESTRA OF
    CLEVELAND, 1133
CROCKER ART MUSEUM, 149
CROOKED TREE ARTS COUNCIL, 688
CROSS AND SWORD AMPHITHEATRE, 357
CROSSROADS THEATRE COMPANY, 828
CRS NATIONAL FESTIVAL FOR THE PERFORMING
    ARTS, 1198
CRYSTAL BALLROOM CONCERT ASSOCIATION, 444
CSC REPERTORY, 967
CSC REPERTORY LTD., 996
CUESTA COLLEGE AUDITORIUM, 189
CULTURAL ACTIVITIES CENTER, 1389, 1390
CULTURAL RESOURCES COUNCIL OF SYRACUSE AND
    ONONDAGA COUNTY, 1032
CUMBERLAND COUNTY CIVIC CENTER, 583, 1056
CUMBERLAND COUNTY FRIENDS OF THE ORCHESTRA, 1055
CUMBERLAND COUNTY PLAYHOUSE, 1280
CUMBERLAND UNIVERSITY AUDITORIUM, 1288
CUMSTON HALL, 579
CURRAN THEATRE, 181
CURTIS INSTITUTE - CURTIS HALL, 1226
CURTIS THEATRE, 66
CURTISS HALL, 446
CUYAHOGA COMMUNITY COLLEGE - WESTERN CAMPUS
    THEATRE, 1144
CUYAHOGA VALLEY YOUTH BALLET, 1128
CYNTHIA WOODS MITCHELL PAVILION, 1393
DA CAPO CHAMBER PLAYERS, INCORPORATED, 942
DA VINCI QUARTET, 229
DADE COUNTY AUDITORIUM, 343
DAEMEN COLLEGE - DAEMEN THEATRE, 862
DALE SCHOLL DANCE ART, 147
DALE WARLAND SINGERS, 710
DALLAS BACH SOCIETY, 1324
DALLAS BLACK DANCE THEATRE, 1323
DALLAS BRASS, 1351
DALLAS CHAMBER MUSIC SOCIETY, 1332
DALLAS CHAMBER ORCHESTRA, 1324
DALLAS CHILDREN'S THEATER, 1329
DALLAS CLASSIC GUITAR SOCIETY, 1325
DALLAS CONVENTION CENTER, 1334
DALLAS CONVENTION CENTER - ARENA, 1334
DALLAS CONVENTION CENTER - THEATER, 1334
DALLAS DANCE COUNCIL, 1323
DALLAS METROPOLITAN BALLET, 1324
DALLAS OPERA, THE, 1327
DALLAS PUPPET THEATER, 1329
DALLAS REPERTORY THEATRE, 1329, 1334
DALLAS SUMMER MUSICALS, 1329
DALLAS SYMPHONY ASSOCIATION, INC., 1325
DALLAS SYMPHONY CHORUS, 1327
DALLAS SYMPHONY ORCHESTRA, 1325
DALLAS THEATER CENTER, 1330
DALLAS THEATER CENTER - ARTS DISTRICT, 1335
DALLAS THEATER CENTER - KALITA HUMPHREYS
    THEATER, 1335
DAN WAGONER AND DANCERS, 915
DANBURY MUSIC CENTRE, INC., 258
DANCE AFFILIATES OF AMERICAN BALLET
    COMPETITION, 1216
DANCE ALIVE!, 328
DANCE ALLOY, 1229
DANCE ART CENTER, 775

DANCE ASPEN, 221
DANCE ASPEN FESTIVAL, THE, 222
DANCE ASSOCIATION/RUTH LANGRIDGE DANCE
    COMPANY, THE, 58
DANCE BRIGADE, 130
DANCE CENTER OF COLUMBIA COLLEGE, THE, 423
DANCE COLLECTIVE, 915
DANCE CONNECTION, THE, 245
DANCE EXCHANGE, 297
DANCE GALLERY COMPANY, 657
DANCE - JUNE LEWIS AND COMPANY, 915
DANCE KALEIDOSCOPE, 494
DANCE NETWORK, THE, 292
DANCE ON THE EDGE, 598
DANCE PLACE, 298
DANCE PROJECTS INC./BETH SOLL AND COMPANY, 605
DANCE REPERTORY THEATRE, 83
DANCE SAINT LOUIS, 754
DANCE SOLOS, INC., 1024
DANCE THEATER WORKSHOP'S BESSIE SCHONBERG
    THEATRE, 996
DANCE THEATRE DAYTON, 1128
DANCE THEATRE IN WESTCHESTER, 1040
DANCE THEATRE OF HARLEM, 916
DANCE THEATRE WORKSHOP, 916
DANCE 2000: THE FELICE LESSER DANCE THEATER, 915
DANCE UMBRELLA, 1307
DANCE UMBRELLA, BOSTON, INC., 618
DANCEBRAZIL, 916
DANCECIRCUS LIMITED, 1503
DANCECLEVELAND, 1109
DANCELLINGTON, INC., 917
DANCERS' GROUP, 162
DANCES FOR 2, 266
DANCES WE DANCE, 402
DANCEWAVE, INC. (THE DIANE JACOBOWITZ DANCE
    THEATER), 870
DANCING IN THE KITCHEN SERIES, 917
DANCING IN THE STREETS, INC., 917
DANMARI LTD./YASS HAKOSHIMA MIME THEATRE, 825
DANSE MIRAGE, INC./ELINOR COLEMAN DANCE
    EMSEMBLE, 917
DANSPACE PROJECT, INC., THE, 918
DANSWINTER/DANSUMMER, 232
DANVILLE SYMPHONY ORCHESTRA, 448
DAS PUPPENSPIEL PUPPET THEATER, INC., 1038
DAVID ADLER CULTURAL CENTER, 460
DAVID GORDON/PICK UP COMPANY, 918
DAVID PARSONS DANCE COMPANY, 918
DAVID TAYLOR DANCE THEATRE, 250
DAVIS ART CENTER, 76
DAVIS DISCOVERY CENTER - AGNES JEFFREY SHEDD
    THEATRE, 1125
DAVIS DISCOVERY CENTER - HENRY VAN FLEET
    THEATRE, 1126
DAWSON THEATRE GUILD, 1387
DAYTON BALLET, 1128
DAYTON CONTEMPORARY DANCE COMPANY, 1129
DAYTON CONVENTION AND EXHIBITION CENTER, 1131
DAYTON OPERA ASSOCIATION, 1130
DAYTON PHILHARMONIC ORCHESTRA ASSOCIATION, 1129
DAYTON PHILHARMONIC YOUTH ORCHESTRA, 1129
DAYTON PLAYHOUSE, 1131
DAYTONA BEACH COMMUNITY COLLEGE - THEATRE
    CENTER, 321
DAYTONA BEACH SYMPHONY SOCIETY, 320
DAYTONA PLAYHOUSE, 320, 321
D.C. CONTEMPORARY DANCE THEATRE, 297
D.C. YOUTH ORCHESTRA PROGRAM, INC., 300
DE ANZA COLLEGE - FLINT CENTER FOR THE
    PERFORMING ARTS, 76
DE PAUL UNIVERSITY - BLACKSTONE THEATRE, 446
DEBORAH HAY DANCE COMPANY, 1308
DEBORAH SLATER AND COMPANY, 163
DEBRA WEISS DANCE COMPANY, 1011
DECATUR CIVIC CENTER, 450
DECATUR CIVIC CENTER - ARENA, 450
DECATUR CIVIC CENTER - THEATER, 450

DECORAH COMMUNITY CONCERT ASSOCIATION, 513
DEE EVENTS CENTER, 1397
DEL-SE-NANGO OLDE TYME FIDDLERS ASSOCIATION,
    INC., 907
DELACORTE THEATRE IN CENTRAL PARK, 997
DELAWARE DANCE COMPANY, 292
DELAWARE REGIONAL BALLET, 291
DELAWARE SINGERS, THE, 293
DELAWARE SYMPHONY ASSOCIATION, 293
DELAWARE THEATRE COMPANY, 295
DELAWARE VALLEY OPERA, 907
DELIA STEWART DANCE COMPANY, THE, 1355
DELL' ARTE PLAYERS COMPANY, 66
DELLA DAVIDSON DANCE COMPANY, 163
DELRAY BEACH PLAYHOUSE, 322
DELTA FESTIVAL BALLET, 561
DENNOS MUSEUM CENTER - MILLIKEN AUDITORIUM, 695
DENTON COMMUNITY THEATRE, 1338
DENVER AUDITORIUM - ARENA, 240
DENVER AUDITORIUM - CURRIGAN EXHIBITION HALL, 240
DENVER AUDITORIUM - MCNICHOLS SPORTS ARENA, 241
DENVER AUDITORIUM - THEATRE, 241
DENVER CENTER THEATER COMPANY, 238
DENVER CHAMBER CHOIR, THE, 237
DENVER CHAMBER ORCHESTRA, 235
DENVER COLISEUM, 241
DENVER MUNICIPAL BAND, 236
DENVER PERFORMING ARTS COMPLEX - BUELL
    THEATRE, 241
DEPOT, SAINT LOUIS COUNTY HERITAGE AND ARTS
    CENTER, THE, 703
DEPOT THEATRE, 731
DERBY DINNER PLAYHOUSE, 486
DES MOINES METRO OPERA, 518
DES MOINES SYMPHONY, 514
DES MOINES WOMEN'S CLUB, 514
DES PLAINES THEATRE GUILD, 451
DESERT DANCE THEATRE, 35
DESERT FOOTHILLS MUSIC FEST, 25
DESERT OPERA THEATRE, 137
DETROIT CENTER FOR THE PERFORMING ARTS, 671
DETROIT CHAMBER WINDS, 695
DETROIT CONCERT BAND, INC., 33
DETROIT JAZZ ORCHESTRA, 667
DETROIT REPERTORY THEATRE, 669
DETROIT SYMPHONY CHORALE, 695
DETROIT SYMPHONY CHORUS, 696
DETROIT SYMPHONY ORCHESTRA, 667
DETROIT SYMPHONY ORCHESTRA HALL, 671
DEVILS LAKE COMMUNITY ORCHESTRA, 1083
DIABLO LIGHT OPERA COMPANY, 216
DIABLO SYMPHONY ORCHESTRA, THE, 215
DIAMOND HEAD THEATRE, 405
DIAMOND STATE CHORUS OF SWEET ADELINES
    INTERNATIONAL, 291
DICKENS OPERA HOUSE, 250
DICKINSON THEATRE ORGAN SOCIETY, 293
DIE MEISTERSINGERS, 790
DILLER STREET THEATER, 478
DILLON STREET PLAYERS, 109
DIMENSIONS DANCE THEATER, 130
DINIZULU AFRICAN DANCERS, DRUMMERS AND
    SINGERS, 899
DINOSAUR ANNEX MUSIC ENSEMBLE, 607
DINOSAUR DANCE COMPANY, 918
DISCOVER HOUSTON COUNTY VISITORS CENTER -
    MUSEUM, 1323
DISCOVER JAZZ FESTIVAL, 1412
DISCOVERY DANCE GROUP AND TRAINING CENTER, 1355
DISTRICT CURATORS, INC., 302
DIXIE COLLEGE - DIXIE CENTER, 1400
DIXIE COLLEGE - DIXIE CENTER PROSCENIUM STAGE, 1400
DIXIE COLLEGE FINE ARTS CENTER, 1400
DIXIE COLLEGE FINE ARTS CENTER - ARENA
    THEATRE, 1401
DIXIE COLLEGE FINE ARTS CENTER - PROSCENIUM
    THEATRE, 1401
DIXON CENTER FOR THE PERFORMING ARTS, 1

DOBAMA THEATRE, 1119, 1120
DOCK STREET THEATRE, 1259
DOCTORS' ORCHESTRAL SOCIETY OF NEW YORK, THE, 942
DODGE CITY CIVIC CENTER, 526
DOLLY HAND CULTURAL ARTS CENTER, 315
DOLPHIN PLAYERS, 1184
DOMINICAN COLLEGE - AUDITORIUM, 192
DON QUIJOTE CHILDREN'S THEATRE, 967
DONALD BYRD DANCE FOUNDATION, INC., THE, 919
DORE THEATRE - CALIFORNIA STATE UNIVERSITY, BAKERSFIELD, 58
DORIAN OPERA THEATRE, 513
DORSET THEATRE FESTIVAL, 1414
DOTHAN CIVIC CENTER, 5
DOUBLE EDGE THEATRE PRODUCTIONS INC., 601
DOUG ELKINS DANCE COMPANY, 919
DOUGLAS DUNN AND DANCERS, 919
DOVER LITTLE THEATRE, 818
DOWLING ENTERTAINMENT CORPORATION, 967
DOWNERS GROVE CONCERT ASSOCIATION, 451
DOWNEY SYMPHONIC SOCIETY, 77
DOWNRIVER COUNCIL FOR THE ARTS, 697
DOWNTOWN ART CO., INC., 968
DOWNTOWN CABARET THEATRE, 256
DOWNTOWN DANCE COMPANY, 586
DOWNTOWN MUSIC PRODUCTIONS, 943
DRAKE UNIVERSITY - HALL OF PERFORMING ARTS, HARMON FINE ARTS CENTER, 515
DRAKE UNIVERISTY - OLD MAIN AUDITORIUM, 515
DRAMA CIRCLE THEATRE, 1330
DRAMALITES, 285
DRAWING LEGION, THE, 510
DREISKE PERFORMANCE COMPANY, 436
DREW UNIVERSITY - BOWNE THEATRE, 824
DRURY LANE OAKBROOK TERRACE, 466
DUBUQUE SYMPHONY ORCHESTRA, 515
DULUTH BALLET, THE, 702
DULUTH ENTERTAINMENT CONVENTION CENTER, 703
DULUTH-SUPERIOR SYMPHONY ORCHESTRA, 702
DULUTH-SUPERIOR YOUTH ORCHESTRA AND SINFONIA, 702
DUMAS AREA ARTS COUNCIL, INC., 43
DUMBARTON CONCERT SERIES, 307
DUNBAR PERFORMING ARTS CENTER, 591
DUPAGE SYMPHONY, 456
DUQUESNE UNIVERSITY TAMBURITZANS, 1230
DURANGO CHORAL SOCIETY, 243
DURHAM CIVIC CHORAL SOCIETY, 1053
EAGLE-REED AMERICAN THEATER, 747
EARLVILLE OPERA HOUSE, 886
EARLY MUSIC AMERICA, INC., 943
EARLY MUSIC CENTER, THE, 1152
EARLY MUSIC GUILD OF SEATTLE, 1455
EARLY MUSIC NOW, 1504
EARPLAY, 135
EARTHLY PLEASURES, 1326
EAST CENTRAL UNIVERSITY - DOROTHY I. SUMMERS THEATER, 1157
EAST COUNTY PERFORMING ARTS CENTER - THEATRE EAST, 78
EAST TEXAS STATE UNIVERSITY - UNIVERSITY PLAYHOUSE STAGE, 1320
EAST TEXAS SYMPHONY ORCHESTRA, 1390
EAST WEST PLAYERS, 109, 118
EAST-WEST FUSION THEATRE, 278
EASTERN ARTS ETHNIC DANCE COMPANY, 1401
EASTERN BRASS QUINTET, 261
EASTERN CONNECTICUT SYMPHONY, 273
EASTERN MUSIC FESTIVAL, 1059
EASTERN SLOPE PLAYHOUSE, 811
EASTMAN SCHOOL OF MUSIC - KILBOURN HALL, 1022
EBONY SHOWCASE THEATRE, 110
ECCENTRIC CIRCLES THEATRE, 968
ECHO THEATRE, 1189
ED LARKIN OLD-TIME CONTRA DANCERS, 1418
EDEN'S EXPRESSWAY, 997
EDISON THEATRE AT WASHINGTON UNIVERSITY, 760
EDITH STEPHEN ELECTRIC CURRENTS, 920

EDWARD VILLELLA AND DANCERS, 920
EGYPTIAN THEATRE, 449
EIKO AND KOMA, 920
EISNER-LUBIN AUDITORIUM, 997
E.J. THOMAS HALL, 1092
E.J. THOMAS PERFORMING ARTS HALL, 1093
EL CAMINO COLLEGE - COMMUNITY ORCHESTRA, 209
EL CAMINO COLLEGE - SOUTH BAY CENTER FOR THE ARTS, 210
EL CENTRO SU TEATRO, 238
EL DORADO MUNICIPAL AUDITORIUM, 44
EL PASO CIVIC CENTER - EXHIBITION HALL, 1342
EL PASO CIVIC CENTER - THEATRE, 1342
EL PASO PRO-MUSICA, 1341
EL PASO SYMPHONY ORCHESTRA, 1341
EL TEATRO CAMPESINO, 188
EL TEATRO DE LA ESPERANZA, 173
ELEO POMARE DANCE COMPANY, 920
ELGIN AREA YOUTH ORCHESTRA, 452
ELGIN SYMPHONY ORCHESTRA, 452
ELISA MONTE DANCE COMPANY, 920
ELIZA R. SNOW PERFORMING ARTS CENTER, 416
ELKHART CIVIC THEATRE, 485
ELKHART CONCERT CLUB, 487
ELKHORN MUSIC FESTIVAL, INC., 417
ELKIN BIG BAND, 1054
ELLEN KOGAN SOLO DANCE, 869
ELLEN WEBB DANCE FOUNDATION, 131
ELLIOTT HALL OF MUSIC, 505
ELMIRA SYMPHONY AND CHORAL SOCIETY, 888
ELMWOOD PLAYHOUSE, 1011
ELNA M. SMITH FOUNDATION, 44
EMBASSY THEATRE, 491
EMELIN THEATRE FOR THE PERFORMING ARTS, THE, 906
EMERALD CHAMBER PLAYERS, 1178
EMERGENCE DANCE THEATRE, 449
EMERSON MAJESTIC THEATRE, 615
EMMY GIFFORD CHILDREN'S THEATER, 791
EMPIRE STATE PERFORMING ARTS CENTER, THE, 861
EMPIRE STATE PERFORMING ARTS CENTER - KITTY CARLISLE HART THEATER, THE, 861
EMPIRE STATE PERFORMING ARTS CENTER- LEWIS A. SWYER THEATER, THE, 861
EMPIRE THEATRE COMPLEX, THE, 1438
EMPIRE THEATRE COMPLEX - EMPIRE STAGE, THE, 1438
EMPIRE THEATRE COMPLEX - LITTLE THEATRE STAGE, THE, 1438
EMPTY SPACE THEATRE, THE, 1459
EN GARDE ARTS, INC., 968
ENCHANTED HILLS PLAYHOUSE, 487
ENCORE PLAYERS, 461
ENID-PHILLIPS SYMPHONY ORCHESTRA, 1160
ENSEMBLE, THE, 1361
ENSEMBLE ESPANOL, 437
ENSEMBLE MUSIC SOCIETY, THE, 494
ENSEMBLE OF SANTA FE, THE, 853
ENSEMBLE STUDIO THEATRE, 997
ENSEMBLE STUDIO THEATRE, THE, 968
ENTERTAINMENT BRANCH, CRD, 1449
EPHRATA CLOISTER CHORUS, 1200
EPHRATA PERFORMING ARTS CENTER - EPHRATA COMMUNITY PARK, 1200
ERICK HAWKINS DANCE COMPANY, 921
ERIE CIVIC CENTER, 1201
ERIE CIVIC CENTER - L.J. TULLIO CONVENTION HALL, 1201
ERIE CIVIC CENTER - WARNER THEATRE, 1202
ERIE CIVIC MUSIC ASSOCIATION, 1201
ERIE PHILHARMONIC, 1201
ERNESTA CORVINO'S DANCE CIRCLE COMPANY, 921
ESTYRE BRINDLE DANCE THEATRE, 724
ETA CREATIVE ARTS FOUNDATION, 437
ETHEL BARRYMORE THEATRE, 997
ETHERREDGE CENTER - UNIVERSITY OF SOUTH CAROLINA AT AIKEN, 1256
ETHICAL SOCIETY AUDITORIUM, 761
ETHNIC DANCE THEATRE, THE, 707
EUGENE BALLET COMPANY, 1178
EUGENE JAMES DANCE COMPANY, 921

EUGENE O'NEILL THEATER, 997
EUGENE OPERA, 1179
EUGENE SYMPHONY, 1179
EUNICE PLAYERS THEATRE, 557
EUREKA THEATRE COMPANY, 173
EVA ANDERSON DANCERS LTD., 593
EVANSVILLE ARTIST EDUCATION COUNCIL, 488
EVANSVILLE DANCE THEATRE, 488
EVANSVILLE PHILHARMONIC ORCHESTRA, 488
EVERETT CIVIC AUDITORIUM, 1449
EXPERIMENTAL INTERMEDIA FOUNDATION, 943
EZIBU MUNTU AFRICAN DANCE COMPANY, 1436
FABULOUS FOX THEATRE, THE, 762
FAIR PARK BANDSHELL, 1335
FAIRBANKS CHORAL SOCIETY, CHILDREN'S CHOIR AND
    CHORUS!, 18
FAIRBANKS LIGHT OPERA THEATRE, 19
FAIRBANKS SUMMER ARTS FESTIVAL, 19
FAIRBANKS SYMPHONY ASSOCIATION, 18
FAIRFAX SYMPHONY ORCHESTRA, 1422
FAIRFIELD COUNTY STAGE COMPANY, THE, 288
FAIRFIELD ORCHESTRA, THE, 269
FAIRMONT CHAMBER MUSIC SOCIETY, INC., 1480
FAIRMONT OPERA HOUSE, THE, 704
FAIRMOUNT FINE ARTS CENTER, 1143
FAIRMOUNT THEATRE OF THE DEAF, 1113
FALLON HOUSE THEATRE, 70
FALMOUTH PLAYHOUSE, 637
FAR-OFF BROADWAY PLAYERS, THE, 542
FARGO-MOORHEAD CIVIC OPERA COMPANY, 1085
FARGO-MOORHEAD COMMUNITY THEATRE, 1085
FARGO-MOORHEAD ORCHESTRAL ASSOCIATION, 1084
FARGO-MOORHEAD SYMPHONY ORCHESTRA, 1084
FARM SHOW ARENA, 1206
FARMINGTON CIVIC CENTER, 852
FARTHING AUDITORIUM, 1045
FAYETTE COUNTY FINE ARTS COUNCIL, 1484
FEDERATED ARTS, 821
FELD BALLETS/NY, 921
FERGUS FALLS SUMMER COMMUNITY THEATRE, 705
FERMILAB ARTS SERIES, 420
FERNDALE REPERTORY THEATRE, 79
FESTIVAL AT ROUND TOP/INTERNATIONAL
    FESTIVAL-INSTITUTE AT ROUND TOP, 1381
FESTIVAL AT SANDPOINT, 417
FESTIVAL BALLET, 1247
FESTIVAL CHOIR, THE, 1497
FESTIVAL CONCERT HALL, 1086
FESTIVAL DANCE AND PERFORMING ARTS, 415
FESTIVAL OF THE ARTS, 675, 1012, 1414
FESTIVAL OF NEW AMERICAN MUSIC, 150
FESTIVAL OUTDOOR THEATER, 1370
FESTIVAL PLAYERS OF CALIFORNIA, 115
FESTIVAL THEATRE, 626
FIDDLE PUPPET DANCERS, THE, 596
FIGURES OF SPEECH THEATRE, 577
FIJI COMPANY, THE, 968
FILIPINIANA ARTS AND CULTURAL CENTER, 1453
FINE ARTS CHAMBER PLAYERS, 1326
FINE ARTS CHORALE, 645
FINE ARTS CONCERT HALL, 45
FINE ARTS THEATRE, 1515
FINEST ASIAN PERFORMING ARTS, INC., 150
FIREFLY FESTIVAL FOR THE PERFORMING ARTS, 503
FIREHOUSE DINNER THEATRE, 793
FIREHOUSE THEATRE/NOODLES COMEDY CLUB, 791
FIRST NIGHT HARTFORD, INC., 264
FIRST NIGHT, INC., 612
FIRST NIGHT PROVIDENCE, 1251
FIRST PRESBYTERIAN THEATER, 490
FIVE FLAGS CENTER, 516
FIVE FLAGS CENTER - ARENA, 516
FIVE FLAGS CENTER - THEATRE, 516
FIVE SEASONS CENTER ARENA, 510
FLAGSTAFF FESTIVAL OF THE ARTS, 26
FLAGSTAFF SYMPHONY ORCHESTRA, 26
FLAMENCO FANTASY DANCE THEATRE/GYPSY
    PRODUCTIONS INC., 235

FLAT ROCK PLAYHOUSE, 1056
FLATHEAD FESTIVAL OF THE ARTS, 779
FLICKINGER CENTER FOR THE PERFORMING ARTS, 847
FLINT CENTER FOR THE PERFORMING ARTS, 75
FLINT INSTITUTE OF MUSIC, THE, 673
FLINT SYMPHONY ORCHESTRA, 672
FLORAL HALL, 525
FLORENCE GOULD THEATRE IN THE CALIFORNIA PALACE
    OF THE LEGION OF HONOR, 181
FLORENCE SCHWIMLEY LITTLE THEATRE, 61
FLORENTINE OPERA COMPANY, 1506
FLORIDA A & M UNIVERSITY - CHARLES WINTER WOOD
    THEATRE, 366
FLORIDA BALLET AT JACKSONVILLE, 331
FLORIDA BRASS QUINTET, 358
FLORIDA DANCE ASSOCIATION INC., 340
FLORIDA INTERNATIONAL FESITVAL, 321
FLORIDA KEYS COMMUNITY COLLEGE - TENNESSEE
    WILLIAMS THEATRE, 334
FLORIDA LYRIC OPERA, 357
FLORIDA NATIONAL PAVILION, 332
FLORIDA ORCHESTRA, THE, 367
FLORIDA SHAKESPEARE FESTIVAL, 319
FLORIDA SOUTHERN COLLEGE - BUCKNER THEATRE, 336
FLORIDA STATE OPERA AT FLORIDA STATE
    UNIVERSITY, 365
FLORIDA STUDIO THEATRE, 361, 363
FLORIDA SUNCOAST PUPPET GUILD, 368
FLORIDA SYMPHONY ORCHESTRA, 349
FLORIDA THEATRE PERFORMING ARTS CENTER, 332
FLORIDA WEST COAST CHAMBER ORCHESTRA, 359
FLORIDA WEST COAST SYMPHONY, 362
FLORIDA WEST COAST SYMPHONY ORCHESTRA, 359
FLORIDA WEST COAST YOUTH ORCHESTRAS, 359
FLORIDA WIND QUINTET, 360
FLORIDA'S CROSS AND SWORD, 356
FLS ENTERTAINMENT, 492
FLUTE FORCE, 943
FLYNN THEATRE FOR THE PERFORMING ARTS, 1412
F.M. KIRBY CENTER FOR THE PERFORMING ARTS, 1242
FOELLINGER THEATER IN FRANKE PARK, 491
FOLLY, 749
FOND DU LAC SYMPHONIC BAND, 1490
FONTANA CONCERT SOCIETY, 681
FONTANA PERFORMING ARTS CENTER, 80
FOOLS COMPANY, INC.: THE INTERNATIONAL
    OFFESTIVAL, 991
FOOTHILLS COMMUNITY THEATRE, 1065
FOOTLIGHT CLUB, THE, 630
FOOTLIGHT PLAYERS, 1258
FOOTLIGHT PLAYERS THEATRE, 1259
FORD'S THEATRE, 310
FORD'S THEATRE SOCIETY, 304
FORREST THEATRE, 1226
FORT COLLINS SYMPHONY ORCHESTRA, 245
FORT DODGE AREA SYMPHONY ORCHESTRA, 517
FORT EUSTIS MUSIC AND VIDEO CENTER, 1426
FORT EUSTIS MUSIC AND VIDEO CENTER - JACOBS
    THEATRE, 1426
FORT EUSTIS MUSIC AND VIDEO CENTER - SOLDIER
    THEATRE, 1426
FORT GRIFFIN FANDANGLE ASSOCIATION, 1304
FORT GRIFFIN FANDANGLE OUTDOOR THEATRE, 1304
FORT HAYS STATE UNIVERSITY-FELTON - START
    THEATRE, 527
FORT HOOD COMMUNITY MUSIC AND THEATER - FORT
    HOOD COMMUNITY PLAYERS, 1343
FORT HOOD MUSIC AND THEATER - THEATER #1, 1343
FORT LAUDERDALE CHILDREN'S THEATRE, 324
FORT LAUDERDALE OPERA, 323
FORT MASON CENTER - COWELL THEATRE, 181
FORT MYERS HARBORSIDE 3 BUILDINGS, 326
FORT SMITH CIVIC CENTER, 46
FORT SMITH CIVIC CENTER - EXHIBITION HALL, 46
FORT SMITH CIVIC CENTER - THEATER, 47
FORT SMITH LITTLE THEATRE, 46, 47
FORT SMITH SYMPHONY, 46
FORT TOTTEN LITTLE THEATRE, 1086

FORT WAYNE BALLET, 489
FORT WAYNE CIVIC THEATRE, 490
FORT WAYNE DANCE COLLECTIVE, 489
FORT WAYNE PHILHARMONIC ORCHESTRA, 490
FORT WORTH BALLET COMPANY, 1343
FORT WORTH OPERA ASSOCIATION, 1344
FORT WORTH SYMPHONY, 1344
FORT WORTH THEATRE, 1347
FORT WORTH/TARRANT COUNTY CONVENTION CENTER -
    CONVENTION CENTER THEATER, 1349
46TH STREET THEATRE, 993
FORUM, THE, 48
FOSTORIA FOOTLIGHTERS, 1132
FOSTORIA FOOTLIGHTERS, INC., 1133
FOUND THEATRE, THE, 98
FOUNDATION FOR BAROQUE MUSIC, 893
FOUNTAIN SQUARE PLAYERS, 540
FOUNTAIN STREET CHURCH, 676
451ST ARMY BAND, 724
14TH ANNUAL CHICAGO JAZZ FESTIVAL, 444
14TH STREET DANCE CENTER AT EDUCATIONAL
    ALLIANCE, 908
14TH STREET PLAYHOUSE, 386
FOX THEATRE, 386, 671
FOX VALLEY SYMPHONY, 1501
FRANCIS SCOTT KEY AUDITORIUM, 585
FRANCISCAN LIFE CENTER, 1146
FRANCISCO MARTINEZ DANCE THEATRE, THE, 212
FRAUENTHAL CENTER FOR THE PERFORMING ARTS, 687
FRAUENTHAL FOUNDATION FINE ARTS CENTER, 687
FREDDICK BRATCHER AND COMPANY, 319
FREDERICK DOUGLASS CREATIVE ARTS CENTER, INC., 969
FREDERICKSBURG CHAMBER MUSIC FESTIVAL, 1426
FREDONIA CHAMBER PLAYERS, 890
FREE STREET THEATER, 438
FREEDOM HALL, NATHAN MANILOW THEATRE, 467
FREMONT-NEWARK PHILHARMONIC, 80
FRESNO BALLET, 80
FRESNO CONVENTION CENTER THEATRE, 82
FRESNO PHILHARMONIC ASSOCIATION, 81
FRESNO PHILHARMONIC ORCHESTRA, 81
FRIEDRICH SCHORR MEMORIAL PERFORMANCE PRIZE IN
    VOICE, 655
FRIENDS AND ARTISTS THEATRE ENSEMBLE, 87
FRIENDS OF CHAMBER MUSIC, 236, 1177
FRIENDS OF CHAMBER MUSIC KANSAS CITY, 745
FRIENDS OF THE CONCORD CITY AUDITORIUM, THE, 804
FRIENDS OF HISTORIC BOONVILLE, 741
FRIENDS OF MUSIC AND ART OF HUDSON COUNTY, 822
FRIENDS OF MUSIC OF WAYNE, INC., 842
FRIENDS OF MUSIC ORCHESTRA AT SAINT MICHAEL'S, 891
FRIENDS OF THE PERFORMING ARTS IN CONCORD -
    51 WALDEN, THE, 623
FULLERTON CIVIC LIGHT OPERA, 83
FULTON OPERA HOUSE, 1209
FULTON OPERA HOUSE FOUNDATION, 1210
FURMAN UNIVERSITY - MCALISTER AUDITORIUM, 1263
GABBIES PUPPETS, 377
GAILLARD MUNICIPAL AUDITORIUM, 1259
GAINES CHAPEL, AGNES SCOTT COLLEGE, 392
GAINESVILLE BALLET, THE, 392
GAINESVILLE SYMPHONY ORCHESTRA, THE, 393
GALA HISPANIC THEATRE, 304
GALLERY THEATRE OF OREGON, 1183
GARDE ARTS CENTER, 275
GARDEN STATE ARTS CENTER, 821
GARDEN STATE BALLET, 830
GARDEN STATE PHILHARMONIC CHORUS, 839
GARDEN STATE PHILHARMONIC SYMPHONY
    ORCHESTRA, 839
GARDEN STATE PHILHARMONIC YOUTH ORCHESTRA, 839
GARLAND CENTER FOR THE PERFORMING ARTS, 1353
GARLAND CENTER FOR THE PERFORMING ARTS -
    THEATER #1, 1353
GARLAND CENTER FOR THE PERFORMING ARTS -
    THEATER #2, 1353
GARLAND CIVIC THEATRE, 1352
GARLAND SUMMER MUSICALS, 1352

GARLAND SYMPHONY ORCHESTRA, 1351
GARTH FAGAN DANCE, 1020
GARTH NEWEL MUSIC CENTER, 1428
GARY BEARD CHORALE, THE, 1289
GAS LIGHT PLAYERS, THE, 570
GASLAMP QUARTER THEATRE, 156, 159
GASTON HALL, 310
GATEWAY BALLET OF SAINT LOUIS, 753
GATEWAY PERFORMANCE PRODUCTIONS, 381
GATEWAY PLAYERS, THE, 626
GAY PERFORMANCES COMPANY, 969
GEARY AUDITORIUM, 1480
GENE DYNARSKI THEATER ENSEMBLE, 110
GENERIC THEATRE, 1433
GENERIE THEATER, 1434
GENESEO CHAMBER SYMPHONY, 892
GENESIS ARTS/KENTUCKY INC., 546
GENESIUS PLAYERS, 1309
GENEVA CONCERTS, INC., 892
GEORGE COATES PERFORMANCE WORKS, 174
GEORGE MASON UNIVERSITY CENTER FOR THE ARTS, 1426
GEORGE STREET PLAYHOUSE, 829
GEORGE WASHINGTON UNIVERSITY - LISNER
    AUDITORIUM, 310
GEORGETOWN CHILDREN'S THEATRE, 542
GEORGIA SHAKESPEARE FESTIVAL, 384
GEORGIA SOUTHERN UNIVERSITY - FOY FINE ARTS
    RECITAL HALL, 398
GEORGIA SOUTHERN UNIVERSITY - PUPPET THEATRE, 398
GERMANTOWN THEATRE GUILD, 1222
GERMINAL STAGE DENVER, 238, 241
GERSHWIN THEATRE, 998
GETTYSBURG SYMPHONY ORCHESTRA, 587
GEVA THEATRE, 1020
GILL COLISEUM, 1178
GINA BACHAUER INTERNATIONAL PIANO FOUNDATION,
    THE, 1406
GIRAULT AUDITORIUM, 736
GLACIER CHORALE, 776
GLACIER ORCHESTRA, 775
GLASSBORO CENTER FOR THE ARTS, 820
GLEN ELLYN CHILDREN'S CHORUS, 457
GLENDALE COMMUNITY COLLEGE PERFORMING ARTS
    CENTER, 27
GLENDALE SYMPHONY, 85
GLENN MEMORIAL AUDITORIUM, 386
GLIMMERGLASS OPERA, 883
GLINES, THE, 969
GLOBE OF THE GREAT SOUTHWEST, 1378
GLOUCESTER STAGE COMPANY, 627
GO FOR BAROQUE, 1164
GOLD BAR ROOM THEATRE, IMPERIAL HOTEL, 233
GOLD COAST MIME COMPANY, 345
GOLD COAST OPERA, 355
GOLDEN APPLE DINNER THEATRE, 362
GOLDEN GATE THEATRE, 181
GOLDEN ISLES CHAMBER MUSIC FESTIVAL, INC., 398
GOLDEN THESPIANS, THE, 329
GOLDEN WEST COLLEGE - MAINSTAGE THEATRE, 90
GOLIARD CHAMBER SOLOISTS, 862
GONZAGA UNIVERSITY - GENE RUSSELL THEATRE, 1467
GOOD COMPANY PLAYERS, 81
GOODFELLOW HALL (JACK BENNY CENTER FOR THE
    ARTS), 477
GOODMAN CHAMBER CHOIR, 954
GOODMAN THEATRE, 438
GOODSPEED-AT-CHESTER/THE NORMA TERRIS
    THEATRE, 257, 258
GOODSPEED OPERA HOUSE, 259
GOOSEBERRY PARK PLAYERS, 1089
GOPHERWOOD MUSIC SOCIETY, 663
GOSHEN COLLEGE - JOHN S. UMBLE CENTER, 493
GOTHENBURG COMMUNITY PLAYHOUSE, 782
GOTHENBURG COMMUNITY PLAYHOUSE - SUN
    THEATRE, 782
GRAMERCY ARTS THEATER, 998
GRANBURY OPERA HOUSE, 1353
GRAND 1894 OPERA HOUSE, 1351

GRAND 1894 OPERA HOUSE, THE, 1350
GRAND CANYON CHAMBER MUSIC FESTIVAL, 27
GRAND CENTER - AUDITORIUM, 676
GRAND CENTER - DEVOS HALL, 676
GRAND JUNCTION MUSICAL ARTS ASSOCIATION, 247
GRAND OLE OPRY HOUSE, 1298
GRAND OPERA HOUSE, 296, 393, 1512
GRAND PRAIRIE FESTIVAL OF THE ARTS, 53
GRAND PRAIRIE WAR MEMORIAL AUDITORIUM, 53
GRAND RAPIDS BALLET, THE, 674
GRAND RAPIDS SYMPHONY ORCHESTRA, 674
GRAND RAPIDS YOUTH SYMPHONY, 675
GRAND TETON MUSIC FESTIVAL, 1523
GRANDE OLDE PLAYERS, 791
GRANDINELE LITHUANIAN FOLK DANCERS, 1138
GRANITE YOUTH SYMPHONY, 1402
GRANT PARK MUSIC FESTIVAL, 444
GRANTHAM ORATORIO SOCIETY, 1203
GREAT AMERICAN CHILDREN'S THEATRE COMPANY,
    THE, 1507
GREAT AMERICAN HISTORY THEATRE, 725
GREAT AMERICAN PEOPLE SHOW, THE, 421
GREAT FALLS CENTER FOR THE PERFORMING ARTS, 772
GREAT FALLS CIVIC CENTER THEATER, 772
GREAT FALLS SYMPHONY ASSOCIATION, 772
GREAT LAKES THEATER FESTIVAL, 1115
GREAT NORTH AMERICAN HISTORY THEATRE, 726
GREAT RIVER FESTIVAL OF ARTS, 1493
GREAT WESTERN FORUM, THE, 91
GREAT WOODS CENTER FOR THE PERFORMING ARTS, 632
GREATER AKRON MUSICAL ASSOCIATION, 1092
GREATER BOSTON YOUTH SYMPHONY ORCHESTRAS, 608
GREATER BRIDGEPORT SYMPHONY, 256
GREATER BRIDGEPORT SYMPHONY YOUTH
    ORCHESTRA, 260
GREATER BUFFALO OPERA COMPANY, 877
GREATER DALLAS YOUTH ORCHESTRA ASSOCIATION, 1326
GREATER FALL RIVER SYMPHONY SOCIETY, 626
GREATER LANSING SYMPHONY ORCHESTRA, 683
GREATER MIAMI MERRY MUMMERS STRING BAND, 341
GREATER MIAMI OPERA ASSOCIATION, THE, 342
GREATER NEW BRITAIN OPERA ASSOCIATION, 268
GREATER PALM BEACH SYMPHONY, 351
GREATER TRENTON SYMPHONY ORCHESTRA, 840
GREATER TWIN CITIES YOUTH SYMPHONIES, 709
GREECE PERFORMING ARTS SOCIETY, 1009
GREECE SYMPHONY ORCHESTRA, 1019
GREEK THEATRE, 115, 118
GREELEY CHORALE, THE, 248
GREEN BAY SYMPHONY ORCHESTRA, 1491
GREEN EARTH PLAYERS, 706
GREEN LAKE FESTIVAL OF MUSIC, 1491
GREEN MOUNTAIN GUILD, 1416
GREENBRIER VALLEY THEATRE, THE, 1483
GREENSBORO CHILDREN'S THEATRE, 1059
GREENSBORO CONCERT BAND, 1057
GREENSBORO OPERA COMPANY, 1058
GREENSBORO SYMPHONY ORCHESTRA, 1058
GREENSBORO WAR MEMORIAL AUDITORIUM, 1060
GREENVILLE CHORALE, THE, 1263
GREENVILLE COMMUNITY THEATER, 1025
GREENVILLE MEMORIAL AUDITORIUM, 1264
GREENVILLE SYMPHONY ASSOCIATION, 1263
GREENVILLE SYMPHONY SOCIETY, 1203
GREENWICH CHORAL SOCIETY, 261
GREENWICH SYMPHONY ORCHESTRA, 260
GREENWOOD CIVIC CENTER, 1264
GREENWOOD LEFLORE CIVIC CENTER, 733
GREENWOOD PLAYERS CHILDREN'S THEATER, 1502
GREER GARSON THEATRE CENTER - COLLEGE OF SANTA
    FE, 856
GREGG SMITH SINGERS, INC., 954
GRETNA PRODUCTIONS, 1214
GROSSE POINTE SUMMER FESTIVAL, 677
GROSSMONT COMMUNITY CONCERTS, 94
GROUNDLING THEATRE, THE, 110
GROUP MOTION MULTI MEDIA DANCE THEATER, 1216
GROUP REPERTORY THEATRE, 128

GROUP THEATRE COMPANY, THE, 1459
GROVE SHAKESPEARE, 84
GROVE SHAKESPEARE FESTIVAL, THE, 84
GRUPO FOLKLORICO MEXICANA, 364
GUADALUPE CULTURAL ARTS CENTER, 1384
GUADALUPE FOLK DANCE COMPANY, 1383
GUATEQUE FOLKLORIC BALLET OF PUERTO RICO, 1525
GUEST ARTIST SERIES, 850
GUILD OPERA COMPANY, INC., 106
GULF COAST OPERA THEATRE, 731
GULF COAST SYMPHONY, 733
GULFCOAST DANCE, 326
GUNN HIGH SCHOOL - SPANGENBERG THEATRE, 139
GUS GIORDANO JAZZ DANCE CHICAGO, 453
GUSMAN CENTER FOR THE PERFORMING ARTS, 343
GUSTAVUS ADOLPHUS COLLEGE - SCHAEFFER FINE ARTS
    COMPLEX, 728
GUSTAVUS ADOLPHUS COLLEGE - SCHAEFFER FINE ARTS
    COMPLEX - EVELYN E. ANDERSON THEATRE, 728
GUSTAVUS ADOLPHUS COLLEGE - SCHAEFFER FINE ARTS
    COMPLEX - JUSSI BJORLING CONCERT HALL, 728
GUTHRIE THEATER, THE, 718
GUTHRIE THEATRE, THE, 713
HAAGE CONCERTS/HARRIS PRESENTS, 1237
HADDONFIELD SYMPHONY, 821
HAINES ARTS COUNCIL, 20
HALL OF NATIONS BLACK BOX THEATRE, 311
HAMILTON COLLEGE - MINOR THEATRE, 882
HAMPTON ARTS COMMISSION, 1427
HAMPTON COLISEUM, 1427
HAMPTON PLAYHOUSE, 806
HAMPTON PLAYHOUSE THEATRE ARTS WORKSHOP, 806
HAMPTON ROADS CIVIC BALLET, 1427
HANDEL AND HAYDN SOCIETY, 608
HANGAR THEATRE, 898
HANGAR THEATRE, THE, 897
HANNAH KAHN DANCE COMPANY, 79
HARDIN COUNTY PLAYHOUSE, 552
HARLEM ARTISTS' DEVELOPMENT LEAGUE ESPECIALLY
    FOR YOU (HADLEY PLAYERS), 969
HARLINGEN CULTURAL ARTS CENTER - AUDITORIUM, 1354
HARRISBURG COMMUNITY THEATRE, 1205
HARRISBURG SYMPHONY ASSOCIATION, 1204
HARRISBURG YOUTH SYMPHONY ORCHESTRA, 1204
HARTFORD BALLET, 262
HARTFORD CHORALE, INC., THE, 255
HARTFORD CIVIC CENTER, 265
HARTFORD JAZZ SOCIETY, 255
HARTFORD STAGE COMPANY, 264, 265
HARTFORD SYMPHONY ORCHESTRA INC., THE, 262
HARTSVILLE COMMUNITY PLAYERS, 1264
HARTT SUMMER YOUTH MUSIC FESTIVAL, 287
HARVARD SUMMER DANCE CENTER, 618
HASTINGS SYMPHONY ORCHESTRA, 782
HAUGH PERFORMING ARTS CENTER, 85
HAWAII CHAMBER ORCHESTRA, 403
HAWAII CONCERT SOCIETY, 401
HAWAII ECUMENICAL CHORALE, 404
HAWAII OPERA THEATRE, 405
HAWAII STATE BALLET, 402
HAWAII YOUTH SYMPHONY ASSOCIATION, 403
HAYS SYMPHONY ORCHESTRA, 527
H.B. PLAYWRIGHTS FOUNDATION THEATRE HOUSE, 998
HEADWATERS COUNCIL, PERFORMING ARTS, 1487
HEARTLAND MEN'S CHORUS, 746
HEDGEROW THEATRE, 1238
HEIGHTS CHAMBER ORCHESTRA, 1119
HEINZ HALL FOR THE PERFORMING ARTS, 1236
HELEN HAYES THEATRE, 998
HELENA CIVIC CENTER, 774
HELENA CIVIC CENTER - AUDITORIUM, 774
HELENA CIVIC CENTER - BALLROOM, 775
HELENA PRESENTS, 774
HELENA SYMPHONY SOCIETY, 773
HELENA YOUTH CHOIRS, INC., 773
HENDRIX THEATRE, 1061
HENNEPIN CENTER FOR THE ARTS, 718
HENRY J. KAISER CONVENTION CENTER, 133

HENRY J. KAISER CONVENTION CENTER - ARENA, 133
HENRY J. KAISER CONVENTION CENTER - CALVIN
    SIMMONS THEATRE, 133
HERITAGE ARTISTS, 883
HERITAGE BRASS QUINTET, THE, 1141
HERITAGE DAYS, 787
HERITAGE SQUARE MUSIC HALL, 247
HERSHELL CARROUSEL FACTORY MUSEUM, 1010
HERSHEY THEATRE, 1206
HESPERUS, 1423
HESSTON PERFORMING ARTS SERIES, 527
HEXAGON, 1411
HEYMANN PERFORMING ARTS AND CONVENTION
    CENTER, 558
HIBBING COLLEGE - COMMUNITY BAND, 705
HICKORY COMMUNITY THEATRE, 1061
HIGH POINT COMMUNITY THEATRE, 1062
HIGH POINT THEATRE AND EXHIBITION
    CENTER, 1062, 1063
HIGHFIELD THEATRE, 627
HIGHLAND BRITISH BRASS BAND ASSOCIATION, 1055
HIGHLANDS CHAMBER MUSIC FESTIVAL, 1063
HIGHLANDS PLAYHOUSE, 1063
HIGHLIGHTS IN JAZZ, 944
HILL COUNTRY ARTS FOUNDATION, 1368
HILO COMMUNITY PLAYERS, 401
HINGHAM CIVIC MUSIC THEATRE, 629
HINGHAM HIGH SCHOOL - AUDITORIUM, 629
HIP POCKET THEATRE, 1347
HIPPODROME, 328, 1391
HIPPODROME STATE THEATRE, 328
HIPPODROME THEATRE, 1391
HIRSCH MEMORIAL COLISEUM, 571
HIS IMAGE, SACRED DANCE, 317
HIS MAJESTIE'S CLERKES, 453
HISPANIC ORGANIZATION OF LATIN ACTORS (HOLA), 970
HISTORIC IRONWOOD THEATRE, 679
HISTORY MAKING PRODUCTIONS, 649
HOBSON MEMORIAL UNION - PROGRAM BOARD, 700
HOLE IN THE WALL THEATRE, 269
HOLLYWOOD BOWL, 89
HOLLYWOOD BOWL SUMMER FESTIVAL, 115
HOLLYWOOD PALLADIUM, 89
HOLLYWOOD PLAYHOUSE, 329
HOLLYWOOD THEATER COMPANY, 207
HOMEMADE JAM, 773
HONOLULU CHILDREN'S OPERA CHORUS, 405
HONOLULU SYMPHONY SOCIETY, 403
HONOLULU THEATRE FOR YOUTH, 405
HOPE COLLEGE ORCHESTRA AND SYMPHONETTE, 677
HOPE COLLEGE THEATRE DEPARTMENT, 678
HOPE MARTIN THEATRE, 521
HOPKINS CENTER SUMMER, 806
HORACE A. MOSES BUILDING, 650
HORACE BUSHNELL MEMORIAL HALL, 265
HORIZON CONCERTS INC., 944
HORIZONS THEATRE, 305
HORN IN THE WEST, 1044
HORSE CAVE THEATRE, 544
HOT SPRINGS CONVENTION AND VISITORS' BUREAU, 47
HOTFOOT QUARTET, 1145
HOUGHTON COLLEGE - WESLEY CHAPEL, 897
HOUGHTON COLLEGE ARTIST SERIES, 896
HOUSTON BALLET, 1356
HOUSTON CIVIC CENTER, 1364
HOUSTON CIVIC CENTER-GEORGE R. BROWN
    CONVENTION CENTER, 1364
HOUSTON CIVIC CENTER-GEORGE R. BROWN
    CONVENTION CENTER - BALLROOM, 1364
HOUSTON CIVIC CENTER-GEORGE R. BROWN
    CONVENTION CENTER - EXHIBITION HALL, 1365
HOUSTON CIVIC CENTER-GEORGE R. BROWN
    CONVENTION CENTER - GENERAL ASSEMBLY
    HALL, 1365
HOUSTON CIVIC CENTER-GUS WORTHAM THEATER
    CENTER, 1365
HOUSTON CIVIC CENTER-GUS WORTHAM THEATER
    CENTER - ALICE AND GEORGE BROWN THEATER, 1365

HOUSTON CIVIC CENTER-GUS WORTHAM THEATER
    CENTER - LILLY AND ROY CULLEN THEATER, 1365
HOUSTON CIVIC CENTER - JESSE H. JONES HALL FOR THE
    PERFORMING ARTS, 1366
HOUSTON CIVIC CENTER - THE MUSIC HALL, 1366
HOUSTON CIVIC CENTER - SAM HOUSTON COLISEUM, 1366
HOUSTON CIVIC SYMPHONY ORCHESTRA, 1357
HOUSTON FINE ARTS CENTER, 241
HOUSTON FRIENDS OF MUSIC, 1358
HOUSTON GRAND OPERA, 1358
HOUSTON HARPSICHORD SOCIETY, 1358
HOUSTON INTERNATIONAL FESTIVAL, THE, 1363
HOUSTON SHAKESPEARE FESTIVAL, 1363
HOUSTON SYMPHONY, 1358
HOUSTON SYMPHONY CHORUS, 1359
HOWARD COLLEGE AT BIG SPRING - HOWARD COLLEGE
    AUDITORIUM, 1316
HOWARD COLLEGE AT BIG SPRING - HOWARD COLLEGE
    COLISEUM, 1316
HOWARD HANGER JAZZ FANTASY, 1043
HUBBARD STREET DANCE COMPANY, 423
HUDSON GUILD THEATRE, 970
HUDSON THEATRE, 213
HUDSON VALLEY PHILHARMONIC, 1017
HULT CENTER FOR THE PERFORMING ARTS, 1181
HULT CENTER FOR THE PERFORMING ARTS - SILVA
    CONCERT HALL, 1181
HULT CENTER FOR THE PERFORMING ARTS - SORENG
    THEATRE, 1181
HUMAN ARMS, 1027
HUMBOLDT STATE UNIVERSITY, 56
HUMBOLDT STATE UNIVERSITY - EAST GYMNASIUM, 57
HUMBOLDT STATE UNIVERSITY - FULKERSON RECITAL
    HALL, 57
HUMBOLDT STATE UNIVERSITY - JOHN VAN DUZER
    THEATRE, 57
HUMBOLDT STATE UNIVERSITY - KATE BUCHANAN
    ROOM, 57
HUNGARIAN OPERA WORKSHOP, 430
HUNTINGTON BEACH PLAYHOUSE, 89
HUNTINGTON CHAMBER ORCHESTRA, 1480
HUNTINGTON CIVIC CENTRE, THE, 1481
HUNTINGTON MUSEUM OF ART - AMPHITHEATRE, 1481
HUNTINGTON MUSEUM OF ART - AUDITORIUM, 1481
HUNTINGTON PARK CIVIC THEATRE, 90
HUNTINGTON PLAYHOUSE, 1096
HUNTINGTON THEATRE, 1096
HUNTINGTON THEATRE COMPANY, 611
HUNTSVILLE CIVIC BALLET, 5
HUNTSVILLE LITTLE THEATRE, 7
HUNTSVILLE OPERA THEATER, 6
HUNTSVILLE SYMPHONY ORCHESTRA, 6
HUNTSVILLE YOUTH ORCHESTRA, 6
HURON MUNICIPAL BAND, 1269
HURON PLAYHOUSE, THE, 1097
HUTCHINSON SYMPHONY, 528
I CANTORI DI NEW YORK, 954
I. SHERMAN GREENE CHORALE, INC., 1432
ICE THEATER OF NEW YORK, INC., 922
IDAHO FALLS SYMPHONY, 413
IDAHO REPERTORY THEATRE COMPANY, 414
IDAHO SHAKESPEARE FESTIVAL, 412
IDAHO STATE UNIVERSITY - FRAZIER AUDITORIUM, 416
IDAHO STATE UNIVERSITY - GORANSON HALL, 416
IDAHO STATE UNIVERSITY - POWELL LITTLE THEATRE, 416
IDAHO THEATER FOR YOUTH, 412
IDYLLWILD SCHOOL OF MUSIC AND THE ARTS, 90
IGLOO, THE THEATRICAL GROUP, 970
IL PICCOLO TEATRO DELL'OPERA, INC., 871
ILLINOIS CHAMBER SYMPHONY, 473
ILLINOIS PHILHARMONIC ORCHESTRA ASSOCIATION, 466
ILLINOIS SHAKESPEARE FESTIVAL, 464
ILLINOIS THEATRE CENTER, 466, 467
ILLINOIS WESLEYAN SCHOOL OF DRAMA - MCPHERSON
    HALL, 421
ILLINOIS WESLEYAN UNIVERSITY - WESTBROOK
    AUDITORIUM, 421
ILLUSION THEATER, 713

ILLUSTRATED STAGE COMPANY, 174
IMAGINATION THEATER, 438
IMAGO, THE THEATRE MASK ENSEMBLE, 1014
IMPERIAL PLAYERS, 233
IMPERIAL SYMPHONY, 335
IMPERIAL THEATRE, 389, 998
IMPOSSIBLE PLAYERS, THE, 251
IMPROVISATIONALMUSICCO, INC., 1193
IN THE HEART OF THE BEAST PUPPET AND MASK
     THEATRE, 713
INDEPENDENT EYE, THE, 1210
INDIANA JAZZ, 495
INDIANA REPERTORY THEATRE, 496
INDIANA UNIVERSITY AUDITORIUM, 484
INDIANA UNIVERSITY MUSICAL ARTS CENTER, 484
INDIANA UNIVERSITY PERFORMING ARTS SERIES, 484
INDIANA UNIVERSITY THEATRE, 485
INDIANAPOLIS BALLET THEATRE, 494
INDIANAPOLIS OPERA, 496
INDIANAPOLIS SYMPHONY ORCHESTRA, 495
INDIANOLA LITTLE THEATRE, 734
INLAND EMPIRE SYMPHONY ASSOCIATION, 151
INNER CITY CULTURAL CENTER, 116
INSPIRATION POINT FINE ARTS COLONY, 44
INSTITUTE FOR DANCE, INC., THE, 1442
INSTITUTE FOR READERS THEATRE, 156
INSTITUTE OF OUTDOOR DRAMA, 1047
INTERBOROUGH REPERTORY THEATER (IRT), 873
INTERLOCHEN ARTS CAMP, 678
INTERLOCHEN ARTS FESTIVAL, 678
INTERLOCHEN CENTER FOR THE ARTS - CORSON
     AUDITORIUM, 678
INTERLOCHEN CENTER FOR THE ARTS - DENDRINOS
     CHAPEL/RECITAL HALL, 679
INTERLOCHEN CENTER FOR THE ARTS - KRESGE
     AUDITORIUM, 679
INTERMOUNTAIN CULTURAL CENTER AND MUSEUM, 418
INTERMOUNTAIN OPERA COMPANY, 771
INTERNATIONAL ARTS RELATIONS DBA INTAR HISPANIC
     AMERICAN ARTS CENTER, 971
INTERNATIONAL ASSOCIATION OF JAZZ APPRECIATION,
     THE, 104
INTERNATIONAL BALLET FOLKLORICO, 1340
INTERNATIONAL CHILDREN'S FESTIVAL, 1422
INTERNATIONAL CONCERTS EXCHANGE, 65
INTERNATIONAL CREATIVE MUSIC ORCHESTRA, 167
INTERNATIONAL FESTIVAL OF PUPPETRY, 971
INTERNATIONAL FESTIVAL-INSTITUTE AT ROUND TOP -
     FESTIVAL CONCERT HALL, 1381
INTERNATIONAL MUSIC CAMP, 1087
INTERNATIONAL SYMPHONY ORCHESTRA OF SARNIA
     AND PORT HURON, 689
INTIMAN THEATRE COMPANY, 1459
INTUITION THEATRE COMPANY, 1104
INVISIBLE THEATRE, 38
IOWA DANCE THEATRE, 514
IOWA STATE UNIVERSITY - BENTON AUDITORIUM, 508
IOWA STATE UNIVERSITY - C.Y. STEPHENS
     AUDITORIUM, 508
IOWA STATE UNIVERSITY - HILTON COLISEUM, 508
IOWA STATE UNIVERSITY - IOWA STATE CENTER, 508
IOWA STATE UNIVERSITY - J.W. FISHER AUDITORIUM, 508
IRINE FOKINE BALLET COMPANY, 836
IRISH ARTS CENTRE THEATRE, 971
IRVING ARTS CENTER, 1370
IRVING BALLET COMPANY, 1368
IRVING COMMUNITY CONCERT ASSOCIATION, 1369
IRVING COMMUNITY THEATRE, 1369
IRVING S. GILMORE INTERNATIONAL KEYBOARD
     FESTIVAL, 682
IRVING SYMPHONY ORCHESTRA, 1369
ISABELLA STEWART GARDNER MUSEUM, 613, 615
ISADORA DUNCAN DANCE CENTER, 163
ISLAND MOVING COMPANY, 1246
ISLAND PLAYERS, 315
ISLAND PLAYERS THEATRE, 315
ISLIP ARTS COUNCIL, 888
ITHACA BALLET (BALLET GUILD OF ITHACA, INC.), 897

ITHACA COLLEGE - DILLINGHAM CENTER FOR THE
     PERFORMING ARTS, 898
ITHACA COLLEGE - DILLINGHAM CENTER FOR THE
     PERFORMING ARTS - ARENA, 898
ITHACA COLLEGE - DILLINGHAM CENTER FOR THE
     PERFORMING ARTS - HOERNER AUDITORIUM, 898
ITHACA OPERA ASSOCIATION, 897
I.U. DONS, INC., 492
IVY GREEN THEATER, 12
JACKIE GLEASON THEATER, 345
JACKSON AUDITORIUM, 1388
JACKSON CIVIC CENTER, 1282
JACKSON COUNTY COMMUNITY THEATRE, 486
JACKSON MARIONETTE PRODUCTIONS, 714
JACKSON MUNICIPAL AUDITORIUM, 736
JACKSON RECREATION CHILDREN'S THEATRE, 1281
JACKSON SYMPHONY ASSOCIATION, 1281
JACKSON SYMPHONY YOUTH ORCHESTRA, 734
JACKSON THEATRE GUILD, 1281
JACKSONVILLE BALLET THEATRE, 331
JACKSONVILLE CIVIC AUDITORIUM, 332
JACKSONVILLE CIVIC AUDITORIUM - EXHIBITION
     HALL, 333
JACKSONVILLE CIVIC AUDITORIUM - LITTLE
     THEATER, 333
JACKSONVILLE SYMPHONY ORCHESTRA, 331
JACOB'S PILLOW DANCE FESTIVAL, 603
JAM AND COMPANY, 971
JAMAICA ARTS CENTER, 900
JAMES A. DOOLITTLE THEATRE, 89
JAMES C. PETRILLO MUSIC SHELL, 446
JAMES E. BUFFAN GOLD COAST BAND, THE, 316
JAMES H. WHITING AUDITORIUM, 673
JAMES L. KNIGHT CENTER, 343
JAMESTOWN CONCERT ASSOCIATION, 900
JAN ERKERT AND COMPANY, 423
JAN JUSTIS DANCE COMPANY, 223
JANE FRANKLIN AND DANCERS, 1425
JANIS BRENNER AND DANCERS, 922
JAPAN AMERICA THEATER, 118
JASPER CIVIC AUDITORIUM, 498
JAZZ ARTS GROUP OF COLUMBUS, THE, 1123
JAZZ COMPOSERS ALLIANCE, 617
JAZZ DANCE THEATRE SOUTH, 394
JAZZ DANCERS, INC., 68
JAZZ IN JUNE, INC., 1162
JAZZ REVIVAL ORCHESTRA, THE, 1150
JAZZ TAP ENSEMBLE, 100
JAZZMOBILE INCORPORATED, 991
JEAN COCTEAU REPERTORY, 972
JEFFERSON PERFORMING ARTS SOCIETY, 562
JEFFERSON SYMPHONY ORCHESTRA, 247
JEKYLL ISLAND AMPHITHEATER, 393
JEKYLL ISLAND MUSICAL THEATRE FESTIVAL, 399
JENNIFER MULLER-THE WORKS, 923
JEWEL BOX THEATRE, 1165
JEWISH COMMUNITY CENTER - JOE FRANK THEATRE, 1366
JEWISH COMMUNITY CENTER - KAPLAN THEATRE, 1366
JEWISH COMMUNITY CENTER OF CLEVELAND, 1120
JEWISH COMMUNITY CENTER OF CLEVELAND - BLANCHE
     R. HALLE THEATER, 1126
JEWISH COMMUNITY CENTER OF HOUSTON, 1363
JEWISH COMMUNITY CENTER OF METROPOLITAN NEW
     JERSEY, 844
JEWISH REPERTORY THEATRE, 972
JO EMERY DANCE COMPANY, 1468
JOAN KARFF'S NEW DANCE, 1356
JOAN MILLER'S DANCE PLAYERS, 923
JOE LOUIS ARENA, 671
JOEL HALL DANCERS, 424
JOFFREY BALLET, 923
JOFFREY II DANCERS, THE, 923
JOHN A. WALKER COMMUNITY CENTER, 1076
JOHN A. WALKER EVENTS, INC., 1075
JOHN ADDISON CONCERT HALL, 594
JOHN CHOOKASIAN FOLK ENSEMBLE-KING TUT REVUE
     BELLY DANCE, 81
JOHN DREW THEATER OF GUILD HALL, THE, 887

JOHN F. KENNEDY CENTER FOR THE PERFORMING
ARTS, 307, 311
JOHN F. KENNEDY CENTER FOR THE PERFORMING ARTS -
AMERICAN FILM INSTITUTE THEATER, 311
JOHN F. KENNEDY CENTER FOR THE PERFORMING ARTS -
CONCERT HALL, 311
JOHN F. KENNEDY CENTER FOR THE PERFORMING ARTS -
EISENHOWER THEATER, 311
JOHN F. KENNEDY CENTER FOR THE PERFORMING ARTS -
OPERA HOUSE, 311
JOHN F. KENNEDY CENTER FOR THE PERFORMING ARTS -
TERRACE THEATER, 312
JOHN F. KENNEDY CENTER FOR THE PERFORMING ARTS -
THEATER LAB, 312
JOHN GAMBLE/JAN VAN DYKE DANCE COMPANY, 1057
JOHN GOLDEN THEATRE, 999
JOHN HARMS CENTER FOR THE ARTS, 819
JOHN MICHAEL KOHLER ARTS CENTER, 1515
JOHN PAUL THEATRE, 31
JOHN PAULSON JAZZ QUARTET, 729
JOHNS HOPKINS UNIVERSITY - THE MERRICK BARN,
THE, 591
JOHNSON CITY CIVIC CHORALE, 1282
JOHNSTOWN SYMPHONY ORCHESTRA, 1208
JOMANDI PRODUCTIONS, 381
JONESBOROUGH REPERTORY THEATRE, 1283
JOPPA JAZZ DANCE COMPANY, 635
JORDAN HALL AT NEW ENGLAND CONSERVATORY, 615
JORDAN THEATRE, 98
JOSE LIMON DANCE COMPANY, 924
JOSE MOLINA BAILES ESPANOLES, 1013
JOSEPH HOLMES CHICAGO DANCE THEATRE, 424
JOSEPH PAPP PUBLIC THEATER, THE, 999
JOYCE THEATER, THE, 999
JUBILATION DANCE COMPANY, 870
JUBILLEE MENS CHORUS, 346
JUILLIARD DANCE ENSEMBLE, 924
JUILLIARD OPERA CENTER, 954
JULIAN THEATRE, THE, 174
JULIE ROGERS THEATRE FOR THE PERFORMING ARTS, 1315
JUMP-START PERFORMANCE COMPANY, 1384
JUNEAU FOLK ENSEMBLE, 17
JUNEAU JAZZ AND CLASSICS, 21
JUNEBUG PRODUCTIONS INC., 566
JUNIOR BLACK ACADEMY OF ARTS AND LETTERS, 1333
JUNIOR THEATRE, 512
JUPITER SYMPHONY, 944
JUST US THEATER COMPANY, 382
KAHILU THEATRE, 408
KALAMAZOO BALLET COMPANY, 679
KALAMAZOO CIVIC AUDITORIUM, 682
KALAMAZOO CIVIC PLAYERS, 680
KALAMAZOO COLLEGE, 682
KALAMAZOO JUNIOR SYMPHONY SOCIETY, THE, 680
KALAMAZOO SYMPHONY ORCHESTRA, 680
KALEIDOSCOPE DANCE THEATRE BALLET, 352
KALEIDOSCOPE THEATRE, 337
KANAWHA PLAYERS, 1479
KANOPY DANCE THEATRE, 1494
KANSAS CITY JAZZ FESTIVAL COMMITTEE, 748
KANSAS CITY MUNICIPAL AUDITORIUM, 749
KANSAS CITY MUNICIPAL AUDITORIUM - ARENA, 749
KANSAS CITY MUNICIPAL AUDITORIUM - MUSIC HALL, 749
KANSAS CITY SYMPHONY, 746
KANSAS STATE FAIR - GRANDSTAND, 528
KANSAS STATE UNIVERSITY - MCCAIN AUDITORIUM, 530
KANSAS UNIVERSITY SYMPHONY ORCHESTRA, 529
KARAMU HOUSE, 1113
KARAMU HOUSE PERFORMING ARTS THEATRE, 1117
KARAMU HOUSE PERFORMING ARTS THEATRE -
AMPHITHEATRE, 1117
KARAMU HOUSE PERFORMING ARTS THEATRE -
ARENA, 1117
KARAMU HOUSE PERFORMING ARTS THEATRE -
PROSCENIUM, 1117
KARPATOK HUNGARIAN FOLK ENSEMBLE, 67
KAST AND COMPANY, 424
KATHARINE CORNELL MEMORIAL THEATRE, 647

KATHY BURKS MARIONETTES, 1330
KAUFMANN CONCERT HALL, 999
KAZUKO HIRABAYASHI DANCE THEATRE, 924, 999
KEAN COLLEGE OF NEW JERSEY - WILKINS THEATRE, 840
KEARNEY COMMUNITY THEATRE, 783
KEI TAKEI'S MOVING EARTH (MOVING EARTH INC.), 925
KEITH-ALBEE THEATRE, 1481
KELLOGG CENTER ARENA, 662
KEMPER ARENA, 750
KENDRICK AMPHITHEATER, 1318
KENNETH C. BECK CENTER FOR THE PERFORMING
ARTS, 1135
KENNETH KING AND DANCERS, 925
KENOSHA SYMPHONY ASSOCIATION, INC., 1492
KENTUCKY CENTER CHAMBER PLAYERS, 547
KENTUCKY CENTER FOR THE ARTS, 549
KENTUCKY CENTER FOR THE ARTS - BOMHARD
THEATER, 550
KENTUCKY CENTER FOR THE ARTS - BOYD MARTIN
EXPERIMENTAL THEATER, 550
KENTUCKY CENTER FOR THE ARTS - WHITNEY HALL, 550
KENTUCKY OPERA, 548
KENWOOD CHAMBER ORCHESTRA, THE, 709
KERRVILLE FESTIVALS, 1370
KERRVILLE PERFORMING ARTS SOCIETY, 1370
KETCHIKAN THEATRE BALLET SCHOOL, 22
KEY WEST PLAYERS, 333
KHADRA INTERNATIONAL FOLK BALLET, 163
KIDS INTO DRAMA, 809
KIEL CENTER, THE, 762
KIEL CENTER - ARENA, THE, 762
KIEL CENTER - OPERA HOUSE, THE, 762
KILLINGTON MUSIC FESTIVAL, 1417
KINCAID REGIONAL THEATRE, 542
KING'S CHAPEL CONCERT SERIES, 613
KINGSPORT SYMPHONY ORCHESTRA, 1283
KIRKLAND ART CENTER, 882
KIRKLAND FINE ARTS CENTER, 450
KITKA, 131
KLEIN MEMORIAL AUDITORIUM, 256
KLEINHANS MUSIC HALL, 880
KLEZMER CONSERVATORY BAND, 619
KLINGENSMITH PARK AMPHITHEATRE, 1159
KNOX COLLEGE - ELEANOR ABBOTT FORD CENTER FOR
THE FINE ARTS, 456
KNOX GALESBURG SYMPHONY, 456
KNOXVILLE BALLET COMPANY, THE, 1284
KNOXVILLE CIVIC AUDITORIUM AND COLISEUM -
AUDITORIUM, 1287
KNOXVILLE METROPOLITAN DANCE THEATRE, 1284
KNOXVILLE OPERA COMPANY, 1285
KNOXVILLE SYMPHONY ORCHESTRA, 1285
KNOXVILLE SYMPHONY YOUTH ORCHESTRA, 1285
KODACTORS, 1021
KODIAK ARTS COUNCIL, 22
KOHAV THEATRE FOUNDATION, 992
KOHLER FOUNDATION, INC., 1492
KOKOMO SYMPHONY, 498
"KOROYAR" FOLKLORE ENSEMBLE, 104
KRANNERT CENTER FOR THE PERFORMING ARTS, 476
KRANNERT CENTER FOR THE PERFORMING ARTS -
COLWELL PLAYHOUSE, 476
KRANNERT CENTER FOR THE PERFORMING ARTS -
FESTIVAL THEATRE, 476
KRANNERT CENTER FOR THE PERFORMING ARTS -
FOELLINGER GREAT HALL, 477
KRANNERT CENTER FOR THE PERFORMING ARTS - STUDIO
THEATRE, 476
KREEGER FINE ARTS AUDITORIUM, 597
KRONOS QUARTET, 167
K2 DANCE AND ARTS COMPANY, INC., 924
KUTZTOWN UNIVERSITY - SCHAEFFER AUDITORIUM, 1209
KUUMBWA JAZZ CENTER, 197
LA ARTS, 577
LA COMPANIA DE TEATRO DE ALBURQUERQUE, 849
LA CROSSE BOYCHOIR, THE, 1493
LA CROSSE CENTER, 1494
LA CROSSE SYMPHONY ORCHESTRA, 1493

LA FAMILLE BEAUDOIN - FAMILY GROUP, 1411
LA JOLLA CHAMBER MUSIC SOCIETY, 93
LA JOLLA PLAYHOUSE, 93
LA MAMA EXPERIMENTAL THEATRE CLUB, 972
LA MARCA AMERICAN VARIETY SINGERS, 209
LA MIRADA THEATRE FOR THE PERFORMING ARTS, 95
LA PENA CULTURAL CENTER, 62
LA SELLS STEWART CENTER, 1178
LABAN/BARTENIEFF INSTITUTE OF MOVEMENT
    STUDIES, 925
LACE/LOS ANGELES CONTEMPORARY EXHIBITIONS, 100
LADIES MUSICAL CLUB (LMC), 1462
LAFAYETTE COMMUNITY THEATRE, 558
LAFAYETTE CONCERT BAND, 558
LAFAYETTE SYMPHONY, 499
LAGOON OPERA HOUSE, 1395
LAGUNA CHAMBER MUSIC SOCIETY, 96
LAGUNA PLAYHOUSE, 96
LAKE CHARLES BALLET SOCIETY, 559
LAKE CHARLES CIVIC CENTER, 560
LAKE CHARLES CIVIC CENTER - COLISEUM, 560
LAKE CHARLES CIVIC CENTER - EXHIBITION HALL, 560
LAKE CHARLES CIVIC CENTER - ROSA HART THEATRE, 560
LAKE CHARLES LITTLE THEATRE, 560
LAKE CHARLES SOCIETY FOR BALLET JOYEUX, 559
LAKE CHELAN BACH FESTIVAL, 1448
LAKE FOREST SYMPHONY ASSOCIATION, INC., 460
LAKE GEORGE DINNER THEATRE, 902, 903
LAKE GEORGE JAZZ WEEKEND, 903
LAKE GEORGE OPERA FESTIVAL, 893
LAKE PLACID CENTER FOR THE ARTS, 903
LAKE PLACID CENTER FOR THE ARTS - THEATER, 903
LAKE SAINT CLAIR SYMPHONY ORCHESTRA, 692
LAKELAND CIVIC CENTER, 336
LAKELAND CIVIC CENTER - ARENA, 336
LAKELAND CIVIC CENTER - EXHIBITION HALL, 337
LAKELAND CIVIC CENTER - THEATRE, 337
LAKESHORE PLAYERS, 729
LAKESHORE PLAYHOUSE, 729
LAKESIDE ASSOCIATION, THE, 1134
LAKESIDE SYMPHONY, 1134
LAKEWOOD THEATRE COMPANY, 1182
LAMAR UNIVERSITY - LAMAR UNIVERSITY PROSCENIUM
    THEATRE, 1315
LAMAR UNIVERSITY - LAMAR UNIVERSITY STUDIO
    THEATRE, 1315
LAMB'S PLAYERS THEATRE, THE, 127
LAMB'S THEATRE, THE, 1000
LAMB'S THEATRE COMPANY LTD., THE, 972
LAMBUTH COLLEGE - LAMBUTH THEATRE, 1282
LAMP-LITE THEATER, 1377
LAMPLIGHTERS/OPERA WEST FOUNDATION, 169
LANCASTER CHORALE, THE, 1135
LANCASTER NEW YORK OPERA HOUSE, 904
LANDERS THEATRE, 766
LANEY COLLEGE THEATRE, 133
LANGFORD AUDITORIUM, 1298
LANSING CIVIC ARENA, 684
LAR LUBOVITCH DANCE COMPANY, 925
LAREDO PHILHARMONIC ORCHESTRA, 1371
LARIMER CHORAL SOCIETY, THE, 245
LARK SOCIETY FOR CHAMBER MUSIC, 581
LARRY RICHARDSON DANCE FOUNDATION, 926
LAS CRUCES COMMUNITY THEATRE, 852
LAS MASCARAS THEATRE, 342
LAS VEGAS CONVENTION AND VISITORS
    AUTHORITY-CASHMAN'S FIELD CENTER, 798
LAS VEGAS LITTLE THEATRE, 797
LATIN AMERICAN THEATRE ENSEMBLE, 973
LAUBINS, THE, 1522
LAURA DEAN DANCERS AND MUSICIANS, 926
LAURA INGALLS WILDER PAGEANT SOCIETY, 1268
LAUREL ARTS, INC./THE PHILIP DRESSLER CENTER FOR
    THE ARTS, 1239
LAUREL FESTIVAL OF THE ARTS, 1207
LAWRENCE ACADEMY THEATRE, 628
LAWRENCE UNIVERSITY - MUSIC-DRAMA CENTER, 1487
LAWRENCE WELK RESORT THEATRE, 79

LAWTON PHILHARMONIC ORCHESTRA, 1160
LE BALLET PETIT GUILD, 424
LE PETIT THEATRE DU VIEUX CARRE, 566
LEAGUE OF OFF-BROADWAY THEATRES AND
    PRODUCERS, 992
LEE CIVIC CENTER, 347
LEE CIVIC CENTER - ARENA, 347
LEE CIVIC CENTER - SMALL THEATER, 347
LEE HALL AUDITORIUM, 737
LEES MCRAE COLLEGE - HAYES AUDITORIUM, 1044
LEHIGH VALLEY CHAMBER ORCHESTRA, 1210
LEHMAN CENTER FOR THE PERFORMING ARTS, 1000
LENNOX MUNICIPAL BAND, 1269
L'ENSEMBLE, 860
L'ENSEMBLE DU MUSIQUE, 880
LES BALLETS TROCKADERO DE MONTE CARLO, 926
LESTER E. PALMER AUDITORIUM, 1310
LEVITT PAVILION FOR THE PERFOMING ARTS, 289
LEVITT PAVILION FOR THE PERFORMING ARTS, 289
LEWITZKY DANCE COMPANY, 101
LEXINGTON BALLET, 544
LEXINGTON CHILDREN'S THEATRE, 545
LEXINGTON OPERA HOUSE, 545
LEXINGTON PHILHARMONIC SOCIETY, 544
LIBERTY CENTER, 764
LIBERTY FREMONT CHAMBER SINGERS, 459
LIBRARY OF CONGRESS, 312
LIED CENTER FOR PERFORMING ARTS, THE, 786
LIED CENTER FOR THE PERFORMING ARTS, 787
LIEDERKRANZ OPERA THEATRE, 955
LIFELINE THEATRE, 438
LIGHT OPERA OF MANHATTAN, 955
LIGHT OPERA WORKS, 453
LILLIPUT ORCHESTRA, 1477
LIMA SYMPHONY ORCHESTRA, 1136
LIME KILN ARTS INCORPORATED, 1429
LIMELIGHT DINNER THEATRE, 356
LINCOLN ARTS COUNCIL, 1064
LINCOLN CENTER, 246
LINCOLN CENTER FOR THE CULTURAL ARTS, 509
LINCOLN CENTER FOR THE PERFORMING ARTS, 1000
LINCOLN CENTER FOR THE PERFORMING ARTS - ALICE
    TULLY HALL, 1000
LINCOLN CENTER FOR THE PERFORMING ARTS - AVERY
    FISHER HALL, 1000
LINCOLN CENTER FOR THE PERFORMING ARTS - THE
    JUILLIARD OPERA CENTER, 1000
LINCOLN CENTER FOR THE PERFORMING ARTS - THE
    JUILLIARD SCHOOL DRAMA WORKSHOP, 1001
LINCOLN CENTER FOR THE PERFORMING ARTS -
    METROPOLITAN OPERA HOUSE, 1001
LINCOLN CENTER FOR THE PERFORMING ARTS - MITZI E.
    NEWHOUSE THEATER, 1001
LINCOLN CENTER FOR THE PERFORMING ARTS - NEW
    YORK PUBLIC LIBRARY AUDITORIUM, 1001
LINCOLN CENTER FOR THE PERFORMING ARTS - NEW
    YORK STATE THEATER, 1001
LINCOLN CENTER FOR THE PERFORMING ARTS - PAUL
    RECITAL HALL, 1001
LINCOLN CENTER FOR THE PERFORMING ARTS - VIVIAN
    BEAUMONT THEATER, 1002
LINCOLN CENTER OUT-OF-DOORS, 992
LINCOLN CENTER THEATER, 973
LINCOLN CENTER'S MOSTLY MOZART FESTIVAL, 992
LINCOLN CITY BALLET COMPANY, 784
LINCOLN CIVIC EXPERIENCE/LINCOLN CIVIC
    ORCHESTRA, 784
LINCOLN COMMUNITY PLAYHOUSE, 786
LINCOLN FRIENDS OF CHAMBER MUSIC, 787
LINCOLN MIDWEST BALLET COMPANY, 784
LINCOLN OPERA, 431
LINCOLN SYMPHONY, 785
LINCOLN THEATER, 287
LINCOLN THEATRE CENTRE, 1451
LINCOLN YOUTH SYMPHONY ORCHESTRA, 785
LIONEL HAMPTON, CHEVRON JAZZ FESTIVAL, 415
LITHUANIAN FOLK DANCE GROUP OF BOSTON, 629
LITTLE BALLET THEATRE, 1176

LITTLE BROADWAY PRODUCTIONS, INC., 124
LITTLE COUNTRY THEATRE, 1085
LITTLE LYRIC OPERA THEATRE, 1220
LITTLE ORCHESTRA SOCIETY OF NEW YORK, THE, 944
LITTLE STAR THEATRE ASSOCIATION, THE, 1087
LITTLE THEATRE OF GASTONIA, 1056
LITTLE THEATRE OF NORFOLK, 1433, 1434
LITTLE THEATRE OF OWATONNA, 721
LITTLE THEATRE OF WINSTON-SALEM, THE, 1079
LIVE THEATRE, 454
LIVELY ARTS AT STANFORD UNIVERSITY, THE, 204
LIVESTOCK PLAYERS MUSICAL THEATRE, 1059
LIVING MASTERS SUBSCRIPTION SERIES, 1234
LIVING STAGE, 305
LIVING THEATRE, INC., THE, 973
LIZ LERMAN EXCHANGE, 298
LOBERO THEATRE, 195
LOEB DRAMA CENTER, 621
LOLA MONTES AND HER SPANISH DANCERS, 101
LONE STAR BALLET, 1305
LONG BEACH CIVIC LIGHT OPERA, 97
LONG BEACH COMMUNITY PLAYHOUSE - STAGE, 98
LONG BEACH CONVENTION AND ENTERTAINMENT
    CENTER, 99
LONG BEACH JEWISH COMMUNITY CENTER YOUTH
    SUMMER STOCK, 98
LONG BEACH OPERA, 97
LONG BEACH PLAYHOUSE - MAINSTAGE THEATRE, 99
LONG BEACH PLAYHOUSE - STUDIO THEATRE, 99
LONG BEACH SYMPHONY ORCHESTRA, 97
LONG CENTER FOR THE PERFORMING ARTS, 499
LONG ISLAND BAROQUE ENSEMBLE, 905
LONG ISLAND DANCE COMPANY, 1029
LONG ISLAND PHILHARMONIC, 906
LONG ISLAND UNIVERSITY - FINE ARTS THEATRE, 1028
LONG WHARF THEATRE, 272
LONG WHARF THEATRE - STAGE II, 273
LONGACRE THEATRE, 1002
LONGVIEW SYMPHONY ORCHESTRA, 1372
LONGWOOD GARDENS, 1208
LOOKING GLASS THEATRE, 1250
L'OPERA FRANCAIS DE NEW YORK, 954
LORETTA LIVINGSTON AND DANCERS, 101
LORRAINE HANSBERRY THEATER, 175
LOS ALAMOS CIVIC AUDITORIUM, 853
LOS ANGELES CHAMBER BALLET, 101
LOS ANGELES CHAMBER ORCHESTRA, 105
LOS ANGELES CHOREOGRAPHERS AND
    DANCERS, 102
LOS ANGELES CIVIC LIGHT OPERA, 110
LOS ANGELES CLASSICAL BALLET, 96
LOS ANGELES CONCERT OPERA ASSOCIATION, 64
LOS ANGELES COUNTY MUSEUM OF ART - LEO S. BING
    THEATER, 118
LOS ANGELES COUNTY MUSEUM OF ART: MUSIC
    PROGRAMS, 116
LOS ANGELES DOCTORS SYMPHONY, 64
LOS ANGELES FESTIVAL, 116
LOS ANGELES MASTER CHORALE ASSOCIATION, 106
LOS ANGELES MUSIC CENTER OPERA, 106
LOS ANGELES PHILHARMONIC ASSOCIATION, 105
LOS ANGELES THEATRE ACADEMY, THE, 111
LOS ANGELES THEATRE CENTER, 111, 118
LOS ANGELES THEATRE CENTER - THEATRE 2, 119
LOS ANGELES THEATRE CENTER - THEATRE 3, 119
LOS ANGELES THEATRE CENTER - THEATRE 4, 119
LOS ANGELES THEATRE CENTER - TOM BRADLEY
    THEATRE, 119
LOS ANGELES THEATRE WORKS, 213
LOTTE GOSLAR AND COMPANY, 286
LOUISIANA JAZZ FEDERATION, 563
LOUISIANA TECH - HOWARD AUDITORIUM CENTER FOR
    THE PERFORMING ARTS, 568
LOUISVILLE BACH SOCIETY, 547
LOUISVILLE BALLET, 546
LOUISVILLE CHORUS, THE, 548
LOUISVILLE MEMORIAL AUDITORIUM, 550
LOUISVILLE ORCHESTRA, THE, 547

LOUISVILLE YOUTH ORCHESTRA, 547
LOYOLA UNIVERSITY - LOUIS J. ROUSSEL PERFORMANCE
    HALL, 567
LOYOLA UNIVERSITY - MARQUETTE THEATRE, 567
LSU UNION THEATER, 556
LUBBOCK MEMORIAL CIVIC CENTER, 1373
LUBBOCK MEMORIAL CIVIC CENTER - BANQUET
    HALL, 1373
LUBBOCK MEMORIAL CIVIC CENTER - COLISEUM, 1373
LUBBOCK MEMORIAL CIVIC CENTER - EXHIBIT HALL, 1373
LUBBOCK MEMORIAL CIVIC CENTER - MUNICIPAL
    AUDITORIUM, 1373
LUBBOCK MEMORIAL CIVIC CENTER - THEATER, 1373
LUBBOCK SYMPHONY ORCHESTRA, 1372
LUCILLE BALL LITTLE THEATRE BUILDING, 901
LUCILLE LORTEL THEATRE, 1002
LUCINDA CHILDS DANCE COMPANY, 926
LUIS RIVERA SPANISH DANCE COMPANY, 927
LULA WASHINGTON CONTEMPORARY DANCE
    FOUNDATION, 102
LUNT-FONTANNE THEATRE, 1002
LUTCHER THEATER, 1378
LUTHER BURBANK CENTER FOR THE ARTS, 200
LUTHER BURBANK CENTER FOR THE ARTS - CONCERT
    CHAMBER, 201
LUTHER BURBANK CENTER FOR THE ARTS - EAST
    AUDITORIUM, 201
LUTHER BURBANK CENTER FOR THE ARTS - GOLD
    ROOM, 201
LUTHER BURBANK CENTER FOR THE ARTS - RUTH FINLEY
    PERSON MEMORIAL THEATRE, 201
LYCEUM REPERTORY COMPANY, 741
LYCEUM THEATRE, 741, 1002
LYNCHBURG FINE ARTS CENTER, 1429
LYNDHURST, 1034
LYNN CANAL COMMUNITY PLAYERS, 20
LYNN CITY HALL MEMORIAL AUDITORIUM, 631
LYNN DANCE COMPANY, 1494
LYNWOOD PERFORMING ARTS, 71
LYRIC CHAMBER ENSEMBLE, 693
LYRIC INC./LYRIC OPERA HOUSE, 592
LYRIC OPERA CENTER FOR AMERICAN ARTISTS, 431
LYRIC OPERA CLEVELAND, 1112
LYRIC OPERA OF CHICAGO, 431
LYRIC OPERA OF DALLAS, THE, 1327
LYRIC OPERA OF KANSAS CITY, 746
LYRIC STAGE, 611
LYRIC THEATRE, 750, 1396
LYRIC THEATRE OF OKLAHOMA, 1165
MABEL TAINTER MEMORIAL THEATER, 1502
MABEL TAINTER MEMORIAL THEATER BUILDING, 1502
MABOU MINES, 974
MACALLISTER, 496
MACAULEY THEATRE, 550
MACHIAS BAY CHAMBER CONCERTS, INC., 578
MACOMB CENTER FOR THE PERFORMING ARTS, 686
MACON SYMPHONY ORCHESTRA, INCORPORATED, 393
MACPHAIL CENTER FOR THE ARTS, 716, 718
MAD HATTERS EDUCATIONAL THEATRE, THE, 681
MAD RIVER THEATER WORKS, 1150 - 1151
MADAME CADILLAC DANCE THEATRE, 666
MADCAP PRODUCTIONS, 1104
MADISON AREA ARTS COUNCIL, 1270
MADISON BOYCHOIR, THE, 1498
MADISON CIVIC CENTER, 1500
MADISON CIVIC CENTER - ISTHMUS PLAYHOUSE, 1500
MADISON CIVIC CENTER - OSCAR MAYER THEATRE, 1500
MADISON JAZZ SOCIETY, 1496
MADISON - MORGAN CULTURAL CENTER, 394
MADISON MUSIC COLLECTIVE, 1496
MADISON OPERA, 1498
MADISON REPERTORY THEATRE, 1499
MADISON SCOTTISH COUNTRY DANCERS, 1495
MADISON SQUARE GARDEN, 1002
MADISON SYMPHONY ORCHESTRA, 1496
MADISON THEATRE GUILD, 1499
MADRIGAL SINGERS OF WILMINGTON, 294
MAELSTROM PERCUSSION ENSEMBLE, LTD., 877

MAGIC CIRCLE THEATER, THE, 633
MAGIC THEATRE, 175
MAGIC VALLEY SYMPHONY, 418
MAGICAL THEATRE COMPANY, 1095
MAIN SQUARE PLAYERS, 493
MAIN STREET THEATER, 1361
MAINE FESTIVAL, THE, 582
MAINE STATE MUSIC THEATER, 575
MAINSTAGE THEATRE COMPANY, 1180
MAJESTIC THEATRE, 822, 1003, 1335
MAKE A CIRCUS, 175
MALASHOCK DANCE AND COMPANY, 152
MALINI'S DANCES OF INDIA, 657
MAMOU CAJUN MUSIC FESTIVAL ASSOCIATION, 561
MANATEE PLAYERS/RIVERFRONT THEATRE, 317
MANCHESTER COLLEGE - CORDIER AUDITORIUM, 501
MANCHESTER MUSIC FESTIVAL, 1040, 1414
MANCHESTER MUSICAL PLAYERS, 266
MANCHESTER PIPE BAND, 279
MANCHESTER SYMPHONY ORCHESTRA/CHORALE, 266
MANDALA FOLK DANCE ENSEMBLE, 618
MANDELL WEISS PERFORMING ARTS CENTER, 94
MANHATTAN ARTS COUNCIL, 530
MANHATTAN BALLET FOUNDATION, 927
MANHATTAN MARIMBA QUARTET, 871
MANHATTAN THEATRE CLUB, 974, 1003
MANKATO STATE UNIVERSITY - ELIAS J. HALLING
    RECITAL HALL, 706
MANKATO SYMPHONY ORCHESTRA, 706
MANN MUSIC CENTER, 1227
MANN MUSIC CENTER, INC., 1225
MANNONI PERFORMING ARTS CENTER, 733
MANSFIELD PLAYHOUSE, 1138
MANSFIELD SYMPHONY SOCIETY, INC., 1138
MANTI TEMPLE GROUNDS AMPHITHEATRE, 1397
MAPLEWOOD COMMUNITY CENTER, 673
MARATHON COMMUNITY THEATRE, 338
MARCUS SCHULKIND DANCE COMPANY, 605
MARGARET JENKINS DANCE COMPANY, 164
MARGOLIS BROWN ADAPTORS, 873
MARGOT GRIMMER AMERICAN DANCE COMPANY, 458
MARIA BENITEZ SPANISH DANCE COMPANY, 853
MARIE HITCHCOCK PUPPET THEATRE IN BALBOA PARK,
    THE, 159
MARIEMONT PLAYERS, 1104
MARIETTA COLLEGE/CIVIC SYMPHONETTE, 1139
MARIN BALLET, THE, 190
MARIN CENTER, 192
MARIN CENTER - SHOWCASE THEATRE, 192
MARIN CENTER - VETERANS MEMORIAL AUDITORIUM, 192
MARIN COMMUNITY COLLEGE SYMPHONY, 92
MARIN SYMPHONY ASSOCIATION, 191
MARIN SYMPHONY YOUTH ORCHESTRA, 191
MARIN THEATRE COMPANY, 123
MARION COMMUNITY THEATER, 1140
MARION CULTURAL AND CIVIC CENTER, 462
MARION PHILHARMONIC ORCHESTRA, 500
MARK DE GARMO AND DANCERS, 927
MARK MORRIS DANCE GROUP, 927
MARK TWO DINNER THEATER, 350
MARKET HOUSE THEATRE, 552
MARKET SQUARE CONCERTS, 1206
MARLBORO CULTURAL AFFAIRS, 632
MARLBORO MUSIC FESTIVAL, 1414
MARLBORO SCHOOL OF MUSIC, 1218
MARQUIS, 1003
MARRIOTT'S LINCOLNSHIRE THEATRE, 460
MARSH ISLAND STAGE, 580
MARSHALL ARTISTS SERIES, 1481
MARSHALL CIVIC CENTER, 1375
MARSHALL PHILHARMONIC ORCHESTRA, 750
MARSHALL REGIONAL ARTS COUNCIL, 1374
MARSHALL SYMPHONY ORCHESTRA, 1374
MARSHALL THEATER AT THE CIVIC CENTER, 1375
MARSHALL UNIVERSITY - JOAN C. EDWARDS
    PLAYHOUSE, 1482
MARSHALL UNIVERSITY - SMITH RECITAL HALL, 1482
MARSHFIELD-WOOD COMMUNITY SYMPHONY, 1500

MARTHA BOWERS' DANCE THEATRE, 870
MARTHA GRAHAM DANCE COMPANY, 928
MARTHA GUINSBERG PAVILION, 886
MARTIN BECK THEATER, 1003
MARTIN COMMUNITY PLAYERS, 1076
MARTIN LUTHER KING JR. PERFORMING AND CULTURAL
    ARTS COMPLEX, 1126
MARTINSVILLE-HENRY COUNTY FESTIVAL OF OPERA, 1430
MARWICK - BOYD AUDITORIUM, 1199
MARY ANTHONY DANCE THEATRE-PHOENIX, 928
MARY GREEN SINGERS, THE, 1207
MARYCREST COLLEGE - UPHAM AUDITORIUM, 513
MARYLAND BALLET, THE, 587
MARYLAND HALL FOR THE CREATIVE ARTS, 585
MARYLAND HANDEL FESTIVAL, 593
MARYLAND SYMPHONY ORCHESTRA, 595
MARYLAND THEATRE, 595
MARYMOUNT MANHATTAN COLLEGE - MARYMOUNT
    MANHATTAN THEATRE, 1003
MARYVILLE COLLEGE, 1288
MASK AND BAUBLE DRAMATIC SOCIETY THEATER, 312
MASQUERADERS, THE, 1192
MASSACHUSETTS YOUTH WIND ENSEMBLE, 608
MASTER CHORALE OF ORANGE COUNTY, 72
MASTER SINGERS, THE, 630
MASTERWORKS CHORALE, 636
MATCHBOX CHILDREN'S THEATRE, 699
MATEEL COMMUNITY CENTER, INC., 144
MATTHEWS OPERA HOUSE, 1275
MATTHEWS OPERA HOUSE SOCIETY, 1274
MAUI ACADEMY OF PERFORMING ARTS, 407
MAUI SYMPHONY ORCHESTRA, 408
MAURICE LEVIN THEATER, 844
MAVERICK CONCERT HALL, 1040
MAVERICK CONCERTS, INC., 1039
MAXWELL C. KING CENTER FOR THE PERFORMING
    ARTS, 339
MAY BONFILS STANTON CENTER FOR THE PERFORMING
    ARTS, 242
MAY BONFILS STANTON CENTER FOR THE PERFORMING
    ARTS - LITTLE AUDITORIUM, 242
MAY BONFILS STANTON CENTER FOR THE PERFORMING
    ARTS - PROSCENIUM THEATRE, 242
MAY BONFILS STANTON CENTER FOR THE PERFORMING
    ARTS - STAGE 2, 242
MAYFAIR THEATRE/"SHEAR MADNESS", 439
MAYO CIVIC CENTER, 722
MAYO CIVIC CENTER - ARENA, 722
MAYO CIVIC CENTER - AUDITORIUM, 722
MAYO CIVIC CENTER - THEATRE, 722
MCALLEN PERFORMING ARTS, INC., 1376
MCCADDEN PLACE THEATRE, 88
MCCARTER THEATRE, 834
MCCLELLAND ARTS CENTER, 1451
MCHENRY COUNTY YOUTH ORCHESTRA, 448
MCKAY AUDITORIUM AT BRIGHAM YOUNG UNIVERSITY
    HAWAII, 408
MCMAHON MEMORIAL AUDITORIUM, 1161
MCMORRAN PLACE, 690
MCPHERSON COLLEGE - BROWN AUDITORIUM, 531
MEADOW BROOK MUSIC FESTIVAL, 690
MEADOW BROOK THEATRE, 690
MEANY HALL, 1464
MEANY HALL FOR THE PERFORMING ARTS, 1453
MEASURED BREATHS THEATRE COMPANY, 955
MECHANICS HALL, 652
MEDFORD CIVIC BALLET, 1183
MEET THE COMPOSER INC., 945
MELBOURNE AUDITORIUM, 339
MELBOURNE CHAMBER MUSIC SOCIETY, 330
MELBOURNE CIVIC THEATRE, 339
MELROSE MOTION COMPANY, 1495
MELROSE ORCHESTRAL ASSOCIATION, 633
MELROSE THEATRE ASSOCIATION, 111
MEMORIAL AUDITORIUM, 525, 1393
MEMORIAL AUDITORIUM AND CONVENTION
    CENTER, 532
MEMPHIS CHILDREN'S THEATRE, 1290, 1292

MEMPHIS COMMUNITY PLAYERS, 751
MEMPHIS COOK CONVENTION CENTER COMPLEX, 1292
MEMPHIS COOK CONVENTION CENTER COMPLEX - DIXON-MYERS HALL, 1292
MEMPHIS COOK CONVENTION CENTER COMPLEX - VINCENT DEFRANK HALL, 1292
MEMPHIS IN MAY INTERNATIONAL FESTIVAL, 1291
MEMPHIS SYMPHONY, 1289
MEMPHIS YOUTH SYMPHONY ORCHESTRA, 1289
MENDOCINO ART CENTER - HELEN SCHOENI THEATER, 123
MENDOCINO DANCE SERIES, 122
MENDOCINO MUSIC FESTIVAL ASSOCIATION, 122
MENDOTA COMMUNITY THEATRE, 463
MERCE CUNNINGHAM DANCE COMPANY, 928
MERCE CUNNINGHAM DANCE STUDIO, 1003
MERCY COLLEGE - LECTURE HALL, 886
MEREDITH MONK - THE HOUSE FOUNDATION FOR THE ARTS, 928
MERIDIAN COMMUNITY COLLEGE - THEATRE, 737
MERKIN CONCERT HALL AT ELAINE KAUFMAN CONCERT CENTER, 1004
MEROLA OPERA PROGRAM, 170
MERRIAM THEATER, 1227
MERRIMACK REPERTORY THEATRE, 631
MERRY-GO-ROUND PLAYHOUSE, 863
MESA COLLEGE - WALTER WALKER AUDITORIUM, 248
MESA COMMUNITY CENTER, 27
MESA COMMUNITY CENTER - AMPHITHEATRE, 28
MESA COMMUNITY CENTER - CENTENNIAL HALL, 28
MESA COMMUNITY CENTER - CONFERENCE CENTER, 28
MESOGHIOS DANCE TROUP, 1503
MESQUITE COMMUNITY BAND, 1376
MESQUITE COMMUNITY THEATRE, 1377
MESSIAH FESTIVAL OF MUSIC, 529
METRO DANCERS, 1185
METRO LYRIC OPERA, 815
METRO THEATER COMPANY/THE CENTER FOR CREATIVE ARTS, 758
METROPOLITAN GREEK CHORALE, THE, 956
METROPOLITAN MUSEUM CONCERTS AND LECTURES, 992
METROPOLITAN OPERA, 956
METROPOLITAN ORCHESTRA OF SAINT LOUIS, 755
METROPOLITAN PERFORMING ARTS CENTER, THE, 1467
METTAWEE THEATRE COMPANY, 1024
MIAMI BALLET COMPANY, 364
MIAMI CHAMBER SYMPHONY, 341
MIAMI CITY BALLET, 344
MIAMI DANCE THEATRE, 340
MIAMI WIND QUINTET, 1144
MICHELLE AVA AND COMPANY, 298
MICHIGAN BACH FESTIVAL, 666
MICHIGAN OPERA THEATRE, 667
MICHIGAN RENAISSANCE FESTIVAL, 663
MICHIGAN THEATER, 660
MID AMERICA DANCE COMPANY, 754
MID-ATLANTIC CENTER FOR THE ARTS, 817
MID-COLUMBIA SYMPHONY, 1452
MID HUDSON BALLET COMPANY, 889
MID-HUDSON CIVIC CENTER, 1017
MIDDLEBURY COLLEGE - WRIGHT THEATRE, 1415
MIDLAND CENTER FOR THE ARTS, 685
MIDLAND COMMUNITY CONCERT SOCIETY, 685
MIDLAND-ODESSA SYMPHONY AND CHORALE, INC., 1377
MIDLAND SYMPHONY ORCHESTRA, 684
MIDSUMMER MOZART, 179
MIDWAY THEATRE, 472
MILL MOUNTAIN THEATRE, 1440
MILL MOUNTAIN THEATRE COMPANY, 1439
MILL VALLEY CHAMBER MUSIC SOCIETY, 123
MILLBROOK PLAYHOUSE, 1212
MILLER AUDITORIUM, 1238
MILLER OUTDOOR THEATRE, 1366
MILLIGAN COLLEGE - DERTHICK THEATRE, 1293
MILLIGAN COLLEGE - SEEGER CHAPEL CONCERT HALL, 1293
MILLIKIN UNIVERSITY OPERA THEATRE, 450
MILLS COLLEGE CONCERT HALL, 134

MILWAUKEE AREA TECHNICAL COLLEGE - COOLEY AUDITORIUM, 1510
MILWAUKEE BALLET, 1504
MILWAUKEE CHAMBER ORCHESTRA, 1504
MILWAUKEE CHAMBER THEATRE, 1508
MILWAUKEE OPERA COMPANY, 1506
MILWAUKEE PERFORMING ARTS CENTER, 1510
MILWAUKEE PUBLIC THEATRE, 1508
MILWAUKEE REPERTORY THEATER, 1508
MILWAUKEE SYMPHONY ORCHESTRA, 1505
MILWAUKEE YOUTH SYMPHONY ORCHESTRA, 1505
MIMI GARRARD DANCE COMPANY, 929
MINETTA LANE THEATRE, 1004
MINNEAPOLIS CHAMBER SYMPHONY, 709
MINNEAPOLIS POPS ORCHESTRA, 709
MINNESOTA CHORALE, THE, 711
MINNESOTA DANCE THEATRE AND SCHOOL, 707
MINNESOTA OPERA, THE, 711
MINNESOTA ORCHESTRA, 717
MINNESOTA ORCHESTRAL ASSOCIATION, 710
MINNESOTA STATE BAND, 724
MINNESOTA YOUTH SYMPHONIES, 710
MINOT CHAMBER CHORALE, 1088
MINOT COMMUNITY OPERA, 1088
MINOT SYMPHONY ASSOCIATION, 1087
MINSKOFF THEATRE, 1004
MIRANA MIDDLE EASTERN DANCE COMPANY, 51
MIRROR REPERTORY COMPANY, 974
MISHLER THEATRE, 1195
MISSISSIPPI OPERA ASSOCIATION, 735
MISSISSIPPI SYMPHONY ORCHESTRA, 734
MISSOULA MENDELSSOHN CLUB, 777
MISSOULA SYMPHONY ASSOCIATION, 776
MISSOURI REPERTORY THEATRE, 747
MISSOURI SYMPHONY SOCIETY, 743
MISSOURI THEATRE, 743
MITCHELL MUNICIPAL BAND, 1270
MITKOF MUMMERS, 23
MIXED BLOOD THEATRE COMPANY, 714
MJT DANCE COMPANY, 605
M.K. BROWN AUDITORIUM, 1379
M.M. COLBERT, 1495
MOBERLY COMMUNITY THEATRE, 752
MOBILE CIVIC CENTER, 9
MOBILE CIVIC CENTER - ARENA, 9
MOBILE CIVIC CENTER - EXPOSITION HALL, 9
MOBILE CIVIC CENTER - THEATRE, 9
MOBILE OPERA, 8
MOBILE THEATRE GUILD, 8, 9
MODESTO CIVIC BALLET THEATRE, 124
MODESTO JUNIOR COLLEGE CABARET, 125
MODESTO SYMPHONY, 124
MOHAWK PLAYERS, 863
MOHAWK TRAIL CONCERTS, 643
MOHAWK VALLEY CENTER FOR THE ARTS, 905
MOLE END PUPPETRY PRODUCTIONS INC., 602
MOLINE BOYS CHOIR, THE, 463
MOMENTUM DANCE COMPANY, 340
MOMIX, 929
MONADNOCK MUSIC, 811
MONMOUTH CIVIC CHORUS, 835
MONROE CIVIC CENTER, 563
MONROE CIVIC CENTER - ARENA, 563
MONROE CIVIC CENTER - THEATER, 563
MONROE SYMPHONY ORCHESTRA, 562
MONTANA BALLET COMPANY, 770
MONTANA CHORALE, 772
MONTANA REP, THE, 777
MONTCLAIR CIVIC CENTER - STARLITE PATIO THEATRE, 125
MONTCLAIR STATE COLLEGE - MEMORIAL AUDITORIUM, 841
MONTCLAIRE STRING QUARTET, 1477
MONTEREY COUNTY SYMPHONY, 69
MONTEREY JAZZ FESTIVAL, 126
MONTGOMERY BALLET, 9
MONTGOMERY COUNTY'S MEMORIAL HALL, 1132
MONTGOMERY SYMPHONY ORCHESTRA, 10

MONTICELLO OPERA HOUSE, 345
MONTPELIER THEATRE GUILD, 1416
MONTREUX ATLANTA MUSIC FESTIVAL, 384
MONTREUX DETROIT JAZZ FESTIVAL - DETROIT
   RENAISSANCE FOUNDATION, 670
MOODY CIVIC CENTER - EXHIBITION HALL, 1351
MOORE AUDITORIUM, 1065
MOORE COMMUNITY BAND, 1045
MOORESVILLE COMMUNITY THEATRE, 1066
MOORHEAD STATE UNIVERSITY, 719
MORCA FOUNDATION OF THE DANCE, 1445
MORDINE AND COMPANY DANCE THEATRE, 425
MORGAN-WIXSON THEATRE, 200
MORMON MIRACLE PAGEANT, 1397
MORMON TABERNACLE CHOIR, 1403
MORRIS CIVIC AUDITORIUM, 504
MORRISTOWN THEATRE GUILD, 1293
MORTON H. MEYERSON SYMPHONY CENTER - EUGENE
   MCDERMOTT CONCERT HALL, THE, 1335
MOSAIC, 230
MOUNT AIRY FINE ARTS CENTER/ANDY GRIFFITH
   PLAYHOUSE, 1067
MOUNT BAKER THEATRE, 1446
MOUNT DESERT FESTIVAL OF CHAMBER MUSIC, 579
MOUNT WASHINGTON VALLEY THEATRE COMPANY, 811
MOUNTAIN PLAYHOUSE, 1207
MOUSE RIVER PLAYERS, 1088
MOVEMENT THEATRE INTERNATIONAL, 1222
MOZART FESTIVAL ORCHESTRA, 945
MOZART ON THE SQUARE, 1212
MUCKENTHALER CULTURAL CENTER, 83
MUHLENBERG COMMUNITY THEATRE, 543
MULE BARN THEATRE, 766
MULE BARN THEATRE OF TARKIO COLLEGE, 766
MULTI-CULTURAL MUSIC AND ART FOUNDATION OF
   NORTHRIDGE, 129
MULTIGRAVITATIONAL AERODANCE GROUP, 929
MUNCIE SYMPHONY ORCHESTRA, 500
MUNICIPAL ART GALLERY - GALLERY THEATER, 119
MUNICIPAL AUDITORIUM, 1386
MUNICIPAL THEATER ASSOCIATION OF SAINT LOUIS, 761
MUNSON-WILLIAMS-PROCTOR INSTITUTE PERFORMING
   ARTS DIVISION, 1036
MUNTU DANCE THEATRE, 425
MUNY, THE, 762
MURRAY CIVIC MUSIC ASSOCIATION, 551
MURRAY STATE UNIVERSITY - LOVETT AUDITORIUM, 551
MUSIC ACADEMY OF THE WEST, 193
MUSIC AND ARTS INSTITUTE, 181
MUSIC AT GRETNA, 1213
MUSIC BEFORE 1800, INC., 945
MUSIC BOX, 1004
MUSIC CENTER OF LOS ANGELES COUNTY, THE, 116, 119
MUSIC CENTER OF LOS ANGELES COUNTY - AHMANSON
   THEATER, THE, 120
MUSIC CENTER OF LOS ANGELES COUNTY - DOROTHY
   CHANDLER PAVILION, THE, 120
MUSIC CENTER OF LOS ANGELES COUNTY - MARK TAPER
   FORUM, THE, 120
MUSIC FESTIVAL OF ARKANSAS, 45
MUSIC FROM ANGEL FIRE, 851
MUSIC FROM BEAR VALLEY, 58
MUSIC FROM SALEM, 880
MUSIC FROM STAN HYWET, 1092
MUSIC HALL, 1367
MUSIC HALL, THE, 813
MUSIC HALL ARTIST SERIES, 353
MUSIC HALL AT FAIR PARK, 1336
MUSIC HALL CENTER FOR THE PERFORMING ARTS, 671
MUSIC IN DEERFIELD, 624
MUSIC IN THE MOUNTAINS, 127
MUSIC IN THE MOUNTAINS, FESTIVAL OF MUSIC AT
   PURGATORY, 243
MUSIC MOUNTAIN, 260
MUSIC OF THE BAROQUE, 428
MUSIC PROJECTS HONOLULU, 403
MUSIC SOCIETY, MIDLAND CENTER FOR THE ARTS, 685
MUSIC TENT, 222

MUSIC THEATRE GROUP AT LENOX ARTS CENTER, 974
MUSIC-THEATRE GROUP, INC., 956
MUSIC THEATRE OF WICHITA, 536
MUSICA ANTIGUA DE ALBUQUERQUE, 848
MUSICA DE CAMARA, INC., 945
MUSICA SACRA, 956
MUSICAL AMERICA, 127
MUSICAL THEATRE WORKS, 975
MUSICAL TRADITIONS INC., 175
MUSICORDA SUMMER STRING PROGRAM AND FESTIVAL,
   THE, 644
MUSKOGEE LITTLE THEATRE, 1161
NAJWA DANCE CORPS, 425
NANCY HAUSER DANCE COMPANY AND SCHOOL, 707
NANCY KARP AND DANCERS, 78
NANETTE BEARDEN CONTEMPORARY DANCE THEATRE,
   THE, 930
NAPA VALLEY OPERA HOUSE, 126
NAPA VALLEY SYMPHONY, 126
NAPERVILLE-NORTH CENTRAL COLLEGE PERFORMING
   ARTS ASSOCIATION, 464
NAROPA INSTITUTE, THE, 227
NASHVILLE ACADEMY THEATRE, 1296
NASHVILLE BALLET, 1294
NASHVILLE CITY BALLET, 1294
NASHVILLE CONTEMPORARY BALLET COMPANY, 1294
NASHVILLE CONVENTION CENTER, 1298
NASHVILLE OPERA, 1295
NASHVILLE SYMPHONY ASSOCIATION, 1295
NASHVILLE YOUTH SYMPHONY, 1295
NASSAU SYMPHONY SOCIETY, INC., 1035
NAT HORNE MUSICAL THEATRE, 975
NATIONAL - LOUIS UNIVERSITY'S WEINSTEIN CENTER
   FOR THE PERFORMING ARTS, 455
NATIONAL BALLET/NEW JERSEY, 828
NATIONAL BLACK ARTS FESTIVAL, 384
NATIONAL BLACK THEATRE, 975
NATIONAL BLACK TOURING CIRCUIT, 976
NATIONAL CHAMBER ORCHESTRA SOCIETY, INC., 597
NATIONAL DANCE INSTITUTE, 930
NATIONAL GALLERY OF ART/CONCERT SERIES, 308
NATIONAL GALLERY ORCHESTRA, 300
NATIONAL GRAND OPERA, 891
NATIONAL IMPROVISATIONAL THEATRE, 976
NATIONAL LUTHERAN CHOIR, 711
NATIONAL LYRIC OPERA COMPANY, 302
NATIONAL MARIONETTE THEATRE, 1410
NATIONAL MUSICAL ARTS, 300
NATIONAL OPERA COMPANY, 1068
NATIONAL ORCHESTRAL ASSOCIATION INC., 946
NATIONAL REPERTORY ORCHESTRA, 236
NATIONAL SHAKESPEARE COMPANY, 976
NATIONAL SYMPHONY ORCHESTRA ASSOCIATION, 300
NATIONAL THEATRE, 305, 312
NATIONAL THEATRE OF THE DEAF, THE, 257
NAZARETH COLLEGE - NAZARETH ARTS CENTER, 1022
NAZARETH COLLEGE ARTS CENTER, 1021
NEAL S. BLAISDELL CENTER, 406
NEAL S. BLAISDELL CENTER - ARENA, 406
NEAL S. BLAISDELL CENTER - CONCERT HALL, 406
NEAL S. BLAISDELL CENTER - WAIKIKI SHELL, 406
NEBRASKA CHAMBER ORCHESTRA, 785
NEBRASKA REPERTORY THEATRE, 786
NEBRASKA THEATRE CARAVAN, 792
NEBRASKA WIND SYMPHONY, 788
NEDERLANDER THEATRE, 1004
NEGRO ENSEMBLE COMPANY, 976
NEIGHBORHOOD PLAYHOUSE, 391
NEIL SIMON THEATRE, 1004
NEODESHA ARTS ASSOCIATION, 531
NETA PULVERMACHER AND DANCERS, 930
NETTLE CREEK PLAYERS, 493
NEVA RUSSIAN DANCE ENSEMBLE, 164
NEVADA DANCE THEATRE, 796
NEVADA OPERA ASSOCIATION, 799
NEVADA SYMPHONY ORCHESTRA, 796, 797
NEVERS' 2ND REGIMENT BAND, 803
NEW AMERICAN THEATER, 472

NEW AMSTERDAM SINGERS, 957
NEW ARTISTS PIANO QUARTET, 360
NEW ARTISTS STRING QUARTET, 360
NEW ARTS PROGRAM, 1209
NEW BALLET SCHOOL, THE, 930
NEW BRITAIN SYMPHONY ORCHESTRA, 268
NEW BRUNSWICK CULTURAL CENTER, INC., 829
NEW CENTURY PLAYERS, 211
NEW CITY THEATER, THE, 1459
NEW CLEVELAND OPERA COMPANY, 1112
NEW CONSERVATORY CHILDRENS THEATRE COMPANY
    AND SCHOOL, THE, 175
NEW DANCE GROUP STUDIO INC., 931
NEW DANCE PERFORMANCE LAB, 708
NEW DAY REPERTORY COMPANY, INC., 1017
NEW DRAMATISTS, 977, 1005
NEW ENGLAND LYRIC OPERETTA, 281
NEW ENGLAND PHILHARMONIC, 619
NEW FEDERAL THEATRE, 977
NEW FREEDOM THEATRE, 1223
NEW HAMPSHIRE MUSIC FESTIVAL, 803
NEW HAMPSHIRE PERFORMING ARTS CENTER, 808
NEW HAMPSHIRE PHILHARMONIC ORCHESTRA, 807
NEW HAMPSHIRE SYMPHONY ORCHESTRA, 808
NEW HAVEN CIVIC ORCHESTRA, 270
NEW HAVEN SYMPHONY ORCHESTRA, 271
NEW HOPE OUTDOOR THEATRE, 719
NEW JERSEY BALLET COMPANY, 844
NEW JERSEY CHAMBER MUSIC SOCIETY, 826
NEW JERSEY DANCE THEATRE, 824
NEW JERSEY SHAKESPEARE FESTIVAL, 824
NEW JERSEY STATE MUSEUM AUDITORIUM, 840
NEW JERSEY STATE OPERA, 831
NEW JERSEY SYMPHONY ORCHESTRA, 831
NEW LONDON BARN PLAYHOUSE, 810
NEW LONDON PLAYERS, 810
NEW MEXICO BALLET COMPANY, THE, 847
NEW MEXICO GAY MEN'S CHORUS, 849
NEW MEXICO REP, 856
NEW MEXICO REPERTORY THEATRE, 850
NEW MEXICO STATE UNIVERSITY - AMERICAN
    SOUTHWEST THEATRE, 852
NEW MEXICO SYMPHONY ORCHESTRA, 848
NEW MUSIC CONSORT, INC., 946
NEW MUSIC-THEATER ENSEMBLE, 714
NEW MUSIK DIRECTIONS, 573
NEW ORCHESTRA OF WESTCHESTER, THE, 895
NEW ORLEANS BALLET ASSOCIATION, 563
NEW ORLEANS CONCERT BAND, 564
NEW ORLEANS FRIENDS OF MUSIC, 564
NEW ORLEANS JAZZ AND HERITAGE FESTIVAL, 566
NEW ORLEANS MUNICIPAL AUDITORIUM, 567
NEW ORLEANS OPERA ASSOCIATION, 565
NEW ORLEANS THEATRE OF THE PERFORMING ARTS, 567
NEW PERFORMANCE GALLERY OF SAN FRANCISCO, 182
NEW PERFORMANCE SERIES/NORTHWEST NEW
    WORKS, 1454
NEW PERFORMING DANCE COMPANY, 1053
NEW PHOENIX, THE, 651
NEW PLAYWRIGHTS' PROGRAM - UNIVERSITY OF
    ALABAMA, 11
NEW RAFT THEATER COMPANY, THE, 977
NEW REPERTORY DANCE COMPANY, 1284
NEW ROSE THEATRE, 1189
NEW SONG QUINTET (PROJECT), THE, 946
NEW STAGE THEATRE, 735
NEW THEATER COMPANY, THE, 532
NEW THEATRE, 319, 611
NEW THEATRE, THE, 759
NEW TUNERS THEATRE, 439
NEW WORLD SYMPHONY, 344
NEW YEAR'S FEST, 682
NEW YORK BAROQUE DANCE COMPANY, THE, 931
NEW YORK CHAMBER ENSEMBLE, 946
NEW YORK CHORAL SOCIETY, 957
NEW YORK CITY BALLET, 931
NEW YORK CITY OPERA, 957
NEW YORK CITY OPERA NATIONAL COMPANY, 958

NEW YORK CONCERT SINGERS, THE, 958
NEW YORK CONSORT OF VIOLS, 946
NEW YORK GILBERT AND SULLIVAN PLAYERS, 958
NEW YORK HARP ENSEMBLE, 947
NEW YORK INTERNATIONAL FESTIVAL OF THE ARTS,
    THE, 993
NEW YORK NEW MUSIC ENSEMBLE, 947
NEW YORK PHILHARMONIC, 947
NEW YORK PHILOMUSICA CHAMBER ENSEMBLE, 948
NEW YORK POPS ORCHESTRA, 948
NEW YORK SHAKESPEARE FESTIVAL, 977
NEW YORK STATE OFFICE OF GENERAL SERVICES, 1037
NEW YORK STATE THEATER INSTITUTE, THE, 860
NEW YORK STREET THEATRE CARAVAN, 900
NEW YORK THEATRE WORKSHOP, 978
NEW YORK VIRTUOSO SINGERS, THE, 1028
NEW YORK YOUTH SYMPHONY, 948
NEW YORK'S ENSEMBLE FOR EARLY MUSIC, 948
NEWARK BOYS CHORUS, 831
NEWARK PERFORMING ARTS CORPORATION/NEWARK
    SYMPHONY HALL, 831
NEWARK SYMPHONY HALL, 832
NEWARK SYMPHONY ORCHESTRA, 292
NEWBERRY COLLEGE THEATRE, 1265
NEWBURYPORT FAMILY YMCA, 635
NEWGATE THEATER, 1250
NEWINGTON CHILDREN'S THEATRE, 275
NEWPORT MUSIC FESTIVAL, 1247
NEWTON SYMPHONY ORCHESTRA, 636
NEXT ACT THEATRE, 1509
NEXT THEATRE COMPANY, 454
NIKOLAIS AND MURRAY LOUIS DANCE COMPANY, 931
NINE O'CLOCK PLAYERS, 111
NINETY MILES OFF BROADWAY, 908
NKYIMKYIM STORY THEATRE, 39
NO THEATRE, 637
NOB HILL MASONIC CENTER, 182
NORFOLK CHAMBER CONSORT, 1431
NORFOLK CHAMBER MUSIC FESTIVAL - YALE SUMMER
    SCHOOL OF MUSIC, 276
NORFOLK SCOPE CULTURAL AND CONVENTION
    CENTER, 1434
NORFOLK SCOPE CULTURAL AND CONVENTION CENTER -
    ARENA, 1434
NORFOLK SCOPE CULTURAL AND CONVENTION CENTER -
    CHRYSLER HALL, 1434
NORRIS CULTURAL ARTS CENTER, 473
NORRIS THEATRE FOR THE PERFORMING ARTS, 147
NORTH AMERICAN NEW MUSIC FESTIVAL, 879
NORTH CAROLINA BLACK REPERTORY COMPANY, 1079
NORTH CAROLINA BLUMENTHAL PERFORMING ARTS
    CENTER, 1051
NORTH CAROLINA DANCE THEATER, 1048
NORTH CAROLINA JAZZ FESTIVAL, 1077
NORTH CAROLINA SCHOOL OF THE ARTS - ROGER L.
    STEVENS CENTER FOR THE PERFORMING ARTS,
    THE, 1080
NORTH CAROLINA SHAKESPEARE FESTIVAL, THE, 1062
NORTH CAROLINA SYMPHONY, 1068
NORTH CAROLINA THEATRE, THE, 1069
NORTH CENTRAL ARKANSAS CONCERT ASSOCIATION, 47
NORTH COAST REPERTORY THEATRE, 203
NORTH COUNTRY CENTER FOR THE ARTS, 807
NORTH COUNTRY CHAMBER PLAYERS, 805
NORTH COUNTRY CHORUS, 1419
NORTH IOWA COMMUNITY AUDITORIUM, 519
NORTH LAKE TAHOE SYMPHONY ASSOCIATION, 795
NORTH SHORE MUSIC THEATRE, 604
NORTH SHORE PHILHARMONIC ORCHESTRA, 632
NORTH STAR DANCE FOUNDATION, 17
NORTH STAR OPERA, 725
NORTH/SOUTH CONSONANCE, INC., 949
NORTHEAST LOUISIANA UNIVERSITY CONCERTS, 562
NORTHEASTERN JUNIOR COLLEGE THEATRE, 252
NORTHEASTERN PENNSYLVANIA PHILHARMONIC, 1195
NORTHERN ARIZONA AUDITORIUM - ARDREY MEMORIAL
    AUDITORIUM, 26
NORTHERN DELAWARE ORATORIO SOCIETY, 294

NORTHLAND PINES HIGH SCHOOL, 1488
NORTHLIGHT THEATRE AT THE CORONET, 454
NORTHROP DANCE SERIES, 717
NORTHSIDE THEATRE COMPANY, THE, 186
NORTHWEST CHAMBER ORCHESTRA, 1455
NORTHWEST FLORIDA BALLET, 327
NORTHWEST FOLKLIFE, 1462
NORTHWEST INDIANA SYMPHONY SOCIETY, 500
NORTHWEST MISSOURI STATE UNIVERSITY - CHARLES
    JOHNSON THEATRE, 751
NORTHWEST MISSOURI STATE UNIVERSITY - MARY LINN
    PERFORMING ARTS CENTER, 751
NORTHWEST MISSOURI STATE UNIVERSITY PERFORMING
    ARTS SERIES, 751
NORTHWEST SYMPHONIC POPS ORCHESTRA, 338
NORTHWEST SYMPHONY ORCHESTRA, 451
NORTHWESTERN COLLEGE, 519
NORTHWOOD ORCHESTRA, 685
NORTON CENTER FOR THE ARTS, 541
NORWALK SYMPHONY SOCIETY, 276
NORWALK YOUTH SYMPHONY, 276
NUTMEG BALLET COMPANY, 283
NW PUPPET CENTER, 1460
OAK ACRES AMPHITHEATRE, 1349
OAK PARK CIVIC BALLET COMPANY, 465
OAK PARK FESTIVAL THEATRE, 465
OAK RIDGE CIVIC MUSIC ASSOCIATION, 1300
OAK RIDGE COMMUNITY PLAYHOUSE, 1299, 1300
OAK RIDGE SYMPHONY ORCHESTRA, 1299
OAKDALE THEATRE, 284
OAKLAND BALLET, 131
OAKLAND CIVIC THEATRE, 132
OAKLAND ENSEMBLE THEATRE, 132
OAKLAND FESTIVAL BALLET COMPANY, 691
OAKLAND JAZZ ALLIANCE, 133
OAKLAND SUMMER THEATRE, 132
OAKLAND YOUTH CHORUS, 131
OBERLIN BAROQUE ENSEMBLE, 1143
OBERLIN COMMUNITY CHAMBER SINGERS, 1143
OCCIDENTAL COLLEGE - THORNE HALL, 120
OCCIDENTAL COLLEGE ARTIST SERIES, 117
OCEAN CENTER, 321
OCEAN CENTER - ARENA, 322
OCEAN CENTER - CONFERENCE CENTER, 322
OCEAN CITY CONVENTION CENTER, 596
OCEAN COUNTY CENTER FOR THE ARTS - STRAND
    THEATRE, 822
OCHEAMI, 1454
ODC/SAN FRANCISCO, 164
ODYSSEY CHAMBER PLAYERS, INC., 949
ODYSSEY THEATRE ENSEMBLE, 112
OFF-BROADWAY MUSICAL THEATRE, 719
OFFICE OF CULTURAL AFFAIRS, 1424
OFFICE OF PUBLIC EVENTS, 140
OFFSTAGE THEATRE, 1425
OGDENSBURG COMMAND PERFORMANCES, 1011
OGLEBAY INSTITUTE, 1485
OGUNQUIT PLAYHOUSE, 580
OHIO BALLET, 1091
OHIO CHAMBER ORCHESTRA, 1111
OHIO LYRIC THEATRE, 1146
OHIO OUTDOOR HISTORICAL DRAMA ASSOCIATION, 1141
OHIO STATE UNIVERSITY - STADIUM II THEATRE, 1126
OHIO STATE UNIVERSITY - THURBER THEATRE, 1126
OHIO THEATRE, 978, 1127, 1149
OHIO UNIVERSITY - PATIO THEATER, 1095
OHIO UNIVERSITY - SCHOOL OF MUSIC, 1095
OHIO VALLEY BRASS QUINTET, 1137
OINKARI BASQUE DANCERS, 411
OJAI FESTIVAL BOWL, 134
OJAI FESTIVALS, 134
OK MOZART INTERNATIONAL FESTIVAL, 1158
OKLAHOMA CITY PHILHARMONIC ORCHESTRA, 1164
OKLAHOMA CITY UNIVERSITY, 1166
OKLAHOMA CITY UNIVERSITY - BURG THEATRE, 1166
OKLAHOMA CITY UNIVERSITY - KIRKPATRICK
    AUDITORIUM, 1166
OKLAHOMA CITY ZOO AMPHITHEATRE, 1166

OKLAHOMA COMMUNITY THEATRE ASSOCIATION, 1165
OKLAHOMA FESTIVAL BALLET, 1162
OKLAHOMA OPERA AND MUSIC THEATER
    COMPANY, 1164
OKOBOJI SUMMER THEATRE, 520
OLD AUDITORIUM, 509
OLD BASTROP OPERA HOUSE, 1312
OLD COLONY PLAYERS, 1075
OLD CREAMERY THEATRE, THE, 517
OLD CREAMERY THEATRE COMPANY, THE, 517
OLD FORT RUGER THEATRE, 406
OLD GLOBE THEATRE, 156
OLD JAIL ART CENTER, 1305
OLD LOG THEATER, 704
OLD OPERA HOUSE COMPANY, THE, 1476
OLD OPERA HOUSE PLAYERS, 1269
OLD SLOCUM HOUSE THEATRE COMPANY, 1471
OLD TIMERS CONCERT, 778
OLD TOWN PLAYHOUSE, 694
OLDCASTLE THEATRE COMPANY, 1409
OLE OLSEN MEMORIAL THEATRE, 501
OLGA DUNN DANCE COMPANY, 628
OLNEY THEATRE/NATIONAL PLAYERS, 596
OLYMPIA SYMPHONY ORCHESTRA, 1452
OLYMPIC BALLET THEATRE, 1448
OMAHA AREA YOUTH ORCHESTRAS, 789
OMAHA BALLET COMPANY AND SCHOOL, 788
OMAHA CIVIC AUDITORIUM - MUSIC HALL, 793
OMAHA COMMUNITY PLAYHOUSE, 792
OMAHA INTERNATIONAL FOLK DANCERS, 794
OMAHA MAGIC THEATRE, 792
OMAHA MODERN DANCE COLLECTIVE, 788
OMAHA SYMPHONY ASSOCIATION, 789
OMILAMI PRODUCTIONS/PEOPLE'S SURVIVAL
    THEATRE, 382
OMNI AUDITORIUM - BROWARD COMMUNITY
    COLLEGE, 318
ONE O'CLOCK LAB BAND, 1338
ONE REID STREET THEATRE, 560
1000 ISLANDS FESTIVAL BALLET COMPANY, INC., 1036
ONE WAY PUPPETS, 324
O'NEILL THEATER CENTER, 286
ONTOLOGICAL-HYSTERIC THEATRE, INC., 978
OPEN AIR THEATRE, 1208
OPEN BOOK, THE, 978
OPEN EYE: NEW STAGINGS, 1005
OPEN EYE: NEW STAGINGS, THE, 979
OPEN STAGE OF HARRISBURG, 1205
OPENSTAGE THEATRE AND COMPANY, INC., 246
OPERA AT FLORHAM, 823
OPERA CAROLINA, 1049
OPERA CLASSICS OF NEW JERSEY, 819
OPERA COLORADO, 237
OPERA/COLUMBUS, 1124
OPERA COMPANY OF BOSTON, 609
OPERA COMPANY OF MID-MICHIGAN, 683
OPERA COMPANY OF PHILADELPHIA, 1221
OPERA DELAWARE, 294
OPERA EBONY, 958
OPERA FACTORY, THE, 432
OPERA FESTIVAL AUDITORIUM, 893
OPERA FESTIVAL OF NEW JERSEY, 835
OPERA FOR THE YOUNG, 1498
OPERA GRAND RAPIDS, 675
OPERA GUILD, 324
OPERA HOUSE THEATRE COMPANY, 1077
OPERA! LEWANEE, 655
OPERA LITE, 667
OPERA MEMPHIS, 1290
OPERA NEW ENGLAND, 610, 620
OPERA NORTH, 1221, 1416
OPERA NORTHEAST, 959
OPERA/OMAHA, 790
OPERA ORCHESTRA OF NEW YORK, 959
OPERA PACIFIC, 72
OPERA ROANOKE, 1439
OPERA SAN JOSE, 186
OPERA THEATER OF PITTSBURGH, INC., 1232

OPERA THEATRE AT WILDWOOD PARK FOR THE
    PERFORMING ARTS, 49
OPERA THEATRE OF NORTHERN VIRGINIA, 1423
OPERA THEATRE OF SAINT LOUIS, 757
ORANGE COAST COLLEGE, 73
ORANGE COUNTY BALLET THEATRE, 908
ORANGE COUNTY CIVIC CENTER, 351
ORANGE COUNTY PERFORMING ARTS CENTER, 74
ORANGE COUNTY PERFORMING ARTS CENTER -
    FOUNDERS HALL, 74
ORANGE COUNTY PERFORMING ARTS CENTER -
    SEGERSTROM HALL, 74
ORANGE COUNTY PHILHARMONIC SOCIETY, 91
ORANGE COUNTY SYMPHONY, 84
ORANGE PARK COMMUNITY THEATRE, 348
ORATORIO SINGERS OF CHARLOTTE, 1050
ORATORIO SOCIETY OF NEW YORK, 959
ORATORIO SOCIETY OF UTAH, 1404
ORCHESTRA HALL, 446, 718
ORCHESTRA NEW ENGLAND, 271
ORCHESTRA OF SAINT LUKE'S, 949
ORCHESTRA OF SANTA FE, 854
ORCHESTRA SEATTLE/ SEATTLE CHAMBER SINGERS, 1457
ORDWAY MUSIC THEATRE, 727
ORDWAY MUSIC THEATRE - MCKNIGHT THEATRE, 727
ORDWAY MUSIC THEATRE - THE MAIN HALL, 727
OREGON BACH FESTIVAL, 1180
OREGON BALLET THEATRE, 1185
OREGON COAST MUSIC ASSOCIATION, 1177
OREGON FANTASY THEATRE, 1180
OREGON MOZART PLAYERS, 1179
OREGON REPERTORY SINGERS, 1187
OREGON SHAKESPEARE FESTIVAL - ANGUS BOWMER
    THEATRE, 1175
OREGON SHAKESPEARE FESTIVAL - BLACK SWAN
    THEATRE, 1175
OREGON SHAKESPEARE FESTIVAL - ELIZABETHAN
    STAGE, 1175
OREGON SHAKESPEAREAN FESTIVAL ASSOCIATION, 1174
OREGON STATE UNIVERSITY - GILL COLISEUM, 1178
OREGON STATE UNIVERSITY - MILAN AUDITORIUM, 1178
OREGON SYMPHONY ASSOCIATION, 1191
OREGON SYMPHONY ORCHESTRA, 1186
ORGANIC THEATER COMPANY, 439
ORLANDO OPERA, 349
OROVILLE STATE THEATER, 135
ORPHEUM THEATER, 182, 567, 793
ORPHEUM THEATRE, 615, 1005, 1292
ORPHEUS CHAMBER ORCHESTRA, INC., 950
ORPHEUS MALE CHORUS OF PHOENIX, 30
ORPHEUS MALE CHORUS OF TACOMA, 1470
ORRIE DE NOOYER AUDITORIUM, 821
OSCEOLA CENTER FOR THE ARTS, 335
OSCEOLA PLAYERS, 335
OSHKOSH SYMPHONY ORCHESTRA, 1511
OTERO JUNIOR COLLEGE - HUMANITIES CENTER
    THEATRE, 249
OTIS A. SINGLETARY CENTER FOR THE ARTS, 545
OTRABANDA COMPANY, 979
OTTAWA MUNICIPAL AUDITORIUM, 531
OTTER TAIL VALLEY COMMUNITY ORCHESTRA, 704
OUACHITA BAPTIST UNIVERSITY - DEPARTMENT OF
    THEATRE & ARTS, 43
OUACHITA LITTLE THEATRE, 50
OUT NORTH THEATRE COMPANY, 15
OUTDOOR DRAMA GROUP ASSOCIATION, THE, 1389
OVENS AUDITORIUM, 1051
OWENSBORO SYMPHONY ORCHESTRA, 551
OXNARD CIVIC AUDITORIUM, 135
OYSTER BAY CONTEMPORARY BALLET, 1013
PABST THEATER, 1510
PACE DOWNTOWN THEATER, 1005
PACIFIC AMPHITHEATRE, 73
PACIFIC CHORALE, 91
PACIFIC CONSERVATORY OF THE PERFORMING ARTS, 199
PACIFIC NORTHWEST BALLET, 1454
PACIFIC NORTHWEST FESTIVAL, 1462
PACIFIC SYMPHONY ASSOCIATION, 91

PACIFIC UNIVERSITY - TOM MILES THEATRE, 1182
PACIFIC UNIVERSITY COMMUNITY ORCHESTRA, 1181
PACT-RUTH ECKERD HALL AT THE BAUMGARDNER
    PERFORMING ARTS CENTER, 318
PADDYWHACK, 1074
PADUA HILLS PLAYWRIGHTS WORKSHOP, 112
PAINTED BRIDE, 1227
PALA OPERA ASSOCIATION, 960
PALACE CIVIC CENTER, 1137
PALACE OF FINE ARTS, 182
PALACE OF FINE ARTS THEATRE, 182
PALACE THEATRE, 273, 861, 1005, 1100, 1127, 1140
PALACE THEATRE - STAMFORD CENTER FOR THE
    ARTS, 282
PALACE THEATRE OF THE ARTS, 281
PALESTINE CIVIC CENTER COMPLEX, 1379
PALISADES SYMPHONY ORCHESTRA, 135
PALM BEACH COMMUNITY COLLEGE - WATSON B.
    DUNCAN, III, THEATRE, 335
PALM BEACH OPERA, 372
PALM SPRINGS DESERT MUSEUM/ANNENBERG
    THEATER, 137
PALM SPRINGS OPERA GUILD OF THE DESERT, 136
PALO ALTO CHILDREN'S THEATRE, 138
PAMPA CIVIC BALLET, 1379
PAN AMERICAN CENTER, 852
PAN-AMERICAN SOCIETY OF ARTISTS INC., 345
PAN ASIAN REPERTORY THEATRE, 979
PANIDA THEATER, 416
PANOLA PLAYHOUSE, 738
PAPER BAG PLAYERS, THE, 980
PAPER MILL PLAYHOUSE, 824, 825
PARADISE AREA ARTS COUNCIL, 139
PARAMOUNT ARTS CENTER, 539
PARAMOUNT ARTS CENTRE, 419
PARAMOUNT CENTER FOR THE ARTS, 1015
PARAMOUNT THEATER FOR THE PERFORMING ARTS, 1311
PARAMOUNT THEATRE, 134
PARAMOUNT THEATRE FOR THE PERFORMING ARTS, 511
PARENTHESIS THEATRE CLUB, 394
PARIS JUNIOR COLLEGE, 1380
PARK ARTS FESTIVAL - SUMMER SEASON, 1120
PARK COLLEGE - ALUMNI HALL THEATRE, 752
PARK COLLEGE - GRAHAM TYLER MEMORIAL CHAPEL, 750
PARK PERFORMING ARTS CENTER, 841
PARK PLACE HOTEL, 695
PARK RIVER COMMUNITY THEATRE, 1089
PARK SQUARE THEATRE COMPANY, 726
PARK THEATRE PERFORMING ARTS CENTRE, 841
PARK THEATRE PERFORMING ARTS CENTRE - MAIN
    THEATRE, 841
PARKER PLAYHOUSE, 325
PARKERSBURG WHEELING BALLET COMPANY, 1484
PARKWAY PLAYHOUSE, 446
PASADENA CIVIC AUDITORIUM, 141
PASADENA CIVIC BALLET, 139
PASADENA DANCE THEATRE, 204
PASADENA PLAYHOUSE - BALCONY THEATRE, 141
PASADENA PLAYHOUSE - MAINSTAGE THEATRE, 141
PASADENA SYMPHONY, 140
PASCUAL OLIVERA AND ANGELA DEL MORAL'S
    CELEBRATION OF SPANISH DANCE, 473
PASSAGE THEATRE, 212
PAT CANNON FOOT AND FIDDLE DANCE COMPANY, 1014
PAUL BUNYAN PLAYHOUSE, 700
PAUL DRESHER ENSEMBLE, 170
PAUL HILL CHORALE/THE WASHINGTON SINGERS, THE, 302
PAUL MADORE CHORALE, 642
PAUL MASSON SUMMER SERIES, 201
PAUL MELLON ARTS CENTER, 284
PAUL ROBESON THEATRE, 877
PAUL TAYLOR DANCE COMPANY, 932
PAWLING CONCERT SERIES, 1014
PCPA THEATERFEST, 198
PEABODY AUDITORIUM, 322
PEACOCK PLAYERS CHILDREN'S THEATRE, 808
PEARL LANG DANCE COMPANY AND FOUNDATION, 932
PEARL THEATRE COMPANY, THE, 980

PEARSON AUDITORIUM, 853
PEGASUS PLAYERS, 439
PEGASUS THEATRE, 1331
PEMBROKE STATE UNIVERSITY - GIVENS PERFORMING
    ARTS CENTER, 1067
PENGUIN REPERTORY COMPANY, 1029
PENINSULA BALLET THEATRE, 190
PENINSULA DANCE THEATRE, 1447
PENINSULA FESTIVAL, 1490
PENINSULA PLAYERS, 326
PENINSULA PLAYERS, THE, 1490
PENNSYLVANIA BALLET, 1216
PENNSYLVANIA CENTRE STAGE, 1240
PENNSYLVANIA DANCE THEATRE, 1239
PENNSYLVANIA OPERA THEATER, THE, 1221
PENNSYLVANIA STAGE COMPANY, 1193
PENNSYLVANIA STATE UNIVERSITY - EISENHOWER
    AUDITORIUM, 1241
PENNSYLVANIA STATE UNIVERSITY - PAVILION
    THEATRE, 1241
PENNSYLVANIA STATE UNIVERSITY - PLAYHOUSE
    THEATRE, 1241
PENNSYLVANIA STATE UNIVERSITY - SCHWAB
    AUDITORIUM, 1241
PENNYRILE PLAYERS, 543
PENOBSCOT THEATRE COMPANY, 574
PENSACOLA CIVIC CENTER, 354
PENSACOLA JUNIOR COLLEGE, MUSIC AND DRAMA
    DEPARTMENT, 354
PENSACOLA LITTLE THEATRE, 353
PENSACOLA SYMPHONY ORCHESTRA, 352
PENUMBRA THEATRE COMPANY, 726
PEOPLE'S LIGHT AND THEATRE COMPANY, THE, 1211
PEORIA CIVIC BALLET, 467
PEORIA CIVIC CENTER, 468
PEORIA CIVIC CENTER - ARENA, 469
PEORIA CIVIC CENTER - EXHIBITION HALL, 469
PEORIA CIVIC CENTER - THEATRE, 469
PEORIA CIVIC OPERA, 468
PEORIA PLAYERS THEATRE, 468, 469
PEORIA SYMPHONY ORCHESTRA, 467
PEPPERDINE UNIVERSITY - AMPHITHEATRE, FINE ARTS
    DIVISION, 122
PEPPERDINE UNIVERSITY - MINI-THEATRE, FINE ARTS
    DIVISION, 122
PEPPERDINE UNIVERSITY - SMOTHERS THEATRE, 122
PERFORMANCE CIRCLE, THE, 1450
PERFORMANCE SPACE 122 INC., 932
PERFORMING ARTS ASSOCIATION, 1251
PERFORMING ARTS CENTER, 491, 1074
PERFORMING ARTS CHICAGO, 429
PERFORMING ARTS PRESENTATIONS, 146
PERFORMING ARTS PROGRAMS IN DANCE, 1121
PERFORMING ARTS SERIES OF MOUNTAIN HOME, 415
PERFORMING COMPANY OF PIONEER DANCE ARTS, 1465
PERFORMING GARAGE, 1005
PERIDANCE ENSEMBLE, 932
PERIWINKLE NATIONAL THEATRE, 906
PERMIAN PLAYHOUSE OF ODESSA INC., 1378
PEROT THEATRE, 1390
PERRY PLAYERS, INC., 396
PERSEVERANCE THEATRE, 17
PERSHING AUDITORIUM, 787
PERSONA GRATA PRODUCTIONS, INC., 176
PETERBOROUGH PLAYERS, 811
PETERSBURG BALLET, 1435
PETRILLO MUSIC SHELL, 447
PETRUCCI'S DINNER THEATRE, 596
PHEASANT RUN THEATRE, 473
PHELPS - STOKES AUDITORIUM, 540
PHILADELPHIA CHAMBER MUSIC SOCIETY, 1218
PHILADELPHIA CIVIC CENTER, 1227
PHILADELPHIA CIVIC CENTER - CONVENTION HALL, 1227
PHILADELPHIA CIVIC CENTER - EXHIBITION HALLS, 1227
PHILADELPHIA CIVIC CENTER - PENNSYLVANIA
    HALL, 1228
PHILADELPHIA DRAMA GUILD, 1223
PHILADELPHIA FESTIVAL THEATRE FOR NEW PLAYS, 1223

PHILADELPHIA ORCHESTRA ASSOCIATION, 1219
PHILADELPHIA RENAISSANCE WIND BAND, 1219
PHILADELPHIA SINGERS, THE, 1222
PHILADELPHIA STRING QUARTET, 1455
PHILADELPHIA THEATRE COMPANY, THE, 1223
PHILADELPHIA YOUTH ORCHESTRA, 1219
PHILADELPHOIA RENAISSANCE WIND BAND, 1220
PHILDANCE/PHILADELPHIA DANCE COMPANY, 1217
PHILHARMONIA BAROQUE ORCHESTRA, 167
PHILHARMONIA VIRTUOSI CORPORATION, 886
PHILHARMONIC ORCHESTRA OF FLORIDA, 323
PHILHARMONIC ORCHESTRA OF INDIANAPOLIS, 495
PHILHARMONIC ORCHESTRA OF NEW JERSEY, 842
PHIPPS CENTER FOR THE ARTS, 1492
PHOENIX BOYS CHOIR ASSOCIATION, 30
PHOENIX CHAMBER MUSIC SOCIETY, 29
PHOENIX CIVIC PLAZA, 31
PHOENIX CIVIC PLAZA - CONVENTION CENTER AND
    SYMPHONY HALL, 32
PHOENIX CIVIC PLAZA - EXHIBITION HALLS, 32
PHOENIX CIVIC PLAZA - GRAND BALLROOM, 32
PHOENIX DANCE THEATRE, 28
PHOENIX LITTLE THEATRE, 31
PHOENIX SYMPHONY, 29
PHOENIX SYMPHONY YOUTH ORCHESTRA, 29
PHOENIX THEATRE, 497
PHYLLIS LAMHUT DANCE COMPANY, 933
PHYLLIS ROSE DANCE COMPANY, THE, 1023
PICCADILLY PUPPETS COMPANY, THE, 392
PICCOLO OPERA COMPANY, 315
PICKARD THEATRE, 576
PICKETWIRE PLAYERS, 249
PICKETWIRE PLAYERS AND COMMUNITY THEATRE, 249
PICKLE FAMILY CIRCUS AND PICKLE FAMILY CIRCUS
    SCHOOL, 176
PICK - STAIGER CONCERT HALL, 455
PIEDMONT OPERA THEATRE, 1078
PIEDMONT PLAYERS THEATRE, 1072
PIER ONE THEATRE, 21
PIERRE MONTEUX SCHOOL, THE, 577
PIERRE PLAYERS, 1271
PIKES PEAK CENTER, 232
PILOBOLUS DANCE THEATRE, 285
PINE BLUFF CONVENTION CENTER, 51
PINE BLUFF CONVENTION CENTER - ARENA, 51
PINE BLUFF CONVENTION CENTER - AUDITORIUM, 52
PINESONG/SPOKANE FALLS COMMUNITY COLLEGE, 1467
PIONEER AMPHITHEATRE, 1318
PIONEER CENTER FOR THE PERFROMING ARTS, 799
PIONEER PLAYHOUSE OF KENTUCKY, 541
PIONEER THEATRE COMPANY, 1405
PIPELINE, INC., 112
PIPER'S OPERA HOUSE, 801
PIRATE PLAYHOUSE, 358
PISGAH PLAYERS, 1043
PITTSBURGH BALLET THEATRE, 1229
PITTSBURGH BOYCHOIR, INC., 1232
PITTSBURGH CHAMBER MUSIC SOCIETY, 1230
PITTSBURGH CIVIC ARENA, 1236
PITTSBURGH CIVIC LIGHT OPERA, 1233
PITTSBURGH DANCE COUNCIL INC., 1230
PITTSBURGH NEW MUSIC ENSEMBLE, THE, 1231
PITTSBURGH OPERA, 1233
PITTSBURGH PUBLIC THEATER, 1234
PITTSBURGH SYMPHONY ORCHESTRA, 1231
PITTSBURGH YOUTH SYMPHONY ORCHESTRA
    ASSOCIATION, INC., 1231
PIVEN THEATRE WORKSHOP, 455
PLANO REPERTORY THEATRE, 1380
PLANTATION THEATRE COMPANY, 355
PLAYBOY JAZZ FESTIVAL, 65
PLAYERS GUILD OF CANTON, 1100
PLAYERS OF SARASOTA, THE, 362
PLAYERS OF SARASOTA THEATRE, THE, 363
PLAYERS THEATRE COLUMBUS, 1124, 1127
PLAYHOUSE 412, 701
PLAYHOUSE ON THE SQUARE, 1291
PLAYHOUSE SQUARE CENTER, 1117

PLAYHOUSE SQUARE CENTER - OHIO THEATRE, 1118
PLAYHOUSE SQUARE CENTER - PALACE THEATRE, 1118
PLAYHOUSE SQUARE CENTER - STATE THEATRE, 1118
PLAYHOUSE SQUARE FOUNDATION, 1114
PLAYHOUSE THEATRE, THE, 296
PLAYMAKERS, 368
PLAYMAKERS CHILDREN'S ACADEMY OF THEATRE
    ARTS, 1398
PLAYMAKERS REPERTORY COMPANY, 1047
PLAYWRIGHTS' CENTER, 440
PLAYWRIGHTS' CENTER, THE, 714
PLAYWRIGHTS' CENTER OF CHICAGO, 447
PLAYWRIGHTS HORIZONS, 980
PLOWSHARES THEATRE, 669
PLUMMER AUDITORIUM, 83
PLYMOUTH MUSIC SERIES OF MINNESOTA, 717
PLYMOUTH PHILHARMONIC ORCHESTRA, 640
PLYMOUTH THEATRE, 1006
POCKET SANDWICH THEATRE, 1331
POCONO PLAYHOUSE, 1213
POLISH AMERICAN FOLK DANCE COMPANY, 933
POLISH NATIONAL ALLIANCE DANCERS, 1086
POMERIUM MUSICES, INCORPORATED, 960
POMPANO PLAYERS, INC., 355
PONCA PLAYHOUSE, 1166, 1167
PONTIAC-OAKLAND SYMPHONY, 688
PONTINE MOVEMENT THEATRE, 812
POOBLEY GREEGY PUPPET THEATRE, 641
POOH KAYE/ECCENTRIC MOTIONS INC., 933
POPLAR PIKE PLAYHOUSE, 1280
PORT HURON CIVIC THEATRE, 689
PORTAGE AREA COMMUNITY THEATRE, 1513
PORTHOUSE THEATRE COMPANY, 1134
PORTLAND BLACK REPERTORY, 1188
PORTLAND CENTER FOR THE PERFORMING ARTS -
    PORTLAND CIVIC AUDITORIUM, 1189
PORTLAND EXPOSITION BUILDING, 583
PORTLAND FESTIVAL SYMPHONY, 1182
PORTLAND OPERA, 1187
PORTLAND PERFORMING ARTS CENTER, 583
PORTLAND PERFORMING ARTS CENTER, INC., 583
PORTLAND STAGE COMPANY, 582
PORTLAND SYMPHONIC CHOIR, 1187
PORTLAND SYMPHONY ORCHESTRA, 582
PORTLAND YOUTH PHILHARMONIC ASSOCIATION, 1186
POSEY DANCE EDUCATION SERVICE, 1010
POSEY SCHOOL OF DANCE, 1010
POSSUM POINT PLAYERS, 291
POTOMAC THEATRE PROJECT, 1415
POUGHKEEPSIE CIVIC BALLET, 1016
POWELL SYMPHONY HALL AT GRAND CENTER, 762
POWER CENTER FOR THE PERFORMING ARTS, 660
PRAIRIE DANCE THEATRE, 1163
PRAIRIE PLAYERS, INC., 528
PRAIRIE PLAYERS CIVIC THEATRE, 456
PRATT INSTITUTE - AUDITORIUM, 876
PREGONES THEATER, 868
PRESCOTT PARK ARTS FESTIVAL, 813
PRESENT MUSIC, INCORPORATED, 1505
PRESENTATIONS OF THE ELAINE KAUFMAN CULTURAL
    CENTER, 993
PRESIDENTIAL JAZZ WEEKEND, 1226
PRIMARY STAGES COMPANY, 981
PRINCESS THEATER, 732
PRINCESS THEATRE, 5, 25
PRINCETON BALLET, 828
PRINCETON PRO MUSICA, 834
PRISCILLA BEACH THEATER SCHOOL, 650
PRO ARTE CHAMBER ORCHESTRA, 620
PRO ARTE CHAMBER SINGERS OF CONNECTICUT, 281
PRO MUSICA, INC., 677
PRO MUSICA CHAMBER ORCHESTRA OF COLUMBUS, 1123
PRO MUSICIS FOUNDATION, INC., 960
PROCESS STUDIO THEATRE, 981
PROCTOR'S THEATRE, 1026
PROJECT INTERACT - ZACHARY SCOTT THEATRE
    CENTER, 1309
PROMENADE THEATRE, 1006

PROSCENIUM PLAYERS, 795
PROVIDENCE CIVIC CENTER, 1252
PROVIDENCE PERFORMING ARTS CENTER, 1252
PROVINCETOWN PLAYHOUSE, 1006
PROVO THEATRE COMPANY, 1399
PTG-FLORIDA, INC./PARKER PLAYHOUSE, 324
PUBLICK THEATRE, THE, 611
PUEBLO BALLET, 250
PUEBLO SYMPHONY ORCHESTRA, 251
PUERTO RICAN TRAVELING THEATRE COMPANY, 981
PUGET SOUND CHAMBER MUSIC SOCIETY, 1456
PULL-TIGHT PLAYERS, 1280
PUPPET ARTS THEATRE, 735
PUPPET HOUSE THEATRE, 282
PUPPET SHOWPLACE THEATRE, 616
PURDUE PROFESSIONAL SUMMER THEATRE, 505
PYRAMID ARTS CENTER, 1022
QRS ARTS FOUNDATION, 879
QUAD CITY ARTS, 471
QUAD CITY SYMPHONY ORCHESTRA, 511
QUAD CITY YOUTH SYMPHONY ORCHESTRA, 512
QUAIGH THEATRE, 981
QUARTET PROGRAM, THE, 1021
QUARTZ THEATRE, 1174
QUEENS COLLEGE - COLDEN CENTER FOR THE
    PERFORMING ARTS, 889
QUEENS OPERA ASSOCIATION, 872
QUEENS SYMPHONY ORCHESTRA, 1019
QUEENSBOROUGH CHORUS, THE, 864
QUEENSBOROUGH COMMUNITY COLLEGE
    THEATER, 864
QUINCY SYMPHONY ORCHESTRA, 469
QUINTET OF THE AMERICAS, 950
RACINE SYMPHONY ORCHESTRA, 1513
RACKHAM SYMPHONY CHOIR, 676
RADCLIFFE COLLEGE - AGASSIZ THEATER, 622
RADCLIFFE COLLEGE - LYMAN COMMON ROOM, 622
RADFORD UNIVERSITY THEATRE, 1435
RADIO CITY MUSIC HALL, 1006
RADOST FOLK EMSEMBLE, 1454
RAINBO CHILDREN'S THEATRE COMPANY, 726
RAJAH THEATRE, 1238
RALEIGH BOYCHOIR, 1069
RALEIGH CIVIC CENTER, 1070
RALEIGH CIVIC CENTER - ARENA, 1070
RALEIGH CIVIC CENTER - THEATRE, 1071
RALEIGH LITTLE THEATRE, 1071
RALPH LEMON COMPANY, 933
RAM ISLAND DANCE, 581
RAMONA BOWL, 87
RAMONA HILLSIDE PLAYERS, 86
RAMONA PAGEANT ASSOCIATION, 86
RAVEN THEATRE COMPANY, 440
RAVINIA FESTIVAL, 459
READING COMMUNITY PLAYERS, 1237
READING SYMPHONY ORCHESTRA, 1236
REALITY THEATRE, THE, 1125
REARDON AUDITORIUM, 483
RECITAL HALL-BALBOA PARK, THE, 159
RED BARN THEATRE, 334
RED EYE COLLABORATION, 715
RED HACKLE PIPE BAND, 18
RED RIVER DANCE AND PERFORMING COMPANY, 1084
RED ROCKS AMPHITHEATRE - MORRISON COLORADO, 242
REDDING CIVIC AUDITORIUM - TRADE AND CONVENTION
    CENTER, 143
REDLANDS BOWL SUMMER MUSIC FESTIVAL, 143
REDLANDS COMMUNITY MUSIC ASSOCIATION, INC., 144
REDLANDS SYMPHONY ASSOCIATION, 143
REED COLLEGE - REED THEATRE, 1189
REED MARIONETTES, INC., 1516
REED WHIPPLE CULTURAL ARTS CENTER, 797, 798
REGINA OPERA COMPANY, 872
REGIONAL CENTER FOR THE ARTS, 216
REICHHOLD CENTER FOR THE ARTS, 1527
REIF ARTS COUNCIL, THE, 705
RELACHE ENSEMBLE, 1220
REMAINS THEATRE, 440

RENAISSANCE AND BAROQUE SOCIETY OF
    PITTSBURGH, 1232
RENAISSANCE CITY CHOIR, 1233
RENAISSANCE DANCE COMPANY OF DETROIT, 666
RENAISSANCE THEATER COMPANY, 272
RENAISSANCE THEATRE, THE, 1139
RENATE BOUE DANCE COMPANY, 825
RENO CHAMBER ORCHESTRA, 798
RENO LITTLE THEATER, 799
RENSSELAER NEWMAN FOUNDATION CHAPEL AND
    CULTURAL CENTER, 1034
REPERTORY DANCE THEATRE, 1402
REPERTORY PEOPLE OF EVANSVILLE, 488
REPERTORY THEATER OF AMERICA, 1380
REPERTORY THEATRE OF SAINT LOUIS, THE, 759
RESTON COMMUNITY CENTER THEATRE, 1435
REUNION ARENA, 1336
REVELS INC., 621
REYNOLDS MEMORIAL AUDITORIUM, 1080
RHAPSODY IN TAPS, 102
RHODE ISLAND CIVIC CHORALE AND ORCHESTRA, 1249
RHODE ISLAND PHILHARMONIC ORCHESTRA, 1248
RHODE ISLAND SHAKESPEARE THEATRE, THE, 1247
RIALTO SQUARE THEATRE, 460
RICE UNIVERSITY - HAMMAN HALL, 1367
RICHARD BURTON PERFORMING ARTS CENTER TRITON
    COLLEGE, 470
RICHARDSON AUDITORIUM, 1322
RICHARDSON AUDITORIUM IN ALEXANDER HALL, 834
RICHMOND BALLET - THE STATE BALLET OF
    VIRGINIA, 1436
RICHMOND CHILDREN'S THEATRE, 553
RICHMOND CIVIC THEATRE, 502
RICHMOND MEMORIAL CONVENTION CENTER, 145
RICHMOND SYMPHONY, 1436
RICHMOND SYMPHONY ORCHESTRA, 502
RIDER COLLEGE - FINE ARTS THEATER, 823
RIDGE THEATER, 982
RIDGEFIELD SYMPHONY ORCHESTRA, 277
RIDGEWOOD GILBERT AND SULLIVAN OPERA
    COMPANY, 837
RIDGEWOOD SYMPHONY ORCHESTRA, 836
RIDICULOUS THEATRICAL COMPANY, THE, 982
RIO GRANDE VALLEY BALLET, 1375
RIO GRANDE VALLEY INTERNATIONAL MUSIC
    FESTIVAL, 1376
RIO HONDO COLLEGE - MERTON WRAY THEATRE, 218
RIO HONDO SYMPHONY ASSOCIATION, 217
RIPON COLLEGE - DEMMER RECITAL HALL, 1514
RIPON COLLEGE/CAESTECKER FINE ARTS SERIES, 1513
RIRIE-WOODBURY DANCE COMPANY, 1402
RISA JAROSLOW AND DANCERS, 934
RITES AND REASON, 1250
RIVER ARTS REPERTORY, 864
RIVER CITY BRASS BAND, 1232
RIVERBEND MUSIC CENTER, 1107
RIVERBEND-CINCINNATI SYMPHONY AND POPS
    ORCHESTRA CONCERTS, 1106
RIVERSIDE BALLET THEATRE, 145
RIVERSIDE CENTROPLEX, 556
RIVERSIDE CENTROPLEX - ARENA, 556
RIVERSIDE CENTROPLEX - EXHIBITION HALL, 556
RIVERSIDE CENTROPLEX - THEATRE FOR PERFORMING
    ARTS, 557
RIVERSIDE CONVENTION CENTER AT RAINCROSS
    SQUARE, 146
RIVERSIDE COUNTY PHILHARMONIC, 145
RIVERSIDE MUNICIPAL AUDITORIUM, 146
RIVERSIDE SHAKESPEARE COMPANY, 982
RIVERSIDE SYMPHONY, THE, 950
RIVERSIDE THEATRE, 372, 518
RIVERTOWN PLAYERS, 499
ROAD COMPANY, THE, 1283
ROADSIDE THEATER, 553
ROANOKE CIVIC CENTER, 1440
ROANOKE ISLAND HISTORICAL ASSOCIATION INC., 1064
ROANOKE SYMPHONY SOCIETY, 1439
ROANOKE VALLEY CHAMBER MUSIC SOCIETY, 1438 - 1439

ROANOKE VALLEY PLAYERS, 1071
ROBBINS - ZUST FAMILY MARIONETTES, 641
ROBERT C. SMITHWICK THEATRE, 99
ROBERT IVEY BALLET, 1257
ROBERT MORRIS COLONIAL THEATER, 1199
ROBERT W. WOODRUFF ARTS CENTER, 386
ROBERT W. WOODRUFF ARTS CENTER - ALLIANCE
    THEATRE, 386
ROBERT W. WOODRUFF ARTS CENTER - ALLIANCE
    THEATRE-STUDIO THEATRE, 387
ROBERT W. WOODRUFF ARTS CENTER - RICHARD H. RICH
    AUDITORIUM, 387
ROBERT W. WOODRUFF ARTS CENTER - SYMPHONY
    HALL, 387
ROBERTS CENTER THEATRE, 287
ROBINSON CENTER MUSIC HALL, 50
ROCHESTER CHAMBER ORCHESTRA, 1020
ROCHESTER CIVIC MUSIC, 721
ROCHESTER CIVIC THEATRE, 722
ROCHESTER PHILHARMONIC ORCHESTRA, 1020
ROCHESTER SYMPHONY ORCHESTRA, 721
ROCKFORD DANCE COMPANY, 471
ROCKFORD SYMPHONY ORCHESTRA, 472
ROCKPORT CHAMBER MUSIC FESTIVAL, 641
ROCKPORT OPERA HOUSE - TOWN OF ROCKPORT, 583
ROCKY MOUNTAIN BRASSWORKS, 221
ROCKY RIDGE MUSIC CENTER, 787
ROGER FURMAN THEATRE, 982
ROLAND HAYES CONCERT HALL, 1279
ROLLINS COLLEGE - ANNIE RUSSELL THEATRE, 374
ROME CITY AUDITORIUM, 396
ROOSEVELT UNIVERSITY - PATRICK L. O'MALLEY
    THEATRE, 447
ROQUE OPERA, 1173
ROSALIE GERUT AND FRIENDS, 633
ROSALIND NEWMAN AND DANCERS, 934
ROSCOE'S SURPRISE ORCHESTRA, 1289
ROSEWOOD CHAMBER ENSEMBLE, INC., 1030
ROULETTE INTERMEDIUM, INC., 950
ROUND HOUSE THEATRE, 598
ROUNDABOUT THEATRE COMPANY, 983
ROWAN COMMUNITY CONCERT ASSOCIATION, 1072
ROXBURY CHAMBER PLAYERS, 1437
ROXY THEATER, 1279
ROYAL ARTS COUNCIL, THE, 766
ROYALE THEATRE, 1006
RUBY VALLEY CHORALE, 779
RUDY PEREZ PERFORMANCE ENSEMBLE, 102
RUMBLE SEAT FOUR QUARTET, THE, 1359
RUSHMORE PLAZA CIVIC CENTER, 1272
RUSSIAN RIVER JAZZ FESTIVAL, INC., 85
RUTGERS ARTS CENTER, 830
RUTGERS SUMMERFEST, 829
RUTGERS UNIVERSITY CONCERT SERIES, 829
RUTH MITCHELL DANCE COMPANY, THE, 377
RUTH ST. DENIS FOUNDATION, 103
RYAN REPERTORY COMPANY AT HARRY WARREN
    THEATRE, 874
SACRAMENTO BALLET, 147
SACRAMENTO COMMUNITY CENTER EXHIBITION
    HALL, 150
SACRAMENTO COMMUNITY CENTER THEATER, 150
SACRAMENTO COMMUNITY CONVENTION
    CENTER, 151
SACRAMENTO MEN'S CHORUS, 148
SACRAMENTO MUSIC CIRCUS, 149
SACRAMENTO OPERA, 148
SACRAMENTO SYMPHONY ASSOCIATION, 148
SACRAMENTO THEATRE COMPANY, 149
SAEKO OCHINOHE AND COMPANY, INC., 934
SAENGER PERFORMING ARTS CENTER, 567
SAENGER THEATRE, 354, 733
SAENGER THEATRE FOR THE PERFORMING ARTS, 731
SAGINAW CIVIC CENTER - HERITAGE THEATER, 692
SAGINAW SYMPHONY ORCHESTRA, 691
SAGINAW SYMPHONY SCHOOL OF MUSIC AND YOUTH
    ORCHESTRA, 691
SAINT AMBROSE COLLEGE - ALLAERT HALL, 513

SAINT AMBROSE COLLEGE - GALVIN FINE ARTS CENTER, 512
SAINT BART'S PLAYHOUSE, 983
SAINT CLEMENT'S CHURCH, 1006
SAINT JAMES THEATER, 1007
SAINT JOHN THEATRE, 568
SAINT JOHN'S RENAISSANCE DANCERS, 826
SAINT JOHN'S UNIVERSITY, 900
SAINT JOSEPH CIVIC CENTER, 753
SAINT JOSEPH CIVIC CENTER - ARENA, 753
SAINT JOSEPH CIVIC CENTER - MISSOURI THEATRE, 754
SAINT JOSEPH SYMPHONY SOCIETY, THE, 753
SAINT LOUIS BLACK REPERTORY COMPANY, 759
SAINT LOUIS CENTER FOR THE PERFORMING ARTS - THE MAMIYA THEATRE, 407
SAINT LOUIS CHAMBER CHORUS, 757
SAINT LOUIS CULTURAL FLAMENCO SOCIETY, 755
SAINT LOUIS PHILHARMONIC ORCHESTRA, 756
SAINT LOUIS SYMPHONY CHAMBER ORCHESTRA, 756
SAINT LOUIS SYMPHONY CHORUS, 758
SAINT LOUIS SYMPHONY ORCHESTRA, 756
SAINT LOUIS SYMPHONY QUEENY POPS, 761
SAINT LOUIS SYMPHONY YOUTH ORCHESTRA, 757
SAINT LUCIE COUNTY CIVIC CENTER, 327
SAINT LUCIE COUNTY CIVIC CENTER - AUDITORIUM, 327
SAINT LUCIE COUNTY CIVIC CENTER - THEATER, 327
SAINT LUKES CHAMBER ENSEMBLE, INC., 951
SAINT MARY COLLEGE - XAVIER HALL THEATRE, 529
SAINT PAUL CHAMBER ORCHESTRA, THE, 724
SAINT PAUL CIVIC CENTER, 727
SAINT PAUL CIVIC CENTER - ARENA, 728
SAINT PAUL CIVIC CENTER - AUDITORIUM, 728
SAINT SAVA FREE SERBIAN ORTHODOX CHURCH, 1109
SAINT SEBASTIAN PLAYERS, 441
SAINT THOMAS CHOIR OF MEN AND BOYS, THE, 960
SALEM CIVIC CENTER, 1440
SALEM THEATER OF PERFORMING ARTS, 1191
SALINA BICENTENNIAL CENTER, 533
SALINA COMMUNITY THEATRE, 533
SALISBURY SYMPHONY ORCHESTRA, 1072
SALT AND PEPPER MIME COMPANY, INC., 983
SALT LAKE ACTING COMPANY, THE, 1405
SALT LAKE OPERA THEATRE, 1404
SALT LAKE SYMPHONIC CHOIR, 1404
SALTWORKS, 1234
SAM HOUSTON STATE UNIVERSITY-THEATRE AND DANCE DIVISION, 1368
SAM HOUSTON STATE UNIVERSITY-THEATRE AND DANCE DIVISION - MAIN STAGE THEATRE, 1367
SAM HOUSTON STATE UNIVERSITY-THEATRE AND DANCE DIVISION - STUDIO THEATRE, 1368
SAMAHAN PHILIPPINE DANCE COMPANY, 77
SAN ANGELO CITY AUDITORIUM, 1382
SAN ANGELO SYMPHONY ORCHESTRA AND CHORALE, 1381
SAN ANTONIO BALLET, 1383
SAN ANTONIO CHAMBER MUSIC SOCIETY, 1383
SAN ANTONIO CONVENTION CENTER, 1386
SAN ANTONIO CONVENTION CENTER - LILA COCKRELL THEATRE, 1387
SAN ANTONIO LITTLE THEATRE, 1385
SAN ANTONIO PERFORMING ARTS ASSOCIATION, 1386
SAN ANTONIO SYMPHONY, 1383
SAN BERNARDINO CIVIC LIGHT OPERA ASSOCIATION, 151
SAN DIEGO CHAMBER ORCHESTRA, 142
SAN DIEGO COMIC OPERA, 154
SAN DIEGO CONCOURSE, 159
SAN DIEGO CONCOURSE - CIVIC THEATRE, 160
SAN DIEGO CONCOURSE - GOLDEN HALL, 160
SAN DIEGO FOUNDATION FOR THE PERFORMING ARTS, 153
SAN DIEGO GUILD OF PUPPETRY, 204
SAN DIEGO JUNIOR THEATRE, 157
SAN DIEGO MEN'S CHORUS, 155
SAN DIEGO OPERA ASSOCIATION, 155
SAN DIEGO REPERTORY THEATRE, 157
SAN DIEGO SYMPHONY ORCHESTRA, 154
SAN DIEGO YOUTH SYMPHONY, 154
SAN FRANCISCO ARTS COMMISSION, 179
SAN FRANCISCO BALLET ASSOCIATION, 164

SAN FRANCISCO CHANTICLEER, INC., 170
SAN FRANCISCO CHILDREN'S OPERA ASSOCIATION, 171
SAN FRANCISCO CHORAL ARTISTS, 171
SAN FRANCISCO CIVIC AUDITORIUM, 182
SAN FRANCISCO CONSERVATORY OF MUSIC, 168
SAN FRANCISCO CONTEMPORARY MUSIC PLAYERS, 168
SAN FRANCISCO COUNTY FAIR BUILDING, 183
SAN FRANCISCO EARLY MUSIC SOCIETY, 60
SAN FRANCISCO GIRLS CHORAL ASSOCIATION, 171
SAN FRANCISCO JAZZ DANCE COMPANY, 165
SAN FRANCISCO JAZZ FESTIVAL, 179
SAN FRANCISCO MIME TROUPE, 176
SAN FRANCISCO OPERA ASSOCIATION, 171
SAN FRANCISCO OPERA CENTER, 172
SAN FRANCISCO PERFORMANCES, 165
SAN FRANCISCO POCKET OPERA, 172
SAN FRANCISCO SYMPHONY CHORUS, 172
SAN FRANCISCO SYMPHONY ORCHESTRA, 168
SAN FRANCISCO SYMPHONY YOUTH ORCHESTRA, 168
SAN FRANCISCO WAR MEMORIAL AND PERFORMING ARTS CENTER, 183
SAN FRANCISCO WAR MEMORIAL AND PERFORMING ARTS CENTER - GREEN ROOM, 183
SAN FRANCISCO WAR MEMORIAL AND PERFORMING ARTS CENTER - HERBST THEATRE, 183
SAN FRANCISCO WAR MEMORIAL AND PERFORMING ARTS CENTER - LOUISE M. DAVIES SYMPHONY HALL, 183
SAN FRANCISCO WAR MEMORIAL AND PERFORMING ARTS CENTER - WAR MEMORIAL OPERA HOUSE, 184
SAN FRANCISCO'S BALLET CELESTE-INTERNATIONAL, 165
SAN GABRIEL CIVIC AUDITORIUM, 184
SAN JOSE CITY COLLEGE, 187
SAN JOSE CIVIC LIGHT OPERA ASSOCIATION INC., 186
SAN JOSE CLEVELAND BALLET, 184
SAN JOSE CONVENTION AND CULTURAL FACILITIES, 187
SAN JOSE CONVENTION AND CULTURAL FACILITIES - CENTER FOR THE PERFORMING ARTS, 187
SAN JOSE CONVENTION AND CULTURAL FACILITIES - CIVIC AUDITORIUM, 188
SAN JOSE CONVENTION AND CULTURAL FACILITIES - MONTGOMERY THEATER, 188
SAN JOSE DANCE THEATRE, 185
SAN JOSE REPERTORY THEATRE, 186
SAN JOSE STATE UNIVERSITY - CONCERT HALL, 188
SAN JOSE STATE UNIVERSITY - UNIVERSITY THEATRE, 188
SAN JOSE SYMPHONY, 185
SAN JOSE TAIKO GROUP, 185
SAN JUAN COMMUNITY THEATRE AND ARTS CENTER, 1450
SAN LUIS OBISPO COUNTY SYMPHONY, 189
SAN LUIS OBISPO MOZART FESITVAL, 189
SAN MATEO PERFORMING ARTS CENTER, 190
SANDERS THEATRE, 622
SANDHILLS LITTLE THEATRE, 1074
SANGAMON STATE UNIVERSITY AUDITORIUM, 475
SANGRE DE CRISTO ARTS AND CONFERENCE CENTER, 251, 252
SANTA BARBARA CHILDREN'S THEATRE, 194
SANTA BARBARA SYMPHONY ORCHESTRA, 193
SANTA CLARA BALLET, 196
SANTA CRUZ BAROQUE FESTIVAL, 197
SANTA CRUZ BRASS QUINTET, 196
SANTA CRUZ CIVIC AUDITORIUM, 198
SANTA CRUZ COUNTY SYMPHONY, 197
SANTA FE CHAMBER MUSIC FESTIVAL, 855
SANTA FE COMMUNITY THEATRE, 855
SANTA FE CONVENTION AND VISITORS BUREAU AT SWEENEY CENTER, 856
SANTA FE DESERT CHORALE, THE, 854
SANTA FE OPERA, THE, 855
SANTA FE SYMPHONY, 854
SANTA MARIA SYMPHONY SOCIETY, 198
SANTA MONICA CIVIC AUDITORIUM, 200
SANTA MONICA PLAYHOUSE AND GROUP THEATRE, 199
SANTA ROSA SYMPHONY, 200
SANTUARIO DE GUADALUPE, 856
SARASOTA MUSIC FESTIVAL, 363
SARASOTA OPERA ASSOCIATION, 361

SARASOTA OPERA HOUSE, 363
SARASOTA-MANATEE COMMUNITY ORCHESTRA, 337
SARATOGA PERFORMING ARTS CENTER, 1024, 1025
SARATOGA PERFORMING ARTS CENTER -
    AMPHITHEATRE, 1025
SARATOGA PERFORMING ARTS CENTER - LITTLE
    THEATRE, 1025
SATURDAY BRASS QUNITET, 951
SAVANNAH CIVIC CENTER, 397
SAVANNAH CIVIC CENTER - ARENA, 397
SAVANNAH CIVIC CENTER - THEATRE, 397
SAVANNAH SYMPHONY, 396
SCANDINAVIAN DANCERS, 778
SCHENECTADY CIVIC PLAYERS, THE, 1026
SCHENECTADY CIVIC PLAYERS, INC., THE, 1026
SCHENECTADY LIGHT OPERA COMPANY, 1026
SCHOENBRUNN AMPHITHEATRE, 1142
SCHOLA CANTORUM OF TEXAS, 1345
SCHOOL OF HARD KNOCKS, 934
SCOTT HARRIS BIG BAND, THE, 197
SCOTT JOPLIN RAGTIME FESTIVAL, 763
SCOTTISH RITE AUDITORIUM, 491, 1098
SCOTTSDALE CENTER FOR THE ARTS, 34
SCOTTSDALE CENTER FOR THE ARTS - CINEMA, 34
SCOTTSDALE CENTER FOR THE ARTS - THEATER, 34
SCOTTSDALE SYMPHONY ORCHESTRA, 33
SCRANTON CULTURAL CENTER AT THE MASONIC
    TEMPLE, 1238
SEA CLIFF CHAMBER PLAYERS, THE, 1027
SEACOAST REPERTORY COMPANY, 812
SEASIDE CIVIC AND CONVENTION CENTER, 1192
SEASIDE MUSIC THEATER, 320
SEATTLE CENTER ARENA, 1464
SEATTLE CENTER COLISEUM, 1464
SEATTLE CENTER OPERA HOUSE, 1464
SEATTLE CHAMBER MUSIC FESTIVAL, 1456
SEATTLE CHILDREN'S THEATRE, 1460
SEATTLE INTERNATIONAL CHILDREN'S FESTIVAL, 1462
SEATTLE MEN'S CHORUS, 1457
SEATTLE MIME THEATRE, 1460
SEATTLE OPERA ASSOCIATION, 1458
SEATTLE PUBLIC LIBRARY-DOWNTOWN LIBRARY, 1465
SEATTLE REPERTORY THEATRE, 1461
SEATTLE SYMPHONY ORCHESTRA, 1456
SEATTLE YOUTH SYMPHONY ORCHESTRA, 1456
SEAVER COLLEGE COMMUNITY SYMPHONY, 121
SECOND CITY, THE, 441
SECOND STAGE THEATRE, THE, 983
SEDONA JAZZ ON THE ROCKS, 34
S.E.M. ENSEMBLE, 871
SENIOR BARN PLAYERS, THE, 534
SEVEN STAGES, 382, 387
SEVENARS CONCERTS, 653
SEVENTH SIGN THEATRE COMPANY, INC., 984
7TH STREET THEATRE, 1450
SEVERAL DANCERS CORE, 1356
SEVERANCE HALL, 1118
SEWANEE SUMMER MUSIC CENTER, 1300
SHADOW BOX THEATRE, THE, 984
SHADY LANE THEATER, 462
SHAKER SYMPHONY ORCHESTRA, 1119
SHAKER SYMPHONY ORCHESTRA, THE, 1140
SHAKESPEARE FESTIVAL OF DALLAS, 1333
SHAKESPEARE IN CENTRAL PARK - KENTUCKY
    SHAKESPEARE FESTIVAL, 549
SHAKESPEARE REPERTORY, 441
SHAKESPEARE '70, 840
SHAKESPEARE THEATRE, THE, 305, 312
SHAKESPEARE-IN-THE-PARK, 1348
SHALHAVET, 1120
SHALHEVET INTERNATIONAL FOLK ENSEMBLE, 1118
SHARIR DANCE COMPANY, 1308
SHARON COMMUNITY THEATRE, INC., 642
SHASTA COLLEGE - FINE ARTS THEATRE, 143
SHASTA SYMPHONY, 142
SHATTERED GLOBE THEATER, 441
SHAWANO COUNTY ARTS COUNCIL, 1514
SHEBOYGAN COMMUNITY PLAYERS, 1514

SHEBOYGAN SYMPHONY ORCHESTRA, 1514
SHEELY CENTER FOR THE PERFORMING ARTS, 464
SHENANDOAH VALLEY MUSIC FESTIVAL, 1443
SHERIDAN CIVIC THEATRE GUILD, 1522
SHERIDAN OPERA HOUSE, 253
SHERMAN PLAYERS, 278
SHERMAN PLAYHOUSE, 279
SHERMAN SYMPHONY ORCHESTRA, 1388
SHERWOOD AUDITORIUM, 94
SHIRIM KLEZMER ORCHESTRA, 608
SHODA MOVING THEATRE (M.O.V.E. CO.), 1245
SHOESTRING PRODUCTIONS, LIMITED, 295
SHOWBOAT DINNER THEATRE, 318
SHOWBOAT MAJESTIC, 1107
SHOWBOAT TROUPE, 218
SHREVEPORT CIVIC THEATRE, 571
SHREVEPORT LITTLE THEATRE, 570
SHREVEPORT METROPOLITAN BALLET, 569
SHREVEPORT MUNICIPAL AUDITORIUM, 571
SHREVEPORT OPERA, 569
SHREVEPORT SYMPHONY ORCHESTRA, 569
SHRINE AUDITORIUM AND EXPOSITION CENTER, 120
SHUBERT PERFORMING ARTS CENTER, 273
SHUBERT THEATRE, 120, 447, 616, 1007
SIDE BY SIDE, 1069
SIERRA WIND QUINTET, 797
SIKESTON LITTLE THEATRE, 764
SILICON VALLEY GAY MEN'S CHORUS OF SAN JOSE, 208
SILK AND BAMBOO ENSEMBLE, THE, 480
SILO CONCERT DANCERS, 256
SILVER CULTURAL ARTS CENTER, 812
SILVER LAKE COLLEGE, 1500
SIMON EDISON CENTER FOR THE PERFORMING ARTS, 160
SIMON EDISON CENTER FOR THE PERFORMING ARTS -
    CASSIUS CARTER CENTRE STAGE, 160
SIMON EDISON CENTER FOR THE PERFORMING ARTS -
    LOWELL DAVIES FESTIVAL THEATRE, 160
SIMON EDISON CENTER FOR THE PERFORMING ARTS -
    OLD GLOBE THEATRE, 161
SINGING BOYS OF PENNSYLVANIA, 1242
SIOUX CITY COMMUNITY THEATRE, 520
SIOUX CITY SYMPHONY ORCHESTRA, 520
SIOUX FALLS COLISEUM, 1274
SIOUX FALLS COMMUNITY PLAYHOUSE, 1274
SIOUX FALLS MASTER SINGERS, 1273
SIOUX FALLS MUNICIPAL BAND, 1272
SIOUXLAND CIVIC DANCE ASSOCIATION, 519
SISKIYOU BAROQUE ENSEMBLE, 1177
SITKA CENTENNIAL BUILDING, 23
SITKA SUMMER MUSIC FESTIVAL, 16
SKANEATELES FESTIVAL, 1027
SKYLIGHT COMIC OPERA LIMITED, 1507
SKYLIGHT OPERA THEATRE, 1510
SKYSAVER PRODUCTIONS, 984
SLOCOMB AUDITORIUM, 1380
SMITH OPERA HOUSE FOR THE PERFORMING
    ARTS, 893
SMITH-RITCH POINT THEATRE, 1368
SMITHSONIAN INSTITUTION - BAIRD AUDITORIUM, 313
SMITHSONIAN INSTITUTION - CARMICHAEL
    AUDITORIUM, 313
SMITHSONIAN INSTITUTION RESIDENT ASSOCIATE
    PROGRAM, 308
SMOKY MOUNTAIN BRITISH BRASS, 1052
SMOKY MOUNTAIN PASSION PLAY, 1277
SMOKY MOUNTAIN REPERTORY THEATRE, 1043
SNUG HARBOR CULTURAL CENTER, 1028
SOCIETY FOR THE PERFORMING ARTS, 1356
SOCIETY HILL PLAYHOUSE, 1224, 1228
SOCIETY OF THE FOUR ARTS GALLERY - THEATER,
    THE, 351
SOHO REP, 1007
SOJOURNER TRUTH PLAYERS, 1347
SOLARIS DANCE THEATRE, 934
SOLID BRASS, 817
SOLOMONS COMPANY-DANCE, THE, 935
SOLVANG THEATERFEST, 199
SONG OF NORWAY FESTIVAL, 1511

SONO ARTS CELEBRATION, INC., 277
SOON 3 THEATER, 177
SOONER THEATRE OF NORMAN, INC., THE, 1163
SOUHEGAN VALLEY THEATRE, 809
SOUNDSCAPES, 230
SOUPSTONE PROJECT, 984
SOURCE THEATRE COMPANY, 306
SOUTH ARKANSAS ARTS CENTER, 44
SOUTH ARKANSAS SYMPHONY, 43
SOUTH BEND SYMPHONY, 503
SOUTH BROADWAY CULTURAL CENTER, 851
SOUTH CAROLINA PHILHARMONIC AND CHAMBER
    ORCHESTRAS, 1260
SOUTH CAROLINA THEATRE COMPANY, THE, 1256
SOUTH COAST REPERTORY, 73, 74
SOUTH COAST REPERTORY - SECOND STAGE, 74
SOUTH COAST REPERTORY - SEGERSTROM AUDITORIUM,
    MAINSTAGE, 75
SOUTH COAST SYMPHONY, 192
SOUTH DAKOTA ART MUSEUM, 1268
SOUTH DAKOTA STATE UNIVERSITY CIVIC SYMPHONY,
    1268
SOUTH DAKOTA SYMPHONY, 1273
SOUTH DALLAS CULTURAL CENTER, 1336
SOUTH FLORIDA YOUTH SYMPHONY, 341
SOUTH JACKSON CIVIC CENTER, 1301
SOUTH JERSEY REGIONAL THEATRE, 837
SOUTH JERSEY SYMPHONY ORCHESTRA, 833
SOUTH MOUNTAIN ASSOCIATION, 640
SOUTH TEXAS SYMPHONY ASSOCIATION, 1339
SOUTHEAST ALABAMA COMMUNITY THEATRE, 5
SOUTHEAST COMMUNITY THEATRE, 157
SOUTHEAST IOWA SYMPHONY ORCHESTRA, 519
SOUTHEAST MISSOURI STATE UNIVERSITY - ACADEMIC
    HALL AUDITORIUM, 742
SOUTHEAST MISSOURI STATE UNIVERSITY - CULTURAL
    PROGRAMS, 742
SOUTHEAST MISSOURI STATE UNIVERSITY - SHOW ME
    CENTER, 742
SOUTHEASTERN LOUISIANA UNIVERSITY - VONNIE
    BORDEN THEATRE, 557
SOUTHEASTERN MUSIC CENTER, 390
SOUTHEASTERN SAVOYARDS, THE, 383
SOUTHERN APPALACHIAN REPERTORY THEATRE, 1065
SOUTHERN BALLET THEATRE, 348
SOUTHERN BAPTIST THEOLOGICAL SEMINARY - ALUMNI
    MEMORIAL CHAPEL, 550
SOUTHERN BAPTIST THEOLOGICAL SEMINARY - HEEREN
    RECITAL HALL, 551
SOUTHERN DANCEWORKS, 1
SOUTHERN ILLINOIS UNIVERSITY-EDWARDSVILLE, 452
SOUTHERN METHODIST UNIVERSITY - BOB HOPE
    THEATRE, 1336
SOUTHERN METHODIST UNIVERSITY - CARUTH
    AUDITORIUM, 1336
SOUTHERN METHODIST UNIVERSITY - MARGO JONES
    THEATRE, 1337
SOUTHERN METHODIST UNIVERSITY - MCFARLIN
    MEMORIAL AUDITORIUM, 1337
SOUTHINGTON COMMUNITY THEATRE, 279
SOUTHWEST JAZZ BALLET COMPANY, 1357
SOUTHWEST MICHIGAN SYMPHONY ORCHESTRA, 693
SOUTHWEST REPERTORY ORGANIZATION, 1341
SOUTHWEST SYMPHONY ORCHESTRA, 1400
SOUTHWESTERN BAPTIST THEOLOGICAL SEMINARY -
    REYNOLDS AUDITORIUM, 1350
SOUTHWESTERN OKLAHOMA STATE UNIVERSITY - FINE
    ARTS CENTER, 1172
SPANISH DANCE THEATRE, 606
SPANISH LYRIC THEATRE, 368
SPANISH THEATRE REPERTORY CO., LTD., 935
SPANISH THEATRE REPERTORY COMPANY, 985
SPARTANBURG MEMORIAL AUDITORIUM, 1266
SPARTANBURG MEMORIAL AUDITORIUM - ARENA, 1266
SPARTANBURG MEMORIAL AUDITORIUM - THEATRE, 1266
SPECTRUM, THE, 1228
SPECULUM MUSICAE, INC., 951
SPINGOLD THEATER CENTER, 648

SPIRIT SQUARE CENTER FOR THE ARTS, 1052
SPOKANE BALLET, 1465
SPOKANE CIVIC THEATRE, 1466
SPOKANE COLISEUM, 1467
SPOKANE CONVENTION CENTER, 1468
SPOKANE INTERPLAYERS ENSEMBLE, 1466
SPOKANE OPERA HOUSE, 1468
SPOKANE SYMPHONY ORCHESTRA, 1466
SPOLETO FESTIVAL USA, 1258
SPRAGUE - GRISWOLD CULTURAL ART CENTER, 646
SPRECKELS ORGAN PAVILION, 161
SPRING MUSIC FESTIVAL, 212
SPRING WIND QUARTET, 404
SPRINGER OPERA HOUSE - THE STATE THEATRE OF
    GEORGIA, 390
SPRINGER OPERA HOUSE/THE STATE THEATER OF
    GEORGIA, 390
SPRINGFIELD BALLET, 764
SPRINGFIELD BALLET COMPANY, 474
SPRINGFIELD CIVIC CENTER, 646
SPRINGFIELD COLLEGE - MUSIC HALL, 475
SPRINGFIELD LITTLE THEATRE, 765
SPRINGFIELD ORCHESTRA ASSOCIATION, 645
SPRINGFIELD REGIONAL OPERA, 765
SPRINGFIELD SYMPHONY ASSOCIATION, 765
SPRINGFIELD SYMPHONY HALL, 646
SPRINGFIELD SYMPHONY ORCHESTRA, 475, 1145
SPRINGSTEAD THEATRE, THE, 364
SPRUCE STREET SINGERS, 1214
STAGE FRONT: THE ARTS DOWNEAST, 578
STAGE LEFT THEATRE, 442
STAGE ONE THE LOUISVILLE CHILDREN'S THEATRE, 549
STAGE WEST, 1348
STAGECENTER, 1319
STAGECRAFTERS, 1105
STAGES REPERTORY THEATRE, 1361, 1367
STAGES THEATRE, 88
STAGES THEATRE CENTER, 113
STAGEWEST, 646
STAGEWORKS TOURING COMPANY, 820
STAGEWRIGHTS, INC., 985
STAMBAUGH AUDITORIUM, 1153
STAMFORD SYMPHONY ORCHESTRA, 280
STAMFORD THEATRE WORKS, 281
STAN MCDONALD'S BLUE HORIZON JAZZ BAND, 643
STANFORD UNIVERSITY - ANNENBURG AUDITORIUM, 205
STANFORD UNIVERSITY - BRAUN RECITAL HALL, 205
STANFORD UNIVERSITY - CAMBLE RECITAL HALL, 205
STANFORD UNIVERSITY - COVERLY AUDITORIUM, 205
STANFORD UNIVERSITY - DINKELSPIEL
    AUDITORIUM, 205
STANFORD UNIVERSITY - MEMORIAL AUDITORIUM, 205
STANLEY PERFORMING ARTS CENTER, 1036
STAR SERIES OF READING, 1237
STARLIGHT BOWL, 161
STARLIGHT MUSICAL THEATRE/SAN DIEGO CIVIC LIGHT
    OPERA ASSOCIATION, 155
STARLIGHT-SAN DIEGO CIVIC LIGHT OPERA
    ASSOCIATION, 158
STARLITE PATIO THEATER SUMMER SERIES, 125
STATE BALLET OF MISSOURI, 745
STATE BALLET OF RHODE ISLAND, 1246
STATE OF ALABAMA BALLET/BALLET SOUTH, THE, 2
STATE THEATRE, 737
STATE THEATRE CENTER FOR THE ARTS, 1240
STATE UNIVERSITY AGRICULTURAL AND TECHNICAL
    COLLEGE - LITTLE THEATRE, 886
STATE UNIVERSITY OF NEW YORK - CORTLAND CAMPUS
    ARTIST AND LECTURE SERIES, 885
STATE UNIVERSITY OF NEW YORK COLLEGE-BROCKPORT-
    TOWER FINE ARTS CENTER, 868
STATE UNIVERSITY OF NEW YORK-ALBANY - ALBANY
    PERFORMING ARTS CENTER, 861
STATE UNIVERSITY OF NEW YORK-ALBANY - ARENA, 861
STATE UNIVERSITY OF NEW YORK-ALBANY - MAIN
    THEATRE, 862
STATE UNIVERSITY OF NEW YORK-ALBANY - RECITAL
    HALL, 862

STATE UNIVERSITY OF NEW YORK-BINGHAMPTON - CHAMBER HALL, 866
STATE UNIVERSITY OF NEW YORK-BINGHAMPTON - CONCERT THEATRE, 867
STATE UNIVERSITY OF NEW YORK-BUFFALO - DEPARTMENT OF THEATRE AND DANCE, 880
STATE UNIVERSITY OF NEW YORK-FREDONIA - MICHAEL C. ROCKEFELLER ARTS CENTER, 890
STATE UNIVERSITY OF NEW YORK-FREDONIA - MICHAEL C. ROCKEFELLER ARTS CENTER - CONCERT HALL, 890
STATE UNIVERSITY OF NEW YORK-FREDONIA - MICHAEL C. ROCKEFELLER ARTS CENTER - EXPERIMENTAL THEATRE, 890
STATE UNIVERSITY OF NEW YORK-FREDONIA - MICHAEL C. ROCKEFELLER ARTS CENTER - THEATRE, 890
STATE UNIVERSITY OF NEW YORK-PURCHASE - PERFORMING ARTS CENTER, 1018
STATE UNIVERSITY OF NEW YORK-PURCHASE - THEATER A, 1018
STATE UNIVERSITY OF NEW YORK-PURCHASE - THEATRE B, 1018
STATE UNIVERSITY OF NEW YORK-PURCHASE - THEATRE C, 1018
STATE UNIVERSITY OF NEW YORK-PURCHASE - THEATRE D, 1018
STATESVILLE COMMUNITY THEATRE, 1074
STEPHEN FOSTER DRAMA ASSOCIATION, 539
STEPHEN FOSTER STATE FOLK CULTURE CENTER - AMPHITHEATRE, 373
STEPHEN PETRONIO DANCE COMPANY, 935
STEPPENWOLF THEATRE COMPANY, 442
STERN GROVE FESTIVAL ASSOCIATION, 180
STEVE MCGRAW'S, 1007
STEVE SILVER PRODUCTIONS, 177
STOCKBRIDGE CHAMBER CONCERTS, 647
STOCKTON CIVIC THEATRE, 206
STOCKTON STATE COLLEGE - PERFORMING ARTS CENTER, 833
STOCKTON SYMPHONY ASSOCIATION, 205
STOP-GAP, 193
STRAND THEATRE, 571
STRAND THEATRE, THE, 1262
STRAND-CAPITOL PERFORMING ARTS CENTER - CAPITOL THEATRE, 1243
STRAND-CAPITOL PERFORMING ARTS CENTER - STRAND THEATRE, 1243
STREET MINSTRELS JAZZ SOCIETY, 429
STREET THEATER, THE, 1038
STRING ORCHESTRA OF THE ROCKIES, 776
STRINGS IN THE MOUNTAINS, 252
STROLLERS STUDENT THEATRICS, 1125
STUART PIMSLER DANCE & THEATER, 1121
STUDEBAKER MOVEMENT THEATER COMPANY, 644
STUDIO ARENA THEATRE, 878
STUDIO E THEATRE ENSEMBLE, 239
STUDIO THEATRE, 905
STUDIO THEATRE, THE, 306
STUDIO X PLAYHOUSE, 1174
SU TEATRO, INC., 239
SUBURBAN SYMPHONY ORCHESTRA, 1096
SUE BENNETT COLLEGE, APPALACHIAN FOLK FESTIVAL, 546
SUFFOLK COUNTY COMMUNITY COLLEGE - SAQTIKOS THEATRE, 867
SUGAR VALLEY CHAPTER OF SWEET ADELINES, 778
SULLIVAN STREET PLAYHOUSE, 1007
SUMMER MUSIC, INC., 274
SUMMER MUSIC ASSOCIATES, 810
SUMMER MUSIC THEATRE, 461
SUMMER OPERA THEATRE COMPANY, 303
SUMMER STRINGS ON THE MEHERRIN, 1060
SUMMIT SYMPHONY, 838
SUMTER COUNTY CULTURAL CENTER, 1266
SUN CITIES CHAMBER MUSIC SOCIETY, 35
SUN VALLEY CENTER FOR THE ARTS AND HUMANITIES, 417
SUNDANCE CHILDREN'S THEATRE, THE, 1407
SUNDANCE INSTITUTE, 1405

SUNFEST OF PALM BEACH COUNTY, INC., 372
SUNSET CENTER THEATRE, 69
SUNSET PLAYHOUSE, 1489
SUPPER CLUB, THE, 1007
SURFLIGHT SUMMER THEATRE, 816
SURFLIGHT THEATRE, 816
SURRY ARTS COUNCIL, 1066
SUSAN MARSHALL & COMPANY, 935
SUSHI PERFORMANCE AND VISUAL ART, 153
SWAMP FOX PLAYERS, 1262
SWARTHMORE MUSIC AND DANCE FESTIVAL, 1240
SWEENEY CONVENTION CENTER, 857
SWEET BRIAR COLLEGE - BABCOCK AUDITORIUM, 1441
SYLVAN WINDS, INCORPORATED, 951
SYMPHONY FOR UNITED NATIONS, 951
SYMPHONY HALL, 616, 1194, 1406
SYMPHONY OF SOUTHEAST TEXAS, 1313
SYMPHONY SOCIETY OF NORTH ARKANSAS, 45
SYNCHRONIA, 757
SYNTHAXIS THEATRE COMPANY, 128
SYRACUSE AREA LANDMARK THEATRE, 1033
SYRACUSE OPERA COMPANY, 1032
SYRACUSE SOCIETY FOR NEW MUSIC, 1031
SYRACUSE STAGE, 1032
SYRACUSE SYMPHONY ORCHESTRA, 1031
SYRACUSE SYMPHONY YOUTH ORCHESTRA, 1031
T. DANIEL MIME/MOVEMENT THEATRE, 478
TACOMA ACTORS GUILD, 1471
TACOMA CONCERT BAND, 1469
TACOMA OPERA ASSOCIATION, 1470
TACOMA PERFORMING DANCE COMPANY, 1468
TACOMA PHILHARMONIC, 1469
TACOMA SYMPHONY ORCHESTRA, 1469
TACOMA YOUTH SYMPHONY, 1470
TAGHKANIC CHORALE, THE, 1041
TALENTO BILINGUE DE HOUSTON, 1361
TALKING BAND, 985
TALLAHASSEE BALLET COMPANY, 365
TALLAHASSEE SYMPHONY ORCHESTRA, 365
TALLAHASSEE-LEON COUNTY CIVIC CENTER, 366
TAMPA BAY CHAMBER ORCHESTRA, 367
TAMPA BAY PERFORMING ARTS CENTER, 369
TAMPA BAY PERFORMING ARTS CENTER - FESTIVAL HALL, 369
TAMPA BAY PERFORMING ARTS CENTER - JAEB THEATER, 369
TAMPA BAY PERFORMING ARTS CENTER - PLAYHOUSE, 369
TAMPA PLAYERS, THE, 368
TAMPA THEATRE, 369
TANCE DANZ, 166
TANDY BEAL AND COMPANY, 196
TANGLEWOOD FESTIVAL, 613
TAOS SCHOOL OF MUSIC, INC., 857
TAP-IT DANCING AND THEATRICAL COMPANY, LTD., 1495
TAPROOT THEATRE COMPANY, 1461
TEATRO AVANTE, 343
TEATRO DEL SERENTA INC., 1525
TEATRO HISPANO DE DALLAS, 1331
TEATRO VISION, 187
TECUMSEH CIVIC AUDITORIUM, 694
TELLURIDE JAZZ CELEBRATION, 253
TEMPLE CIVIC THEATRE, 1389, 1390
TEMPLE THEATRE COMPANY, 1073
TEMPLE THEATRE COMPANY INC., 1073
TEMPLE THEATRE ORGAN CLUB, 692
TENNESSEE ASSOCIATION OF DANCE, 1282
TENNESSEE CHILDREN'S DANCE ENSEMBLE, 1285
TENNESSEE DANCE THEATRE, 1294
TENNESSEE PERFORMING ARTS CENTER, 1298
TENNESSEE PERFORMING ARTS CENTER - ANDREW JACKSON HALL, 1298
TENNESSEE PERFORMING ARTS CENTER - ANDREW JOHNSON THEATER, 1298
TENNESSEE PERFORMING ARTS CENTER - JAMES K. POLK THEATER, 1299
TENNESSEE PERFORMING ARTS CENTER MANAGEMENT CORPORATION, 1297
TENNESSEE REPERTORY THEATRE, 1296

TENNESSEE THEATER, 1287
TENNESSEE WILLIAMS FINE ARTS CENTER, 334
TERRE HAUTE SYMPHONY ORCHESTRA, 504
TERRI LEWIS DANCE ENSEMBLE, 139
TEXAS BACH CHOIR, 1384
TEXAS BAROQUE ENSEMBLE, 1352
TEXAS BOYS CHOIR, THE, 1345
TEXAS CHRISTIAN UNIVERSITY - ED LANDRETH
    AUDITORIUM, 1350
TEXAS GIRLS CHOIR, THE, 1345
TEXAS JAZZ FESTIVAL SOCIETY, 1322
TEXAS - THE MUSICAL DRAMA, 1318
TEXAS OPERA THEATER, 1359
TEXAS TECH UNIVERSITY CENTER - ALLEN THEATRE, 1374
TEXAS TECH UNIVERSITY CENTER - MUSIC BUILDING, 1374
TEXAS WESLEYAN COLLEGE - TEXAS WESLEYAN FINE
    ARTS AUDITORIUM, 1350
TEXAS WOMAN'S UNIVERSITY - REDBUD THEATRE, 1339
THALIA SPANISH THEATRE, 1030
THALIAN HALL - THALIAN HALL CENTER FOR THE
    PERFORMING ARTS, 1077
THANKS-GIVING SQUARE, 1337
THANKS-GIVING SQUARE - CHAPEL OF
    THANKSGIVING, 1337
THANKS-GIVING SQUARE - COURTYARD AT
    THANKS-GIVING SQUARE, 1337
THANKS-GIVING SQUARE - HALL OF WORLD
    THANKSGIVING, 1337
THAYER SYMPHONY ORCHESTRA, 644
THE. ART. RE. GRUP, INC./THE LAB, 169
THEATER ARTAUD, 166
THEATER AT MONMOUTH, THE, 579
THEATER BRISTOL, 1277
THEATER CHAMBER PLAYERS OF THE KENNEDY
    CENTER, 301
THEATER FACTORY SAINT LOUIS, 760
THEATER FOR THE NEW CITY, 985
THEATER GROTTESCO, 669
THEATER KNOXVILLE, 1286
THEATER OF THE STARS, 384
THEATER ON THE SQUARE, 1098
THEATER RHINOCERUS, INC., 177
THEATRE 40, 65
THEATRE ALBANY, 375, 376
THEATRE ARLINGTON, 1306, 1307
THEATRE BALLET OF SAN FRANCISCO, 166
THEATRE BUILDING, 447
THEATRE-BY-THE-SEA, 1246
THEATRE CHAMBER PLAYERS OF THE KENNEDY
    CENTER, 301
THEATRE CHARLOTTE, 1051
THEATRE CLUB OF THE PALM BEACHES, 338
THEATRE DE LA JEUNE LUNE, 715
THEATRE DU GRAND-GUIGNOL DE PARIS
    (GRAND-GUIGNOL THEATRE OF PARIS), 986
THEATRE EAST, 207
THEATRE EXCHANGE, 129
THEATRE FANTASTIQUE, 1014
THEATRE FIRST, 442
THEATRE FOR A NEW AUDIENCE, 986
THEATRE IV, 1437
THEATRE GAEL, 383
THEATRE GEMINI, 1331
THEATRE GUILD, 1293
THEATRE II COMPANY, 443
THEATRE IN THE GROVE, 1182
THEATRE IN THE PARK, 1069, 1071
THEATRE IN THE ROUND, 719
THEATRE IN THE ROUND PLAYERS, 715
THEATRE IN THE SQUARE, 395, 396
THEATRE-IN-THE-WORKS, 350
THEATRE MEMPHIS, 1291, 1292
THEATRE OF THE ENCHANTED FOREST, 580
THEATRE OF THE PERFORMING ARTS, 570
THEATRE OF THE RIVERSIDE CHURCH, 936
THEATRE OF UNIVERSAL IMAGES, 832
THEATRE OF WESTERN SPRINGS, 477
THEATRE OF YOUTH CO., 878

THEATRE OFF PARK, 986
THEATRE ON THE RIDGE, 1020
THEATRE ON THE SQUARE, 177
THEATRE ON WHEELS, 1362
THEATRE PROJECT, 590, 592
THEATRE RAPPORT/HOLLYWOOD THEATRE CLUB, 88
THEATRE ROCOCO, 961
THEATRE SUBURBIA, 1362, 1367
THEATRE THREE, 1332, 1337
THEATRE THREE PRODUCTIONS, 1016
THEATRE THREE PRODUCTIONS - MAINSTAGE, 1016
THEATRE THREE PRODUCTIONS - SECOND STAGE, 1016
THEATRE TULSA, 1169
THEATRE UNDER THE STARS, 1362
THEATRE VIRGINIA, 1437
THEATRE WEST, 113
THEATRE WEST VIRGINIA, INC., 1475
THEATRE WINTER HAVEN, 373
THEATRE WORKSHOP OF NANTUCKET, INC., THE, 634
THEATRE WORKSHOP OF OWENSBORO, 552
THEATRE X, 1509
THEATREMOVES, INC./RAJECKAS AND INTRAUB
    MOVEMENT THEATER, 986
THEATREWORKS, 138
THEATREWORKS/USA, 987
THEATRICAL OUTFIT, 383
THESPIAN THEATRICAL CLUB, THE, 178
THIEL COLLEGE - PASSAVANT MEMORIAL
    CENTER, 1204
THOMASTON-UPSON ARTS COUNCIL, 398
THOMASVILLE CULTURAL CENTER AUDITORIUM, 399
THREE ARTS THEATRE, 391
THREE RIVERS SHAKESPEARE FESTIVAL, 1235
THROUGH THE OPERA GLASS, 1418
THUNDER BAY ARTS COUNCIL, 656
THUNDER BAY ENSEMBLE, 987
THUNDER BAY THEATRE, 656
THURSDAY MUSICALE, THE, 346
TIBBITS OPERA AND ARTS COUNCIL, 665
TIBBITS OPERA HOUSE, 665
TICONDEROGA FESTIVAL GUILD, INC., 1034
TIMBERS DINNER THEATER, 1212, 1213
TISCH CENTER FOR THE ARTS, 952
TITAS - THE INTERNATIONAL THEATRICAL ARTS
    SOCIETY, 1333
TIVOLI THEATRE, 1279
TNR-MOEBIUS, 103
TOBY'S DINNER THEATRE, 594
TOCCOA SYMPHONY ORCHESTRA GUILD, 399
TOKUNAGA DANCE COMPANY, 936
TOLEDO BALLET SCHOOL, THE, 1147
TOLEDO JAZZ SOCIETY, 1147
TOLEDO MASONIC AUDITORIUM, 1149
TOLEDO MUSEUM OF ART, THE, 1148
TOLEDO MUSEUM OF ART - PERISTYLE, THE, 1149
TOLEDO OPERA, 1148
TOLEDO REP, THE, 1148
TOLEDO SYMPHONY, THE, 1147
TOM EVERT DANCE COMPANY, THE, 1132
TOMOV FOLK DANCE ENSEMBLE, 1039
TOP BRASS QUARTET, THE, 1130
TOPEKA CIVIC THEATRE, 534
TOPEKA JAZZ WORKSHOP, 534
TOPEKA PERFORMING ARTS CENTER, 535
TORRANCE COMMUNITY THEATRE, 210
TORRANCE CULTURAL ARTS CENTER, 210
TORRINGTON CIVIC THEATRE, 283
TOTEM POLE PLAYHOUSE, 1202
TOUCH, 1046
TOUCHSTONE THEATRE, 1196
TOURING CONCERT OPERA CO. INC. - BERKSHIRE-HUDSON
    VALLEY FESTIVAL OF OPERA AND BALLET, 885
TOURING CONCERT OPERA COMPANY, 961
TOWER THEATRE FOR THE PERFORMING ARTS, 82
TOWN AND GOWN THEATER, 3
TOWN PLAYERS, 1276
TOWNE AND COUNTRY PLAYERS, 1142
TOWNSEND OPERA PLAYERS, 125

TOWSON STATE UNIVERSITY FINE ARTS CENTER, 599
TOWSON STATE UNIVERSITY FINE ARTS CENTER - CONCERT HALL, 599
TOWSON STATE UNIVERSITY FINE ARTS CENTER - MAIN STAGE, 599
TOWSON STATE UNIVERSITY FINE ARTS CENTER - STUDIO THEATRE, 599
TOWSON STATE UNIVERSITY - STEPHENS AUDITORIUM, 599
TRANSYLVANIA UNIVERSITY, 545
TRAVELING JEWISH THEATRE, A, 173
TRAVELING PLAYHOUSE, 1039
TRAVERSE SYMPHONY ORCHESTRA, 694
TREMONT STRING QUARTET, INC., 892
TRI LAKES COMMUNITY THEATRE, 742
TRIANGLE CULTURAL CENTER, 739
TRIANGLE OPERA THEATER, 1054
TRI-C JAZZFEST, 1115
TRI-CITIES OPERA COMPANY, 866
TRINITY ARTS CENTER, 1252
TRINITY REPERTORY COMPANY, 1251
TRINITY SQUARE ENSEMBLE, 455
TRINITY UNIVERSITY - DEPARTMENT OF SPEECH AND DRAMA, 1387
TRINITY UNIVERSITY - LAURIE AUDITORIUM, 1387
TRINKLE BRASS WORKS, 1064
TRISHA BROWN COMPANY, 936
TROUPE AMERICA INC., 716
TROY ARENA, 1035
TROY CHROMATICS CONCERTS, INC., 1034
TROY - HAYNER CULTURAL CENTER, 1035
TROY SAVINGS BANK MUSIC HALL, 1035
TRUMAN COLLEGE - O'ROURKE CENTER FOR THE PERFORMING ARTS, 448
TRUMBULL NEW THEATRE, 1142
TRUSTEES AUDITORIUM - ASIAN ART MUSEUM, 184
TRUSTUS, 1260
TRYON FINE ARTS CENTER, 1075
TUCSON ARIZONA BOYS CHORUS, 37
TUCSON CONVENTION CENTER, 39
TUCSON CONVENTION CENTER - ARENA, 40
TUCSON CONVENTION CENTER - EXHIBITION HALL, 40
TUCSON CONVENTION CENTER - LITTLE THEATRE, 40
TUCSON CONVENTION CENTER - MUSIC HALL, 40
TUCSON CONVENTION CENTER - THEATRE, 40
TUCSON FESTIVAL SOCIETY, 39
TUCSON JAZZ SOCIETY, INC., 36
TUCSON SYMPHONY ORCHESTRA, 36
TUESDAY EVENING CONCERT SERIES, 1425
TUESDAY MUSICAL CONCERT SERIES, 793
TUFTS UNIVERSITY - BALCH ARENA THEATER, 633
TULANE UNIVERSITY - ALBERT I. LUPIN MEMORIAL EXPERIMENTAL THEATRE, 568
TULARE COUNTY SYMPHONY ORCHESTRA, 214
TULSA BALLET THEATRE, 1167
TULSA OPERA, 1169
TULSA PERFORMING ARTS CENTER, 1170
TULSA PERFORMING ARTS CENTER - CHAPMAN MUSIC HALL, 1170
TULSA PERFORMING ARTS CENTER - JOHN H. WILLIAMS THEATRE, 1171
TULSA PERFORMING ARTS CENTER - STUDIO I, 1171
TULSA PERFORMING ARTS CENTER - STUDIO II, 1171
TULSA PHILHARMONIC, 1168
TULSA YOUTH SYMPHONY ORCHESTRA, 1168
TUPELO SYMPHONY, 738
TURTLE CREEK CHORALE, 1328
TUSCARAWAS CAMPUS OF KENT STATE UNIVERSITY - AUDITORIUM, 1142
TUSCARAWAS PHILHARMONIC, 1141
12TH STREET JAZZ SERIES, 748
TWENTIETH CENTURY CONSORI, 1423
24TH STREET EXPERIMENT, 1384
TWIN CITIES GAY MEN'S CHORUS, 711
TWIN LAKES PLAYHOUSE, 51
TWIN MOUNTAIN TONESMEN, 1382
TWYLA THARP DANCE FOUNDATION, 936
UBU REPERTORY THEATER, 987

UCI CULTURAL EVENTS, 92
UKIAH PLAYERS THEATRE, 211
ULSTER PERFORMING ARTS CENTER, 902
UMPQUA SYMPHONY ASSOCIATION, 1190
UNDERGROUND RAILWAY THEATER, 602
UNDERMAIN THEATRE, 1332
UNICORN PLAYERS INC., 88
UNICORN THEATRE, 748, 750
UNION COLONY CIVIC CENTER, 248
UNION COUNTY ARTS CENTER, 835
UNION SYMPHONY ORCHESTRA, 1066
UNITARIAN PLAYERS, 1145
UNITED ARTISTS OF RALEIGH AND WAKE COUNTY, 1070
UNITED BLACK ARTISTS, USA, INC., 670
UNITED JEWISH YS OF LONG ISLAND, 1015
UNITED STATES AIR FORCE BAND, THE, 301
UNITY CONCERTS, 827
UNIVERSITY ARTISTS SERIES, 1488
UNIVERSITY CENTER AUDITORIUM, 316
UNIVERSITY CENTER CULTURAL EVENTS, 1372
UNIVERSITY CENTER THEATRE COMPLEX AND CONFERENCE TOWER, 1319
UNIVERSITY CENTER THEATRE COMPLEX AND CONFERENCE TOWER - RUDDER AUDITORIUM, 1319
UNIVERSITY CENTER THEATRE COMPLEX AND CONFERENCE TOWER - RUDDER FORUM, 1319
UNIVERSITY CENTER THEATRE COMPLEX AND CONFERENCE TOWER - RUDDER THEATRE, 1319
UNIVERSITY CIRCLE CHAMBER ORCHESTRA, 1111
UNIVERSITY DANCE COMPANY, 1121
UNIVERSITY MUSICAL SOCIETY OF THE UNIVERSITY OF MICHIGAN, 660
UNIVERSITY OF ALABAMA - CONCERT HALL, 12
UNIVERSITY OF ALABAMA - GALLAWAY THEATRE, 12
UNIVERSITY OF ALABAMA - HUEY RECITAL HALL, 12
UNIVERSITY OF ALABAMA - MORGAN AUDITORIUM, 12
UNIVERSITY OF ALASKA - CHARLES W. DAVIS CONCERT HALL, 19
UNIVERSITY OF ARIZONA - CENTENNIAL HALL, 40
UNIVERSITY OF ARIZONA - CROWDER HALL, 41
UNIVERSITY OF ARKANSAS-LITTLE ROCK - STELLA BOYLE SMITH CONCERT HALL, 50
UNIVERSITY OF BRIDGEPORT - BERNHARD CENTER, 256
UNIVERSITY OF CALIFORNIA-BERKELEY - ALFRED HERTZ MEMORIAL HALL, 63
UNIVERSITY OF CALIFORNIA-BERKELEY - CALIFORNIA PERFORMANCES, 62
UNIVERSITY OF CALIFORNIA-BERKELEY - HEARST GREEK THEATRE, 63
UNIVERSITY OF CALIFORNIA-BERKELEY - ZELLERBACH HALL, 63
UNIVERSITY OF CALIFORNIA-BERKELEY - ZELLERBACH PLAYHOUSE, 63
UNIVERSITY OF CALIFORNIA-DAVIS - UC DAVIS PRESENTS, 76
UNIVERSITY OF CALIFORNIA-IRVINE - VILLAGE THEATRE, 92
UNIVERSITY OF CALIFORNIA-LOS ANGELES - ROYCE HALL, 121
UNIVERSITY OF CALIFORNIA-LOS ANGELES - WADSWORTH THEATER, 121
UNIVERSITY OF CALIFORNIA-RIVERSIDE - UNIVERSITY THEATRE, 146
UNIVERSITY OF CALIFORNIA-SAN DIEGO - MANDEVILLE AUDITORIUM, 94
UNIVERSITY OF CALIFORNIA-SAN DIEGO UNIVERSITY EVENTS OFFICE, 93
UNIVERSITY OF CALIFORNIA -SANTA BARBARA - ARTS & LECTURES, 195
UNIVERSITY OF CALIFORNIA-SANTA CRUZ - PERFORMING ARTS CENTER, 198
UNIVERSITY OF CINCINNATI - CORBETT AUDITORIUM, 1107
UNIVERSITY OF CINCINNATI - CORBETT CENTER FOR THE PERFORMING ARTS, 1107
UNIVERSITY OF CINCINNATI - PATRICIA CORBETT THEATER, 1108
UNIVERSITY OF CINCINNATI - WATSON HALL, 1108

UNIVERSITY OF COLORADO - MACKY AUDITORIUM CONCERT HALL, 227
UNIVERSITY OF CONNECTICUT - HARRIET S. JORGENSEN THEATRE, 282
UNIVERSITY OF CONNECTICUT - STUDIO THEATRE, 283
UNIVERSITY OF DAYTON ARTS SERIES, THE, 1131
UNIVERSITY OF HAWAII - HILO THEATRE, 402
UNIVERSITY OF HAWAII AT MANOA, COLLEGE OF CONTINUING EDUCATION AND COMMUNITY SERVICE, 404
UNIVERSITY OF IOWA - HANCHER AUDITORIUM, THE, 518
UNIVERSITY OF KANSAS - CRAFTON-PREYER THEATRE, 529
UNIVERSITY OF LOWELL - CENTER FOR THE ARTS, 631
UNIVERSITY OF MAINE - MAINE CENTER FOR THE ARTS, 581
UNIVERSITY OF MAINE AT MACHIAS - STAGE FRONT, 579
UNIVERSITY OF MARYLAND INTERNATIONAL PIANO FESTIVAL AND WILLIAM KAPELL COMPETITION, 593
UNIVERSITY OF MASSACHUSETTS - BOWKER AUDITORIUM, 602
UNIVERSITY OF MASSACHUSETTS - CONCERT HALL, 602
UNIVERSITY OF MICHIGAN, UNIVERSITY PRODUCTIONS, 659
UNIVERSITY OF MICHIGAN - MENDELSSOHN THEATRE, 660
UNIVERSITY OF MICHIGAN - TRUEBLOOD THEATRE, 660
UNIVERSITY OF MICHIGAN CHORAL UNION, 658
UNIVERSITY OF MICHIGAN GILBERT AND SULLIVAN SOCIETY, 659
UNIVERSITY OF MISSISSIPPI - FULTON CHAPEL, 737
UNIVERSITY OF MISSISSIPPI - MEEK AUDITORIUM, 738
UNIVERSITY OF MISSISSIPPI - STUDIO THEATRE, 738
UNIVERSITY OF MISSOURI- COLUMBIA - JESSE AUDITORIUM, 744
UNIVERSITY OF MONTANA - MONTANA THEATRE, 777
UNIVERSITY OF NEBRASKA - UNIVERSITY THEATRE, 784
UNIVERSITY OF NEBRASKA-LINCOLN - KIMBALL RECITAL HALL, 787
UNIVERSITY OF NEVADA-LAS VEGAS - ARTEMUS HAM CONCERT HALL, 798
UNIVERSITY OF NEVADA-RENO - CHURCH FINE ARTS CENTER, 800
UNIVERSITY OF NEVADA-RENO - CHURCH FINE ARTS CENTER - FINE ARTS THEATRE, 800
UNIVERSITY OF NEVADA-RENO - CHURCH FINE ARTS CENTER - NIGHTINGALE HALL, 800
UNIVERSITY OF NEVADA-RENO - CHURCH FINE ARTS CENTER - REDFIELD STUDIO THEATRE, 800
UNIVERSITY OF NEVADA-RENO - LAWLOR EVENTS CENTER, 800
UNIVERSITY OF NEW HAMPSHIRE - DURHAM, 804
UNIVERSITY OF NEW HAMPSHIRE-DURHAM - BRATTON RECITAL HALL, 804
UNIVERSITY OF NEW HAMPSHIRE-DURHAM - HENNESSY THEATER, 804
UNIVERSITY OF NEW HAMPSHIRE-DURHAM - JOHNSON THEATER, 805
UNIVERSITY OF NEW MEXICO - POPEJOY HALL, 851
UNIVERSITY OF NEW ORLEANS PERFORMING ARTS CENTER, 568
UNIVERSITY OF NEW ORLEANS RESIDENT ACTING COMPANY, 566
UNIVERSITY OF NORTH CAROLINA-WILMINGTON - SARAH GRAHAM KENAN MEMORIAL AUDITORIUM, 1078
UNIVERSITY OF NORTH DAKOTA - CHESTER FRITZ AUDITORIUM, 1087
UNIVERSITY OF NORTH TEXAS - CONCERT HALL, 1339
UNIVERSITY OF NORTH TEXAS - DEPARTMENT OF DANCE AND DRAMA, 1339
UNIVERSITY OF NORTHERN COLORADO - HELEN LANGWORTHY THEATRE, 249
UNIVERSITY OF NORTHERN IOWA - RUSSELL HALL, 509
UNIVERSITY OF NORTHERN IOWA - STRAYER-WOOD THEATRE, 509
UNIVERSITY OF NORTHERN IOWA - STRAYER-WOOD THEATRE-BLACK BOX, 509
UNIVERSITY OF NORTHERN IOWA - STRAYER-WOOD THEATRE-MAIN STAGE, 510
UNIVERSITY OF OKLAHOMA THEATRE, 1163

UNIVERSITY OF OREGON - BEALL CONCERT HALL, 1181
UNIVERSITY OF THE PACIFIC - DE MARCUS BROWN STUDIO THEATRE, 206
UNIVERSITY OF THE PACIFIC - FAYE SPANOS CONCERT HALL, 206
UNIVERSITY OF THE PACIFIC - LONG THEATRE, 207
UNIVERSITY OF THE PACIFIC - RECITAL HALL, 207
UNIVERSITY OF RHODE ISLAND FINE ARTS CENTER, 1245
UNIVERSITY OF RHODE ISLAND FINE ARTS CENTER - J STUDIO, 1245
UNIVERSITY OF RHODE ISLAND FINE ARTS CENTER - ROBERT E. WILL THEATRE, 1246
UNIVERSITY OF RICHMOND - JAMES L. CAMP MEMORIAL THEATRE, 1438
UNIVERSITY OF ROCHESTER THEATRE PROGRAM, 1021
UNIVERSITY OF ROCHESTER-RIVER CAMPUS - STRONG AUDITORIUM, 1022
UNIVERSITY OF SOUTH CAROLINA - DRAYTON HALL THEATRE, 1261
UNIVERSITY OF SOUTH CAROLINA - LONGSTREET THEATRE, 1261
UNIVERSITY OF SOUTH CAROLINA BEAUFORT ARTS CENTER, 1257
UNIVERSITY OF SOUTH CAROLINA-COASTAL CAROLINA COLLEGE - LITTLE THEATRE, 1261
UNIVERSITY OF SOUTH CAROLINA-COASTAL CAROLINA COLLEGE - WHEELWRIGHT PERFORMING ARTS CENTER, 1262
UNIVERSITY OF SOUTH DAKOTA - SLAGLE AUDITORIUM, 1275
UNIVERSITY OF SOUTH DAKOTA - WARREN M. LEE CENTER FOR THE FINE ARTS, 1275
UNIVERSITY OF SOUTH FLORIDA - STUDIO THEATRE, 370
UNIVERSITY OF SOUTH FLORIDA - THEATRE I, 370
UNIVERSITY OF SOUTH FLORIDA - THEATRE II, 370
UNIVERSITY OF SOUTHERN CALIFORNIA - BOVARD AUDITORIUM, 121
UNIVERSITY OF SOUTHERN CALIFORNIA OPERA, 107
UNIVERSITY OF TENNESSEE MUSIC HALL, 1287
UNIVERSITY OF TEXAS AT ARLINGTON - MAINSTAGE THEATER, 1307
UNIVERSITY OF TEXAS AT ARLINGTON - STUDIO THEATER, 1307
UNIVERSITY OF TEXAS AT AUSTIN - B. IDEN PAYNE THEATRE, 1311
UNIVERSITY OF TEXAS AT AUSTIN - THEATRE ROOM, 1311
UNIVERSITY OF TEXAS AT AUSTIN PERFORMING ARTS CENTER, 1311
UNIVERSITY OF TEXAS AT AUSTIN PERFORMING ARTS CENTER - THE BASS CONCERT HALL, 1311
UNIVERSITY OF TEXAS AT AUSTIN PERFORMING ARTS CENTER - BATES RECITAL HALL, 1311
UNIVERSITY OF TEXAS AT AUSTIN PERFORMING ARTS CENTER - THE MCCULLOUGH THEATRE, 1312
UNIVERSITY OF TEXAS AT EL PASO - MAIN PLAYHOUSE, 1342
UNIVERSITY OF TEXAS-PAN AMERICAN - FINE ARTS AUDITORIUM, 1340
UNIVERSITY OF TEXAS-PAN AMERICAN - THEATER, 1340
UNIVERSITY OF TULSA - KENDALL HALL, 1171
UNIVERSITY OF TULSA - TYRRELL HALL, 1171
UNIVERSITY OF UTAH - KINGSBURY HALL, 1406
UNIVERSITY OF VERMONT - RECITAL HALL, 1413
UNIVERSITY OF WEST FLORIDA CENTER FOR THE PERFORMING ARTS, 354
UNIVERSITY OF WISCONSIN CENTER - FOX VALLEY, 1501
UNIVERSITY OF WISCONSIN LECTURES AND FINE ARTS SERIES, 1501
UNIVERSITY OF WISCONSIN-PLATTEVILLE - PERFORMING ARTS SERIES, 1512
UNIVERSITY OF WISCONSIN-SUPERIOR - PAUL E. HOLDEN FINE AND APPLIED ARTS CENTER, 1516
UNIVERSITY OF WYOMING - ARENA AUDITORIUM, 1521
UNIVERSITY OF WYOMING - ARTS AND SCIENCES AUDITORIUM, 1521
UNIVERSITY OF WYOMING - FINE ARTS CONCERT HALL, 1521
UNIVERSITY SETTLEMENT, 1008

UP WITH PEOPLE, 37
UPPER ARLINGTON CULTURAL ARTS COMMISSION, 1149
UPPER CATSKILL COMMUNITY COUNCIL OF THE
    ARTS, 1012
UPSALA COLLEGE - WORKSHOP 90 THEATER, 818
UPSTAGE!, 1463
URBAN BUSH WOMEN, 937
USA INTERNATIONAL BALLET COMPETITION, 736
UTAH CLASSICAL GUITAR SOCIETY, 1398
UTAH OPERA COMPANY, 1404
UTAH REGIONAL BALLET, 1395
UTAH SHAKESPEAREAN FESTIVAL, 1395
UTAH STATE UNIVERSITY - CHASE FINE ARTS
    CENTER, 1396
UTAH STATE UNIVERSITY - KENT CONCERT HALL, 1396
UTAH STATE UNIVERSITY - MORGAN THEATRE, 1396
UTAH SYMPHONY, 1403
UTAH VALLEY SYMPHONY, 1398
UTAH VALLEY YOUTH SYMPHONY, 1399
UTAH YOUTH SYMPHONY, 1403
UTICA MEMORIAL AUDITORIUM, 1036
VAL A. BROWNING CENTER FOR THE PERFORMING
    ARTS, 1397
VALDOSTA STATE COLLEGE - SAWYER THEATRE, 400
VALDOSTA STATE COLLEGE - WHITEHEAD
    AUDITORIUM, 400
VALENCIA COMMUNITY COLLEGE - BLACK BOX
    THEATRE, 351
VALENCIA COMMUNITY COLLEGE - PERFORMING ARTS
    CENTER, 351
VALENTINA OUMANSKY DRAMATIC DANCE
    FOUNDATION, 103
VALLEY COMMUNITY THEATER, 418
VALLEY FORGE MUSIC FAIR, 1200
VALLEY FORGE MUSIC FAIR PRODUCTIONS, INC., 1199
VALLEY LIGHT OPERA, 601
VALLEY PERFORMING ARTS, 22
VALLEY SYMPHONY ORCHESTRA & CHORALE AND
    VALLEY SINFONETTE, 1375
VAN CLIBURN FOUNDATION, 1348
VAN WEZEL AUDITORIUM, 364
VANAVER CARAVAN, THE, 1023
VANDERBURGH AUDITORIUM CONVENTION
    CENTER, 489
VAUDEVILLE PALACE, 358
VEERA WIBAUX MIME THEATRE, 178
VENETIAN THEATRE, 901
VENICE COMMUNITY CENTER, 371
VENICE LITTLE THEATRE, THE, 370
VENTI DA CAMERA, 1097
VENTURA COUNTY SYMPHONY ASSOCIATION, 213
VERMONT BALLET THEATRE, 1410
VERMONT MOZART FESTIVAL, 1412
VERMONT OPERA THEATER, 1409
VERMONT SYMPHONY ORCHESTRA, 1411
VERMONT YOUTH ORCHESTRA, 1411
VERO BEACH THEATRE GUILD, 371
VETERANS MEMORIAL, 1127
VETERAN'S MEMORIAL AUDITORIUM, 75
VETERANS MEMORIAL AUDITORIUM, 1252
VETERANS MEMORIAL CIVIC AND CONVENTION
    CENTER, 1137
VETERANS MEMORIAL CIVIC AND CONVENTION CENTER -
    CROUSE PERFORMANCE HALL, 1137
VETERANS MEMORIAL HALL, 1028
VETERANS' MEMORIAL THEATRE, 76
VICTOR VALLEY COLLEGE PERFORMING ARTS
    CENTER, 214
VICTORIA BACH FESTIVAL ASSOCIATION, 1391
VICTORIA MARKS PERFORMANCE COMPANY, 937
VICTORIAN THEATRE, 239, 242
VICTORY GARDENS THEATER, 443, 448
VICTORY PARK AUDITORIUM, 347
VICTORY THEATRE, 67
VIGILANTE THEATRE COMPANY, 771
VIKLARBO CHAMBER EMSEMBLE, 105
VILLA JULIA COLLEGE - INSCAPE THEATRE, 598
VILLA MONTALVO CENTER FOR THE ARTS, 202

VILLA MONTALVO CENTER FOR THE ARTS - CARRIAGE
    HOUSE THEATRE, 202
VILLA MONTALVO CENTER FOR THE ARTS - LILIAN
    FONTAINE GARDEN THEATRE, 202
VILLAGE BACH FESTIVAL, 664
VILLAGE GATE, 1008
VILLAGE LIGHT OPERA GROUP, 961
VILLAGE PLAYERS, 783
VILLAGE PLAYERS, THE, 347
VILLAGE PLAYERS (OAK PARK-RIVER FOREST CIVIC
    THEATRE, INC.), 465
VINCENNES UNIVERSITY SUMMER THEATRE, 505
VINEYARD THEATRE, 987
VIRGINIA BALLET THEATRE, 1431
VIRGINIA BEACH PAVILION CONVENTION CENTER, 1441
VIRGINIA BEACH PAVILION CONVENTION CENTER -
    EXHIBIT HALL, 1442
VIRGINIA BEACH PAVILION CONVENTION CENTER -
    PAVILION THEATER, 1442
VIRGINIA CHORAL SOCIETY, 1431
VIRGINIA OPERA, 1432
VIRGINIA SHAKESPEARE FESTIVAL, 1442
VIRGINIA STAGE COMPANY, 1433
VIRGINIA SYMPHONY, THE, 1431
VIRGINIA THEATER, 1008
VIRTUOSI DELLA ROSA, INC., 1187
VISALIA CONVENTION CENTER - EXHIBIT HALL, 214
VISALIA CONVENTION CENTER - L.J. WILLIAMS
    THEATRE, 214
VISALIA CONVENTION CENTER - ROTARY THEATRE, 215
VIVA EL PASO!, 1342
VIVE LES ARTS SOCIETE AND THEATRE, 1371
VIVE LES ARTS THEATRE, 1371
VOCAL ARTS ENSEMBLE OF CINCINNATI, 1103
VOICES OF CHANGE, 1326
VON BRAUN CIVIC CENTER, 7
VON BRAUN CIVIC CENTER - ARENA, 7
VON BRAUN CIVIC CENTER - CONCERT HALL, 7
VON BRAUN CIVIC CENTER - EXHIBIT HALL, 7
VON BRAUN CIVIC CENTER - PLAYHOUSE, 8
VORSPIEL DRAMA EPHRATA CLOISTER ASSOCIATES, 1200
VORTEX REPERTORY COMPANY, 1310
WACO CONVENTION CENTER, 1392
WACO CONVENTION CENTER - CHISHOLM HALL, 1392
WADSWORTH AUDITORIUM, 892
WAIMEA COMMUNITY THEATRE, 408
WALDORF COMMUNITY ARTISTS SERIES, 516
WALKER ART CENTER, 716
WALLA WALLA SYMPHONY, 1472
WALLINGFORD SYMPHONY ORCHESTRA, 284
WALNUT STREET THEATRE, 1228
WALNUT STREET THEATRE - MAINSTAGE, 1228
WALNUT STREET THEATRE - STUDIO FIVE, 1229
WALNUT STREET THEATRE - STUDIO THREE, 1229
WALNUT STREET THEATRE COMPANY, 1224
WALTER KERR THEATRE, 1008
WALTON CREEK PLAYHOUSE, 1108
WANG CENTER FOR THE PERFORMING ARTS, THE, 616
WAR MEMORIAL AUDITORIUM, 325
WAREHOUSE LIVING ARTS CENTER, 1323
WARNER THEATRE, 313
WARNOR'S THEATER, 82
WARREN CIVIC MUSIC ASSOCIATION, 1150
WARREN PERFORMING ARTS CENTER, 498
WARREN PERFORMING ARTS CENTER - ESCH
    AUDITORIUM, 498
WARREN PERFORMING ARTS CENTER - STUDIO
    THEATER, 498
WARREN SYMPHONY ORCHESTRA, 696
WARTBURG COLLEGE - NEUMANN AUDITORIUM, 522
WARTBURG COLLEGE ARTISTS SERIES, 522
WARWICK PLAYERS, 1252
WASHINGTON AND LEE UNIVERSITY CONCERT GUILD,
    1429
WASHINGTON BACH CONSORT, 303
WASHINGTON BALLET, THE, 298
WASHINGTON BLUEGRASS ASSOCIATION, 1471
WASHINGTON CENTER FOR THE PERFORMING ARTS, 1452

WASHINGTON CHAMBER SYMPHONY, 301
WASHINGTON IDAHO SYMPHONY, 414
WASHINGTON OPERA, 303
WASHINGTON PERFORMING ARTS SOCIETY, 309
WASHINGTON SINGERS, 304
WASHINGTON STAGE GUILD, THE, 306
WASHINGTON UNIVERSITY - EDISON THEATRE, 763
WATER MUSIC, 620
WATERBURY SYMPHONY ORCHESTRA, 286
WATERLOO COMMUNITY PLAYHOUSE/BLACK HAWK
    CHILDREN'S THEATRE, 521
WATERLOO MUSIC FESTIVAL, 842
WATERLOO-CEDAR FALLS SYMPHONY ORCHESTRA, 521
WATERTOWN LYRIC THEATER PRODUCTIONS, 1037
WATERTOWN MUNICIPAL BAND, 1276
WATERVILLE OPERA HOUSE, 535
WATERVILLE SUMMER THEATRE CORPORATION, 535
WATERVILLE VALLEY FOUNDATION, 814
WAUKESHA CIVIC THEATRE, 1517
WAUKESHA SYMPHONY, 1516
WAUPACA FINE ARTS FESTIVAL, 1517
WAVERLY CONSORT, INC., 952
WAYNE CHAMBER ORCHESTRA, 843
WAYNE STATE UNIVERSITY HILBERRY AND BONSTELLE
    THEATRES, 669
WAYSIDE THEATRE, 1430
WEATHERVANE THEATRE, 814
WEBSTER COMMUNITY EDUCATION, 1276
WEBSTER UNIVERSITY-LORETTO - HILTON CENTER FOR
    THE PERFORMING ARTS, 763
WECKESSER STUDIO THEATRE, 857
WEIDNER CENTER FOR THE PERFORMING ARTS, 1491
WEIDNER CENTER FOR THE PERFROMING ARTS, 1491
WELLS THEATRE, 1434
WENDY ROGERS/CHOREOGRAPHICS, 59
WESLEYAN COLLEGE - PORTER AUDITORIUM, 394
WESLEYAN UNIVERSITY CENTER FOR THE ARTS, 267
WESLEYAN UNIVERSITY CENTER FOR THE ARTS -
    CINEMA, 267
WESLEYAN UNIVERSITY CENTER FOR THE ARTS -
    CROWELL CONCERT HALL, 267
WESLEYAN UNIVERSITY CENTER FOR THE ARTS -
    THEATER, 267
WESLEYAN UNIVERSITY CENTER FOR THE ARTS - WORLD
    MUSIC HALL, 268
WEST BAY OPERA, 138
WEST COAST CHAMBER ORCHESTRA, 194
WEST COAST OPERA THEATRE, 136
WEST COAST SYMPHONY, 194
WEST END DRAMA MINISTRIES, 1297
WEST JERSEY CHAMBER MUSIC SOCIETY, 827
WEST PALM BEACH AUDITORIUM, 373
WEST SHORE SYMPHONY, 686
WEST SHORE YOUTH SYMPHONY ORCHESTRA, 686
WEST TEXAS STATE UNIVERSITY - BRANDING IRON
    THEATER, 1318
WEST VALLEY CHAMBER ORCHESTRA, THE, 218
WEST VALLEY SYMPHONY, DIVISION OF THE LOS
    ANGELES CIVIC ORCHESTRA, 68
WEST VIRGINIA STATE COLLEGE - CAPITOL CENTER, 1480
WEST VIRGINIA STATE COLLEGE - F.S. BELCHER
    THEATRE, 1482
WEST VIRGINIA SYMPHONY, 1477
WEST VIRGINIA SYMPHONY ORCHESTRA, 1477
WEST VIRGINIA UNIVERSITY CREATIVE ARTS
    CENTER, 1483
WEST VIRGINIA UNIVERSITY CREATIVE ARTS CENTER -
    CHORAL RECITAL HALL, 1483
WEST VIRGINIA UNIVERSITY CREATIVE ARTS CENTER -
    CLASSROOM THEATRE, 1484
WEST VIRGINIA UNIVERSITY CREATIVE ARTS CENTER -
    CONCERT THEATRE, 1484
WEST VIRGINIA UNIVERSITY CREATIVE ARTS CENTER -
    OPERA THEATRE, 1484
WEST VIRGINIA UNIVERSITY CREATIVE ARTS CENTER -
    STUDIO THEATER, 1484
WEST VIRGINIA WESLEYAN COLLEGE - ATKINSON
    AUDITORIUM, 1475

WESTARK COMMUNITY COLLEGE - BREEDLOVE
    AUDITORIUM, 47
WESTBETH THEATRE CENTER, 988, 1008
WESTBETH THEATRE CENTER - BIG ROOM, 1008
WESTBETH THEATRE CENTER - SECOND FLOOR
    THEATRE, 1009
WESTBETH THEATRE CENTER - STUDIO THEATRE, 1009
WESTBURY MUSIC FAIR, 1037, 1038
WESTCHESTER BALLET COMPANY, 1013
WESTCHESTER BROADWAY THEATRE, 889
WESTCHESTER CHORAL SOCIETY, INC., 1038
WESTCHESTER ELEMENTARY ORCHESTRA, 895
WESTCHESTER JUNIOR STRING ORCHESTRA, 895
WESTCHESTER YOUTH SYMPHONY, 896
WESTERN ARTS MUSIC FESTIVAL, 1521
WESTERN ILLINOIS UNIVERSITY - HAINLINE THEATRE, 461
WESTERN MASSACHUSETTS YOUNG PEOPLE'S
    SYMPHONY/PHILHARMONIA, 645
WESTERN MICHIGAN UNIVERSITY - JAMES W. MILLER
    AUDITORIUM, 683
WESTERN MICHIGAN UNIVERSITY - LAURA V. SHAW
    THEATRE, 683
WESTERN OKLAHOMA BALLET THEATRE, 1159
WESTERN OREGON STATE COLLEGE, 1184
WESTERN WASHINGTON UNIVERSITY - CONCERT
    HALL, 1446
WESTERN WASHINGTON UNIVERSITY - EXPERIMENTAL
    THEATER, 1446
WESTERN WASHINGTON UNIVERSITY - MAIN STAGE, 1446
WESTERN WASHINGTON UNIVERSITY - OLD MAIN
    THEATER, 1446
WESTERN WIND VOCAL ENSEMBLE, 952
WESTERVILLE CIVIC SYMPHONY, 1151
WESTFIELD SYMPHONY, THE, 845
WESTMINSTER COLLEGE - BEEGHLY THEATER, 1215
WESTMINSTER COLLEGE - WESTMINSTER CHAMP
    AUDITORIUM, 744
WESTMINSTER COLLEGE - WILL W. ORR AUDITORIUM, 1215
WESTMINSTER COLLEGE - WINSTON CHURCHILL
    MEMORIAL AND LIBRARY IN THE UNITED STATES, 744
WESTMINSTER COMMUNITY ARTIST SERIES, 254
WESTMORELAND SYMPHONY ORCHESTRA, 1203
WESTPORT COMMUNITY THEATRE, 288, 289
WESTPORT COUNTRY PLAYHOUSE, 288, 289
WESTSIDE ARTS THEATRE, 1009
WESTSIDE COMMUNITY REPERTORY, 988
WESTWOOD PLAYHOUSE, THE, 113
WESTWOOD TOWN HALL, 1108
WESTWOOD WIND QUARTET, 1465
WEXNER CENTER FOR THE ARTS/MERSHON
    AUDITORIUM, 1127
WHEATLAND CHAMBER PLAYERS, 1191
WHEATON COLLEGE - ARENA THEATER, 478
WHEATON COLLEGE - EDMAN CHAPEL, 478
WHEATON SYMPHONY ORCHESTRA, 477
WHEELER OPERA HOUSE, 223
WHEELER OPERA HOUSE ASSOCIATION, 222
WHEELING CIVIC CENTER, 1486
WHEELING SYMPHONY, 1485
WHIDBEY PLAYHOUSE, 1452
WHISTLE STOP PLAYHOUSE, 731
WHITE BIRD PRODUCTIONS, INC., 988
WHITE MOUNTAIN SUMMER DANCE FESTIVAL, 805
WHITEWATER OPERA COMPANY, 502
WHITMAN COLLEGE - CORDINER HALL, 1472
WHITTIER JUNIOR THEATRE, 217
WHOLE ART THEATER, 681
WICHITA COMMUNITY THEATRE, 536
WICHITA FALLS BACKDOOR PLAYERS, 1393
WICHITA FALLS BALLET THEATRE, 1392
WICHITA FALLS SYMPHONY ORCHESTRA, 1392
WICHITA SYMPHONY, 535
WICHITA YOUTH ORCHESTRA, 536
WICOMICO YOUTH AND CIVIC CENTER, 597
WIDENER UNIVERSITY-ALUMNI AUDITORIUM - BERT
    MUSTIN THEATRE, 1198
WILKES UNIVERSITY - DOROTHY DICKSON DARTE
    CENTER FOR THE PERFORMING ARTS, 1242

WILKES-BARRE BALLET THEATRE, 1242
WILL GEER THEATRICUM BOTANICUM, THE, 209
WILLIAM A. EGAN CIVIC AND CONVENTION CENTER, 16
WILLIAM A. EGAN CIVIC AND CONVENTION CENTER - EXPLORERS HALL, 16
WILLIAM A. EGAN CIVIC AND CONVENTION CENTER - SUMMIT HALL, 16
WILLIAM EDRINGTON SCOTT THEATRE, 1350
WILLIAM PATERSON COLLEGE - THE JAZZ ROOM SERIES, 843
WILLIAM WOODS COLLEGE - CAMPUS CENTER, 744
WILLIAM WOODS COLLEGE - DULANY AUDITORIUM, 744
WILLIAMS CENTER FOR THE ARTS - THE RIVOLI, 837
WILLIAMS COLLEGE - CHAPIN HALL, 652
WILLIAMS TRIO, THE, 651
WILLIAMSON THEATRE, 1029
WILLIAMSTOWN THEATRE FESTIVAL, 651
WILLOW...A DANCE CONCERN, 1496
WILLOWBROOK JAZZ FESTIVAL, 843
WILLOWS THEATRE, 72
WILMA THEATER, 1229
WILMA THEATER, THE, 1224
WILMINGTON DRAMA LEAGUE, 295
WILMINGTON SYMPHONY ORCHESTRA, 1076
WILSON CENTER FOR THE PERFORMING ARTS, 1189
WILSON HALL AUDITORIUM, 1428
WILSON SYMPHONY, 1078
WILTON PLAYSHOP, THE, 289
WINDWARD THEATRE GUILD, 407
WINSTON-SALEM SYMPHONY ASSOCIATION, 1078
WINTER GARDEN THEATRE, 1009
WINTHROP COLLEGE - JAMES F. BYRNES AUDITORIUM, 1265
WISCONSIN CHAMBER ORCHESTRA, 1497
WISCONSIN DANCE ENSEMBLE, 1511
WISCONSIN UNION THEATER, 1499
WISCONSIN YOUTH SYMPHONY ORCHESTRAS, 1497
WISDOM BRIDGE THEATRE, 443
WITTENBERG UNIVERSITY - WITTENBERG SERIES, 1146
W.L. ZORN ARENA, 1489
WOLF TRAP FARM FOUNDATION, 1441
WOLF TRAP FARM PARK FOR THE PERFORMING ARTS, 1441
WOMEN'S GUILD OF THE NEW ORLEANS OPERA ASSOCIATION, 565
WOMEN'S INTERART CENTER, 988
WOMEN'S PHILHARMONIC, 169
WOMEN'S PROJECT AND PRODUCTIONS, 989
WOOD JUNIOR COLLEGE - THEATRE, 736
WOODLAND OPERA HOUSE, 218
WOODROW WILSON HIGH SCHOOL, 99
WOODSTOCK OPERA HOUSE, 480
WOODWARD ARTS AND THEATRE COUNCIL, 1172
WOOLLY MAMMOTH THEATRE COMPANY, 307
WOOSTER GROUP, THE, 989
WOOSTER SYMPHONY ORCHESTRA, 1151
WORCESTER CHILDREN'S THEATRE, 652
WORCESTER FOOTHILLS THEATRE COMPANY, 652
WORCESTER MEMORIAL AUDITORIUM, 653
WORKING THEATRE COMPANY, INC., THE, 989
WORLD DANCE SERIES, 1455
WORLD MUSIC INSTITUTE INC., 937
WORLD TREE PUPPET THEATER, THE, 716
WORLD'S FIRST INNER-MUSICAL THEATRE, THE, 113

WORTHINGTON CIVIC BALLET AND JAZZ NORTH DANCE COMPANIES, 1122
WPA THEATRE, 989
WRIGHT AUDITORIUM, 1061
WYNMOOR RECITAL HALL, 318
WYO THEATER, INC., 1522
WYOMING ARTS COUNCIL, 1520
XIPE TOTEC AZTEC DANCERS/VIRGINIA CARMELO, 55
YADKIN PLAYERS/YADKIN YOUTH THEATRE, 1080
YAKIMA SYMPHONY ORCHESTRA, 1473
YAKIMA YOUTH ORCHESTRA, 1473
YALE REPERTORY THEATRE, 272, 273
YALE SYMPHONY ORCHESTRA, 271
YANKTON AREA SUMMER BAND, 1275
YARD, THE, 993
YASS HAKOSHIMA MIME THEATRE, 826
YATES PERFORMING ARTS SERIES, 1015
YAVAPI SYMPHONY ASSOCIATION, 32
YELLOW BARN, 1417
YELLOW BARN MUSIC FESTIVAL, 1417
YELLOWSTONE CHAMBER PLAYERS, 769
YORK THEATRE COMPANY, THE, 990
YOUNG ACTORS THEATRE, 366
YOUNG ARTISTS PHILHARMONIC, THE, 280
YOUNG ARTISTS SERIES, 705
YOUNG ARTISTS SYMPHONY ORCHESTRA, 215
YOUNG AUDIENCES OF BEAUMONT, 1314
YOUNG AUDIENCES OF MARYLAND, 590
YOUNG AUDIENCES OF WESTERN MONTANA, 777
YOUNG CIRCLE PARK AND BANDSHELL, 330
YOUNG PEOPLES SYMPHONY OF RHODE ISLAND, 1248
YOUNG SINGERS OF CALLANWOLDE, INC., 391
YOUNGSTOWN MUSICA SACRA, 1153
YOUNGSTOWN PLAYHOUSE, THE, 1153
YOUNGSTOWN STATE UNIVERSITY - BLISS RECITAL HALL, 1153
YOUNGSTOWN STATE UNIVERSITY - FORD THEATRE, 1154
YOUNGSTOWN STATE UNIVERSITY - SPOTLIGHT ARENA THEATRE, 1154
YOUNGSTOWN SYMPHONY CENTER - POWERS AUDITORIUM, 1154
YOUNGSTOWN SYMPHONY ORCHESTRA, 1153
YOUTH ORCHESTRA OF GREATER FORT WORTH, 1344
YOUTH PRO MUSICA, 649
YOUTH SYMPHONY OF KANSAS CITY, 532
YOUTH SYMPHONY WEST, 77
YOUTHEATRE, 1062
YREKA COMMUNITY THEATRE CENTER, 219
YUEH LUNG SHADOW THEATRE, 899
YUMA BALLET THEATRE, 41
YUMA CIVIC AND CONVENTION CENTER - YUMA ROOM, 41
ZAMIR CHORALE OF BOSTON, 636
ZANESVILLE ART CENTER, 1155
ZANESVILLE CHAMBER ORCHESTRA, 1154
ZAPPED TAPS/ALFRED DESIO, 103
ZE'EVA COHEN AND DANCERS, 937
ZEITERION THEATRE, 634, 635
ZENON DANCE COMPANY AND SCHOOL, INC., 708
ZEPHYR THEATRE, 114
ZERO MOVING DANCE COMPANY, 1217
ZION PASSION PLAY, 481
ZIVILI: DANCES AND MUSIC OF THE SOUTH SLAVS, 1133